ROTHMANS FOOTBALL YEARBOOK 1981–82

EDITOR: JACK ROLLIN

QUEEN ANNE PRESS
MACDONALD FUTURA PUBLISHERS
LONDON

Front Cover: Ipswich Town v Aston Villa, FA Cup, January 1981
(Photograph courtesy of Guinness Superlatives Ltd)

ISBN 0362 02044 2 (hardcover)
0362 02046 9 (limp)

Published by Queen Anne Press,
Macdonald Futura Publishers,
Paulton House, 8 Shepherdess Walk, London N1 7LW

Typeset, printed and bound in Great Britain by
Hazell Watson & Viney Ltd, Aylesbury, Bucks

CONTENTS

OTHER COMPETITIONS

SCOTTISH FOOTBALL

BRITISH INTERNATIONAL FOOTBALL

IRISH AND WELSH FOOTBALL

WORLD FOOTBALL

EUROPEAN FOOTBALL

RECORDS SECTION

OTHER LEAGUE, YOUTH AND SCHOOLS FOOTBALL

INFORMATION SECTION

FOREWORD FROM ROTHMANS OF PALL MALL

This year, the 12th consecutive edition of *Rothmans Football Yearbook* coincides with a major new innovation in the Football League – three points for a win.

While it is customary to reflect here on the season past, we find this an irresistible opportunity to echo the desires of everyone concerned with this great game for the promotion of attacking football and the style, grace and enthusiasm that accompany such ambition. We at Rothmans helped to sow the seeds for this development in the early seventies when, with the help of *avant garde* thinking, teams in the Hellenic, Isthmian, Northern and Western Leagues were rewarded with three points for winning their respective matches.

We wish Mr Jack Dunnett, the new Chairman of the Football League, and Mr Bert Millichip, the new Chairman of the Football Association, every success in achieving their declared intent to work together for the good of our international reputation in football, both on and off the field. If the Football League gives the England administration its support, and accepts the fact that a successful national side creates a financially rewarding atmosphere for the game in this country, we can look forward to a more cheerful season. A season which we hope will also bring rewards for Britain's other national teams.

There is nothing wrong with British football at its best. It was seen last season in the FA Cup Final replay, even if we needed two Argentines to add a little extra sparkle, while both Aston Villa and Ipswich Town were often superb.

We certainly hope that the next edition of the incomparable *Rothmans Football Yearbook* gives Jack Rollin and his wonderful team of compilers the opportunity to chronicle a wealth of goals, higher attendances and the phenomenon – almost forgotten in recent years – of attacking football.

INTRODUCTION

The twelfth edition of *Rothmans Football Yearbook* includes the results of all World Cup qualifying matches played up to the time of publication. The full list of teams and goal-scorers for the entire qualifying competition and the finals themselves will appear in the next edition.

In addition, there is full coverage of domestic football with line-ups, goalscorers and attendances of matches played in the Football League and Scottish League, as well as the League Cup, FA Cup, Scottish League Cup and Scottish Cup. Transfers affecting players being signed by Football League clubs are given, together with any transfer fee noted at the time. As there is no official figure for such moves, the fees quoted are estimated, and with the addition of levies, including VAT, they are merely a guide to the value of the players in question.

This year's edition also marks the return of the Milestones of soccer which appeared in early issues of *Rothmans Football Yearbook*. Accompanying this is a more concise Diary of main events covering the 1980–81 season.

The Editor would like to thank Norman Barrett, Lionel Francis and Alan Elliott respectively for their assistance in the compilation of the Diary, Non-League Football and the Scottish season; also the invaluable assistance rendered in the completion of the book by Graeme Wright.

The Editor would also like to pay tribute to the various organisations who have helped to make this edition complete, especially Mrs Sandra Whiteside of the Football League, Mike McNamara of the Football Association, and the secretaries of all the Football League and Scottish League clubs for their kind cooperation. The ready availability of Football League secretary Graham Kelly and his staff to answer queries was as usual most appreciated. Thanks are also due to Jim Farry, the Scottish League secretary, and his staff.

ACKNOWLEDGEMENTS

The Editor would like to express his appreciation of the following individuals and organisations for their cooperation: Jill C. Ingram, Sheila Cheetham, Glynis Firth, Mike Foster, Chris J. Whalley (all from the Football League); Adrian Titcombe (The Football Association); The Scottish Football Association, The Welsh Football Association, Tom Cairns of The Scottish League, the secretaries of all Football League and Scottish League clubs, Alan Dick, Barry Hugman, Malcolm Brodie, A. Rice (The English Schools FA), W. P. Goss (AFA), Maurice Golesworthy, Ken Goldman, Peter Fay, Peter Dunk, Karen Spink, Christine Forrest, Christine Phillips, Elaine Morgan and Margaret Skinner.

EDITORIAL

The slump in League attendances of almost 2¾ millions during the 1980–81 season to a new post-war low of 21,907,569 is not due solely to the economic recession, which has certainly hit the game as badly as many another industry. Watching the game has become an expensive pastime, and in the scramble for that ever-elusive quality, success, the product, so often designed to achieve it, loses vital eye appeal. Thus, in seeking one and missing out on the other, clubs have added to the desertion of spectators.

Dwindling personal finances have led to many would-be spectators deciding to give football a miss, though not completely as there are attractive alternatives encompassing the sport. The retreat to the armchair and the extensive coverage available on television enables former devotees of the live audience to keep in touch. Indeed, the medium increasingly appears to have become a source of relatively cheap entertainment at the flick of a switch in inflationary times.

The fireside fan may still retain his interest in the game rather than take his viewing in the same detached and uncommitted way that he would watch any soap opera. But many of the genuine followers of the sport, especially those of an older generation, have tended to disappear from active participation at grounds for a variety of reasons. They have been driven away by modern annoyances, including hooliganism, obscene language, the spiralling cost of attending matches and the realisation that the game probably no longer represents the one they once knew.

Certainly it is true that people invariably remember the last result rather than the quality of the game it might have represented. But this failing allows the modern trend towards association with success to flourish whatever the quality. For there is evidence that the fan is being forced away by this pandering to the prize of success as a stimulus for a greater following.

And it is at a considerable cost to the game. In the 1955–56 season, for example, the top average attendance for a club in the First Division was 42,000; the lowest 20,000. In 1980–81, the best supported team had just over 45,000 while the lowest was just under 16,000. Moreover, there were eight First Division teams who failed to reach an average of 20,000. It could be argued that the gap between the winners and losers is widening to an alarming degree. Indeed, the structure of the game will not allow the luxury of simply following the winners, for no club can guarantee success. Only the fortunate few will enjoy that. But what they all can do, and should be ensuring, is that entertainment is provided.

It is a sickness of modern society that nobody wants to be seen to be associated with a losing team, but unless there are sufficient spectators prepared to show their loyalty to the unsuccessful clubs, the professional game will not exist in its present form. Naturally it is all too easy to blame the Football League, in its present size, for all the ills of the game. However, if the leagues were sliced to half their present number, the problems of winning and losing teams would remain the same.

It is frequently said that the Football League is the best in the world. It may be. What it certainly represents is the most competitive and longest-running, and it has continued to produce teams capable of winning honours outside this country. The 1980–81 season was no exception to this impressive record. Liverpool won the European Cup for the third time – in another tediously boring final – and Ipswich Town claimed the UEFA Cup. Though Liverpool also achieved the League Cup, a trophy which had previously eluded the Anfield sideboard, it was probably not looked upon as a vintage season on Merseyside, such has been the dominance they have provided in the First Division. The club also suffered at the turnstiles, with their lower-than-usual average of 37,547 reflecting the crippling effects of the recession in their area as much as anything else. Yet it was still the second-best figure in the Football League.

Ipswich were victims of the overcrowded fixture list, and in chasing a treble of League, FA Cup and UEFA Cup they might have failed in all three. In the First Division they see-sawed nervously in the closing stages as their apparently almost unassailable lead was shredded in a sequence which produced just one win in five games – this solitary success, incredibly enough, coming at Villa Park against the eventual champions. Indeed, Ipswich beat Villa three times, twice in the League and also in the FA Cup. They were also the only club in the Football League with as many as four players reaching double figures of goals scored.

Villa, not burdened by other commitments, kept within measurable striking distance and made few changes that were not affected by injury or the odd suspension. They had seven ever-present players, one who missed only two League games, and another absent three times among only 14 players used. Even so the League Championship remained in doubt until their last fixture, at Highbury against Arsenal. However, there was something of an anti-climax about the proceedings when, on the same day, Ipswich – with a match in hand – were beaten at Middlesbrough. This made Villa's own defeat of academic interest.

Underlining the fierce competitiveness of the divisions, the other issues throughout the League remained unresolved until the last few vital games. Leicester City, despite the achievement of a rare double over Liverpool, were relegated along with Norwich City and Crystal Palace, who had languished for much of the term. Brighton and Hove Albion escaped the drop by winning their last four matches, one of them at Sunderland who themselves retrieved what appeared a desperate situation. They had to win at Liverpool and did so by the only goal of the game.

West Ham United were aristocratic in achieving their 13 points' lead at the top of the Second Division and finishing with a club record 66 points. The other two promotion places were less obvious, and Notts County and Swansea City finally achieved elevation at the expense of a handful of others, including Blackburn Rovers, Luton Town, Derby County and Grimsby Town. Chelsea, regarded as early contenders, scored in only three of their last 22 matches.

At the bottom of the Second Division the two Bristol clubs, who had been among the chief strugglers during the season, went down with Preston North End, while Cardiff City extricated themselves at the eleventh hour.

Yorkshire clubs dominated the challenge for the promotion places in Division Three, with Rotherham United and Barnsley succeeding, along with Charlton Athletic who arrested the late slide that threatened to end their hopes as it finally did those of Huddersfield Town. Rotherham set a new divisional record, conceding only 32 goals. One of the other hopefuls, Chesterfield, had had the earlier consolation of winning the last Anglo-Scottish Cup, the competition being replaced for 1981–82 by a pre-season cup for 32 clubs outside the First Division.

Probably the most dramatic end came at the foot of the Third Division, with Walsall winning at Sheffield United on the last day and United missing a penalty that would have saved them from accompanying Colchester United, Blackpool and Hull City into Division Four.

Southend United and record breakers Lincoln City, who let in a mere 25 goals, were consistent in the Fourth Division and not surprisingly finished well ahead of the rest of the field. In the eventual shake-out, Doncaster Rovers and Wimbledon progressed with them.

The oddest event of the season came near the depths of the division on 25 April in a bout of freak weather. Stockport County visited Bury but found that several snowbound players had been unable to reach the ground. Playing the entire first half with nine men they held Bury, and with a full side after the interval they actually won 1-0 – a result which helped them climb out of the re-election zone.

The other major domestic honour went to Tottenham Hotspur, who maintained their impressive record of six victories in six FA Cup finals. Their replayed success against Manchester City was a fitting climax to the 100th competition.

While the crowded domestic programme is of no real assistance to clubs aiming to achieve more than one honour, it does little to help the international teams either. The unique situation of two bodies often operating in a manner which, to an outsider, must seem to be at variance with the aims of the other, is one of the root causes. However many the problems of demarcation for the Football Association and the Football League, there will have to be a move to centralise interests wherever the affairs of the two overlap.

It may be argued that the performances of the England team in 1980–81 were largely unimpressive because of the stranglehold on players' time caused by the demands of the League system. But the Football League clubs cannot be made responsible for the material at their disposal. This continues to mirror the far from satisfactory situation which often has promising young players regimented into tactics designed to win competitions when they should be devoting their formative years to developing individual skills.

JACK ROLLIN

ROTHMANS FOOTBALL AWARDS 1981

The following six special awards have been made by Rothmans to mark a worthwhile contribution to the game in season 1980–81.

JOHN BOND. When John Bond was persuaded to leave Norwich City for Maine Road, Manchester City were languishing so badly in the lower reaches of the First Division that salvation seemed an unlikely outcome, even under a new administration. Yet with the instilment of confidence and some judicious deals in the transfer market, he fashioned a side which proved itself not only capable of escaping danger but possessing the ability to reach the FA Cup final and provide a fitting finale to the 100th competition, even though City had to be content with the runners-up medals after the replay.

ENFIELD. Giant-killing has been one of the essential ingredients in the success of the FA Cup and the 100th competition proved to be no exception to this rule. Enfield emerged with traditionally excellent credentials, taking on Football League opposition and beating it in the process. Both Port Vale and Hereford United succumbed to the Berger Isthmian League side before Barnsley were faced in the fourth round. After battling to a draw at Oakwell, Enfield won a replay which was switched to White Hart Lane to accommodate a crowd of 35,244 – and defeat there brought no disgrace to the part-timers.

TONY KELLOW. Although he made his name as a prolific goalscorer outside the League with Falmouth Town, Tony Kellow has also established himself in the national competition in a few seasons. In 1980–81 he enjoyed his best campaign, finishing as the League's top marksman with 25 League goals plus another eight in cup games. After a couple of seasons with Blackpool he returned to his first League club, Exeter City, towards the end of 1979–80 and by the conclusion of last season had taken his overall total to 93 for his two clubs – an average of nearly one goal for every two matches.

JIM McLEAN. Dundee United's long-serving manager Jim McLean has established a reputation for both success and attractiveness – an almost elusive combination in the modern game. In 1980–81 United were able to retain the League Cup won the previous season, and they also reached the Scottish Cup final where they were beaten by Rangers in a replay. In the Premier Division Dundee United were freely acknowledged to be the team to catch the eye, often providing a challenge to Celtic, Rangers and Aberdeen – the dominating teams in recent years.

MICK MILLS. Ipswich Town owed much to captain Mick Mills during the 1980–81 season as they chased a treble of honours involving the League title, FA Cup and UEFA Cup. In the final reckoning they managed only the European prize, but it in no way diminished their gallant attempt. Throughout they owed much to the leadership of their captain, who acted as the interpreter on the field to the guidance of manager Bobby Robson. A full England international capable of playing either at full-back or in midfield, Mills has been a one-club man.

BRYAN ROBSON. The most consistent player to have emerged during the past year for the full England team is arguably Bryan Robson, of West Bromwich Albion, who has proved able to acquit himself either in midfield or defence and at any level of the game. A product of the fertile North-East, he has been with the Albion since his youth, and despite a nightmare season early in his development when he experienced the trauma of breaking his leg three times, he has graduated to become one of the most talented professionals in the Football League.

MILESTONES/DIARY 1980–81

1848
The first rules drawn up at Cambridge University.

1855
Sheffield, the oldest soccer club still in existence, founded.

1857
Sheffield start playing on a regular basis.

1862
Notts County, the oldest Football League club, founded.

1863
Football Association formed in London on 26 October.

1865
Tape to be stretched across the goals 8ft (2·4m) from the ground.

1866
Offside rule altered to allow a player to be onside when three of opposing team are nearer their own goal-line.
Fair catch rule omitted.

1867
Queen's Park, the oldest Scottish club, founded.

1869
Kick-out rule altered and goalkicks introduced.

1871
Start of the FA Cup. Goalkeepers first mentioned in Laws.

1872
First official international, between Scotland and England at Glasgow, drawn 0-0.
The Wanderers win the first FA Cup final.
Corner-kick introduced.

1873
Scottish FA formed and the start of the Scottish Cup.

1874
Umpires first mentioned in Laws.
Shinguards introduced.

1875
The cross-bar replaces tape on the goalposts.

1876
FA of Wales formed.
The first international between Scotland and Wales.

1877
The London Association and the Sheffield Association agree to use the same rules.
A player may be charged by an opponent if he is facing his own goal.

1878
Referees use a whistle for the first time.

1879
First international between England and Wales.
Cliftonville, the oldest Irish club, founded.

1880
Irish FA formed and the start of the Irish Cup.

1882
Ireland's first internationals with Wales and England.
International Football Association Board set up.
Two-handed throw-in introduced.

1883
First international between Scotland and Ireland.
The first British International Championship.

1885
Professionalism legalised in England.
Arbroath beat Bon Accord 36-0 in Scottish Cup; still a record score for an official first-class match.

1886
International caps first awarded.

1888
Football League formed.

1889
Preston North End achieve the League and FA Cup 'double'.

1890
Irish League formed.
First hat-trick in the FA Cup final, by Blackburn's William Townley.
Goal nets invented.
Scottish League formed.

1891
Referees and linesmen replace umpires.
Introduction of the penalty-kick.

1892
Penalty taker must not play the ball twice.
Extra time allowed for taking a penalty.
Goal nets used in FA Cup final for the first time.
Division Two of the Football League formed.

1893
Scotland adopts professionalism.

1894
First FA Amateur Cup final.
Division Two of Scottish League formed.
Referee given complete control of the game.
Unnecessary for players in future to appeal to him for a decision.
Goalkeeper can only be charged when playing the ball or obstructing an opponent.

1895
FA Cup stolen from a Birmingham shop window and never recovered.
Goalposts and cross-bars must not exceed 5in (127mm) in width.
Player taking throw-in must stand on touchline.

1897
Aston Villa win both the League and FA Cup.
The Corinthians tour South America.
The word 'intentional' introduced into the law on handling.

1898
Players' Union first formed.

1899
Promotion and relegation first used in the Football League, replacing 'test matches'.

1901
Tottenham Hotspur win the FA Cup as members of the Southern League.

1902
Terracing collapses during the Scotland–England match at Ibrox Park, killing 25.

1904
FIFA formed in Paris, on 21 May.

1905
First £1000 transfer. Alf Common moves from Sunderland to Middlesbrough.
First international in South America, between Argentina and Uruguay.
England joins FIFA.

1907
Amateur FA formed.
Players' Union (now Professional Footballers' Association – PFA) re-formed.

1908
England play in Vienna, their first international against a foreign side.
The first official Olympic soccer tournament in London, won by the United Kingdom.

1910
Scotland, Wales and Ireland join FIFA.

1912
Goalkeeper not permitted to handle ball outside his own penalty area.

1913
Defending players not to approach within ten yards of the ball at a free-kick.

1914
Defending players not to approach within ten yards of ball at corner-kick.

1916
The South American Championship first held.

1920
Division Three (Southern Section) of the Football League formed.
Players cannot be offside at throw-in.

1921
Division Three (Northern Section) formed.

1922
Promotion and relegation introduced in the Scottish League.

1923
First FA Cup final at Wembley: Bolton Wanderers beat West Ham United before a record crowd.

1924
A goal may be scored direct from a corner-kick.

1925
Offside law changed to require two instead of three defenders between attacker and goal.
Player taking throw-in must have both feet on touch-line.

1926
Huddersfield Town achieve the first hat-trick of League Championships.

1927
Cardiff City take the FA Cup out of England for the first time.
Mitropa Cup begins.
J. C. Clegg, President of the FA, knighted.

1928
British associations leave FIFA over broken-time payments to amateurs.
First £10,000 transfer: David Jack goes from Bolton to Arsenal.
Dixie Dean scores 60 goals for Everton in Division One, a Football League record.

1929
England lose 4-3 to Spain in Madrid, their first defeat on the Continent.
Goalkeeper compelled to stand still on his goal-line at penalty-kick.

1930
Uruguay win the first World Cup, in Montevideo, Uruguay.
F. J. Wall, Secretary of the FA, knighted.

1931
Goalkeeper permitted to carry ball four steps instead of two.
Instead of free-kick after a foul throw-in, the throw reverts to opposing side.
Scotland lose 5-0 to Austria in Vienna, their first defeat on the Continent.

1933
Numbers worn for the first time in the FA Cup final, but from 1 to 22.

1934
Italy win the second World Cup, in Rome.

1935
Arsenal equal Huddersfield's hat-trick of League Championships.

1936
Defending players not permitted to tap the ball into goalkeeper's hands from a goalkick.
Luton centre-forward Joe Payne scores ten goals against Bristol Rovers, a Football League record.
Dixie Dean overhauls Steve Bloomer's 352 goals in the Football League.

1937
A record crowd of 149,547 watch the Scotland v England match at Hampden Park.
Defending players not permitted to tap the ball into goalkeeper's hands from free-kick inside penalty area.
Weight of ball increased from 13–15oz to 14–16oz.
Arc of circle 10yd radius from penalty spot to be drawn outside penalty area.

1938
Italy retain the World Cup, in Paris.
Laws of the Game rewritten.
Scotland's Jimmy McGrory retires, having scored 550 goals in first-class football, a British record.

1946
British associations rejoin FIFA.
The Burnden Park tragedy: 33 killed and more than 400 injured during an FA Cup tie between Bolton Wanderers and Stoke City.

1949
Aircraft carrying Italian champions Torino crashes at Superga near Turin, killing all on board.
England are beaten 2-0 by Republic of Ireland at Goodison Park, so losing their unbeaten home record against sides outside the home countries.
Rangers win the first 'treble' – Scottish League, Scottish Cup and League Cup.
S. F. Rous, Secretary of the FA, knighted.

1950
Uruguay win the fourth World Cup, in Rio de Janeiro.
England, entering for the first time, lose 1-0 to USA.
Scotland's unbeaten home record against foreign opposition ends in a 1-0 defeat by Austria at Hampden Park.

1951
Obstruction included as an offence punishable by indirect free-kick.
Studs must project ¾in instead of ½in.

1952
Billy Wright overhauls Bob Crompton's record of 42 caps.
Newcastle United retain the FA Cup, the first club to do so in the 20th century.
England lose their unbeaten home record against Continental opposition, going down 6-3 to Hungary at Wembley.

1954
West Germany win the fifth World Cup, in Berne.
England suffer their heaviest international defeat, beaten 7-1 by Hungary at Budapest.
The Union of European Football Associations (UEFA) formed.
Ball not to be changed during the game unless authorised by the referee.

1955
European Cup of the Champions and Inter-Cities Fairs Cup started.

1956
Real Madrid win the first European Cup final.
First floodlit match in the Football League: Portsmouth v Newcastle United on 22 February.

1957
George Young retires with a record 53 Scottish caps.
John Charles of Leeds United becomes the first British player to be transferred to a foreign club for a substantial fee (to Juventus, Italy).

1958
Manchester United lose eight players in the Munich air disaster on 6 February.
Brazil win the sixth World Cup, in Stockholm.
Sunderland, continuously in Division One, relegated.
Football League reorganisation: Division Three and Division Four started.

1959
Billy Wright plays his 100th game for England, against Scotland, and retires at the end of the season with a world record 105 appearances.

1960
USSR win the first European Nations Cup, in Paris.
Real Madrid win the European Cup for fifth consecutive time.

1961
Sir Stanley Rous becomes President of FIFA.
Tottenham Hotspur win the League and Cup, the first 'double' of the 20th century.
The Professional Football Association (PFA) succeed in achieving the abolition of the maximum wage.

Fiorentina win the first European Cup-Winners' Cup final.

1962
Brazil retain the seventh World Cup in Santiago.
Denis Law is transferred from Torino to Manchester United, the first transfer over £100,000 paid by a British club.

1963
The centenary of the FA. England beat the Rest of the World 2-1, at Wembley.
The Football League's 'retain and transfer' system declared illegal.
Tottenham Hotspur win the European Cup-Winners' Cup, the first British success in Europe.

1964
Spain win the European Nations' Cup, in Madrid.
More than 300 killed and 500 injured in rioting during an Olympic qualifying game between Peru and Argentina at Lima, Peru.
Jimmy Dickinson (Portsmouth) becomes the first player to make 700 Football League appearances.

1965
Stanley Matthews becomes the first footballer to be knighted.
Arthur Rowley retires having scored a record 434 Football League goals.
The Football League agree to substitutes for one injured player.

1966
England win the eighth World Cup, at Wembley.
The Football League allow substitutes for any reason.

1967
Alf Ramsey, England's team manager, knighted.
Celtic become the first British club to win the European Cup.

1968
Italy win the European Football Championship, in Rome.
A world record transfer: Pietro Anastasi moves from Varese to Juventus for £440,000.
Manchester United win the European Cup: Matt Busby knighted.
Leeds United become the first British club to win the Fairs Cup.

1969
Leeds United win the Football League Championship with a record 67 points.

1970
Brazil win the ninth World Cup, in Mexico City and win the Jules Rimet Trophy outright.
Bobby Charlton wins his 106th England cap in the quarter-finals to overhaul Billy Wright's record.
The first £200,000 transfer in Britain: Martin Peters moves from West Ham United to Tottenham Hotspur.

1971
Britain's worst-ever crowd disaster: 66 killed at a match between Rangers and Celtic at Ibrox Park.
Arsenal achieve the League and Cup 'double'.
Barcelona win the Fairs Cup outright (to be replaced by the UEFA Cup) after beating the holders Leeds United 2-1.

1972
Tottenham Hotspur defeat Wolverhampton Wanderers in the first all-British European club competition final – the UEFA Cup.
West Germany win the European Football Championship, in Brussels.

1973
Ajax win the European Cup for the third consecutive time.
Bobby Moore makes his 108th appearance for England, a new record.
Johan Cruyff becomes the first £1 million transfer, moving from Ajax to Barcelona for £922,300.

1974
Joao Havelange of Brazil replaces Sir Stanley Rous as President of FIFA.
West Germany win the tenth World Cup in Munich.
Denis Law makes his 55th appearance for Scotland, a new record.

1975
Leeds United banned from competing in Europe for any of two seasons in the next four, after their fans rioted at the European Cup final in Paris.
Terry Paine overhauls Jimmy Dickinson's record of 764 League games.

1976
Bayern Munich win the European Cup for the third consecutive time.
Czechoslovakia win the European Football Championship in Belgrade, beating West Germany.
Pat Jennings makes his 60th appearance for Northern Ireland, a new record.
The Football League abandon 'goal average', introducing 'goal difference'.
Liverpool win their ninth League title, overhauling Arsenal's record.

1977
Liverpool win their 10th League title as well as the European Cup.
Kevin Keegan transferred from Liverpool to SV Hamburg for £500,000, the highest fee involving a British club.
Kenny Dalglish transferred from Celtic to Liverpool for £440,000, a record fee between British clubs.
First World Youth Cup, held in Tunisia and won by USSR.

1978
Argentina win the eleventh World Cup in Buenos Aires.
Liverpool retain the European Cup.
Nottingham Forest, the only Football League club not a limited company, win their first Championship title. Forest also win the League Cup.
Ipswich Town become the 40th different team to win the FA Cup.
Kenny Dalglish makes his 56th appearance for Scotland to overhaul Denis Law's record.

1979
David Mills transferred from Middlesbrough to West Bromwich Albion for £516,000, a record fee between British clubs.
Trevor Francis, transferred from Birmingham City to Nottingham Forest for £1 million, breaks the record for a single transfer involving British clubs.
Liverpool win their eleventh League title.
Nottingham Forest become the third English club to win the European Cup.
Andy Gray, transferred from Aston Villa to Wolverhampton Wanderers, breaks the record for a single transfer involving British clubs at £1,469,000.
Argentina win the Second World Youth Cup in Japan.

1980
Liverpool retain the League Championship for their 12th League honour.
Nottingham Forest retain the European Cup.
West Germany regain their European Championship title, beating Belgium in Rome.
Steve Archibald joins Tottenham Hotspur from Aberdeen in an £800,000 deal which makes him the most expensive transfer from a Scottish club.
John Trollope overhauls Jimmy Dickinson's record of 764 League appearances for one club, reaching a total of 770.

1981
Uruguay win the Gold Cup in Montevideo.
Liverpool win the European Cup and the League Cup.

Soccer – The Fight for Survival

On 11 August 1980, the Secretaries, Managers and Coaches Association announced their charter 'Soccer – The Fight for Survival'. A 'blueprint for the future', it was drawn up by a study group comprising Ken Friar, Alan Dicks, Harry Haslam, Ron Saunders, Graham Taylor, Terry Venables and Bill Nicholson. It was then discussed at Solihull by the representatives (mainly chairmen) of the 92 League clubs in a two-day seminar (26–27 October). This, in turn, was followed by an extraordinary general meeting on 9 February 1981, in which votes were taken and resolutions passed or rejected.

The resolutions passed included the following:

A new points system for the League – 3 points for a win, 1 for a draw – to be introduced in 1981–82.

A maximum of six League matches allowed each weekend on Fridays or Sundays (see below, Sunday Soccer).

No players to be bought by a club until previous transfer debts settled. (Rejected was the proposal that half a transfer fee be paid immediately, with the rest within 12 months.)

No club official (director or secretary) to be involved in the management or administration of more than one club at the same time.

Voting power of Third and Fourth Divisions to be increased from six to eight.

Apprentice players to receive compulsory instruction in the laws of the game.

A 'gentlemen's agreement' not to poach another club's manager during the course of a season.

Among the proposals rejected were a reduction in the majority vote required to pass a resolution from three-quarters to two-thirds; all 92 clubs to vote on re-election and election to the League; extension of the half-time interval to 15 minutes; and a ban on any player rejoining a club within 12 months of leaving them.

In addition, the meeting recommended that a proposal to allow each club one paid director be put to the FA.

Several other suggestions made in the original charter were either rejected at the first seminar (restructuring of the League by reduction in size of Divisions 1 and 2 and regionalizing of 3 and 4), implemented before the extraordinary general meeting (see below, 1981–82 Season Put Back and End of Red and Yellow Cards), or required further discussion, perhaps with the FA (appointment of 'supremo' to co-ordinate the administration of the game in England; the setting up of a 'think tank' composed of members from the various bodies; setting up of a commercial section; introduction of professional referees; and scrapping of the assessor system).

Sunday Soccer

First-class Sunday soccer was staged in England for the first time since 1974, when Sunday League and Cup fixtures were allowed from January to March owing to the power crisis and the three-day week. This time, however, despite the club chairmen's recommendations for Sunday football in the League, the FA firmly rejected Port Vale's request to stage their First Round FA Cup tie against Bradford City on the Sunday and reasserted their strong opposition to Sunday ties.

The first match played on Sunday in the 1980–81 season took place on 15 February at Feethams Ground, where Fourth Division Darlington entertained Mansfield Town in front of a crowd of 5932, trebling their average home gate. Sunday soccer continued for the rest of the season, with matches played in Divisions 2, 3, and 4. Most gates were well above average at first, but as the season progressed the increases were less significant.

In order to switch a fixture to Sunday, the home club (having first, of course, reached agreement with their visitors) had to apply to the League management committee. Admission procedure on Sunday involved the sale of a single-sheet programme priced the same as normal admission, together with a complimentary admission ticket (different colours for different parts of the ground). The regular match programme was on sale inside the ground.

End of Red and Yellow Cards

An FA directive ended the system of referees' displaying yellow and red cards for cautions and sending-offs, respectively. A unanimous decision of the FA Council, but by no means popular with the majority of referees, the directive took effect as from Monday 19 January

1981, and applied to all English leagues, competitions, and friendlies. The system had originally been introduced in 1975–76.

1981–82 Season Put Back

In February, the League announced changes in scheduling for the 1981–82 season. The League programme has been put back a fortnight, to avoid the clash with end-of-August holidays, and will now run from 29 August to 15 May, with the FA Cup final on 22 May.

Football League Cup

In accordance with the rescheduling of the Football League programme, the Football League Cup has also been rearranged, with the first round starting in the first week of September and the second round reverting to a one-leg system.

In April, League secretary Graham Kelly announced that the Football League Cup was open to sponsorship, and invited applications.

British International Championship

The British International Championship has been rescheduled for the 1981–82 season, with half the fixtures to be played in midweek in February and April, and the other half at the end of the season in the week following the Cup final, only the Scotland–England fixture being played on a Saturday (29 May).

In September 1980, the Football Association announced that there would be no allocation of tickets for the 1981 England–Scotland match at Wembley 'north of the border'. The Scottish Supporters' Club later challenged this decision in law on the grounds that it contravened the Race Relations Act, but they were unsuccessful. The FA made it clear that if these severe measures still did not curtail the vandalism and hooliganism associated with the traditional Scottish 'invasion' of London for the game, they might have to terminate what is the oldest international fixture in football.

Other Competitions

The formation was announced in December 1980 of the Semi-Professional Football League (South) for the 1982–83 season, an amalgamation of the Southern and Isthmian Leagues, with the Athenian, Hellenic, and Western Leagues serving as feeders. The Alliance Premier League announced its extension to 22 clubs for the 1981–82 season with the addition of Dagenham and Enfield. The Alliance also took steps to amend their rules to allow for the defection of the Southern League, one of their feeder leagues.

The Anglo-Scottish Cup Committee decided to scrap the competition after the Scottish League withdrew its clubs. They felt they had to take this decision owing to the continued absence of English First Division clubs.

New Scheme Announced by Football Trust

In January 1981, the Football Trust (which derives its income from spot-the-ball competitions run by the football pools) announced a new scheme to provide some £2 million to assist depressed areas. Administered by the Sports Council, the scheme was designed to provide more and better soccer-playing facilities in the heavily populated areas by assisting clubs and local councils. The Sports Council pointed out that there was nothing to prevent major clubs benefiting from the scheme provided any proposed developments were to the advantage of the local community. They would have to apply through their councils.

New Football League President

Newcastle United chairman Lord Westwood resigned as Football League president in March, and Burnley chairman Bob Lord took over as acting president.

Annual General Meeting

Jack Dunnett, 58, Labour MP for Nottingham East and the Chairman of Notts County, was elected President of the Football League, winning on a second ballot from John Smith, the Liverpool chairman, by 28 votes to 24. Ernie Clay (Fulham) and Jack Wiseman (Birmingham City) had been eliminated on the first ballot.

Altrincham, who had failed by only one vote to obtain election from the Alliance Premier League the previous year, received only 17 votes this time compared with Halifax Town 41, Hereford United 46, York City 46 and Tranmere Rovers 48 who were all re-elected.

Attendances fell by 11 per cent on the previous season, the aggregate being returned at 21,907,569 compared with 24,623,975 – a drop of 2,716,406 and considered to represent a loss of £6 million in attendance money.

There was a move to pressure the Football Association to reverse its controversial decision to forbid paid directors, clarify the lines of demarcation with the FA and attempt to curtail television coverage without infringing the present contract.

Everton successfully introduced a proposal to allow a single loan transfer to any club at any time from 1981–82.

Takeover at Crystal Palace

Crystal Palace had a traumatic season both on and off the field, and the eventual takeover of the club led to a change in the League's rules. On 17 December, Fulham chairman Ernie Clay announced that he had made an offer for a controlling interest in Crystal Palace. The following day Palace chairman Raymond Bloye admitted that he had received several offers for part or whole of his share holdings but strongly denied that he was leaving the club or selling his shares. Fulham's financial director Brian Dalton, however, claimed that Fulham had been negotiating a deal with Palace but that there were a number of other people attempting to outbid them. Among those who denied that they were bidding was Wimbledon chairman Ron Noades, who dismissed any such suggestions as a 'joke'. After weeks of rumour and denials, on 23 January Bloye sold his 75 per cent stake in Palace to a consortium headed by Noades for £600,000. One of the decisions of the meeting of the Football League chairmen on 9 February was that no club official could be involved in the administration of more than one club at a time, and as a result Noades stated that he was prepared to give up his shares in Wimbledon. On 19 February, however, he changed his mind and decided to retain his shares, while maintaining that he would play no part in the future plans of the club.

During the season, Palace had four managers. They started off with Terry Venables, but he left in mid-October to take over Tommy Docherty's job at Queen's Park Rangers. Ernie Walley was placed in temporary and then 'permanent' charge, but in early December, Malcolm Allison, sacked by Manchester City, was appointed joint manager with Walley and then sole manager. But when Ron Noades took over the club, he replaced Allison with Wimbledon manager Dario Gradi.

All-Seater Stadiums and Other Rebuilding

Following in the footsteps of Aberdeen and Clydebank north of the border, both Charlton (20,000) and Coventry (20,000) began construction of all-seater stadiums, the first English clubs to do so. Tottenham began the reconstruction of their main stand, and Chelsea announced plans for a £14m redevelopment, including the replacement of the 'Shed' terracing with a new stand.

Artificial Pitch for QPR

QPR chairman Jim Gregory announced plans on 23 March for a synthetic, all-weather pitch. Neither the Football League nor the FA raised objections, although they expressed reservations about the scheme. Work started on the laying of the £350,000 pitch as soon as Rangers' fixtures were completed. The new surface is manufactured in Canada.

Crowd Disturbances and Hooliganism

The FA's committee set up to deal with the problem of crowd disturbances met three times in September and October 1980 and prepared a memorandum. It proposed limitations on the sale of alcohol, new methods for the identification of trouble-makers, and stronger measures against premeditated foul play, and discussed matters over which the FA has no jurisdiction (such as attendance centres, stiffer penalties for offenders, and the sale of alcohol in various places). Five members of the FA visited the Home Secretary on 15 December to put their recommendations, and received both approval and appreciation of the measures being taken by the FA and the Football League in co-operation. The FA is preparing a code of conduct, and one item of behaviour they criticize is the overexuberant clenched-fist gesture employed by players after scoring goals. Many clubs objected to the proposed ban on the sale of alcohol inside grounds and its implementation was delayed pending further investigation.

The need for further measures was underlined during the season by several incidents. Aggravating the rapidly declining reputation of British soccer fans abroad, the drunken behaviour of a number of West Ham followers at the Bernabeu Stadium, Madrid, on 17 September forced UEFA to take serious action. The incidents occurred at the first leg of West Ham's European Cup-Winners' Cup match with Castilla, and in addition to a heavy fine, West Ham had to play the return leg behind closed doors.

Domestic incidents were no less serious, and included a riot of Sheffield Wednesday fans at Oldham on 6 September which reduced their manager Jackie Charlton to tears. Hurling bricks, bottles, and anything else available when the referee sent off Terry Curran, the hooligans scaled barriers and surged onto the pitch. The referee led the players off, and they were unable to return for nearly half an hour.

Oldham were inadvertently involved in another serious incident when they played at Kenilworth Road on 26 April. With their team 2-1 down and their hopes of promotion fading, hundreds of young Luton fans invaded the pitch with three minutes to go, in what was a blatant attempt to have the game abandoned. The referee took the players off for ten minutes, and according to Oldham manager Jimmy Frizzell advised him to leave striker Rodger Wylde in the dressing-room. In the event, he did not, although Wylde had been the object of much abuse from the terraces after an early foul and he had scored both Oldham goals.

The most tragic occurrence, however, was the death of a 17-year-old Middlesbrough supporter, who was found in the road near Ayresome Park with severe head injuries after Middlesbrough's game with Nottingham Forest on 6 September, the same Saturday as the riot at Oldham.

On the bright side, it should be noted that, at the same time as West Ham were playing their European tie to empty stands and terraces, Ipswich were visiting Aris Salonika in the UEFA Cup and both their players and their fans drew strong praise from a top UEFA official at the match. West German Hubert Claessen remarked on the sportsmanship of the players, the exemplary behaviour of the fans, and the admirable organization of the trip by the club.

Rugby League

Fulham's experiment with Rugby League at Craven Cottage proved a success. With matches on Sundays in the Second Division of the League, Fulham opened their programme with a 24 points to 5 win over Wigan on 14 September in front of a 9554 crowd, much higher than their average home gate for soccer. They achieved promotion to Division 1 in their first season. Both Cardiff and Carlisle entered teams in Division 2 of the Rugby League for 1981–82.

Advertising and Sponsorship

Advertising on shirts continued to be a thorny problem with the TV companies. ATV planned to show highlights of the Aston Villa v Brighton League match (22 October) on a news programme, but withdrew their cameras when Brighton refused to change their shirts bearing the name of their sponsors, British Caledonian. In February, Nottingham Forest were fined £7000 by UEFA for displaying advertising material on their shirts, and a month later they, Bolton, and Newcastle were each fined £1000 by the FA for shirt advertising in televised FA Cup ties in January. Writing in *FA Today*, FA Secretary Ted Croker suggested that, if the government were prepared to put back into the game some of the millions they were 'creaming off' from football pools, clubs would be prepared to discontinue raising revenue by such controversial means as 'using players as mobile bill-boards'.

In August, Coventry City announced plans for a £250,000 sponsorship deal with Talbot, and that they would be known in the 1981–82 season as 'Coventry-Talbot', but the FA rejected the idea. The Football League proposed to find a sponsor for the League Cup (see above).

FIFA's Ultimatum to the NASL

In an exercise in brinkmanship, the NASL resisted FIFA's demand that they should drop the 35-yard offside line and the three substitutes rule until the very last moment. Most club owners were furious at FIFA's ultimatum, and a major row developed between NASL Commissioner Phil Woosnam and Gene Edwards, President of the US Soccer Federation, who backed FIFA and were accused by Woosnam of blocking an attempted compromise. A couple of hours before the opening of the NASL season on 28 March, the NASL backed down and temporarily suspended the offending practices so that the League would operate under FIFA rules pending further discussions, only for FIFA to allow them to carry on at the last minute.

British International Championship

With England declining to play Northern Ireland in Belfast because of the political unrest in the province and Wales deciding to follow their example, the 1980–81 British International Championship was declared null and void at a meeting of the Home Associations on 13 June, 1981, though the other four fixtures had been completed. Scotland had been the only country to play all three of its matches.

SPORT AND THE LAW

Sport and the law in 1980–81 moved on from the previous season's experiences with charities and violence, to companies, contracts and commercial causes.

The Crystal Palace–Wimbledon boardroom shuffles before Christmas exposed gaps in the Football League–FA Regulations and Rules, and these were further emphasised with the end-of-season managerial merry-go-round. West Bromwich Albion threatened to take legal action for compensation concerning Ron Atkinson's contract termination on moving to Old Trafford, and newly promoted Rotherham United were reported to have 'taken urgent legal advice' after Ian Porterfield accepted Sheffield United's managerial offer. Contract breakages are not as dramatic as leg breakages, but the law protects them equally effectively. These two examples pinpoint an issue long overdue for investigation: to what extent can company club football directors create a damages claim for directly or indirectly interfering with another club's existing contract with its manager?

Such action is a remedy well known to the courts. If written specifically into Football League and FA conditions, it would go a long way to making more acceptable the face of football capitalism. For the law of the land is as acceptable to football company boardroom violation of contracts as it is to penalising violence on and off the field.

On that recurring unhappy theme, the season ended almost as it began. The minority disgrace of England's supporters at Basle on the occasion of the end-of-season international against Switzerland threw the mind back to the opening explosions of violence both on and off the field at its commencement. Vince Hilaire of Crystal Palace pushed over a referee and was found guilty by a disciplinary tribunal of bringing the game into disrepute. Charlie George of Southampton was disciplined by his club and fined by local magistrates for assaulting a photographer at the Norwich City ground; and the law and sport merged dramatically when a police officer marched onto the field at Colchester to remonstrate about a defender's verbal chastisement of his own goalkeeper. This occasion was not without precedent. In the late 1960s, a visiting player at Portsmouth made rude signs during an FA Cup tie which could have incited crowd disturbance. A local policeman, on that occasion, attempted to object too. Each time the referee complained, but forgot how the law of the land transcends the field of play; and both referees could have been at risk for obstructing the respective police officers in the execution of their duty.

Crowd violence doubtless reflected the minority elements which have wreaked so much havoc to the game's image. Unhappily they cannot be ignored, however disproportionate they are numerically to the genuine followers. At the beginning of the season, on 17 August, 1980, 16 police were injured and 63 arrests were made at Hillsborough when Sheffield Wednesday played Newcastle United. Three weeks later, when Oldham Athletic entertained Sheffield Wednesday, the crowd invaded the pitch. Both clubs were charged domestically with bringing the game into disrepute; and Wednesday were found guilty because of misbehaviour by a minority of their supporters.

In due course the FA blamed the Government, the Government through the Minister with special responsibility for sport blamed the football authorities, and what has become accepted is the reality of how a game reflects the society and conditions of the times within which it is played. Alcohol was recognised as one element causing the problems, and so legislation was passed by Parliament against drink at football matches in Scotland and on British Rail respectively under the Criminal Justice (Scotland) Act and a bye-law approved by the Minister of Transport.

Against this background, the election of Mr Jack Dunnett, MP, chairman of Notts County, as the Football League's new president, and the election of Mr Bert Millichip, chairman of West Bromwich Albion, to the chairmanship of the FA, take on a special significance. Each is a practising solicitor and brings to the game's administration a wealth of legal experience and expertise, which this review of last season suggests will be welcome at all levels. Not least will be the problems at the international levels. From distances as far afield as Belfast and Johannesburg, British clubs and players found themselves involved in legal wrangles.

The Northern Ireland FA claimed compensation from the Welsh and English FAs after each had withdrawn from the Home International fixtures in Belfast because of the political violence in that city; and the fully integrated and multi-racial Football Council of South Africa (FCSA), through its black president, Mr George Thabe, claimed after a FIFA ban on an English players' coaching/playing tour: 'We have no alternative but to try to breach the isolation effects of FIFA's expulsion of South Africa whenever and wherever possible. We have endeavoured with a good deal of success to rid South Africa of racism and race discrimination, and we cannot let the sport suffer because of the laws of the country.' Indeed, nearer home, in London's Westminster County Court, the FA successfully resisted a complaint that it had racially discriminated against Scottish soccer fans by banning ticket sales to them in seeking to protect the world's oldest soccer international, between the two countries, from possible closure because of recent lawless violence on the terraces.

At school and for the millions of club players throughout the world, soccer is still and always will be a game of fun and joy. But when money and international politics become involved, the law is the ultimate referee.

EDWARD GRAYSON

CROWD VIOLENCE

Sam Phillips was banned from attending Ledbury Town's home matches in 1980–81 for allegedly assaulting a referee. But he still watched his team through a hedge surrounding the ground. Mr Phillips, variously described as aged between 77 and 82, had apparently rendered the shirt of a referee to a condition 'torn beyond repair'.

AWARDS 1980–81

FOOTBALLER OF THE YEAR

The Football Writers' Association award for the Footballer of the Year went to Frans Thijssen, the Dutch international midfield player of Ipswich Town. Ipswich players dominated the voting, with captain Mick Mills finishing as runner-up and John Wark being placed third. Billy Bonds (West Ham U) and Dennis Mortimer (Aston Villa) tied for fourth place, and another Ipswich player, Arnold Muhren, a Dutch international himself, came fifth.

Award Winners
1947–48 Stanley Matthews (Blackpool), 1948–49 Johnny Carey (Manchester U), 1949–50 Joe Mercer (Arsenal), 1950–51 Harry Johnston (Blackpool), 1951–52 Billy Wright (Wolverhampton W), 1952–53 Nat Lofthouse (Bolton W), 1953–54 Tom Finney (Preston NE), 1954–55 Don Revie (Manchester C), 1955–56 Bert Trautmann (Manchester C), 1956–57 Tom Finney (Preston NE), 1957–58 Danny Blanchflower (Tottenham H), 1958–59 Syd Owen (Luton T), 1959–60 Bill Slater (Wolverhampton W), 1960–61 Danny Blanchflower (Tottenham H), 1961–62 Jimmy Adamson (Burnley), 1962–63 Stanley Matthews (Stoke C), 1963–64 Bobby Moore (West Ham U), 1964–65 Bobby Collins (Leeds U), 1965–66 Bobby Charlton (Manchester U), 1966–67 Jackie Charlton (Leeds U), 1967–68 George Best (Manchester U), 1968–69 Dave Mackay (Derby Co) shared with Tony Book (Manchester C), 1969–70 Billy Bremner (Leeds U), 1970–71 Frank McLintock (Arsenal), 1971–72 Gordon Banks (Stoke C), 1972–73 Pat Jennings (Tottenham H), 1973–74 Ian Callaghan (Liverpool), 1974–75 Alan Mullery (Fulham), 1975–76 Kevin Keegan (Liverpool), 1976–77 Emlyn Hughes (Liverpool), 1977–78 Kenny Burns (Nottingham F), 1978–79 Kenny Dalglish (Liverpool), 1979–80 Terry McDermott (Liverpool), 1980–81 Frans Thijssen (Ipswich T).

THE PFA AWARDS 1981

Player of the Year – John Wark (Ipswich T)
Previous Winners – Andy Gray (Aston V); Pat Jennings (Tottenham H); Colin Todd (Derby Co); Norman Hunter (Leeds U); Peter Shilton (Nottingham F); Liam Brady (Arsenal); Terry McDermott (Liverpool).
Young Player of the Year – Gary Shaw (Aston Villa)
Previous Winners – Andy Gray (Aston V); Peter Barnes (Manchester C); Mervyn Day (West Ham U); Kevin Beattie (Ipswich T); Tony Woodcock (Nottingham F); Cyrille Regis (WBA); Glenn Hoddle (Tottenham H).
PFA Merit Award – John Trollope
Previous Winners – Jack Taylor; George Eastham; Denis Law; Bobby Charlton; Bill Shankly; Tom Finney; Sir Matt Busby.

The following four teams were selected by the Professional Footballers' Association to represent the divisions of the Football League.

Division 1: Peter Shilton (Nottingham F); Kenny Swain (Aston Villa), Russell Osman (Ipswich T), Allan Evans (Aston Villa), Kenny Sansom (Arsenal), Frans Thijssen (Ipswich T), John Wark (Ipswich T), Graeme Souness (Liverpool), Paul Mariner (Liverpool), Kenny Dalglish (Liverpool), Gary Shaw (Aston Villa).

Division 2: Phil Parkes (West Ham U); Ray Stewart (West Ham U), Alvin Martin (West Ham U), Billy Bonds (West Ham U), Ray O'Brien (Notts Co), Trevor Brooking (West Ham U), Tony Currie (QPR), Alan Devonshire (West Ham U), Paul Goddard (West Ham U), David Cross (West Ham U), Terry Curran (Sheffield Wednesday).

Division 3: Nicky Johns (Charlton Ath); Malcolm Brown (Huddersfield T), John Breckin (Rotherham U), Ian Evans (Barnsley), Mike McCarthy (Barnsley), Ronnie Glavin (Barnsley), Alan Birch (Chesterfield), Danny Wilson (Chesterfield), David Kemp (Plymouth Arg), Derek Hales (Charlton Ath), Tony Kellow (Exeter C).

Division 4: Mervyn Cawston (Southend U); Cec Podd (Bradford C), Steve Sherlock (Stockport Co), Trevor Peake (Lincoln C), Dave Cusack (Southend U), Billy Kellock (Peterborough U), Alan Little (Doncaster R), Anton Otulakowski (Southend U), Robbie Cooke (Peterborough U), Derek Spence (Southend U), Steve Phillips (Northampton T).

BELL'S FOOTBALL MANAGER OF THE YEAR 1980–81

Ron Saunders was elected Manager of the Year in the Bell's Scotch Whisky award. Aston Villa won the League Championship under his guidance, their first such honour since

1910. Other winners were West Ham United's John Lyall (Second Division), Ian Porterfield of Rotherham United (Third Division) and Southend United's Dave Smith (Fourth Division). The special award went to Swansea City's player-manager, John Toshack.

AUGUST
Manager of the Month: **Bobby Robson** (Ipswich T); *Division Two:* **Howard Kendall** (Blackburn R); *Division Three:* **Frank Burrows** (Portsmouth); *Division Four:* **Colin Murphy** (Lincoln C)

SEPTEMBER
Manager of the Month: **Gordon Lee** (Everton); *Division 2:* **John Lyall** (West Ham U); *Division Three:* **Bobby Saxton** (Plymouth Arg); *Division Four:* **Billy Bremner** (Doncaster R)

OCTOBER
Manager of the Month: **Ron Saunders** (Aston Villa); *Division Two:* **Geoff Hurst** (Chelsea); *Division Three:* **Mike Bailey** (Charlton Ath); *Division Four:* **Dave Smith** (Southend U)

NOVEMBER
Manager of the Month: **John Bond** (Manchester C); *Division Two:* **Geoff Hurst** (Chelsea); *Division Three:* **Norman Hunter** (Barnsley); *Division Four:* **George Mulhall** (Bradford C)

DECEMBER
Manager of the Month: **John Bond** (Manchester C); *Division Two:* **David Pleat** (Luton T); *Division Three:* **Norman Hunter** (Barnsley); *Division Four:* **Dario Gradi** (Wimbledon)

JANUARY
Manager of the Month: **Lawrie McMenemy** (Southampton); *Division Two:* **Arthur Cox** (Newcastle U); *Division Three:* **Mike Bailey** (Charlton Ath); *Division Four:* **Peter Morris** (Peterborough U)

FEBRUARY
Manager of the Month: **Bobby Robson** (Ipswich T); *Division Two:* **John Lyall** (West Ham U); *Division Three:* **Malcolm Macdonald** (Fulham); *Division Four:* **David Webb** (AFC Bournemouth)

MARCH
Manager of the Month: **Bobby Robson** (Ipswich T); *Division Two:* **George Kerr** (Grimsby T); *Division Three:* **Frank Barlow** (Chesterfield); *Division Four:* **Dave Bassett** (Wimbledon)

APRIL
Manager of the Month: **Bob Paisley** (Liverpool); *Division Two:* **John Toshack** (Swansea C); *Division Three:* **Norman Hunter** (Barnsley); *Division Four:* **Dave Smith** (Southend U)

MECCA LOYALTY AWARDS 1980–81

During the last eighteen months, one of the most worthy of awards to players has come from Mecca Promotions in their Loyalty Awards to those who have reached a milestone of League appearances with one club. In 1980–81 a total of 59 awards was made.

Aldershot: Glen Johnson 300; *Arsenal:* Pat Rice 400, Frank Stapleton 200; *AFC Bournemouth:* John Impey 200; *Brighton & HA:* Brian Horton 200; *Bristol R:* David Williams 200, Phil Bater 200; *Bradford C:* Gary Watson 200; *Bolton W:* Peter Reid 200; *Chester:* Grenville Millington 200; *Clacton:* Peter Cooper 200; *Colchester U:* Mike Packer 300, Steve Leslie 300, Ian Allinson 200, Bobby Gough 200; *Crewe Alex:* David Davies 200; *Coventry C:* Mick Coop 400; *Chelsea:* Micky Droy 200; *Cardiff C:* Phil Dwyer 300; *Carlisle U:* George McVitie 200; *Crystal Palace:* Jim Cannon 300, Paul Hinshelwood 200; *Exeter C:* Peter Hatch 300, John Hore 200; *Gillingham:* Damien Richardson 300, Danny Westwood 200; *Grimsby T:* Mike Brolly 200, Bob Cumming 200, Joe Waters 200; *Ipswich T:* Paul Cooper 200; *Leeds U:* Trevor Cherry 300; *Mansfield T:* Kevin Bird 300; *Manchester U:* Sammy McIlroy 200; *Middlesbrough:* Tony McAndrew 200; *Norwich C:* Duncan Forbes 300; *Notts Co:* Pedro Richards 200; *Nottingham F:* Viv Anderson 200, John Robertson 300, John McGovern 300; *Oxford U:* Roy Burton 300, Peter Foley 200, Les Taylor 200; *Plymouth Arg:* Brian Johnson 200; *Port Vale:* Neil Griffiths 200; *Preston NE:* Alex Bruce 200; *Reading:* Steve Hetzke 200; *Swindon T:* John Trollope 749 (subsequently 770); *Swansea C:* Robbie James 300; *Stockport Co:* John Rutter 200; *Shrewsbury T:* Colin Griffin 200, Ian Atkins 200; *Tranmere R:* Eddie Flood 300; *Walsall:* Dave Serella 200; *WBA:* John Wile 400, Ally Brown 200; *Wolverhampton W:* John McAlle 400, Willie Carr 200; *Wrexham:* Graham Whittle 400; *West Ham U:* Billy Bonds 500*.

** Awaiting presentation at the start of 1981–82 season.*

DIVISION 1 LEAGUE POSITION PROGRESS CHART

1980 (Aug–Dec) — 1981 (Jan–May)

	Aug	Sept				Oct				Nov					Dec				Jan				Feb				Mar					Apr				May	Final Position
	31	7	14	21	28	5	12	19	26	2	9	16	23	30	7	14	21	28	4	11	18	25	1	8	15	22	1	8	15	22	29	5	12	19	26	3	
Arsenal	8	9	5	9	8	5	9	9	8	5	4	5	4	5	4	6	4	4	4	4	5	5	6	6	6	8	6	7	7	7	7	7	7	5	3	3	3
Aston Villa	3	4	10	6	4	4	3	2	1	1	1	1	1	1	2	1	2	2	2	1	2	2	2	2	2	2	2	2	2	2	2	1	1	1	1	1	1
Birmingham C	13	15	14	15	14	15	15	14	14	11	9	10	10	9	10	12	13	14	14	14	14	14	18	17	14	13	14	14	14	10	10	11	11	11	13	13	13
Brighton & HA	13	18	17	14	16	16	18	18	20	22	22	19	20	20	20	20	20	18	18	19	19	19	19	19	19	19	19	19	19	19	19	19	20	20	18	18	19
Coventry C	15	11	8	12	15	13	14	15	15	12	13	13	15	15	16	15	16	15	15	15	15	15	15	15	17	16	16	16	16	18	18	18	18	18	15	15	16
Crystal Palace	19	21	22	22	22	22	22	21	22	20	21	21	21	21	22	22	22	22	22	21	21	21	22	22	22	22	22	22	22	22	22	22	22	22	22	22	22
Everton	17	13	11	5	3	3	4	4	7	8	8	4	7	7	7	5	6	9	9	10	10	10	10	12	13	12	10	10	12	15	15	15	15	15	16	17	15
Ipswich T	1	1	1	1	1	1	1	1	2	2	2	2	2	3	3	3	3	3	3	2	1	1	1	1	1	1	1	1	1	1	1	2	2	2	2	2	2
Leeds U	20	22	21	19	21	20	16	17	16	17	19	17	19	19	17	16	17	16	16	18	16	16	14	14	15	15	12	12	10	12	11	10	10	10	10	10	9
Leicester C	11	14	18	20	17	18	19	20	19	21	20	22	22	22	21	21	21	21	21	22	22	22	21	21	21	20	21	20	20	21	20	21	21	21	21	21	21
Liverpool	5	5	3	4	2	2	2	3	3	4	5	3	3	2	1	2	1	1	1	3	3	3	3	3	3	3	3	4	5	5	6	5	5	6	8	8	5
Manchester C	21	19	20	21	20	21	21	22	21	18	18	18	16	17	15	18	14	13	13	12	11	11	11	11	12	11	13	13	11	13	14	12	14	13	12	12	12
Manchester U	10	10	6	7	9	6	7	7	5	7	7	6	5	6	6	4	5	7	7	8	9	9	9	9	9	9	9	9	9	9	9	9	8	7	7	7	8
Middlesbrough	16	16	13	11	12	11	13	13	12	15	12	15	13	13	13	13	12	12	12	13	13	13	12	10	11	10	11	11	13	16	13	14	13	14	14	14	14
Norwich C	18	20	16	18	18	19	20	19	18	19	17	20	18	18	19	19	19	20	20	20	20	20	20	20	20	21	20	21	21	20	21	20	19	19	19	20	20
Nottingham F	5	6	4	2	5	8	6	5	4	3	3	7	8	8	8	8	7	5	5	7	8	8	8	8	8	6	5	5	3	5	3	6	6	8	4	5	7
Southampton	2	2	2	3	7	9	10	10	11	14	15	14	12	12	9	10	9	8	8	6	6	6	4	4	5	5	7	6	6	3	4	4	4	3	6	6	6
Stoke C	22	17	19	16	13	14	12	12	13	13	14	12	11	11	11	11	11	11	11	11	12	12	13	13	10	14	15	15	15	11	12	13	12	12	11	11	11
Sunderland	4	3	7	8	6	10	8	8	9	10	11	11	14	16	18	17	18	17	17	16	18	18	17	18	16	17	17	17	17	14	16	17	17	16	17	16	17
Tottenham H	7	8	9	10	11	12	11	11	10	9	10	9	9	10	12	9	10	10	10	9	7	7	7	7	7	7	8	8	8	8	8	8	9	9	9	9	10
WBA	12	7	12	13	10	7	5	6	6	6	6	8	6	4	5	7	8	6	6	5	4	4	5	5	4	4	4	3	4	4	5	3	3	4	5	4	4
Wolverhampton W	9	12	15	17	19	17	17	16	17	16	16	16	17	14	14	14	15	19	19	17	17	17	16	16	18	18	18	18	18	17	17	16	16	17	20	19	18

DIVISION 2 LEAGUE POSITION PROGRESS CHART

	1980																		1981																		
	Aug 31	7	Sept 14	21	28	5	Oct 12	19	26	2	9	Nov 16	23	30	7	Dec 14	21	28	4	Jan 11	18	25	1	Feb 8	15	22	1	8	Mar 15	22	29	5	Apr 12	19	26	May 3	Final Position
Blackburn R	1	1	1	1	1	1	3	3	5	5	5	6	7	6	7	8	7	7	7	7	6	7	5	7	4	5	5	5	4	3	4	5	3	3	3	4	4
Bolton W	15	8	9	12	13	16	13	14	12	10	12	16	17	13	10	12	15	14	14	16	17	14	15	14	15	16	15	15	15	18	15	15	15	15	15	18	18
Bristol C	18	21	22	22	22	22	21	21	21	21	20	21	21	21	21	21	21	21	21	21	21	21	21	21	21	21	21	21	21	21	21	21	21	21	21	21	21
Bristol R	20	22	21	21	21	21	22	22	22	22	22	22	22	22	22	22	22	22	22	22	22	22	22	22	22	22	22	22	22	22	22	22	22	22	22	22	22
Cambridge U	4	10	15	18	20	17	10	8	11	14	11	8	8	9	8	9	9	10	10	11	9	10	10	12	10	11	9	11	10	10	9	11	11	12	17	13	13
Cardiff C	11	16	13	10	14	12	16	18	18	20	21	15	14	14	16	16	19	17	17	17	16	17	18	19	19	20	17	17	18	19	19	19	19	20	19	19	19
Chelsea	16	20	14	14	11	9	6	6	3	3	3	3	2	2	2	2	2	3	3	3	4	4	3	3	3	3	7	4	6	5	6	10	9	9	10	12	12
Derby Co	2	2	2	6	7	5	8	9	8	9	8	11	9	8	5	6	8	5	5	4	5	5	6	4	5	6	6	6	8	9	5	9	8	8	6	6	6
Grimsby T	5	12	16	19	19	14	18	16	19	18	19	20	19	18	12	11	11	11	11	10	8	9	7	8	6	4	4	8	3	4	3	4	6	7	7	7	7
Luton T	12	11	18	11	12	13	19	19	14	11	13	10	11	11	11	10	10	6	6	6	7	8	8	6	8	10	11	9	7	8	7	8	5	5	5	5	5
Newcastle U	21	14	8	9	8	10	9	10	9	8	9	9	10	10	13	14	13	16	16	15	13	13	13	13	13	13	13	14	12	13	12	13	12	11	11	10	11
Notts Co	6	3	4	3	3	2	2	1	1	1	1	2	3	3	3	3	4	4	4	5	3	3	2	2	2	2	2	2	2	2	2	2	2	2	2	2	2
Oldham Ath	10	6	5	7	6	8	11	11	16	16	18	19	20	20	20	19	18	20	20	20	20	20	17	16	16	17	18	19	17	17	17	17	17	18	18	15	15
Orient	9	5	10	13	9	6	7	7	7	7	7	7	5	7	9	7	5	8	8	9	10	11	12	11	12	12	12	12	13	14	13	12	13	14	16	17	17
Preston NE	19	13	17	16	15	18	17	12	15	13	10	13	12	15	18	20	20	18	18	18	19	19	20	18	18	19	19	18	19	20	20	20	20	19	20	20	20
QPR	8	15	19	20	17	19	12	13	20	19	17	12	13	12	17	17	14	12	12	12	12	12	11	9	11	8	10	10	11	11	10	7	10	10	8	8	8
Sheffield W	3	9	6	5	4	4	4	5	6	6	6	4	4	4	6	5	6	9	9	8	11	6	9	10	9	7	3	3	5	6	8	6	7	6	9	9	10
Shrewsbury T	22	18	20	17	16	15	20	20	17	17	16	14	15	16	14	15	17	19	19	19	18	18	19	20	20	18	20	20	20	16	18	18	18	17	14	14	14
Swansea C	13	7	7	4	5	7	5	4	4	4	4	5	6	5	4	4	3	2	2	2	2	2	4	5	7	9	8	7	9	7	11	3	4	4	4	3	3
Watford	14	19	12	15	18	20	15	15	13	15	15	17	18	19	19	18	16	15	15	14	14	15	14	15	14	14	14	13	14	12	14	14	16	13	12	11	9
West Ham U	7	4	3	2	2	3	1	2	2	2	2	1	1	1	1	1	1	1	1	1	1	1	1	1	1	1	1	1	1	1	1	1	1	1	1	1	1
Wrexham	17	17	11	8	10	11	14	17	10	12	14	18	16	17	15	13	12	13	13	13	15	16	16	17	17	15	16	16	16	15	16	16	14	16	13	16	16

DIVISION 3 LEAGUE POSITION PROGRESS CHART

	1980																		1981																	
	Aug	Sept				Oct				Nov					Dec				Jan				Feb				Mar					Apr				May	Final Position
	31	7	14	21	28	5	12	19	26	2	9	16	23	30	7	14	21	28	4	11	18	25	1	8	15	22	1	8	15	22	29	5	12	19	26	3	
Barnsley	9	17	10	6	11	12	12	10	7	8	3	3	3	2	2	2	2	2	2	2	2	2	2	4	4	4	5	4	5	5	4	4	3	2	3	2	2
Blackpool	12	10	10	18	17	10	7	8	13	15	16	16	16	16	17	17	19	22	22	22	22	22	22	23	23	23	23	23	23	23	23	23	23	23	23	23	23
Brentford	11	8	13	9	9	9	6	10	12	9	11	12	12	14	13	13	14	14	13	14	13	11	11	10	11	10	10	10	10	11	12	11	10	9	9	9	9
Burnley	20	18	14	12	5	4	3	5	4	4	7	6	6	6	4	4	3	4	4	5	5	5	7	6	7	7	7	7	7	7	8	8	7	7	8	8	8
Carlisle U	23	23	24	20	23	24	24	24	23	22	22	22	22	23	21	21	23	23	23	23	23	23	23	22	21	22	22	22	22	20	16	15	14	19	16	18	19
Charlton Ath	3	5	1	10	12	13	9	6	2	1	1	1	1	1	1	1	1	1	1	1	1	1	1	2	2	1	1	1	1	1	1	2	2	3	2	3	3
Chester	21	19	22	22	20	18	13	13	14	17	15	14	14	15	12	11	12	10	10	10	11	12	13	12	12	12	14	12	14	13	13	13	16	14	20	19	18
Chesterfield	10	6	8	4	2	3	1	1	1	2	2	2	2	5	3	3	4	6	6	6	6	6	5	7	6	6	6	6	5	4	5	5	5	6	7	6	5
Colchester U	22	22	21	15	15	20	17	17	19	18	18	15	15	13	15	15	13	12	14	12	15	14	15	16	15	14	12	14	17	14	17	19	21	21	22	22	22
Exeter C	2	3	3	3	3	5	7	12	10	13	12	10	10	9	10	10	10	8	8	9	8	8	9	9	10	11	11	11	11	10	10	9	9	10	11	11	11
Fulham	6	8	5	5	10	15	20	21	18	20	19	19	19	19	18	18	18	15	17	18	20	21	20	19	18	17	13	16	13	16	14	14	13	11	12	12	13
Gillingham	15	14	12	17	16	21	18	19	16	16	17	17	17	17	19	19	17	21	20	21	19	17	17	18	19	19	20	19	21	19	19	17	17	18	13	14	15
Huddersfield T	16	12	16	13	13	8	4	2	6	5	6	5	5	4	5	5	6	5	5	4	4	4	4	3	3	3	3	3	3	3	3	3	4	4	4	4	4
Hull C	14	20	20	19	18	19	22	23	24	24	24	24	24	24	24	24	24	24	24	24	24	24	24	24	24	24	24	24	24	24	24	24	24	24	24	24	24
Millwall	16	13	18	16	19	17	14	18	20	21	20	21	21	21	22	22	20	19	18	16	16	16	16	15	16	15	18	13	12	12	11	12	11	12	14	15	16
Newport Co	7	11	15	21	24	22	19	20	21	14	14	18	18	18	16	16	16	17	15	17	17	18	19	17	17	18	16	15	16	17	21	20	20	20	15	16	12
Oxford U	18	21	19	23	21	16	21	16	17	19	21	20	20	20	20	20	22	20	21	20	18	20	18	20	22	21	21	21	20	18	15	18	19	17	19	13	14
Plymouth Arg	8	4	4	1	1	1	2	3	3	7	8	8	8	8	8	8	9	11	12	13	10	9	8	8	8	9	8	8	8	8	7	7	8	8	5	7	7
Portsmouth	1	2	7	6	4	6	11	7	8	10	5	7	7	7	7	7	7	7	7	7	7	7	6	5	5	5	4	5	4	6	6	6	6	5	6	5	6
Reading	5	7	6	11	7	7	10	14	11	11	10	11	11	11	11	12	11	13	11	8	9	10	10	11	9	8	9	9	9	9	9	10	12	13	10	10	10
Rotherham U	19	16	17	8	6	2	5	4	5	3	4	4	4	3	6	6	5	3	3	3	3	3	3	1	1	2	2	2	2	2	2	1	1	1	1	1	1
Sheffield U	4	1	2	2	8	11	15	9	9	6	9	9	9	10	9	9	8	9	9	11	12	13	14	13	14	16	15	18	15	15	18	16	15	15	17	21	21
Swindon T	24	24	23	24	22	23	23	22	22	23	23	23	23	22	23	23	21	18	19	19	21	19	21	21	20	20	19	20	19	21	22	21	18	16	18	17	17
Walsall	13	14	9	14	14	14	16	15	15	12	13	13	13	12	14	14	15	16	16	15	14	15	12	14	13	13	17	17	18	22	20	22	22	22	21	20	20

DIVISION 4 LEAGUE POSITION PROGRESS CHART

	1980																		1981																		
	Aug 31	7	Sept 14	21	28	5	Oct 12	19	26	2	9	Nov 16	23	30	7	Dec 14	21	28	4	Jan 11	18	25	1	Feb 8	15	22	1	Mar 8	15	22	29	5	Apr 12	19	26	May 3	Final Position
Aldershot	6	5	3	1	1	2	3	4	4	4	5	4	4	5	5	5	7	7	6	7	7	7	7	7	7	6	7	5	5	5	7	7	5	7	6	6	6
Bournemouth	17	17	15	11	7	15	9	12	16	9	15	17	17	14	17	17	20	17	19	16	12	12	10	9	8	8	5	7	7	9	9	9	8	10	11	12	13
Bradford C	14	11	16	8	11	7	14	11	14	12	9	7	7	7	7	7	8	8	10	9	9	10	12	12	13	15	15	10	11	13	13	14	15	15	15	14	14
Bury	18	23	17	24	22	21	22	23	23	22	22	22	22	22	22	22	22	20	21	19	19	20	20	20	19	18	18	18	18	18	18	17	17	12	13	13	12
Crewe Alex	22	22	23	17	13	13	7	10	8	11	11	10	10	12	11	12	11	12	13	13	16	17	17	18	16	16	16	16	16	14	16	15	16	17	18	18	18
Darlington	9	13	10	15	19	19	21	21	21	15	17	12	12	17	14	16	13	10	9	10	10	9	9	11	10	13	13	14	12	8	8	8	9	8	8	9	8
Doncaster R	23	14	13	5	4	5	5	6	6	6	6	8	8	8	8	8	6	5	5	5	4	5	5	5	4	4	3	3	3	3	3	4	3	4	4	4	3
Halifax T	12	15	14	19	23	24	24	24	24	23	23	23	23	23	23	23	24	23	23	23	23	22	22	22	23	23	23	23	23	23	22	22	23	24	23	22	23
Hartlepool U	6	9	6	6	10	6	8	7	9	5	4	3	3	3	4	4	3	4	4	4	6	4	4	4	5	5	6	9	10	10	10	10	10	9	9	7	9
Hereford U	21	24	24	23	21	20	23	22	22	24	24	24	24	24	24	24	23	24	24	24	24	24	23	24	24	24	24	24	24	24	24	24	24	23	24	24	22
Lincoln C	1	1	1	2	3	1	2	2	2	2	2	2	2	2	2	2	2	2	2	2	2	2	2	2	2	2	2	2	2	2	2	2	2	2	2	2	2
Mansfield T	4	3	7	7	5	9	6	5	3	3	3	6	6	4	3	3	4	3	3	3	3	3	3	3	3	3	4	4	4	4	5	6	7	6	7	8	7
Northampton T	24	18	19	20	20	23	17	13	15	13	14	18	18	15	12	13	9	13	11	11	11	11	13	14	12	14	14	15	14	15	14	13	13	14	12	10	10
Peterborough U	5	4	4	4	6	4	4	3	5	7	7	5	5	6	6	6	5	6	7	6	5	6	6	6	6	7	9	8	8	7	4	5	6	5	5	5	5
Port Vale	16	20	21	22	24	22	16	20	17	18	21	21	21	21	21	21	21	22	22	22	22	23	24	23	22	22	22	21	22	21	19	19	20	19	20	20	19
Rochdale	11	6	5	14	18	16	18	15	13	14	13	13	13	11	15	9	10	11	8	8	8	8	8	8	11	11	12	11	15	16	15	16	14	13	14	15	15
Scunthorpe U	20	21	22	16	15	11	13	18	18	20	18	19	19	20	20	20	18	19	20	20	20	19	18	17	18	17	17	17	17	17	17	18	18	18	17	16	16
Southend U	2	2	2	3	2	3	1	1	1	1	1	1	1	1	1	1	1	1	1	1	1	1	1	1	1	1	1	1	1	1	1	1	1	1	1	1	1
Stockport Co	13	8	10	9	12	14	15	19	11	16	12	16	16	13	16	18	19	21	18	21	21	21	21	21	21	20	19	20	20	19	20	20	21	21	19	19	20
Torquay U	8	10	8	12	8	10	20	14	12	19	16	14	14	10	10	11	15	15	15	18	15	14	14	15	15	12	10	12	9	12	12	12	12	16	16	17	17
Tranmere R	15	19	20	20	17	8	12	8	7	8	8	11	11	16	13	15	17	16	16	17	14	16	15	16	17	19	20	19	19	20	21	21	19	20	21	21	21
Wigan Ath	19	16	18	10	16	18	11	17	19	17	20	20	20	19	19	14	16	14	14	15	18	15	16	13	14	10	11	13	13	11	11	11	11	11	10	11	11
Wimbledon	9	12	9	13	9	12	10	9	10	10	10	9	9	9	9	10	12	9	12	12	13	13	11	10	9	9	8	6	6	6	6	3	4	3	3	3	4
York C	3	7	12	18	14	17	18	16	20	21	19	15	15	18	18	19	14	18	17	14	17	18	19	19	20	21	21	22	21	22	23	23	22	22	22	23	24

THE FOOTBALL LEAGUE

Featuring full details of each of the 92 clubs in the Football League.

Officials, statistics, ground information, full 1980–81 League record and career details of the players.

THE FOOTBALL LEAGUE OFFICIALS

President

J. J. Dunnett MA (Cantab), LLB, MP
(*Notts County*)

Vice-Presidents

R. W. Lord (*Burnley*)
R. Wragg (*Sheffield United*)

Management Committee

J. F. Wiseman (*Birmingham City*)
Sir Matt Busby (*Manchester United*)
Dr C. S. Grossmark (*Gillingham*)
G. H. C. Needler (*Hull City*)
R. Daniel (*Plymouth Argyle*)
Sir Arthur South JP (*Norwich City*)
B. B. Winston (*Orient*)

Life Members

F. A. Would (*Grimsby Town*)
E. M. Gliksten (*Charlton Athletic*)
L. T. Shipman CBE (*Leicester City*)
Lord Westwood

Secretary

R. H. G. Kelly FCIS

Deputy Secretary

G. E. Readle MBE

Assistant Secretary

N. J. Thomas FCA

INTRODUCTION TO CLUB SECTION

For the first time in the history of *Rothmans Football Yearbook*, there is a major alteration in the listing of career totals for Football League players. On the fourth page of each club's section, the accumulative figures of League appearances include both full appearances and those made as a substitute.

However, in order that these figures can be broken down each season, they will continue to be split on the third page of the club's section as in previous years. For example, the 29+1s will still be shown on page three, but will go forward to page four as 30 – to be added to any previous total for that particular player.

It should be stressed that these substitute appearances are confined only to those players who actually appeared in the match in question and not to nominated substitutes who did not get on to the field of play during the game.

The actual players' appearances have been checked and re-checked while this change has been effected. Wherever discovered, alterations from previous years, including changes in goalscorers, have been included.

Over the years there have been a number of queries raised concerning the attendance figures which appear on these club pages. Those which feature on page two of each club are taken either from press sources at the time of the match or from estimated figures. But the final attendance figures for the season, which also incorporate the club's average crowd at home, are those officially supplied by the Football League.

On page four of the club section, the asterisk * which appears with the name of a player means that he was given a free transfer by that club at the end of the 1980–81 season. The list of players on the club's page four is based on the retained list. Any subsequent transfers appear under the section provided elsewhere in the yearbook, and the record of such players will appear under their former club. The asterisk against a number on page three of the club section denotes the player substituted. In the Scottish League, the additional dagger refers to the second substituted player.

Because of the pressure of space, it is not possible to include a list of apprentices, non-contract players and associated schoolboys retained by clubs, but those under these categories who made appearances in the Football League during 1980–81 are included.

ALDERSHOT — Division 4

Chairman: R. J. Driver.

Vice-Chairman: F. G. Wiltshire FSVA.

Directors: R. H. Lamarre, A. English, L. Kennett.

Team Manager: Len Walker.

Secretary/Commercial Manager: M. A. Cosway.

Assistant Manager: Dave Turner.

Year Formed: 1926. *Turned Professional:* 1927.

Limited Company: 1927

Football League Record:
1932 Elected to Division 3(S); 1958–73 Division 4; 1973–76 Division 3; 1976– Division 4.

Honours: *Football League:* best season: 8th, Division 3, 1973–74. *FA Cup* best season: 5th rd, 1932–33, 5th rd replay, 1978–79. *Football League Cup:* never past 2nd rd.

Record Victory: 8-1 v Gateshead, Division 4, 13 Sept, 1958.

Record Defeat: 0-9 v Bristol C, Division 3(S), 28 Dec, 1946.

Most League Points: 57, Division 4, 1978–79.

Most League Goals: 83, Division 4, 1963–64.

Highest League Scorer in Season: John Dungworth, 26, Division 4, 1978–79.

Most League Goals in Total Aggregate: Jack Howarth, 171, 1965–71; 1972–77.

Most Capped Player: Peter Scott, 1 (10), Northern Ireland.

Most League Appearances: Len Walker, 450, 1964–76.

Record Transfer Fee Received: £100,000 from Shrewsbury T for John Dungworth, Nov 1979.

Record Transfer Fee Paid: £54,000 to Portsmouth for Colin Garwood, Feb 1980.

Previous Managers since the War: Bill McCracken, Gordon Clark, Harry Evans, Dave Smith, Tommy McAnearney, Jimmy Melia, Cliff Huxford, Tommy McAnearney.

Address of Supporters Club: 213 High St, Aldershot.

Recreation Ground, High St, Aldershot GU11 1TW. Telephone Aldershot 20211. *Record attendance:* 19,138 v Carlisle U, FA Cup 4th rd replay, 28 January, 1970. *Record receipts:* £11,850 v Shrewsbury T, FA Cup 5th rd, 20 February, 1979. *Ground capacity:* 16,000 (14,000 under cover).

How to get there: Aldershot railway station is on the main line from London's Waterloo; the ground is five minutes walk from the station. Many buses run from the town centre on match days.

Match tickets: Can be booked in advance by telephoning ground. Available 2 weeks prior to match.

Car parking: Car parks within ¾ mile of the ground.

Entertainments/catering facilities: Members' club, Sportsman's club.

Club shop: Run by Supporters' Club; sells all types of souvenirs.

Handbooks/programmes: Programmes only available on sale.

Extra information: Harry Brooks scored five goals for Aldershot in each of two successive FA Cup ties in the 1945–46 season.

Club Colours: Red and blue striped shirts, blue edge on collar and cuffs, blue shorts, red stockings with two blue hoops.

Change Colours: White shirts, red edge on collar and cuffs, white shorts with blue stripe, white stockings with two blue hoops.

Club Captain: Joe Jopling.

Trainer: John Anderson.

Coach:

Club Nickname: Shots.

ALDEF ˉHOT 1980–81 LEAGUE RECORD

Match No.	Date	Venue	Opponents	Result	H/T Score	Goalscorers	Attendance
1	Aug 16	A	Scunthorpe U	D 2-2	0-1	Brodie, Garwood	1325
2	19	H	Wimbledon	W 2-0	1-0	Brodie 2	2922
3	23	H	Crewe Alex	W 2-0	2-0	Brodie 2	2640
4	30	A	Wigan Ath	L 0-1	0-1		4300
5	Sept 5	H	Bury	W 1-0	1-0	Brodie	3100
6	13	A	Port Vale	W 1-0	1-0	McGregor	2370
7	17	A	Lincoln C	W 1-0	1-0	Garwood	4331
8	20	H	Mansfield T	W 1-0	1-0	Robinson	3607
9	27	A	Darlington	W 2-1	2-1	Brodie, Garwood	1933
10	30	H	Lincoln C	D 0-0	0-0		4970
11	Oct 4	A	Hartlepool U	L 0-1	0-1		2844
12	7	H	AFC Bournemouth	D 0-0	0-0		3780
13	11	H	Rochdale	D 0-0	0-0		3017
14	17	A	Tranmere R	L 1-3	1-1	Jopling	2312
15	21	A	Northampton T	L 0-2	0-0		3194
16	25	H	Doncaster R	W 1-0	1-0	Robinson	2988
17	28	H	Torquay U	W 2-1	2-0	Garwood, French	2892
18	Nov 1	A	Bradford C	L 0-1	0-1		2279
19	4	A	AFC Bournemouth	W 2-0	0-0	Crosby, Brodie	3477
20	8	H	Peterborough U	D 0-0	0-0		3057
21	11	A	Wimbledon	L 0-4	0-1		2538
22	15	H	Scunthorpe U	D 0-0	0-0		2512
23	29	A	Stockport Co	L 0-1	0-0		1818
24	Dec 6	H	Halifax T	W 2-1	1-0	Robinson, Sanford	2335
25	20	A	York C	L 1-4	0-1	Sanford	1583
26	26	H	Hereford U	W 4-0	1-0	Sanford 4	3094
27	27	A	Southend U	L 0-3	0-2		6828
28	Jan 3	H	Northampton T	D 0-0	0-0		2992
29	10	A	Doncaster R	L 1-3	0-1	Crosby	4502
30	17	H	Stockport Co	W 3-0	1-0	Hampshire 2, McGregor	2020
31	24	H	Wigan Ath	L 0-1	0-1		2932
32	31	A	Crewe Alex	D 0-0	0-0		2455
33	Feb 7	H	Port Vale	D 0-0	0-0		2598
34	14	A	Bury	D 0-0	0-0		2576
35	21	H	Darlington	W 2-1	1-0	Garwood (pen), Lucas	2046
36	Mar 7	H	Hartlepool U	W 2-1	2-0	Robinson, Garwood	2252
37	14	A	Rochdale	W 2-0	0-0	Sanford, Garwood	1832
38	22	H	Tranmere R	W 3-2	2-1	Sanford, Lucas, Garwood	4493
39	29	A	Torquay U	L 0-2	0-2		2086
40	Apr 4	H	Bradford C	D 1-1	0-0	Robinson	2255
41	6	A	Mansfield T	W 2-1	0-0	Sanford, Robinson	2748
42	11	A	Peterborough U	D 0-0	0-0		4783
43	18	H	Southend U	L 1-2	0-2	Bennett	4433
44	20	A	Hereford U	D 0-0	0-0		2946
45	25	H	York C	D 1-1	1-0	Sanford	1813
46	May 2	A	Halifax T	L 0-1	0-1		1587

Final League Position: 6

Goalscorers

League (43): Sanford 10, Brodie 8, Garwood 8 (1 pen), Robinson 6, Crosby 2, Hampshire 2, Lucas 2, McGregor 2, Bennett 1, French 1, Jopling 1.
League Cup (3): Garwood 2, Brodie.
F.A. Cup (0).

League Cup	First Round	Wimbledon (h)	2-0
		(a)	1-4
FA Cup	First Round	Oxford U (a)	0-1

Johnson	Edwards	Wooler	Briley	Bennett	Jopling	Lucas	Brodie	Garwood	Crosby	Robinson	McGregor	Sanford	French	Scott	Horn	Youlden	Tomlin	Hampshire	*Match No.*
1	2	3	4	5	6	7	8	9	10	11									1
1	2	3	4	5	6		8	9	10	11	7								2
1	2	3	4	5	6		8	9*	10	11	7	12							3
1	2	3	4	5	6	11*	8		10		7		9	12					4
1	2	3	4	5	6	12	8		10	11*	7		9						5
1	2	3	4	5	6*	11	10	9	8		7			12					6
1	2	3	4	5	6		8	9	10	11*	7			12					7
1	2	3	4	5	6	12	8	9*	10	11	7								8
1	2	3	4	5*	6		8	9	10	11	7			12					9
1	2	3	4		6		8	9	10	11	7			5					10
1	2	3	4		6		8	9	10	11	7			5					11
1	2	3	4		6	11	8	9	10		7			5					12
1	2	3	4		6		8	9	10	11	7			5					13
1	2	3	4		6		8	9	10	11	7			5					14
	2	3	4		6		8*	9	10	11	7			5	1	12			15
	2*	3	4		6			9	10	11	7		8	5	1	12			16
1		3	4	12	6			9	10	11	7*		8	2		5			17
		3	4	5	6	7		9	10	11			8	2	1				18
		3	4	6			11	9	10	12			8	2	1	5	7*		19
1		3	4	6		7*	11	9	10		12		8	2		5			20
1		3	4	6		7	11	9	10				8	2		5			21
1	2	3	4	5	6	7	11	9	10				8						22
1	2	3	4		6		8		10	11	7		9			5			23
1	2	3	4		6			9	10	11		8				5	7		24
1	2	3	4	6				9	10	11		8		12		5*	7		25
1	2	3	4*	5	6	12		9	10	11		8					7		26
1	2	3		5	6	7		9	10	11		8		4					27
1	2	3	4	5	6	12		9*	10	11		8					7		28
1	2	3	4	5	6	9			10	11		8*		7		12			29
1	2	3	4	5	6	7			10		11	9						8	30
1	2	3	4	5	6	7			10	11*		9				12		8	31
1	2	3	4		6	7		8*	10			9		11		5		12	32
1	2	3	4		6	7			10		12	9*		11		5		8	33
1	2	3	4		6	7		11	10			9		8		5			34
1	2	3	4		6	7		11	10			9		8		5			35
1	2	3	4		6	7		11		10		9		8		5			36
1	2	3	4		6	7		11		10		9		8		5			37
1	2*	3	4		6	7		11		10		9		8		5			38
1	2*	3	4		6	7		11	12	10		9		8		5			39
1		3	4		6	7		11	2	10		9		8		5			40
1	2	3	4	5	6	7			10	11		9		8					41
1	2	3	4	5	6	7*		12	10	11		9		8					42
1	2	3	4	5	6	7		12	10*	11		9		8					43
1	2	3		5	6	7	10		8	11*	12	9		4					44
1	2	3	11	5	6	7	10		8*		12	9		4					45
1	2	3	11	5	6	7	10		8		12	9		4*					46
42	39	46	44	27	42	27	23	33	43	32	18	23	10	29	4	16	5	3	
				+ 1s		+ 4s		+ 2s	+ 1s	+ 1s	+ 6s	+ 1s		+ 5s		+ 4s		+ 1s	

ALDERSHOT

	Ht	Wt	Birthplace	Clubs	League App.	League Gls
Goalkeepers						
Glen Johnson	6 2	13 6	Barrow	Arsenal	—	—
				Doncaster R	95	—
				Walsall (on loan)	3	—
				Aldershot	334	—
Graham Horn	6 2	14 1	Westminster	Arsenal	—	—
				Portsmouth (on loan)	22	—
				Luton T	58	—
				Brentford (on loan)	3	—
				Charlton Ath	—	—
				Kettering T	(not known)	
				Southend U	9	—
				Aldershot	7	—
Defenders						
Tommy Youlden*	6 1	12 9	London	Arsenal	—	—
				Portsmouth	90	1
				Reading	163	3
				Aldershot	123	1
Joe Jopling	6 0	12 13	South Shields	Aldershot	35	2
				Leicester C	3	—
				Torquay U (on loan)	6	—
				Aldershot	235	8
Alan Wooler	6 0	11 0	Poole	Reading	38	—
(Contract cancelled April 1981)				West Ham	4	—
				Aldershot	204	3
Peter Scott	5 10	11 4	Liverpool	Everton	44	1
(N. Ireland)				Southport (on loan)	4	—
				York C	100	4
				Aldershot	54	1
Nigel Edwards	5 11	11 10	Wrexham	Chester	290	15
				Rotherham U (on loan)	—	—
				Aldershot	95	5
Paul Bennett	6 0	12 6	Southampton	Southampton	116	1
				Reading	105	3
				Aldershot	67	1
Midfield						
Malcolm Crosby	5 9	11 0	South Shields	Aldershot	280	21
Les Briley	5 6	9 11	London	Chelsea	—	—
				Hereford U	61	2
				Wimbledon	61	2
				Aldershot	56	—
Stuart Robinson	5 7	10 5	Middlesbrough	Newcastle U	12	2
				Aldershot	33	6
Forwards						
Colin Garwood	5 9	10 13	Heacham	Peterborough U	66	31
				Oldham Ath	92	36
				Huddersfield T	28	8
				Colchester U	87	25
				Portsmouth	71	34
				Aldershot	51	18
Murray Brodie	6 0	12 13	Glasgow	Leicester C	3	2
				Aldershot	398	78
Alex McGregor	5 10	10 8	Glasgow	Ayr U	29	1
				Hibernian	—	—
				Shrewsbury T	49	7
				Aldershot	170	17
Andy Needham	5 11	11 6	Oldham	Birmingham C	3	1
(Contract cancelled Oct 1980)				Blackburn R	5	—
				Aldershot	95	29
David Tomlin*	5 10	11 9	Nuneaton	Leicester C	27	2
				Torquay U	38	2
				Aldershot	30	2
Brian Lucas	5 7	10 12	Farnborough	Aldershot	44	3
Mickey French	6 0	12 4	Eastbourne	QPR	—	—
				Brentford	65	16
				Swindon T	10	1
				Doncaster R	36	5
				Aldershot	43	6
Paul Hampshire	5 6	10 7	Guildford	Aldershot	4	2
Mark Sanford	6 0	11 8	London	Aldershot	30	10
Michael Milsom*			Basingstoke	Aldershot	—	—

ARSENAL Division 1

Chairman: D. J. C. Hill-Wood MC, MA.

Directors: Sir Robert Bellinger CBE,DSC, S. C. McIntyre MBE, FCIS, The Rev N. F. Bone TD, P. D. Hill-Wood, A. Wood, R. G. Gibbs, C. E. B. L. Carr, R. C. L. Carr.

Manager: Terry Neill. *Secretary:* K. J. Friar.

Assistant Manager/Chief Scout: Wilf Dixon.

Chief Coach: Don Howe.

Year Formed: 1886. *Turned Professional:* 1891. *Limited Company:* 1893.

Former Names: 1886–91, Royal Arsenal; 1891–1914, Woolwich Arsenal.

Former Grounds: 1886–87, Plumstead Common; 1887–88, Sportsman Ground; 1888–90, Manor Ground; 1890–93, Invicta Ground; 1893–1913, Manor Ground; 1913– Highbury.

Football League Record:
1893 Elected to Division 2; 1904–13 Division 1; 1913–19 Division 2; 1919– Division 1.

Honours: *Football League:* Division 1 – Champions 1930–31, 1932–33, 1933-34, 1934–35, 1937–38, 1947–48, 1952–53, 1970–71; Runners-up 1925–26, 1931–32, 1972–73; Division 2 – Runners-up 1903–04. *FA Cup:* Winners 1929–30, 1935–36, 1949–50, 1970–71, 1978–79; Runners-up 1926–27, 1931–32, 1951–52, 1971–72, 1977–78, 1979–80. *Double Performed:* 1970–71. *League Cup:* Runners-up 1967–68, 1968–69. **European Competitions:** *Fairs Cup:* 1963–64, 1969–70 (winners), 1970–71. *European Cup:* 1971–72. *UEFA Cup:* 1978–79. *European Cup-Winners' Cup:* 1979–80 (runners-up).

Record Victory: 12–0 v Loughborough T, Division 2, 12 Mar, 1900.

Record Defeat: 0-8 v Loughborough T, Division 2, 12 Dec, 1896.

Most League Points: 66, Division 1, 1930–31.

Most League Goals: 127, Division 1, 1930–31.

Highest League Scorer in Season: Ted Drake, 42, 1934–35.

Most League Goals in Total Aggregate: Cliff Bastin, 150, 1930–47.

Most Capped Player: Pat Rice, 49, Northern Ireland.

Most League Appearances: George Armstrong, 500, 1960–77.

Record Transfer Fee Received: £1,250,000 from Crystal Palace for Clive Allen, August 1980.

Record Transfer Fee Paid: £1,250,000 to QPR for Clive Allen, June 1980.

Previous Managers since the War: George Allison, Tom Whittaker, Jack Crayston, George Swindin, Billy Wright, Bertie Mee.

Address of the Club Shop or Boutique: Gunners Shop, Arsenal Stadium, Highbury, N5.

Arsenal Stadium, Highbury, London N5. Telephone 01-226 0304. *Ground capacity:* 60,000. *Record attendance:* 73,295 v Sunderland, Div 1, 9 March, 1935. *Record receipts:* £116,498 v Juventus, Cup-Winners' Cup semi-final, 9 April, 1980. *Telegraphs:* 'Gunneretic London N5.' *Pitch measurements:* 110yd×71yd.

How to get there: Arsenal Underground Station (Piccadilly Line) is within one minute of the ground. Finsbury Park (Piccadilly and Victoria) and Drayton Park (Northern) are also within walking distance. Buses 4a, 19, 106, 141a, 236.

Match tickets: Postal application one calendar month prior to the match. Prices and availability of tickets can be checked with the club on their Ansafone Service 01-359 0131.

Car parking: Parking is allowed in the adjacent streets under the control of the Police.

Entertainments/catering facilities: West Stand restaurant is open Mon–Fri for the general public and on match days for ticket holders in the West Stand Upper tier. East Stand restaurant is open on match days only for ticket holders in the East Stand Upper tier. Reservations for both restaurants can be made by telephoning 01-226 4968. There are also extensive refreshment bars around the ground.

Club shop: Shop in Avenell Road, Highbury, is open Mon–Fri 9.30 am–5 pm. On Saturday first team matches it is open from 1.00 pm–5.30 pm. Other shops in the ground are open on match days.

Handbooks/programmes: Handbooks and programmes can be obtained from the club shop. Programmes available on subscription.

Club Colours: Red shirts with white sleeves, white shorts, red and white stockings.

Change Colours: Yellow shirts with blue shorts, yellow stockings.

Club Captain: David O'Leary.

Club Nickname: Gunners.

ARSENAL 1980–81 LEAGUE RECORD

Match No.	Date	Venue	Opponents	Result	H/T Score	Goalscorers	Attendance
1	Aug 16	A	WBA	W 1-0	1-0	Stapleton	22,364
2	19	H	Southampton	D 1-1	1-0	Stapleton	43,050
3	23	A	Coventry C	L 1-3	0-0	Stapleton	15,399
4	30	H	Tottenham H	W 2-0	0-0	Price, Stapleton	54,045
5	Sept 6	A	Manchester C	D 1-1	0-0	Young	32,233
6	13	H	Stoke C	W 2-0	0-0	Hollins, Sansom	27,183
7	20	A	Middlesbrough	L 1-2	1-1	Rix	14,680
8	27	H	Nottingham F	W 1-0	0-0	Rix	37,584
9	Oct 4	H	Leicester C	W 1-0	1-0	Stapleton	28,490
10	7	A	Birmingham C	L 1-3	1-2	Sunderland	15,511
11	11	A	Manchester U	D 0-0	0-0		49,036
12	18	H	Sunderland	D 2-2	1-0	Gatting, Young	32,135
13	21	H	Norwich C	W 3-1	1-0	Talbot, McDermott, Sansom	21,839
14	25	A	Liverpool	D 1-1	0-0	Sunderland	40,310
15	Nov 1	H	Brighton & HA	W 2-0	0-0	Rix, McDermott	28,569
16	8	A	Leeds U	W 5-0	2-0	Hollins 2, Gatting, Talbot, Sunderland	20,855
17	11	A	Southampton	L 1-3	1-0	Rix	21,244
18	15	H	WBA	D 2-2	0-1	Sunderland, Batson (og)	25,855
19	22	H	Everton	W 2-1	2-0	McDermott, Stapleton	30,911
20	29	A	Aston Villa	D 1-1	0-0	Talbot	30,140
21	Dec 6	H	Wolverhampton W	D 1-1	1-1	Stapleton	26,050
22	13	A	Sunderland	L 0-2	0-1		21,595
23	20	H	Manchester U	W 2-1	1-0	Rix, Vaessen	33,730
24	26	A	Crystal Palace	D 2-2	1-1	Stapleton, McDermott	29,850
25	27	H	Ipswich T	D 1-1	1-0	Sunderland	42,818
26	Jan 10	A	Everton	W 2-1	0-0	Gatting, Vaessen	29,360
27	17	A	Tottenham H	L 0-2	0-1		32,994
28	31	H	Coventry C	D 2-2	1-1	Talbot, Stapleton	24,876
29	Feb 7	A	Stoke C	D 1-1	0-1	Stapleton	14,400
30	21	A	Nottingham F	L 1-3	1-2	Stapleton	25,357
31	24	H	Manchester C	W 2-0	0-0	Talbot, Sunderland	24,790
32	28	H	Middlesbrough	D 2-2	2-1	Stapleton, Hollins (pen)	24,504
33	Mar 7	A	Leicester C	L 0-1	0-1		20,198
34	21	A	Norwich C	D 1-1	0-1	Talbot	19,569
35	28	H	Liverpool	W 1-0	1-0	Sunderland	47,058
36	31	H	Birmingham C	W 2-1	1-0	Stapleton, O'Leary	17,431
37	Apr 4	A	Brighton & HA	W 1-0	1-0	Hollins	21,015
38	11	H	Leeds U	D 0-0	0-0		29,339
39	18	A	Ipswich T	W 2-0	1-0	Nicholas, Sansom	30,935
40	20	H	Crystal Palace	W 3-2	1-1	Talbot, Davis, Young	24,346
41	25	A	Wolverhampton W	W 2-1	1-1	Berry (og), Stapleton	15,160
42	May 2	H	Aston Villa	W 2-0	2-0	Young, McDermott	57,472

Final League Position: 3

Goalscorers

League (61): Stapleton 14, Sunderland 7, Talbot 7, Hollins 5 (1 pen), McDermott 5, Rix 5, Young 4, Gatting 3, Sansom 3, Vaessen 2, Davis 1, Nicholas 1, O'Leary 1, Price 1, own goals 2.
League Cup (7): Hollins 2 (1 pen), Stapleton 2, Sunderland 2, Walford 1.
F.A. Cup (0).

League Cup	Second Round	Swansea C (a)	1-1
		(h)	3-1
	Third Round	Stockport Co (a)	3-1
	Fourth Round	Tottenham H (a)	0-1
FA Cup	Third Round	Everton (a)	0-2

Jennings	Devine	Sansom	Talbot	O'Leary	Young	Vaessen	Price	Stapleton	Hollins	Rix	McDermott	Sunderland	Wood	Gatting	Walford	Rice	Davis	Nicholas	Nelson	*Match No.*
1	2	3	4	5	6	7	8	9	10	11										1
1	2	3	4*	5	6	8	10	9	7	11	12									2
1	2	3	4	5	6		10*	9	7	11		8				12				3
1	2	3	4	5	6		10	9	7	11		8								4
1	2	3	4	5	6		10	9	7	11		8								5
1	2	3	4	5	6		10	9	7	11		8								6
	2	3	4	5	6		10	9	7	11		8	1							7
	2	3	4	5	6			9	7	11		8	1	10						8
	2	3	4		6			9	7	11		8	1	10	5					9
	2	3	4		6			9	7	11		8	1	10	5					10
	2	3	4		6			9	7	11		8	1	10	5					11
	2	3	4*		6			9	7	11	12	8	1	10	5					12
	2	3	4		6			9	7*	11	12	8	1	10	5					13
	2	3	4		6		10*	9	7	11		8	1		5	12				14
	2	3	4		6			9	7	11	10	8	1		5					15
	2	3	4		6				7	11	10	8	1	9	5					16
	2	3	4		6		12		7	11	10	8	1	9*	5					17
1	2	3	4	5	6			9	7	11		8		10						18
1	2	3*	4	5				9	7	11	10	8		12	6					19
1	2	3	4		5			9	7	11		8		10	6					20
1	2	3	4		6	12		9	7*	11	8			10	5					21
1	2	3	4		6	12	7	9			8			10*	5		11			22
1	2	3	4		6	7		9		11	8			10	5					23
1	2	3	4		6	8		9	7	11	10				5					24
1	2	3	4		6			9	7	11		8		10	5					25
1	2	3			6	8	12	9	7*		11			10	5		4			26
1	2	3			6			9	7	11	4	8		10	5					27
1		3	4		6			9	2	11	7	8		10	5					28
1		3	4	5	6			9	2	11	7	8		10						29
1	12	3	4	5	6			9	2	11	10	8		7*						30
1	2	3	4	5	6			9	7	11		8		10						31
1	2	3	4	5				9	7	11	12	8*		10	6					32
1	2	3	4	5	6		12	9	7*	11		8		10						33
1	2	3	4	5	6			9		11	10	8						7		34
1	2	3	4	5	6			9	7*	11		8					12	10		35
1	2*	3	4	5	6			9		11	12	8					7	10		36
1	2	3	4	5	6			9	7	11		8					10			37
1	2	3	4	5	6			9	7*		12	8					11	10		38
1	2	3	4	5	6			9	7			8					11	10		39
1	2	3	4	5	6			9	7		12	8*					11	10		40
1	2	3	4	5	6			9	7		8						11	10		41
1		3	4*	5	6			9	2		7	8					11	10	12	42
31	38	42	40	24	40	5	9	40	38	35	16	34	11	22	20	—	9	8	—	
	+ 1s					+ 2s	+ 3s				+ 7s			+ 1s		+ 2s	+ 1s		+ 1s	

ARSENAL

	Ht	*Wt*	*Birthplace*	*Clubs*	*League App.*	*League Gls*
Goalkeepers						
Pat Jennings	6 0	12 6	Newry,	Watford	48	—
(N. Ireland)			Co. Down	Tottenham H	472	—
				Arsenal	149	—
Rhys Wilmot	6 1	12 0	Wales	Arsenal	—	—
George Wood	6 3	14 0	Douglas	East Stirling	22	—
(Scotland)				Blackpool	117	—
				Everton	103	—
				Arsenal	11	—
Defenders						
Sammy Nelson	5 10	11 0	Belfast	Arsenal	255	10
(N. Ireland)						
Willie Young	6 3	12 10	Edinburgh	Aberdeen	132	10
				Tottenham H	54	3
				Arsenal	160	11
David O'Leary	5 11	11 3	London	Arsenal	196	7
(Eire)						
John Devine	5 10½	12 1	Dublin	Arsenal	69	—
(Eire)						
Steve Gatting	5 11	11 11	Middlesex	Arsenal	58	5
Chris Whyte	6 1	11 10	London	Arsenal	—	—
Nicky Law*	5 11	12 7	London	Arsenal	—	—
Michael Pittaway*	5 10	11 0	London	Arsenal	—	—
Kenny Sansom	5 6	11 8	Camberwell	Crystal Palace	172	3
(England)				Arsenal	42	3
Midfield						
Graham Rix	5 9	11 0	Doncaster	Arsenal	158	15
(England)						
Richie Powling*	5 7	11 6	Barking	Arsenal	55	3
Liam Brady	5 7	10 7	Dublin	Arsenal	235	43
(Eire) (Transferred to Juventus July 1980)						
Brian Talbot	5 10	12 0	Ipswich	Ipswich T	177	25
(England)				Arsenal	102	8
John Hollins	5 8	11 7	Guildford	Chelsea	436	47
(England)				QPR	151	5
				Arsenal	64	6
Peter Nicholas	5 8½	11 8	Newport,	Crystal Palace	127	7
(Wales)			Gwent	Arsenal	8	1
Forwards						
Frank Stapleton	5 11	12 7	Dublin	Arsenal	225	75
(Eire)						
Alan Sunderland	5 9	11 6¼	Mexborough	Wolverhampton W	158	29
(England)				Arsenal	131	34
Brian McDermott	5 8	9 12	London	Arsenal	26	5
Paul Vaessen			Bermondsey	Arsenal	22	4
Brian Sparrow	5 7	10 2	London	Arsenal	—	—
Paul Davis	5 8	9 7	London	Arsenal	12	1

John Smith (Contract cancelled March 1981)
Also retained: David Cork, Paul Gorman, Raphael Meade, Danny O'Shea.
Free transfer: Chris Evans*.

ASTON VILLA — Division 1

Chairman: R. F. Bendall.
Vice Chairman: J. H. Kartz.
Directors: D. J. Bendall, A. T. Gill.
Manager: Ron Saunders. *Secretary:* Steven Stride.
Commercial Manager: Sue Walker. *Year Formed:* 1874.
Turned Professional: 1885. *Limited Company:* 1896.
Previous Grounds: 1874–76, Aston Park; 1876–97, Perry Barr; 1897– Villa Park.

Football League Record:
1888 Original Member of the League; 1936–38 Division 2; 1938–59 Division 1; 1959–60 Division 2; 1960–67 Division 1; 1967–70 Division 2; 1970–72 Division 3; 1972–75 Division 2; 1975– Division 1.

Honours: *Football League:* Division 1 – Champions 1893–94, 1895–96, 1896–97, 1898–99, 1899–1900, 1909–10, 1980–81; Runners-up 1888–89, 1902–03, 1907–08, 1910–11, 1912–13, 1913–14, 1930–31, 1932–33; Division 2 – Champions 1937–38, 1959–60; Runners-up 1974–75; Division 3 – Champions 1971–72. *FA Cup:* Winners 1887, 1895, 1897, 1905, 1913, 1920, 1957 (7 wins stands as the record); Runners-up 1892, 1924. *Double Performed:* 1896–97. *Football League Cup:* Winners 1961, 1975, 1977; Runners-up 1963, 1971. **European Competitions:** *UEFA Cup:* 1975–76, 1977–78.

Record Victory: 13-0 v Wednesbury Old Athletic, FA Cup 1st rd, 1886.

Record Defeat: 1-8 v Blackburn R, FA Cup 3rd rd, 1888–89.

Most League Points: 70, Division 3, 1971–72.

Most League Goals: 128, Division 1, 1930–31.

Highest League Scorer in Season: 49, 'Pongo' Waring, Division 1, 1930–31.

Most League Goals in Total Aggregate: 213, Harry Hampton, 1904–20, and Billy Walker, 1919–34.

Most Capped Player: Peter McParland, 33 (34), Northern Ireland.

Most League Appearances: 560, Charlie Aitken, 1961–76.

Record Transfer Fee Received: £1,469,000 (£1,175,000 basic fee) from Wolverhampton W for Andy Gray, Sept 1979.

Record Transfer Fee Paid: £500,000 to Newcastle U for Peter Withe, May 1980.

Previous Managers since the War: Alex Massie, George Martin, Eric Houghton, Joe Mercer, Dick Taylor, Tommy Cummings, Tommy Docherty, Vic Crowe.

Address of the Club Shop or Boutique: c/o Villa Park.

Villa Park, Trinity Rd, Birmingham B6 6HE. Telephone 021-327 6604. 24-hour answering service 021-328 1722. *Telegraphic Address:* 'Villa, Birmingham 6'. *Ground capacity:* 48,000. *Record attendance:* 76,588 v Derby Co, FA Cup 6th rd, 2 March, 1946. *Record receipts:* £167,753, FA Cup semi-final, Everton v West Ham U, 12 April, 1980. *Club record:* £90,000 UEFA Cup quarter-final v Barcelona, 1 Mar, 1978. *Pitch measurements:* 115yd×75yd.

How to get there: Bus 5 from Corporation Street to Witton Square. Special buses from Priory Ringway and Hall of Memory (city centre). Birmingham New Street railway station is near the centre. The ground is ½ mile from link to the motorway.

Match tickets: Applications for any games can be made by post or in person, any time during the season.

Car parking: Asda Car Park in Aston Hall Road. Side-street parking also available.

Entertainments/catering facilities: Many refreshment points around the ground.

Club shop: Adjacent to the ground; sells all types of souvenirs.

Handbooks/programmes: Programmes available on seasonal subscription.

Club Colours: Claret shirts with light blue trim, white shorts, blue stockings. *Change Colours:* White shirts with claret and light blue collar and cuffs, blue shorts, white stockings.
Club Nickname: The Villans.

ASTON VILLA 1980–81 LEAGUE RECORD

Match No.	Date	Venue	Opponents	Result	H/T Score	Goalscorers	Attendance
1	Aug 16	A	Leeds U	W 2-1	1-1	Morley, Shaw	23,401
2	20	H	Norwich C	W 1-0	0-0	Shaw	25,970
3	23	A	Manchester C	D 2-2	1-0	Withe 2	30,017
4	30	H	Coventry C	W 1-0	0-0	Shaw	20,050
5	Sept 6	A	Ipswich T	L 0-1	0-0		23,192
6	13	H	Everton	L 0-2	0-2		25,673
7	20	H	Wolverhampton W	W 2-1	1-0	Hughes (og), Geddis	26,881
8	27	A	Crystal Palace	W 1-0	0-0	Shaw	18,398
9	Oct 4	H	Sunderland	W 4-0	1-0	Evans 2, Morley, Shaw	26,914
10	8	A	Manchester U	D 3-3	1-2	Withe, Cowans (pen), Shaw	38,831
11	11	A	Birmingham C	W 2-1	1-0	Cowans (pen), Evans	33,879
12	18	H	Tottenham H	W 3-0	1-0	Morley 2, Withe	30,940
13	22	H	Brighton & HA	W 4-1	1-1	Mortimer, Withe, Bremner, Shaw	27,367
14	25	A	Southampton	W 2-1	1-0	Morley, Withe	21,249
15	Nov 1	H	Leicester C	W 2-0	0-0	Shaw, Cowans	29,953
16	8	A	WBA	D 0-0	0-0		34,001
17	12	A	Norwich C	W 3-1	0-1	Shaw 2, Evans	17,050
18	15	H	Leeds U	D 1-1	1-1	Shaw	29,106
19	22	A	Liverpool	L 1-2	0-0	Evans	48,114
20	29	H	Arsenal	D 1-1	0-0	Morley	30,140
21	Dec 6	A	Middlesbrough	L 1-2	0-0	Shaw	15,579
22	13	H	Birmingham C	W 3-0	0-0	Geddis 2, Shaw	41,101
23	20	A	Brighton & HA	L 0-1	0-1		16,425
24	26	H	Stoke C	W 1-0	1-0	Withe	34,658
25	27	A	Nottingham F	D 2-2	1-1	Lloyd (og), Shaw	33,930
26	Jan 10	H	Liverpool	W 2-0	1-0	Withe, Mortimer	47,960
27	17	A	Coventry C	W 2-1	0-0	Morley, Withe	27,020
28	31	H	Manchester C	W 1-0	1-0	Shaw	33,682
29	Feb 7	A	Everton	W 3-1	2-1	Morley, Mortimer, Cowans (pen)	31,434
30	21	H	Crystal Palace	W 2-1	1-0	Withe 2	27,203
31	28	A	Wolverhampton W	W 1-0	0-0	Withe	34,693
32	Mar 7	A	Sunderland	W 2-1	2-0	Evans, Mortimer	27,278
33	14	H	Manchester U	D 3-3	2-0	Withe 2, Shaw	42,182
34	21	A	Tottenham H	L 0-2	0-1		35,091
35	28	H	Southampton	W 2-1	2-1	Morley, Geddis	32,467
36	Apr 4	A	Leicester C	W 4-2	2-2	Withe 2, Bremner, Morley	26,032
37	8	H	WBA	W 1-0	0-0	Withe	47,998
38	14	H	Ipswich T	L 1-2	0-1	Shaw	47,495
39	18	H	Nottingham F	W 2-0	2-0	Cowans (pen), Withe	34,707
40	20	A	Stoke C	D 1-1	1-1	Withe	23,500
41	25	H	Middlesbrough	W 3-0	1-0	Shaw, Withe, Evans	38,018
42	May 2	A	Arsenal	L 0-2	0-2		57,472

Final League Position: 1

Goalscorers

League (72): Withe 20, Shaw 18, Morley 10, Evans 7, Cowans 5 (4 pens), Mortimer 4, Geddis 4, Bremner 2, own goals 2.
League Cup (5): Morley 2, Shaw 2, Withe 1.
F.A. Cup (0).

League Cup	Second Round	Leeds U (h)	1-0
		(a)	3-1
	Third Round	Cambridge U (a)	1-2
FA Cup	Third Round	Ipswich T (a)	0-1

Rimmer	Swain	Deacy	Williams	McNaught	Mortimer	Bremner	Shaw	Withe	Cowans	Morley	Gibson	Evans	Geddis	*Match No.*
1	2	3	4	5	6	7	8	9	10	11				1
1	2			5	6	7	8	9	10	11	3	4		2
1	2			5	6	7	8	9	10	11	3	4		3
1	2			5	6	7	8	9	10	11	3	4		4
1	2			5	6	7	8	9	10	11	3	4		5
1	2			5	6	7	8	9	10	11	3	4		6
1	2			5	6	7		9	10	11	3	4	8	7
1	2			5	6	7	8	9	10	11	3	4		8
1	2	12		5	6	7	8	9	10	11	3*	4		9
1	2	3		5	6	7	8	9	10	11		4		10
1	2	3		5	6	7	8	9	10	11		4		11
1	2			5	6	7	8	9	10	11	3	4		12
1	2			5	6	7	8	9	10	11	3	4		13
1	2	12		5	6	7	8	9	10	11*	3	4		14
1	2	3*	12	5	6	7	8	9	10	11		4		15
1	2		3	5	6	7	8	9	10	11		4		16
1	2		3	5	6	7	8	9	10	11		4		17
1	2		3	5	6	7	8	9	10	11		4		18
1	2		3	5	6	7	8	9	10	11		4		19
1	2		3	5	6	7	8	9	10	11		4		20
1	2		3	5	6	7	8		10	11		4	9	21
1	2		3	5	6	7	8		10	11		4	9	22
1	2	12	3	5	6	7	8		10	11		4	9*	23
1	2		3	5	6	7	8	9	10	11		4		24
1	2		3	5	6	7	8		10	11		4	9	25
1	2			5	6	7	8	9	10	11	3	4		26
1	2			5	6	7	8	9	10	11	3	4		27
1	2	3		5*	6	7	8	9	10	11		4	12	28
1	2		3	5	6	7	8	9	10	11		4		29
1	2		3*	5	6	7	8	9	10	11	12	4		30
1	2		3	5	6	7	8	9	10	11		4		31
1	2		3	5*	6	7	8	9	10	11	12	4		32
1	2		3	5	6	7	8	9	10	11		4		33
1	2		3	5	6	7	8		10	11		4	9	34
1	2		3	5	6	7	8		10	11		4	9	35
1	2		3	5	6	7	8	9	10	11		4		36
1	2			5	6	7		9	10	11	3	4	8	37
1	2		4	5	6	7	8	9	10	11	3			38
1	2		4	5	6	7	8	9	10	11	3			39
1	2	12		5	6	7	8*	9	10	11	3	4		40
1	2			5	6	7	8	9	10	11	3	4		41
1	2			5	6	7	8	9	10	11	3	4		42
42	42	5	21	42	42	42	40	36	42	42	19	39	8	
		+ 4s	+ 1s								+ 2s		+ 1s	

ASTON VILLA

	Ht	*Wt*	*Birthplace*	*Clubs*	*League App.*	*League Gls*
Goalkeepers						
Nigel Spink	6 1	13 10	Chelmsford	Aston V	1	—
Jimmy Rimmer	5 11	11 12	Southport	Manchester U	34	—
(England)				Swansea C (on loan)	17	—
				Arsenal	124	—
				Aston V	167	—
Mark Kendall	6 0	12 10	Nuneaton	Aston V	—	—
Defenders						
Colin Gibson	5 8	10 10	Bridport	Aston V	64	2
Kenneth McNaught	5 11	11 1	Kirkcaldy	Everton	66	3
				Aston V	144	4
Allan Evans	6 0	11 12	Dunfermline	Dunfermline Ath	116	15
				Aston V	120	22
Gary Williams	5 9	11 7	Wolverhampton	Aston V	47	—
				Walsall (on loan)	9	—
Noel Blake	6 0	13 5	Jamaica	Aston V	3	—
Mark Jones	5 6	10 5½	Warley	Aston V	—	—
Mike Pejic	5 7	11 3	Chesterton	Stoke C	274	6
(England)				Everton	76	2
				Aston V	10	—
Ken Swain	5 11	11 7	Liverpool	Chelsea	119	26
				WBA (on loan)	—	—
				Aston V	107	2
Midfield						
Dennis Mortimer	5 10	12 0	Liverpool	Coventry C	193	10
				Aston V	203	20
Alex Cropley	5 8	10 0	Aldershot	Hibernian	114	24
(Scotland)				Arsenal	30	5
				Aston V	67	7
				Newcastle U (on loan)	3	—
Gordon Cowans	5 8	9 2	County Durham	Aston V	172	25
Gary Shelton	5 7	10 0	Nottingham	Walsall	24	—
				Aston V	23	7
				Notts Co (on loan)	8	—
Brendan Ormsby	5 10½	11 3	Birmingham	Aston V	25	—
Gary Stirland	5 8½	10 2	Middlesbrough	Aston V	—	—
Eamonn Deacy	5 8½	10 10	Galway	Aston V	12	—
Des Bremner	5 10	11 11	Aberchider	Hibernian	199	18
(Scotland)				Aston V	78	5
Terry Bullivant	5 7½	10 11	London	Fulham	101	2
				Aston V	6	—
Pat Heard	5 10	11 0½	Hull	Everton	11	—
				Aston V	9	—
Robert Hopkins	5 7	10 5	Birmingham	Aston V	2	1
Forwards						
Brian Little	5 8	11 2	Durham	Aston V	247	60
(England)						
Ivor Linton	5 10	10 13	West Bromwich	Aston V	26	—
Gary Shaw	5 10	11 9	Birmingham	Aston V	71	27
William Young	5 7	11 7	Glasgow	Aston V	3	—
Kevin Ready	5 11½	11 11½	Wymondham	Aston V	—	—
(To Bromsgrove Nov 1980)				Hereford U (on loan)	—	—
Terry Donovan	5 11	10 12	Liverpool	Grimsby T	64	23
(Eire)				Aston V	9	2
David Geddis	5 10½	12 2	Carlisle	Ipswich T	43	5
				Luton T (on loan)	13	4
				Aston V	29	6
Tony Morley	5 8½	11 8½	Ormskirk	Preston NE	84	15
				Burnley	91	5
				Aston V	60	13
Peter Withe	6 2	12 0	Liverpool	Southport	3	—
(England)				Barrow	1	—
				Arcadia Shepherds	(not known)	
				Wolverhampton W	17	3
				Birmingham C	35	9
				Nottingham F	75	28
				Newcastle U	76	25
				Aston V	36	20

Also retained: Paul Birch, David Mail.

BARNSLEY Division 2

Chairman: G. Buckle LLB.
Directors: A. Raynor JP, R. F. Potter, G. Pallister, N. W. B. Moody JP, C. Williams.
General Manager: Johnny Steele.
Secretary: Michael Spinks.
Team Manager: Norman Hunter.
Year Formed: 1887. *Turned Professional:* 1888.
Limited Company: 1899.
Previous Name: Barnsley St Peter's.
Football League Record:
1898 Elected to Division 2; 1932–34 Division 3(N); 1934–38 Division 2; 1938–39 Division 3(N); 1946–53 Division 2; 1953–55 Division 3(N); 1955–59 Division 2; 1959–65 Division 3; 1965–68 Division 4; 1968–72 Division 3; 1972–79 Division 4; 1979–81 Division 3; 1981– Division 2.

Honours: *Football League:* best season: 3rd, Division 2, 1914–15, 1921–22; Division 3(N) – Champions 1933–34, 1938–39, 1954–55; Runners-up 1953–54; Division 3 – Runners-up 1980–81; Division 4 – Runners-up 1967–68; Promoted 1978–79. *FA Cup:* Winners 1912; Runners-up 1910. *Football League Cup* best season: 4th rd, 1980–81.
Record Victory: 9-0 v Loughborough T, Division 2, 28 Jan, 1899 and v Accrington Stanley, Division 3(N), 3 Feb, 1934.
Record Defeat: 0-9 v Notts Co, Division 2, 19 Nov, 1927.
Most League Points: 67, Division 3(N), 1938–39.
Most League Goals: 118, Division 3(N), 1933–34.
Highest League Scorer in Season: Cecil McCormack, 33, Division 2, 1950–51.
Most League Goals in Total Aggregate: Ernest Hine, 123, 1921–26, 1934–38.
Most Capped Player: Eddie McMorran, 9 (15), Ireland.
Most League Appearances: Barry Murphy, 514, 1962-78.
Record Transfer Fee Received: £60,000 from West Ham U for Anton Otulakowski, Oct 1976.
Record Transfer Fee Paid: £95,000 to Crystal Palace for Ian Evans, March 1980.
Previous Managers since the War: Angus Seed, Tim Ward, Johnny Steele, John McSeveney, Jim Iley, Allan Clarke.

Oakwell Ground, Grove St, Barnsley. Telephone Barnsley (0226) 295353. *Ground capacity:* 38,500 (15,000 under cover). *Record attendance:* 40,255 v Stoke C, 15 Feb, 1936, FA Cup 5th rd. *Record receipts:* £16,146 v Rotherham U, 16 Dec, 1978, FA Cup 2nd rd. *Pitch measurements:* 111yd×75yd.
How to get there: Fairly frequent train service from Sheffield and Leeds to Exchange Station Barnsley. No special buses, just the normal services, and no buses from town centre because the ground is so close.
Match tickets: Stand seats bookable two weeks in advance.
Car parking: Two official club parks adjacent to the ground holding 1200 cars; parking fee 25p. There is a free public park in Queens Road, two minutes from the ground. The M1 runs approximately two miles from the ground.
Entertainments/catering facilities: Football club social club is adjacent to the ground. Seven tea bars sited around the ground sell refreshments; six of them sell alcoholic drinks.
Club shop: Inside the ground; sells all types of souvenirs.
Handbooks/programmes: Programmes available on subscription.
Extra information: For post-match entertainment, there is Rebeccas night club in Queens Road.
Club Colours: Red shirts, white shorts, white stockings.
Change Colours: White shirts, black shorts, black stockings.
Club Captain: Phil Chambers.
Club Nickname: The Tykes.

BARNSLEY 1980–81 LEAGUE RECORD

Match No.	Date	Venue	Opponents	Result	H/T Score	Goalscorers	Attendance
1	Aug 16	H	Portsmouth	L 1-2	0-1	Parker	10,253
2	19	A	Hull C	W 2-1	2-0	Banks, Glavin	6978
3	23	A	Gillingham	D 1-1	1-1	Banks (pen)	5195
4	30	H	Sheffield U	W 2-1	1-1	Glavin, Evans	17,478
5	Sept 6	A	Rotherham U	L 0-2	0-0		10,766
6	13	H	Huddersfield T	W 1-0	0-0	Glavin	13,819
7	15	A	Brentford	D 1-1	0-0	Banks	6900
8	20	H	Swindon T	W 2-0	0-0	Glavin (pen), Parker	9747
9	27	A	Reading	L 2-3	2-2	Banks, Parker	5380
10	30	H	Brentford	L 0-1	0-1		11,227
11	Oct 4	H	Charlton Ath	D 0-0	0-0		9305
12	7	A	Carlisle U	D 2-2	1-2	Lester, Riley	2828
13	11	A	Colchester U	D 2-2	2-1	Parker, Glavin	2749
14	18	H	Millwall	W 2-0	1-0	Aylott, Banks	8693
15	21	H	Oxford U	D 1-1	1-1	Downes	8991
16	25	A	Plymouth Arg	W 3-1	0-1	Lester, Riley, Glavin	8911
17	Nov 1	H	Chester	W 2-0	1-0	Aylott, Glavin	9330
18	4	H	Carlisle U	W 3-1	2-0	Glavin, Aylott, Lester	9191
19	8	A	Exeter C	W 1-0	0-0	Riley	4019
20	11	H	Hull C	W 5-0	2-0	Aylott 3, Riley, Banks	11,628
21	15	A	Portsmouth	W 1-0	1-0	Riley	14,732
22	29	H	Fulham	D 2-2	1-2	Lester, Banks	9940
23	Dec 2	A	Burnley	W 1-0	0-0	Banks	9094
24	6	A	Newport Co	D 0-0	0-0		5537
25	20	H	Blackpool	W 2-0	1-0	Aylott, Parker	10,862
26	26	A	Chesterfield	D 0-0	0-0		17,146
27	27	H	Walsall	W 3-0	2-0	Glavin 2, Aylott	14,958
28	Jan 10	H	Plymouth Arg	W 2-1	1-0	Lester, Aylott	12,355
29	16	A	Fulham	W 3-2	1-1	Aylott 2, Banks	5265
30	31	H	Gillingham	D 3-3	1-2	Banks, Parker, Riley	13,703
31	Feb 7	A	Huddersfield T	L 0-1	0-1		28,901
32	21	H	Reading	L 2-3	0-2	McCarthy, Aylott	13,304
33	28	A	Swindon T	L 0-2	0-1		7819
34	Mar 7	A	Charlton Ath	D 1-1	1-1	Banks	9371
35	21	A	Millwall	D 1-1	0-1	Glavin	4901
36	24	A	Oxford U	D 1-1	0-0	Glavin	4705
37	28	H	Burnley	W 3-2	1-2	Glavin, Banks 2 (1 pen)	13,689
38	31	A	Sheffield U	D 1-1	1-0	Riley	20,369
39	Apr 4	A	Chester	D 2-2	1-1	Parker, Glavin	4680
40	7	H	Colchester U	W 3-0	2-0	McHale, Parker 2	13,283
41	10	H	Exeter C	W 1-0	0-0	Cooper	13,445
42	18	A	Walsall	D 1-1	1-0	Cooper	6026
43	20	H	Chesterfield	D 1-1	0-0	Banks	17,019
44	25	A	Blackpool	L 0-1	0-1		7648
45	28	H	Rotherham U	W 1-0	1-0	Glavin	25,935
46	May 2	H	Newport Co	W 4-1	1-0	Parker, Glavin 3	15,559

Final League Position: 2

Goalscorers

League (72): Glavin 18 (1 pen), Banks 14 (2 pens), Aylott 12, Parker 10, Riley 7, Lester 5, Cooper 2, Downes 1, Evans 1, McCarthy 1, McHale 1.
League Cup (11): Glavin 5 (2 pens), Banks 2, Parker 2, Evans, Riley.
F.A. Cup (10): Aylott 3, Parker 3, Banks (pen), Cooper, Glavin, Lester.

League Cup	First Round	Scunthorpe U (a)	1-0
		(h)	2-1
	Second Round	Mansfield T (a)	0-0
		(h)	4-2
	Third Round	Cardiff C (h)	3-2
	Fourth Round	West Ham U (h)	1-2
FA Cup	First Round	Chester (a)	2-1
	Second Round	Rotherham U (a)	1-0
	Third Round	Torquay U (h)	2-1
	Fourth Round	Enfield (h)	1-1
		(a)	3-0
	Fifth Round	Middlesbrough (a)	1-2

New	Cooper	Chambers	Glavin	Banks	McCarthy	Evans	Parker	Aylott	Lester	Downes	Riley	Boyd	Hunter	Joyce	Pierce	Barrowclough	Campbell	McHale	Walker	Match No.
1	2	3	4	5	6	7	8	9*	10	11	12									1
1	2	3	4*	5	6	7	8		10	11	9	12								2
1	2	3		5	6	7	8		10	11	9	4								3
1	2	3	4	5	6	7	8		10	11	9									4
1	2	3	4	5		7	8		10	11	9		6							5
1	2	3	4	5		7	8	12	10	11*	9		6							6
1	2	3	4	5		7	8		10	11	9		6							7
1	2	3	4	5	6	7	8		10	11	9									8
1	2	3	4	5	6	7	8	12	10	11	9*									9
1	2	3	4	5	6	7	8	12	10	11*	9									10
1	2	3	4	5	6	7	8	9	10		11									11
1	2	3	4*	5	6	7	8	9	10		11		12							12
1	2	3	4*	5	6	7	8	9	10		11		12							13
1		3		5	6	7	8	9	10	11			4	2						14
1		3	4	5	6	7	8	9	10	11				2						15
1		3	4	5	6	7	8*	9	10	11	12			2						16
1		3	4	5	6	7		9	10	11	8			2						17
1		3	4	5	6	7		9	10	11	8			2						18
1		3	4	5	6	7		9	10	11	8			2						19
1	12	3	4	5*	6	7		9	10	11	8			2						20
1	4	3		5	6	7		9	10	11	8			2						21
	4	3		5	6	7		9	10	11	8			2	1					22
	4	3		5	6	7	8	9	10	11				2	1					23
	4	3		5	6	7	8	9	10	11				2	1					24
	10	3	4	5	6	7	8	9		11				2	1					25
	10	3	4	5	6	7	8	9		11				2	1					26
	10	3	4	5	6	7	8	9		11				2	1					27
		3	4	5	6	7	8	9	10	11				2	1					28
		3	4	5	6	7	8	9	10	11	12			2	1*					29
1		3	4	5	6	7	8	9*	10	11	12			2						30
1	12	3	4	5*	6	7	8		10	11	9			2						31
1	7	3	4	5	6			9	10	11	8			2						32
	4	3			6	7		9	10	11	8*			2	1	5	12			33
		3	4	5	6	7	8	9						2	1	11		10		34
		3	4	5	6	7	8	9						2	1	11		10		35
		3	4*	5	6	7	8	9			12			2	1	11		10		36
		3*	4	5	6	7	8	9			12			2	1	11		10		37
			4	5	6	7	8	9			3			2	1	11		10		38
	12		4	5	6	7*	8	9			3			2	1	11		10		39
	7		4	5	6		8	9	11		3			2	1			10		40
	4	3		5	6	7	8	9						2	1	11		10		41
	4	3	12	5	6	7	8	9*						2	1	11		10		42
	4	3		5	6	7	8*	9						2	1	11		10	12	43
	4*	3	9	5	6	7	8							2	1	11		10	12	44
		3	4	5	6	7	8	9*			12			2	1	11		10		45
		3	4	5	6	7	8				9			2	1	11		10		46
24	27	43	36	45	43	44	38	34	31	30	25	1	4	33	22	13	—	13	—	
	+ 3s		+ 1s					+ 3s			+ 7s	+ 1s	+ 2s				+ 1s		+ 2s	

BARNSLEY

	Ht	Wt	Birthplace	Clubs	League App.	League Gls
Goalkeepers						
Gary Pierce	6 1	12 9	Bury	Huddersfield T	23	—
				Wolverhampton W	98	—
				Barnsley	59	—
Martin New	5 11	13 5	Swindon	Arsenal	—	—
				Mansfield T	21	—
				Barnsley	24	—
Robert Horn	5 10½	14 1	Westminster	Crystal Palace	—	—
				Barnsley	—	—
Defenders						
Philip Chambers	5 7½	11 1	Barnsley	Barnsley	317	7
Mike McCarthy	6 1½	13 3	Barnsley	Barnsley	179	5
Norman Hunter	5 11½	12 6	Eighton Banks	Leeds U	541	18
(England)				Bristol C	108	4
(Contract cancelled Nov 1980)				Barnsley	30	—
Neil Cooper	5 10½	11 1	Aberdeen	Aberdeen	12	1
				Barnsley	50	5
Joe Joyce	5 9	10 5	Consett	Barnsley	41	—
Ian Evans	6 2½	12 6	Egham	QPR	39	2
(Wales)				Crystal Palace	137	14
				Barnsley	60	2
Midfield						
Brett Mellor	6 0	12 0	Huddersfield T	Huddersfield T	1	—
(Contract cancelled April 1981)				Barnsley	—	—
Ray McHale	5 8	12 6	Sheffield	Chesterfield	124	27
				Halifax T	86	21
				Swindon T	173	33
				Brighton & HA	11	—
				Barnsley	13	1
Ian Banks	5 10½	12 2	Mexborough	Barnsley	85	17
Ronnie Glavin	5 10	12 6	Glasgow	Partick T	126	34
(Scotland)				Celtic	102	36
				Barnsley	79	38
Mike Lester	5 9½	11 8	Manchester	Oldham Ath	27	1
				Manchester C	2	—
				Stockport Co (on loan)	9	1
				Washington D	(Not known)	
				Grimsby T	48	10
				Barnsley	64	11
Bobby Downes	5 7½	11 4	Bloxwich	WBA	—	—
				Peterborough	26	3
				Rochdale	174	10
				Watford	199	19
				Barnsley	43	1
Gordon Boyd	5 7	10 5	Glasgow	Glasgow R	—	—
				Fulham	3	—
				Glasgow R	—	—
				Barnsley	2	—
Stewart Barrowclough	5 9	10 5	Barnsley	Barnsley	9	—
				Newcastle U	219	20
				Birmingham C	29	2
				Bristol R	61	14
				Barnsley	13	—
Winston Campbell	5 8	11 6	Sheffield	Barnsley	2	—
Gary Walters	5 7	10 0	Doncaster	Barnsley	—	—
Forwards						
Glyn Riley	5 10	11 11	Barnsley	Doncaster R (on loan)	8	2
				Barnsley	115	16
Allan Clarke	6 0	11 1	Willenhall	Walsall	72	41
(England)				Fulham	85	45
(Contract cancelled Sept 1980)				Leicester C	36	12
				Leeds U	273	110
				Barnsley	47	15
Derrick Parker	5 9½	11 8	Wallsend	Burnley	6	2
				Southend U	129	43
				Barnsley	57	14
Trevor Aylott	6 1½	14 0	London	Chelsea	29	2
				QPR (on loan)	—	—
				Barnsley	55	16
Colin Walker	5 8	11 8	Rotherham	Barnsley	2	—

Free transfer: Nigel Bentley *.
Contracts cancelled April 1981: Barry Tyerman, David Whyte.

BIRMINGHAM CITY Division 1

President:

Chairman: C. K. Coombs.

Directors: J. F. Wiseman, N. Bosworth LLB, D. M. Coombs, R. Burman, J. Carrot.

Manager: Jim Smith. *Limited Company:* 1888.

Secretary: Alan Instone. *Coach:* Norman Bodell.

Physiotherapist: K. Walters.

Year Formed: 1875. *Turned Professional:* 1885.

Previous Grounds: Waste ground near Arthur St, 1875; Muntz St, Small Heath, 1877; St Andrew's, 1906.

Previous Names: 1875–88, Small Heath Alliance; 1888, dropped 'Alliance'; became Birmingham 1905; became Birmingham City 1945.

Football League Record:
Division One: 1894–96; 1901–02; 1903–08; 1921–39; 1948–50; 1955–65; 1972–79; 1980–
Division Two: 1892–94; 1896–1901; 1902–03; 1908–21; 1946–48; 1950–55; 1965–72; 1979–80.

Honours: *Football League:* Division 1 best season: 6th, 1955–56; Division 2 – Champions 1892–93, 1920–21, 1947–48, 1954–55; Runners-up 1893–94, 1900–01, 1902–03, 1971–72. *FA Cup:* Runners-up 1931, 1956. *Football League Cup:* Winners 1963. **European Competitions:** *European Fairs Cup:* 1955–58, 1958–60 (runners-up), 1960–61 (runners-up), 1960–62.

Record Victory: 12-0 v Walsall Town Swifts, Division 2, 17 Dec, 1892 and v Doncaster R, Division 2, 11 April, 1903.

Record Defeat: 1-9 v Sheffield W, Division 1, 13 Dec, 1930.

Most League Points: 59, Division 2, 1947–48.

Most League Goals: 103, Division 2, 1893–94 (only 28 games).

Highest League Scorer in Season: Joe Bradford, 29, Division 1, 1927–28.

Most League Goals in Total Aggregate: Joe Bradford, 249, 1920–35.

Most Capped Player: Malcolm Page, 28, Wales.

Most League Appearances: Gil Merrick, 486, 1946–60.

Record Transfer Fee Received: £975,000 from Nottingham F for Trevor Francis, Feb 1979.

Record Transfer Fee Paid: £350,000 to Derby Co for David Langan, June 1980.

Previous Managers since the War: Ted Goodier, Harry Storer, Bob Brocklebank, Arthur Turner, Pat Beasley, Gil Merrick, Joe Mallett, Stan Cullis, Fred Goodwin, Willie Bell, Sir Alf Ramsey.

Address of Supporters Club: St Andrew's Club, St Andrew's, Birmingham 9.

Address of the Club Shop or Boutique: The Beautique, 26 Cattell Road, Birmingham 9.

St Andrews, Birmingham B9 4NH. Telephone 021-772 0101/2689. *Ground capacity:* 44,500 (9,009 seats). *Record Attendance:* 66,844 v Everton, FA Cup 5th rd, 11 Feb, 1939. *Record Receipts:* £48,505 v Aston Villa, Division 1, 11 Oct, 1980. *Pitch measurements:* 115yd×75yd.

How to get there: Buses 97 from Carr's Lane, City Centre, 98, 99 from Bus Station, 58, 60 from High Street; Specials from Albert Street and Hall of Memory, Broad Street. Nearest railway station, Birmingham New Street. By road; via M1, M45, and A45 to Small Heath area of Birmingham and via Cattell Road (sixth turning on the right past Small Heath Park) to the ground; via M6 (exit 6, Gravelly Hill) and A38M (Aston Expressway), leave Expressway at first exit, left into Dartmouth Street, and then via Lawley Street and Watery Lane onto the Coventry Road. Turn left and then take left fork into Cattell Road.

Match tickets: Bookable three weeks in advance.

Car parking: Public car park in Coventry Road and Cattell Road.

Entertainments/catering facilities: Catering points inside the ground.

Club shop: Sells all types of souvenirs.

Handbooks/programmes: Programmes on sale on match days in and outside the ground; subscription rates available on request.

Extra information: In their away League programme in 1947–48, Birmingham let in only 11 goals; this is the best away performance in Division 2 since World War II.

Club Colours: Royal blue shirts, three vertical stripes on sleeves, white shorts blue trim, white stockings with blue hoops on turnover.

Change Colours: Yellow shirts, three blue vertical stripes on sleeves, yellow shorts blue trim, yellow stockings with blue hoops on turnover.

Club Captain: Archie Gemmill. *Chief Scout:* Don Dorman. *Club Nickname:* Blues.

BIRMINGHAM CITY 1980–81 LEAGUE RECORD

Match No.	Date	Venue	Opponents	Result	H/T Score	Goalscorers	Attendance
1	Aug 16	H	Coventry C	W 3-1	2-0	Curbishley 2, Dillon	21,907
2	20	A	Nottingham F	L 1-2	1-1	Worthington	26,561
3	23	H	Manchester U	D 0-0	0-0		28,661
4	30	A	Southampton	L 1-3	0-3	Worthington	21,683
5	Sept 6	H	Liverpool	D 1-1	0-0	Worthington	27,042
6	13	A	Brighton & HA	D 2-2	1-1	Curbishley, Bertschin	15,788
7	20	H	WBA	D 1-1	0-0	Givens	22,016
8	27	A	Norwich C	D 2-2	1-2	Ainscow, Worthington	13,801
9	Oct 4	A	Wolverhampton W	L 0-1	0-1		22,777
10	7	H	Arsenal	W 3-1	2-1	Lynex, Worthington, Dillon	15,511
11	11	H	Aston Villa	L 1-2	0-1	Worthington (pen)	33,879
12	18	A	Manchester C	W 1-0	0-0	Gemmill (pen)	30,041
13	25	H	Stoke C	D 1-1	0-0	Bertschin	16,535
14	Nov 1	A	Middlesbrough	W 2-1	0-1	Worthington 2	14,061
15	8	H	Crystal Palace	W 1-0	1-0	Bertschin	16,910
16	11	H	Nottingham F	W 2-0	1-0	Worthington 2	22,433
17	15	A	Coventry C	L 1-2	1-1	Curbishley	18,758
18	22	H	Tottenham H	W 2-1	1-1	Curbishley, Ainscow	24,817
19	29	A	Everton	D 1-1	1-1	Ainscow	22,258
20	Dec 6	H	Leicester C	L 1-2	0-2	Scott (og)	18,479
21	13	A	Aston Villa	L 0-3	0-0		41,101
22	20	H	Ipswich T	L 1-3	0-1	Ainscow	16,161
23	26	A	Leeds U	D 0-0	0-0		19,214
24	27	H	Sunderland	W 3-2	2-1	Gemmill, Bertschin, Worthington	19,005
25	Jan 10	A	Tottenham H	L 0-1	0-0		24,909
26	13	A	Ipswich T	L 1-5	1-3	Worthington	21,158
27	17	H	Southampton	L 0-3	0-1		16,491
28	31	A	Manchester U	L 0-2	0-1		39,081
29	Feb 7	H	Brighton & HA	W 2-1	1-0	Evans, Curbishley	13,691
30	14	A	Liverpool	D 2-2	1-2	Evans, Ainscow	32,199
31	20	H	Norwich C	W 4-0	0-0	Ainscow, Evans 2, Gemmill	14,686
32	28	A	WBA	D 2-2	2-1	Worthington, Ainscow	24,853
33	Mar 17	H	Wolverhampton W	W 1-0	0-0	Worthington	20,005
34	21	H	Manchester C	W 2-0	2-0	Worthington, Evans	16,160
35	28	A	Stoke C	D 0-0	0-0		14,624
36	31	A	Arsenal	L 1-2	0-1	Worthington	17,431
37	Apr 4	H	Middlesbrough	W 2-1	1-0	Evans, Broadhurst	12,472
38	11	A	Crystal Palace	L 1-3	1-0	Ainscow	9820
39	18	A	Sunderland	L 0-3	0-2		20,158
40	21	H	Leeds U	L 0-2	0-1		14,505
41	25	A	Leicester C	L 0-1	0-0		13,666
42	May 2	H	Everton	D 1-1	1-1	Evans	12,863

Final League Position: 13

Goalscorers

League (50): Worthington 16 (1 pen), Ainscow 8, Curbishley 6, Evans 7, Bertschin 4, Gemmill 3 (1 pen), Dillon 2, Broadhurst 1, Givens 1, Lynex 1, own goal 1.
League Cup (6): Ainscow 2, Bertschin, Gallagher, Gemmill (pen), Worthington (pen).
F.A. Cup (5): Bertschin 2, Ainscow, Evans, Worthington (pen).

League Cup	Second Round	Bristol C (h)	2-1
		(a)	0-0
	Third Round	Blackburn R (h)	1-0
	Fourth Round	Ipswich T (h)	2-1
	Fifth Round	Liverpool (a)	1-3
FA Cup	Third Round	Sunderland (h)	1-1
		(a)	2-1 (aet)
	Fourth Round	Coventry C (a)	2-3

Wealands	Langan	Dennis	Curbishley	Gallagher	Givens	Ainscow	Bertschin	Worthington	Gemmill	Dillon	Todd	Page	Lynex	Evans	Hawker	Lees	Coton	Handysides	Broadhurst	Van Den Hauwe	Ivey	Goode	*Match No.*
1	2	3	4	5	6	7	8	9	10	11													1
1	2	3	4	5	12	7*	8	9	10	11	6												2
1	2		4	5		7	9	8	10	11	6	3											3
1	2	3	4*	5		7	8	9	10	11	6		12										4
1	2	3	4	5		7	8	9	10	11	6												5
1	2		4	5	12	7	8	9*	10	11	6	3											6
1	2	3	4	5	12	7	8*	9	10	11	6												7
1	2	3	4	5	8*	7		9	10	11	6		12										8
1	2	3	4	5	8	7*		9	10	11	6		12										9
1	2	3	4	5		7		9	10	11	6		8										10
1	2	3	4	5		7		9	10	11	6		8										11
1	2	3	4	5	12	7		9*	10	11	6		8										12
1	2	3	4	5			8	9	10	11	6		7										13
1	2	3	4	5		7	8	9	10	11	6												14
1	2	3*	4	5		7	8	9	10	11	6			12									15
1	2		4	5		7	8	9	10	11	6				3								16
1	2		4	5		7	8	9	10	11*	6		12		3								17
1	2		4	5		7	8	9	10	11	6				3								18
1	2		4	5		7	8	9	10	11	6				3								19
1	2		4*	5		7	8	9	10	11	6		12		3								20
1	2		4	5		7	8	9	10	11*	6		12		3								21
1	2		4	5	11*	7	8	9	10	12	6				3								22
1	2		4	5		7	8	9	10	11	6					3							23
	2		4	5		7	8	9	10	11	6					3	1						24
1	2		4	5		7	8	9	10		6		3	11									25
1	2		4	5		7	8	9	10		6		12	11*	3								26
	2		4	5		7	8	9	10*	11	6				3		1	12					27
1	2		4	5		7	8*	9	10	11	6		12						3				28
1	2		4*	5		7	12	9	10		6		11	8					3				29
1	2			5	12	7		9*	10	4	6			8				11	3				30
1	2			5		7		9	10	4	6			8				11	3				31
1	2			5	12	7		9		4	6			8	10*			11	3				32
1	2	3		5		7		9	10	4	6			8					11				33
1	2	3		5		7		9	10	4	6			8*				12	11				34
1	2	3		5		7		9	10	4	6			8					11				35
1	2	3		5		7	12	9	10	4	6			8*					11				36
1	2	3		5		7	9		10	4	6			8					11				37
1	2			5		7	9		10	4	6			8	3*				11	12			38
1	2					7	9		10	4	6			8				11	3	5			39
	2			5		7	9		10	4				8*			1	11	3	6	12		40
1	2			5		7	9		10	4	6			8					3	11*		12	41
1	2	3		5					10	4	6			8				7	11		9*	12	42
39	42	19	29	41	4	40	28	36	41	38	40	2	6	16	11	2	3	6	15	3	1	—	
					+ 6s		+ 2s			+ 1s			+ 8s	+ 1s				+ 2s		+ 1s	+ 1s	+ 2s	

BIRMINGHAM CITY

	Ht	*Wt*	*Birthplace*	*Clubs*	*League App.*	*League Gls*
Goalkeepers						
Tony Coton	6 1	11 8	Tamworth	Birmingham C	3	—
				Hereford U (on loan)	—	—
Neil Freeman	6 2	14 4	Northampton	Arsenal	—	—
				Northampton (on loan)	—	—
				Grimsby T	33	—
				Southend U	69	—
				Birmingham C	31	—
				Walsall (on loan)	8	—
				Huddersfield T (on loan)	18	—
Jeff Wealands	6 0½	12 0	Darlington	Wolverhampton W	—	—
				Northampton T (on loan)	—	—
				Darlington	28	—
				Hull C	240	—
				Birmingham C	79	—
Defenders						
Joe Gallagher	6 2	11 3	Liverpool	Birmingham C	286	17
Jimmy Calderwood	5 9	11 0	Glasgow	Birmingham C	145	4
(Contract cancelled July 1980)				Cambridge U (on loan)	8	—
Mark Dennis	5 9	10 8	Streatham	Birmingham C	90	—
Pat Van den Hauwe	5 10	10 6	Dendermonde, Belgium	Birmingham C	13	—
Paul Brady*	5 10	10 8	Birmingham	Birmingham C	—	—
Kevan Broadhurst	5 9½	11 2	Dewsbury	Birmingham C	67	4
				Walsall (on loan)	3	—
Colin Todd	5 9	11 5	Chester-le-Street	Sunderland	173	3
(England)				Derby Co	293	6
				Everton	32	1
				Birmingham C	74	—
Terry Lees*	5 8	11 0	Stoke	Stoke C	24	—
				Crewe Alex (on loan)	6	—
				Port Vale	41	2
				Roda	(not known)	
				Birmingham C	12	—
David Langan	5 10	11 2	Dublin	Derby Co	143	1
(Eire)				Birmingham C	42	—
Phil Hawker	6 1	11 6	Solihull	Birmingham C	11	—
Les Phillips			Lambeth	Birmingham C	—	—
Midfield						
Kevin Dillon	5 11	10 13	Sunderland	Birmingham C	123	11
Tony Towers	5 8½	11 2½	Manchester	Manchester C	122	10
(England)				Sunderland	108	19
(Contract cancelled February 1981)				Birmingham C	92	4
Alan Ainscow	5 6½	9 3½	Bolton	Blackpool	192	28
				Birmingham C	108	16
Archie Gemmill	5 5	11 2	Paisley	St Mirren	67	9
(Scotland)				Preston NE	99	13
				Derby Co	261	18
				Nottingham F	58	4
				Birmingham C	78	11
Alan Curbishley	5 9	11 6	Forest Gate	West Ham U	85	4
				Birmingham C	71	9
Carl Francis			West Ham	Birmingham C	—	—
Alex Gibson			Nottingham	Birmingham C	—	—
Greg King			Australia	Birmingham C	—	—
(Contract cancelled April 1981)						
Forwards						
Keith Bertschin	6 1	11 8	Enfield	Ipswich T	32	8
				Birmingham C	118	29
Trevor Dark	5 9	10 9	Surrey	Birmingham C	5	1
(Contract cancelled March 1981)						
Paul Ivey	5 11	10 8	Westminster	Birmingham C	7	—
Frank Worthington	5 10½	11 10	Halifax	Huddersfield T	171	42
(England)				Leicester C	210	72
(Contract cancelled April 1981)				Bolton W	84	35
				Birmingham C	55	21
Tony Evans	5 8	11 7	Liverpool	Blackpool	6	—
				Cardiff C	124	47
				Birmingham C	30	11
Ian Handysides	5 6	10 6	Jarrow	Birmingham C	8	—
Terry Goode	5 8	11 3	Islington	Birmingham C	2	—
Mike Sturridge			Birmingham	Birmingham C	—	—

Also Retained: Tony Hinchey, David Linney.
Free Transfer: Alan Kurila*.

BLACKBURN ROVERS Division 2

President: W. H. Bancroft.

Chairman: D. Brown.

Vice-Chairman: W. Fox.

Directors: T. W. Ibbotson LLB, A. Sharples, R. D. Coar BSC, Dr M. Jeffries TD.

Secretary: John W. Howarth AAAI.

Manager: Bobby Saxton. *Year Formed:* 1875.

Limited Company: 1897. *Turned Professional:* 1880.

Previous Grounds: 1875, Brookhouse Ground; 1876, Alexandra Meadows; 1881, Leamington Road; 1890, Ewood Park.

Previous Name: Blackburn Grammar School OB.

Football League Record:
1888 Original Member of the League; 1936–39 Division 2; 1946–47 Division 1; 1947–57 Division 2; 1957–66 Division 1; 1966–71 Division 2; 1971–75 Division 3; 1975–79 Division 2; 1979–80 Division 3; 1980– Division 2.

Honours: *Football League:* Division 1 – Champions 1911–12, 1913–14; Division 2 – Champions 1938–39; Runners-up 1957–58; Division 3 – Champions 1974–75; Runners-up 1979–80. *FA Cup:* Winners 1884, 1885, 1886, 1890, 1891, 1928; Runners-up 1882, 1960. *Football League Cup:* Semi-final 1961–62.

Record Victory: 11-0 v Rossendale U, FA Cup, 1884–85.

Record Defeat: 0-8 v Arsenal, Division 1, 25 Feb, 1933.

Most League Points: 60, Division 3, 1974–75.

Most League Goals: 114, Division 2, 1954–55.

Highest League Scorer in Season: Ted Harper, 43, Division 1, 1925–26.

Most League Goals in Total Aggregate: Tommy Briggs, 140, 1952–58.

Most Capped Player: Bob Crompton, 41, England.

Most League Appearances: Ronnie Clayton, 580, 1950–69 (and 57 FA Cup games).

Record Transfer Fee Received: £357,000 from Leeds U for Kevin Hird, Feb 1979.

Record Transfer Fee Paid: £100,000 to Chelsea for Duncan McKenzie, March 1979.

Previous Managers since the War: Eddie Hapgood, Will Scott, Jack Bruton, Jackie Bestall, John Carey, Dally Duncan, Jack Marshall, Eddie Quigley, John Carey, Ken Furphy, Gordon Lee, Jim Smith, Jim Iley, Howard Kendall.

Ewood Park, Blackburn BB2 4JF. Telephone Blackburn 55432/55433. *Telegraphic Address:* 'Rovers, Blackburn'. *Ground capacity:* 25,000. *Record attendance:* 61,783 v Bolton W, FA Cup 6th rd, 2 Mar, 1929. *Record receipts:* £40,686 v Aston Villa, FA Cup 5th rd, 16 Feb, 1980. *Pitch measurements:* 166yd 2ft×72yd 2ft.

How to get there: Blackburn is the nearest railway station and Corporation buses run from there to the ground.

Club shop: Open every day selling all types of souvenirs.

Handbooks/programmes: No handbook. Programmes available on subscription from the club shop.

Extra information: In 1881–82, Blackburn Rovers were unbeaten for 35 successive matches.

Club Colours: Blue and white halved shirts, white shorts, blue stockings with red and white tops.

Change Colours:

Reserve Team Manager: Jim Furnell

Club Nickname: Blue and Whites.

BLACKBURN ROVERS 1980–81 LEAGUE RECORD

Match No.	Date	Venue	Opponents	Result	H/T Score	Goalscorers	Attendance
1	Aug 16	A	Cardiff C	W 2-1	1-1	Brotherston, Crawford	6908
2	20	H	Oldham Ath	W 1-0	0-0	Keeley	10,831
3	23	A	Orient	D 1-1	0-1	Speight	5057
4	30	H	Shrewsbury T	W 2-0	1-0	Kendall (pen), Garner	8465
5	Sept 6	A	Derby Co	D 2-2	2-0	Kendall (pen), Garner	18,159
6	13	H	Luton T	W 3-0	0-0	Garner 2, Stonehouse	9076
7	20	H	Grimsby T	W 2-0	2-0	Garner, Stonehouse	10,338
8	27	A	Wrexham	W 1-0	0-0	McKenzie	10,913
9	Oct 4	H	QPR	W 2-1	0-0	Stonehouse 2 (1 pen)	12,209
10	7	A	Sheffield W	L 1-2	1-2	Stonehouse	16,707
11	11	A	West Ham U	L 0-2	0-1		32,402
12	18	H	Chelsea	D 1-1	1-1	Stonehouse	15,503
13	22	H	Cambridge U	W 2-0	0-0	Garner, Kendall	9438
14	25	A	Notts Co	L 0-2	0-2		13,500
15	Nov 1	H	Swansea C	D 0-0	0-0		10,846
16	8	A	Bristol C	L 0-2	0-0		8773
17	11	A	Oldham Ath	L 0-1	0-0		7748
18	15	H	Cardiff C	L 2-3	0-0	Stonehouse, Keeley	7854
19	22	A	Watford	D 1-1	0-0	McKenzie	13,436
20	29	H	Bristol R	W 2-0	0-0	Brotherston, Stonehouse	8025
21	Dec 13	H	West Ham U	D 0-0	0-0		13,279
22	20	A	Cambridge U	D 0-0	0-0		4389
23	26	H	Preston NE	D 0-0	0-0		17,726
24	27	A	Bolton W	W 2-1	0-0	Stonehouse, Burke	18,184
25	Jan 10	H	Watford	D 0-0	0-0		9466
26	17	A	Shrewsbury T	D 1-1	0-1	Burke	5212
27	31	H	Orient	W 2-0	2-0	Burke, Lowey	9091
28	Feb 7	A	Luton T	L 1-3	1-0	Burke	9350
29	14	H	Derby Co	W 1-0	1-0	Brotherston	12,533
30	21	H	Wrexham	D 1-1	0-0	Garner	10,147
31	28	A	Grimsby T	D 0-0	0-0		12,210
32	Mar 7	A	QPR	D 1-1	0-0	Speight	9513
33	14	H	Sheffield W	W 3-1	2-0	Speight, Kendall, Busby	19,222
34	21	A	Chelsea	D 0-0	0-0		14,314
35	28	H	Notts Co	D 0-0	0-0		14,451
36	Apr 4	A	Swansea C	L 0-2	0-0		12,011
37	11	H	Bristol C	W 1-0	0-0	Burke	9970
38	15	A	Newcastle U	D 0-0	0-0		15,339
39	18	H	Bolton W	D 0-0	0-0		16,357
40	21	A	Preston NE	D 0-0	0-0		18,742
41	25	H	Newcastle U	W 3-0	2-0	Lowey (pen), Burke, Speight	10,609
42	May 2	A	Bristol R	W 1-0	0-0	Speight	9078

Final League Position: 4

Goalscorers

League (42): Stonehouse 9 (1 pen), Garner 7, Burke 6, Speight 5, Kendall 4 (2 pens), Brotherston 3, Keeley 2, Lowey 2 (1 pen), McKenzie 2, Busby 1, Crawford 1.
League Cup (3): Garner, McKenzie, Stonehouse (pen).
F.A. Cup (1): Burke.

League Cup	First Round	Huddersfield T (h)	0-0
		(a)	1-1
	Second Round	Gillingham (h)	0-0
		(a)	2-1
	Third Round	Birmingham C (a)	0-1
FA Cup	Third Round	Notts Co (a)	1-2

Butcher	Branagan	Devries	Kendall	Keeley	Fazackerley	Brotherston	Crawford	Garner	McKenzie	Parkes	Speight	Rathbone	Arnold	Craig	Stonehouse	Coughlin	Comstive	Lowey	Burke	Hamilton	Round	Busby	*Match No.*
1	2	3	4	5	6	7	8	9	10	11*	12												1
1	2		4	5	6	7	8	9	10		11	3											2
	2		4	5	6	7	8	9	10		11	3	1										3
	2		4*	5	6	7	8	9	10		11	3	1	12									4
1	2	3	4	5	6	7	8*	9	10		11				12								5
	2	3	4	5	6	7		9	10		11		1		8								6
	2	3	4	5	6	7		9	10		11		1		8								7
1	2	3	4	5	6	7		9	10	12	11				8*								8
1	2	3	4*	5	6	7		9	10	12	11				8								9
1	2	3*		5	6	7		9		11					8	4	10				12		10
1	2	3		5	6	7*		9		11		12			8	4	10						11
1	2	3		5	6	7		9		11	10				8	4							12
1	2		4	5	6	7		9		11	10	3			8								13
1	2		4	5	6	7		9	8	11	10	3											14
1	2		4	5	6	7		9	8		10	3			11								15
1	2			5	6	7		9	8	4	10	3			11								16
1	2		4	5	6	7		9	8	10	3				11								17
1	2		4	5	6*	7		9	10		11	3			8		12						18
1	2		4	5		7		9	10	6	11	3			8								19
1	2		4	5		7			10	6	11	3			8			9					20
1	3		4	5	6	7			10*	11	2				8			9	12				21
1	3		4	5	6	7	8		10	11	2*							9	12				22
1	2	3	4	5	6	7	8		10	11					12			9*					23
1	2	3	4	5	6	7	9			11					8				10				24
1	2	3	4*	5	6	7		9			11				8				10	12			25
1	2	3	4*	5	6	7		9			11				8				10	12			26
	2		4	5	6	7		8			11	3	1					9	10				27
	2		4	5	6*	7		8			11	3	1		12			9	10				28
	2		4	5		7		12		11	6	3	1					9	10			8*	29
	2		4	5		7		12		11*	6	3	1					9	10			8	30
	2		4	5	6	7		9			11	3	1						10			8	31
	2		4	5	6	7					11	3	1					9	10			8	32
	2		4	5	6	7*					11	3	1					9	10	12		8	33
	2		4	5	6			7			11	3	1					9	10			8	34
	2		4	5	6			7			11	3	1					9	10			8	35
	2		4	5	6			7			11	3	1		12			9			10*	8	36
	2		4	5	6		8	7			11	3	1					9	10				37
	2		4	5	6		8	7			11	3	1					9	10				38
	2		4	5	6			7			11	3	1		8			9	10				39
	2		4	5	6			7			11	3	1		8			9	10				40
	2		4	5	6		8				11	3	1		10			9	7				41
	2		4	5	6		8				11	3	1		10			9	7				42
22	42	13	38	42	38	33	12	31	19	16	37	26	20	—	22	3	2	19	18	—	1	8	
								+ 2s		+ 2s	+ 1s	+ 1s		+ 1s	+ 4s		+ 1s		+ 2s	+ 3s	+ 1s		

BLACKBURN ROVERS

	Ht	*Wt*	*Birthplace*	*Clubs*	*League App.*	*League Gls*
Goalkeepers						
John Butcher	6 2	12 3	Newcastle	Blackburn R	98	—
Jim Arnold	6 1	11 5	Stafford	Stafford R	(not known)	´
				Blackburn R	58	—
Chris Pearce	6 0	11 4	Newport	Wolverhampton W	—	—
				Rochdale (on loan)	5	—
				Blackburn R	—	—
Defenders						
Derek Fazackerley	5 11	11 6	Preston	Blackburn R	397	13
Glenn Keeley	5 10	12 0	Barking	Ipswich T	4	—
				Newcastle U	44	2
				Blackburn R	173	5
Mike Rathbone	5 10	11 13	Birmingham	Birmingham C	20	—
				Blackburn R	70	1
Brian Morley	5 7	11 3	Fleetwood	Blackburn R	20	—
(Contract cancelled April 1981)						
Jim Branagan	5 10	11 5	Barton	Oldham Ath	27	—
				Huddersfield T	38	—
				Blackburn R	73	1
Paul Round	6 0	11 0	Blackburn	Blackburn R	51	5
(Contract cancelled April 1981)						
Roger De Vries*	5 8½	11 5	Hull	Hull C	318	—
				Blackburn R	13	—
David Hamilton	5 7½	9 12	South Shields	Sunderland	—	—
				Blackburn R	3	—
Jimmy Hall	5 9	9 3	Bootle	Blackpool	1	—
(Contract cancelled April 1981)				Blackburn R	—	—
Colin James				Blackburn R	—	—
(Contract cancelled March 1981)						
Andrew Morley				Blackburn R	—	—
(Contract cancelled January 1981)						
Midfield						
Kim Walters			Pilsley	Heanor T	(not known)	
				Blackburn R	—	—
Tony Parkes	5 7½	11 2	Sheffield	Blackburn R	350	38
Howard Kendall	5 7	10 13	Ryton-on-Tyne	Preston NE	104	13
				Everton	230	21
				Birmingham C	115	16
				Stoke C	82	9
				Blackburn R	79	6
Noel Brotherston	5 8½	10 8	Belfast	Tottenham H	1	—
(N. Ireland)				Blackburn R	149	23
Mick Speight	5 10½	12 7	Upton	Sheffield U	199	14
				Blackburn R	38	5
Paul Comstive			Southport	Blackburn R	3	—
Forwards						
Simon Garner	5 8	11 3	Boston	Blackburn R	86	21
Joe Craig	5 9	11 2	Alloa	Partick T	112	44
(Scotland)				Celtic	55	23
(Transferred to Hamilton A March 1981)				Blackburn R	48	8
Duncan McKenzie	5 9	11 0	Luton	Nottingham F	111	41
(Contract cancelled March 1981)				Mansfield T (on loan)	16	10
				Leeds U	66	27
				Anderlecht	30	16
				Everton	48	14
				Chelsea	15	4
				Blackburn R	74	16
Kevin Stonehouse	5 11	11 10	Bishop Auckland	Shildon	(not known)	
				Blackburn R	33	11
Andy Crawford	5 7	10 4	Filey	Derby Co	21	4
				Blackburn R	48	19
Viv Busby	6 0	11 12	Slough	Luton T	77	16
				Newcastle U (on loan)	4	2
				Fulham	118	29
				Norwich C	22	11
				Sheffield U (on loan)	3	1
				Stoke C	50	9
				Tulsa R	(not known)	
				Blackburn R	8	1
John Lowey	5 11	12 7	Manchester	Manchester U	—	—
				California S	(not known)	
				Blackburn R	—	—
				Port Vale	—	—
				Sheffield W	42	4
				Blackburn R	19	2
Marshall Burke	5 7	9 1	Glasgow	Burnley	24	5
				Leeds U	—	—
				Blackburn R	20	6

Also retained: Phil Williamson.

BLACKPOOL Division 4

President: L. Moore.

Chairman: K. Chadwick LLB.

Directors: G. Bloor, F. J. Hessey, B. A. Pemberton, T. White.

Manager: Allan Brown. *Secretary:* D. Johnson.

Year Formed: 1887. *Limited Company:* 1896.

Turned Professional: 1887.

Previous Grounds: 1887, Raikes Hall Gardens; 1897, Athletic Grounds; 1899, Raikes Hall Gardens; 1899, Bloomfield Road.

Previous Name: 'South Shore' combined with Blackpool in 1899, twelve years after the latter had been formed on the breaking up of the old 'Blackpool St John's club.

Football League Record:
1896 Elected to Division 2; 1899 Failed Re-election; 1900 Re-elected; 1900–30 Division 2; 1930–33 Division 1; 1933–37 Division 2; 1937–67 Division 1; 1967–70 Division 2; 1970–71 Division 1; 1971–78 Division 2; 1978–81 Division 3; 1981– Division 4.

Honours: *Football League:* Division 1 – Runners-up 1955–56; Division 2 – Champions 1929–30; Runners-up 1936–37, 1969–70. *FA Cup:* Winners 1953; Runners-up 1948, 1951. *Football League Cup:* Semi-final 1962. *Anglo-Italian Cup:* Winners 1971; Runners-up 1972.

Record Victory: 10-0 v Lanerossi Vicenza, Anglo-Italian tournament, 10 June, 1972.

Record Defeat: 1-10 v Small Heath, Division 2, 2 March, 1901 and 1-10 v Huddersfield, Division 1, 13 Dec, 1930.

Most League Points: 58, Division 2, 1929–30 and 1967–68.

Most League Goals: 98, Division 2, 1929–30.

Highest League Scorer in Season: Jimmy Hampson, 45, Division 2, 1929–30.

Most League Goals in Total Aggregate: Jimmy Hampson, 247, 1927–38.

Most Capped Player: Jimmy Armfield, 43, England.

Most League Appearances: Jimmy Armfield, 568, 1952–71.

Record Transfer Fee Received: £325,000 from Everton for Mickey Walsh, August 1978.

Record Transfer Fee Paid: £105,000 to Sunderland for Jackie Ashurst, Oct 1979 and £105,000 to Exeter C for Tony Kellow, Nov 1978.

Previous Managers since the War: Joe Smith, Ron Suart, Stan Mortensen, Les Shannon, Jimmy Meadows, Bob Stokoe, Harry Potts, Allan Brown, Jimmy Meadows, Bob Stokoe, Stan Ternent, Alan Ball Jnr.

Address of Supporters Club: Blackpool FC Supporters' Club, Bloomfield Road, Blackpool, Lancs. (*Shop:* Same address as ground.)

Bloomfield Rd Ground, Blackpool FY1 6JJ. Telephone Blackpool 404331. *Telegraphic address:* 'Football Blackpool'. *Ground capacity:* 18,000. *Record attendance:* 39,118 v Manchester U, Division 1, 19 April, 1952. *Record receipts:* £28,986.52 v Everton, League Cup 2nd rd, 2nd leg, 3 Sept, 1980. *Pitch measurements:* 111yd×73yd.

How to get there: Coliseum bus station, Lytham Road, 10 minutes' walk. Railway: South station (a few minutes' walk from ground) and North station.

Match tickets: Bookable four weeks in advance of the match.

Car parking: Car park for 1,000 cars. Street parking available.

Entertainments/catering facilities: Refreshment and licensed bars. Entertainment after the game at the Supporters' Club by prior arrangement.

Club shop: In Bloomfield Road sells all types of souvenirs.

Handbooks/programmes: Progtammes available from the development shop.

Extra information: When England lost 6-3 to Hungary in November 1953, there were four Blackpool players – Stanley Matthews, Stan Mortensen, Harry Johnston, and Ernie Taylor – in the team.

Club Colours: Tangerine shirts with white stripe on sleeves, collars and cuffs, white shorts, tangerine with white trim stockings.

Change Colours: White shirts, tangerine shorts and tangerine stockings.

Club Captain: Peter Noble. *First Team Coach:* Bobby Smith.

Club Nickname: The Seasiders.

BLACKPOOL 1980–81 LEAGUE RECORD

Match No.	Date	Venue	Opponents	Result		H/T Score	Goalscorers	Attendance
1	Aug 16	A	Swindon T	W	2-1	1-0	Hockaday, Fletcher	7108
2	20	H	Rotherham U	D	0-0	0-0		10,427
3	23	A	Huddersfield T	D	1-1	1-1	Morris	9490
4	30	H	Portsmouth	L	0-2	0-1		8352
5	Sept 5	A	Fulham	W	2-1	2-1	Sbragia, Morris	4940
6	13	H	Hull C	D	2-2	1-0	Morris, Harrison	6138
7	16	A	Sheffield U	L	2-4	1-2	Hockaday, Gardner	13,331
8	20	H	Brentford	L	0-3	0-2		6738
9	27	A	Walsall	D	2-2	1-1	Morris 2	4227
10	Oct 1	H	Sheffield U	W	2-1	0-0	Thompson 2	8995
11	4	H	Gillingham	W	4-0	1-0	Thompson, Morris 2, Hockaday	6588
12	7	A	Millwall	D	0-0	0-0		3363
13	11	A	Plymouth Arg	W	2-0	1-0	Morris 2	10,698
14	18	H	Colchester U	D	1-1	1-0	Williams	6997
15	22	H	Chesterfield	L	0-3	0-1		8062
16	25	A	Charlton Ath	L	1-2	1-2	Morgan	6838
17	28	A	Carlisle U	L	0-2	0-2		3588
18	Nov 1	H	Newport Co	L	2-4	1-2	McEwan (pen), Ashurst	4556
19	8	A	Oxford U	W	2-0	0-0	Ball 2 (2 pens)	3038
20	11	A	Rotherham U	L	0-4	0-2		6367
21	15	H	Swindon T	D	1-1	1-0	Entwistle	3758
22	29	A	Reading	L	0-3	0-2		3968
23	Dec 6	H	Exeter C	D	0-0	0-0		3597
24	20	A	Barnsley	L	0-2	0-1		10,862
25	26	H	Chester	L	2-3	2-0	Morgan, Bamber	4878
26	27	A	Burnley	L	1-4	0-2	Bamber	10,667
27	Jan 10	A	Colchester U	L	2-3	1-1	Morris, Ball	2378
28	17	H	Reading	D	0-0	0-0		3273
29	24	A	Portsmouth	D	3-3	0-2	Morris, Hockaday, Thompson	13,265
30	31	H	Huddersfield T	L	1-2	1-1	Ball (pen)	9431
31	Feb 7	A	Hull C	L	1-2	0-0	Ball	5315
32	14	H	Fulham	L	0-2	0-1		3792
33	21	H	Walsall	W	1-0	0-0	Ashurst	3895
34	28	A	Brentford	L	0-2	0-1		5580
35	Mar 4	H	Millwall	D	0-0	0-0		4534
36	7	A	Gillingham	L	1-3	1-1	Ashurst	3424
37	14	H	Plymouth Arg	W	1-0	0-0	Morris	3933
38	21	A	Chesterfield	L	2-3	1-2	Thompson, Noble	5959
39	25	H	Charlton Ath	L	0-2	0-1		4230
40	28	H	Carlisle U	L	0-1	0-0		4531
41	Apr 4	A	Newport Co	L	1-3	0-1	Williams	4514
42	12	H	Oxford U	D	1-1	1-1	Bamber	3188
43	17	A	Chester	L	1-2	0-0	Entwistle	2804
44	18	H	Burnley	D	0-0	0-0		7198
45	25	H	Barnsley	W	1-0	1-0	Entwistle	7648
46	May 2	A	Exeter C	D	0-0	0-0		3864

Final League Position: 23

Goalscorers

League (45): Morris 12, Ball 5 (3 pens), Thompson 5, Ashurst 3, Bamber 3, Entwistle 3, Hockaday 4, Morgan 2, Williams 2, Fletcher 1, Gardner 1, Harrison 1, McEwan 1 (pen), Noble 1, Sbragia 1.
League Cup (8): McEwan 3 (2 pens), Morris 3, Ashurst, Fletcher.
F.A. Cup (5): Hockaday 2, Entwistle, Morris, Williams.

League Cup	First Round	Walsall (a)	3-2
		(h)	3-1
	Second Round	Everton (a)	0-3
		(h)	2-2
FA Cup	First Round	Fleetwood (a)	4-0
	Second Round	Doncaster R (a)	1-2

Hesford	Gardner	Williams	Doyle	McEwan	Ashurst	Morris	Hockaday	Fletcher	Ball	Harrison	Noble	Brockbank	Greenall	MacDougall	Welsh	Sbragia	Deary	Bamber	Pashley	Simmonite	Morgan	Thompson	Rush	Entwistle	Conn	*Match No.*
1	2	3	4	5	6	7	8	9	10	11																1
1	2	3	4	5	6	7	8		10*	11	9	12														2
1	2	3	4	5		7	8	9*		11	10		6	12												3
1	2	3	4	5		7	8	9*			10		6	12	11											4
1	2	3	4	5		7	8			11				9		6	10									5
1	2	3	4	5		7	8			11				9		6	10									6
1	2	3	4	5		7	8		10					9*		6		12	11							7
1		3	4	5			8		10	7						6		9	11	2						8
1		3		6		10	8	9*	4							5	11			2	7	12				9
1		3		11		9	7		4							5	10			2	6	8				10
1		3		6		10	8		4							5	11			2	7	9				11
1		3		6		10	8		4							5	11			2	7	9				12
1		3		6	9	10	8		4							5	11			2	7					13
1		3		6	9	10	8		4							5*	11			2	7	12				14
1		3		6	5	10	8		4								11			2	7	9				15
		3		6	4	9	10		8				5				11*			2	7	12	1			16
		3		8	5	10	9		4				6							2	7	11	1			17
		11		6	5	10	9		4			3	12					8		2*	7		1			18
1		3	9		2	10	8		4				6			5			11		7					19
1		3	9		2	10	11*		7	12			5			4			6					8		20
1		3	8	5	2	10			4				6						11		7			9		21
1		3		6	2	10	8		4				5						11		7			9		22
1		3		6	2	10	8		4	7									11			5		9		23
1		3		6	2	10			4			12						8	11		7*	5		9		24
1	2	3		6		10			4									8	11		7	5		9		25
1	2	3		6		10			4									8	11		7	5		9		26
1	2				6	10	8		4	9*		12				5			3	11	7					27
1	2				6	10	8		4	9						5			3	11	7					28
1	2				6	10	8		4	9									3	11*	7	5		12		29
					6	10	8		4	9								12	3	2*	7	5	1	11		30
1	2								4	9		11				6		8	3		7	5		10		31
1					6	10	11		4	9									3	2	7	5		8		32
1	12				6	10	11		4	9									3	2*	7	5		8		33
1	2				6	10	8		4	9		11							3		7*	5		12		34
1	2			7	6	10	11			9		8*				4			3			5		12		35
1		3		7	6	10	11*			9	4	8				5			2					12		36
1	2			4	6	10					11					5		12	3		7	9*			8	37
1	2	12		4	6	10				8	11					5			3			9		7*		38
1	2	11		4	6	10	12			7	8					5*			3			9				39
1				6	2	10	8			9	4					12			3		7	5			11*	40
1		8		6	2	10	7			9	4							11	3			5				41
1	2			6		10	12			9	4		5					11	3		7				8*	42
1	2			6		10				8	4					5		11	3		7			9		43
1	2	4		6		10	12			8						5*		11	3		7			9		44
1	2			6		10				8	4		5					11	3		7			9		45
1	2			6		10				8	4		5					11	3	7				9		46
42	23	30	11	36	28	44	33	4	30	26	13	5	11	3	1	22	10	12	30	18	30	21	4	16	3	
	+ 1s	+ 1s					+ 3s			+ 1s		+ 3s	+ 1s	+ 2s		+ 1s		+ 3s				+ 3s		+ 4s		

BLACKPOOL

	Ht	*Wt*	*Birthplace*	*Clubs*	*League App.*	*League Gls*
Goalkeepers						
Iain Hesford	6 1½	14 2½	Noola, Kenya	Blackpool	119	—
Jon Rush	6 0	12 9	Wellington, NZ	Blackpool	4	—
Defenders						
Ian McWilliams			Glasgow	Blackpool	—	—
(Contract cancelled Feb 1981)						
Ricky Sbragia	6 0	11 0	Lennoxtown	Birmingham C	15	1
				Morton (on loan)	4	—
				Walsall	77	4
				Blackpool	23	1
Paul Gardner	5 9	12 6	Southport	Blackpool	140	1
Max Thompson	6 1	13 12	Liverpool	Liverpool	1	—
				Blackpool	99	6
Terry Pashley	5 8	12 0	Chesterfield	Burnley	18	—
				Blackpool	109	3
Jack Ashurst	6 0	11 10½	Renton	Sunderland	140	4
				Blackpool	53	3
Mark Davies	5 9	10 5	Salford	Blackpool	—	—
(Transferred to Northwich V Dec 1980)						
Gary Williams	5 11	11 8	Nantwich	Tranmere R	1	—
				Djurgaarden	(not known)	
				Blackpool	31	2
Gordon Simmonite	5 10	11 4	Sheffield	Sheffield W	1	—
				Boston U	(not known)	
				Blackpool	18	—
Colin Greenall			Billinge	Blackpool	12	—
Midfield						
Peter Noble	5 9	10 7½	Newcastle	Newcastle U	25	7
				Swindon T	216	62
				Burnley	243	63
				Blackpool	27	3
Keith Bowey*	5 6	9 8	Newcastle	Blackpool	3	1
Wayne Harrison	5 6	10 2	Whitehaven	Workington	4	—
				Blackpool	51	4
Andy Brockbank	5 10	10 9½	Havering	Blackpool	9	—
John Deary	5 8	11 2	Ormskirk	Blackpool	10	—
Willie Morgan	5 8½	10 8	Glasgow	Burnley	183	19
(Scotland)				Manchester U	238	24
				Burnley	13	—
				Bolton W	134	7
				Blackpool	30	2
Alfie Conn	5 10	11 5	Kirkcaldy	Rangers	94	21
(Scotland)				Tottenham H	38	6
(Contract cancelled April 1981)				Celtic	37	8
				Hartford	(not known)	
				Hearts	17	3
				Blackpool	3	—
Stan McEwan	5 11	12 8	Cambusrethan	Blackpool	189	19
Forwards						
David Hockaday	5 10	10 9½	Billingham	Blackpool	66	9
Dave Bamber	6 3	13 10	St Helens	Blackpool	22	4
Colin Morris	5 7	10 5½	Blyth	Burnley	10	—
				Southend U	133	25
				Blackpool	65	16
Paul Fletcher	5 9½	12 10	Bolton	Bolton W	36	5
				Burnley	293	71
				Blackpool	19	8
Phil Smith	5 9	11 6	Fleetwood	Blackpool	1	—
(Contract cancelled Dec 1980)						
Gary Seward*	5 7	9 11½	Paddington	Blackpool	1	—
Andy Welsh	5 5	8 10	Fleetwood	Blackpool	1	—
Ted MacDougall	5 10	11 13	Inverness	Liverpool	—	—
(Scotland)				York C	84	34
(Contract cancelled October 1980)				Bournemouth	146	103
				Manchester U	18	5
				West Ham U	24	5
				Norwich C	112	51
				Southampton	86	42
				Bournemouth	52	16
				Blackpool	13	—
Alan McAvoy	5 6	9 12	Wigton	Blackpool	—	—
Gerry Hendrick	5 11	10 6	Dublin	St Patrick's Ath	(not known)	
				Blackpool	—	—
Wayne Entwistle	5 11	11 8	Bury	Bury	31	7
				Sunderland	45	12
				Leeds U	11	2
				Blackpool	20	3
Phil Williams			Swansea	Arsenal	—	—
(Contract cancelled April 1981)				Blackpool	—	—

BOLTON WANDERERS Division 2

President: J. Battersby.

Chairman: G. Warburton.

Vice-Chairman and Chief Executive: B. Turnbull.

Directors: G. Ashworth, S. Jones, J. Lightbown, H. D. Warburton.

Manager: George Mulhall.

Secretary: Des McBain. *Year Formed:* 1874.

Turned Professional: 1880. *Limited Company:* 1895.

Previous Grounds: Park Recreation Ground and Cockle's Field before moving to Pike's Lane Ground 1881; Burnden Park 1895.

Previous Name: 1874–77, Christ Church FC; 1877 became Bolton Wanderers.

Football League Record:
1888 Founder Member of the League; 1899–1900 Division 2; 1900–03 Division 1; 1903–05 Division 2; 1905–08 Division 1; 1908–09 Division 2; 1909–10 Division 1; 1910–11 Division 2; 1911–33 Division 1; 1933–35 Division 2; 1935–64 Division 1; 1964–71 Division 2; 1971–73 Division 3; 1973–78 Division 2; 1978–80 Division 1; 1980– Division 2.

Honours: *Football League:* Division 1 best season: 3rd 1891–92, 1920–21, 1924–25. Division 2 – Champions 1908–09, 1977–78; Runners-up 1899–1900, 1904–05, 1910–11, 1934–35. Division 3 – Champions 1972–73. *FA Cup:* Winners 1923, 1926, 1929, 1958; Runners-up 1894, 1904, 1953. *Football League Cup:* Semi-final 1976–77.

Record Victory: 13-0 v Sheffield U, FA Cup, 2nd rd, 1 Feb, 1890.

Record Defeat: 0-7 v Manchester C, Division 1, 21 Mar, 1936.

Most League Points: 61, Division 3, 1972–73.

Most League Goals: 96, Division 2, 1934–35.

Highest League Scorer in Season: Joe Smith, 38, Division 1, 1920–21.

Most League Goals in Total Aggregate: Nat Lofthouse, 255, 1946–61.

Most Capped Player: Nat Lofthouse, 33, England.

Most League Appearances: Eddie Hopkinson, 519, 1956–70.

Record Transfer Fee Received: £250,000 from Everton for Jim McDonagh, June 1980.

Record Transfer Fee Paid: £350,000 to WBA for Len Cantello, May 1979.

Previous Managers since the War: Walter Rowley, Bill Ridding, Nat Lofthouse, Jimmy McIlroy, Jimmy Meadows, Nat Lofthouse, Jimmy Armfield, Ian Greaves, Stan Anderson.

Address of Supporters Club: Supporters Club, Burnden Park, Manchester Road, Bolton.

Address of the Club Shop or Boutique: 'The Happy Shop', Burnden Park, Bolton.

Burnden Park, Bolton BL3 2QR. Telephone Bolton 389200. Information Service: Bolton 21101. *Ground capacity:* 43,000. *Record attendance:* 69,912 v Manchester C, FA Cup 5th rd, 18 Feb, 1933. *Record receipts:* £53,931 v Everton, League Cup, semi-final 2nd leg, 15 Feb, 1977. *Pitch measurements:* 113yd×76yd.

How to get there: Local buses 8, 524, 523, 542, 543. The nearest station is Trinity St in the town centre.
Match tickets: Bookable in advance.
Car parking: Private car parking only on Burnden forecourt. Large park only 200 yards from the ground. Limited street parking in the vicinity. Multi-storey parks in the town centre.
Entertainments/catering facilities: Prerecorded programmes of news, interviews, and record requests. Burnden Sporting Club not now available to the general public. Refreshment bars in each section of the ground and in the Sporting Club.
Club shop: On main car park. Open Mon-Sat. Send SAE for mail order list.
Handbooks/programmes: Programmes available on subscription from club shop.
Extra information: History of club written by Dr Percy Young.
Club Colours: White shirts, navy blue shorts, white stockings.
Change Colours: Red shirts, white shorts, red stockings white trim.
Club Captain: Mike Walsh. *Club Coach:* Walter Joyce.
Reserve Team Coach: Charlie Wright. *Physiotherapist/Trainer:* Jim Headrige.
Club Nickname: Trotters.

BOLTON WANDERERS 1980–81 LEAGUE RECORD

Match No.	Date	Venue	Opponents	Result	H/T Score	Goalscorers	Attendance
1	Aug 16	A	Notts Co	L 1-2	1-2	Whatmore	7459
2	19	H	Sheffield W	D 0-0	0-0		15,926
3	23	H	Newcastle U	W 4-0	2-0	Kidd 3, Whatmore	11,835
4	30	A	Derby Co	L 0-1	0-1		17,738
5	Sept 6	H	Bristol R	W 2-0	0-0	Griffiths (og), Gowling (pen)	8712
6	13	A	Cardiff C	D 1-1	1-1	Walsh	6649
7	20	H	Swansea C	L 1-4	0-3	Whatmore	9419
8	27	A	Oldham Ath	D 1-1	1-0	Cantello	10,174
9	Oct 4	H	Chelsea	L 2-3	0-1	Thompson, Gowling	11,888
10	7	A	Shrewsbury T	W 2-1	0-0	Carter, Kidd	5077
11	11	A	QPR	L 1-3	0-1	Kidd	8641
12	18	H	Bristol C	D 1-1	1-1	Gowling	8988
13	21	H	Preston NE	W 2-1	2-1	Carter, Whatmore	10,713
14	25	A	West Ham U	L 1-2	0-1	Kidd	25,257
15	Nov 1	H	Cambridge U	W 6-1	1-0	Kidd 3, Whatmore, Hoggan, Cantello	8016
16	8	A	Watford	L 1-3	1-1	Hoggan	11,296
17	11	A	Sheffield W	L 0-2	0-1		16,262
18	22	H	Grimsby T	D 1-1	0-0	Hoggan	9031
19	25	H	Notts Co	W 3-0	1-0	Wilson 2, Kidd	7344
20	29	A	Luton T	D 2-2	0-1	Whatmore 2	8300
21	Dec 6	H	Orient	W 3-1	2-0	Whatmore, Kidd 2	8228
22	13	A	Bristol C	L 1-3	1-1	Gowling (pen)	7384
23	19	H	QPR	L 1-2	1-1	Gowling	6315
24	26	A	Wrexham	W 1-0	1-0	Whatmore	7635
25	27	H	Blackburn R	L 1-2	0-0	Hoggan	18,184
26	Jan 10	A	Grimsby T	L 0-4	0-1		9320
27	24	H	Derby Co	W 3-1	2-1	Gowling 2, Thomas	9937
28	31	A	Newcastle U	L 1-2	0-1	Bennett	19,108
29	Feb 7	H	Cardiff C	W 4-2	1-1	Thomas 2, Wilson, Nikolic	8115
30	14	A	Bristol R	L 1-2	0-1	Gowling	5368
31	24	H	Oldham Ath	W 2-0	1-0	Whatmore, Thomas	9641
32	28	A	Swansea C	L 0-3	0-1		9468
33	Mar 7	A	Chelsea	L 0-2	0-1		12,948
34	14	H	Shrewsbury T	L 0-2	0-1		7900
35	24	A	Preston NE	W 2-1	1-0	Reid, Gowling	8505
36	28	H	West Ham U	D 1-1	1-0	Whatmore	13,271
37	Apr 4	A	Cambridge U	W 3-2	1-1	Reid, Nikolic, Whatmore	4512
38	11	H	Watford	W 2-1	0-0	Thomas, Whatmore	8461
39	18	A	Blackburn R	D 0-0	0-0		16,357
40	20	H	Wrexham	D 1-1	0-1	Kidd (pen)	7594
41	26	A	Orient	D 2-2	1-2	Gowling, Whatmore	3824
42	May 2	H	Luton T	L 0-3	0-0		7268

Final League Position: 18

Goalscorers

League (61): Whatmore 14, Kidd 13 (1 pen), Gowling 10 (1 pen), Thomas 5, Hoggan 4, Wilson 3, Cantello 2, Carter 2, Nikolic 2, Reid 2, Bennett 1, Thompson 1, Walsh 1, own goal 1.
League Cup (1): Kidd.
F.A. Cup (3): Hoggan 2, Whatmore.

League Cup	Second Round	Crystal Palace (h)	0-3
		(a)	1-2
FA Cup	Third Round	Nottingham F (a)	3-3
		(h)	0-1 (aet)

Peacock	Graham	Burke	Wilson	Jones	Walsh	Gowling	Whatmore	Carter	Kidd	Cantello	Clement	Hoggan	McElhinney	Nowak	Poole	Thompson	Nikolic	Nicholson	Reid	Moores	Brennan	Thomas	Bennett	*Match No.*
1	2	3	4	5	6	7	8	9	10	11														1
1	2	3	7	5	6	11	8	9	10	4														2
1	2	3	4	5	6	7	8	9	10	11														3
1		3		5	6	7	8	9	10	4	2	11												4
1		3	12		6*	7	8	9	10	4	2	11	5											5
1		3	12	5*	6	9	8		10	4	2	11		7										6
1		3	9		6	5	8		10	4	2	11		7										7
	2	3		5	6	9	8		10	4		11			1	7								8
	2	3		5	6	9	8		10	4*		12			1	7	11							9
	12	3	7	5	6	9		8	10*	4					1		11	2						10
		3	7	5	6	9	8	11	10	4					1			2						11
	2	11		5	6	9		8	10	4					1			3	7					12
	2	3		5	6	11	8	9	10	4					1				7					13
	2	3		5	6	11	8	9	10	4					1				7					14
		3		5	6	11	8	9*	10	4		12			1			2	7					15
		3		5	6	11	8		10	4		9			1			2	7					16
	2	3	12	5*	6	11	8		10			9			1	4			7					17
	2	3		5	6	4	8	9	10*			11			1				7	12				18
	2		4	5	6	11	8		10			9	3		1				7					19
	2		4	5	6	11	8		10			9	3		1			7						20
	2		4	5	6*	11	8		10			9	3		1			7				12		21
	2		4	5		11	8		10			9	3		1			7*			6	12		22
	2	3	4	5		11	8*		10			9	6		1	12		7						23
	2		4			11	8		10			9	3		1		5	7					6	24
1	2		4			11		12	10			9	3				7				5	8	6*	25
1	2		4			5			10			9	3				7*	12			6	8	11	26
1	2		6	4		8*			11			9	3			12	7				5	10		27
1	2		4	5			8		10			9	3				7				6		11	28
1	2		4	5		11						9	3				7				6	8	10	29
	2		12	5		11	8					9	3		1		7				6	10	4*	30
	2	4		5		11	8					9	3		1		7				6	10		31
	2	4		5		11	8					9*	3		1	12	7				6	10		32
	2*				5	11	8		10	4		12	3		1		7		9		6			33
	2	3*			5	11	8		10	4		12	6		1		7		9					34
				5	3	11	8		12	6		9			1		7*	2	4			10		35
				5	3	11	8			6		10			1		7	2	4			9		36
				5	3	11	8			6		10			1		7	2	4			9		37
			6*	5	3	11	8		12			10			1		7	2	4			9		38
				5	3	11	8			6		10			1		7	2	4			9		39
				5		11	8		12	6		10*			1		7	2	4		3	9		40
				5	3	11	8			6		10			1		7*	2	4		12	9		41
1				5	6	11	8	12		4							7	2	10*		3	9		42
13	26	22	18	35	30	41	36	12	30	25	4	29	17	2	29	3	21	18	18	—	12	15	6	
	+ 1s		+ 4s					+ 2s	+ 3s			+ 4s				+ 3s		+ 1s		+ 1s	+ 1s	+ 2s		

BOLTON WANDERERS

	Ht	*Wt*	*Birthplace*	*Clubs*	*League App.*	*League Gls*
Terry Poole*	6 1	13 0	Chesterfield	Huddersfield T	207	—
				Sheffield U (on loan)	7	—
				Bolton W	29	—
Dennis Peacock	6 2	14 1	Lincoln	Nottingham F	22	—
				Walsall (on loan)	10	—
				Doncaster R	199	—
				Bolton W	13	—
Defenders						
Paul Jones	6 1½	12 9	Ellesmere Port	Bolton W	370	35
Mike Walsh	6 0	12 0	Manchester	Bolton W	177	4
Mike Graham*	5 10	11 13	Lancaster	Bolton W	46	—
Peter Nicholson	6 0	12 0	Cleator Moor	Blackpool	6	—
				Bolton W	310	12
Roy Heaney	5 7½	11 11	Liverpool	Bolton W	—	—
(Contract cancelled Feb 1981)						
Michael Bennett	5 7	10 0	Bolton	Bolton W	14	1
David Burke*	5 10	10 7	Liverpool	Bolton W	69	1
Gerry McElhinney	6 2	13 0	Londonderry	Distillery	(not known)	
				Bolton W	17	—
Ian Brennan	5 10½	11 11	Easington	Burnley	175	11
				Bolton W	13	—
Neil Berry	5 11	10 4	Edinburgh	Bolton W	—	—
Midfield						
Peter Reid	5 7	11 5	Huyton	Bolton W	198	21
Philip Wilson*	5 6	10 4	Hemsworth	Bolton W	39	4
Tadeusz Nowak	6 0	11 2	Trzcinsko,	Legia	—	—
(Poland)			Poland	Bolton W	24	1
(Contract cancelled Dec 1980)						
Len Cantello	5 10	11 13	Newton Heath	WBA	301	13
				Bolton W	56	2
John McGlynn	5 9	10 10	Musselburgh	Bolton W	—	—
(Transferred to Berwick Dec 1980)						
Dusan Nikolic	5 8	11 10	Belgrade	Red Star	(not known)	
(Yugoslavia)				Bolton W	21	2
Barry Taylor	5 7½	10 2	Bolton	Bolton W	—	—
Brian Atherton	5 6	9 0	Bolton	Bolton W	—	—
Forwards						
Neil Whatmore	5 9½	11 8	Ellesmere Port	Bolton W	277	102
Chris Thompson	5 10	11 6	Walsall	Bolton W	21	2
Alan Gowling	6 1	12 0	Stockport	Manchester U	71	18
				Huddersfield T	128	58
				Newcastle U	92	30
				Bolton W	109	26
John Keighley*	5 7½	10 5	Ribchester	Bolton W	—	—
James Moores*	5 7	9 10	Macclesfield	Bolton W	1	—
David Hoggan	5 9	10 0	Falkirk	Bolton W	36	4
Geoff Langley	5 8	10 8	Gateshead	Bolton W	—	—
Brian Kidd	6 0	13 0	Manchester	Manchester U	203	53
(England)				Arsenal	77	30
(Contract cancelled April 1981)				Manchester C	98	44
				Everton	40	11
				Bolton W	33	13
Mike Carter	5 9	10 7	Warrington	Bolton W	36	7
				Mansfield T (on loan)	18	4
John Thomas	5 8	11 3	Birmingham	Everton	—	—
				Halifax T (on loan)	5	—
				Tranmere R (on loan)	11	2
				Bolton W	17	5

AFC BOURNEMOUTH Division 4

Chairman: H. G. Walker LLB.

Directors: E. G. Keep, P. W. Hayward, W. J. L. Mackeen, D. R. Lever, G. P. Pound, S. A. Latter.

Secretary: G. H. MacKrell ACCA.

Manager: David Webb.

Commercial Manager: D. Dowsett.

Year Formed: 1899.

Turned Professional: 1912. *Limited Company:* 1914.

Previous Names: Boscombe St Johns, 1890–99; Boscombe FC, 1899–1923; Bournemouth & Boscombe Ath FC, 1923–71.

Previous Grounds: 1899–1910, Castlemain Road, Pokesdown; 1910, Dean Court.

Football League Record:
Elected to Division 3(S), 1923. Remained a Third Division Club for record number of years until 1970; 1970–71 Division 4; 1971–75, Division 3; 1975– Division 4.

Honours: *Football League:* Division 3 best season: 3rd, 1961–62, 1971–72; Division 3(S) – Runners-up 1947–48. Promotion from Division 4 1970–71 (2nd). *FA Cup* best season: 6th rd, 1956–57. *Football League Cup* best season: 4th rd, 1962, 1964.

Record Victory: 11-0 v Margate, FA Cup 1st rd, 20 Nov, 1971.

Record Defeat: 1-8 v Bradford C, Division 3, 24 Jan, 1970.

Most League Points: 62, Division 3, 1971–72.

Most League Goals: 88, Division 3(S), 1956–57.

Highest League Scorer in Season: Ted MacDougall, 42, 1970–71.

Most League Goals in Total Aggregate: Ron Eyre, 202, 1924–33.

Most Capped Player: Tommy Godwin, 4 (13), Eire.

Most League Appearances: Ray Bumstead, 412, 1958–70.

Record Transfer Fee Received: £195,000 from Manchester U for Ted MacDougall, Sept 1972.

Record Transfer Fee Paid: £70,000 to Cardiff C for Brian Clark, Oct 1972.

Previous Managers since the War: Harry Kinghorn, Harry Lowe, Jack Bruton, Freddie Cox, Don Welsh, Bill McGarry, Reg Flewin, Freddie Cox, John Bond, Trevor Hartley, John Benson, Alec Stock.

Address of Supporters Club Shop: The Cherry Bees Shop, Dean Court, Bournemouth, BH7 7AF.

Dean Court Ground, Bournemouth. Telephone Bournemouth 35381. *Telegraphic address:* 'Football Bournemouth'. *Ground capacity:* 19,175. *Record attendance:* 28,799 v Manchester U, FA Cup 6th rd, 2 March, 1957. *Record Receipts:* £15,466 v Portsmouth, Division 4, 2 Oct, 1979. *Pitch measurements:* 118yd×75yd.

How to get there: Nearest station Bournemouth on the main line from London (Waterloo). Corporation bus 25.
Car parking: Adequate parking for 1500 cars.
Entertainments/catering facilities: Refreshment points around the ground.
Club shop: Sells all types of souvenirs.
Handbooks/programmes: No handbook. Programmes available on subscription.
Extra information: The club did not compete in the FA Cup in 1923–24, their first League season, because their election came too late for them to be exempt from the preliminary rounds.
Club Colours: All red with single white stripe under arm and down side.
Change Colours: All white with single red stripe under arm and down side.
Club Captain: John Impey.
Trainer: John Kirk. *Coach:* Harry Redknapp.
Club Nickname: Cherries.

AFC BOURNEMOUTH 1980–81 LEAGUE RECORD

Match No.	Date	Venue	Opponents	Result	H/T Score	Goalscorers	Attendance
1	Aug 16	A	York C	L 0-4	0-2		2195
2	19	H	Hereford U	W 1-0	1-0	Elliott	2991
3	23	H	Northampton T	D 0-0	0-0		2875
4	30	A	Torquay U	L 0-2	0-0		2532
5	Sept 6	A	Bradford C	D 1-1	1-1	Heffernan	3389
6	13	H	Tranmere R	W 1-0	0-0	Massey	2642
7	16	H	Hartlepool U	W 1-0	1-0	Massey	2413
8	20	A	Peterborough U	L 0-1	0-0		3774
9	27	H	Rochdale	W 2-1	1-1	Morgan, Massey	2557
10	30	A	Hartlepool U	L 0-1	0-1		2405
11	Oct 4	H	Scunthorpe U	D 2-2	0-1	Massey, Heffernan	3079
12	7	A	Aldershot	D 0-0	0-0		3780
13	11	A	Darlington	W 2-1	1-1	Massey 2	2363
14	18	H	Mansfield T	L 0-1	0-0		3335
15	21	H	Crewe Alex	D 0-0	0-0		2632
16	24	A	Stockport Co	L 1-2	0-1	Massey	2012
17	27	A	Port Vale	W 2-0	1-0	Massey, Morgan	3009
18	Nov 1	H	Wigan Ath	W 3-0	0-0	Moore, Massey, Ferns	2983
19	4	H	Aldershot	L 0-2	0-0		3477
20	8	A	Bury	L 0-3	0-2		2202
21	12	A	Hereford U	L 0-1	0-0		1640
22	15	H	York C	D 1-1	0-0	Moore	2203
23	29	A	Halifax T	W 2-1	1-0	Morgan 2	987
24	Dec 6	H	Doncaster R	L 1-2	1-1	Spackman	2495
25	20	A	Lincoln C	L 0-2	0-1		3391
26	26	H	Southend U	W 2-1	0-0	Cusack (og), Spackman	4381
27	27	A	Wimbledon	L 0-2	0-1		2681
28	Jan 3	H	Stockport Co	L 0-1	0-1		2822
29	10	A	Crewe Alex	W 2-0	2-0	Mooney 2	3087
30	17	H	Halifax T	W 2-1	2-0	Morgan, Ferns	2413
31	24	H	Torquay U	D 1-1	0-0	Mooney	3256
32	31	A	Northampton T	W 1-0	0-0	Smith	2140
33	Feb 6	A	Tranmere R	W 1-0	0-0	Ferns	2480
34	14	H	Bradford C	W 4-0	1-0	Mooney 2, Hebditch (og), Morgan	3561
35	21	A	Rochdale	D 0-0	0-0		1846
36	28	H	Peterborough U	W 4-1	1-1	Mooney, Morgan 2, Ferns	5334
37	Mar 6	A	Scunthorpe U	D 1-1	1-0	Mooney	2392
38	14	H	Darlington	D 3-3	2-3	Mooney 2, Ferns	4995
39	21	A	Mansfield T	D 1-1	1-1	Mooney	2606
40	28	H	Port Vale	D 0-0	0-0		4665
41	Apr 4	A	Wigan Ath	W 1-0	0-0	Spackman	3750
42	11	H	Bury	D 2-2	1-0	Morgan, Pugh	4204
43	17	A	Southend U	L 1-2	0-1	Morgan	7355
44	18	H	Wimbledon	L 0-1	0-1		5048
45	25	H	Lincoln C	L 0-1	0-1		3542
46	May 2	A	Doncaster R	L 1-2	1-1	Dawtry	11,373

Final League Position: 13

Goalscorers

League (47): Mooney 10, Morgan 10, Massey 9, Ferns 5, Spackman 3, Heffernan 2, Moore 2, Dawtry 1, Elliott 1, Pugh 1, Smith 1, own goals 2.
League Cup (1): Massey.
F.A. Cup (4): Morgan 2, Massey, Webb.

League Cup	First Round	Swindon T (h)	1-1
		(a)	0-2
FA Cup	First Round	Wycombe W (a)	3-0
	Second Round	Charlton Ath (a)	1-2

Allen	Cunningham	Ferns	Impey	Townsend	Hefferman	McGrath	Spackman	Prudham	Massey	Evanson	Elliott	Prosser	Morgan	Webb	Smeulders	Moore	Compton	Bailey	Butler	Mooney	Smith	Chambers	Whittle	Sulley	Dawtry	Pugh	*Match No.*
1	2	3	4	5	6	7	8	9	10	11*	12																1
1	2	3	4	5	6	12	8		10	11	7	9*															2
1	2	3	4	5	6	9	7	12	10	11	8*																3
1	2	3	4	5	6	9	7		10	11	8																4
1	2	3	4	5	6	8	7		10*	11	12		9														5
1	2	3	4		5	8	7		10	11			9	6													6
1	2	3	4		5	8	7		10	11			9	6													7
1	2	3	4		6	8	7		10	11			9	5													8
1	2	3	4		5	8	7		10	11			9	6													9
1	2	3	4		5	8	7		10*	11	12		9	6													10
1	2	3	4		5	8	7		10	11			9	6													11
1	2	3	4		5	8	7	10		11			9	6													12
1	2	3	4		5	8	7	12	10*	11			9	6													13
	2		4		5	8	7		10	11			9	6	1	3											14
1	2	11	4		6	8	7		10*		12		9			3	5										15
1	2	7	4		6	8			10	11			9			3	5										16
1	2	8	4		6		7		10	11			9			3	5										17
1	2	7	4		6		8		10	11			9			3	5										18
1	2	8	4		6	12	7		10	11*			9			3	5										19
1	2	8	4		6		7		10		11		9			3	5										20
1		7	4		6	2	8		10		11		9*			3	5	12									21
1		2	4		6		7		10	11			9	8		3	5										22
1	2	11	4		6	8	7		10				9			3	5										23
1	2	11	4		6	12	7		10	8*			9			3	5										24
1	2		4		6		7		10		11	12	9			3	5	8*									25
1	2		4		6		7		10	11*	12		9				5		3	8							26
1	2		4		6	12	7		10				9			3	5		11*	8							27
	2	11			6	12	7		10				9*		1	3	5			8	4						28
1	2	11			6		7		10				8			3	5			9	4						29
1	2	11			6		7		10				8			3*	5			9	4	12					30
1		11	2		6		7						8				5		3	9	4		10				31
1		11	2		6		7						8				5		3	9	4		10				32
1		11	2		6		7						8				5		3	9	4		10				33
1		11	2		6		7						8				5		3	9	4		10				34
1		11	2		6		7						8				5		3	9	4		10				35
1		11	2		6		7						8				5		3	9	4		10				36
1		11	2		6		7						8				5		3	9	4		10				37
1		11	2		6								8				5		3*	9	4		10	12	7		38
1		5	2		6		10						8						3	9	4		12	11*	7		39
1			2		6		10						8				5		3	9	4			11	7		40
1	2*				6		10						8				5		3	9	4			11	7	12	41
1		3			6		10		11*				8				5		2	9	4				7	12	42
1		3	2		6		10						8				5			9	4			11	7		43
1			2		6		10*						8				5		3	9	4			11	7	12	44
1		3	2		6		10						8				5			9	4			11	7		45
1			2		6		10		4				8				5		3	9				11	7		46
44	29	38	41	5	46	17	44	2	31	21	6	1	42	10	2	16	31	1	16	21	18	—	8	7	9	—	
						+ 5s		+ 2s			+ 5s	+ 1s						+ 1s				+ 1s	+ 1s	+ 1s		+ 3s	

AFC BOURNEMOUTH

	Ht	*Wt*	*Birthplace*	*Clubs*	*League App.*	*League Gls*
Goalkeepers						
Ken Allen	6 4	13 8	Thornaby on Tees	Bournemouth	124	—
Ian Leigh	5 11	12 3	Ilfracombe	Bournemouth	—	—
John Smeulders	5 10	13 0	Hackney	Orient	—	—
(Contract cancelled Jan 1981)				Bournemouth	14	—
Defenders						
John Impey	5 11	11 12	Exeter	Cardiff C	21	—
				Bournemouth	214	5
Ian Cunningham*	5 11	10 11	Glasgow	Bournemouth	188	4
Phil Ferns	5 11	11 4	Liverpool	Bournemouth	95	6
Jon Moore	5 10	11 3	Cardiff	Bristol R	—	—
(Contract cancelled March 1981)				Millwall	119	5
				Bournemouth	36	2
Neil Townsend*	6 0½	12 10	Long Buckby	Northampton T	67	1
				Southend U	157	7
				Norwich C (on loan)	—	—
				Weymouth	(not known)	
				Bournemouth	34	2
David Webb	5 10½	12 11	London	Orient	62	3
				Southampton	75	2
				Chelsea	230	21
				QPR	116	7
				Leicester C	33	—
				Derby Co	26	1
				Bournemouth	10	—
Paul Compton	6 1½	13 1	Stroud	Trowbridge T	(not known)	
				Bournemouth	31	—
Geoff Butler	5 8	11 0	Middlesbrough	Middlesbrough	55	1
(non-contract)				Chelsea	9	—
				Sunderland	2	—
				Norwich C	153	1
				Bournemouth	129	1
Midfield						
Tom Heffernan	6 2	12 7	Dublin	Tottenham H	—	—
				Bournemouth	66	4
Philip Holder*	5 6	11 0	Kilburn	Tottenham H	13	1
				Crystal Palace	95	5
				Bournemouth	58	4
Billy Elliott	5 10	11 6	Poole	Plymouth Arg	—	—
				Bournemouth	11	1
Martin McGrath	5 8½	11 9	Finchley	Southampton	1	—
(Transferred to Oxford C March 1981)				Bournemouth	22	—
Brian Smith	5 7	11 8	Bolton	Bolton W	49	3
				Bradford C (on loan)	8	—
				Blackpool	19	1
				Bournemouth	18	1
Gary Pugh	6 1	12 10	Ramsgate	Dover	(not known)	
				Bournemouth	3	1
Forwards						
Steve Massey*	5 11	10 7	Denton	Stockport Co	101	20
				Bournemouth	97	19
John Evanson	5 10	11 7	Newcastle-under-Lyme	Oxford U	158	10
				Blackpool	67	—
(Contract cancelled March 1981)				Fulham	95	5
				Bournemouth	53	2
Nigel Spackman	6 1	12 4	Romsey	Bournemouth	44	3
Eddie Prudham	5 10	11 0	Gateshead	Sheffield W	19	2
(Contract cancelled January 1981)				Carlisle U	17	2
				Hartlepool U (on loan)	3	—
				Partick T (on loan)	4	3
				Workington (on loan)	15	6
				Stockport Co	87	22
				Bournemouth	4	—
Danny Bailey (Apprentice)			Leyton	Bournemouth	2	—
Neil Prosser	5 7	10 10	Edmonton	Harlow T	(not known)	
				Bournemouth	2	—
Dean Mooney	6 2	12 12	Paddington	Orient	22	3
				Walthamstow A	(not known)	
				Haugar	(not known)	
				Gais (Sweden)	(not known)	
				Bournemouth	21	10
Trevor Morgan	6 1	13 1	Forest Gate	Leytonstone	(not known)	
				Bournemouth	42	10
Kevin Dawtry	5 6	9 10	Hythe	Southampton	1	—
				Crystal Palace	—	—
				Bournemouth	9	1
Chris Sulley	5 8	10 0	Camberwell	Chelsea	—	—
				Bournemouth	8	—
Alan Whittle	5 7	10 4	Liverpool	Everton	74	21
(Non-contract)				Crystal Palace	108	19
				Sheffield U	—	—
				Orient	50	6
				Bournemouth	9	—

BRADFORD CITY — Division 4

Chairman: R. Martin.

Vice-Chairman: J. H. Garside.

Directors: W. McGrath, E. Sutcliffe, R. Stead.

Manager: Roy McFarland.

Secretary: T. F. Newman.

Year Formed: 1903.

Turned Professional: 1903.

Limited Company: 1908.

Football League Record:
1903 Elected to Division 2; 1908–22 Division 1; 1922–27 Division 2; 1927–29 Division 3(N); 1929–37 Division 2; 1937–61 Division 3; 1961–69 Division 4; 1969–72 Division 3; 1972–77 Division 4; 1977–78 Division 3; 1978– Division 4.

Honours: *Football League:* Division 1 best season: 5th, 1910–11; Division 2 – Champions 1907–08; Division 3(N) – Champions 1928–29. *FA Cup:* Winners 1911 (first holders of the present trophy). *Football League Cup* best season: 5th rd, 1965.

Record Victory: 11-1 v Rotherham U, Division 3(N), 25 Aug, 1928.

Record Defeat: 1-9 v Colchester U, Division 4, 30 Dec, 1961.

Most League Points: 63, Division 3(N), 1928–29.

Most League Goals: 128, Division 3(N), 1928–29.

Highest League Scorer in Season: David Layne, 34, Division 4, 1961–62.

Most League Goals in Total Aggregate: Frank O'Rourke, 88, 1906–13.

Most Capped Player: Harry Hampton, 9, Ireland.

Most League Appearances: Ian Cooper, 443, 1965–77.

Record Transfer Fee Received: £50,000 from Walsall for Stephen Baines, July 1980.

Record Transfer Fee Paid: £31,000 to Burnley for Billy Ingham, Aug 1980.

Previous Managers since the War: Jack Barker, John Milburn, David Steele, Ivor Powell, Peter Jackson, Bob Brocklebank, Bill Harris, Willie Watson, Grenville Hair, Jimmy Wheeler, Bryan Edwards, Bobby Kennedy, John Napier, George Mulhall.

Valley Parade Ground, Bradford BD8 7DY. Telephone Bradford 306062. *Ground capacity:* 16,000. *Record attendance:* 39,146 v Burnley, FA Cup 4th rd, 11 March, 1911. *Record receipts:* £27,000 v Southampton, FA Cup 6th rd, 6 March, 1976. *Pitch measurements:* 110yd×76yd.

How to get there: Ground situated approximately ¾ mile from city centre along Manningham Lane. Corporation buses 23–26 from Cheapside plus specials. West Yorkshire buses from Chester St bus station. The nearest railway station is Bradford Exchange. By road, the ground is approximately ¼ mile from Ring Road towards Bradford.

Car parking: Street parking in most side-streets. No parking in Valley Parade or South Parade.

Entertainments/catering facilities: Hot drinks, pies, crisps, etc. available at snack bars in the ground.

Club shop: Adjacent to ground entrance; sells all types of souvenirs.

Handbooks/programmes: Programmes will be sent on receipt of remittance and SAE c/o City Shop, Valley Parade.

Extra information: A Bradford firm designed the present FA Cup, the third actual trophy, in 1910. The first club to win it was Bradford City in 1911.

Club Colours: White shirts with amber and claret trimmings, white shorts, with amber and claret stripe, white with amber and claret trim stockings.

Change Colours: Amber shirts with maroon shorts, amber stockings.

Club Captain: Terry Dolan.

Coach: Mick Jones. *First Team Trainer:* Brian Edwards.

Club Nickname: The Paraders.

BRADFORD CITY 1980–81 LEAGUE RECORD

Match No.	Date	Venue	Opponents	Result	H/T Score	Goalscorers	Attendance
1	Aug 16	A	Wimbledon	D 2-2	1-1	Dolan (pen), Gallagher	2161
2	20	H	Stockport Co	D 1-1	0-0	Galvin (og)	3660
3	23	H	Scunthorpe U	D 0-0	0-0		3177
4	30	A	Peterborough U	D 2-2	0-1	McNiven, Staniforth	4009
5	Sept 6	H	AFC Bournemouth	D 1-1	1-1	Hutchins	3389
6	13	A	Torquay U	L 0-2	0-2		2611
7	17	H	Northampton T	W 3-1	0-0	Staniforth 2, Hutchins	2765
8	20	A	Rochdale	W 2-0	2-0	McNiven 2	3221
9	27	H	Tranmere R	L 0-3	0-1		3628
10	30	A	Northampton T	W 1-0	1-0	Cooper	2293
11	Oct 4	H	Crewe Alex	D 2-2	2-0	Staniforth 2	3111
12	7	A	Darlington	L 1-2	0-1	Campbell	2158
13	11	A	Mansfield T	L 0-1	0-1		3234
14	18	H	Port Vale	W 2-1	2-1	Campbell 2 (1 pen)	2843
15	22	H	Lincoln C	L 1-2	0-1	Campbell	2832
16	25	A	Bury	D 2-2	1-0	Campbell 2	3281
17	28	A	Halifax T	L 0-2	0-1		2365
18	Nov 1	H	Aldershot	W 1-0	1-0	Dolan	2279
19	4	H	Darlington	W 3-0	1-0	Watson, Campbell 2	2053
20	8	A	Wigan Ath	W 1-0	1-0	Dolan	5155
21	10	A	Stockport Co	W 2-1	0-0	Watson 2	3248
22	15	H	Wimbledon	W 2-0	1-0	Watson 2	3327
23	Dec 6	H	York C	D 1-1	0-0	Dolan	3638
24	12	A	Southend U	L 1-3	1-1	Campbell	4476
25	20	A	Hereford U	L 0-4	0-2		2114
26	26	H	Doncaster R	D 1-1	1-0	Dolan (pen)	4356
27	27	A	Hartlepool U	D 2-2	2-1	Ingham 2	3670
28	Jan 10	A	Lincoln C	D 1-1	1-0	Wood	4670
29	28	H	Peterborough U	D 1-1	1-0	Campbell	3305
30	31	A	Scunthorpe U	L 0-1	0-1		2558
31	Feb 7	H	Torquay U	W 2-0	2-0	Campbell 2	2872
32	11	H	Halifax T	D 0-0	0-0		3056
33	14	A	AFC Bournemouth	L 0-4	0-1		3561
34	Mar 4	H	Southend U	W 2-1	1-0	Gallagher, Jackson	2369
35	7	A	Crewe Alex	L 0-1	0-0		2487
36	8	H	Rochdale	W 2-1	1-0	McNiven, Staniforth	2926
37	10	A	Tranmere R	D 1-1	0-1	Campbell (pen)	1300
38	14	H	Mansfield T	L 0-2	0-0		2986
39	28	H	Bury	L 0-2	0-0		2242
40	Apr 4	A	Aldershot	D 1-1	0-0	Ingham	2255
41	11	H	Wigan Ath	D 3-3	2-2	Campbell 3	2069
42	14	A	Port Vale	L 1-2	0-1	Campbell	2221
43	19	H	Hartlepool U	W 2-0	2-0	Staniforth, Black	1614
44	21	A	Doncaster R	L 0-2	0-1		8856
45	May 2	A	York C	W 3-0	0-0	Campbell 2, Ellis	1481
46	15	H	Hereford U	L 0-1	0-1		1249

Final League Position: 14

Goalscorers

League (53): Campbell 19 (2 pens), Staniforth 7, Dolan 5 (2 pens), Watson 5, McNiven 4, Ingham 3, Gallagher 2, Hutchins 2, Black 1, Cooper 1, Ellis 1, Jackson 1, Wood 1, own goal 1.
League Cup (4): Campbell 3, Gallagher.
F.A. Cup (2): Chapman, Wood.

League Cup	First Round	Rotherham U (a)	3-1
		(h)	0-0
	Second Round	Liverpool (h)	1-0
		(a)	0-4
FA Cup	First Round	Port Vale (a)	2-4

Smith	Podd	Watson	Dolan	Jackson	Wood	Gallagher	Staniforth	Campbell	Ingham	Chapman	Cooper	McNiven	Hutchins	Robertson	Hanson	Thompson	Black	Ramsbottom	Hebditch	Ellis	*Match No.*
1	2	3	4	5	6*	7	8	9	10	11	12										1
1	2	3		5		7	8	9	4	11	6	10									2
1	2		3	5		7*	8	9	4	11	6	10	12								3
1	2		7	5	3		8	9		11	6	10		4							4
1	2*		12	5	3		8	9		7	6	10	11	4							5
1	2			5	3		8	9		7	6	10	11	4							6
1	2		4	5	3		8		10	7	6	12	11		9*						7
1	2		7	5	3		8		11	9	6	10				4					8
1	2		7*	5	3		8	12	6	9		10	11			4					9
1	2		7	5	3		8		11	9	6	10				4					10
1	2		7	5	3		8*		11	9	6	10	12			4					11
1	2		7	5	3			9	11	8*	6	10	12			4					12
1	2	12	7	5	3			9	11	8	6	10				4*					13
1	2	3		5	7		8	9	4		6	10	11								14
1	2	3		5	6		8	9	4	7		10	11								15
1	2	3		5	4		8	9		7	6	10	11								16
1	2	3		5	6		8	9	4	7		10	11								17
1	2	3	10	5	6		8	9	4	7			11								18
1		3	10	5	6		8	9	4	7			11			2					19
1		3	10	5	6		8	9	4	7			11			2					20
1	11*	3	10	5	6		8	9	4	7		12				2					21
1		3	10	5	6		8	9	4	7			11			2					22
1		3	10	5	6			9	4	7		8*	11			2	12				23
1		3	10	5	6*		8	9	4	7		12				2	11				24
1		3	10	5	6		8	9	4	7		12				2	11*				25
		3	12	5*	6		8	9	4	7		10	11			2		1			26
			3		6			9	4	7	5	10	8			2	11	1			27
	2		10	5	3		8	9	4	7		12	11*			6		1			28
	2	6	10	5	3		8	9	4	7							11	1			29
	2	6	10*	5	3		8	9	4	7		12					11	1			30
		6		5	3	10	8	9	4	7						2	11	1			31
		3		5		10	8*	9	4	7		12		2			11	1	6		32
		6		5			8	9	4	7		10	11			2		1	3		33
	2			5	3	11	8	9	4	7		10				6		1			34
	2			5	3	11	8*	9	4	7		10				6	12	1			35
	2			5	3	11	8	9	4	7		10				6		1			36
	2			5	3	11	8	9	4	7		10				6		1			37
	2			5	3	11*	8	9	4	7.		10				6	12	1			38
	2			5	3	11	8	9	4	7*		10	12			6		1			39
	2			5	3		8	9	4	7		10				6	11	1			40
	2			5	3		8	9	4	7		10				6*	11	1		12	41
	2	6		5	3		8	9	4	7		10					11	1			42
	2	3		5	6	12	8	9	4	7			11*				10	1			43
	2	6		5	3		8	9	4	7							10	1		11	44
	2	6		5	3		8	9	4	7							10	1		11	45
1	2*			5	3		8	9	4	7		12				6	10			11	46
26	35	24	22	45	42	11	42	41	42	45	14	28	18	4	1	27	14	20	2	3	
		+ 1s	+ 2s			+ 1s		+ 1s			+ 1s	+ 8s	+ 4s				+ 3s			+ 1s	

BRADFORD CITY

	Ht	Wt	Birthplace	Clubs	League App.	League Gls
Goalkeepers						
Steve Smith	6 0	12 5	Lydney	Birmingham C	2	—
				Bradford C	93	—
Neil Ramsbottom	6 1	13 0	Blackburn	Bury	174	—
				Blackpool	13	—
				Crewe Alex (on loan)	3	—
				Coventry C	51	—
				Sheffield W	18	—
				Plymouth Arg	39	—
				Blackburn R	10	—
				Sheffield U	2	—
				Bradford C	20	—
Defenders						
Cec Podd	5 9	10 0	St Kitts, W Indies	Bradford C	389	1
Mick Wood	5 11	10 13	Bury	Blackburn R	147	2
				Bradford C	131	8
Peter Jackson	6 1		Bradford	Bradford C	66	2
Terry Cooper*	5 9	11 7	Cwmbran	Newport Co	68	1
				Notts Co	9	—
				Lincoln C	270	12
				Scunthorpe U (on loan)	4	—
				Bradford C	48	2
Alan Thompson	5 11	12 0	Liverpool	Sheffield W	156	3
				Stockport Co	94	17
				Bradford C	29	—
Alan Hebditch (Non-contract)			Wigan	Bradford C	2	—
Midfield						
Gary Watson	5 8	10 6	Bradford	Bradford C	209	28
Barry Gallagher			Bradford	Bradford C	15	3
Les Chapman	5 7	10 4	Oldham	Oldham Ath	76	9
				Huddersfield T	133	8
				Oldham Ath	187	11
				Stockport Co	32	1
				Bradford C	59	2
Billy Ingham	5 5½	9 10	Stakeford	Burnley	212	22
				Bradford C	42	3
John Black	5 8	10 10½	Glasgow	Wolverhampton W	6	—
				Bradford C	23	5
Forwards						
Don Hutchins*	5 7	10 2	Leicester	Leicester C	4	—
				Plymouth Arg	96	23
				Blackburn R	41	6
				Bradford C	256	45
Terry Dolan	6 1	11 3	Bradford	Bradford C	—	—
				Bradford PA	48	—
				Huddersfield T	162	14
				Bradford C	195	43
David McNiven	5 6	11 4	Stonehouse	Leeds U	22	6
				Bradford C	142	41
Lammie Robertson*	5 10	11 2	Paisley	Burnley	—	—
				Bury	5	—
				Halifax T	149	20
				Brighton	46	9
				Exeter C	133	25
				Leicester C	7	—
				Peterborough U	15	1
				Bradford C	43	3
David Staniforth	6 0	12 1	Chesterfield	Sheffield U	26	3
				Bristol R	153	31
				Bradford C	81	18
Bobby Campbell	5 11	12 7	Belfast	Aston V	10	1
				Halifax T (on loan)	15	—
				Huddersfield T	31	9
				Sheffield U	37	11
				Huddersfield T	7	3
				Halifax T	22	3
				Bradford C	63	27
John Hanson	5 11	11 9	Bradford	Bradford C	1	—
Mark Ellis (Non-contract)	5 7	10 5	Bradford	Bradford C	4	1

BRENTFORD Division 3

Chairman: Dan Tana.

Directors: R. J. J. Blindell LLB, E. J. Radley-Smith MS, FRCS, LRCP, M. M. Lange.

Manager: Fred Callaghan.

Chief Administrator/Secretary: D. R. Piggott.

Year Formed: 1889.

Turned Professional: 1899. *Limited Company:* 1901.

Previous Grounds: Clifden Road 1889–91; Benns Fields, Little Ealing 1891–95; Shotters Field 1895–98; Cross Road, S. Ealing 1898–1900; Boston Park 1900–04; Griffin Park 1904.

Football League Record:
1920 Original Member of Division 3; 1921–33 Division 3(S); 1933–35 Division 2; 1935–47 Division 1; 1947–54 Division 2; 1954–62 Division 3(S); 1962–63 Division 4; 1963–66 Division 3; 1966–72 Division 4; 1972–73 Division 3; 1973–78 Division 4; 1978– Division 3.

Honours: *Football League:* Division 1 best season: 5th, 1935–36; Division 2 – Champions 1934–35; Division 3(S) – Champions 1932–33; Runners-up 1929–30, 1957–58; Division 4 – Champions 1962–63. *FA Cup* best season: 6th rd, 1938, 1946, 1949. *Football League Cup* best season: 3rd rd, 1961, 1969.

Record Victory: 9-0 v Wrexham, Division 3, 15 Oct, 1963.

Record Defeat: 0-7 v Swansea T, Division 3(S), 8 Nov, 1924; 0-7 v Walsall, Division 3(S), 19 Jan, 1957.

Most League Points: 62, Division 3(S), 1932–33; 62, Division 4, 1962–63.

Most League Goals: 98, Division 4, 1962–63.

Highest League Scorer in Season: Jack Holliday, 38, Division 3(S), 1932–33.

Most League Goals in Total Aggregate: Jim Towers, 153, 1954–61.

Most Capped Player: Idris Hopkins, 12, Wales.

Most League Appearances: Ken Coote, 514, 1949–64.

Record Transfer Fee Received: £60,000 from Sheffield W for Andy McCulloch, June 1979.

Record Transfer Fee Paid: £50,000 to Gillingham for Tony Funnell, March 1980.

Previous Managers since the War: Harry Curtis, Jackie Gibbons, Jimmy Bain, Tom Lawton, Bill Dodgin (Snr), Malcolm McDonald, Tommy Cavanagh, Billy Gray, Jimmy Sirrel, Frank Blunstone, Mike Everitt, John Docherty, Bill Dodgin (Jnr).

Address of Supporters Club: Same as Football Club.

Address of the Club Shop or Boutique: c/o the Club.

Griffin Park, Braemar Rd, Brentford, Middlesex TW8 0NT. Telephone 01-560 2021. *Ground capacity:* 37,000 (30,500 under cover). *Record attendance:* 39,626 v Preston NE, FA Cup 6th rd, 5 March, 1938. *Record receipts:* £16,799 v Fulham, Division 3, 13 Sept, 1980. *Pitch measurements:* 114yd×75yd.

How to get there: South Ealing (Underground, Piccadilly line). Southern Region trains from Waterloo to Brentford Central. Buses 91, 65, 117, E1, E2, 267. The ground is within a mile of the M4 and A4 roads.

Match tickets: Admission mainly by cash through the turnstiles on the day but tickets for Block B only are available at £2.60 each a fortnight prior to each match. Postal applications should include SAE.

Car parking: Confined to streets around the ground.

Entertainments/catering facilities: Catering kiosks in the ground. A members' social club, the 'Centre Circle' in Braemar Road.

Club shop: Applications for price lists, etc., should be sent to the Commercial Manager, Brentford FC, Braemar Road, Brentford, Middlesex, TW8 0NT, accompanied by SAE.

Handbooks/programmes: Programmes not available on subscription.

Extra information: One of only six clubs to win all their home games in a season; Brentford accomplished this feat in 1929–30.

Club Colours: Red and white striped shirts, black shorts, black stockings with red and white hoop tops.

Change Colours: All blue.

Physiotherapist: A. E. Lyons. *Player-Coach:* Ron Harris.

Club Nickname: Bees.

BRENTFORD 1980–81 LEAGUE RECORD

Match No.	Date	Venue	Opponents	Result	H/T Score	Goalscorers	Attendance
1	Aug 16	A	Charlton Ath	L 1-3	0-2	Hill	5125
2	18	H	Millwall	W 1-0	1-0	Funnell	6520
3	23	H	Reading	L 1-2	1-1	Funnell	6720
4	30	A	Walsall	W 3-2	1-1	Walker, Hill, Funnell	4586
5	Sept 6	A	Portsmouth	W 2-0	0-0	Booker, Funnell	16,971
6	13	H	Fulham	L 1-3	1-1	Booker	11,600
7	15	H	Barnsley	D 1-1	0-0	Funnell	6900
8	20	A	Blackpool	W 3-0	2-0	Crown 2, Walker	6738
9	27	H	Hull C	D 2-2	1-2	Jenkins, Funnell	6300
10	30	A	Barnsley	W 1-0	1-0	Walker	11,227
11	Oct 4	H	Newport Co	L 0-1	0-1		7309
12	8	A	Exeter C	D 0-0	0-0		4665
13	11	A	Carlisle U	W 2-1	0-0	Walker, Silkman (pen)	3030
14	18	H	Chester	L 0-1	0-1		6600
15	20	H	Gillingham	D 3-3	2-1	Crown, Hurlock, Smith	6790
16	25	A	Burnley	L 0-2	0-1		7297
17	28	A	Plymouth Arg	W 1-0	0-0	Smith	7249
18	Nov 1	H	Oxford U	W 3-0	1-0	Hill, Crown 2	6550
19	3	H	Exeter C	L 0-1	0-1		6590
20	8	A	Chesterfield	L 1-2	1-1	Graham	7186
21	11	A	Millwall	D 2-2	0-2	Booker, Hurlock	4274
22	15	H	Charlton Ath	L 0-1	0-0		8180
23	29	A	Huddersfield T	L 0-3	0-1		8871
24	Dec 6	H	Swindon T	D 1-1	1-0	Kruse	5730
25	20	A	Rotherham U	L 1-4	0-2	Johnson	5913
26	26	H	Colchester U	W 2-1	1-1	Kruse, Hurlock	6240
27	27	A	Sheffield U	D 0-0	0-0		13,130
28	Jan 3	H	Burnley	D 0-0	0-0		6380
29	10	A	Chester	D 0-0	0-0		2041
30	17	H	Huddersfield T	D 0-0	0-0		5830
31	24	H	Walsall	W 4-0	3-0	Frost, Johnson 2, Shrubb	5500
32	31	A	Reading	D 0-0	0-0		6129
33	Feb 7	A	Fulham	D 1-1	0-1	Roberts	8721
34	14	H	Portsmouth	D 2-2	2-1	Tucker (pen), Roberts	10,160
35	21	A	Hull C	D 0-0	0-0		4535
36	28	H	Blackpool	W 2-0	1-0	Johnson, Frost	5580
37	Mar 7	A	Newport Co	D 1-1	0-1	Crown	5224
38	14	H	Carlisle U	D 1-1	0-0	Frost	6211
39	21	A	Gillingham	L 0-2	0-0		3916
40	28	H	Plymouth Arg	L 0-1	0-1		5870
41	Apr 4	A	Oxford U	D 1-1	0-0	Booker	3873
42	11	H	Chesterfield	W 3-2	1-1	Roberts, Johnson, Ridley (og)	4880
43	18	H	Sheffield U	D 1-1	0-1	Booker	5620
44	20	A	Colchester U	W 2-0	2-0	Shrubb, Booker	2609
45	25	H	Rotherham U	W 2-1	0-0	Booker, Hurlock	6910
46	May 2	A	Swindon T	D 0-0	0-0		8725

Final League Position: 9

Goalscorers

League (52): Booker 7, Crown 6, Funnell 6, Johnson (G) 5, Hurlock 4, Walker 4, Frost 3, Hill 3, Roberts 3, Kruse 2, Shrubb 2, Smith 2, Graham 1, Jenkins 1, Silkman 1 (pen), Tucker 1 (pen), own goal 1.
League Cup (3): Crown, Smith, Walker.
F.A. Cup (4): Funnell 2 (1 pen), Booker, Crown.

League Cup	First Round	Charlton Ath (h)	3-1
		(a)	0-5
FA Cup	First Round	Addlestone (a)	2-2
		(h)	2-0
	Second Round	Fulham (a)	0-1

McCullough	Shrubb	Hill	Jenkins	Kruse	Harris	Salman	Silkman	Booker	Walker	Crown	Funnell	Hurlock	McKellar	McNichol	Smith	Roberts	Graham	Tucker	Frost	Johnson G	Johnson R	Teer	*Match No.*
1	2	3	4*	5	6	7	8	9	10	11	12												1
1	2	3		5	6	4	8	9	10	11	7												2
1	2	3		5	6	4	8	9	10	11	7												3
1		3		5	2	4	8	9	10	11	7	6											4
1	2	3		5		4	8	9	10	11	7	6											5
1	2	3		5		4	8	9	10	11	7	6											6
1	2	3*	12	5		4	8	9	10	11	7	6											7
	3		2*	5		4	8	9	10	11	7	6	1	12									8
	3		2	5		4	8	9	10	11	7	6	1										9
	3		2	5		4	8	9	10	11	7	6	1										10
	3		2*	5		4	8	9	10	11	7	6	1		12								11
	3		2	5		4	8	9	10	11	7	6	1										12
	3	12	2	5		4	8	9	10	11		6	1			7*							13
	3		12	5	2	4	8	9	10	11		6	1			7*							14
		3		5	2	4			10	11	7	6	1		9		8						15
	2	3		5	8	4			10	11*	7	6	1	12	9								16
	2	3		5	8	4		9	10	11		6	1		7								17
	2	3		5	8	4			10	11	7	6	1		9								18
	2	3	12	5*	8	4			10	11	7	6	1		9								19
	12	3	2			4		9*	10	11	7	6	1	5			8						20
	12	3	2			4		9	10*	11	7	6	1	5			8						21
	12	3	2			4		9	10	11	7*	6	1	5			8						22
	2	3		5		4		9	10*	11	7	6	1	12			8						23
	2			5	8	4			10*	11	7	6	1		9	12		3					24
	12	3	5			4*			10	11		6	1			7		2	8	9			25
		2		5		4			10	11		6	1			7		3	8	9			26
	10	3		5	7	4				11		6	1					2	8	9			27
	7	3		5	10	4				11	12	6	1					2	8*	9			28
	7	3		5	10	4				11		6	1					2	8	9			29
	7	3		5	10	4				11		6	1					2	8	9			30
	7	3		5	10	4				11*		6	1			12		2	8	9			31
	7	3		5	10	4				11		6	1					2	8	9			32
	7	3		5	10	4				11*		6	1			12		2	8	9			33
	7	3		5	10							6	1	4		11		2	8	9			34
	7	3		5	10							6	1	4		11		2	8	9			35
	7	3		5	10							6	1	4		11		2	8	9			36
	7	3		5	10					11		6	1	4		12		2	8*	9			37
	7	3		5	10					11		6	1	4				2	8	9			38
	7*	3		5	10	4				11		6	1			12		2	8	9			39
		3		5		4		12	10	11*	7	6	1			8		2		9			40
	7	3		5	6	4		8	10				1			11		2		9			41
	7	3		5	10	4*		8		12		6	1			11		2		9			42
	7	3		5	10			8				6	1	4		11		2		9			43
	7			5	10			8				6	1	4		11		2		9	3		44
	7	3		5	10			8				6	1	4		11		2		9			45
	7	3		5		4		8	10			6	1			11*		2		9		12	46
7	38	37	11	42	29	38	14	25	29	37	21	42	39	11	6	14	5	23	15	22	1	—	
	+ 4s	+ 1s	+ 3s					+ 1s		+ 1s	+ 2s			+ 3s	+ 1s	+ 5s						+ 1s	

BRENTFORD

	Ht	*Wt*	*Birthplace*	*Clubs*	*League App.*	*League Gls*
Paul McCullough*	6 0	12 5	Birmingham	Reading	—	—
				Dawlish	(not known)	
				Brentford	7	—
David McKellar	6 0	11 8	Irvine	Ipswich T	—	—
				Colchester U (on loan)	—	—
				Peterborough U (on loan)	—	—
				Derby Co	41	—
				Brentford	39	—
Defenders						
Danis Salman	5 10	11 8	Famagusta	Brentford	180	5
Barry Tucker	5 6	10 12	Swansea	Northampton T	214	3
				Brentford	126	1
John Fraser	5 10	10 7	London	Fulham	55	1
(Contract cancelled Aug 1980)				Brentford	123	6
Pat Kruse	5 11	12 10	Biggleswade	Leicester C	2	—
				Mansfield T (on loan)	6	1
				Torquay U	79	4
				Brentford	185	12
Jim McNichol	6 0	12 10	Glasgow	Ipswich T	—	—
				Luton T	15	—
				Brentford	77	12
Ron Harris	5 8	11 7	Hackney	Chelsea	655	13
				Brentford	29	—
Iori Jenkins	5 11	11 6	Neath	Chelsea	—	—
(Contract cancelled Jan 1981)				Brentford	15	1
Robbie Johnson	5 8	10 13	London	Arsenal	—	—
				Brentford	1	—
Mark Hill	6 0	12 0	Perivale	QPR	—	—
				Brentford	38	3
Midfield						
Paul Walker	5 6	10 10	London	Brentford	46	4
Paul Shrubb	5 7¾	10 4	Guildford	Fulham	1	—
				Hellenic (S Africa)	(not known)	
				Brentford	178	8
Willie Graham	5 8½	10 7	Co Armagh	Northampton T	—	—
(Contract cancelled Feb 1981)				Brentford	48	3
Billy Holmes	5 10	10 10	Balham	Millwall	1	—
(Contract cancelled July 1980)				Luton T	1	—
				Wimbledon	15	5
				Hereford U	31	5
				Brentford	15	2
Terry Hurlock	5 9	13 2	Hackney	Leytonstone	(not known)	
				Brentford	42	4
Forwards						
Bob Booker	6 2½	12 4	Watford	Brentford	41	13
Dean Smith	5 10	11 9	Leicester	Leicester C	10	1
(Contract cancelled Feb 1981)				Brentford	54	16
Lee Holmes	6 0	12 7	Aveley	Harringey	(not known)	
(Contract cancelled Oct 1980)				Brentford	28	6
Tony Funnell	5 6¼	10 10	Eastbourne	Southampton	17	8
				Gillingham	33	10
				Brentford	32	8
Gary Roberts	6 0	11 6	Rhyl	Wembley	(not known)	
				Brentford	19	3
Lee Frost*	5 8½	10 7	Woking	Chelsea	14	5
				Brentford	21	3
Gary Johnson	5 11¾	11 8	Camberwell	Chelsea	19	9
				Brentford	22	5
David Crown	5 10	11 0	Enfield	Walthamstow A	(not known)	
				Brentford	38	6
Kevin Teer (Apprentice)				Brentford	1	—

BRIGHTON & HOVE ALBION Division 1

Chairman: M. K. Bamber.
Vice-Chairman: K. Wickenden.
Directors: N. J. Hyams, D. Sizen, T. Appleby.
Manager: Mike Bailey.
Secretary: Kenneth Calver. *Year Formed:* 1900.
Turned Professional: 1900. *Limited Company:* 1901.
Previous Name: Brighton & Hove Rangers.
Previous Grounds: 1900, Withdean; 1901, County Ground; 1902, Goldstone Ground.

Football League Record:
1920 Original Member of Division 3; 1921–58 Division 3(S); 1958–62 Division 2; 1962–63 Division 3; 1963–65 Division 4; 1965–72 Division 3; 1972–73 Division 2; 1973–77 Division 3; 1977–79 Division 2; 1979– Division 1.

Honours: *Football League:* Division 1 best season: 16th, 1979–80; Division 3(S) – Champions 1957–58; Runners-up 1953–54, 1955–56; Division 3 – Runners-up 1971–72, 1976–77; Division 4 – Champions 1964–65. *FA Cup* best season: 5th rd, 1929–30, 1932–33, 1945–46, 1959–60; old 3rd rd 1913–14, 1923–24. *Football League Cup* best season: 5th rd, 1978–79.

Record Victory: 10-1 v Wisbech, FA Cup 1st rd, 13 Nov, 1965.
Record Defeat: 0-9 v Middlesbrough, Division 2, 23 Aug, 1958.
Most League Points: 65, Division 3(S), 1955–56, and Division 3, 1971–72.
Most League Goals: 112, Division 3(S), 1955–56.
Highest League Scorer in Season: Peter Ward, 32, Division 3, 1976–77.
Most League Goals in Total Aggregate: Tommy Cook, 113, 1922–29.
Most Capped Player: Mark Lawrenson, 13 (14), Eire.
Most League Appearances: 'Tug' Wilson, 509, 1922–36.
Record Transfer Fee Received: £400,000 from Nottingham F for Peter Ward, Oct 1980.
Record Transfer Fee Paid: £400,000 to Glasgow Rangers for Gordon Smith, June 1980.
Previous Managers since the War: Tommy Cook, Don Welsh, Billy Lane, George Curtis, Archie Macaulay, Freddie Goodwin, Pat Saward, Brian Clough, Peter Taylor, Alan Mullery MBE.
Address of Supporters Club: Albion Shop, Goldstone Ground, Hove.

Goldstone Ground, Old Shoreham Rd, Hove, Sussex BN3 7DE. Telephone Brighton 739535. *Ground capacity:* 32,500. *Record attendance:* 36,747 v Fulham, Division 2, 27 December, 1958. *Pitch measurements:* 112yd×75yd.

How to get there: Buses 5, B5, 9, 26, 40, 55, 19 from Old Steyne and 11 via Brighton station and Old Shoreham Rd. Hove station is five minutes walk from the ground.
Match tickets: Postal bookings for tickets four weeks in advance if available.
Car parking: Car parking facilities are available a few minutes away at the Greyhound Stadium, Neville Road, and in Hove Station Goods Yard, Sackville Road. There is limited parking adjacent to the stadium.
Entertainments/catering facilities: Bars and tea stands around the ground.
Club shop: At the ground; sells all types of souvenirs.
Handbooks/programmes: Programmes available by post from the club shop.
Extra information: In 1933–34 Oliver Brown was Brighton's leading scorer with 12 goals; yet he played in only 8 matches! Missed promotion to Division 1, 1977–78 on goal difference.
Club Colours: All blue.
Change Colours: All yellow.
Physiotherapist: M. Yaxley.
First Team Coach: John Collins.
Club Nickname: The Seagulls.

BRIGHTON & HOVE ALBION 1980–81 LEAGUE RECORD

Match No.	Date	Venue	Opponents	Result	H/T Score	Goalscorers	Attendance
1	Aug 16	H	Wolverhampton W	W 2-0	0-0	Smith, Gregory	19,307
2	19	A	Ipswich T	L 0-2	0-1		21,568
3	23	A	Tottenham H	D 2-2	1-1	Smith 2	39,763
4	30	H	WBA	L 1-2	1-0	Robinson	18,162
5	Sept 6	A	Southampton	L 1-3	0-2	Smith	22,225
6	13	H	Birmingham C	D 2-2	1-1	McNab, Lawrenson	15,788
7	20	H	Norwich C	W 2-0	0-0	Robinson, Stevens	14,877
8	27	A	Liverpool	L 1-4	0-1	Horton (pen)	35,836
9	Oct 4	A	Coventry C	D 3-3	0-2	Smith 3	11,462
10	7	H	Everton	L 1-3	0-0	Ward	16,523
11	11	H	Nottingham F	L 0-1	0-1		17,420
12	18	A	Stoke C	D 0-0	0-0		13,079
13	22	A	Aston Villa	L 1-4	1-1	Gregory	27,367
14	25	H	Manchester C	L 1-2	0-0	Robinson	18,368
15	Nov 1	A	Arsenal	L 0-2	0-0		28,569
16	8	H	Middlesbrough	L 0-1	0-0		12,112
17	11	H	Ipswich T	W 1-0	0-0	Robinson	17,055
18	15	A	Wolverhampton W	W 2-0	1-0	Robinson 2	15,946
19	22	H	Manchester U	L 1-4	0-3	Ritchie	23,277
20	29	A	Leeds U	L 0-1	0-0		14,333
21	Dec 6	H	Sunderland	W 2-1	1-0	Robinson, Ritchie	13,903
22	13	A	Everton	L 3-4	2-2	O'Sullivan, Ritchie, Robinson	19,157
23	20	H	Aston Villa	W 1-0	1-0	Robinson	16,425
24	26	A	Leicester C	W 1-0	0-0	Gregory	19,570
25	27	H	Crystal Palace	W 3-2	1-1	O'Sullivan, Robinson 2	27,367
26	Jan 10	A	Manchester U	L 1-2	0-1	Ritchie	42,208
27	17	A	WBA	L 0-2	0-1		15,643
28	31	H	Tottenham H	L 0-2	0-1		23,354
29	Feb 7	A	Birmingham C	L 1-2	0-1	Robinson	13,691
30	21	H	Liverpool	D 2-2	2-1	Robinson, Smith	23,275
31	24	H	Southampton	W 2-0	0-0	Williams (pen), Stille	23,715
32	28	A	Norwich C	L 1-3	0-2	Robinson	16,199
33	Mar 7	H	Coventry C	W 4-1	2-1	Robinson 2, Stille, Smith	14,063
34	14	A	Nottingham F	L 1-4	1-2	Stille	20,688
35	21	H	Stoke C	D 1-1	1-1	Robinson	13,583
36	28	A	Manchester C	D 1-1	0-0	Gregory	30,122
37	Apr 4	H	Arsenal	L 0-1	0-1		21,015
38	11	A	Middlesbrough	L 0-1	0-0		11,076
39	18	A	Crystal Palace	W 3-0	2-0	Gregory 2, Smith	18,792
40	20	H	Leicester C	W 2-1	0-1	Robinson, Gregory	21,176
41	25	A	Sunderland	W 2-1	1-0	Robinson, Williams	22,317
42	May 2	H	Leeds U	W 2-0	1-0	Foster, Ritchie	27,577

Final League Position: 19

Goalscorers

League (54): Robinson 19, Smith 10, Gregory 7, Ritchie 5, Stille 3, O'Sullivan 2, Williams 2 (1 pen), Foster 1, Horton 1 (pen), Lawrenson 1, McNab 1, Stevens 1, Ward 1.
League Cup (8): Robinson 3, Foster 2, Ryan, Ward, Williams.
F.A. Cup (2): Horton, Ritchie.

League Cup	Second Round	Tranmere R (h)	3-1
		(a)	4-2
	Third Round	Coventry C (h)	1-2
FA Cup	Third Round	Manchester U (a)	2-2
		(h)	0-2

Moseley	Gregory	Williams	Horton	Foster	Lawrenson	McHale	Ward	Robinson	Smith	McNab	Ryan	Gariani	Stevens	Stille	Cohen	O'Sullivan	Ritchie	Clark	Phillips	Digweed	Vessey	Ramsey	*Match No.*
1	2	3	4	5	6	7	8	9	10	11													1
1	2	3	4	5	6	7	8	9	10	11													2
1	2	3	4	5	6	7	8	9	10	11													3
1	2	3	4	5	6	7*	8	9	10	11	12												4
1	2	3		5		7	8	9	10	11	4*	12	6										5
1	2	3	4	5	6	7*	8	9	10	11				12									6
1	2	3	4	5	6		8	9	10	11			7										7
1	2	3	4	5	6		8	9	10*	11	12		7										8
1	2	3	4	5	6	12	8	9	10	11			7*										9
1	2	3	4	5	6	12	8	9	10	11			7*										10
1	2	3	4	5	6		8	9	10	11			7										11
1	2	3	4	5	6	8		9	10		11*		7		12								12
1	2	3*	4	5	6	11		9	10				7			12	8						13
1	2		4	5	6	11*		9	10				7		3	12	8						14
1	2		4	5	6			9	10				7		3	11	8						15
1	2		4	5	6			9	10	7			12		3*	11	8						16
1	2		4	5	6			9	10	7			3			11	8						17
1	2		4	5	6			9	10	7			3			11	8						18
1	2		4	5	6			9	10*	7	12		3			11	8						19
1	2		4	5	6			9	10*	7			3		12	11	8						20
1	2		4	5	6			9	10*	7			3		12	11	8						21
1	2		4	5	6			9	10	7			3			11	8						22
1	2		4	5	6			9		7			3			11	8	10					23
1	2		4	5	6			9		7			3			11	8	10					24
	2		4	5	6			9		7			3			11	8	10	1				25
1	2		4	5	6			9	10	7			3			11	8						26
	2		4	5	6			9		7			3			11	8	10		1			27
	2		4	5	6			9	12	7*			3			11	8	10		1			28
	2		4	5*	6			9	10	7			3			11	8	12		1			29
	2*	8		5	6			9	10		12		3	7		11		4		1			30
		2		5	6			9	10	7			3	8		11		4		1			31
		2		5	6			9	10	7	12		3	8		11*		4		1			32
		2	4	5	6			9	10	7	12		3	8						1	11*		33
	11*	2	4	5	6			9	10	7			3	8			12			1			34
	7	3	4	5				9	10	11			2	8			6			1			35
	7	3	4	5	6*			9	8	11			2	10			12			1			36
	7	3	4	5	6			9	10	11			2	8*			12			1			37
	7	3	4	5	6			9	12	11*			2	8			10			1			38
	7	3	4	5	6			9	11		12					8	10			1		2*	39
1	7	3	4	5	6			9	10				2			11	8						40
	7	3	4	5	6			9	10		12					11	8*			1		2	41
	7	3	4	5	6			9	10							11	8			1		2	42
26	39	26	38	42	40	9	11	42	36	33	2	—	33	9	3	22	23	8	1	15	1	3	
						+ 2s			+ 2s		+ 8s	+ 1s	+ 1s	+ 1s	+ 3s	+ 2s	+ 3s	+ 1s					

BRIGHTON & HOVE ALBION

	Ht	*Wt*	*Birthplace*	*Clubs*	*League App.*	*League Gls*
Goalkeepers						
Graham Moseley	6 0	11 8	Manchester	Blackburn R	—	—
				Derby Co	32	—
				Aston V (on loan)	3	—
				Walsall (on loan)	3	—
				Brighton	80	—
Tony Knight*	6 1	11 0	Romford	Dover	(not known)	
				Swindon T (on loan)	—	—
				Brighton	—	—
John Phillips*	6 0	10 8	Shrewsbury	Shrewsbury T	51	—
(Wales)				Aston V	15	—
				Chelsea	125	—
				Swansea C (on loan)	—	—
				Crewe Alex (on loan)	6	—
				Brighton	1	—
Perry Digweed	6 0½	11 4	London	Fulham	15	—
				Brighton	15	—
Defenders						
Mark Lawrenson	5 10	10 10	Preston	Preston NE	73	2
(Eire)				Brighton	152	5
Gary Williams	5 10	11 0	Liverpool	Preston NE	112	2
				Brighton	144	6
John Gregory	6 1	11 0	Scunthorpe	Northampton T	187	8
				Aston V	65	10
				Brighton	72	7
Tony Vessey	5 9	11 10	Derby	Brighton	1	—
Gary Stevens	5 11	11 10	Ipswich	Ipswich T	—	—
				Brighton	60	2
Peter Suddaby	5 11	12 2	Stockport	Blackpool	332	9
				Brighton	23	—
Steve Foster	6 0	12 8	Portsmouth	Portsmouth	109	6
				Brighton	80	2
Jacob Cohen			Israel	Maccabi Tel Aviv	(not known)	
(Israel)				Brighton	6	—
Chris Ramsey			Birmingham	Bristol C	—	—
				Brighton	3	—
Midfield						
Glen Geard	5 7	10 3	Brighton	Brighton	—	—
(Contract cancelled Feb 1981)						
Brian Horton	5 10	11 4	Hednesford	Port Vale	236	33
				Brighton	218	33
Peter O'Sullivan*	5 6	10 0	Colwyn Bay	Manchester U	—	—
(Wales)				Brighton	435	38
Paul Clark	5 10	12 5	S Benfleet	Southend U	33	1
				Brighton	79	9
Giles Stille	5 9	11 9	London	Brighton	11	3
Neil McNab	5 7	10 10	Greenock	Morton	14	—
				Tottenham H	72	3
				Bolton W	35	4
				Brighton	49	1
Moshe Gariani			Israel	Maccabi Nathanya	(not known)	
(Israel)				Brighton	1	—
Wayne Orton			Bognor	Littlehampton	(not known)	
(Contract cancelled March 1981)				Brighton	—	—
Forwards						
Mike Ring	5 10	10 6	Brighton	Brighton	—	—
Gerry Ryan	5 10	10 12	Dublin	Bohemians	—	—
(Eire)				Derby Co	30	4
				Brighton	80	14
Andy Ritchie	5 9½	11 11	Manchester	Manchester U	33	13
				Brighton	26	5
Mick Robinson	6 0	13 4	Leicester	Preston NE	48	15
(Eire)				Manchester C	30	8
				Brighton	42	19
Gordon Smith	5 11	12 0	Kilwinning	Kilmarnock	163	36
				Rangers	98	35
				Brighton	38	10

BRISTOL CITY Division 3

Chairman: A. W. Gooch.
Vice-Chairman: E. J. Kingston.
Directors: W. G. Garland, H. Bissex, D. Callow, P. D. West, M. G. Fox, W. I. Williams, S. F. Kew.
Manager: Bob Houghton.
Secretary: J. Lillington.
Year Formed: 1894.
Turned Professional: 1897. *Limited Company:* 1897.
Previous Grounds: 1894, St John's Lane; 1904, Ashton Gate.
Previous Name: 1894–97, Bristol South End.

Football League Record:
1901 Elected to Division 2; 1906–11 Division 1; 1911–22 Division 2; 1922–23 Division 3(S); 1923–24 Division 2; 1924–27 Division 3(S); 1927–32 Division 2; 1932–55 Division 3(S); 1955–60 Division 2; 1960–65 Division 3; 1965–76 Division 2; 1976–80 Division 1; 1980–81 Division 2; 1981– Division 3.

Honours: *Football League:* Division 1 – Runners-up 1906–07; Division 2 – Champions 1905–06; Runners-up 1975–76; Division 3(S) – Champions 1922–23, 1926–27, 1954–55; Runners-up 1937–38; Division 3 – Runners-up 1964–65. *FA Cup:* Runners-up 1909. *Football League Cup:* Semi-final 1970–71. *Welsh Cup:* Winners 1934. *Anglo-Scottish Cup:* Winners 1977–78.
Record Victory: 11-0 v Chichester, FA Cup, 1st rd, 5 Nov, 1960.
Record Defeat: 0-9 v Coventry C, Division 3(S), 28 Apr, 1934.
Most League Points: 70, Division 3(S), 1954–55.
Most League Goals: 104, Division 3(S), 1926–27.
Highest League Scorer in Season: Don Clark, 36, Division 3(S), 1946–47.
Most League Goals in Total Aggregate: John Atyeo, 315, 1951–66.
Most Capped Player: Billy Wedlock, 26, England.
Most League Appearances: John Atyeo, 597, 1951–1966 (+48 cup ties).
Record Transfer Fee Received: £325,000 from Coventry C for Gary Collier, July 1979.
Record Transfer Fee Paid: £235,000 to St Mirren for Tony Fitzpatrick, July 1979.
Previous Managers since the War: Bob Hewison, Bob Wright, Pat Beasley, Peter Doherty, Fred Ford, Alan Dicks.
Address of Supporters Club: Supporters Club, Bristol City FC, Ashton Gate, Bristol BS3 2EJ.
Address of the Club Shop or Boutique: City Shop, Ashton Gate, Bristol BS3 2EJ.

Ashton Gate, Bristol BS3 2EJ. Telephone Bristol 632812 (5 lines). *Telegraphic address:* 'City Bristol'. *Ground capacity:* 30,868. *Record attendance:* 43,335 v Preston NE, FA Cup 5th rd, 16 Feb, 1935. *Record receipts:* £30,000 v Tottenham H, Division 1, 13 Jan, 1979. *Pitch measurements:* 115yd×75yd.
How to get there: Buses 79, 59. Parsons St station is available within walking distance for special trains. Also certain scheduled trains stop there.
Match tickets: Tickets can be booked any length of time before the match; Postal application must include remittance and SAE. Personal applications not accepted until 4 weeks before the match.
Car parking: Season-ticket holders can obtain season car park parking tickets. Coach parking at Cannons Marsh. There is limited street parking around the ground.
Entertainments/catering facilities: Social club in the main stands. Tea bars in the ground. Alcoholic beverages only obtainable by members of a bona-fide Supporters' Club. There is a wide variety of pre-match entertainment, and some matches are sponsored, so throw-away gifts to the crowd, and programme prizes, are a regular feature.
Club shop: One of the biggest in the country, sells all types of souvenirs, clothing and many other items.
Handbooks/programmes: Programmes not available on subscription but postal applications are accepted.
Extra information: Indoor bowling area in the main stand. Large room available for functions caters for 200 people.
Club Colours: Red shirts, white shorts, red stockings.
Change Colours: White shirts, black shorts, black stockings.
Club Captain: Gerry Sweeney.
Club Nickname: Robins.

BRISTOL CITY 1980–81 LEAGUE RECORD

Match No.	Date	Venue	Opponents	Result	H/T Score	Goalscorers	Attendance
1	Aug 16	A	Preston NE	D 1-1	0-0	Mann	6058
2	19	H	West Ham U	D 1-1	1-1	Ritchie	13,554
3	23	H	Bristol R	D 0-0	0-0		16,937
4	30	A	Watford	L 0-1	0-0		10,450
5	Sept 6	H	Swansea C	L 0-1	0-1		9528
6	13	A	Sheffield W	L 1-2	1-1	Ritchie	15,054
7	20	H	Notts Co	L 0-1	0-0		7485
8	27	A	QPR	L 0-4	0-2		8551
9	Oct 4	A	Grimsby T	L 0-1	0-0		8781
10	7	H	Luton T	W 2-1	0-1	Ritchie (pen), Mabbutt	7014
11	11	H	Newcastle U	W 2-0	0-0	Ritchie 2 (1 pen)	10,539
12	18	A	Bolton W	D 1-1	1-1	Mabbutt	8988
13	21	A	Wrexham	L 0-1	0-0		4179
14	25	H	Derby Co	D 2-2	1-0	Mabbutt 2	12,020
15	Nov 1	A	Orient	L 1-3	1-1	Mabbutt	4689
16	8	H	Blackburn R	W 2-0	0-0	Garland, Tainton	8773
17	11	A	West Ham U	L 0-5	0-2		25,210
18	15	H	Preston NE	D 0-0	0-0		8042
19	22	A	Cambridge U	L 1-2	0-2	Mann	4922
20	29	H	Oldham Ath	D 1-1	0-1	Fitzpatrick	8037
21	Dec 6	A	Shrewsbury T	L 0-4	0-1		4435
22	13	H	Bolton W	W 3-1	1-1	Mabbutt 2, Aitken	7384
23	20	A	Newcastle U	D 0-0	0-0		14,100
24	26	H	Cardiff C	D 0-0	0-0		14,921
25	27	A	Chelsea	D 0-0	0-0		18,514
26	Jan 10	H	Cambridge U	L 0-1	0-1		9727
27	17	H	Watford	D 0-0	0-0		8746
28	31	A	Bristol R	D 0-0	0-0		10,087
29	Feb 7	H	Sheffield W	W 1-0	0-0	Pritchard	11,639
30	21	H	QPR	L 0-1	0-0		10,988
31	28	A	Notts Co	L 1-2	1-2	Nicholls	7609
32	Mar 10	H	Grimsby T	D 1-1	0-1	Tainton	5881
33	14	A	Luton T	L 1-3	1-2	Pritchard	8745
34	17	A	Swansea C	D 0-0	0-0		10,832
35	21	H	Wrexham	L 0-2	0-1		6667
36	28	A	Derby Co	L 0-1	0-0		15,008
37	Apr 4	H	Orient	W 3-1	0-0	Hay, Mann, Mabbutt	5803
38	11	A	Blackburn R	L 0-1	0-0		9970
39	18	H	Chelsea	D 0-0	0-0		9764
40	20	A	Cardiff C	W 3-2	1-1	Mabbutt, Mann 2	5579
41	25	H	Shrewsbury T	D 1-1	1-0	Mann	5698
42	May 2	A	Oldham Ath	L 0-2	0-0		4785

Final League Position: 21

Goalscorers

League (29): Mabbutt 9, Mann 6, Ritchie 5 (2 pens), Pritchard 2, Tainton 2, Aitken 1, Garland 1, Hay 1, Fitzpatrick 1, Nicholls 1.
League Cup (1): Ritchie.
F.A. Cup (9): Mabbutt 5, Ritchie 3 (1 pen), Mann.

League Cup	Second Round	Birmingham C (a)	1-2
		(h)	0-0
FA Cup	Third Round	Derby Co (a)	0-0
		(h)	2-0
	Fourth Round	Carlisle U (a)	1-1
		(h)	5-0
	Fifth Round	Nottingham F (a)	1-2

Cashley	Sweeney	Hay	Tainton	Rodgers	Merrick	Whitehead	Fitzpatrick	Mabbutt	Ritchie	Mann	Garland	Baddeley	Gow	Pritchard	Doyle	Smith	Marshall	Shaw	Aitken	Moller	Chandler	Stevens	Nicholls	Musker	Williams	*Match No.*
1	2	3	4	5	6*	7	8	9	10	11	12															1
1	2		4	5*	6	11	7	8	9	10	12	3														2
1	2		4		6	3	7	8	9	10			5	11												3
1	2	5	7		6	3		9	8	10	12		4	11*												4
1	2	5	3		6	7		9	8		11*		4	12	10											5
1	2	3	4	5	6	9	7	11	10				8													6
1	2	3	4	5	6	9		11	10	7			8													7
1	3		2		6	5	8	9	10	7			4	11*		12										8
1	2	3	7	5*	6	11	8	10	9	12			4													9
1	2	3	7		6	5	8	9	10				4			11										10
1	2	3	7		6	5	8	9	10				4			11										11
1	2	3	7		6	5	8	9	10				4			11										12
1	2	3	7		6	5	8	9	10		12		4			11*										13
1	2	3	7		6	5	8	9	10	4*	11					12										14
1	2	3	7		6	5	8	9	10	4	11															15
1	2	3	7			5	8	9*	10	4	11			12			6									16
1	2	3	7*		6	9	8		10	4				11		12	5									17
1	2	3	7		12	6	8*		10	4	9			11			5									18
1	2	3	7			6	8		10	4	9			11			5									19
1	2	3	7	5	6*	4	8	9	10		11			12												20
	2	3	7	5		11	8	9	10								6	1	4							21
	2	3	7	5		11*	8	9	10		12						6	1	4							22
	2	3	7	5			8	9	10		11*			12			6	1	4							23
	2	3	7	5			8	9	10		11						6		4	1						24
	2	3	7	5			8		10		9*			11		12	6		4	1						25
	2	3	7	5			8	9	10					11			6		4	1						26
	2	3	7	5			8	9	10*					11			6	1	4		12					27
	2	3	7	5*		11	8	9		10				12			6	1	4							28
	3		7			11		9		8				10			5		4	1		2	6			29
		3	7			11	8	9		10*				12			5		4	1		2	6			30
		3	7			11	8	9						10			5		4	1		2	6			31
		3	7			11		9		8				10*		12	5		4	1		2	6			32
		3	7*			6	8	9		12				10		11	5		4	1		2				33
	6	3	7			11	8	9						10			5		4	1		2				34
	6	3	7			11	8	9						10			5		4	1		2				35
	6	3	7				8*	9		12						11	5		4	1	10	2				36
	6	3	7					9		8						11	5		4	1	10	2				37
	6	3	7				8	9		10							5		4	1	11	2				38
	6	3					8	9		10							5		4	1	11	2		7		39
	6	3	12				8	9		10							5		4	1	11	2		7*		40
	6		8			3*		9		10						12	5		4	1	11	2		7		41
	6		7					9		10*						12	5		4	1	11	2		8	3	42
20	38	36	40	14	17	31	34	38	27	22	10	1	11	15	1	7	26	5	22	17	7	14	4	4	1	
			+ 1s		+ 1s					+ 3s	+ 5s			+ 6s		+ 7s					+ 1s					

BRISTOL CITY

	Ht	Wt	Birthplace	Clubs	League App.	League Gls
Goalkeepers						
Ray Cashley*	5 10	11 0	Bristol	Bristol C	227	1
				Hereford U (on loan)	20	—
John Shaw	6 1	13 7	Stirling	Leeds U	—	—
				Bristol C	147	—
David Mogg	5 9½	10 5	Bristol	Bristol C	—	—
(Contract cancelled April 1981)						
Jan Moller			Sweden	Malmo	(not known)	
(Sweden)				Bristol C	17	—
Defenders						
Geoff Merrick	5 9	11 0	Bristol	Bristol C	364	10
David Rodgers	6 1¼	13 2	Bristol	Bristol C	174	15
Gerry Sweeney	5 10	10 10	Glasgow	Celtic	—	—
				Morton	139	16
				Bristol C	396	22
Paul Stevens	5 7	9 9½	Bristol	Bristol C	15	—
Allan Hay	5 11	11 3	Scotland	Bolton W	—	—
				Bristol C	40	1
Kevin Baddeley	5 10	11 0	Swindon	Bristol C	1	—
Alan Nicholls	6 2	12 0	Plymouth	Bristol C	4	1
Julian Marshall	6 3	12 0	Swansea	Hereford U	92	4
				Bristol C	26	—
Peter Aitken	5 11	12 1	Penarth	Bristol R	234	3
				Bristol C	22	1
Gary Williams			Bristol	Bristol C	1	—
Midfield						
Trevor Tainton	5 8	11 7	Bristol	Bristol C	468	23
James Mann	5 6	11 1	Poole	Leeds U	2	—
				Bristol C	209	25
Ricky Chandler	5 10	11 1	Bristol	Bristol C	8	—
Pertti Jantunen	5 8½	11 7	Lahti, Finland	Eskilstuna, Sweden	(not known)	
(Finland)				Bristol C	8	1
(Contract cancelled Jan 1981)						
Joe Economou	5 6	10 6	London	Bristol C	—	—
Tony Fitzpatrick	5 7	10 7	Glasgow	St Mirren	160	9
				Bristol C	75	1
Forwards						
Kevin Mabbutt	5 7	10 2	Bristol	Bristol C	118	28
Clive Whitehead	5 9	10 7	Birmingham	Bristol C	223	10
Chris Garland	5 9½	11 12	Bristol	Bristol C	142	32
(Contract cancelled April 1981)				Chelsea	92	22
				Leicester C	55	15
				Bristol C	53	9
Howard Pritchard	5 10	10 8	Cardiff	Bristol C	38	2
Ian Doyle	5 9½	11 4	Torquay	Barnstaple	—	—
(Contract cancelled Feb 1981)				Bristol C	3	—
Russell Musker	5 7	10 0	Plymouth	Bristol C	4	—
Gary Smith	5 9	11 2	Warminster	Bristol C	14	—

BRISTOL ROVERS Division 3

President: Duke of Beaufort. *Vice-Presidents:* E. W. H. Godfrey, H. E. L. Brown.

Chairman: G. A. W. Holmes.

Directors: C. A. L. Stevens, Dr W. T. Cussen, D. Mearns Milne, A. I. Seager, G. H. Hole, N. Roydon, B. W. Bradshaw, M. R. Flook.

Manager: Terry Cooper.

Secretary: Mrs M. D. Hall.

Chief Executive: G. J. Bennett.

Year Formed: 1883. *Turned Professional:* 1897.

Limited Company: 1896.

Previous Names: 1883, Black Arabs; 1884, Eastville Rovers; 1897, Bristol Eastville Rovers; 1898, Bristol Rovers.

Previous Grounds: Purdown, Ashley Hill and Ridgeway Ground.

Football League Record:
1920 Original Member of Division 3; 1921–53 Division 3(S); 1953–62 Division 2; 1962–74 Division 3; 1974–81 Division 2; 1981– Division 3.

Honours: *Football League:* Division 2 best season: 6th, 1955–56, 1958–59; Division 3(S) – Champions 1952–53; Division 3 – Runners-up 1973–74. *FA Cup* best season: 6th rd, 1950–51, 1957–58. *Football League Cup* best season: 5th rd, 1970–71, 1971–72.

Record Victory: 7-0 v Swansea T, Division 2, 2 Oct, 1954, v Brighton, Division 3(S), 29 Nov, 1952 and v Shrewsbury T, Division 3, 21 Mar, 1964.

Record Defeat: 0-12 v Luton T, Division 3(S), 13 Apr, 1936.

Most League Points: 64, Division 3(S), 1952–53.

Most League Goals: 92, Division 3(S), 1952–53.

Highest League Scorer in Season: Geoff Bradford, 33, Division 3(S), 1952–53.

Most League Goals in Total Aggregate: Geoff Bradford, 245, 1949–64.

Most Capped Player: Matt O'Mahoney, 6, Eire, and 1, Ireland.

Most League Appearances: Stuart Taylor, 545, 1966–80.

Record Transfer Fee Received: £200,000 from Luton T for Steve White, Dec 1979.

Record Transfer Fee Paid: £100,000 to Birmingham C for Stewart Barrowclough, July 1979.

Previous Managers since the War: Brough Fletcher, Bert Tann, Fred Ford, Bill Dodgin (Snr), Don Megson, Bobby Campbell, Harold Jarman.

Address of Supporters Club: 468 Stapleton Road, Bristol.

Address of the Club Shop or Boutique: The Rovers Shop, 468 Stapleton Road, Bristol 5.

Bristol Stadium, Eastville, Bristol BS5 6NN. Telephone Bristol 511050. *Ground capacity:* 12,500 (7,500 covered). *Record attendance:* 38,472 v Preston NE, FA Cup 4th rd, 30 Jan, 1960. *Record receipts:* £23,275 v Southampton, FA Cup 4th rd, 28 Jan, 1978. *Pitch measurements:* 110yd×70yd.

How to get there: Buses 51 from Temple Meads Station to Stapleton Rd, five minutes from ground. By car, leave M4 or M5 at M32 junction; M32 runs direct to the ground.

Match tickets: Stand tickets available two weeks prior to the match.

Car parking: Large car parks at Stapleton Rd and Muller Rd entrances.

Entertainments/catering facilities: Bar open to the public in stand. Tea bar on the terraces.

Club shop: In Stapleton Rd; sells all types of souvenirs.

Handbooks/programmes: Handbooks and programmes available from club shop; programmes can be ordered on subscription.

Extra information: Bristol Rovers went 27 games without defeat in 1952–53, a Division 3 (South) record, and 27 games in Division 3 from the start of the season 1973–74 (a Division 3 record).

Club Colours: Blue and white quartered shirts, blue shorts, white stockings with two blue rings on top.

Change Colours: Green and black.

Club Nickname: The Pirates.

BRISTOL ROVERS 1980–81 LEAGUE RECORD

Match No.	*Date*	*Venue*	*Opponents*	*Result*	*H/T Score*	*Goalscorers*	*Attendance*
1	Aug 16	H	Orient	D 1-1	1-1	Williams D.	5831
2	19	A	QPR	L 0-4	0-0		9731
3	23	A	Bristol C	D 0-0	0-0		16,937
4	30¶	H	Grimsby T	D 2-2	2-1	McCaffery, Moore (og)	4461
5	Sept 6	A	Bolton W	L 0-2	0-0		8712
6	13¶	H	Oldham Ath	D 0-0	0-0		3808
7	20	A	Cardiff C	L 1-2	1-1	Lee	6122
8	27¶	H	Newcastle U	D 0-0	0-0		5171
9	Oct 4	H	Cambridge U	L 0-1	0-0		5231
10	8	A	Chelsea	L 0-2	0-0		13,108
11	11	A	Notts Co	L 1-3	0-0	Mabbutt	7292
12	18	H	Sheffield W	D 3-3	1-2	Mabbutt, Barrett, Bates	4401
13	25	A	Preston NE	D 0-0	0-0		5807
14	Nov 1	H	West Ham U	L 0-1	0-1		6328
15	4	H	Watford	W 3-1	2-1	Bates, McCaffery, Mabbutt	5450
16	8	A	Shrewsbury T	L 1-3	1-1	Williams G.	4446
17	11	H	QPR	L 1-2	0-2	Barrowclough (pen)	6636
18	15	A	Orient	D 2-2	0-1	McCaffery 2	5100
19	22	H	Derby Co	D 1-1	1-1	McCaffery	6258
20	29	A	Blackburn R	L 0-2	0-0		8025
21	Dec 6	H	Wrexham	L 0-1	0-0		4862
22	13	A	Sheffield W	L 1-4	0-1	Jones (pen)	14,008
23	19	H	Notts Co	D 1-1	1-1	Williams S.	3552
24	26	A	Swansea C	L 1-2	0-2	Emmanuel	15,135
25	27	H	Luton T	L 2-4	2-3	Barrowclough, Mabbutt	7010
26	Jan 10	A	Derby Co	L 1-2	0-1	Lee	15,018
27	17	A	Grimsby T	L 0-2	0-1		9601
28	31	H	Bristol C	D 0-0	0-0		10,087
29	Feb 7	A	Oldham Ath	L 0-1	0-1		5552
30	14	H	Bolton W	W 2-1	1-0	Randall 2	5368
31	21	A	Newcastle U	D 0-0	0-0		14,180
32	28	H	Cardiff C	L 0-1	0-1		7525
33	Mar 7	A	Cambridge U	W 3-1	1-0	Randall, Williams D., Penny	4060
34	14	H	Chelsea	W 1-0	0-0	Williams D.	7565
35	21	A	Watford	L 1-3	0-2	Hughes	10,162
36	28	H	Preston NE	W 2-0	1-0	Mabbutt, Penny	4427
37	Apr 4	A	West Ham U	L 0-2	0-1		23,544
38	11	H	Shrewsbury T	D 1-1	1-1	Penny	4151
39	18	A	Luton T	L 0-1	0-1		9009
40	21	H	Swansea C	L 1-2	0-2	Barrett	8250
41	25	A	Wrexham	L 1-3	0-2	Barrett	3220
42	May 2	H	Blackburn R	L 0-1	0-0		9078

Final League Position: 22

¶ Played at Ashton Gate, Bristol

Goalscorers

League (34): Mabbutt 5, McCaffery 5, Barrett 3, Penny 3, Randall 3, Williams D. 3, Barrowclough 2 (1 pen), Bates 2, Lee 2, Emmanuel 1, Hughes 1, Jones 1 (pen), Williams G. 1, Williams S. 1, own goal 1.
League Cup (4): Bates 2, McCaffery, own goal.
F.A. Cup (5): Williams G. 2, Barrett, Barrowclough, Mabbutt.

League Cup	First Round	Exeter C (a)	1-1
		(h)	1-1 (won on pens)
	Second Round	York C (a)	1-2
		(h)	1-0
	Third Round	Portsmouth (h)	0-0
		(a)	0-2
FA Cup	Third Round	Preston NE (a)	4-3
	Fourth Round	Southampton (a)	1-3

Thomas	Gillies	Bater	Mabbutt	Cooper	Williams D	Hughes	Griffiths	Barrowclough	Bates	Penny	McCaffery	Jones	Lee	Pulis	Barrett	Brown	Williams G	Emmanuel	Williams S	Kite	Routledge	Randall	McAlister	Slatter	Westaway	Holloway	Match No.
1	2	3	4	6	9	5	11	8	10	7																	1
1	2	3	4	6	9*	5	11	8	10		7	12															2
1	2	3	4		9	5		8	10	11*	7		6	12													3
1	2	3	5		8	6		7*	9	10	4		11	12													4
1		3	6		8	5	7		9		4	2	11	10													5
1	2	3	5		8	6			9*	10	4	12	11	7													6
1	2*	3	5		8	6		9	12	10	4		11	7													7
1		3	5		8	6		9*	12	10	4	2	11	7													8
1		3	5		8	6	2	9		10	4*	12	11		7												9
1	2		5	3	8	6		11		10	4		9		7												10
1	7	2	5	3	8	6				10*	4		12		11	9											11
1		2	5	3	8	6		7	12		4		10*		11		9										12
1	8	2	5	3		6		7	10		4				11		9										13
1	2	3	9	6		5		7*	10		4				11		8	12									14
1	2	3	9	6		5		7	10		4				11		8										15
1	2	3	9	6		5		7	10		4				11		8										16
1	2	3	9	6		5		7	10		4				11		8										17
1	2	3	9	6*		5			10	7	4				11		8	12									18
1	2	3	9	6		5			10	7*	4				11		8	12									19
1	2	3	9	6*		5			10		4		7		11		8	12									20
1	2	3	9						10		4		5		11		8	6	7								21
1		3	9	6	10						4	2	5		11		8		7								22
1			9	6	10			8			4	2	5	3	11				7								23
1		3	5		10			12			4	2	9	8	11			6	7*								24
1	12	3	9	6	10	5*		8				2			11			4	7								25
	2		10	12		5		8			4	3	9		11*		7	6		1							26
	2		10			5*	11	8			4	3	9				7	6		1	12						27
	2		11	4		5		7				3	9				8	6		1		10					28
	2		11	4		5		7		12		3	9*				8	6		1		10					29
			10	3		5		7			4	2	12				8	6*	11			9	1				30
			10	3		5		7			4	2	12				8	6	11			9*	1				31
			10	3		5					4	2	12		11		8	6	7*			9	1				32
	3		10		11	5				7	4	2					8	6				9	1				33
	2		10		11	5				7	4	3					8	6				9	1				34
	2		11		8	5	12			10	4	3					7	6				9*	1				35
	2		11	12	7	5				10	4	3*					8	6				9	1				36
	2		11	12	8	5				10	4	3					7*	6				9	1				37
	2		11	3		5				10*	4				8		7	6				9	1	12			38
	2		11		12	5					4		10		8		7*	6				9	1	3			39
	2*		11		7	5				10	4				8		12	6				9	1	3			40
			11		8	5*				10	4				7		6					9	1	3	2	12	41
	2	3	11	8	6	5				10*	4						12	7				9	1				42
25	30	24	42	23	24	38	5	22	15	20	38	18	19	6	23	1	26	19	8	4	—	15	13	3	1	—	
	+1s			+3s	+1s		+1s	+1s	+3s	+1s		+3s	+4s	+2s			+2s	+4s			+1s			+1s		+1s	

BRISTOL ROVERS

	Ht	Wt	Birthplace	Clubs	League App.	League Gls
Goalkeepers						
Martin Thomas	6 1	12 11	Senghenydd	Bristol R	143	—
Phillip Kite	6 1	13 12	Bristol	Bristol R	4	—
Defenders						
Phil Bater	5 10½	12 12	Cardiff	Bristol R	212	2
Vaughan Jones	5 8½	11 11	Tonyrefail	Bristol R	67	3
Steve Harding*	6 1	14 4	Bristol	Bristol C	2	—
				Southend U (on loan)	2	—
				Grimsby T (on loan)	8	—
				Brentford (on loan)	4	—
				Bristol R	38	1
Mike England*	6 0	10 10	Bristol	Bristol R	1	—
David Palmer (Contract cancelled Jan 1981)	5 9	11 0	Bristol	Bristol R	1	—
Terry Cooper (England)	5 7½	10 9	Castleford	Leeds U	249	7
				Middlesbrough	105	1
				Bristol C	11	—
				Bristol R	51	—
Mark Hughes	6 0	11 4	Port Talbot	Bristol R	39	1
Don Gillies	5 10	11 5	Glencoe	Morton	47	23
				Bristol C	200	26
				Bristol R	31	—
Aidan McCaffery	5 11	11 2	Newcastle	Newcastle U	59	4
				Derby Co	37	4
				Bristol R	38	5
Kevin Westaway	5 8	11 4	Bristol	Bristol R	1	—
Midfield						
David Williams	5 9	11 12	Cardiff	Bristol R	220	37
Tony Pulis*	5 10	11 8	Newport	Bristol R	85	3
Ashley Griffiths*	5 9	10 6	Barry	Bristol R	7	—
Gary Emmanuel	5 9	10 8	Birmingham	Birmingham C	71	6
				Bristol R	65	2
Geraint Williams	5 7	10 8	Treorchy	Bristol R	28	1
Steve Dean (Contract cancelled Dec 1980)	5 7	9 10	Poole	Poole T	(not known)	
				Bristol R	—	—
Gary Mabbutt	5 10	10 6	Bristol	Bristol R	86	5
Alan Routledge	5 9	11 5	Wallsend	Bristol R	1	—
Ian Holloway			Kingswood	Bristol R	1	—
Forwards						
Keith Brown (Contract cancelled Jan 1981)	5 9	11 13	Bristol	Bristol R	7	—
Shaun Penny	5 8	10 13	Bristol	Bristol C	—	—
				Bristol R	54	12
Mike Barrett	5 10	10 6	Bristol	Bristol R	26	3
Bob Lee	6 1½	14 0	Leicester	Leicester C	63	17
				Doncaster R (on loan)	14	4
				Sunderland	109	32
				Bristol R	23	2
David Wilcox (Transferred to Frome T March 1981)			Bristol	Portaway	(not known)	
				Bristol R	—	—
Paul Randall	5 11	12 6	Liverpool	Bristol R	52	33
				Stoke C	46	7
				Bristol R	15	3
Mark Stevens*			Bristol	Bristol R	—	—
Steve Williams	5 10	10 10	Barry	Bristol R	8	1
Neil Slatter (Apprentice)			Cardiff	Bristol R	4	—

BURNLEY Division 3

Chairman: R. W. Lord.

Directors: Dr R. D. Iven MRCS (Eng), LRCP (Lond), MRCGP, J. E. Jackson, J. Wilde MBE, J. Eglin, J. Harrison.

Team Manager: Brian Miller.

Secretary: Albert Maddox. *Deputy Secretary:* Robert Bradshaw.

Commercial Manager: Bill Read.

Year Formed: 1882. *Turned Professional:* 1883.

Limited Company: 1897.

Previous Name: 1881–82, Burnley Rovers.

Previous Grounds: 1881, Calder Vale; 1882 Turf Moor.

Football League Record:
1888 Original Member of the Football League; 1897–98 Division 2; 1898–1900 Division 1; 1900–13 Division 2; 1913–30 Division 1; 1930–47 Division 2; 1947–71 Division 1; 1971–73 Division 2; 1973–76 Division 1; 1976–80 Division 2; 1980– Division 3.

Honours: *Football League:* Division 1 – Champions 1920–21, 1959–60; Runners-up 1919–20, 1961–62; Division 2 – Champions 1897–98, 1972–73; Runners-up 1912–13, 1946–47. Record 30 consecutive Division 1 games without defeat 1920–21. *FA Cup:* Winners 1913–14; Runners-up 1946–47, 1961–62. *Football League Cup:* semi-final 1960–61, 1968–69. *Anglo-Scottish Cup:* Winners 1978–79. **European Competitions:** *European Cup:* 1960–61; *European Fairs Cup:* 1966–67.

Record Victory: 9-0 v Darwen, Division 1, 9 Jan, 1892; v C Palace, FA Cup 2nd rd replay 1908–09; v New Brighton, FA Cup 4th rd, 26 Jan, 1957.

Record Defeat: 0-10 v Aston Villa, Division 1, 29 Aug, 1925 and v Sheffield U, Division 1, 19 Jan, 1929.

Most League Points: 62, Division 2, 1972–73.

Most League Goals: 102, Division 1, 1960–61.

Highest League Scorer in Season: George Beel, 35, Division 1, 1927–28.

Most League Goals in Total Aggregate: George Beel, 178, 1923–32.

Most Capped Player: Jimmy McIlroy, 52 (55) Northern Ireland.

Most League Appearances: Jerry Dawson, 530, 1906–29.

Record Transfer Fee Received: £300,000 from Everton for Martin Dobson, Aug 1974; and from Derby Co for Leighton James, Nov 1975.

Record Transfer Fee Paid: £165,000 to QPR for Leighton James, Sept 1978.

Previous Managers since the War: Cliff Britton, Frank Hill, Alan Brown, Billy Dougall, Harry Potts, Jimmy Adamson, Joe Brown, Harry Potts.

Address of the Club Shop or Boutique: The Claret and Blue Shop, Brunshaw Road, Burnley, Lancs.

Turf Moor, Burnley BB10 4BX. *Telephone: Office:* Burnley (0282) 27777/38021; *Ticket Office and Shop:* Burnley 27777 and 38021. *Ground capacity:* 23,000. *Record attendance:* 54,775 v Huddersfield T, FA Cup 3rd rd, 23 Feb, 1924. *Pitch measurements:* 115yd×73yd.

How to get there: Central bus station and the Central railway station are both within 5 minutes' walk of the ground, which is near the town centre.

Match tickets: None. Pay at turnstiles £3.75 and £3.25.

Car parking: Parks in Church St and Fulledge Recreation Ground are both chargeable. Each holds about 500 cars, and both are about 5 minutes' walk from stadium.

Entertainments/catering facilities: 'Centre Spot' Social Club underneath Bob Lord Stand open every night. Seating for 300. Members and bona-fide guests only on match days. Snack, licensed bars are sited around the ground and under the stands.

Club shop: Attached to the Development Office in Brunshaw Rd, Burnley. Telephone: Burnley 27777 and 38021.

Handbooks/programmes: No handbooks. There is a subscription list for League programmes on a seasonal basis; enquiries c/o Club shop.

Club Colours: Claret shirts with light blue sleeves, white shorts, blue stockings.

Change Colours: All yellow.

Club Captain: Martin Dobson.

First Team Trainer: Frank Casper.

Physiotherapist: Jimmy Holland MCSP

Club Nickname: Clarets.

BURNLEY 1980–81 LEAGUE RECORD

Match No.	Date	Venue	Opponents	Result	H/T Score	Goalscorers	Attendance
1	Aug 16	H	Newport Co	D 1-1	1-1	Cassidy	6715
2	20	A	Walsall	L 1-3	0-0	Taylor	4714
3	23	H	Chesterfield	W 1-0	1-0	Dobson (pen)	5855
4	30	A	Charlton Ath	L 0-2	0-0		5445
5	Sept 6	H	Colchester U	W 1-0	1-0	Hamilton	4391
6	13	A	Exeter C	D 0-0	0-0		4534
7	16	H	Hull C	W 2-0	0-0	Young, Taylor	4925
8	20	A	Chester	D 0-0	0-0		3402
9	27	H	Millwall	W 5-0	1-0	Hamilton, Dobson, Taylor 3 (1 pen)	5643
10	30	A	Hull C	D 0-0	0-0		5497
11	Oct 4	A	Fulham	W 2-0	1-0	Laws, Potts	4683
12	7	H	Sheffield U	W 3-2	2-1	Taylor 2, Hamilton	7305
13	11	H	Rotherham U	D 1-1	0-0	Dobson	9691
14	18	A	Portsmouth	L 2-4	1-3	Scott 2	13,459
15	21	A	Huddersfield T	D 0-0	0-0		15,741
16	25	H	Brentford	W 2-0	1-0	Dobson (pen), Cavener	7297
17	Nov 1	A	Swindon T	W 3-0	1-0	Carter (og), Scott 2	6191
18	4	A	Sheffield U	D 0-0	0-0		14,585
19	8	H	Reading	L 1-2	1-1	Hamilton	6910
20	11	H	Walsall	D 0-0	0-0		5570
21	15	A	Newport Co	W 2-1	2-0	Hamilton, Taylor	5370
22	29	H	Gillingham	W 3-2	2-0	Scott, Taylor, Weatherly (og)	5767
23	Dec 2	H	Barnsley	L 0-1	0-0		9094
24	6	A	Oxford U	W 2-0	1-0	Scott, Young	3305
25	20	H	Plymouth Arg	W 2-1	1-0	Taylor 2	5678
26	26	A	Carlisle U	L 2-3	0-3	Scott, Taylor	7137
27	27	H	Blackpool	W 4-1	2-0	Taylor, Potts, Laws, Holt	10,667
28	Jan 3	A	Brentford	D 0-0	0-0		6380
29	27	H	Portsmouth	L 1-3	1-1	Hamilton	6683
30	31	A	Chesterfield	L 0-3	0-2		8635
31	Feb 7	H	Exeter C	W 1-0	1-0	Dobson (pen)	5585
32	14	A	Colchester U	L 1-2	0-1	Hamilton	3082
33	17	H	Charlton Ath	L 0-1	0-1		5781
34	21	A	Millwall	D 2-2	0-0	Taylor, Hamilton	4691
35	28	H	Chester	W 1-0	0-0	Young	4993
36	Mar 7	H	Fulham	W 3-0	2-0	Hamilton, Dobson 2 (1 pen)	5465
37	28	A	Barnsley	L 2-3	2-1	Phelan, Scott	13,689
38	31	A	Rotherham U	L 0-1	0-0		9762
39	Apr 4	H	Swindon T	D 0-0	0-0		4726
40	7	A	Gillingham	D 0-0	0-0		4362
41	11	A	Reading	W 3-1	1-0	Taylor 2, Phelan	3728
42	14	H	Huddersfield T	W 4-2	3-1	Brown (og), Scott, Overson, Potts	11,259
43	18	A	Blackpool	D 0-0	0-0		7198
44	21	H	Carlisle U	L 0-3	0-1		5100
45	25	A	Plymouth Arg	L 1-2	0-1	Cavener	4331
46	May 2	H	Oxford U	D 1-1	1-0	Potts	3938

Final League Position: 8

Goalscorers

League (60): Taylor 16 (1 pen), Scott 9, Hamilton 9, Dobson 7 (4 pens), Potts 4, Young 3, Cavener 2, Laws 2, Phelan 2, Cassidy 1, Holt 1, Overson 1, own goals 3.
League Cup (5): Cassidy, Dobson (pen), Scott, Thomson, own goal.
F.A. Cup (2): Hamilton Potts.

League Cup	First Round	Wrexham (a)	3-1
		(h)	2-1
	Second Round	West Ham U (h)	0-2
		(a)	0-4
FA Cup	First Round	Scarborough (h)	1-0
	Second Round	Port Vale (h)	1-1
		(a)	0-2

Stevenson	Wood	Holt	Scott	Thomson	Rodaway	Cassidy	Dobson	Hamilton	Taylor	Cavener	Young	Laws	Overson	Robertson	Potts	Anderson	Wharton	O'Rourke	Phelan	Steven	Wardrobe	*Match No.*
1	2	3	4	5	6	7	8	9	10	11												1
1	2	3	4	5	6	7	8	9	10	11												2
1	2	3	4	5	6		8	9	10	11	7											3
1		3	4			7	6	9	10	11	8	2	5									4
1		3				7	6	9	10	11	8	2	5	4								5
1		3	4			7	6	9	10	11	8	2	5									6
1	12	3	4			7	6	9*	10	11	8	2	5									7
1		3	4			7	6	9	10	11		2	5		8							8
1		3	4			7	6	9	10	11		2	5		8							9
1		3	4			7	6	9	10	11		2	5		8							10
1		3	4*			7	6	9	10	11		2	5		8	12						11
1		3	4			7	6	9	10	11		2	5		8							12
1	12	3*	4			7	6	9	10	11		2	5		8							13
1	3		4			7	6	9	10	11		2	5		8							14
1	3		4			7	6	9	10	11		2	5		8							15
1	3		4			7	6	9	10	11		2	5		8							16
1		3	4			7	6	9	10	11		2	5		8							17
1		3	4			7	6	9	10	11		2	5		8							18
1		3	4			7	6	9	10	11		2	5		8							19
1		3				8	6	9	10	7	11	2	5		4							20
1		3	4			7	6	9	10	11		2	5		8							21
1			4				6	9	10	11	7	2	5		8		3					22
1			4				6	9	10	11	7	2	5		8		3					23
1			4				6	9	10	11	7	2	5		8		3					24
1		3	4			7	6	9	10	11		2	5		8							25
1		3	4			7	6	9	10	11		2	5		8							26
1		3	4*			7	6	9	10	11	12	2	5		8							27
		3				7	6	9	10	11	4	2	5		8			1				28
	4	3			5		6	9	10	11	7	2			8			1				29
1	4	3			5		6	9	10*		7	2			8	11			12			30
1	4	3					6	9		11	7	2		10	8				5			31
1		3					6	9	12	11	7	8	5	10*			2		4			32
1		3					6	9	10	11	7	4		8			2		5			33
1		3					6	9	10	11	7	2	4	8					5			34
1		3					6	9	10	11	7	2	4	8					5			35
1		3	10				6	9		11*	7	2	4	8	12				5			36
1		3	10				6	9		12	7		5	8	11		2		4*			37
1		3					6	9	10		7	2	5	8	11				4			38
1		3					6	9	10	12	7	2	5	8	11*				4			39
1		3					6	9	10	4	7	2	5	8	11							40
1	12	3*					6	9	10		7	2	5	8	11				4			41
1	2		10*				6	9			7	3	5	8	11				4	12		42
1	2		10				6	9			7	3	5	8	11				4			43
1	2					10	6	9			7*	3	5	8	11				4		12	44
1	2					10	6	9		12	7	3	5	8	11				4*			45
1	3*					4	6	9		12	7	2	5	8	11				10			46
44	14	35	29	3	5	27	46	46	37	36	28	42	39	17	34	1	6	2	15	—	—	
	+ 3s								+ 1s	+ 4s	+ 1s				+ 1s	+ 1s			+ 1s	+ 1s	+ 1s	

BURNLEY

	Ht	Wt	Birthplace	Clubs	League App.	League Gls
Goalkeepers						
Alan Stevenson	6 1	12 2½	Staveley	Chesterfield	104	—
				Burnley	360	—
Billy O'Rourke	6 0	12 7	Nottingham	Burnley	4	—
Dave Reynolds	6 0	13 0	Belfast	Burnley	—	—
Defenders						
Jim Thomson*	5 11½	12 0	Glasgow	Chelsea	39	1
				Burnley	297	3
Derek Scott	5 8	11 12	Gateshead	Burnley	151	15
William Rodaway*	5 9	12 12	Liverpool	Burnley	203	1
Peter Robinson	6 1	12 6	Ashington	Burnley	55	3
(Contract cancelled July 1980)						
Ian Wood	5 9	12 0	Radcliffe	Oldham Ath	525	22
				Burnley	17	—
Brian Laws	5 8	11 0	Wallsend	Burnley	43	2
Vince Overson	6 0	13 0	Kettering	Burnley	61	1
Dean Walker*	5 9	11 0	Newcastle	Burnley	—	—
David Holt	5 10	11 0	Padiham	Bury	178	9
				Oldham Ath	142	1
				Burnley	35	1
Garnett Cromie			Belfast	Crusaders	(not known)	
				Burnley	—	—
Midfield						
Stuart Robertson	5 4	10 0	Glasgow	Burnley	26	—
Paul Dixon	5 10½	10 10	Burnley	Burnley	15	1
Martin Dobson	5 9	11 7	Blackburn	Bolton W	—	—
(England)				Burnley	224	43
				Everton	190	29
				Burnley	75	12
Tom Cassidy	5 11	12 5	Belfast	Coleraine	(not known)	
(N Ireland)				Newcastle U	180	22
				Burnley	27	1
Eric Potts	5 6	10 5	Liverpool	Sheffield W	159	21
				Brighton	33	5
				Preston NE	57	5
				Burnley	35	4
Mike Phelan			Nelson	Burnley	16	2
Kevin Young	5 8	9 11	Burnley	Burnley	55	3
Forwards						
Philip Cavener	5 8	10 7	S Shields	Burnley	54	4
Billy Hamilton	6 1	12 0	Belfast	Linfield	(not known)	
(N Ireland)				QPR	12	2
				Burnley	71	16
Micky Wardrobe*	5 10	11 7	Newcastle	Burnley	1	—
Billy Gray*	5 7	10 7	Glasgow	Burnley	—	—
Colin Anderson	5 7	10 0	Newcastle	Burnley	2	—
Andrew Wharton	5 5	10 10	Burnley	Burnley	6	—
Steve Taylor	5 10	10 8	Oldham	Bolton W	40	16
				Port Vale (on loan)	4	2
				Oldham Ath	47	25
				Luton T	20	1
				Mansfield T	37	7
				Burnley	38	16
Geoff Smith*			Wallsend	Burnley	—	—
William Wright			Corbridge	Burnley	—	—
Trevor Steven			Berwick	Burnley	1	—
(Apprentice)						

BURY — Division 4

Chairman: R. A. Clarke BSC TECH, FIOB.

Vice-Chairman: Canon J. R. Smith MA.

Directors: G. A. Black, A. Metcalfe, Mrs A. Allen.

Team Manager: Jim Iley.

Secretary: John Heap.

Year Formed: 1885. *Turned Professional:* 1885.

Limited Company: 1897.

Football League Record:
1894 Elected to Division 2; 1895–1912 Division 1; 1912–24 Division 2; 1924–29 Division 1; 1929–57 Division 2; 1957–61 Division 3; 1961–67 Division 2; 1967–68 Division 3; 1968–69 Division 2; 1969–71 Division 3; 1971–74 Division 4; 1974–80 Division 3; 1980– Division 4.

Honours: *Football League:* Division 1 best season: 4th, 1925–26; Division 2 – Champions 1894–95; Runners-up 1923–24; Division 3 – Champions 1960–61; Runners-up 1967–68. *FA Cup:* Winners 1900, 1903. *Football League Cup:* Semi-final 1963.

Record Victory: 12-1 v Stockton, FA Cup 1st rd replay, 1896–97.

Record Defeat: 0-10 v Blackburn R, FA Cup, 1887–88.

Most League Points: 68, Division 3, 1960–61.

Most League Goals: 108, Division 3, 1960–61.

Highest League Scorer in Season: Norman Bullock, 31, Division 1, 1925–26.

Most League Goals in Total Aggregate: Norman Bullock, 124, 1920–35.

Most Capped Player: Bill Gorman, 11 (14), Eire, and (4), Ireland.

Most League Appearances: 506, Norman Bullock, 1920–35.

Record Transfer Fee Received: £85,000 from Swindon T for Andy Rowland, Sept 1978.

Record Transfer Fee Paid: £30,000 to Stoke C for David Gregory and £30,000 to Port Vale for Ken Beamish, Sept 1978.

Previous Managers since the War: Norman Bullock, John McNeil, Dave Russell, Bob Stokoe, Bert Head, Les Shannon, Jack Marshall, Les Hart, Colin McDonald, Tommy McAnearney, Allan Brown, Bobby Smith, Bob Stokoe, Dave Hatton, Dave Connor.

Address of the Club Shop or Boutique: Bury FC Souvenir Shop, Gigg Lane.

Gigg Lane, Bury BL9 9HR. Telephone 061-764 4881/2. *Ground capacity:* 35,000. *Record attendance:* 35,000 v Bolton, FA Cup 3rd rd, 9 Jan, 1960. *Record receipts:* £22,200 v Nottingham F, League Cup quarter-final, 17 Jan, 1978. *Pitch measurements:* 112yd×72yd.

How to get there: Buses 35, 472, 481, 487, 488, 524 from Kay Gardens to within walking distance. The nearest railway station is Bury. Buses run from the station to the ground.

Match tickets: 500 seats in the Reserved Chair section of the main stand may be booked two weeks before the match.

Car parking: Season-ticket holders only may use the car park on match days. But there is ample parking space in the side-streets around the ground.

Entertainments/catering facilities: Social club open during normal licensing hours.

Club shop: At the ground; sells all types of souvenirs.

Handbooks/programmes: Programmes available from club shop.

Extra information: The social club has large dance hall, lounge, and cocktail bars. These facilities may be hired for private functions; tel: 061-764 6771.

Club Colours: White shirts, royal blue shorts, royal blue stockings with white band.

Change Colours: Yellow shirts, yellow shorts, yellow stockings.

Club Captain:

First Team Trainer:

Club Nickname: Shakers.

BURY 1980–81 LEAGUE RECORD

Match No.	Date	Venue	Opponents	Result	H/T Score	Goalscorers	Attendance
1	Aug 16	H	Southend U	L 1-2	0-0	Hilton	2647
2	19	A	Hartlepool U	W 2-1	0-0	Hilton 2	3643
3	23	A	Halifax T	L 2-4	1-3	Whitehead, Johnson	1861
4	30	H	Darlington	L 1-2	1-1	Whitehead	2268
5	Sept 5	A	Aldershot	L 0-1	0-1		3100
6	13	H	Mansfield T	W 4-1	1-0	Madden, Butler, Johnson, Hilton	2668
7	16	H	Crewe Alex	L 1-3	0-3	Madden	2810
8	20	A	Wigan Ath	L 1-2	0-1	Johnson (pen)	6239
9	27	H	Port Vale	W 2-1	0-0	Johnson, Madden	2341
10	Oct 1	A	Crewe Alex	D 2-2	1-1	Prophett (og), Johnson	3436
11	4	A	Peterborough U	L 0-2	0-1		4080
12	7	H	Northampton T	L 1-2	1-1	Johnson	1779
13	11	H	Torquay U	W 3-0	0-0	Trainer, Farley, Butler	2145
14	18	A	Rochdale	L 1-2	0-2	Farley	4306
15	21	A	Doncaster R	L 0-1	0-0		3529
16	25	H	Bradford C	D 2-2	0-1	Hilton, Gore	3281
17	28	H	Hereford U	W 2-1	1-1	Hilton, Tully	2268
18	31	A	Tranmere R	L 1-3	0-2	Madden	2426
19	Nov 4	A	Northampton T	L 3-5	1-3	Hilton 2, Butler	2229
20	8	H	AFC Bournemouth	W 3-0	2-0	Johnson 2 (1 pen), Impey (og)	2202
21	11	H	Hartlepool U	D 0-0	0-0		2301
22	15	A	Southend U	L 0-1	0-0		4312
23	29	H	Wimbledon	W 1-0	1-0	Hilton	2392
24	Dec 6	A	Lincoln C	L 1-2	1-2	Carr (og)	3545
25	19	A	Stockport Co	W 2-1	0-1	Cruickshank, Johnson	1941
26	26	H	York C	W 2-0	2-0	Hilton, Butler	3224
27	27	A	Scunthorpe U	D 2-2	0-2	Hilton, Mullen	2360
28	Jan 10	A	Hereford U	W 1-0	1-0	Hilton	2382
29	24	A	Darlington	L 1-2	0-1	Whitehead	1914
30	31	H	Halifax T	D 0-0	0-0		3144
31	Feb 7	A	Mansfield T	L 0-2	0-1		3514
32	14	H	Aldershot	D 0-0	0-0		2576
33	21	A	Port Vale	W 3-1	2-0	Gore 2, Butler	2831
34	28	H	Wigan Ath	D 0-0	0-0		4700
35	Mar 7	H	Peterborough U	D 1-1	0-1	Johnson	2522
36	14	A	Torquay U	L 1-3	1-1	Butler	1635
37	21	H	Rochdale	W 3-1	0-0	Johnson 3 (2 pens)	3931
38	28	A	Bradford C	W 2-0	0-0	Madden 2	2242
39	31	H	Doncaster R	W 2-0	1-0	Howard, Cruickshank	3394
40	Apr 4	H	Tranmere R	D 2-2	2-1	Whitehead, Mullen	2425
41	11	A	AFC Bournemouth	D 2-2	0-1	Madden, Johnson	4204
42	14	A	York C	W 1-0	1-0	Johnson	1786
43	18	H	Scunthorpe U	W 6-1	2-0	Whitehead, Johnson 2 (1 pen), Madden 2, Butler	2357
44	25	H	Stockport Co	L 0-1	0-0		2862
45	May 2	A	Wimbledon	W 4-2	1-0	Johnson (pen), Whitehead, Madden, Jakub	2293
46	4	H	Lincoln C	D 1-1	0-0	Hilton	2968

Final League Position: 12

Goalscorers

League (70): Johnson 18 (6 pens), Hilton 13, Madden 10, Butler 7, Whitehead 6, Gore 3, Cruickshank 2, Farley 2, Mullen 2, Howard 1, Jakub 1, Trainer 1, Tully 1, own goals 3.
League Cup (6): Johnson 3, Butler 2, Bradley.
F.A. Cup (5): Hilton 2, Butler, Jakub, Mullen.

League Cup	First Round	Halifax T (h)	2-2
		(a)	1-0
	Second Round	Newcastle U (a)	2-3
		(h)	1-0
	Third Round	Nottingham F (h)	0-7
FA Cup	First Round	Darlington (a)	2-0
	Second Round	Lincoln C (h)	2-0
	Third Round	Fulham (h)	1-1
		(a)	0-0 (aet)
			0-1 (at WBA)

Forrest	Howard	Kennedy	Waldron	Waddington	Whitehead	Mullen	Halford	Johnson	Butler	Madden	Hilton	Goodwin	Bradley	Phillips	Tully	Southall	Farley	Trainer	Jakub	Cruickshank	Gore	Mooney	Betts	Graham	Constantine	*Match No.*
1	2	3	10	6	5	7*	4	9	8	11	12															1
1	2	3	10	6	5	7	4*	9	8	11	12															2
1	2	3	10	6	5	7*	4	9	8	11	12															3
1	2	3	10	6	5	7	4	9	8	11*	12															4
1	2*	3	10	6		7	4	9	8	11		12	5													5
1		3	10	6		7		9	8*	11	12		5	2	4											6
1		3	10	6		7		9	8	11			5	2	4											7
	2	3		12	4	7*	6	9		8	10		5			1	11									8
	2*	3	10	5	4	7	6	9		8	12					1	11									9
		3	10	6	5	7	8	9		4				2		1	11									10
		3	10	6*	5	7	8	9	12	4				2		1	11									11
		3			5	7	8	9	12	4	10*		6	2		1	11									12
		3			5	7		9	8	4				2		1	11	6	10							13
		3		6	5	7		9	8*	4				2		1	11		10	12						14
		3			5	7		9	8	4			6*	2		1	11		10	12						15
		3			5	7		9		4	12			2		1	11*		10	8	6					16
	2	3			5			9		4	11				7	1			10	8	6					17
	2	3			5*	7		9		8	11				12	1			10	6	4					18
	2					7		9	6	8*	11				12	1			10		4	3	5			19
	6	3				7		9	8		5			2		1	11		10		4					20
	6	3				7*		9	8		5			2		1	11		10	12	4					21
	6	3						9	8*		5			2		1	11		10	7	4			12		22
	6	3				7		9	8		5			2		1	11		10		4					23
	6	3				7		9	8		5			2		1	11		10		4					24
	2	3			6	7*		9	8		5	11				1			10	12	4					25
	2	3			6	7		9*	8		5					1	11		10	12	4					26
	2	3			6	7			8	11*	5	9				1				10	4			12		27
	2	3			6	7		9	8		5					1			10	11	4					28
	2	3			6	7		9	8		5					1	12		10	11*	4					29
	2	3			6	7*		9	8		5					1	11		10	12	4					30
	2	3			6			9	8	7	5					1	11		10		4					31
	2	3			6	7		9	8		5				11	1			10		4					32
	2	3			6	7*		9	8		5				11	1			10	12	4					33
	2	3			6	7		9	8		5				11	1			10		4					34
	2	3			6	7		9	8				5		11*	1			10	12	4					35
	2	3			6	7		9	8				5*			1			10	11	4			12		36
		3			6	7		9	8		5					1			10	11	4				2	37
		3			6	7*			8	9	5	12				1			10	11	4				2	38
	5	3			6	8			7	9						1			10	11	4				2	39
	5	3			6	7		12	8	9						1			10	11	4*				2	40
	6	3			5			7	8	9						1			10	11	4				2	41
	6	3			5	12		7	8	9						1			10	11	4				2*	42
	6	3			5	12		7	8*	9						1			10	11	4				2	43
	6*	3			5	8		7		9	12					1			10	11	4				2	44
	2	3			5			7	8	9	6					1			10	11	4					45
	2	3			5	4		7	8	9*	6				12	1			10	11						46
7	35	45	10	11	37	39	10	42	37	30	24	2	8	14	7	39	17	1	33	18	30	1	1	—	8	
				+ 1s		+ 2s		+ 1s	+ 2s		+ 8s	+ 2s			+ 3s		+ 1s			+ 8s				+ 3s		

BURY

	Ht	Wt	Birthplace	Clubs	League App.	League Gls
Goalkeepers						
John Forrest*	5 9	11 6	Bury	Bury	430	—
Neville Southall	6 1	12 0	Llandudno	Winsford U	(not known)	
				Bury	39	—
Defenders						
John Hughes	5 7	10 6	Manchester	Bury	—	—
Mike Spencer	5 6	10 0	Manchester	Bury	—	—
Ben Phillips*			Hazelgrove	Bury	14	—
Brian Edwards	5 11	11 0	Manchester	Bury	—	—
Keith Kennedy	5 7	10 8	Sunderland	Newcastle U	1	—
				Bury	360	4
Dave Constantine	5 8	10 3	Dukinfield	Hyde U	—	—
				Bury	53	2
Alan Whitehead	6 3	12 0	Bury	Bury	99	13
John Ritson	5 9	10 5	Liverpool	Bolton W	324	9
(Contract cancelled Jan 1981)				Bury	41	2
Pat Howard	5 11	12 0	Dodworth	Barnsley	178	6
				Newcastle U	184	7
				Arsenal	16	—
				Birmingham C	40	—
				Bury	73	3
John Waddington	5 11	11 7	Darwen	Liverpool	—	—
(Contract cancelled April 1981)				Blackburn R	148	18
				Bury	47	—
Dave Bradley*	6 0	13 0	Manchester	Manchester U	—	—
				Wimbledon (on loan)	7	—
				Doncaster R	67	5
				Bury	8	—
Kevin Mooney*			Liverpool	Bangor C	(not known)	
				Bury	1	—
Mike Betts			Barnsley	Blackpool	7	—
(Non-contract)				Northwich V	(not known)	
				Bury	1	—
Midfield						
Carl Halford	5 6	10 10	Oldham	Manchester C	—	—
(Contract cancelled March 1981)				Stockport Co	74	5
				Bury	31	2
Don Graham*	5 10	11 2	Oldham	Hyde U	(not known)	
				Bury	7	—
Alan Waldron*	5 7½	9 8	Royton	Bolton W	140	6
				Blackpool	23	1
				Bury	34	—
Craig Madden	5 8	10 2	Manchester	Bury	82	21
Joe Jakub	5 6	9 6	Falkirk	Burnley	42	—
				Bury	33	1
Jack Trainer	6 2½	12 5	Glasgow	Cork Hibs	(not known)	
(Contract cancelled Nov 1980)				Halifax T	105	5
				Hong Kong	(not known)	
				Bury	1	1
Tommy Gore	5 7	11 8	Liverpool	Liverpool	—	—
				Tranmere R	—	—
				Wigan Ath	102	14
				Bury	30	3
Forwards						
Paul Hilton	6 1	11 6	Oldham	Bury	69	19
Steve Johnson	6 0	12 9	Liverpool	Bury	89	29
Steve Mullen	5 7	10 2	Glasgow	Darwen	—	—
				Bury	71	5
Paul Cruickshank	5 11	11 1	Oldham	Blackpool	—	—
				Bury	29	2
Dave Goodwin*	5 11	11 7	Nantwich	Stoke C	26	3
				Workington (on loan)	7	—
				Mansfield T	46	5
				Bury	4	—
Mick Butler	5 9	10 0	Barnsley	Barnsley	120	57
				Huddersfield T	79	21
				Bournemouth	69	19
				Bury	39	7
Kevin Tully*	5 10	12 4	Manchester	Blackpool	11	—
				Cambridge U	44	8
				Crewe Alex	86	4
				Port Vale	13	2
				Chorley	(not known)	
				Bury	10	1
John Farley*	5 7	9 12	Stockton	Watford	104	8
				Halifax T (on loan)	6	3
				Wolverhampton W	40	—
				Blackpool (on loan)	1	—
				Hull C	60	5
				Bury	18	2

CAMBRIDGE UNITED Division 2

Chairman: D. A. Ruston.

Vice-Chairman: A. R. Douglas.

Directors: C. R. Brett, J. E. Cooke, S. W. Cutter, A. E. Harris, B. Peacock.

Manager: John Docherty. *Secretary:* L. S. Holloway.

Year Formed: 1919. *Turned Professional:* 1946.

Limited Company: 1948.

Previous Name: Abbey United until 1949.

Football League Record:
1970 Elected to Division 4; 1973–74 Division 3; 1974–77 Division 4; 1977-78 Division 3; 1978– Division 2.

Honours: *Football League:* Division 2 best season: 8th, 1979–80. Division 3 – Runners-up 1977–78; Division 4 – Champions 1976–77. *FA Cup* best season: 4th rd, 1979–80. *Football League Cup:* 4th rd, 1980–81.

Record Victory: 6-0 v Darlington, 18 Sept, 1971.

Record Defeat: 0-6 v Aldershot, Division 3, 13 April, 1974, and v Darlington, Division 4, 28 Sept, 1974.

Most League Points: 65, Division 4, 1976–77.

Most League Goals: 87, Division 4, 1976–77.

Highest League Scorer in Season: Alan Biley, 21, 1977–78.

Most League Goals in Total Aggregate: Alan Biley, 75, 1975–80.

Most Capped Player: Tom Finney, 7 (14), Northern Ireland.

Most League Appearances: Terry Eades, 248, 1970–77.

Record Transfer Fee Received: £350,000 from Derby Co for Alan Biley, Jan 1980.

Record Transfer Fee Paid: £140,000 to Northampton T for George Reilly, Nov 1979.

Previous Managers since the War: Bill Whittaker, Gerald Williams, Bert Johnson, Roy Kirk, Alan Moore, Bill Leivers, Ron Atkinson.

Address of Supporters Club: 530 Newmarket Rd, Cambridge.

Abbey Stadium, Newmarket Rd, Cambridge. Telephone Teversham (02205) 2170/3555. *Ground capacity:* 12,500. *Record attendance:* 14,000 v Chelsea, Friendly, 1 May, 1970. *Record receipts:* £18,811 v Aston Villa, FA Cup 4th rd, 26 Jan, 1980. *Pitch measurements:* 115yd×75yd.

How to get there: Nearest railway station: Cambridge. Buses 180 and 181 run from the station to the town centre; then buses 182 and 183 to the ground, which is situated on the east side of the city.

Match tickets: Reserved seats bookable 14 days in advance. Postal applications must be accompanied by remittance and SAE.

Car parking: Limited parking at main entrance; off-street parking allowed, and at Coldhams Common.

Entertainments/catering facilities: Entertainments each evening organised by Supporters' Club. Three canteens open in the ground on match days.

Club shop: Two shops, one at the main entrance, the other inside the ground.

Handbooks/programmes: Handbooks not available.

Extra information: Cambridge are the third youngest professional club in the Football League; they turned professional in 1946.

Club Colours: Shirts amber with black trim, shorts amber with black trim, stockings black with amber trim.

Change Colours: White.

Club Captain:

CAMBRIDGE UNITED 1980–81 LEAGUE RECORD

Match No.	Date	Venue	Opponents	Result	H/T Score	Goalscorers	Attendance
1	Aug 16	H	Derby Co	W 3-0	2-0	Reilly 2, Christie	9558
2	19	A	Orient	L 0-3	0-2		5109
3	23	H	Watford	W 3-1	1-0	Finney, Christie, Spriggs (pen)	6546
4	30	A	Swansea C	D 1-1	0-1	Finney	11,112
5	Sept 6	A	Preston NE	L 0-2	0-2		5515
6	13	H	Chelsea	L 0-1	0-0		9474
7	20	A	Shrewsbury T	L 1-2	0-1	Gibbins	4465
8	27	H	West Ham U	L 1-2	1-1	Finney	8591
9	Oct 4	A	Bristol R	W 1-0	0-0	Fallon	5231
10	7	H	Wrexham	W 1-0	1-0	Smith	4431
11	11	H	Oldham Ath	W 3-1	2-0	Christie, Lyons, Spriggs (pen)	4564
12	17	A	Cardiff C	W 2-1	0-1	Lyons, Spriggs	4059
13	22	A	Blackburn R	L 0-2	0-0		9438
14	25	H	Luton T	L 1-3	1-1	Reilly	7218
15	Nov 1	A	Bolton W	L 1-6	0-1	Taylor	8016
16	8	H	Newcastle U	W 2-1	1-0	Gibbins, Spriggs	5684
17	11	H	Orient	W 1-0	1-0	Spriggs	5072
18	15	A	Derby Co	W 3-0	1-0	Gibbins, Christie, Lyons	15,179
19	22	H	Bristol C	W 2-1	2-0	Lyons 2	4922
20	29	A	Grimsby T	L 1-3	0-2	Reilly	7592
21	Dec 6	H	QPR	W 1-0	0-0	Taylor	6349
22	13	A	Wrexham	D 0-0	0-0		5049
23	20	H	Blackburn R	D 0-0	0-0		4389
24	Jan 10	A	Bristol C	W 1-0	1-0	Marshall (og)	9727
25	17	H	Swansea C	W 3-1	1-1	Spriggs 2 (1 pen), Streete	5121
26	24	H	Sheffield W	L 0-2	0-2		9231
27	31	A	Watford	D 0-0	0-0		11,944
28	Feb 7	A	Chelsea	L 0-3	0-1		16,704
29	14	H	Preston NE	W 1-0	1-0	Reilly	4228
30	21	A	West Ham U	L 2-4	1-2	Reilly, Spriggs	36,002
31	28	H	Shrewsbury T	W 3-1	1-0	Smith, Streete, Spriggs	4007
32	Mar 7	H	Bristol R	L 1-3	0-1	O'Neill	4060
33	15	A	Oldham Ath	D 2-2	1-2	Lyons, Reilly	4836
34	21	H	Cardiff C	W 2-0	0-0	Reilly, Christie	3790
35	28	A	Luton T	D 0-0	0-0		9412
36	Apr 4	H	Bolton W	L 2-3	1-1	Fallon, O'Neill	4512
37	11	A	Newcastle U	L 1-2	1-1	Goldsmith	10,987
38	18	A	Sheffield W	L 1-4	1-0	Streete	14,315
39	20	H	Notts Co	L 1-2	0-1	Gibbins	5507
40	25	A	QPR	L 0-5	0-2		6668
41	May 2	H	Grimsby T	W 5-1	3-0	Evans 2, Streete, Fallon, O'Neill	4528
42	5	A	Notts Co	L 0-2	0-1		12,489

Final League Position: 13

Goalscorers

League (53): Spriggs 9 (3 pens), Reilly 8, Lyons 6, Christie 5, Gibbins 4, Streete 4, Fallon 3, Finney 3, O'Neill 3, Evans 2, Smith 2, Taylor 2, Goldsmith 1, own goals 1.
League Cup (7): Finney 2, Reilly 2, Spriggs, Streete, Taylor.
F.A. Cup (0).

League Cup	Second Round	Wolverhampton W (h)	3-1
		(a)	1-0
	Third Round	Aston Villa (h)	2-1
	Fourth Round	Coventry C (a)	1-1
		(h)	0-1
FA Cup	Third Round	Norwich C (a)	0-1

Webster	Donaldson	Smith	Murray	Fallon	Gibbins	Streete	Spriggs	Reilly	Finney	Christie	O'Neill	Evans	Stringer	Buckley	Key	Lyons	Taylor	Turner	Goldsmith	Pyle	*Match No.*
1	2	3	4	5	6	7	8	9	10	11											1
1	2	3	4	5	6	7	8	9	10	11											2
1	2	3	4	5	6	7	8	9	10	11											3
1	2	4	3	5	6	7		9*	10	11	8	12									4
1	2	4	3	5	6	7	8		10	11*	9		12								5
1		4	3	5	6		8	9	10	11	7	2									6
1	2	4	3	5	6		8		10	11	7*	9	12								7
1	2	4		5	6		8	9	10	11	12	7		3*							8
1	2	4	3	5	6		8	9	10	11			7								9
1	2	4	3	5	6		8	9	10	11			7								10
	2	4*	3	5	6		8	9	10	11			12		1	7					11
	2	4	3	5	6		8	9	10	11					1	7					12
	2	4	3	5	6		8	9	10	11	12				1	7*					13
	2	4	3	5	6		8	9	10	11	7				1						14
	2	4		5	6*		8	9	12	11	7			3	1		10				15
	2	4	3	5	6		8	9		11	7				1	10					16
	2	4	3	5	6		8	9		11	7				1	10					17
	2	4	3	5	6		8	9		11	7				1	10					18
	2	4	3	5	6		8	9		11	7				1	10					19
	2	4	3	5	6		8	9	12	11	7*				1	10					20
	2	4	3	5			8	9	6	11	7				1		10				21
	2	4	3	5			8	9	6	11	7				1		10				22
	2	4	3	5			8	9	6	11	7				1		10				23
	2	4	3	5		7	8	9	6	11					1		10				24
	2	4	3	5		7	8	9	6	11					1		10				25
	2	4	3	5		7	8	9*	6	11	12				1		10				26
	2	4	3	5	11	7	8	9	6						1			10			27
	2	4	3	5		7	8	9*	6		12				1		10	11			28
	2	4	3	5		7	8	9	6	11					1	10					29
	2*	4	3	5	11	7	8	9	6		12				1	10					30
	2	4	3	5	11	7	8		6		9				1	10					31
	2	4	3	5	11	7	8		6		9				1	10					32
	2*		3	5		7	8	9	6	11	12				1	10		4			33
		4	3	5		7*	8	9	6	11	12	2			1	10					34
		4	3	5		7	8	9	6	11		2			1	10					35
	2	4	3	5		7	8	9	6		11				1	10					36
		4	3		6	7	8	9			11	2			1			5	10*	12	37
	2	5	3		6	7	8			9*	11				1	10		4	12		38
	2	4	3	5	6		8	9			11	7			1	10*		12			39
		5	3	2	6		8	9			11	7			1	10*		4	12		40
1	4		3	5	6	10	8	9			11	7						2			41
1	4		3	5	6	10	8	9*	12		7	2						11			42
12	37	39	40	40	30	22	41	37	30	31	23	10	2	2	30	19	8	8	1	—	
									+ 3s		+ 7s	+ 1s	+ 3s					+ 1s	+ 2s	+ 1s	

CAMBRIDGE UNITED

	Ht	*Wt*	*Birthplace*	*Clubs*	*League App.*	*League Gls*
Goalkeepers						
Malcolm Webster	5 10½	12 6	Rossington	Arsenal	3	—
				Fulham	95	—
				Southend	96	—
				Cambridge U	176	—
Richard Key	6 0	12 4	Coventry	Coventry C	—	—
				Exeter C	109	—
				Cambridge U	31	—
Defenders						
David Stringer*	5 10	11 9	Gt Yarmouth	Norwich C	419	19
				Cambridge U	157	1
Steve Fallon	6 1	12 7	Whittlesey	Cambridge U	255	18
Jamie Murray	5 9	10 12	Scotland	Cambridge U	121	3
Lindsay Smith	5 11	12 0	London	Colchester U	212	16
				Cambridge U	141	5
				Charlton Ath (on loan)	1	—
				Millwall (on loan)	5	—
Dave Donaldson	5 10	13 0	London	Arsenal	—	—
				Millwall	216	1
				Cambridge U	51	—
Chris Turner	6 1	14 0	St Neots	Peterborough U	312	37
				Luton T	30	5
				Cambridge U	19	—
				New England TM	(not known)	
				Swindon T	3	—
				Cambridge U	9	—
Midfield						
Floyd Streete	6 1	13 11	West Indies	Cambridge U	80	10
Steven Bailey*			Ely	Cambridge U	—	—
Stephen Spriggs	5 3	10 2	Doncaster	Huddersfield T	4	—
				Cambridge U	245	36
Ian Buckley	5 8	11 0	Oldham	Oldham Ath	5	—
(Contract cancelled Jan 1981)				Rochdale (on loan)	6	—
				Stockport Co	65	2
				Cambridge U	57	2
Doug Evans	5 10	11 10	Swansea	Norwich C	18	1
				Cambridge U	12	2
Roger Gibbins	5 11	11 11	Enfield	Tottenham H	—	—
				Oxford U	19	2
				Norwich C	48	12
				New England	(not known)	
				Cambridge U	65	8
Ian Hendry	5 8	10 12	Glasgow	Aston Villa	—	—
(Contract cancelled Dec 1980)				Hereford U	21	—
				Cambridge U	—	—
Nigel Jalland*			London	Coventry C	—	—
				Cambridge U	—	—
Graham Cox	5 8	9 11	Hitchin	Cambridge U	—	—
Forwards						
Tom Finney	5 10	11 8	Belfast	Luton T	14	5
(N Ireland)				Sunderland	15	1
				Cambridge U	188	53
Tom O'Neill	5 7	10 11	Glasgow	Cambridge U	61	6
Derrick Christie	5 8	11 0	Bletchley	Northampton T	138	18
				Cambridge U	83	13
Martin Goldsmith	6 0	10 11	Wales	Cambridge U	3	1
George Reilly	6 3	13 5	Bellshill	Northampton T	127	46
				Cambridge U	62	19
Graham Watson	5 10	11 6	Doncaster	Doncaster R	48	11
				Rotherham U	13	—
				Doncaster R	109	23
				Cambridge U	209	24
				Lincoln C	43	2
				Cambridge U	1	—
John Lyons	5 10	11 6	Buckley	Wrexham	86	23
				Millwall	55	20
				Cambridge U	19	6
Alan Taylor	5 9	10 6	Lancaster	Rochdale	55	7
(Contract cancelled Feb 1981)				West Ham U	98	25
				Norwich C	24	5
				Vancouver W	(not known)	
				Cambridge U	8	2
Steve Pyle	5 7	10 3	Newcastle	Cambridge U	1	—
(Apprentice)						

CARDIFF CITY — Division 2

Chairman: R. Grogan C Eng, MIEE, MI Gas E, AMBIM.
Vice-Chairman: J. A. Clemo, Dip PE.
Directors: C. Griffiths, J. P. Leonard.
Executive Director: J. D. Evans, MA (Cantab).
Team Manager: Richie Morgan.
Asst. Manager:
General Manager: Ron Jones.
Secretary:
Year Formed: 1899. *Turned Professional:* 1910.
Limited Company: 1910.
Previous Grounds: Riverside, Sophia Gardens, Old Park and Fir Gardens. Moved to Ninian Park, 1910.
Previous Name: 1899–1910, Riverside.

Football League Record:
1920 Elected to Division 2; 1921–29 Division 1; 1929–31 Division 2; 1931–47 Division 3(S); 1947–52 Division 2; 1952–57 Division 1; 1957–60 Division 2; 1960–62 Division 1; 1962–75 Division 2; 1975–76 Division 3; 1976– Division 2.

Honours: *Football League:* Division 1 – Runners-up 1923–24; Division 2 – Runners-up 1920–21, 1951–52, 1959–60; Division 3(S) – Champions 1946–47; Division 3 – Runners-up 1975–76. *FA Cup:* Winners 1926–27 (only occasion the Cup has been won by a club outside England); Runners-up 1925. *Football League Cup:* semi-final 1965–66. *Welsh Cup:* Winners 20 times. *Charity Shield:* 1927. **European Competitions:** *European Cup-Winners' Cup:* 1964–65, 1965–66, 1967–68, 1968–69, 1969–70, 1970–71, 1971–72, 1973–74, 1974–75, 1976–77, 1977–78.

Record Victory: 9-2 v Thames, Division 3(S), 6 Feb, 1932.
Record Defeat: 2-11 v Sheffield U, Division 1, 1 Jan, 1926.
Most League Points: 66, Division 3(S), 1946–47.
Most League Goals: 93, Division 3(S), 1946–47.
Highest League Scorer in Season: Stan Richards, 31, Division 3(S), 1946–47.
Most League Goals in Total Aggregate: Len Davies, 127, 1921–29.
Most Capped Player: Alf Sherwood, 39 (41), Wales.
Most League Appearances: Tom Farquharson, 445, 1922–35.
Record Transfer Fee Received: £110,000 for John Toshack from Liverpool, Nov 1970.
Record Transfer Fee Paid: £130,000 to Blackpool for Billy Ronson, July 1979.
Previous Managers since the War: Bill McCandless, Cyril Spiers, Trevor Morris, Bill Jones, George Swindin, Jimmy Scoular, Frank O'Farrell, Jimmy Andrews.
Address of Supporters Club: Bluebirds Club, Bluebirds Office, Ninian Park, Cardiff CF1 8SX.
Address of the Club Shop or Boutique: Bluebirds Shop, Ninian Park, Cardiff CF1 8SX.

Ninian Park, Cardiff CF1 8SX. Telephone Cardiff 398636/7/8. *Telegraphic address:* 'Soccer Cardiff'. *Ground capacity:* 43,000. *Record attendance:* 61,566, Wales v England, 14 Oct, 1961. *Club record:* 57,800 v Arsenal, Division 1, 22 April, 1953. *Record receipts:* £31,728 v Everton, FA Cup 5th rd, 26 Feb, 1977. *Pitch measurements:* 114yd×78yd.
How to get there: Corporation bus 2 runs past the ground; special buses run to Ninian Park from the bus station, returning after the match. Nearest railway station: Cardiff Central.
Match tickets: Bookable 14 days in advance by postal application. Details from Ticket Office (tel: Cardiff 398636/7/8).
Entertainments/catering facilities: Refreshment points around the ground.
Club shop: Open on match days; souvenirs available during the week from the Pools Office.
Handbooks/programmes: No handbook. Back numbers of programmes available from Programme Dept, Ninian Park.
Extra information: In 1928–29 Cardiff conceded the fewest number of goals in the First Division – but were relegated.
Club Colours: Blue shirts, blue shorts and white stockings.
Change Colours: All yellow.
Club Nickname: Bluebirds.

CARDIFF CITY 1980–81 LEAGUE RECORD

Match No.	Date	Venue	Opponents	Result	H/T Score	Goalscorers	Attendance
1	Aug 16	H	Blackburn R	L 1-2	1-1	Stevens	6908
2	19	A	Wrexham	W 1-0	0-0	Bishop	7771
3	23	A	Oldham Ath	L 0-2	0-0		5690
4	30	H	Orient	W 4-2	2-2	Stevens 2, Dwyer, Buchanan	5649
5	Sept 6	A	Newcastle U	L 1-2	0-2	Kitchen	15,804
6	13	H	Bolton W	D 1-1	1-1	Stevens	6649
7	20	H	Bristol R	W 2-1	1-1	Ronson, Pontin	6122
8	27	A	Notts Co	L 2-4	1-2	Dwyer, Kitchen	7229
9	Oct 4	H	Watford	W 1-0	1-0	Micallef	6407
10	7	A	West Ham U	L 0-1	0-0		20,402
11	11	A	Sheffield W	L 0-2	0-1		15,396
12	17	H	Cambridge U	L 1-2	1-0	Smith (og)	4059
13	22	H	QPR	W 1-0	1-0	Grapes	4489
14	25	A	Shrewsbury T	L 0-2	0-0		4466
15	31	H	Chelsea	L 0-1	0-1		8489
16	Nov 8	A	Preston NE	L 1-3	1-0	Kitchen	5458
17	12	H	Wrexham	W 1-0	0-0	Kitchen (pen)	4562
18	15	A	Blackburn R	W 3-2	0-0	Kitchen 2, Buchanan	7854
19	22	H	Luton T	W 1-0	0-0	Buchanan	6064
20	29	A	Derby Co	D 1-1	0-0	Clark (og)	15,581
21	Dec 6	H	Grimsby T	D 1-1	0-1	Kitchen (pen)	6063
22	26	A	Bristol C	D 0-0	0-0		14,921
23	27	H	Swansea C	D 3-3	1-2	Stevens, Kitchen, Buchanan	21,239
24	Jan 10	A	Luton T	D 2-2	1-1	Kitchen, Giles	9013
25	17	A	Orient	D 2-2	0-0	Maddy 2	3838
26	31	H	Oldham Ath	L 0-2	0-1		5687
27	Feb 3	A	QPR	L 0-2	0-0		9834
28	7	A	Bolton W	L 2-4	1-1	Buchanan 2	8115
29	20	H	Notts Co	L 0-1	0-0		4987
30	25	H	Newcastle U	W 1-0	1-0	Kitchen	4235
31	28	A	Bristol R	W 1-0	1-0	Grapes	7525
32	Mar 4	H	Sheffield W	D 0-0	0-0		7002
33	7	A	Watford	L 2-4	1-2	Kitchen, Jones	10,014
34	21	A	Cambridge U	L 0-2	0-0		3790
35	28	H	Shrewsbury T	D 2-2	1-2	Lewis, Dwyer	5201
36	Apr 4	A	Chelsea	W 1-0	0-0	Stevens	11,589
37	11	H	Preston NE	L 1-3	1-0	Dwyer	4991
38	18	A	Swansea C	D 1-1	0-1	Kitchen	19,038
39	20	H	Bristol C	L 2-3	1-1	Grapes, Kitchen	5579
40	25	A	Grimsby T	W 1-0	1-0	Stevens	7377
41	May 2	H	Derby Co	D 0-0	0-0		7585
42	6	H	West Ham U	D 0-0	0-0		10,558

Final League Position: 19

Goalscorers

League (44): Kitchen 13 (2 pens), Stevens 7, Buchanan 6, Dwyer 4, Grapes 3, Maddy 2, Bishop 1, Giles 1, Jones 1, Lewis 1, Micallef 1, Pontin 1, Ronson 1, own goals 2.
League Cup (6): Bishop 2, Buchanan, Kitchen, Lewis, Stevens.
F.A. Cup (0).

League Cup	First Round	Torquay U (a)	0-0
		(h)	2-1
	Second Round	Chelsea (h)	1-0
		(a)	1-1
	Third Round	Barnsley (a)	2-3
FA Cup	Third Round	Leicester C (a)	0-3

Grotier	Grapes	Lewis	Dwyer	Pontin	Thomas	Bishop	Micallef	Stevens	Ronson	Buchanan	Campbell	Kitchen	Maddy	Roberts	Hughes	Jones	Healey	Giles	Davies	Gilbert	Sullivan	*Match No.*
1	2	3	4	5	6	7	8	9	10	11*	12											1
1	2	11	3	5	6	7		9	10	8	4											2
1	2	11	3	5	6	7		9	10	8*	4	12										3
1	2	3	6	5		7		9	10	11	4	8										4
1	2	3	6	5		7		9	10	11	4	8										5
1	2	3	6	5		7		9	10	11	4	8										6
1	2	3	6*	5		7		9	10	11	12	8	4									7
1	2	3	6	5	12		7	9	10	11		8	4*									8
1	2	3	6	5			7	9	10	11		8	4*	12								9
1	2			5	3		7	9	10	11		8		6	4							10
1	2		12	5	3	11*	7	9	10		4	8		6								11
1	2	11*	12	5			7	9	10		4	8		6		3						12
1	4*	3	6	5		7		12	8	10		9	11			2						13
1	4	3	6	5		7		12	10	9		8	11*			2						14
1	4*	3	6	5		7	12	9	10	11		8				2						15
1		3	6	5		7		9	10	11		8			4	2						16
	12	3	6	5			7*	9	10	11		8			4	2	1					17
			6	5	3			9	10	11		8			4	2	1	7				18
		12	6	5	3			9	10	11*		8			4	2	1	7				19
			6	5	3			9	10	11		8			4	2	1	7				20
		12	6	5	3			9	10	11		8			4	2	1	7*				21
		7	6	5				9	10	11		8		3	4	2	1					22
		3	6*	5		7		9	10	11		8			4	2	1	12				23
			6	5	3		12	9	10	11*		8		2	4		1	7				24
				5	3			9	10	11		8	6	2	4		1	7				25
			4*	5	3				10	11		8	6		12	2	1	7	9			26
			6*	5	3		9		10	11		8	12		4	2	1	7				27
				5	3		6	9	10	11		8		4		2	1	7				28
	4			5	6		7	9	10	11		8				2	1			3		29
1	4	7		5	6			9	10	11		8				2				3		30
1	4	7		5	6			9	10	11		8				2				3		31
1	4	7		5	6			9	10	11		8				2				3		32
1	4	7		5	6			9	10	11		8				2				3		33
1		7	3	5	6			9	10	11		8			4	2						34
1		7	3	5	6		4	9	10	11		8				2						35
	4	7	6	5				9	10	11		8				2	1				3	36
	4	7	6	5				9	10	11		8				2	1				3	37
	4	7	6	5			12	9	10			8				2	1	11*			3	38
	4	7	6	5			11	9	10			8				2	1				3	39
	4	7	6	5			11	9	10			8				2	1				3	40
	4	7	6	5			11	9	10			8				2	1				3	41
	4*	7	6	5	12		11	9	10			8				2	1				3	42
22	27	30	32	42	21	13	15	38	42	35	7	39	7	7	13	29	20	10	1	5	7	
	+ 1s	+ 2s	+ 2s		+ 2s		+ 3s	+ 2s			+ 2s	+ 1s	+ 1s	+ 1s	+ 1s			+ 1s				

CARDIFF CITY

	Ht	*Wt*	*Birthplace*	*Clubs*	*League App.*	*League Gls*
Goalkeepers						
Ron Healey	5 11	13 0	Manchester	Manchester C	30	—
(Eire)				Coventry C (on loan)	3	—
				Preston NE (on loan)	6	—
				Cardiff C	184	—
Peter Grotier	5 11	12 10	West Ham	West Ham U	50	—
				Cardiff C (on loan)	2	—
				Lincoln C	233	—
				Cardiff C	29	—
Defenders						
Colin Sullivan	5 8	11 4	Saltash	Plymouth Arg	230	7
				Norwich C	157	3
				Cardiff C	56	1
Phil Dwyer	6 0	13 0	Cardiff	Cardiff C	335	31
(Wales)						
Keith Pontin	6 1½	12 7	Pontyclun	Cardiff C	149	5
(Wales)						
Rod Thomas	6 2½	13 1	Glyncorrwg	Swindon T	296	5
(Wales)				Derby Co	89	2
				Cardiff C	92	—
Linden Jones	5 6	10 8	New Tredegar	Cardiff C	60	2
Dave Roberts*	5 11	12 5	Southampton	Fulham	22	—
(Wales)				Oxford U	161	8
				Hull C	86	4
				Cardiff C	41	2
Gary Harris*	5 9½	13 0	Birmingham	Cardiff C	4	—
Craig Richards	5 7	10 2	Neath	QPR	—	—
(Contract cancelled Sept 1980)				Wimbledon	2	—
				Cardiff C	—	—
Andy Dyson*			Stourport	Cardiff C	—	—
Andy Wood*			Usk	Cardiff C	—	—
Martin Thomas*			Clevedon	Cardiff C	—	—
Mike Lewis*			Pembroke	Cardiff C	—	—
Tim Gilbert	5 9	11 12	South Shields	Sunderland	36	3
				Cardiff C	5	—
Midfield						
John Buchanan	5 8	11 0	Dingwall	Northampton T	114	25
				Cardiff C	228	54
Steve Grapes	5 7	10 11	Norwich	Norwich C	41	3
				Bournemouth (on loan)	7	1
				Cardiff C	122	6
John Lewis	5 9	11 3	Tredegar	Cardiff C	76	3
Wayne Hughes	6 0	12 5	Port Talbot	WBA	6	2
				Tulsa R	(not known)	
				Cardiff C	22	1
Billy Ronson	5 6	9 9	Fleetwood	Blackpool	128	12
				Cardiff C	83	3
Paul Maddy			Cwycarn	Cardiff C	8	2
Paul Giles			Cardiff	Cardiff C	11	1
Miah Dennehy	5 9	10 13	Cork	Nottingham F	41	4
(Eire) (Contract cancelled September 1980)				Walsall	128	22
				Bristol R	52	6
				Cardiff C	—	—
Dave Haskell*			Newport	Cardiff C	—	—
Forwards						
Paul Davies	5 11	12 9	Kidderminster	Cardiff C	2	—
Gary Stevens	6 1	12 0	Birmingham	Cardiff C	112	31
Constantinous Micallef	5 5	11 4	Cardiff	Cardiff C	28	2
Richard Elliott*				Brighton	3	—
				Cardiff C	7	—
				Bournemouth (on loan)	4	—
Peter Kitchen	5 8	11 1	Mexborough	Doncaster R	228	89
				Ipswich T (on loan)	—	—
				Orient	65	28
				Fulham	24	6
				Cardiff C	40	13
Neil Baldock*			Barry	Cardiff C	—	—
Steve James*			Carleon	Cardiff C	—	—
Adrian Powell*			Builth Wells	Cardiff C	—	—
Kevin Davies*			Swansea	Milford U	(not known)	
				Cardiff C	—	—

CARLISLE UNITED Division 3

President: H. Sherrard.

Vice-Presidents: J. Johnstone JP, J. W. Cullen, T. L. Gibson.

Chairman: J. A. Bendall.

Directors: J. C. Monkhouse, H. A. Jenkins, J. R. Sheffield, R. S. Liddell, I. Ward, Dr T. Gardner MB, CHB.

General Manager: Colin Hutchinson.

Team Manager: Bob Stokoe.

Secretary: E. Morrison. *Asst Manager:* Bryan Robson

Year Formed: 1904. *Limited Company:* 1921.

Previous Grounds: 1903–5, Milholme Bank; 1906–9, Devonshire Park; 1910– Brunton Park.

Football League Record:
1928 Elected to Division 3(N); 1958–62 Division 4; 1962–63 Division 3; 1963–64 Division 4; 1964–65 Division 3; 1965–74 Division 2; 1974–75 Division 1; 1975–77 Division 2; 1977– Division 3.

Honours: *Football League:* Division 1 best season: 22nd, 1974–75; Promoted from Division 2 (3rd) 1973–74; Division 3 – Champions 1964–65; Division 4 – Runners-up 1963–64. *FA Cup:* 6th rd, 1974–75. *Football League Cup:* Semi-final 1969–70.

Record Victory: 8-0 v Hartlepools U, Division 3(N), 1 Sept, 1928 and v Scunthorpe U, Division 3(N), 25 Dec, 1952.

Record Defeat: 1-11 v Hull C, Division 3(N), 14 Jan, 1939.

Most League Points: 62, Division 3(N), 1950–51.

Most League Goals: 113, Division 4, 1963–64.

Highest League Scorer in Season: Jimmy McConnell, 42, Division 3(N), 1928–29.

Most League Goals in Total Aggregate: Jimmy McConnell, 126, 1928–32.

Most Capped Player: Eric Welsh, 4, Ireland.

Most League Appearances: Alan Ross, 466, 1963–79.

Record Transfer Fee Received: £150,000 from Hull C for Mick Tait, Sept 1979 and £150,000 from Chesterfield for Phil Bonnyman, March 1980.

Record Transfer Fee Paid: £120,000 to York C for Gordon Staniforth, Oct 1979.

Previous Managers since the War: W. Clark, Ivor Broadis, Bill Shankly, Fred Emery, Andy Beattie, Ivor Powell, Alan Ashman, Tim Ward, Bob Stokoe, Ian MacFarlane, Alan Ashman, Dick Young, Bobby Moncur, Martin Harvey.

Brunton Park, Carlisle CA1 1LL. Telephone Carlisle (0228) 26237. *Record attendance:* 27,500 v Birmingham C, FA Cup 3rd rd, 5 Jan, 1957, and v Middlesbrough, FA Cup 5th rd, 7 Feb, 1970. *Record receipts:* £20,506 v Manchester U, FA Cup 3rd rd, 7 Jan, 1978. *Ground capacity:* 25,000. *Pitch measurements:* 117yd×78yd.

How to get there: City centre one mile away. Ribble buses from the Town Hall. Nearest railway station, Carlisle. By road – exit 43 from the M6, ground ¾ mile away; this avoids the town centre.

Match tickets: Bookable 1–2 weeks in advance by post or personal application.

Car parking: Car park holding 1500 vehicles adjacent to the ground. Limited street parking available.

Entertainments/catering facilities: Supporters Club with extensive bar facilities. Refreshment points around the ground.

Club shop: Caravan in car park open on match days.

Handbooks/programmes: No handbook. Programmes available on subscription.

Extra information: In 1949, Carlisle's player-manager Ivor Broadis transferred himself to Sunderland for £18,000.

Club Colours: Blue shirts with red and white trim, blue shorts, white stockings with red and white trim.

Change Colours: Yellow shirts, blue shorts, yellow stockings.

Club Trainer: John Pickering.

Club Nickname: Cumbrians.

CARLISLE UNITED 1980–81 LEAGUE RECORD

Match No.	Date	Venue	Opponents	Result	H/T Score	Goalscorers	Attendance
1	Aug 16	H	Sheffield U	L 0-3	0-1		5248
2	19	A	Huddersfield T	D 1-1	1-1	Houghton	7674
3	23	A	Chester	L 0-1	0-0		2007
4	30	H	Newport Co	L 1-4	1-2	Hamilton	2859
5	Sept 6	A	Plymouth Arg	L 1-4	1-2	Staniforth	4854
6	13	H	Gillingham	D 0-0	0-0		3029
7	16	H	Millwall	W 2-1	2-1	Tagg (og), Metcalfe	3400
8	20	A	Oxford U	W 2-1	1-1	Staniforth, Beardsley	2712
9	27	H	Chesterfield	L 2-6	2-3	Staniforth (pen), Coady	4256
10	30	A	Millwall	L 0-3	0-1		3168
11	Oct 4	A	Walsall	L 3-4	1-2	Hamilton, Staniforth, MacDonald	3815
12	7	H	Barnsley	D 2-2	2-1	Bannon, Cooper (og)	2828
13	11	H	Brentford	L 1-2	0-0	Beardsley	3030
14	18	A	Swindon T	D 1-1	0-0	McAuley	5789
15	21	A	Hull C	W 1-0	0-0	Metcalfe	3603
16	28	H	Blackpool	W 2-0	2-0	Bannon 2	3588
17	Nov 1	A	Portsmouth	L 1-2	0-1	Beardsley	13,913
18	4	A	Barnsley	L 1-3	0-2	Metcalfe	9191
19	8	H	Fulham	D 2-2	1-0	Staniforth (pen), Wilson (og)	3665
20	11	H	Huddersfield T	D 1-1	1-0	Coughlin	3998
21	15	A	Sheffield U	D 2-2	2-1	Staniforth, Bannon	11,031
22	29	A	Exeter C	L 0-2	0-2		3940
23	Dec 6	H	Colchester U	W 4-0	2-0	Brown, Beardsley 2, Staniforth	3196
24	20	A	Charlton Ath	L 1-2	1-0	Brown	5444
25	26	H	Burnley	W 3-2	3-0	Campbell, Beardsley, Coughlin	7137
26	27	A	Rotherham U	L 0-3	0-2		8450
27	Jan 10	A	Reading	L 1-3	1-2	Coughlin	3957
28	31	H	Chester	W 3-0	3-0	Campbell, Staniforth 2	3282
29	Feb 7	A	Gillingham	W 1-0	0-0	Staniforth (pen)	4927
30	10	H	Reading	D 0-0	0-0		3889
31	14	H	Plymouth Arg	W 2-0	0-0	Staniforth, Beardsley	3924
32	21	A	Chesterfield	L 0-1	0-1		5750
33	28	H	Oxford U	D 0-0	0-0		3552
34	Mar 7	H	Walsall	D 1-1	1-0	Robson	4485
35	14	A	Brentford	D 1-1	0-0	Staniforth (pen)	6211
36	17	H	Swindon T	W 2-1	2-1	Robson 2	4104
37	21	H	Hull C	W 2-0	0-0	Robson, Beardsley	4098
38	28	A	Blackpool	W 1-0	0-0	Beardsley	4531
39	31	H	Exeter C	D 1-1	1-0	Robson	4385
40	Apr 4	H	Portsmouth	D 0-0	0-0		4299
41	11	A	Fulham	W 3-2	1-1	Beardsley, Staniforth, Robson	4193
42	18	H	Rotherham U	L 0-1	0-1		6798
43	21	A	Burnley	W 3-0	1-0	Staniforth 3	5100
44	25	H	Charlton Ath	L 1-2	0-2	Bannon	4397
45	May 2	A	Colchester U	L 0-1	0-1		1430
46	5	A	Newport Co	L 0-4	0-2		3747

Final League Position: 19

Goalscorers

League (56): Staniforth 16 (4 pens), Beardsley 10, Robson 6, Bannon 5, Coughlin 3, Metcalfe 3, Brown 2, Campbell 2, Hamilton 2, Coady 1, Houghton 1, MacDonald 1, McAuley 1, own goals 3.
League Cup (5): Brown 2, Hamilton 2, Bannon.
F.A. Cup (12): Beardsley 5, Brown 3, Bannon, Coady, MacDonald, own goal.

League Cup	First Round	Rochdale (h)	2-0
		(a)	1-1
	Second Round	Charlton Ath (h)	1-2
		(a)	1-2
FA Cup	First Round	Workington (a)	0-0
		(h)	4-1
	Second Round	Walsall (h)	3-0
	Third Round	Mansfield T (a)	2-2
		(h)	2-1
	Fourth Round	Bristol C (h)	1-1
		(a)	0-5

Swinburne	Coady	Watson	MacDonald	Houghton	Parker	McVitie	Metcalfe	Bannon	Hamilton	Brown	Beardsley	Collins	Staniforth	Hoolickin	McAuley	McGrogan	Coughlin	Haigh	Harrison	Campbell	Robson	Mossop	*Match No.*
1	2	3	4	5	6	7	8	9	10	11*	12												1
1	6	3	4	5		7	8	9	10		12	2	11*										2
1	2	3	4	5	6	7	8	9	10				11										3
1			4	5	6	7	8	12	10*		9	3	11	2									4
1	12		4	5	6	7	8		10		9*	3	11	2									5
1	5	3	4		6	7	8	9	10		12		11*	2									6
1	5	3	4		6	7	8	9	10		12		11*	2									7
1	5	3*	4		6	7	8	9	10		12		11	2									8
1	5		4		6	7	8	9*	3		10		11	2	12								9
1	5	3	4		6	7	8	9*	10		12		11	2									10
1	10	3	4		5	6	7	12	9		8		11*	2									11
1	5	3	4		6	7	8	9	10		11			2									12
1	5*	3	4		6	7	8	12	10		9		11	2									13
1	3		4		6	7	8		10		9		11	2	12	5*							14
1	3		4		6	7	8	9	5		10			2	11								15
1	3		4		6		8	9	5		10		7	2	11								16
1	3		4		6		8	9	5		10		7	2	11*		12						17
1	3		4		6		8	9	5		10		7	2*	11		12						18
1	3		4		6		8		5		9		11		7		10	2					19
	3		4		6			9	5		8		11				10	2	1	7			20
	5		4		6*	12		9	10		8		11	2			7	3	1				21
	2		4		6			9	10		8	12	11				7*	3	1	5			22
	3		4		6		8			9	10		11				7	2	1	5			23
	3		4		6	12	8			9*	10		11				7	2	1	5			24
	3		4*		6		8	9	12		10		11				7	2	1	5			25
	3		4		6		8		9		10		11				7	2	1	5			26
	3		4	5	6		12	9*			10		11				7	2	1	8			27
1	3			5	6			9	4		10		11			12	7*	2		8			28
1	3			5	6			9	4		10		11				7	2		8			29
1	3			5	6			9	4		10		11				7	2		8			30
1	3			5	6				4	9	10		11				7	2		8			31
1	3			5	6			9	4		10		11				7	2		8			32
1	3			5	6				4		10	2	11				7	9		8			33
1	3	12		5	6				4		10	2*	11				7	8			9		34
1	2	3		5	6				4		10		11					7		8	9		35
1	2	3		5	6				4		10		11					7		8	9		36
1	2	3		5	6				4		10		11					7		8	9		37
1	2	3		5	6			11	4		10							7		8	9		38
1	2	3		5	6				4		10		11					7		8	9		39
1	2	3		5	6				4		10		11				8	7			9		40
1	2	3*		5	6				4		10		11				12	7		8	9		41
1	2			5	6			12	4		10		11				7	3		8	9*		42
1	2			5	6			9	4		10		11				7	3		8			43
1	3		12	5*	6			9	4		10		11				7	2		8			44
1	3		5		6			9	4			12	11				7	2		8*		10	45
1	8		4	5	6		12		9			3	11*				7	2				10	46
38	44	17	29	24	45	15	23	26	42	4	37	6	42	16	5	1	22	28	8	23	9	2	
	+ 1s	+ 1s	+ 1s			+ 2s	+ 2s	+ 4s	+ 1s		+ 6s	+ 2s			+ 2s	+ 1s	+ 3s						

CARLISLE UNITED

	Ht	*Wt*	*Birthplace*	*Clubs*	*League App.*	*League Gls*
Goalkeepers						
Trevor Swinburne	6 0	12 12	East Rainton	Sunderland	10	—
				Sheffield U (on loan)	—	—
				Carlisle U	160	—
Tony Harrison	6 1	13 0	Gateshead	Southport	48	—
				Carlisle U	8	—
Defenders						
Bob Parker	5 9	10 12	Coventry	Coventry C	81	—
				Carlisle U	264	5
Ian MacDonald	6 1	12 4	Rinteln,	St Johnstone	108	2
			W Germany	Carlisle U	187	7
Andy Collins	5 10	10 9	Carlisle	Carlisle U	51	1
Gary Watson	6 2	11 7	Easington	Oxford U	24	—
				Carlisle U	18	—
Graham Winstanley	5 11	11 3	Croxdale	Newcastle U	7	—
(Contract cancelled June 1980)				Carlisle U	166	8
				Brighton	64	4
				Carlisle U	33	1
Mike Coady	5 11	11 0	Dipton	Sunderland	6	—
				Carlisle U	45	1
Paul Haigh	5 10	11 6	Scarborough	Hull C	180	8
				Carlisle U	28	—
Midfield						
Jimmy Hamilton	5 11½	11 4	Uddingston	Sunderland	17	2
				Plymouth Arg	8	—
				Bristol R	20	1
				Carlisle U	153	12
Graham Mossop*	5 8	11 1	Carlisle	Workington	1	—
				Carlisle U	2	—
Keith Houghton	6 2	12 4	Newcastle	Carlisle U	40	1
Stuart Metcalfe	5 7	9 0	Blackburn	Blackburn R	386	21
				Carlisle U	25	3
Russell Coughlin	5 8	11 6	Swansea	Manchester C	—	—
				Blackburn R	24	—
				Carlisle U	25	3
Alan Campbell	5 8	11 7	Arbroath	Charlton Ath	198	28
				Birmingham C	175	12
				Cardiff C	167	2
				Carlisle U	23	—
Forwards						
Paul Bannon	6 2	11 2	Dublin	Carlisle U	76	24
George McVitie	5 9¾	11 1	Carlisle	Carlisle U	128	21
				WBA	42	5
				Oldham Ath	113	19
				Carlisle U	198	20
Hugh McGrogan	5 9	11 0	Dunbarton	Oxford U	126	13
				Carlisle U	2	—
Peter Beardsley	5 8	11 4	Newcastle	Carlisle U	82	18
(Contract cancelled April 1981)						
Gordon Staniforth	5 6	9 12	Hull	Hull C	12	2
				York C	128	33
				Carlisle U	63	20
Hugh McAuley	5 7	9 7	Bootle	Liverpool	—	—
(Contract cancelled April 1981)				Tranmere R (on loan)	13	1
				Plymouth Arg	77	7
				Charlton Ath	55	9
				Tranmere R	43	—
				Carlisle U	17	1
Owen Brown	5 10¼	11 10	Liverpool	Liverpool	—	—
(Contract cancelled April 1981)				Carlisle U	4	2
Bryan Robson	5 7	11 8	Sunderland	Newcastle U	206	81
				West Ham U	120	47
				Sunderland	90	34
				West Ham U	107	47
				Sunderland	52	23
				Carlisle U	9	6

CHARLTON ATHLETIC Division 2

Chairman: E. M. Gliksten.

Directors: W. J. Jenner, C. W. Wheeler, R. D. Collins, G. E. Neighbour, W. F. Whitehead, N. E. Madsen.

Secretary: John Stacey.

Manager: Alan Mullery MBE. *Asst. Secretary:* Mrs J. P. Doble.

Assistant Manager: Benny Fenton.

Year Formed: 1905. *Turned Professional:* 1920.

Limited Company: 1919.

Previous Grounds: 1906, Siemen's Meadow; 1907, Woolwich Common; 1909, Pound Park; 1913, Horn Lane; 1920, The Valley; 1922, Catford; 1922, The Valley.

Football League Record:
1921 Elected to Division 3(S); 1929–33 Division 2; 1933–35 Division 3(S); 1935–36 Division 2; 1936–57 Division 1; 1957–72 Division 2; 1972–75 Division 3; 1975–80 Division 2; 1980–81 Division 3; 1981– Division 2.

Honours: *Football League:* Division 1 – Runners-up 1936–37; Division 2 – Runners-up 1935–36; Division 3(S) – Champions 1928–29, 1934–35; Promoted from Division 3 (3rd) 1974–75, 1980–81. *FA Cup:* Winners 1947; Runners-up 1946. *Football League Cup* best season: 4th rd, 1962–63, 1964–65, 1978–79.

Record Victory: 8-1 v Middlesbrough, Division 1, 12 Sept, 1953.

Record Defeat: 1-11 v Aston Villa, Division 2, 14 Nov, 1959.

Most League Points: 61, Division 3(S), 1934–35.

Most League Goals: 107, Division 2, 1957–58.

Highest League Scorer in Season: Ralph Allen, 32, Division 3(S), 1934–35.

Most League Goals in Total Aggregate: Stuart Leary, 153, 1953–62.

Most Capped Player: John Hewie, 19, Scotland.

Most League Appearances: Sam Bartram, 583, 1934–56.

Record Transfer Fee Received: £650,000 from Crystal Palace for Mike Flanagan, Aug 1979.

Record Transfer Fee Paid: £135,000 to Tampa Bay for Nicky Johns, Aug 1979.

Previous Managers since the War: Jimmy Seed, Jimmy Trotter, Frank Hill, Bob Stokoe, Eddie Firmani, Theo Foley, Andy Nelson, Mike Bailey.

Address of Supporters Club: Same address as Club.

Address of the Club Shop or Boutique: 'The Valley Shop', The Valley, Floyd Road, London SE7 8AW. 01-858 6006.

The Valley, Floyd Rd, Charlton, London SE7 8AW. Telephone 01-858 3711/2. *Ground capacity:* 20,000. *Record attendance:* 75,031 v Aston Villa, FA Cup 5th rd, 12 Feb, 1938. *Record receipts:* £31,120 v West Ham U, League Cup 3rd rd, 23 Sept, 1980. *Pitch measurements:* 114yd×78yd.

How to get there: Buses 53, 54, 75, 177, 180. Nearest railway station, Charlton, is on the line from London from Charing Cross and Waterloo East. The ground is 3 minutes walk from the station.

Car parking: In ground for season-ticket holders only. Off-street parking available.

Entertainments/catering facilities: The Valley Club, Harvey Gardens (01-858 1495), and Beer and Snack Bars in the ground.

Club shop: The Valley Shop in ground is open on match days.

Handbooks/programmes: Both available in shops, and programmes on subscription.

Extra information: Charlton are the only club to go from the third to the first division in successive seasons (1934–36) and then finish runners-up.

Club Colours: Red shirts, white shorts, red stockings.

Change Colours: Yellow and blue.

Club Captain:

Club Coach: Ken Craggs.

First Team Trainer/Physiotherapist: Charlie Hall.

Club Nickname: Haddicks, Robins, or Valiants.

CHARLTON ATHLETIC 1980–81 LEAGUE RECORD

Match No.	Date	Venue	Opponents	Result	H/T Score	Goalscorers	Attendance
1	Aug 16	H	Brentford	W 3-1	2-0	Powell, Hales, Robinson	5125
2	19	A	Newport Co	W 2-1	0-0	Robinson, Powell	8062
3	23	A	Plymouth Arg	D 1-1	1-1	Berry	6023
4	30	H	Burnley	W 2-0	0-0	Walker, Robinson	5445
5	Sept 6	A	Millwall	L 0-2	0-1		6893
6	13	H	Chester	W 1-0	0-0	Hales (pen)	4422
7	16	A	Portsmouth	L 0-1	0-0		12,796
8	20	H	Colchester U	L 1-2	1-1	Hales (pen)	4323
9	27	A	Exeter C	L 3-4	2-3	Hales, Robinson 2	4916
10	Oct 4	A	Barnsley	D 0-0	0-0		9305
11	7	H	Walsall	W 2-0	2-0	Walker, Walsh	3352
12	11	H	Sheffield U	W 2-0	1-0	Hales, Robinson	5602
13	18	A	Hull C	W 2-0	1-0	Walker, Hales	3551
14	21	A	Swindon T	W 3-0	1-0	Hales 2, Walsh	5672
15	25	H	Blackpool	W 2-1	2-1	Walsh, Hales (pen)	6838
16	28	H	Reading	W 4-2	2-0	Walsh 2, Robinson, Powell	6162
17	Nov 1	A	Huddersfield T	W 1-0	0-0	Walker	11,329
18	4	A	Walsall	D 2-2	2-0	Lazarus, Hales	4287
19	8	H	Rotherham U	W 2-0	1-0	Hales, Smith	7338
20	11	H	Newport Co	W 3-0	3-0	Berry, Robinson, Hales	6991
21	15	A	Brentford	W 1-0	0-0	Shaw	8180
22	29	H	Chesterfield	W 1-0	1-0	Walker	8120
23	Dec 6	A	Gillingham	W 1-0	1-0	Hales	8775
24	20	H	Carlisle U	W 2-1	0-1	Powell, MacDonald (og)	5444
25	26	A	Oxford U	L 0-1	0-1		5717
26	27	H	Fulham	D 1-1	1-0	Walker	11,070
27	Jan 10	H	Hull C	W 3-2	3-0	Tydeman, Hales, Walker	6494
28	17	A	Chesterfield	W 1-0	1-0	Hales	9563
29	31	H	Plymouth Arg	D 1-1	1-0	Walsh	8127
30	Feb 7	A	Chester	L 0-4	0-3		2461
31	17	A	Burnley	W 1-0	1-0	Powell	5781
32	21	H	Exeter C	W 1-0	0-0	Walker	7245
33	28	A	Colchester U	L 0-2	0-2		4864
34	Mar 7	H	Barnsley	D 1-1	1-1	Walsh	9371
35	14	A	Sheffield U	L 2-3	1-2	Walsh, Hales (pen)	11,687
36	17	H	Millwall	D 0-0	0-0		12,700
37	21	H	Swindon T	D 0-0	0-0		6495
38	25	A	Blackpool	W 2-0	1-0	Smith, Robinson	4230
39	28	A	Reading	W 3-1	1-1	Powell, Hales, Walsh	6989
40	Apr 4	H	Huddersfield T	L 1-2	1-0	Madden	8878
41	11	A	Rotherham U	L 0-3	0-2		13,515
42	14	H	Portsmouth	L 1-2	0-0	Warman	8863
43	18	A	Fulham	L 0-1	0-1		7102
44	21	H	Oxford U	D 0-0	0-0		7634
45	25	A	Carlisle U	W 2-1	2-0	Walsh, Robinson	4397
46	May 2	H	Gillingham	W 2-1	1-1	Walsh, Smith	9367

Final League Position: 3

Goalscorers

League (63): Hales 17 (4 pens), Walsh 11, Robinson 10, Walker 8, Powell 6, Smith 3, Berry 2, Lazarus 1, Madden 1, Shaw 1, Tydeman 1, Warman 1, own goal 1.
League Cup (11): Walsh 6, Hales 2, Robinson 2, Walker.
F.A. Cup (8): Hales 4, Powell, Robinson, Shaw, Walsh.

League Cup	First Round	Brentford (a)	1-3
		(h)	5-0
	Second Round	Carlisle U (a)	2-1
		(h)	2-1
	Third Round	West Ham U (h)	1-2
FA Cup	First Round	Harlow (a)	2-0
	Second Round	Bournemouth (h)	2-1
	Third Round	Plymouth Arg (a)	2-1
	Fourth Round	Fulham (a)	2-1
	Fifth Round	Ipswich T (a)	0-2

Wood	Gritt	Warman	Shaw	Berry	Tydeman	Powell	Walsh	Hales	Smith	Robinson	Ostergaard	Walker	Hazell	Johns	Madden	Lazarus	Naylor	Ambrose	*Match No.*
1	2*	3	4	5	6	7	8	9	10	11		12							1
1	2	3	4	5	6	7	8	9	10	11									2
1	2	3	4	5	6	7	8		10	11	9*	12							3
1	2	3	4	5	6	7	8	12	10	11		9*							4
1	2	3	4	5	6	7	8	9	10*	11		12							5
1	2	3		5	6	7*	8	9	10	11		12	4						6
1	2	3	4	5	6	7	8	9	10	11*		12							7
1	2	3	4	5	6	7	8	9	10*	11		12							8
1	2	3	4	5	6	7	8	9	10*	11		12							9
	2	3	4	5	6	7	8	9		11		10		1					10
	2	3	4	5	6	7	8	9		11		10		1					11
	2	3	4	5	6	7	8	9*	12	11		10		1					12
	2	3	4	5	6	7	8*	9	12	11		10		1					13
	2	3*	4	5	6	7	8	9	12	11		10		1					14
	2		4	5	6	7	8	9		11		10		1	3				15
	2		4	5	6	7	8*	9	12	11		10		1	3				16
	2		4	5	6	7		9		11		10		1	3	8			17
			4	5	6	7		9	12	11		10	2	1	3	8*			18
	2		4	5	6	7		9	8	11		10		1	3				19
	2		4	5	6*	7		9	8	11	12	10		1	3				20
	2		4	5		7		9	8	11*	12	10		1	3		6		21
	2		4	5	6	7	8	9*	10			11		1	3		12		22
	2		4	5	6	7	8	9	10					1	3			11	23
	2		4	5	6	7	8	9	10*			11		1	3		12		24
	2		4	5	6	7	8	9	10			11*		1	3		12		25
	2		4	5		7	8	9	12			11		1	3		6	10*	26
	2		4	5*	6	7	8	9		11		10		1	3		12		27
	2		4	5	6	7		9		11		10		1	3		8		28
	2		4	5	6	7	9			11		10		1	3		8		29
	2		4	5	6	7	9		12	11		10		1	3		8*		30
	12	3	4		6	7*	8	9		11		10		1	5		2		31
		3	4		6	7	8	9		10		11		1	5		2		32
		3	4	5	6	7	8*	9		11		10		1	12		2		33
		3	4	5		7	8	9		11		10	6	1			2		34
	12	3	4	5	6	7	8	9		11*			10	1			2		35
	12	3	4	5	6	7	8	9	10	11*				1			2		36
	12	3	4*	5	6	7	8	9	10			11		1			2		37
		3		5	6	7	8	9	10	12		11*		1	4		2		38
	12	3		5	6	7	8	9*	10	11				1	4		2		39
	12	3		5	6	7	8		10*	9		11		1	4		2		40
	2	3		5	6	7	9			10		11		1	4		8		41
	2*	3		5	6	7	8	9		11		12		1	4		10		42
	2	3		5	6	7	9	11		10				1	4		8		43
	9	3		5	6	7	8		10	11*	12			1	4		2		44
		3		5	6	7	8	9	10	11				1	4		2		45
	12	3		5	6	7	8	9	10	11				1	4		2*		46
9	33	30	36	44	43	46	40	39	24	39	1	29	4	37	27	2	21	2	
	+ 7s							+ 1s	+ 7s	+ 1s	+ 3s	+ 8s			+ 1s		+ 4s		

CHARLTON ATHLETIC

	Ht	Wt	Birthplace	Clubs	League App.	League Gls
Goalkeepers						
Jeff Wood	6 1	10 9	London	Charlton Ath	147	—
(Contract cancelled April 1981)						
Nicky Johns	6 3½	11 8	Bristol	Millwall	50	—
				Tampa Bay R	(not known)	
				Charlton Ath (on loan)	10	—
				Sheffield U (on loan)	1	—
				Charlton Ath	71	—
Defenders						
Phil Warman*	5 6½	10 1	Bromley	Charlton Ath	316	19
Leslie Berry	6 2	12 5	Plumstead	Charlton Ath	219	10
Peter Shaw	6 2½	13 11	Northolt	Charlton Ath	105	5
Lawrie Madden	5 11	12 6½	London	Arsenal	—	—
				Mansfield T	10	—
				Charlton Ath	106	5
Tony Hazell	5 10	12 12½	High Wycombe	QPR	369	4
				Millwall	153	6
				Crystal Palace	5	—
				Charlton Ath	37	—
Kevin Dickenson	5 5	10 3½	London	Tottenham H	—	—
				Charlton Ath	1	—
Terry Naylor	5 10	11 10	Islington	Tottenham H	243	—
				Charlton Ath	25	—
Paul Elliott	6 1½	11 11½	London	Charlton Ath	—	—
Frank Clark	6 0	11 7½	Bromley	Charlton Ath	—	—
Midfield						
Dick Tydeman	6 2	12 6	Gillingham	Gillingham	295	12
				Charlton Ath	158	7
Steven Gritt	5 10	10 10	Bournemouth	Bournemouth	6	3
				Charlton Ath	144	13
Gary Churchouse*	5 9	11 8	Wembley	Windsor & Eton	—	—
				Charlton Ath	18	—
Phil Walker	5 9½	12 1	London	Millwall	146	16
				Charlton Ath	75	12
Kevin Smith	5 8	10 7	St Paul's Cray, Kent	Charlton Ath	36	4
Viggo Jacobsen	5 6	9 11½	Denmark	Kastrup	(not known)	
				Charlton Ath	9	—
Martin Taylor*			London	Arsenal	—	—
				Charlton Ath	—	—
Forwards						
Colin Powell	5 10	11 13½	Hendon	Stevenage	(not known)	
				Barnet	(not known)	
				New England TM	(not known)	
				Charlton Ath	321	30
Martin Robinson	5 8½	11 5½	Ilford	Tottenham H	6	2
				Charlton Ath	124	39
Leroy Ambrose	5 9	10 11	St Vincent, W Indies	Charlton Ath	11	—
Derek Hales	5 9½	11 8½	Lower Halstow	Luton T	7	1
				Charlton Ath	129	73
				Derby Co	23	4
				West Ham U	24	10
				Charlton Ath	83	33
Johnny Ostergaard	5 10½	13 2½	Denmark	Ikast	(not known)	
				Charlton Ath	12	1
Richard Wilson	5 8	10 7	Orpington	Chelsea	—	—
(Contract cancelled April 1981)				Orient (on loan)	—	—
				Charlton Ath	17	1
Paul Walsh	5 7	10 1	London	Charlton Ath	49	11
(Contract cancelled April 1981)						
Paul Lazarus			London	Charlton Ath	2	1
(Contract cancelled April 1981)						

CHELSEA Division 2

President: The Right Hon Earl Cadogan MC, DL.
Chairman: Viscount Chelsea. *Vice-Chairman:* D. Mears BSC.
Directors: G. M. Thomson, Sir R. S. Attenborough CBE, Major A. Dobson, MBE.
Chief Executive: Martin Spencer FCA.
Manager: John Neal. *Asst Manager:* Ian McNeill.
Secretary: Sheila Marson.
Marketing Executive: Mike Barker.
Year Formed: 1905. *Turned Professional:* 1905.
Limited Company: 1905.

Football League Record:
1905 Elected to Division 2; 1907–10 Division 1; 1910–12 Division 2; 1912–24 Division 1; 1924–30 Division 2; 1930–62 Division 1; 1962–63 Division 2; 1963–75 Division 1; 1975–77 Division 2; 1977–79 Division 1; 1979– Division 2.

Honours: *Football League:* Division 1 – Champions 1954–55; Division 2 – Runners-up 1906–07, 1911–12, 1929–30, 1962–63, 1976–77. *FA Cup*; Winners 1970; Runners-up 1914–15, 1966–67. *Football League Cup:* Winners 1964–65, Runners-up 1971–72. **European Competitions:** *European Fairs Cup:* 1958–60, 1965–66, 1968–69. *European Cup-Winners' Cup:* 1970-71 (winners), 1971–72.

Record Victory: 13-0 v Jeunesse Hautcharage, European Cup-Winners' Cup 1st rd, 29 Sept, 1971.
Record Defeat: 1-8 v Wolverhampton W, Division 1, 26 Sept, 1953.
Most League Points: 57, Division 2, 1906–07.
Most League Goals: 98, Division 1, 1960–61.
Highest League Scorer in Season: Jimmy Greaves, 41, 1960–61.
Most League Goals in Total Aggregate: Bobby Tambling, 164, 1958–70.
Most Capped Player: Ray Wilkins, 24 (42) England.
Most League Appearances: Ron Harris, 655, 1962–80.
Record Transfer Fee Received: £825,000 from Manchester U for Ray Wilkins, Aug 1979.
Record Transfer Fee Paid: £225,000 to Celtic for David Hay, July 1974.
Previous Managers since the War: Billy Birrell, Ted Drake, Tommy Docherty, Dave Sexton, Ron Suart, Eddie McCreadie, Ken Shellito, Danny Blanchflower, Geoff Hurst.
Address of Supporters Club: Same as Football Club.
Address of the Club Shop or Boutique: Stamford Bridge, SW6.

Stamford Bridge, London SW6. Telephone 01-385 5545/6. *Telegraphic address:* 'Chelstam, London SW6.' *Ground capacity:* 45,000 (21,500 covered). *Record attendance:* 82,905 v Arsenal, Division 1, 12 Oct, 1935. *Record receipts:* £147,225, FA Cup semi-final, Orient v Arsenal, 8 April, 1978. *Pitch measurements:* 114yd×71yd.

How to get there: Nearest station is Fulham Broadway on the Underground (District Line). London Transport regular buses to Fulham Broadway, Kings Road, Fulham Road, or Stamford Bridge.
Match tickets: Advance tickets available by postal or personal application. No telephone bookings.
Car parking: Street parking only.
Entertainments/catering facilities: Licensed bars at all points of the ground.
Club shop: Run by the Football Club; sells all types of souvenirs.
Handbooks/programmes: Programmes available on subscription.
Club Colours: All royal blue with white stripe on shorts. White stockings.
Change Colours: Yellow, blue, yellow.
Youth Team Coach: Mick Leach.
First Team Trainer: Norman Medhurst.
Physiotherapist: Eddie Franklin, MCSP.
Club Nickname: Blues.

CHELSEA 1980–81 LEAGUE RECORD

Match No.	Date	Venue	Opponents	Result		H/T Score	Goalscorers	Attendance
1	Aug 16	H	Wrexham	D	2-2	1-2	Rhoades-Brown, Fillery	20,001
2	20	A	Derby Co	L	2-3	1-1	Walker, Johnson	20,353
3	23	A	Shrewsbury T	D	2-2	2-1	Walker, Fillery	6672
4	30	H	QPR	D	1-1	0-1	Chivers	23,381
5	Sept 6	H	West Ham U	L	0-1	0-0		32,669
6	13	A	Cambridge U	W	1-0	0-0	Lee	9474
7	20	H	Preston NE	D	1-1	0-0	Lee	13,755
8	27	A	Watford	W	3-2	0-0	Walker 2, Lee	19,802
9	Oct 4	A	Bolton W	W	3-2	1-0	Lee 2, Fillery	11,888
10	8	H	Bristol R	W	2-0	0-0	Lee (og), Walker	13,108
11	11	H	Grimsby T	W	3-0	2-0	Lee 2, Walker	16,206
12	18	A	Blackburn R	D	1-1	1-1	Walker	15,503
13	21	A	Orient	W	1-0	1-0	Fillery	11,950
14	25	H	Newcastle U	W	6-0	3-0	Lee 3, Fillery, Walker, Chivers	22,912
15	31	A	Cardiff C	W	1-0	1-0	Hutchings	8489
16	Nov 8	H	Oldham Ath	W	1-0	0-0	Lee	19,327
17	12	H	Derby Co	L	1-3	0-1	Lee	19,449
18	15	A	Wrexham	W	4-0	1-0	Britton, Driver, Walker, Lee	7953
19	22	H	Sheffield W	W	2-0	0-0	Lee, Walker	24,947
20	29	A	Notts Co	D	1-1	0-0	Bumstead	14,419
21	Dec 6	H	Swansea C	D	0-0	0-0		20,067
22	13	A	Grimsby T	L	0-2	0-2		14,708
23	20	H	Orient	L	0-1	0-1		15,943
24	26	A	Luton T	L	0-2	0-0		16,006
25	27	H	Bristol C	D	0-0	0-0		18,514
26	Jan 10	A	Sheffield W	D	0-0	0-0		25,113
27	17	A	QPR	L	0-1	0-0		22,873
28	31	H	Shrewsbury T	W	3-0	2-0	Mayes, Lee (pen), Fillery	14,673
29	Feb 7	H	Cambridge U	W	3-0	1-0	Droy, Mayes 2	16,704
30	14	A	West Ham U	L	0-4	0-1		35,164
31	21	H	Watford	L	0-1	0-0		19,153
32	28	A	Preston NE	L	0-1	0-1		8129
33	Mar 7	H	Bolton W	W	2-0	1-0	Walker, Mayes	12,948
34	14	A	Bristol R	L	0-1	0-0		7565
35	21	H	Blackburn R	D	0-0	0-0		14,314
36	28	A	Newcastle U	L	0-1	0-1		17,392
37	Apr 4	H	Cardiff C	L	0-1	0-0		11,569
38	11	A	Oldham Ath	D	0-0	0-0		6740
39	18	A	Bristol C	D	0-0	0-0		9764
40	20	H	Luton T	L	0-2	0-1		12,868
41	25	A	Swansea C	L	0-3	0-2		16,063
42	May 2	H	Notts Co	L	0-2	0-1		13,324

Final League Position: 12

Goalscorers

League (46): Lee 15 (1 pen), Walker 11, Fillery 6, Mayes 4, Chivers 2, Britton 1, Bumstead 1, Driver 1, Droy 1, Hutchings 1, Johnson 1, Rhoades-Brown 1, own goal 1.
League Cup (1): Droy.
F.A. Cup (1): Lee.

League Cup	Second Round	Cardiff C (a)	0-1
		(h)	1-1
FA Cup	Third Round	Southampton (a)	1-3

Borota	Wilkins	Rofe	Bumstead	Droy	Chivers	Britton	Fillery	Johnson	Walker	Rhoades-Brown	Viljoen	Nutton	Pates	Lee	Driver	Hutchings	Locke	Elmes	Mayes	Clare	*Match No.*
1	2	3	4	5	6	7	8	9*	10	11	12										1
1	2	3	4	5	6	7	8	9	10	11											2
1	2	3	4	5	6	7	8	9*	10	12		11									3
1	2	3	12		6	7	8		10*		4	11	5	9							4
1	2	3	4*		12	7	8		10		11	5	6	9							5
1	2	3	4	5	11	7	8		10			6		9							6
1	2	3	4	5	11	7	8*		10	12		6		9							7
1	2	3	4	5	6	7	8		10	11				9							8
1	2	3	4		6	7	8		10*	11			5	9						12	9
1	2	3	4		6	7*	8		10	11			5	9	12						10
1	2	3	4		6	7	8		10	11			5*	9	12						11
1		3	4		6	7*	8		10	11		2	5	9	12						12
1		3	4		6		8		10	11		2	5	9	7						13
1		3	4	5	6	12	8		10*	11		2		9	7						14
1		3	4	5	6		8*		10	11		2		9	7	12					15
1		3	4	5	6				10	11		2		9	7	8					16
1		3	4	5	6*	8			10	11		2		9	7	12					17
1	2	3	4	5		7			10	11		6*		9	12	8					18
1		3	4	5	6	7			10	11		2*		9	12	8					19
1		3	4	5	6	8			10	11				9	7		2				20
1		3	4	5	6	8			10	11				9	7		2				21
1		3	4	5	6	7	8		10	11*				9	12		2				22
1		3*	4	5	6	7	8		10	11				9	12		2				23
1		3	6				7					5*	4	10	9	8	2	12	11		24
1		3	4		6		8		12	11			5	9		7*	2		10		25
1		3		5	6	7	8		10	11*				9	12		2	4			26
1		3	4	5	6	7	8		10	11*							2	12	9		27
1		3	4	5	6		8		10		7			9			2		11		28
1		3	4	5	6		8		10		7			9			2		11		29
1		3	4	5	6		8			11				9	12		2	7*	10		30
1		3	4*	5	6		8		12	11	7			9			2		10		31
1		3	4	5	6	7	8		10	9			11*			12	2				32
1		3	4	5	6	7*	8		10	11					12		2		9		33
1		3	4	5	6	7	8		10	11*					12		2		9		34
1		3	4	5	6	7	8		10	11*				12			2		9		35
1		3	4	5	6		8*		10	11				9	7	12	2				36
1		3	4	5	6		8		10	11				9	7		2				37
1			4	5	6		8					2	3	9	7	11			10		38
1			4	5*	2		8					6	3	9	7	11	12		10		39
1		3	4		6		8			12		5	2	9		11	7		10*		40
1	3		4		6	8	12		10	11		5*	2	9			7				41
1	3		4		6	7	8		10	12	11		5	9			2*				42
42	14	38	40	30	39	27	35	3	35	30	6	18	15	34	12	8	21	2	13	—	
			+ 1s		+ 1s	+ 1s	+ 1s		+ 2s	+ 4s	+ 1s			+ 1s	+ 11s	+ 4s	+ 1s	+ 2s		+ 1s	

CHELSEA

	Ht	*Wt*	*Birthplace*	*Clubs*	*League App.*	*League Gls*
Goalkeepers						
Petar Borota (Yugoslavia)	6 0	12 7	Yugoslavia	Belgrade SC	—	—
				Partizan	—	—
				Chelsea	95	—
Bob Iles	6 1	12 7	Leicester	Weymouth	—	—
				Chelsea	8	—
Defenders						
Gary Locke	5 11	11 5	Park Royal	Chelsea	235	2
Micky Droy	6 4½	15 5	Highbury	Chelsea	216	8
Graham Wilkins	5 6½	10 2	Hayes	Chelsea	126	1
Michael Nutton	5 11	10 12	St John's Wood	Chelsea	52	—
Gary Chivers	5 11	11 5	Stockwell	Chelsea	74	4
Kevin Hales	5 7	10 4	Dartford	Chelsea	7	—
Colin Pates	5 11	11 0	Carshalton	Chelsea	31	—
Dennis Rofe	5 7	10 11	Fulham	Orient	171	6
				Leicester C	290	5
				Chelsea	52	—
Paul Williams	6 0	11 7	Lambeth	Chelsea	—	—
Midfield						
John Bumstead	5 7	10 0	Rotherhithe	Chelsea	77	5
Mike Fillery	5 10	11 12	Mitcham	Chelsea	84	17
Ian Britton	5 5	9 7	Dundee	Chelsea	245	33
Colin Viljoen (England)	5 8	10 10	Johannesburg	Ipswich T	305	46
				QPR (on loan)	—	—
				Manchester C	27	—
				Chelsea	11	—
Chris Hutchings	5 10	11 0	Winchester	Harrow B	(not known)	
				Chelsea	12	1
Timmy Elmes	5 10	12 0	Thornton Heath	Chelsea	4	—
Forwards						
Clive Walker	5 8½	11 4	Oxford	Chelsea	127	35
Jimmy Clare*	5 7	10 0	Islington	Chelsea	1	—
Colin Lee	6 1	11 9	Plymouth	Bristol C	—	—
				Hereford U (on loan)	9	—
				Torquay U	35	14
				Tottenham H	62	18
				Chelsea	40	16
Peter Rhoades-Brown	5 9	10 6	Hampton	Chelsea	38	1
Phil Driver	5 10	10 12	Huddersfield	Luton T	—	—
				Wimbledon	16	3
				Chelsea	23	1
Andy Cook*			Lyndhurst	Chelsea	—	—
Alan Mayes	5 7	10 10	London	QPR	—	—
				Watford	133	31
				Northampton T (on loan)	10	4
				Swindon T	89	38
				Chelsea	13	4
Nigel MacLaren (Contract cancelled April 1981)			Southall	Chelsea	—	—

CHESTER Division 3

President: Duke of Westminster. *Chairman:* R. Rowlands.
Vice-Chairman: C. Thompson.
Directors: L. Lloyd, E. J. Owen, R. S. Tresidder.
Team Manager: Alan Oakes. *Secretary:* S. Gandy.
Assistant Manager: Cliff Sear.
Year Formed: 1884. *Turned Professional:* 1902.
Limited Company: 1909.
Previous Grounds: Faulkner Street; Old Showground; 1904, Whipcord Lane; 1906, Sealand Road.

Football League Record:
1931 Elected Division 3(N); 1958–75 Division 4; 1975– Division 3.

Honours: *Football League:* Division 3 best season: 5th, 1977–78; Division 3(N) – Runners-up 1935–36. *FA Cup* best season: 5th rd, 1976–77, 1979–80. *Football League Cup:* Semi-final 1974–75. *Welsh Cup:* Winners 1908, 1933, 1947. *Debenhams Cup:* Winners 1977.

Record Victory: 12-0 v York C, Division 3(N), 1 Feb, 1936.
Record Defeat: 2-11 v Oldham Ath, Division 3(N), 19 Jan, 1952.
Most League Points: 56, Division 3(N), 1946–47; Division 4, 1964–65.
Most League Goals: 119, Division 4, 1964–65.
Highest League Scorer in Season: Dick Yates, 36, Division 3(N), 1946–47.
Most League Goals in Total Aggregate: Gary Talbot, 83, 1963–67, 1968–70.
Most Capped Player: Bill Lewis, 9 (30), Wales.
Most League Appearances: Ray Gill, 408, 1951–62.
Record Transfer Fee Received: £300,000 from Liverpool for Ian Rush, May 1980.
Record Transfer Fee Paid: £45,000 to Carlisle U for Steve Ludlam, May 1980.
Previous Managers since the War: Frank Brown, Louis Page, John Harris, Stan Pearson, Bill Lambton, Peter Hauser, Ken Roberts.
Address of the Club Shop or Boutique: 18 Grosvenor St, Chester.

The Stadium, Sealand Rd, Chester CH1 4LW. Telephone Chester 371376. *Ground capacity:* 20,000. *Record attendance:* 20,500 v Chelsea, FA Cup 3rd rd replay, 16 Jan, 1952. *Record receipts:* £15,854 v Aston Villa, FL Cup semi-final first leg, 15 Jan, 1975. *Pitch measurements:* 114yd×76yd.

How to get there: Nearest railway station, Chester. Corporation bus to Town Hall Square, where special buses run from the Odeon Cinema to the ground.
Match tickets: No advance booking.
Car parking: Extensive parking at ground.
Entertainments/catering facilities: Catering facilities on ground.
Club shop: In town centre, stocks all types of souvenirs.
Handbooks/programmes: Programmes not available on subscription.
Extra information: Additional programme shop inside the ground.
Club Colours: Royal blue shirts with white stripes, royal blue shorts with red and white trim, white stockings with red and blue ringed top.
Change Colours: All yellow.
First Team Trainer: Vincent Pritchard.
Club Nickname: The Seals.

CHESTER 1980–81 LEAGUE RECORD

Match No.	Date	Venue	Opponents	Result	H/T Score	Goalscorers	Attendance
1	Aug 16	H	Oxford U	L 0-1	0-1		2203
2	19	A	Plymouth Arg	L 0-2	0-0		4823
3	23	H	Carlisle U	W 1-0	0-0	Oakes	2007
4	30	A	Millwall	L 0-1	0-0		3264
5	Sept 6	H	Exeter C	W 1-0	0-0	Cooke	1974
6	13	A	Charlton Ath	L 0-1	0-0		4422
7	20	H	Burnley	D 0-0	0-0		3402
8	27	A	Colchester U	D 1-1	0-0	Jones	2147
9	Oct 4	A	Swindon T	W 2-1	0-0	Howat, Ludlam	5577
10	8	H	Hull C	W 4-1	2-0	Phillips T. 2, Ludlam, Howat	1964
11	11	H	Reading	W 1-0	0-0	Phillips T.	2444
12	18	A	Brentford	W 1-0	1-0	Howat	6600
13	21	A	Rotherham U	D 0-0	0-0		6635
14	25	H	Fulham	L 0-1	0-0		3169
15	29	H	Huddersfield T	L 0-2	0-2		4331
16	Nov 1	A	Barnsley	L 0-2	0-1		9330
17	4	A	Hull C	D 0-0	0-0		3335
18	8	H	Sheffield U	W 3-2	0-0	Phillips T. 2, Sutcliffe	4563
19	12	H	Plymouth Arg	W 1-0	0-0	Ludlam	2247
20	15	A	Oxford U	L 0-1	0-0		2526
21	29	A	Portsmouth	L 0-2	0-1		10,515
22	Dec 3	H	Newport Co	D 1-1	0-1	Sutcliffe	1640
23	6	H	Walsall	W 1-0	0-0	Phillips T.	2215
24	13	A	Newport Co	D 1-1	1-1	Cottam	4169
25	20	H	Gillingham	L 1-2	1-1	Ludlam	1740
26	26	A	Blackpool	W 3-2	0-2	Fear, Ludlam, Cooke	4878
27	27	H	Chesterfield	W 2-1	1-0	Cooke, Fear	4222
28	Jan 2	A	Reading	L 0-3	0-0		3804
29	10	H	Brentford	D 0-0	0-0		2041
30	17	A	Walsall	L 1-2	1-0	Jones	3483
31	24	H	Millwall	L 0-1	0-1		2114
32	31	A	Carlisle U	L 0-3	0-3		3282
33	Feb 7	H	Charlton Ath	W 4-0	3-0	Phillips T., Jones, Howat, Raynor (pen)	2461
34	21	H	Colchester U	D 0-0	0-0		1778
35	28	A	Burnley	L 0-1	0-0		4993
36	Mar 7	H	Swindon T	W 1-0	1-0	Rollings (og)	1810
37	17	A	Fulham	W 1-0	1-0	Phillips T.	3387
38	21	H	Rotherham U	L 0-1	0-1		3945
39	28	A	Huddersfield T	D 0-0	0-0		11,117
40	Apr 4	H	Barnsley	D 2-2	1-1	Ludlam 2	4680
41	7	A	Sheffield U	L 0-2	0-2		10,027
42	17	H	Blackpool	W 2-1	0-0	Cooke 2	2804
43	18	A	Chesterfield	L 0-2	0-2		3850
44	25	A	Gillingham	L 1-2	0-2	Oakes	3228
45	29	A	Exeter C	D 2-2	0-1	Jones, Howat	3056
46	May 2	H	Portsmouth	L 0-1	0-0		2153

Final League Position: 18

Goalscorers

League (38): Phillips T. 8, Ludlam 7, Cooke 5, Howat 5, Jones 4, Fear 2, Oakes 2, Sutcliffe 2, Cottam 1, Raynor 1 (pen), own goal 1.
League Cup (1): Oakes.
F.A. Cup (1): Birch.

League Cup	First Round	Stockport Co (h)	1-1
		(a)	0-1
FA Cup	First Round	Barnsley (h)	1-2

Millington	Jeffries	Walker	Storton	Cottam	Oakes	Burns	Kearney	Birch	Jones	Ludlam	Fear	Raynor	Zelem	Sutcliffe	Phillips T	Cooke	Phillips R	Gendall	Howat	Needham	*Match No.*
1	2	3	4	5	6	7*	8	9	10	11	12										1
1	2	3	4	5*	6	7	8	9	10	11							12				2
1		3	4		6		8		10	11		2	5	7	9						3
1		3	4	5	6		8		10	11		2		7	9						4
1		3	4	5	6		8		10	11*		2		7	9	12					5
1		3	4	5	6		9	7	8	10		2			12	11*					6
1		3	4	5			9	7	8	10		2				11*	6	12			7
1		3	4	5			9	7	10	11	6	2							8		8
1		3	4	5			9	7	10	11	6	2							8		9
1		3	4	5				7	8	11	6	2			10				9		10
1		3	4	5				7	10	11	6	2			8				9		11
1		3	4	5		12		7	8	11	6*	2			10				9		12
1		3	4	5				7	10	11		2			8		6		9		13
1		3*	4	5		12		7	10	11	6	2			8				9		14
1		3	4	5		12		7*	10	11		2			8			6	9		15
1		3	4	5				7	10	11		2			8			6	9		16
1	6	3	4	5		11		9	10			2		7	8						17
1	5	3	4			11		9	10	6		2		7	8						18
1	4			5		3		9	10	6		2		7	8			11			19
1	2		4	5		3		9	10	6				7	8			11*		12	20
1	2	3	4	5	6	11		9	10		7				8						21
1	2	3	4	5*	6	11		9		10	7			12	8						22
1	5	3	4		6			9		10	2			7	8				11		23
1	2	3	4	5	6					10	9			7	8				11		24
1	2	3	4	5	6				12	10	9			7	8				11*		25
1	2	3	4	5	6				10	11	9			7	8*	12					26
1	2	3	4	5	6				8	11	9			7		10					27
1	2	3	4	5	6				8	11	9			7		10					28
1	2	3	4	5	6				8	11*	9			7	12	10					29
1	2	3	4	5	6			9	8		10			7		11					30
1	5	3	4		6	11		9	8		7	2*			12	10					31
1	2	3	4	5		6		9	8		7*		12		10	11					32
1	6	3	4	5		11			8			2		7	10				9		33
1	6	3*	4	5		11			8	12		2		7	10				9		34
1	2		4	5					8	6	11	3		7	10*				9	12	35
1	2*		4	5	6				8	11	9	3	12	7	10						36
1			4	5	6				8	11	9	3		7	10					2	37
1			4	5	6			12	8	11	9	3		7	10*					2	38
1			4	5	6			10	8	11	9	3		7						2	39
1			4	5	6			10	8	11	9	3		7						2	40
1			4	5	6			10	8	11	9	3		7						2	41
1			4	5	6			10	8	11	9	3		7		12				2*	42
1			4	5	6	3		9*		11	7	2	12		8	10					43
1			4	5	6	3		10	8	11	9	2		7*		12					44
1			4	5	6*	3		9	8	11	7	2	12						10		45
1				5	6				8	11	7	3	4			10			9	2	46
46	22	32	44	42	28	15	9	30	41	39	30	32	2	26	28	10	2	4	17	7	
						+ 3s		+ 1s	+ 1s	+ 1s	+ 1s		+ 4s	+ 1s	+ 3s	+ 4s	+ 1s	+ 1s		+ 2s	

CHESTER

	Ht	Wt	Birthplace	Clubs	League App.	League Gls
Goalkeepers						
Gren Millington	5 10	11 6	Queensferry	Chester	1	—
				Brighton	—	—
				Chester	242	—
Brian Lloyd* (Wales)	6 2	12 7	Rhyl	Stockport Co	32	—
				Southend U	46	—
				Wrexham	266	—
				Port Vale (on loan)	16	—
				Chester	94	—
Defenders						
Trevor Storton	6 1	12 4	Keighley	Tranmere R	118	9
				Liverpool	5	—
				Chester	299	13
Jim Walker	5 10	10 10	Northwich	Derby Co	42	3
				Hartlepool U (on loan)	10	—
				Brighton	28	4
				Peterborough U	31	1
				Chester	172	4
Paul Raynor	5 11	11 0	Chester	Chester	157	8
Ian Edwards*	6 0	11 10	Chester	Chester	—	—
Paul Needham	5 10	11 0	Chester	Chester	9	—
John Cottam	5 10	11 10	Nottingham	Nottingham F	95	4
				Mansfield T (on loan)	2	1
				Lincoln C (on loan)	1	—
				Chesterfield	120	7
				Chester	87	1
David Burns	5 8	10 6	Ellesmere Pt	Chester	46	1
Peter Zelem	5 11	10 12	Manchester	Chester	6	—
Midfield						
Alan Oakes	6 0	12 10	Winsford	Manchester C	565	26
				Chester	186	14
Ron Phillips (Contract cancelled Jan 1981)	5 6½	10 3	Worsley	Bolton W	145	17
				Chesterfield (on loan)	5	—
				Bury	72	5
				Chester	130	21
Derek Jeffries*	5 10¼	11 3	Manchester	Manchester C	73	—
				Crystal Palace	107	1
				Peterborough U (on loan)	7	—
				Millwall (on loan)	11	—
				Chester	121	2
Richard Gendall*	5 11	11 6	Wrexham	Chester	5	—
Keith Fear*	5 7	10 8	Bristol	Bristol C	151	33
				Blackburn R (on loan)	5	2
				Hereford U (on loan)	6	—
				Plymouth Arg	45	9
				Brentford (on loan)	8	2
				Chester	44	3
Trevor Birch*	5 11	11 13	Ormskirk	Liverpool	—	—
				Shrewsbury T	25	4
				Chester	31	—
Steve Ludlam	5 6	9 11	Chesterfield	Sheffield U	27	1
				Carlisle U	96	11
				Chester	40	7
Forwards						
David Prestidge*	5 9	10 6	Queensferry	Chester	—	—
Ian Howat	5 8	10 7	Wrexham	Chester	52	10
Bryn Jones	5 8	10 0	St Asaph	Chester	128	14
Peter Sutcliffe	5 6	9 0	Manchester	Manchester U	—	—
				Stockport Co	27	2
				Port Vale	50	6
				Chester	76	5
Trevor Phillips	5 6	10 3	Rotherham	Rotherham U	322	81
				Hull C	22	3
				Chester	43	9
Terry Cooke	5 10	11 0	Wrexham	Chester	14	5
John Anderson (Transferred to Northwich V Oct 1980)	5 9	10 3	Manchester	Everton	—	—
				Chester	—	—

CHESTERFIELD Division 3

President: His Grace the Duke of Devonshire MC, DL, JP.
Vice-President: G. Kenning DFC, TD, MA.
Chairman: E. I. Gaunt.
Vice-Chairman: A. Bates.
Directors: F. Tuckley, E. Brocklehurst, P. C. J. T. Kirkman OBE, J. Leedham.
Team Manager: Frank Barlow.
Secretary: R. F. Pepper.
Year Formed: 1866. *Turned Professional:* 1891.
Limited Company: 1871.
Previous Name: Chesterfield Town, 1904.

Football League Record:
1899 Elected to Division 2; 1909 failed re-election; 1921–31 Division 3(N); 1931–33 Division 2; 1933–36 Division 3(N); 1936–51 Division 2; 1951–58 Division 3(N); 1958–61 Division 3; 1961–70 Division 4; 1970– Division 3.

Honours: *Football League:* Division 2 best season: 4th, 1946–47; Division 3(N) – Champions 1930–31, 1935–36; Runners-up 1933–34; Division 4 – Champions 1969–70. *FA Cup* best season: 5th rd, 1932–33, 1937–38, 1949–50. *Football League Cup* best season: 4th rd, 1964–65. *Anglo-Scottish Cup:* Winners 1980–81.

Record Victory: 10-0 v Glossop North End, Division 2, 17 Jan, 1903.
Record Defeat: 1-9 v Port Vale, Division 2, 24 Sept, 1932.
Most League Points: 64, Division 4, 1969–70.
Most League Goals: 102, Division 3(N), 1930–31.
Highest League Scorer in Season: Jimmy Cookson, 44, Division 3(N), 1925–26.
Most League Goals in Total Aggregate: Ernie Moss, 127, 1969–76; 1979–81.
Most Capped Player: Walter McMillen, 4(7), Ireland.
Most League Appearances: Dave Blakey, 613, 1948–67.
Record Transfer Fee Received: £80,000 from Newcastle U for Steve Hardwick, Feb 1977.
Record Transfer Fee Paid: £150,000 to Carlisle U for Phil Bonnyman, March 1980.
Previous Managers since the War: Bob Brocklebank, Bob Marshall, Ted Davison, Duggie Livingstone, Tony McShane, Jimmy McGuigan, Joe Shaw, Arthur Cox.
Address of Supporters Club: 132 Saltergate, Chesterfield. Contact secretary P. Tooley (0246) 853162 or chairman H. Borrell (0246) 75862.
Address of the Club Shop or Boutique: 132 Saltergate, Chesterfield.

Recreation Ground, Chesterfield S40 4SX. Telephone Chesterfield 32318. *Ground capacity:* 22,000 (12,000 covered). *Record attendance:* 30,968 v Newcastle U, Division 2, 7 April, 1939. *Record receipts:* £24,640 v Barnsley, Division 3, 26 Dec, 1980. *Pitch measurements:* 114yd×72yd.
How to get there: Chesterfield railway station is one mile from the ground, via Corporation St, Holywell St, to Saltergate.
Match tickets: Seats in the Centre and Wing Stands may be booked in advance.
Car parking: Street parking permitted around the ground. Also car parks in Saltergate within ½ mile of the ground.
Entertainments/catering facilities: A social club (members only) is sited on the ground at the Saltergate entrance. Refreshment bars around the ground.
Club shop: A wide range of souvenirs available as well as programmes.
Handbooks/programmes: Programmes available on subscription from Commercial Manager, Alan Humphreys. A yearly handbook with review of previous season. 1981–82 edition available by post, 60p + postage.
Extra information: Arnold Birch, Chesterfield's goalkeeper, scored five goals in 1923–24, all from penalties.
Club Colours: Royal blue shirts, white shorts, white stockings with two blue rings.
Change Colours: Red shirts, black shorts, red stockings.
Club Player/Coach: Bill Green.
Second and Third Team Coach: Billy Dearden.
Physiotherapist: Steve Wanless. *Scout:* Syd Lancashire.
Club Nickname: Blues or Spireites.

CHESTERFIELD 1980–81 LEAGUE RECORD

Match No.	Date	Venue	Opponents	Result	H/T Score	Goalscorers	Attendance
1	Aug 16	H	Huddersfield T	W 2-1	1-0	Birch (pen), Bonnyman	7819
2	19	A	Sheffield U	L 0-2	0-1		18,390
3	23	A	Burnley	L 0-1	0-1		5855
4	30	H	Gillingham	W 2-0	2-0	Crawford, Bonnyman	5535
5	Sept 6	A	Oxford U	W 3-0	1-0	Walwyn 2, Wilson	3273
6	13	H	Plymouth Arg	D 2-2	1-1	Hunter, Walker	5561
7	16	A	Colchester U	D 1-1	1-0	Green	2171
8	20	H	Newport Co	W 3-2	1-0	Birch 2 (1 pen), Ridley	5277
9	27	A	Carlisle U	W 6-2	3-2	Birch 3, Moss 2, Walker	4256
10	30	H	Colchester U	W 3-0	3-0	Moss, Walker, Birch	6674
11	Oct 4	A	Portsmouth	L 0-1	0-1		14,953
12	7	H	Rotherham U	W 2-0	0-0	Birch 2 (1 pen)	10,638
13	11	H	Hull C	W 1-0	0-0	Walker	7126
14	18	A	Reading	W 3-2	1-0	Birch, Moss, Salmons	5904
15	22	A	Blackpool	W 3-0	1-0	Wilson, Moss, Salmons	8062
16	25	H	Walsall	L 1-2	0-2	Birch	7870
17	Nov 1	A	Fulham	D 1-1	0-1	Birch	4706
18	4	A	Rotherham U	D 0-0	0-0		11,093
19	8	H	Brentford	W 2-1	1-1	Bonnyman 2	7186
20	11	H	Sheffield U	W 1-0	0-0	Bonnyman	15,992
21	15	A	Huddersfield T	L 0-2	0-1		12,828
22	29	A	Charlton Ath	L 0-1	0-1		8120
23	Dec 6	H	Millwall	W 3-0	1-0	Bonnyman, Birch 2	5930
24	20	A	Exeter C	D 2-2	1-0	Birch, Crawford	4075
25	26	H	Barnsley	D 0-0	0-0		17,146
26	27	A	Chester	L 1-2	0-1	Birch (pen)	4222
27	Jan 10	A	Swindon T	W 1-0	0-0	Moss	6717
28	17	H	Charlton Ath	L 0-1	0-1		9563
29	24	A	Gillingham	L 0-1	0-0		5122
30	31	H	Burnley	W 3-0	2-0	Hunter, Kowalski, Birch	8635
31	Feb 7	A	Plymouth Arg	L 0-1	0-0		6305
32	14	H	Oxford U	W 2-1	0-1	Birch, Wilson	6451
33	21	H	Carlisle U	W 1-0	1-0	Birch	5750
34	28	A	Newport Co	L 1-5	0-1	Birch	5340
35	Mar 7	H	Portsmouth	W 3-0	1-0	Salmons, Simpson, Birch	6985
36	14	A	Hull C	D 0-0	0-0		5488
37	21	H	Blackpool	W 3-2	2-1	Entwistle (og), Bonnyman, Walker	5959
38	28	A	Walsall	L 3-4	1-2	Moss 3	4044
39	Apr 4	H	Fulham	D 0-0	0-0		6756
40	7	H	Swindon T	D 2-2	0-1	Crawford, Birch	5222
41	11	A	Brentford	L 2-3	1-1	Moss, Kowalski	4880
42	18	H	Chester	W 2-0	2-0	Moss, Crawford	3850
43	20	A	Barnsley	D 1-1	0-0	Crawford	17,019
44	May 2	A	Millwall	W 2-0	1-0	Kowalski, Moss	3522
45	5	H	Reading	W 3-2	3-1	Moss 2, Bonnyman	3059
46	8	H	Exeter C	W 1-0	0-0	Tartt	3448

Final League Position: 5

Goalscorers

League (72): Birch 22 (4 pens), Moss 14, Bonnyman 8, Crawford 5, Walker 5, Kowalski 3, Salmons 3, Wilson 3, Walwyn 2, Hunter 2, Green 1, Ridley 1, Simpson 1, Tartt 1, own goal 1.
League Cup (6): Moss 2, Bonnyman, Crawford, Walker, Wilson.
F.A. Cup (8): Birch (pen), Crawford, Green, Hunter, Salmons, Simpson, Tartt, Wilson.

League Cup	First Round	Darlington (h)	1-0
		(a)	2-1
	Second Round	Oxford U (h)	3-1
		(a)	0-3
FA Cup	First Round	Wigan Ath (a)	2-2
		(h)	2-0
	Second Round	Sheffield U (a)	1-1
		(h)	1-0
	Third Round	Peterborough U (a)	1-1
		(h)	1-2

Turner	Kowalski	O'Neill	Wilson	Green	Ridley	Birch	Moss	Bonnyman	Salmons	Walker	Hunter	Crawford	Stirk	Walwyn	Tartt	Pollard	Tingay	Simpson	Gregory	Bellamy	Windridge	*Match No.*
1	2	3	4	5	6	7	8	9	10	11												1
1	2	3	4	5	6	7	8	9	10	11												2
1	2	3	4	5	6	7	8	9	10	11												3
1		3	4	5	2	7	8	9	10		6	11										4
1		3	4	5	10	7		8		11	6		2	9								5
1		3	4*	5	10	7	12	8		11	6		2	9								6
1		3	4	5	10	7	8	9		11	6				2							7
1		3		5	4	7	8	9	10	11	6				2*	12						8
1		3	4	5	6	7	8	9	10	11	12				2*							9
1		3	4	5	6	7	8	9	10	11					2							10
1		3	4	5	6	7	8	9	10	11					2							11
1			4	5	6	7	8	9	10	11					2	3						12
1			4	5	6	7	8	9	10	11					2	3						13
1			4	5	6	7	8	9	10	11					2	3						14
1			4	5	6	7	8	9	10	11					2	3						15
			4	5	6	7	8	9	10	11		12			2*	3	1					16
1			4	5	6	7	8	9	10	11					2	3						17
1			4	5	6	7	8	9	10	11					2	3						18
1			4	5	6	7	8	9		10		11			2	3						19
1			4	5	6	7	8	9		10		11			2	3						20
1			4	5	6	7	8	9		10		11			2	3						21
1	12		4	5	6	7	8	9	10	11*					2	3						22
1			4	5	6	7	8	9	10			11	3		2							23
1	4			5		7	8*	9	10		6	11			2	3		12				24
1	4			5		7		9	10		6	11			2	3		8				25
1	4			5		7		9	10		6	11		8	2	3						26
1	4			5	6	7	8	9	10						2	3		11				27
1	4			5	6	7	8	9	10			12			2	3*		11				28
1	9	3	4	5		7	8		10	11	6				2							29
1	9	3	4	5		7	8		10	11	6				2							30
1	9	3	4	5	12	7	8		10*	11	6				2							31
1	9	3	4	5		7	8	12	10	11*	6				2							32
1	9	3	4	5	6	7		10		11					2			8				33
1	9	3	4	5	6	7		10		11					2			8				34
1		3	4	5	6	7		10	9	11			2					8				35
1		3	4	5	6	7		9	10	11			2					8				36
1	12	3	4	5	6	7	8	9*	10	11			2									37
1	9	3		5	6	7	8		10	11*		12	2		4							38
	4	3		5	6	7	8	9	10*	11		12	2						1			39
	4	3		5	6	7	8	9	10	11*		12	2						1			40
1	4	11		5	6	7	8	9	10*			2	3		12							41
1	4	3		5	6	7	8	9				11	2		10							42
1	4	3		5	6	7	8	9				11	2		10							43
1	10	3	4	5	6		8	9				11			2			7*		12		44
1	10	3*	4	5	6	7	8	9				11								2	12	45
1	4	3		5	6	7	8	9							10					2	11	46
43	23	29	33	46	39	45	38	41	33	33	12	13	12	3	33	16	1	8	2	2	1	
	+ 2s				+ 1s		+ 1s	+ 1s			+ 1s	+ 5s			+ 1s	+ 1s		+ 1s		+ 1s	+ 1s	

CHESTERFIELD

	Ht	Wt	Birthplace	Clubs	League App.	League Gls
Goalkeepers						
Philip Tingay*	5 11	12 0	Chesterfield	Chesterfield	181	—
				Barnsley (on loan)	8	—
Paul Gregory		11 7	Sheffield	Chesterfield	2	—
John Turner	5 11	12 8	Peterlee	Derby Co	—	—
				Doncaster R (on loan)	4	—
				Brighton (on loan)	—	—
				Peterborough U (on loan)	—	—
				Huddersfield T (on loan)	1	—
				Reading	31	—
				Torquay U	76	—
				Chesterfield	55	—
Defenders						
Sean O'Neill	5 9	12 2	Belfast	Leeds U	—	—
				Chesterfield	262	3
Leslie Hunter	6 2	11 10	Middlesbrough	Chesterfield	153	7
Glyn Chamberlain*	5 9	11 4	Chesterfield	Burnley	—	—
				Chesterfield	18	—
Bill Green	6 3	12 8	Newcastle	Hartlepool U	131	9
				Carlisle U	119	4
				West Ham U	35	1
				Peterborough U	30	—
				Chesterfield	81	2
John Stirk	5 6	11 1	Consett	Ipswich T	6	—
				Watford	46	—
				Chesterfield	23	—
Gary Bellamy	6 1¾	11 5	Worksop	Chesterfield	3	—
John Partridge	5 11	11 8	Chesterfield	Chesterfield	—	—
Midfield						
Colin Tartt	5 11	11 8	Liverpool	Port Vale	175	7
				Chesterfield	182	7
Geoff Salmons	5 10¾	10 11½	Mexborough	Sheffield U	180	8
				Stoke C	118	14
				Sheffield U (on loan)	5	—
				Leicester C	26	4
				Chesterfield	116	15
Phil Bonnyman	6 0	12 0	Glasgow	Rangers	—	—
				Hamilton A	71	7
				Carlisle U	152	26
				Chesterfield	53	11
John Ridley	6 1½	12 6	Consett	Port Vale	156	3
				Leicester C	24	—
				Chesterfield	86	4
Danny Wilson	5 7	10 3	Wigan	Wigan Ath	(not known)	
				Bury	90	8
				Chesterfield	33	3
Forwards						
Phil Walker	6 0	12 1	Kirby	Chesterfield	128	29
Andrew Kowalski	5 10	11 0	Mansfield	Chesterfield	286	27
Gary Simpson	6 0	12 0	Chesterfield	Chesterfield	43	8
Gary Pollard	6 1	11 10	Staveley	Chesterfield	38	—
Ernie Moss	6 1	12 11	Chesterfield	Chesterfield	271	94
				Peterborough U	35	9
				Mansfield T	57	21
				Chesterfield	107	33
Alan Crawford	5 7½	9 10	Rotherham	Rotherham U	237	49
				Mansfield T (on loan)	2	—
				Chesterfield	53	15
David Windridge	5 9	11 0	Atherstone	Sheffield U	—	—
				Chesterfield	2	—
Alan Birch	5 5	10 2	West Bromwich	Walsall	171	23
				Chesterfield	90	35
Keith Walwyn	6 1	13 2	Jamaica	Winterton	(not known)	
				Chesterfield	3	2
Russ Athersych	5 9	11 4	Sheffield	Chesterfield	—	—

COLCHESTER UNITED Division 4

Patron: A. Buck QC, MP.
President: R. G. R. Chapman FRICS.
Chairman: M. J. Cadman. *Vice-Chairman:* H. R. Piper.
Directors: N. F. Fitch, R. T. Jackson, J. W. Rippingale.
Manager: Bobby Roberts. *Secretary:* Martin R. Bennet.
Year Formed: 1937. *Turned Professional:* 1937.
Limited Company: 1937.

Football League Record:

1950 Elected to Division 3(S); 1958–61 Division 3; 1961–62 Division 4; 1962–65 Division 3; 1965–66 Division 4; 1966–68 Division 3; 1968–74 Division 4; 1974–76 Division 3; 1976–77 Division 4; 1977–81 Division 3; 1981– Division 4.

Honours: *Football League:* Division 3(S) best season: 3rd, 1956–57; Division 4 – Runners-up 1961–62. *FA Cup* best season: 1970–71, 6th rd (record for a Fourth Division club shared with Oxford United and Bradford City). *Football League Cup* best season: 5th rd, 1974–75.

Record Victory: 9-1 v Bradford C, Division 4, 30 Dec, 1961.

Record Defeat: 0-7 v Leyton Orient, Division 3(S), 5 Jan, 1952; 0-7 v Reading, Division 3(S), 18 Sept, 1957.

Most League Points: 60, Division 4, 1973–74.

Most League Goals: 104, Division 4, 1961–62.

Highest League Scorer in Season: Bobby Hunt, 37, Division 4, 1961–62.

Most League Goals in Total Aggregate: Martyn King, 131, 1959–65.

Most Capped Player: None.

Most League Appearances: Micky Cook, 490, 1969–81.

Record Transfer Fee Received: £90,000 from Gillingham for Trevor Lee, Jan 1981.

Record Transfer Fee Paid: £25,000 to Ipswich T for Roger Osborne, Feb 1981.

Previous Managers since the War: Ted Fenton, Jimmy Allen, Jack Butler, Benny Fenton, Neil Franklin, Dick Graham, Jim Smith.

Layer Rd Ground, Colchester. Telephone (0206) 74042. *Telegraphic address:* 'United Colchester'. *Ground capacity:* 16,150. *Record attendance:* 19,072 v Reading, FA Cup 1st rd, 27 Nov, 1948. *Record receipts:* £20,265 v Manchester U, FA Cup 5th rd, 20 Feb, 1979. *Pitch measurements:* 110yd×71yd.

How to get there: Buses from Osborne Street in Colchester, which is about 2 miles from the railway station.

Match tickets: Stand seats can be booked two weeks in advance (Ticket Office tel: Colchester 72202 or 74042.) All bookings will be accepted and held, *provided* the tickets are *paid for* and *collected* at least 48 hours before kick-off. During the 48 hours prior to the game, tickets will be available *only* to cash customers at the ground. This method should not affect people who live outside the immediate area of Layer Road, for postal applications with the appropriate remittance will still be accepted up to 72 hours before kick-off provided that such applications are accompanied by a stamped (first class) addressed envelope.

Car parking: Parking facilities in Butt Road and Layer Road, approximately 150 yards past the ground on the south side of Colchester. Free parking in Army Barracks (150 yards).

Entertainments/catering facilities: Refreshment points on the ground.

Club shop: Sells all types of souvenirs; mailing list on request.

Handbooks/programmes: Back numbers of CUFC programmes can be ordered from the club shop.

Extra information: In 1947–48, Colchester, then a non-League side, reached the 5th round of the FA Cup.

Club Colours: Blue and white vertical stripes, blue shorts, white stockings.

Change Colours: Red shirts, black shorts, black stockings.

Club Trainer/Coach: Ray Harford.

Club Nickname: The U's.

COLCHESTER UNITED 1980–81 LEAGUE RECORD

Match No.	Date	Venue	Opponents	Result	H/T Score	Goalscorers	Attendance
1	Aug 16	H	Plymouth Arg	D 2-2	0-1	Hodge, Gough	2061
2	20	A	Fulham	L 0-1	0-0		4250
3	23	H	Walsall	D 1-1	0-1	Rowles	1979
4	30	A	Exeter C	L 0-4	0-1		3918
5	Sept 6	A	Burnley	L 0-1	0-1		4391
6	13	H	Millwall	W 3-0	1-0	Foley, Lee, Rowles	2724
7	16	H	Chesterfield	D 1-1	0-1	Lee	2171
8	20	A	Charlton Ath	W 2-1	1-1	Foley, Hodge	4323
9	27	H	Chester	D 1-1	0-0	Lee	2147
10	30	A	Chesterfield	L 0-3	0-3		6674
11	Oct 4	A	Huddersfield T	L 0-2	0-0		8400
12	7	H	Portsmouth	W 1-0	0-0	Lee	2702
13	11	H	Barnsley	D 2-2	1-2	Gough, Hodge	2749
14	18	A	Blackpool	D 1-1	0-1	Allinson	6997
15	22	A	Reading	L 0-1	0-1		3935
16	25	H	Rotherham U	D 0-0	0-0		2623
17	28	H	Hull C	W 2-0	1-0	Allinson, Lee	2239
18	Nov 1	A	Sheffield U	L 0-3	0-2		12,810
19	4	A	Portsmouth	L 1-2	1-1	Lee	10,895
20	8	H	Swindon T	W 1-0	0-0	Hodge (pen)	2153
21	11	H	Fulham	W 3-2	2-1	Wignall, Allinson 2	2543
22	15	A	Plymouth Arg	D 1-1	1-0	Bremner	4905
23	29	H	Oxford U	W 3-0	0-0	Hodge (pen), Bremner 2	2114
24	Dec 6	A	Carlisle U	L 0-4	0-2		3196
25	20	H	Newport Co	W 1-0	1-0	Hodge (pen)	2160
26	26	A	Brentford	L 1-2	1-1	Bremner	6240
27	27	H	Gillingham	W 2-1	1-1	Packer (pen), Lee	3879
28	Jan 10	H	Blackpool	W 3-2	1-1	Foley, Gough 2	2378
29	17	A	Oxford U	L 1-2	0-1	Foley	3498
30	31	A	Walsall	L 1-3	0-2	Allinson	3195
31	Feb 3	H	Exeter C	L 1-2	1-2	Bremner	2357
32	7	A	Millwall	L 1-3	1-1	Bremner	4565
33	14	H	Burnley	W 2-1	1-0	McDonough, Bremner	3082
34	21	A	Chester	D 0-0	0-0		1778
35	28	H	Charlton Ath	W 2-0	2-0	Foley, Packer (pen)	4864
36	Mar 7	H	Huddersfield T	L 1-2	1-1	Packer	3644
37	17	A	Hull C	W 1-0	1-0	Cotton	3586
38	22	H	Reading	L 1-2	1-2	Bremner	3705
39	28	A	Rotherham U	L 0-2	0-1		7956
40	Apr 4	H	Sheffield U	D 1-1	1-0	Allinson	2439
41	7	A	Barnsley	L 0-3	0-2		13,283
42	11	A	Swindon T	L 0-3	0-1		6120
43	18	A	Gillingham	D 0-0	0-0		4408
44	20	H	Brentford	L 0-2	0-2		2609
45	25	A	Newport Co	L 0-1	0-1		4619
46	May 2	H	Carlisle U	W 1-0	1-0	McDonough	1430

Final League Position: 22

Goalscorers

League (45): Bremner 8, Lee 7, Allinson 6, Hodge 6 (3 pens), Foley 5, Gough 4, Packer 3 (2 pens), McDonough 2, Rowles 2, Cotton 1, Wignall 1.
League Cup (1): Gough.
F.A. Cup (6): Bremner 2, Lee 2, Allinson, Wignall.

League Cup	First Round	Gillingham (h)	0-2
		(a)	1-2
FA Cup	First Round	Portsmouth (h)	3-0
	Second Round	Yeovil T (h)	1-1
		(a)	2-0
	Third Round	Watford (h)	0-1

Walker	Cook	Allinson	Gough	Wignall	Packer	Hodge	Rowles	Foley	Lee	Cotton	Leslie	Harvey	Evans	Crouch	Longhorn	Bremner	Wright	Osborne	McDonough	Coleman	Adcock	*Match No.*
1	2	3	4	5	6	7	8*	9	10	11	12											1
1	2	3	8	5	6			9	12	11	4	7*	10									2
1	2	11	4*	5	6	7	8	9	10		3		12									3
1		3		5	6	7		9	10	11	4	8	2									4
1	2	3		5	6	7	11	9	10		4		8*	12								5
1	2	8		5	6		11	9	10	7	4			3								6
1	2	11		5	6	7	8	9	10		4			3								7
1	2	11		5	6	7	8	9	10		4			3								8
1	2	11		5	6	7	8	9	10		4			3								9
1	2	3		5	6	7	8	9	10		4			11								10
1	2	11		5	6	7			10	9	4		12	3	8*							11
1	2	11	8	5	6	7	9		10		4			3								12
1	2	11	8	5	6	7	9		10		4			3*		12						13
1	2	11	8	5	6	7	9				4		3			10						14
1	2	11	8	5	6		3		10	7	4					9						15
1	2	11	8		6		3		9	7	4				5	10						16
1	2	11	8	5	6	7	3		9		4					10						17
1	2	11		5	6				10	8	4		7		3	9						18
1	2	11		5	6				10	8	4		7		3	9						19
1	2	11	8*	5	6	7	3		10		4				12	9						20
1	2	11		5	6	7	3	12	10		4				8*	9						21
1	2	11		5	6	7	3	8	10		4					9						22
1	2	11		5	6	7	3	8	10		4					9						23
1	2	11		5	6	7	3	8	10		4					9						24
1	2	11	8	5		7	3		10		4				6	9						25
1	2	11		5	6	7*	3		10	12	4				8	9						26
1	2	11	8	5	6	12			10		4				7	9	3*					27
1	2	11	10	5	6			8			4				3	9	7					28
1	2	11	10	5	6	12		8			4				3	9	7*					29
1	2	11		5	3			10		8	4				7	9	6					30
1	2	11	10	5		7		8			4				3	9	6					31
1	2	11		5		9		10		7	4				3	8	6					32
1	2	11			6			8		4					3	9	5	7	10			33
1	2	11			6			10		4						9	5	7	8	3		34
1	2	11			6			8			4					9	5	7	10	3		35
1	2	11		5	6			8			4					9		7	10	3		36
1	2	12		3	6			8		11*	4					9	5	7	10			37
1	2	12		3	6			8*		11	4					9	5	7	10			38
1	2	12		5	6			8		11*	4					9	3	7	10			39
1	2	11		5	6						4				8	9	3	7	10			40
1	2	11		5	6			10		7	4				8	9	3*		12			41
1	2	11		5	6			3			4				8	9		7	10			42
1	2	11		5	6			10			4			3	8	9	7					43
1	2	11		5	6*			7			4				8	9		12	10	3		44
1	2	11		5	6			7		4					8	9	3	10				45
1	2	11		5	6						12				8*	9	3	4	10		7	46
46	45	43	15	42	43	22	21	30	25	18	41	2	6	9	21	33	17	11	11	4	1	
		+ 3s				+ 2s		+ 1s	+ 1s	+ 1s	+ 2s		+ 2s	+ 1s	+ 1s	+ 1s		+ 1s	+ 1s			

COLCHESTER UNITED

	Ht	Wt	Birthplace	Clubs	League App.	League Gls
Goalkeepers						
Mike Walker	6 1	13 2	Colwyn Bay	Reading	—	—
				Shrewsbury T	6	—
				York C	60	—
				Watford	137	—
				Charlton Ath (on loan)	1	—
				Colchester U	363	—
Bobby Hamilton*	5 10	12 7	Irvine	Colchester U	—	—
Defenders						
Micky Cook	5 7	10 11	Enfield	Colchester U	490	14
Mick Packer	5 10	11 0	London	Watford	67	2
				Crewe Alex (on loan)	12	—
				Colchester U	318	19
Steve Wignall	5 11	11 11	Liverpool	Doncaster R	130	1
				Nottingham F (on loan)	—	—
				Colchester U	158	10
Steve Wright	6 0	10 11	Clacton	Colchester U	79	2
Nigel Crouch*	5 8	10 7	Ardleigh	Ipswich T	—	—
				Lincoln C (on loan)	7	—
				Colchester U	10	—
Phil Coleman	5 11	11 9	Woolwich	Millwall	36	1
				Colchester U	4	—
Midfield						
Steve Leslie	5 10	11 0	Brentwood	Colchester U	344	36
Russell Cotton	5 10	11 8	Wellington	Colchester U	26	1
Bobby Hodge*	5 9½	11 0	Exeter	Exeter C	128	18
				Colchester U	92	14
Dennis Longhorn	5 11	11 0	Southampton	Bournemouth	30	1
				Mansfield T	96	5
				Sunderland	40	3
				Sheffield U	36	1
				Aldershot	53	3
				Colchester U	22	—
Roger Osborne	5 9	10 11	Otley	Ipswich T	124	9
				Colchester U	12	—
Calogero Cusenza*			Edmonton	Colchester U	—	—
Tony Adcock (Non-contract)	5 10	10 8	Bethnal Green	Colchester U	1	—
Forwards						
Stephen Foley	6 0	11 4	Clacton	Colchester U	281	54
Bobby Gough	5 7	11 0	Birmingham	Walsall	1	—
(Contract cancelled March 1981)				Port Vale	210	33
				Stockport Co (on loan)	6	—
				Southport	61	16
				Colchester U	196	65
Ian Allinson	5 10	11 0	Hitchin	Colchester U	220	26
Eddie Rowles	5 9	11 2	Gosport	Bournemouth	66	12
				York C	67	14
				Torquay U	59	13
				Darlington	103	21
				Colchester U	85	17
Tony Evans	5 8	10 8	Colchester	Colchester U	30	2
(To Kongsvinger, Norway, Dec 1980)						
Gary Harvey	5 7	11 2	Colchester	Colchester U	6	2
(To Kongsvinger, Norway, Dec 1980)						
Kevin Bremner	5 9½	12 3	Banff	Keith	(not known)	
				Colchester U	34	8
Roy McDonough	6 1	11 11	Solihull	Birmingham C	2	1
				Walsall	82	15
				Chelsea	—	—
				Colchester U	12	2

COVENTRY CITY Division 1

Life President: Derrick H. Robins.
President: J. R. Mead JP.
Chairman: J. W. T. Hill.
Directors: M. F. French FCA, J. W. Jamieson, P. D. H. Robins, T. Sergeant FRCS.
Chief Executive: Gordon Milne.
Team Manager: Dave Sexton.
Asst. Manager: Ron Wylie.
General Secretary: J. D. Dent.
Commercial Manager: George Curtis.
Year Formed: 1883. *Turned Professional:* 1908.
Limited Company: 1907. *Former Names:* 1883–98 Singers FC; 1898 Coventry City FC.

Football League Record:
1919 Elected to Division 2; 1925–26 Division 3(N); 1926–36 Division 3(S); 1936–52 Division 2; 1952–58 Division 3(S); 1958–59 Division 4; 1959–64 Division 3; 1964–67 Division 2; 1967– Division 1.

Honours: *Football League:* Division 1 best season: 6th, 1969–70; Division 2 – Champions 1966–67; Division 3 – Champions 1963–64; Division 3(S) – Champions 1935–36; Runners–up 1933–34. Division 4 – Runners-up 1958–59. *FA Cup* best season: 6th rd, 1962–63, 1966–67, 1972–73; old 4th rd, 1909–10. *Football League Cup* best season: Semi-final 1980–81. **European Competition:** *European Fairs Cup:* 1970–71.
Record Victory: 9-0 v Bristol C, Division 3(S), 28 Apr, 1934.
Record Defeat: 2-10 v Norwich C, Division 3(S), 15 Mar, 1930.
Most League Points: 60, Division 4, 1958–59; and Division 3, 1963–64.
Most League Goals: 108, Division 3(S), 1931–32.
Highest League Scorer in Season: Clarrie Bourton, 49, Division 3(S), 1931–32.
Most League Goals in Total Aggregate: 171, Clarrie Bourton, 1931–37.
Most Capped Player: Dave Clements, 21 (48), Northern Ireland.
Most League Appearances: George Curtis, 486, 1956–70.
Record Transfer Fee Received: £365,000 from Portland Timbers for Gary Collier, March 1980.
Record Transfer Fee Paid: £325,000 to Bristol C for Gary Collier, July 1979.
Previous Managers since the War: Dick Bayliss, Billy Frith, Harry Storer, Jack Fairbrother, Jesse Carver, Harry Warren, Billy Frith, Jimmy Hill, Noel Cantwell, Bob Dennison, Gordon Milne.
Address of Supporters Club: Freehold St, Coventry. Telephone: 26268.
Address of Club Shop: 'Sky Blue Shop', Highfield Road, Coventry.

Highfield Road Stadium, King Richard Street, Coventry CV2 4GU. Telephone Coventry 57171. *Telex:* 312132, answer back code COV AFC. *Telegraphic address:* 'City Football Coventry'. *Ground capacity:* 20,000 all-seater stadium. *Record attendance:* 51,455 v Wolverhampton W, Division 2, 29 April, 1967. *Record receipts:* £68,029·70 v West Ham U, League Cup semi-final 1st leg, 27 Jan, 1981. *Pitch measurements:* 110yd×75yd.
How to get there: Buses from Coventry railway station to town centre (Pool Meadow bus station). Then buses 16, 17 (Hospital), 32 (Potters Green), 33 (Bell Green) to ground. Also taxi service from station.
Match tickets: Stand seat tickets can be booked 21 days in advance of any home League fixture. Postal applications accepted if sent with correct remittance to the Ticket Office Manager, Coventry City FC, Highfield Rd Stadium, Coventry.
Car parking: Street parking permitted all around the ground. Special coach/car park situated at Gosford Green (200 yards from stadium) on Walsgrave Road (A46).
Entertainments/catering facilities: Pre-match entertainment at all League and Cup games by Radio Sky Blue; live entertainment from groups and bands at special matches. The Sky Blue Buttery is open for hot and cold snacks before matches for main stand patrons. There are 16 licensed refreshment rooms and lounges, and 11 unlicensed refreshment rooms and lounges around the ground; all are open before the game, at half-time, and after the match. The Grandstand restaurant, recommended by Egon Ronay, is open for lunch Mon. to Fri. and is available in the evening for private dinner parties. On match days it is used as the Vice-Presidents' Club. An executive suite, with accommodation for 60 and full buffet facilities, can also be hired on match days, during the afternoon. Mr T. Caluori, catering mgr, Grandstand Restaurant, Highfield Road, Coventry.
Club shop: Sited in the main stand; sells all types of souvenirs. There is a similar shop at the Thackhall St side of the stadium, attached to the Sky Blue Pools Office.
Handbooks/programmes: Programmes available through a postal service.
Extra information: Coventry City Supporters' Club under the Sky Blue stand, Thackhall St, welcomes visiting supporters on production of the membership card of their own club. They can attend the evening entertainment if they give 48-hours' notice by post to the secretary, Frank Fountaine, Coventry City SC, Thackhall St, Coventry.
Club Colours: Sky blue shirts and shorts with navy and white trim, sky blue stockings.
Change Colours: Red shirts and shorts with navy and white trim, red stockings.
Club Nickname: Sky Blues.

COVENTRY CITY 1980–81 LEAGUE RECORD

Match No.	Date	Venue	Opponents	Result	H/T Score	Goalscorers	Attendance
1	Aug 16	A	Birmingham C	L 1-3	0-2	Blair	21,907
2	19	H	Liverpool	D 0-0	0-0		22,807
3	23	H	Arsenal	W 3-1	0-0	Thompson, English, Gillespie	15,399
4	30	A	Aston Villa	L 0-1	0-0		20,050
5	Sept 6	H	Crystal Palace	W 3-1	0-0	Daly 2, Blair	13,091
6	13	A	Wolverhampton W	W 1-0	1-0	Bodak	18,115
7	20	A	Ipswich T	L 0-2	0-0		20,507
8	27	H	Everton	L 0-5	0-3		14,810
9	Oct 4	H	Brighton & HA	D 3-3	2-0	Dyson, Thompson, Hutchison	11,462
10	8	A	WBA	L 0-1	0-0		16,377
11	11	A	Leicester C	W 3-1	1-1	Dyson, Gooding, English	17,104
12	18	H	Norwich C	L 0-1	0-1		12,235
13	21	H	Sunderland	W 2-1	1-0	Hunt, Thompson	13,115
14	25	A	Tottenham H	L 1-4	0-1	Gooding	25,484
15	Nov 1	H	Leeds U	W 2-1	2-0	Hunt, Bodak	13,970
16	8	A	Manchester U	D 0-0	0-0		42,794
17	11	A	Liverpool	L 1-2	0-1	Thomas	26,744
18	15	H	Birmingham C	W 2-1	1-1	Blair, Hunt	18,758
19	22	A	Manchester C	L 0-3	0-2		30,047
20	29	H	Nottingham F	D 1-1	0-1	Daly (pen)	15,171
21	Dec 6	A	Southampton	L 0-1	0-1		18,847
22	13	H	WBA	W 3-0	1-0	Blair, Daly (pen), Hunt	16,027
23	20	A	Norwich C	L 0-2	0-2		12,630
24	26	H	Middlesbrough	W 1-0	1-0	Daly	16,066
25	27	A	Stoke C	D 2-2	1-0	Hateley, Thompson	17,765
26	Jan 10	H	Manchester C	D 1-1	0-0	Hunt	18,248
27	17	H	Aston Villa	L 1-2	0-0	Hateley	27,020
28	31	A	Arsenal	D 2-2	1-1	Bodak, Daly	24,876
29	Feb 7	H	Wolverhampton W	D 2-2	2-0	Hunt, Hateley	18,243
30	17	A	Crystal Palace	W 3-0	3-0	English 2, Bannister	12,868
31	21	A	Everton	L 0-3	0-1		26,731
32	28	H	Ipswich T	L 0-4	0-1		17,557
33	Mar 7	A	Brighton & HA	L 1-4	1-2	Bannister	14,063
34	14	H	Leicester C	W 4-1	2-1	English 3, Thompson	21,430
35	21	A	Sunderland	L 0-3	0-1		20,622
36	28	H	Tottenham H	L 0-1	0-1		18,666
37	Apr 4	A	Leeds U	L 0-3	0-1		15,882
38	11	H	Manchester U	L 0-2	0-2		20,175
39	18	H	Stoke C	D 2-2	2-0	Daly, Thompson	12,766
40	21	A	Middlesbrough	W 1-0	0-0	Daly	11,371
41	25	H	Southampton	W 1-0	0-0	Thompson	18,213
42	May 2	A	Nottingham F	D 1-1	1-1	Thompson	21,511

Final League Position: 16

Goalscorers

League (48): Daly 8 (2 pens), Thompson 8, English 7, Hunt 6, Blair 4, Bodak 3, Hateley 3, Bannister 2, Dyson 2, Gooding 2, Gillespie 1, Hutchison 1, Thomas 1.
League Cup (16): Thompson 6, English 2, Hateley 2, Hunt 2, Blair, Bodak, Daly, Hutchison.
F.A. Cup (6): Daly 2 (1 pen), Blair, English, Thomas, Thompson.

League Cup	Second Round	Manchester U (a)	1-0
		(h)	1-0
	Third Round	Brighton (a)	2-1
	Fourth Round	Cambridge U (h)	1-1
		(a)	1-0
	Fifth Round	Watford (h)	2-2
		(a)	5-0
	Semi-final	West Ham U (h)	3-2
		(a)	0-2
FA Cup	Third Round	Leeds U (a)	1-1
		(h)	1-0
	Fourth Round	Birmingham C (h)	3-2
	Fifth Round	Tottenham H (a)	1-3

Blyth	Coop	McDonald	Blair	Dyson	Gillespie	Van Gool	English	Thompson	Gooding	Hunt	Roberts	Jones	Daly	Thomas	Haywood	Hateley	Bodak	Jacobs	Sealey	Hutchison	Bannister	Ferguson	Whitton	*Match No.*
1	2	3	4	5	6	7*	8	9	10	11	12													1
1	2		4	5	6	7*	8	9		11	3	12	10											2
1	2		4	5	6	7	10	9		11	3		8											3
1	2		4	5	6*		10			11	3		8	12	7	9								4
1	2		4	5			10	9*		11	3	6	8			12	7							5
1	2		4	5			10			11	3		8			9	7	6						6
	2		4	5			12			11	3		8			9	7*	6	1	10				7
1	2		4	5			10			11	3		8			9	12	6		7*				8
	2		4	5				10		11	3		8			9		6	1	7				9
	2		4*	5	6		10	9		11	3		8					12	1	7				10
	2			5	6	7	10	9	4	11	3		8						1					11
	2			5	6	7	10	9	4*	11	3		8						1		12			12
	2			5	6	10*		9	4	11	3		8				7	12	1					13
	2		8	5	6		12	9	4	11	3						7		1		10*			14
	2		8	5	6	10			4*	11	3			12		9	7		1					15
	2		4	5	6	8*	12			11	3			10		9	7		1					16
	2		4	5	6	8*	12			11	3			10		9	7		1					17
	2		8	5	6			10		11	3			4		9	7		1					18
			4	5	6*			8		11	3		12	10		9	7	2	1					19
			4	5	6		10*	12		11	3		8	2			7		1			9		20
			4	5	6			9		11	3		8	2		10	7		1					21
			4	5	6			9		11	3		8	2		10	7		1					22
			4	5	6			9	8*	11	3	12		2		10	7		1					23
			4	5	6			9		11	3		8	2		10	7		1					24
			4	5	6			9		11	3		8	2		10			1		7			25
	2		4	5	6			9		11*	3		8	7			12		1			10		26
	2		4	5	6			9		11	3		8	7		12			1			10*		27
			4	5	6			9		11	3		8	2		10	7*	12	1					28
			4	5	6			9		11	3		8	2		10	7		1					29
			4		6		10	9		11	3		8	2				5	1		7			30
				5	6*		10	9		11	3	12	8	2				4	1		7			31
				5	6		10	9		11	3		8	2			7	4	1					32
			4	5	6		10	9			3		8	2			7		1		11			33
			4	5	6		10	9			3		8	2			7		1		11			34
			4	5	6		10	9		11	3		8	2					1		7			35
	7		4*	5	6		10	9		11	3		8	2					1				12	36
	2			5	6		10	9		11	3		8	4			7*		1		12			37
	2			5	6		10	9		11	3		8	4					1		7			38
	2		4	5	6		10	9		11	3		8						1		7			39
	2		4	5	6		10	9	7	11	3		8						1					40
	2		4	5	6		10	9	7	11	3		8						1					41
	2		4	5	6		10	9	7	11	3		8						1					42
7	27	1	35	41	37	9	24	34	10	40	41	1	34	23	1	17	21	8	35	4	9	3	—	
							+ 4s	+ 1s			+ 1s	+ 3s	+ 1s	+ 2s		+ 2s	+ 2s	+ 3s			+ 2s		+ 1s	

COVENTRY CITY

	Ht	*Wt*	*Birthplace*	*Clubs*	*League App.*	*League Gls*
Goalkeepers						
Jim Blyth	6 1¼	13 3	Perth	Preston NE	1	—
(Scotland)				Coventry C	124	—
				Hereford U (on loan)	7	—
Les Sealey	6 1	11 6½	Bethnal Green	Coventry C	104	—
Steve Murcott	6 0	12 0	Birmingham	Coventry C	1	—
Defenders						
Mick Coop	5 11	11 5½	Leamington	Coventry C	424	18
				York C (on loan)	4	—
Brian Roberts	5 8¼	11 3½	Manchester	Coventry	113	—
				Hereford U (on loan)	5	—
Jim Holton*	6 1¼	13 7	Lesmahagow	WBA	—	—
(Scotland)				Shrewsbury T	67	4
				Manchester U	63	5
				Sunderland	15	—
				Coventry C	91	—
Paul Dyson	6 2	13 7	Birmingham	Coventry C	61	4
Kevin Cooper	6 0	12 7	London	Coventry C	—	—
(Contract cancelled Jan 1981)						
Steve Jacobs	5 8	11 0	London	Coventry C	12	—
David Jones	5 10	12 7	Liverpool	Everton	86	1
(Contract cancelled March 1981)				Coventry C	11	—
Gary Gillespie	6 2	12 1	Scotland	Falkirk	22	—
				Coventry C	90	2
David Barnes	5 10	10 8	London	Coventry C	3	—
Peter Hormantschuk	5 10	10 8	Coventry	Coventry C	—	—
Danny Thomas	5 7	11 0	Worksop	Coventry C	28	1
Midfield						
Andy Blair	5 8½	10 10	Bedworth	Coventry C	93	6
Ray Gooding	5 8	11 4½	Hartlepool	Coventry C	48	5
Nick Phillips	5 10	11 2	London	Coventry C	5	—
(Contract cancelled Feb 1981)						
Steve Whitton	6 0	12 7	London	Coventry C	8	—
Gerry Daly	5 10	10 6	Dublin	Bohemians	(not known)	
(Eire)				Manchester U	111	23
				Derby Co	112	31
				Coventry C	35	8
Gary Howlett	5 8	10 4	Dublin	Home Farm	(not known)	
				Coventry C	—	—
Martin Singleton	5 9	10 0	Banbury	Coventry C	—	—
Forwards						
Mick Ferguson	6 1¾	12 8½	Newcastle	Coventry C	127	51
Gary Barnett	5 5	9 4	Stratford	Coventry C	—	—
Garry Thompson	6 0	12 9	Birmingham	Coventry C	78	24
Gary Bannister	5 7½	10 1	Warrington	Coventry C	22	3
Steve Hunt	5 7	10 11	Birmingham	Aston V	7	1
				New York C	—	—
				Coventry C	99	12
Mark Hateley	6 1	11 7	Liverpool	Coventry C	24	3
Clive Haywood	5 9	11 7	Kent	Coventry C	1	—
(Contract cancelled April 1981)						
Tom English	5 9	11 6	Cirencester	Coventry C	58	17
Roger van Gool	5 9	11 10	Belgium	FC Bruges	(not known)	
(Belgium)				Cologne	(not known)	
				Coventry C	17	—
Gordon Buchanan			Glasgow	Coventry C	—	—
(Contract cancelled Oct 1980)						
Peter Bodak	5 8	9 10	Birmingham	Coventry C	23	3

CREWE ALEXANDRA Division 4

President: D. Plastow.

Chairman: N. Rowlinson.

Directors: J. McHugh, K. Potts, E. Tagg, D. Rowlinson, L. Williams, N. Hassall, R. Clayton, J. McMillan, J. Bowler, R. Wadsley.

Manager:

Secretary: Mrs Gill Palin.

Year Formed: 1877. *Turned Professional:* 1893.

Limited Company: 1892.

Football League Record:
1892 Original Member of Division 2; 1896 Failed re-election; 1921 Re-entered Division 3(N); 1958–63 Division 4; 1963–64 Division 3; 1964–68 Division 4; 1968–69 Division 3; 1969– Division 4.

Honours: *Football League:* Division 2 best season: 10th, 1892–93. *FA Cup* best season: semi-final 1888. *Football League Cup* best season: 3rd rd, 1974–75, 1975–76, 1978–79.

Record Victory: 8-0 v Rotherham U, Division 3(N), 1 Oct, 1932.

Record Defeat: 2-13 v Tottenham H, FA Cup 4th rd replay, 3 Feb, 1960.

Most League Points: 59, Division 4, 1962–63.

Most League Goals: 95, Division 3(N), 1931–32.

Highest League Scorer in Season: Terry Harkin, 34, Division 4, 1964–65.

Most League Goals in Total Aggregate: Bert Swindells, 126, 1928–37.

Most Capped Player: Bill Lewis, 12 (30), Wales.

Most League Appearances: Tommy Lowry, 436, 1966–78.

Record Transfer Fee Received: £40,000 from Port Vale for Paul Bowles, Sept 1979.

Record Transfer Fee Paid: £10,000 to Derby Co for Colin Chesters, Sept 1979, and to Sheffield U for Mike Guy, Sept 1979.

Previous Managers since the War: George Lillycrop, Frank Hill, Arthur Turner, Harry Catterick, Ralph Ward, Maurice Lindley, Harry Ware, Jimmy McGuinan, Ernie Tagg, Dennis Viollet, Jimmy Melia, Ernie Tagg, Harry Gregg, Warwick Rimmer, Tony Waddington.

Address of Supporters Club: Registered Office, Crewe Alexandra Supporters' Association, 131 Edleston Road, Crewe, Cheshire.

Address of the Club Shop or Boutique: Gresty Road, Crewe.

Football Ground, Gresty Rd, Crewe. Telephone Crewe 213014. *Telegraphic address:* 'Alex Football Crewe'. *Ground capacity:* 17,000. *Record attendance:* 20,000 v Tottenham H, FA Cup 4th rd, 30 Jan, 1960. *Record receipts:* £5,388 v Wigan Ath, League Cup 1st rd, 13 Aug, 1980. *Pitch measurements:* 112yd×74yd.

How to get there: Local bus services from outlying districts. The ground is situated just five minutes' walk from Crewe railway station.

Match tickets: Advance booking for important cup ties only.

Car parking: Parking at the ground for 200 cars.

Entertainments/catering facilities: The Alexandra Club adjoining the ground is owned by the club. Refreshment points inside the ground.

Club shop: Situated at the ground; sells all types of souvenirs.

Handbooks/programmes: Handbooks on sale at matches.

Extra information: In 1956–57 the club set an unenviable League record of playing 30 consecutive games without a win.

Club Colours: Red shirts, white shorts, red and white stockings.

Change Colours: Sky blue shirts and stockings, black shorts.

Club Nickname: The Railwaymen.

CREWE ALEXANDRA 1980–81 LEAGUE RECORD

Match No.	Date	Venue	Opponents	Result	H/T Score	Goalscorers	Attendance
1	Aug 16	H	Torquay U	L 0-1	0-0		1962
2	18	A	Tranmere R	W 1-0	1-0	Palios	2246
3	23	A	Aldershot	L 0-2	0-2		2640
4	30	H	Lincoln C	L 0-3	0-1		2121
5	Sept 6	A	Scunthorpe U	D 1-1	1-0	Davies	1516
6	13	H	Wimbledon	L 0-3	0-2		1881
7	16	A	Bury	W 3-1	3-0	Davies, Conroy 2	2810
8	20	H	Halifax T	W 2-1	1-1	McMahon, Conroy	2102
9	26	A	Stockport Co	W 3-1	3-1	Coyne, Palios, Sunley (og)	3536
10	Oct 1	H	Bury	D 2-2	1-1	Coyne, Palios	3436
11	4	A	Bradford C	D 2-2	0-2	Coyne, Scott	3111
12	7	H	Hereford U	W 5-0	1-0	Coyne 4, Hunter	3033
13	11	H	Doncaster R	D 0-0	0-0		4033
14	17	A	Northampton T	L 1-4	1-1	Palios	2179
15	21	A	AFC Bournemouth	D 0-0	0-0		2632
16	25	H	Rochdale	W 1-0	0-0	Guy	3391
17	29	H	Southend U	D 1-1	1-1	Bowers	4217
18	Nov 1	A	Hartlepool U	L 2-6	1-5	Coyne 2	3089
19	5	A	Hereford U	D 0-0	0-0		1476
20	8	H	York C	D 1-1	1-1	Hunter	2798
21	12	H	Tranmere R	W 3-0	0-0	Coyne 2, Scott	3173
22	15	A	Torquay U	L 0-1	0-0		1858
23	29	H	Mansfield T	L 1-2	0-2	Hunter	2482
24	Dec 5	A	Port Vale	D 2-2	0-0	Davies, Hunter	4154
25	13	H	Wigan Ath	L 1-2	1-0	Prophett	2829
26	20	H	Darlington	D 1-1	0-1	Greenhoff	3282
27	26	A	Wigan Ath	D 0-0	0-0		5026
28	27	H	Peterborough U	W 1-0	1-0	Coyne	4132
29	Jan 3	A	Rochdale	L 0-2	0-1		2540
30	10	H	AFC Bournemouth	L 0-2	0-2		3087
31	17	A	Mansfield T	L 1-4	0-3	Greenhoff	3202
32	24	A	Lincoln C	L 1-2	1-1	Greenhoff	4925
33	31	H	Aldershot	D 0-0	0-0		2455
34	Feb 7	A	Wimbledon	L 0-2	0-2		2782
35	14	H	Scunthorpe U	W 1-0	1-0	Greenhoff	2231
36	21	H	Stockport Co	W 2-0	1-0	Palios, Nelson	2598
37	Mar 7	H	Bradford C	W 1-0	0-0	Palios	2487
38	13	A	Doncaster R	D 1-1	0-1	Davies	7167
39	21	H	Northampton T	W 3-1	1-0	Chesters, Coyne, Davies	2120
40	24	A	Halifax T	L 0-1	0-1		2266
41	27	A	Southend U	L 0-3	0-1		5878
42	Apr 3	H	Hartlepool U	W 2-0	0-0	Palios, Conroy	2419
43	11	A	York C	L 0-2	0-1		1602
44	18	A	Peterborough U	L 1-2	0-1	Bowers	3743
45	25	A	Darlington	L 1-2	0-0	Nelson	1304
46	May 1	H	Port Vale	D 0-0	0-0		4634

Final League Position: 18

Goalscorers

League (48): Coyne 13, Palios 7, Davies 5, Conroy 4, Greenhoff 4, Hunter 4, Bowers 2, Nelson 2, Scott 2, Chesters 1, Guy 1, McMahon 1, Prophett 1, own goal 1.
League Cup (3): Conroy 2, Hunter.
F.A. Cup (0).

League Cup	First Round	Wigan Ath (a)	1-2
		(h)	2-2
FA Cup	First Round	Mossley (a)	0-1

Mulhearn	Wilkinson	Lewis	Hunter	Scott	Prophett	McMahon	Guy	Mountford	Palios	Bowers	Davies	Conroy	Coyne	Nelson	Hanlon	Chesters	Glendon	Greenhoff	*Match No.*
1	2	3	4	5	6	7	8	9*	10	11	12								1
1	2	3	4	5	6	7	8*		10	11	12	9							2
1	2	3	4*	5	6	7	8		10	11	12	9							3
1	2	3	4	5	6	7	8		10*	11	12	9							4
1		3	4	5	6	2	8		10	11	7	9							5
1	12	3	4	5	6	2	8		10	11	7*	9							6
1		3	4	5	6	2			10	11	7	9	8						7
1	12	3	4	5	6	2			10	11*	7	9	8						8
1		3	4	5	6	2		9	10	11			8	7					9
1		3	4	5	6	2			10	11		9	8	7					10
1		3	4	5	6	2	12		10	11		9	8	7*					11
1		3	4	5	6	2	7		10	11		9	8						12
1		3	4	5	6	2	7		10	11		9*	8	12					13
1	3	5	4		6	2		9*	10	11	7		8	12					14
1		3	4	5	6	2	7		10	11	9		8						15
1		3	4	5	6	2	7		10	11*	12	9	8						16
1		3	4	5	6	2	7		10	11		9	8						17
1		3	4	5	6	2*	7		10	11	9		8	12					18
1		2	4	5	6		7		10	3	12	9*	8	11					19
1		2	4	5	6		7		10	3	9		8	11					20
1		2	4	5	6				10	3	7	9	8	11					21
1	12	2	4	5	6		9		10*	3	7		8	11					22
1	2	3	4	5	6		10*			11		9		8	7	12			23
1	12	2	4	5	6					3	7	9		11	8*		10		24
1	12	2	4	5	6					3	7	9	8	11			10*		25
1		2	4	5	6	7				3	12	9	10	11*				8	26
1		3	4	5	6	2				11	7	9	8					10	27
1		3	4	5	6	2				11	7	9	8					10	28
1		3	4	5	6	2				11	7	9	8*	12				10	29
1		3	4	5	6	2			9	11*	7		8				12	10	30
1		2	4	5	6	7			9	3		8		12			11*	10	31
1		3	4	5	6	2			9	12		7	8	11				10*	32
1		3	4	5	6	2			9	11	12	7*		8				10	33
1		3	4	5	6	2	8*		9	7	12			11				10	34
1		2*	4	5	6	7			9	3	8			11	12			10	35
1		3	4	5	6	2			9	11	8			7				10	36
1		3	4	5	6	2			10	11	8			7		9			37
1		3	4	5	6	2			10	11	8		12	7*		9			38
1		3*	4	5	6	2			10	11	8		12	7		9			39
1		3	4	5	6	2			10	11*	8		12	7		9			40
1		3	4	5	6	2			10	11	8		12	7		9*			41
1		3*	4	5	6	2			10	11	8	7	12			9			42
1		3	4	5	6	2			10		8	7	12	11*		9			43
1		3	4	5	6	2			10	11	8	9*	12			7			44
1		3	4	5	6	2			10	11*	8	9	12	7					45
1		3	4	5	6	2			10	11	8	9*	12	7					46
46	6	46	46	45	46	39	17	3	39	44	28	30	23	24	2	8	3	11	
	+ 5s						+ 1s			+ 1s	+ 9s		+ 9s	+ 5s	+ 1s	+ 1s	+ 1s		

CREWE ALEXANDRA

	Ht	*Wt*	*Birthplace*	*Clubs*	*League App.*	*League Gls*
Goalkeepers						
Ken Mulhearn	6 0	13 11	Liverpool	Everton	—	—
				Stockport Co	100	—
				Manchester C	50	—
				Shrewsbury T	370	—
				Crewe Alex	46	—
Defenders						
Kevin Lewis	5 9	11 13	Hull	Manchester U	—	—
				Stoke C	15	—
				Crewe Alex	76	—
Bob Scott*	6 2½	13 4	Liverpool	Wrexham	19	—
				Reading (on loan)	5	—
				Hartlepool U	37	—
				Rochdale	71	3
				Crewe Alex	88	4
Neil Wilkinson	5 7	10 4	Blackburn	Blackburn R	30	—
(Contract cancelled March 1981)				Port Vale	7	—
				Crewe Alex	75	—
Danny Bowers	5 8¾	10 2	Stoke	Stoke C	39	2
				Shrewsbury T (on loan)	6	—
				Crewe Alex	90	2
John McMahon	5 9	11 2	Manchester	Preston NE	257	7
				Southend U (on loan)	3	—
				Chesterfield (on loan)	1	—
				Crewe Alex	67	2
Colin Prophett	5 11	12 2	Crewe	Sheffield W	117	7
				Norwich C	35	—
				Swindon T	160	10
				Chesterfield	37	1
				Crewe Alex	79	1
Duncan Heath	5 9	10 13	Stoke	Aston Villa	—	—
				Crewe Alex	—	—
Midfield						
Geoff Hunter	5 9	10 5	Hull	Manchester U	—	—
				Crewe Alex	87	8
Paul Mayman*	5 8	10 0	Crewe	Crewe Alex	43	3
David Davies*	6 0	13 5	Rhondda Valley	Swansea C	1	—
				Crewe Alex	209	26
Kevin Glendon*	5 9	10 2	Manchester	Manchester C	—	—
				Crewe Alex	4	—
Steve Hanlon (Apprentice)	5 10	10 6	Chester	Crewe Alex	3	—
Forwards						
Mark Palios	5 8	10 13	Birkenhead	Tranmere R	190	25
				Crewe Alex	60	11
Peter Coyne*	5 8¾	10 7	Hartlepool	Manchester U	2	1
				Crewe Alex	134	47
Dennis Nelson*	5 8	10 4	Edinburgh	Dunfermline Ath	48	17
				Crewe Alex	71	18
				Reading	59	6
				Crewe Alex	107	15
Terry Conroy* (Eire)	5 9¾	11 11	Dublin	Stoke C	271	49
				Crewe Alex	37	5
Colin Chesters*	5 11	11 0	Crewe	Derby Co	9	1
				Crewe Alex	25	4
Mike Guy*	5 9	11 2	Limavady	Coleraine	(not known)	
				Sheffield U	18	2
				Crewe Alex	55	7
Jimmy Greenhoff	5 9	12 0	Barnsley	Leeds U	96	19
(Contract cancelled March 1981)				Birmingham C	31	14
				Stoke C	274	76
				Manchester U	97	26
				Crewe Alex	11	4

CRYSTAL PALACE Division 2

Chairman: R. G. Noades.

Deputy Chairman: B. Bishop. *Vice-Chairman:* J. C. C. M. Rose.

Directors: B. Coleman, R. J. Easterby, A. S. C. DeSouza, R. O. Faulkner, P. Lazenby, C. D. Richards, R. R. Varey, P. Zetter.

Team Manager: Dario Gradi.

Secretary: Alan Leather.

Year Formed: 1905. *Limited Company:* 1905.

Turned Professional: 1905.

Previous Grounds: 1905, Crystal Palace; 1915, Herne Hill; 1919, The Nest; 1924, Selhurst Park.

Football League Record:
1920 Original Members of Division 3; 1921–25 Division 2; 1925–58 Division 3(S); 1958–61 Division 4; 1961–64 Division 3; 1964–69 Division 2; 1969–73 Division 1; 1973–74 Division 2; 1974–77 Division 3; 1977–79 Division 2; 1979–81 Division 1; 1981– Division 2.

Honours: *Football League:* Division 1 best season: 13th, 1979–80; Division 2 – Champions 1978–79; Runners-up 1968–69; Division 3 – Runners-up 1963–64; Division 3(S) – Champions 1920–21; Runners-up 1928–29, 1930–31, 1938–39; Division 4 – Runners-up 1960–61. *FA Cup* best season: semi-final 1975–76. *Football League Cup* best season: 5th rd, 1968–69, 1970–71.

Record Victory: 9-0 v Barrow, Division 4, 10 Oct 1959.

Record Defeat: 4-11 v Manchester C, FA Cup 5th rd, 20 Feb, 1926.

Most League Points: 64, Division 4, 1960–61.

Most League Goals: 110, Division 4, 1960–61.

Highest League Scorer in Season: Peter Simpson, 46, Division 3(S), 1930–31.

Most League Goals in Total Aggregate: Peter Simpson, 154, 1930–36.

Most Capped Player: Ian Evans, 13, Wales.

Most League Appearances: Terry Long, 432, 1956–69.

Record Transfer Fee Received: £800,000 (nett) from Arsenal for Kenny Sansom, Aug 1980.

Record Transfer Fee Paid: £800,000 (nett) to Arsenal for Clive Allen, Aug 1980.

Previous Managers since the War: George Irwin, Jack Butler, Ronnie Rooke, Fred Dawes, Charlie Slade, Laurie Scott, Cyril Spiers, George Smith, Arthur Rowe, Dick Graham, Bert Head, Malcolm Allison, Terry Venables, Ernie Walley, Malcolm Allison.

Address of Supporters Club: Social Hall, Selhurst Park, SE25, 6PU.

Address of Club Shop: Palace Shop; Programme Shop in Old Stand.

Selhurst Park, London, SE25 6PU. Telephone 01-653 4462. *Ground capacity:* 38,500 (18,000 covered). *Record attendance:* 51,482 v Burnley, Division 2, 11 May, 1979. *Record receipts:* £74,868 v Tottenham H, Division 1, 6 Oct, 1979. *Pitch measurements:* 112yd×74yd.

How to get there: Ground served by three stations – Selhurst (5 minutes walk), Norwood Junction (7 minutes) and Thornton Heath (10 minutes). Buses 68, 75, 154, 157, 12 (to Norwood Junction).

Information service: 01-653 2223.

Match tickets: Seats bookable in advance, postal applications accepted one month in advance and personal application two weeks in advance. Postal applications must be accompanied by SAE and the correct remittance. Cheques must be made payable to Crystal Palace FC and name and address must be written on the back. Separate application must be made for each match.

Car parking: Large car park at the ground.

Entertainments/catering facilities: A social hall and catering facilities within the ground.

Club shop: Sells all types of souvenirs.

Handbooks/programmes: Programmes available on subscription.

Extra information: Vic Rouse, the Crystal Palace goalkeeper, was the first Fourth Division player to be capped when he played for Wales v Ireland in 1959.

Club Colours: White shirts with 4-inch diagonal band red over blue, white shorts, white stockings.

Change Colours: Light blue shirts with 4-inch diagonal red band from left shoulder; light blue shorts; light blue stockings.

Assistant Team Manager: Mike Kelly.

Club Captain: Jim Cannon.

Club Nickname: The Eagles.

CRYSTAL PALACE 1980–81 LEAGUE RECORD

Match No.	Date	Venue	Opponents	Result	H/T Score	Goalscorers	Attendance
1	Aug 16	A	Liverpool	L 0-3	0-2		42,777
2	19	H	Tottenham H	L 3-4	1-3	Hilaire, Smillie, Cannon	27,102
3	23	H	Middlesbrough	W 5-2	1-2	Allen 3 (1 pen), Sealy, Francis	16,713
4	30	A	Wolverhampton W	L 0-2	0-1		20,601
5	Sept 6	A	Coventry C	L 1-3	0-0	Allen	13,091
6	13	H	Ipswich T	L 1-2	0-1	Lovell	24,282
7	20	A	Everton	L 0-5	0-0		26,950
8	27	H	Aston Villa	L 0-1	0-0		18,398
9	Oct 4	H	WBA	L 0-1	0-0		16,081
10	11	A	Sunderland	L 0-1	0-1		25,444
11	18	H	Leicester C	W 2-1	1-0	Hilaire, Allen (pen)	16,387
12	21	H	Southampton	W 3-2	1-1	Flanagan 3	20,630
13	25	A	Leeds U	L 0-1	0-1		19,208
14	29	A	Norwich C	D 1-1	1-1	Francis	15,782
15	Nov 1	H	Manchester U	W 1-0	1-0	Nicholas	31,181
16	8	A	Birmingham C	L 0-1	0-1		16,910
17	12	A	Tottenham H	L 2-4	1-1	Hilaire, Walsh	25,777
18	15	H	Liverpool	D 2-2	0-1	Francis (pen), Walsh	31,154
19	22	A	Stoke C	L 0-1	0-0		13,422
20	29	H	Manchester C	L 2-3	0-2	Walsh, Sealy	16,575
21	Dec 6	A	Nottingham F	L 0-3	0-0		20,223
22	13	H	Norwich C	W 4-1	3-1	Allen 2, Murphy, Francis	15,257
23	20	A	Southampton	L 2-4	0-2	Sealy, Allen	19,332
24	26	H	Arsenal	D 2-2	1-1	Sealy 2	29,850
25	27	A	Brighton & HA	L 2-3	1-1	Murphy, Gregory (og)	27,367
26	Jan 10	H	Stoke C	D 1-1	1-0	Boyle	14,154
27	17	H	Wolverhampton W	D 0-0	0-0		15,080
28	31	A	Middlesbrough	L 0-2	0-0		16,099
29	Feb 7	A	Ipswich T	L 2-3	1-0	Walsh, Mariner (og)	25,036
30	17	H	Coventry C	L 0-3	0-3		12,868
31	21	A	Aston Villa	L 1-2	0-1	Hinshelwood	27,203
32	28	H	Everton	L 2-3	1-1	Allen (pen), Hilaire	14,594
33	Mar 7	A	WBA	L 0-1	0-0		15,599
34	14	H	Sunderland	L 0-1	0-1		16,748
35	21	A	Leicester C	D 1-1	0-0	Price	15,176
36	28	H	Leeds U	L 0-1	0-1		15,053
37	Apr 4	A	Manchester U	L 0-1	0-0		37,974
38	11	H	Birmingham C	W 3-1	0-1	Langley 2, Lovell	9820
39	18	H	Brighton & HA	L 0-3	0-2		18,792
40	20	A	Arsenal	L 2-3	1-1	Price, Langley	24,346
41	25	H	Nottingham F	L 1-3	0-2	Smillie	12,138
42	May 2	A	Manchester C	D 1-1	0-1	Walsh	31,017

Final League Position: 22

Goalscorers

League (47): Allen 9 (3 pens), Sealy 5, Walsh 5, Francis 4 (1 pen), Hilaire 4, Flanagan 3, Langley 3, Lovell 2, Murphy 2, Price 2, Smillie 2, Boyle 1, Cannon 1, Hinshelwood 1, Nicholas 1, own goals 2.
League Cup (6): Allen 2 (1 pen), Murphy 2, Flanagan, Francis.
F.A. Cup (0).

League Cup	Second Round	Bolton W (a)	3-0
		(h)	2-1
	Third Round	Tottenham H (a)	0-0
		(h)	1-3
FA Cup	Third Round	Manchester C (a)	0-4

Barron	Hinshelwood	Fenwick	Nicholas	Cannon	Gilbert	Smillie	Francis	Allen	Flanagan	Hilaire	Murphy	Sealy	Leahy	Lovell	Brooks	Walsh	Boyle	Fry	Gennoe	Carter	Goodchild	Dare	Banfield	Price	Bason	Langley	Paul	*Match No.*
1	2*	3	4	5	6	7	8	9	10	11	12																	1
1		3	2	5	6	7*	8	9	10	11	4	12																2
1		3	2	5	6	7	8	9	10		4	12	11*															3
1		3		5	6		8	9	10	11	4	12	7*	2														4
1	2	3		5	6	7	8	9	10	11	4																	5
1	2	3		5	6	7	8	9	10	11*		12		4														6
1	2	3		5	6*	7	8	9	10		11			4	12													7
1	2	3	4	5	6	7		9	10		11	8																8
1	2	3	4	5	6	7*	8	9	10	11						12												9
1	2	3	4	5	6		8	9	7	11						10												10
1	2	3	4	5	6	12	8	9	7	11*						10												11
1	2	3	4	5	6		8	9	7	11						10												12
1	2	3	4	5	6		8*	9	7	11				12		10												13
1	2	3	4	5	6	11*	8		10			12		7		9												14
1	2	3	4	5	6	11	8		10					7		9												15
1	2	3	4	5	6	11			10*		8			7		9	12											16
1	2	3	4	5	6		8		10	11				7		9												17
1	2	3	4	5	6		8		10*	11		12		7		9												18
1		3	4	5	6		8		10	11				7		9	2											19
1	4	3		2	6		8*		10	11		12		7		9	5											20
1	2	3	4	5	6		8	10		11		7				9												21
1	2		4	5	6		8	9		11	7*	10				12	3											22
	2		4	5	6		8	9		11	7	10					3	1										23
	2		4	5	6	12	8	9		11*	7	10					3	1										24
	2		4	5		11	8	9			7	10		6*	12		3	1										25
	2		4	5	6	12	8			11*		9		7			3		1	10								26
	2		4	5	6	11	8	10			7	9					3		1									27
	2		4	5	6	11		10				9		7	8*		3		1		12							28
1	3		8		4	7		9			10			2	6	11	5											29
	2		4			8		9		10	7*				6	11	5	1				3	12					30
	2		4			7		9		11		10			8		5	1				3	6					31
1	2		4		6	7*		9		11		10		3	8		5			12								32
1	2		4		6					11		9		7	8	10	5						3					33
1	2			5*	7	6				11				3	8	9								4	12	10		34
1	2				6					11				3	8	9	5							4	7	10		35
1	3				6					11	12			2*	8	9	5							4	7	10		36
1	3				6					11				2	8	9	5							4	7	10		37
	3				6					11				2	8	9	5	1						4*	7	10	12	38
1	3			6	12					11				2	8	9*	5							4	7	10		
1	3			5	6			9*		11	12			2	8									4	7	10		40
1	3			5	6	11					4			2	8	9									7	10		41
1	3			5	6	7				11*	12				8	9								4	2	10		42
33	38	21	28	33	38	21	25	25	20	31	15	12	2	24	15	23	19	6	3	1	—	2	2	8	8	9	—	
					+ 1s	+ 3s					+ 4s	+ 7s		+ 1s	+ 2s	+ 2s	+ 1s			+ 1s	+ 1s		+ 1s		+ 1s		+ 1s	

CRYSTAL PALACE

	Ht	*Wt*	*Birthplace*	*Clubs*	*League App.*	*League Gls*
Goalkeepers						
David Fry	6 1	12 7	Bournemouth	Crystal Palace	13	—
Paul Barron	6 2	13 5	London	Plymouth Arg	44	—
				Arsenal	8	—
				Crystal Palace	33	—
Defenders						
Jim Cannon	6 0	13 0	Glasgow	Crystal Palace	294	18
Kevin Dare	5 9	11 13	Finchley	Crystal Palace	2	—
Billy Gilbert	5 11	12 0	Lewisham	Crystal Palace	138	2
Terry Boyle	5 10	12 4	Ammerford	Tottenham H	—	—
(Wales)				Crystal Palace	26	1
Chris Sparks*	5 10	10 8	Islington	Crystal Palace	—	—
				Reading (on loan)	3	—
Paul Hinshelwood	6 0	12 6	Bristol	Crystal Palace	214	14
Neil Banfield	5 11	12 0	London	Crystal Palace	3	—
David Boulter	5 8	11 3	London	Crystal Palace	—	—
Steve Lovell	5 9	11 3	Swansea	Crystal Palace	25	2
				Stockport Co (on loan)	12	—
Midfield						
Jerry Murphy	5 9	11 10	Stepney	Crystal Palace	106	10
(Eire)						
Tony Paul	5 9	11 0	Islington	Crystal Palace	1	—
(Contract cancelled April 1981)						
Shaun Brooks	5 7	11 0	London	Crystal Palace	18	—
David Price	5 11	12 0	Caterham	Arsenal	126	16
				Peterborough U (on loan)	6	1
				Crystal Palace	8	2
Brian Bason	5 9	11 0	Epsom	Chelsea	19	1
				Plymouth Arg	130	10
				Crystal Palace	9	—
Steve Leahy	5 7	10 9	Battersea	Crystal Palace	2	—
Forwards						
Neil Smillie	5 6	10 7	Barnsley	Crystal Palace	42	4
				Brentford (on loan)	3	—
Les Carter	5 9	11 2	Farnborough	Crystal Palace	2	—
Vince Hilaire	5 6	10 0	Forest Hill	Crystal Palace	137	17
Ian Walsh	5 10	11 5	St Davids, Pem.	Crystal Palace	104	21
(Wales)						
Mike Elwiss	6 0	12 6	Doncaster	Doncaster R	97	30
				Preston NE	192	60
				Crystal Palace	20	7
				Preston NE (on loan)	10	3
Gary Goodchild	6 0	12 3	Chelmsford	Arsenal	—	—
(Contract cancelled March 1981)				Hereford U	4	—
				Sheffield W (on loan)	—	—
				Reading	1	—
				Crystal Palace	2	—
Clive Allen	5 10	11 0	London	QPR	49	32
				Arsenal	—	—
				Crystal Palace	25	9
Tommy Langley	5 11	11 7	Elephant and Castle	Chelsea	142	40
				QPR	25	8
				Crystal Palace	9	3
Gary Grabban*			Croydon	Crystal Palace	—	—

DARLINGTON Division 4

Chairman: J. L. T. Moore.
Directors: D. Mason, A. Brown, J. B. Hadley, B. J. H. Richardson, E. W. A. McMahon, K. Warne, C. Parias.
Manager: Billy Elliott.
Secretary: David Thorne.
Year Formed: 1883. *Turned Professional:* 1908.
Limited Company: 1891.
Football League Record:
1921 Original Member Division 3(N); 1925–27 Division 2; 1927–58 Division 3(N); 1958–66 Division 4; 1966–67 Division 3; 1967– Division 4.
Honours: *Football League:* Division 2 best season: 15th, 1925–26; Division 3(N) – Champions 1924–25; Runners-up 1921–22; Division 4 – Runners-up 1965–66. *FA Cup* best season: 3rd rd, 1910–11, 5th rd, 1957–58. *Football League Cup* best season: 5th rd, 1967–68.
Record Victory: 9-2 v Lincoln C, Division 3(N), 7 Jan, 1928.
Record Defeat: 0-10 v Doncaster R, Division 4, 25 Jan, 1964.
Most League Points: 59, Division 4, 1965–66.
Most League Goals: 108, Division 3(N), 1929–30.
Highest League Scorer in Season: David Brown, 39, Division 3(N), 1924–25.
Most League Goals in Total Aggregate: David Brown, 74, 1923–26.
Most Capped Player: None.
Most League Appearances: Ron Greener, 442, 1955–68.
Record Transfer Fee Received: £15,555 from Lincoln C for Alan Harding, March 1973.
Record Transfer Fee Paid: £17,000 to Notts Co for Eric Probert, Oct 1978.
Previous Managers since the War: Bill Forrest, George Irwin, Bob Gurney, Dick Duckworth, Eddie Carr, Lol Morgan, Jimmy Greenhalgh, Ray Yeoman, Len Richley, Frank Brennan, Allan Jones, Ralph Brand, Dick Conner, Billy Horner, Peter Madden, Len Walker.
Address of Supporters Club: Same as Football Club.

Feethams Ground, Darlington. Telephone Darlington (0325) 65097/67712. *Ground capacity:* 20,000. *Record attendance:* 21,023 v Bolton W, League Cup 3rd rd, 14 Nov, 1960. *Record receipts:* £8,264.80 v Hartlepool U, Division 4, 26 Dec, 1980. *Pitch measurements:* 110yd×74yd.
How to get there: Darlington railway station, five minutes walk.
Match tickets: Postal and telephone bookings accepted in advance of the match.
Car parking: Ample parking in surrounding side-streets.
Entertainments/catering facilities: Three nearby cafés. Three snack bars in the ground.
Club shop: Shop inside the ground sells all types of souvenirs.
Handbooks/programmes: No handbook. Programmes available on subscription.
Extra information: The club will make every effort to cater for the disabled, the blind, or any person who has some difficulty seeking entrance because of illness.
Club Colours: White shirts with black collar and cuffs, black shorts, black stockings with white hoop round top.
Change Colours: All royal blue or all red.
First Team Trainer/Coach: George Herd.
Club Nickname: The Quakers.

DARLINGTON 1980–81 LEAGUE RECORD

Match No.	Date	Venue	Opponents	Result	H/T Score	Goalscorers	Attendance
1	Aug 16	H	Northampton T	W 1-0	1-0	Stalker	1763
2	19	A	Doncaster R	L 0-2	0-1		3157
3	23	H	Stockport Co	D 2-2	1-0	Hamilton, Walsh	1920
4	30	A	Bury	W 2-1	1-1	Charlton, Skipper	2268
5	Sept 6	A	Mansfield T	L 0-1	0-0		3001
6	13	H	Wigan Ath	W 3-1	1-1	Stalker 3	2321
7	16	H	Scunthorpe U	L 0-1	0-1		2663
8	20	A	Port Vale	L 2-4	1-3	Walsh 2	2158
9	27	H	Aldershot	L 1-2	1-2	Walsh	1933
10	30	A	Scunthorpe U	L 0-3	0-2		2106
11	Oct 4	A	Hereford U	W 1-0	1-0	Walsh	2934
12	7	H	Bradford C	W 2-1	1-0	McLean, Walsh	2158
13	11	H	AFC Bournemouth	L 1-2	1-1	Walsh	2363
14	18	A	Peterborough U	L 0-1	0-0		4217
15	21	A	York C	W 2-1	0-1	Stalker, Hamilton	2534
16	25	H	Southend U	L 0-2	0-1		2013
17	28	H	Rochdale	D 4-4	2-2	McLean 2 (2 pens), Speedie, Walsh	1579
18	Nov 1	A	Torquay U	W 2-0	1-0	Hamilton, Stalker	2122
19	4	A	Bradford C	L 0-3	0-1		2053
20	8	H	Tranmere R	W 2-0	1-0	Stalker, Walsh	1645
21	11	H	Doncaster R	W 5-0	0-0	Stalker, Walsh, Hawker, Charlton, Hamilton (pen)	2092
22	15	A	Northampton T	D 2-2	1-0	Walsh, Stalker	1656
23	Dec 6	A	Wimbledon	D 1-1	1-0	Hawker	1811
24	20	A	Crewe Alex	D 1-1	1-0	Stalker	3282
25	26	H	Hartlepool U	W 3-0	2-0	Stalker, Walsh, Hamilton	7152
26	27	A	Halifax T	W 2-1	2-0	Walsh, Skipper	1805
27	Jan 3	H	York C	D 0-0	0-0		3209
28	9	A	Southend U	L 0-1	0-0		5066
29	24	H	Bury	W 2-1	1-0	Stalker, Walsh	1914
30	30	A	Stockport Co	W 1-0	1-0	Walsh	2011
31	Feb 7	A	Wigan Ath	L 1-3	0-0	Hamilton	3626
32	15	H	Mansfield T	D 2-2	1-1	Hamilton (pen), Walsh	5932
33	21	A	Aldershot	L 1-2	0-1	Walsh	2046
34	Mar 8	H	Hereford U	W 2-1	1-1	Stalker 2	3491
35	10	H	Lincoln C	D 0-0	0-0		2436
36	14	A	AFC Bournemouth	D 3-3	3-2	Walsh, Wicks, Speedie	4995
37	17	H	Wimbledon	W 4-1	2-1	Speedie, Hamilton, Charlton, Walsh	2091
38	21	H	Peterborough U	W 2-0	1-0	Stalker, Walsh	2522
39	28	A	Rochdale	D 0-0	0-0		1843
40	Apr 5	H	Torquay U	W 1-0	0-0	Smith	3631
41	10	A	Tranmere R	L 1-3	0-1	Stalker	1225
42	17	A	Hartlepool U	L 0-2	0-0		5531
43	18	H	Halifax T	W 3-1	3-0	Stalker, Walsh 2	2015
44	25	H	Crewe Alex	W 2-1	0-0	Smith, Speedie	1304
45	May 2	A	Lincoln C	L 0-1	0-0		3888
46	5	H	Port Vale	D 1-1	0-0	McLean	1576

Final League Position: 8

Goalscorers

League (65): Walsh 22, Stalker 17, Hamilton 8 (2 pens), McLean 4 (2 pens), Speedie 4, Charlton 3, Hawker 2, Skipper 2, Smith 2, Wicks 1.
League Cup (1): Walsh.
F.A. Cup (0).

League Cup	First Round	Chesterfield (a)	0-1
		(h)	1-2
FA Cup	First Round	Bury (h)	0-2

Cuff	Kamara	McLean	Ball	Skipper	Speedie	Hawker	Charlton	Stalker	Hamilton	Walsh	Barry	Smith	Wilson	Siddall	Stell	Glendinning	Wicks	*Match No.*
1	2	3	4	5	6	7	8	9	10	11								1
	2	3	4	5	6	7	8	9	10	11	1							2
	2	3	4	5	6	7	8	9	10	11	1							3
	2	3	4	5	6	7	8	9*	10	11	1	12						4
	2	3	4	5	6	7*	8	9	10	11	1	12						5
	2	10	4	5	6	7	8	9		11	1		3					6
1	2	10	4	5	6	7	8	9		11			3					7
	2	9	4	5	6	7	8		10	11	1		3					8
	2	12	4*	5	6		8	9	10	11	1	7	3					9
	2	7		5	6		8	9	10	11	1	4	3					10
	2	7		5	6		8	9	10	11		4	3	1				11
	2	7		5	6		8	9	10	11		4	3	1				12
	2	7		5	6	12	8	9	10*	11		4	3	1				13
	2	7	8	5	6	10	12	9		11		4*	3	1				14
	2	7	8	5	6			9	10	11		4	3	1				15
	2	7	8*	5	6		12	9	10	11		4	3	1				16
	2	3		5	6	7	8	9	10	11		4		1				17
	2	3		5	6	7	8	9	10	11		4		1				18
1	2	3		5	6	7	8*	9	10	11		4	12					19
1	2	8*		5	6	7	12	9	10	11		4	3					20
1	2			5	6	7	8	9	10	11		4	3					21
1	2	8*		5	6	7		9	10	11		4	3		12			22
1	2	8	12	5	6	7		9*	10	11		4	3					23
1	2	8		5	6	7		9	10	11		4	3					24
1	2	8		5	6	7		9	10	11		4	3					25
1	2	8		5	6	7		9	10	11		4	3					26
1	2		12	5	6	7	8*	9	10	11		4	3					27
1	2	8	3	5	6	7		9	10	11		4						28
1	2		7	5			8	9	10	11		4			6	3		29
1	2		7	5			8	9	10	11		4			6	3		30
1	2		7	5	9			10	8	11		4			6	3		31
1	2	8	4	5	6			9	10	11					7	3*	12	32
1	2	8	3	5	6			9	10	11		4			7*		12	33
1	2	8	3*	5	6		7	9	10	11		4					12	34
1	2	3		5	6		7	9	10	11		4					8	35
1	2	3		5	6		7	9	10	11		4*			12		8	36
1	2	3		5	6		7	9*	10	11		4	12				8	37
1	2	3		5	6	7		9	10	11		4					8	38
1	2	3		5	6	7		9	10	11		4					8	39
1	2	3		5	6	7		9	10	11		4					8	40
1	2	3		5	6	7		9	10	11		4					8	41
1	2	3		5	6	7	8*	9	10	11		4	12					42
1		2		5	6	7		9	10	11		4	3		8			43
1	10	3		5	6	7		9		11		4	2		8			44
1	2	8		5	6	7		9	10	11		4	3					45
1	2	8		5	6	7		9	10	11		4	3					46
30	45	40	19	46	44	30	25	45	42	46	8	37	23	8	7	4	7	
		+ 1s	+ 2s			+ 1s	+ 3s					+ 2s	+ 3s		+ 2s		+ 3s	

DARLINGTON

	Ht	Wt	Birthplace	Clubs	League App.	League Gls
Goalkeepers						
Kevin Barry	5 10	11 7	Newcastle	Nottingham F	—	—
				Darlington	18	—
Pat Cuff	6 0	12 6	Middlesbrough	Middlesbrough	31	—
				Grimsby T (on loan)	2	—
				Millwall	42	—
				Darlington	30	—
Defenders						
Kevan Smith	6 3	11 9	Eaglescliffe	Darlington	74	3
Keith Coleman	5 9	11 5	Washington	Sunderland	49	2
(Contract cancelled Aug 1980)				West Ham U	101	—
				Racing Malines	(not known)	
				Darlington	25	—
Donald Ball	5 11	11 3	Barnard Castle	Darlington	56	2
Peter Skipper	5 11	12 6½	Hull	Hull C	23	2
				Scunthorpe U (on loan)	1	—
				Darlington	46	2
Alan Kamara	5 9	10 12	Sheffield	York C	10	—
				Darlington	45	—
Kevin Glendinning			Corbridge	Darlington	4	—
Harry Wilson	5 9½	10 12	Hetton-le-Hole	Burnley	10	—
				Brighton	130	4
				Preston NE	42	—
				Darlington	26	—
David McLean	5 8	11 0	Newcastle	Newcastle U	9	—
				Carlisle U	15	—
				Darlington	77	8
Midfield						
David Hawker	5 7	9 12	Hull	Hull C	35	2
				Darlington	39	2
Harry Charlton	5 7¾	10 8	Newcastle	Middlesbrough	10	—
				Hartlepool U (on loan)	3	—
				Chesterfield	21	—
				Buxton	(not known)	
				Darlington	71	4
David Speedie	5 7	10 4	Glenrothes	Barnsley	23	—
				Darlington	44	4
Scott Duncan			Darlington	Scarborough	(not known)	
				Darlington	—	—
Barry Stell	5 8½	10 10	Felling	Sheffield W	—	—
(Non-contract)				Darlington	9	—
Roger Wicks	6 0	11 0	Warrington	Darlington	10	1
(Non-contract)						
Forwards						
Alan Walsh	6 0	11 0	Hartlepool	Middlesbrough	3	—
				Darlington	122	46
Ken Ellis	5 9½	11 6	Sunderland	Hartlepool U	34	4
(Contract cancelled Nov 1980)				Racing Jet	(not known)	
				Ostend	(not known)	
				Varna	(not known)	
				Scarborough	(not known)	
				Darlington	21	—
John Stalker	5 11	11 7	Musselburgh	Leicester C	—	—
				Darlington	75	29
Ian Hamilton	5 7½	10 7	S Shields	Darlington	65	11

Free Transfers: Scott Milford*, David Thompson*.

DERBY COUNTY Division 2

Chairman: R. J. Moore.

Vice-Chairman: W. Stevenson.

Directors: A. B. Atkins, R. J. Mulholland, R Stone, E. Strachan.

Manager: Colin Addison.

Assistant Manager: John Newman.

Secretary: Michael Dunford.

Year Formed: 1884. *Turned Professional:* 1884.

Limited Company: 1896.

Former Grounds: 1884–95, Racecourse Ground; 1895, Baseball Ground.

Football League Record:
1888 Founder Member of the Football League; 1907–12 Division 2; 1912–14 Division 1; 1914–15 Division 2; 1915–21 Division 1; 1921–26 Division 2; 1926–53 Division 1; 1953–55 Division 2; 1955–57 Division 3(N); 1957–69 Division 2; 1969–80 Division 1; 1980– Division 2.

Honours: *Football League:* Division 1 – Champions 1971–72, 1974–75; Runners-up 1895–96, 1929–30, 1935–36; Division 2 – Champions 1911-12, 1914–15, 1968–69; Runners-up 1925–26; Division 3(N) – Champions 1956–57; Runners-up 1955–56. *FA Cup:* Winners 1945–46; Runners-up 1897–98, 1898–99, 1902–03. *Football League Cup:* Semi-final 1967–68. **European Competitions:** *European Cup:* 1972–73, 1975–76; *UEFA Cup:* 1974–75, 1976–77.

Record Victory: 12-0 v Finn Harps, UEFA Cup 3rd rd, 1st leg, 15 Sept, 1976.

Record Defeat: 2-11 v Everton, FA Cup 1st rd, 1889–90.

Most League Points: 63, Division 2, 1968–69 and 63, Division 3(N), 1955–56, 1956–57.

Most League Goals: 111, Division 3(N), 1956–57.

Highest League Scorer in Season: Jack Bowers, 37, Division 1, 1930–31 and Ray Straw, 37, Division 3(N), 1956–57.

Most League Goals in Total Aggregate: Steve Bloomer, 291, 1892–1906 and 1910–14.

Most Capped Player: Roy McFarland, 28, England.

Most League Appearances: Jack Parry, 478, 1949–66.

Record Transfer Fee Received: £400,000 from Southampton for Charlie George, Dec 1978.

Record Transfer Fee Paid: £410,000 to Crystal Palace for Dave Swindlehurst, April 1980.

Previous Managers since the War: Stuart McMillan, Jack Barker, Harry Storer, Tim Ward, Brian Clough, Dave Mackay, Colin Murphy, Tommy Docherty.

Address of Supporters Club: Baseball Ground, Derby.

Address of the Club Shop or Boutique: The Ramtique, 39 Osmaston Road, Derby.

Baseball Ground, Shaftesbury Crescent, Derby DE3 8NB. Telephone Derby 40105. *Telegraphic address:* 'Football Derby'. *Ground capacity:* 33,000 (16,000 seats.) *Record attendance:* 41,826 v Tottenham H, Division 1, 20 Sept, 1969. *Record receipts:* £65,000 v Juventus, European Cup semi-final, 25 April, 1973. *Pitch measurements:* 110yd×71yd.

How to get there: Buses from town centre 159, 188 and 189. Nearest railway station Derby Midland.

Match tickets: Available 14 days prior to game (£2.70, £3.30, £3.80).

Car parking: Eight car parks within half a mile of the ground run by the club in connection with the local corporation. Street parking half a mile from the ground.

Entertainments/catering facilities: Sportsmen's Club (members only). Licensed and refreshment bars in all parts of the ground. Executive Box complex.

Club shop: The Ramtique, 39 Osmaston Road.

Programmes: The Ram Newspaper, the official club programme, is available on match days priced 40p and on subscription care of the Programme Editor, Derby County Football Club, or from local newsagents.

Club Colours: White shirts, blue shorts, white stockings.

Change Colours: Orange, blue, orange.

Club Captain: Steve Powell.

Club Nickname: The Rams.

DERBY COUNTY 1980–81 LEAGUE RECORD

Match No.	Date	Venue	Opponents	Result		H/T Score	Goalscorers	Attendance
1	Aug 16	A	Cambridge U	L	0-3	0-2		9558
2	20	H	Chelsea	W	3-2	1-1	Biley, Powell B. (pen), Chivers (og)	20,353
3	23	A	Luton T	W	2-1	1-1	Osgood, Swindlehurst	11,025
4	30	H	Bolton W	W	1-0	1-0	Swindlehurst	17,378
5	Sept 6	H	Blackburn R	D	2-2	0-2	Biley 2	18,159
6	13	A	Grimsby T	W	1-0	1-0	Swindlehurst	15,052
7	20	H	Wrexham	L	0-1	0-0		16,823
8	27	A	Orient	L	0-1	0-1		5490
9	Oct 4	H	Sheffield W	W	3-1	2-0	Grant (og), Emson, Biley	18,554
10	7	A	Watford	D	1-1	0-1	Osgood	11,703
11	11	A	Swansea C	L	1-3	0-1	Osgood (pen)	13,323
12	18	H	QPR	D	3-3	1-1	Sheridan 2, Emson	16,021
13	25	A	Bristol C	D	2-2	0-1	Wilson, Emson	12,020
14	Nov 1	H	Shrewsbury T	D	1-1	0-1	Biley	15,784
15	8	A	Notts Co	D	0-0	0-0		16,650
16	12	A	Chelsea	W	3-1	1-0	Wilson, Clark, Reid	19,449
17	15	H	Cambridge U	L	0-3	0-1		15,179
18	22	A	Bristol R	D	1-1	1-1	Emson	6258
19	26	H	West Ham U	W	2-0	1-0	Biley, Clark	18,446
20	29	H	Cardiff C	D	1-1	0-0	Wilson	15,581
21	Dec 6	A	Preston NE	W	3-0	1-0	Hector, Swindlehurst, Biley	6118
22	13	H	Watford	D	1-1	1-0	Hector	16,464
23	20	A	West Ham U	L	1-3	1-1	Swindlehurst (pen)	24,071
24	26	H	Oldham Ath	W	4-1	2-1	Biley 2, Swindlehurst 2	16,958
25	27	A	Newcastle U	W	2-0	2-0	Boam (og), McFarland	20,858
26	Jan 10	H	Bristol R	W	2-1	1-0	Gillies (og), Biley	15,018
27	24	A	Bolton W	L	1-3	1-2	Wilson	9937
28	31	H	Luton T	D	2-2	1-0	Wilson, Hector	16,477
29	Feb 7	H	Grimsby T	W	2-1	1-0	Swindlehurst, Emery	19,691
30	14	A	Blackburn R	L	0-1	0-1		12,533
31	21	H	Orient	D	1-1	1-0	McFarland	15,709
32	28	A	Wrexham	D	2-2	1-0	Sheridan, Swindlehurst (pen)	6485
33	Mar 7	A	Sheffield W	D	0-0	0-0		28,301
34	21	A	QPR	L	1-3	1-1	Powell B.	8905
35	28	H	Bristol C	W	1-0	0-0	Swindlehurst	15,008
36	31	H	Swansea C	L	0-1	0-0		16,210
37	Apr 4	A	Shrewsbury T	L	0-1	0-1		6668
38	11	H	Notts Co	D	2-2	2-1	Osgood (pen), Wilson	17,922
39	18	H	Newcastle U	W	2-0	1-0	Wilson, McFarland	14,139
40	20	A	Oldham Ath	W	2-0	1-0	Buckley, Clayton	6194
41	May 2	A	Cardiff C	D	0-0	0-0		7585
42	6	H	Preston NE	L	1-2	0-0	Swindlehurst	15,050

Final League Position: 6

Goalscorers

League (57): Swindlehurst 11 (2 pens), Biley 10, Wilson 7, Emson 4, Osgood 4 (2 pens), Hector 3, Sheridan 3, McFarland 3, Clark 2, Powell B. 2 (1 pen), Buckley 1, Clayton 1, Emery 1, Reid 1, own goals 4.
League Cup (0).
F.A. Cup (0).

League Cup	Second Round	QPR (a)	0-0
		(h)	0-0 (lost on pens)
FA Cup	Third Round	Bristol C (h)	0-0
		(a)	0-2

Jones	Emery	Buckley	Powell S	McFarland	Ramage	Clark	Powell B	Biley	Swindlehurst	Emson	Osgood	Wilson	Skivington	Hector	Sheridan	Reid	Clayton	Richards	Duncan	Gibson	Spooner	*Match No.*
1	2	3	4	5	6	7	8	9	10	11												1
1	2	3	4		6	8	7	9	10	11	5											2
1	2	3	4		6	8	7	9	10	11*	5							12				3
1	2	3	4		6	7	8	9	10*	11	5	12										4
1	2	3	4		6	7	8	9		11	5	10										5
1	2	3	4		6		8	9	10	11	5		7									6
1	2	3	4		6		8	9	10	11	5		7									7
1	2	3	4	5	12		8	9	10	11	6		7*									8
1	2	3	4	5		7	8	9	10	11	6											9
1	2	3	4	5	7*	12	8	9	10	11	6											10
1	2	3	4	5*		7	8		10	11	6		12	9								11
1	2	3	5				8			11	6	9	7	10	4							12
1	2	3	5			8		9		11	6	12	7*	10	4							13
1	2	3	5			7		9	10	11	6			8	4							14
1	2	3	5			7		9	8	11	6	10	4									15
1	2		5		6	7		9	8	11*	3.	10	4			12						16
1			5		6	4	7*	9	8		3	10	2			12	11					17
1			5		4	7	3	9	8	11	6	10	2									18
1			2	5	6	4	7	9	8	11		10						3				19
1			2	5	6	4	7*	9	8	11	12	10						3				20
1			2	5	6	4		9	10	11				8		7		3				21
1			2	5*	6	4		9	10	11		12		8		7		3				22
1	2		7		6	4		9	10	11	5			8				3				23
1	2		7	5	6	4		9	10	11				8*		12		3				24
1	2		7	5	6	4		9	10	11				8				3				25
1	2	3	4	5	6		8	9	10	11						7						26
1	2	3	4	5			7	9		11	6	10		8								27
1	2	3	4	5			7	9		11	6	10		8								28
1	2	3	4	5			7	9	6*	11	12	10		8								29
1	2	3		5	6		7	9	4	11	12	10*		8								30
1	2	3		5*	6		7	9	10		12	11		8		4						31
1	2	3			6	12			10		5	9		8	4	7	11*					32
1	2*	3		5	6				10	12		9		8	4	7	11					33
1	2	3	6	5			7		10	12		9		8	4		11*					34
1	2	3	4	5			6		10	11		7		8					9			35
1	2	3	4	5*			6		10	11		7		8	12				9			36
1	2	3	4				6		10			9*		8	5	7	11			12		37
1	2	3	4				6			11	5	10		8		7			9			38
1		3	4	5			6			11	2	10		8		7	9					39
1		3	4				6			11	2	10		8	5	7	9					40
1		4							10	11	2	9*		8	5	7	12	3			6	41
1		3		5					10	11	2	9*		8	4	7	12				6	42
42	32	32	36	23	23	20	29	29	34	36	26	24	9	25	10	12	7	8	3	—	2	
					+ 1s	+ 2s				+ 2s	+ 4s	+ 3s	+ 1s		+ 1s	+ 3s	+ 2s	+ 1s		+ 1s		

DERBY COUNTY

	Ht	*Wt*	*Birthplace*	*Clubs*	*League App.*	*League Gls*
Goalkeepers						
John Middleton	6 2	13 7	Lincoln	Nottingham F	90	—
(Retired, injury)				Derby Co	73	—
Steve Cherry	5 11	11 0	Nottingham	Derby Co	4	—
				Port Vale (on loan)	4	—
Roger Jones	5 10	12 12	Upton-on-Severn	Bournemouth	160	—
				Blackburn R	242	—
				Newcastle U	5	—
				Stoke C	101	—
				Derby Co	42	—
Yakka Banovic	5 10	11 8	Yugoslavia	Heidelberg U	(not known)	
(Yugoslavia)				Derby Co	—	—
Defenders						
Roy McFarland*	5 11½	11 4	Liverpool	Tranmere R	35	—
(England)				Derby Co	434	44
Steve Buckley	5 11	12 4	Brinsley	Luton T	123	9
				Derby Co	134	6
Frank Sheridan	6 0	11 0	London	Derby Co	11	3
Steve Spooner	5 9	12 3	London	Derby Co	4	—
Keith Osgood	6 0	12 0	Ealing	Tottenham H	113	13
				Coventry C	25	1
				Derby Co	62	7
John Lovatt	5 7	10 0	Newcastle	Derby Co	—	—
Wayne Richards	5 8	11 0	Scunthorpe	Derby Co	10	—
Alan Ramage	6 2	13 8	Guisborough	Middlesbrough	71	2
				Derby Co	24	—
Steve Emery	5 10	11 10	Hereford	Hereford U	204	10
				Derby Co	59	3
David Tarry			Greenwich	Derby Co	—	—
(Contract cancelled April 1981)						
Ian Dalziel	5 8	11 10	Sunderland	Derby Co	—	—
Steve Powell	5 9	12 0	Derby	Derby Co	251	17
Midfield						
Robert Bowers	5 7	10 0	Dublin	Cliftonville	—	—
(Contract cancelled April 1981)				Derby Co	—	—
Jonathan Clark	5 9	10 11	Swansea	Manchester U	1	—
				Derby Co	53	3
Barry Powell	5 7½	10 2	Kenilworth	Wolverhampton W	64	7
(Contract cancelled April 1981)				Coventry C	164	28
				Derby Co	52	5
Glen Skivington	5 10	11 3	Barrow	Barrow	(not known)	
				Derby Co	10	—
Kevin Murray	5 10	12 0	Dundee	Derby Co	—	—
(Contract cancelled April 1981)						
David King	5 9	10 7	Colchester	Derby Co	—	—
Tony Reid	5 9	10 10	Nottingham	Derby Co	15	1
Kevin Hector	5 8	11 6	Leeds	Bradford PA	176	113
(England)				Derby Co	430	147
				Vancouver W	(not known)	
				Burton A	(not known)	
				Derby Co	25	3
Forwards						
Paul Bartlett*	5 6	10 1	Grimsby	Derby Co	13	—
John Duncan*	5 11	11 4	Lochee	Dundee	124	62
				Tottenham H	103	53
				Derby Co	36	12
Steve Carter*	5 8	10 10	Gt Yarmouth	Manchester C	6	2
				Notts Co	188	21
				Derby Co	33	—
John Clayton	5 11	11 7	Elgin	Derby Co	10	1
Paul Emson	5 11	11 3	Lincoln	Brigg T	—	—
				Derby Co	70	8
Alan Biley	5 8	10 9	Leighton Buzzard	Luton T	—	—
				Cambridge U	165	75
				Derby Co	47	19
David Swindlehurst	6 2	13 3	Edgware	Crystal Palace	237	73
				Derby Co	46	15
Keith Wilson	5 7	10 7	Banbury	Derby Co	31	7
Aidan Gibson			Clayton	Derby Co	1	—
(Apprentice)						

Also retained: Colin Murphy.

DONCASTER ROVERS Division 3

Doncaster Rovers Football Club Ltd.
(Founded 1879)

President: J. C. Morris.
Chairman: I. M. Jones.
Directors: H. Bates, A. Phillips, K. Jackson, B. Boldry, J. Burke, G. Smith.
Vice-Presidents: B. Bailey, R. Jones.
Manager: Billy Bremner.
Secretary: Roger Reade.
Promotions Manager: Roy Gregory.
Year Formed: 1879. *Turned Professional:* 1885.
Limited Company: 1905 and 1920.
Previous Grounds: 1880–1916, Intake Ground; 1920–22, Benetthorpe Ground; 1922, Low Pasture, Belle Vue.

Football League Record:
1901 Elected to Division 2; 1903 Failed re-election; 1904 Re-elected;
1905 Failed re-election; 1923 Re-elected to Division 3(N); 1935–37 Division 2; 1937–47 Division 3(N); 1947–48 Division 2; 1948–50 Division 3(N); 1950–58 Division 2; 1958–59 Division 3; 1959–66 Division 4; 1966–67 Division 3; 1967–69 Division 4; 1969–71 Division 3; 1971–81 Division 4; 1981– Division 3.

Honours: *Football League:* Division 2 best season: 7th, 1901–02; Division 3(N) – Champions 1934–35, 1946–47, 1949–50; Runners-up 1937–38, 1938–39; Division 4 – Champions 1965–66, 1968–69; Promoted 1980–81 (3rd). *FA Cup* best season: 5th rd, 1951–52, 1953–54, 1954–55, 1955–56. *Football League Cup* best season: 5th rd, 1975–76.

Record Victory: 10-0 v Darlington, Division 4, 25 Jan, 1964.
Record Defeat: 0-12 v Small Heath, Division 2, 11 Apr, 1903.
Most League Points: 72, Division 3(N), 1946–47.
Most League Goals: 123, Division 3(N), 1946–47.
Highest League Scorer in Season: Clarrie Jordan, 42, Division 3(N), 1946–47.
Most League Goals in Total Aggregate: Tom Keetley, 180, 1923–29.
Most Capped Player: Len Graham, 14, Ireland.
Most League Appearances: Fred Emery, 406, 1925–36.
Record Transfer Fee Received: £70,000 from Preston NE for Mike Elwiss, Feb 1974 and £70,000 from Bolton W for Dennis Peacock, March 1980.
Record Transfer Fee Paid: £30,000 to Barnsley for Alan Little, Dec 1979.
Previous Managers since the War: Bill Marsden, Jackie Bestall, Peter Doherty, Jack Hodgson, Syd Bycroft, Jack Crayston, Jack Bestall, Norman Curtis, Danny Malloy, Oscar Hold, Bill Leivers, Keith Kettleborough, George Raynor, Lawrie McMenemy, Maurice Setters, Stan Anderson.
Address of Supporters Club: Secretary, K. J. Avis, 64 Harrowden Road, Doncaster.
Address of the Club Shop or Boutique: On ground.

Belle Vue Ground, Doncaster. Telephone Doncaster 55281. *Telegraphic address:* 'Rovers Doncaster'. *Ground capacity:* 21,150. *Record attendance:* 37,149 v Hull C, Division 3(N), 2 Oct, 1948. *Record receipts:* £12,655.70 v Bournemouth, Division 4, 2 May, 1981. *Pitch measurements:* 110yd×77yd.

How to get there: Buses from town centre (Duke St) – Race Course, Hyde Park, and Cantley Estate services. Doncaster railway station is near the town centre.
Match tickets: No advance booking except for Cup ties.
Car parking: Very large car and coach park adjoining the ground. Entrance direct from Great North Road.
Entertainments/catering facilities: Refreshment bars in Main Stand and around the ground, including licensed bars. Social club adjoining ground.
Club shop: In Main Stand, stocks all types of souvenirs.
Handbooks/programmes: Annual handbook on sale at 20p post free or at shop or Supporters Club office. Programmes on sale at shop but not on subscription.
Extra information: Development Association office on ground. Supporters Club office on ground – minimum subscription 15p (Children and OAPs 10p). Handbook free to members. Phone 59679.
Club Colours: White shirts with red trim on sleeves, white shorts with red stripes on side, red with white turnover stockings.
Change Colours: Green shirts with white sleeves, green shorts, green stockings, all with white trim.
Coach: Dave Bentley. *Physiotherapist:* Gerry Delahunt. *Club Nickname:* Rovers.

DONCASTER ROVERS 1980–81 LEAGUE RECORD

Match No.	Date	Venue	Opponents	Result	H/T Score	Goalscorers	Attendance
1	Aug 16	A	Port Vale	L 0-3	0-2		2846
2	19	H	Darlington	W 2-0	1-0	Nimmo 2	3157
3	23	H	Peterborough U	L 0-4	0-1		3536
4	30	A	Hartlepool U	L 0-1	0-0		2110
5	Sept 6	H	Hereford U	W 5-1	3-0	Warboys 2 (1 pen), Little, Nimmo 2	2186
6	13	A	Northampton T	W 2-0	1-0	Little, Pugh	2280
7	16	A	Torquay U	W 3-2	0-0	Nimmo 2, Snodin G.	2533
8	19	H	Southend U	W 1-0	1-0	Little	6044
9	27	A	York C	W 1-0	1-0	Mell	4641
10	30	H	Torquay U	W 2-0	1-0	Warboys, Lister	6916
11	Oct 4	H	Lincoln C	L 0-1	0-0		9693
12	8	A	Wigan Ath	L 0-3	0-2		3608
13	11	A	Crewe Alex	D 0-0	0-0		4033
14	18	H	Halifax T	D 0-0	0-0		4044
15	21	H	Bury	W 1-0	0-0	Warboys (pen)	3529
16	25	A	Aldershot	L 0-1	0-1		2988
17	28	A	Scunthorpe U	D 1-1	1-1	Nimmo	4053
18	Nov 1	H	Wimbledon	W 2-1	0-0	Brown (og), Mell	3245
19	4	H	Wigan Ath	D 1-1	1-0	Little	3625
20	7	A	Stockport Co	L 1-2	0-2	Nimmo	2474
21	11	A	Darlington	L 0-5	0-0		2092
22	15	H	Port Vale	W 2-0	1-0	Harle, Flanagan	2422
23	29	H	Rochdale	L 1-2	1-0	Snodin G.	2502
24	Dec 6	A	AFC Bournemouth	W 2-1	1-1	Swan, Nimmo	2495
25	19	H	Mansfield T	W 2-1	1-0	Little, Pugh	3620
26	26	A	Bradford C	D 1-1	0-1	Mell	4356
27	27	H	Tranmere R	W 1-0	0-0	Little	5530
28	Jan 10	H	Aldershot	W 3-1	1-0	Saunders, Lister, Little (pen)	4502
29	17	A	Rochdale	D 2-2	1-0	Snodin I., Pugh	3021
30	24	H	Hartlepool U	L 1-2	0-0	Nimmo	6814
31	31	A	Peterborough U	W 1-0	0-0	Nimmo	6146
32	Feb 6	H	Northampton T	D 1-1	1-1	Nimmo	5680
33	14	A	Hereford U	W 3-1	1-1	Snodin I., Nimmo 2	2806
34	20	H	York C	W 3-2	3-0	Russell, Nimmo, Dawson	5839
35	27	A	Southend U	D 0-0	0-0		5942
36	Mar 7	A	Lincoln C	D 1-1	0-1	Nimmo	8832
37	13	H	Crewe Alex	D 1-1	1-0	Dawson	7167
38	21	A	Halifax T	W 3-0	2-0	Saunders, O'Neil (og), Nimmo	3762
39	27	H	Scunthorpe U	W 1-0	1-0	Dawson	8001
40	31	A	Bury	L 0-2	0-1		3394
41	Apr 4	A	Wimbledon	L 0-1	0-1		3595
42	10	H	Stockport Co	W 2-1	0-0	Dawson 2	6120
43	17	A	Tranmere R	D 1-1	0-0	Warboys (pen)	2919
44	21	H	Bradford C	W 2-0	1-0	Lister, Snodin G.	8856
45	May 2	H	AFC Bournemouth	W 2-1	1-1	Warboys, Nimmo	11,373
46	6	A	Mansfield T	D 1-1	1-0	Dawson	4506

Final League Position: 3

Goalscorers

League (59): Nimmo 18, Little 7 (1 pen), Dawson 6, Warboys 6 (3 pens), Lister 3, Mell 3, Pugh 3, Snodin G. 3, Saunders 2, Snodin I. 2, Flanagan 1, Harle 1, Russell 1, Swan 1, own goals 2.
League Cup (2): Nimmo, Snodin G.
F.A. Cup (4): Dowd, Lally, Little, Mell.

League Cup	First Round	Mansfield T (h)	1-1
		(a)	1-2
FA Cup	First Round	Sutton Coldfield (a)	2-0
	Second Round	Blackpool (h)	2-1
	Third Round	Hull C (a)	0-1

Boyd	Russell	Lally	Lister	Saunders	Dowd	Pugh	Mell	Nimmo	Snodin G	Little	Bates	Flanagan	Warboys	Dowie	Harle	Snodin I	Shipley	Bremner	Swan	Bennett	Dawson	Aldridge	Wilcox	Humphries	*Match No.*
1	2	3	4	5	6	7	8	9*	10	11	12														1
1	2	5	4		6	7		8	10		11	3	9												2
1	2	5	4		6	7	12	8	10		11*	3	9												3
1	2		4	5	6	7	8		10	11	3		9												4
1	2		4		6	7		8	10	11			9	3	5										5
1	2		4	12	6*	7		8	10	11			9	3	5										6
1	2		4	6		7		8	10	11			9	3	5										7
1	2		4	6		7		8	10	11			9	3	5										8
1	2			4	6*	7	9	8	10	11				3	5	12									9
1	2		4	6		7		8	10	11			9	3	5										10
1	2		4	6		7		8	10	11			9	3	5*	12									11
1	2		3	4*	6	7		8	10	11			9		5	12									12
	2		4		6		8*	12	10	11			9	3	5	7	1								13
1	2		4		6	7*		8		11		10	9	3	5	12									14
1	2		3	4	5		7	8	10*	11			9		12	6									15
1	2		4	5	6	12	8		10	11			9		3	7*									16
1	2	3*	4		6		7	8	10	11			9	5	12										17
1	2	3	4		6	12	7	8	10	11			9*	5											18
1	2	3	4		6	12	7	8	10	11			9*	5											19
1	2	3	4		6	7*	9	8	10	11					5	12									20
1	2	3	4	5	6		12	8	10	11					9*	7									21
1	2	3	4		6	7			10	11*		8	9		5			12							22
1	2	3	4		6	7		12	10	11		8*	9			5									23
1	2	3*			6	7	12	8	10	11			9			4			5						24
1	2				6	7	3	8	10*	11			9		12	4			5						25
1	2		3		6*	7	10	8		11			9		12	4			5						26
1	2		6			7	3	8	10*	11			9		12	4			5						27
1	2		6	9		7	3	8	10	11						4			5						28
1	2	3	6	9		7		8	10	11						4			5						29
1	2	12	6*	3		7		8	10	11			9			4			5						30
1	2	3		5		7		8	10	11			9		6	4									31
1	2	3	9	5		7		8	10	11*					6	4				12					32
1	2	3	12	5		7		8	10	11					6*	4					9				33
1	2	3		5	6*	7		8	10	11					12	4					9				34
1	2	3		5		7		8	10	11			9		6	4									35
1	2	3*		5		7		8	10	11			9		6	4					12				36
1	2		12	5		7		8	10	11			9		6*	4					3				37
1	2	6	12	5		7		8*	10	11			9			4					3				38
1	2	3	8	5		7			10	11*			9		12	4					6				39
1	2	3	11	5		7		8	10						6	4					9				40
1	2		6			7		8*	10				9		11	4		3	5		12				41
1	2		6			7			10				9		11*	4		12	5		3	8			42
1	2		5		6*	7		8	10				9		11	4			12		3				43
1	2		8	5		7			10				9		11	4			6		3				44
1	2		11	5		7		8	10				9		12	4*			6		3				45
1	2		8	5		7			10				9		11				6		3		4*	12	46
45	46	21	36	27	24	39	14	37	44	37	3	5	36	12	26	27	1	1	12	—	11	1	1	—	
		+ 1s	+ 3s	+ 1s		+ 3s	+ 3s	+ 2s			+ 1s				+ 8s	+ 5s		+ 2s	+ 1s	+ 1s	+ 2s			+ 1s	

DONCASTER ROVERS

	Ht	Wt	Birthplace	Clubs	League App.	League Gls
Goalkeepers						
Willie Boyd	5 10	11 4	Bellshill	Hull C	—	—
				Doncaster R	56	—
Mark Shipley*	5 10	11 8	Hemsworth	Blackburn R	—	—
				Doncaster R	6	—
Defenders						
Shaun Flanagan*	5 4½	11 0	Doncaster	Doncaster R	50	3
Hugh Dowd*	6 1	13 0	Lurgan	Glenavon	(not known)	
(N Ireland)				Sheffield W	113	—
				Doncaster R	61	2
Billy Russell	5 10	11 4	Glasgow	Everton	—	—
				Celtic	—	—
				Doncaster R	88	1
Stephen Daniels*	5 7	9 7	Leeds	Doncaster R	1	—
Stewart Mell	5 10	11 0	Doncaster	Doncaster R	26	5
John Saunders*	6 0½	11 12	Worksop	Mansfield T	90	2
				Huddersfield T	121	1
				Barnsley	149	7
				Lincoln C	26	1
				Doncaster R	28	2
Carl Swan	6 2	11 10	Sheffield	Burton A	(not known)	
				Doncaster R	13	1
Midfield						
Steve Lister	6 1	11 10	Doncaster	Doncaster R	88	15
Pat Lally	5 10	10 9	Paddington	Millwall	1	—
				York C	72	5
				Swansea C	160	10
				Aldershot (on loan)	3	—
				Doncaster R	90	—
John Dowie*	6 0½	11 9	Hamilton	Fulham	37	2
				Celtic	14	—
				Doncaster R	21	—
Dave Harle	5 8	9 10	Doncaster	Doncaster R	35	1
Ian Snodin	5 7	8 11½	Rotherham	Doncaster R	41	3
Mick Bates	5 7	10 7	Doncaster	Leeds U	122	4
(Contract cancelled Nov 1980)				Walsall	85	4
				Bradford C	56	1
				Doncaster R	4	—
Steve Aldridge			Armthorpe	Sheffield U	—	—
(Non-contract)				Doncaster R	1	—
Forwards						
Glynn Snodin	5 6	9 5	Rotherham	Doncaster R	145	9
Daral Pugh	5 8	10 7	Sunderland	Doncaster R	103	9
Alan Little	5 11½	12 12	Newcastle	Aston V	3	—
				Southend U	103	12
				Barnsley	91	14
				Doncaster R	59	9
Ian Nimmo	5 11	11 12	Boston	Sheffield W	45	10
				Peterborough (on loan)	4	1
				Doncaster R	78	28
Alan Warboys	6 0½	14 0	Goldthorpe	Doncaster R	39	11
				Sheffield W	71	13
				Cardiff C	60	27
				Sheffield U	7	—
				Bristol R	144	53
				Fulham	19	2
				Hull C	49	9
				Doncaster R	75	17
Billy Bremner	5 5½	10 7	Stirling	Leeds U	586	92
(Scotland)				Hull C	61	6
(Non-contract)				Doncaster R	4	—
Richard Dawson	5 9	11 12	Chesterfield	Rotherham U	24	3
				Doncaster R	13	6
Des Bennett			Doncaster	Doncaster R	1	—
(Apprentice)						
Russell Wilcox			Hemsworth	Doncaster R	1	—
(Apprentice)						
Glenn Humphries			Hull	Doncaster R	1	—
(Apprentice)						

EVERTON Division 1

Chairman: P. D. Carter.
Vice-Chairman: T. H. W. Scott.
Directors: A. W. Waterworth, G. A. Watts, K. M. Tamlin, J. Search, D. A. B. Newton.
Manager: Howard Kendall.
Secretary: Jim Greenwood.
Year Formed: 1878. *Limited Company:* 1892.
Turned Professional: 1885.
Former Grounds: 1878, Stanley Park; 1882, Priory Road; 1884, Anfield Road; 1892, Goodison Park.

Football League Record:
1888 Founder Member of the Football League; 1930–31 Division 2; 1931–51 Division 1; 1951–54 Division 2; 1954– Division 1.

Honours: *Football League:* Division 1 – Champions 1890–91, 1914–15, 1927–28, 1931–32, 1938–39, 1962–63, 1969–70; Runners-up 1889–90, 1894–95, 1901–02, 1904–05, 1908–09, 1911–12; Division 2 – Champions 1930–31; Runners-up 1953–54. *FA Cup:* Winners 1906, 1933, 1966; Runners-up 1893, 1897, 1907, 1968. *Football League Cup:* Runners-up 1976–77. **European Competitions:** *European Cup:* 1963–64, 1970–71; *European Cup-Winners' Cup:* 1966–67. *European Fairs Cup:* 1962–63, 1964–65, 1965–66. *UEFA Cup:* 1975–76, 1978–79, 1979–80.
Record Victory: 11-2 v Derby Co, FA Cup 1st rd, 1889–90.
Record Defeat: 4-10 v Tottenham H, Division 1, 11 Oct, 1958.
Most League Points: 66, Division 1, 1969–70.
Most League Goals: 121, Division 2, 1930–31.
Highest League Scorer in Season: Dixie Dean, 60, 1927–28.
Most League Goals in Total Aggregate: Dixie Dean, 349, 1925–37.
Most Capped Player: Alan Ball, 39 (72), England.
Most League Appearances: Ted Sagar, 465, 1929–53.
Record Transfer Fee Received: £325,000 from Wolverhampton W for Dave Thomas, Oct 1979.
Record Transfer Fee Paid: £650,000 to Aston Villa for John Gidman, Oct 1979.
Previous Managers since the War: Theo Kelly, Cliff Britton, Ian Buchan, John Carey, Harry Catterick, Billy Bingham, Gordon Lee.
Address of Supporters Club: 38 City Road, Liverpool 4.

Goodison Park, Liverpool L4 4EL. Telephone 051-521 2020. *Match ticket information:* 051-523 6642 (24 hr. service). *Ground capacity:* 54,709 (25,000 seats). *Record attendance:* 78,299 v Liverpool, Division 1, 18 Sept, 1948. *Record receipts:* £174,945, Liverpool v Manchester U, FA Cup semi-final replay, 4 April, 1979. *Pitch measurements:* 112yd×78yd.

How to get there: Corporation buses 19 and 44 from Pierhead, 68 from Old Swan, 3, 22, 25, 500 from South End of the City and 30, 92, 92a, 92b, 93 from City centre. Nearest railway station, Liverpool Lime Street.

Match tickets: Reserved stand seats are available for all home fixtures (except the match v Liverpool) at any time during the season, either by post or by personal application to the Box Office at the Goodison Rd side of the ground. The Box Office is open each weekday from 9 am to 5 pm. Postal applications should be addressed to the Box Office manager and contain the correct remittance and SAE.

Car parking: Extensive parking facilities on site at the corner of Priory Rd and Utting Ave.

Entertainments/catering facilities: Royal Blue Restaurant open to the public for lunch on Mondays to Fridays but restricted to members on match days.

Club shop: All souvenirs available from The Toffee Shop in Goodison Rd; send SAE for mail order list.

Handbooks/programmes: Match-day magazine available on seasonal subscription.
Club Colours: Royal blue shirts with white trim, white shorts, blue trim, blue stockings.
Change Colours: Amber shirts, blue trim, amber shorts, blue trim, amber stockings.
Club Coach: Mike Heaton.
Team Captain: Mick Lyons.
Club Nickname: Toffeemen or Blues.

EVERTON 1980–81 LEAGUE RECORD

Match No.	Date	Venue	Opponents	Result		H/T Score	Goalscorers	Attendance
1	Aug 16	A	Sunderland	L	1-3	0-2	Eastoe	32,005
2	19	H	Leicester C	W	1-0	1-0	Eastoe	23,337
3	23	H	Nottingham F	D	0-0	0-0		25,981
4	30	A	Ipswich T	L	0-4	0-2		20,879
5	Sept 6	H	Wolverhampton W	W	2-0	1-0	Eastoe, Wright	21,820
6	13	A	Aston Villa	W	2-0	2-0	Lyons, Eastoe	25,673
7	20	H	Crystal Palace	W	5-0	0-0	Latchford 3, Gidman (pen), Eastoe	26,950
8	27	A	Coventry C	W	5-0	3-0	Eastoe, Latchford 2, McBride 2	14,810
9	Oct 4	H	Southampton	W	2-1	1-1	McBride 2 (2 pens)	36,544
10	7	A	Brighton & HA	W	3-1	0-0	McMahon, Lyons, McBride	16,523
11	11	A	Leeds U	L	0-1	0-0		25,601
12	18	H	Liverpool	D	2-2	2-1	Hartford, McBride	52,565
13	21	H	WBA	D	1-1	1-1	Eastoe	24,046
14	25	A	Manchester U	L	0-2	0-1		54,260
15	Nov 1	H	Tottenham H	D	2-2	1-1	Eastoe, McMahon	26,174
16	8	A	Norwich C	L	1-2	0-0	Latchford	14,557
17	12	A	Leicester C	W	1-0	0-0	Eastoe	15,511
18	15	H	Sunderland	W	2-1	1-1	O'Keefe, Hartford	24,099
19	22	A	Arsenal	L	1-2	0-2	Wright	30,911
20	29	H	Birmingham C	D	1-1	1-1	O'Keefe	22,258
21	Dec 6	A	Stoke C	D	2-2	1-1	McBride, Varadi	15,650
22	13	H	Brighton & HA	W	4-3	2-2	Eastoe 2, McMahon, Varadi	19,157
23	26	H	Manchester C	L	0-2	0-0		36,194
24	27	A	Middlesbrough	L	0-1	0-1		20,210
25	Jan 10	H	Arsenal	L	1-2	0-0	O'Keefe	29,360
26	17	H	Ipswich T	D	0-0	0-0		25,516
27	31	A	Nottingham F	L	0-1	0-1		25,611
28	Feb 7	H	Aston Villa	L	1-3	1-2	Ross (pen)	31,434
29	21	H	Coventry C	W	3-0	1-0	Ross, McMahon, Eastoe	26,731
30	28	A	Crystal Palace	W	3-2	1-1	Eastoe, McMahon, Varadi	14,594
31	Mar 14	H	Leeds U	L	1-2	1-0	Varadi	23,014
32	17	A	Southampton	L	0-3	0-1		20,829
33	21	A	Liverpool	L	0-1	0-0		49,743
34	28	H	Manchester U	L	0-1	0-1		25,854
35	31	A	WBA	L	0-2	0-1		14,833
36	Apr 4	A	Tottenham H	D	2-2	2-0	Hartford, Varadi	27,208
37	11	H	Norwich C	L	0-2	0-1		16,254
38	18	H	Middlesbrough	W	4-1	2-1	Hartford 2 (1 pen), Megson, Eastoe	15,706
39	20	A	Manchester C	L	1-3	0-0	Varadi	34,434
40	25	H	Stoke C	L	0-1	0-0		15,352
41	May 2	A	Birmingham C	D	1-1	1-1	Eastoe	12,863
42	4	A	Wolverhampton W	D	0-0	0-0		16,269

Final League Position: 15

Goalscorers

League (55): Eastoe 15, McBride 7 (2 pens), Latchford 6, Varadi 6, Hartford 5 (1 pen), McMahon 5, O'Keefe 3, Lyons 2, Ross 2 (1 pen), Wright 2, Gidman 1 (pen), Megson 1.
League Cup (6): Latchford 3, Eastoe, Gidman, McBride.
F.A. Cup (8): Eastoe 2, Lyons, O'Keefe, Ross (pen), Varadi, own goals 2.

League Cup	Second Round	Blackpool (h)	3-0
		(a)	2-2
	Third Round	WBA (h)	1-2
FA Cup	Third Round	Arsenal (h)	2-0
	Fourth Round	Liverpool (h)	2-1
	Fifth Round	Southampton (a)	0-0
		(h)	1-0
	Sixth Round	Manchester C (h)	2-2
		(a)	1-3

McDonagh	Gidman	Ratcliffe	Wright	Lyons	Megson	McMahon	Sharp	Latchford	Hartford	McBride	Eastoe	Stanley	O'Keefe	Bailey	Ross	Higgins	Varadi	Hodge	Lodge	Telfer	Barton	*Match No.*
1	2	3	4	5	6	7*	8	9	10	11	12											1
1	2	3	4	5		7		9	10	11	8	6										2
1	2	3	4	5		7		9	10	11	8	6										3
1	2	3	4	5		7		9	8	11*	10	6	12									4
1	2		4	5		7		9*	10	11	8	6	12	3								5
1	2		4	5		7		9	10	11	8*	6	12	3								6
1	2		4	5		7		9	10	11	8	6		3								7
1	2		4	5		7		9	10*	11	8	6	12	3								8
1	2		4	5	10	7		9		11	8	6		3								9
1	2		4	5		7		9	10	11	8*	6	12	3								10
1	2		4	5		7		9	10	11	8	6*	12	3								11
1	2*		4	5		7		9	8	11	10	6	12	3								12
1			4	5		7		9	10	11	8	6		3	2							13
1	2		4	5		7		9	10	11	8	6*	12	3								14
1	2		4	5		7		9*	10	11	8	6	12	3								15
1	2		4	5*		7		9	10	11	8	6	12	3								16
1	2		4			7		9	10	11	8	5	6	3								17
1	2		4		12	7		9*	10	11	8	5	6	3								18
1	2		4		6	7			10	11	8	5	9	3								19
1	2		4		6	7			10	11	8	5	9	3								20
1			2			7			10	11	8	5	6	3		4	9					21
1			2	12		7			10	11	8	4	6*	3		5	9					22
1	2	5	4	12		7			10	11*	8		6	3			9					23
1	2	5	4	12		7			10	11	8			3	6		9*					24
1	2	5	4			7			10		8		11	3	6		9					25
1		2	4	5		7			10	12	8		11*	3	6		9					26
		2	4	5		7			10	12	8		11*	3	6		9	1				27
		2	4	5	7				10		8		11*	3	6		9	1	12			28
1	2*	3	4	5		7			10		8		11		6		9		12			29
1	2	3	4	5		7			10		8		11		6*		9		12			30
1	2		4	5		7			10	11	8			3	6		9					31
1	2	3	4	5*		7			10	12	8	6			11		9					32
1	2		4			7				12	10	5	11	3	6		9*		8			33
1	2	12	4			7					8	5	11	3*	6		9		10			34
1	2	3	4			7*			10		8	5			6		12		11	9		35
1	2		4	7					11		8	5		3	6		9*		10	12		36
1	2	3	4	5	12				10		8*	6			7		9		11			37
1	2	3	4	5	7		12		10		8	6*					9		11			38
1	2	3	4	5	7		12		10	11	8*						9		6			39
1		4		5	7		9		10	11*	8			3			12		6		2	40
1	6	4	7	5					10		8			3	11		9				2	41
1	6	4	7	5				12	10		8*			3	11		9				2	42
40	35	20	41	30	8	34	2	18	39	27	41	28	15	31	17	2	20	2	8	1	3	
		+ 1s		+ 3s	+ 2s		+ 2s	+ 1s		+ 4s	+ 1s		+ 10s				+ 2s		+ 3s	+ 1s		

EVERTON

	Ht	*Wt*	*Birthplace*	*Clubs*	*League App.*	*League Gls*
Goalkeepers						
Martin Hodge	6 0	13 4	Southport	Plymouth Arg	43	—
				Everton	25	—
Jim McDonagh (Eire)	6 0	13 7	Rotherham	Rotherham U	121	—
				Manchester U (on loan)	—	—
				Bolton W	161	—
				Everton	40	—
Defenders						
Billy Wright	5 9	11 6	Liverpool	Everton	125	5
Mike Lyons	6 0	12 2	Liverpool	Everton	363	45
Mark Higgins	6 1	13 3	Buxton	Everton	70	2
Ray Deakin*	5 8	11 1	Liverpool	Everton	—	—
John Barton	5 10	11 0	Birmingham	Everton	20	—
Kevin Ratcliffe (Wales)	5 11	12 7	Mancot	Everton	23	—
John Gidman (England)	5 10½	12 2	Liverpool	Liverpool	—	—
				Aston V	197	9
				Everton	64	2
Brian Borrows	5 10	10 11	Liverpool	Everton	—	—
John Bailey	5 8	11 4	Liverpool	Blackburn R	120	1
				Everton	73	2
Kevin Richardson	5 11	11 5	Newcastle	Everton	—	—
Midfield						
Steve McMahon	5 7	10 9	Liverpool	Everton	34	5
Trevor Ross	5 9½	11 10	Ashton-u-Lyne	Arsenal	58	5
				Everton	96	15
Paul Lodge	5 8½	10 10	Liverpool	Everton	11	—
Gary Megson	5 10	11 3	Manchester	Plymouth Arg	78	10
				Everton	22	2
Brian Quinn*	5 7½	11 2	Belfast	Larne	(not known)	
				Everton	—	—
Gary Stanley	5 10	12 2	Burton upon Trent	Chelsea	109	15
				Everton	52	1
Asa Hartford (Scotland)	5 7	11 4	Clydebank	WBA	213	18
				Manchester C	185	22
				Nottingham F	3	—
				Everton	74	6
Gary Stevens	5 11	10 11	Barrow	Everton	—	—
Forwards						
Bob Latchford (England)	6 0	12 1	Birmingham	Birmingham C	159	68
				Everton	236	106
George Telfer*	5 10	11 5	Liverpool	Everton	99	20
Joe McBride	5 8	10 0	Glasgow	Everton	49	8
Imre Varadi	5 8½	10 6	Paddington	Letchworth	—	—
				Sheffield U	10	4
				Everton	26	6
Peter Eastoe	5 9	11 1	Tamworth	Wolverhampton W	6	—
				Swindon T	91	43
				QPR	72	15
				Everton	76	21
Dean Kelly	5 7	10 2	Liverpool	Everton	—	—
Eamon O'Keefe (Eire)	5 7	11 5	Manchester	Stalybridge C	(not known)	
				Plymouth Arg	—	—
				Hyde U	(not known)	
				Saudi Arabia	(not known)	
				Mossley	(not known)	
				Everton	29	3
Graeme Sharp	6 1	11 8	Glasgow	Dumbarton	40	16
				Everton	6	—
Mark Ward*			Huyton	Everton	—	—
Gerry Mullan			Limavady	Ballymena U	(not known)	
				Everton	—	—

EXETER CITY Division 3

President: F. E. J. Dart.
Chairman: L. G. Vallance.
Vice-Chairman: W. O. Rice MA (Cantab), AIB, FRGS.
Directors: F. E. J. Dart, C. Hill, I. Webb ICMA, S. J. West FIB.
Manager: Brian Godfrey.
Secretary: P. R. Wakeham.
Commercial Manager: E. R. Ellis.
Year Formed: 1904. *Turned Professional:* 1908.
Limited Company: 1908.

Football League Record:
1920 Elected Division 3; 1921–1958 Division 3(S); 1958–64 Division 4; 1964–66 Division 3; 1966–77 Division 4; 1977– Division 3.

Honours: *Football League:* Division 3 best season: 8th, 1979–80; Division 3(S) – Runners-up 1932–33; Division 4 – Runners-up 1976–77. *FA Cup* best season: 6th rd replay, 1931. *Football League Cup:* never beyond 4th rd. *Division 3(S) Cup:* Winners 1934.

Record Victory: 8-1 v Coventry C, Division 3(S), 4 Dec, 1926 and v Aldershot, Division 3(S), 4 May, 1935.

Record Defeat: 0-9 v Notts Co, Division 3(S), 16 Oct, 1948 and v Northampton T, Division 3(S), 12 Apr, 1958.

Most League Points: 62, Division 4, 1976–77.

Most League Goals: 88, Division 3(S), 1932–33.

Highest League Scorer in Season: Fred Whitlow, 34, Division 3(S), 1932–33.

Most League Goals in Total Aggregate: Alan Banks, 105, 1963–66, 1967–73.

Most Capped Player: Dermot Curtis, 1 (17), Eire.

Most League Appearances: Arnold Mitchell, 495, 1952–66.

Record Transfer Fee Received: £105,000 from Blackpool for Tony Kellow, Nov 1978.

Record Transfer Fee Paid: £65,000 to Blackpool for Tony Kellow, March 1980.

Previous Managers since the War: George Roughton, Norman Kirkman, Norman Dodgin, Bill Thompson, Frank Broome, Glen Wilson, Cyril Spiers, Jack Edwards, Ellis Stuttard, Jock Basford, Frank Broome, John Newman, Bobby Saxton.

Address of Supporters Club: Same as Football Club.

Address of the Club Shop or Boutique: The 'Near Post', 2 Blackbury Road, Exeter.

St James Park, Exeter EX4 6PX. Telephone Exeter 54073. *Ground capacity:* 17,500. *Record attendance:* 20,984 v Sunderland, FA Cup 6th rd replay, 4 March, 1931. *Record receipts:* £32,007 v Newcastle U, FA Cup 5th rd replay, 18 Feb, 1981. *Pitch measurements:* 114yd×73yd.

How to get there: City buses A, D, J, K, S from city centre to The Fountain (one-minute walk to the ground). Routes G and J pass both railway stations – Exeter St David's and Exeter Central.

Match tickets: Tickets may be booked in advance usually two weeks before home matches.

Car parking: No car park at the ground. Limited street parking permitted.

Entertainments/catering facilities: Members social club. Subscription £1.25; joint membership £2.50. The club is situated at the ground.

Club shop: Sells all types of souvenir.

Handbooks/programmes: Programmes can be ordered on subscription.

Extra information: Membership of the Supporters Association at 25p per year.

Club Colours: Red and white vertical stripes, black shorts, black stockings with red and white turnover.

Change Colours: Green shirts, green shorts, green stockings.

Coaches: Alan Beer, Malcolm Musgrove.

Club Nickname: The Grecians.

EXETER CITY 1980–81 LEAGUE RECORD

Match No.	Date	Venue	Opponents	Result	H/T Score	Goalscorers	Attendance
1	Aug 16	H	Gillingham	W 2-1	1-0	Kellow, Neville	3630
2	20	A	Oxford U	W 2-1	1-0	Neville, Kellow	3751
3	23	A	Hull C	D 3-3	1-0	Neville 2, Hatch	3559
4	30	H	Colchester U	W 4-0	1-0	Neville, Giles, Delve, Kellow (pen)	3918
5	Sept 6	A	Chester	L 0-1	0-0		1974
6	13	H	Burnley	D 0-0	0-0		4534
7	17	H	Fulham	W 1-0	0-0	Kellow	5300
8	20	A	Millwall	L 0-1	0-0		3638
9	27	H	Charlton Ath	W 4-3	3-2	Kellow 3, Prince	4916
10	Oct 1	A	Fulham	W 1-0	0-0	Rogers P.	4509
11	4	A	Rotherham U	L 1-3	1-1	Giles	6889
12	8	H	Brentford	D 0-0	0-0		4665
13	11	H	Huddersfield T	L 1-4	1-3	Rogers P.	4769
14	18	A	Sheffield U	L 1-3	0-0	Kellow	10,608
15	21	A	Walsall	W 3-1	2-0	Rogers P., Kellow, Pratt	3703
16	25	H	Swindon T	L 3-4	1-2	Kellow 2 (1 pen), Pratt	4688
17	Nov 1	A	Reading	L 1-2	0-1	Kellow	4622
18	3	A	Brentford	W 1-0	1-0	Kellow	6590
19	8	H	Barnsley	L 0-1	0-0		4019
20	12	H	Oxford U	D 1-1	1-0	Delve	3241
21	15	A	Gillingham	W 5-1	1-0	Delve, Kellow 3, Pullar	3725
22	29	H	Carlisle U	W 2-0	2-0	Rogers P., Forbes	3940
23	Dec 6	A	Blackpool	D 0-0	0-0		3597
24	20	H	Chesterfield	D 2-2	0-1	Rogers P., Pratt	4075
25	26	A	Plymouth Arg	W 2-0	2-0	Kellow (pen), Pullar	14,792
26	27	H	Newport Co	D 2-2	1-2	Pullar, Kellow (pen)	6295
27	Jan 10	H	Walsall	L 0-3	0-1		4590
28	14	H	Portsmouth	W 2-0	1-0	Pearson, Pullar	3722
29	31	H	Hull C	L 1-3	1-1	Hoolickin (og)	5022
30	Feb 3	A	Colchester U	W 2-1	2-1	Forbes, Pullar	2357
31	7	A	Burnley	L 0-1	0-1		5585
32	10	A	Portsmouth	L 0-5	0-1		12,743
33	21	A	Charlton Ath	L 0-1	0-0		7245
34	28	H	Millwall	W 2-0	2-0	Kellow, Hatch	5408
35	Mar 18	H	Rotherham U	W 2-1	0-1	Sparrow, Delve	4494
36	21	H	Sheffield U	D 1-1	0-0	Kellow	4224
37	28	A	Swindon T	D 2-2	1-1	Pearson, Kellow	6509
38	31	A	Carlisle U	D 1-1	0-1	Rogers P.	4385
39	Apr 4	H	Reading	W 3-1	1-0	Pearson 2, Kellow	3890
40	7	A	Huddersfield T	L 0-5	0-1		12,009
41	10	A	Barnsley	L 0-1	0-0		13,445
42	18	A	Newport Co	L 1-2	1-0	Kellow (pen)	5231
43	21	H	Plymouth Arg	D 1-1	0-0	Kellow	8491
44	29	H	Chester	D 2-2	1-0	Kellow, Pratt	3056
45	May 2	H	Blackpool	D 0-0	0-0		3864
46	8	A	Chesterfield	L 0-1	0-0		3448

Final League Position: 11

Goalscorers

League (62): Kellow 25 (5 pens), Rogers P. 6, Neville 5, Pullar 5, Delve 4, Pearson 4, Pratt 4, Forbes 2, Giles 2, Hatch 2, Prince 1, Sparrow 1, own goal 1.
League Cup (2): Kellow 2.
F.A. Cup (19): Kellow 6 (1 pen), Pullar 3, Rogers P. 3, Pearson 2, Roberts L. 2, Hatch, Rogers M., own goal.

League Cup	First Round	Bristol R (h)	1-1
		(a)	1-1 (lost on pens)
FA Cup	First Round	Leatherhead (h)	5-0
	Second Round	Millwall (a)	1-0
	Third Round	Maidstone (a)	4-2
	Fourth Round	Leicester C (a)	1-1
		(h)	3-1
	Fifth Round	Newcastle U (a)	1-1
		(h)	4-0
	Sixth Round	Tottenham H (a)	0-2

Main	Ireland	Hatch	Prince	Giles	Roberts P	Pearson	Neville	Kellow	Delve	Pullar	Rogers P	Rogers M	Forbes	Bond	Pratt	Roberts L	Sparrow	Mitchell	Nute	Fisher	*Match No.*
1	2	3	4	5	6	7*	8	9	10	11	12										1
1	2	3	4	5	6	7	8	9*	10	11	12										2
1	2	3	4	5	6	7	8	9	10	11											3
1	2	3	4	5	6	7	8	9*	10	11	12										4
1	2*	3	4	5	6	7	8	9	10	11	12										5
1	2	3	4	5	6	7	8	9	10	11											6
1	2	3	4	5	6	7	8	9	10	11											7
1	2*	3	4	5	6	7	8	9	10	11	12										8
1		3	4	5	6	7	8	9	10		11	2									9
1		3	4	5	6	7	8	9	10		11	2									10
1		3	4	5	6	7	8	9	10		11	2									11
1		3	4	5	6	7	8	9	10		11	2									12
1		3	4	5	6	7*	8	9	10		11	2	12								13
1		3	4	5	6		8	9	10		11	2	7								14
		3	4	5	6			9	10	11	8*	2	7	1	12						15
		3	4*	5	6	12		9	10	11		2	7	1	8						16
		3		5	6	7		9	10	11	8	2	4	1							17
		3		5	6	7		9	10	11	8	2	4	1							18
	3			5	6	7		9	10	11*	8	2	4	1	12						19
		3			6	7		9	10		11	2	4	1	8	5					20
		3			6	7		9	10	11	8	2	4	1		5					21
	10	3			6	7		9		11	8	2	4	1		5					22
	10	3			6	7		9		11	8	2	4	1		5					23
		3			6	7*		9	10	11	8	2	4	1	12	5					24
		3			6	7		9	10	11	8	2	4	1		5					25
		3			6	7		9	10	11	8	2	4	1		5					26
		3			6	7*		9	10	11	8	2	4	1	12	5					27
		3			6	7		9	10	11	8	2	4	1		5					28
1		3			6	7		9	10	11	8	2	4		12	5*					29
1		3		5	6	7		9	10	11	8	2	4								30
1		3		5	6	7		9	10	11*	8	2	4			12					31
1		11	10	5	6	7		9*			8	2	4			12	3				32
		11				7		9	10			2	4	1	8	5	3	6			33
		11			6*	7		9	10		8	2	4	1	12	5	3				34
		11			6	7		9	10		8	2	4	1		5	3				35
1		11			6	7		9	10		8	2	4			5	3				36
1		11			6	7		9	10		8	2	4*		12	5	3				37
1	10	11			6	7		9			8	2	4			5	3				38
	10	11			6	7		9			8	2	4			5	3		1		39
	10*	11			6	7		9			8	2	4		12	5	3		1		40
	12	11			6	7		9	10			2	4*		8	5	3		1		41
	12	11			6	7		9			8	2	4*		10	5	3		1		42
1		11	7		6			9	10*		8	2	4		12	5	3				43
1		11	4		6			9			8	2	12		10	5	3			7*	44
1		11	4		6	8		9			12				10	5	3	2		7*	45
		11	4					9		12	8*	2			10	5	3	6	1	7	46
24	14	45	21	22	44	40	14	46	36	24	34	37	30	17	8	24	15	3	5	3	
	+ 2s					+ 1s				+ 1s	+ 6s		+ 2s		+ 9s	+ 2s					

EXETER CITY

	Ht	Wt	Birthplace	Clubs	League App.	League Gls
Goalkeepers						
Ian Main	6 0	13 2	Gloucester	Gloucester C	(not known)	
				Exeter C	63	—
Steve Nute*	6 2	11 6	Saltash	Exeter C	5	—
Len Bond	6 0	11 9	Ilminster	Bristol C	30	—
				Exeter C (on loan)	30	—
				Cardiff C (on loan)	—	—
				Torquay U (on loan)	3	—
				Scunthorpe U (on loan)	8	—
				Colchester U (on loan)	3	—
				Brentford	122	—
				Exeter C	17	—
Defenders						
Peter Hatch	5 10	11 7	Reading	Oxford U	19	2
				Exeter C	324	15
John Hore	5 8	10 11	St Austell	Plymouth Arg	398	17
(Contract cancelled Dec 1980)				Exeter C	193	—
Jimmy Giles	6 0	13 3	Kidlington	Swindon T	13	—
(Contract cancelled Feb 1981)				Aldershot	81	3
				Exeter C	183	6
				Charlton Ath	93	6
				Exeter C	130	5
Phil Roberts	6 0	12 6	Bristol	Bristol R	176	6
(Wales)				Portsmouth	153	1
				Hereford U	3	—
				Exeter C	78	—
Richard Forbes*	5 8	10 7	London	Exeter C	59	5
Martyn Rogers	5 10	11 7	Bristol	Bristol C	—	—
				Bath C	(not known)	
				Exeter C	48	—
Tony Mitchell	5 10	11 2	London	Exeter C	47	—
Lee Roberts	5 11	11 10	Wolverhampton	Shrewsbury T	15	1
				Exeter C	117	8
John Sparrow	5 10	12 0	Bethnal Green	Chelsea	69	2
				Millwall (on loan)	7	—
				Exeter C	15	1
Jon May	5 11	11 4	Crosby	Blackpool	4	—
(Contract cancelled Dec 1980)				Exeter C	—	—
Midfield						
John Delve	5 8	10 12	Hanworth	QPR	15	—
				Plymouth Arg	132	6
				Exeter C	131	12
David Pullar	5 11	11 4	London	Portsmouth	93	4
				Exeter C	68	15
Roy Ireland*	5 9	10 12	Exeter	Exeter C	21	—
Frankie Prince	5 9	11 7	Cardiff	Bristol R	361	23
				Exeter C	21	1
Forwards						
Peter Rogers	5 7	10 12	Bristol	Bath C	(not known)	
				Exeter C	95	14
Ian Pearson	5 11	11 3	Leeds	Plymouth Arg	12	—
				Millwall	44	9
				Exeter C	69	10
Tony Kellow	5 11	12 4	Falmouth	Falmouth	(not known)	
				Exeter C	107	40
				Blackpool	57	23
				Exeter C	56	30
Ray Pratt	5 11	11 6	Merthyr	Merthyr T	(not known)	
				Exeter C	24	6
Phil Fisher			Carmarthen	Exeter C	3	—
Ian Cole*			Exeter	Exeter C	—	—

FULHAM Division 3

Life-President: Tommy Trinder CBE.
Chairman: E. Clay.
Directors: G. Clay, B. Dalton, E. Drake, A. Price.
Manager: Malcolm Macdonald.
Club Secretary: George Noyce. *Year Formed:* 1879.
Turned Professional: 1898. *Limited Company:* 1903.
Previous Name: 1879–98, Fulham St Andrew's.
Previous Grounds: Lillie Road, Fulham Cross; Barn Elms, Barnes; Ranelagh House; Stansfield's Field, Fulham Road; Half-Moon Cricket Ground, Putney; 1896, Craven Cottage.

Football League Record:
1907 Elected to Division 2; 1928–32 Division 3(S); 1932–49 Division 2; 1949–52 Division 1; 1952–59 Division 2; 1959–68 Division 1; 1968–69 Division 2; 1969–71 Division 3; 1971–80 Division 2; 1980– Division 3.

Honours: *Football League:* Division 1 best season: 10th, 1959–60; Division 2 – Champions 1948–49; Runners-up 1958–59; Division 3(S) – Champions 1931–32; Division 3 – Runners-up 1970–71. *FA Cup:* Runners-up 1974–75. *Football League Cup* best season: 5th rd, 1967–68, 1970–71.

Record Victory: 10-1 v Ipswich T, Division 1, 26 Dec, 1963.
Record Defeat: 0-9 v Wolverhampton W, Division 1, 16 Sept, 1959.
Most League Points: 60, Division 2 1958–59, and Division 3, 1970–71.
Most League Goals: 111, Division 3(S), 1931–32.
Highest League Scorer in Season: Frank Newton, 41, Division 3(S), 1931–32.
Most League Goals in Total Aggregate: Bedford Jezzard, 154, 1948–56.
Most Capped Player: Johnny Haynes, 56, England.
Most League Appearances: Johnny Haynes, 594, 1952–70.
Record Transfer Fee Received: £333,333 from Liverpool for Richard Money, May 1980.
Record Transfer Fee Paid: £150,000 to Orient for Peter Kitchen, Feb 1979 and £150,000 to Brighton & HA for Teddy Maybank, Dec 1979.
Previous Managers since the War: Jack Peart, Frank Osborne, Doug Livingstone, Bill Dodgin (Snr), Bedford Jezzard, Vic Buckingham, Bobby Robson, Johnny Haynes, Bill Dodgin (Jnr), Alec Stock, Bobby Campbell.
Address of Supporters Club: Fulham Travel Club, Craven Cottage, Stevenage Road, SW6.

Craven Cottage, Stevenage Rd, Fulham, London SW6. Telephone 01-736 6561/2/3. Pools Office: 01-736 4634. *Telegraphic address:* 'Fulhamish, London SW6'. *Ground capacity:* 20,000. *Record attendance:* 49,335 v Millwall, Division 2, 8 Oct, 1938. *Record receipts:* £44,763 v Manchester U, FA Cup 4th rd, 27 Jan, 1979. *Pitch measurements:* 110yd×75yd.

How to get there: Underground stations, Putney Bridge (District Line) and Hammersmith (District, Metropolitan, Piccadilly). Then by bus – 30, 74, 85, 93, 220.
Match tickets: The Box Office is now computerised, and seats are bookable at any time during the season. Closed all day Monday.
Car parking: Parking in streets around the ground.
Entertainments/catering facilities: Social amenities available. Snack bars and licensed bars around the ground. The Riverside Suite is available for conferences, weddings, parties, etc.
Club shop: Sells all types of souvenir. Open only on match days.
Handbooks/programmes: Programmes available.
Extra information: Fulham Travel Club runs trips to away matches.
Club Colours: White shirts with black collar, black shorts, white stockings with three black hoops on turnover.
Change Colours: Red shirts, red shorts, black stockings with three red hoops on turnover.
Club Captain: Tony Gale.
First Team Trainer: John Clinkard.
Club Nickname: Cottagers.

FULHAM 1980–81 LEAGUE RECORD

Match No.	Date	Venue	Opponents	Result		H/T Score	Goalscorers	Attendance
1	Aug 16	A	Rotherham U	D	2-2	1-1	Beck, Lock	4436
2	20	H	Colchester U	W	1-0	0-0	Lock (pen)	4250
3	23	A	Swindon T	W	4-3	1-2	Davies 2, Wilson, Mahoney	6473
4	29	H	Hull C	D	0-0	0-0		4592
5	Sept 5	H	Blackpool	L	1-2	1-2	Davies	4940
6	13	A	Brentford	W	3-1	1-1	O'Driscoll, Brown, Davies	11,600
7	17	A	Exeter C	L	0-1	0-0		5300
8	20	H	Walsall	W	2-1	1-0	Davies, Lock (pen)	4573
9	27	A	Portsmouth	L	0-1	0-0		16,460
10	Oct 1	H	Exeter C	L	0-1	0-0		4509
11	4	H	Burnley	L	0-2	0-1		4683
12	7	A	Plymouth Arg	L	1-2	1-2	Beck	11,547
13	11	A	Gillingham	L	0-1	0-1		4730
14	18	H	Oxford U	L	0-4	0-2		3817
15	22	H	Millwall	D	1-1	1-0	Davies	4115
16	25	A	Chester	W	1-0	0-0	Davies	3169
17	28	A	Newport Co	L	1-2	0-2	Beck (pen)	6029
18	Nov 1	H	Chesterfield	D	1-1	1-0	Wilson	4706
19	4	H	Plymouth Arg	D	0-0	0-0		3507
20	8	A	Carlisle U	D	2-2	0-1	Beck, Hatter	3665
21	11	A	Colchester U	L	2-3	1-2	Beck, Davies	2543
22	15	H	Rotherham U	D	1-1	0-1	O'Driscoll	4011
23	29	A	Barnsley	D	2-2	2-1	Peters, Goodlass	9940
24	Dec 6	H	Huddersfield T	D	2-2	1-0	Davies 2	4513
25	20	A	Reading	D	0-0	0-0		4455
26	26	H	Sheffield U	W	2-1	1-0	Lock (pen), Davies	6029
27	27	A	Charlton Ath	D	1-1	0-1	Greenaway	11,070
28	Jan 10	A	Millwall	L	1-3	1-1	Davies	6002
29	16	H	Barnsley	L	2-3	1-1	Mahoney, Wilson	5265
30	31	H	Swindon T	W	2-0	0-0	Davies, Mahoney	4785
31	Feb 7	H	Brentford	D	1-1	1-0	Beck	8721
32	14	A	Blackpool	W	2-0	1-0	Mahoney, Goodlass	3792
33	21	H	Portsmouth	W	3-0	1-0	Davies, Doyle (og), Lock (pen)	9921
34	Mar 1	A	Walsall	W	2-1	2-1	Beck, Peters	4958
35	7	A	Burnley	L	0-3	0-2		5465
36	14	H	Gillingham	W	3-2	1-1	Davies 2, Gale	5445
37	17	H	Chester	L	0-1	0-1		3387
38	21	A	Oxford U	L	0-2	0-1		3646
39	28	H	Newport Co	W	2-1	1-0	Davies, O'Driscoll	4570
40	Apr 4	A	Chesterfield	D	0-0	0-0		6756
41	7	A	Hull C	W	1-0	0-0	Brown	3152
42	11	H	Carlisle U	L	2-3	1-1	Banton, Coney	4193
43	18	H	Charlton Ath	W	1-0	1-0	Coney	7102
44	21	A	Sheffield U	W	2-1	1-0	Coney, Greenaway	10,898
45	25	H	Reading	L	1-2	0-1	Strong	4601
46	May 2	A	Huddersfield T	L	2-4	1-2	Beck (pen), Davies	6965

Final League Position: 13

Goalscorers

League (57): Davies 18, Beck 8 (2 pens), Lock 5 (4 pens), Mahoney 4, Coney 3, O'Driscoll 3, Wilson 3, Brown 2, Goodlass 2, Greenaway 2, Peters 2, Banton 1, Gale 1, Hatter 1, Strong 1, own goal 1.
League Cup (3): Davies, Gale, Strong.
F.A. Cup (6): Davies 3, Mahoney 2, Greenaway.

League Cup	First Round	Peterborough U (a)	2-3
		(h)	1-1
FA Cup	First Round	Reading (a)	2-1
	Second Round	Brentford (h)	1-0
	Third Round	Bury (a)	1-1
		(h)	0-0 (aet)
			1-0 (at WBA)
	Fourth Round	Charlton Ath (h)	1-2

Peyton	Peters	Strong	Beck	Brown	Gale	Greenaway	Wilson	O'Driscoll	Davies	Lock	Mahoney	Hatter	Goodlass	Clement	Digweed	Corner	Banton	Lewington	Stannard	Day	Tempest	Coney	Parker	Hopkins	*Match No.*
1	2	3	4	5	6	7	8	9	10	11															1
1	2	3	4	5	6	7	8	9	10	11															2
1	2	3	4	5	6		10	8	9	11	7														3
1	2	3	4	5	6		10	8	9	11	7														4
1	2	3	4	5	6	12	10	8	9	11*	7														5
1	2	3	4	5	6	10		8	9	11	7*	12													6
1	2	3	4	5*	6	12	10	8	9	11	7														7
1	2	3	4	5	6		10	8	9	11	7														8
1	2*	3	4	5	6	12	10	8	9	11	7														9
1	2*	3	4	5	6	12		8	9	10	7		11												10
1		3	4	5	6			8	9	10	7		11	2											11
1		3	4	5	7	12		8	9	10*		6	11	2											12
1		3	4	5	6		10	8	9		7		11	2											13
1		3	4	5	9	10	2	7	8	6			11												14
1		3	4	5	9	12	10*	7	8	6			11	2											15
1		3	4	5	6	9	10	7	8				11	2											16
	12	3	4	5	6	9*	10	7	8				11	2	1										17
1	12	2	4	5	6		10	7	8	3	9*		11												18
1	9	3	4	5	6	12	10	7	8				11	2*											19
1	2	3	4	5	9		10	8	7			6*	11			12									20
1	2	3	4*	5	9		10	7	8			6	11			12									21
1	2	3	4	5	9		8	10	7				11			6									22
1	9	2	4	5	10		12	8		3	7	6*	11												23
1	9	2		5	4	10		8	7	3		6	11												24
1	9	2			4	10		8	7*	3		6	11				5	12							25
1	12	2			4	10		8	7	3	5	6	11*				9								26
1		2			4	10		8	7	3	9	6					5	11							27
1		2						8	7	3	9	6	11	4			5	10							28
1		6		5	4		12	8	7	3*	9		11	2				10							29
	3		4	5	6	11	12	8*	7		9			2				10	1						30
	2	3	4	5	6	11*	12	8	7		9							10	1						31
	12	3	4	5	6		10	8	7	2*	9		11						1						32
	12	2	4	5	6		10		7	3	9			8*				11	1						33
	8	3	4	5	6		10	9	7*	2								11	1	12					34
	8	3	4	5	6		10	9*	7									11	1	2	12				35
	8	3	4	5	6		10	9*	7					2				11	1	12					36
	8	3	4	5	6		10	9	7					2				11*	1	12					37
	4	3		5	6		10	8	7		9*			2				11	1	12					38
		3		5	6	4	10	8*	7	2								11	1	12		9			39
		3	8	5	6	4	10		7	2								11	1			9			40
		3	8	5	6*	4	10		7	2				12				11	1			9			41
	2	3	8			4	10		7					6			5	11	1			9			42
	4	3	8	5			10	12	7	2*				6				11	1			9			43
	8	3		5		4	10	12	7					2			6	11	1			9*			44
	6	3	4			8		10*	7				12				5	11	1			9	2		45
	6	3	4			8		12	7		9		10*				5	11	1					2	46
28	29	45	37	39	40	19	31	39	45	29	22	9	21	17	1	1	8	19	17	1	—	7	1	1	
	+ 5s					+ 7s	+ 4s	+ 3s				+ 1s	+ 1s	+ 1s		+ 2s		+ 1s		+ 5s	+ 1s				

FULHAM

	Ht	Wt	Birthplace	Clubs	League App.	League Gls
Goalkeepers						
Gerry Peyton	6 2	13 11	Birmingham	Burnley	30	—
(Eire)				Fulham	164	—
Doug Hatcher*	5 11	11 10	Surrey	Fulham	—	—
Jim Stannard			London	Fulham	17	—
Defenders						
Les Strong	5 9	10 7	London	Crystal Palace	—	—
				Fulham	323	5
Steve Hatter	6 2	13 0	London	Fulham	26	1
(Contract cancelled April 1981)						
Tony Gale	6 1½	12 4	London	Fulham	156	15
Kevin Lock	6 0	11 6	London	West Ham U	132	2
				Fulham	106	13
Geoff Banton	5 11	11 7	Ashton-u-Lyne	Bolton W	—	—
				Plymouth Arg	7	—
				Fulham	37	3
Brian Corner*	5 7	9 3	Scotland	Fulham	3	—
Tommy Mason*	5 8	10 6	London	Fulham	6	—
Gary Peters	5 11	11 12	Surrey	Reading	156	7
				Fulham	63	2
Robert Wilson	5 10	11 2	London	Fulham	37	3
Roger Brown	6 1	11 10	Tamworth	Bournemouth	63	3
				Norwich C	16	—
				Fulham	40	2
David Clement	6 0	12 5	Battersea	QPR	405	22
(England)				Bolton W	33	—
				Fulham	18	—
Paul Parker			London	Fulham	1	—
(Apprentice)						
Jeff Hopkins			Swansea	Fulham	1	—
(Apprentice)						
Midfield						
John Beck	5 10½	11 9	Edmonton	QPR	40	1
				Coventry C	69	6
				Fulham	109	12
Clive Day	6 0	11 0	Essex	Fulham	6	—
Ray Lewington	5 6	10 5	London	Chelsea	85	4
				Wimbledon	23	—
				Fulham	30	1
Sean O'Driscoll	5 8	10 6	Birmingham	Fulham	52	4
Brian Gibson*	5 9	10 0	Scotland	Fulham	—	—
Ron Goodlass	5 7	10 12	Liverpool	Everton	35	2
				Den Haag	(not known)	
				Fulham	22	2
Tony Finnigan			Wimbledon	Crystal Palace	—	—
				Fulham		
Cliff Cant	5 11	11 11	London	Arsenal	—	—
(Contract cancelled Dec 1980)				Fulham	—	—
Forwards						
Brian Greenaway	5 9	10 1	London	Fulham	85	8
Tony Mahoney	6 0	11 12	Barking	Fulham	59	10
Gordon Davies	5 7	10 6	S Wales	Fulham	121	43
(Wales)						
Peter Marinello	5 8	10 9	Edinburgh	Hibernian	45	5
(Contract cancelled July 1980)				Arsenal	37	3
				Portsmouth	95	7
				Motherwell	89	12
				Fulham	27	1
Mark Lovell*	5 9	11 9	London	Fulham	5	—
Teddy Maybank	5 10	10 12	London	Chelsea	28	6
(Contract cancelled Aug 1980)				Fulham	27	14
				Brighton	64	16
				Fulham	19	3
Peter Nott			London	Fulham	—	—
(Contract cancelled March 1981)						
Dale Tempest			Leeds	Fulham	1	—
(Apprentice)						
Dean Coney			Dagenham	Fulham	7	3
(Apprentice)						

Also retained: Hilton Phillips.

GILLINGHAM Division 3

Chairman: Dr C. S. Grossmark.

Vice-Chairman: C. A. L. Cox.

Directors: J. W. Leech, S. H. Martin, B. B. Moore.

Manager: Keith Peacock. *Club Secretary:* M. A. Bramley.

Assistant Manager: Alan Hodgkinson.

Year Formed: 1893. *Turned Professional:* 1894.

Limited Company: 1893.

Previous Name: New Brompton, 1893–1913.

Football League Record:
1920 Original Member of Division 3; 1921 Division 3(S); 1938 Failed re-election; 1950 Re-elected to Division 3(S); 1958–64 Division 4; 1964–71 Division 3; 1971–74 Division 4; 1974– Division 3.

Honours: *Football League:* Division 3 best season: 4th, 1978–79; Division 4 – Champions 1963–64; Runners-up 1973–74. *FA Cup* best season: 5th rd, 1969–70. *Football League Cup* best season: 4th rd, 1964.

Record Victory: 10-1 v Gorleston, FA Cup 1st rd, 16 Nov, 1957.

Record Defeat: 2-9 v Nottingham F, Division 3(S), 18 Nov, 1950.

Most League Points: 62, Division 4, 1973–74.

Most League Goals: 90, Division 4, 1973–74.

Highest League Scorer in Season: Ernie Morgan, 31, Division 3(S), 1954–55; Brian Yeo, 31, Division 4, 1973–74.

Most League Goals in Total Aggregate: Brian Yeo, 135, 1963–75.

Most Capped Player: Fred Fox, 1, England; Damien Richardson, 1 (2), Eire.

Most League Appearances: John Simpson, 571, 1957–72.

Record Transfer Fee Received: £60,000 from Charlton Ath for Dick Tydeman, Dec 1976.

Record Transfer Fee Paid: £90,000 to Colchester U for Trevor Lee, Jan 1981.

Previous Managers since the War: Archie Clark, Harry Barratt, Freddie Cox, Basil Hayward, Andy Nelson, Len Ashurst, Gerry Summers.

Address of Supporters Club: Gillingham FC Supporters' Association, Gordon Road, Gillingham.

Priestfield Stadium, Gillingham. Telephone 0634 51854/52100. *Telegraphic address:* 'Football Gillingham, Kent'. *Ground capacity:* 22,000. *Record attendance:* 23,002 v QPR, FA Cup 3rd rd, 10 Jan, 1948. *Record receipts:* £13,500 v Shrewsbury T, Division 3, 28 April, 1979. *Pitch measurements:* 114yd×75yd.

How to get there: Gillingham railway station (six or seven minutes' walk). Bus services are 10 minutes from ground.

Match tickets: Can be reserved by postal application enclosing correct remittance and SAE.

Car parking: Park for 500 cars adjoining the ground, entrance in Toronto Rd.

Entertainments/catering facilities: A club house, and several bars around the ground.

Club shop: Sells all types of souvenir.

Handbooks/programmes: Programmes available on subscription. Handbooks also available.

Extra information: Enquiries about supporters association to Gillingham FC Supporters Association, Gordon Rd, Gillingham.

Club Colours: Blue shirts, white shorts, blue stockings, white and blue trim.

Change Colours: White shirts with red sash, red shorts and stockings.

Club Captain: Andy Ford.

Club Nickname: The Gills.

GILLINGHAM 1980–81 LEAGUE RECORD

Match No.	Date	Venue	Opponents	Result		H/T Score	Goalscorers	Attendance
1	Aug 16	A	Exeter C	L	1-2	0-1	Ford	3630
2	19	H	Reading	W	2-0	1-0	Henderson, Richardson	5192
3	23	H	Barnsley	D	1-1	1-1	Henderson	5195
4	30	A	Chesterfield	L	0-2	0-2		5535
5	Sept 6	H	Newport Co	W	3-2	2-1	Hughes, Price, Henderson	4712
6	13	A	Carlisle U	D	0-0	0-0		3029
7	16	H	Huddersfield T	D	0-0	0-0		5092
8	20	A	Plymouth Arg	L	1-4	1-2	Price	6719
9	27	H	Oxford U	D	1-1	0-0	Burton (og)	4137
10	30	A	Huddersfield T	L	0-1	0-1		7716
11	Oct 4	A	Blackpool	L	0-4	0-1		6588
12	7	H	Swindon T	D	0-0	0-0		4066
13	11	H	Fulham	W	1-0	1-0	Westwood	4730
14	18	A	Rotherham U	L	0-2	0-0		5903
15	20	A	Brentford	D	3-3	1-2	Price 2, Westwood	6790
16	25	H	Hull C	W	2-0	1-0	Bruce, Westwood	4100
17	28	H	Sheffield U	D	2-2	2-2	Bruce, Westwood	4976
18	Nov 1	A	Walsall	D	3-3	2-3	Nicholl, Westwood, Price	4060
19	4	A	Swindon T	D	0-0	0-0		4719
20	8	H	Portsmouth	L	0-1	0-0		6623
21	12	A	Reading	W	1-0	0-0	Hughes	4648
22	15	H	Exeter C	L	1-5	0-1	Westwood	3725
23	29	A	Burnley	L	2-3	0-2	White, Nicholl	5767
24	Dec 6	H	Charlton Ath	L	0-1	0-1		8775
25	20	A	Chester	W	2-1	1-1	Crabbe, Price	1740
26	26	H	Millwall	L	1-2	0-1	Weatherly	4603
27	27	A	Colchester U	L	1-2	1-1	Price	3879
28	Jan 3	H	Rotherham U	D	0-0	0-0		3748
29	17	A	Sheffield U	W	1-0	0-0	Ford (pen)	8778
30	24	H	Chesterfield	W	1-0	0-0	Bruce	5122
31	31	A	Barnsley	D	3-3	2-1	White, Lee, Price	13,703
32	Feb 7	H	Carlisle U	L	0-1	0-0		4927
33	14	A	Newport Co	D	1-1	1-1	Lee	5152
34	21	A	Oxford U	D	1-1	0-1	Lee	3641
35	28	H	Plymouth Arg	L	0-1	0-1		4396
36	Mar 7	H	Blackpool	W	3-1	1-1	White 2, Price	3424
37	14	A	Fulham	L	2-3	1-1	Price, Ford	5445
38	21	H	Brentford	W	2-0	0-0	Overton, White (pen)	3916
39	28	A	Hull C	D	2-2	2-1	Lee 2	3309
40	Apr 3	H	Walsall	W	1-0	1-0	Price	4112
41	7	H	Burnley	D	0-0	0-0		4362
42	11	A	Portsmouth	D	0-0	0-0		9172
43	18	H	Colchester U	D	0-0	0-0		4408
44	20	A	Millwall	D	0-0	0-0		4214
45	25	H	Chester	W	2-1	2-0	Bruce, Raynor (og)	3228
46	May 2	A	Charlton Ath	L	1-2	1-1	Lee	9367

Final League Position: 15

Goalscorers

League (48): Price 11, Lee 6, Westwood 6, White 5 (1 pen), Bruce 4, Ford 3 (1 pen), Henderson 3, Hughes 2, Nicholl 2, Crabbe 1, Overton 1, Richardson 1, Weatherly 1, own goals 2.
League Cup (5): Bruce 3, Ford, Price.
F.A. Cup (2): Ford, Price.

League Cup	First Round	Colchester U (a)	2-0
		(h)	2-1
	Second Round	Blackburn R (a)	0-0
		(h)	1-2
FA Cup	First Round	Dagenham (h)	2-1
	Second Round	Maidstone (h)	0-0
		(a)	0-0 (aet)
		(h)	0-2

Hillyard	Sharpe	Ford	Overton	Weatherly	Crabbe	Duncan	Dunn	Price	Henderson	Bruce	Walker	Richardson	Adams	White	Westwood	Hughes	Nicholl	Lloyd	Bottiglieri	Sutton	Lee	Young	*Match No.*
1	2	3	4	5	6	7	8*	9	10	11	12												1
1	2	3	4	5	6	8			10	7		9	11										2
1	2	3	4	5	6	8*			10	7	12	9	11										3
1	2	3	4		6	8			10	5		11*		7	9	12							4
1	2	3	4	5		8		9*	10	7	12		11			6							5
1	2	3	4	5		8		9	10	7			11*		12	6							6
1	2*	3	4	5		8		9	12	7		10	11			6							7
1		3	4	5		8	11*	9		7	2				10	6			12				8
1		3	4	5	6	8		9		7	2	12			10*	11							9
1		3	4	5	6	8		9		7	2	10				11							10
1	2	3	4	5	6	8				7	12	9			10*	11							11
1	2	3	4	5				9		7	11			6		10	8						12
1		3		5	6			9		4	2			7	10	11	8						13
1	2	3		5	6			9		4				7	10	11	8						14
1	2	3	5		6			9		4				7	10	11	8						15
1	2	3		5	6			9		4				7	10	11	8						16
1	2	3		5	6			9		4				7	10	11	8						17
1	2	3	4	5	6			9						7	10	11	8						18
1	2	3	4	5	6			9						7	10	11	8						19
1	2	3	4	5	6			9						7	10	11	8						20
1	2	3		5	6			9		4				7	10	11	8						21
1	2	3		5		6		9		4				7	10	11	8*	12					22
1	2	3	4	5	6	8		9						11		12	7		10*				23
1	2	3	4	5	6			9						11	10		7		8				24
1	2	3	4	5*	6			9		12				11	10	8	7						25
1	2	3	4	5	6			9		8		12	11				7		10*				26
	2	3		5	6	8		9		4		10		11			7			1			27
		3		5	6					4	2	9		11	10	8	7			1			28
	2	3		5	6	8		9		4				11			7			1	10		29
1		3		5	6	8		9		4	2*	12		11			7				10		30
1		3		5	6	8		9		4	2			11			7				10		31
		3		5	6	8		9		4*	2	11	12				7			1	10		32
		3		5	6	8		10		4	2			9			7			1	11		33
		3		5	6	8		9		4	2			11			7			1	10		34
		3		5		8		9		4	2	12	11	6			7*			1	10		35
		3		5	6	8		9		4	2			11			7			1	10		36
		3*		5	6	8		9		4	2		12	11			7			1	10		37
1			3	5	6	8		9		4	2			11			7				10		38
1			3	5	6	8		9		4	2*			11		12	7				10		39
1	2	3		5	6	8		9		4				11			7				10		40
1			3	5	6	8		9		4				11			7				10	2	41
1		3	5		6	8		9		4				11			7				10	2	42
1			3*	5	6	8		9		4			12	11			7				10	2	43
1		3		5		8		9		4	2		6	11			7				10		44
1		3		5		8		9		4	2		6	11			7				10		45
1	2	3		5		8		9		4	7		6	11							10		46
37	26	42	25	43	36	32	2	41	6	40	19	9	10	34	17	20	34	—	3	9	18	3	
									+ 1s	+ 1s	+ 4s	+ 4s	+ 3s		+ 1s	+ 3s		+ 1s	+ 1s				

GILLINGHAM

	Ht	Wt	Birthplace	Clubs	League App.	League Gls
Goalkeepers						
Ron Hillyard	5 11	11 4	Rotherham	York C	61	—
				Hartlepool (on loan)	23	—
				Bury (on loan)	—	—
				Brighton (on loan)	—	—
				Gillingham	288	—
Steve Wheatley	5 10½	11 0	Durham	Gillingham	4	—
(Contract cancelled June 1980)						
Gary Sutton	5 10½	11 0	Folkestone	Gillingham	9	—
Defenders						
Charles Young	6 1	11 12	Nicosia	Aston V	10	—
				Gillingham	26	1
Mickey Barker	5 11	11 6	Newcastle	Newcastle U	23	—
(Contract cancelled Jan 1981)				Gillingham	64	2
John Sharpe	5 11	11 5	Portsmouth	Southampton	21	—
				Gillingham	99	1
Andy Ford	5 11	12 0	Minehead	Bournemouth	—	—
				Southend U	138	3
				Swindon T	98	—
				Gillingham	42	3
Mark Weatherly	6 0	11 12	Ramsgate	Gillingham	198	14
Midfield						
Billy Hughes*	5 10	10 8	Folkestone	Gillingham	126	8
Terry Nicholl*	5 9½	10 12	Wilmslow	Crewe Alex	46	7
				Sheffield U	22	1
				Southend U	50	3
				Gillingham	184	11
John Overton	5 11	10 10	Rotherham	Aston V	3	—
				Halifax T (on loan)	14	2
				Gillingham	178	10
John Crabbe*	5 8	10 6	Weymouth	Southampton	12	—
				Gillingham	181	12
Steve Bruce	6 0	11 2	Durham	Gillingham	81	9
Nigel Donn	5 10	10 8	Maidstone	Gillingham	2	—
Steve Dudley*	5 9	10 12	Ramsgate	Gillingham	—	—
Colin Duncan	5 10½	11 0	Plymouth	Oxford U	189	6
				Gillingham	51	1
Trevor Lee	5 11	11 7	London	Millwall	108	23
				Colchester U	96	35
				Gillingham	18	6
Forwards						
Damien Richardson*	6 0	12 0	Dublin	Shamrock R	(not known)	
(Eire)				Gillingham	323	91
Danny Westwood	5 10½	11 5	Dagenham	QPR	1	1
				Gillingham	208	73
Terry Jolley	5 11	10 6	London	Gillingham	21	5
(Contract cancelled Sept 1980)						
Ken Price	5 10½	11 3	Dudley	Southend U	1	—
				Gillingham	196	66
Pat Walker	5 9½	11 2	Dublin	Gillingham	51	3
Dean White	5 10	11 4	Hastings	Chelsea	—	—
				Gillingham	70	11
Mick Adams	5 6	10 4	Sheffield	Gillingham	17	—
Tony Bottiglieri	5 9½	10 4	Gillingham	Gillingham	5	—
Kevin Lloyd*			Wolverhampton	Cardiff C	1	—
				Gillingham	1	—
Peter Henderson	6 0	12 4	Berwick on Tweed	Witton A	(not known)	
				Chester	64	10
				Gillingham	7	3
David Young	5 10½	11 0	Rochester	Gillingham	—	—

GRIMSBY TOWN Division 2

Chairman: R. K. Middleton.

Vice-Chairman: M. McGarry.

Directors: T. J. Lindley, T. Wilkinson, T. W. Bygott, D. B. Ramsden, W. R. Ramsden, M. Skipwith, P. Sheffield.

Manager: George Kerr. *Secretary:* D. J. Dowse.

Year Formed: 1878. *Turned Professional:* 1890.

Limited Company: 1890. *Previous Name:* Grimsby Pelham.

Previous Grounds: Clee Park; Abbey Park.

Football League Record:
1892 Original Member Division 2; 1901–03 Division 1; 1903 Division 2; 1910 Failed Re-election; 1911 Re-elected Division 2; 1920–21 Division 3; 1921–26 Division 3(N); 1926–29 Division 2; 1929–32 Division 1; 1932–34 Division 2; 1934–48 Division 1; 1948–51 Division 2; 1951–56 Division 3(N); 1956–59 Division 2; 1959–62 Division 3; 1962–64 Division 2; 1964–68 Division 3; 1968–72 Division 4; 1972–77 Division 3; 1977–79 Division 4; 1979–80 Division 3; 1980– Division 2.

Honours: *Football League:* Division 1 best season: 5th, 1934–35; Division 2 – Champions 1900–01, 1933–34; Runners-up 1928–29; Division 3(N) – Champions 1925–26, 1955–56; Runners-up 1951–52; Division 3 – Champions 1979–80; Runners-up 1961–62; Division 4 – Champions 1971–72; Runners-up 1978–79. *FA Cup:* Semi-finals, 1936, 1939. *Football League Cup* best season: 5th rd, 1979–80.

Record Victory: 9-2 v Darwen, Division 2, 15 Apr, 1899.

Record Defeat: 1-9 v Arsenal, Division 1, 28 Jan, 1931.

Most League Points: 68, Division 3(N), 1955–56.

Most League Goals: 103, Division 2, 1933–34.

Highest League Scorer in Season: Pat Glover, 42, Division 2, 1933–34.

Most League Goals in Total Aggregate: Pat Glover, 182, 1930–39.

Most Capped Player: Pat Glover, 7, Wales.

Most League Appearances: Keith Jobling, 448, 1953–69.

Record Transfer Fee Received: £75,000 from Aston Villa for Terry Donovan, July 1979.

Record Transfer Fee Paid: £80,000 to Vancouver Whitecaps for Trevor Whymark, Dec 1980.

Previous Managers since the War: Charlie Spencer, Bill Shankly, Billy Walsh, Allenby Chilton, Tim Ward, Tom Johnston, Jimmy McGuigan, Don McEvoy, Bill Harvey, Bobby Kennedy, Lawrie McMenemy, Ron Ashman, Tommy Casey, John Newman.

Address of Supporters Club: Souvenir Shop, Blundell Park, Cleethorpes.

Blundell Park, Cleethorpes, South Humberside DN35 7PY. Telephone Cleethorpes 61420 and 61803. *Telegraphic address:* 'Football Grimsby'. *Ground capacity:* 21,500. *Record attendance:* 31,657 v Wolverhampton W, FA Cup 5th rd, 20 Feb, 1937. *Record receipts:* £29,228, v Wolverhampton W, FL Cup 5th rd, 4 Dec, 1979. *Pitch measurements:* 111yd×74yd.

How to get there: Buses 3A, 3F, 9 run to the ground; also football specials from the town centre. Nearest railway stations are Cleethorpes and Grimsby Town.
Match tickets: Seating can be booked two weeks in advance.
Car parking: Parking permitted in all side streets around the ground.
Entertainments/catering facilities: A licensed bar and several snack bars.
Club shop: There are 5 club shops, around the ground, selling all types of souvenir.
Handbooks/programmes: Programmes on sale at matches, and souvenir shops.
Extra information: Grimsby have played in all six divisions of the Football League – First, Second, Third, Third South, Third North and Fourth.
Club Colours: Black and white striped shirts, black shorts, white stockings.
Change Colours: Red shirts, red shorts and red stockings.
Club Captain: Joe Waters.
Coach: David Booth.
Club Nickname: The Mariners.

GRIMSBY TOWN 1980–81 LEAGUE RECORD

Match No.	Date	Venue	Opponents	Result	H/T Score	Goalscorers	Attendance
1	Aug 16	A	Shrewsbury T	D 1-1	1-1	Drinkell	4998
2	19	H	Preston NE	D 0-0	0-0		10,461
3	23	H	Wrexham	W 1-0	1-0	Ford	9175
4	30	A	Bristol R	D 2-2	1-2	Cumming 2	4461
5	Sept 6	A	Orient	L 0-2	0-1		4506
6	13	H	Derby Co	L 0-1	0-1		15,052
7	20	A	Blackburn R	L 0-2	0-2		10,338
8	27	H	Luton T	D 0-0	0-0		9044
9	Oct 4	H	Bristol C	W 1-0	0-0	Drinkell	8781
10	7	A	Notts Co	D 0-0	0-0		8017
11	11	A	Chelsea	L 0-3	0-2		16,206
12	18	H	Watford	D 1-1	1-0	Moore	8906
13	21	H	Sheffield W	D 0-0	0-0		10,298
14	24	A	Swansea C	L 0-1	0-0		12,928
15	Nov 1	H	QPR	D 0-0	0-0		10,015
16	8	A	West Ham U	L 1-2	0-1	Stone	25,468
17	15	H	Shrewsbury T	W 1-0	0-0	Cumming	8737
18	22	A	Bolton W	D 1-1	0-0	Stone	9031
19	29	H	Cambridge U	W 3-1	2-0	Waters, Brolly, Cumming	7592
20	Dec 2	A	Preston NE	W 4-2	2-1	Cumming, Ford, Brolly 2	5289
21	6	A	Cardiff C	D 1-1	1-0	Waters (pen)	6063
22	13	H	Chelsea	W 2-0	2-0	Whymark, Ford	14,708
23	20	A	Watford	L 1-3	0-2	Kilmore	10,209
24	26	H	Newcastle U	D 0-0	0-0		17,623
25	27	A	Oldham Ath	W 2-1	1-1	Waters, Ford	7183
26	Jan 10	H	Bolton W	W 4-0	1-0	Cumming, Drinkell 2, Waters	9320
27	17	H	Bristol R	W 2-0	1-0	Cumming, Drinkell	9601
28	31	A	Wrexham	W 2-0	1-0	Cumming 2	5619
29	Feb 7	A	Derby Co	L 1-2	0-1	Waters (pen)	19,691
30	14	H	Orient	W 2-0	0-0	Waters 2 (2 pens)	10,190
31	21	A	Luton T	W 2-0	1-0	Cumming, Waters	9217
32	28	H	Blackburn R	D 0-0	0-0		12,210
33	Mar 10	A	Bristol C	D 1-1	1-0	Cumming	5881
34	14	H	Notts Co	W 2-1	0-1	Whymark, Brolly	12,184
35	28	H	Swansea C	W 1-0	0-0	Whymark	12,166
36	Apr 4	A	QPR	L 0-1	0-1		8906
37	11	H	West Ham U	L 1-5	0-1	Waters (pen)	17,924
38	18	H	Oldham Ath	D 0-0	0-0		10,634
39	20	A	Newcastle U	D 1-1	1-0	Drinkell	13,215
40	25	H	Cardiff C	L 0-1	0-1		7377
41	28	A	Sheffield W	W 2-1	2-0	Drinkell, Kilmore	16,747
42	May 2	A	Cambridge U	L 1-5	0-3	Waters (pen)	4528

Final League Position: 7

Goalscorers

League (44): Cumming 11, Waters 10 (6 pens), Drinkell 7, Brolly 4, Ford 4, Whymark 3, Kilmore 2, Stone 2, Moore 1.
League Cup (1): Waters.
F.A. Cup (0).

League Cup	First Round	Notts Co (h)	1-0
		(a)	0-3
FA Cup	Third Round	WBA (a)	0-3

Batch	Stone	Moore K	Waters	Wigginton	Crombie	Brolly	Ford	Drinkell	Mitchell	Cumming	Liddell	Kilmore	Czuczman	Crosby	Steeples	Whymark	Moore D	Beacock	*Match No.*
1	2	3	4	5	6	7	8	9	10	11									1
1	2	3	4	5	6	7	8	9	10	11									2
1	2	3	4	5	6	7	8		10	11	9*	12							3
1	2	3	4	5	6	7	8	9	10	11									4
1	2	3	4	5	6	7	8*	9	10	11	12								5
1	2	3	4	5	6	7		9	10	11	12	8*							6
1	2	3	4	5	6	7*	12	9	10	11	8								7
1		6	4	5			7	9	10	11	8		2	3					8
1		6	4	5		12	7	9	10	11		8*	2	3					9
1		6	4	5		12	7	9	10	11		8*	2	3					10
1		6	4	5		12	7	9	10	11*		8	2	3					11
1	2	6	4	5		12	7*	9	10	11		8		3					12
1	2	6	4	5		7	8	9	10	11				3					13
1	2	6	4	5		7	8	9	10	11				3					14
1	2	6	4	5		7*	8	9	10	11		12		3					15
1	2	6	4	5		7		9	10		11*	8		3	12				16
1	2	6	4	5	3	7	8*	9	10	11		12							17
1	2	6	4	5	3	7*	8	9	10	11		12							18
1	2	6	4	5	3	7	8*	9	10	11		12							19
1	2	6	4	5	3	7	8	9	10	11*		12							20
1	2	6	4	5	3	7	11	9	10			12				8*			21
1		6	4	5	3	7	11	9	10			12				8*	2		22
1		6	4	5	3	7	11*	9	10			12				8	2		23
1	2	6	4		3	7	11*	9	10	12			5			8			24
1	2		4		6	7*	8	9	10	11			5	3		12			25
1	2	6	4	5	3	7	8	9	10	11*	12								26
1	2	6	4	5	3	7*	8	9	10	11						12			27
1	2	6	4	5	3	7		9	10	11						8			28
1	2	6	4	5	3	7*		9	10	11		12				8			29
1	2	6	4	5	3	7		9	10	11						8			30
1	2	6	4	5	3	7		9*	10	11		12				8			31
1		6	4	5	3	7		9	10	11						8	2		32
1		6	4	5	3	7		9	10	11						8	2		33
1	2	6	4	5	3	7		9	10			11*			12	8			34
1	2	6	4	5	3	7		9	10			12			11*	8			35
1	2	6	4	5	3	7*		9	10	11		12				8			36
1	2	6	4	5	3*	7	12	9	10	11						8			37
1	2	6	4	5	3	7	12	9	10						11*	8			38
1	2	6	4	5	3	11	7	9*	10			12				8			39
1	2	6	4	5	3			9	10	11		12			7*	8			40
1	2	6	4	5	3	11		9*	10			7				8		12	41
1		6	4	5	3	11		9	10			7*				8	2	12	42
42	33	41	42	40	33	36	25	41	42	31	4	9	6	10	3	19	5	—	
						+ 4s	+ 3s			+ 1s	+ 3s	+ 15s			+ 2s	+ 2s		+ 2s	

GRIMSBY TOWN

	Ht	*Wt*	*Birthplace*	*Clubs*	*League App.*	*League Gls*
Goalkeepers						
Harry Wainman*	6 0	13 6	Hull	Grimsby T	420	—
				Rochdale (on loan)	9	—
Nigel Batch	5 10	12 5	Huddersfield	Grimsby T	152	—
Len Robinson	5 10	12 0	Bridlington	Brigg T	(not known)	
				Grimsby T	—	—
Defenders						
Kevin Moore	5 11	11 7	Grimsby	Grimsby T	198	11
David Moore	5 10	12 13	Grimsby	Grimsby T	64	—
Shaun Mawer	5 7	10 8	Ulceby	Grimsby T	60	1
(Contract cancelled April 1981)						
Clive Wigginton	6 0	12 1	Sheffield	Grimsby T	171	6
				Scunthorpe U	88	7
				Lincoln C	60	6
				Grimsby T	102	1
Dean Crombie	5 11	11 7	Lincoln	Lincoln C	33	—
				Grimsby T	118	1
John Stone	6 0	12 5	Saltburn, Yorks	Middlesbrough	2	—
				York C	86	5
				Darlington	120	14
				Grimsby T	61	2
Phil Crosby			Leeds	Grimsby T	14	—
Graham Cawthorne	6 2	13 12	Doncaster	Grimsby T	1	—
Mike Czuczman	6 1	12 8	Carlisle	Preston NE	—	—
				Grimsby T	114	6
				Scunthorpe U	116	1
				Stockport Co	36	7
				San Jose E	(not known)	
				Grimsby T	6	—
Jimmy Fell	5 10	12 0	Newcastle	Grimsby T	—	—
Midfield						
Bob Cumming	5 8	11 4	Airdrie	Grimsby T	211	39
Joe Waters	5 5	10 5	Limerick	Leicester C	13	1
(Eire)				Grimsby T	244	43
Bob Mitchell	5 10	11 0	S Shields	Sunderland	3	—
				Blackburn R	29	6
				Grimsby T	112	4
Andy O'Dell	5 8	10 8	Hull	Grimsby T	—	—
Forwards						
Tony Ford	5 9	12 2	Grimsby	Grimsby T	164	26
Mike Brolly	5 9	10 4	Kilmarnock	Chelsea	8	1
				Bristol C	30	2
				Grimsby T	216	24
Gary Liddell	5 9½	11 2	Bannockburn	Leeds U	3	—
(Contract cancelled Feb 1981)				Grimsby T	105	24
Kevin Drinkell	5 10	11 10	Grimsby	Grimsby T	132	37
Peter Wainwright	6 0	12 0	Brigg, Lincs	Grimsby T	—	—
(Contract cancelled March 1981)						
Kevin Kilmore	5 9	11 10	Scunthorpe	Scunthorpe U	102	28
				Grimsby T	54	17
Garry Beacock	5 10	11 10	Scunthorpe	Grimsby T	2	—
John Steeples	5 10	11 13	Doncaster	Grimsby T	5	—
Trevor Whymark	6 0	11 0	Norfolk	Ipswich T	260	74
(England)				Vancouver W	(not known)	
				Sparta Rotterdam	(not known)	
				Derby Co	2	—
				Grimsby T	21	3

HALIFAX TOWN Division 4

Chairman: S. J. Rorke. *Vice-Chairman:* J. S. Crowther.
Directors: D. Sharp, M INST BM, P. Dawson, A. Hodgson, J. Robinson.
Manager: Mickey Bullock.
Secretary: Mrs Carol Bell.
Commercial Manager: Tony Thwaites.
Year Formed: 1911. *Turned Professional:* 1911.
Limited Company: 1911.
Previous Grounds: Sandhall and Exley.

Football League Record:
1921 Original Member; Division 3(N); 1958–63 Division 3; 1963–69 Division 4; 1969–76 Division 3; 1976– Division 4.

Honours: *Football League:* Division 3 best season: 3rd, 1970–71; Division 3(N) – Runners-up 1934–35; Division 4 – Runners-up 1968–69. *FA Cup* best season: 5th rd, 1932–33, 1952–53. *Football League Cup* best season: 4th rd, 1964.
Record Victory: 7-0 v Bishop Auckland, FA Cup 2nd rd replay, 10 Jan, 1967.
Record Defeat: 0-13 v Stockport Co, Division 3(N), 6 Jan, 1934.
Most League Points: 57, Division 4, 1968–69.
Most League Goals: 83, Division 3(N), 1957–58.
Highest League Scorer in Season: Albert Valentine, 34, Division 3(N), 1934–35.
Most League Goals in Total Aggregate: Ernest Dixon, 129, 1922–30.
Most Capped Player: None.
Most League Appearances: John Pickering, 367, 1965–74.
Record Transfer Fee Received: £55,000 from Huddersfield T for Mick Kennedy, Aug 1980.
Record Transfer Fee Paid: £25,000 to Huddersfield T for Kevin Johnson, Aug 1978.
Previous Managers since the War: Jack Breedon, W. Wootton, Jimmy Thomson, Gerald Henry, Bobby Browne, Willie Watson, Billy Burnicle, Harry Hooper, Willie Watson, Vic Metcalfe, Alan Ball (Snr), George Kirby, Ray Henderson, George Mulhall, John Quinn, Alan Ball (Snr), Jimmy Lawson, George Kirby.
Address of Supporters Club: Same as Football Club.
Address of the Club Shop or Boutique: Club Shop, 11 Horton Street, Halifax, Yorks.

Shay Ground, Halifax HX1 2YS. Telephone Halifax 53423. *Ground capacity:* 16,500. *Record attendance:* 36,885 v Tottenham H, FA Cup 5th rd, 14 Feb, 1953. *Record receipts:* £14,000 v Manchester C, FA Cup 3rd rd, 4 Jan, 1980. *Pitch measurements:* 110yd×70yd.
How to get there: Near the town centre within a few minutes walking distance of the bus station and railway station.
Match tickets: Advance booking on application to the secretary.
Car parking: Car park is available; entrance in Shaw Hill.
Entertainments/catering facilities: High-class restaurant and social club adjacent to club office.
Club shop: Shop on ground and also in town centre. Programmes, souvenirs, etc (wide range always available) from the Promotions Office, 11 Horton Street, Halifax. P & p must always accompany requests.
Handbooks/programmes: Handbooks and programmes available from Supporters Club, c/o Halifax Town AFC.
Extra information: In 1929, Halifax played a goalkeeper, Bob Suter, who was 47 years old.
Club Colours: Royal blue shirts with white trim, collar and cuffs, white shorts, blue trim, blue stockings with white tops.
Change Colours: Yellow and blue vertical stripes.
Team Captain: Dave Evans.
Club Nickname: The Shaymen.

HALIFAX TOWN 1980–81 LEAGUE RECORD

Match No.	Date	Venue	Opponents	Result		H/T Score	Goalscorers	Attendance
1	Aug 16	H	Mansfield T	L	0-2	0-0		1682
2	20	A	Peterborough U	D	2-2	0-0	Ward, Firth	3885
3	23	H	Bury	W	4-2	3-1	Firth 2, Dunleavy, Allatt	1861
4	29	A	Stockport Co	D	1-1	0-0	Firth	2487
5	Sept 6	A	Lincoln C	L	0-3	0-0		3720
6	13	H	Scunthorpe U	W	1-0	1-0	Firth	1226
7	16	H	Wigan Ath	L	0-1	0-0		2052
8	20	A	Crewe Alex	L	1-2	1-1	Nattress	2102
9	27	H	Wimbledon	L	0-1	0-0		1407
10	Oct 1	A	Wigan Ath	L	1-4	0-2	Firth	4247
11	4	A	Torquay U	L	0-1	0-0		1849
12	7	H	York C	W	3-1	1-0	Nattress, Hendrie, O'Neil	1088
13	11	H	Southend U	L	1-5	0-2	O'Neil	1609
14	18	A	Doncaster R	D	0-0	0-0		4044
15	20	A	Tranmere R	L	0-2	0-0		2314
16	25	H	Hereford U	D	0-0	0-0		1288
17	28	H	Bradford C	W	2-0	1-0	Graham, Hendrie	2365
18	31	A	Northampton T	L	1-2	1-1	McIlwraith (pen)	2226
19	Nov 4	A	York C	D	1-1	0-0	Evans	1837
20	8	H	Hartlepool U	L	1-2	0-1	Goodman	1692
21	11	H	Peterborough U	L	2-3	1-2	McIlwraith (pen), Nattress	1151
22	15	A	Mansfield T	W	1-0	0-0	McIlwraith (pen)	2561
23	29	H	AFC Bournemouth	L	1-2	0-1	Bullock	987
24	Dec 6	A	Aldershot	L	1-2	0-1	Burton	2335
25	20	H	Port Vale	D	2-2	2-2	Dunleavy, Nattress	1215
26	26	A	Rochdale	D	1-1	0-1	Nattress	2623
27	27	H	Darlington	L	1-2	0-2	Graham	1805
28	Jan 10	H	Tranmere R	D	1-1	1-0	Graham	1268
29	17	A	AFC Bournemouth	L	1-2	0-2	Firth (pen)	2413
30	24	H	Stockport Co	W	2-0	1-0	Allatt, Graham	3286
31	31	A	Bury	D	0-0	0-0		3144
32	Feb 7	A	Scunthorpe U	D	2-2	1-2	Ayre, Hendrie	2073
33	11	A	Bradford C	D	0-0	0-0		3056
34	14	H	Lincoln C	L	1-3	0-1	Firth (pen)	4444
35	21	A	Wimbledon	L	0-3	0-2		2501
36	Mar 7	H	Torquay U	W	2-1	1-0	Graham 2	2008
37	13	A	Southend U	L	1-5	0-2	Graham	5542
38	21	H	Doncaster R	L	0-3	0-2		3762
39	24	H	Crewe Alex	W	1-0	1-0	McIlwraith (pen)	2266
40	28	A	Hereford U	W	1-0	0-0	Allatt	2588
41	Apr 4	H	Northampton T	L	0-1	0-1		1996
42	11	A	Hartlepool U	L	0-3	0-2		1576
43	18	A	Darlington	L	1-3	0-3	McIlwraith (pen)	2015
44	20	H	Rochdale	W	2-0	0-0	Graham 2	2278
45	26	A	Port Vale	D	0-0	0-0		2301
46	May 2	H	Aldershot	W	1-0	1-0	Chambers	1587

Final League Position: 23

Goalscorers

League (44): Graham 9, Firth 8 (2 pens), McIlwraith 5 (5 pens), Nattress 5, Allatt 3, Hendrie 3, Dunleavy 2, O'Neil 2, Ayre 1, Bullock 1, Burton 1, Chambers 1, Evans 1, Goodman 1, Ward 1.
League Cup (2): Evans, Firth.
F.A. Cup (1): Firth.

League Cup	First Round	Bury (a)	2-2
		(h)	0-1
FA Cup	First Round	Hull C (a)	1-2

Kilner	Nattress	Dunleavy	Evans	Harris	Goodman	Firth	Hendrie	Allatt	Ward	O'Neil	Stafford	Burton	Johnson	Whiteley	Graham	McIlwraith	Bullock	Ayre	Flavell	Turner	Chambers	*Match No.*
1	2	3	4	5*	6	7	8	9	10	11	12											1
1	2	3	4	5	6	7	8	9	10	11												2
1	2*	3	4	5	6	7	8	9	10	11		12										3
1	2	3	4	5	6	7	8	9	10	11												4
1	2	3	4	5	6	7	8	9		11		10										5
1	2	6	4	5		7	8	9	10	11		3										6
1	2	6	4	5		7	8	9	10	11		3										7
1	2	6	4*	5		7	8	9	10	11	12	3										8
1	2	6		5		7	8	9	4	11		3	10									9
1	2	6		5	12	7	8	9	4	11		3	10*									10
1	2	6		5	10	7	8	9	4*		11	3		12								11
1	2		4	5		7	6	8		10		3			9	11						12
1	2		4	5		7	6	8		10		3	12		9	11*						13
1	2	3	4		5	7	6		12	10	11				8	9*						14
1	2	3	4		5	7	6		11*	10				12	8	9						15
1	2*	3	4	5	6	7	9			11				12	8	10						16
1		2	4	5	3	7	6			10			9*	12	8	11						17
1	9	2	4		5*	7	6			11		3		12	8	10						18
1		2	4	5	3	7*	6			10	11			12	8	9						19
1		2*	4	5	3		6			10	11		7	12	8	9						20
1	2		4	5	3*		6		12	10			7		8	9	11					21
1	2		4		5		6		7		11	3			8	9	10					22
1	2		4		5	7			11*	6		3	12		8	9	10					23
1		10	4		5	7				2	11*	3		6	8	9	12					24
1	8	6	4		5	7		10		2		3	12			9	11*					25
1	8*		4		5	7	6	10		2		3			12	9	11					26
1	8		4		5	7			6	2		3	12		10	9*	11					27
1					4	7	6		2			3			8	9	11	5	10			28
1	10			12	4	7	6		2			3			8	9*	11	5				29
	11		4		10	7	6	9	3	2					8			5		1		30
	11		4		10	7	6	9	3	2					8			5		1		31
	11		4		10	7	6	9	3	2					8			5		1		32
	11		4		10	7	6	9	3	2					8			5		1		33
	11		4		10	7	6	9	3	2					8			5		1		34
1	11		4		12	7	6	9*	2			3			8	10		5				35
1	10			4		7	6		2			3			8	11		5			9	36
1	10			4		7	6		2			3			8	11		5			9	37
1	11		2	12		7	6	10	3	4*					8			5			9	38
1	11		4	3		7		9	2						8	10		5			6	39
1	10		4	3		7		9	2						8	11		5			6	40
1	10		4	3		7		9	2						8	11		5			6	41
1	10		4	3*		7		9	2			8			12	11		5			6	42
1			4			7		9	2			3		10	8	11		5			6	43
1			4			7		9	2			3		10	8	11		5			6	44
1			4	3		7		9	2			8		6	10	11		5				45
1			4			7		9	2			3		10	8	11		5			6	46
41	37	20	39	25	27	43	34	30	33	31	6	26	5	5	32	29	8	19	1	5	10	
				+ 2s	+ 2s				+ 2s		+ 2s	+ 1s	+ 4s	+ 7s	+ 2s		+ 1s					

HALIFAX TOWN

	Ht	*Wt*	*Birthplace*	*Clubs*	*League App.*	*League Gls*
Goalkeepers						
John Kilner	6 0	11 7	Bolton	Preston NE	—	—
				Halifax T	102	—
Defenders						
Bill Ayre	5 10	12 0	Crookhills	Scarborough	(not known)	
				Hartlepool U	141	27
				Halifax T	19	1
Chris Dunleavy	5 10	11 6	Liverpool	Everton	—	—
(Contract cancelled Jan 1981)				Southport	147	9
				Chester	76	—
				Halifax T	181	13
Malcolm Goodman	6 0	12 0	Bromsgrove	Halifax T	51	1
David Harris*	6 2	12 4	Stoke	Port Vale	176	8
				Halifax T	71	3
David Evans	5 10	12 1	West Bromwich	Aston V	2	—
				Halifax T	84	4
Clive Nattress	6 0	12 4½	Durham	Blackpool	—	—
				Darlington	302	15
				Halifax T	37	5
Ken Burton	5 7½	11 8	Sheffield	Sheffield W	56	2
				Peterborough U (on loan)	4	—
				Chesterfield	237	6
				Halifax T	27	1
Bobby Flavell	5 7	9 10	Berwick	Burnley	—	—
(Non-contract)				Halifax T	91	7
				Chesterfield	29	2
				Barnsley	25	—
				Halifax T	1	—
Midfield						
Franny Firth	5 10	11 0	Dewsbury	Huddersfield T	27	4
				Halifax T	131	18
Paul Hendrie	5 6	9 8	Glasgow	Birmingham C	23	1
				Bristol R	30	1
				Halifax T	68	6
Steve Ward	6 0	12 5	Derby	Brighton	—	—
				Northampton T	15	2
				Halifax T	35	1
Tom O'Neil	5 6½	10 4	St Helens	Manchester U	53	—
				Blackpool (on loan)	7	—
				Southport	197	16
				Tranmere R	74	10
				Halifax T	31	2
Brian Chambers*	5 9½	11 3	Newcastle	Sunderland	63	5
				Arsenal	1	—
				Luton T	76	9
				Millwall	59	9
				Bournemouth	42	7
				Halifax T	10	1
Forwards						
Andy Stafford*	6 2	11 12	Littleborough	Halifax T	41	1
Andrew Whiteley	5 10	11 0	Halifax	Halifax T	21	1
Carl Dryhurst*	5 11	12 8	Sutton	Halifax T	8	—
Vernon Allatt	5 11	11 8	Hednesford	Halifax T	46	3
Simon Bullock	5 11	11 9	Stoke	Stoke C	—	—
				Halifax T	9	1
Tommy Graham	5 9	10 10	Glasgow	Aston V	—	—
				Barnsley	38	13
				Halifax T	34	9
Jimmy McIlwraith	5 8	10 4	Troon	Motherwell	28	2
				Bury	89	21
				Portsmouth	19	—
				Bury	29	3
				Halifax T	29	5

HARTLEPOOL UNITED — Division 4

President: S. Spaldin.

Chairman: J. V. Barker.

Vice-Chairman: B. H. Crosby.

Directors: B. Maxwell, S. I. Levinson.

Manager: Billy Horner. *Secretary:* W. P. Hillan.

Year Formed: 1908. *Turned Professional:* 1908.

Limited Company: 1908.

Previous Names: Hartlepools United until 1968; Hartlepool until 1977.

Football League Record:
1921 Original Member of Division 3(N); 1958–68 Division 4; 1968–69 Division 3; 1969– Division 4.

Honours: *Football League:* Division 3 best season: 22nd, 1968–69; Division 3(N) – Runners-up 1956–57. *FA Cup* best season: 4th rd, 1954–55, 1977–78. *Football League Cup* best season: 4th rd, 1974–75.

Record Victory: 10-1 v Barrow, Division 4, 4 Apr, 1959.

Record Defeat: 1-10 v Wrexham, Division 4, 3 Mar, 1962.

Most League Points: 60, Division 4, 1967–68.

Most League Goals: 90, Division 3(N), 1956–57.

Highest League Scorer in Season: William Robinson, 28, Division 3(N), 1927–28.

Most League Goals in Total Aggregate: Ken Johnson, 98, 1949–64.

Most Capped Player: Ambrose Fogarty, 1 (11), Eire.

Most League Appearances: Wattie Moore, 448, 1948–64.

Record Transfer Fee Received: £60,000 from Brighton for Malcolm Poskett, Feb 1978.

Record Transfer Fee Paid: £10,000 to Sunderland for Ambrose Fogarty, Nov 1963.

Previous Managers since the War: Fred Westgarth, Ray Middleton, Bill Robinson, Allenby Chilton, Bob Gurney, Alvan Williams, Geoff Twentyman, Brian Clough, Angus McLean, John Simpson, Len Ashurst, Ken Hale.

Club Shop: On ground.

The Victoria Ground, 18 Scarborough Street, Hartlepool Telephone Hartlepool 72584; (Office) 73492. *Ground capacity:* 18,000. *Record attendance:* 17,426 v Manchester U, FA Cup 3rd rd, 5 Jan, 1957. *Record receipts:* £17,000 v Leeds U, FA Cup 3rd rd, 18 Jan, 1979. *Pitch measurements:* 113yd×77yd.

How to get there: Hartlepool railway station is only a few hundred yards from the ground. Local bus services run scheduled services to Hartlepool.

Match tickets: No pre-booking of tickets.

Car parking: Ample side-street parking.

Entertainments/catering facilities: Two refreshment kiosks inside the ground.

Club shop: Open on match days; stocks all types of souvenirs.

Handbooks/programmes: No handbooks. Programmes available on subscription.

Extra information: Just three years after finishing second in Division 3(N) in 1956–57, the club conceded a Fourth Division record 109 goals.

Club Colours: Blue shirts, white shorts, blue stockings.

Change Colours: All red with white stripe on shirt and emblem, red shorts and stockings.

Club Nickname: The Pool.

HARTLEPOOL UNITED 1980–81 LEAGUE RECORD

Match No.	Date	Venue	Opponents	Result		H/T Score	Goalscorers	Attendance
1	Aug 16	A	Wigan Ath	W	3-0	0-0	Forster 2, Houchen	5233
2	19	H	Bury	L	1-2	0-0	Forster	3643
3	23	A	Rochdale	D	1-1	0-1	Brown	2803
4	30	H	Doncaster R	W	1-0	0-0	Bird	2110
5	Sept 6	H	Northampton T	L	2-3	1-1	Hogan, Forster	2410
6	13	A	York C	W	1-0	1-0	Houchen	2504
7	16	A	AFC Bournemouth	L	0-1	0-1		2413
8	20	H	Hereford U	W	2-0	1-0	Houchen, Ayre	2320
9	26	A	Southend U	L	0-4	0-2		5112
10	30	H	AFC Bournemouth	W	1-0	1-0	Lawrence	2405
11	Oct 4	H	Aldershot	W	1-0	1-0	Linacre	2844
12	7	A	Scunthorpe U	D	3-3	2-0	Newton 2, Houchen	2900
13	11	A	Wimbledon	L	0-5	0-3		1971
14	18	H	Lincoln C	W	2-0	1-0	Bird, Newton	2689
15	21	H	Mansfield T	L	0-1	0-1		3369
16	25	A	Port Vale	D	1-1	0-1	Kerr	3072
17	27	A	Stockport Co	W	2-0	1-0	Newton, Houchen	2066
18	Nov 1	H	Crewe Alex	W	6-2	5-1	Kerr, Houchen 2, Newton 2, Hampton	3089
19	4	H	Scunthorpe U	W	2-0	2-0	Sweeney, Hampton	4357
20	8	A	Halifax T	W	2-1	1-0	Kilner (og), Hogan	1692
21	11	A	Bury	D	0-0	0-0		2301
22	15	H	Wigan Ath	W	3-1	1-0	Hogan, Houchen 2	5020
23	29	H	Torquay U	L	0-2	0-0		3408
24	Dec 5	A	Tranmere R	D	2-2	1-1	Houchen, Hamilton (og)	1366
25	20	H	Peterborough U	D	1-1	1-0	Hampton	3100
26	26	A	Darlington	L	0-3	0-2		7152
27	27	H	Bradford C	D	2-2	1-2	Hampton, Hogan	3670
28	Jan 10	H	Port Vale	W	3-0	1-0	Newton 2 (1 pen), Hogan	3058
29	17	A	Torquay U	L	1-2	1-1	Newton	1745
30	24	A	Doncaster R	W	2-1	0-0	Hogan, Hampton	6814
31	31	H	Rochdale	D	2-2	1-0	Houchen 2 (1 pen)	3819
32	Feb 7	H	York C	W	1-0	0-0	Bird	3119
33	14	A	Northampton T	L	1-3	0-2	Hampton	2032
34	21	H	Southend U	L	1-3	0-2	Bird	3751
35	28	A	Hereford U	L	0-3	0-2		2313
36	Mar 7	A	Aldershot	L	1-2	0-2	Houchen	2252
37	14	H	Wimbledon	L	2-3	0-2	Houchen, Newton	2329
38	16	A	Mansfield T	W	1-0	1-0	Harding	3737
39	21	A	Lincoln C	L	0-2	0-0		3856
40	28	H	Stockport Co	W	1-0	0-0	Harding	1928
41	Apr 3	A	Crewe Alex	L	0-2	0-0		2419
42	11	H	Halifax T	W	3-0	2-0	Hogan, Houchen, Lawrence	1576
43	17	H	Darlington	W	2-0	0-0	Howard, Linacre J.	5531
44	19	A	Bradford C	L	0-2	0-2		1614
45	25	A	Peterborough U	D	1-1	1-0	Lawrence	3560
46	May 2	H	Tranmere R	W	3-0	1-0	Houchen 2 (1 pen), Sweeney	1802

Final League Position: 9

Goalscorers

League (64): Houchen 17 (2 pens), Newton 10 (1 pen), Hogan 7, Hampton 6, Bird 4, Forster 4, Lawrence 3, Harding 2, Kerr 2, Linacre 2, Sweeney 2, Ayre 1, Brown 1, Howard 1, own goals 2.
League Cup (1): Forster.
F.A. Cup (1): Hampton.

League Cup	First Round	York C (a)	1-2
		(h)	0-0
FA Cup	First Round	Scunthorpe U (a)	1-3

Burleigh	Brown	Sweeney	Hogan	Bird	Fagan	Linacre J	Kerr	Houchen	Forster	Hampton	Ayre	Lawrence	Richardson	Harding	Newton	Linacre P	Johnson	Normanton	Granycombe	Stimpson	Linighan	Howard	Staff	*Match No.*
1	2	3	4	5	6	7	8	9	10	11														1
1	2	3	4	5		7	8	9	10*	11	6	12												2
	3		4	5	2	7	8		10	11*	6	12	1	9										3
	3		4	5	2	7	8	12	9*		6	11	1	10										4
	3		4	5	2	7	8	12	10		6	9	1	11*										5
	3	2	4	5	6*		8	9	10	12		7	1	11										6
	3	2	4	5			7	10	12		6	8*	1	11	9									7
	3	2	4	5			8	10	12		6	7	1	11	9*									8
	3	2	4	5			7	10	12		6	8	1	11*	9									9
	3	2	4	5			7	10	11		6	8	1		9									10
	3	2	4	5		6	7	10	11			8	1		9									11
	3	2	4	5		6	7	10	11*	12		8	1		9									12
	3	2	4	5		6	7	10	11			8	1		9									13
1	3	2	4	5		6	7	10		11		8			9									14
1	3	2	4*	5		6	7	10	12	11		8			9									15
1	3	2	4	5		6	7	10		11		8			9									16
1	3	2	4	5		6	7	10		11		8			9									17
1	3	2	4	5		6	7	10		11		8			9									18
1	3	2	4	5		6	7	10		11		8			9									19
1	3	2	4	5		6	7	10		11		8			9									20
1	3	2	4	5		6	7	10		11		8			9									21
1	3	2	4	5		6	7	10		11		8			9									22
1	3	2	4	5		6	7	10		11		8		12	9*									23
1	3	2	4	5		6	7	10		11		8			9									24
1	3	2	4		5	6	7	10		11		8				9								25
1	3		4	5		6	7	10		11	2	8		9										26
1	3		4	5	12	6*	7	10		11	2	8			9									27
	3		4	5	2	6	7	10		11*		8	1		9		12							28
	3		4	5	2	6	7*	10		11		8	1		9		12							29
	3	8	4	5	6	2	7	12		11			1		9		10*							30
	3	8	4	5	6	2	7	9		11		12	1				10*							31
	3	8	4	5	6	2	7	9		11		12	1				10*							32
	3	8	4*	5	6	2	7	9		11		10	1				12							33
	3	2	4	5			7	9		11		8	1				12	6	10*					34
	2	3	4	5			7	10		12		8*	1		9		11	6						35
	6	3		5	8	2	7	10					1	4	9		11							36
	6	3	12	5	8	2	7	10					1	4*	9		11							37
	6		11	5	8	2	7	10				3	1	4*	9		12							38
	6		4	5	8	2	7	10				3	1	11	9									39
	6			5		2	7	10		12		4	1	11			9*			3	8			40
	6			5		2	7	10		12		4	1	11			9*			3	8			41
	6		11	5		2	7	10				4	1							3	8	9*	12	42
	6		11	5		2	7	10				4	1							3	8	9		43
	6	3	11	5	8	2	7	10		9*		4	1				12							44
	6	3	11*	5		2	7	10		12		4	1								8		9	45
	6	3	11	5		2	7	10				4	1								8	12	9*	46
16	46	33	42	45	17	39	46	42	10	25	10	38	30	14	27	1	8	2	1	4	6	2	2	
			+ 1s		+ 1s			+ 3s	+ 4s	+ 6s		+ 4s		+ 1s			+ 6s					+ 1s	+ 1s	

HARTLEPOOL UNITED

	Ht	Wt	Birthplace	Clubs	League App.	League Gls
Goalkeepers						
Graham Richardson	5 10	11 4	Sedgefield	Hartlepool U	89	—
John Watson	6 1	13 1	Huddersfield	Huddersfield T	—	—
				Hartlepool U	20	—
Martin Burleigh	5 11	12 10	Newcastle	Newcastle U	11	—
				Darlington	30	—
				Carlisle U	26	—
				Darlington	71	—
				Hartlepool U	48	—
Trevor Ramshaw	5 11	12 2	Durham	Hartlepool U	—	—
Defenders						
George Smith*	5 8	10 12	Newcastle	Barrow	92	11
				Portsmouth	64	3
				Middlesbrough	74	—
				Birmingham C	39	—
				Cardiff C	45	1
				Swansea C	88	8
				Hartlepool U	85	2
Steve Brookes	6 0	11 8	Southport	Southport	65	3
(Transferred to Barrow Aug 1980)				Hartlepool U	63	2
Graham Normanton*	5 10	11 10	Hartlepool	Hartlepool U	18	—
Edward Leighton	6 0	11 4	Hartlepool	Hartlepool U	—	—
Michael Fagan	5 11	12 0	Newcastle	Carlisle U	—	—
				Hartlepool U	25	—
Alan Sweeney	5 7	11 10	Glasgow	Huddersfield T	66	1
				Hartlepool U	65	2
John Bird	6 1	13 0	Doncaster	Doncaster R	50	3
				Preston NE	166	9
				Newcastle U	87	5
				Hartlepool U	45	4
Andy Linighan	6 6	12 6	Hartlepool	Smiths BC	(not known)	
				Hartlepool U	6	—
Barrie Stimpson (Apprentice)			Billingham	Hartlepool U	4	—
Phillip Brown	5 11	11 6	Hartlepool	Hartlepool U	56	1
Neil Black	5 11	11 0	Blaydon	Hartlepool U	—	—
Midfield						
Roy Hogan	5 8	10 6	Hartlepool	Hartlepool U	77	8
Derek Loadwick	5 7	12 0	Middlesbrough	Leeds U	—	—
				Stockport Co	84	—
				Hartlepool U	51	1
Ken Lowe	5 10	11 4	Hartlepool	Hartlepool U	—	—
David Norton			Gateshead	Hartlepool U	17	1
(Contract cancelled Aug 1980)						
Bobby Kerr	5 4½	9 3	Alexandria	Sunderland	368	57
				Blackpool	22	2
				Hartlepool U	46	2
Philip Linacre	6 0	11 0	Middlesbrough	Coventry C	—	—
				Hartlepool U	1	—
Harry Clarke	5 10	11 7	Sunderland	Middlesbrough	—	—
				Hartlepool U	—	—
Neal Granycombe			Middlesbrough	South Bank	(not known)	
(Non-contract)				Hartlepool U	1	—
Mark Lawrence	6 0	11 2	Middlesbrough	Hartlepool U	126	18
John Linacre	5 9	11 10	Middlesbrough	Hartlepool U	154	9
Forwards						
Keith Houchen	6 2	11 4	Middlesbrough	Hartlepool U	138	47
Bob Newton	5 11	12 6	Chesterfield	Huddersfield T	42	7
(Contract cancelled March 1981)				York C (on loan)	—	—
				Hartlepool U	113	33
Alan Harding	5 9	11 4	Sunderland	Darlington	129	38
				Lincoln C	209	38
				Hartlepool U	70	6
David Evans	5 10	11 10	Sunderland	Hartlepool U	4	—
(Contract cancelled Oct 1980)						
Derek Hampton	5 10	11 4	Middlesbrough	Whitby	(not known)	
				Hartlepool U	57	13
Paul Staff	5 9	10 12	Hartlepool	Hartlepool U	9	—
Kevin Johnson	5 9	10 12	Doncaster	Sheffield W	1	—
				Southend U	17	1
				Gillingham (on loan)	1	—
				Workington	15	1
				Hartlepool U	61	9
				Huddersfield T	81	23
				Halifax T	57	10
				Hartlepool U	14	—
Geoff Forster			Middlesbrough	Rochdale	1	—
(Contract cancelled March 1981)				Whitley Bay	(not known)	
				Hartlepool U	14	4
David Howard			Hartlepool	Newcastle U	—	—
(Non-contract)				Hartlepool U	3	1
Gerry McNamee	5 11	11 4	Consett	Hartlepool U	3	1

Also retained: Mike Spelman.

HEREFORD UNITED Division 4

Chairman: P. S. Hill FRICS.

Vice-Chairman: M. B. Roberts.

Directors: D. Vaughan, R. Tidball JP, A. J. Phillips, G. Rivers, J. E. Jackson, G. C. E. Hales.

Manager: Frank Lord. *Secretary:* P. J. Grange.

Chief Executive: Charles Harrold.

Year Formed: 1924. *Turned Professional:* 1924.

Limited Company: 1939.

Ground: Edgar Street Athletic Ground.

Football League Record:
1972 Elected to Division 4; 1973–76 Division 3; 1976–77 Division 2; 1977–78 Division 3; 1978– Division 4.

Honours: *Football League:* Division 3 – Champions 1975–76; Division 4 – Runners-up 1972–73. *FA Cup* best season: 4th rd, 1971–72, 1976–77. *Football League Cup* best season: 3rd rd, 1974–75.

Record Victory: 11-0 v Thynnes (FA Cup), Sept 1947.

Record Defeat: 0-5 v Wrexham, 22 Dec, 1973; 1-6 v Tranmere R, 29 Nov, 1975; 1-6 v Wolverhampton W, 2 Oct, 1976.

Most League Points: 63, Division 3, 1975–76.

Most League Goals: 86, Division 3, 1975–76.

Highest League Scorer in Season: Dixie McNeil, 35, 1975–76.

Most League Goals in Total Aggregate: Dixie McNeil, 85, 1974–77.

Most Capped Player: Brian Evans, 1 (7) Wales.

Most League Appearances: Tommy Hughes, 222, 1973–80.

Record Transfer Fee Received: £100,000 from Derby Co for Steve Emery, Sept 1979.

Record Transfer Fee Paid: £25,000 to Aston Villa for David Cunningham, Aug 1979.

Previous Managers since the War: George Tranter, Alex Massie, Joe Wade, Ray Daniel, Bob Dennison, John Charles, Colin Addison, John Sillett, Tony Ford, Mike Bailey.

Address of Supporters Club: Edgar Street, Hereford.

Address of the Club Shop or Boutique: Edgar Street, Hereford.

Edgar Street, Hereford. Telephone Hereford (0432) 4037. *Ground capacity:* 17,500. *Record attendance:* 18,114 v Sheffield W, FA Cup 3rd rd, 4 Jan, 1958. *Record receipts:* £12,666 v Bristol C, FA Cup 4th rd, 26 Jan, 1974. *Pitch measurements:* 111yd×80yd.

How to get there: Ground very close to town centre, within five minutes walking distance from Hereford railway station and the bus station.

Match tickets: Tickets can be booked in advance.

Car parking: Parking is available around the ground for approximately 1,000 vehicles.

Entertainments/catering facilities: Canteens on the ground. A social club next to ground.

Club shop: All types of souvenirs sold.

Handbooks/programmes: Programmes available on application to the club shop.

Extra information: As a non-League Club, Hereford reached the first round proper of the FA Cup for 21 consecutive seasons.

Club Colours: White shirts with red and black trim, black shorts, white with red and black top stockings.

Change Colours: Red shirts, white and black trim, white shorts, red stockings, white and black trim.

Club Trainer: Peter Isaac. *Club Nickname:* United.

HEREFORD UNITED 1980–81 LEAGUE RECORD

Match No.	Date	Venue	Opponents	Result	H/T Score	Goalscorers	Attendance
1	Aug 16	H	Tranmere R	D 1-1	0-1	Harvey	3034
2	19	A	AFC Bournemouth	L 0-1	0-1		2991
3	23	A	Mansfield T	L 0-4	0-1		3103
4	30	H	York C	D 1-1	0-0	Jones G.	2757
5	Sept 6	A	Doncaster R	L 1-5	0-3	White	2186
6	13	H	Southend U	D 0-0	0-0		2464
7	17	H	Rochdale	W 3-0	1-0	Jones G., Price, Hicks	2475
8	20	A	Hartlepool U	L 0-2	0-1		2320
9	27	H	Northampton T	W 4-1	1-1	White (pen), Jones G., Price, Bartley	2693
10	30	A	Rochdale	D 0-0	0-0		2328
11	Oct 4	H	Darlington	L 0-1	0-1		2934
12	7	A	Crewe Alex	L 0-5	0-1		3033
13	10	A	Stockport Co	D 0-0	0-0		2303
14	18	H	Wimbledon	D 1-1	1-0	Jones G.	2369
15	22	H	Port Vale	L 2-3	0-1	Dobson 2	2101
16	25	A	Halifax T	D 0-0	0-0		1288
17	28	A	Bury	L 1-2	1-1	Hunt	2268
18	Nov 1	H	Lincoln C	L 0-2	0-0		2755
19	5	H	Crewe Alex	D 0-0	0-0		1476
20	8	A	Scunthorpe U	L 1-3	1-0	Phillips	1539
21	12	H	AFC Bournemouth	W 1-0	0-0	Bartley	1640
22	29	H	Wigan Ath	D 1-1	1-1	Bartley	2358
23	Dec 6	A	Peterborough U	L 0-3	0-0		3281
24	20	H	Bradford C	W 4-0	2-0	McGrellis 3, Showers	2114
25	26	A	Aldershot	L 0-4	0-1		3094
26	27	H	Torquay U	L 0-1	0-1		3412
27	Jan 10	H	Bury	L 0-1	0-1		2382
28	24	A	York C	W 2-1	2-1	Showers, McGrellis	1924
29	31	H	Mansfield T	W 2-1	2-0	Showers, White (pen)	2672
30	Feb 6	A	Southend U	L 0-2	0-1		5229
31	11	A	Wigan Ath	L 0-1	0-0		3370
32	14	H	Doncaster R	L 1-3	1-1	White	2806
33	28	H	Hartlepool U	W 3-0	2-0	Laidlaw, White (pen), McGrellis	2313
34	Mar 8	A	Darlington	L 1-2	1-1	McGrellis	3491
35	16	A	Port Vale	L 0-4	0-1		2379
36	22	A	Wimbledon	D 0-0	0-0		3898
37	28	H	Halifax T	L 0-1	0-0		2588
38	Apr 4	A	Lincoln C	L 0-1	0-0		3655
39	11	H	Scunthorpe U	W 2-1	2-1	McGrellis, Cornes	2009
40	14	A	Northampton T	D 0-0	0-0		1380
41	18	A	Torquay U	W 1-0	0-0	McGrellis	1865
42	20	H	Aldershot	D 0-0	0-0		2946
43	29	A	Tranmere R	L 1-2	0-1	Bartley	1136
44	May 2	H	Peterborough U	D 1-1	1-0	McGrellis	2102
45	6	H	Stockport Co	W 2-0	1-0	Showers, Spiring	1707
46	15	A	Bradford C	W 1-0	1-0	McGrellis	1249

Final League Position: 22

Goalscorers

League (38): McGrellis 10, White 5 (3 pens), Bartley 4, Jones D. 4, Showers 4, Dobson 2, Price 2, Cornes 1, Harvey 1, Hicks 1, Hunt 1, Laidlaw 1, Phillips 1, Spiring 1.
League Cup (1): Bartley.
F.A. Cup (1): Jones G.

League Cup	First Round	Newport Co (h)	1-0
		(a)	0-5
FA Cup	First Round	Southend U (a)	1-0
	Second Round	Enfield (a)	0-2

Hugnes	Pejic	Musial	Spiring	Dobson	Price	Harvey	Bartley	McGrellis	Jones G	Lane	Binney	Cornes	Hunt	Overson	Lowe	White	Phillips	Brand	Thomas	Hicks	Morris	Ames	Strong	Laidlaw	Showers	Cashley	*Match No.*
1	2	3	4	5	6	7	8	9*	10	11	12																1
1	2	6	4	5	3	7	8		10	11	9*	12															2
1	2*	6	4		3	7	8		10	11	9	5	12														3
1		3	4	5	2*		8		10	11				12	6	7	9										4
		3	11	5			8		10*	12					6	7	9	1	2	4							5
		3	2	5			8		9	11					6	7		1		4	10						6
		3	2	5	7		8		10	11*					6	9		1		4	12						7
		3*	2	5	9	7	8		10	12					6	11		1		4							8
		3	2	5	9		8		10	7					6	11		1		4							9
		3	4*	5	2		10		9	11			12		8	7		1		6							10
		3	2	5	7		8		10	11*			12	4	6	9		1									11
		3	2	5	7		8		10				12		6*	9		1		4		11					12
			2	5	6		3		10	7						11		1		4		9	8				13
			2	5	6	12	3		10	7						11		1		4		9	8*				14
			2	5	6	7	3		10				12			11		1		4*		9	8				15
			2	5	9		3		10			4	6			11		1	7				8				16
			2	5	9		3		10			4	6			11		1	7				8				17
			2			6	3		10			4	7			9		1	11	5		12	8*				18
					2	6	11				12	5	7			10	8	1	3	4		9*					19
				9*	2	6	11		12			5	7			10	8	1	3	4							20
					2	6	8		10			5	7			11	9	1	3	4							21
			6		2	8*	11		10			5	7			9	12	1	3	4							22
			6		2		11		10			5	12			9*		1	3	4				7	8		23
		3	6		2		7	10				5				11		1		4				8	9		24
		3	6		2		7	10	12			5				11*		1		4				8	9		25
		3	6		2		7	10				5				11		1		4				8	9		26
		3	6		2		7	10*				5				11	12			4				8	9	1	27
			6		2	8	3	10				5				11				4				7	9	1	28
			6		2	7	3	10				5				11				4				8	9	1	29
			6		2	7	3	10				5				11				4				8	9	1	30
			11		2	6	3	9				5	12			10*				4				7	8	1	31
			6		2	7*	3	10	12			5				11				4				8	9	1	32
	2		6			7	3	10				5				11				4				8	9	1	33
			6		2	7	3	10				5				11				4				8	9	1	34
			6		2	7	3	10*	12			5				11				4				8	9	1	35
	3				2	7	6	10				5				11				4				8	9	1	36
	3		12		2	7	6	10*				5				11				4				8	9	1	37
	3		8		2	7	6	10				5	9	12		11*				4						1	38
	3		8		2	7	6	10				5	12			11	9*			4						1	39
	3		8		2	7	6	10				5				11				4					9	1	40
	3		8		2	7	6	10				5				11				4					9	1	41
	3		6		2	7		10				5				11				4				8	9	1	42
	3		6		2	7	8	10				5				11				4				12	9*	1	43
	3				2	7	6	10				5				11				4				8	9	1	44
			6		2	7	3	10				5				11				4				8	9	1	45
			6		2	7	3	10				5				11				4				8	9	1	46
4	13	16	40	17	42	29	45	24	21	11	2	32	8	1	9	43	6	22	9	39	1	5	6	19	22	20	
			+ 1s			+ 1s			+ 4s	+ 2s	+ 2s	+ 1s	+ 8s	+ 2s			+ 2s				+ 1s	+ 1s		+ 1s			

Players continued from following page.

Derek Showers (Wales)	5 11	11 4	Merthyr Tydfil	Cardiff C	83	10
				Bournemouth	60	19
				Portsmouth	39	8
				Hereford U	22	4
Trevor Ames	6 0	11 1	Poole	Aston V	—	—
				Hereford U	6	—

HEREFORD UNITED

	Ht	Wt	Birthplace	Clubs	League App.	League Gls
Goalkeepers						
Tommy Hughes	6 1	12 4	Dalmuir	Chelsea	11	—
				Aston V	16	—
				Brighton (on loan)	3	—
				Hereford U	226	—
Drew Brand	6 1	11 1	Edinburgh	Everton	2	—
				Crewe Alex (on loan)	15	—
				Hereford U	22	—
				Sheffield U (on loan)	—	—
Defenders						
John Layton	6 0	13 2	Hereford	Hereford U	200	13
(Contract cancelled Sept 1980)						
Phil Burrows	5 8	10 6	Stockton	Manchester C	—	—
(Contract cancelled Aug 1980)				York C	337	14
				Plymouth Arg	81	2
				Hereford U	110	2
				Gillingham (on loan)	5	—
Stuart Cornes	6 0	11 1	Usk	Hereford U	86	3
Chris Price	5 7	10 2	Hereford	Hereford U	128	2
Paul Hunt*	5 9	11 3	Hereford	Coventry C	—	—
				Hereford U	51	4
Valmore Thomas*	5 8	10 6	Worksop	Coventry C	—	—
				Hereford U	32	1
Steve Strong*	5 11	11 4	Bristol	Hereford U	16	—
Danny Bartley	5 8½	11 4½	Paulton	Bristol C	100	7
				Swansea C	199	8
				Hereford U	56	4
Richard Overson	5 11	12 2	Kettering	Burnley	6	—
				Hereford U	3	—
Ian Dobson	5 10	11 1	Hull	Hull C	92	7
				Hereford U	17	2
Mel Pejic	5 7½	10 6	Stoke	Stoke C	1	—
				Hereford U	13	—
Adam Musial	5 8	10 10	Poland	Arka Gydnia	(not known)	
(Poland)				Hereford U	16	—
Keith Hicks	6 0	13 2	Oldham	Oldham Ath	242	11
				Hereford U	39	1
Midfield						
Andy Feeley*	5 9		Hereford	Hereford U	51	3
				Chelsea (on loan)	—	—
Winston White	5 10½	10 12	Leicester	Leicester C	12	1
				Hereford U	92	10
Paul Gilchrist	5 11	11 6	Dartford	Charlton Ath	7	—
				Fulham (on loan)	—	—
				Doncaster R	22	8
				Southampton	107	17
				Portsmouth	39	3
				Swindon T	17	6
				Hereford U	11	1
Jimmy Harvey	5 9½	11 4	Lurgan	Glenavon	(not known)	
				Arsenal	3	—
				Hereford U	41	1
Gary Lowe	5 11	11 10	Manchester	Crystal Palace	—	—
				Manchester C	—	—
				Hereford U	9	—
Sean Lane			Bristol	Hereford U	13	—
Forwards						
Peter Spiring	5 8	11 0	Glastonbury	Bristol C	61	16
				Liverpool	—	—
				Luton T	15	2
				Hereford U	180	18
Stuart Phillips	6 0½	11 7	Halifax	Hereford U	28	3
David Jones*	6 2	14 0	Ruabon	Hereford U	47	11
Frank McGrellis	5 10	11 6	Falkirk	Coventry C	—	—
				Huddersfield T (on loan)	5	—
				Hereford U	76	23
Paul Morris	6 0	12 0	Llanelli	Hereford U	4	1
(Contract cancelled Nov 1980)						
Fred Binney*	5 10	11 7	Plymouth	Torquay U	12	1
				Exeter C (on loan)	17	11
				Torquay U	22	9
				Exeter C	160	79
				Brighton	70	35
				Plymouth Arg	71	39
				Hereford U	23	4
Ian Bray			Neath	Hereford U	—	—
Garry Jones*	5 9	10 2	Manchester	Bolton W	203	42
				Sheffield U (on loan)	3	1
				Blackpool	27	5
				Hereford U	25	4
Joe Laidlaw	5 8½	11 12	Wallsend	Middlesbrough	111	20
				Carlisle U	151	44
				Doncaster R	128	27
				Portsmouth	60	19
				Hereford U	20	1

Note: Players continued on previous page.

HUDDERSFIELD TOWN Division 3

Chairman: K. S. Longbottom.
Directors: S. Kinder OBE, J. Christie, K. C. Padley, C. Senior, M. Ryan, E. A. Lodge, C. Hodgkinson.
Manager: Mick Buxton.
Secretary: G. S. Binns.
Year Formed: 1908.
Turned Professional: 1908. *Limited Company:* 1908.

Football League Record:
1910 Elected to Division 2; 1920–52 Division 1; 1952–53 Division 2; 1953–56 Division 1; 1956–70 Division 2; 1970–72 Division 1; 1972–73 Division 2; 1973–75 Division 3; 1975–80 Division 4; 1980– Division 3.

© 1973

Honours: *Football League:* Division 1 – Champions 1923–24, 1924–25, 1925–26; Runners-up 1926-27, 1927–28, 1933–34; Division 2 – Champions 1969–70; Runners-up 1919–20, 1952–53; Division 4 – Champions 1979–80. *FA Cup:* Winners 1922; Runners-up 1920, 1928, 1930, 1938. *Football League Cup:* Semi-final, 1967–68.
Record Victory: 10-1 v Blackpool, Division 1, 13 Dec, 1930.
Record Defeat: 0-8 v Middlesbrough, Division 1, 30 Sept, 1950.
Most League Points: 66, Division 4, 1979–80.
Most League Goals: 101, Division 4, 1979–80.
Highest League Scorer in Season: Sam Taylor, 35, Division 2, 1919–20; George Brown, 35, Division 1, 1925–26.
Most League Goals in Total Aggregate: George Brown, 142, 1921–29.
Most Capped Player: Jimmy Nicholson, 31 (41), Northern Ireland.
Most League Appearances: Billy Smith, 520, 1914–34.
Record Transfer Fee Received: £100,000 from Leeds U for Trevor Cherry, June 1972.
Record Transfer Fee Paid: £110,000 to Mansfield T for Terry Austin, Dec 1980.
Previous Managers since the War: David Steele, George Stephenson, Andy Beattie, Bill Shankly, Eddie Boot, Tom Johnston, Ian Greaves, Bobby Collins, Tom Johnston.
Address of Supporters Club: Supporters Club Offices, 286 Leeds Road, Huddersfield, Yorkshire.
Address of the Club Shop or Boutique: The Terriers Souvenir Shop, 286 Leeds Road, Huddersfield.

Leeds Rd., Huddersfield HD1 6PE. Telephone Huddersfield 20335/6. *Ground capacity:* 48,000. *Record attendance:* 67,037 v Arsenal, FA Cup 6th rd, 27 Feb, 1932. *Record receipts:* £36,997 v Barnsley, Division 3, 7 Feb, 1981. *Pitch measurements:* 115yd×75yd.

How to get there: The ground is one mile from the town centre via Corporation buses 40, 41, 42. On match days special buses run from the centre. By road, the ground can be reached along Leeds Road either from the town centre or from Leeds.
Match tickets: Admission to all parts is by payment at the turnstiles except for special matches (Tel: Huddersfield 36100).
Car parking: Ample parking accommodation on all four sides of the ground; in the region of 6000 cars can be parked within 200 yards of the turnstiles.
Entertainments/catering facilities: Licensed Presidents Club – members only. 11 unlicensed snack bars around the ground.
Club shop: Close to the ground; sells all types of souvenirs (Tel: Huddersfield 31028). Open match days.
Handbooks/programmes: Programmes available on subscription from the club shop.
Extra information: In 1952–53 the club fielded an unchanged defensive line-up throughout the season.
Club Colours: Blue and white striped shirts, white shorts, white stockings.
Change Colours: All yellow.
Club Captain: David Sutton.
Coach: Jim Robson.
Physiotherapist/Coach: John Haselden.
Club Nickname: The Terriers.

HUDDERSFIELD TOWN 1980–81 LEAGUE RECORD

Match No.	Date	Venue	Opponents	Result	H/T Score	Goalscorers	Attendance
1	Aug 16	A	Chesterfield	L 1-2	0-1	Kindon	7819
2	19	H	Carlisle U	D 1-1	1-1	Robinson	7674
3	23	H	Blackpool	D 1-1	1-1	Laverick	9490
4	30	A	Rotherham U	D 0-0	0-0		6961
5	Sept 6	H	Reading	W 4-1	1-0	Death (og), Kennedy (pen), Laverick, Stanton	7312
6	13	A	Barnsley	L 0-1	0-0		13,819
7	16	A	Gillingham	D 0-0	0-0		5092
8	20	H	Sheffield U	W 1-0	1-0	Stanton	14,721
9	27	A	Swindon T	L 0-1	0-0		5856
10	30	H	Gillingham	W 1-0	1-0	Kindon	7716
11	Oct 4	H	Colchester U	W 2-0	0-0	Kindon (pen), Brown	8400
12	8	A	Oxford U	W 2-0	0-0	Robins, Cowling	3373
13	11	A	Exeter C	W 4-1	3-1	Kindon 3, Stanton	4769
14	18	H	Plymouth Arg	W 2-0	0-0	Robins, Kennedy	11,655
15	21	H	Burnley	D 0-0	0-0		15,741
16	25	A	Newport Co	L 2-3	1-2	Kindon 2 (1 pen)	6403
17	29	A	Chester	W 2-0	2-0	Kindon, Robins	4331
18	Nov 1	H	Charlton Ath	L 0-1	0-0		11,329
19	4	H	Oxford U	W 2-0	2-0	Kindon, Robins	7543
20	8	A	Millwall	L 1-2	0-0	Robins	3529
21	11	A	Carlisle U	D 1-1	0-1	Kindon	3998
22	15	H	Chesterfield	W 2-0	1-0	Kindon, Brown	12,828
23	29	H	Brentford	W 3-0	1-0	Robins, Kindon (pen), Stanton	8871
24	Dec 6	A	Fulham	D 2-2	0-1	Lillis, Stanton	4513
25	20	H	Portsmouth	D 0-0	0-0		10,869
26	26	A	Walsall	D 2-2	0-1	Austin 2	5906
27	27	H	Hull C	W 5-0	2-0	Stanton, Austin, Cowling, Lillis, Robins	13,240
28	Jan 10	H	Newport Co	W 4-1	2-1	Stanton 2, Austin, Cowling	9063
29	17	A	Brentford	D 0-0	0-0		5830
30	24	H	Rotherham U	W 1-0	0-0	Stanton	16,687
31	31	A	Blackpool	W 2-1	1-1	Austin 2	9431
32	Feb 7	H	Barnsley	W 1-0	1-0	Cowling	28,901
33	14	A	Reading	L 1-2	0-0	Lillis	5290
34	21	H	Swindon T	L 0-2	0-2		10,655
35	28	A	Sheffield U	D 2-2	0-1	Kindon 2	14,426
36	Mar 7	A	Colchester U	W 2-1	1-1	Robins, Lillis	3644
37	17	A	Plymouth Arg	D 0-0	0-0		5433
38	28	H	Chester	D 0-0	0-0		11,117
39	Apr 4	A	Charlton Ath	W 2-1	0-1	Brown, Kindon	8878
40	7	H	Exeter C	W 5-0	1-0	Hanvey, Lillis 2, Stanton 2	12,009
41	11	H	Millwall	L 0-1	0-0		13,353
42	14	A	Burnley	L 2-4	1-3	Kindon, Stanton	11,259
43	18	A	Hull C	L 1-2	0-0	Robins	6328
44	21	H	Walsall	D 1-1	1-0	Lillis	9463
45	25	A	Portsmouth	W 2-1	1-1	Austin 2	10,238
46	May 2	H	Fulham	W 4-2	2-1	Robins 2, Kindon, Sutton	6965

Final League Position: 4

Goalscorers

League (71): Kindon 18 (3 pens), Stanton 12, Robins 11, Austin 8, Lillis 7, Cowling 4, Brown 3, Kennedy 2 (1 pen), Laverick 2, Hanvey 1, Robinson 1, Sutton 1, own goal 1.
League Cup (1): Kindon.
F.A. Cup (10): Robins 4, Stanton 4, Hanvey, Laverick.

League Cup	First Round	Blackburn R (a)	0-0
		(h)	1-1
FA Cup	First Round	Northwich Vic (a)	1-1
		(h)	6-0
	Second Round	Tranmere R (a)	3-0
	Third Round	Shrewsbury T (h)	0-3

Rankin	Brown	Robinson	Stanton	Sutton	Hanvey	Laverick	Kindon	Purdie	Robins	Cowling	Kennedy	Davison	Lillis	Topping	Austin	Freeman	*Match No.*
1	2	3	4*	5	6	7	8	9	10	11	12						1
1	2	3	4	5	6	7	8		10	11	9						2
1	2	3	4	5	6	7	8*	12	10	11	9						3
1	2	3		5	6	7		8	10	11	9	4					4
1	2	3	4	5	6	7		9*	10	11	8		12				5
1	2	3	4	5	6	7			10	11	8		9				6
1	2	3	4	5	6	7			10	11	8		9				7
1	2	3	4	5	6	7	9		10	11	8						8
1	2	3	4	5*	6	7	9		10	11	8		12				9
1	2	3	4		6	7	9		10	11	8		5				10
1	2	3	4		6	7	9		10	11	8			5			11
1	2	3	4		6	7	9		10	11	8			5			12
1	2	3	4		6	7	9		10	11	8			5			13
1	2	3	4		6	7	9		10	11	8			5			14
1	2	3	4		6	7	9		10	11	8			5			15
1	2	3	4		6	7	9		10	11	8			5			16
1	2	3	4	5	6	7	9		10	11	8						17
1	2	3	4*	5	6	7	9		10	11	8		12				18
1	2	3	4	5	6	7	9*		10	11	8		12				19
1	2	3	4	5	6	7	9		10	11*	8		12				20
1	2	3	4	5	6	7*	9		10		8	12	11				21
1	2	3	4	5	6		9		10	11	8		7				22
1	2	3	4	5	6		9		10	11	8		7				23
1	2	3	4	5	6		9		10	11	8		7				24
1	2	3	4	5	6		9		10	11	8		7				25
1	2	3	4	5	6*		12		10	11	8		7		9		26
1	2	3	4*	5	6	8	10		12	11			7		9		27
	2	3	4	5			10			11	8		7	6	9	1	28
	2	3	4	5	6		10			11	8		7		9	1	29
	2	3	4	5	6		10			11	8		7		9	1	30
	2	3	4	5	6	11	10				8		7		9	1	31
	2	3	4	5	6		10			11	8		7		9	1	32
	2	3	4	5	6		10	8*	12	11			7		9	1	33
	2	3	4	5	6*	8	10		12	11			7		9	1	34
	2		4	5	6		12	3	10	11*	8		7		9	1	35
	2		4	5	6			3	10	11	8		7		9	1	36
	2	3	4	5	6				10	11	8		7		9	1	37
	2	3	4	5	6		12		10	11	8		7		9*	1	38
1	2	3	4	5	6		9		10	11	8		7				39
	2	3	4	5	6		9		10	11	8		7			1	40
	2	3	4	5	6		9		10	11	8		7			1	41
	2	3	4	5	6		9		10	11*	8		7		12	1	42
	2	3	4	5	6	8*	9		10	11			7		12	1	43
	2	3	4	5	6		10		12	11*	8		7		9	1	44
	2			5	6		9	3	10	11	4		7		8	1	45
	2		11	5	6		9	3	10		4		7		8	1	46
28	46	42	44	39	45	25	37	8	37	43	41	1	29	7	16	18	
							+ 3s	+ 1s	+ 4s		+ 1s	+ 1s	+ 5s		+ 2s		

HUDDERSFIELD TOWN

	Ht	*Wt*	*Birthplace*	*Clubs*	*League App.*	*League Gls*
Goalkeepers						
Richard Taylor	6 0½	12 9	Huddersfield	Huddersfield T	92	—
				Wolverhampton W (on loan)	—	—
				Sunderland (on loan)	—	—
				York C (on loan)	2	—
Alan Starling	6 1	13 4	Barking	Luton T	7	—
				Torquay U (on loan)	1	—
				Northampton T	238	1
				Huddersfield T	112	—
Andy Rankin	6 0	12 0	Bootle	Everton	85	—
				Watford	299	—
				Huddersfield T	52	—
Robert Picton	6 2	13 0	Barnsley	Huddersfield T	—	—
Defenders						
Malcolm Brown	6 2	13 0	Salford	Bury	11	—
				Huddersfield T	164	6
Chris Topping*	6 1	12 10	Bubwith	York C	412	11
				Huddersfield T	43	1
David Sutton	6 1	12 2	Tarleton	Plymouth Arg	61	—
				Reading (on loan)	9	—
				Huddersfield T	138	8
Keith Hanvey	6 0	12 7	Manchester	Manchester C	—	—
				Swansea C	11	—
				Rochdale	121	10
				Grimsby T	54	2
				Huddersfield T	110	5
Mark Lillis	6 0	12 2	Manchester	Huddersfield T	46	7
Fred Robinson	5 10	11 4	Rotherham	Doncaster R	119	3
				Huddersfield T	72	2
Stephen Vass*	5 10	12 2	Leicester	Hartlepool U	4	—
				Huddersfield T	—	—
Midfield						
Paul Gibson*	5 8	10 6	Huddersfield	Huddersfield T	—	—
David Cowling	5 7	10 6	Doncaster	Mansfield T	—	—
				Huddersfield T	109	15
Mickey Laverick	5 9	10 9	Trimdon	Mansfield T	89	13
				Southend U	110	18
				Huddersfield T	70	6
Brian Stanton	5 7	10 7	Liverpool	Bury	83	14
				Huddersfield T	85	21
Steve Johnston (Contract cancelled Aug 1980)				Huddersfield T	—	—
Micky Kennedy	5 10	10 6	Salford	Halifax T	76	4
				Huddersfield T	42	2
Peter Valentine	5 10	12 0	Huddersfield	Huddersfield T	—	—
Forwards						
Ian Robins	5 9	11 4	Bury	Oldham Ath	220	40
				Bury	49	5
				Huddersfield T	124	52
Peter Fletcher	6 1	12 0	Manchester	Manchester U	7	—
				Hull C	36	5
				Stockport Co	51	13
				Huddersfield T	73	30
Tommy Smith*	5 10	11 7	Wolverhampton	Sheffield U	3	1
				Huddersfield T	1	—
Bernard Purdie	5 9	11 0	Wrexham	Wrexham	10	3
				Chester	63	14
				Crewe Alex	213	44
				Huddersfield T	31	—
Steve Kindon	6 0	12 12	Warrington	Burnley	109	28
				Wolverhampton W	138	28
				Burnley	76	18
				Huddersfield T	63	32
Bobby Davison	5 9	11 7	South Shields	Seaham CW	(not known)	
				Huddersfield T	2	—
Paul Wormley (Contract cancelled)			Leeds	Barnsley	1	—
				Huddersfield T	—	—
Terry Austin	6 1	12 6	Isleworth	Crystal Palace	—	—
				Ipswich T	19	1
				Plymouth Arg	58	18
				Walsall	47	19
				Mansfield T	84	31
				Huddersfield T	18	8

HULL CITY — Division 4

Chairman: G. H. C. Needler BA, ACA.
Vice-Chairman: M. J. Kay DIP ARCH, JP.
Directors: P. J. Carver JP, C. A. Maxsted, J. Needler, G. Needler FRICS, JP, T. G. C. Thomas MA, ACA.

Team Manager: Mike Smith.
Assistant Manager/Coach: Cyril Lea.
Secretary: M. T. Stone.
General Manager (Development): G. H. Dimbleby.
Year Formed: 1904. *Turned Professional:* 1905.
Limited Company: 1905.
Previous Grounds: 1904, Boulevard Ground (Hull RFC); 1905, Anlaby Road (Hull CC); 1946, Boothferry Park.

Football League Record:
1905 Elected to Division 2; 1930–33 Division 3(N); 1933–36 Division 2; 1936–49 Division 3(N); 1949–56 Division 2; 1956–58 Division 3(N); 1958–59 Division 3; 1959–60 Division 2; 1960–66 Division 3; 1966–78 Division 2; 1978–81 Division 3; 1981– Division 4.

Honours: *Football League:* Division 2 best season: 3rd, 1909–10; Division 3(N) – Champions 1932–33, 1948–49; Division 3 – Champions 1965–66; Runners-up 1958–59. *FA Cup* best season: Semi-final, 1930. *Football League Cup* best season: 4th rd, 1973–74, 1975–76, 1977–78.

Record Victory: 11-1 v Carlisle U, Division 3(N), 14 Jan, 1939.
Record Defeat: 0-8 v Wolverhampton W, Division 2, 4 Nov, 1911.
Most League Points: 69, Division 3, 1965–66.
Most League Goals: 109, Division 3, 1965–66.
Highest League Scorer in Season: Bill McNaughton, 39, Division 3(N), 1932–33.
Most League Goals in Total Aggregate: Chris Chilton, 195, 1960–71.
Most Capped Player: Terry Neill, 15 (59), Northern Ireland.
Most League Appearances: Andy Davidson, 511, 1952–67.
Record Transfer Fee Received: £200,000 from Manchester U for Stuart Pearson, May 1974.
Record Transfer Fee Paid: £150,000 to Carlisle U for Mick Tait, Sept 1979.
Previous Managers since the War: Ernest Blackburn, Major Frank Buckley, Raich Carter, Bob Jackson, Bob Brocklebank, Cliff Britton, Terry Neill, John Kaye, Bobby Collins, Ken Houghton.
Club Shop: Club Shop, Boothferry Park, Hull. On match days, in main car park. Also in South Stand. Weekdays; articles may be purchased from the Development Association, 101 Boothferry Road, Hull. (0482) 51119.

Boothferry Park, Hull HU4 6EU. Telephone (0482) 52195. *Telegraphic address:* 'Tigers Hull'. *Ground capacity:* 42,000. *Record attendance:* 55,019 v Manchester U, FA Cup 6th rd, 26 Feb, 1949. *Record receipts:* £22,229 v Stoke City, FA Cup 6th rd, 6 March, 1971. *Pitch measurements:* 112yd×75yd.

How to get there: Buses 55, 57, 43, 48 from coach station, Ferensway, Hull. Nearest railway stations, Hull and Boothferry Park Halt. Special trains on match days from Hull Paragon to Boothferry Park Halt; admittance to ground through turnstiles on station. Ground situated on A63 to the west of the city.
Car parking: Official car park at ground for season passholders only. Public car park, Kempton Road park three minutes walk away; coach parking on Main Car Park.
Entertainments/catering facilities: Catering facilities at points around the ground.
Handbooks/programmes: Programmes available on subscription.
Extra information: The club's 31 wins in 1965–66 was a Third Division record.
Club Colours: Black and amber striped shirts, black shorts, black stockings.
Change Colours: All white.
Club Nickname: The Tigers.

HULL CITY 1980–81 LEAGUE RECORD

Match No.	Date	Venue	Opponents	Result	H/T Score	Goalscorers	Attendance
1	Aug 16	A	Millwall	D 1-1	1-0	Edwards	3831
2	19	H	Barnsley	L 1-2	0-2	McCarthy (og)	6978
3	23	H	Exeter C	D 3-3	0-1	Moss, Edwards, Deacy	3559
4	29	A	Fulham	D 0-0	0-0		4592
5	Sept 6	H	Walsall	L 0-1	0-0		4121
6	13	A	Blackpool	D 2-2	0-1	Haigh 2	6138
7	16	A	Burnley	L 0-2	0-0		4925
8	20	H	Portsmouth	W 2-1	1-1	Edwards, Swann	4613
9	27	A	Brentford	D 2-2	2-1	Edwards, Swann	6300
10	30	H	Burnley	D 0-0	0-0		5497
11	Oct 4	H	Oxford U	L 0-1	0-0		4211
12	8	A	Chester	L 1-4	0-2	Edwards	1964
13	11	A	Chesterfield	L 0-1	0-0		7126
14	18	H	Charlton Ath	L 0-2	0-1		3551
15	21	H	Carlisle U	L 0-1	0-0		3603
16	25	A	Gillingham	L 0-2	0-1		4100
17	28	A	Colchester U	L 0-2	0-1		2239
18	Nov 1	H	Plymouth Arg	W 1-0	1-0	Deacy	3367
19	4	H	Chester	D 0-0	0-0		3335
20	8	A	Newport Co	L 0-4	0-2		5495
21	11	A	Barnsley	L 0-5	0-2		11,628
22	15	H	Millwall	W 3-1	1-0	Edwards, Marwood, Roberts G.	3210
23	29	A	Swindon T	L 1-3	1-1	Marwood	5275
24	Dec 6	H	Reading	W 2-0	2-0	Edwards, Roberts G.	3130
25	20	A	Sheffield U	L 1-3	1-2	Edwards (pen)	10,720
26	26	H	Rotherham U	L 1-2	0-1	Edwards	8618
27	27	A	Huddersfield T	L 0-5	0-2		13,240
28	Jan 10	A	Charlton Ath	L 2-3	0-3	Roberts J., Edwards	6494
29	31	A	Exeter C	W 3-1	1-1	Marwood, McClaren, Mutrie	5022
30	Feb 7	H	Blackpool	W 2-1	0-0	Whitehurst, Edwards	5315
31	14	A	Walsall	D 1-1	0-0	Roberts G.	3914
32	21	H	Brentford	D 0-0	0-0		4535
33	28	A	Portsmouth	L 1-2	1-1	Mutrie	13,596
34	Mar 7	A	Oxford U	D 1-1	0-1	Roberts D.	2934
35	14	H	Chesterfield	D 0-0	0-0		5488
36	17	H	Colchester U	L 0-1	0-1		3586
37	21	A	Carlisle U	L 0-2	0-0		4098
38	28	H	Gillingham	D 2-2	1-2	Mutrie, Richards	3309
39	Apr 4	A	Plymouth Arg	D 0-0	0-0		4668
40	7	H	Fulham	L 0-1	0-0		3152
41	14	H	Swindon T	D 0-0	0-0		2789
42	18	H	Huddersfield T	W 2-1	0-0	Marwood, Deacy	6328
43	20	A	Rotherham U	D 1-1	0-0	Edwards	11,602
44	25	H	Sheffield U	D 1-1	1-1	Deacy	4895
45	May 2	A	Reading	L 0-2	0-1		3159
46	7	H	Newport Co	W 3-1	1-0	Mutrie 2, Edwards (pen)	2059

Final League Position: 24

Goalscorers

League (40): Edwards 13 (2 pens), Mutrie 5, Deacy 4, Marwood 4, Roberts G. 3, Haigh 2, Swann 2, McClaren 1, Moss 1, Richards 1, Roberts D. 1, Roberts J. 1, Whitehurst 1, own goal 1.
League Cup (0).
F.A. Cup (8): Edwards 4, Norrie 2, Croft, Deacy.

League Cup	First Round	Lincoln C (a)	0-5
		(h)	0-2
FA Cup	First Round	Halifax T (h)	2-1
	Second Round	Blyth Spartans (h)	1-1
		(a)	2-2 (aet)
			2-1 (aet, at Elland Road)
	Third Round	Doncaster R (h)	1-0
	Fourth Round	Tottenham H (a)	0-2

Norman	Nisbet	Horswill	Roberts J	Haigh	Booth	Norrie	Roberts G	Edwards	Moss	Deacy	Kilgallon	Swann	McClaren	Roberts D	McNeil	Croft	Kynman	Flounders	Richards	Marwood	Whitehurst	Hoolickin	Ferguson	Mutrie	Davies	Eccleston	*Match No.*
1	2	3	4	5	6	7	8	9	10	11																	1
1	2	3	5	6	4	7*	8	9	10	11	12																2
1	2	3	5	6	4	7	8*	9	10	11		12															3
1	2	3	5	6	4			9	10	11		8	7*	12													4
1	2	3	5	6	4			9	10	11		8		7													5
1	8	3	5	6	4			9	10	11*		7		12	2												6
1	7	3	5	11	4			9	10*	12		8		6	2												7
1	7	3	5	11	4			9	10			8		6	2												8
1	7	3	5	6	4			9	10	11		8			2												9
1	7	3*	5	6	4			9	10	11		8		12	2												10
1	2		4	11	6			9	10	7*					3	5	8	12									11
1	2		5	10	4			9	7	8					3*	6	11	12									12
1	2		5	3	4	12	7	9*		11								10	6	8							13
1	2		5	3	4	10			9*	11						6		8	12	7							14
1	2		5	3*	4			9	10	12		11						8	6	7							15
1	2		5	3	4	12				11		8					10*		6	7	9						16
1	2		5	3		12		9	8	11		4		6						7	10*						17
1	2		5	3				9	8	11		4		6						7	10						18
1	2		5					9	8	11*		4	12	6	3					7	10						19
1	2		5				4	12	8	11			9	6	3					7	10*						20
1	2		5		10		4	9		11			8*	6	3					7	12						21
1	2		5				4	9		11			10	6	3					7	8						22
1	2		5*		12	11	4	9					8	6	3					7	10						23
1	5						6	10		9			8	4		3				7	11	2					24
1			6				5	9		11*			8		3	4			12	7	10	2					25
1			6				5	9		11			8			4				7		2	3	10			26
1					7*	12	6	9		11			8			4			5			2	3	10			27
1			5					9		11			6						4	7	10	2	3	8			28
1					3		5	9		11			8	6					4	7		2		10			29
					3		5	10		9*			8	6					4	7	12	2		11	1		30
					3		5	9		11			8	6					4	7	12	2		10*	1		31
					3		5	9*		11			8	6					4	7	12	2		10	1		32
					3		5	9		11			8	6					4	7		2		10	1		33
1					3		5	9		11			8*	6					4	7		2	12	10			34
1*					3	12	5	9		11				6					4		7	2	8	10			35
1					3	12	5	9		11				6*					4		7	2	8	10			36
1					3	9				11			6						4	7*	12	2	8	10		5	37
1					3			9		11			8*						6	7	12	2	4	10		5	38
1					3					11		8							6	7	9	2	4	10		5	39
1					3					11*		12	8						4	7	10	2	6	9		5	40
1					3	12				11		8		5					4	7	9*	2	6	10			41
1					3			12		11		8*							4	7	9	2	6	10		5	42
1		6			3	10*		9		11		12							4	7	8	2				5	43
1		6			3			9		11									4	7	8	2		10		5	44
1					3			9				6							4	7	10	2	8	11		5	45
1		6			3			9				8			2				4	7	11			10		5	46
42	24	13	26	18	36	7	20	38	18	40	—	17	19	20	14	7	3	3	23	31	20	22	12	20	4	9	
					+ 1s	+ 7s		+ 2s		+ 2s	+ 1s	+ 3s	+ 1s	+ 3s				+ 2s	+ 2s		+ 6s		+ 1s				

HULL CITY

	Ht	Wt	Birthplace	Clubs	League App.	League Gls
Goalkeepers						
Tony Norman	6 1½	12 8	Mancot	Burnley	—	—
				Hull C	59	—
John Davies	6 3	13 2	Llandyssul	Cardiff C	7	—
				Hull C	4	—
Defenders						
John Roberts (Wales)	6 0	12 2	Swansea	Swansea C	37	16
				Northampton T	62	11
				Arsenal	59	4
				Birmingham C	66	1
				Wrexham	145	5
				Hull C	26	1
Robert McDonald	6 3	13 5	Hull	Hull C	25	2
(Contract cancelled Aug 1980)						
Dale Roberts	5 10½	11 5	Newcastle	Ipswich T	18	—
				Hull C	36	2
Steve Richards	6 0	12 0	Hull	Hull C	26	1
Ian Bennyworth*	6 0	12 4	Hull	Hull C	1	—
Bob McNeil	5 8½	10 9	Bellshill	Hull C	14	—
Steve Hoolickin	5 11	11 2	Manchester	Oldham Ath	8	—
				Bury	140	5
				Carlisle U	143	2
				Hull C	22	—
Stuart Eccleston	5 11	11 5	Stoke	Stoke C	—	—
				Hull C	9	—
Midfield						
Steve McClaren	5 7½	9 4	York	Hull C	21	1
Brian Marwood	5 7	9 13	Easington	Hull C	37	4
Mike Horswill*	5 10½	11 0	Annfield Plain	Sunderland	69	3
				Manchester C	14	—
				Plymouth Arg	102	3
				Hull C	66	6
Garreth Roberts	5 4	10 2	Hull	Hull C	83	8
Paul Moss	5 7	10 2	Birmingham	Wolverhampton W	—	—
				Hull C	54	7
Dennis Booth	5 7½	10 5	Stenley Common	Charlton Ath	77	5
				Blackpool	12	—
				Southend U	78	1
				Lincoln C	162	9
				Watford	100	2
				Hull	37	—
David Kynman	5 10	9 12	Hull	Hull C	3	—
Gary Swann	5 8¾	10 10	Hull	Hull C	20	2
Brian Ferguson	5 10	10 6	Irvine	Mansfield T	—	—
				Newcastle U	5	1
				Hull C	13	—
Forwards						
Keith Edwards	5 7	10 3	Stockton	Sheffield U	70	29
				Hull C	127	56
Craig Norrie	5 10½	10 11½	Hull	Hull C	30	4
Nick Deacy (Wales)	6 0½	12 7	Cardiff	Merthyr T	(not known)	
				Hereford U	17	2
				Workington (on loan)	5	2
				PSV Eindhoven	(not known)	
				Beringen	(not known)	
				Vitesse	(not known)	
				Hull C	57	5
Billy Whitehurst	6 0	13 0	Rotherham	Mexborough	(not known)	
				Hull C	26	1
Andy Smith*			London	Hull C	—	—
Les Mutrie	6 1	11 6	Newcastle	Gateshead	(not known)	
				Carlisle U	5	—
				Blyth S	(not known)	
				Hull C	20	5
Mark Kilgallon			Glasgow	Ipswich T	—	—
(Contract cancelled March 1981)				Hull C	1	—
Andy Flounders (Apprentice)			Hull	Hull C	5	—

IPSWICH TOWN — Division 1

President: Lady Blanche Cobbold.

Chairman: P. M. Cobbold.

Directors: W. Kerr, H. R. Smith, J. M. Sangster, K. H. Brightwell, J. C. Cobbold.

Manager: Bobby Robson.

Secretary: D. C. Rose.

PRO: Mel Henderson.

Year Formed: 1887. *Turned Professional:* 1936.

Limited Company: 1936.

Football League Record:
1938 Elected to Division 3(S); 1954–55 Division 2; 1955–57 Division 3(S); 1957–61 Division 2; 1961–64 Division 1; 1964–68 Division 2; 1968– Division 1.

Honours: *Football League:* Division 1 – Champions 1961–62; Runners-up 1980–81; Division 2 – Champions 1960–61, 1967–68; Division 3(S) – Champions 1953–54, 1956–57. *FA Cup:* Winners 1977–78. *Football League Cup* best season: 5th rd, 1966, 1974. **European Competitions:** *European Cup:* 1962–63. *European Cup-Winners' Cup:* 1978–79. *UEFA Cup:* 1973–74, 1974–75, 1975–76, 1977–78, 1979–80, 1980–81 (winners).

Record Victory: 10-0 v Floriana, Malta, European Cup 1st rd, 25 Sept, 1962.

Record Defeat: 1-10 v Fulham, Division 1, 26 Dec, 1963.

Most League Points: 64, Division 3(S), 1953–54, 1955–56.

Most League Goals: 106, Division 3(S), 1955–56.

Highest League Scorer in Season: Ted Phillips, 41, Division 3(S), 1956–57.

Most League Goals in Total Aggregate: Ray Crawford, 203, 1958–63, 1966–69.

Most Capped Player: Allan Hunter, 45 (51), Northern Ireland.

Most League Appearances: Mick Mills, 538, 1966–81.

Record Transfer Fee Received: £450,000 from Arsenal for Brian Talbot, Jan 1979.

Record Transfer Fee Paid: £250,000 to Millwall for Kevin O'Callaghan, Jan 1980.

Previous Managers since the War: A. Scott Duncan, Alf Ramsey, Jackie Milburn, Bill McGarry.

Address of Supporters Club: Same as Football Club.

Address of the Club Shop or Boutique: Same as Football Club.

Portman Road, Ipswich, Suffolk IP1 2DA. Telephone: Ipswich 219211 (4 lines). *Ground capacity:* 32,000. *Record attendance:* 38,010 v Leeds U, FA Cup 6th rd, 8 March, 1975. *Record receipts:* £105,950 v AZ 67 Alkmaar, UEFA Cup final 1st leg, 6 May, 1981. *Pitch measurements:* 112yd×72yd.

How to get there: The ground is central and only two minutes walk from Ipswich railway station; the town centre is five minutes away. Local buses run past the ground.

Match tickets: All seats sold as season tickets.

Car parking: Large parks in Portman Road, Portman's Walk, and off Princess Street at Greyfriars Park.

Entertainments/catering facilities: 'Centre Spot' bar and restaurant in Portman Road. Bars around the ground. Executive boxes available.

Club shop: Four on the ground stock all types of souvenirs.

Handbooks/programmes: Programmes available on subscription and an Annual is published.

Extra information: When Ipswich won the First Division title in 1962, five of the side – Bailey, Carberry, Phillips, Elsworthy, and Leadbetter – had been regulars in the Third Division side of the middle fifties.

Club Colours: Blue shirts with three white stripes down each arm, white shorts with three blue stripes, blue stockings with three white stripes.

Change Colours: White shirts with three black stripes down each arm, black shorts with three white stripes, white stockings with three black stripes.

Club Captain: Mick Mills.

First Team Trainer: Bobby Ferguson.

Club Nickname: Town or Blues.

IPSWICH TOWN 1980–81 LEAGUE RECORD

Match No.	Date	Venue	Opponents	Result	H/T Score	Goalscorers	Attendance
1	Aug 16	A	Leicester C	W 1-0	0-0	Wark	21,640
2	19	H	Brighton & HA	W 2-0	1-0	Wark, Gates	21,568
3	23	A	Stoke C	D 2-2	2-1	Brazil, Gates	10,722
4	30	H	Everton	W 4-0	2-0	Brazil, Wark, Butcher, Mariner	20,879
5	Sept 6	H	Aston Villa	W 1-0	0-0	Thijssen	23,192
6	13	A	Crystal Palace	W 2-1	1-0	Wark, Gates	24,282
7	20	H	Coventry C	W 2-0	0-0	Wark 2	20,507
8	27	A	Wolverhampton W	W 2-0	2-0	Brazil, Mariner	18,503
9	Oct 4	H	Leeds U	D 1-1	0-0	Wark	24,087
10	11	A	Liverpool	D 1-1	1-1	Thijssen	48,084
11	18	H	Manchester U	D 1-1	0-0	Mariner	28,451
12	25	A	Sunderland	W 2-0	1-0	Muhren, Brazil	32,368
13	Nov 1	H	WBA	D 0-0	0-0		23,043
14	8	A	Southampton	D 3-3	2-1	Gates, Wark, Mariner	21,261
15	11	A	Brighton & HA	L 0-1	0-0		17,055
16	15	H	Leicester C	W 3-1	1-0	Gates, Williams (og), D'Avray	19,852
17	22	A	Nottingham F.	W 2-1	1-0	Brazil, Wark (pen)	24,423
18	Dec 6	A	Manchester C	D 1-1	1-0	Muhren	35,215
19	13	H	Liverpool	D 1-1	1-0	Brazil	32,274
20	17	A	Tottenham H	L 3-5	1-2	Mariner 2, Gates	22,741
21	20	A	Birmingham C	W 3-1	1-0	Mariner, Wark, Brazil	16,161
22	26	H	Norwich C	W 2-0	1-0	Brazil, Wark	27,890
23	27	A	Arsenal	D 1-1	0-1	Wark (pen)	42,818
24	Jan 10	H	Nottingham F	W 2-0	0-0	Mariner, Muhren	25,701
25	13	H	Birmingham C	W 5-1	3-1	Wark, Butcher, Mariner, Muhren, Brazil	21,158
26	17	A	Everton	D 0-0	0-0		25,516
27	31	H	Stoke C	W 4-0	2-0	Wark (pen), Brazil 2, Gates	23,843
28	Feb 7	H	Crystal Palace	W 3-2	0-1	Mariner, Wark (pen), Gilbert (og)	25,036
29	17	H	Middlesbrough	W 1-0	1-0	Brazil	24,781
30	21	H	Wolverhampton W	W 3-1	2-1	Wark, Gates, Beattie	24,218
31	28	A	Coventry C	W 4-0	1-0	Brazil, Gates, McCall, Osman	17,557
32	Mar 14	H	Tottenham H	W 3-0	2-0	Gates, Wark (pen), Brazil	32,052
33	21	A	Manchester U	L 1-2	1-1	Butcher	46,685
34	28	H	Sunderland	W 4-1	1-1	Muhren, Mariner 2, Thijssen	25,450
35	31	A	Leeds U	L 0-3	0-2		26,462
36	Apr 4	A	WBA	L 1-3	1-2	Brazil	22,216
37	14	A	Aston Villa	W 2-1	1-0	Brazil, Gates	47,495
38	18	H	Arsenal	L 0-2	0-1		30,935
39	20	A	Norwich C	L 0-1	0-0		26,083
40	25	H	Manchester C	W 1-0	0-0	Butcher	22,684
41	May 2	A	Middlesbrough	L 1-2	1-0	Mariner	15,503
42	13	H	Southampton	L 2-3	2-3	Brazil, Wark	19,504

Final League Position: 2

Goalscorers

League (77): Wark 18 (5 pens), Brazil 17, Mariner 13, Gates 11, Muhren 5, Butcher 4, Thijssen 3, Beattie 1, D'Avray 1, McCall 1, Osman 1, own goals 2.
League Cup (9): Mariner 4, Osman 2, Wark 2 (1 pen), Muhren.
F.A. Cup (10): Mariner 3, Gates 2, Wark 2, Muhren, Thijssen, own goal.

League Cup	Second Round	Middlesbrough (a)	1-3
		(h)	3-0
	Third Round	Norwich C (h)	1-1
		(a)	3-1
	Fourth Round	Birmingham C (a)	1-2
FA Cup	Third Round	Aston Villa (h)	1-0
	Fourth Round	Shrewsbury T (a)	0-0
		(h)	3-0
	Fifth Round	Charlton Ath (h)	2-0
	Sixth Round	Nottingham F (a)	3-3
		(h)	1-0
	Semi-final	Manchester C	0-1 (at Villa Park)

Cooper	Burley	Mills	Thijssen	Osman	Butcher	Wark	McCall	Mariner	Gates	O'Callaghan	Muhren	Brazil	Beattie	D'Avray	Turner	Sivell	Hunter	Osborne	Parkin	Steggles	*Match No.*
1	2	3	4	5	6	7	8	9	10	11											1
1	2	3	4	5	6	7		9	10	11	8										2
1	2	3	4	5	6	7		9	11	12	8	10*									3
1	2	3	4	5	6	7		9	11		8	10									4
1	2		4	5	6	7	3	9	11		8	10									5
1	2	3	4	5		7		9	11		8	10	6								6
1	2	3	4	5	6	7		9	10	12	8	11*									7
1	2	3	4	5	6	7		9	11		8	10									8
1	2	3	4	5	6	7		9	11	12	8*	10									9
1	2	3	4	5	6	7	11	9	10		8										10
1	2	3	4*	5	6	7	12	9	11		8	10									11
1	2	4		5	3		7	9*	11		8	10	6	12							12
1*	2	3	4	5	6	7	11		9		8	10			12						13
	2	4		5	3	7	11	9	10		8		6			1					14
	2*	4		6		7	3	9	11		8			12	10	1	5				15
		2		5	6	7	3	9	11*		8	10		12		1		4			16
		2	4	5	6	7	3	9	11		8	10				1					17
1	2		4	5	6	7	3	9	11	12	8	10*									18
1	2		4	5	6	7	3	9	11		8	10									19
1	2		4	5	6	7	3*	9	11	12	8	10									20
1	2		4	5	6	7	3	9		11	8	10									21
1	2		4	5	6	7	3	9	11*	12	8	10									22
1		2	4	5	6	7	3*	9	11	12	8	10									23
1	2	3	4	5	6	7		9		11	8	10									24
1	2	3	4	5	6	7		9		11	8	10									25
1	2	3	4	5	6	7		9	11		8	10									26
1		2	4	5	6	7	3	9*	11	12	8	10									27
1			4	2	6	7	3	9	11		8	10	5								28
1		2	4	5	3	7			11	9	8	10	6								29
1		2		5	3	7	4	9	11	10	8		6								30
1		2	4	5	3		7	9	11		8	10	6								31
1		2*	4	5	6	7	3	9	11	12	8	10									32
1			4	5	6	7	3	9	11	10	8									2	33
1			4	5	6	7	3	9	11	12	8*	10								2	34
1		2	4	5	6	7	3*	9	11	12	8	10									35
1		4		5	6	7	3		11	9	8	10							12	2*	36
1		2	4	5	6	7	3	9	11		8	10									37
1		2		5	6	7	3	9	11*	4	8	10							12		38
1		3		5	6	7	11				8	10		12	9				4	2*	39
1		4		5	6	7	3			11	8	10			9					2	40
1		4		5	6	7	3	9	11	12	8	10								2*	41
1		2		5	6	7	3		11	12	8	10		9*					4		42
38	23	33	31	42	40	40	30	36	37	11	41	35	7	1	3	4	1	1	2	6	
							+			+				+	+				+		
							1s			13s				4s	1s				2s		

IPSWICH TOWN

	Ht	*Wt*	*Birthplace*	*Clubs*	*League App.*	*League Gls*
Goalkeepers						
Paul Cooper	5 11	12 7	Brierley Hill	Birmingham C	17	—
				Ipswich T	236	—
Laurie Sivell	5 8	11 0	Lowestoft	Ipswich T	119	—
				Lincoln C (on loan)	2	—
Scott Endersby*	5 10	12 4	Lewisham	Ipswich T	—	—
Gary Westwood	6 0	13 0	Barrow	Ipswich T	—	—
Defenders						
George Burley (Scotland)	5 9½	11 0	Cumnock	Ipswich T	263	4
Terry Butcher (England)	6 4	14 0	Singapore	Ipswich T	100	8
Allan Hunter (N Ireland)	6 0	12 8	Sion Mills	Oldham Ath	83	1
				Blackburn R	84	1
				Ipswich T	280	8
Mick Mills (England)	5 7½	11 10	Godalming	Ipswich T	538	19
Kevin Beattie (England)	5 10½	12 4	Carlisle	Ipswich T	228	24
Russell Osman (England)	6 0	11 10	Repton	Ipswich T	151	5
Don Souter	5 11	11 8	Hammersmith	Ipswich T	—	—
Kevin Steggles	6 0	11 1	Ditchingham	Ipswich T	6	—
Adam Nichols*	6 1	12 0	Dagenham	Ipswich T	—	—
Ron Burns	5 8	10 7	Londonderry	Coleraine	—	—
				Ipswich T	—	—
Tony Hall*			Jarrow	Ipswich T	—	—
Fred Gernon	6 2	11 13½	Birmingham	Ipswich T	—	—
Peter Shields (Transferred to Hearts Sept 1980)	5 7	10 11	Glasgow	Ipswich T	—	—
Midfield						
John Wark (Scotland)	5 10½	11 12	Glasgow	Ipswich T	180	51
Tommy Parkin	5 7	10 4	Gateshead	Ipswich T	9	—
				Grimsby T (on loan)	6	—
				Peterborough U (on loan)	3	—
Bryan Klug	5 8	10 10	Coventry	Ipswich T	—	—
				Wimbledon (on loan)	11	—
Steve McCall	5 11	11 3	Carlisle	Ipswich T	41	1
Arnold Muhren (Holland)	5 11	11 1	Volendam	Twente	(not known)	
				Ipswich T	119	17
Frans Thijssen (Holland)	5 11	11 2	Heumen	Twente	(not known)	
				Ipswich T	84	6
Jim King	5 7	11 0	Dumfries	Ipswich T	—	—
Robert Hutchison*	6 0	11 8	Maybole	Ipswich T	—	—
Colin Clarke*			Newry	Ipswich T	—	—
Mark Lomas	5 9	11 7	Manchester	Ipswich T	—	—
Forwards						
Eric Gates (England)	5 6	10 4	Ferryhill	Ipswich T	156	35
Robin Turner	5 9	10 8	Carlisle	Ipswich T	30	—
Paul Mariner (England)	6 0	12 2	Bolton	Plymouth Arg	135	56
				Ipswich T	175	64
Alan Brazil (Scotland)	6 0	12 4	Glasgow	Ipswich T	91	38
Tony Wharton (Contract cancelled May 1980)	5 9	10 8	Beverley	Ipswich T	—	—
Mich D'Avray	6 1	12 0	Johannesburg	Ipswich T	7	1
Kevin O'Callaghan (Eire)	5 8½	10 9	London	Millwall	20	3
				Ipswich T	28	—
Trevor Putney	5 9½	10 3	Harold Hill	Brentwood & W	(not known)	
				Ipswich T	—	—
Russell Irving	5 8	11 2½	Wallsend	Ipswich T	—	—

LEEDS UNITED Division 1

President: The Right Hon The Earl of Harewood LLD.
Chairman: M. Cussins.
Vice-Chairman: R. Barker MCIT, MBIM.
Directors: B. Woodward, J. W. G. Marjason, S. G. Simon, W. J. Fotherby, G. Maxwell-Holmes, L. Silver.
Manager: Allan Clarke.
General Manager/Secretary: Keith Archer.
Year Formed: 1919, as Leeds United after disbandment (by FA order) of Leeds City in 1904.
Turned Professional: 1920. *Limited Company:* 1920.

Football League Record:
1920 Elected to Division 2; 1924–27 Division 1; 1927–28 Division 2; 1928–31 Division 1; 1931–32 Division 2; 1932–47 Division 1; 1947–56 Division 2; 1956–60 Division 1; 1960–64 Division 2; 1964– Division 1.

Honours: *Football League:* Division 1 – Champions 1968–69, 1973–74; Runners-up 1964–65, 1965–66, 1969–70, 1970–71, 1971–72; Division 2 – Champions 1923–24, 1963–64; Runners-up 1927–28, 1931–32, 1955–56. *FA Cup:* Winners 1972; Runners-up 1965, 1970, 1973. *Football League Cup:* Winners 1967–68. **European Competitions:** *European Cup:* 1969–70, 1974–75 (runners-up). *European Cup-Winners' Cup:* 1972–73 (runners-up). *European Fairs Cup:* 1965–66, 1966–67 (runners-up), 1967–68 (winners), 1968–69, 1970–71 (winners). *UEFA Cup:* 1971–72, 1973–74, 1979–80.

Record Victory: 10-0 v Lyn Oslo, European Cup 1st rd 1st leg, 17 Sept, 1969.
Record Defeat: 1-8 v Stoke C, Division 1, 27 Aug, 1934.
Most League Points: 67, Division 1, 1968–69.
Most League Goals: 98, Division 2, 1927–28.
Highest League Scorer in Season: John Charles, 42, Division 2, 1953–54.
Most League Goals in Total Aggregate: John Charles, 154, 1948–57 and 1962.
Most Capped Player: Billy Bremner, 54, Scotland.
Most League Appearances: Jack Charlton, 629, 1953–73.
Record Transfer Fee Received: £500,000 from Nottingham F for Frank Gray, July 1979.
Record Transfer Fee Paid: £400,000 to Sheffield U for Alex Sabella, May 1980.
Previous Managers since the War: Billy Hampson, Willis Edwards, Major Frank Buckley, Raich Carter, Bill Lambton, Jack Taylor, Don Revie OBE, Brian Clough, Jimmy Armfield, Jock Stein, Jimmy Adamson.
Address of Supporters Club: Leeds United Supporters Club, Fullerton Park, Elland Road, Leeds 11.
Address of the Club Shop or Boutique: Leeds United Club Shop, Elland Road, Leeds 11.

Elland Road, Leeds LS11 0ES. Telephone Leeds 716037 (3 lines). *Telegraphic Address:* 'Football Leeds'. *Ground capacity:* 43,900. *Record attendance:* 57,892 v Sunderland, FA Cup 5th rd replay, 15 March, 1967. *Record receipts:* £146,483, FA Cup semi-final replay, Everton v West Ham U, 16 April, 1980. *Pitch measurements:* 117yd×76yd.
How to get there: Nearest railway station, Leeds. The city centre is within walking distance from the station and then by Corporation buses to the ground.
Match tickets: Computer installed for sale of match-by-match tickets.
Car parking: Within one minute of the ground there is a large park owned by the Leeds Greyhound Association; this holds about 1000 cars. Large park on the Beeston Ring road owned and operated by the club.
Entertainments/catering facilities: Supporters' social club adjacent to the ground. Snack bars around the ground.
Club shop: This operates at the ground next to the Pools Office and stocks all types of souvenirs.
Handbooks/programmes: Both handbooks and programmes are available from the club shop; programmes are available on subscription.
Extra information: The club have a Robotphone Answering System – the Leeds United Information Service: Leeds 702621. New Football League record established in 1973–74 with a 29-game run of matches without defeat from beginning of the season. Leeds United now have an official fan club aimed at young supporters aged 6–16.
Club Colours: All white with blue and yellow stripe.
Change Colours: All yellow with blue and white trim.
Club Captain: Trevor Cherry.
Deputy Manager: Martin Wilkinson.

LEEDS UNITED 1980–81 LEAGUE RECORD

Match No.	Date	Venue	Opponents	Result	H/T Score	Goalscorers	Attendance
1	Aug 16	H	Aston Villa	L 1-2	1-1	Stevenson (pen)	23,401
2	19	A	Middlesbrough	L 0-3	0-1		19,470
3	23	A	Norwich C	W 3-2	1-0	Hart, Graham, Connor	17,890
4	30	H	Leicester C	L 1-2	0-0	Hart	18,530
5	Sept 6	A	Stoke C	L 0-3	0-3		12,729
6	13	H	Tottenham H	D 0-0	0-0		21,947
7	20	H	Manchester U	D 0-0	0-0		32,539
8	27	A	Sunderland	L 1-4	0-2	Parlane	29,619
9	Oct 4	A	Ipswich T	D 1-1	0-0	Sabella	24,087
10	8	H	Manchester C	W 1-0	0-0	Harris	19,134
11	11	H	Everton	W 1-0	0-0	Curtis	25,601
12	18	A	Wolverhampton W	L 1-2	1-1	Connor	20,699
13	22	A	Nottingham F	L 1-2	1-2	Harris	25,033
14	25	H	Crystal Palace	W 1-0	1-0	Connor	19,208
15	Nov 1	A	Coventry C	L 1-2	0-2	Connor	13,970
16	8	H	Arsenal	L 0-5	0-2		20,855
17	12	H	Middlesbrough	W 2-1	0-0	Hird 2 (1 pen)	17,382
18	15	A	Aston Villa	D 1-1	1-1	Sabella	29,106
19	22	A	Southampton	L 1-2	1-2	Graham	20,278
20	29	H	Brighton & HA	W 1-0	0-0	Harris	14,333
21	Dec 6	A	WBA	W 2-1	1-1	Harris, Graham	17,771
22	13	H	Nottingham F	W 1-0	0-0	Greenhoff	21,882
23	20	A	Manchester C	L 0-1	0-0		31,866
24	26	H	Birmingham C	D 0-0	0-0		19,214
25	27	A	Liverpool	D 0-0	0-0		44,086
26	Jan 10	H	Southampton	L 0-3	0-1		21,007
27	17	A	Leicester C	W 1-0	0-0	Hart	16,094
28	31	H	Norwich C	W 1-0	0-0	Harris	15,836
29	Feb 7	A	Tottenham H	D 1-1	0-1	Harris	32,372
30	14	H	Stoke C	L 1-3	1-1	Flynn	16,530
31	21	H	Sunderland	W 1-0	0-0	Harris	23,236
32	28	A	Manchester U	W 1-0	0-0	Flynn	45,733
33	Mar 14	A	Everton	W 2-1	0-1	Parlane, Harris	23,014
34	21	H	Wolverhampton W	L 1-3	1-1	Harris	19,252
35	28	A	Crystal Palace	W 1-0	1-0	Parlane	15,053
36	31	H	Ipswich T	W 3-0	2-0	Hird, Harris, Hart	26,462
37	Apr 4	H	Coventry C	W 3-0	1-0	Stevenson, Parlane, Flynn	15,882
38	11	A	Arsenal	D 0-0	0-0		29,339
39	18	H	Liverpool	D 0-0	0-0		39,206
40	21	A	Birmingham C	W 2-0	1-0	Parlane, Hird (pen)	14,505
41	May 2	A	Brighton & HA	L 0-2	0-1		27,577
42	6	H	WBA	D 0-0	0-0		17,218

Final League Position: 9

Goalscorers

League (39): Harris 10, Parlane 5, Connor 4, Hart 4, Hird 4 (2 pens), Flynn 3, Graham 3, Sabella 2, Stevenson 2 (1 pen), Curtis 1, Greenhoff 1.
League Cup (1): Graham.
F.A. Cup (1): Hird (pen).

League Cup	Second Round	Aston Villa (a)	0-1
		(h)	1-3
FA Cup	Third Round	Coventry C (h)	1-1
		(a)	0-1

Lukic	Cherry	Stevenson	Flynn	Hart	Greenhoff	Gray	Harris	Curtis	Sabella	Graham	Parlane	Connor	Chandler	Madeley	Hamson	Thomas	Hird	Firm	Parkinson	Butterworth	Dickinson	*Match No.*
1	2	3	4	5	6	7*	8	9	10	11	12											1
1	2	3	4	5	6	7		9		11	12	8*	10									2
1	2		4	5	3				10	11		9	7	6	8*	12						3
1	2		4	5	3				10	11		9	7	6	8							4
1	2		4	5	3		12		10	11	7	9		6*	8							5
1	4	3		5					10	11	8	9*	7		12		2	6				6
1	7	3	4	5		10				11	9	8					2	6				7
1	7	3	4	5		10	12			11	9	8					2	6*				8
1	6		4	5	2	3	7	8	10	11	9											9
1	6		4	5	2	3	7	8	10	11	9*				12							10
1	6		4	5	2	3	7	8	10	11					9							11
1	6		4	5	2	3*	7	8	10			11			9		12					12
1	6		4	5	2	3	7*		10			9	11			12	8					13
1	6		4	5	2	10	7			11		9		3			8					14
1	6		4	5	2	10	7			11		9		3			8					15
1	6		4	5	2	10	12			11	7	9		3*			8					16
1	6		4	5	2	3	7		10	11		9					8					17
1	6		4	5	2	3	7		10	11		9*			12		8					18
1	6		4	5	2	3	7		10	11					9		8					19
1	6		4	5	2	3	7		10	11		9					8					20
1	6		4	5	2	3	7		10	11		9					8					21
1	6		4	5	2	3	7		10	11	12	9*					8					22
1	6		4	5	2	3	7		10	11		9					8					23
1	6		4	5	2	3	7		10	11*	12	9					8					24
1	6		4	5		3	7		10	11	8	9*			12		2					25
1	6		4	5		3	12		10	11	7*		9		8		2					26
1	6		4	5	2	3	7		10*	11		9	12				8					27
1	6		4	5	2	3	7		10	11		9					8					28
1	6	12	4	5	2	3	7			11		9	10*				8					29
1	6		4	5	2	3	7		12	11	10	9*					8					30
1	6	10	4	5	2	3	7			11	9						8					31
1	6	10	4	5	2	3	7			11	9						8					32
1	6	10	4		2	3	7			11	9						8		5			33
1	6	10	4		2	3	7			11	9	12	8*						5			34
1	6	10	4	5		3	8			11	9						7		2			35
1	6	10	4	5	2	3	7			11	9						8					36
1		10	4	5	2	3	7			11	9*						8	6		12		37
1	6	10	4	5	2	3	7			11	9						8					38
1	6	10	4	5	2	3	7			11	9						8					39
1	6	10	4	5*	2	3	7			11	9						8	12				40
1	6	10	4		2	3	7*			11	9	12					8	5				41
1	6	10*	4		2	3	7			11	9	5					8				12	42
42	41	17	41	38	36	38	33	6	22	40	22	25	8	6	7	—	32	5	3	—	—	
		+ 1s					+ 4s		+ 1s		+ 4s	+ 2s	+ 1s		+ 4s	+ 2s	+ 1s	+ 1s		+ 1s	+ 1s	

LEEDS UNITED

	Ht	*Wt*	*Birthplace*	*Clubs*	*League App.*	*League Gls*
Goalkeepers						
David Harvey	5 11	12 3	Leeds	Leeds U	276	—
(Scotland) (Contract cancelled March 1981)						
Henry Smith*	6 2	12 0	Lanarkshire	Leeds U	—	—
John Lukic	6 4	13 7	Chesterfield	Leeds U	75	—
Kevin Seggie*	6 2	14 0	Bury St Edmunds	Leeds U	—	—
Defenders						
Paul Madeley* (England)	6 0	12 6	Leeds	Leeds U	534	24
Byron Stevenson (Wales)	6 1	11 0	Llanelli	Leeds U	76	3
Paul Hart	6 2	12 8	Manchester	Stockport Co	88	5
				Blackpool	143	17
				Leeds U	120	12
Keith Parkinson	6 1	12 6	Preston	Leeds U	31	—
Kevin Hird	5 7	10 6	Colne	Blackburn R	132	20
				Leeds U	86	12
Neil Parker*	5 6	10 3	Blackburn	Leeds U	1	—
Neil Firm	6 3	13 7	Bradford	Leeds U	9	—
Gary Fozzard*	6 0	11 5	Leeds	Leeds U	—	—
Phil Porthouse*	5 9	10 0	Jarrow	Leeds U	—	—
Brian Greenhoff (England)	5 10	12 2	Barnsley	Manchester U	221	13
				Leeds U	60	1
Tony Arins	5 11	11 8	Chesterfield	Burnley	29	2
				Leeds U	—	—
Trevor Cherry (England)	5 9	11 6	Huddersfield	Huddersfield T	186	10
				Leeds U	345	22
Paul Harrisskitt*			Hartlepool	Leeds U	—	—
Midfield						
Brian Flynn (Wales)	5 3¼	12 3	Port Talbot	Burnley	120	8
				Leeds U	135	10
David Bennett*	5 9	9 6	Rotherham	Leeds U	—	—
Eddie Gray (Scotland)	5 11	12 6	Glasgow	Leeds U	398	51
Gary Hamson	5 8	10 12	Nottingham	Sheffield U	108	8
				Leeds U	30	1
Jeff Chandler (Eire)	5 7	10 1	Hammersmith	Blackpool	37	7
				Leeds U	26	2
Craig Howard*	5 4	9 9	Worksop	Leeds U	—	—
Aiden Butterworth			Leeds	Leeds U	1	—
Forwards						
Carl Harris (Wales)	5 9	11 0	Neath	Leeds U	135	26
Gwyn Thomas	5 8	11 0	Swansea	Leeds U	18	2
Arthur Graham (Scotland)	5 8	11 10	Glasgow	Aberdeen	220	34
				Leeds U	146	23
Martin Dickinson	5 10	11 0	Leeds	Leeds U	7	—
Alex Sabella	5 8	10 13	Buenos Aires	River Plate	(not known)	
				Sheffield U	76	8
				Leeds U	23	2
Derek Parlane (Scotland)	6 0	11 10	Helensburgh	Queen's Park	—	—
				Rangers	218	80
				Leeds U	37	8
Terry Connor	5 7	10 0	Leeds	Leeds U	50	10
Steve Balcombe	6 1	11 0	Bangor	Leeds U	—	—
David Matthews	5 11	11 4	Shipley	Leeds U	—	—
Alan Clarke	5 9	10 0	Dublin	Leeds U	—	—

Free transfer: Edward Burrows*.

LEICESTER CITY — Division 2

Chairman: T. W. Shipman.

Vice-Chairman: T. E. Bloor.

Directors: W. G. Page, D. E. Sharp, W. K. Shooter FCA, T. Smeaton.

Manager: Jock Wallace. *Gen Secretary:* A. K. Bennett.

PRO: Graham Clark.

Year Formed: 1884.

Previous Grounds: 1884, Victoria Park; 1887, Belgrave Road; 1888, Victoria Park; 1891, Filbert Street.

Previous Name: 1884–1919, Leicester Fosse.

Football League Record:
1894 Elected to Division 2; 1908–09 Division 1; 1909–25 Division 2; 1925–35 Division 1; 1935–37 Division 2; 1937–39 Division 1; 1946–54 Division 2; 1954–55 Division 1; 1955–57 Division 2; 1957–69 Division 1; 1969–71 Division 2; 1971–78 Division 1; 1978–80 Division 2; 1980–81 Division 1; 1981– Division 2.

Honours: *Football League:* Division 1 – Runners-up 1928–29; Division 2 – Champions 1924–25, 1936–37, 1953–54, 1956–57, 1970–71, 1979–80; Runners-up 1907–08. *FA Cup:* Runners-up 1949, 1961, 1963, 1969. *Football League Cup:* Winners 1964; Runners-up 1965. **European Competitions:** *European Cup-Winners' Cup:* 1961–62.

Record Victory: 10-0 v Portsmouth, Division 1, 20 Oct, 1928.

Record Defeat: 0-12 (as Leicester Fosse) v Nottingham F, Division 1, 21 Apr, 1909.

Most League Points: 61, Division 2, 1956–57.

Most League Goals: 109, Division 2, 1956–57.

Highest League Scorer in Season: Arthur Rowley, 44, Division 2, 1956–57.

Most League Goals in Total Aggregate: Arthur Chandler, 262, 1923–35.

Most Capped Player: Gordon Banks, 37 (73), England.

Most League Appearances: Adam Black, 530, 1920–35.

Record Transfer Fee Received: £325,000 from Stoke C for Peter Shilton, Nov 1974.

Record Transfer Fee Paid: £250,000 to FC Bruges, Belgium, for Roger Davies, Dec 1977; to Oldham Ath for Alan Young, July 1979; to Partick T for Jim Melrose, July 1980.

Previous Managers since the War: Johnny Duncan, Norman Bullock, David Halliday, Matt Gillies, Frank O'Farrell, Jimmy Bloomfield, Frank McLintock.

Address of Supporters Club: Leicester City Promotions, Club Shop, City Stadium, Filbert Street, Leicester. Remittance and SAE for price list.

City Stadium, Filbert St, Leicester, LE2 7FL. Telephone Leicester 555000 (Match information Leicester 551155). *Ground capacity:* 32,000. *Record attendance:* 47,298 v Tottenham H, FA Cup 5th rd, 18 Feb, 1928. *Record receipts:* £57,740 v Liverpool, Division 1, 23 Aug, 1980. *Pitch measurements:* 112yd×75yd.

How to get there: Corporation buses from Humberstone Gate and Waterloo St (opposite railway station) in city centre. Nearest station Leicester. Midland Red run bus services to the town centre from outlying districts.

Match tickets: Seats can be booked from 2 months prior to the date of match & SAE.

Car parking: Parking adjacent to the ground is for season-ticket holders only. There is nearby street parking and also a public car park about five minutes walk from the ground.

Entertainments/catering facilities: A private season-ticket members bar in the main stand, and catering bars in all sections of the ground.

Club shop: Situated under the main stand; sells all types of souvenirs.

Handbooks/programmes: Both handbooks and programmes are available from the club shop.

Extra information: A League inquiry after Leicester's record defeat discovered that the players had been celebrating a team-mate's wedding!

Club Colours: Blue shirts with white collar and cuffs, white shorts with LCFC initials on thigh, white stockings with blue tops.

Club Captain: Mark Wallington.

Physiotherapist: John McVey.

Club Nickname: Filberts or Foxes.

LEICESTER CITY 1980–81 LEAGUE RECORD

Match No.	Date	Venue	Opponents	Result	H/T Score	Goalscorers	Attendance
1	Aug 16	H	Ipswich T	L 0-1	0-0		21,640
2	19	A	Everton	L 0-1	0-1		23,337
3	23	H	Liverpool	W 2-0	1-0	Peake, Henderson	28,455
4	30	A	Leeds U	W 2-1	0-0	O'Neill, Henderson	18,530
5	Sept 6	H	Sunderland	L 0-1	0-1		20,638
6	13	A	Manchester U	L 0-5	0-2		43,222
7	20	A	Nottingham F	L 0-5	0-1		27,145
8	27	H	Tottenham H	W 2-1	0-0	Smith, Buchanan	22,616
9	Oct 4	A	Arsenal	L 0-1	0-1		28,490
10	8	H	Stoke C	D 1-1	1-1	Wilson	14,549
11	11	H	Coventry C	L 1-3	1-1	Lineker	17,104
12	18	A	Crystal Palace	L 1-2	0-1	Young	16,387
13	21	A	Middlesbrough	L 0-1	0-0		13,137
14	25	H	Wolverhampton W	W 2-0	1-0	Henderson, Young	18,133
15	Nov 1	A	Aston Villa	L 0-2	0-0		29,953
16	8	H	Manchester C	D 1-1	1-0	Young	19,104
17	12	H	Everton	L 0-1	0-0		15,511
18	15	A	Ipswich T	L 1-3	0-1	Williams	19,852
19	22	A	WBA	L 1-3	0-1	Lineker	17,752
20	29	H	Norwich C	L 1-2	1-2	Young	13,958
21	Dec 6	A	Birmingham C	W 2-1	2-0	Melrose 2	18,479
22	13	H	Middlesbrough	W 1-0	1-0	MacDonald (pen)	13,998
23	20	A	Stoke C	L 0-1	0-1		13,433
24	26	H	Brighton & HA	L 0-1	0-0		19,570
25	27	A	Southampton	L 0-4	0-4		21,886
26	Jan 10	H	WBA	L 0-2	0-2		17,778
27	17	H	Leeds U	L 0-1	0-0		16,094
28	31	A	Liverpool	W 2-1	0-1	Byrne, Melrose	35,154
29	Feb 7	H	Manchester U	W 1-0	0-0	Melrose	26,085
30	14	A	Sunderland	L 0-1	0-1		22,569
31	21	A	Tottenham H	W 2-1	1-1	Lynex, Byrne	26,126
32	28	H	Nottingham F	D 1-1	1-0	Lynex	26,608
33	Mar 7	H	Arsenal	W 1-0	1-0	Williams	20,198
34	14	A	Coventry C	L 1-4	1-2	Young	21,430
35	21	H	Crystal Palace	D 1-1	0-0	O'Neill	15,176
36	28	A	Wolverhampton W	W 1-0	0-0	Melrose	21,694
37	31	A	Manchester C	D 3-3	0-1	Williams, Young, Melrose	26,141
38	Apr 4	H	Aston Villa	L 2-4	2-2	Lynex 2 (1 pen)	26,032
39	18	H	Southampton	D 2-2	0-0	Young, Lynex (pen)	21,349
40	20	A	Brighton & HA	L 1-2	1-0	MacDonald	21,176
41	25	H	Birmingham C	W 1-0	0-0	Williams	13,666
42	May 2	A	Norwich C	W 3-2	2-1	Melrose 3	25,307

Final League Position: 21

Goalscorers

League (40): Melrose 9, Young 7, Lynex 5 (2 pens), Williams 4, Henderson 3, Byrne 2, Lineker 2, MacDonald 2 (1 pen), O'Neill 2, Buchanan 1, Peake 1, Smith 1, Wilson 1.
League Cup (0).
F.A. Cup (5): Melrose 2, Buchanan, Henderson, Lineker.

League Cup	Second Round	WBA (a)	0-1
		(h)	0-1
FA Cup	Third Round	Cardiff C (h)	3-0
	Fourth Round	Exeter C (h)	1-1
		(a)	1-3

Wallington	Williams	Gibson	Peake	May	O'Neill	Edmunds	Melrose	Young	Wilson	Smith	Henderson	Goodwin	Grewcock	Welsh	Carr	Scott	Buchanan	Lineker	Byrne	Hamill	MacDonald	Friar	Lynex	Ramsey	Leet	*Match No.*
1	2	3	4	5	6	7*	8	9	10	11	12															1
1	2	3	4	5	6		8	9	10	11		7														2
1	2	3	4	5	6		8*	9	10	11	12	7														3
1	2	3	4	5	6		8*	9	10		11	7	12													4
1	2	3		5	6		12	9	10	8	11	4	7*													5
1	2	3		5	6		12	9	10	11	8	4	7*													6
1	2	3		5	6*			9	10	11	8	4	7	12												7
1	4	3		5				9		10	8	7		12	2*	6	11									8
1	4	3		5				9		10	8	7		2		6	11									9
1	2	3		5				12	10	11	9	4				6	8*	7								10
1	2	3		5				12	10	11	9	4				6	8*	7								11
1	2			5			12	9	10	11	8	7*			3	6			4							12
1	4	3		5			7	9	10	11	8				2	6										13
1	4	3		5			7	9	10	11	8*				2	6	12									14
1	4	3		5			7	9	10	11	8				2	6										15
1	11		4	5	6			9	10		12				2	3		8		7*						16
1	11		4	5	6			9	10			12			2	3		8		7*						17
1	11		4	5	6			9	10		12				2	3		8*		7						18
1	11		4	5	6			9	10		12				2*	3		8		7						19
1	2	3	4		6		8	9	10	11						5				7*	12					20
1	2	3	4		6		8	9*	10					12		5				7	11					21
1	2	3	4		6		8		10			12				5		9		7*	11					22
1	2	3	4		6		8	9	10			12				5				7*	11					23
1	2	3	4		6		8	9	10			7*		12		5					11					24
1	2		4		6		8	9	10		7			3		5					11					25
1	2	3	4*		6		9		10			12				5	8	7			11					26
1	4		7*		6		12		10	11	9	2				5	8					3				27
1	2		4	5	6		8	9	10			12							7*		11	3				28
1	2		4	5	6		8	9	10			12							7		11*	3				29
1	2		4*	5	6		8	9	10										7		12	3	11			30
1	2		4	5	6		8*	9	10										12		11	3	7			31
1	2		4	5	6		8	9	10										12		11	3	7*			32
1	2		4	5	6		8*	9	10										7		11	3		12		33
1	2		4	5	6		8	9	10												11	3	7			34
1	2			5	6		8	9	10*	12									4		11	3	7			35
1	2			5	6*		8	9	10	12									4		11	3	7			36
1	2			5			8	9	10				11	6					4*		12	3	7			37
1	2			5			8	9	10				11			6			4			3	7			38
1	2			5	6			9	10	11	8*								4		12	3	7			39
1	2			5	6		8	9	10				11*						12		4	3	7			40
1	2		4	5	6		8*		10		11							9				3	7	12		41
1	2			5	6		8	9	10		12										11		7	4	3*	42
42	42	20	24	34	32	1	28	36	40	17	16	13	6	3	9	21	6	9	10	8	16	15	12	1	1	
							+ 4s	+ 2s		+ 2s	+ 6s	+ 6s	+ 1s	+ 4s			+ 1s		+ 3s		+ 4s			+ 2s		

LEICESTER CITY

	Ht	Wt	Birthplace	Clubs	League App.	League Gls
Goalkeepers						
Mark Wallington	6 1	14 2½	Sleaford	Walsall	11	—
				Leicester C	288	—
Nicky Walker	6 2½	12 10¼	Aberdeen	Elgin	(not known)	
				Leicester C	—	—
Steve Humphries*	5 11	12 10	Hull	Leicester C	—	—
Defenders						
Tommy Williams	5 10¼	10 12	West Lothian	Leicester C	149	10
Larry May	6 0¼	12 6	Sutton Coldfield	Leicester C	118	8
John O'Neill (N Ireland)	5 11¾	13 3	Derry	Leicester C	88	2
Billy Gibson	5 9¾	11 6	Lanark	Leicester C	20	—
Nigel Hart*	6 0	12 3	Golbourne	Wigan Ath	1	—
				Leicester C	—	—
Geoff Scott	5 10¼	12 4¾	Birmingham	Stoke C	78	3
				Leicester C	32	—
Peter Welsh	6 0¾	13 2¼	Coatbridge	Leicester C	25	—
Norman Leet	6 2½	13 12	Leicester	Leicester C	1	—
Paul Friar	5 8	10 1	Glasgow	Leicester C	15	—
Paul Geddes	6 1½	12 2	Paisley	Leicester C	—	—
(Transferred to Hibs April 1981)						
Mark Ratcliffe	6 10¾	10 13½	Coventry	Leicester C	—	—
(Free transfer May 1980)						
Midfield						
Andy Peake	5 9½	11 2½	Market Harborough	Leicester C	67	6
Colin Bell	5 9¼	10 10½	Braunstone	Leicester C	—	—
Everton Carr*	5 7	11 6	Antigua	Leicester C	12	—
Bobby Smith	5 7	11 7¾	Dalkeith	Hibernian	152	19
				Leicester C	71	19
Mike Dûffy*	5 10	12 1	Leicester	Leicester C	12	1
Ian Wilson	5 7¼	10 10½	Aberdeen	Leicester C	64	3
Pat Byrne*	5 7	11 3	Dublin	Shelbourne	(not known)	
				Leicester C	36	3
Michael Higginbottom*	5 9	11 0	Sheffield	Leicester C	—	—
Paul Ramsey	5 10	12 0	Derry	Leicester C	3	—
Mike Page*			Swindon	Swindon T	—	—
				Leicester C	—	—
Andy Geddes	5 9½	11 10	Paisley	Leicester C	—	—
(Transferred to Dundee Nov 1980)						
Forwards						
Gary Lineker	5 9¾	11 10½	Leicester	Leicester C	35	6
Neil Grewcock	5 5½	11 3	Leicester	Leicester C	8	1
Alan Lee	5 11	12 10	Weoberg	Leicester C	6	—
(Contract cancelled April 1981)						
Martin Henderson	6 0	12 9	Kirkcaldy	Rangers	33	10
				Hibernian (on loan)	6	—
				Philadelphia F	(not known)	
				Leicester C	91	12
Paul Edmunds*	5 8	10 10	Leicester	Leicester C	8	2
Dave Buchanan	5 7¼	11 0	Newcastle	Leicester C	28	6
Gavin Drummond	5 10¾	10 13½	Derry	Leicester C	—	—
Kevin MacDonald	6 0¼	11 11¼	Inverness	Inverness Caley	(not known)	
				Leicester C	20	2
Richard Pell	5 7½	11 0	Leicester	Leicester C	—	—
Greg Shelton*	5 11	10 8	Corby	Leicester C	—	—
Derek Strickland*	5 8	10 2	Stoneyburn	Rangers	1	—
				Leicester C	7	2
Alan Young	6 0	12 7	Kirkcaldy	Oldham Ath	122	30
				Leicester C	80	21
Jim Melrose	5 9	10 1	Glasgow	Partick T	122	31
				Leicester C	32	9
Stewart Hamill	5 9	10 8	Glasgow	Pollock	(not known)	
				Leicester C	8	—
Steve Lynex	5 9	11 5	West Bromwich	WBA	—	—
				Shamrock R	(not known)	
				Birmingham C	46	10
				Leicester C	12	5

LINCOLN CITY Division 3

Chairman: D. W. Houlston.
Vice-Chairman: M. J. Green.
Directors: G. T. Blades, H. W. Dove, A. C. Davey, H. C. Sills.
Manager: Colin Murphy.
Secretary: J. H. Sorby FAAI.
Year Formed: 1883. *Turned Professional:* 1892.
Limited Company: 1892.
Previous Grounds: 1883, John O'Gaunt's; 1894, Sincil Bank.

Football League Record:
1892 Original Member of Division 2. Remained in Division 2 until 1920 when they failed re-election but also missed seasons 1908–09 and 1911–12, when not re-elected. 1921–32 Division 3(N); 1932–34 Division 2; 1934–48 Division 3(N); 1948–49 Division 2; 1949–52 Division 3(N); 1952–61 Division 2; 1961–62 Division 3; 1962–76 Division 4; 1976–79 Division 3; 1979–81 Division 4; 1981– Division 3.

Honours: *Football League:* Division 2 best season: 5th, 1901–02; Division 3(N) – Champions 1931–32, 1947–48, 1951–52; Runners-up 1927–28, 1930–31, 1936–37; Division 4 – Champions 1975–76; Runners-up 1980–81. *FA Cup* best season: 1st rd of Second Series (5th rd equivalent), 1886–87, 2nd rd (5th rd equivalent), 1889–90, 1901–02. *Football League Cup* best season: 4th rd, 1967–68.
Record Victory: 11-1 v Crewe Alex, Division 3(N), 29 Sept, 1951.
Record Defeat: 3-11 v Manchester C, Division 2, 23 Mar, 1895.
Most League Points: 74, Division 4, 1975–76 (League record).
Most League Goals: 121, Division 3(N), 1951–52.
Highest League Scorer in Season: Allan Hall, 42, Division 3(N), 1931–32.
Most League Goals in Total Aggregate: Andy Graver, 144, 1950–55 and 1958–61.
Most Capped Player: David Pugh, 3 (7), Wales; Con Moulson, 3 (6) Eire; George Moulson, 3, Eire.
Most League Appearances: Tony Emery, 402, 1946–59.
Record Transfer Fee Received: £180,000 from Newcastle U for Mick Harford, Dec 1980.
Record Transfer Fee Paid: £45,000 to Southampton for George Shipley, Jan 1980.
Previous Managers since the War: Bill Anderson, Bob Chapman, Ron Gray, Bert Loxley, David Herd, Graham Taylor, George Kerr, Willie Bell.
Address of the Club Shop or Boutique: Red Imps Shop on ground.

Sincil Bank, Lincoln. Telephone Lincoln 22224 and 22225. *Ground capacity:* 16,225. *Record attendance:* 23,196 v Derby Co, League Cup 4th rd, 15 Nov, 1967. *Record receipts:* £10,007 v Doncaster R, Division 4, 7 Mar, 1981. *Pitch Measurements:* 110yd×75yd.
How to get there: There is a regular bus service from Lincoln Central Station to the ground, although there are no special buses. Nearest stations are Lincoln Central and Lincoln St Marks.
Match tickets: Car parking: Limited to 150 cars at the ground.
Entertainments/catering facilities: Social club at the ground with light catering before and after the match.
Club shop: Sited on the ground; sells all types of souvenirs.
Handbooks/programmes: Programmes available at each game or by subscription.
Extra information: Frank Keetley scored six times in 21 minutes for Lincoln against Halifax Town, 16 January 1932. Most points, most wins, fewest defeats and fewest goals against in a season in Division 4.
Club Colours: Red with white vertical striped shirts, black shorts, red and white stockings.
Change Colours: All white.
Club Coach: Lennie Lawrence.
Assistant Manager: John Sheridan.
Physiotherapist: Bert Loxley.
Club Nickname: The Red Imps.

LINCOLN CITY 1980–81 LEAGUE RECORD

Match No.	Date	Venue	Opponents	Result		H/T Score	Goalscorers	Attendance
1	Aug 16	H	Peterborough U	D	1-1	1-1	Harford	5131
2	20	A	Torquay U	W	2-1	2-1	Harford 2	3568
3	23	H	Wigan Ath	W	2-0	1-0	Hobson, Cunningham	3939
4	30	A	Crewe Alex	W	3-0	1-0	Hobson 2, Prophett (og)	2121
5	Sept 6	H	Halifax T	W	3-0	0-0	Hobson 2, Thompson S.	3720
6	13	A	Stockport Co	D	0-0	0-0		3289
7	17	H	Aldershot	L	0-1	0-1		4331
8	20	A	Wimbledon	W	1-0	1-0	Hobson	2320
9	27	H	Scunthorpe U	D	2-2	1-1	Harford, Hughes	4209
10	30	A	Aldershot	D	0-0	0-0		4970
11	Oct 4	A	Doncaster R	W	1-0	0-0	Hobson	9693
12	8	H	Rochdale	W	3-0	3-0	Neale, Hobson, Peake	3523
13	11	H	York C	D	1-1	1-0	Hobson	4026
14	18	A	Hartlepool U	L	0-2	0-1		2689
15	22	A	Bradford C	W	2-1	1-0	Harford, Neale	2832
16	25	H	Northampton T	W	8-0	2-0	Hobson 4, Harford 2, Shipley 2 (2 pens)	4031
17	29	H	Tranmere R	W	2-0	0-0	Neale, Thompson T.	4628
18	Nov 1	A	Hereford U	W	2-0	0-0	Neale 2	2755
19	4	A	Rochdale	L	0-1	0-0		2257
20	8	H	Southend U	W	2-1	1-0	Neale, Hobson	7218
21	12	H	Torquay U	W	5-0	1-0	Harford 3, Shipley, Neale	5050
22	15	A	Peterborough U	L	0-1	0-1		5817
23	Dec 6	H	Bury	W	2-1	2-1	Turner, Neale	3545
24	20	H	AFC Bournemouth	W	2-0	1-0	Hobson, Shipley (pen)	3391
25	26	A	Port Vale	W	1-0	0-0	Turner	4239
26	27	H	Mansfield T	D	1-1	1-1	Carr	8522
27	Jan 10	H	Bradford C	D	1-1	0-1	Turner	4670
28	24	H	Crewe Alex	W	2-1	1-1	Neale, Thompson S.	4925
29	31	A	Wigan Ath	W	2-0	0-0	Cunningham, Turner	5190
30	Feb 7	H	Stockport Co	W	1-0	0-0	Cunningham	4315
31	14	A	Halifax T	W	3-1	1-0	Hobson 2, Shipley (pen)	4444
32	21	A	Scunthorpe U	D	2-2	1-0	Hobson 2	4848
33	28	H	Wimbledon	D	0-0	0-0		3988
34	Mar 3	A	Tranmere R	D	0-0	0-0		1538
35	7	H	Doncaster R	D	1-1	1-0	Cunningham	8832
36	10	A	Darlington	D	0-0	0-0		2436
37	14	A	York C	L	0-1	0-0		2222
38	21	H	Hartlepool U	W	2-0	0-0	Biggins, Shipley	3856
39	28	A	Northampton T	D	1-1	1-1	Hobson	2424
40	Apr 4	H	Hereford U	W	1-0	0-0	Hobson	3655
41	11	A	Southend U	D	0-0	0-0		11,955
42	18	A	Mansfield T	L	0-2	0-0		4771
43	20	H	Port Vale	W	1-0	0-0	Cunningham	3665
44	25	A	AFC Bournemouth	W	1-0	1-0	Shipley	3542
45	May 2	H	Darlington	W	1-0	0-0	Cunningham	3888
46	4	A	Bury	D	1-1	0-0	Shipley	2968

Final League Position: 2

Goalscorers

League (66): Hobson 21, Harford 10, Neale 9, Shipley 8 (4 pens), Cunningham 6, Turner 4, Thompson S. 2, Biggins 1, Carr 1, Hughes 1, Peake 1, Thompson T. 1, own goal 1.
League Cup (8): Harford 5, Shipley 2, Bell.
F.A. Cup (1): Turner.

League Cup	First Round	Hull C (h)	5-0
		(a)	2-0
	Second Round	Swindon T (h)	1-2
		(a)	0-2
FA Cup	First Round	Gateshead (h)	1-0
	Second Round	Bury (a)	0-2

Boulton	Thompson T	Keeley	Thompson S	Peake	Carr	Turner	Harford	Cunningham	Hughes	Shipley	Hobson	Ramsey	Felgate	Neale	Bell	Hibberd	Biggins	Creane	Gilbert	*Match No.*
1	2	3	4	5	6	7	8	9	10	11										1
1	2	3	9	5	6	7	4	10	8	11										2
1	2	3	8	5	6	7	9	10		11	4									3
1*	2	3	4	5	6	7	8		10	11	9	12								4
	2	3	4	5	6	7	8		10	11	9		1							5
	2	3	4	5	6	7	8		10	11	9		1							6
	2	3*		5	6		8	10	4	11	9		1	7	12					7
	2	3		5	6		8	10	4	11	9		1	7						8
	2	3	8*	5	6		10	12	4	11	9		1	7						9
	2	3	8	5	6		10		4	11	9		1	7						10
	2	3	8	5	6		10		4	11	9		1	7						11
	2	3	8	5	6		10	12	4*	11	9		1	7						12
	2	3	8	5	6		10		4	11	9		1	7						13
	2	3	8	5	6			10	4*	11	9		1	7	12					14
		3	8	5	6	2	10		4	11	9		1	7						15
		3	8*	5	6	2	10	12	4	11	9		1	7						16
	2	3		5	6	8	10	12	4	11	9*		1	7						17
	2	3		5	6	8	10		4	11	9		1	7						18
	2	3		5	6	8	10	12	4*	11	9		1	7						19
	2	3		5	6	8	10		4	11	9		1	7						20
	2	3		5	6	8	10	12	4*	11	9		1	7						21
	2	3	12	5	6	8		10	4	11*	9		1	7						22
	2	3	4	5	6	8		10		11	9		1	7						23
	2	3	4	5	6	8	10			11	9		1	7						24
	2	3		5	6	8		10	4	11	9		1	7						25
	2	3		5	6	8		10	4	11	9		1	7						26
	2	3*	5		6	8		10	4	11	9		1	7	12					27
	2	3*	5		6	8		10	4	11	9		1	7	12					28
	2	3		5	6	8		10	4	11	9		1	7						29
	2	3		5	6	8		10	4	11	9		1	7						30
	2	3		5	6	8		10	4	11	9		1	7						31
	2	3		5	6	8		10	4	11	9		1	7						32
	2	3		5	6	8		10	4	11	9		1	7						33
	2	3	6	5		8		10	4	11	9		1	7						34
	2	3*		5	6	8		10	4	11	9		1	7	12					35
	2		6	5	3	8		10	4	11	9		1	7						36
	2		6	5	3	8		10	4*	11	9		1		7	12				37
	2		6	5	3	8			4	11	9		1	7			10			38
			6	5	2	8			4	11	9		1	7		3	10			39
	2		6	5	4	8		12		11	9		1	3		7*	10			40
	2		6	5	4	8		7		11	9		1	3	12		10*			41
	2		6	5	4	8		7		11	9		1	3	12		10*			42
	2		6	5	4*	8		7		11	9		1	3	12		10			43
	2		6	5	4	8		7		11	9		1	3			10			44
	2		6	5*	4	8		7	12	11	9		1	3			10			45
	2		6		3	8		7	4	11	9	10*	1					5	12	46
4	43	35	30	43	45	38	21	27	37	46	44	1	42	38	1	2	8	1	—	
			+ 1s					+ 7s	+ 1s			+ 1s			+ 8s	+ 1s			+ 1s	

LINCOLN CITY

	Ht	*Wt*	*Birthplace*	*Clubs*	*League App.*	*League Gls*
Goalkeepers						
Kevin Fox*	5 11	11 2	Sheffield	Lincoln C	4	—
				Hull C (on loan)	—	—
Kevin Rose	5 10½	12 11½	Evesham	Ledbury T	(not known)	
(Contract cancelled Sept 1980)				Lincoln C	—	—
Colin Boulton	5 10	13 1	Cheltenham	Derby Co	273	—
				Southampton (on loan)	5	—
				Los Angeles A	(not known)	
				Lincoln C	4	—
David Felgate	6 1	13 13	Blaenau Ffestiniog	Bolton W	—	—
				Rochdale (on loan)	47	—
				Bradford C (on loan)	—	—
				Crewe Alex (on loan)	14	—
				Lincoln C	42	—
Stuart Naylor	6 2	11 13	Leeds	Lincoln C	—	—
Defenders						
Phil Neale	5 10	11 5	Scunthorpe	Lincoln C	199	18
Steve Ward	6 0	10 13	Sheffield	Lincoln C	2	—
David Carr	5 11	11 0	Aylesham	Luton T	43	—
				Lincoln C	91	3
Trevor Peake	6 0	12 9	Nuneaton	Nuneaton B	(not known)	
				Lincoln C	88	2
Steve Thompson	6 0	14 7½	Sheffield	Boston U	(not known)	
				Lincoln C	31	2
Trevor Thompson	5 9	11 13¾	Newcastle	WBA	20	—
				Newport Co	35	2
				Lincoln C	68	1
Nolan Keeley	5 11	11 2	East Barsham	Scunthorpe U	259	37
				Lincoln C	52	3
Gerry Creane	6 0	13 12	Lincoln	Lincoln C	4	—
Midfield						
David Hughes	5 9	12 5	Birmingham	Aston V	4	1
				Lincoln C	62	1
George Shipley	5 7	10 2¾	Newcastle	Southampton	3	—
				Reading (on loan)	12	1
				Blackpool (on loan)	—	—
				Lincoln C	69	10
Phil Turner	5 8	10 7	Sheffield	Lincoln C	52	5
Stuart Hibberd	6 0	11 13½	Sheffield	Lincoln C	3	—
Forwards						
Gordon Hobson	5 8	10 5	Sheffield	Lincoln C	125	39
Dave Burrows*	5 7	9 4	Bilsthorpe	Lincoln C	1	—
Tony Cunningham	6 1	13 2½	Kingston, Jamaica	Lincoln C	72	18
Derek Bell	5 8	10 4½	Wyberton	Derby Co	—	—
				Halifax T	112	21
				Sheffield W (on loan)	5	1
				Barnsley	46	20
				Lincoln C	34	5
Craig Ramsey	5 7	11 13½	Dunfermline	Lincoln C	5	2
Wayne Biggins*	5 1	11 0	Sheffield	Lincoln C	8	1
David Gilbert (Apprentice)				Lincoln C	1	—

Ian Travis (Contract cancelled November 1980)

LIVERPOOL Division 1

Chairman: J. W. Smith JP

Directors: C. J. Hill, Coun. S. J. Moss JP, S. C. Reakes JP, H. Cartwright, J. T. Cross, W. D. Corkish.

Team Manager: Bob Paisley. *Asst. Manager:* Joe Fagan.

General Secretary: P. B. Robinson.

Year Formed: 1892. *Turned Professional:* 1892.

Limited Company: 1892.

Football League Record:
1893 Elected to Division 2; 1894–95 Division 1; 1895–96 Division 2; 1896–1904 Division 1; 1904–05 Division 2; 1905–54 Division 1; 1954–62 Division 2; 1962– Division 1.

Honours: *Football League:* Division 1 – Champions 1900–01, 1905–06, 1921–22, 1922–23, 1946–47, 1963–64, 1965–66, 1972–73, 1975–76, 1976–77, 1978–79, 1979–80 (Liverpool have a record number of 12 League Championship wins); Runners-up 1898–99, 1909–10, 1968–69, 1973–74, 1974–75, 1977–78; Division 2 – Champions 1893–94, 1895–96, 1904–05, 1961–62; *FA Cup:* Winners 1965, 1974; Runners-up 1914, 1950, 1971, 1977; *Football League Cup:* Winners 1981; Runners-up 1977–78. **European Competitions:** *European Cup:* 1964–65, 1966–67, 1973–74, 1976–77 (winners), 1977–78 (winners), 1978–79, 1979–80, 1980–81 (winners); *European Cup-Winners' Cup:* 1965–66 (runners-up), 1971–72, 1974–75; *European Fairs Cup:* 1967–68, 1968–69, 1969–70, 1970–71; *UEFA Cup:* 1972–73 (winners), 1975–76 (winners); *Super Cup:* 1977 (winners), 1978.

Record Victory: 11-0 v Strömsgodset, European Cup-Winners' Cup, 17 Sept, 1974.

Record Defeat: 1-9 v Birmingham C, Division 2, 11 Dec, 1954.

Most League Points: 68, Division 1, 1978–79 (First Division record).

Most League Goals: 106, Division 2, 1895–96.

Highest League Scorer in Season: Roger Hunt, 41, Division 2, 1961–62.

Most League Goals in Total Aggregate: Roger Hunt, 245, 1959–69.

Most Capped Player: Emlyn Hughes, 59 (62) England.

Most League Appearances: Ian Callaghan, 640, 1960–78.

Record Transfer Fee Received: £500,000 from Hamburg SV for Kevin Keegan, June 1977.

Record Transfer Fee Paid: £440,000 to Celtic for Kenny Dalglish, Aug 1977.

Previous Managers since the War: George Kay, Don Welsh, Phil Taylor, Bill Shankly.

Address of Supporters Club: 212 Lower Breck Road.

Address of the Club Shop or Boutique: Same as ground.

Anfield Road, Liverpool 4. Telephone 051-263 2361. *Telegraphic address:* 'Goalkeeper Liverpool'. *Ground capacity:* 52,518. *Record attendance:* 61,905 v Wolverhampton W, FA Cup 4th rd, 2 Feb, 1952. *Record receipts:* £154,000 Wales v Scotland, World Cup qualifying tie, 12 Oct, 1977. *Pitch measurements:* 110yd×75yd.

How to get there: Buses 17d from Pier Head and 26, 27 from Castle Street. Nearest stations, Bankhall and Kirkdale.

Match tickets: Postal applications 19 days before the match.

Car parking: Limited street parking around the ground. Large privately owned car park in Priory Road within five minutes walk of the ground.

Entertainments/catering facilities: Licensed refreshment bars in all parts of the ground.

Club shop: Main shop run by the Development Association open Monday–Saturday. Small kiosks in the ground open on match days only.

Handbooks/programmes: No handbook. Programmes available on subscription from the secretary.

Extra information: Liverpool's defensive record of only 16 goals conceded in 1978–79 is the best in First Division history.

Club Colours: All red with white facings.

Change Colours: White shirts with red collars and cuffs, black shorts, white stockings.

Captain: Phil Thompson. *First Team Trainer:* Ron Moran.

Club Nickname: Reds or Pool.

LIVERPOOL 1980–81 LEAGUE RECORD

Match No.	Date	Venue	Opponents	Result	H/T Score	Goalscorers	Attendance
1	Aug 16	H	Crystal Palace	W 3-0	2-0	Dalglish, Kennedy R., Kennedy A.	42,777
2	19	A	Coventry C	D 0-0	0-0		22,807
3	23	A	Leicester C	L 0-2	0-1		28,455
4	30	H	Norwich C	W 4-1	1-0	Hansen, McDermott, Kennedy A., Johnson	35,315
5	Sept 6	A	Birmingham C	D 1-1	0-0	Dalglish	27,042
6	13	H	WBA	W 4-0	2-0	McDermott (pen), Souness, Fairclough 2	36,792
7	20	A	Southampton	D 2-2	1-2	Souness, Fairclough	24,085
8	27	H	Brighton & HA	W 4-1	1-0	Souness 2, McDermott (pen), Fairclough	35,836
9	Oct 4	A	Manchester C	W 3-0	1-0	Dalglish, Souness, Lee	41,022
10	7	H	Middlesbrough	W 4-2	1-0	McDermott 2 (1 pen), Kennedy R., Dalglish	28,204
11	11	H	Ipswich T	D 1-1	1-1	McDermott (pen)	48,084
12	18	A	Everton	D 2-2	1-2	Lee, Dalglish	52,565
13	25	H	Arsenal	D 1-1	0-0	Souness	40,310
14	Nov 1	A	Stoke C	D 2-2	1-0	Johnson, Dalglish	22,864
15	8	H	Nottingham F	D 0-0	0-0		43,143
16	11	H	Coventry C	W 2-1	1-0	Johnson 2	26,744
17	15	A	Crystal Palace	D 2-2	1-0	Kennedy R., McDermott	31,154
18	22	H	Aston Villa	W 2-1	0-0	Dalglish 2	48,114
19	25	A	Wolverhampton W	L 1-4	1-1	Neal	25,497
20	29	A	Sunderland	W 4-2	2-0	Johnson, McDermott, Lee 2	32,340
21	Dec 6	H	Tottenham H	W 2-1	1-1	Johnson, Kennedy R.	39,545
22	13	A	Ipswich T	D 1-1	0-1	Case	32,274
23	20	H	Wolverhampton W	W 1-0	1-0	Kennedy R.	33,563
24	26	A	Manchester U	D 0-0	0-0		57,073
25	27	H	Leeds U	D 0-0	0-0		44,086
26	Jan 10	A	Aston Villa	L 0-2	0-1		47,960
27	17	A	Norwich C	W 1-0	1-0	McDermott	23,829
28	31	H	Leicester C	L 1-2	1-0	Young (og)	35,154
29	Feb 7	A	WBA	L 0-2	0-1		27,905
30	14	H	Birmingham C	D 2-2	2-1	Johnson, Neal	32,199
31	21	A	Brighton & HA	D 2-2	1-2	Johnson, McDermott	23,275
32	28	H	Southampton	W 2-0	1-0	Kennedy R., McDermott	41,575
33	Mar 21	H	Everton	W 1-0	0-0	Bailey (og)	49,743
34	28	A	Arsenal	L 0-1	0-1		47,058
35	Apr 3	H	Stoke C	W 3-0	1-0	Whelan, McDermott 2	33,308
36	11	A	Nottingham F	D 0-0	0-0		27,363
37	14	H	Manchester U	L 0-1	0-1		31,276
38	18	A	Leeds U	D 0-0	0-0		39,206
39	25	A	Tottenham H	D 1-1	1-1	Gayle	35,334
40	May 2	H	Sunderland	L 0-1	0-1		40,337
41	5	A	Middlesbrough	W 2-1	2-1	Kennedy R., Irwin	19,102
42	19	H	Manchester C	W 1-0	1-0	Kennedy R.	24,462

Final League Position: 5

Goalscorers

League (62): McDermott 13 (4 pens), Dalglish 8, Johnson 8, Kennedy R. 8, Souness 6, Fairclough 4, Lee 4, Kennedy A. 2, Neal 2, Case 1, Gayle 1, Hansen 1, Irwin 1, Whelan 1, own goals 2.
League Cup (21): Dalglish 7, Johnson 4, Fairclough 2, Kennedy R. 2, Lee 2, Hansen, Kennedy A., McDermott, Souness.
F.A. Cup (5): Dalglish 2, Case, Kennedy R., McDermott.

League Cup	Second Round	Bradford C (a)	0-1
		(h)	4-0
	Third Round	Swindon T (h)	5-0
	Fourth Round	Portsmouth (h)	4-1
	Fifth Round	Birmingham C (h)	3-1
	Semi-final	Manchester C (a)	1-0
		(h)	1-1
	Final	West Ham U	1-1 (at Wembley)
	Replay		2-1 (at Villa Park)
FA Cup	Third Round	Altrincham (h)	4-1
	Fourth Round	Everton (a)	1-2

Clemence	Neal	Kennedy A	Thompson	Kennedy R	Hansen	Dalglish	Case	Johnson	McDermott	Souness	Ogrizovic	Fairclough	Lee	Cohen	Money	Irwin	Gayle	Rush	Heighway	Sheedy	Whelan	Russell	*Match No.*
1	2	3	4	5	6	7*	8	9	10	11		12											1
	2	3	4	5	6	7	8*	9	10	11	1	12											2
1	2	3	4	5	6	7		9	10	11		12	8*										3
1	2	3	4	5	6	7	8	9	10	11													4
1	2	3	4	5	6	7	8	9*	10	11				12									5
1	2		4	5	6*	7			10	11		9	8	3	12								6
1	2		4	5	6	7			10*	11		9	8	3		12							7
1	2		4	5	6	7			10	11		9	8	3									8
1	2		4	5	6	7			10	11		9*	8	3			12						9
1	2		4	5	6	7	12	9*	10	11			8	3									10
1	2		4	5	6	7		9	10	11			8	3									11
1	2		4	5	6	7		9	10	11			8	3									12
1	2	3	4	5	6	7	12	9*	10	11			8										13
1	2	3	4	5	6	7		9	10	11			8										14
1	2		4	5	6	7		9	10	11			8	3									15
1	2		4	5	6	7		9	10	11			8		3								16
1	2		4*	5	6	7	12	9	10	11			8	3									17
1	2			5	6	7		9	10	11			8	3		4							18
1	2			5	6	7	12	9	10	11			8*	3		4							19
1	2	3		5	6	7		9	10	11			8			4							20
1	2	3		5	6	7*	12	9	10	11			8			4							21
1	2	3		5	6		12	9*	10	11			8			4		7					22
1	2	3		5	6			9	10	11			8			4			7				23
1	2	3		5	6*	7	11	9	10				8		12	4							24
1	2	3		5		7*	11	9	10				8		6	4			12				25
1	2	3		5		7		9	10	11			8		6	4							26
1	2	3	4	5		7	12		10	11		9*	8			6							27
1	2		4	5			12	9	10*	11			8	3		6			7				28
1	2			5	6		7	9		11		10*	8		3	4			12				29
1	2			5		7	12	9	10*	11			8		3	4				6			30
1	2			5		7	6	9	10	11			8	3		4							31
1	2	3	4	5	6	7		9*	10	11			8			12							32
1	2			5	6	7	10			11			8		3	4			9				33
1	2	3		5	6	7	12		10	11*			8			4			9				34
1	2	3	4		6	7	11		10				8					9			5		35
1	2		4	5	6	7	11		10				8		3			9					36
1	2		4	5	6	7	11		10				8		3			9					37
1	2		4	5	6	7		9	10	11			8		3								38
1	2			5	6				10	11			8		3	4	7	9					39
1	2			5	6				10	11			8		3	4	7*	9				12	40
1	2			5	6		7		10	11			8		3	4		9					41
1	2	3	4	5	6		8	9	10	11							7						42
41	42	19	25	41	36	34	14	29	40	37	1	6	37	13	12	19	3	7	4	1	1	—	
							+ 10s					+ 3s		+ 1s	+ 2s	+ 2s	+ 1s		+ 2s			+ 1s	

LIVERPOOL

	Ht	Wt	Birthplace	Clubs	League App.	League Gls
Goalkeepers						
Ray Clemence (England)	5 11½	12 9	Skegness	Scunthorpe U	48	—
				Liverpool	470	—
Steve Ogrizovic	6 3	14 7	Mansfield	Chesterfield	16	—
				Liverpool	4	—
Bruce Grobbelaar (Zimbabwe)			Rhodesia	Crewe Alex	24	1
				Vancouver W	(not known)	
				Liverpool	—	—
Defenders						
Phil Neal (England)	5 11	12 2	Irchester	Northampton T	186	29
				Liverpool	275	25
Phil Thompson (England)	6 0	11 8	Liverpool	Liverpool	282	7
Jeff Ainsworth (Contract cancelled Sept 1980)	5 9	11 7	Liverpool	Liverpool	—	—
Colin Irwin	6 0	12 6	Liverpool	Liverpool	29	3
Alan Hansen (Scotland)	6 1	13 0	Alloa	Partick T	86	6
				Liverpool	126	6
Alan Harper	5 8	9 7	Liverpool	Liverpool	—	—
Alan Kennedy	5 9	10 7	Sunderland	Newcastle U	158	9
				Liverpool	93	6
Michael Halsall	5 10	11 4	Liverpool	Liverpool	—	—
Avi Cohen (Israel)	5 11½	11 11	Tel Aviv	Maccabi	(not known)	
				Liverpool	18	1
Richard Money	5 11½	11 5	Lowestoft	Scunthorpe U	173	4
				Fulham	106	3
				Liverpool	14	—
Mark Hodder*	5 8½	10 6	Liverpool	Liverpool	—	—
Tim Bredbury			Hong Kong	Liverpool	—	—
Midfield						
Terry McDermott (England)	5 9	12 13	Kirkby	Bury	90	8
				Newcastle U	56	6
				Liverpool	201	40
Ray Kennedy (England)	5 11	13 4	Seaton Delavel	Arsenal	158	53
				Liverpool	260	49
Howard Gayle	5 10½	10 9	Liverpool	Liverpool	4	1
				Fulham (on loan)	14	—
Bob Savage	5 7	11 1	Liverpool	Liverpool	—	—
Graeme Souness (Scotland)	5 11	12 13	Edinburgh	Tottenham H	—	—
				Middlesbrough	176	22
				Liverpool	134	17
Kevin Sheedy	5 7	9 2	Hereford	Hereford U	51	4
				Liverpool	1	—
Ron Whelan (Eire)	5 9	10 13	Dublin	Home Farm	(not known)	
				Liverpool	1	1
Eric Vasco*			Liverpool	Liverpool	—	—
Craig Johnston	5 9	11 2	Johannesburg	Lake McQuarrie	(not known)	
				Sydney C	(not known)	
				Middlesbrough	64	16
				Liverpool	—	—
Forwards						
Steve Heighway (Eire) (Contract cancelled April 1981)	5 10½	11 2	Dublin	Liverpool	331	49
Jimmy Case	5 9	12 7	Liverpool	Liverpool	186	23
David Fairclough	5 9	11 0	Liverpool	Liverpool	90	31
Sammy Lee	5 7	10 1	Liverpool	Liverpool	48	5
David Johnson (England)	5 10	12 4	Liverpool	Everton	50	11
				Ipswich T	137	35
				Liverpool	134	53
Kenny Dalglish (Scotland)	5 8	11 13	Glasgow	Celtic	204	112
				Liverpool	160	65
Colin Russell	5 7	10 7	Liverpool	Liverpool	1	—
Jim Williams (Contract cancelled Nov 1980)	5 6½	9 2	Liverpool	Liverpool	—	—
Karl Green (Contract cancelled Nov 1980)	5 8½	10 7	Liverpool	Liverpool	—	—
Ian Rush (Wales)	6 0½	12 6	Flint	Chester	34	14
				Liverpool	7	—
Steven Foley			Liverpool	Liverpool	—	—

LUTON TOWN — Division 2

President: T. Hodgson.

Chairman: D. Mortimer.

Directors: H. Richardson, R. J. Smith, E. S. Pearson LLM, BSC, R. L. Banks, J. R. Yates, D. J. Evans.

Club Secretary: J. S. Wilkinson.

Company Secretary/Chief Executive: J. R. Smith.

Team Manager: David Pleat.

Year Formed: 1885. *Turned Professional:* 1890.

Limited Company: 1897.

Previous Grounds: 1885, Excelsior, Dallow Lane; 1897, Dunstable Road; 1905, Kenilworth Road.

Football League Record:
1897 Elected to Division 2; 1900 failed re-election; 1920 Division 3; 1921 Division 3(S); 1937–55 Division 2; 1955–60 Division 1; 1960–63 Division 2; 1963–65 Division 3; 1965–68 Division 4; 1968–70 Division 3; 1970–74 Division 2; 1974–75 Division 1; 1975– Division 2.

Honours: *Football League:* Division 1 best season: 8th, 1957–58; Division 2 – Runners-up 1954–55, 1973–74; Division 3 – Runners-up 1969–70; Division 4 – Champions 1967–68. Division 3(S) – Champions 1936–37; Runners-up 1935–36. *FA Cup:* Runners-up 1959. *Football League Cup* best season: 5th rd, 1978–79.

Record Victory: 12-0 v Bristol R, Division 3(S), 13 Apr, 1936.

Record Defeat: 1-9 v Swindon T, Division 3(S), 28 Aug, 1920.

Most League Points: 66, Division 4, 1967–68 (equalled Division 4 record).

Most League Goals: 103, Division 3(S), 1936–37.

Highest League Scorer in Season: Joe Payne, 55, Division 3(S), 1936–37.

Most League Goals in Total Aggregate: 243, Gordon Turner, 1949–64.

Most Capped Player: George Cummins, 19, Eire.

Most League Appearances: Bob Morton, 494, 1948–64.

Record Transfer Fee Received: £350,000 from Manchester C for Paul Futcher, June 1978.

Record Transfer Fee Paid: £200,000 to Mansfield T for Mike Saxby, July 1979 and £200,000 to Bristol R for Steve White, Dec 1980.

Previous Managers since the War: George Martin, Dally Duncan, Syd Owen, Sam Bartram, Bill Harvey, Allan Brown, Alec Stock, Harry Haslam.

Address of Supporters Club: Bobbers Club, Beech Hill Path, Luton.

70–72 Kenilworth Rd, Luton. Telephone Luton (0582) 411622. 24-hour answering service: 0582-33010. *Telegraphic address:* 'Football Luton'. *Ground capacity:* 22,741 (17,000 covered). *Record attendance:* 30,069 v Blackpool, FA Cup 6th rd replay, 4 March, 1959. *Record receipts:* £31,233.25 v West Ham U, Division 2, 1 March, 1980. *Pitch measurements:* 112yd×72yd.

How to get there: Nearest railway station, Luton (six minutes walk). There is also a frequent bus service to and from the town centre to the ground, but the ground is central.

Match tickets: Seats can be booked two weeks before the game.

Car parking: Ample parking facilities adjacent to the ground entrance in Maple Road.

Entertainments/catering facilities: Licensed bars and refreshment bars on ground.

Club shop: Sells all types of souvenirs.

Programmes: Programmes can be obtained from club shop.

Extra information: Joe Payne scored 10 goals against Bristol Rovers in April 1936, a record individual score in a Football League match.

Club Colours: White shirt with orange collar and cuffs, with two orange and three navy blue stripes down left side, white shorts with two orange and three navy blue stripes on sides, white stockings with white, orange, and navy blue turnover.

Change Colours: White shirts, white, orange or navy shorts, white stockings.

Club Captain:

First Team Trainer: John Sheridan.

Club Nickname: Hatters.

LUTON TOWN 1980–81 LEAGUE RECORD

Match No.	Date	Venue	Opponents	Result	H/T Score	Goalscorers	Attendance
1	Aug 16	A	West Ham U	W 2-1	0-0	Moss 2 (2 pens)	27,933
2	19	H	Watford	W 1-0	1-0	White	13,887
3	23	H	Derby Co	L 1-2	1-1	Stein	11,025
4	30	A	Newcastle U	L 1-2	1-0	Stein	13,164
5	Sept 6	H	Wrexham	D 1-1	0-0	Bunn	8244
6	13	A	Blackburn R	L 0-3	0-0		9076
7	20	H	Orient	W 2-1	0-0	Stein, Hill	8506
8	27	A	Grimsby T	D 0-0	0-0		9044
9	Oct 4	H	Notts Co	L 0-1	0-1		8786
10	7	A	Bristol C	L 1-2	1-0	Saxby	7014
11	11	A	Preston NE	L 0-1	0-1		5620
12	18	H	Shrewsbury T	D 1-1	0-1	White	8014
13	21	H	Swansea C	D 2-2	1-1	Stein, Moss	8402
14	25	A	Cambridge U	W 3-1	1-1	Moss (pen), Goodyear, Stein	7218
15	Nov 1	H	Sheffield W	W 3-0	0-0	Moss 2 (1 pen), White	12,092
16	8	A	QPR	L 2-3	2-2	Stein, Moss	10,082
17	11	A	Watford	W 1-0	1-0	White	16,939
18	15	H	West Ham U	W 3-2	2-1	Stein 2, Moss	17,031
19	22	A	Cardiff C	L 0-1	0-0		6064
20	29	H	Bolton W	D 2-2	1-0	Hill, Stein	8300
21	Dec 6	A	Oldham Ath	D 0-0	0-0		4720
22	13	H	Preston NE	W 4-2	1-0	Moss 2 (1 pen), Fuccillo, Ingram	7874
23	19	A	Shrewsbury T	W 1-0	0-0	Ingram	4521
24	26	H	Chelsea	W 2-0	0-0	Stein 2	16,006
25	27	A	Bristol R	W 4-2	3-2	Stein 3, Hill	7010
26	Jan 10	H	Cardiff C	D 2-2	1-1	Moss, Price	9013
27	17	H	Newcastle U	L 0-1	0-1		10,774
28	31	A	Derby Co	D 2-2	0-1	Moss, Ingram	16,477
29	Feb 7	H	Blackburn R	W 3-1	0-1	Price, Hill, Moss	9350
30	21	H	Grimsby T	L 0-2	0-1		9217
31	Mar 1	A	Orient	D 0-0	0-0		8074
32	7	A	Notts Co	W 1-0	1-0	Stein	8075
33	14	H	Bristol C	W 3-1	2-1	White 2, Moss (pen)	8745
34	28	H	Cambridge U	D 0-0	0-0		9412
35	31	A	Wrexham	D 0-0	0-0		4157
36	Apr 4	A	Sheffield W	L 1-3	0-1	Ingram	17,006
37	11	H	QPR	W 3-0	1-0	Ingram, Stein, Antic	12,112
38	18	H	Bristol R	W 1-0	1-0	Moss (pen)	9009
39	20	A	Chelsea	W 2-0	1-0	Moss, Hill	12,868
40	25	H	Oldham Ath	L 1-2	0-1	Stein	10,305
41	27	A	Swansea C	D 2-2	1-2	Hill 2	21,354
42	May 2	A	Bolton W	W 3-0	0-0	Stein, White, Stephens	7268

Final League Position: 5

Goalscorers

League (61): Stein 18, Moss 16 (7 pens), Hill 7, White 7, Ingram 5, Price 2, Antic 1, Bunn 1, Fuccillo 1, Goodyear 1, Saxby 1, Stephens 1.
League Cup (4): Antic, Moss, Saxby, Stein.
F.A. Cup (4): Ingram 2, Moss 2 (1 pen).

League Cup	Second Round	Reading (a)	2-0
		(h)	1-1
	Third Round	Manchester C (h)	1-2
FA Cup	Third Round	Orient (a)	3-1
	Fourth Round	Newcastle U (a)	1-2

Findlay	Stephens	Donaghy	Grealish	Saxby	Price	Hill	Stein	White	Antic	Moss	West	Bunn	Aizlewood	Ingram	Harrow	Goodyear	Judge	Fuccillo	Turner	*Match No.*
1	2	3	4	5	6	7	8	9*	10	11	12									1
1	2	3	4	5	6	7	8	9	10*	11	12									2
1	2	3	4	5	6	7	8		10	11		9*	12							3
1	2	3	4	5*	6	7	8		10	11		9	12							4
1	2	3	4	5	6	7	8		10*	11	12	9								5
1	2	3	4	5	6	7	8	12		11*	10			9						6
1	2	3	4	5	6	7	8		10	11	9									7
1		2	4	5	6	7	8		10*	11	9		3		12					8
1	2	3	4	5	6	7	8		12	11	10*				9					9
1	2	3	4	5	6	7	8			11	10				9					10
1	2	3	4	5	6	7	8	11			10		12		9*					11
1	2	3	4		6	7	8	9		11			10			5				12
1	2	3	4		6	7	8	9		11			10			5				13
1	2	3	4		6	7	8	9	12	11*			10			5				14
	2	3	4		6	7	8	9		11			10			5	1			15
	2	3	4		6	7	8	9		11			10			5	1			16
1	2	3	4	5	6	7	8	9		11	12		10*							17
1	2	3	4	5	6	7	8	9		11	12		10*							18
1	2	3*	4	5	6	7	8	9		11	12		10							19
1	2	3	4*	5	6	7	8	9		11	12		10							20
1	2*	3	4	5	6	7	8	9		11	12		10							21
1	2	3		5*	6	7	8		12	11			10	9				4		22
1	2	3	4	5		7	8		12	11	6		10	9*						23
1	2	3	6		4	7	9			11	8		5	10						24
1	2*	3	4		6	7	8		12	11	5		10	9						25
1		3	4	5	6	7	8			11	2		10	9						26
1	2	3	4		6	7	8			11	5		10	9*				12		27
1	2	3			6	7	8			11	5			9				10	4	28
1	2	3	4		6	7	8			11	5		10	9						29
1	2	3	6		4*	8	10	12		11	7		5	9						30
1	2	3	4	5*	6	7	8		12	11				9				10		31
1	2	3	4	5	6	7	8	9	10	11										32
1	2	3	4	5	6	7	8	9	10	11										33
1	2	3		5	6	7	8	9	10	11	4									34
1	2	3	4	5	6	7	8	9*	10	11				12						35
1	2	9	4	5	6	7*	8		10	11			3	12						36
1	2	3	4	5	6	7	8		10	11				9						37
1	2	3	4	5	6	7	8		10	11				9						38
1	2	3	4	5	6	7	8		10	11				9						39
1	2	3	4	5	6	7	8		10*	11	12			9						40
1	2	3		5	6	7	8	9	10	11	4									41
1	2	3		5	6	7	8	9	10	11								4		42
40	40	42	37	31	41	42	42	19	18	41	16	3	20	15	3	5	2	4	1	
								+ 2s	+ 6s		+ 9s		+ 3s	+ 2s	+ 1s			+ 1s		

LUTON TOWN

	Ht	Wt	Birthplace	Clubs	League App.	League Gls
Goalkeepers						
Alan Judge	5 11	11 5½	Kingsbury	Luton T	3	—
Jake Findlay	6 1	14 1	Blairgowrie	Aston V	14	—
				Luton T	104	—
Defenders						
Paul Price (Wales)	5 11	11 12	St Albans	Luton T	207	8
Wayne Turner	5 9	11 5	Luton	Luton T	4	—
Mal Donaghy (N. Ireland)	5 10	12 7	Belfast	Larne	—	—
				Luton T	124	1
Kirk Stephens	5 9	11 8	Coventry	Luton T	105	2
Mark Aizlewood	6 0	11 4	Newport	Newport Co	38	1
				Luton T	72	—
Mike Saxby	6 0	13 10	Mansfield	Mansfield T	79	5
				Luton T	70	5
John Woodward (Contract cancelled Nov 1980)	5 5¾	8 13½	London	Luton T	—	—
Midfield						
Pasqualle Fuccillo	5 11	11 4	Bedford	Luton T	122	22
Ricky Hill	5 9	11 10	London	Luton T	173	26
Alan West	5 9	10 8	Hyde	Burnley	44	3
				Luton T	285	16
Les Harriott (Contract cancelled Dec 1980)	5 7	11 9	Luton	Luton T	—	—
Clive Goodyear	5 11	11 4	Lincoln	Luton T	6	1
Tony Grealish (Eire)	5 7	11 7	Paddington	Orient	171	10
				Luton T	78	2
Robert Johnson	5 6	9 12	Bedford	Luton T	—	—
Neil Madden	5 6	9 4	Luton	Luton T	1	—
Raddy Antic (Yugoslavia)			Yugoslavia	Zaragoza	(not known)	
				Luton T	24	1
Forwards						
Godfrey Ingram	5 7	10 3	Luton	Luton T	24	6
				Northampton T (on loan)	10	4
Brian Stein	5 10	11 8	South Africa	Luton T	142	39
Dave Moss	5 9	11 7	Witney	Swindon T	230	60
				Luton T	111	53
Seamus Heath	5 9	10 5	Belfast	Luton T	—	—
Andy Pearson (Contract cancelled Jan 1981)	5 5	9 9	Newmarket	Luton T	2	—
Michael Small (Contract cancelled Oct 1980)	6 0	12 4	Birmingham	Luton T	—	—
William Smith (Contract cancelled Feb 1981)	6 1	14 3	London	Luton T	—	—
Steve White	5 11	11 10	Chipping Sodbury	Bristol R	50	20
				Luton T	30	7
Frankie Bunn	5 11	10 6	Birmingham	Luton T	3	1
Andy Harrow (Transferred to Aberdeen Jan 1981)	5 10	11 6	Kirkcaldy	Cowdenbeath	95	18
				Raith R	149	42
				Luton T	4	—

MANCHESTER CITY — Division 1

Chairman: P. J. Swales.
Executive President: S. H. Cussons.
Directors: S. S. Rose MB, FRCS, A. E. Alexander MSIA, R. Harris, J. B. Muir, I. L. G. Niven, M. T. Horwich, W. C. Adams.
Secretary: J. B. Halford.
Team Manager: John Bond.
Assistant Team Manager: John Benson.
Year Formed: 1887 as Ardwick FC; 1895 as Manchester City.
Limited Company: 1894.
Turned Professional: 1887 as Ardwick FC.
Previous Names: 1887–94, Ardwick FC (Formed through the amalgamation of West Gorton and Gorton Athletic, the latter having been formed in 1880).

Previous Grounds: 1880–81, Clowes Street; 1881–82, Kirkmanshulme Cricket Ground; 1882–84, Queens Road; 1884–87, Pink Bank Lane; 1887–1923, Hyde Road (1894–1923, as City); 1923, Maine Road.

Football League Record:
1892 Ardwick elected founder member of Division 2; 1894 Newly-formed Manchester C elected to Division 2; Division 1 1899–1902, 1903–09, 1910–26, 1928–38, 1947–50, 1951–63, 1966– ; Division 2 1902–03, 1909–10, 1926–28, 1938–47, 1950–51, 1963–66.

Honours: *Football League:* Division 1 – Champions 1936–37, 1967–68; Runners-up 1903–04, 1920–21, 1976–77; Division 2 – Champions 1898–99, 1902–03, 1909–10, 1927–28, 1946–47, 1965–66; Runners-up 1895–96, 1950–51. *FA Cup:* Winners 1904, 1934, 1956, 1969; Runners-up 1926, 1933, 1955, 1981. *Football League Cup:* Winners 1970, 1976; Runners-up 1973–74. **European Competitions:** *European Cup:* 1968–69. *European Cup-Winners' Cup:* 1969–70 (winners), 1970–71. *UEFA Cup:* 1972–73, 1976–77, 1977–78, 1978–79.
Record Victory: 11-3 v Lincoln C, Division 2, 23 Mar, 1895.
Record Defeat: 1-9 v Everton, Division 1, 3 Sept, 1906.
Most League Points: 62, Division 2, 1946–47.
Most League Goals: 108, Division 2, 1926–27.
Highest League Scorer in Season: Tommy Johnson, 38, Division 1, 1928–29.
Most League Goals in Total Aggregate: Tommy Johnson, 158, 1919–30.
Most Capped Player: Colin Bell, 48, England.
Most League Appearances: Alan Oakes, 565, 1959–76.
Record Transfer Fee Received: £748,000 from WBA for Peter Barnes, July 1979.
Record Transfer Fee Paid: £1,437,500 to Wolverhampton W for Steve Daley, Sept 1979. (£1,150,000 basic fee).
Previous Managers since the War: Wilf Wild, Sam Cowan, Jock Thomson, Les McDowall, George Poyser, Joe Mercer, Malcolm Allison, John Hart, Ron Saunders, Tony Book, Malcolm Allison.
Address of Supporters Club: OK Souvenir Sports Ltd, Maine Road, Moss Side, Manchester M14 7WN.

Maine Road, Moss Side, Manchester M14 7WN. Telephone 061-226 1191/2. *Telegraphic address:* 'Football, Manchester 14'. *Ground capacity:* 52,500. *Record attendance:* 84,569 v Stoke C, FA Cup 6th rd, 3 March, 1934 (British record for any game outside London or Glasgow). *Record receipts:* £165,000 Liverpool v Manchester U, FA Cup semi-final, 31 March, 1979. *Pitch measurements:* 119yd×79yd.
How to get there: Corporation specials from Aytoun Street, Piccadilly, in centre of city. Nearest railway station, Manchester Piccadilly.
Match tickets: Advance booking 14 days prior to the match.
Car parking: Kippax Street car park holds approximately 400 cars. Also street parking.
Entertainments/catering facilities: Social club can be used by visiting supporters (contact Mr Roy Clarke). Licensed refreshment points around the ground.
Club shop: Open all week at the ground.
Handbooks/programmes: Handbook available. Programmes can be obtained on a mailing list.
Extra information: Manchester City scored more goals in 1937–38 than any other First Division side – but were relegated!
Club Colours: Sky blue shirts with white collar and cuffs, white stripe down sleeve, sky blue shorts with white trimmings, sky blue stockings with white rings on top.
Change Colours: White shirts with red/black stripe diagonally across chest, black shorts, black stockings.
Club Captain: Joe Corrigan. *Team Captain:* Paul Power.
Club Nickname: Citizens.

MANCHESTER CITY 1980–81 LEAGUE RECORD

Match No.	Date	Venue	Opponents	Result		H/T Score	Goalscorers	Attendance
1	Aug 16	A	Southampton	L	0-3	0-2		23,320
2	20	H	Sunderland	L	0-4	0-1		33,271
3	23	H	Aston Villa	D	2-2	0-1	Tueart (pen), Ranson	30,017
4	30	A	Middlesbrough	D	2-2	2-1	Reeves, MacKenzie	15,761
5	Sept 6	H	Arsenal	D	1-1	0-0	Tueart (pen)	32,233
6	13	A	Nottingham F	L	2-3	2-1	Bennett, Henry	23,184
7	20	H	Stoke C	L	1-2	1-2	Tueart	29,507
8	27	A	Manchester U	D	2-2	1-1	Reeves, Palmer	55,926
9	Oct 4	H	Liverpool	L	0-3	0-1		41,022
10	8	A	Leeds U	L	0-1	0-0		19,134
11	11	A	WBA	L	1-3	0-2	Daley	19,515
12	18	H	Birmingham C	L	0-1	0-0		30,041
13	22	H	Tottenham H	W	3-1	2-0	Reeves, Daley, MacKenzie	28,788
14	25	A	Brighton & HA	W	2-1	0-0	Tueart 2	18,368
15	Nov 1	H	Norwich C	W	1-0	0-0	Power	33,056
16	8	A	Leicester C	D	1-1	0-1	Tueart	19,104
17	12	A	Sunderland	L	0-2	0-0		23,387
18	15	H	Southampton	W	3-0	0-0	Gow, Bennett, Reeves	32,661
19	22	H	Coventry C	W	3-0	2-0	Reeves, Power, Bennett	30,047
20	29	A	Crystal Palace	W	3-2	2-0	Reeves, Gow 2	16,575
21	Dec 6	H	Ipswich T	D	1-1	0-1	Gow	35,215
22	13	A	Tottenham H	L	1-2	1-1	Boyer	23,883
23	20	H	Leeds U	W	1-0	0-0	Reeves	31,866
24	26	A	Everton	W	2-0	0-0	Gow, Power	36,194
25	27	H	Wolverhampton W	W	4-0	0-0	McDonald, Hutchison 2, Reeves	37,817
26	Jan 10	A	Coventry C	D	1-1	0-0	MacKenzie	18,248
27	17	H	Middlesbrough	W	3-2	2-1	Reeves, Hutchison, McDonald	30,774
28	31	A	Aston Villa	L	0-1	0-1		33,682
29	Feb 7	H	Nottingham F	D	1-1	1-0	Power	39,524
30	21	H	Manchester U	W	1-0	0-0	MacKenzie	50,114
31	24	A	Arsenal	L	0-2	0-0		24,790
32	Mar 14	H	WBA	W	2-1	2-0	McDonald, Tueart	36,581
33	18	A	Stoke C	L	1-2	1-1	McDonald	15,842
34	21	A	Birmingham C	L	0-2	0-2		16,160
35	28	H	Brighton & HA	D	1-1	0-0	MacKenzie	30,122
36	31	H	Leicester C	D	3-3	1-0	Reeves 2, Henry	26,141
37	Apr 4	A	Norwich C	L	0-2	0-2		17,957
38	18	A	Wolverhampton W	W	3-1	1-1	Tueart, Bennett 2	17,371
39	20	H	Everton	W	3-1	0-0	Bennett, Reeves, MacKenzie	34,434
40	25	A	Ipswich T	L	0-1	0-0		22,684
41	May 2	H	Crystal Palace	D	1-1	1-0	Bennett	31,017
42	19	A	Liverpool	L	0-1	0-1		24,462

Final League Position: 12

Goalscorers

League (56): Reeves 12, Tueart 8 (2 pens), Bennett 7, MacKenzie 6, Gow 5, McDonald 4, Power 4, Hutchison 3, Daley 2, Henry 2, Boyer 1, Palmer 1, Ranson 1.
League Cup (14): Bennett 5, Henry 4, Tueart 4, Reeves.
F.A. Cup (20): Power 5, Reeves 4 (2 pens), McDonald 3, Gow 2, MacKenzie 2, Bennett, Booth, Boyer, Hutchison.

League Cup	Second Round	Stoke C (a)	1-1
		(h)	3-0
	Third Round	Luton T (a)	2-1
	Fourth Round	Notts Co (h)	5-1
	Fifth Round	WBA (h)	2-1
	Semi-final	Liverpool (h)	0-1
		(a)	1-1
FA Cup	Third Round	Crystal Palace (h)	4-0
	Fourth Round	Norwich C (h)	6-0
	Fifth Round	Peterborough U (a)	1-0
	Sixth Round	Everton (a)	2-2
		(h)	3-1
	Semi-final	Ipswich T	1-0 (at Villa Park)
	Final	Tottenham H	1-1 (at Wembley)
	Replay		2-3 (at Wembley)

Corrigan	Ranson	Caton	Reid	Booth	Henry	Tueart	Daley	Sugrue	Power	Reeves	Stepanovic	MacKenzie	Palmer	MacRae	Bennett	Deyna	Buckley	McDonald	Hutchison	Gow	Boyer	Williams	Kinsey	May	*Match No.*
1	2	3	4	5	6	7	8	9	10	11															1
1		3	2	5	6	7	8	9	10	11	4														2
1	2	5	3	4		7	8	9*	10	11		6	12												3
	2	5	3	4	6		8		10	11		9		1	7										4
		5	2	4	6	7	8		3	11		9		1	10										5
		5	2	4	6	7	8		3	11		9		1	10										6
1		5	2	4	6*	7	8		3			9	12		10	11									7
1	2	5	3	4	6		8	12	7	11			9		10*										8
1	2	5	3	4	6		8		7	11		9	10												9
1	2	5	3	4	6		8		7	11		9	10*			12									10
1	2	5	3	4	6		8		7	11		9				10									11
1	2	5	4	6	7		8		3	11		9			10										12
1	12	6	2	5*	4	7	8		3	11		9					10								13
1	2	6	4			7	8		5	11		9						3	10						14
1	2	5	4			7	12		6			8			11			3	10*	9					15
1	2	5*	4			9			11	10		6			12			3	7	8					16
1	2		4	6		7*			5	11		9			12			3	10	8					17
1	2		4	6					5	11		9			7			3	10	8					18
1	2		4	6	12				5	11		9			7*			3	10	8					19
1	2		4	6					5	11		9			7			3	10	8					20
1	2		4	6		10*			5	11		9						3	7	8	12				21
1	2		4	6					5	11		9*			12			3	10	8	7				22
1	2		4	6*	12				5	11		9						3	10	8	7				23
1	2	6	4						5	11		9						3	10	8	7				24
1	2	6	4						5	11		9						3	10	8	7				25
1	2	6	4						5	11		9						3	10	8	7				26
1	2*	6	4						5	11		9			12			3	10	8	7				27
1		5		4	2				6	11		9			7			3	10	8					28
1		6		4	2	7			5	11		9						3	10	8					29
1			4	6	2				5	11		9			7			3	10	8					30
1	2	6	4			12			5	11		9			7			3*	10	8					31
	2	6	4		10	7			5	11		9					12	3		8*		1			32
1	2	12	4	6	10	7			5	11		9*					8	3							33
1	2*	6		4	8	7			5	11		9			12			3	10						34
1	2	6	4		8	7*			5	11		9			12			3	10						35
1	2	6	4		8				5	11		9			7			3	10						36
1	2		4	6	8				5	11		9			7			3	10						37
1		6*		4	2	8			5	11		9			7		12	3					10		38
1			4	6	2	8		11*	5	12		9			7		10	3							39
1	2		4	6	3	8			5	11		9			7		10*							12	40
1	2	6			4				5	11		9			7			3	10	8					41
	2		4	6		11			5			9			7			3	10	8		1			42
37	32	29	37	30	25	21	14	4	42	38	1	39	3	3	20	2	4	28	24	20	6	2	1	—	
	+ 1s	+ 1s			+ 2s	+ 1s	+ 1s	+ 1s		+ 1s			+ 2s		+ 6s	+ 1s	+ 2s				+ 1s			+ 1s	

MANCHESTER CITY

	Ht	*Wt*	*Birthplace*	*Clubs*	*League App.*	*League Gls*
Goalkeepers						
Joe Corrigan	6 4½	15 11	Manchester	Manchester C	412	—
(England)						
Keith MacRae	6 0	11 9	Glasgow	Motherwell	111	—
(Contract cancelled March 1981)				Manchester C	56	—
Alex Williams	6 2	12 8	Manchester	Manchester C	2	—
Defenders						
Tommy Booth	6 1	11 13	Manchester	Manchester C	381	25
Noel Bradley*	5 11½	11 4	Manchester	Manchester C	—	—
				Bury (on loan)	9	—
Ray Ranson	5 10	11 5	St Helens	Manchester C	81	1
Nicky Reid	5 9½	11 10	Manchester	Manchester C	68	—
Tommy Caton	6 1	12 1	Liverpool	Manchester C	72	—
Gary Bennett*	6 1	12 1	Manchester	Manchester C	—	—
Gary Fitzgerald*	5 5	8 12	Ashton-under-Lyne	Manchester C	—	—
Bobby McDonald	5 9	11 6	Aberdeen	Aston V	39	3
				Coventry C	161	14
				Manchester C	28	4
Kevin Budd			Hillingdon	Bournemouth	—	—
(Contract cancelled March 1981)				Norwich C	—	—
				Manchester C	—	—
Midfield						
Paul Sugrue*	5 7	9 10	Coventry	Nuneaton B	(not known)	
				Manchester C	6	—
Steve Daley	5 10	12 0	Barnsley	Wolverhampton W	212	37
(Contract cancelled Feb 1981)				Manchester C	48	4
Tony Henry	5 11	11 12	Newcastle	Manchester C	77	6
Paul Power	5 11	10 13	Manchester	Manchester C	192	20
Kazimierz Deyna	5 10½	12 2	Starograd	Legia Warsaw	(not known)	
(Poland) (Contract cancelled Jan 1981)				Manchester C	38	12
Dragoslav Stepanovic*	6 0	12 5	Rekovac	Wormatia W, W Germany	(not known)	
(Yugoslavia)				Manchester C	15	—
Steve MacKenzie	5 10	11 3	Romford	Crystal Palace	—	—
				Manchester C	58	8
Gary Bees*			Ton Pentre	Manchester C	—	—
Gerry Gow	5 8	10 8	Glasgow	Bristol C	375	47
				Manchester C	20	5
Tommy Hutchison	5 11½	11 2	Cardenden	Alloa	68	4
(Scotland)				Blackpool	165	10
				Coventry C	314	24
				Manchester C	24	3
Forwards						
Gary Buckley	5 4	9 6	Manchester	Manchester C	6	—
Dave Bennett	5 10	10 2	Manchester	Manchester C	52	9
Dennis Tueart	5 8	11 0	Newcastle	Sunderland	178	46
(England)				Manchester C	140	59
				New York Cosmos	(not known)	
				Manchester C	33	13
Kevin Reeves	5 10	11 4	Burley	Bournemouth	63	20
(England)				Norwich C	119	37
				Manchester C	48	14
Steve Kinsey	5 7	8 7	Manchester	Manchester C	1	—
Dave Wiffill	6 1	10 12	Bristol	Bath C	(not known)	
				Manchester C	—	—
Clive Wilson	5 5	9 6	Manchester	Manchester C	—	—
Dick Cunningham*			Halifax	Manchester C	—	—
Phil Boyer	5 8	11 2	Nottingham	Derby Co	—	—
(England)				York C	109	27
				Bournemouth	141	46
				Norwich C	116	34
				Southampton	138	49
				Manchester C	7	1
Andy May	5 7½	10 7	Manchester	Manchester C	1	—
(Apprentice)						

MANCHESTER UNITED Division 1

President: Sir Matt Busby CBE, KCSG.
Chairman: C. M. Edwards. *Vice-Chairman:* J. A. Gibson.
Directors: W. A. Young, D. D. Haroun JP, Sir Matt Busby CBE, KCSG, J. G. Gulliver.
Manager: Ron Atkinson. *Secretary:* R. L. Olive.
Year Formed: 1878 as Newton Heath; 1902, Manchester United.
Turned Professional: 1885. *Limited Company:* 1907.
Previous Name: Newton Heath, 1880–1902.
Previous Grounds: 1880–93, North Road, Monsall Road; 1893, Bank Street; 1910, Old Trafford (Played at Maine Rd 1941-49).

Football League Record:
1892 Newton Heath elected to Division 1; 1894–1906 Division 2; 1906–22 Division 1; 1922–25 Division 2; 1925–31 Division 1; 1931–36 Division 2; 1936–37 Division 1; 1937–38 Division 2; 1938–74 Division 1; 1974–75 Division 2; 1975– Division 1.

Honours: *Football League:* Division 1 – Champions 1907–08, 1910–11, 1951–52, 1955–56, 1956–57, 1964–65, 1966–67; Runners-up 1946–47, 1947–48, 1948–49, 1950–51, 1958–59, 1963–64, 1967–68, 1979–80; Division 2 – Champions 1935–36, 1974–75; Runners-up 1896–97, 1905–06, 1924–25, 1937–38. *FA Cup:* Winners 1909, 1948, 1963, 1977; Runners-up 1957, 1958, 1976, 1979. *Football League Cup:* Semi-final 1969–70, 1970–71, 1974–75, 1978–79. **European Competitions:** *European Cup:* 1956–57 (s-f), 1957–58 (s-f), 1965–66 (s-f)1967–68 (winners), 1968–69 (s-f). *European Cup-Winners' Cup:* 1963–64, 1977–78. *European Fairs Cup:* 1964–65. *UEFA Cup:* 1976–77, 1980–81.
Record Victory: 10-0 v Anderlecht, European Cup preliminary rd, 26 Sept, 1956.
Record Defeat: 0-7 v Aston Villa, Division 1, 27 Dec, 1930.
Most League Points: 64, Division 1, 1956–57.
Most League Goals: 103, Division 1, 1956–57 and 1958–59.
Highest League Scorer in Season: Dennis Viollet, 32, 1959–60.
Most League Goals in Total Aggregate: Bobby Charlton, 198, 1956–73.
Most Capped Player: Bobby Charlton, 106, England.
Most League Appearances: Bobby Charlton, 606, 1956–73.
Record Transfer Fee Received: £500,000 from Brighton & HA for Andy Ritchie, Oct 1980.
Record Transfer Fee Paid: £1,250,000 to Nottingham F for Garry Birtles, Oct 1980.
Previous Managers since the War: Matt Busby, Wilf McGuinness, Sir Matt Busby, Frank O'Farrell, Tommy Docherty, Dave Sexton.
Address of Supporters Club: Football Ground, Old Trafford (sae for details). Tel: 061-872 6000.
Address of the Club Shop or Boutique: Red Devils Souvenir Shop, Old Trafford. Tel: 061-872 3398.

Old Trafford, Manchester M16 0RA. Telephone 061-872 1661/2. *Telegraphic address:* 'Stadium Manchester'. *Ground capacity:* 58,504. *Record attendance:* 76,962 Wolverhampton W v Grimsby T, FA Cup semi-final, 25 March, 1939. *Club record:* 70,504 v Aston Villa, Division 1, 27 Dec, 1920. *Record receipts:* £124,441, League Cup Final replay, Liverpool v Nottingham F, 22 March, 1978; £91,466.12 v Tottenham H, FA Cup 3rd rd replay, 9 Jan, 1980. *Pitch measurements:* 116yd×76yd.
How to get there: Special buses from Aytoun Street, Cannon Street, and various points in Manchester and Salford. Frequent train service from Manchester Oxford Road station direct to the Football Ground station, returning after the match. Schedule services from Oxford Road and Knott Mill, Manchester, or from Altrincham, Timperley, and intermediate stations, run to Warwick Road station, only a few minutes walk from the ground.
Match tickets: Seats can be booked from one calendar month before the match. Any not sold by Monday before a Saturday match can be reserved by personal application. For up-to-date ticket information, tel: 061-872 7771 (24 hour service). Tickets for over-subscribed matches are allocated by ballot.
Car parking: Large car parks within easy reach of the ground at Lancashire County Cricket Ground, Talbot Rd and Great Stone Rd (1,200). White City Stadium, Chester Rd (900). Alternatively, cars can be parked in Manchester, Altrincham, or at outside intermediate stations and the rest of the journey made by the above train services.
Entertainments/catering facilities: Licensed bars around the ground. Restaurant in conference complex (not match days).
Club shop: The souvenir shop alongside the ticket office is open throughout the week. Price lists sent on receipt of SAE.
Programmes: Available on subscription and application with remittance can be sent to the ground for individual matches. The supporters' club publishes an annual handbook and newsletters.
Extra information: The Manchester United Development Association has monthly draws for special prizes and a weekly draw. New agents are always welcome; tel: 061-872 4676/5208 for full details. There is a travel club for away matches. The club also run their own lottery.
Club Colours: Red shirts with red and white trim, white shorts, black stockings with red tops and three white bands.
Change Colours: White shirts with black trim, black shorts with red stripes, black stockings with red and white top.
Club Nickname: Red Devils.

MANCHESTER UNITED 1980–81 LEAGUE RECORD

Match No.	*Date*	*Venue*	*Opponents*	*Result*	*H/T Score*	*Goalscorers*	*Attendance*
1	Aug 16	H	Middlesbrough	W 3-0	1-0	Macari, Grimes, Thomas	54,394
2	19	A	Wolverhampton W	L 0-1	0-0		31,955
3	23	A	Birmingham C	D 0-0	0-0		28,661
4	30	H	Sunderland	D 1-1	0-0	Jovanovic	51,498
5	Sept 6	A	Tottenham H	D 0-0	0-0		40,995
6	13	H	Leicester C	W 5-0	2-0	Coppell, Grimes, Jovanovic 2, Macari	43,222
7	20	A	Leeds U	D 0-0	0-0		32,539
8	27	H	Manchester C	D 2-2	1-1	Coppell, Albiston	55,926
9	Oct 4	A	Nottingham F	W 2-1	1-1	Macari, Coppell	29,801
10	8	H	Aston Villa	D 3-3	2-1	McIlroy 2 (1 pen), Coppell	38,831
11	11	H	Arsenal	D 0-0	0-0		49,036
12	18	A	Ipswich T	D 1-1	0-0	McIlroy (pen)	28,451
13	22	A	Stoke C	W 2-1	0-0	Jordan, Macari	22,000
14	25	H	Everton	W 2-0	1-0	Jordan, Coppell	54,260
15	Nov 1	A	Crystal Palace	L 0-1	0-1		31,181
16	8	H	Coventry C	D 0-0	0-0		42,794
17	12	H	Wolverhampton W	D 0-0	0-0		37,959
18	15	A	Middlesbrough	D 1-1	0-0	Jordan	20,606
19	22	A	Brighton & HA	W 4-1	3-0	Jordan 2, McIlroy, Duxbury	23,277
20	29	H	Southampton	D 1-1	0-0	Jordan	46,840
21	Dec 6	A	Norwich C	D 2-2	2-0	Bond (og), Coppell	19,228
22	13	H	Stoke C	D 2-2	1-2	Macari, Jordan	39,568
23	20	A	Arsenal	L 1-2	0-1	Macari	33,730
24	26	H	Liverpool	D 0-0	0-0		57,073
25	27	A	WBA	L 1-3	0-2	Jovanovic	30,033
26	Jan 10	H	Brighton & HA	W 2-1	1-0	McQueen, Macari	42,208
27	28	A	Sunderland	L 0-2	0-1		31,910
28	31	H	Birmingham C	W 2-0	1-0	Jordan, Macari	39,081
29	Feb 7	A	Leicester C	L 0-1	0-0		26,085
30	17	H	Tottenham H	D 0-0	0-0		40,282
31	21	A	Manchester C	L 0-1	0-0		50,114
32	28	H	Leeds U	L 0-1	0-0		45,733
33	Mar 7	A	Southampton	L 0-1	0-1		22,698
34	14	A	Aston Villa	D 3-3	0-2	Jordan 2, McIlroy (pen)	42,182
35	18	H	Nottingham F	D 1-1	1-1	Burns (og)	38,205
36	21	H	Ipswich T	W 2-1	1-1	Thomas, Nicholl	46,685
37	28	A	Everton	W 1-0	1-0	Jordan	25,854
38	Apr 4	H	Crystal Palace	W 1-0	0-0	Duxbury	37,974
39	11	A	Coventry C	W 2-0	2-0	Jordan 2	20,175
40	14	A	Liverpool	W 1-0	1-0	McQueen	31,276
41	18	H	WBA	W 2-1	2-0	Jordan, Macari	44,442
42	25	H	Norwich C	W 1-0	0-0	Jordan	40,165

Final League Position: 8

Goalscorers

League (51): Jordan 15, Macari 9, Coppell 6, McIlroy 5 (3 pens), Jovanovic 4, Duxbury 2, Grimes 2, McQueen 2, Thomas 2, Albiston 1, Nicholl 1, own goals 2.
League Cup (0).
F.A. Cup (4): Birtles, Duxbury, Nicholl, Thomas.

League Cup	Second Round	Coventry C (h)	0-1
		(a)	0-1
FA Cup	Third Round	Brighton & HA (h)	2-2
		(a)	2-0
	Fourth Round	Nottingham F (a)	0-1

Bailey	Nicholl	Albiston	McIlroy	Moran	Buchan	Coppell	Greenhoff	Jordan	Macari	Thomas	Grimes	Roche	Ritchie	Duxbury	McGrath	Jovanovic	McGarvey	McQueen	Sloan	Birtles	Whelan	Wilkins	*Match No.*
1	2	3	4	5	6	7	8	9*	10	11	12												1
	2	3	4	5	6	9	8		10	11	7*	1	12										2
	2	3	4	5*	6	8			10	11		1	9	12	7								3
1	2	3	4		6	7	8		10	11			9			5							4
1	2	3	4		6	7	8		10	11			9*	12		5							5
1	2	3	4		6	9	8		10*	11	7					5	12						6
1	2	3	4		6	9	8		10*	11	7			12		5							7
1	2	3	4		6	9	8			11	7			10*				5	12				8
1	2	3	4	6		8		9	10	11				7		5							9
1	2	3	4	6		8	12	9	10*	11				7		5							10
1	2	3	4	6		8		9		11	7			10		5							11
1	2	3	4	6		7		9	10	11				8		5							12
1	2	3	4	6		7		9	10	11				12		5*				8			13
1	2	3	4	5		7		9	10	11				6						8			14
1	2	3	4	6		7		9	10	11						5				8			15
1	2	3	4	6		7		9	10	11						5*			12	8			16
1	2	3	4	5		7		9	10	11				6						8			17
1	2	3	4	5		7		9	10	11				6						8			18
1	2	3	4	6		7		9		11	12			10		5				8*			19
1		3	4	5*		7		9	10		11			6		2				8	12		20
1	2	3	4		6	7	8	9	10					11		5							21
1	2	3	4	6		7		9	10	11				8		5							22
1	2	3	4	6		7		9	10	11				8		5							23
1	2	3	4	6		7		9	10	11				8		5							24
1	2	3	4	6		7		9	10	11				8		5							25
1	2	3			6	7		9	10	11				12				5		8		4*	26
1	2	3			6	7		9	10	11				4				5		8			27
1	2	3	12		6	7		9	10	11*				4				5		8			28
1	2	3			6	7		9	10	11				4		5*				8		12	29
1	2	3	11	5	6	7			10					9						8		4	30
1	2	3	11	5	6	7			10					4*			12			9		8	31
1	2	3	11	5	6	7		9	10											8		4	32
1	2	3	11	5	6	7		9	10											8		4	33
1	2	3	11	5	6	7		9	10											8		4	34
1	2	3	11*	5	6	7		9	10					12						8		4	35
1	2	3		4	6	7		9		11				10				5		8			36
1	2*	3		4	6	7		9	12	11				10				5		8			37
1		3		4	6	7		9	10	11*				2				5		8		12	38
1		3		4	6	7		9	10					2				5		8		11	39
1		3		4	6	7		9	10					2				5		8		11	40
1		3		4	6	7		9	10					2				5		8		11	41
1		3		4	6	7		9	10					2				5		8		11	42
40	36	42	31	32	26	42	8	33	37	30	6	2	3	27	1	19	—	11	—	25	—	11	
			+ 1s				+ 1s		+ 1s		+ 2s		+ 1s	+ 6s			+ 2s		+ 2s		+ 1s	+ 2s	

MANCHESTER UNITED

	Ht	*Wt*	*Birthplace*	*Clubs*	*League App.*	*League Gls*
Goalkeepers						
Paddy Roche	6 1½	11 4	Dublin	Shelbourne	(not known)	
(Eire)				Manchester U	43	—
Gary Bailey	6 1½	12 4	Ipswich	Manchester U	110	—
Stephen Pears*	5 11	11 10	Brandon	Manchester U	—	—
Defenders						
Martin Buchan	5 10	12 4	Aberdeen	Aberdeen	131	10
(Scotland)				Manchester U	346	4
Arthur Albiston	5 7½	11 1	Scotland	Manchester U	150	1
James Nicholl	5 9½	11 12	Canada	Manchester U	196	3
(N Ireland)						
Gordon McQueen	6 3	13 8	Kilbirnie	St Mirren	57	5
(Scotland)				Leeds U	140	15
				Manchester U	94	18
Martin Lane	5 9	11 2	Altrincham	Manchester U	—	—
David Jeffrey	5 11	11 7	Newtonards	Manchester U	—	—
Nikola Jovanovic	6 3	13 4	Cetinje	Red Star	(not known)	
(Yugoslavia)				Manchester U	21	4
Gareth Orritt	5 6	9 10	Middlesbrough	Manchester U	—	—
Tom Connell	5 9½	10 9½	Newry	Coleraine	—	—
(N Ireland)				Manchester U	2	—
Nigel Keen*	5 9	11 4	Barrow	Manchester U	—	—
Chris Roberts*	5 7	10 8	Bangor	Manchester U	—	—
Kevin Moran	5 10½	12 9	Dublin	Manchester U	42	1
(Eire)						
Barry Knox*	5 7½	10 5	Gateshead	Sunderland	—	—
				Manchester U	—	—
Tony Whelan	5 11	11 6	Dublin	Bohemians	(not known)	
				Manchester U	1	—
Shaun Williams	5 3½	9 12	Trebanog	Manchester U	—	—
Midfield						
Mike Duxbury	5 9½	10 7	Accrington	Manchester U	33	2
Alan Davies*	5 8	10 4	Manchester	Manchester U	—	—
Ray Wilkins	5 8	11 4	Hillingdon	Chelsea	179	30
(England)				Manchester U	50	2
Lou Macari	5 6½	10 11	Edinburgh	Celtic	56	27
(Scotland)				Manchester U	304	74
David Haggett*	6 0	10 11½	Merthyr	Manchester U	—	—
Danny Keough	5 7½	9 10	Bacup	Manchester U	—	—
Alan Stevenson	5 6	9 7	Rotherham	Manchester U	—	—
David Wynn	5 6½	10 3	Ormskirk	Manchester U	—	—
Kel McDermott	5 6½	9 5	Belfast	Manchester U	—	—
Mickey Thomas	5 6	10 6	Mochdre	Wrexham	230	33
(Wales)				Manchester U	90	11
Tom Sloan	5 6	9 9	Ballymena	Ballymena	—	—
(N Ireland)				Manchester U	11	—
Forwards						
Sammy McIlroy	5 9½	11 4	Belfast	Manchester U	330	54
(N Ireland)						
Steve Coppell	5 9½	10 13	Liverpool	Tranmere R	38	10
(England)				Manchester U	257	40
Chris McGrath	5 9½	10 12	Belfast	Tottenham H	38	5
(N Ireland)				Millwall (on loan)	15	3
(Contract cancelled Feb 1981)				Manchester U	28	1
Ashley Grimes	5 11	11 1	Dublin	Manchester U	63	7
(Eire)						
Joe Jordan	6 1	12 0	Carluke	Morton	10	1
(Scotland)				Leeds U	169	35
				Manchester U	109	37
Gary Worrall	5 9½	10 12	Salford	Manchester U	—	—
Chris Lynam	5 6	9 9	Manchester	Manchester U	—	—
Andy Reynolds	5 4	9 4	Neath	Manchester U	—	—
Scott McGarvey	5 11½	10 11	Glasgow	Manchester U	2	—
Garry Birtles	6 0	12 0	Nottingham	Nottingham F	87	32
(England)				Manchester U	25	—
Mark Hughes	5 8	11 5	Wrexham	Manchester U	—	—
Steve Paterson	6 1½	13 2½	Elgin	Manchester U	6	—
(Contract cancelled July 1980)						

MANSFIELD TOWN — Division 4

President: A. F. Patrick.

Chairman: J. B. Almond. *Vice-Chairman:* J. W. Pratt.

Directors: J. A. Brown, Dr S. S. Scott MB, CHB, MRCGP.

Player-Manager: Stuart Boam. *Secretary:* J. D. Eaton.

Year Formed: 1905.

Turned Professional: 1905. *Limited Company:* 1905.

Football League Record:
1931 Elected to Division 3(S); 1932–37 Division 3(N); 1937–47 Division 3(S); 1947–58 Division 3(N); 1958–60 Division 3; 1960–63 Division 4; 1963–72 Division 3; 1972–75 Division 4; 1975–77 Division 3; 1977–78 Division 2; 1978–80 Division 3; 1980– Division 4.

Honours: *Football League:* Division 3 – Champions 1976–77; Division 4 – Champions 1974–75; Division 3(N) – Runners-up 1950–51. *FA Cup* best season: 6th rd, 1968–69. *Football League Cup* best season: 5th rd, 1975–76.

Record Victory: 9-2 v Rotherham U, Division 3(N), 27 Dec, 1932 and v Hounslow T, FA Cup 1st rd replay, 5 Nov 1962.

Record Defeat: 1-8 v Walsall, Division 3(N), 19 Jan, 1933.

Most League Points: 68, Division 4, 1974–75.

Most League Goals: 108, Division 4, 1962–63.

Highest League Scorer in Season: Ted Harston, 55, Division 3(N), 1936–37.

Most League Goals in Total Aggregate: Harry Johnson, 104, 1931–36.

Most Capped Player: John McClelland, 6 (8) Northern Ireland.

Most League Appearances: Don Bradley, 417, 1949–62.

Record Transfer Fee Received: £200,000 from Luton T for Mike Saxby, July 1979.

Record Transfer Fee Paid: £75,000 to Luton T for Steve Taylor, July 1979.

Previous Managers since the War: Roy Goodall, Freddie Steele, Stan Mercer, Charlie Mitten, Sam Weaver, Raich Carter, Tommy Cummings, Tommy Eggleston, Jock Basford, Danny Williams, David Smith, Peter Morris, Billy Bingham, Mick Jones.

Address of Supporters Club: Club Shop, c/o the ground.

Field Mill Ground, Quarry Lane, Mansfield. Telephone Mansfield 23567. *Telegraphic address:* 'Football Mansfield'. *Ground capacity:* 23,500. *Record attendance:* 24,467 v Nottingham F, FA Cup 3rd rd, 10 Jan, 1953. *Record receipts:* £19,227 v Sheffield W, Division 3, 15 Mar, 1980. *Pitch measurements:* 115yd×72yd.

How to get there: Buses from town centre to within 300 yards of the ground. Nearest railway station, Alfreton and Mansfield Parkway.

Match tickets: Advance booking 5 days prior to match.

Car parking: Room for 500 cars at the ground and another 3,000 within 500 yards.

Entertainments/catering facilities: No club room. Licensed tea bars in the ground.

Club shop: Adjacent to the ground; sells all types of souvenirs.

Handbooks/programmes: Both on sale at the club shop.

Extra information: Mansfield became famous giant-killers as a non-League side in 1929. They went to Molineux in the FA Cup 3rd round and beat Wolves 1-0.

Club Colours: Amber shirts, blue shorts, amber stockings.

Change Colours: White shirts with blue and amber trimmings, white shorts, white stockings.

Club Trainer/Coach: Geoff Allen.

Club Nickname: The Stags.

MANSFIELD TOWN 1980–81 LEAGUE RECORD

Match No.	Date	Venue	Opponents	Result	H/T Score	Goalscorers	Attendance
1	Aug 16	A	Halifax T	W 2-0	0-0	Austin 2	1682
2	18	H	York C	L 0-1	0-1		4080
3	23	H	Hereford U	W 4-0	1-0	Bird, Burrows, Austin, Caldwell	3103
4	30	A	Port Vale	D 0-0	0-0		2558
5	Sept 6	H	Darlington	W 1-0	0-0	Hamilton	3001
6	13	A	Bury	L 1-4	0-1	McClelland	2668
7	15	H	Wimbledon	W 1-0	1-0	McClelland	2903
8	20	A	Aldershot	L 0-1	0-1		3607
9	27	H	Wigan Ath	W 3-1	2-0	Pollard, Hamilton, Allen	3402
10	30	A	Wimbledon	L 1-2	1-1	Austin	2052
11	Oct 3	A	Southend U	L 0-2	0-1		4443
12	6	H	Tranmere R	D 1-1	1-0	Allen	1925
13	11	H	Bradford C	W 1-0	1-0	Bird	3234
14	18	A	AFC Bournemouth	W 1-0	0-0	Bird	3335
15	21	A	Hartlepool U	W 1-0	1-0	McClelland	3369
16	25	H	Peterborough U	W 2-1	1-1	Parkinson (pen), Allen	4883
17	27	H	Northampton T	W 2-0	1-0	Parkinson (pen), Allen	3560
18	Nov 1	A	Rochdale	W 4-1	2-0	Mann, Austin 3 (1 pen)	2636
19	3	A	Tranmere R	L 0-1	0-0		2048
20	8	H	Torquay U	D 1-1	0-1	Bird	3266
21	11	A	York C	L 0-2	0-1		2204
22	15	H	Halifax T	L 0-1	0-0		2561
23	29	A	Crewe Alex	W 2-1	2-0	Caldwell, Parkinson (pen)	2482
24	Dec 6	H	Stockport Co	W 1-0	1-0	Allen	2873
25	19	A	Doncaster R	L 1-2	0-1	Caldwell	3620
26	26	H	Scunthorpe U	W 1-0	0-0	Allen	4261
27	27	A	Lincoln C	D 1-1	1-1	Thompson (og)	8522
28	Jan 10	A	Northampton T	W 1-0	1-0	McClelland	2985
29	17	H	Crewe Alex	W 4-1	3-0	Lumby, Caldwell, Wood, Mann	3202
30	24	H	Port Vale	W 5-0	5-0	Wood 2, Caldwell 2, McClelland	3864
31	31	A	Hereford U	L 1-2	0-2	Lumby (pen)	2672
32	Feb 7	H	Bury	W 2-0	1-0	Bird, Caldwell	3514
33	15	A	Darlington	D 2-2	1-1	Allen, McClelland	5932
34	21	A	Wigan Ath	L 0-2	0-1		4032
35	Mar 7	H	Southend U	L 0-1	0-1		4379
36	14	A	Bradford C	W 2-0	0-0	Parkinson (pen), Allen	2986
37	16	H	Hartlepool U	L 0-1	0-1		3737
38	21	H	AFC Bournemouth	D 1-1	1-1	Heffernan (og)	2606
39	28	A	Peterborough U	L 0-1	0-1		4904
40	Apr 4	H	Rochdale	D 2-2	1-1	Wood, Lumby	2597
41	6	H	Aldershot	L 1-2	0-0	Burrows	2748
42	12	A	Torquay U	D 1-1	1-1	Burrows	1699
43	18	H	Lincoln C	W 2-0	0-0	Thomson, Caldwell	4771
44	20	A	Scunthorpe U	L 0-2	0-2		1850
45	May 1	A	Stockport Co	L 1-2	1-0	Allen	2236
46	6	H	Doncaster R	D 1-1	0-1	Lumby (pen)	4506

Final League Position: 7

Goalscorers

League (58): Allen 9, Austin 7 (1 pen), Caldwell 8, McClelland 6, Bird 5, Lumby 4 (2 pens), Parkinson 4 (4 pens), Wood 4, Burrows 3, Hamilton 2, Mann 2, Pollard 1, Thomson 1, own goals 2.
League Cup (5): Austin, Caldwell, McClelland, Parkinson (pen), Pollard.
F.A. Cup (9): Parkinson 3 (2 pens), Caldwell 2, Allen (pen), Bird, Pollard, Thomson.

League Cup	First Round	Doncaster R (a)	1-1
		(h)	2-1
	Second Round	Barnsley (h)	0-0
		(a)	2-4
FA Cup	First Round	Rochdale (h)	3-1
	Second Round	Mossley (a)	3-1
	Third Round	Carlisle U (h)	2-2
		(a)	1-2

Arnold	Dawkins	Mann	Bird	McClelland	Burrows	Phillips	Caldwell	Austin	Parkinson	Pollard	Hamilton	Allen	Thomson	McJannet	Foster	Wood	Johnson	Lumby	Sutton	Woodhead	*Match No.*
1	2	3	4	5	6	7	8	9	10	11											1
1	2	3	4	5	6	7	8	9	10	11											2
1	2	3	4	5	6	7	8	9	10	11											3
1	2	3	4	5	6	7	8	9	10	11											4
1	2	3		5	6	7	8*	9	10	11	4	12									5
1	2	3	4	5	6*	7	8	9	10	11	12										6
1	2	3	6	5		8		9	10	11	4	7									7
1	2*	3	6	5		8		9	10	11	4	7	12								8
1	2	3	6	5		8		9	10	11	4	7									9
1	2	3	6	5		8		9	10	11	4	7									10
1	2	3	6	5		8	12	9	10	11	4*	7									11
1	2	3	6	5		8	12	9	10	11	4	7*									12
1		8	6	5				9	10	11	4	7		2	3						13
1		8	6	5				9	10	11	4	7		2*	3	12					14
1		8	6	5				9	10	11	4	7		2	3						15
1		8	6	5			12	9	10	11	4	7*		2	3						16
1		8	6	5				9	10	11	4	7		2	3						17
1		8	6	5				9	10	11	4	7*		2	3	12					18
1			6	5				9	10	11	4	7	12	2	3	8*					19
1		8	6	5				9	10	11	4	7		2	3						20
1		8	6	5				9	10	11	4	7		2	3						21
1		8	6	5			12	9*	10		4	7	11	2	3						22
1		8	6	5			9		10	12	4	7*	11	2	3						23
1		8	6	5			9		10		4	7	11	2	3						24
1		8	6	5		10	9			12	4	7	11	2	3*						25
1		8	6	5			9		10		4	7	11	2			3				26
1		8	6	5			9		10	12	4	7*	11	2		3					27
1		8	6	5		10	9				4		11	2		3		7			28
1		8	6	5		7	9				4		11	2		3		10			29
1		8	6	5		7	9				4		11	2		3		10			30
1		8	6	5		7	9			12	4*		11	2		3		10			31
1		8	6*	5	12		9		10		4	7	11	2		3					32
1		8		5	6		9		10		4	7	11	2		3					33
1		8		5	6		9		10*	12	4	7	11	2		3					34
1		8	6	5					10	9	4	7	11	2		3					35
1		8	6	5	4				10	9		7	11	2		3					36
1		6		5	4		9		10	12		7*	11	2		3		8			37
1		8	6	5	4				10			7	11	2		3		9			38
		8	6	5	4		7		10*		12		11	2		3		9	1		39
		8	6	5	4		9		10*			7	11	2		3		12	1		40
		8	4	6	5					11	10	7		2		3		9	1		41
		8	4	6	5		12				10	7	11	2		3		9*	1		42
		8	4	6	5		9			12	10	7	11	2		3*			1		43
		8	4	6	5		9			12	10*	7	11	2		3			1		44
		8*	4	6	5					12	10	7	11	2		3		9	1		45
			4	6	5					8	10	7	11*	2		3		9	1	12	46
38	12	44	42	46	19	17	23	22	35	25	36	35	24	34	13	21	1	11	8	—	
					+ 1s		+ 5s			+ 9s	+ 2s	+ 1s	+ 2s			+ 2s		+ 1s		+ 1s	

MANSFIELD TOWN

	Ht	*Wt*	*Birthplace*	*Clubs*	*League App.*	*League Gls*
Goalkeepers						
Rod Arnold	5 10	11 4	Wolverhampton	Wolverhampton W	—	—
				Mansfield T	341	—
Colin King*	6 0	11 8	Edinburgh	Blackpool	—	—
				Clydebank	6	—
				Notts Co	—	—
				Rotherham (on loan)	—	—
				Mansfield T	—	—
Defenders						
Kevin Bird	5 9	10 12	Doncaster	Doncaster R	—	—
				Mansfield T	322	51
Barry Foster	5 9	10 4	Worksop	Mansfield T	259	—
Ian Wood	5 10	10 7	Kirkby in Ashfield	Mansfield T	113	5
John McClelland (N Ireland)	6 1	11 4	Belfast	Portadown	—	—
				Cardiff C	4	1
				Bangor	—	—
				Mansfield T	125	8
Derek Dawkins*	5 10	11 1	Edmonton	Leicester C	3	—
				Mansfield T	73	—
Leslie McJannet		10 4	Cumnock	Mansfield T	36	—
Adrian Burrows	5 11	11 12	Sutton	Mansfield T	37	3
Brian Thompson (Contract cancelled Sept 1980)	5 10	10 12	Sunderland	Yeovil	(not known)	
				Sunderland	—	—
				Mansfield T	9	—
Steve Johnson*	5 9	10 10	Mansfield	Mansfield T	1	—
Brendon Phillips (Contract cancelled Feb 1981)			West Indies	Leicester C	—	—
				Peterborough U	1	—
				Kettering T	(not known)	
				Boston U	(not known)	
				Mansfield T	17	—
Andy Bircumshaw*			Gladwell	Mansfield T	—	—
Iain Jamieson	5 10	10 9	Ayr	Mansfield T	—	—
Midfield						
John Lathan (Contract cancelled Jan 1981)	5 7	11 0	Sunderland	53	14	
				Mansfield T	74	14
				Carlisle U	61	8
				Barnsley (on loan)	7	—
				Portsmouth	58	4
				Mansfield T	29	1
Neville Hamilton*	5 8	10 0	Leicester	Leicester C	4	—
				Mansfield T	89	4
Arthur Mann	5 9	10 8	Burntisland	Hearts	32	—
				Manchester C	35	—
				Blackpool (on loan)	3	—
				Notts Co	253	21
				Shrewsbury T	8	1
				Mansfield T	79	2
Noel Parkinson	5 8	10 7	Hull	Ipswich T	—	—
				Bristol R (on loan)	5	1
				Brentford (on loan)	10	—
				Mansfield T	35	4
Phil Saunders*			Nottingham	Mansfield T	—	—
Forwards						
Russell Allen*	5 9	11 7	Smethwick	Arsenal	—	—
				WBA	—	—
				Cambridge U (on loan)	—	—
				Tranmere R	156	44
				Mansfield T	116	18
Brian Thomson	5 8	10 2	Morecambe	West Ham U	—	—
				Mansfield T	34	1
Brian Pollard*	5 8	10 6	York	York C	163	34
				Watford	71	8
				Mansfield T	54	5
David Caldwell	5 10	11 6	Aberdeen	Mansfield T	31	8
Simon Woodhead	5 10	11 0	Wakefield	Mansfield T	1	—
Jim Lumby	5 11	11 4	Grimsby	Grimsby T	31	12
				Boston U	(not known)	
				Gainsborough T	(not known)	
				Brigg T	(not known)	
				Scunthorpe U	55	28
				Carlisle U	27	7
				Tranmere R	46	21
				Mansfield T	12	4

MIDDLESBROUGH Division 1

Chairman: C. Amer.
Vice-Chairman: G. T. Kitching.
Directors: Dr U. N. Phillips, E. Varley, J. D. Hatfield, M. McCullagh, K. Amer, E. K. Varley.
Manager: Bobby Murdoch.
Asst Manager: Harold Shepherdson MBE.
Secretary: T. H. C. Green FAAI.
Year Formed: 1876.
Turned Professional: 1889; became amateur 1892, and professional again, 1899.
Limited Company: 1892.
Previous Grounds: 1877, Old Archery Ground, Linthorpe Rd; 1903, Ayresome Park.

Football League Record:
1899 Elected to Division 2; 1902–24 Division 1; 1924–27 Division 2; 1927–28 Division 1; 1928–29 Division 2; 1929–54 Division 1; 1954–66 Division 2; 1966–67 Division 3; 1967–74 Division 2; 1974– Division 1.

Honours: *Football League:* Division 1 best season: 3rd, 1913–14. Division 2 – Champions 1926–27, 1928–29, 1973–74; Runners-up 1901–02. Division 3 – Runners-up 1966–67. *FA Cup* best season: 6th rd, 1935–36, 1946–47, 1969–70, 1974–75, 1976–77, 1977–78; old last eight 1900–01, 1903–04. *Football League Cup:* Semi-final 1975–76. *Amateur Cup:* Winners 1895, 1898. *Anglo-Scottish Cup:* Winners 1975–76.

Record Victory: 9-0 v Brighton & HA, Division 2, 23 Aug, 1958.
Record Defeat: 0-9 v Blackburn R, Division 2, 6 Nov, 1954.
Most League Points: 65, Division 2, 1973–74.
Most League Goals: 122, Division 2, 1926–27.
Highest League Scorer in Season: George Camsell, 59, Division 2, 1926–27 (record for Division 2).
Most League Goals in Total Aggregate: George Camsell, 326, 1925–39.
Most Capped Player: Wilf Mannion, 26, England.
Most League Appearances: Tim Williamson, 563, 1902–23.
Record Transfer Fee Received: £575,000 from Liverpool for Craig Johnston, April 1981.
Record Transfer Fee Paid: £475,000 to Newcastle U for Irving Nattrass, Aug 1979.
Previous Managers since the War: David Jack, Walter Rowley, Bob Dennison, Raich Carter, Stan Anderson, Jack Charlton OBE, John Neal.
Address of the Club Shop or Boutique: Warwick Street, Middlesbrough.

Ayresome Park, Middlesbrough, Teesside. Telephone Middlesbrough 89659/85996. Special Answering Service available on 0642-825383. *Telegraphic address:* 'Football, Middlesbrough'. *Ground capacity:* 42,000. *Record attendance:* 53,596 v Newcastle U, Division 1, 27 Dec, 1949. *Record receipts:* £57,710 v Barnsley, FA Cup 5th rd, 14 Feb, 1981. *Pitch measurements:* 115yd×75yd.

How to get there: Regular buses from the Exchange in Middlesbrough to the ground. Buses also from bus station next to Middlesbrough railway station.
Match tickets: By postal or personal application two weeks prior to the match.
Car parking: Off-street parking near the ground.
Entertainments/catering facilities: Social club (members only); refreshment bars around the ground.
Handbooks/programmes: Programmes available on subscription.
Extra information: When Middlesbrough bought Alf Common from Sunderland in 1905, they paid the first £1,000 transfer fee.
Club Colours: Red shirts with three narrow stripes down sleeve in white; red shorts with same markings and white stockings.
Change Colours: All white.
Club Captain: Tony McAndrew.
First Team Trainer: Lew Clayton. *Club Coaches:* John Coddington and Cyril Knowles.
Club Nickname: The Boro.

MIDDLESBROUGH 1980–81 LEAGUE RECORD

Match No.	Date	Venue	Opponents	Result	H/T Score	Goalscorers	Attendance
1	Aug 16	A	Manchester U	L 0-3	0-1		54,394
2	19	H	Leeds U	W 3-0	1-0	Johnston, Nattrass, Armstrong	19,470
3	23	A	Crystal Palace	L 2-5	2-1	Ashcroft, Johnston	16,713
4	30	H	Manchester C	D 2-2	1-2	MacKenzie (og), Jankovic	15,761
5	Sept 6	H	Nottingham F	D 0-0	0-0		17,119
6	13	A	Sunderland	W 1-0	1-0	Jankovic	32,745
7	20	H	Arsenal	W 2-1	1-1	Proctor, Armstrong	14,680
8	27	A	Stoke C	L 0-1	0-1		11,847
9	Oct 4	H	Norwich C	W 6-1	2-0	McAndrew, Armstrong, Jankovic 2, Woods (og), Johnston	12,837
10	7	A	Liverpool	L 2-4	0-1	Johnston, Jankovic	28,204
11	11	A	Tottenham H	L 2-3	1-0	Hodgson, Johnston	27,380
12	18	H	Southampton	D 1-1	1-0	Jankovic	15,858
13	21	H	Leicester C	W 1-0	0-0	Armstrong	13,137
14	25	A	WBA	L 0-3	0-1		16,162
15	Nov 1	H	Birmingham C	L 1-2	1-0	Jankovic	14,061
16	8	A	Brighton & HA	W 1-0	0-0	Johnston	12,112
17	12	A	Leeds U	L 1-2	0-0	Jankovic	17,382
18	15	H	Manchester U	D 1-1	0-0	Johnston	20,606
19	22	H	Wolverhampton W	W 2-0	0-0	Johnston, Shearer	13,562
20	Dec 6	H	Aston Villa	W 2-1	0-0	Johnston, Shearer	15,579
21	13	A	Leicester C	L 0-1	0-1		13,998
22	20	H	Tottenham H	W 4-1	2-1	Hodgson 3, Johnston	15,992
23	26	A	Coventry C	L 0-1	0-1		16,066
24	27	H	Everton	W 1-0	1-0	Ashcroft	20,210
25	Jan 10	A	Wolverhampton W	L 0-3	0-1		16,253
26	17	A	Manchester C	L 2-3	1-2	Hodgson, McAndrew	30,774
27	31	H	Crystal Palace	W 2-0	0-0	Armstrong, McAndrew (pen)	16,099
28	Feb 7	H	Sunderland	W 1-0	1-0	Hedley	35,065
29	17	A	Ipswich T	L 0-1	0-1		24,781
30	21	H	Stoke C	W 3-1	1-0	Jankovic 2 (1 pen), Cochrane	15,142
31	28	A	Arsenal	D 2-2	1-2	Armstrong, Shearer	24,504
32	Mar 3	A	Nottingham F	L 0-1	0-0		19,690
33	17	A	Norwich C	L 0-2	0-2		14,549
34	21	A	Southampton	L 0-1	0-0		20,651
35	28	H	WBA	W 2-1	1-0	Batson (og), Shearer	13,288
36	Apr 4	A	Birmingham C	L 1-2	0-1	Bell	12,472
37	11	H	Brighton & HA	W 1-0	0-0	Shearer	11,076
38	18	A	Everton	L 1-4	1-2	Shearer	15,706
39	21	H	Coventry C	L 0-1	0-0		11,371
40	25	A	Aston Villa	L 0-3	0-1		38,018
41	May 2	H	Ipswich T	W 2-1	0-1	Jankovic 2	15,503
42	5	H	Liverpool	L 1-2	1-2	Shearer	19,102

Final League Position: 14

Goalscorers

League (53): Jankovic 12 (1 pen), Johnston 10, Shearer 7, Armstrong 6, Hodgson 5, McAndrew 3 (1 pen), Ashcroft 2, Bell 1, Cochrane 1, Hedley 1, Nattrass 1, Proctor 1, own goals 3.
League Cup (3): Shearer 2, Proctor.
F.A. Cup (10): Hodgson 3, Cochrane 2, Angus, Ashcroft, Bailey, Jankovic, Proctor.

League Cup	Second Round	Ipswich T (h)	3-1
		(a)	0-3
FA Cup	Third Round	Swansea C (a)	5-0
	Fourth Round	WBA (h)	1-0
	Fifth Round	Barnsley (h)	2-1
	Sixth Round	Wolverhampton W (h)	1-1
		(a)	1-3

Platt	Craggs	Bailey	Johnston	Ashcroft	McAndrew	Shearer	Hedley	Hodgson	Nattrass	Armstrong	Burns	Proctor	Jankovic	Cochrane	Askew	Angus	Stewart	MacDonald	Bell	Blackburn	Ross	Woof	Nobbs	*Match No.*
1	2	3	4	5	6	7	8*	9	10	11	12													1
1	2	3	4	5	6	10	8	9	7	11														2
1	2	3	4*	5	6	7	8	9	10	11	12													3
1	2	3	4	5		10	8	9	6	11*		7	12											4
1	2	3	4	5	6		12	9				8	10	7	11*									5
1	2	3	4		6			9				8	10	7	11	5								6
	2	3	4		6			9	12	11		8	10	7*		5	1							7
	2	3	4		6		12	9	7*	11		8	10			5	1							8
1	2	3	4		6	9		7		11		8	10			5								9
1	2	3	4	12	6	9		7*		11		8	10			5								10
1	2	3	4	12	6	9*		7		11		8	10			5								11
1	2	3	4		6			9	12	11		8	10	7*		5								12
1	2		4*	12	6			9	3	11	7	8	10			5								13
1	2	3	4	12	6			9		11	7*	8	10			5								14
1	2	3	4		6		7	9		11		8	10			5								15
1	2		4	5	6			9	3	11		8	10					7						16
1	2		4	5	6		12	9	3	11		8	10					7*						17
1		3	4	5*	6	10	12	9	2	11		8		7										18
1		3	4	5	6	10		9	2	11		8		7										19
1	2	3	4	5		10		9	6	11		8		7										20
1	2	3	4	5		10		9	6	11		8		7										21
1	2	3	4	5		10		9	6	11		8		7										22
1	2	3	4	5	12	10		9	6	11		8*		7										23
1	2	3		5	4	10		9	6	11		8		7										24
1	2	3		5*	4	10		9	6	11		8		7		12								25
1		3			4	10*		9	2	11		8	12	7		5			6					26
1		3		5*	6	12	4	9	2	11		8	10	7										27
1		3		5	6		4	9	2	11		8	10	7										28
1	7	3	4	5	6	10		9	2	11		8												29
1		3	4	5	6			9	2	11		8	10	7										30
1	12	3	4	5*	6	9			2	11		8	10	7										31
1	2	3				9	4		6	11		8	10*			5		12		7				32
1		3	4	5	6*	10		9	2	11		8		7		12								33
1		3		12	6	10			2			8		7*	11	5		9			4			34
1		3		12	6	10		9	2*	11		8		7		5					4			35
1		3		12	6	10			2	11					4	5		9*	8			7		36
1		3			6	10			2	11		8				5		9	4			7		37
1		3		12	6	10			2*	11	7	8				5		9	4					38
1		3			6	10				11	9*	8		7	12	5			4				2	39
1	2	3		5	6	9				11		8	10	7							4			40
1	2	3			6	9				11		8	10	7		5					4			41
1	2	3			6	9				11		8	10	7		5					4			42
40	28	39	27	22	36	29	8	32	29	39	4	38	21	24	4	20	2	6	5	1	5	2	1	
	+ 1s			+ 8s	+ 1s	+ 1s	+ 4s		+ 2s		+ 2s		+ 2s		+ 1s	+ 2s		+ 1s						

MIDDLESBROUGH

	Ht	*Wt*	*Birthplace*	*Clubs*	*League App.*	*League Gls*
Goalkeepers						
Jim Platt	6 1	12 10	Ballymoney	Middlesbrough	336	—
(N Ireland)				Hartlepool U (on loan)	13	—
				Cardiff C (on loan)	4	—
Jim Stewart	6 1	13 8	Kilwinning	Kilmarnock	175	—
(Scotland)				Middlesbrough	34	—
(Transferred to Rangers March 1981)						
Kelham O'Hanlon	6 0	11 0	Saltburn	Middlesbrough	—	—
Defenders						
John Craggs	5 8½	12 4	Flinthill	Newcastle U	52	1
				Middlesbrough	386	12
Ian Bailey	5 9	11 2	Middlesbrough	Middlesbrough	119	—
				Carlisle U (on loan)	7	1
				Doncaster R (on loan)	9	—
Mike Angus	5 10	12 3	Middlesbrough	Middlesbrough	23	—
Jeff Peters	5 6	10 2	Wideopen	Middlesbrough	6	—
Irving Nattrass	5 11	12 0	Fishburn	Newcastle U	238	16
				Middlesbrough	44	1
Keith Nobbs	5 10	11 10	Bishop Auckland	Middlesbrough	1	—
Billy Ashcroft	6 1	14 4	Liverpool	Wrexham	219	72
				Middlesbrough	138	17
Tony McAndrew	5 10	12 6	Lanark	Middlesbrough	208	9
Midfield						
Dave Armstrong (England)	5 8	11 3	Durham	Middlesbrough	359	59
Bill Askew	5 6½	10 2	Lumley	Middlesbrough	6	—
Mark Proctor	5 10	11 9	Middlesbrough	Middlesbrough	109	12
Graeme Hedley	5 10	10 4	Easington	Middlesbrough	47	6
				Sheffield W (on loan)	6	1
				Darlington (on loan)	14	1
Charles Bell*	5 9	10 10	Middlesbrough	Middlesbrough	10	1
Terry Cochrane	5 7½	10 9	Killyleagh	Coleraine	—	—
(N Ireland)				Burnley	67	13
				Middlesbrough	72	5
Andy McCreesh			Billingham	Middlesbrough	—	—
Colin Ross			Dailly	Middlesbrough	5	—
Mark Robinson	5 10	11 8	Middlesbrough	Middlesbrough	—	—
Forwards						
Billy Woof	5 10	11 9	Gateshead	Middlesbrough	23	2
				Brighton (on loan)	—	—
				Peterborough U (on loan)	3	—
David Shearer	5 10	12 0	Inverness	Middlesbrough	44	11
				Wigan Ath (on loan)	11	9
Micky Burns*	5 7	11 1	Blackpool	Blackpool	179	53
				Newcastle U	145	39
				Cardiff C	6	—
				Middlesbrough	61	24
David Hodgson	5 10	11 8	Gateshead	Middlesbrough	91	13
Bozo Jankovic	6 0	13 4	Sarajevo	Zeljeznicar	495	(gls not known)
(Yugoslavia)				Middlesbrough	50	16
Gary MacDonald	6 0	11 12	Middlesbrough	Middlesbrough	7	—
Ray Pirie	5 10;4	11 8	Aberdeen	Middlesbrough	—	—
(Contract cancelled Jan 1981)						
Colin Blackburn	5 9	10 9	Richmond	Middlesbrough	1	—

MILLWALL Division 3

Chairman: Allan A. Thorne.

Directors: H. T. J. Burnige FRICS, R. I. Burr, L. C. Eppel, P. J. Martinelli, W. J. Nelan.

General Secretary: G. I. S. Hortop.

Player-Manager: Peter Anderson.

Assistant Manager: Terry Long.

Year Formed: 1885. *Turned Professional:* 1893.

Limited Company: 1894.

Previous Grounds: 1885, Glengall Road, Millwall; 1886, Back of 'Lord Nelson'; 1890, East Ferry Road; 1901, North Greenwich; 1910, The Den.

Previous Names: 1885, Millwall Rovers; 1889, Millwall Athletic.

Football League Record:
1920 Original Members of Division 3; 1921 Division 3(S); 1928–34 Division 2; 1934–38 Division 3(S); 1938–48 Division 2; 1948–58 Division 3(S); 1958–62 Division 4; 1962–64 Division 3; 1964–65 Division 4; 1965–66 Division 3; 1966–75 Division 2; 1975–76 Division 3; 1976–79 Division 2; 1979– Division 3.

Honours: *Football League:* Division 2 best season: 3rd, 1971–72; Division 3(S) – Champions 1927–28, 1937–38; Division 3 – Runners-up 1965–66; Division 4 – Champions 1961–62; Runners-up 1964–65. *FA Cup:* semi-final 1900, 1903, 1937 (first Division 3 side to reach semi-final). *Football League Cup* best season: 5th rd, 1973–74, 1976–77.

Record Victory: 9-1 v Torquay U, Division 3(S), 29 Aug, 1927; v Coventry C, Division 3(S), 19 Nov, 1927.

Record Defeat: 1-9 v Aston Villa, FA Cup 4th rd, 28 Jan, 1946.

Most League Points: 65, Division 3(S), 1927–28; Division 3, 1965–66.

Most League Goals: 127, Division 3(S), 1927–28.

Highest League Scorer in Season: Richard Parker, 37, Division 3(S), 1926–27.

Most League Goals in Total Aggregate: Derek Possee, 79, 1967–73.

Most Capped Player: Eamonn Dunphy, 22 (23), Eire.

Most League Appearances: Barry Kitchener, 520, 1967–81.

Record Transfer Fee Received: £250,000 from Ipswich T for Kevin O'Callaghan, Jan 1980.

Record Transfer Fee Paid: £100,000 to Fulham for John Mitchell, July 1978; £100,000 to Crystal P for Nick Chatterton, Nov 1978; £100,000 to Fulham for Chris Guthrie, March 1980.

Previous Managers since the War: Jack Cock, Charlie Hewitt, Ron Gray, Jimmy Seed, Reg Smith, Ron Gray, Billy Gray, Benny Fenton, Gordon Jago, George Petchey.

Address of Supporters Club: 470 New Cross Road, Deptford, London, SE8.

Address of the Club Shop or Boutique: Same.

The Den, Cold Blow Lane, London, SE14 5RH. Telephone 01-639 3143/4,/1474. *Ground capacity:* 32,000. *Record attendance:* 48,672 v Derby Co, FA Cup 5th rd, 20 Feb, 1937. *Record receipts:* £21,756 v Ipswich T, FA Cup 6th rd, 11 Mar, 1978. *Pitch measurements:* 112yd×74yd.

How to get there: Buses from Central London and West End: 36, 36A, 36B, 53, 141, 171, 177, 182. From City: 21. Nearest Underground stations, New Cross or New Cross Gate (Metropolitan Line). Also New Cross Gate British Rail station.

Match tickets: Bookable 10–14 days in advance from club office.

Car parking: Car park near the ground. Also ample street parking.

Entertainments/catering facilities: Several licensed refreshment points around the ground.

Club shop: Three shops at the ground open on match days.

Programmes: Programmes available on subscription.

Extra information: Millwall went unbeaten for 59 successive League matches at The Den between 24 Aug 1964 and 14 Jan 1967.

Club Colours: Blue shirts, white trim, white shorts, blue stockings.

Change Colours: Red shirts, white trim, red shorts, red stockings.

Club Captain: Barry Kitchener.

First Team Physiotherapist: R. Adams.

Club Nickname: Lions.

MILLWALL 1980–81 LEAGUE RECORD

Match No.	Date	Venue	Opponents	Result	H/T Score	Goalscorers	Attendance
1	Aug 16	H	Hull C	D 1-1	0-1	Lyons	3831
2	18	A	Brentford	L 0-1	0-1		6520
3	23	A	Newport Co	L 1-2	0-1	Mitchell	6620
4	30	H	Chester	W 1-0	0-0	Chatterton	3264
5	Sept 6	H	Charlton Ath	W 2-0	1-0	Lyons, Mitchell	6893
6	13	A	Colchester U	L 0-3	0-1		2724
7	16	A	Carlisle U	L 1-2	1-2	Chatterton	3400
8	20	H	Exeter C	W 1-0	0-0	Gregory	3638
9	27	A	Burnley	L 0-5	0-1		5643
10	30	H	Carlisle U	W 3-0	1-0	Mitchell 2, Gregory	3168
11	Oct 4	A	Reading	L 1-4	0-3	Dibble	5690
12	7	H	Blackpool	D 0-0	0-0		3363
13	11	H	Swindon T	W 3-1	0-0	Chatterton, Kinsella, Dibble	3571
14	18	A	Barnsley	L 0-2	0-1		8693
15	22	A	Fulham	D 1-1	0-1	McKenna	4115
16	25	H	Sheffield U	L 1-4	1-3	McKenna	5261
17	28	H	Walsall	L 0-1	0-0		2785
18	Nov 1	A	Rotherham U	L 0-3	0-2		5742
19	8	H	Huddersfield T	W 2-1	0-0	Tagg, Chatterton	3529
20	11	H	Brentford	D 2-2	2-0	Mehmet, Chatterton	4274
21	15	A	Hull C	L 1-3	0-1	Chatterton (pen)	3210
22	29	H	Plymouth Arg	D 1-1	0-1	Mehmet	3385
23	Dec 6	A	Chesterfield	L 0-3	0-1		5930
24	20	H	Oxford U	W 2-1	0-1	Chatterton, Bartley	2781
25	26	A	Gillingham	W 2-1	1-0	Bartley, McKenna	4603
26	27	H	Portsmouth	D 0-0	0-0		8422
27	Jan 3	A	Walsall	D 0-0	0-0		3918
28	10	H	Fulham	W 3-1	1-1	Chatterton, Mehmet, Bartley	6002
29	17	A	Plymouth Arg	L 0-2	0-2		4847
30	24	A	Chester	W 1-0	1-0	Anderson	2114
31	31	H	Newport Co	D 0-0	0-0		4913
32	Feb 7	H	Colchester U	W 3-1	1-1	Bartley, Martin, Horrix	4565
33	21	H	Burnley	D 2-2	0-0	Bartley 2	4691
34	28	A	Exeter C	L 0-2	0-2		5408
35	Mar 4	A	Blackpool	D 0-0	0-0		4534
36	8	H	Reading	W 2-1	0-1	Kitchener, Bartley	7535
37	14	A	Swindon T	D 0-0	0-0		6966
38	17	A	Charlton Ath	D 0-0	0-0		12,700
39	21	H	Barnsley	D 1-1	1-0	Horrix	4901
40	28	A	Sheffield U	W 3-2	0-2	Hayes 2, Mitchell	10,350
41	Apr 4	H	Rotherham U	L 0-1	0-1		5041
42	11	A	Huddersfield T	W 1-0	0-0	Horrix	13,353
43	18	A	Portsmouth	L 1-2	1-1	Horrix	13,115
44	20	H	Gillingham	D 0-0	0-0		4214
45	29	A	Oxford U	L 0-1	0-1		3690
46	May 2	H	Chesterfield	L 0-2	0-1		3522

Final League Position: 16

Goalscorers

League (43): Chatterton 8 (1 pen), Bartley 7, Mitchell 5, Horrix 4, McKenna 3, Mehmet 3, Dibble 2, Gregory 2, Hayes 2, Lyons 2, Anderson 1, Kinsella 1, Kitchener 1, Martin 1, Tagg 1.
League Cup (1): Lyons.
F.A. Cup (2): Chatterton, own goal.

League Cup	First Round	Watford (a)	1-2
		(h)	0-2
FA Cup	First Round	Kidderminster (a)	1-1
		(h)	1-0
	Second Round	Exeter C (h)	0-1

Gleasure	Gregory	Sitton	Kitchener	Blyth	Chatterton	Mehmet	Martin	Mitchell	Lyons	Kinsella	Roberts	Tagg	Massey	Coleman	McKenna	Dibble	Jackson	Robinson	Bartley	Horrix	Anderson	Hayes	Stevens	*Match No.*
1	2	3*	4	5	6	7	8	9	10	11	12													1
1	3	2	5	6	4	8	7*	9	10	11	12													2
1	3	2*		6	4	8	7	9	10	11	12	5												3
1	3	2		6	4	8	7	9	10	11		5												4
1	3	2		5	6			9	10	11	8	4	7											5
1	3	2		6	4			9	10	11	7	5	8											6
1	3	2	12	6*	4		7	9	10	11	8	5												7
1	3	2			4		7*	9	10	11	8	5		6	12									8
1	3	2*			4	11	7	9	10		8	5		6		12								9
	3	12			4	7*		9	10	11	2	5		6	8		1							10
	3			6	4	7		9		11	2	5			8	10	1							11
		3		6	4	7*	12	9		11	2	5			8	10	1							12
		3		5*	6	7	12	9		11	2	4			8	10	1							13
		3			4	9	7			11	2	5		6	8	10	1							14
		3		6	4	7	9			11	2	5			8	10	1							15
		3		6	4	9	7			11	2	5			8	10	1							16
		3		6	4	9*	7			11	2	5		12	8	10	1							17
		6			4		11			7	2	5			8	10	1	3	9					18
		6			4	8	11			7	2	5			12	10	1	3	9*					19
		6			4	8	11			7	2	5				10	1	3	9					20
		6			4	8	11			7	2	5			12	10	1	3	9*					21
		6	5	4		8	11*			7	2				12	10	1	3	9					22
	2	6		11		8				7	4	5	9		12	10	1	3*						23
			5	6	4	8				7	2		11		9		1	3	10					24
			5	6		8*	2	11		7	3		4	12	9		1		10					25
	3		5	6			4	8		7	2		11		9*		1		10	12				26
				6	4	8*	2	9		7	3	5	11		12		1		10					27
				6	4	8	2	9		7	3	5	11				1		10					28
				6	4	8	2	9		7	3	5	11			12	1		10*					29
				6		8	2	9		7	3	5	11				1		10		4			30
					4	8	2	9		7	3	5	11	6			1		10					31
						8	2			7	3	5	11	6			1		10	9	4			32
			5	6*	4	8	2			7	3						1		10	12	9	11		33
		6	5		4*	8	2			7	3		12				1		10		9	11		34
		6	5		4	8				7	3		9				1		10		2	11		35
		2	6		4	8					3	5	7				1		10		9	11		36
		2	6		4						3	5	7				1		10	8	9	11		37
		2	5		4						3	6*	7			12	1		10	9	8	11		38
		2	5		4*						3	6	12			7	1		10	9	8	11		39
		2	5		4			12			3	6				7	1		10*	9	8	11		40
		2	5		4			10*			3	6				7	1		12	9	8	11		41
			6		4		2	10			3	5				7	1		11	9	8			42
1			6		4		2	10			3	5				7			11	9	8*	12		43
1			6		4		2	10			3	5	8			7			11	9				44
1		6			4		8				3	5	12			7			11*	9		10	2	45
1		12		5	6		2				3	4*	8			7			10	9		11		46
13	13	30	18	24	40	30	31	24	10	34	42	37	18	6	12	21	33	7	27	11	13	11	1	
		+ 2s	+ 1s				+ 2s	+ 1s			+ 3s		+ 3s	+ 2s	+ 6s	+ 3s			+ 1s	+ 2s		+ 1s		

MILLWALL

	Ht	*Wt*	*Birthplace*	*Clubs*	*League App.*	*League Gls*
Goalkeepers						
Peter Gleasure	5 11	12 13	Luton	Millwall	13	—
John Jackson*	6 0	13 13	Hammersmith	Crystal Palace	346	—
				Orient	226	—
				Millwall	79	—
Paul Sansome	5 11	11 10	New Addington	Millwall	—	—
Defenders						
Barry Kitchener	6 1½	14 9	Dagenham	Millwall	520	24
Tony Tagg	6 2½	12 11	Epsom	QPR	4	—
				Millwall	122	4
David Gregory	5 7	10 10	Essex	Millwall	52	2
Mel Blyth*	6 0	11 13	Norwich	Scunthorpe U	27	3
				Crystal Palace	216	9
				Southampton	105	7
				Crystal Palace (on loan)	6	—
				Millwall	75	—
Paul Roberts	5 8	11 5	London	Millwall	74	—
John Sitton	5 11	12 4	Hackney	Chelsea	13	—
				Millwall	45	1
Paul Robinson	5 10	11 1	Hampstead	Millwall	8	—
Keith Stevens (Apprentice)	5 11	11 1	Wimbledon	Millwall	1	—
Midfield						
Tony Kinsella (Contract cancelled March 1981)	5 8	10 4	Essex	Millwall	61	1
Nicky Chatterton	5 9	11 0	Norwood	Crystal Palace	151	31
				Millwall	110	22
Andy Massey	5 10	10 9	London	Millwall	21	—
David Mehmet (Contract cancelled March 1981)	5 9	11 9	London	Millwall	114	15
David Martin	5 11	10 11	East Ham	Millwall	36	1
Andy Mavin*			London	Barking	(not known)	
				Millwall	—	—
Mark Dennehy	5 7	10 1	Stratford	Millwall	—	—
David Rose	5 9	11 2	Redhill	Millwall	—	—
Peter Anderson	5 9½	11 4	Hendon	Hendon	(not known)	
				Luton T	181	34
				Royal Antwerp	(not known)	
				Tampa Bay	(not known)	
				Sheffield U (on loan)	30	12
				Millwall	13	1
Forwards						
Chris Dibble	5 10	10 6	Surrey	Millwall	37	2
Austin Hayes (Eire)	5 4½	9 12	London	Southampton	31	5
				Millwall	12	2
Dean Horrix	5 10	10 8	Slough	Millwall	13	4
Alan McKenna	5 10	11 4	Edinburgh	Millwall	24	3
John Mitchell	5 11	12 4	London	Fulham	169	56
				Millwall	81	18
Chris Guthrie	6 1	13 6	Dilston	Newcastle U	3	—
				Southend U	108	35
				Sheffield U	60	15
				Swindon T	45	12
				Fulham	50	15
				Millwall	7	1
Jimmy Sweetzer (Contract cancelled March 1981)	5 8	11 1	Woking	Oxford U	8	1
				Millwall	3	1
Keith Soundy*			Stepney	Orient	—	—
				Millwall	—	—
John Bartley	5 9	12 1	London	Welling U	(not known)	
				Millwall	28	7

NEWCASTLE UNITED Division 2

President: Rt Hon Lord Westwood JP, FCIS.
Chairman: S. Seymour. *Vice-Chairman:* R. Mackenzie.
Directors: F. Braithwaite OBE, J. Rush AFC, W. G. McKeag, Sir G. Bowman, W. P. Catesby.
Manager: Arthur Cox. *Asst Manager:* Tommy Cavanagh.
Secretary: R. Cushing.
Assistant Secretary: A. J. Garvie.
Year Formed: 1882. *Turned Professional:* 1889.
Limited Company: 1890.
Previous Name: Newcastle East End until Newcastle U in 1892.
Previous Ground: Chillingham Road, Heaton, until 1892.

Football League Record:
1893 Elected to Division 2; 1898–1934 Division 1; 1934–48 Division 2; 1948–61 Division 1; 1961–65 Division 2; 1965–78 Division 1; 1978– Division 2.

Honours: *Football League:* Division 1 – Champions 1904–05, 1906–07, 1908–09, 1926–27; Division 2 – Champions 1964–65; Runners-up 1897–98, 1947–48. *FA Cup:* Winners 1910, 1924, 1932, 1951, 1952, 1955; Runners-up 1905, 1906, 1908, 1911, 1974. *Football League Cup:* Runners-up 1975–76. *Texaco Cup:* Winners 1973–74, 1974–75. **European Competitions:** *European Fairs Cup:* 1968–69 (winners), 1969–70, 1970–71. *UEFA Cup:* 1977–78. *Anglo-Italian Cup:* Winners 1973.

Record Victory: 13-0 v Newport Co, Division 2, 5 Oct, 1946.
Record Defeat: 0-9 v Burton Wanderers, Division 2, 15 April, 1895.
Most League Points: 57, Division 2, 1964–65.
Most League Goals: 98, Division 1, 1951–52.
Highest League Scorer in Season: Hughie Gallacher, 36, Division 1, 1926–27.
Most League Goals in Total Aggregate: Jackie Milburn, 178, 1946–57.
Most Capped Player: Alf McMichael, 40, Ireland.
Most League Appearances: Jim Lawrence, 432, 1904–22.
Record Transfer Fee Received: £500,000 from Aston Villa for Peter Withe, May 1980.
Record Transfer Fee Paid: £250,000 to WBA for John Trewick, Dec 1980.
Previous Managers since the War: George Martin, Duggie Livingstone, Charlie Mitten, Norman Smith, Joe Harvey, Gordon Lee, Richard Dinnis, Bill McGarry.
Address of the Club Shop or Boutique: 7 Prudhoe Place, Haymarket, Newcastle-upon-Tyne 1.

St James' Park, Newcastle-upon-Tyne NE1 4ST Telephone Newcastle 28361. Information service 611571. *Telegraphic address:* 'Football, Newcastle-upon-Tyne'. *Ground capacity:* 40,480. *Record attendance:* 68,386 v Chelsea, Division 1, 3 Sept, 1930. *Record receipts:* £42,415 v Ujpest Dozsa, European Fairs Cup Final, 29 May, 1969. *Pitch measurements:* 115yd×75yd.
How to get there: The ground is central and within walking distance of the railway station and the town centre.
Match tickets: Personal applications accepted 10 days before a match and postal applications accepted 14 days before a match.
Car parking: Car park on the north side of the ground. Street parking available.
Entertainments/catering facilities: Excellent facilities in the New East Stand. Refreshments available in all parts of the ground.
Club shop: Open daily (except Sundays). Kiosk in St James' Park open match days 9.30 am–3.00 pm. Run by Supporters' Club.
Handbooks/programmes: Handbook, *Magpie*, published by Supporters' Club. Programmes if available can be ordered from the secretary price 30p, old programmes from the Supporters' Club shop/club office.
Extra information: United's 13-0 win over Newport County in 1946 was a second Division record score.
Club Colours: Black and white striped shirts, black shorts, black stockings with two white hoops on turnover.
Change Colours: All yellow.
First Team Trainer/Coach: Iam McFaul.
Club Nickname: Magpies.

NEWCASTLE UNITED 1980–81 LEAGUE RECORD

Match No.	Date	Venue	Opponents	Result	H/T Score	Goalscorers	Attendance
1	Aug 16	A	Sheffield W	L 0-2	0-0		26,164
2	20	H	Notts Co	D 1-1	0-0	Shoulder	17,249
3	23	A	Bolton W	L 0-4	0-2		11,835
4	30	H	Luton T	W 2-1	0-1	Hibbitt, Koenen	13,164
5	Sept 6	H	Cardiff C	W 2-1	2-0	Clarke, Shoulder (pen)	15,804
6	13	A	QPR	W 2-1	1-0	Boam, Hibbitt	10,865
7	20	H	Oldham Ath	D 0-0	0-0		19,700
8	27	A	Bristol R	D 0-0	0-0		5171
9	Oct 4	H	West Ham U	D 0-0	0-0		24,848
10	7	A	Preston NE	W 3-2	2-0	Rafferty, Shinton 2	5301
11	11	A	Bristol C	L 0-2	0-0		10,539
12	18	H	Swansea C	L 1-2	0-1	Rafferty	16,392
13	22	H	Shrewsbury T	W 1-0	0-0	Shinton	11,973
14	25	A	Chelsea	L 0-6	0-3		22,912
15	Nov 1	H	Watford	W 2-1	2-1	Hibbitt, Shinton	14,619
16	8	A	Cambridge U	L 1-2	0-1	Shinton	5684
17	11	A	Notts Co	D 0-0	0-0		8093
18	15	H	Sheffield W	W 1-0	1-0	Shinton	19,161
19	22	H	Wrexham	L 0-1	0-1		15,953
20	29	A	Orient	D 1-1	0-0	Shinton	5800
21	Dec 13	A	Swansea C	L 0-4	0-3		11,672
22	20	H	Bristol C	D 0-0	0-0		14,100
23	26	A	Grimsby T	D 0-0	0-0		17,623
24	27	H	Derby Co	L 0-2	0-2		20,858
25	Jan 10	A	Wrexham	D 0-0	0-0		6437
26	17	A	Luton T	W 1-0	1-0	Harford	10,774
27	31	H	Bolton W	W 2-1	1-0	Clarke, Martin	19,108
28	Feb 7	H	QPR	W 1-0	0-0	Waddle	20,442
29	21	H	Bristol R	D 0-0	0-0		14,180
30	25	A	Cardiff C	L 0-1	0-1		4235
31	28	A	Oldham Ath	D 0-0	0-0		5887
32	Mar 7	A	West Ham U	L 0-1	0-1		26,274
33	14	H	Preston NE	W 2-0	1-0	Harford 2	11,946
34	21	A	Shrewsbury T	L 0-1	0-0		4975
35	28	H	Chelsea	W 1-0	1-0	Halliday	17,392
36	Apr 4	A	Watford	D 0-0	0-0		10,986
37	11	H	Cambridge U	W 2-1	1-1	Turner (og), Shoulder	10,987
38	15	H	Blackburn R	D 0-0	0-0		15,339
39	18	A	Derby Co	L 0-2	0-1		14,139
40	20	H	Grimsby T	D 1-1	0-1	Shoulder	13,215
41	25	A	Blackburn R	L 0-3	0-2		10,609
42	May 2	H	Orient	W 3-1	1-0	Walker, Trewick, Harford	11,376

Final League Position: 11

Goalscorers

League (30): Shinton 7, Harford 4, Shoulder 4 (1 pen), Hibbitt 3, Clarke 2, Rafferty 2, Boam 1, Halliday 1, Koenen 1, Martin 1, Trewick 1, Waddle 1, Walker 1, own goal 1.
League Cup (3): Rafferty 2, Shoulder.
F.A. Cup (5): Waddle 2, Clarke, Martin, Shoulder.

League Cup	Second Round	Bury (h)	3-2
		(a)	0-1
FA Cup	Third Round	Sheffield W (h)	2-1
	Fourth Round	Luton T (h)	2-1
	Fifth Round	Exeter C (h)	1-1
		(a)	0-4

Carr	Kelly	Davies	Cartwright	Boam	Carney	Rafferty	Shinton	Clarke	Wharton	Koenen	Shoulder	Barton	Hardwick	Walker	Nicholson	Hibbitt	Mitchell	Martin	Withe	Waddle	Halliday	Johnson	Trewick	Harford	Brownlie	*Match No.*
1	2	3	4	5	6	7	8	9	10	11																1
1	2	3	12	5		7	8*	9	10	11	4	6														2
1	2	3	12	5		7	8	9	10	11*	4	6														3
		3		5	2	9			12	11	7	6*	1	4	8	10										4
		3		5	2	8		9		11	7		1	4		10	6									5
		3	12	5	2	8		9		11	7		1	4		10*	6									6
		3		5	2	8		9		11	7		1	4		10	6									7
1	2	3		5	6	8		9		11	7			4		10										8
1	2	3		5		10	9			11	7			4		8	6									9
1	2	3		5		10	9				7			4		11	6	8								10
1	2	3	12	5		10	9		8		7*					11	6	4								11
1	2	3		5		10	9		8		7					11	6	4								12
1				5	2	10	7		8							11	6	4	3	9						13
1			8	5	2	10	7		11	12								4	3	9*	6					14
1				5	2		7	9	8		10					11	6	4				3				15
1				5	2		7	9	8		10					11	6	4				3				16
1				5	2		7	9	8		10					11	6	4				3				17
1				5	2		7	9	8		10					11	6	4				3				18
1				5	2		7	9	8		10					11	6	4				3				19
1				5	2	9	7		8	11	10						6	4				3				20
1			9	5	2		7		8	11*	10				12		6	4				3				21
1				5	2		7		11		10						6	4		9		3	8			22
1				5	2		7		10								6	4		11		3	8	9		23
1				5	2		7		10							12	6*	4		11		3	8	9		24
1				5	2		7		10									4		11	6	3	8	9		25
1				5	2		7		10									4		11	6	3	8	9		26
1				5	2		7	9	10									4		11	6	3	8			27
1				5	2		7	9	10									4*		11	6	3	8	12		28
1				5	4				10		7									11	6	3	8	9	2	29
1		7	4	5					10*					12						11	6	3	8	9	2	30
1		3		5	12				10		7							4		11*	6		8	9	2	31
1		3			12				10		7	5						4		11*	6		8	9	2	32
1		3							10		7	5		11				4			6		8	9	2	33
1		3			12				10		7	5*		11				4			6		8	9	2	34
1		3			12				10		7	5		11				4*			6		8	9	2	35
1		3							10		7	5		11				4			6		8	9	2	36
1		3							10		7	5		11				4			6		8	9	2	37
1		3							10		7	5		11				4			6		8	9	2	38
1		3							10		7	5		11				4			6		8	9	2	39
1		3							10		7	5		11				4			6		8	9	2	40
1		3							10		7	5		11				4			6		8	9	2	41
1		3							10		7	5		11				4			6		8	9	2	42
38	8	25	4	31	23	15	23	14	35	11	32	14	4	17	1	15	18	31	2	13	19	16	21	18	14	
			+ 4s		+ 4s				+ 1s	+ 1s				+ 1s	+ 1s	+ 1s								+ 1s		

NEWCASTLE UNITED

	Ht	*Wt*	*Birthplace*	*Clubs*	*League App.*	*League Gls*
Goalkeepers						
Steve Hardwick	5 11	13 0	Mansfield	Chesterfield	38	—
				Newcastle U	85	—
Kevin Carr	6 2	13 6	Ashington	Newcastle U	56	—
Simon Smith	5 9	11 5½	Newton Aycliffe	Newcastle U	—	—
Defenders						
David Barton	6 0	11 7	Bishop Auckland	Newcastle U	82	4
Peter Kelly*	5 8	9 10	Lothian	Newcastle U	33	—
John Brownlie	5 10	11 10	Calder-Cruix	Hibernian	211	14
(Scotland)				Newcastle U	86	—
Bruce Halliday	5 10	11 3	Sunderland	Newcastle U	19	1
Stuart Boam	6 1	13 5	Kirkby	Mansfield T	175	2
				Middlesbrough	320	14
				Newcastle U	69	1
Stephen Carney	5 10	11 5	Wallsend	Blyth S	(not known)	
				Newcastle U	38	—
Ian Davies	5 8	10 8	Bristol	Norwich C	32	2
				Newcastle U	62	1
Peter Haddock	5 10	11 5	Newcastle	Newcastle U	—	—
Philip Leaver	5 9½	11 3	Derbyshire	Newcastle U	—	—
Peter Johnson	5 8	10 4	Harrogate	Middlesbrough	43	—
				Newcastle U	16	—
Chris Withe	5 10	11 3	Speke	Newcastle U	2	—
Midfield						
Kevin Pugh	5 1	10 13	Newburn	Newcastle U	—	—
Ken Wharton	5 7½	8 10	Newcastle	Newcastle U	39	—
Colin Suggett*	5 8	11 4	Washington	Sunderland	86	24
				WBA	128	20
				Norwich C	203	21
				Newcastle U	23	—
Mick Martin	5 10	10 11	Belfast	Manchester U	40	2
(Eire)				WBA	89	11
				Newcastle U	73	2
Peter Cartwright	5 7	10 0	Newcastle	N Shields	(not known)	
				Newcastle U	44	3
Frans Koenen	5 8	11 2	Waalwijk	NEC Nijmegen	(not known)	
				Newcastle U	12	1
John Trewick	5 9	10 10	Bedlington	WBA	96	11
				Newcastle U	21	1
Forwards						
Mick Harford	6 1	12 4	Sunderland	Lincoln C	115	41
				Newcastle U	19	4
Chris Waddle	6 0	11 5	Gateshead	Tow Law T	(not known)	
				Newcastle U	13	1
Gary Walton	5 11	11 9	Coundon	Newcastle U	—	—
Ken Mitchell*	5 11	11 12	Sunderland	Newcastle U	66	2
Nigel Walker	5 10	11 11	Gateshead	Newcastle U	65	3
Terry Hibbitt*	5 7	10 5	Bradford	Leeds U	47	9
				Newcastle U	138	7
				Birmingham C	110	11
				Newcastle U	90	5
John Connolly	5 11	11 7	Glasgow	St Johnstone	96	41
(Scotland) (Contract cancelled Aug 1980)				Everton	108	16
				Birmingham C	57	9
				Newcastle U	49	10
Gary Nicholson	5 7½	9 11	Newcastle	Newcastle U	12	—
Alan Shoulder	5 5	10 5	Bishop Auckland	Blyth S	—	—
				Newcastle U	97	35
Sam Montgomerie*	5 11	11 7	Irvine Central	Saltcoats V	(not known)	
				Newcastle U	—	—
Bobby Shinton	5 10	11 12	West Bromwich	Walsall	79	20
				Cambridge U	99	25
				Wrexham	128	37
				Manchester C	5	—
				Millwall (on loan)	5	3
				Newcastle U	33	8
Ray Clarke	6 0	11 7	London	Tottenham H	1	—
				Swindon T	14	2
				Mansfield T	91	52
				Sparta	(not known)	
				Ajax	(not known)	
				FC Bruges	(not known)	
				Brighton	30	8
				Newcastle U	14	2

NEWPORT COUNTY Division 3

President: S. Jenkins.

Chairman: R. Ford.

Vice-Chairman: G. C. Thorneycroft.

Directors: J. Ford, A. O. Menzies.

Manager: Len Ashurst.

Secretary: Mr P. Dauncey.

Year Formed: 1912.

Turned Professional: 1912.

Limited Company: 1912.

Football League Record:
1920 Original Member of Division 3; 1921 Division 3(S); dropped out of the Football League in 1931 but re-elected 1932; 1932–39 Division 3(S); 1946–47 Division 2; 1947–58 Division 3(S); 1958–62 Division 3; 1962–80 Division 4; 1980– Division 3.

Honours: *Football League:* Division 3 best season: 12th, 1980–81; Division 3(S) – Champions 1938–39. *FA Cup* best season: 5th rd, 1948–49. *Football League Cup:* never past 3rd rd. *Welsh Cup:* winners 1979–80. **European Competitions:** *European Cup-Winners' Cup:* 1980–81 (quarter-finalists).

Record Victory: 10-0 v Merthyr Town, Division 3(S), 10 Apr, 1930.

Record Defeat: 0-13 v Newcastle U, Division 2, 5 Oct, 1946.

Most League Points: 61, Division 4, 1979–80.

Most League Goals: 85, Division 4, 1964–65.

Highest League Scorer in Season: Tudor Martin, 34, Division 3(S), 1929–30.

Most League Goals in Total Aggregate: Reg Parker, 99, 1948–54.

Most Capped Player: Fred Cook, 2 (8), Jack Nicholls, 2 (4), Alf Sherwood, 2 (41), Bill Thomas, 2, Harold Williams, 2 (4), (all for Wales).

Most League Appearances: Ray Wilcox, 530, 1946–60.

Record Transfer Fee Received: £50,000 from Luton T for Mark Aizlewood, March 1978.

Record Transfer Fee Paid: £80,000 to Swansea C for Alan Waddle, Jan 1981.

Previous Managers since the War: Billy McCandless, Tom Bromilow, Fred Stansfield, Bill Lucas, Bobby Evans, Bill Lucas, Trevor Morris, Les Graham, Bob Ferguson, Bill Lucas, Brian Harris, Dave Elliot, Jimmy Scoular, Colin Addison.

Address of Supporters Club: Same as Football Club.

Somerton Park, Newport, Gwent. Telephone 277543/277271/277472. *Ground capacity:* 18,000 (seating 1,200). *Record attendance:* 24,268 v Cardiff C, Division 3(S), 16 Oct, 1937. *Record receipts:* £28,050 v Carl Zeiss Jena, European Cup-Winners' Cup quarter-final 2nd leg, 18 Mar, 1981. *Pitch measurements:* 110yd×75yd.

How to get there: Nearest railway station, Newport. By bus: the Chepstow Road bus to Beechwood and walk down over Somerton Hill; the Corporation Road bus to Cromwell Road and Somerton Park. All buses from bus centre in Dock Street.

Match tickets: Seats can be reserved from the club secretary.

Car parking: Street parking under police control.

Entertainments/catering facilities: Licensed bar in Supporters' Club. Licensed bar in the Social Club at Cromwell Road; both membership only. Licensed bars on both sides of ground.

Club shop: Sells all types of souvenirs, including 1979–80 promotion book. Souvenir list available from Commercial Department.

Handbooks/programmes: Back issues of programmes available from programme shop. Match programmes available on subscription from Commercial Department.

Club Colours: Amber shirts, black shorts, amber stockings.

Change Colours: White shirts, black shorts, white stockings.

First Team Trainer: Jimmy Goodfellow. *Asst Trainer:* Dave Williams.

Club Nickname: The Ironsides.

NEWPORT COUNTY 1980–81 LEAGUE RECORD

Match No.	Date	Venue	Opponents	Result	H/T Score	Goalscorers	Attendance
1	Aug 16	A	Burnley	D 1-1	1-1	Aldridge	6715
2	19	H	Charlton Ath	L 1-2	0-0	Tynan	8062
3	23	H	Millwall	W 2-1	1-0	Tynan 2 (2 pens)	6620
4	30	A	Carlisle U	W 4-1	2-1	Aldridge, Elsey, Gwyther, Moore	2859
5	Sept 6	A	Gillingham	L 2-3	1-2	Lowndes, Oakes	4712
6	13	H	Oxford U	L 0-1	0-1		5256
7	20	A	Chesterfield	L 2-3	0-1	Gwyther, Tynan	5277
8	27	H	Plymouth Arg	L 0-2	0-0		6878
9	Oct 4	A	Brentford	W 1-0	1-0	Lowndes	7309
10	7	H	Reading	D 0-0	0-0		5545
11	11	H	Portsmouth	W 2-1	2-0	Oakes 2	7003
12	14	A	Sheffield U	L 0-2	0-1		9776
13	18	A	Walsall	L 0-1	0-0		4335
14	25	H	Huddersfield T	W 3-2	2-1	Oakes, Lowndes, Gwyther	6403
15	28	H	Fulham	W 2-1	2-0	Aldridge, Clement (og)	6029
16	Nov 1	A	Blackpool	W 4-2	2-1	Aldridge, Gwyther, Oakes 2	4556
17	8	H	Hull C	W 4-0	2-0	Oakes, Gwyther, Bailey, Lowndes	5495
18	11	A	Charlton Ath	L 0-3	0-3		6991
19	15	H	Burnley	L 1-2	0-2	Tynan (pen)	5370
20	29	A	Rotherham U	L 0-1	0-0		5512
21	Dec 3	A	Chester	D 1-1	1-0	Lowndes	1640
22	6	H	Barnsley	D 0-0	0-0		5537
23	13	H	Chester	D 1-1	1-1	Gwyther	4169
24	20	A	Colchester U	L 0-1	0-1		2160
25	26	H	Swindon T	L 0-2	0-1		7086
26	27	A	Exeter C	D 2-2	2-1	Tynan (pen), Gwyther	6295
27	Jan 3	H	Sheffield U	W 4-0	1-0	Waddle, Lowndes, Moore, Tynan	6630
28	10	A	Huddersfield T	L 1-4	1-2	Lowndes	9063
29	16	H	Rotherham U	L 0-1	0-0		4783
30	31	A	Millwall	D 0-0	0-0		4913
31	Feb 7	A	Oxford U	W 1-0	1-0	Gwyther	4440
32	14	H	Gillingham	D 1-1	1-1	Gwyther	5152
33	18	A	Reading	D 1-1	1-1	Lowndes	3876
34	21	A	Plymouth Arg	L 2-3	1-0	Tynan, Gwyther	4315
35	28	H	Chesterfield	W 5-1	1-0	Gwyther, Oakes, Lowndes, Tynan 2	5340
36	Mar 7	H	Brentford	D 1-1	1-0	Tynan	5224
37	14	A	Portsmouth	D 0-0	0-0		13,208
38	28	A	Fulham	L 1-2	0-1	Gwyther	4570
39	Apr 4	H	Blackpool	W 3-1	1-0	Waddle, Aldridge 2	4514
40	7	H	Walsall	D 1-1	1-1	Moore	5446
41	18	H	Exeter C	W 2-1	0-1	Tynan, Waddle	5231
42	20	A	Swindon T	D 1-1	0-0	Waddle	8435
43	25	H	Colchester U	W 1-0	1-0	Aldridge	4619
44	May 2	A	Barnsley	L 1-4	0-1	Gwyther	15,559
45	5	H	Carlisle U	W 4-0	2-0	Gwyther 2, Tynan, Vaughan	3747
46	7	A	Hull C	L 1-3	0-1	Elsey	2059

Final League Position: 12

Goalscorers

League (64): Gwyther 15, Tynan 13 (4 pens), Lowndes 9, Oakes 8, Aldridge 7, Waddle 4, Moore 3, Elsey 2, Bailey 1, Vaughan 1, own goal 1.
League Cup (6): Aldridge 2, Tynan 2, Gwyther, Vaughan.
F.A. Cup (0).

League Cup	First Round	Hereford U (a)	0-1
		(h)	5-0
	Second Round	Notts Co (h)	1-1
		(a)	0-2
FA Cup	First Round	Plymouth Arg (a)	0-2

Plumley	Walden	Relish	Bruton	Oakes	Tynan	Vaughan	Lowndes	Gwyther	Aldridge	Moore	Elsey	Dowler	Kendall	Bailey	Davies	Warriner	Ward	Waddle	Bishop	*Match No.*
1	2	3	4	5	6	7	8	9	10	11										1
1	2	3*	4	5	6	7	8	9	10	11	12									2
1	2	3	4	5	6	7	8	9*	10	11	12									3
1	2	3	4*	5	6	7	8	9	10	11	12									4
	2	3	4	5	6	7	8	9	10*	11	12	1								5
	2*	3	4	5	6	7	8	9	10	11	12	1								6
	2	3	4	5	6	7	8	9	10	11		1								7
	2	3*	4	5	6	7	8	9	10	11	12	1								8
	2			5	6	7	8	9		11	10		1	3	4					9
	2			5	6	7	8	9		11	10		1	3	4					10
	2			5	6*	7	8	9	12	11	10		1	3	4					11
	2			5	6	7	8	9	12	11*	10		1	3	4					12
	2		4	5	12	7	8	9	10	11	6		1	3*						13
	2		4	5	6	7	8	9	10	11			1	3						14
	2		4	5	6	7	8	9	10	11			1	3						15
	2		4	5	6	7	8	9	10	11			1	3						16
	2		4	5	6	7	8	9	10*	11	12		1	3						17
	2		4	5	6	7	8	9	10*	11	12		1	3						18
	2		4	5	6	7	8	9	10	11			1	3						19
	2	3	4	5	10	12	8	9			7		1	6		11*				20
	2*	3		5	6	12	8	9	10		7		1	11	4					21
		3		5	6	2	8	9	10	11	7		1		4					22
1	2*	3		5	6	12	8	9	10	11	7				4					23
1		3		5	6	7	8	9		11	10				4	2				24
1	2	3			6	7	8	9		11	10				4	5				25
1	2	3*			6	7	8	9		11	10				4	5	12			26
1	2			5	6	3	8	9		11	7				4	12		10*		27
	2			5	6	3	8	9		11	7		1		4			10		28
	2	12		5	6	3	8	9*		11	7		1		4			10		29
	2	3		5	6	7	8	9		11	10		1		4					30
	2	3		5	6	7	8	9		11	10		1		4					31
	2	3		5	6	7	8	9		11	10		1		4					32
	2	3		5	6	7	8	9		11	10		1		4					33
1	2	3*		5	6	7	8	9		11	10				4	12				34
1	2*	3		5	6	7	8	9		11	10				4				12	35
1	2	3		5	6	7	8	9		11	10				4					36
1	2	3		5	6*	7	8	9		11	10				4				12	37
1	2	3	5		6	7	8	9		11	10*				4				12	38
	2	3		5		7	8		12	11			1	6	4			9	10*	39
	2	3		5	8	7			10	11			1	6	4			9		40
	2	3		5	8	7			10*	11			1	6	4			9	12	41
	2	3		5	8	7	12		10	11*			1	6	4			9		42
	2	3		5	8	7			10	11			1	6	4			9		43
	2	3		5	8			9		11	7		1	6	4				10	44
	2	3		5	8	7		9	12	11*			1	6	4				10	45
	2*	3		5	8	7		9	10		11		1	6	4			12		46
14	44	32	17	43	44	42	39	41	23	43	26	4	28	21	30	4	—	8	3	
		+ 1s			+ 1s	+ 3s	+ 1s		+ 4s		+ 8s					+ 2s	+ 1s	+ 1s	+ 4s	

NEWPORT COUNTY

	Ht	*Wt*	*Birthplace*	*Clubs*	*League App.*	*League Gls*
Goalkeepers						
Mike Dowler	5 8	11 0	Caldicot	Newport Co	19	—
(Contract cancelled Jan 1981)						
Gary Plumley*	6 0	12 0	Leicester	Leicester C	—	—
				Newport Co	182	—
Mark Kendall	6 0	12 4	Blackwood	Tottenham H	29	—
				Chesterfield (on loan)	9	—
				Newport Co	28	—
Defenders						
Grant Davies	5 10	11 4	Barrow	Preston NE	—	—
				Newport Co	100	1
John Relish	5 8	12 0	Liverpool	Chester	11	1
				Bury (on loan)	—	—
				Newport Co	196	6
David Bruton*	6 2	14 0	Gloucester	Bristol C	17	—
				Swansea C	193	19
				Newport Co	88	10
Richard Walden	6 0	12 0	Hereford	Aldershot	405	16
				Sheffield W	100	1
				Newport Co	128	2
Keith Oakes	5 10	12 2	Bedworth	Peterborough U	62	2
				Newport Co	122	24
Shane Carey			Carleon	Newport Co	—	—
(Contract cancelled Jan 1981)						
Midfield						
Nigel Vaughan	5 5	8 10	Newport	Newport Co	130	17
Steve Warriner*	5 7	10 0	Liverpool	Liverpool	—	—
				Newport Co	36	2
Bobby Ward	5 9	10 2	Glasgow	Celtic	—	—
(Contract cancelled March 1981)				Newport Co	3	—
Neil Bailey	5 9	11 0	Wigan	Burnley	—	—
				Newport Co	71	3
Karl Elsey	5 10	11 6	Pembroke	QPR	7	—
				Newport Co	34	2
Forwards						
John Aldridge	5 11	10 4	Liverpool	Newport Co	65	21
Howard Goddard	5 9	12 0	Over Wallop	Bournemouth	64	18
				Swindon T	13	—
				Newport Co	101	41
Steve Lowndes	5 7	10 7	Cwmbran	Newport Co	134	24
Kevin Moore	5 9	11 4	Blackpool	Blackpool	38	3
				Swansea C	55	6
				Bury (on loan)	4	—
				Newport Co	105	11
Tommy Tynan	5 10	13 0	Liverpool	Liverpool	—	—
				Swansea (on loan)	6	2
				Sheffield W	91	31
				Lincoln C	9	1
				Newport Co	99	28
Dave Gwyther	5 10	13 4	Birmingham	Swansea	217	59
				Halifax T	104	26
				Rotherham U	162	45
				Newport Co	60	23
David Cunningham	5 5	9 5	Kirkcaldy	Brechin C	49	6
(Contract cancelled Jan 1981)				Southend U	60	4
				Hartlepool U (on loan)	12	1
				Swindon T	23	3
				Peterborough U (on loan)	4	1
				Aston V	—	—
				Hereford U	30	2
				Newport Co	—	—
Keith Armstrong	5 8	11 5	Corbridge	Sunderland	11	—
(Contract cancelled Nov 1980)				Carlisle U	—	—
				Newport Co (on loan)	4	—
				Scunthorpe U (on loan)	1	—
				Oulu	(not known)	
				Newcastle U	—	—
				Newport Co	—	—
Alan Waddle	6 3	12 6	Wallsend	Workington	(not known)	
				Halifax T	39	4
				Liverpool	16	1
				Leicester C	11	1
				Swansea C	90	34
				Newport Co	9	4
Ray Bishop	5 10	11 0	Hengoed	Cardiff C	101	26
				Newport Co	7	—

NORTHAMPTON TOWN Division 4

Vice-President: W. R. Penn.

Chairman: N. J. Ronson.

Vice-Chairman: S. Wilson.

Directors: E. P. Northover, G. Taylor, L. Jaffa, Dr R. Gunn, B. Johnson, G. Pointon, W. M. Griggs.

Secretary/General Manager: Dave Bowen.

Team Manager: Bill Dodgin (Jnr).

Commercial Executive: G. Moody.

Year Formed: 1897. *Turned Professional:* 1901.

Limited Company: 1901.

Football League Record:
1920 Original Member of Division 3; 1921 Division 3(S); 1958–61 Division 4; 1961–63 Division 3; 1963–65 Division 2; 1965–66 Division 1; 1966–67 Division 2; 1967–68 Division 3; 1968–76 Division 4; 1976–77 Division 3; 1977– Division 4.

Honours: *Football League:* Division 1 best season: 21st, 1965–66; Division 2 – Runners-up 1964–65; Division 3 – Champions 1962–63; Division 3(S) – Runners-up 1927–28, 1949–50; Division 4 – Promoted 1960–61 (3rd); Runners-up 1975–76. *FA Cup* best season: 5th rd, 1933–34, 1949–50, 1969–70. *Football League Cup* best season: 5th rd, 1964–65, 1966–67.

Record Victory: 10-0 v Walsall, Division 3(S), 5 Nov, 1927.

Record Defeat: 0-10 v Bournemouth, Division 3(S), 2 Sept, 1939.

Most League Points: 68, Division 4, 1975–76.

Most League Goals: 109, Division 3, 1962–63; Division 3(S), 1952–53.

Highest League Scorer in Season: Cliff Holton, 36, Division 3, 1961–62.

Most League Goals in Total Aggregate: Jack English, 135, 1947–60.

Most Capped Player: E. Lloyd Davies, 12 (16), Wales.

Most League Appearances: Tommy Fowler, 521, 1946–61 (39 FA Cup ties).

Record Transfer Fee Received: £140,000 from Cambridge U for George Reilly, Nov 1979.

Record Transfer Fee Paid: £40,000 to Brentford for Steve Phillips, Aug 1980.

Previous Managers since the War: T. Smith, Bob Dennison, David Smith, Dave Bowen, Tony Marchi, Ron Flowers, Bill Baxter, Bill Dodgin (Jnr), Pat Crerand, John Petts, Mike Keen, Clive Walker.

Address of Supporters Club: 195, Abington Avenue, Northampton.

County Ground, Abington Avenue, Northampton NN1 4PS. Telephone Northampton 31553. *Ground capacity:* 17,000 (seating 1,400). *Record attendance:* 24,523 v Fulham, Division 1, 23 April, 1966. *Record receipts:* £17,438 v Manchester U. *Pitch measurements:* 120yd×75yd.

How to get there: Nearest railway station, Northampton. Any bus to the town centre, then from Mercer's Row, buses 1, 21, 2 and 14, though only 2 goes right to the ground.

Match tickets: No pre-match booking.

Car parking: No car park, but ample space in nearby side-streets.

Entertainments/catering facilities: Refreshment in hotel and tea bars on ground.

Club shop: 195 Abington Ave – opposite club. Run by the Supporters Club; sells all types of souvenirs.

Handbooks/programmes: Programmes available from the Supporters Club.

Extra information: Ground is shared with Northamptonshire County Cricket Club.

Club Colours: White shirts, claret trim, white shorts, white stockings.

Change Colours: Yellow shirts, claret trim, yellow shorts, yellow stockings.

Club Nickname: Cobblers.

NORTHAMPTON TOWN 1980–81 LEAGUE RECORD

Match No.	Date	Venue	Opponents	Result	H/T Score	Goalscorers	Attendance
1	Aug 16	A	Darlington	L 0-1	0-1		1763
2	23	A	AFC Bournemouth	D 0-0	0-0		2875
3	Sept 6	A	Hartlepool U	W 3-2	1-1	Bowen, Farmer, Phillips	2410
4	13	H	Doncaster R	L 0-2	0-1		2280
5	17	A	Bradford C	L 1-3	0-0	Phillips	2765
6	19	H	York C	W 2-0	1-0	Phillips, Saxby	1843
7	23	H	Southend U	W 2-0	1-0	Carlton, Phillips	2337
8	27	A	Hereford U	L 1-4	1-1	Phillips (pen)	2693
9	30	H	Bradford C	L 0-1	0-1		2293
10	Oct 3	H	Stockport Co	L 0-1	0-1		1902
11	7	A	Bury	W 2-1	1-1	Denyer, Waldock	1779
12	11	A	Scunthorpe U	W 2-0	2-0	Phillips 2	2650
13	17	H	Crewe Alex	W 4-1	1-1	Phillips 2, Farmer 2	2179
14	21	H	Aldershot	W 2-0	0-0	Gage, Heeley	3194
15	25	A	Lincoln C	L 0-8	0-2		4031
16	27	A	Mansfield T	L 0-2	0-1		3560
17	31	H	Halifax T	W 2-1	1-1	Phillips 2	2226
18	Nov 4	H	Bury	W 5-3	3-1	Denyer 3 (1 pen), Saunders 2	2229
19	8	A	Wimbledon	L 0-1	0-1		2029
20	12	A	Wigan Ath	L 0-3	0-1		3375
21	15	H	Darlington	D 2-2	0-1	Denyer, Phillips	1656
22	29	H	Tranmere R	W 3-1	0-1	Phillips 2, Sandy	1487
23	Dec 6	A	Torquay U	D 3-3	0-1	Bowen 2, Williams	2065
24	20	H	Rochdale	W 3-2	2-1	Phillips, Denyer, Bowen	1705
25	26	A	Peterborough U	L 0-3	0-2		6265
26	27	H	Port Vale	W 5-1	1-0	Farmer, Bowen 2, Sandercock, Denyer	2978
27	Jan 3	A	Aldershot	D 0-0	0-0		2992
28	10	H	Mansfield T	L 0-1	0-1		2985
29	16	A	Tranmere R	L 2-3	1-1	Bramhall (og), Bowen	1254
30	23	A	Southend U	D 0-0	0-0		5854
31	31	H	AFC Bournemouth	L 0-1	0-0		2140
32	Feb 3	H	Wigan Ath	D 1-1	0-0	Farmer	1708
33	6	A	Doncaster R	D 1-1	1-1	Bowen	5680
34	14	H	Hartlepool U	W 3-1	2-0	Bowen 2, Denyer	2032
35	Mar 6	A	Stockport Co	W 2-1	1-1	Phillips, Cooke	1945
36	13	H	Scunthorpe U	D 3-3	3-1	Denyer 3 (1 pen)	2046
37	21	A	Crewe Alex	L 1-3	0-1	Williams	2120
38	28	H	Lincoln C	D 1-1	1-1	Heeley	2424
39	Apr 4	A	Halifax T	W 1-0	1-0	Phillips	1996
40	11	H	Wimbledon	D 1-1	1-0	Bowen	2121
41	14	H	Hereford U	D 0-0	0-0		1380
42	18	A	Port Vale	D 1-1	0-1	Farmer	2371
43	21	H	Peterborough U	D 2-2	1-0	Denyer, Phillips	3800
44	May 1	H	Torquay U	W 1-0	0-0	Bowen	1562
45	3	A	Rochdale	W 1-0	0-0	Denyer	1474
46	5	A	York C	W 2-1	0-0	Bowen, Phillips	1167

Final League Position: 10

Goalscorers

League (65): Phillips 19 (1 pen), Bowen 13, Denyer 13 (2 pens), Farmer 6, Heeley 2, Saunders 2, Williams 2, Carlton 1, Cooke 1, Gage 1, Sandercock 1, Sandy 1, Saxby 1, Waldock 1, own goal 1.
League Cup (3): Phillips 2 (1 pen), Denyer.
F.A. Cup (1): Phillips.

League Cup	First Round	Reading (h)	0-2
		(a)	3-2
FA Cup	First Round	Peterborough U (h)	1-4

Poole	Walker	Sandercock	Byatt	Gage	Heeley	Denyer	Sargent	Phillips	Bowen	Farmer	Saunders	Sandy	Williams	Carlton	Saxby	Waldock	Leonard	Cooke	*Match No.*
1	2	3	4	5	6	7	8*	9	10	11	12								1
1			4	5	6	2		9	10	11	3	7	8						2
1			4	5	6	2		9	10	11	3	7	8						3
1			4	5	6	2		9	10	11*	3	12	8	7					4
1		4		5	6	2		9	10	11	3		8	7					5
1		4		5	6	2		9		11	3	10	8*	7	12				6
1		4		5		2		9		11	3	10	8	7	6				7
1		4		5	6*	2		9	10	12	3	7		8	11				8
1		4		5	11*	2		9	10	12	3		8	7	6				9
1		4		5	6*	2	10	9		11			8	7	12	3			10
1		6		5	8	4	10*	9		11		12		7	2	3			11
1		4		5	6	8		9		11			10	7	2	3			12
1		4		5	6	8		9		11	3		10	7	2				13
1		3		5	7	10		9		11		12		8	2	4	6*		14
1				5	6	8		9		11	3	10*		7	2	4		12	15
1	3			5	6	8		9		11			10	7	2	4			16
1		3		5	6	8		9		11			10	7	2	4			17
1		3	5			8		9		11*	12	6	10	7	2	4			18
1		3	5			8		9	11			6	10	7	2	4			19
1		3	5		12	8		9			11*	6	10	7	2	4			20
1		3	5	7	11	8		9				6	10		2	4			21
1		3		12	11	5		9	7	10*		6	2	8		4			22
1		3		5	11	10		9	7			6	2	8		4			23
1		3		5	11*	6		9	10			8	2	7	12	4			24
1		3	5			10		9	7			6	11	8	2	4			25
1		3	5			6		9	10	11		8	7			4		2	26
1		3	5			6		9	10	11		2	8	7		4			27
1		3	5			6		9	10	11*		2	8	7	12	4			28
1		3	5		11*	6		9	10	12		8	2	7		4			29
1		3	5*		11	2		9	10	4		8	6	7	12				30
1		3			11*	2		9	10	4		8	6	7	12	5			31
1		3				11		9	10	4	12	8*	6	7	2	5			32
1		3				11		9	10	4	5	8	6	7	2				33
1		3		12	7*	11		9	10	4	5	8	6		2				34
1		3			12	6		9		4	5	10	8*	7	2			11	35
1		3				6		9	10	4	5	8		7	2			11	36
1					12	6		9	10	4	5	11	3	7	2			8*	37
1				3	11	6		9	10	4	5	2	8	7					38
1				3	11	6		9	10	4	5	12	8	7*	2				39
1				3	11	6		9	10	4	5		8	7	2				40
1				3	11	6			10	4	5	9	8	7	2				41
1				3	11	6		9	10	4	5	8		7	2				42
1				3	11	6		9	10	4	5		8	7	2				43
1				3	11	6		9	10	4	5	7	8		2				44
1				3	11	6		9	10		5	4	8	7		2			45
1				3*	11			9	10	4	5	6	8	7	2	12			46
46	2	31	14	29	33	45	3	45	32	36	25	32	39	39	28	22	1	4	
				+ 2s	+ 3s					+ 3s	+ 3s	+ 4s			+ 6s	+ 1s		+ 1s	

NORTHAMPTON TOWN

	Ht	*Wt*	*Birthplace*	*Clubs*	*League App.*	*League Gls*
Goalkeepers						
Andy Poole	6 0	12 2	Chesterfield	Mansfield T	—	—
				Northampton T	95	—
Paul Overton*	6 0	12 0	Ely	Ipswich T	1	—
				Peterborough U	—	—
				Northampton T	—	—
Defenders						
Keith Williams*	5 9	11 10	Burtwood	Aston V	—	—
				Northampton T	131	6
Paul Saunders	5 10	11 10	Watford	Watford	—	—
				Northampton T	68	3
Ricky Walker*	5 9	11 2	Northampton	Coventry C	—	—
				Northampton T	53	—
Dennis Byatt	5 11	12 0	Hillingdon	Fulham	—	—
(Contract cancelled March 1981)				Peterborough U	3	—
				Northampton T	47	3
Phil Sandercock	5 10	11 0	Hollymouth	Torquay U	205	13
(Contract cancelled March 1981)				Huddersfield T	81	1
				Northampton T	69	3
Des Waldock	5 11	11 6	Northampton	Northampton T	54	4
Wakeley Gage	6 4	13 7	Northampton	Northampton T	52	2
Peter Cooke	6 0	12 0	Northampton	Northampton T	5	1
Gary Saxby	5 8	10 3	Mansfield	Mansfield T	16	1
				Northampton T	34	1
Midfield						
Peter Denyer	5 11	11 9	Haslemere	Portsmouth	131	15
				Northampton T	91	18
Adam Sandy	5 10	11 4	Peterborough	Northampton T	58	1
Russ Townsend	5 8	11 0	Barnet	Arsenal	—	—
(Contract cancelled July 1980)				Barnet	(not known)	
				Northampton T	13	—
Gary Leonard	5 8	10 10	Northampton	Northampton T	2	—
David Carlton	5 10½	11 2	London	Fulham	9	—
				Northampton T	104	6
				Brentford	140	7
				Northampton T	39	1
Forwards						
Keith Bowen	6 1	11 4	Northampton	Northampton T	62	24
(Non-contract)						
Kevin Farmer	6 0	12 0	Kent	Leicester C	1	—
				Northampton T	73	12
Gary Sargent	5 9	11 0	Bedford	Norwich C	1	—
(Contract cancelled Nov 1980)				Scunthorpe U	15	1
				Bedford T	(not known)	
				Peterborough U	34	5
				Northampton T	43	4
Mark Heeley	5 6	9 6	Peterborough	Peterborough U	17	3
				Arsenal	15	1
				Northampton T	44	2
Steve Phillips	5 6	10 6	Edmonton	Birmingham C	20	1
				Torquay U (on loan)	6	—
				Northampton T	51	8
				Brentford	157	65
				Northampton T	45	19

NORWICH CITY Division 2

President: J. L. Hanly JP. *Chairman:* Sir A. South JP.
Vice-Chairman: G. C. Watling.
Directors: D. S. McCall, E. A. Burrell, I. D. Coutts FCA.
Manager: Ken Brown.
Company Secretary/Accountant: R. C. W. Jackson FCA.
Commercial Manager: N. S. MacKay.
Football Secretary: N. S. Pleasants.
Year Formed: 1905. *Turned Professional:* 1905.
Limited Company: 1905.
Previous Grounds: 1905, Newmarket Road; 1908, The Nest, Rosary Road; 1935, Carrow Road.

NORWICH CITY FC

Football League Record:
1920 Original Member of Division 3; 1921 Division 3(S); 1934–39 Division 2; 1946–60 Division 3; 1960–72 Division 2; 1972–74 Division 1; 1974–75 Division 2; 1975–81 Division 1; 1981– Division 2.

Honours: *Football League:* Division 1 best season: 10th, 1975–76; Division 2 – Champions 1971–72; Division 3(S) – Champions 1933–34; Division 3 – Runners-up 1959–60. *FA Cup:* semi-finals 1959. *Football League Cup:* Winners 1962; Runners-up 1973, 1975.

Record Victory: 10-2 v Coventry C, Division 3(S), 15 Mar, 1930.
Record Defeat: 2-10 v Swindon T, Southern League, 5 Sept, 1908.
Most League Points: 64, Division 3(S), 1950–51.
Most League Goals: 99, Division 3(S), 1952–53.
Highest League Scorer in Season: Ralph Hunt, 31, Division 3(S), 1955–56.
Most League Goals in Total Aggregate: Johnny Gavin, 122, 1945–54; 1955–58.
Most Capped Player: David Jones, 8, Wales.
Most League Appearances: Ron Ashman, 590, 1947–64 (plus 72 Cup games).
Record Transfer Fee Received: £1,000,000 from Manchester C for Kevin Reeves, March 1980.
Record Transfer Fee Paid: £300,000 to Hajduk Split for Drazen Muzinic, Sept 1980.
Previous Managers since the War: Cyril Spiers, Dugald Lockhead, Norman Low, Tom Parker, Archie Macauley, Willie Reid, George Swindin, Ron Ashman, Lol Morgan, Ron Saunders, John Bond.
Address of Supporters Club: 50 King Street, Norwich.
Address of the Club Shop or Boutique: Norwich City Promotions, Carrow Road, Norwich.

Carrow Road, Norwich NR1 1JE. Telephone Norwich 612131. *Match information:* Norwich 612591. *Telegraphic address:* 'Football, Norwich'. *Ground capacity:* 29,000. *Record attendance:* 43,984 v Leicester C, FA Cup 6th rd, 30 March, 1963. *Record receipts:* £56,894.35 v Ipswich T, League Cup 3rd rd replay, 8 Oct, 1980. *Pitch measurements:* 114yd×74yd.

How to get there: Norwich railway station is eight minutes walk from the ground; British Rail run trains from outlying districts on match days. Coach firms also operate special services from surrounding parts. Any scheduled bus to the station and then walk.

Match tickets: Personal or postal applications to the Box Office on the ground, 14 days before the match. (Postal applications must include sae.)

Car parking: Several private car parks within walking distance of the ground. Multi-storey parks in Malt House Road and St Andrews Street. Street parking in Rouen Road, Carrow Hill, Kerrison Road, Cousins Road, and side streets off King Street. Coaches may park at Lower Clarence Road Car Park.

Entertainments/catering facilities: Norwich City have their own Public House, The Nest, in the River End Complex at Carrow road (NB: closed match days). Numerous licensed bars in the ground.

Club shop: Sells all types of souvenirs.

Programmes: Programmes available on subscription (from Carrow Road).

Extra information: In 1958–59 Norwich became one of only four clubs (now five) from the Third Division to reach the FA Cup semi-final.

Club Colours: Yellow shirts, green pinstripe, green shorts yellow trim, yellow stockings.

Change Colours: White shirts, green pinstripe, white shorts, green stockings.

Team Captain: Graham Paddon.

Club Nickname: Canaries.

NORWICH CITY 1980–81 LEAGUE RECORD

Match No.	Date	Venue	Opponents	Result	H/T Score	Goalscorers	Attendance
1	Aug 16	H	Stoke C	W 5-1	4-1	Downs, Fashanu 3, Woods	14,616
2	20	A	Aston Villa	L 0-1	0-0		25,970
3	23	H	Leeds U	L 2-3	0-1	Fashanu, Woods	17,890
4	30	A	Liverpool	L 1-4	0-1	Bennett	35,315
5	Sept 6	A	WBA	L 0-3	0-0		15,414
6	13	H	Southampton	W 1-0	1-0	Fashanu	18,158
7	20	A	Brighton & HA	L 0-2	0-0		14,877
8	27	H	Birmingham C	D 2-2	2-1	Paddon, Fashanu	13,801
9	Oct 4	A	Middlesbrough	L 1-6	0-2	Fashanu	12,837
10	11	H	Wolverhampton W	D 1-1	0-1	Fashanu	12,993
11	18	A	Coventry C	W 1-0	1-0	Downs	12,235
12	21	A	Arsenal	L 1-3	0-1	Barham	21,839
13	25	H	Nottingham F	D 1-1	0-0	Royle	17,849
14	29	H	Crystal Palace	D 1-1	1-1	Fashanu	15,782
15	Nov 1	A	Manchester C	L 0-1	0-0		33,056
16	8	H	Everton	W 2-1	0-0	Fashanu, Royle	14,557
17	12	H	Aston Villa	L 1-3	1-0	Paddon	17,050
18	15	A	Stoke C	L 1-3	0-1	Royle	11,207
19	22	H	Sunderland	W 1-0	1-0	Goble	15,024
20	29	A	Leicester C	W 2-1	2-1	Fashanu, Royle	13,958
21	Dec 6	H	Manchester U	D 2-2	0-2	Jovanovic (og), Fashanu	19,228
22	13	A	Crystal Palace	L 1-4	1-3	Royle	15,257
23	20	H	Coventry C	W 2-0	2-0	Royle, Paddon	12,630
24	26	A	Ipswich T	L 0-2	0-1		27,890
25	27	H	Tottenham H	D 2-2	1-1	Fashanu, Bond (pen)	23,898
26	Jan 10	A	Sunderland	L 0-3	0-2		17,749
27	17	H	Liverpool	L 0-1	0-1		23,829
28	31	A	Leeds U	L 0-1	0-0		15,836
29	Feb 7	A	Southampton	L 1-2	0-0	Watson	20,454
30	14	H	WBA	L 0-2	0-1		15,218
31	20	A	Birmingham C	L 0-4	0-0		14,686
32	28	H	Brighton & HA	W 3-1	2-0	McGuire, Watson, Fashanu	16,199
33	Mar 14	A	Wolverhampton W	L 0-3	0-1		21,605
34	17	H	Middlesbrough	W 2-0	2-0	Royle 2	14,549
35	21	H	Arsenal	D 1-1	1-0	Fashanu	19,569
36	28	A	Nottingham F	L 1-2	1-0	Fashanu	22,353
37	Apr 4	H	Manchester C	W 2-0	2-0	McGuire, McDowell (pen)	17,957
38	11	A	Everton	W 2-0	1-0	Royle, Fashanu	16,254
39	18	A	Tottenham H	W 3-2	2-2	O'Neill, Watson, Roberts (og)	34,413
40	20	H	Ipswich T	W 1-0	0-0	Fashanu	26,083
41	25	A	Manchester U	L 0-1	0-0		40,165
42	May 2	H	Leicester C	L 2-3	1-2	McGuire, Fashanu	25,307

Final League Position: 20

Goalscorers

League (49): Fashanu 19, Royle 9, Paddon 3, McGuire 3, Watson 3, Downs 2, Woods 2, Barham 1, Bennett 1, Bond 1 (pen), Goble 1, McDowell 1 (pen), O'Neill 1, own goals 2.
League Cup (5): Fashanu 3, Powell, Royle.
F.A. Cup (1): Downs.

League Cup	Second Round	Shrewsbury T (a)	1-1
		(h)	2-0
	Third Round	Ipswich T (a)	1-1
		(h)	1-3
FA Cup	Third Round	Cambridge U (h)	1-0
	Fourth Round	Manchester C (a)	0-6

Hansbury	McDowell	Bond	Powell	Downs	Mendham	Woods, Clive	Paddon	Fashanu	Royle	Goble	Nightingale	Barham	Forbes	Bennett	Symonds	Hoadley	Muzinic	Jack	McGuire	Baker	Watson	Robson	O'Neill	Woods, Chris	Walford	*Match No.*
1	2	5	6	3	4	7	10	8	9	11																1
1	2	5	6	3	4	7	10	8	9	11*	12															2
1	2*	5	6	3	4	7	10	8	9	11		12														3
1		2	6	3		7	10	8	9			4	5	11												4
1		2	6	12		7	10	8	9			4	5*	11	3											5
1		2	6		12	7	10	8		11	3	4*				5	9									6
1		2	6			7	10	8	12	11	3*	4				5	9									7
1		2	6	3		7*	10	8		11		4				12	9	5								8
1		2	6			7	10	8	12	11		4			3		9	5*								9
1		2		3*	12		10	8	9	11	6	4	5				7									10
1		2		3			10	8	9	11	6	7				5			4							11
1		2		3			10	8	9	11	6	7				5			4							12
1		2		3			10	8	9	11	6	7				5			4							13
1		2		3			10	8	9	11	6	7				5			4							14
1		2	12	3			10	8	9	11	6	7				5*			4							15
1		2		3			10	8	9	11	6	7				5			4							16
1	5	2		3			10	8	9	11*	6	7						12	4							17
1	5	2		3		11*	10	8	9		6	7		12					4							18
		2	6	3			10	8	9	11		7				5		12	4*	1						19
		2	3				10	8	9	11	6	7*				5	12		4	1						20
		3	6				10	8	9	11	2	7				5	12		4*	1						21
		2	5	3			10	8	9	11	6	7					4			1						22
	6	2	12		7		10	8	9	11						5	3*		4	1						23
		2	3		7	12	10	8	9	11						5			4*	1	6					24
	6	2		3*	7	12	10	8	9	11						5			4	1						25
	2				7		10	8	9					12	3	5*		11	4	1	6					26
	5	2			11		9		8			3		10				12	4*	1	6	7				27
		2	5		7		10	8	9			3		11				4		1	6					28
1	2		3*		7		10	8	9	11		4				5	12				6					29
1	2		3			12	10		9*	11		4					5	7			6	8				30
1		2			5		10	8	9	11		7					3*	12	4		6					31
1	2			3			10	8	9			11				5			4		6		7			32
	2*			3			10	8	9			11		12					4		6		7	1	5	33
	2			3			10	8	9			11							4		6		7	1	5	34
	2			3			10	8	9*			11							4		6	12	7	1	5	35
	2			3			10	8	9			11			12				4		6		7*	1	5	36
	2			3			10	8	9			11		12					4		6		7*	1	5	37
	2			3			10	8	9			11							4		6		7	1	5	38
	2*			3			10	8	9			11				12			4		6		7	1	5	39
				3			10	8	9			11*			2			12	4		6		7	1	5	40
				3			10	8*	9		12			11	2				4		6		7	1	5	41
	2*			3			10	8	9			11						12	4		6		7	1	5	42
22	20	28	17	28	11	10	42	40	38	25	14	34	3	5	5	17	9	5	28	10	18	2	11	10	10	
			+ 2s	+ 1s	+ 2s	+ 3s			+ 2s		+ 2s	+ 1s		+ 4s	+ 1s	+ 2s	+ 3s	+ 6s				+ 1s				

NORWICH CITY

	Ht	Wt	Birthplace	Clubs	League App.	League Gls
Goalkeepers						
Roger Hansbury	5 11	12 0	Barnsley	Norwich C	78	—
				Bolton W (on loan)	—	—
				Cambridge U (on loan)	11	—
				Orient (on loan)	—	—
Clive Baker	5 9	11 0	N Walsham	Norwich C	14	—
Duncan Steward*	5 10	12 4	Norwich	Norwich C	—	—
Defenders						
David Jones	6 1	12 8	Gosport	Bournemouth	134	5
(Wales)				Nottingham F	36	1
(Contract cancelled April 1980)				Norwich C	123	4
Mark Halsey*	5 6	10 1	Romford	Norwich C	3	—
Tony Powell	5 11	10 3	Bristol	Bournemouth	219	10
(Contract cancelled March 1981)				Norwich C	237	3
Duncan Forbes*	5 11	11 7	Edinburgh	Colchester U	270	2
				Norwich C	293	10
				Torquay U (on loan)	7	—
Kevin Bond	6 0	12 4	London	Norwich C	142	12
(Contract cancelled Feb 1981)						
Phil Hoadley	5 11	12 2	Battersea	Crystal Palace	73	1
				Orient	255	9
				Norwich C	73	—
John McDowell	5 10	12 4	East Ham	West Ham U	249	8
				Norwich C	41	1
Greg Downs	5 9½	10 7	Carlton	Norwich C	51	2
				Torquay U (on loan)	1	1
Richard Symonds	6 1	11 5	Langham	Norwich C	40	—
Mark Nightingale	5 10	10 7	Salisbury	Bournemouth	49	4
				Crystal Palace	—	—
				Norwich C	26	—
Drazen Muzinic			Yugoslavia	Hajduk Split	(not known)	
(Yugoslavia)				Norwich C	12	—
David Watson	5 11¼	11 12	Liverpool	Liverpool	—	—
				Norwich C	18	3
Adrian Harris*	6 1	12 11	Gorleston	Norwich C	—	—
Paul Haylock	5 8	11 0	Lowestoft	Norwich C	—	—
Steve Walford	6 1	11 7	Highgate	Tottenham H	2	—
				Arsenal	77	3
				Norwich C	10	—
Midfield						
Mick McGuire	5 7	10 5	Blackpool	Coventry C	72	1
				Norwich C	128	9
Graham Paddon	5 9	11 7	Manchester	Coventry C	5	1
				Norwich C	162	19
				West Ham U	115	11
				Norwich C	120	6
Peter Mountford	5 10	10 6	Stoke	Norwich C	—	—
Mark Barham	5 7	11 0	Folkestone	Norwich C	39	1
Clive Woods	5 9	10 10	Norwich	Ipswich T	268	23
				Norwich C	24	3
Peter Mendham	5 10	11 6	King's Lynn	Norwich C	41	2
Andrew Hart	5 8	11 0	Gt Yarmouth	Norwich C	—	—
Martin O'Neill	5 10	11 3	Kilrea	Distillery	(not known)	
(N Ireland)				Nottingham F	285	48
				Norwich C	11	1
Forwards						
Keith Robson	5 10	10 4	Hetton-le-Hole	Newcastle U	14	3
				West Ham U	68	13
				Cardiff C	21	5
				Norwich C	65	13
Dave Bennett	5 11	11 7	Oldham	Manchester C	—	—
				Norwich C	14	1
Justin Fashanu	6 1	12 7	London	Norwich C	90	35
Steve Goble	5 11	10 6	Wells	Norwich C	30	2
Greig Shepherd	6 1	12 0	Edinburgh	Norwich C	1	—
Gary Butcher*	5 10	11 6	Norwich	Norwich C	—	—
Ross Jack	5 10	11 2	Inverness	Everton	1	1
				Cardiff C (on loan)	—	—
				Norwich C	11	—
Peter Fishenden			Tottenham	Woodford T	(not known)	
(Contract cancelled April 1981)				Norwich C	—	—
Joe Royle	6 1	13 8	Liverpool	Everton	231	102
(England)				Manchester C	99	23
				Bristol C	101	18
				Norwich C	40	9
William Murphy			Hamilton	Norwich C	—	—
John Fashanu			Kensington	Cambridge U	—	—
				Norwich C	—	—

NOTTINGHAM FOREST Division 1

Chairman: G. E. Macpherson JP.

Vice-Chairman: F. Reacher.

Committee: H. W. Alcock FCA, B. J. Appleby QC, G. T. Thorpe, F. T. C. Pell FCA, D. C. Pavis, Dr I. Loch, M. R. Roworth.

Manager: Brian Clough. *Sec/Treasurer:* K. Smales.

Assistant Manager: Peter Taylor.

Year Formed: 1865. *Turned Professional:* 1889.

This is a club (200 members), *not* a limited company.

Previous Grounds: 1865, Forest Racecourse; 1879, The Meadows; 1880, Trent Bridge Cricket Ground; 1882, Parkside, Lenton; 1885, Gregory, Lenton; 1890, Town Ground; 1898, City Ground.

Football League Record:
1892 Elected to Division 1; 1906 Division 2; 1907 Division 1; 1911–22 Division 2; 1922–25 Division 1; 1925–49 Division 2; 1949–51 Division 3(S); 1951–57 Division 2; 1957–72 Division 1; 1972–77 Division 2; 1977– Division 1.

Honours: *Football League:* Division 1 – Champions 1977–78; Runners-up 1966–67, 1978–79. Division 2 – Champions 1906–07, 1921–22; Runners-up 1956–57; Division 3(S) – Champions 1950–51. *FA Cup:* Winners 1898, 1959. *Anglo-Scottish Cup:* Winners 1976–77. *Football League Cup:* Winners 1977–78, 1978–79; Runners-up 1979–80. **European Competitions:** *Fairs Cup:* 1961–62, 1967–68. *European Cup:* 1978–79 (winners), 1979–80 (winners), 1980–81. *Super Cup:* 1979–80 (winners), 1980–81 (runners-up). *World Club Championship:* 1980–81 (runners-up).

Record Victory: 14-0 v Clapton, FA Cup, 1st rd, 1890–91.

Record Defeat: 1-9 v Blackburn R, Division 2, 10 Apr, 1937.

Most League Points: 70, Division 3(S), 1950–51.

Most League Goals: 110, Division 3(S), 1950–51.

Highest League Scorer in Season: Wally Ardron, 36, Division 3(S), 1950–51.

Most League Goals in Total Aggregate: Grenville Morris, 199, 1898–1913.

Most Capped Player: Martin O'Neill, 36 (40), Northern Ireland.

Most League Appearances: Bob McKinlay, 614, 1951–70.

Record Transfer Fee Received: £1,250,000 from Manchester U for Garry Birtles, Oct 1980.

Record Transfer Fee Paid: £975,000 to Birmingham C for Trevor Francis, Feb 1979.

Previous Managers since the War: Billy Walker, Andy Beattie, John Carey, Matt Gillies, Dave Mackay, Allan Brown.

Address of Supporters Club: S. Dewar, c/o City Ground, Nottingham.

Address of the Club Shop or Boutique: Pools Office, City Ground, Nottingham NG2 5FJ. Forest Sports Shop, Clinton Street West, Nottingham.

City Ground, Nottingham NG2 5FJ. Telephone Nottingham 868236-7-8. Information Desk: 860232. *Telegraphic Address:* 'Forestball, Nottingham'. *Telex:* 377207 Answer back code 'Forest G'. *Ground capacity:* 35,000 (14,200 seats). *Record attendance:* 49,945 v Manchester U, Division 1, 28 Oct, 1967. *Record receipts:* £132,500 v Ajax, European Cup semi-final first leg, 9 April, 1980. *Pitch measurements:* 115yd×78yd.

How to get there: From Nottingham station any bus marked 'Trent Bridge'. Corporation specials from Parliament Street.

Match tickets: Bookable 14 days in advance of the match (personal) and 12 days (postal).

Car parking: Room for 300 cars in the East Stand car park and street parking off the Loughborough and Radcliffe Roads.

Entertainments/catering facilities: Only match-day refreshment bars. Social club situated just outside the ground. Jubilee club on ground (members only).

Club shop: Three shops on the ground sell all types of souvenirs. Also sports shop in city centre.

Handbooks/programmes: Programmes available on subscription from Carrington Publications Ltd, Wilford Crescent East, Trent Bridge, Nottingham.

Extra information: Forest hold the record for the highest away win in the FA Cup proper; they beat Clapton 14-0 in 1890-91. They were also the first club to adopt shinguards (1874), the Referee's whistle (1878), three half-backs (1885), the crossbar instead of tape (1891), and oval section goal-posts. Nottingham Forest are the only club to have played against clubs from all four home countries in the FA Cup. They are the only club in the Football League which is not a limited company. They hold the Football League record with 42 successive League matches without defeat. They are the only club to have been in three successive League Cup Finals and the only club to have done the League Championship and League Cup double.

Club Colours: Red shirts with white pinstripe, white shorts, red stockings. *Change Colours:* All yellow.

Club Captain: John McGovern. *First Team Trainer:* Ron Fenton. *Second Team:* Liam O'Kane.

Club Nickname: Reds.

NOTTINGHAM FOREST 1980–81 LEAGUE RECORD

Match No.	Date	Venue	Opponents	Result	H/T Score	Goalscorers	Attendance
1	Aug 16	A	Tottenham H	L 0-2	0-0		43,270
2	20	H	Birmingham C	W 2-1	1-1	Birtles, Ponte	26,561
3	23	A	Everton	D 0-0	0-0		25,981
4	30	H	Stoke C	W 5-0	2-0	Wallace 2, Birtles 2, Robertson (pen)	21,915
5	Sept 6	A	Middlesbrough	D 0-0	0-0		17,119
6	13	H	Manchester C	W 3-2	1-2	Birtles, Bowyer, Wallace	23,184
7	20	H	Leicester C	W 5-0	1-0	Gray, Birtles 2, Robertson (pen), Mills	27,145
8	27	A	Arsenal	L 0-1	0-0		37,584
9	Oct 4	H	Manchester U	L 1-2	1-1	Wallace	29,801
10	8	A	Sunderland	D 2-2	0-2	Mills, Bowyer	30,515
11	11	A	Brighton & HA	W 1-0	1-0	Wallace	17,420
12	18	H	WBA	W 2-1	2-1	Bowyer, Mills	25,096
13	22	H	Leeds U	W 2-1	2-1	Burns, Wallace	25,033
14	25	A	Norwich C	D 1-1	0-0	Robertson	17,849
15	Nov 1	H	Southampton	W 2-1	2-1	Ward, Robertson (pen)	24,669
16	8	A	Liverpool	D 0-0	0-0		43,143
17	11	A	Birmingham C	L 0-2	0-1		22,433
18	15	H	Tottenham H	L 0-3	0-0		25,400
19	22	H	Ipswich T	L 1-2	0-1	Wallace	24,423
20	29	A	Coventry C	D 1-1	1-0	Wallace	15,171
21	Dec 6	H	Crystal Palace	W 3-0	0-0	Gray (pen), Walsh, Ward	20,223
22	13	A	Leeds U	L 0-1	0-0		21,882
23	20	H	Sunderland	W 3-1	2-0	Ponte, Walsh, Francis	23,151
24	26	A	Wolverhampton W	W 4-1	1-0	Brazier (og), Gray (pen), Palmer (og), Ponte	31,588
25	27	H	Aston Villa	D 2-2	1-1	Francis, O'Neill	33,930
26	Jan 10	A	Ipswich T	L 0-2	0-0		25,701
27	31	H	Everton	W 1-0	1-0	Burns	25,611
28	Feb 7	A	Manchester C	D 1-1	0-1	Francis	39,524
29	18	A	Stoke C	W 2-1	1-0	Doyle (og), Walsh	17,305
30	21	H	Arsenal	W 3-1	2-1	O'Neill 2, Burns	25,357
31	28	A	Leicester C	D 1-1	0-1	Walsh	26,608
32	Mar 3	H	Middlesbrough	W 1-0	0-0	Burns	19,690
33	14	H	Brighton & HA	W 4-1	2-1	Robertson (pen), Wallace, Mills, Burns	20,688
34	18	A	Manchester U	D 1-1	1-1	Wallace	38,205
35	21	A	WBA	L 1-2	0-1	Mills	19,269
36	28	H	Norwich C	W 2-1	0-1	Francis 2	22,353
37	Apr 4	A	Southampton	L 0-2	0-2		22,712
38	11	H	Liverpool	D 0-0	0-0		27,363
39	18	A	Aston Villa	L 0-2	0-2		34,707
40	20	H	Wolverhampton W	W 1-0	1-0	Francis	19,711
41	25	A	Crystal Palace	W 3-1	2-0	Gray S., Wallace, Aas	12,138
42	May 2	H	Coventry C	D 1-1	1-1	Robertson (pen)	21,511

Final League Position: 7

Goalscorers

League (62): Wallace 11, Birtles 6, Francis 6, Robertson 6 (5 pens), Burns 5, Mills 5, Walsh 4, Bowyer 3, Gray F. 3 (2 pens), O'Neill 3, Ponte 3, Ward 2, Aas 1, Gray S. 1, own goals 3.
League Cup (12): Birtles 3, Ponte 3, Mills 2, Anderson, Gray F., Robertson (pen), Wallace.
F.A. Cup (10): Francis 5, Robertson 2 (2 pens), Ponte, Wallace, Walsh.

League Cup	Second Round	Peterborough U (h)	3-0
		(a)	1-1
	Third Round	Bury (a)	7-0
	Fourth Round	Watford (a)	1-4
FA Cup	Third Round	Bolton W (h)	3-3
		(a)	1-0 (aet)
	Fourth Round	Manchester U (h)	1-0
	Fifth Round	Bristol C (h)	2-1
	Sixth Round	Ipswich T (h)	3-3
		(a)	0-1

Shilton	Gunn	Gray F	McGovern	Needham	Burns	Ponte	Bowyer	Birtles	Wallace	Robertson	Anderson	O'Neill	Lloyd	Mills	Ward	Sutton	Walsh	Francis	Gray S	Smelt	Aas	*Match No.*
1	2	3	4	5	6	7	8	9	10	11												1
1		3*	4	5	6	8	12	9	10	11	2	7										2
1		3	4	5	6	7	8	9	10	11	2											3
1		3	4	6			8	9	10	11	2	7	5									4
1		3	4	5	6		8	9	10	11	2	7										5
1		3	4	5	6		8	9	10	11	2	7										6
1		3	4	5	6	8		9	10*	11	2	7		12								7
1		3	4	5	6	8*	12	9		11	2	7		10								8
1		3	4	6			8	9	10	11	2*	7	5	12								9
1	2	3	4	6			8		10	11		7	5	9								10
1	2	3	4	6			8		10	11		7	5	9								11
1	2	3			6	4	8		10	11		7	5	9								12
1	2	3			6	4	8		10	11		7*	5	12	9							13
	2	3	4		6		8		10	11		7	5		9	1						14
1		3			6	4	8		10	11	2	7	5		9							15
1		3	4		6		8		10	11	2	7	5		9							16
1	2	3	4		6		8		10	11		7	5		9							17
1		3			6	4*	8		10	11	2	12	5	7	9							18
1		3	4		6		8		10	11	2		5	7	9							19
1	6	3				4	8		10	11*	2		5	7	9		12					20
1	6	3	4				8*		10		2	12	5	7	9		11					21
1	6	3	4			12			10		2	8	5	7*	9		11					22
1	6	3	4			8			10		2	7	5				11	9				23
1	6	3	4			8			10		2	7	5	12			11	9*				24
1	6	3	4			7			10	11	2	8	5					9				25
1		3	4	5	6		10			11	2	7			8			9				26
1	6	3	4		5	7			8	11	2						10	9				27
1	6	3			5				8	11	2			7			10	9	4			28
1	6	3			5				8	11	2	12		7			10*	9	4			29
1	6	3			5				10	11	2	8		7				9	4			30
1	6	3			5	12			8	11	2			7*			10	9	4			31
1	6	3			5	12			8	11	2			7*			10	9	4			32
1	2	3		5	6	7			8	11				9	12		10		4*			33
1	2	3		5	6	7*			8	11				9	12		10		4			34
	2	3		5	6	12			8	11				7			10*	9	4	1		35
1		3		5*	6	7			8	11	2						10	9	4		12	36
1		3			6				8	11	2			7			10	9	4		5	37
1		3	4		5					11	2			7	8			9	10		6	38
1	3		4	6						11	2			7	8			9	10		5	39
1	6	3	4							11	2			7	8		10	9			5	40
1	3		4		5				8	11	2			7				9	10		6	41
1	2	3	4		5				8	11				7				9	10		6	42
40	26	40	27	17	30	17	19	9	37	38	31	21	18	23	14	1	15	18	14	1	6	
						+ 4s	+ 2s					+ 3s		+ 4s	+ 2s		+ 1s				+ 1s	

NOTTINGHAM FOREST

	Ht	*Wt*	*Birthplace*	*Clubs*	*League App.*	*League Gls*
Goalkeepers						
Peter Shilton	6 0	12 10	Leicester	Leicester C	286	1
(England)				Stoke C	110	—
				Nottingham F	161	—
Lee Smelt			Edmonton	Colchester U	—	—
				Gravesend	(not known)	
				Nottingham F	1	—
Steve Sutton			Derby	Nottingham F	1	—
				Mansfield T (on loan)	8	—
Defenders						
Viv Anderson	5 11	10 4	Nottingham	Nottingham F	224	8
(England)						
Bryn Gunn	5 9	10 5	Corby	Nottingham F	40	—
Kenny Burns	5 10½	11 0	Glasgow	Birmingham C	170	45
(Scotland)				Nottingham F	130	12
David Needham	6 1	12 7	Leicester	Notts Co	429	32
				QPR	18	3
				Nottingham F	69	7
Frank Gray	5 9½	11 10	Glasgow	Leeds U	193	17
(Scotland)				Nottingham F	81	5
Stuart Gray			Withernsea	Nottingham F	14	1
Einar Aas			Moss, Norway	Bayern Munich	(not known)	
(Norway)				Nottingham F	7	1
Midfield						
John McGovern	5 10	10 13	Montrose	Hartlepool	71	5
				Derby Co	190	16
				Leeds U	4	—
				Nottingham F	223	6
John Robertson	5 8	10 9	Uddinston	Nottingham F	316	53
(Scotland)						
Colin Walsh	5 9	11 0		Nottingham F	16	4
Raimondo Ponte			Naples	Grasshoppers	(not known)	
(Switzerland)				Nottingham F	21	3
Calvin Plummer			Nottingham	Nottingham F	—	—
Forwards						
John O'Hare*	5 8½	11 7	Renton	Sunderland	51	14
(Scotland)				Derby Co	248	65
				Leeds U	6	1
				Nottingham F	101	14
Trevor Francis	5 10	11 7	Plymouth	Birmingham C	280	118
(England)				Nottingham F	68	26
Gary Mills	5 8	11 1	Northampton	Nottingham F	44	7
Ian Wallace	5 7½	10 9½	Glasgow	Dumbarton	34	11
(Scotland)				Coventry C	130	57
				Nottingham F	37	11
Peter Ward	5 7	10 3	Lichfield	Burton A	(not known)	
(England)				Brighton	178	79
				Nottingham F	16	2
Steve Wigley			Ashton-under Lyne	Curzon Ashton	(not known)	
				Nottingham F	—	—
Steve Hodge			Nottingham	Nottingham F	—	—

NOTTS COUNTY Division 1

Chairman: J. J. Dunnett MA, LLB (CANTAB), MP.
Directors: L. S. Levin JP, R. C. Hartley, J. Mounteney.
Manager: Jimmy Sirrel.
Commercial Manager: Stuart J. Burgan A INST M.
Secretary: Dennis Marshall FAAI, AMBIM.
Year Formed: 1862 (the oldest club in the Football League).
Turned Professional: 1885. *Limited Company:* 1888.
Previous Grounds: 1862, The Park; 1863, The Meadows; 1881, Trent Bridge; 1910, Meadow Lane.

Football League Record:
1888 Founder Member of the Football League; 1893–97 Division 2; 1897–1913 Division 1; 1913–14 Division 2; 1914–20 Division 1; 1920–23 Division 2; 1923–26 Division 1; 1926–30 Division 2; 1930–31 Division 3(S); 1931–35 Division 2; 1935–50 Division 3(S); 1950–58 Division 2; 1958–59 Division 3; 1959–60 Division 4; 1960–64 Division 3; 1964–71 Division 4; 1971–73 Division 3; 1973–81 Division 2; 1981– Division 1.

Honours: *Football League:* Division 1 best season: 3rd, 1890–91, 1900–01; Division 2 – Champions 1896–97, 1913–14, 1922–23; Runners-up 1894–95, 1980–81; Division 3(S) – Champions 1930–31, 1949–50; Runners-up 1936–37; Division 4 – Champions 1970–71; Runners-up 1959–60. *FA Cup:* Winners 1893–94; Runners-up 1890–91. *Football League Cup* best season: 5th rd, 1963–64, 1972–73, 1975–76.

Record Victory: 15-0 v Thornhill U, FA Cup 1st rd, 24 Oct, 1885.
Record Defeat: 1-9 v Blackburn R, Division 1, 16 Nov, 1889; v Aston Villa, Division 1, 29 Sept, 1888; v Portsmouth, Division 2, 9 Apr, 1927.
Most League Points: 69, Division 4, 1970–71.
Most League Goals: 107, Division 4, 1959–60.
Highest League Scorer in Season: Tom Keetley, 39, Division 3(S), 1930–31.
Most League Goals in Total Aggregate: Les Bradd, 125, 1967–78.
Most Capped Player: Bill Fallon, 7 (9), Eire.
Most League Appearances: Albert Iremonger, 564, 1904–26.
Record Transfer Fee Received: £150,000 from Wrexham for Mick Vinter, June 1979.
Record Transfer Fee Paid: £200,000 to NK Rijeka for Radojko Avramovic, Aug 1979.
Previous Managers since the War: Arthur Stollery, Eric Houghton, George Poyser, Tommy Lawton, Frank Hill, Tim Coleman, Eddie Lowe, Jack Burkitt, Andy Beattie, Billy Gray, Jimmy Sirrel, Ron Fenton.
Address of Supporters Club: c/o Club.
Address of the Club Shop or Boutique: Souvenir Sales, c/o the Ground.

County Ground, Meadow Lane, Nottingham NG2 3HJ. *Telegraphic address:* 'Notts County FC Nottingham'. Telephone General Office: Nottingham 868494; Commercial Manager: Nottingham 868177. Information Service tel: 864152. Sports Hall 865198. *Ground capacity:* 24,654. *Record attendance:* 47,310 v York C, FA Cup 6th rd, 12 March, 1955. *Record receipts:* £23,215.62 v Leeds U, FA Cup 3rd rd, 3 Jan, 1976. *Pitch measurements:* 117yd×76yd.
How to get there: Nearest railway station Nottingham from there any bus marked 'Trent Bridge'.
Match tickets: Advance bookings can be accepted by post or by personal application 14 days before each home game. SAE must be sent with remittance in postal applications.
Car parking: No street parking around the ground, but ample space in the City of Nottingham Corporation car park on the Cattle Market, Meadow Lane, just 400 yards from the main entrances.
Entertainments/catering facilities: No social club. Tea bars and refreshment points on all sides of the ground.
Club shop: Open daily; situated at the ground.
Programmes: Back copies and subscription rates available from the club.
Extra information: When Notts County won the FA Cup in 1893–94, they became the first winners from the Second Division. The club has recently had a Sports Hall built on the Iremonger Road car park. This is available, for hire, to the public at certain times of the day.
Club Colours: Black and white striped shirts, black shorts, white stockings.
Change Colours: Yellow shirts with blue trim, yellow shorts, yellow stockings; (or all blue).
Club Captain: Don Masson *First Team Trainer:* Jack Wheeler.
Club Nickname: Magpies.

NOTTS COUNTY 1980–81 LEAGUE RECORD

Match No.	Date	Venue	Opponents	Result	H/T Score	Goalscorers	Attendance
1	Aug 16	H	Bolton W	W 2-1	2-1	Christie, Hooks	7459
2	20	A	Newcastle U	D 1-1	0-0	Masson	17,249
3	23	H	Sheffield W	W 2-0	1-0	Christie, McCulloch	10,246
4	30	A	West Ham U	L 0-4	0-1		21,769
5	Sept 6	H	QPR	W 2-1	2-0	Christie, Hunt	7197
6	13	A	Swansea C	D 1-1	0-1	Kilcline	10,921
7	20	A	Bristol C	W 1-0	0-0	Masson	7485
8	27	H	Cardiff C	W 4-2	2-1	Kelly, McCulloch, O'Brien (pen), Hooks	7229
9	Oct 4	A	Luton T	W 1-0	1-0	Hunt	8786
10	7	H	Grimsby T	D 0-0	0-0		8017
11	11	H	Bristol R	W 3-1	0-0	Harkouk, Hooks, Christie	7292
12	18	A	Orient	W 2-0	1-0	Gray (og), McCulloch	5829
13	21	A	Oldham Ath	W 1-0	0-0	McCulloch	5876
14	25	H	Blackburn R	W 2-0	2-0	McCulloch 2	13,500
15	Nov 1	A	Wrexham	D 1-1	1-1	Hooks	6221
16	8	H	Derby Co	D 0-0	0-0		16,650
17	11	H	Newcastle U	D 0-0	0-0		8093
18	22	A	Shrewsbury T	D 1-1	0-0	Christie	5352
19	25	A	Bolton W	L 0-3	0-1		7344
20	29	H	Chelsea	D 1-1	0-0	Harkouk	14,419
21	Dec 6	A	Watford	L 0-2	0-2		11,133
22	13	H	Oldham Ath	L 0-2	0-0		6565
23	19	A	Bristol R	D 1-1	1-1	McCulloch	3552
24	27	A	Preston NE	D 2-2	1-2	Harkouk, Manns	6547
25	Jan 10	H	Shrewsbury T	D 0-0	0-0		7139
26	17	H	West Ham U	D 1-1	0-1	Hooks	13,718
27	31	A	Sheffield W	W 2-1	1-0	Christie, McCulloch	22,449
28	Feb 7	H	Swansea C	W 2-1	2-0	Masson, McCulloch	8628
29	14	A	QPR	D 1-1	0-0	McCulloch	11,457
30	20	A	Cardiff C	W 1-0	0-0	Christie	4987
31	28	H	Bristol C	W 2-1	2-1	O'Brien (pen), Christie	7609
32	Mar 7	H	Luton T	L 0-1	0-1		8075
33	14	A	Grimsby T	L 1-2	1-0	Christie	12,184
34	21	H	Orient	W 1-0	0-0	O'Brien	6846
35	28	A	Blackburn R	D 0-0	0-0		14,451
36	Apr 5	H	Wrexham	D 1-1	1-0	Hunt	10,959
37	11	A	Derby Co	D 2-2	1-2	Goodwin, Christie	17,922
38	18	H	Preston NE	D 0-0	0-0		8485
39	20	A	Cambridge U	W 2-1	1-0	Christie 2	5507
40	25	H	Watford	L 1-2	0-1	Goodwin	10,345
41	May 2	A	Chelsea	W 2-0	1-0	Christie, Harkouk	13,324
42	5	H	Cambridge U	W 2-0	1-0	Christie, McCulloch	12,489

Final League Position: 2

Goalscorers

League (49): Christie 14, McCulloch 11, Hooks 5, Harkouk 4, Hunt 3, Masson 3, O'Brien 3 (2 pens), Goodwin 2, Kelly 1, Kilcline 1, Manns 1, own goal 1.
League Cup (11): Christie 4, Kelly 2, O'Brien 2 (2 pens), Hooks, Hunt, Mair.
F.A. Cup (2): Christie, Manns.

League Cup	First Round	Grimsby T (a)	0-1
		(h)	3-0
	Second Round	Newport Co (a)	1-1
		(h)	2-0
	Third Round	QPR (h)	4-1
	Fourth Round	Manchester C (a)	1-5
FA Cup	Third Round	Blackburn R (h)	2-1
	Fourth Round	Peterborough U (h)	0-1

Avramovic	Benjamin	O'Brien	Kelly	Kilcline	Richards	McCulloch	Masson	Christie	Hunt	Hooks	Wood	Mair	Harkouk	Doherty	Manns	Leonard	McParland	Beavon	Goodwin	*Match No.*
1	2	3	4	5	6	7	8	9	10	11										1
1	2	3*	4	5	6	7	8	9	10	11	12									2
1	2	3	4	5	6	7	8	9	10	11*		12								3
1	2	3	4	5	6	7	8	9*	10	11		12								4
1	2	3	4*	5	6	7	8	9	10	12		11								5
1	2	3	4	5	6	7	8	9	10	12		11*								6
1	2	3	4*	5	6	7	8		10	11	12		9							7
1	2	3	4	5	6	7		9	10	11			8							8
1	2	3	4	5	6	7	8	9	10	11										9
1	2	3	4	5	6	7	8	9	10	11										10
1	2	3	4*	5	6	7	8	9	10	11			12							11
1	2	3	4	5	6	7	8	9*	10	11			12							12
1	2	3		5	6	7	8	9	10	11			4							13
1	2	3		5	6	7	8	9	10	11			4							14
1	2	3	12	5	6	7	8	9	10	11*			4							15
1	2	3	4	5	6	7		9	10	11			8							16
1	2	3	4	5	6	7*		9	10	11	12		8							17
1	2	3	4	5	6	7*		9	10	11			8		12					18
1	2	3	4	5	6	7	8	9	10	11*			12							19
1	2	3	4	5	6	7*	8	9	10	11			12							20
1	2	3	4*	5	6	7	8	9	10	12			11							21
1	2	3		5	6		8		10		11		9	4	7					22
	2	3	4*	5	6	9	8		10		11		7	12		1				23
	2			5			8	9	6		3		10	4*	7	1	12	11		24
	2			5			8	9	4	11	3*		10		7	1	12	6		25
1	2	3	4	5	6	7	8	9	10	11										26
1	2	3	4*	5	6	7	8	9	10	11			12							27
	2	3	4	5	6	7	8	9	10	11						1				28
1	2	3	4	5	6	7	8	9	10	11										29
1	2	3	4	5	6	7	8	9	10*	11			12							30
1	2	3	4*	5	6	7	8	9	10	11			12							31
1	2	3	4	5	6	7	8	9*	10	11			12							32
1	2	3		5	6	7	8	9	10									11	4	33
1	2	3		5	6	7	8	9	10	11									4	34
1	2	3		5	6	7	8	9	10	11									4	35
1	2	3		5	6	7	8	9	10	11									4	36
1	2	3		5	6	7	8	9	10									11	4	37
1	2	3		5	6	7	8	9	10				12					11*	4	38
1	2	3		5	6	7	8	9	10	11									4	39
1	2	3		5	6	7	8*	9	10	11			12						4	40
1	2	3		5	6	7		9	10	11			8						4	41
1	2	3		5	6	7		9	10	11			8						4	42
38	42	40	26	42	40	39	36	39	42	33	4	2	15	2	3	4	—	5	10	
			+ 1s							+ 3s	+ 3s	+ 2s	+ 10s	+ 1s	+ 1s		+ 2s			

NOTTS COUNTY

	Ht	*Wt*	*Birthplace*	*Clubs*	*League App.*	*League Gls*
Goalkeepers						
Mike Leonard	5 11	11 0	Carshalton	Halifax T	69	—
				Notts Co	13	—
Radojko Avramovic	6 0	12 0	Yugoslavia	NK Rijeka	(not known)	
(Yugoslavia)				Notts Co	71	—
Defenders						
Pedro Richards	5 8	10 8	London	Notts Co	228	2
Brian Stubbs	6 2	12 0	Keyworth	Notts Co	426	21
Tristan Benjamin	6 0	11 1	St Kitts	Notts Co	133	4
Ray O'Brien	5 9	11 0	Sherborne	Manchester U	—	—
(Eire)				Notts Co	279	29
Gary Wood	5 10	11 3	Corby	Notts Co	11	—
Brian Kilcline	6 2	12 0	Nottingham	Notts Co	58	2
David Beavon	5 9	10 9	Nottingham	Notts Co	5	—
Midfield						
Gordon Mair	5 9	10 6	Coatbridge	Notts Co	55	6
David Hunt	5 11	11 0	Leicester	Derby Co	5	—
				Notts Co	129	9
Don Masson	5 8	10 12	Banchory	Middlesbrough	54	6
(Scotland)				Notts Co	273	81
(Contract cancelled April 1981)				QPR	116	18
				Derby Co	23	1
				Notts Co	113	10
Rachid Harkouk	6 0½	12 5	Chelsea	Crystal Palace	54	21
				QPR	20	3
				Notts Co	25	4
Eddie Kelly*	5 9½	12 4	Glasgow	Arsenal	175	13
				QPR	28	1
				Leicester C	85	4
				Notts Co	27	1
Mark Goodwin	5 9¾	10 9	Sheffield	Leicester C	91	8
				Notts Co	10	2
Forwards						
Paul Hooks	5 8	10 11	Wallsend	Notts Co	128	24
Paul Manns	5 6	10 7	Staffs	Cardiff C	—	—
				Notts Co	7	1
Jim Doherty	5 10	11 0	Lanarkshire	Cumnock	(not known)	
				Notts Co	8	—
Ian McCulloch	5 10	11 0	Kilmarnock	Kilmarnock	106	12
				Notts Co	119	25
David Millar*	5 9	11 0	Stirlingshire	Notts Co	—	—
Trevor Christie	6 2	12 0	Newcastle	Leicester C	31	8
				Notts Co	80	23
Ian McParland	5 8	10 8	Edinburgh	Ormiston Primrose	(not known)	
				Notts Co	2	—

OLDHAM ATHLETIC Division 2

Chairman: H. Wilde.

Vice-Chairman: R. Schofield.

Directors: J. Kershaw, F. D. Whitehead, I. H. Stott, G. T. Butterworth, D. A. Brierley, G. Knight.

Manager: Jimmy Frizzell.

Asst Manager/Chief Coach: Bill Taylor.

Secretary: T. Finn.

Year Formed: 1894. *Turned Professional:* 1899.

Limited Company: 1906.

Previous Names: 1894, Pine Villa; 1899, Oldham Athletic.

Previous Ground: Sheepfoot Lane; 1905, Boundary Park.

Football League Record:
1907 Elected to Division 2; 1910–23 Division 1; 1923–35 Division 2; 1935–53 Division 3(N); 1953–54 Division 2; 1954–58 Division 3; 1958–63; Division 4; 1963–69 Division 3; 1969–71 Division 4; 1971–74 Division 3; 1974– Division 2.

Honours: *Football League:* Division 1 – Runners-up 1914–15; Division 2 – Runners-up 1909–10; Division 3(N) – Champions 1952–53; Division 3 – Champions 1973–74; Division 4 – Runners-up 1962–63. *FA Cup:* semi-final 1913. *Football League Cup:* never past 3rd rd.

Record Victory: 11-0 v Southport, Division 4, 26 Dec, 1962.

Record Defeat: 4-13 v Tranmere R, Division 3(N), 26 Dec, 1935.

Most League Points: 62, Division 3, 1973–74.

Most League Goals: 95, Division 4, 1962–63.

Highest League Scorer in Season: Tom Davis, 33, Division 3(N), 1936–37.

Most League Goals in Total Aggregate: Eric Gemmell, 110, 1947–54.

Most Capped Player: Albert Gray, 9 (23), Wales.

Most League Appearances: Ian Wood, 525, 1966–80.

Record Transfer Fee Received: £275,000 from QPR for Simon Stainrod, Nov 1980.

Record Transfer Fee Paid: £200,000 to Manchester C for Kenny Clements, Sept 1979.

Previous Managers since the War: Bob Mellor, Frank Womack, Billy Wooton, George Hardwick, Ted Goodier, Peter McKennan, Norman Dodgin, Jack Rowley, Les McDowall, Gordon Hurst, Jimmy McIlroy, Jack Rowley.

Address of Supporters Club: Same as club.

Address of the Club Shop or Boutique: 'Latique', Boundary Park, Oldham OL1 2PA.

Boundary Park, Oldham. Telephone 061-624 4972. *Ground capacity:* 26,324. *Record attendance:* 47,671 v Sheffield W, FA Cup 4th rd, 25 Jan, 1930. *Record receipts:* £18,125 v Tottenham H, FA Cup 5th rd, 28 Feb, 1979. *Pitch measurements:* 110yd×74yd.

How to get there: Oldham Werneth is the nearest railway station; ordinary bus routes and specials link the station to the ground at Boundary Park.

Match tickets: Tickets can be purchased in advance 12 days before the day of the match by either personal or postal application from the ticket office.

Car parking: Parking for 800 cars on site adjacent to ground.

Entertainments/catering facilities: Social club (members only); refreshment bars around the ground. Licensed bars in seated sections.

Club shop: A new shop has been opened and sells all the usual souvenirs.

Handbooks/programmes: Programmes on sale at the ground or through the post for cover price plus postage and packing.

Extra information: Oldham's record victory in 1962 is the record for the Fourth Division.

Club Colours: Blue shirts with white trim on sleeves, white shorts with blue stripe down side, white stockings.

Change Colours: Tangerine shirts, blue shorts, tangerine stockings.

Physiotherapist: R. Jay. *Commercial Manager:* M. Twiss.

Club Nickname: The Latics.

OLDHAM ATHLETIC 1980–81 LEAGUE RECORD

Match No.	Date	Venue	Opponents	Result	H/T Score	Goalscorers	Attendance
1	Aug 16	H	QPR	W 1-0	1-0	Kowenicki	6986
2	20	A	Blackburn R	L 0-1	0-0		10,831
3	23	H	Cardiff C	W 2-0	0-0	Kowenicki, Stainrod	5690
4	30	A	Wrexham	L 2-3	1-1	Wylde 2	5176
5	Sept 6	H	Sheffield W	W 2-0	1-0	Stainrod, Futcher	11,700
6	13	A	Bristol R	D 0-0	0-0		3808
7	20	A	Newcastle U	D 0-0	0-0		19,700
8	27	H	Bolton W	D 1-1	0-1	Stainrod	10,174
9	Oct 4	H	Shrewsbury T	D 0-0	0-0		6093
10	7	A	Swansea C	L 0-3	0-2		8624
11	11	A	Cambridge U	L 1-3	0-2	Stainrod	4564
12	18	H	West Ham U	D 0-0	0-0		8344
13	21	H	Notts Co	L 0-1	0-0		5876
14	25	A	Watford	L 1-2	1-1	Stainrod	10,853
15	Nov 1	H	Preston NE	D 1-1	1-1	Keegan	6739
16	8	A	Chelsea	L 0-1	0-0		19,327
17	11	H	Blackburn R	W 1-0	0-0	Steel	7748
18	15	A	QPR	L 0-2	0-1		8223
19	22	H	Orient	L 0-1	0-0		5707
20	29	A	Bristol C	D 1-1	1-0	Heaton	8037
21	Dec 6	H	Luton T	D 0-0	0-0		4720
22	13	A	Notts Co	W 2-0	0-0	Palmer, McDonough	6565
23	20	H	Swansea C	D 2-2	1-2	Steel, Wylde	5486
24	26	A	Derby Co	L 1-4	1-2	Wylde	16,958
25	27	H	Grimsby T	L 1-2	1-1	Wylde	7183
26	Jan 10	A	Orient	W 3-2	2-1	Palmer 2, Keegan	4048
27	31	A	Cardiff C	W 2-0	1-0	Palmer, Nuttall	5687
28	Feb 7	H	Bristol R	W 1-0	1-0	McDonough	5552
29	14	A	Sheffield W	L 0-3	0-2		16,679
30	17	H	Wrexham	L 1-2	1-2	McDonough	5042
31	24	A	Bolton W	L 0-2	0-1		9641
32	28	H	Newcastle U	D 0-0	0-0		5887
33	Mar 7	A	Shrewsbury T	D 2-2	0-0	Palmer, Wylde	4191
34	15	H	Cambridge U	D 2-2	2-1	Wylde (pen), Palmer	4836
35	21	A	West Ham U	D 1-1	0-0	Wylde	24,394
36	28	H	Watford	W 2-1	2-1	Atkinson, Steel	4802
37	Apr 4	A	Preston NE	W 2-1	2-1	Wylde, Atkinson	6154
38	11	H	Chelsea	D 0-0	0-0		6740
39	18	A	Grimsby T	D 0-0	0-0		10,634
40	20	H	Derby Co	L 0-2	0-1		6194
41	25	A	Luton T	W 2-1	1-0	Wylde 2	10,305
42	May 2	H	Bristol C	W 2-0	0-0	Wylde, Heaton	4785

Final League Position: 15

Goalscorers

League (39): Wylde 12 (1 pen), Palmer 6, Stainrod 5, McDonough 3, Steel 3, Atkinson 2, Heaton 2, Keegan 2, Kowenicki 2, Futcher 1, Nuttall 1.
League Cup (3): Keegan, Kowenicki, Stainrod.
F.A. Cup (0).

League Cup	Second Round	Portsmouth (h)	3-2
		(a)	0-1
FA Cup	Third Round	Wimbledon (a)	0-0
		(h)	0-1

McDonnell	Hoolickin	Blair	Kowenicki	Clements	Hurst	Wylde	Futcher	Stainrod	Keegan	Atkinson	Heaton	Steel	Sinclair	Hilton	Platt	Gardner	Palmer	McDonough	Edwards	Nuttall	*Match No.*
1	2	3	4	5	6	7	8	9	10	11											1
1	2	3	4	5	6	7	8	9	10*	11	12										2
1	2	3	4	5	6	7	8	9	10	11*	12										3
1	2	3	4	5*	6	7	8	9	10	11		12									4
1	2	3*	4	5	6	7	8	9	10	11	12										5
1	2	3	4	5	6	7	8	9	10	11											6
1	2	3	4	5	6	7	8	9	10	11											7
1	2	3	4	5	6	7	8	9	10	11											8
1		4	5	3	6	7	8	9*	10	11		12	2								9
1		3	4*	5	6	7	8	9	10	11		12	2								10
1		3	4	5	6		8	9	10	11*	12	7	2								11
1		3	4*	5	6		8	10	7	12	11	9	2								12
1		3	4	5	6		8	10	7		11	9	2								13
1		3	4*	5	6		8	10	7	12	11	9	2								14
1		3	4	5	6	9		8	10		11		2	7							15
	2	3		5	6	9*		8	10	11	12			4	1	7					16
	2	3		5	6	7	8	10	4			9		11	1						17
	2	3		5	6	7*	8	9	4		11			10	1	12					18
	2	3		5	6		8		4	11	7				1	9	10				19
	2*	3		5	6		8		4	11	7	9	12		1		10				20
		3	12	5	6		8		4		7	9	2	11*	1		10				21
	12	3		5	6	7	8		4			9	2		1		10*	11			22
		3		5	6	7	8		4			9	2		1	10		11			23
		3		5	6	7	8		4			9	2		1	10		11			24
		3	4	5	6	7	8		10	11		9*	2		1	12					25
		3		5	6				4				2	8	1		10	11	7	9	26
		3		5	6				4				2	8	1		10	11	7	9	27
		3		5	6				4				2	8	1		10	11	7	9	28
		3		5	6	12			4				2	8*	1		10	11	7	9	29
		3		5	6		8		4	7			2		1		10	11		9	30
1		3		5	6		8		4	7			2				10	11		9	31
		3		5	6	9	8		4	7	11				1		10		2		32
		3		5	6	7	8		4	11		9			1		10		2		33
		3	12		6*	7	8			11		9		4	1		10	5	2		34
		3				7	6		4	11	8	9			1		10	5	2		35
		3		5		7	6		4	11	8	9			1		10		2		36
1		3		5		7	6		4	11*	8	9					10	12	2		37
1		3		5			6		4	11	8*	9					10	12	2	7	38
1		3		5		7	6		4	11		9					10	8	2		39
1		3		5		7*	6		4	11	12	9	2				10	8			40
1		3		5		7	6		4	11	8	9	2				10				41
1		3		5		7	6		4	11	8	9	2				10				42
22	13	42	16	40	34	28	36	18	41	28	15	21	21	10	20	4	21	13	12	7	
	+		+			+				+	+	+	+			+		+			
	1s		2s			1s				2s	6s	3s	1s			2s		2s			

OLDHAM ATHLETIC

	Ht	*Wt*	*Birthplace*	*Clubs*	*League App.*	*League Gls*
Goalkeepers						
John Platt	5 10	11 7	Ashton	Oldham Ath	109	—
Peter McDonnell	6 0½	13 7	Kendal	Bury	1	—
				Liverpool	—	—
				Oldham Ath	98	—
Defenders						
Gary Hoolickin	5 11	11 1	Middleton	Oldham Ath	37	1
John Hurst*	5 10	12 9	Blackpool	Everton	349	29
				Oldham Ath	170	2
Stephen Edwards	5 9	11 0	Birkenhead	Oldham Ath	51	—
Nick Sinclair	5 11	11 7	Manchester	Oldham Ath	23	—
Kenny Clements	6 1	12 6	Manchester	Manchester C	119	—
				Oldham Ath	76	1
Paul Futcher	6 0	12 3	Chester	Chester	20	—
				Luton T	131	1
				Manchester C	37	—
				Oldham Ath	36	1
John Ryan	5 10	11 7	Oldham	Oldham Ath	—	—
Midfield						
Ronnie Blair*	5 9	11 0	Coleraine	Oldham Ath	76	1
(N Ireland)				Preston NE (on loan)	—	—
				Rochdale	71	3
				Oldham Ath	295	22
Steve Gardner	5 10	10 5	Hemsworth	Ipswich T	—	—
(Contract cancelled April 1981)				Oldham Ath	53	2
Mark Hilton*	5 9	10 3	Middleton	Oldham Ath	50	2
Gerard Keegan	5 6½	10 9	Manchester	Manchester C	37	2
				Oldham Ath	83	2
Ryszard Kowenicki*	5 10	11 0	Poland	Widzew Lodz	(not known)	
(Poland)				Oldham Ath	42	5
Darren McDonough	5 9	10 0	Manchester	Oldham Ath	15	3
Douglas Anderson	5 11½	9 5	Hong Kong	Port Glasgow	(not known)	
				Oldham Ath	—	—
Forwards						
Paul Heaton	5 9	10 2	Hyde	Oldham Ath	68	11
Jim Steel	6 3	11 0	Dumfries	Oldham Ath	64	17
Tim Jordan	5 9	10 6	Littleborough	Oldham Ath	5	—
(Contract cancelled April 1981)						
Paul Atkinson	5 10	11 5	Pudsey	Oldham Ath	68	8
Rodger Wylde	6 1½	12 0	Sheffield	Sheffield W	169	54
				Burnley (on loan)	—	—
				Oldham Ath	39	16
Roger Palmer	5 10	10 10	Manchester	Manchester C	31	9
				Oldham Ath	21	6
John Bowden	6 0	11 7	Stockport	Oldham Ath	—	—
Martin Nuttall	5 9	11 2	Oldham	Oldham Ath	7	1

ORIENT Division 2

Chairman: Brian B. Winston.
Directors: H. S. Zussman, A. J. Harding.
Manager: Jimmy Bloomfield.
Secretary: Peter Barnes.
Administration Executive: Rod Erridge.
Asst Secretary: Mrs Carol Stokes.
Assistant Manager: Paul West.
Year Formed: 1881. *Turned Professional:* 1903.
Limited Company: 1906.
Previous Names: 1881–86, Glyn Cricket and Football Club; 1886–88, Eagle Football Club; 1888–98, Orient Football Club; 1898–1946, Clapton Orient; 1946–66, Leyton Orient.
Previous Grounds: Glyn Road (1884–96), Whittles Athletic Ground (1896–1900), Millfields Road (1900–30), and Lea Bridge Road (1930–37).

Football League Record:
1905 Elected to Division 2; 1929–56 Division 3(S); 1956–62 Division 2; 1962–63 Division 1; 1963–66 Division 2; 1966–70 Division 3; 1970– Division 2.

Honours: *Football League:* Division 1 best season: 22nd, 1962–63; Division 2 – Runners-up 1961–62; Division 3 – Champions 1969–70; Division 3(S) – Champions 1955–56; Runners-up 1954–55. *FA Cup:* Semi-final 1977–78. *Football League Cup* best season: 5th rd, 1963.
Record Victory: 9-2 v Aldershot, Division 3(S), 10 Feb, 1934 and v Chester, League Cup 3rd rd, 15 Oct, 1962.
Record Defeat: 0-8 v Aston Villa, FA Cup 4th rd, 30 Jan, 1929.
Most League Points: 66, Division 3(S), 1955–56.
Most League Goals: 106, Division 3(S), 1955–56.
Highest League Scorer in Season: Tom Johnston, 35, Division 2, 1957–58.
Most League Goals in Total Aggregate: Tom Johnston, 121, 1956–58, 1959–61.
Most Capped Player: Tony Grealish, 8 (25), Eire.
Most League Appearances: Peter Allen, 431, 1965–78.
Record Transfer Fee Received: £210,000 from QPR for Glenn Roeder, Aug 1978.
Record Transfer Fee Paid: £150,000 to Tottenham H for Peter Taylor, Nov 1980.
Previous Managers since the War: Charles Hewitt, Neil McBain, Alec Stock, Les Gore, Alec Stock, John Carey, Benny Fenton, Dave Sexton, Dick Graham, Jimmy Bloomfield, George Petchey.
Address of Supporters Club: Same as Ground.
Address of the Club Shop or Boutique: Orient Shop, 369 High Road, Leyton E10.

Leyton Stadium, Brisbane Road, Leyton, London E10 5NE. Telephone 01-539 2223/4. *Telegraphic address:* 'The Orient', Leyton E10. *Ground capacity:* 26,500 (7,171 seats). *Record attendance:* 34,345 v West Ham U, FA Cup 4th rd, 25 Jan, 1964. *Record receipts:* £41,765.20 v West Ham U, FA Cup 4th rd, 26 Jan, 1980. *Pitch measurements:* 110yd×75yd.
How to get there: Buses 69, 58, 278, 241 pass the ground. From the centre of London, journey by underground (Central Line) to Leyton station; the ground is a few minutes' walk. Nearest BR station is Leyton Midland Road (10 minutes' walk).
Match tickets: Can be booked at least two weeks in advance.
Car parking: Street parking around the ground. A National Car Park five minutes from Brisbane Road (off Oliver Road).
Entertainments/catering facilities: Supporters' Section Club and snack bar points around the ground.
Club shop: Sells all types of souvenirs and sportswear.
Handbooks/programmes: Programmes can be obtained on subscription, and back numbers can be ordered from the club shop. Official centenary handbook available from club shop, £1.20 including p & p, limited edition only.
Extra information: The club operates a Pools Section and Travel Service. All enquiries to Mr P. Couldrige, commercial manager, 369 High Road, Leyton, E10 (01-539 4483/4). Club's official historian – Neil Kaufman – can answer queries connected with the history of the club; c/o the Secretary.
Club Colours: White shirts two red vertical stripes, white shorts, white stockings.
Change Colours: Red shirts, two white vertical stripes, red shorts, red stockings.
Club Captain: Tommy Taylor. *Reserve Team Coach:* Ralph Coates.
Club Nickname: The O's.

ORIENT 1980–81 LEAGUE RECORD

Match No.	Date	Venue	Opponents	Result	H/T Score	Goalscorers	Attendance
1	Aug 16	A	Bristol R	D 1-1	1-1	Chiedozie	5831
2	19	H	Cambridge U	W 3-0	2-0	Jennings, Parsons, Chiedozie	5109
3	23	H	Blackburn R	D 1-1	1-0	Bowles	5057
4	30	A	Cardiff C	L 2-4	2-2	Parsons, Jennings	5649
5	Sept 6	H	Grimsby T	W 2-0	1-0	Moores, Bowles (pen)	4506
6	13	A	Wrexham	L 1-3	1-1	Bowles	5356
7	20	A	Luton T	L 1-2	0-0	Moores	8506
8	27	H	Derby Co	W 1-0	1-0	Moores	5490
9	Oct 4	H	Preston NE	W 4-0	2-0	Moores, Parsons, Chiedozie, Bowles	4295
10	7	A	QPR	D 0-0	0-0		9627
11	11	A	Shrewsbury T	W 2-1	1-1	Chiedozie, Moores	4300
12	18	H	Notts Co	L 0-2	0-1		5829
13	21	H	Chelsea	L 0-1	0-1		11,950
14	25	A	Sheffield W	D 2-2	0-1	Moores, Chiedozie	18,018
15	Nov 1	H	Bristol C	W 3-1	1-1	Chiedozie, Parsons, Moores	4689
16	8	A	Swansea C	W 2-0	0-0	Moores, Chiedozie	10,922
17	11	A	Cambridge U	L 0-1	0-1		5072
18	15	H	Bristol R	D 2-2	1-0	Moores, Taylor P.	5100
19	22	A	Oldham Ath	W 1-0	0-0	Parsons	5707
20	29	H	Newcastle U	D 1-1	0-0	Taylor P.	5800
21	Dec 6	A	Bolton W	L 1-3	0-2	Taylor P.	8228
22	13	H	Shrewsbury T	W 1-0	0-0	Taylor P.	4801
23	20	A	Chelsea	W 1-0	1-0	Mayo	15,943
24	26	H	Watford	D 1-1	1-1	Taylor P.	10,041
25	27	A	West Ham U	L 1-2	0-0	Chiedozie	34,408
26	Jan 10	H	Oldham Ath	L 2-3	1-2	Jennings, Bowles (pen)	4048
27	17	H	Cardiff C	D 2-2	0-0	Mayo, Taylor P.	3838
28	31	A	Blackburn R	L 0-2	0-2		9091
29	Feb 7	H	Wrexham	W 2-1	1-1	Bowles (pen), Parsons	4057
30	14	A	Grimsby T	L 0-2	0-0		10,190
31	21	A	Derby Co	D 1-1	0-1	Margerrison	15,709
32	Mar 1	H	Luton T	D 0-0	0-0		8074
33	7	A	Preston NE	L 0-3	0-3		5448
34	21	A	Notts Co	L 0-1	0-0		6846
35	28	H	Sheffield W	W 2-0	0-0	Jennings, Taylor P.	6561
36	31	H	QPR	W 4-0	1-0	Chiedozie, Jennings 2, Taylor P.	6724
37	Apr 4	A	Bristol C	L 1-3	0-0	Jennings	5803
38	11	H	Swansea C	D 1-1	0-1	Godfrey	4984
39	17	A	Watford	L 0-2	0-0		12,459
40	18	H	West Ham U	L 0-2	0-2		14,592
41	26	H	Bolton W	D 2-2	2-1	Mayo, Godfrey	3824
42	May 2	A	Newcastle U	L 1-3	0-1	Mayo	11,376

Final League Position: 17

Goalscorers

League (52): Chiedozie 9, Moores 9, Taylor P. 8, Jennings 7, Bowles 6 (3 pens), Parsons 6, Mayo 4, Godfrey 2, Margerrison 1.
League Cup (1): Jennings.
F.A. Cup (1): Jennings.

League Cup	Second Round	Tottenham H (h)	0-1
		(a)	1-3
FA Cup	Third Round	Luton T (h)	1-3

Day	Fisher	Roffey	Taylor T	Gray	Bowles	Chiedozie	Parsons	Mayo	Jennings	Coates	Moores	Margerrison	Hughton	Godfrey	Taylor P	Rafter	*Match No.*
1	2	3	4	5	10	7*	6	9	8	11	12						1
1	2	3	4	5	10	7	6	9	8	11							2
1	2	3	4	5	10	7	6	9	8	11							3
1	2	3	4	5	10	7	6	9	8	11*		12					4
1	2	3	4	5	10	7	6	9			8	11					5
1	2	3		5	10	7	6*	9			8	11	4	12			6
1	2	3	4	5	10	7	6	9			8	11					7
1	2	3	4	5	10	7	6	9			8	11					8
1	2	3	4	5	10	7	6	9			8	11					9
1	2	3	4	5	10	7	6	9			8	11					10
1	2	3	4	5	10	7	6	9			8	11					11
1	2	3	4	5	10	7	6	9			8	11					12
1	2	3	4	5	10	7	6*	9	12		8	11					13
1	2	3	4*	5	10	7	6	9			8	11	12				14
1	2	3	4	5	10	7	6	9			8	11					15
1	2	3	4	5		7	6	9			8	11	10				16
1	2	3	4	5	10	7	6	9			8	11					17
1	2	3	4	5	10	7	6	9			8				11		18
1	2	3	4	5	10	7	6	9			8				11		19
1	2	3	4	5	10	7	6	9			8*		12		11		20
1	2	3	4	5	10		6		9		8		7		11		21
1	2	3	4	5	10	7	6	9			8				11		22
1	2	3	4	5	10		6	9			8			7	11		23
1	2	3	4	5	10	7	6	9			8				11		24
1	2	3	4	5	10	7	6	9			8				11		25
1		3	4	5	10	7	6	8	9				2		11		26
1	2	3	4	5	10	7	6	8	9						11		27
1	2	3	4		10	7	6		9		5	8			11		28
1	2	3	4		10	7	6		9*		5	8	12		11		29
1	2	3	4		10	7	6*		9		5	8		12	11		30
1	2	3	4	5	10	7			9		6	8			11		31
1	2	3	4	5	10	7			9		6	8			11		32
1	2	3	4	5	10	7		12	9		6	8*			11		33
1	2	3	4	5		7		10	9		6	8*		12	11		34
1	2	3	4	5	8	7		10	9		6				11		35
1	2	3	4	5	8	7*			9		6		10	12	11		36
1	2	3	4	5	8	7*		12	9		6		10		11		37
1	2	3	4	5	10			9	8		6			7	11		38
1	2	3	4	5	10			9	8		6			7	11		39
1	2	3	4*	5	10	7		12	9		6		8		11		40
	2	3	4	5	10			9	8		6			7	11	1	41
	2	3	4	5				9	8		6	10	7	11		1	42
40	41	42	41	39	39	36	30	32	22	4	36	21	8	5	24	2	
								+ 3s	+ 1s		+ 1s	+ 1s	+ 3s	+ 4s			

ORIENT

	Ht	Wt	Birthplace	Clubs	League App.	League Gls
Goalkeepers						
Mervyn Day	6 2	14 12	Chelmsford	West Ham U	194	—
				Orient	82	—
Sean Rafter*	6 1¼	12 12	Rochford	Southend U	23	—
				Leicester C	—	—
				Orient	2	—
Lloyd Scott	6 0	12 3	Stepney	Orient	—	—
Jeff Fielding	6 0	11 7	Stevenage	Orient	—	—
Defenders						
Bill Roffey	5 11	12 13	Stepney	Crystal Palace	24	—
				Orient	239	5
Nigel Gray	6 3	13 4	Fulham	Orient	165	1
Bobby Fisher	5 8	11 2	Wembley	Orient	281	4
Paul Went*	6 0	12 10	Bromley by Bow	Orient	50	5
				Charlton Ath	163	15
				Fulham	58	3
				Portsmouth	92	5
				Cardiff C	72	11
				Orient	45	3
Tommy Taylor	6 1	13 7	Hornchurch	Orient	114	4
				West Ham U	340	8
				Orient	83	5
Mark Penfold*	5 7	10 1	Woolwich	Charlton Ath	70	—
				Manchester U (on loan)	—	—
				Orient	3	1
Mark Smith*	6 0	12 0	Carlisle	Orient	3	—
Robert Waterfall	5 11	10 7	Ilford	Orient	—	—
Midfield						
Tunji Banjo (Nigeria)	5 8	11 0	Kensington	Orient	24	1
Henry Hughton	5 8½	11 10	Stratford	Orient	84	2
Ralph Coates (England)	5 7½	12 2	Hetton-le-Hole	Burnley	216	26
				Tottenham H	188	14
				Orient	76	12
Jimmy Hallybone	5 6	10 0	Leytonstone	Orient	—	—
Mark Kane*	5 6	9 12	Hackney	Orient	—	—
John Margerrison	5 10	12 2	Bushey	Tottenham H	—	—
				Fulham	71	9
				Orient	46	3
Tony Mercer*	5 9	10 10	Forest Gate	Crystal Palace	—	—
				Orient	—	—
Peter Moles	5 7	9 5	Basildon	Orient	—	—
Stan Bowles (England)	5 10	11 4	Manchester	Manchester C	17	2
				Bury	5	—
				Crewe Alex	51	18
				Carlisle U	33	12
				QPR	255	70
				Nottingham F	19	2
				Orient	39	6
Peter Taylor (England)	5 9	11 7	Southend	Southend U	75	12
				Crystal Palace	122	33
				Tottenham H	123	31
				Orient	24	8
Forwards						
Kevin Godfrey	5 10	10 11	Kennington	Orient	31	3
John Chiedozie (Nigeria)	5 7	10 10	Owerri, Nigeria	Orient	145	20
Billy Hurley	5 9½	12 6	Leytonstone	Orient	2	—
Joe Mayo	6 2½	13 6	Tipton	Walsall	7	1
				WBA	73	16
				Orient	154	35
Ian Moores	6 2	13 8	Chesterton	Stoke C	50	14
				Tottenham H	29	6
				Orient	93	22
Mark Blackhall*	6 0	12 2	Upney	Orient	—	—
Steve Parsons	6 0	12 7	London	Wimbledon	94	19
				Orient	36	6
Billy Jennings	5 9	10 2	Hackney	Watford	92	33
				West Ham U	99	33
				Orient	57	18
Mark McNeil	5 10	10 5	Bethnal Green	Orient	—	—
Nigel Meeking*	6 0	12 0	Barking	Orient	—	—
Gary Elphick (Contract cancelled Oct 1980)			Brighton	Coventry C	—	—
				Orient	—	—
John McFarlane*			Leytonstone	Orient	—	—

OXFORD UNITED Division 3

President: The Duke of Marlborough.
Chairman: W. H. Reeves BDS, LDS, RCS.
Vice-Chairman: Dr D Morris BSC, D PHIL.
Directors: G. Coppock, H. Kimber, P. Marsh, P. Reeves, J. Devaney.
Manager: Ian Greaves.
Secretary: Jim Hunt.
Year Formed: 1896. *Turned Professional:* 1949.
Limited Company: 1949.
Previous Names: Headington United; 1960, Oxford United.

Football League Record:
1962 Elected to Division 4; 1965–68 Division 3; 1968–76 Division 2; 1976– Division 3.

Honours: *Football League:* Division 2 best season: 8th, 1972–73; Division 3 – Champions 1967–68; Division 4 – Promoted 1964–65 (4th). *FA Cup* best season: 6th rd, 1963–64 (record for 4th Division club). *Football League Cup* best season: 5th rd, 1969–70.
Record Victory: 7-1 v Barrow, Division 4, 19 Dec, 1964.
Record Defeat: 0-5 v Cardiff C, Division 2, 8 Feb, 1969, and v Cardiff C, Division 2, 12 Sept, 1973.
Most League Points: 61, Division 4, 1964–65.
Most League Goals: 87, Division 4, 1964–65.
Highest League Scorer in Season: Colin Booth, 23, Division 4, 1964–65.
Most League Goals in Total Aggregate: Graham Atkinson, 73, 1962–73.
Most Capped Player: David Roberts, 6 (17), Wales.
Most League Appearances: John Shuker, 480, 1962–77.
Record Transfer Fee Received: £100,000 from Watford for Les Taylor, Nov 1980.
Record Transfer Fee Paid: £75,000 to Cardiff C for Andy McCulloch, July 1974.
Previous Managers since the War: Arthur Turner, Ron Saunders, Gerry Summers, Mike Brown, Bill Asprey.
Address of Supporters Club: Supporters Club Offices, Manor Ground, Headington, Oxford.
Address of the Club Shop or Boutique: On ground on match days.

Manor Ground, Headington, Oxford. Telephone Oxford 61503. *Ground capacity:* 17,350. *Record attendance:* 22,730 v Preston NE, FA Cup 6th rd, 29 Feb, 1964. *Record receipts:* £13,825 v Nottingham F, League Cup 3rd rd, 6 Oct, 1978. *Pitch measurements:* 112yd×78yd.

How to get there: Bus 580/1/2 from the city centre. Nearest railway station is Oxford General. From the station take Bus 1 to Queens Lane and then take Bus 581/2/3. By road, take Oxford ring road to the east of the city, following the signs for Headington. Leave the ring road at Green Road roundabout into London Road; the ground is on the right after going straight across at the traffic lights.
Match tickets: Subject to availability tickets may be booked 14 days prior to the match.
Car parking: Parking is available in certain streets around the ground.
Entertainments/catering facilities: Public houses, and cafés, all just minutes from the ground. Refreshments available inside the ground.
Club shop: On ground, offering all types of souvenirs and programmes (open match days only).
Handbooks/programmes: Programmes available from the club shop.
Extra information: In five years from joining the Fourth Division, Oxford reached Division Two.
Club Colours: Yellow shirts with blue trim, blue shorts, yellow stockings.
Change Colours: All red.
Club Captain: Billy Jeffrey.
First Team Trainer: Ken Fish.
Club Nickname: The U's.

OXFORD UNITED 1980–81 LEAGUE RECORD

Match No.	Date	Venue	Opponents	Result	H/T Score	Goalscorers	Attendance
1	Aug 16	A	Chester	W 1-0	1-0	Brock	2203
2	20	H	Exeter C	L 1-2	0-1	Shotton (pen)	3751
3	23	A	Sheffield U	L 0-1	0-0		13,632
4	30	H	Plymouth Arg	D 0-0	0-0		3398
5	Sept 6	H	Chesterfield	L 0-3	0-1		3273
6	13	A	Newport Co	W 1-0	1-0	Brock	5256
7	16	A	Swindon T	L 0-1	0-0		7709
8	20	H	Carlisle U	L 1-2	1-1	Lythgoe	2712
9	27	A	Gillingham	D 1-1	0-0	Lythgoe	4137
10	Oct 1	H	Swindon T	D 0-0	0-0		6071
11	4	A	Hull C	W 1-0	0-0	Brock	4211
12	8	H	Huddersfield T	L 0-2	0-0		3373
13	11	H	Walsall	D 1-1	1-1	Cooke	3123
14	18	A	Fulham	W 4-0	2-0	Lythgoe, Brock 2, Jeffrey	3817
15	21	A	Barnsley	D 1-1	1-1	Briggs	8991
16	25	H	Portsmouth	L 1-2	1-0	Cooke	6217
17	29	H	Rotherham U	D 1-1	0-0	Shotton (pen)	3064
18	Nov 1	A	Brentford	L 0-3	0-1		6550
19	4	A	Huddersfield T	L 0-2	0-2		7543
20	8	H	Blackpool	L 0-2	0-0		3038
21	12	A	Exeter C	D 1-1	0-1	Foley	3241
22	15	H	Chester	W 1-0	0-0	Cooke	2526
23	29	A	Colchester U	L 0-3	0-0		2114
24	Dec 6	H	Burnley	L 0-2	0-1		3305
25	20	A	Millwall	L 1-2	1-0	Cooke	2781
26	26	H	Charlton Ath	W 1-0	1-0	Berry	5717
27	27	A	Reading	W 1-0	0-0	Cooke	7019
28	Jan 10	A	Rotherham U	D 0-0	0-0		6705
29	17	H	Colchester U	W 2-1	1-0	Shotton, Jeffrey	3498
30	24	A	Plymouth Arg	L 0-3	0-2		5121
31	31	H	Sheffield U	W 2-0	1-0	Thomas, Foley	4427
32	Feb 7	H	Newport Co	L 0-1	0-1		4440
33	14	A	Chesterfield	L 1-2	1-0	Foley	6451
34	21	H	Gillingham	D 1-1	1-0	Shotton	3641
35	28	A	Carlisle U	D 0-0	0-0		3552
36	Mar 7	H	Hull C	D 1-1	1-0	Cooke	2934
37	14	A	Walsall	W 3-0	1-0	Jones, Cassells, Foley	3185
38	21	H	Fulham	W 2-0	1-0	Shotton (pen), Seacole	3646
39	24	H	Barnsley	D 1-1	0-0	Cassells	4705
40	29	A	Portsmouth	D 1-1	1-1	Cassells	13,243
41	Apr 4	H	Brentford	D 1-1	0-0	Fogg (pen)	3873
42	12	A	Blackpool	D 1-1	1-1	Foley	3188
43	18	H	Reading	W 2-1	2-1	Page, Smithers	5386
44	21	A	Charlton Ath	D 0-0	0-0		7634
45	29	H	Millwall	W 1-0	1-0	Smithers	3690
46	May 2	A	Burnley	D 1-1	0-1	Smithers	3938

Final League Position: 14

Goalscorers

League (39): Cooke 6, Brock 5, Foley 5, Shotton 5 (3 pens), Cassells 3, Lythgoe 3, Smithers 3, Jeffrey 2, Berry 1, Briggs 1, Fogg 1 (pen), Jones 1, Page 1, Seacole 1, Thomas 1.
League Cup (6): Lythgoe 2, Shotton 2 (1 pen), Brock, Foley.
F.A. Cup (1): Foley.

League Cup	First Round	Southend U (a)	0-1
		(h)	2-0
	Second Round	Chesterfield (a)	1-3
		(h)	3-0
	Third Round	Preston NE (a)	0-1
FA Cup	First Round	Aldershot (h)	1-0
	Second Round	Plymouth Arg (a)	0-3

Brown	Fogg	Smithers	Jeffrey	Briggs	Shotton	Brock	Taylor	O'Dowd	Foley	Seacole	Kingston	Lythgoe	Cooke	Berry	Burton	Thomas	Jones	Graydon	McIntosh	Cassells	Doyle	Page	Match No.
1	2	3	4	5	6	7	8	9	10	11*	12												1
1	2	3	4	5	6	7	8	9*	10	11		12											2
1		3	4*	2	6	7	8		10	12		11	5	9									3
	2	3	4	5	6	7	8		10*	12		11	9		1								4
		3	4*	2	6	7	8		9			11	5		1	12	10						5
	3		4		6	7	8		9		2	11	5		1		10						6
	3		4		6	7	8		9		2	11	5		1		10						7
	3		4		6	7	8		9*		2	11	5	12	1		10						8
	3		4	2	6	7	8		9			11	5	10	1								9
	3		4	2	6	7	8		9			11	5	10	1								10
	3		4	2	6	7	8					11	5	9	1		10						11
	3		4*	2	6	7	8		10			11	5	9	1		12						12
	3		4	2	6	7	8					11	5	10*	1		9	12					13
	3		4	2	6	7	8					11	5	9	1		10						14
	3		4	2	6	7	8*		12			11	5	9	1		10						15
	3		4	2	6	7	8		12			11	5	9	1		10*						16
	3		4	2	6	7	8		10			11*	5	9	1			12					17
	3		4	2	6		8				12	11	5	9*	1		10		7				18
	3	12	4	5	6*		8				2	11	9		1		10		7				19
	2	3	4	5	6	7			10				9	11	1				8				20
	3		4	5		7			10		2		9	11	1				6	8			21
	3		4	5		7			10		2		9	11	1				6	8			22
	3	12	4	5		7			10		2	11*			1		9		6	8			23
	3*	12	4	5	6	7			10		2	11			1		9			8			24
	3*	11	4	5	6	12							9	10	1		7		2	8			25
	3	11	4	5	6				8				9	10	1		7		2				26
	3	11	4	5	6				8				9	10	1		7		2				27
	3	11	4	5	6				8					10	1	9	7				2		28
	3	11	4	5	6				8					10	1	9	7				2		29
	3	11	4	6					10			12	5	8	1	9*	7				2		30
	3	11	4	6					8			10	5		1	9	7				2		31
	3	11	4	6					8			10	5		1	9	7			12	2*		32
	3	11	4	6		12			8				5		1	9	7*			10	2		33
	3	11	4*	6	5				8					9	1	12	7				2	10	34
	3	11		5	6	4			8					9	1		7			10	2		35
	3	11	4	5		10			8				6	9	1		7				2		36
	3		4	5	6				8				10*	9	1		7			12	2	11	37
	3	9	4	5	6				8	12				11	1		7			10*	2		38
	3	9	4	5	6				8	12				11*	1		7			10	2		39
	3	9	4	5	6				8	12				11*	1		7			10	2		40
	2	3	4	5	6				8	11*					1	9	7	12		10			41
	3	9	4	5	6				8						1		7			10	2	11	42
	3	9	4	5	6				8						1		7			10	2	11	43
	3	9	4	5	6				8						1		7			10	2	11	44
	3	9	4		6				8				5		1		7			10	2	11	45
	3	9	4	5	6				8						1		7			10	2	11	46
3	44	27	45	42	38	24	19	2	38	3	8	21	30	27	43	7	35	—	9	16	18	7	
		+ 3s				+ 2s			+ 2s	+ 5s	+ 2s	+ 2s		+ 1s		+ 2s	+ 1s	+ 3s		+ 2s			

OXFORD UNITED

	Ht	Wt	Birthplace	Clubs	League App.	League Gls
Goalkeepers						
Roy Burton	5 10	12 2	Wantage	Oxford U	339	—
Steve Foyster	6 3	12 0	Carlton, Collivell	Oxford U	—	—
David Brown	6 1	12 8	Hartlepool	Middlesbrough	10	—
				Oxford U	21	—
				Plymouth Arg (on loan)	5	—
Defenders						
Andy Bodel (Contract cancelled Aug 1980)	5 11	11 13	Clydebank	Oxford U	128	11
David Fogg	5 10½	11 0	Liverpool	Wrexham	161	—
				Oxford U	209	8
Andy Kingston	5 11	11 2	Oxford	Oxford U	47	—
John Doyle	5 9	10 7	Oxford	Oxford U	36	—
Gary Briggs	6 3	12 7	Leeds	Middlesbrough	—	—
				Oxford U	147	4
Malcolm McIntosh*	5 8	11 0	Oxford	Oxford U	56	—
Joe Cooke	5 11	12 7	Dominica	Bradford C	204	62
				Peterborough U	18	5
				Oxford U	72	13
David Simms*	5 9	10 10	Oxford	Oxford U	—	—
Timothy Smithers	5 11	11 0	Ramsgate	Nuneaton B	(not known)	
				Oxford U	30	3
Malcolm Shotton	6 3	13 7	Newcastle	Nuneaton B	(not known)	
				Oxford U	38	5
Mark Wright			Dorchester	Oxford U	—	—
Midfield						
Billy Jeffrey	5 10	11 6	Clydebank	Oxford U	279	21
Kevin Brock	5 9	10 10	Middleton Stoney	Oxford U	45	7
Martin Wood*	5 9	10 12	Stanton Harcourt	Oxford U	—	—
Phil Lythgoe	5 9	11 0	Norwich	Norwich C	12	1
				Bristol R (on loan)	6	—
				Oxford U	23	3
Malcolm Page (Wales)	5 9	10 11	Knucklas	Birmingham C	338	9
				Oxford U	7	1
Forwards						
Peter Foley	5 11	10 7	Bicester	Oxford U	225	58
Jason Seacole	5 9½	11 0	Oxford	Oxford U	116	21
Paul Berry	6 0	12 7	Oxford	Oxford U	106	20
Ray Graydon*	5 8	11 0	Bristol	Bristol R	134	27
				Aston V	193	67
				Coventry C	20	5
				Washington D	—	—
				Oxford U	42	10
Mark Jones	5 8	9 3	Berinsfield	Oxford U	38	1
Adrian O'Dowd (Contract cancelled Oct 1980)	5 11	11 7	Solihull	Aston V	—	—
				Oxford U	10	1
Keith Cassells	5 10	11 2	London	Watford	12	—
				Peterborough U (on loan)	8	—
				Oxford U	18	3
Andrew Thomas			Oxford	Oxford U	9	1

Also retained: David Burn.

PETERBOROUGH UNITED Division 4

Chairman: H. W. Wright.

Vice-Chairman: W. O'Neill Wilde.

Directors: S. E. Nicholas, A. Hand, C. Duddington.

Manager: Peter Morris.

General Manager/Secretary: A. V. Blades.

Commercial Manager: E. Stafford.

Year Formed: 1923.

Turned Professional: 1934.

Limited Company: 1934.

Previous Name: Peterborough and Fletton United until 1934.

Football League Record:
1960 Elected to Division 4; 1961–68 Division 3, when they were demoted for financial irregularities; 1968–74 Division 4; 1974–79 Division 3; 1979– Division 4.

Honours: *Football League:* Division 3 best season: 4th, 1977–78. Division 4 – Champions 1960–61, 1973–74. *FA Cup* best season: 6th rd, 1965. *Football League Cup:* semi-final 1966.

Record Victory: 8-1 v Oldham Ath, Division 4, 26 Nov, 1969.

Record Defeat: 1-8 v Northampton T, FA Cup 2nd rd (2nd replay), 1946–47.

Most League Points: 66, Division 4, 1960–61.

Most League Goals: 134, Division 4, 1960–61.

Highest League Scorer in Season: Terry Bly, 52, Division 4, 1960–61.

Most League Goals in Total Aggregate: Jim Hall, 120, 1967–75.

Most Capped Player: Ollie Conmy, 5, Eire.

Most League Appearances: Tommy Robson, 482, 1968–81.

Record Transfer Fee Received: £110,000 from Blackpool for Bob Doyle, July 1979.

Record Transfer Fee Paid: £60,000 to West Ham U, for Bill Green, July 1978.

Previous Managers since Election to Football League: Jimmy Hagan, Jack Fairbrother, Gordon Clark, Norman Rigby, Jim Iley, Noel Cantwell, John Barnwell, Billy Hails.

Address of Supporters Club: Same as Football Club.

London Road Ground, Peterborough PE2 8AL. Telephone Peterborough (0733) 63947. *Ground capacity:* 30,000. *Record attendance:* 30,096 v Swansea T, FA Cup 5th rd, 20 Feb, 1965. *Record receipts:* £44,157.83 v Manchester C, FA Cup 5th rd, 14 Feb, 1981. *Pitch measurements:* 112yd×76yd.

How to get there: Peterborough Station (20 minutes' walking distance). Bus terminal 400 yards.

Match tickets: Bookable 14 days in advance.

Car parking: Ample parking available at the ground.

Entertainments/catering facilities: Supporters' Club provides entertainments. Licensed refreshment kiosks in the ground.

Club shop: Sells all types of souvenirs (postal requests to Commercial Manager).

Handbooks/programmes: Handbooks available and programmes can be ordered on subscription.

Extra information: Upon joining the Football League in 1960 Peterborough United set up a record in Division Four of scoring 134 goals in their first season.

Club Colours: Blue shirts, white shorts, blue stockings with white top.

Change Colours: All yellow with Royal blue trim.

Team Captain: Billy Kellock.

First Team Trainer/Coach:

Club Nickname: The Posh.

PETERBOROUGH UNITED 1980–81 LEAGUE RECORD

Match No.	Date	Venue	Opponents	Result	H/T Score	Goalscorers	Attendance
1	Aug 16	A	Lincoln C	D 1-1	1-1	Cooke	5131
2	20	H	Halifax T	D 2-2	0-0	Cooke, Kellock (pen)	3885
3	23	A	Doncaster R	W 4-0	1-0	Slack, Syrett, Kellock, McVay	3536
4	30	H	Bradford C	D 2-2	1-0	Cooke, Foster	4009
5	Sept 5	A	Tranmere R	W 2-1	0-0	Cooke, Slack	1772
6	13	H	Rochdale	D 2-2	0-1	Cooke, Quow	3906
7	15	A	Southend U	L 0-1	0-1		5609
8	20	H	AFC Bournemouth	W 1-0	0-0	Cooke	3774
9	27	A	Torquay U	L 0-2	0-1		2090
10	Oct 1	H	Southend U	W 5-2	1-1	Cooke 2, Otulakowski (og), Kellock, Quow	4228
11	4	H	Bury	W 2-0	1-0	Syrett 2	4080
12	6	A	Stockport Co	W 4-3	4-2	Kellock, Sword (og), Winters, Cooke	1794
13	11	A	Wigan Ath	D 1-1	1-1	Gallagher	4851
14	18	H	Darlington	W 1-0	0-0	Cooke	4217
15	22	H	Scunthorpe U	L 0-2	0-0		4262
16	25	A	Mansfield T	L 1-2	1-1	Cooke	4883
17	28	A	Wimbledon	L 1-2	0-0	Quow	1901
18	Nov 1	H	Port Vale	D 1-1	1-0	Kellock	3643
19	4	H	Stockport Co	L 1-2	1-0	Cliss	2772
20	8	A	Aldershot	D 0-0	0-0		3057
21	11	A	Halifax T	W 3-2	2-1	Cooke, Gynn, Kellock	1151
22	15	H	Lincoln C	W 1-0	1-0	Kellock	5817
23	Dec 6	H	Hereford U	W 3-0	0-0	Cooke, Robson 2	3281
24	20	A	Hartlepool U	D 1-1	0-1	Gynn	3100
25	26	H	Northampton T	W 3-0	2-0	Kellock, Cooke, Robson	6265
26	27	A	Crewe Alex	L 0-1	0-1		4132
27	Jan 10	A	Scunthorpe U	D 1-1	1-0	Robson	2064
28	17	H	York C	W 3-0	2-0	Hodgson, Slack, Kellock	3954
29	28	A	Bradford C	D 1-1	0-1	Kellock	3305
30	31	H	Doncaster R	L 0-1	0-0		6146
31	Feb 7	A	Rochdale	W 3-2	0-2	Gynn 2, Quow	2865
32	21	H	Torquay U	L 1-3	1-2	Cooke	4172
33	28	A	AFC Bournemouth	L 1-4	1-1	Kellock	5334
34	Mar 4	H	Wimbledon	D 1-1	0-0	Cooke	3201
35	7	A	Bury	D 1-1	1-0	Syrett	2522
36	13	H	Wigan Ath	D 0-0	0-0		3455
37	18	H	Tranmere R	W 4-1	3-0	Gynn, Kellock 2, Slack	3034
38	21	A	Darlington	L 0-2	0-1		2522
39	24	A	York C	W 2-1	2-1	Cooke 2	1725
40	28	H	Mansfield T	W 1-0	1-0	Gynn	4904
41	Apr 4	A	Port Vale	D 1-1	0-0	Cooke	2982
42	11	H	Aldershot	D 0-0	0-0		4783
43	18	H	Crewe Alex	W 2-1	1-0	Cooke, Gynn	3743
44	21	A	Northampton T	D 2-2	0-1	Cooke, Foster	3800
45	25	H	Hartlepool U	D 1-1	0-1	Foster	3560
46	May 2	A	Hereford U	D 1-1	0-1	Cooke	2102

Final League Position: 5

Goalscorers

League (68): Cooke 22, Kellock 13 (1 pen), Gynn 7, Quow 4, Robson 4, Slack 4, Syrett 4, Foster 3, Cliss 1, Gallagher 1, Hodgson 1, McVay 1, Winters 1, own goals 2.
League Cup (5): Cooke 3, Kellock, Syrett.
F.A. Cup (9): Cooke 4, Robson 3, Quow, Slack.

League Cup	First Round	Fulham (h)	3-2
		(a)	1-1
	Second Round	Nottingham F (a)	0-3
		(h)	1-1
FA Cup	First Round	Northampton T (a)	4-1
	Second Round	Barnet (a)	1-0
	Third Round	Chesterfield (h)	1-1
		(a)	2-1
	Fourth Round	Notts Co (a)	1-0
	Fifth Round	Manchester C (h)	0-1

Waugh	McVay	Phillips	Hodgson	Slack	Foster	Quow	Kellock	Cooke	Syrett	Cliss	Gallagher	Robson	Lambert	Slough	Barron	Winters	Guy	Gynn	Smith	Collins	*Match No.*
1	2	3	4	5	6	7	8	9	10	11											1
1	2	3	4	5	6	7	8	9	10*	11	12										2
1	2	3	4	5	6	7	8	9	10	11											3
1	2	3	4*	5	6	7	8	9	10	11		12									4
1	2	3	4	5	6	7	8	9	10	11*			12								5
1	2	3	4	5	6	7	8	9	10*	12			11								6
1	2	3	4		6	7	8	9*	10	11			12	5							7
1	2	3	4		6	7	8	9	10		12		11*	5							8
1	2	3	4		6	7	8	9	10				11	5							9
		3	4		6	7	8	9	10		11			5	1	2					10
1		3	4		6	7	8	9	10*	12	11			5		2					11
1		3	4		6	7	8	9	10		11			5		2					12
1		3	4		6	7	8	9	10		11*			5		2	12				13
1		3	4		6	7	8	9	10		11			5		2					14
1		3	4*		6	7	8	9	10		11			5		2	12				15
1		3	4		6	7	8	9	10	11				5		2					16
1			4		6	7	8	9	10		11*	3		5		2	12				17
1		3	4*	6		7	8	9	10	11				5		2		12			18
1	2	3		5		7	8	9	10	11				6				4			19
1	2	3	10	5		7	8	9		11				6				4			20
1	2	3	10	5		7	8	9				11		6				4			21
1	2	3	10	5		7	8	9				11		6				4			22
1	2	3	10	5		7	8	9*		12		11		6				4			23
1	2	3	10	5		7	8	9				11		6				4			24
1	2	3	10	5		7*	8	9		12		11		6				4			25
1	2	3*	10	5			8	9		12		11		6			7	4			26
1	2	3	10	5		7	8	9				11		6				4			27
1	2	3	10*	5		7	8	9	12			11		6				4			28
1	2	3	10	5		7	8	9	12			11*		6				4			29
1	2	3	10*	5		7	8	9	12			11		6				4			30
1	2	3		5*		7	8	9	10	12		11		6				4			31
1	2	3	10	5		7	8	9				11		6				4			32
1	2		10	5		7	8*	9		12	11	3		6				4			33
1			10	5		7	8*	9		12	11	3				2		4	6		34
1			10	5		7	8	9	11			3				2		4	6		35
1		3	10	5		7	8	9	11							2		4	6		36
1		3	10	5		7	8	9	11							2		4	6		37
1		3	10	5		7	8	9	11	12						2		4	6*		38
1		3	10	5	6	7	8	9	11							2		4			39
1		3	10	5	6	7	8	9	11							2		4			40
1		3	10	5	6	7	8	9	11							2		4			41
1		3	10	5	6	7	8	9	11*	12						2		4			42
1		3	10	5	6	7	8	9	11*			12				2		4			43
1		3	10	5	6	7*	8	9		12		11				2		4			44
1		3*	10	5	6		8	9		12	7	11				2		4			45
1			10*	5	6	7	8	9	11			12				2		4		3	46
45	24	41	44	35	25	44	46	46	30	10	10	18	3	27	1	22	1	28	5	1	
									+ 3s	+ 12s	+ 2s	+ 3s	+ 2s				+ 3s	+ 1s			

PETERBOROUGH UNITED

	Ht	*Wt*	*Birthplace*	*Clubs*	*League App.*	*League Gls*
Goalkeepers						
Keith Waugh	6 1	12 0	Sunderland	Sunderland	—	—
				Peterborough U	195	—
Jim Barron	5 11½	11 7	Durham	Wolverhampton W	8	—
(Non-contract)				Chelsea	1	—
				Oxford U	152	—
				Nottingham F	155	—
				Swindon T	79	—
				Peterborough U	21	—
Defenders						
John Winters	5 8	11 8	Wisbech	Peterborough U	22	1
David McVay*	6 1	12 11	Workington	Notts Co	113	2
				Torquay U (on loan)	8	—
				Peterborough U	49	1
Ian Phillips	5 8	12 2	Edinburgh	Mansfield T	23	—
				Peterborough U	80	1
Colin Foster*	5 9	12 2	Nottingham	Mansfield T	205	17
				Peterborough U	71	4
Trevor Slack	6 1¾	12 0	Peterborough	Peterborough U	35	4
Steve Collins	5 8	11 4	Stamford	Peterborough U	14	—
Midfield						
Mick Gynn	5 5	10 6	Peterborough	Peterborough U	67	10
Tommy Robson*	5 8	10 0	Gateshead	Northampton T	74	20
				Chelsea	7	—
				Newcastle U	48	11
				Peterborough U	482	112
Alan Slough	5 10	12 5	Luton	Luton T	275	28
(Contract cancelled April 1981)				Fulham	154	13
				Peterborough U	105	10
Phil Chard	5 8	11 3	Corby	Peterborough U	26	3
Tony Smith	5 10	11 11	Sunderland	Newcastle U	2	—
				Peterborough U	29	2
Pat Sharkey*	5 10	11 12	Omagh	Portadown	(not known)	
(N Ireland)				Ipswich T	18	1
				Millwall (on loan)	7	—
				Mansfield T	32	5
				Colchester U	6	—
				Peterborough U	15	—
Billy Kellock	5 10	11 10	Glasgow	Aston V	—	—
				Cardiff C	35	2
				Norwich C	3	—
				Millwall	—	—
				Chelmsford	(not known)	
				Kettering T	(not known)	
				Peterborough U	91	32
Ricky Heppolette	5 9	12 3	India	Preston NE	154	13
(Contract cancelled Nov 1980)				Orient	113	10
				Crystal Palace	15	—
				Chesterfield	47	3
				Peterborough U	5	—
Gordon Hodgson	5 11	10 7	Newcastle under Lyne	Newcastle U	9	—
				Mansfield T	184	23
				Oxford U	67	3
				Peterborough U	44	1
Forwards						
Tony Cliss	5 9	11 0	March	Peterborough U	78	11
Trevor Quow			Peterborough	Peterborough U	81	7
Alan Guy*	5 9	11 10	Jarrow	Newcastle U	4	—
				Peterborough U	53	5
Dave Syrett	5 11	11 13	Salisbury	Swindon T	122	30
				Wolverhampton W (on loan)	—	—
				Mansfield T	65	20
				Walsall	11	3
				Peterborough U	62	15
Jackie Gallacher	5 10½	12 9	Wisbech	King's Lynn	(not known)	
				Lincoln C	1	—
				Peterborough U	13	1
Mick Lambert	5 8	10 12	Cambridge	Ipswich T	211	39
(Contract cancelled Nov 1980)				Peterborough U	21	2
Tim Gale	5 7	11 0½	Peterborough	Peterborough U	—	—
Robbie Cooke	5 9	10 8	Rotherham	Mansfield T	15	1
				Grantham T	(not known)	
				Peterborough U	46	22

PLYMOUTH ARGYLE Division 3

President: G. H. Gillin. *Chairman:* R. Daniel.
Vice-Chairman: P. W. Skinnard LLB.
Directors: B. S. Williams, S. J. Williams, B. Ford, P. L. Riley FCA.
Team Manager: Bobby Moncur.
Asst Manager: Martin Harvey.
Secretary: Graham Little.
Year Formed: 1886. *Turned Professional:* 1903.
Limited Company: 1903.
Previous Name: 1886–1903, Argyle Athletic Club.

Football League Record:
1920 Original Member of Division 3; 1921–30 Division 3(S); 1930–50 Division 2; 1950–52 Division 3(S); 1952–56 Division 2; 1956–58 Division 3(S); 1958–59 Division 3; 1959–68 Division 2; 1968–75 Division 3; 1975–77 Division 2; 1977– Division 3.

Honours: *Football League:* Division 2 best season: 4th, 1931–32, 1952–53; Division 3(S) – Champions 1929–30, 1951–52; Runners-up 1921–22, 1922–23, 1923–24, 1924–25, 1925–26, 1926–27 (record of six consecutive years); Division 3 – Champions 1958–59; Runners-up 1974–75. *FA Cup* best season: 5th rd, 1952–53. *Football League Cup:* semi-final, 1965, 1974.

Record Victory: 8-1 v Millwall, Division 2, 16 Jan, 1932.
Record Defeat: 0-9 v Stoke C, Division 2, 17 Dec, 1960.
Most League Points: 68, Division 3(S), 1929–30.
Most League Goals: 107, Division 3(S), 1925–26 and 1951–52.
Highest League Scorer in Season: Jack Cock, 32, Division 3(S), 1925–26.
Most League Goals in Total Aggregate: Sammy Black, 180, 1924–38.
Most Capped Player: Moses Russell, 20 (23) Wales.
Most League Appearances: Sammy Black, 470, 1924–38.
Record Transfer Fee Received: £250,000 from Everton for Gary Megson, Feb 1980.
Record Transfer Fee Paid: £75,000 to Carlisle U for David Kemp, Sept 1979.
Previous Managers since the War: Jack Tresadern, Jimmy Rae, Jack Rowley, Neil Dougall, Ellis Stuttard, Andy Beattie, Malcolm Allison, Derek Ufton, Billy Bingham, Ellis Stuttard, Tony Waiters, Mike Kelly, Malcolm Allison, Bobby Saxton.
Address of Supporters Club: Same as Football Club.
Address of the Club Shop or Boutique: The Pilgrim Shop, Home Park, Plymouth, Devon.

Home Park Plymouth, Devon PL2 3DQ. Telephone Plymouth (0752) 52561/2/3. Lottery Shop: 51041. *Ground capacity:* 38,000 (20,000 covered). *Record attendance:* 43,596 v Aston Villa, Division 2, 10 Oct, 1936. *Record receipts:* over £10,000 (official figure not disclosed by club) v Manchester C, League Cup semi-final, 23 Jan, 1974. *Pitch measurements:* 112yd×75yd.

How to get there: Special City buses from the Plymouth bus station at Bretonside. Nearest railway station Plymouth.
Match tickets: Grand Stand and Mayflower Stand tickets are available 2–3 weeks before each first-team game.
Car parking: Car park adjoining the ground holds 2000 cars.
Entertainments/catering facilities: Eight refreshment bars around the ground.
Club shop: Situated on the ground; sells all types of souvenirs.
Handbooks/programmes: Programmes sent to all parts of the world.
Extra information: In 1920–21, Plymouth Argyle established a Third Division record by drawing 21 matches.
Club Colours: Green shirts, white shorts, white stockings.
Change Colours: Green shirts, white trim, yellow shorts, green trim.
Club Nickname: The Pilgrims.

PLYMOUTH ARGYLE 1980–81 LEAGUE RECORD

Match No.	Date	Venue	Opponents	Result	H/T Score	Goalscorers	Attendance
1	Aug 16	A	Colchester U	D 2-2	1-0	Kemp, Murphy	2061
2	19	H	Chester	W 2-0	0-0	Kemp, Bason	4823
3	23	H	Charlton Ath	D 1-1	1-1	Murphy	6023
4	30	A	Oxford U	D 0-0	0-0		3398
5	Sept 6	H	Carlisle U	W 4-1	2-1	Kemp 3, Murphy	4854
6	13	A	Chesterfield	D 2-2	1-1	Graves, Kemp	5561
7	17	A	Reading	D 1-1	0-1	Murphy	5859
8	20	H	Gillingham	W 4-1	2-1	Kemp 2, Hodges, Bason	6719
9	27	A	Newport Co	W 2-0	0-0	Sims, Kemp	6878
10	30	H	Reading	W 2-1	1-1	Bason, Kemp	11,480
11	Oct 4	A	Sheffield U	D 0-0	0-0		12,401
12	7	H	Fulham	W 2-1	2-1	Sims, Bason	11,547
13	11	H	Blackpool	L 0-2	0-1		10,698
14	18	A	Huddersfield T	L 0-2	0-0		11,655
15	21	A	Portsmouth	W 3-1	1-1	Kemp 2, Sims	15,635
16	25	H	Barnsley	L 1-3	1-0	Sims	8911
17	28	H	Brentford	L 0-1	0-0		7249
18	Nov 1	A	Hull C	L 0-1	0-1		3367
19	4	A	Fulham	D 0-0	0-0		3507
20	8	H	Walsall	W 2-0	0-0	Kemp 2	5022
21	12	A	Chester	L 0-1	0-0		2247
22	15	H	Colchester U	D 1-1	0-1	Kemp	4905
23	29	A	Millwall	D 1-1	1-0	Hodges	3385
24	Dec 6	H	Rotherham U	W 3-1	1-0	Murphy 2 (1 pen), Kemp	6155
25	20	A	Burnley	L 1-2	0-1	Murphy (pen)	5678
26	26	H	Exeter C	L 0-2	0-2		14,792
27	27	A	Swindon T	L 0-3	0-0		9710
28	Jan 10	A	Barnsley	L 1-2	0-1	Kemp	12,355
29	17	H	Millwall	W 2-0	2-0	Murphy, Cooper	4847
30	24	H	Oxford U	W 3-0	2-0	Cooper 2, Kemp	5121
31	31	A	Charlton Ath	D 1-1	0-1	Kemp	8127
32	Feb 7	H	Chesterfield	W 1-0	0-0	Johnson	6305
33	14	A	Carlisle U	L 0-2	0-0		3924
34	21	H	Newport Co	W 3-2	0-1	Johnson (pen), Hodges, Sims	4315
35	28	A	Gillingham	W 1-0	1-0	Sims	4396
36	Mar 14	A	Blackpool	L 0-1	0-0		3933
37	17	H	Huddersfield T	D 0-0	0-0		5433
38	21	H	Portsmouth	W 1-0	1-0	Murphy	6042
39	28	A	Brentford	W 1-0	1-0	Kemp	5870
40	Apr 4	H	Hull C	D 0-0	0-0		4668
41	11	A	Walsall	W 3-1	1-0	Hodges, Kemp 2	3556
42	14	H	Sheffield U	W 1-0	0-0	Hodges	4897
43	18	H	Swindon T	D 0-0	0-0		6369
44	21	A	Exeter C	D 1-1	0-0	Sims	8491
45	25	H	Burnley	W 2-1	1-0	Kemp 2	4331
46	May 2	A	Rotherham U	L 1-2	1-1	Sims	11,497

Final League Position: 7

Goalscorers

League (56): Kemp 24, Murphy 9 (2 pens), Sims 8, Hodges 5, Bason 4, Cooper 3, Johnson 2 (1 pen), Graves 1.
League Cup (1): Kemp.
F.A. Cup (6): Kemp 3, Murphy 2 (1 pen), Sims.

League Cup	First Round	Portsmouth (h)	0-1
		(a)	1-2
FA Cup	First Round	Newport Co (h)	2-0
	Second Round	Oxford U (h)	3-0
	Third Round	Charlton Ath (h)	1-2

Crudgington	Harrison	Uzzell	Cooper	Foster	Phillipson-Masters	Hodges	Kemp	Graves	Bason	Murphy	Sims	Randell	James	Johnson	McNeill	Nisbet	Collins	Peachey	*Match No.*
1	2	3	4	5	6	7	8*	9	10	11								12	1
1	2	3	4	5	6	7	8	9	10	11									2
1	2	3	4	5	6	7	8	9*	10	11	12								3
1	2	3		5	6	7	8		10	11	9	4							4
1	2	3		5	6	7	8	12	10	11	9*	4							5
1	2	3		5		7	8	9*	10	11		4	6					12	6
1	2	3		5	6	7	8	12	10	11	9*	4							7
1	2	3		5	6	7	8		10	11	9	4							8
1	2	3		5	6	7	8		10	11	9	4							9
1	2	3		5	6	7	8		10	11	9	4							10
1	2	3		5	6	7	8		10	11	9	4							11
1	2	3		5	6	7	8		10	11	9	4							12
1	2	3*	11	5	6	7	8		10		9	4		12					13
1	2	3*	7	5	6		8		10	11	9	4	12						14
1	2		7	5	6		8		10	11	9	4	3						15
1	2*		7	5	6	12	8		10	11	9	4	3						16
1	2*		7	5	6		8	12	10	11	9	4	3						17
1	2		7	5	6		8		10	11	9	4	3						18
1	3		7	5	6	11	8		10		9	4	2						19
1	3		7	5	6		8		10	11	9	4	2						20
1	2		7	5	6	12	8		10	11*	9	4	3						21
1	3		7	5	6	4	8		10	11	9				2				22
1	3		7	5	6	4	8		10	11	9				2				23
1		3	7	5	6	4	8		10	11	9				2				24
1	3		7	6	5	4	8		10	11	9				2				25
1	3		7	5	6	4	8		10	11	9			12	2*				26
1	3*			5	6	7	8		10	11	9	4	2	12					27
1	3		7	5	6	4	8		10	11	9					2			28
1	3		7	5	6	4	8			11	9			10		2			29
1	3		7	5	6	4	8		12	11*	9			10		2			30
1	3		7	5	6	4	8			12	9			11		2	10*		31
1	3		7	5	6	4	8			11	9			10		2			32
1	3		7	5	6	4	8			11	9			10		2			33
1	3		7	5	6	4	8				9	10		11		2			34
1	3		7	5	6	4	8				9	10		11		2			35
1	3*		7	5	6	4	8			12	9	10		11		2			36
1	3		7	5	6	4	8			10	9			11		2			37
1	3		7*	5	6	4	8	12		11	9					2		10	38
1	3			5	6	4	8			11	9	10				2	7		39
1	3			5	6	4	8			11	9	10				2	7		40
1	3			5	6	4	8			11	9	10		7		2			41
1	3			5	6	4	8			11	9	10		7		2			42
1	3			5	6	4	8			11	9	10		7		2			43
1	3			5	6	4	8			11	9	10		7		2			44
1	3	6		5		4	8			11	9	10		7		2			45
1	3			5	6	4	8			11	9	10		7		2			46
46	45	16	28	46	44	39	46	4	28	40	42	30	9	15	5	19	3	1	
						+ 2s		+ 4s	+ 1s	+ 2s	+ 1s		+ 1s	+ 3s				+ 2s	

PLYMOUTH ARGYLE

	Ht	*Wt*	*Birthplace*	*Clubs*	*League App.*	*League Gls*
Goalkeepers						
Geoff Crudgington	6 0	12 12	Wolverhampton	Aston V	4	—
				Bradford C (on loan)	1	—
				Preston NE	—	—
				Crewe Alex	250	—
				Swansea C	52	—
				Plymouth Arg	83	—
Neil Hards	6 0	12 7	Portsmouth	Plymouth Arg	4	—
Defenders						
John Uzzell	5 10	11 0	Plymouth	Plymouth Arg	82	1
Tyrone James	6 2	11 0	Paddington	Fulham	20	—
				Plymouth Arg	75	—
Brian McNeill*	5 9	10 12	Newcastle	Bristol C	3	—
				Plymouth Arg	47	—
George Foster	5 10	11 2	Plymouth	Plymouth Arg	202	6
				Torquay U (on loan)	6	3
Steven Morris*	6 0	11 0	Swansea	Swansea C	39	1
				Plymouth Arg	—	—
Forbes Phillipson-Masters	6 1	12 10	Bournemouth	Southampton	9	—
				Exeter C (on loan)	6	—
				Bournemouth (on loan)	7	2
				Luton T (on loan)	10	—
				Plymouth Arg	82	—
Vaughan Powell			Slough	Plymouth Arg	—	—
Chris Jefferis			Plymouth	Plymouth Arg	—	—
Midfield						
Kevin Hodges	5 7	10 0	Bridport	Plymouth Arg	97	10
Chris Harrison	5 8	10 6	Launceston	Plymouth Arg	163	4
Leigh Cooper	5 8	10 9	Reading	Plymouth Arg	42	3
Jeremy Collins	5 8	10 0	Plymouth	Plymouth Arg	3	—
Colin Randell	5 9	10 8	Skewen	Coventry C	—	—
				Plymouth Arg	139	9
				Exeter C	78	4
				Plymouth Arg	72	5
Denis Murphy			Dublin	Plymouth Arg	—	—
Gordon Nisbet	5 10	12 2	Wallsend	WBA	136	—
				Hull C	193	1
				Plymouth Arg	19	—
Forwards						
Brian Johnson	5 10	11 6	London	Plymouth Arg	197	40
				Torquay U (on loan)	5	2
Mark Graves	5 9	10 11	Middlesex	Plymouth Arg	33	3
Colin Upton*	5 7	10 9	Reading	Plymouth Arg	3	—
David Kemp	5 9	11 0	Harrow	Crystal Palace	35	10
				Portsmouth	64	30
				Carlisle U	61	22
				Plymouth Arg	75	39
John Sims	6 0	12 10	Belper	Derby Co	3	—
				Luton T (on loan)	3	1
				Oxford U (on loan)	7	1
				Colchester U (on loan)	2	—
				Notts Co	61	13
				Exeter C	34	11
				Plymouth Arg	74	15
Donal Murphy	5 11	11 0	Dublin	Coventry C	43	10
				Millwall (on loan)	3	—
				Torquay U	85	20
				Plymouth Arg	42	9
John Peachey	6 0	12 1	Cambridge	York C	8	3
				Barnsley	127	31
				Darlington	26	7
				Plymouth Arg	3	—
Kelvin Howe			Calstock	Plymouth Arg	—	—

PORTSMOUTH Division 3

Vice-Presidents: R. Vernon Stokes, Sir A. L. Blake MC, LLB, KCVO.

Chairman: B. J. Deacon.

Vice-Chairman: J. R. Parkhouse.

Directors: D. K. Deacon, S. W. Sloan, G. G. Gauntlett.

Manager: Frank Burrows.

Company Secretary: W. J. B. Davis.

Chief Executive: J. W. Dickinson MBE.

Year Formed: 1898.

Turned Professional: 1898. *Limited Company:* 1898.

Football League Record:
1920 Original Member of Division 3; 1921 Division 3(S); 1924–27 Division 2; 1927–59 Division 1; 1959–61 Division 2; 1961–62 Division 3; 1962–76 Division 2; 1976–78 Division 3; 1978–80 Division 4; 1980– Division 3.

Honours: *Football League:* Division 1 – Champions 1948–49, 1949–50; Division 2 – Runners-up 1926–27; Division 3(S) – Champions 1923–24; Division 3 – Champions 1961–62. *FA Cup:* Winners 1939; Runners-up 1929, 1934. *Football League Cup* best season: 5th rd, 1961.

Record Victory: 9-1 v Notts Co, Division 2, 9 Apr, 1927.

Record Defeat: 0-10 v Leicester C, Division 1, 20 Oct, 1928.

Most League Points: 65, Division 3, 1961–62.

Most League Goals: 91, Division 4, 1979–80.

Highest League Scorer in Season: Billy Haines, 40, Division 2, 1926–27.

Most League Goals in Total Aggregate: Peter Harris, 194, 1946–60.

Most Capped Player: Jimmy Dickinson, 48, England.

Most League Appearances: 764, Jimmy Dickinson, 1946–65.

Record Transfer Fee Received: £130,000 from Brighton for Steve Foster, June 1979.

Record Transfer Fee Paid: £155,000 to Fulham for Paul Went, Dec 1973.

Previous Managers since the War: Jack Tinn, Bob Jackson, Eddie Lever, Freddie Cox, George Smith, John Mortimore, Ron Tindall, Ian St John, Jimmy Dickinson MBE.

Address of Supporters Club: Frogmore Road, Portsmouth.

Address of the Club Shop or Boutique: The Club Shop, Portsmouth, 42 Frogmore Road, Portsmouth.

Fratton Park, Frogmore Rd, Portsmouth PO4 8RA. Telephone Portsmouth 731204/5. *Telegraphic address:* 'Pompey Portsm'th'. *Ground capacity:* 40,000 (14,200 covered). *Record attendance:* 51,385 v Derby Co, FA Cup 6th rd, 26 Feb, 1949. *Record receipts:* £39,521 v Middlesbrough, FA Cup 3rd rd, 9 Jan, 1980. *Pitch measurements:* 116yd×73yd.

How to get there: Fratton station on main line from London Waterloo is just four minutes walk from the ground. Buses 17 and 18 from Portsmouth Harbour station and Gosport Ferry Terminal to the ground. Buses also from Portsmouth station.

Match tickets: South Stand centre section (the best seats) bookable 10 days in advance.

Car parking: Only side-street parking.

Entertainments/catering facilities: The Pompey public house and reception rooms adjoin the ground and are owned by the club. There are also several bars around the ground.

Club shop: 42 Frogmore Road.

Handbooks/programmes: No handbook. The match-day magazine available on subscription.

Extra information: Portsmouth were the first club to come out of the Third Division to win the League Championship.

Club Colours: Blue shirts with white collars and cuffs, white shorts, red socks.

Change Colours: Red shirts with white collar and cuffs, red shorts, white stockings.

Club Captain: Peter Mellor.

Club Nickname: Pompey.

PORTSMOUTH 1980–81 LEAGUE RECORD

Match No.	Date	Venue	Opponents	Result	H/T Score	Goalscorers	Attendance
1	Aug 16	A	Barnsley	W 2-1	1-0	Aizlewood, Rogers	10,253
2	19	H	Swindon T	W 1-0	0-0	Laidlaw	15,810
3	23	H	Rotherham U	W 3-1	1-1	Gregory, Showers, Bryant	14,767
4	30	A	Blackpool	W 2-0	1-0	Gregory, Showers	8352
5	Sept 6	H	Brentford	L 0-2	0-0		16,971
6	13	A	Walsall	L 0-2	0-1		5738
7	16	H	Charlton Ath	W 1-0	0-0	Laidlaw	12,796
8	20	A	Hull C	L 1-2	1-1	Brisley	4613
9	27	H	Fulham	W 1-0	0-0	Gregory	16,460
10	Oct 4	H	Chesterfield	W 1-0	1-0	Rogers	14,953
11	7	A	Colchester U	L 0-1	0-0		2702
12	11	A	Newport Co	L 1-2	0-2	Garner	7003
13	18	H	Burnley	W 4-2	3-1	Tait, Gregory (pen), Rogers, Showers	13,459
14	21	H	Plymouth Arg	L 1-3	1-1	Garner	15,635
15	25	A	Oxford U	W 2-1	0-1	Gregory, Barnard	6217
16	Nov 1	H	Carlisle U	W 2-1	1-0	Gregory, Showers	13,913
17	4	H	Colchester U	W 2-1	1-1	Gregory 2	10,895
18	8	A	Gillingham	W 1-0	0-0	Gregory	6623
19	11	A	Swindon T	W 2-0	0-0	Laidlaw, Showers	8164
20	15	H	Barnsley	L 0-1	0-1		14,732
21	29	H	Chester	W 2-0	1-0	Storton (og), Tait	10,515
22	Dec 6	A	Sheffield U	L 0-1	0-0		12,158
23	20	A	Huddersfield T	D 0-0	0-0		10,869
24	26	H	Reading	D 0-0	0-0		17,412
25	27	A	Millwall	D 0-0	0-0		8422
26	Jan 10	H	Sheffield U	W 1-0	1-0	Gregory (pen)	14,321
27	14	A	Exeter C	L 0-2	0-1		3722
28	24	H	Blackpool	D 3-3	2-0	Hemmerman, Rafferty, Tait	13,265
29	27	A	Burnley	W 3-1	1-1	Tait, Bryant, Hemmerman	6683
30	31	A	Rotherham U	L 0-3	0-1		7588
31	Feb 7	H	Walsall	W 2-0	1-0	Doyle (pen), Tait	11,921
32	10	H	Exeter C	W 5-0	1-0	Bryant, Tait 3, Rafferty	12,743
33	14	A	Brentford	D 2-2	1-2	Rafferty 2	10,160
34	21	A	Fulham	L 0-3	0-1		9921
35	28	H	Hull C	W 2-1	1-1	Rafferty, Doyle (pen)	13,596
36	Mar 7	A	Chesterfield	L 0-3	0-1		6985
37	14	H	Newport Co	D 0-0	0-0		13,208
38	21	A	Plymouth Arg	L 0-1	0-1		6042
39	29	H	Oxford U	D 1-1	1-1	Gregory	13,243
40	Apr 4	A	Carlisle U	D 0-0	0-0		4299
41	11	H	Gillingham	D 0-0	0-0		9172
42	14	A	Charlton Ath	W 2-1	0-0	Croft, Rafferty	8863
43	18	H	Millwall	W 2-1	1-1	Doyle (pen), Gregory	13,115
44	20	A	Reading	L 1-2	0-2	Perrin	7061
45	25	H	Huddersfield T	L 1-2	1-1	Doyle (pen)	10,238
46	May 2	A	Chester	W 1-0	0-0	Gregory	2153

Final League Position: 6

Goalscorers

League (55): Gregory 13 (2 pens), Tait 8, Rafferty 6, Showers 5, Doyle 4 (4 pens), Bryant 3, Laidlaw 3, Rogers 3, Garner 2, Hemmerman 2, Aizlewood 1, Barnard 1, Brisley 1, Croft 1, Perrin 1, own goal 1.
League Cup (9): Laidlaw 3 (1 pen), Gregory 2, Garner, Perrin, Rogers, own goal.
F.A. Cup (0).

League Cup	First Round	Plymouth Arg (a)	1-0
		(h)	2-1
	Second Round	Oldham Ath (a)	2-3
		(h)	1-0
	Third Round	Bristol R (a)	0-0
		(h)	2-0
	Fourth Round	Liverpool (a)	1-4
FA Cup	First Round	Colchester U (a)	0-3

Mellor	McLaughlin	Viney	Brisley	Aizlewood	Garner	Gregory	Laidlaw	Tait	Bryant	Rogers	Showers	Ayrton	Perrin	Barnard	Davey	Ellis	Hemmerman	Doyle	Rafferty	Knight	Bartlett	Croft	*Match No.*
1	2	3	4	5	6	7	8	9	10	11													1
1	2	3	4	5	6	7	8	9	10	11													2
1	2	3*	4	5	6	7	8	9	10	11	12												3
1	2	3	4	5	6	7	8	12	10	11	9*												4
1	2	3	4*	5	6	7	8		10	11	9	12											5
1	2	3	4	5	6	7	8		10	11	9*		12										6
1	2	3	4	5	6	7	8		10	11			9										7
1	2	3	4	5	6	7	8	12	10*	11			9										8
1	2	3	4	5	6	7	8		10	11			9										9
1	2	3	4	5	6	7*	8		10	11	12		9										10
1	2	3	4	5	6	7	8		10	11			9										11
1	2	3	4*	5	6	7		8	10	11	9			12									12
1	2	3	4	5	6	7		8	10	11	9												13
1	2	3	4*	5	6	7		8	10	11	9			12									14
1	2	3		5	6	7		8	10	11	9			4									15
1	2	3			6	7		8	10	11	9			4	5								16
1	2	3			6	7	4	8	10	11	9				5								17
1	2	3		5	6	7	4	8	10	11	9												18
1	2	3		5	6	7	4	8	10	11	9												19
1	2	3		5	6	7	4	8	10	11	9												20
1	2	3		5				8	10	11			9	4	12	6	7*						21
1		3		5				8	10	11			9	12	6	2	7*	4					22
1	2	3		5		7		8	10	11					6			4	9				23
1	2	3		5		7		8	10	11					6			4	9				24
1	2	3		5		7		8	10	11					6			4	9				25
1	2	3		5		7		8	10	11			9		6			4					26
1	2	3		5		7		8	10*	11					6		12	4	9				27
1	2	3		5*		12		8	10	11						6	7	4	9				28
1	2	3						8	10	11					6	5	7	4	9				29
1	2	3		5				8*	10	11					12	6	7	4	9				30
1	2*	3		5		12		8	10	11						6	7	4	9				31
		3		5				8	10	11					6	2	7	4	9	1			32
1		3		5		12		8	10*	11					6	2	7	4	9				33
1		3		5		12		8	10	11					6*	2	7	4	9				34
1	2	3		5					10*	11				8		6	7	4	9		12		35
1	2	3*		5	6				10	11				8		12	7	4	9				36
1	2	3		5		7		8		11				10		6		4	9				37
1	2	3		5		7		8		11*			12	10		6		4	9				38
1	2	3		5		7		8				11*		10		6	12	4	9				39
1	2	3			6	7		8		11				10				4	9			5	40
1	2	3			6	7*		8		11				10				4	9		12	5	41
1	2			5		7		8	3	11				10				4	9			6	42
1	2			5		7		8	3	11				10				4	9			6	43
1	2			5		7		8*	3	11			12	10			9	4				6	44
1	2			5		7		8	3	11				10				4	9			6	45
1	2			5		7		8	3	11				10		6		4	9				46
45	42	41	14	41	23	35	15	36	41	45	12	1	8	15	12	14	12	25	22	1	—	6	
						+ 4s		+ 2s			+ 2s	+ 1s	+ 3s	+ 3s	+ 2s	+ 1s	+ 2s				+ 2s		

PORTSMOUTH

	Ht	*Wt*	*Birthplace*	*Clubs*	*League App.*	*League Gls*
Goalkeepers						
Peter Mellor	6 2	14 0	Presbury	Manchester C	—	—
				Burnley	69	—
				Chesterfield (on loan)	4	—
				Fulham	189	—
				Hereford U	32	—
				Portsmouth	129	—
Alan Knight	6 1	13 1½	Balham	Portsmouth	10	—
Defenders						
Stuart Croft*	5 11	11 5	Ashington	Hull C	190	4
				Portsmouth	6	1
John McLaughlin	5 8	10 10	Edmonton	Colchester U	66	2
				Swindon T	202	8
				Portsmouth	71	1
Alan Garner	6 0	12 4	Lambeth	Millwall	2	—
				Luton T	88	3
				Watford	200	15
				Portsmouth	26	2
Peter Ellis	5 11	11 2	Portsmouth	Portsmouth	177	—
Keith Viney	5 11	11 12	Portsmouth	Portsmouth	142	3
Keith James (Contract cancelled Feb 1981)				Portsmouth	6	—
Archie Styles	5 9	11 0	Liverpool	Everton	23	—
				Birmingham C	74	3
				Peterborough U	32	1
				Portsmouth	28	—
Steve Aizlewood	5 11	13 7	Newport	Newport Co	197	18
				Swindon T	112	10
				Portsmouth	75	3
Kevin Bartlett			Portsmouth	Portsmouth	2	—
Midfield						
Leigh Barnard	5 7½	9 10	Worsley	Portsmouth	62	8
Steve Piper	5 10	11 10	Brighton	Brighton	162	9
(Retired, injury)				Portsmouth	29	2
Terry Brisley*	5 6	10 6½	Stepney	Orient	142	10
				Southend U (on loan)	8	—
				Millwall	107	15
				Charlton Ath	48	5
				Portsmouth	55	13
Ken Todd	5 7	9 9	Co Durham	Wolverhampton W	5	1
				Port Vale	44	9
				Portsmouth	3	1
Steve Bryant	5 8	10 6	Islington	Birmingham C	36	1
				Sheffield W (on loan)	3	—
				Northampton T	97	5
				Portsmouth	100	5
Ian Purdie	5 8½	11 0	Motherwell	Aberdeen	39	10
(Contract cancelled April 1981)				Dundee U	59	7
				Motherwell	16	3
				Wigan Ath	55	12
				Portsmouth	5	1
David Gregory	5 9	11 6	Peterborough	Peterborough U	142	32
				Stoke C	23	3
				Blackburn R (on loan)	5	3
				Bury	52	13
				Portsmouth	60	18
Neil Ayrton			Lewisham	Maidstone U	(not known)	
				Portsmouth	2	—
Bobby Doyle	5 11	12 0	Dunbarton	Barnsley	149	16
				Peterborough U	130	10
				Blackpool	49	2
				Portsmouth	25	4
Forwards						
Jeff Hemmerman	5 11	11 0	Hull	Hull C	59	10
				Scunthorpe U (on loan)	5	1
				Port Vale	15	5
				Portsmouth	89	29
Steve Davey*	5 7	10 3	Plymouth	Plymouth Arg	226	48
				Hereford U	107	32
				Portsmouth	92	8
Alan Rogers	5 10	11 4	Plymouth	Plymouth Arg	117	5
				Portsmouth	87	12
Steve Perrin*	6 1	12 3	London	Crystal Palace	48	11
				Plymouth Arg	35	6
				Portsmouth	28	3
Mick Tait	5 11	11 8	Wallsend	Oxford U	64	23
				Carlisle U	106	20
				Hull C	33	3
				Portsmouth	38	8
Billy Rafferty	5 10	10 7	Pt Glasgow	Coventry C	27	3
				Blackpool	36	9
				Plymouth Arg	90	35
				Carlisle U	72	27
				Wolverhampton W	44	6
				Newcastle U	39	6
				Portsmouth	22	6

Also retained: Gary Juryeff, Steve Berry, David Leworthy, Graham Marriner.

PORT VALE — Division 4

Chairman: D. Ratcliffe JP.

Vice-Chairman: J. D. Lloyd.

Directors: L. W. Cliff, D. S. Jones, A. McPherson, D. Leese, J. Lloyd, J. Burgess (President).

Manager: John McGrath. *Secretary:* Andrew Waterhouse.

Chief Coach: John Rudge.

Year Formed: 1876. *Turned Professional:* 1885.

Limited Company: 1911.

Previous Name: Burslem Port Vale; became Port Vale, 1913.

Previous Grounds: 1876, Limekin Lane, Longport; 1881, Westport; 1884, Moorland Road, Burslem; 1886, Athletic Ground, Cobridge; 1913, Recreation Ground, Hanley; 1950, Vale Park.

Football League Record:
Original Member Division 2, 1892–96; Failed re-election in 1896; Re-elected 1898; Resigned 1907; Returned in Oct, 1919, when they took over the fixtures of Leeds City; 1929–30 Division 3(N); 1930–36 Division 2; 1936–38 Division 3(N); 1938–52 Division 3(S); 1952–54 Division 3(N); 1954–57 Division 2; 1957–58 Division 3(S); 1958–59 Division 4; 1959–65 Division 3; 1965–70 Division 4; 1970–78 Division 3; 1978– Division 4.

Honours: *Football League:* Division 2 best season: 5th, 1930–31; Division 3(N) – Champions 1929–30, 1953–54; Runners-up 1952–53; Division 4 – Champions 1958–59; Promoted 1969–70 (4th). *FA Cup:* semi-final 1954, when in Division 3. *Football League Cup:* never past 2nd rd.

Record Victory: 9-1 v Chesterfield, Division 2, 24 Sept, 1932.

Record Defeat: 0-10 v Sheffield U, Division 2, 10 Dec, 1892 and v Notts Co, Division 2, 26 Feb, 1895.

Most League Points: 69, Division 3(N), 1953–54.

Most League Goals: 110, Division 4, 1958–59.

Highest League Scorer in Season: Wilf Kirkham, 38, Division 2, 1926–27.

Most League Goals in Total Aggregate: Wilf Kirkham, 154, 1923–29, 1931–33.

Most Capped Player: Sammy Morgan, 7 (18) Northern Ireland.

Most League Appearances: Roy Sproson, 761, 1950–72.

Record Transfer Fee Received: £55,000 from Leicester C for John Ridley, Sept 1978.

Record Transfer Fee Paid: £40,000 to Bury for Peter Farrell, Nov 1978; £40,000 to Wolverhampton W for Ken Todd, Aug 1978.

Previous Managers since the War: Billy Frith, Gordon Hodgson, Ivor Powell, Freddie Steele, Norman Low, Freddie Steele, Jackie Mudie, Sir Stanley Matthews, Gordon Lee, Roy Sproson, Colin Harper, Bob Smith, Dennis Butler, Alan Bloor.

Address of Supporters Club: Hamil Rd, Burslem, Stoke-on-Trent ST6 1AW.

Vale Park, Burslem, Stoke-on-Trent. Telephone Stoke-on-Trent 814134. *Ground capacity:* 35,000. *Record attendance:* 50,000 v Aston Villa, FA Cup 5th rd, 20 Feb, 1960. *Record receipts:* £11,991 v Burnley, FA Cup 4th rd, 29 Jan, 1977. *Pitch measurements:* 116yd×76yd.

How to get there: Nearest railway station, Stoke-on-Trent; there are frequent bus services from the town centre to Burslem.

Match tickets: Not bookable in advance.

Car parking: Parking is available behind the Railway Stand on Hamil Road, and on the Lorne Street side of the ground.

Entertainments/catering facilities: Light refreshments served on the ground. Social club on the Hamil Road side of the ground provides entertainment on certain evenings; membership by subscription.

Club shop: Sells all types of souvenirs.

Handbooks/programmes: Programmes are available on application to the club office or to the club shop.

Extra information: Port Vale are one of only five clubs to reach the FA Cup semi-final while in the Third Division; they did so in the 1953–54 season.

Club Colours: White shirts with black trim, black shorts, black stockings.

Change Colours: Yellow shirts, green shorts, yellow stockings.

Trainer: Lol Hamlett.

Club Nickname: Valiants.

PORT VALE 1980–81 LEAGUE RECORD

Match No.	Date	Venue	Opponents	Result	H/T Score	Goalscorers	Attendance
1	Aug 16	H	Doncaster R	W 3-0	2-0	Jones, Griffiths, Chamberlain N.	2846
2	18	A	Southend U	L 1-5	1-3	Chamberlain N.	3948
3	23	A	Wimbledon	L 0-1	0-1		1775
4	30	H	Mansfield T	D 0-0	0-0		2558
5	Sept 6	A	Wigan Ath	L 0-1	0-1		4678
6	13	H	Aldershot	L 0-1	0-1		2370
7	15	A	Stockport Co	L 1-2	0-1	Chamberlain N.	3480
8	20	H	Darlington	W 4-2	3-1	Keenan 2, Allen, Farrell	2158
9	27	A	Bury	L 1-2	0-0	Keenan	2341
10	29	H	Stockport Co	W 2-0	1-0	Beech, Allen	2835
11	Oct 4	A	York C	L 1-4	0-3	Griffiths	2025
12	6	H	Torquay U	W 3-1	0-0	Hayes (og), Beech, Griffiths (pen)	2091
13	11	H	Tranmere R	W 5-1	2-0	Bromage 2, Allen, Chamberlain M. 2	2820
14	18	A	Bradford C	L 1-2	1-2	Bromage	2843
15	22	A	Hereford U	W 3-2	1-0	Beech, Chamberlain M. 2	2101
16	25	H	Hartlepool U	D 1-1	1-0	Bromage	3072
17	27	H	AFC Bournemouth	L 0-2	0-1		3009
18	Nov 1	A	Peterborough U	D 1-1	0-1	Waugh (og)	3643
19	5	A	Torquay U	L 0-4	0-2		1370
20	8	H	Rochdale	D 1-1	0-0	Bowles	2774
21	10	H	Southend U	W 1-0	0-0	Allen	2780
22	15	A	Doncaster R	L 0-2	0-1		2422
23	Dec 5	H	Crewe Alex	D 2-2	0-0	Beech, Chamberlain N.	4154
24	20	A	Halifax T	D 2-2	2-2	Dunleavy (og), Woolfall	1215
25	26	H	Lincoln C	L 0-1	0-0		4239
26	27	A	Northampton T	L 1-5	0-1	Chamberlain N.	2978
27	Jan 10	A	Hartlepool U	L 0-3	0-1		3058
28	24	A	Mansfield T	L 0-5	0-5		3864
29	31	H	Wimbledon	L 2-3	1-1	Miller 2	2372
30	Feb 7	A	Aldershot	D 0-0	0-0		2598
31	14	H	Wigan Ath	W 3-0	2-0	Bowles, Miller, Chamberlain N.	3214
32	21	H	Bury	L 1-3	0-2	Chamberlain N.	2831
33	24	A	Scunthorpe U	D 1-1	0-0	Chamberlain M.	1946
34	Mar 3	H	Scunthorpe U	D 2-2	2-0	Miller, Chamberlain M.	2277
35	7	H	York C	W 2-0	1-0	Bennett (pen), Chamberlain M.	2319
36	16	H	Hereford U	W 4-0	1-0	Bowles 2, Chamberlain M., Armstrong	2379
37	24	A	Tranmere R	W 2-1	1-0	Beech, Chamberlain N.	1479
38	28	A	AFC Bournemouth	D 0-0	0-0		4665
39	Apr 4	H	Peterborough U	D 1-1	0-0	Armstrong	2982
40	12	A	Rochdale	L 1-2	0-1	Bowles	2590
41	14	H	Bradford C	W 2-1	1-0	Chamberlain N., Bowles	2221
42	18	H	Northampton T	D 1-1	1-0	Sproson	2371
43	20	A	Lincoln C	L 0-1	0-0		3665
44	26	H	Halifax T	D 0-0	0-0		2301
45	May 1	A	Crewe Alex	D 0-0	0-0		4634
46	5	A	Darlington	D 1-1	0-0	Chamberlain M.	1576

Final League Position: 19

Goalscorers

League (57): Chamberlain M. 9, Chamberlain N. 9, Bowles 6, Beech 5, Allen 4, Bromage 4, Miller 4, Griffiths 3 (1 pen), Keenan 3, Armstrong 2, Bennett 1 (pen), Farrell 1, Jones 1, Sproson 1, Woolfall 1, own goals 3.
League Cup (3): Chamberlain N. 2, Bromage.
F.A. Cup (8): Beech 2, Chamberlain N. 2, Bennett (pen), Chamberlain M., Farrell, Miller.

League Cup	First Round	Tranmere R (h)	2-3
		(a)	1-0
FA Cup	First Round	Bradford C (h)	4-2
	Second Round	Burnley (a)	1-1
		(h)	2-0
	Third Round	Enfield (h)	1-1
		(a)	0-3

Dance	Keenan	Griffiths	Beech	Harwood	Sproson	Jones	Farrell	Allen	Chamberlain N	Bromage	Brissett	Woolfall	Harrison	Bowles	Elsby	Miller	Chamberlain M	Bennett	Cherry	Jenkins	Higgins	Armstrong	Lloyd	*Match No.*
1	2*	3	4	5	6	7	8	9	10	11	12													1
1	2	3	4	5*	6	7	8		10	11	12	9												2
	2	3	4		6	7*	8	9	10	11	12		1	5										3
	2	3	4		6	7	8	9*	10	11			1	5	12									4
	2	3	4		6	7	8		10	11	9*		1	5	12									5
	2	3	4		6	7*	8		10	11		9	1	5	12									6
	2	3	4		6		8		10	11	7	9	1	5										7
	2	3	4		6		8	9	10	11*	7	12	1	5										8
	2	3	4		6	7	8	9	10	12	11*		1	5										9
	2*	3	4		6		8	9	10	11	7	12	1	5										10
		3	4		6		8	9	10*	11	2	12	1	5	7									11
		3	4		6		8	9		11		10	1	5	2		7							12
		3	4		6		8	9		11*	2		1	5	12	7	10							13
		3	4		6		8	9		11	2		1	5		7	10							14
		3	4		6		8	9		11	2		1	5		7	10							15
		3	4		6		8	9		11	2		1	5		7	10							16
		3	4		6		8	9*		11	2		1	5	12	7	10							17
	8*		4		6			9		11	2		1	5	3	7.	10	12						18
		3	4		6				9	11	2		1	5	8	7	10							19
			4		6				9	11	2		1	5	3	7	10	8						20
		11	4		6			9			2		1	5	3	7	10	8						21
		12	4		6			9*		11	2		1	5	3	7	10	8						22
			4		6		7		9	11	2			5	3		10	8	1					23
			4		6		7		9	11	2	10		5	12	3*		8	1					24
			4		6		7		9	11	2	10		5				8	1	3				25
		7			6		8	10	9	3	2			5	4			11	1					26
	10		4			3	7	8	9	11	2		1	5	6									27
			4			7	8		9	3	12		1	5	6	11*	10	2						28
			4		6	11	8		9	3	2		1	5		7	10							29
			4		6				9	3	2		1	5			10	11			7	8		30
			4		6				9	3	2			5		7	10	11				8	1	31
			4		6				9	3	2			5		7	10	11*			12	8	1	32
			4		6					3	2	9		5		12	10	11			7*	8	1	33
			4		6					3	2	9*		5		7	10	11			12	8	1	34
			4		6				9	3	2			5		7	10	11				8	1	35
			4		6				9	3	2			5		7	10	11				8	1	36
			4		6				9	3	2			5			10	11			7	8	1	37
			4		6				9	3	2			5			10	11			7	8	1	38
			4		6				9	3				5		7	10	11			2	8	1	39
			4	7*	6				9	3	2			5		12	10	11				8	1	40
			4		6				9	3	2			5		7	10	11				8	1	41
			4		6				9	3	2			5		7	10	11				8	1	42
			4	7*	6				9	3				5		12	10	11			2	8	1	43
			4*		6		12		9	3	2			5		7	10	11				8	1	44
			4		6				9	3	2			5		12	10*	11			7	8	1	45
			4		6				9	3	2			5			10	11			7	8	1	46
2	12	20	45	4	44	10	24	18	35	44	37	8	24	44	11	22	31	25	4	1	8	17	16	
		+ 1s					+ 1s			+ 1s	+ 4s	+ 3s			+ 6s	+ 4s		+ 1s			+ 2s			

PORT VALE

	Ht	*Wt*	*Birthplace*	*Clubs*	*League App.*	*League Gls*
Goalkeepers						
Trevor Dance	5 11	11 10	Durham	Port Vale	84	—
(Contract cancelled Sept 1980)				Stoke C (on loan)	—	—
Mark Harrison	6 0½	12 7	Derby	Nottingham F	—	—
				Southampton	—	—
				Port Vale	24	—
Defenders						
Gerry Keenan	5 9	11 0	Liverpool	Bury	71	3
				Port Vale	85	6
Neil Griffiths*	5 11	11 10	Stoke	Chester	90	4
				Port Vale	218	13
Phil Sproson	6 0	12 0	Trent Vale	Port Vale	108	4
Lee Harwood*	6 1	13 0	Perivale	Southampton	—	—
				Wimbledon	1	—
				Leatherhead	(not known)	
				Port Vale	19	1
Paul Bowles	6 1	12 11	Manchester	Manchester U	—	—
				Crewe Alex	178	20
				Port Vale	54	6
				Southampton (on loan)	—	—
Trevor Brissett	5 10½	11 7	Stoke	Stoke C	—	—
				Port Vale	41	—
Andrew Higgins	6 3	12 4	Bolsover	Chesterfield	1	—
				Port Vale	10	—
Midfield						
Paul Bennett	5 9	9 9	Liverpool	Port Vale	26	1
Peter Farrell	5 7	10 9	Liverpool	Bury	54	9
				Port Vale	85	10
Felix Healy	5 11	12 0	Londonderry	Finn Harps	(not known)	
				Port Vale	41	2
Ian Elsby*	5 9	9 0	Stoke	Port Vale	43	1
Steven Jones*	6 1	10 7	Liverpool	Manchester U	—	—
				Port Vale	25	3
Ken Beech	5 7	10 2	Stoke	Port Vale	175	17
Russell Bromage	5 11	11 5	Blurton	Port Vale	100	7
Lee Jenkins*	5 10	12 0	Birmingham	Aston V	3	—
				Port Vale	1	—
Terry Armstrong	5 10	12 2	Barnsley	Huddersfield T	40	2
				Port Vale	17	2
Forwards						
Neville Chamberlain	5 7½	11 5	Stoke	Port Vale	106	28
Mark Chamberlain	5 8½	9 8	Stoke	Port Vale	50	10
Alan Woolfall*	5 6	10 0	Liverpool	Bury	57	11
				Port Vale	18	3
John Allen*	6 0	13 3	Coventry	Leicester C	—	—
				Port Vale	18	4
John Miller	5 10	12 10	Ipswich	Ipswich T	50	2
				Norwich C	23	3
				Mansfield T	113	14
				Port Vale	26	4

PRESTON NORTH END Division 3

President: Tom Finney OBE, JP.
Chairman: Alan R. W. Jones JP, FRICS.
Vice-Chairman: T. J. Hemmings.
Directors: T. W. S. Croft, K. W. Leeming, T. H. Gore, E. Griffith, M. H. McCann, A. C. Pilkington.
Team Manager: Tommy Docherty.
Secretary: Ron Severs FIM Ent. *Asst Manager:* Ken Shellito.
Year Formed: 1881. *Turned Professional:* 1885.
Limited Company: 1893.

Football League Record:
1888 Original Member of League; 1901–04 Division 2; 1904–12 Division 1; 1912–13 Division 2; 1913–14 Division 1; 1914–15 Division 2; 1919–25 Division 1; 1925–34 Division 2; 1934–49 Division 1; 1949–51 Division 2; 1951–61 Division 1; 1961–70 Division 2; 1970–71 Division 3; 1971–74 Division 2; 1974–78 Division 3; 1978–81 Division 2; 1981– Division 3.

Honours: *Football League:* Division 1 – Champions 1888–89 (first champions), 1889–90; Runners-up 1890–91, 1891–92, 1892–93, 1905–06, 1952–53, 1957–58; Division 2 – Champions 1903–04, 1912–13, 1950–51; Runners-up 1914–15, 1933–34; Division 3 – Champions 1970–71. *FA Cup:* Winners 1889, 1938; Runners-up 1888, 1922, 1937, 1954, 1964. *Double Performed:* 1888–89. *Football League Cup* best season: 4th rd, 1963, 1966, 1972, 1981.

Record Victory: 26-0 v Hyde, FA Cup 1st Series, 1st rd, 15 Oct, 1887.
Record Defeat: 0-7 v Blackpool, Division 1, 1 May, 1948.
Most League Points: 61, Division 3, 1970–71.
Most League Goals: 100, Division 2, 1927–28 and Division 1, 1957–58.
Highest League Scorer in Season: Ted Harper, 37, Division 2, 1932–33.
Most League Goals in Total Aggregate: Tom Finney, 187, 1946–60.
Most Capped Player: Tom Finney, 76, England.
Most League Appearances: Alan Kelly, 447, 1961–75.
Record Transfer Fee Received: £765,000 from Manchester C for Mick Robinson, June 1979.
Record Transfer Fee Paid: £95,000 to Nottingham F for Steve Elliott, March 1979.
Previous Managers since the War: W. Scott, Scot Symon, Frank Hill, Cliff Britton, Jimmy Milne, Bobby Seith, Alan Ball Snr, Bobby Charlton CBE, Harry Catterick, Nobby Stiles.
Address of Supporters Club: c/o Preston North End FC, Deepdale, Preston.
Address of the Club Shop or Boutique: Lilywhite Shop, Deepdale, Preston.

Deepdale, Preston PR1 6RU. Telephone Preston 795919. *Telegraphic address:* 'Football Preston'. *Ground capacity:* 25,000. *Record attendance:* 42,684 v Arsenal, Division 1, 23 Apr, 1938. *Record receipts:* £28,303.40 v Blackburn R, Division 2, 21 April, 1981. *Pitch measurements:* 112yd×78yd.

How to get there: Special buses to Deepdale from outlying areas and town centre bus station. Nearest railway station: Preston.

Match tickets: Postal applications, including remittance and SAE, may be made 14 days before the match.

Car parking: Club car park on the Deepdale Road (West Stand) side of the ground, holds 500 vehicles. Only limited off-street parking.

Entertainments/catering facilities: The ground is well-equipped for normal match-day refreshments.

Club shop: Open on match days. All postal enquiries to: The Commercial Manager, Preston North End Development Association, Deepdale Road, Preston (Tel: Preston 795465). Shop items also available from Mon-Fri 9am-5pm at the Lottery Office, Deepdale Road.

Handbooks/programmes: No handbook. Programmes available on subscription from the Commercial Manager.

Extra information: The first club to do the League and FA Cup double, accomplishing this feat in 1888–89.

Club Colours: White shirts, with navy blue collars and cuffs, navy blue shorts with white stripes, white stockings with navy blue rings.

Change Colours: Yellow shirts, royal blue shorts, yellow stockings.

Club Captain: Francis Burns.

First Team Trainer: Harry Hubbick.

Club Nickname: The Lilywhites or North End.

PRESTON NORTH END 1980–81 LEAGUE RECORD

Match No.	Date	Venue	Opponents	Result	H/T Score	Goalscorers	Attendance
1	Aug 16	H	Bristol C	D 1-1	0-0	Elliott	6058
2	19	A	Grimsby T	D 0-0	0-0		10,461
3	23	H	West Ham U	D 0-0	0-0		9063
4	30	A	Sheffield W	L 0-3	0-2		16,724
5	Sept 6	H	Cambridge U	W 2-0	2-0	McGee 2	5516
6	13	A	Watford	L 1-2	0-1	Coleman	11,275
7	20	A	Chelsea	D 1-1	0-0	Elliott	13,755
8	27	H	Shrewsbury T	D 0-0	0-0		6309
9	Oct 4	A	Orient	L 0-4	0-2		4295
10	7	H	Newcastle U	L 2-3	0-2	Coleman, Bruce	5301
11	11	H	Luton T	W 1-0	1-0	Elliott	5620
12	18	A	Wrexham	W 1-0	0-0	Bruce	5775
13	21	A	Bolton W	L 1-2	1-2	Bruce	10,713
14	25	H	Bristol R	D 0-0	0-0		5807
15	Nov 1	A	Oldham Ath	D 1-1	1-1	Bruce	6739
16	8	H	Cardiff C	W 3-1	0-1	Baxter, Bruce, Stevens (og)	5458
17	15	A	Bristol C	D 0-0	0-0		8042
18	22	H	QPR	W 3-2	1-0	Naughton 2, Baxter	6725
19	28	A	Swansea C	L 0-3	0-1		9115
20	Dec 2	H	Grimsby T	L 2-4	1-2	Elliott (pen), Baxter	5289
21	6	H	Derby Co	L 0-3	0-1		6118
22	13	A	Luton T	L 2-4	0-1	Elliott, Bruce	7874
23	20	H	Wrexham	D 1-1	1-0	Elliott	4746
24	26	A	Blackburn R	D 0-0	0-0		17,726
25	27	H	Notts Co	D 2-2	2-1	Baxter, Elliott (pen)	6547
26	Jan 10	A	QPR	D 1-1	0-0	Bell	8415
27	31	A	West Ham U	L 0-5	0-2		26,413
28	Feb 7	H	Watford	W 2-1	2-1	McGee, Coleman	5107
29	14	A	Cambridge U	L 0-1	0-1		4228
30	21	A	Shrewsbury T	L 0-3	0-3		4660
31	28	H	Chelsea	W 1-0	1-0	Bruce	8129
32	Mar 7	H	Orient	W 3-0	3-0	Taylor (og), Doyle, McGee	5448
33	14	A	Newcastle U	L 0-2	0-1		11,946
34	24	H	Bolton W	L 1-2	0-1	Bruce	8505
35	28	A	Bristol R	L 0-2	0-1		4427
36	Apr 4	H	Oldham Ath	L 1-2	1-2	Bruce	6154
37	11	A	Cardiff C	W 3-1	0-1	Haslegrave, Bruce, Elliott	4991
38	14	H	Sheffield W	W 2-1	0-0	Elliott, Houston	9537
39	18	A	Notts Co	D 0-0	0-0		8485
40	21	H	Blackburn R	D 0-0	0-0		18,742
41	May 2	H	Swansea C	L 1-3	0-2	Bruce	18,970
42	6	A	Derby Co	W 2-1	0-0	Bruce 2	15,050

Final League Position: 20

Goalscorers

League (41): Bruce 13, Elliott 9 (2 pens), Baxter 4, McGee 4, Coleman 3, Naughton 2, Bell 1, Doyle 1, Haslegrave 1, Houston 1, own goals 2.
League Cup (6): Coleman 2, McGee 2, Bell, Bruce.
F.A. Cup (3): Bruce, Houston, McGee.

League Cup	Second Round	Wigan Ath (h)	1-0
		(a)	2-1
	Third Round	Oxford U (h)	1-0
	Fourth Round	WBA (a)	0-0
		(h)	1-1
		(a)	1-2 (aet)
FA Cup	Third Round	Bristol R (h)	3-4

Tunks	Taylor	Cameron	Burns	Baxter	Blackley	Bell	Coleman	Elliott	Potts	McGee	Doyle	McAteer	Bruce	Sayer	O'Riordan	Houston	Westwell	Haslegrave	Naughton	Anderson	Litchfield	*Match No.*
1	2	3	4	5	6	7	8	9	10	11												1
1	2*	3	4	5	6	7	8	9	10	11	12											2
1		2	4	5	6*	7	8	9	10	11	12	3										3
1		2	4*	5	6	7	8			11	12	3	9	10								4
1		2	4	5		7	8			9		3	11		6	10						5
1		2	4	5		7	8	12		9		3	11	10*	6							6
1		3		5		7	8	10		9	4				6	11	2					7
1				5		7	8	12		9	4	3		10	6	11	2*					8
1	2			5	12		8	10		9	4	3		7	6	11*						9
1	2	3	4	5			8	9		12	7		10		6	11*						10
1		3	4	5	6		8	9		11	7		10		2							11
1		3	4	5	6		8	9		11	7		10		2							12
1			4	5	6	8		9		11	7	3	10		2							13
1	2		4	5	6		8	9		11	7*		10		3			12				14
1			4	5	6	7	8	9*		11		3	10		12		2					15
1	12		4	5		7	8			9		3	11		6		2		10*			16
1	12		4	5	6	7	8*	9		11		3	10				2					17
1	8		4	5	6	7		9		11		3					2		10			18
1	8	3	4	5	6	7		9		11			10				2					19
1	8	3	4	5	6*	7		9		11			10				2		12			20
1	4	3*		5		7		9		11	8		10	12			2			6		21
1	2		4	5		7		9		11*	8		10	12			3			6		22
1	2		4	5			8	9			7	3	10		6	11						23
1	2		4	5			7	9			8	3	10		6	11						24
1	2			5		4	7	9		12	8	3	10*		6	11						25
1				5		4	8	9		10	7	3			6	11	2					26
1				5		4	7	9		10*	8	3		12	6	11	2					27
1				5		4	8	9		10	7	3			6		2		11			28
1				5		4	8	9		10	7	3			6		2		11			29
1				5		4	8	9		10	7*	3	12		6		2		11			30
			3	5		4	8			10	7		12	9*			2		11	6	1	31
			3	5		4	8			10	7		9				2		11	6	1	32
			3	5		4	8	12		10	7		9*				2		11	6	1	33
1			3	5	12	4	8			10	7		9				2		11	6*		34
1				5	6	12	8	9		11	7	3	10				2*	4				35
1	2			5	6	8	3			9	7		11			10		4				36
1	2		3	5	6	8	7	9					11			10		4				37
1	2		3	5	6	8	7	9					11			10		4				38
1	2		3	5	6	8	7	9					11			10		4				39
1	2		3	5	6	8	7	9					11			10		4				40
1	2		3*	5	6	8	7	9					11			10		4		12		41
1	2			5	6	8	7	9					11		12	10*		4		3		42
39	20	13	29	42	21	34	36	32	3	32	24	20	29	5	19	17	20	8	9	7	3	
	+ 2s				+ 2s	+ 1s		+ 3s		+ 2s	+ 3s		+ 2s	+ 3s	+ 2s			+ 1s	+ 1s	+ 1s		

PRESTON NORTH END

	Ht	Wt	Birthplace	Clubs	League App.	League Gls
Goalkeepers						
Roy Tunks	6 1	13 11	Wuppertall	Rotherham U	138	—
				York C (on loan)	4	—
				Ipswich T (on loan)	—	—
				Newcastle U (on loan)	—	—
				Preston NE	277	—
Peter Litchfield	6 2	13 7	Manchester	Droylsden	—	—
				Preston NE	3	—
Defenders						
Michael Baxter	6 2	12 6	Birmingham	Preston NE	210	17
Daniel Cameron	5 6½	11 3	Dundee	Sheffield W	31	1
				Colchester U (on loan)	5	—
				Preston NE	122	—
Brian Taylor	5 10	11 7	Gateshead	Coventry C	—	—
				Walsall	216	25
				Plymouth Arg	35	5
				Preston NE	87	1
Donald O'Riordan	6 0	11 12	Dublin	Derby Co	6	1
				Tulsa R	(not known)	
				Doncaster R (on loan)	2	—
				Preston NE	71	—
Simon Westwell	5 9½	9 6	Clitheroe	Preston NE	20	—
John Anderson (Eire)	5 11	11 6	Dublin	WBA	—	—
				Preston NE	13	—
John Blackley (Scotland)	5 10	13 0	Falkirk	Hibernian	263	6
				Newcastle U	46	—
				Preston NE	50	—
Andrew McAteer	5 9½	10 12	Preston	Preston NE	41	—
Jimmy Bell	6 1	12 7	Glasgow	Preston NE	—	—
Midfield						
Francis Burns (Scotland)	5 9	10 10	Coatbridge	Manchester U	120	6
				Southampton	21	—
				Preston NE	273	9
Stephen Doyle	5 9½	11 1	Neath	Preston NE	161	5
Gordon Coleman	5 9	10 12	Nottingham	Preston NE	236	24
Alan Spavin (Non-contract)	5 8	11 4	Lancaster	Preston NE	426	26
Sean Haslegrave*	5 8	10 7	Stoke	Stoke C	113	5
				Nottingham F	7	1
				Preston NE	113	2
Graham Bell	5 9	10 6	Middleton	Oldham Ath	170	9
				Preston NE	81	4
Ian Rothwell (Contract cancelled Feb 1981)	6 0	11 0	Preston	Preston NE	—	—
Peter Sayer (Wales)	5 6	10 2	Cardiff	Cardiff C	82	14
				Brighton	55	6
				Preston NE	8	—
Mark Walsh	5 10	10 7	Preston	Preston NE	—	—
Forwards						
Alex Bruce	5 8	11 0	Dundee	Preston NE	62	22
				Newcastle U	20	3
				Preston NE	228	110
Ricky Thomson	5 8	10 10	Edinburgh	Preston NE	71	20
Graham Houston	5 8	10 6	Gibraltar	Preston NE	18	1
Stephen Elliott	5 11	11 10	Haltwistle, North'land	Nottingham F	4	—
				Preston NE	84	25
Gary Corless (Contract cancelled Oct 1980)	5 5½	10 7	Preston	Preston NE	—	—
Paul McGee (Eire)	5 10	12 0	Sligo	Sligo R	(not known)	
				Toronto M	(not known)	
				QPR	39	7
				Preston NE	56	12
Willie Naughton	5 11	12 6	Catrine	Preston NE	13	2
Mike Imlach*			Croydon	Everton	—	—
				Preston NE	—	—

QUEEN'S PARK RANGERS Division 2

President: Sir Stanley Rous CBE
Chairman: J. A. Gregory. *Vice-Chairman:* J. C. Gregory.
Directors: B. A. V. Henson FCA, S. P. Daverin, I. S. W. Simpson, A. Williamson.
Team Manager: Terry Venables.
Secretary: R. J. Phillips FAAI.
Assistant Team Manager: Alan Harris.
Year Formed: 1885. *Turned Professional:* 1898.
Limited Company: 1899.
Previous Name: 1885–87, St Jude's; 1887, became Queen's Park Rangers.
Previous Grounds: 1885, Welford's Fields; 1888, London Scottish Ground, Brondesbury: Home Farm: Kensal Rise Green: Gun Club, Wormwood Scrubs: Kilburn Cricket Ground; 1899, Kensal Rise Athletic Ground; 1901, Latimer Road, Notting Hill; 1904, Agricultural Society, Park Royal; 1907, Park Royal Ground; 1917, Loftus Road; 1931, White City; 1933, Loftus Road; 1962, White City; 1963, Loftus Road.
Football League Record:
1920 Original Members of Division 3; 1921 Division 3(S); 1948–52 Division 2; 1952–58 Division 3(S); 1958–67 Division 3; 1967–68 Division 2; 1968–69 Division 1; 1969–73 Division 2; 1973–79 Division 1; 1979– Division 2.
Honours: *Football League:* Division 1 – Runners-up 1975–76; Division 2 – Runners-up 1967–68, 1972–73; Division 3(S) – Champions 1947–48; Runners-up 1946–47; Division 3 – Champions 1966–67. *FA Cup* best season: 6th rd (or equivalent) 1910, 1914, 1923, 1948, 1970, 1974. *Football League Cup*: Winners 1966–67. (In 1966–67 won Division 3 and Football League Cup.) **European Competition:** *UEFA Cup:* 1976–77.
Record Victory: 9-2 v Tranmere R, Division 3, 3 Dec, 1960.
Record Defeat: 1-8 v Mansfield T, Division 3, 15 Mar, 1965, and 1-8 v Manchester U, Division 1, 19 Mar, 1969.
Most League Points: 67, Division 3, 1966–67.
Most League Goals: 111, Division 3, 1961–62.
Highest League Scorer in Season: George Goddard, 37, Division 3(S), 1929–30.
Most League Goals in Total Aggregate: George Goddard, 172, 1926–34.
Most Capped Player: Don Givens, 21 (51), Eire.
Most League Appearances: Tony Ingham, 519, 1950–63.
Record Transfer Fee Received: £1,250,000 from Arsenal for Clive Allen, June 1980.
Record Transfer Fee Paid: £400,000 to Leeds U for Tony Currie, Aug 1979.
Previous Managers since the War: Dave Mangnall, Jack Taylor, Alec Stock, Tommy Docherty, Les Allen, Gordon Jago, Dave Sexton, Frank Sibley, Steve Burtenshaw, Tommy Docherty.
Address of Supporters Club: c/o Football Club.
Address of the Club Shop or Boutique: Supporters Club Shop, Queen's Park Rangers FC, South Africa Road, London W12.

South Africa Road, W12 7PA. Telephone 01-743 0262/3/4/5. *Telegraphic address:* 'Queu Pear'. *Ground capacity:* 30,000 (23,000 covered). *Record attendance:* 35,353 v Leeds U, Division 1, 28 April, 1974. *Record receipts:* £79,660 v Tottenham H, FA Cup 3rd rd, 3 Jan, 1981. *Pitch measurements:* 112yd×72yd.
How to get there: Buses 12 and 207. Nos 11, 49, 72, 88, 105, 220 go near Shepherd's Bush (Metropolitan and Central Lines) and White City (Central Line – five to ten minutes walk).
Match tickets: Seats bookable one month in advance of the match.
Car parking: No club car park, but the White City park, adjacent to the ground, is recommended. Limited parking in side-streets.
Entertainments/catering facilities: Various bars around the ground.
Club shop: Programme shop in South Africa Road and kiosks inside the ground.
Handbooks/programmes: Available from programme shop.
Extra information: Queen's Park Rangers have had more home grounds than any other present Football League club; 12 in all, plus one game at Highbury in 1930.
Club Colours: Blue and white hooped shirts, white shorts, white stockings.
Change Colours: Red and white halved shirts, black shorts, black socks.
Club Captain: Glenn Roeder. *First Team Trainer:* Alan Harris.
Club Nickname: Rangers or R's.

QUEEN'S PARK RANGERS 1980–81 LEAGUE RECORD

Match No.	*Date*	*Venue*	*Opponents*	*Result*	*H/T Score*	*Goalscorers*	*Attendance*
1	Aug 16	A	Oldham Ath	L 0-1	0-1		6986
2	19	H	Bristol R	W 4-0	0-0	Shanks, Fereday 2, Hazell	9731
3	23	H	Swansea C	D 0-0	0-0		10,854
4	30	A	Chelsea	D 1-1	1-0	Langley	23,381
5	Sept 6	A	Notts Co	L 1-2	0-2	Hill (pen)	7197
6	13	H	Newcastle U	L 1-2	0-1	Hazell	10,865
7	20	A	Sheffield W	L 0-1	0-1		15,195
8	27	H	Bristol C	W 4-0	2-0	Neal 2, Shanks, Langley	8551
9	Oct 4	A	Blackburn R	L 1-2	0-0	Neal	12,209
10	7	H	Orient	D 0-0	0-0		9627
11	11	H	Bolton W	W 3-1	1-0	Langley, Burke (pen), Neal	8641
12	18	A	Derby Co	D 3-3	1-1	King 2, Langley	16,021
13	22	A	Cardiff C	L 0-1	0-1		4489
14	25	H	Wrexham	L 0-1	0-1		9050
15	Nov 1	A	Grimsby T	D 0-0	0-0		10,015
16	8	H	Luton T	W 3-2	2-2	Neal 2, King	10,082
17	11	A	Bristol R	W 2-1	2-0	King, Langley	6636
18	15	H	Oldham Ath	W 2-0	1-0	Silkman (pen), Neal	8223
19	22	A	Preston NE	L 2-3	0-1	Roeder, Neal	6725
20	29	H	Shrewsbury T	D 0-0	0-0		7982
21	Dec 6	A	Cambridge U	L 0-1	0-0		6349
22	19	A	Bolton W	W 2-1	1-1	Stainrod, Flanagan	6315
23	26	H	West Ham U	W 3-0	1-0	Silkman, Currie, Stainrod	23,811
24	27	A	Watford	D 1-1	1-0	King	22,911
25	Jan 10	H	Preston NE	D 1-1	0-0	Stainrod	8415
26	17	H	Chelsea	W 1-0	0-0	Langley	22,873
27	31	A	Swansea C	W 2-1	2-1	Langley, King	12,518
28	Feb 3	H	Cardiff C	W 2-0	0-0	Fenwick, Langley	9834
29	7	A	Newcastle U	L 0-1	0-0		20,442
30	14	H	Notts Co	D 1-1	0-0	Howe	11,457
31	21	A	Bristol C	W 1-0	0-0	Waddock	10,988
32	28	H	Sheffield W	L 1-2	0-0	Stainrod	15,104
33	Mar 7	H	Blackburn R	D 1-1	0-0	Francis	9513
34	21	H	Derby Co	W 3-1	1-1	Francis 2 (1 pen), Flanagan	8905
35	28	A	Wrexham	D 1-1	1-0	Waddock	5887
36	31	A	Orient	L 0-4	0-1		6724
37	Apr 4	H	Grimsby T	W 1-0	1-0	Francis (pen)	8906
38	11	A	Luton T	L 0-3	0-1		12,112
39	18	H	Watford	D 0-0	0-0		10,571
40	21	A	West Ham U	L 0-3	0-2		24,599
41	25	H	Cambridge U	W 5-0	2-0	Roeder, Sealy 2, Muir 2	6668
42	May 2	A	Shrewsbury T	D 3-3	2-1	Fenwick, Waddock, Flanagan	5714

Final League Position: 8

Goalscorers

League (56): Langley 8, Neal 8, King 6, Francis 4 (2 pens), Stainrod 4, Flanagan 3, Waddock 3, Fenwick 2, Fereday 2, Hazell 2, Roeder 2, Sealy 2, Shanks 2, Silkman 2 (1 pen), Muir 2, Burke 1 (pen), Currie 1, Hill 1 (pen), Howe 1.
League Cup (1): Langley.
F.A. Cup (1): Stainrod.

League Cup	Second Round	Derby Co (h)	0-0
		(a)	0-0 (won on pens)
	Third Round	Notts Co (a)	1-4
FA Cup	Third Round	Tottenham H (h)	0-0
		(a)	1-3

Woods	McCreery	Gillard	Waddock	Wicks	Roeder	Hill	Shanks	Walsh	Currie	Burke	Neal	Fereday	Hazell	Langley	King	Stewart	Howe	Wilkins	Silkman	Micklewhite	Stainrod	Fenwick	Flanagan	Burridge	Francis	Sealy	Neill	Muir	Hucker	*Match No.*
1	2	3	4	5	6	7	8	9*	10	11	12																			1
1	2	3	4	5	6	12	8		10	11		7	9*																	2
1	2	3	4	5	6		8		9	10		7*	12	11																3
1	2	3	4	5	6		8		10	11*		7		9													12			4
1	2	3	4	5	6	11	8					7*	12	9													10			5
1	2	3	4		6	12	8		10	11		7*	5	9																6
1	7	3*	4	5	6	11	2		10	12				9	8															7
1	2	3	4	5	6		8		10	11	7			9																8
1	2	3	4	5	6		8		10		11			9*	7	12														9
1	11	3	4	5	6		2		10		9			8	7															10
1	4	3	12	5			2		10	11	9		6	8*	7															11
1	7	3	4	5	6		2			11	9			10	8															12
1	7	3	4	5	6		2			11*	9		12	10	8															13
1	7	3	4	5	6		2			11*	9	12		10	8															14
1		3	4	5	7*		2				9			10	8		6	12	11											15
1	12	3	4	5	7		2				9			10	8*		6		11											16
1		3	4	5	7		2				9			10	8		6		11											17
1		3	4	5	7		2*				9			10	8		6		11	12										18
1		3	4	5	7		2				9				8		6		11		10									19
1		3	4	5	7		2				9			6	8				11		10									20
1		3	4	5	7		2		6		9				8				11		10									21
1		3		5	6		2		10						8				11		9	4	7							22
		3	12	5	6		2		10*						8				11		9	4	7	1						23
		3	10	5	6		2								8				11		9	4	7	1						24
		3		5	6		2		10		7				8				11		9	4		1						25
		3		5	6		2		10					7	8				11		9	4		1						26
		3	12	5	6		2		10					7	8				11		9*	4		1						27
		3		5	6		2		10					7	8				11		9	4		1						28
		3		5	6		2		10					7	8				11		9	4		1						29
		3					2		10				5	7	8		6		11		9	4		1						30
		3	12	5			2		10				6*	7	8				11		9	4		1						31
		3		5	6		2		10					7					11*		9	4	12	1	8					32
		3		5	6		2		10*					12					11		9	4	7	1	8					33
		3		5	6		2		10						12				11*			4	7	1	8	9				34
		3	11*	5	6		2		10						12							4	9	1	8	7				35
		3*	11	5	6		2		10										12			4	7	1	8	9				36
		3	11	5	6		2		10										4				7	1	8	9				37
		3*	11	5	6		2		10	12									4				7	1	8	9				38
		3	7	5	6				10	11												4	9	1	8		2			39
		3	7	5*	6				10	12												4	9	1	8	11	2			40
		3	4		6				10								5					2	9	1	8	7		11		41
		3	8		6				7								5	4				2	9			11		10	1	42
22	14	42	29	38	39	3	38	1	31	11	15	5	5	24	24	—	8	1	22	—	15	19	13	19	10	8	3	2	1	
	+ 1s		+ 4s			+ 2s				+ 3s	+ 1s	+ 1s	+ 3s	+ 1s	+ 2s	+ 1s		+ 1s	+ 1s	+ 1s			+ 1s				+ 1s			

Players continued from following page.

Ian Muir	5 6½	10 12	Coventry	QPR	2	2
			QPR			
Mike Flanagan	5 10½	11 10	Ilford	Tottenham H	—	—
				Charlton Ath	254	85
				Crystal Palace	56	8
				QPR	14	3
Simon Stainrod	6 1	11 13	Sheffield	Sheffield U	67	14
				Oldham Ath	69	21
				QPR	15	4
Ian Dawes			Croydon	QPR	—	—

QUEEN'S PARK RANGERS

	Ht	*Wt*	*Birthplace*	*Clubs*	*League App.*	*League Gls*
Goalkeepers						
Peter Hucker	6 4	13 1	London	QPR	1	—
				Cambridge U (on loan)	—	—
Andy Pape*	6 2	14 1	London	QPR	1	—
				Charlton Ath (on loan)	—	—
Chris Woods	6 2	12 8	Lincs	Nottingham F	—	—
				QPR	63	—
				Norwich C (on loan)	10	—
John Burridge	5 10	12 4	Workington	Workington	27	—
				Blackpool	134	—
				Aston V	65	—
				Southend U (on loan)	6	—
				Crystal Palace	88	—
				QPR	19	—
Defenders						
Martyn Rogers*	5 9	11 6	Nottingham	Manchester U	1	—
				QPR	2	—
Ian Gillard (England)	6 1¾	13 7	London	QPR	373	8
Don Shanks	5 11	10 8	London	Luton T	90	2
				QPR	180	10
Ernie Howe	6 2¾	12 12	London	Crystal Palace	—	—
				Fulham	70	10
				QPR	73	3
Glenn Roeder	6 2	12 9	Woodford	Orient	115	4
				QPR	106	15
Bob Hazell	6 1	14 7	Jamaica	Wolverhampton W	33	1
				QPR	37	3
Steve Wicks	6 2	13 2	Reading	Chelsea	118	5
				Derby Co	24	—
				QPR	73	—
Dean Wilkins	5 8½	11 8	London	QPR	2	—
Mark O'Connor			Rochford	QPR	—	—
Warren Neill	5 10	12 6	London	QPR	4	—
Midfield						
Gary Waddock (Eire)	5 10	11 12	Kingsbury	QPR	49	4
Tony Currie (England)	5 11	12 9	Edgware	Watford	18	9
				Sheffield U	313	55
				Leeds U	102	11
				QPR	59	4
David McCreery (N Ireland) (Contract cancelled March 1981)	5 6½	10 7	Belfast	Manchester U	87	7
				QPR	57	4
Andy King	5 9½	10 13	Luton	Luton T	33	9
				Everton	151	38
				QPR	26	6
Gerry Francis (England)	5 10½	12 1½	London	QPR	293	53
				Crystal Palace	59	7
				QPR	10	4
Barry Silkman	5 8	10 14	London	Hereford U	37	2
				Crystal Palace	48	7
				Plymouth Arg	14	2
				Luton T (on loan)	3	—
				Manchester C	19	3
				Brentford	14	1
				QPR	23	2
Terry Fenwick	5 10	10 10	Camden, Durham	Crystal Palace	70	—
				QPR	19	2
Forwards						
Martyn Busby	6 2	12 3	Slough	QPR	78	6
				Portsmouth (on loan)	6	1
				Notts Co	37	4
				Burnley (on loan)	4	1
				QPR	66	11
Mickey Walsh (Eire) (Contract cancelled Sept 1980)	5 10	11 6	Chorley	Blackpool	180	72
				Everton	20	1
				QPR	18	3
Gordon Hill (England) (Contract cancelled Jan 1981)	5 7	10 9	Sunbury-on-Thames	Millwall	86	20
				Manchester U	101	39
				Derby Co	24	5
				QPR	14	1
Steve Burke	5 9½	12 5	Nottingham	Nottingham F	—	—
				QPR	45	5
Dean Neal (Contract cancelled March 1981)	5 10½	12 0	London	QPR	23	8
Gary Micklewhite	5 6½	9 10½	Southwark	Manchester U	—	—
				QPR	1	—
Ian Stewart	5 6½	11 10	Belfast	QPR	1	—
Wayne Fereday	5 9¼	11 8	Birmingham	QPR	6	2
Tony Sealy	5 8	10 12	London	Southampton	7	—
				Crystal Palace	24	5
				Port Vale (on loan)	17	6
				QPR	8	2

Note: Players continued on previous page.

READING | Division 3

Chairman: F. V. Waller.

Directors: L. Davies, J. Brooks, K. Darvall, F. J. Briggs.

Manager: Maurice Evans.

Secretary/Manager: Roy Bentley.

Year Formed: 1871. *Turned Professional:* 1895.

Limited Company: 1895.

Previous Grounds: 1871, Reading Recreation; Reading Cricket Ground; 1882, Coley Park; 1889, Caversham Cricket Ground; 18[illegible]5, Elm Park.

Football League Record:
1920 Original Member of Division 3; 1921–26 Division 3(S); 1926–31 Division 2; 1931–58 Division 3(S); 1958–71 Division 3; 1971–76 Division 4; 1976–77 Division 3; 1977–79 Division 4; 1979– Division 3.

Honours: *Football League:* Division 2 best season: 14th, 1926–27; Division 3(S) – Champions 1925–26; Runners-up 1931–32, 1934–35, 1948–49, 1951–52; Division 4 – Champions 1978–79. *FA Cup:* semi-final 1927. *Football League Cup* best season: 4th rd, 1965, 1966, 1978.
Record Victory: 10-2 v Crystal Palace, Division 3(S), 4 Sept, 1946.
Record Defeat: 0-18 v Preston NE, FA Cup, 1st rd, 1893–94.
Most League Points: 65, Division 4, 1978–79.
Most League Goals: 112, Division 3(S), 1951–52.
Highest League Scorer in Season: Ronnie Blackman, 39, Division 3(S), 1951–52.
Most League Goals in Total Aggregate: Ronnie Blackman, 156, 1947–54.
Most Capped Player: Pat McConnell, 8, Ireland.
Most League Appearances: Steve Death, 468, 1969–81.
Record Transfer Fee Received: £60,000 from Southampton for Tommy Jenkins, Dec 1969.
Record Transfer Fee Paid: £50,000 to Charlton Ath for Dave Shipperley, Sept 1979.
Previous Managers since the War: Joe Edelston, Ted Drake, Jack Smith, Harry Johnston, Roy Bentley, Jack Mansell, Charlie Hurley.
Address of Supporters Club: Reading Football Supporters Club, Elm Park, Norfolk Road, Reading.

Elm Park, Norfolk Road, Reading. Telephone Reading 57878/9/0. *Ground capacity:* 27,200. *Record attendance:* 33,042 v Brentford, FA Cup 5th rd, 19 Feb, 1927. *Record receipts:* £25,972 v Southampton, League Cup 4th rd, 8 Nov, 1978. *Pitch measurements:* 112yd×77yd.
How to get there: Corporation specials from St Mary's Butts (town centre) and from Northumberland Avenue. Usual buses within a few minutes of the ground. Nearest railway station, Reading.
Match tickets: Stand tickets are bookable in advance for all first-team matches 14 days before the match.
Car parking: Space is available for approximately 300 cars adjoining the ground entrance in Norfolk Road and Tilehurst Road.
Entertainments/catering facilities: Catering is available in each of the five stands and also on the terraces.
Club shop: Shops in Norfolk Road and on the West Terrace are open on match days selling all types of souvenirs.
Handbooks/programmes: The Supporters' Club produces a handbook and these are available on application to the club. Unsold programmes are available after each match at the programme shop on the West Terrace.
Extra information: Reading first appeared in the FA Cup 1st rd in 1877; only Notts County of the present League clubs played so long ago.
Club Colours: Blue and white hoops, white shorts, white stockings, two blue rings.
Change Colours: Yellow.
First Team Trainer: Stewart Henderson.
Club Nickname: The Royals.

READING 1980–81 LEAGUE RECORD

Match No.	Date	Venue	Opponents	Result	H/T Score	Goalscorers	Attendance
1	Aug 16	H	Walsall	W 2-0	1-0	Mower (og), Beavon	4369
2	19	A	Gillingham	L 0-2	0-1		5192
3	23	A	Brentford	W 2-1	1-1	Earles, Dixon	6720
4	30	H	Swindon T	W 4-1	1-0	Earles, Webb, Bowman (pen), Dixon	6405
5	Sept 6	A	Huddersfield T	L 1-4	0-1	Wanklyn	7312
6	13	H	Sheffield U	W 1-0	1-0	Beavon	7249
7	17	H	Plymouth Arg	D 1-1	1-0	Sanchez	5859
8	20	A	Rotherham U	L 0-2	0-2		4461
9	27	H	Barnsley	W 3-2	2-2	Earles 2, Webb	5380
10	30	A	Plymouth Arg	L 1-2	1-1	Beavon	11,480
11	Oct 4	H	Millwall	W 4-1	3-0	Bowman, Hicks, Webb, Dibble (og)	5690
12	7	A	Newport Co	D 0-0	0-0		5545
13	11	A	Chester	L 0-1	0-0		2444
14	18	H	Chesterfield	L 2-3	0-1	Webb, Dixon	5904
15	22	H	Colchester U	W 1-0	1-0	Williams	3935
16	28	A	Charlton Ath	L 2-4	0-2	Earles, Webb	6162
17	Nov 1	H	Exeter C	W 2-1	1-0	Hicks, Williams	4622
18	8	A	Burnley	W 2-1	1-1	Webb, Dixon	6910
19	12	H	Gillingham	L 0-1	0-0		4648
20	15	A	Walsall	D 2-2	1-2	Williams, Webb	3583
21	29	H	Blackpool	W 3-0	2-0	Earles 2, Kearney	3968
22	Dec 6	A	Hull C	L 0-2	0-2		3130
23	20	H	Fulham	D 0-0	0-0		4455
24	26	A	Portsmouth	D 0-0	0-0		17,412
25	27	H	Oxford U	L 0-1	0-0		7019
26	Jan 2	H	Chester	W 3-0	0-0	Kearney, Sanchez, Dixon	3804
27	10	H	Carlisle U	W 3-1	2-1	Hetzke 2 (1 pen), Dixon	3957
28	17	A	Blackpool	D 0-0	0-0		3273
29	24	A	Swindon T	L 1-3	0-1	Bowman	8100
30	31	H	Brentford	D 0-0	0-0		6129
31	Feb 7	A	Sheffield U	L 0-2	0-1		8601
32	10	A	Carlisle U	D 0-0	0-0		3889
33	14	H	Huddersfield T	W 2-1	0-0	Beavon 2	5290
34	18	H	Newport Co	D 1-1	1-1	Heale	3876
35	21	A	Barnsley	W 3-2	2-0	Earles, Dixon 2	13,304
36	28	H	Rotherham U	D 1-1	0-1	Earles	5630
37	Mar 8	A	Millwall	L 1-2	1-0	Beavon	7535
38	22	A	Colchester U	W 2-1	2-1	Heale 2	3703
39	28	H	Charlton Ath	L 1-3	1-1	Hetzke	6989
40	Apr 4	A	Exeter C	L 1-3	0-1	Kearney	3890
41	11	H	Burnley	L 1-3	0-1	Laws (og)	3728
42	18	A	Oxford U	L 1-2	1-2	Hetzke	5386
43	20	H	Portsmouth	W 2-1	2-0	Dixon, Hetzke	7061
44	25	A	Fulham	W 2-1	1-0	Dixon 2	4601
45	May 2	H	Hull C	W 2-0	1-0	Dixon 2	3159
46	5	A	Chesterfield	L 2-3	1-3	Heale, Kearney	3059

Final League Position: 10

Goalscorers

League (62): Dixon 13, Earles 9, Webb 7, Beavon 6, Hetzke 5 (1 pen), Heale 4, Kearney 4, Bowman 3 (1 pen), Williams 3, Hicks 2, Sanchez 2, Wanklyn 1, own goals 3.
League Cup (5): Heale 2, Hetzke 2, Earles.
F.A. Cup (1): Earles.

League Cup	First Round	Northampton T (a)	2-0
		(h)	2-3
	Second Round	Luton T (h)	0-2
		(a)	1-1
FA Cup	First Round	Fulham (h)	1-2

Death	Joslyn	White	Bowman	Hetzke	Shipperley	Earles	Heale	Dixon	Sanchez	Beavon	Webb	Henderson	Williams	Cheetham	Hicks	Wanklyn	Lewis	Moreline	Kearney	Alexander	Barnes	Fearon	Wood	Cullen	*Match No.*
1	2	3	4	5	6	7	8	9	10	11															1
1	2	3	4	5	6	7	8	9*	10	11	12														2
1	2	3	4	5	6	7	8	9	10	11															3
1	2		4	5	6*	7		9	10	11	8	3	12												4
1	2		4	6		7		9	10	11				3	5	8									5
1	2		4	6		7		9	10	11		3			5	8									6
1	2		4	6		7		9	10	11		3			5	8									7
1	2		4	6		7		9	10	11*	8	3			5	12									8
1	2		4	6		7*		9	10	11	8	3			5	12									9
1	2		4	6				9	10	11	8	3			5		7								10
1	2		4	6		7		9		11	8	3			5		10								11
1	2		4	6		7		9	12	11	8*				5		10	3							12
1	2		4	6		7		9	12	11	8*				5		10	3							13
1			4	6		7		9	2	11	8	3			5		10								14
1	2			6		7		9	10	11	4		8		5		3								15
1	2		4	6		7		9	10	11	8				5		3								16
1	2		4	6		7		9	10*	11	8		12		5		3								17
1	2		4	6				9	10	11	8		7		5		3								18
1	2		4	6				9	10	11	8		7		5		3								19
1	2		4*	6		12		9	10	11	8		7		5		3								20
1			4	6		7			10	11		2	9		5		3		8						21
1			4	6		7			10	11*	12	2	9		5		3		8						22
1			4	6		7			10	11	9	2			5		3		8						23
1			4	6		7			10	11	9	2			5		3		8						24
1			4	6		7	12		10	11*	9	2			5		3		8						25
1	11		4*	6		7		12	10		9		2		5		3		8						26
1	10			6		7*		9	11		4		2		5		3		8	12					27
1	10		4	6		7		9	11				2		5		3		8						28
1	10		4	6		7		9	11		12		2		5*		3		8						29
1	10		4	6		7*	8	9		12	11		2				3		5						30
1	10*		4	6		7	12	9		8			2	11			3		5						31
1	10		4	6		7	12	9		8			2	11			3		5*						32
1	3		4	6		7	10	9		8			2	11					5						33
1	3		4	6		7*	10	9		8	12		2	11					5						34
1	3		4	6		7	10	9		8	12		2	11*					5						35
1	3		4	6		7	10	9	12	8			2	11*					5						36
1	3		4			7	10	9	11	8			2		6				5						37
1	3		4	6		7	9		11	10			2		5				8						38
1	3		4	6		7	9	8	11	10			2						5						39
1	7*		4	6		11	9	12	10				2				3		8		5				40
	10		4	6		7	9*		11	8			2				3		5			1	12		41
			4	6			10	9	11	7			2				3		8			1	5		42
	7		4	6			9	10	11				2				3		8			1	5		43
	7		4	6			9	10	11				2				3		8			1	5		44
	11		4	6			10	9			7						3		8			1	5	2	45
	11		4	6		12	10*	9			7						3		8			1	5	2	46
40	39	3	44	45	4	37	18	37	34	36	22	13	25	7	27	3	30	2	26	—	1	6	5	2	
						+ 2s	+ 3s	+ 2s	+ 3s	+ 1s	+ 5s		+ 2s			+ 2s				+ 1s			+ 1s		

READING

	Ht	*Wt*	*Birthplace*	*Clubs*	*League App.*	*League Gls*
Goalkeepers						
Steve Death	5 8	11 7	Elmswell	West Ham U	1	—
				Reading	468	—
Ron Fearon	5 11	12 0	Romford	QPR	—	—
				Reading	6	—
Defenders						
Martin Hicks	6 3	13 6	Stratford-upon-Avon	Charlton Ath	—	—
				Reading	93	5
Dave Moreline*	5 9	10 8	Stepney	Fulham	70	—
				Reading	166	—
Stewart Henderson	5 8	11 8	Bridge of Allan	Chelsea	—	—
				Brighton	198	1
				Reading	159	6
Steve Hetzke	6 2	11 10	Marlborough	Reading	229	21
Mark White	5 9	11 0	Sheffield	Sheffield W	—	—
				Reading	119	—
Dave Shipperley	6 3	14 0	Hillingdon	Charlton Ath	100	8
				Plymouth Arg (on loan)	1	—
				Gillingham	144	11
				Charlton Ath	53	6
				Reading	19	—
John Cullen	5 7½	10 10	Oxford	Reading	3	—
Steve Wood	6 0	11 9	Bracknell	Reading	8	—
Mike Barnes (Apprentice)			Reading	Reading	1	—
Midfield						
Wayne Wanklyn*	5 7	10 7	Hull	Reading	54	3
Richie Bowman	5 6	10 7	Lewisham	Charlton Ath	96	7
				Reading	194	30
Alan Lewis	5 8	10 12	Oxford	Derby Co	2	—
				Peterborough U (on loan)	10	1
				Brighton	3	—
				Sheffield W (on loan)	—	—
				Reading	113	5
Hughie Cheetham*	5 8	11 0	Manchester	Crewe Alex	96	—
				Reading	12	—
Roger Joslyn	5 10	11 2	Colchester	Colchester U	98	4
				Aldershot	186	17
				Watford	182	17
				Reading	67	1
Stuart Beavon	5 6½	10 4	Oxford	Tottenham H	4	—
				Notts Co (on loan)	6	—
				Reading	37	6
Neil Webb	5 11	11 6	Reading	Reading	32	7
Forwards						
Pat Earles	5 7	11 6	Titchfield	Southampton	12	1
				Reading	183	54
Jerry Williams	5 11	11 10	Didcot	Reading	61	7
Ollie Kearns*	6 0	12 0	Banbury	Reading	86	40
Mike Kearney	6 0	12 0	Glasgow	Shrewsbury T	149	41
				Chester	38	5
				Reading	87	24
				Chester	9	—
				Reading	26	4
Lawrie Sanchez	5 11	11 7	Reading	Reading	130	12
John Alexander*	5 11	10 11	Liverpool	Millwall	15	2
				Reading	25	9
Gary Heale	5 11	11 6¾	Canvey	Luton T	7	1
				Exeter C (on loan)	4	—
				Reading	58	12
Kerry Dixon	6 0	13 0	Luton	Dunstable	(not known)	
				Reading	39	13

ROCHDALE Division 4

Joint Chairmen: D. H. Wrigley LL B, J. B. Faulks FRICS.
Directors: T. Butterworth, G. Morris FCA, D. Kilpatrick, C. W. Walkden, W. H. C. Dronsfield.
Manager: Peter Madden.
Secretary: T. Nichol.
Year Formed: 1907.
Turned Professional: 1907.
Limited Company: 1910.

Football League Record:
1921 Elected to Division 3(N); 1958–59 Division 3; 1959–69 Division 4; 1969–74 Division 3; 1974– Division 4.

Honours: *Football League:* Division 3 best season: 9th, 1969–70; Division 3(N) – Runners-up 1923–24, 1926–27. *FA Cup* best season: 4th rd, 1970–71. *Football League Cup:* Runners-up 1962 (record for 4th Division club).

Record Victory: 8-1 v Chesterfield, Division 3(N), 18 Dec, 1926.
Record Defeat: 0-8 v Wrexham, Division 3(N), 28 Dec, 1929.
Most League Points: 62, Division 3(N), 1923–24.
Most League Goals: 105, Division 3(N), 1926–27.
Highest League Scorer in Season: Albert Whitehurst, 44, Division 3(N), 1926–27.
Most League Goals in Total Aggregate: Albert Whitehurst, 117, 1923–28.
Most Capped Player: None.
Most League Appearances: Graham Smith, 317, 1966–74.
Record Transfer Fee Received: £40,000 plus Malcolm Darling from Norwich C for David Cross, Oct 1971.
Record Transfer Fee Paid: £12,000 to Sunderland for Alan Weir, June 1979.
Previous Managers since the War: Ted Goodier, Jack Warner, Harry Catterick, Jack Marshall, Tony Collins, Bob Stokoe, Len Richley, Dick Conner, Walter Joyce, Brian Green, Mike Ferguson, Doug Collins, Bob Stokoe.
Address of Supporters Club: Rochdale AFC Soccer Shop, Spotland, Sandy Lane, Rochdale.

Spotland, Willbutts Lane, Rochdale. Telephone 0706-44648/9. *Ground capacity:* 28,000. *Record attendance:* 24,231 v Notts County, FA Cup 2nd rd, 10 Dec, 1949. *Record receipts:* £3996.83 v Coventry C, FA Cup 3rd rd, 11 Jan, 1971. *Pitch measurements:* 113yd×75yd.
How to get there: Bus station – Norden for Churchill Street; Greave for ground.
Match tickets: Seats can be reserved in advance.
Car parking: Car parking at the ground and in the adjacent side-streets.
Entertainments/catering facilities: A social club in the car park.
Club shop: Sells all types of souvenirs and programmes.
Handbooks/programmes: Programmes available on subscription.
Extra information: Social club.
Club Colours: Royal blue shirts with white collar and trim, white shorts with blue trim, blue stockings with white ring.
Change Colours: Red and green striped shirts, red shorts with green trim, red stockings.
Club Nickname: The Dale.

ROCHDALE 1980–81 LEAGUE RECORD

Match No.	Date	Venue	Opponents	Result	H/T Score	Goalscorers	Attendance
1	Aug 16	A	Stockport Co	D 2-2	2-1	Hilditch, Esser	2739
2	19	H	Scunthorpe U	W 4-0	2-0	Hilditch 2, Burke, Taylor	2427
3	23	H	Hartlepool U	D 1-1	1-0	Hilditch	2803
4	29	A	Tranmere R	L 1-3	0-2	Esser	1826
5	Sept 6	H	Torquay U	W 2-1	1-1	Martinez, Wann	1777
6	13	A	Peterborough U	D 2-2	1-0	Hilditch, Wellings	3906
7	17	A	Hereford U	L 0-3	0-1		2475
8	20	H	Bradford C	L 0-2	0-2		3221
9	27	A	AFC Bournemouth	L 1-2	1-1	Hilditch	2557
10	30	H	Hereford U	D 0-0	0-0		2328
11	Oct 4	H	Wigan Ath	W 3-0	1-0	Wann 2, Hilditch	3479
12	8	A	Lincoln C	L 0-3	0-3		3523
13	11	A	Aldershot	D 0-0	0-0		3017
14	18	H	Bury	W 2-1	2-0	Hilditch, Wellings	4306
15	21	H	Wimbledon	W 2-0	2-0	O'Loughlin, Wellings	2391
16	25	A	Crewe Alex	L 0-1	0-0		3391
17	28	A	Darlington	D 4-4	2-2	Taylor, Esser, Jones, Wellings	1579
18	Nov 1	H	Mansfield T	L 1-4	0-2	O'Loughlin	2636
19	4	H	Lincoln C	W 1-0	0-0	Hilditch	2257
20	8	A	Port Vale	D 1-1	0-0	Esser	2774
21	11	A	Scunthorpe U	D 1-1	0-1	Wellings	2019
22	29	A	Doncaster R	W 2-1	0-1	Wellings, Lister (og)	2502
23	Dec 6	H	Southend U	L 0-2	0-0		2214
24	12	H	Stockport Co	W 2-1	1-1	Martinez, Wellings	1291
25	20	A	Northampton T	L 2-3	1-2	Wellings 2	1705
26	26	H	Halifax T	D 1-1	1-0	Wellings (pen)	2623
27	27	A	York C	W 2-1	0-1	Wellings, Martinez	2828
28	Jan 3	H	Crewe Alex	W 2-0	1-0	Jones 2	2540
29	17	H	Doncaster R	D 2-2	0-1	Taylor, Wellings (pen)	3021
30	24	H	Tranmere R	W 3-1	2-1	Wann, Seal, Wellings	2731
31	31	A	Hartlepool U	D 2-2	0-1	Taylor, Esser	3819
32	Feb 7	H	Peterborough U	L 2-3	2-0	Wann, Burke	2865
33	14	A	Torquay U	L 0-2	0-0		1724
34	21	H	AFC Bournemouth	D 0-0	0-0		1846
35	Mar 7	A	Wigan Ath	W 1-0	0-0	Taylor	6029
36	8	A	Bradford C	L 1-2	0-1	Esser	2926
37	14	H	Aldershot	L 0-2	0-0		1832
38	21	A	Bury	L 1-3	0-0	Hilditch	3931
39	28	H	Darlington	D 0-0	0-0		1845
40	Apr 4	A	Mansfield T	D 2-2	1-1	Hilditch, Wellings	2597
41	12	H	Port Vale	W 2-1	1-0	Martinez, Esser	2590
42	18	H	York C	W 3-2	1-0	Taylor, Hilditch, Jones	1651
43	20	A	Halifax T	L 0-2	0-0		2278
44	28	A	Wimbledon	L 1-4	1-2	Wann	3884
45	May 1	A	Southend U	D 1-1	1-0	Jones	10,668
46	3	H	Northampton T	L 0-1	0-0		1474

Final League Position: 15

Goalscorers

League (60): Wellings 14 (2 pens), Hilditch 12, Esser 7, Taylor 6, Wann 6, Jones 5, Martinez 4, Burke 2, O'Loughlin 2, Seal 1, own goal 1.
League Cup (1): Martinez.
F.A. Cup (1): Jones.

League Cup	First Round	Carlisle U (a)	0-2
		(h)	1-1
FA Cup	First Round	Mansfield T (a)	1-3

Pearce	Jones	Snookes	Esser	Cliff	Taylor	Wann	O'Loughlin	Hilditch	Wellings	Martinez	Burke	Weir	Crawford	Hoy	Seal	Higgins	*Match No.*
1	2	3	4	5	6	7	8	9	10	11							1
1	2	3	4		6	7	8	9	10	11	5						2
1	2	3	4		6	7	8	9	10	11	5						3
1	2		8	3	6	7	4	10	9	11		5					4
1	2	3	4		6	7	8	9	10	11	5						5
	2	3	8		6	7	4	9	10	11	5		1				6
	2	3	8		6	7	4	9	10	11	5		1				7
	2	3	4*		6	7	8	9	10	11	5		1	12			8
	2	3	4		6	7	8	9	10	11	5		1				9
	2	3	4*		6	7	8	9	10	11	5		1		12		10
	2	3	4		6	7	8	9	10	11	5		1				11
	2	3	4*		6	7	8	9	10	11	5	12	1				12
	2	3	4		6	7*	8	9	10	11	5	12	1				13
	2	3	4		6		8	9	10	11	5		1	7			14
	2	3*	4		6		8	9	10	11	5		1	7	12		15
	2		4		6	12	8	9	10	11	5	3	1	7*			16
	2		4		6	7	8	9	10	11	5	3	1				17
	2	3	4*		6	7	8	9	10	11	5		1		12		18
	7	3			6		8	9	10	11	5	2	1		4		19
	7	2	12		6		8	9	10	11	5	3	1		4*		20
	7*	3	12				8	9	10	11	5	2	1		4	6	21
		3	4		6*		8	9	10	11	5	2	1		7	12	22
	12	3	7				8	9	10*	11	5	2	1		4	6	23
		3	4			7	8	9	10	11	5	2	1			6	24
	12	3*	4			7	8	9	10	11	5	2	1			6	25
	12	3	4*		5	7	8	9	10	11	6	2	1				26
	2	3			6	7	8	9	10	11	5		1		4		27
	2	3			6*	7	8	9	10	11	5	12	1		4		28
	2	3			6	7	8	9	10	11	5		1		4		29
	2	3			6	7	8	9*	10	11	5	12	1		4		30
	2	3	4		6	7	8		10	11	5		1		9		31
	2	3	4		6	7		9	10	11	5		1		8		32
	2	3	4		6	7		9	10	11	5*	8	1		12		33
	2	3	4		6	7	8	9	10	11	5		1				34
	2		4	3	6	7	8		10	11	5		1		9		35
	2		4	3	6	7	8	9	10		5		1		11		36
	2	3	4*		6	7	8	9	10		5	12	1		11		37
	12	3		5	6	7	8	9	10	11	2*	4	1				38
	2	3	4		6	7	8	9	10	11		5	1				39
	2	3	4*		6	7	8	9	10	11		5	1		12		40
	2	3	4*		6	7	8	9	10	11	5		1		12		41
	2	3			6*	7	8	9	10	11	5	12	1		4		42
	2	3				7	8	9	10	11	5	6	1		4		43
	2	3			6	7	8	9	10	11	5	4	1				44
	2	3			6	7	8	9	10	11	5	4	1				45
	2	3	4		5*	7	8	9	10	11		6	1		12		46
5	40	41	34	5	41	38	44	44	46	44	41	19	41	3	16	4	
	+ 4s		+ 2s			+ 1s						+ 6s		+ 1s	+ 7s	+ 1s	

ROCHDALE

	Ht	Wt	Birthplace	Clubs	League App.	League Gls
Goalkeeper						
Graeme Crawford	6 2	13 0	Falkirk	E Stirling	2	—
				Sheffield U	2	—
				Mansfield T (on loan)	2	—
				York C	235	—
				Scunthorpe U	104	—
				York C	17	—
				Rochdale	41	—
Defenders						
Eddie Cliff*	5 10	11 5	Liverpool	Burnley	21	—
				Notts Co	5	—
				Lincoln C (on loan)	3	—
				Chicago S	(not known)	
				Tranmere R	50	4
				Rochdale	26	—
Ted Oliver*	5 6	9 6	Manchester	Rochdale	22	1
Eric Snookes	5 7	10 0	Birmingham	Preston NE	20	—
				Crewe Alex	34	—
				Southport	110	2
				Rochdale	106	1
Brian Taylor	5 11	11 9	Hodthorpe	Middlesbrough	18	1
				Doncaster R	119	12
				Rochdale	103	10
Alan Weir	5 9	10 0	S Shields	Sunderland	1	—
				Rochdale	64	3
Peter Burke	6 0	11 10	Rotherham	Barnsley	35	1
				Halifax T	85	9
				Rochdale	41	2
Alan Jones*	5 6	10 11	Grimethorpe	Huddersfield T	32	—
				Halifax T	109	6
				Chesterfield	39	6
				Lincoln C	26	4
				Bradford C	19	1
				Rochdale	44	5
Midfield						
Nigel O'Loughlin	5 8½	10 10	Denbigh	Shrewsbury T	33	7
				Rochdale	212	12
Dennis Wann	5 8	10 11	Blackpool	Blackpool	17	—
				York C	66	7
				Southend U (on loan)	—	—
				Chesterfield (on loan)	3	—
				Hartlepool (on loan)	2	—
				Darlington	121	13
				Rochdale	67	7
Eric Probert	5 7½	10 9½	South Kirby	Burnley	67	11
(Contract cancelled Sept 1980)				Notts Co	122	14
				Huddersfield T (on loan)	—	—
				Darlington	21	—
				Rochdale	—	—
Bob Higgins*	6 2	13 6	Bolsover	Burnley	3	—
				Hartlepool U (on loan)	2	—
				Rochdale	5	—
Eugene Martinez	5 8	10 10	Chelmsford	Bradford C	52	5
				Rochdale	44	4
Forwards						
David Esser	5 6	10 2	Bowden	Everton	—	—
				Rochdale	156	24
Bobby Hoy	5 7½	10 0	Halifax	Huddersfield T	144	20
(Contract cancelled Feb 1981)				Blackburn R	19	—
				Halifax T	30	7
				York C	14	1
				Rochdale	66	12
Mark Hilditch	5 11	11 8	Shaw	Rochdale	118	19
Jimmy Seal*	5 10	11 8	Pontefract	Wolverhampton W	1	—
				Walsall (on loan)	40	14
				Barnsley	43	12
				York C	161	43
				Darlington	122	19
				Rochdale	53	4
Barry Wellings	5 7	11 0	Liverpool	Everton	—	—
				York C	47	9
				Rochdale	46	14
Nick Stanley*			Bolton	Rochdale	—	—

ROTHERHAM UNITED Division 2

Chairman: Anton Johnson.

Directors: D. G. Travell, C. R. Wright.

Player-Manager: Emlyn Hughes. *Secretary:* J. E. Bennison.

Year Formed: 1884. *Turned Professional:* 1905.

Limited Company: 1920.

Previous Names: 1884, Thornhill United; 1905, Rotherham County; 1925, amalgamated with Rotherham Town under Rotherham United.

Previous Grounds: Red House Ground; 1907, Millmoor.

Football League Record:
1893 Rotherham Town elected to Division 2; 1896 Failed re-election; 1919 Rotherham County elected to Division 2; 1923–51 Division 3(N); 1951–68 Division 2; 1968–73 Division 3; 1973–75 Division 4; 1975–81 Division 3; 1981– Division 2.

Honours: *Football League:* Division 2 best season: 3rd, 1954–55 (equal points with champions and runners-up); Division 3 – Champions 1980–81; Division 3(N) – Champions 1950–51; Runners-up 1946–47, 1947–48, 1948–49. *FA Cup* best season: 5th rd, 1953, 1968. *Football League Cup:* Runners-up 1961.

Record Victory: 8-0 v Oldham Ath, Division 3(N), 26 May, 1947.

Record Defeat: 1-11 v Bradford C, Division 3(N), 25 Aug, 1928.

Most League Points: 71, Division 3(N), 1950–51.

Most League Goals: 114, Division 3(N), 1946–47.

Highest League Scorer in Season: Wally Ardron, 38, Division 3(N), 1946–47.

Most League Goals in Total Aggregate: Gladstone Guest, 130, 1946–56.

Most Capped Player: Harold Millership, 6, Wales.

Most League Appearances: Danny Williams, 459, 1946–62.

Record Transfer Fee Received: £100,000 from Sunderland for Dave Watson, Dec 1970.

Record Transfer Fee Paid: £30,000 to Peterborough U for Billy McEwan, Aug 1979.

Previous Managers since the War: Reg Freeman, Andy Smailes, Tom Johnston, Danny Williams, Jack Mansell, Tommy Docherty, Jimmy McAnearney, Jimmy McGuigan, Ian Porterfield.

Address of Supporters Club: Red and White Shop, c/o Millmoor, Rotherham.

Millmoor Ground, Rotherham. Telephone Rotherham 562434. *Telegraphic address:* 'Holmes Millmoor, Rotherham'. *Ground capacity:* 19,000. *Record attendance:* 25,000 v Sheffield U, Division 2, 13 Dec, 1952 and v Sheffield W, Division 2, 26 Jan, 1952. *Record receipts:* £23,977 v Sheffield U, Division 3, 6 Oct, 1979. *Pitch measurements:* 115yd×76yd.

How to get there: Corporation buses from town centre. Also regular service buses from Sheffield to town centre. Nearest railway station, Rotherham on the line from Sheffield. Station across road from ground.

Match tickets: Seats can be reserved one month before the match.

Car parking: There are parks in Kimberworth Road and Main St (the municipal car park); both are within easy reach of the ground.

Entertainments/catering facilities: There are refreshment kiosks on all four sides of the ground and also behind the grandstand, and the Windmill where meals may be obtained if booked in advance and drinks are served during licensing hours.

Club shop: Sited on the forecourt of the ground; stocks all types of souvenirs.

Handbooks/programmes: No handbook, but programmes may be obtained from the club or the club shop.

Extra information: Rotherham full-back Irvine Rhodes scored twice on his début for Rotherham against Hartlepools in March 1937.

Club Colours: Red shirts, white collar, white sleeves, white (or black) shorts, red stockings.

Change Colours: Yellow shirts with blue trim, blue shorts with yellow trim, yellow stockings.

Club Coach:

Club Nickname: The Merry Millers.

ROTHERHAM UNITED 1980–81 LEAGUE RECORD

Match No.	Date	Venue	Opponents	Result	H/T Score	Goalscorers	Attendance
1	Aug 16	H	Fulham	D 2-2	1-1	Forrest, Moore	4436
2	20	A	Blackpool	D 0-0	0-0		10,427
3	23	A	Portsmouth	L 1-3	1-1	Gooding	14,767
4	30	H	Huddersfield T	D 0-0	0-0		6961
5	Sept 6	H	Barnsley	W 2-0	0-0	Finney, Moore	10,766
6	13	A	Swindon T	L 1-2	1-0	Towner	5498
7	16	A	Walsall	W 2-0	2-0	Halom, Towner	4500
8	20	H	Reading	W 2-0	2-0	Moore 2	4461
9	27	A	Sheffield U	W 2-1	1-0	Finney, Rhodes	17,955
10	30	H	Walsall	W 2-1	1-0	Moore, Seasman	6842
11	Oct 4	H	Exeter C	W 3-1	1-1	Henson, Seasman, Moore	6889
12	7	A	Chesterfield	L 0-2	0-0		10,638
13	11	A	Burnley	D 1-1	0-0	Towner (pen)	9691
14	18	H	Gillingham	W 2-0	0-0	Forrest, Winn	5903
15	21	H	Chester	D 0-0	0-0		6635
16	25	A	Colchester U	D 0-0	0-0		2623
17	29	A	Oxford U	D 1-1	0-0	Moore (pen)	3064
18	Nov 1	H	Millwall	W 3-0	2-0	Moore 2 (1 pen), Henson	5742
19	4	H	Chesterfield	D 0-0	0-0		11,093
20	8	A	Charlton Ath	L 0-2	0-1		7338
21	11	H	Blackpool	W 4-0	2-0	Moore 3 (1 pen), Gooding	6367
22	15	A	Fulham	D 1-1	1-0	Fern	4011
23	29	H	Newport Co	W 1-0	0-0	Moore	5512
24	Dec 6	A	Plymouth Arg	L 1-3	0-1	Fern	6155
25	20	H	Brentford	W 4-1	2-0	Moore, Fern, Towner 2	5913
26	26	A	Hull C	W 2-1	1-0	Gooding, Henson	8618
27	27	H	Carlisle U	W 3-0	2-0	Moore 2, Fern	8450
28	Jan 3	A	Gillingham	D 0-0	0-0		3748
29	10	H	Oxford U	D 0-0	0-0		6705
30	16	A	Newport Co	W 1-0	0-0	Fern	4783
31	24	A	Huddersfield T	L 0-1	0-0		16,687
32	31	H	Portsmouth	W 3-0	1-0	Seasman 2, Towner	7588
33	Feb 7	H	Swindon T	W 1-0	0-0	Gooding	7162
34	21	H	Sheffield U	W 2-1	0-1	Towner, Moore	11,905
35	28	A	Reading	D 1-1	1-0	Fern	5630
36	Mar 18	A	Exeter C	L 1-2	1-0	Moore	4494
37	21	A	Chester	W 1-0	1-0	Fern	3945
38	28	H	Colchester U	W 2-0	1-0	Moore 2	7956
39	31	H	Burnley	W 1-0	0-0	Moore	9762
40	Apr 4	A	Millwall	W 1-0	1-0	Fern	5041
41	11	H	Charlton Ath	W 3-0	2-0	Seasman, Mullen, Fern	13,515
42	18	A	Carlisle U	W 1-0	1-0	Fern	6798
43	20	H	Hull C	D 1-1	0-0	Seasman	11,602
44	25	A	Brentford	L 1-2	0-0	Moore	6910
45	28	A	Barnsley	L 0-1	0-1		25,935
46	May 2	H	Plymouth Arg	W 2-1	1-1	Moore, Fern	11,497

Final League Position: 1

Goalscorers

League (62): Moore 23 (3 pens), Fern 11, Towner 7 (1 pen), Seasman 6, Gooding 4, Henson 3, Finney 2, Forrest 2, Halom 1, Mullen 1, Rhodes 1, Winn 1.
League Cup (1): Forrest.
F.A. Cup (4): Moore 2, Carr, Taylor.

League Cup	First Round	Bradford C (h)	1-3
		(a)	0-0
FA Cup	First Round	Boston U (a)	4-0
	Second Round	Barnsley (h)	0-1

Brown	Forrest	Breckin	Halom	Stancliffe	Vaughan	Towner	Gooding	Moore	Seasman	Finney	Mullen	Carr	Tiler	Henson	Rhodes	Winn	Mountford	Fern	Taylor	*Match No.*
1	2	3	4	5	6	7	8	9	10	11										1
1	2	3	4	5		7	8	9	10	11*	6	12								2
1	2	3	4	5		7	8	9	10		6	11								3
1	2	3	4	5		7	8	9	10	11	6									4
1	2	3		5		7	8	9	10	11	6		4							5
1	2	3		5		7	8	9*	10	11	6		4	12						6
1	2	3	9	5		7	8		10	11	6				4					7
1	2	3		5		7	8	9	10	11	6				4					8
1	2	3		5		7	8	9	10	11	6				4					9
1	2	3		5		7	8	9	10	11	6				4					10
1	2	3		5		7	8	9	10	11*	6			12	4					11
1	2	3		5		7	8	9	10		6			11	4					12
1	2	3		5		7	8	9	10		6		4	11						13
1	2	3		5		7*	8	9	10				6	11	4	12				14
1	2	3		5			8	9	10		6		7	11	4					15
	2	3		5			8	9	10		6		7	11	4		1			16
	2*	3		5			8	9	10		6		7	11	4	12	1			17
		3		5			8*	9	10		6		2	11	4	12	1	7		18
		3		5			8	9	10		6		2	11	4		1	7		19
	2	3		5			8	9			6		10	11	4		1	7		20
	2	3		5			8	9			6	10		11	4		1	7		21
	2	3		5			8*	9			6	10		11	4	12	1	7		22
	2	3		5			8	9			6	10		11	4		1	7*	12	23
	2	3		5			8	9*			6	10		11	4	12	1	7		24
	2	3		5		7	8	9			6			11	4		1	10		25
	2	3		5		7	8	9			6			11	4		1	10		26
	2	3		5		7	8*	9			6	12		11	4		1	10		27
	2	3		5		7	8	9			6			11	4		1	10		28
	2	3		5		7	8	9			6			11	4		1	10		29
	2	3		5		7	8	9			6			11	4		1	10		30
	2	3		5		7	8	9			6			11	4		1	10		31
	2	3		5		7		9	8		6			11	4		1	10		32
	2	3				7	10	9	8		6		5	11	4		1			33
	2	3			5	7		9	8		6			11	4		1	10		34
	2	3		5	6	7		9	8					11	4		1	10		35
	2	3		5		7		9	8		6			11	4		1	10		36
	2	3		5		7		9	8		6			11	4		1	10		37
	2	3		5		7		9	8		6			11	4		1	10		38
	2	3		5		7		9	8		6			11	4		1	10		39
	2	3		5		7		9	8		6			11	4		1	10		40
	2	3		5		7	12	9	8		6			11*	4		1	10		41
	2	3		5		7	11	9	8		6				4		1	10		42
	2	3		5		7	11	9	8		6				4		1	10		43
	2	3		5		7	11	9	8		6				4		1	10		44
	2	3		5		7		9	8		6			11	4		1	10		45
	2	3		5		7	4	9	8		6			11			1	10		46
15	44	46	5	44	3	36	36	45	34	10	43	5	11	32	38	—	31	28	—	
							+ 1s					+ 2s		+ 2s		+ 5s			+ 1s	

ROTHERHAM UNITED

	Ht	*Wt*	*Birthplace*	*Clubs*	*League App.*	*League Gls*
Goalkeepers						
Ray Mountford	6 3	12 7	Mexborough	Manchester U	—	—
				Notts Co (on loan)	—	—
				Rotherham U	59	—
Graham Brown	6 1	12 7	Matlock	Millwall	—	—
				Brighton	—	—
				Crawley T	(not known)	
				Watford	—	—
				Mansfield T	142	—
				Doncaster R	53	—
				Swansea C	4	—
				Southport	—	—
				York C	69	—
				Rotherham U	31	—
Defenders						
John Breckin	5 9½	11 9	Rotherham	Rotherham U	361	7
				Darlington (on loan)	4	—
Gerald Forrest	5 11	10 7	Stockton	Rotherham U	177	6
John Green	5 10	12 1	Rotherham	Rotherham U	170	4
Paul Stancliffe	6 0	11 10	Sheffield	Rotherham U	230	6
Ashley Taylor	5 10	10 4	Conisborough	Rotherham U	13	—
Ken Tiler*	5 11	10 12½	Sheffield	Chesterfield	139	1
				Brighton	130	—
				Rotherham U	46	1
Jimmy Mullen	5 10½	11 12½	Jarrow	Sheffield W	230	10
				Rotherham U	43	1
Mark Wilkinson*			Mexborough	Rotherham U	—	—
Andy Brolly*			York	Rotherham U	—	—
Midfield						
Mark Rhodes	5 9	10 11	Sheffield	Rotherham U	177	11
Peter Carr	5 9	9 12½	Rawmarsh	Rotherham U	34	3
Phil Henson	5 10	9 12	Manchester	Manchester C	17	—
				Swansea C (on loan)	1	—
				Sheffield W	72	9
				Stockport Co	67	13
				Rotherham U	51	6
Billy McEwan	5 10	11 2	Cleveland	Hibernian	61	2
				Blackpool	4	—
				Brighton	27	3
				Chesterfield	80	7
				Mansfield T	32	3
				Peterborough U	63	3
				Rotherham U	32	7
Tony Towner	5 6	10 0	Brighton	Brighton	162	24
				Millwall	68	13
				Rotherham U	36	7
John Seasman	5 9	11 3	Liverpool	Tranmere R	17	—
				Luton T	8	2
				Millwall	158	35
				Rotherham U	34	6
Forwards						
Richard Finney	5 7	10 4	Rotherham	Rotherham U	236	67
Steve Winn	5 10½	11 5	Thornaby	Rotherham U	24	3
Ian Vaughan	5 10	10 0	Rotherham	Rotherham U	4	—
Ian Parkin*	5 6	10 3	Sheffield	Rotherham U	—	—
Rodney Fern	5 11	11 0	Burton	Leicester C	149	31
				Luton T	39	5
				Chesterfield	152	54
				Rotherham U	65	16
Ian Porterfield	5 11	12 8	Dunfermline	Raith R	117	17
				Sunderland	228	17
				Reading (on loan)	5	—
				Sheffield W	106	3
				Rotherham U	—	—
Vic Halom (Contract cancelled)	5 10	12 10	Burton	Charlton Ath	12	—
				Orient	53	12
				Fulham	71	22
				Luton T	59	17
				Sunderland	113	35
				Oldham Ath	123	43
				Rotherham U	20	2
Steve Fleetwood	5 10½	10 0	Sheffield	Rotherham U	—	—
Mick Gooding	5 7	10 7½	Newcastle	Bishop Auckland	(not known)	
				Rotherham U	71	7
Ronnie Moore	6 0	12 13½	Liverpool	Tranmere R	249	72
				Cardiff C	56	6
				Rotherham U	45	23
Tony Ellis*			Wickersley	Rotherham U	—	—

SCUNTHORPE UNITED Division 4

President: Sir Reginald Sheffield, Bt. *Chairman:* J. T. Empson.

Vice-Chairman: W. H. Archer.

Directors: G. E. Johnson, D. J. Wraith, T. E. Belton.

Manager: Ron Ashman. *Player-Manager:* John Duncan.

Secretary: Mrs S. Louth.

Year Formed: 1904. *Turned Professional:* 1912.

Limited Company: 1912.

Previous Name: Amalgamated with Lindsey United to become Scunthorpe United, 1910.

Football League Record:
1950 Elected to Division 3(N); 1958–64 Division 2; 1964–68 Division 3; 1968–72 Division 4; 1972–73 Division 3; 1973– Division 4.

Honours: *Football League:* Division 2 best season: 4th, 1961–62; Division 3(N) – Champions 1957–58. *FA Cup* best season: 5th rd, 1957–58, 1969–70. *Football League Cup:* never past 3rd rd.

Record Victory: 9-0 v Boston U, FA Cup 1st rd, 21 Nov, 1953.

Record Defeat: 0-8 v Carlisle U, Division 3(N), 25 Dec, 1952.

Most League Points: 66, Division 3(N), 1957–58.

Most League Goals: 88, Division 3(N), 1957–58.

Highest League Scorer in Season: Barrie Thomas, 31, Division 2, 1961–62.

Most League Goals in Total Aggregate: Barrie Thomas, 92, 1959–62, 1964–66.

Most Capped Player: None.

Most League Appearances: Jack Brownsword, 600, 1050–65.

Record Transfer Fee Received: £60,000 from Grimsby T for Kevin Kilmore, Sept 1979.

Record Transfer Fee Paid: £20,000 to Newcastle U for Barrie Thomas, Nov 1964.

Previous Managers since the War: Leslie Jones, Bill Corkhill, Ron Suart, Tony McShane, Bill Lambton (3 days, shortest ever term of office), Frank Soo, Dick Duckworth, Freddie Goodwin, Ron Ashman, Ron Bradley, Dickie Rooks.

Address of Supporters Club: Scunthorpe U Supporters and Social Club at Ground.

Old Show Ground, Scunthorpe, South Humberside. Telephone Scunthorpe 842954. *Ground capacity:* 27,000. *Record attendance:* 23, 935 v Portsmouth, FA Cup 4th rd, 30 Jan, 1954. *Record receipts:* £7895 v Newcastle U, FA Cup 4th rd replay, 30 Jan, 1974. *Pitch measurements:* 112yd×78yd.

How to get there: Buses 118, 106, 309, 300, 301, 306 run near the ground. Nearest railway station is Scunthorpe. By road along A18 from Doncaster via Berkeley Circle, Doncaster Road Hill, and Henderson Avenue; A18 from Grimsby; A15 from Lincoln via Queensway Circle, Ashby Road, Station Roundabout, Church Lane, Exeter Road, and Doncaster Road; via A1 on A638 to Retford, A620 to Gainsborough, A159 to Scunthorpe.

Match tickets: Tickets are bookable up to the day of the match unless advertised otherwise in the local press. No telephone bookings accepted.

Car parking: Club car park adjoining the ground holds 40–50 cars. Ample street parking around the ground.

Entertainments/catering facilities: Catering sub-let to an outside firm; hot drinks and light refreshments served on first-team match days.

Club shop: Three club shops and Development Office on the ground sell all types of souvenirs.

Handbooks/programmes: Programmes available on match days.

Extra information: The club song, 'Scunthorpe United', is available on record.

Club Colours: All red, with white trims on jersey.

Change Colours: All yellow.

Club Captain: Vince Grimes. *Club Coach:* Phil McLoughlin.

Physiotherapist: Charles Strong.

Club Nickname: The Irons.

SCUNTHORPE UNITED 1980–81 LEAGUE RECORD

Match No.	Date	Venue	Opponents	Result	H/T Score	Goalscorers	Attendance
1	Aug 16	H	Aldershot	D 2-2	1-0	Grimes, Cammack	1325
2	19	A	Rochdale	L 0-4	0-2		2427
3	23	A	Bradford C	D 0-0	0-0		3177
4	30	H	Wimbledon	L 1-2	0-0	O'Berg	1624
5	Sept 6	H	Crewe Alex	D 1-1	0-1	Partridge	1516
6	13	A	Halifax T	L 0-1	0-1		1226
7	16	A	Darlington	W 1-0	1-0	Cammack	2663
8	19	H	Stockport Co	W 2-0	2-0	Cammack, O'Berg	1985
9	27	A	Lincoln C	D 2-2	1-1	Ashworth, Thompson S. (og)	4209
10	30	H	Darlington	W 3-0	2-0	Cammack 2, Partridge (pen)	2106
11	Oct 4	A	AFC Bournemouth	D 2-2	1-0	Lambert, O'Berg	3079
12	7	H	Hartlepool U	D 3-3	0-2	Ashworth 2, Cammack	2900
13	11	H	Northampton T	L 0-2	0-2		2650
14	17	A	Southend U	L 0-2	0-0		5271
15	22	A	Peterborough U	W 2-0	0-0	Lambert, Partridge	4262
16	25	H	Torquay U	L 0-2	0-1		2254
17	28	H	Doncaster R	D 1-1	1-1	Cammack	4053
18	Nov 1	A	York C	L 0-1	0-1		1959
19	4	A	Hartlepool U	L 0-2	0-2		4357
20	8	H	Hereford U	W 3-1	0-1	Stewart 2, Cammack	1539
21	11	H	Rochdale	D 1-1	1-0	Stewart	2019
22	15	A	Aldershot	D 0-0	0-0		2512
23	Dec 6	A	Wigan Ath	D 1-1	1-0	Partridge (pen)	3672
24	20	H	Tranmere R	W 2-0	1-0	Lambert, Stewart	1664
25	26	A	Mansfield T	L 0-1	0-0		4261
26	27	H	Bury	D 2-2	2-0	Boxall, Cammack	2360
27	Jan 10	H	Peterborough U	D 1-1	0-1	Green	2064
28	19	A	Wimbledon	D 2-2	1-0	Green, O'Berg	2112
29	31	H	Bradford C	W 1-0	1-0	Cammack	2558
30	Feb 4	A	Torquay U	L 1-2	0-2	Green	1760
31	7	H	Halifax T	D 2-2	2-1	Stewart, Grimes	2073
32	14	A	Crewe Alex	L 0-1	0-1		2231
33	21	H	Lincoln C	D 2-2	0-1	O'Berg, Pilling	4848
34	24	H	Port Vale	D 1-1	0-0	Cammack (pen)	1946
35	27	A	Stockport Co	L 0-2	0-0		1675
36	Mar 3	A	Port Vale	D 2-2	0-2	Partridge (pen), Cammack	2277
37	6	H	AFC Bournemouth	D 1-1	0-1	Partridge (pen)	2392
38	13	A	Northampton T	D 3-3	1-3	Grimes, O'Berg, Green	2046
39	22	H	Southend U	W 2-1	0-0	Pilling, Green	3605
40	27	A	Doncaster R	L 0-1	0-1		8001
41	Apr 4	H	York C	W 3-2	3-2	Green 2, Stewart	1694
42	11	A	Hereford U	L 1-2	1-2	Price (og)	2009
43	18	A	Bury	L 1-6	0-2	Stewart	2357
44	20	H	Mansfield T	W 2-0	2-0	O'Berg, Cammack	1850
45	24	A	Tranmere R	W 2-1	0-1	Stewart, Pilling	1063
46	May 2	H	Wigan Ath	D 4-4	3-1	O'Berg 2, Cammack 2	1704

Final League Position: 16

Goalscorers

League (60): Cammack 15 (1 pen), O'Berg 9, Stewart 8, Green 7, Partridge 6 (4 pens), Ashworth 3, Grimes 3, Lambert 3, Pilling 3, Boxall 1, own goals 2.
League Cup (1): Cammack.
F.A. Cup (3): Green, Grimes, Partridge (pen).

League Cup	First Round	Barnsley (h)	0-1
		(a)	1-2
FA Cup	First Round	Hartlepool U (h)	3-1
	Second Round	Altrincham (h)	0-0
		(a)	0-1

Neenan	Davy	Jarvis	Grimes	Dall	Oates	Pugh	Cammack	Lambert	Partridge	O'Berg	Ashworth	Pilling	Boxall	Stewart	Gordon	Cowling	Wood	Green	Duffy	*Match No.*
1	2	3	4	5	6	7	8	9	10	11										1
1	2*	3	4	5	6	7	8	9	10	11	12									2
1	2		4		6	7	8	9	10			3	5	11						3
			4	2	6	7	8	9	10*	12		3	5	11	1					4
			4	5	6	2	8	9	10	12		3		11	1	7*				5
1			4	5	6	2	8	9*	10	12	7	3		11						6
1	2		4	5	6	7	8	9	12	11*	10	3								7
1	2		4	5	6	7	8	9		11	10	3								8
1	2*		4	5	6	7	8	9	12	11	10	3								9
1			4	5	6	7	8	9	2	11	10	3*		12						10
1			4	5	6	7	8	9	2	11	10*	3		12						11
1			4	5	6	7	8	9	2	11	10	3								12
1			4	5	6	7	8	9	2	11	10	3*		12						13
1		3	4	5	6	7*	8		2	11	10			9			12			14
1		3	4	5	6	7	8	9	2	11								10		15
1		3	4	5	6	7	8	9	2	11	12							10*		16
1		3	4	5	6	7	8	9	2	11	12							10*		17
1		3	4	5	6	7	8	9	2	11*	12							10		18
1		3	4	5	6	7	8	9*	2	11	10							12		19
1	2	3	4		6		8	12	7	11			5	9				10*		20
1	2	3	4		6		8		7	11			5	9				10		21
1	2	3	4		6		8		7	11			5	9				10		22
1	2	3	4		6	12	8		7	11*			5	9				10		23
1	2	3	4		6	10	8	7	9				5	12				11*		24
1	2	3	4		6	10	8	7*	9		12		5	11						25
1	2	3	4		6	10	8	7*	9	12			5	11						26
1	2	3	4		6	10	8			7			5	11				9		27
1	2	3	4	5	6	10	8		12	7				11*				9		28
1	2	3			6	10	8		4	7			5	11				9		29
1	2	3	4	5	6	10	8		11*	7				12				9		30
1	2	3	4		6	10	8			7			5	11				9		31
1	2		4		6	10	8			7		3	5	11				9		32
1			4		6	10	8		2	7	12	3	5	11				9*		33
1			4		6	10	8		2*	7		3	5	11				9	12	34
1	2*		4		6	10	8		9	7	12	3	5	11						35
1	2		4		6	10*	8		9	7	12	3	5	11						36
1	2		4		6		8		9	7	10*	3	5	11				12		37
1	2		4		6		8		9	7		3	5	11				10		38
1	2		4		6		8		9	7		3	5	11				10		39
1	2		4		6		8		9	7		3	5	11				10		40
1	2		4			6	8		9	7		3	5	11				10		41
1	2		4	6		9	8			7		3	5	11				10		42
1	2		4	6		9	8			7	12	3	5*	11				10		43
1	2	3	4			10	8	12	5	7*	6	11						9		44
1	2		4			10	8		5	7	6	3		11				9		45
1	2		4				8	10	5	7	6	3		11		9				46
44	31	21	45	22	40	37	46	22	37	39	14	26	24	29	2	2	—	25	—	
						+ 1s		+ 2s	+ 3s	+ 4s	+ 9s			+ 5s			+ 1s	+ 2s	+ 1s	

SCUNTHORPE UNITED

	Ht	*Wt*	*Birthplace*	*Clubs*	*League App.*	*League Gls*
Goalkeepers						
Jimmy Gordon*	5 11	12 5	Stretford	Luton T	—	—
				Lincoln C	4	—
				Reading	—	—
				Scunthorpe U	34	—
Joe Neenan	6 3	11 13	Manchester	York C	56	—
				Scunthorpe U	46	—
Defenders						
Stuart Pilling	5 9	10 2	Sheffield	Hull C	—	—
				Scunthorpe U	244	26
Steve Davy	5 8½	10 2	Grantham	Scunthorpe U	106	1
David Dall	6 3	12 7	Scotland	Grantham T	(not known)	
				Scunthorpe U	49	—
Graham Pugh*	5 7½	11 3	Hoole	Sheffield W	139	8
				Huddersfield T	80	1
				Chester	69	3
				Barnsley	130	8
				Scunthorpe U	55	—
Robert Oates	5 11½	11 7	Leeds	Scunthorpe U	258	15
Nick Jarvis*	5 9	11 0	Mansfield	Grantham T	(not known)	
				Scunthorpe U	21	—
Alan Boxall	6 3¾	14 2	Woolwich	Barton T	(not known)	
				Scunthorpe U	24	1
Midfield						
David Stewart (N Ireland)	5 9	10 12	Belfast	Hull C	51	7
				Chelsea	—	—
				Scunthorpe U	57	13
Vincent Grimes	5 9½	11 10	Scunthorpe	Hull C	89	9
				Scunthorpe U	109	10
				Bradford C (on loan)	7	1
Paul O'Berg	5 5	9 4	Hull	Bridlington T	(not known)	
				Scunthorpe U	61	12
Ian Botham (Non-contract)			Cheshire	Scunthorpe U	2	—
Hugh Wood*	5 9¼	11 1	Nottingham	Grantham T	(not known)	
				Scunthorpe U	1	—
Vince Duffy	5 6½	9 6	Nottingham	Nottingham F	—	—
				Scunthorpe U	1	—
Anton Lambert	6 0	11 7	Nottingham	Long Eaton	(not known)	
				Scunthorpe U	24	3
Forwards						
Malcolm Partridge	6 0½	12 0	Calow	Mansfield T	69	20
				Leicester C	35	4
				Charlton Ath (on loan)	2	—
				Grimsby T	138	24
				Scunthorpe U	84	19
Steve Cammack	5 10¼	11 9	Sheffield	Sheffield U	36	5
				Chesterfield	113	21
				Scunthorpe U	84	27
Chris Cowling	6 1½	11 0	Scunthorpe	Scunthorpe U	17	—
Rick Green	6 1½	13 2	Scunthorpe	Scunthorpe U	66	19
				Chesterfield	48	13
				Notts Co	9	—
				Scunthorpe U	53	16
Phil Ashworth*	6 0½	12 7	Burnley	Blackburn R	—	—
				Bournemouth	31	2
				Workington	39	7
				Southport	24	9
				Rochdale	11	—
				Portsmouth	4	4
				Scunthorpe U	23	3
Daniel Anderson (Contract cancelled Nov 1980)			Nottingham	Long Eaton	(not known)	
				Scunthorpe U	—	—

SHEFFIELD UNITED Division 4

Chairman: R. J. Brealey.

Vice-Chairman: A. A. Bramall.

Directors: A. H. Laver, A. H. Barrington, R. Wragg M INST BM.

Manager: Ian Porterfield.

Secretary: Richard Chester FAAI.

Commercial Manager: Derek Dooley.

Year Formed: 1889. *Turned Professional:* 1889.

Limited Company: 1899.

Football League Record:
1892 Elected to Division 2; 1893–1934 Division 1; 1934–39 Division 2; 1946–49 Division 1; 1949–53 Division 2; 1953–56 Division 1; 1956–61 Division 2; 1961–68 Division 1; 1968–71 Division 2; 1971–76 Division 1; 1976–79 Division 2; 1979–81 Division 3; 1981– Division 4.

Honours: *Football League:* Division 1 – Champions 1897–98; Runners-up 1896–97. 1899–1900; Division 2 – Champions 1952–53; Runners-up 1892–93; 1938–39, 1960–61, 1970–71. *FA Cup:* Winners 1899, 1902, 1915, 1925; Runners-up: 1901, 1936. *Football League Cup* best season: 5th rd, 1961–62, 1966–67.

Record Victory: 11-2 v Cardiff C, Division 1, 1 Jan, 1926.

Record Defeat: 0-13 v Bolton W, FA Cup, 2nd rd, 1 Feb, 1890.

Most League Points: 60, Division 2, 1952–53.

Most League Goals: 102, Division 1, 1925–26.

Highest League Scorer in Season: Jimmy Dunne, 41, Division 1, 1930–31.

Most League Goals in Total Aggregate: Harry Johnson, 205, 1919–30.

Most Capped Player: Billy Gillespie, 25, Ireland.

Most League Appearances: Joe Shaw, 629, 1948–66.

Record Transfer Fee Received: £400,000 from Leeds U for Alex Sabella, May 1980.

Record Transfer Fee Paid: £160,000 to River Plate for Alex Sabella, July 1978.

Previous Managers since the War: Ted Davison, Reg, Freeman, Joe Mercer, John Harris, Arthur Rowley, John Harris, Ken Furphy, Jimmy Sirrel, Harry Haslam, Martin Peters.

Address of Supporters Club: Secretary, c/o SUFC, Bramall Lane, Sheffield S2 4SU.

Address of the Club Shop or Boutique: Lane Souvenir Shop, John Street, Sheffield S2 4SU.

Bramall Lane Ground, Sheffield, S2 4SU. Telephone Sheffield (0742) 738955/6/7. *Telegraphic address:* 'United, Sheffield'. *Ground capacity:* 49,000 (15,300 seats). *Record attendance:* 68,287 v Leeds U, FA Cup 5th rd, 15 Feb, 1936. *Record receipts:* £65,092 v Sheffield W, Division 3, 5 Apr, 1980. *Pitch measurements:* 117yd×75yd.

How to get there: Buses 34, 35, 38, 42, 45 from the central bus station. Sheffield railway station is within walking distance of the town centre.

Match tickets: Tickets bookable 14 days prior to the match.

Car parking: The ground is five minutes from car parks in the city centre. Ample parking in side-streets around Bramall Lane.

Entertainments/catering facilities: Numerous bars and buffets in the ground.

Club shop: Sells all types of souvenirs.

Handbooks/programmes: Mail order service available through the club shop.

Extra information: Lane Social Club offers lounge bars and bier keller.

Club Colours: White shirts with wide red band down front and thin red and black stripes down side, black shorts with red and white trim, white stockings with black and red turnovers.

Change Colours: White shirt, red shortstripe down left hand side edged with thin black stripe, black shorts, white stockings with red and black top.

Club Captain:

Chief Coach:

Club Nickname: Blades.

SHEFFIELD UNITED 1980–81 LEAGUE RECORD

Match No.	Date	Venue	Opponents	Result	H/T Score	Goalscorers	Attendance
1	Aug 16	A	Carlisle U	W 3-0	1-0	Hatton 2, Peters	5248
2	19	H	Chesterfield	W 2-0	1-0	Butlin, Peters	18,390
3	23	H	Oxford U	W 1-0	0-0	Hatton	13,632
4	30	A	Barnsley	L 1-2	1-1	Butlin	17,478
5	Sept 6	H	Swindon T	W 3-0	1-0	Kenworthy (pen), Trusson, Peters	12,089
6	13	A	Reading	L 0-1	0-1		7249
7	16	H	Blackpool	W 4-2	2-1	Butlin, Kenworthy (pen), Charles, Hatton	13,331
8	20	A	Huddersfield T	L 0-1	0-1		14,721
9	27	H	Rotherham U	L 1-2	0-1	Ryan	17,955
10	Oct 1	A	Blackpool	L 1-2	0-0	Wiggan	8995
11	4	H	Plymouth Arg	D 0-0	0-0		12,401
12	7	A	Burnley	L 2-3	1-2	Trusson, Jones	7305
13	11	A	Charlton Ath	L 0-2	0-1		5602
14	14	H	Newport Co	W 2-0	1-0	Trusson, Hatton	9776
15	18	H	Exeter C	W 3-1	0-0	Charles, Peters, Hatton	10,608
16	25	A	Millwall	W 4-1	3-1	Charles, Ryan, Neville, Sitton (og)	5261
17	28	A	Gillingham	D 2-2	2-2	Trusson, Charles	4976
18	Nov 1	H	Colchester U	W 3-0	2-0	Kenworthy (pen), Trusson, Charles	12,810
19	4	H	Burnley	D 0-0	0-0		14,585
20	8	A	Chester	L 2-3	0-0	Butlin, Hatton	4563
21	11	A	Chesterfield	L 0-1	0-0		15,992
22	15	H	Carlisle U	D 2-2	1-2	Kenworthy 2 (1 pen)	11,031
23	29	A	Walsall	D 4-4	1-0	Butlin, Kenworthy (pen), Hatton 2	4931
24	Dec 6	H	Portsmouth	W 1-0	0-0	Trusson	12,158
25	20	H	Hull C	W 3-1	2-1	Hatton 2, Tibbott	10,720
26	26	A	Fulham	L 1-2	0-1	Hatton	6029
27	27	H	Brentford	D 0-0	0-0		13,130
28	Jan 3	A	Newport Co	L 0-4	0-1		6630
29	10	A	Portsmouth	L 0-1	0-1		14,321
30	17	H	Gillingham	L 0-1	0-0		8778
31	31	A	Oxford U	L 0-2	0-1		4427
32	Feb 7	H	Reading	W 2-0	1-0	Hatton, Neville	8601
33	14	A	Swindon T	L 2-5	0-3	Kenworthy (pen), Hatton	6305
34	21	A	Rotherham U	L 1-2	1-0	Trusson	11,905
35	28	H	Huddersfield T	D 2-2	1-0	Hatton, Wiggan	14,426
36	Mar 14	H	Charlton Ath	W 3-2	2-1	Hatton, Garner, Givens	11,687
37	21	A	Exeter C	D 1-1	0-0	Charles	4224
38	28	H	Millwall	L 2-3	2-0	Garner, Hatton	10,350
39	31	H	Barnsley	D 1-1	0-1	Matthews	20,369
40	Apr 4	A	Colchester U	D 1-1	0-1	Wiggan	2439
41	7	H	Chester	W 2-0	2-0	Garner, Givens	10,027
42	14	A	Plymouth Arg	L 0-1	0-0		4897
43	18	A	Brentford	D 1-1	1-0	Givens	5620
44	21	H	Fulham	L 1-2	0-1	Hatton	10,898
45	25	A	Hull C	D 1-1	1-1	Trusson	4895
46	May 2	H	Walsall	L 0-1	0-0		16,001

Final League Position: 21

Goalscorers

League (65): Hatton 18, Trusson 8, Kenworthy 7 (6 pens), Charles 6, Butlin 5, Peters 4, Garner 3, Givens 3, Wiggan 3, Neville 2, Ryan 2, Jones 1, Matthews 1, Tibbott 1, own goal 1.
League Cup (1): Hatton.
F.A. Cup (4): Charles, Hatton, Kenworthy, own goal.

League Cup	First Round	Sheffield W (a)	0-2
		(h)	1-1
FA Cup	First Round	Stockport Co (a)	0-0
		(h)	3-2
	Second Round	Chesterfield (h)	1-1
		(a)	0-1

Richardson	Cutbush	Houston	Kenworthy	McPhail	Jones	Tibbott	Trusson	Butlin	Hatton	Peters	Garner	Matthews	Charles	Wiggan	Ryan	Moore	Neville	Conroy	Keeley	Brazil	Flood	Givens	Casey	Match No.
1	2	3	4	5	6	7*	8	9	10	11	12													1
1	2	3	4	5	7	6	8	9	10	11														2
1	2	3	4	5	7	6	8	9	10	11														3
1	2	3	4	5	7	6	8	9	10	11														4
1	2	3	4	5		7	8	9	10	11*	12	6												5
1	2	3	4	5		6	8	9	10	11		7												6
1	2	3	4	5		7	8	9*	10	11		6	12											7
1	2	3	4	5		7	8			11		6	10	9										8
1	2*	3	4	5		7	8		10	11		6		12	9									9
1	2	3	4	5		7	8*		10	12		6		9	11									10
1		3	4	5		7	8		10	11		6		9	2									11
1			4	5	3	7	8		10	11		6			9	2								12
1			4	5	3	7	8		10	11		6			9	2								13
1			4	5		3	8*		10	11	7	6	12	9		2								14
1			4	5		3*	8		10	11	7		12	9	6	2								15
1			4	5*	12		6		10	11	3		9		7	2	8							16
1		5	4				6		10	11	3		9		7	2	8							17
1			4	5			6		10	11	3		9		7	2	8							18
1			4	5			6	11	10		3		9		7	2	8							19
1			4	5			6	11	10		3		9		7	2	8							20
1	2		4	5			6		10	11	3		9		7		8							21
1	2*		4	5			6	12	10	11	3		9		7		8							22
1			4	5	8		7	6	10		3		9		2		11							23
1			4	5	7		6	11	10		3		9		2		8							24
		4		5	7*	9	6	11	10		3		12		2		8	1						25
		4		5		9	6	11	10		3		7		2		8	1						26
		4	6	5	7*	9		10		11	3		12		2		8	1						27
		7	4	5			6		10.	11	3		12		2		8*	1	9					28
		4		5		8	6	9	10	11	3		7		2			1						29
		4		5		8	6	9*	10	11	3				2		7	1		12				30
	2	5	4		11		6		10		3			12	9		8	1			7*			31
			4	5		3	6		10		9				8	2	11	1		7				32
1			4	5			6		10		3		9		11	2	8			7				33
		4		5			6		10		3		9	7	11	2	8	1						34
		4	6	5				8	10		3		9	7	11	2		1						35
		4	6	5					10		3		9	7	11	2		1				8		36
		4	6	5					10		3		9	7	11	2		1				8		37
		4	6		5		12		10		3		9	7	11	2*		1				8		38
		4	6	5			2*		10		3	12	9	7	11			1				8		39
		4	6	5					10		3		9	7	11			1				8	2	40
		4	6	5					10		3		9	7	11			1				8	2	41
		4				5	6		10		3		9	7	11			1				8	2	42
	2	4				5	6		10		3		9	7	11			1				8		43
	2*	4	5			6			10		3	12	9	7	11			1				8		44
		4				5	7		10		3	6	9		11			1				8	2	45
		4		5		9	6*		10		3	7			11		12	1				8	2	46
25	15	32	37	39	12	26	38	17	44	23	33	12	25	16	37	16	18	21	1	2	1	11	5	
					+ 1s		+ 1s	+ 1s		+ 1s	+ 2s	+ 2s	+ 6s	+ 2s			+ 1s			+ 1s				

Players continued from following page.

Stewart Evans	6 4	11 5	Maltby	Rotherham U Gainsborough T Sheffield U	— (not known) —
Don Givens* (Eire)	6 0	12 2	Limerick	Manchester U Luton T QPR Bournemouth (on loan) Birmingham C Sheffield U	8 83 242 5 59 11

Second figures column for Stewart Evans: —, (not known), —; for Don Givens: 1, 19, 76, 4, 10, 3.

SHEFFIELD UNITED

	Ht	*Wt*	*Birthplace*	*Clubs*	*League App.*	*League Gls*
Goalkeepers						
Steve Conroy	6 0¼	12 2½	Chesterfield	Sheffield U	85	—
Derek Richardson	6 2½	15 0	London	Chelsea	—	—
				QPR	31	—
				Sheffield U	42	—
Keith Soloman			Truro	Truro C	(not known)	
(Deceased)				Sheffield U	—	—
Defenders						
Craig Renwick	5 10	11 2½	Lanark	East Stirling	11	—
(Contract cancelled Nov 1980)				Sheffield U	9	—
John Cutbush*	5 8	10 7	Malta	Tottenham H	—	—
				Fulham	135	3
				Sheffield U	129	1
Paul Garner	5 8¾	10 8	Doncaster	Huddersfield T	96	2
				Sheffield U	158	6
Andy Keeley*	5 9¼	11 4	Basildon	Tottenham H	6	—
				Sheffield U	28	—
Phil Jones	6 0½	12 4	Mansfield	Sheffield U	28	1
Leslie Tibbott	5 10	11 7	Oswestry	Ipswich T	54	—
				Sheffield U	75	2
John MacPhail	6 0½	12 3	Dundee	Dundee	68	—
				Sheffield U	98	6
John Matthews	6 0	12 6	London	Arsenal	45	2
				Sheffield U	78	11
Tony Moore	5 9	10 12	Burton	Burton A	(not known)	
				Sheffield U	25	—
Mick Jones	5 8	10 11		Sheffield U	—	—
(Contract cancelled April 1981)						
Tony Kenworthy	5 10	10 7	Leeds	Sheffield U	178	15
John Burke	5 7	10 8	Motherwell	Motherwell	—	—
				Sheffield U	—	—
Stewart Houston	5 11	12 3	Dunoon	Chelsea	9	—
(Scotland)				Brentford	77	9
				Manchester U	205	13
				Sheffield U	32	—
John Ryan	5 11	11 8	Lewisham	Fulham	45	1
				Luton T	266	10
				Norwich C	116	26
				Seattle S	(not known)	
				Sheffield U	37	2
Midfield						
Leendert de Goey	5 11	11 5	Amsterdam	Sparta	(not known)	
(Contract cancelled Oct 1980)				Sheffield U	33	5
Stephen Charles	5 9	10 7	Sheffield	Sheffield U	45	7
Paul Casey	5 7	10 2	Worksop	Sheffield U	13	1
Mike Trusson	5 10	12 4	Northolt	Plymouth Arg	73	15
				Stoke C (on loan)	—	—
				Sheffield U	39	8
Gary Brazil			Tunbridge Wells	Crystal Palace	—	—
				Sheffield U	3	—
Gary Marrow			Worksop	Sheffield U	—	—
Martin Peters	5 11	12 4	Plaistow	West Ham U	302	80
(England)				Tottenham H	189	46
				Norwich C	207	44
				Sheffield U	24	4
Forwards						
Pedro Verde	5 11	12 2	Buenos Aires	Hercules	(not known)	
				Sheffield U	10	3
Dougie Brown	5 9	12 4	Airdrie	Clydebank	12	—
(Contract cancelled Oct 1980)				Sheffield U	25	2
John Flood	5 7	9 8½	Glasgow	Sheffield U	19	1
(Transferred to Airdrieonians Feb 1981)						
Mark Smith	5 9	12 0	Sheffield	Sheffield U	—	—
Barry Butlin*	5 11½	11 10	Roslington	Notts Co	30	13
				Derby Co	7	—
				Luton T	57	24
				Nottingham F	74	17
				Brighton (on loan)	5	2
				Reading (on loan)	5	1
				Peterborough U	64	12
				Sheffield U	53	12
Trenton Wiggan			West Indies	Sheffield U	19	3
Bob Hatton	5 11	12 10	Hull	Wolverhampton W	10	7
				Bolton W	28	2
				Northampton T	33	8
				Carlisle U	93	38
				Birmingham C	175	58
				Blackpool	75	32
				Luton T	82	29
				Sheffield U	44	18
Steve Neville	5 9½	11 0	Walthamstow	Southampton	5	1
				Exeter C	93	22
				Sheffield U	19	2

Note: Players continued on previous page.

SHEFFIELD WEDNESDAY Division 2

Vice-Presidents: R. R. Gunstone, S. Ashton, A. Broomhead, C. Turner.
Chairman: H. E. McGee.
Vice-Chairman: M. Sheppard JP, FCA.
Directors: S. L. Speight OBE, C. Woodward, K. T. Addy, E. Barron, G. K. Hulley.
Manager: Jack Charlton OBE.
Secretary: Eric England FAAI.
Commercial Manager: D. Woodhead.
Year Formed: 1867 (fifth oldest League Club).
Turned professional: 1887. *Limited Company:* 1899.
Previous Grounds: 1867, Highfield; 1869, Myrtle Road; 1877, Sheaf House; 1887, Olive Grove; 1899, Owlerton (since 1912 known as Hillsborough). Some games were played at Endcliffe in the 1880s. Until 1895 Bramall Lane was used for some games.
Football League Record:
1892 Elected to Division 1; 1899–1900 Division 2; 1900–20 Division 1; 1920–26 Division 2; 1926–37 Division 1; 1937–50 Division 2; 1950–51 Division 1; 1951–52 Division 2; 1952–55 Division 1; 1955–56 Division 2; 1956–58 Division 1; 1958–59 Division 2; 1959–70 Division 1; 1970–75 Division 2; 1975–80 Division 3; 1980– Division 2.
Honours: *Football League:* Division 1 – Champions 1902–03, 1903–04, 1928–29, 1929–30; Runners-up 1960–61; Division 2 – Champions 1899–1900, 1925–26, 1951–52, 1955–56, 1958–59; Runners-up 1949–50; Division 3 – Runners-up 1979–80. *FA Cup:* Winners 1896, 1907, 1935; Runners-up 1890, 1966. *Football League Cup* best season: 4th rd, 1967–68, 1976–77, 1977–78. **European Competitions:** *Fairs Cup:* 1961–62, 1963–64.
Record Victory: 12-0 v Halliwell, FA Cup 1st rd, 17 Jan, 1891.
Record Defeat: 0-10 v Aston Villa, Division 1, 5 Oct, 1912.
Most League Points: 62, Division 2, 1958–59.
Most League Goals: 106, Division 2, 1958–59.
Highest League Scorer in Season: Derek Dooley, 46, Division 2, 1951–52.
Most League Goals in Total Aggregate: Andy Wilson, 200, 1900–20.
Most Capped Player: Ron Springett, 33, England.
Most League Appearances: Andy Wilson, 502, 1900–20.
Record Transfer Fee Received: £120,000 from Newcastle U for Tommy Craig, Jan 1975.
Record Transfer Fee Paid: £100,000 to Aberdeen for Tommy Craig, May 1969, and £100,000 to Southampton for Terry Curran, March 1979.
Previous Managers since the War: Secretary/Manager Eric Taylor, Harry Catterick, Vic Buckingham, Alan Brown, Jack Marshall, Danny Williams, Derek Dooley, Steve Burtenshaw, Len Ashurst.
Address of Supporters Club: Same as Football Club.
Address of the Club Shop or Boutique: Owl Shop, Hillsborough, Sheffield S6 1SW.
Club Restaurant: Adjoining South Stand.

Hillsborough, Sheffield, S6 1SW. Telephone Sheffield 343123. Box Office: Sheffield 343122. *Telegraphic address:* 'Wednesday, Sheffield 6'. *Ground capacity:* 50,174. *Record attendance:* 72,841 v Manchester C, FA Cup 5th rd, 17 Feb, 1934. *Record receipts:* £192,159, Liverpool v Arsenal, FA Cup semi-final, 12 Apr, 1980 (record for FA Cup-tie other than the Final). *Pitch measurements:* 115yd×75yd.
How to get there: Buses 42, 53, 81, 2 from the city centre. Sheffield railway station is close to the centre.
Match tickets: Seats can be booked in advance in the South and North Stands. Postal applications to the Box Office not more than 21 days before the match. Tickets are offered subject to being unsold when the application is received. Remittance and SAE must be enclosed.
Car parking: Street parking available. Also a park at the training ground in Middlewood Road.
Entertainments/catering facilities: Refreshment bars in all parts of the ground.
Club shop: Two shops in the ground sell all types of souvenirs.
Handbooks/programmes: Handbooks available from the secretary. Programmes available on subscription.
Extra information: When Sheffield Wednesday won the First Division title in 1929–30, they finished 10 points ahead of the runners-up.
Club Colours: Royal blue/white striped shirts, royal blue shorts, white stockings.
Change Colours: Yellow shirts with blue trim, white shorts, yellow socks with blue band.
Club Nickname: Owls.

SHEFFIELD WEDNESDAY 1980–81 LEAGUE RECORD

Match No.	*Date*	*Venue*	*Opponents*	*Result*	*H/T Score*	*Goalscorers*	*Attendance*
1	Aug 16	H	Newcastle U	W 2-0	0-0	McCulloch, Taylor	26,164
2	19	A	Bolton W	D 0-0	0-0		15,926
3	23	A	Notts Co	L 0-2	0-1		10,246
4	30	H	Preston NE	W 3-0	2-0	McCulloch 2, King	16,724
5	Sept 6	A	Oldham Ath	L 0-2	0-1		11,700
6	13	H	Bristol C	W 2-1	1-1	Pearson, King	15,054
7	20	H	QPR	W 1-0	1-0	Pearson	15,195
8	27	A	Swansea C	W 3-2	1-1	Hornsby, Pearson, McCulloch	9764
9	Oct 4	A	Derby Co	L 1-3	0-2	McCulloch	18,554
10	7	H	Blackburn R	W 2-1	2-1	Hornsby, Curran	16,707
11	11	H	Cardiff C	W 2-0	1-0	Hornsby, McCulloch	15,396
12	18	A	Bristol R	D 3-3	2-1	Blackhall, McCulloch, Grant	4401
13	21	A	Grimsby T	D 0-0	0-0		10,298
14	25	H	Orient	D 2-2	1-0	McCulloch, Mirocevic	18,018
15	Nov 1	A	Luton T	L 0-3	0-0		12,092
16	8	H	Wrexham	W 2-1	0-0	Curran 2 (1 pen)	15,736
17	11	H	Bolton W	W 2-0	1-0	Curran (pen), Jones (og)	16,262
18	15	A	Newcastle U	L 0-1	0-1		19,161
19	22	A	Chelsea	L 0-2	0-0		24,947
20	29	H	Watford	W 1-0	1-0	McCulloch	14,761
21	Dec 6	A	West Ham U	L 1-2	1-2	Mirocevic	30,476
22	13	H	Bristol R	W 4-1	1-0	Smith, Curran, McCulloch 2	14,008
23	26	H	Shrewsbury T	D 1-1	0-0	Pearson	22,863
24	Jan 10	H	Chelsea	D 0-0	0-0		25,113
25	24	A	Cambridge U	W 2-0	2-0	Sterland, Leman	9231
26	31	H	Notts Co	L 1-2	0-1	Mirocevic	22,449
27	Feb 7	A	Bristol C	L 0-1	0-0		11,639
28	14	H	Oldham Ath	W 3-0	2-0	Curran 2, McCulloch	16,679
29	21	H	Swansea C	W 2-0	1-0	Sterland, McCulloch	17,887
30	28	A	QPR	W 2-1	0-0	Taylor 2	15,104
31	Mar 4	A	Cardiff C	D 0-0	0-0		7002
32	7	H	Derby Co	D 0-0	0-0		28,301
33	14	A	Blackburn R	L 1-3	0-2	McCulloch	19,222
34	28	A	Orient	L 0-2	0-0		6561
35	Apr 4	H	Luton T	W 3-1	1-0	Mirocevic, Curran 2	17,006
36	11	A	Wrexham	L 0-4	0-1		8001
37	14	A	Preston NE	L 1-2	0-0	McCulloch	9537
38	18	H	Cambridge U	W 4-1	0-1	McCulloch 3, Taylor	14,315
39	21	A	Shrewsbury T	L 0-2	0-1		8118
40	28	H	Grimsby T	L 1-2	0-2	Mirocevic	16,747
41	May 2	A	Watford	L 1-2	1-1	Taylor	12,351
42	8	H	West Ham U	L 0-1	0-0		21,087

Final League Position: 10

Goalscorers

League (53): McCulloch 18, Curran 9 (2 pens), Mirocevic 5, Taylor 5, Pearson 4, Hornsby 3, King 2, Sterland 2, Blackhall 1, Grant 1, Leman 1, Smith 1, own goal 1.
League Cup (8): Curran 2, Owen 2, Grant, Johnson, Pearson, Taylor.
F.A. Cup (1): Pearson.

League Cup	First Round	Sheffield U (h)	2-0
		(a)	1-1
	Second Round	Wimbledon (a)	1-2
		(h)	3-1
	Third Round	Watford (h)	1-2
FA Cup	Third Round	Newcastle U (a)	1-2

Bolder	Blackhall	Williamson	Smith	Pickering	King	Taylor	Johnson	Mellor	McCulloch	Curran	Owen	Grant	Oliver	Campbell	Pearson	Cox	Hornsby	Leman	Shirtliff, Peter	Sterland	Mirocevic	Shirtliff, Paul	Matthewson	*Match No.*
1	2	3	4	5	6	7	8	9	10	11														1
1	2	3	4	5	6	7	8	9	10	11														2
1	2	3	4	5	6	7	8	9*	10	11	12													3
1	2		4	5	6	7	8		10	11	9	3												4
1	2		4	5	6	7	8	10*		11	9	3	12											5
1	2		4	5	6	7	8	11			9*	3		12	10									6
1	2		4	5	6	7	8*	11			9	3	12		10									7
	2		4	5		7		8	10			3			11	1	6	9						8
	2		4	5	6	8			10	11		3			12	1	7*	9						9
	2		4	5*	9	7	8	12	10	11		3				1	6							10
1	2		4		9	7	8		10	11		3					6		5					11
1	2		4	5	9*	7	8		10	11		3					6			12				12
1	2		4			7	8	12	10	11*		3					6		5	9				13
1	2		4			7	8	12	10*			3					6		5	9	11			14
1	2		4	5		7*	8		10	11		3					6			9	12			15
1	2		4	5*	9		8	12	10	7		3					6				11			16
1	2		4		9		8		10	7		3					6		5		11			17
1	2		4		9		8	12	10	7		3					6		5		11*			18
1	2	3	4				8		10	11					12			9	5	6	7*			19
1	2		4				8		10	11		3						9	5	6	7			20
1	2		4				8		10	11	12	3						9	5	6	7*			21
1	2		4				8		10	11		3			12			9*	5	6	7			22
1	2		4				8		10	11		3			12			9	5	6	7*			23
1	2		4				8		10	11		3			7			9	5	6				24
1	2	3	4			8			10	11					7			9	5	6				25
1	2	3	4				8		10	11					7			9*	5	6	12			26
1	2		4				8*		10	11		3			12			9	5	6	7			27
1	2		4			8*			10	11		3			12			9	5	6	7			28
1	2		4		11	8			10			3*			12			9	5	6	7			29
1	2		4		11	8			10			3						9	5	6	7			30
1		2	4		11*	8			10	12		3						9	5	6	7			31
1	2		4		9	8			10	11		3							5	6	7			32
1	2	3	4			8	12		10	11								9	5	6	7*			33
1	2		4			8*	9		10	11		3					12		5	6	7			34
1	2		4			9*	8	6	10	11		3					12		5		7			35
1	2		4			9	8	6	10	11		3							5	7*	12			36
1	2		4			9	6	7	10	11		3			8				5					37
1	2		4	5		8	6	7	10	11		3									9			38
1	2		4	6*		12	8	7	10	11		3							5		9			39
1	2				6		8		10	11		3					9*		5	4	7	12		40
1	2		4			8*	6	12	10	11		3							5		9		7	41
1	2		4		9*	8	6	7	10	11		3			12				5					42
39	41	8	41	15	20	29	33	13	39	35	4	35	—	—	7	3	12	16	28	21	22	—	1	
						+ 1s	+ 1s	+ 6s		+ 1s	+ 2s		+ 2s	+ 1s	+ 8s		+ 2s			+ 1s	+ 3s	+ 1s		

SHEFFIELD WEDNESDAY

	Ht	Wt	Birthplace	Clubs	League App.	League Gls
Goalkeepers						
Bob Bolder	6 1	14 8	Dover	Dover	(not known)	
				Sheffield W	112	—
Brian Cox	6 0	13 3	Sheffield	Sheffield W	22	—
Defenders						
David Grant	6 0	12 8½	Sheffield	Sheffield W	129	4
Mark Smith	6 0½	12 0	Sheffield	Sheffield W	108	10
Ray Blackhall	5 10	11 7	Ashington	Newcastle U	37	—
				Sheffield W	97	1
Mike Pickering	5 11	12 8	Mirfield	Barnsley	100	1
				Southampton	44	—
				Sheffield W	82	—
Peter Shirtliff	5 11	12 2	Chapeltown	Sheffield W	57	1
Charles Williamson	5 10	10 11	Sheffield	Sheffield W	11	—
Gavin Oliver	5 11	12 11	Felling	Sheffield W	2	—
Kevin Matthewson	6 1	12 0	Sheffield	Sheffield W	1	—
Midfield						
Dennis Leman	5 5	11 4	Newcastle	Manchester C	17	1
				Sheffield W	102	9
Jeff Johnson	5 8	11 12	Cardiff	Manchester C	6	—
				Swansea C (on loan)	39	4
				Crystal Palace	87	4
				Sheffield W	180	6
Kevin Taylor	5 8	11 6	Wakefield	Sheffield W	56	11
Jeff King	5 8	10 2	Fauld House	Albion R	42	7
				Derby Co	15	—
				Notts Co (on loan)	3	—
				Portsmouth (on loan)	4	—
				Walsall	51	4
				Sheffield W	55	5
Brian Hornsby	5 8	11 0	Shellford	Arsenal	26	5
				Shrewsbury T	75	16
				Sheffield W	105	25
Melvyn Sterland	5 11	12 7	Sheffield	Sheffield W	26	3
Paul Shirtliff	5 5	8 8	Barnsley	Sheffield W	1	—
Ante Mirocevic (Yugoslavia)	5 8	11 0	Titograd	Budocnost	(not known)	
				Sheffield W	25	5
Forwards						
Gordon Owen	5 8	10 7	Barnsley	Sheffield W	35	4
				Rotherham U (on loan)	9	—
Terry Curran	5 10	12 4	Kinsley	Doncaster R	68	11
				Nottingham F	48	12
				Bury (on loan)	2	—
				Derby Co	26	2
				Southampton	26	—
				Sheffield W	89	32
Brian Strutt*	5 9½	10 7	Malta	Sheffield W	2	—
Philip Campbell*	5 9		Barnsley	Sheffield W	1	—
Andy McCulloch	6 2	13 9	Northampton	QPR	42	10
				Cardiff C	58	24
				Oxford U	41	9
				Brentford	117	48
				Sheffield W	69	30
Ian Mellor	6 2	11 12	Sale	Manchester C	40	7
				Norwich C	29	2
				Brighton	122	31
				Chester	40	11
				Sheffield W	56	11
John Pearson (Apprentice)	6 1	11 9½	Sheffield	Sheffield W	15	4
Mick Bentley*			Barnsley	Sheffield W	—	—

SHREWSBURY TOWN Division 2

President: L. Tudor-Owen.

Chairman: H. S. Yates. *Vice-Chairman:* K. R. Woodhouse.

Directors: L. Tudor-Owen, A. C. Williams, F. C. G. Fry, P. W. Newbrook.

Player/Manager: Graham Turner.

Secretary: M. J. Starkey.

Year Formed: 1886. *Turned Professional:* 1905 (approx).

Limited Company: 1936.

Previous Ground: Old Shrewsbury Racecourse.

Football League Record:
1950 Elected to Division 3(N); 1951–58 Division 3(S); 1958–59 Division 4; 1959–74 Division 3; 1974–75 Division 4; 1975–79 Division 3; 1979– Division 2.

Honours: *Football League:* Division 2 best season: 13th, 1979–80; Division 3 – Champions 1978–79; Division 4 – Runners-up 1974–75. *FA Cup* best season: 6th rd, 1978–79. *Football League Cup:* semi-final 1961. *Welsh Cup:* Winners 1891, 1938, 1977, 1979.

Record Victory: 7-0 v Swindon T, Division 3(S), 6 May, 1955.

Record Defeat: 1-8 v Norwich C, Division 3(S), 1952–53 and v Coventry C, Division 3, 22 Oct, 1963.

Most League Points: 62, Division 4, 1974–75.

Most League Goals: 101, Division 4, 1958–59.

Highest League Scorer in Season: Arthur Rowley, 38, Division 4, 1958–59.

Most League Goals in Total Aggregate: Arthur Rowley, 152, 1958–65 (While with Shrewsbury T, Arthur Rowley completed his League scoring record of 434 goals).

Most Capped Player: Jimmy McLaughlin, 5 (12) Ireland.

Most League Appearances: Ken Mulhearn, 370, 1971–80.

Record Transfer Fee Received: £262,000 from Stoke C for Paul Maguire, Sept 1980.

Record Transfer Fee Paid: £100,000 to Aldershot for John Dungworth, Nov 1979.

Previous Managers since the War: Sam Crooks, Walter Rowley, Harry Potts, John Spuhler, Arthur Rowley, Harry Gregg, Maurice Evans, Alan Durban, Richie Barker.

Address of Supporters Club: c/o Football Club.

Gay Meadow, Shrewsbury. Telephone Shrewsbury 60111. *Match information:* 8040. *Ground capacity:* 18,000. *Record attendance:* 18,917 v Walsall, Division 3, 26 Apr, 1961. *Record receipts:* £32,740 v Ipswich T, FA Cup 4th rd, 24 Jan, 1981. *Pitch measurements:* 116yd×76yd.

How to get there: Midland Red schedule bus services from main bus station in Barker Street to the ground. Special coach facilities are arranged by local companies from neighbouring districts. Shrewsbury railway station is 10 minutes walk from the ground.

Car parking: A park adjacent to the ground and a free public car park five minutes walk away.

Entertainments/catering facilities: Buffets are situated on each side of the ground.

Club shop: Sells all types of souvenirs.

Handbooks/programmes: No handbook. Programmes can be obtained through the post at 30p each plus sae to Promotions Office, Gay Meadow, Shrewsbury.

Extra information: In 1960–61 Shrewsbury met Swindon Town six times in League, FA Cup, and League Cup and did not lose once.

Club Colours: Amber shirts with blue stripes, blue shorts, amber stockings.

Change Colours: Red or white.

Club Nickname: Town.

SHREWSBURY TOWN 1980–81 LEAGUE RECORD

Match No.	Date	Venue	Opponents	Result	H/T Score	Goalscorers	Attendance
1	Aug 16	H	Grimsby T	D 1-1	1-1	King	4998
2	19	A	Swansea C	L 1-2	0-0	King	12,754
3	23	H	Chelsea	D 2-2	1-2	Atkins, Biggins	6672
4	30	A	Blackburn R	L 0-2	0-1		8465
5	Sept 6	H	Watford	W 2-1	1-1	Dungworth 2	5500
6	13	A	West Ham U	L 0-3	0-1		22,339
7	20	H	Cambridge U	W 2-1	1-0	King, Dungworth	4465
8	27	A	Preston NE	D 0-0	0-0		6309
9	Oct 4	A	Oldham Ath	D 0-0	0-0		6093
10	7	H	Bolton W	L 1-2	0-0	Turner	5077
11	11	H	Orient	L 1-2	1-1	Keay	4300
12	18	A	Luton T	D 1-1	1-0	Turner	8014
13	22	A	Newcastle U	L 0-1	0-0		11,973
14	25	H	Cardiff C	W 2-0	0-0	Keay (pen), Biggins	4466
15	Nov 1	A	Derby Co	D 1-1	1-0	Keay (pen)	15,784
16	8	H	Bristol R	W 3-1	1-1	Atkins, Biggins, Cross	4446
17	11	H	Swansea C	D 0-0	0-0		5863
18	15	A	Grimsby T	L 0-1	0-0		8737
19	22	H	Notts Co	D 1-1	0-0	Biggins	5352
20	29	A	QPR	D 0-0	0-0		7982
21	Dec 6	H	Bristol C	W 4-0	1-0	Biggins, Tong, Atkins, Edwards	4435
22	13	A	Orient	L 0-1	0-0		4801
23	19	H	Luton T	L 0-1	0-0		4521
24	26	A	Sheffield W	D 1-1	0-0	Atkins	22,863
25	27	H	Wrexham	L 1-2	1-2	Keay (pen)	8320
26	Jan 10	A	Notts Co	D 0-0	0-0		7139
27	17	H	Blackburn R	D 1-1	1-0	Bates	5212
28	31	A	Chelsea	L 0-3	0-2		14,673
29	Feb 7	H	West Ham U	L 0-2	0-1		9201
30	14	A	Watford	L 0-1	0-1		11,034
31	21	H	Preston NE	W 3-0	3-0	Keay (pen), Turner, Biggins	4660
32	28	A	Cambridge U	L 1-3	0-1	Bates	4007
33	Mar 7	H	Oldham Ath	D 2-2	0-0	Keay (pen), King	4191
34	14	A	Bolton W	W 2-0	1-0	Dungworth, Walsh (og)	7900
35	21	H	Newcastle U	W 1-0	0-0	Turner	4975
36	28	A	Cardiff C	D 2-2	2-1	Atkins, Keay (pen)	5201
37	Apr 4	H	Derby Co	W 1-0	1-0	King	6668
38	11	A	Bristol R	D 1-1	1-1	Biggins	4151
39	18	A	Wrexham	W 2-1	1-0	Biggins, Atkins	8416
40	21	H	Sheffield W	W 2-0	1-0	Biggins, Smith (og)	8118
41	25	A	Bristol C	D 1-1	0-1	Cross	5698
42	May 2	H	QPR	D 3-3	1-2	Dungworth, Keay (pen), King	5714

Final League Position: 14

Goalscorers

League (46): Biggins 9, Keay 8 (7 pens), Atkins 6, King 6, Dungworth 5, Turner 4, Bates 2, Cross 2, Edwards 1, Tong 1, own goals 2.
League Cup (1): Biggins.
F.A. Cup (3): Bates, Cross, own goal.

League Cup	Second Round	Norwich C (h)	1-1
		(a)	0-2
FA Cup	Third Round	Huddersfield T (a)	3-0
	Fourth Round	Ipswich T (h)	0-0
		(a)	0-3

Wardle	King	Leonard	Turner	Griffin	Keay	Tong	Atkins	Biggins	Dungworth	Petts	Lindsay	Cross	Edwards	Larkin	MacLaren	Bates	McNally	*Match No.*
1	2	3	4	5	6	7	8	9	10	11								1
1	2	3	4	5	6	7	8	9	10	11								2
1	2	3	4	5	6	7	8*	9	10	11	12							3
1	2	3*	4	5	6	7		9	10	11	8	12						4
1	2	3		5	6	7	8*		10	11	4	12	9					5
1	2	3		5	6	7	8		9	11	4		10					6
1	2		4	5	6	7		9*	10	11	8	12		3				7
1	2		4	5	6	7	12	9	10	11	8*			3				8
1	2		4	5	6	7	8		10			11	9	3				9
1	2		4	5	6	7	8		10	11		12	9*	3				10
1	2	3	4	5	6	7	8		10	11		9						11
1	2	3	4	5		7	8	9	10		12	11		6*				12
1	2	3	4	5	6	7	8	9	10			11						13
1	2	3		5	6	7	8	10	11	4		9						14
1	2	3	12	5	6	7	8	9	10	4*		11						15
1	2	3		5	6	7	8	9	10	4		11						16
1	2	3*		5	6	7	8	9	10	4		11			12			17
1	2			5	6	7	8	9	10	4		11		3				18
1	2			5	6	7	8	9	10*	4	12	11		3				19
1	2		4	5	6	7	8	9			10	11		3				20
1	2		4*	5	6	7	8	9		10		11	12	3				21
1	2		4*	5	6	7	8	9	10			11	12	3				22
1	2			5*	6	7	8	12	10	4		11		3		9		23
1	2	3	4	5	6	7	8			10		11				9		24
1	2	3	4	5	6	7	8*	12		10		11				9		25
1	2	3	4	5	6	7	8			10		11				9		26
1	2	3	4*	5	6	7	8	12		10		11				9		27
1	2	3	4	5	6	7	8		12			11*			10	9		28
1	2	3		5	6	7	8	10		12		11			4*	9		29
1	2	3	4	5	6	7*		10			8	11		12		9		30
1	2	3	4	5	6	7	8	10	9							12	11*	31
1	2	3	4	5	6	7	8	10	9	11*						12		32
1	2	3*	4	5	6	7	8	10	12			11				9		33
1	2	3	4		6	7	8*	10	9			11		5		12		34
1	2	3	4	5		7	8	10	9			11		6				35
1	2	3	4	5	6	7	8	10	9			11						36
1	2	3	4	5	6	7	8	10	9			11*				12		37
1	2	3	4	5	6	7	8	10	9			11						38
1	2	3	4	5	6	7	8	10	9			11						39
1	2	3	4	5	6	7	8	10	9			11						40
1	2	3	4	5	6	7	8	10*	9			11				12		41
1	2	3	4	5	6	7	8*		9			11			12	10		42
42	42	32	32	41	40	42	38	30	32	23	7	31	4	13	2	10	1	
			+ 1s				+ 1s	+ 3s	+ 2s	+ 1s	+ 3s	+ 4s	+ 2s	+ 1s	+ 2s	+ 5s		

SHREWSBURY TOWN

	Ht	*Wt*	*Birthplace*	*Clubs*	*League App.*	*League Gls*
Goalkeepers						
Bob Wardle	5 11	11 2	Leeds	Bristol C	—	—
				Shrewsbury T	89	—
Stephen Perks	6 0	11 3½	Shrewsbury	Shrewsbury T	—	—
Glyn Jones*	6 0	13 1	Newport	Bristol R	9	—
				Shrewsbury T	—	—
Defenders						
Colin Griffin	6 0	11 7	Dudley	Derby Co	—	—
				Shrewsbury T	227	6
Jake King	5 10	11 0	Glasgow	Shrewsbury T	304	20
Carleton Leonard	5 9	10 3	Oswestry	Shrewsbury T	185	1
Jack Keay	6 0	12 6	Glasgow	Celtic	—	—
				Shrewsbury T	131	20
Steve Cross	5 10	10 6	Wolverhampton	Shrewsbury T	79	4
Anthony Larkin*	5 11	11 12	Wrexham	Wrexham	—	—
				Shrewsbury	55	—
Mark Adams	5 11	10 4½	Shrewsbury	Shrewsbury T	—	—
Midfield						
Ian Atkins	5 10	11 0	Birmingham	Shrewsbury T	238	41
Graham Turner	5 10	11 13	Ellesmere Port	Wrexham	77	—
				Chester	218	5
				Shrewsbury T	311	22
Jimmy Lindsay*	5 7½	12 0	Hamilton	West Ham U	36	2
				Watford	65	12
				Colchester U	45	6
				Hereford U	79	6
				Shrewsbury T	86	—
David Tong	5 8	10 1	Blackpool	Blackpool	78	7
				Shrewsbury T	120	7
Brian Coyne	5 10	11 0	Glasgow	Celtic	—	—
(Contract cancelled March 1981)				Shrewsbury T	1	—
Ross MacLaren			Edinburgh	Rangers	—	—
				Shrewsbury T	4	—
Bernard McNally	5 7	9 11	Shrewsbury	Shrewsbury T	1	—
Forwards						
Steve Biggins	6 0	11 12	Walsall	Shrewsbury T	124	38
Geoff Croft (Contract cancelled Oct 1980)				Shrewsbury T	—	—
John Dungworth	6 0	10 7	Rotherham	Huddersfield T	23	1
				Barnsley (on loan)	3	1
				Oldham Ath	4	—
				Rochdale (on loan)	14	3
				Aldershot	105	58
				Shrewsbury T	62	12
Dean Edwards	5 10	10 6	Wolverhampton	Shrewsbury T	10	1
Paul Petts	5 9	10 11	Hackney	Bristol R	13	—
				Shrewsbury T	24	—
Chic Bates	6 0	11 12	West Bromwich	Stourbridge	(not known)	
				Shrewsbury T	160	45
				Swindon T	63	15
				Bristol R	29	4
				Shrewsbury T	15	2
Charles Gibson	5 10	11 8	Dunbarton	Shrewsbury T	—	—

SOUTHAMPTON Division 1

President: H. G. Blagrave. *Chairman:* A. A. Woodford.
Directors: J. Corbett, Lt-Col Sir George Meyrick (Bart) MC, TD, B. G. W. Bowyer JP, F. G. Askham FCA, E. T. Bates.
Manager: Lawrie McMenemy.
Assistant Manager: John Mortimore.
Secretary: Brian Truscott.
Year Formed: 1885.
Turned Professional: 1894. *Limited Company:* 1897.
Previous Name: Southampton St Mary's until 1885.
Previous Grounds: 1885, Antelope Ground; 1897, County Cricket Ground; 1898, The Dell.

Football League Record:
1920 Original Members of Division 3; 1921 Division 3(S); 1922–53 Division 2; 1953–58 Division 3(S); 1958–60 Division 3; 1960–66 Division 2; 1966–74 Division 1; 1974–78 Division 2; 1978– Division 1.

Honours: *Football League:* Division 1 best season: 6th, 1980–81; Division 2 – Runners-up 1965–66, 1977–78; Division 3(S) – Champions 1921–22; Runners-up 1920–21; Division 3 – Champions 1959–60. *FA Cup:* Winners 1975–76; Runners-up 1900, 1902. *Football League Cup:* Runners-up 1978–79. **European Competitions:** *European Fairs Cup:* 1969–70. *UEFA Cup:* 1971-72. *European Cup-Winners' Cup:* 1976–77.

Record Victory: 11-0 v Northampton T, Southern League, 28 Dec, 1901.
Record Defeat: 0-8 v Tottenham H, Division 2, 28 Mar, 1936, and v Everton, Division 1, 20 Nov, 1971.
Most League Points: 61, Division 3(S), 1921–22, and Division 3, 1959–60.
Most League Goals: 112, Div 3(S), 1957–58.
Highest League Scorer in Season: Derek Reeves, 39, Division 3, 1959–60.
Most League Goals in Total Aggregate: Mike Channon, 175, 1966–77, 1979–81.
Most Capped Player: Mike Channon, 45 (46), England.
Most League Appearances: Terry Paine, 713, 1956–74.
Record Transfer Fee Received: £300,000 from Manchester C for Mike Channon, July 1977.
Record Transfer Fee Paid: £400,000 to Derby Co for Charlie George, Dec 1978.
Previous Managers since the War: Bill Dodgin (Snr), Sid Cann, George Roughton, Ted Bates.
Address of Supporters Club: Same as Football Club.

The Dell, Milton Road, Southampton SO9 4XX. Telephone Southampton 39445 and 39633. *Ground capacity:* 25,000. *Record attendance:* 31,044 v Manchester U, Division 1, 8 Oct, 1969. *Record receipts:* £63,574 v Everton, FA Cup 5th rd, 14 Feb, 1981. *Pitch measurements:* 110yd×72yd.

How to get there: The ground is 10 minutes' walk from Southampton Central station via Hill Lane. Buses 2 and 5 from the city centre pass the ground, which is only 10 minutes walk from the centre.
Match tickets: No seats available, all seats being sold to season-ticket holders. Room on the terraces for 8,800 standing, and admission is by purchasing tickets in advance.
Car parking: Only street parking in the vicinity of the ground. Municipal car parks in the city centre.
Entertainments/catering facilities: Licensed bars inside the ground.
Club shop: Situated in Milton Road, and at Hanover Buildings in City Centre.
Handbooks/programmes: Handbooks not published annually. Programmes available on subscription.
Extra information: In 1921–22, Southampton lost only four league games and conceded only 21 goals, both Division Three(South) records.
Club Colours: Red and white broad-striped shirts, black shorts, white stockings.
Change Colours: Light blue/dark blue shirts, dark blue shorts, light blue stockings.
Club Captain: Kevin Keegan.
Physiotherapist: Don Taylor MCSP, SRP.
First Team Trainer: Lew Chatterley *Club Nickname:* Saints.

SOUTHAMPTON 1980–81 LEAGUE RECORD

Match No.	Date	Venue	Opponents	Result	H/T Score	Goalscorers	Attendance
1	Aug 16	H	Manchester C	W 2-0	2-0	Channon 2	23,320
2	19	A	Arsenal	D 1-1	0-1	Baker	43,050
3	23	A	Sunderland	W 2-1	2-1	Nicholl, George	41,141
4	30	H	Birmingham C	W 3-1	3-0	Baker, Channon, Keegan	21,683
5	Sept 6	H	Brighton & HA	W 3-1	2-0	Williams, Baker, Golac	22,225
6	13	A	Norwich C	L 0-1	0-1		18,158
7	20	H	Liverpool	D 2-2	2-1	Nicholl, Boyer	24,085
8	27	A	WBA	L 1-2	0-0	George	20,845
9	Oct 4	A	Everton	L 1-2	1-1	Channon	36,544
10	7	H	Wolverhampton W	W 4-2	1-2	McCartney (pen), Nicholl, Baker, Moran	21,712
11	11	H	Stoke C	L 1-2	1-0	George (pen)	19,473
12	18	A	Middlesbrough	D 1-1	0-1	Watson	15,858
13	21	A	Crystal Palace	L 2-3	1-1	Moran 2	20,630
14	25	H	Aston Villa	L 1-2	0-1	Moran	21,249
15	Nov 1	A	Nottingham F	L 1-2	1-2	Moran	24,669
16	8	H	Ipswich T	D 3-3	1-2	Williams, Boyer, Moran	21,261
17	11	H	Arsenal	W 3-1	0-1	Moran, Watson, Holmes	21,244
18	15	A	Manchester C	L 0-3	0-0		32,661
19	22	H	Leeds U	W 2-1	2-1	George, Channon	20,278
20	29	A	Manchester U	D 1-1	0-0	Holmes	46,840
21	Dec 6	H	Coventry C	W 1-0	1-0	Holmes	18,847
22	13	A	Wolverhampton W	D 1-1	0-0	Moran	18,147
23	20	H	Crystal Palace	W 4-2	2-0	Gilbert (og), Channon, Moran, George	19,332
24	26	A	Tottenham H	D 4-4	2-2	Baker, George, Moran 2	28,792
25	27	H	Leicester C	W 4-0	4-0	Keegan, Baker (pen), George, Moran	21,886
26	Jan 10	A	Leeds U	W 3-0	1-0	Channon, Holmes 2	21,007
27	17	A	Birmingham C	W 3-0	1-0	Moran, Channon, Keegan	16,491
28	31	H	Sunderland	W 2-1	2-0	Keegan 2	21,345
29	Feb 7	H	Norwich C	W 2-1	0-0	Williams, George	20,454
30	21	H	WBA	D 2-2	1-1	Golac, Moran	21,910
31	24	A	Brighton & HA	L 0-2	0-0		23,715
32	28	A	Liverpool	L 0-2	0-1		41,575
33	Mar 7	H	Manchester U	W 1-0	1-0	Keegan	22,698
34	14	A	Stoke C	W 2-1	1-0	Keegan 2	14,828
35	17	H	Everton	W 3-0	1-0	Keegan, Baker, Williams	20,829
36	21	H	Middlesbrough	W 1-0	0-0	Moran	20,651
37	28	A	Aston Villa	L 1-2	1-2	Evans (og)	32,467
38	Apr 4	H	Nottingham F	W 2-0	2-0	Keegan, Channon	22,712
39	18	A	Leicester C	D 2-2	0-0	Baker, Moran	21,349
40	20	H	Tottenham H	D 1-1	1-0	Channon	23,735
41	25	A	Coventry C	L 0-1	0-0		18,213
42	May 13	A	Ipswich T	W 3-2	3-2	Keegan, Moran 2	19,504

Final League Position: 6

Goalscorers

League (76): Moran 18, Keegan 11, Channon 10, Baker 8 (1 pen), George 8 (1 pen), Holmes 5, Williams 4, Nicholl 3, Boyer 2, Golac 2, Watson 2, McCartney 1 (pen), own goals 2.
League Cup (5): George 2, Holmes 2, own goal.
F.A. Cup (6): Moran 3, Baker, Keegan, Williams.

League Cup	Second Round	Watford (h)	4-0
		(a)	1-7
FA Cup	Third Round	Chelsea (h)	3-1
	Fourth Round	Bristol R (h)	3-1
	Fifth Round	Everton (h)	0-0
		(a)	0-1

Katalinic	Golac	McCartney	Williams	Watson	Nicholl	Keegan	Channon	George	Holmes	Baker G	Hebberd	Wells	Boyer	Moran	Waldron	Pratt	Agboola	Wallace	Rogers	Ball	Puckett	Baker S	*Match No.*
1	2	3	4	5	6	7	8	9	10	11													1
1	2*	3	4	5	6	7	8	9	10	11	12												2
1	2	3	4	5	6	7	8	9	10	11													3
1	2*	3	4	5	6	7	8	9	10	11	12												4
	2	3	4	5	6		8		10	11	7	1	9										5
	2	3*	4	5	6		8	9	10	11	12	1	7										6
	2	3	4	5	6	7	8		10	11		1	9										7
	2	3		5	6	7	8	4	10	11		1	9										8
1	2	3	4	5	6	7*	8	9	10	11	12												9
1	2	3	4	5	6		8*		10	11	7		9	12									10
1	2	3*	4	5	6		8	7	10	11	12		9										11
1	2	3	4	5	6		8		10	11			9	7									12
1	2	3	4	5	6		8		10	11			9	7									13
1	2		4	5	6	7	8		10				9	11	3								14
1	2		4	5	6		8		10	7			9	11	3								15
1	2		4	5	6	7	8		3	11			9	10									16
	2		4	5	6	7	8		3	11		1	9	10									17
	2		4	5	6	7*	8		3	11	12	1	9	10									18
	2	3			6		8	9	10	11		1		7	5	4							19
	2	3		5	6		8	9	10	11		1					4	7					20
	2	3			6		8		10	11		1		9	5		4	7					21
	2	3		5	6		8		10	11	7	1		9			4						22
	2	3	4	5	6		8	9	10	11		1		7									23
	2		4	5	6		8	9	10	11		1		7			3						24
	2		4		6	7	8	9	3	11		1		10			5						25
	2		4	5	6	7	8	9	3	11		1		10									26
	2		4	5*	6	7	8	9	3	11		1		10			12						27
	2		4	5	6	7	8	9	3			1		10	11								28
	2		4		6	7	8	9	3	11		1		10	5								29
	2		4	5	6	7*	8	9	3	11	12	1		10									30
	2		4	5	6		8	9		11	7*	1		10	3				12				31
	2	3		5	6	7	8	9	4	11		1		10									32
	2			5	6	7	8	9	3	11		1		10						4			33
	2		4	5	6	7	8	9	3			1		10						11			34
	2		4	5	6	7	8*		3	9		1		10						11	12		35
	2		4	5	6	7	8		3	9*		1		10						11	12		36
	2		4	5	6	7	8		3	9		1		10						11*	12		37
	2		4	5	6	7	8*		3	9		1		10						11	12		38
	2		4	5	6	7	8		3	9		1		10						11			39
	2	4		5	6	7*	8		3	9		1		10						11	12		40
	2	4*	7	5	6		8		3	9		1		10						11	12		41
		4		5	6	7	8*		3	9		1		10						11	12	2	42
12	41	22	33	38	42	27	42	22	41	39	4	30	13	30	7	1	5	2	—	10	—	1	
											+ 7s			+ 1s			+ 1s		+ 1s		+ 7s		

SOUTHAMPTON

	Ht	Wt	Birthplace	Clubs	League App.	League Gls
Goalkeepers						
Peter Wells	6 1	13 4	Nottingham	Nottingham F	27	—
				Southampton	128	—
Terence Gennoe	6 2½	13 5	Shrewsbury	Bury	3	—
				Blackburn R (on loan)	—	—
				Leeds U (on loan)	—	—
				Halifax T	78	—
				Everton (on loan)	—	—
				Crystal Palace (on loan)	3	—
				Southampton	36	—
Ivan Katalinic	6 0½	12 3	Yugoslavia	Red Star Belgrade	(not known)	
(Yugoslavia)				Southampton	16	—
Defenders						
Malcolm Waldron	6 0	12 4	Emsworth	Southampton	141	8
(Contract cancelled April 1981)						
Chris Nicholl	6 2	12 13	Wilmslow	Burnley	—	—
(N Ireland)				Witton A	(not known)	
				Halifax T	42	3
				Luton T	98	6
				Aston V	210	11
				Southampton	152	8
Mark Whitlock	5 11	12 2½	Portsmouth	Southampton	—	—
Ivan Golac	5 10	13 1	Yugoslavia	Partizan	—	—
(Yugoslavia)				Southampton	108	4
Reuben Agboola	5 9½	11 7	London	Southampton	6	—
Stephen Baker	5 5	10 2	Newcastle	Southampton	1	—
Steven Richardson	5 6	10 1	Slough	Southampton	—	—
Dave Watson	5 11½	12 0	Nottingham	Notts Co	23	1
(England)				Rotherham U	121	20
				Sunderland	177	27
				Manchester C	146	4
				Werder Bremen	(not known)	
				Southampton	68	6
Mike McCartney	5 7	10 12	Edinburgh	WBA	—	—
				Carlisle U	156	17
				Southampton	22	1
Chris Hodge*			London	Southampton	—	—
Midfield						
Nick Holmes	5 11	12 2	Southampton	Southampton	262	45
Graham Baker	5 9	10 8	Southampton	Southampton	87	18
Alan Ball	5 6	10 5	Farnworth	Blackpool	116	41
(England)				Everton	208	66
				Arsenal	177	45
				Southampton	132	9
				Blackpool	30	5
				Southampton	10	—
Steve Williams	5 10½	10 11	London	Southampton	177	11
Wayne Pratt*	5 8	9 9	Southampton	Southampton	1	—
Trevor Hebberd	5 11½	11 4	Winchester	Southampton	93	7
(Contract cancelled April 1981)						
Russell Burtenshaw*			Horley	Southampton	—	—
David Madden	6 0	11 3	London	Southampton	—	—
David Wallace			London	Southampton	2	—
(Apprentice)						
Forwards						
Charlie George	5 11	12 7	London	Arsenal	133	31
(England)				Derby Co	106	34
				Nottingham F (on loan)	2	—
				Southampton	44	11
David Puckett	5 7	10 2	Southampton	Southampton	7	—
Mike O'Donoghue	5 9	11 9	London	Southampton	—	—
(Contract cancelled Feb 1981)				Northampton T (on loan)	4	1
Mike Channon	6 0½	12 11	Orcheston	Southampton	392	155
(England)				Manchester C	72	24
				Southampton	79	20
Joe Blochel	5 10½	11 11	Chalfont St Giles	Southampton	—	—
Steve Moran	5 8	10 11	Croydon	Southampton	32	19
Andy Rogers	5 8¾	9 7	Chatteris	Peterborough U	29	1
				Southampton	3	—
Kevin Keegan	5 8	11 7	Armthorpe	Scunthorpe U	124	18
(England)				Liverpool	230	68
				Hamburg	(not known)	
				Southampton	27	11
Martin Foyle			Salisbury	Southampton	—	—
George Lawrence	5 10	12 2	London	Southampton	—	—
Ian Juryeff	5 10½	11 6	Gosport	Southampton	—	—

SOUTHEND UNITED Division 3

President: N. L. Mitchell. *Chairman:* Frank Walton.

Directors: J. N. Woodcock, L. H. Lesser FCA, D. A. Smith, G. C. Janes, F. Bonfield, M. D. Rubin, A. R. Rubin.

Manager: David Smith. *Secretary:* K. Holmes FAAI, F INST CM.

Year Formed: 1906. *Turned Professional:* 1906.

Limited Company: 1919.

Previous Grounds: 1906, Roots Hall, Prittlewell; 1920, Kursaal; 1934, Southend Stadium; 1955, Roots Hall Football Ground.

Football League Record:
1920 Original Member of Division 3; 1921 Division 3(S); 1958–66 Division 3; 1966–72 Division 4; 1972–76 Division 3; 1976–78 Division 4; 1978–80 Division 3; 1980–81 Division 4; 1981– Division 3.

Honours: *Football League:* Division 3(S) best season: 3rd, 1931–32, 1949–50; Division 4 – Champions 1980–81; Runners-up 1971–72, 1977–78. *FA Cup* best season: old 3rd rd, 1920–21, 5th rd, 1925–26, 1951–52, 1975–76. *Football League Cup:* never past 3rd rd.

Record Victory: 10-1 v Golders Green, FA Cup 1st rd, 24 Nov, 1934, 10-1 v Brentwood, FA Cup 2nd rd, 7 Dec, 1968.

Record Defeat: 1-11 v Northampton T, Southern League, 30 Dec, 1909.

Most League Points: 67, Division 4, 1980–81.

Most League Goals: 92, Division 3(S), 1950–51.

Highest League Scorer in Season: Jim Shankly, 31, 1928–29 and Sammy McCrory, 1957–58, both in Division 3(S).

Most League Goals in Total Aggregate: Roy Hollis, 122, 1953–60.

Most Capped Player: George Mackenzie, 9, Eire.

Most League Appearances: Sandy Anderson, 451, 1950–63.

Record Transfer Fee Received: £111,111 from Blackpool for Colin Morris, Dec 1979.

Record Transfer Fee Paid: £111,111 to Blackpool for Derek Spence, Dec 1979.

Previous Managers since the War: Harry Warren, Eddie Perry, Frank Broome, Ted Fenton, Alvan Williams, Ernie Shepherd, Geoff Hudson, Arthur Rowley.

Address of Supporters Club: 374 Victoria Ave, Southend-on-Sea, Essex.

Address of the Club Shop or Boutique: 374 Victoria Avenue, Southend-on-Sea.

Roots Hall Football Ground, Victoria Avenue, Southend-on-Sea. Telephone Southend 40707. *Ground capacity:* 32,000 (16,000 covered). *Record attendance:* 31,033 v Liverpool, FA Cup 3rd rd, 10 Jan, 1979. *Record receipts:* £36,599 v Liverpool, FA Cup 3rd rd, 10 Jan, 1979. *Pitch measurements:* 110yd×74yd.

How to get there: Regular buses from Southend Central station in the High Street; the station is on the London line from Fenchurch Street. Southend Victoria, five minutes walk from the ground, is served by trains from Liverpool Street, London.

Match tickets: Seats can be purchased 14 days before the match.

Car parking: Two car parks at the ground hold approximately 700 cars. Ample parking in side-streets.

Entertainments/catering facilities: Tea bars all around the ground. There is a social club for members and *bona fide* visitors.

Club shop: Situated in Victoria Avenue opposite the ground; sells all types of souvenirs.

Handbooks/programmes: Programmes are available from the club shop; programmes are available on subscription.

Extra information: In 1921–22 full-back Jimmy Evans topped Southend's scorers' list with 10 penalties.

Club Colours: White shirts with blue sleeves and blue V-neck, blue shorts, blue stockings.

Change Colours: Red shirts with black trim, black shorts, black stockings.

Club Captain: Micky Stead.

Club Trainer/Coach: Brian Beckett.

Club Nickname: The Shrimpers.

SOUTHEND UNITED 1980–81 LEAGUE RECORD

Match No.	Date	Venue	Opponents	Result	H/T Score	Goalscorers	Attendance
1	Aug 16	A	Bury	W 2-1	0-0	Mercer, Hull	2647
2	18	H	Port Vale	W 5-1	3-1	Gray 2, Spence 2, Hadley	3948
3	22	H	Tranmere R	W 2-0	1-0	Mungall (og), Mercer	4623
4	Sept 5	H	York C	W 3-0	1-0	Spence 3	5124
5	13	A	Hereford U	D 0-0	0-0		2464
6	15	H	Peterborough U	W 1-0	1-0	Spence	5609
7	19	A	Doncaster R	L 0-1	0-1		6044
8	23	A	Northampton T	L 0-2	0-1		2337
9	26	H	Hartlepool U	W 4-0	2-0	Gray, Otulakowski, Mercer, Pountney	5112
10	Oct 1	A	Peterborough U	L 2-5	1-1	Spence, Gray	4228
11	3	H	Mansfield T	W 2-0	1-0	Mercer 2	4443
12	7	A	Wimbledon	W 1-0	1-0	Spence	2117
13	11	A	Halifax T	W 5-1	2-0	Spence, Moody, Cusack, Gray 2	1609
14	17	H	Scunthorpe U	W 2-0	0-0	Spence, Hadley	5271
15	20	H	Wigan Ath	W 1-0	1-0	Hadley	5643
16	25	A	Darlington	W 2-0	1-0	Mercer, Spence	2013
17	29	A	Crewe Alex	D 1-1	1-1	Spence	4217
18	31	H	Stockport Co	W 2-0	1-0	Gray, Mercer	5716
19	Nov 3	H	Wimbledon	W 1-0	0-0	Spence	4935
20	8	A	Lincoln C	L 1-2	0-1	Spence	7218
21	10	A	Port Vale	L 0-1	0-0		2780
22	15	H	Bury	W 1-0	0-0	Cusack (pen)	4312
23	Dec 6	A	Rochdale	W 2-0	0-0	Mercer, Spence	2214
24	12	H	Bradford C	W 3-1	1-1	Pountney, Gray, Thompson (og)	4476
25	19	H	Torquay U	W 3-1	1-1	Otulakowski, Gray, Cusack (pen)	4205
26	26	A	AFC Bournemouth	L 1-2	0-0	Polycarpou	4381
27	27	H	Aldershot	W 3-0	2-0	Pountney, Gray, Mercer	6828
28	Jan 3	A	Wigan Ath	W 1-0	0-0	McAdam (og)	5267
29	9	H	Darlington	W 1-0	0-0	Cusack	5066
30	23	H	Northampton T	D 0-0	0-0		5854
31	30	A	Tranmere R	D 2-2	1-1	Bramhall (og), Nelson	2127
32	Feb 6	H	Hereford U	W 2-0	1-0	Pountney, Spence	5229
33	14	A	York C	W 1-0	1-0	Spence	2129
34	21	A	Hartlepool U	W 3-1	2-0	Spence 2, Gray	3751
35	27	H	Doncaster R	D 0-0	0-0		5942
36	Mar 4	A	Bradford C	L 1-2	0-1	Gray	2369
37	7	A	Mansfield T	W 1-0	1-0	Gray	4379
38	13	H	Halifax T	W 5-1	2-0	Moody, Cusack (pen), Spence, Pountney, Gray	5542
39	22	A	Scunthorpe U	L 1-2	0-0	Hadley	3605
40	27	H	Crewe Alex	W 3-0	1-0	Gray 2, Mercer	5878
41	Apr 3	A	Stockport Co	L 0-1	0-1		2278
42	11	H	Lincoln C	D 0-0	0-0		11,955
43	17	H	AFC Bournemouth	W 2-1	1-0	Hadley, Spence	7355
44	18	A	Aldershot	W 2-1	2-0	Nelson, Gray	4433
45	25	A	Torquay U	W 3-0	3-0	Nelson, Hadley, Cusack (pen)	1767
46	May 1	H	Rochdale	D 1-1	0-1	Hadley	10,668

Final League Position: 1

Goalscorers

League (79): Spence 21, Gray 17, Mercer 10, Hadley 7, Cusack 6 (4 pens), Pountney 5, Nelson 3, Moody 2, Otulakowski 2, Hull 1, Polycarpou 1, own goals 4.
League Cup (1): Pountney.
F.A. Cup (0).

League Cup	First Round	Oxford U (h)	1-0
		(a)	0-2
FA Cup	First Round	Hereford U (h)	0-1

Cawston	Stead	Moody	Cusack	Yates	Hadley	Pountney	Hull	Gray	Spence	Mercer	Dudley	Otulakowski	Nelson	Polycarpou	Walker	Pennyfather	Match No.
1	2	5	6	3	4	8	11	7	9	10							1
1	2	5	6	3	4	8*	11	7	9	10	12						2
1	2	5	6	3	4		11	7	9	10		8					3
1	2	5	6	3	4	8		7	9	10		11					4
1	2	5	6	3	4	8		7	9	10		11					5
1	2	5	6	3	4	8	12	7	9	10		11*					6
1	2	5	6	3	4	8		7	9	10		11					7
1	2	5	6	3	4	8	12	7	9*	10		11					8
1	2	5	6*	3	4	8		7	9	10		11	12				9
1	2*	5		3	4	8		7	9	10	6	11	12				10
1		5	6	3	4	8		7	9	10	2	11					11
1		5	6	3	4	8		7*	9	10	2	11	12				12
1		5	6	3	4	8		7	9	10	2	11					13
1		5	6	3	4	8		7	9	10*	2	11	12				14
1		5	6	3	4			7	9		2	11	10	8			15
1			6	3	4	8		7	9	10	2	11			5		16
1		5	6	3	4	8		7	9		2	11		10			17
1	2		6	3	4	8		7	9	10	5	11*		12			18
1	3	5*	6		4	8		7	9	10	2	11	12				19
1	3		6		4	8		7	9	10	2	11			5		20
1	3				4	8		7	9	10	2	11	6		5		21
1	2		6	3	4*	8		7	9	10		11	12		5		22
1	2		6	3	4	8		7	9	10		11			5		23
1	2		6	3*	4	8		7	9	10		11		12	5		24
1	2		6	3	4	8		7	9	10		11			5		25
1	2		6	3	4*	8		7	9			11	10	12	5		26
1	2		6	3	4	8		7	9	10		5	11				27
1	2		6	3		8		7	9	10		4	11		5		28
1			5	3		7		6*	8	9	2	11	10	12	4		29
1			6	3	4	8		7	9	10*	2	11	12		5		30
1	2		6	3	4	8		7	9			11	10		5		31
1	2		6	3	4	8		7	9			11	10		5		32
1	2		6	3	4	8		7	9	10		11			5		33
1	2	6		3	4	8		7	9	10		11			5		34
1		6			4	8		7	9	10	2	11			5	3	35
1	2	5	6	3	4	8		7	9	10		11					36
1		6	5	3	4	8		7	9	10		11			2		37
1	2	5	6	3	4	8		7	9	10		11					38
1	2	5	6	3	4	8		7	9	10			11				39
1	2	5	6	3	4	8		7	9	10		11					40
1	2	5	6	3	4*	8		7	9	10		11	12				41
1	2	5	6	3	4	8		7	9	10*		11	12				42
1	2	5	6	3	4	8		7	9	10*		11	12				43
1	2	5	6	3	4	8		7	9			11	10				44
1	2	5	6	3	4	8		7	9			11	10				45
1	2	5	6	3	4	8		7	9			11	10				46
46	35	30	42	42	44	44	3	46	46	38	15	43	12	2	17	1	
							+ 2s				+ 1s		+ 10s	+ 4s			

SOUTHEND UNITED

	Ht	Wt	Birthplace	Clubs	League App.	League Gls
Goalkeepers						
Mervyn Cawston	6 1	12 12	Norwich	Norwich C	4	—
				Southend U (on loan)	10	—
				Leicester C (on loan)	—	—
				Newport Co (on loan)	4	—
				Gillingham	19	—
				Chicago S	—	—
				Southend U	127	—
John Keeley	6 0	12 0	Plaistow	Southend U	4	—
Defenders						
Alan Moody	5 11	11 10	Middlesbrough	Middlesbrough	46	—
				Southend U	355	38
Tony Hadley	6 0	12 2	Rochford	Southend U	206	15
John Walker	5 10	11 9	Rochford	Southend U	47	—
Phil Dudley	5 7	9 10	Basildon	Southend U	102	3
Steve Yates	6 0	12 13	Burton upon Trent	Leicester C	19	—
				Southend U	142	2
David Cusack	6 1½	13 13	Rotherham	Sheffield W	95	1
				Southend U	115	8
Glenn Pennyfather			Billericay	Southend U	1	—
Midfield						
Ron Pountney	5 6	9 13	Bilston	Walsall	1	—
				Port Vale	—	—
				Southend U	200	15
Anton Otulakowski	5 7	10 10	Dewsbury	Barnsley	42	2
				West Ham U	17	—
				Southend U	94	2
Mickey Stead	5 8	11 10	West Ham	Tottenham H	15	—
				Swansea C (on loan)	5	1
				Southend U	115	4
Jeff Hull*	5 6	9 11	Rochford	Southend U	15	1
Steve Goodwin	5 8	11 2	Chadderton	Norwich C	3	—
(Contract cancelled Oct 1980)				Scunthorpe U (on loan)	2	—
				Southend U	75	10
Jon Watson*	5 7	10 5	Upminster	Southend U	—	—
Keith Mercer	5 10	11 7	Lewisham	Watford	134	46
				Southend U	52	14
Forwards						
Graham Franklin	5 9	11 3	Bicester	Southend U	6	1
Andy Polycarpou*	5 9	11 3	Bicester	Southend U	63	10
Terry Gray	5 8	10 0	Bradford	Chelsea	—	—
				Huddersfield T	163	36
				Southend U	87	24
Garry Nelson	5 10	10 7	Braintree	Southend U	44	5
Derek Spence	5 10	11 3	Belfast	Oldham Ath	6	—
(N Ireland)				Bury	140	44
				Olympiakos	(not known)	
				Blackpool	85	20
				Southend U	68	26
Mickey Tuohy	6 1	12 2	West Bromwich	Redditch	(not known)	
(Contract cancelled Feb 1981)				Southend U	21	4
Danny Greaves			Upminster	Southend U	—	—

STOCKPORT COUNTY Division 4

President/Chairman: A. N. Kirk.
Directors: P. Lukic, A. M. Barlow, J. Lewis, A. Pownall.
Chief Executive/Secretary: T. R. McCreery FAAI.
Manager: Jimmy McGuigan.
Commercial Manager: Roger Fielding.
Year Formed: 1883. *Turned Professional:* 1891.
Limited Company: 1908.
Previous Names: Heaton Norris Rovers 1883–88, Heaton Norris 1888–90.
Previous Grounds: 1883 Heaton Norris Recreation Ground, 1884 Heaton Norris Wanderers Cricket Ground, 1885 Chorlton's Farm, Chorlton's Lane, 1886 Heaton Norris Cricket Ground, 1887 Wilkes' Field, Belmont Street, 1889 Nursery Inn, Green Lane, 1902 Edgeley Park.

Football League Record:
1900 Elected to Division 2; 1904 failed re-election; 1905–21 Division 2; 1921–22 Division 3(N); 1922–26 Division 2; 1926–37 Division 3(N); 1937–38 Division 2; 1938–58 Division 3(N); 1958–59 Division 3; 1959–67 Division 4; 1967–70 Division 3; 1970– Division 4.

Honours: *Football League:* Division 2 best season: 17th, 1905–06; Division 3(N) – Champions 1921–22, 1936–37; Runners-up 1928–29, 1929–30; Division 4 – Champions 1966–67. *FA Cup* best season: 5th rd, 1935, 1950. *Football League Cup* best season: 4th rd, 1972–73.
Record Victory: 13-0 v Halifax T, Division 3(N), 6 Jan, 1934.
Record Defeat: 1-8 v Chesterfield, Division 2, 19 Apr, 1902.
Most League Points: 64, Division 4, 1966–67.
Most League Goals: 115, Division 3(N), 1933–34.
Highest League Scorer in Season: Alf Lythgoe, 46, Division 3(N), 1933–34.
Most League Goals in Total Aggregate: Jack Connor, 132, 1951–56.
Most Capped Player: Harry Hardy, 1, England.
Most League Appearances: Bob Murray, 465, 1952–63.
Record Transfer Fee Received: £80,000 from Manchester C for Stuart Lee, Sept 1979.
Record Transfer Fee Paid: £25,000 to Albion Rovers for Tony Coyle, Dec 1979.
Previous Managers since the War: Bob Marshall, Andy Beattie, Dick Duckworth, Willie Moir, Reg Flewin, Trevor Porteous, Bert Trautmann, Eddie Quigley, Jimmy Meadows, Walter Galbraith, Matt Woods, Brian Doyle, Jimmy Meadows, Roy Chapman, Eddie Quigley, Alan Thompson, Mike Summerbee.
Programme Editor: Howard Jones.
Address of Supporters Club: A. Flitcroft, 8 Vine Street, Hazel Grove, Stockport, Cheshire SK7 4JS.
Address of Club Shop: Office at the ground.

Edgeley Park, Hardcastle Road, Stockport, Cheshire SK3 9DD. Telephone: 061-480 8888. *Ground capacity:* 16,500. *Record attendance:* 27,833 v Liverpool, FA Cup 5th rd, 11 Feb, 1950. *Record receipts:* £19,382 v Arsenal, League Cup 3rd rd, 22 Sept, 1980. *Pitch measurements:* 110yd×75yd.
How to get there: Edgeley Park is situated within a mile of the Mersey Square, the town centre; a few minutes walk via Wellington Road South and Greek Street. The main line railway station lies just off Greek Street and is only a five minute walk to the Ground.
Match tickets: Seats can be reserved in the Main Stand by post or telephone two weeks before the match.
Car parking: Ample street parking around the ground.
Entertainments/catering facilities: Top class cabaret club next to the ground; four refreshment bars around the ground (not licensed).
Club shop: Small kiosk situated on Popular side of ground.
Handbooks/programmes: The *Matchday Magazine* is available outside the ground. It is also available on subscription to the Programme Editor and by post.
Extra information: In 1934 Stockport County created a record which is still unsurpassed in a Football League game when they defeated Halifax Town 13-0, eleven goals coming in the second half.
Club Colours: Sky blue and white stripes, black shorts, white stockings with three sky blue bands at top.
Change Colours: Yellow shirts with green sleeves, green shorts, yellow stockings with three green bands at top.
Club Captain:
Club Nickname: County.

STOCKPORT COUNTY 1980–81 LEAGUE RECORD

Match No.	Date	Venue	Opponents	Result	H/T Score	Goalscorers	Attendance
1	Aug 16	H	Rochdale	D 2-2	1-2	Booth, Sword (pen)	2739
2	20	A	Bradford C	D 1-1	0-0	Williams	3660
3	23	A	Darlington	D 2-2	0-1	Sword, Bradd	1920
4	29	H	Halifax T	D 1-1	0-0	Sword	2487
5	Sept 6	A	Wimbledon	W 2-1	0-0	Rutter, Bradd	2018
6	13	H	Lincoln C	D 0-0	0-0		3289
7	15	H	Port Vale	W 2-1	1-0	Williams, Sword (pen)	3480
8	19	A	Scunthorpe U	L 0-2	0-2		1985
9	26	H	Crewe Alex	L 1-3	1-3	Prophett (og)	3536
10	29	A	Port Vale	L 0-2	0-1		2835
11	Oct 3	A	Northampton T	W 1-0	1-0	Williams	1902
12	6	H	Peterborough U	L 3-4	2-4	Galvin, Sunley, Williams	1794
13	10	H	Hereford U	D 0-0	0-0		2303
14	18	A	York C	L 0-1	0-0		2135
15	22	A	Torquay U	W 2-1	0-0	Williams, Sunley	1792
16	24	H	AFC Bournemouth	W 2-1	1-0	Sherlock, Williams	2012
17	27	H	Hartlepool U	L 0-2	0-1		2066
18	31	A	Southend U	L 0-2	0-1		5716
19	Nov 4	A	Peterborough U	W 2-1	0-1	Fowler, Booth	2772
20	7	H	Doncaster R	W 2-1	2-0	Mountford 2	2474
21	10	H	Bradford C	L 1-2	0-0	Galvin	3248
22	29	H	Aldershot	W 1-0	0-0	Fowler	1818
23	Dec 6	A	Mansfield T	L 0-1	0-1		2873
24	12	A	Rochdale	L 1-2	1-1	Mountford	1291
25	19	H	Bury	L 1-2	1-0	Thorpe	1941
26	26	A	Tranmere R	L 0-1	0-1		2531
27	27	H	Wigan Ath	L 0-1	0-1		3062
28	Jan 3	A	AFC Bournemouth	W 1-0	1-0	Leigh	2822
29	17	A	Aldershot	L 0-3	0-1		2020
30	24	A	Halifax T	L 0-2	0-1		3286
31	30	H	Darlington	L 0-1	0-1		2011
32	Feb 7	A	Lincoln C	L 0-1	0-0		4315
33	13	H	Wimbledon	D 0-0	0-0		1772
34	16	H	Torquay U	W 4-1	0-0	Sword (pen), Coyle, Sherlock, Bradd	1431
35	21	A	Crewe Alex	L 0-2	0-1		2598
36	27	H	Scunthorpe U	W 2-0	0-0	Bradd 2	1675
37	Mar 6	H	Northampton T	L 1-2	1-1	Sunley	1945
38	20	H	York C	W 2-0	0-0	Bradd 2	1903
39	28	A	Hartlepool U	L 0-1	0-0		1928
40	Apr 3	H	Southend U	W 1-0	1-0	Bradd	2278
41	10	A	Doncaster R	L 1-2	0-0	Bradd	6120
42	18	A	Wigan Ath	L 1-2	0-1	Bradd	3980
43	20	H	Tranmere R	W 1-0	0-0	Galvin	2311
44	25	A	Bury	W 1-0	0-0	Fowler	2862
45	May 1	H	Mansfield T	W 2-1	0-1	Rutter, Park	2236
46	6	A	Hereford U	L 0-2	0-1		1707

Final League Position: 20

Goalscorers

League (44): Bradd 10, Williams 6, Sword 5 (2 pens), Fowler 3, Galvin 3, Mountford 3, Sunley 3, Booth 2, Rutter 2, Sherlock 2, Coyle 1, Leigh 1, Park 1, Thorpe 1, own goal 1.
League Cup (6): Sunley 3, Sword 2 (1 pen), Bradd.
F.A. Cup (2): Coyle, Sunley.

League Cup	First Round	Chester (a)	1-1
		(h)	1-0
	Second Round	Sunderland (h)	1-1
		(a)	2-1
	Third Round	Arsenal (h)	1-3
FA Cup	First Round	Sheffield U (h)	0-0
		(a)	2-3

Lawson	Rutter	Sherlock	Thorpe	Sword	Uzelac	Williams	Sunley	Bradd	Galvin	Booth	Fowler	Coyle	Rogan	Power	Mountford	Leigh	Park	Smith	*Match No.*
1	2	3	4	5	6	7	8	9	10	11									1
1	2	3		5	6	7	8	9	10		4	11							2
1	2	3		5	6	7	8	9	10		4	11							3
1	2	3		5	6	7	8	9	10		4	11							4
1	2	3		5	6	7	8	9	10		4	11							5
1	2	3		5	6	7	8	9	10		4	11							6
1	2	3		5	6	7		9	10	8	4	11							7
1	2	3		5	6	7	8	9	10		4	11							8
	2	3		5	6	7	8		10	9	4	11	1						9
	2	3	12	5	6	7	8		10	9	4	11*	1						10
1	2	3	10	5	6*	7	8	9	11	12	4								11
1	2	3	11	5		7	8	6	10		4			9					12
1	2	3	10	5		9	8	6	11		4	7*		12					13
1	2	3	10	5		7	8	6	11		4			9					14
1	2	3	10	5		7	8	6	11		4	9							15
1	2	3	10	5		7	8	6	11		4	9							16
1	2	3	10	5		7	8	6	11		4	9							17
1	2	3	10	5		7	8	6	11		4	9							18
1	2		10	5	3	7	8	6	11*	12	4	9							19
1	2		10	5	3	7	8	6			4	11			9				20
1	2		10	5	3	7	8	6	11*	12	4				9				21
1	2		3	5	6	7	8	9	10		4	11							22
1	2		3	5	6	7*	8	9	10		4	11			12				23
1	2	3	10	5			8	6		7	4	11			9				24
1	2	3	10	5			8	6		7	4	11			9				25
1	2	3	10	5			8	6		7	4	11			9				26
1	2	3	10	5			8	6		7*	4	11			9	12			27
1	2	3	5		6		8	9	10		4	11				7			28
1	2	3	5				8	6	10		4	11		9		7			29
1	2	3	5			7	8	6	10	12	4	11		9*					30
1	2	3	5	6		7	8	9	10		4	11							31
1	2	3	5	6		7	8	9	10		4*	11				12			32
1	2	3	5	6		7	8	9	10		4	11							33
1	2	3	5	6		7	8	9	10		4	11							34
1	2	3	5	6		7	8	9	10		4	11							35
1	2	3	5	6			8	9	10		4	11				7			36
1	2	3	5	6			8	9	10		4	11				7			37
1	2	3	5	6			8	9	10		4	11					7		38
1	2	3	5	6			8	9	10		4						7	11	39
1	2	3	5	6		7	8	9	11		4						10		40
1	2	3	5	6		7	8	9	11		4						10		41
1	2	3	5	6		7	8	9	11		4						10		42
1	2	3	5	6		7	8	9	11		4						10		43
1	2	3	5	6		7	8		10		4	11						9	44
1	2	3	5	6		7	8	9	11		4						10		45
1	2	3	5	6		7	8	9	10		4						11		46
44	46	41	37	43	17	36	45	43	41	8	45	34	2	4	6	4	8	2	
			+ 1s							+ 4s				+ 1s	+ 1s	+ 2s			

STOCKPORT COUNTY

	Ht	Wt	Birthplace	Clubs	League App.	League Gls
Goalkeepers						
Mike Rogan*	5 11	12 0	Fleetwood	Workington	390	—
				Stockport Co	73	—
				Crewe Alex (on loan)	3	—
Dave Lawson*	6 0¾	11 0	Newcastle	Newcastle U	—	—
				Shrewsbury T	—	—
				Bradford PA	13	—
				Huddersfield T	51	—
				Everton	124	—
				Luton T	5	—
				Stockport Co	106	—
Defenders						
John Rutter	5 9	10 10	Warrington	Wolverhampton W	—	—
				Bournemouth	4	—
				Exeter C	32	1
				Stockport Co	225	8
Andy Thorpe	5 11	11 4	Stockport	Stockport Co	116	2
Steve Sherlock	5 9	11 8	Birmingham	Manchester C	—	—
				Luton T	2	—
				Stockport Co	80	4
Steve Uzelac	5 11	11 4	Doncaster	Doncaster R	185	9
				Mansfield T (on loan)	2	—
				Liverpool	—	—
				Preston NE	9	—
				Stockport Co	26	—
Nigel Smith (Non-contract)			Manchester	Blackburn R	—	—
				Stockport Co	2	—
Midfield						
Chris Galvin*	5 10	12 3	Huddersfield	Leeds U	8	—
				Hull C	143	11
				York C (on loan)	22	6
				Stockport Co	68	3
Terry Park	5 11¾	11 6	Liverpool	Wolverhampton W	—	—
				Minnesota	(not known)	
				Stockport Co	98	9
Oshor Williams	5 10	11 8	Stockton	Manchester U	—	—
				Gateshead	(not known)	
				Southampton	6	—
				Exeter C (on loan)	3	—
				Stockport Co	64	7
Tony Coyle	5 9	11 0	Glasgow	Albion R	46	5
				Stockport Co	48	1
David Booth	6 0	11 4	Manchester	Stockport Co	28	4
Martin Fowler	5 11	12 10	York	Huddersfield T	73	2
				Norwich C (on loan)	—	—
				Hartlepool U (on loan)	6	—
				Blackburn R	38	—
				Stockport Co	45	3
Mark Leigh (Non-contract)			Manchester	Manchester C	—	—
				Stockport Co	6	1
Forwards						
Les Bradd*	6 1	13 0	Buxton	Rotherham U	3	—
				Notts Co	398	125
				Stockport Co	117	31
Tommy Sword	6 2	13 0	Newcastle	Bishop Auckland	(not known)	
				Stockport Co	68	13
David Sunley	5 9	11 0	Shelton	Sheffield W	133	21
				Nottingham F (on loan)	1	—
				Hull C	69	11
				Lincoln C	41	6
				Stockport Co	52	4
Bob Mountford (Contract cancelled Jan 1981)	5 11	10 10	Stoke	Port Vale	81	9
				Scunthorpe U (on loan)	3	—
				Crewe Alex (on loan)	5	—
				Rochdale	98	37
				Huddersfield T	14	4
				Halifax T	62	11
				Crewe Alex	3	—
				Stockport Co	7	3
Mike Power (Non-contract)			Stockport	Stockport Co	5	—

STOKE CITY Division 1

Chairman: P. Axon.

Directors: J. A. M. Humphreys, A. W. Clubb, A. A. Henshall, F. Edwards.

Manager: Richie Barker.

Secretary: M. J. Potts. *Coach:* Wally Gould.

Year Formed: 1863 (second oldest League Club).

Turned Professional: 1885. *Limited Company:* 1908.

Previous Grounds: 1875, Sweeting's Field; 1878, Victoria Ground (previously known as the Athletic Club Ground).

Football League Record:
1888 Founder Members of Football League; 1890 Not re-elected; 1891 Re-elected; Relegated in 1907, and after one year in Division 2, resigned for financial reasons; Re-elected to Division 2 in 1919; 1922–23 Division 1; 1923–26 Division 2; 1926–27 Division 3(N); 1927–33 Division 2; 1933–53 Division 1; 1953–63 Division 2; 1963–77 Division 1; 1977–79 Division 2; 1979– Division 1.

Honours: *Football League:* Division 1 best season: 4th, 1935–36, 1946–47; Division 2 – Champions 1932–33, 1962–63; Runners-up 1921–22; Promoted 1978–79 (3rd); Division 3(N) – Champions 1926–27. *FA Cup:* Semi-finals 1899, 1971, 1972. *Football League Cup:* Winners 1971–72. **European Competitions:** *UEFA Cup:* 1972–73, 1974–75.

Record Victory: 10-3 v WBA, Division 1, 4 Feb, 1937.

Record Defeat: 0-10 v Preston NE, Division 1, 14 Sept, 1889.

Most League Points: 63, Division 3(N), 1926–27.

Most League Goals: 92, Division 3(N), 1926–27.

Highest League Scorer in Season: Freddie Steele, 33, Division 1, 1936–37.

Most League Goals in Total Aggregate: Freddie Steele, 142, 1934–49.

Most League Appearances: Eric Skeels, 506, 1958–76.

Most Capped Player: Gordon Banks 36 (73), England.

Record Transfer Fee Received: £600,000 from Tottenham H for Garth Crooks, July 1980.

Record Transfer Fee Paid: £325,000 to Leicester C for Peter Shilton, Nov 1974.

Previous Managers since the War: Bob McGrory, Frank Taylor, Tony Waddington, George Eastham, Alan A'Court, Alan Durban.

Address of Social Club: c/o Football Club.

Victoria Ground, Stoke-on-Trent. Telephone Stoke-on-Trent 413511. *Telegraphic address:* 'Football, Stoke-on-Trent'. *Ground capacity:* 35,000. *Record attendance:* 51,380 v Arsenal, Division 1, 29 Mar, 1937. *Record receipts:* £33,739 v Liverpool, Division 1, 23 Apr, 1980. *Pitch measurements:* 116yd×75yd.

How to get there: Stoke-on-Trent railway station, on the main line from London, is five minutes walk from the ground. No special buses from the town centre because the ground is central. By road, Stoke is well served by the M6 which passes just two miles from the city.

Match tickets: Bookable two weeks before the match. Ticket office tel: Stoke-on-Trent 413961.

Car parking: The official car park in Wheildon Road holds 2,000 cars. Street parking permitted.

Entertainments/catering facilities: Social club. Refreshments obtainable on the ground.

Handbooks/programmes: Programmes available on subscription.

Extra information: Neville Coleman scored seven goals for Stoke against Lincoln City in 1957, a record for a winger in English senior football.

Club Colours: Red and white striped shirts, white shorts and stockings.

Change Colours: All sky blue.

Club Captain: Ray Evans.

Club Nickname: Potters.

STOKE CITY 1980–81 LEAGUE RECORD

Match No.	*Date*	*Venue*	*Opponents*	*Result*	*H/T Score*	*Goalscorers*	*Attendance*
1	Aug 16	A	Norwich C	L 1-5	1-4	Heath	14,616
2	20	H	WBA	D 0-0	0-0		14,085
3	23	H	Ipswich T	D 2-2	1-2	Ursem, Chapman	10,722
4	30	A	Nottingham F	L 0-5	0-2		21,915
5	Sept 6	H	Leeds U	W 3-0	3-0	Ursem, Maguire, Heath	12,729
6	13	A	Arsenal	L 0-2	0-0		27,183
7	20	A	Manchester C	W 2-1	2-1	Ursem, Chapman	29,507
8	27	H	Middlesbrough	W 1-0	1-0	Ursem	11,847
9	Oct 4	H	Tottenham H	L 2-3	0-2	Hampton, O'Callaghan	18,511
10	8	A	Leicester C	D 1-1	1-1	Chapman	14,549
11	11	A	Southampton	W 2-1	0-1	Munro, Hampton	19,473
12	18	H	Brighton & HA	D 0-0	0-0		13,079
13	22	H	Manchester U	L 1-2	0-0	O'Callaghan	22,000
14	25	A	Birmingham C	D 1-1	0-0	Doyle	16,535
15	Nov 1	H	Liverpool	D 2-2	0-1	Chapman, Randall	22,864
16	8	A	Sunderland	D 0-0	0-0		21,483
17	15	H	Norwich C	W 3-1	1-0	Chapman 3	11,207
18	22	H	Crystal Palace	W 1-0	0-0	O'Callaghan	13,422
19	25	A	WBA	D 0-0	0-0		15,922
20	29	A	Wolverhampton W	L 0-1	0-0		18,786
21	Dec 6	H	Everton	D 2-2	1-1	Chapman, O'Callaghan	15,650
22	13	A	Manchester U	D 2-2	2-1	Randall, Chapman	39,568
23	20	H	Leicester C	W 1-0	1-0	Chapman	13,433
24	26	A	Aston Villa	L 0-1	0-1		34,658
25	27	H	Coventry C	D 2-2	0-1	Doyle, Griffiths	17,765
26	Jan 10	A	Crystal Palace	D 1-1	0-1	Doyle	14,154
27	31	A	Ipswich T	L 0-4	0-2		23,843
28	Feb 7	H	Arsenal	D 1-1	1-0	Ursem	14,400
29	14	A	Leeds U	W 3-1	1-1	Chapman 3	16,530
30	18	H	Nottingham F	L 1-2	0-1	Heath	17,305
31	21	A	Middlesbrough	L 1-3	0-1	Maguire	15,142
32	Mar 11	A	Tottenham H	D 2-2	1-0	O'Callaghan, Heath	28,742
33	14	H	Southampton	L 1-2	0-1	Heath	14,828
34	18	H	Manchester C	W 2-1	1-1	Doyle, O'Callaghan	15,842
35	21	A	Brighton & HA	D 1-1	1-1	Ursem	13,583
36	28	H	Birmingham C	D 0-0	0-0		14,624
37	Apr 3	A	Liverpool	L 0-3	0-1		33,308
38	11	H	Sunderland	W 2-0	0-0	Chapman, Dodd	11,501
39	18	A	Coventry C	D 2-2	0-2	Chapman, Maguire (pen)	12,766
40	20	H	Aston Villa	D 1-1	1-1	O'Callaghan	23,500
41	25	A	Everton	W 1-0	0-0	Heath	15,352
42	May 2	H	Wolverhampton W	W 3-2	1-1	Bracewell 2, Ursem	14,929

Final League Position: 11

Goalscorers

League (51): Chapman 15, O'Callaghan 7, Ursem 7, Heath 6, Doyle 4, Maguire 3 (1 pen), Bracewell 2, Hampton 2, Randall 2, Dodd 1, Griffiths 1, Munro 1.
League Cup (1): Chapman.
F.A. Cup (3): Bracewell, Chapman, Heath.

League Cup	Second Round	Manchester C (h)	1-1
		(a)	0-3
FA Cup	Third Round	Wolverhampton W (h)	2-2
		(a)	1-2

Fox	Evans	Hampton	Doyle	Dodd	Richardson	Ursem	Heath	Chapman	Cook	Bracewell	Johnson P A	Thorley	Johnson P	McAughtrie	Sheldon	Randall	Maguire	O'Callaghan	Munro	Griffiths	Match No.
1	2	3	4	5	6	7	8*	9	10	11	12										1
1	2	3		4	6	7		9	10	11	8	5									2
1	2	3		4	6	7		9	10	11	8*	5				12					3
1	2			5	6			9		11	10		3	4	7	8					4
1	2	3	6	4		10	8*	9		11	12	5					7				5
1	2	3	6	4			8	9		11		5					7	10			6
1	2	3	6	4		8	7	9		11		10						5			7
1	2	3	6	4		8	7	9		11		10						5			8
1	2	3	6	4	10*	8	7	9		11						12		5			9
1	2	3	6	4	10	8*	7	9		11		12						5			10
1	2	3	6	4	10	8	7	9										5	11		11
1	2	3	6	4	10*	8	7	9		12								5	11		12
1	2	3	6	4	10	8*	7	9		12								5	11		13
1	2	3	6	4	10*		8	9		12						7		5	11		14
1	2	3	6*	4	10		8	9		7						12		5	11		15
1	2*	3	6	4	10		8	9		7						12		5	11		16
1	2	3	6	4	10		8	9		7								5	11		17
1	2	3	6	4	10		8	9*		7								5	11	12	18
1	2	3	6	4	10		8	9		12						7*		5	11		19
1	2	3	6		10		8	9				4						5	11	7	20
1	2	3	6	4		7*	8	9		10								5	11	12	21
1	2	3	6	4			8	9		10						7		5	11		22
1	2	3		4			8	9	12	10		6				7*		5	11		23
1	2	3	6	4			8	9		10						7*		5	11	12	24
1	2		6	4	11	7*	8			10		12						5	3	9	25
1	2	3	6	4	10	12		9		7*								5	11	8	26
1		3	2	4		12	10	9		7							11	5	6	8*	27
1		3	6	4		7	10	9		8	2							5	11		28
1		3	6	4		7	10	9		8	2							5	11		29
1		3	6	4		10*	8	9		7	2							5	11	12	30
1			6*	4		7	8	9		10	2	12					11	5	3		31
1		3	6	4			7	9		8	2						11	5	10		32
1		3	6	4		12	7	9		8							11	5	10*	2	33
1		3*	6	4		12	8	9		10	2						11	5	7		34
1			6	4		7	10	9		8	2						11	5	3		35
1			6	4		7	10*	9		8	2						11	5	3	12	36
1	2		6	4		7	10	9		8							11	5	3		37
1	2		6	4		7	10	9		8							11	5	3		38
1	2	7	6	4			10	9		8							11	5	3		39
1	2		6	4		7	10	9		8							11	5	3		40
1	2	12	6	4		7*	10	9		8							11	5	3		41
1	2		6	4		7	10	9		8							11	5	3		42
42	32	32	38	41	18	24	38	41	3	36	11	8	1	1	1	6	15	37	32	5	
		+ 1s				+ 4s			+ 1s	+ 4s	+ 2s	+ 3s				+ 4s				+ 5s	

STOKE CITY

	Ht	*Wt*	*Birthplace*	*Clubs*	*League App.*	*League Gls*
Goalkeepers						
Peter Fox	5 10½	12 4	Scunthorpe	Sheffield W	49	—
				West Ham U (on loan)	—	—
				Barnsley (on loan)	1	—
				Stoke C	66	—
Eric McManus	6 1	12 12	Limavady	Coventry C	6	—
				Notts Co	229	—
				Lincoln C (on loan)	21	—
				Stoke C	—	—
Defenders						
Paul Johnson	5 9	11 3	Stoke	Stoke C	34	—
Denis Smith	6 0	12 2	Stoke	Stoke C	390	30
Alan Dodd	5 10¼	12 3	Stoke	Stoke C	313	3
Mike Doyle	6 0	12 2	Manchester	Manchester C	448	32
(England)				Stoke C	107	5
Ray Evans	5 10	12 8	Edmonton	Tottenham H	136	2
				Millwall	74	3
				Fulham	86	6
				Stoke C	72	1
Stephen Kirk	5 11½	10 8	Kirkcaldy	East Fife	25	2
				Stoke C	—	—
Dennis Thorley	6 0	11 4	Stoke	Stoke C	13	—
				Blackburn R (on loan)	4	—
David McAughtrie	6 1	12 3	Newcumnock	Stoke C	1	—
Peter Hampton	5 7½	10 9	Teeside	Leeds U	68	2
				Stoke C	33	2
Midfield						
Kevin Sheldon*	5 5½	9 4	Stoke	Stoke C	15	—
Paul Richardson	5 10	11 12	Nottingham	Nottingham F	221	18
				Chester	28	2
				Stoke C	127	10
Paul A. Johnson	5 6½	11 12	Stoke	Stoke C	43	—
Sammy Irvine	5 6	11 2	Glasgow	Shrewsbury T	207	18
(Retired, injury)				Stoke C	67	11
Adrian Heath	5 6	10 1	Stoke	Stoke C	78	11
Loek Ursem	5 9	11 4	Amsterdam	AZ Sportlaan	(not known)	
				Stoke C	35	7
John Lumsden	5 8½	11 5	Edinburgh	East Fife	22	7
				Stoke C	1	—
Paul Bracewell	5 8	10 9	Stoke	Stoke C	46	2
Iain Munro	5 7½	10 5	Uddingston	St Mirren	104	16
(Scotland)				Hibernian	61	11
				Rangers	5	—
				St Mirren	89	3
				Stoke C	32	1
Forwards						
Jeff Cook	5 9	11 3	Hartlepool	Stoke C	29	5
				Bradford C (on loan)	8	1
				Plymouth Arg (on loan)	7	5
Bren O'Callaghan	6 2½	14 0	Bradford	Doncaster R	187	65
(Eire)				Stoke C	129	34
Lee Chapman	6 1½	13 5	Lincoln	Stoke C	58	18
				Plymouth Arg (on loan)	4	—
Paul Maguire	5 8	11 6	Glasgow	Shrewsbury T	151	35
				Stoke C	15	3
Stephen Bould	6 2½	11 13	Stoke	Stoke C	—	—
Peter Griffiths	5 6	10 8	Barnstaple	Bideford	(not known)	
				Stoke C	10	1

SUNDERLAND Division 1

Chairman: T. Cowie.

Vice-Chairman: K. I. Collings.

Directors: E. M. Evans, F. Stewart, F. S. Cronin, J. M. Ditchburn, I. T. S. Fraser, P. J. Heyward.

Manager: Alan Durban. *Secretary:* R. M. Linney.

Assistant Manager:

Year Formed: 1879. *Turned Professional:* 1886.

Limited Company: 1906.

Previous Grounds: 1879, Blue House Field, Hendon; 1881, Ashbrooke; 1883, site of Cooper Street; 1884, Abbs Field, Fulwell; 1886, Newcastle Road; 1898, Roker Park.

Previous Name: 1879–81, Sunderland and District Teachers' AFC.

Football League Record:
1890 Elected to Division 1 (record run of 57 seasons); 1958–64 Division 2; 1964–70 Division 1; 1970–76 Division 2; 1976–77 Division 1; 1977–80 Division 2; 1980– Division 1.

Honours: *Football League:* Division 1 – Champions 1891–92, 1892–93, 1894–95, 1901–02, 1912–13, 1935–36; Runners-up 1893–94, 1897–98, 1900–01, 1922–23, 1934–35; Division 2 – Champions 1975–76; Runners-up 1963–64, 1979–80. *FA Cup:* Winners 1937, 1973; Runners-up 1913. *Football League Cup:* semi-finals: 1963. **European Competitions:** *European Cup-Winners' Cup:* 1973–74.

Record Victory: 11-1 v Fairfield, FA Cup 1st rd, 1894–95.

Record Defeat: 0-8 v West Ham U, Division 1, 19 Oct, 1968.

Most League Points: 61, Division 2, 1963–64.

Most League Goals: 109, Division 1, 1935–36.

Highest League Scorer in Season: Dave Halliday, 43, Division 1, 1928–29.

Most League Goals in Total Aggregate: Charlie Buchan, 209, 1911–25.

Most Capped Player: Jim Montgomery, 537, 1962–77.

Most League Appearances: Billy Bingham, 33 (56), Northern Ireland; Martin Harvey, 33, Northern Ireland.

Record Transfer Fee Received: £275,000 from Manchester C for Dennis Tueart, March 1974.

Record Transfer Fee Paid: £320,000 to San Lorenzo for Claudio Marangoni, Dec 1979.

Previous Managers since the War: Bill Murray, Alan Brown, George Hardwick, Ian McColl, Alan Brown, Bob Stokoe, Jimmy Adamson, Billy Elliott, Ken Knighton.

Address of Supporters Club: c/o Football Club.

Roker Park Ground, Sunderland. Telephone Sunderland 40332. *Telegraphic address:* 'Football, Sunderland'. *Ground capacity:* 47,000. *Record attendance:* 75,118 v Derby Co, FA Cup 6th rd replay, 8 Mar, 1933. *Record receipts:* £63,211 v Southampton, Division 1, 23 Aug, 1980. *Pitch measurements:* 113yd×74yd.

How to get there: From Sunderland railway station and Seaburn railway station take buses 123 and 124 to Redby Community Centre: the ground is five minutes walk away. Special buses from the town centre. By road via M1, A690 to Sunderland, and then route to Roker Park is signed.

Match tickets: Seats may be booked 10 days prior to the match.

Car parking: Parking for 1500 cars, 200 yards from ground.

Entertainments/catering facilities: Hot and cold drinks, pies, sandwiches, etc. available in the ground.

Club shop: Open daily; sells all types of souvenirs.

Handbooks/programmes: Programmes are obtainable on subscription; details from the Club Shop.

Extra information: Sunderland share the highest First Division away win, beating Newcastle United 9-1 in 1908; Newcastle went on to win the League that season.

Club Colours: Red and white striped shirts, black shorts, red stockings with white tops.

Change Colours: Blue shirts with red trim, red shorts with white trim, blue stockings with red tops.

Club Coach:

Club Nickname: Rokerites.

SUNDERLAND 1980–81 LEAGUE RECORD

Match No.	Date	Venue	Opponents	Result	H/T Score	Goalscorers	Attendance
1	Aug 16	H	Everton	W 3-1	2-0	Hawley (pen), Cummins, Lyons (og)	32,005
2	20	A	Manchester C	W 4-0	1-0	Cummins, Hawley 3 (1 pen)	33,271
3	23	H	Southampton	L 1-2	1-2	Allardyce	41,141
4	30	A	Manchester U	D 1-1	0-0	Brown	51,498
5	Sept 6	A	Leicester C	W 1-0	1-0	Hawley	20,638
6	13	H	Middlesbrough	L 0-1	0-1		32,745
7	20	A	Tottenham H	D 0-0	0-0		32,030
8	27	H	Leeds U	W 4-1	2-0	Robson 2, Rowell, Brown	29,619
9	Oct 4	A	Aston Villa	L 0-4	0-1		26,914
10	8	H	Nottingham F	D 2-2	2-0	Rowell, Brown	30,515
11	11	H	Crystal Palace	W 1-0	1-0	Rowell	25,444
12	18	A	Arsenal	D 2-2	0-1	Rowell, Cummins	32,135
13	21	A	Coventry C	L 1-2	0-1	Cummins	13,115
14	25	H	Ipswich T	L 0-2	0-1		32,368
15	Nov 1	A	Wolverhampton W	L 1-2	1-2	Allardyce	18,816
16	8	H	Stoke C	D 0-0	0-0		21,483
17	12	H	Manchester C	W 2-0	0-0	Arnott, Cooke	23,387
18	15	A	Everton	L 1-2	1-1	Robson	24,099
19	22	A	Norwich C	L 0-1	0-1		15,024
20	29	H	Liverpool	L 2-4	0-2	Brown, Cummins	32,340
21	Dec 6	A	Brighton & HA	L 1-2	0-1	Chisholm	13,903
22	13	H	Arsenal	W 2-0	1-0	Hawley, Arnott	21,595
23	20	A	Nottingham F	L 1-3	0-2	Rowell	23,151
24	26	H	WBA	D 0-0	0-0		28,296
25	27	A	Birmingham C	L 2-3	1-2	Hawley, Rowell	19,005
26	Jan 10	H	Norwich C	W 3-0	2-0	Rowell 2, Cummins	17,749
27	28	H	Manchester U	W 2-0	1-0	Chisholm, Rowell (pen)	31,910
28	31	A	Southampton	L 1-2	0-2	Chisholm	21,345
29	Feb 7	A	Middlesbrough	L 0-1	0-1		35,065
30	14	H	Leicester C	W 1-0	1-0	Cummins	22,569
31	21	A	Leeds U	L 0-1	0-0		23,236
32	28	H	Tottenham H	D 1-1	0-1	Bowyer	22,382
33	Mar 7	H	Aston Villa	L 1-2	0-2	Hinnigan	27,278
34	14	A	Crystal Palace	W 1-0	1-0	Hinnigan	16,748
35	21	H	Coventry C	W 3-0	1-0	Hinnigan 2, Cummins (pen)	20,622
36	28	A	Ipswich T	L 1-4	1-1	Rowell	25,450
37	Apr 4	H	Wolverhampton W	L 0-1	0-0		20,138
38	11	A	Stoke C	L 0-2	0-0		11,501
39	18	H	Birmingham C	W 3-0	2-0	Ritchie 3 (1 pen)	20,158
40	20	A	WBA	L 1-2	1-1	Ritchie (pen)	15,243
41	25	H	Brighton & HA	L 1-2	0-1	Brown	22,317
42	May 2	A	Liverpool	W 1-0	1-0	Cummins	40,337

Final League Position: 17

Goalscorers

League (52): Rowell 10 (1 pen), Cummins 9 (1 pen), Hawley 7 (2 pens), Brown 5, Hinnigan 4, Ritchie 4 (2 pens), Robson 3, Chisholm 3, Allardyce 2, Arnott 2, Bowyer 1, Cooke 1, own goal 1.
League Cup (2): Arnott, Cummins.
F.A. Cup (2): Chisholm, Rowell.

League Cup	Second Round	Stockport Co	(a)	1-1
			(h)	1-2
FA Cup	Third Round	Birmingham C	(a)	1-1
			(h)	1-2 (aet)

Turner	Whitworth	Bolton	Allardyce	Elliott	Hindmarch	Arnott	Buckley	Hawley	Brown	Cummins	Chisholm	Robson	Hinnigan	Marangoni	Rowell	Dunn	Cooke	Bowyer	Siddall	Ritchie	Vincent	Match No.
1	2	3	4	5	6	7	8	9	10	11												1
1	2	3	4	5	6		8*	9	10	11	7	12										2
1	2	3	4	5	6		8*	9	10	11	7	12										3
1		3	4	5		8		9	10	11	7		2	6								4
1		3	4	5		8		9	10	11	7		2	6								5
1		3	4	5		8		9*	10	11	7		2	6	12							6
1		3	4	5		7			10	11	6	9	2*		8	12						7
1	2	3	4	5		7			10	11	6	9			8							8
1	2	3	4	5		7			9	11	6*	10			8	12						9
1	2	3	4	5		7			10	11	6	9			8							10
1	2	3	4	5		7			10	11	6	9			8							11
1	2	3	4	5		7			10	11	6				8		9					12
1	2	3	4	5		7			10	11	6				8		9					13
1	2	3	4	5		7			10	11	6				8		9					14
1	2	3	4	5		7	6		10	11					8		9					15
1	2	3	4	5		7	6		10*	11		12			8		9					16
1	2	3		5*	4	7	6			11		10		12	8		9					17
1	2	3	5		4	7	6			11		10			8		9					18
1	2	3	4		5	7	6		12	11		10*				8	9					19
1	2	3	5	6	4	7			8	11	12	10					9*					20
1	2	3	5	6	4	7			8*	11	10				12		9					21
1	2	3	5	6	4	7		9	8*	11	10						12					22
1	2	3		5	4	7		9	8*	11	10				6		12					23
1	2	3		5	4	7		9	12	11*	10				6		8					24
1	2	3		5	4	7		9		11	10				6		8					25
1	2	3		5	4	7		9	8	11	10				6							26
1	2	3		5	4	7		9*	12	11	10				6			8				27
	2	3		5	4	7*		9		11	10				6			8	1	12		28
	2	3		5	4			9		11	10				6			8	1	7		29
	2			5	4			9		11	10		3		6			8	1	7		30
	2			5	4			9	12	11	10		3		6*			8	1	7		31
	2			5	4	7			12	11	10*		3		6			8	1	9		32
		3		5	4	7				11	10		2		6		12	8*	1	9		33
		3		5	4	7	6		12	11	10		2				8*		1	9		34
		3		5	4	7	6			11	10		2				8		1	9		35
		3		5	4	7	6		8	11			2		12			10	1	9*		36
	2	3		5	4	7			8*	11	6				12			10	1	9		37
		3	5		4	7			8	11	6		2		10				1	9		38
		3	5	6*	4	7	8		10	11			2		12				1	9		39
		3	5		4		8		10	11	7		2						1	9	6	40
		3		5	4		8		10*	11	7		2		6				1	9	12	41
		3	12	5	4		8		10	11	7*		2		6				1	9		42
27	29	39	24	38	29	34	15	16	28	42	33	9	16	3	26	1	14	9	15	14	1	
			+ 1s						+ 6s		+ 1s	+ 3s		+ 1s	+ 5s	+ 2s	+ 3s			+ 1s	+ 1s	

SUNDERLAND

	Ht	*Wt*	*Birthplace*	*Clubs*	*League App.*	*League Gls*
Goalkeepers						
Barry Siddall	6 0½	14 3½	Ellesmere Port	Bolton W	137	—
				Sunderland	144	—
				Darlington (on loan)	8	—
Ian Watson*	6 0	12 0	North Shields	Sunderland	1	—
				Rochdale (on loan)	33	—
Chris Turner	5 10½	11 11	Sheffield	Sheffield W	91	—
				Lincoln C (on loan)	5	—
				Sunderland	57	—
Robert Crooks*	6 0	13 1	Durham	Sunderland	—	—
Jim Montgomery	5 10	11 9	Sunderland	Sunderland	537	—
				Southampton (on loan)	5	—
				Birmingham C	66	—
				Nottingham F	—	—
				Sunderland	—	—
Defenders						
Joe Bolton	5 11½	12 11	Birley	Sunderland	273	11
Jeff Clarke	6 0½	13 8	Pontefract	Manchester C	13	—
				Sunderland	155	6
Steve Whitworth	6 0	12 0	Coalville	Leicester C	353	—
(England)				Sunderland	81	—
Joe Hinnigan	6 0½	12 10	Liverpool	Wigan Ath	66	10
				Sunderland	30	4
Robert Hindmarch	6 1½	13 4½	Stannington	Sunderland	52	—
Gordon Chisholm	6 0¾	12 0	Glasgow	Sunderland	74	4
Sam Allardyce	6 1½	14 0	Dudley	Bolton W	184	21
				Sunderland	25	2
Paul Brown			Blackhill	Sunderland	—	—
Colin West			Wallsend	Sunderland	—	—
Midfield						
Kevin Arnott	5 10	11 12	Bensham	Sunderland	127	16
Mike Buckley	5 6	10 7	Manchester	Everton	135	10
				Sunderland	64	2
Ian Hughes*	5 9	11 1	Sunderland	Sunderland	1	—
Stan Cummins	5 6	9 1	Durham	Middlesbrough	44	9
(Contract cancelled April 1981)				Sunderland	68	21
Robert Vincent	5 10½	12 1	Newcastle	Sunderland	2	—
Stewart Sherwood*	5 2½	9 6	Houghton-le-Spring	Sunderland	—	—
John Main	5 9	9 9	Glasgow	Sunderland	—	—
(Contract cancelled August 1980)						
Shaun Elliott	6 0	11 6½	Haydon Bridge	Sunderland	168	9
(Contract cancelled April 1981)						
Peter McMullen*	5 8	10 0	Middlesbrough	Sunderland	—	—
Peter Embleton*			Gosforth	Sunderland	—	—
Ian Bowyer	5 11	11 2½	Ellesmere Port	Manchester C	50	13
				Orient	78	18
				Nottingham F	239	49
				Sunderland	9	1
Forwards						
Gary Rowell	5 10	11 3	Seaham	Sunderland	155	55
Alan Brown	5 11½	12 10½	Easington	Sunderland	106	20
Roland Gregoire	5 9	10 7	Liverpool	Halifax T	5	—
(Contract cancelled July 1980)				Sunderland	9	1
Colin Crawford	5 7	11 4	Doagh, Co Antrim	Bangor	—	—
				Sunderland	—	—
Claudio Marangoni	6 1	13 0	Argentina	San Lorenzo	(Not known)	
(Contract cancelled Dec 1980)				Sunderland	20	3
John Hawley	6 0	13 12	Withernsea	Hull C	114	22
				Leeds U	33	16
				Sunderland	25	11
Barry Dunn	5 8½	10 4½	Sunderland	Blue Star	(not known)	
				Sunderland	23	2
John Cooke	5 8	11 0	Salford	Sunderland	21	2
Mike Whitfield			Sunderland	Sunderland	—	—
Tom Ritchie	5 11	12 8	Scotland	Bristol C	321	77
				Sunderland	15	4
Tom Wardrobe			Newcastle	Sunderland	—	—

Free Transfer: Tim Benson*.

Stewart	Marustik	Rushbury	Attley	Stevenson	Phillips	Giles	James R	James L	Charles	Robinson	Mahoney	Craig	Toshack	Evans	Hadziabdic	Waddle	Loveridge	Curtis	Lewis	Rajkovic	*Match No.*
1	2	3	4	5	6	7*	8	9	10	11	12										1
1	2	3	4	5	6	7	8	9	10*	11		12									2
1		3	4	5	6	7	8	9		2		11	10								3
1		3	4	5	6	7	8	9		11	12		10*	2							4
1			2	5	6	7	8	9	10	11*	4				3	12					5
1			2	5	6	7	8	9	10	11	4				3						6
1			2	5	6	7		9	10	11	4	12			3	8*					7
1	4*		2	5	6	7		9	10	11	12				3	8					8
1			2	5	6	7	12	9	10	11	4				3	8*					9
1			2	5	6	7		9	10	11	4				3	8					10
1			2	5	6	7*	12	9	10	11	4				3	8					11
1			2	5	6	7		9	10	11	4				3	8					12
1			2	5	6	7*	12	9	10	11	4				3	8					13
1			2*	5	6	7	12	9	10	11	4				3	8					14
1		5	2		6	7*	12	9	10	11	4				3	8					15
1			2	5	6	7		9	10	11*	4	12			3	8					16
1		8	2	5	6	7		9*	10	11	4	12			3						17
1		4	2		6		9		5	11	10	7			3*	8	12				18
1			2	5	6		7	9	10	11	4				3	8					19
1			2	5	6		7	9	10	11	4				3	8					20
1		4	2	5	6		8	9*	10	11	7	12			3						21
1		4	2	5	6		8	9*	10	11	7				3			12			22
1			2	5	6		8	9	10	11	4				3			7			23
1		4	2	5	6		8	9*	10	11	7				3			12			24
1			2	5	6		8	9	10	11	4				3			7			25
1			2	5	6	12	7	9*	10	11	4				3			8			26
1		12	2	5	6	7	8		10	11*	4				3			9			27
1			2	6		7*	8	11	5	12	4		10		3			9			28
1			2	5	6	12		10*		11	8	7			3			9	4		29
1		4		12	6	7*	8	10	5	2	11				3			9			30
1				6			8	10	5		11	7		2	3			9	4		31
1				6			8	10	5	12	11	7		2	3			9*	4		32
1				6			8	10	5	12	11	7		2	3			9*		4	33
1				5		12	7	9	4	11*	10			2	3			8	6		34
1			4	5		7	8	9	10			11		2	3*			12	6		35
1			4	5		7	8	9	10			11		2	3				6		36
1			4	5		7*	8	9	10			11		2	3			12	6		37
1				5			8	9	10			11		2	3			7	6	4	38
1				5		4	8	9	10*		12	11		2	3			7	6		39
1				5			8	9		4	10	11		2	3			7	6		40
1				5			8	9	12	4	10	11*		2	3			7	6		41
1				5			8	9	10	4		11		2	3			7	6		42
42	3	11	32	39	29	24	30	40	37	33	31	14	3	13	38	13	—	16	12	2	
		+ 1s		+ 1s		+ 3s	+ 5s		+ 1s	+ 3s	+ 4s	+ 5s				+ 1s	+ 1s	+ 4s			

SWANSEA CITY

	Ht	Wt	Birthplace	Clubs	League App.	League Gls
Goalkeepers						
David Stewart	6 1½	13 0	Glasgow	Ayr U	157	—
(Scotland)				Leeds U	55	—
				WBA	—	—
				Swansea C	57	—
Chris Sander	5 11½		Swansea	Swansea C	—	—
Glan Letheran*	6 2	13 10	Llanelli	Leeds U	1	—
				Scunthorpe U (on loan)	27	—
				Chelsea (on loan)	—	—
				Notts Co (on loan)	—	—
				Chesterfield	63	—
				Swansea C	21	—
Defenders						
Wyndham Evans	5 9½	12 11½	Llanelli	Swansea C	347	19
Nigel Stevenson	6 2	11 0	Swansea	Swansea C	115	10
Brian Attley	5 9	9 12	Cardiff	Cardiff C	79	1
				Swansea C	85	6
Leighton Phillips	5 10	10 11	Briton Ferry	Cardiff C	180	11
(Wales)				Aston V	140	4
				Swansea C	97	—
Neil Robinson	5 8	10 12	Liverpool	Everton	16	1
				Swansea C	52	6
Dudley Lewis	5 9½	10 5	Swansea	Swansea C	12	—
Cameron Medwin	5 11	11 10	London	Swansea C	—	—
(Contract cancelled Oct 1980)						
David Rushbury	5 10	11 4	Wolverhampton	WBA	28	—
				Sheffield W	112	7
				Swansea C	52	—
Dzemal Hadziabdic			Yugoslavia	Velez Mostar	(not known)	
(Yugoslavia)				Swansea C	38	1
Midfield						
Leslie Chappell	5 8	10 5	Nottingham	Rotherham U	111	36
				Blackburn R	7	—
				Reading	201	81
				Doncaster R	58	10
				Swansea C	67	5
Tony James	5 8	10 0	Swansea	Swansea C	11	1
(Contract cancelled Dec 1980)						
Phil Boersma	5 10	11 7	Liverpool	Liverpool	83	18
Retired April 1981)				Wrexham (on loan)	5	—
				Middlesbrough	47	3
				Luton T	36	8
				Swansea C	18	1
Chris Marustik	5 8	11 11½	Swansea	Swansea C	19	—
Ian Callaghan	5 7	11 11	Liverpool	Liverpool	640	49
(England) (Contract cancelled Jan 1981)				Swansea C	76	1
John Mahoney	5 7½	11 4	Cardiff	Crewe Alex	18	5
(Wales)				Stoke C	284	25
				Middlesbrough	77	1
				Swansea C	61	1
Tommy Craig	5 8	11 9	Aberdeen	Aberdeen	45	8
(Scotland)				Sheffield W	214	38
				Newcastle U	124	23
				Aston V	27	2
				Swansea C	52	9
Neil Henson			Swansea	Swansea C	—	—
Ante Rajkovic			Yugoslavia	Sarajevo	(not known)	
(Yugoslavia)				Swansea C	2	—
Forwards						
Robbie James	5 10	12 1½	Swansea	Swansea C	312	76
(Wales)						
Jeremy Charles	6 1	12 0	Swansea	Swansea C	192	49
(Wales)						
John Toshack	6 1	12 0	Cardiff	Cardiff C	162	75
(Wales)				Liverpool	172	74
				Swansea C	60	24
Mark Baker	5 9	11 4½	Swansea	Swansea C	11	2
(Contract cancelled Oct 1980)						
David Giles	5 7	10 4½	Cardiff	Cardiff C	59	3
(Wales)				Wrexham	38	2
				Swansea C	52	13
Leighton James	5 9	11 0	Llwchwr, Glam.	Burnley	181	44
(Wales)				Derby Co	68	15
				QPR	28	4
				Burnley	76	9
				Swansea C	41	16
Jimmy Loveridge	5 7	10 12½	Swansea	Swansea C	3	—
Pat McQuillan			Belfast	Pembroke B	(not known)	
				Swansea C	—	—
Darren Gale			Port Talbot	Swansea C	—	—
Alan Curtis	5 11	12 3	Rhondda	Swansea C	248	72
(Wales)				Leeds U	28	5
				Swansea C	20	6

SWINDON TOWN Division 3

President: W. H. Castle. *Chairman:* C. J. Green.

Directors: C. Day, C. Cowley, T. J. R. Kearsley, R. Stephenson, M. W. Earle, W. H. Dore, L. Smart, G. Whittock.

Team Manager: John Trollope.

Admin Manager/Secretary: R. Jefferies.

Finance Manager: R. A. Morse.

Year Formed: 1881. *Turned Professional:* 1894.

Limited Company: 1894. *Previous Ground:* 1881–96, The Croft.

Football League Record:
1920 Original Member of Division 3; 1921–58 Division 3(S); 1958–63 Division 3; 1963–65 Division 2; 1965–69 Division 3; 1969–74 Division 2; 1974– Division 3.

Honours: *Football League:* Division 2 best season: 5th, 1969–70. Division 3 – Runners-up 1962–63, 1968–69. *FA Cup:* semi-finals 1910, 1912. *Football League Cup:* Winners 1968–69. *Anglo-Italian Cup:* Winners 1970.

Record Victory: 10-1 v Farnham United Breweries, FA Cup 1st rd, 28 Nov, 1925.

Record Defeat: 1-10 v Manchester C, FA Cup 4th rd replay, 25 Jan, 1930.

Most League Points: 64, Division 3, 1968–69.

Most League Goals: 100, Division 3(S), 1926–27.

Highest League Scorer in Season: Harry Morris, 47, Division 3(S), 1926–27.

Most League Goals in Total Aggregate: Harry Morris, 216, 1926–33.

Most Capped Player: Rod Thomas, 30 (50), Wales.

Most League Appearances: John Trollope, 770, 1960–80.

Record Transfer Fee Received: £175,000 from Chelsea for Alan Mayes, Dec 1980.

Record Transfer Fee Paid: £150,000 to Southampton for David Peach, March 1980.

Previous Managers since the War: Louis Page, Maurice Lindley, Bert Head, Danny Williams, Fred Ford, Dave Mackay, Les Allen, Danny Williams, Bob Smith.

Address of Supporters Club: Swindon Town Supporters Club, County Ground, Swindon, Wilts.

Address of the Club Shop or Boutique: Souvenir and Sports Shop, Swindon Town FC, County Ground, Swindon.

County Ground, Swindon, Wiltshire. Telephone Swindon 22118. *Ground capacity:* 26,000 (6500 seats). *Record attendance:* 32,000 v Arsenal, FA Cup 3rd rd, 15 Jan, 1972. *Record receipts:* £56,024 v Tottenham H, FA Cup 4th rd, 26 Jan, 1980. *Pitch measurements:* 114yd×72yd.

How to get there: Both Swindon bus and railway stations are half a mile from the ground.

Match tickets: Available 3 weeks in advance.

Car parking: Corporation car park adjacent to the west end of the ground, off County Road.

Entertainments/catering facilities: The Supporters' Club Rendezvous Club and Squash Club in the North Stand. Refreshment kiosks in all parts of the ground. No licensed bars on terraces or stands.

Club shop: Postal enquiries welcome. All types of souvenirs are stocked.

Handbooks/programmes: Programmes available by postal application, or subscription.

Extra information: Harold Fleming of Swindon Town played 11 times for England before World War I when the club were still a non-League side. Separate terrace enclosure available for adults and accompanied children only.

Club Colours: Red shirts with white trimmings, white shorts, red stockings.

Change Colours: All blue.

Club Coach: Geoff Butler

Club Nickname: Robins.

SWINDON TOWN 1980–81 LEAGUE RECORD

Match No.	Date	Venue	Opponents	Result	H/T Score	Goalscorers	Attendance
1	Aug 16	H	Blackpool	L 1-2	0-1	Rowland	7108
2	19	A	Portsmouth	L 0-1	0-0		15,810
3	23	H	Fulham	L 3-4	2-1	Rollings, Peach (pen), Mayes	6473
4	30	A	Reading	L 1-4	0-1	Mayes	6405
5	Sept 6	A	Sheffield U	L 0-3	0-1		12,089
6	13	H	Rotherham U	W 2-1	0-1	Greenwood, Rowland	5498
7	16	H	Oxford U	W 1-0	0-0	Miller	7709
8	20	A	Barnsley	L 0-2	0-0		9747
9	27	H	Huddersfield T	W 1-0	0-0	Rowland	5856
10	Oct 1	A	Oxford U	D 0-0	0-0		6071
11	4	H	Chester	L 1-2	0-0	Mayes	5577
12	7	A	Gillingham	D 0-0	0-0		4066
13	11	A	Millwall	L 1-3	0-0	Mayes	3571
14	18	H	Carlisle U	D 1-1	0-0	Mayes	5789
15	21	H	Charlton Ath	L 0-3	0-1		5672
16	25	A	Exeter C	W 4-3	2-1	Mayes, Rowland 2, Miller	4688
17	Nov 1	H	Burnley	L 0-3	0-1		6191
18	4	H	Gillingham	D 0-0	0-0		4719
19	8	A	Colchester U	L 0-1	0-0		2153
20	11	H	Portsmouth	L 0-2	0-0		8164
21	15	A	Blackpool	D 1-1	0-1	Mayes	3758
22	29	H	Hull C	W 3-1	1-1	Stroud, Lewis, Rideout	5275
23	Dec 6	A	Brentford	D 1-1	0-1	Peach	5730
24	19	H	Walsall	W 3-1	1-0	Carter, Mayes, Greenwood	4523
25	26	A	Newport Co	W 2-0	1-0	Kamara, Lewis	7086
26	27	H	Plymouth Arg	W 3-0	0-0	Carter, Greenwood, Rowland	9710
27	Jan 10	H	Chesterfield	L 0-1	0-0		6717
28	24	H	Reading	W 3-1	1-0	Greenwood, Carter, Rowland	8100
29	31	A	Fulham	L 0-2	0-0		4785
30	Feb 7	A	Rotherham U	L 0-1	0-0		7162
31	14	H	Sheffield U	W 5-2	3-0	Miller, Rowland 3, Williams (pen)	6305
32	21	A	Huddersfield T	W 2-0	2-0	Kamara 2	10,655
33	28	H	Barnsley	W 2-0	1-0	Hughes, Williams (pen)	7819
34	Mar 7	A	Chester	L 0-1	0-1		1810
35	14	H	Millwall	D 0-0	0-0		6966
36	17	A	Carlisle U	L 1-2	1-2	Carter	4104
37	21	A	Charlton Ath	D 0-0	0-0		6495
38	28	H	Exeter C	D 2-2	1-1	Rideout, Rowland	6509
39	Apr 4	A	Burnley	D 0-0	0-0		4726
40	7	A	Chesterfield	D 2-2	1-0	Kamara, Carter	5222
41	11	H	Colchester U	W 3-0	1-0	Rideout 2, Rowland	6120
42	14	A	Hull C	D 0-0	0-0		2789
43	18	A	Plymouth Arg	D 0-0	0-0		6369
44	20	H	Newport Co	D 1-1	0-0	Williams (pen)	8435
45	25	A	Walsall	L 1-2	0-0	Miller	3429
46	May 2	H	Brentford	D 0-0	0-0		8725

Final League Position: 17

Goalscorers

League (51): Rowland 12, Mayes 8, Carter 5, Greenwood 4, Kamara 4, Miller 4, Rideout 4, Williams 3 (3 pens), Lewis 2, Peach 2 (1 pen), Hughes 1, Rollings 1, Stroud 1.
League Cup (6): Mayes 3, Rowland, Rollings, own goal.
F.A. Cup (3): Kamara, Lewis, Mayes.

League Cup	First Round	Bournemouth (a)	1-1
		(h)	2-0
	Second Round	Lincoln C (a)	1-1
		(h)	2-0
	Third Round	Liverpool (a)	0-5
FA Cup	First Round	Weymouth (h)	3-2
	Second Round	Wimbledon (a)	0-2

Allan	Barrett	Peach	Kamara	Rollings	Walsh	Miller	Cockerill	Rowland	Mayes	Carter	Hamilton	Templeman	Greenwood	Lewis	Hughes	Henry	Trollope	Turner	Williams	Stroud	Rideout	McAlister	Abbey	*Match No.*
1	2	3	4	5	6	7	8	9	10	11														1
1	2	3	4	5	6	7	8	9	10	11*	12													2
1	2	3	4	5		7	8	9*	10	6		12	11											3
1		3	4	5	6	7			10	11			9	2	8*	12								4
1		3	4	5		7		9*	10	6	8		11	2		12								5
1			4			7	8	9	10	6			11	5		2	3							6
1			4			7	8	9	10	6			11	5		2	3							7
1			4			7	8	9	10	6			11	5		2	3							8
1			4			7	8	9	10	6			11	5		2	3							9
1			4			7*	8	9	10	6			11	5		2	3	12						10
1			4				8*	9	10	6			11	5	7	2	3	12						11
1			4					9	10	6			11	5	7	2	3		8					12
1			4			12		9	10	6			7	5	8*	2	3		11					13
1			4				8	9	10	6		2	7	5			3		11					14
1		3	4			7	11*	9	10	6				5	8		2	12						15
1		3	4			7	8	9	10	6				5			2		11					16
1		3	4*	12		7	8	9	10	6				5			2		11					17
1		3	4			7		9	10	8				5			2		11	6				18
1		3	4			7		9	10	8				5			2		11	6				19
1		3	4	5		7		9	10	8				2					11	6				20
1		3	4			7		9	10	8				5		2			11	6				21
1		3	4		2	7			10	8				5					11	6	9			22
1		3	4		2	7			10	8			12	5					11	6	9*			23
1		3	4			7			10	8			9	5		2			11	6				24
1*		3	4			7		9		8			10	5	12	2			11	6				25
		3	4			7		9		8			10	5	11*	2				6	12	1		26
1			4		3*	7		9		8			10	5		2			11	6			12	27
1			4		3	7		9		8*			10	5		2			11	6	12			28
1		3	4			7*		9		8			10	5		2			11	6			12	29
1		3	4	5		7	8*	9					10			2			11	6	12			30
1		3	4	5		7		9							8	2			11	6	10			31
1		3	4	5		7		9					10		8	2			11	6				32
1		3	4	5		7		9					10		8	2			11	6				33
1		3	4*	5		7	12	9					10		8	2			11	6				34
1		3	12			7	4	9		5			10*		8	2				6			11	35
1		3	4			7		9		11			10	5	8	2				6				36
1		3				7		9		4			10*	5	8	2			11	6	12			37
1			4			7		9		3				5	8	2			11	6	10			38
1			4			7		9		3				5	8	2			11	6	10			39
1		12	4			7		9		3				5	8*	2			11	6	10			40
1		3	4			7		9		8				5		2			11	6	10			41
1		3	4			7		9		8				5		2			11	6	10			42
1		3	4			7		9		8				5		2			11	6	10			43
1		3	4			7		9		8				5		2			11	6	10			44
1		3	4			7		9		2				5	8				11	6	10			45
1		3	4			7		9		2				5	8				11	6	10			46
45	3	32	44	11	7	42	15	42	24	41	1	1	25	37	18	30	14	—	31	29	12	1	1	
		+ 1s	+ 1s	+ 1s		+ 1s	+ 1s				+ 1s	+ 1s	+ 1s		+ 1s	+ 2s		+ 3s			+ 4s		+ 2s	

SWINDON TOWN

	Ht	Wt	Birthplace	Clubs	League App.	League Gls
Goalkeepers						
Jimmy Allan	6 0	12 3	Inverness	Swindon T	272	—
Tom McAlister	6 0	11 1	Clydebank	Sheffield U	63	—
				Rotherham U	159	—
				Blackpool	16	—
				Bristol R (on loan)	13	—
				Swindon T	1	—
Defenders						
John Templeman	5 11	11 8	Yapton	Brighton	226	16
(Contract cancelled Nov 1980)				Exeter C	206	7
				Swindon T	21	—
Russell Lewis	5 10½	12 13	Neath	Swindon T	95	5
John Trollope	6 0½	12 3	Wroughton	Swindon T	770	22
(Contract cancelled Nov 1980)						
Kenneth Stroud	5 11	12 0	London	Swindon T	281	16
David Peach	5 9	11 6	Bedford	Gillingham	187	30
				Southampton	224	34
				Swindon T	43	2
Andy Rollings	6 1	12 0	Portishead	Norwich C	4	—
				Brighton	168	10
				Swindon T	12	1
Billy Tucker*	6 0	12 5	Kidderminster	Hereford U	137	12
				Bury	96	8
				Swindon T	35	4
Colin Barrett	5 11	11 7	Stockport	Manchester C	53	—
				Nottingham F	69	4
				Swindon T	3	—
Charles Henry			Acton	Swindon T	32	—
Brendon Guest	5 10½	10 9	Nottingham	Lincoln C	104	2
(Contract cancelled)				Swindon T	—	—
Midfield						
Roy Carter	6 0½	10 12	Torpoint	Hereford U	71	9
				Swindon T	152	20
Chris Kamara	6 1	12 0	Middlesbrough	Portsmouth	63	7
				Swindon T	147	21
Brian Williams	5 9	12 1	Manchester	Bury	159	19
				QPR	19	—
				Swindon T	99	8
Glenn Cockerill	6 0	11 13	Grimsby	Lincoln C	71	10
				Swindon T	26	1
Roy Walsh*	5 10	11 13	Belfast	Glentoran	(not known)	
				Swindon T	7	—
Jack Carmichael	5 10	12 11½	Newcastle	Arsenal	—	—
(Contract cancelled March 1981)				Peterborough U	352	5
				Swindon T	—	—
Martin Blackler			Swindon	Swindon T	—	—
David Round			Sedgley	Swindon T	—	—
Forwards						
Andy Rowland	5 11	12 0	Derby	Derby Co	—	—
				Bury	174	58
				Swindon T	114	45
Ian Miller	5 9	11 7	Perth	Bury	15	—
				Nottingham F	—	—
				Doncaster R	124	14
				Swindon T	127	9
Stephen Abbley	5 11	10 8	Liverpool	Swindon T	8	—
Roy Greenwood	5 9	10 3	Leeds	Hull C	124	24
				Sunderland	56	9
				Derby Co	31	1
				Swindon T	30	4
Mike Russtell			Frome	Swindon T	—	—
(Contract cancelled Dec 1980)						
Brian Hughes			Ludgershall	Swindon T	19	1
Paul Rideout			Bournemouth	Swindon T	16	4
(Apprentice)						

TORQUAY UNITED Division 4

Chairman: A. J. Boyce.
Vice-Chairman: M. C. Spedding.
Directors: D. C. Hair MRCVS, J. H. Perry, Lt-Col W. J. Elliot MBE, FCIS, L. W. Leppington ERD, L. W. Pope, W. G. Standley, W. W. Rogers, A. Loze.
Manager: Frank O'Farrell. *Secretary:* D. J. Easton.
Year Formed: 1898. *Turned Professional:* 1921.
Limited Company: 1921.
Previous Name: 1910, Torquay Town; 1921, Torquay United.
Previous Grounds: 1898, Teignmouth Road; 1901, Torquay Recreation Ground; 1905, Cricket Field Road; 1907, Torquay Cricket Ground; 1910, Plainmoor.

Football League Record:
1927 Elected to Division 3(S); 1958–60 Division 4; 1960–62 Division 3; 1962–66 Division 4; 1966–72 Division 3; 1972– Division 4.

Honours: *Football League:* Division 3 best season: 4th, 1967–68. Division 3(S) – Runners-up 1956–57; Division 4 – Promoted 1959–60 (3rd), 1965–66 (3rd). *FA Cup* best season: 4th rd, 1949, 1955, 1971. *Football League Cup:* never past 3rd rd.
Record Victory: 9-0 v Swindon T, Division 3(S), 8 March, 1952.
Record Defeat: 2-10 v Fulham, Division 3(S), 7 Sept, 1931 and v Luton T, Division 3(S), 2 Sept, 1933.
Most League Points: 60, Division 4, 1959–60.
Most League Goals: 89, Division 3(S), 1956–57.
Highest League Scorer in Season: Sammy Collins, 40, Division 3(S), 1955–56.
Most League Goals in Total Aggregate: Sammy Collins, 204, 1948–58.
Most Capped Player: None.
Most League Appearances: Dennis Lewis, 443, 1947–59.
Record Transfer Fee Received: £80,000 from Tottenham H for Colin Lee, Oct 1977.
Record Transfer Fee Paid: £25,000 to Exeter C for Vince O'Keefe, March 1980.
Previous Managers since the War: Jack Butler, John McNeil, Bob John, Alex Massie, Eric Webber, Frank O'Farrell, Allan Brown, Jack Edwards, Malcolm Musgrove, Frank O'Farrell, Mike Green.
Address of Supporters Association: Plainmoor, Torquay, Devon.
Address of Club Shop: The Gull Shop, Torquay United Supporters Association, Plainmoor, Torquay, Devon.

Plainmoor Ground, Torquay, Devon TQ1 3PS. Telephone Torquay (0803) 38666/7. *Ground capacity:* 22,000. *Record attendance:* 21,908 v Huddersfield T, FA Cup 4th rd, 29 Jan, 1955. *Record receipts:* £10,326 v Tottenham H, FL Cup 3rd rd, 6 Oct, 1971. *Pitch measurements:* 112yd×74yd.
How to get there: Train to Torquay railway station. Bus 30 runs every 12 minutes from the station to the ground.
Match tickets: Stand seats available a fortnight before the match. Postal applications accepted provided correct remittance and sae are enclosed.
Car parking: Some street parking. Coaches park at Lymington Road coach station.
Entertainments/catering facilities: 200 Club – a match day venue luxury club – membership £6 (48 hours notice required for membership). Supporters' Social Club – open all week – now completely up-dated with luxury furnishings – membership £1, OAPs 50p (48 hours notice required).
Club shop: Sells all types of souvenirs.
Handbooks/programmes: For programmes contact the club shop.
Extra information: Running commentaries of home matches to local hospitals. Twelve free seats supplied to members of the local Rehabilitation Centre of the Royal National Institute for the Blind who can listen to the hospital commentary while experiencing the match atmosphere.
Club Colours: White shirts with blue and yellow vertical stripes on sleeve, blue shorts with yellow and white stripes on side, white stockings with blue and yellow ring on turnover.
Change Colours: Yellow shirts with blue and white vertical stripes on sleeve, yellow shorts with blue and white stripes on side, yellow stockings with blue turnover and yellow ring on turnover.
Club Captain: Albert Larmour. *Team Captain:* Tommy Sermanni.
Player-Coach: Bruce Rioch.
Club Nickname: Gulls.

TORQUAY UNITED 1980–81 LEAGUE RECORD

Match No.	Date	Venue	Opponents	Result	H/T Score	Goalscorers	Attendance
1	Aug 16	A	Crewe Alex	W 1-0	0-0	Lawrence	1962
2	20	H	Lincoln C	L 1-2	1-2	Fell	3568
3	23	A	York C	D 0-0	0-0		2892
4	30	H	AFC Bournemouth	W 2-0	0-0	Bourne, Fell	2532
5	Sept 6	A	Rochdale	L 1-2	1-1	Taylor (og)	1777
6	13	H	Bradford C	W 2-0	2-0	Lawrence, Cooper	2611
7	16	H	Doncaster R	L 2-3	0-0	Cooper, Bourne	2533
8	19	A	Tranmere R	L 0-1	0-0		1564
9	27	H	Peterborough U	W 2-0	1-0	Cooper, Fell (pen)	2080
10	30	A	Doncaster R	L 0-2	0-1		6916
11	Oct 4	H	Halifax T	W 1-0	0-0	Wilson	1849
12	6	A	Port Vale	L 1-3	0-0	Wilson	2091
13	11	A	Bury	L 0-3	0-0		2145
14	18	H	Wigan Ath	W 2-0	1-0	Bowker, Cooper	2013
15	22	H	Stockport Co	L 1-2	0-0	Fell (pen)	1792
16	25	A	Scunthorpe U	W 2-0	1-0	Wilson, Fell	2254
17	28	A	Aldershot	L 1-2	0-2	Coffill	2892
18	Nov 1	H	Darlington	L 0-2	0-1		2122
19	5	H	Port Vale	W 4-0	2-0	Sermanni 2, Cooper, Fell	1370
20	8	A	Mansfield T	D 1-1	1-0	Rioch	3266
21	12	A	Lincoln C	L 0-5	0-1		5050
22	15	H	Crewe Alex	W 1-0	0-0	Jones	1858
23	29	A	Hartlepool U	W 2-0	0-0	Cooper, Twitchin	3408
24	Dec 6	H	Northampton T	D 3-3	1-0	Bowker, Fell (pen), Cooper	2065
25	19	A	Southend U	L 1-3	1-1	Cooper	4205
26	26	H	Wimbledon	L 2-3	1-2	Lawrence, Fell (pen)	3191
27	27	A	Hereford U	W 1-0	1-0	Cox	3412
28	Jan 17	H	Hartlepool U	W 2-1	1-1	Cooper, Lawrence	1745
29	24	A	AFC Bournemouth	D 1-1	0-0	Cooper	3256
30	Feb 4	H	Scunthorpe U	W 2-1	2-0	Lawrence, Cooper	1760
31	7	A	Bradford C	L 0-2	0-2		2872
32	14	H	Rochdale	W 2-0	0-0	Bowker, Rioch	1724
33	16	A	Stockport Co	L 1-4	0-0	Cox	1431
34	21	A	Peterborough U	W 3-1	2-1	Bowker, Fell, Cox	4172
35	Mar 1	H	Tranmere R	W 2-1	0-1	Fell, Sermanni	2484
36	7	A	Halifax T	L 1-2	0-1	Fell	2008
37	14	H	Bury	W 3-1	1-1	Bowker 3	1635
38	21	A	Wigan Ath	L 0-2	0-0		3376
39	29	H	Aldershot	W 2-0	2-0	Jones, Cox	2086
40	Apr 5	A	Darlington	L 0-1	0-0		3631
41	8	H	York C	L 1-2	0-0	Cox	1406
42	12	H	Mansfield T	D 1-1	1-1	Fell (pen)	1699
43	18	H	Hereford U	L 0-1	0-0		1865
44	20	A	Wimbledon	L 0-1	0-1		3190
45	25	H	Southend U	L 0-3	0-3		1767
46	May 1	A	Northampton T	L 0-1	0-0		1562

Final League Position: 17

Goalscorers

League (55): Fell 12 (5 pens), Cooper 11, Bowker 7, Cox 5, Lawrence 5, Semanni 3, Wilson 3, Bourne 2, Jones 2, Rioch 2, Coffill 1, Twitchin 1, own goal 1.
League Cup (1): Fell.
F.A. Cup (8): Fell 4 (2 pens), Cooper 2, Lawrence, Weston

League Cup	First Round	Cardiff C (h)	0-0
		(a)	1-2
FA Cup	First Round	Barton R (h)	2-0
	Second Round	St Albans (a)	1-1
		(h)	4-1
	Third Round	Barnsley (a)	1-2

O'Keefe	Jones	Pethard	Twitchin	Bourne	Hayes	Fell	Lawrence	Cooper	Bowker	Weston	Wilson	Coffill	Cochrane	Sermanni	Cox	Rioch	Larmour	*Match No.*
1	2	3	4	5	6	7	8	9	10	11*	12							1
1	2	3	4*	5	6	7	8	9	10			12	11					2
1	2	3		5	6	7	8	9	10	11			4					3
1	4	2		5	6	7	8	9	10	11			3					4
1	4	2	12	5	6	7	8	9	10	11*			3					5
1	4	2	12	5	6	7	8	9	10				3	11*				6
1	4	2		5	6	7	8	9	10				3	11				7
1	4	2*	12	5	6	7	8	9	10				3	11				8
1	4	2			6	7		9	10		5		3	11	8			9
1	4	2	11		6	7	8	9*	10		5		3		12			10
1	4	2			6	7*	12	9	10	11	5		3		8			11
1	4	2			6		12	9	10	11*	5	7	3		8			12
1	2	4	6	5		7	8	9	10	11			3					13
1	4	2	10	5		7		9	8	11			3	6				14
1	2	4	10	5		7		9	8	11	12		3*	6				15
1	4	2	10	5		7		9	8		6	11	3					16
1	4	2	10	5		7	12	8	9		6*	11	3					17
1	2	4	3	5		7	8	9	10	11		12		6*				18
1	2	3		5		7		9	10	11	8			4		6		19
1	2	3	8	5		7	12		10	11*	9			4		6		20
1	2	3	8*	5		7	12		10	11	9			4		6		21
1	2	3	10	5		7	8		9*	11		12		4		6		22
1	2	3	10	5		7		9	8	11		4				6		23
1	2	3	10	5		7		9	8	11		4				6		24
1	2	3	10	12	6	7	8*	9		11	5	4						25
1	2	3	10	5*		7	8	9		11		4		12		6		26
1	2	3				7	8			11	5	4		10	9	6		27
1	2	3		5		7	8	9		11	10	4				6		28
1	2	3		5	10	7*	8	9		11		4		12		6		29
1	2	3		5*		7	8	9	12	11	10	4				6		30
1	2	3				7	8*	9	5	11	10	4		12		6		31
1	2	3			5	7			8	11	10	4			9	6		32
1	2	3			5	7			8	11	10	4			9	6		33
1	2	3			5	7			8	11	10	4			9	6		34
1	2	3			5	7			8	11	6	4		10	9			35
1	2	3	6		5	7	8*		9	11		4		10	12			36
1	2	3	10		5	7			9	11	6	4			8			37
1	2	3	10	12	5	7*			9	11	6	4			8			38
1	2	3	7		5			10	8	11	6	4			9			39
1	2	3	11		5	7		9	8		6	4			10			40
1	2	3	10		5	7		12	8*	11	6	4			9			41
1	2	3	12	5		7		9	8		6	4		11*	10			42
1	2	3		5		7		9	8	11	6	4			10			43
1	2	3	10	5		7		9	12		11	4*			8		6	44
1	2	3	10	5		7		9		11	6	4			8			45
1	2	3*	10	5	6	7	12		9	11		4			8			46
46	46	46	25	29	25	44	20	33	38	35	27	27	16	15	18	15	1	
			+ 4s	+ 2s			+ 6s	+ 1s	+ 2s		+ 2s	+ 3s		+ 3s	+ 2s			

TORQUAY UNITED

	Ht	*Wt*	*Birthplace*	*Clubs*	*League App.*	*League Gls*
Goalkeepers						
Vince O'Keefe	6 0	11 0	Birmingham	Birmingham C	—	—
				Peterborough U (on loan)	—	—
				Walsall	—	—
				AP Leamington	(not known)	
				Exeter C	53	—
				Torquay U	62	—
Defenders						
Ian Twitchin*	5 6	10 0	Teignmouth	Torquay U	403	14
Richard Bourne	6 0	12 0	Colchester	Colchester U	4	—
				Bath C	(not known)	
				Torquay U	66	6
Freddie Pethard	5 9	11 0	Glasgow	Celtic	—	—
				Cardiff C	171	—
				Torquay U	86	—
Brian Wilson	5 9	10 5	Newcastle	Blackpool	31	6
				Torquay U	55	3
Albert Larmour	5 10	10 7	Belfast	Linfield	(not known)	
				Cardiff C	154	—
				Torquay U	28	3
Steve Hayes*	5 10	11 6	Smethwick	Shrewsbury T	72	—
				Torquay U	26	—
Jimmy Cochrane	5 9	11 0	Glasgow	Middlesbrough	3	—
(Contract cancelled Jan 1981)				Darlington	223	5
				Torquay U	16	—
Graham Jones	6 0	13 0	Worsley	Luton T	39	—
				Torquay U	50	3
Midfield						
Dave Smith	5 5	10 7	Nottingham	Notts Co	50	—
(Contract cancelled Jan 1981)				Torquay U	23	1
Tommy Sermanni	5 8	11 2	Glasgow	Albion R	151	38
				Blackpool	10	—
				Torquay U	50	9
Jimmy Weston	5 9	11 0	Liverpool	Blackpool	105	8
				Torquay U	35	—
Bruce Rioch	5 11	12 5	Aldershot	Luton T	149	47
(Scotland) (Contract cancelled Feb 1981)				Aston V	156	34
				Derby Co	106	34
				Everton	30	3
				Birmingham C (on loan)	3	—
				Sheffield U (on loan)	8	1
				Derby Co	41	4
				Torquay U	15	2
Forwards						
Peter Coffill	5 8	10 7	Romford	Watford	63	6
				Torquay U	122	[illegible]
Les Lawrence	6 3	11 0	Wolverhampton	Shrewsbury T	14	—
				Torquay U	147	[illegible]
Steve Cooper	5 11	11 0	Stourbridge	Torquay U	121	[illegible]
Maurice Cox	5 10	10 7	Torquay	Torquay U	31	[illegible]
Gerry Fell	6 0	12 0	Newark	Brighton	79	19
				Southend U	45	[illegible]
				Torquay U	44	[illegible]
Keith Bowker	5 10	11 5	West Bromwich	Birmingham C	21	[illegible]
				Exeter C	110	[illegible]
				Cambridge U	17	1
				Northampton T (on loan)	4	—
				Exeter C	102	28
				Torquay U	40	7
Ken Norman	5 9	10 6	Longlevens	Swindon T	—	—
(Contract cancelled Jan 1981)				Torquay U	—	—

TOTTENHAM HOTSPUR Division 1

Chairman: A. Richardson.

Directors: G. A. Richardson, D. W. Kennard, D. A. Alexiou.

Manager: Keith Burkinshaw. *Secretary:* G. W. Jones.

First Team Coach: P. Shreeves.

Year Formed: 1882. *Turned Professional:* 1895.

Limited Company: 1898.

Previous Grounds: 1882, Tottenham Marshes; 1885, Northumberland Park; 1898, White Hart Lane.

Previous Name: 1882–85, Hotspur Football Club.

Football League Record:
1908 Elected to Division 2; 1909–15 Division 1; 1919–20 Division 2; 1920–28 Division 1; 1928–33 Division 2; 1933–35 Division 1; 1935–50 Division 2; 1950–77 Division 1; 1977–78 Division 2; 1978– Division 1.

Honours: *Football League:* Division 1 – Champions 1950–51, 1960–61; Runners-up 1921–22, 1951–52, 1956–57, 1962–63; Division 2 – Champions 1919–20, 1949–50; Runners-up 1908–09, 1932–33; Promoted 1977–78 (3rd). *FA Cup:* Winners 1901 (as non-League club), 1921, 1961, 1962, 1967, 1981. *Football League Cup:* Winners 1970–71, 1972–73. **European Competitions:** *European Cup:* 1961–62. *European Cup-Winner's Cup:* 1962–63 (winners), 1963–64, 1967–68. *UEFA Cup:* 1971–72 (winners), 1972–73, 1973–74 (runners-up).

Record Victory: 13-2 v Crewe Alex, FA Cup 4th rd replay, 3 Feb, 1960.

Record Defeat: 0-7 v Liverpool, Division 1, 2 Sept, 1978.

Most League Points: 70, Division 2, 1919–20.

Most League Goals: 115, Division 1, 1960–61.

Highest League Scorer in Season: Jimmy Greaves, 37, Division 1, 1962–63.

Most League Goals in Total Aggregate: Jimmy Greaves, 220, 1961–70.

Most Capped Player: Pat Jennings, 66 (87), Northern Ireland.

Most League Appearances: Pat Jennings, 472, 1964–77.

Record Transfer Fee Received: £250,000 for Neil McNab from Bolton W, Nov 1978.

Record Transfer Fee Paid: £800,000 to Aberdeen for Steve Archibald, May 1980.

Previous Managers since the War: Joe Hulme, Arthur Rowe, Jimmy Anderson, Bill Nicholson, Terry Neill.

Address of Supporters Club: 744 High Road, N17.

---

748 High Rd, Tottenham, London, N17. Telephone 01-801 6451. *Ground capacity:* 50,000. *Record attendance:* 75,038 v Sunderland, FA Cup 6th rd, 5 March, 1938. *Record receipts:* £49,920 v Feyenoord, UEFA Cup Final 1st leg, 21 May, 1974. *Pitch measurements:* 110yd×73yd.

How to get there: Underground to Manor House (Piccadilly line), or Seven Sisters (Victoria line). From Manor House, buses 279, 259; from Seven Sisters 67, 149, 171, 243, 259, 123, 279. White Hart Lane station is three minutes' walk from the ground and is served by trains from Liverpool St.

Match tickets: For League matches, seats can be booked not earlier than 21 days before the match. At the Park Lane and Paxton Road ends, there are seats available at the turnstiles.

Car parking: No street parking within a ¼ mile radius of the ground.

Entertainments/catering facilities: Hot food available at snack and chicken bars in the ground.

Club shop: There are shops on the corner of Park Lane and High Road, and Paxton Road and High Road.

Handbooks/programmes: Programmes available on subscription to shop.

Extra information: Supporters' Club with a present membership of over 7000 is open to new members; information from the Secretary, Mrs M. Ellam (Tel: 808 7430).

Club Colours: White shirts, blue shorts, white stockings.

Change Colours: All yellow with blue trims.

Club Captain: Steve Perryman.

Club Nickname: Spurs.

TOTTENHAM HOTSPUR 1980–81 LEAGUE RECORD

Match No.	Date	Venue	Opponents	Result	H/T Score	Goalscorers	Attendance
1	Aug 16	H	Nottingham F	W 2-0	0-0	Hoddle (pen), Crooks	43,270
2	19	A	Crystal Palace	W 4-3	3-1	Crooks 2, Hoddle, Archibald	27,102
3	23	H	Brighton & HA	D 2-2	1-1	Crooks, Hoddle	39,763
4	30	A	Arsenal	L 0-2	0-0		54,045
5	Sept 6	H	Manchester U	D 0-0	0-0		40,995
6	13	A	Leeds U	D 0-0	0-0		21,947
7	20	H	Sunderland	D 0-0	0-0		32,030
8	27	A	Leicester C	L 1-2	0-0	Villa	22,616
9	Oct 4	A	Stoke C	W 3-2	2-0	Taylor (pen), Archibald, Hughton	18,511
10	11	H	Middlesbrough	W 3-2	0-1	Villa, Crooks, Archibald	27,380
11	18	A	Aston Villa	L 0-3	0-1		30,940
12	22	A	Manchester C	L 1-3	0-2	Hoddle	28,788
13	25	H	Coventry C	W 4-1	1-0	Hoddle 2, Archibald 2	25,484
14	Nov 1	A	Everton	D 2-2	1-1	Archibald 2	26,174
15	8	H	Wolverhampton W	D 2-2	2-1	Hoddle (pen), Crooks	29,244
16	12	H	Crystal Palace	W 4-2	1-1	Crooks 3, Archibald	25,777
17	15	A	Nottingham F	W 3-0	0-0	Archibald 2, Ardiles	25,400
18	22	A	Birmingham C	L 1-2	1-1	Ardiles	24,817
19	29	H	WBA	L 2-3	0-3	Lacy, Perryman	27,371
20	Dec 6	A	Liverpool	L 1-2	1-1	Archibald	39,545
21	13	H	Manchester C	W 2-1	1-1	Archibald, Hoddle	23,883
22	17	H	Ipswich T	W 5-3	2-1	Crooks, Hoddle, Perryman, Archibald, Ardiles	22,741
23	20	A	Middlesbrough	L 1-4	1-2	Lacy	15,992
24	26	H	Southampton	D 4-4	2-2	Archibald, Brooke 2, Crooks	28,792
25	27	A	Norwich C	D 2-2	1-1	Archibald, Hoddle	23,898
26	Jan 10	H	Birmingham C	W 1-0	0-0	Crooks	24,909
27	17	H	Arsenal	W 2-0	1-0	Archibald 2	32,994
28	31	A	Brighton & HA	W 2-0	1-0	Ardiles, Crooks	23,354
29	Feb 7	H	Leeds U	D 1-1	1-0	Archibald	32,372
30	17	A	Manchester U	D 0-0	0-0		40,282
31	21	H	Leicester C	L 1-2	1-1	Archibald	26,126
32	28	A	Sunderland	D 1-1	1-0	Crooks	22,382
33	Mar 11	H	Stoke C	D 2-2	0-1	Ardiles, Brooke	28,742
34	14	A	Ipswich T	L 0-3	0-2		32,052
35	21	H	Aston Villa	W 2-0	1-0	Crooks, Archibald	35,091
36	28	A	Coventry C	W 1-0	1-0	Roberts (og)	18,666
37	Apr 4	H	Everton	D 2-2	0-2	Crooks, Galvin	27,208
38	18	H	Norwich C	L 2-3	2-2	Hoddle (pen), Miller	34,413
39	20	A	Southampton	D 1-1	0-1	Miller	23,735
40	25	H	Liverpool	D 1-1	1-1	Hoddle	35,334
41	30	A	Wolverhampton W	L 0-1	0-1		18,530
42	May 2	A	WBA	L 2-4	0-2	Falco, Smith	20,429

Final League Position: 10

Goalscorers

League (70): Archibald 20, Crooks 16, Hoddle 12 (3 pens), Ardiles 5, Brooke 3, Lacy 2, Miller 2, Perryman 2, Villa 2, Falco 1, Galvin 1, Hughton 1, Smith 1, Taylor 1 (pen), own goal 1.
League Cup (8): Archibald 2, Crooks 2, Ardiles, Hoddle, Lacy, Villa.
F.A. Cup (19): Crooks 4, Archibald 3, Villa 3, Hoddle 2, Ardiles, Brooke, Galvin, Hughton, Miller, Roberts, own goal.

League Cup	Second Round	Orient (a)	1-0
		(h)	3-1
	Third Round	Crystal Palace (h)	0-0
		(a)	3-1
	Fourth Round	Arsenal (h)	1-0
	Fifth Round	West Ham U (h)	0-1
FA Cup	Third Round	QPR (a)	0-0
		(h)	3-1
	Fourth Round	Hull C (h)	2-0
	Fifth Round	Coventry C (h)	3-1
	Sixth Round	Exeter C (h)	2-0
	Semi-final	Wolverhampton W	2-2 (at Hillsborough)
			3-0 (at Highbury)
	Final	Manchester C	1-1 (at Wembley)
	Replay		3-2 (at Wembley)

Kendall	Smith	Hughton	Yorath	Lacy	Perryman	Ardiles	Archibald	Villa	Hoddle	Crooks	Armstrong	Taylor	Daines	Roberts	Miller	McAllister	Brooke	Aleksic	O'Reilly	Mazzon	Galvin	Hazard	Falco	*Match No.*
1	2	3	4	5	6	7*	8	9	10	11	12													1
1	2	3	4	5	6	7	8	9	10	11														2
1	2	3	4	5	6	7	8	9	10	11														3
1	2*	3	4	5	6	7	8	9	10	11		12												4
	2	3	4*	5	6	7	8	9	10	11		12	1											5
	2	3		5	6	7	8	9	10	11		4	1											6
	2	3		5	6	7	8	9	10	11	12	4*	1											7
	2	3	4	5	6	7	8	9	10	11			1											8
	2	3	4	5	6	7	8	9		11*		10	1	12										9
	2	3	4	5	6	7*	8	9	10	11		12	1											10
	2	3	4*	5	6		8	9	10	11	12	7	1											11
	2	3		5	6	7	8	9	10	11*	12	4	1											12
	2	3		5	6	7	8	9	10	11			1		4									13
	2	3		5	6	7	8	9	10	11			1		4									14
	2	3*		5	6	7	8	9	10	11			1	12	4									15
		3		5	6	7	8	9	10	11			1	12	4	2*								16
		2		5	6	7	8	9	10	11			1		4	3								17
		3		5	6	7	8	9	10	11			1		4	2								18
		3		5	6	7*	8	9	10	11			1		4	2	12							19
		3		5	6	7	8	9	10	11			1	4		2								20
		3	12	5	6	7*	8	9	10	11			1	4		2								21
		3	12	5	6	7	8	9*	10	11			1	4		2								22
		3	12	5	6	7	8	9	10	11				4*		2		1						23
		3*	2	5	6		8	9	10	11				4			7	1	12					24
			4	5	6		8	9*	10	11				2	12		7	1	3					25
				5	6		8		10	11			1	4	3	2	7*			12	9			26
			12	5*	6		8		10	11			1	4	3	2	7				9			27
				5	6	7*	8		10	11			1	4	3	2	12				9			28
				5	6	7	8		10	11*			1	4	3	2	12				9			29
		2		5	6	7	8		10	11			1	4	3						9			30
		2		5	6	7	8		10	11*			1	4	3		12				9			31
	12	2			6	7	8*		10	11			1	4	3					5	9			32
		2*			6	7	8		10	11			1	4	3	5	12				9			33
		2			6	7*	8		10	11			1	4	3	5	12				9			34
		2			6	7	8		10	11				4	3		5	1			9			35
	12	2			6	7	8		10	11				4	3		5*	1			9			36
		2			6	7	8	12	10	11				4	3		5*	1			9			37
		2			6	7	8		10	11				4	3		5*	1			9	12		38
		2			5	7		6		11*					4	3	12	1			10	9	8	39
	2				6	7	8	5*	10	11					3	4	12	1			9			40
	2				6	7	8						1	4	3*	10	5				9	12	11	41
	2				6		12	5						10*	3	4	7	1			9	8	11	42
4	18	34	11	31	42	36	40	28	38	40	—	5	28	21	24	18	10	10	1	1	17	2	3	
	+ 2s		+ 4s				+ 1s	+ 1s			+ 4s	+ 3s		+ 3s	+ 1s		+ 8s		+ 1s	+ 1s		+ 2s		

TOTTENHAM HOTSPUR

	Ht	*Wt*	*Birthplace*	*Clubs*	*League App.*	*League Gls*
Goalkeepers						
Barry Daines	5 11½	11 8	Whitham	Tottenham H	146	—
Milija Aleksic	6 0	13 11	Stafford	Plymouth Arg	32	—
				Ipswich T (on loan)	—	—
				Oxford U (on loan)	—	—
				Luton T	77	—
				Tottenham H	23	—
				Sheffield U (on loan)	—	—
Tony Parks	5 10½	10 8	Hackney	Tottenham H	—	—
Mark Hughes	6 0	11 0	West Ham	Tottenham H	—	—
Defenders						
Don McAllister	5 10	11 2	Radcliffe	Bolton W	156	2
				Tottenham H	172	9
James Holmes	5 9	11 7	Dublin	Coventry C	128	7
(Eire) (Contract cancelled Feb 1981)				Tottenham H	81	2
Chris Hughton (Eire)	5 7¾	11 5	West Ham	Tottenham H	73	2
John Lacy	6 1	12 4	Liverpool	Fulham	168	7
				Tottenham H	70	2
Gordon Smith	5 9	12 1	Glasgow	St Johnstone	118	11
				Aston V	79	—
				Tottenham H	36	1
Giorgio Mazzon	5 10	11 5	London	Tottenham H	2	—
Peter Southey	5 9	11 0	Putney	Tottenham H	1	—
Alex Hamill	5 8	10 1	Coatbridge	Tottenham H	—	—
(Transferred to Hearts Nov 1980)						
John Cooper	5 11	11 0	London	Tottenham H	—	—
Paul Miller	6 1	12 2	London	Tottenham H	59	4
Graham Roberts	5 10	12 12	Southampton	Weymouth	(not known)	
				Tottenham H	24	—
Pat Corbett	6 0	11 0	Hackney	Tottenham H	—	—
Midfield						
Steve Perryman	5 8	10 10	Ealing	Tottenham H	474	26
Glenn Hoddle (England)	6 0	11 6	Hayes	Tottenham H	201	55
Mike Hazard	5 7	10 5	Sunderland	Tottenham H	7	—
Osvaldo Ardiles	5 6	9 10	Cordoba	Huracan	(not known)	
(Argentina)				Tottenham H	114	11
Ricardo Villa	6 0	12 5	Buenos Aires	Racing	(not known)	
(Argentina)				Tottenham H	83	8
Terry Yorath	6 0	12 3	Cardiff	Leeds U	143	10
(Wales) (Contract cancelled Feb 1981)				Coventry C	99	3
				Tottenham H	48	1
Paul Grayling*	5 8	10 3	Salisbury	Tottenham H	—	—
Gary O'Reilly	5 11		Isleworth	Tottenham H	2	—
Ian Crook	5 8	10 6	Romford	Tottenham H	—	—
Allan Cockram	5 7	10 6	Kensington	Tottenham H	—	—
Garry Brooke	5 6	10 5	Bethnal Green	Tottenham H	18	3
Forwards						
Tony Galvin	5 9	11 5	Huddersfield	Tottenham H	28	5
Chris Jones	5 11	10 7	Jersey	Tottenham H	157	37
Mark Falco	6 0	12 0	Hackney	Tottenham H	13	4
Terry Gibson	5 5	10 0	London	Tottenham H	1	—
Anthony Chambers*	5 9	11 6	Jamaica	Tottenham H	—	—
Steve Archibald	5 10	11 2	Scotland	Clyde	65	7
(Scotland)				Aberdeen	76	29
				Tottenham H	41	20
Garth Crooks	5 8	11 6	Stoke	Stoke C	147	48
				Tottenham H	40	16
James Bolton*			Kensington	Tottenham H	—	—
Chris Harvey*			Barking	Tottenham H	—	—

TRANMERE ROVERS Division 4

Chairman: H. B. Thomas.

Directors: H. A. Bainbridge FCA, G. A. Gould FCA, G. T. H. Kemp. A. J. Adams.

General Manager/Secretary: Jack Butterfield.

Team Manager: Bryan Hamilton.

Year Formed: 1883. *Turned Professional:* 1912.

Limited Company: 1920.

Commercial Department: 051-608 3677/4194.

Football League Record:
1921 Original Member of Division 3(N); 1938–39 Division 2; 1946–58 Division 3(N); 1958–61 Division 3; 1961–67 Division 4; 1967–75 Division 3; 1975–76 Division 4; 1976–79 Division 3; 1979– Division 4.

Honours: *Football League:* Division 2 best season: 22nd, 1938–39; Division 3(N) – Champions 1937–38; Promotion to 3rd Division: 1966–67, 1975–76. *FA Cup* best season: 5th rd, 1967–68. *Football League Cup* best season: 4th rd, 1961. *Welsh Cup:* Winners 1935.

Record Victory: 13-4 v Oldham Ath, Division 3(N), 26 Dec, 1935.

Record Defeat: 1-9 v Tottenham H, FA Cup 3rd rd replay, 14 Jan, 1953.

Most League Points: 60, Division 4, 1964–65.

Most League Goals: 111, Division 3(N), 1930–31.

Highest League Scorer in Season: Bunny Bell, 35, Division 3(N), 1933–34.

Most League Goals in Total Aggregate: Bunny Bell, 104, 1931–36.

Most Capped Player: Albert Gray, 3 (23), Wales.

Most League Appearances: Harold Bell, 595, 1946–64 (including League record of 401 consecutive appearances).

Record Transfer Fee Received: £120,000 from Cardiff C for Ronnie Moore, Feb 1979.

Record Transfer Fee Paid: £20,000 to Charlton Ath for Hugh McAuley, Aug 1978.

Previous Managers since the War: Ernie Blackburn, Noel Kelly, Peter Farrell, Walter Galbraith, Dave Russell, Jackie Wright, Ron Yeats, John King.

Address of Supporters Club: Supporters Assn, Prenton Park, Birkenhead.

Prenton Park, Prenton Road West, Birkenhead. Telephone 051-608 3677/4194. *Ground capacity:* 18,000. *Record attendance:* 24,424 v Stoke C, FA Cup 4th rd, 5 Feb, 1972. *Record receipts:* £8982 v Stoke C, FA Cup 4th rd, 5 Feb, 1972. *Pitch measurements:* 112yd×74yd.

How to get there: Special buses from railway stations, Hamilton Square and Rock Ferry. Mersey Railway Liverpool, to Hamilton Square, then buses 80 to 90 or 64.

Match tickets: Seats can be booked in advance.

Car parking: Large car park at the back of the stand.

Entertainments/catering facilities: Snack bars in ground. Social club with bar facilities.

Club shop: Prenton Road West.

Handbooks/programmes: Programmes available on subscription.

Extra information: Tranmere's record victory equals the highest score in a League game; in the 13-4 win over Oldham, centre-forward Bunny Bell scored nine goals and missed a penalty.

Club Colours: Royal blue shirts, white collar and cuffs, white shorts, royal blue stockings.

Change Colours: All yellow.

First Team Trainer/Coach: Eddie Robertson.

Club Nickname: Rovers.

TRANMERE ROVERS 1980–81 LEAGUE RECORD

Match No.	Date	Venue	Opponents	Result		H/T Score	Goalscorers	Attendance
1	Aug 16	A	Hereford U	D	1-1	1-0	Lumby	3034
2	18	H	Crewe Alex	L	0-1	0-1		2246
3	22	A	Southend U	L	0-2	0-1		4623
4	29	H	Rochdale	W	3-1	2-0	Lumby 2, Evans	1826
5	Sept 5	H	Peterborough U	L	1-2	0-0	Lumby	1772
6	13	A	AFC Bournemouth	L	0-1	0-0		2642
7	19	H	Torquay U	W	1-0	0-0	Beamish	1564
8	23	A	York C	L	1-4	0-2	Lumby	2322
9	27	A	Bradford C	W	3-0	1-0	Beamish, Lumby 2	3628
10	29	H	York C	W	5-0	3-0	Beamish, Peplow, Lumby 3	1595
11	Oct 3	H	Wimbledon	W	3-0	2-0	Evans, Beamish (pen), Lumby	2507
12	6	A	Mansfield T	D	1-1	0-1	Lumby	1925
13	11	A	Port Vale	L	1-5	0-2	Peplow	2820
14	17	H	Aldershot	W	3-1	1-1	Peplow, Mungall, Kerr	2312
15	20	H	Halifax T	W	2-0	0-0	Lumby, Mungall	2314
16	25	A	Wigan Ath	D	1-1	0-1	Lumby	5421
17	29	A	Lincoln C	L	0-2	0-0		4628
18	31	H	Bury	W	3-1	2-0	Evans, Lumby 2	2426
19	Nov 3	H	Mansfield T	W	1-0	0-0	Lumby	2048
20	8	A	Darlington	L	0-2	0-1		1645
21	12	A	Crewe Alex	L	0-3	0-0		3173
22	29	A	Northampton T	L	1-3	1-0	Craven	1487
23	Dec 5	H	Hartlepool U	D	2-2	1-1	Kerr, Lumby	1366
24	20	A	Scunthorpe U	L	0-2	0-1		1664
25	26	H	Stockport Co	W	1-0	1-0	Kerr	2531
26	27	A	Doncaster R	L	0-1	0-0		5530
27	Jan 10	A	Halifax T	D	1-1	0-1	Kelly	1268
28	16	H	Northampton T	W	3-2	1-1	Parry, Kelly, Beamish	1254
29	24	A	Rochdale	L	1-3	1-2	Kerr	2731
30	30	H	Southend U	D	2-2	1-1	Evans, Kelly	2127
31	Feb 6	H	AFC Bournemouth	L	0-1	0-0		2480
32	Mar 1	A	Torquay U	L	1-2	1-0	Powell	2484
33	3	H	Lincoln C	D	0-0	0-0		1538
34	7	A	Wimbledon	L	1-2	0-0	Evans	2394
35	10	H	Bradford C	D	1-1	1-0	Jackson (og)	1300
36	18	A	Peterborough U	L	1-4	0-3	Bramhall	3034
37	22	A	Aldershot	L	2-3	1-2	Kerr, Beamish	4493
38	24	H	Port Vale	L	1-2	0-1	Evans	1479
39	29	H	Wigan Ath	L	2-3	1-2	Mungall, Kelly	3437
40	Apr 4	A	Bury	D	2-2	1-2	Parry, Evans	2425
41	10	H	Darlington	W	3-1	1-0	Evans 2, Williams	1225
42	17	H	Doncaster R	D	1-1	0-0	Craven	2919
43	20	A	Stockport Co	L	0-1	0-0		2311
44	24	H	Scunthorpe U	L	1-2	1-0	Williams	1063
45	29	H	Hereford U	W	2-1	1-0	Peplow, Kelly	1136
46	May 2	A	Hartlepool U	L	0-3	0-1		1802

Final League Position: 21

Goalscorers

League (59): Lumby 18, Evans 9, Beamish 6 (1 pen), Kelly 5, Kerr 5, Peplow 4, Mungall 3, Craven 2, Parry 2, Williams 2, Bramhall 1, Powell 1, own goal 1.
League Cup (6): Bramhall, Craven, Edwards (pen), Evans, Kelly, Kerr.
F.A. Cup (2): Beamish, Craven.

League Cup	First Round	Port Vale (a)	3-2
		(h)	0-1
	Second Round	Brighton & HA (a)	1-3
		(h)	2-4
FA Cup	First Round	York C (h)	0-0
		(a)	2-1
	Second Round	Huddersfield T (h)	0-3

Johnson	Parry	Mathias	Bramhall	Edwards	Mungall	Kelly	Craven	Lumby	Beamish	Peplow	Evans	Kerr	Williams	Flood	Griffiths	Hamilton	Le Cornu	Powell	Whittingham	Mountfield	*Match No.*
1	2	3	4	5	6	7	8*	9	10	11			12								1
1	2	3	4	5	6	7	8	9	10	11*	12										2
1	2	3	4	5	7	11	8*	9	10		6	12									3
1	2	3	4	5	7	11		9	10		6	8									4
1	2	3	4	5	7	11		9	10		6	8*	12								5
1	2	3	4	5	7	11		9	10		6	8*		12							6
1	5	2	4		8	11*		9	10	7	6			3	12						7
1	5	2	4*		8	11		9	10	7	6			3	12						8
1	5	2			8	11		9	10	7	6		4	3							9
1	5	2			8	11		9	10	7	6		4	3							10
1	5	2			8	11*		9	10	7	6		4	3		12					11
1	5	2	12		8			9	10	7*	6		4	3		11					12
1	5	2	12		8			9	10*	7	6		4	3		11					13
1	5	2			8			9	10*	7	6	12	4	3		11					14
1	5	2			8			9	10	7	6		4	3		11					15
1		2	5		8			9	10	7	6		4	3		11					16
1		2	5	7	8			10*	11	12	6		4	3		9					17
1		2*	5		8			9	10	7	6		4	3	12	11					18
1		2	5		8			9	10	7	6		4	3	11						19
1		2	5		8			9	10	7	6		4	3	11*	12					20
1	2	3	5		8			9	10	12	6		4		11	7*					21
1	4			2	8		7	9	10		6		5	3*	11	12					22
1	5	3		2	8*		7	9			12	10	4		11	6					23
1		3		2	8*	12	7	9				10	4	5	11	6					24
1	5			2		7			9		8	10	4	3	11*	6	12				25
1	5	2	4		8	9					6	10		3	11	12	7*				26
1	5		4	2		7	9				6	10		3	11	8					27
1	5		4	2		7	9*		12		6	10		3	11	8					28
1	5		4	2		7	9*		12		6	10		3	11	8					29
1	5	2	4		8	7			9		6	10		3	11						30
1	5	2	4		8	7			9*		6	10		3	11		12				31
1	5	2	4		8*	9					6	10		3	11	12		7			32
1	5	2	4			10					6	9		3	11	8		7			33
1	5	2	4	3		9					6	10			11	8		7			34
1	5	2	4	3		7					6	10	9		11	8					35
1		2	4	3*							6	10	9		11	8		7	12	5	36
1		2	4		12				9		6	10		3	11	8*		7		5	37
1	3	2	4		8				9		6	10			11			7		5	38
1	5*		4		8	11			9	7	6	10		3	12	2					39
1	5		4		2	8			9*	12	6	10		3	11	7					40
1	5	3	4		2	7	10		9*	11	6		12			8					41
1	5	3	4		2		7*				6	10	9		11	8	12				42
1	5	3	4		2						6	10	9		11	8	7				43
1	5	2	4		3	12					6	10*	9		11	8	7				44
1	5		4		2	9				7			10	3	11	8				6	45
1	5		4		2	10				7	12		9	3	11*	8				6	46
46	38	37	35	17	37	27	11	24	30	19	40	24	24	30	26	27	3	6	—	5	
			+ 2s		+ 1s	+ 2s			+ 2s	+ 3s	+ 3s	+ 2s	+ 3s	+ 1s	+ 4s	+ 5s	+ 3s		+ 1s		

TRANMERE ROVERS

	Ht	Wt	Birthplace	Clubs	League App.	League Gls
Goalkeepers						
Dickie Johnson	6 1	12 10	Liverpool	Tranmere R	352	—
Defenders						
Ray Mathias	5 9	11 4	Liverpool	Tranmere R	541	5
John Bramhall	6 2	13 6	Warrington	Tranmere R	135	4
Eddie Flood*	5 7	10 0	Liverpool	Liverpool	—	—
				Tranmere R	315	6
Leslie Parry	5 11	11 0	Wallasey	Tranmere R	210	4
Steve Mungall	5 8	10 12	Bellshill	Motherwell	20	—
				Tranmere R	62	3
Elfyn Edwards*	5 11	12 3	Aberystwyth	Wrexham	—	—
				Tranmere R	62	1
Derek Mountfield	6 1	12 7	Liverpool	Tranmere R	5	—
Midfield						
Steve Craven	5 10	11 0	Birkenhead	Tranmere R	75	9
Clive Evans	5 10	10 9	Birkenhead	Tranmere R	178	27
Ian Griffiths	5 6	10 2	Birkenhead	Tranmere R	35	—
Bryan Hamilton (N Ireland)	5 9	11 4	Belfast	Ipswich T	153	43
				Everton	41	5
				Millwall	49	6
				Swindon T	24	1
				Tranmere R	32	—
Craig Le Cornu*	5 8	10 12	Birkenhead	Liverpool	—	—
				Tranmere R	6	—
Forwards						
Steve Peplow*	5 8	10 13	Liverpool	Liverpool	2	—
				Swindon T	40	11
				Nottingham F	3	—
				Mansfield T (on loan)	4	3
				Tranmere R	248	44
John Kerr	6 1	12 5	Birkenhead	Tranmere R	81	17
John Williams	6 2	13 6	Liverpool	Tranmere R	31	2
Steve Whittingham*	5 10	11 8	Birkenhead	Tranmere R	2	—
Ken Beamish*	6 0	12 6	Bebbington	Tranmere R	177	49
				Brighton & HA	96	27
				Blackburn R	86	18
				Port Vale	85	29
				Bury	49	20
				Tranmere R	59	15
John Kelly	5 10	10 9	Bebbington	Tranmere R	57	9
Neville Powell (Apprentice)	5 7	9 12	Flint	Tranmere R	6	1

WALSALL — Division 3

Chairman: K. E. Wheldon.

Directors: J. A. Harris, S. E. Boler, R. Homden, B. E. Bradnack.

General-Manager: Neil Martin.

Player-Manager: Alan Buckley.

Secretary: H. J. Westmancoat LAAI.

Year Formed: 1888.

Turned Professional: 1888.

Limited Company: 1921.

Previous Names: Walsall Swifts (Founded 1877) and Walsall Town (Founded 1879) amalgamated in 1888 and were known as Walsall Town Swifts until 1895.

Football League Record:
1892 Elected to Division 2; 1895 failed re-election; 1896–1901 Division 2; 1901 failed re-election; 1921 Original Member of Division 3(N); 1927–31 Division 3(S); 1931–36 Division 3(N); 1936–58 Division 3(S); 1958–60 Division 4; 1960–61 Division 3; 1961–63 Division 2; 1963–79 Division 3; 1979–80 Division 4; 1980– Division 3.

Honours: *Football League:* Division 2 best season: 6th, 1898–99; Division 3 – Runners-up 1960–61; Division 4 – Champions 1959–60; Runners-up 1979–80. *FA Cup* best season: 5th rd, 1939, 1975, 1978, and last 16 1888–89. *Football League Cup* best season: 4th rd, 1966–67.

Record Victory: 10-0 v Darwen, Division 2, 4 Mar, 1899.

Record Defeat: 0-12 v Small Heath, 17 Dec, 1892 and v Darwen, 26 Dec, 1896, both Division 2.

Most League Points: 65, Division 4, 1959–60.

Most League Goals: 102, Division 4, 1959–60.

Highest League Scorer in Season: Gilbert Alsop, 40, Division 3(N), 1933–34 and 1934–35.

Most League Goals in Total Aggregate: Tony Richards, 184, 1954–63, and Colin Taylor, 184, 1958–63, 1964–68, 1969–73.

Most Capped Player: Mick Kearns, 15 (17), Eire.

Most League Appearances: Colin Harrison, 466, 1964–81.

Record Transfer Fee Received: £175,000 from Birmingham C for Alan Buckley, Oct 1978.

Record Transfer Fee Paid: £175,000 to Birmingham C for Alan Buckley, June 1979.

Previous Managers since the War: Harry Hibbs, Tony McPhee, Brough Fletcher, Major Buckley, John Love, Billy Moore, Alf Wood, Ray Shaw, Ron Lewin, Dick Graham, Billy Moore, John Smith, Ronnie Allen, Doug Fraser, Dave Mackay, Alan Ashman, Frank Sibley.

Address of Supporters Club: Saddlers Club, Wallows Lane, Walsall, Staffs.

Fellows Park, Walsall. Telephone 0922 22791. *Telegraphic address:* 'Walsall FC, Walsall'. *Ground capacity:* 24,100. *Record attendance:* 25,453 v Newcastle U, Division 2, 29 Aug, 1961. *Record receipts:* £12,775.35 v Newcastle U, FA Cup 4th rd, 25 Jan, 1975. *Pitch measurements:* 113yd×73yd.

How to get there: Corporation specials from Bradford Place. Buses 237 and 238 within walking distance of the ground. Nearest railway stations, Bescot (10 minutes' walk from ground) and Walsall.

Match tickets: Seats can be booked at any time by postal, personal, or telephone application to the ticket office; tel: 0922 22791.

Car parking: Car park in Hillary Street for 100 cars. Side-street parking available.

Entertainments/catering facilities: Supporters' club adjacent to ground. Tea bars and licensed bars inside the ground.

Club shop: The Boutique, is open on match days.

Extra information: In 1947, Walsall set a Division 3(S) record by winning 8-0 away at Northampton.

Club Colours: Red shirts, white shorts, red stockings with two white bands on turnover.

Change Colours: Blue shirts, black trim, black shorts, black stockings.

Club Captain: Peter Hart.

Club Nickname: Saddlers.

WALSALL 1980–81 LEAGUE RECORD

Match No.	Date	Venue	Opponents	Result	H/T Score	Goalscorers	Attendance
1	Aug 16	A	Reading	L 0-2	0-1		4369
2	20	H	Burnley	W 3-1	0-0	Penn, Baines, Buckley	4714
3	23	A	Colchester U	D 1-1	1-0	O'Kelly	1979
4	30	H	Brentford	L 2-3	1-1	Hill (og), Buckley	4586
5	Sept 6	A	Hull C	W 1-0	0-0	Buckley	4121
6	13	H	Portsmouth	W 2-0	1-0	Rees, Buckley	5738
7	16	H	Rotherham U	L 0-2	0-2		4500
8	20	A	Fulham	L 1-2	0-1	Buckley	4573
9	27	H	Blackpool	D 2-2	1-1	Rees, McDonough	4227
10	30	A	Rotherham U	L 1-2	0-1	Paul	6842
11	Oct 4	H	Carlisle U	W 4-3	2-1	Penn 2, McVitie (og), Baines	3815
12	7	A	Charlton Ath	L 0-2	0-2		3359
13	11	A	Oxford U	D 1-1	1-1	Penn	3123
14	18	H	Newport Co	W 1-0	0-0	Hart	4335
15	21	H	Exeter C	L 1-3	0-2	Rees	3703
16	25	A	Chesterfield	W 2-1	2-0	O'Kelly, Baines	7870
17	28	A	Millwall	W 1-0	0-0	O'Kelly	2785
18	Nov 1	H	Gillingham	D 3-3	3-2	Hart, Paul, O'Kelly	4060
19	4	H	Charlton Ath	D 2-2	0-2	Waddington S., Smith	4287
20	8	A	Plymouth Arg	L 0-2	0-0		5022
21	11	A	Burnley	D 0-0	0-0		5570
22	15	H	Reading	D 2-2	2-1	Paul 2	3583
23	29	H	Sheffield U	D 4-4	0-1	Buckley (pen), Penn 2, Mower	4931
24	Dec 6	A	Chester	L 0-1	0-0		2215
25	19	A	Swindon T	L 1-3	0-1	Buckley	4523
26	26	H	Huddersfield T	D 2-2	1-0	Buckley, O'Kelly	5906
27	27	A	Barnsley	L 0-3	0-2		14,958
28	Jan 3	H	Millwall	D 0-0	0-0		3918
29	10	A	Exeter C	W 3-0	1-0	O'Kelly, Hart, Buckley	4590
30	17	H	Chester	W 2-1	0-1	Waddington S., Baines	3483
31	24	A	Brentford	L 0-4	0-3		5500
32	31	H	Colchester U	W 3-1	2-0	Waddington S., Mower, Smith	3195
33	Feb 7	A	Portsmouth	L 0-2	0-1		11,921
34	14	H	Hull C	D 1-1	0-0	Buckley	3914
35	21	A	Blackpool	L 0-1	0-0		3895
36	Mar 1	H	Fulham	L 1-2	1-2	Smith	4958
37	7	A	Carlisle U	D 1-1	0-1	Hart	4485
38	14	H	Oxford U	L 0-3	0-1		3185
39	28	H	Chesterfield	W 4-3	2-1	Rees 2, O'Kelly, Hart	4044
40	Apr 3	A	Gillingham	L 0-1	0-1		4112
41	7	A	Newport Co	D 1-1	1-1	Caswell	5446
42	11	H	Plymouth Arg	L 1-3	0-1	Penn	3556
43	18	H	Barnsley	D 1-1	0-1	Buckley (pen)	6026
44	21	A	Huddersfield T	D 1-1	0-1	Waddington S.	9463
45	25	H	Swindon T	W 2-1	0-0	Penn, Rees	3429
46	May 2	A	Sheffield U	W 1-0	0-0	Penn (pen)	16,001

Final League Position: 20

Goalscorers

League (59): Buckley 11 (2 pens), Penn 9 (1 pen), O'Kelly 7, Rees 6, Hart 5, Baines 4, Paul 4, Waddington S. 4, Smith 3, Mower 2, Caswell 1, McDonough 1, own goals 2.
League Cup (3): Buckley, McDonough, Penn.
F.A. Cup (3): Buckley, Penn, Waddington S.

League Cup	First Round	Blackpool (h)	2-3
		(a)	1-3
FA Cup	First Round	Stafford R (h)	3-0
	Second Round	Carlisle U (a)	0-3

Turner	Macken	Mower	Serella	Baines	Hart	Penn	O'Kelly	McDonough	Buckley	Caswell	Waddington S	Freeman	Rees	Paul	Conneally	Smith	Harrison	Horne	Green	Waddington P	Preece	*Match No.*
1	2*	3	4	5	6	7	8	9	10	11	12											1
	2	3	4	5	6	7	8*	9	10	11	12	1										2
	2	3	4	5	6	7	8	9	10	11*	12	1										3
	2	3	4	5	6	7	8	9	10		11	1										4
	2	3	4	5	6	7	8		10	11		1	9									5
	2	3	4	5	6	7	8		10	11		1	9									6
	2	3	4	5	6	7*	8	12	10	11		1	9									7
	2	3*	4	5	6	7	8		10	11		1	9	12								8
	2*		4	5	6	7	8	9	10	11		1	12	3								9
		3	4	5	6	9	8		10	2			11	7	1							10
	2	12	4	5	6	7	8		10	3*			9	11	1							11
	2	3	4	5	6	7	8		10				9	11	1							12
1	2	3	4		6	7	8		10		5		9	11								13
1	2	3	4	5*	6	7	8		10		11		9			12						14
1	2	3	4	5	6	7			10*		8		9	11		12						15
1	2		4	5	6		8		10	3	7			11		9						16
1	2		4	5	6	7	8		10	11						9	3					17
1	2		4	5	6		8		10	3	7			11		9						18
1	2		4	5	6		8		10	3	7			11		9						19
1	2		4	5	6		8		10	3*	7			11		9	12					20
1	2		4		6	10	8				7		12	11		9*	3	5				21
1	2		4		6	9	8				7			11		10	3	5				22
	2*	3	4		6	12	8		10		7			11		9	5		1			23
	2	3	4	5	6	8			10		7			11		9			1			24
	2	3	5			7	6		10	11	8		12			9*	4		1			25
	2	3	4	5	6	7*	9		10	11	8		12						1			26
	2	3	4	5	6		9		10	11	8*		7						1	12		27
	2	3*	4	5	6		12		10	11	8					9			1	7		28
	2*		4	5	6		9		10	8	7						3	12	1	11		29
			4	5	6	10	9			3	8		7*				2		1	11	12	30
			4	5	6		9			3	7		8*				2	12	1	11	10	31
		3	4	5	6				10	2	7					9			1	11	8	32
		3	4	5	6	12			10	8	7					9*	2		1	11		33
		3		5	6	9	12		10	8	7						2		1	11*	4	34
			4	5	6	7	9		10	3	8						2		1		11	35
			4	5	6*	7	8		10	3						9	2		1	11	12	36
		3	5		6	7*	12		10							9	2	4	1	11	8	37
		3	5		6	12			10	4	7					9*	2		1	11	8	38
	2	3		5	6	10	9			8	12		7				4		1	11*		39
	2	3	5	9	6	10	8				12		7*				4		1	11		40
	2	3	5	12	6	10	9			8			7				4		1	11*		41
	2	3	5		6	10	9		12	8*			7				4		1	11		42
	2	3	4*	5	6	9	11		10		8		7					12	1			43
	2	3		5	6	9			10	11	8		7					4	1			44
	2	3		5	6	9			10	11	8		7					4	1			45
	2	3	4	5	6*	9			10	11	8		7					12	1			46
11	36	32	42	37	45	34	35	5	38	34	28	8	21	14	3	16	18	5	24	14	6	
		+ 1s		+ 1s		+ 3s	+ 3s	+ 1s	+ 1s		+ 5s		+ 4s	+ 1s		+ 2s	+ 1s	+ 4s		+ 1s	+ 2s	

WALSALL

	Ht	Wt	Birthplace	Clubs	League App.	League Gls
Goalkeepers						
Ronald Green	6 2	12 10	Birmingham	Walsall	65	—
Ian Turner	6 0	12 0	Middlesbrough	Huddersfield T	—	—
				Grimsby T	26	—
				Walsall (on loan)	3	—
				Southampton	77	—
				Newport Co (on loan)	7	—
				Lincoln C (on loan)	7	—
				Luton T (on loan)	—	—
				Halifax T (on loan)	5	—
				Walsall	39	—
Martin Conneally	6 0	12 0	Lichfield	Walsall	3	—
Defenders						
Tony Macken	5 8	12 6	Waterford	Derby Co	23	1
(Eire)				Portsmouth (on loan)	10	1
				Walsall	150	1
Colin Harrison	5 10	11 8	Pelsall	Walsall	466	33
David Serella	5 9	10 10	King's Lynn	Nottingham F	68	—
				Walsall	221	10
Brian Caswell	5 10	10 7	Wednesbury	Walsall	253	14
Ian Paul	5 9	11 0	Wolverhampton	Walsall	70	9
Ken Mower	6 0¾	11 11	Walsall	Walsall	78	3
John Horne	6 0	11 6	Netherton	Walsall	11	—
Stephen Baines	6 0	12 12	Newark	Nottingham F	2	—
				Huddersfield T	114	10
				Bradford C	99	17
				Walsall	38	4
Peter Hadland	5 10	11 5	Birmingham	Walsall	—	—
Midfield						
James Kelly	5 6	10 2	Aldergrove	Wolverhampton W	22	—
(Contract cancelled Oct 1980)				Wrexham (on loan)	4	—
				Walsall	26	3
Steve Waddington	5 4	9 3	Crewe	Stoke C	52	5
				Walsall	104	11
Richard O'Kelly	5 10	11 0	West Bromwich	Walsall	38	7
Peter Hart	5 10	12 7	Mexborough	Huddersfield T	210	7
				Walsall	45	5
David Preece	5 5	9 0	Bridgnorth	Walsall	8	—
Forwards						
Donald Penn	5 10	12 0	Smethwick	Walsall	96	37
Paul Waddington	5 8	9 12	Oldbury	Walsall	17	—
Jimmy Williams	5 9	11 2	Wolverhampton	Walsall	38	2
(Contract cancelled July 1980)						
Mark Rees	5 10	11 10	Smethwick	Walsall	53	9
Alan Buckley	5 6	10 9	Mansfield	Nottingham F	18	1
				Walsall	241	125
				Birmingham C	28	8
				Walsall	84	27
Steve Round	6 1	12 2	Bridgnorth	Walsall	—	—
Steve Smith	5 10	11 6	Birmingham	Bromsgrove R	(not known)	
				Walsall	18	3

WATFORD Division 2

Chairman: E. John.

Directors: J. Harrowell, H. M. Stratford, G. A. Smith, J. Reid.

Chief Executive & Company Secretary: Eddie Plumley FAAI.

General Manager: Graham Taylor.

Assistant Manager: Bertie Mee.

Marketing Manager: Caroline Gillies.

Year Formed: 1891. *Turned Professional:* 1897.

Limited Company: 1909.

Previous Grounds: 1899, Cassio Road; 1919, Vicarage Road.

Football League Record:
1920 Original Member of Division 3; 1921–58 Division 3(S); 1958–60 Division 4; 1960–69 Division 3; 1969–72 Division 2; 1972–75 Division 3; 1975–78 Division 4; 1978–79 Division 3; 1979– Division 2.

Honours: *Football League:* Division 2 best season: 11th, 1980–81; Division 3 – Champions 1968–69; Runners-up 1978–79; Division 4 – Champions 1977–78; Promoted 1959–60 (4th). *FA Cup:* semi-final 1970. *Football League Cup:* semi-final 1978–79.

Record Victory: 10-1 v Lowestoft Town, FA Cup 1st rd, 27 Nov, 1926.

Record Defeat: 0-10 v Wolverhampton W, FA Cup 1st rd replay, 13 Jan, 1912.

Most League Points: 71, Division 4, 1977–78.

Most League Goals: 92, Division 4, 1959–60.

Highest League Scorer in Season: Cliff Holton, 42, Division 4, 1959–60.

Most League Goals in Total Aggregate: Tom Barnett, 144, 1928–39.

Most Capped Player: Gerry Armstrong, 4 (32), Northern Ireland.

Most League Appearances: Duncan Welbourne, 411, 1963–74.

Record Transfer Fee Received: £110,00 from West Ham U for Billy Jennings, Sept 1974.

Record Transfer Fee Paid: £250,000 to Tottenham H for Gerry Armstrong, Nov 1980.

Previous Managers since the War: Jack Bray, Eddie Hapgood, Haydn Green, Ron Gray, Len Goulden, Neil McBain, Ron Burgess, Bill McGarry, Ken Furphy, George Kirby, Mike Keen.

Address of Supporters Club: Watford FC Supporters Club, Vicarage Road, Watford.

Address of Club Shop: 85 Vicarage Road, Watford.

Vicarage Road Stadium, Watford WD1 8ER. Telephone Watford 49747–9. *Ground capacity:* 30,000. *Record attendance:* 34,099 v Manchester U, FA Cup 4th rd, 3 Feb, 1969. *Record receipts:* £48,743 v Coventry C, League Cup 5th rd, 2 Dec, 1980. *Pitch measurements:* 113yd×73yd.

How to get there: Bus 385 from Watford Junction. This and Watford High Street Station are both within walking distance from the ground. Trains from London leave Euston Station.

Match tickets: Stand seats bookable 10 days before each League match. Visiting terrace supporters will be guided by Police to special visitors enclosure (admission £2.00).

Car parking: Parking for season ticket holders only at the ground, but several multi-storey car parks a few minutes away.

Entertainments/catering facilities: Pre-match entertainment at all League and Cup games by Radio Hornet. Tea kiosks and hot dog stands inside the ground.

Club shop: Shops on the ground and 'Hornet Shop' at 85 Vicarage Road, Watford sell all type of souvenirs and programmes.

Handbooks/programmes: Programmes are available on subscription. Price 30p, plus postage. Handbook, 50p, will be available for season 1981–82 with full statistics and interesting information and action pictures.

Extra information: Answerphone Service – Watford 44930 for information. In 1968–69 Watford conceded only 34 goals, a record for the Third Division.

Club Colours: Yellow shirts with black-red facings, red shorts, red stockings with black and yellow tops.

Change Colours: White shirts, black shorts, black stockings with red and yellow tops.

WATFORD 1980–81 LEAGUE RECORD

Match No.	Date	Venue	Opponents	Result	H/T Score	Goalscorers	Attendance
1	Aug 16	H	Swansea C	W 2-1	1-1	Poskett 2	11,316
2	19	A	Luton T	L 0-1	0-1		13,887
3	23	A	Cambridge U	L 1-3	0-1	Poskett	6546
4	30	H	Bristol C	W 1-0	0-0	Patching	10,450
5	Sept 6	A	Shrewsbury T	L 1-2	1-1	Jenkins	5500
6	13	H	Preston NE	W 2-1	1-0	Bolton (pen), Jenkins	11,275
7	20	A	West Ham U	L 2-3	1-0	Poskett, Jackett	24,288
8	27	H	Chelsea	L 2-3	0-0	Callaghan, Bolton (pen)	19,802
9	Oct 4	A	Cardiff C	L 0-1	0-1		6407
10	7	H	Derby Co	D 1-1	1-0	Poskett	11,703
11	11	H	Wrexham	W 1-0	0-0	Sims	10,694
12	18	A	Grimsby T	D 1-1	0-1	Train	8906
13	25	H	Oldham Ath	W 2-1	1-1	Blissett 2 (1 pen)	10,853
14	Nov 1	A	Newcastle U	L 1-2	1-2	Poskett	14,619
15	4	A	Bristol R	L 1-3	1-2	Jackett	5450
16	8	H	Bolton W	W 3-1	1-1	Poskett, Ward, Rostron	11,296
17	11	H	Luton T	L 0-1	0-1		16,939
18	22	H	Blackburn R	D 1-1	0-0	Blissett	13,436
19	29	A	Sheffield W	L 0-1	0-1		14,761
20	Dec 6	H	Notts Co	W 2-0	2-0	Callaghan, Jenkins	11,133
21	13	A	Derby Co	D 1-1	0-1	Blissett	16,464
22	16	A	Swansea C	L 0-1	0-0		13,305
23	20	H	Grimsby T	W 3-1	2-0	Taylor, Armstrong, Poskett	10,209
24	26	A	Orient	D 1-1	1-1	Blissett	10,041
25	27	H	QPR	D 1-1	0-1	Ward	22,911
26	Jan 10	A	Blackburn R	D 0-0	0-0		9466
27	17	A	Bristol C	D 0-0	0-0		8746
28	31	H	Cambridge U	D 0-0	0-0		11,944
29	Feb 7	A	Preston NE	L 1-2	1-2	Jenkins	5107
30	14	H	Shrewsbury T	W 1-0	1-0	Bolton	11,034
31	21	A	Chelsea	W 1-0	0-0	Poskett	19,153
32	28	H	West Ham U	L 1-2	0-0	Poskett	20,786
33	Mar 7	H	Cardiff C	W 4-2	2-1	Poskett 2, Blissett, Pritchett	10,014
34	21	H	Bristol R	W 3-1	2-0	Armstrong, Ward, Blissett	10,162
35	28	A	Oldham Ath	L 1-2	1-2	Ward	4802
36	Apr 4	H	Newcastle U	D 0-0	0-0		10,986
37	11	A	Bolton W	L 1-2	0-0	Armstrong	8461
38	17	H	Orient	W 2-0	0-0	Jackett, Bolton	12,459
39	18	A	QPR	D 0-0	0-0		10,571
40	25	A	Notts Co	W 2-1	1-0	Blissett 2 (1 pen)	10,345
41	May 2	H	Sheffield W	W 2-1	1-1	Poskett, Blissett	12,351
42	4	A	Wrexham	W 1-0	0-0	Blissett	4659

Final League Position: 9

Goalscorers

League (50): Poskett 13, Blissett 11 (2 pens), Bolton 4 (2 pens), Jenkins 4, Ward 4, Armstrong 3, Jackett 3, Callaghan 2, Patching 1, Pritchett 1, Rostron 1, Sims 1, Taylor 1, Train 1.
League Cup (19): Poskett 6, Jenkins 5, Blissett 2 (1 pen), Armstrong, Bolton (pen), Callaghan, Patching, Sims, Train.
F.A. Cup (3): Poskett 2, Armstrong.

League Cup	First Round	Millwall (h)	2-1
		(a)	2-0
	Second Round	Southampton (a)	0-4
		(h)	7-1
	Third Round	Sheffield W (a)	2-1
	Fourth Round	Nottingham F (h)	4-1
	Fifth Round	Coventry C (h)	2-2
		(a)	0-5
FA Cup	Third Round	Colchester U (a)	1-0
	Fourth Round	Wolverhampton W (h)	1-1
		(a)	1-2

Steele	Henderson	Jackett	Patching	Sims	Bolton	Blissett	Poskett	Jenkins	Train	Rostron	Cassells	Callaghan	Harrison	Pritchett	Ward	Taylor	Rice	Armstrong	Terry	Sherwood	*Match No.*
1	2	3	4	5	6	7	8	9	10	11											1
1	2	3	4	5	6	7	8	9	10	11											2
1	2	3	4	5	6	7	8	9	10	11											3
1	2	3	4	5	6	7	8	9	10	11											4
1	2	3	4	5	6	7*	8	9	10	11	12										5
1	2	3	4*	5	6	7	8	9	10	11		12									6
1	2	3		5	6	4	8	9	10	11		7*	12								7
1	2	3		5	6	4	8	9	10	11		7									8
1	2	6		5		4	8	9	10	11		7*	3·	12							9
1	2	6		5		4	8	9	10	11		7*	3	12							10
1	2	6		5		4	8	9	10	11		7*	3	12							11
1	2	6		5		4	8	9	10	11*			3	7	12						12
1	2	6		5		4	7	9	10	11*			3	12	8						13
1	2	6		5		4	7	9	10	11			3		8						14
1	2	6		5		4	7	9	10	11*	8	12	3								15
1	2	6		5		4	8		10	11		7	3		9						16
1	2	6		5		4	8	9	10	11		7*	3			12					17
1		6		5		4	8	12	10	11			3			7*	2	9			18
1	12	6		5		4	7	9	10	11			3				2	8*			19
1		6				4	8	9	10	11		7	3				2		5		20
		6				8	11		10			7*	3		12	4	2	9	5	1	21
		6		5		8	11	12	10				3		7*	4	2	9		1	22
		6		5		8	11		10			7	3			4	2	9		1	23
		6		5		8			11	10		7	3			4	2	9		1	24
		6		5		8	11		10	7*			3		12	4	2	9		1	25
		6				8	11		10			7	3			4	2	9	5	1	26
		6		5		8	11		10			7	3			4	2	9		1	27
		6		5		11	8	9	10				3			4	2	7		1	28
		6		5		11	8	9	10*	12			3			4	2	7		1	29
		10		5	6	8	11					7		3		4	2	9		1	30
		10		5	6	8	11							3	7	4	2	9		1	31
		10		5	6	8	11							3	7	4	2	9		1	32
		10		5	6	8	11							3	7	4	2	9		1	33
		10		5	6	8	11							3	7	4	2	9		1	34
		10		5	6	8	11			12				3	7*	4	2	9		1	35
		10		5	6	8	11							3	7	4	2	9		1	36
		10		5	6	8	11			12				3*	7	4	2	9		1	37
		10			6	8	11					12	3		7*	4	2	9	5	1	38
		10			6	8				11		7	3			4	2	9	5	1	39
		10		5	6	8	11					7	3			4	2	9		1	40
		3		5	6	8	11			10		7				4	2	9		1	41
	3	10		5	6	8	11					7				4	2	9		1	42
20	18	42	6	37	21	42	40	20	29	24	1	18	24	9	12	23	25	24	5	22	
	+ 1s							+ 2s		+ 3s	+ 1s	+ 3s	+ 1s	+ 4s	+ 3s	+ 1s					

WATFORD

	Ht	Wt	Birthplace	Clubs	League App.	League Gls
Goalkeepers						
Steve Sherwood	6 4	14 7	Selby	Chelsea	16	—
				Brighton (on loan)	—	—
				Millwall (on loan)	1	—
				Brentford (on loan)	62	—
				Watford	66	—
Eric Steele	6 0	12 8½	Newcastle	Newcastle U	—	—
				Peterborough U	124	—
				Brighton	87	—
				Watford	48	—
Defenders						
Keith Pritchett	5 9¼	11 5	Glasgow	Wolverhampton W	—	—
				Doncaster R	6	—
				QPR	4	—
				Brentford	11	1
				Watford	122	9
Trevor How	5 10	12 2	Amersham	Watford	91	2
(Contract cancelled March 1981)						
Steve Sims	6 1½	13 9	Lincoln	Leicester C	79	3
				Watford	85	4
Ian Bolton	6 1½	12 7	Leicester	Notts Co	70	4
				Lincoln C (on loan)	1	—
				Watford	147	23
Steve Harrison*	5 7	11 1½	Blackpool	Blackpool	148	—
				Vancouver W	(not known)	
				Watford	83	—
Steve Terry	6 1½	13 3	Enfield	Watford	7	—
Mick Henderson	5 10	11 4½	Gosforth	Sunderland	84	2
				Watford	47	—
Kenny Jackett	5 10½	11 3	Watford	Watford	44	3
Pat Rice	5 9½	12 7	Belfast	Arsenal	397	11
(N Ireland)				Watford	25	—
Midfield						
Ray Train	5 5	10 5	Nuneaton	Walsall	73	11
				Carlisle U	155	8
				Sunderland	32	1
				Bolton W	51	—
				Watford	92	3
Martin Patching	6 0	12 9½	Rotherham	Wolverhampton W	90	10
				Watford	21	2
Gary Donnellan	5 8	11 12	London	Chelsea	—	—
				Watford	—	—
Les Taylor	5 8	11 7	North Shields	Oxford U	219	15
				Watford	24	1
Nigel Callaghan	5 9	10 9	Singapore	Watford	22	2
Forwards						
Wilf Rostron	5 7	11 1½	Sunderland	Arsenal	17	2
				Sunderland	76	17
				Watford	58	4
Ross Jenkins	6 2	12 2	Kensington	Crystal Palace	15	2
(Contract cancelled April 1981)				Watford	286	100
Luther Blissett	5 10½	11 13½	Jamaica	Watford	165	49
Malcolm Poskett	6 0	11 7	Middlesbrough	Middlesbrough	1	—
				Hartlepool U	51	20
				Brighton	45	16
				Watford	56	16
John Ward*	5 8	10 7	Lincoln	Lincoln C	240	91
				Workington (on loan)	11	3
				Watford	27	6
Gerry Armstrong	5 11¾	13 0	Belfast	Tottenham H	84	10
(N Ireland)				Watford	24	3

WEST BROMWICH ALBION Division 1

President: J. W. Gaunt.
Chairman: F. A. Millichip.
Vice-Chairman: J. Gordon.
Directors: C. I. Edwards, D. B. Boundy, J. S. Lucas, A. Everiss.
Manager: Ronnie Allen. *Secretary:* A. E. Rance.
Assistant Manager:
Assistant Secretary: Ray Fairfax.
Statistician: Tony Matthews.
Year Formed: 1879. *Turned Professional:* 1885.
Limited Company: 1891.
Previous Grounds: 1879, Coopers Hill; 1879, Dartmouth Park; 1881, Bunns Field, Walsall Street; 1882, Four Acres (Dartmouth Cricket Club); 1885, Stoney Lane; 1900, The Hawthorns. *Previous Name:* 1879–80, West Bromwich Strollers.
Football League Record:
1888 Founder Member of Football League; 1901–02 Division 2; 1902–04 Division 1; 1904–11 Division 2; 1911–27 Division 1; 1927–31 Division 2; 1931–38 Division 1; 1938–49 Division 2; 1949–73 Division 1; 1973–76 Division 2; 1976– Division 1.
Honours: *Football League:* Division 1 – Champions 1919–20; Runners-up 1924–25, 1953–54. Division 2 – Champions 1901–02, 1910–11; Runners-up 1930–31, 1948–49; Promoted to Division 1 1975–76 (3rd). *FA Cup:* Winners 1888, 1892, 1931, 1954, 1968; Runners-up 1886, 1887, 1895, 1912, 1935. *Football League Cup:* Winners 1965–66; Runners-up 1966–67, 1969–70. **European Competitions:** *European Cup-Winners' Cup:* 1968–69. *European Fairs Cup:* 1966–67. *UEFA Cup:* 1978–79, 1979–80.
Record Victory: 12-0 v Darwen, Division 1, 4 April, 1892.
Record Defeat: 3-10 v Stoke C, Division 1, 4 Feb, 1937.
Most League Points: 60, Division 1, 1919–20.
Most League Goals: 105, Division 2, 1929–30.
Highest League Scorer in Season: William 'Ginger' Richardson, 39, Division 1, 1935–36.
Most League Goals in Total Aggregate: Tony Brown, 218, 1963–79.
Most Capped Player: Stuart Williams, 33 (43), Wales.
Most League Appearances: Tony Brown, 574, 1963–80.
Record Transfer Fee Received: £995,000 from Real Madrid for Laurie Cunningham, June 1979.
Record Transfer Fee Paid: £748,000 to Manchester C for Peter Barnes, July 1979.
Previous Managers since the War: Jack Smith, Vic Buckingham, Gordon Clark, Archie Macaulay, Jimmy Hagan, Alan Ashman, Don Howe, John Giles, Ronnie Allen, Ron Atkinson.
Address of Supporters Club: Throstle Club, Birmingham Road, West Bromwich, Staffs.
Address of the Club Shop or Boutique: Albion Club Shop, same address as club.

The Hawthorns, West Bromwich B71 4LF. Telephone 021-553 0095 and 021-525 5666. Box Office 021-553 5472. *Ground capacity:* 38,600 (seats 12,500). *Record attendance:* 64,815 v Arsenal, FA Cup 6th rd, 6 Mar, 1937. *Record receipts:* £74,594 v Red Star Belgrade, UEFA Cup, 21 Mar, 1979. *Pitch measurements:* 115½yd×75½yd.
How to get there: Buses 72, 74, 75, and 79 from outside Birmingham New Street station run directly to the ground. A special bus service from the centre of West Bromwich to the ground runs every three minutes on match days.
Match tickets: Advance bookings for Centre and Wing Stands accepted six weeks in advance by post including remittance and sae. Telephone bookings are accepted but not before two days prior to the match; tickets reserved by telephone must be collected at least 30 minutes before kick-off. A limited number of unreserved seats in the Paddock is available at Door E1 on the day of the match.
Car parking: Street parking permitted in certain areas, all within 10 minutes' walk of the ground.
Entertainments/catering facilities: Post-match entertainment in the Supporters Club adjoining the ground; several restaurants within walking distance of the ground. Snack bars in the ground. Excellent facilities at The Hawthorns Throstle Club alongside the ground include a full-course lunch.
Club shop: Situated in the Pools Office in Birmingham Rd, and open from 9–5 Mon–Sat. Stocks over 200 different articles. Excellent mailing service. Price list available on request.
Handbooks/programmes: Handbook and programmes available on subscription.
Extra information: There are 3 Throstle Clubs in the surrounding areas, and the club runs a Junior Throstle Club for the under-15s.
Club Colours: Navy blue and white striped shirts, white shorts and white stockings.
Change Colours: Yellow and green striped shirts, green shorts, yellow stockings.
Player-Coach: John Wile.
Club Nickname: Baggies, Throstles and Albion.

WEST BROMWICH ALBION 1980–81 LEAGUE RECORD

Match No.	Date	Venue	Opponents	Result		H/T Score	Goalscorers	Attendance
1	Aug 16	H	Arsenal	L	0-1	0-1		22,364
2	20	A	Stoke C	D	0-0	0-0		14,085
3	23	H	Wolverhampton W	D	1-1	0-1	Regis	25,409
4	30	A	Brighton & HA	W	2-1	0-1	Regis, Owen	18,162
5	Sept 6	H	Norwich C	W	3-0	0-0	Barnes (pen), Owen, Brown	15,414
6	13	A	Liverpool	L	0-4	0-2		36,792
7	20	A	Birmingham C	D	1-1	0-0	Brown	26,881
8	27	H	Southampton	W	2-1	0-0	Brown 2	20,845
9	Oct 4	A	Crystal Palace	W	1-0	0-0	Regis	16,081
10	8	H	Coventry C	W	1-0	0-0	Barnes	16,377
11	11	H	Manchester C	W	3-1	2-0	Regis, Robson, Trewick	19,515
12	18	A	Nottingham F	L	1-2	1-2	Moses	25,096
13	21	A	Everton	D	1-1	1-1	Wile	24,046
14	25	H	Middlesbrough	W	3-0	1-0	Regis 2, Brown	16,162
15	Nov 1	A	Ipswich T	D	0-0	0-0		23,043
16	8	H	Aston Villa	D	0-0	0-0		34,001
17	15	A	Arsenal	D	2-2	1-0	Barnes, Owen (pen)	25,855
18	22	H	Leicester C	W	3-1	1-0	Robson, Moses, Owen (pen)	17,752
19	25	H	Stoke C	D	0-0	0-0		15,922
20	29	A	Tottenham H	W	3-2	3-0	Brown, Robson, Barnes	27,371
21	Dec 6	H	Leeds U	L	1-2	1-1	Moses	17,771
22	13	A	Coventry C	L	0-3	0-1		16,027
23	26	A	Sunderland	D	0-0	0-0		28,296
24	27	H	Manchester U	W	3-1	2-0	Owen (pen), Barnes, Regis	30,033
25	Jan 10	A	Leicester C	W	2-0	2-0	Bennett, Deehan	17,778
26	17	H	Brighton & HA	W	2-0	1-0	Regis, Barnes	15,643
27	31	A	Wolverhampton W	L	0-2	0-0		29,764
28	Feb 7	H	Liverpool	W	2-0	1-0	Robson, Regis	27,905
29	14	A	Norwich C	W	2-0	1-0	Regis, Owen (pen)	15,218
30	21	A	Southampton	D	2-2	1-1	Robson, Regis	21,910
31	28	H	Birmingham C	D	2-2	1-2	Moses, Brown	24,853
32	Mar 7	H	Crystal Palace	W	1-0	0-0	Robson	15,599
33	14	A	Manchester C	L	1-2	0-2	Robson	36,581
34	21	H	Nottingham F	W	2-1	1-0	Gunn (og), Deehan	19,269
35	28	A	Middlesbrough	L	1-2	0-1	Robson	13,288
36	31	H	Everton	W	2-0	1-0	Robson, Brown	14,833
37	Apr 4	H	Ipswich T	W	3-1	2-1	Brown, Batson, Barnes	22,216
38	8	A	Aston Villa	L	0-1	0-0		47,998
39	18	A	Manchester U	L	1-2	0-2	Regis	44,442
40	20	H	Sunderland	W	2-1	1-1	Regis 2	15,243
41	May 2	H	Tottenham H	W	4-2	2-0	Brown, Barnes, Robson, Cross	20,429
42	6	A	Leeds U	D	0-0	0-0		17,218

Final League Position: 4

Goalscorers

League (60): Regis 14, Brown 10, Robson 10, Barnes 8 (1 pen), Owen 6 (4 pens), Moses 4, Deehan 2, Batson 1, Cross 1, Bennett 1, Trewick 1, Wile 1, own goal 1.
League Cup (8): Regis 3, Barnes, Brown, Moses, Robertson, own goal.
F.A. Cup (3): Barnes, Cowdrill, Robson.

League Cup	Second Round	Leicester C (h)	1-0
		(a)	1-0
	Third Round	Everton (a)	2-1
	Fourth Round	Preston NE (h)	0-0
		(a)	1-1
		(h)	2-1
	Fifth Round	Manchester C (a)	1-2
FA Cup	Third Round	Grimsby T (h)	3-0
	Fourth Round	Middlesbrough (a)	0-1

Godden	Trewick	Statham	Moses	Wile	Robertson	Robson	Deehan	Regis	Owen	Barnes	Batson	Brown	Monaghan	Benjamin	Mills	Cowdrill	Bennett	Cross	*Match No.*
1	2	3	4	5	6	7	8	9	10	11									1
1	2	3	4	5	6	7	8	9	10	11									2
1		3	4	5*	6	7	8	9	10	11	2	12							3
1	2	3	4	5	6	7		9	10	11		8							4
1	2	3	4	5	6	7*	12	9	10	11		8							5
1	12	3	4	5	6	7		9	10*	11	2	8							6
1	10	3	4	5	6	7		9		11	2	8							7
1	7	3	4	5	6			9	10	11	2	8							8
1	7	3	4	5	6			9	10	11	2	8							9
1	12	3	4*	5	6	7			10	11	2	8	9						10
1	4	3		5	6	7		9	10	11	2	8							11
1	12	3	4	5	6	7		9	10	11*	2	8							12
1	10	3	4	5	6	7		9			2	8	11						13
1	10	3	4	5	6	7		9			2	8	11*		12				14
1	2	3*	4	5	6	7		9				8	11	12	10				15
1			4	5	6	7		9	10	11	2	8				3			16
1			4	5	6	7		9	10	11*	2	8			12	3			17
1			4	5	6	7		9	10	11	2	8				3			18
1			4	5	6	7		9	10	11	2	8				3			19
1	3		4	5		7		9	10	11	2	8					6		20
1			4	5		7		9	10	11	2	8*			12	3	6		21
1			4	5	6	7	12	9	10	11*	2	8				3			22
1			4	5		7		9	10	11	2	8				3	6		23
1			4	5		7		9	10	11	2	8				3	6		24
1			4	5		7	9		10	11	2	8				3	6		25
1			4	5	2	7		9	10	11		8				3	6		26
1		3	4	5		7		9	10	11	2				8		6		27
1		3	4	5		7*	8	9	10	11	2	12					6		28
1		3	4	5		7	8	9	10	11	2						6		29
1		3	4	5		7	8	9	10	11	2						6		30
1		3	4	5		7	8	9*	10	11	2	12					6		31
1		3	4	5		7	9		10	11	2*	8			12		6		32
1		3	4	5	2	7	9		10*	11		8			12		6		33
1		3	4	5		7	8	9		11	2				10		6		34
1		3	4	5		7	8*	9		11	2	12			10		6		35
1		3	4	5		7	8	9		11	2	12			10		6*		36
1		3	4	5	6	7		9	10	11	2	8							37
1		3	4	5	6	7		9	10	11	2	8							38
1		3	4	5	6	7		9	10	11	2	8*						12	39
1		3	4	5	6	7		9	10	11	2	8							40
1		3	4	5	6	7		9	10*	11	2	8						12	41
1		3	4	5	6	7		9		11	2	8		10					42
42	12	31	41	42	28	40	13	38	34	39	35	31	4	1	5	10	16	—	
	+ 3s						+ 2s					+ 5s		+ 1s	+ 5s			+ 2s	

WEST BROMWICH ALBION

	Ht	Wt	Birthplace	Clubs	League App.	League Gls
Goalkeepers						
Tony Godden	6 1	12 2	Gillingham	Gillingham	—	—
				Preston NE (on loan)	—	—
				WBA	174	—
Mark Grew	5 10	11 2	Bilston	WBA	—	—
				Notts Co (on loan)	—	—
				Wigan Ath (on loan)	4	—
Gary Phillips	5 10	11 1	London	WBA	—	—
(Contract cancelled Jan 1981)						
Defenders						
Alistair Robertson	5 9	12 0	Philipstown	WBA	373	5
David Arthur	5 8	11 0	Bushbury	WBA	—	—
John Wile	6 1	11 12	Sherburn	Sunderland	—	—
				Peterborough U	118	7
				WBA	427	24
Derek Statham	5 5	11 0	Wolverhampton	WBA	142	2
Brendon Batson	5 10	11 7	Grenada	Arsenal	10	—
				Cambridge U	163	6
				WBA	121	1
Martyn Bennett	6 0	12 11	Birmingham	WBA	21	1
Alan Webb	5 9	12 0	Birmingham	WBA	—	—
Gary Pendrey*	5 10	12 0	Birmingham	Birmingham C	304	4
				WBA	18	—
Barry Cowdrill	5 11	11 5	Birmingham	WBA	19	—
Phil Danks	5 9	12 1	Kidderminster	WBA	—	—
Nigel Conniff	5 9	10 10	Birmingham	WBA	—	—
Midfield						
Bryan Robson	5 9	11 1	Chester-le-Street	WBA	192	39
(England)						
John Loveridge*	5 7	10 10	Wolverhampton	WBA	—	—
David Mills	5 8	11 0	Whitby	Middlesbrough	295	76
				WBA	45	3
Remi Moses	5 7	10 10	Manchester	WBA	59	5
Ian Benjamin	5 11	12 4	Nottingham	Sheffield U	5	3
				WBA	2	—
Gary Owen	5 9	11 2	St Helens	Manchester C	103	19
				WBA	71	11
Tony Lowery	5 10	10 10	Wallsend	Ashington	(not known)	
				WBA	—	—
Forwards						
Alistair Brown	6 0	11 0	Musselburgh	Leicester C	101	31
(Contract cancelled April 1981)				WBA	237	64
Tony Brown	5 7	11 2	Oldham	WBA	574	218
(England) (Contract cancelled March 1981)						
Kevin Summerfield	5 11	11 0	Walsall	WBA	5	2
Derek Monaghan	5 9	11 2	Bromsgrove	WBA	8	—
Cyrille Regis	6 0	13 0	French Guyana	WBA	137	45
Nicky Cross	5 9	11 0	Birmingham	WBA	2	1
Peter Barnes	5 10	11 0	Manchester	Manchester C	115	15
(England)				WBA	77	23
John Deehan	6 0	11 3	Solihull	Aston V	110	42
				WBA	43	5
Tony Dawson*			Tynemouth	WBA	—	—

WEST HAM UNITED Division 1

President: R. H. Pratt.

Chairman: L. C. Cearns.

Directors: W. F. Cearns, B. R. Cearns FCIS, J. Petchey, M. W. Cearns AIB.

Manager: John Lyall.

Chief Executive and Secretary: Eddie Chapman FAAI.

PRO: Jack Helliar. *Year Formed:* 1900.

Turned Professional: 1900. *Limited Company:* 1900.

Previous Grounds: Memorial Recreation Ground, Canning Town; 1904 Boleyn Ground.

Football League Record:
1919 Elected to Division 2; 1923–32 Division 1; 1932–58 Division 2; 1958–78 Division 1; 1978–81 Division 2; 1981– Division 1.

Honours: *Football League:* Division 1 best season: 6th, 1926–27, 1958–59, 1972–73. Division 2 – Champions 1957–58, 1980–81; Runners-up 1922–23. *FA Cup:* Winners 1964, 1975, 1980; Runners-up 1922–23. *Football League Cup:* Runners-up 1966, 1981. **European Competitions:** *European Cup-Winners' Cup:* 1964–65 (winners), 1965–66, 1975–76 (runners-up), 1980–81.

Record Victory: 8-0 v Rotherham U, Division 2, 8 Mar, 1958 and v Sunderland, Division 1, 19 Oct, 1968.

Record Defeat: 2-8 v Blackburn R, Division 1, 26 Dec, 1963.

Most League Points: 66, Division 2, 1980–81.

Most League Goals: 101, Division 2, 1957–58.

Highest League Scorer in Season: Vic Watson, 41, Division 1, 1929–30.

Most League Goals in Total Aggregate: Vic Watson, 306, 1920–35.

Most Capped Player: Bobby Moore, 108, England.

Most League Appearances: Bobby Moore, 544, 1958–74.

Record Transfer Fee Received: £225,000 from Birmingham C for Alan Curbishley, June 1979.

Record Transfer Fee Paid: £800,000 (nett) to QPR for Paul Goddard, Aug 1980.

Previous Managers since the War: Charlie Paynter, Ted Fenton, Ron Greenwood.

Address of Supporters Club: Castle Street, Upton Park, E13.

Address of the Club Shop or Boutique: Hammers Shop, Boleyn Ground, Green Street, Upton Park, London E13.

Boleyn Ground, Green Street, Upton Park, London E13. Telephone 01-472 2740. Answerphone 01-470 1325. *Ground capacity:* 35,500. *Record attendance:* 42,322 v Tottenham H, Division 1, 17 Oct, 1970. *Record receipts:* £71,455 v Aston Villa, FA Cup 6th rd, 8 Mar, 1980. *Pitch measurements:* 110yd×72yd.

How to get there: Nearest station Upton Park (Underground, District Line) – five minutes' walk. Buses from Barking Road, Romford Road and Green Street.

Match tickets: Advance booking, by personal application or by post 21 days prior to League matches.

Car parking: Ample side-street parking available.

Entertainments/catering facilities: Refreshment points around the ground.

Club shop: Situated on the ground; sells all types of souvenirs.

Handbooks/programmes: Programmes and handbook available by post from either Sales Service c/o West Ham United FC or from Helliar & Sons, 237 Barking Road, London E13 8EQ.

Extra information: Vic Watson's 306 League goals for West Ham is the fourth highest total scored with one club in the history of the competition.

Club Colours: Claret shirts with blue sleeves and three claret stripes down sleeves, white shorts with three claret stripes, white stockings.

Change Colours: White shirts with three claret stripes down sleeves, blue shorts with three claret stripes, blue stockings.

Club Captain: Billy Bonds.

Physiotherapist: Rob Jenkins.

Club Nickname: Hammers.

WEST HAM UNITED 1980–81 LEAGUE RECORD

Match No.	*Date*	*Venue*	*Opponents*	*Result*	*H/T Score*	*Goalscorers*	*Attendance*
1	Aug 16	H	Luton T	L 1-2	0-0	Stewart (pen)	27,933
2	19	A	Bristol C	D 1-1	1-1	Cross	13,554
3	23	A	Preston NE	D 0-0	0-0		9063
4	30	H	Notts Co	W 4-0	1-0	Cross, Goddard 2, Stewart (pen)	21,769
5	Sept 6	A	Chelsea	W 1-0	0-0	Wilkins (og)	32,669
6	13	H	Shrewsbury T	W 3-0	1-0	King (og), Goddard, Cross	22,339
7	20	H	Watford	W 3-2	0-1	Cross, Barnes, Brooking	24,288
8	27	A	Cambridge U	W 2-1	1-1	Goddard, Cross	8591
9	Oct 4	A	Newcastle U	D 0-0	0-0		24,848
10	7	H	Cardiff C	W 1-0	0-0	Neighbour	20,402
11	11	H	Blackburn R	W 2-0	1-0	Cross 2	32,402
12	18	A	Oldham Ath	D 0-0	0-0		8344
13	25	H	Bolton W	W 2-1	1-0	Walsh (og), Pike	25,257
14	Nov 1	A	Bristol R	W 1-0	1-0	Goddard	6328
15	8	H	Grimsby T	W 2-1	1-0	Cross 2	25,468
16	11	H	Bristol C	W 5-0	2-0	Goddard 2, Martin, Brooking, Cross	25,210
17	15	A	Luton T	L 2-3	1-2	Brooking 2	17,031
18	22	H	Swansea C	W 2-0	0-0	Cross, Goddard	27,376
19	26	A	Derby Co	L 0-2	0-1		18,446
20	29	A	Wrexham	D 2-2	1-1	Devonshire, Goddard	8941
21	Dec 6	H	Sheffield W	W 2-1	2-1	Brooking, Holland	30,476
22	13	A	Blackburn R	D 0-0	0-0		13,279
23	20	H	Derby Co	W 3-1	1-1	Cross, Goddard, Brooking	24,071
24	26	A	QPR	L 0-3	0-1		23,811
25	27	H	Orient	W 2-1	0-0	Holland, Allen	34,408
26	Jan 10	A	Swansea C	W 3-1	2-0	Brooking, Pike, Cross	22,110
27	17	A	Notts Co	D 1-1	1-0	Holland	13,718
28	31	H	Preston NE	W 5-0	2-0	Goddard, Pike, Lampard, Devonshire 2	26,413
29	Feb 7	A	Shrewsbury T	W 2-0	1-0	Devonshire, Cross	9201
30	14	H	Chelsea	W 4-0	1-0	Brooking 2, Cross, Devonshire	35,164
31	21	H	Cambridge U	W 4-2	2-1	Devonshire, Stewart 2 (1 pen), Goddard	36,002
32	28	A	Watford	W 2-1	0-0	Cross 2	20,786
33	Mar 7	H	Newcastle U	W 1-0	1-0	Cross	26,274
34	21	H	Oldham Ath	D 1-1	0-0	Goddard	24,394
35	28	A	Bolton W	D 1-1	0-1	Brooking	13,271
36	Apr 4	H	Bristol R	W 2-0	1-0	Pike, Goddard	23,544
37	11	A	Grimsby T	W 5-1	1-0	Cross 4, Pike	17,924
38	18	A	Orient	W 2-0	2-0	Neighbour, Pike	14,592
39	21	H	QPR	W 3-0	2-0	Goddard 3	24,599
40	May 2	H	Wrexham	W 1-0	1-0	Stewart (pen)	30,515
41	6	A	Cardiff C	D 0-0	0-0		10,558
42	8	A	Sheffield W	W 1-0	0-0	Morgan	21,087

Final League Position: 1

Goalscorers

League (79): Cross 22, Goddard 17, Brooking 10, Devonshire 6, Pike 6, Stewart 5 (4 pens), Holland 3, Neighbour 2, Allen 1, Barnes 1, Lampard 1, Martin 1, Morgan 1, own goals 3.
League Cup (17): Cross 5, Goddard 4, Stewart 2 (2 pens), Bonds, Martin, Neighbour, Pike, own goals 2.
F.A. Cup (1): Stewart (pen).

League Cup	Second Round	Burnley (a)	2-0
		(h)	4-0
	Third Round	Charlton Ath (a)	2-1
	Fourth Round	Barnsley (a)	2-1
	Fifth Round	Tottenham H (a)	1-0
	Semi-final	Coventry C (a)	2-3
		(h)	2-0
	Final	Liverpool	1-1 (at Wembley)
	Replay		1-2 (at Villa Park)
FA Cup	Third Round	Wrexham (h)	1-1
		(a)	0-1 (aet)

Parkes	Stewart	Brush	Bonds	Martin	Devonshire	Holland	Goddard	Brooking	Pike	Cross	Lampard	Neighbour	Morgan	Barnes	Allen	Pearson	Match No.
1	2	3	4	5	6	7	8*	10	11	9	12						1
1	2	3	4	5	6	7	8	10	11	9							2
1	4	3		5	6	7	8	10	11	9	2						3
1	2		4	5	6	7	8	10	11	9	3						4
1	2		4	5	6	7	8	10	11	9	3						5
1	2		4	5	6		8	10	11	9	3	7*	12				6
1	2		4	5	6		8	10	11	9	3			7			7
1	2		4	5	6	7	8	10	11	9	3						8
1	2	12	4	5	6	7	8*		11	9	3	10					9
1	2		4	5	6	7			11	9	3	10	8				10
1	2		4	5	6	7	8		11	9	3	10					11
1	2		4	5	6*	7			11	9	3	10	8	12			12
1	2	3	4	5	6	7	8		11	9		10					13
1	2	12	4	5	6*	7	8		11	9	3	10					14
1		2	4	5		7	8	10	11	9	3	6					15
1	2		4	5	6	7	8	10	11	9	3						16
1	2		4	5	6	7	8	10	11	9	3						17
1	2		4	5	6*	7	8	10	11	9	3	12					18
1	2		4	5	6	7	8	10	11	9	3						19
1	2		4	5	6	7	8	10	11	9	3						20
1	2		4	5	6	7	8	10	11	9	3						21
1	2		4	5	6	7	8	10	11	9	3						22
1	2		4	5	6	7	8	10	11	9	3						23
1	2		4	5	6	7	8	10	11	9*	3	12					24
1	2		4	5	6	7	8	10	11		3*		9		12		25
1	2		4	5	6	7	8	10	11	9	3						26
1	2	3	4	5	6	7*	8	10	11	9					12		27
1	2		4	5	6		8	10	11	9	3	7					28
1	2		4	5	6		8*	10	11	9	3	7		12			29
1	2		4	5	6		8	10	11	9	3	7					30
1	2		4	5	6		8	10	11	9	3	7					31
1	2		4	5	6		8	10	11	9	3	7					32
1	2		4	5			8	10	11	9	3	7			6*	12	33
1	2	6*	4	5			8	10	11	9	3			12		7	34
1	2		4	5*	6		8	10	11	9	3	7				12	35
1	2	5	4		6		8	10	11	9	3	7					36
1	2		4	5	6		8	10	11	9	3	7					37
1	2		4	5	6			10	11	9	3	7		12		8*	38
1	2		4	5	6		8	10*	11	9	3	7		12			39
1	2		4	5	6		8*	10	11	9	3	7				12	40
1	2		4	5	6			10	11	9	3	7	8				41
1	2	12	4	5*	6			10	11	9	3	7	8				42
42	41	8	41	41	39	25	37	36	42	41	38	22	5	1	1	2	
		+ 3s									+ 1s	+ 2s	+ 1s	+ 5s	+ 2s	+ 3s	

WEST HAM UNITED

	Ht	Wt	Birthplace	Clubs	League App.	League Gls
Goalkeepers						
Bobby Ferguson*	5 11	12 12	Ardrossan	Kilmarnock	73	—
(Scotland)				West Ham U	240	—
				Sheffield W (on loan)	5	—
				Leicester C (on loan)	—	—
				Cardiff C (on loan)	—	—
Gary Moseley*	6 0	13 0	Westerham	West Ham U	—	—
Phil Parkes	6 3	14 9	Sedgeley	Walsall	52	—
(England)				QPR	344	—
				West Ham U	100	—
Defenders						
Frank Lampard	5 11	12 9	West Ham	West Ham U	468	16
(England)						
Paul Brush	5 11	11 12	London	West Ham U	104	—
Alvin Martin	6 1	13 0	Bootle	West Ham U	110	5
(England)						
Phil Brignull*	6 1	11 2	Stratford	West Ham U	1	—
Ray Stewart	5 11	12 0	Perthshire	Dundee U	44	5
(Scotland)				West Ham U	79	15
Steve Hibbert*	5 8	10 8	Southend	West Ham U	—	—
Mark Smith				West Ham U	1	—
Billy Bonds	6 0½	13 2	Woolwich	Charlton Ath	95	1
				West Ham U	512	41
Adrian Keith			Colchester	West Ham U	—	—
Everald Laronde			East Ham	West Ham U	—	—
Midfield						
Mike McGiven	6 0	11 13	Newcastle	Sunderland	113	9
				West Ham U	48	—
Trevor Brooking	6 0½	13 0	Barking	West Ham U	458	73
(England)						
Geoff Pike	5 6	11 3	Clapton	West Ham U	138	20
Georgie Cowie	5 9	11 0	Findochty	Buckie R	(not known)	
				West Ham U	—	—
Dale Banton	5 10	10 5	Kensington	West Ham U	4	—
Paul Allen	5 7	9 12	Averley	West Ham U	34	3
Ray Houghton	5 7	10 10	Scotland	West Ham U	—	—
David Barnes			Kingston	West Ham U	6	1
Glen Burvill			Canning Town	West Ham U	—	—
Forwards						
Nicky Morgan	5 10	12 8	East Ham	West Ham U	14	2
Alan Devonshire	5 10½	11 0	London	West Ham U	176	19
(England)						
Pat Holland	5 10	11 7	Poplar	West Ham U	245	23
				Bournemouth (on loan)	10	—
Billy Lansdowne*	6 0	11 6	Epping	West Ham U	9	1
Jimmy Neighbour	5 7½	10 8	Chingford	Tottenham H	119	8
				Norwich C	106	5
				West Ham U	47	3
Stuart Pearson	5 8½	11 12	Hull	Hull C	129	44
(England)				Manchester U	139	55
				West Ham U	30	5
David Cross	6 1	12 2	Bury	Rochdale	59	21
				Norwich C	84	21
				Coventry C	91	29
				WBA	38	18
				West Ham U	141	62
Paul Goddard	5 9½	11 5	Harlington	QPR	70	23
				West Ham U	37	17
Steve Milton			Fulham	West Ham U	—	—
Tony Laronde*			West Ham	West Ham U	—	—
Jason Wright*			Stepney	West Ham U	—	—

WIGAN ATHLETIC — Division 4

Chairman: F. Pye.

Vice-Chairman:

Directors: J. Albert Eckersley, John H. Farrimond, A. Muir, R. Charlton, OBE, E. Barnes, F. Summers, A. O. Horrocks (president/director).

Company Secretary: Colin Burke.

Secretary: G. Jones.

Asst Secretary: J. H. Farrimond.

Player-Manager: Larry Lloyd.

Year Formed: 1932.

Football League Record:
1978 Elected to Division 4.

Honours: *Northern Premier League:* Champions 1970–71, 1974–75. *Northern Premier Cup:* Winners 1971–72. *Northern Premier Shield:* Winners 1972–73, 1973–74, 1975–76. *Cheshire League:* Champions 1933–34, 1934–35, 1935–36, 1964–65. *Lancashire Combination:* Champions 1947–48, 1950–51, 1952–53, 1953–54.
Record Victory: 4-1 v Bradford C, Division 4, 29 Sept, 1979; v Darlington, Division 4, 3 Nov, 1979; v Scunthorpe U, Division 4, 17 Nov, 1979; v Halifax T, Division 4, 1 Oct, 1980.
Record Defeat: 0-4 v Huddersfield T, Division 4, 9 Oct, 1979 and 0-4 v Lincoln C, Division 4, 29 Feb, 1980.
Most League Points: 55, Division 4, 1978–79 and 1979–80.
Most League Goals: 76, Division 4, 1979–80.
Highest League Scorer in Season: Peter Houghton, 15, Division 4, 1979–80.
Most League Goals in Total Aggregate: Peter Houghton, 34, 1978–81.
Most Capped Player: None.
Most League Appearances: Jeff Wright, 130, 1978–81.
Record Transfer Fee Received: £135,000 from Sunderland for Joe Hinnigan, February 1980.
Previous Managers of Note: Ted Goodier, Allan Brown, Gordon Milne, Ian McNeill.
Address of Social Club: Springfield Park, Wigan.

Springfield Park, Wigan. Telephone: 0942 44433. *Telegraphic address:* Springfield, Wigan. *Ground capacity:* 30,000. *Record attendance:* 27,500 v Hereford U, 12 Dec, 1953. *Record receipts:* £16,752 v Blackpool, FA Cup 1st rd, 28 Nov, 1979. *Pitch measurements:* 117yd×73yd.
How to get there: Wigan Wallgate and Wigan North West Railway Stations. Wigan is served by three motorways, the M6, the M61 and the M62, with convenient access and exit points. Wigan also enjoys the facilities of the main London to Scotland railway line.
Match tickets: Stand – available 14 days prior to game.
Car parking: On ground and within close proximity to ground.
Entertainments/catering facilities: Licensed bar and tea bar in Main Stand, tea bars on ground, Social Club on ground.
Extra information: Springfield Park covers approximately nine acres and is owned by Wigan Athletic AFC Ltd. The ground will hold over 30,000 spectators with seating accommodation for 1069 and additional covered standing accommodation for 10,000.
There are terraces on all four sides of the excellent playing area, surrounded by four 114 feet high pylons with 36 lights on each.
The dressing rooms are equipped with plunge baths, slipper baths, showers and medical and physiotherapy equipment. There are parking facilities for 200 cars.
A lively Social Club and a productive Development Association office are located on the ground.
Wigan has a population of over 300,000 within a radius of 5 miles from the town centre. The actual town population is 89,000.
Club Colours: Blue and white striped shirts, blue shorts, white stockings.
Change Colours: White shirts, blue shorts, red stockings.
First Team Trainer: Ken Banks.
Club Captain: Colin Methven.
Club Nickname: The Latics.

WIGAN ATHLETIC 1980–81 LEAGUE RECORD

Match No.	Date	Venue	Opponents	Result		H/T Score	Goalscorers	Attendance
1	Aug 16	H	Hartlepool U	L	0-3	0-0		5233
2	23	A	Lincoln C	L	0-2	0-1		3939
3	30	H	Aldershot	W	1-0	1-0	Wright	4300
4	Sept 6	H	Port Vale	W	1-0	1-0	Gore	4678
5	13	A	Darlington	L	1-3	1-1	McLean (og)	2321
6	16	A	Halifax T	W	1-0	0-0	Quinn T.	2052
7	20	H	Bury	W	2-1	1-0	Gore 2 (1 pen)	6239
8	27	A	Mansfield T	L	1-3	0-2	Hutchinson	3402
9	Oct 1	H	Halifax T	W	4-1	2-0	Quinn M. 2, Kettle, Urquhart G.	4247
10	4	A	Rochdale	L	0-3	0-1		3479
11	8	H	Doncaster R	W	3-0	2-0	Quinn M. 3	3608
12	11	H	Peterborough U	D	1-1	1-1	Corrigan	4851
13	18	A	Torquay U	L	0-2	0-1		2013
14	20	A	Southend U	L	0-1	0-1		5643
15	25	H	Tranmere R	D	1-1	1-0	Quinn M.	5421
16	29	H	York C	W	1-0	1-0	Urquhart G.	3668
17	Nov 1	A	AFC Bournemouth	L	0-3	0-0		2983
18	4	A	Doncaster R	D	1-1	0-1	Quinn M.	3625
19	8	H	Bradford C	L	0-1	0-1		5155
20	12	H	Northampton T	W	3-0	1-0	Quinn M. 2, Urquhart B.	3375
21	15	A	Hartlepool U	L	1-3	0-1	Houghton	5020
22	29	A	Hereford U	D	1-1	1-1	Houghton	2358
23	Dec 6	H	Scunthorpe U	D	1-1	0-1	McMullen	3672
24	13	A	Crewe Alex	W	2-1	0-1	Quinn T., Houghton	2829
25	26	H	Crewe Alex	D	0-0	0-0		5026
26	27	A	Stockport Co	W	1-0	1-0	Quinn T.	3062
27	Jan 3	H	Southend U	L	0-1	0-0		5267
28	10	A	York C	L	1-2	0-1	Urquhart B.	2028
29	24	A	Aldershot	W	1-0	1-0	Quinn T.	2932
30	31	H	Lincoln C	L	0-2	0-0		5190
31	Feb 3	A	Northampton T	D	1-1	0-0	Quinn M.	1708
32	7	H	Darlington	W	3-1	0-0	Methven, Wright, Quinn M.	3626
33	11	H	Hereford U	W	1-0	0-0	Wright	3370
34	14	A	Port Vale	L	0-3	0-2		3214
35	21	H	Mansfield T	W	2-0	1-0	Quinn M., Wright	4032
36	28	A	Bury	D	0-0	0-0		4700
37	Mar 7	H	Rochdale	L	0-1	0-0		6029
38	13	A	Peterborough U	D	0-0	0-0		3455
39	21	H	Torquay U	W	2-0	0-0	Hutchinson, Wilson (og)	3376
40	29	A	Tranmere R	W	3-2	2-1	Houghton 3	3437
41	31	H	Wimbledon	L	0-1	0-1		2638
42	Apr 4	H	AFC Bournemouth	L	0-1	0-0		3750
43	11	A	Bradford C	D	3-3	2-2	Wright 2 (2 pens), Quinn M.	2069
44	18	H	Stockport Co	W	2-1	1-0	Hutchinson, Quinn T.	3980
45	25	H	Wimbledon	W	1-0	0-0	Methven	3381
46	May 2	A	Scunthorpe U	D	4-4	1-3	Quinn M., Wright (pen), Glenn 2	1704

Final League Position: 11

Goalscorers

League (51): Quinn M. 14, Wright 7 (3 pens), Houghton 6, Quinn T. 5, Gore 3 (1 pen), Hutchinson 3, Urquhart B. 2, Urquhart G. 2, Glenn 2, Methven 2, Corrigan 1, Kettle 1, McMullen 1, own goals 2.
League Cup (5): Gore 3 (1 pen), Hutchinson, Wright.
F.A. Cup (2): Houghton 2.

League Cup	First Round	Crewe Alex (h)	2-1
		(a)	2-2
	Second Round	Preston NE (a)	0-1
		(h)	1-2
FA Cup	First Round	Chesterfield (h)	2-2
		(a)	0-2

Brown	Fretwell	Whittle	Gore	Methven	Davids	McMullen	Wright	Houghton	Hutchinson	Quinn T	Quinn M	Curtis	Glenn	Corrigan	Kettle	Oliver	Ward	Urquhart G	Tierney	Cribley	Urquhart B	McAdam	Wignall	Lloyd	*Match No.*
1	2	3	4	5	6	7	8	9	10	11*	12														1
1	3	11	4	5	6	12	8	9	10		7*	2													2
1	2	3	4	5	6	7	8	9	10	12	11*														3
1	2	3	4	5	6	7	8	9*	10				12	11											4
1	2		4	5	6	7	8		10				12	11	3	9*									5
1			4	5	6	7	8		9	10		2		11	3										6
			4	5	6	7	8		9*	10	12	2		11	3		1								7
			4	5	6	7*	8		9	10		2		11	3		1	12							8
			4	5	6		8		9		10	2		11	3		1	7							9
			4	5	6		8	12	9		10	2		11*	3		1	7							10
				5	6	7	8		9		10	2		12	3		1	4	11*						11
				5	6	7	8		9		10	2		11	3		1	4*	12						12
				5	6	7*	8		9		10	2		11	3		1	4	12						13
	4			5	6		8	12	9		10	2		11	3		1		7*						14
				5	6	7*	8	12	9		10	2		11	3		1	4							15
	6			5			8		9		10	2	7	11*	3	12	1	4							16
	6			5			8		9*		10	2	7	12	3		1	11		4					17
	3			5		12	8	9			10	2	7		11*		1		4	6					18
	3			5		12			11*		10	2	7				1	8	4	6	9				19
	2			5			8				10		7	11			1	4		6	9	3			20
1	3			5		12	8	7			10*			11				4		6	9	2			21
1	3			5		8		7	9		10	2		11				4		6					22
1	2			5		8		7	9		10			11				4		6		3			23
	2			5		7		9	10	12				11			1	4		6	8*	3			24
	2			5		7		9	10	8				11*			1	4		6	12	3			25
	2			5		7		9	10	8				11			1	4		6		3			26
	2			5		7		9	10	8*				11			1	4		6	12	3			27
	2			5		7	11*	9	10	8							1	4		6	12	3			28
	2			5		7*	11	9	10	8	12						1	4		6		3			29
	2			5		7*	11	9	10	8	12						1	4		6		3			30
	2			5			11	9	10	8	7						1	4*	12	6		3			31
	2			5			11	9	10	8	7						1			6		3	4		32
	2			5			11	9	10*	8	7		12				1			6		3	4		33
	2			5		12	11	9	4	8	7						1			6	10	3*			34
	6			5			11	10		8	9	2					1			4	12	3	7*		35
	6			5			11	10		8	9	2					1			7		3	4		36
	12			5			11	10		8	9*	2					1			4		3	7	6	37
				5			8	10			9	2		11			1	7		4		3		6	38
				5			8	10	12		9	2		11			1	7*		4		3		6	39
				5			8	10			9	2		11			1	7		4		3		6	40
				5			8	10			9	2		11			1	7		4		3		6	41
	2			5			8			10*	9			11			1	7		4	12	3		6	42
	6			5			8	10		12	9		7	11*			1			2		3	4		43
	2			5					10	9			7	11			1			4		3	8	6	44
	2			5			11	10	7	12	9						1			4		3*	8	6	45
	3			5			8	10	11	12	9		7				1			2			4	6*	46
9	32	4	10	46	15	20	38	29	34	19	32	23	8	27	14	1	37	26	4	30	5	25	9	9	
	+ 1s					+ 5s		+ 3s	+ 1s	+ 5s	+ 4s		+ 3s	+ 2s		+ 1s		+ 1s	+ 3s		+ 5s				

WIGAN ATHLETIC

	Ht	*Wt*	*Birthplace*	*Clubs*	*League App.*	*League Gls*
Goalkeepers						
John Brown	5 11	13 0	Bradford	Preston NE	67	—
				Stockport Co	41	—
				Wigan Ath	87	—
Bob Ward	6 1	12 0	West Bromwich	WBA	9	—
				Northampton T (on loan)	8	—
				Blackpool	41	—
				Wigan Ath	37	—
Defenders						
Larry Lloyd	6 2	14 0	Bristol	Bristol R	43	1
(England)				Liverpool	150	4
				Coventry C	50	5
				Nottingham F	148	6
				Wigan Ath	9	—
John Curtis*	5 8	10 0	Poulton	Blackpool	102	—
				Blackburn R	10	—
				Wigan Ath	32	—
Noel Ward	6 2½	12 10	Londonderry	Portadown	—	—
				Aberdeen	7	—
				Wigan Ath	48	4
Neil Davids	6 0¾	13 9	Bingley	Leeds U	—	—
				Norwich C	2	—
				Northampton T (on loan)	9	—
				Stockport Co (on loan)	5	1
				Swansea	9	—
				Wigan Ath	68	1
Dave Fretwell*	5 9	10 9	Normanton	Bradford C	253	5
				Wigan Ath	112	—
Colin Methven	6 2	12 7	Kirkcaldy	East Fife	154	15
				Wigan Ath	81	4
Maurice Whittle	5 9	11 0	Wigan	Blackburn R	7	—
(Contract cancelled Oct 1980)				Oldham Ath	312	39
				Wigan Ath	21	1
Brian Kettle	5 9	12 13	Prescot	Liverpool	3	—
				Wigan Ath	14	1
Alex Cribley	5 11¼	12 9	Liverpool	Liverpool	—	—
				Wigan Ath	30	—
Steven McAdam	6 0½	11 2	Portadown	Portadown	(not known)	
				Burnley	5	—
				Oldham Ath	—	—
				Barnsley	—	—
				Wigan Ath	25	—
Midfield						
Jeff Wright	5 11	11 7	Alston	Wigan Ath	130	19
Frank Corrigan	5 10	11 7	Liverpool	Blackpool	—	—
				Walsall	1	—
				Wigan Ath	116	12
Dave McMullen*	5 5	10 0	Denny	Wigan Ath	27	1
Lawrie Tierney*	5 9	12 0	Leith	Hearts	49	2
				Hibernian	8	—
				Wigan Ath	7	—
Mark Wignall	5 6	10 7	Preston	Wigan Ath	9	—
Jeff Ainsworth	5 9	11 7	Liverpool	Liverpool	—	—
(Contract cancelled Oct 1980)				Wigan Ath	—	—
Forwards						
Peter Houghton	5 11	12 7	Liverpool	Wigan Ath	99	34
Tony Quinn	5 9½	10 7	Liverpool	Wigan Ath	43	14
Mike Quinn	5 10½	11 0	Liverpool	Wigan Ath	40	15
George Urquhart	5 11	12 0	Glasgow	Wigan Ath	68	6
Bobby Hutchinson*	5 8	10 7	Glasgow	Montrose	41	8
				Dundee	88	25
				Hibernian	67	13
				Wigan Ath	35	3
Billy Urquhart	5 10	12 0	Inverness	Inverness Caley	(not known)	
				Rangers	14	6
				Wigan Ath	10	2
Jim Oliver	5 11	13 0	Fearn	Montrose	28	10
(Contract cancelled April 1981)				Wigan Ath	2	—
David Glenn	5 10	10 10	Wigan	Wigan Ath	11	2

WIMBLEDON Division 3

President: Rt Hon Sir Michael Havers QC, MP.

Chairman: J. J. McElligott.

Vice-Chairman: W. Unwin.

Directors: S. Hammam, P. Cork, M. Dell, E. C. Gush, D. Miller, Q. Spicer, P. Turner.

Manager: Dave Bassett.

Secretary: Adrian Cook.

Year Formed: 1889. *Turned Semi-Professional:* 1964.

Limited Company: 1964.

Football League Record:
1977–79 Division 4; 1979–80 Division 3; 1980–81 Division 4; 1981– Division 3.

Honours: *Southern League:* Champions 1974–75, 1975–76, 1976–77. *Southern League Cup:* Winners 1969–70, 1975–76. Division 4: Promoted 1978–79 (3rd), 1980–81 (4th). *FA Cup* best season: 4th rd, 1974–75. *Football League Cup* best season: 4th rd, 1979–80.

Record Victory: 15-2 v Polytechnic, FA Cup Preliminary rd, 7 Feb, 1929.

Record Defeat: 0-8 v Everton, League Cup 2nd rd, 29 Aug, 1978.

Most League Points: 61, Division 4, 1978–79.

Most League Goals: 78, Division 4, 1978–79.

Highest League Scorer in Season: Alan Cork, 23, 1980–81.

Most League Goals in Total Aggregate: Alan Cork, 60, 1978–81.

Most Capped Player: None.

Most League Appearances: John Leslie, 173, 1977–81.

Record Transfer Fee Received: £42,000 from Orient for Steve Parsons, Mar 1980.

Record Transfer Fee Paid: £45,000 to QPR for Tommy Cunningham, Mar 1979.

Previous Managers since 1955: Les Henley, Mike Everitt, Dick Graham, Allen Batsford, Dario Gradi.

Address of Supporters Club and Club Shop: Plough Lane Ground, Durnsford Road.

Plough Lane Ground, Durnsford Road, Wimbledon, London SW19 (first used in 1912). Telephone: 01-946 6311. *Ground capacity:* 15,000. *Record attendance:* 18,000 v HMS Victory in FA Amateur Cup 3rd rd, 1934–35. *Record receipts:* £30,600 v Leeds U, FA Cup 4th rd replay at Crystal Palace, 1974–75. *Pitch measurements:* 110yd×85yd.

How to get there: Nearest station Wimbledon or Haydons Road (SR), South Wimbledon Underground. Buses: 77a from Wimbledon, 189 from Tooting.

Match tickets: Available 14 days prior to game for important matches.

Car parking: On ground and in streets quarter mile from ground.

Entertainments/catering facilities: Four licensed bars and two tea bars in main stand. Sportsman Public House adjacent to ground and owned by club.

Club shop: Two shops, one in Durnsford Road open weekdays, one in ground open matchdays. Sell all types of souvenirs.

Handbooks/programmes: Supporters Club Handbook published annually. Programmes available on subscription.

Club Colours: Blue shirts with yellow trim, blue shorts with yellow trim, blue stockings.

Change Colours: Yellow shirts with blue trim, yellow shorts with blue trim, yellow stockings.

Club Captain:

Club Nickname: The Dons.

WIMBLEDON 1980–81 LEAGUE RECORD

Match No.	Date	Venue	Opponents	Result	H/T Score	Goalscorers	Attendance
1	Aug 16	H	Bradford C	D 2-2	1-1	Cork, Downes	2161
2	19	A	Aldershot	L 0-2	0-1		2922
3	23	H	Port Vale	W 1-0	1-0	Cork	1775
4	30	A	Scunthorpe U	W 2-1	0-0	Driver 2	1624
5	Sept 6	H	Stockport Co	L 1-2	0-0	Leslie	2018
6	13	A	Crewe Alex	W 3-0	2-0	Cork 3	1881
7	15	A	Mansfield T	L 0-1	0-1		2903
8	20	H	Lincoln C	L 0-1	0-1		2320
9	27	A	Halifax T	W 1-0	0-0	Leslie	1407
10	30	H	Mansfield T	W 2-1	1-1	Hubbick, Leslie	2052
11	Oct 3	A	Tranmere R	L 0-3	0-2		2507
12	7	H	Southend U	L 0-1	0-1		2117
13	11	H	Hartlepool U	W 5-0	3-0	Galliers, Leslie 2, Cork, Ketteridge	1971
14	18	A	Hereford U	D 1-1	0-1	Hubbick	2369
15	21	A	Rochdale	L 0-2	0-2		2391
16	25	H	York C	W 3-0	2-0	Hodges, Cork, Kay (og)	2082
17	28	H	Peterborough U	W 2-1	0-0	Leslie, Cork	1901
18	Nov 1	A	Doncaster R	L 1-2	0-0	Cork (pen)	3245
19	3	A	Southend U	L 0-1	0-0		4935
20	8	H	Northampton T	W 1-0	1-0	Cork	2029
21	11	H	Aldershot	W 4-0	1-0	Leslie, Cork (pen), Cunningham 2	2538
22	15	A	Bradford C	L 0-2	0-1		3327
23	29	A	Bury	L 0-1	0-1		2392
24	Dec 6	H	Darlington	D 1-1	0-1	Joseph	1811
25	26	A	Torquay U	W 3-2	2-1	Leslie, Hubbick, Cork	3191
26	27	H	AFC Bournemouth	W 2-0	1-0	Cork, Hubbick	2681
27	Jan 19	H	Scunthorpe U	D 2-2	0-1	Cork (pen), Galliers	2112
28	31	A	Port Vale	W 3-2	1-1	Cork, Hodges, Smith	2372
29	Feb 7	H	Crewe Alex	W 2-0	2-0	Cork 2	2782
30	13	A	Stockport Co	D 0-0	0-0		1772
31	21	H	Halifax T	W 3-0	2-0	Galliers, Downes, Cork	2501
32	28	A	Lincoln C	D 0-0	0-0		3988
33	Mar 4	A	Peterborough U	D 1-1	0-0	Cork	3201
34	7	H	Tranmere R	W 2-1	0-0	Leslie, Hodges	2394
35	14	A	Hartlepool U	W 3-2	2-0	Cork 2, Downes	2329
36	17	A	Darlington	L 1-4	1-2	Smith	2091
37	22	H	Hereford U	D 0-0	0-0		3898
38	28	A	York C	W 1-0	1-0	Cork	2026
39	31	H	Wigan Ath	W 1-0	1-0	Hodges	2638
40	Apr 4	H	Doncaster R	W 1-0	1-0	Cork	3595
41	11	A	Northampton T	D 1-1	0-1	Cunningham	2121
42	18	A	AFC Bournemouth	W 1-0	1-0	Downes	5048
43	20	H	Torquay U	W 1-0	1-0	Cunningham	3190
44	25	A	Wigan Ath	L 0-1	0-0		3381
45	28	H	Rochdale	W 4-1	2-1	Leslie 2, Hodges, Galliers	3884
46	May 2	H	Bury	L 2-4	0-1	Goddard (pen), Denny	2293

Final League Position: 4

Goalscorers

League (64): Cork 23 (3 pens), Leslie 11, Hodges 5, Cunningham 4, Downes 4, Galliers 4, Hubbick 4, Driver 2, Smith 2, Denny 1, Goddard 1 (pen), Joseph 1, Ketteridge 1, own goal 1.
League Cup (7): Leslie 3, Cork, Cunningham, Denny, Downes.
F.A. Cup (11): Hubbick 3, Cork 2, Denny 2, Smith 2, Cunningham, Leslie.

League Cup	First Round	Aldershot (a)	0-2
		(h)	4-1
	Second Round	Sheffield W (h)	2-1
		(a)	1-3
FA Cup	First Round	Windsor (h)	7-2
	Second Round	Swindon T (h)	2-0
	Third Round	Oldham Ath (h)	0-0
		(a)	1-0
	Fourth Round	Wrexham (a)	1-2

Goddard	Jones	Armstrong	Galliers	Smith	Cunningham	Ketteridge	Downes	Leslie	Cork	Denny	Davies	Brown	Perkins	Driver	Beasant	Hubbick	Hodges	Joseph	Belfield	Gage	*Match No.*
1	2	3*	4	5	6	7	8	9	10	11	12										1
1			4	5	6	7	8	9	10	11		2	3								2
1			4	5	6	7*	8	9	10		12	2	3	11							3
1			4	5	6		8	9	10		7	2	3	11							4
1			4	5	6		8	9	10	12	7*	2	3	11							5
		11	4	5*	6		8	9	10	7		2	3	12	1						6
		3	4	12	6		8*	9	10	7		2	5	11	1						7
		3*	4	5	6		8	9	10	7	12	11	2		1						8
			4	5	6		8	9	10		7	2	3		1	11*	12				9
			4	5		7	6	9	10		8	2	3		1	11					10
			4	5	6	12	8*	9	10		7	2	3		1	11					11
			4	5	6		8	9	10		7*	2	3		1	11	12				12
		3	4	5	6	7		9	10			2			1	11	8				13
		3	4	5	6	11		8	10			2			1	9	7				14
		3	4	5	6	7		9	10			2			1	11	8				15
	12	3	4	5	6	7		9*	10			2			1	11	8				16
		3	4	5	6	7		9	10			2			1	11	8				17
		3	4	5	6	7		9	10			2			1	11	8				18
	12	3	4	5	6	7		9	10			2			1	11*	8				19
	2	3		5	6	7	4	9	10			12			1	11*	8				20
	2	3		5	6	7		9	10	4					1	11	8				21
	2	3		5	6	7		9	10	4		12			1	11*	8				22
	2	3*	4	5	6	7		9	10	12					1	11	8				23
	3		4	5	6	7*		9	10	8		2			1	11		12			24
	2	3	4	5	6	7		9	10	8					1	11					25
	2	3	4	5	6	7	10		9	8					1	11					26
	2	3	4	5		7	11		10	9		6*			1	12	8				27
	2	3	4	5	6	7	11	9*	10	12					1		8				28
	2	3	4	5	6	7	11	9	10						1		8*	12			29
	2	3	4	5	6	7	11	9*	10						1		8	12			30
	2	3	4	5	6	7*	11	9	10						1		8	12			31
	2	3	4	5	6	7	11	9	10	12					1		8*				32
	2	3	4	5	6	7	11	9	10						1		8				33
	2	3	4	5	6	7	11	9	10*						1	12	8				34
	2	3	4	5	6	7	11	9	10	12					1		8*				35
	2	3	4	5	6	7	11	9	10						1		8				36
1	2	3		5		7	6	9	10	4						11*	8	12			37
1	2	3		5	6	7	11	9	10	4							8				38
1	2	3		5	6	7	11	9	10	4							8*	12			39
1		3		5	6	7	11	9	10	4		2					8				40
1		3		5	6	7	11	9	10*	4		2						12	8		41
1		3	4	5	6	7	11	9		8		2						10			42
	2	3	4	5	6	7	11	9		8					1			10			43
		3*	4	5	6	7	11	9		8		2			1		12	10			44
	2		4	5	6	7	11	9		8		3			1		10				45
1	5				6	7	3	12		8		2				11*	9	10		4	46
12	24	35	37	44	43	38	34	43	41	21	6	26	11	4	34	20	27	4	1	1	
	+ 2s			+ 1s		+ 1s		+ 1s		+ 5s	+ 3s	+ 2s		+ 1s		+ 2s	+ 3s	+ 7s			

WIMBLEDON

	Ht	*Wt*	*Birthplace*	*Clubs*	*League App.*	*League Gls*
Goalkeepers						
Ray Goddard*	5 11	11 12	Fulham	Orient	279	—
				Morton (on loan)	1	—
				Millwall	80	—
				Wimbledon	119	1
Dave Beasant	6 4	13 0	Willesden	Wimbledon	36	—
Defenders						
Steve Perkins	5 11	11 0	London	Chelsea	—	—
(Contract cancelled Jan 1981)				QPR	2	—
				Wimbledon	52	—
Tommy Cunningham	6 0	11 3	London	Chelsea	—	—
				QPR	30	2
				Wimbledon	97	12
Gary Armstrong	5 8	10 7	London	Gillingham	86	2
				Wimbledon	40	—
Mick Smith	6 0½	11 9	Sunderland	Lincoln C	25	—
				Wimbledon	65	2
Steve Jones	6 1	12 1	Eastbourne	QPR	—	—
				Walsall	15	—
				Wimbledon	65	—
Wally Downes	5 10	10 11	London	Wimbledon	63	8
Peter Brown	5 10	11 0	Hemel Hempstead	Chelsea	—	—
				Wimbledon	28	—
Midfield						
Paul Denny	5 9	10 8	Croydon	Southend U	9	2
				Wimbledon	103	11
Mark Dziadulewicz	5 7	9 12	Wimbledon	Southend U	—	—
(Contract cancelled March 1981)				Wimbledon	28	1
Steve Ketteridge	5 8½	10 7	Stevenage	Wimbledon	90	8
Steve Galliers	5 6	9 7	Chorley	Wimbledon	144	10
Roy Davies	5 8	11 7	London	Reading	37	2
(Contract cancelled Dec 1980)				Torquay U	70	6
				Wimbledon	9	—
Kevin Gage	5 9	11 2	Chiswick	Wimbledon	1	—
(Apprentice)						
Glyn Hodges	5 10	12 3	Streatham	Wimbledon	30	5
(Contract cancelled April 1981)						
Forwards						
Alan Cork	6 0	12 0	Derby	Derby Co	—	—
				Lincoln C (on loan)	5	—
				Wimbledon	145	60
John Leslie	5 8	11 2	London	Charlton Ath	—	—
				Wimbledon	173	55
Mick Belfield	5 9	10 7	London	Wimbledon	2	—
(Contract cancelled April 1981)						
Terry Emms			London	Tottenham H	—	—
(Contract cancelled March 1981)				Wimbledon	—	—
Dave Hubbick	5 7	10 7	South Shields	Ipswich T	—	—
				Wimbledon	22	4
Mark Morris			Carshalton	Wimbledon	—	—
(Contract cancelled March 1981)						
Francis Joseph	5 10	12 0	London	Hillingdon B	(not known)	
				Wimbledon	11	1

WOLVERHAMPTON WANDERERS

Division 1

President: J. R. Ireland.

Chairman: Harry J. Marshall.

Vice-Chairman: W. C. Sproson.

Directors: G. S. Clark, M. A. Goody, G. P. Devine.

Manager: John Barnwell. *Secretary:* P. A. Shaw.

Assistant Manager.

Year Formed: 1877. *Turned Professional:* 1888.

Limited Company: 1923.

Previous Grounds: 1877, Goldthorn Hill; 1884, Dudley Road; 1889, Molineux.

Previous Name: 1880, St Luke's, Blakenhall combined with The Wanderers to become Wolverhampton Wanderers.

Football League Record:
1888 Founder Members of Football League; 1906–23 Division 2; 1923–24 Division 3(N); 1924–32 Division 2; 1932–65 Division 1; 1965–67 Division 2; 1967–76 Division 1; 1976–77 Division 2; 1977– Division 1.

Honours: *Football League:* Division 1 – Champions 1953–54, 1957–58, 1958–59; Runners-up 1937–38, 1938–39, 1949–50, 1954–55, 1959–60; Division 2 – Champions 1931–32, 1976–77; Runners-up 1966–67; Division 3(N) – Champions 1923–24. *FA Cup:* Winners 1893, 1908, 1949, 1960; Runners-up 1889, 1896, 1921, 1939. *Football League Cup:* Winners 1973–74, 1979–80. **European Competitions:** *European Cup:* 1958–59, 1959–60. *European Cup-Winners' Cup:* 1960–61. *UEFA Cup:* 1971–72 (runners-up), 1973–74, 1974–75, 1980–81.

Record Victory: 14-0 v Crosswell's Brewery, FA Cup 2nd rd, 1886–87.

Record Defeat: 1-10 v Newton Heath, Division 1, 15 Oct, 1892.

Most League Points: 64, Division 1, 1957–58.

Most League Goals: 115, Division 2, 1931–32.

Highest League Scorer in Season: Dennis Westcott, 37, Division 1, 1946–47.

Most League Goals in Total Aggregate: Bill Hartill, 164, 1928–35.

Most Capped Player: Billy Wright, 105, England (70 consecutive).

Most League Appearances: Billy Wright, 491, 1946–59.

Record Transfer Fee Received: £1,150,000 from Manchester C for Steve Daley, Sept 1979.

Record Transfer Fee Paid: £1,175,000 to Aston Villa for Andy Gray, Sept 1979.

Previous Managers since the War: Ted Vizard, Stan Cullis, Andy Beattie, Ron Allen, Bill McGarry, Sammy Chung.

Address of the Club Shop or Boutique: 'The Lair', Wolverhampton W FC, Molineux Grounds, Wolverhampton, West Midlands.

Molineux Grounds, Wolverhampton WV1 4QR. Telephone Admin office – Wolverhampton 712181; Ticket office – 711457/711432. *Telegraphic address:* 'Wanderers, Wolverhampton'. *Ground capacity:* 41,074. *Record attendance:* 61,315 v Liverpool, FA Cup 5th rd, 11 Feb, 1939. *Record receipts:* £80,839 v Swindon T, League Cup semi-final, 12 Feb, 1980. *Pitch measurements:* 115yd×72yd.

How to get there: The ground is within easy walking distance of both Wolverhampton High Level railway station and the town centre. For this reason the local bus company does not operate special services on match days.

Match tickets: Seats are bookable by post one month before the match.

Car parking: Parking is available around 'The West Park', in various side streets, and at the Molineux Hotel.

Entertainments/catering facilities: Entertainment at the Wolves Sporting Club a few yards from the ground. Bars are provided all around the ground.

Club shop: The club shop is situated on the official car park at the ground.

Handbooks/programmes: No handbook. Programmes available on subscription.

Extra information: Wolves scored over 100 First Division goals in four successive seasons (1957–58 to 1960–61).

Club Colours: Old gold shirts, black collar and cuffs, black shorts, old gold stockings.

Change Colours: White shirts, white shorts, white stockings.

Club Captain:

Club Nickname: Wolves.

WOLVERHAMPTON WANDERERS 1980–81 LEAGUE RECORD

Match No.	Date	Venue	Opponents	Result	H/T Score	Goalscorers	Attendance
1	Aug 16	A	Brighton & HA	L 0-2	0-0		19,307
2	19	H	Manchester U	W 1-0	0-0	Berry	31,955
3	23	A	WBA	D 1-1	1-0	Gray	25,409
4	30	H	Crystal Palace	W 2-0	1-0	Gray, Richards	20,601
5	Sept 6	A	Everton	L 0-2	0-1		21,820
6	13	H	Coventry C	L 0-1	0-1		18,115
7	20	A	Aston Villa	L 1-2	0-1	Eves	26,881
8	27	H	Ipswich T	L 0-2	0-2		18,503
9	Oct 4	H	Birmingham C	W 1-0	1-0	Richards	22,777
10	7	A	Southampton	L 2-4	2-1	Richards, Gray	21,712
11	11	A	Norwich C	D 1-1	1-0	Hibbitt	12,993
12	18	H	Leeds U	W 2-1	1-1	Hughes, Richards	20,699
13	25	A	Leicester C	L 0-2	0-1		18,133
14	Nov 1	H	Sunderland	W 2-1	2-1	Clarke 2	18,816
15	8	A	Tottenham H	D 2-2	1-2	Atkinson, Richards	29,244
16	12	A	Manchester U	D 0-0	0-0		37,959
17	15	H	Brighton & HA	L 0-2	0-1		15,946
18	22	A	Middlesbrough	L 0-2	0-0		13,562
19	25	H	Liverpool	W 4-1	1-1	Eves, Richards, Bell, Hughes	25,497
20	29	H	Stoke C	W 1-0	0-0	Bell	18,786
21	Dec 6	A	Arsenal	D 1-1	1-1	Richards	26,050
22	13	H	Southampton	D 1-1	0-0	Bell	18,147
23	20	A	Liverpool	L 0-1	0-1		33,563
24	26	H	Nottingham F	L 1-4	0-1	Richards (pen)	31,588
25	27	A	Manchester C	L 0-4	0-0		37,817
26	Jan 10	H	Middlesbrough	W 3-0	1-0	Hibbitt, Eves 2	16,253
27	17	A	Crystal Palace	D 0-0	0-0		15,080
28	31	H	WBA	W 2-0	0-0	Eves, Gray	29,764
29	Feb 7	A	Coventry C	D 2-2	0-2	Richards, Gray	18,243
30	21	A	Ipswich T	L 1-3	1-2	Gray	24,218
31	28	H	Aston Villa	L 0-1	0-0		34,693
32	Mar 14	H	Norwich C	W 3-0	1-0	Richards, McDowell (og), Palmer	21,605
33	17	A	Birmingham C	L 0-1	0-0		20,005
34	21	A	Leeds U	W 3-1	1-1	Richards, Clarke, Gray	19,252
35	28	H	Leicester C	L 0-1	0-0		21,694
36	Apr 4	A	Sunderland	W 1-0	0-0	Gray	20,138
37	18	H	Manchester C	L 1-3	1-1	Richards	17,371
38	20	A	Nottingham F	L 0-1	0-1		19,711
39	25	H	Arsenal	L 1-2	1-1	Richards	15,160
40	30	H	Tottenham H	W 1-0	1-0	Gray	18,530
41	May 2	A	Stoke C	L 2-3	1-1	Evans (og), Hibbitt	14,929
42	4	H	Everton	D 0-0	0-0		16,269

Final League Position: 18

Goalscorers

League (43): Richards 13 (1 pen), Gray 9, Eves 5, Bell 3, Clarke 3, Hibbitt 3, Hughes 2, Atkinson 1, Berry 1, Palmer 1, own goals 2.
League Cup (1): Daniel (pen).
F.A. Cup (16): Richards 4 (1 pen), Bell 3, Eves 3, Hibbitt 3, Carr (pen), Gray, Parkin.

League Cup	Second Round	Cambridge U (a)	1-3
		(h)	0-1
FA Cup	Third Round	Stoke C (a)	2-2
		(h)	2-1
	Fourth Round	Watford (a)	1-1
		(h)	2-1
	Fifth Round	Wrexham (h)	3-1
	Sixth Round	Middlesbrough (a)	1-1
		(h)	3-1
	Semi-final	Tottenham H	2-2 (at Hillsborough)
			0-3 (at Highbury)

Bradshaw	Palmer	Parkin	Daniel	Hughes	Berry	Brazier	Carr	Gray	Richards	Eves	Clarke	Hibbitt	Villazan	Atkinson	Bell	Humphrey	Hollifield	McAlle	Teasdale	Moss	Kearns	Matthews	*Match No.*
1	2	3	4	5	6	7	8	9	10	11*	12												1
1	2	3*	4	5	6	7	8	9	10	11	12												2
1	2		4	5	6	3	8	9*	10	11	12	7											3
1	2		4	5	6	3*	8	9	10	11	12		7										4
1	2	3	4	5	6		8	9	10	11	12		7*										5
1	2	3	4*	5	6		8	9	10	11	7		12										6
1	2			5	6	3	8		10	11	12		7	4	9*								7
1	2	3	4	5		6		9	12	11	10*		7	8									8
1	2	3	4	5		12	8	9	10	11		7*	6										9
1		3*	4	5			8	9	10	11		7	6		12	2							10
1			4	5		3	8	9	10	11		7	6			2							11
1	3		4	5			8	9	10	11		7	6			2							12
1	3		4		5	12	8*		10	11	9	7	6			2							13
1	3		4			5	12		10	11	9*	7	6	8		2							14
1			4			5	12		10	11	9	7	6*	8		2	3						15
1			4	6		5			10	11	9	7		8		2	3						16
1	2		4*	6		5	12		10	11	9	7		8			3						17
1	11*		4	5		6			10	12	9	7		8		2	3						18
1			4	6		5			10	11		7		8	9	2	3						19
1			4	6		5			10	11		7		8	9	2	3						20
1			4	6		5			10	11		7		8	9	2	3						21
1	2		4	6		5			10	11		7		8	9		3						22
1	2		4	6		5			10	11		7		8	9		3						23
1	2		4	6		5		12	10	11		7		8*	9		3						24
1	2			6	4	5	8*	11	10			7		12	9		3						25
1	2		4		6				10	11		7		8	9		3	5					26
1	2	12	4*		6				10	11		7		8	9		3	5					27
1	2	3	4*		6			9	10	11		7		8	12			5					28
1	2	3			6			9	10	11*	4	7		8	12			5					29
1	2	3	4*		6			9	10	11		7		8	12			5					30
1	2	3	4*		6		8	9	10	11		7			12			5					31
1	2	3			6		8	9	10	11	4	7						5					32
1	2	3		7	6		8	9	10	11	4*				12			5					33
1	2	3			6		8	9	10	11*	4	7			12			5					34
1	2	3			6		8	9	10	11	4*	7			12			5					35
1	2	3			6		8	12		11*	4			7	9			5	10				36
1		3			6				10		4*	7		8	9	2		5	12	11			37
1	2	3			6		8	9	10	11*	4	7						5	12				38
	2	3			6		8	9	10		4	7						5	11		1		39
	2				6	4	8	9*	10			7		12			3	5	11		1		40
	2				6	4*	8	9	10			7		12			3	5	11		1		41
	2					6		9	10		4	7					3	5	11		1	8	42
38	34	19	28	23	25	22	23	25	40	35	18	33	11	20	12	12	16	17	5	1	4	1	
		+ 1s				+ 2s	+ 3s	+ 2s	+ 1s	+ 1s	+ 6s		+ 1s	+ 3s	+ 8s				+ 2s				

WOLVERHAMPTON WANDERERS

	Ht	*Wt*	*Birthplace*	*Clubs*	*League App.*	*League Gls*
Goalkeepers						
Paul Bradshaw	6 2½	12 1	Altrincham	Blackburn R	78	—
				Wolverhampton W	148	—
Mick Kearns	6 4½	14 0	Banbury	Oxford U	67	—
(Eire)				Plymouth Arg (on loan)	1	—
				Charlton Ath (on loan)	4	—
				Walsall	249	—
				Wolverhampton W	9	—
Stephen Lowe	6 0	11 13	West Bromwich	Aston Villa	—	—
				Wolverhampton W	—	—
Defenders						
Derek Parkin	5 8½	11 0	Newcastle	Huddersfield T	61	1
				Wolverhampton W	480	6
Geoff Palmer	5 10	10 5	Cannock	Wolverhampton W	281	6
George Berry	6 0¾	11 12	Germany	Ipswich T	—	—
(Wales)				Wolverhampton W	104	4
John McAlle	6 0	11 3	Liverpool	Wolverhampton W	407	—
Colin Brazier	6 1½	10 13	Birmingham	Wolverhampton W	66	1
Peter Daniel	5 8½	11 3	Hull	Hull C	113	9
				Wolverhampton W	105	11
John Humphrey	5 9½	10 13	Wembley	Wolverhampton W	14	—
Gary Cutler*	5 9	9 12	Blackheath	Wolverhampton W	—	—
Robert Coy	5 11	11 12	Birmingham	Wolverhampton W	—	—
Rafael Villazan	5 10	12 3	Montevideo	Huelva	(not known)	
				Wolverhampton W	12	—
Emlyn Hughes*	5 10	12 6	Barrow-in-	Blackpool	28	—
(England)			Furness	Liverpool	474	35
				Wolverhampton W	58	2
Ian Ross	5 10	12 0	Glasgow	Liverpool	46	2
				Aston V	175	3
				Peterborough U (on loan)	21	—
				Northampton T (on loan)	2	—
				Notts Co (on loan)	4	1
				Peterborough U	91	1
				Wolverhampton W	—	—
Mike Hollifield	5 10½	11 0	Middlesbrough	Wolverhampton W	16	—
Midfield						
Willie Carr	5 6¾	10 7½	Glasgow	Coventry C	252	32
(Scotland)				Wolverhampton W	218	21
Kenny Hibbitt	5 10	12 0	Bradford	Bradford PA	15	—
				Wolverhampton W	378	82
Hugh Atkinson	6 0	11 9	Dublin	Wolverhampton W	30	2
Frank Hayes*	5 7	9 10	Waterford	Waterford	(not known)	
				Wolverhampton W	—	—
Anthony Kernan	5 8	9 13	Letterkenny, Co Donegal	Wolverhampton W	—	—
Forwards						
Norman Bell	6 0¼	13 2	Sunderland	Wolverhampton W	75	17
Michael Matthews	5 7½	10 12	Hull	Wolverhampton W	1	—
John Richards	5 9	11 1	Warrington	Wolverhampton W	347	141
(England)						
Mel Eves	5 10½	10 1	Wednesbury	Wolverhampton W	98	16
Chris Fleming	5 8	9 10	Bangor	Wolverhampton W	—	—
(Contract cancelled Nov 1980)						
Wayne Clarke	5 11¼	10 6¼	Wolverhampton	Wolverhampton W	49	6
Craig Moss	5 7½	10 8	Birmingham	Wolverhampton W	3	—
David Butler	5 11	12 0	West Midlands	Wolverhampton W	—	—
Andy Gray	5 11	11 7	Glasgow	Dundee U	62	36
(Scotland)				Aston V	113	54
				Wolverhampton W	62	21
Dave Thomas	5 8	10 8	Kirkby-in-	Burnley	157	19
(England)			Ashfield	QPR	182	29
(Contract cancelled Dec 1980)				Everton	71	4
				Wolverhampton W	10	—
John Teasdale	5 9	10 7	Glasgow	Nairn	(not known)	
				Wolverhampton W	7	—

Also retained: Peter Knowles

WREXHAM Division 2

President: F. Wellum.

Chairman: F. J. Tomlinson.

Directors: G. Mytton, H. G. Phillips, A. W. Gaade, G. Morris, R. E. A. Clark, A. Morris, P. Griffiths.

Manager: Mel Sutton. *Asst Manager:* Mick Evans.

General Secretary: C. N. Wilson FAAI.

Year Formed: 1873 (oldest Club in Wales).

Turned Professional: 1912. *Limited Company:* 1912.

Previous Ground: Acton Park.

Football League Record:
1921 Original Members of Division 3(N); 1958–60 Division 3; 1960–62 Division 4; 1962–64 Division 3; 1964–70 Division 4; 1970–78 Division 3; 1978– Division 2.

Honours: *Football League:* Division 2 best season: 15th, 1978–79; Division 3 – Champions 1977–78; Division 3(N) – Runners-up 1932–33; Division 4 – Runners-up 1969–70. *FA Cup* best season: 6th rd, 1973–74, 1977–78. *Football League Cup* best season: 5th rd, 1961, 1978. *Welsh Cup:* Winners 21 times.
European Competition: *European Cup-Winners' Cup:* 1972–73, 1975–76, 1978–79, 1979–80.

Record Victory: 10-1 v Hartlepools U, Division 4, 3 Mar, 1962.

Record Defeat: 0-9 v Brentford, Division 3, 15 Oct, 1963.

Most League Points: 61, Division 4, 1969–70, Division 3, 1977–78.

Most League Goals: 106, Division 3(N), 1932–33.

Highest League Scorer in Season: Tom Bamford, 44, Division 3(N), 1933–34.

Most League Goals in Total Aggregate: Tom Bamford, 175, 1928–34.

Most Capped Player: Dai Davies, 28 (44), Wales.

Most League Appearances: Arfon Griffiths, 592, 1959–61; 1962–79.

Record Transfer Fee Received: £300,000 from Manchester U for Mickey Thomas, Nov 1978 and £300,000 from Manchester C for Bobby Shinton, July 1979.

Record Transfer Fee Paid: £210,000 to Liverpool for Joey Jones, Oct 1978.

Previous Managers since the War: Tom Williams, Les McDowell, Peter Jackson, Cliff Lloyd, John Love, Bill Morris, Ken Barnes, Bill Morris, Jack Rowley, Alvan Williams, John Neal, Arfon Griffiths MBE.

Address of Supporters Club: Secretary, Lyn Williams, c/o Centre Spot, Mold Rd, Wrexham.

Racecourse Ground, Mold Road, Wrexham. Telephone Wrexham (0978) 262129. *Telegraphic address:* 'Football, Wrexham'. *Ground capacity:* 30,000 (18,000 covered). *Record attendance:* 34,445 v Manchester U, FA Cup 4th rd, 26 Jan, 1957. *Record receipts:* £25,107 v Anderlecht, European Cup-Winners' Cup quarter-final, 17 Mar, 1976. *Pitch measurements:* 117yd×75yd.

How to get there: Wrexham General railway station is only 200 yards from the ground. Trains run from Chester and Shrewsbury. Bus services from outlying districts to town.

Match tickets: Stand tickets bookable in advance.

Car parking: Berse Field Main Car Park plus parking grounds at St Marks, Bodhyfryd Square, Eagles Meadows, Old Guild Hall, Hill Street, Holt Street, and Town Hill, Hill Street.

Entertainments/catering facilities: A social club and four catering kiosks at the ground.

Club shop: Situated on Mold Road.

Handbooks/programmes: Handbooks and programmes available on subscription.

Extra information: Season tickets available for all parts of the ground and all stands.

Club Colours: Red shirts with white facings, white shorts with red stripe, red stockings.

Change Colours: White shirts, red trim, black shorts, black stockings with white/red tops.

Club Captain: Dixie McNeil.

Club Nickname: The Robins.

WREXHAM 1980–81 LEAGUE RECORD

Match No.	Date	Venue	Opponents	Result	H/T Score	Goalscorers	Attendance
1	Aug 16	A	Chelsea	D 2-2	2-1	McNeil, Vinter	20,001
2	19	H	Cardiff C	L 0-1	0-0		7771
3	23	A	Grimsby T	L 0-1	0-1		9175
4	30	H	Oldham Ath	W 3-2	1-1	McNeil 2, Vinter	5176
5	Sept 6	A	Luton T	D 1-1	0-0	Edwards	8244
6	13	H	Orient	W 3-1	1-1	McNeil, Vinter, Moores (og)	5356
7	20	A	Derby Co	W 1-0	0-0	Edwards	16,823
8	27	H	Blackburn R	L 0-1	0-0		10,913
9	Oct 4	H	Swansea C	D 1-1	1-1	Edwards	8544
10	7	A	Cambridge U	L 0-1	0-1		4431
11	11	A	Watford	L 0-1	0-0		10,694
12	18	H	Preston NE	L 0-1	0-0		5775
13	21	H	Bristol C	W 1-0	0-0	McNeil	4179
14	25	A	QPR	W 1-0	1-0	Vinter	9050
15	Nov 1	H	Notts Co	D 1-1	1-1	McNeil	6221
16	8	A	Sheffield W	L 1-2	0-0	Sutton	15,736
17	12	A	Cardiff C	L 0-1	0-0		4562
18	15	H	Chelsea	L 0-4	0-1		7953
19	22	A	Newcastle U	W 1-0	1-0	McNeil	15,953
20	29	H	West Ham U	D 2-2	1-1	Cartwright, Edwards	8941
21	Dec 6	A	Bristol R	W 1-0	0-0	Edwards	4862
22	13	H	Cambridge U	D 0-0	0-0		5049
23	20	A	Preston NE	D 1-1	0-1	Edwards	4746
24	26	H	Bolton W	L 0-1	0-1		7635
25	27	A	Shrewsbury T	W 2-1	2-1	McNeil, Jones	8320
26	Jan 10	H	Newcastle U	D 0-0	0-0		6437
27	31	H	Grimsby T	L 0-2	0-1		5619
28	Feb 7	A	Orient	L 1-2	1-1	Fox	4057
29	17	A	Oldham Ath	W 3-1	2-1	Cartwright, Vinter, McNeil	5042
30	21	A	Blackburn R	D 1-1	0-0	McNeil	10,147
31	28	H	Derby Co	D 2-2	0-1	McNeil 2	6485
32	Mar 6	A	Swansea C	L 1-3	1-1	McNeil	12,103
33	21	A	Bristol C	W 2-0	1-0	Carrodus, Fox	6667
34	28	H	QPR	D 1-1	0-1	Buxton (pen)	5887
35	31	H	Luton T	D 0-0	0-0		4157
36	Apr 5	A	Notts Co	D 1-1	0-1	Fox	10,959
37	11	H	Sheffield W	W 4-0	1-0	Vinter 2, Fox 2	8001
38	18	H	Shrewsbury T	L 1-2	0-1	Hill	8416
39	20	A	Bolton W	D 1-1	1-0	Buxton	7594
40	25	H	Bristol R	W 3-1	2-0	Vinter 2, Fox	3220
41	May 2	A	West Ham U	L 0-1	0-1		30,515
42	4	H	Watford	L 0-1	0-0		4659

Final League Position: 16

Goalscorers

League (43): McNeil 13, Vinter 9, Fox 6, Edwards 6, Buxton 2 (1 pen), Cartwright 2, Carrodus 1, Hill 1, Jones 1, Sutton 1, own goal 1.
League Cup (2): Edwards, Vinter.
F.A. Cup (5): Fox 2, McNeil 2, Davis.

League Cup	First Round	Burnley (h)	1-3
		(a)	1-2
FA Cup	Third Round	West Ham U (a)	1-1
		(h)	0-0 (aet)
		(h)	1-0 (aet)
	Fourth Round	Wimbledon (h)	2-1
	Fifth Round	Wolverhampton W (a)	1-3

Davies	Hill	Dwyer	Jones F	Jones J	Carrodus	Vinter	Arkwright	Edwards	McNeil	Cartwright	Sutton	Fox	Davis	Cegielski	Buxton	Salathiel	Whittle	Kenworthy	Dowman	Williams	Jones S	*Match No.*
1	2	3	4	5	6	7	8	9	10	11												1
1	2	3	4	5	6	7	8*	9	10	11							12					2
1	2	3	4	5	6	7		9	10	11	8											3
1	2	3	4	5	6	7		9*	10	11	8	12										4
1		3		2	6	7		9	10	11	8		4	5								5
1		3*		2	6	7		9	10	11	8	12	4	5								6
1	12			3	6	7		9	10*	11	2	8	4	5								7
1	10			3	6	7		9		11	2	8	4	5								8
1	12			3	6	7*		9	10	11	2	8	4	5								9
1	12			3	6	7*		9	10	11	2	8	4	5								10
1	2			3	6	12		9*	10	11	8	7	4	5								11
1	2			3	6	10			9	11*	8	7	4	5	12							12
1	2			3	6	10			9	11	8	7	4	5								13
1				3	6	10			9	11	8	7	4	5		2						14
1	12			3	6	10			9	11	8	7	4	5		2*						15
1	9			3	6	10		12		11	8	7	4	5		2*						16
1	2			3	6	10	12	9		11*	8	7	4	5								17
1					6		11*	9	10		8	7	4	5	12	2	3					18
1					6	12	8	9*	10	11	2	7	4	5				3				19
1					6		8	9	10	11	2	7	4	5				3				20
1				2	6			9	10	11	8	7	4	5				3				21
1				2	6*	12		9	10	11	8	7	4	5				3				22
1				2		12		9	10	11	8	7	4	5	6*			3				23
1	12			2		6		9	10	11	8	7	4	5				3*				24
1	2			3			6	9	10	11	8	12	4	5	7*							25
1	2			3		12	6	9*	10	11	8	7	4	5								26
1	2			4		12	6	9	10	11	8	7		5*				3				27
1	12	3		4	8*		6	9	10	11	2	7		5								28
1	2	3		4	6	9			10	11	8	7		5								29
1	2	3		4		9	6*		10	11	8	7		5	12							30
1	2	3		4	6	9			10	11	8	7		5								31
1	12	3		4	6	9			10	11*	8	7		5					2			32
1	2	3		4	6	9	8			11		7		5	10							33
1	2	3		4	6	9	8			11		7		5	10							34
1	2	3		4	6	9	8					7		5	10					12	11*	35
1	2	3		4	11	9	8					7	6	5	10							36
1	11	3		2	6	9	8		10			7	4	5								37
1	11	3		2	6*	9	8		10			7	4	5	12							38
1	11	3		2	6	9			10			7	4	5	8							39
1	11	3			6	9			10			7	4	5	8				2			40
1	11	3			6	9		12	10			7	4	5	8*				2			41
1	11	3		4	6	9		12	10			7		5	8*				2			42
42	26	21	4	37	36	31	16	23	35	33	30	35	28	38	10	4	1	7	4	—	1	
	+ 7s					+ 6s	+ 1s	+ 3s				+ 3s			+ 4s		+ 1s			+ 1s		

WREXHAM

	Ht	*Wt*	*Birthplace*	*Clubs*	*League App.*	*League Gls*
Goalkeepers						
Eddie Niedzwiecki	6 0	11 0	Wrexham	Wrexham	27	—
Dai Davies	6 1	13 3½	Ammanford	Swansea C	9	—
(Wales)				Everton	82	—
				Swansea C (on loan)	6	—
				Wrexham	144	—
Defenders						
Gareth Davis	5 10½	11 7	Bangor	Wrexham	470	9
(Wales)						
Alan Hill	5 11	11 4	Chester	Wrexham	146	5
Wayne Cegielski	6 0	12 0	Bedwellty	Tottenham H	—	—
				Northampton T (on loan)	11	—
				Wrexham	88	—
Steve Kenworthy*	6 1	12 0	Wrexham	Wrexham	20	—
Joey Jones	5 10	11 7	Llandudno	Wrexham	98	2
(Wales)				Liverpool	72	3
				Wrexham	103	6
Terry Darracott	5 9	11 6	Liverpool	Everton	148	—
				Wrexham	22	—
Frank Jones*	5 11	11 0		Wrexham	8	—
Steve Dowman	5 11	12 4	Manor Park	Colchester U	154	21
				Wrexham	4	—
Neil Salathiel			Wrexham	Sheffield W	—	—
(Non-contract)				Wrexham	4	—
Midfield						
Mel Sutton	5 10	10 10	Birmingham	Cardiff C	138	5
				Wrexham	360	21
Alan Dwyer*	5 7	10 7	Liverpool	Wrexham	180	2
Les Cartwright	5 9	10 13	Aberdare	Coventry C	68	3
(Wales)				Wrexham	111	6
Frank Carrodus	5 9	10 11	Manchester	Manchester C	42	1
				Aston V	151	7
				Wrexham	56	2
Ian Arkwright	5 8¼	10 8	Shafton	Wolverhampton W	4	—
				Wrexham	27	—
Bill Fleming			Newmarket	Wrexham	—	—
(Contract cancelled March 1981)						
Forwards						
Graham Whittle	5 9	10 3	Liverpool	Wrexham	306	91
(Contract cancelled March 1981)						
Dixie McNeil	5 10	11 12	Melton Mowbray	Leicester C	—	—
				Exeter C	31	11
				Northampton T	86	33
				Lincoln C	97	53
				Hereford U	129	85
				Wrexham	127	44
Steve Buxton	5 5	9 8	Birmingham	Wrexham	41	5
Steve Fox	5 7¾	11 2	Tamworth	Birmingham C	29	1
				Wrexham	98	9
Peter Williams*	5 8	10 11	Wrexham	Wrexham	10	1
Ian Edwards	6 1	12 5	Wrexham	WBA	16	3
(Wales)				Chester	104	36
				Wrexham	46	9
Mick Vinter	5 9	11 0	Boston	Notts Co	166	53
				Wrexham	72	20
David Palmer			New Cross	Wrexham	—	—
(Contract cancelled Feb 1981)						
Steven Jones			Wrexham	Wrexham	1	—
(Associated Schoolboy)						

YORK CITY — Division 4

President: F. H. Magson.

Chairman: M. D. B. Sinclair.

Directors: D. M. Craig JP, BSC, FICE, FI, MUN E, FCI ARB, M CONS E, B. A. Houghton, R. B. Strachan MA, LLB, FCIS, C. Webb.

Team Manager: Barry Lyons. *Sales Executive:* S. B. Winship.

Medical Officer: Dr A. I. MacLeod.

Year Formed: 1922. *Turned Professional:* 1922.

Limited Company: 1922.

Previous Grounds: 1922, Fulfordgate; 1932, Bootham Crescent.

Football League Record:
1929 Elected to Division 3(N); 1958–59 Division 4; 1959–60 Division 3; 1960–65 Division 4; 1965–66 Division 3; 1966–71 Division 4; 1971–74 Division 3; 1974–76 Division 2; 1976–77 Division 3; 1977– Division 4.

Honours: *Football League:* Division 2 best season: 15th, 1974–75; Division 3 – Promoted 1973–74 (3rd); Division 4 – Promoted 1958–59 (3rd), 1964–65 (3rd), 1970–71 (4th). *FA Cup:* semi-finals 1955, when in Division 3. *Football League Cup* best season: 5th rd, 1962.

Record Victory: 9-1 v Southport, Division 3(N), 2 Feb, 1957.

Record Defeat: 0-12 v Chester, Division 3(N), 1 Feb, 1936.

Most League Points: 62, Division 4, 1964–65.

Most League Goals: 92, Division 3(N), 1954–55.

Highest League Scorer in Season: Bill Fenton, 31, Division 3(N), 1951–52; Arthur Bottom, 31, Division 3(N), 1955–56.

Most League Goals in Total Aggregate: Norman Wilkinson, 125, 1954–66.

Most Capped Player: Peter Scott, 7 (10), Northern Ireland.

Most League Appearances: Barry Jackson, 481, 1958–70.

Record Transfer Fee Received: £100,000 from Carlisle U for Gordon Staniforth, Oct 1979.

Record Transfer Fee Paid: £18,000 to AFC Bournemouth for Micky Cave, August 1974.

Previous Managers since the War: Tom Mitchell, Dick Duckworth, Charlie Spencer, Jimmy McCormack, Sam Bartram, Tom Lockie, Joe Shaw, Tom Johnston, Wilf McGuinness, Charlie Wright.

Address of Supporters Club: G. J. Mortimer, Secretary, 2 Plantation Grove, Boroughbridge Road, York.

Bootham Crescent, York. Telephone: York 24447. *Telegraphic address:* 'City Football, York'. *Ground capacity:* 16,529. *Record attendance:* 28,123 v Huddersfield T, FA Cup 5th rd, 5 Mar, 1938. *Record receipts:* £9856 v Arsenal, FA Cup 3rd rd replay, 7 Jan, 1975. *Pitch measurements:* 115yd×75yd.

How to get there: Buses 2, 2a, and 8 every 10 minutes from York railway station to the ground.

Match tickets: On sale 14 days prior to match.

Car parking: Ample parking in side-streets.

Entertainments/catering facilities: Licensed Social Club open to members only. Three tea bars on the ground.

Club shop: Selling all types of souvenirs.

Handbooks/programmes: Programmes available on subscription, details available from the Secretary. Programme shop at the ground stocking a wide variety of English, Scottish and non-League programmes.

Extra information: One of only five Third Division clubs to reach the semi-finals of the FA Cup (in 1954–55).

Club Colours: Red shirts with red and blue collar and cuffs, navy blue shorts with white and red stripe. Stockings white with blue and red hoops on turnover.

Change Colours: White shirts with red and blue collar and cuffs, white shorts with red and blue stripe, white stockings with red and blue hoops on turnover.

Club Captain: Ian McDonald.

Youth team coach: Kevin Randall.

Physiotherapist: John Simpson.

Club Nickname: Minster Men.

YORK CITY 1980–81 LEAGUE RECORD

Match No.	Date	Venue	Opponents	Result	H/T Score	Goalscorers	Attendance
1	Aug 16	H	AFC Bournemouth	W 4-0	2-0	Eccles, McDonald, Ford, Byrne	2195
2	18	A	Mansfield T	W 1-0	1-0	Eccles	4080
3	23	H	Torquay U	D 0-0	0-0		2892
4	30	A	Hereford U	D 1-1	0-0	Ford	2757
5	Sept 5	A	Southend U	L 0-3	0-1		5124
6	13	H	Hartlepool U	L 0-1	0-1		2504
7	19	A	Northampton T	L 0-2	0-1		1843
8	23	H	Tranmere R	W 4-1	2-0	Kay, Ford, Faulkner, Eccles	2322
9	27	H	Doncaster R	L 0-1	0-1		4641
10	29	A	Tranmere R	L 0-5	0-3		1595
11	Oct 4	H	Port Vale	W 4-1	3-0	McDonald 2, Byrne, Eccles	2025
12	7	A	Halifax T	L 1-3	0-1	Smith	1088
13	11	A	Lincoln C	D 1-1	0-1	Smith	4026
14	18	H	Stockport Co	W 1-0	0-0	McDonald	2135
15	21	H	Darlington	L 1-2	1-0	Smith	2534
16	25	A	Wimbledon	L 0-3	0-2		2082
17	29	A	Wigan Ath	L 0-1	0-1		3668
18	Nov 1	H	Scunthorpe U	W 1-0	1-0	Eccles	1959
19	4	H	Halifax T	D 1-1	0-0	Eccles	1837
20	8	A	Crewe Alex	D 1-1	1-1	McGhie	2798
21	11	H	Mansfield T	W 2-0	1-0	Smith, Byrne	2204
22	15	A	AFC Bournemouth	D 1-1	0-0	Clements	2203
23	Dec 6	A	Bradford C	D 1-1	0-0	Watson (og)	3638
24	20	H	Aldershot	W 4-1	1-0	McDonald, Eccles 2, Ford	1583
25	26	A	Bury	L 0-2	0-2		3224
26	27	H	Rochdale	L 1-2	1-0	Smith	2828
27	Jan 3	A	Darlington	D 0-0	0-0		3209
28	10	H	Wigan Ath	W 2-1	1-0	McDonald, Richards	2028
29	17	A	Peterborough U	L 0-3	0-2		3954
30	24	H	Hereford U	L 1-2	1-2	Craig	1924
31	Feb 7	A	Hartlepool U	L 0-1	0-0		3119
32	14	H	Southend U	L 0-1	0-1		2129
33	20	A	Doncaster R	L 2-3	0-3	Russell (og), Eccles	5839
34	Mar 7	A	Port Vale	L 0-2	0-1		2319
35	14	H	Lincoln C	W 1-0	0-0	Pugh	2222
36	20	A	Stockport Co	L 0-2	0-0		1903
37	24	H	Peterborough U	L 1-2	1-2	Randall	1725
38	28	H	Wimbledon	L 0-1	0-1		2026
39	Apr 4	A	Scunthorpe U	L 2-3	2-3	Byrne, Randall	1694
40	8	A	Torquay U	W 2-1	0-0	Smith, McDonald	1406
41	11	H	Crewe Alex	W 2-0	1-0	McDonald (pen), Byrne	1602
42	14	H	Bury	L 0-1	0-1		1786
43	18	A	Rochdale	L 2-3	0-1	McDonald 2 (1 pen)	1651
44	25	A	Aldershot	D 1-1	0-1	McDonald	1813
45	May 2	H	Bradford C	L 0-3	0-0		1481
46	5	H	Northampton T	L 1-2	0-0	Byrne	1167

Final League Position: 24

Goalscorers

League (47): McDonald 11 (2 pens), Eccles 9, Byrne 6, Smith 6, Ford 4, Randall 2, Clements 1, Craig 1, Faulkner 1, Kay 1, McGhie 1, Pugh 1, Richards 1, own goals 2.
League Cup (4): Ford, McDonald, Richards, own goal.
F.A. Cup (1): Byrne.

League Cup	First Round	Hartlepool U (h)	2-1
		(a)	0-0
	Second Round	Bristol R (h)	2-1
		(a)	0-1
FA Cup	First Round	Tranmere R (a)	0-0
		(h)	1-2

Blackburn	Kay	Faulkner	Craig	Ford	Richards	McGhie	McDonald	Eccles	Byrne	Walsh	Smith	Hood	Ferebee	Millar	Clements	Astbury	Stanley	Randall	Pugh	Senior	Match No.
1	2	5	6	7	4	10	11	9	8	3											1
1	2	5	6	7	4	10	11	9		3	8										2
1	2	5	6	7	4	10	11	9		3	8										3
1	2	5	6	7	4	10	11	9		3	8										4
1	2	5	6	7	4		11	9*	12	3	8	10									5
1	2	5	6	7	4		11	9	8*	3		10	12								6
1	2	5	6	7*	4		11	9		3	8	10		12							7
1	3	5	6	7	4		11	9			8	2		10							8
1	3	5	6	7	4		11	9			8	2		10							9
1	3	5	6	7	4		11	9			8	2		10*	12						10
1	3		6	7			11	9	8*	12	4	2		10	5						11
1	3		6	7			11	9	8	12	4	2*		10	5						12
1	3		6	7			11	9*	8	12	4	2		10	5						13
1	3		6	7			11		8*	12	4	2	9	10	5						14
1	3		6	7			11		8	12	4	2	9*	10	5						15
1	3		6				11	9	8	7	4	2		10	5						16
1	3		6	12			11*	9	8	7	4	2		10	5						17
1	3		6	4	11		10	9	8	7		2			5						18
1	3		6	4	11		10	9	8	7		2			5						19
1	3		6	12		7*	10	9	8	11	4	2			5						20
1	3		6			11	10	9	8	12	4*	2		7	5						21
	3		6	7		11	10	9	8	4		2			5	1					22
1	3		6	7		4*	10	9	8	11	12	2			5						23
1	3		6	7		4	10	9		11	8	2			5						24
1	3		6	7*		4	10	9	12	11	8	2			5						25
1	3		6	7			10	9	8	11	4	2			5						26
1	3		6	7	12	4	10		8	11	9*	2			5						27
1	3		6	7	9	4	10		8	11		2			5						28
1	3		6	7*	9	4	10		8	11	12	2			5						29
1	3		6	7	9	4	10		8	11*	12	2			5						30
1	3		6	7		4	10	9	8		11	2			5						31
1	3		6	7	4		10	9	8		11	2			5						32
1	3	4	6				10	9	8	11	7	2			5						33
1		4	6	7	11		10	9	8	3		2			5						34
1		5	6*	7		12	10		8	3		2					4	9	11		35
1		5	6	7			10		8	3		2					4	9	11		36
1		5	6	7			10		8	3		2					4	9	11		37
1			6	7			10		8	3		2			5		4	9	11		38
1			6	7		12	10		8	3		2			5		4*	9	11		39
1			6	7		4	10		8	3	12	2			5			9*	11		40
1			6	7		4	10		8	3	12	2			5			9*	11		41
1			6	7		4	10		8	3	12	2			5*			9	11		42
1			6	7		4	10		8*	3	12	2			5			9	11		43
1	5		6	7		11*	10		8	3	9	2					4			12	44
1	2		6	7			10*		8	3	9	5					4		11	12	45
1	3		6	7			10		8		9	5					4		11	2	46
45	36	15	46	41	17	20	46	28	36	34	27	42	2	11	30	1	8	9	11	1	
				+ 2s	+ 1s	+ 2s			+ 2s	+ 6s	+ 7s		+ 1s	+ 1s	+ 1s					+ 2s	

YORK CITY

	Ht	Wt	Birthplace	Clubs	League App.	League Gls
Goalkeepers						
Edwin Blackburn	5 9	10 5	Houghton-le-Spring	Hull C	68	—
				York C	45	—
Mike Astbury (Apprentice)			Leeds	York C	1	—
Defenders						
Steve Faulkner	6 3	13 5	Sheffield	Sheffield U	15	—
				Stockport Co (on loan)	4	—
				York C	90	7
Andy Clements (Contract cancelled April 1981)	5 11	11 2	Swinton	Bolton W	1	—
				Port Vale (on loan)	3	—
				York C	148	6
Jimmy Walsh (Contract cancelled April 1981)	5 9	11 0	London	Watford	65	—
				York C	99	2
Roy Kay	5 9	11 0	Edinburgh	Hearts	143	1
				Celtic	5	—
				York C	123	4
Derek Hood	5 10½	11 4	Washington	WBA	—	—
				Hull C	24	—
				York C	58	1
Andy Leaf (Contract cancelled March 1981)	5 10	11 3	York	York C	1	—
Derek Craig	6 0	11 9	Durham	Newcastle U	—	—
				Darlington	187	10
				York C	46	1
Richard Dawson	5 11	11 3	York	York C	—	—
Steve Senior (Apprentice)	5 10	11 4	Sheffield	York C	3	—
Midfield						
Tom Stanley	5 7	10 6	Hemsworth	York C	8	—
Ian McDonald	5 7	10 5	Barrow	Barrow	35	2
				Workington	42	4
				Liverpool	—	—
				Colchester U (on loan)	5	2
				Mansfield T	56	4
				York C	165	27
David Pugh*	5 10½	11 7	Markham	Newport Co	78	9
				Chesterfield	213	12
				Halifax T	96	3
				Rotherham U	58	—
				York C	77	2
Gary Ford	5 9	10 7	York	York C	105	10
John Harrison (Contract cancelled Oct 1980)	5 9	10 7	York	York C	8	—
Billy McGhie	5 9	11 0	Lanark	Leeds U	2	1
				York C	40	1
Lloyd Richards (Contract cancelled April 1981)	5 8	11 0	Derby	Notts Co	9	—
				York C	18	1
Ally Millar (Contract cancelled Jan 1981)	5 9	10 7	Glasgow	Barnsley	289	17
				York C	12	—
Forwards						
Kevin Randall (Non-contract)	5 11	12 9	Ashton under Lyne	Bury	4	—
				Chesterfield	258	97
				Notts Co	121	38
				Mansfield T	66	20
				York C	107	27
John Byrne	5 11	11 6	Manchester	York C	47	8
Terry Eccles (Contract cancelled April 1981)	6 1	13 0	Leeds	Blackburn R	46	6
				Mansfield T	118	47
				Huddersfield T	46	6
				Ethnikos	(not known)	
				York C	64	18
Stewart Ferebee (Contract cancelled April 1981)	5 10	11 5	Carshalton	York C	13	—
Tony Robb (Contract cancelled Oct 1980)				York C	—	—
Malcolm Smith	5 8	11 0	Stockton	Middlesbrough	56	11
				Bury (on loan)	5	1
				Blackpool (on loan)	8	5
				Burnley	85	17
				York C	34	6
John Bentham	5 7	10 8	Pontefract	York C	—	—

FOOTBALL LEAGUE 1980–81

DIVISION 1

		Home					Away					
	P	W	D	L	F	A	W	D	L	F	A	Pts
1. Aston Villa	42	16	3	2	40	13	10	5	6	32	27	60
2. Ipswich T	42	15	4	2	45	14	8	6	7	32	29	56
3. Arsenal	42	13	8	0	36	17	6	7	8	25	28	53
4. WBA	42	15	4	2	40	15	5	8	8	20	27	52
5. Liverpool	42	13	5	3	38	15	4	12	5	24	27	51
6. Southampton	42	15	4	2	47	22	5	6	10	29	34	50
7. Nottingham F	42	15	3	3	44	20	4	9	8	18	24	50
8. Manchester U	42	9	11	1	30	14	6	7	8	21	22	48
9. Leeds U	42	10	5	6	19	19	7	5	9	20	28	44
10. Tottenham H	42	9	9	3	44	31	5	6	10	26	37	43
11. Stoke C	42	8	9	4	31	23	4	9	8	20	37	42
12. Manchester C	42	10	7	4	35	25	4	4	13	21	34	39
13. Birmingham C	42	11	5	5	32	23	2	7	12	18	38	38
14. Middlesbrough	42	14	4	3	38	16	2	1	18	15	45	37
15. Everton	42	8	6	7	32	25	5	4	12	23	33	36
16. Coventry C	42	9	6	6	31	30	4	4	13	17	38	36
17. Sunderland	42	10	4	7	32	19	4	3	14	20	34	35
18. Wolverhampton W	42	11	2	8	26	20	2	7	12	17	35	35
19. Brighton & HA	42	10	3	8	30	26	4	4	13	24	41	35
20. Norwich C	42	9	7	5	34	25	4	0	17	15	48	33
21. Leicester C	42	7	5	9	20	23	6	1	14	20	44	32
22. Crystal Palace	42	6	4	11	32	37	0	3	18	15	46	19

DIVISION 2

		Home					Away					
	P	W	D	L	F	A	W	D	L	F	A	Pts
1. West Ham U	42	19	1	1	53	12	9	9	3	26	17	66
2. Notts Co	42	10	8	3	26	15	8	9	4	23	23	53
3. Swansea C	42	12	5	4	39	19	6	9	6	25	25	50
4. Blackburn R	42	12	8	1	28	7	4	10	7	14	22	50
5. Luton T	42	10	6	5	35	23	8	6	7	26	23	48
6. Derby Co	42	9	8	4	34	26	6	7	8	23	26	45
7. Grimsby T	42	10	8	3	21	10	5	7	9	23	32	45
8. QPR	42	11	7	3	36	12	4	6	11	20	34	43
9. Watford	42	13	5	3	34	18	3	6	12	16	27	43
10. Sheffield W	42	14	4	3	38	14	3	4	14	15	37	42
11. Newcastle U	42	11	7	3	22	13	3	7	11	8	32	42
12. Chelsea	42	8	6	7	27	15	6	6	9	19	26	40
13. Cambridge U	42	13	1	7	36	23	4	5	12	17	42	40
14. Shrewsbury T	42	9	7	5	33	22	2	10	9	13	25	39
15. Oldham Ath	42	7	9	5	19	16	5	6	10	20	32	39
16. Wrexham	42	5	8	8	22	24	7	6	8	21	21	38
17. Orient	42	9	8	4	34	20	4	4	13	18	36	38
18. Bolton W	42	10	5	6	40	27	4	5	12	21	39	38
19. Cardiff C	42	7	7	7	23	24	5	5	11	21	36	36
20. Preston NE	42	8	7	6	28	26	3	7	11	13	36	36
21. Bristol C	42	6	10	5	19	15	1	6	14	10	36	30
22. Bristol R	42	4	9	8	21	24	1	4	16	13	41	23

DIVISION 3

		Home					Away					
	P	W	D	L	F	A	W	D	L	F	A	Pts
1. Rotherham U	46	17	6	0	43	8	7	7	9	19	24	61
2. Barnsley	46	15	5	3	46	19	6	12	5	26	26	59
3. Charlton Ath	46	14	6	3	36	17	11	3	9	27	27	59
4. Huddersfield T	46	14	6	3	40	11	7	8	8	31	29	56
5. Chesterfield	46	17	4	2	42	16	6	6	11	30	32	56
6. Portsmouth	46	14	5	4	35	19	8	4	11	20	28	53
7. Plymouth Arg	46	14	5	4	35	18	5	9	9	21	26	52
8. Burnley	46	13	5	5	37	21	5	9	9	23	27	50
9. Brentford	46	7	9	7	30	25	7	10	6	22	24	47
10. Reading	46	13	5	5	39	22	5	5	13	23	40	46
11. Exeter C	46	9	9	5	36	30	7	4	12	26	36	45
12. Newport Co	46	11	6	6	38	22	4	7	12	26	39	43
13. Fulham	46	8	7	8	28	29	7	6	10	29	35	43
14. Oxford U	46	7	8	8	20	24	6	9	8	19	23	43
15. Gillingham	46	9	8	6	23	19	3	10	10	25	39	42
16. Millwall	46	10	9	4	30	21	4	5	14	13	39	42
17. Swindon	46	10	6	7	35	27	3	9	11	16	29	41
18. Chester	46	11	5	7	25	17	4	6	13	13	31	41
19. Carlisle U	46	8	9	6	32	29	6	4	13	24	41	41
20. Walsall	46	8	9	6	43	43	5	6	12	16	31	41
21. Sheffield U	46	12	6	5	38	20	2	6	15	27	43	40
22. Colchester U	46	12	7	4	35	22	2	4	17	10	43	39
23. Blackpool	46	5	9	9	19	28	4	5	14	26	47	32
24. Hull C	46	7	8	8	23	22	1	8	14	17	49	32

DIVISION 4

		Home					Away					
	P	W	D	L	F	A	W	D	L	F	A	Pts
1. Southend U	46	19	4	0	47	6	11	3	9	32	25	67
2. Lincoln C	46	15	7	1	44	11	10	8	5	22	14	65
3. Doncaster R	46	15	4	4	36	20	7	8	8	23	29	56
4. Wimbledon	46	15	4	4	42	17	8	5	10	22	29	55
5. Peterborough U	46	11	8	4	37	21	6	10	7	31	33	52
6. Aldershot	46	12	9	2	28	11	6	5	12	15	30	50
7. Mansfield T	46	13	5	5	36	15	7	4	12	22	29	49
8. Darlington	46	13	6	4	43	23	6	5	12	22	36	49
9. Hartlepool U	46	14	3	6	42	22	6	6	11	22	39	49
10. Northampton T	46	11	7	5	42	26	7	6	10	23	41	49
11. Wigan Ath	46	13	4	6	29	16	5	7	11	22	39	47
12. Bury	46	10	8	5	38	21	7	3	13	32	41	45
13. Bournemouth	46	9	8	6	30	21	7	5	11	17	27	45
14. Bradford C	46	9	9	5	30	24	5	7	11	23	36	44
15. Rochdale	46	11	6	6	33	25	3	9	11	27	45	43
16. Scunthorpe U	46	8	12	3	40	31	3	8	12	20	38	42
17. Torquay U	46	13	2	8	38	26	5	3	15	17	37	41
18. Crewe Alex	46	10	7	6	28	20	3	7	13	20	41	40
19. Port Vale	46	10	8	5	40	23	2	7	14	17	47	39
20. Stockport Co	46	10	5	8	29	25	6	2	15	15	32	39
21. Tranmere R	46	12	5	6	41	24	1	5	17	18	49	36
22. Hereford U	46	8	8	7	29	20	3	5	15	9	42	35
23. Halifax T	46	9	3	11	28	32	2	9	12	16	39	34
24. York C	46	10	2	11	31	23	2	7	14	16	43	33

FOOTBALL LEAGUE 1888–89 to 1980–81

FOOTBALL LEAGUE

	First	*Pts*	*Second*	*Pts*	*Third*	*Pts*
1888–89*a*	Preston NE	40	Aston Villa	29	Wolverhampton W	28
1889–90*a*	Preston NE	33	Everton	31	Blackburn R	27
1890–91*a*	Everton	29	Preston NE	27	Notts Co	26
1891–92*b*	Sunderland	42	Preston NE	37	Bolton W	36

FIRST DIVISION

Maximum points: a 44; *b* 52; *c* 60; *d* 68; *e* 76; *f* 84.

1892–93*c*	Sunderland	48	Preston NE	37	Everton	36
1893–94*c*	Aston Villa	44	Sunderland	38	Derby Co	36
1894–95*c*	Sunderland	47	Everton	42	Aston Villa	39
1895–96*c*	Aston Villa	45	Derby Co	41	Everton	39
1896–97*c*	Aston Villa	47	Sheffield U	36	Derby Co	36
1897–98*c*	Sheffield U	42	Sunderland	37	Wolverhampton W	35
1898–99*d*	Aston Villa	45	Liverpool	43	Burnley	39
1899–1900*d*	Aston Villa	50	Sheffield U	48	Sunderland	41
1900–01*d*	Liverpool	45	Sunderland	43	Notts Co	40
1901–02*d*	Sunderland	44	Everton	41	Newcastle U	37
1902–03*d*	The Wednesday	42	Aston Villa	41	Sunderland	41
1903–04*d*	The Wednesday	47	Manchester C	44	Everton	43
1904–05*d*	Newcastle U	48	Everton	47	Manchester C	46
1905–06*e*	Liverpool	51	Preston NE	47	The Wednesday	44
1906–07*e*	Newcastle U	51	Bristol C	48	Everton	45
1907–08*e*	Manchester U	52	Aston Villa	43	Manchester C	43
1908–09*e*	Newcastle U	53	Everton	46	Sunderland	44
1909–10*e*	Aston Villa	53	Liverpool	48	Blackburn R	45
1910–11*e*	Manchester U	52	Aston Villa	51	Sunderland	45
1911–12*e*	Blackburn R	49	Everton	46	Newcastle U	44
1912–13*e*	Sunderland	54	Aston Villa	50	Sheffield W	49
1913–14*e*	Blackburn R	51	Aston Villa	44	Middlesbrough	43
1914–15*e*	Everton	46	Oldham Ath	45	Blackburn R	43
1919–20*f*	WBA	60	Burnley	51	Chelsea	49
1920–21*f*	Burnley	59	Manchester C	54	Bolton W	52
1921–22*f*	Liverpool	57	Tottenham H	51	Burnley	49
1922-23*f*	Liverpool	60	Sunderland	54	Huddersfield T	53
1923–24*f*	Huddersfield T*	57	Cardiff C	57	Sunderland	53
1924–25*f*	Huddersfield T	58	WBA	56	Bolton W	55
1925–26*f*	Huddersfield T	57	Arsenal	52	Sunderland	48
1926–27*f*	Newcastle U	56	Huddersfield T	51	Sunderland	49
1927–28*f*	Everton	53	Huddersfield T	51	Leicester C	48
1928–29*f*	Sheffield W	52	Leicester C	51	Aston Villa	50
1929–30*f*	Sheffield W	60	Derby Co	50	Manchester C	47
1930–31*f*	Arsenal	66	Aston Villa	59	Sheffield W	52
1931–32*f*	Everton	56	Arsenal	54	Sheffield W	50
1932–33*f*	Arsenal	58	Aston Villa	54	Sheffield W	51
1933–34*f*	Arsenal	59	Huddersfield T	56	Tottenham H	49
1934–35*f*	Arsenal	58	Sunderland	54	Sheffield W	49
1935–36*f*	Sunderland	56	Derby Co	48	Huddersfield T	48
1936–37*f*	Manchester C	57	Charlton Ath	54	Arsenal	52
1937–38*f*	Arsenal	52	Wolverhampton W	51	Preston NE	49
1938–39*f*	Everton	59	Wolverhampton W	55	Charlton Ath	50
1946–47*f*	Liverpool	57	Manchester U	56	Wolverhampton W	56
1947–48*f*	Arsenal	59	Manchester U	52	Burnley	52
1948–49*f*	Portsmouth	58	Manchester U	53	Derby Co	53
1949–50*f*	Portsmouth*	53	Wolverhampton W	53	Sunderland	52
1950–51*f*	Tottenham H	60	Manchester U	56	Blackpool	50
1951–52*f*	Manchester U	57	Tottenham H	53	Arsenal	53
1952–53*f*	Arsenal*	54	Preston NE	54	Wolverhampton W	51
1953–54*f*	Wolverhampton W	57	WBA	53	Huddersfield T	51
1954–55*f*	Chelsea	52	Wolverhampton W	48	Portsmouth	48
1955–56*f*	Manchester U	60	Blackpool	49	Wolverhampton W	49
1956–57*f*	Manchester U	64	Tottenham H	56	Preston NE	56
1957–58*f*	Wolverhampton W	64	Preston NE	59	Tottenham H	51
1958–59*f*	Wolverhampton W	61	Manchester U	55	Arsenal	50

* *Won on goal average.*

	First	Pts	Second	Pts	Third	Pts
1959–60*f*	Burnley	55	Wolverhampton W	54	Tottenham H	53
1960–61*f*	Tottenham H	66	Sheffield W	58	Wolverhampton W	57
1961–62*f*	Ipswich T	56	Burnley	53	Tottenham H	52
1962–63*f*	Everton	61	Tottenham H	55	Burnley	54
1963–64*f*	Liverpool	57	Manchester U	53	Everton	52
1964–65*f*	Manchester U*	61	Leeds U	61	Chelsea	56
1965–66*f*	Liverpool	61	Leeds U	55	Burnley	55
1966–67*f*	Manchester U	60	Nottingham F	56	Tottenham H	56
1967–68*f*	Manchester C	58	Manchester U	56	Liverpool	55
1968–69*f*	Leeds U	67	Liverpool	61	Everton	57
1969–70*f*	Everton	66	Leeds U	57	Chelsea	55
1970–71*f*	Arsenal	65	Leeds U	64	Tottenham H	52
1971–72*f*	Derby Co	58	Leeds U	57	Liverpool	57
1972–73*f*	Liverpool	60	Arsenal	57	Leeds U	53
1973–74*f*	Leeds U	62	Liverpool	57	Derby Co	48
1974–75*f*	Derby Co	53	Liverpool	51	Ipswich T	57
1975–76*f*	Liverpool	60	QPR	59	Manchester U	56
1976–77*f*	Liverpool	57	Manchester C	56	Ipswich T	52
1977–78*f*	Nottingham F	64	Liverpool	57	Everton	55
1978–79*f*	Liverpool	68	Nottingham F	60	WBA	59
1979–80*f*	Liverpool	60	Manchester U	58	Ipswich T	53
1980–81*f*	Aston Villa	60	Ipswich T	56	Arsenal	53

No competition during 1915–19 and 1939–46.

SECOND DIVISION

Maximum points: a 44; *b* 56; *c* 60; *d* 68; *e* 76; *f* 84.

	First	Pts	Second	Pts	Third	Pts
1892–93*a*	Small Heath	36	Sheffield U	35	Darwen	30
1893–94*b*	Liverpool	50	Small Heath	42	Notts Co	39
1894–95*c*	Bury	48	Notts Co	39	Newton Heath	38
1895–96*c*	Liverpool*	46	Manchester C	46	Grimsby T	42
1896–97*c*	Notts Co	42	Newton Heath	39	Grimsby T	38
1897–98*c*	Burnley	48	Newcastle U	45	Manchester C	39
1898–99*d*	Manchester C	52	Glossop NE	46	Leicester Fosse	45
1899–1900*d*	The Wednesday	54	Bolton W	52	Small Heath	46
1900–01*d*	Grimsby T	49	Small Heath	48	Burnley	44
1901–02*d*	WBA	55	Middlesbrough	51	Preston NE	42
1902–03*d*	Manchester C	54	Small Heath	51	Woolwich A	48
1903–04*d*	Preston NE	50	Woolwich A	49	Manchester U	48
1904–05*d*	Liverpool	58	Bolton W	56	Manchester U	53
1905–06*e*	Bristol C	66	Manchester U	62	Chelsea	53
1906–07*e*	Nottingham F	60	Chelsea	57	Leicester Fosse	48
1907–08*e*	Bradford C	54	Leicester Fosse	52	Oldham Ath	50
1908–09*e*	Bolton W	52	Tottenham H*	51	WBA	51
1909–10*e*	Manchester C	54	Oldham Ath*	53	Hull C	53
1910–11*e*	WBA	53	Bolton W	51	Chelsea	49
1911–12*e*	Derby Co*	54	Chelsea	54	Burnley	52
1912–13*e*	Preston NE	53	Burnley	50	Birmingham	46
1913–14*e*	Notts Co	53	Bradford PA	49	Woolwich A	49
1914–15*e*	Derby Co	53	Preston NE	50	Barnsley	47
1919–20*f*	Tottenham H	70	Huddersfield T	64	Birmingham	56
1920–21*f*	Birmingham*	58	Cardiff C	58	Bristol C	51
1921–22*f*	Nottingham F	56	Stoke C	52	Barnsley	52
1922–23*f*	Notts Co	53	West Ham U*	51	Leicester C	51
1923–24*f*	Leeds U	54	Bury*	51	Derby Co	51
1924–25*f*	Leicester C	59	Manchester U	57	Derby Co	55
1925–26*f*	Sheffield W	60	Derby Co	57	Chelsea	52
1926–27*f*	Middlesbrough	62	Portsmouth*	54	Manchester C	54
1927–28*f*	Manchester C	59	Leeds U	57	Chelsea	54
1928–29*f*	Middlesbrough	55	Grimsby T	53	Bradford	48
1929–30*f*	Blackpool	58	Chelsea	55	Oldham Ath	53
1930–31*f*	Everton	61	WBA	54	Tottenham H	51
1931–32*f*	Wolverhampton W	56	Leeds U	54	Stoke C	52
1932–33*f*	Stoke C	56	Tottenham H	55	Fulham	50
1933–34*f*	Grimsby T	59	Preston NE	52	Bolton W	51
1934–35*f*	Brentford	61	Bolton W*	56	West Ham U	56
1935–36*f*	Manchester U	56	Charlton Ath	55	Sheffield U	52
1936–37*f*	Leicester C	56	Blackpool	55	Bury	52

* *Won on goal average.*

	First	Pts	Second	Pts	Third	Pts
1937–38*f*	Aston Villa	57	Manchester U*	53	Sheffield U	53
1938–39*f*	Blackburn R	55	Sheffield U	54	Sheffield W	53
1946–47*f*	Manchester C	62	Burnley	58	Birmingham C	55
1947–48*f*	Birmingham C	59	Newcastle U	56	Southampton	52
1948–49*f*	Fulham	57	WBA	56	Southampton	55
1949–50*f*	Tottenham H	61	Sheffield W*	52	Sheffield U	52
1950–51*f*	Preston NE	57	Manchester C	52	Cardiff C	50
1951–52*f*	Sheffield W	53	Cardiff C*	51	Birmingham C	51
1952–53*f*	Sheffield U	60	Huddersfield T	58	Luton T	52
1953–54*f*	Leicester C*	56	Everton	56	Blackburn R	55
1954–55*f*	Birmingham C*	54	Luton T*	54	Rotherham U	54
1955–56*f*	Sheffield W	55	Leeds U	52	Liverpool	48
1956–57*f*	Leicester C	61	Nottingham F	54	Liverpool	53
1957–58*f*	West Ham U	57	Blackburn R	56	Charlton Ath	55
1958–59*f*	Sheffield W	62	Fulham	60	Sheffield U	53
1959–60*f*	Aston Villa	59	Cardiff C	58	Liverpool	50
1960–61*f*	Ipswich T	59	Sheffield U	58	Liverpool	52
1961–62*f*	Liverpool	62	Leyton O	54	Sunderland	53
1962–63*f*	Stoke C	53	Chelsea*	52	Sunderland	52
1963–64*f*	Leeds U	63	Sunderland	61	Preston NE	56
1964–65*f*	Newcastle U	57	Northampton T	56	Bolton W	50
1965–66*f*	Manchester C	59	Southampton	54	Coventry C	53
1966–67*f*	Coventry C	59	Wolverhampton W	58	Carlisle U	52
1967–68*f*	Ipswich T	59	QPR*	58	Blackpool	58
1968–69*f*	Derby Co	63	Crystal Palace	56	Charlton Ath	50
1969–70*f*	Huddersfield T	60	Blackpool	53	Leicester C	51
1970–71*f*	Leicester C	59	Sheffield U	56	Cardiff C	53
1971–72*f*	Norwich C	57	Birmingham C	56	Millwall	55
1972–73*f*	Burnley	62	QPR	61	Aston Villa	50
1973–74*f*	Middlesbrough	65	Luton T	50	Carlisle U	49
1974–75*f*	Manchester U	61	Aston Villa	58	Norwich C	53
1975–76*f*	Sunderland	56	Bristol C	53	WBA	53
1976–77*f*	Wolverhampton W	57	Chelsea	55	Nottingham F	52
1977–78*f*	Bolton W	58	Southampton	57	Tottenham H	56
1978–79*f*	Crystal Palace	57	Brighton	56	Stoke C	56
1979–80*f*	Leicester C	55	Sunderland	54	Birmingham C	53
1980–81*f*	West Ham U	66	Notts Co	53	Swansea C*	50

No competition during 1915–19 and 1939–46.

THIRD DIVISION

Maximum points: 92

	First	Pts	Second	Pts	Third	Pts
1958–59	Plymouth Arg	62	Hull C	61	Brentford	57
1959–60	Southampton	61	Norwich C	59	Shrewsbury T	52
1960–61	Bury	68	Walsall	62	QPR	60
1961–62	Portsmouth	65	Grimsby T	62	Bournemouth	59
1962–63	Northampton T	62	Swindon T	58	Port Vale	54
1963–64	Coventry C*	60	Crystal Palace	60	Watford	58
1964–65	Carlisle U	60	Bristol C*	59	Mansfield T	59
1965–66	Hull C	69	Millwall	65	QPR	57
1966–67	QPR	67	Middlesbrough	55	Watford	54
1967–68	Oxford U	57	Bury	56	Shrewsbury T	55
1968–69	Watford*	64	Swindon T	64	Luton T	61
1969–70	Orient	62	Luton T	60	Bristol R	56
1970–71	Preston NE	61	Fulham	60	Halifax T	56
1971–72	Aston Villa	70	Brighton	65	Bournemouth	62
1972–73	Bolton W	61	Notts Co	57	Blackburn R	55
1973–74	Oldham Ath	62	Bristol R	61	York C	61
1974–75	Blackburn R	60	Plymouth Arg	59	Charlton Ath	55
1975–76	Hereford U	63	Cardiff C	57	Millwall	56
1976–77	Mansfield T	64	Brighton & HA	61	Crystal Palace	59
1977–78	Wrexham	61	Cambridge U	58	Preston NE	56
1978–79	Shrewsbury T	61	Watford	60	Swansea C	60
1979–80	Grimsby T	62	Blackburn R	59	Sheffield W	58
1980–81	Rotherham U	61	Barnsley*	59	Charlton Ath	59

**Won on goal average.*

FOURTH DIVISION

Maximum points: 92.

	First	Pts	Second	Pts	Third	Pts	Fourth	Pts
1958–59	Port Vale	64	Coventry C	60	York C	60	Shrewsbury T	58
1959–60	Walsall	65	Notts Co	60	Torquay U	60	Watford	57
1960–61	Peterborough U	66	Crystal Palace	64	Northampton T	60	Bradford PA	60
1961–62†	Millwall	56	Colchester U	55	Wrexham	53	Carlisle U	52
1962–63	Brentford	62	Oldham Ath	59	Crewe Alex	59	Mansfield T	57
1963–64	Gillingham*	60	Carlisle U	60	Workington T	59	Exeter C	58
1964–65	Brighton	63	Millwall	62	York C	62	Oxford U	61
1965–66	Doncaster R*	59	Darlington	59	Torquay U	58	Colchester U	56
1966–67	Stockport Co	64	Southport	59	Barrow	59	Tranmere R	58
1967–68	Luton T	66	Barnsley	61	Hartlepools U	60	Crewe Alex	58
1968–69	Doncaster R	59	Halifax T	57	Rochdale	56	Bradford C	56
1969–70	Chesterfield	64	Wrexham	61	Swansea C	60	Port Vale	59
1970–71	Notts Co	69	Bournemouth	60	Oldham Ath	59	York C	56
1971–72	Grimsby T	63	Southend U	60	Brentford	59	Scunthorpe U	57
1972–73	Southport	62	Hereford U	58	Cambridge U	57	Aldershot*	56
1973–74	Peterborough U	65	Gillingham	62	Colchester U	60	Bury	59
1974–75	Mansfield T	68	Shrewsbury T	62	Rotherham U	59	Chester	57
1975–76	Lincoln C	74	Northampton T	68	Reading	60	Tranmere R	58
1976–77	Cambridge U	65	Exeter C	62	Colchester U	59	Bradford C	59
1977–78	Watford	71	Southend U	60	Swansea C	56	Brentford	56
1978–79	Reading	65	Grimsby T	61	Wimbledon	61	Barnsley	61
1979–80	Huddersfield T	66	Walsall	64	Newport Co	61	Portsmouth	60
1980–81	Southend U	67	Lincoln C	65	Doncaster R	56	Wimbledon	55

†*Maximum points:* 88 owing to Accrington Stanley's resignation.

THIRD DIVISION—SOUTH (1921–1958)

Maximum points: a 84; *b* 76; *c* 80; *d* 92.

	First	Pts	Second	Pts	Third	Pts
1920–21*a*	Crystal Palace	59	Southampton	54	QPR	53
1921–22*a*	Southampton*	61	Plymouth Arg	61	Portsmouth	53
1922–23*a*	Bristol C	59	Plymouth Arg	53	Swansea T	53
1923–24*a*	Portsmouth	59	Plymouth Arg	55	Millwall	54
1924–25*a*	Swansea T	57	Plymouth Arg	56	Bristol C	53
1925–26*a*	Reading	57	Plymouth Arg	56	Millwall	53
1926–27*a*	Bristol C	62	Plymouth Arg	60	Millwall	56
1927–28*a*	Millwall	65	Northampton T	55	Plymouth Arg	53
1928–29*a*	Charlton Ath*	54	Crystal Palace	54	Northampton T	52
1929–30*a*	Plymouth Arg	68	Brentford	61	QPR	51
1930–31*a*	Notts Co	59	Crystal Palace	51	Brentford	50
1931–32*a*	Fulham	57	Reading	55	Southend U	53
1932–33*a*	Brentford	62	Exeter C	58	Norwich C	57
1933–34*a*	Norwich C	61	Coventry C	54	Reading	54
1934–35*a*	Charlton Ath	61	Reading	53	Coventry C	51
1935–36*a*	Coventry C	57	Luton T	56	Reading	54
1936–37*a*	Luton T	58	Notts Co	56	Brighton	53
1937–38*a*	Millwall	56	Bristol C	55	QPR	53
1938–39*a*	Newport Co	55	Crystal Palace	52	Brighton	49
1939–46	Competition cancelled owing to war.					
1946–47*a*	Cardiff C	66	QPR	57	Bristol C	51
1947–48*a*	QPR	61	Bournemouth	57	Walsall	51
1948–49*a*	Swansea T	62	Reading	55	Bournemouth	52
1949–50*a*	Notts Co	58	Northampton T	51	Southend U	51
1950–51*d*	Nottingham F	70	Norwich C	64	Reading	57
1951–52*d*	Plymouth Arg	66	Reading	61	Norwich C	61
1952–53*d*	Bristol R	64	Millwall	62	Northampton T	62
1953–54*d*	Ipswich T	64	Brighton	61	Bristol C	56
1954–55*d*	Bristol C	70	Leyton O	61	Southampton	59
1955–56*d*	Leyton O	66	Brighton	65	Ipswich T	64
1956–57*d*	Ipswich T*	59	Torquay U	59	Colchester U	58
1957–58*d*	Brighton	60	Brentford	58	Plymouth Arg	58

* *Won on goal average.*

THIRD DIVISION—NORTH (1921–1958)

Maximum points: a 84; b 76; c 80; d 92.

	First	Pts	Second	Pts	Third	Pts
1921–22*b*	Stockport Co	56	Darlington	50	Grimsby T	50
1922–23*b*	Nelson	51	Bradford PA	47	Walsall	46
1923–24*a*	Wolverhampton W	63	Rochdale	62	Chesterfield	54
1924–25*a*	Darlington	58	Nelson	53	New Brighton	53
1925–26*a*	Grimsby T	61	Bradford PA	60	Rochdale	59
1926–27*a*	Stoke C	63	Rochdale	58	Bradford PA	55
1927–28*a*	Bradford PA	63	Lincoln C	55	Stockport Co	54
1928–29*a*	Bradford C	63	Stockport Co	62	Wrexham	52
1929–30*a*	Port Vale	67	Stockport Co	63	Darlington	50
1930–31*a*	Chesterfield	58	Lincoln C	57	Wrexham	54
1931–32*c*	Lincoln C*	57	Gateshead	57	Chester	50
1932–33*a*	Hull C	59	Wrexham	57	Stockport Co	54
1933–34*a*	Barnsley	62	Chesterfield	61	Stockport Co	59
1934–35*a*	Doncaster R	57	Halifax T	55	Chester	54
1935–36*a*	Chesterfield	60	Chester	55	Tranmere R	55
1936–37*a*	Stockport Co	60	Lincoln C	57	Chester	53
1937–38*a*	Tranmere R	56	Doncaster R	54	Hull C	53
1938–39*a*	Barnsley	67	Doncaster R	56	Bradford C	52
1939–46	Competition cancelled owing to war.					
1946–47*a*	Doncaster R	72	Rotherham U	64	Chester	56
1947–48*a*	Lincoln C	60	Rotherham U	59	Wrexham	50
1948–49*a*	Hull C	65	Rotherham U	62	Doncaster R	50
1949–50*a*	Doncaster R	55	Gateshead	53	Rochdale	51
1950–51*d*	Rotherham U	71	Mansfield T	64	Carlisle U	62
1951–52*d*	Lincoln C	69	Grimsby T	66	Stockport Co	59
1952–53*d*	Oldham Ath	59	Port Vale	58	Wrexham	56
1953–54*d*	Port Vale	69	Barnsley	58	Scunthorpe U	57
1954–55*d*	Barnsley	65	Accrington S	61	Scunthorpe U	58
1955–56*d*	Grimsby T	68	Derby Co	63	Accrington S	59
1956–57*d*	Derby Co	63	Hartlepools U	59	Accrington S	58
1957–58*d*	Scunthorpe U	66	Accrington S	59	Bradford C	57

* *Won on goal average.*

LEAGUE TITLE WINS

LEAGUE DIVISION 1 – Liverpool 12, Arsenal 8, Manchester U 7, Everton 7, Aston Villa 7, Sunderland 6, Newcastle U 4, Sheffield W 4, Huddersfield T 3, Wolverhampton W 3, Blackburn R 2, Portsmouth 2, Preston NE 2, Burnley 2, Manchester C 2, Tottenham H 2, Leeds U 2, Derby Co 2, Chelsea 1, Sheffield U 1, WBA 1, Ipswich T 1, Nottingham F 1.

LEAGUE DIVISION 2 – Leicester C 6, Manchester C 6, Sheffield W 5, Birmingham C (one as Small Heath) 4, Liverpool 4, Notts Co 3, Preston NE 3, Derby Co 3, Middlesbrough 3, Grimsby T 2, Nottingham F 2, Tottenham H 2, WBA 2, Aston Villa 2, Stoke C 2, Leeds U 2, Ipswich T 2, Burnley 2, Manchester U 2, West Ham U 2, Wolverhampton W 2, Bolton W 2, Huddersfield T 1, Bristol C 1, Brentford 1, Bury 1, Bradford C 1, Everton 1, Fulham 1, Sheffield U 1, Newcastle U 1, Coventry C 1, Blackpool 1, Blackburn R 1, Norwich C 1, Sunderland 1, Crystal Palace 1.

LEAGUE DIVISION 3 – Plymouth Arg, Southampton, Bury, Portsmouth, Northampton T, Coventry C, Carlisle U, Hull C, QPR, Oxford U, Watford, Leyton O, Preston NE, Aston Villa, Bolton W, Oldham Ath, Blackburn R, Hereford U, Mansfield T, Wrexham, Shrewsbury T, Grimsby T, Rotherham U 1 each.

LEAGUE DIVISION 4 – Doncaster R 2, Peterborough U 2; Port Vale, Walsall, Millwall, Brentford, Gillingham, Brighton, Stockport Co, Luton T, Chesterfield, Notts Co, Grimsby T, Southport, Mansfield T, Lincoln C, Cambridge U, Watford, Reading, Huddersfield T, Southend U, 1 each.

To 1957–58

DIVISION 3 (South) – Bristol C 3; Charlton Ath, Ipswich T, Millwall, Notts Co, Plymouth Arg, Swansea T 2; Brentford, Bristol R, Cardiff C, Crystal Palace, Coventry C, Fulham, Leyton O, Luton T, Newport Co, Nottingham F, Norwich C, Portsmouth, QPR, Reading, Southampton, Brighton 1.

DIVISION 3 (North) – Barnsley, Doncaster R, Lincoln C 3; Chesterfield, Grimsby T, Hull C, Port Vale, Stockport Co 2; Bradford PA, Bradford C, Darlington, Derby Co, Nelson, Oldham Ath, Rotherham U, Stoke C, Tranmere R, Wolverhampton W, Scunthorpe U 1.

RELEGATED CLUBS

1891–92 League extended. Newton Heath, Sheffield W and Nottingham F admitted. *Second Division formed* including Darwen.

1892–93 In Test matches, Sheffield U and Darwen won promotion in place of Notts Co and Accrington S.

1893–94 In Tests, Liverpool and Small Heath won promotion. Newton Heath and Darwen relegated.

1894–95 After Tests, Bury promoted, Liverpool relegated.

1895–96 After Tests, Liverpool promoted, Small Heath relegated.

1896–97 After Tests, Notts Co promoted, Burnley relegated.

1897–98 Test system abolished after success of Stoke C and Burnley. League extended. Blackburn R and Newcastle U elected to First Division. *Automatic promotion and relegation introduced.*

DIVISION 1 TO DIVISION 2

1898–99 Bolton W and Sheffield W
1899–1900 Burnley and Glossop
1900–01 Preston NE and WBA
1901–02 Small Heath and Manchester C
1902–03 Grimsby T and Bolton W
1903–04 Liverpool and WBA
1904–05 League extended. Bury and Notts Co, two bottom clubs in First Division, re-elected.
1905–06 Nottingham F and Wolverhampton W
1906–07 Derby Co and Stoke C
1907–08 Bolton W and Birmingham C
1908–09 Manchester C and Leicester Fosse
1909–10 Bolton W and Chelsea
1910–11 Bristol C and Nottingham F
1911–12 Preston NE and Bury
1912–13 Notts Co and Woolwich Arsenal
1913–14 Preston NE and Derby Co
1914–15 Tottenham H and Chelsea*
1919–20 Notts Co and Sheffield W
1920–21 Derby Co and Bradford
1921–22 Bradford C and Manchester U
1922–23 Stoke C and Oldham Ath
1923–24 Chelsea and Middlesbrough
1924–25 Preston NE and Nottingham F
1925–26 Manchester C and Notts Co
1926–27 Leeds U and WBA
1927–28 Tottenham H and Middlesbrough
1928–29 Bury and Cardiff C
1929–30 Burnley and Everton
1930–31 Leeds U and Manchester U
1931–32 Grimsby T and West Ham U
1932–33 Bolton W and Blackpool
1933–34 Newcastle U and Sheffield U
1934–35 Leicester C and Tottenham H
1935–36 Aston Villa and Blackburn R
1936–37 Manchester U and Sheffield W
1937–38 Manchester C and WBA
1938–39 Birmingham C and Leicester C
1946–47 Brentford and Leeds U
1947–48 Blackburn R and Grimsby T
1948–49 Preston NE and Sheffield U
1949–50 Manchester C and Birmingham C
1950–51 Sheffield W and Everton
1951–52 Huddersfield and Fulham
1952–53 Stoke C and Derby Co
1953–54 Middlesbrough and Liverpool
1954–55 Leicester C and Sheffield W
1955–56 Huddersfield and Sheffield U
1956–57 Charlton Ath and Cardiff C
1957–58 Sheffield W and Sunderland
1958–59 Portsmouth and Aston Villa
1959–60 Luton T and Leeds U
1960–61 Preston NE and Newcastle U
1961–62 Chelsea and Cardiff C
1962–63 Manchester C and Leyton O
1963–64 Bolton W and Ipswich T
1964–65 Wolverhampton W and Birmingham C
1965–66 Northampton T and Blackburn R
1966–67 Aston Villa and Blackpool
1967–68 Fulham and Sheffield U
1968–69 Leicester C and QPR
1969–70 Sunderland and Sheffield W
1970–71 Burnley and Blackpool
1971–72 Huddersfield T and Nottingham F
1972–73 Crystal Palace and WBA
1973–74 Southampton, Manchester U, Norwich C
1974–75 Luton T, Chelsea, Carlisle U
1975–76 Wolverhampton W, Burnley, Sheffield U
1976–77 Sunderland, Stoke C, Tottenham H
1977–78 West Ham U, Newcastle U, Leicester C
1978–79 QPR, Birmingham C, Chelsea
1979–80 Bristol C, Derby Co, Bolton W
1980–81 Norwich C, Leicester C, Crystal Palace

*Subsequently re-elected to Division 1 when League was extended after the War.

DIVISION 2 TO DIVISION 3

1920–21 Stockport Co
1921–22 Bradford and Bristol C
1922–23 Rotherham C and Wolverhampton W
1923–24 Nelson and Bristol C
1924–25 Crystal Palace and Coventry C
1925–26 Stoke C and Stockport Co
1926–27 Darlington and Bradford C
1927–28 Fulham and South Shields
1928–29 Port Vale and Clapton O
1929–30 Hull C and Notts Co
1930–31 Reading and Cardiff C
1931–32 Barnsley and Bristol C
1932–33 Chesterfield and Charlton Ath
1933–34 Millwall and Lincoln C
1934–35 Oldham Ath and Notts Co
1935–36 Port Vale and Hull C
1936–37 Doncaster R and Bradford C
1937–38 Barnsley and Stockport Co
1938–39 Norwich C and Tranmere R
1946–47 Swansea T and Newport Co
1947–48 Doncaster R and Millwall
1948–49 Nottingham F and Lincoln C
1949–50 Plymouth Arg and Bradford
1950–51 Grimsby T and Chesterfield
1951–52 Coventry C and QPR
1952–53 Southampton and Barnsley
1953–54 Brentford and Oldham Ath
1954–55 Ipswich T and Derby Co
1955–56 Plymouth Arg and Hull C
1956–57 Port Vale and Bury
1957–58 Doncaster R and Notts Co
1958–59 Barnsley and Grimsby T
1959–60 Bristol C and Hull C
1960–61 Lincoln C and Portsmouth
1961–62 Brighton and Bristol R
1962–63 Walsall and Luton T
1963–64 Grimsby T and Scunthorpe U
1964–65 Swindon T and Swansea T
1965–66 Middlesbrough and Leyton O
1966–67 Northampton T and Bury
1967–68 Plymouth Arg and Rotherham U
1968–69 Fulham and Bury
1969–70 Preston NE and Aston Villa
1970–71 Blackburn R and Bolton W
1971–72 Charlton Ath and Watford
1972–73 Huddersfield T and Brighton
1973–74 Crystal Palace, Preston NE, Swindon T
1974–75 Millwall, Cardiff C, Sheffield W
1975–76 Oxford U, York C, Portsmouth
1976–77 Carlisle U, Plymouth Arg, Hereford U
1977–78 Blackpool, Mansfield T, Hull C
1978–79 Sheffield U, Millwall, Blackburn R
1979–80 Fulham, Burnley, Charlton Ath
1980–81 Preston NE, Bristol C, Bristol R

DIVISION 3 TO DIVISION 4

1958–59 Rochdale, Notts Co, Doncaster R and Stockport Co
1959–60 Accrington S, Wrexham, Mansfield T and York C
1960–61 Chesterfield, Colchester U, Bradford C and Tranmere R
1961–62 Newport Co, Brentford, Lincoln C and Torquay U
1962–63 Bradford, Brighton, Carlisle U and Halifax T
1963–64 Millwall, Crewe Alex, Wrexham and Notts Co
1964–65 Luton T, Port Vale, Colchester U and Barnsley
1965–66 Southend U, Exeter C, Brentford and York C
1966–67 Doncaster R, Workington T, Darlington and Swansea T
1967–68 Scunthorpe U, Colchester U, Grimsby T and Peterborough U (demoted)
1968–69 Oldham Ath, Crewe Alex, Hartlepool and Northampton T
1969–70 Bournemouth, Southport, Barrow, Stockport Co
1970–71 Reading, Bury, Doncaster R, Gillingham
1971–72 Mansfield T, Barnsley, Torquay U, Bradford C
1972–73 Rotherham U, Brentford, Swansea C, Scunthorpe U
1973–74 Cambridge U, Shrewsbury T, Southport, Rochdale
1974–75 AFC Bournemouth, Tranmere R, Watford, Huddersfield T
1975–76 Aldershot, Colchester U, Southend U, Halifax T
1976–77 Reading, Northampton T, Grimsby T, York C
1977–78 Port Vale, Bradford C, Hereford U, Portsmouth
1978–79 Peterborough U, Walsall, Tranmere R, Lincoln C
1979–80 Bury, Southend U, Mansfield T, Wimbledon
1980–81 Sheffield U, Colchester U, Blackpool, Hull C

APPLICATIONS FOR RE-ELECTION

FOURTH DIVISION

Nine: Hartlepool.
Six: Barrow (lost League place to Hereford U 1972), Southport (lost League place to Wigan Ath 1978), York C
Five: Darlington, Crewe Alex, Lincoln C, Workington (lost League place to Wimbledon 1977)
Four: Bradford PA (lost League place to Cambridge United 1970), Chester, Halifax T, Newport Co, Rochdale, Stockport Co
Three: Doncaster R
Two: Bradford C, Hereford U, Northampton T, Oldham Ath
One: Aldershot, Colchester U, Exeter C, Gateshead (lost League place to Peterborough U 1960), Grimsby T, Scunthorpe U, Swansea C, Tranmere R, Wrexham
Accrington S resigned and Oxford U were elected 1962.
Port Vale were forced to re-apply following expulsion in 1968.

THIRD DIVISIONS NORTH & SOUTH

Seven: Walsall.
Six: Exeter C, Halifax T, Newport Co.
Five: Accrington S, Barrow, Gillingham, New Brighton, Southport.
Four: Rochdale, Norwich C.
Three: Crystal Palace, Crewe Alex, Darlington, Hartlepool, Merthyr T, Swindon T.
Two: Aberdare Ath, Aldershot, Ashington, Bournemouth, Brentford, Chester, Colchester U, Durham C, Millwall, Nelson, QPR, Rotherham U, Southend U, Tranmere R, Watford, Workington
One: Bradford C, Bradford PA, Brighton, Bristol R, Cardiff C, Carlisle U, Charlton Ath, Gateshead, Grimsby T, Mansfield T, Shrewsbury T, Torquay U, York C.

CHESTERFIELD'S RECORD

In 1980–81 Chesterfield created a record for a team outside the top two divisions by playing 65 competitive matches, 46 in the League, four in the League Cup, six in the FA Cup and nine in the Anglo-Scottish Cup, which they won. In addition, their Reserve team won the North Midlands League for the first time as well as the North Midlands League Cup.

SOUTHEND'S RECORD

Southend United created 17 club records in 1980–81. They recorded 42 home points; 30 wins including 19 at home; 18 successive home wins; 15 successive home wins from the start of the season; 32 unbeaten home games; 31 goals against; 11 away wins; 25 clean sheets including 17 at home, ten of them successively; ten 'doubles' against other teams; six goals against at home (a new Fourth Division record); goalkeeper Mervyn Cawston completed 982 minutes without conceding a home goal between August and December; they were undefeated throughout the season at home; had fewest defeats in a season; and no team completed the 'double' against them.

LEADING GOALSCORERS 1980–81

Listed in order of League goals scored.

DIVISION 1

	League	*League Cup*	*FA Cup*	*Total*
Steve Archibald (Tottenham H)	20	2	3	25
Peter Withe (Aston Villa)	20	1	–	21
Justin Fashanu (Norwich C)	19	3	–	22
Mick Robinson (Brighton & HA)	19	3	–	22
John Wark (Ipswich T)	18	2	2	22
Steve Moran (Southampton)	18	–	3	21
Gary Shaw (Aston Villa)	18	2	–	20
Alan Brazil (Ipswich T)	17	–	–	17
Garth Crooks (Tottenham H)	16	2	4	22
Frank Worthington (Birmingham C)	16	1	1	18
Peter Eastoe (Everton)	15	1	2	18
Lee Chapman (Stoke C)	15	1	1	17
Joe Jordan (Manchester U)	15	–	–	15
Cyrille Regis (WBA)	14	3	–	17
Frank Stapleton (Arsenal)	14	2	–	16
Paul Mariner (Ipswich T)	13	4	3	20
John Richards (Wolverhampton W)	13	–	4	17
Terry McDermott (Liverpool)	13	1	1	15
Kevin Reeves (Manchester C)	12	1	4	17
Glenn Hoddle (Tottenham H)	12	1	2	15
Bosco Jankovic (Middlesbrough)	12	–	1	13
Ian Wallace (Nottingham F)	11	1	1	13
Eric Gates (Ipswich T)	11	–	2	13
Kevin Keegan (Southampton)	11	–	1	12
Tommy Langley (Crystal Palace)	11	1	–	12
(inc 8 for QPR plus 1 League Cup)				
Tony Morley (Aston Villa)	10	2	–	12
Ally Brown (WBA)	10	1	–	11
Bryan Robson (WBA)	10	–	1	11
Gary Rowell (Sunderland)	10	–	1	11
Mike Channon (Southampton)	10	–	–	10
Carl Harris (Leeds U)	10	–	–	10
Craig Johnston (Middlesbrough)	10	–	–	10
Gordon Smith (Brighton & HA)	10	–	–	10

DIVISION 2

	League	*League Cup*	*FA Cup*	*Total*
David Cross (West Ham U)	22	5	–	27
Brian Stein (Luton T)	18	1	–	19
Paul Goddard (West Ham U)	17	4	a1–	21
Andy McCulloch (Sheffield W)	18	–	–	18
David Moss (Luton T)	16	1	2	19
Leighton James (Swansea C)	15	1	–	16
Colin Lee (Chelsea)	15	–	1	16
Trevor Christie (Notts Co)	14	4	1	19
Mick Harford (Newcastle U)	14	5	–	19
(inc 10 for Lincoln C in League, 5 in League Cup)				
Neil Whatmore (Bolton W)	14	–	1	15
Malcolm Poskett (Watford)	13	6	2	21
Alex Bruce (Preston NE)	13	1	1	15
Dixie McNeil (Wrexham)	13	–	2	15
Brian Kidd (Bolton W)	13	1	–	14
Peter Kitchen (Cardiff C)	13	1	–	14
Alan Mayes (Chelsea)	12	3	1	16
(inc 8 for Swindon T plus League Cup, FA Cup)				
Rodger Wylde (Oldham Ath)	12	–	–	12
Luther Blissett (Watford)	11	2	–	13
Bob Cumming (Grimsby T)	11	–	–	11
Iain McCulloch (Notts Co)	11	–	–	11
Dave Swindlehurst (Derby Co)	11	–	–	11
Clive Walker (Chelsea)	11	–	–	11
Joe Waters (Grimsby T)	10	1	–	11
Alan Biley (Derby Co)	10	–	–	10
Trevor Brooking (West Ham U)	10	–	–	10
Alan Gowling (Bolton W)	10	–	–	10

DIVISION 3

	League	*League Cup*	*FA Cup*	*Total*
Tony Kellow (Exeter C)	25	2	6	33
David Kemp (Portsmouth)	24	1	3	28
Ronnie Moore (Rotherham U)	23	–	2	25
Alan Birch (Chesterfield)	22	–	1	23
Ronnie Glavin (Barnsley)	18	5	1	24
Gordon Davies (Fulham)	18	1	3	22
Bob Hatton (Sheffield U)	18	1	1	20
Steve Kindon (Huddersfield T)	18	1	–	19
Derek Hales (Charlton Ath)	17	2	4	23
Gordon Staniforth (Carlisle U)	16	–	–	16
Steve Taylor (Burnley)	16	–	–	16
Terry Austin (Huddersfield T)	15	1	–	16
(inc 7 for Mansfield T plus 1 League Cup)				
Dave Gwyther (Newport Co)	15	1		16
Ian Banks (Barnsley)	14	2	1	17
Ernie Moss (Chesterfield)	14	2	–	16
Keith Edwards (Hull C)	13	–	4	17
David Gregory (Portsmouth)	13	2	–	15
Tommy Tynan (Newport Co)	13	2	–	15
Trevor Lee (Gillingham)	13	–	2	15
(inc 7 for Colchester U, plus 2 FA Cup)				
Kerry Dixon (Reading)	13	–	–	13
Colin Morris (Blackpool)	12	3	1	16
Brian Stanton (Huddersfield T)	12	–	4	16
Trevor Aylott (Barnsley)	12	–	3	15
Andy Rowland (Swindon T)	12	1	–	13
Paul Walsh (Charlton Ath)	11	6	1	18
Ian Robins (Huddersfield T)	11	–	4	15
Alan Buckley (Walsall)	11	1	1	13
Ken Price (Gillingham)	11	1	1	13
Rodney Fern (Rotherham U)	11	–	–	11
Alan Waddle (Newport Co)	11	–	–	11
(inc 7 for Swansea C)				
Peter Beardsley (Carlisle U)	10	–	5	15
Derrick Parker (Barnsley)	10	2	3	15
Martin Robinson (Charlton Ath)	10	2	1	13

DIVISION 4

	League	*League Cup*	*FA Cup*	*Total*
Alan Cork (Wimbledon)	23	1	2	26
Robbie Cooke (Peterborough U)	22	3	4	29
Alan Walsh (Darlington)	22	1	–	23
Jim Lumby (Mansfield T)	22	–	–	22
(inc 18 for Tranmere R)				
Graham Hobson (Lincoln C)	21	–	–	21
Derek Spence (Southend U)	21	–	–	21
Bobby Campbell (Bradford C)	19	3	1	23
Steve Phillips (Northampton T)	19	2	1	22
Steve Johnson (Bury)	18	3	–	21
Ian Nimmo (Doncaster R)	18	1	–	19
Terry Gray (Southend U)	17	–	–	17
Keith Houchen (Hartlepool U)	17	–	–	17
John Stalker (Darlington)	17	–	–	17
Steve Cammack (Scunthorpe U)	15	1	–	16
Mick Quinn (Wigan Ath)	14	–	–	14
Barry Wellings (Rochdale)	14	–	–	14
Paul Hilton (Bury)	13	–	2	15
Billy Kellock (Peterborough U)	13	1	–	14
Keith Bowen (Northampton T)	13	–	–	13
Peter Coyne (Crewe Alex)	13	–	–	13
Peter Denyer (Northampton T)	13	–	–	13
Gerry Fell (Torquay U)	12	1	4	17
Mark Hilditch (Rochdale)	12	–	–	12
John Leslie (Wimbledon)	11	3	1	15
Steve Cooper (Torquay U)	11	–	2	13
Ian McDonald (York C)	11	1	–	12
Trevor Morgan (Bournemouth)	10	–	2	12
Les Bradd (Stockport Co)	10	1	–	11
Frank McGrellis (Hereford U)	10	–	–	10
Dean Mooney (Bournemouth)	10	–	–	10
Craig Madden (Bury)	10	–	–	10
Keith Mercer (Southend U)	10	–	–	10
Bob Newton (Hartlepool U)	10	–	–	10

LEADING SCORERS IN LEAGUE SINCE 1946–47

1946–47

Division 1

D. Westcott (Wolverhampton W)	37
D. Reid (Portsmouth)	29
F. Steele (Stoke C)	29
R. Lewis (Arsenal)	28
S. Mortensen (Blackpool)	28

Division 3 (South)

D. Clark (Bristol C)	36
M. G. McPhee (Reading)	31
S. Richards (Cardiff C)	31
A. Garrett (Northampton T)	26
J. W. Stephens (Swindon T)	25

Division 2

C. Wayman (Newcastle U)	30
D. J. Walsh (WBA)	28
G. Lowrie (Coventry C)	26
G. Robledo (Barnsley)	24

Division 3 (North)

C. Jordan (Doncaster R)	42
W. Ardron (Rotherham U)	38
R. Yates (Chester)	36
P. M. Cheetham (Lincoln C)	28

1947–48

Division 1

a1R.Rooke(Arsenal)	33
M. Fenton (Middlesbrough)	28
A. Stubbins (Liverpool)	26
J. Rowley (Manchester U)	23
S. Mortensen (Blackpool)	21

Division 3 (South)

L. Townsend (Bristol C)	29
D. Milligan (Bournemouth & BA)	26
D. Massart (Walsall)	23
C. Hatton (QPR)	21

Division 2

E. Quigley (Sheffield W)	23
A. J. Wakefield (Leeds U)	22
D. J. Walsh (WBA)	22
J. Milburn (Newcastle U)	21
J. Downie (Bradford)	19

Division 3 (North)

J. Hutchinson (Lincoln C)	32
W. Ardron (Rotherham U)	27
J. Lindsay (Carlisle U)	26
T. Wyles (Southport)	26
W. F. Tunnicliffe (Wrexham)	20

1948–49

Division 1

W. Moir (Bolton W)	25
F. Bowyer (Stoke C)	21
R. Bentley (Chelsea)	20
J. Rowley (Manchester U)	20
C. Vaughan (Charlton Ath)	20

Division 3 (South)

D. McGibbon (Bournemouth & BA)	30
S. Richards (Swansea T)	26
J. Sewell (Notts County)	26
P. E. Chapman (Walsall)	25
W. M. Jones (Swindon T)	25

Division 2

C. Wayman (Southampton)	32
T. Briggs (Grimsby T)	26
D. Massart (Bury)	25
R. Thomas (Fulham)	23
D. J. Walsh (WBA)	23

Division 3 (North)

W. Ardron (Rotherham U)	29
A. Patrick (York C)	26
A. Quinn (Darlington)	23
N. W. Moore (Hull C)	22
E. Gemmell (Oldham Ath)	19

1949–50

Division 1

D. Davis (Sunderland)	25
S. Mortensen (Blackpool)	22
J. Stamps (Derby Co)	22
H. Goring (Arsenal)	21
J. Rowley (Manchester U)	20

Division 3 (South)

T. Lawton (Notts Co)	31
W. Ardron (Nottingham F)	25
A. J. Wakefield (Southend U)	23
R. Blackman (Reading)	22
J. Devlin (Walsall)	22

Division 2

T. Briggs (Grimsby T)	35
C. Wayman (Southampton)	24
W. Robinson (West Ham U)	23
J. Lee (Leicester C)	22
L. Medley (Tottenham H)	18

Division 3 (North)

P. Doherty (Doncaster R)	26
R. Phillips, (Crewe Alex)	26
A. C. Burgess (Chester)	24
E. Dodds (Lincoln C)	21
D. Travis (Accrington Stanley)	20

1950–51

Division 1

S. Mortensen (Blackpool)	30
J. Lee (Derby Co)	28
N. Lofthouse (Bolton W)	21
A. McCrae (Middlesbrough)	21
D. Reid (Portsmouth)	21

Division 3 (South)

W. Ardron (Nottingham F)	36
R. Blackman (Reading)	35
J. Constantine (Millwall)	27
M. Tadman (Plymouth Arg)	23

Division 2

J. McCormack (Barnsley)	33
A. Rowley (Leicester C)	28
C. Wayman (Preston NE)	27
W. Robinson (West Ham U)	26

Division 3 (North)

J. Shaw (Rotherham U)	37
R. Crosbie (Bradford)	27
L. E. Wildon (Hartlepools U)	26
A. Burgess (Chester)	22
J. Nuttall (Southport)	22

1951–52

Division 1		Division 2	
G. Robledo (Newcastle U)	33	D. Dooley (Sheffield W)	46
R. Allen (WBA)	32	A. Rowley (Leicester C)	38
J. Rowley (Manchester U)	30	W. Ardron (Nottingham F)	29
J. Dixon (Aston Villa)	26	W. Grant (Cardiff C)	26
C. Wayman (Preston NE)	24	**Division 3 (North)**	
Division 3 (South)		A. Graver (Lincoln C)	36
R. Blackman (Reading)	39	W. Cairns (Grimsby T)	32
V. Lambden (Bristol R)	29	W. Fenton (York C)	31
M. Tadman (Plymouth Arg)	27	E. Gemmell (Oldham Ath)	28
F. Ramscar (Northampton T)	24	D. Frost (Halifax T)	24

1952–53

Division 1		Division 2	
C. Wayman (Preston NE)	24	A. Rowley (Leicester C)	39
P. Harris (Portsmouth)	23	B. Jezzard (Fulham)	34
D. Lishman (Arsenal)	23	J. Glazzard (Huddersfield T)	30
		J. Charles (Leeds U)	26
		J. Pye (Luton T)	24
Division 3 (South)		**Division 3 (North)**	
G. Bradford (Bristol R)	33	J. Whitehouse (Carlisle U)	29
R. Collins (Torquay U)	27	J. Connor (Stockport Co)	26
J. English (Northampton T)	26	W. Fenton (York C)	24
A. W. Rodgers (Bristol C)	26	E. Gemmell (Oldham Ath)	24
W. O'Donnell (Northampton T)	26	D. Travis (Chester)	24

1953–54

Division 1		Division 2	
J. Glazzard (Huddersfield T)	29	J. Charles (Leeds U)	42
J. Nicholls (WBA)	29	B. Jezzard (Fulham)	38
R. Allen (WBA)	25	T. Briggs (Blackburn R)	32
J. Hancocks (Wolverhampton W)	25	R. Burke (Rotherham U)	32
D. Wilshaw (Wolverhampton W)	25	J. W. Parker (Everton)	31
Division 3 (South)		**Division 3 (North)**	
J. English (Northampton T)	28	J. Connor (Stockport Co)	31
R. Blackman (Reading)	27	G. Ashman (Carlisle U)	30
E. Day (Southampton)	26	C. Done (Tranmere R)	25
L. Graham (Newport Co)	24	R. Brown (Barnsley)	24
J. Atyeo (Bristol C)	23	K. Murray (Mansfield T)	22

1954–55

Division 1		Division 2	
R. Allen (WBA)	27	T. Briggs (Blackburn R)	33
J. Glazzard (Huddersfield T)	26	G. Turner (Luton T)	32
E. Firmani (Charlton Ath)	25	W. Liddell (Liverpool)	30
J. Hancocks (Wolverhampton W)	25	J. Evans (Liverpool)	29
		G. Bradford (Bristol R)	27
Division 3 (South)		**Division 3 (North)**	
E. Morgan (Gillingham)	31	A. Bottom (York C)	30
J. Atyeo (Bristol C)	28	J. Connor (Stockport Co)	30
E. Day (Southampton)	27	D. Travis (Oldham Ath)	30
R. Hollis (Southend U)	27	G. Stewart (Accrington S)	28
		J. Whitehouse (Carlisle U)	25

1955–56

Division 1		Division 2	
N. Lofthouse (Bolton W)	33	W. Gardiner (Leicester C)	34
C. Fleming (Sunderland)	28	R. Shiner (Sheffield W)	33
V. Keeble (Newcastle U)	26	T. Briggs (Blackburn R)	31
T. Taylor (Manchester U)	25	J. Atyeo (Bristol C)	30
		J. Charles (Leeds U)	30
Division 3 (South)		**Division 3 (North)**	
R. Collins (Torquay U)	40	R. Crosbie (Grimsby T)	36
R. A. R. Hunt (Norwich C)	31	G. Stewart (Accrington S)	35
T. Parker (Ipswich T)	30	W. Sowden (Chesterfield)	32
K. McCurley (Colchester U)	29	A. Bottom (York C)	31
A. Mundy (Brighton & HA)	27	J. Connor (Stockport Co)	30

1956–57

Division 1

J. Charles (Leeds U)	38
J. Mudie (Blackpool)	32
G. Turner (Luton T)	30
N. Lofthouse (Bolton W)	28

Division 3 (South)

E. Phillips (Ipswich T)	41
R. Collins (Torquay U)	30
S. Newsham (Bournemouth & BA)	30
T. Dixon (Reading)	28
B. Edwards (Swindon T)	25

Division 2

A. Rowley (Leicester C)	44
B. Clough (Middlesbrough)	38
T. Briggs (Blackburn R)	32
J. Barrett (Nottingham F)	27
T. Johnston (Leyton O)	27

Division 3 (North)

R. Straw (Derby Co)	37
G. Stewart (Accrington S)	33
W. Tulip (Darlington)	32
R. Smith (Bradford)	28
W. Gordon (Barrow)	27

1957–58

Division 1

R. Smith (Tottenham H)	36
T. Thompson (Preston NE)	34
G. Turner (Luton T)	33
J. Murray (Wolverhampton W)	29
T. Finney (Preston NE)	26

Division 3 (South)

S. McCrory (Southend U)	31
D. Reeves (Southampton)	31
E. Towers (Brentford)	29
W. Carter (Plymouth Arg)	26
T. Dixon (Reading)	24

Division 2

T. Johnston (Leyton O 35, plus 8 for Blackburn R)	43
B. Clough (Middlesbrough)	40
J. Summers (Charlton Ath)	28
R. Rafferty (Grimsby T)	26
J. Atyeo (Bristol C)	23

Division 3 (North)

A. Ackerman (Carlisle U)	35
K. Williams (Tranmere R)	28
G. Stewart (Accrington Stanley)	27
B. Jepson (Chester)	25
J. Parker (Bury)	25

1958–59

Division 1

J. Greaves (Chelsea)	32
R. Smith (Tottenham H)	32
R. Charlton (Manchester U)	29
N. Lofthouse (Bolton W)	29

Division 3

E. Towers (Brentford)	32
W. Bradbury (Hull C)	30
J. McCole (Bradford C)	28
C. Smith (Hull C)	26
T. Rowley (Tranmere R)	25

Division 2

B. Clough (Middlesbrough)	42
R. Shiner (Sheffield W)	28
R. Froggatt (Sheffield W)	26
D. Pace (Sheffield U)	26
D. Ward (Bristol R)	26

Division 4

A. Rowley (Shrewsbury T)	37
A. Woan (Northampton T)	32
A. Richards (Walsall)	28
E. Calland (Exeter C)	27
R. Straw (Coventry C)	27

1959–60

Division 1

D. Viollet (Manchester U)	32
J. Greaves (Chelsea)	29
J. Murray (Wolverhampton W)	29
L. White (Newcastle U)	28
D. Kevan (WBA)	26

Division 3

D. Reeves (Southampton)	39
R. Hunt (Grimsby T)	33
A. Rowley (Shrewsbury T)	32
M. King (Colchester U)	30
D. Price (Southend U)	28

Division 2

B. Clough (Middlesbrough)	39
E. Phillips (Ipswich T)	24
T. Johnston (Leyton Orient)	24
W. Curry (Brighton & HA)	23
G. Hitchens (Aston Villa)	23

Division 4

C. Holton (Watford)	42
E. Uphill (Watford)	30
J. Allan (Bradford)	27
H. Llewellyn (Crewe Alex)	25

1960–61

Division 1

J. Greaves (Chelsea)	41
D. Herd (Arsenal)	29
G. Hitchens (Aston Villa)	29
J. Farmer (Wolverhampton W)	28
R. Smith (Tottenham H)	28

Division 3

A. Richards (Walsall)	36
B. Bedford (QPR)	33
C. Taylor (Walsall)	33
C. Holton (Watford)	32
J. Wheeler (Reading)	31

Division 2

R. Crawford (Ipswich T)	39
B. Clough (Middlesbrough)	34
E. Phillips (Ipswich T)	30

Division 4

T. Bly (Peterborough U)	52
G. Hudson (Accrington Stanley)	35
P. Burridge (Millwall)	34
J. Byrne (Crystal Palace)	30
R. Summersby (Crystal Palace)	25

1961–62

Division 1

R. Crawford (Ipswich T)	33
D. Kevan (WBA)	33
R. Charnley (Blackpool)	30
E. Phillips (Ipswich T)	28
T. R. Vernon (Everton)	28

Division 3

C. Holton (Northampton T 36, plus 1 for Watford)	37
D. Bedford (QPR)	36
R. Rafferty (Grimsby T)	34
T. Bly (Peterborough U)	30
J. Atyeo (Bristol C)	26

Division 2

R. Hunt (Liverpool)	41
B. Thomas (Scunthorpe U)	31
B. Clough (Sunderland)	29
G. O'Brien (Southampton)	28
A. Peacock (Middlesbrough)	24

Division 4

R. R. Hunt (Colchester U)	37
D. Layne (Bradford C)	34
M. King (Colchester U)	31
F. Lord (Crewe Alex)	30
J. Weir (York C)	28

1962–63

Division 1

J. Greaves (Tottenham H)	37
J. Baker (Arsenal)	29
D. Layne (Sheffield W)	29
R. Crawford (Ipswich T)	25

Division 3

G. Hudson (Coventry C)	30
D. Ward (Watford)	29
M. King (Colchester U)	26
A. Ashworth (Northampton T)	25

Division 2

R. Tambling (Chelsea)	35
A. Peacock (Middlesbrough)	31
T. Allcock (Norwich C)	26
J. Storrie (Leeds U)	25
B. Clough (Sunderland)	24

Division 4

K. Wagstaff (Mansfield T)	34
C. Booth (Doncaster R)	34
R. Chapman (Mansfield T)	31
H. Lister (Oldham Ath)	30
F. Lord (Crewe Alex)	30

1963–64

Division 1

J. Greaves (Tottenham H)	35
M. McEvoy (Blackburn R)	32
R. Hunt (Liverpool)	31
D. Law (Manchester U)	30
R. Crawford (Wolverhampton W 26, plus 2 for Ipswich T)	28

Division 3

A. Biggs (Bristol R)	30
K. Wagstaff (Mansfield T)	29
D. Coughlin (Bournemouth & BA)	28
G. Hudson (Coventry C)	25

Division 2

R. Saunders (Portsmouth)	33
A. Dawson (Preston NE)	31
D. Kevan (Manchester C)	30
R. T. Davies (Norwich C)	26
J. Crossan (Sunderland)	22

Division 4

H. McIlmoyle (Carlisle U)	39
H. Green (Bradford C)	29
A. Spence (Southport)	27
J. Dyson (Tranmere R)	26
J. Bonson (Newport Co)	25

1964–65

Division 1

J. Greaves (Tottenham H)	29
A. McEvoy (Blackburn R)	29
D. Law (Manchester U)	28
F. Pickering (Everton)	27

Division 3

K. Wagstaff (Mansfield T 8, plus 23 for Hull C)	31
C. Chilton (Hull C)	27
J. Atyeo (Bristol C)	23
B. Bedford (QPR)	23
A. Clarke (Walsall)	23

Division 2

G. O'Brien (Southampton)	34
A. Dawson (Preston NE)	26
B. Godfrey (Preston NE)	25
A. Bennett (Rotherham U)	24
F. Lee (Bolton W)	23

Division 4

A. Jeffrey (Doncaster R)	36
T. Harkin (Crewe Alex)	35
R. Stubbs (Torquay U)	31
K. Hector (Bradford)	29

1965–66

Division 1

R. Hunt (Liverpool)	30
W. Irvine (Burnley)	29
T. Hateley (Aston Villa)	27
D. Herd (Manchester U)	24
G. Hurst (West Ham U)	23

Division 3

L. Allen (QPR)	30
M. Tees (Grimsby T)	28
K. Wagstaff (Hull C)	27
B. Gibbs (Gillingham)	23

Division 2

M. Chivers (Southampton)	30
G. Vowden (Birmingham C)	21
P. Knowles (Wolverhampton W)	20
J. Atyeo (Bristol C)	19

Division 4

K. Hector (Bradford)	44
J. O'Rourke (Luton T)	32
J. Dyson (Tranmere R)	29
L. Sheffield (Doncaster R)	28

1966–67

Division 1		Division 2	
R. Davies (Southampton)	37	R. Gould (Coventry C)	24
G. Hurst (West Ham U)	29	F. Lee (Bolton W)	22
J. Greaves (Tottenham H)	25	R. Crawford (Ipswich T)	21
A. Clarke (Fulham)	24	K. Wagstaff (Hull C)	21
D. Law (Manchester U)	23	E. Hunt (Wolverhampton W)	20
Division 3		**Division 4**	
R. Marsh (QPR)	30	E. Phythian (Hartlepools U)	23
J. O'Rourke (Middlesbrough	27	E. Chapman (Lincoln C)	20
I. Towers (Oldham Ath)	27	J. Mulvaney (Hartlepools U)	19
D. Rogers (Swindon T)	25	R. Smith (Southend U)	19

1967–68

Division 1		Division 2	
G. Best (Manchester U)	28	J. Hickton (Middlesbrough)	24
R. Davies (Southampton)	28	B. Bridges (Birmingham C)	23
J. Astle (WBA)	25	K. Hector (Derby Co)	21
R. Hunt (Liverpool)	25	G. Ingram (Blackpool)	18
J. Greaves (Tottenham H)	23	R. Woodruff (Crystal Palace)	18
Division 3		**Division 4**	
D. Rogers (Swindon T)	25	R. Chapman (Port Vale)	25
R. Owen (Bury)	25	L. Massie (Halifax T)	25
J. Fryatt (Torquay U 2 plus 22 for Stockport County)	24	B. Rioch (Luton T)	24
K. Napier (Brighton & HA)	24	E. Loyden (Chester)	22
G. Yardley (Tranmere R)	23	K. Randall (Chesterfield)	21

1968–69

Division 1		Division 2	
J. Greaves (Tottenham H)	27	J. Toshack (Cardiff C)	22
G. Hurst (West Ham U)	25	K. Wagstaff (Hull C)	20
J. Royle (Everton)	22	J. Hickton (Middlesbrough)	18
J. Astle (WBA)	21		
B. Robson (Newcastle U)	21		
Division 3		**Division 4**	
B. Lewis (Luton T)	22	G. Talbot (Chester)	22
D. Rogers (Swindon T)	22	W. Best (Southend U)	20
G. Andrews (Southport)	19	J. Howarth (Aldershot)	19
W. Atkins (Stockport Co)	18	E. MacDougall (York C)	19

1969–70

Division 1		Division 2	
J. Astle (WBA)	25	J. Hickton (Middlesbrough)	24
P. Osgood (Chelsea)	23	B. Bridges (QPR)	22
J. Royle (Everton)	23	J. Byrom (Bolton W)	20
B. Robson (Newcastle U)	22		
H. Curran (Wolverhampton W)	20		
Division 3		**Division 4**	
G. Jones (Bury)	26	A. Kinsey (Wrexham)	27
M. Macdonald (Luton T)	25	S. Brace (Grimsby T)	25
L. Chappell (Reading)	24	J. Hall (Peterborough U)	24
S. Earle (Fulham)	22		
E. MacDougall (Bournemouth & BA)	21		

1970–71

Division 1		Division 2	
A. Brown (WBA)	28	J. Hickton (Middlesbrough)	25
M. Chivers (Tottenham H)	21	M. Macdonald (Luton T)	24
A. Clarke (Leeds U)	19	C. Chilton (Hull C)	21
R. Kennedy (Arsenal)	19	R. Marsh (QPR)	21
		R. Hatton (Carlisle U)	18
Division 3		**Division 4**	
G. Ingram (Preston NE)	22	E. MacDougall (Bournemouth & BA)	42
D. Roberts (Mansfield T)	22	P. Aimson (York C)	26
K. Randall (Chesterfield)	19	R. Crawford (Colchester U)	25
		J. Fryatt (Oldham Ath)	24

1971–72

Division 1

F. Lee (Manchester C)	33
M. Chivers (Tottenham H)	25
P. Lorimer (Leeds U)	23
M. Macdonald (Newcastle U)	23
P. Osgood (Chelsea)	19

Division 3

E. MacDougall (Bournemouth & BA)	35
A. Wood (Shrewsbury T)	35
C. Gilbert (Rotherham U)	22
L. Bradd (Notts Co)	21
A. Lochhead (Aston Villa)	19

Division 2

R. Latchford (Birmingham C)	23
J. Galley (Bristol C)	22
R. Hatton (Carlisle U 7 plus 15 for Birmingham C)	22
B. Clark (Cardiff C)	21
F. Casper (Burnley)	18

Division 4

P. Price (Peterborough U)	28
R. McNeil (Lincoln C 13 plus 14 for Northampton T)	27
M. Tees (Grimsby T)	27
W. Garner (Southend U)	25
J. O'Mara (Brentford)	25

1972–73

Division 1

B. Robson (West Ham U)	28
J. Richards (Wolverhampton W)	27
W. Dearden (Sheffield U)	20
R. Latchford (Birmingham C)	19

Division 3

B. Bannister (Bristol R)	25
A. Horsfield (Charlton Ath)	25
J. Byrom (Bolton W)	20
E. Loyden (Tranmere R)	19
K. Randall (Notts Co)	19

Division 2

D. Givens (QPR)	23
G. Bolland (Millwall)	19
S. Bowles (QPR)	17
A. Gowling (Huddersfield T)	17
S. Pearson (Hull C)	11

Division 4

F. Binney (Exeter C)	28
J. Hall (Peterborough U)	21
R. McNeil (Lincoln C)	21
A. Provan (Southport)	21
J. Fairbrother (Mansfield T)	20

1973–74

Division 1

M. Channon (Southampton)	21
F. Worthington (Leicester C)	20
S. Bowles (QPR)	19
K. Hector (Derby Co)	18

Division 3

W. Jennings (Watford)	26
J. Howarth (Aldershot)	25
A. Gowling (Huddersfield T)	24
A. Warboys (Bristol R)	22
A. Buckley (Walsall)	21

Division 2

D. McKenzie (Nottingham F)	26
A. Wood (Millwall)	21
T. Brown (WBA)	19
A. Foggon (Middlesbrough)	19

Division 4

B. Yeo (Gillingham)	31
F. Binney (Exeter C)	25
L. Chappell (Reading)	24
R. Svarc (Colchester U)	24

1974–75

Division 1

M. Macdonald (Newcastle U)	21
B. Kidd (Arsenal)	19
F. Worthington (Leicester C)	18
K. Hibbitt (Wolverhampton W)	17
R. Latchford (Everton)	17

Division 3

R. McNeil (Hereford U)	31
P. Eastoe (Swindon T)	26
R. Svarc (Colchester U)	24
W. Rafferty (Plymouth Arg)	23

Division 2

B. Little (Aston Villa)	20
M. Channon (Southampton)	19
R. Graydon (Aston Villa)	19
B. Robson (Sunderland)	19

Division 4

R. Clarke (Mansfield T)	28
R. Habbin (Rotherham U 10 plus 12 for Reading)	22
R. Haywood (Shrewsbury T)	21
P. Kitchen (Doncaster R)	21
E. Woods (Newport County)	21

1975–76

Division 1

E. MacDougall (Norwich C)	23
J. Duncan (Tottenham H)	20
M. Macdonald (Newcastle U)	19
J. Richards (Wolverhampton W)	17
T. Francis (Birmingham C)	17

Division 3

R. McNeil (Hereford U)	35
A. Buckley (Walsall)	34
R. Clarke (Mansfield T)	24
F. Binney (Brighton & HA)	23
T. Evans (Cardiff C)	21

Division 2

D. Hales (Charlton Ath)	28
M. Channon (Southampton)	19
T. Ritchie (Bristol C)	18
M. Walsh (Blackpool)	17
L. Bradd (Notts Co)	16

Division 4

R. Moore (Tranmere R)	34
J. Ward (Lincoln C)	24
N. Freeman (Lincoln C)	23

1976–77

Division 1

A. Gray (Aston Villa)	25
M. Macdonald (Arsenal)	25
B. Kidd (Manchester C)	21
T. Francis (Birmingham C)	21

Division 2

M. Walsh (Blackpool)	26
N. Whatmore (Bolton W)	25
S. Finnieston (Chelsea)	24
E. MacDougall (Southampton)	23
M. Flanagan (Charlton Ath)	23

Division 3

P. Ward (Brighton & HA)	32
G. Whittle (Wrexham)	28
A. Bruce (Preston NE)	24
A. Crawford (Rotherham U)	23

Division 4

B. Joicey (Barnsley)	25
P. Kitchen (Doncaster R)	23
J. Charles (Swansea C)	23
G. Sweetzer (Brentford)	23

1977–78

Division 1

R. Latchford (Everton)	30
T. Francis (Birmingham C)	25
K. Dalglish (Liverpool)	20
I. Wallace (Coventry C)	20
R. Hankin (Leeds U)	20

Division 2

R. Hatton (Blackpool)	22
P. Kitchen (Orient)	21
P. Randall (Bristol R)	20
S. Taylor (Oldham Ath)	20

Division 3

A. Bruce (Preston NE)	27
A. Buckley (Walsall)	24
A. Biley (Cambridge U)	21
J. Lumby (Carlisle U 1, plus 20 for Scunthorpe U)	21

Division 4

S. Phillips (Brentford)	32
A. Curtis (Swansea C)	32
J. Dungworth (Aldershot)	23
A. McCulloch (Brentford)	22

1978–79

Division 1

F. Worthington (Bolton W)	24
K. Dalglish (Liverpool)	21
A. Brown (WBA)	18
F. Stapleton (Arsenal)	17

Division 2

B. Robson (West Ham U)	24
A. Bruce (Preston NE)	21
G. Rowell (Sunderland)	21
A. Biley (Cambridge U)	20

Division 3

R. Jenkins (Watford)	29
F. Binney (Plymouth Arg)	26
K. Edwards (Hull C)	24
L. Blissett (Watford)	21

Division 4

J. Dungworth (Aldershot)	26
A. Cork (Wimbledon)	22
D. Bell (Barnsley 18, plus 3 for Halifax T)	21
S. Lee (Stockport Co)	20

1979–80

Division 1

P. Boyer (Southampton)	23
D. Johnson (Liverpool)	21
A. Biley (Derby Co 9, plus 12 for Cambridge U)	21
G. Hoddle (Tottenham H)	19

Division 2

C. Allen (QPR)	28
D. Moss (Luton T)	24
B. Robson (Sunderland)	20
A. Shoulder (Newcastle U)	20

Division 3

T. Curran (Sheffield W)	22
A. Rowland (Swindon T)	20
R. Glavin (Barnsley)	20

Division 4

C. Garwood (Aldershot 10, plus 17 for Portsmouth)	27
I. Robins (Huddersfield T)	25
D. Penn (Walsall)	25
W. Kellock (Peterborough U)	19

THE MANAGERS

A directory of Football League managers with biographical details. In some entries information has been at the discretion of individuals.

ADDISON, Colin. *Manager:* Hereford U (player-manager), Durban C, Notts Co (assistant), Newport Co, West Bromwich Albion (assistant), Derby Co July 1979– . *Honours:* Promotion to Division 3 1973. *Player:* York C, Nottingham F, Arsenal, Sheffield U, Hereford U.

ALLEN, Ronnie. *Manager:* Wolverhampton W, Athletic Bilbao, Sporting Lisbon, Walsall, WBA, Saudi Arabia, Panathinaikos, WBA July 1981– . *Player:* Port Vale, WBA, Crystal Palace. *Honours:* FA Cup winners medal 1954. Five full England caps.

ANDERSON, Peter. *Player-Manager:* Millwall Dec 1980– . *Player:* Hendon, Luton T, San Diego, Antwerp, Tampa Bay R, Sheffield U, Millwall.

ASHURST, Len. *Manager:* Hartlepool, Gillingham, Sheffield W, Newport Co June 1978– . *Player:* Sunderland 1957–1971; Hartlepool 1971–1973. *Honours:* One Under-23 cap for England. Promotion to Div 3 1980.

ATKINSON, Ron. *Manager:* Kettering T, Cambridge U, WBA, Manchester U June 1981– . *Honours:* Division 4 Champions 1977. *Player:* Aston Villa, Oxford U, Kettering T. *Honours:* Promotion to Division 3 1965; Division 3 Championship medal 1968.

BAILEY, Mike. *Manager:* Charlton Ath, Brighton & HA June 1981– . *Honours:* Promotion to Division 2, 1981. *Player-Manager:* Hereford U. *Player-Coach:* Minnesota Kicks. *Player:* Charlton Ath, Wolverhampton W. *Honours:* Five Under-23 and two full England caps.

BARKER, Richie. *Manager:* Stoke C June 1981– . Formerly assistant-manager Wolverhampton W. *Player:* Derby Co, Notts Co.

BARLOW, Frank. *Manager:* Chesterfield 1980– . *Honours:* Anglo-Scottish Cup 1981. *Player:* Sheffield U, Chesterfield. *Coach:* Chesterfield.

BARNWELL, John. *Manager:* Peterborough U, Wolverhampton W November 1978– . *Player:* Bishop Auckland, Arsenal, Nottingham F, Sheffield U. *Honours:* Youth international, one Under-23 cap for England. League Cup winners 1980.

BASSETT, Dave. *Manager:* Wimbledon Jan 1981– . *Honours:* Promotion to Division 3 1981. *Player:* Watford, Chelsea, Wimbledon.

BLOOMFIELD, Jimmy. *Manager:* Orient 1969, Leicester C 1971, Orient September 1977– . *Player:* Brentford, Arsenal, Birmingham C, West Ham U, Plymouth Arg, Orient (player-manager). *Honours:* Two Under-23 caps for England.

BOAM, Stuart. *Player-Manager:* Mansfield T July 1981– . *Player:* Mansfield T, Middlesbrough, Newcastle U. *Honours:* Division 2 championship medal 1974.

BOND, John. *Manager:* AFC Bournemouth, Norwich C, Manchester C Oct 1980– . *Honours:* AFC Bournemouth, Promotion to Division 3; Norwich C, Promotion to Division 1 1975; Manchester C FA Cup runners-up 1981. *Player:* West Ham U (17 years), Torquay U (3 years). *Honours:* West Ham U Division 2 Championship medal 1958; FA Cup winners medal 1964; Torquay U, Promotion to Division 3 1966.

BREMNER, Billy. *Manager:* Doncaster R, November 1978– . *Honours:* Promotion to Division 3, 1981. *Player:* Leeds U, Hull C. *Honours:* FA Cup winners medal 1972, runners-up 1965, 1970, 1973. League Cup winners medal 1968; European Cup runners-up medal 1975; UEFA Cup winners medal 1968, 1971; runners-up 1967. Footballer of the Year 1970. Fifty-four full Scottish caps.

BROWN, Allan. *Manager:* Luton T 1967; Torquay U 1969; Bury 1972; Nottingham F 1974; Southport 1976; Blackpool, Southport, Blackpool 1981– . *Honours:* Luton T, Division 4 Champions 1968. *Player:* East Fife 1944–1950; Blackpool 1950–1956; Luton T 1956–1960; Portsmouth 1960–1964. *Honours:* East Fife, League Cup winners medal 1950; Scottish Cup runners-up medal 1950; Blackpool, FA Cup finals (injured) 1951, 1953. Luton T, FA Cup runners-up medal 1959.

BROWN, Ken. *Manager:* Norwich C Nov 1980– . Formerly assistant manager. *Player:* West Ham U, Torquay U, Hereford U. Trainer-coach Bournemouth. *Honours:* West Ham U, Division 2 Championship 1958. FA Cup winners medal 1964, European Cup-Winners' Cup winners medal 1965, League Cup runners-up medal 1966.

BUCKLEY, Alan. *Player-Manager:* Walsall 1980– . *Player:* Walsall, Birmingham C, Walsall. *Honours:* Promotion to Division Three 1980.

BULLOCK, Mickey. *Manager:* Halifax T July 1981– (formerly Coach). *Player:* Birmingham C, Oxford U, Orient, Halifax T.

BURKINSHAW, Keith. *Manager:* Tottenham H July 1976– . *Honours:* Promotion to Division 1 1978, FA Cup winners 1981. *Coach:* Newcastle U 1968–1975; Tottenham H 1975–1976. *Honours:* FA Cup finalists 1974. *Player:* Liverpool 1954–1958; Workington 1958–1965; Scunthorpe U 1965–1968.

BURROWS, Frank. *Manager:* Portsmouth May 1979– . *Assistant Manager:* Swindon T. *Coach:* Portsmouth 1978. *Player:* Raith R, Scunthorpe U, Swindon T, Mansfield T (on loan). *Honours:* Promotion Div 3 1980.

BUXTON, Mick. *Manager:* Huddersfield T October 1978– . *Coach:* Huddersfield T, Southend U. *Player:* Burnley, Halifax T. *Honours:* Div 4 Champions 1980.

CALLAGHAN, Fred. *Manager:* Woking, Brentford 1980– . *Player:* Fulham. *Coach:* Brentford.

CHARLTON, Jack, OBE. *Manager:* Middlesbrough, Sheffield W October 1977– . *Honours:* 'Manager of the Year' 1974. *Player:* Leeds U 1952–1973. *Honours:* Division 2 Championship medal 1964; FA Cup runners-up medal 1965; World Cup winners medal 1966; Fairs Cup runners-up medal 1967; 'Footballer of the Year' 1967; League Cup winners medal 1968; Fairs Cup winners medal 1968; Division 1 championship medal 1969; FA Cup runners-up medal 1970; Fairs Cup winners medal 1971; FA Cup winners medal 1972. Promotion Div 2 1980.

CLARKE, Allan. *Manager:* Barnsley, Leeds U Sept 1980– . *Player:* Walsall, Fulham, Leicester C, Leeds U. *Honours:* Promotion Barnsley 1979; Division 1 championship medal 1974; FA Cup winners medal 1972; runners-up medals 1970, 1973; European Cup runners-up medal 1975; UEFA Cup winners medal 1971. Six Under-23 and nineteen full England caps.

CLOUGH, Brian. *Manager:* Hartlepool, Derby Co, Brighton & HA, Leeds U, Nottingham F January 1975– . *Honours:* Division 2 Championship 1969; Division 1 Championship 1972; Promotion to Division 1 1977; Division 1 Championship 1978; League Cup winners 1978, 1979; European Cup winners 1979, 1980; Division 1 runners-up 1979. *Player:* Middlesbrough, Sunderland. *Honours:* Three Under-23 caps and two full caps for England.

COOPER, Terry. *Player-Manager:* Bristol R 1980– . *Player:* Leeds U, Bristol R. *Coach:* Bristol R. *Honours:* 20 full England caps.

COX, Arthur. *Manager:* Chesterfield, Newcastle U Sept 1980– . *Coach:* Youth coach Coventry C, chief coach Walsall, Aston Villa, Preston NE, Halifax T. *Assistant Manager:* Sunderland. *Honours:* Preston NE Division 3 Championship; Sunderland Division 2 Championship; FA Cup winners 1973. *Player:* Coventry C 1955–1958 (broken leg ended career at 18). Joined coaching staff.

DODGIN, Bill. *Manager:* QPR, Fulham, Northampton T, Brentford, Northampton T Oct 1980– . *Honours:* Fulham to Division 2 1971, Northampton T Division 3 1976, Brentford Division 3 1978. *Player:* Fulham 1949–1952; Arsenal 1952–1961; Fulham 1961–1965. *Honours:* Under-23 cap for England.

DOCHERTY, John. *Manager:* Brentford, Cambridge U January 1978– . *Coach:* Cambridge U. *Player:* Brentford 1959–1961; 1965–1968; 1970–1974; Sheffield U 1961–1965; Reading 1968–1970; QPR player/coach 1974–1975.

DOCHERTY, Tommy. *Manager:* Chelsea 1962; Rotherham U 1967; Aston Villa 1969; Porto FC; Scottish Team Manager; Manchester U 1973; Derby Co 1977; QPR 1979, Sydney Olympic 1980; Preston NE June 1981– . *Honours:* Qualified for 1974 World Cup with Scotland; Manchester U, Division 2 Champions 1975; FA Cup winners 1977. *Player:* Celtic 1949; Preston NE 1949–1958; Arsenal 1958–1962. *Honours:* Division 2 Championship medal 1951; 25 full caps for Scotland.

DUNCAN, John. *Player-Manager* Scunthorpe U June 1981– . *Player: Dundee, Tottenham H, Derby Co.*

DURBAN, William Alan. *Manager:* Shrewsbury T, Stoke C, Sunderland June 1981– . *Honours:* Division 4 runners-up 1975. *Player:* Cardiff C 1959–1963; Derby Co 1963–1973; Shrewsbury T 1973–1978. *Honours:* 27 full caps for Wales; Division 2 Championship medal 1969; Division 1 Championship medal 1972; promotion to Division 3 1975; promotion to Division 1 1979.

ELLIOTT, Billy. *Manager:* Sunderland, Darlington June 1979– . *Coach:* Brann (Norway), Sunderland. *Player:* Bradford Park Avenue, Burnley, Sunderland. Five full England caps.

EVANS, Maurice. *Manager:* Shrewsbury T 1972–1974; Reading May 1977– . *Coach:* Shrewsbury T 1968–1972; Reading 1974–1977. *Honours:* Promotion to Division 3 1968. *Player:* Reading 1953–1967. *Honours:* Football Combination team 1957; Division 3 South team 1957.

FRIZZELL, James. *Manager:* Oldham Ath March 1970– . *Honours:* Winners of Ford Sporting League; Division 3 champions 1974. *Player:* Morton 1957–1960; Oldham Ath 1960–1970. *Honours:* Promotion to Division 3 1963.

GODFREY, Brian. *Manager:* Exeter C January 1979– . *Player:* Everton, Scunthorpe U, Preston NE, Aston Villa, Bristol R, Newport Co. *Honours:* One Under-23 and three full Welsh caps.

GRADI, Dario. *Manager:* Wimbledon, Crystal Palace Jan 1981– . *Honours:* Promotion to Division 3 1979. *Coach:* Chelsea, Derby Co, Wimbledon. *Player:* Sutton U.

GREAVES, Ian. *Manager:* Huddersfield T 1968–1974; Bolton W 1974, Hereford U (assistant) 1980; Oxford U Dec 1980– . *Honours:* Huddersfield T, Division 2 Champions 1970. *Player:* Manchester U 1952–1960; Lincoln C 1960–1961; Oldham Ath 1961–1963. *Honours:* Manchester U, Division 1 Championship medal 1956, FA Cup runners-up medal 1958.

HAMILTON, Bryan. *Manager:* Tranmere Rovers Oct 1980– . *Player:* Linfield, Ipswich T, Everton, Millwall, Swindon T. *Honours:* 50 full Northern Ireland caps.

HORNER, Billy. *Manager:* Darlington, Hartlepool U November 1976– . *Player:* Middlesbrough, Darlington.

HOUGHTON, Bob. *Manager:* Bristol C Oct 1980– . Formerly Malmo (Sweden), Ethnikos (Greece). *Honours:* European Cup runners-up 1979. *Player:* Fulham, Brighton & HA, Maidstone U (player-manager). *Coach:* In South Africa and Ipswich T youth team.

HUGHES, Emlyn. *Player-Manager* Rotherham U July 1981– . *Player:* Blackpool, Liverpool, Wolverhampton W. *Honours:* Division 1 championship medals 1973, 1976, 1977, 1979. FA Cup winners medal 1974; runners-up medals 1971, 1977. League Cup winners medal 1980; runners-up medal 1978. UEFA Cup winners medals 1973, 1976. European Cup winners medals 1977, 1978. 62 full England caps.

HUNTER, Norman. *Manager:* Barnsley Sept 1980– . *Honours:* Promotion to Division 2 1981. *Player:* Leeds U, Bristol C, Barnsley (player-manager). *Honours:* 1972 FA Cup winners medal; 1965, 1970, 1973 FA Cup runners-up medals; 1968 League Cup winners medal; 1975 European Cup runners-up medal; 1973 European Cup-Winners' Cup runners-up medal; 1968, 1971 UEFA Cup winners medals; 1967 UEFA Cup runners-up medal. Under-23 and 28 full England caps.

ILEY, Jim. *Manager:* Peterborough U 1969; Barnsley 1973; Blackburn R, Bury 1980– . *Honours:* Watney Cup entry 1973, 1974. *Player:* Sheffield U 1953–1957; Tottenham H 1958–1959; Nottingham F 1959–1963; Newcastle U 1963–1969; Peterborough U 1969–1973. *Honours:* Football League XI with Sheffield U, Tottenham H. Under-23 cap for England and FA XI representative team.

KENDALL, Howard. *Player/Manager:* Blackburn R, Everton May 1981– . *Player:* Preston NE, Everton. While with Preston, he was the youngest player ever to appear in the FA Cup final. *Honours:* Promotion to Div 2 1980.

KERR, George. *Manager:* Lincoln C (previously assistant manager), Grimsby T 1979– . *Player:* Barnsley, Bury, Oxford U. *Honours:* Div 3 Promotion 1980.

LLOYD, Larry. *Player-Manager:* Wigan Ath March 1981– . *Player:* Bristol R, Liverpool, Coventry C, Nottingham F. *Honours:* 1971 FA Cup runners-up medal; 1973 UEFA Cup winners medal; European Cup winners medals 1979, 1980; League Cup winners medals 1978, 1979. Under 23 and three full England caps.

LORD, Frank. *Manager:* Cape Town (South Africa), Hereford U 1980– . *Player:* Rochdale, Blackburn R, Plymouth Arg. *Player/Coach:* Plymouth Arg. *Coach:* Crystal Palace.

LYALL, John. *Manager:* West Ham U August 1974– . Previously Assistant Manager 1971. *Honours:* FA Cup winners 1975, 1980; Division 2 champions 1981; League Cup runners-up 1981. *Player:* West Ham U 1957. *Honours:* Youth International.

LYONS, Barry. *Manager:* York C 1980– . *Youth coach:* York C 1978–80. *Player:* Rotherham, Nottingham F, York C, Darlington.

MACDONALD, Malcolm. *Manager:* Fulham Nov 1980– . Formerly Chief Marketing Executive. *Player:* Tonbridge, Fulham, Luton T, Newcastle U, Arsenal. *Honours:* FA Cup runners-up medal 1974, League Cup runners-up medal 1976, FA Cup runners-up medal 1978. Under-23 and 14 full England caps.

McFARLAND, Roy. *Player-Manager:* Bradford C May 1981– . *Player:* Tranmere R, Derby Co. *Honours:* Division 2 Championship 1969, Division 1 Championship 1972. Under-23 and 28 full England caps.

McGRATH, John. *Manager:* Southampton youth side 1975–79, Port Vale 1980– . *Coach:* Southampton. *Player:* Bury, Newcastle U, Southampton.

McGUIGAN, Jimmy. *Manager:* Crewe Alex 1960; Grimsby T 1964; Chesterfield 1967; Rotherham U May 1973. *Honours:* Crewe Alex promotion to Division 3 1963; Chesterfield promotion to Division 3 1970; Rotherham U promotion to Division 3 1975. Division 4 Manager of the Year. *Player:* Hamilton Acad, Sunderland, Stockport Co, Crewe Alex, Rochdale.

McMENEMY, Lawrie. *Manager:* Doncaster R 1968–1971; Grimsby T 1971–1973; Southampton June 1973– . *Honours:* Doncaster R, Division 4 Championship 1969; Grimsby T, Division 4 Championship 1972; Southampton, FA Cup Winners 1976. League Cup runners-up 1979. *Player:* Newcastle U, Gateshead.

MADDEN, Peter. *Manager:* Darlington, Rochdale 1980– . *Assistant Manager:* Rochdale. *Player:* Rotherham U 1955–66, Bradford PA 1966–67, Aldershot 1967–68, Skegness 1968–70. *Honours:* Rotherham U League Cup runners-up medal 1961. Two Lincolnshire Cup medals with Skegness.

MILLER, Brian. *Manager:* Burnley 1979– . *Player:* Burnley. *Coach:* Burnley.

MONCUR, Bobby. *Manager:* Carlisle U, Hearts, Plymouth Arg June 1981– . *Honours:* Scottish Division 1 championship 1980. *Player:* Newcastle U, Sunderland. *Honours:* One Under-23 and 16 full Scottish caps; UEFA Cup winners medal 1969; FA Cup runners-up medal 1974; Division 2 championship 1965; Anglo-Italian Cup winners medal 1973; Division 2 championship 1976.

MORGAN, Richie. *Manager:* Cardiff C, December 1978– . *Player:* Cardiff C (14 years); One Under-23 cap for Wales.

MORRIS, Peter. *Manager:* Mansfield T (player-manager), Peterborough U February 1979– . *Honours:* Division 3 Championship 1977. *Coach:* Norwich C reserve team coach, Newcastle U. *Player:* Mansfield T, Ipswich T, Norwich C, Mansfield T. *Honours:* Mansfield T Division 3 and Division 4 promotion; Norwich C and Ipswich T promotion to Division 1.

MULHALL, George. *Manager:* Halifax T, Bradford C, Bolton W June 1981 (formerly assistant). *Coach:* Halifax T, Bolton W (assistant-manager). *Player:* Aberdeen, Sunderland, South Africa (player-coach). *Honours:* Three full Scottish caps.

MULLERY, Alan. *Manager:* Brighton & HA, Charlton Ath July 1981– . *Honours:* Promotion to Division 2 1977; Promotion to Division 1 1979. *Player:* Fulham 1959–1964; Tottenham H 1964–1972; Fulham 1972–1976. *Honours:* 35 England caps; FA Cup winners medal 1967; FA Cup runners-up medal 1975; League Cup winners medal 1971; UEFA Cup winners medal 1972; Footballer of the Year 1975; Played for Great Britain XI.

MURDOCH, Bobby. *Manager:* Middlesbrough May 1981– . Formerly youth team coach. *Player:* Celtic, Middlesbrough. *Honours:* Regular member of Celtic first team squad during eight of their nine successive Scottish League championship successes 1966–1972. Division 2 Championship medal with Middlesbrough 1974. Scottish international 12 caps. European Cup winners medal 1967, runners-up 1970.

MURPHY, Colin. *Manager:* Derby Co, Lincoln C November 1978– . *Coach:* Derby Co (reserve team), Nottingham F (reserve team), Notts Co (assistant manager). *Player:* Cork Hibs, Wimbledon, Hastings U, Crystal Palace. *Honours:* Derby Co Central League runners-up 1974–75; Lincoln C Division 4 runners-up 1981.

NEAL, John. *Manager:* Wrexham, Middlesbrough, Chelsea May 1981– . *Honours:* Promotion to Division 3 1970; Welsh Cup winners 1972, 1975; Qualified for Cup-Winners' Cup 1973, 1976 (quarter-finalists). *Player:* Hull C 1949–1955; Swindon T 1956–1958; Aston Villa 1959–1963; Southend U 1964–1967. *Honours:* Aston Villa, Division 2 championship medal 1960; League Cup winners medal 1961.

NEILL, Terry. *Manager:* Hull C, N Ireland, Tottenham H, 1974–76; Arsenal July 1976– . *Honours:* FA Cup Winners 1979; Runners-up 1978; 1980. *Player:* Arsenal 1959–1970; Hull C 1970–1974. *Honours:* Schoolboy, Youth, Under-23, 'B' and 59 full caps for N Ireland.

OAKES, Alan. *Manager:* Chester September 1976– . *Honours:* Debenhams Cup 1977. *Player:* Manchester C 1959–1976 (565 League appearances – a club record). *Honours:* Division 2 Championship medal 1966; Division 1 Championship 1968; FA Cup winners medal 1969; League Cup winners medal 1970; European Cup-Winners' Cup medal 1970; Football League representative honours.

O'FARRELL, Frank. *Manager:* Weymouth, Torquay U, Leicester C, Manchester U, Iran national team, Cardiff C, Torquay U as Consultant Manager, Torquay U June 1981– . *Honours:* Leicester C Division 2 Championship 1971, FA Cup runners-up 1969. *Player:* Cork, West Ham U, Preston NE, Weymouth (player-manager). *Honours:* Nine caps for Republic of Ireland.

PAISLEY, Robert. *Manager:* Liverpool July 1974– . *Honours:* Division 1 Champions 1976, 1977, 1979 and 1980, runners-up 1978; UEFA Cup winners 1976; European Cup winners 1977, 1978. *Player:* Bishop Auckland 1938–1939; Liverpool 1939–1954. *Honours:* Amateur Cup winners medal 1939; Division 1 Championship medal 1947.

PEACOCK, Keith. *Manager:* Charlton Ath July 1981– . *Assistant Manager:* Tampa Bay Rowdies. *Player:* Charlton Ath.

PLEAT, David. *Manager:* Nuneaton B, Luton T January 1978– . *Coach:* Luton T. *Player:* Nottingham F, Luton T, Shrewsbury T, Exeter C, Peterborough U. *Honours:* England schools and youth international.

PORTERFIELD, Ian. *Player/Manager:* Rotherham U, Sheffield U June 1981– . *Honours:* Division 3 Championship 1981. *Player:* Raith R, Sunderland, Reading, Sheffield W. Scored the goal for Sunderland which beat Leeds U in the 1973 FA Cup final.

ROBERTS, Bobby. *Manager:* Colchester U June 1975– . Promotion to Division 3 1977. *Player:* Motherwell, Leicester C, Mansfield T. *Honours:* One Under-23 cap for Scotland; Scottish League.

ROBSON, Bobby. *Manager:* Fulham 1968; Ipswich T January 1969– . *Honours:* Ipswich T, Texaco Cup winners 1973, FA Cup winners 1978, Division 1 runners-up 1981, UEFA Cup winners 1981. *Player:* Fulham 1950–1956; WBA 1956–1962; Fulham 1962–1968. *Honours:* Under-23 and 20 full England caps; (World Cups 1958 and 1962); Football League.

SAUNDERS, Ron. *Manager:* Yeovil 1967; Oxford U 1969; Norwich C 1969; Manchester C 1973; Aston Villa June 1974– . *Honours:* Norwich C Champions Division 2 1972; League Cup runners-up 1973; Manchester C League Cup runners-up 1974; Aston Villa League Cup winners 1975 and 1977; Runners-up Division 2 1975, Division 1 Championship 1981; Manager of the Year 1975. *Player:* Everton, Tonbridge, Gillingham, Portsmouth, Watford, Charlton Ath.

SAXTON, Bobby. *Manager:* Exeter C (player-manager), Plymouth Arg, Blackburn R May 1981– . *Honours:* Promotion to Division 3 1977. *Player:* Derby Co 1962–1968; Plymouth Arg 1968–1975; Exeter C 1975– . *Honours:* Promotion to Division 2 Plymouth Arg 1975.

SEXTON, David. *Manager:* Orient 1965–1966; Chelsea 1967–1974; QPR 1974–1977; Manchester U July 1977–April 1981; Coventry C May 1981– . *Honours:* FA Cup winners 1970, runners-up 1979; European Cup-Winners' Cup 1971; League Cup runners-up 1972, 1976. *Player:* Chelmsford 1950–51; Luton T 1951–53; West Ham U 1953–56; Orient 1956–57; Brighton & HA 1957–59; Crystal Palace 1959–61. *Honours:* FA XI v RAF; Third Division South v Third Division North.

SIRREL, Jimmy. *Manager:* Brentford 1965–1969; Notts Co 1969–1975; Sheffield U 1975–1977; Notts Co October 1977– . *Honours:* Notts Co, Division 4 Champions 1971; Division 3 runners-up 1973; Division 2 runners-up 1981. *Player:* Glasgow Celtic 1945–1949; Bradford PA 1949–1951; Brighton & HA 1951–1954; Aldershot 1954–1955 (later trainer).

SMITH, Dave. *Manager:* Mansfield T 1974–1976; Southend U 1976– . *Honours:* Division 4 Championship 1975, runners-up 1978; Anglo-Scottish Cup semi-finalists 1976; League Cup quarter-finalists 1976, Division 4 Championship 1981. *Coach:* Chief coach Sheffield W 1965–1968; Chief coach Newcastle U 1968–1971; Reserve team manager Arsenal 1971–1974. *Honours:* FA Cup runners-up 1966 Sheffield W; Fairs Cup winners 1969. *Player:* Burnley 1950–1961; Brighton & HA 1961–1962; Bristol C 1962–1963.

SMITH, Jimmy. *Manager:* Boston U 1968–1972; Colchester U 1972–1975; Blackburn R 1975–1978; Birmingham C March 1978– . *Honours:* Boston U Eastern Professional Floodlight Cup winners; Colchester U promoted from Division 4 1974. Promoted Div 1 1980. *Player:* Sheffield U 1957–1961; Aldershot 1961–1964; Halifax T 1964–1967; Lincoln C 1967–1968; Boston U 1968–1972.

SMITH, Mike. *Manager:* Hull C 1979– . *Player:* Great Britain Olympic team 1960. Director of Coaching, Welsh FA Welsh national team manager 1974–79.

STOKOE, Bob. *Manager:* Charlton Ath, Rochdale, Carlisle U, Blackpool, Sunderland, Bury, Blackpool, Rochdale, Carlisle U 1980– . *Honours:* Sunderland FA Cup winners 1973. Division 2 champions 1976. *Player:* Newcastle U (13 years), Bury (player-manager). *Honours:* FA Cup winners medal 1955.

SUTTON, Mel. *Manager:* Wrexham June 1981– . Former player-coach. *Player:* Aston Villa (amateur), Cardiff C, Wrexham.

TAYLOR, Graham. *Manager:* Lincoln C, Watford June 1977– . *Honours:* Division 4 Championship 1976, 1978; Division 3 runners-up 1979. *Player:* Grimsby T 1962–1968; Lincoln C 1968–1972.

TOSHACK, John. *Player-Manager:* Swansea C February 1978– . *Honours:* Promotion to Division 3 1978, Division 2 1979, Division 1 1981. *Player:* Cardiff C, Liverpool, Swansea C. *Honours:* Three Under-23 and 39 full Welsh caps.

TROLLOPE, John, MBE. *Manager:* Swindon T Nov 1980– . *Player:* Swindon T 1960–1980 making record 770 League appearances.

TURNER, Graham. *Player-Manager:* Shrewsbury T December 1978– . *Player:* Wrexham, Chester, Shrewsbury T. *Honours:* Promotion 1979.

VENABLES, Terry. *Manager:* Crystal Palace June 1976– (formerly coach), QPR Oct 1980– . *Honours:* Promotion to Division 2 1976, Division 2 Championship 1979. *Player:* Chelsea, Tottenham H, QPR, Crystal Palace. *Honours:* capped at all levels by England schools, youth, Amateur, Under-23 and two full honours; Promotion to Division 1 1963 Chelsea; League Cup winners medal 1965 Chelsea; FA Cup winners medal 1967 Tottenham H.

WALKER, Len. *Manager:* Darlington, Aldershot April 1981– . *Player:* Spennymoor, Middlesbrough, Newcastle U, Aldershot, Darlington (player-coach).

WALLACE, Jock. *Manager:* Rangers, Leicester C June 1978– . *Coach:* Hearts, Rangers. *Player-Manager:* Berwick R. *Player:* Airdrieonians, WBA, Workington T, Hereford U, Bedford T. *Honours:* Champions Div 2 1980.

WEBB, David. *Manager:* AFC Bournemouth 1980– . Formerly coach. *Player:* Orient, Southampton, Chelsea, QPR, Leicester C, Derby Co, Bournemouth. *Honours:* FA Cup winners medal 1970. League Cup runners-up medal 1972, European Cup-Winners' Cup winners medal 1971.

TRANSFERS 1980–81

** Denotes nett figure excluding levies*

	From	To	Fee if known
June 1980			
Clive Allen	Queen's Park Rangers	Arsenal	£1,250,000
John Allen	Leicester City	Port Vale	
Colin Barrett	Nottingham Forest	Swindon Town	
Owen Brown	Liverpool	Carlisle United	
Pat Cuff	Millwall	Darlington	
Moshe Gariani	Maccabi Nathanya	Brighton	£40,000
Don Gillies	Bristol City	Bristol Rovers	
Rachid Harkouk	Queen's Park Rangers	Notts County	£50,000
Jimmy Harvey	Arsenal	Hereford United	
Garry Lowe	Manchester City	Hereford United	
Donal Murphy	Torquay United	Plymouth Argyle	£65,000
Paul Overton	Peterborough United	Northampton Town	
Lloyd Richards	Notts County	York City	
Alex Sabella	Sheffield United	Leeds United	£400,000
Lee Smelt	Gravesend	Nottingham Forest	£15,000
Gordon Smith	Rangers	Brighton	£400,000
David Speedie	Barnsley	Darlington	
Mick Tait	Hull City	Portsmouth	£100,000
John Thomas	Everton	Bolton Wanderers	
Jimmy Weston	Blackpool	Torquay United	
July 1980			
Sam Allardyce	Bolton Wanderers	Sunderland	£150,000
John Anderson	Everton	Chester	
Stephen Baines	Bradford City	Walsall	£50,000
Mike Beavon	Tottenham Hotspur	Reading	
Trevor Birch	Shrewsbury Town	Chester	
John Bird	Newcastle United	Hartlepool United	
Stan Bowles	Nottingham Forest	Orient	£100,000
Liam Brady	Arsenal	Juventus	£600,000
Tommy Cassidy	Newcastle United	Burnley	
Ray Clarke	Brighton	Newcastle United	£180,000
Mike Coady	Sunderland	Carlisle United	£20,000
Garth Crooks	Stoke City	Tottenham Hotspur	£600,000
Nigel Crouch	Ipswich Town	Colchester United	
John Davies	Cardiff City	Hull City	£12,000
Kerry Dixon	Dunstable	Reading	£20,000
Steve Dowman	Colchester United	Wrexham	£75,000
Andy Ford	Swindon Town	Gillingham	£30,000
Brendan Guest	Lincoln City	Swindon Town	
Bob Hatton	Luton Town	Sheffield United	£75,000
Peter Henderson	Chester	Gillingham	£40,000
David Holt	Oldham Athletic	Burnley	£40,000
Stewart Houston	Manchester United	Sheffield United	
Chris Hutchings	Harrow	Chelsea	
Kevin Keegan	Hamburg	Southampton	£400,000
Glyn Jones	Bristol Rovers	Shrewsbury Town	
Roger Jones	Stoke City	Derby County	£20,000
Mike Kearney	Reading	Chester	
Nicky Jarvis	Grantham	Scunthorpe United	£2,300
Eddie Kelly	Leicester City	Notts County	
Bobby Kerr	Blackpool	Hartlepool United	
David Langan	Derby County	Birmingham City	£350,000
Steve Ludlam	Carlisle United	Chester	£45,000
Mike McCartney	Carlisle United	Southampton	£50,000
Jim McDonagh	Bolton Wanderers	Everton	£250,000
Jim Melrose	Partick Thistle	Leicester City	£250,000
Ally Millar	Barnsley	York City	
Stuart Metcalfe	Blackburn Rovers	Carlisle United	£35,000
Noel Parkinson	Ipswich Town	Mansfield Town	£35,000
John Peachey	Darlington	Plymouth Argyle	
Frankie Prince	Bristol Rovers	Exeter City	
Alan Ramage	Middlesbrough	Derby County	
Mike Robinson	Manchester City	Brighton	£400,000
Stuart Robinson	Newcastle United	Aldershot	
Ricky Sbragia	Walsall	Blackpool	£35,000
Micky Speight	Sheffield United	Blackburn Rovers	
Steve Taylor	Mansfield Town	Burnley	£35,000
Mike Trusson	Plymouth Argyle	Sheffield United	£60,000
Ian Wallace	Coventry City	Nottingham Forest	£1,250,000
Danny Wilson	Bury	Chesterfield	£100,000

August 1980

Clive Allen	Arsenal	Crystal Palace	*£800,000
Paul Barron	Arsenal	Crystal Palace	£400,000
Keith Bowker	Exeter City	Torquay United	
Mick Butler	AFC Bournemouth	Bury	£30,000
Gerry Daly	Derby County	Coventry City	£300,000
Paul Futcher	Manchester City	Oldham Athletic	£150,000
Paul Goddard	Queen's Park Rangers	West Ham United	£800,000
Dzemal Hadziabdic	Velez Mostar	Swansea City	£160,000
Peter Hampton	Leeds United	Stoke City	£175,000
Peter Hart	Huddersfield Town	Walsall	£70,000
Gerry Hendrick	St Patrick's Athletic	Blackpool	
Gordon Hodgson	Oxford United	Peterborough United	£10,000
Billy Ingham	Burnley	Bradford City	£30,000
Graham Jones	Luton Town	Torquay United	
Mick Kennedy	Halifax Town	Huddersfield Town	£50,000
Peter Kitchen	Fulham	Cardiff City	£100,000
Tommy Langley	Chelsea	Queen's Park Rangers	£400,000
Bob Lee	Sunderland	Bristol Rovers	£70,000
Phil Lythgoe	Norwich City	Oxford United	£15,000
Aidan McCaffery	Derby County	Bristol Rovers	£70,000
Ronnie Moore	Cardiff City	Rotherham United	£100,000
Jimmy Mullen	Sheffield Wednesday	Rotherham United	£25,000
Jim Oliver	Montrose	Wigan Athletic	
Martin Peters	Norwich City	Sheffield United	
Paul Petts	Bristol Rovers	Shrewsbury Town	
Brendon Phillips	Boston United	Mansfield Town	£15,000
Steve Phillips	Brentford	Northampton Town	£40,000
Raimondo Ponte	Grasshoppers	Nottingham Forest	£230,000
John Roberts	Wrexham	Hull City	£20,000
Joe Royle	Bristol City	Norwich City	£60,000
Kenny Sansom	Crystal Palace	Arsenal	*£800,000
Peter Sayer	Brighton	Preston North End	£85,000
John Seasman	Millwall	Rotherham United	£85,000
Barry Silkman	Manchester City	Brentford	£50,000
Cliff Smith	Bromsgrove Rovers	Walsall	£10,000
Tony Towner	Millwall	Rotherham United	£100,000
Tony Whelan	Bohemians	Manchester United	
Gary Williams	Djurgaarden	Blackpool	£40,000
George Wood	Everton	Arsenal	£150,000

Temporary transfers

Neil Freeman	Birmingham City	Walsall
Chris Pearce	Blackburn Rovers	Rochdale

September 1980

Yakka Banovic	Heidelberg	Derby County	£40,000
Phil Driver	Wimbledon	Chelsea	
Andy Harrow	Raith Rovers	Luton Town	
David Hubbick	Ipswich Town	Wimbledon	£10,000
Brian Kettle	Liverpool	Wigan Athletic	£25,000
Andy King	Everton	Queen's Park Rangers	£400,000
Gerry McElhinney	Distillery	Bolton Wanderers	£25,000
Paul Maguire	Shrewsbury Town	Stoke City	£262,000
Drazen Muzinic	Hajduk Split	Norwich City	£300,000
Trevor Morgan	Leytonstone/Ilford	AFC Bournemouth	£3000
Eric Potts	Preston North End	Burnley	£20,000
Peter Shields	Ipswich Town	Hearts	
Gordon Simmonite	Boston United	Blackpool	£15,000

Temporary transfers

Graeme Crawford	York City	Rochdale
David Felgate	Bolton Wanderers	Lincoln City
Terry Gennoe	Southampton	Everton
Mark Kendall	Tottenham Hotspur	Newport County
David McKellar	Derby County	Brentford

October 1980

John Bartley	Welling	Millwall	£6000
Garry Birtles	Nottingham Forest	Manchester United	£1,250,000
Len Bond	Brentford	Exeter City	
Kevin Bremner	Keith	Colchester United	£40,000
David Clement	Bolton Wanderers	Fulham	
Russell Coughlin	Blackburn Rovers	Carlisle United	£20,000
Graeme Crawford	York City	Rochdale	
Paul Compton	Trowbridge Town	AFC Bournemouth	£10,000
David Felgate	Bolton Wanderers	Lincoln City	£25,000
Tommy Gore	Wigan Athletic	Bury	
Gerry Gow	Bristol City	Manchester City	£175,000
Tommy Graham	Barnsley	Halifax Town	£20,000
Tommy Hutchison	Coventry City	Manchester City	£47,000
Joe Jakub	Burnley	Bury	£15,000
Peter Johnson	Middlesbrough	Newcastle United	£60,000

Mike Kearney	Chester	Reading	
Mark Kendall	Tottenham Hotspur	Newport County	£45,000
John Lyons	Millwall	Cambridge United	£100,000
Bobby McDonald	Coventry City	Manchester City	£250,000
Roy McDonough	Walsall	Chelsea	£15,000
David McKellar	Derby County	Brentford	£30,000
Gerry Mullan	Ballymena United	Everton	
Iain Munro	St Mirren	Stoke City	£250,000
Steve Neville	Exeter City	Sheffield United	£80,000
Andy Ritchie	Manchester United	Brighton	£500,000
Gary Roberts	Wembley	Brentford	£6000
Barry Silkman	Brentford	Queen's Park Rangers	£20,000
Alan Taylor	Vancouver Whitecaps	Cambridge United	£130,000
Chris Turner	Swindon Town	Cambridge United	
Peter Ward	Brighton	Nottingham Forest	£400,000
Temporary transfer			
Barry Siddall	Sunderland	Darlington	
November 1980			
Gerry Armstrong	Tottenham Hotspur	Watford	£250,000
Phil Boyer	Southampton	Manchester City	£220,000
Alan Campbell	Cardiff City	Carlisle United	£35,000
Keith Cassells	Watford	Oxford United	
Gary Donnellan	Chelsea	Watford	
Wayne Entwistle	Leeds United	Blackpool	£60,000
Andy Geddes	Leicester City	Dundee	£20,000
Peter Griffiths	Bideford	Stoke City	£15,000
Paul Haigh	Hull City	Carlisle United	£100,000
Alex Hamill	Tottenham Hotspur	Hearts	
Duncan Heath	Aston Villa	Crewe Alexandra	
Robert Horn	Crystal Palace	Barnsley	
John Lowey	Sheffield Wednesday	Blackburn Rovers	£25,000
Roger Palmer	Manchester City	Oldham Athletic	£70,000
Pat Rice	Arsenal	Watford	
Simon Stainrod	Oldham Athletic	Queen's Park Rangers	£275,000
Les Taylor	Oxford United	Watford	£100,000
Peter Taylor	Tottenham Hotspur	Orient	£150,000
Billy Urquhart	Rangers	Wigan Athletic	
David Watson	Liverpool	Norwich City	£50,000
Temporary transfer			
Steve Cherry	Derby County	Port Vale	
December 1980			
Terry Austin	Mansfield Town	Huddersfield Town	£110,000
Chic Bates	Bristol Rovers	Shrewsbury Town	
Ian Brennan	Burnley	Bolton Wanderers	£25,000
Marshall Burke	Leeds United	Blackburn Rovers	
John Burridge	Crystal Palace	Queen's Park Rangers	£200,000
Alan Curtis	Leeds United	Swansea City	£175,000
Bob Doyle	Blackpool	Portsmouth	£90,000
Terry Fenwick	Crystal Palace	Queen's Park Rangers	£100,000
Brian Ferguson	Newcastle United	Hull City	
Mike Flanagan	Crystal Palace	Queen's Park Rangers	£150,000
Lee Frost	Chelsea	Brentford	£30,000
Mick Harford	Lincoln City	Newcastle United	£180,000
Steve Hoolickin	Carlisle United	Hull City	
Gary Johnson	Chelsea	Brentford	
Joe Laidlaw	Portsmouth	Hereford United	£15,000
John McGlynn	Bolton Wanderers	Berwick Rangers	
Alan Mayes	Swindon Town	Chelsea	£175,000
Dean Mooney	Gais	AFC Bournemouth	£15,000
Jan Moller	Malmo	Bristol City	£120,000
Gordon Nisbet	Hull City	Plymouth Argyle	£30,000
Billy Rafferty	Newcastle United	Portsmouth	£80,000
Derek Showers	Portsmouth	Hereford United	£13,000
Carl Swan	Burton Albion	Doncaster Rovers	£7000
John Trewick	West Bromwich Albion	Newcastle United	£250,000
Alan Waddle	Swansea City	Newport County	£80,000
Trevor Whymark	Vancouver Whitecaps	Grimsby Town	£80,000
January 1981			
Bill Ayre	Hartlepool United	Halifax Town	
Ian Bowyer	Nottingham Forest	Sunderland	£250,000
Perry Digweed	Fulham	Brighton	£150,000
David Hamilton	Sunderland	Blackburn Rovers	
Andy Harrow	Luton Town	Aberdeen	£65,000
Kevin Johnson	Halifax Town	Hartlepool United	
Trevor Lee	Colchester United	Gillingham	£90,000
Jim Lumby	Tranmere Rovers	Mansfield Town	£50,000
Paul Randall	Stoke City	Bristol Rovers	£55,000

Tom Ritchie	Bristol City	Sunderland	£185,000
John Sparrow	Chelsea	Exeter City	£5000
Stephen Vass	Hartlepool United	Huddersfield Town	
Temporary transfers			
Ray Cashley	Bristol City	Hereford United	
Neil Freeman	Birmingham City	Huddersfield Town	
Terry Gennoe	Southampton	Crystal Palace	
Ian Turner	Walsall	Halifax Town	
February 1981			
Terry Armstrong	Huddersfield Town	Port Vale	
Stewart Barrowclough	Bristol Rovers	Barnsley	£50,000
Ray Bishop	Cardiff City	Newport County	£10,000
Phil Coleman	Millwall	Colchester United	£15,000
Richard Dawson	Rotherham United	Doncaster Rovers	
John Flood	Sheffield United	Airdrieonians	
Gerry Francis	Crystal Palace	Queen's Park Rangers	£150,000
Tim Gilbert	Sunderland	Cardiff City	
Austin Hayes	Southampton	Millwall	£25,000
Andy Higgins	Chesterfield	Port Vale	
Steve Lynex	Birmingham City	Leicester City	£60,000
Roy McDonough	Chelsea	Colchester United	
Martin O'Neill	Nottingham Forest	Norwich City	£250,000
Roger Osborne	Ipswich Town	Colchester United	£25,000
Malcolm Page	Birmingham City	Oxford United	
Temporary transfers			
Tony Knight	Brighton	Swindon Town	
Brian Lloyd	Chester	Port Vale	
Tom McAlister	Swindon Town	Bristol Rovers	
Andy Pape	Queen's Park Rangers	Charlton Athletic	
March 1981			
Einar Aas	Bayern Munich	Nottingham Forest	£250,000
Brian Bason	Plymouth Argyle	Crystal Palace	£80,000
Brian Chambers	AFC Bournemouth	Halifax Town	
Joe Craig	Blackburn Rovers	Hamilton Academical	£10,000
Kevin Dawtry	Crystal Palace	AFC Bournemouth	
Don Givens	Birmingham City	Sheffield United	£20,000
Mark Goodwin	Leicester City	Notts County	£50,000
Bruce Grobbelaar	Vancouver Whitecaps	Liverpool	£250,000
Tommy Langley	Queen's Park Rangers	Crystal Palace	£200,000
Tony Lowery	Ashington	West Bromwich Albion	£3500
Ray McHale	Brighton	Barnsley	£50,000
Peter Nicholas	Crystal Palace	Arsenal	£400,000
David Price	Arsenal	Crystal Palace	£150,000
Ante Rajkovic	Sarajevo	Swansea City	£100,000
Bryan Robson	Sunderland	Carlisle United	
Tony Sealy	Crystal Palace	Queen's Park Rangers	£75,000
Jim Stewart	Middlesbrough	Rangers	£100,000
Chris Sulley	Chelsea	AFC Bournemouth	
Steve Walford	Arsenal	Norwich City	175,000
Temporary transfers			
Kevin Fox	Lincoln City	Hull City	
Steve Sutton	Nottingham Forest	Mansfield Town	
Chris Woods	Queen's Park Rangers	Norwich City	
April 1981			
Paul Geddes	Leicester City	Hibernian	
Craig Johnston	Middlesbrough	Liverpool	£575,000
May 1981			
Frank Gray	Nottingham Forest	Leeds United	£300,000
Paul Johnson	Stoke City	Shrewsbury Town	£20,000
Tom McAlister	Swindon Town	West Ham United	
John McClelland	Mansfield Town	Rangers	£90,000
Temporary transfers			
Mark Harrison	Port Vale	Stoke City	
John Turner	Chesterfield	Everton	

June 1981

Clive Allen	Crystal Palace	Queen's Park Rangers	‡£700,000
Kevin Baddeley	Bristol City	Swindon Town	
Joe Cooke	Oxford United	Exeter City	£25,000
Tony Fitzpatrick	Bristol City	St Mirren	£170,000
John Gregory	Brighton	Queen's Park Rangers	£300,000
David Hughes	Lincoln City	Scunthorpe United	
Tommy Mason	Fulham	Brighton	
Ernie Moss	Chesterfield	Port Vale	£16,000
Martin O'Neill	Norwich City	Manchester City	£275,000
Peter O'Sullivan	Brighton	Fulham	
Paul Price	Luton Town	Tottenham Hotspur	£250,000
Mark Stevens	Bristol Rovers	Swindon Town	
Steve Wicks	Queen's Park Rangers	Crystal Palace	£275,000
Clive Woods	Queen's Park Rangers	Norwich City	£225,000

July 1981

Alan Biley	Derby County	Everton	£350,000
Peter Coffill	Torquay United	Northampton Town	
Billy Lansdowne	West Ham United	Charlton Athletic	
Tony Larkin	Shrewsbury Town	Carlisle United	
Ian MacDonald	Carlisle United	Dundee	
Neville Southall	Bury	Everton	
Alan West	Luton Town	Millwall	£45,000
Nigel Worthington	Ballymena United	Notts County	£10,000
Ian Bell	Middlesbrough	Mansfield Town	
Stuart Boam	Newcastle United	Mansfield Town	
Joe Bolton	Sunderland	Middlesbrough	£150,000
Steve Cammack	Scunthorpe United	Lincoln City	£20,000
Mick Coop	Coventry City	Derby County	
Gary Emmanuel	Bristol Rovers	Swindon Town	
Tony Grealish	Luton Town	Brighton	£100,000
Bob Latchford	Everton	Swansea City	£125,000
David McClurg	Distillery	Middlesbrough	
Joe Jordan	Manchester United	AC Milan	£170,000
Bill Rodaway	Burnley	Peterborough United	
Brian Williams	Swindon Town	Bristol Rovers	

August 1981 (up to the time of going to press)

David Armstrong	Middlesbrough	Southampton	†£600,000
Gary Bannister	Coventry City	Sheffield Wednesday	
Andy Blair	Coventry City	Aston Villa	£300,000
Glyn Chamberlain	Chesterfield	Halifax Town	
John Gidman	Everton	Manchester United	
Mickey Thomas	Manchester United	Everton	

†*Record fee for Southampton.*
‡*Exchange deal involving Steve Wicks.*

FOOTBALL LEAGUE REFEREES 1980–81

Allison, D. B. (Lancaster)
Ashley N. J. (Rugby)
Axcell D. J. (Southend)
Baker K. W. (Wolverhampton)
Baker M. R. (Wolverhampton)
Banks R. A. (Manchester)
Barratt K. P. (Coventry)
Bates S. G. (Bristol)
Bodenham M. J. (Brighton)
Borrett I. J. (Diss)
Bray J. E. (Hinckley, Leics)
Bridges R. (Deeside)
Bune T. G. (Billingshurst)
Burden L. F. (Corfe Mullen, Dorset)
Callow V. G. (Solihull)
Chadwick R. (Darwen)
Challinor A. (Rotherham)
Civil D. W. (Birmingham)
Courtney G. (Spennymoor)
Daniels B. H. (Brentwood)
Deakin J. C. (Bedford)
Dimblebee M. (Stevenage)
Downey C. (Hounslow)
Fitzharris T. (Bolton)
Flint G. E. (Kirkby-in-Ashfield)
Glasson A. R. (Salisbury)
Glover N. H. (Chorley)
Grey A. W. (Great Yarmouth)
Gunn A. (Burgess Hill, Sussex)
Hackett K. S. (Sheffield)
Hamil A. J. (Wolverhampton)
Heath M. J. (Stoke)
Hedges D. A. (Oxford)
Hill B. (Wellingborough)
Hough J. D. (Macclesfield)
Hunting J. (Leicester)
Hutchinson D.(Bourn, Cambs)
James M. L. (Horsham)
Key J. M. (Rotherham)
King H. W. (Merthyr Tydfil)
Letts D. (Basingstoke)
Lewis R. S. (Great Bookham, Surrey)
Lloyd D. W. (Fernhill Heath)
Lovatt J. (Crewe)
Lowe M. (Sheffield)
Martin B. (Keyworth, Notts)
Martin J. E. (Alton, Hants)
Maskell C. A. (Cambridge)
Midgley N. (Salford)
Milford R. G. (Bristol)
Mills T. (Barnsley)
Morris T. L. (Leeds)
Moules J. A. (Ongar)
Napthine G. J. (Loughborough)
Newsome C. L. (Broseley)
Nixon R. F. (Stockport)
Owen D. (Wirral)
Owen G. P. (Anglesey)
Peck M. G. (Doncaster)
Read E. A. (Bristol)
Redfern K. A. (Whitley Bay)
Reeves D. V. (Uxbridge)
Richardson D. (Great Harwood)
Richardson P. J. (Lincoln)
Roberts F. (Prestatyn)
Robinson A. (Portsmouth)
Robinson, Arthur (Manchester)
Robinson L. M. (Sutton Coldfield)
Salmon K. G. (Barnet)
Saunders A. (Newcastle)
Scott D. (Burnley)
Scott M. P. (Nottingham)
Seel C. N. (Carlisle)
Seville A. (Birmingham)
Shapter L. C. (Newton Abbot)
Shaw D. (Sandbach)
Spencer T. D. (Salisbury)
Stevens B. T. (Stonehouse)
Taylor H. (Leicester)
Taylor M. J.(Deal)
Thomas C. (Porthcawl)
Tyldesley P. A. (Stockport)
Tyson G. M. (Sunderland)
Vickers D. S. (Ilford)
Walmsley K. (Thornton)
Ward A. W. (London)
Webb D. A.(Radcliffe)
White C. B. (Harrow)
Willis P. N. (Meadowfield)
Wilson N. (Morecambe)
Worral J. B. (Warrington)

FOOTBALL LEAGUE ATTENDANCES 1980–81

FIRST DIVISION

	Home	*Home avge*
Arsenal	682,077	32,480
Aston Villa	706,465	33,641
Birmingham C	404,199	19,248
Brighton & HA	398,660	18,984
Coventry C	354,986	16,904
Crystal Palace	404,877	19,280
Everton	548,211	26,105
Ipswich T	517,002	24,619
Leeds U	448,925	21,377
Leicester C	408,993	19,476
Liverpool	788,490	37,547
Manchester C	705,328	33,587
Manchester U	946,401	45,071
Middlesbrough	345,076	16,432
Norwich C	359,943	17,140
Nottingham F	514,133	24,483
Southampton	451,114	21,481
Stoke C	327,183	15,580
Sunderland	556,010	26,477
Tottenham H	645,198	30,724
WBA	426,954	20,331
Wolverhampton W	452,570	21,551
TOTAL	11,392,894	

SECOND DIVISION

	Home	*Home avge*
Blackburn R	245,357	11,684
Bolton W	206,796	9847
Bristol C	205,063	9765
Bristol R	124,509	5929
Cambridge U	121,711	5796
Cardiff C	142,098	6767
Chelsea	375,832	17,897
Derby Co	350,320	16,682
Grimsby T	230,175	10,961
Luton T	216,106	10,291
Newcastle U	336,015	11,239
Notts Co	200,580	9551
Oldham Ath	136,712	6510
Orient	127,591	6076
Preston NE	160,246	7631
QPR	229,663	10,936
Sheffield W	391,104	18,624
Shrewsbury T	117,945	5616
Swansea C	276,008	13,143
Watford	275,268	13,108
West Ham U	569,948	27,140
Wrexham	136,395	6495
TOTAL	5,175,442	

THIRD DIVISION

	Home	*Home avge*
Barnsley	294,407	12,800
Blackpool	134,848	5863
Brentford	155,297	6752
Burnley	148,791	6469
Carlisle U	93,467	4064
Charlton Ath	165,739	7206
Chester	66,518	2892
Chesterfield	168,616	7331
Colchester U	60,840	2645
Exeter C	104,859	4559
Fulham	116,377	5060
Gillingham	107,547	4676
Huddersfield T	265,602	11,548
Hull C	99,339	4319
Millwall	103,355	4494
Newport Co	130,701	5683
Oxford U	95,043	4132
Plymouth Arg	155,626	6766
Portsmouth	310,830	13,514
Reading	125,090	5439
Rotherham U	183,662	7985
Sheffield U	293,758	12,772
Swindon T	159,449	6933
Walsall	98,093	4265
TOTAL	3,637,854	

FOURTH DIVISION

	Home	*Home avge*
Aldershot	68,748	2989
AFC Bournemouth	77,731	3380
Bradford C	65,741	2858
Bury	63,200	2748
Crewe Alex	66,904	2909
Darlington	58,350	2537
Doncaster R	124,471	5412
Halifax T	44,258	1924
Hartlepool U	71,637	3115
Hereford U	56,216	2444
Lincoln C	108,449	4715
Mansfield T	78,204	3400
Northampton T	53,024	2305
Peterborough U	95,148	4137
Port Vale	62,973	2738
Rochdale	56,576	2460
Scunthorpe U	54,213	2357
Southend U	140,196	6095
Stockport Co	53,711	2335
Torquay U	47,151	2050
Tranmere R	43,726	1901
Wigan Ath	101,985	4434
Wimbledon	57,133	2484
York C	51,634	2245
TOTAL	1,701,379	

ATTENDANCES AT FOOTBALL LEAGUE MATCHES

Season	*Matches*	*Total*	*Div. 1*	*Div. 2*	*Div. 3 (S)*	*Div. 3 (N)*
1946–47	1848	35,604,606	15,005,316	11,071,572	5,664,004	3,863,714
1947–48	1848	40,259,130	16,732,341	12,286,350	6,653,610	4,586,829
1948–49	1848	41,271,414	17,914,667	11,353,237	6,998,429	5,005,081
1949–50	1848	40,517,865	17,278,625	11,694,158	7,104,155	4,440,927
1950–51	2028	39,584,967	16,679,454	10,780,580	7,367,884	4,757,109
1951–52	2028	39,015,866	16,110,322	11,066,189	6,958,927	4,880,428
1952–53	2028	37,149,966	16,050,278	9,686,654	6,704,299	4,708,735
1953–54	2028	36,174,590	16,154,915	9,510,053	6,311,508	4,198,114
1954–55	2028	34,133,103	15,087,221	8,988,794	5,996,017	4,051,071
1955–56	2028	33,150,809	14,108,961	9,080,002	5,692,479	4,269,367
1956–57	2028	32,744,405	13,803,037	8,718,162	5,622,189	4,601,017
1957–58	2028	33,562,208	14,468,652	8,663,712	6,097,183	4,332,661
					Div. 3	*Div. 4*
1958–59	2028	33,610,985	14,727,691	8,641,997	5,946,600	4,276,697
1959–60	2028	32,538,611	14,391,227	8,399,627	5,739,707	4,008,050
1960–61	2028	28,619,754	12,926,948	7,033,936	4,784,256	3,874,614
1961–62	2015	27,979,902	12,061,194	7,453,089	5,199,106	3,266,513
1962–63	2028	28,885,852	12,490,239	7,792,770	5,341,362	3,261,481
1963–64	2028	28,535,022	12,486,626	7,594,158	5,419,157	3,035,081
1964–65	2028	27,641,168	12,708,752	6,984,104	4,436,245	3,512,067
1965–66	2028	27,206,980	12,480,644	6,914,757	4,779,150	3,032,429
1966–67	2028	28,902,596	14,242,957	7,253,819	4,421,172	2,984,648
1967–68	2028	30,107,298	15,289,410	7,450,410	4,013,087	3,354,391
1968–69	2028	29,382,172	14,584,851	7,382,390	4,339,656	3,075,275
1969–70	2028	29,600,972	14,868,754	7,581,728	4,223,761	2,926,729
1970–71	2028	28,194,146	13,954,337	7,098,265	4,377,213	2,764,331
1971–72	2028	28,700,729	14,484,603	6,769,308	4,697,392	2,749,426
1972–73	2028	25,448,642	13,998,154	5,631,730	3,737,252	2,081,506
1973–74	2027	24,982,203	13,070,991	6,326,108	3,421,624	2,163,480
1974–75	2028	25,577,977	12,613,178	6,955,970	4,086,145	1,992,684
1975–76	2028	24,896,053	13,089,861	5,798,405	3,948,449	2,059,338
1976–77	2028	26,182,800	13,647,585	6,250,597	4,152,218	2,132,400
1977–78	2028	25,392,872	13,255,677	6,474,763	3,332,042	2,330,390
1978–79	2028	24,540,627	12,704,549	6,153,223	3,374,558	2,308,297
1979–80	2028	24,623,975	12,163,002	6,112,025	3,999,328	2,349,620
1980–81	2028	21,907,569	11,392,894	5,175,442	3,637,854	1,701,379

FOOTBALL LEAGUE CUP 1980–81

FIRST ROUND, FIRST LEG

8 AUG

Northampton T (0) 0

Reading (2) 2 *(Hetzke, Earles)* 3294

Northampton T: Poole; Walker, Sandercock, Byatt, Waldock, Saxby, Denyer, Sandy (Farmer), Sargent, Phillips, Bowen.
Reading: Death; Joslyn, Moreline, Bowman, Hetzke, Shipperley, Earles, Heale, Dixon, Sanchez, Beavon.

9 AUG

Aldershot (1) 2 *(Garwood 2)*

Wimbledon (0) 0 3023

Aldershot: Johnson; Edwards, Wooler, Briley, Bennett, Jopling, Lucas, Sanford, Garwood, Scott, Robinson (Tomlin).
Wimbledon: Goddard; Jones, Armstrong, Galliers, Smith, Cunningham, Ketteridge (Denny), Downes, Leslie, Cork, Davies.

Blackburn R (0) 0

Huddersfield T (0) (0) 8670

Blackburn R: Arnold; Branagan, De Vries, Speight, Keeley, Fazackerley, Brotherston, Crawford, Garner, McKenzie, Parkes.
Huddersfield T: Rankin; Brown, Robinson, Stanton (Kennedy), Sutton, Hanvey, Laverick, Kindon, Purdie, Robins, Cowling.

Bournemouth (1) 1 *(Massey)*

Swindon T (0) 1 *(Rowland)* 5121

Bournemouth: Allen; Cunningham, Ferns, Impey, Townsend, Heffernan, McGrath, Spackman, Prudham, Massey, Evanson.
Swindon T: Allan; Barrett, Peach, Kamara, Rollings, Walsh, Miller, Cockerill, Rowland, Mayes, Carter.

Brentford (1) 3 *(Crown, Smith, Walker)*

Charlton Ath (1) 1 *(Walsh)* 5850

Brentford: McCulloch; Shrubb, Hill, Kruse, Jenkins, Silkman, Harris, Walker, Crown, Booker, Smith D.
Charlton Ath: Wood; Gritt, Warman, Berry, Shaw, Tydeman, Powell, Walsh, Hales, Smith (Walker), Robinson.

Bury (2) 2 *(Butler, Johnson)*

Halifax T (1) 2 *(Firth, Evans)* 3029

Bury: Forrest; Howard, Kennedy, Halford, Whitehead, Waddington, Mullen, Butler, Johnson, Madden, Farley.
Halifax T: Kilner; Nattress, Burton, Evans, Goodman (Harris), Dunleavy, Firth, Hendrie, Allatt, Ward, Stafford.

Carlisle U (1) 2 *(Bannon, Brown)*

Rochdale (0) 0 2257

Carlisle U: Swinburne; Collins, Watson, Macdonald, Coady, Parker, McGrogan (Brown), Metcalfe, Bannon, Hamilton, Beardsley.
Rochdale: Pearce; Jones, Snookes, Esser, Weir, Taylor, Wann, O'Loughlin, Hilditch, Wellings, Martinez.

Chester (0) 1 *(Oakes)*

Stockport Co (0) 1 *(Sword)* 2468

Chester: Millington; Rayner, Walker, Storton, Cottam, Oakes, Anderson, Kearney, Birch, Jones, Ludlam (Phillips).
Stockport Co: Lawson; Rutter, Sherlock, Thorpe, Sword, Uzelac, Williams, Sunley, Bradd, Galvin, Coyle.

Chesterfield (1) 1 *(Walker)*

Darlington (0) 0 4489

Chesterfield: Turner; Tartt (Kowalski), O'Neill, Wilson, Pollard, Ridley, Birch, Moss, Bonnyman, Salmons, Walker.
Darlington: Cuff; Kamara, McLean, Ball, Skipper, Speedie, Hawker, Charlton, Stalker, Hamilton, Walsh.

Colchester U (0) (0)

Gillingham (1) 2 *(Price, Bruce)* 2514

Colchester U: Walker; Crouch, Cusenza, Longhorn (Evans), Wignall, Packer, Hodge, Rowles, Foley, Lee, Allinson.
Gillingham: Hillyard; Sharpe, Ford, Overton, Weatherley, Hughes, Donn, Duncan, Price, Henderson, Bruce.

Doncaster R (1) 1 *(Snodin)*

Mansfield T (0) 1 *(Caldwell)* 4201

Doncaster R: Shipley; Russell, Flanagan, Lister (Bates), Saunders, Dowd, Pugh, Mell, Warboys, Little, Snodin G.
Mansfield T: Arnold; Dawkins, Mann, Bird, McClelland, Burrows, Phillips, Caldwell, Austin, Parkinson, Pollard.

Exeter C (0) 1 *(Kellow)*

Bristol R (1) 1 *(Bates)* 4702

Exeter C: Main; Ireland, Hatch, Prince, Giles, Roberts P., Pearson, Rogers P. (Neville), Kellow, Delve, Fuller.
Bristol R: Thomas; Gillies, Bater, Mabbutt, Hughes, Cooper, Emmanuel, Barrowclough, Williams G., Bates, Barrett.

Grimsby T (0) 1 *(Waters)*

Notts Co (0) 0 7402

Grimsby T: Batch; Stone, Moore, Waters, Wigginton, Crombie, Brolly, Ford, Drinkell, Mitchell, Cumming.
Notts Co: Avramovic; Benjamin, O'Brien, Kelly (Mair), Kilcline, Richards, McCulloch, Masson, Christie, Hunt, Hooks.

Hereford U (0) 1 *(Bartley)*

Newport Co (0) 0 7745

Hereford U: Hughes; Pejic, Price, Spiring, Dobson, Lowe, Bartley, Harvey, McGrellis (Hunt), Jones, Lane.
Newport Co: Plumley; Walden, Relish, Bruton, Oakes, Bailey, Tynan, Lowndes, Gwyther, Aldridge (Vaughan), Moore.

Lincoln C (0) 5 *(Harford 3, Bell, Shipley)*

Hull C (0) 0 3538

Lincoln C: Boulton; Thompson T., Keeley, Thompson S., Peake, Carr, Turner, Bell, Cunningham, Harford, Shipley.
Hull C: Norman; Nisbet, Haigh, Booth (McLaren), Roberts J., Richards, Marwood, Roberts G., Edwards, Norrie, Moss.

Peterborough U (0) 3 *(Cooke, Kellock, Syrett)*

Fulham (1) 2 *(Strong, Gale)* 3662

Peterborough U: Waugh; McVay, Phillips, Dobson, Slack, Foster (Gallagher), Quow, Kellock, Cooke, Syrett, Cliss.
Fulham: Peyton; Peters, Brown, Gale, Strong, Beck, Lewington, O'Driscoll (Hatter), Greenaway, Mahoney, Davies.

Plymouth Arg (0) 0

Portsmouth (1) 1 *(Laidlaw)* 7036

Plymouth Arg: Crudgington; James, McNeil, Randell, Foster, Phillipson-Masters, Hodges, Kemp, Sims, Bason, Johnson (Graves).
Portsmouth: Mellor; McLaughlin, Viney, Barnard, Aizlewood, Garner, Gregory, Laidlaw, Tait, Brisley, Rogers.

Port Vale (2) 2 *(Chamberlain 2)*

Tranmere R (2) 3 *(Edwards pen, Kelly, Craven)* 2651

Port Vale: Dance; Keenan, Griffiths, Beech, Harwood, Sproson, Jones (Elsby), Farrell, Allen, Chamberlain N., Bromage.
Tranmere R: Johnson; Parry, Mathias, Bramhall, Edwards (Mungall), Evans, Kelly, Craven, Lumby, Beamish, Peplow.

Rotherham U (0) 1 *(Forrest)*

Bradford C (0) 3 *(Campbell 2, Gallagher)* 3881

Rotherham U: Brown; Forrest, Breckin, Henson, Stancliffe, Vaughan, Gooding, Fern, Halom, Carr, Finney.
Bradford C: Smith; Podd, Watson, Robertson, Jackson, Wood, Gallagher, Stainforth, Campbell, McNiven, Chapman.

Scunthorpe U (0) 0

Barnsley (0) 1 *(Parker)* 4550

Scunthorpe U: Neenan; Davy, Jarvis, Grimes, Dall, Oates, Pugh, Cammack, Lambert (O'Berg), Partridge, Stewart.
Barnsley: New; Cooper, Chambers, Glavin, Banks (Joyce), McCarthy, Evans, Parker, Aylott, Lester, Downes.

Sheffield W (2) 2 *(Taylor, Johnson)*

Sheffield U (0) 0 23,989

Sheffield W: Bolder; Blackhall, Grant, Smith, Pickering, King, Taylor, Johnson, Owen, McCulloch, Curran.
Sheffield U: Richardson; Cutbush, Houston, Kenworthy, MacPhail, Matthews (Tibbott), Wiggan, Trusson, Charles, Hatton, Peters.

Southend U (1) 1 *(Pountney)*

Oxford U (0) 0 3023

Southend U: Cawston; Stead, Cusack, Moody, Yates, Pountney, Hadley, Otulakowski, Gray, Spence, Mercer.
Oxford U: Brown; Briggs, Smithers, Jeffrey, Cooke, Shotton, Brock, Taylor, Berry (Fogg), Foley, Seacole.

Torquay U (0) 0

Cardiff C (0) 0 3441

Torquay U: O'Keefe; Jones, Pethard, Sermanni, Bourne, Hayes, Fell, Lawrence, Cooper, Bowker, Weston.
Cardiff C: Grotier; Grapes, Lewis, Jones, Pontin, Roberts, Bishop, Micallef (Hughes), Stevens, Ronson, Buchanan.

Walsall (1) 2 *(McDonough, Penn)*

Blackpool (1) 3 *(McEwan 2 [1 pen], Morris)* 5496

Walsall: Turner; Paul, Mower, Serella, Baines, Hart, Penn, O'Kelly (Waddington), McDonough, Buckley, Caswell.
Blackpool: Hesford; Gardner, Pashley, Doyle, McEwan, Ashurst, Morris, Hockaday, MacDougall, Ball, Welsh.

Watford (1) 2 *(Poskett 2)*

Millwall (1) 1 *(Lyons)* 9050

Watford: Steele; Henderson, Harrison (Jackett), Patching, Sims, Bolton, Blissett, Poskett, Jenkins, Train, Rostron.
Millwall: Gleasure; Sitton, Gregory, Chatterton, Kitchener, Blyth, Martin (Roberts), Mehmet, Mitchell, Lyons, Kinsella.

Wigan Ath (1) 2 *(Gore 2)*

Crewe Alex (0) 1 *(Hunter)* 5512

Wigan Ath: Brown; Fretwell, Whittle, Gore, Methven, Davids, McMullen (Quinn T.), Wright, Hutchinson, Morton, Tierney.
Crewe Alex: Mulhearn; Wilkinson, Lewis (Mountford), Hunter, Scott, Prophett, McMahon, Guy, Conroy, Palios, Bowers.

Wrexham (1) 1 *(Vinter)*

Burnley (1) 3 *(Davis og, Cassidy, Thomson)* 5126

Wrexham: Davies; Hill, Davis, Jones, Dwyer, Sutton (Whittle), Arkwright, McNeil, Cartwright, Edwards, Vinter.
Burnley: Stevenson; Wood, Rodaway, Thomson, Holt, Scott, Dobson, Cassidy, Cavener, Taylor, Hamilton.

York C (1) 2 *(Ford, McDonald)*

Hartlepool U (1) 1 *(Forster)* 2444

York C: Blackburn; Kay, Walsh, Richards, Faulkner, Craig, Ford, Smith, Eccles, McGhie, McDonald.
Hartlepool U: Burleigh; Brown, Vass, Lawrence, Bird, Fagan, Linacre, Kerry, Houchen, Foster, Hampton.

FIRST ROUND, SECOND LEG

11 AUG

Stockport Co (0) 1 *aet (Sunley)*

Chester (0) 0 2720

Stockport Co won 2-1

Stockport Co: Lawson; Rutter, Sword, Uzelac, Sherlock, Williams, Thorpe, Galvin, Coyle, Sunley, Bradd.
Chester: Millington; Jeffries, Walker, Storton, Cottam, Oakes, Jones, Kearney, Birch, Phillips, Ludlam.

12 AUG

Barnsley (1) 2 *(Banks, Glavin)*

Scunthorpe U (0) 1 *(Cammack)* 8430

Barnsley won 3-1

Barnsley: New; Cooper, Chambers, Glavin, Banks, McCarthy, Evans, Parker, Aylott, Boyd, Downes.
Scunthorpe U: Neenan; Davy, Jarvis, Grimes, Dall, Oates, Pugh, Cammack, Lambert, Partridge, Stewart (O'Berg).

Bristol R (1) 1 *aet (Bates)*

Exeter C (1) 1 *(Kellow)* 4070

Aggregate 2-2; Bristol R won 7-6 on penalties

Bristol R: Thomas; Gillies, Hughes, Mabbutt, Bater, Emmanuel, Williams G., Cooper, Barrowclough, Bates, Barrett (Jones).
Exeter C: Main; Ireland, Hatch, Prince, Giles, Roberts P., Forbes, Neville, Kellow, Delve, Pullar.

Burnley (1) 2 *(Scott, Dobson pen)*

Wrexham (1) 1 *(Edwards)* 4439

Burnley won 5-2

Burnley: Stevenson; Laws, Holt, Scott, Rodaway, Thomson, Young, Dobson, Hamilton, Cavener, Taylor.
Wrexham: Davies; Hill, Dwyer, Jones F., Jones J., Carrodus (Whittle), Vinter, Arkwright, Edwards, McNeil, Cartwright.

Charlton Ath (2) 5 *(Walsh 3, Hales 2)*

Brentford (0) 0 3764

Charlton Ath won 6-3

Charlton Ath: Wood; Gritt, Warman, Shaw, Berry, Tydeman, Powell, Walsh, Hales, Smith, Robinson.
Brentford: McCulloch; Shrubb, Hill, Kruse (Salman), Jenkins, Silkman, Harris, Walker, Crown, Booker, Smith.

Darlington (1) 1 *(Walsh)*

Chesterfield (0) 2 *(Wilson, Moss)* 2500

Chesterfield won 3-1

Darlington: Cuff; Kamara, McLean (Smith), Ball, Skipper, Speedie, Hawker, Charlton, Stalker, Hamilton, Walsh.
Chesterfield: Turner; Kowalski, O'Neill, Wilson, Green, Ridley, Birch, Moss, Bonnyman, Salmons, Walker.

Fulham (0) 1 *aet (Davies)*

Peterborough U (0) 1 *(Cooke)* 3157

Peterborough U won 4-3

Fulham: Peyton; Peters, Strong, Beck, Brown, Gale, Greenaway, Lewington (Wilson), Mahoney, Davies, Lock.
Peterborough U: Waugh; McVay, Phillips, Dobson, Slack, Foster, Quow (Gallagher), Kellock, Cooke, Syrett, Cliss.

Gillingham (0) 2 *(Ford, Bruce)*

Colchester U (0) 1 *(Gough)* 5220

Gillingham won 4-1

Gillingham: Hillyard; Sharpe, Ford, Overton, Weatherley, Crabbe, Donn, Duncan, Price, Henderson, Bruce.
Colchester U: Walker; Cook (Evans), Cotton, Gough, Wignall, Packer, Hodge, Rowles, Foley, Lee, Allinson.

Halifax T (0) 0

Bury (0) 1 *(Johnson)* 2268

Bury won 3-2

Halifax T: Kilner; Nattress, Dunleavy, Evans, Harris, Goodman, Firth, Hendrie, Allatt, Ward, Stafford.
Bury: Forrest; Howard, Kennedy, Halford, Whitehead, Waddington, Mullen, Butler, Johnson, Waldron, Madden.

Hartlepool U (0) 0

York C (0) 0 3496

York C won 2-1

Hartlepool U: Burleigh; Brown, Sweeney, Lawrence, Bird, Fagan, Linacre, Kerry, Houchen, Foster, Hampton.
York C: Blackburn; Kay, Walsh, Richards, Faulkner, Craig, Ford, Smith, Eccles, McGhie, McDonald.

Huddersfield T (0) 1 *aet (Kindon)*

Blackburn R (0) 1 *(Garner)* 9500

Aggregate 1-1; Blackburn R won on away goals rule

Huddersfield T: Rankin; Brown, Robinson, Stanton, Sutton, Hanvey, Laverick, Kindon, Purdie (Kennedy), Robins, Cowling.
Blackburn R: Arnold; Branagan, De Vries, Kendall, Keeley, Fazackerley, Brotherston, Speight, Garner, Crawford, Parkes.

Hull C (0) 0

Lincoln C (0) 2 *(Harford 2)* 2933

Lincoln C won 7-0

Hull C: Norman; Nisbet, Horswill, Booth, Roberts J., Haigh, Norrie, Roberts G., Edwards, Moss (McClaren), McDonald.
Lincoln C: Boulton; Thompson T., Keeley, Thompson S., Peake, Carr, Turner, Harford, Cunningham, Bell (Hughes), Shipley.

Mansfield T (0) 2 *aet (Austin, Pollard)*

Doncaster R (1) 1 *(Nimmo)* 3420

Mansfield T won 3-2

Mansfield T: Arnold; Dawkins, Mann, Bird, McClelland, Burrows, Phillips, Caldwell, Austin, Parkinson, Pollard.
Doncaster R: Boyd; Russell, Lally, Lister, Saunders, Dowd, Pugh, Mell, Nimmo, Little, Snodin G.

Millwall (0) 0

Watford (1) 2 *(Sims, Blissett)* 5210

Watford won 4-1

Millwall: Gleasure; Gregory, Sitton, Chatterton, Kitchener, Blyth, Mehmet, Martin, Mitchell, Lyons, Kinsella.
Watford: Steele; Henderson, Jackett, Patching, Sims, Bolton, Blissett, Poskett, Jenkins (Callaghan), Train, Rostron.

Newport Co (2) 5 *(Tynan 2, Aldridge 2, Gwyther)*

Hereford U (0) 0 5683

Newport Co won 5-0

Newport Co: Plumley; Walden, Relish (Elsey), Bruton, Oakes, Tynan, Vaughan, Lowndes, Gwyther, Aldridge, Moore.
Hereford U: Hughes; Pejic, Price, Spiring, Dobson, Layton, Harvey, Bartley, Lowe, Jones, Lane.

Notts Co (1) 3 *(Christie, Kelly, Mair)*

Grimsby T (0) 0 4718

Notts Co won 3-1

Notts Co: Avramovic; Benjamin, O'Brien, Kelly, Kilcline, Richards, McCulloch, Masson, Christie, Hunt, Hooks (Mair).
Grimsby T: Bach; Stone, Moore K., Waters, Wigginton, Crombie, Brolly, Ford, Drinkell, Mitchell, Cumming.

Portsmouth (1) 2 *(Gregory, Rogers)*

Plymouth Arg (1) 1 *(Kemp)* 11,997

Portsmouth won 3-1

Portsmouth: Mellor; McLaughlin, Viney, Brisley, Aizlewood, Garner, Gregory, Laidlaw, Tait, Barnard, Rogers.
Plymouth Arg: Crudgington; James, Harrison, Randell, Foster, Phillipson-Masters, Hodges, Kemp, Sims, Bason (Graves), Murphy.

Rochdale (0) 1 *(Martinez)*

Carlisle U (0) 1 *(Brown)* 1806

Carlisle U won 3-1

Rochdale: Pearce; Jones, Snookes, Esser, Burke, Weir (Seal), Wann, O'Laughlin, Hilditch, Wellings, Martinez.
Carlisle U: Swinburne; Collins, Watson, Macdonald, Coady, Parker, McAuley (Brown), Metcalfe, Bannon, Hamilton, Beardsley.

Sheffield U (1) 1 *(Hatton)*
Sheffield W (0) 1 *(Curran)* 25,588
Sheffield W won 3-1
Sheffield U: Richardson; Cutbush, Houston, Kenworthy, MacPhail, Tibbott, Wiggan (Butlin), Trusson, Charles, Hatton, Peters.
Sheffield W: Bolder; Blackhall, Williamson, Smith, Pickering, King, Taylor, Owen, Mellor, McCulloch, Curran.

Swindon T (0) *aet (McGrath* og, *Mayes)*
Bournemouth (0) 0 5814
Swindon T won 3-1
Swindon T: Allan; Barrett, Peach, Kamara, Rollings, Walsh, Miller, Cockerill, Rowland, Mayes, Carter.
Bournemouth: Allen; Cunningham, Ferns, Impey, Townsend, Heffernan, McGrath, Spackman (Elliott), Prudham, Massey, Evanson.

Tranmere R (0) 0 *aet*
Port Vale (0) 1 *(Bromage)* 2386
Aggregate 3-3; Tranmere R won on away goals rule
Tranmere R: Johnson; Parry, Mathias, Bramhall, Edwards, Evans, Kelly, Craven, Lumby (Williams), Beamish, Peplow.
Port Vale: Dance; Brissett, Griffiths, Beech, Harwood, Sproson, Jones, Farrell, Allen, Chamberlain N., Bromage.

Wimbledon (3) 4 *(Leslie 2, Denny, Downes)*
Aldershot (0) 1 *(Brodie)* 2444
Wimbledon won 4-3
Wimbledon: Goddard; Jones, Armstrong, Galliers, Smith, Cunningham, Ketteridge, Downes, Leslie, Cork, Denny.
Aldershot: Johnson; Edwards, Wooler, Briley, Bennett, Jopling, Lucas, Brodie, Garwood, Crosby, Sanford.

13 AUG

Blackpool (1) 3 *(Morris, Fletcher, Ashurst)*
Walsall (0) 1 *(Buckley)* 9781
Blackpool won 6-3
Blackpool: Hesford; Gardner, Williams, Doyle (Wells), McEwan, Ashurst, Morris, Hockaday, Fletcher, Ball, Harrison.
Walsall: Turner; Macken, Mower, Serella, Paul (O'Kelly), Baines, Hart, Caswell, Penn, McDonough, Buckley.

Bradford C (0) 0
Rotherham U (0) 0 4431
Bradford C won 3-1
Bradford C: Smith; Podd, Watson (Cooper), Billingham, Jackson, Wood, Gallagher, Staniforth, Campbell, McNiven, Chapman.
Rotherham U: Brown; Forrest, Breckin, Halom, Stancliffe, Vaughan, Towner, Gooding, Moore, Seasman (Carr), Finney.

Cardiff C (0) 2 *(Bishop, Stevens)*
Torquay U (0) 1 *(Fell)* 3149
Cardiff C won 2-1
Cardiff C: Grotier; Grapes, Dwyer, Jones, Pontin, Roberts, Bishop, Micallef, Stevens, Ronson, Buchanan.
Torquay U: O'Keefe; Jones, Pethard, Sermanni (Twitchin), Bourne, Hayes, Fell, Lawrence, Cooper, Bowker, Weston.

Crewe Alex (1) 2 *aet (Conroy 2)*
Wigan Ath (0) 2 *(Hutchinson, Gore* pen*)* 4063
Wigan Ath won 4-3
Crewe Alex: Mulhearn; Wilkinson, Lewis, Hunter, Scott, Prophett, McMahon, Guy, Conroy, Palios, Bowers.
Wigan Ath: Brown; Fretwell, Whittle, Gore, Methven, Davids, Quinn T., Wright, Houghton, Hutchinson, Tierney.

Oxford U (1) 2 *(Foley, Shotton)*
Southend U (0) 0 2989
Oxford U won 2-1
Oxford U: Brown; Briggs, Smithers, Jeffrey, Cooke, Shotton, Brock, Taylor, O'Dowd, Foley, Seacole.
Southend U: Cawston; Stead, Yates, Hadley, Moody, Cusack, Gray, Pountney, Spence, Mercer, Otulakowski.

Reading (2) 2 *(Heale 2)*
Northampton T (1) 3 *(Phillips 2* [1 pen], *Denyer)* 4357
Reading won 4-3
Reading: Death; Joslyn, White, Bowman (Webb), Hetzke, Shipperley, Earles, Heale, Dixon, Sanchez, Beavon.
Northampton T: Poole; Walker, Sandercock, Byatt, Gage, Sargent, Denyer, Heeley, Farmer, Phillips, Bowen.

SECOND ROUND, FIRST LEG

26 AUG

Birmingham C (1) 2 *(Ainscow, Gemmill* pen*)*
Bristol C (0) 1 *(Ritchie)* 12,163
Birmingham C: Wealands; Langan, Dennis, Curbishley, Gallagher, Todd, Ainscow, Worthington, Bertschin, Gemmill, Dillon.
Bristol C: Cashley; Sweeney, Whitehead, Tainton, Gow, Merrick, Fitzpatrick (Hay), Ritchie, Mabbutt, Mann, Pritchard.

Bolton W (0) 0
Crystal Palace (2) 3 *(Murphy 2, Flanagan)* 9913
Bolton W: Peacock; Graham, Burke, Wilson (Nowak), Jones, Walsh, Gowling, Whatmore, Carter, Kidd, Hoggan.
Crystal Palace: Barron; Nicholas, Fenwick, Murphy (Sealy), Cannon, Gilbert, Leahy, Francis, Flanagan, Allen, Hilaire.

Burnley (0) 0
West Ham U (2) 2 *(Goddard, Cross)* 6818
Burnley: Stevenson; Wood, Thomson, Rodaway, Laws, Scott, Dobson, Cassidy, Cavener, Hamilton, Taylor.
West Ham U: Parkes; Stewart, Lampard, Bonds, Martin, Devonshire, Holland, Goddard, Cross, Brooking, Pike.

Brighton & HA (3) 3 *(Foster, Robinson, Ward)*
Tranmere R (0) 1 *(Evans)* 10,055
Brighton & HA: Moseley; Gregory, Williams, Horton, Foster, Lawrenson, McHale, Ward, Robinson, Smith, McNab.
Tranmere R: Johnson; Parry, Mathias, Bramall, Evans, Edwards, Mungall, Kerr, Lumby, Beamish, Kelly.

Cambridge U (1) 3 *(Reilly 2, Finney)*
Wolverhampton W (0) 1 *(Daniel* pen*)* 7234
Cambridge U: Webster; Donaldson, Murray, Smith, Fallon, Gibbins, Streete, Spriggs, Reilly, Finney, Christie (O'Neill).
Wolverhampton W: Bradshaw; Palmer, Brazier, Daniel, Hughes, Berry, Hibbitt, Carr, Gray, Richards, Eves.

Carlisle U (1) 1 *(Hamilton)*

Charlton Ath (1) 2 *(Robinson, Walker)* 2673

Carlisle U: Swinburne; Coady, Collins, MacDonald, Houghton, Parker, McVitie, Metcalfe, Bannon (Beardsley), Hamilton, Staniforth.
Charlton Ath: Wood; Gritt, Warman, Shaw, Berry, Tydeman, Powell, Walsh, Walker, Smith, Robinson.

Chesterfield (2) 3 *(Crawford, Bonnyman* pen, *Moss)*

Oxford U (1) 1 *(Lythgoe)* 4856

Chesterfield: Turner; Kowalski (Walwyn), O'Neill, Wilson, Hunter, Ridley, Crawford, Moss, Bonnyman, Salmons, Walker.
Oxford U: Brown; Briggs, Smithers, Jeffrey, Cooke, Shotton, Brock, Taylor, Berry, Foley, Lythgoe.

Everton (1) 3 *(Eastoe, Latchford, McBride)*

Blackpool (0) 0 20,156

Everton: McDonagh; Gidman, Ratcliffe, Wright, Lyons, Stanley, McMahon, Eastoe, Latchford, Hartford, McBride.
Blackpool: Hesford; Gardner, Williams, Doyle, McEwan, Greenall, Morris, Hockaday, Fletcher, Noble, Harrison.

Mansfield T (0) 0

Barnsley (0) 0 6294

Mansfield T: Arnold; Dawkins, Mann, Bird, McClelland, Burrows, Phillips, Caldwell, Austin, Parkinson, Pollard.
Barnsley: New; Joyce, Chambers, Glavin, Banks, Cooper, Evans, Parker, Riley, Lester, Downes.

Middlesbrough (3) 3 *(Shearer 2, Proctor)*

Ipswich T (1) 1 *(Wark)* 14,459

Middlesbrough: Platt; Craggs, Bailey, Johnston (Jankovic), Ashcroft, Nattrass, Proctor, Hedley, Hodgson, Shearer, Armstrong.
Ipswich T: Cooper; Mills, McCall, Thijssen, Osman, Butcher, Wark, Muhren, Mariner, Gates, O'Callaghan.

Newport Co (1) 1 *(Vaughan)*

Notts Co (1) 1 *(Hunt)* 6708

Newport Co: Plumley; Walden, Relish, Bruton, Oakes, Tynan, Vaughan, Lowndes, Gwyther, Aldridge, Cunningham (Elsey).
Notts Co: Avramovic; Benjamin, O'Brien, Kelly, Kilcline, Richards, McCulloch, Masson, Christie, Hunt, Hooks (Mair).

Oldham Ath (2) 3 *(Keegan, Kowenicki, Stainrod)*

Portsmouth (0) 2 *(Garner, Laidlaw* pen*)* 5251

Oldham Ath: McDonnell; Hoolickin, Blair, Kowenicki, Clements, Hurst, Wylde, Futcher, Stainrod, Keegan, Atkinson.
Portsmouth: Mellor; McLaughlin, Bryant, Brisley, Aizlewood, Garner, Gregory, Laidlaw, Showers, Tait, Rogers.

Preston NE (0) 1 *(McGee)*

Wigan Ath (0) 0 8073

Preston NE: Tunks; Cameron, McAteer, Burns, Baxter, O'Riordan, Bell, Coleman, Elliott (Doyle), Houston, McGee.
Wigan Ath: Brown; Curtis (Quinn T.), Fretwell, Gore, Methven, Davids, McMullen, Wright, Houghton, Hutchinson, Whittle.

QPR (0) 0

Derby Co (0) 0 11,244

QPR: Woods; McCreery, Gillard, Waddock, Wicks, Roeder, Hazell, Shanks, Langley, Currie, Burke.
Derby Co: Jones; Emery (Richards), Buckley, Powell S., Osgood, Ramage, Clark, Powell B., Biley, Swindlehurst, Emson.

Shrewsbury T (0) 1 *(Biggins)*

Norwich C (1) 1 *(Fashanu)* 5536

Shrewsbury T: Wardle; King, Leonard, Turner, Griffin, Keay, Tong, Lindsay, Biggins, Dungworth, Petts.
Norwich C: Hansbury; Bond, Downs, Barham, Forbes, Powell, Woods, Fashanu, Royle, Paddon, Bennett.

Southampton (2) 4 *(George 2, Holmes 2)*

Watford (0) 0 16,659

Southampton: Katalinic; Golac, McCartney, Williams, Watson, Nicholl, Keegan, Channon, George, Holmes, Baker.
Watford: Steele; Henderson, Harrison, Patching, Sims, Bolton, Blissett, Poskett, Rostron, Train, Jackett (Jenkins).

Swansea C (0) 1 *(James L.)*

Arsenal (0) 1 *(Stapleton)* 17,036

Swansea C: Stewart; Marustik (Toshack), Rushbury, Mahoney, Stevenson, Phillips, Giles, James R., James L., Craig, Robinson.
Arsenal: Jennings; Devine, Sansom, Talbot, O'Leary, Young, Hollins, Sunderland, Stapleton, Price, Rix.

WBA (1) 1 *(Barnes)*

Leicester C (0) 0 13,810

WBA: Godden; Trewick, Statham, Moses, Wile, Robertson, Robson, Brown, Regis, Owen, Barnes.
Leicester C: Wallington; Carr, Gibson, Peake, May, O'Neill, Goodwin, Melrose, Young, Wilson, Smith (Henderson).

Wimbledon (2) 2 *(Cunningham, Leslie)*

Sheffield W (1) 1 *(Owen)* 3549

Wimbledon: Goddard; Brown, Perkins, Galliers, Smith, Cunningham, Davies, Downes, Leslie, Cork, Driver.
Sheffield W: Bolder; Blackhall, Grant, Smith, Pickering, King, Owen, Johnson, Lowey, McCulloch, Curran.

27 AUG

Aston Villa (1) 1 *(Morley)*

Leeds U (0) 0 24,238

Aston Villa: Rimmer; Swain, Gibson, Evans, McNaught, Mortimer, Bremner, Shaw, Withe, Cowans, Morley.
Leeds U: Lukic; Cherry, Greenhoff, Flynn, Hart, Madeley, Chandler, Thomas, Connor, Sabella, Graham.

Blackburn R (0) 0

Gillingham (0) 0 7316

Blackburn R: Arnold; Branigan, Rathbone, Kendall, Keeley, Fazackerley, Brotherston, Crawford, Garner (Craig), McKenzie, Speight.
Gillingham: Hillyard; Sharpe, Ford, Overton, Weatherley, Crabbe, Bruce, Duncan, Westwood, Henderson, Richardson.

Bradford C (0) 1 *(Campbell)*

Liverpool (0) 0 16,232

Bradford C: Smith; Podd, Wood, Robertson, Jackson, Cooper, Dolan, Staniforth, Campbell, McNiven, Chapman.
Liverpool: Clemence; Neal, Kennedy A., Thompson, Kennedy R., Hansen, Fairclough, Case, Johnson, McDermott, Souness.

Cardiff C (1) 1 *(Bishop)*

Chelsea (0) 0 6549

Cardiff C: Grotier; Grapes, Lewis, Campbell, Pontin, Dwyer, Bishop, Kitchen, Stevens, Ronson, Buchanan (Thomas).
Chelsea: Borota; Wilkins, Rofe, Bumstead, Droy, Chivers, Britton, Fillery, Johnson (Lee), Walker, Nutton.

Lincoln C (0) 1 *(Shipley)*

Swindon T (0) 1 *(Rollings)* 4940

Lincoln C: Boulton; Thompson T., Keeley, Hobson, Peake, Carr, Turner, Thompson S., Harford, Cunningham, Shipley.
Swindon T: Allen; Lewis, Peach, Kamara, Rollings, Walsh, Miller, Hughes, Mayes, Carter, Greenwood.

Manchester U (0) 0

Coventry C (0) 1 *(English)* 31,656

Manchester U: Bailey; Nicholl, Albiston, McIlroy, Jovanovic, Buchan, Coppell, Greenhoff (Sloan), Ritchie, Macari, Thomas.
Coventry C: Blyth; Coop, Roberts, Blair, Dyson, Van Gool, Daly, Thompson (McDonald), English, Hunt, Gillespie.

Newcastle U (1) 3 *(Rafferty 2, Shoulder* pen*)*

Bury (1) 2 *(Butler, Johnson)* 9069

Newcastle U: Carr; Kelly, Davies, Barton, Boam, Leaver (Cartwright), Koenen, Hibbitt, Shoulder, Rafferty, Nicholson.
Bury: Forrest; Howard, Kennedy, Halford, Whitehead, Waddington, Mullen, Butler (Hilton), Johnson, Madden, Farley.

Nottingham F (0) 3 *(Robertson* pen*, Birtles, Gray)*

Peterborough U (0) 0 16,117

Nottingham F: Shilton; Anderson, Gray, O'Hare, Lloyd, Needham, O'Neill, Bowyer, Birtles, Wallace, Robertson.
Peterborough U: Waugh; McVay, Phillips, Hodgson, Slack, Foster, Quow, Kellock, Cooke, Syrett (Gallagher), Cliss.

Orient (0) 0

Tottenham H (1) 1 *(Lacy)* 20,087

Orient: Day; Fisher, Roffey, Taylor, Gray, Parsons, Chiedozie, Jennings, Mayo, Bowles, Coates.
Tottenham H: Kendall; Smith, Hughton, Yorath, Lacy, Perryman, Ardiles, Archibald, Villa, Hoddle, Crooks.

Reading (0) 0

Luton T (1) 2 *(Moss, Stein)* 5778

Reading: Death; Joslyn, White (Webb), Bowman, Shipperley, Moreline, Earles, Heale, Dixon, Sanchez, Beavon.
Luton T: Findlay; Stephens, Donaghy, Grealish, Saxby, Price, Hill, Stein, Bunn (White), Antic, Moss.

Stockport Co (1) 1 *(Sunley)*

Sunderland (0) 1 *(Arnott)* 6108

Stockport Co: Lawson; Rutter, Sherlock, Fowler, Sword, Uzelac, Williams, Sunley, Bradd, Galvin, Coyle.
Sunderland: Turner; Whitworth, Bolton, Allardyce, Elliott, Hindmarch, Arnott, Chisholm, Hawley (Robson), Brown, Cummins.

Stoke C (1) 1 *(Chapman)*

Manchester C (0) 1 *(Henry)* 13,176

Stoke C: Fox; Evans, Hampton, Dodd, Thorley, Richardson, Ursem, Johnson P.A., Chapman, Cook (Randall), Bracewell.
Manchester C: Corrigan (Palmer); Ranson, Reid, Booth, Caton, Henry, Tueart, Daley, MacKenzie, Power, Reeves.

York C (1) 2 *(Richards, Pulis* og*)*

Bristol R (0) 1 *(McCaffery)* 3405

York C: Blackburn; Kay, Walsh, Richards, Faulkner, Craig, Ford, Smith, Eccles, McGhie (Byrne), McDonald.
Bristol R: Thomas; Gillies, Bater, McCaffery, Mabbutt, Lee, Barrowclough, Williams, Bates, Penny, Hughes (Pulis).

SECOND ROUND, SECOND LEG

2 SEPT

Arsenal (1) 3 *(Hollins* pen*, Sunderland, Walford)*

Swansea C (1) 1 *(Charles)* 26,399

Arsenal won 4-2

Arsenal: Jennings; Devine, Sansom, Talbot, Walford, Young, Hollins, Sunderland, Stapleton, Price, Rix.
Swansea C: Stewart; Attley, Haziabdic, Rushbury, Stevenson, Phillips, Giles, James R., James L., Charles, Toshack.

Barnsley (0) 4 *aet (Riley, Glavin 3* [1 pen]*)*

Mansfield T (1) 2 *(Parkinson* pen*, McClelland)* 10,566

Barnsley won 4-2

Barnsley: New; Cooper, Chambers, Glavin, Banks, McCarthy, Evans, Parker, Riley, Lester, Downes.
Mansfield T: Arnold; Dawkins (Hamilton), Mann, Bird, McClelland, Burrows, Phillips, Caldwell, Austin, Parkinson, Pollard.

Bristol C (0) 0

Birmingham C (0) 0 6958

Birmingham C won 2-1

Bristol C: Cashley; Sweeney, Tainton, Gow, Hay, Merrick, Whitehead, Ritchie, Mabbutt, Doyle (Jantunen), Garland.
Birmingham C: Wealands; Langan, Dennis, Curbishley, Gallagher, Todd, Ainscow, Bertschin, Worthington, Gemmill, Dillon.

Bury (1) 1 *(Bradley)*

Newcastle U (0) 0 4348

Aggregate 3-3; Bury won on away goals rule

Bury: Forrest; Howard, Waddington, Bradley, Kennedy, Waldron, Halford, Mullen, Butler, Johnson, Madden.
Newcastle U: Hardwick; Carney, Boam, Wharton (Mitchell), Davies, Walker, Koenen, Hibbitt, Shinton, Shoulder, Rafferty.

Charlton Ath (1) 2 *(Walsh 2)*

Carlisle U (1) 1 *(Hamilton)* 5160

Charlton Ath won 4-2

Charlton Ath: Wood; Gritt, Warman, Shaw, Berry, Tydeman, Powell, Hales, Walsh, Smith, Robinson (Walker).
Carlisle U: Swinburne; Hoolickin, Collins (Bannon), MacDonald, Houghton, Parker, McVitie, Metcalfe, Beardsley, Hamilton, Staniforth.

Coventry C (0) 1 *(Blair)*

Manchester U (0) 0 18,705

Coventry C won 2-0

Coventry C: Blyth; Coop, Roberts, Blair, Dyson, Jones, Bannister, Thompson, Daly (Thomas), English, Hunt.
Manchester U: Bailey; Nicholl, Albiston, McIlroy, Jovanovic, Buchan, Coppell, Greenhoff, Ritchie, Macari, Thomas.

Crystal Palace (0) 2 *(Allen, Francis)*

Bolton W (1) 1 *(Kidd)* 14,764

Crystal Palace won 5-1

Crystal Palace: Barron; Lovell, Fenwick, Murphy (Brooks), Cannon, Gilbert, Smillie, Francis, Allen, Flanagan, Hilaire.
Bolton W: Peacock; Clement, Burke, Cantello, Jones (Nowak), Walsh, Gowling, Whatmore, Carter, Kidd, Hoggan.

Gillingham (0) 1 *aet (Bruce)*

Blackburn R (0) 2 *(McKenzie, Stonehouse pen)* 6315

Blackburn R won 2-1

Gillingham: Hillyard; Sharpe, Ford, Overton (Westwood), Weatherley, Hughes, Bruce, Duncan, Price, Henderson, Adams.
Blackburn R: Butcher; Branagan, DeVries, Round, Keeley, Fazackerley, Brotherston, Crawford (Stonehouse), Garner, McKenzie, Speight.

Ipswich T (2) 3 *(Osman, Mariner 2)*

Middlesbrough (0) 0 14,780

Ipswich T won 4-3

Ipswich T: Cooper; Burley, Mills, Thijssen, Osman, Butcher, Wark, Muhren, Mariner, Brazil, Gates.
Middlesbrough: Platt; Craggs, Bailey, Angus, Nattrass (Jankovic), McAndrew, Proctor, Hedley, Hodgson, Shearer, Armstrong.

Liverpool (3) 4 *(Dalglish 2, Kennedy R., Johnson)*

Bradford C (0) 0 21,107

Liverpool won 4-1

Liverpool: Clemence; Neal, Kennedy A., Thompson, Hansen, Kennedy R., Case, Souness, McDermott, Johnson (Fairclough), Dalglish.
Bradford C: Smith; Podd, Wood, Robertson, Jackson, Cooper, Dolan, Staniforth, Campbell, McNiven, Chapman.

Luton T (0) 1 *(Saxby)*

Reading (0) 1 *(Hetzke)* 5707

Luton T won 3-1

Luton T: Findlay; Stephens, Donaghy, Grealish, Saxby, Aizlewood, Hill, Stein, White, Antic, Heath (Ingram).
Reading: Death; Joslyn, Cheetham, Bowman, Hetzke, Hicks, Earles, Wanklyn, Dixon, Sanchez, Beavon.

Notts Co (1) 2 *(O'Brien pen, Christie)*

Newport Co (0) 0 4714

Notts Co won 3-1

Notts Co: Avramovic; Benjamin, O'Brien, Kelly, Kilcline, Richards, McCulloch, Masson, Christie, Hunt, Mair.
Newport Co: Plumley; Walden, Relish, Davies, Oakes, Tynan, Vaughan, Lowndes, Gwyther (Elsey), Aldridge, Moore.

Portsmouth (1) 1 *aet (Laidlaw)*

Oldham Ath (0) 0 18,548

Aggregate 3-3; Portsmouth won on away goals rule

Portsmouth: Mellor; McLaughlin, Viney, Brisley, Aizlewood, Garner, Gregory, Laidlaw, Showers, Bryant, Rogers.
Oldham Ath: McDonnell; Hoolickin, Blair, Kowenicki (Heaton), Clements, Hurst, Wylde, Futcher, Stainrod, Keegan, Atkinson.

Sheffield W (1) 3 *(Owen, Grant, Curran)*

Wimbledon (1) 1 *(Cork)* 15,151

Sheffield W won 4-3

Sheffield W: Cox; Blackhall, Grant, Smith, Pickering, King, Taylor, Johnson, Owen, McCulloch, Curran.
Wimbledon: Goddard; Brown, Perkins, Galliers, Smith, Cunningham, Davies, Downes, Leslie, Cork, Driver.

Swindon T (0) 2 *(Mayes 2)*

Lincoln C (0) 0 4907

Swindon T won 3-1

Swindon T: Allan; Lewis, Peach, Kamara, Rollings, Carter, Miller, Hughes, Henry, Mayes, Greenwood.
Lincoln C: Fox; Thompson T., Keeley, Thompson S., Peake, Carr, Turner, Harford, Hobson, Bell, Shipley.

Watford (2) 7 *aet (Poskett 2, Train, Patching, Bolton pen, Jenkins, Callaghan)*

Southampton (0) 1 *(Sims og)* 15,992

Watford won 7-5

Watford: Steele; Henderson, Jackett, Patching, Sims, Bolton, Blissett, Poskett, Jenkins, Train (Callaghan), Rostron.
Southampton: Katalinic; Waldron, McCartney, Williams, Watson, Nicholl, Hebberd, Channon, George (Moran), Holmes, Baker.

West Ham U (1) 4 *(Stewart pen, Goddard, Wood og, Pike)*

Burnley (0) 0 15,216

West Ham U won 6-0

West Ham U: Parkes; Stewart, Lampard, Bonds, Martin, Devonshire, Holland, Goddard, Cross, Brooking, Pike (Allen).
Burnley: Stevenson; Laws, Holt, Scott (Wood), Dobson, Overson, Cassidy, Young, Hamilton, Taylor, Cavener.

Wolverhampton W (0) 0

Cambridge U (1) 1 *(Streete)* 19,939

Cambridge U won 4-1

Wolverhampton W: Bradshaw; Palmer, Parkin, Daniel, Hughes, Berry (Clarke), Villazan, Carr, Gray, Richards, Eves.
Cambridge U: Webster; Donaldson, Smith, Murray, Fallon, Gibbins, Streete, Spriggs, Stringer, Finney, Christie.

3 SEPT

Blackpool (0) 2 *(McEwan pen, Morris)*

Everton (0) 2 *(Latchford 2)* 10,579

Everton won 5-2

Blackpool: Hesford; Gardner, Williams, Doyle, McEwan, Sbragia, Morris, Hockaday, MacDougall, Ball, Harrison.
Everton: McDonagh; Gidman, Ratcliffe (Bailey), Wright, Lyons, Stanley, McMahon, Eastoe, Latchford, Hartford, McBride.

Bristol R (1) 1 *aet (Faulkner og)*

York C (0) 0 3047

Aggregate 2-2; Bristol R won on away goals rule

Bristol R: Thomas; Gillies, Bater, McCaffery, Mabbutt, Hughes, Barrowclough (Jones), Williams, Bates, Lee, Pulis.
York C: Blackburn; Kay, Walsh, Richards, Faulkner, Craig, Ford (Byrne), Smith, Eccles, Hood, McDonald.

Chelsea (1) 1 *(Droy)*

Cardiff C (0) 1 *(Kitchen)* 12,959

Cardiff C won 2-1

Chelsea: Borota; Wilkins, Rofe, Droy (Walker), Chivers, Bumstead, Britton, Fillery, Viljoen, Frost, Lee.
Cardiff C: Grotier; Grapes, Lewis, Campbell, Pontin, Dwyer, Bishop, Kitchen, Stevens, Ronson, Buchanan.

Derby Co (0) 0 *aet*

QPR (0) 0 16,728

Aggregate 0-0; QPR won 5-3 on penalties

Derby Co: Jones; Emery, Osgood, Ramage, Buckley, Powell S., Clark, Powell B., Biley, Swindlehurst (Wilson), Emson.
QPR: Woods; McCreery, Gillard, Waddock, Wicks, Roeder, Fereday, Shanks, Langley, Currie (Neal), Hill.

Leeds U (1) 1 *(Graham)*

Aston Villa (2) 3 *(Withe, Shaw 2)* 12,236

Aston Villa won 4-1

Leeds U: Lukic; Cherry, Greenhoff, Flynn, Hart, Madeley, Parlane, Hamson (Harris), Connor, Sabella, Graham.
Aston Villa: Rimmer; Swain, Gibson, Evans, McNaught, Mortimer, Bremner, Shaw (Deacy), Withe, Cowans, Morley.

Leicester C (0) 0

WBA (0) 1 *(Regis)* 17,081

WBA won 2-0

Leicester C: Wallington; Williams, Gibson, Peake (Grewcock), May, O'Neill, Goodwin, Melrose, Young, Wilson, Henderson.
WBA: Godden; Trewick, Statham, Moses, Wile, Robertson, Bennett, Brown, Regis, Owen, Barnes.

Manchester C (2) 3 *(Henry, Bennett 2)*

Stoke C (0) 0 21,356

Manchester C won 4-1

Manchester C: MacRae; Ranson, Reid, Booth, Caton, Henry, Bennett, Daley, MacKenzie, Power, Reeves.
Stoke C: Fox; Evans, Hampton, Dodd, Thorley, Richardson, Johnson P. A., Bracewell, Chapman, Heath (Randall), Maguire.

Norwich C (0) 2 *aet (Royle, Fashanu)*

Shrewsbury T (0) 0 9185

Norwich C won 3-1

Norwich C: Hansbury; Bond, Downs, Barham, Forbes, Powell, Woods, Fashanu, Royle, Paddon, Bennett.
Shrewsbury T: Wardle; King, Larkin, Turner, Griffin, Keay, Tong, Atkins, Biggins (Lindsay), Dungworth, Petts.

Oxford U (1) 3 *(Shotton* pen, *Brock, Lythgoe)*

Chesterfield (0) 0 3085

Oxford U won 3-0

Oxford U: Burton; Briggs, Smithers, Jeffrey, Cooke, Shotton, Brock, Taylor, Foley, Jones, Lythgoe.
Chesterfield: Turner; Ridley, O'Neill, Wilson, Green, Hunter, Birch, Moss, Bonnyman, Salmons, Crawford.

Peterborough U (1) 1 *(Cooke)*

Nottingham F (1) 1 *(Mills)* 11,503

Nottingham F won 4-1

Peterborough U: Waugh; McVay, Phillips, Hodgson, Slack, Foster, Quow, Kellock, Cooke, Syrett, Cliss (Lambert).
Nottingham F: Shilton; Anderson, Gray, McGovern, Needham, Burns, Ponte, Bowyer, Birtles, Mills, Robertson.

Sunderland (0) 1 *(Cummins)*

Stockport Co (0) 2 *(Sunley, Sword* pen*)* 17,346

Stockport Co won 3-2

Sunderland: Turner; Hinnigan, Bolton, Allardyce, Elliott, Marangoni (Rowell), Chisholm, Arnott, Hawley, Brown, Cummins.
Stockport Co: Lawson; Rutter, Sherlock, Fowler, Sword, Uzelec, Williams, Sunley, Bradd, Galvin, Coyle.

Tottenham H (1) 3 *(Archibald 2, Crooks)*

Orient (0) 1 *(Jennings)* 25,443

Tottenham H won 4-1

Tottenham H: Daines; Smith, Hughton, Yorath, Lacy, Perryman, Ardiles (Taylor), Archibald, Villa, Hoddle, Crooks.
Orient: Day; Fisher, Roffey, Taylor, Gray, Parsons, Chiedozie, Jennings (Moores), Mayo, Bowles, Margerrison.

Tranmere R (1) 2 *(Kerr, Bramhall)*

Brighton & HA (1) 4 *(Robinson 2, Foster, Williams)* 4390

Brighton & HA won 7-3

Tranmere R: Johnson; Parry, Mathias, Bramhall, Edwards, Evans, Mungall, Kerr, Lumby, Beamish, Kelly.
Brighton & HA: Moseley; Gregory, Williams, Horton, Foster, Lawrenson, McHale, Ward, Robinson, Smith, McNab.

Wigan Ath (1) 1 *(Wright)*

Preston NE (2) 2 *(McGee, Coleman)* 9692

Preston NE won 3-1

Wigan Ath: Brown; Fretwell, Whittle, Gore, Methven, Davids, McMullen, Wright, Houghton, Hutchinson, Quinn M., (Quinn T.).
Preston NE: Tunks; Cameron, McAteer, Burns, Baxter, O'Riordan, Bell, Coleman, McGee, Houston, Bruce (Elliott).

THIRD ROUND

22 SEPT

Stockport Co (0) 1 *(Bradd)*

Arsenal (1) 3 *(Hollins, Sunderland, Stapleton)* 11,635

Stockport Co: Lawson; Rutter, Sherlock, Fowler, Sword, Uzelac, Williams, Sunley, Bradd, Galvin, Coyle.
Arsenal: Wood; Devine, Sansom, Talbot, O'Leary, Young, Hollins, Sunderland, Stapleton, Gatting, Rix.

23 SEPT

Barnsley (1) 3 *(Glavin* pen, *Parker, Banks)*

Cardiff C (0) 2 *(Buchanan, Lewis)* 13,135

Barnsley: New; Cooper, Chambers, Glavin, Banks, McCarthy, Evans, Parker, Riley, Lester, Downes.
Cardiff C: Grotier; Grapes, Lewis, Campbell, Pontin, Thomas, Bishop, Kitchen, Stevens, Ronson, Buchanan.

Birmingham C (0) 1 *(Gallagher)*

Blackburn R (0) 0 14,580

Birmingham C: Wealands; Langan, Dennis, Curbishley, Gallagher, Todd, Ainscow, Givens, Worthington, Gemmill, Dillon.
Blackburn R: Butcher; Branagan, Rathbone, Kendall, Keeley, Fazackerley, Brotherston, Stonehouse, Garner, McKenzie, Speight.

Brighton & HA (1) 1 *(Ryan)*

Coventry C (1) 2 *(English, Hutchison)* 14,426

Brighton & HA: Moseley; Gregory, Williams, Horton, Foster, Lawrenson, Stevens, Ward, Robinson, Smith, Ryan.
Coventry C: Blyth; Coop, Roberts, Blair, Dyson, Jacobs, Hutchison, Daly, Hateley, English, Hunt.

Bristol R (0) 0

Portsmouth (0) 0 6982

Bristol R: Thomas; Jones, Bater, McCaffery, Mabbutt, Hughes, Pulis, Williams, Barrowclough, Penny (Bates), Lee.
Portsmouth: Mellor; McLaughlin, Viney, Brisley, Aizlewood, Garner, Gregory, Laidlaw, Perrin, Bryant, Rogers.

Bury (0) 0

Nottingham F (3) 7 *(Ponte 3, Mills, Anderson, Birtles 2)* 8828

Bury: Forrest; Howard, Waddington, Whitehead, Kennedy, Mullen, Waldron, Halford (Hilton), Madden, Johnson, Farley.
Nottingham F: Shilton; Anderson, Needham, Burns, Gray, McGovern, Ponte, O'Neill, Birtles, Mills, Robertson.

Cambridge U (2) 2 *(Finney, Spriggs)*

Aston Villa (1) 1 *(Morley)* 7628

Cambridge U: Webster; Donaldson, Murray, Smith, Fallon, Gibbins, Evans (Buckley), Spriggs, Reilly, Finney, Christie.
Aston Villa: Rimmer; Swain, Gibson, Evans, McNaught, Mortimer, Bremner, Geddis, Withe, Cowans, Morley (Shaw).

Charlton Ath (1) 1 *(Robinson)*

West Ham U (1) 2 *(Cross 2)* 17,884

Charlton Ath: Wood; Gritt, Warman, Shaw, Berry, Tydeman, Powell, Walsh, Hales, Smith, Robinson.
West Ham U: Parkes; Stewart, Lampard, Bonds, Martin, Devonshire, Barnes, Goddard, Cross, Brush, Pike.

Ipswich T (1) 1 *(Osman)*

Norwich C (0) 1 *(Fashanu)* 26,462

Ipswich T: Cooper; Burley, Mills, Thijssen, Osman, Butcher, Wark, Muhren, Mariner, Gates, Brazil (O'Callaghan).
Norwich C: Hansbury; Bond, Muzinic, Barham, Hoadley, Powell, Woods, Fashanu, Jack (Royle), Paddon, Goble.

Liverpool (2) 5 *(Lee 2, Dalglish, Fairclough 2)*

Swindon T (0) 0 16,566

Liverpool: Clemence; Neal, Cohen, Thompson, Kennedy R., Hansen, Dalglish, Lee, Fairclough, McDermott, Souness.
Swindon T: Allan; Henry, Trollope, Kamara, Lewis, Carter, Miller, Cockerill, Rowland, Mayes, Greenwood.

Luton T (1) 1 *(Antic)*

Manchester C (2) 2 *(Bennett, Henry)* 10,030

Luton T: Findlay; Stephens, Donaghy, Grealish (Smith), Saxby, Price, Hill, Stein, West, Antic, Moss.
Manchester C: Corrigan; Ranson, Reid, Booth, Caton, Henry, Power, Daley, Palmer, Bennett, Reeves.

Notts Co (1) 4 *(O'Brien pen, Christie, Kelly, Hooks)*

QPR (0) 1 *(Langley)* 6644

Notts Co: Avramovic; Benjamin, O'Brien, Kelly, Kilcline, Richards, McCulloch, Masson, Christie, Hunt, Hooks.
QPR: Woods; McCreery, Burke, Waddock, Wicks, Roeder, King, Shanks, Langley, Currie (Hazell), Neal.

Preston NE (0) 1 *(Coleman)*

Oxford U (0) 0 5722

Preston NE: Tunks; Westwell, Cameron, Doyle, Baxter, O'Riordan, Bell, Coleman, McGee, Elliott (Sayer), Houston.
Oxford U: Burton; Kingston, Fogg, Jeffrey, Cooke, Shotton, Brock, Taylor, Foley, Jones (Berry), Lythgoe.

Sheffield W (0) 1 *(Pearson)*

Watford (0) 2 *(Poskett, Jenkins)* 14,085

Sheffield W: Cox; Blackhall, Grant, Smith, Pickering, King (Oliver), Taylor, Mellor, Owen, McCulloch, Pearson.
Watford: Steele; Henderson, Harrison, Blissett, Sims, Jackett, Cassells, Poskett, Jenkins, Train, Rostron.

24 SEPT

Everton (1) 1 *(Gidman)*

WBA (1) 2 *(Moses, Robertson)* 23,436

Everton: McDonagh; Gidman, Bailey, Wright, Lyons, Stanley, McMahon (O'Keefe), Eastoe, Latchford, Hartford, McBride.
WBA: Godden; Batson, Statham, Moses, Wile, Robertson, Trewick, Brown, Regis, Owen, Barnes (Monaghan).

Tottenham H (0) 0

Crystal Palace (0) 0 29,654

Tottenham H: Daines; Smith, Hughton, Yorath, Lacy, Perryman, Ardiles, Archibald, Villa, Hoddle, Crooks.
Crystal Palace: Barron; Hinshelwood, Fenwick, Nicholas, Cannon, Gilbert, Smillie, Francis, Allen, Flanagan, Murphy.

THIRD ROUND REPLAY

30 SEPT

Crystal Palace (0) 1 *(Allen pen)*

Tottenham H (0) 3 *(Hoddle, Crooks, Villa)* 26,409

Crystal Palace: Barron; Hinshelwood, Fenwick, Nicholas, Cannon, Gilbert, Smillie (Sealy), Francis, Allen, Flanagan, Murphy.
Tottenham H: Daines; Smith, Hughton, Yorath, Lacy, Perryman, Ardiles (Taylor), Archibald, Villa, Hoddle, Crooks.

Portsmouth (1) 2 *(Gregory, Perrin)*

Bristol R (0) 0 18,965

Portsmouth: Mellor; McLaughlin, Viney, Brisley, Aizlewood, Garner, Gregory, Laidlaw, Perrin, Bryant, Rogers.
Bristol R: Thomas; Jones, Bater, Barrowclough, Mabbutt, Hughes, Pulis, Williams D., Bates, Penny, Lee.

8 OCT

Norwich C (0) 1 *(Powell)*

Ipswich T (1) 3 *(Mariner 2, Muhren)* 24,523

Norwich C: Hansbury; Bond, Hoadley, Barham, Jack (Symonds), Powell, Woods, Fashanu, Muzinic, Paddon, Goble.
Ipswich T: Cooper; Burley, Mills, Thijssen, Osman, Butcher, Wark, Muhren, Mariner, Brazil, Gates.

FOURTH ROUND

28 OCT

Birmingham C (1) 2 *(Worthington pen, Ainscow)*

Ipswich T (1) 1 *(Wark pen)* 18,968

Birmingham C: Wealands; Page, Dennis, Curbishley, Gallagher, Todd, Ainscow, Bertschin, Worthington, Gemmill, Givens.
Ipswich T: Cooper; Burley, McCall, Mills, Osman, Butcher, Wark, Muhren, D'Avray, Brazil, Gates.

Coventry C (1) 1 *(Thompson)*

Cambridge U (0) 1 *(Taylor)* 17,049

Coventry C: Sealey; Coop, Roberts, Gooding, Dyson, Gillespie, Bodak, Blair, Thompson, English, Hunt.
Cambridge U: Key; Donaldson, Murray, Smith, Fallon, Gibbins, O'Neill, Spriggs, Reilly, Taylor, Christie.

Liverpool (2) 4 *(Dalglish, Johnson 2, Souness)*

Portsmouth (1) 1 *(Kennedy A. og)* 32,021

Liverpool: Clemence; Neal, Irwin, Hansen, Kennedy A., Lee, McDermott, Souness, Kennedy R., Dalglish, Johnson.
Portsmouth: Mellor; McLaughlin, Davey, Garner, Viney, Barnard, Gregory (Laidlaw), Tait, Bryant, Showers, Rogers.

Watford (2) 4 *(Blissett pen, Jenkins 3)*

Nottingham F (0) 1 *(Wallace)* 22,597

Watford: Steele; Henderson, Harrison, Blissett, Sims, Jackett, Poskett, Ward, Jenkins, Train, Rostron.
Nottingham F: Sutton; Gunn, Gray F., Ponte, Lloyd, Burns, O'Neill, Bowyer, Mills, Wallace, Robertson.

West Ham U (0) 2 *(Martin, Cross)*

Barnsley (0) 1 *(Evans)* 21,548

West Ham U: Parkes; Stewart, Lampard (Allen), Brush, Martin, Devonshire, Holland, Goddard, Cross, Neighbour, Pike.
Barnsley: New; Joyce, Chambers, Glavin, Banks, McCarthy, Evans, Riley, Aylott, Lester, Downes.

29 OCT

Manchester C (2) 5 *(Tueart 4, Bennett)*

Notts Co (0) 1 *(Christie)* 26,363

Manchester C: Corrigan; Ranson, Power, Reid, Henry, Caton, Tueart, Buckley, MacKenzie, Bennett, Reeves (Sugrue).
Notts Co: Avramovic; Benjamin, O'Brien, Harkouk, Kilcline, Richards, McCulloch, Masson, Christie (Wood), Hunt, Hooks.

WBA (0) 0

Preston NE (0) 0 17,579

WBA: Godden; Batson, Statham, Moses, Wile, Robertson, Robson, Brown, Regis, Trewick, Barnes (Mills).
Preston NE: Hunt; Westwell, McAteer, Burns, Baxter, Blackley, Doyle (Bell), Coleman, Elliott, Bruce, McGee.

4 NOV

Tottenham H (1) 1 *(Ardiles)*

Arsenal (0) 0 42,551

Tottenham H: Daines; Smith, Hughton, Miller, Lacy, Perryman, Ardiles (Roberts), Archibald, Villa, Hoddle, Crooks.
Arsenal: Wood; Devine, Sansom, Talbot, Walford, Young, Hollins (McDermott), Sunderland, Stapleton, Gatting, Rix.

FOURTH ROUND REPLAY

4 NOV

Cambridge U (0) 0

Coventry C (1) 1 *(Hunt)* 10,171

Cambridge U: Key; Donaldson (Taylor), Murray, Smith, Fallon, Gibbins, O'Neill, Spriggs, Reilly, Finney, Christie.
Coventry C: Sealey; Coop, Roberts, Blair, Dyson, Gillespie, Bodak, Van Gool, Hateley, Thomas, Hunt.

Preston NE (0) 1 *(Bell)*

WBA (1) 1 *(Brown)* 14,420

Preston NE: Tunks; Westwell, McAteer, Burns, Baxter, Blackley, Bell, Coleman, McGee, Bruce, Naughton (Taylor).
WBA: Godden; Batson, Cowdrill, Moses, Wile, Robertson, Robson, Brown, Regis, Owen (Trewick), Mills.

FOURTH ROUND SECOND REPLAY

12 NOV

WBA (0) 2 *(Regis 2)*

Preston NE (1) 1 *(Bruce)* 15,218

WBA: Godden; Batson, Cowdrill, Moses, Wile, Robertson, Robson, Brown, Regis, Owen, Barnes (Mills).
Preston NE: Tunks; Westwell, McAteer, Burns (Taylor), Baxter, Blackley, Bell, Coleman, Elliott, Bruce, McGee.

QUARTER-FINALS

2 DEC

Liverpool (1) 3 *(Dalglish, McDermott, Johnson)*

Birmingham C (1) 1 *(Bertschin)* 30,236

Liverpool: Clemence; Neal, Kennedy A., Irwin, Kennedy R., Hansen, Dalglish, Lee, Johnson, McDermott, Souness.
Birmingham C: Wealands; Langan, Hawker, Curbishley, Gallagher, Todd, Ainscow (Givens), Bertschin, Lynex, Gemmill, Dillon.

Watford (2) 2 *(Poskett, Armstrong)*

Coventry C (2) 2 *(Thompson 2)* 27,542

Watford: Steele; Rice, Sims, Jackett, Harrison, Blissett, Train, Rostron, Poskett, Armstrong, Jenkins.
Coventry C: Sealey; Thomas, Dyson, Gillespie, Roberts, Blair, Daly, Bodak, Thompson, Hateley, Hunt.

West Ham U (0) 1 *(Cross)*

Tottenham H (0) 0 36,235

West Ham U: Parkes; Stewart, Lampard, Bonds, Martin, Devonshire, Holland, Goddard, Cross, Brooking, Pike.
Tottenham H: Daines; McAllister, Hughton, Yorath, Lacy, Perryman, Ardiles, Archibald, Villa, Hoddle, Crooks.

3 DEC

Manchester C (1) 2 *(Bennett, Henry)*

WBA (1) 1 *(Booth og)* 35,011

Manchester C: Corrigan; Ranson, Power, Reid, Booth, Henry, Tueart, Bennett, MacKenzie, Boyer, Reeves.
WBA: Godden; Batson, Trewick, Moses, Wile, Bennett, Robson, Brown, Regis, Owen, Barnes.

QUARTER-FINAL REPLAY

9 DEC

Coventry C (3) 5 *(Bodak, Hateley 2, Thompson, Hunt)*

Watford (0) 0 30,348

Coventry C: Sealey; Thomas, Roberts, Blair, Dyson, Gillespie, Bodak, Daly (Jacobs), Thompson, Hateley, Hunt.
Watford: Sherwood; Rice, Harrison, Blissett, Terry, Jackett, Callaghan, Armstrong, Jenkins (Henderson), Train, Poskett.

SEMI-FINAL, FIRST LEG

14 JAN

Manchester C (0) 0

Liverpool (0) 1 *(Kennedy R.)* 48,045

Manchester C: Corrigan; Ranson, Power, Reid, Caton, Henry, Boyer, Bennett, MacKenzie, Tueart, Reeves.
Liverpool: Clemence; Neal, Kennedy A., Thompson, Kennedy R., Irwin, Dalglish, Lee, Fairclough, McDermott, Souness.

27 JAN

Coventry C (0) 3 *(Thompson 2, Daly)*

West Ham U (2) 2 *(Bonds, Thompson og)* 35,468

Coventry C: Sealey; Thomas, Roberts, Blair, Dyson, Gillespie, Bodak, Daly (Jacobs), Thompson, Hateley, Hunt.
West Ham U: Parkes; Stewart, Brush, Bonds, Martin, Devonshire, Allen, Goddard, Cross, Brooking, Pike.

SEMI-FINAL, SECOND LEG

10 FEB

Liverpool (1) 1 *(Dalglish)*

Manchester C (0) 1 *(Reeves)* 46,711

Liverpool won 2-1

Liverpool: Clemence; Neal, Money, Thompson, Kennedy R., Hansen, Dalglish, Lee, Johnson, McDermott, Souness.
Manchester C: Corrigan; Ranson (Henry), Caton, Reid, Power, Booth, Tueart, Buckley, MacKenzie, Bennett, Reeves.

West Ham U (0) 2 *(Goddard, Neighbour)*

Coventry C (0) 0 36,511

West Ham U won 4-3

West Ham U: Parkes; Stewart, Lampard, Bonds, Martin, Devonshire, Neighbour, Goddard, Cross, Brooking, Pike.
Coventry C: Sealey; Thomas, Roberts, Blair, Dyson, Gillespie, Bodak (Jacobs), Daly, Thompson, Hateley, Hunt.

FINAL (at Wembley)

14 MAR

Liverpool (0) 1 *aet (Kennedy A.)*

West Ham U (0) 1 *(Stewart* pen*)* 100,000

Liverpool: Clemence; Neal, Kennedy A., Irwin, Kennedy R., Hansen, Dalglish, Lee, Heighway (Case), McDermott, Souness.
West Ham U: Parkes; Stewart, Lampard, Bonds, Martin, Devonshire, Neighbour, Goddard (Pearson), Cross, Brooking, Pike.

FINAL REPLAY (at Villa Park)

6 APR

Liverpool (2) 2 *(Dalglish, Hansen)*

West Ham U (1) 1 *(Goddard)* 36,693

Liverpool: Clemence; Neal, Kennedy A., Thompson, Kennedy R., Hansen, Dalglish, Lee, Rush, McDermott, Case.
West Ham U: Parkes; Stewart, Lampard, Bonds, Martin, Devonshire, Neighbour, Goddard, Cross, Brooking, Pike (Pearson).

FOOTBALL LEAGUE CUP 1960–61

Home team shown first; where a tie was replayed, the team given second was the home team in the replay.

First Round

Middlesbrough v Cardiff C	3-4
Colchester U v Newcastle U	4-1
Newport Co v Southampton	2-2,2-2,3-5
Chester v Leyton O	2-2, 0-1
Preston NE v Peterborough U	4-1
Lincoln C v Bradford	2-2, 0-1
Plymouth Arg v Southport	2-0
York C v Blackburn R	1-3
Rochdale v Scunthorpe U	1-1, 1-0
Exeter C v Manchester U	1-1, 1-4
Watford v Derby Co	2-5
Ipswich T v Barnsley	0-2
Oldham Ath v Hartlepools U	2-1
QPR v Port Vale	2-2, 1-3
Everton v Accrington S	3-1
Darlington v Crystal Palace	2-0
West Ham U v Charlton Ath	3-1
Hull C v Bolton W	0-0, 1-5
Leicester C v Mansfield T	4-0
Bristol R v Fulham	2-1
Coventry C v Barrow	4-2
Stockport Co v Carlisle U	2-0
Millwall v Chelsea	1-7

(All the rest byes, except Arsenal, Tottenham H, Sheffield W, WBA, and Wolverhampton W, who did not compete).

Second Round

Liverpool v Luton T	1-1, 5-2
Colchester U v Southampton	0-2
Leyton O v Chesterfield	0-1
Leeds U v Blackpool	0-0, 3-1
Brentford v Sunderland	4-3
Cardiff C v Burnley	0-4
Nottingham F v Halifax T	2-0
Aldershot v Bristol C	1-1, 0-3
Gillingham v Preston NE	1-1, 0-3
Aston Villa v Huddersfield T	4-1
Bradford v Birmingham C	0-1
Plymouth Arg v Torquay U	1-1, 2-1
Swansea T v Blackburn R	1-2
Rochdale v Southend U	5-2
Notts Co v Brighton	1-3
Northampton T v Wrexham	1-1, 0-2
Darlington v West Ham U	3-2
Bolton W v Grimsby T	6-2
Leicester C v Rotherham U	1-2
Reading v Bristol R	3-5
Portsmouth v Coventry C	2-0
Manchester C v Stockport Co	3-0
Doncaster R v Stoke C	3-1
Chelsea v Workington	4-2
Swindon T v Shrewsbury T	1-1, 2-2, 0-2
Bradford C v Manchester U	2-1
Derby Co v Barnsley	3-0
Norwich C v Oldham Ath	6-2
Port Vale v Tranmere R	0-2
Bournemouth v Crewe Alex	1-1, 0-2
Everton v Walsall	3-1
Bury v Sheffield U	3-1

Third Round

Liverpool v Southampton	1-2
Chesterfield v Leeds U	0-4
Brentford v Burnley	1-1, 1-2
Nottingham F v Bristol C	2-1
Preston NE v Aston Villa	3-3, 1-3
Birmingham C v Plymouth Arg	0-0, 1-3
Blackburn R v Rochdale	2-1
Brighton v Wrexham	0-2
Darlington v Bolton W	1-2
Rotherham U v Bristol R	2-0
Portsmouth v Manchester C	2-0
Doncaster R v Chelsea	0-7
Shrewsbury T v Bradford C	2-1
Derby Co v Norwich C	1-4
Tranmere R v Crewe Alex	2-0
Everton v Bury	3-1

Fourth Round

Southampton v Leeds U	5-4
Burnley v Nottingham F	2-1
Aston Villa v Plymouth Arg	3-3, 0-0, 5-3
Blackburn R v Wrexham	1-1, 1-3
Bolton W v Rotherham U	0-2
Portsmouth v Chelsea	1-0
Shrewsbury T v Norwich C	1-0
Tranmere R v Everton	0-4

Fifth Round

Southampton v Burnley	2-4
Aston Villa v Wrexham	3-0
Rotherham U v Portsmouth	3-0
Shrewsbury T v Everton	2-1

Semi-Final

Burnley v Aston Villa	1-1, 2-2, 1-2
(Replay, Manchester U)	
Aston Villa won 5-4 on aggregate	
Rotherham U v Shrewsbury T	3-2, 1-1
Rotherham U won 4-3 on aggregate	

Final

Rotherham U 2, Aston Villa 0

(First leg, Rotherham, 12,226, 22 August, 1961)

Rotherham U: Ironside; Perry, Morgan; Lambert, Madden, Waterhouse; Webster, Weston, Houghton, Kirkman, Bambridge.

Aston Villa: Sims; Lynn, Lee; Crowe, Dugdale, Deakin; McEwan, Thomson, Brown, Wylie, McParland.

Scorers: Rotherham U – Webster, Kirkman.

Aston Villa 3, Rotherham U 0 (aet)

(Second leg, Villa Park, 27,000, 5 September, 1961)

Aston Villa: Sidebottom; Neal, Lee; Crowe, Dugdale, Deakin; McEwan, O'Neill, McParland, Thomson, Burrows.

Rotherham U: Ironside; Perry, Morgan; Lambert, Madden, Waterhouse; Webster, Weston, Houghton, Kirkman, Bambridge.

Scorers: Aston Villa – O'Neill, Burrows, McParland.

Aston Villa won on aggregate 3-2

FOOTBALL LEAGUE CUP 1961–62

Home team shown first; where a tie was replayed, the team given second was the home team in the replay.

First Round

Barnsley v Southport	3-2
Barrow v Portsmouth	0-2
Birmingham C v Swindon T	1-1, 0-2
Blackpool v Port Vale	2-1
Bolton W v Sunderland	1-1, 0-1
Bournemouth v Torquay U	2-2, 1-0
Bradford C v Aston Villa	3-4
Bristol R v Hartlepools U	2-1
Bury v Brighton	5-1
Cardiff C v Wrexham	2-0
Carlisle U v Huddersfield T	1-1, 0-3
Chesterfield v Norwich C	2-3
Colchester U v Crewe Alex	1-2
Darlington v Rotherham U	0-1
Doncaster R v Grimsby T	3-2
Fulham v Sheffield U	1-1, 0-4
Hull C v Bradford PA	4-2
Ipswich T v Manchester C	4-2
Leeds U v Brentford	4-1
Lincoln C v Accrington S	1-0
Luton T v Northampton T	2-1
Millwall v Walsall	1-2
Mansfield T v Exeter C	5-2
Newcastle U v Scunthorpe U	2-0
Newport Co v Shrewsbury T	0-0, 1-3
Notts Co v Derby Co	2-2, 2-3
Nottingham F v Gillingham	4-1
Oldham Ath v Charlton Ath	1-4
Peterborough U v Blackburn R	1-3
Preston NE v Aldershot	3-1
QPR v Crystal Palace	5-2
Reading v Chester	4-2
Southampton v Rochdale	0-0, 1-2
Southend U v Stoke C	0-1
Stockport Co v Leyton O	0-1
Tranmere R v Middlesbrough	3-6
Watford v Halifax T	3-0
West Ham U v Plymouth Arg	3-2
Workington v Coventry C	3-0
York C v Bristol C	3-0

Byes: Leicester C and Swansea T

Second Round

Barnsley v Workington	1-3
Bristol R v Blackburn R	1-1, 0-4
Bury v Hull C	3-4
Charlton Ath v Stoke C	4-1
Leeds U v Huddersfield T	3-2
Leyton O v Blackpool	1-1, 1-5
Luton T v Rotherham U	0-0, 0-2
Mansfield T v Cardiff C	1-1, 1-2
Middlesbrough v Crewe Alex	3-2
Norwich C v Lincoln C	3-2
Portsmouth v Derby Co	1-1, 4-2
QPR v Nottingham F	1-2
Preston NE v Swindon T	3-1
Rochdale v Doncaster R	4-0
Sheffield U v Newcastle U	2-2, 2-0
Shrewsbury T v Bournemouth	1-3
Swansea T v Ipswich T	3-3, 2-3
Sunderland v Walsall	5-2
Watford v Reading	3-1
West Ham U v Aston Villa	1-3
York C v Leicester C	2-1

Third Round

Norwich C v Middlesbrough	3-2
Workington v Blackpool	0-1
Aston Villa v Ipswich T	2-3
Bournemouth v Cardiff C	3-0
Preston NE v Rotherham U	0-0, 0-3
Sheffield U v Portsmouth	1-0
Sunderland v Hull C	2-1
York C v Watford	1-1, 2-2, 3-2
Nottingham F v Blackburn R	1-2
Rochdale v Charlton Ath	1-0

Bye: Leeds U

Fourth Round

Blackburn R v Ipswich T	4-1
Rotherham U v Leeds U	1-1, 2-1
York C v Bournemouth	1-0

Byes: Sunderland, Blackpool, Norwich C, Sheffield U and Rochdale

Fifth Round

Sunderland v Norwich C	1-4
Blackpool v Sheffield U	0-0, 2-0
Rotherham U v Blackburn R	0-1
Rochdale v York C	2-1

Semi-Final

Norwich C v Blackpool	4-1, 0-2
Norwich C won 4-3 on aggregate	
Rochdale v Blackburn R	3-1, 1-2
Rochdale won 4-3 on aggregate	

Final

Rochdale 0, Norwich C 3

(First leg, Rochdale, 11,123, 26 April, 1962)

Rochdale: Burgin; Milburn, Winton; Bodell, Aspden, Thompson; Wragg, Hepton, Bimpson, Cairns, Whitaker.
Norwich C: Kennon; McCrohan, Ashman; Burton, Butler, Mullett; Mannion, Lythgoe, Scott, Hill, Punton.
Scorers: Norwich C – Lythgoe 2, Punton.

Norwich C 1, Rochdale 0

(Second leg, Norwich, 19,708, 1 May, 1962)

Norwich C: Kennon; McCrohan, Ashman; Burton, Butler, Mullett; Mannion, Lythgoe, Scott Hill, Punton.
Rochdale: Burgin; Milburn, Winton; Bodell, Aspden, Thompson; Whyke, Richardson, Bimpson, Cairns, Whitaker.
Scorer: Norwich C – Hill.

Norwich C won on aggregate 4-0

FOOTBALL LEAGUE CUP 1962–63

Home team shown first; where a tie was replayed, the team given second was the home team in the replay.

First Round

Aldershot v Exeter C	2-0
Barrow v Workington	3-2
Bradford C v Doncaster R	2-2, 0-2
Brentford v Wrexham	3-0
Chester v Stockport Co	2-0
Crewe Alex v Oldham Ath	2-3
Darlington v Chesterfield	1-0
Halifax T v Mansfield T	2-3
Hartlepools U v Barnsley	1-1, 1-2
Newport Co v Gillingham	2-1
Shrewsbury T v Millwall	3-1
Southport v Rochdale	0-0, 2-1
Torquay U v Oxford U	2-0
Tranmere R v Carlisle U	2-3
Watford v Colchester U	1-2
York C v Lincoln C	2-2, 0-2

Second Round

Aldershot v Newport Co	0-3
Aston Villa v Peterborough U	6-1
Barnsley v Grimsby T	3-2
Barrow v Shrewsbury T	3-1
Birmingham C v Doncaster R	5-0
Bradford PA v Huddersfield T	3-1
Brentford v Sheffield U	1-4
Brighton v Portsmouth	1-5
Bristol C v Rotherham U	1-2
Bristol R v Port Vale	2-0
Bury v Lincoln C	2-2, 3-2
Cardiff C v Reading	5-1
Chester v Mansfield T	2-2, 1-0
Coventry C v Swansea T	3-2
Derby Co v Blackburn R	1-1, 1-3
Fulham v Bournemouth	4-0
Hull C v Middlesbrough	2-2, 1-1, 3-0
Leeds U v Crystal Palace	2-1
Leicester C v Charlton Ath	4-4, 1-2
Newcastle U v Leyton O	1-1, 2-4
Northampton T v Colchester U	2-0
Norwich C v Bolton W	4-0
Manchester C v Blackpool	0-0, 3-3, 4-2
QPR v Preston NE	1-2
Southampton v Scunthorpe U	1-1, 2-2, 0-3
Southend U v Notts Co	2-3
Southport v Luton T	1-3
Sunderland v Oldham Ath	7-1
Swindon T v Darlington	4-0
Torquay U v Carlisle U	1-2
Walsall v Stoke C	1-2
West Ham U v Plymouth Arg	6-0

Third Round

Barrow v Birmingham C	1-1, 1-5
Notts Co v Swindon T	5-0
Newport Co v Manchester C	1-2
Barnsley v Luton T	1-2
Leyton O v Chester	9-2
Bradford PA v Charlton Ath	2-2, 0-1
Bury v Sheffield U	3-1
Bristol R v Cardiff C	2-0
Portsmouth v Coventry C	5-1
Sunderland v Scunthorpe U	2-0
Blackburn R v Leeds U	4-0
Rotherham U v West Ham U	3-1
Carlisle U v Norwich C	1-1, 0-5
Hull C v Fulham	1-2
Aston Villa v Stoke C	3-1
Northampton T v Preston NE	1-1, 1-2

Fourth Round

Birmingham C v Notts Co	3-2
Manchester C v Luton T	1-0
Leyton O v Charlton Ath	3-2
Bury v Bristol R	3-1
Portsmouth v Sunderland	0-0, 1-2
Blackburn R v Rotherham U	4-1
Norwich C v Fulham	1-0
Aston Villa v Preston NE	6-2

Fifth Round

Birmingham C v Manchester C	6-0
Leyton O v Bury	0-2
Sunderland v Blackburn R	3-2
Aston Villa v Norwich C	4-1

Semi-Final

Birmingham C v Bury	3-2, 1-1
Birmingham C won 4-3 on aggregate	
Sunderland v Aston Villa	1-3, 0-0
Aston Villa won 3-1 on aggregate	

Final

Birmingham C 3, Aston Villa 1

(First leg, St Andrews, 31,850, 23 May, 1963)

Birmingham C: Schofield; Lynn, Green; Hennessey, Smith, Beard; Hellawell, Bloomfield, Harris, Leek, Auld.
Aston Villa: Sims, Fraser, Aitken; Crowe, Sleeuwenhoek, Lee; Baker, Graham, Thomson, Wylie, Burrows.
Scorers: Birmingham C – Leek 2, Bloomfield; Aston Villa – Thomson.

Aston Villa 0, Birmingham C 0

(Second leg, Villa Park, 37,921, 27 May, 1963)

No change in teams.

Birmingham C won on aggregate 3-1

FOOTBALL LEAGUE CUP 1963–64

Home team shown first; where a tie was replayed, the team given second was the home team in the replay.

First Round

Aldershot v QPR	3-1
Bradford PA v Bradford C	7-3
Carlisle U v Crewe Alex	3-2
Chesterfield v Halifax T	0-1
Darlington v Barnsley	2-2, 2-6
Doncaster R v York C	0-0, 0-3
Gillingham v Bristol C	4-2
Lincoln C v Hartlepools U	3-2
Mansfield T v Watford	2-1
Newport Co v Millwall	3-4
Oldham Ath v Workington T	3-5
Oxford U v Exeter C	0-1
Reading v Brentford	1-1, 0-2
Rochdale v Chester	1-1, 5-2
Shrewsbury T v Bristol R	1-1, 2-6
Southport v Barrow	2-1
Torquay U v Brighton	1-2
Tranmere R v Stockport Co	2-0

Second Round

Aston Villa v Barnsley	3-1
Blackpool v Charlton Ath	7-1
Bradford PA v Middlesbrough	2-2, 3-2
Brentford v Bournemouth	0-0, 0-2
Brighton v Northampton T	1-1, 2-3
Bristol R v Crystal Palace	2-0
Cardiff C v Wrexham	2-2, 1-1, 0-3
Colchester U v Fulham	5-3
Gillingham v Bury	3-0
Grimsby T v Rotherham U	1-3
Halifax T v Rochdale	4-2
Hull C v Exeter C	1-0
Ipswich T v Walsall	0-0, 0-1
Leeds U v Mansfield T	5-1
Leicester C v Aldershot	2-0
Luton T v Coventry C	3-4
Manchester C v Carlisle U	2-0
Millwall v Peterborough U	3-2
Newcastle U v Preston NE	3-0
Norwich C v Birmingham C	2-0
Notts Co v Blackburn R	2-1
Plymouth Arg v Huddersfield T	2-2, 3-3, 1-2
Portsmouth v Derby Co	3-2
Scunthorpe U v Stoke C	2-2, 3-3, 0-1
Sheffield U v Bolton W	1-2
Southend U v Port Vale	2-1
Swansea T v Sunderland	3-1
Swindon T v Chelsea	3-0
Tranmere R v Southampton	2-0
West Ham U v Leyton O	2-1
Workington v Southport	3-0
York C v Lincoln C	1-1, 0-2

Third Round

Stoke C v Bolton W	3-0
Bournemouth v Newcastle U	2-1
Rotherham U v Coventry C	4-2
Millwall v Lincoln C	1-1, 2-1
Notts Co v Bradford PA	3-2
Wrexham v Portsmouth	3-5
Hull C v Manchester C	0-3
Leeds U v Swansea T	2-0
Swindon T v Southend U	3-0
Aston Villa v West Ham U	0-2
Workington v Huddersfield T	1-0
Colchester U v Northampton T	4-1
Halifax T v Walsall	2-0
Norwich C v Blackpool	1-0
Tranmere R v Leicester C	1-2
Bristol R v Gillingham	1-1, 1-3

Fourth Round

Stoke C v Bournemouth	2-1
Rotherham U v Millwall	5-2
Notts Co v Portsmouth	3-2
Manchester C v Leeds U	3-1
Swindon T v West Ham U	3-3, 1-4
Workington v Colchester U	2-1
Halifax T v Norwich C	1-7
Leicester C v Gillingham	4-1

Fifth Round

Stoke C v Rotherham U	3-2
Notts Co v Manchester C	0-1
West Ham U v Workington	6-0
Norwich C v Leicester C	1-1, 1-2

Semi-Final

Stoke C v Manchester C	2-0, 0-1
Stoke C won 2-1 on aggregate	
Leicester C v West Ham U	4-3, 2-0
Leicester C won 6-3 on aggregate	

Final

Stoke C 1, Leicester C 1

(First leg, Stoke, 22,309, 15 April, 1964)

Stoke C: Leslie; Asprey, Allen; Palmer, Kinnell, Skeels; Dobing, Viollet, Ritchie, McIlroy, Bebbington.
Leicester C: Banks; Sjoberg, Appleton; Dougan, King, Cross; Riley, Heath, Keyworth, Gibson, Stringfellow.
Scorers: Stoke C – Bebbington; Leicester C – Gibson.

Leicester C 3, Stoke C 2

(Second leg, Leicester, 25,372, 22 April, 1964)

No change in teams.
Scorers: Leicester C – Stringfellow, Gibson, Riley; Stoke C – Viollet, Kinnell.

Leicester C won on aggregate 4-3

FOOTBALL LEAGUE CUP 1964–65

Home team shown first; where a tie was replayed, the team given second was the home team in the replay.

First Round

Barnsley v Lincoln C	2-1
Bradford C v York C	2-0
Brentford v Southend U	0-2
Brighton v Millwall	2-2, 0-1
Chester v Wrexham	3-0
Chesterfield v Hartlepools U	3-0
Colchester U v Torquay U	1-1, 0-3
Doncaster R v Bradford PA	1-0
Exeter C v Gillingham	2-0
Halifax T v Darlington	1-3
Notts Co v Newport Co	3-2
Port Vale v Luton T	0-1
QPR v Aldershot	5-2
Southport v Carlisle U	0-0, 0-1
Stockport Co v Rochdale	1-3
Tranmere R v Crewe Alex	2-0
Walsall v Oxford U	1-1, 1-6
Workington v Barrow	9-1

Second Round

Birmingham C v Chelsea	0-3
Blackpool v Newcastle U	3-0
Bolton W v Blackburn R	1-5
Bristol R v Chesterfield	0-2
Bournemouth v Northampton T	0-2
Bury v Darlington	1-0
Carlisle U v Bristol C	4-1
Charlton Ath v Middlesbrough	2-1
Chester v Derby Co	5-4
Coventry C v Ipswich T	4-1
Doncaster R v Preston NE	1-0
Exeter C v Bradford C	3-5
Fulham v Oxford U	2-0
Grimsby T v Oldham Ath	3-1
Hull C v Southend U	0-0, 1-3
Leeds U v Huddersfield T	3-2
Leicester C v Peterborough U	0-0, 2-0
Leyton O v Barnsley	3-0
Luton T v Aston Villa	0-1
Manchester C v Mansfield T	3-5
Millwall v Norwich C	1-2
Plymouth Arg v Sheffield U	2-1
Reading v QPR	4-0
Rotherham U v Rochdale	2-0
Scunthorpe U v Workington	0-1
Southampton v Cardiff C	3-2
Stoke C v Shrewsbury T	1-1, 1-0
Sunderland v West Ham U	4-1
Swansea T v Swindon T	3-1
Torquay U v Notts Co	1-2
Tranmere R v Crystal Palace	0-2
Watford v Portsmouth	2-2, 1-2

Third Round

Leeds U v Aston Villa	2-3
Reading v Fulham	1-1, 3-1
Charlton Ath v Leyton O	2-1
Doncaster R v Bradford C	2-3
Workington v Blackburn R	0-0, 5-1
Norwich C v Chester	5-3
Chelsea v Notts Co	4-0
Rotherham U v Swansea T	2-2, 0-2
Stoke C v Southend U	3-1
Bury v Plymouth Arg	0-1
Northampton T v Portsmouth	2-1
Chesterfield v Carlisle U	3-1
Coventry C v Mansfield T	3-2
Sunderland v Blackpool	4-1
Grimsby T v Leicester C	0-5
Crystal Palace v Southampton	2-0

Fourth Round

Aston Villa v Reading	3-1
Charlton Ath v Bradford C	0-1
Workington v Norwich C	3-0
Chelsea v Swansea T	3-2
Stoke C v Plymouth Arg	1-1, 1-3
Northampton T v Chesterfield	4-1
Coventry C v Sunderland	4-2
Leicester C v Crystal Palace	0-0, 2-1

Fifth Round

Aston Villa v Bradford C	7-1
Workington v Chelsea	2-2, 0-2
Plymouth Arg v Northampton T	1-0
Coventry C v Leicester C	1-8

Semi-Final

Aston Villa v Chelsea	2-3, 1-1
Chelsea won 4-3 on aggregate	
Leicester C v Plymouth Arg	3-2, 1-0
Leicester C won 4-2 on aggregate	

Final

Chelsea 3, Leicester C 2

(First leg, Stamford Bridge, 20,690, 15 March, 1965)

Chelsea: Bonetti; Hinton, Harris; Hollins, Young, Boyle; Murray, Graham, McCreadie, Venables, Tambling.
Leicester C: Banks; Sjoberg, Norman; Chalmers, King, Appleton; Hodgson, Cross, Goodfellow, Gibson, Sweenie.
Scorers: Chelsea – Tambling, Venables (pen), McCreadie; Leicester C – Appleton, Goodfellow.

Leicester C 0, Chelsea 0

(Second leg, Leicester, 26,957, 5 April, 1965)

No changes in teams.

Chelsea won on aggregate 3-2

FOOTBALL LEAGUE CUP 1965–66

Home team shown first; where a tie was replayed, the team given second was the home team in the replay.

First Round

Barrow v Rochdale	1-1, 1-3
Bournemouth v Aldershot	0-0, 1-2
Bradford PA v Halifax T	1-0
Colchester U v Exeter C	2-1
Crewe Alex v Southport	2-0
Doncaster R v Barnsley	2-2, 2-1
Hartlepools U v Bradford C	1-0
Luton T v Brighton	1-1, 0-2
Lincoln C v York C	2-2, 2-4
Newport Co v Southend U	2-2, 1-3
Notts Co v Chesterfield	0-0, 1-2
Oldham Ath v Tranmere R	3-2
Oxford U v Millwall	0-1
Port Vale v Reading	2-2, 0-1
QPR v Walsall	1-1, 2-3
Scunthorpe U v Darlington	0-2
Shrewsbury T v Torquay U	3-0
Stockport Co v Workington	2-3
Wrexham v Chester	5-2

Second Round

Blackburn R v Northampton T	0-1
Brighton v Ipswich T	1-2
Bristol R v West Ham U	3-3, 2-3
Bury v Huddersfield T	0-2
Charlton Ath v Carlisle U	4-1
Swansea T v Aston Villa	2-3
Blackpool v Gillingham	5-2
Bolton W v Aldershot	3-0
Chesterfield v Bradford PA	3-0
Colchester U v Middlesbrough	2-4
Crewe Alex v Cardiff C	1-1, 0-3
Crystal Palace v Grimsby T	0-1
Darlington v Swindon T	2-1
Doncaster R v Burnley	0-4
Hull C v Derby Co	2-2, 3-4
Leeds U v Hartlepools U	4-2
Leyton O v Coventry C	0-3
Manchester C v Leicester C	3-1
Mansfield T v Birmingham C	2-1
Millwall v York C	4-1
Newcastle U v Peterborough U	3-4
Oldham Ath v Portsmouth	1-2
Preston NE v Plymouth Arg	1-0
Reading v Southend U	5-1
Rotherham U v Watford	2-0
Shrewsbury T v Bristol C	1-0
Southampton v Rochdale	3-0
Stoke C v Norwich C	2-1
Sunderland v Sheffield U	2-1
WBA v Walsall	3-1
Workington v Brentford	0-0, 2-1
Wrexham v Fulham	1-2

Third Round

Leeds U v WBA	2-4
Manchester C v Coventry C	2-3
Fulham v Northampton T	5-0
Sunderland v Aston Villa	1-2
Middlesbrough v Millwall	0-0, 1-3
Peterborough U v Charlton Ath	4-3
Chesterfield v Stoke C	2-2, 1-2
Burnley v Southampton	3-2
Cardiff C v Portsmouth	2-0
Derby Co v Reading	1-1, 0-2
Workington v Ipswich T	1-1, 1-3
Blackpool v Darlington	1-2
Grimsby T v Bolton W	4-2
Huddersfield T v Preston NE	0-1
Shrewsbury T v Rotherham U	2-5
West Ham U v Mansfield T	4-0

Fourth Round

Coventry C v WBA	1-1, 1-6
Fulham v Aston Villa	1-1, 0-2
Millwall v Peterborough U	1-4
Stoke C v Burnley	0-0, 1-2
Cardiff C v Reading	5-1
Ipswich T v Darlington	2-0
Grimsby T v Preston NE	4-0
Rotherham U v West Ham U	1-2

Fifth Round

WBA v Aston Villa	3-1
Peterborough U v Burnley	4-0
Cardiff C v Ipswich T	2-1
Grimsby T v West Ham U	2-2, 0-1

Semi-Final

WBA v Peterborough U	2-1, 4-2
WBA won 6-3 on aggregate	
West Ham U v Cardiff C	5-2, 5-1
West Ham U won 10-3 on aggregate	

Final

West Ham U 2, WBA 1

(First leg, Upton Park, 28,341, 9 March, 1966)

West Ham United: Standen; Burnett, Burkett, Peters, Brown, Moore, Brabrook, Boyce, Byrne, Hurst, Dear.
WBA: Potter; Cram, Fairfax, Fraser, Campbell, Williams, Brown, Astle, Kaye, Lovett, Clark.
Scorers: West Ham U – Moore, Byrne; WBA – Astle.

WBA 4, West Ham U 1

(Second leg, WBA, 31,925, 23 March, 1966)

WBA: Potter; Cram, Fairfax, Fraser, Campbell, Williams, Brown, Astle, Kaye, Hope, Clark.
West Ham U: Standen; Burnett, Peters, Bovington, Brown, Moore, Brabrook, Boyce, Byrne, Hurst, Sissons.
Scorers: WBA – Kaye, Brown, Clark, Williams; West Ham U – Peters.

WBA won on aggregate 5-3

FOOTBALL LEAGUE CUP 1966–67

Home team shown first; where a tie was replayed, the team given second was the home team in the replay.

First Round

Aldershot v Luton T	2-2, 2-1
Barnsley v Grimsby T	1-2
Barrow v Oldham Ath	2-1
Bradford PA v Hartlepools U	2-2, 2-1
Brentford v Millwall	0-0, 1-0
Brighton v Leyton O	1-0
Bury v Rochdale	2-0
Bradford C v Doncaster R	1-1, 2-5
Cardiff C v Bristol R	1-0
Chester v Tranmere R	2-5
Chesterfield v Scunthorpe U	2-1
Crewe Alex v Stockport Co	1-0
Exeter C v Torquay U	2-2, 2-1
Halifax T v Darlington	0-0, 0-4
Lincoln C v Hull C	1-0
Middlesbrough v York C	0-0, 1-2
Newport Co v Swansea T	1-2
Notts Co v Mansfield T	1-1, 0-3
Peterborough U v Oxford U	2-1
Southend U v Gillingham	0-0, 0-2
Southport v Workington	0-1
Shrewsbury T v Wrexham	6-1
Swindon T v Bournemouth	2-1
Port Vale v Walsall	1-3
QPR v Colchester U	5-0
Watford v Reading	1-1, 0-1

Second Round

Aldershot v QPR	1-1, 0-2
Arsenal v Gillingham	1-1, 1-1, 5-0
Blackburn R v Barrow	4-1
Blackpool v Manchester U	5-1
Bradford PA v Grimsby T	0-0, 1-3
Brentford v Ipswich T	2-4
Bristol C v Swansea T	1-1, 1-2
Bury v Workington	2-3
Cardiff C v Exeter C	0-1
Carlisle U v Tranmere R	1-1, 2-0
Chelsea v Charlton Ath	5-2
Coventry C v Derby Co	2-1
Darlington v Doncaster R	1-1, 0-2
Fulham v Crystal Palace	2-0
Leeds U v Newcastle U	1-0
Leicester C v Reading	5-0
Lincoln C v Huddersfield	2-1
Manchester C v Bolton W	3-1
Northampton T v Peterborough U	2-2, 2-0
Norwich C v Brighton	0-1
Nottingham F v Birmingham C	1-1, 1-2
Preston NE v Crewe Alex	2-0
Southampton v Plymouth Arg	4-3
Sheffield W v Rotherham U	0-1
Shrewsbury T v Burnley	1-1, 1-5
Sunderland v Sheffield U	1-1, 0-1
Swindon T v Portsmouth	4-1
WBA v Aston Villa	6-1
West Ham U v Tottenham H	1-0
Wolverhampton W v Mansfield T	2-1
Walsall v Stoke C	2-1
York C v Chesterfield	3-1

Third Round

Swansea T v QPR	1-2
Leicester C v Lincoln C	5-0
Southampton v Carlisle U	3-3, 1-2
York C v Blackburn R	0-2
Sheffield U v Burnley	2-0
Exeter C v Walsall	1-2
Grimsby T v Workington	3-0
Birmingham C v Ipswich T	2-1
Brighton v Coventry C	1-1, 3-4
Northampton T v Rotherham U	2-1
Doncaster R v Swindon T	1-1, 2-0
WBA v Manchester C	4-1
Blackpool v Chelsea	1-1, 3-2
Fulham v Wolverhampton W	5-1
Arsenal v West Ham U	1-3
Preston NE v Leeds U	1-1, 0-3

Fourth Round

QPR v Leicester C	4-2
Carlisle U v Blackburn R	4-0
Sheffield U v Walsall	2-1
Grimsby T v Birmingham C	2-4
Brighton v Northampton T	1-1, 0-8
Swindon T v WBA	0-2
Blackpool v Fulham	4-2
West Ham U v Leeds U	7-0

Fifth Round

QPR v Carlisle U	2-1
Sheffield U v Birmingham C	2-3
Northampton T v WBA	1-3
Blackpool v West Ham U	1-3

Semi-Final

Birmingham C v QPR	1-4, 1-3
QPR won 7-2 on aggregate	
WBA v West Ham U	4-0, 2-2
WBA won 6-2 on aggregate	

Final

QPR 3, WBA 2

(Wembley, 97,952, receipts £57,000, 4 March, 1967)

QPR: Springett; Hazell, Langley, Sibley, Hunt, Keen, Lazarus, Sanderson, Allen, Marsh, Morgan R.

WBA: Sheppard; Cram, Williams, Collard, Clarke D., Fraser, Brown, Astle, Kaye, Hope, Clark C.

Scorers: QPR – Morgan R., Marsh, Lazarus; WBA – Clark C. 2.

FOOTBALL LEAGUE CUP 1967–68

Home team shown first; where a tie was replayed, the team given second was the home team in the replay.

First Round

Aldershot v Cardiff C	2-3
Barrow v Southport	1-0
Bournemouth v Watford	1-1, 0-0, 1-2
Brighton v Colchester U	4-0
Crewe Alex v Stockport Co	1-1, 0-3
Darlington v York C	1-0
Doncaster R v Scunthorpe U	1-2
Grimsby T v Chesterfield	1-0
Halifax T v Bradford PA	5-0
Hartlepools U v Bradford C	2-0
Luton T v Charlton Ath	1-1, 2-1
Mansfield T v Lincoln C	2-3
Middlesbrough v Barnsley	4-1
Northampton T v Peterborough U	3-2
Notts Co v Rotherham U	0-1
Orient v Gillingham	1-3
Oxford U v Swansea T	3-1
Port Vale v Chester	3-0
Reading v Bristol R	3-0
Rochdale v Bury	0-1
Southend U v Brentford	1-0
Swindon T v Newport Co	1-1, 0-2
Torquay U v Exeter C	0-0, 3-0
Tranmere R v Wrexham	2-1
Walsall v Shrewsbury T	4-2
Workington v Oldham Ath	1-1, 1-1, 2-1

Second Round

Barrow v Crystal Palace	1-0
Blackburn R v Brighton	3-1
Bristol C v Everton	0-5
Burnley v Cardiff C	2-1
Carlisle U v Workington	0-2
Coventry C v Arsenal	1-2
Derby Co v Hartlepools U	4-0
Fulham v Tranmere R	1-0
Gillingham v Torquay U	2-2, 0-2
Grimsby T v Bury	2-2, 0-2
Huddersfield T v Wolverhampton W	1-0
Ipswich T v Southampton	5-2
Leeds U v Luton T	3-1
Lincoln C v Newcastle U	2-1
Liverpool v Bolton W	1-1, 2-3
Manchester C v Leicester C	4-0
Middlesbrough v Chelsea	2-1
Millwall v Sheffield U	3-2
Newport Co v Blackpool	0-1
Northampton T v Aston Villa	3-1
Norwich C v Rotherham U	1-1, 2-0
Oxford U v Preston NE	2-1
Portsmouth v Port Vale	3-1
Plymouth Arg v Birmingham C	0-2
QPR v Hull C	2-1
Scunthorpe U v Nottingham F	0-1
Reading v WBA	3-1
Southend U v Darlington	1-2
Stockport Co v Sheffield W	3-5
Stoke C v Watford	2-0
Sunderland v Halifax T	3-2
Walsall v West Ham U	1-5

Third Round

Arsenal v Reading	1-0
Blackburn R v Middlesbrough	3-2
QPR v Oxford U	5-1
Burnley v Nottingham F	3-0
Workington v Fulham	2-2, 2-6
Manchester C v Blackpool	1-1, 2-0
Norwich C v Huddersfield T	0-1
West Ham U v Bolton W	4-1
Derby Co v Birmingham C	3-1
Lincoln C v Torquay U	4-2
Darlington v Portsmouth	4-1
Northampton T v Millwall	0-0, 1-5
Everton v Sunderland	2-3
Leeds U v Bury	3-0
Sheffield W v Barrow	3-1
Stoke C v Ipswich T	2-1

Fourth Round

Arsenal v Blackburn R	2-1
QPR v Burnley	1-2
Fulham v Manchester C	3-2
Huddersfield v West Ham U	2-0
Derby Co v Lincoln C	1-1, 3-0
Darlington v Millwall	2-0
Sunderland v Leeds U	0-2
Sheffield W v Stoke C	0-0, 1-2

Fifth Round

Burnley v Arsenal	3-3, 1-2
Fulham v Huddersfield T	1-1, 1-2
Derby Co v Darlington	5-4
Leeds U v Stoke C	2-0

Semi-Final

Arsenal v Huddersfield	3-2, 3-1
Arsenal won 6-3 on aggregate	
Derby Co v Leeds U	0-1, 2-3
Leeds U won 4-2 on aggregate	

Final

Leeds U 1, Arsenal 0

(Wembley, 97,887, receipts £95,000, 2 March, 1968)

Leeds U: Sprake; Reaney, Cooper; Bremner, Charlton, Hunter; Greenhoff, Lorimer, Madeley, Giles, Gray (Belfitt).
Arsenal: Furnell; Storey, McNab; McLintock, Simpson, Ure; Radford, Jenkins, Graham, Sammels, Armstrong.
Scorer: Leeds U – Cooper.

FOOTBALL LEAGUE CUP 1968–69

Home team shown first; where a tie was replayed, the team given second was the home team in the replay.

First Round

Aldershot v Brentford	2-4
Bournemouth v Southend U	1-6
Bradford PA v Darlington	0-3
Bradford C v Hartlepool	3-2
Brighton v Oxford U	2-0
Bristol C v Newport Co	2-0
Bristol R v Swansea T	0-2
Bury v Stockport Co	1-1, 0-1
Chester v Tranmere R	0-0, 2-2, 1-1, 1-2
Colchester U v Reading	2-0
Derby Co v Chesterfield	3-0
Doncaster R v Peterborough U	0-0, 0-1
Gillingham v Orient	2-2, 0-3
Grimsby T v Notts Co	0-0, 1-0
Halifax T v Hull C	0-3
Lincoln C v Mansfield T	2-1
Luton T v Watford	3-0
Northampton T v Crewe Alex	1-1, 0-1
Plymouth Arg v Exeter C	0-0, 0-0, 0-1
Preston NE v Oldham Ath	1-1, 1-0
Scunthorpe U v Rotherham U	2-1
Southport v Barrow	2-2, 3-1
Swindon T v Torquay U	2-1
Walsall v Shrewsbury T	2-0
Workington v Rochdale	2-1
Wrexham v Port Vale	2-0
York C v Barnsley	3-4

Second Round

Arsenal v Sunderland	1-0
Aston Villa v Tottenham H	1-4
Barnsley v Millwall	1-1, 1-3
Birmingham C v Chelsea	0-1
Blackburn R v Stoke C	1-1, 1-0
Bradford C v Swindon T	1-1, 3-4
Brentford v Hull C	3-0
Brighton v Luton T	1-1, 2-4
Bristol C v Middlesbrough	1-0
Carlisle U v Cardiff C	2-0
Colchester U v Workington	0-1
Coventry C v Portsmouth	2-0
Crystal Palace v Preston NE	3-1
Darlington v Leicester C	1-2
Derby Co v Stockport Co	5-1
Everton v Tranmere R	4-0
Exeter C v Sheffield W	3-1
Grimsby T v Burnley	1-1, 0-6
Huddersfield T v Manchester C	0-0, 0-4
Ipswich T v Norwich C	2-4
Leeds U v Charlton Ath	1-0
Liverpool v Sheffield U	4-0
Peterborough U v QPR	4-2
Nottingham F v WBA	2-3
Orient v Fulham	1-0
Scunthorpe U v Lincoln C	2-1
Southampton v Crewe Alex	3-1
Southport v Newcastle U	0-2
West Ham U v Bolton W	7-2
Wolverhampton W v Southend U	1-0
Wrexham v Blackpool	1-1, 0-3
Walsall v Swansea T	1-1, 2-3

Third Round

Scunthorpe U v Arsenal	1-6
Liverpool v Swansea T	2-0
Blackpool v Manchester C	1-0
Wolverhampton W v Millwall	5-1
Tottenham H v Exeter C	6-3
Peterborough U v WBA	2-1
Brentford v Norwich C	0-2
Southampton v Newcastle U	4-1
Workington v Burnley	0-1
Carlisle U v Leicester C	0-3
Orient v Crystal Palace	0-1
Leeds U v Bristol C	2-1
Everton v Luton T	5-1
Chelsea v Derby Co	0-0, 1-3
West Ham U v Coventry C	0-0, 2-3
Swindon T v Blackburn R	1-0

Fourth Round

Arsenal v Liverpool	2-1
Blackpool v Wolverhampton W	2-1
Tottenham H v Peterborough U	1-0
Norwich C v Southampton	0-4
Burnley v Leicester C	4-0
Crystal Palace v Leeds U	2-1
Everton v Derby Co	0-0, 0-1
Coventry C v Swindon T	2-2, 0-3

Fifth Round

Arsenal v Blackpool	5-1
Tottenham H v Southampton	1-0
Burnley v Crystal Palace	2-0
Derby Co v Swindon T	0-0, 0-1

Semi-Final

Arsenal v Tottenham H	1-0, 1-1
Arsenal won 2-1 on aggregate	
Burnley v Swindon T	1-2, 2-1, 2-3
(Replay at the Hawthorns)	
Swindon T won 6-5 on aggregate	

Final

Arsenal 1, Swindon T 3

(Wembley, 98,189, receipts £104,000, 15 March, 1969)

Arsenal: Wilson; Storey, McNab; McLintock, Ure, Simpson (Graham); Radford, Sammels, Court, Gould, Armstrong.

Swindon T: Downsborough; Thomas, Trollope; Butler, Burrows, Harland; Heath, Smart, Smith, Noble (Penman), Rogers.

Scorers: Arsenal – Gould; Swindon T – Smart, Rogers 2.

FOOTBALL LEAGUE CUP 1969–70

Home team shown first; where a tie was replayed, the team given second was the home team in the replay.

First Round

Aldershot v Gillingham	0-1
Barnsley v Halifax T	0-1
Bolton W v Rochdale	6-3
Bournemouth v Bristol R	3-0
Bradford PA v Rotherham U	0-2
Bradford C v Chesterfield	1-1, 1-0
Brighton v Portsmouth	1-0
Chester v Aston Villa	1-2
Colchester U v Reading	1-1, 3-0
Crewe Alex v Wrexham	0-0, 0-1
Darlington v York C	3-0
Exeter C v Bristol C	1-1, 2-3
Grimsby T v Doncaster R	0-2
Mansfield T v Notts Co	3-1
Newport Co v Swansea T	2-3
Orient v Fulham	0-0, 1-3
Oxford U v Northampton T	2-0
Peterborough U v Luton T	1-1, 2-5
Plymouth Arg v Torquay U	2-2, 0-1
Preston NE v Bury	0-1
Port Vale v Tranmere R	0-1
Scunthorpe U v Hartlepool	0-2
Shrewsbury T v Walsall	1-0
Southend U v Brentford	2-2, 0-0, 3-2
Southport v Oldham Ath	5-1
Stockport Co v Blackburn R	0-2
Watford v Lincoln C	2-1
Workington v Barrow	0-0, 1-3

Second Round

Aston Villa v WBA	1-2
Barrow v Nottingham F	1-2
Blackburn R v Doncaster R	4-2
Blackpool v Gillingham	3-1
Bolton W v Rotherham U	0-0, 3-3, 0-1
Brighton v Birmingham C	2-0
Bristol C v Leicester C	0-0, 0-0, 1-3
Carlisle U v Huddersfield	2-0
Charlton Ath v Wrexham	0-2
Coventry C v Chelsea	0-1
Crystal Palace v Cardiff C	3-1
Darlington v Everton	0-1
Fulham v Leeds U	0-1
Hartlepool v Derby Co	1-3
Hull C v Norwich C	1-0
Ipswich T v Colchester U	4-0
Luton T v Millwall	2-2, 1-0
Manchester U v Middlesbrough	1-0
Mansfield T v QPR	2-2, 0-4
Oxford U v Bury	4-1
Sheffield U v Newcastle U	2-0
Sheffield W v Bournemouth	1-1, 0-1
Shrewsbury T v Southend U	2-2, 0-2
Southampton v Arsenal	1-1, 0-2
Southport v Manchester C	0-3
Stoke C v Burnley	0-2
Sunderland v Bradford C	1-2
Swansea T v Swindon T	1-3
Tranmere R v Torquay U	2-1
Watford v Liverpool	1-2
West Ham U v Halifax T	4-2
Wolverhampton W v Tottenham H	1-0

Third Round

Arsenal v Everton	0-0, 0-1
Manchester C v Liverpool	3-2
QPR v Tranmere R	6-0
Brighton v Wolverhampton W	2-3
Rotherham U v Burnley	1-1, 0-2
Manchester U v Wrexham	2-0
Crystal Palace v Blackpool	2-2, 1-0
Derby Co v Hull C	3-1
Nottingham F v West Ham U	1-0
Oxford U v Swindon T	1-0
Carlisle U v Blackburn R	2-1
Leeds U v Chelsea	1-1, 0-2
Bournemouth v Leicester C	0-2
Sheffield U v Luton T	3-0
Bradford C v Southend U	2-1
Ipswich T v WBA	1-1, 0-2

Fourth Round

Manchester C v Everton	2-0
QPR v Wolverhampton W	3-1
Burnley v Manchester U	0-0, 0-1
Crystal Palace v Derby Co	1-1, 0-3
Nottingham F v Oxford U	0-1
Carlisle U v Chelsea	1-0
Leicester C v Sheffield U	2-0
WBA v Bradford C	4-0

Fifth Round

Manchester C v QPR	3-0
Manchester U v Derby Co	0-0, 1-0
Oxford U v Carlisle U	0-0, 0-1
Leicester C v WBA	0-0, 1-2

Semi-Final

Manchester C v Manchester U	2-1, 2-2
Manchester C won 4-3 on aggregate	
Carlisle U v WBA	1-0, 1-4
WBA won 4-2 on aggregate	

Final

Manchester C 2, WBA 1

(Wembley, 97,963, receipts £123,000, 7 March, 1970)

Manchester C: Corrigan; Book, Mann; Doyle, Booth, Oakes; Heslop, Bell, Summerbee (Bowyer), Lee, Pardoe.
WBA: Osborne; Fraser, Wilson; Brown, Talbut, Kaye; Cantello, Suggett, Astle, Hartford (Krzywicki), Hope.
Scorers: Manchester C – Doyle, Pardoe; WBA – Astle.

FOOTBALL LEAGUE CUP 1970–71

Home team shown first; where a tie was replayed, the team given second was the home team in the replay.

First Round

Aldershot v Brentford	1-0
Aston Villa v Notts Co	4-0
Barnsley v Rotherham U	0-1
Chester v Shrewsbury T	2-1
Colchester U v Cambridge U	5-0
Doncaster R v Darlington	1-1, 1-3
Fulham v Orient	1-0
Gillingham v Luton T	0-1
Halifax T v Bradford C	3-2
Hartlepool v York C	2-3
Lincoln C v Grimsby T	2-1
Mansfield T v Chesterfield	6-2
Newport Co v Reading	2-1
Portsmouth v Plymouth Arg	2-0
Rochdale v Southport	1-0
Rotherham U v Barnsley	1-0
Scunthorpe U v Northampton T	2-3
Stockport Co v Preston NE	0-1
Torquay U v Bournemouth	1-1, 2-1
Watford v Peterborough U	2-0
Workington v Barrow	2-0
Birmingham C v Wrexham	3-3, 3-2
Bristol R v Brighton	1-0
Bury v Oldham Ath	1-3
Charlton Ath v Southend U	3-0
Crewe Alex v Tranmere R	2-2, 0-4
Exeter C v Swansea C	0-0, 2-4
Port Vale v Walsall	0-1

Second Round

Carlisle U v Manchester C	2-1
QPR v Cardiff C	4-0
Crystal Palace v Rochdale	3-3, 3-1
Lincoln C v Sunderland	2-1
Torquay U v Preston NE	1-3
Norwich C v Chester	0-0, 2-1
Sheffield W v Chelsea	1-1, 1-2
WBA v Charlton Ath	3-1
Stoke C v Millwall	0-0, 1-2
Oldham Ath v Middlesbrough	2-4
Tranmere R v Coventry C	1-1, 1-2
Derby Co v Halifax T	3-1
Luton T v Workington	3-0
Bristol R v Newcastle U	2-1
Darlington v Fulham	0-4
Bolton W v Blackburn R	1-0
Mansfield T v Liverpool	0-0, 2-3
Colchester U v Birmingham C	1-1, 1-2
York C v Northampton T	0-0, 1-1, 1-2
Swindon T v Watford	4-2
Sheffield U v Leeds U	1-0
Leicester C v Southampton	3-2
Ipswich T v Arsenal	0-0, 0-4
Portsmouth v Walsall	1-0
Aldershot v Manchester U	1-3
West Ham U v Hull C	1-0
Aston Villa v Burnley	2-0
Oxford U v Wolverhampton W	1-0
Rotherham U v Bristol C	0-0, 0-4
Tottenham H v Swansea C	3-0
Blackpool v Newport Co	4-1
Huddersfield T v Nottingham F	0-0, 0-2

Third Round

Bolton W v Leicester C	1-1, 0-1
Derby Co v Millwall	4-2
Preston NE v WBA	0-1
Crystal Palace v Lincoln C	4-0
Tottenham H v Sheffield U	2-1
Northampton T v Aston Villa	1-1, 0-3
Coventry C v West Ham U	3-1
Birmingham C v Nottingham F	2-1
Luton T v Arsenal	0-1
Norwich C v Bristol R	1-1, 1-3
Carlisle U v Oxford U	3-1
Blackpool v Bristol C	0-1
Manchester U v Portsmouth	1-0
Fulham v QPR	2-0
Swindon T v Liverpool	2-0
Chelsea v Middlesbrough	3-2

Fourth Round

Bristol R v Birmingham C	3-0
Leicester C v Bristol C	2-2, 1-2
Manchester U v Chelsea	2-1
Crystal Palace v Arsenal	0-0, 2-0
Aston Villa v Carlisle U	1-0
Coventry C v Derby Co	1-0
Tottenham H v WBA	5-0
Fulham v Swindon T	1-0

Fifth Round

Bristol R v Aston Villa	1-1, 0-1
Fulham v Bristol C	0-0, 0-1
Tottenham H v Coventry C	4-1
Manchester U v Crystal Palace	4-2

Semi-Final

Bristol C v Tottenham H	1-1, 0-2
Tottenham H won 3-1 on aggregate	
Manchester U v Aston Villa	1-1, 1-2
Aston Villa won 3-2 on aggregate	

Final

Aston Villa 0, Tottenham H 2

(Wembley, 100,000, receipts £132,000, 27 February, 1971)

Aston Villa: Dunn; Bradley, Aitken; Godfrey, Turnbull, Tiler; McMahon, Rioch, Lochhead, Hamilton, Anderson.
Tottenham H: Jennings; Kinnear, Knowles; Mullery, Collins, Beal; Gilzean, Perryman, Chivers, Peters, Neighbour.
Scorer: Tottenham H – Chivers 2.

FOOTBALL LEAGUE CUP 1971–72

Home team shown first; where a tie was replayed, the team given second was the home team in the replay.

First Round

Aldershot v Southend U	1-1, 2-1
Aston Villa v Wrexham	2-2, 1-1, 4-3
Barnsley v Hartlepool	0-0, 1-0
Barrow v Preston NE	0-2
Blackburn R v Workington	2-0
Bournemouth v Portsmouth	2-1
Bradford C v Bolton W	1-1, 1-2
Charlton Ath v Peterborough U	5-1
Chesterfield v Mansfield T	0-0, 5-0
Colchester U v Brentford	3-1
Crewe Alex v Southport	0-1
Darlington v York C	0-1
Exeter C v Bristol R	0-3
Fulham v Cambridge U	4-0
Gillingham v Reading	4-0
Grimsby T v Doncaster R	4-3
Halifax T v Rochdale	1-1, 2-2, 2-0
Newport Co v Torquay U	1-2
Oldham Ath v Bury	1-0
Orient v Notts Co	1-1, 1-3
Plymouth Arg v Bristol C	1-0
Port Vale v Shrewsbury T	0-2
Rotherham U v Sheffield W	0-2
Scunthorpe U v Lincoln C	0-1
Stockport Co v Walsall	1-0
Swansea C v Brighton	0-1
Tranmere R v Chester	1-1, 3-1
Watford v Northampton T	2-0

Second Round

Arsenal v Barnsley	1-0
Blackburn R v Lincoln C	0-0, 1-4
Bournemouth v Blackpool	0-2
Bristol R v Sunderland	3-1
Carlisle U v Sheffield W	5-0
Charlton Ath v Leicester C	3-1
Chelsea v Plymouth Arg	2-0
Chesterfield v Aston Villa	2-3
Colchester U v Swindon T	4-1
Coventry C v Burnley	0-1
Crystal Palace v Luton T	2-0
Derby Co v Leeds U	0-0, 0-2
Grimsby T v Shrewsbury T	2-1
Huddersfield T v Bolton W	0-2
Ipswich T v Manchester U	1-3
Liverpool v Hull C	3-0
Manchester C v Wolverhampton W	4-3
Newcastle U v Halifax T	2-1
Norwich C v Brighton	2-0
Nottingham F v Aldershot	5-1
Notts Co v Gillingham	1-2
Oxford U v Millwall	1-0
QPR v Birmingham C	2-0
Sheffield U v Fulham	3-0
Southampton v Everton	2-1
Southport v Stoke C	1-2
Stockport Co v Watford	0-1
Torquay U v Oldham Ath	2-1
Tranmere R v Preston NE	0-1
WBA v Tottenham H	0-1
West Ham U v Cardiff C	1-1, 2-1
York C v Middlesbrough	2-2, 2-1

Third Round

Arsenal v Newcastle U	4-0
Blackpool v Colchester U	4-0
Bolton W v Manchester C	3-0
Bristol R v Charlton Ath	2-1
Crystal Palace v Aston Villa	2-2, 0-2
Gillingham v Grimsby T	1-1, 0-1
Liverpool v Southampton	1-0
Manchester U v Burnley	1-1, 1-0
Norwich v Carlisle U	4-1
Nottingham F v Chelsea	1-1, 1-2
Oxford U v Stoke C	1-1, 0-2
QPR v Lincoln C	4-2
Sheffield U v York C	3-2
Torquay U v Tottenham H	1-4
Watford v Preston NE	1-1, 1-2
West Ham U v Leeds U	0-0, 1-0

Fourth Round

Arsenal v Sheffield U	0-0, 0-2
Blackpool v Aston Villa	4-1
Chelsea v Bolton W	1-1, 6-0
Grimsby T v Norwich C	1-1, 1-3
Manchester U v Stoke C	1-1, 0-0, 1-2
QPR v Bristol R	1-1, 0-1
Tottenham H v Preston NE	1-1, 2-1
West Ham U v Liverpool	2-1

Fifth Round

Bristol R v Stoke C	2-4
Norwich C v Chelsea	0-1
Tottenham H v Blackpool	2-0
West Ham U v Sheffield U	5-0

Semi-Final

Chelsea v Tottenham H *Chelsea won 5-4 on aggregate*	3-2, 2-2
Stoke C v West Ham U *Stoke C won 5-4 on aggregate*	1-2, 1-0, 0-0, 3-2

Final

Chelsea 1, Stoke C 2

(Wembley, 100,000, receipts £132,000, 4 March, 1972)

Chelsea: Bonetti; Mulligan (Baldwin), Harris, Hollins, Dempsey, Webb, Cooke, Garland, Osgood, Hudson, Houseman.
Stoke C: Banks; Marsh, Pejic, Bernard, Smith, Bloor, Conroy, Greenhoff (Mahoney), Ritchie, Dobing, Eastham.
Scorers: Chelsea – Osgood; Stoke C – Conroy, Eastham.

FOOTBALL LEAGUE CUP 1972–73

Home team shown first; where a tie was replayed, the team given second was the home team in the replay.

First Round

Aston Villa v Hereford U	4-1
Barnsley v Grimsby T	0-0, 0-2
Blackburn R v Rochdale	0-1
Bolton W v Oldham Ath	3-0
Bradford C v Stockport Co	1-1, 1-1, 0-2
Brentford v Cambridge U	1-0
Brighton v Exeter C	2-1
Cardiff C v Bristol R	2-2, 1-3
Chester v Shrewsbury T	4-3
Darlington v Rotherham U	0-1
Gillingham v Colchester U	1-0
Halifax T v Bury	1-2
Hartlepool v Doncaster R	1-0
Mansfield T v Lincoln C	3-1
Northampton T v Charlton Ath	0-3
Notts Co v York C	3-1
Orient v Watford	2-0
Oxford U v Peterborough U	4-0
Plymouth Arg v Bournemouth	0-2
Reading v Fulham	1-1, 1-1, 0-1
Scunthorpe U v Chesterfield	0-0, 0-5
Southend U v Aldershot	2-1
Southport v Walsall	4-1
Swansea C v Newport Co	1-1, 0-3
Torquay U v Portsmouth	1-2
Tranmere R v Port Vale	0-1
Workington v Preston NE	1-0
Wrexham v Crewe Alex	4-0

Second Round

Arsenal v Everton	1-0
Birmingham C v Luton T	1-1, 1-1, 1-0
Bournemouth v Blackpool	0-0, 1-1, 1-2
Bristol R v Brighton	4-0
Bury v Grimsby T	1-0
Carlisle U v Liverpool	1-1, 1-5
Charlton Ath v Mansfield T	4-3
Coventry C v Hartlepool	1-0
Crystal Palace v Stockport Co	0-1
Gillingham v Millwall	0-2
Hull C v Fulham	1-0
Leeds U v Burnley	4-0
Manchester C v Rochdale	4-0
Middlesbrough v Wrexham	2-0
Newport Co v Ipswich T	0-3
Norwich C v Leicester C	2-1
Notts Co v Southport	3-2
Nottingham F v Aston Villa	0-1
Oxford U v Manchester U	2-2, 1-3
Portsmouth v Chesterfield	0-1
Port Vale v Newcastle U	1-3
Rotherham U v Brentford	2-0
Sheffield W v Bolton W	2-0
Southampton v Chester	0-0, 2-2, 2-0
Southend U v Chelsea	0-1
Stoke C v Sunderland	3-0
Swindon T v Derby Co	0-1
Tottenham H v Huddersfield T	2-1
WBA v QPR	2-1
West Ham U v Bristol C	2-1
Wolverhampton W v Orient	2-1
Workington v Sheffield U	0-1

Third Round

Arsenal v Rotherham U	5-0
Aston Villa v Leeds U	1-1, 0-2
Birmingham C v Coventry C	2-1
Bristol R v Manchester U	1-1, 2-1
Bury v Manchester C	2-0
Derby Co v Chelsea	0-0, 2-3
Hull C v Norwich C	1-2
Ipswich T v Stoke C	1-2
Middlesbrough v Tottenham H	1-1, 0-0, 1-2
Millwall v Chesterfield	2-0
Newcastle U v Blackpool	0-3
Sheffield U v Charlton Ath	0-0, 2-2, 1-0
Southampton v Notts Co	1-3
Stockport Co v West Ham U	2-1
WBA v Liverpool	1-1, 1-2
Wolverhampton W v Sheffield W	3-1

Fourth Round

Blackpool v Birmingham C	2-0
Bury v Chelsea	0-1
Liverpool v Leeds U	2-2, 1-0
Notts Co v Stoke C	3-1
Sheffield U v Arsenal	1-2
Stockport Co v Norwich C	1-5
Tottenham H v Millwall	2-0
Wolverhampton W v Bristol R	4-0

Fifth Round

Arsenal v Norwich C	0-3
Chelsea v Notts Co	3-1
Wolverhampton W v Blackpool	1-1, 1-0
Liverpool v Tottenham H	1-1, 1-3

Semi-Final

Chelsea v Norwich C	0-2, 0-1
Norwich C won 3-0 on aggregate	
Wolverhampton W v Tottenham H	1-2, 2-2
Tottenham H won 4-3 on aggregate	

Final

Tottenham H 1, Norwich C 0

(Wembley, 100,000, receipts £132,000, 3 March, 1973)

Tottenham H: Jennings; Kinnear, Knowles, Pratt (Coates), England, Beal, Gilzean, Perryman, Chivers, Peters, Pearce.
Norwich C: Keelan; Payne, Butler, Stringer, Forbes, Briggs, Livermore, Blair (Howard), Cross, Paddon, Anderson.
Scorer: Tottenham H – Coates.

FOOTBALL LEAGUE CUP 1973–74

Home team shown first; where a tie was replayed, the team given second was the home team in the replay.

First Round

Aldershot v Cambridge U	1-1, 0-3
Bolton W v Preston NE	1-1, 2-0
AFC Bournemouth v Bristol R	1-0
Brentford v Orient	1-2
Brighton v Charlton Ath	1-2
Bury v Oldham Ath	0-0, 3-2
Cardiff C v Hereford U	2-0
Carlisle U v Workington	2-2, 1-0
Chester v Wrexham	0-2
Chesterfield v Mansfield T	1-1, 1-0
Darlington v Bradford C	2-1
Gillingham v Colchester U	4-2
Grimsby T v Northampton T	2-1
Halifax T v Barnsley	1-1, 1-0
Notts Co v Doncaster R	3-4
Peterborough U v Scunthorpe U	2-2, 1-2
Portsmouth v Southend U	2-1
Reading v Watford	2-2, 3-2
Rochdale v Hartlepool	5-3
Rotherham U v Lincoln C	2-1
Southport v Blackburn R	1-1, 1-3
Stockport Co v Port Vale	2-0
Swansea C v Exeter C	1-1, 1-2
Swindon T v Newport Co	3-3, 2-1
Torquay U v Plymouth Arg	0-2
Tranmere R v Crewe Alex	3-3, 1-0
Walsall v Shrewsbury T	6-1
York C v Huddersfield T	1-0

Second Round

Arsenal v Tranmere R	0-1
Blackpool v Birmingham C	1-1, 2-4
AFC Bournemouth v Sheffield W	0-0, 2-2, 1-2
Bury v Cambridge U	2-0
Cardiff C v Burnley	2-2, 2-3
Chesterfield v Swindon T	1-0
Coventry C v Darlington	5-1
Derby Co v Sunderland	2-2, 1-1, 0-3
Everton v Reading	1-0
Gillingham v Carlisle U	1-2
Halifax T v Wolverhampton W	0-3
Ipswich T v Leeds U	2-0
Leicester C v Hull C	3-3, 2-3
Luton T v Grimsby T	1-1, 0-0, 2-0
Manchester U v Middlesbrough	0-1
Millwall v Nottingham F	0-0, 3-1
Newcastle U v Doncaster R	6-0
Norwich C v Wrexham	6-2
Orient v Blackburn R	2-0
Oxford U v Fulham	1-1, 0-3
Plymouth Arg v Portsmouth	4-0
QPR v Tottenham H	1-0
Rochdale v Bolton W	0-4
Rotherham U v Exeter C	1-4
Scunthorpe U v Bristol C	0-0, 1-2
Southampton v Charlton Ath	3-0
Stockport Co v Crystal Palace	1-0
Stoke C v Chelsea	1-0
WBA v Sheffield U	2-1
West Ham U v Liverpool	2-2, 0-1
Walsall v Manchester C	0-0, 0-0, 0-4
York C v Aston Villa	1-0

Third Round

Birmingham C v Newcastle U	2-2, 1-0
Bristol C v Coventry C	2-2, 1-2
Burnley v Plymouth Arg	1-2
Carlisle U v Manchester C	0-1
Everton v Norwich C	0-1
Fulham v Ipswich T	2-2, 1-2
Hull C v Stockport Co	4-1
Luton T v Bury	0-0, 3-2
Millwall v Bolton W	1-1, 2-1
Orient v York C	1-1, 1-2
QPR v Sheffield W	8-2
Southampton v Chesterfield	3-0
Stoke C v Middlesbrough	1-1, 2-1
Sunderland v Liverpool	0-2
Tranmere R v Wolverhampton W	1-1, 1-2
WBA v Exeter C	1-3

Fourth Round

Coventry C v Stoke C	2-1
Hull C v Liverpool	0-0, 1-3
Ipswich T v Birmingham C	1-3
Millwall v Luton T	3-1
QPR v Plymouth Arg	0-3
Southampton v Norwich C	0-2
Wolverhampton W v Exeter C	5-1
York C v Manchester C	0-0, 1-4

Fifth Round

Birmingham C v Plymouth Arg	1-2
Coventry C v Manchester C	2-2, 2-4
Millwall v Norwich C	1-1, 1-2
Wolverhampton W v Liverpool	1-0

Semi-Final

Norwich C v Wolverhampton W	1-1, 0-1
Wolverhampton W won 2-1 on aggregate	
Plymouth Arg v Manchester C	1-1, 0-2
Manchester C won 3-1 on aggregate	

Final

Wolverhampton W 2, Manchester C 1

(Wembley, 100,000, receipts £165,500, 2 March, 1974)

Wolverhampton W: Pierce; Palmer, Parkin, Bailey, Munro, McAlle, Sunderland, Hibbitt, Richards, Dougan, Wagstaffe (Powell).

Manchester C: MacRae; Pardoe, Donachie, Doyle, Booth, Towers, Summerbee, Bell, Lee, Law, Marsh.

Scorers: Wolverhampton W – Hibbitt, Richards; Manchester C – Bell.

FOOTBALL LEAGUE CUP 1974–75

Home team shown first; where a tie was replayed, the team given second was the home team in the replay.

First Round

Barnsley v Halifax T	0-1
Bradford C v Darlington	2-1
Brentford v Aldershot	3-0
Bristol C v Cardiff C	2-1
Bristol R v Plymouth Arg	0-0, 1-0
Bury v Oldham Ath	2-0
Charlton Ath v Peterborough U	4-0
Chester v Walsall	2-1
Chesterfield v Grimsby T	3-0
Colchester U v Oxford U	1-0
Doncaster R v Mansfield T	2-1
Exeter C v Swansea C	3-1
Gillingham v AFC Bournemouth	1-1, 1-1, 1-2
Hereford U v Shrewsbury T	1-1, 1-0
Newport Co v Torquay U	1-0
Northampton T v Port Vale	1-0
Preston NE v Rochdale	1-0
Reading v Brighton & HA	0-0, 2-2, 0-0, 3-2
Rotherham U v Lincoln C	1-1, 1-1, 2-1
Scunthorpe U v Sheffield W	1-0
Southend U v Cambridge U	2-0
Southport v Tranmere R	0-2
Stockport Co v Blackburn R	0-2
Swindon T v Portsmouth	0-1
Watford v Crystal Palace	1-1, 1-5
Workington v Hartlepool	1-2
Wrexham v Crewe Alex	1-2
York C v Huddersfield T	0-2

Second Round

Arsenal v Leicester C	1-1, 1-2
Aston Villa v Everton	1-1, 3-0
Bolton W v Norwich C	0-0, 1-3
AFC Bournemouth v Hartlepool	1-1, 2-2, 1-1, 0-1
Bradford C v Carlisle U	0-1
Bury v Doncaster R	2-0
Chelsea v Newport Co	4-2
Chester v Blackpool	3-1
Crystal Palace v Bristol C	1-4
Coventry C v Ipswich T	1-2
Crewe Alex v Birmingham C	2-1
Exeter C v Hereford U	0-1
Huddersfield T v Leeds U	1-1, 1-1, 1-2
Hull C v Burnley	1-2
Liverpool v Brentford	2-1
Luton T v Bristol R	1-0
Manchester C v Scunthorpe U	6-0
Manchester U v Charlton Ath	5-1
Northampton T v Blackburn R	2-2, 0-1
Nottingham F v Newcastle U	1-1, 0-3
Portsmouth v Derby Co	1-5
Preston NE v Sunderland	2-0
QPR v Orient	1-1, 3-0
Reading v Rotherham U	4-2
Sheffield U v Chesterfield	3-1
Southampton v Notts Co	1-0
Southend U v Colchester U	0-2
Stoke C v Halifax T	3-0
Tottenham H v Middlesbrough	0-4
Tranmere R v West Ham U	0-0, 0-6
WBA v Millwall	1-0
Wolverhampton W v Fulham	1-3

Third Round

Bristol C v Liverpool	0-0, 0-4
Bury v Leeds U	1-2
Chelsea v Stoke C	2-2, 1-1, 2-6
Chester v Preston NE	1-0
Colchester U v Carlisle U	2-0
Crewe Alex v Aston Villa	2-2, 0-1
Fulham v West Ham U	2-1
Hartlepool v Blackburn R	1-1, 2-1
Ipswich T v Hereford U	4-1
Manchester U v Manchester C	1-0
Middlesbrough v Leicester C	1-0
QPR v Newcastle U	0-4
Reading v Burnley	1-2
Sheffield U v Luton T	2-0
Southampton v Derby Co	5-0
WBA v Norwich C	1-1, 0-2

Fourth Round

Chester v Leeds U	3-0
Colchester U v Southampton	0-0, 1-0
Hartlepool v Aston Villa	1-1, 1-6
Ipswich T v Stoke C	2-1
Liverpool v Middlesbrough	0-1
Manchester U v Burnley	3-2
Newcastle U v Fulham	3-0
Sheffield U v Norwich C	2-2, 1-2

Fifth Round

Colchester U v Aston Villa	1-2
Middlesbrough v Manchester U	0-0, 0-3
Norwich C v Ipswich T	1-1, 2-1
Newcastle U v Chester	0-0, 0-1

Semi-Final

Chester v Aston Villa	2-2, 2-3
Aston Villa won 5-4 on aggregate	
Manchester U v Norwich C	2-2, 0-1
Norwich C won 3-2 on aggregate	

Final

Aston Villa 1, Norwich C 0

(Wembley, 100,000, receipts £196,000, 1 March, 1975)

Aston Villa: Cumbes; Robson, Aitken, Ross, Nicholl, McDonald, Graydon, Little, Leonard, Hamilton, Carrodus.

Norwich C: Keelan; Machin, Sullivan, Morris, Forbes, Stringer, Miller, MacDougall, Boyer, Suggett, Powell.

Scorer: Aston Villa – Graydon.

FOOTBALL LEAGUE CUP 1975–76

Home team shown first; where a tie was replayed, the team given second was the home team in the replay.

First Round

Aldershot v Portsmouth	1-1, 1-2
Bradford C v York C	2-0, 0-3
Brentford v Brighton & HA	2-1, 1-1
Bury v Rochdale	2-0, 2-0
Cambridge U v Charlton Ath	1-1, 0-3
Cardiff C v Bristol R	1-2, 1-1
Crystal Palace v Colchester U	3-0, 1-3
Crewe Alex v Tranmere R	2-1, 1-2
Darlington v Sheffield W	0-2, 2-0, 5-3
Doncaster R v Grimsby T	3-1, 0-0
Halifax T v Hartlepool	4-1, 1-2
Huddersfield T v Barnsley	2-1, 1-1
Lincoln C v Chesterfield	4-2, 2-3
Mansfield T v Scunthorpe U	4-0, 2-0
Newport Co v Exeter C	1-1, 0-2
Oldham Ath v Workington	3-0, 3-1
Plymouth Arg v AFC Bournemouth	2-0, 2-1
Port Vale v Hereford U	4-2, 0-2, 0-1
Preston NE v Blackburn R	2-0, 0-0
Reading v Gillingham	0-1, 1-1
Rotherham U v Nottingham F	1-2, 1-5
Southend U v Peterborough U	2-0, 0-3
Southport v Stockport Co	3-1, 2-1
Swansea C v Torquay U	1-2, 3-5
Swindon T v Millwall	2-1, 1-0
Walsall v Shrewsbury T	0-0, 1-2
Watford v Northampton T	2-0, 1-1
Wrexham v Chester	3-0, 0-0

Second Round

Aston Villa v Oldham Ath	2-0
Birmingham C v Orient	4-0
Bolton W v Coventry C	1-3
Bury v Middlesbrough	1-2
Carlisle U v Gillingham	2-0
Charlton Ath v Oxford U	3-3, 1-1, 3-2
Crewe Alex v Chelsea	1-0
Darlington v Luton T	2-1
Derby Co v Huddersfield T	2-1
Doncaster R v Crystal Palace	2-1
Everton v Arsenal	2-2, 1-0
Halifax T v Sheffield U	2-4
Hereford U v Burnley	1-4
Hull C v Preston NE	4-2
Leeds U v Ipswich T	3-2
Lincoln C v Stoke C	2-1
Manchester U v Brentford	2-1
Norwich C v Manchester C	1-1, 2-2, 1-6
Notts Co v Sunderland	2-1
Nottingham F v Plymouth Arg	1-0
Peterborough U v Blackpool	2-0
Portsmouth v Leicester C	1-1, 0-1
Shrewsbury T v QPR	1-4
Southampton v Bristol R	0-1
Southport v Newcastle U	0-6
Swindon T v Wolverhampton W	2-2, 2-3
Torquay U v Exeter C	1-1, 2-1
Watford v Tottenham H	0-1
WBA v Fulham	1-1, 0-1
West Ham U v Bristol C	0-0, 3-1
Wrexham v Mansfield T	1-2
York C v Liverpool	0-1

Third Round

Aston Villa v Manchester U	1-2
Birmingham C v Wolverhampton W	0-2
Bristol R v Newcastle U	1-1, 0-2
Crewe Alex v Tottenham H	0-2
Everton v Carlisle U	2-0
Fulham v Peterborough U	0-1
Hull C v Sheffield U	2-0
Leeds U v Notts Co	0-1
Leicester C v Lincoln C	2-1
Liverpool v Burnley	1-1, 0-1
Manchester C v Nottingham F	2-1
Mansfield T v Coventry C	2-0
Middlesbrough v Derby Co	1-0
QPR v Charlton Ath	1-1, 3-0
Torquay U v Doncaster R	1-1, 0-3
West Ham U v Darlington	3-0

Fourth Round

Burnley v Leicester C	2-0
Doncaster R v Hull C	2-1
Everton v Notts Co	2-2, 0-2
Manchester C v Manchester U	4-0
Mansfield T v Wolverhampton W	1-0
Middlesbrough v Peterborough U	3-0
QPR v Newcastle U	1-3
Tottenham H v West Ham U	0-0, 2-0

Fifth Round

Burnley v Middlesbrough	0-2
Manchester C v Mansfield T	4-2
Newcastle U v Notts Co	1-0
Tottenham H v Doncaster R	7-2

Semi-Final

Middlesbrough v Manchester C	1-0, 0-4
Manchester C won 4-1 on aggregate	
Tottenham H v Newcastle U	1-0, 1-3
Newcastle U won 3-2 on aggregate	

Final

Manchester C 2, Newcastle U 1

(Wembley, 100,000, receipts £299,601.16, 28 February, 1976)

Manchester C: Corrigan; Keegan, Donachie, Doyle, Watson, Oakes, Barnes, Booth, Royle, Hartford, Tueart.

Newcastle U: Mahoney; Nattrass, Kennedy, Barrowclough, Keeley, Howard, Burns, Cassidy, Macdonald, Gowling, Craig.

Scorers: Manchester C – Barnes, Tueart; Newcastle U – Gowling.

FOOTBALL LEAGUE CUP 1976–77

Home team shown first; where a tie was replayed, the team given second was the home team in the replay.

First Round

Aldershot v Gillingham	1-1, 0-2
AFC Bournemouth v Torquay U	0-0, 0-1
Bradford C v Oldham Ath	1-1, 3-1
Bury v Preston NE	2-1, 1-1
Cardiff C v Bristol R	2-1, 4-4
Chester v Hereford U	2-0, 3-4
Chesterfield v Rotherham U	3-1, 0-3
Crewe Alex v Tranmere R	2-1, 1-3
Crystal Palace v Portsmouth	2-2, 1-0
Doncaster R v Lincoln C	1-1, 1-1, 2-2
Doncaster R won on penalties	
Grimsby T v Sheffield W	0-3, 0-0
Halifax T v Darlington	0-0, 1-1, 1-2
Huddersfield T v Hartlepool	2-0, 2-1
Mansfield T v Scunthorpe U	2-0, 0-2, 1-2
Millwall v Colchester U	2-1, 1-2, 4-4
Millwall won on penalties	
Oxford U v Cambridge U	1-0, 0-2
Plymouth Arg v Exeter C	0-1, 0-1
Port Vale v Wrexham	1-1, 0-1
Reading v Peterborough U	2-3, 1-0, 1-3
Rochdale v Blackburn R	0-1, 1-4
Shrewsbury T v Walsall	0-1, 0-1
Southend U v Brighton & HA	1-1, 1-2
Southport v Carlisle U	1-2, 1-0, 2-3
Swansea C v Newport Co	4-1, 0-1
Swindon T v Northampton T	3-2, 0-2
Watford v Brentford	1-1, 2-0
Workington v Stockport Co	0-0, 0-0, 0-2
York C v Barnsley	0-0, 0-0, 1-2

Second Round

Arsenal v Carlisle U	3-2
Aston Villa v Manchester C	3-0
Blackburn R v Stockport Co	1-3
Blackpool v Birmingham C	2-1
Bradford C v Bolton W	1-2
Bristol C v Coventry C	0-1
Bury v Darlington	2-1
Cardiff C v QPR	1-3
Chelsea v Sheffield U	3-1
Chester v Swansea C	2-3
Crystal Palace v Watford	1-3
Doncaster R v Derby Co	1-2
Everton v Cambridge U	3-0
Exeter C v Norwich C	1-3
Fulham v Peterborough U	1-1, 2-1
Gillingham v Newcastle U	1-2
Ipswich T v Brighton & HA	0-0, 1-2
Liverpool v WBA	1-1, 0-1
Manchester U v Tranmere R	5-0
Middlesbrough v Tottenham H	1-2
Northampton T v Huddersfield T	0-1
Orient v Hull C	1-0
Rotherham U v Millwall	1-2
Scunthorpe U v Notts Co	0-2
Southampton v Charlton Ath	1-1, 1-2
Stoke C v Leeds U	2-1
Sunderland v Luton T	3-1
Torquay U v Burnley	1-0
Walsall v Nottingham F	2-4
West Ham U v Barnsley	3-0
Wolverhampton W v Sheffield W	1-2
Wrexham v Leicester C	1-0

Third Round

Aston Villa v Norwich C	2-1
Blackpool v Arsenal	1-1, 0-0, 0-2
Charlton Ath v West Ham U	0-1
Chelsea v Huddersfield T	2-0
Derby Co v Notts Co	1-1, 2-1
Fulham v Bolton W	2-2, 2-2, 1-2
Manchester U v Sunderland	2-2, 2-2, 1-0
Millwall v Orient	0-0, 0-0, 3-0
Newcastle U v Stoke C	3-0
Nottingham F v Coventry C	0-3
QPR v Bury	2-1
Sheffield W v Watford	3-1
Stockport Co v Everton	0-1
Tottenham H v Wrexham	2-3
Torquay U v Swansea C	1-2
WBA v Brighton & HA	0-2

Fourth Round

Arsenal v Chelsea	2-1
Aston Villa v Wrexham	5-1
Brighton & HA v Derby Co	1-1, 1-2
Everton v Coventry C	3-0
Manchester U v Newcastle U	7-2
Millwall v Sheffield W	3-0
Swansea C v Bolton W	1-1, 1-5
West Ham U v QPR	0-2

Fifth Round

Aston Villa v Millwall	2-0
Derby Co v Bolton W	1-2
Manchester U v Everton	0-3
QPR v Arsenal	2-1

Semi-Finals

Everton v Bolton W	1-1, 1-0
Everton won 2-1 on aggregate	
QPR v Aston Villa	0-0, 2-2, 0-3
Aston Villa won 5-2 on aggregate	

Final

Aston Villa 0, Everton 0

(Wembley, 100,000, receipts £301,000, 12 March, 1977)

Aston Villa: Burridge; Gidman, Robson, Phillips, Nicholl, Mortimer, Deehan, Little, Gray, Cropley, Carrodus.

Everton: Lawson; Jones, Darracott, Lyons, McNaught, King, Hamilton, Dobson, Latchford, McKenzie, Goodlass.

Final, Replay

Aston Villa 1, Everton 1 (aet)

(Hillsborough, 55,000, 16 March, 1977)

Aston Villa: Burridge; Gidman, Robson, Phillips, Nicholl, Mortimer, Deehan, Little, Gray, Cowans, Carrodus.

Everton: Lawson; Bernard, Darracott, Lyons, McNaught, King, Hamilton (Pearson), Kenyon, Latchford, McKenzie, Goodlass.

Scorers: Aston Villa – Kenyon og; Everton – Latchford

Final, Second Replay

Everton 2, Aston Villa 3 (aet)

(Old Trafford, 54,749, 13 April, 1977)

Aston Villa: Burridge; Gidman (Smith), Robson, Phillips, Nicholl, Mortimer, Graydon, Little, Deehan, Cropley, Cowans.

Everton: Lawson; Robinson, Darracott, Lyons, McNaught, King, Hamilton, Dobson, Latchford, Pearson (Seargeant), Goodlass.

Scorers: Everton – Latchford, Lyons; Aston Villa – Little 2, Nicholl.

FOOTBALL LEAGUE CUP 1977–78

Home team shown first; where a tie was replayed, the team given second was the home team in the replay.

First Round

Aldershot v Colchester U	1-1, 1-4
Brentford v Crystal Palace	2-1, 1-5
Bristol R v Walsall	1-2, 0-1
Burnley v Chester	2-0, 0-1
Bury v Crewe Alex	3-0, 1-1
Cambridge U v Brighton & HA	0-0, 0-0, 0-3
Chesterfield v Barnsley	4-1, 0-3, 2-0
Darlington v Scunthorpe U	0-0, 1-3
Exeter C v Plymouth Arg	2-2, 0-0, 1-0
Gillingham v Wimbledon	1-1, 1-3
Grimsby T v Hartlepool U	3-0, 2-1
Hereford U v AFC Bournemouth	2-0, 2-4, 1-2
Huddersfield T v Carlisle U	1-1, 2-2, 2-1
Mansfield T v Lincoln C	0-1, 0-0
Orient v Fulham	2-0, 1-2
Oxford U v Shrewsbury T	3-0, 2-2
Peterborough U v Bradford C	4-1, 1-1
Portsmouth v Newport Co	3-1, 2-3
Port Vale v Preston NE	2-1, 1-2, 1-2
Rochdale v Halifax T	1-1, 2-1
Rotherham U v York C	3-0, 0-3, 1-1
Rotherham U won on penalties	
Sheffield W v Doncaster R	5-2, 3-0
Southend U v Northampton T	2-3, 1-2
Swansea C v Swindon T	1-3, 1-2
Torquay U v Cardiff C	1-0, 2-3, 1-2
Tranmere R v Southport	0-1, 2-2
Watford v Reading	2-1, 0-1, 5-0
Wrexham v Stockport Co	1-0, 1-1

Second Round

Arsenal v Manchester U	3-2
Birmingham C v Notts Co	0-2
Blackburn R v Colchester U	1-1, 0-4
Blackpool v Sheffield W	2-2, 1-3
Bolton W v Lincoln C	1-0
Brighton & HA v Oldham Ath	0-0, 2-2, 1-2
Bristol C v Stoke C	1-0
Burnley v Norwich C	3-1
Charlton Ath v Wrexham	1-2
Chesterfield v Manchester C	0-1
Crystal Palace v Southampton	0-0, 1-2
Derby Co v Orient	3-1
Exeter C v Aston Villa	1-3
Grimsby T v Watford	1-2
Huddersfield T v Coventry C	0-2
Ipswich T v Northampton T	5-0
Liverpool v Chelsea	2-0
Newcastle U v Millwall	0-2
Nottingham F v West Ham U	5-0
Oxford U v Bury	1-1, 0-1
Peterborough U v Scunthorpe U	1-1, 1-0
Portsmouth v Leicester C	2-0
QPR v AFC Bournemouth	2-0
Rochdale v Leeds U	0-3
Sheffield U v Everton	0-3
Southport v Hull C	2-2, 0-1
Sunderland v Middlesbrough	2-2, 0-1
Swindon T v Cardiff C	5-1
Tottenham H v Wimbledon	4-0
Walsall v Preston NE	0-0, 1-0
WBA v Rotherham U	4-0
Wolverhampton W v Luton T	1-3

Third Round

Arsenal v Southampton	2-0
Aston Villa v QPR	1-0
Bolton W v Peterborough U	3-1
Burnley v Ipswich T	1-2
Everton v Middlesbrough	2-2, 2-1
Hull C v Oldham Ath	2-0
Leeds U v Colchester U	4-0
Liverpool v Derby Co	2-0
Luton T v Manchester C	1-1, 0-0, 2-3
Millwall v Bury	1-1, 0-2
Nottingham F v Notts Co	4-0
Portsmouth v Swindon T	1-1, 3-4
Sheffield W v Walsall	2-1
Tottenham H v Coventry C	2-3
WBA v Watford	1-0
Wrexham v Bristol C	1-0

Fourth Round

Arsenal v Hull C	5-1
Bolton W v Leeds U	1-3
Bury v WBA	1-0
Ipswich T v Manchester C	1-2
Liverpool v Coventry C	2-2, 2-0
Nottingham F v Aston Villa	4-2
Sheffield W v Everton	1-3
Wrexham v Swindon T	2-0

Fifth Round

Bury v Nottingham F	0-3
Leeds U v Everton	4-1
Manchester C v Arsenal	0-0, 0-1
Wrexham v Liverpool	1-3

Semi-Final

Leeds U v Nottingham F	1-3, 2-4
Nottingham F won 7-3 on aggregate	
Liverpool v Arsenal	2-1, 0-0
Liverpool won 2-1 on aggregate	

Final

Nottingham F 0, Liverpool 0 (aet)

(Wembley, 100,000, 18 March, 1978)

Nottingham F: Woods; Anderson, Clark, McGovern (O'Hare), Lloyd, Burns, O'Neill, Bowyer, Withe, Woodcock, Robertson.

Liverpool: Clemence; Neal, Smith, Thompson, Kennedy (Fairclough), Hughes, Dalglish, Case, Heighway, McDermott, Callaghan.

Final, Replay

Nottingham F 1, Liverpool 0

(Old Trafford, 54,375, 22 March, 1978)

Nottingham F: Woods; Anderson, Clark, O'Hare, Lloyd, Burns, O'Neill, Bowyer, Withe, Woodcock, Robertson.

Liverpool: Clemence; Neal, Smith, Thompson, Kennedy, Hughes, Dalglish, Case (Fairclough), Heighway, McDermott, Callaghan.

Scorer: Nottingham F – Robertson (pen).

FOOTBALL LEAGUE CUP 1978–79

Home team shown first; where a tie was replayed, the team given second was the home team in the replay.

First Round

Aldershot v Millwall	0-1, 0-1
Barnsley v Chesterfield	1-2, 0-0
AFC Bournemouth v Exeter C	0-1, 1-1
Bradford C v Lincoln C	2-0, 1-1
Bristol R v Hereford U	2-1, 0-4
Cambridge U v Northampton T	2-2, 1-2
Cardiff C v Oxford U	1-2, 1-2
Carlisle U v Blackpool	2-2, 1-2
Colchester U v Charlton Ath	2-3, 0-0
Crewe Alex v Rochdale	1-0, 4-2
Doncaster R v Sheffield W	0-1, 1-0, 0-1
Grimsby T v York C	2-0, 3-0
Hull C v Peterborough U	0-1, 2-1, 0-1
Mansfield T v Darlington	0-1, 2-2
Newport Co v Swansea C	2-1, 0-5
Plymouth Arg v Torquay U	1-1, 2-1
Portsmouth v Swindon T	0-0, 2-4
Port Vale v Chester	0-3, 1-1
Preston NE v Huddersfield T	3-0, 2-2
Reading v Gillingham	3-1, 2-1
Rotherham U v Hartlepool U	5-0, 1-1
Scunthorpe U v Notts Co	0-1, 0-3
Southend U v Wimbledon	1-0, 1-4
Tranmere R v Wigan Ath	1-1, 1-2
Walsall v Halifax T	2-1, 2-0
Watford v Brentford	4-0, 3-1
Wrexham v Bury	2-0, 2-1
Shrewsbury T v Stockport Co	1-0, 1-3

Second Round

Birmingham C v Southampton	2-5
Bolton W v Chelsea	2-1
Brighton v Millwall	1-0
Bristol C v Crystal Palace	1-2
Burnley v Bradford C	1-1, 3-2
Everton v Wimbledon	8-0
Exeter C v Blackburn R	2-1
Fulham v Darlington	2-2, 0-1
Luton T v Wigan Ath	2-0
Manchester C v Grimsby T	2-0
Middlesbrough v Peterborough U	0-0, 0-1
Northampton T v Hereford U	0-0, 1-0
Oldham Ath v Nottingham F	0-0, 2-4
Orient v Chesterfield	1-2
Preston NE v QPR	1-3
Rotherham U v Arsenal	3-1
Sheffield U v Liverpool	1-0
Swansea C v Tottenham H	2-2, 3-1
Walsall v Charlton Ath	1-2
Watford v Newcastle U	2-1
WBA v Leeds U	0-0, 0-0, 0-1
Wrexham v Norwich C	1-3
Aston Villa v Sheffield W	1-0
Blackpool v Ipswich T	2-0
Chester v Coventry C	2-1
Crewe Alex v Notts Co	2-0
Leicester C v Derby Co	0-1
Oxford U v Plymouth Arg	1-1, 2-1
Reading v Wolverhampton W	1-0
Stockport Co v Manchester U	2-3
Sunderland v Stoke C	0-2
West Ham U v Swindon T	1-2

Third Round

Burnley v Brighton	1-3
Everton v Darlington	1-0
Luton T v Crewe Alex	2-1
Northampton T v Stoke C	1-3
Peterborough U v Swindon T	1-1, 2-0
QPR v Swansea C	2-0
Rotherham U v Reading	2-2, 0-1
Southampton v Derby Co	1-0
Blackpool v Manchester C	1-1, 0-3
Chester v Norwich C	0-2
Chesterfield v Charlton Ath	4-5
Exeter C v Bolton W	2-1
Manchester U v Watford	1-2
Oxford U v Nottingham F	0-5
Aston Villa v Crystal Palace	1-1, 0-0, 3-0
Sheffield U v Leeds U	1-4

Fourth Round

Brighton v Peterborough U	1-0
Charlton Ath v Stoke C	2-3
Everton v Nottingham F	2-3
QPR v Leeds U	0-2
Aston Villa v Luton T	0-2
Exeter C v Watford	0-2
Norwich C v Manchester C	1-3
Reading v Southampton	0-0, 0-2

Fifth Round

Southampton v Manchester C	2-1
Leeds U v Luton T	4-1
Nottingham F v Brighton	3-1
Stoke C v Watford	0-0, 1-3

Semi-Final

Nottingham F v Watford	3-1, 0-0
Nottingham F won 3-1 on aggregate	
Leeds U v Southampton	2-2, 0-1
Southampton won 3-2 on aggregate	

Final

Nottingham F 3, Southampton 2

(Wembley, 100,000, 17 March, 1979)

Nottingham F: Shilton; Barrett, Clark, McGovern, Lloyd, Needham, O'Neill, Gemmill, Birtles, Woodcock, Robertson.

Southampton: Gennoe; Golac, Peach, Williams, Nicholl, Waldron, Ball, Boyer, Hayes (Sealy), Holmes, Curran.

Scorers: Nottingham F – Birtles 2, Woodcock; Southampton – Peach, Holmes.

FOOTBALL LEAGUE CUP 1979–80

Home team shown first; where a tie was replayed, the team given second was the home team in the replay.

First Round

Blackpool v Rochdale	1-1, 1-0
Bradford C v Darlington	0-2, 3-0
Bury v Blackburn R	0-3, 2-3
Chester v Walsall	2-1, 0-0
Chesterfield v Hartlepool U	5-1, 1-2
Colchester U v Watford	2-0, 1-2
Gillingham v Luton T	3-0, 1-1
Grimsby T v Scunthorpe U	2-0, 0-0
Halifax T v Shrewsbury T	2-2, 0-1
Hereford U v Exeter C	1-3, 1-2
Huddersfield T v Crewe Alex	2-1, 3-1
Leicester C v Rotherham U	1-2, 0-3
Lincoln C v Barnsley	2-1, 1-2
Mansfield T v York C	1-0, 2-3
Newport Co v Plymouth Arg	1-0, 0-2
Northampton T v Millwall	2-1, 2-2
Oxford U v Reading	1-5, 1-2
Peterborough U v Charlton Ath	3-1, 1-1
Portsmouth v Swindon T	1-1, 0-2
Port Vale v Tranmere R	1-2, 0-1
Sheffield U v Doncaster R	1-1, 1-3
Sheffield W v Hull C	1-1, 2-1
Stockport Co v Wigan Ath	2-1, 0-0
Swansea C v AFC Bournemouth	4-1, 0-0
Torquay U v Bristol R	1-2, 3-1
Wimbledon v Aldershot	4-1, 2-1
Wrexham v Carlisle U	1-1, 2-1
Southend U v Brentford	2-1, 4-1

Second Round

Birmingham C v Preston NE	2-1, 1-0
Bolton W v Southend U	1-2, 0-0
Brighton & HA v Cambridge U	2-0, 2-1
Bristol C v Rotherham U	1-0, 1-1
Burnley v Wolverhampton W	1-1, 0-2
Chesterfield v Shrewsbury T	3-0, 0-0
Colchester U v Aston Villa	0-2, 2-0
Aston Villa won 9-8 on penalties.	
Doncaster R v Exeter C	3-1, 1-5
Everton v Cardiff C	2-0, 0-1
Gillingham v Norwich C	1-1, 2-4
Grimsby T v Huddersfield T	1-0, 4-1
Northampton T v Oldham Ath	3-0, 1-3
Notts Co v Torquay U	0-0, 1-0
QPR v Bradford C	2-1, 2-0
Plymouth Arg v Chelsea	2-2, 2-1
Sheffield W v Manchester C	1-1, 1-2
Southampton v Wrexham	5-0, 3-0
Swindon T v Chester	1-0, 1-1
West Ham U v Barnsley	3-1, 2-0
Blackburn R v Nottingham F	1-1, 1-6
Derby Co v Middlesbrough	0-1, 1-1
Ipswich T v Coventry C	0-1, 0-0
Leeds U v Arsenal	1-1, 0-7
Orient v Wimbledon	2-2, 2-2
Wimbledon won 5-4 on penalties.	
Peterborough U v Blackpool	0-0, 1-0
Reading v Mansfield T	4-3, 2-4
Stockport Co v Crystal Palace	1-1, 0-7
Stoke C v Swansea C	1-1, 3-1
Sunderland v Newcastle U	2-2, 2-2
Sunderland won 7-6 on penalties.	
Tottenham H v Manchester U	2-1, 1-3
Tranmere R v Liverpool	0-0, 0-4
WBA v Fulham	1-1, 1-0

Third Round

Arsenal v Southampton	2-1
Aston Villa v Everton	0-0, 1-4
Crystal Palace v Wolverhampton W	1-2
Grimsby T v Notts Co	3-1
Liverpool v Chesterfield	3-1
Mansfield T v QPR	0-3
Middlesbrough v Nottingham F	1-3
Northampton T v Brighton & HA	0-1
Plymouth Arg v Wimbledon	0-0, 0-1
West Ham U v Southend U	1-1, 0-0, 5-1
Birmingham C v Exeter C	1-2
Manchester C v Sunderland	1-1, 0-1
Norwich C v Manchester U	4-1
Peterborough U v Bristol C	1-1, 0-4
Stoke C v Swindon T	2-2, 1-2
WBA v Coventry C	2-1

Fourth Round

Brighton & HA v Arsenal	0-0, 0-4
Bristol C v Nottingham F	1-1, 0-3
Grimsby T v Everton	2-1
Liverpool v Exeter C	2-0
QPR v Wolverhampton W	1-1, 0-1
Wimbledon v Swindon T	1-2
Sunderland v West Ham U	1-1, 1-2
WBA v Norwich C	0-0, 0-3

Fifth Round

Arsenal v Swindon T	1-1, 3-4
Grimsby T v Wolverhampton W	0-0, 1-1, 0-2
West Ham U v Nottingham F	0-0, 0-3
Norwich C v Liverpool	1-3

Semi-Final

Nottingham F v Liverpool	1-0, 1-1
Nottingham F won 2-1 on aggregate.	
Swindon T v Wolverhampton W	2-1, 1-3
Wolverhampton W won 4-3 on aggregate.	

Final

Nottingham F 0, Wolverhampton W 1

(Wembley, 100,000, 15 March, 1981)

Nottingham F: Shilton; Anderson, Gray, McGovern, Needham, Burns, O'Neill, Bowyer, Birtles, Francis, Robertson.
Wolverhampton W: Bradshaw; Palmer, Parkin, Daniel, Berry, Hughes, Carr, Hibbitt, Gray, Richards, Eves.
Scorer: Wolverhampton W – Gray.

THE FA CUP

THE FOOTBALL ASSOCIATION OFFICIALS

Patron: HER MAJESTY THE QUEEN

President: HRH THE DUKE OF KENT

Honorary Vice-Presidents

His Grace the Duke of Marlborough; The Rt Hon The Earl of Derby MC; Air Vice-Marshal D. P. Hall CBE, AFC; Lt-General Sir James Wilson KBE, MC; Admiral Sir Anthony Morton KCB; Right Hon Earl of Harewood LLD; Sir Stanley Rous CBE; Sir Cyril Hawker; Sir Walter Winterbottom CBE; Sir Denis Follows CBE; Rt Hon Lord Westwood FCIS, JP

Chairman of the Council

F. A. Millichip (West Bromwich Albion FC)

Vice-Chairman of the Council

A. D. McMullen MBE (Bedfordshire FA)

Life Vice-Presidents

I. Robinson (Liverpool County FA);
R. V. Stokes OBE (Hampshire FA);
E. D. Smith MBE, JP (Cumberland FA);
Sir Harold Thompson CBE, FRS (Oxford University);
S. W. Jacobs (Oxfordshire FA);
G. T. Dorrington (Lincs FA)

Vice-Presidents

A. D. McMullen MBE (Bedfordshire FA);
W. H. Webster CBE (Cambridge University);
E. Kangley (Sheffield and Hallamshire FA);
E. A. Brown (Suffolk County FA);
R. Wragg (Football League);
R. H. Speake

Secretary

E. Croker, 16 Lancaster Gate, London W2 3LW

FA CUP 1980–81

QUALIFYING ROUNDS

Preliminary Round

Peterlee Newtown v West Auckland Town	1-1
Carlisle City v Farsley Celtic	1-4
Netherfield v Washington	3-2
Bridlington Trinity v Eppleton CW	3-0
Whitby Town v Yorkshire Amateur	3-1
Easington CW v South Bank	0-2
Thackley v Wingate	1-1
Consett v Crook Town	0-2
New Brighton v Worsboro Bridge MW	1-3
Emley v Fleetwood Town	0-3
Prescot Cables v South Liverpool	2-1
Formby v Glossop	0-2
Porthmadog v Skelmersdale United	1-1
Caernarvon Town v Chorley	0-2
Rossendale United v Worksop Town	1-1
Denaby United v Frickley Athletic	1-3
Nantwich Town v Winterton Rangers	0-0
Buxton v Eastwood Town	1-2
Normanby PW v Sutton Town	0-0
Desborough Town v Friar Lane OB	2-1
March Town United v Stamford	2-1
Gainsborough Trinity v Heanor Town	3-1
Walsall Wood v Winsford United	0-3
Bilston v Congleton Town	3-2
Redditch United v Witton Albion	0-0
Gresley Rovers v Highgate United	1-1
Tamworth v Wolverton Town	3-0
Histon v Irthlingborough Diamonds	3-0
Racing Club Warwick v VS Rugby	1-2
Brierley Hill Alliance v Darlaston	0-2
Oxford City v Cheltenham Town	0-2
Cinderford Town v Forest Green Rovers	0-0
Brereton Social v Evesham United	1-1
St Neots Town v Thetford Town	3-1
Chatteris Town v Great Yarmouth Town	1-1
Potton United v Wisbech Town	0-1
Bury Town v Felixstowe Town	2-1
Tiptree United v Wootton Blue Cross	3-0
Edgware v Hoddesdon Town	4-3
Newmarket Town v Wellingborough Town	1-0
Hayes v Hemel Hempstead	2-0
Milton Keynes City v Southall	0-2
Dulwich Hamlet v Hampton	3-1
Staines Town v Willesden	0-1
Carshalton Athletic v Feltham	2-0
Walton & Hersham v Woodford Town	3-0
Chertsey Town v Dunstable	2-1
Rainham Town v Uxbridge	3-4
Epping Town v Haringey Borough	2-1
Worthing v Basingstoke Town	0-1
Egham Town v Molesey	3-1
Arundel v Kingstonian	0-2
Hornchurch v Walthamstow Avenue	2-3
Cheshunt v Clapton	0-1
Peacehaven & Telscombe v Tilbury (*at Tilbury FC*)	0-1
Cray Wanderers v Dorking Town	1-1
Haywards Heath v Whitstable Town	1-0
Crawley Town v Deal Town	2-1
Herne Bay v Tonbridge AFC	0-3
Chatham Town v Eastbourne United	2-1
Ringmer v Tunbridge Wells	3-1
Horsham v Lewes	1-6
Three Bridges v Wokingham Town	0-1
Bracknell Town v Poole Town	1-5
Newbury Town v Pagham	1-0
Chichester City v Devizes Town	1-1
Lye Town v Mangotsfield United (*at Mangotsfield United FC*)	2-0
Calne Town v Chippenham Town	0-1
Paulton Rovers v Weston-super-Mare	0-3
Bath City v Glastonbury	7-1
Shepton Mallet Town v Welton Rovers	2-1
Chard Town v Clevedon Town	1-1
Saltash United v Wadebridge Town	5-0
Newquay v Ottery St Mary	8-0

Preliminary Round – Replays

West Auckland Town v Peterlee Newtown	aet 3-4
Wingate v Thackley	0-1
Skelmersdale United v Porthmadog	3-1
Worksop Town v Rossendale United	3-1
Winterton Rangers v Nantwich Town	0-1
Sutton Town v Normanby PW	2-3
Witton Albion v Redditch United	5-1
Highgate United v Gresley Rovers	3-1
Forest Green Rovers v Cinderford Town	0-0
Evesham United v Brereton Social	aet 3-2
Great Yarmouth Town v Chatteris Town	3-2
Dorking Town v Cray Wanderers	0-2
Devizes Town v Chichester City	1-3
Clevedon Town v Chard Town	4-1

Preliminary Round – Second Replay

Cinderford Town v Forest Green Rovers (*at Gloucester City FC*)	1-2

First Round Qualifying

Guisborough Town v Gateshead	2-3
Annfield Plain v Billingham Synthonia	2-3
North Shields v Tow Law Town	0-0
Peterlee Newtown v Farsley Celtic	0-2
Ferryhill Athletic v Evenwood Town	2-2
Ashington v Bishop Auckland	0-3
Brandon United v Shildon	0-0
Netherfield v Bridlington Trinity	1-2
Wallsend Town v Spennymoor United (*at Spennymoor United FC*)	0-2
Barrow v Boldon CA	8-1
Horden CW v Willington	1-0
Whitby Town v South Bank	3-0
Penrith v Durham City	6-0
Blue Star v Bridlington Town	3-1
Goole Town v Whitley Bay	1-0
Thackley v Crook Town	1-0
Lytham v Leyland Motors	0-2
Accrington Stanley v Darwen	2-0
Southport v St Helens Town	1-3
Worsboro' Bridge MW v Fleetwood Town	0-4
Lancaster City v Hyde United	1-1
Clitheroe v Curzon Ashton	1-1
Burscough v Prestwich Heys	2-1
Prescot Cables v Glossop	2-0
Oswestry Town v Colwyn Bay	0-1
Bangor City v Bootle	0-2
Marine v Rhyl	3-0
Skelmersdale United v Chorley	0-1
North Ferriby United v Horwich RMI	1-0
Appleby Frodingham v Ashby Institute	5-0
Droylsden v Stalybridge Celtic	1-1
Worksop Town v Frickley Athletic	3-2
Mexboro' Town Athletic v Leek Town (*at Leek Town FC*)	1-2
Alfreton Town v Brigg Town	2-1
Northwich Victoria v New Mills	1-0
Nantwich Town v Eastwood Town	0-0
Long Eaton United v Grantham	0-0
Arnold v Barton Town	0-1
Boston United v Skegness Town	3-0
Normanby PW v Desborough Town	0-4
Ilkeston Town v Holbeach United	0-0
Corby Town v Ely City	1-0
Boston v Spalding United	6-1
March Town United v Gainsboro' Trinity	1-2
Stourbridge v Macclesfield Town	6-2
Armitage v Belper Town	1-2
Burton Albion v Willenhall Town	2-2
Winsford United v Bilston (*at Middlewich Athletic FC*)	4-2
Oldbury United v Matlock Town	4-0
Bedworth United v Gornal Athletic	2-0
Sutton Coldfield Town v Telford United	1-0

Witton Albion v Highgate United	3-1
Soham Town Rangers v King's Lynn	1-1
Coventry Sporting v Hinckley Athletic	2-3
Enderby Town v Tividale	3-1
Tamworth v Histon	3-0
Moreton Town v Dudley Town	0-1
Alvechurch v Banbury U	0-2
Moor Green v Rothwell Town	4-0
VS Rugby v Darlaston	3-1
Halesowen Town v Didcot Town	1-1
Evesham United v Buckingham Town	0-1
Kidderminster Harriers v Hednesford Town	3-0
Cheltenham Town v Forest Green Rovers	3-2
Lowestoft Town v Harwich & Parkeston	0-2
Bourne Town v Cambridge City	0-0
Parson Drove v Stowmarket	0-1
St Neots Town v Great Yarmouth Town	0-1
Haverhill Rovers v Gorleston	2-3
Bedford Town v Bishop's Stortford	3-2
Hitchin Town v Rushden Town	3-0
Wisbech Town v Bury Town	1-2
Sudbury Town v Letchworth Garden City	0-3
Chelmsford City v Clacton Town	0-0
Leytonstone & Ilford v Wembley	0-1
Tiptree United v Edgware	0-1
Kempston Rovers v Hertford Town	3-0
Berkhamsted Town v Finchley	1-2
Witney Town v Ruislip Manor	2-1
Newmarket Town v Hayes	1-1
Marlow v Harrow Borough	1-2
Billericay Town v Chalfont St Peter	1-1
Chesham United v St Albans City	0-1
Southall v Dulwich Hamlet	0-8
Leyton-Wingate v Harefield United	0-3
Addlestone & Weybridge Town v Boreham Wood	2-2
Maidenhead United v Thame United	1-0
Willesden v Carshalton Athletic	0-2
Metropolitan Police v Hounslow	2-3
Barton Rovers v Camberley Town	3-0
Slough Town v Ware	5-1
Walton & Hersham v Chertsey Town	1-0
Hillingdon Borough v Hendon	0-0
Aylesbury United v Burnham	2-0
Woking v Tring Town	2-1
Uxbridge v Epping Town	1-0
Waterlooville v Horsham YMCA	2-0
Kingstonian v Banstead Athletic	1-0
Tooting & Mitcham Utd v Windsor & Eton	0-3
Basingstoke Town v Egham Town	2-3
Grays Athletic v Erith & Belvedere	0-0
Aveley v Basildon United	2-0
Dartford v Saffron Walden Town	4-1
Walthamstow Avenue v Clapton	5-0
Faversham Town v Dover	0-2
Burgess Hill Town v Canterbury City	1-2
Welling United v Sheppey United	4-2
Tilbury v Cray Wanderers	4-1
Epsom & Ewell v Eastbourne Town	1-0
Ashford Town v Corinthian Casuals	4-1
Margate v Sittingbourne	1-1
Haywards Heath v Crawley Town	0-1
Folkestone v East Grinstead	6-2
Bexhill Town v Bromley (*at Hastings United FC*)	0-7
Maidstone United v Ramsgate	6-0
Tonbridge AFC v Chatham Town	1-1
Redhill v Littlehampton Town	0-2
Gosport Borough v Hastings United	0-0
Croydon v Southwick	1-0
Ringmer v Lewes	3-3
Sutton United v Steyning	3-1
Alton Town v Andover	0-3
Hungerford Town v Wick	5-1
Wokingham Town v Poole Town	0-1
Frome Town v Farnborough Town	1-1
Bognor Regis Town v Bridport	3-1
Fareham Town v Newport IOW	2-0
Newbury Town v Chichester City	2-0
Llanelli v Clandown	2-0
Barry Town v Bromsgrove Rovers	1-0
Worcester City v Malvern Town	1-1
Lye Town v Chippenham Town	1-1
Melksham Town v Ilminster Town	7-0
Almondsbury Greenway v Barnstaple Town	0-1
Bridgend Town v Ton Pentre	0-1
Weston-super-Mare v Bath City (*at Bath City FC*)	1-2
Gloucester City v Dorchester Town	1-0
Bideford v Bridgwater Town	1-0
Salisbury v Trowbridge Town	1-1
Shepton Mallet Town v Clevedon Town	0-4
St Blazey v Penzance	1-2
Falmouth Town v Liskeard Athletic	1-1
Tiverton Town v Taunton Town	0-5
Saltash United v Newquay	4-0

First Round Qualifying – Replays

Tow Law Town v North Shields	aet 4-2
Evenwood Town v Ferryhill Athletic	2-1
Shildon v Brandon United	aet 1-0
Hyde United v Lancaster City	3-1
Curzon Ashton v Clitheroe	2-2
Stalybridge Celtic v Droylsden	2-1
Eastwood Town v Nantwich Town	1-0
Grantham v Long Eaton United	2-2
Holbeach United v Ilkeston Town	1-0
Willenhall Town v Burton Albion	1-2
King's Lynn v Soham Town Rangers	2-1
Didcot Town v Halesowen Town	0-1
Cambridge City v Bourne Town	0-1
Clacton Town v Chelmsford City	1-2
Hayes v Newmarket Town	5-0
Chalfont St Peter v Billericay Town	0-3
Boreham Wood v Addlestone & Weybridge Town	0-2
Hendon v Hillingdon Borough	3-2
Erith & Belvedere v Grays Athletic	1-3
Sittingbourne v Margate	3-4
Chatham Town v Tonbridge AFC	1-0
Hastings United v Gosport Borough	aet 3-4
Lewes v Ringmer	6-2
Farnborough Town v Frome Town	1-0
Malvern Town v Worcester City	0-2
Chippenham Town v Lye Town	0-2
Trowbridge Town v Salisbury	2-1
Liskeard Athletic v Falmouth Town	2-3

First Round Qualifying – Second Replays

Clitheroe v Curzon Ashton (*at Burscough FC*)	0-1
Long Eaton United v Grantham (*at Grantham FC*)	0-3

Second Round Qualifying

Billingham Synthonia v Farsley Celtic	2-0
Gateshead v Tow Law Town	2-0
Bishop Auckland v Bridlington Trinity	1-0
Evenwood Town v Shildon	2-0
Barrow v Whitby Town	1-1
Spennymoor United v Horden CW	1-2
Blue Star v Thackley	2-0
Penrith v Goole Town	2-0
Accrington Stanley v Fleetwood Town	1-1
Leyland Motors v St Helens Town	0-4
Curzon Ashton v Prescot Cables	1-4
Hyde United v Burscough	1-2
Bootle v Chorley	0-1
Colwyn Bay v Marine	2-2
Appleby Frodingham v Worksop Town	0-2
North Ferriby Utd v Stalybridge Celtic	0-0
Alfreton Town v Eastwood Town	1-0
Leek Town v Northwich Victoria	1-1
Barton Town v Desborough Town	4-1
Grantham v Boston United	1-3
Corby Town v Gainsborough Trinity	2-0
Holbeach United v Boston	0-3
Belper Town v Winsford United	2-2
Stourbridge v Burton Albion	1-1
Bedworth United v Witton Albion	1-2
Oldbury United v Sutton Coldfield Town	0-3
Hinckley Athletic v Tamworth	2-1
King's Lynn v Enderby Town	2-0
Banbury United v VS Rugby	3-3
Dudley Town v Moor Green	0-0
Buckingham Town v Cheltenham Town	2-1
Halesowen Town v Kidderminster Harriers	1-4
Bourne Town v Great Yarmouth Town	0-2
Harwich & Parkeston v Stowmarket	2-1

Bedford Town v Bury Town 4-0
Gorleston v Hitchin Town 0-1
Chelmsford City v Edgware 3-1
Letchworth Garden City v Wembley 0-0
Finchley v Hayes 0-1
Kempston Rovers v Witney Town 2-1
Billericay Town v Dulwich Hamlet 1-2
Harrow Borough v St Albans City 3-4
Addlestone & Weybridge Town v Carshalton Athletic 1-0
Harefield United v Maidenhead United 0-0
Barton Rovers v Walton & Hersham 1-0
Hounslow v Slough Town 1-3
Aylesbury United v Uxbridge 6-0
Hendon v Woking 1-1
Kingstonian v Egham Town 2-1
Waterlooville v Windsor & Eton 0-0
Aveley v Walthamstow Avenue 2-0
Grays Athletic v Dartford 2-0
Canterbury City v Tilbury 2-1
Dover v Welling United 2-0
Ashford Town v Crawley Town 3-0
Epsom & Ewell v Margate 3-1
Bromley v Chatham Town 4-0
Folkestone v Maidstone United 0-2
Gosport Borough v Lewes 2-1
Littlehampton Town v Croydon 0-3
Andover v Poole Town 0-2
Sutton United v Hungerford Town 2-0
Bognor Regis Town v Newbury Town 1-2
Farnborough Town v Fareham Town 1-0
Barry Town v Lye Town 1-1
Llanelli v Worcester City 0-3
Barnstaple Town v Bath City 0-1
Melksham Town v Ton Pentre 0-3
Bideford v Clevedon Town 2-1
Gloucester City v Trowbridge Town 0-1
Falmouth Town v Saltash United 2-1
Penzance v Taunton Town 2-3

Second Round Qualifying – Replays

Whitby Town v Barrow 1-2
Fleetwood Town v Accrington Stanley 3-2
Marine v Colwyn Bay 4-0
Stalybridge Celtic v North Ferriby Utd 3-0
Northwich Victoria v Leek Town 1-0
Winsford United v Belper Town 5-0
Burton Albion v Stourbridge 2-1
VS Rugby v Banbury United 1-3
Moor Green v Dudley Town 2-1
Wembley v Letchworth Garden City 3-1
Maidenhead United v Harefield United 5-1
Woking v Hendon 1-4
Windsor & Eton v Waterlooville 4-1
Lye Town v Barry Town 1-2

Third Round Qualifying

Gateshead v Billingham Synthonia 3-0
Evenwood Town v Bishop Auckland 0-1
Horden CW v Barrow 0-0
Penrith v Blue Star 1-0
St Helens Town v Fleetwood Town 0-1
Burscough v Prescot Cables 4-0
Marine v Chorley 3-0
Stalybridge Celtic v Worksop Town 0-0
Northwich Victoria v Alfreton Town 3-2
Boston United v Barton Town 2-0
Boston v Corby Town 0-1
Burton Albion v Winsford United 2-2
Sutton Coldfield Town v Witton Albion 2-1
King's Lynn v Hinckley Athletic 5-1
Moor Green v Banbury United 0-2
Kidderminster Harriers v Buckingham Town 2-1
Harwich & Parkeston v Gt Yarmouth Town 1-0
Hitchin Town v Bedford Town 3-2
Wembley v Chelmsford City 3-1
Kempston Rovers v Hayes 0-2
St Albans City v Dulwich Hamlet 2-1
Maidenhead United v Addlestone & Weybridge Town 0-0
Slough Town v Barton Rovers 0-1
Hendon v Aylesbury United 1-1
Windsor & Eton v Kingstonian 1-1
Grays Athletic v Aveley 0-1
Dover v Canterbury City 2-2
Epsom & Ewell v Ashford Town 1-0
Maidstone United v Bromley 2-0
Croydon v Gosport Borough 0-1
Sutton United v Poole Town 4-1
Farnborough Town v Newbury Town 4-1
Worcester City v Barry Town 1-1
Ton Pentre v Bath City 1-3
Trowbridge Town v Bideford 2-3
Taunton Town v Falmouth Town 1-0

Third Round Qualifying – Replays

Barrow v Horden CW aet 2-3
Worksop Town v Stalybridge Celtic 1-2
Winsford United v Burton Albion 1-3
Addlestone & Weybridge Town v Maidenhead United 5-0
Aylesbury United v Hendon aet 1-0
Kingstonian v Windsor & Eton 2-3
Canterbury City v Dover 3-3
Barry Town v Worcester City 2-3

Third Round Qualifying – Second Replay

Canterbury City v Dover 0-2
(*at Canterbury City FC*)

Fourth Round Qualifying

Northwich Victoria v Runcorn 2-1
Marine v Gateshead 1-0
(*Match awarded to Gateshead; as Marine played an ineligible player*)
Workington v Bishop Auckland 4-1
Blyth Spartans v Horden CW 7-0
Fleetwood Town v Stalybridge Celtic 1-0
Burton Albion v Penrith 1-0
Burscough v Morecambe 2-0
King's Lynn v Stafford Rangers 1-3
Kettering Town v Banbury United 3-0
Corby Town v Boston United 0-1
Hitchin Town v Sutton Coldfield Town 0-1
Worcester City v Wycombe Wanderers 1-1
AP Leamington v Barton Rovers 0-1
Kidderminster Har. v Nuneaton Borough 1-0
Maidstone United v Barking 2-0
Aylesbury United v Barnet 1-1
Enfield v Epsom & Ewell 5-0
Harlow Town v Wealdstone 1-1
Harwich & Parkeston v St Albans City 2-2
Wembley v Dover 1-1
Gravesend & Northfleet v Aveley 4-0
Addlestone & Weybridge Town v Bideford 3-0
Hayes v Yeovil Town 1-1
Windsor & Eton v Gosport Borough 2-0
Minehead v Sutton United 2-0
Merthyr Tydfil v Farnborough Town 0-1
Weymouth v Taunton Town 0-0
Leatherhead v Bath City 1-0

Fourth Round Qualifying – Replays

Wycombe Wanderers v Worcester City 1-0
Barnet v Aylesbury United 0-0
Wealdstone v Harlow Town 0-1
St Albans City v Harwich & Parkeston 3-0
Dover v Wembley 2-3
Yeovil Town v Hayes 2-0
Taunton Town v Weymouth 0-3

Fourth Round Qualifying – Second Replay

Aylesbury United v Barnet 0-1
(*at Barnet FC*)

FA CUP 1980–81

FIRST ROUND

22 NOV

Addlestone and Weybridge (1) 2 *(Morris, Donaldson)*
Brentford (2) 2 *(Booker, Funnell* pen*)* 6540
Addlestone and Weybridge: Able; Steer, Braithwaite, Donaldson, Harvey, Cassidy, Grout, Graham, Morris, Bennett (Van Den Berg), Finniston.
Brentford: McKellar; Shrubb, Hill, McNichol, Kruse, Hurlock, Funnell, Harris, Booker, Walker, Crown.

Barnet (0) 2 *(Walker og, Hughes* pen*)*
Minehead (0) 2 *(Chick, Brown)* 1529
Barnet: Steel; Hardman, Foody, Millett, Robinson, Townsend, Brinkman, Roberts, Clayton, Hughes (French), Turner.
Minehead: Lee; Clausen, Impey, Darke, Walker, Boulton, Guscott (Bruce), Chick, Richardson, Brown, Hodgson.

Blyth Spartans (1) 2 *(Walker P., Mutrie)*
Burton (1) 1 *(Kent)* 3500
Blyth Spartans: Clarke; Grierson, Walker A., Varty, Mitchinson, Dixon, Walker P., Johnson, Hogan, Mutrie, Barker (Boylan).
Burton: Bradwell; Hindley (Moore), Kent, Fletcher, Swan, Chapman, Fern, Davison, Nixon, Blair, Harrison.

Boston (0) 0
Rotherham U (1) 4 *(Taylor, Moore 2, Carr)* 6004
Boston: Blackwell; Leigh, Peacock, Poplar, Annable, Adamson, Callery, Mallender, Brown, Kabia, Simpson.
Rotherham U: Mountford; Forrest, Breckin, Rhodes, Stancliffe, Mullen, Fern, Taylor, Moore, Carr, Henson.

Burnley (0) 1 *(Hamilton)*
Scarborough (0) 0 7789
Burnley: Stevenson; Laws, Holt, Scott, Overson, Dobson, Young, Potts (Wharton), Hamilton, Taylor, Cavener.
Scarborough: Springett; Marshall, Dennis, Magee, Dixey, Smith T., Harris, Donoghue, Smith I., Sellers, Lewis (Gauden).

Burscough (1) 1 *(Perry)*
Altrincham (2) 2 *(Johnson, Rogers)* 1207
Burscough: Hamilton, Blakeman (Griffiths), Waugh, Crisp, Stokes, Durnin, McFerran, Perry, Gamble, Jaycock, Gray.
Altrincham: Connaughton; Allen, Davison, Owens, Bailey, King, Heathcote (Whitbread), Barrow, Johnson, Rogers, Howard.

Chester (1) 1 *(Birch)*
Barnsley (1) 2 *(Cooper, Banks)* 7135
Chester: Millington; Jeffries, Raynor, Storton, Cottam, Ludlam, Sutcliffe (Howat), Phillips, Birch, Jones, Burns.
Barnsley: New; Joyce, Chambers, Cooper, Banks, McCarthy, Evans, Riley, Aylott, Lester, Downes.

Colchester U (1) 3 *(Lee, Allinson, Bremner)*
Portsmouth (0) 0 5387
Colchester U: Walker; Cook, Rowles, Leslie, Wignall, Packer, Hodge, Foley, Bremner, Lee, Allinson.
Portsmouth: Mellor; McLaughlin, Viney, Barnard, Aizlewood, Garner, Perrin, Tait, Showers, Bryant, Rogers.

Darlington (0) 0
Bury (1) 2 *(Jakub, Butler)* 2912
Darlington: Cuff; Kamara, Wilson, Smith, Skipper, Speedie, Hawker, McLean, Stalker, Hamilton, Walsh.
Bury; Southall; Phillips, Kennedy, Gore, Hilton, Howard, Mullen, Butler (Cruickshank), Johnson, Jakub, Farley.

Enfield (2) 3 *(Holmes, Wade, Jennings)*
Wembley (0) 0 852
Enfield: Jacobs; Barratt, Tone, Jennings, Oliver, Wade, Ashford, Bishop, Burton (Waite), Holmes, King.
Wembley: Sambridge; Joughis, Hatton, Murphy, Lakey, Schools, Ward, Bensted, Jackson, Cerasoli, Read (Odunoye).

Exeter C (2) 5 *(Kellow 2, Pearson, Roberts L., Hinshelwood og)*
Leatherhead (0) 0 4607
Exeter C: Bond; Rogers, Hatch, Forbes, Roberts L., Roberts P., Pearson, Rogers, Kellow, Delve (Pratt), Pullar.
Leatherhead: Caswell; Dixon, Brooks, Davies, Dyer, Malley, Cox (Page), Hinshelwood, Kelly, Crook, Doyle.

Fleetwood (0) 0
Blackpool (1) 4 *(Entwistle, Morris, Hockaday 2)* 10,897
Fleetwood: Newman; Whitehouse, Mudie, Thomas, Robinson S., Tuson, Brown, Owen, Atherton (Moran), Robinson G., Brownwood.
Blackpool: Hesford; Ashurst, Williams, Ball, Greenall, McEwan, Morgan, Doyle, Entwistle, Morris, Pashley (Hockaday).

Gillingham (2) 2 *(Price, Ford)*
Dagenham (1) 1 *(Kidd)* 4390
Gillingham: Hillyard; Sharpe, Ford, Overton, Weatherly, Crabbe, Nicholl, Duncan, Price, Bottiglieri, Walker.
Dagenham: Cotter; Wright, Scales, Moore, Ellen, Binks (Horan), Ballard, Kidd, Duck, Maycock, Jones.

Gravesend (0) 1 *(Stonebridge)*
St Albans (0) 2 *(Whitehead* 2 pens*)* 1659
Gravesend: Lewington; Idle, Jacks, Barrett, Galvin, Stonebridge, Dyer (Brown), Gregory, Bryant, Busby, Dudman.
St Albans: Plumley; Whitehead, Levy, Droy, Leonard, Sille, Dear, Cooper, Lawrence, Mayles, Butterfield.

Harlow (0) 0
Charlton Ath (2) 2 *(Robinson, Hales)* 6073
Harlow: Kitson; Wickendon, Griffiths, Gough, Clarke (Twigg), Carrington, Mann, Carretta, Hardy, Parker, MacKenzie.
Charlton Ath: Johns; Gritt, Madden, Shaw, Berry, Hazell, Powell, Smith, Hales, Walker, Robinson (Ostergaard).

Hull C (0) 2 *(Edwards 2)*
Halifax T (0) 1 *(Firth)* 4024
Hull C: Norman; Nisbet, Horswill, Roberts G., Roberts J., Roberts D., Marwood, Norrie, Edwards, McClaren, Deacy (Flounders).
Halifax T: Kilner; Nattress, Burton, Evans, Goodman, Hendrie (O'Neil), Ward, Graham, Firth, Bullock, Stafford.

Kettering (0) **1** *(Guy C.)*

Maidstone (0) **1** *(Ovard)* 2880

Kettering: Walters; Duggan, Easthall, Curtis (Guy), Suddards, Haverson, Phipps, Evans, Hofbauer, Martin, Flanagan.
Maidstone: Guy; Thompson, Kinnear, Hill, Hutton, Hamberger, Wiltshire, Ovard (Daubney), Woon, Aitken, Newson.

Kidderminster (1) **1** *(Wright)*

Millwall (1) **1** *(Williams og)* 2500

Kidderminster: Parry; Travis, Kirby, James, Nicholls, Chambers, Powell, Williams, Wright, Fleet (Mullen), Gavin.
Millwall: Jackson; Roberts, Robinson, Chatterton, Tagg, Sitton, Kinsella, Mehmet, McKenna, Dibble, Martin.

Lincoln C (0) **1** *(Turner)*

Gateshead (0) **0** 4543

Lincoln C: Felgate; Thompson T., Keeley, Thompson S. (Bell), Peake, Carr, Neale, Turner, Hobson, Cunningham, Shipley.
Gateshead: Dodds; Waterson, McLeod, Parnaby, Harrison, Cramer, Davies, Mitchell, Topping, Hulse, Gill.

Mansfield T (1) **3** *(Parkinson* 2 pens, *Caldwell)*

Rochdale (0) **1** *(Jones* pen*)* 3280

Mansfield T: Arnold; McJannet, Foster, Hamilton, McClelland, Bird, Allen, Mann, Caldwell, Parkinson, Thomson.
Rochdale: Crawford; Weir, Snookes, Esser, Higgins, Taylor, Jones, O'Loughlin, Hilditch, Wellings, Martinez.

Mossley (0) **1** *(Mobley)*

Crewe Alex (0) **0** 3822

Mossley: Fitton; Brown, Mobley, Gorman, Vaughan, Gibson, Summerbee (Szabo), Geelan, Skeete, O'Connor, Garmory.
Crewe Alex: Mulhearn; Lewis, Bowers, Hunter, Scott, Prophett, Davies (Chesters), Wilkinson, Conroy, Guy, Nelson.

Northampton T (1) **1** *(Phillips)*

Peterborough U (2) **4** *(Robson 2, Quow, Slack)* 5542

Northampton T: Poole; Saxby, Sandercock, Waldock, Gage, Sandy, Bowen, Denyer, Phillips, Williams, Heeley.
Peterborough U: Waugh; McVay, Phillips, Gynn, Slack, Slough, Quow, Kellock, Cooke, Hodgson, Robson.

Northwich Victoria (0) **1** *(Denham)*

Huddersfield T (1) **1** *(Stanton)* 6685

Northwich Victoria: Ryan; Eaton, Murphy, Mayman, Forshaw, Jones, Anderson, Hall, Williams, Wilson, Denham.
Huddersfield T: Rankin; Brown, Robinson, Stanton, Sutton, Hanvey, Lillis, Kennedy, Kindon, Robins, Cowling.

Oxford U (1) **1** *(Foley)*

Aldershot (0) **0** 4153

Oxford U: Burton; Kingston, Fogg, Jeffrey, Briggs, McIntosh, Brock, Cassells, Berry, Foley, Lythgoe.
Aldershot: Johnson; Edwards, Wooler, Briley, Bennett, Jopling, McGregor, Brodie, French, Crosby, Robinson.

Plymouth Arg (0) **2** *(Kemp, Murphy)*

Newport Co (0) **0** 6719

Plymouth Arg: Crudgington; McNeil, Harrison, Hodges, Foster, Phillipson-Masters, Cooper, Kemp, Sims, Bason, Murphy.
Newport Co: Kendall; Walden, Relish (Aldridge), Davies, Oakes, Tynan, Bailey, Lowndes, Gwyther, Elsey, Moore.

Port Vale (1) **4** *(Bennett* pen, *Chamberlain N. 2, Beech)*

Bradford C (1) **2** *(Wood, Chapman)* 4022

Port Vale: Harrison; Brissett, Elsby, Beech, Bowles, Sproson, Miller, Bennett, Chamberlain N., Chamberlain M., Bromage.
Bradford C: Smith; Thompson, Watson, Bingham, Jackson, Wood, Chapman, McNiven, Campbell, Dolan, Hutchins.

Reading (0) **1** *(Earles)*

Fulham (0) **2** *(Davies, Mahoney)* 7485

Reading: Death; Joslyn, Lewis, Webb, Hicks, Hetzke, Earles, Williams, Dixon (Kearney), Sanchez, Beavon.
Fulham: Peyton; Peters, Strong, Lock, Brown, Hatter, Davies, O'Driscoll, Gale, Mahoney, Goodlass.

Scunthorpe U (1) **3** *(Grimes, Green, Partridge* pen*)*

Hartlepool U (1) **1** *(Hampton)* 5165

Scunthorpe U: Neenan; Davy, Jarvis, Grimes, Boxall, Oates, Partridge, Cammack, Stewart, Green, O'Berg.
Hartlepool U: Burleigh; Sweeney, Brown, Hogan, Bird, Linacre, Kerr, Lawrence, Newton, Houchen, Hampton.

Southend U (0) **0**

Hereford U (1) **1** *(Jones)* 4922

Southend U: Cawston; Pennyfather, Yates, Hadley, Walker, Cusack, Gray, Pountney (Nelson), Spence, Mercer, Otulakowski.
Hereford U: Brand; Price, Cornes, Hicks, Thomas, Spiring, Hunt, Harvey, Bartley, White, Jones.

Stockport Co (0) **0**

Sheffield U (0) **0** 7179

Stockport Co: Lawson; Uzelac, Rutter, Fowler, Sword, Bradd, Williams, Sunley, Mountford, Thorpe, Coyle.
Sheffield U: Richardson; Ryan, Garner, Kenworthy, McPhail, Trusson, Jones, Neville, Charles, Hatton, Tibbott.

Sutton Coldfield (0) **0**

Doncaster R (0) **2** *(Dowd, Lally)* 2250

Sutton Coldfield: Burton; Evans, O'Connell, Parsons, Mason, Perkins, Kenning, Hickson, Casey, Yates (Wilson), Rhodes.
Doncaster R: Boyd; Russell, Dowd, Lister, Snodin, Lally, Little, Harle, Flanagan, Warboys, Pugh.

Swindon T (1) **3** *(Mayes, Kamara, Lewis)*

Weymouth (1) **2** *(Iannone, Dove* pen*)* 5477

Swindon T: Allan; Henry, Peach, Kamara, Lewis, Stroud, Miller, Carter, Rowland, Mayes, Williams.
Weymouth: Roberts; Lawrence, Byrne, Dyer, Merrick, Joseph, McCafferty, Courtney, Iannone, Dove, Johnson.

Torquay U (1) **2** *(Weston, Cooper)*

Barton R (0) **0** 2495

Torquay U: O'Keefe; Jones, Pethard, Sermanni (Coffill), Bourne, Rioch, Fell, Bowker, Cooper, Twitchin, Weston.
Barton R: Taylor, Smith, Baldry, Bevis (Brown), O'Dell, Lawson D., Dunn, Lawson R., Hodge, Singfield, Nicholls.

Tranmere R (0) **0**

York C (0) **0** 2687

Tranmere R: Johnson; Mathias, Flood, Parry, Williams, Evans, Peplow (Hamilton), Mungall, Beamish, Lumby, Griffiths.
York C: Blackburn; Hood, Kay, Walsh, Clements, Craig, Ford, Byrne, Eccles, McDonald, McGhie.

Walsall (1) 3 *(Waddington, Buckley, Penn)*

Stafford Rangers (0) 0 6898

Walsall: Green; Macken, Mower, Serella, Harrison, Hart, Waddington S., O'Kelly, Penn, Buckley, Paul.
Stafford Rangers: Dance; Wood, Dulson, Brindle, Nieman, Chapman, Brownbill, Bailey, Kersley, Fenoughty, Secker (Smith).

Wigan Ath (0) 2 *(Houghton 2)*

Chesterfield (2) 2 *(Wilson, Green)* 8896

Wigan Ath: Brown; Fretwell, Methven, Cribley, McAdam, Hutchinson, Wright, Corrigan, Urquhart, Houghton, Quinn M. (McMullen).
Chesterfield: Turner; Tartt, Green, Ridley, Pollard, Wilson, Bonnyman, Salmons, Walker, Moss, Birch.

Wimbledon (2) 7 *(Smith M. 2, Hubbick 3, Cunningham, Cork)*

Windsor & Eton (1) 2 *(McCulloch, Hill)* 3087

Wimbledon: Beasant; Jones, Armstrong, Galliers, Smith M., Cunningham, Ketteridge, Hodges, Leslie, Cork, Hubbick.
Windsor & Eton: Mitchell K.; Mitchell J., Edwards (Beckett), Richardson, Smith C., King, Hill, Harris, McCulloch, Cadogan, Yates.

Workington (0) 0

Carlisle U (0) 0 8000

Workington: Fisher; Kisby, Rosethorn, Breach, Roberts, Hill, Handley, Smith, Gill, Darling (Diamond), Armstrong.
Carlisle U: Harrison; Watson, Haigh, MacDonald, Coady, Parker, Coughlin, Beardsley, Bannon (McVitie), Hamilton, Staniforth.

Wycombe Wanderers (0) 0

Bournemouth (2) 3 *(Massey, Morgan 2)* 4768

Wycombe Wanderers: Lester; Birdseye, Borg, Davies, Hardwick, Dell (Toll), Long, Jacobs, Glynn, Price, Holifield.
Bournemouth: Allen; Cunningham, Moore, Impey, Heffernan, Webb, Ferns, Spackman, Morgan, Massey, Evanson.

Yeovil (0) 2 *(Morrall, Ritchie)*

Farnborough (0) 1 *(Parkin pen)* 2396

Yeovil: Parker; Ryan, Ritchie, Borthwick, Payne, Gold (William), Morrall, Bell, Green, Durbin, Brown.
Farnborough: Smith; Gosnell, Richardson, Turner, Blount, Hill, Brune, Parkin, Waughman (Gunn), Saunders, Painter.

FIRST ROUND REPLAYS

25 NOV

Brentford (0) 2 *(Crown, Funnell)*

Addlestone & Weybridge (0) 0 7680

Brentford: McKellar; Shrubb, Hill, Salman, Kruse, Hurlock, Funnell, Harris, Booker, Walker, Crown.
Addlestone & Weybridge: Abel; Steer (Van Den Berg), Braithwaite, Donaldson, Harvey, Cassidy, Grout, Graham, Morris, Bennett, Finnieston.

Chesterfield (2) 2 *(Salmons, Tartt)*

Wigan Ath (0) 0 8372

Chesterfield: Turner; Tartt, Pollard, Wilson, Green, Ridley, Birch, Walwyn, Bonnyman, Salmons, Walker.
Wigan Ath: Brown; Fretwell, McAdam, Hutchinson, Methven, Cribley, Houghton, Wright, Urquhart B. (McMullen), Urquhart G., Corrigan.

Huddersfield T (4) 6 *(Stanton 2, Robins 2, Hanvey, Laverick)*

Northwich Victoria (0) 0 9849

Huddersfield T: Rankin; Brown, Robinson, Stanton, Sutton, Hanvey, Laverick (Lillis), Kennedy, Kindon, Robins, Cowling.
Northwich Victoria: Ryan; Eaton, Murphy, Mayman, Forshaw, Jones, Anderson, Hall, Williams, Denham, Wilson.

Millwall (0) 1 *(Chatterton)*

Kidderminster (0) 0 4197

Millwall: Jackson; Roberts, Robinson, Chatterton, Tagg, Sitton, Kinsella, Mehmet, McKenna, Dibble, Martin.
Kidderminster: Parry; Travis, Kirby, James, Nicholls, Chambers, Powell, Williams (Mullen), Wright, Fleet, Gavin.

Minehead (0) 1 *(Druce)*

Barnet (0) 2 *(Roberts 2)* 770

Minehead: Lee; Clawson, Impey, Darke, Walker, Boulton, Bruce, Chick, Brown, Richardson, Hodgson (Hyett).
Barnet: Steel; Pearce, Foody, Millet, Robinson, Townsend, Brickman, Roberts, Clayton, Turner, French.

Sheffield U (0) 3 *aet (Sherlock og, Charles, Kenworthy)*

Stockport Co (0) 2 *(Coyle, Sunley)* 10,428

Sheffield U: Richardson; Ryan, Garner, Kenworthy, MacPhail, Sutton, Charles, Neville, Butlin, Hatton, Jones.
Stockport Co: Lawson; Rutter, Sherlock, Fowler, Sword, Uzelac, Williams, Sunley, Bradd, Thorpe, Coyle (Galvin).

York C (1) 1 *aet (Byrne)*

Tranmere R (0) 2 *(Craven, Beamish)* 3036

York C: Blackburn; Hood, Clements, Craig, Kay, Ford, McGhie, Walsh, McDonald, Eccles, Byrne (Millar).
Tranmere R: Johnson; Mathias, Flood, Parry, Williams, Evans, Hamilton, Mungall, Lumby, Beamish, Griffiths (Craven).

26 NOV

Maidstone (0) 0 *aet*

Kettering (0) 0 3156

Maidstone: Guy; Thompson, Hill, Hutton, Kinnear, Newson, Hamberger, Wiltshire, Aitken, Ovard, Woon.
Kettering: Walters, Duggan, Haverson, Suddards, Easthall, Martin, Pownall (Hofbauer), Flanagan, Phipps, Evans, Guy.

1 DEC

Carlisle U (2) 4 *(Brown 2, Beardsley 2)*

Workington (0) 1 *(Gill)* 5356

Carlisle U: Harrison; Collins, Haigh, MacDonald, Coady, Parker, Coughlin, Metcalfe, Brown, Beardsley, Staniforth.
Workington: Fisher; Kisby, Rosethorn, Reach, Roberts, Hill, Handley, Smith, Gill, Darling (Diamond), Armstrong.

FIRST ROUND SECOND REPLAY

1 DEC

Maidstone (0) 3 *(Woon 2, Newson pen)*

Kettering (0) 1 *(Middleton)* 3098

Maidstone: Guy; Thompson, Kinnear, Hill, Hutton, Hamberger, Daubney, Ovard, Woon, Aitken, Newson.
Kettering: Walters; Duggan, Easthall, Pownall (Middleton), Suddard, Haverson, Pitts, Hofbauer, Guy, Martin, Flanagan.

SECOND ROUND

13 DEC

Barnet (0) 0
Peterborough U (1) 1 *(Robson)* 4498

Barnet: Steel; Foody, Pearce, Millett, Robinson, Hardman (Barnes), Brinkman, Roberts, Sargent, Turner, Clayton.
Peterborough U: Waugh; McVay, Phillips, Gynn, Slack, Slough, Quow, Kellock, Cooke, Hodgson, Robson.

Burnley (0) 1 *(Potts)*
Port Vale (0) 1 *(Miller)* 7497

Burnley: Stevenson; Laws, Holt, Scott, Overson, Dobson, Young, Potts, Hamilton, Wardrobe, Cavener.
Port Vale: Cherry; Brissett, Bromage, Beech, Bowles, Sproson, Farrell, Bennett, Chamberlain N., Chamberlain M., Miller (Elsby).

Bury (1) 2 *(Hilton, Mullen)*
Lincoln C (0) 0 3375

Bury: Southall; Howard, Hilton, Whitehead, Kennedy, Mullen, Gore, Jakub, Butler, Johnson, Farley.
Lincoln C: Felgate; Thompson T., Carr, Peake, Keeley, Neale, Thompson S., Turner (Cunningham), Shipley, Hobson, Harford.

Carlisle U (1) 3 *(Brown, Beardsley 2)*
Walsall (0) 0 4778

Carlisle U: Harrison; Haigh, Coady, MacDonald, Campbell, Parker, Coughlin, Metcalfe, Brown, Beardsley, McVitie.
Walsall: Green; Macken, Mower, Serella, Baines, Hart, Waddington S., Penn, Caswell, Buckley, Paul (Rees).

Charlton Ath (0) 2 *(Walsh, Hales)*
Bournemouth (0) 1 *(Webb)* 7226

Charlton Ath: Johns; Gritt, Madden, Shaw, Berry, Tydeman, Powell, Walsh, Hales, Smith, Walker.
Bournemouth: Allen; Cunningham, Moore, Impey, Heffernan, Webb, Spackman, Ferns, Morgan, Massey, Elliott.

Colchester U (0) 1 *(Wignall)*
Yeovil (1) 1 *(Green)* 3394

Colchester U: Walker; Cook, Rowles, Leslie, Wignall, Packer, Hodge (Longhorn), Gough, Bremner, Lee, Allinson.
Yeovil: Parker; Ryan, Ritchie, Borthwick, Payne, Broom, Morrall, Bell, Green, Durbin, Brown.

Doncaster R (0) 2 *(Little, Mell)*
Blackpool (1) 1 *(Williams)* 6398

Doncaster R: Boyd; Russell, Mell, Snodin I., Lister, Dowd, Pugh, Nimmo, Warboys, Snodin G., Little.
Blackpool: Hesford; Ashurst, Williams, Ball, Thompson, McEwan, Harrison, Hockaday, Entwistle, Morris, Pashley.

Enfield (1) 2 *(Burton 2)*
Hereford U (0) 0 2263

Enfield: Jacobs; Barrett, Tone, Jennings, Waite, Howell, Oliver, Holmes, Burton, Ashford, King.
Hereford U: Brand; Price, Thomas (Dobson), Hicks, Cornes, Spiring, Hunt, Harvey, White, Jones, Bartley.

Fulham (1) 1 *(Greenaway)*
Brentford (0) 0 11,261

Fulham: Peyton; Strong, Lock, Gale, Banton, Hatter, Davies, O'Driscoll (Day), Peters, Greenaway, Goodlass.
Brentford: McKellar; Shrubb, Tucker, Salman, Kruse, Hurlock, Smith, Harris, Booker (Funnell), Walker, Crown.

Gillingham (0) 0
Maidstone (0) 0 9099

Gillingham: Hillyard; Sharpe, Ford, Overton, Weatherley, Crabbe, Nicholl, Bottiglieri (Hughes), Price, Westwood, White.
Maidstone: Guy; Thompson, Kinnear, Hill, Hutton, Hamberger, Daubney, Ovard, Woon (Shield), Aitken, Newson.

Hull C (1) 1 *(Edwards)*
Blyth Spartans (0) 1 *(Mutrie)* 6050

Hull C: Norman; Nisbet, McNeil, Croft, Roberts G., Richards, Marwood, McClaren, Edwards, Norrie, Deacy.
Blyth Spartans: Clarke; Grierson, Walker A., Boylan (Roff), Mitchinson, Dixon, Walker P., Johnson, Hogan, Mutrie, Barker.

Millwall (0) 0
Exeter C (0) 1 *(Rogers P.)* 3426

Millwall: Jackson; Roberts, Robinson, Chatterton, Kitchener, Blyth, Kinsella, Mehmet, McKenna, Dibble, Massey.
Exeter C: Bond; Rogers M., Hatch, Forbes, Roberts L., Roberts P., Pearson, Rogers P., Kellow, Delve, Pullar.

Mossley (0) 1 *(Skeete)*
Mansfield T (2) 3 *(Allen* pen, *Thomson, Caldwell)* 3680

Mossley: Fitton; Brown, Mobley, Gorman, Vaughan, Salter, Tinsley, Keelan (Gibson), Skeete, O'Connor, Garmory.
Mansfield T: Arnold; McJannett, Foster, Hamilton, McClelland, Bird, Allen, Mann, Caldwell, Phillips, Thomson.

Plymouth Arg (0) 3 *(Sims, Kemp, Murphy* pen*)*
Oxford U (0) 0 7264

Plymouth Arg: Crudgington; McNeill, Harrison, Hodges, Phillipson-Masters, Foster, Cooper, Kemp, Sims, Bason, Murphy.
Oxford U: Burton; Briggs, Smithers, Jeffrey, Wright, Shotton, Brock, Cassells, Cooke, Graydon, Lythgoe.

Rotherham U (0) 0
Barnsley (1) 1 *(Parker)* 15,426

Rotherham U: Mountford; Forrest, Breckin, Rhodes, Stancliffe, Mullen, Fern, Gooding, Moore, Seasman, Henson.
Barnsley: Pierce; Joyce, Chambers, Cooper, Banks, McCarthy, Evans, Parker, Aylott, Lester, Downes.

St Albans (0) 1 *(Mayles)*
Torquay U (1) 1 *(Fell)* 4500

St Albans: Plumley; Whitehead, Levy, Droy, Leonard, Silley, Cooper G., Dear, Mayles, O'Donoghue, Lawrence.
Torquay U: O'Keefe; Jones, Pethard, Coffill, Bourne, Rioch (Wilson), Fell, Bowker, Cooper S., Twitchin, Weston.

Scunthorpe U (0) 0
Altrincham (0) 0 3672

Scunthorpe U: Neenan; Davy, Jarvis, Grimes, Boxall, Oates, Partridge, Cammack, Stewart, Green, O'Berg (Pugh).
Altrincham: Connaughton; Allan, Davison, Bailey, Owens, King, Barrow, Whitbread, Johnson, Rogers, Howard.

Sheffield U (0) 1 *(Hatton)*

Chesterfield (0) 1 *(Birch pen)* 18,101

Sheffield U: Richardson; Ryan, Garner, Houston, McPhail, Trusson, Jones, Neville, Tibbott, Hatton, Butlin.
Chesterfield: Turner; Tartt, Pollard (Simpson), Wilson, Green, Ridley, Birch, Moss, Bonnyman, Salmons, Crawford.

Tranmere R (0) 0

Huddersfield T (1) 3 *(Stanton, Robins 2)* 6763

Tranmere R: Johnson; Edwards, Mathias, Williams, Parry, Hamilton, Craven, Mungall, Lumby, Kerr, Griffiths.
Huddersfield T: Rankin; Brown, Robinson, Sutton, Hanvey, Stanton, Lillis, Kennedy (Laverick), Kindon, Robins, Cowling.

Wimbledon (2) 2 *(Denny, Leslie)*

Swindon T (0) 0 3470

Wimbledon: Beasant; Brown, Jones, Galliers, Smith, Cunningham, Ketteridge (Hubbick), Hodges, Leslie, Cork, Denny.
Swindon T: Allan; Walsh (Hughes), Peach, Kamara, Lewis, Stroud, Miller, Carter, Greenwood, Mayes, Williams.

SECOND ROUND REPLAYS

15 DEC

Altrincham (1) 1 *(Davison pen)*

Scunthorpe U (0) 0 5176

Altrincham: Connaughton; Allan, Davison, Bailey, Owens, King, Barrow, Whitbread (Heathcote), Johnson, Rogers, Howard.
Scunthorpe U: Neenan; Davy, Jarvis, Grimes, Boxall, Oates, Pugh, Cammack, Stewart (Ashworth), Green, Lambert.

16 DEC

Blyth Spartans (2) 2 *aet (Mutrie, Young)*

Hull C (1) 2 *(Norrie, Edwards)* 6000

Blyth Spartans: Clarke; Grierson, Walker A., Young, Mitchinson, Dixon, Walker P., Johnson, Hogan (Ross), Mutrie, Barker.
Hull C: Norman; Nisbet, McNeil, Croft, Roberts, Richards, Marwood, McClaren, Edwards, Norrie, Deacy.

Port Vale (2) 2 *(Farrell, Chamberlain M.)*

Burnley (0) 0 7684

Port Vale: Cherry; Brissett, Miller (Elsby), Beech, Bowles, Sproson, Farrell, Bennett, Chamberlain M., Bromage, Chamberlain N.
Burnley: Stevenson; Laws, Holt, Scott, Overson, Dobson, Cassidy, Potts, Hamilton, Taylor (Young), Cavener.

Chesterfield (0) 1 *(Simpson)*

Sheffield U (0) 0 14,706

Chesterfield: Turner; Tartt, Pollard, Wilson (Simpson), Green, Ridley, Birch, Moss, Bonnyman, Salmons, Crawford.
Sheffield U: Conroy; Ryan, Garner, Houston, McPhail, Trusson, Jones (Charles), Neville, Tibbott, Hatton, Butlin.

Maidstone (0) 0 *aet*

Gillingham (0) 0 7465

Maidstone: Guy; Thompson, Kinnear, Hill, Hutton, Hamberger, Daubney, Ovard, Woon, Wiltshire (Shield), Newson.
Gillingham: Hillyard; Sharpe, Ford, Overton, Weatherly, Crabbe, Nicholl, Hughes, Price, Westwood, White.

17 DEC

Torquay U (3) 4 *(Cooper, Fell 3* [2 pens])

St Albans (0) 1 *(Whitehead pen)* 2638

Torquay U: O'Keefe; Jones, Pethard, Coffill, Wilson, Hayes, Fell, Bowker, Cooper, Twitchin, Weston.
St Albans: Plumley; Whitehead, Levy, Droy, Leonard, Sille, Cooper, Dear (Wood), Mayles, O'Donoghue, Lawrence.

Yeovil (0) 0

Colchester U (0) 2 *(Lee, Bremner)* 5803

Yeovil: Parker; Ryan, Ritchie, Borthwick, Payne, Broom, Morall, Bell (Williams), Green, Durbin, Brown.
Colchester U: Walker; Cook, Bowles, Leslie, Wignall, Parker, Longhorn, Foley, Bremner, Lee, Allinson.

SECOND ROUND SECOND REPLAYS

22 DEC

Gillingham (0) 0

Maidstone (0) 2 *(Newson, Ovard)* 7941

Gillingham: Hillyard; Sharpe, Ford, Bruce, Overton, Crabbe, Nicholl, Hughes, Price, Westwood, White (Lloyd).
Maidstone: Guy; Thompson, Kinnear, Hill, Hutton, Hamberger, Daubney, Ovard, Woon, Wiltshire, Newson.

Hull C (0) 2 *aet (Norrie, Croft)*

Blyth Spartans (0) 1 *(Mutrie pen)* 5914

Hull C: Norman; Booth, McNeil, Croft, Roberts G., Roberts J., Marwood (Moss), McClaren, Edwards, Norrie, Deacy.
Blyth Spartans: Clarke; Grierson, Walker A., Young, Mitchinson, Dixon, Walker P. (Boylan), Johnson, Hogan, Mutrie, Barker.

THIRD ROUND

3 JAN

Barnsley (1) 2 *(Parker 2)*

Torquay U (1) 1 *(Lawrence)* 14,431

Barnsley: Pierce; Joyce, Chambers, Glavin, Banks, McCarthy, Evans, Parker, Aylott, Lester, Downes.
Torquay U: O'Keefe; Jones, Pethard, Coffill (Sermanni), Wilson, Rioch, Fell, Lawrence, Cooper, Twitchin, Weston.

Birmingham C (1) 1 *(Bertschin)*

Sunderland (0) 1 *(Chisholm)* 23,098

Birmingham C: Wealands; Langan, Lees, Curbishley, Gallagher, Todd, Ainscow, Bertschin, Worthington, Gemmill, Dillon.
Sunderland: Turner; Whitworth, Bolton, Hindmarch, Elliott, Rowell, Arnott, Cooke (Brown), Hawley, Chisholm, Cummins.

Bury (0) 1 *(Hilton)*

Fulham (0) 1 *(Mahoney)* 5360

Bury: Southall; Howard, Hilton, Whitehead, Kennedy, Mullen, Gore, Jakub, Butler, Johnson, Farley.
Fulham: Peyton; Strong, Hatter, Banton, Lock, O'Driscoll, Greenaway, Gale, Goodlass, Davies, Mahoney.

Colchester U (0) 0

Watford (1) 1 *(Poskett)* 7769

Colchester U: Walker; Cook, Longhorn, Leslie, Wignall, Packer, Hodge (Gough), Foley, Bremner, Lee, Allinson.
Watford: Sherwood; Rice, Harrison, Taylor, Sims, Jackett, Callaghan, Armstrong, Blissett, Train, Poskett.

Derby Co (0) 0

Bristol C (0) 0 19,071

Derby Co: Jones; Emery, Richards, Clark (Reid), McFarland, Ramage, Powell S., Hector, Biley, Swindlehurst, Emson.
Bristol C: Shaw; Sweeney, Hay, Aitken, Rodgers, Marshall, Tainton, Fitzpatrick, Mabbutt, Garland, Pritchard.

Everton (0) 2 *(Sansom og, Lyons)*

Arsenal (0) 0 34,240

Everton: McDonagh; Gidman, Bailey, Wright, Ratcliffe, Ross, McMahon, Eastoe, Varadi (Lyons), Hartford, McBride.
Arsenal: Jennings; Devine, Sansom, Talbot (McDermott), O'Leary, Young, Hollins, Sunderland, Stapleton, Gatting, Rix.

Huddersfield T (0) 0

Shrewsbury T (1) 3 *(Topping og, Cross, Bates)* 14,712

Huddersfield T: Rankin (Robins); Brown, Robinson, Stanton, Sutton, Topping, Lillis, Kennedy, Austin, Kindon, Cowling.
Shrewsbury T: Wardle; King, Leonard, Turner, Griffin, Keay, Tong, Atkins, Bates, Petts (McClaren), Cross.

Hull C (0) 1 *(Deacy)*

Doncaster R (0) 0 10,709

Hull C: Norman; Hoolickin, Croft, Richards, Ferguson, Roberts G., Marwood, McClaren, Edwards, Norrie, Deacy.
Doncaster R: Boyd; Russell, Snodin I., Lister, Saunders, Mell, Pugh, Snodin G., Nimmo, Warboys, Little.

Ipswich T (1) 1 *(Mariner)*

Aston Villa (0) 0 27,721

Ipswich T: Cooper; Burley, Mills, Thijssen, Osman, Butcher, Wark, Muhren, Mariner, Brazil, Gates.
Aston Villa: Rimmer; Swain, Williams, Evans, McNaught, Mortimer, Bremner, Shaw, Withe, Cowans, Morley (Geddis).

Peterborough U (0) 1 *(Cooke)*

Chesterfield (0) 1 *(Crawford)* 8631

Peterborough U: Waugh; McVay, Phillips, Gynn, Slack, Slough, Guy (Cliss), Kellock, Cooke, Hodgson, Robson.
Chesterfield: Turner; Tartt, Pollard, Wilson, Green, Hunter, Birch, Simpson, Bonnyman, Salmons, Crawford.

Plymouth Arg (1) 1 *(Kemp)*

Charlton Ath (0) 2 *(Powell, Hales)* 9499

Plymouth Arg: Crudgington; McNeill, Harrison, Hodges, Phillipson-Masters, Foster, Cooper, Kemp, Sims, Bason, Murphy.
Charlton Ath: Johns; Gritt, Madden, Shaw, Berry, Tydeman (Robinson), Powell, Walker, Hales, Walsh, Naylor.

Port Vale (0) 1 *(Beech)*

Enfield (1) 1 *(Bishop)* 5538

Port Vale: Cherry; Griffiths, Miller, Beech, Bowles, Elsby, Farrell, Bennett (Jones S.), Chamberlain N., Chamberlain M., Bromage.
Enfield: Jacobs; Wade, Tone, Jennings, Waite (Holmes), Howell, Oliver, Ashford, Burton, Bishop, King.

Preston NE (0) 3 *(Houston, Bruce, McGee)*

Bristol R (4) 4 *(Mabbutt, Barrowclough, Barrett, Williams)* 6248

Preston NE: Tunks; Taylor, McAteer, Burns (McGee), Baxter, O'Riordan, Doyle, Coleman, Elliott, Bruce, Houston.
Bristol R: Kite; Gillies, Jones, Hughes, McCaffery, Emmanuel, Williams G., Barrowclough, Lee, Mabbutt, Barrett.

QPR (0) 0

Tottenham H (0) 0 28,829

QPR: Burridge; Shanks, Gillard, Fenwick, Wicks, Roeder, Flanagan, King, Stainrod, Waddock, Silkman.
Tottenham H: Daines; Yorath, Miller, Roberts, Lacy, Perryman, Brooke, Archibald, Villa (Galvin), Hoddle, Crooks.

Southampton (2) 3 *(Moran, Keegan, Baker)*

Chelsea (0) 1 *(Lee)* 23,694

Southampton: Wells; Golac, Holmes, Williams, Watson, Nicholl, Keegan (Hebbard), Channon, George, Moran, Baker.
Chelsea: Borota; Locke, Rofe, Bumstead (Driver), Droy, Chivers, Britton, Fillery, Lee, Walker, Rhoades-Brown.

Stoke C (1) 2 *(Chapman, Bracewell)*

Wolverhampton W (2) 2 *(Eves, Hibbitt)* 24,737

Stoke C: Fox; Evans, Hampton, Dodd, O'Callaghan, Doyle, Bracewell, Heath, Chapman, Richardson, Munro.
Wolverhampton W: Bradshaw; Palmer, Hollifield, Daniel, Brazier, Berry, Hibbitt, Atkinson, Bell, Richards, Eves.

Swansea C (0) 0

Middlesbrough (2) 5 *(Ashcroft, Angus, Hodgson 2, Cochrane)* 18,015

Swansea C: Stewart; Attley, Hadziabdic, Rushbury, Stevenson, Phillips, Mahoney, James, Curtis, Charles (Giles), Robinson.
Middlesbrough: Platt; Craggs, Bailey, Angus, Ashcroft, Nattrass, Cochrane, Proctor, Hodgson, Shearer, McAndrew.

WBA (1) 3 *(Robson, Cowdrill, Barnes)*

Grimsby T (0) 0 22,477

WBA: Godden; Batson, Cowdrill, Moses, Wile, Bennett, Robson, Brown A. (Mills), Regis, Owen, Barnes.
Grimsby T: Batch; Stone, Crombie, Waters, Wigginton, Moore, Brolly (Ford), Whymark, Drinkell, Mitchell, Cumming.

West Ham U (0) 1 *(Stewart pen)*

Wrexham (0) 1 *(Davis)* 30,137

West Ham U: Parkes; Stewart, Lampard, Bonds, Martin, Devonshire, Holland, Goddard, Cross, Brooking, Pike.
Wrexham: Davies; Hill, Jones, Davis, Cegielski, Arkwright, Buxton (Fox), Sutton, Edwards, McNeil, Cartwright.

Wimbledon (0) 0

Oldham Ath (0) 0 4693

Wimbledon: Beasant; Jones, Armstrong, Galliers, Smith, Cunningham (Downes), Ketteridge, Denny, Leslie, Cork, Hubbick.
Oldham Ath: Platt; Edwards, Blair, Keegan, Clements, Hurst, Wylde, Futcher, Steel, Palmer, Kowenicki.

Leeds U (0) 1 *(Hird* pen*)*

Coventry C (1) 1 *(Thomas)* 24,523

Leeds U: Lukic; Greenhoff (Hamson), Gray, Flynn, Hart, Cherry, Parlane, Hird, Connor, Sabella, Graham.
Coventry C: Sealey; Thomas, Roberts, Blair, Dyson, Gillespie, Bannister (Jacobs), Daly, Thompson, Hateley, Hunt.

Leicester C (1) 3 *(Lineker, Buchanan, Melrose)*

Cardiff C (0) 0 17,527

Leicester C: Wallington; Williams, Gibson, Peake, Scott, O'Neill, Lineker, Buchanan D. (Melrose), Young, Wilson, MacDonald.
Cardiff C: Healey; Jones, Lewis, Hughes, Pontin, Thomas (Micallef), Giles, Kitchen, Stevens, Ronson, Buchanan J.

Liverpool (2) 4 *(McDermott, Dalglish 2, Kennedy R.)*

Altrincham (0) 1 *(Heathcote* pen*)* 37,170

Liverpool: Clemence; Neal, Kennedy A., Irwin, Kennedy R., Money, Dalglish, Lee, Johnson, McDermott, Case.
Altrincham: Connaughton; Allan, Davison, Bailey (Whitbread), Owens, King, Barrow, Heathcote, Johnson, Rogers, Howard.

Maidstone (0) 2 *(Woon, Ovard)*

Exeter C (1) 4 *(Pullar 2, Kellow, Rogers P.)* 6310

Maidstone: Guy; Thompson, Kinnear, Hill (Shield), Hutton, Hamberger, Daubney, Ovard, Woon, Wiltshire, Newson.
Exeter C: Bond; Rogers M., Hatch, Forbes, Roberts L., Roberts P., Rogers P., Kellow, Pearson, Delve, Pullar.

Manchester C (0) 4 *(Reeves 2* [1 pen], *Power, Boyer)*

Crystal Palace (0) 0 39,347

Manchester C: Corrigan; Ranson, McDonald, Reid, Power, Caton, Boyer, Gow, MacKenzie, Hutchison, Reeves.
Crystal Palace: Fry; Hinshelwood, Boyle, Nicholas (Goodchild), Cannon, Gilbert, Murphy, Lovell, Sealy, Walsh, Smillie.

Manchester U (0) 2 *(Duxbury, Thomas)*

Brighton & HA (2) 2 *(Horton, Ritchie)* 42,199

Manchester U: Bailey; Nicholl, Albiston, McIlroy (Duxbury), Jovanovic, Moran, Coppell, Birtles, Jordan, Macari, Thomas.
Brighton & HA: Moseley; Gregory, Stevens, Horton, Foster, Lawrenson, McNab, Ritchie, Robinson, Clark, O'Sullivan.

Mansfield T (1) 2 *(Bird, Parkinson)*

Carlisle U (0) 2 *(Bannon, Bird og)* 5598

Mansfield T: Arnold; McJannet, Wood, Hamilton, McClelland, Bird, Pollard, Mann, Caldwell, Parkinson, Thomson.
Carlisle U: Harrison; Haigh, Coady, McDonald, Campbell, Parker, Coughlin, Metcalfe, Bannon, Beardsley, Staniforth.

Newcastle U (1) 2 *(Waddle 2)*

Sheffield W (1) 1 *(Pearson)* 22,499

Newcastle U: Carr; Carney, Johnson, Martin, Boam, Halliday, Shinton, Trewick, Clarke, Wharton, Waddle.
Sheffield W: Bolder; Blackhall, Grant (Mirocevic), Smith, Shirtliff, Sterland, Pearson, Johnson, Leman, McCulloch, Curran.

Norwich C (0) 1 *(Downs)*

Cambridge U (0) 0 18,420

Norwich C: Baker; McDowell, Downs, McGuire, Hoadley, Watson, Mendham, Fashanu, Royle, Paddon, Goble.
Cambridge U: Key; Donaldson, Murray, Smith, Fallon, Finney, Streete, Spriggs, Reilly, Taylor, Christie (Gibbins).

Nottingham F (1) 3 *(Francis 2, Ponte)*

Bolton W (1) 3 *(Hoggan 2, Whatmore)* 22,920

Nottingham F: Shilton; Anderson, Gray, McGovern, Lloyd, Gunn, O'Neill, Ponte, Francis, Wallace, Robertson.
Bolton W: Peacock; Graham, McElhinney, Wilson, Jones (Nicholson), Brennan, Nikolic, Whatmore, Hoggan, Kidd, Gowling.

Notts Co (1) 2 *(Manns, Christie)*

Blackburn R (1) 1 *(Burke)* 7885

Notts Co: Leonard; Benjamin, Wood, Hunt, Kilcline, Beavon, Manns, Masson, Christie, Harkouk, Hooks.
Blackburn R: Butcher; Branagan, De Vries, McKenzie, Keeley, Fazackerley, Brotherston, Stonehouse, Crawford, Burke, Parkes (Garner).

Orient (0) 1 *(Jennings)*

Luton T (0) 3 *(Moss 2* [1 pen], *Ingram)* 9891

Orient: Day; Hughton, Roffey, Taylor T., Gray, Parsons, Chiedozie, Moores, Jennings, Bowles, Taylor P.
Luton T: Findlay; West, Donaghy, Grealish, Saxby, Price, Hill, Stein, Ingram, Aizlewood, Moss.

THIRD ROUND REPLAYS

6 JAN

Bolton W (0) 0 *aet*

Nottingham F (0) 1 *(Francis)* 22,779

Bolton W: Peacock; Graham, Brennan, Wilson, Nicholson, McElhinney, Nikolic, Whatmore, Hoggan, Kidd, Gowling.
Nottingham F: Shilton; Anderson, Gray, McGovern, Lloyd, Burns, O'Neill, Bowyer, Francis, Ward, Robertson.

Carlisle U (0) 2 *(Beardsley, MacDonald)*

Mansfield T (1) 1 *(Pollard)* 6929

Carlisle U: Harrison; Haigh, Coady, MacDonald, Campbell, Parker, Coughlin, Metcalfe, Bannon, Beardsley, Staniforth.
Mansfield T: Arnold; McJannet, Wood, Hamilton, McClelland, Bird, Pollard (Burrows), Mann, Caldwell, Phillips, Thomson.

Chesterfield (1) 1 *(Hunter)*

Peterborough U (2) 2 *(Cooke 2)* 8216

Chesterfield: Turner; Tartt, Pollard, Kowalski, Green, Hunter (Walwyn), Birch, Simpson, Bonnyman, Salmons, Crawford.
Peterborough U: Waugh; McVay, Phillips, Gynn, Slack, Slough, Quow, Kellock, Cooke, Hodgson, Robson.

Coventry C (0) 1 *(Thompson)*

Leeds U (0) 0 22,057

Coventry C: Sealey; Coop, Roberts, Blair, Dyson, Gillespie, Bodak, Daly, Thompson, Hateley, Bannister.
Leeds U: Lukic; Hird, Gray, Flynn, Hart, Cherry, Parlane, Chandler, Hamson, Sabella, Graham.

Enfield (2) 3 *(Bishop, King, Howell)*

Port Vale (0) 0 6449

Enfield: Jacobs; Wade, Tone, Jennings, Oliver, Howell, Ashford (Holmes), Barrett, Burton, Bishop, King.
Port Vale: Cherry; Griffiths, Miller, Beech, Bowles, Sproson, Farrell, Jones, Chamberlain N., Chamberlain M. (Elsby), Bromage.

Fulham (0) 0 *aet*

Bury (0) 0 6582

Fulham: Peyton; Strong, Lock, Gale, Banton, Hatter, Davies, O'Driscoll, Mahoney, Greenaway (Lewington), Goodlass.
Bury: Southall; Howard, Kennedy, Gore, Hilton, Whitehead, Mullen, Butler, Johnson, Jakub, Cruickshank (Farley).

Oldham Ath (0) 0

Wimbledon (0) 1 *(Cork)* 6789

Oldham Ath: Platt; Edwards, Blair, Keegan, Clements, Hurst, Wylde, Atkinson (Hilton), Steel, Palmer, Kowenicki.
Wimbledon: Beasant; Jones, Armstrong, Galliers, Smith, Brown, Ketteridge, Denny, Leslie, Cork, Hubbick (Hodges).

Wolverhampton W (0) 2 *(Eves, Hibbitt)*

Stoke C (1) 1 *(Heath)* 22,892

Wolverhampton W: Bradshaw; Palmer, Hollifield, Daniel, McAlle, Berry, Hibbitt, Atkinson, Bell, Richards, Eves.
Stoke C: Fox; Evans, Hampton, Dodd, Cook, Doyle, Bracewell, Heath, Chapman, Maguire (Richardson), Munroe.

Wrexham (0) 0 *aet*

West Ham U (0) 0 13,643

Wrexham: Davies; Sutton, Kenworthy, Davis, Cegielski, Carrodus, Fox, Arkwright, Edwards, McNeil, Cartwright.
West Ham U: Parkes; Stewart, Lampard, Bonds, Martin, Devonshire, Holland, Goddard, Cross, Brooking, Pike.

7 JAN

Sunderland (1) 1 *aet (Rowell)*

Birmingham C (0) 2 *(Bertschin, Evans)* 27,793

Sunderland: Turner; Whitworth, Bolton, Hindmarch, Elliott, Rowell, Arnott (Cooke), Brown, Hawley, Chisholm, Cummins.
Birmingham C: Wealands; Langan, Lees, Curbishley, Gallagher (Evans), Todd, Ainscow, Bertschin, Worthington, Gemmill, Lynex.

Brighton & HA (0) 0

Manchester U (1) 2 *(Nicholl, Birtles)* 26,928

Brighton & HA: Moseley; Gregory, Stevens, Horton, Foster, Lawrenson, McNab, Ritchie, Robinson, Clark (Smith), O'Sullivan.
Manchester U: Bailey; Nicholl, Albiston, Wilkins (Duxbury), McQueen, Buchan, Coppell, Birtles, Jordan, Macari, Thomas.

Bristol C (1) 2 *(Mabbutt, Ritchie)*

Derby Co (0) 0 13,649

Bristol C: Shaw; Sweeney, Hay, Aitken, Rodgers, Marshall, Tainton, Fitzpatrick, Mabbutt, Ritchie, Pritchard.
Derby Co: Jones; Emery, Richards, Clark, Osgood, Ramage, Powell, Hector, Biley, Swindlehurst, Reid (Emson).

Tottenham H (2) 3 *(Crooks, Galvin, Hoddle)*

QPR (0) 1 *(Stainrod)* 36,294

Tottenham H: Daines; McAllister, Miller, Roberts, Lacy, Perryman, Brooke, Archibald, Galvin, Hoddle, Crooks.
QPR: Burridge; Shanks, Gillard, Fenwick, Wicks, Roeder, Flanagan (McCreery), King, Stainrod, Currie, Silkman.

THIRD ROUND SECOND REPLAYS

12 JAN

Bury (0) 0

Fulham (0) 1 *(Davies)* 2468

At West Bromwich Albion

Bury: Southall; Howard, Kennedy, Gore, Hilton, Whitehead, Mullen, Butler, Johnson, Jakub, Cruickshank.
Fulham: Peyton; Clement, Lock, Gale, Brown, Strong, Davies, O'Driscoll, Mahoney, Lewington, Goodlass.

19 JAN

Wrexham (0) 1 *aet (McNeil)*

West Ham U (0) 0 14,615

Wrexham: Davies; Hill, Jones, Davis (Vinter), Cegielski, Arkwright, Fox, Sutton, Edwards, McNeil, Cartwright.
West Ham U: Parkes; Stewart, Brush, Bonds, Martin, Devonshire, Allen (Neighbour), Goddard, Cross, Brooking, Pike.

FOURTH ROUND

24 JAN

Barnsley (1) 1 *(Aylott)*

Enfield (0) 1 *(Burton)* 24,251

Barnsley: New; Joyce, Chambers, Glavin, Banks, McCarthy, Evans, Parker, Aylott, Lester, Downes.
Enfield: Jacobs; Wade, Tone, Jennings, Barrett, Howell (Holmes), Ashford, Bishop, Burton, Oliver, King.

Carlisle U (1) 1 *(Coady)*

Bristol C (0) 1 *(Mabbutt)* 10,057

Carlisle U: Swinburne; Haigh, Coady, MacDonald, Houghton, Parker, Coughlin, Campbell, Bannon (Hamilton), Beardsley, Staniforth.
Bristol C: Moller; Sweeney, Hay, Aitken, Rodgers, Marshall, Tainton, Fitzpatrick, Mabbutt, Ritchie (Pritchard), Whitehead.

Coventry C (2) 3 *(Daly 2 [1 pen], Blair)*

Birmingham C (0) 2 *(Worthington pen, Ainscow)* 29,500

Coventry C: Sealey; Coop, Roberts, Blair, Dyson, Gillespie, Bodak (Thomas), Daly, Thompson, Ferguson, Hunt.
Birmingham C: Coton; Langan, Lees, Curbishley, Gallagher, Todd, Ainscow, Bertschin, Worthington, Gemmill, Dillon.

Everton (1) 2 *(Cohen og, Varadi)*

Liverpool (0) 1 *(Case)* 53,084

Everton: Hodge; Wright, Bailey, Lyons, Ratcliffe, O'Keefe, Hartford, Eastoe, Varadi, McMahon, Ross.
Liverpool: Clemence; Neal, Thompson, Irwin, Cohen, Souness, McDermott, Lee, Fairclough, Dalglish (Case), Kennedy R.

Fulham (0) 1 *(Davies)*

Charlton Ath (1) 2 *(Shaw, Hales)* 17,050

Fulham: Peyton; Clement, Lock (Wilson), Beck, Brown, Banton, Davies, O'Driscoll, Mahoney, Lewington, Greenaway.
Charlton Ath: Johns; Gritt, Madden, Shaw, Berry, Tydeman, Powell, Naylor, Hales, Walker (Hazell), Robinson.

Leicester C (1) 1 *(Henderson)*

Exeter C (0) 1 *Pullar)* 20,996

Leicester C: Wallington; Williams, Scott, Burns, May, O'Neill, Melrose (Buchanan), Henderson, Young, Wilson, Smith.
Exeter C: Bond; Rogers M., Hatch, Forbes, Roberts L., Roberts P., Prince, Rogers P., Kellow, Delve, Pullar.

Manchester C (2) 6 *(Reeves, Gow, MacKenzie, Bennett, Power, McDonald)*

Norwich C (0) 0 38,919

Manchester C: Corrigan; Henry, McDonald, Booth, Power, Caton, Boyer (Bennett), Gow, MacKenzie, Hutchison, Reeves.
Norwich C: Baker; Bond, Barham, Powell, McDowell, Watson, Mendham (Robson), Fashanu, Royle, Paddon, Bennett.

Middlesbrough (1) 1 *(Bailey)*

WBA (0) 0 28,285

Middlesbrough: Platt; Nattrass, Bailey, Johnston (Angus), Ashcroft, McAndrew, Cochrane, Proctor, Shearer, Jankovic, Armstrong.
WBA: Godden; Robertson, Cowdrill, Moses, Wile, Bennett, Robson, Brown (Mills), Regis, Owen, Barnes.

Newcastle U (1) 2 *(Clarke, Martin)*

Luton T (0) 1 *(Ingram)* 29,202

Newcastle U: Carr; Carney, Johnson, Martin, Boam, Halliday, Shinton, Trewick, Clarke, Wharton, Waddle.
Luton T: Findlay; Stephens, Donaghy, Grealish, West, Price, Hill, Stein, Ingram, Aizlewood, Moss.

Nottingham F (1) 1 *(Francis)*

Manchester U (0) 0 34,110

Nottingham F: Shilton; Anderson, Gray, McGovern, Burns, Gunn, Ponte, Wallace, Francis, Walsh, Robertson.
Manchester U: Bailey; Nicholl, Albiston, Wilkins, McQueen, Buchan, Coppell, Birtles, Jordan, Macari, Thomas.

Notts Co (0) 0

Peterborough U (0) 1 *(Cooke)* 11,714

Notts Co: Avramovic; Benjamin (Harkouk), O'Brien, Kelly, Kilcline, Richards, McCulloch, Masson, Christie, Hunt, Hooks.
Peterborough U: Waugh; McVay, Phillips, Gynn, Slack, Slough, Quow, Kellock, Cooke, Hodgson, Robson.

Shrewsbury T (0) 0

Ipswich T (0) 0 18,000

Shrewsbury T: Wardle; King, Leonard, Turner, Griffin, Keay, Tong, Atkins, Bates, Biggins, Cross.
Ipswich T: Cooper; Burley, Mills, Thijssen, Osman, Butcher, Wark, Muhren, Mariner, Brazil (O'Callaghan), Gates.

Tottenham H (0) 2 *(Brooke, Archibald)*

Hull C (0) 0 37,432

Tottenham H: Daines; McAllister, Miller, Roberts, Yorath, Perryman, Ardiles (Brooke), Archibald, Galvin, Hoddle, Crooks.
Hull C: Norman; Hoolickin, McNeil, Richards, Booth, Roberts, Marwood, McClaren, Edwards, Norrie, Deacy.

Watford (1) 1 *(Armstrong)*

Wolverhampton W (0) 1 *(Richards)* 24,228

Watford: Sherwood; Rice, Harrison, Taylor, Sims, Jackett, Callaghan (Ward), Blissett, Armstrong, Train, Poskett.
Wolverhampton W: Bradshaw; Palmer, Hollifield, Daniel, McAlle, Berry, Hibbitt, Atkinson (Parkin), Gray, Richards, Eves.

Wrexham (1) 2 *(Fox, McNeil)*

Wimbledon (0) 1 *(Denny)* 12,267

Wrexham: Davies; Hill, Kenworthy, Jones J., Cegielski, Arkwright, Fox, Sutton, Edwards, McNeil, Cartwright.
Wimbledon: Beasant; Jones S., Armstrong, Galliers, Smith, Cunningham, Ketteridge, Hodges (Hubbick), Denny, Cork, Downes.

Southampton (1) 3 *(Moran 2, Williams)*

Bristol R (0) 1 *(Williams)* 23,597

Southampton: Wells; Golac, Nicholl, Watson, Holmes, Baker, Williams, Keegan, Channon, Moran, George.
Bristol R: Kite; Gillies, Hughes, McCaffery, Cooper, Jones, Williams G., Mabbutt, Emmanuel, Barrowclough, Lee.

FOURTH ROUND REPLAYS

27 JAN

Ipswich T (1) 3 *(Gates 2, Wark)*

Shrewsbury T (0) 0 27,543

Ipswich T: Cooper; Mills, McCall, Thijssen, Osman, Butcher, Wark, Muhren, Mariner, Brazil (O'Callaghan), Gates.
Shrewsbury T: Wardle; King, Leonard, Turner, Griffin, Keay, Tong, Atkins, Bates, Biggins (Dungworth), Cross.

Wolverhampton W (0) 2 *(Richards* pen, *Parkin)*

Watford (0) 1 *(Poskett)* 30,854

Wolverhampton W: Bradshaw; Palmer, Hollifield, Daniel, McAlle, Berry, Hibbitt, Parkin, Gray, Richards, Eves.
Watford: Sherwood; Rice, Harrison, Taylor, Sims, Jackett, Jenkins, Blissett, Armstrong, Train, Rostron (Poskett).

28 JAN

Bristol C (0) 5 *(Mabbutt 2, Ritchie 2* [1 pen], *Mann)*

Carlisle U (0) 0 12,801

Bristol C: Moller; Sweeney, Hay, Aitken, Rodgers, Marshall, Tainton (Mann), Fitzpatrick, Mabbutt, Ritchie, Whitehead.
Carlisle U: Swinburne; Haigh, Coady, McDonald, Houghton, Parker, Coughlin, Campbell, Bannon, Beardsley, Staniforth (Hamilton).

Enfield (0) 0

Barnsley (1) 3 *(Aylott 2, Glavin)* 35,244

At White Hart Lane, Tottenham

Enfield: Jacobs; Wade (Holmes), Tone, Jennings, Barrett, Howell, Ashford, Bishop, Burton, Oliver, King.
Barnsley: New; Joyce, Chambers, Glavin, Banks (Riley), McCarthy, Evans, Parker, Aylott, Lester, Downes.

Exeter C (1) 3 *(Kellow 3* [1 pen]*)*

Leicester C (0) 1 *(Melrose)* 15,268

Exeter C: Main; Rogers M., Hatch, Forbes, Roberts L., Roberts P., Pearson, Rogers P., Kellow, Delve, Pullar.
Leicester C: Wallington; Williams, Friar, Peake (Goodwin), May, O'Neill, Byrne, Melrose, Young, Wilson, MacDonald.

FIFTH ROUND

14 FEB

Ipswich T (0) 2 *(Wark, Mariner)*

Charlton Ath (0) 0 30,221

Ipswich T: Cooper; Osman, McCall, Thijssen, Beattie, Butcher, Wark, Muhren, Mariner, Brazil, Gates.
Charlton Ath: Johns; Naylor, Warman, Shaw, Berry (Smith), Tydeman, Powell, Walsh, Hales, Robinson, Walker.

Middlesbrough (2) 2 *(Proctor, Jankovic)*

Barnsley (1) 1 *(Lester)* 37,557

Middlesbrough: Platt; Nattrass, Bailey, Johnston, Ashcroft, McAndrew, Cochrane, Proctor, Hodgson, Jankovic, Armstrong.
Barnsley: New; Joyce, Chambers, Glavin, Banks, McCarthy, Cooper, Riley, Aylott, Lester, Downes.

Newcastle U (0) 1 *(Shoulder)*

Exeter C (0) 1 *(Roberts L.)* 37,420

Newcastle U: Carr; Carney, Johnson, Walker, Boam, Halliday, Shinton (Shoulder), Trewick, Clarke, Wharton, Waddle.
Exeter C: Bond; Rogers M., Sparrow, Forbes (Pratt), Roberts L., Roberts P., Pearson, Rogers P., Kellow, Delve, Hatch.

Nottingham F (0) 2 *(Robertson* pen, *Wallace)*

Bristol C (1) 1 *(Mabbutt)* 26,732

Nottingham F: Shilton; Anderson, Gray F., Gray S., Burns, Gunn, Mills, Wallace, Francis, Walsh, Robertson.
Bristol C: Moller; Stevens, Sweeney, Aitken, Marshall, Nicholls, Tainton, Mann, Mabbutt, Pritchard, Whitehead.

Peterborough U (0) 0

Manchester C (1) 1 *(Booth)* 27,780

Peterborough U: Waugh; McVay, Phillips (Syrett), Gynn, Slack, Slough, Quow, Kellock, Cooke, Hodgson, Robson.
Manchester C: Corrigan; Henry, McDonald, Reid, Power, Booth, Bennett, Gow, MacKenzie, Hutchison, Reeves.

Southampton (0) 0

Everton (0) 0 24,152

Southampton: Wells; Golac, Waldron, Williams, Watson, Nicholl, Keegan, Channon, George, Moran (Hebberd), Holmes.
Everton: McDonagh; Ratcliffe, Bailey, Wright, Lyons, Gidman, Ross, Eastoe, Varadi, Hartford, O'Keefe.

Tottenham H (2) 3 *(Ardiles, Archibald, Hughton)*

Coventry C (1) 1 *(English)* 26,688

Tottenham H: Daines; Hughton, Miller, Roberts, Lacy, Perryman, Ardiles (Brooke), Archibald, Galvin, Hoddle, Crooks.
Coventry C: Sealey; Thomas, Roberts, Blair, Dyson (Hateley), Gillespie, Jacobs, Daly, Thompson, English, Hunt.

Wolverhampton W (0) 3 *(Bell 2, Richards)*

Wrexham (1) 1 *(Fox)* 33,788

Wolverhampton W: Bradshaw; Palmer, Parkin, Clarke, McAlle, Berry, Hibbitt, Atkinson, Gray, Richards, Eves (Bell).
Wrexham: Davies; Hill, Dwyer, Jones, Cegielski, Arkwright, Fox, Sutton, Edwards, McNeil, Cartwright.

FIFTH ROUND REPLAYS

17 FEB

Everton (0) 1 *aet (O'Keefe)*

Southampton (0) 0 49,192

Everton: McDonagh; Gidman, Ratcliffe, Wright, Lyons, Ross, McMahon, Eastoe, Varadi, Hartford, O'Keefe.
Southampton: Wells; Golac (Hebberd), Waldron, Williams, Watson, Nicholl, Keegan, Channon, George, Holmes, Baker.

18 FEB

Exeter C (3) 4 *(Hatch, Pearson, Rogers P., Rogers M.)*

Newcastle U (0) 0 17,668

Exeter C: Bond; Rogers M., Sparrow, Forbes, Roberts L., Roberts P., Pearson, Rogers P., Kellow, Delve, Hatch.
Newcastle U: Carr; Carney, Johnson, Walker, Boam, Halliday, Shoulder, Trewick, Clarke, Wharton (Brownlie), Waddle.

SIXTH ROUND

7 MAR

Everton (1) 2 *(Eastoe, Ross* pen*)*

Manchester C (1) 2 *(Gow, Power)* 52,791

Everton: McDonagh; Gidman, Ratcliffe, Wright, Lyons, Ross, McMahon, Eastoe, Varadi, Hartford, O'Keefe (Stanley).
Manchester C: Corrigan; Ranson, McDonald, Reid, Power, Caton, Tueart, Gow, MacKenzie, Hutchison, Reeves.

Nottingham F (2) 3 *(Francis, Walsh, Robertson* pen*)*

Ipswich T (2) 3 *(Mariner, Anderson og, Thijssen)* 34,796

Nottingham F: Shilton; Anderson (Ponte), Gunn, Burns, Gray F., Mills G., Gray S., Walsh, Wallace, Francis, Robertson.
Ipswich T: Cooper; Mills, Osman, Butcher, McCall (O'Callaghan), Thijssen, Gates, Wark, Muhren, Mariner, Brazil.

Middlesbrough (1) 1 *(Cochrane)*

Wolverhampton W (1) 1 *(Gray)* 36,382

Middlesbrough: Platt; Nattrass, Bailey, Johnston, Ashcroft, McAndrew, Cochrane, Proctor, Hodgson, Jankovic (Shearer), Armstrong.
Wolverhampton W: Bradshaw; Palmer, Parkin, Clarke (Bell), McAlle, Berry, Hibbitt, Carr, Gray, Richards, Eves.

Tottenham H (0) 2 *(Roberts G., Miller)*

Exeter C (0) 0 40,629

Tottenham H: Daines; Hughton, Miller, Roberts G., Mazzon, Perryman, Ardiles, Archibald, Galvin, Hoddle, Crooks.
Exeter C: Bond; Rogers M., Sparrow, Forbes, Roberts L., Roberts P., Pearson (Pratt), Rogers P., Kellow, Delve, Hatch.

SIXTH ROUND REPLAYS

10 MAR

Ipswich T (0) 1 *(Muhren)*

Nottingham F (0) 0 31,060

Ipswich T: Cooper; Mills, McCall, Thijssen, Osman, Butcher, Wark, Muhren, Mariner, Brazil (O'Callaghan), Gates.
Nottingham F: Shilton; Gunn, Gray F., Gray S., Burns, Needham, Mills, Wallace, Francis (Ponte), Walsh, Robertson.

Wolverhampton W (1) 3 *aet (Eves, Richards, Bell)*

Middlesbrough (0) 1 *(Hodgson)* 40,524

Wolverhampton W: Bradshaw; Palmer, Parkin, Clarke (Bell), McAlle, Berry, Hibbitt, Carr, Gray, Richards, Eves.
Middlesbrough: Platt; Nattrass, Bailey, Johnston, Ashcroft, McAndrew, Cochrane (Shearer), Proctor, Hodgson, Jankovic, Armstrong.

11 MAR

Manchester C (0) 3 *(McDonald 2, Power)*

Everton (0) 1 *(Eastoe)* 52,532

Manchester C: Corrigan; Ranson, McDonald, Reid, Power, Caton, Tueart, Gow, MacKenzie, Hutchison, Reeves.
Everton: McDonagh; Gidman, Bailey, Wright, Lyons, Ross, McMahon, Eastoe, Varadi, Hartford, McBride.

SEMI-FINALS

11 APRIL

Manchester C (0) 1 *aet (Power)*

Ipswich T (0) 0 46,537

At Villa Park

Manchester C: Corrigan; Ranson, McDonald, Reid, Power, Caton, Bennett, Gow, MacKenzie, Hutchison, Reeves.
Ipswich T: Cooper; Mills, Butcher, Thijssen, Osman, Beattie (McCall), Wark, Muhren, Mariner, Brazil, Gates.

Tottenham H (2) 2 *aet (Archibald, Hoddle)*

Wolverhampton W (1) 2 *(Hibbitt, Carr* pen*)* 50,174

At Hillsborough

Tottenham H: Aleksic; Hughton, Miller, Roberts, Perryman, Ardiles, Archibald, Galvin, Hoddle, Crooks, Villa (Brooke).
Wolverhampton W: Bradshaw; Palmer, Parkin, Clarke (Bell), McAlle, Berry, Hibbitt, Carr, Gray, Richards, Hughes.

SEMI-FINAL REPLAY

15 APRIL

Tottenham H (2) 3 *(Crooks 2, Villa)*

Wolverhampton W (0) 0 52,539

At Highbury

Tottenham H: Aleksic; Hughton, Miller, Roberts, Villa, Perryman, Ardiles (Brooke), Archibald, Galvin, Hoddle, Crooks.
Wolverhampton W: Bradshaw; Palmer, Parkin, Hughes (Clarke), McAlle, Berry, Hibbitt, Carr, Bell, Richards, Eves.

FINAL (at Wembley)

9 MAY

Manchester C (1) 1 *aet (Hutchison)*

Tottenham H (0) 1 *(Hutchison og)* 99,500

Manchester C: Corrigan; Ranson, McDonald, Reid, Power, Caton, Bennett, Gow, MacKenzie, Hutchison (Henry), Reeves.
Tottenham H: Aleksic; Hughton, Miller, Roberts, Perryman, Villa (Brooke), Ardiles, Archibald, Galvin, Hoddle, Crooks.

FINAL REPLAY (at Wembley)

14 MAY

Manchester C (1) 2 *(MacKenzie, Reeves* pen*)*

Tottenham H (1) 3 *(Villa 2, Crooks)* 92,000

Manchester C: Corrigan; Ranson, McDonald (Tueart), Caton, Reid, Gow, Power, MacKenzie, Reeves, Bennett, Hutchison.
Tottenham H: Aleksic; Hughton, Miller, Roberts, Perryman, Villa, Ardiles, Archibald, Galvin, Hoddle, Crooks.

FA CUP FINALS 1872–1981

1872 and 1874–92	Kennington Oval	1911	Replay at Old Trafford
1873	Lillie Bridge	1912	Replay at Bramall Lane
1893	Fallowfield, Manchester	1915	Old Trafford, Manchester
1894	Everton	1920–22	Stamford Bridge
1895–1914	Crystal Palace	1923 to date	Wembley
1901	Replay at Bolton	1970	Replay at Old Trafford
1910	Replay at Everton	1981	Replay at Wembley

Year	*Winners*	*Runners-up*	*Score*
1872	Wanderers	Royal Engineers	1-0
1873	Wanderers	Oxford University	2-0
1874	Oxford University	Royal Engineers	2-0
1875	Royal Engineers	Old Etonians	2-0 (after 1-1 draw)
1876	Wanderers	Old Etonians	3-0 (after 0-0 draw)
1877	Wanderers	Oxford University	2-1 (aet)
1878	Wanderers*	Royal Engineers	3-1
1879	Old Etonians	Clapham R	1-0
1880	Clapham R	Oxford University	1-0
1881	Old Carthusians	Old Etonians	3-0
1882	Old Etonians	Blackburn R	1-0
1883	Blackburn Olympic	Old Etonians	2-1 (aet)
1884	Blackburn R	Queen's Park, Glasgow	2-1
1885	Blackburn R	Queen's Park, Glasgow	2-0
1886	Blackburn R†	WBA	2-0 (after 0-0 draw)
1887	Aston Villa	WBA	2-0
1888	WBA	Preston NE	2-1
1889	Preston NE	Wolverhampton W	3-0
1890	Blackburn R	Sheffield W	6-1
1891	Blackburn R	Notts Co	3-1
1892	WBA	Aston Villa	3-0
1893	Wolverhampton W	Everton	1-0
1894	Notts Co	Bolton W	4-1
1895	Aston Villa	WBA	1-0
1896	Sheffield W	Wolverhampton W	2-1
1897	Aston Villa	Everton	3-2
1898	Nottingham F	Derby Co	3-1
1899	Sheffield U	Derby Co	4-1
1900	Bury	Southampton	4-0
1901	Tottenham H	Sheffield U	3-1 (after 2-2 draw)
1902	Sheffield U	Southampton	2-1 (after 1-1 draw)
1903	Bury	Derby Co	6-0
1904	Manchester C	Bolton W	1-0
1905	Aston Villa	Newcastle U	2-0
1906	Everton	Newcastle U	1-0
1907	Sheffield W	Everton	2-1
1908	Wolverhampton W	Newcastle U	3-1
1909	Manchester U	Bristol C	1-0
1910	Newcastle U	Barnsley	2-0 (after 1-1 draw)
1911	Bradford C	Newcastle U	1-0 (after 0-0 draw)
1912	Barnsley	WBA	1-0 (aet)
1913	Aston Villa	Sunderland	1-0 (after 0-0 draw)
1914	Burnley	Liverpool	1-0
1915	Sheffield U	Chelsea	3-0
1920	Aston Villa	Huddersfield T	1-0 (aet)
1921	Tottenham H	Wolverhampton W	1-0
1922	Huddersfield T	Preston NE	1-0
1923	Bolton W	West Ham U	2-0
1924	Newcastle U	Aston Villa	2-0
1925	Sheffield U	Cardiff C	1-0
1926	Bolton W	Manchester C	1-0
1927	Cardiff C	Arsenal	1-0
1928	Blackburn R	Huddersfield T	3-1
1929	Bolton W	Portsmouth	2-0
1930	Arsenal	Huddersfield T	2-0
1931	WBA	Birmingham	2-1
1932	Newcastle U	Arsenal	2-1
1933	Everton	Manchester C	3-0
1934	Manchester C	Portsmouth	2-1
1935	Sheffield W	WBA	4-2
1936	Arsenal	Sheffield U	1-0
1937	Sunderland	Preston NE	3-1
1938	Preston NE	Huddersfield T	1-0 (aet)
1939	Portsmouth	Wolverhampton W	4-1
1946	Derby Co	Charlton Ath	4-1 (aet)
1947	Charlton Ath	Burnley	1-0 (aet)
1948	Manchester U	Blackpool	4-2
1949	Wolverhampton W	Leicester C	3-1
1950	Arsenal	Liverpool	2-0
1951	Newcastle U	Blackpool	2-0
1952	Newcastle U	Arsenal	1-0

Year	Winners	Runners-up	Score
1953	Blackpool	Bolton W	4-3
1954	WBA	Preston NE	3-2
1955	Newcastle U	Manchester C	3-1
1956	Manchester C	Birmingham C	3-1
1957	Aston Villa	Manchester U	2-1
1958	Bolton W	Manchester U	2-0
1959	Nottingham F	Luton T	2-1
1960	Wolverhampton W	Blackburn R	3-0
1961	Tottenham H	Leicester C	2-0
1962	Tottenham H	Burnley	3-1
1963	Manchester U	Leicester C	3-1
1964	West Ham U	Preston NE	3-2
1965	Liverpool	Leeds U	2-1 (aet)
1966	Everton	Sheffield W	3-2
1967	Tottenham H	Chelsea	2-1
1968	WBA	Everton	1-0 (aet)
1969	Manchester C	Leicester C	1-0
1970	Chelsea	Leeds U	2-1 (aet)
	(after 2-2 draw, after extra time, at Wembley)		
1971	Arsenal	Liverpool	2-1 (aet)
1972	Leeds U	Arsenal	1-0
1973	Sunderland	Leeds U	1-0
1974	Liverpool	Newcastle U	3-0
1975	West Ham U	Fulham	2-0
1976	Southampton	Manchester U	1-0
1977	Manchester U	Liverpool	2-1
1978	Ipswich T	Arsenal	1-0
1979	Arsenal	Manchester U	3-2
1980	West Ham U	Arsenal	1-0
1981	Tottenham H	Manchester C	3-2
	(after 1-1 draw, after extra time, at Wembley)		

* *Won outright, but restored to the Football Association.*

† *A special trophy was awarded for third consecutive win.*

FA CUP WINS

Aston Villa 7, Blackburn R 6, Newcastle U 6, Tottenham H 6, Arsenal 5, The Wanderers 5, WBA 5, Sheffield U 4, Bolton W 4, Wolverhampton W 4, Manchester C 4, Manchester U 4, Sheffield W 3, Everton 3, West Ham U 3, Bury 2, Old Etonians 2, Preston NE 2, Nottingham F 2, Sunderland 2, Liverpool 2, Barnsley 1, Blackburn Olympic 1, Blackpool 1, Bradford C 1, Burnley 1, Cardiff C 1, Charlton Ath 1, Chelsea 1, Clapham R 1, Derby Co 1, Huddersfield T 1, Notts Co 1, Old Carthusians 1, Oxford University 1, Portsmouth 1, Royal Engineers 1, Leeds U 1, Southampton 1, Ipswich T 1.

APPEARANCES IN FINALS

Arsenal 11, Newcastle U 11, WBA 10, Aston Villa 9, Blackburn R 8, Manchester C 8, Manchester U 8, Wolverhampton W 8, Bolton W 7, Preston NE 7, Everton 7, Liverpool 6, Old Etonians 6, Sheffield U 6, *Tottenham H 6, Huddersfield T 5, *The Wanderers 5, Sheffield W 5, Derby Co 4, Oxford University 4, Royal Engineers 4, Leeds U 4, Leicester C 4, West Ham U 4, Blackpool 3, Burnley 3, Chelsea 3, Portsmouth 3, Sunderland 3, Southampton 3, Barnsley 2, Birmingham C 2, *Bury 2, Cardiff C 2, Charlton Ath 2, Clapham R 2, Notts Co 2, Queen's Park (Glasgow) 2, *Nottingham F 2, *Blackburn Olympic 1, *Bradford C 1, Bristol C 1, *Old Carthusians 1, Luton T 1, Fulham 1, *Ipswich T 1.

* *Denotes undefeated.*

APPEARANCES IN SEMI-FINALS

Everton 18, WBA 18, Aston Villa 17, Blackburn R 16, Arsenal 15, Manchester U 15, Sheffield W 13, Derby Co 13, Liverpool 13, Newcastle U 13, Wolverhampton W 13, Bolton W 12, Sunderland 10, Preston NE 10, Manchester C 10, Tottenham H 10, Sheffield U 10, Chelsea 10, Nottingham F 9, Birmingham C 9, Burnley 8, Southampton 8, Huddersfield T 7, Leeds U 7, Old Etonians 6, Oxford University 6, Leicester C 6, The Wanderers 5, Notts Co 5, Fulham 5, West Ham U 5, Portsmouth 4, Queen's Park (Glasgow) 4, Royal Engineers 4, Blackpool 3, Cardiff C 3, Clapham R 3, Millwall 3, Old Carthusians 3, The Swifts 3, Stoke C 3, Ipswich T 3, Barnsley 2, Blackburn Olympic 2, Bristol C 2, Bury 2, Charlton Ath 2, Grimsby T 2, Swansea T 2, Swindon T 2, Crystal Palace 2, Bradford C 1, Cambridge University 1, Crewe Alex 1, Darwen 1, Derby Junction 1, Glasgow R 1, Hull C 1, Marlow 1, Old Harrovians 1, Oldham Ath 1, Port Vale 1, Reading 1, Shropshire W 1, York C 1, Luton T 1, Norwich C 1, Watford 1, Orient 1.

FA CHALLENGE CUP 1960–61 – 1979–80

Home team shown first; where a tie was replayed, the team given second was the home team in the replay.

FA CUP 1960–61

Third Round

Leicester C v Oxford U	3-1
Plymouth Arg v Bristol C	0-1
Nottingham F v Birmingham C	0-2
Rotherham U v Watford	1-0
Wolverhampton W v Huddersfield T	1-1, 1-2
Reading v Barnsley	1-1, 1-3
Luton T v Northampton T	4-0
Cardiff C v Manchester C	1-1, 0-0, 0-2
Newcastle U v Fulham	5-0
Stockport Co v Southport	3-1
West Ham U v Stoke C	2-2, 0-1
Aldershot v Shrewsbury T	1-1, 2-2, 2-0
Everton v Sheffield U	0-1
Lincoln C v WBA	3-1
Hull C v Bolton W	0-1
Chesterfield v Blackburn R	0-0, 0-3
Southampton v Ipswich T	7-1
Gillingham v Leyton O	2-6
Sheffield W v Leeds U	2-0
Manchester U v Middlesbrough	3-0
Brighton v Derby Co	3-1
Burnley v Bournemouth	1-0
Swansea T v Port Vale	3-0
Preston NE v Accrington S	1-1, 4-0
Scunthorpe U v Blackpool	6-2
York C v Norwich C	1-1, 0-1
Liverpool v Coventry C	3-2
Sunderland v Arsenal	2-1
Portsmouth v Peterborough U	1-2
Bristol R v Aston Villa	1-1, 0-4
Chelsea v Crewe Alex	1-2
Tottenham H v Charlton Ath	3-2

Fourth Round

Leicester C v Bristol C	5-1
Birmingham C v Rotherham U	4-0
Huddersfield T v Barnsley	1-1, 0-1
Luton T v Manchester C	3-1
Newcastle U v Stockport Co	4-0
Stoke C v Aldershot	0-0, 0-0, 3-0
Sheffield U v Lincoln C	3-1
Bolton W v Blackburn R	3-3, 0-4
Southampton v Leyton O	0-1
Sheffield W v Manchester U	1-1, 7-2
Brighton v Burnley	3-3, 0-1
Swansea T v Preston NE	2-1
Scunthorpe U v Norwich C	1-4
Liverpool v Sunderland	0-2
Peterborough U v Aston Villa	1-1, 1-2
Tottenham H v Crewe Alex	5-1

Fifth Round

Birmingham C v Leicester C	1-1, 1-2
Barnsley v Luton T	1-0
Newcastle U v Stoke C	3-1
Sheffield U v Blackburn R	2-1
Leyton O v Sheffield W	0-2
Burnley v Swansea T	4-0
Norwich C v Sunderland	0-1
Aston Villa v Tottenham H	0-2

Sixth Round

Leicester C v Barnsley	0-0, 2-1
Newcastle U v Sheffield U	1-3
Sheffield W v Burnley	0-0, 0-2
Sunderland v Tottenham H	1-1, 0-5

Semi-Final

Leicester C v Sheffield U	[1]0-0, 0-0, 2-0
Burnley v Tottenham H	[2]0-3

Final

Leicester C 0, Tottenham H 2

[1] At Leeds, replay at Nottingham Forest, 2nd replay at Birmingham. [2] At Villa Park.

FA CUP 1961–62

Third Round

Burnley v QPR	6-1
Brentford v Leyton O	1-1, 1-2
Everton v King's Lynn	4-0
Notts Co v Manchester C	0-1
Newcastle U v Peterborough U	0-1
Bury v Sheffield U	0-0, 2-2, 0-2
Norwich C v Wrexham	3-1
Ipswich T v Luton T	1-1, 1-1, 5-1
Fulham v Hartlepools U	3-1
Bristol C v Walsall	0-0, 1-4
Southampton v Sunderland	2-2, 0-3
Port Vale v Northampton T	3-1
Leicester C v Stoke C	1-1, 2-5
Brighton v Blackburn R	0-3
Southport v Shrewsbury T	1-3
Middlesbrough v Cardiff C	1-0
Bristol R v Oldham Ath	1-1, 0-2
Liverpool v Chelsea	4-3
Preston NE v Watford	3-2
Morecambe v Weymouth	0-1
Manchester U v Bolton W	2-1
Arsenal v Bradford C	3-0
Workington v Nottingham F	1-2
Sheffield W v Swansea T	1-0
Aston Villa v Crystal Palace	4-3
Huddersfield T v Rotherham U	4-3
Charlton Ath v Scunthorpe U	1-0
Leeds U v Derby Co	2-2, 1-3
Wolverhampton W v Carlisle U	3-1
Blackpool v WBA	0-0, 1-2
Plymouth Arg v West Ham U	3-0
Birmingham C v Tottenham H	3-3, 2-4

Fourth Round

Burnley v Leyton O	1-1, 1-0
Everton v Manchester C	2-0
Peterborough U v Sheffield U	1-3
Norwich C v Ipswich T	1-1, 2-1
Fulham v Walsall	2-2, 2-0
Sunderland v Port Vale	0-0, 1-3
Stoke C v Blackburn R	0-1
Shrewsbury T v Middlesbrough	2-2, 1-5
Oldham Ath v Liverpool	1-2
Preston NE v Weymouth	2-0
Manchester U v Arsenal	1-0
Nottingham F v Sheffield W	0-2
Aston Villa v Huddersfield T	2-1
Charlton Ath v Derby Co	2-1
Wolverhampton W v WBA	1-2
Plymouth Arg v Tottenham H	1-5

Fifth Round

Burnley v Everton	3-1
Sheffield U v Norwich C	3-1
Fulham v Port Vale	1-0
Blackburn R v Middlesbrough	2-1
Liverpool v Preston NE	0-0, 0-0, 0-1
Manchester U v Sheffield W	0-0, 2-0
Aston Villa v Charlton Ath	2-1
WBA v Tottenham H	2-4

Sixth Round

Sheffield U v Burnley	0-1
Fulham v Blackburn R	2-2, 1-0
Preston NE v Manchester U	0-0, 1-2
Tottenham H v Aston Villa	2-0

Semi-Final

Burnley v Fulham	[1]1-1, 2-1
Manchester U v Tottenham H	[2]1-3

Final

Burnley 1, Tottenham H 3

[1] At Villa Park, replay at Leicester. [2] At Hillsborough.

FA CUP 1962–63

Third Round

Grimsby T v Leicester C	1-3
Mansfield T v Ipswich T	2-3
Leyton O v Hull C	1-1, 2-0
Derby Co v Peterborough U	2-0
Walsall v Manchester C	0-1
Birmingham C v Bury	3-3, 0-2
Norwich C v Blackpool	1-1, 3-1
Bradford C v Newcastle	1-6
Arsenal v Oxford U	5-1
Shrewsbury T v Sheffield W	1-1, 1-2
Tottenham H v Burnley	0-3
Wrexham v Liverpool	0-3
West Ham U v Fulham	0-0, 2-1
Swansea T v QPR	2-0
Luton T v Swindon T	0-2
Barnsley v Everton	0-3
Plymouth Arg v WBA	1-5
Nottingham F v Wolverhampton W	4-3
Blackburn R v Middlesbrough	1-1, 1-3
Leeds U v Stoke C	3-1
Southampton v York C	5-0
Watford v Rotherham U	2-0
Gillingham v Port Vale	2-4
Sheffield U v Bolton W	3-1
Portsmouth v Scunthorpe U	1-1, 2-1
Lincoln C v Coventry C	1-5
Carlisle U v Gravesend	0-1
Preston NE v Sunderland	1-4
Charlton Ath v Cardiff C	1-0
Tranmere R v Chelsea	2-2, 1-3
Bristol C v Aston Villa	1-1, 2-3
Manchester U v Huddersfield T	5-0

Fourth Round

Leicester C v Ipswich T	3-1
Leyton O v Derby Co	3-0
Manchester C v Bury	1-0
Norwich C v Newcastle U	5-0
Arsenal v Sheffield W	2-0
Burnley v Liverpool	1-1, 1-2
West Ham U v Swansea T	1-0
Swindon T v Everton	1-5
WBA v Nottingham F	0-0, 1-2
Middlesbrough v Leeds U	0-2
Southampton v Watford	3-1
Port Vale v Sheffield U	1-2
Portsmouth v Coventry C	1-1, 2-2, 1-2
Gravesend v Sunderland	1-1, 2-5
Charlton Ath v Chelsea	0-3
Manchester U v Aston Villa	1-0

Fifth Round

Leyton O v Leicester C	0-1
Manchester C v Norwich C	1-2
Arsenal v Liverpool	1-2
West Ham U v Everton	1-0
Nottingham F v Leeds U	3-0
Southampton v Sheffield U	1-0
Coventry C v Sunderland	2-1
Manchester U v Chelsea	2-1

Sixth Round

Norwich C v Leicester C	0-2
Liverpool v West Ham U	1-0
Nottingham F v Southampton	1-1, 3-3, 0-5
Coventry C v Manchester U	1-3

Semi-Final

Leicester C v Liverpool	[1]1-0
Southampton v Manchester U	[2]0-1

Final

Leicester C 1, Manchester U 3

[1] At Hillsborough. [2] At Villa Park.

FA CUP 1963–64

Third Round

West Ham U v Charlton Ath	3-0
Leicester C v Leyton O	2-3
Aston Villa v Aldershot	0-0, 1-2
Swindon T v Manchester C	2-1
Burnley v Rotherham U	1-1, 3-2
Newport Co v Sheffield W	3-2
Tottenham H v Chelsea	1-1, 0-2
Plymouth Arg v Huddersfield T	0-1
Sunderland v Northampton T	2-0
Doncaster R v Bristol C	2-2, 0-2
Cardiff C v Leeds U	0-1
Hull C v Everton	1-1, 1-2
Scunthorpe U v Barnsley	2-2, 2-3
Yeovil v Bury	0-2
Southampton v Manchester U	2-3
Bristol R v Norwich C	2-1
Ipswich T v Oldham Ath	6-3
Stoke C v Portsmouth	4-1
Lincoln C v Sheffield U	0-4
Swansea T v Barrow	4-1
WBA v Blackpool	2-2, 1-0
Arsenal v Wolverhampton W	2-1
Liverpool v Derby Co	5-0
Birmingham C v Port Vale	1-2
Oxford U v Chesterfield	1-0
Brentford v Middlesbrough	2-1
Blackburn R v Grimsby T	4-0
Fulham v Luton T	4-1
Newcastle U v Bedford T	1-2
Carlisle U v QPR	2-0
Bath C v Bolton W	1-1, 0-3
Nottingham F v Preston NE	0-0, 0-1

Fourth Round

Leyton O v West Ham U	1-1, 0-3
Aldershot v Swindon T	1-2
Burnley v Newport Co	2-1
Chelsea v Huddersfield T	1-2
Sunderland v Bristol C	6-1
Leeds U v Everton	1-1, 0-2
Barnsley v Bury	2-1
Manchester U v Bristol R	4-1
Ipswich T v Stoke C	1-1, 0-1
Sheffield U v Swansea T	1-1, 0-4
WBA v Arsenal	3-3, 0-2
Liverpool v Port Vale	0-0, 2-1
Oxford U v Brentford	2-2, 2-1
Blackburn R v Fulham	2-0
Bedford T v Carlisle U	0-3
Bolton W v Preston NE	2-2, 1-2

Fifth Round

Swindon T v West Ham U	1-3
Burnley v Huddersfield T	3-0
Sunderland v Everton	3-1
Barnsley v Manchester U	0-4
Stoke C v Swansea T	2-2, 0-2
Arsenal v Liverpool	0-1
Oxford U v Blackburn R	3-1
Preston NE v Carlisle U	1-0

Sixth Round

West Ham U v Burnley	3-2
Manchester U v Sunderland	3-3, 2-2, 5-1
Liverpool v Swansea T	1-2
Oxford U v Preston NE	1-2

Semi-Final

West Ham U v Manchester U	[1]3-1
Swansea T v Preston NE	[2]1-2

Final

Preston NE 2, West Ham U 3

[1] At Hillsborough. [2] At Villa Park.

FA CUP 1964–65

Third Round
Liverpool v WBA 2-1
Bristol R v Stockport Co 0-0, 2-3
Bolton W v Workington 4-1
Barnet v Preston NE 2-3
Leicester C v Blackburn R 2-2, 2-1
Plymouth Arg v Derby Co 4-2
Middlesbrough v Oldham Ath 6-2
Cardiff C v Charlton Ath 1-2
Chelsea v Northampton T 4-1
West Ham U v Birmingham C 4-2
Torquay U v Tottenham H 3-3, 1-5
Swindon T v Ipswich T 1-2
Chesterfield v Peterborough U 0-3
Darlington v Arsenal 0-2
Swansea T v Newcastle U 1-0
Doncaster R v Huddersfield T 0-1
Portsmouth v Wolverhampton W 0-0, 2-3
Rotherham U v Lincoln C 5-1
Bristol C v Sheffield U 1-1, 0-3
Aston Villa v Coventry C 3-0
Stoke C v Blackpool 4-1
Manchester U v Chester 2-1
Reading v Newport Co 2-2, 1-0
Burnley v Brentford 1-1, 2-0
Southampton v Leyton O 3-1
Crystal Palace v Bury 5-1
Luton T v Sunderland 0-3
Nottingham F v Norwich C 1-0
Fulham v Millwall 3-3, 0-2
Manchester C v Shrewsbury T 1-1, 1-3
Everton v Sheffield W 2-2, 3-0
Leeds U v Southport 3-0

Fourth Round
Liverpool v Stockport Co 1-1, 2-0
Preston NE v Bolton W 1-2
Leicester C v Plymouth Arg 5-0
Charlton Ath v Middlesbrough 1-1, 1-2
West Ham U v Chelsea 0-1
Tottenham H v Ipswich T 5-0
Peterborough U v Arsenal 2-1
Swansea T v Huddersfield T 1-0
Wolverhampton W v Rotherham U 2-2, 3-0
Sheffield U v Aston Villa 0-2
Stoke C v Manchester U 0-0, 0-1
Reading v Burnley 1-1, 0-1
Southampton v Crystal Palace 1-2
Sunderland v Nottingham F 1-3
Millwall v Shrewsbury T 1-2
Leeds U v Everton 1-1, 2-1

Fifth Round
Bolton W v Liverpool 0-1
Middlesbrough v Leicester C 0-3
Chelsea v Tottenham H 1-0
Peterborough U v Swansea T 0-0, 2-0
Aston Villa v Wolverhampton W 1-1, 0-0, 1-3
Manchester U v Burnley 2-1
Crystal Palace v Nottingham F 3-1
Leeds U v Shrewsbury T 2-0

Sixth Round
Leicester C v Liverpool 0-0, 0-1
Chelsea v Peterborough U 5-1
Wolverhampton W v Manchester U 3-5
Crystal Palace v Leeds U 0-3

Semi-Final
Liverpool v Chelsea [1]2-0
Manchester U v Leeds U [2]0-0, 0-1

Final
Leeds U 1, Liverpool 2

[1] At Villa Park. [2] At Hillsborough, replay at Nottingham Forest.

FA CUP 1965–66

Third Round
Everton v Sunderland 3-0
Bedford T v Hereford U 2-1
Swindon T v Coventry C 1-2
Folkestone v Crewe Alex 1-5
Blackpool v Manchester C 1-1, 1-3
Grimsby T v Portsmouth 0-0, 3-1
Birmingham C v Bristol C 3-2
Aston Villa v Leicester C 1-2
Derby Co v Manchester U 2-5
Rotherham U v Southend U 3-2
Wolverhampton W v Altrincham 5-0
Sheffield U v Fulham 3-1
Bolton W v WBA 3-0
Charlton Ath v Preston NE 2-3
Tottenham H v Middlesbrough 4-0
Bournemouth v Burnley 1-1, 0-7
Liverpool v Chelsea 1-2
Leeds U v Bury 6-0
QPR v Shrewsbury T 0-0, 0-1
Carlisle U v Crystal Palace 3-0
Hull C v Southampton 1-0
Northampton T v Nottingham F 1-2
Southport v Ipswich T 0-0, 3-2
Cardiff C v Port Vale 2-1
Leyton O v Norwich C 1-3
Stoke C v Walsall 0-2
Oldham Ath v West Ham U 2-2, 1-2
Blackburn R v Arsenal 3-0
Plymouth Arg v Corby T 6-0
Huddersfield T v Hartlepools U 3-1
Chester v Newcastle U 1-3
Reading v Sheffield W 2-3

Fourth Round
Bedford T v Everton 0-3
Crewe Alex v Coventry C 1-1, 1-4
Manchester C v Grimsby T 2-0
Birmingham C v Leicester C 1-2
Manchester U v Rotherham U 0-0, 1-0
Wolverhampton W v Sheffield U 3-0
Bolton W v Preston NE 1-1, 2-3
Tottenham H v Burnley 4-3
Chelsea v Leeds U 1-0
Shrewsbury T v Carlisle U 0-0, 1-1, 4-3
Hull C v Nottingham F 2-0
Southport v Cardiff C 2-0
Norwich C v Walsall 3-2
West Ham U v Blackburn R 3-3, 1-4
Plymouth Arg v Huddersfield T 0-2
Newcastle U v Sheffield W 1-2

Fifth Round
Everton v Coventry C 3-0
Manchester C v Leicester C 2-2, 1-0
Wolverhampton W v Manchester U 2-4
Preston NE v Tottenham H 2-1
Chelsea v Shrewsbury T 3-2
Hull C v Southport 2-0
Norwich C v Blackburn R 2-2, 2-3
Huddersfield T v Sheffield W 1-2

Sixth Round
Manchester C v Everton 0-0, 0-0, 0-2
Preston NE v Manchester U 1-1, 1-3
Chelsea v Hull C 2-2, 3-1
Blackburn R v Sheffield W 1-2

Semi-Final
Everton v Manchester U [1]1-0
Chelsea v Sheffield W [2]0-2

Final
Everton 3, Sheffield W 2

[1] At Bolton. [2] At Villa Park.

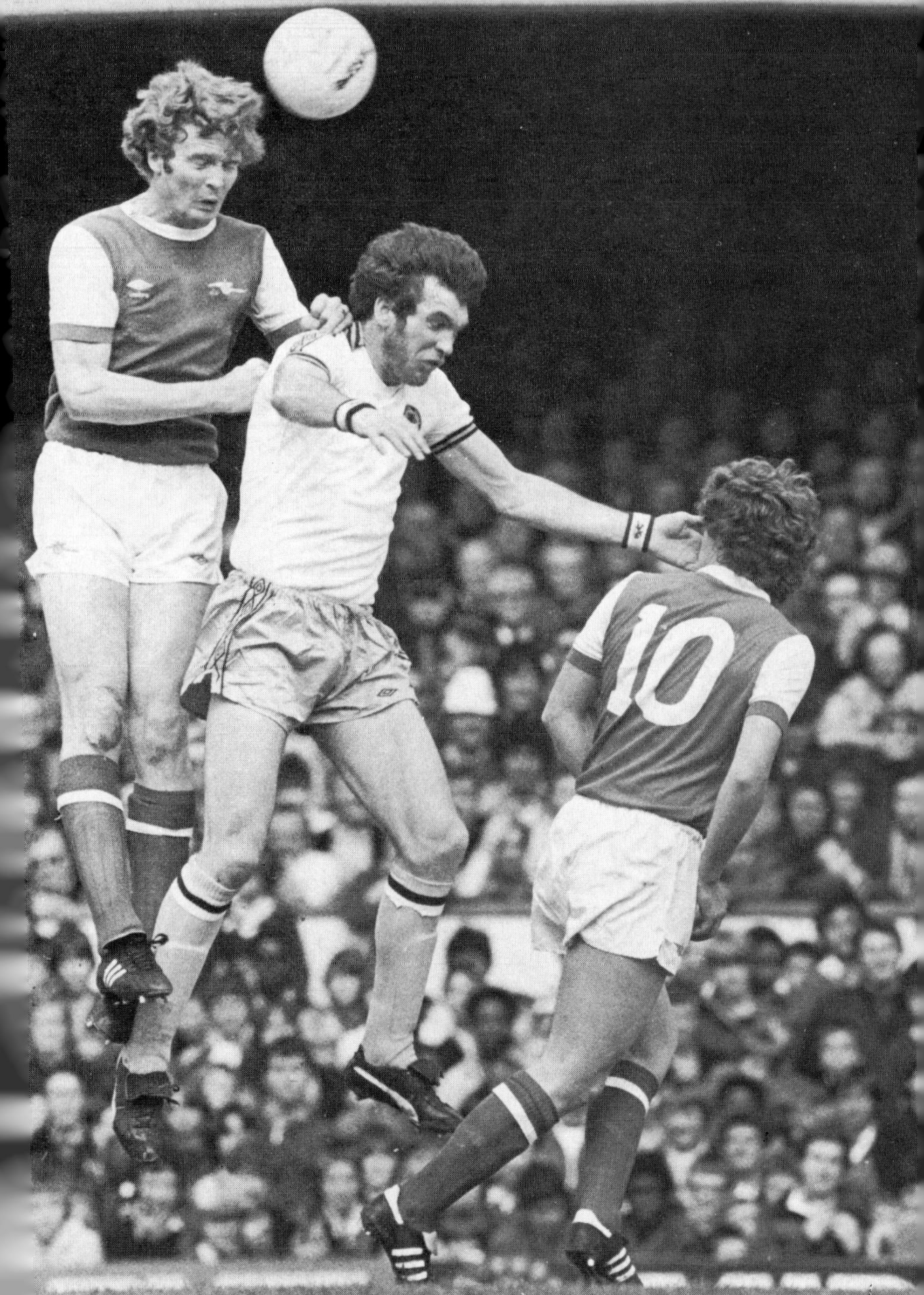

Aston Villa were confirmed as League Champions on the last day of the season despite losing 2-0 at Highbury. Villa striker Peter Withe is seen here in a tussle with Arsenal's Willie Young.

Ricky Villa will long remember the centenary FA Cup Final. Substituted at Wembley after an indifferent performance, he capped a superb display in the replay with the goal of the final for Tottenham Hotspur.

West Ham United manager John Lyall makes a point to Frank Lampard during the break before extra time in the League Cup Final against Liverpool. The Merseysiders were taken to a replay before winning 2-1.

Alan Kennedy (left) and Phil Neal celebrate Liverpool's 1-0 win over Real Madrid in the European Champions Cup Final. Kennedy scored the goal which enabled Liverpool to win the Cup for the third time in five years.

John Wark, scorer of fourteen goals in the competition, played a major part in Ipswich Town's UEFA Cup success. Ipswich won an exciting two-leg final against AZ67 Alkmaar by 5-4 on aggregate.

Runners-up in the previous season, Celtic won the Scottish Premier Division Championship with a handsome seven point margin over Aberdeen. Tommy Burns (no. 10) rounded off a fine season for Celtic by winning his first international cap.

Bobby Russell of Rangers evades a tackle in the Scottish FA Cup Final replay. Rangers went on to beat Dundee United 4-1 after a 0-0 draw first time round.

A shot from Graeme Payne (Dundee United) is touched over the bar by Dundee's keeper Bobby Geddes during the Scottish League Cup Final, which United went on to win 3-0.

FA CUP 1966–67

Third Round

Huddersfield T v Chelsea	1-2
Aldershot v Brighton	0-0, 1-3
Bradford v Fulham	1-3
Charlton Ath v Sheffield U	0-1
Manchester U v Stoke C	2-0
Norwich C v Derby Co	3-0
Sheffield W v QPR	3-0
Mansfield T v Middlesbrough	2-0
Sunderland v Brentford	5-2
Bedford T v Peterborough U	2-6
Leeds U v Crystal Palace	3-0
Northampton T v WBA	1-3
Barnsley v Cardiff C	1-1, 1-2
Manchester C v Leicester C	2-1
Ipswich T v Shrewsbury T	4-1
Blackburn R v Carlisle U	1-2
Nuneaton T v Rotherham U	1-1, 0-1
Birmingham C v Blackpool	2-1
Bolton W v Crewe Alex	1-0
Bristol R v Arsenal	0-3
Millwall v Tottenham H	0-0, 0-1
Hull C v Portsmouth	1-1, 2-2, 1-3
Halifax T v Bristol C	1-1, 1-4
Barrow v Southampton	2-2, 0-3
Nottingham F v Plymouth Arg	2-1
Coventry C v Newcastle U	3-4
West Ham U v Swindon T	3-3, 1-3
Bury v Walsall	2-0
Oldham Ath v Wolverhampton W	2-2, 1-4
Burnley v Everton	0-0, 1-2
Watford v Liverpool	0-0, 1-3
Preston NE v Aston Villa	0-1

Fourth Round

Brighton v Chelsea	1-1, 0-4
Fulham v Sheffield U	1-1, 1-3
Manchester U v Norwich C	1-2
Sheffield W v Mansfield T	4-0
Sunderland v Peterborough U	7-1
Leeds U v WBA	5-0
Cardiff C v Manchester C	1-1, 1-3
Ipswich T v Carlisle U	2-0
Rotherham U v Birmingham C	0-0, 1-2
Bolton W v Arsenal	0-0, 0-3
Tottenham H v Portsmouth	3-1
Bristol C v Southampton	1-0
Nottingham F v Newcastle U	3-0
Swindon T v Bury	2-1
Wolverhampton W v Everton	1-1, 1-3
Liverpool v Aston Villa	1-0

Fifth Round

Chelsea v Sheffield U	2-0
Norwich C v Sheffield W	1-3
Sunderland v Leeds U	1-1, 1-1, 1-2
Manchester C v Ipswich T	1-1, 3-0
Birmingham C v Arsenal	1-0
Tottenham H v Bristol C	2-0
Nottingham F v Swindon T	0-0, 1-1, 3-0
Everton v Liverpool	1-0

Sixth Round

Chelsea v Sheffield W	1-0
Leeds U v Manchester C	1-0
Birmingham C v Tottenham H	0-0, 0-6
Nottingham F v Everton	3-2

Semi-Final

Chelsea v Leeds U	[1]1-0
Tottenham H v Nottingham F	[2]2-1

Final

Chelsea 1, Tottenham H 2

[1] At Villa Park. [2] At Hillsborough.

FA CUP 1967–68

Third Round

Newcastle U v Carlisle U	0-1
Southport v Everton	0-1
Coventry C v Charlton Ath	3-0
Tranmere R v Huddersfield T	2-1
Aston Villa v Millwall	3-0
Rotherham U v Wolverhampton W	1-0
Manchester C v Reading	0-0, 7-0
Barrow v Leicester C	1-2
Leeds U v Derby Co	2-0
Nottingham F v Bolton W	4-2
Middlesbrough v Hull C	1-1, 2-2, 1-0
Bristol C v Bristol R	0-0, 2-1
Stoke C v Cardiff C	4-1
Burnley v West Ham U	1-3
Watford v Sheffield U	0-1
Blackpool v Chesterfield	2-1
Doncaster R v Swansea T	0-2
Shrewsbury T v Arsenal	1-1, 0-2
Halifax T v Birmingham C	2-4
Orient v Bury	1-0
Sheffield W v Plymouth Arg	3-0
Swindon T v Blackburn R	1-0
Chelsea v Ipswich T	3-0
Norwich C v Sunderland	1-1, 1-0
Fulham v Macclesfield	4-2
Peterborough U v Portsmouth	0-1
Colchester U v WBA	1-1, 0-4
Southampton v Newport Co	1-1, 3-2
Manchester U v Tottenham H	2-2, 0-1
QPR v Preston NE	1-3
Walsall v Crystal Palace	1-1, 2-1
Bournemouth v Liverpool	0-0, 1-4

Fourth Round

Carlisle U v Everton	0-2
Coventry C v Tranmere R	1-1, 0-2
Aston Villa v Rotherham U	0-1
Manchester C v Leicester C	0-0, 3-4
Leeds U v Nottingham F	2-1
Middlesbrough v Bristol C	1-1, 1-2
Stoke C v West Ham U	0-3
Sheffield U v Blackpool	2-1
Swansea T v Arsenal	0-1
Birmingham C v Orient	3-0
Sheffield W v Swindon T	2-1
Chelsea v Norwich C	1-0
Fulham v Portsmouth	0-0, 0-1
WBA v Southampton	1-1, 3-2
Tottenham H v Preston NE	3-1
Walsall v Liverpool	0-0, 2-5

Fifth Round

Everton v Tranmere R	2-0
Rotherham U v Leicester C	1-1, 0-2
Leeds U v Bristol C	2-0
West Ham U v Sheffield U	1-2
Arsenal v Birmingham C	1-1, 1-2
Sheffield W v Chelsea	2-2, 0-2
Portsmouth v WBA	1-2
Tottenham H v Liverpool	1-1, 1-2

Sixth Round

Everton v Leicester C	3-1
Leeds U v Sheffield U	1-0
Birmingham C v Chelsea	1-0
WBA v Liverpool	0-0, 1-1, 2-1

Semi-Final

Everton v Leeds U	[1]1-0
WBA v Birmingham C	[2]2-0

Final

Everton 0, WBA 1

[1] At Old Trafford. [2] At Villa Park.

FA CUP 1968–69

Third Round

Manchester C v Luton T	1-0
Newcastle U v Reading	4-0
Blackburn R v Stockport Co	2-0
Portsmouth v Chesterfield	3-0
Walsall v Tottenham H	0-1
Hull C v Wolverhampton W	1-3
Oxford U v Southampton	1-1, 0-2
Aston Villa v QPR	2-1
Sheffield W v Leeds U	1-1, 3-1
Birmingham C v Lincoln C	2-1
Exeter C v Manchester U	1-3
Watford v Port Vale	2-0
Bolton W v Northampton T	2-1
Bristol R v Kettering	1-1, 2-1
Coventry C v Blackpool	3-1
Everton v Ipswich T	2-1
WBA v Norwich C	3-0
Sunderland v Fulham	1-4
Cardiff C v Arsenal	0-0, 0-2
Charlton Ath v Crystal Palace	0-0, 2-0
Preston NE v Nottingham F	3-0
Chelsea v Carlisle U	2-0
York C v Stoke C	0-2
Swansea T v Halifax T	0-1
Mansfield T v Sheffield U	2-1
Swindon T v Southend U	0-2
Bury v Huddersfield T	1-2
West Ham U v Bristol C	3-2
Liverpool v Doncaster R	2-0
Burnley v Derby Co	3-1
Middlesbrough v Millwall	1-1, 0-1
Barnsley v Leicester C	1-1, 1-2

Fourth Round

Newcastle U v Manchester C	0-0, 0-2
Blackburn R v Portsmouth	4-0
Tottenham H v Wolverhampton W	2-1
Southampton v Aston Villa	2-2, 1-2
Sheffield W v Birmingham C	2-2, 1-2
Manchester U v Watford	1-1, 2-0
Bolton W v Bristol R	1-2
Everton v Coventry C	2-0
WBA v Fulham	2-1
Arsenal v Charlton Ath	2-0
Preston NE v Chelsea	0-0, 1-2
Stoke C v Halifax T	1-1, 3-0
Mansfield T v Southend U	2-1
Huddersfield T v West Ham U	0-2
Liverpool v Burnley	2-1
Millwall v Leicester C	0-1

Fifth Round

Blackburn R v Manchester C	1-4
Tottenham H v Aston Villa	3-2
Birmingham C v Manchester U	2-2, 2-6
Bristol R v Everton	1-0
WBA v Arsenal	1-0
Chelsea v Stoke C	3-2
Mansfield T v West Ham U	3-0
Liverpool v Leicester C	0-0, 0-1

Sixth Round

Manchester C v Tottenham H	1-0
Manchester U v Everton	0-1
Chelsea v WBA	1-2
Mansfield T v Leicester C	0-1

Semi-Final

Manchester C v Everton	[1]1-0
WBA v Leicester C	[2]0-1

Final

Leicester C 0, Manchester C 1

[1] At Villa Park. [2] At Hillsborough.

FA CUP 1969–70

Third Round

Chelsea v Birmingham	3-0
Burnley v Wolverhampton W	3-0
Bradford C v Tottenham H	2-2, 0-5
Crystal Palace v Walsall	2-0
Aston Villa v Charlton Ath	1-1, 0-1
QPR v South Shields	4-1
Preston NE v Derby Co	1-1, 1-4
Sheffield U v Everton	2-1
Bolton W v Watford	1-2
Oxford U v Stoke C	0-0, 2-3
Gillingham v Newport Co	1-0
Rotherham U v Peterborough U	0-1
Coventry C v Liverpool	1-1, 0-3
Norwich C v Wrexham	1-2
Southampton v Newcastle U	3-0
Leicester C v Sunderland	1-0
Middlesbrough v West Ham U	2-1
York C v Cardiff C	1-1, 1-1, 3-1
Nottingham F v Carlisle U	0-0, 1-2
Huddersfield T v Aldershot	1-1, 1-3
Ipswich T v Manchester U	0-1
Hull C v Manchester C	0-1
Portsmouth v Tranmere R	1-2
Brentwood v Northampton T	0-1
Blackburn R v Swindon T	0-4
Chester v Bristol C	2-1
Sheffield W v WBA	2-1
Scunthorpe U v Millwall	2-1
Arsenal v Blackpool	1-1, 2-3
Mansfield T v Barnsley	3-2
Hillingdon v Sutton	0-0, 1-4
Leeds U v Swansea C	2-1

Fourth Round

Chelsea v Burnley	2-2, 3-1
Tottenham H v Crystal Palace	0-0, 0-1
Charlton Ath v QPR	2-3
Derby Co v Sheffield U	3-0
Watford v Stoke C	1-0
Gillingham v Peterborough U	5-1
Liverpool v Wrexham	3-1
Southampton v Leicester C	1-1, 2-4
Middlesbrough v York C	4-1
Carlisle U v Aldershot	2-2, 4-1
Manchester U v Manchester C	3-0
Tranmere R v Northampton T	0-0, 1-2
Swindon T v Chester	4-2
Sheffield W v Scunthorpe U	1-2
Blackpool v Mansfield T	0-2
Sutton v Leeds U	0-6

Fifth Round

Crystal Palace v Chelsea	1-4
QPR v Derby Co	1-0
Watford v Gillingham	2-1
Liverpool v Leicester C	0-0, 2-0
Carlisle v Middlesbrough	1-2
Northampton T v Manchester U	2-8
Swindon T v Scunthorpe U	3-1
Leeds U v Mansfield T	2-0

Sixth Round

QPR v Chelsea	2-4
Watford v Liverpool	1-0
Middlesbrough v Manchester U	1-1, 1-2
Swindon T v Leeds U	0-2

Semi-Final

Chelsea v Watford	[1]5-1
Manchester U v Leeds U	[2]0-0, 0-0, 0-1

Final

Chelsea 2, Leeds U 2
Chelsea 2, Leeds U 1[3]
(*in replay after extra time*)

[1] At White Hart Lane. [2] At Hillsborough, replay at Villa Park, 2nd replay at Bolton. [3] Final replay at Old Trafford.

FA CUP 1970–71

Third Round

Yeovil T v Arsenal	0-3
Portsmouth v Sheffield U	2-0
Crystal Palace v Chelsea	2-2, 0-2
Manchester C v Wigan Ath	1-0
Leicester C v Notts Co	2-0
Torquay U v Lincoln C	4-3
Oxford U v Burnley	3-0
Watford v Reading	5-0
Cardiff C v Brighton	1-0
Workington v Brentford	0-1
Hull C v Charlton Ath	3-0
Blackpool v West Ham U	4-0
Stoke C v Millwall	2-1
Huddersfield T v Birmingham C	1-1, 2-0
WBA v Scunthorpe U	0-0, 3-1
Newcastle U v Ipswich T	1-1, 1-2
Rochdale v Coventry C	2-1
Barnet v Colchester U	0-1
Rotherham U v Leeds U	0-0, 2-3
QPR v Swindon T	1-2
Everton v Blackburn R	2-0
Manchester U v Middlesbrough	0-0, 1-2
Southend U v Carlisle U	0-3
Tottenham H v Sheffield W	4-1
Chester v Derby Co	1-2
Wolverhampton W v Norwich C	5-1
Nottingham F v Luton T	1-1, 4-3
Sunderland v Orient	0-3
York C v Bolton W	2-0
Southampton v Bristol C	3-0
Swansea C v Rhyl	6-1
Liverpool v Aldershot	1-0

Fourth Round

Portsmouth v Arsenal	1-1, 2-3
Chelsea v Manchester C	0-3
Leicester C v Torquay U	3-0
Oxford U v Watford	1-1, 2-1
Cardiff C v Brentford	0-2
Hull C v Blackpool	2-0
Stoke C v Huddersfield T	3-3, 0-0, 1-0
WBA v Ipswich T	1-1, 0-3
Rochdale v Colchester U	3-3, 0-5
Leeds U v Swindon T	4-0
Carlisle U v Tottenham H	2-3
Derby Co v Wolverhampton W	2-1
Everton v Middlesbrough	3-0
Nottingham F v Orient	1-1, 1-0
York C v Southampton	3-3, 2-3
Liverpool v Swansea C	3-0

Fifth Round

Manchester C v Arsenal	1-2
Leicester C v Oxford U	1-1, 3-1
Hull C v Brentford	2-1
Stoke C v Ipswich T	0-0, 1-0
Colchester U v Leeds U	3-2
Everton v Derby Co	1-0
Tottenham H v Nottingham F	2-1
Liverpool v Southampton	1-0

Sixth Round

Leicester C v Arsenal	0-0, 0-1
Hull C v Stoke C	2-3
Everton v Colchester U	5-0
Liverpool v Tottenham H	0-0, 1-0

Semi-Final

Arsenal v Stoke C	[1]2-2, 2-0
Everton v Liverpool	[2]1-2

Final

Arsenal 2, Liverpool 1
(*After extra time*)

[1] At Hillsborough, replay at Villa Park. [2] At Old Trafford.

FA CUP 1971–72

Third Round

Birmingham C v Port Vale	3-0
Blackpool v Chelsea	0-1
Blyth Spartans v Reading	2-2, 1-6
Bolton W v Torquay U	2-1
Boston U v Portsmouth	0-1
Burnley v Huddersfield T	0-1
Bury v Rotherham U	1-1, 1-2
Charlton Ath v Tranmere R	0-0, 2-4
Crystal Palace v Everton	2-2, 2-3
Derby Co v Shrewsbury T	2-0
Leeds U v Bristol R	4-1
Manchester C v Middlesbrough	1-1, 0-1
Millwall v Nottingham F	3-1
Norwich C v Hull C	0-3
Orient v Wrexham	3-0
Oxford U v Liverpool	0-3
Peterborough U v Ipswich T	0-2
Preston NE v Bristol C	4-2
QPR v Fulham	1-1, 1-2
Sheffield U v Cardiff C	1-3
Southampton v Manchester U	1-1, 1-4
Stoke C v Chesterfield	2-1
Sunderland v Sheffield W	3-0
Swansea C v Gillingham	1-0
Swindon T v Arsenal	0-2
Tottenham H v Carlisle U	1-1, 3-1
Walsall v Bournemouth	1-0
Watford v Notts Co	1-4
WBA v Coventry C	1-2
West Ham U v Luton T	2-1
Wolverhampton W v Leicester C	1-1, 0-2
Newcastle U v Hereford U	2-2, 1-2

Fourth Round

Liverpool v Leeds U	0-0, 0-2
Cardiff C v Sunderland	1-1, 1-1, 3-1
Everton v Walsall	2-1
Tottenham H v Rotherham U	2-0
Birmingham C v Ipswich T	1-0
Portsmouth v Swansea C	2-0
Huddersfield T v Fulham	3-0
Hereford U v West Ham U	0-0, 1-3
Preston NE v Manchester U	0-2
Millwall v Middlesbrough	2-2, 1-2
Tranmere R v Stoke C	2-2, 0-2
Coventry C v Hull C	0-1
Leicester C v Orient	0-2
Chelsea v Bolton W	3-0
Derby Co v Notts Co	6-0
Reading v Arsenal	1-2

Fifth Round

Cardiff C v Leeds U	0-2
Everton v Tottenham H	0-2
Birmingham C v Portsmouth	3-1
Huddersfield T v West Ham U	4-2
Manchester U v Middlesbrough	0-0, 3-0
Stoke C v Hull C	4-1
Orient v Chelsea	3-2
Derby Co v Arsenal	2-2, 0-0, 0-1

Sixth Round

Leeds U v Tottenham H	2-1
Birmingham C v Huddersfield T	3-1
Manchester U v Stoke C	1-1, 1-2
Orient v Arsenal	0-1

Semi-Final

Leeds U v Birmingham C	[1]3-0
Arsenal v Stoke C	[2]1-1, [3]2-1

Final

Leeds U 1, Arsenal 0

[1] At Hillsborough. [2] At Villa Park. [3] At Old Trafford.

FA CUP 1972–73

Third Round

Arsenal v Leicester C	2-2, 2-1
Bradford C v Blackpool	2-1
Brighton & HA v Chelsea	0-2
Burnley v Liverpool	0-0, 0-3
Carlisle U v Huddersfield T	2-2, 1-0
Charlton Ath v Bolton W	1-1, 0-4
Chelmsford C v Ipswich T	1-3
Crystal Palace v Southampton	2-0
Everton v Aston Villa	3-2
Grimsby T v Preston NE	0-0, 1-0
Luton T v Crewe Alex	2-0
Manchester C v Stoke C	3-2
Margate v Tottenham H	0-6
Millwall v Newport Co	3-0
Newcastle U v Bournemouth	2-0
Norwich C v Leeds U	1-1, 1-1, 0-5
Notts Co v Sunderland	1-1, 0-2
Orient v Coventry C	1-4
Peterborough U v Derby Co	0-1
Plymouth Arg v Middlesbrough	1-0
Portsmouth v Bristol C	1-1, 1-4
Port Vale v West Ham U	0-1
QPR v Barnet	0-0, 3-0
Reading v Doncaster R	2-0
Sheffield W v Fulham	2-0
Scunthorpe U v Cardiff C	2-3
Stockport Co v Hull C	0-0, 0-2
Swindon T v Birmingham C	2-0
Watford v Sheffield U	0-1
WBA v Nottingham F	1-1, 0-0, 3-1
Wolverhampton W v Manchester U	1-0
York C v Oxford U	0-1

Fourth Round

Arsenal v Bradford C	2-0
Bolton W v Cardiff C	2-2, 1-1, 1-0
Carlisle U v Sheffield U	2-1
Chelsea v Ipswich T	2-0
Coventry C v Grimsby T	1-0
Derby Co v Tottenham H	1-1, 5-3
Everton v Millwall	0-2
Hull C v West Ham U	1-0
Leeds U v Plymouth Arg	2-1
Liverpool v Manchester C	0-0, 0-2
Newcastle U v Luton T	0-2
Oxford U v QPR	0-2
Sheffield W v Crystal Palace	1-1, 1-1, 3-2
Sunderland v Reading	1-1, 3-1
WBA v Swindon T	2-0
Wolverhampton W v Bristol C	1-0

Fifth Round

Bolton W v Luton T	0-1
Carlisle U v Arsenal	1-2
Coventry C v Hull C	3-0
Derby Co v QPR	4-2
Leeds U v WBA	2-0
Manchester C v Sunderland	2-2, 1-3
Sheffield W v Chelsea	1-2
Wolverhampton W v Millwall	1-0

Sixth Round

Chelsea v Arsenal	2-2, 1-2
Derby Co v Leeds U	0-1
Sunderland v Luton T	2-0
Wolverhampton W v Coventry C	2-0

Semi-Final

Arsenal v Sunderland	[1]1-2
Leeds U v Wolverhampton W	[2]1-0

Final

Leeds U 0, Sunderland 1

[1] At Hillsborough. [2] At Maine Road.

FA CUP 1973–74

Third Round

Aston Villa v Chester	3-1
Birmingham C v Cardiff C	5-2
Bolton W v Stoke C	3-2
Bradford C v Alvechurch	4-2
Bristol C v Hull C	1-1, 1-0
Cambridge U v Oldham Ath	2-2, 3-3, 1-2
Carlisle U v Sunderland	0-0, 1-0
Chelsea v QPR	0-0, 0-1
Crystal Palace v Wrexham	0-2
Derby Co v Boston U	0-0, 6-1
Everton v Blackburn R	3-0
Fulham v Preston NE	1-0
Grantham v Middlesbrough	0-2
Grimsby T v Burnley	0-2
Ipswich T v Sheffield U	3-2
Leicester C v Tottenham H	1-0
Liverpool v Doncaster R	2-2, 2-0
Manchester U v Plymouth Arg	1-0
Millwall v Scunthorpe U	1-1, 0-1
Newcastle U v Hendon	1-1, 4-0
Norwich C v Arsenal	0-1
Nottingham F v Bristol R	4-3
Orient v Bournemouth	2-1
Oxford U v Manchester C	2-5
Peterborough U v Southend U	3-1
Port Vale v Luton T	1-1, 2-4
Portsmouth v Swindon T	3-3, 1-0
Sheffield W v Coventry C	0-0, 1-3
Southampton v Blackpool	2-1
WBA v Notts Co	4-0
West Ham U v Hereford U	1-1, 1-2
Wolverhampton W v Leeds U	1-1, 0-1

Fourth Round

Arsenal v Aston Villa	1-1, 0-2
Coventry C v Derby Co	0-0, 1-0
Everton v WBA	0-0, 0-1
Fulham v Leicester C	1-1, 1-2
Hereford U v Bristol C	0-1
Liverpool v Carlisle U	0-0, 2-0
Luton T v Bradford C	3-0
Manchester U v Ipswich T	0-1
Newcastle U v Scunthorpe U	1-1, 3-0
Nottingham F v Manchester C	4-1
Oldham Ath v Burnley	1-4
Peterborough U v Leeds U	1-4
Portsmouth v Orient	0-0, 1-1, 2-0
QPR v Birmingham C	2-0
Southampton v Bolton W	3-3, 2-0
Wrexham v Middlesbrough	1-0

Fifth Round

Bristol C v Leeds U	1-1, 1-0
Burnley v Aston Villa	1-0
Coventry C v QPR	0-0, 2-3
Liverpool v Ipswich T	2-0
Luton T v Leicester C	0-4
Nottingham F v Portsmouth	1-0
Southampton v Wrexham	0-1
WBA v Newcastle U	0-3

Sixth Round

Bristol C v Liverpool	0-1
Burnley v Wrexham	1-0
Newcastle U v Nottingham F	4-3*, 0-0, 1-0
QPR v Leicester C	0-2

* FA ordered replay because of crowd invasion. Second and third games both played at Goodison Park

Semi-Final

Burnley v Newcastle U	[1]0-2
Leicester C v Liverpool	[2]0-0, [3]1-3

Final

Liverpool 3, Newcastle U 0

[1] At Hillsborough. [2] At Old Trafford. [3] At Villa Park.

FA CUP 1974–75

Third Round

Notts Co v Portsmouth	3-1
Arsenal v York C	1-1, 3-1
Blackburn R v Bristol R	1-2
Bolton W v WBA	0-0, 0-4
Brighton & HA v Leatherhead	0-1
Burnley v Wimbledon	0-1
Bury v Millwall	2-2, 1-1, 2-0
Chelsea v Sheffield W	3-2
Coventry C v Norwich C	2-0
Everton v Altrincham	1-1, 2-0
Fulham v Hull C	1-1, 2-2, 1-0
Leeds U v Cardiff C	4-1
Leicester C v Oxford U	3-1
Liverpool v Stoke C	2-0
Luton T v Birmingham C	0-1
Manchester U v Walsall	0-0, 2-3
Mansfield T v Cambridge U	1-0
Newcastle U v Manchester C	2-0
Nottingham F v Tottenham H	1-1, 1-0
Oldham Ath v Aston Villa	0-3
Orient v Derby Co	2-2, 1-2
Peterborough U v Tranmere R	1-0
Plymouth Arg v Blackpool	2-0
Preston NE v Carlisle U	0-1
Sheffield U v Bristol C	2-0
Southampton v West Ham U	1-2
Southend U v QPR	2-2, 0-2
Stafford R v Rotherham U	0-0, 2-0
Sunderland v Chesterfield	2-0
Swindon T v Lincoln C	2-0
Wolverhampton W v Ipswich T	1-2
Wycombe W v Middlesbrough	0-0, 0-1

Fourth Round

QPR v Notts Co	3-0
Aston Villa v Sheffield U	4-1
Bury v Mansfield T	1-2
Carlisle U v WBA	3-2
Chelsea v Birmingham C	0-1
Coventry C v Arsenal	1-1, 3-0
Ipswich T v Liverpool	1-0
Leatherhead v Leicester C	2-3
Leeds U v Wimbledon	0-0, 1-0
Middlesbrough v Sunderland	3-1
Plymouth Arg v Everton	1-3
Stafford R v Peterborough U	1-2
Walsall v Newcastle U	1-0
West Ham U v Swindon T	1-1, 2-1
Derby Co v Bristol R	2-0
Fulham v Nottingham F	0-0, 1-1, 1-1, 2-1

Fifth Round

Arsenal v Leicester C	0-0, 1-0
Birmingham C v Walsall	2-1
Everton v Fulham	1-2
Ipswich T v Aston Villa	3-2
Mansfield T v Carlisle U	0-1
Peterborough U v Middlesbrough	1-1, 2-0
West Ham U v QPR	2-1
Derby Co v Leeds U	0-1

Sixth Round

Arsenal v West Ham U	0-2
Birmingham C v Middlesbrough	1-0
Carlisle U v Fulham	0-1
Ipswich T v Leeds U	0-0, 1-1, 0-0, 3-2

Semi-Final

Fulham v Birmingham C	[1]1-1, [3]1-0
West Ham U v Ipswich T	[2]0-0, [4]2-1

Final

Fulham 0, West Ham U 2

[1] At Hillsborough. [2] At Villa Park. [3] At Maine Road. [4] At Stamford Bridge.

FA CUP 1975–76

Third Round

Chelsea v Bristol R	1-1, 1-0
Nottingham F v Peterborough U	0-0, 0-1
Aldershot v Lincoln C	1-2
Blackpool v Burnley	1-0
Brentford v Bolton W	0-0, 0-2
Charlton Ath v Sheffield W	2-1
Coventry C v Bristol C	2-1
Derby Co v Everton	2-1
Fulham v Huddersfield T	2-3
Hull C v Plymouth Arg	1-1, 4-1
Ipswich T v Halifax T	3-1
Leicester C v Sheffield U	3-0
Luton T v Blackburn R	2-0
Manchester C v Hartlepool	6-0
Manchester U v Oxford U	2-1
Middlesbrough v Bury	0-0, 2-3
Norwich C v Rochdale	1-1, 0-0, 2-1
Notts Co v Leeds U	0-1
Orient v Cardiff C	0-1
Portsmouth v Birmingham C	1-1, 1-0
QPR v Newcastle U	0-0, 1-2
Scarborough v Crystal Palace	1-2
Shrewsbury T v Bradford C	1-2
Southampton v Aston Villa	1-1, 2-1
Southend U v Brighton & HA	2-1
Sunderland v Oldham Ath	2-0
Swindon T v Tooting & Mitcham U	2-2, 1-2
Tottenham H v Stoke C	1-1, 1-2
WBA v Carlisle U	3-1
West Ham U v Liverpool	0-2
Wolverhampton W v Arsenal	3-0
York C v Hereford U	2-1

Fourth Round

Bradford C v Tooting & Mitcham U	3-1
Charlton Ath v Portsmouth	1-1, 3-0
Coventry C v Newcastle U	1-1, 0-5
Derby Co v Liverpool	1-0
Huddersfield T v Bolton W	0-1
Ipswich T v Wolverhampton W	0-0, 0-1
Leeds U v Crystal Palace	0-1
Leicester C v Bury	1-0
Manchester U v Peterborough U	3-1
Norwich C v Luton T	2-0
Southampton v Blackpool	3-1
Southend U v Cardiff C	2-1
Stoke C v Manchester C	1-0
Sunderland v Hull C	1-0
WBA v Lincoln C	3-2
York C v Chelsea	0-2

Fifth Round

Bolton W v Newcastle U	3-3, 0-0, 1-2
Chelsea v Crystal Palace	2-3
Derby Co v Southend U	1-0
Leicester C v Manchester U	1-2
Norwich C v Bradford C	1-2
Stoke C v Sunderland	0-0, 1-2
WBA v Southampton	1-1, 0-4
Wolverhampton W v Charlton Ath	3-0

Sixth Round

Bradford C v Southampton	0-1
Derby Co v Newcastle U	4-2
Manchester U v Wolverhampton W	1-1, 3-2
Sunderland v Crystal Palace	0-1

Semi-Final

Manchester U v Derby Co	[1]2-0
Southampton v Crystal Palace	[2]2-0

Final

Southampton 1, Manchester U 0

[1] At Hillsborough. [2] At Stamford Bridge.

FA CUP 1976–77

Third Round

Birmingham C v Portsmouth	1-0
Blackpool v Derby Co	0-0, 2-3
Burnley v Lincoln C	2-2, 1-0
Cardiff C v Tottenham H	1-0
Carlisle U v Matlock T	5-1
Charlton Ath v Blackburn R	1-1, 0-2
Coventry C v Millwall	1-0
Darlington v Orient	2-2, 0-0, 0-3
Everton v Stoke C	2-0
Fulham v Swindon T	3-3, 0-5
Halifax T v Luton T	0-1
Hereford U v Reading	1-0
Hull C v Port Vale	1-1, 1-3
Ipswich T v Bristol C	4-1
Kettering T v Colchester U	2-3
Leeds U v Norwich C	5-2
Leicester C v Aston Villa	0-1
Liverpool v Crystal Palace	0-0, 3-2
Manchester C v WBA	1-1, 1-0
Manchester U v Walsall	1-0
Northwich Vic v Watford	3-2
Nottingham F v Bristol R	1-1, 1-1, 6-0
Notts Co v Arsenal	0-1
Oldham Ath v Plymouth Arg	3-0
QPR v Shrewsbury T	2-1
Sheffield U v Newcastle U	0-0, 1-3
Southampton v Chelsea	1-1, 3-0
Southend U v Chester	0-4
Sunderland v Wrexham	2-2, 0-1
West Ham U v Bolton W	2-1
Wimbledon v Middlesbrough	0-0, 0-1
Wolverhampton W v Rotherham U	3-2

Fourth Round

Arsenal v Coventry C	3-1
Aston Villa v West Ham U	3-0
Birmingham C v Leeds U	1-2
Blackburn R v Orient	3-0
Cardiff C v Wrexham	3-2
Chester v Luton T	1-0
Colchester U v Derby Co	1-1, 0-1
Ipswich T v Wolverhampton W	2-2, 0-1
Liverpool v Carlisle U	3-0
Manchester U v QPR	1-0
Middlesbrough v Hereford U	4-0
Northwich Vic v Oldham Ath (*played at Maine Road*)	1-3
Port Vale v Burnley	2-1
Swindon T v Everton	2-2, 1-2
Nottingham F v Southampton	3-3, 1-2
Newcastle U v Manchester C	1-3

Fifth Round

Aston Villa v Port Vale	3-0
Cardiff C v Everton	1-2
Derby Co v Blackburn R	3-1
Leeds U v Manchester C	0-1
Liverpool v Oldham Ath	3-1
Middlesbrough v Arsenal	4-1
Southampton v Manchester U	2-2, 1-2
Wolverhampton W v Chester	1-0

Sixth Round

Everton v Derby Co	2-0
Liverpool v Middlesbrough	2-0
Manchester U v Aston Villa	2-1
Wolverhampton W v Leeds U	0-1

Semi-Final

Everton v Liverpool	[1]2-2, 0-3
Leeds U v Manchester U	[2]1-2

Final

Liverpool 1, Manchester U 2

[1] Both games at Maine Road. [2] At Hillsborough.

FA CUP 1977–78

Third Round

Orient v Norwich C	1-1, 1-0
Birmingham C v Wigan Ath	4-0
Blackburn R v Shrewsbury T	2-1
Blyth Spartans v Enfield	1-0
Brighton & HA v Scarborough	3-0
Bristol C v Wrexham	4-4, 0-3
Burnley v Fulham	1-0
Cardiff C v Ipswich T	0-2
Carlisle U v Manchester U	1-1, 2-4
Charlton Ath v Notts Co	0-2
Chelsea v Liverpool	4-2
Derby Co v Southend U	3-2
Everton v Aston Villa	4-1
Exeter C v Wolverhampton W	2-2, 1-3
Grimsby T v Southampton	0-0, 0-0, 1-4
Hartlepool U v Crystal Palace	2-1
Hull C v Leicester C	0-1
Leeds U v Manchester C	1-2
Luton T v Oldham Ath	1-1, 2-1
Mansfield T v Plymouth Arg	1-0
Middlesbrough v Coventry C	3-0
Nottingham F v Swindon T	4-1
Peterborough U v Newcastle U	1-1, 0-2
QPR v Wealdstone	4-0
Rotherham U v Millwall	1-1, 0-2
Sheffield U v Arsenal	0-5
Stoke C v Tilbury	4-0
Sunderland v Bristol R	0-1
Tottenham H v Bolton W	2-2, 1-2
Walsall v Swansea C	4-1
WBA v Blackpool	4-1
West Ham U v Watford	1-0

Fourth Round

Arsenal v Wolverhampton W	2-1
Bolton W v Mansfield T	1-0
Brighton & HA v Notts Co	1-2
Bristol R v Southampton	2-0
Chelsea v Burnley	6-2
Derby Co v Birmingham C	2-1
Ipswich T v Hartlepool U	4-1
Manchester U v WBA	1-1, 2-3
Middlesbrough v Everton	3-2
Millwall v Luton T	4-0
Newcastle U v Wrexham	2-2, 1-4
Nottingham F v Manchester U	2-1
Orient v Blackburn R	3-1
Stoke C v Blyth Sp	2-3
Walsall v Leicester C	1-0
West Ham U v QPR	1-1, 1-6

Fifth Round

Arsenal v Walsall	4-1
Bristol R v Ipswich T	2-2, 0-3
Derby Co v WBA	0-2
Orient v Chelsea	0-0, 2-1
Middlesbrough v Bolton W	2-0
Millwall v Notts Co	2-1
QPR v Nottingham F	1-1, 1-3
Wrexham v Blyth Sp	1-1, 2-1

Sixth Round

Middlesbrough v Orient	0-0, 1-2
Millwall v Ipswich T	1-6
WBA v Nottingham F	2-0
Wrexham v Arsenal	2-3

Semi-Final

Arsenal v Orient	[1]3-0
Ipswich v WBA	[2]3-1

Final

Arsenal 0, Ipswich T 1

[1] At Stamford Bridge. [2] At Highbury.

FA CUP 1978–79

Third Round

Birmingham C v Burnley	0-1
Brighton & HA v Wolverhampton W	2-3
Bristol C v Bolton W	3-1
Charlton Ath v Maidstone	1-1, 2-1
Coventry C v WBA	2-2, 0-4
Darlington v Colchester U	0-1
Fulham v QPR	2-0
Middlesbrough v Crystal Palace	1-1, 0-1
Newport Co v West Ham U	2-1
Notts Co v Reading	4-2
Orient v Bury	3-2
Sheffield U v Aldershot	0-0, 0-1
Leicester C v Norwich C	3-0
Sheffield W v Arsenal	1-1, 1-1, 2-2, 3-3, 0-2
Shrewsbury T v Cambridge U	3-1
Swansea C v Bristol R	0-1
Swindon T v Cardiff C	3-0
Wimbledon v Southampton	0-2
York C v Luton T	2-0
Ipswich T v Carlisle U	3-2
Millwall v Blackburn R	1-2
Nottingham F v Aston Villa	2-0
Southend U v Liverpool	0-0, 0-3
Sunderland v Everton	2-1
Tottenham H v Altrincham	1-1, 3-0
Manchester C v Rotherham U	0-0, 4-2
Manchester U v Chelsea	3-0
Newcastle U v Torquay U	3-1
Preston NE v Derby Co	3-0
Stoke C v Oldham Ath	0-1
Hartlepool U v Leeds U	2-6
Wrexham v Stockport Co	6-2

Fourth Round

Arsenal v Notts Co	2-0
Ipswich T v Orient	0-0, 2-0
Newcastle U v Wolverhampton W	1-1, 0-1
Nottingham F v York C	3-1
Shrewsbury T v Manchester C	2-0
Crystal Palace v Bristol C	3-0
Aldershot v Swindon T	2-1
Liverpool v Blackburn R	1-0
Newport Co v Colchester U	0-0, 0-1
Fulham v Manchester U	1-1, 0-1
Bristol R v Charlton Ath	1-0
Preston NE v Southampton	0-1
Tottenham H v Wrexham	3-3, 3-2
Burnley v Sunderland	1-1, 3-0
WBA v Leeds U	3-3, 2-0
Oldham Ath v Leicester C	3-1

Fifth Round

Aldershot v Shrewsbury T	2-2, 1-3
Colchester U v Manchester U	0-1
Crystal Palace v Wolverhampton W	0-1
Ipswich T v Bristol R	6-1
Nottingham F v Arsenal	0-1
Liverpool v Burnley	3-0
Oldham Ath v Tottenham H	0-1
WBA v Southampton	1-1, 1-2

Sixth Round

Ipswich T v Liverpool	0-1
Tottenham H v Manchester U	1-1, 0-2
Wolverhampton W v Shrewsbury T	1-1, 3-1
Southampton v Arsenal	1-1, 0-2

Semi-Final

Arsenal v Wolverhampton W	[1]2-0
Liverpool v Manchester U	[2]2-2, [3]0-1

Final

Arsenal 3, Manchester U 2

[1] At Villa Park. [2] At Maine Road. [3] At Goodison Park.

FA CUP 1979–80

Third Round

Altrincham v Orient	1-1, 1-2
Bristol C v Derby Co	6-2
Bristol R v Aston Villa	1-2
Birmingham C v Southampton	2-1
Burnley v Stoke C	1-0
Cardiff C v Arsenal	0-0, 1-2
Carlisle U v Bradford C	3-2
Chesham U v Cambridge U	0-2
Everton v Aldershot	4-1
Halifax T v Manchester C	1-0
Leeds U v Nottingham F	1-4
Leicester C v Harlow T	1-1, 0-1
Liverpool v Grimsby T	5-0
Luton T v Swindon T	0-2
Mansfield T v Brighton & HA	0-2
Millwall v Shrewsbury T	5-1
Newcastle U v Chester	0-2
Notts Co v Wolverhampton W	1-3
Oldham Ath v Coventry C	0-1
Preston NE v Ipswich T	0-3
QPR v Watford	1-2
Reading v Colchester U	2-0
Sunderland v Bolton W	0-1
Swansea C v Crystal Palace	2-2, 3-3, 2-1
Tottenham H v Manchester U	1-1, 1-0
WBA v West Ham U	1-1, 1-2
Wrexham v Charlton Ath	6-0
Yeovil T v Norwich C	0-3
Blackburn R v Fulham	1-1, 1-0
Rochdale v Bury	1-1, 2-3
Portsmouth v Middlesbrough	1-1, 0-3
Chelsea v Wigan Ath	0-1

Fourth Round

Arsenal v Brighton & HA	2-0
Birmingham C v Middlesbrough	2-1
Blackburn R v Coventry C	1-0
Bolton W v Halifax T	2-0
Bradford C v Ipswich T	1-2
Bury v Burnley	1-0
Cambridge U v Aston Villa	1-1, 1-4
Carlisle U v Wrexham	0-0, 1-3
Chester v Millwall	2-0
Everton v Wigan Ath	3-0
Nottingham F v Liverpool	0-2
Orient v West Ham U	2-3
Swansea C v Reading	4-1
Swindon T v Tottenham H	0-0, 1-2
Watford v Harlow T	4-3
Wolverhampton W v Norwich C	1-1, 3-2

Fifth Round

Blackburn R v Aston Villa	1-1, 0-1
Bolton W v Arsenal	1-1, 0-3
Everton v Wrexham	5-2
Ipswich T v Chester	2-1
Liverpool v Bury	2-0
Tottenham H v Birmingham C	3-1
West Ham U v Swansea C	2-0
Wolverhampton W v Watford	0-3

Sixth Round

Everton v Ipswich T	2-1
Tottenham H v Liverpool	0-1
Watford v Arsenal	1-2
West Ham U v Aston Villa	1-0

Semi-Final

Arsenal v Liverpool	[1]0-0, [3]1-1, [5]1-0
West Ham U v Everton	[2]1-1, [4]2-1

Final

Arsenal 0, West Ham U 1

[1] At Hillsborough. [2] At Villa Park. [3] Replay at Villa Park. [4] Replay at Elland Road. [5] 2nd replay at Coventry.

FA CUP FINALISTS 1872–1980

Some goalscorers in the early years are not available.
R: replay; aet: after extra time.

1871–72 THE WANDERERS R. de C. Welch; C. W. Alcock, M. P. Betts, A. G. Bonsor, E. E. Bowen, W. P. Crake, T. C. Hooman, E. Lubbock, A. C. Thompson, R. W. S. Vidal, C. H. R. Wollaston. (In alphabetical order.) *Scorer:* 'A. H. Chequer' (M. P. Betts).

1-0 ROYAL ENGINEERS Capt. Marindin; Capt. Merriman, Lieut. Addison; Lieut. Creswell, Lieut. Mitchell, Lieut. Renny-Tailyour; Lieut. Rich, Lieut. Goodwyn, Lieut. Muirhead, Lieut. Cotter, Lieut. Bogle.

1872–73 THE WANDERERS E. E. Bowen; C. M. Thompson, R. de C. Welch; Hon. A. F. Kinnaird, L. S. Howell, C. H. R. Wollaston; J. R. Sturgiss, Rev. H. H. Stewart, W. S. Kenyon-Slaney, R. K. Kingsford, A. G. Bonsor. *Scorers:* Wollaston, Kinnaird.

2-0 OXFORD UNIVERSITY A. Kirke-Smith; A. J. Leach, C. C. Mackarness; F. H. Birley, C. J. Longman, F. B. Chappell-Maddison; H. B. Cixon, W. B. Paton, R. W. S. Vidal, W. E. Sumner, C. J. Ottaway.

1873–74 OXFORD UNIVERSITY C. E. B. Neapean; C. C. Mackarness, F. H. Birley; F. T. Green, R. W. S. Vidal, C. J. Ottaway; R. H. Benson, F. J. Patton, W. S. Rawson, F. B. Chappell-Maddison, Rev. A. H. Johnson. *Scorers:* Mackarness, Patton.

2-0 ROYAL ENGINEERS Capt. Merriman; Major Marindin, Lieut. G. W. Addison; Lieut. G. C. Onslow, Lieut. H. G. Oliver, Lieut. T. Digby; Lieut. H. W. Renny-Tailyour, Lieut. H. E. Rawson, Lieut. J. E. Blackman, Lieut. A. K. Wood, Lieut. P. G. von Donop.

1874–75 ROYAL ENGINEERS Capt. Merriman; Lieut. G. H. Sim, Lieut. G. Onslow; Lieut. R. M. Ruck, Lieut. P. G. von Donop, Lieut. C. K. Wood; Lieut. H. E. Rawson, Lieut. R. H. Stafford, Capt. H. W. Renny-Tailyour, Lieut. Mein, Lieut. C. Wingfield Stratford.

1-1 OLD ETONIANS Capt. E. H. Drummond-Moray; M. Farrer, E. Lubbock; F. H. Wilson, Hon. A. F. Kinnaird, J. H. Stronge; F. J. Patton, C. E. Farmer, A. G. Bonsor, A. Lubbock, T.
***R*:2-0** Hammond. (C. J. Ottaway, W. S. Kenyon-Slaney, R. H. Benson and A. G. Thompson took part in the first match in place of A. Lubbock, T. Hammond, M. Farrer and Capt. E. H. Drummond-Moray.)

1875–76 THE WANDERERS W. D. O. Greig; A. Stratford, W. Lindsay; F. B. C. Maddison, F. H. Birley, C. H. R. Wollaston; H. Heron, F. Heron, J. H. Edwards, J. Kenrick, T. Hughes. *Scorers:* Wollaston, Hughes 2.

0-0 OLD ETONIANS Q. Hogg; E. Lubbock, Hon. E. Lyttelton; M. G. Faner, Hon. A. F. Kinnaird, J. H. Stronge; W. S. Kenyon-Slaney, Hon. A. Lyttelton, J. R. Sturgis, A. G. Bonsor, H. P.
***R*:3-0** Allene. (C. Meysey, A. C. Thompson and J. E. C. Welldon took part in the first match in place of J. H. Stronge, M. G. Faner and E. Lubbock.)

1876–77 THE WANDERERS F. H. Bitley; C. A. Denton, F. T. Green; H. Heron, T. Hughes, J. Kenrick; Hon. A. F. Kinnaird, W. Lindsay, A. Stratford, H. Wace, C. H. R. Wollaston. (In
2-1 alphabetical order.)
aet OXFORD UNIVERSITY E. H. Allington; J. Bain, O. R. Dunnell; J. H. Savory, A. H. Todd, E. W. Waddington; P. H. Fernandez, A. F. Hills, H. S. Otter, E. H. Parry, W. S. Rawson.

1877–78 THE WANDERERS J. Kirkpatrick; A. Stratford, W. Lindsay; Hon. A. F. Kinnaird, F. T. Green, C. H. R. Wollaston; H. Heron, J. G. Wylie, H. Wace, C. A. Denton, J. Kenrick.

3-1 ROYAL ENGINEERS L. B. Friend; J. H. Cowan, W. J. Morris; C. B. Mayne, F. C. Heath, C. E. Haynes; M. Lindsay, R. B. Hedley, F. G. Bond, H. H. Barnet, O. E. Ruck.

1878–79 OLD ETONIANS J. P. Hawtrey; E. Christian, L. Bury; Hon. A. F. Kinnaird, E. Lubbock, C. J. Clerke; N. Pares, H. C. Goodhart, H. Whitfield, J. B. T. Chevallier, H. Beaufoy.

1-0 CLAPHAM ROVERS R. H. Birkett; R. A. Ogilvie, E. Field; N. C. Bailey, J. F. M. Prinsep, F. L. Rawson; A. J. Stanley, S. W. Scott, H. S. Bevington, E. F. Growse, C. Keith-Falconer.

1879–80 CLAPHAM ROVERS R. H. Birkett; R. A. Ogilvie, E. Field; A. Weston, N. C. Bailey, H. Brougham; A. J. Stanley, F. Barry, F. J. Sparks, C. A. Lloyd-Jones, E. A. Ram. *Scorer:* Lloyd-Jones.

1-0 OXFORD UNIVERSITY P. C. Parr; C. W. Wilson, C. J. S. King; F. A. H. Phillips, B. Rogers, R. T. Heygate; G. B. Childs, J. Eyre, F. D. Crowdy, E. H. Hill, J. B. Lubbock.

1880–81 OLD CARTHUSIANS L. F. Gillett; W. H. Norris, E. G. Colvin; J. F. M. Prinsep, A. J. Vintcent, W. E. Hansell; L. M. Richards, W. R. Page, E. G. Wynyard, E. H. Parry, A. H. Todd.

3-0 OLD ETONIANS J. F. P. Rawlinson; C. W. Foley, C. H. French; Hon. A. F. Kinnaird, R. B. Farrer, J. B. T. Chevallier; W. J. Anderson, H. C. Goodhart, R. H. Macaulay, H. Whitfield, P. C. Novelli.

1881–82 OLD ETONIANS J. F. P. Rawlinson; T. H. French, P. J. de Paravicini; Hon. A. F. Kinnaird, C. W. Foley, P. C. Novelli; A. T. R. Dunn, R. H. Macaulay, H. C. Goodhart, W. J. Anderson, J. B. T. Chevallier. *Scorer:* Anderson.

1-0 BLACKBURN ROVERS R. Howarth; H. McIntyre, F. Suter; H. Sharples, F. W. Hargreaves, J. Duckworth; J. Douglas, T. Strachan, J. Brown, G. Avery, J. Hargreaves.

1882–83 BLACKBURN OLYMPIC T. Hacking; J. T. Ward, S. A. Warburton; T. Gibson, W. Astley, J. Hunter; T. Dewhurst, A. Matthews, G. Wilson, J. Costley, J. Yates. *Scorers:* Costley, Matthews.

2-1 OLD ETONIANS J. F. P. Rawlinson, T. H. French, P. J. de Paravicini, Hon. A. F. Kinnaird,
aet C. W. Foley, J. B. T. Chevallier, W. J. Anderson, R. H. Macaulay, H. C. Goodhart, A. T. B. Dunn, H. W. Bainbridge. *Scorer:* Goodhart.

1883–84 BLACKBURN ROVERS H. J. Arthur; J. Beverley, F. Suter; H. McIntyre, J. Hargreaves, J. H. Forrest; J. M. Lofthouse, J. Douglas, J. Sowerbutts, J. Inglis, J. Brown. *Scorers:* Brown, Forrest.
2-1 QUEEN'S PARK G. Gillespie; W. Arnott, J. MacDonald; C. Campbell, J. J. Gow, W. Anderson; W. W. Watt, Dr Smith, W. Harrower, D. S. Allan, R. M. Christie. *Scorer:* Christie.

1884–85 BLACKBURN ROVERS H. J. Arthur; R. G. Turner, F. Suter; H. McIntyre, G. Haworth, J. H. Forrest; J. M. Lofthouse, J. Douglas, J. Brown, H. E. Fecitt, J. Sowerbutts. *Scorers:* Forrest, Brown.
2-0 QUEEN'S PARK G. Gillespie; W. Arnott, W. Macleod; C. Campbell, J. MacDonald, A. Hamilton; W. Anderson, W. Sellar, W. Gray, N. McWhannel, D. S. Allan.

1885–86 BLACKBURN ROVERS H. J. Arthur; Turner, Suter; Douglas, Forrest, McIntyre; Walton, Strachan, Brown, Fecitt, J. Sowerbutts. (Heyes played in the first match at the Oval, but Walton
0-0 took his place in the replay.) *Scorers:* Sowerbutts, Brown.
***R*:2-0** WEST BROMWICH ALBION Roberts; H. Green, H. Bell; Horton, Perry, Timmins; Woodhall, T. Green, Bayliss, Loach, G. Bell.

1886–87 ASTON VILLA Warner; Coulton, Simmonds; Yates, Dawson, Burton; Davis, Brown, Hunter, Vaughton, Hodgetts. *Scorers:* Hodgetts, Hunter.
2-0 WEST BROMWICH ALBION Roberts; H. Green, Aldridge; Horton, Perry, Timmins; Woodhall, T. Green, Bayliss, Paddock, Pearson.

1887–88 WEST BROMWICH ALBION Roberts; Aldridge, Green; Horton, Perry, Timmins; Bassett, Woodhall, Bayliss, Wilson, Pearson. *Scorers:* Bayliss, Woodhall.
2-1 PRESTON NORTH END Dr R. H. Mills-Roberts; Howarth, N. J. Ross; Holmes, Russell, Graham; Gordon, J. Ross, J. Goodall, F. Dewhurst, Drummond. *Scorer:* Goodall.

1888–89 PRESTON NORTH END Dr R. H. Mills-Roberts; Howarth, Holmes; Drummond, Russell, Graham; Gordon, Ross, J. Goodall, F. Dewhurst, Thompson. *Scorers:* Dewhurst, Ross, Thompson.
3-0 WOLVERHAMPTON WANDERERS Baynton; Baugh, Mason; Fletcher, Allen, Lowder; Hunter, Wykes, Broodie, Wood, Knight.

1889–90 BLACKBURN ROVERS J. K. Horne; Southworth (Jas.), Forbes; Barton, Dewar, Forrest; Lofthouse, Campbell, Southworth (John), Walton, Townley. *Scorer:* Dewar, Southworth (John), Lofthouse, Townley 3.
6-1 SHEFFIELD WEDNESDAY Smith (J.); Brayshaw, H. Morley; Dungworth, Betts, Waller; Ingram, Woodhouse, Bennett, Mumford, Cawley. *Scorer:* Bennett.

1890–91 BLACKBURN ROVERS Pennington; Brandon, J. Forbes; Barton, Dewar, Forrest; Lofthouse, Walton, Southworth (John), Hall, Townley. *Scorers:* Dewar, Southworth, Townley.
3-1 NOTTS COUNTY Thraves; Ferguson, Hendry; H. Osborne, Calderhead, Shelton; A. McGregor, McInnes, Oswald, Locker, H. B. Daft. *Scorer:* Oswald.

1891–92 WEST BROMWICH ALBION Reader; Nicholson, McCulloch, Reynolds, Perry, Groves; Bassett, McLeod, Nicholls, Pearson, Geddes. *Scorers:* Geddes, Nicholls, Reynolds.
3-0 ASTON VILLA Warner; Evans, Cox; H. Devey, Cowan, Baird; Athersmith, J. Devey, Dickson, Campbell, Hodgetts.

1892–93 WOLVERHAMPTON WANDERERS Rose; Baugh, Swift; Malpass, Allen, Kinsey; R. Topham, Wykes, Butcher, Wood, Griffin. *Scorer:* Allen.
1-0 EVERTON Williams; Howarth, Kelso; Stewart, Holt, Boyle; Latta, Gordon, Maxwell, Chadwick, Milward.

1893–94 NOTTS COUNTY Toone; Harper, Hendry; Bramley, Calderhead, A. Shelton; Watson, Donnelly, Logan, Bruce, H. B. Daft. *Scorers:* Watson, Logan 3.
4-1 BOLTON WANDERERS Sutcliffe; Somerville, Jones; Gardiner, Paton, Hughes; Dickinson, Wilson, Tannahill, Bentley, Cassidy. *Scorer:* Cassidy.

1894–95 ASTON VILLA Wilkes; Spencer, Welford; Reynolds, Cowan (Jas.), Russell; Athersmith, Chatt, J. Devey, Hodgetts, S. Smith. *Scorer:* Chatt.
1-0 WEST BROMWICH ALBION Reader; Williams, Horton; Taggart, Higgins, T. Perry; Bassett, McLeod, Richards, Hutchinson, Banks.

1895–96 SHEFFIELD WEDNESDAY Massey; Earp, Langley; H. Brandon, Crawshaw, Petrie; Brash, Brady, L. Bell, Davis, Spiksley. *Scorer:* Spiksley 2.
2-1 WOLVERHAMPTON WANDERERS Tennant; Baugh, Dunn; Owen, Malpass, Griffiths; Tonks, Henderson, Beats, Wood, Black. *Scorer:* Black.

1896–97 ASTON VILLA Whitehouse; Spencer, Evans; Reynolds, Cowan (Jas.), Crabtree; Athersmith, J. Devey, Campbell, Wheldon, Cowan (John). *Scorers:* Campbell, Wheldon, Crabtree.
3-2 EVERTON Menham; Meecham, Storrier; Boyle, Holt, Stewart; Taylor, Bell, Hartley, Chadwick, Milward. *Scorers:* Bell, Boyle.

1897–98 NOTTINGHAM FOREST Allsop; Richie, Scott; Forman (Frank), McPherson, Wragg; McInnes, Richards, Benbow, Capes, Spouncer. *Scorers:* Capes 2, McPherson.
3-1 DERBY COUNTY Fryer; Methven, Leiper; Cox, A. Goodall, Turner; J. Goodall, Bloomer, Boag, Stevenson, McQueen. *Scorer:* Bloomer.

1898–99 SHEFFIELD UNITED Foulke; Thickett, Boyle; Johnson, Morren, Needham; Bennett, Beers, Hedley, Almond, Priest. *Scorers:* Bennett, Beers, Almond, Priest.
4-1 DERBY COUNTY Fryer; Methven, Staley; Cox, Paterson, May; Arkesden, Bloomer, Boag, McDonald, Allen. *Scorer:* Boag.

1899– BURY Thompson; Darrock, Davidson; Pray, Leeming, Ross; Richards, Wood, McLuckie, Sagar, Plant.
1900 *Scorers:* McLuckie 2, Wood, Plant.
4-0 SOUTHAMPTON Robinson; Meehan, Durber; Meston, Chadwick, Petrie; Turner, Yates, Farrell, Wood, Milward.

1900–01 TOTTENHAM HOTSPUR Clawley; Erentz, Tait; Norris, Hughes, Jones; Smith, Cameron, Brown, Copeland, Kirwan. *Scorers:* (First match) Brown 2; (Second match), Cameron, Smith, Brown.

2-2 SHEFFIELD UNITED Foulke; Thickett, Boyle; Johnson, Morren, Needham; Bennett, Field,
***R:*3-1** Hedley, Priest, Lipsham. *Scorers:* (First match) Bennett, Priest; (Second match) Priest.

1901–02 SHEFFIELD UNITED Foulke; Thickett, Boyle; Needham, Wilkinson, Johnson; Barnes, Common, Hedley, Priest, Lipsham. (Bennett was injured in the first match and Barnes took his place in the replay.) *Scorers:* (First match) Common; (Second match) Hedley, Barnes.

1-1 SOUTHAMPTON Robinson; C. B. Fry, Molyneux; Meston, Bowman, Lee; A. Turner, Wood,
***R:*2-1** Brown, Chadwick, J. Turner. *Scorers:* (First match) Wood; (Second match) Brown.

1902–03 BURY Monteith; Lindsey, McEwen; Johnson, Thorpe, Ross; Richards, Wood, Sagar, Leeming, Plant. *Scorers:* Ross, Sagar, Leeming 2, Wood, Plant.

6-0 DERBY COUNTY Fryer; Methven, Morris; Warren, A. Goodall, May; Warrington, York, Boag, Richards, Davis.

1903–04 MANCHESTER CITY Hillman; McMahon, Burgess; Frost, Hynds, S. B. Ashworth; Meredith, Livingstone, Gillespie, A. Turnbull, Booth. *Scorer:* Meredith.

1-0 BOLTON WANDERERS D. Davies; Brown, Struthers; Clifford, Greenhaigh, Freebairn; Stokes, Marsh, Yenson, White, Taylor.

1904–05 ASTON VILLA George; Spencer, Miles; Pearson, Leake, Windmill; Brawn, Garratty, Hampton, Bache, Hall. *Scorer:* Hampton 2.

2-0 NEWCASTLE UNITED Lawrence; McCombie, Carr; Gardner, Aitken, McWilliam; Rutherford, Howie, Appleyard, Veitch, Gosnell.

1905–06 EVERTON Scott; W. Balmer, Crelly; Makepeace, Taylor, Abbott; Sharp, Bolton, Young, Settle, H. P. Hardman. *Scorer:* Young.

1-0 NEWCASTLE UNITED Lawrence; McCombie, Carr; Gardner, Aitken, McWilliam; Rutherford, Howie, Veitch, Orr, Gosnell.

1906–07 SHEFFIELD WEDNESDAY Lyall; Layton, Burton; Brittleton, Crawshaw, Bartlett; Chapman, Bradshaw, Wilson, Stewart, Simpson. *Scorers:* Stewart, Simpson.

2-1 EVERTON Scott; W. Balmer, R. Balmer; Makepeace, Taylor, Abbott; Sharp, Bolton, Young, Settle, H. P. Hardman. *Scorer:* Sharp.

1907–08 WOLVERHAMPTON WANDERERS Lunn; Jones, Collins; Rev. K. R. G. Hunt, Wooldridge, Bishop; Harrison, Shelton, Hedley, Radford, Pedley. *Scorers:* Hunt, Hedley, Harrison.

3-1 NEWCASTLE UNITED Lawrence; McCracken, Pudan; Gardner, Veitch, McWilliam; Rutherford, Howie, Appleyard, Speedie, Wilson. *Scorer:* Howie.

1908–09 MANCHESTER UNITED Moger; Stacey, Hayes; Duckworth, Roberts, Bell; Meredith, Halse, J. Turnbull, A. Turnbull, Wall. *Scorer:* A. Turnbull.

1-0 BRISTOL CITY Clay; Annan, Cottle; Hanlin, Wedlock, Spear; Staniforth, Hardy, Gilligan, Burton, Hilton.

1909–10 NEWCASTLE UNITED Lawrence; McCracken, Carr; Veitch, Low, McWilliam; Rutherford, Howie, Shepherd, Higgins, Wilson. (Whitson was injured in first match and Carr took his place in the replay.) *Scorers:* (First match) Rutherford; (Second match) Shepherd 2 (1 pen).

1-1 BARNSLEY Mearns; Downs, Ness; Glendinning, Boyle, Utley; Bartrop, Gadsby, Lillycrop,
***R:*2-0** Tuffnell, Forman. *Scorer:* (First match) Tuffnell.

1910–11 BRADFORD CITY Mellors; Campbell, Taylor; Robinson, Torrance, McDonald; Logan, Spiers, O'Rourke, Devine, Thompson. (Gildea played centre-half in the first match.) *Scorer:* Spiers.

0-0 NEWCASTLE UNITED Lawrence; McCracken, Whitson; Veitch, Low, Willis; Rutherford,
***R:*1-0** Jobey, Stewart, Higgins, Wilson.

1911–12 BARNSLEY Cooper; Downs, Taylor; Glendinning, Bratley, Utley; Bartrop, Tuffnell,
0-0 Lillycrop, Travers, Moore. *Scorer:* Tuffnell.
***R:*2-0** WEST BROMWICH ALBION Pearson; Cook, Pennington; Baddeley, Buck, McNeal;
aet Jephcott, Wright, Pailor, Bowser, Shearman.

1912–13 ASTON VILLA Hardy; Lyons, Weston; Barber, Harrop, Leach; Wallace, Halse, Hampton, C. Stephenson, Bache. *Scorer:* Barber.

1-0 SUNDERLAND Butler; Gladwin, Ness; Cuggy, Thompson, Low; Mordue, Buchan, Richardson, Holley, Martin.

1913–14 BURNLEY Sewell; Bamford, Taylor; Halley, Boyle, Watson; Nesbit, Lindley, Freeman, Hodgson, Mosscrop. *Scorer:* Freeman.

1-0 LIVERPOOL Campbell; Longworth, Pursell; Fairfoul, Ferguson, McKinlay; Sheldon, Metcalf, Miller, Lacey, Nicholl.

1914–15 SHEFFIELD UNITED Gough; Cook, English; Sturgess, Brelsford, Utley; Simmons, Fazackerley, Kitchen, Masterman, Evans. *Scorers:* Simmons, Fazackerley, Kitchen.

3-0 CHELSEA Molyneux; Bettridge, Harrow; Taylor, Logan, Walker; Ford, Halse, Thompson, Croal, McNeil.

1919–20 ASTON VILLA Hardy; Smart, Weston; Ducat, Barson, Moss; Wallace, Kirton, Walker, C. Stephenson, Dorrell. *Scorer:* Kirton.

1-0 HUDDERSFIELD TOWN Mutch; Wood, Bullock; Slade, Wilson, Watson; Richardson,
aet Mann, Taylor, Swan, Islip.

1920–21 TOTTENHAM HOTSPUR Hunter; Clay, McDonald; Smith, Walters, Grimsdell; Banks, Seed, Cantrell, Bliss, Dimmock. *Scorer:* Dimmock.

1-0 WOLVERHAMPTON WANDERERS George; Woodward, Marshall; Gregory, Hodnet, Riley; Lea, Burrill, Edmonds, Potts, Brooks.

1921–22 HUDDERSFIELD TOWN Mutch; Wood, Wadsworth; Slade, Wilson, Watson; Richardson, Mann, Islip, Stephenson, W. H. Smith. *Scorer:* Smith (pen).

1-0 PRESTON NORTH END J. F. Mitchell; Hamilton, Doolan; Duxbury, McCall, Williamson; Rawlings, Jefferis, Roberts, Woodhouse, Quinn.

1922–23 BOLTON WANDERERS Pym; Haworth, Finney; Nuttall, Seddon, Jennings; Butler, Jack, J. R. Smith, J. Smith, Vizard. *Scorers:* Jack, J. R. Smith.

2-0 WEST HAM UNITED Hufton; Henderson, Young; Bishop, Kay, Tresadern, Richards, Brown, V. Watson, Moore, Ruffell.

1923–24 NEWCASTLE UNITED Bradley; Hampson, Hudspeth; Mooney, Spencer, Gibson; Low, Cowan, Harris, McDonald, Seymour. *Scorers:* Harris, Seymour.

2-0 ASTON VILLA Jackson; Smart, Mort; Moss, Dr V. E. Milne, Blackburn; York, Kirton, Capewell, Walker, Dorrell.

1924–25 SHEFFIELD UNITED Sutcliffe; Cook, Milton; Pantling, King, Green; Mercer, Boyle, Johnson, Gillespie, Tunstall. *Scorer:* Tunstall.

1-0 CARDIFF CITY Farquharson; Nelson, Blair; Wake, Keenor, Hardy; W. Davies; Gill, Nicholson, Beadles, J. Evans.

1925–26 BOLTON WANDERERS Pym; Haworth, Greenhalgh; Nuttall, Seddon, Jennings; Butler, Jack, J. R. Smith, J. Smith, Vizard. *Scorer:* Jack.

1-0 MANCHESTER CITY Goodchild; Cookson, McCloy; Pringle, Cowan, McMullan; Austin, Browell, Roberts, Johnson, Hicks.

1926–27 CARDIFF CITY Farquharson; Nelson, Watson; Keenor, Sloan, Hardy; Curtis, Irving, Ferguson, L. Davies, McLachlan. *Scorer:* Ferguson.

1-0 ARSENAL Lewis; Parker, Kennedy; Baker, Butler, John; Hulme, Buchan, Brain, Blyth, Hoar.

1927–28 BLACKBURN ROVERS Crawford; Hutton, Jones; Healless, Rankin, Campbell; Thornewell, Puddefoot, Roscamp, McLean, Rigby. *Scorers:* Roscamp 2, McLean.

3-1 HUDDERSFIELD TOWN Mercer; Goodall, Barkas; Redfern, Wilson, Steele; A. Jackson, Kelly, Brown, Stephenson, W. H. Smith. *Scorer:* Jackson.

1928–29 BOLTON WANDERERS Pym; Haworth, Finney; Kean, Seddon, Nuttall; Butler, McClelland, Blackmore, Gibson, W. Cook. *Scorers:* Butler, Blackmore.

2-0 PORTSMOUTH Gilfillan; Mackie, Bell; Nichol, McIlwaine, Thackeray; Forward, J. Smith, Weddle, Watson, F. Cook.

1929–30 ARSENAL Preedy; Parker, Hapgood; Baker, Seddon, John; Hulme, Jack, Lambert, James, Bastin. *Scorers:* James, Lambert.

2-0 HUDDERSFIELD TOWN Turner; Goodall, Spence; Naylor, Wilson, Campbell; A. Jackson, Kelly, Davies, Raw, W. H. Smith.

1930–31 WEST BROMWICH ALBION Pearson; Shaw, Trentham; Magee, W. Richardson, Edwards; Glidden, Carter, W. G. Richardson, Sandford, Wood. *Scorer:* W. G. Richardson 2.

2-1 BIRMINGHAM Hibbs; Liddell, Barkas; Cringan, Morrall, Leslie; Briggs, Crosbie, Bradford, Gregg, Curtis. *Scorer:* Bradford.

1931–32 NEWCASTLE UNITED McInroy; Nelson, Fairhurst; McKenzie, Davidson, Weaver; Boyd, Richardson, Allen, McMenemy, Lang. *Scorer:* Allen 2.

2-1 ARSENAL Moss; Parker, Hapgood; C. Jones, Roberts, Male; Hulme, Jack, Lambert, Bastin, John. *Scorer:* John.

1932–33 EVERTON Sagar; Cook, Cresswell; Britton, White, Thomson; Geldard, Dunn, Dean, Johnson, Stein. *Scorers:* Stein, Dean, Dunn.

3-0 MANCHESTER CITY Langford; Cann, Dale; Busby, Cowan, Bray; Toseland, Marshall, Herd, McMullan, Brook.

1933–34 MANCHESTER CITY Swift; Barnett, Dale; Busby, Cowan, Bray; Toseland, Marshall, Tilson, Herd, Brook. *Scorer:* Tilson 2.

2-1 PORTSMOUTH Gilfillan; Mackie, W. Smith; Nichol, Allen, Thackeray; Worrall, J. Smith, Weddle, Easson, Rutherford. *Scorer:* Rutherford.

1934–35 SHEFFIELD WEDNESDAY Brown; Nibloe, Catlin; Sharp, Millership, Burrows; Hooper, Surtees, Palethorpe, Starling, Rimmer. *Scorers:* Rimmer 2, Palethorpe, Hooper.

4-2 WEST BROMWICH ALBION Pearson; Shaw, Trentham; Murphy, W. Richardson, Edwards; Glidden, Carter, W. G. Richardson, Sandford, Boyes. *Scorers:* Boyes, Sandford.

1935–36 ARSENAL Wilson; Male, Hapgood; Crayston, Robertson, Copping; Hulme, Bowden, Drake, James, Bastin. *Scorer:* Drake.

1-0 SHEFFIELD UNITED Smith; Hooper, Wilkinson; Jackson, Johnson, McPherson; Barton, Barclay, Dodds, Pickering, Williams.

1936–37 SUNDERLAND Mapson; Gorman, Hall; Thomson, Johnson, McNab; Duns, Carter, Gurney, Gallacher, Burbanks. *Scorers:* Gurney, Carter, Burbanks.

3-1 PRESTON NORTH END Burns; Gallimore, A. Beattie; Shankly, Tremelling, Milne; Dougal, Beresford, F. O'Donnell, Fagan, H. O'Donnell. *Scorer:* F. O'Donnell.

1937–38 PRESTON NORTH END Holdcroft; Gallimore, A. Beattie; Shankly, Smith, Batey; Watmough, Mutch, Maxwell, R. Beattie, H. O'Donnell. *Scorer:* Mutch (pen).

1-0 aet HUDDERSFIELD TOWN Hesford; Craig, Mountford; Willingham, Young, Boot; Hulme, Isaac, McFadyen, Barclay, Beasley.

1938–39 PORTSMOUTH Walker; Morgan, Rochford; Guthrie, Rowe, Wharton; Worrall, McAlinden, Anderson, Barlow, Parker. *Scorers:* Parker 2, Barlow, Anderson.
4-1 WOLVERHAMPTON WANDERERS Scott; Morris, Taylor; Galley, Cullis, Gardiner; Burton, McIntosh, Westcott, Dorsett, Maguire. *Scorer:* Dorsett.

1945–46 DERBY COUNTY Woodley; Nicholas, Howe; Bullions, Leuty, Musson; Harrison, Carter, Stamps, Doherty, Duncan. *Scorers:* H. Turner og, Doherty, Stamps 2.
4-1 aet CHARLTON ATHLETIC Bartram; Phipps, Shreeve; H. Turner, Oakes, Johnson; Fell, Brown, A. A. Turner, Welsh, Duffy. *Scorer:* H. Turner.

1946–47 CHARLTON ATHLETIC Bartram; Crocker, Shreeve; Johnson, Phipps, Whittaker; Hurst, Dawson, W. Robinson, Welsh, Duffy. *Scorer:* Duffy.
1-0 aet BURNLEY Strong; Woodruff, Mather; Attwell, Brown, Bray; Chew, Morris, Harrison, Potts, F. P. Kippax.

1947–48 MANCHESTER UNITED Crompton; Carey, Aston; Anderson, Chilton, Cockburn; Delaney, Morris, Rowley, Pearson, Mitten. *Scorers:* Rowley 2, Pearson, Anderson.
4-2 BLACKPOOL Robinson; Shimwell, Crosland; Johnston, Hayward, Kelly; Matthews, Munro, Mortensen, Dick, Rickett. *Scorers:* Shimwell (pen), Mortensen.

1948–49 WOLVERHAMPTON WANDERERS Williams; Pritchard, Springthorpe; W. Crook, Shorthouse, Wright; Hancock, Smyth, Pye, Dunn, Mullen. *Scorers:* Pye 2, Smyth.
3-1 LEICESTER CITY Bradley; Jelly, Scott; W. Harrison, Plummer, King; Griffiths, Lee, J. Harrison, Chisholm, Adam. *Scorer:* Griffiths.

1949–50 ARSENAL Swindin; Scott, Barnes; Forbes, L. Compton, Mercer; Cox, Logie, Goring, Lewis, D. Compton. *Scorer:* Lewis 2.
2-0 LIVERPOOL Sidlow; Lambert, Spicer; Taylor, Hughes, Jones; Payne, Baron, Stubbins, Fagan, Liddell.

1950–51 NEWCASTLE UNITED Fairbrother; Cowell, Corbett; Harvey, Brennan, Crowe; Walker, Taylor, Milburn, G. Robledo, Mitchell. *Scorer:* Milburn 2.
2-0 BLACKPOOL Farm; Shimwell, Garrett; Johnston, Hayward, Kelly; Matthews, Mudie, Mortensen; W. J. Slater, Perry.

1951–52 NEWCASTLE UNITED Simpson; Cowell, McMichael; Harvey, Brennan, E. Robledo, Walker, Foulkes, Milburn, G. Robledo, Mitchell. *Scorer:* G. Robledo.
1-0 ARSENAL Swindin; Barnes, L. Smith; Forbes, Daniel, Mercer; Cox, Logie, Holton, Lishman, Roper.

1952–53 BLACKPOOL Farm; Shimwell, Garrett; Fenton, Johnston, Robinson; Matthews, Taylor, Mortensen, Mudie, Perry. *Scorers:* Mortensen 3, Perry.
4-3 BOLTON WANDERERS Hanson; Ball, R. Banks; Wheeler, Barass, Bell; Holden, Moir, Lofthouse, Hassall, Langton. *Scorers:* Lofthouse, Moir, Bell.

1953–54 WEST BROMWICH ALBION Sanders; Kennedy, Millard; Dudley, Dugdale, Barlow; Griffin, Ryan, Allen, Nicholls, Lee. *Scorers:* Allen 2 (1 pen), Griffin.
3-2 PRESTON NORTH END Thompson; Cunningham, Walton; Docherty, Marston, Forbes; Finney, Foster, Wayman, Baxter, Morrison. *Scorers:* Morrison, Wayman.

1954–55 NEWCASTLE UNITED Simpson; Cowell, Batty; Scoular, Stokoe, Casey; White, Milburn, Keeble, Hannah, Mitchell. *Scorers:* Milburn, Mitchell, Hannah.
3-1 MANCHESTER CITY Trautmann; Meadows, Little; Barnes, Ewing, Paul; Spurdle, Hayes, Revie, Johnstone, Fagan. *Scorer:* Johnstone.

1955–56 MANCHESTER CITY Trautmann; Leivers, Little; Barnes, Ewing, Paul; Johnstone, Hayes, Revie, Dyson, Clarke. *Scorers:* Hayes, Dyson, Johnstone.
3-1 BIRMINGHAM CITY Merrick; Hall, Green; Newman, Smith, Boyd; Astall, Kinsey, Brown, Murphy, Govan. *Scorer:* Kinsey.

1956–57 ASTON VILLA Sims; Lynn, Aldis; Crowther, Dugdale, Saward; Smith, Sewell, Myerscough, Dixon, McParland. *Scorer:* McParland 2.
2-1 MANCHESTER UNITED Wood; Foulkes, Byrne; Colman, J. Blanchflower, Edwards; Berry, Whelan, T. Taylor, R. Charlton, Pegg. *Scorer:* Taylor.

1957–58 BOLTON WANDERERS Hopkinson; Hartle, Banks; Hennin, Higgins, Edwards; Birch, Stevens, Lofthouse, Parry, Holden. *Scorer:* Lofthouse 2.
2-0 MANCHESTER UNITED Gregg; Foulkes, Greaves; Goodwin, Cope, Crowther; Dawson, E. Taylor; R. Charlton, Viollet, Webster.

1958–59 NOTTINGHAM FOREST Thomson; Whare, McDonald; Whitefoot, McKinlay, Burkitt; Dwight, Quigley, Wilson, Gray, Imlach. *Scorers:* Dwight, Wilson.
2-1 LUTON TOWN Baynham; McNally, Hawkes; Groves, Owen, Pacey; Bingham, Brown, Morton, Cummins, Gregory. *Scorer:* Pacey.

1959–60 WOLVERHAMPTON WANDERERS Finlayson; Showell, Harris; Clamp, Slater, Flowers; Deeley, Stobart, Murray, Broadbent, Horne. *Scorers:* McGrath og, Deeley 2.
3-0 BLACKBURN ROVERS Leyland; Bray, Whelan; Clayton, Woods, McGrath; Bimpson, Dobing, Dougan, Douglas, McLeod.

1960–61 TOTTENHAM HOTSPUR Brown; Baker, Henry; D. Blanchflower, Norman, Mackay; Jones, White, Smith, Allen, Dyson. *Scorers:* Smith, Dyson.
2-0 LEICESTER CITY Banks; Chalmers, Norman; McLintock, King, Appleton; Riley, Walsh, McIlmoyle, Keyworth, Cheesebrough.

1961–62 TOTTENHAM HOTSPUR Brown; Baker, Henry; D. Blanchflower, Norman, Mackay; Medwin, White, Smith, Greaves, Jones. *Scorers:* Greaves, Smith, Blanchflower (pen).
3-1 BURNLEY Blacklaw; Angus, Elder; Adamson, Cummings, Miller; Connelly, McIlroy, Pointer, Robson, Harris. *Scorer:* Robson.

1962–63 MANCHESTER UNITED Gaskell; Dunne, Cantwell; Crerand, Foulkes, Setters; Giles, Quixall, Herd, Law, R. Charlton. *Scorers:* Law, Herd 2.
3-1 LEICESTER CITY Banks; Sjoberg, Norman; McLintock, King, Appleton; Riley, Cross, Keyworth, Gibson, Stringfellow. *Scorer:* Keyworth.

1963–64 WEST HAM UNITED Standen; Bond, Burkett; Bovington, Brown, Moore; Brabrook, Boyce, Byrne, Hurst, Sissons. *Scorers:* Sissons, Hurst, Boyce.
3-2 PRESTON NORTH END Kelly; Ross, Smith; Lawton, Singleton, Kendall; Wilson, Ashworth, Dawson, Spavin, Holden. *Scorers:* Holden, Dawson.

1964–65 LIVERPOOL Lawrence; Lawler, Byrne; Strong, Yeats, Stevenson; Callaghan, Hunt, St John, Smith, Thompson. *Scorers:* Hunt, St John.
2-1 aet LEEDS UNITED Sprake; Reaney, Bell; Bremner, J. Charlton, Hunter; Giles, Storrie, Peacock, Collins, Johanneson. *Scorer:* Bremner.

1965–66 EVERTON West; Wright, Wilson; Gabriel, Labone, Harris; Scott, Trebilcock, Young, Harvey, Temple. *Scorers:* Trebilcock 2, Temple.
3-2 SHEFFIELD WEDNESDAY Springett; Smith, Megson; Eustace, Ellis, Young; Pugh, Fantham, McCalliog, Ford, Quinn. *Scorers:* McCalliog, Ford.

1966–67 TOTTENHAM HOTSPUR Jennings; Kinnear, Knowles; Mullery, England, Mackay; Robertson, Greaves, Gilzean, Venables, Saul. *Scorers:* Robertson, Saul.
2-1 CHELSEA Bonetti; A. Harris, McCreadie; Hollins, Hinton, R. Harris; Cooke, Baldwin, Hateley, Tambling, Boyle. *Scorer:* Tambling.

1967–68 WEST BROMWICH ALBION Osborne; Fraser, Williams; Brown, Talbut, Kaye (Clarke); Lovett, Collard, Astle, Hope, Clark. *Scorer:* Astle.
1-0 aet EVERTON West; Wright, Wilson; Kendall, Labone, Harvey; Husband, Ball, Royle, Hurst, Morrisey.

1968–69 MANCHESTER CITY Dowd; Book, Pardoe; Doyle, Booth, Oakes; Summerbee, Bell, Lee, Young, Coleman. *Scorer:* Young.
1-0 LEICESTER CITY Shilton; Rodrigues, Nish; Roberts, Woollett, Cross; Fern, Gibson, Lochhead, Clarke, Glover (Manley).

1969–70 CHELSEA Bonetti; Webb, McCreadie; Hollins, Dempsey, R. Harris (Hinton); Baldwin, Houseman, Osgood, Hutchinson, Cooke. *Scorers:* Houseman, Hutchinson.
2-2 aet LEEDS UNITED Sprake; Madeley, Cooper; Bremner, J. Charlton, Hunter; Lorimer, Clarke, Jones, Giles, E. Gray. *Scorers:* Charlton, Jones.
Replay (at Old Trafford, Manchester)
***R:*2-1 aet** CHELSEA Bonetti; R. Harris, McCreadie; Hollins, Dempsey, Webb; Baldwin, Cooke, Osgood (Hinton), Hutchinson, Houseman. *Scorers:* Osgood, Webb.
LEEDS UNITED Harvey; Madeley, Cooper; Bremner, J. Charlton, Hunter; Lorimer, Clarke, Jones, Giles, E. Gray. *Scorer:* Jones.

1970–71 ARSENAL Wilson; Rice, McNab; Storey (Kelly), McLintock, Simpson; Armstrong, Graham, Radford, Kennedy, George. *Scorers:* Kelly, George.
2-1 aet LIVERPOOL Clemence; Lawler, Lindsay; Smith, Lloyd, Hughes; Callaghan, Evans (Thompson), Heighway, Toshack, Hall. *Scorer:* Heighway.

1971–72 LEEDS UNITED Harvey; Reaney, Madeley; Bremner, J. Charlton, Hunter; Lorimer, Clarke, Jones, Giles, E. Gray. *Scorer:* Clarke.
1-0 ARSENAL Barnett; Rice, McNab; Storey, McLintock, Simpson; Armstrong, Ball, George, Radford (Kennedy), Graham.

1972–73 SUNDERLAND Montgomery; Malone, Guthrie; Horswill, Watson, Pitt; Kerr, Hughes, Halom, Porterfield, Tueart. *Scorer:* Porterfield.
1-0 LEEDS UNITED Harvey; Reaney, Cherry; Bremner, Madeley, Hunter; Lorimer, Clarke, Jones, Giles, E. Gray (Yorath).

1973–74 LIVERPOOL Clemence; Smith, Lindsay, Thompson, Cormack, Hughes, Keegan, Hall, Heighway, Toshack, Callaghan. *Scorers:* Keegan 2, Heighway.
3-0 NEWCASTLE UNITED McFaul; Clark, Kennedy, McDermott, Howard, Moncur, Smith (Gibb), Cassidy, Macdonald, Tudor, Hibbitt.

1974–75 WEST HAM UNITED Day; McDowell, T. Taylor, Lock, Lampard, Bonds, Paddon, Brooking, Jennings, A. Taylor, Holland. *Scorer:* A. Taylor 2.
2-0 FULHAM Mellor; Cutbush, Lacy, Moore, Fraser, Mullery, Conway, Slough, Mitchell, Busby, Barrett.

1975–76 SOUTHAMPTON Turner; Rodrigues, Peach; Holmes, Blyth, Steele; Gilchrist, Channon, Osgood, McCalliog, Stokes. *Scorer:* Stokes.
1-0 MANCHESTER UNITED Stepney; Forsyth, Houston; Daly, Greenhoff, Buchan; Coppell, McIlroy, Pearson, Macari, Hill (McCreery).

1976–77 MANCHESTER UNITED Stepney; Nicholl, Albiston; McIlroy, B. Greenhoff, Buchan; Coppell, J. Greenhoff, Pearson, Macari, Hill (McCreery). *Scorers:* Pearson, J. Greenhoff.
2-1 LIVERPOOL Clemence; Neal, Jones; Smith, Kennedy, Hughes; Keegan, Case, Heighway, Johnson (Callaghan), McDermott. *Scorer:* Case.

1977–78 IPSWICH TOWN Cooper; Burley, Mills; Osborne (Lambert), Hunter, Beattie, Talbot, Wark, Mariner, Geddis, Woods. *Scorer:* Osborne.

1-0 ARSENAL Jennings; Rice, Nelson, Price, Young, O'Leary, Brady (Rix), Hudson, Macdonald, Stapleton, Sunderland.

1978–79 ARSENAL Jennings; Rice, Nelson, Talbot, O'Leary, Young, Brady, Sunderland, Stapleton, Price (Walford), Rix. *Scorers:* Talbot, Stapleton, Sunderland.

3-2 MANCHESTER UNITED Bailey; Nicholl, Albiston, McIlroy, McQueen, Buchan, Coppell, J. Greenhoff, Jordan, Macari, Thomas. *Scorers:* McQueen, McIlroy.

1979–80 WEST HAM UNITED Parkes; Stewart, Lampard, Bonds, Martin, Devonshire, Allen, Pearson, Cross, Brooking, Pike. *Scorer:* Brooking.

1-0 ARSENAL Jennings; Rice, Devine (Nelson), Talbot, O'Leary, Young, Brady, Sunderland, Stapleton, Price, Rix

FA CHARITY SHIELD WINNERS 1908–80

Year	*Winners*	*Runners-up*	*Score*
1908	Manchester U	QPR	4-0 after 1-1 draw
1909	Newcastle U	Northampton T	2-0
1910	Brighton	Aston Villa	1-0
1911	Manchester U	Swindon T	8-4
1912	Blackburn R	QPR	2-1
1913	Professionals	Amateurs	7-2
1919	WBA	Tottenham H	2-0
1920	Tottenham H	Burnley	2-0
1921	Huddersfield	Liverpool	1-0
1922	Not played		
1923	Professionals	Amateurs	2-0
1924	Professionals	Amateurs	3-1
1925	Amateurs	Professionals	6-1
1926	Amateurs	Professionals	6-3
1927	Cardiff C	Corinthians	2-1
1928	Everton	Blackburn R	2-1
1929	Professionals	Amateurs	3-0
1930	Arsenal	Sheffield W	2-1
1931	Arsenal	WBA	1-0
1932	Everton	Newcastle U	5-3
1933	Arsenal	Everton	3-0
1934	Arsenal	Manchester C	4-0
1935	Sheffield W	Arsenal	1-0
1936	Sunderland	Arsenal	2-1
1937	Manchester C	Sunderland	2-0
1938	Arsenal	Preston NE	2-1
1948	Arsenal	Manchester U	4-3
1949	Portsmouth	Wolverhampton W	1-1*
1950	World Cup Team	Canadian Touring Team	4-2
1951	Tottenham H	Newcastle U	2-1
1952	Manchester U	Newcastle U	4-2
1953	Arsenal	Blackpool	3-1
1954	Wolverhampton W	WBA	4-4*
1955	Chelsea	Newcastle U	3-0
1956	Manchester U	Manchester C	1-0
1957	Manchester U	Aston Villa	4-0
1958	Bolton W	Wolverhampton W	4-1
1959	Wolverhampton W	Nottingham F	3-1
1960	Burnley	Wolverhampton W	2-2*
1961	Tottenham H	FA XI	3-2
1962	Tottenham H	Ipswich T	5-1
1963	Everton	Manchester U	4-0
1964	Liverpool	West Ham U	2-2*
1965	Manchester U	Liverpool	2-2*
1966	Liverpool	Everton	1-0
1967	Manchester U	Tottenham H	3-3*
1968	Manchester C	WBA	6-1
1969	Leeds U	Manchester C	2-1
1970	Everton	Chelsea	2-1
1971	Leicester C	Liverpool	1-0
1972	Manchester C	Aston Villa	1-0
1973	Burnley	Manchester C	1-0
1974	Liverpool†	Leeds	1-1
1975	Derby Co	West Ham U	2-0
1976	Liverpool	Southampton	1-0
1977	Liverpool	Manchester U	0-0*
1978	Nottingham F	Ipswich T	5-0
1979	Liverpool	Arsenal	3-1

* *Each club retained shield for six months.* † *Won on penalties.*

FA CHARITY SHIELD 1980

Liverpool (1) 1 West Ham U (0) 0

At Wembley, 9 August, 1980. Attendance 90,000

Liverpool: Clemence; Neal, Kennedy A., Thompson, Kennedy R., Hansen, Dalglish, Case, Johnson, McDermott, Souness.

West Ham U: Parkes; Stewart, Brush, Bonds, Martin, Devonshire, Allen, Holland, Cross, Brooking, Pike (Morgan).

Scorer: Liverpool – McDermott.

THE SCOTTISH SEASON 1980–81

Football in Scotland continues to attract fewer spectators as the years go by. There are plenty who seek the reasons – the pull of television, the call of many other growing sports, fear of bad behaviour in the crowds, lack of reasonable facilities at the grounds, and so on. There are doubtless many reasons why our crowds decrease, and there is no immediate answer, no instant remedy which will bring the masses flocking back. This is a pity, for there was much to talk about in this season, much to discuss, much to enthuse about; and not a little to complain about, too.

The home season was full of incident. In the League Cup we had the unprecedented spectacle of two Dundee teams contesting the final at a Dundee ground and with a Dundee referee. That may seem a little parochial, but substitute 'Glasgow' for 'Dundee' – and how often have we seen that! Anyway, a Dundee final it was, and if United were well ahead on the day, nothing could take away from some stirring results from the First Division side, which included the dismissal of Aberdeen, then Premier Division leaders.

The Premier was in many ways the least interesting of the divisions: Aberdeen started in fine form, but they faltered in mid-stream and Celtic swept through to win by a substantial margin in the end. It did not pass without notice that Aberdeen's decline coincided almost with the injury to Gordon Strachan; and Aberdeen had other injury problems too. This undoubtedly upset their rhythm but it would be unfair to Celtic to make too much of this. After all, a team must have the resilience and depth to ride its injuries if it is to dwell in the halls of greatness. Celtic looked a good deal more mature this year, and deservedly won after the usual long and gruelling season. Dundee United, surely recognised now as one of our top teams, had the ability to demolish opposition, and on occasions they were unstoppable and even almost ready to receive the public plaudits of their perfection-demanding manager. Rangers were inconsistent in the League, and St Mirren never quite recaptured the previous season's high form. For the rest, it was mostly the scuttle away from relegation, but too soon it was obvious that Kilmarnock and Hearts were this year's appointed candidates and by Christmas they were almost resigned to it.

In Division One there were spirited struggles at both ends of the table. Hibs were out to assert their divine right to ascend and they did this in fairly regal fashion – though not without the odd stutter. Dundee started abysmally, and new manager Donald Mackay must have had nightmares as his team fumbled at the foot of the table. However, in time they began to gain some confidence and started to move upwards. For a long while Raith Rovers looked certainties for promotion, but there were other candidates – Ayr, Motherwell and, notably, St Johnstone. With only a few games left, there were still five teams in the hunt and all games were crucial. In the end Dundee just pipped St Johnstone, but they needed points from the last game on the last day to do it. In the relegation area, Berwick were always in danger; as the season progressed, Dunfermline and Stirling Albion were likely to join them. For a while, Berwick looked as if they might avoid the drop, but in the end they succumbed and were joined by Stirling, who failed to score in their last 13 League matches.

There are always many who like to see Queen's Park doing well. This was their season in the Second Division, and they finished as champions after leading the field for a considerable period. In fact, they were never out of the top group throughout the season. Good luck to them! They will need it in the new season, for undoubtedly this great amateur club with a great tradition will have again been the training ground for future professionals and will need to start team building all over again. Alloa looked strong for some time, Brechin had a long climb from the lower end to achieve third position at one time, but their challenge came to nothing, and Cowdenbeath all but reached promotion before losing the last vital game. It was left to Queen of the South to take five points from the final possible six and thus to clinch a berth in Division One. It was all interesting and exciting and, taken with the last-match decisions in the First Division, meant as good a last day to the League season as there has been.

So to the Cup. It is always good to see Highland League clubs making progress in this competition, and this year Buckie Thistle and Inverness Thistle both reached the third round, disposing of three Second Division clubs on the way. Ultimately Division One opposition proved too strong, but it is worth noting that more than 3,000 turned out to see Stirling win at Buckie. St Mirren made a quick exit at the hands of Dumbarton, and in the fourth round Clydebank beat Kilmarnock after two drawn games; but the real shock in that round was averted by seconds when Rangers scored an injury-time goal to draw 3-3 with St Johnstone – and subsequently won the replay comfortably. There were four First

Division teams in the last eight, but they were all eliminated. Rangers won a rather heavy semi-final against Morton, while Dundee United and Celtic needed two games before the former took the other place in the final. A no-score draw was barely a fair reflection of United's superiority in the final, though the game all but went Rangers' way in the end, the last-minute penalty being missed. The replay saw Rangers in a completely different mood. They took good chances when they came and cruised to victory, with United's rather light ball-players given little chance by a firm Rangers defence.

International results were, for the most part, encouraging and (dare it be said) there looks to be a reasonable chance of reaching Spain in 1982. Jock Stein wisely remains sphinx-like: some of his experiments – for example, at Swansea – did not work out well, but some new, young players were given their chance, and others reached full maturity in their international careers. The Wembley result was sweet, but we are under no delusions about the standards of World Cup opposition. There is hope, but this time the fans are keeping their feet firmly on the ground.

There have been more ominous rumbles about the demise of Hampden, and a decision looks to be not far away. I hope that matters may be satisfactorily concluded: international football without the home inspiration of Hampden is hard to think about and no other ready-made headquarters obviously available.

There did seem some chance of a reorganisation in the Leagues, and there were three proposals debated: in the end, however, we are back as we were. Can the game survive in its present shape? We shall see.

ALAN ELLIOTT

SCOTTISH LEAGUE REFEREES 1980–81

H. Alexander (Irvine)
W. Anderson (East Kilbride)
R. R. Cuthill (Winchburgh)
M. Delaney (Cleland)
D. S. Downie (Edinburgh)
J. Duncan (Gorebridge)
A. Ferguson (Giffnock)
I. M. D. Foote (Glasgow)
D. M. Galloway (Pitlessie)
A. C. Harris (Liff)
K. J. Hope (Clarkston)
W. P. Knowles (Inverurie)
A. G. M. McFaull (Knightswood)
B. R. McGinlay (Balfron)
A. McGunnigle (Glasgow)
F. McKenzie (Wishaw)
W. McLeish (Stonehouse)
T. Muirhead (Stenhousemuir)
E. H. Pringle (Edinburgh)
D. Ramsay (Edinburgh)
J. R. S. Renton (Cowdenbeath)
B. Robertson (East Kilbride)
G. B. Smith (Edinburgh)
K. Stewart (Glasgow)
D. F. T. Syme (Rutherglen)
L. B. Thow (Ayr)
J. J. Timmons (Kilwinning)
R. B. Valentine (Dundee)
A. W. Waddell (Penicuik)
J. A. R. Wales (Condorrat)
C. J. White (Clarkston)

FLOODLIGHTS AT STRANRAER

Stranraer lost their status of being the only Scottish League club without floodlights when work was completed on a £20,000 system at Stair Park in June 1981.

SCOTTISH LEAGUE 1980–81

PREMIER DIVISION

		Home					Away					
	P	*W*	*D*	*L*	*F*	*A*	*W*	*D*	*L*	*F*	*A*	*Pts*
1. Celtic	36	12	3	3	47	18	14	1	3	37	19	56
2. Aberdeen	36	11	4	3	39	16	8	7	3	22	10	49
3. Rangers	36	12	3	3	33	10	4	9	5	27	22	44
4. St Mirren	36	9	6	3	28	20	9	2	7	28	27	44
5. Dundee U	36	8	5	5	34	24	9	4	5	32	18	43
6. Partick T	36	6	6	6	17	17	4	4	10	15	31	30
7. Airdrieonians	36	6	5	7	19	25	4	4	10	17	30	29
8. Morton	36	7	2	9	24	28	3	6	9	12	30	28
9. Kilmarnock	36	3	5	10	14	31	2	4	12	9	34	19
10. Hearts	36	3	4	11	10	27	3	2	13	17	44	18

FIRST DIVISION

1. Hibernian	39	14	4	2	38	9	10	5	4	29	15	57
2. Dundee	39	14	4	2	42	18	8	4	7	22	22	52
3. St Johnstone	39	12	3	5	31	21	8	8	3	33	24	51
4. Raith R	39	11	7	1	26	11	9	3	8	23	21	50
5. Motherwell	39	14	5	1	41	20	5	6	8	24	31	49
6. Ayr U	39	11	5	3	34	17	6	6	8	25	25	45
7. Hamilton A	39	9	5	6	39	27	6	2	11	22	30	37
8. Dumbarton	39	8	5	6	23	22	5	6	9	26	28	37
9. Falkirk	39	7	4	8	24	29	6	4	10	15	23	34
10. Clydebank	39	8	6	5	31	25	2	7	11	17	34	33
11. East Stirling	39	4	10	6	20	24	2	7	10	21	32	29
12. Dunfermline Ath	39	6	3	11	17	28	4	4	11	24	30	27
13. Stirling Albion	39	4	6	9	13	21	2	5	13	5	27	23
14. Berwick R	39	5	6	8	18	27	0	6	14	13	55	22

SECOND DIVISION

1. Queen's Park	39	9	9	2	30	19	7	9	3	32	24	50
2. Queen of the S	39	7	8	4	31	29	9	6	5	35	24	46
3. Cowdenbeath	39	12	3	4	35	20	6	6	8	28	28	45
4. Brechin C	39	10	7	3	29	18	5	7	7	23	28	44
5. Forfar Ath	39	9	3	7	34	32	8	6	6	29	25	43
6. Alloa	39	10	4	6	29	25	5	8	6	32	29	42
7. Montrose	39	9	4	6	31	24	7	4	9	35	31	40
8. Clyde	39	10	6	4	45	31	4	6	9	23	32	40
9. Arbroath	39	3	9	8	20	29	10	3	6	38	25	38
10. Stenhousemuir	39	4	7	8	27	32	9	4	7	36	26	37
11. East Fife	39	6	9	4	21	21	4	6	10	23	32	35
12. Albion R	39	9	3	8	37	41	4	6	9	22	31	35
13. Meadowbank T	39	6	2	11	17	35	5	5	10	25	29	29
14. Stranraer	39	4	5	11	20	41	3	3	13	16	42	22

HIGHLAND LEAGUE 1980–81

	P	*W*	*D*	*L*	*F*	*A*	*Pts*
Keith	30	17	8	5	52	26	42
Fraserburgh	30	17	7	6	55	31	41
Elgin City	30	17	6	7	63	32	40
Clachnacuddin	30	14	9	7	55	42	37
Buckie Thistle	30	15	6	9	63	43	36
Peterhead	30	14	8	8	50	35	36
Rothes	30	14	7	9	55	40	35
Inverness Thistle	30	15	4	11	62	42	34
Inverness Caledonian	30	11	8	11	48	44	30
Brora Rangers	30	12	6	12	49	47	30
Ross County	30	13	3	14	51	59	29
Huntly	30	10	8	12	63	65	28
Deveronvale	30	6	10	14	40	68	22
Nairn County	30	6	8	16	49	74	20
Lossiemouth	30	2	6	22	30	70	10
Forres Mechanics	30	3	4	23	31	98	10

ABERDEEN Premier Division

Year Formed: 1903.
Ground: Pittodrie Stadium. *Size:* 110yd×71yd. *Capacity:* 24,000 (all seated and all covered).
Telephone: Aberdeen 632328, 633497.
Manager: Alec Ferguson. *Assistant-Manager:* Archie Knox.
Secretary: I. J. Taggart. *Trainer:* Teddy Scott. *Physiotherapist:* Roland Arnott.
Club Colours: Red shirts, red shorts, red stockings.
Club Nickname: The Dons.
Record Attendance: 45,061 v Hearts, Scottish Cup 4th rd, March 13, 1954.
(Present Aberdeen FC have had no other home but Pittodrie.)
European Competitions: *Fairs Cup* 1968–69; *European Cup-Winners' Cup* 1967–68, 1970–71, 1978–79; *UEFA Cup* 1971–72, 1972–73, 1973–74, 1977–78, 1979–80; *European Cup* 1980–81.
Record Transfer Fee Received: £800,000 from Tottenham H for Steve Archibald, May 1980.

1980–81 LEAGUE RECORD

Match No.	Date	Venue	Opponents	Result	H/T Score	League Pos'n	Goalscorers	Attendance
1	Aug 9	A	St Mirren	W 1-0	1-0	—	Jarvie	7000
2	16	H	Dundee U	D 1-1	1-1	4	Strachan	12,000
3	23	A	Airdrieonians	W 4-0	2-0	2	McGhee, Cowan, Jarvie, Scanlon	6000
4	Sept 6	H	Morton	W 6-0	1-0	1	Miller, Strachan, Scanlon 2, Hewitt, McMaster	10,000
5	13	A	Rangers	D 1-1	1-1	1	Strachan (pen)	32,000
6	20	A	Partick T	W 1-0	0-0	2	McGhee	6000
7	27	H	Celtic	D 2-2	0-2	2	McGhee, McAdam (og)	23,000
8	Oct 4	A	Hearts	W 1-0	0-0	2	Rougvie	10,873
9	11	H	Kilmarnock	W 2-0	0-0	2	Scanlon, Jarvie	12,000
10	18	H	St Mirren	W 3-2	1-0	1	McMaster, McGhee 2	8000
11	25	A	Dundee U	W 3-1	2-1	1	Strachan, McGhee, Hewitt	10,043
12	Nov 1	H	Airdrieonians	W 4-1	3-0	1	McCall 3, McGhee	9000
13	8	A	Celtic	W 2-0	1-0	1	McCall 2	29,000
14	15	H	Partick T	W 2-1	0-0	1	Strachan, Bell	10,000
15	22	A	Kilmarnock	D 1-1	0-1	1	McLeish	3500
16	Dec 6	A	Morton	L 0-1	0-0	1		7000
17	13	H	Rangers	W 2-0	0-0	1	McGhee, Johnston (og)	20,000
18	20	A	Partick T	D 1-1	1-1	1	McCall	4000
19	27	H	Celtic	W 4-1	2-0	1	McLeish, Miller, McCall, Strachan	24,000
20	30	H	Dundee U	D 1-1	0-1	—	Scanlon (pen)	22,000
21	Jan 3	A	St Mirren	D 1-1	0-0	1	Scanlon (pen)	11,100
22	10	A	Hearts	W 2-0	1-0	1	McCall, McGhee	7999
23	31	A	Rangers	L 0-1	0-0	2		32,500
24	Feb 7	H	Morton	L 0-1	0-0	2		11,000
25	21	A	Airdrieonians	D 0-0	0-0	2		5000
26	28	H	St Mirren	L 1-2	1-1	2	Jarvie	8000
27	Mar 7	H	Hearts	W 4-1	2-0	2	McCall, Jarvie, Angus, Hamilton (og)	11,000
28	14	A	Kilmarnock	L 0-1	0-0	2		2500
29	28	A	Celtic	D 1-1	1-0	2	Harrow	35,200
30	Apr 1	H	Partick T	W 3-1	1-0	—	Simpson, McLeish, McGhee	9000
31	4	A	Morton	W 3-1	1-0	2	McGhee, Simpson, Rougvie	5500
32	11	H	Hearts	W 1-0	0-0	2	Rougvie	6000
33	18	H	Airdrieonians	W 3-0	2-0	2	McGhee 2, McCall	7000
34	22	H	Rangers	D 0-0	0-0	—		15,000
35	25	A	Dundee U	D 0-0	0-0	2		6369
36	May 2	H	Kilmarnock	L 0-2	0-0	2		6300

Final League Position: 2

Goalscorers

League (61): McGhee 13, McCall 10, Scanlon 6 (2 pen), Strachan 6 (1 pen), Jarvie 5, McLeish 3, Rougvie 3, Hewitt 2, McMaster 2, Miller 2, Simpson 2, Angus 1, Bell 1, Cowan 1, Harrow 1, own goals 3.
League Cup (15): McGhee 3, Strachan 3 (2 pens), Jarvie 2, Watson 2, Bell 1, de Clerck 1, Hewitt 1, Kennedy 1, McMaster 1.
Scottish Cup (2): Jarvie 2.

Honours
Scottish League – Division 1 Champions 1954–55; Runners-up: 1910–11, 1936–37, 1955–56, 1970–71, 1971–72; Premier Division Champions 1979–80; Runners-up 1977–78, 1980–81.
Scottish Cup – Winners: 1947, 1970; Runners-up: 1937, 1953, 1954, 1959, 1967, 1978.
Scottish League Cup – Winners: 1955–56, 1976–77; Runners-up: 1946–47, 1978–79, 1979–80.
Drybrough Cup – Winners 1971.
Record Victory: 13-0 v Peterhead, Scottish Cup, 9 Feb, 1923.
Record Defeat: 0-8 v Celtic, Division 1, 30 Jan, 1965.
Most League Points: 61, Division 1, 1935–36.
Most Individual League Goals in Season: Benny Yorston, 38, Division 1, 1929–30.
Most Capped Player: Bobby Clark, 17, Scotland.

Leighton J	de Clerck M	Kennedy S	Rougvie D	Considine D	Hamilton D	Watson A	McLeish A	Miller W	McMaster J	Cooper N	Angus I	Strachan G	Simpson N	Bell D	Jarvie A	Cowan S	Hewitt J	Scanlon I	McGhee M	Harrow A	Dornan A	McCall W	Davidson D	Garner W	Harper J	*Match No.*
1		2				4	5	6	3			7			10	12	8*	11	9							1
1		2				4*	5	6	3			7		12	10†	8	13	11	9							2
1		2		12		4*	5	6	3			7			10	8†	13	11	9							3
1		2	3			4*	5	6	8			7		12	10†		13	11	9							4
1		2	3		12	4	5	6	8			7		13			10†	11	9*							5
1		2	3		12		5	6	8			7		4			10*	11	9							6
1		2	5		3*	4		6	8			7		10			11†	12	9			13				7
1		2	3			12		6	11			7		4	10			13	9			8†		5*		8
	1	2	3			4		6	8	5*		7		12	10	13		11	9†							9
1		2	3			4	5	6	8			7			10			11	9							10
1		2	3				5	6				7		4	10	8*	12	11	9							11
1			3			4	5*	6		12		7			10			11	9†		2	8	13			12
1			3	12		4	5			6		7		10			13	11	9†		2*	8				13
1			2	3		4	5	6				7		10			12	11*	9			8				14
1		2		3	13	4	5	6				7			10		12	11†	9			8*				15
1		2		3		4	5	6			13	7			10†		8*	11	9			12				16
1		2		3		4	5	6			10	7						11	9			8				17
1		2		3			4	6			10	7	12					11†	9			8	13	5*		18
1		2	12	3		4	5	6				7		10*				11	9			8				19
1		2		3		4	5	6			13	7		10†			12	11	9			8*				20
1		2	3			4	5	6			10		7				12	11	9			8*				21
1		2	3*	12		4	5	6			10		7		13			11	9†			8				22
1			3	13	2	4*	5			6†	10				7			11	9	12		8				23
1			6	3	2	12	5				10		4	7*				11	9	8†		13				24
1		2	3			4*	5	6			12		7		10			11†	9	8			13			25
1		2	3			4	5	6			12		7		10		13	11	9†	8*						26
1		2	12		3*		5	6			4		7		10		13	11	9	8†						27
1		2	12		3*	13	5	6			4		7		10			11	9	8†						28
1		2	3			4	5	6					7	8*	12			11	9	10†		13				29
1		2	3			4	5	6			8		7					11	9	10						30
1		2	3			4	5	6			8		7		12			11†	9	10*			13			31
1		2	3			4*		6		5†	8		7		12		13	11	9	10						32
1		2	3				5	6			10*		7	4	12		11		9			8				33
1		2	3				5	6			10		7	4			11	8*	9	12						34
1		2	3				5	6			10*		7	4	12		11	8	9							35
1		2	3			4*	5	6			10†		7		12		11		8	13					9	36
35	1	31	25	8	5	26	32	33	10	4	15	20	15	13	16	3	9	32	36	9	2	13	0	2	1	
			+ 3s	+ 4s	+ 3s	+ 3s				+ 1s	+ 4s		+ 1s	+ 4s	+ 7s	+ 2s	+ 12s	+ 2s		+ 3s		+ 4s	+ 4s			

AIRDRIEONIANS Premier Division

Year Formed: 1878.
Ground: Broomfield Park. *Size:* 112yd×68yd. *Capacity:* 26,000 (2000 seats).
Telephone: Airdrie 62067.
Manager: Bobby Watson. *Coaches:* W. Humphries and D. McLindon. *Second team:* R. Morrison.
Secretary: George W. Peat CA.
Club Colours: White shirt with red diamond, white shorts, red stockings and white diamond tops.
Club Nickname: Diamonds or Waysiders.
Record Attendance: 24,000 v Hearts, Scottish Cup, 8 March, 1952.

1980–81 LEAGUE RECORD

Match No.	*Date*	*Venue*	*Opponents*	*Result*	*H/T Score*	*League Pos'n*	*Goalscorers*	*Atten-dance*
1	Aug 9	H	Rangers	D 1-1	0-1	—	Walker	16,000
2	16	A	Hearts	W 2-0	0-0	3	Clark, McGuire	6711
3	23	H	Aberdeen	L 0-4	0-2	5		6000
4	Sept 6	A	St Mirren	D 2-2	1-0	5	Clark (pen), Erwin	5220
5	13	H	Dundee U	D 0-0	0-0	4		3000
6	20	A	Celtic	D 1-1	0-0	4	Clark	18,000
7	27	H	Kilmarnock	W 1-0	0-0	4	McGuire	2000
8	Oct 4	A	Partick T	L 1-2	1-0	4	Erwin	5000
9	11	H	Morton	W 1-0	0-0	4	Clark	4000
10	18	A	Rangers	D 0-0	0-0	4		22,000
11	25	H	Hearts	W 3-0	3-0	4	March 2, Thompson	3500
12	Nov 1	A	Aberdeen	L 1-4	0-3	5	Miller	9000
13	8	A	Kilmarnock	D 1-1	0-1	5	McCulloch	2300
14	15	H	Celtic	L 1-4	0-3	6	McGuire	15,000
15	22	A	Morton	L 1-3	0-1	6	Walker	3500
16	29	H	Partick T	D 0-0	0-0	6		3500
17	Dec 6	H	St Mirren	L 1-2	0-2	7	Clark (pen)	4000
18	13	A	Dundee U	L 0-1	0-0	8		4700
19	20	A	Celtic	L 1-2	0-1	8	Clark	11,900
20	Jan 1	A	Hearts	W 3-2	0-0	—	Rodger, McCulloch 2	8086
21	3	H	Rangers	D 1-1	1-0	8	McCloy (og)	12,000
22	10	A	Partick T	L 0-1	0-1	8		3000
23	31	H	Dundee U	L 0-5	0-0	8		3000
24	Feb 21	H	Aberdeen	D 0-0	0-0	8		5000
25	28	A	Rangers	L 0-2	0-0	8		12,200
26	Mar 4	A	St Mirren	L 1-2	0-1	—	Flood	3649
27	7	H	Partick T	W 2-0	1-0	8	Flood, Campbell (og)	3000
28	11	H	Kilmarnock	W 3-0	3-0	—	McGuire, Rodger, Flood	3500
29	14	A	Morton	W 1-0	0-0	6	Thompson	3500
30	21	H	Celtic	L 1-2	0-1	6	Thompson	13,000
31	28	A	Kilmarnock	W 1-0	1-0	6	Anderson G.	1849
32	Apr 4	H	St Mirren	L 0-2	0-1	6		3500
33	18	A	Aberdeen	L 0-3	0-2	8		7000
34	25	H	Hearts	L 1-2	0-1	8	Clark	2000
35	29	A	Dundee U	L 1-4	1-1	—	Clark	3133
36	May 2	H	Morton	W 3-2	1-1	7	Clark 2, March	1600

Final League Position: 7

Goalscorers

League (36): Clark 10 (2 pens), McGuire 4, Flood 3, McCulloch 3, March 3, Thompson 3, Erwin 2, Rodger 2, Walker 2, Anderson G. 1, Miller 1, own goals 2.
League Cup (0).
Scottish Cup (0).

Honours

Scottish League – Division 1 Runners-up: 1922–23, 1923–24, 1924–25, 1925–26, 1979–80; Division 2 Champions: 1902–03, 1954–55, 1973–74; Runners-up: 1900–1901, 1946–47, 1949–50, 1965–66.
Scottish Cup – Winners 1924; Runners-up 1975.
Scottish League Cup – None.
Spring Cup – Winners 1975–76.
Record Victory: 15-1 v Dundee Wanderers, Division 2, 1 Dec, 1894.
Record Defeat: 1-11 v Hibernian, Division 1, 24 Oct, 1959.
Most League Points: 60, Division 2, 1973–74.
Most Individual League Goals in Season: H. G. Yarnall, 45, Division 1, 1916–17.
Most Capped Player: Jimmy Crapnell, 9, Scotland.
Highest goalscorers in British league football 1973–74 with 102 goals.

McGarr E	Martin J	Gardiner J	Erwin H	Walker T	Cairney H	Rodger J	Anderson G	March J	Hamilton G	Anderson N	McCulloch W	McKeown B	McCluskey P	Flood J G	Thompson D	McClymont J	Russell R	Clark A	McGuire W	Gordon I	McVeigh J	Davidson A	McCafferty T	Burnett A	*Match No.*
1			2	4		3		5		6		7			12		9	8	11	10*					1
1			2	4		3*		5	12	6	10	7					9	8	11						2
1			2	4		3		5		6		7					9	8	11	10					3
	1		2	4		3		5*	12	6	13	7†					9	8	11	10					4
	1		2	4		3	5			6	9*				7			8	11	10	12				5
	1		2	4		3	5			6	11				7*			8	12	10	9				6
	1		2	4		3*	5			6	11	12			13			8	7	10	9†				7
	1		2	4		3	5	6			11				12		9	8	7*	10					8
	1			2	5*	3		12			4	7	6					8	11	10	9				9
	1		12	4	2*	3		5				7	6		11			8	13	10	9†				10
	1			2		3		5		6		7	4		11		9	8		10					11
	1			2		3	12	5		6		11	4		7*		9	8		10					12
	1			2	13	3	5			6	10	7	4		11†		9*	8	12						13
	1		2	4		3*	5			6	12	7	11†				13	8	9	10					14
	1		2	4		3*	5			6	7	12			9			8	11	10					15
	1		2*	4		3		5		6	12		11		7†		9	8	13	10					16
	1			2		3		5		6	4	13	11†		12		9*	8	7	10					17
	1			4*	2	3		5		6	12	7	11		13		9†	8		10					18
	1			4*	2	3	5			6	12	7†	9				11	8	13	10					19
	1			4	2	3	5			6			9				7	8	11	10					20
	1			6	2	3		5			9	13	4		12		7*	8	11†	10					21
	1			10	2	3		5			6	9	4		12		7	8	11*						22
	1		12	4	2*		3	5				7†	6		13		11	8	9	10					23
		1		4	2	3	5	12		9			6	7			8*	11		10					24
		1		4	2	3		5		9		11	6	7	12			8		10*					25
		1	2	4*		3		5		9		11	6	7		12		8		10					26
		1	2	4		3		5		9			6	7*	12	13	11†	8		10					27
		1	2	4		3		5		9		10	6	7				8	11						28
		1	2	4		3	11†	5		9		10	6	7*	12			8	13						29
		1	2	4*		3	6	5		9		12	11	7	13			8	10†						30
		1		4	2	3	5			9		10	6	7*	12			8	11						31
		1	2	4		3	5			9		10	6	7*	12			8	11						32
		1	4		2*	3	5			9		10	6	7	12			8†	11				13		33
	1		2*	4	12	3	5			9		10	6	11				8	7						34
				12	2	3	4	5		9		10*	6	7				8	13			1		11†	35
	1			10	2	3	4	5		9		11	6	7				8							36
3	22	10	19	34	14	35	19	22	0	30	11	24	27	13	8	0	18	36	21	24	4	1	0	1	
			+ 2s	+ 1s	+ 2s		+ 1s	+ 2s	+ 2s		+ 5s	+ 5s			+ 15s	+ 2s	+ 1s		+ 7s		+ 1s		+ 1s		

ALBION ROVERS Division 2

Year Formed: 1882. *Ground:* Cliftonhill Park. *Capacity:* 10,000 (580 seats). *Size:* 110yd×74yd. *Telephone:* Coatbridge 32350.
Manager: *Secretary:* David Forrester CA.
Club Colours: Primrose shirts, with red trim and number, red shorts, primrose stockings.
Record Attendance: 27,381 v Rangers, Scottish Cup 2nd rd, 8 Feb, 1936.
Previous Grounds: Meadow Park, Whifflet, 1881–1919.
Club Nickname: The Wee Rovers.

1980–81 LEAGUE RECORD

Match No.	Date	Venue	Opponents	Result	H/T Score	League Pos'n	Goalscorers	Attendance
1	Aug 9	A	Forfar Ath	D 1-1	0-1	—	Franchetti (pen)	1000
2	16	A	Stenhousemuir	L 1-3	0-1	—	Campbell	500
3	24	H	Meadowbank T	W 3-1	0-1	—	Hamill, Franchetti, Campbell	350
4	Sept 6	A	Montrose	W 1-0	0-0	7	Ross	350
5	10	H	Queen of the S	L 0-4	0-2	—		250
6	13	H	Cowdenbeath	W 2-0	2-0	7	Campbell, Higgins	344
7	17	A	East Fife	D 1-1	1-0	—	Hill H.	542
8	20	H	Brechin C	L 2-3	0-1	10	Houston, Mulvaney	350
9	27	A	Alloa	L 0-1	0-0	11		650
10	Oct 1	A	Clyde	D 1-1	1-1	—	Brogan (og)	650
11	4	H	Arbroath	L 1-6	0-3	—	Mulvaney	360
12	11	A	Stranraer	W 4-1	2-1	—	Houston, Hill H., Campbell 2	400
13	18	H	Queen's Park	D 2-2	1-1	11	Allan, Hill H. (pen)	750
14	25	A	Cowdenbeath	L 1-2	1-1	11	Meikle	845
15	Nov 1	H	Montrose	W 2-1	0-0	11	Campbell, Franchetti	400
16	8	H	East Fife	D 0-0	0-0	11		400
17	15	A	Brechin C	D 2-2	0-2	10	Campbell, Ross	400
18	22	H	Alloa	W 3-1	2-0	10	Houston, McPherson, Hannigan	1000
19	Dec 6	H	Stranraer	L 1-3	0-1	10	Campbell	350
20	13	A	Arbroath	D 2-2	1-1	10	Campbell, Ross	487
21	20	A	Queen's Park	L 0-2	0-1	11		850
22	Jan 1	H	Meadowbank T	W 2-1	0-0	—	Hill H. 2 (1 pen)	700
23	10	H	Clyde	D 3-3	0-1	9	Campbell, Houston, Meikle	500
24	24	H	Forfar Ath	L 2-4	1-2	9	Hill H., Hannigan	300
25	31	A	Queen's Park	L 1-3	0-1	10	Campbell	500
26	Feb 14	H	East Fife	W 3-2	0-0	11	Franchetti 2 (1 pen), Gillespie	500
27	21	A	Brechin C	L 1-2	1-0	11	Ross	400
28	24	A	Stenhousemuir	W 3-0	1-0	—	Gillespie, Mulvaney, Ross	450
29	28	H	Arbroath	L 2-4	1-2	9	Gillespie, Mackie	300
30	Mar 11	A	Alloa	W 1-0	0-0	—	Ross	610
31	14	H	Queen of the S	W 1-0	0-0	8	Clark (og)	450
32	17	H	Stranraer	W 5-0	2-0	—	Ross 2, Franchetti, Burgess, Hill H. (pen)	300
33	21	A	Clyde	L 0-4	0-3	—		450
34	28	H	Cowdenbeath	L 0-2	0-0	9		250
35	Apr 4	A	Meadowbank T	L 1-2	0-0	11	Gillespie	150
36	11	H	Forfar Ath	W 3-2	0-1	12	Ross, Mulvaney, Campbell	300
37	18	H	Stenhousemuir	L 0-2	0-0	12		250
38	25	A	Montrose	D 1-1	1-0	11	Hill H.	300
39	May 2	A	Queen of the S	L 0-3	0-1	12		1500

Final League Position: 12

Goalscorers

League (59): Campbell 12, Ross 9, Hill H. 8 (3 pens), Franchetti 6 (2 pens), Gillespie 4, Houston 4, Mulvaney 4, Hannigan 2, Meikle 2, Allan 1, Burgess 1, Hamill 1, Higgins 1, Mackie 1, McPherson 1, own goals 2.
League Cup (1): Campbell 1.
Scottish Cup (1): Campbell 1.

Honours
Scottish League – Division 2 Champions 1933–34; Runners-up 1913-14, 1937–38, 1947–48.
Scottish Cup – Finalists 1920.
Record Victory: 12-0 v Airdriehill, Scottish Cup, 3 Sept, 1887.
Record Defeat: 1-9 v Motherwell, Division 1, 2 Jan, 1937.
Most League Points: 54, Division 2, 1929–30.
Most Individual League Goals in Season: Jim Renwick, 41, 1932–33.
Most Capped Player: Jock White, 1(2), Scotland.

Hill M	Balavage J	Allan P	Hannigan S	Martin B	Main D	Hamill P	Mackie G S	Meikle H	Docherty J	McPherson A F	Campbell I	Franchetti R	Burgess S R	Higgins J	Ross A R	Hill H	Gillespie I	Leishman W	Walker C	Dempsey J	Mulvaney F	Egan C	McDougall J	Houston P	Brand D	Boyle F	Murray T	Gardiner V	*Match No.*
1				2	6	3		4			8	10			11*		7	5			12			9					1
1			9	2*	6	3		5	11†		10	4		12	13		7							8					2
1		2	10			6		5	3		7	4					8							9	11				3
1			10*	2		3		5		6	8	4			12	7	11							9					4
1			10	2	6	3		5			8	4			11		7							9					5
	1	2				3		4		5	8	13		11†	9*	6	7				12			10					6
	1	2				3		6	11	5	10			7		4	8							9					7
1		2				3		5	11*	4	10	7				8	13		6†		12			9					8
	1	2		13		3		6†	4	5	10*			12		7	9				8			11					9
	1	2	9*			3		6	4	5	10			12		7					8			11					10
	1	2	11†			3		6		5	7*	9		12	13	8	4				10								11
	1	2	3	11*		5		6		4	7				12	8	9							10					12
	1	2	3		6*	5				4	7	12			11	8	9							10					13
	1	2	3		6	5		4	11						10	8	7							9					14
	1	2	3		11	5				6	9	4				8					7			10					15
	1	2	3		11	5		12		6*	9	4			13	8					7†			10					16
	1	2	3	7†	11	5		4		6*	9			13	12	8								10					17
	1	2	3	7	11	5		4		6	9					8								10					18
	1	2			4	6		5	3*	8†	9			12	10	7					13			11					19
	1	2			6			5	3	4	7				10	8*	13				12			9		11†			20
	1	2			3			6		5	7			12	9	4	8				11*			10					21
	1	2			6	3*	4	5	12		7				9†	8	11						13	10					22
	1	2*			6	3	4	5	12		7				9†	8	11						13	10					23
	1		3*		6		4	5			7	13	9†		12	8	2						11	10					24
	1		3*		11		6			5	10	4	12			8†	2					7	13	9					25
	1			2	6		4	5	3		9	12			10*	7	11							8					26
	1				6		4	5	3	2	9	12			10*	7	11							8					27
	1				6		4	5	3	2	9*				10	7	11				12			8					28
	1			2*	6		4	12	3		13		5		9	7	11				10†			8					29
	1				3		4				10†	13	5		9	7	11			6	12			8*			2		30
	1				3			4			10*		5		9	7	11			6	12			8			2		31
	1				3			4				10	5		9	7	11			6				8			2		32
	1	2*			3		4	12			10	13	5		9†	7	11			6				8					33
	1	12			3*		4	2			9*	10	5			7	11			6	12			8					34
	1				3		4	2			9	10	5			7	11			6				8					35
	1		3		6		4	2			9	12	5		10*		7				11			8					36
	1		3					2			8		5		9	12	11			6	10*			7				4	37
	1	2	3		8	13	12				10		5*		9	4	11†			6				7					38
12	1*	2	3		6		8	13			10				9	4	7†			5				11					39
6	33	22	19	9	29	21	14	30	13	19	36	13	11	2	22	33	31	1	1	9	9	1	1	38	1	1	3	1	
+ 1s		+ 1s		+ 1s		+ 1s	+ 1s	+ 4s	+ 2s		+ 1s	+ 8s	+ 1s	+ 7s	+ 7s	+ 1s	+ 2s				+ 9s		+ 3s						

ALLOA Division 2

Year Formed: 1883. *Ground:* Recreation Ground. *Size:* 110yd×75yd. *Capacity:* 9000.
Telephone: Alloa 722695. *Manager:* Alex Totten.
Secretary: George Ormiston.
Club Colours: Gold with black trim, black shorts, gold socks with black tops.
Club Nickname: The Wasps.
Record Attendance: 13,000 v Dunfermline Ath, Scottish Cup 3rd rd replay, 26 Feb, 1939.

1980–81 LEAGUE RECORD

Match No.	Date	Venue	Opponents	Result	H/T Score	League Pos'n	Goalscorers	Attendance
1	Aug 9	A	Meadowbank T	W 3-0	2-0	—	McComb, McIntosh, Rae	300
2	16	H	Cowdenbeath	D 1-1	1-1	3	McNab	650
3	23	A	Stenhousemuir	D 1-1	1-0	3	McComb	300
4	Sept 2	A	Queen of the S	D 1-1	1-0	—	McIntosh	1000
5	6	H	Clyde	W 2-0	1-0	3	McComb, McIntosh	750
6	9	H	Forfar Ath	W 1-0	0-0	—	Holt	800
7	13	A	Arbroath	D 1-1	0-0	2	Shields	615
8	17	H	Stranraer	W 3-1	1-1	—	Morrison, Purdie, Shields	700
9	20	A	Montrose	L 1-2	0-0	2	McComb	500
10	27	H	Albion R	W 1-0	0-0	1	Holt	650
11	Oct 4	A	Queen's Park	D 1-1	0-1	2	Holt (pen)	700
12	11	H	Brechin C	W 5-0	1-0	1	McComb, McIntosh, McNab, Holt, Grant	610
13	18	A	East Fife	D 1-1	0-1	1	Holt	720
14	25	H	Arbroath	D 1-1	0-0	1	Holt	950
15	Nov 1	A	Clyde	W 3-0	1-0	1	Grant, Holt, Morrison	685
16	8	A	Stranraer	W 3-1	1-1	1	McComb, McNab 2	400
17	15	H	Montrose	L 0-4	0-1	1		950
18	22	A	Albion R	L 1-3	0-2	2	Morrison	1000
19	29	H	Queen's Park	W 5-2	3-2	1	McComb 2, Grant 3	1050
20	Dec 6	A	Brechin C	D 1-1	0-0	1	McNab	400
21	20	H	East Fife	W 2-1	2-1	1	Holt, Morrison	700
22	Jan 1	H	Stenhousemuir	W 3-2	2-1	—	McComb, McIntosh, Morrison	1100
23	10	H	Meadowbank T	W 2-1	1-1	1	McComb, McIntosh	755
24	24	A	Meadowbank T	W 4-0	3-0	1	McComb 2, McIntosh, Smith	300
25	31	H	East Fife	D 0-0	0-0	1		325
26	Feb 7	H	Brechin C	L 0-2	0-0	1		675
27	14	A	Stranraer	D 2-2	0-0	1	Headley, Holt	350
28	21	H	Montrose	W 1-0	0-0	1	Holt (pen)	510
29	28	A	Queen's Park	L 1-2	0-0	1	Headley	1300
30	Mar 4	H	Queen of the S	L 1-3	0-2	—	Clark (og)	500
31	11	H	Albion R	L 0-1	0-0	—		610
32	14	H	Stenhousemuir	D 0-0	0-0	1		570
33	21	A	Cowdenbeath	L 2-5	1-1	2	Holt 2 (1 pen)	500
34	28	A	Arbroath	W 3-0	0-0	2	Spence, Grant, McIntosh	500
35	Apr 4	H	Forfar Ath	L 0-1	0-1	2		660
36	11	A	Clyde	D 0-0	0-0	2		430
37	15	A	Cowdenbeath	L 2-4	0-1	—	Holt 2 (1 pen)	800
38	18	H	Queen of the S	L 1-5	0-3	4	Grant	650
39	May 2	A	Forfar Ath	L 1-4	0-1	6	Spence	722

Final League Position: 6

Goalscorers

League (61): Holt 14 (4 pens), McComb 12, McIntosh 8, Grant 7, McNab 5, Morrison 5, Headley 2, Shields 2, Spence 2, Purdie 1, Rae 1, Smith 1, own goal 1.
League Cup (1): McIntosh 1.
Scottish Cup (3): Holt 2, Grant 1.

Honours

Scottish League – Division 2 Champions 1921–22; Runners-up: 1938–39, 1976–77.
Record Victory: 9-2 v Forfar, Division 2, 18 March, 1933.
Record Defeat: 0-10 v Dundee, Division 2, 8 March, 1947.
Most League Points: 60, 1921–22.
Most Individual League Goals in Season: Wee Crilley, 49, Division 2, 1931–32.
Most Capped Player: Jock Hepburn, 1, Scotland.

Drummond S A	McBain G	Robertson J	Abel G	Haggart L	Rae D	Purdie B	Stewart J B	Holt A	Scott D	Hamilton L	Grant A	McIntosh C	Morrison W	McComb L K	McNab R	Shields A	Smith I	Headley G L	Ward R C	Spence C	Henry A	*Match No.*
	1	2			3	4	5	6				7	8	9	10	11						1
1		2*	12		3	4	5	6	13			7	8	9	10	11†						2
1			2		3	4	5	6	12			7*	8	9	10	11						3
1		2	3			4	5	6				7	8	9	10	11						4
1		2	3			4	5	6*	12		13	7	8†	9	10	11						5
1		2	3			4	5	6				7	8	9	10	11						6
1		2	3			4*	5	6		12	13	7†	8	9	10	11						7
1		2			3	4	5	6		13	12	7	8	9*	10†	11						8
1		2			3	4	5	6			12	7	8	9	10	11*						9
1		2			3	4	5	6	12		7	9	8	13	10*	11†						10
1		2	3*			4	5	6			12	7	8	9	10	11						11
1		2			3	4	5	6				7	8*	9	10	11			12			12
1		2			3	4	5	6			12	7*	8	9	10	11						13
1		2			3	4	5	6			13	7	8*	9	10	11†			12			14
1		2			3*	4	5	6		12	7	9	8		10	11						15
1		2			3	4	5	6			7	11	8	9	10							16
1		2			3	4	5	6			7	11*	8	9	10	12						17
1		2			3	4	5	6			7	11	8	9	10							18
1		2			3	4	5	6			7		8	9	10	11						19
1		2			3	4	5	6			7*		8	9	10	11	12					20
1		2		3		4	5	6			11	7*	8	9	10	12						21
1		2*		3	12		5	4			7†	11	6	9	10	13	8					22
1		2		3	13		5	4	11†		7*	10	6	9		12	8					23
1		2		3		4	5	6				11	8	9	10		7					24
1		2		3*	12	4	5	6			13	11†	8	9	10		7					25
1		2		3	13	4	5	6			7*	11	8†	9	10			12				26
1				2	3	4	5	6				12	8*	9	10		7	11				27
1				2	3	4	5	6				12	13	9	10†	11	7	8*				28
1				2	3		5	4			10	11	8		6	12	7	9*				29
1				2	3	4	5	6					8	9		11	7	10				30
				2	3		5	6		4		12	11		9	10	7	8*			1	31
1		2		3		4	5	6			12	9	8*		10	11	7					32
1		2		3		4		5				12	6	9	10	11*	7			8		33
1		2		3				5		4	7	12	8	9*	10		6			11		34
1		2		3			5	6		4	7		8	9	10					11		35
1		2		3			5	6		4	7	12		9	10		8			11*		36
1		2		3			5	6		4	7	11		9	10		8					37
1		2			3	8	5	6		4	7	10				11*		12		9		38
1		2*		3†	10	4	5	6			7	12	8		11	13				9		39
37	1	33	6	18	22	31	37	39	1	6	18	28	35	32	36	23	14	5	0	6	1	
			+		+				+	+	+	+	+	+		+	+	+	+			
			1s		4s				4s	3s	9s	7s	1s	1s		6s	1s	2s	2s			

ARBROATH Division 2

Year Formed: 1878. *Ground:* Gayfield Park. *Size:* 115yd×73yd. *Capacity:* 15,000. *Telephone:* Arbroath 72157.
Manager: Ian J. Stewart.
Trainer: Dave Ewen. *Club Colours:* Maroon shirts, white shorts, maroon stockings.
Club Nickname: Red Lichties.
Record Attendance: 13,510 v Rangers, Scottish Cup 3rd rd, 23 Feb, 1952.
Record Transfer Fee Received: £50,000 from Motherwell for Jeo Carson, Jan 1980 and £50,000 from Motherwell for Albert Kidd, Jan 1980.

1980–81 LEAGUE RECORD

Match No.	*Date*	*Venue*	*Opponents*	*Result*	*H/T Score*	*League Pos'n*	*Goalscorers*	*Attendance*
1	Aug 9	A	Cowdenbeath	L 1-2	0-0	—	Russell (og)	400
2	16	A	Queen of the S	D 2-2	1-1	9	Harley, Shaw	1250
3	20	A	Meadowbank T	W 4-1	2-0	—	Mylles S. 2, Yule, Harley	300
4	23	H	Forfar Ath	L 2-3	2-1	5	Harley, Downie (pen)	1431
5	Sept 3	H	Montrose	L 1-4	0-1	—	Forsyth	742
6	9	A	Stenhousemuir	W 2-1	2-1	—	Mylles T., Gillespie	500
7	13	H	Alloa	D 1-1	0-0	10	Mylles S.	615
8	17	H	Queen's Park	L 1-4	1-3	—	Gavine	584
9	20	A	Stranraer	W 2-0	1-0	9	Mylles S., Yule	500
10	27	H	Brechin C	D 2-2	0-1	8	Mylles T. 2 (2 pens)	895
11	Oct 4	A	Albion R	W 6-1	3-0	5	Docherty, Mylles S., Young, Mylles T. (pen), Gillespie, Shaw	360
12	11	H	East Fife	D 1-1	0-0	6	Harley	779
13	18	A	Clyde	W 2-0	0-0	5	Harley, Young	650
14	25	A	Alloa	D 1-1	0-0	5	Mylles T.	950
15	Nov 1	H	Meadowbank T	L 0-1	0-0	5		599
16	8	A	Queen's Park	D 2-2	1-1	7	Hyslop, Harley	851
17	15	H	Stranraer	W 3-1	1-1	6	Harley, Yule, Hyslop (og)	630
18	22	A	Brechin C	L 1-5	1-1	8	Harley	800
19	Dec 6	A	East Fife	L 1-2	0-0	9	McKenzie	353
20	13	H	Albion R	D 2-2	1-1	8	Harley, McDowell	487
21	20	H	Clyde	D 2-2	0-0	8	Hyslop, Gavine	537
22	27	H	Queen of the S	L 1-2	0-1	9	Hyslop	600
23	Jan 10	A	Montrose	W 2-1	0-0	8	McKenzie, Harley	950
24	31	A	Clyde	L 0-1	0-0	9		1200
25	Feb 7	A	East Fife	W 2-0	1-0	8	Shaw, Harley	449
26	14	H	Queen's Park	D 0-0	0-0	8		682
27	21	H	Stranraer	W 1-0	1-0	6	Harley	420
28	28	A	Albion R	W 4-2	2-1	5	Harley 2, Lees, Gavine	300
29	Mar 4	H	Cowdenbeath	L 0-1	0-1	—		600
30	7	H	Brechin C	D 0-0	0-0	5		993
31	14	H	Forfar Ath	D 0-0	0-0	5		915
32	21	A	Meadowbank T	W 2-1	1-1	5	Gavine, Harley	250
33	28	H	Alloa	L 0-3	0-0	7		500
34	Apr 4	A	Montrose	W 3-0	2-0	7	Hyslop 2, Lees (pen)	450
35	8	A	Forfar Ath	L 1-2	1-0	—	Lees	1000
36	11	H	Stenhousemuir	L 0-1	0-0	8		320
37	18	A	Cowdenbeath	L 0-1	0-1	10		500
38	25	H	Queen of the S	D 1-1	1-1	10	Lees	463
39	May 2	H	Stenhousemuir	W 2-0	1-0	9	Docherty, Kydd	400

Final League Position: 9

Goalscorers

League (58): Harley 15, Hyslop 5, Mylles S. 5, Mylles T. 5 (3 pens), Gavine 4, Lees 4 (1 pen), Shaw 3, Yule 3, Docherty 2, Gillespie 2, McKenzie 2, Young 2, Downie 1 (pen), Forsyth 1, Kydd 1, McDowell 1, own goals 2.
League Cup (0).
Scottish Cup (3): Harley 2, Young 1.

Honours

Scottish League – Division 2 Runners-up: 1934–35, 1958–59, 1967–68, 1971–72.
Record Victory: 36-0 v Bon Accord, Scottish Cup 1st rd, 12 Sept, 1885.
Record Defeat: 0-8 v Kilmarnock, Division 2, 3 Jan, 1949.
Most League Points: 57, Division 2, 1966–67.
Most League Goals: 87, Division 2, 1967–68.
Most Individual League Goals in Season: Dave Easson, 45, Division 2, 1958–59.
Most League Goals in Aggregate: Jimmy Jack, 120, 1966–71.
Most Capped Player: Ned Doig, 2(5), Scotland.

Lister J	Martin E	McKenzie A W	Forsyth S	Rylance D	Scrimgeour E N	Downie C	Young D	Docherty B	Cargill T	Hyslop D	Durno D W	Gavine W J	Harley J	Mylles T	Kydd L	Yule T	Casey J	Wells W J	Barrowman J	Mylles S	McDowell D F	Donald J	Peden A N	Gillespie R J	Shaw G	Lees D G	Henderson D B	Anderson G R	*Match No.*
1		2	7†	3		4		6*				8	9		10	13		5		12					11				1
1		2		3		4		8	5			6	7			11				9					10				2
1		2		3		4		8	5			6	7			11				9					10				3
1		2	12	3		4		8	5			6	7*		13	11				9					10†				4
1		5	2	3		4		7*				6		8		11						12		9	10				5
1		5	2		3			6				4		8		11*				7		12		9	10				6
1		3*	2	12			5	6				4		8	13	11				9†				7	10				7
1			2	3			5	6				4		8		11				9				7	10				8
1			2		3		5	6				4		12	8	11				9				7	10*				9
1			2		3		5	6				4		8		11				9*			12	7	10				10
1			2		3		5	6				4		8		11				9			12	7*	10				11
1			2		3		5	6				4	12	8		11				9				7*	10				12
1			2*	12	3		5	6				4	7	8		11				9†					10		13		13
	1		2	13	3		5	6				4	7	8		11				9*					10†		12		14
	1		2	3			5	6		9		4	7	8	12	11†											13	10*	15
	1		2	12	3		5	6		9		4	7	8*	10	11†											13		16
	1		2		3*		5	6		9	12	8	7		4†	11				13					10				17
	1		2	12	3		5	6		9		4*	7	8†		11				13					10				18
	1	2	4*		3		5	6		9			7		11	12					8				10				19
	1	5	2	3	13			6		9			7	10	4*	12					8				11†				20
	1	5	2	3				6		9		4	7	12		13					11				10†	8*			21
	1	3	2				5	6		9	13	4	7			12					11†				10	8*			22
	1	8	2		3		5	6		9		4	7												10	11			23
1		2		6	3		5			9		8	7				4								10	11			24
1		2		6	3		5	12		9		8*	7				4								10	11			25
1		2		6	3		5	8*		9		12	7				4								10	11			26
1			8*	6	3		5	2		9		12	7				4								10	11			27
1				6	3		5	2		9		8	7				4								10	11			28
1				6*	3		5	2		9		8	7	13			4				12				10†	11			29
1				6	3		5	2		9		8	7				4								10	11			30
1				6	3*		5	2		9		8	7†				4			13	12				10	11			31
1					3		5	2		9*		6	7	8		12	4				10					11			32
1		13			3		5	2		9*		6	7			12	4				10†				8	11			33
1		8	2				5	4		9	3	6	7												10	11			34
1		8	2		3		5	4		9	10	6	7													11			35
1		8	2		3		5	4		9	10	6*	7†			12				13						11			36
1		8	2				5	6		9	3	10	7		4											11			37
1		4	2				5	6			3	10†	9*		8	11				12					13	7			38
1			2					6			3	10	9†		8	11	5*		4						13	7		12	39
29	10	20	27	17	24	5	30	37	3	23	6	35	31	14	9	19	11	1	1	12	6	0	0	8	31	19	0	1	
		+ 1s	+ 1s	+ 5s	+ 1s			+ 1s			+ 2s	+ 2s	+ 1s	+ 3s	+ 3s	+ 8s				+ 6s	+ 2s	+ 2s	+ 2s		+ 2s		+ 4s	+ 1s	

AYR UNITED Division 1

Year Formed: 1910.
Ground: Somerset Park. *Size:* 111yd×75yd. *Capacity:* 18,500 (1500 seats).
Telephone: Ayr (0292) 263 435.
Manager: Willie McLean. *Asst Manager:* George Caldwell.
Secretary: John Robertson.
Club Colours: White shirts with black facings, black shorts, white stockings.
Club Nickname: The Honest Men.
Record Attendance: 25,225 v Rangers, Division 1, 13 Sept, 1969.

1980–81 LEAGUE RECORD

Match No.	*Date*	*Venue*	*Opponents*	*Result*	*H/T Score*	*League Pos'n*	*Goalscorers*	*Atten-dance*
1	Aug 9	H	Motherwell	W 5-0	2-0	—	Frye, Nicol, Fleeting, Cashmore, Carson (og)	3782
2	16	A	Dundee	D 0-0	0-0	3		7000
3	23	H	Stirling Albion	D 0-0	0-0	3		2850
4	Sept 6	A	Berwick R	W 2-1	1-1	2	Morris, Christie	713
5	13	H	Hibernian	L 1-3	1-0	8	Morris	3960
6	17	H	Hamilton A	W 2-1	0-0	—	Connor, Christie	3500
7	20	A	Clydebank	D 2-2	1-1	5	Connor, Frye	1000
8	27	H	Dunfermline Ath	W 2-0	1-0	5	Frye, Larnach	3170
9	Oct 1	H	Raith R	W 1-0	0-0	—	Frye	2498
10	4	A	Falkirk	L 1-3	0-1	3	Love	2000
11	11	H	St Johnstone	D 0-0	0-0	3		2649
12	13	A	East Stirling	W 2-0	1-0	—	Morris, Christie	800
13	18	A	Dumbarton	W 1-0	0-0	2	Morris	1000
14	25	A	Hibernian	L 0-1	0-0	3		4500
15	Nov 1	H	Berwick R	W 4-1	1-0	3	Christie, Morris, Connor (pen), Frye	2086
16	8	A	Hamilton A	L 0-1	0-1	3		1885
17	15	H	Clydebank	W 1-0	0-0	3	Morris	2279
18	22	A	Dunfermline Ath	W 3-2	0-1	3	Frye 2, Love	2200
19	29	H	Falkirk	W 3-1	0-0	3	Frye, Shanks (pen), Connor	2204
20	Dec 6	A	St Johnstone	L 0-1	0-0	3		1792
21	13	H	Dumbarton	D 0-0	0-0	3		1875
22	20	A	Raith R	L 1-2	1-0	4	Morris	2000
23	27	H	Dundee	W 1-0	1-0	3	Fleeting	4036
24	Jan 1	A	Stirling Albion	D 1-1	1-0	—	Fleeting	2000
25	3	H	East Stirling	D 3-3	1-0	3	Armour, Frye, Connor	2339
26	10	A	Motherwell	L 2-3	1-3	3	Christie, Love	2554
27	17	H	St Johnstone	D 3-3	0-2	3	Connor, Nicol, McCutcheon	2364
28	31	A	Dundee	W 4-2	1-1	3	McCutcheon, Reilly 2, Morris	4724
29	Feb 21	H	Clydebank	W 4-1	2-0	3	Reilly 2, Nicol, McCutcheon	1440
30	28	A	Falkirk	L 1-2	0-0	3	Connor (pen)	2000
31	Mar 4	A	Hamilton A	D 0-0	0-0	—		1000
32	7	H	Dunfermline Ath	W 2-1	0-1	3	McAllister, Frye	1697
33	14	A	Berwick R	D 1-1	0-0	3	McCutcheon	570
34	21	A	Raith R	D 1-1	0-0	4	Connor	2300
35	28	H	Hibernian	L 0-1	0-1	5		2997
36	Apr 4	A	East Stirling	W 3-1	3-0	5	Christie 2, Morris	850
37	11	A	Motherwell	L 0-1	0-0	6		2068
38	18	H	Stirling Albion	W 1-0	0-0	6	McCutcheon (pen)	1220
39	25	H	Dumbarton	L 1-2	0-2	6	Morris	998

Final League Position: 6

Goalscorers

League (59): Frye 10, Morris 10, Connor 8 (2 pens), Christie 7, McCutcheon 5 (1 pen), Reilly 4, Fleeting 3, Love 3, Nicol 3, Armour 1, Cashmore 1, Larnach 1, McAllister 1, Shanks 1 (pen), own goal 1.
League Cup (20): Connor 4 (1 pen), Frye 4, Morris 4, Christie 3, Cashmore 2, Armour 1, McColl 1, own goal 1.
Scottish Cup (1): Hendry 1.

Honours
Scottish League – Division 2 Champions 1911–12, 1912–13, 1927–28, 1936–37, 1958–59, 1965–66; Runners-up 1910–11, 1955–56, 1968–69.
Scottish Cup – None.
Scottish League Cup – None.
Record Victory: 11-1 v Dumbarton, League Cup, 13 Aug, 1952.
Record Defeat: 0-9 v Rangers, Division 1, 16 Nov, 1929, and Hearts, Division 1, 28 Feb, 1931.
Most League Points: 60, Division 2, 1958–59.
Most Individual League Goals in Season: Jimmy Smith, 66, 1927–28.
Most Capped Player: Jim Nisbet, 3, Scotland.

Rennie S	Shanks J M	Nicol S	McAllister I	Aitken I	McSherry J	Larnach M	Hendry W	McColl W	Fleeting J	Frye J F	Cashmore I	Armour D	Love A	Reilly R	Christie G	McCutcheon D	Morris E	Connor R	McInally A	McGee L	*Match No.*
1	2	3	5		4				6	7	12		8		11*		9	10			1
1	2	3			4		5		6	7	13	12	8*		11†		9	10			2
1	2	3			4*		5		6	7	13	10	8		11†		9	12			3
1	2	3			4		5		6		7		8		11		9	10			4
1	2	3	5		4*		12		6	7†	13		8		11		9	10			5
1	2	3	5		4				6	7			8		11		9	10			6
1	2	3	5		8*		4		6	7	13	12			11†		9	10			7
1	2	3	5		13	12	4		6	7*		8†			11		9	10			8
1	2	3	5				4		6	7		8			11		9	10			9
1		3	5		12	4	2		6	7			8		11*		9	10			10
1	2	3			13	12	5	4*	6	7			8		11†		9	10			11
1	2	3	5				4		6	7			8		11		9	10			12
1	2	3				12	5	4	6		7*		8		11		9	10			13
1	2	3			12	7†	5	4*	6	13			8		11		9	10			14
1	2	3				12	5	4*	6	7			8		11		9	10			15
1	2	3				12	5	4*	6	7†	13		8		11		9	10			16
1	2	3				5		12	6		7	4	8*		11		9	10			17
1	2	3				11†	5	4	6	7		12	8		13		9*	10			18
1	2	3				9	5	4	6	7	13	8*	12		11†			10			19
1	2	3				9	5	4	6	7		12	8		11*			10			20
1	2	3				9*	5	4	6	7	12	8			11			10			21
1	2	3					5*	4	6	7†	11	8	12		13		9	10			22
1	2	3					5	4	6	7		8	12		11*		9	10			23
1	2	3					5	4	6	13	12	8	7*		11		9†	10			24
1	2	3					5	4	6	7		8*	12		11		9	10			25
1	2	3				12	5		6	7		8*	4		11†	13	9	10			26
1	2	3					5	4*	6	7†		12	8		13	11	9	10			27
1	2	3					5	4	6				8*	11		7	9	10		12	28
1	2	3					5	4	6					8	11	7	9*	10	12		29
1	2	3					5	4	6					8	11*	7	9	10	12		30
1	2*	3					5	4	6					8	11	7	9	10	12		31
1*		3	2				5		6	12				4	11	7	9	10	8		32
1		3	2*		12		5		6	7			13	4†	11	8	9	10			33
1		3		2	4		5		6	7*			12	11†	13	8	9	10			34
1		3		2	4*		5		6		12		8†	13	11	7	9	10			35
1	2	3		4	12		5		6					8*	11	7	9	10			36
1	2	3		4*			5		6	12			8		11	7	9	10			37
1	2	3					5	4	6	12					11	8	9	10	7*		38
1	2	3			12		5*		6	7				13	11	4	9	10	8†		39
39	34	39	10	4	9	7	35	19	39	25	4	11	22	8	34	13	36	38	3	0	
					+ 7s	+ 6s	+ 1s	+ 1s		+ 5s	+ 10s	+ 5s	+ 6s	+ 2s	+ 4s	+ 1s		+ 1s	+ 3s	+ 1s	

BERWICK RANGERS Division 2

Year Formed: 1881. *Ground:* Shielfield Park. *Size:* 112yd×76yd. *Capacity:* 10,673 (1473 seats).
Telephone: Berwick (0289) 7424/2554.
Manager: Frank Connor. *Commercial Manager:* Ian Davison. *Assistant Manager:* Roy McDowell.
Secretary: Dennis McCleary. *Limited Company:* 1952.
Club Colours: Gold shirts with black vertical stripes, black shorts with gold trim.
Record Attendance: 13,365 v Rangers, Scottish Cup 1st rd, 28 Jan, 1967.
Club Nickname: The Borderers.

1980–81 LEAGUE RECORD

Match No.	*Date*	*Venue*	*Opponents*	*Result*		*H/T Score*	*League Pos'n*	*Goalscorers*	*Attendance*
1	Aug 9	A	Hamilton A	L	1-9	0-3	—	Egan	1471
2	16	H	Dunfermline Ath	D	1-1	0-0	13	Smith G. (pen)	1204
3	23	A	Hibernian	L	0-3	0-2	14		4000
4	Sept 3	A	Falkirk	L	0-6	0-1	—		1500
5	6	H	Ayr U	L	1-2	1-1	14	Tait	713
6	9	H	St Johnstone	L	0-1	0-1	—		847
7	13	A	Dundee	D	2-2	2-0	13	Smith D., Deakin	3782
8	17	A	Dumbarton	L	0-2	0-1	—		1250
9	20	H	Motherwell	W	3-2	1-1	13	Egan, Hamilton, Tait	1191
10	27	A	East Stirling	L	1-5	0-3	14	McDowell	500
11	Oct 4	H	Stirling Albion	W	1-0	1-0	14	Tait	640
12	11	A	Clydebank	L	1-2	1-1	14	McLeod	600
13	18	H	Raith R	L	1-4	1-2	14	Wallace	961
14	25	H	Dundee	L	0-1	0-1	14		1080
15	Nov 1	A	Ayr U	L	1-4	0-1	14	Tait	2086
16	8	H	Dumbarton	D	2-2	0-0	14	Hamilton 2 (2 pens)	659
17	15	A	Motherwell	L	1-2	0-0	14	Smith G.	1890
18	22	H	East Stirling	L	1-2	1-0	14	McLeod	750
19	29	A	Stirling Albion	L	0-1	0-0	14		500
20	Dec 6	H	Clydebank	L	0-1	0-0	14		550
21	13	A	Raith R	L	0-3	0-2	14		1700
22	20	H	Falkirk	L	0-4	0-2	14		682
23	Jan 1	H	Hibernian	L	0-2	0-2	—		2110
24	3	A	St Johnstone	L	0-1	0-0	14		2365
25	10	H	Hamilton A	W	1-0	0-0	14	Tait	647
26	31	H	Hibernian	D	0-0	0-0	14		2019
27	Feb 7	H	Motherwell	D	2-2	2-0	14	Black, Dixon	928
28	14	A	Raith R	D	1-1	0-1	14	Black	1500
29	21	A	Dumbarton	D	1-1	1-0	14	Hamilton	400
30	28	H	Stirling Albion	W	1-0	1-0	14	Hamilton (pen)	510
31	Mar 14	H	Ayr U	D	1-1	0-0	14	Hamilton	570
32	21	A	St Johnstone	L	2-6	1-3	14	Tait, Thomson	2048
33	28	A	Dundee	D	0-0	0-0	14		4000
34	Apr 4	H	Dunfermline Ath	W	1-0	0-0	14	Thomson	710
35	7	A	East Stirling	D	0-0	0-0	—		600
36	11	A	Clydebank	L	0-2	0-2	14		350
37	18	H	Falkirk	L	1-2	0-1	14	Tait (pen)	812
38	22	A	Dunfermline Ath	D	1-1	1-0	—	Tait	1500
39	25	A	Hamilton A	L	1-4	0-1	14	Brown	1000

Final League Position: 14

Goalscorers

League (30): Tait 8 (1 pen), Hamilton 6 (3 pens), Black 2, Egan 2, McLeod 2, Smith G. 2 (1 pen), Thomson 2, Brown 1, Deakin 1, Dixon 1, McDowell 1, Smith D. 1, Wallace 1.
League Cup (1): Egan 1.
Scottish Cup (0).

Honours
Scottish League – Division 2 Champions 1978–79.
East of Scotland FA Shield – Winners 1981.
Record Victory: 8-1 v Forfar Athletic, Division 2, 25 Dec, 1965 and 8-1 v Vale of Leithen, Scottish Cup, Dec, 1966.
Record Defeat: 1-9 v Hamilton A, Division 2, 9 Aug, 1980.
Most League Points: 54, Division 2, 1978–79.
Most Individual League Goals in Season: Ken Bowron, 38, Division 2, 1963–64.
Most League Goals: 83, Division 2, 1961–62.
Most League Appearances: Eric Tait, 309, 1970–81.
Best Cup Run: 1963 League Cup Semi-Final 1-3 v Rangers (Hampden Park).
Extra Information: Only Scottish League club with home ground in England.
Previous grounds: Bull Stob Close, Pier Field, Meadow Field, Union Park and Old Shielfield.

Davidson K	McLaren I	McGarr E	McDonald M	Glynn M	McCann H	Moyes D	Deakin J	Henderson I	Hamilton G	Dixon S	McDowell R	Smith D	Muir L	Marshall B	Davidson P	Romaines S	McLeod I	Smith G	Tait E	Egan C	McGlynn J	Brown D	Duncan A R	Wallace G	Lumsdaine C	Thomson A J	Scott J A	McKenna M	Black I G	Carlyle R	McDougall J	*Match No.*
1							3			5	12	6		4*	7	10	8	9		11								2				1
1						6	3			2	5				7	8		9	10	11											4	2
1					2	6	12			3*	5	9			7	8		13	10	11†											4	3
1					2	6	3				5	7				8		9	10	11							4					4
	1				2	6	3*					5			7	4	8	12	10	11							9					5
	1				2	6	3		5			8			7	4			10	11							9					6
	1				2		3	12				5			7	4	8*	9	10	11							6					7
	1				2		3					5			7	4	8	9	10	11							6					8
	1				2		3	4	5			8			7	12	10		9	11							6*					9
	1				2*		3	4	5		12	11			7	8		9†	13	10							6					10
	1				2	7	3	4	5		6	8				12	9		10	11*												11
		1			2	7	3	4	5		6	8				12	9		10	11*												12
		1			2	3			4		5	6			8	7	11*		9	12				10								13
		1			2*	9	3			4	5	7		12	6	8			10	11†			13									14
		1				9	3		8	4	5	6		2	7		12		10*				11									15
		1			12	2	3		8	6	5	7			9†	4*			10				11	13								16
			1			2	3*		8	6	5	7		12	13	4			10				11†	9								17
			1			3	12		8	6	5			2*		4	9		10				11	7†			13					18
			1		2		9	3		5				6	7†	4*	8		10				11	13					12			19
			1				11			5			6	2	7*	4	9		10		8		12						3			20
			1			2	8*		4	5			6	12		7	13	9	10†		11								3			21
		1				2	12		5				6	4	8		13	9	10†		11					7*			3			22
			1		3	2	8		4	5			6		12	9	7				10*	11†				13						23
			1		3	2	8*		4	5			6		12	9	7				10	11†				13						24
			1		3	2	11†		4	5			6		7	9	13		10*		8	12										25
			1		3	2			4	5			6	13	7	9	12		10*		8								11†			26
			1		3	2			4	5			6	12	7	9	10†				8*	13							11			27
			1		3	2			4	5			6		7*	9	10†				8	12			13				11			28
			1		3	2			4	5			6		12	9	8				7	11*							10			29
			1		3	2			4	5			6		12	9	7*		10†		8					13			11			30
			1		3				4	5			6	2*	7	9†	12		10		8					13			11			31
				1	3	2			4	5			6		7	9*	12		10†		8					13			11			32
				1	2				4	5			6	12	7*	8	10				11†				13	9			3			33
				1	2				4	5			6	10	7	8									11	9			3			34
				1	2				4	5			6	10	7	8									11	9			3			35
			1		3				4	5			6	2	7*	8	13		10						11†	9				12		36
				1	3	4	13			5			6	2		7*	11		10		12				8†	9						37
				1	3	2				5			6	9		4	8		10						11	7						38
				1	3	2				5			6	9*		10†	8				11	12			4	7				13		39
4	7	6	15	7	30	27	21	5	26	28	11	16	20	13	26	34	21	8	28	13	15	3	5	3	6	8	7	1	13	0	2	
					+ 1s		+ 4s	+ 1s			+ 2s			+ 6s	+ 5s	+ 3s	+ 8s	+ 2s	+ 1s	+ 1s	+ 1s	+ 4s	+ 2s	+ 2s	+ 2s	+ 5s	+ 1s		+ 1s	+ 2s		

BRECHIN CITY Division 2

Year Formed: 1906. *Ground:* Glebe Park. *Size:* 110yd×67yd. *Capacity:* 7500. *Telephone:* Brechin 2856. *Manager:* Doug Houston. *Secretary:* George Johnston. *Club Colours:* Red shirts, shorts and stockings. *Club Nickname:* City. *Record Attendance:* 8123 v Aberdeen, Scottish Cup, 3rd rd, 3 Feb, 1973.

1980–81 LEAGUE RECORD

Match No.	Date	Venue	Opponents	Result	H/T Score	League Pos'n	Goalscorers	Attendance
1	Aug 9	A	Queen of the S	L 2-3	0-2	—	Paterson, Elvin	1500
2	16	A	Clyde	L 0-3	0-3	14		680
3	23	H	Montrose	D 1-1	0-0	14	Paterson	500
4	Sept 3	H	Stenhousemuir	W 2-1	2-1	—	Henderson, Campbell R.	400
5	6	A	Cowdenbeath	L 1-2	1-1	13	Paterson	350
6	9	A	Meadowbank T	L 0-2	0-0	—		300
7	13	H	Queen's Park	D 0-0	0-0	14		400
8	17	H	Forfar Ath	D 1-1	0-1	—	Graham	1100
9	20	A	Albion R	W 3-2	1-0	12	Clark 2, Cormack	350
10	27	A	Arbroath	D 2-2	1-0	13	Henderson, Kyles	895
11	Oct 4	H	East Fife	L 0-1	0-0	13		400
12	11	A	Alloa	L 0-5	0-1	13		610
13	18	H	Stranraer	W 1-0	1-0	12	McLeod	400
14	25	A	Queen's Park	D 1-1	0-1	12	Campbell I.	910
15	Nov 1	H	Cowdenbeath	L 0-2	0-0	12		400
16	8	A	Forfar Ath	D 0-0	0-0	12		811
17	15	H	Albion R	D 2-2	2-0	12	Cormack, Campbell I.	400
18	22	H	Arbroath	W 5-1	1-1	12	Lorimer, Campbell I. 2, Graham, Scrimgeour (og)	800
19	29	A	East Fife	W 2-0	1-0	11	Lorimer, Cormack	567
20	Dec 6	H	Alloa	D 1-1	0-0	11	Graham	400
21	20	A	Stranraer	W 1-0	0-0	10	Keating	200
22	27	H	Clyde	W 3-1	0-1	7	Henderson, Graham, Paterson	500
23	Jan 1	H	Montrose	W 3-1	1-1	—	Paterson, Campbell I. 2	1200
24	31	A	Stranraer	D 1-1	0-1	7	Rodger (og)	450
25	Feb 7	A	Alloa	W 2-0	0-0	5	Campbell I. 2	675
26	14	H	Forfar Ath	D 0-0	0-0	4		600
27	21	H	Albion R	W 2-1	0-1	4	Graham, Paterson	400
28	28	A	East Fife	D 2-2	1-0	4	Kyles, Graham	398
29	Mar 7	A	Arbroath	D 0-0	0-0	4		993
30	14	H	Clyde	W 2-1	2-0	4	Graham 2	400
31	18	A	Stenhousemuir	W 3-0	0-0	—	Lesslie 2, Kyles	300
32	24	H	Queen of the S	W 2-1	1-0	—	Graham 2	500
33	28	A	Queen's Park	L 0-1	0-0	3		1135
34	Apr 4	H	Cowdenbeath	L 1-2	1-1	4	Kyles	400
35	11	H	Meadowbank T	D 0-0	0-0	4		400
36	14	H	Queen of the S	W 1-0	1-0	—	Campbell I. (pen)	400
37	18	A	Montrose	L 2-3	1-0	5	Kyles, Campbell I.	950
38	25	A	Stenhousemuir	D 1-1	0-1	5	Campbell I.	150
39	May 2	H	Meadowbank T	W 2-1	1-0	4	Elvin, Lesslie	400

Final League Position: 4

Goalscorers

League (52): Campbell I. 11 (1 pen), Graham 10, Paterson 6, Kyles 5, Cormack 3, Henderson 3, Lesslie 3, Clark 2, Elvin 2, Lorimer 2, Campbell R. 1, Keating 1, McLeod 1, own goals 2.
League Cup (1): Campbell I. 1.
Scottish Cup (5): Campbell I. 1, Cormack 1, Graham 1, Keating 1, Paterson 1.

Honours
Record Victory: 12-1 v Thornhill, Scottish Cup, 1st rd, 28 Jan, 1926.
Record Defeat: 1-10 v Dunfermline Ath, Division 2, 14 Dec, 1929.
Most League Points: 44, Division 2, 1980–81.
Most Individual Goals: Willie McIntosh, 26, 1959–60.
Highest League Placing: 4th, Division 2, 1980–81.

Neilson D	Ritchie J B	Watt D C	Keating A	Simpson D	Glover S	Reid B	Sime J	McLeod D	Lowe M	Henderson A S	Campbell R	Lorimer R	Elvin C	Cormack R	Kyles J	Lesslie G	Scullion D	Campbell I	Paterson I A	Graham S	Burnside D P	Match No.
	1	2	3	4*	12		5	6	10†	11			8	13				7	9			1
1		2	3		12	4	5*	6	10	11			8	13				7	9†			2
1		2	3		5	8		4	6		12		10	11				7	9*			3
1		2	3		5	12		6*	4	11	8		10					7	9			4
1		2	3		5	6*			4	11	8		10		12			7	9			5
1		2	3*		5			4	6	10	8		13	12	11†			7	9			6
1		2	3		5	6			4	9*	8		10	11	12			7				7
1		2	3		5	6*			4	13	8		10	11	12			7†		9		8
1		2	3		5	6*			4	7	8		10	11				12		9		9
1		2	3		5	6			4	7	8*		10	11	12			13		9†		10
1		2	3	12	5		13	6*	4	9	8			11†	10			7				11
1		2	3		5	6			4	13	12		8	11	10†			7		9*		12
1		2	3		5	10		6	4	9			8	11				7				13
1		2	3		5	10†		4	6*	9	13		8	11	12			7				14
1		2	3		5	13		4		9	6*		8	11†	12			7		10		15
1		2	3		5			4			6	10	8	11				7		9		16
1		2	3			6		4		12	5	10	8	11				7		9*		17
1		2	3			6		4			5	10	8	11				7		9		18
1		2	3		5			4			6	10	8	11				7		9		19
1		2	3		5			4			6	10	8*	11	12			7		9		20
1		2	3		5				4		6	10	8	11				7		9		21
1		2	3		5				4		6	10	8*	11				7	12	9		22
1		2	3		5					11	6	10	12		4*			7	8	9		23
1		2	3		5					4	6	10	13	11†	12			7	8	9*		24
1		2	3		5					4	6	10	11		9			7	8			25
1		2	3		5					4	6	10	11		9			7	8			26
1		2	3*		5					4	6	10	8†	11	12			7	9	13		27
1		2	3		5					4	6	10		12	8*			7	9	11		28
1		2	3		.5					4*	6	10	12		8			7	9	11		29
1		2	3							12	6	10	7	11		4	5*		8	9		30
1		2	3								6	10	8	11	12	4	5	7	9*			31
1		2	3					6		12		10	7		11*	4	5		8	9		32
1		2	3					6		12		10	7	13	11†	4	5		8	9*		33
1		2	3					6		13		7	10	12	11	4*	5		8	9†		34
1		2	3					7*		13	6	10	11		12	5	4		8†	9		35
1		2	3							4	6	10			11	5		7	8	9		36
1		2	3			13				4	6	10†	12		11	5		7	8*	9		37
1		2	3							4	6	10†	8		7	5	12	11	13	9*		38
1		2	3							10†	6	12	8		7*	5	4	9		13	11	39
38	1	39	39	1	25	12	2	18	16	23	30	23	31	21	15	10	7	32	21	24	1	
				+ 1s	+ 2s	+ 3s	+ 1s			+ 8s	+ 3s	+ 1s	+ 5s	+ 6s	+ 11s		+ 1s	+ 2s	+ 2s	+ 2s		

CELTIC — Premier Division

Year Formed: 1888. *Ground:* Celtic Park. *Size:* 115yd×75yd. *Capacity:* 67,500 (9000 seats). *Telephone:* 041-554 2710. *Manager:* Billy McNeill. *Secretary:* Desmond White CA. *Asst Manager:* John Clark. *Commercial Manager:* Jack McGinn. *Club Colours:* Green and white hooped shirts, white shorts. *Club nickname:* The Bhoys. *Record Attendance:* 92,000 v Rangers, Division 1, 1 Jan, 1938. *European Competitions:* European Cup, 1966–67 (winners), 1967–68, 1969–70 (finalists), 1970–71, 1971–72, 1972–73, 1973–74, 1974–75, 1976–77, 1979–80; European Cup-Winners' Cup, 1963–64, 1965–66, 1975–76, 1980–81; Fairs Cup, 1962–63, 1964–65; UEFA Cup, 1976–77. *Coronation Cup:* 1953. *Empire Exhibition Cup:* 1938.

1980–81 LEAGUE RECORD

Match No.	*Date*	*Venue*	*Opponents*	*Result*	*H/T Score*	*League Pos'n*	*Goalscorers*	*Attendance*
1	Aug 9	H	Morton	W 2-1	0-0	—	McCluskey, MacLeod	20,000
2	16	A	Kilmarnock	W 3-0	3-0	1	McGarvey 2, Sullivan	13,800
3	23	H	Rangers	L 1-2	0-0	3	Burns	58,000
4	Sept 6	H	Partick T	W 4-1	2-1	3	McGarvey, Nicholas 2, MacLeod (pen)	20,000
5	13	A	Hearts	W 2-0	1-0	2	Provan, Nicholas	17,169
6	20	H	Airdrieonians	D 1-1	0-0	3	Nicholas	18,000
7	27	A	Aberdeen	D 2-2	2-0	3	Nicholas, Burns	23,000
8	Oct 4	H	Dundee U	W 2-0	1-0	3	McGarvey, Nicholas	21,000
9	11	A	St Mirren	W 2-0	2-0	3	MacDonald, Stark (og)	18,601
10	18	A	Morton	W 3-2	2-0	3	Provan, Aitken, Nicholas	16,000
11	25	H	Kilmarnock	W 4-1	2-1	2	McGarvey 2, Nicholas 2 (1 pen)	18,000
12	Nov 1	A	Rangers	L 0-3	0-2	3		53,000
13	8	H	Aberdeen	L 0-2	0-1	3		29,000
14	15	A	Airdrieonians	W 4-1	3-0	3	Aitken, McGarvey, Nicholas, McAdam	15,000
15	22	H	St Mirren	L 1-2	0-0	3	McCluskey (pen)	16,000
16	29	A	Dundee U	W 3-0	0-0	3	McAdam, Weir, Hegarty (og)	15,000
17	Dec 6	A	Partick T	W 1-0	0-0	2	McCluskey	12,436
18	13	H	Hearts	W 3-2	2-1	2	MacDonald, McCluskey, McGarvey	13,800
19	20	H	Airdrieonians	W 2-1	1-0	2	McAdam, McCluskey	11,900
20	27	A	Aberdeen	L 1-4	0-2	2	Nicholas	24,000
21	Jan 1	A	Kilmarnock	W 2-1	2-1	—	McGarvey 2	8000
22	3	H	Morton	W 3-0	3-0	2	McGarvey 2, Provan	14,900
23	10	H	Dundee U	W 2-1	2-0	2	Nicholas, McGarvey	22,000
24	31	A	Hearts	W 3-0	1-0	1	Burns, McGarvey, Sullivan	14,596
25	Feb 21	H	Rangers	W 3-1	0-1	1	Nicholas 2, Aitken	52,800
26	28	A	Morton	W 3-0	2-0	1	McGarvey 2, Provan	14,000
27	Mar 14	H	St Mirren	W 7-0	3-0	1	Aitken, Nicholas, McGarvey 3, McCluskey 2	18,100
28	18	H	Partick T	W 4-1	2-1	—	MacLeod 2, McGarvey, Sullivan	15,000
29	21	A	Airdrieonians	W 2-1	1-0	1	McGarvey, MacLeod	13,000
30	28	H	Aberdeen	D 1-1	0-1	1	McCluskey	35,200
31	Apr 1	H	Hearts	W 6-0	3-0	—	McCluskey 2, MacLeod 2, Provan, McGarvey	13,300
32	5	A	Partick T	W 1-0	0-0	—	McAdam	17,196
33	18	A	Rangers	W 1-0	0-0	1	Nicholas	34,000
34	22	A	Dundee U	W 3-2	2-1	—	MacLeod, McGarvey, Burns	15,349
35	25	H	Kilmarnock	D 1-1	1-0	1	Provan	23,300
36	May 2	A	St Mirren	L 1-3	0-1	1	Provan	14,806

Final League Position: 1

Goalscorers

League (84): McGarvey 23, Nicholas 16 (1 pen), McCluskey 10 (1 pen), MacLeod 8 (1 pen), Provan 7, Aitken 4, Burns 4, McAdam 4, Sullivan 3, MacDonald 2, Weir 1, own goals 2.
League Cup (17): Nicholas 6 (1 pen), Burns 5, McGarvey 2, Doyle 1, MacDonald 1, Provan 1, Sullivan 1.
Scottish Cup (9): Nicholas 3 (1 pen), Burns 2, Conroy 1, McCluskey 1, McGarvey 1, MacLeod 1.

Honours

Scottish League: Division 1 Champions: 1892–93, 1893–94, 1895–96, 1897–98, 1904–05, 1905–06, 1906–07, 1907–08, 1908–09, 1909–10, 1913–14, 1914–15, 1915–16, 1916–17, 1918–19, 1921–22, 1925–26, 1935–36, 1937–38, 1953–54, 1965–66, 1966–67, 1967–68, 1968–69, 1969–70, 1970–71, 1971–72, 1972–73, 1973–74; Runners-up: 16 times; Premier Division Champions: 1977, 1979, 1981; Runners-up 1976, 1980. *Scottish Cup.* Winners: 1892, 1899, 1900, 1904, 1907, 1908, 1911, 1912, 1914, 1923, 1925, 1927, 1931, 1933, 1937, 1951, 1954, 1965, 1967, 1969, 1971, 1972, 1974, 1975, 1977, 1980; Runners-up: 14 times. *Scottish League Cup:* Winners: 1956–57, 1957–58, 1965–66, 1966–67, 1967–68, 1968–69, 1969–70, 1974–75; Runners-up: 7 times. *Record Victory:* 11-0 v Dundee, Division 1, 26 Oct, 1895. *Record Defeat:* 0-8 v Motherwell, Division 1, 30 April, 1937. *Most League Points:* 67, 1915–16, 1921–22. *Most Individual League Goals in Season:* 50, James McGrory, 1935–36. *Most Goals in Total Aggregate:* 397, James McGrory, 1922–39. *Most Capped Player:* Danny McGrain, 55, Scotland.

Bonner P J	McGrain D	Reid M	Sneddon A	MacLeod M	Aitken R	McAdam T	Conroy M	MacDonald R	Sullivan D	Weir J	Provan D	Burns T	McCluskey G	McGarvey F	Nicholas C	Doyle J	*Match No.*
1	3		2	10	4	5	6*		8		7	12	11	9			1
1	3		2	6	4	5			8		7	10	11	9*	12		2
1	3		2	6	4	5			8		7	10	11	9			3
1	3		2	6	4	5			8		7	10	12	9*	11		4
1	3		2	6*	4	5	12		8		7	10	9		11		5
1	3		2			5	4		8	6	7	10	9*		11	12	6
1	3		2	13		4	6	5	8		7	10†		9*	11	12	7
1	3		2	10		6	4	5	8				7	9	11		8
1	3		2		4	6		5	8		7		10	9	11		9
1	3		2	12	4	6		5	8		7*			9	11	10	10
1	3		2		4	6		5	8		7	10		9	11		11
1	3		2		4	6		5	8		7	10	12	9*	11†	13	12
1	3		2		4	5	6*		8		7	10	12	9†	11	13	13
1	2	3			4	5				6	7	10	8	9	11		14
1	2	3			4	6		5	7	8		10	12	9	11*		15
1	2	3			4	6		5	7	8		10	11	9			16
1		3	2		4	6		5	7*	8	12	10	11	9			17
1		3	2		4	6		5		8	7	10	11	9			18
1	2	3			4	6		5		8	7	10	11	9			19
1	2	3			4	6	7*	5		8	12	10	11†	9	13		20
1	2	3			6	5			4	8	7	10		9	11		21
1	2	3			6	5			4	8	7	10		9	11		22
1	2	3			6	5			4	8	7	10		9	11		23
1	2	3			6	5	8		4		7	10	12	9	11*		24
1	2	3			6	5	8		4		7	10		9	11		25
1	2	3			6	5	8		4		7	10		9	11		26
1	2	3		12	6	5	8*		4		7	10	13	9	11†		27
1	2	3		12	6	5	8*		4		7	10		9	11		28
1	2	3		8	6	5			4		7	10		9	11		29
1	2	3		8	6	5			4		7	10	12	9	11*		30
1	2	3		8	6	5			4		7	10	11	9			31
1		3		2	6	5	8		4		7	10	11	9*	12		32
1	2			3	6	5	8	4			7	10		9	11		33
1	2	3		4	6	5	8				7	10		9	11		34
1	2	3		8	6	5			4		7	10		9	11		35
1	2	3		8	6			5	4		7	10		9	11		36
36	33	22	15	14	33	35	14	14	30	11	31	32	15	34	26	1	
				+ 4s			+ 1s				+ 2s	+ 1s	+ 7s		+ 3s	+ 4s	

CLYDE Division 2

Year Formed: 1878.
Ground: Shawfield Stadium, Glasgow C5. *Size:* 110yd×70yd. *Capacity:* 25,000 (2000 seats).
Telephone: 041-647 6329.
Manager: Craig Brown BA, DPE.
Secretary: John F. McBeth ARICS.
Club Colours: White shirts with red facings, black shorts, red stockings.
Club Nickname: The Bully Wee.
Record Attendance: 52,000 v Rangers, Division 1, 21 Nov, 1908.

1980–81 LEAGUE RECORD

Match No.	Date	Venue	Opponents	Result	H/T Score	League Pos'n	Goalscorers	Attendance
1	Aug 9	H	East Fife	W 3-1	1-0	—	Masterton 2, Dolan	600
2	16	H	Brechin C	W 3-0	3-0	1	Ahern, Dolan, Masterton	680
3	23	A	Queen's Park	W 1-0	1-0	—	O'Neill	1430
4	Sept 6	A	Alloa	L 0-2	0-1	4		750
5	9	A	Stranraer	L 0-1	0-0	—		400
6	13	H	Montrose	W 4-3	2-2	4	O'Neill, Masterton 3	550
7	15	H	Stenhousemuir	D 2-2	1-1	—	Masterton 2	600
8	20	A	Meadowbank T	W 2-0	2-0	3	Kean J., Masterton	300
9	27	H	Forfar Ath	W 2-1	1-0	3	Masterton, Edgar	600
10	Oct 1	H	Albion R	D 1-1	1-1	—	Edgar	650
11	4	A	Queen of the S	W 3-1	1-1	1	Ahern, Dolan, Brogan	1500
12	11	A	Cowdenbeath	L 2-4	2-2	2	McAlpine 2	900
13	18	H	Arbroath	L 0-2	0-0	3		650
14	25	A	Montrose	L 0-1	0-0	4		500
15	Nov 1	H	Alloa	L 0-3	0-1	4		685
16	8	A	Stenhousemuir	L 0-3	0-2	9		700
17	15	H	Meadowbank T	W 2-1	2-1	8	Dempster, O'Neill	500
18	22	A	Forfar Ath	L 2-3	0-1	9	Ahern (pen), O'Neill	800
19	Dec 6	H	Cowdenbeath	D 2-2	0-1	7	Ahern (pen), Kean J.	550
20	20	A	Arbroath	D 2-2	0-0	9	Dempster, Masterton	537
21	27	A	Brechin C	L 1-3	1-0	10	Kinnear	500
22	Jan 10	A	Albion R	D 3-3	1-0	10	Dempster 2, Ahern (pen)	500
23	31	H	Arbroath	W 1-0	0-0	8	Masterton	1200
24	Feb 14	A	Stenhousemuir	D 3-3	3-2	10	O'Neill, Kean J., Evans	350
25	22	H	Meadowbank T	L 1-4	1-2	—	Brogan	750
26	28	A	Queen of the S	D 0-0	0-0	11		1000
27	Mar 4	H	Queen's Park	D 1-1	0-0	—	Miller	500
28	7	H	Forfar Ath	W 3-1	2-0	7	Dempster, Ahern (pen), Masterton	500
29	14	A	Brechin C	L 1-2	0-2	10	Ahern (pen)	400
30	18	A	Cowdenbeath	L 0-2	0-1	—		400
31	21	H	Albion R	W 4-0	3-0	9	Masterton 2, O'Neill, Ahern (pen)	450
32	24	A	East Fife	W 1-0	0-0	—	Edgar	477
33	28	H	Montrose	W 6-0	2-0	6	McAlpine, O'Neill, Masterton, Evans, Ahern, Dolan	400
34	Apr 1	H	Queen of the S	L 1-4	0-1	—	Ahern (pen)	500
35	4	A	Queen's Park	D 1-1	1-0	8	Evans	1740
36	11	H	Alloa	D 0-0	0-0	7		430
37	18	A	Stranraer	D 1-1	1-0	7	Masterton	250
38	25	H	East Fife	W 6-2	6-2	8	Ahern (pen), Dempsey 2, Kean J., Masterton, Evans	350
39	May 2	H	Stranraer	D 3-3	0-0	8	Kean J., Masterton, Ahern	400

Final League Position: 8

Goalscorers

League (68): Masterton 19, Ahern 12 (8 pens), O'Neill 7, Dempster 5, Kean J. 5, Dolan 4, Evans 4, Edgar 3, McAlpine 3, Brogan 2, Dempsey 2, Kinnear 1, Miller 1.
League Cup (3): Dolan 2, Ahern 1 (pen).
Scottish Cup (9): Masterton 5, O'Neill 2, Evans 1, own goal 1.

Honours
Scottish League – Division 2 Champions: 1904–05, 1951–52, 1956–57, 1961–62, 1972–73, 1977–78; Runners-up: 1903–04, 1905–06, 1925–26, 1963–64.
Scottish FA Cup: Winners: 1939, 1955, 1958; Runners-up 1910, 1912, 1949.
Scottish League Cup: None.
Record Victory: 11-1 v Cowdenbeath, Division 2, 6 Oct, 1951.
Record Defeat: 0-11 v Dumbarton, Scottish Cup 4th rd, 22 Nov, 1879; 0-11 v Rangers, Scottish Cup 4th rd, 13 Nov, 1880.
Most League Points: 64, Division 2, 1956–57.
Most Individual League Goals in Season: 32, Bill Boyd, 1932–33.
Most Capped Player: Tommy Ring, 12, Scotland.

McWilliams D	Campbell A	Young G	Brogan J	Filippi J	Kinnear B	Dempsey J	Ahern B	McArthur P	Edgar R	Boyd J	Miller J	Kean J	Dempster J	Masterton D	Coutts T	Kean P	O'Neill T	Dolan P	McAlpine J	Boyd A	Wells W J	Evans S	Daly P	Hyslop D	Thorburn R	Murray E S	Brown C	Nelson J	McGregor J G	*Match No.*
1			2	3	5	6*	4					8		9			10	11	7			12								1
1			2	3	5*	6	4					8†		9			10	11	7	12		13								2
1			2	3		5	4					8†		9			10	11	6			12		7*	13					3
1			2	3	5		4				8	12		9			10	11	6								7*			4
1			2	3	5		4*				8	12		9			10	11	6					7						5
1			2	3	5		4				8	12		9			10	11*	6								7*	12		6
1				3	5	6	4					8		9			10		11						2		12	7*		7
1			2	3	5		4		12			7*		9		6	10	8	11											8
1			2	3			6		7	5		8		9		4	10		11*					12						9
1			2	3*	5		4		7		12	8		9		6	10	11												10
1			2	3			4		12	5*	7	8		9		6	10	13	11†											11
1			2	3			6			5	7	8		9		4	10	12	11*											12
1			2	12	5		6			3	8*	7		9		4	10		11											13
1				3	5		4		7		2	8		9		6	10*	11†	12			13								14
1				3	5	4	6	2	7*		8†	10		9		13			11			12								15
	1		4	3	5		6	2	12		8	7		9*					10			11								16
	1		2		5		4			3	8	11	7	9			10		6											17
	1		2	3	5		4			6*	8	9†	7				10		11			12							13	18
1			2	7	5		6			3*	8	12	11	9		4	10													19
1			2	3	5		4				6*	8	7	9		13	10					11†	12							20
		1	2	3	5		6				8*	4	7	9			10		11				12							21
		1	2	3	5	4	6				8		7	9			10					11								22
		1	2	3	5*	4	6				13	8	7	9†		12	10					11								23
		1	2	3		12	6		5		8	9			7	4*	10					11								24
		1	2	3		4	6		5		8	9			7		10					11								25
		1	2	3	5		6				8		7	9	4		10					11								26
		1	2	3	5		6				8		7	9	4		10					11								27
		1	2	3*		12	6				8†	4	7	9	13		10				5	11								28
		1	2	3		12	6					8	7†	9	13		10			4	5*	11								29
		1	2	3		5	6		12			8*	7	9	4		10					11								30
		1	2	3		5	6		12		8*		7	9†	4		10					11				13				31
		1	2	3		5	6		4		8		7	9			10					11								32
		1		3		5	6		8†		2			9	4*	12	10	13	7			11								33
		1		3		5	6		8		2			9	4		10		7			11								34
		1	2	3		5	6				4	8	7*	9	12		10					11								35
		1	2	3		5	6	13	8		4*			9			10†	7	12			11								36
		1	2			5	4	3	7			8		9			10		6			11								37
		1	2	3		5	4		6		8	7		9			10					11								38
		1	4			5	6	3	8		2	7		9	12		10					11*								39
17	3	19	34	35	21	18	39	4	13	7	28	27	15	36	8	9	37	10	20	1	2	20	0	2	1	0	2	1	0	
				+ 1s		+ 3s		+ 1s	+ 5s		+ 2s	+ 4s			+ 4s	+ 4s		+ 3s	+ 2s	+ 1s		+ 6s	+ 2s	+ 1s	+ 1s	+ 1s	+ 1s	+ 1s	+ 1s	

CLYDEBANK — Division 1

Year Formed: 1965. *Ground:* Kilbowie Park. *Size:* 110yd×68yd. *Capacity:* 10,000 (all seated).
Telephone: 041-952 2887. *Secretary:* I. C. Steedman. *Team Manager:* W. Munro.
Club Colours: White shirts with red and black vertical stripes on the left breast and red stripe on sleeves, white shorts with red and black vertical stripe and white stockings with red and black tops.
Club Nickname: The Bankies.
Record Attendance: 14,900 v Hibernian, Scottish Cup 1st rd, 10 Feb, 19[illegible]5.

1980–81 LEAGUE RECORD

Match No.	*Date*	*Venue*	*Opponents*	*Result*	*H/T Score*	*League Pos'n*	*Goalscorers*	*Atten-dance*
1	Aug 9	H	East Stirling	W 3-2	1-0	—	Given (pen), Miller, McGorm	800
2	16	A	Raith R	W 4-0	2-0	1	McGorm 2, Miller, McCabe	1800
3	23	H	Dumbarton	L 1-4	0-2	6	McGorm	2000
4	Sept 6	H	Dundee	W 3-0	2-0	3	Sweeney 2, Houston	1240
5	9	H	Motherwell	D 2-2	2-2	—	Gervaise, Given	1500
6	13	A	Falkirk	L 2-3	0-2	7	Sweeney, Given (pen)	2600
7	17	A	St Johnstone	D 1-1	0-1	—	Miller	1597
8	20	H	Ayr U	D 2-2	1-1	6	Miller, McGorm	1000
9	27	A	Hibernian	L 1-4	1-1	8	Fallon	5000
10	Oct 1	A	Stirling Albion	D 0-0	0-0	—		500
11	4	H	Hamilton A	W 3-1	1-0	5	Given, McGorm, Miller	1000
12	11	H	Berwick R	W 2-1	1-1	4	McLaughlin, Harkins	600
13	18	A	Dunfermline Ath	L 1-3	0-0	6	Miller	2100
14	25	H	Falkirk	W 2-1	1-0	5	Evans, McLaughlin	600
15	Nov 1	A	Dundee	L 1-2	1-1	6	Miller	4700
16	8	H	St Johnstone	L 0-2	0-0	8		400
17	15	A	Ayr U	L 0-1	0-0	10		2279
18	22	H	Hibernian	D 1-1	0-0	9	Miller	1300
19	29	A	Hamilton A	L 0-3	0-1	9		1516
20	Dec 6	A	Berwick R	W 1-0	0-0	9	Evans	550
21	13	H	Dunfermline Ath	L 2-3	1-1	9	Given, Sweeney	420
22	20	A	Motherwell	L 0-3	0-0	9		1671
23	Jan 1	A	Dumbarton	D 1-1	1-1	—	Sharkey	2900
24	3	H	Stirling Albion	D 1-1	1-0	9	Miller	500
25	31	A	Falkirk	D 0-0	0-0	10		2500
26	Feb 21	A	Ayr U	L 1-4	0-2	10	Miller	1440
27	28	H	Hamilton A	L 1-2	1-0	11	Miller	600
28	Mar 21	H	Motherwell	D 0-0	0-0	11		900
29	24	H	St Johnstone	L 1-3	0-1	—	Miller	500
30	28	A	Stirling Albion	D 0-0	0-0	11		600
31	Apr 1	A	Dunfermline Ath	L 1-2	0-2	—	Miller	1550
32	4	A	Raith R	D 1-1	1-0	11	McGorm	2500
33	11	H	Berwick R	W 2-0	2-0	10	Miller 2	350
34	15	A	Hibernian	L 0-3	0-3	—		3691
35	18	A	Dundee	L 0-1	0-1	11		4771
36	22	H	Raith R	W 3-0	1-0	—	Miller, McGorm, Given (pen)	400
37	25	H	East Stirling	W 2-0	1-0	10	McKeown, Miller	400
38	29	A	East Stirling	D 2-2	2-2	—	Miller, Given	1300
39	May 2	H	Dumbarton	D 0-0	0-0	10		500

Final League Position: 10

Goalscorers

League (48): Miller 18, McGorm 8, Given 7 (3 pens), Sweeney 4, Evans 2, McLaughlin 2, Fallon 1, Gervaise 1, Houston 1, Harkins 1, McCabe 1, McKeown 1, Sharkey 1.
League Cup (11): Houston 3, Miller 3, Given 2 (1 pen), McGorm 2, own goal 1.
Scottish Cup (7): Miller 4, Evans 1, Given 1 (pen), Houston 1.

Honours
Scottish League – Division 1 Runners-up 1976–77; Division 2 Champions 1975–76.
Spring Cup – Runners-up 1975–76.
Record Victory: 8-1 v Arbroath, Division 1, 3 Jan, 1977.
Record Defeat: 1-9 v Gala Fairydean, Scottish Cup qualifying rd, 15 Sept, 1965.
Most League Points: 58, Division 1, 1976–77.
Most Individual Goals in Season: Blair Miller, 28, Division 1, 1978–79.

Gallacher J	Kenny D	Gervaise A	Treanor M	Colgan G D	Fallon J	McLaughlin G	Evans B D	Sharkey G	Given J C	Ronald G	Houston D	Miller B	McGorm T	Harkins T	Sweeney J J	McCabe G	McKeown C R	McIntyre J F	Jones D M	O'Rourke H	Williamson R	McBride J	*Match No.*
1		2		3	12	4	5*		6	7	8	9	10			11							1
1		2		3		4		5	6	7	8*	9	10		12	11							2
1		2		3		4	5		6	7*	8	9	10		12	11							3
1		2		3		12	5		6	7*	8	11	10		9					4			4
1		2		3			5		6		8	9	10		7	11				4			5
1		2		3		4	5		6	7	8	10			9	11							6
1		2		3*	12	4	5		6	7	8	9	13		10†	11							7
1		2			3	4	5		6	7	8	9*	10		12	11							8
1*		2		12	3	4	5		6	7	8	9	10		13	11†							9
1		2			3	4	5		6	7	8	9	10			11							10
1		2			3	4	5		6	7	8	9	10			11							11
1		2		3	5	4			6		8	9*	10	7		11					12		12
1		2		12	3	4	5*		6		8	9	7†	13	10	11							13
1		2			3	4	5		6	7*	8	9	10		12	11							14
1		2			3	4	5		6	7		10	12		9*	11						8	15
1			2		3	4	5	12	10	7		9*	11†	13		6						8	16
1		8	2		3	4	5	6	10†	7		9*	12	13		11							17
1		8	2		4	3	9	5	6			13	7*	12	10†	11							18
1		8	2		4	3		5	6	7*		9†	13	12	10	11							19
1			2		4	3	9	5	6		8	12	7*		10†	11						13	20
1			2		4	3*	9	5	6		8	7	12		10	11							21
1		2			3		4	5	6	7	8	9	11*		12	10							22
1		2			3		4	5	6	7	8	9	10*	12		11							23
1		6	2		3		4	5		7*	8	9	12	10		11							24
	1		2		4	3	5		6	12	8	10				11	9*	7					25
	1	2			4	3	5		6	12	8	9	7*	10		11							26
	1	10	2		4	3	5		6	7	8	9				11*		12					27
1			2		4	3	9	5	6	7*	8	10				11		12					28
1		5	2		4	3	9*		6	7	8	10				11		12					29
1		2			4	3	5	12	6	7*	8	9	10			11							30
1			2		4	3	5		6	7	8	9	10			11							31
1			2		4	3	5	12	6	7	8	9*	10†			11					13		32
1			2		4	3	5		6	7	8	9	10			11							33
1		8	2		4	3	5		6	7		9	10			11							34
1		2	12		4	3		5	6	7	8*	9	10			11							35
1		2			4	3	12	5	6		8	9	7			11			10*				36
1		2			4	3		5	6		8	9	7			11*	12		10				37
1		2			4	3		5	6		8	9	7			11			10				38
1		2			4	3		5	6	7*	8	9	12			11			10				39
36	3	31	15	8	32	34	31	15	38	28	33	37	27	3	10	38	1	1	4	2	0	2	
			+ 1s	+ 2s	+ 2s	+ 1s	+ 1s	+ 3s		+ 2s		+ 2s	+ 7s	+ 6s	+ 6s		+ 1s	+ 3s			+ 2s	+ 1s	

COWDENBEATH Division 2

Year Formed: 1881. *Ground:* Central Park. *Size:* 110yd×70yd. *Telephone:* Cowdenbeath 511205.
Manager: Andrew Rolland.
Secretary: W. Foster. *Club Colours:* Royal blue shirt, white shorts, white stockings with blue and white tops. *Club Nickname:* Cowden.
Record Attendance: 25,586 v Rangers, League Cup Quarter Final, 21 Sept, 1949.
Previous Grounds: North End Park, 1881–1917.

1980–81 LEAGUE RECORD

Match No.	*Date*	*Venue*	*Opponents*	*Result*	*H/T Score*	*League Pos'n*	*Goalscorers*	*Attendance*
1	Aug 9	H	Arbroath	W 2-1	0-0	—	Tierney, Marshall	400
2	16	A	Alloa	D 1-1	1-1	6	Forrest	650
3	23	A	East Fife	L 2-3	1-2	7	Marshall, Rolland	635
4	Sept 3	H	Stranraer	D 1-1	1-1	—	Steele W.	200
5	6	H	Brechin C	W 2-1	1-1	5	Steele W., Liddle	350
6	9	A	Queen's Park	D 1-1	0-0	—	Rolland (pen)	964
7	13	A	Albion R	L 0-2	0-2	5		344
8	17	H	Montrose	W 2-1	0-1	—	Hunter, Rolland (pen)	300
9	20	A	Stenhousemuir	D 1-1	1-0	6	Liddle	400
10	27	H	Meadowbank T	W 1-0	0-0	5	Stewart	400
11	Oct 4	A	Forfar Ath	W 2-1	1-0	4	Forrest 2	950
12	11	H	Clyde	W 4-2	2-2	3	Liddle 2, Marshall, Rolland (pen)	900
13	18	A	Queen of the S	L 0-1	0-0	4		1200
14	25	H	Albion R	W 2-1	1-1	2	Ferguson, Forrest	845
15	Nov 1	A	Brechin C	W 2-0	0-0	2	Steele W., Marshall	400
16	8	A	Montrose	L 2-3	1-0	3	Forrest, Liddle	300
17	15	H	Stenhousemuir	L 0-1	0-0	3		500
18	22	A	Meadowbank T	W 4-1	1-1	3	Hunter 2, Steele W. 2	300
19	Dec 6	A	Clyde	D 2-2	1-0	4	Liddle 2	550
20	Jan 1	H	East Fife	D 1-1	0-0	—	Halley (og)	1000
21	31	H	Queen of the S	D 1-1	1-1	6	Marshall	750
22	Feb 21	H	Stenhousemuir	L 1-2	0-2	9	Steele W.	300
23	Mar 4	A	Arbroath	W 1-0	1-0	—	Duncan	600
24	11	A	Forfar Ath	L 0-1	0-0	—		745
25	14	A	East Fife	L 0-1	0-0	12		501
26	18	H	Clyde	W 2-0	1-0	—	Brogan (og), Hunter	400
27	21	H	Alloa	W 5-2	1-1	7	Steele W. 2, Liddle 3	500
28	24	H	Stranraer	W 3-0	0-0	—	Forrest, Liddle, Steele W.	300
29	28	A	Albion R	W 2-0	0-0	5	Liddle, Forrest	250
30	Apr 1	H	Forfar Ath	L 1-2	0-1	—	Hunter	500
31	4	A	Brechin C	W 2-1	1-1	5	Liddle 2	400
32	8	A	Queen of the S	D 2-2	0-1	—	Hunter, Marshall	1734
33	11	A	Stranraer	L 2-3	2-0	6	Hay (og), Liddle	250
34	15	H	Alloa	W 4-2	1-0	—	Forrest 2, Liddle 2	350
35	18	H	Arbroath	W 1-0	1-0	3	Forrest	800
36	22	A	Montrose	L 1-3	0-1	—	Markey	300
37	25	A	Queen's Park	D 1-1	1-0	3	Wallace	2051
38	29	H	Meadowbank T	W 1-0	1-0	—	Steele W.	300
39	May 2	H	Queen's Park	L 1-2	1-1	3	Liddle	1965

Final League Position: 3

Goalscorers

League (63): Liddle 18, Forrest 10, Steele W. 10, Hunter 6, Marshall 6, Rolland 4 (3 pens), Duncan 1, Ferguson 1, Markey 1, Stewart 1, Tierney 1, Wallace 1, own goals 3.
League Cup (1): Liddle 1.
Scottish Cup (11): Liddle 3, Steele W. 3, Forrest 2, McGhee 2, Marshall 1.

Honours

Scottish League – Division 2 Champions: 1913–14, 1914–15, 1938–39; Runners-up: 1921–22, 1923–24, 1969–70.
Record Victory: 12-0 v St Johnstone, Scottish Cup 1st rd, 21 Jan, 1928.
Record Defeat: 1-11 v Clyde, Division 2, 6 Oct, 1951.
Most League Points: 60, Division 2, 1938–39.
Most Individual League Goals in Season: Willie Devlin, 40, Division 1, 1925–26.
Most Capped Player: Jim Paterson, 3, Scotland.

Allan R	Rolland A	Markey J	Ferguson K	Stewart G	Russell R	Hunter D	Tierney G	Duncan A R	Steele W	Marshall J	Ferrier B	Liddle J	Forrest G	Fleming J M	Wallace G	McCathie N	Hunter G	Steele T	McGhee A J	Park D G	Murray W	*Match No.*
1	4	3	2		5		6			10	8	9	11					7				1
1	4	3	2		5	6*	10			11	8	9	7	12								2
1	4	3	2		5	10	6			11	8	9	7*					12				3
1	2	3			5	4	6		11	10	8	9	7									4
1	2	3	7		5	4	6		11	10	8*	9	12									5
1	2	3	7		5	4	6		11	10	8	9										6
1	2	3	7		5	4	6		11	10	8	9										7
1	2	3	7		5	4	6		11	10		9	8									8
1	2		7		5	4	6			10	8	9	12	3*				11				9
1	2	3	7	4	5				11	10	6*	9	8			12						10
1	2	3		4	5	6	12			9			11			8*		10			7	11
1	2	3		4	5	6				8		9	11					10			7	12
1	2	3		4	5	6			11*	10		9	8			12					7	13
1		3	2	4	5	6			11	10		9	7			8						14
1	2	3		4	5	6			11	10		9	7*			8	12					15
1	2	3		4	5	6			11	10		9	7*			8	12					16
1	2	3		4	5	6			11	10	12	9	7*				8					17
1	2	3	8		5	6	4		11	10		9							7			18
1	2	3	8		5	6*	4		11	10		9					12		7			19
1	2	3	8		5	6	4		11	10		9							7			20
1	2	3	7	5		6	4	13	8*	10		9	11†						12			21
1	2	3		5		6	4	11	7	12		9	10							8*		22
1	2	3	7	5			4	11	10	6		9								8		23
1	2	3	7	5			4		10	6		9	11		12					8*		24
1	2	3	7	5		6	4		11*	10		9	12		8							25
1	2	3			5	6	4		11	10		9	12		7*					8		26
1	2	3	7*		5	6	4	11†	8	10		9	12							13		27
1	2	3	7		5	6	4	11*	8	10		9	12									28
1	2*	3	7		5	6	4		8	10		9†	11		12					13		29
1		3	2		5	6	4		7	10			11		9	12				8*		30
1		3	2		5	6	4			10		8	11		9	7						31
1		3	2		5	6	4		8†	10		9	11		12	7*		13				32
1	2	3	7		5	6*	4		8	10		9	11			12						33
1	2	3	7		5		4		8	6		9	11							10		34
1	2	3	7		5		4		8			9	11		6*	12				10		35
1		3	2		5	6	4		8			9	11		7					10		36
1		3	2		5	6	4		8			9	11*		7			12		10		37
1	2	3			5	6	4		8			9	11		7					10		38
1	2	3			5	6	4		8	7		9	11							10		39
39	33	38	28	13	34	33	31	4	32	34	9	37	27	1	8	6	1	4	3	11	3	
							+ 1s	+ 1s		+ 1s	+ 1s		+ 6s	+ 1s	+ 3s	+ 5s	+ 3s	+ 3s	+ 1s	+ 2s		

DUMBARTON — Division 1

Year Formed: 1872. *Ground:* Boghead Park. *Size:* 112yd×74yd. *Capacity:* 18,000. *Telephone:* Dumbarton 62569.
Manager: Billy Lamont.
Secretary: John Hosie.
Club Colours: White with gold horizontal band between two black bands, white shorts and stockings.
Club Nickname: Sons.
Record Attendance: 18,000 v Raith Rovers, Scottish Cup 7th rd, 2 Mar, 1957.
Previous Name: Dumbarton Athletic.

1980–81 LEAGUE RECORD

Match No.	Date	Venue	Opponents	Result	H/T Score	League Pos'n	Goalscorers	Attendance
1	Aug 9	A	Falkirk	W 5-0	1-0	—	Brown, MacLeod (pen), Rankin, Blair 2	2500
2	16	H	St Johnstone	L 0-3	0-2	5		1000
3	23	A	Clydebank	W 4-1	2-0	2	Gallagher B., Blair 2, Coyle J.	2000
4	Sept 6	A	Hamilton A	D 1-1	0-0	5	Rankin	1800
5	9	A	Dunfermline Ath	D 1-1	0-0	—	Brown	2500
6	13	H	East Stirling	D 2-2	0-1	6	Gallagher B., MacLeod	600
7	17	H	Berwick R	W 2-0	1-0	—	Coyle J., MacLeod	1250
8	20	A	Raith R	L 1-4	0-2	7	Coyle J.	1400
9	27	H	Motherwell	L 1-2	1-0	7	Gallagher B.	1000
10	Oct 1	H	Hibernian	W 2-0	0-0	—	Gallagher B., Rankin	1000
11	4	A	Dundee	L 1-3	0-2	7	Schaedler (og)	3553
12	11	A	Stirling Albion	W 1-0	1-0	6	Donnelly	700
13	18	H	Ayr U	L 0-1	0-0	8		1000
14	25	A	East Stirling	L 1-2	0-1	9	Gallagher B.	550
15	Nov 1	H	Hamilton A	W 2-1	1-0	8	Gallagher B. 2	500
16	8	A	Berwick R	D 2-2	0-0	7	Donnelly, Brown	659
17	15	H	Raith R	D 2-2	1-1	8	Donnelly, McGowan P.	700
18	22	A	Motherwell	L 2-4	2-2	8	Jackson, Smith (og)	2223
19	29	H	Dundee	L 1-2	1-0	8	Gallagher B.	958
20	Dec 6	H	Stirling Albion	W 2-0	1-0	8	Clougherty, Gallagher B.	400
21	13	A	Ayr U	D 0-0	0-0	8		1875
22	20	H	Dunfermline Ath	W 1-0	1-0	7	Gallagher B.	400
23	27	A	St Johnstone	L 0-2	0-1	8		2018
24	Jan 1	H	Clydebank	D 1-1	1-1	—	Brown	2900
25	3	A	Hibernian	L 0-1	0-1	8		5546
26	10	H	Falkirk	L 0-1	0-0	8		700
27	31	H	East Stirling	W 1-0	1-0	8	MacLeod	450
28	Feb 7	A	Raith R	L 0-1	0-0	8		1500
29	21	H	Berwick R	D 1-1	0-1	8	Donnelly	400
30	Mar 11	A	Dundee	L 1-2	1-2	—	Gallagher B.	2812
31	14	A	Stirling Albion	D 0-0	0-0	9		500
32	21	H	Hibernian	L 1-4	1-1	9	Rankin	1000
33	28	A	St Johnstone	L 1-2	1-1	9	Gallagher B.	2647
34	Apr 4	H	Hamilton A	W 2-1	2-0	9	Gallagher B., Brown	300
35	8	H	Motherwell	D 0-0	0-0	—		1500
36	11	A	Falkirk	W 3-1	0-0	8	Blair 2, Brown	1500
37	18	H	Dunfermline Ath	W 2-1	0-0	8	Brown, Gallagher B.	350
38	25	A	Ayr U	W 2-1	2-0	8	Blair 2	998
39	May 2	A	Clydebank	D 0-0	0-0	8		500

Final League Position: 8

Goalscorers

League (49): Gallagher B. 14, Blair 8, Brown 7, Donnelly 4, MacLeod 4 (1 pen), Rankin 4, Coyle J. 3, Clougherty 1, Jackson 1, McGowan P. 1, own goals 2.
League Cup (1): Gallagher B. 1.
Scottish Cup (3): Coyle J. 2, Donnelly 1.

Honours

Original members of Scottish League 1890.
Scottish League: Division 1 Champions 1890–91 (shared with Rangers), 1891–92; Division 2 Champions 1910–11, 1971–72; Runners-up 1907–08.
Scottish Cup: Winners 1883; Finalists 1881, 1882, 1887, 1891, 1897.
Record Victory: 13-1 v Kirkintilloch Central, Scottish Cup 1st rd, 1 Sept, 1888.
Record Defeat: 1-11 v Albion Rovers, Division 2, 30 Jan, 1926; 1-11 v Ayr United, League Cup, 13 August, 1952.
Most League Points: 52, Division 2, 1971–72.
Most Individual League Goals in Season: Kenny Wilson, 38, Division 2, 1971–72.
Most Capped Player: John Lindsay, 8, Scotland; James McAulay, 8, Scotland.

Carson T	Hunter D	Sinclair G	MacLeod A	Campbell R	Clougherty M	Gallacher J	Coyle T	Jackson D	Hutchison W	McNeil D	Martin J	McGowan M	Coyle J	McGrain T	Rankin M	Kennedy J	Blair R	Gallagher B	Donnelly M	Brown A D	Brannigan G	Mailer J	Gibson I	Marshall G	McGowan P	Sweeney S	O'Donnell J	Armstrong S	Match No.
1		2	3	12		4				5	10		6*	11†	8		9			7				13					1
1		2	3	12	4	5				6*			10		7		9			8			13	11†					2
1		2	3		4	5							6	8	11		10	9		7									3
1		2*	3		4		5				13	12	6		11		10	9		8	7†								4
1		2	3	4			5						6	11	8		10	9		7									5
1		2	3	12	4*		5				13		6	8†	11		10	9		7									6
1		2	3		4		5						6	8	11		10	9		7									7
1		2	3	12	4	5*	8				13		6		11		10†	9		7									8
1		2	8	3	4				5				6	11		10	12	9		7*									9
1		2	3		4		8		5		12		6*	11	13	10†		9		7									10
1		2	3		4				5		13			11	12	10	8†	9	6*	7									11
1		2	6	3	4			5			10			8	7			9	11*						12				12
1		2	10	3	4			5			6			7	12		13	9	11†	8*									13
1		2	6	3	4			5			11			8*	12			9	10	7									14
	1	2	3	5	6		4							8*	7	12		9	11†	10					13				15
	1	2	3*	5	6		4				12			13	7†			9	11	10					8				16
	1	2	3		6*		4	5						12	7	10		9	11						8				17
	1	2	3				4	5						6	7		12	9	11			10*			8				18
	1		3	2	6	5	4							11	7			9				10			8				19
1			3	2	6	5	4							11	7		12	9				10*			8				20
1		2	3		6	5	4							11	7*	12		9				10			8				21
1		2	3		6	5	4							11	7	12		9				10*			8				22
1		2	3		6	5	4							11	7		12	9				10*			8				23
1		2	3		7	5	4						6				11			9		10*	12		8				24
1		2	3		7	5	4						6				11			9		10*	12		8				25
1		2	3		11	5	4				7*		6					9		10					8	12			26
1		2	3				4	5					6	11	7		12	9	10*						8				27
1		2	3	13			4	5					6	11	7*		12	9	10†						8				28
1		2	3			5	4						6	11	12		7		10			9*			8				29
1		2	3		11	5	4						6	8*	7		13		10†			9			12				30
1		2	3			5	4						6	10			11	7	12			9*			8				31
1		2	3		10	5	4				12		6		7		11*	9							8				32
1		2	3		10	5	4						6	8†	7*		11	9	12						13				33
1		2	3		10	5	4						6				11	9		7					8				34
1		2	3		10	5	4						6				11	9		7					8				35
1		2	3		10	5†	4*	13			12		6				11	9		7					8				36
1		2	3		10	5	4										11	9	6	7					8				37
1		2	3		10	5	4						6				11	9	8	7*								12	38
	1		3		10	5	4						6				11	9		7*					8		2	12	39
33	6	36	39	9	32	23	31	7	3	2	5	0	25	24	23	4	21	33	14	24	1	11	0	1	21	0	1	0	
				+ 5s				+ 1s			+ 8s	+ 1s		+ 2s	+ 5s	+ 3s	+ 8s		+ 2s				+ 3s	+ 1s	+ 4s	+ 1s		+ 2s	

DUNDEE — Premier Division

Year Formed: 1893.
Ground: Dens Park. *Size:* 113yd×73yd. *Capacity:* 21,000 (12,100 seats).
Telephone: Dundee 826104.
Manager: Donald MacKay. *Coaches:* Frank Upton, Jocky Scott.
Secretary: Ian Gellatly. *Physiotherapist:* Eric Ferguson.
Club Colours: Dark blue shirts with red and white stripes, white shorts with red/white flashing, red stockings.
Club Nickname: Dark Blues or The Dee.
Record Attendance: 43,024 v Rangers, Scottish Cup, 1953.
Previous Name: East End and Our Boys amalgamated to become Dundee in 1893.
Previous Ground: Carolina Port, 1893–98.
European Competitions: European Cup, 1962–63 (semi-final); European Cup-Winners' Cup, 1964–65; Fairs Cup, 1967–68 (semi-final); UEFA Cup 1971–72, 1974–75.
Record Transfer Fee Received: £210,000 from Rangers for Ian Redford, Feb 1980.

1980–81 LEAGUE RECORD

Match No.	Date	Venue	Opponents	Result	H/T Score	League Pos'n	Goalscorers	Attendance
1	Aug 9	A	Dunfermline Ath	L 0-1	0-1	—		3660
2	16	H	Ayr U	D 0-0	0-0	12		5328
3	23	A	St Johnstone	L 0-1	0-0	12		4197
4	Sept 6	A	Clydebank	L 0-3	0-2	13		1296
5	9	H	Hibernian	L 1-2	1-1	—	Scrimgeour	5304
6	13	H	Berwick R	D 2-2	0-2	14	Fraser, Shirra (pen)	3782
7	17	A	Motherwell	L 2-3	2-1	—	Fraser, McGeachie	2300
8	20	H	Falkirk	W 4-0	2-0	14	Sinclair 2, Mackie, Fletcher	3993
9	27	A	Stirling Albion	D 1-1	0-1	13	Shirra (pen)	1557
10	Oct 4	H	Dumbarton	W 3-1	2-0	12	Fleming, Shirra, Sinclair	3553
11	11	A	Raith R	D 0-0	0-0	12		3255
12	14	H	Hamilton A	W 2-0	0-0	—	Fraser, Sinclair	3170
13	18	H	East Stirling	W 2-0	1-0	9	Murphy, Sinclair	3771
14	25	A	Berwick R	W 1-0	1-0	7	Sinclair	1080
15	Nov 1	H	Clydebank	W 2-1	1-1	4	Fraser, Stephen	4700
16	8	H	Motherwell	W 2-1	0-0	4	Shirra (pen), Ferguson (pen)	5112
17	15	A	Falkirk	W 3-0	0-0	4	McGeachie, Sinclair 2	2800
18	22	H	Stirling Albion	W 5-1	1-0	4	Stephen 2, Mackie 2, Sinclair	4815
19	29	A	Dumbarton	W 2-1	0-1	4	Stephen 2	958
20	Dec 13	A	East Stirling	W 2-0	0-0	4	Geddes A., Murphy	1026
21	20	H	Hibernian	W 1-0	1-0	3	Sinclair	7454
22	27	A	Ayr U	L 0-1	0-1	4		4036
23	Jan 1	H	St Johnstone	D 2-2	1-1	—	Sinclair, Stephen	8500
24	3	A	Hamilton A	L 2-4	1-2	4	Stephen, Geddes A.	2500
25	31	H	Ayr U	L 2-4	1-1	5	Sinclair, Scrimgeour	4724
26	Feb 7	A	Hibernian	D 0-0	0-0	5		4989
27	21	A	Motherwell	L 1-4	1-2	5	Williamson	2072
28	Mar 11	H	Dumbarton	W 2-1	2-1	—	Scrimgeour, Sinclair	2812
29	14	H	Raith R	W 3-1	0-0	5	Geddes A. 2, Scrimgeour	6350
30	18	H	Dunfermline Ath	W 2-0	1-0	—	Geddes A. 2	3153
31	21	A	Hamilton A	W 3-1	1-1	5	Sinclair 2, Murphy	1500
32	24	A	Stirling Albion	W 1-0	0-0	—	Murphy	700
33	28	H	Berwick R	D 0-0	0-0	4		4000
34	Apr 1	H	Raith R	W 2-1	1-0	—	Sinclair, Fraser	6178
35	4	H	St Johnstone	W 4-1	0-0	4	Sinclair 2, Mackie, Scrimgeour	8586
36	11	A	Dunfermline Ath	D 1-1	1-0	4	Mackie	2629
37	18	H	Clydebank	W 1-0	1-0	3	Geddes A.	4771
38	25	A	Falkirk	W 2-1	0-0	3	Murphy, Stephen	4500
39	May 2	A	East Stirling	W 1-0	1-0	2	Sinclair	5762

Final League Position: 2

Goalscorers

League (64): Sinclair 19, Stephen 8, Geddes A. 7, Fraser 5, Mackie 5, Murphy 5, Scrimgeour 5, Shirra 4 (3 pens), McGeachie 2, Ferguson 1 (pen), Fleming 1, Fletcher 1, Williamson 1.
League Cup (10): Fletcher 3, Sinclair 3, Fraser 2, MacLaren 1, Williamson 1.
Scottish Cup (0).

Honours
Scottish League – Division 1 Champions: 1961–62, 1978–79; Runners-up 1902–03, 1906–07, 1908–09, 1948–49, 1980–81; Division 2 Champions: 1946–47.
Scottish Cup – Winners: 1910; Runners-up: 1925, 1952, 1964.
Scottish League Cup – Winners: 1951–52, 1952–53, 1973–74; Runners-up: 1967–68, 1980–81.
Record Victory: 10-0 v Alloa, Division 2, 8 Mar 1947 and v Dunfermline, Division 2, 22 Mar, 1947.
Most League Points: 55, Division 1, 1978–79.
Most Individual League Goals in Season: 38, Dave Halliday, 1923–24.
Most Capped Player: Alex Hamilton, 24, Scotland.

Geddes R	Williams L	Blair A	Barr L	Schaedler E	Fraser C	McGeachie G	MacLaren S	Glennie R	McKimmie S	Scrimgeour B	Mackie P	Shirra J	Williamson W	Murphy J	Fleming I	Ferguson I	Corrigan D	Fletcher J	Sinclair E	Stephen R	Geddes A	Scott J	Davidson G	*Match No.*
1			2	3		6	4	5			7	12		11*	8	9	10							1
1			2	3		6	4*	5			7†	10		11	8	9	12	13						2
1			2*	3		6	4	5			7	10		11	12	8†	13		9					3
1				3		2	4	5		8	7	6		12				11	9			10*		4
1			2	3		6		5		4	7	11	12	13		10†			9			8*		5
1			2	3	4	6		5		10*	12	11†	8	13				7	9					6
1			2	3	4	6	8	5		10			11					7	9					7
1			2	3	4	6	8	5			10*	13	11†	12				7	9					8
1			2	3	4		6	5		8	7	11		12				10*	9					9
1			2	13	4*		6	5		8†	7	11	3	12	10				9					10
1			2	3*	4	8	6	5			7†	11	12	13	10				9					11
1			2		4*	8	6	5	3		12	11†	13	7	10				9					12
1			2*		4	8	6	5	3		13	12	11	7	10†				9					13
1			2		4	8*	6	5	3		13	12	11	7	10†				9					14
1			2	3	4	8†	6	5			10	13	11	7*					9	12				15
1			2	3	4		6	5		13		10†	11			12		7*	9	8				16
1			2*	3	4	12	6	5			7†	10	11	13					9	8				17
1			2	3	4	6		5			7		10	12					9	8*	11			18
1			2	3	4	6		5			7		10						9	8	11			19
1			2	3	4	6		5			7	10		11					9		8			20
	1		2	3	4	6		5			7*	10		12					9	8	11			21
	1		2*	3	4	6		5			7	10	13	12					9	8	11†			22
	1		2	3	4*		6	5†		13	7		12	11					9	8	10			23
	1		2*	3				5		6	12	10†	4	11		13			9	8	7			24
		1	2	3	4		6	5		8	7		10*	11					9	12				25
		1		3*	4	2	6	5	12	8	7†		10	11		13			9					26
		1		3	4	2*	6	5	12	8	7		10	11†		9				13				27
		1		3		2	6	5	4	8	7					11*			9	10			12	28
		1		3		2	6	5	4	8	7			12					9	10	11*			29
		1		3		2*	6	5	4	8	7			12		13			9	10†	11			30
		1		3	4	2	6	5	10		7*			12					9	8	11			31
		1		3	4	2	6	5	10					7					9	8	11			32
		1	2	3*	4		6	5	10	12	13			7					9	8†	11			33
		1	2	3	4		6	5	10					7					9	8	11			34
		1	2	3	4		6	5	10†	13	12			7*					9	8	11			35
		1	2		4	13	6	5	3	10	7*			12					9	8	11†			36
		1			4	2*	6	5	3	10	12			7		8			9	13	11†			37
		1			4	2	6	5	3	10				7					9	8	11			38
		1	2		4	13	6	5	3	10	12			7					9	8*	11†			39
20	4	15	29	31	30	27	31	39	15	17	25	15	15	20	7	7	1	6	36	19	18	2	0	
				+ 1s		+ 3s			+ 2s	+ 4s	+ 9s	+ 5s	+ 5s	+ 15s	+ 1s	+ 4s	+ 2s	+ 1s		+ 4s			+ 1s	

DUNDEE UNITED Premier Division

Year Formed: 1910 as Dundee Hibernians, became Dundee U in 1923.
Ground: Tannadice Park. *Size:* 110yd×74yd. *Capacity:* 18,912 (2,204 seats).
Telephone: Dundee 86289.
Manager: Jim McLean.
Secretary: Mrs Helen Lindsay. *Physiotherapist:* Andy Dickson.
Club Colours: Tangerine shirts/black trim, black shorts/tangerine trim.
Club Nickname: Terrors.
Record Attendance: 28,000 v Barcelona, Fairs Cup, 1966.
European Competitions: Fairs Cup: 1966–67, 1969–70, 1970–71; European Cup-Winners' Cup: 1974–75; UEFA Cup: 1975–76, 1977–78, 1978–79, 1980–81.
Record Transfer Fee Received: £400,000 from West Ham U for Ray Stewart, Sept 1979.

1980–81 LEAGUE RECORD

Match No.	Date	Venue	Opponents	Result		H/T Score	League Pos'n	Goalscorers	Atten-dance
1	Aug 9	H	Kilmarnock	D	2-2	1-0	—	Payne, Sturrock	5788
2	16	A	Aberdeen	D	1-1	1-1	6	Hegarty	12,000
3	23	H	Morton	D	1-1	1-1	4	Bannon	5339
4	Sept 6	H	Rangers	L	2-4	0-4	7	Dodds, Payne	15,000
5	13	A	Airdrieonians	D	0-0	0-0	5		3000
6	20	A	St Mirren	L	0-2	0-1	8		5700
7	27	H	Hearts	D	1-1	0-1	8	Dodds	6263
8	Oct 4	A	Celtic	L	0-2	0-1	9		21,000
9	11	H	Partick T	D	0-0	0-0	7		4706
10	18	A	Kilmarnock	W	1-0	0-0	6	Pettigrew	2700
11	25	H	Aberdeen	L	1-3	1-2	7	Sturrock	10,043
12	Nov 1	A	Morton	W	2-0	0-0	6	Kirkwood 2	4000
13	8	A	Hearts	W	3-0	2-0	6	Hegarty, Sturrock 2	5800
14	15	H	St Mirren	W	2-0	1-0	5	Dodds, Sturrock	5000
15	22	A	Partick T	W	3-2	1-1	4	Pettigrew, Sturrock, Bannon	4000
16	29	A	Celtic	L	0-3	0-0	4		15,000
17	Dec 13	H	Airdrieonians	W	1-0	0-0	5	Dodds	4700
18	20	A	St Mirren	D	3-3	2-0	5	Dodds, Payne, Pettigrew	5300
19	27	H	Hearts	W	4-1	1-1	4	Sturrock 2, Milne 2	6928
20	30	A	Aberdeen	D	1-1	1-0	—	Dodds	22,000
21	Jan 3	H	Kilmarnock	W	7-0	2-0	4	Gibson, Kirkwood 2, Addison, Dodds, Bannon Milne	6474
22	10	A	Celtic	L	1-2	0-2	4	Milne	22,000
23	31	A	Airdrieonians	W	5-0	0-0	4	Bannon (pen), Dodds 3, Sturrock	3000
24	Feb 7	H	Rangers	W	2-1	1-1	4	Kirkwood, Dodds	14,328
25	21	H	Morton	W	1-0	1-0	4	Hegarty	4886
26	28	A	Kilmarnock	W	1-0	0-0	4	Dodds	2100
27	Mar 14	A	Partick T	W	2-0	2-0	3	Pettigrew, Milne	3500
28	18	A	Rangers	W	4-1	2-1	—	Bannon 2, Sturrock, Kirkwood	12,000
29	21	H	St Mirren	L	1-2	0-0	3	Pettigrew	5808
30	28	A	Hearts	W	4-0	2-0	3	Sturrock 2, Kirkwood 2	3776
31	Apr 4	A	Rangers	L	1-2	1-1	4	Milne	14,000
32	18	A	Morton	L	0-2	0-2	5		3000
33	22	H	Celtic	L	2-3	1-2	—	Pettigrew, Sturrock	15,349
34	25	H	Aberdeen	D	0-0	0-0	5		6369
35	29	H	Airdrieonians	W	4-1	1-1	—	Bannon, Milne, Kirkwood 2	3133
36	May 2	H	Partick T	W	3-2	1-1	5	Dodds 2, Bannon	4124

Final League Position: 5

Goalscorers

League (66): Dodds 14, Sturrock 13, Kirkwood 10, Bannon 8 (1 pen), Milne 7, Pettigrew 6, Hegarty 3, Payne 3, Addison 1, Gibson 1.
League Cup (34): Sturrock 9 (1 pen), Ward 7, Bannon 4, Hegarty 4, Milne 3, Dodds 2, Addison 1, Holt 1, Narey 1, Payne 1, Pettigrew 1.
Scottish Cup (13): Dodds 5, Hegarty 2, Kirkwood 2, Addison 1, Bannon 1, Narey 1, Sturrock 1.

Honours

Scottish League: Division 2, Champions: 1924–25, 1928–29; Runners-up: 1930–31, 1959–60.
Scottish Cup: Runners-up 1973–74, 1980–81.
Scottish League Cup: Winners: 1979–80, 1980–81.
Record Victory: 14-0 v Nithsdale Wanderers, Scottish Cup, 1st rd, 17 Jan, 1931.
Record Defeat: 1-12 v Motherwell, Division 2, 23 Jan, 1954.
Most League Points: 51, Division 2, 1928–29.
Most Individual League Goals in Season: 41, John Coyle, Division 2, 1955–56.
Most Capped Player: Dave Narey, 10, Scotland.

McAlpine H	Stark D	Kopel F	Kirkwood W	Holt J	Phillip I	Hegarty P	Narey D	Bannon E	Gibson I	Pettigrew W	Payne G	Milne R	Sturrock P	Addison D	Campbell C	Ward J	Smith W	Dodds D	Reilly J	Gough	Murray	*Match No.*
1	3		2	12	4	5	6	7*			9	11†	8	10		13						1
1	3	12	2		4	5	6	11			9	7*	8	10								2
1	3		2		12	5	6	4			9	7*	8	10		11†			13			3
1	2	3	4		13	5	6	7*			9	12	8	10†				11				4
1	2	3	4		6	5		7			9*	12	8	10				11				5
1	2	3	4	13		5	6	7			9*		8		12		10	11†				6
1	3	13	2	4		5	6	7†		9*	10	12	8					11				7
1	2	3	12	10	4*	5	6			7	9		8		13			11†				8
1	2	3	12	4		5	6	7		9*	11		8		10							9
1	2	3			4	5	6		8	7	9		10		11							10
1		3	2	4		5	6	11	8*	7	9†	12	10			13						11
1	2	3	12		4	5	6	7	8		9*		10			11†		13				12
1	2	3	9		4	5	6	7	8	12			10			11*						13
1		3		2	4	5	6	7	8	9*	12		10					11				14
1		3	12	2	4	5		7	6	9	8*		10					11				15
1		3	13	2	4*	5	6	7		9	12		10	8†				11				16
1		3		2	4	5	6	7		9	8		10					11				17
1		3		2	4	5	6*	7	9	12	8		10					11				18
1		3		2	4	5	6	7	9			8	10					11				19
1		3		2	4	5	6	7	9			8	10					11				20
1		3	2		4	5	6	7	9*	12		8	10	13				11†				21
1		3	2		4	5	6	7	9†	8*		12	10	13				11				22
1		3	9		2	5	6	7			8		10	4				11				23
1	2	3	9			5	6	7			8		10	4				11				24
1		12	9	2	3	5	6	7				8	10	4*				11				25
1		12	9	2	3	5	6	7†	4*	13		8	10					11				26
1	12	3	9	2	4	5*	6	7		10		8						11				27
1	3	12	9	2	4	5	6	7		13		8*	10					11†				28
1		3	9	2	4	5	6	7		11	8		10									29
1	2	3	9		4	5*	6	7			12		10	8		11						30
1	3	12	9	2	4	5	6	7	11*			8	10									31
1	5*	3	9†	2	4		6	7		12		8	10	13				11				32
1	6	3		2	4	5		7		9		8	10	11*						12		33
1	6		4	2		5*		7	13	9	11†	8	10							12	3	34
1	5	3	9	2	4*		6	7				8	10					11		12		35
1	5	3	9	2*	4		6	7				8	10					11		12		36
36	21	27	24	22	28	33	32	34	13	14	19	16	35	11	2	4	1	23	0	0	1	
	+ 1s	+ 6s	+ 5s	+ 2s	+ 2s				+ 1s	+ 6s	+ 3s	+ 5s		+ 3s	+ 2s	+ 2s		+ 1s	+ 1s	+ 4s		

DUNFERMLINE ATHLETIC Division 2

Year Formed: 1885.
Ground: East End Park. *Size:* 114yd×72yd. *Capacity:* 27,500 (3000 seats).
Telephone: Dunfermline 24295.
Manager: Pat Stanton. *Physiotherapist:* Jim Stevenson.
Secretary: Jim McColville JP.
Club Colours: White and black vertical striped shirts, black shorts.
Club Nickname: The Pars.
Record Attendance: 27,816 v Celtic, Division 1, 1968.
European Competitions: *European Cup-Winners' Cup* 1961–62, 1968–69; *Fairs Cup* 1962–63, 1964–65, 1965–66, 1966–67, 1969–70.

1980–81 LEAGUE RECORD

Match No.	Date	Venue	Opponents	Result	H/T Score	League Pos'n	Goalscorers	Attendance
1	Aug 9	H	Dundee	W 1-0	1-0	—	Leonard	4000
2	16	A	Berwick R	D 1-1	0-0	4	Bowie	1204
3	23	H	Raith R	L 0-2	0-2	8		4200
4	Sept 6	A	East Stirling	W 4-0	3-0	6	Salton, McNaughton 3 (1 pen)	1059
5	9	H	Dumbarton	D 1-1	0-0	—	O'Brien	2500
6	13	H	Stirling Albion	W 2-0	1-0	3	McNaughton (pen), Leonard	2350
7	17	A	Falkirk	L 1-2	1-0	—	O'Brien	3500
8	20	H	St Johnstone	L 0-2	0-1	8		3100
9	27	A	Ayr U	L 0-2	0-1	9		3170
10	Oct 1	A	Motherwell	L 0-2	0-2	—		1848
11	4	H	Hibernian	L 0-2	0-0	11		5650
12	11	A	Hamilton A	D 1-1	1-1	11	McNaughton	2000
13	18	H	Clydebank	W 3-1	0-0	11	McFarlane, O'Brien, Leonard	2100
14	25	A	Stirling Albion	D 3-3	2-0	11	McNaughton 2, Donnelly	1100
15	Nov 1	H	East Stirling	W 1-0	1-0	10	McNaughton	1900
16	8	H	Falkirk	L 0-1	0-1	11		2250
17	15	A	St Johnstone	W 4-2	3-1	9	McNaughton 3, McFarlane	2129
18	22	H	Ayr U	L 2-3	1-0	10	Donnelly, Salton	2200
19	29	A	Hibernian	L 0-1	0-1	10		4350
20	Dec 6	H	Hamilton A	L 0-1	0-0	11		1650
21	13	A	Clydebank	W 3-2	1-1	10	McNaughton 2, Leonard	420
22	20	A	Dumbarton	L 0-1	0-1	10		400
23	Jan 1	A	Raith R	L 0-1	0-0	—		1750
24	31	H	Stirling Albion	L 0-1	0-0	13		2500
25	Feb 14	A	Hamilton A	W 4-1	2-0	11	Dunlop, McNaughton 2 (1 pen), Hutt	1000
26	21	A	St Johnstone	L 1-4	1-0	12	McNaughton	2282
27	28	H	Hibernian	L 0-5	0-1	12		3000
28	Mar 4	H	Falkirk	L 0-1	0-1	—		1500
29	7	A	Ayr U	L 1-2	1-0	12	McNaughton	1697
30	18	A	Dundee	L 0-2	0-1	—		3153
31	21	A	East Stirling	D 0-0	0-0	12		5088
32	28	H	Motherwell	L 1-3	0-3	13	Jenkins	1800
33	Apr 1	H	Clydebank	W 2-1	2-0	—	McNaughton 2	1550
34	4	A	Berwick R	L 0-1	0-0	12		710
35	11	H	Dundee	D 1-1	0-1	12	McFarlane	3200
36	15	H	Motherwell	W 2-1	1-1	—	Hegarty, Wark (og)	1870
37	18	A	Dumbarton	L 1-2	0-0	12	Jenkins	350
38	22	H	Berwick R	D 1-1	0-1	—	McNaughton	1500
39	25	A	Raith R	L 0-1	0-0	12		2535

Final League Position: 12

Goalscorers

League (41): McNaughton 20 (3 pens), Leonard 4, McFarlane 3, O'Brien 3, Donnelly 2, Jenkins 2, Salton 2, Bowie 1, Dunlop 1, Hegarty 1, Hutt 1, own goal 1.
League Cup (1): McNaughton 1.
Scottish Cup (2): Leonard 1, McNaughton 1.

Honours
Scottish League – Division 2 Champions: 1925–26; Runners-up: 1912–13, 1933–34, 1954–55, 1957–58, 1972–73, 1978–79.
Scottish Cup – Winners: 1961, 1968; Finalists: 1965.
Scottish League Cup – Finalists 1949–50.
Record Victory: 11-2 v Stenhousemuir, Division 2, 27 Sept, 1930.
Record Defeat: 0-10 v Dundee, Division 2, 22 Mar, 1947.
Most League Points: 59, Division 2, 1925–26.
Most Individual League Goals in Season: Bobby Skinner, 55, Division 2, 1925–26.
Most Capped Player: Andy Wilson, 6(12), Scotland.

Whyte H	Thomson K	Mercer B	Robertson R	Hutt G	Dunlop R	Robertson A	Salton J	Leishman W	Muir J	Borthwick W	Hegarty K	McNaughton A	Leonard M	Donnelly P	Bowie J	O'Brien C	Jenkins G R	McFarlane C	Wilson T	Williams M	Gillespie R	Robb D	McGovern D	*Match No.*
1	2	3	8				4		5		6	7	9		10	11								1
1	2	3*	8†		13		4	5			6	7	9		10	12				11				2
1	3		8			12	4	2	5*		6	7	9		10					11				3
1	2	3	8				4	5			6	7	9		10	11								4
1	2	3	8				4	5			6	7	9		10	11								5
1	2	3	8			4		5*		12	6	7	9		10	11								6
1	2	3	8				4,	5			6	7	9		10	11								7
1	2	3	8		12	5	4				6	7	9		10*	11								8
1	2	3	8		12	13	4*	5†			6	7	9	10		11								9
1	2	3	8			5	4		9		6	7		10		11								10
1	5	3	8	12	2*		4				6	7	13	10		11		9†						11
1	5	3	8		2*	12	4				6	7	13	10		11		9†						12
1	4	3	8		2			5			6	7	12	10		11		9*						13
1	2	3	8			12	4*	5			6	7		10		11		9						14
1	2		8		12	3	4*	5			6	7		10		11		9						15
1	2		8	10	12	3*	4	5			6	7	13			11		9†						16
1	2	3	8	6			4	5				7		10		11		9						17
1	2	3	8	6		12	4			5*		7		10		11†		9			13			18
1	2	3	8	6*			4			5	11	7		10		12		9						19
1	2		8	12		3	4*	5			6	7	13	10		11†					9			20
1	4	3	2	8				5			6	7	9	10		11								21
1	4	3	2	8	10			5*			6	7	9			11					12			22
1	4	3	2	6	8			5				7	9	10		11								23
1	4	3	2	6	8		5				13	7	12	10		11†		9*						24
1	4	3	2	6	8			5				7		11				9				10		25
1	4	3	2	6	8			5				7		11		12		9*				10		26
1	4	3	2	6	8			5				7	12	11*			9					10		27
1	3		8	12	6		4*	5				7	13	10			9	11†					2	28
1	4	3	8	6				5				7	12	10		11*		9					2	29
1	2	3	8				5*	4			6	7	13	10		11	12	9†						30
1	4	3	2	6				5			10	7	9	8		11								31
1	4	3	2	8				5			6	7	9*	10		11†	12		13					32
1	4	3	5	2	8*							7	12	10	6		9		11					33
1	4	3	5	2	8*			12				7	13	10	6		9		11†					34
1	4	3	5	2							6	7			8		9	11	10					35
1	4	3	5	2							6*	7		12	8		9	11	10					36
1	4	3	5	2		12					6	7			8		9	11*	10					37
1	4	3	5	2				12			6	7		13	8		9	11†	10*					38
1	4	3	8	2				5			6	7			10		9		11					39
39	39	34	39	21	12	6	21	25	3	2	28	39	14	24	15	25	9	19	7	2	1	3	2	
				+ 3s	+ 5s	+ 6s		+ 2s		+ 1s	+ 1s		+ 12s	+ 2s		+ 3s	+ 2s		+ 1s		+ 2s			

EAST FIFE

Division 2

Year Formed: 1903.
Address: Bayview Park, Methil, Fife KY8 3AG, Scotland. *Size:* 110yd×75yd. *Capacity:* 20,000.
Telephone: Leven 26323.
Manager: David Clarke.
Secretary: Tom Clark.
Club Colours: Gold jerseys, black shorts, black stockings.
Record Attendance: 22,515 v Raith R, Division 1, 2 Jan, 1950.
Club Nickname: The Fifers.

1980–81 LEAGUE RECORD

Match No.	Date	Venue	Opponents	Result	H/T Score	League Pos'n	Goalscorers	Attendance
1	Aug 9	A	Clyde	L 1-3	0-1	—	Mitchell	600
2	16	A	Forfar Ath	L 2-3	1-1	—	Scott, Mitchell	1100
3	23	H	Cowdenbeath	W 3-2	2-1	—	Herd, Scott, Thomson R. (pen)	635
4	Sept 3	H	Meadowbank T	W 2-1	1-1	11	Clarke, Mitchell	511
5	6	A	Stenhousemuir	L 0-2	0-1	—		400
6	9	A	Montrose	L 0-1	0-0	—		400
7	13	H	Stranraer	W 3-1	0-1	8	Harvey (og), Thomson R. 2	530
8	17	H	Albion R	D 1-1	0-1	—	Scott	542
9	20	A	Queen's Park	L 1-2	0-1	11	Scott G.	800
10	27	H	Queen of the S	D 1-1	0-1	10	Mitchell	603
11	Oct 4	A	Brechin C	W 1-0	0-0	—	Mackie	400
12	11	A	Arbroath	D 1-1	0-0	—	Scott G.	779
13	18	H	Alloa	D 1-1	1-0	10	Scott G.	720
14	Nov 1	H	Stenhousemuir	D 1-1	1-0	10	Thomson R.	590
15	8	A	Albion R	D 0-0	0-0	—		400
16	15	H	Queen's Park	L 0-2	0-1	11		563
17	22	A	Queen of the S	D 1-1	1-1	11	Thomson R. (pen)	1000
18	29	H	Brechin C	L 0-2	0-1	12		567
19	Dec 6	H	Arbroath	W 2-1	0-0	12	Burt 2	353
20	20	A	Alloa	L 1-2	1-2	12	Duncan	700
21	27	H	Forfar Ath	D 0-0	0-0	12		616
22	Jan 1	A	Cowdenbeath	D 1-1	0-0	—	Burt	1000
23	31	A	Alloa	D 0-0	0-0	12		325
24	Feb 7	H	Arbroath	L 0-2	0-1	12		449
25	11	A	Meadowbank T	W 3-1	1-1	—	Scott J., McGinn, Mitchell	270
26	14	A	Albion R	L 2-3	0-0	12	Thomson R. (pen), Huskie	500
27	21	H	Queen's Park	D 1-1	1-0	12	Thomson R.	390
28	28	H	Brechin C	D 2-2	0-1	12	Halley, Thomson R. (pen)	398
29	Mar 7	A	Queen of the S	L 1-2	1-1	12	Halley	1000
30	11	H	Stranraer	W 2-1	1-0	—	Neilson, Halley	500
31	14	H	Cowdenbeath	W 1-0	0-0	11	Caithness	501
32	21	A	Forfar Ath	W 2-1	1-0	—	Wedderburn, Scott	700
33	24	H	Clyde	L 0-1	0-0	—		477
34	28	A	Stranraer	D 1-1	1-1	12	Thomson R. (pen)	200
35	Apr 4	A	Stenhousemuir	W 3-1	3-0	9	Halley, Tait, Caithness	350
36	11	H	Montrose	D 1-1	1-0	11	Tait	303
37	18	A	Meadowbank T	L 0-1	0-0	11		150
38	25	A	Clyde	L 2-6	2-6	12	Caithness, Thomson R.	350
39	May 2	H	Montrose	D 0-0	0-0	11		339

Final League Position: 11

Goalscorers

League (44): Thomson R. 10 (5 pens), Scott G. 7, Mitchell 5, Halley 4, Burt 3, Caithness 3, Tait 2, Clarke 1, Duncan 1, Herd 1, Huskie 1, McGinn 1, Mackie 1, Neilson 1, Scott J. 1, Wedderburn 1, own goal 1.
League Cup (2): Herd 1, Thomson R. 1.
Scottish Cup (8): Scott G. 4, Halley 2, Huskie 1, Mitchell 1.

Honours

Scottish League – Division 2 Champions 1947–48; Runners-up: 1929–30, 1970–71.
Scottish Cup – Winners: 1938 (only Second Division winners); Runners-up: 1927, 1950.
Scottish League Cup – Winners: 1947–48 (only Second Division winners), 1949–50, 1953–54.
Record Victory: 13-2 v Edinburgh City, Division 2, 11 Dec, 1937.
Record Defeat: 0-9 v Hearts, Division 1, 5 Oct, 1957.
Most League Points: 57, Division 2, 1929–30.
Most Individual League Goals in a Season: Henry Morris, 41, Division 2, 1947–48.
Most Capped Player: George Aitken, 5 (8), Scotland.

Gorman D	Scott J	Beveridge G	Duncan A	Clarke D	Cairns R	Halley K	Thomson R	Mitchell M	McLaren J	Tait C	Burt P	Wedderburn W	Huskie J	Mackie K	Black J	MacNicol D J	Thomson A	Honeyman A	Kelly D	McGinn R	Neilson G	Caithness M	Marnoch W	Kerr G	Scott G	Herd W	Huggins D	Mellon S	*Match No.*
1	12	5	3		10		6	8	4	13				9		2*	7									11			1
1	2			3	6	5	10	8	4	7*		13						12							11	9†			2
1	2			3	10†	5	6	8	4	7		13						12							11	9*			3
1		2		3		5	10	8	4	7		6													11	9			4
1		13		2		5	10	8†	4	7		6*			3		12				11				9				5
1	2			3	10	5		7	4		9						6							8	11				6
1	2*	12		3	10	5	6	7	4		11													8	9				7
1	2			3	10	5	6	7	4		11*		12											8	9				8
1	2			3	6	5	10	7		12	11				4									8*	9				9
1		13		2	6	5	10	8	4†	7	12			11	3*										9				10
1			3	2	6	5	10	8	4	7*				9†					12		13				11				11
1	2	12	3*	4	6		10	8	5	7†	13										11				9				12
1	2	4		3	6		10	8	5	7	12										11*				9				13
1		4	3*	2	6		11	7	5	8	12		13	9†											10				14
1		7	3	4	6		10	8	5	2				11											9				15
1	11		3	4	6	5	10	8	2	7*		13	12	9†															16
1		2			6*	5	3	8	4	12	9†	10	11					13		7									17
1		11		2		5	3	8	4			6								7					10			9	18
1		2	3	8		5	6	7	4	10	12		11*								9								19
1	10		3	4		5	7	2*	6	8	11†		12								13				9				20
1	10		3	2		5	6		4	8			11								7				9				21
1	10		3	2		5	6		4	8	12		11								7*				9				22
1	8			3		5	6	2	4	10	13		11	9†						12					7*				23
1	8	13		3		5	6	2	4	10	12		7*	9†											11				24
1	8	2		3		5	6	10	4		7									11					9				25
1	10	2		3		5	6	8	4		7*		12							11					9				26
1	8	2		3		5	6		4	10	12		11*									9			7				27
1	8	2*		3		5	6	12	4	10											11	7			9				28
1	8	4*		3		5	6	12	2	10†			13								7	11			9				29
1	10	2*		3		5	6		4	8			11†							12	7	13			9				30
1	2			3		5	6	8*	4	10										12	11	7			9				31
1				3		5	6	7	4	2		8	12								11*	10			9				32
1	8	4		3		5	6			2		10									11	7			9				33
1	10*	5	3	4			6	2		8		12									7	11			9				34
1	2	4		3		5	6	10		8											7	11			9				35
1	2			3		5	6		4	8			12								11*	10	7		9				36
1	2		13	3		5	6		4	10			12								7*	11	8†		9				37
1			3	2		5	6*		4	8	13	10	7†								12	11			9				38
		2		3		5	6		4	8		10									7	11			9		1		39
38	26	18	12	37	15	33	38	28	35	30	8	8	9	8	3	1	2	0	0	4	17	12	2	4	35	4	1	1	
	+ 1s	+ 5s	+ 1s					+ 2s		+ 3s	+ 10s	+ 4s	+ 9s				+ 1s	+ 3s	+ 1s	+ 3s	+ 3s	+ 1s							

EAST STIRLING Division 1

Year Formed: 1881. *Ground:* Firs Park. *Size:* 112yd×72yd. *Capacity:* 12,000.
Telephone: Falkirk 23583. *Secretary:* P. I. McKay. *Manager:* Martin Ferguson.
Club Colours: Black and white 1-inch hoops, black shorts, red stockings. *Club Nickname:* The Shire.
Record Attendance: 11,500 v Hibernian, Scottish Cup, 10 Feb, 1969.

1980–81 LEAGUE RECORD

Match No.	Date	Venue	Opponents	Result	H/T Score	League Pos'n	Goalscorers	Attendance
1	Aug 9	A	Clydebank	L 2-3	0-1	—	Grant (pen), Rennie	800
2	16	H	Hamilton A	D 1-1	1-0	11	McCaig	855
3	23	A	Falkirk	D 1-1	0-0	10	Lamont	2000
4	Sept 3	A	St Johnstone	W 2-0	1-0	—	Lamont, Craig	1258
5	6	H	Dunfermline Ath	L 0-4	0-3	10		1059
6	13	A	Dumbarton	D 2-2	1-0	10	Coyle T. (og), McCulley (pen)	600
7	17	A	Hibernian	D 2-2	1-1	—	Grant 2	3000
8	20	H	Stirling Albion	W 2-0	1-0	9	McCaig, Grant	750
9	27	H	Berwick R	W 5-1	3-0	6	Rennie, McCaig 2, Sharp, Robertson	500
10	Oct 4	A	Raith R	L 1-2	0-0	9	Blair	1500
11	11	H	Motherwell	D 1-1	1-0	9	McCulley	1200
12	13	H	Ayr U	L 0-2	0-1	—		800
13	18	A	Dundee	L 0-2	0-1	10		3771
14	25	H	Dumbarton	W 2-1	1-0	10	Lamont, Rennie	550
15	Nov 1	A	Dunfermline Ath	L 0-1	0-1	11		1900
16	8	H	Hibernian	D 1-1	1-1	10	Robertson	1963
17	15	A	Stirling Albion	L 2-4	2-1	10	McCulley, McCaig	500
18	22	A	Berwick R	W 2-1	0-1	11	Rennie, Grant	750
19	Dec 6	A	Motherwell	D 1-1	1-0	10	Lamont	1999
20	13	H	Dundee	L 0-2	0-0	11		1026
21	20	H	St Johnstone	D 1-1	0-0	11	McCaig	750
22	27	A	Hamilton A	L 0-1	0-0	11		1670
23	Jan 1	H	Falkirk	D 0-0	0-0	—		3200
24	3	A	Ayr U	D 3-3	0-1	10	Lamont, McCulley, Kelly	2339
25	31	A	Dumbarton	L 0-1	0-1	11		450
26	Feb 21	H	Falkirk	D 1-1	0-0	11	Renwick	2000
27	28	A	Raith R	D 0-0	0-0	10		1200
28	Mar 14	A	Motherwell	L 1-2	0-0	10	Ashwood	1800
29	21	H	Dunfermline Ath	D 0-0	0-0	10		5088
30	24	H	Raith R	L 0-1	0-0	—		1800
31	28	A	Hamilton A	D 2-2	1-0	10	Lamont, Gourlay	1200
32	Apr 1	H	Stirling Albion	W 1-0	0-0	—	McCaig	800
33	4	H	Ayr U	L 1-3	0-3	10	Sharp	850
34	7	H	Berwick R	D 0-0	0-0	—		600
35	11	A	Hibernian	L 0-2	0-1	11		3500
36	18	H	St Johnstone	D 2-2	1-0	10	Lamont, Ashwood	2000
37	25	A	Clydebank	L 0-2	0-1	11		400
38	29	H	Clydebank	D 2-2	2-2	—	Hunter, Rennie	1300
39	May 2	H	Dundee	L 0-1	0-1	11		5762

Final League Position: 11

Goalscorers

League (41): Lamont 7, McCaig 7, Grant 5 (1 pen), Rennie 5, McCulley 4 (1 pen), Ashwood 2, Robertson 2, Sharp 2, Blair 1, Craig 1, Gourlay 1, Hunter 1, Kelly 1, Renwick 1, own goal 1.
League Cup (0).
Scottish Cup (6): McCaig 2, Ashwood 1, Blair 1, Grant 1, Rennie 1.

Honours
Scottish League – Division 2 Champions 1931–32; Runners-up: 1962–63, 1979–80.
Record Victory: 10-1 v Stenhousemuir, Scottish Cup 1st rd, 1 Sept, 1888.
Record Defeat: 1-12 v Dundee U, Division 2, 13 April, 1936.
Most League Points: 55, Division 2, 1931–32.
Most Individual League Goals in a Season: Malcolm Morrison, 36, Division 2, 1938–39.
Most Capped Player: Humphrey Jones, 5, Wales.

Kelly C	Gourlay I	Renwick C	McRitchie R	Blair J	McCulley R	Rennie I	Watt D	Lamont P	Robertson I	Grant A	Ashwood W	McCaig D	Sharp R	Bennett A	Taylor G	Simpson G	Goodall J T	Daly P	Brown C	Hunter G H	*Match No.*
1	2			3	8	5	13	6*	11	7		9		10†		4		12			1
1	3			2	4	5	6	8	10	9		7	12		11*						2
1	2		12	3	4	5	6	10	11	7		9*	8								3
1	2			3	4	5	6	7*	10	11		9	8	12							4
1	2		12	5	7		3	9	10	11			8	4		6*					5
1	8		2	3	7*	5	4	6	10	9		13	11†	12							6
1	8		2	3	7	5	4	6	10	9		12	11*								7
1	10		2	3	8	5	4	6*	12	7	13	11	9†								8
1	2		3	12	8	5	6	10	4	7	13	11†	9*								9
1	8		2	3	7†	5	4	6*	10	11	12	13	9								10
1	3		2	12	4	5*	6	8	10	7	11		9								11
1	3		2		7	5	4	6	10	11		8	9								12
1	4		2	3*		5	6	7	10		11		9	8	12						13
1	4		2	3	8	5	6	7	10		11		9								14
1	8		2*	3	4	5	6	7	10†	12	11	13	9								15
1			2	3	4	5	6	7	10	8	11	9									16
1		3	2	12	4	5*	6	7	10	8	11	9									17
1	4	2		3	12	5	6		10	7	11	13	9†						8*		18
1	8	2		3	4	5	6	7	10	9	11										19
1	8*	2		3	4	5	6	7		9	11	13	12						10†		20
1	2	12		3	4*	5	6	8	10	7	11†	9	13								21
1	8	2		3		5	6	7†	10	9	13	11	12						4*		22
1	8	2		3	4*	5	6	12	10	7	9	11									23
1	8	2	4	3	10	5		6*	11	7	9	12									24
1	4	2	12	3		5	6	8	10	7		9*	11†	13							25
1	2	3		12	4	5	6	10	13	7	9	11†		8*							26
1	2	3		5	4		6	8	11	7			12	10			9*				27
1	4	2		3	8	5	6*			7	9	13	12	10			11†				28
1	2			3	8	5	6	10	4	7*	9	11					12				29
1	2			3	8	5	6		4	7	9*	11		10			12				30
1	4	2		3		5	6	10	11	13		7	9†	12						8*	31
1		2		3		5	6	10	8	7		11	9	4							32
1		2	12	3*		5	6	8	4		11	7†	9	10			13				33
1		2		3		5	6	8	10		11	7	9	4							34
1		3	4	2	10	5		6	11	7*	9	12		8							35
1	2	3		5	4		6	8	9		11			10			7*			12	36
1	2	5	3		4*			7	9		11	6		10			8			12	37
1	2		3			5		7	9		11	6		10			8			4	38
1	2	3		5	8		6	10	11		9	7†	13				12			4*	39
39	33	19	16	32	30	34	34	35	35	29	23	23	19	14	1	2	5	0	3	3	
		+ 1s	+ 4s	+ 4s	+ 1s		+ 1s	+ 1s	+ 2s	+ 2s	+ 4s	+ 9s	+ 7s	+ 4s	+ 1s		+ 4s	+ 1s		+ 2s	

FALKIRK

Division 1

Year Formed: 1876.
Ground: Brockville Park. *Size:* 100yd×70yd. *Capacity:* 22,000 (2750 seats).
Telephone: Falkirk 24121.
Manager: John Hagart. *Physiotherapist/Trainer:* Tom Logan.
Secretary: R. Shaw. *PRO:* William McFarlane.
Club Colours: Navy blue shirts with white trimmings and white motif, white shorts, red stockings.
Club Nickname: The Bairns.
Record Attendance: 23,100 v Celtic, Scottish Cup, 3rd rd, 21 Feb, 1953.

1980–81 LEAGUE RECORD

Match No.	*Date*	*Venue*	*Opponents*	*Result*		*H/T Score*	*League Pos'n*	*Goalscorers*	*Attendance*
1	Aug 9	H	Dumbarton	L	0-5	0-1	—		2500
2	16	A	Motherwell	L	0-3	0-1	14		2531
3	23	H	East Stirling	D	1-1	0-0	13	Spence	2000
4	Sept 3	H	Berwick R	W	6-0	1-0	—	Spence, Hay 3, Perry, Brown	1500
5	6	A	Stirling Albion	L	0-1	0-0	11		1500
6	9	A	Raith R	L	1-2	0-1	—	Mackin	1500
7	13	H	Clydebank	W	3-2	2-0	9	Mackin, Perry, Conn	2600
8	17	H	Dunfermline Ath	W	2-1	0-1	—	Spence, Perry (pen)	3500
9	20	A	Dundee	L	0-4	0-2	10		3993
10	27	A	St Johnstone	D	0-0	0-0	11		2065
11	Oct 4	H	Ayr U	W	3-1	1-0	10	McAllister (og), Thompson, Herd	2000
12	11	A	Hibernian	L	0-2	0-1	10		6947
13	18	H	Hamilton A	L	2-3	1-2	12	Thompson, Spence	1200
14	25	A	Clydebank	L	1-2	0-1	12	Hay	600
15	Nov 1	H	Stirling Albion	D	0-0	0-0	12		2000
16	8	A	Dunfermline Ath	W	1-0	1-0	12	Spence	2250
17	15	H	Dundee	L	0-3	0-0	12		2800
18	22	H	St Johnstone	L	0-3	0-1	12		2000
19	29	A	Ayr U	L	1-3	0-0	12	McRoberts	2204
20	Dec 6	H	Hibernian	L	0-2	0-1	12		3400
21	13	A	Hamilton A	W	1-0	0-0	13	Mackin	1200
22	20	A	Berwick R	W	4-0	2-0	12	Oliver A. 2, Kettings 2	682
23	Jan 1	A	East Stirling	D	0-0	0-0	—		3200
24	3	H	Raith R	W	1-0	0-0	11	Oliver A.	1500
25	10	A	Dumbarton	W	1-0	0-0	9	Brown	700
26	17	A	Hibernian	L	0-1	0-0	9		4670
27	31	H	Clydebank	D	0-0	0-0	9		2500
28	Feb 21	A	East Stirling	D	1-1	0-0	9	Hoggan	2000
29	28	H	Ayr U	W	2-1	0-0	9	Smith, Brown	2000
30	Mar 4	A	Dunfermline Ath	W	1-0	1-0	—	Smith	1500
31	7	A	St Johnstone	L	1-2	1-1	8	Smith	2325
32	14	H	Hamilton A	W	2-1	1-1	8	Brown, Mackin	1800
33	18	H	Motherwell	L	0-1	0-1	—		1500
34	21	H	Stirling Albion	D	0-0	0-0	8		1700
35	28	A	Raith R	D	0-0	0-0	8		3000
36	Apr 4	A	Motherwell	L	0-1	0-0	8		2045
37	11	H	Dumbarton	L	1-3	0-0	9	Smith	1500
38	18	A	Berwick R	W	2-1	1-0	9	Hoggan (pen), Perry	812
39	25	H	Dundee	L	1-2	0-0	9	Fowler	4500

Final League Position: 9

Goalscorers

League (39): Spence 5, Brown 4, Hay 4, Mackin 4, Perry 4 (1 pen), Smith 4, Oliver A. 3, Hoggan 2 (1 pen), Kettings 2, Thompson 2, Conn 1, Fowler 1, Herd 1, McRoberts 1, own goal 1.
League Cup (2): Leetion 1, Perry 1.
Scottish Cup (1): Hay 1.

Honours

Scottish League: Division 1 Runners-up: 1907–08, 1909–10; Division 2 Champions: 1935–36, 1969–70, 1974–75, 1979–80; Runners-up: 1904–05, 1951–52, 1960–61.
Scottish Cup: Winners: 1913, 1957. *Scottish League Cup:* Runners-up 1947–48.
Record Victory: 12-1 v Laurieston, Scottish Cup 2nd rd, 23 March, 1893.
Record Defeat: 1-11 v Airdrieonians, Division 1, 28 Apr, 1951.
Most League Points: 59, Division 2, 1935–36.
Most Individual League Goals in Season: 43, Evelyn Morrison, Division 1, 1928–29.
Most Capped Player: Alec Parker, 14 (15), Scotland.

Watson G	Allan T	Rose A	Burrell A	Stevenson W	Nicol A	Hoggan W	Oliver M	Brown B	Watson D	McRoberts A	Mackin A	Hay J	Thompson G	Herd W	Oliver A	Perry J	Leetion P	Kettings P	Conn S	Spence C	Mitchell J	McDowell D	Smith G J	Gillon J	Fowler C	Buchanan G	*Match No.*
1				2	3	7	13	5	8	10		6			4	11†				9*		12					1
1			2	3		7	13	5	4*	10		6			12	9	8				11†						2
	1	3		10	2	4*		5		9		6				7	8			12	11						3
	1	2		10	3	7		4	8		5	6				11				9							4
	1	2*		10	3	7		4	13	12	5	6		8		11				9†							5
	1			8	3	2	6*	4	12	10†	5			9		7	11			13							6
	1			10	3	2		6	4*		5			8		7	12		11	9							7
	1			10	3	2		6	4		5			8		7			11	9							8
	1			10	3†	2*		4	6	12	5			8		7	13		11	9							9
	1			2	3		12	4		6	5*		9	8		7	10		11								10
	1			10	3	2		4		6	5		9	8		7	12		11*								11
	1			10	3*	2	5	4	13	6			9	8			7†		11	12							12
	1		3	10		2	12	4*	13	6	5		9	8†					11	7							13
	1	12	3*	10		2		4		8	5	6	9			7			11†	13							14
1		3		10		2*	12		13	4	5	6	9†			7			11	8							15
1		3		8			2		4*	12	5	6†	13			7			11	9	10						16
1		3		4*		7	2			12	5		8†			13			11	9	10					6	17
1		3*				2	12	5		4			9	8		7†			11	13	10					6	18
1					3	2	4			12	5	6	9*	8	7			10	11								19
1				12	3	2			7	4*	5	6		8	9		10		11								20
1		2	3	10†		7		4		13	5	6	12	8	9*			11									21
1		2*	3	10†		7		4		12	5	6		8	9	13		11									22
1		2	3			7		4		10	5	6		8	9*	12		11									23
1		2	3			7		4		10	5	6		8	9*	12		11									24
1		2	3			7*		4		10	5	6		8	9	12		11									25
1			3	7		2	13	4		10	5	6		8*	9	12		11†									26
1		3				2		4		10	5	6	12	8	9	13		11†	7*								27
1		2	3	11		7		4			5	6	12	8*	10					9							28
1		2*	3	11			13	4		7	5	6		8	9†			12					10				29
1		2	3	11		7		4		8	5	6			9								10				30
1		2	3			7	8*	4			5	6			9	13	12	11					10†				31
1		2	3	11		7	13	4			5	6		8*		9†		12					10				32
1		2	3	11		7		4			5	6*		8	12			10					9				33
1		2	3	11†		7		4			5	6*	13	8	9				12				10				34
1		2	3*	12		7		4			5	13	6	8	9†			11					10				35
1		2			3	7*	13	4			5		6	8†	9			11					10	12			36
1		2	3			7		4			5	13	6			9	8*	11†					10	12			37
1			3	11		2	4				5	6	8			7		10					9				38
1			3		2	7	5	4				6*	8			10			12				9	11†	13		39
27	12	23	20	27	15	36	8	33	8	19	33	26	14	26	17	19	7	14	15	11	5	0	11	1	0	2	
		+ 1s		+ 2s			+ 10s		+ 5s			+ 2s	+ 5s		+ 2s	+ 8s	+ 4s	+ 2s	+ 2s	+ 5s		+ 1s		+ 2s	+ 1s		

FORFAR ATHLETIC Division 2

Year Formed: 1884. *Ground:* Station Park. *Size:* 116yd×69yd. *Capacity:* 10,000 (850 seated). *Telephone:* Forfar 63576 and 62817. *Manager:* Alex Rae. *Secretary:* James Robertson.
Assistant Manager and Trainer-coach: Alex Carswell. *Commercial Manager:* Brian C. Rankin. *Telephone:* Forfar 67849.
Club Colours: Sky blue shirts, sky blue shorts, sky blue stockings with navy tops.
Club Nickname: Loons.
Record Attendance: 10,780 v Rangers, Scottish Cup 2nd rd, 2 Feb, 1970.

1980–81 LEAGUE RECORD

Match No.	*Date*	*Venue*	*Opponents*	*Result*	*H/T Score*	*League Pos'n*	*Goalscorers*	*Attendance*
1	Aug 9	H	Albion R	D 1-1	1-0	—	Clark	1000
2	16	H	East Fife	W 3-2	1-1	5	Watt 2, Farningham	1100
3	23	A	Arbroath	W 3-2	1-2	2	Robb, Watt, Gillies	1431
4	Sept 3	H	Queen's Park	D 1-1	0-0	—	Clark (pen)	498
5	6	A	Stranraer	W 4-0	3-0	1	Clark 2, Gillies, Gallacher	450
6	9	A	Alloa	L 0-1	0-0	—		800
7	13	H	Meadowbank T	W 3-2	2-0	1	Clark (pen), Watt 2	1000
8	17	A	Brechin C	D 1-1	1-0	—	Gallacher	1100
9	20	H	Queen of the S	L 1-2	0-0	4	McPhee	1000
10	27	A	Clyde	L 1-2	0-1	4	Wildridge	600
11	Oct 4	H	Cowdenbeath	L 1-2	0-1	6	Clark	950
12	11	A	Stenhousemuir	W 1-0	0-0	5	Brown	350
13	18	H	Montrose	L 0-4	0-1	8		1000
14	25	A	Meadowbank T	L 2-4	2-2	9	Brash (pen), Clark	150
15	Nov 1	H	Stranraer	W 3-0	0-0	7	Rae (pen), Brash (pen), Mitchell	900
16	8	H	Brechin C	D 0-0	0-0	8		811
17	15	A	Queen of the S	D 1-1	1-0	9	Laurie	1000
18	22	H	Clyde	W 3-2	1-0	5	Clark 2, Watt	800
19	Dec 6	H	Stenhousemuir	W 2-1	2-1	5	Brash (pen), Mitchell	600
20	13	H	Queen of the S	L 3-4	3-1	5	Mitchell 2, Brash	600
21	27	A	East Fife	D 0-0	0-0	6		616
22	Jan 10	A	Queen's Park	W 3-1	2-0	5	Brash (pen), Gallacher, Clark	906
23	24	A	Albion R	W 4-2	2-1	4	Brash (pen), Laurie, Bennett, Robb	300
24	31	A	Montrose	L 0-4	0-1	5		1000
25	Feb 7	H	Stenhousemuir	L 1-4	0-2	6	Leitch	750
26	14	A	Brechin C	D 0-0	0-0	6		600
27	Mar 7	A	Clyde	L 1-3	0-2	10	Farningham	500
28	11	H	Cowdenbeath	W 1-0	0-0	—	Brash (pen)	745
29	14	A	Arbroath	D 0-0	0-0	7		915
30	21	H	East Fife	L 1-2	0-1	10	Gallacher	700
31	24	A	Montrose	D 0-0	0-0	—		350
32	28	H	Meadowbank T	W 3-1	2-0	8	Farningham 2, Watt	800
33	Apr 1	A	Cowdenbeath	W 2-1	1-0	—	Watt 2	500
34	4	A	Alloa	W 1-0	1-0	6	Watt	660
35	8	H	Arbroath	W 2-1	0-1	—	Watt, Brash (pen)	1000
36	11	A	Albion R	L 2-3	1-0	5	Allan, Meikle (og)	300
37	18	H	Queen's Park	L 1-2	0-0	6	Brash	1000
38	25	A	Stranraer	W 3-0	1-0	6	Mitchell, Watt, Gallacher	200
39	May 2	H	Alloa	W 4-1	1-0	5	Leitch, Mitchell, Gallacher, Watt	722

Final League Position: 5

Goalscorers

League (63): Watt 13, Clark 10 (2 pens), Brash 9 (7 pens), Gallacher 6, Mitchell 6, Farningham 4, Gillies 2, Laurie 2, Leitch 2, Robb 2, Allan 1, Bennett 1, Brown 1, McPhee 1, Rae 1 (pen), Wildridge 1, own goal 1.
League Cup (1): Robb 1.
Scottish Cup (0).

Honours

Scottish League Cup – Semi-Finalists 1977–78.
Forfarshire Cup – Winners 4 times.
Record Victory: 14-1 v Lindertis, Scottish Cup 1st rd, 1 Sept, 1888.
Record Defeat: 2-12 v King's Park, Division 2, 2 Jan, 1930.
Most League Points: 47, Division 2, 1968–69, 1979–80.
Most Individual League Goals in Season: Davie Kilgour, 45, Division 2, 1929–30.

Kennedy S	Boardley I	Bennett W	McPhee I	Cameron J	Beattie	Stewart I B	Gillies W	Brown K	Laurie R J	Morris R M	Brash A Y	Clark J G	Rankin B	Robb R	Gallacher W	Leitch G R	McLeod D C	Allan J	Wildridge I	Rae A	Farningham R P	Watt N J	Gibson J	Mitchell J	Duncan A R	*Match No.*
1		4	10	3	2	5*			6†			9		12		11			13		7	8				1
1		2	6	3*			12	4			5	9		11		10					7	8				2
1		2	3				6	4	5*			9		11	12	8					7	10				3
1		2	3		8		6	4	5*			9		11	7	12						10				4
1		2	3	13			6	4	12		5*	9		11	7	8†						10				5
1		2	3				6	4			5	9		11	7	8						10				6
1		2	3				6	4	5			9		11		8*			12		7	10				7
1		2	3	13			6	4	5*			12		11	7	10†					8	9				8
1		2	10	3			6*	4				5		12	11	7			13		8	9†				9
1		2	3			8	6	4			5	9†		13	11	7*			10			12				10
1		2	3			8	6	4			5	10			9*	12			11		7					11
1		2	3			8	6	4			5	10*			11	7			12		9					12
1			3			2	6	4			5				9	8*			10†		7	12		13	11	13
1			10	3		2	6	4*			5	11			8†	12					7	13		9		14
1		2	3				6				5	11		13	10†	12	7			4*	8			9		15
1		2					3			4	5	11		12		10†	7			6	8	13		9*		16
1		2	6				3	12	10	4	5	11†				13	7*				8	9				17
1		2	6				3			4	5	10		11	8						7	9				18
1		2	6				3*	12		4	5	11			9						7	8		10		19
	1	2	6					12	3	4	5	11			10						7	8		9*		20
	1		6	2			3			4	5			11*	10	8					7	12		9		21
	1	2	3					8	6	4	5	9			12	11					7			10*		22
	1	2	3			12		8*	6	4	5			13	10	11					7	9†				23
	1	2	3			8			6	4	5			13	10	11†					7	9*		12		24
	1	2	3				6	12	5*	4				11	9	8					7	10				25
1		2				10	5		3*	4				9	12	11	7			6	8					26
1		2	3			8				4		9*	6	12	10	11		5			7					27
1		2*	10			12	3			4	5	11	6		9	13					8		7†			28
1		2	10				3			4	5	11	6		9	12					8		7*			29
1		2	10			8†	3			4	5	9	6	7*	11		13						12			30
1		2	3							4	5	13			10	11	8*	6			7	9†	12			31
1		2	3					12		4	5	13				11		6			8	9	7*	10†		32
1		2	3					7		4	5					11		6			8	9		10		33
1		2	3					7		4	5					11		6			8	9		10		34
1		2	3					7		4	5	12				11		6			8	9		10*		35
1		2	3			12	11			4	5	10				7		6*			8	9†	13			36
1		2	3				12	8		4	5	13			10			6*			7	9	11†			37
1								4		2		11	3		7	6		5			8	10		9		38
1								4		2		11	3		7	6		5			8	10	12	9*		39
33	6	34	35	5	2	10	24	21	12	24	28	26	6	12	26	27	5	10	3	3	34	25	4	13	1	
				+ 2s		+ 3s	+ 2s	+ 5s				+ 5s		+ 8s	+ 3s	+ 7s	+ 1s		+ 4s			+ 5s	+ 4s	+ 2s		

HAMILTON ACADEMICAL Division 1

Year Formed: 1875.
Ground: Douglas Park (since 1888). *Size:* 104yd×72yd. *Capacity:* 18,000 (1600 seated).
Telephone: Hamilton 286103.
Manager: David McParland.
Secretary: Joseph Friel. *PRO:* Alan Dick. *Physiotherapist:* R. Reid. *Coach:* P. Barkey.
Club Colours: Red and white hooped shirts, white shorts with white stockings.
Club Nickname: The Accies.
Record Attendance: 28,281 v Hearts, Scottish Cup, 3rd rd, 3 Mar, 1937.
Previous Grounds: Bent Farm, South Avenue, South Haugh.
Record Transfer Fee Received: £30,000 from Dundee United for Paul Hegarty, Nov 1974.
Record Transfer Fee Paid: £15,000 to Motherwell for Bobby Graham, July 1977.

1980–81 LEAGUE RECORD

Match No.	Date	Venue	Opponents	Result	H/T Score	League Pos'n	Goalscorers	Attendance
1	Aug 9	H	Berwick R	W 9-1	3-0	—	Brown 3, McGrogan, Graham, Fairlie, Deeney 2, McDowall	1471
2	16	A	East Stirling	D 1-1	0-1	2	McDowall	855
3	23	H	Motherwell	W 4-2	1-1	1	McGrogan, Fairlie 2 (1 pen), McDowall	3936
4	Sept 6	H	Dumbarton	D 1-1	0-0	1	Fairlie	1800
5	9	H	Stirling Albion	W 2-0	1-0	—	Fairlie 2	1600
6	13	A	St Johnstone	L 0-1	0-0	2		1574
7	17	A	Ayr U	L 1-2	0-0	—	Wright	3500
8	20	H	Hibernian	D 1-1	0-0	4	Graham	5197
9	27	H	Raith R	W 3-1	2-0	4	McDowall, Wright, McDougall	1500
10	Oct 4	A	Clydebank	L 1-3	0-1	6	Brown	1000
11	11	H	Dunfermline Ath	D 1-1	1-1	7	McDowall	2000
12	13	A	Dundee	L 0-2	0-1	—		3170
13	18	A	Falkirk	W 3-2	2-1	4	Howie, Wright, Marshall	1200
14	25	H	St Johnstone	L 0-3	0-2	6		2000
15	Nov 1	A	Dumbarton	L 1-2	0-1	9	Fairlie	500
16	8	H	Ayr U	W 1-0	1-0	6	McManus	1885
17	15	A	Hibernian	D 3-3	1-1	7	Graham, Wright, Howie	4000
18	22	A	Raith R	L 0-1	0-0	7		2200
19	29	H	Clydebank	W 3-0	1-0	7	Fairlie 2 (1 pen), McManus	1516
20	Dec 6	A	Dunfermline Ath	W 1-0	0-0	7	Wright	1650
21	13	H	Falkirk	L 0-1	0-0	7		1200
22	20	H	East Stirling	W 1-0	0-0	7	Fairlie	1670
23	Jan 1	A	Motherwell	W 3-1	2-1	—	McManus, Wright, Howie	4000
24	3	H	Dundee	W 4-2	2-1	6	Brown, Howie, McDowall, Deeney	2500
25	10	A	Berwick R	L 0-1	0-0	6		647
26	31	A	St Johnstone	L 1-2	0-1	6	Fairlie	2122
27	Feb 14	H	Dunfermline Ath	L 1-4	0-2	7	Fairlie (pen)	1000
28	21	A	Hibernian	L 0-4	0-1	7		4000
29	28	A	Clydebank	W 2-1	0-1	7	Alexander 2	600
30	Mar 4	H	Ayr U	D 0-0	0-0	—		1000
31	7	H	Raith R	L 0-2	0-1	7		1500
32	11	A	Stirling Albion	W 2-0	0-0	—	Fairlie, Howie	350
33	14	A	Falkirk	L 1-2	1-1	7	Alexander	1800
34	21	H	Dundee	L 1-3	1-1		Alexander	1500
35	28	H	East Stirling	D 2-2	0-1	7	Brown, Craig	1200
36	Apr 4	A	Dumbarton	L 1-2	0-2	7	McDowall	300
37	11	A	Stirling Albion	W 1-0	0-0	7	Craig	500
38	18	H	Motherwell	L 1-2	0-0	7	Alexander	2601
39	25	H	Berwick R	W 4-1	1-0	7	McManus, Craig, Deeney, Alexander	1000

Final League Position: 7

Goalscorers

League (61): Fairlie 13 (3 pens), McDowall 7, Alexander 6, Brown 6, Wright 6, Howie 5, Deeney 4, McManus 4, Craig 3, Graham 3, McGrogan 2, Marshall 1, McDougall 1.
League Cup (9): McDowall 3, Fairlie 2, McAdams 1, McGrogan 1, McManus 1, Wright 1.
Scottish Cup (0).

Honours

Scottish League: Division 2 Champions: 1903–04; Runners-up: 1952–53, 1964–65.
Scottish Cup: Runners-up: 1911, 1935. *Lanarkshire Cup:* 9 times winners.
Record Victory: 10-2 v Cowdenbeath, Division 1, 15 Oct, 1932.
Record Defeat: 1-11 v Hibernian, Division 1, 6 Nov, 1965.
Most League Points: 55, Division 2, 1973–74.
Most League Goals: 92, Division 1, 1932–33.
Most Individual League Goals in a Season: 34, David Wilson, 1936–37.
Highest Scorer in Total Aggregate: 246, David Wilson, 1928–39.
Most Capped Players: Jimmy King, 2, Bobby Howe, 2, Scotland.
Best Season: 4th in Division 1, 1934–35.
Extra Information: The hat-trick by John Brown v Berwick R, 9 Aug, 1980, is the only one (without the aid of a penalty) by a full-back in Scottish League history.

Ferguson R	Muir J	Frew J	Brown J	Alexander E	Kellachan D	Marshall G	Colgan G	Wright B	McDougall A	Dailly G	McGrogan J	McDowall G	McManus M	Young A	Dempsey J	Gormley J	Fairlie J	Smith D	Mitchell G	Howie N	Deeney J	Dunsmore G	Graham R	McAdams P	Craig J	*Match No.*
1		2	3	6				4*	5		11	7	13				8				9†		12	10		1
1		2	3	6				4	5*		11	7	13	12			8				9†			10		2
1		2	3	6				4	5		11	7	8				9							10		3
1		2	3	12		6		4*	5		11	7					9			8†		13		10		4
1		2	3	4		6			5		11	7	8				9							10		5
1		2	3	4*		6		12	5		11†	7	8				9			13				10		6
1		2	3	4		6†		7	5		13		11	8*			9						12	10		7
1		2	3	4		6		10	5		12	7	11*				9						8			8
1		2				3		4	5		11	7	8*			6	9						12	10		9
	1	2	13	12		3		4	5		11†	7	8			6*	9							10		10
1		2	3	6				4	5		11*	7	8				9			12				10		11
1		2	3	6				4			11	7	8*		5		9			10				12		12
1			3	2		12		4	6			7			5		9			11			8	10*		13
1			3	2		12		4	6		13	7			5*		9			11			8†	10		14
1			3	2		10†		7	6	4*	12		11		5	8	9							13		15
1		2	3	6				4	5		11		9				7						8	10		16
1		2	3	6			11†	4	5				9*		12		7			13			8	10		17
1		2	3	6				4	5		11	12	9*				7			13			8	10†		18
1		2	3	6				4	5		11		9				7						8	10		19
1		2	3	6			11	4	5			9					7			12			8*	10		20
1		2	3	6			11†	4	5			9	13				7			12			8*	10		21
1		2	3	6				4	5		13	8*	11				7			10	9†			12		22
1		2	3	6		12		4	5			9	11				7			8				10*		23
1		2	3	6				4	5			9	11				7			8*	12			10		24
1		2	3	6				4	5		13	9	11				7			8*	12			10†		25
1			3	6	2		11*	4	5		12	8					7			10	9					26
1		12	6	2	3*			4	5			8	11				7			9	13			10†		27
1			10	2	3		12†	4	5			8	11*				7	6		9				13		28
1			3	2				4	5		11*	8					7	6		9	12			10		29
1			3	2				4	5		11*	8	12				7	6		9†	13			10		30
1			3	2				4	5			8	11				7	6*	12	13	9†			10		31
1		2	3	4					5		12	8					7	6		9	11*			10		32
1		2	3	4				12	5			8					7*	6		11	13			10†	9	33
1		12	3	2		6*		10	5			4	11							7	9				8	34
1		2	10	4		6*	3		5			12	7†						11	8	13				9	35
1			10	4*			3	2	6		11	5	12			7				13	9†				8	36
1		2	10	6			3	4	5			7	12							9	11*				8	37
1		2	3	6		13			5		12	7	11†			4			10*		8				9	38
1		2	10	6			3	4	5			7*	11†						12	13	9				8	39
38	1	28	37	36	3	10	8	33	38	1	16	32	25	1	4	5	33	6	2	18	11	0	9	27	7	
		+ 2s	+ 1s	+ 2s		+ 4s	+ 1s	+ 2s			+ 9s	+ 2s	+ 6s	+ 1s	+ 1s				+ 2s	+ 9s	+ 7s	+ 1s	+ 3s	+ 4s		

HEART OF MIDLOTHIAN Division 1

Year Formed: 1874.
Ground: Tynecastle Park, Gorgie Road, Edinburgh EH11 2NL. *Size:* 110yd×76yd. *Capacity:* 23,450 (7000 seats).
Telephone: 031-337 6132.
Manager: Tony Ford.
Secretary: L. W. Porteous. *Trainer:* Andy Stevenson.
Club Colours: Maroon shirts, white collar and cuffs, white shorts, maroon stockings with white tops.
Club Nickname: Jam Tarts.
Record Attendance: 53,496 v Rangers, Scottish Cup 3rd rd, 13 Feb, 1932.
Previous Grounds: The Meadows, 1873–78; Powderhall, 1878–81; Tynecastle, 1881–86; Tyneside Park, 1886–
European Competitions: *European Cup* 1958–59, 1960–61; *Fairs Cup* 1961–62, 1963–64, 1965–66. *European Cup-Winners' Cup* 1976–77.
Record Transfer Fee Received: £200,000 from Chelsea for Eamonn Bannon, Jan 1979.
Record Transfer Fee Paid: £30,000 to Glasgow Rangers for Jim Denny, 1979 and £30,000 to Glasgow Rangers for Alex MacDonald, July 1980.

1980–81 LEAGUE RECORD

Match No.	Date	Venue	Opponents	Result	H/T Score	League Pos'n	Goalscorers	Attendance
1	Aug 9	A	Partick T	L 2-3	0-1	—	Liddell, Fraser (pen)	4000
2	16	H	Airdrieonians	L 0-2	0-0	9		6711
3	23	A	St Mirren	W 3-1	1-1	8	Conn, O'Connor 2	7553
4	Sept 6	A	Kilmarnock	W 1-0	0-0	4	Gibson	4000
5	13	H	Celtic	L 0-2	0-1	6		17,169
6	20	H	Morton	L 0-1	0-1	7		5996
7	27	A	Dundee U	D 1-1	1-0	7	O'Connor	6263
8	Oct 4	H	Aberdeen	L 0-1	0-0	8		10,873
9	11	A	Rangers	L 1-3	0-0	9	MacDonald	23,700
10	18	H	Partick T	L 0-1	0-0	9		5905
11	25	A	Airdrieonians	L 0-3	0-3	9		3500
12	Nov 1	H	St Mirren	D 1-1	0-0	9	Conn	5707
13	8	H	Dundee U	L 0-3	0-2	9		5800
14	15	A	Morton	D 2-2	1-0	9	Conn, O'Connor	3500
15	22	H	Rangers	D 0-0	0-0	9		16,000
16	Dec 6	H	Kilmarnock	W 2-0	0-0	9	MacDonald, O'Brien	5183
17	13	A	Celtic	L 2-3	1-2	9	MacDonald, Gibson	13,800
18	20	H	Morton	D 0-0	0-0	9		5900
19	27	A	Dundee U	L 1-4	1-1	9	Gibson	6928
20	Jan 1	H	Airdrieonians	L 2-3	0-0	—	Gibson, O'Brien	8086
21	3	A	Partick T	L 0-1	0-1	9		3500
22	10	H	Aberdeen	L 0-2	0-1	9		7999
23	31	H	Celtic	L 0-3	0-1	9		14,596
24	Feb 21	A	St Mirren	L 1-2	0-1	9	McShane	3412
25	28	H	Partick T	D 1-1	1-1	9	Kidd	3491
26	Mar 7	A	Aberdeen	L 1-4	0-2	9	Hamill	11,000
27	14	H	Rangers	W 2-1	1-1	9	Redford (og), Liddell	11,500
28	21	A	Morton	L 0-3	0-1	9		3500
29	24	A	Kilmarnock	L 0-2	0-1	—		1445
30	28	H	Dundee U	L 0-4	0-2	10		3776
31	Apr 1	A	Celtic	L 0-6	0-3	—		13,300
32	4	H	Kilmarnock	W 1-0	1-0	9	Bowman	1866
33	11	A	Aberdeen	L 0-1	0-0	9		6000
34	18	H	St Mirren	L 1-2	1-1	9	Maxwell	2500
35	25	A	Airdrieonians	W 2-1	1-0	9	Liddell 2	2000
36	May 2	A	Rangers	L 0-4	0-3	10		7000

Final League Position: 10

Goalscorers

League (27): Gibson 4, Liddell 4, O'Connor 4, Conn 3, MacDonald 3, O'Brien 2, Bowman 1, Fraser 1 (pen), Hamill 1, Kidd 1, McShane 1, Maxwell 1, own goal 1.
League Cup (7): Robertson C. 5, Bowman 1, MacDonald 1.
Scottish Cup (1): MacDonald 1.

Honours

Scottish League – Division 1 Champions: 1894–95, 1896–97, 1957–58, 1959–60, 1979–80; Runners-up: 1893–94, 1898–99, 1903–04, 1905–06, 1914–15, 1937–38, 1953–54, 1956–57, 1958–59, 1964–65, 1977–78.
Scottish Cup – Winners: 1891, 1896, 1901, 1906, 1956; Runners-up: 1903, 1907, 1968, 1976.
Scottish League Cup – Winners: 1954–55, 1958–59, 1959–60, 1962–63; Runners-up 1961–62.
Record Victory: 15-0 v King's Park, Scottish Cup 2nd rd, 13 Feb, 1937.
Record Defeat: 0-7 v Hibernian, Division 1, 1 Jan, 1973.
Most League Points: 62, Division 1, 1957–58.
Most League Goals: 132, Division 1, 1957–58. (Record for Division 1.)
Most Individual Goals in Season: Barney Battles, 44, 1930–31.
Highest Scorer in Total Aggregate: Jimmy Wardhaugh, 206, 1946–59.
Most Capped Player: Bobby Walker, 29, Scotland.

Brough J	Hamilton S	Jefferies J	Shields P	Denny J	Robinson R	Liddell F	More C D	Kidd W	Hamill A	Boyd C	Bowman D	Fraser C	Gibson W	Conn A J	Robertson C	McVie W	Westwater I	MacDonald A	O'Connor D	Mackay G	Masterton R	White A	O'Brien P	McShane P	Liddell G	Robertson M	Docherty J	Maxwell S	*Match No.*
1				3	2	5	4	6				12		7*	10			8	9							11			1
1		3			2	5				4	8			7	10			6	9							11*	12		2
1		3			2	5	13	6		4	7		12	8*	10			11	9†										3
1		3			2	5	12	6		4	7*		8		10			11	9										4
1		3			2	5		6		4	7*		8	12	10			11	9										5
1		2	3		6	5				4	7		8*	12	10†			11	9							13			6
1		2	3	4	12			6			7		8		10*	5		11	9										7
1		2	3	4*	12			6			7		8		10	5		11	9										8
1		2	3	4	13			6			7*		8†	12	10	5		11	9										9
1		2	3	4				6			7		8		9	5		11								10			10
1		2	3	4	12			6			7*		8†	13		5		11	9							10			11
		2	3	4	8	5		6			7*		10	9			1	11			12								12
		2	3	4		5		6*			7†		10	9			1	11		12	8	13							13
1	2		3		6	4							8	9		5		11	10		7								14
1	2*		3		6	5	12						8	9		4		11	10		7								15
1			3	4	6		2		12				8	9		5		11			7*		10						16
1			3	4	6		2		7				8	9*		5		11	13		12		10†						17
1			3	4	6		2		7				8*	9		5		11†	12		13		10						18
1			3	4	6		2		7				8			5			9		11		10						19
1			3	4			2		7				8	9		5		11			6		10						20
1	2*		3		12	5	4		7				8	9				11			6		10						21
1	2		3		12	5	4		7				8	9†				11	13		6*		10						22
1	2		3			5	4	7	10				9†					8		6*		12	11	13					23
1	2					5	4	11	3		6		8							7				9	10				24
1	2		3			5	4	11	6				8							7				9	10				25
1	2		3			5	4	11	6		12		8							7*			13	9†	10				26
1	2		3			5	4	11	6				8					10		7					9				27
1	2		3			5	4	11	6				8					10		7			12		9*				28
1	2		3			5	4	11	6				8					10					7		9				29
1	2		3			5	4	11	6				8					10					7		9				30
1			3	2			5	4	6		10		8					11		7					9				31
1			3	2			5	11	6		4		8*		12			10		7					9				32
1			3	2		5		11	6		4		8		10					7					9				33
1			3	2		5	4	11	6						8								10		9			7	34
1			3	2		5	4	11	6						8					7			10		9				35
1		12	3	2		5	4	11	6				13		8					7*			10†		9				36
34	12	12	30	19	13	24	21	25	20	5	16	0	30	13	14	12	2	28	13	11	8	0	13	3	13	4	0	1	
		+ 1s			+ 6s		+ 3s		+ 1s		+ 1s	+ 1s	+ 2s	+ 4s	+ 1s				+ 3s	+ 1s	+ 3s	+ 2s	+ 2s	+ 1s		+ 1s	+ 1s		

HIBERNIAN Premier Division

Year Formed: 1875. *Ground:* Easter Road Park. *Size:* 112yd×74yd. *Capacity:* 29,464 (6636 seats).
Telephone: 031-661 2159.
Manager: Bertie Auld. *Secretary:* C. F. Graham. *Assistant Manager:* Pat Quinn. *Trainer:* John Lambie.
Club Colours: Green shirts with white collars and sleeves, white shorts, green and white stockings.
Club Nickname: Hi-Bees.
Record Attendance: 65,840 v Hearts, Division 1, 2 Jan, 1950.
Previous Name: Edinburgh Hibernians. *Previous Ground:* Mayfield 1875–80.
European Competitions: *European Cup* 1955–56. *European Cup-Winners' Cup* 1972–73; *Fairs Cup* 1960–61, 1961–62, 1962–63, 1965–66, 1967–68, 1968–69; *UEFA Cup* 1973–74, 1974–75, 1975–76, 1976–77, 1978–79.
Record Transfer Fee Received: £275,000 from Aston Villa for Des Bremner, Sept 1979.
Record Transfer Fee Paid: £120,000 to Everton for Joe Harper, Feb 1974.

1980–81 LEAGUE RECORD

Match No.	Date	Venue	Opponents	Result	H/T Score	League Pos'n	Goalscorers	Attendance
1	Aug 9	H	Raith R	L 0-1	0-0	—		4500
2	16	A	Stirling Albion	W 2-0	1-0	7	Cormack, Rae	2500
3	23	H	Berwick R	W 3-0	2-0	4	MacLeod 2 (2 pens), Paterson	4000
4	Sept 6	H	Motherwell	W 1-0	0-0	4	Jamieson	4390
5	9	A	Dundee	W 2-1	1-1	—	MacLeod, Rae	5304
6	13	A	Ayr U	W 3-1	0-1	1	MacLeod, Rae, Jamieson	3960
7	17	H	East Stirling	D 2-2	1-1	—	Jamieson 2	3000
8	20	A	Hamilton A	D 1-1	0-0	1	Connolly	5197
9	27	H	Clydebank	W 4-1	1-1	1	Wilson, Connolly, Rae, MacLeod	5000
10	Oct 1	A	Dumbarton	L 0-2	0-0	—		1000
11	4	A	Dunfermline Ath	W 2-0	0-0	1	MacLeod 2	5650
12	11	H	Falkirk	W 2-0	1-0	1	Connolly, Jamieson	6947
13	18	A	St Johnstone	W 2-1	0-0	1	Jamieson, MacLeod	4318
14	25	H	Ayr U	W 1-0	0-0	1	Brazil	4500
15	Nov 1	A	Motherwell	L 0-2	0-0	1		3855
16	8	A	East Stirling	D 1-1	1-1	2	Jamieson	1963
17	15	H	Hamilton A	D 3-3	1-1	2	MacLeod 2 (1 pen), Rae	4000
18	22	A	Clydebank	D 1-1	0-0	2	Brown J. A.	1300
19	29	H	Dunfermline Ath	W 1-0	1-0	1	MacLeod	4350
20	Dec 6	A	Falkirk	W 2-0	1-0	1	MacLeod, Rae	3400
21	13	H	St Johnstone	W 4-0	0-0	1	Callachan 2 (2 pens), Rae 2	5000
22	20	A	Dundee	L 0-1	0-1	1		7454
23	27	H	Stirling Albion	W 3-0	3-0	1	MacLeod 2, Connolly	5600
24	Jan 1	A	Berwick R	W 2-0	2-0	—	MacLeod, Duncan	2110
25	3	H	Dumbarton	W 1-0	1-0	1	Murray G.	5546
26	10	A	Raith R	L 0-2	0-1	1		10,000
27	17	H	Falkirk	W 1-0	0-0	1	Paterson	4670
28	31	A	Berwick R	D 0-0	0-0	1		2019
29	Feb 7	H	Dundee	D 0-0	0-0	1		4989
30	21	H	Hamilton A	W 4-0	1-0	1	Brown (og), Connolly, Jamieson 2	4000
31	28	A	Dunfermline Ath	W 5-0	1-0	1	Rae (pen), Jamieson 2, Connolly 2	3000
32	Mar 18	H	St Johnstone	L 1-2	1-1	—	McNamara	3000
33	21	A	Dumbarton	W 4-1	1-1	1	Rae 2, Murray G. 2	1000
34	28	A	Ayr U	W 1-0	1-0	1	Jamieson	2997
35	Apr 4	H	Stirling Albion	D 0-0	0-0	1		3500
36	11	H	East Stirling	W 2-0	1-0	1	Connolly, Callachan	3500
37	15	H	Clydebank	W 3-0	3-0	—	Rae 2, Paterson	3691
38	18	H	Raith R	W 2-0	1-0	1	Murray G., Callachan	8071
39	25	A	Motherwell	D 1-1	0-1	1	Murray G.	3478

Final League Position: 1

Goalscorers

League (67): MacLeod 15 (3 pens), Rae 13 (1 pen), Jamieson 12, Connolly 8, Murray G. 5, Callachan 4 (2 pens), Paterson 3, Brown J. A. 1, Brazil 1, Cormack 1, Duncan 1, McNamara 1, Wilson 1, own goal 1.
League Cup (9): MacLeod 3, Jamieson 2, Rae 2, Hamill 1, Wilson 1.
Scottish Cup (5): Callachan 2, MacLeod 1, McNamara 1, Rae 1.

Honours

Scottish League – Division 1 Champions: 1902–03, 1947–48, 1950–51, 1951–52, 1980–81; Runners-up: 1896–97, 1946–47, 1949–50, 1952–53, 1973–74, 1974–75; Division 2 Champions: 1893–94, 1894–95, 1932–33.
Scottish Cup – Winners: 1887, 1902; Runners-up: 1896, 1914, 1923, 1924, 1947, 1958, 1972, 1979.
Scottish League Cup – Winners: 1972–73; Runners-up: 1950–51, 1968–69, 1974–75.
Drybrough Cup – Winners: 1972–73, 1973–74.
Record Victory: 15-1 v Peebles Rovers, Scottish Cup 2nd rd, 11 Feb, 1961.
Record Defeat: 1-9 v Dumbarton, Scottish Cup 2nd rd, 27 Sept, 1890.
Most League Points: 57, Division 1, 1980–81.
Most Individual League Goals in Season: Joe Baker, 42, Division 1, 1959–60.
Most Capped Player: Lawrie Reilly, 38, Scotland.

McArthur J	Kelly C	Brown J	Rodier D	McGlinchey P	Byrne G	Sneddon A	Duncan A	Black I	Stewart G	McNamara J	Wilson T	McLaren W	Paterson C	Brazil A	Cormack P	Callachan R	Rae G	Brown J A	Murray G	Torrance R	MacLeod A	Hamill H	Rice B	Jamieson W	Connolly J	Best G	Hendry I	Brown S	Murray W	*Match No.*
1		2					3		4	10			5	6	12	8				9	11*								7	1
1		2					11	3		4			5	10	6	8	9			7*	12									2
1		2	13				11	3		4			5		6	7	10†				9	8*							12	3
1		2	8				3			4			5			6	9					7*	12	11	10					4
1		2					3		5	4						6	8				9	7			10	11				5
1		2					3			4			5		12	6	8				9	7*		10	11					6
1		2					3			4			5	12	7*	6	8				9			10	11					7
1		2					3			4			5			6	8				9			7	10	11				8
1		2	12				3			4	11*		5			6	8				9			7	10					9
1		2	13				3			4	11†		5	12		6	8				9			7*	10					10
1		2					3			4	12		5			6	8				9			7*	10	11				11
1		2					3			4	7*		5			6	8				9			12	10	11				12
1		2					3			4*	12		5	10	13	6†	8				9			7	11					13
	1	2					3			4			5	10		6	8				9			7	11					14
	1	2	12				3			4			5	10*		6	8				9			7	11					15
1		2					3			4	12		5			6	8	11*			9			7	10					16
1		2*	12				3			4			5			6	10	8			7			9	11					17
1		2					3			4	11*		5			8	6	12			9			7	10					18
1		12		2*			3			4			5			7	8	6			9				10			11		19
1		2		11			3					4	5			7	8*	6			10			12	9					20
1		2*		4	12		3					6	5			7	8	11			10				9					21
1		2		4			3					6	5			7	8	11			10			12	9*					22
1				2			3			4		6	5			7		11	10		8*			12	9					23
1		12		2*			3			6		4	5			7		11	10†		8			13	9					24
1				2			3			4		6	5			7		11	10		8				9					25
1				13		2	3			4		6	5			7		11†	10		8			12	9*					26
1				11*		2	3			4		6	5			7	8		10		9			12						27
1						2	3			4		6	5			7	8		9		10	12					11*			28
1						2	3			4			5			7	8	6	10*		9	11†		12	13					29
1		4				2	3			6			5			7	8	10						9	11					30
1						2	3			4		6	5				8	11	9*			7		10	12					31
1						2	3			6		4*	5			7	8	10	9					12	11					32
1		2				3	11			6		4	5			7	9		10					8						33
1		2				3	11			6		4	5			7	9		10					8						34
1		3	13			2	11			6		4	5			7	8		10†					9*	12					35
1		2				3	10			6		4	5			7	8				12			9*	11					36
1		3				2	10			6		4	5			7	9		8						11					37
1		3				2	10			6		4	5			7	8		9						11					38
1		3				2	10			6		4	5			7	9		8		12				11*					39
37	2	29	1	8	0	14	39	2	2	36	4	18	38	5	3	38	34	14	15	2	27	6	0	19	29	4	1	1	1	
		+ 2s	+ 6s	+ 1s	+ 1s						+ 3s			+ 2s	+ 3s			+ 1s			+ 3s	+ 1s	+ 1s	+ 9s	+ 3s				+ 1s	

KILMARNOCK Division 1

Year Founded: 1869.
Ground: Rugby Park. *Size:* 115yd×75yd. *Capacity:* 18,500 (4200 seats).
Telephone: Kilmarnock 25184.
Manager: Jim Clunie. *Secretary/General Manager:* Walter W. McCrae.
Trainer/Physiotherapist: Hugh Allan.
Club Colours: Blue and white hoops, blue shorts.
Club Nickname: The Killies.
Record Attendance: 34,246 v Rangers, League Cup, Aug 1963.
European Competitions: *European Cup* 1965–66; *Fairs Cup* 1964–65, 1966–67, 1969–70.
Record Transfer Fee Received: £120,000 from Celtic for David Provan, Sept 1978.

1980–81 LEAGUE RECORD

Match No.	Date	Venue	Opponents	Result	H/T Score	League Pos'n	Goalscorers	Attendance
1	Aug 9	A	Dundee U	D 2-2	0-1	—	Street, Mauchlen	4000
2	16	H	Celtic	L 0-3	0-3	8		13,800
3	23	A	Partick T	W 1-0	0-0	6	McBride	4000
4	Sept 6	H	Hearts	L 0-1	0-0	8		4000
5	13	A	Morton	L 0-2	0-1	9		5000
6	20	H	Rangers	L 1-8	0-3	10	Bourke	20,000
7	27	A	Airdrieonians	L 0-1	0-0	10		2000
8	Oct 4	H	St Mirren	L 1-6	0-4	10	Cramond	4000
9	11	A	Aberdeen	L 0-2	0-0	10		12,000
10	18	H	Dundee U	L 0-1	0-0	10		2700
11	25	A	Celtic	L 1-4	1-2	10	Cramond	18,000
12	Nov 1	H	Partick T	L 0-1	0-0	10		2500
13	8	H	Airdrieonians	D 1-1	1-0	10	Houston	2300
14	15	A	Rangers	L 0-2	0-1	10		16,000
15	22	H	Aberdeen	D 1-1	1-0	10	Street	3500
16	29	A	St Mirren	L 0-2	0-1	10		5200
17	Dec 6	A	Hearts	L 0-2	0-0	10		5183
18	13	H	Morton	D 3-3	2-1	10	Armstrong, Bourke, Hughes	2490
19	20	H	Rangers	D 1-1	1-0	10	Bourke	9500
20	Jan 1	H	Celtic	L 1-2	1-2	—	Hughes	8000
21	3	A	Dundee U	L 0-7	0-2	10		6474
22	10	H	St Mirren	W 2-0	1-0	10	Mauchlen, Doherty	4900
23	31	A	Morton	L 0-1	0-1	10		4000
24	Feb 21	A	Partick T	D 1-1	1-0	10	Bourke	1600
25	28	H	Dundee U	L 0-1	0-0	10		2100
26	Mar 7	A	St Mirren	D 1-1	0-1	10	Bourke	4203
27	11	A	Airdrieonians	L 0-3	0-3	—		3500
28	14	H	Aberdeen	W 1-0	0-0	10	Doherty	2500
29	21	A	Rangers	L 0-2	0-1	10		8500
30	24	H	Hearts	W 2-0	1-0	—	Mauchlen, McLean	1445
31	28	H	Airdrieonians	L 0-1	0-1	9		1849
32	Apr 4	A	Hearts	L 0-1	0-1	10		1866
33	15	H	Morton	D 0-0	0-0	—		973
34	18	H	Partick T	L 0-1	0-1	10		1250
35	25	A	Celtic	D 1-1	0-1	10	Eadie	23,300
36	May 2	A	Aberdeen	W 2-0	0-0	9	McDicken, McCready	6300

Final League Position: 9

Goalscorers

League (23): Bourke 5, Mauchlen 3, Cramond 2, Doherty 2, Hughes 2, Street 2, Armstrong 1, Eadie 1, Houston 1, McBride 1, McCready 1, McDicken 1, McLean 1.
League Cup (4): Cramond 2, Clark P. 1, McBride 1.
Scottish Cup (3): Bourke 1, Hughes 1, McDicken 1.

Honours

Scottish League – Division 1 Champions 1964–65; Runners-up: 1959–60, 1960–61, 1962–63, 1963–64, 1975–76, 1978–79; Division 2 Champions: 1897–98, 1898–99; Runners-up: 1953–54, 1973–74.
Scottish Cup – Winners: 1920, 1929; Runners-up: 1898, 1932, 1938, 1957, 1960.
Record Victory: 13-2 v Saltcoats Victoria, Scottish Cup 2nd rd, 12 Sept, 1896.
Record Defeat: 0-8 v Hibernian, Division 1, 22 Aug, 1925, and v Rangers, Division 1, 27 Feb, 1937.
Most League Points: 54, Division 1, 1978–79.
Most Individual League Goals in Season: Peerie Cunningham, 35, Division 1, 1927–28.
Most Capped Player: Joe Nibloe, 11, Scotland.

McCulloch A	Brown J	Wilson A	McLean S	Robertson A	Cockburn J	Robin K	Maxwell S	Mauchlen A	Clark J	McDicken D	Clarke P	Black S	Bourke J	Cramond G	McBride J	McClurg J	Bryce T	Armstrong K	Houston R	Street R	Hughes J	Gibson I	Doherty J	Eadie K W	Cairney J	Wilson G	McCready G	Morrison A	*Match No.*
1			2	3				4		6	5			10					7	11*		8	12		9				1
1			2	3				4		6	5		9	10						7		8	12		11*				2
1			2	3			8	4		6	5				9					11		7						10	3
1			2	3	12		8	4		6	5*			10	9					7†	13	11							4
1*			2	3			12	8	4	6				10	9†			5		11		7					13		5
	1		2	3			13	8	4	6			9	10†				5	7*	11		12							6
	1		2	3			8	4	12	6	5		9	10				13		11†		7*							7
	1		2	3			8	4*	12	6	5		9	10					7	11†		13							8
	1			2	3			8	4	6	5			10†					7	11		9*	12			13			9
	1		13	2	3		8†		4	6	5		9	10						7*		11	12						10
	1		12	2	3			8	4	6	5			10	9				7				11*						11
	1		10*	2	3			8	4	6	5			11	9				7		12								12
	1		2	3	12		8	4		6	5		10	11*	9				7										13
	1		2	3			8	4	12	6	5		10	11*	9				7										14
		1	2	3			8	4		6	5			10	9				7	11									15
		1	2	3				4	8	6	5		12	10	9				7	11*									16
		1	2		3		10	8	4*	6	5	12	9		7				13						11†				17
		1	2		3			4	8	6			9		12			5	7		11*					10			18
		1	2		3		12				5		9†		13	4		6	7		11	8*				10			19
		1	2		3						6		9			4		5	7		11	8				10			20
		1	2		3		12	8			5		9†		13	4*		6	7		11					10			21
		1	2		3			10	4	6	8		9					5			11		7						22
1			2		3			10	4	6	8		9					5			11	12	7*						23
1			8	2*	3		12		4	6			9		13		10	5			7†				11				24
1			2		3			10	4	8	6		9		12		13	5		7*					11†				25
1			2*		3		12	10	4	8†	6		9		7		13	5			11								26
1					3	2		10	4	8	6		9		7			5			11								27
1			8		3	2		10	4	6			9		7			5					11						28
1			8		3	2		10	4*	6			9		7		12	5			13		11†						29
1			8		3	2		10	4	6			9		7			5					11						30
1			8		3	2		10	4	6			9		7*			5			12		11						31
1			8		3	2*		10	4	6				12	9†		11	5					7	13					32
1			2		3			8	4	6			9	11				5						10			7		33
1			2		3*	12		8	4	6			9	13			11†	5						10			7		34
1			8	3	10	2			4	6			9					5						11			7		35
1			8	12	3	2*		10	4	6			9					5						11			7		36
19	9	8	32	18	24	8	9	31	24	33	23	0	26	16	17	3	3	21	14	13	9	10	8	4	5	4	4	1	
			+ 2s	+ 1s	+ 2s	+ 1s	+ 6s		+ 3s			+ 1s	+ 1s	+ 2s	+ 5s		+ 3s	+ 1s	+ 1s		+ 4s	+ 3s	+ 4s	+ 1s		+ 1s	+ 1s		

MEADOWBANK THISTLE Division 2

Year Formed: 1974. (Previously called Ferranti Thistle, founded 1943.) *Ground:* Meadowbank Stadium.
Size: 105yd×72yd. *Capacity:* 16,000 (at present only main stand, 7500 seats, is used for football).
Telephone: (Secretary's office) 031-337 2442, ext 3666.
Manager: Terry Christie. *Secretary:* William L. Mill.
Club Colours: Amber with black trim shirts, black shorts, amber stockings.
Record Attendance: 4000 v Albion Rovers, Scottish League Cup, 9 Aug, 1974.

1980–81 LEAGUE RECORD

Match No.	*Date*	*Venue*	*Opponents*	*Result*	*H/T Score*	*League Pos'n*	*Goalscorers*	*Attendance*
1	Aug 9	H	Alloa	L 0-3	0-2	—		300
2	16	A	Stranraer	W 3-1	1-1	8	Jobson 2 (1 pen), Murdoch	500
3	20	H	Arbroath	L 1-4	0-2	—	McCallan	300
4	24	A	Albion R	L 1-3	1-0	—	McCallan	350
5	Sept 3	A	East Fife	L 1-2	1-1	—	Downie	511
6	9	H	Brechin C	W 2-0	0-0	—	McQuade 2	300
7	13	A	Forfar Ath	L 2-3	0-2	13	Jobson (pen), Sprott	1000
8	17	A	Queen of the S	D 1-1	0-1	—	Jobson	1225
9	20	H	Clyde	L 0-2	0-2	14		300
10	27	A	Cowdenbeath	L 0-1	0-0	14		400
11	Oct 4	H	Montrose	L 0-2	0-1	14		150
12	11	A	Queen's Park	D 1-1	1-0	14	Sprott	950
13	18	H	Stenhousemuir	L 0-3	0-2	14		150
14	25	H	Forfar Ath	W 4-2	2-2	14	Sprott 2, McCallan 2	150
15	Nov 1	A	Arbroath	W 1-0	0-0	13	Jobson	599
16	8	H	Queen of the S	L 0-2	0-1	13		250
17	15	A	Clyde	L 1-2	1-2	13	McCallan	500
18	22	H	Cowdenbeath	L 1-4	1-1	13	McCallan	300
19	Dec 6	H	Queen's Park	D 1-1	0-1	14	McCallan	250
20	27	H	Stranraer	L 0-1	0-0	14		250
21	Jan 1	A	Albion R	L 1-2	0-0	—	McCallan	700
22	3	A	Queen's Park	D 1-1	1-0	14	Jobson	750
23	10	A	Alloa	L 1-2	1-1	14	Georgeson	755
24	24	H	Alloa	L 0-4	0-3	14		300
25	31	H	Stenhousemuir	W 1-0	1-0	14	Jobson	470
26	Feb 11	H	East Fife	L 1-3	1-1	—	Jobson	270
27	14	H	Queen of the S	D 0-0	0-0	14		400
28	22	A	Clyde	W 4-1	2-1	—	Jobson 3, Sprott	750
29	28	H	Montrose	W 2-1	0-0	13	Sprott, Jobson	250
30	Mar 14	A	Stranraer	W 2-1	0-1	13	Boyd, McCallan	300
31	18	A	Montrose	W 2-1	2-0	—	Davidson, McCallan	250
32	21	H	Arbroath	L 1-2	1-1	13	Scrimgeour (og)	250
33	28	A	Forfar Ath	L 1-3	0-2	13	Sprott	800
34	31	A	Stenhousemuir	D 1-1	0-0	—	Boyd	300
35	Apr 4	H	Albion R	W 2-1	0-0	13	McCallan, Sprott	150
36	11	A	Brechin C	D 0-0	0-0	13		400
37	18	H	East Fife	W 1-0	0-0	13	Conroy	150
38	29	A	Cowdenbeath	L 0-1	0-1	—		300
39	May 2	A	Brechin C	L 1-2	0-1	13	Georgeson	400

Final League Position: 13

Goalscorers

League (42): Jobson 12 (2 pens), McCallan 11, Sprott 8, Boyd 2, Georgeson 2, McQuade 2, Conroy 1, Davidson 1, Downie 1, Murdoch 1, own goal 1.
League Cup (2): Downie 1, Jobson 1.
Scottish Cup (4): McCallan 2, Davidson 1, Georgeson 1.

Honours
East of Scotland Qualifying Cup – Winners 1963–64.
Scottish Qualifying Cup (South) – Winners 1973–74.
Record Victory: 4-1 v Forfar Athletic, League Cup, 23 Aug, 1975; v Albion Rovers, Division 2, 17 Jan, 1976; v Clyde, 22 Feb, 1981.
Record Defeat: 0-8 v Hamilton A, Division 2, 14 Dec, 1974.
Most League Points: 32, Division 2, 1976–77, 1979–80.
Most Individual League Goals in a Season: John Jobson, 17, Division 2, 1979–80.

McKell R	Conroy D	Dunn L	Henderson I	Leetion M	Downie T	Fraser G	Boyd W	Brown D	Wight D	Smith D	McQuade J	Davidson K	Sprott A	Godfrey P	Georgeson R	Hendrie T	McCallan J	Watson J M	Jobson J	Grant A	*Match No.*
1	12	2		7	6	3*	4	5			13	11			9†		8		10		1
1	11	2		7	6*	3	4	5							8	12	9		10		2
1	8	2		7	6	3	4	5							9		10		11		3
1	8	2		10	6	3	4	5					7				9		11		4
1	3	2		6	8		4	5			11		7			10			9		5
1	3	2		6	10		4	5			11	8	7						9		6
1	3			8	2		4	5			11*	6	7		10	12			9		7
1	3			8	2		4	5			11	6	7		10				9		8
1	3	2		7	10*		4	5			12	6	11			8			9		9
1	3	11*		8	2	12	4	5				6	9		7				10		10
1	3	7		6			4	2	5			10			11	8			9		11
1	3	2		6			4	8	5		11*	10	7			12			9		12
1	10†	2		6		3	4		5		11	8	7*		12			9		13	13
1	3	11		2			10	6	5	4		8	7				9				14
1		11†		2		3	8	10	5	4	12	6	7				9*		13		15
1		11		2		3	8	10	5	4		6	7				9				16
1	3			2			6	11	5	4	7*				12	13	10	8†	9		17
1	3	12		2			10	4*	5	6		13			11	7	9		8†		18
1	3	2		7	8*		6	5		4	12	13	11†		10		9				19
1	13	2		7*	6	3	8		5	4		11†			12		9		10		20
1	3	2		7			6		5*	4		12	13		11†	8	9		10		21
1	3	2		7			6		5	4			12		11*	8	9		10		22
1	3	2*		7			6		5	4			12		11	8	9		10		23
1	3	2		6†		13	10		5*	4			7		12	8	9		11		24
1	3	2		10			4	6	5			11	7			8			9		25
1	3	2		10			4	6	5			11	7			8			9		26
1	10	2	3	6			4	5				11			7	8			9		27
1	10	2	3	6			4	5				11	7			8			9		28
1	6		12	2		3*	4	5				11†	7		10	8	13		9		29
1	6		2	7*		3	4	5				13	11		10†	8	12		9		30
1	6		2	12		3	4	5				7	11*			8	10		9		31
1	6		2	12		3	4	5				7*	11			8	10		9		32
1	6		2	7		3	4	5				11†	12		13	8*	10		9		33
1	10		2	7		3	6	5					11	4			8		9		34
1	10		2	7		3	6	5					11	4			8		9		35
1	10	2	3	7		4	6	5				12	11		8*		13		9†		36
1	6	2	3	7		4	8	5					11		10				9		37
1	6	2	3	7			4	5					11		10	8			9		38
1	10	2	3	7*		4	6	5					11		8		12		9		39
39	35	28	12	37	12	18	39	33	15	11	7	21	27	2	19	18	20	2	34	0	
	+	+	+	+		+					+	+	+		+	+	+		+	+	
	2s	1s	1s	2s		2s					4s	5s	4s		5s	4s	4s		1s	1s	

MONTROSE Division 2

Year Formed: 1879. *Ground:* Links Park. *Size:* 114yd×66yd. *Capacity:* 9000. *Telephone:* Montrose 3200.
Manager: Bobby Livingstone.
Secretary: William Coull.
Club Colours: Royal blue and white shirts, blue shorts, white stockings with royal blue tops.
Club Nickname: Gable Endies.
Record Attendance: 8983 v Dundee, Scottish Cup 3rd rd, 17 Mar, 1973.
Record Transfer Fee Received: £50,000 from Hibernian for Gary Murray, Dec 1980.

1980–81 LEAGUE RECORD

Match No.	Date	Venue	Opponents	Result	H/T Score	League Pos'n	Goalscorers	Attendance
1	Aug 9	H	Stranraer	D 0-0	0-0	—		400
2	16	H	Queen's Park	L 1-3	0-0	—	Murray	450
3	23	A	Brechin C	D 1-1	0-0	—	Taylor	500
4	Sept 3	A	Arbroath	W 4-1	1-0	12	Murray 2, Taylor, Forrest	742
5	6	H	Albion R	L 0-1	0-0	—		350
6	9	H	East Fife	W 1-0	0-0	—	Robb	400
7	13	A	Clyde	L 3-4	2-2	11	McDonald, Markland, Taylor	550
8	17	A	Cowdenbeath	L 1-2	1-0	—	Murray	300
9	20	H	Alloa	W 2-1	0-0	8	Murray, Robb	500
10	27	H	Stenhousemuir	L 1-3	0-2	9	Robb	400
11	Oct 4	A	Meadowbank T	W 2-0	1-0	—	Bain, Beedie	150
12	11	H	Queen of the S	D 1-1	0-0	—	Taylor	350
13	18	A	Forfar Ath	W 4-0	1-0	7	Beedie 2, Robb 2	1000
14	25	H	Clyde	W 1-0	0-0	6	Murray	500
15	Nov 1	A	Albion R	L 1-2	0-0	6	Robb	400
16	8	H	Cowdenbeath	W 3-2	0-1	—	Wright, Taylor, Murray (pen)	300
17	15	A	Alloa	W 4-0	1-0	4	Murray 2, Robb, Wright	950
18	22	A	Stenhousemuir	W 2-1	1-0	4	Robb 2	350
19	Dec 6	A	Queen of the S	W 5-1	2-0	3	Clark (og), Wright, Murray 3	900
20	Jan 1	A	Brechin C	L 1-3	1-1	—	Johnston H.	1200
21	10	H	Arbroath	L 1-2	0-0	7	Hair	950
22	24	A	Stranraer	W 3-0	1-0	5	Pirie, Beedie 2	350
23	31	H	Forfar Ath	W 4-0	1-0	4	Beedie, Robb, Guyan, Forrest	1000
24	Feb 7	A	Queen of the S	L 1-4	0-1	4	Wright	1000
25	21	A	Alloa	L 0-1	0-0	5		510
26	28	A	Meadowbank T	L 1-2	0-0	7	Johnston H.	250
27	Mar 11	H	Stenhousemuir	W 2-1	1-0	—	Beedie, Robb	350
28	14	A	Queen's Park	D 1-1	0-0	6	Wright	972
29	18	H	Meadowbank T	L 1-2	0-2	—	Beedie	250
30	24	H	Forfar Ath	D 0-0	0-0	—		350
31	28	A	Clyde	L 0-6	0-2	10		400
32	Apr 1	A	Queen's Park	L 0-1	0-0	—		976
33	4	H	Arbroath	L 0-3	0-2	12		450
34	8	H	Stranraer	W 6-1	3-1	—	Allan 3, Sheran, Forrest, Robb	300
35	11	A	East Fife	D 1-1	0-1	9	Allan	303
36	18	H	Brechin C	W 3-2	0-1	8	Hair, Taylor, Wright	950
37	22	H	Cowdenbeath	W 3-1	1-0	—	Beedie, Forrest, Taylor	300
38	25	H	Albion R	D 1-1	0-1	7	Forbes	300
39	May 2	A	East Fife	D 0-0	0-0	7		339

Final League Position: 7

Goalscorers

League (66): Murray 12 (1 pen), Robb 12, Beedie 9, Taylor 7, Wright 6, Allan 4, Forrest 4, Hair 2, Johnston H. 2, Bain 1, Forbes 1, Guyan 1, McDonald 1, Markland 1, Pirie 1, Sheran 1, own goal 1.
League Cup (2): Milne 1, Robb 1.
Scottish Cup (4): Murray 2, Johnston H. 1, Wright 1.

Honours

Record Victory: 12-0 v Vale of Leithen, Scottish Cup 2nd rd, 4 Jan, 1975.
Record Defeat: 0-13 v Aberdeen, 17 Mar, 1951.
Most League Points: 53, Division 2, 1974–75.
Most Capped Player: Alexander Keillor, 2 (6), Scotland.

Moffat J	Charles R M	Forbes N	Taylor K	Hair I	Milne M	Johnston D	Markland S	Sheran W J	Forrest A	Clark G	Robb D	Beedie S	Johnston H	Murray G	Wright A	Donald J	Livingstone R	McDonald I J	Guyan C	Turnbull M C	Pirie R	Allan C	Bain M	Finney	Nicol D	Joss K	*Match No.*
1		2	6			3	4	5	10		12	8	7*	9	11												1
1		2*	12			3	4	5	7		13	6	8	10	11								9†				2
1		4	2		8	3		5	6		10†	7*	13	9	11	12											3
1			2		3		10	5	6		11	8		9			7									4	4
1		2	10		3		4	5	6		7	8	11*	9	12												5
1		10	2*		3		4	5	6		7	11	12	9				8									6
1		2	8		3		4	5	6		7	11		9				10									7
1		2	10		3		4	5	6		7	11		9				8									8
1		2	10		3		4	5	6		7			11				8					9				9
1		2	10		3		4	5*	6		11		12	9	13			8					7†				10
1		2			3		4		6	5	7	10		11				8					9				11
1		2	12					5	3	4	7	8	6	11†	13			10					9*				12
1		3	8	2				5		4	7	10	6	9	11												13
1		3	8*	2				5	12	4	7	10	6	9	11												14
1		3	8	2				5	12	4	7	10	6	9	11*												15
1		3	10	2*				5	12	4	11	8	6	9	7												16
1		2	8	3				5		4	7	10	6	11	9												17
1		2	8	3				5	12	4	7	10	6	11	9*												18
1		2	8	3				5	12	4	9	10	6	11	7*												19
1		3	8	2	12			5	9*	4	7		6		11†			10							13		20
1		2		10	3			5	12	4	9	7*	6		11				13		8†						21
1		3		2				5	11	4	10	8	6					7*	12		9						22
1		3		2				5	7	4	11	8	6						10		9						23
1		3		2				5	10†	4	9*	8	6		7			13	11		12						24
	1	2	8	10	3			5	12	4	9*	13	6		11†				7								25
	1	2	10		3			5	12	4	9†	8	6		11				7*		13						26
1		2	12	8	3			5		4	7	10	6		11							9*					27
1		3	8*	2	12			5	11†	4	9	10	6		7						13						28
1		2	13		3			5	7	4	9†	10	6		11			12			8*						29
	1	2	12		3			5	13	4*	9	8	10		7				11†	6							30
	1	2	4		3			5	10	8	7*	11	6		9				12								31
	1	4	2					5	3		9	8	6		11			7		10							32
	1	4	2					5	3		7	8	6		11			10			9						33
	1	2	12		3*			5	6	4	7	8	13		11					10†		9					34
	1	2		8	3			5	6	4	11	10			7							9					35
	1	2	12	8	3*			5	7	4		10	6		11			9									36
		2	12	8	3			5	7	4		10	6*		11			9						1			37
	1	2	12	8†	3			5	7*	4		10	6		11			9			13						38
	1	2	11		3			5	6	4	7	10						9			8						39
27	11	38	24	19	22	3	10	38	27	27	34	35	28	19	27	0	1	15	5	3	6	3	5	1	0	1	
			+ 9s		+ 2s				+ 9s		+ 2s	+ 1s	+ 4s		+ 3s	+ 1s		+ 2s	+ 3s		+ 4s				+ 1s		

MORTON — Premier Division

Year Formed: 1874. *Limited Company:* 1896.
Ground: Cappielow Park, Greenock PA15 2TY. *Size:* 110yd×71yd. *Capacity:* 18,000 (5000 seats).
Telephone: Greenock 23571.
Manager: Benny Rooney.
Secretary: Tom Robertson.
Club Colours: Blue and white hooped shirts, white shorts and stockings.
Club Nickname: Ton.
Record Attendance: 23,500 v Celtic, Division 1, 1922.
European Competitions: *Fairs Cup*, 1968–69.
Record Transfer Fee Received: £150,000 from Newcastle U for Mark McGhee, Dec 1977.

1980–81 LEAGUE RECORD

Match No.	*Date*	*Venue*	*Opponents*	*Result*	*H/T Score*	*League Pos'n*	*Goalscorers*	*Atten-dance*
1	Aug 9	A	Celtic	L 1-2	0-0	—	Ritchie	20,000
2	16	H	St Mirren	L 1-4	1-1	10	Hutchison	8000
3	23	A	Dundee U	D 1-1	1-1	10	Anderson	5339
4	Sept 6	A	Aberdeen	L 0-6	0-1	10		10,000
5	13	H	Kilmarnock	W 2-0	1-0	10	Cochrane, McNeil	5000
6	20	A	Hearts	W 1-0	1-0	6	McNeil	5996
7	27	H	Partick T	L 1-2	0-0	9	Ritchie	5000
8	Oct 4	H	Rangers	D 2-2	2-1	7	Busby, Ritchie (pen)	15,000
9	11	A	Airdrieonians	L 0-1	0-0	8		4000
10	18	H	Celtic	L 2-3	0-2	8	Ritchie, Cochrane	16,000
11	25	A	St Mirren	D 1-1	0-0	8	Rooney (pen)	7000
12	Nov 1	H	Dundee U	L 0-2	0-0	8		4000
13	8	A	Partick T	D 0-0	0-0	8		3000
14	15	H	Hearts	D 2-2	0-1	8	McLaughlin, Rooney	3500
15	22	H	Airdrieonians	W 3-1	1-0	8	Tolmie, Ritchie 2 (1 pen)	3500
16	29	A	Rangers	W 1-0	0-0	8	Tolmie	16,000
17	Dec 6	H	Aberdeen	W 1-0	0-0	8	Rooney	7000
18	13	A	Kilmarnock	D 3-3	1-2	7	Thomson 2, Busby	2490
19	20	A	Hearts	D 0-0	0-0	7		5900
20	27	H	Partick T	W 2-0	0-0	6	Tolmie, Hutchison	6000
21	Jan 1	H	St Mirren	L 1-3	0-3	—	Ritchie (pen)	8000
22	3	A	Celtic	L 0-3	0-3	7		14,900
23	10	H	Rangers	L 0-2	0-1	7		13,000
24	31	H	Kilmarnock	W 1-0	1-0	7	Rooney	4000
25	Feb 7	A	Aberdeen	W 1-0	0-0	7	Busby	11,000
26	21	A	Dundee U	L 0-1	0-1	7		4886
27	28	H	Celtic	L 0-3	0-2	7		14,000
28	Mar 14	H	Airdrieonians	L 0-1	0-0	8		3500
29	21	H	Hearts	W 3-0	1-0	7	McNeil 2, Busby	3500
30	28	A	Partick T	L 1-3	1-1	8	Rooney	2000
31	Apr 1	A	Rangers	L 0-4	0-2	—		2500
32	4	H	Aberdeen	L 1-3	0-1	8	Tolmie	5500
33	15	A	Kilmarnock	D 0-0	0-0	—		973
34	18	H	Dundee U	W 2-0	2-0	7	Busby, Tolmie	3000
35	25	A	St Mirren	L 0-2	0-1	7		4345
36	May 2	A	Airdrieonians	L 2-3	1-1	8	Hutchison, Ritchie (pen)	1600

Final League Position: 8

Goalscorers

League (36): Ritchie 8 (4 pens), Busby 5, Rooney 5 (1 pen), Tolmie 5, McNeil 4, Hutchison 3, Cochrane 2, Thomson 2, Anderson 1, McLaughlin 1.
League Cup (2): Hutchison 1, Ritchie 1.
Scottish Cup (11): Thomson 4, Ritchie 2 (1 pen), Rooney 2, Tolmie 2, McNeil 1.

Honours
Scottish League – Division 1 Champions: 1977–78; Runners-up: 1916–17; Division 2 Champions: 1949–50, 1963–64, 1966–67; Runners-up: 1899–1900, 1928–29, 1936–37.
Scottish Cup – Winners: 1922; Runners-up: 1948.
Scottish League Cup – Runners-up: 1964.
Southern League Cup – Runners-up: 1941-42.
Renfrewshire Cup: 37 times winners.
War Shield winners: 1914.
Record Victory: 11-0 v Carfin Shamrock, Scottish Cup 1st rd, 13 Nov, 1886.
Record Defeat: 1-10 v Port Glasgow Ath, Division 2, 5 May, 1894.
Most League Points: 69, Division 2, 1966–67.
Most League Goals: 135, Division 2, 1963–64.
Most Individual League Goals in Season: 41, Allan McGraw, Division 2, 1963–64.
Most Capped Player: Jimmy Cowan, 25, Scotland.

Baines R	Hayes A D M	Holmes J B	Wilkie J	Rooney J	McLaughlin J	Orr N I	McLaren W R	McNeil J	Cochrane I	Thomson R	Busby A D	Tolmie J	Hutchison R	Ritchie A	Anderson G	Houston R J	Craig J V	Marr J	Bryce T	McNab E	Scott A	Mauchlen J S	Docherty D	*Match No.*
1		3		9	5	2	6	12				10	8*	11	4						7			1
1		2		8	5	3	6*			9†		10	7	11	4		12				13			2
1		3	2	8		5	6	7		9			10	11	4									3
1		3	2	8		5	6	7	10	9		13	12	11†	4*									4
1	2	3		4	5	6		7	8	9		12	10	11*										5
1	2	3		4	5	6	11	7*	8	9		12	10†									13		6
1	2*	3		4	5	6	12	7	8	9		13	10†	11										7
1	2	3		4	5	6		7	8	9	10	12		11*										8
1	2	3		4	5	6		7*	8	9	10			11						12				9
1	2	3		4	5	6		7*	8	9	10	12		11										10
1	2	3		10	5	6	4	12	8		9	7		11*										11
1	2	3		4	5	6		12	8	9*	10†	7	13	11										12
1	2	3		4	5	6	11		8	9		7	10											13
1	2	3		4	5	6		12	8	9		7	10*	11										14
1	2	3		4	5	6		7	8	9		10		11										15
1	2	3		4	5	6		7	8	9	11	10												16
1	2	3		4	5	6		7*	8	9	11	10		12										17
1	2	3		4	5	6			8	9	7	10	12	11*										18
1	2	3		4	5	6		7		9	8	10		11*					12					19
1	2	3		4	5	6		7		9	8*	10	12	11										20
1	2	3		4	5	6		7		9	8	10		11										21
1	2	3		4	5	6		7*		9	8	10	11†	13					12					22
1	2	3		4	5	6		7*	13		9	10		12		11†		8						23
1	2	3		4	5	6			12	9	7	10†		11		13		8*						24
1	2	3		4	5	6				9	7	10		11				8						25
1		3	2	4	5	6		12		9*	7	10		11				8						26
1	2	3		4	5	6		12			7	10		11		9*		8						27
1	2	3		4	5	6		7		9	8	10		11										28
1	2	3		4*	5	6		7	13	9	8	10		11†		12								29
1	2	3		4	5				7*	9	8	10	13	11†		12		6						30
1	2	3		4	5	6*		7		9	8	10		11		13		12†						31
1	2	3	6	4	5			7		9	8	10		11*						12				32
1	2		3	4	5	6			9		8	10		11		7								33
1	2	3		4	5	6			7	9*	8	10		11†		13				12				34
1	2	3	7	4	5				8		9	10	6							11				35
1	2			4	5	6			8		7	10*	9	11						12			3	36
36	31	34	6	36	34	33	7	20	20	29	26	28	11	29	4	3	0	6	0	1	1	0	1	
							+ 1s	+ 6s	+ 3s			+ 6s	+ 5s	+ 3s		+ 5s	+ 1s	+ 1s	+ 2s	+ 4s	+ 1s	+ 1s		

MOTHERWELL — Division 1

Year Formed: 1886.
Ground: Fir Park. *Size:* 110yd×72yd. *Capacity:* 22,600 (3200 seats).
Telephone: Motherwell 61437.
Manager: Ally MacLeod.
Secretary: Jack McGraw. *Asst Manager:* David Hay.
Club Colours: Amber with claret.
Club Nickname: Well.
Record Attendance: 35,632 v Rangers, Scottish Cup 4th rd replay, 12 Mar, 1952.
Previous Names: Club formed following the amalgamation of Alpha and Glencairn, known as Wee Alpha for a year before becoming Motherwell in 1886.
Previous Grounds: Roman Park, Dalziel Park.

1980–81 LEAGUE RECORD

Match No.	Date	Venue	Opponents	Result	H/T Score	League Pos'n	Goalscorers	Attendance
1	Aug 9	A	Ayr U	L 0-5	0-2	—		3782
2	16	H	Falkirk	W 3-0	1-0	9	McLelland S., McKeever, Kidd	2531
3	23	A	Hamilton A	L 2-4	1-1	11	McLelland S., Kidd (pen)	3936
4	Sept 6	A	Hibernian	L 0-1	0-0	12		4390
5	9	A	Clydebank	D 2-2	2-2	—	Clinging, Carson	1500
6	13	H	Raith R	D 1-1	1-1	12	Kidd	2230
7	17	H	Dundee	W 3-2	1-2	—	Kidd, Irvine, McKeever	2300
8	20	A	Berwick R	L 2-3	1-1	11	Clinging, Kidd	1191
9	27	A	Dumbarton	W 2-1	0-1	10	Kidd (pen), McKeever	1000
10	Oct 1	H	Dunfermline Ath	W 2-0	2-0	—	McLaughlin, McKeever	1848
11	4	H	St Johnstone	D 2-2	2-2	8	Kidd, Caldwell (og)	2470
12	11	A	East Stirling	D 1-1	0-1	8	Kidd	1200
13	18	H	Stirling Albion	W 2-1	0-0	7	Carson, Rafferty	1996
14	25	A	Raith R	L 0-2	0-2	8		2000
15	Nov 1	H	Hibernian	W 2-0	0-0	7	Kidd (pen), Irvine	3855
16	8	A	Dundee	L 1-2	0-0	9	Carson	5112
17	15	H	Berwick R	W 2-1	0-0	6	Irvine, MacLeod	1890
18	22	H	Dumbarton	W 4-2	2-2	6	Forbes, Cleland, Soutar, McLelland S.	2223
19	29	A	St Johnstone	D 2-2	1-1	6	Kidd, Irvine	2135
20	Dec 6	H	East Stirling	D 1-1	0-1	6	Cleland	1999
21	13	A	Stirling Albion	L 0-2	0-0	6		1000
22	20	H	Clydebank	W 3-0	0-0	6	Forbes, Cleland 2	1671
23	Jan 1	H	Hamilton A	L 1-3	1-2	—	McLaughlin	4000
24	10	H	Ayr U	W 3-2	3-1	7	Irvine 2, McLaughlin	2554
25	31	H	Raith R	D 0-0	0-0	7		2953
26	Feb 7	A	Berwick R	D 2-2	0-2	6	McLaughlin, Irvine	928
27	21	H	Dundee	W 4-1	2-1	6	Cleland 2, Irvine, McLaughlin (pen)	2072
28	28	H	St Johnstone	W 3-2	1-1	5	Forbes 2, Cleland	2646
29	Mar 14	H	East Stirling	W 2-1	0-0	6	Soutar (pen), Rafferty	1800
30	18	A	Falkirk	W 1-0	1-0	—	Irvine	1500
31	21	A	Clydebank	D 0-0	0-0	6		900
32	28	A	Dunfermline Ath	W 3-1	3-0	6	Gahagan, Kidd (pen), Irvine	1800
33	Apr 4	H	Falkirk	W 1-0	0-0	6	Kidd (pen)	2045
34	8	A	Dumbarton	D 0-0	0-0	—		1500
35	11	H	Ayr U	W 1-0	0-0	5	Kidd (pen)	2068
36	15	A	Dunfermline Ath	L 1-2	1-1	—	Irvine	1870
37	18	A	Hamilton A	W 2-1	0-0	5	Soutar, Cleland	2600
38	25	H	Hibernian	D 1-1	1-0	5	Irvine	3478
39	May 2	A	Stirling Albion	W 3-0	1-0	5	Soutar 2, McLaughlin	500

Final League Position: 5

Goalscorers

League (65): Kidd 13 (6 pens), Irvine 12, Cleland 8, McLaughlin 6 (1 pen), Soutar 5 (1 pen), Forbes 4, McKeever 4, Carson 3, McLelland S. 3, Clinging 2, Rafferty 2, Gahagan 1, MacLeod 1, own goal 1.
League Cup (10): Clinging 4, McLaughlin 3, Irvine 1, Kidd 1, McKeever 1.
Scottish Cup (6): Gahagan 2, Forbes 1, McLaughlin 1, McLelland S. 1, Soutar 1.

Honours

Scottish League – Division 1 Champions 1931–32; Runners-up: 1926–27, 1929–30, 1932–33, 1933–34; Division 2 Champions: 1953–54, 1968–69; Runners-up: 1894–95, 1902–03.
Scottish Cup – Winners 1952; Finalists: 1931, 1933, 1939, 1951.
Scottish League Cup – Winners 1950–51; Finalists 1954–55.
Record Victory: 12-1 v Dundee U, Division 2, 23 Jan, 1954.
Record Defeat: 0-8 v Aberdeen, Premier Division, 26 March, 1979.
Most League Points: 66, Division 1, 1931–32.
Most Individual League Goals in Season: Willie McFadyen, 52, 1931–32.
Highest Scorer in Total Aggregate: Hugh Ferguson, 283, 1916–25.
Most Capped Player: George Stevenson, 12, Scotland.

Sproat H	MacLean A	Williams L	Wark J	McLelland C	O'Rourke T	MacLeod I	Mackay J	Smith J	Carberry R	McLelland S	Carson J	Kidd A	Forbes G	Larnach M	Soutar G	Gahagan J	Irvine W	McLaughlin B	Clinging I	McKeever J	Kane A	Cleland B	Mills P	Rafferty S	Coyne B	Williams D	*Match No.*
1				3	2	4				9*	5	6		8		11†	12	10	7	13							1
1				3	2			4		7	5	6	13	8		12		10†	11	9*							2
1				3	2			4		11†	5	10	6	8*		13	9	12	7								3
1				3	2				4	7*	5	8	12	6		13		10	11	9†							4
1				3	2				4	7	5	8		6				10	11	9							5
1				3	2				4	7	5	8		6	13	11†	12	10*	9								6
1				3	2				4	7	5	8			6		12	10*	11	9							7
1				3		2			4	7*	5	8	10†		6	12	9		11	13							8
1			6	12	2*	3		4		7	5	8				10	9		11								9
1			2			3		4			5	6				7	9	10	11	8							10
1			2			3		4			5	6			12	7*	9	10	11	8							11
	1		2			3		4			5	8			6	7	9	10*	11					12			12
		1	2			3		4			5	8			6	7	9	12	11*					10			13
		1	2			3		4			5	8			6	7*	9	12	11					10			14
		1	2	3		10		4*			5	8	6				9	7	11				12				15
		1	2	3		10		4			5	8	6				9	7	11								16
1			2	3		10		4			5	7	6*			12	9	8†	11			13					17
1			2	3		10		4			5	8	7*		6	12	9					11					18
1			2	3		10†		4			5	8	7*		6	12	9	13				11					19
1			2	3*		11		4			5	10	7†		6	13		8		9		12					20
1			2	3		11		4			5	8*	7			13		10		9†	6	12					21
1						3	2			4	5	8	6*			7	9	11			12	10					22
1				12		3*	2			4	5	8	6			7	9†	11			13	10					23
1			2			3				4	5	8	6			7	9	11				10					24
1			2			3				4	5	8	6		10		9	7				12				11*	25
1			2			3		4		5		8	6		10	11	9	7									26
1			2			3		5		4			6		10	11	9	7				8					27
1			2			3		5		4			6		10	11	9	7				8					28
1			2			3				4	5	10			6	11	9	7				8*		12			29
1			2			3				4	5	8	6		10	11	9	7									30
1			2			3		10†		4	5	8*	6			11	9	7						12	13		31
1			3		2					4	5	10	6			11	9*	7				12			8		32
1			3		2*		12			4	5	10	6			11	9	7		13					8†		33
1			3				2			4	5	8	6		10	11	9	7									34
1			2				3			4	5	8	6		10	11	9	7*		12							35
1			2				3			4	5	8	6		10	11	9	7									36
1			2				3*			4	5	8†	6		10	11	9	7		12		13					37
1			2				3			4	5	8*	6		10	11	9	7†		12		13					38
1			2				3			4	5	8	6		10	11	9	7									39
34	1	4	29	15	10	25	8	19	5	27	36	37	26	6	20	25	31	32	17	8	1	8	0	2	2	1	
				+ 2s			+ 1s						+ 2s		+ 2s	+ 9s	+ 3s	+ 4s		+ 6s	+ 2s	+ 7s	+ 1s	+ 3s	+ 1s		

PARTICK THISTLE Premier Division

Year Formed: 1876. *Team Manager:* Peter Cormack. *Admin. Manager:* Scot Symon. *Secretary:* L. J. McIntyre, CA. *Address:* Firhill Park, Glasgow, N.W. *Size:* 110yd×71yd. *Capacity:* 36,000 (3500 seated). *Telephone:* 041-946 2673. *Previous Grounds:* Kelvingrove, 1876–81; Jordanvale Park, 1881–83; Muirpark 1883–85; Meadowside Park, 1891–1908; Firhill Park, 1909 (1908–9, Ibrox was used by Partick T when they had no ground of their own, but some 'home games' still had to be played away). *Nickname:* The Jags. *Colours:* Red and yellow shirts with broad vertical stripes, red shorts, red stockings with black and yellow tops.
Record Attendance: 49,838 v Rangers, Division 1, 18 Feb, 1922.
European Competitions: *Fairs Cup* 1963–64; *UEFA Cup* 1973–74.

1980–81 LEAGUE RECORD

Match No.	*Date*	*Venue*	*Opponents*	*Result*	*H/T Score*	*League Pos'n*	*Goalscorers*	*Attendance*
1	Aug 9	H	Hearts	W 3-2	1-0	—	Higgins, Gibson, Liddell (og)	4000
2	16	A	Rangers	L 0-4	0-3	7		26,000
3	23	H	Kilmarnock	L 0-1	0-0	9		4000
4	Sept 6	A	Celtic	L 1-4	1-2	9	Gibson	20,000
5	13	H	St Mirren	W 1-0	1-0	7	Clark	4000
6	20	H	Aberdeen	L 0-1	0-0	9		6000
7	27	A	Morton	W 2-1	0-0	5	O'Hara, Watson	5000
8	Oct 4	H	Airdrieonians	W 2-1	0-1	5	Higgins 2	5000
9	11	A	Dundee U	D 0-0	0-0	5		4706
10	18	A	Hearts	W 1-0	0-0	5	Jardine	5905
11	25	H	Rangers	D 1-1	0-0	5	Park	14,000
12	Nov 1	A	Kilmarnock	W 1-0	0-0	4	O'Hara	2500
13	8	H	Morton	D 0-0	0-0	4		3000
14	15	A	Aberdeen	L 1-2	0-0	4	O'Hara	10,000
15	22	H	Dundee U	L 2-3	1-1	5	Clark, O'Hara	4000
16	29	A	Airdrieonians	D 0-0	0-0	5		3500
17	Dec 6	H	Celtic	L 0-1	0-1	6		12,436
18	13	A	St Mirren	L 0-1	0-0	6		5626
19	20	H	Aberdeen	D 1-1	1-1	6	Watson (pen)	4000
20	27	A	Morton	L 0-2	0-0	7		6000
21	Jan 1	A	Rangers	D 1-1	0-1	—	O'Hara	17,000
22	3	H	Hearts	W 1-0	1-0	6	Watson (pen)	3500
23	10	H	Airdrieonians	W 1-0	1-0	6	Park	3000
24	31	H	St Mirren	D 0-0	0-0	6		4000
25	Feb 21	H	Kilmarnock	D 1-1	0-1	6	McDonald	1600
26	28	A	Hearts	D 1-1	1-1	6	Higgins	3491
27	Mar 7	A	Airdrieonians	L 0-2	0-1	6		3000
28	14	H	Dundee U	L 0-2	0-2	7		3500
29	18	A	Celtic	L 1-4	1-2	—	Park	15,000
30	28	H	Morton	W 3-1	1-1	7	Watson, Higgins, Rooney (og)	2000
31	Apr 1	A	Aberdeen	L 1-3	0-1	—	Watson	9000
32	5	H	Celtic	L 0-1	0-0	—		17,196
33	11	A	St Mirren	L 2-3	2-0	7	Higgins 2	4445
34	18	A	Kilmarnock	W 1-0	1-0	6	Clark	1250
35	25	H	Rangers	D 1-1	0-1	6	Whittaker	9000
36	May 2	A	Dundee U	L 2-3	1-1	6	O'Hara 2	4124

Final League Position: 6

Goalscorers

League (32):Higgins 7, O'Hara 7, Watson 5 (2 pens), Clark 3, Park 3, Gibson 2, Jardine 1, McDonald 1, Whittaker 1, own goals 2.
League Cup (7): Gibson 2, Higgins 2, O'Hara 2, Watson 1.
Scottish Cup (6): Clark 3, O'Hara 2, Whittaker 1.

Honours
Scottish League – Division 1 Champions: 1975–76; Division 2 Champions: 1896–97, 1899–1900, 1970–71; Runners-up 1901–02.
Scottish Cup – Winners 1921; Runners-up 1930.
Scottish League Cup – Winners 1971–72; Runners-up: 1953–54, 1956–57, 1958–59.
Glasgow Cup – 1980-81.
Most Capped Player: Alan Rough, 42, Scotland.
Most League Points: 56, Division 2, 1970–71.
Record Victory: 16-0 v Royal Albert, Scottish Cup 1st rd, 17 Jan, 1931.
Record Defeat: 0-10 v Queen's Park, Scottish Cup 5th rd, 3 Dec, 1881.
Most Individual League Goals in Season: Alec Hair, 41, Division 1, 1926–27.

Rough A	McNab D	McKinnon D	Whittaker B	Lapsley J	Doyle J	Welsh F	Anderson A	Campbell J	Marr J	Gibson I	Park D	O'Hara A	Torrance R	Jardine I	McDonald I	Sweeney J	Higgins A	Watson K	Clark G	Murray J	Scott A	McLeod W	*Match No.*
1			3			5		4		10	12	9*			11		8	6		2		7	1
1			3	13		5		4		10	12	9			11†		8	6		2*		7	2
1			3	13	2	6		5		4	7	8*		12	11†		9	10					3
1			3	12	2	6		5*		8	7†	9		4			10	11			13		4
1			3		2	5		6		8	7	9		4			10	11					5
1			3	13	2	6		4		8	7	5*			11†		9	10			12		6
1			3		2	6		5		4	7	8		11			9	10					7
1			3		2	6		5		4	7	8		11			9	10					8
1			6	3		2		5	12		7	8	9		11*		4	10					9
1			3			6		4			7	5	9	11	12		8*	10		2			10
1			5	3			6		4		7	8	12	11				10	9*	2			11
1			5	3	12	6	4				7	8	9	11				10†	13	2*			12
1			5	3	2		6	4			7	9	12	11				10	8*				13
1			5	3*	2	6		4†			7	8	12	11	13			10	9				14
1			5	3*		2	6†	4	13		7	9		11	12			10	8				15
1				3	8	4		5	6		7	9	13		12			10*	11†	2			16
1			3	11	2		4	5			7	9		8				6	10				17
1			3	11*	2	4		5			7	9		8	12			6	10				18
1			3	12	2		5	4			7	10	9*	8				6	11				19
1			3		2		5	4			7*	10	9	8	12			6	11				20
1			3		10	2	5	4			7	11		8		9		6					21
1			3		10	2	5	4			7	11		8		9*		6	12				22
1			3		10	2*	4	5			7			8	12	9		6	11				23
1		2	3				5	4			7	9		8	10			6	11				24
1		2	3	12	10*		5	4				9		8	7			6	11				25
1		2	3	12			5	4*				9		8	7		10	6	11				26
1		2*	3	13		12	5	4				8			7	9†	10	6	11				27
1		2	3	6			5	4			7	9			8		11*	10	12				28
1			3	6		2	5	4			7	10		12	8*		9		11				29
	1	13		3		2	5*	4			7			10	8	12	9	6†	11				30
	1	2	3	10		4		5			7				8		9	6	11				31
	1		3	10	6	2	5	4			7				8		9		11				32
1		2	3		6	5		4			7	11		13	8*		9	10†	12				33
1			3		6	2	5	4			7*	10		8	12		9		11				34
1			3	12	6	2	5	4			7*	10		8			9	13	11†				35
1			3		7	2*	5	4			6	11			8		10	9	12				36
33	3	7	34	14	22	26	21	34	2	8	31	32	5	23	16	4	21	32	20	6	0	2	
		+ 1s		+ 9s	+ 1s	+ 1s			+ 2s		+ 2s		+ 4s	+ 3s	+ 8s	+ 1s		+ 1s	+ 5s		+ 2s		

QUEEN OF THE SOUTH — Division 1

Year Formed: 1919. *Ground:* Palmerston Park. *Size:* 111yd×73yd. *Capacity:* 20,000.
Telephone: Dumfries 4853.
Secretary: Lewis Russell.
Club Colours: Royal blue shirts with white facings, white shorts, royal blue stockings with two white hoops on top.
Club Nickname: Queens or The Doonhamers.
Record Attendance: 24,500 v Hearts, Scottish Cup 3rd rd, 23 Feb, 1952.

1980–81 LEAGUE RECORD

Match No.	*Date*	*Venue*	*Opponents*	*Result*	*H/T Score*	*League Pos'n*	*Goalscorers*	*Attendance*
1	Aug 9	H	Brechin C	W 3-2	2-0	—	Phillips 2, Proudfoot	1500
2	16	H	Arbroath	D 2-2	1-1	—	Learmont, Phillips	1250
3	23	A	Stranraer	L 0-1	0-0	—		750
4	Sept 2	H	Alloa	D 1-1	0-1	9	Dickson	1000
5	6	A	Queen's Park	L 1-5	1-2	—	Alexander	640
6	10	A	Albion R	W 4-0	2-0	—	McCann, Roddy, Robertson, Alexander	250
7	13	H	Stenhousemuir	D 4-4	3-1	6	Dickson, Learmont, Coughlin, Roddy (pen)	850
8	17	H	Meadowbank T	D 1-1	1-0	—	Robertson	1225
9	20	A	Forfar Ath	W 2-1	0-0	5	Cameron (og), Robertson M.	1000
10	27	A	East Fife	D 1-1	1-0	6	Coughlin	603
11	Oct 4	H	Clyde	L 1-3	1-1	—	Robertson	1500
12	11	A	Montrose	D 1-1	0-0	—	Forbes (og)	350
13	18	H	Cowdenbeath	W 1-0	0-0	6	Alexander	1200
14	25	A	Stenhousemuir	D 1-1	1-1	7	Robertson J. (pen)	400
15	Nov 1	H	Queen's Park	L 0-3	0-2	7		1000
16	8	A	Meadowbank T	W 2-0	1-0	—	Alexander, Robertson J. (pen)	250
17	15	H	Forfar Ath	D 1-1	0-1	7	Robertson G.	1000
18	22	H	East Fife	D 1-1	1-1	6	Alexander	1000
19	Dec 6	H	Montrose	L 1-5	0-2	8	Robertson J.	900
20	13	A	Forfar Ath	W 4-3	1-3	6	Robertson J., Gordon, Learmont, Robertson G.	600
21	27	A	Arbroath	W 2-1	1-0	5	McCann, Robertson J.	600
22	Jan 1	H	Stranraer	W 3-0	1-0	—	Gordon, Alexander, Robertson	1471
23	24	H	Queen's Park	W 1-0	0-0	3	Coughlin	900
24	31	A	Cowdenbeath	D 1-1	1-1	3	Coughlin	750
25	Feb 7	H	Montrose	W 4-1	1-0	3	Scott, Coughlin, Alexander 2	1000
26	14	A	Meadowbank T	D 0-0	0-0	3		400
27	28	H	Clyde	D 0-0	0-0	3		1000
28	Mar 4	A	Alloa	W 3-1	2-0	—	Robertson 3	500
29	7	H	East Fife	W 2-1	1-1	3	Coughlin, Robertson	1000
30	14	A	Albion R	L 0-1	0-0	3		450
31	24	A	Brechin C	L 1-2	0-1	—	Alexander	500
32	28	H	Stenhousemuir	L 0-2	0-2	4		1000
33	Apr 1	A	Clyde	W 4-1	1-0	—	Gordon, Phillips, Alexander, Robertson (pen)	500
34	4	A	Stranraer	W 2-1	1-0	3	Alexander, Coughlin	400
35	8	H	Cowdenbeath	D 2-2	1-0	—	Robertson J. 2 (1 pen)	1734
36	14	A	Brechin C	L 0-1	0-1	—		400
37	18	A	Alloa	W 5-1	3-0	2	Robertson J., Phillips, Coughlin, Alexander 2	650
38	25	A	Arbroath	D 1-1	1-1	2	Phillips	463
39	May 2	H	Albion R	W 3-0	1-0	2	Robertson J. 2, Alexander	1500

Final League Position: 2

Goalscorers

League (66): Robertson J. 19 (5 pens), Alexander 14, Coughlin 8, Phillips 6, Gordon 3, Learmont 3, Dickson 2, McCann 2, Robertson G. 2, Roddy 2 (1 pen), Proudfoot 1, Robertson M. 1, Scott 1, own goals 2.
League Cup (1): Alexander 1.
Scottish Cup (1): Gordon 1.

Honours

Scottish League – Division 2 Champions 1950–51; Runners-up: 1932–33, 1961–62, 1974–75, 1980–81.
Record Victory: 11-1 v Stranraer, Scottish Cup 1st rd, 16 Jan, 1932.
Record Defeat: 2-10 v Dundee, Division 1, 1 Dec, 1962.
Most League Points: 53, Division 2, 1961–62.
Most Individual League Goals in Season: Jimmy Gray, 33, Division 2, 1927–28.
Most Capped Player: Billy Houliston, 3, Scotland.

Ball A	Dunlop R	McChesney I	Brown R	Proudfoot T	Clark R	Robertson M	McCann K	Dickson P	Mitchell I	Roddy J	Gordon W	Alexander R	Robertson G	Learmont D	Phillips G	Coughlin J	Robertson J	Malone R	Boyd C	McLure B	Scott A B	Veitch T	*Match No.*
	1	3		8	5		12	2		6	4*			7	9	10	11						1
	1	3		8†	5			2		6	4*	12	13	7	9	10	11						2
	1	3		12	5			2	4	6		8		7	9	10*	11						3
	1	3			5	2	4	7	10	6	8	9					11						4
	1	3		12	5		10	2		6	8	9	4*	13			11			7†			5
	1	3		8	5			2	4	6		9	10	7			11						6
	1	3		2	5		4*	9		6	8		10	7		12	11						7
	1			2	5		4	9		6	7	3	8			11	10						8
	1	3		2	5	13	8	9†	7*		4	10				12	11	6					9
	1	2	3		5		7	9			4	8				10	11	6					10
	1	2	3		5		7	9			4	8	12			10	11	6					11
	1		3	2	5		4	7			8	9				10	11	6					12
	1		3	2	5		4	7			8	9	12			10*	11	6					13
	1		3	2	5		4*	7†		12	8	9	10	13			11	6					14
	1		3	2	5		4	7*			8	9	13	12		10†	11	6					15
	1		3	2	5		10			7	8	9	4				11	6					16
	1		3	2	5		10	12		7	8*	9	4				11	6					17
	1		3	2	5		10†	13	7*		8	9	4	12			11	6					18
	1	12	3	2*	5		10			4	8†	9	13	7			11	6					19
1		2	3		5		7			4*	8	9	13	12		10	11†	6					20
1		2			5		4	3	7		8	9				10	11	6					21
1		3			5		4	2	7*		8	9			12	10	11	6					22
1		2	3		5		4				8	9			7	10	11	6					23
1		2	3		5		4		12		8	9			7*	10	11	6					24
1		3			5		4	2			8	9				10*	11	6			7	12	25
1		3			5		4	2			8	9			10*		11	6			7	12	26
1		3			5		4*	2			8	9			12		11	6			10	7	27
1		3			5		4	2			8	9			10		11	6			7		28
1		3			5			2	12		4				9	10	11	6*	8		7		29
1		3			5			2			4	9			7	10	11	6	8				30
1		3			5		4	2			8	9			7	10	11		6				31
1			3		5		12	2			8	9				10	11	6	4		7*		32
1			3		5		4	2			8	9			7	10	11	6					33
1			3		5		4	2			8	9			7	10	11	6					34
1			3		5		4	2			8	9			7	10	11	6					35
1		3			5			2			8	9			7	10	11	6	4				36
1					5		4	2			8	9			7	10	11	6	3				37
1					5		4	2			8	9			7	10	11	6	3				38
1					5		4	2			8	9			7	10	11	6	3				39
20	19	23	17	14	39	1	31	32	7	12	37	35	8	6	17	26	39	30	8	1	6	1	
		+		+		+	+	+	+	+		+	+	+	+	+						+	
		1s		2s		1s	2s	2s	2s	1s		1s	6s	5s	2s	2s						2s	

QUEEN'S PARK Division 1

Year Formed: 1867. *Ground:* Hampden Park, Glasgow G42. *Size:* 115yd×75yd. *Telephone:* 041-632 1275 (ground).
Coach: Eddie Hunter.
Secretary: W. Frank Campbell.
Club Colours: Black and white hooped shirts, white shorts, white stockings with two black hoops on top.
Club Nickname: Spiders.
Only amateur club in British senior football.
Record Attendance: 97,000 v Rangers, Scottish Cup 2nd rd, 18 Feb, 1933. (Record for ground – 149,547, Scotland v England, 1937.) *Capacity:* 88,000.
Previous Grounds: Queen's Park Recreation Ground 1867–73; 'First' Hampden (site: approx Florida Ave) 1873–83; 'Second' Hampden (renamed Cathkin Park and used by Third Lanark FC until 1967) 1883–1903.

1980–81 LEAGUE RECORD

Match No.	*Date*	*Venue*	*Opponents*	*Result*	*H/T Score*	*League Pos'n*	*Goalscorers*	*Attendance*
1	Aug 9	H	Stenhousemuir	W 2-1	1-0	—	Gillespie, Niven	610
2	16	A	Montrose	W 3-1	0-0	—	Nicholson 2, McGregor	450
3	23	H	Clyde	L 0-1	0-1	—		1430
4	Sept 3	A	Forfar Ath	D 1-1	0-0	4	McGregor	498
5	6	H	Queen of the S	W 5-1	2-1	—	Nicholson 2, McCoy 3	640
6	9	H	Cowdenbeath	D 1-1	0-0	—	McCoy	964
7	13	A	Brechin C	D 0-0	0-0	3		400
8	17	A	Arbroath	W 4-1	3-1	—	McGregor 2 (1 pen), McNiven, Irvine	584
9	20	H	East Fife	W 2-1	1-0	1	Irvine, McCoy	800
10	27	A	Stranraer	L 1-2	1-2	2	McCoy	450
11	Oct 4	H	Alloa	D 1-1	1-0	—	Irvine	700
12	11	H	Meadowbank T	D 1-1	0-1	—	McGregor	950
13	18	A	Albion R	D 2-2	1-1	2	McCoy, McNiven	750
14	25	H	Brechin C	D 1-1	1-0	3	Watt (og)	910
15	Nov 1	A	Queen of the S	W 3-0	2-0	3	Gillespie, McCoy, Malone (og)	1000
16	8	H	Arbroath	D 2-2	1-1	—	McCoy, McGregor	851
17	15	A	East Fife	W 2-0	1-0	2	Dickson, McCoy	563
18	22	H	Stranraer	W 1-0	1-0	1	McSkimming	750
19	29	A	Alloa	L 2-5	2-3	2	McGregor, Crawley	1050
20	Dec 6	A	Meadowbank T	D 1-1	1-0	2	McCoy	250
21	20	H	Albion R	W 2-0	1-0	2	McGregor, Grant	850
22	Jan 3	H	Meadowbank T	D 1-1	0-1	2	Nicholson	750
23	10	H	Forfar Ath	L 1-3	0-2	2	McGregor (pen)	906
24	24	A	Queen of the S	L 0-1	0-0	2		900
25	31	H	Albion R	W 3-1	1-0	2	Dickson, McCoy 2	500
26	Feb 10	A	Stenhousemuir	D 2-2	2-1	—	McCoy, Dickson	300
27	14	A	Arbroath	D 0-0	0-0	2		682
28	21	A	East Fife	D 1-1	0-1	2	McGregor	390
29	28	H	Alloa	W 2-1	0-0	2	McGregor, Nicholson	1300
30	Mar 4	A	Clyde	D 1-1	0-0	—	McFarlane	500
31	7	A	Stranraer	D 1-1	1-1	2	Nicholson	400
32	14	H	Montrose	D 1-1	0-0	2	McGregor	972
33	21	A	Stenhousemuir	W 4-3	1-3	—	McCoy, Irvine, McGregor (pen), Crawley	350
34	28	H	Brechin C	W 1-0	0-0	1	McSkimming	1135
35	Apr 1	H	Montrose	W 1-0	0-0	—	McCoy	976
36	4	H	Clyde	D 1-1	0-1	1	Dickson	1740
37	18	A	Forfar Ath	W 2-1	0-0	1	Nicholson, Crawley (pen)	1000
38	25	H	Cowdenbeath	D 1-1	0-1	1	McCoy	2051
39	May 2	A	Cowdenbeath	W 2-1	1-1	1	Nicholson, McFarlane	1965

Final League Position: 1

Goalscorers

League (62): McCoy 17, McGregor 13 (3 pens), Nicholson 9, Dickson 4, Irvine 4, Crawley 3 (1 pen), McNiven 3, Gillespie 2, McFarlane 2, McSkimming 2, Grant 1, own goals 2.
League Cup (7): McCoy 3, Nicholson 2, Dickson 1, Irvine 1.
Scottish Cup (2): Irvine 1, McCoy 1.

Honours
Scottish League – Division 2 Champions: 1922–23, 1955–56, 1980–81.
Scottish Cup – Winners: 1874, 1875, 1876, 1880, 1881, 1882, 1884, 1886, 1890, 1893; Finalists 1892, 1900.
FA Cup – Finalists: 1884, 1885.
Record Victory: 16-0 v St Peters, Scottish Cup 1st rd, Sept, 1885.
Record Defeat: 0-9 v Motherwell, Division 1, 26 April, 1930.
Most League Points: 57, Division 2, 1922–23.
Most Individual League Goals in Season: Peter Buchanan, 32, Division 2, 1962–63.
Most Capped Player: Watty Arnott, 14, Scotland.

Atkins D	McSkimming R	Dickson R	Wilson T	Rennie A	McGregor J	McFarlane R	Grant A	Gillespie M	McNiven J	Irvine A	Sinclair J	Wood D	Crawley G M	Nicholson J	Cook S	McCoy G	Falconer R	Mackay G B	Melrose F	Cairns W	*Match No.*
1	2	3		4	5	7		6	8					9		10	11				1
1	2	3		4	5	6		8	11	7				9		10					2
1	2	3		4	5	6		8		9	7			10		11					3
1	2	3		4	5	6		8		9	7			10		11					4
1	2	3		4	5	6*		8†	12	9	7			10	13	11					5
1	2	3		4	5	6		8		9	7			10		11					6
1		3		4	5	2		8	6	9	7			10		11					7
1		3		4	5	2		8	6	9	7			10		11					8
1		3		4	5	2		8	6	9	7			10		11					9
1		3		4	5	2		8	6	9	7			10		11					10
1		3		4	5	2		8	6*	9	7	12		10		11					11
1		3		4	5	2		6	8*	9	7		12	10		11					12
1		3*		4	5	2		6	8	9	7			10	12	11					13
1		3		4	5	2		6	8*	9	7		12	10†		11		13			14
1	2	3		4	5	8		6*	12	9	7			10		11					15
1	2	3		4	5	8			6*	9	7		12	10		11					16
1	2	3			5	8				9	7		6	10	4	11					17
1	2	3		4	5	8*	13			9	7		6	10	12				11†		18
1	2	3		4	5	8				9	7		6	10		11					19
1		3	2		5		12		8	9	7		6	10*	4	11					20
1		3		4	5	2	10*	8		9	7	12	6	11							21
1		3		4	5	2		8		9	7		6	11		10					22
1	2	3		4*	5	6		7†	12	9	13		8	11		10					23
1	2	3			5			8*	12	9	7		6	11	4	10					24
1	2	3			5	6*			12	9	7	13	8	11†	4	10					25
1	2	3			5	6				9	7		8	11	4	10					26
1	2	3			5	6				9	7		8	11	4	10*			12		27
1	2	3		4	5	6				9	7		8	11		10					28
1	2	3		4	5	6				9	7		8	11		10					29
1	2	3		4	5	6				9	7		8	11		10					30
1	2			4	5	6*		12		9	7		8	11	3	10					31
1	2	3		4	5	6		12		9	7		8	11*		10					32
1	2			4	5	3		6		9	7		8	11		10					33
1	2			4	5	3		7		9	6		8	11		10					34
1	2			4	5	3		7		9	6		8	11		10					35
1	2	3		4	5	6				9	7		8	11		10					36
1	2	3		4		6	12			9	7		8	11*		10				5	37
1	2	3		4	5	6		12		9	7		8*	11		10					38
1	2	3		4	5	6				9	7		8	11		10					39
39	28	35	1	33	38	37	1	22	12	38	36	0	23	39	7	37	1	0	1	1	
							+ 3s	+ 3s	+ 5s		+ 1s	+ 3s	+ 3s		+ 3s			+ 1s	+ 1s		

RAITH ROVERS Division 1

Year Formed: 1883. *Limited Company:* 1907. *Ground:* Stark's Park. *Size:* 113yd×67yd. *Capacity:* 28,000. *Telephone:* Kirkcaldy 3514.
Manager: Gordon Wallace. *Club Secretary:* Mrs M. B. Watters.
Club Colours: Royal blue, white.
Record Attendance: 31,306 v Hearts, Scottish Cup 2nd rd, 7 Feb, 1953.
Previous Grounds: Robbie's Park 1883–89.
Managers since the War: Bert Herdman, Hugh Shaw, Doug Cowie, George Farm, Tommy Walker, Jimmy Millar, Bill Baxter, George Farm, Bert Paton, Andy Matthew, Willie McLean.

1980–81 LEAGUE RECORD

Match No.	*Date*	*Venue*	*Opponents*	*Result*	*H/T Score*	*League Pos'n*	*Goalscorers*	*Attendance*
1	Aug 9	A	Hibernian	W 1-0	0-0	—	Ballantyne	4500
2	16	H	Clydebank	L 0-4	0-2	—		1800
3	23	A	Dunfermline Ath	W 2-0	2-0	—	Candlish, Steen	4200
4	Sept 6	H	St Johnstone	D 0-0	0-0	9		1500
5	9	H	Falkirk	W 2-1	1-0	—	Harrow, Candlish	1500
6	13	A	Motherwell	D 1-1	1-1	5	Harrow	2230
7	17	A	Stirling Albion	W 2-0	2-0	—	Harrow 2	2300
8	20	H	Dumbarton	W 4-1	2-0	2	Harrow, Urquhart, Lawson 2	1400
9	27	A	Hamilton A	L 1-3	0-2	3	Harris	1500
10	Oct 1	A	Ayr U	L 0-1	0-0	—		2498
11	4	H	East Stirling	W 2-1	0-0	—	Harris 2	1500
12	11	H	Dundee	D 0-0	0-0	2		3255
13	18	A	Berwick R	W 4-1	2-1	3	Ballantyne 2, Harris, Moyes (og)	961
14	25	H	Motherwell	W 2-0	2-0	2	Ballantyne 2	2000
15	Nov 1	A	St Johnstone	W 3-0	0-0	2	Ballantyne, Forsyth, Ford	3016
16	8	H	Stirling Albion	W 3-0	2-0	—	Ballantyne 2 (1 pen), Harris	1800
17	15	A	Dumbarton	D 2-2	1-1	1	Ballantyne, Harris	700
18	22	H	Hamilton A	W 1-0	0-0	1	Harris	2200
19	Dec 13	H	Berwick R	W 3-0	2-0	2	Harris, Ballantyne 2	1700
20	20	H	Ayr U	W 2-1	0-1	2	Forsyth, Miller	2000
21	Jan 1	H	Dunfermline Ath	W 1-0	0-0	—	Ballantyne (pen)	1750
22	3	A	Falkirk	L 0-1	0-0	2		1500
23	10	H	Hibernian	W 2-0	1-0	2	Steen, Forsyth (pen)	10,000
24	31	A	Motherwell	D 0-0	0-0	2		2953
25	Feb 7	H	Dumbarton	W 1-0	0-0	2	Jackson (og)	1500
26	14	H	Berwick R	D 1-1	1-0	2	Harris	1500
27	21	A	Stirling Albion	W 1-0	0-0	2	Forsyth	1124
28	28	H	East Stirling	D 0-0	0-0	2		1200
29	Mar 7	A	Hamilton A	W 2-0	1-0	2	Forsyth, Miller	1000
30	14	A	Dundee	L 1-3	0-0	2	Miller	6350
31	21	H	Ayr U	D 1-1	0-0	—	Carroll	2300
32	24	A	East Stirling	W 1-0	0-0	—	Russell	1800
33	28	H	Falkirk	D 0-0	0-0	2		3000
34	Apr 1	A	Dundee	L 1-2	0-1	—	Candlish	6178
35	4	H	Clydebank	D 1-1	0-1	2	Mitchell	2500
36	11	A	St Johnstone	L 0-2	0-1	2		4926
37	18	A	Hibernian	L 0-2	0-1	4		8071
38	22	A	Clydebank	L 0-3	0-1	—		400
39	25	A	Dunfermline Ath	W 1-0	0-0	4	Russell	2535

Final League Position: 4

Goalscorers

League (49): Ballantyne 12 (2 pens), Harris 9, Forsyth 5, Harrow 5, Candlish 3, Miller 3, Lawson 2, Russell 2, Steen 2, Carroll 1, Ford 1, Mitchell 1, Urquhart 1, own goals 2.
League Cup (7): Harrow 2, Ballantyne 1 (pen), Candlish 1, Ford 1, Lawson 1, Steen 1.
Scottish Cup (1): Harris 1.

Honours

Scottish League – Division 2 Champions: 1907–08, 1909–10 (shared), 1937–38, 1948–49; Runners-up: 1908–09, 1926–27, 1966–67, 1975–76, 1977–78.
Scottish Cup – Finalists 1913.
League Cup – Finalists 1948–49.
Record Victory: 10-1 v Coldstream, Scottish Cup 2nd rd, 13 Feb, 1954.
Record Defeat: 2-11 v Morton, Division 2, 18 March, 1936.
Most League Points: 59, Division 2, 1937–38.
Most Individual League Goals in Season: Norman Haywood, 38, Division 2, 1937–38.
Most Capped Player: Dave Morris, 6, Scotland.
Most League Goals: 142, Division 2, 1937–38.
British record goalscorers: 142 goals in 34 Division 2 matches, 1937–38.

McDermott M	Houston T	Candlish C	McDonough B	Ford R	Forsyth A	Thomson D	Steel D	Ballantyne J I	Lawson M	Urquhart D	Steen J	Mitchell J A	Russell R	Harrow A	Miller R	Carroll P	Berry D	Harris C	Duncan R	Match No.
1	2	3		4	5	6		7	11	8				9		10				1
1	2	3		4	5	6		7	11	8				9		10*			12	2
1	2	3		4	5	6		7	11	8	10			9						3
1	2	3		4	5		6	7		8	11			9	12	10*				4
1	2	3		4	5		6	7	12	8	10			9	11*					5
1	2	3		4	5		6	7		8	10			9	11					6
1	2	3		4	5		6	7		8	10			9	11					7
1	2	3		4*	5		6	13	7	8	10			9†	11	12				8
1	2	3		4		5	6	9	7	8	10			12	11*					9
1	2	3		4		5	6	9	7	8	10*				11†	12	13			10
1	5	3	2	4			6	7	9		8			12	11*		10			11
1	2	3		4	5		6	7	11*	8	10				12			9		12
1		3	2	4	5		6	7		8	10				11			9		13
1		3	2	4	5		6	7		8	10				11			9		14
1		3	2	4	5		6	7	12	8	10				11			9*		15
1		3	2	4	5		6	7	12	8	10				11			9*		16
1		3	2	4	5		6	7		8	10				11			9		17
1		3	2	4	5		6	7	13	8	10*				11†	12		9		18
1		3	2	4	5		6	7*	12	8	10				11†	13		9		19
1		3	2	4	5		6	7	12	8	10				11*			9		20
1	2		3	4	5		6	7		8	10				11			9		21
1	2		3	4	5		6	7*	12	8	10				11†	13		9		22
1		3	2	4	5		6		7	8	10	11*				12		9		23
1		3	2	4	5		6	7*	12	8	10	11†				13		9		24
1		3	2	4	5		6	7*	12	8	10†	11				13		9		25
1		3	2	4	5		6	7*	12	8		11				10		9		26
1	2	3		4	5		6	12	7*	8	10	11†			13			9		27
1	2	3		4	5		6	12	7*	8	10				11			9		28
1	2	3		4	5		6	7		8	10				11			9		29
1	2	3		4	5	8*	6	7			10	12			11			9		30
1	2	3			5		6				8		7		11	10	4	9		31
1	2	3*			5	12	6				8		7		11	10	4	9		32
1	2		3	12	5		6		13		8		7		11	10	4*	9†		33
1	2	3	12	4*	5		6				8		7		13	10	11†	9		34
1		3	2	4	5		6		9*	8		12	7		11	10				35
1		3	2	4	5		6	9	12	8	13	11†	7			10*				36
1		3	2	4		5	6	13	9	8	12	11†	7			10*				37
1		3	2	4		5*	6	7		8	10†		9		11	12		13		38
1†	5	3	2*	4			6	7			10	12	9		11	8		13		39
39	23	36	21	36	33	8	36	29	13	32	33	7	9	8	26	12	5	23	0	
			+ 1s	+ 1s		+ 1s		+ 4s	+ 12s		+ 2s	+ 3s		+ 2s	+ 4s	+ 9s	+ 1s	+ 2s	+ 1s	

RANGERS Premier Division

Year Formed: 1873. *Turned Professional:* 1893. *Limited Company:* 1899.
Ground: Ibrox Stadium Glasgow G51 2XD. *Size:* 115yd×75yd. *Capacity:* 44,000 (19,500 seated).
Telephone: 041-427 0159. *Manager:* John Greig MBE. *Secretary:* Frank King.
Club Colours: Royal blue shirts with white shorts, royal blue stockings.
Club Nicknames: Blues or Gers.
Record Attendance: 118,567 v Celtic, Division 1, 2 Jan, 1939.
Previous Grounds: Flesher's Haugh on Glasgow Green was shared with Great Eastern FC; Kinning Park, Burnbank; Ibrox Park since 1887.
European Competitions: *European Cup:* 1956–57, 1957–58, 1959–60, 1961–62, 1963–64, 1964–65, 1975–76, 1976–77; *European Cup-Winners' Cup:* 1960–61 (finalists), 1962–63, 1966–67 (finalists), 1969–70, 1971–72 (winners), 1973–74, 1977–78; *Fairs Cup:* 1967–68, 1968–69, 1970–71.
Record Transfer Fee Received: £140,000 from Coventry C for Colin Stein, Oct 1972.
Record Transfer Fee Paid: £100,000 to Hibernian for Colin Stein, Oct 1968.

1980–81 LEAGUE RECORD

Match No.	Date	Venue	Opponents	Result	H/T Score	League Pos'n	Goalscorers	Attendance
1	Aug 9	A	Airdrieonians	D 1-1	1-0	—	MacDonald	16,000
2	16	H	Partick T	W 4-0	3-0	—	Cooper, McAdam, MacDonald, Jardine	26,000
3	23	A	Celtic	W 2-1	0-0	—	Bett, Miller	58,000
4	Sept 6	A	Dundee U	W 4-2	4-0	2	Cooper, McAdam, MacDonald, Hegarty (og)	15,000
5	13	H	Aberdeen	D 1-1	1-1	3	McAdam	32,000
6	20	A	Kilmarnock	W 8-1	3-0	1	MacDonald 3, Redford 2 (1 pen), McAdam, Jardine, Bett	20,000
7	27	H	St Mirren	W 2-0	0-0	1	Bett, Cooper	25,000
8	Oct 4	A	Morton	D 2-2	1-2	—	Miller (pen), McAdam	15,000
9	11	H	Hearts	W 3-1	0-0	1	McAdam 2, Jefferies (og)	23,700
10	18	H	Airdrieonians	D 0-0	0-0	2		22,000
11	25	A	Partick T	D 1-1	0-0	3	McAdam	14,000
12	Nov 1	H	Celtic	W 3-0	2-0	2	McAdam 2, MacDonald	53,000
13	8	A	St Mirren	D 0-0	0-0	—		17,000
14	15	H	Kilmarnock	W 2-0	1-0	2	Johnston, Jardine	16,000
15	22	A	Hearts	D 0-0	0-0	2		16,000
16	29	H	Morton	L 0-1	0-0	2		16,000
17	Dec 13	A	Aberdeen	L 0-2	0-0	3		20,000
18	20	A	Kilmarnock	D 1-1	0-1	3	Russell	9500
19	Jan 1	H	Partick T	D 1-1	1-0	—	McAdam	17,000
20	3	A	Airdrieonians	D 1-1	0-1	3	Dawson	12,000
21	10	A	Morton	W 2-0	1-0	3	MacDonald, Redford	13,000
22	31	H	Aberdeen	W 1-0	0-0	3	Johnstone	32,500
23	Feb 7	A	Dundee U	L 1-2	1-1	3	MacDonald	14,328
24	21	A	Celtic	L 1-3	1-0	3	Johnstone	52,800
25	28	H	Airdrieonians	W 2-0	0-0	3	MacDonald, Redford	12,200
26	Mar 14	A	Hearts	L 1-2	1-1	4	Redford	11,500
27	18	H	Dundee U	L 1-4	1-2	—	McAdam	12,000
28	21	H	Kilmarnock	W 2-0	1-0	—	Redford, Russell	8500
29	28	A	St Mirren	L 1-2	0-1	4	Dawson	9988
30	Apr 1	H	Morton	W 4-0	2-0	—	Johnstone 2, MacDonald, Redford	2500
31	4	H	Dundee U	W 2-1	1-1	3	Russell, Redford	14,000
32	15	H	St Mirren	W 1-0	1-0	—	Russell	7000
33	18	H	Celtic	L 0-1	0-0	3		34,000
34	22	A	Aberdeen	D 0-0	0-0	—		15,000
35	25	A	Partick T	D 1-1	1-0	3	Russell	9000
36	May 2	H	Hearts	W 4-0	3-0	3	Bett, Redford, Russell, Johnston	7000

Final League Position: 3

Goalscorers

League (60): McAdam 12, MacDonald 11, Redford 9 (1 pen), Russell 6, Bett 4, Johnstone 4, Cooper 3, Jardine 3, Dawson 2, Johnston 2, Miller 2 (1 pen), own goals 2.
League Cup (7): McAdam 5 (1 pen), Johnstone 1, Miller 1 (pen).
Scottish Cup (20): McAdam 4, MacDonald 3, Redford 3, Russell 3, Johnstone 2, Stevens 2, Bett 1, Cooper 1, Jackson 1.

Honours

Scottish League: Division 1 Champions: 1890–91 (shared with Dumbarton), 1898–99, 1899–1900, 1900–01, 1901–02, 1910–11, 1911–12, 1912–13, 1917–18, 1919–20, 1920–21, 1922–23, 1923–24, 1924–25, 1926–27, 1927–28, 1928–29, 1929–30, 1930–31, 1932–33, 1933–34, 1934–35, 1936–37, 1938–39, 1946–47, 1948–49, 1949–50, 1952–53, 1955–56, 1956–57, 1958–59, 1960–61, 1962–63, 1963–64, 1974–75; Runners-up: 21 times; Premier Division: 1975–76, 1977–78; Runners-up: 1976–77, 1978–79.
Scottish Cup: Winners: 1894, 1897, 1898, 1903, 1928, 1930, 1932, 1934, 1935, 1936, 1948, 1949, 1950, 1953, 1960, 1962, 1963, 1964, 1966, 1973, 1976, 1978, 1979, 1981; Runners-up: 12 times.
Scottish League Cup: Winners: 1946–47, 1948–49, 1960–61, 1961–62, 1963–64, 1964–65, 1970–71, 1975–76, 1977–78, 1978–79; Runners-up: 5 times.
Record Victory: 14-2 v Blairgowrie, Scottish Cup, 1st rd, 20 Jan, 1934. *Record Defeat:* 2-10 v Airdrieonians, 1886. *Most League Points:* 76, Division 1, 1920–21. *Most Individual League Goals in Season:* 44, Sam English, Division 1, 1931–32. *Highest Scorer in Total Aggregate:* Bob McPhail, 233, 1927–39. *Most Capped Player:* George Young, 53, Scotland. *Most League Appearances:* John Greig, 496, 1962–78.

McCloy P	Stewart J	Jardine W	Dawson A	Miller A	Forsyth T	Stevens G	Jackson C	Bett J	Johnstone D	Forsyth A	Cooper D	McKay W	Clark R	Johnston W	McLean T	Russell R	McAdam C	MacDonald J	Redford I	*Match No.*
1		2			4		5	6		3	7					8	9	11	10	1
1		2			4		5	6	12		7*			10†	13	8	9	11	3	2
1		2		3	4		5	6	13		12			7		8*	9	11†	10	3
1		2		3	4*	12	5	6			11				7		9	8	10	4
1		2		3	4*		5	6	12		7			11	8†		9	13	10	5
1		2		3	12		5*	6	4		11			13	7		9†	8	10	6
1		2		3	13		5	6	4*		11			12	7		9†	8	10	7
1		2		3		12	5	6	4		7*			13	8		9	11†	10	8
1		2		3	12		5	6	4		7*			11†	13		9	8	10	9
1		2		3	12		5	6	4*		7			13	8†		9	11	10	10
1		2		3	13		5	6	4		11†				7*	12	9	8	10	11
1		2	3				5	6	4					11	7		9	8	10	12
1		2	3		13		5	6	4					11	7*	12	9†	8	10	13
1		2	3		4		5	6	9			13		11†	7	12		8*	10	14
1		2	3				5	6	4					11	7*	12	9	8	10	15
1		2	3		6*		5		4		7			12	13	8	9	11	10†	16
1			3	2			5		4		12	13		11	7†	8	9	10	6*	17
1		2	3				5	6	4*		12	13		11†	7	8	9	10		18
1		2	3	4				6	5		11†	13			7*	8	9	12	10	19
1		4	3	2	5			6			7	12			13	8*	9	11	10†	20
1		4	3	2		5		6			7					8	9	11	10	21
1		2	3			4	5	6	9		12			7		8		11*	10	22
1		2	3	13		4	5	6			12			7	9†	8*		11	10	23
1		2	3	8†			5	6	4		7*			11		12	9	13	10	24
1		4	3	2			5	6			12			7*		8	9	11	10	25
1		2*	3				5	6	4†			12	13	7		8	9	11	10	26
	1		3	2*	13	4	5	6†			12			7		8	9	11	10	27
	1		3	2	4		5	6			11			7*	12	8	9		10	28
	1	13	3	2	4		5	6			12			7*	11†	8	9		10	29
	1		3	2	4		5	6	9						7	8		11	10	30
	1	4	3	2	5			6	9					12	7	8		11*	10	31
	1		3	2			5	6	4					11	7	8	9		10	32
	1	13	3	2			5	6*	4					11†	7	8	9	12	10	33
	1	2		3	5	4		6	9						7	8	11		10	34
	1	2		3	5	4		6	9						7	8	11		10	35
	1	2			5	4		3			7			11	6	8	9		10	36
26	10	29	22	24	15	7	29	34	23	1	17	0	0	21	23	23	31	26	35	
		+ 2s		+ 1s	+ 7s	+ 2s			+ 3s		+ 8s	+ 6s	+ 1s	+ 6s	+ 5s	+ 5s		+ 4s		

ST JOHNSTONE — Division 1

Year Formed: 1884.
Ground: Muirton Park. *Size:* 109yd×74yd. *Capacity:* 24,950 (2415 seats).
Telephone: Perth 26961.
Manager: Alec Rennie.
Secretary: George Bell. *Coach:* T. G. Fleming.
Club Colours: Royal blue with white collar and cuffs, white shorts and white stockings with royal blue tops.
Club Nickname: Saints.
Record Attendance: 29,972 v Dundee, Scottish Cup 2nd rd, 10 Feb, 1952.
Previous Ground: Recreation Ground.
European Competition: *UEFA Cup* 1971–72.

1980–81 LEAGUE RECORD

Match No.	*Date*	*Venue*	*Opponents*	*Result*	*H/T Score*	*League Pos'n*	*Goalscorers*	*Attendance*
1	Aug 9	H	Stirling Albion	L 0-1	0-1	—		1390
2	16	A	Dumbarton	W 3-0	2-0	—	Morton, Brannigan, McCoist	1000
3	23	H	Dundee	W 1-0	0-0	—	McCoist	4197
4	Sept 3	H	East Stirling	L 0-2	0-1	7		1258
5	6	A	Raith R	D 0-0	0-0	—		1500
6	9	A	Berwick R	W 1-0	1-0	—	McCoist	847
7	13	H	Hamilton A	W 1-0	0-0	4	Docherty	1574
8	17	H	Clydebank	D 1-1	1-0	—	Weir	1597
9	20	A	Dunfermline Ath	W 2-0	1-0	3	McCoist 2	3100
10	27	H	Falkirk	D 0-0	0-0	2		2065
11	Oct 4	A	Motherwell	D 2-2	2-2	—	McCoist, Docherty	2470
12	11	A	Ayr U	D 0-0	0-0	5		2649
13	18	H	Hibernian	L 1-2	0-0	5	Docherty	4318
14	25	A	Hamilton A	W 3-0	2-0	4	Pelosi, Morton (pen), Docherty	2000
15	Nov 1	H	Raith R	L 0-3	0-0	5		3016
16	8	A	Clydebank	W 2-0	0-0	—	Fleming, McCoist	400
17	15	H	Dunfermline Ath	L 2-4	1-3	5	Docherty, Salisbury	2129
18	22	A	Falkirk	W 3-0	1-0	5	Morton, Docherty 2	2000
19	29	H	Motherwell	D 2-2	1-1	5	McCoist 2	2135
20	Dec 6	H	Ayr U	W 1-0	0-0	5	McCoist	1792
21	13	A	Hibernian	L 0-4	0-0	5		5000
22	20	A	East Stirling	D 1-1	0-0	5	Morton	750
23	27	H	Dumbarton	W 2-0	1-0	5	Docherty 2	2018
24	Jan 1	A	Dundee	D 2-2	1-1	—	Morton, Pelosi	8500
25	3	H	Berwick R	W 1-0	0-0	5	McCoist	2365
26	10	A	Stirling Albion	W 1-0	1-0	4	Morton	1450
27	17	A	Ayr U	D 3-3	2-0	4	Pelosi, McCoist 2	2364
28	31	H	Hamilton A	W 2-1	1-0	4	McCoist, Morton (pen)	2122
29	Feb 21	H	Dunfermline Ath	W 4-1	0-1	4	Pelosi 2, Docherty, McCoist	2282
30	28	A	Motherwell	L 2-3	1-1	4	Brogan 2	2646
31	Mar 7	H	Falkirk	W 2-1	1-1	4	Brogan 2	2325
32	18	A	Hibernian	W 2-1	1-1	—	Brogan, Docherty	3000
33	21	H	Berwick R	W 6-2	3-1	—	McCoist 4, Brogan, Kilgour	2048
34	24	A	Clydebank	W 3-1	1-0	—	McNeil, Caldwell, McCoist	500
35	28	H	Dumbarton	W 2-1	1-1	3	Brogan, Kilgour	2647
36	Apr 4	A	Dundee	L 1-4	0-0	3	McCoist	8586
37	11	H	Raith R	W 2-0	1-0	3	McNeil, Morton	4926
38	18	A	East Stirling	D 2-2	0-1	2	McCoist, Brogan	2000
39	25	H	Stirling Albion	W 1-0	1-0	2	Morton	3352

Final League Position: 3

Goalscorers

League (64): McCoist 22, Docherty 11, Morton 9 (2 pens), Brogan 8, Pelosi 5, Kilgour 2, McNeil 2, Brannigan 1, Caldwell 1, Fleming 1, Salisbury 1, Weir 1.
League Cup (0).
Scottish Cup (7): Brogan 3, Docherty 2, McCoist 1, Morton 1.

Honours
Scottish League – Division 2 Champions: 1923–24, 1959–60, 1962–63; Runners-up 1931–32.
Scottish League Cup – Runners-up 1969–70.
Record Victory: 8-1 v Partick T, League Cup, 16 Aug, 1969.
Record Defeat: 1-10 v Third Lanark, Scottish Cup 1st rd, 24 Jan, 1903.
Most League Points: 56, Division 2, 1923–24.
Most Individual League Goals in Season: Jimmy Benson, 36, Division 2, 1931–32.
Most Capped Player: Sandy McLaren, 5, Scotland.

Tulloch G	Jenkins A	Mackay J	McNeil T	Kilgour R	Redford G	Weir J	Rutherford D	Caldwell A	Brannigan D	Fleming G	Docherty J	Pelosi J	Brogan J	McCoist A	Salisbury A	Gilchrist A	Morton J	Barron D	Connor P	Match No.
1		2	3		4		5	6	7*	9				8	11	12	10			1
1		2		3	4		5	6	11	9				8		7	10			2
1		2		3	4		5	6	11	9		7		8			10			3
1		2	12	3	4*	13	5	6	11†	9		7		8			10			4
1		2		3		4	5	6	12	9		7		8		11*	10			5
1		2		3		4	5	6		9	11	7		8			10			6
1		2		3		4*	5	6	12	11	9	7		8			10			7
1		2		3		4	5	6	12	11	9	7*		8			10			8
1		2		3		4	5	6		11	9	7		8			10			9
1		2		3		4*	5	6	12	11	9	7		8			10			10
1		2	10	3		4	5	6		11	9	7		8						11
1		2	10	3		4	5	6		11	9	7		8						12
1		2		3		4	5	6		11	9	7		8			10			13
1		2		3		4	5	6		11	9	7		8			10			14
1		2	12	3		4	5	6	7*	11	9			8		13	10†			15
1		2		3		4	5	6	7	11	9			8			10			16
1				3	2*	4		6	7	11	9				12	8	10†	5	13	17
1		2		3		4	5	6	7	11	9			8			10			18
1		2		3		4	5	6	7*	11	9	12		8			10			19
1		2		3		4	5	6		11	9	7		8			10			20
1		2		3		4	5	6		11	9	7		8			10			21
1		2	3				5	6	11	4	9	7		8			10			22
1		2	3				5	6	11	4	9	7		8			10			23
1		2	3				5	6	11	4	9	7*	12	8			10			24
1			3	2			5	6	11*	4	9	7	12	8			10			25
1		2	3				5	6		4	9	7	11	8			10			26
1*		2	3			12	5	6	13	4	9	7	11†	8			10			27
	1	2	3				5	6		4	9	7	11	8			10			28
1		5	3	2	12	10*		6		4	9	7	11	8						29
1		5	3	2		10		6		4	9	7	11	8						30
1		5	3	2		4		6		9		7	11	8			10			31
1		2	3			4	5	6		9	12	7	11*	8			10			32
1			3	2		4	5	6		9		7	11	8			10			33
1			3	2		4	5	6		9		7	11	8			10			34
1				3		4	5	6		10	9	7		8		2	11			35
1			3	2		4*	5	6		9	12	7	11	8			10			36
1			3	2		4	5	6		9		7	11	8			10			37
1			3	2*		4	5	6	12	9†	13	7	11	8			10			38
1		2		3		4	5	6		9	12	7	11	8*			10			39
38	1	31	19	31	5	28	35	39	13	39	26	32	13	38	1	4	35	1	0	
			+ 2s		+ 1s	+ 2s			+ 6s		+ 4s	+ 1s	+ 2s		+ 1s	+ 2s			+ 1s	

ST MIRREN Premier Division

Year Formed: 1876. *Ground:* St Mirren Park (also known as Love Street). *Size:* 115yd×74yd. *Capacity:* 25,800.
Telephone: 041-889 2558 and 840 1337.
Manager: Ricky McFarlane. *Secretary:* L. S. Rew.
Club Colours: Black and white stripes, black shorts and black stockings, with three white bands.
Club Nickname: The Buddies.
Record Attendance: 47,428 v Celtic, Scottish Cup, 4th rd, 7 Mar, 1925.
European Competitions: *UEFA Cup* 1980–81.

1980–81 LEAGUE RECORD

Match No.	*Date*	*Venue*	*Opponents*	*Result*	*H/T Score*	*League Pos'n*	*Goalscorers*	*Attendance*
1	Aug 9	H	Aberdeen	L 0-1	0-1	—		7000
2	16	A	Morton	W 4-1	1-1	5	Somner 3 (2 pens), Stark	8000
3	23	H	Hearts	L 1-3	1-1	7	Somner	7553
4	Sept 6	H	Airdrieonians	D 2-2	0-1	6	Somner 2	5220
5	13	A	Partick T	L 0-1	0-1	8		4000
6	20	H	Dundee U	W 2-0	1-0	5	McDougall, Stark	5700
7	27	A	Rangers	L 0-2	0-0	6		25,000
8	Oct 4	A	Kilmarnock	W 6-1	4-0	6	Somner 3 (1 pen), Abercromby, McDougall, Stark	4000
9	11	H	Celtic	L 0-2	0-2	6		18,601
10	18	A	Aberdeen	L 2-3	0-1	7	Copland, McDougall	8000
11	25	H	Morton	D 1-1	0-0	6	Orr (og)	7000
12	Nov 1	A	Hearts	D 1-1	0-0	7	Somner	5707
13	8	H	Rangers	D 0-0	0-0	7		17,000
14	15	A	Dundee U	L 0-2	0-1	7		5000
15	22	A	Celtic	W 2-1	0-0	7	Richardson, Beckett	16,000
16	29	H	Kilmarnock	W 2-0	1-0	7	Bone, Weir	5200
17	Dec 6	A	Airdrieonians	W 2-1	2-0	4	Stark, McCormack	4000
18	13	H	Partick T	W 1-0	0-0	4	Bone	5626
19	20	H	Dundee U	D 3-3	0-2	4	Bone 2, Somner	5300
20	Jan 1	A	Morton	W 3-1	3-0	—	McCormack, Somner, Weir	8000
21	3	H	Aberdeen	D 1-1	0-0	5	Bone	11,100
22	10	A	Kilmarnock	L 0-2	0-1	5		4900
23	31	A	Partick T	D 0-0	0-0	5		4000
24	Feb 21	H	Hearts	W 2-1	1-0	5	McDougall, Copland	3412
25	28	A	Aberdeen	W 2-1	1-1	5	Richardson, McDougall	8000
26	Mar 4	H	Airdrieonians	W 2-1	1-0	—	Richardson, Stark	3649
27	7	H	Kilmarnock	D 1-1	1-0	5	McDougall	4203
28	14	A	Celtic	L 0-7	0-3	5		18,100
29	21	A	Dundee U	W 2-1	0-0	5	Logan, McCormack	5808
30	28	H	Rangers	W 2-1	1-0	5	Richardson 2	9988
31	Apr 4	A	Airdrieonians	W 2-0	1-0	5	Somner, McDougall	3500
32	11	H	Partick T	W 3-2	0-2	5	Logan 3	4445
33	15	A	Rangers	L 0-1	0-1	—		7000
34	18	A	Hearts	W 2-1	1-1	4	McDougall, Logan	2500
35	25	H	Morton	W 2-0	1-0	4	Bone 2	4345
36	May 2	H	Celtic	W 3-1	1-0	4	McDougall 2, Richardson	14,806

Final League Position: 4

Goalscorers

League (56): Somner 13 (3 pens), McDougall 10, Bone 7, Richardson 6, Logan 5, Stark 5, McCormack 3, Copland 2, Weir 2, Abercromby 1, Beckett 1, own goal 1.
League Cup (7): Somner 3, Richardson 2, Stark 1, own goal 1.
Scottish Cup (0).

Honours

Scottish League – Division 1 Champions 1976–77; Division 2 Champions 1967–68; Runners-up 1935–36.
Scottish Cup – Winners: 1926, 1959; Finalists: 1908, 1934, 1962.
Victory Cup 1919–20.
Scottish Summer Cup 1943–44.
League Cup Finalists 1955–56.
Anglo-Scottish Cup 1979–80.
Record Victory: 15-0 v Glasgow University, Scottish Cup 1st rd, 30 Jan, 1960.
Record Defeat: 2-9 v Dundee, Division 1, 29 Feb, 1964.
Most League Points: 62, Division 2, 1967–68; Division 1, 1976–77.
Most Individual League Goals in Season: Dunky Walker, 45, Division 1, 1921–22.
Most Capped Player: Iain Munro, 7, Scotland.

Thomson W	Young J	Beckett A	McAveety P	Richardson A	Fulton M	McCormack J	Copland J	Abercromby W	Dunlop A	Logan A	Stark W	Somner D	Weir P	Curran J	Spiers D	Munro S D	McDougall F	Bone J	McEachran J	*Match No.*
1	2	3		4	5		6	7		11*	8	9	10				12			1
1	2	3		4	5		6	7		11	8	9	10							2
1	2	3		4	5	12	6*	7		11	8	9	10†				13			3
1	2	3		4			6	7	5	11	8	9						10		4
1	2	3		4		5	6	7*		12	8	9	10					11		5
1	2	3		4		5	6				8	9	10				7	11		6
1	2	3		4		5	6	12			8	9	10				7	11*		7
1	2					5	6	4			8	9	10	12		3	7*	11		8
1	2*		3	4		5	6	11		13	8†	9	10	12			7			9
1	2	3		4		5	6	11			8	9	10				7			10
1	2	3		4		5	6	11			8	9	10				7*	12		11
1	2	3				5	6	11*		7	12	9	10	4				8		12
1	2			4		5	6	3			8	9	10				7	11		13
1	2	3		4		5	6	11				9	10	8				7*	12	14
1		2		4	5	7	6	3			8	9	10					11		15
1		2		10	5	4	6	3			8	9	11					7		16
1	2	3		10	5	4	6				8	9	11					7		17
1	2*	3		10	5	4	6				8	9	11		12			7		18
1	2	3		10	5	4	6				8	9	11					7		19
1	2	3		10	5	4	6				8	9	11					7		20
1	2	3		10	5	4	6				8	9	11					7		21
1	2	3		10	5	4*			6		8	9	11				12	7		22
1	2	3		10	5	4		6		11	8						9	7		23
1		2		10	5	6	4	3		7			11	8			9			24
1		2		4	5	3	6	10			8	9	11				7			25
1		2		4	5	3	6	10			8	9	11				7			26
1		2		4	5	3	6	10		12	8	9*	11				7			27
1	4	2*	12		5	3		6		13	8		11		10		7†	9		28
1			3*	8	5	2	4	6		12	7		11				9	10		29
1			3	8	5	2	4	6		12	7		11*				9	10		30
1	2		3	11	5		4	6			8	9					10	7		31
1	2		3	11	5		4	6		12	8	9					10*	7		32
1	2		3	10	5		4	6		11	8	9						7		33
1	2	12	3	11	5*		4	6		13	8	9†					10	7		34
1	2	3		11	5	4	6	10		12	8*						9	7		35
1	2	3		11	5	4	6	10			8						9	7		36
36	28	27	7	33	25	28	33	28	2	8	33	29	28	3	1	1	20	26	0	
		+ 1s	+ 1s			+ 1s		+ 1s		+ 9s	+ 1s			+ 2s	+ 1s		+ 3s	+ 1s	+ 1s	

STENHOUSEMUIR Division 2

Year Formed: 1884. *Ground:* Ochilview Park. *Size:* 110yd×72yd. *Capacity:* 12,000 (500 seated).
Telephone: Larbert 2992.
Team Manager: Jim Black. *Secretary:* Jim Richardson. *Trainer:* W. Williamson.
Club Colours: Maroon shirts with white trimmings, white shorts and stockings.
Club Nickname: The Warriors.
Record Attendance: 12,500 v East Fife, Scottish Cup 4th rd, 11 Mar, 1950.
Record Receipts: £2,800 v Celtic, Scottish League Cup quarter-final 1st leg, 10 Sept, 1975.

1980–81 LEAGUE RECORD

Match No.	*Date*	*Venue*	*Opponents*	*Result*	*H/T Score*	*League Pos'n*	*Goalscorers*	*Attendance*
1	Aug 9	A	Queen's Park	L 1-2	0-1	—	Hancock	610
2	16	H	Albion R	W 3-1	1-0	—	Hancock, McLeod, Jack	500
3	23	H	Alloa	D 1-1	0-1	—	Hancock	300
4	Sept 3	A	Brechin C	L 1-2	1-2	6	Murray	400
5	6	H	East Fife	W 2-0	1-0	—	Jack, Kirkland	400
6	9	H	Arbroath	L 1-2	1-2	—	Meakin	500
7	13	A	Queen of the S	D 4-4	1-3	9	Bryce, Jack, Graham, Murray	850
8	15	A	Clyde	D 2-2	1-1	—	Jack, Jenkins	600
9	20	H	Cowdenbeath	D 1-1	0-1	7	Jenkins (pen)	400
10	27	A	Montrose	W 3-1	2-0	7	Murray, Jenkins (pen), Dunn	400
11	Oct 4	H	Stranraer	L 1-2	0-1	—	Kirkland	300
12	11	H	Forfar Ath	L 0-1	0-0	—		350
13	18	A	Meadowbank T	W 3-0	2-0	9	Hancock 2, Jack	150
14	25	H	Queen of the S	D 1-1	1-1	8	Hancock	400
15	Nov 1	A	East Fife	D 1-1	0-1	8	Murray	590
16	8	H	Clyde	W 3-0	2-0	—	Hancock, Murray 2	700
17	15	A	Cowdenbeath	W 1-0	0-0	5	Hancock	500
18	22	H	Montrose	L 1-2	0-1	7	Murray	350
19	29	A	Stranraer	W 5-2	3-1	5	Hancock 2, Graham, Murray, Kirkland	350
20	Dec 6	A	Forfar Ath	L 1-2	1-2	6	Hancock	600
21	Jan 1	A	Alloa	L 2-3	1-2	—	Hancock 2	1100
22	31	A	Meadowbank T	L 0-1	0-1	11		470
23	Feb 7	A	Forfar Ath	W 4-1	2-0	10	Bennett (og), Hancock, Meakin, Jenkins	750
24	10	H	Queen's Park	D 2-2	1-2	—	Meakin, Hancock	300
25	14	H	Clyde	D 3-3	2-3	9	Jenkins 2, Jack	350
26	21	A	Cowdenbeath	W 2-1	2-0	8	Hancock, Dunn	300
27	24	H	Albion R	L 0-3	0-1	—		450
28	28	H	Stranraer	W 2-1	0-1	6	Wallace (og), Jack	300
29	Mar 11	A	Montrose	L 1-2	0-1	—	Kirkland	350
30	14	A	Alloa	D 0-0	0-0	9		570
31	18	H	Brechin C	L 0-3	0-0	—		300
32	21	H	Queen's Park	L 3-4	3-1	—	Jack, Jenkins 2	350
33	28	A	Queen of the S	W 2-0	2-0	11	Jack, Hancock	1000
34	31	H	Meadowbank T	D 1-1	0-0	—	Jack	300
35	Apr 4	H	East Fife	L 1-3	0-3	10	Hancock	350
36	11	A	Arbroath	W 1-0	0-0	10	Hancock	320
37	18	A	Albion R	W 2-0	0-0	9	Rennie, Hancock	250
38	25	H	Brechin C	D 1-1	1-0	9	Meakin	150
39	May 2	A	Arbroath	L 0-2	0-1	10		400

Final League Position: 10

Goalscorers

League (63): Hancock 20, Jack 10, Jenkins 8 (2 pens), Murray 8, Kirkland 4, Meakin 4, Dunn 2, Graham 2, Bryce 1, McLeod 1, Rennie 1, own goals 2.
League Cup (1): Kirkland 1.
Scottish Cup (8): Jack 2, Kirkland 2, Meakin 2, Hancock 1, Jenkins 1.

Honours

Scottish Cup – 1902–03 (semi-finalists).
Record Victory: 9-2 v Dundee U, Division 2, 1936–37.
Record Defeat: 2-11 v Dunfermline Ath, Division 2, 1930–31.
Most League Points: 50, Division 2, 1960–61.
Most League Goals: 99, Division 2, 1960–61.
Most Individual Goals in Season: Evelyn Morrison, 29, Division 2, 1927–28 and Bobby Murray, 29, Division 2, 1936–37.
Record Transfer Fee Received: £10,000 from Rangers for Stewart Kennedy, April 1973.

Mulholland R	Howie B	McLaren I	McCraw J	Rennie A	Black J	Meakin J	Frickleton J	Bryce T	Graham R	Mullen T	Jack D	Hancock S	Jenkins B	Murray G	Kirkland B	Downie T	Dunn J	McLeod D	Murdoch W	Sweeney S	Gaines N	Martin B	Smith B	McGonigal A	Harkins J	*Match No.*
	1		3		5	4	6				7	8	10	9	11						2					1
	1		2	3	5	4	6				7	9	10	12	11*			8								2
	1		2	3	5	4	12		8*	6	7	9	10	13						11†						3
	1		2	3	5	4	12			6	7	9	10	11				8*								4
	1		2	3	5	4			12	6	7	9	10	8*	11											5
	1		2	3	5	4		12		6	7	9	10	8	11*											6
	1		2	3	5	4*	6	11†	12		7	9	10	8	13											7
	1		2	3	5	4	6				7	9	10	8	11											8
	1		2	3	5		6	11†	4		7	12	10	9	8*		13									9
	1		2	3	5		6	12	4		7	9	10	8*	13		11†									10
	1		2	3	5	12	6		4		7*	9	10	8†	13		11									11
	1		3	12	5	9	2	13	4*	6	7		10	8			11†									12
	1		3		5	4	2			6	7	9	10	8	11											13
	1		3		5	4	2	12		6	7	9*	10	8	11											14
	1		3		5	4	2			6	7*	9	10	8	11		12									15
	1		2	3	5	4			12	6	7	9	10	8	11*											16
	1		2	3	5	4			12	6	7*	9	10	8	11											17
	1		2	3	5	4			7*	6	12	9	10	8	11											18
	1		2	3	5	4			12	6	7*	9	10	8	11											19
	1		2	3	5	4	6		7*		12	9	10	8	11†		13									20
	1		2	3	5	4	6*		8†	12		9	10		11		7		13							21
	1		2	3	4	5				6	7	9	10		11†	12	13		8*							22
	1		2	3	5	4			12	6	7	9	10			11			8*							23
	1		2	3	5	4			8	6	7	9	10		11											24
	1		2	3	5				7*	6	12	9	10		11†	8	13		4							25
	1		2	3	5				12	6	8	9	10			7*	11		4							26
	1		2	3	5				7*	6	8	9	10		13	12	11†		4							27
1			2	3*	5	4				6	8	9	10		12	7	11									28
1			2	3	5	4			13	6	8	9	10		12	7*	11†									29
		1	2	3	5	4	12			6*	8†	9	10		11	7	13									30
		1	2	3	5	4				6	8	9	10		11	7										31
		1	2	3	5	4	6		7		8	9	10		11											32
		1	2		5	4	10		7	6	8	9			3	11										33
		1	2		5		10		4	6	8	9			3	11								7		34
		1	2		5		10		7	6	8	9			3	11									4	35
		1	2		5	4	10		7	6	8	9			3	11										36
		1	10	3	5	4	12			6	8	9				11	7*					2				37
		1	10	2	5	4			7	6	8	9			3	11										38
		1	10	2	5	4	12			6	8	9			3							7*	11			39
2	27	10	39	30	39	31	18	2	17	29	35	37	32	18	27	13	9	2	5	1	1	2	1	1	1	
				+ 1s		+ 1s	+ 5s	+ 4s	+ 8s	+ 1s	+ 3s	+ 1s		+ 2s	+ 6s	+ 2s	+ 6s		+ 1s							

STIRLING ALBION — Division 2

Year Formed: 1945. *Ground:* Annfield Park. *Size:* 110yd×74yd. *Capacity:* 20,000 (900 seated). *Telephone:* Stirling 3584.
Manager: Alex Smith. *Secretary:* Peter Gardiner.
Club Colours: Red shirts, socks and shorts.
Record Attendance: 26,400 v Celtic, Scottish Cup 4th rd, 14 Mar, 1959.

1980–81 LEAGUE RECORD

Match No.	*Date*	*Venue*	*Opponents*	*Result*	*H/T Score*	*League Pos'n*	*Goalscorers*	*Attendance*
1	Aug 9	A	St Johnstone	W 1-0	1-0	—	Kennedy A.	1390
2	16	H	Hibernian	L 0-2	0-1	—		2500
3	23	A	Ayr U	D 0-0	0-0	—		2850
4	Sept 6	H	Falkirk	W 1-0	0-0	8	McPhee	1500
5	9	A	Hamilton A	L 0-2	0-1	—		1600
6	13	A	Dunfermline Ath	L 0-2	0-1	11		2350
7	17	H	Raith R	L 0-2	0-2	—		2300
8	20	A	East Stirling	L 0-2	0-1	12		750
9	27	H	Dundee	D 1-1	1-0	12	Irvine	1500
10	Oct 1	H	Clydebank	D 0-0	0-0	—		500
11	4	A	Berwick R	L 0-1	0-1	—		640
12	11	H	Dumbarton	L 0-1	0-1	13		700
13	18	A	Motherwell	L 1-2	0-0	13	Armstrong (pen)	1996
14	25	H	Dunfermline Ath	D 3-3	0-2	13	Kennedy J., Armstrong, Duffin	1100
15	Nov 1	A	Falkirk	D 0-0	0-0	13		2000
16	8	A	Raith R	L 0-3	0-2	—		1800
17	15	H	East Stirling	W 4-2	1-2	13	Steele, Kennedy J., Gray 2	500
18	22	A	Dundee	L 1-5	0-1	13	McPhee	4815
19	29	H	Berwick R	W 1-0	0-0	13	Steele	500
20	Dec 6	A	Dumbarton	L 0-2	0-1	13		400
21	13	H	Motherwell	W 2-0	0-0	12	Armstrong, Steele	1000
22	27	A	Hibernian	L 0-3	0-3	13		5600
23	Jan 1	H	Ayr U	D 1-1	0-1	—	Armstrong (pen)	2000
24	3	A	Clydebank	D 1-1	0-1	13	Steele	500
25	10	H	St Johnstone	L 0-1	0-1	13		1450
26	31	A	Dunfermline Ath	W 1-0	0-0	12	McPhee	2500
27	Feb 21	H	Raith R	L 0-1	0-0	13		1124
28	28	A	Berwick R	L 0-1	0-1	13		510
29	Mar 11	H	Hamilton A	L 0-2	0-0	—		350
30	14	H	Dumbarton	D 0-0	0-0	13		500
31	21	A	Falkirk	D 0-0	0-0	—		1700
32	24	H	Dundee	L 0-1	0-0	—		700
33	28	H	Clydebank	D 0-0	0-0	12		600
34	Apr 1	A	East Stirling	L 0-1	0-0	—		800
35	4	A	Hibernian	D 0-0	0-0	13		3500
36	11	H	Hamilton A	L 0-1	0-0	13		500
37	18	A	Ayr U	L 0-1	0-0	13		1220
38	25	A	St Johnstone	L 0-1	0-1	13		3352
39	May 2	H	Motherwell	L 0-3	0-1	13		500

Final League Position: 13

Goalscorers

League (18): Armstrong 4 (2 pens), Steele 4, McPhee 3, Gray 2, Kennedy J. 2, Duffin 1, Irvine 1, Kennedy A. 1.
League Cup (2): Irvine 1, McPhee 1.
Scottish Cup (3): Colquhoun 2, Steele 1.

Honours

Scottish League: Division 2 Champions 1952–53, 1957–58, 1960–61, 1964–65, 1976–77; Runners-up 1948–49, 1950–51.
Record Victory: 7-0 v Albion R, Division 2, 19 Nov, 1947; v Montrose, Division 2, 28 Sept, 1957; v St Mirren, Division 1, 5 March 1960; v Arbroath, Division 2, 11 March 1961.
Record Defeat: 0-9 v Dundee United, Division 1, 30 Dec, 1967.
Most League Points: 59, Division 2, 1964–65.
Most Individual League Goals in Season: Michael Lawson, 26, Division 2, 1975–76.

Arthur G	Nicol G	Steedman A	Skilling A	Young R	Kennedy J	Farmer F	Moffat A	McPhee M	O'Sullivan D	Irvine L	Kennedy A	McCue A R	Gray R	Steele W B	Duffin R	Armstrong G J	Beaton R	O'Connor J	Colquhoun J M	Lindsay J	Fryer J E	McNeil C	Philliben J	McGregor J	Dunlop J	Match No.
1	2	3	10	6	5	12		7		11	9		8				4*									1
1	2	3	4	6	5			7		11	9†		8*				12					13		10		2
1	2	3	4*	6	5	12		11	7†	13	8						10							9		3
1	2		3	6	5	4		7			8						10	11						9		4
1	2	3	4	6	5			7			8						10	11						9		5
1	2*	3	4	6	5		12	7		8	10†					11		13						9		6
1		3	10	6†	5	2*		7	13	4	12					11	8							9		7
1		3	2	8	5		6	7		4	9*					11	10†	12						13		8
1		3	2	4	5		6	7	8*	9				12		11	10									9
1			3	4	5		6	7	8	9						11	10						2			10
1			3*	4	5		6	7	8†	9	13					11	10	12					2			11
1		3		4	5		6	7		10	9†	12		8*		11	13						2			12
1		3	10†	2	5		6	7		4*	13		8	9		11	12									13
1		3		2	5		6	7						9	4	11	10					8				14
1			3	2	5		6	12					7	9	4	11	10					8*				15
1		3*	12	2	5		6	13					7	9	4	11	10					8†				16
1	2	3	6*	4	5			12		8			7	9		11	10									17
1	2	3	8	4	5		6	12					7	9		11	10*									18
1	2	3	10		5		6	7		4			8	9		11										19
1	2	3	10	12	5		6	7		4*	13		8	9†		11										20
1		3	10†	2	5		6	7			12		4	9*	13	11						8				21
1		3*	10	2	5		6	7			13		4	9	12	11						8†				22
1			3	2	5		6	7*		10†	9		8	12	4	11						13				23
1			3*	2	5		6	7		10	9		8	12	4	11										24
1			3	2	5		6	7*		10	9†		8	13	4	11						12				25
1		3	10†	2	5		6	7			8			9*	4	11			12			13				26
1			3	2			6	13			10†		9	8	4	11			12			7*	5			27
1	2		3	4			6	12		8			10	9		11†			7*	13			5			28
1			3	2	5		6	12					10†	9	8	11			13	7*			4			29
1	2		3		5		6					4		9	8				11†	12	13	7*	10			30
1	2	3		12	5		6					8		9	4	13			11			7*	10†			31
1	2*			3	5		6	13				4		9	8	12			11			7†	10			32
1	2			3	5		6	12				4		9	8	13			11†			7*	10			33
1	2			3	5		6	7				4		9	8	11							10			34
1	2	4		3	5		6			7*		10		13	12	11			9†				8			35
1	2	3			5		6	12		7*		10	8	9†		11			13				4			36
1	2	3		10	5		6	7*				4	8†	9		11			13			12				37
1	2	3			5		6	12				10	8	9		11*			7				4			38
1		3			5		6	13				10	4*				8†		9		7	11	2		12	39
39	20	25	27	32	37	2	31	24	4	19	13	10	21	23	14	29	15	2	8	1	1	11	15	6	0	
			+ 1s	+ 2s		+ 2s	+ 1s	+ 12s	+ 1s	+ 1s	+ 6s	+ 1s		+ 5s	+ 3s	+ 3s	+ 3s	+ 3s	+ 5s	+ 2s	+ 1s	+ 5s		+ 1s	+ 1s	

STRANRAER Division 2

Year Formed: 1870. *Ground:* Stair Park. *Size:* 110yd×70yd. *Capacity:* 5,500.
Telephone: Stranraer 3271.
Player-Manager: Gordon Hamilton. *Secretary:* Graham Rodgers.
Club Colours: Royal blue shirts, white shorts, blue stockings with red tops.
Record Attendance: 6,500 v Rangers, Scottish Cup 1st rd, 24 Jan, 1948.

1980–81 LEAGUE RECORD

Match No.	Date	Venue	Opponents	Result	H/T Score	League Pos'n	Goalscorers	Attendance
1	Aug 9	A	Montrose	D 0-0	0-0	—		400
2	16	H	Meadowbank T	L 1-3	1-1	—	Hay	500
3	23	H	Queen of the S	W 1-0	0-0	—	Wilson	750
4	Sept 3	A	Cowdenbeath	D 1-1	1-1	—	Harvey	200
5	6	H	Forfar Ath	L 0-4	0-3	10		450
6	9	H	Clyde	W 1-0	0-0	—	Mitchell	400
7	13	A	East Fife	L 1-3	1-0	12	McLaren (og)	530
8	17	A	Alloa	L 1-3	1-1	—	Murphy	700
9	20	H	Arbroath	L 0-2	0-1	13		500
10	27	H	Queen's Park	W 2-1	2-1	12	Hood, Murphy	450
11	Oct 4	A	Stenhousemuir	W 2-1	1-0	—	Gibb Frickleton (og)	300
12	11	H	Albion R	L 1-4	1-2	—	Hood	400
13	18	A	Brechin C	L 0-1	0-1	13		400
14	25	A	Forfar Ath	L 0-3	0-0	13		900
15	Nov 8	H	Alloa	L 1-3	1-1	—	Hay (pen)	400
16	15	A	Arbroath	L 1-3	1-1	14	Hood	630
17	22	A	Queen's Park	L 0-1	0-1	14		750
18	29	H	Stenhousemuir	L 2-5	1-3	14	Hay, Meakin (og)	350
19	Dec 6	A	Albion R	W 3-1	1-0	13	Gibb, Hay (pen), Brown	350
20	20	H	Brechin C	L 0-1	0-0	13		200
21	27	A	Meadowbank T	W 1-0	0-0	13	Brown	250
22	Jan 1	A	Queen of the S	L 0-3	0-1	—		1471
23	24	H	Montrose	L 0-3	0-1	13		350
24	31	H	Brechin C	D 1-1	1-0	13	Sim	450
25	Feb 14	H	Alloa	D 2-2	0-0	13	McCutcheon, Hood	350
26	21	A	Arbroath	L 0-1	0-1	13		420
27	28	A	Stenhousemuir	L 1-2	1-0	14	Hay (pen)	300
28	Mar 7	H	Queen's Park	D 1-1	1-1	14	Harvey	400
29	11	A	East Fife	L 1-2	0-1	—	Harvey	500
30	14	H	Meadowbank T	L 1-2	1-0	14	Harvey	300
31	17	A	Albion R	L 0-5	0-2	—		300
32	24	A	Cowdenbeath	L 0-3	0-0	—		300
33	28	H	East Fife	D 1-1	1-1	14	Murphy	200
34	Apr 4	H	Queen of the S	L 1-2	0-1	14	Hay (pen)	400
35	8	A	Montrose	L 1-6	1-3	—	Hay (pen)	300
36	11	H	Cowdenbeath	W 3-2	0-2	14	Murphy 2, Harvey	250
37	18	H	Clyde	D 1-1	0-1	14	Murphy	250
38	25	H	Forfar Ath	L 0-3	0-1	14		200
39	May 2	A	Clyde	D 3-3	0-0	14	Murdoch, Rodgers, Neil	400

Final League Position: 14

Goalscorers

League (36): Hay 7 (5 pens), Murphy 6, Harvey 5, Hood 4, Brown 2, Gibb 2, McCutcheon 1, Mitchell 1, Murdoch 1, Neil 1, Rodgers 1, Sim 1, Wilson 1, own goals 3.
League Cup (1): Neil 1.
Scottish Cup (4): Brown 1, Gibb 1, Hay 1, Sim 1.

Honours

Record Victory: 7-0 v Brechin C, Division 2, 6 Feb, 1965.
Record Defeat: 1-11 v Queen of the South, Scottish Cup 1st rd, 16 Jan, 1932.
Most League Points: 44, Division 2, 1960–61, 1971–72.
Most Individual Goals in Season: Derek Frye, 27, Division 2, 1977–78.

Greenhorn W	Taylor J	McClintock D	Hopkins J	Hay H	McDonald D	McCutcheon A	Murdoch H	Hyslop J	Wilson B	Harvey A	Rodgers J	Shields D	Hood N	Gibb I	Neil M	Murphy I	Wallace S	Inglis R	McGuigan I	Mitchell J	Howe S	Sim I	McKie R	Brown D	Cronie A	Millar R	*Match No.*
1			2	4	3	7	6		13			5	9*	8	12				10†			11					1
1			2	4	3	7	6		12			5*	9†	8	11			13	10								2
1			7	3	4	6	2		11			5	12	8	9				10*								3
1			8	4	3	6	2			7	11*	5			9				10			12					4
1			8	4*	3	6	2		12	7	13	5		11	9				10†								5
1			12	3	2	6*	5			4	8			11	13	9				7	10†						6
1				3	2	6	5	8		4*	12			13	11	9†				7	10						7
1			2	3	6	13	5	4		7*	8			11	12	9					10†						8
1				2	3	6	5	4		12	8			11†	13	9				7*	10						9
1			13	3	2	6	5	4		7			11	12	8*	9					10†						10
1				2	3	6	5	4		7	12		11	8		9					10*						11
1				2	3	6	5	4		7*	12		11	8†	13	9						10					12
1				3	2		6	5	12	7	10		11		8	9*									4		13
1			2	10	6	12	5	8	3	4†			11	9*	7	13											14
1			2	4		6		5	3	7*	12		11	9	8†	13	10										15
1			2	4		5		6	3	10	13		7*	9†	8	12								11			16
1			2	3	6	5		4		10	12		7*	9†	8	13								11			17
1			2	10	3	6	5	4					7		8	9								11			18
1				3	4	6	5	2*	12	8	10			9		7								11			19
1				3	4	6	5	2	13	8*	10			9	7	12								11†			20
	1				4	6	5	2	3		10			9	8	12							7*	11			21
	1				4	6	5	2	3	13	10			9	8	12							7*	11†			22
	1		13	6	4	3	5	2	12		8*		9†		7	11						10					23
	1		2	4		8	5	6	3	11*	13		12		7	9†						10					24
	1		2	4	8	10	5	6*	3	11	12		13		7	9†											25
	1		2	4	8	10	5	6*	3	11†	12		13		7	9											26
	1		2	4	3	6*	5	12		9	10				7		8						11				27
	1		8	4	2	6	5	10	3	9					7*	12							11				28
	1		8	4	2	6		5	3	9	10†				7*	13	12						11				29
	1		8	4	2	6		5	3	9*	13				7	12						10†	11				30
		1		4	2			5	3	9	10				12	7	8						11*			6	31
		1	7	3	4	2	5	6		9*					10	11	8						12				32
		1	12	3	4	2	5		13	9	6				7*	11	8					10†					33
		1	12	3	4	2	5			9	6				7	11	8					10*					34
		1	12	2	4		5		3	9	6		13		7*	11	8					10†					35
		1	2	3	4	6	5	13	11*	9	10†				7	12	8										36
		1	12	3	4	2	5	6		9	10*				7	11	8										37
		1	2	3	4	6	5	10		9					7	11	8										38
	1		13	3	4	2	5	6		11*	10		9		7	12	8†										39
20	11	8	21	37	36	34	33	28	15	31	19	5	13	17	31	21	11	0	5	3	6	8	7	7	1	1	
			+ 8s			+ 2s		+ 2s	+ 8s	+ 2s	+ 11s		+ 5s	+ 2s	+ 6s	+ 12s	+ 1s	+ 1s				+ 1s	+ 1s				

SCOTTISH LEAGUE 1890–91 to 1980–81

*On goal average/difference. †Held jointly after indecisive play-off. ‡Won on deciding match.
††Held jointly. ¶Two points deducted for fielding ineligible player.
Competition suspended 1940–45 during war. ‡‡Two points deducted for registration irregularities.

PREMIER DIVISION

Maximum points: 72

	First	*Pts*	*Second*	*Pts*	*Third*	*Pts*
1975–76	Rangers	54	Celtic	48	Hibernian	43
1976–77	Celtic	55	Rangers	46	Aberdeen	43
1977–78	Rangers	55	Aberdeen	53	Dundee U	40
1978–79	Celtic	48	Rangers	45	Dundee U	44
1979–80	Aberdeen	48	Celtic	47	St Mirren	42
1980–81	Celtic	56	Aberdeen	49	Rangers*	44

FIRST DIVISION

Maximum points: 52

1975–76	Partick T	41	Kilmarnock	35	Montrose	30
			Maximum points: 78			
1976–77	St Mirren	62	Clydebank	58	Dundee	51
1977–78	Morton*	58	Hearts	58	Dundee	57
1978–79	Dundee	55	Kilmarnock*	54	Clydebank	54
1979–80	Hearts	53	Airdrieonians	51	Ayr U	44
1980–81	Hibernian	57	Dundee	52	St Johnstone	51

SECOND DIVISION

Maximum points: 52

1975–76	Clydebank*	40	Raith R	40	Alloa	35
			Maximum points: 78			
1976–77	Stirling A	55	Alloa	51	Dunfermline Ath	50
1977–78	Clyde*	53	Raith R	53	Dunfermline Ath	48
1978–79	Berwick R	54	Dunfermline Ath	52	Falkirk	50
1979–80	Falkirk	50	East Stirling	49	Forfar Ath	46
1980–81	Queen's Park	50	Queen of the S	46	Cowdenbeath	45

FIRST DIVISION to 1974–75

Maximum points: a 36; *b* 44; *c* 40; *d* 52; *e* 60; *f* 68; *g* 76; *h* 84.

1890–91*a*††	Dumbarton	29	Rangers	29	Celtic	24
1891–92*b*	Dumbarton	37	Celtic	35	Hearts	30
1892–93*a*	Celtic	29	Rangers	28	St Mirren	23
1893–94*a*	Celtic	29	Hearts	26	St Bernard's	22
1894–95*a*	Hearts	31	Celtic	26	Rangers	21
1895–96*a*	Celtic	30	Rangers	26	Hibernian	24
1896–97*a*	Hearts	28	Hibernian	26	Rangers	25
1897–98*a*	Celtic	33	Rangers	29	Hibernian	22
1898–99*a*	Rangers	36	Hearts	26	Celtic	24
1899–1900*a*	Rangers	32	Celtic	25	Hibernian	24
1900–01*c*	Rangers	35	Celtic	29	Hibernian	25
1901–02*a*	Rangers	28	Celtic	26	Hearts	22
1902–03*b*	Hibernian	37	Dundee	31	Rangers	29
1903–04*d*	Third Lanark	43	Hearts	39	Rangers*	38
1904–05*d*	Celtic‡	41	Rangers	41	Third Lanark	35
1905–06*e*	Celtic	49	Hearts	43	Airdrieonians	38
1906–07*f*	Celtic	55	Dundee	48	Rangers	45
1907–08*f*	Celtic	55	Falkirk	51	Rangers	50
1908–09*f*	Celtic	51	Dundee	50	Clyde	48
1909–10*f*	Celtic	54	Falkirk	52	Rangers	46
1910–11*f*	Rangers	52	Aberdeen	48	Falkirk	44
1911–12*f*	Rangers	51	Celtic	45	Clyde	42
1912–13*f*	Rangers	53	Celtic	49	Hearts*	41

	First	Pts	Second	Pts	Third	Pts
1913–14*g*	Celtic	65	Rangers	59	Hearts*	54
1914–15*g*	Celtic	65	Hearts	61	Rangers	50
1915–16*g*	Celtic	67	Rangers	56	Morton	51
1916–17*g*	Celtic	64	Morton	54	Rangers	53
1917–18*f*	Rangers	56	Celtic	55	Kilmarnock	43
1918–19*f*	Celtic	58	Rangers	57	Morton	47
1919–20*h*	Rangers	71	Celtic	68	Motherwell	57
1920–21*h*	Rangers	76	Celtic	66	Hearts	56
1921–22*h*	Celtic	67	Rangers	66	Raith R	56
1922–23*g*	Rangers	55	Airdrieonians	50	Celtic	46
1923–24*g*	Rangers	59	Airdrieonians	50	Celtic	41
1924–25*g*	Rangers	60	Airdrieonians	57	Hibernian	52
1925–26*g*	Celtic	58	Airdrieonians*	50	Hearts	50
1926–27*g*	Rangers	56	Motherwell	51	Celtic	49
1927–28*g*	Rangers	60	Celtic*	55	Motherwell	55
1928–29*g*	Rangers	67	Celtic	51	Motherwell	50
1929–30*g*	Rangers	60	Motherwell	55	Aberdeen	53
1930–31*g*	Rangers	60	Celtic	58	Motherwell	56
1931–32*g*	Motherwell	66	Rangers	61	Celtic	48
1932–33*g*	Rangers	62	Motherwell	59	Hearts	50
1933–34*g*	Rangers	66	Motherwell	62	Celtic	47
1934–35*g*	Rangers	55	Celtic	52	Hearts	50
1935–36*g*	Celtic	66	Rangers*	61	Aberdeen	61
1936–37*g*	Rangers	61	Aberdeen	54	Celtic	52
1937–38*g*	Celtic	61	Hearts	58	Rangers	49
1938–39*g*	Rangers	59	Celtic	48	Aberdeen	46
1946–47*e*	Rangers	46	Hibernian	44	Aberdeen	39
1947–48*e*	Hibernian	48	Rangers	46	Partick T	36
1948–49*e*	Rangers	46	Dundee	45	Hibernian	39
1949–50*e*	Rangers	50	Hibernian	49	Hearts	43
1950–51*e*	Hibernian	48	Rangers*	38	Dundee	38
1951–52*e*	Hibernian	45	Rangers	41	East Fife	37
1952–53*e*	Rangers*	43	Hibernian	43	East Fife	39
1953–54*e*	Celtic	43	Hearts	38	Partick T	35
1954–55*e*	Aberdeen	49	Celtic	46	Rangers	41
1955–56*f*	Rangers	52	Aberdeen	46	Hearts*	45
1956–57*f*	Rangers	55	Hearts	53	Kilmarnock	42
1957–58*f*	Hearts	62	Rangers	49	Celtic	46
1958–59*f*	Rangers	50	Hearts	48	Motherwell	44
1959–60*f*	Hearts	54	Kilmarnock	50	Rangers*	42
1960–61*f*	Rangers	51	Kilmarnock	50	Third Lanark	42
1961–62*f*	Dundee	54	Rangers	51	Celtic	46
1962–63*f*	Rangers	57	Kilmarnock	48	Partick T	46
1963–64*f*	Rangers	55	Kilmarnock	49	Celtic*	47
1964–65*f*	Kilmarnock*	50	Hearts	50	Dunfermline Ath	49
1965–66*f*	Celtic	57	Rangers	55	Kilmarnock	45
1966–67*f*	Celtic	58	Rangers	55	Clyde	46
1967–68*f*	Celtic	63	Rangers	61	Hibernian	45
1968–69*f*	Celtic	54	Rangers	49	Dunfermline Ath	45
1969–70*f*	Celtic	57	Rangers	45	Hibernian	44
1970–71*f*	Celtic	56	Aberdeen	54	St Johnstone	44
1971–72*f*	Celtic	60	Aberdeen	50	Rangers	44
1972–73*f*	Celtic	57	Rangers	56	Hibernian	45
1973–74*f*	Celtic	53	Hibernian	49	Rangers	48
1974–75*f*	Rangers	56	Hibernian	49	Celtic	45

SECOND DIVISION to 1974–75

Maximum points: a 76; *b* 72; *c* 68; *d* 52; *e* 60; *f* 36; *g* 44; *h* 52.

1893–94*f*[a]	Hibernian	29	Cowlairs	27	Clyde	24
1894–95*f*	Hibernian	30	Motherwell	22	Port Glasgow	20
1895–96*f*	Abercorn	27	Leith Ath	23	Renton	21
1896–97*f*	Partick T	31	Leith Ath	27	Kilmarnock	21
1897–98*f*	Kilmarnock	29	Port Glasgow	25	Morton	22
1898–99*f*	Kilmarnock	32	Leith Ath	27	Port Glasgow	25
1899–1900*f*	Partick T	29	Morton	26	Port Glasgow	20
1900–01*f*	St Bernard's	26	Airdrieonians	23	Abercorn	21
1901–02*g*	Port Glasgow	32	Partick T	31	Motherwell	26
1902–03*g*	Airdrieonians	35	Motherwell	28	Ayr U	27
1903–04*g*	Hamilton A	37	Clyde	29	Ayr U	28
1904–05*g*	Clyde	32	Falkirk	28	Hamilton A	27

	First	Pts	Second	Pts	Third	Pts
1905–06*g*	Leith Ath	34	Clyde	31	Albion R	27
1906–07*g*	St Bernard's	32	Vale of Leven*	27	Arthurlie	27
1907–08*g*	Raith R	30	Dumbarton	‡‡27	Ayr U	27
1908–09*g*	Abercorn	31	Raith R*	28	Vale of Leven	28
1909–10*g*‡	Leith Ath	33	Raith R	33	St Bernard's	27
1910–11*g*	Dumbarton	31	Ayr U	27	Albion R	25
1911–12*g*	Ayr U	35	Abercorn	30	Dumbarton	27
1912–13*h*	Ayr U	34	Dunfermline Ath	33	East Stirling	32
1913–14*g*	Cowdenbeath	31	Albion R	27	Dunfermline Ath	26
1914–15*h*	Cowdenbeath*	37	St Bernard's*	37	Leith Ath	37
1921–22*a*	Alloa	60	Cowdenbeath	47	Armadale	45
1922–23*a*	Queen's Park	57	Clydebank	¶50	St Johnstone	¶45
1923–24*a*	St Johnstone	56	Cowdenbeath	55	Bathgate	44
1924–25*a*	Dundee U	50	Clydebank	48	Clyde	47
1925–26*a*	Dunfermline Ath	59	Clyde	53	Ayr U	52
1926–27*a*	Bo'ness	56	Raith R	49	Clydebank	45
1927–28*a*	Ayr U	54	Third Lanark	45	King's Park	44
1928–29*b*	Dundee U	51	Morton	50	Arbroath	47
1929–30*a*	Leith Ath*	57	East Fife	57	Albion R	54
1930–31*a*	Third Lanark	61	Dundee U	50	Dunfermline Ath	47
1931–32*a*	East Stirling*	55	St Johnstone	55	Raith Rovers*	46
1932–33*c*	Hibernian	54	Queen of the S	49	Dunfermline Ath	47
1933–34*c*	Albion R	45	Dunfermline Ath*	44	Arbroath	44
1934–35*c*	Third Lanark	52	Arbroath	50	St Bernard's	47
1935–36*c*	Falkirk	59	St Mirren	52	Morton	48
1936–37*c*	Ayr U	54	Morton	51	St Bernard's	48
1937–38*c*	Raith R	59	Albion R	48	Airdrieonians	47
1938–39*c*	Cowdenbeath	60	Alloa*	48	East Fife	48
1946–47*d*	Dundee	45	Airdrieonians	42	East Fife	31
1947–48*e*	East Fife	53	Albion R	42	Hamilton A	40
1948–49*e*	Raith R*	42	Stirling Albion	42	Airdrieonians*	41
1949–50*e*	Morton	47	Airdrieonians	44	St Johnstone*	36
1950–51*e*	Queen of the S*	45	Stirling Albion	45	Ayr U*	36
1951–52*e*	Clyde	44	Falkirk	43	Ayr U	39
1952–53*e*	Stirling Albion	44	Hamilton A	43	Queen's Park	37
1953–54*e*	Motherwell	45	Kilmarnock	42	Third Lanark*	36
1954–55*e*	Airdrieonians	46	Dunfermline Ath	42	Hamilton A	39
1955–56*b*	Queen's Park	54	Ayr U	51	St Johnstone	49
1956–57*b*	Clyde	64	Third Lanark	51	Cowdenbeath	45
1957–58*b*	Stirling Albion	55	Dunfermline Ath	53	Arbroath	47
1958–59*b*	Ayr U	60	Arbroath	51	Stenhousemuir	40
1959–60*b*	St Johnstone	53	Dundee U	50	Queen of the S	49
1960–61*b*	Stirling Albion	55	Falkirk	54	Stenhousemuir	50
1961–62*b*	Clyde	54	Queen of the S	53	Morton	44
1962–63*b*	St Johnstone	55	East Stirling	49	Morton	48
1963–64*b*	Morton	67	Clyde	53	Arbroath	46
1964–65*b*	Stirling Albion	59	Hamilton A	50	Queen of the S	45
1965–66*b*	Ayr U	53	Airdrieonians	50	Queen of the S	49
1966–67*b*	Morton	69	Raith R	58	Arbroath	57
1967–68*b*	St Mirren	62	Arbroath	53	East Fife	40
1968–69*b*	Motherwell	64	Ayr U	53	East Fife*	47
1969–70*b*	Falkirk	56	Cowdenbeath	55	Queen of the S	50
1970–71*b*	Partick T	56	East Fife	51	Arbroath	46
1971–72*b*	Dumbarton*	52	Arbroath	52	Stirling Albion	50
1972–73*b*	Clyde	56	Dunfermline Ath	52	Raith R*	47
1973–74*b*	Airdrieonians	60	Kilmarnock	59	Hamilton A	55
1974–75*a*	Falkirk	54	Queen of the S	53	Montrose	53

Elected to First Division: 1894 Clyde; 1897 Partick T; 1899 Kilmarnock; 1900 Partick T; 1902 Partick T; 1903 Airdrieonians; 1905 Falkirk, Aberdeen and Hamilton A; 1906 Clyde; 1910 Raith R; 1913 Ayr U.

RELEGATED FROM PREMIER DIVISION

1975–76 Dundee, St Johnstone
1976–77 Hearts, Kilmarnock
1977–78 Ayr U, Clydebank
1978–79 Hearts, Motherwell
1979–80 Dundee, Hibernian
1980–81 Kilmarnock, Hearts

RELEGATED FROM DIVISION 1

1975–76 Dunfermline Ath, Clyde
1976–77 Raith R, Falkirk
1977–78 Alloa Ath, East Fife
1978–79 Montrose, Queen of the S
1979–80 Arbroath, Clyde
1980–81 Stirling A, Berwick R

RELEGATED FROM DIVISION 1 (to 1973–74)

1921–22*Queen's Park, Dumbarton, Clydebank
1922–23 Albion R, Alloa Ath
1923–24 Clyde, Clydebank
1924–25 Third Lanark, Ayr U
1925–26 Raith R, Clydebank
1926–27 Morton, Dundee U
1927–28 Dunfermline Ath, Bo'ness
1928–29 Third Lanark, Raith R
1929–30 St Johnstone, Dundee U
1930–31 Hibernian, East Fife
1931–32 Dundee U, Leith Ath
1932–33 Morton, East Stirling
1933–34 Third Lanark, Cowdenbeath
1934–35 St Mirren, Falkirk
1935–36 Aidrieonians, Ayr U
1936–37 Dunfermline Ath, Albion R
1937–38 Dundee, Morton
1938–39 Queen's Park, Raith R
1946–47 Kilmarnock, Hamilton A
1947–48 Airdrieonians, Queen's Park
1948–49 Morton, Albion R
1949–50 Queen of the S, Stirling Albion
1950–51 Clyde, Falkirk
1951–52 Morton, Stirling Albion
1952–53 Motherwell, Third Lanark
1953–54 Airdrieonians, Hamilton A
1954–55 No clubs relegated
1955–56 Stirling Albion, Clyde
1956–57 Dunfermline Ath, Ayr U
1957–58 East Fife, Queen's Park
1958–59 Queen of the S, Falkirk
1959–60 Arbroath, Stirling Albion
1960–61 Ayr U, Clyde
1961–62 St Johnstone, Stirling Albion
1962–63 Clyde, Raith R
1963–64 Queen of the S, East Stirling
1964–65 Airdrieonians, Third Lanark
1965–66 Morton, Hamilton A
1966–67 St Mirren, Ayr U
1967–68 Motherwell, Stirling Albion
1968–69 Falkirk, Arbroath
1969–70 Raith R, Partick T
1970–71 St Mirren, Cowdenbeath
1971–72 Clyde, Dunfermline Ath
1972–73 Kilmarnock, Airdrieonians
1973–74 East Fife, Falkirk

*Season 1921–22 – only 1 club promoted, 3 clubs relegated.

The Scottish Football League was reconstructed into three divisions at the end of the 1974–75 season, so the usual relegation statistics do not apply.

SCOTTISH FA CUP FINALS 1874–1981

Year	*Winners*	*Runners-up*	*Score*
1874	Queen's Park	Clydesdale	2-0
1875	Queen's Park	Renton	3-0
1876	Queen's Park	Third Lanark	2-0 after 1-1 draw
1877	Vale of Leven	Rangers	3-2 after 0-0 and 1-1 draws
1878	Vale of Leven	Third Lanark	1-0
1879	Vale of Leven*	Rangers	
1880	Queen's Park	Thornlibank	3-0
1881	Queen's Park†	Dumbarton	3-1
1882	Queen's Park	Dumbarton	4-1 after 2-2 draw
1883	Dumbarton	Vale of Leven	2-1 after 2-2 draw
1884	Queen's Park‡	Vale of Leven	
1885	Renton	Vale of Leven	3-1 after 0-0 draw
1886	Queen's Park	Renton	3-1
1887	Hibernian	Dumbarton	2-1
1888	Renton	Cambuslang	6-1
1889	Third Lanark§	Celtic	2-1
1890	Queen's Park	Vale of Leven	2-1 after 1-1 draw
1891	Hearts	Dumbarton	1-0
1892	Celtic¶	Queen's Park	5-1
1893	Queen's Park	Celtic	2-1
1894	Rangers	Celtic	3-1
1895	St Bernard's	Renton	2-1
1896	Hearts	Hibernian	3-1
1897	Rangers	Dumbarton	5-1
1898	Rangers	Kilmarnock	2-0
1899	Celtic	Rangers	2-0
1900	Celtic	Queen's Park	4-3
1901	Hearts	Celtic	4-3
1902	Hibernian	Celtic	1-0
1903	Rangers	Hearts	2-0 after 1-1 and 0-0 draws
1904	Celtic	Rangers	3-2
1905	Third Lanark	Rangers	3-1 after 0-0 draw
1906	Hearts	Third Lanark	1-0
1907	Celtic	Hearts	3-0
1908	Celtic	St Mirren	5-1
1909	••		
1910	Dundee	Clyde	2-1 after 2-2 and 0-0 draws
1911	Celtic	Hamilton A	2-0 after 0-0 draw
1912	Celtic	Clyde	2-0
1913	Falkirk	Raith R	2-0
1914	Celtic	Hibernian	4-1 after 0-0 draw
1920	Kilmarnock	Albion R	3-2
1921	Partick T	Rangers	1-0
1922	Morton	Rangers	1-0
1923	Celtic	Hibernian	1-0
1924	Airdrieonians	Hibernian	2-0
1925	Celtic	Dundee	2-1
1926	St Mirren	Celtic	2-0
1927	Celtic	East Fife	3-1
1928	Rangers	Celtic	4-0
1929	Kilmarnock	Rangers	2-0
1930	Rangers	Partick T	2-1 after 0-0 draw
1931	Celtic	Motherwell	4-2 after 2-2 draw
1932	Rangers	Kilmarnock	3-0 after 1-1 draw
1933	Celtic	Motherwell	1-0
1934	Rangers	St Mirren	5-0
1935	Rangers	Hamilton A	2-1
1936	Rangers	Third Lanark	1-0
1937	Celtic	Aberdeen	2-1
1938	East Fife	Kilmarnock	4-2 after 1-1 draw
1939	Clyde	Motherwell	4-0
1947	Aberdeen	Hibernian	2-1
1948	Rangers	Morton	1-0 after 1-1 draw
1949	Rangers	Clyde	4-1
1950	Rangers	East Fife	3-0
1951	Celtic	Motherwell	1-0
1952	Motherwell	Dundee	4-0

Year	*Winners*	*Runners-up*	*Score*
1953	Rangers	Aberdeen	1-0 after 1-1 draw
1954	Celtic	Aberdeen	2-1
1955	Clyde	Celtic	1-0 after 1-1 draw
1956	Hearts	Celtic	3-1
1957	Falkirk	Kilmarnock	2-1 after 1-1 draw
1958	Clyde	Hibernian	1-0
1959	St Mirren	Aberdeen	3-1
1960	Rangers	Kilmarnock	2-0
1961	Dunfermline Ath	Celtic	2-0 after 0-0 draw
1962	Rangers	St Mirren	2-0
1963	Rangers	Celtic	3-0 after 1-1 draw
1964	Rangers	Dundee	3-1
1965	Celtic	Dunfermline Ath	3-2
1966	Rangers	Celtic	1-0 after 0-0 draw
1967	Celtic	Aberdeen	2-0
1968	Dunfermline Ath	Hearts	3-1
1969	Celtic	Rangers	4-0
1970	Aberdeen	Celtic	3-1
1971	Celtic	Rangers	2-1 after 1-1 draw
1972	Celtic	Hibernian	6-1
1973	Rangers	Celtic	3-2
1974	Celtic	Dundee U	3-0
1975	Celtic	Airdrieonians	3-1
1976	Rangers	Hearts	3-1
1977	Celtic	Rangers	1-0
1978	Rangers	Aberdeen	2-1
1979	Rangers	Hibernian	3-2 after 0-0 and 0-0 draws
1980	Celtic	Rangers	1-0
1981	Rangers	Dundee U	4-1 after 0-0 draw

*Vale of Leven awarded cup, Rangers failed to appear for replay after 1-1 draw.
†After Dumbarton protested the first game, which Queen's Park won 2-1.
‡Queen's Park awarded cup, Vale of Leven failing to appear.
§Replay by order of Scottish FA because of playing conditions in first match, won 3-0 by Third Lanark.
¶After mutual protested game which Celtic won 1-0.
•• Owing to riot, the cup was withheld after two drawn games – Celtic 2-1, Rangers 2-1.

SCOTTISH ATTENDANCES

Attendances in the Scottish League and League Cup during 1980–81 totalled 2,870,731 – a drop of nearly half a million on 1979–80, when the final figures were 3,361,011.

SCOTTISH LEAGUE CUP FINALS 1946–81

Season	*Winners*	*Runners-up*	*Score*
1946–47	Rangers	Aberdeen	4-0
1947–48	East Fife	Falkirk	4-1 after 0-0 draw
1948–49	Rangers	Raith R	2-0
1949–50	East Fife	Dunfermline Ath	3-0
1950–51	Motherwell	Hibernian	3-0
1951–52	Dundee	Rangers	3-2
1952–53	Dundee	Kilmarnock	2-0
1953–54	East Fife	Partick T	3-2
1954–55	Hearts	Motherwell	4-2
1955–56	Aberdeen	St Mirren	2-1
1956–57	Celtic	Partick T	3-0 after 0-0 draw
1957–58	Celtic	Rangers	7-1
1958–59	Hearts	Partick T	5-1
1959–60	Hearts	Third Lanark	2-1
1960–61	Rangers	Kilmarnock	2-0
1961–62	Rangers	Hearts	3-1 after 1-1 draw
1962–63	Hearts	Kilmarnock	1-0
1963–64	Rangers	Morton	5-0
1964–65	Rangers	Celtic	2-1
1965–66	Celtic	Rangers	2-1
1966–67	Celtic	Rangers	1-0
1967–68	Celtic	Dundee	5-3
1968–69	Celtic	Hibernian	6-2
1969–70	Celtic	St Johnstone	1-0
1970–71	Rangers	Celtic	1-0
1971–72	Partick T	Celtic	4-1
1972–73	Hibernian	Celtic	2-1
1973–74	Dundee	Celtic	1-0
1974–75	Celtic	Hibernian	6-3
1975–76	Rangers	Celtic	1-0
1976–77	Aberdeen	Celtic	2-1
1977–78	Rangers	Celtic	2-1
1978–79	Rangers	Aberdeen	2-1
1979–80	Dundee U	Aberdeen	3-0 after 0-0 draw
1980–81	Dundee U	Dundee	3-0

BELL'S LEAGUE CUP 1980–81

FIRST ROUND FIRST LEG

13 AUG

Ayr U (1) 1 *(Christie)*

Morton (1) 2 *(Ritchie, Hutchison)* 3730

Ayr U: Rennie; Shanks, Nicol, McSherry, McAllister (Hendry), Fleeting, Frye (Cashmore), Love, Morris, Connor, Christie.
Morton: Baines; Holmes, Orr, Anderson, McLaughlin, McLaren, Hutchison, Rooney, Thomson, Tolmie (Scott), Ritchie.

East Fife (1) 2 *(Thomson R. pen, Herd)*

Dundee U (3) 5 *(Milne 2, Ward, Narey, Sturrock pen)* 1992

East Fife: Gorman; Scott J., Clarke, McLaren, Beveridge, Thomson R., Mitchell, Cairns, Herd, Tait (Scott G.), Thomson A. (Huskie).
Dundee U: McAlpine; Kirkwood, Stark, Phillip, Hegarty, Narey, Milne, Sturrock (Bannon), Payne, Addison, Ward.

Kilmarnock (1) 1 *(Cramond)*

Airdrieonians (0) 0 3500

Kilmarnock: McCulloch; Robertson, Cockburn, Mauchlen, Clarke, McDicken, Docherty, Gibson, Cairney, Cramond, Houston (Bourke).
Airdrieonians: McGarr; Erwin, Rodger, Walker, March, Anderson, McKeown, Clark, Russell (Thomson), Gordon, McGuire (McCulloch).

Queen's Park (0) 1 *(Nicholson)*

East Stirling (0) 0 519

Queen's Park: Atkins; McSkimming, Dickson, Rennie, McGregor, Gillespie, McFarlane, McNiven, Nicholson, McCoy, Falconer (Cook).
East Stirling: Kelly; Watt, Blair, Gourlay, Rennie, Simpson, Grant, McCulley, McCaig, Bennett (Lamont), Robertson.

Raith R (2) 3 *(Harrow, Candlish, Ballantyne pen)*

Falkirk (2) 2 *(Leetion, Perry)* 1700

Raith R: McDermott; Houston, Candlish, Ford, Forsyth, Thomson, Ballantyne, Urquhart, Harrow, Carroll, Lawson.
Falkirk: Watson G.; Burrell, Nicol (Oliver M.), Watson D., Brown, Hay, Hoggan, Leetion, Perry, McRoberts, Mitchell (Oliver A.).

St Johnstone (0) 0

Clydebank (1) 2 *(Miller, McGorm)* 1379

St Johnstone: Tulloch; Mackay, Kilgour, Redford, Rutherford, Caldwell, Brannigan (McNeil), McCoist, Fleming, Morton, Gilchrist.
Clydebank: Gallacher; Gervaise, Colgan, McLaughlin, Evans (Sharkey), Given, Ronald, Houston, Miller, McGorm, McCabe.

FIRST ROUND SECOND LEG

19 AUG

East Stirling (0) 0

Queen's Park (2) 4 *(McCoy 3, Nicholson)* 500

East Stirling: Kelly; Watt, Blair, Gourlay, Rennie, Simpson (McCulley), Grant, Lamont (Taylor), Sharp, Robertson, McCaig.
Queen's Park: Atkins; McSkimming, Dickson, Rennie, McGregor, McFarlane, Sinclair, Gillespie, Irvine, Nicholson, McCoy.

20 AUG

Airdrieonians (0) 0

Kilmarnock (0) 1 *(Cramond)* 3000

Airdrieonians: McGarr; Erwin, Rodger, Walker, March, Anderson, McKeown (McCulloch), Clark, Russell, Gordon (Thomson), McGuire.
Kilmarnock: McCulloch; McLean, Robertson, Mauchlen, Clarke, McDicken, Gibson, Maxwell, McBride, Cramond, Street.

Clydebank (0) 0

St Johnstone (0) 0 500

Clydebank: Gallacher; Gervaise, Colgan, McLaughlin, Evans, Given, Ronald, Houston, Miller, McGorm, McCabe.
St Johnstone: Tulloch; Mackay, Kilgour, Redford, Rutherford, Caldwell, Pelosi, McCoist, Fleming, Morton, Brannigan.

Dundee U (1) 4 *(Ward 2, Hegarty, Payne)*

East Fife (0) 0 3227

Dundee U: McAlpine; Stark (Reilly), Murray, Bannon, Hegarty, Narey, Kirkwood, Sturrock, Payne, Addison, Ward.
East Fife: Gorman; Scott J., Clarke, McLaren, Halley, Cairns, Marnoch (Honeyman), Mitchell, Herd (Beveridge), Thomson R., Scott G.

Falkirk (0) 0

Raith R (1) 2 *(Ford, Steen)* 2500

Falkirk: Allan; Hoggan, Rose, Nicol, Brown (Oliver M.), Hay, Perry, Watson D. (Cribbes), Leetion, McRoberts, Oliver A.
Raith R: McDermott; Houston, Candlish, Ford, Forsyth, Thomson, Ballantyne (Carroll), Urquhart (McFarlane), Harrow, Steen, Lawson.

Morton (0) 0

Ayr U (1) 2 *(Morris, Armour)* 2000

Morton: Baines; Miller, Holmes, Anderson, Orr, Rooney, McNeil, Hutchison, Thomson (McLaren), Tolmie, Ritchie.
Ayr U: Rennie; Shanks, Nicol, McColl, Hendry, Armour, Frye, Love, Morris, Connor (Fleeting), Cashmore.

SECOND ROUND FIRST LEG

26 AUG

Albion R (1) 1 *(Campbell)*

St Mirren (0) 2 *(Hamill og, Richardson)* 1400

Albion R: Hill M.; Allan, Docherty, Franchetti, Meikle, Hamill, Campbell, Hill H., Houston, Hannigan (Higgins), Gillespie.
St Mirren: Thomson; Young, Beckett, Richardson, Fulton, Reid, Abercromby, Stark, Somner, McCormack, McDougall.

Dundee (1) 2 *(Fletcher 2)*

Arbroath (0) 0 3745

Dundee: Geddes; MacLaren, Schaedler, Glennie, McGeachie, Shirra, Scott, Fleming, Fletcher, Sinclair, Murphy (Stephen).
Arbroath: Lister; Forsyth, Rylance, Downie, McKenzie, Gavine, Harley, Docherty, Mylles (Donald), Shaw, Yule.

27 AUG

Aberdeen (4) 8 *(McGhee 3, Watson 2, Jarvie 2, Bell)*

Berwick R (0) 1 *(Egan)* 11,800

Aberdeen: Leighton; Kennedy, McMaster, Watson, McLeish, Miller, Strachan (Bell), Cowan (Rougvie), McGhee, Jarvie, Scanlon.
Berwick R: McLaren; McCann, Deakin, McDougall, McDowell, Wheatley, Davidson, Romaines, Smith G., Tait (Dixon), Egan (Smith D.).

Alloa (0) 0

Hibernian (1) 2 *(Rae, MacLeod)* 1750

Alloa: Drummond; Robertson, Rae, Purdie, Stewart, Holt, Smith (Morrison), McIntosh, McComb, McNab (Scott), Shields.
Hibernian: McArthur; Brown, Duncan, McNamara, Paterson, Cormack, Callachan, Hamill, MacLeod, Rae, Murray.

Brechin C (0) 0

Clyde (0) 0 700

Brechin C: Neilson; Watt, Keating, McLeod, Glover, Reid, Campbell I., Campbell R., Paterson, Elvin, Kyles (Henderson).
Clyde: McWilliams; Brogan, Filippi, Ahern, Dempsey, McAlpine, Hyslop, Kean, Masterton, O'Neill, Dolan.

Dumbarton (0) 0

Raith R (0) 1 *(Harrow)* 800

Dumbarton: Carson; Sinclair, MacLeod, McCluskey, Gallacher J., Coyle J., Brown, McGrain, Gallagher B., Blair, Rankin.
Raith R: McDermott; Houston, Candlish, Ford, Forsyth, Thomson, Ballantyne, Urquhart, Harrow, Steen, Lawson.

Dundee U (2) 4 *(Bannon 2, Sturrock, Hegarty)*

Cowdenbeath (0) 0 3401

Dundee U: McAlpine; Kirkwood, Stark, Bannon, Hegarty, Narey, Milne, Sturrock, Payne, Addison, Ward (Dodds).
Cowdenbeath: Allan; Rolland, Markey, Hunter D., Russell, Tierney, Forrest (Ferguson), Ferrier, Liddle, Marshall, Steele.

Forfar Ath (0) 0

Rangers (1) 2 *(McAdam 2)* 4500

Forfar Ath: Kennedy; Bennett, McPhee, Brown, Clark, Gillies, Gallacher, Farningham, Watt (Wildridge), Leitch (Laurie), Robb.
Rangers: McCloy; Jardine, Miller, Forsyth, Jackson, Bett, Cooper, MacDonald, McAdam, Redford, Johnston.

Hamilton A (3) 5 *(Fairlie 2, McDowall 2, McGrogan)*

Stranraer (0) 1 *(Neil)* 1800

Hamilton A: Ferguson; Frew, Brown, Wright, McDougall, Alexander, McDowall, McManus, Fairlie, McAdams, McGrogan.
Stranraer: Greenhorn; Hopkins, McDonald, Hay, Murdoch, McCutcheon (Shields), Harvey, Gibb, Neil, McGuigan, Wilson.

Hearts (1) 2 *(Robertson, MacDonald)*

Montrose (0) 1 *(Robb)* 4211

Hearts: Brough; Robinson, Jefferies, Boyd, Liddell, Kidd, Bowman, Conn (Gibson), O'Connor, Robertson C. (White), MacDonald.
Montrose: Moffat; Taylor, Johnston D. (McDonald), Forbes, Sheran, Beedie, Forrest, Milne, Murray, Robb, Wright (Johnston H.).

Kilmarnock (0) 0

Dunfermline Ath (0) 0 2000

Kilmarnock: McCulloch; McLean, Robertson, Mauchlen, Clarke, McDicken, Street (McReady), Maxwell, McBride, Morrison, Gibson (Bourke).
Dunfermline Ath: Whyte; Thomson, Mercer, Salton, Leishman, Hegarty, McNaughton, Robertson R., Leonard, Bowie (Donnelly), O'Brien.

Meadowbank T (0) 1 *(Downie)*

Clydebank (2) 2 *(Given, Houston)* 350

Meadowbank T: McKell; Dunn, Fraser (Henry), Boyd, Brown, Conroy, Sprott, Downie, Georgeson (McQuade), Leetion, Jobson.
Clydebank: Gallacher; Gervaise, Colgan, McLaughlin, Evans, Given, Ronald, Houston, Miller, McGorm, McCabe.

Partick T (2) 3 *(Higgins 2, O'Hara)*

Queen's Park (0) 1 *(Dickson)* 2000

Partick T: Rough; Doyle, Lapsley, Higgins, Welsh, Whittaker, Park, Jardine, O'Hara, McDonald, Watson (Gibson).
Queen's Park: Atkins; McSkimming, Dickson (Grant), Cook, McGregor, McFarlane, Sinclair, Gillespie, Irvine, Nicholson, McCoy.

Queen of the S (0) 1 *(Alexander)*

Ayr U (0) 2 *(Morris, Christie)* 2198

Queen of the S: Dunlop; Dickson, McChesney, Learmont, Clark, Roddy, Phillips, Mitchell, Alexander, Coughlin (Gordon), Robertson J.
Ayr U: Rennie; Shanks, Nicol, McSherry, Hendry, Fleeting, Frye (Christie), Love, Morris, Connor, Cashmore.

Stenhousemuir (0) 0

Motherwell (0) 0 800

Stenhousemuir: Howie; McCraw, Rennie, Meakin, Black, Mullen, Jack, McLeod, Hancock, Jenkins, Murray (Kirkland).
Motherwell: Sproat; O'Rourke, McLelland C., Smith, Carson, Kidd, Clinging, Larnach, Irvine, McLaughlin, Gahagan (McLelland S.).

Stirling Albion (0) 1 *(Irvine)*

Celtic (0) 0 5800

Stirling Albion: Arthur; Nicol, Steedman, Farmer, Kennedy J., Young, McPhee, Gray, Kennedy A., Beaton, Irvine (McGregor).
Celtic: Bonner; Sneddon, McGrain, Aitken, McAdam, MacLeod (Conroy), Provan, Sullivan, McGarvey, Burns, McCluskey.

SECOND ROUND SECOND LEG

30 AUG

Arbroath (0) 0

Dundee (1) 3 *(McClaren, Fletcher, Sinclair)* 2855

Arbroath: Lister; Docherty, Rylance, Downie, McKenzie, Gavine (Ronald), Forsyth, Kydd, Mylles S., Shaw, Yule (Mylles T.).
Dundee: Geddes; McGeachie, Schaedler, MacLaren, Glennie, Shirra, Mackie (Barr), Fleming, Sinclair (Murphy), Scott, Fletcher.

Ayr U (0) 1 *(Cashmore)*

Queen of the S (0) 0 2660

Ayr U: Rennie; Shanks, Nicol, McSherry, Hendry, Fleeting, Cashmore, Love, Morris, Connor (Armour), Christie.
Queen of the S: Dunlop; Learmont, McChesney, Dickson, Clark, Roddy, Phillips (Gordon), Mitchell, Alexander, Coughlin (Robertson M.), Robertson J.

Berwick R (0) 0

Aberdeen (3) 4 *(Strachan, Hewitt, De Clerck, Kennedy)* 1088

Berwick R: Davidson; McCann, Deakin, Gregson (Smith G.), McDowell, Moyes, Smith D., Romaines, McLeod, Tait, Egan.
Aberdeen: De Clerck; Kennedy, Rougvie, Garner, McLeish (Cowan), Miller, Strachan, Bell, Morrison, Hewitt, Davidson.

Celtic (1) 6 *aet (Sullivan, Burns 2, Provan, Nicholas 2)*

Stirling Albion (1) 1 *(McPhee)* 16,000

Celtic: Bonner; Sneddon, McGrain, Aitken, McAdam, MacLeod, Provan, Sullivan, McGarvey (Conroy), Burns, McCluskey (Nicholas).
Stirling Albion: Arthur; Nicol, Steedman, Farmer (Moffat), Kennedy J., Young, McPhee, Gray, Kennedy A., Beaton, Irvine (McGregor).

Clyde (0) 2 *(Dolan 2)*

Brechin C (0) 1 *(Campbell I.)* 600

Clyde: McWilliams; Brogan, Filippi, Ahern, Dempsey (Kinnear), McAlpine, Brown, Kean, Masterton, O'Neill, Dolan.
Brechin C: Neilson; Watt, Keating, McLeod, Glover, Reid (Henderson), Campbell I., Campbell R., Paterson, Elvin, Kyles.

Clydebank (0) 2 *(Houston, Dunn og)*

Meadowbank T (0) 1 *(Jobson)* 500

Clydebank: Gallacher; Gervaise, Colgan, O'Rourke, Evans, Given, Ronald (Harkins), Houston, Miller, McGorm, McCabe.
Meadowbank T: McKell; Dunn, Conroy, Boyd, Brown, Downie (Davidson), Henry, Leetion, Jobson, Sprott, McQuade (Georgeson).

Cowdenbeath (0) 1 *(Liddle)*

Dundee U (2) 4 *(Hegarty, Ward 2, Sturrock)* 1232

Cowdenbeath: Allan; Rolland, Markey, Hunter D., Russell, Tierney, Forrest, Ferrier, Liddle, Marshall, Steele W. (Ferguson).
Dundee U: McAlpine; Kirkwood, Stark, Phillip, Hegarty, Narey, Milne, Sturrock, Bannon, Addison (Campbell), Ward.

Dunfermline Ath (0) 1 *(McNaughton)*

Kilmarnock (1) 2 *(Clarke, McBride)* 3500

Dunfermline Ath: Whyte; Thomson, Mercer, Salton, Leishman, Hegarty, McNaughton, Robertson R., Leonard (Donnelly), Bowie (Williams), O'Brien.
Kilmarnock: McCulloch; McLean, Robertson, Maxwell, Clarke, McDicken, McCready, Gibson, Bourke (Street), Mauchlen, McBride.

Hibernian (1) 1 *(Hamill)*

Alloa (1) 1 *(McIntosh)* 2500

Hibernian: McArthur; Brown, Duncan, McNamara, Paterson (Torrance), Cormack (Clarke), Callachan, Hamill, MacLeod, Rae, Murray.
Alloa: Drummond; Robertson, Abel, Purdie, Stewart (Hamilton), Holt, McIntosh, Morrison, Scott, McNab (Grant), Shields.

Montrose (0) 1 *(Milne)*

Hearts (3) 3 *(Robertson C. 3)* 1600

Montrose: Moffat; Taylor, Johnston D., Forbes, Sheran, Beedie (McDonald), Forrest, Milne, Murray, Robb, Johnston H.
Hearts: Brough; Robinson, Jefferies, Boyd, Liddell, Kidd, Bowman, Gibson, O'Connor, Robertson C. (Robertson M.), MacDonald.

Motherwell (1) 6 *(Clinging 2, Kidd, McLaughlin 3)*

Stenhousemuir (0) 1 *(Kirkland)* 1839

Motherwell: Sproat; O'Rourke, McLelland C., McLeod, Carson, Larnach, McLelland S., Kidd, McKeever (Irvine) (Gahagan), McLaughlin, Clinging.
Stenhousemuir: Howie; McCraw, Rennie, Meakin, Black, Mullen, Jack (Kirkland), McLeod (Frickleton), Hancock, Jenkins, Murray.

Queen's Park (1) 1 *(Irvine)*

Partick T (0) 1 *(Watson)* 1472

Queen's Park: Atkins, McSkimming, Dickson, Rennie, McGregor, McFarlane (McNiven), Sinclair, Gillespie, Irvine, Nicholson, McCoy.
Partick T: Rough; Murray, Whittaker, Campbell, Welsh, Watson, Park, Doyle, Higgins, O'Hara, Jardine (Gibson).

Raith R (0) 1 *aet (Lawson)*

Dumbarton (0) 1 *(Gallagher)* 1750

Raith R: McDermott; Houston, Candlish, Ford, Forsyth, Thomson, Ballantyne (Miller), Urquhart (Carroll), Harrow, Steen, Lawson.
Dumbarton: Carson; Sinclair, MacLeod, Clougherty, Gallacher, Coyle J., Martin (Marshall), Coyle T., Gallagher, Blair (Rankin), Brown.

Rangers (2) 3 *(Miller* pen, *Johnstone, McAdam* pen*)*

Forfar Ath (1) 1 *(Robb)* 15,000

Rangers: McCloy; Jardine, Miller, Forsyth (Russell), Jackson, Bett, Cooper, Johnstone, McAdam, Redford, Johnston (McLean).
Forfar Ath: Kennedy; Bennett, McPhee, Brown, Clark, Gillies, Gallacher, Farningham, Watt, Leitch (Wildridge), Robb (Laurie).

St Mirren (2) 5 *(Richardson, Somner 3, Stark)*

Albion R (0) 0 3770

St Mirren: Thomson; Young, Beckett, Richardson, Dunlop, Fulton, Abercromby, Stark, Somner, Weir, McDougall.
Albion R: Hill M., Allan (Ross), Hamill, Franchetti, Meikle, McPherson, Campbell, Hill H., Houston, Hannigan (Martin), Gillespie.

Stranraer (0) 0

Hamilton A (1) 2 *(Wright, McAdams)* 500

Stranraer: Greenhorn; Hopkins, Shields, McDonald, Hay, Murdoch, Sim, Harvey, Gibb, Neil, McGuigan.
a1*Hamilton A:* Ferguson; Frew, Brown, Wright, McDougall, Marshall, McDowall, McManus, Fairlie (Howie), Young, McGrogan (McAdams).

THIRD ROUND FIRST LEG

3 SEPT

Clyde (0) 0

Hibernian (1) 2 *(Rae, MacLeod)* 1300

Clyde: McWilliams; Brogan, Filippi, Ahern, Kinnear, McAlpine, Brown, Kean, Masterton, O'Neill, Dolan.
Hibernian: McArthur; Brown J., Duncan, McNamara, Paterson, McGinn, Hamill, Callachan, MacLeod, Rae, Connolly.

Dundee (0) 0

Kilmarnock (0) 0 4388

Dundee: Geddes; McGeachie (Barr), Schaedler, MacLaren, Glennie, Shirra, Scott, Fleming (Murphy), Sinclair, Mackie, Fletcher.
Kilmarnock: McCulloch; McLean, Robertson, Maxwell, Clarke, McDicken, Gibson, McBride, Bourke, Mauchlen, Street.

Hearts (1) 2 *(Robertson, Bowman)*

Ayr U (1) 3 *(Connor 2 [1 pen], Cashmore)* 5364

Hearts: Brough; Robinson, Jefferies, Boyd, Liddell, Kidd (Paterson), Bowman, Gibson, O'Connor, Robertson C., MacDonald.
Ayr U: Rennie; Shanks, Nicol, McSherry, Hendry, Fleeting, Cashmore, Love, Morris, Connor, Christie.

Motherwell (2) 2 *(McKeever, Clinging)*

Dundee U (1) 1 *(Addison)* 3327

Motherwell: Sproat; O'Rourke, McLelland C., Carberry, Carson, Larnach, McLelland S. (Gahagan), Kidd, McKeever, McLaughlin, Clinging.
Dundee U: McAlpine; Kirkwood, Stark (Kopel), Phillip, Hegarty, Narey, Milne, Sturrock, Bannon, Addison, Ward (Payne).

Partick T (2) 2 *(Gibson 2)*

St Mirren (0) 0 4000

Partick T: Rough; Doyle, Whittaker, Jardine, Campbell, Welsh, Park, Gibson, O'Hara, Higgins, Watson.
St Mirren: Thomson; Young, Beckett, Richardson, Fulton, Dunlop, Abercromby, Stark, Somner, McCormack (Bone), Logan (McDougall).

Raith R (0) 0

Clydebank (1) 1 *(Houston)* 2000

Raith R: McDermott; Houston, Candlish, Ford, Forsyth, Thomson, Ballantyne, Urquhart, Harrow, Carroll, Lawson.
Clydebank: Gallacher; Gervaise, Colgan, O'Rourke, Evans, Given, Ronald, Houston, Miller, McGorm, McCabe.

Rangers (1) 1 *(McAdam)*

Aberdeen (0) 0 30,000

Rangers: McCloy; Jardine, Miller, Forsyth T., Jackson, Bett, McLean (Stevens), MacDonald (Johnston), McAdam, Redford, Cooper.
Aberdeen: Leighton; Kennedy, Rougvie, Watson, McLeish, Miller, Strachan, McMaster, McGhee, Jarvie (Hewitt), Scanlon (Bell).

22 SEPT

Hamilton A (0) 1 *(McDowall)*

Celtic (2) 3 *(Doyle, Nicholas, Burns)* 9500

Hamilton A: Ferguson; Frew, Brown (McAdams), Alexander, McDougall, Marshall, McDowall, Graham (McManus), Fairlie, Wright, McGrogan.
Celtic: Bonner; Sneddon, McGrain, Aitken, MacDonald, McAdam, Provan, Sullivan, Doyle, Burns, Nicholas.

THIRD ROUND SECOND LEG

24 SEPT

Aberdeen (2) 3 *(McMaster, Strachan 2 pens)*

Rangers (0) 1 *(McAdam)* 19,000

Aberdeen: Leighton; Kennedy, Rougvie, Watson, McLeish, Miller, Strachan, McMaster, McGhee, Bell (Hewitt), Scanlon.
Rangers: McCloy; Jardine, Miller, Forsyth T., Jackson, Bett, Cooper (McLean), Johnstone, McAdam, Redford, Johnston (MacDonald).

Ayr U (1) 4 *(Connor, Robinson og, Frye, Morris)*

Hearts (0) 0 4484

Ayr U: Rennie; Shanks, Nicol, Hendry, McAllister, Fleeting, Frye, Armour, Morris, Connor, Christie.
Hearts: Brough; Robinson, Shields, Denny, Liddell, Jefferies, Bowman (Mackay), Conn, O'Connor, Robertson C. (Gibson), MacDonald.

Celtic (2) 4 *(Nicholas, Burns, McGarvey 2)*

Hamilton A (0) 1 *(McManus)* 10,000

Celtic: Bonner; Sneddon, McGrain, Aitken, MacDonald, McAdam, Provan, Sullivan, Doyle, Burns, Nicholas (McGarvey).
Hamilton A: Ferguson; Frew, Marshall, Gormley, McDougall, Alexander, McDowall, Graham (McManus), Fairlie, Wright, McAdams.

Clydebank (0) 1 *(Given pen)*

Raith R (0) 0 1000

Clydebank: Gallacher; Gervaise, Fallon, McLaughlin, Evans, Given, Ronald, Houston, Miller, McGorm (Sweeney), McCabe.
Raith R: McDermott; Houston, Candlish, Ford, Thomson, Steel, Lawson (Ballantyne), Urquhart, Harrow, Steen (Carroll), Miller.

Dundee U (1) 4 *(Holt, Sturrock 2, Milne)*

Motherwell (0) 2 *(Irvine, Clinging)* 5628

Dundee U: McAlpine; Stark, Phillip, Smith W. (Milne), Hegarty, Narey, Bannon, Sturrock, Pettigrew (Kirkwood), Holt, Dodds.
Motherwell: Sproat; O'Rourke, McLeod, Smith J., Carson, Soutar, McLelland, Kidd, McKeever (Irvine), Gahagan, Clinging.

Hibernian (0) 2 *(Jamieson 2)*

Clyde (0) 1 *(Ahern pen)* 3773

Hibernian: McArthur; Brown, Duncan, McNamara, Paterson, Callachan, Jamieson, Rae, MacLeod, Connolly, Best.
Clyde: McWilliams; Brogan, Filippi, Dempsey, Boyd, Ahern, Kean, O'Neill (Edgar), Masterton, Hyslop (Dolan), McAlpine.

Kilmarnock (0) 0 *aet*

Dundee (0) 0 2401

Dundee won 5-3 on penalties.

Kilmarnock: Brown; McLean, Robertson, Clarke, Armstrong, McDicken, Gibson (Street), Mauchlen, Bourke, Cramond (Maxwell), Houston.
Dundee: Geddes; Barr, Schaedler, Fraser, Glennie, MacLaren, Mackie (Murphy), Scrimgeour, Sinclair, Fletcher (Williamson), Shirra.

St Mirren (0) 0

Partick T (0) 0 5700

St Mirren: Thomson; Young, Beckett, Richardson, McCormack, Copland, McDougall, Stark, Somner, Weir, Bone.
Partick T: Rough; Doyle, Whittaker, Gibson, Campbell, Welsh, Park, O'Hara, Jardine, Higgins, Watson.

QUARTER-FINALS FIRST LEG

8 OCT

Ayr U (1) 2 *(Frye 2)*

Hibernian (1) 2 *(Wilson, MacLeod)* 4717

Ayr U: Rennie; Shanks, Nicol, McColl, Hendry, Fleeting, Frye, Love, Morris, Connor, Christie.
Hibernian: McArthur; Brown, Duncan, McNamara, Paterson, Callachan, Wilson, Rae, MacLeod, Connolly, Best.

Clydebank (2) 2 *(McGorm, Miller)*

Dundee U (0) 1 *(Bannon)* 1600

Clydebank: Gallacher; Gervaise, Fallon, McLaughlin, Evans, Given, Ronald, Houston, Miller, McGorm, McCabe.
Dundee U: McAlpine; Stark, Kopel, Phillip (Dodds), Hegarty, Narey, Bannon, Sturrock, Pettigrew, Holt, Payne.

Dundee (0) 0

Aberdeen (0) 0 10,300

Dundee: Geddes; Barr, Williamson, Fraser, Glennie, MacLaren, Mackie, McGeachie, Sinclair, Fleming (Murphy), Shirra.
Aberdeen: Leighton; Kennedy, McMaster, Watson, Rougvie, Miller, Strachan, Jarvie, McGhee, Bell (Cowan), Scanlon.

Partick T (0) 0

Celtic (0) 1 *(Nicholas pen)* 18,000

Partick T: Rough; Doyle, Whittaker, Gibson, Campbell, Welsh, Park, O'Hara, Higgins, Watson, Jardine.
Celtic: Bonner; Sneddon, McGrain, Aitken, MacDonald, McAdam, McCluskey, Sullivan, McGarvey, MacLeod, Nicholas.

QUARTER-FINALS SECOND LEG

20 OCT

Celtic (0) 2 *aet (Burns, MacDonald)*

Partick T (1) 1 *(O'Hara)* 12,000

Celtic: Bonner; Sneddon, McGrain (Conroy), Aitken, MacDonald, McAdam, Provan, Sullivan (McGarvey), Doyle, Burns, Nicholas.
Partick T: Rough; Murray, Lapsley, Campbell (McDonald), Whittaker, Welsh, Park, O'Hara, Clark (McLeod), Watson, Jardine.

22 OCT

Hibernian (0) 0 *aet*

Ayr U (0) 2 *(Morris, Frye)* 5500

Hibernian: Kelly; Brown, Duncan, Brazil, Paterson, Callachan, Jamieson (Wilson), Rae, MacLeod, Cormack (Rice), Connolly.
Ayr U: Rennie; Shanks, Nicol, McColl, Hendry, Fleeting, Cashmore (Frye), Love, Morris, Connor, Christie.

29 OCT

Aberdeen (0) 0

Dundee (0) 1 *(Fraser)* 14,060

Aberdeen: Leighton; Kennedy (Watson), Rougvie, Bell, McLeish, Miller, Strachan, Cowan, McGhee, Jarvie, Scanlon.
Dundee: Geddes; Barr, Schaedler, Fraser, Glennie, MacLaren, Murphy, McGeachie, Sinclair, Mackie (Fletcher), Williamson.

Dundee U (2) 4 *(Ward 2, Hegarty, Sturrock)*

Clydebank (0) 1 *(Miller)* 5265

Dundee U: McAlpine; Stark, Kopel, Phillip, Hegarty, Narey, Bannon, Ward, Payne, Sturrock, Dodds (Pettigrew).
Clydebank: Gallacher; Gervaise, Fallon, McLaughlin, Evans, Colgan, Sweeney (McGorm), Houston (Ronald), Miller, Given, McCabe.

SEMI-FINALS FIRST LEG

5 NOV

Ayr U (0) 1 *(Connor)*

Dundee (1) 1 *(Sinclair)* 6801

Ayr U: Rennie; Shanks, Nicol, McColl, Hendry, Fleeting, Frye (Cashmore), Love (McSherry), Morris, Connor, Christie.
Dundee: Geddes; Barr, Schaedler, Fraser, Glennie, MacLaren, Murphy, McGeachie (Shirra), Sinclair, Mackie (Fletcher), Williamson.

12 NOV

Dundee U (1) 1 *(Bannon)*

Celtic (0) 1 *(Nicholas)* 14,000

Dundee U: McAlpine; Stark, Kopel, Phillip, Hegarty, Narey, Bannon, Kirkwood, Pettigrew, Sturrock, Dodds.
Celtic: Bonner; McGrain, Reid, Aitken, MacDonald, McAdam, Provan, Weir, McCluskey (McGarvey), Burns, Doyle (Nicholas).

SEMI-FINALS SECOND LEG

19 NOV

Celtic (0) 0

Dundee U (1) 3 *(Pettigrew, Dodds, Sturrock)* 21,000

Celtic: Bonner; McGrain, Reid, Aitken, McAdam, Weir, Provan, McCluskey (MacDonald), McGarvey (Doyle), Burns, Nicholas.
Dundee U: McAlpine; Holt, Kopel, Phillip, Hegarty, Narey, Bannon, Payne, Pettigrew, Sturrock, Dodds.

Dundee (1) 3 *(Williamson, Sinclair, Fraser)*

Ayr U (0) 2 *(Christie, McColl)* 9438

Dundee: Geddes; McGeachie, Schaedler (Mackie), Fraser, Glennie, MacLaren (Barr), Murphy, Stephen, Sinclair, Williamson, Shirra.
Ayr U: Rennie; Shanks, Nicol, McColl, Hendry, Fleeting, Frye, Armour, Morris, Connor, Christie.

FINAL (at Dens Park, Dundee)

6 DEC

Dundee (0) 0

Dundee U (1) 3 *(Dodds, Sturrock 2)* 24,466

Dundee: Geddes R.; Barr, Schaedler, Fraser, Glennie, McGeachie, Mackie, Stephen, Sinclair, Williamson, Geddes A.
Dundee U: McAlpine; Holt, Kopel, Phillip, Hegarty, Narey, Bannon, Payne, Pettigrew, Sturrock, Dodds.

SCOTTISH CUP 1980–81

FIRST ROUND

13 DEC

Alloa (0) 1 *(Holt)*

Stenhousemuir (1) 1 *(Kirkland)* 1020

Alloa: Drummond; Robertson, Rae, Purdie, Stewart, Holt, Smith (Scott), Morrison, McComb, McNab, Shields (McIntosh).
Stenhousemuir: Howie; McCraw, Rennie, Meakin, Black, Frickleton, Jack, Graham, Hancock, Jenkins, Kirkland.

Brechin C (0) 2 *(Keating, Cormack)*

Keith (1) 1 *(Bavidge)* 770

Brechin C: Neilson; Watt, Keating, MacLeod, Glover, Campbell R., Campbell I., Elvin (Kyles), Graham (Henderson), Lorimer, Cormack.
Keith: Gray; Mackay, Martin, Wilson, Fettes, Wilsey, Winton (Duncan), Fyvie, Bavidge, O'Hara, Craig.

East Fife (1) 2 *(Mitchell, Halley)*

Civil Service Strollers (1) 1 *(Lumsdaine S.)* 483

East Fife: Gorman; Tait, Duncan, McLaren, Halley, Thomson R., Mitchell, Clarke, Scott G., McGinn (Burt), Neilson (Huskie).
Civil Service Strollers: Gordon; Darling, Davidson, Lumsdaine C., Boyd, Rodgers, McGauran, Rutherford, Ashton (Shearer), Lumsdaine S., Clapperton.

Meadowbank T (1) 2 *(Georgeson, Davidson)*

Buckie Thistle (0) 2 *(Duncan, Hunter)* 400

Meadowbank T: McKell; Dunn, Conroy, Smith, Brown, Boyd, Leetion, McQuade (Davidson), McCallan, Downie, Georgeson (Jobson).
Buckie Thistle: Wood; Cowie, Brett, Wilson, Forbes, Scott, Hunter, Soutar, Nicol, Duncan, Christie (Robertson).

Queen's Park (2) 2 *(Irvine, McCoy)*

Montrose (0) 2 *(Murray 2)* 843

Queen's Park: Atkins; Wilson, Dickson, Cook, McGregor, McFarlane, Gillespie (Crawley), Sinclair, Irvine, Nicholson, McCoy.
Montrose: Moffat; Hair, Forbes, Beedie, Sheran (McDonald), Clark, Robb, Taylor, Murray, Johnston H., Wright.

Whitehill Welfare (0) 1 *(Smyth)*

Hawick Royal Albert (0) 1 *(Colville)* 1000

Whitehill Welfare: Heaney; Chapman, Morton, Sutton, Moffat, Clark, Lees, Robertson, Brown, Brydon, Smyth.
Hawick Royal Albert: Nichol; Inglis, Colville, Rutherford, Fairgrieve, Bell A., Kerr, Loughran, Blazyca, Brown, McConnell.

FIRST ROUND REPLAYS

17 DEC

Hawick Royal Albert (2) 4 *(Loughran 2, Kerr, Brown)*

Whitehill Welfare (0) 1 *(Lees)* 200

Hawick Royal Albert: Nichol; Inglis, Colville, Rutherford, Fairgrieve, Bell A., Kerr, Loughran, Blazyca, Brown, McConnell.
Whitehill Welfare: Heaney; Chapman, Morton, Sutton (Stevens), Moffat, Clark (Holmes), Lees, Robertson, Brown, Brydon, Smyth.

Montrose (0) 2 *(Johnston, Wright)*

Queen's Park (0) 0 900

Montrose: Moffat; Hair, Forbes, Clark, Sheran, Johnston H., Robb, Taylor, Murray, McDonald, Wright.
Queen's Park: Atkins; Wilson, Dickson, Rennie, McGregor, McFarlane, Gillespie, Crawley, Irvine, Nicholson, McCoy.

Stenhousemuir (0) 3 *aet (Kirkland, Jenkins, Meakin)*

Alloa (1) 2 *(Holt, Grant)* 350

Stenhousemuir: Howie; McCraw, Rennie, Meakin, Black, Frickleton, Jack, Graham, Hancock, Jenkins, Kirkland.
Alloa: Drummond; Robertson, Haggart, Purdie (Grant), Stewart, Holt, McIntosh, Morrison, McComb, McQuade, Shields.

20 DEC

Buckie Thistle (0) 3 *(Scott, McDonald, Hunter)*

Meadowbank T (1) 2 *(McCallan 2)* 1300

Buckie Thistle: Wood; Cowie, McDonald, Wilson, Forbes, Scott, Hunter, Soutar, Nicol, Duncan, Robertson.
Meadowbank T: McKell; Dunn, Fraser (McQuade), Smith, Brown, Downie, Leetion, Boyd, McCallan, Hendrie, Davidson.

SECOND ROUND

3 JAN

Forfar Ath (0) 0

Brechin C (2) 2 *(Graham, Campbell I.)* 1900

Forfar Ath: Boardley; Bennett, Gillies, Morris, Brash, Cameron, Farningham, Watt (Clark), Mitchell (Leitch), McPhee, Gallacher.
Brechin C: Neilson; Watt, Lorimer, Kyles, Glover, Campbell R., Campbell I., Henderson, Graham, Paterson, Cormack.

Hawick Royal Albert (1) 2 *(Loughran, McConnell)*

Cowdenbeath (0) 2 *(Steele, McGhee)* 1000

Hawick Royal Albert: Nichol; Maclean, Colville, Rutherford, Fairgrieve, Bell A. (Inglis), Kerr, Loughran, Blazyca, Brown, McConnell.
Cowdenbeath: Allan; Rolland, Markey, Tierney, Russell, Hunter D., Steele W., Ferguson (McGhee), Liddle, Marshall, Forrest.

Inverness Thistle (1) 2 *(Black B., Guyan)*

Montrose (0) 0 2000

Inverness Thistle: Gray; Fraser, Black B., Cumming, Bremner, Milroy, Black A. (Smith), Drews, Inglis, Guyan, Ironside.
Montrose: Moffat; Hair, Forbes, Clark, Sheran, Johnston H., Robb, Taylor, Wright, McDonald (Forrest), Milne.

Rothes (0) 1 *(Ross pen)*

Clyde (1) 5 *(Masterton 3, O'Neill, McKen og)* 1200

Rothes: Seivwright; McKen, Noble, Ross, Senff, Gray, Tweedie (Paton), Reid, Simpson, Wales (Whyte), Fraser.
Clyde: Young; Brogan, Filippi, Dempsey, Kinnear (Coutts), Ahern, Dempster (McAlpine), Miller, Masterton, O'Neill, Evans.

Stenhousemuir (0) 0

Spartans (0) 0 600

Stenhousemuir: Howie; McCraw, Rennie, Meakin, Black, Mullen, Dunn, Jack (Graham), Hancock, Jenkins, Kirkland.
Spartans: Napier; Hepburn, Brough, Kirkwood, Beattie, Cuthbert, Dick (Costello), McKinnon, Arnott, Cargill, Morrison (Cruickshank).

Stranraer (2) 2 *(Sim, Gibb)*

Buckie Thistle (1) 2 *(Kennedy, Duncan)* 350

Stranraer: Taylor; Rodger, Wilson, McDonald, Murdoch, McCutcheon, Neil, Hay, Hood (Brown), Sim, Gibb.
Buckie Thistle: Wood; Cowie, Scott, Wilson, Forbes, Robertson, Hunter, Soutar, Nicol, Duncan, Kennedy.

10 JAN

Queen of the S (0) 1 *(Gordon)*

East Fife (0) 2 *(Scott G. 2)* 1950

Queen of the S: Ball; Dickson, McChesney, McCann, Clark, Malone, Mitchell, Gordon, Alexander, Roddy, Robertson J. (Phillips).
East Fife: Gorman; Clarke, Duncan, McLaren, Halley, Thomson R., Huskie (McGinn), Tait, Burt (Mitchell), Scott J., Scott G.

12 JAN

Albion R (0) 1 *(Campbell)*

Arbroath (1) 1 *(Harley)* 450

Albion R: Balavage; Gillespie, Hamill, Mackie, Meikle, Main, Campbell, Hill H., Houston, McDougall, Docherty (Hannigan).
Arbroath: Martin; Forsyth, Scrimgeour, Gavine, Young, Docherty, Harley, McKenzie, Hyslop, Shaw, Yule (Mylles T.).

SECOND ROUND REPLAYS

7 JAN

Spartans (1) 1 *(McKinnon)*

Stenhousemuir (1) 2 *(Hancock, Jack)* 1000

Spartans: Napier; Hepburn, Brough, Kirkwood, Beattie, Cuthbert, Dick, McKinnon, Arnott, Cargill, Morrison.
Stenhousemuir: Howie; McCraw, Rennie, Meakin, Black, Mullen, Jack, Graham, Hancock, Jenkins, Dunn (Kirkland).

10 JAN

Buckie Thistle (2) 3 *(Hunter, Forbes, McDonald og)*

Stranraer (1) 2 *(Brown, Hay)* 2250

Buckie Thistle: Wood; Cowie, Scott, Wilson, Forbes, Robertson, Nicol, Soutar, Hunter, Duncan, Kennedy.
Stranraer: Taylor; Hyslop, McCutcheon, McDonald, Murdoch, Rodger (Murphy), Neil, Hay, Hood, Sim, Brown (Wilson).

12 JAN

Cowdenbeath (1) 3 *(McGhee, Liddle, Marshall)*

Hawick Royal Albert (0) 0 505

Cowdenbeath: Allan; Rolland, Markey, Tierney, Stewart, Hunter D., Forrest, Steele W., Liddle, Marshall, McGhee.
Hawick Royal Albert: Nichol; Maclean, Colville, Rutherford, Fairgrieve, Bell A., Kerr, Loughran, Blazyca, Brown, McConnell.

14 JAN

Arbroath (1) 1 *(Harley)*

Albion R (0) 0 500

Arbroath: Martin; Forsyth, Scrimgeour, Gavine, Young, Docherty, Harley, McKenzie, Hyslop, Shaw, Yule.
Albion R: Balavage; Gillespie (Hannigan), Hamill, Mackie, Meikle, Main, Campbell, Hill H., Houston, McDougall, Docherty (Ross).

THIRD ROUND

24 JAN

Airdrieonians (0) 0

Rangers (2) 5 *(Stevens, Redford, Bett, Johnstone 2)* 16,054

Airdrieonians: Martin; Cairney, March, McCluskey (McKeown), Rodger (Anderson), McCulloch, Walker, Gordon, Clark, McGuire, Russell.
Rangers: McCloy; Jardine, Jackson, Stevens, Dawson, Russell (Cooper), Bett, Redford, Johnston, Johnstone, MacDonald.

Arbroath (1) 1 *(Young)*

Cowdenbeath (0) 1 *(Liddle)* 979

Arbroath: Martin; Forsyth, Scrimgeour (McDowell), Gavine, Young, Docherty (Mylles T.), Harley, McKenzie, Hyslop, Shaw, Yule.
Cowdenbeath: Allan; Rolland, Markey, Tierney, Stewart, Hunter D., Ferguson, Steele W., Liddle, Marshall, Forrest.

Berwick R (0) 0

Celtic (1) 2 *(Nicholas, Burns)* 9676

Berwick R: McDonald; Moyes, Marshall, Muir, McCann, McGlynn, Hamilton, Black, Tait (Brown), Romaines, Davidson P. (McLeod).
Celtic: Bonner; McGrain, McAdam, Aitken, Reid, Sullivan (MacLeod), Weir, Burns, Provan, McGarvey, Nicholas.

Brechin C (0) 1 *(Paterson)*

Dundee U (2) 2 *(Dodds, Kirkwood)* 5791

Brechin C: Neilson; Watt, Keating, Henderson, Glover, Campbell R., Campbell I., Paterson, Graham, Lorimer, Cormack.
Dundee U: McAlpine; Holt, Kopel, Phillip, Hegarty, Narey, Bannon, Addison, Kirkwood, Sturrock, Dodds.

Buckie Thistle (0) 1 *(Duncan pen)*

Stirling Albion (1) 3 *(Steele, Colquhoun 2)* 3480

Buckie Thistle: Wood; Cowie, Brett, Wilson, Forbes, Scott, Hunter, Soutar, Nicol (Thomson), Duncan, Kennedy.
Stirling Albion: Arthur; Young, Steedman, Duffin, Kennedy J., Moffat, McPhee, Kennedy A., Steele, Skilling, Armstrong.

East Fife (0) 0

Clydebank (0) 0 1026

East Fife: Gorman; Clarke, Duncan, McLaren, Halley, Thomson R., Scott G., Scott J., Burt (Neilson), Tait, Huskie (Mitchell).
Clydebank: Hill M.; Treanor, Fallon, McLaughlin, Evans, Gervaise, McIntyre, Houston, Miller, McCabe, Harkins.

East Stirling (1) 4 *(Blair, Grant, McCaig 2)*

Inverness Thistle (0) 1 *(Inglis)* 669

East Stirling: Kelly; Gourlay, Blair, McCulley, Renwick, McRitchie, Grant, Robertson, Ashwood, Sharp, McCaig.
Inverness Thistle: Gray; Fraser, Black B., Cumming, Bremner, Milroy, Black A., Drews, Inglis, Guyan, Ironside.

Falkirk (1) 1 *(Hay)*

Dundee (0) 0 4486

Falkirk: Watson; Hoggan, Rose, Brown, Mackin, Hay, Stevenson, Herd, Oliver M., McRoberts, Kettings.
Dundee: Williams; McGeachie, Schaedler, Fraser, Glennie, MacLaren, Mackie, Ferguson, Sinclair, Stephen, Geddes A.

Hamilton A (0) 0

St Johnstone (0) 3 *(Brogan, Morton, Docherty)* 3059

Hamilton A: Ferguson; Frew, Brown, Wright, McDougall, Alexander (McGrogan), Fairlie, McDowall, Deeney, McAdams (Howie), McManus.
St Johnstone: Jenkins; Mackay, McNeil, Fleming, Rutherford, Caldwell, Pelosi, McCoist, Docherty, Morton, Brogan.

Hibernian (0) 1 *(MacLeod)*

Dunfermline Ath (1) 1 *(Leonard)* 6550

Hibernian: McArthur; Sneddon, Duncan, McNamara, Paterson, McLaren, Callachan, Rae, Jamieson, MacLeod, McGlinchey.
Dunfermline Ath: Whyte; Robertson R., Mercer, Thomson, Leishman, Hutt, McNaughton, Dunlop, Leonard, Donnelly, O'Brien.

Kilmarnock (1) 2 *(McDicken, Hughes)*

Ayr U (0) 1 *(Hendry)* 8200

Kilmarnock: McCulloch; McLean, Cockburn, Gibson, Armstrong, McDicken, Doherty, Clarke P., Bourke, Clark J., Hughes.
Ayr U: Rennie; Shanks, Connor, McColl, Nicol, Fleeting, McCutcheon, Armour (Hendry), Morris, Love, Christie (Frye).

Morton (0) 0

Hearts (0) 0 4773

Morton: Baines; Hayes, Holmes, Rooney, Hutchison, Orr, Houston (Ritchie), Marr, McNeil (Bryce), Tolmie, Cochrane.
Hearts: Brough; Hamilton, Shields, More, Liddell, McKay, Kidd, MacDonald, Gibson, Hamill, O'Brien.

Partick T (0) 2 *(Whittaker, Clark)*

Clyde (0) 2 *(Masterton 2)* 4200

Partick T: Rough; Murray, Lapsley, Whittaker, Anderson, Watson, Park, Jardine, Sweeney, O'Hara, Clark.
Clyde: Young; Brogan, Filippi, Dempsey, Kinnear, Ahern, Dempster, Kean J., Masterton, O'Neill, Evans (McAlpine).

Raith R (0) 1 *(Harris)*

Aberdeen (1) 2 *(Jarvie 2)* 10,000

Raith R: McDermott; McDonough, Candlish, Ford, Forsyth, Steel, Lawson, Urquhart, Harris, Steen, Mitchell.
Aberdeen: Leighton; Rougvie, Considine, Watson, McLeish, Cooper, Bell, McCall, McGhee, Jarvie, Hewitt.

St Mirren (0) 0

Dumbarton (1) 2 *(Donnelly, Coyle J.)* 6209

St Mirren: Thomson; Young, Beckett, McCormack, Dunlop (Abercromby), Fulton, Bone, Stark, Somner, Richardson, Weir (McDougall).
Dumbarton: Carson; Sinclair, MacLeod, Coyle T., Gallacher J. (Campbell), Coyle J., Rankin (Blair), McGowan, Gallagher B., McGrain, Donnelly.

Stenhousemuir (0) 1 *(Jack)*

Motherwell (1) 1 *(Forbes)* 2250

Stenhousemuir: Howie; McCraw, Rennie, Meakin, Black, Mullen, Jack, Graham (Murdoch), Hancock, Jenkins, Kirkland (Dunn).
Motherwell: Sproat; Wark, McLeod, McLelland S., Carson, Forbes, Gahagan, Kidd (Rafferty), Irvine, Cleland, McLaughlin.

THIRD ROUND REPLAYS

28 JAN

Clyde (1) 2 *(O'Neill, Evans)*

Partick T (2) 4 *(O'Hara 2, Clark 2)* 4100

Clyde: Young; Brogan, Filippi, Dempsey, Kinnear, Ahern, Dempster, Kean J., Masterton, O'Neill, Evans.
Partick T: Rough; McKinnon, Whittaker, Campbell, Anderson, Watson, McDonald, Jardine, O'Hara, Doyle, Clark.

Clydebank (2) 5 *aet (Miller 3, Evans, Houston)*

East Fife (2) 4 *(Scott G., Huskie, Halley)* 600

Clydebank: Hill M.; Gervaise (Harkins), McLaughlin, Fallon, Sharkey, Given, Ronald (McIntyre), Houston, Evans, Miller, McCabe.
East Fife: Gorman; Clarke, Mitchell, McLaren, Halley, Thomson R., Huskie, Scott J., Scott G., Mackie (Burt), Tait.

Cowdenbeath (2) 4 *(Liddle, Steele, Forrest 2)*

Arbroath (0) 0 745

Cowdenbeath: Allan; Rolland, Markey, Tierney, Stewart, Hunter D., Ferguson, Steele W., Liddle, Marshall, Forrest.
Arbroath: Martin; Forsyth, Scrimgeour, Gavine, Young, Rylance, Harley (Mylles T.), McKenzie, Hyslop, Shaw, McDowell.

Dunfermline Ath (0) 1 *(McNaughton)*

Hibernian (1) 2 *(Rae, Callachan)* 8552

Dunfermline Ath: Whyte; Robertson R., Mercer, Thomson, Leishman, Hegarty (Hutt), McNaughton, Dunlop, Leonard (McFarlane), Donnelly, O'Brien.
Hibernian: McArthur; Sneddon, Duncan, McNamara, Paterson, McLaren, Callachan, Rae, Hamill, MacLeod, Connolly (Jamieson).

Hearts (0) 1 *(MacDonald)*

Morton (1) 3 *(Tolmie, Rooney, Thomson)* 9762

Hearts: Brough; Hamilton (McShane), Shields, More, Liddell, McKay, Kidd, Gibson, Hamill (White), O'Brien, MacDonald.
Morton: Baines; Hayes, Holmes, Rooney, McLaughlin, Orr, Houston, Marr, Thomson, Tolmie, Ritchie.

Motherwell (2) 2 *(McLelland, Gahagan)*

Stenhousemuir (0) 1 *(Meakin)* 2735

Motherwell: Sproat; Wark, McLeod, McLelland S., Carson, Forbes, Gahagan, Kidd, Irvine, Cleland, McLaughlin.
Stenhousemuir: Howie; McCraw, Rennie, Meakin, Black, Mullen, Jack, Murdoch, Hancock, Jenkins, Kirkland.

FOURTH ROUND

14 FEB

Celtic (1) 3 *(McGarvey, Burns, McCluskey)*

Stirling Albion (0) 0 14,200

Celtic: Bonner; McGrain, Reid, Sullivan, McAdam, Aitken, Provan, Conroy, McGarvey (McCluskey), Burns, Nicholas.
Stirling Albion: Arthur; Young, Skilling, Philliben, Nicol, Moffat, McPhee (Colquhoun), Duffin, Steele, Gray, Armstrong (McNeil).

Cowdenbeath (1) 1 *(Steele)*

East Stirling (0) 2 *(Ashwood, Rennie)* 1012

Cowdenbeath: Allan; Rolland, Markey, Tierney, Stewart, Hunter D., Ferguson, Steele W., Liddle, Marshall, Duncan (McGhee).
East Stirling: Kelly; Renwick, Gourlay, McCulley, Rennie, Watt, Grant, Sharp (Robertson), Ashwood, Lamont, McCaig (Bennett).

Dundee U (0) 1 *(Addison)*

Partick T (0) 0 7758

Dundee U: McAlpine; Phillip, Kopel, Addison, Hegarty, Narey, Bannon, Payne (Pettigrew), Kirkwood, Sturrock, Dodds.
Partick T: Rough; McKinnon, Whittaker, Campbell, Anderson, Watson (Lapsley), McDonald (Sweeney), Jardine, O'Hara, Doyle, Clark.

Hibernian (0) 1 *(Callachan)*

Falkirk (0) 0 6425

Hibernian: McArthur; Sneddon, Duncan, Brown J., Paterson, McNamara, Callachan, Rae, MacLeod, Connolly, McGlinchey (Jamieson).
Falkirk: Watson; Hoggan, Burrell, Brown (Spence), Mackin, Hay, Stevenson, Herd, Perry (Thompson), Oliver M., Kettings.

Kilmarnock (0) 0

Clydebank (0) 0 3000

Kilmarnock: McCulloch; McLean, Cockburn, Clark J., Armstrong, McDicken, McBride, Gibson (Hughes), Bourke, Bryce, Street.
Clydebank: Kenny; Gervaise, McLaughlin, Fallon, Evans, Given, Ronald, Houston, Miller, McGorm, McCabe.

Morton (1) 1 *(Ritchie)*

Aberdeen (0) 0 10,000

Morton: Baines; Hayes, Holmes, Rooney, McLaughlin, Orr, Busby, Marr, Thomson, McNeil, Ritchie (Houston).
Aberdeen: Leighton; Kennedy, Considine, Watson, McLeish, Miller, Bell (Davidson), McCall (Hamilton), McGhee, Harrow, Angus.

Motherwell (1) 2 *(Gahagan, McLaughlin)*

Dumbarton (0) 1 *(Coyle J.)* 4374

Motherwell: Sproat; Wark, McLeod, McLelland S., Smith, Forbes, McLaughlin, Kidd, Irvine, Soutar, Gahagan.
Dumbarton: Carson; Sinclair, MacLeod, Coyle T., Gallacher J. (Jackson), Coyle J., Rankin (Blair), McGowan, Gallagher B., Donnelly, McGrain.

St Johnstone (1) 3 *(Docherty, Brogan 2)*

Rangers (2) 3 *(McAdam, Redford 2)* 17,595

St Johnstone: Tulloch; Mackay, McNeil, Fleming, Rutherford, Caldwell, Pelosi, McCoist, Docherty, Morton, Brogan.
Rangers: McCloy; Jardine, Dawson, Forsyth, Jackson, Bett, Johnston W., Russell (Miller), McAdam, Redford, MacDonald (Cooper).

FOURTH ROUND REPLAYS

18 FEB

Clydebank (0) 1 *aet (Miller)*

Kilmarnock (1) 1 *(Bourke)* 4000

Clydebank: Kenny; Gervaise, McLaughlin, Fallon, Evans, Given, Harkins, Houston, Miller, McGorm, McCabe.
Kilmarnock: McCulloch; McLean, Cockburn, Clark J., Armstrong, McDicken, Maxwell (Cairney), Mauchlen, Bourke, Bryce (Wilson), McBride.

Rangers (1) 3 *(McAdam 2, Stevens)*

St Johnstone (0) 1 *(McCoist)* 23,000

Rangers: McCloy; Jardine, Dawson, Stevens, Jackson, Bett, Johnston, Miller, McAdam, Redford, Johnstone.
St Johnstone: Tulloch; Mackay, McNeil, Fleming, Rutherford (Kilgour), Caldwell, Pelosi, McCoist, Docherty, Morton, Brogan.

FOURTH ROUND SECOND REPLAY

23 FEB

Kilmarnock (0) 0

Clydebank (1) 1 *(Given pen)* 2340

Kilmarnock: McCulloch; McLean, Cockburn, Clark J., Armstrong, McDicken, Maxwell (Cairney), Mauchlen, Bourke, Bryce (Wilson), McBride.
Clydebank: Kenny; Treanor, McLaughlin, Fallon, Evans, Given, Ronald, Houston, Miller, Gervaise, McCabe.

FIFTH ROUND

7 MAR

Dundee U (4) 6 *(Dodds 3, Sturrock, Narey, Kirkwood)*

Motherwell (1) 1 *(Soutar)* 10,236

Dundee U: McAlpine; Holt, Kopel, Phillip (Pettigrew), Hegarty, Narey, Bannon, Milne (Payne), Kirkwood, Sturrock, Dodds.
Motherwell: Sproat; Wark, McLeod, McLelland S., Smith, Forbes, McLaughlin, Cleland (Carson), Irvine, Soutar, Gahagan.

Rangers (2) 3 *(Russell, McAdam, MacDonald)*

Hibernian (1) 1 *(McNamara)* 25,690

Rangers: McCloy; Miller, Dawson, Jardine, Jackson, Bett, Johnston (Cooper), Russell, McAdam, Redford, MacDonald.
Hibernian: McArthur; Brown J., Sneddon, McLaren, Paterson, McNamara, Hamill (Brown J. K.), Jamieson (Rodier), Rae, Duncan, Connolly.

8 MAR

Celtic (1) 2 *(Conroy, MacLeod)*

East Stirling (0) 0 18,500

Celtic: Bonner; McGrain, Reid, Sullivan, McAdam, Aitken, Provan, Conroy, McGarvey, Burns (MacLeod), Nicholas.
East Stirling: Kelly; Blair, Renwick, Watt, Rennie, Lamont, Grant, Gourlay, Ashwood, McCulley, Robertson.

11 MAR

Morton (0) 0

Clydebank (0) 0 5000

Morton: Baines; Hayes, Holmes, Rooney, McLaughlin, Orr, Busby, Marr (McNeil), Thomson, Tolmie, Ritchie.
Clydebank: Kenny; Treanor, McLaughlin, Fallon, Evans, Given, Ronald, Houston, Miller, McCabe, Gervaise.

FIFTH ROUND REPLAY

16 MAR

Clydebank (0) 0

Morton (1) 6 *(Thomson 3, McNeil, Rooney, Tolmie)* 5000

Clydebank: Kenny; Treanor, McLaughlin, Fallon, Evans, Given, Ronald, Houston, Miller, Gervaise (Harkins), McCabe.
Morton: Baines; Hayes, Holmes, Rooney, McLaughlin, Orr, McNeil, Busby, Thomson, Tolmie, Ritchie.

SEMI-FINALS

11 APRIL

Celtic (0) 0

Dundee U (0) 0 40,337

(At Hampden Park)

Celtic: Bonner; MacLeod, Reid, Sullivan, McAdam, Aitken, Provan, Conroy, McCluskey (Doyle), Burns, Nicholas.
Dundee U: McAlpine; Holt, Kopel, Phillip, Hegarty (Stark), Narey, Bannon, Milne, Kirkwood, Sturrock, Dodds.

Morton (0) 1 *(Ritchie* pen*)*

Rangers (1) 2 *(Jackson, Russell)* 27,050

(At Celtic Park)

Morton: Baines; Hayes, Holmes, Rooney, McLaughlin, Orr (Ritchie), McNeil, Busby, Thomson, Tolmie, Cochrane.
Rangers: Stewart; Miller, Dawson, Forsyth, Jackson, Bett (McAdam), McLean, Russell, Johnstone, Redford, Johnston.

SEMI-FINAL REPLAY

15 APRIL

Celtic (2) 2 *(Nicholas 2* [1 pen]*)*

Dundee U (2) 3 *(Hegarty 2, Bannon)* 32,328

(At Hampden Park)

Celtic: Bonner; MacLeod, Reid, Sullivan, McAdam, Aitken, Provan, Conroy, McGarvey, Burns, Nicholas.
Dundee U: McAlpine; Holt, Kopel, Phillip, Hegarty, Narey, Bannon, Milne, Kirkwood, Sturrock, Dodds.

FINAL (at Hampden Park)

9 MAY

Dundee U (0) 0 *aet*

Rangers (0) 0 53,000

Dundee U: McAlpine; Holt, Kopel, Phillip (Stark), Hegarty, Narey, Bannon, Milne (Pettigrew), Kirkwood, Sturrock, Dodds.
Rangers: Stewart; Jardine, Dawson, Stevens, Forsyth, Bett, McLean, Russell, McAdam (Cooper), Redford, Johnston (MacDonald).

FINAL REPLAY (at Hampden Park)

12 MAY

Dundee U (1) 1 *(Dodds)*

Rangers (3) 4 *(Cooper, Russell, MacDonald 2)* 43,099

Dundee U: McAlpine; Holt, Kopel, Phillip (Stark), Hegarty, Narey, Bannon, Milne, Kirkwood, Sturrock, Dodds.
Rangers: Stewart; Jardine, Dawson, Forsyth, Stevens, Bett, Cooper, Russell, Johnstone, Redford, MacDonald.

BRITISH HOME INTERNATIONALS

INTERNATIONAL CHAMPIONSHIP 1883–1981

Year	*Champions*	*Pts*
1883–84	Scotland	6
1884–85	Scotland	5
1885–86	England	5
	Scotland	5
1886–87	Scotland	6
1887–88	England	6
1888–89	Scotland	5
1889–90	Scotland	5
	England	5
1890–91	England	6
1891–92	England	6
1892–93	England	6
1893–94	Scotland	5
1894–95	England	5
1895–96	Scotland	5
1896–97	Scotland	5
1897–98	England	6
1898–99	England	6
1899–1900	Scotland	6
1900–01	England	5
1901–02	Scotland	5
1902–03	England	4
	Ireland	4
	Scotland	4
1903–04	England	5
1904–05	England	5
1905–06	England	4
	Scotland	4
1906–07	Wales	5
1907–08	Scotland	5
	England	5
1908–09	England	6
1909–10	Scotland	4
1910–11	England	5
1911–12	England	5
	Scotland	5
1912–13	England	4
1913–14	Ireland	5
1919–20	Wales	4
1920–21	Scotland	6
1921–22	Scotland	4
1922–23	Scotland	5
1923–24	Wales	6
1924–25	Scotland	6
1925–26	Scotland	6
1926–27	Scotland	4
	England	4
1927–28	Wales	5
1928–29	Scotland	6
1929–30	England	6
1930–31	Scotland	4
	England	4
1931–32	England	6
1932–33	Wales	5
1933–34	Wales	5
1934–35	England	4
	Scotland	4
1935–36	Scotland	4
1936–37	Wales	6
1937–38	England	4
1938–39	England	4
	Scotland	4
	Wales	4
1946–47	England	5
1947–48	England	5
1948–49	Scotland	6
1949–50	England	6
1950–51	Scotland	6
1951–52	Wales	5
	England	5
1952–53	England	4
	Scotland	4
1953–54	England	6
1954–55	England	6
1955–56	England	3
	Scotland	3
	Wales	3
	Ireland	3
1956–57	England	5
1957–58	England	4
	Ireland	4
1958–59	Ireland	4
	England	4
1959–60	England	4
	Scotland	4
	Wales	4
1960–61	England	6
1961–62	Scotland	6
1962–63	Scotland	6
1963–64	Scotland	4
	England	4
	Ireland	4
1964–65	England	5
1965–66	England	5
1966–67	Scotland	5
1967–68	England	5
1968–69	England	6
1969–70	England	4
	Scotland	4
	Wales	4
1970–71	England	5
1971–72	England	4
	Scotland	4
1972–73	England	6
1973–74	England	4
	Scotland	4
1974–75	England	4
1975–76	Scotland	6
1976–77	Scotland	5
1977–78	England	6
1978–79	England	5
1979–80	Ireland	5
1980–81	*Not completed*	

Note: In the results that follow, WC = World Cup, EC = European Championship.

ENGLAND v SCOTLAND

Played: 99; England won 38, Scotland won 39, Drawn 22. *Goals:* England 179, Scotland 165.

		E	*S*
1872	Glasgow	0	0
1873	Kennington Oval	4	2
1874	Glasgow	1	2
1875	Kennington Oval	2	2
1876	Glasgow	0	3
1877	Kennington Oval	1	3
1878	Glasgow	2	7
1879	Kennington Oval	5	4
1880	Glasgow	4	5
1881	Kennington Oval	1	6
1882	Glasgow	1	5
1883	Sheffield	2	3
1884	Glasgow	0	1
1885	Kennington Oval	1	1
1886	Glasgow	1	1
1887	Blackburn	2	3
1888	Glasgow	5	0
1889	Kennington Oval	2	3
1890	Glasgow	1	1
1891	Blackburn	2	1
1892	Glasgow	4	1
1893	Richmond	5	2
1894	Glasgow	2	2
1895	Everton	3	0
1896	Glasgow	1	2
1897	Crystal Palace	1	2
1898	Glasgow	3	1
1899	Birmingham	2	1
1900	Glasgow	1	4
1901	Crystal Palace	2	2
1902	Birmingham	2	2
1903	Sheffield	1	2
1904	Glasgow	1	0
1905	Crystal Palace	1	0
1906	Glasgow	1	2
1907	Newcastle	1	1
1908	Glasgow	1	1
1909	Crystal Palace	2	0
1910	Glasgow	0	2
1911	Everton	1	1
1912	Glasgow	1	1
1913	Chelsea	1	0
1914	Glasgow	1	3
1920	Sheffield	5	4
1921	Glasgow	0	3
1922	Aston Villa	0	1
1923	Glasgow	2	2
1924	Wembley	1	1
1925	Glasgow	0	2
1926	Manchester	0	1
1927	Glasgow	2	1
1928	Wembley	1	5
1929	Glasgow	0	1
1930	Wembley	5	2

	E	S
1931 Glasgow	0	2
1932 Wembley	3	0
1933 Glasgow	1	2
1934 Wembley	3	0
1935 Glasgow	0	2
1936 Wembley	1	1
1937 Glasgow	1	3
1938 Wembley	0	1
1939 Glasgow	2	1
1947 Wembley	1	1
1948 Glasgow	2	0
1949 Wembley	1	3
wc1950 Glasgow	1	0
1951 Wembley	2	3
1952 Glasgow	2	1
1953 Wembley	2	2
wc1954 Glasgow	4	2
1955 Wembley	7	2
1956 Glasgow	1	1
1957 Wembley	2	1
1958 Glasgow	4	0
1959 Wembley	1	0
1960 Glasgow	1	1
1961 Wembley	9	3
1962 Glasgow	0	2
1963 Wembley	1	2
1964 Glasgow	0	1
1965 Wembley	2	2
1966 Glasgow	4	3
EC1967 Wembley	2	3
EC1968 Glasgow	1	1
1969 Wembley	4	1
1970 Glasgow	0	0
1971 Wembley	3	1
1972 Glasgow	1	0
1973 Glasgow	5	0
1973 Wembley	1	0
1974 Glasgow	0	2
1975 Wembley	5	1
1976 Glasgow	1	2
1977 Wembley	1	2
1978 Glasgow	1	0
1979 Wembley	3	1
1980 Glasgow	2	0
1981 Wembley	0	1

ENGLAND v WALES

Played: 94; England won 60, Wales won 13, Drawn 21. *Goals:* England 236, Wales 88.

	E	W
1879 Kennington Oval	2	1
1880 Wrexham	3	2
1881 Blackburn	0	1
1882 Wrexham	3	5
1883 Kennington Oval	5	0
1884 Wrexham	4	0
1885 Blackburn	1	1
1886 Wrexham	3	1
1887 Kennington Oval	4	0
1888 Crewe	5	1
1889 Stoke	4	1
1890 Wrexham	3	1
1891 Sunderland	4	1
1892 Wrexham	2	0
1893 Stoke	6	0
1894 Wrexham	5	1
1894 Queen's Club, Kensington	1	1
1896 Cardiff	9	1
1897 Sheffield	4	0
1898 Wrexham	3	0
1899 Bristol	4	0
1900 Cardiff	1	1
1901 Newcastle	6	0
1902 Wrexham	0	0
1903 Portsmouth	2	1
1904 Wrexham	2	2
1905 Liverpool	3	1
1906 Cardiff	1	0
1907 Fulham	1	1
1908 Wrexham	7	1
1909 Nottingham	2	0
1910 Cardiff	1	0
1911 Millwall	3	0
1912 Wrexham	2	0
1913 Bristol	4	3
1914 Cardiff	2	0
1920 Highbury	1	2
1921 Cardiff	0	0
1922 Liverpool	1	0
1923 Cardiff	2	2
1924 Blackburn	1	2
1925 Swansea	2	1
1926 Crystal Palace	1	3
1927 Wrexham	3	3
1927 Burnley	1	2
1928 Swansea	3	2
1929 Chelsea	6	0
1930 Wrexham	4	0
1931 Liverpool	3	1
1932 Wrexham	0	0
1933 Newcastle	1	2
1934 Cardiff	4	0
1935 Wolverhampton	1	2
1936 Cardiff	1	2
1937 Middlesbrough	2	1
1938 Cardiff	2	4
1946 Manchester	3	0
1947 Cardiff	3	0
1948 Aston Villa	1	0
wc1949 Cardiff	4	1
1950 Sunderland	4	2
1951 Cardiff	1	1
1952 Wembley	5	2
wc1953 Cardiff	4	1
1954 Wembley	3	2
1955 Cardiff	1	2
1956 Wembley	3	1
1957 Cardiff	4	0
1958 Aston Villa	2	2
1959 Cardiff	1	1
1960 Wembley	5	1
1961 Cardiff	1	1
1962 Wembley	4	0
1963 Cardiff	4	0
1964 Wembley	2	1
1965 Cardiff	0	0
EC1966 Wembley	5	1
EC1967 Cardiff	3	0
1969 Wembley	2	1
1970 Cardiff	1	1
1971 Wembley	0	0
1972 Cardiff	3	0
wc1972 Cardiff	1	0
wc1973 Wembley	1	1
1973 Wembley	3	0
1974 Cardiff	2	0
1975 Wembley	2	2
1976 Wrexham	2	1
1976 Cardiff	1	0
1977 Wembley	0	1
1978 Cardiff	3	1
1979 Wembley	0	0
1980 Wrexham	1	4
1981 Wembley	0	0

ENGLAND v IRELAND

Played: 89; England won 69, Ireland won 6, Drawn 14. *Goals:* England 308, Ireland 80.

	E	I
1882 Belfast	13	0
1883 Liverpool	7	0
1884 Belfast	8	1
1885 Manchester	4	0
1886 Belfast	6	1
1887 Sheffield	7	0
1888 Belfast	5	1
1889 Everton	6	1
1890 Belfast	9	1
1891 Wolverhampton	6	1
1892 Belfast	2	0
1893 Birmingham	6	1
1894 Belfast	2	2
1895 Derby	9	0
1896 Belfast	2	0
1897 Nottingham	6	0
1898 Belfast	3	2
1899 Sunderland	13	2
1900 Dublin	2	0
1901 Southampton	3	0
1902 Belfast	1	0
1903 Wolverhampton	4	0
1904 Belfast	3	1
1905 Middlesbrough	1	1
1906 Belfast	5	0
1907 Everton	1	0
1908 Belfast	3	1
1909 Bradford	4	0
1910 Belfast	1	1
1911 Derby	2	1
1912 Dublin	6	1
1913 Belfast	1	2
1914 Middlesbrough	0	3
1919 Belfast	1	1
1920 Sunderland	2	0
1921 Belfast	1	1
1922 West Bromwich	2	0
1923 Belfast	1	2
1924 Everton	3	1

	E	I		E	I		E	I
1925 Belfast	0	0	wc1949 Manchester	9	2	EC1966 Belfast	2	0
1926 Liverpool	3	3	1950 Belfast	4	1	EC1967 Wembley	2	0
1927 Belfast	0	2	1951 Aston Villa	2	0	1969 Belfast	3	1
1928 Everton	2	1	1952 Belfast	2	2	1970 Wembley	3	1
1929 Belfast	3	0	wc1953 Everton	3	1	1971 Belfast	1	0
1930 Sheffield	5	1	1954 Belfast	2	0	1972 Wembley	0	1
1931 Belfast	6	2	1955 Wembley	3	0	1973 Everton	2	1
1932 Blackpool	1	0	1956 Belfast	1	1	1974 Wembley	1	0
1933 Belfast	3	0	1957 Wembley	2	3	1975 Belfast	0	0
1935 Everton	2	1	1958 Belfast	3	3	1976 Wembley	4	0
1935 Belfast	3	1	1959 Wembley	2	1	1977 Belfast	2	1
1936 Stoke	3	1	1960 Belfast	5	2	1978 Wembley	1	0
1937 Belfast	5	1	1961 Wembley	1	1	EC1979 Wembley	4	0
1938 Manchester	7	0	1962 Belfast	3	1	1979 Belfast	2	0
1946 Belfast	7	2	1963 Wembley	8	3	EC1979 Belfast	5	1
1947 Everton	2	2	1964 Belfast	4	3	1980 Wembley	1	1
1948 Belfast	6	2	1965 Wembley	2	1			

SCOTLAND v WALES

Played: 96; Scotland won 57, Wales won 17, Drawn 22. *Goals:* Scotland 232, Wales 108.

	S	W		S	W		S	W
1876 Glasgow	4	0	1908 Dundee	2	1	1951 Glasgow	0	1
1877 Wrexham	2	0	1909 Wrexham	2	3	wc1952 Cardiff	2	1
1878 Glasgow	9	0	1910 Kilmarnock	1	0	1953 Glasgow	3	3
1879 Wrexham	3	0	1911 Cardiff	2	2	1954 Cardiff	1	0
1880 Glasgow	5	1	1912 Tynecastle	1	0	1955 Glasgow	2	0
1881 Wrexham	5	1	1913 Wrexham	0	0	1956 Cardiff	2	2
1882 Glasgow	5	0	1914 Glasgow	0	0	1957 Glasgow	1	1
1883 Wrexham	4	1	1920 Cardiff	1	1	1958 Cardiff	3	0
1884 Glasgow	4	1	1921 Aberdeen	2	1	1959 Glasgow	1	1
1885 Wrexham	8	1	1922 Wrexham	1	2	1960 Cardiff	0	2
1886 Glasgow	4	1	1923 Paisley	2	0	1961 Glasgow	2	0
1887 Wrexham	2	0	1924 Cardiff	0	2	1962 Cardiff	3	2
1888 Edinburgh	5	1	1925 Tynecastle	3	1	1963 Glasgow	2	1
1889 Wrexham	0	0	1926 Cardiff	3	0	1964 Cardiff	2	3
1890 Paisley	5	0	1927 Glasgow	3	0	EC1965 Glasgow	4	1
1891 Wrexham	4	3	1928 Wrexham	2	2	EC1966 Cardiff	1	1
1892 Edinburgh	6	1	1929 Glasgow	4	2	1967 Glasgow	3	2
1893 Wrexham	8	0	1930 Cardiff	4	2	1969 Wrexham	5	3
1894 Kilmarnock	5	2	1931 Glasgow	1	1	1970 Glasgow	0	0
1895 Wrexham	2	2	1932 Wrexham	3	2	1971 Cardiff	0	0
1896 Dundee	4	0	1933 Edinburgh	2	5	1972 Glasgow	1	0
1897 Wrexham	2	2	1934 Cardiff	2	3	1973 Wrexham	2	0
1898 Motherwell	5	2	1935 Aberdeen	3	2	1974 Glasgow	2	0
1899 Wrexham	6	0	1936 Cardiff	1	1	1975 Cardiff	2	2
1900 Aberdeen	5	2	1937 Dundee	1	2	1976 Glasgow	3	1
1901 Wrexham	1	1	1938 Cardiff	1	2	wc1977 Glasgow	1	0
1902 Greenock	5	1	1939 Edinburgh	3	2	1977 Wrexham	0	0
1903 Cardiff	1	0	1946 Wrexham	1	3	wc1977 Liverpool	2	0
1904 Dundee	1	1	1947 Glasgow	1	2	1978 Glasgow	1	1
1905 Wrexham	1	3	wc1948 Cardiff	3	1	1979 Cardiff	0	3
1906 Edinburgh	0	2	1949 Glasgow	2	0	1980 Glasgow	1	0
1907 Wrexham	0	1	1950 Cardiff	3	1	1981 Swansea	0	2

SCOTLAND v IRELAND

Played: 87; Scotland won 60, Ireland won 14, Drawn 13. *Goals:* Scotland 252, Ireland 78.

	S	I		S	I		S	I
1884 Belfast	5	0	1895 Glasgow	3	1	1906 Dublin	1	0
1885 Glasgow	8	2	1896 Belfast	3	3	1907 Glasgow	3	0
1886 Belfast	7	2	1897 Glasgow	5	1	1908 Dublin	5	0
1887 Glasgow	4	1	1898 Belfast	3	0	1909 Glasgow	5	0
1888 Belfast	10	2	1899 Glasgow	9	1	1910 Belfast	0	1
1889 Glasgow	7	0	1900 Belfast	3	0	1911 Glasgow	2	0
1890 Belfast	4	1	1901 Glasgow	11	0	1912 Belfast	4	1
1891 Glasgow	2	1	1902 Belfast	5	1	1913 Dublin	2	1
1892 Belfast	3	2	1903 Glasgow	0	2	1914 Belfast	1	1
1893 Glasgow	6	1	1904 Dublin	1	1	1920 Glasgow	3	0
1894 Belfast	2	1	1905 Glasgow	4	0	1921 Belfast	2	0

	S	I		S	I		S	I
1922 Glasgow	2	1	1946 Glasgow	0	0	1964 Glasgow	3	2
1923 Belfast	1	0	1947 Belfast	0	2	1965 Belfast	2	3
1924 Glasgow	2	0	1948 Glasgow	3	2	1966 Glasgow	2	1
1925 Belfast	3	0	1949 Belfast	8	2	1967 Belfast	0	1
1926 Glasgow	4	0	1950 Glasgow	6	1	1969 Glasgow	1	1
1927 Belfast	2	0	1951 Belfast	3	0	1970 Belfast	1	0
1928 Glasgow	0	1	1952 Glasgow	1	1	1971 Glasgow	0	1
1929 Belfast	7	3	1953 Belfast	3	1	1972 Glasgow	2	0
1930 Glasgow	3	1	1954 Glasgow	2	2	1973 Glasgow	1	2
1931 Belfast	0	0	1955 Belfast	1	2	1974 Glasgow	0	1
1932 Glasgow	3	1	1956 Glasgow	1	0	1975 Glasgow	3	0
1933 Belfast	4	0	1957 Belfast	1	1	1976 Glasgow	3	0
1934 Glasgow	1	2	1958 Glasgow	2	2	1977 Glasgow	3	0
1935 Belfast	1	2	1959 Belfast	4	0	1978 Glasgow	1	1
1936 Edinburgh	2	1	1960 Glasgow	5	2	1979 Glasgow	1	0
1937 Belfast	3	1	1961 Belfast	6	1	1980 Belfast	0	1
1938 Aberdeen	1	1	1962 Glasgow	5	1	wc1981 Glasgow	1	1
1939 Belfast	2	0	1963 Belfast	1	2	1981 Glasgow	2	0

WALES v IRELAND

Played: 87; Wales won 40, Ireland won 27, Drawn 20. *Goals:* Wales 176, Ireland 125.

	W	I		W	I		W	I
1882 Wrexham	7	1	1911 Belfast	2	1	1952 Swansea	3	0
1883 Belfast	1	1	1912 Cardiff	2	3	1953 Belfast	3	2
1884 Wrexham	6	0	1913 Belfast	1	0	wc1954 Wrexham	1	2
1885 Belfast	8	2	1914 Wrexham	1	2	1955 Belfast	3	2
1886 Wrexham	5	0	1920 Belfast	2	2	1956 Cardiff	1	1
1887 Belfast	1	4	1921 Swansea	2	1	1957 Belfast	0	0
1888 Wrexham	11	0	1922 Belfast	1	1	1958 Cardiff	1	1
1889 Belfast	3	1	1923 Wrexham	0	3	1959 Belfast	1	4
1890 Shrewsbury	5	2	1924 Belfast	1	0	1960 Wrexham	3	2
1891 Belfast	2	7	1925 Wrexham	0	0	1961 Belfast	5	1
1892 Bangor	1	1	1926 Belfast	0	3	1962 Cardiff	4	0
1893 Belfast	3	4	1927 Cardiff	2	2	1963 Belfast	4	1
1894 Swansea	4	1	1928 Belfast	2	1	1964 Cardiff	2	3
1895 Belfast	2	2	1929 Wrexham	2	2	1965 Belfast	5	0
1896 Wrexham	6	1	1930 Belfast	0	7	1966 Cardiff	1	4
1897 Belfast	3	4	1931 Wrexham	3	2	EC1967 Belfast	0	0
1898 Llandudno	0	1	1932 Belfast	0	4	EC1968 Wrexham	2	0
1899 Belfast	0	1	1933 Wrexham	4	1	1969 Belfast	0	0
1900 Llandudno	2	0	1934 Belfast	1	1	1970 Swansea	1	0
1901 Belfast	1	0	1935 Wrexham	3	1	1971 Belfast	0	1
1902 Cardiff	0	3	1936 Belfast	2	3	1972 Wrexham	0	0
1903 Belfast	0	2	1937 Wrexham	4	1	1973 Everton	0	1
1904 Bangor	0	1	1938 Belfast	0	1	1974 Wrexham	1	0
1905 Belfast	2	2	1939 Wrexham	3	1	1975 Belfast	0	1
1906 Wrexham	4	4	1947 Belfast	1	2	1976 Cardiff	1	0
1907 Belfast	3	2	1948 Wrexham	2	0	1977 Belfast	1	1
1908 Aberdare	0	1	1949 Belfast	2	0	1978 Swansea	1	0
1909 Belfast	3	2	wc1950 Wrexham	0	0	1979 Belfast	1	1
1910 Wrexham	4	1	1951 Belfast	2	1	1980 Cardiff	0	1

OTHER BRITISH INTERNATIONAL RESULTS 1908–1981

ENGLAND

v ARGENTINA

			E	A
1951	9 May	Wembley	2	1
1953	17 May	Buenos Aires	0	0
		(*abandoned after 21 mins*)		
wc1962	2 June	Rancagua	3	1
1964	6 June	Rio de Janeiro	0	1
wc1966	23 July	Wembley	1	0
1974	22 May	Wembley	2	2
1977	12 June	Buenos Aires	1	1
1980	13 May	Wembley	3	1

v AUSTRALIA

			E	A
1980	31 May	Sydney	2	1

v AUSTRIA

			E	A
1908	6 June	Vienna	6	1
1908	8 June	Vienna	11	1
1909	1 June	Vienna	8	1
1930	14 May	Vienna	0	0
1932	7 Dec	Chelsea	4	3
1936	6 May	Vienna	1	2
1951	28 Nov	Wembley	2	2
1952	25 May	Vienna	3	2
wc1958	15 June	Boras	2	2
1961	27 May	Vienna	1	3
1962	4 Apr	Wembley	3	1
1965	20 Oct	Wembley	2	3
1967	27 May	Vienna	1	0
1973	26 Sept	Wembley	7	0
1979	13 June	Vienna	3	4

v BELGIUM

			E	B
1921	21 May	Brussels	2	0
1923	19 Mar	Highbury	6	1
1923	1 Nov	Antwerp	2	2
1924	8 Dec	West Bromwich	4	0
1926	24 May	Antwerp	5	3
1927	11 May	Brussels	9	1
1928	19 May	Antwerp	3	1
1929	11 May	Brussels	5	1
1931	16 May	Brussels	4	1
1936	9 May	Brussels	2	3
1947	21 Sept	Brussels	5	2
1950	18 May	Brussels	4	1
1952	26 Nov	Wembley	5	0
WC1954	17 June	Basle	4	4*
1964	21 Oct	Wembley	2	2
1970	25 Feb	Brussels	3	1
EC1980	12 June	Turin	1	1

**After extra time.*

v BOHEMIA

			E	B
1908	13 June	Prague	4	0

v BRAZIL

			E	B
1956	9 May	Wembley	4	2
WC1958	11 June	Gothenburg	0	0
1959	13 May	Rio de Janeiro	0	2
WC1962	10 June	Vina del Mar	1	3
1963	8 May	Wembley	1	1
1964	30 May	Rio de Janeiro	1	5
1969	12 June	Rio de Janeiro	1	2
WC1970	7 June	Guadalajara	0	1
1976	23 May	Los Angeles	0	1
1977	8 June	Rio de Janeiro	0	0
1978	19 Apr	Wembley	1	1
1981	12 May	Wembley	0	1

v BULGARIA

			E	B
WC1962	7 June	Rancagua	0	0
1968	11 Dec	Wembley	1	1
1974	1 June	Sofia	1	0
EC1979	6 June	Sofia	3	0
EC1979	22 Nov	Wembley	2	0

v CHILE

			E	C
WC1950	25 June	Rio de Janeiro	2	0
1953	24 May	Santiago	2	1

v COLOMBIA

			E	C
1970	20 May	Bogota	4	0

v CYPRUS

			E	C
EC1975	16 Apr	Wembley	5	0
EC1975	11 May	Limassol	1	0

v CZECHOSLOVAKIA

			E	C
1934	16 May	Prague	1	2
1937	1 Dec	Tottenham	5	4
1963	29 May	Bratislava	4	2
1966	2 Nov	Wembley	0	0
WC1970	11 June	Guadalajara	1	0
1973	27 May	Prague	1	1
EC1974	30 Oct	Wembley	3	0
EC1975	30 Oct	Bratislava	1	2
1978	29 Nov	Wembley	1	0

v DENMARK

			E	D
1948	26 Sept	Copenhagen	0	0
1955	2 Oct	Copenhagen	5	1
WC1956	5 Dec	Wolverhampton	5	2
WC1957	15 May	Copenhagen	4	1
1966	3 July	Copenhagen	2	0
EC1978	20 Sept	Copenhagen	4	3
EC1979	12 Sept	Wembley	1	0

v ECUADOR

			E	Ec
1970	24 May	Quito	2	0

v FIFA

			E	FIFA
1938	26 Oct	Highbury	3	0
1953	21 Oct	Wembley	4	4
1963	23 Oct	Wembley	2	1

v FINLAND

			E	F
1937	20 May	Helsinki	8	0
1956	20 May	Helsinki	5	1
1966	26 June	Helsinki	3	0
WC1976	13 June	Helsinki	4	1
WC1976	13 Oct	Wembley	2	1

v FRANCE

			E	F
1923	10 May	Paris	4	1
1924	17 May	Paris	3	1
1925	21 May	Paris	3	2
1927	26 May	Paris	6	0
1928	17 May	Paris	5	1
1929	9 May	Paris	4	1
1931	14 May	Paris	2	5
1933	6 Dec	Tottenham	4	1
1938	26 May	Paris	4	2
1947	3 May	Highbury	3	0
1949	22 May	Paris	3	1
1951	3 Oct	Highbury	2	2
1955	15 May	Paris	0	1
1957	27 Nov	Wembley	4	0
EC1962	3 Oct	Sheffield	1	1
EC1963	27 Feb	Paris	2	5
WC1966	20 July	Wembley	2	0
1969	12 Mar	Wembley	5	0

v GERMANY

			E	G
1930	10 May	Berlin	3	3
1935	4 Dec	Tottenham	3	0
1938	14 May	Berlin	6	3

v EAST GERMANY

			E	EG
1963	2 June	Leipzig	2	1
1970	25 Nov	Wembley	3	1
1974	29 May	Leipzig	1	1

WEST GERMANY

			E	WG
1954	1 Dec	Wembley	3	1
1956	26 May	Berlin	3	1
1965	12 May	Nuremberg	1	0
1966	23 Feb	Wembley	1	0
WC1966	30 July	Wembley	4	2*
1968	1 June	Hanover	0	1
WC1970	14 June	Leon	2	3*
EC1972	29 Apr	Wembley	1	3
EC1972	13 May	Berlin	0	0
1975	12 Mar	Wembley	2	0
1978	22 Feb	Munich	1	2

**After extra time.*

v GREECE

			E	G
EC1971	21 Apr	Wembley	3	0
EC1971	1 Dec	Athens	2	0

v HUNGARY

			E	H
1908	10 June	Budapest	7	0
1909	29 May	Budapest	4	2
1909	31 May	Budapest	8	2
1934	10 May	Budapest	1	2
1936	2 Dec	Highbury	6	2
1953	25 Nov	Wembley	3	6
1954	23 May	Budapest	1	7
1960	22 May	Budapest	0	2
WC1962	31 May	Rancagua	1	2
1965	5 May	Wembley	1	0
1978	24 May	Wembley	4	1
WC1981	6 June	Budapest	3	1

v REPUBLIC OF IRELAND

			E	*RI*
1946	30 Sept	Dublin	1	0
1949	21 Sept	Everton	0	2
wc1957	8 May	Wembley	5	1
wc1957	19 May	Dublin	1	1
1964	24 May	Dublin	3	1
1976	8 Sept	Wembley	1	1
EC1978	25 Oct	Dublin	1	1
EC1980	6 Feb	Wembley	2	0

v ITALY

			E	*I*
1933	13 May	Rome	1	1
1934	14 Nov	Highbury	3	2
1939	13 May	Milan	2	2
1948	16 May	Turin	4	0
1949	30 Nov	Tottenham	2	0
1952	18 May	Florence	1	1
1959	6 May	Wembley	2	2
1961	24 May	Rome	3	2
1973	14 June	Turin	0	2
1973	14 Nov	Wembley	0	1
1976	28 May	New York	3	2
wc1976	17 Nov	Rome	0	2
wc1977	16 Nov	Wembley	2	0
EC1980	15 June	Turin	0	1

v LUXEMBOURG

			E	*L*
1927	21 May	Luxembourg	5	2
wc1960	19 Oct	Luxembourg	9	0
wc1961	28 Sept	Highbury	4	1
wc1977	30 Mar	Wembley	5	0
wc1977	12 Oct	Luxembourg	2	0

v MALTA

			E	*M*
EC1971	3 Feb	Valletta	1	0
EC1971	12 May	Wembley	5	0

v MEXICO

			E	*M*
1959	24 May	Mexico City	1	2
1961	10 May	Wembley	8	0
wc1966	16 July	Wembley	2	0
1969	1 June	Mexico City	0	0

v NETHERLANDS

			E	*N*
1935	18 May	Amsterdam	1	0
1946	27 Nov	Huddersfield	8	2
1964	9 Dec	Amsterdam	1	1
1969	5 Nov	Amsterdam	1	0
1970	14 Jan	Wembley	0	0
1977	9 Feb	Wembley	0	2

v NORWAY

			E	*N*
1937	14 May	Oslo	6	0
1938	9 Nov	Newcastle	4	0
1949	18 May	Oslo	4	1
1966	29 June	Oslo	6	1
wc1980	10 Sept	Wembley	4	0

v PERU

			E	*P*
1959	17 May	Lima	1	4
1962	20 May	Lima	4	0

v POLAND

			E	*P*
1966	5 Jan	Everton	1	1
1966	5 July	Chorzow	1	0
wc1973	6 June	Chorzow	0	2
wc1973	17 Oct	Wembley	1	1

v PORTUGAL

			E	*P*
1947	25 May	Lisbon	10	0
1950	14 May	Lisbon	5	3
1951	19 May	Everton	5	2
1955	22 May	Oporto	1	3
1958	7 May	Wembley	2	1
wc1961	21 May	Lisbon	1	1
wc1961	25 Oct	Wembley	2	0
1964	17 May	Lisbon	4	3
1964	4 June	São Paulo	1	1
wc1966	26 July	Wembley	2	1
1969	10 Dec	Wembley	1	0
1974	3 Apr	Lisbon	0	0
EC1974	20 Nov	Wembley	0	0
EC1975	19 Nov	Lisbon	1	1

v RUMANIA

			E	*R*
1939	24 May	Bucharest	2	0
1968	6 Nov	Bucharest	0	0
1969	15 Jan	Wembley	1	1
wc1970	2 June	Guadalajara	1	0
wc1980	15 Oct	Bucharest	1	2
wc1981	29 April	Wembley	0	0

v SPAIN

			E	*S*
1929	15 May	Madrid	3	4
1931	9 Dec	Highbury	7	1
wc1950	2 July	Rio de Janeiro	0	1
1955	18 May	Madrid	1	1
1955	30 Nov	Wembley	4	1
1960	15 May	Madrid	0	3
1960	26 Oct	Wembley	4	2
1965	8 Dec	Madrid	2	0
1967	24 May	Wembley	2	0
EC1968	3 Apr	Wembley	1	0
EC1968	8 May	Madrid	2	1
1980	26 Mar	Barcelona	2	0
EC1980	18 June	Naples	2	1
1981	25 Mar	Wembley	1	2

v SWEDEN

			E	*S*
1923	21 May	Stockholm	4	2
1923	24 May	Stockholm	3	1
1937	17 May	Stockholm	4	0
1947	19 Nov	Highbury	4	2
1949	13 May	Stockholm	1	3
1956	16 May	Stockholm	0	0
1959	28 Oct	Wembley	2	3
1965	16 May	Gothenburg	2	1
1968	22 May	Wembley	3	1
1979	10 June	Stockholm	0	0

v SWITZERLAND

			E	*S*
1933	20 May	Berne	4	0
1938	21 May	Zurich	1	2
1947	18 May	Zurich	0	1
1948	2 Dec	Highbury	6	0
1952	28 May	Zurich	3	0
wc1954	20 June	Berne	2	0
1962	9 May	Wembley	3	1
1963	5 June	Basle	8	1
EC1971	13 Oct	Basle	3	2
EC1971	10 Nov	Wembley	1	1
1975	3 Sept	Basle	2	1
1977	7 Sept	Wembley	0	0
wc1980	19 Nov	Wembley	2	1
wc1981	30 May	Basle	1	2

v USA

			E	*USA*
wc1950	29 June	Belo Horizonte	0	1
1953	8 June	New York	6	3
1959	28 May	Los Angeles	8	1
1964	27 May	New York	10	0

v URUGUAY

			E	*U*
1953	31 May	Montevideo	1	2
wc1954	26 June	Basle	2	4
1964	6 May	Wembley	2	1
wc1966	11 July	Wembley	0	0
1969	8 June	Montevideo	2	1
1977	15 June	Montevideo	0	0

v USSR

			E	USSR
1958	18 May	Moscow	1	1
WC1958	8 June	Gothenburg	2	2
WC1958	17 June	Gothenburg	0	1
1958	22 Oct	Wembley	5	0
1967	6 Dec	Wembley	2	2
EC1968	8 June	Rome	2	0
1973	10 June	Moscow	2	1

v YUGOSLAVIA

			E	Y
1939	18 May	Belgrade	1	2
1950	22 Nov	Highbury	2	2
1954	16 May	Belgrade	0	1
1956	28 Nov	Wembley	3	0
1958	11 May	Belgrade	0	5
1960	11 May	Wembley	3	3
1965	9 May	Belgrade	1	1
1966	4 May	Wembley	2	0
EC1968	5 June	Florence	0	1
1972	11 Oct	Wembley	1	1
1974	5 June	Belgrade	2	2

SCOTLAND

v ARGENTINA

			S	A
1977	18 June	Buenos Aires	1	1
1979	2 June	Glasgow	1	3

v AUSTRIA

			S	A
1931	16 May	Vienna	0	5
1933	29 Nov	Glasgow	2	2
1937	9 May	Vienna	1	1
1950	13 Dec	Glasgow	0	1
1951	27 May	Vienna	0	4
WC1954	16 June	Zurich	0	1
1955	19 May	Vienna	4	1
1956	2 May	Glasgow	1	1
1960	29 May	Vienna	1	4
1963	8 May	Glasgow	4	1
		(*abandoned after 79 mins*)		
WC1968	6 Nov	Glasgow	2	1
WC1969	5 Nov	Vienna	0	2
EC1978	20 Sept	Vienna	2	3
EC1979	17 Oct	Glasgow	1	1

v BELGIUM

			S	B
1947	18 May	Brussels	1	2
1948	28 Apr	Glasgow	2	0
1951	20 May	Brussels	5	0
EC1971	3 Feb	Liège	0	3
EC1971	10 Nov	Aberdeen	1	0
1974	2 June	Brussels	1	2
EC1979	21 Nov	Brussels	0	2
EC1979	19 Dec	Glasgow	1	3

v BRAZIL

			S	B
1966	25 June	Glasgow	1	1
1972	5 July	Rio de Janeiro	0	1
1973	30 June	Glasgow	0	1
WC1974	18 June	Frankfurt	0	0
1977	23 June	Rio de Janeiro	0	2

v BULGARIA

			S	B
1978	22 Feb	Glasgow	2	1

v CHILE

			S	C
1977	15 June	Santiago	4	2

v CYPRUS

			S	C
WC1968	17 Dec	Nicosia	5	0
WC1969	11 May	Glasgow	8	0

v CZECHOSLOVAKIA

			S	C
1937	22 May	Prague	3	1
1937	8 Dec	Glasgow	5	0
WC1961	14 May	Bratislava	0	4
WC1961	26 Sept	Glasgow	3	2
WC1961	29 Nov	Brussels	2	4*
1972	2 July	Porto Alegre	0	0
WC1973	26 Sept	Glasgow	2	1
WC1973	17 Oct	Prague	0	1
WC1976	13 Oct	Prague	0	2
WC1977	21 Sept	Glasgow	3	1

**After extra time.*

v DENMARK

			S	D
1951	12 May	Glasgow	3	1
1952	25 May	Copenhagen	2	1
1968	16 Oct	Copenhagen	1	0
EC1970	11 Nov	Glasgow	1	0
EC1971	9 June	Copenhagen	0	1
WC1972	18 Oct	Copenhagen	4	1
WC1972	15 Nov	Glasgow	2	0
EC1975	3 Sept	Copenhagen	1	0
EC1975	29 Oct	Glasgow	3	1

v FINLAND

			S	F
1954	25 May	Helsinki	2	1
WC1964	21 Oct	Glasgow	3	1
WC1965	27 May	Helsinki	2	1
1976	8 Sept	Glasgow	6	0

v FRANCE

			S	F
1930	18 May	Paris	2	0
1932	8 May	Paris	3	1
1948	23 May	Paris	0	3
1949	27 Apr	Glasgow	2	0
1950	27 May	Paris	1	0
1951	16 May	Glasgow	1	0
WC1958	15 June	Orebro	1	2

v GERMANY

			S	G
1929	1 June	Berlin	1	1
1936	14 Oct	Glasgow	2	0

v EAST GERMANY

			S	EG
1974	30 Oct	Glasgow	3	0
1977	7 Sept	East Berlin	0	1

v WEST GERMANY

			S	WG
1957	22 May	Stuttgart	3	1
1959	6 May	Glasgow	3	2
1964	12 May	Hanover	2	2
WC1969	16 Apr	Glasgow	1	1
WC1969	22 Oct	Hamburg	2	3
1973	14 Nov	Glasgow	1	1
1974	27 Mar	Frankfurt	1	2

v HUNGARY

			S	H
1938	7 Dec	Glasgow	3	1
1954	8 Dec	Glasgow	2	4
1955	29 May	Budapest	1	3
1958	7 May	Glasgow	1	1
1960	5 June	Budapest	3	3
1980	31 May	Budapest	1	3

v IRAN

			S	I
WC1978	7 June	Cordoba	1	1

v REPUBLIC OF IRELAND

			S	RI
WC1961	3 May	Glasgow	4	1
WC1961	7 May	Dublin	3	0
1963	9 June	Dublin	0	1
1969	21 Sept	Dublin	1	1

v ISRAEL

			S	I
wc1981	25 Feb	Tel Aviv	1	0
wc1981	28 Apr	Glasgow	3	1

v ITALY

			S	I
1931	20 May	Rome	0	3
wc1965	9 Nov	Glasgow	1	0
wc1965	7 Dec	Naples	0	3

v LUXEMBOURG

			S	L
1947	24 May	Luxembourg	6	0

v NETHERLANDS

			S	N
1929	4 June	Amsterdam	2	0
1938	21 May	Amsterdam	3	1
1959	27 May	Amsterdam	2	1
1966	11 May	Glasgow	0	3
1968	30 May	Amsterdam	0	0
1971	1 Dec	Rotterdam	1	2
wc1978	11 June	Mendoza	3	2

v NORWAY

			S	N
1929	28 May	Oslo	7	3
1954	5 May	Glasgow	1	0
1954	19 May	Oslo	1	1
1963	4 June	Bergen	3	4
1963	7 Nov	Glasgow	6	1
1974	6 June	Oslo	2	1
EC1978	25 Oct	Glasgow	3	2
EC1979	7 June	Oslo	4	0

v PARAGUAY

			S	P
wc1958	11 June	Norrkoping	2	3

v PERU

			S	P
1972	26 Apr	Glasgow	2	0
wc1978	3 June	Cordoba	1	3
1979	12 Sept	Glasgow	1	1

v POLAND

			S	P
1958	1 June	Warsaw	2	1
1960	4 May	Glasgow	2	3
wc1965	23 May	Chorzow	1	1
wc1965	13 Oct	Glasgow	1	2
1980	28 May	Poznan	0	1

v PORTUGAL

			S	P
1950	21 May	Lisbon	2	2
1955	4 May	Glasgow	3	0
1959	3 June	Lisbon	0	1
1966	18 June	Glasgow	0	1
EC1971	21 Apr	Lisbon	0	2
EC1971	13 Oct	Glasgow	2	1
1975	13 May	Glasgow	1	0
EC1978	29 Nov	Lisbon	0	1
EC1980	26 Mar	Glasgow	4	1
wc1980	15 Oct	Glasgow	0	0

v RUMANIA

			S	R
EC1975	1 June	Bucharest	1	1
EC1975	17 Dec	Glasgow	1	1

v SPAIN

			S	Sp
wc1957	8 May	Glasgow	4	2
wc1957	26 May	Madrid	1	4
1963	13 June	Madrid	6	2
1965	8 May	Glasgow	0	0
EC1974	20 Nov	Glasgow	1	2
EC1975	5 Feb	Valencia	1	1

v SWEDEN

			S	Sw
1952	30 May	Stockholm	1	3
1953	6 May	Glasgow	1	2
1975	16 Apr	Gothenburg	1	1
1977	27 Apr	Glasgow	3	1
wc1980	10 Sept	Stockholm	1	0

v SWITZERLAND

			S	Sw
1931	24 May	Geneva	3	2
1948	17 May	Berne	1	2
1950	26 Apr	Glasgow	3	1
wc1957	19 May	Basle	2	1
wc1957	6 Nov	Glasgow	3	2
1973	22 June	Berne	0	1
1976	7 Apr	Glasgow	1	0

v TURKEY

			S	T
1960	8 June	Ankara	2	4

v URUGUAY

			S	U
wc1954	19 June	Basle	0	7
1962	2 May	Glasgow	2	3

v USA

			S	USA
1952	30 Apr	Glasgow	6	0

v USSR

			S	USSR
1967	10 May	Glasgow	0	2
1971	14 June	Moscow	0	1

v YUGOSLAVIA

			S	Y
1955	15 May	Belgrade	2	2
1956	21 Nov	Glasgow	2	0
wc1958	8 June	Vasteras	1	1
1972	29 June	Belo Horizonte	2	2
wc1974	22 June	Frankfurt	1	1

v ZAIRE

			S	Z
wc1974	14 June	Dortmund	2	0

WALES

v AUSTRIA

			W	A
1954	9 May	Vienna	0	2
EC1955	23 Nov	Wrexham	1	2
EC1974	4 Sept	Vienna	1	2
1975	19 Nov	Wrexham	1	0

v BELGIUM

			W	B
1949	22 May	Liège	1	3
1949	23 Nov	Cardiff	5	1

v BRAZIL

			W	B
wc1958	19 June	Gothenburg	0	1
1962	12 May	Rio de Janeiro	1	3
1962	16 May	São Paulo	1	3
1966	14 May	Rio de Janeiro	1	3
1966	18 May	Belo Horizonte	0	1

v CHILE

			W	C
1966	22 May	Santiago	0	2

v CZECHOSLOVAKIA

			W	C
WC1957	1 May	Cardiff	1	0
WC1957	26 May	Prague	0	2
EC1971	21 Apr	Swansea	1	3
EC1971	27 Oct	Prague	0	1
WC1977	30 Mar	Wrexham	3	0
WC1977	16 Nov	Prague	0	1
WC1980	19 Nov	Cardiff	1	0

v DENMARK

			W	D
WC1964	21 Oct	Copenhagen	0	1
WC1965	1 Dec	Wrexham	4	2

v FINLAND

			W	F
EC1971	26 May	Helsinki	1	0
EC1971	13 Oct	Swansea	3	0

v FRANCE

			W	F
1933	25 May	Paris	1	1
1939	20 May	Paris	1	2
1953	14 May	Paris	1	6

v EAST GERMANY

			W	EG
WC1957	19 May	Leipzig	1	2
WC1957	25 Sept	Cardiff	4	1
WC1969	16 Apr	Dresden	1	2
WC1969	22 Oct	Cardiff	1	3

v WEST GERMANY

			W	WG
1968	8 May	Cardiff	1	1
1969	26 Mar	Frankfurt	1	1
1976	6 Oct	Cardiff	0	2
1977	14 Dec	Dortmund	1	1
EC1979	2 May	Wrexham	0	2
EC1979	17 Oct	Cologne	1	5

v GREECE

			W	G
WC1964	9 Dec	Athens	0	2
WC1965	17 Mar	Cardiff	4	1

v HUNGARY

			W	H
WC1958	8 June	Sanviken	1	1
WC1958	17 June	Stockholm	2	1
1961	28 May	Budapest	2	3
EC1962	7 Nov	Budapest	1	3
EC1963	20 Mar	Cardiff	1	1
EC1974	30 Oct	Cardiff	2	0
EC1975	16 Apr	Budapest	2	1

v ICELAND

			W	I
WC1980	2 June	Reykjavik	4	0

v IRAN

			W	I
1978	18 Apr	Teheran	1	0

v REPUBLIC OF IRELAND

			W	RI
1960	28 Sept	Dublin	3	2
1979	11 Sept	Swansea	2	1
1981	24 Feb	Dublin	3	1

v ISRAEL

			W	I
WC1958	15 Jan	Tel Aviv	2	0
WC1958	5 Feb	Cardiff	2	0

v ITALY

			W	I
1965	1 May	Florence	1	4
WC1968	23 Oct	Cardiff	0	1
WC1969	4 Nov	Rome	1	4

v KUWAIT

			W	K
1977	6 Sept	Wrexham	0	0
1977	20 Sept	Kuwait	0	0

v LUXEMBOURG

			W	L
EC1974	20 Nov	Swansea	5	0
EC1975	1 May	Luxembourg	3	1

v MALTA

			W	M
EC1978	25 Oct	Wrexham	7	0
EC1979	2 June	Valletta	2	0

v MEXICO

			W	M
WC1958	11 June	Stockholm	1	1
1962	22 May	Mexico City	1	2

v POLAND

			W	P
WC1973	28 Mar	Cardiff	2	0
WC1973	26 Sept	Katowice	0	3

v PORTUGAL

			W	P
1949	15 May	Lisbon	2	3
1951	12 May	Cardiff	2	1

v RUMANIA

			W	R
EC1970	11 Nov	Cardiff	0	0
EC1971	24 Nov	Bucharest	0	2

v SPAIN

			W	S
WC1961	19 Apr	Cardiff	1	2
WC1961	18 May	Madrid	1	1

v SWEDEN

			W	S
WC1958	15 June	Stockholm	0	0

v SWITZERLAND

			W	S
1949	26 May	Berne	0	4
1951	16 May	Wrexham	3	2

v TURKEY

			W	T
EC1978	29 Nov	Wrexham	1	0
EC1979	21 Nov	Izmir	0	1
WC1980	15 Oct	Cardiff	4	0
WC1981	25 Mar	Ankara	1	0

v REST OF UNITED KINGDOM

			W	UK
1951	5 Dec	Cardiff	3	2
1969	28 July	Cardiff	0	1

v USSR

			W	USSR
WC1965	30 May	Moscow	1	2
WC1965	27 Oct	Cardiff	2	1
WC1981	30 May	Wrexham	0	0

v YUGOSLAVIA

			W	Y
1953	21 May	Belgrade	2	5
1954	22 Nov	Cardiff	1	3
EC1976	24 Apr	Zagreb	0	2
EC1976	22 May	Cardiff	1	1

NORTHERN IRELAND

v ALBANIA

			NI	A
wc1965	7 May	Belfast	4	1
wc1965	24 Nov	Tirana	1	1

v ARGENTINA

			NI	A
wc1958	11 June	Halmstad	1	3

v AUSTRALIA

			NI	A
1980	11 June	Sydney	2	1
1980	15 June	Melbourne	1	1
1980	18 June	Adelaide	2	1

v BELGIUM

			NI	B
wc1976	10 Nov	Liège	0	2
wc1977	16 Nov	Belfast	3	0

v BULGARIA

			NI	B
wc1972	18 Oct	Sofia	0	3
wc1973	26 Sept	Sheffield	0	0
EC1978	29 Nov	Sofia	2	0
EC1979	2 May	Belfast	2	0

v CYPRUS

			NI	C
EC1971	3 Feb	Nicosia	3	0
EC1971	21 Apr	Belfast	5	0
wc1973	14 Feb	Nicosia	0	1
wc1973	8 May	London	3	0

v CZECHOSLOVAKIA

			NI	C
wc1958	8 June	Halmstad	1	0
wc1958	17 June	Malmo	2	1*

**After extra time*

v DENMARK

			NI	D
EC1978	25 Oct	Belfast	2	1
EC1979	6 June	Copenhagen	0	4

v FRANCE

			NI	F
1951	12 May	Belfast	2	2
1952	11 Nov	Paris	1	3
wc1958	19 June	Norrkoping	0	4

v WEST GERMANY

			NI	WG
wc1958	15 June	Malmo	2	2
wc1960	26 Oct	Belfast	3	4
wc1961	10 May	Hamburg	1	2
1966	7 May	Belfast	0	2
1977	27 Apr	Cologne	0	5

v GREECE

			NI	G
wc1961	3 May	Athens	1	2
wc1961	17 Oct	Belfast	2	0

v ICELAND

			NI	I
wc1977	11 June	Reykjavik	0	1
wc1977	21 Sept	Belfast	2	0

v REPUBLIC OF IRELAND

			NI	RI
EC1978	20 Sept	Dublin	0	0
EC1979	21 Nov	Belfast	1	0

v ISRAEL

			NI	I
1968	10 Sept	Jaffa	3	2
1976	3 Mar	Tel Aviv	1	1
wc1980	26 Mar	Tel Aviv	0	0

v ITALY

			NI	I
wc1957	25 Apr	Rome	0	1
1957	4 Dec	Belfast	2	2
wc1958	15 Jan	Belfast	2	1
1961	25 Apr	Bologna	2	3

v MEXICO

			NI	M
1966	22 June	Belfast	4	1

v NETHERLANDS

			NI	N
1962	9 May	Rotterdam	0	4
wc1965	17 Mar	Belfast	2	1
wc1965	7 Apr	Rotterdam	0	0
wc1976	13 Oct	Rotterdam	2	2
wc1977	12 Oct	Belfast	0	1

v NORWAY

			NI	N
EC1974	4 Sept	Oslo	1	2
EC1975	29 Oct	Belfast	3	0

v POLAND

			NI	P
EC1962	10 Oct	Katowice	2	0
EC1962	28 Nov	Belfast	2	0

v PORTUGAL

			NI	P
wc1957	16 Jan	Lisbon	1	1
wc1957	1 May	Belfast	3	0
wc1973	28 Mar	Coventry	1	1
wc1973	14 Nov	Lisbon	1	1
wc1980	19 Nov	Lisbon	0	1
wc1981	29 Apr	Belfast	1	0

v SPAIN

			NI	S
1958	15 Oct	Madrid	2	6
1963	30 May	Bilbao	1	1
1963	30 Oct	Belfast	0	1
EC1970	11 Nov	Seville	0	3
EC1972	16 Feb	Hull	1	1

v SWEDEN

			NI	S
EC1974	30 Oct	Solna	2	0
EC1975	3 Sept	Belfast	1	2
wc1980	15 Oct	Belfast	3	0
wc1981	3 June	Solna	0	1

v SWITZERLAND

			NI	S
wc1964	14 Oct	Belfast	1	0
wc1964	14 Nov	Lausanne	1	2

v TURKEY

			NI	T
wc1968	23 Oct	Belfast	4	1
wc1968	11 Dec	Istanbul	3	0

v URUGUAY

			NI	U
1964	29 Apr	Belfast	3	0

v USSR

			NI	USSR
wc1969	10 Sept	Belfast	0	0
wc1969	22 Oct	Moscow	0	2
EC1971	22 Sept	Moscow	0	1
EC1971	13 Oct	Belfast	1	1

v YUGOSLAVIA

			NI	Y
EC1975	16 Mar	Belfast	1	0
EC1975	19 Nov	Belgrade	0	1

REPUBLIC OF IRELAND

v ARGENTINA

			RI	*A*
1951	13 May	Dublin	0	1
1979	29 May	Dublin	0	0
1980	16 May	Dublin	0	1

v AUSTRIA

			RI	*A*
1952	7 May	Vienna	0	6
1953	25 Mar	Dublin	4	0
1958	14 Mar	Vienna	1	3
1962	8 Apr	Dublin	2	3
EC1963	25 Sept	Vienna	0	0
EC1963	13 Oct	Dublin	3	2
1966	22 May	Vienna	0	1
1968	10 Nov	Dublin	2	2
EC1971	30 May	Dublin	1	4
EC1971	10 Oct	Linz	0	6

v BELGIUM

			RI	*B*
1928	12 Feb	Liège	4	2
1929	30 Apr	Dublin	4	0
1930	11 May	Brussels	3	1
wc1934	25 Feb	Dublin	4	4
1949	24 Apr	Dublin	0	2
1950	10 May	Brussels	1	5
1965	24 Mar	Dublin	0	2
1966	25 May	Liège	3	2
wc1980	15 Oct	Dublin	1	1
wc1981	25 Mar	Brussels	0	1

v BRAZIL

			RI	*B*
1974	5 May	Rio de Janeiro	1	2

v BULGARIA

			RI	*B*
wc1977	1 June	Sofia	1	2
wc1977	12 Oct	Dublin	0	0
EC1979	19 May	Sofia	0	1
EC1979	17 Oct	Dublin	3	0

v CHILE

			RI	*C*
1960	30 Mar	Dublin	2	0
1972	21 June	Recife	1	2
1974	12 May	Santiago	2	1

v CYPRUS

			RI	*C*
wc1980	26 Mar	Nicosia	3	2
wc1980	19 Nov	Dublin	6	0

v CZECHOSLOVAKIA

			RI	*C*
1938	18 May	Prague	2	2
EC1959	5 Apr	Dublin	2	0
EC1959	10 May	Bratislava	0	4
wc1961	8 Oct	Dublin	1	3
1979	26 Sept	Prague	1	4
wc1961	29 Oct	Prague	1	7
EC1967	21 May	Dublin	0	2
EC1967	22 Nov	Prague	2	1
wc1969	4 May	Dublin	1	2
wc1969	7 Oct	Prague	0	3
1981	29 Apr	Dublin	3	1

v DENMARK

			RI	*D*
wc1956	3 Oct	Dublin	2	1
wc1957	2 Oct	Copenhagen	2	0
wc1968	4 Dec	Dublin	1	1
		(*abandoned after 51 mins*)		
wc1969	27 May	Copenhagen	0	2
wc1969	15 Oct	Dublin	1	1
EC1978	24 May	Copenhagen	3	3
EC1979	2 May	Dublin	2	0

v ECUADOR

			RI	*E*
1972	19 June	Natal	3	2

v FINLAND

			RI	*F*
wc1949	8 Sept	Dublin	3	0
wc1949	9 Oct	Helsinki	1	1

v FRANCE

			RI	*F*
1937	23 May	Paris	2	0
1952	16 Nov	Dublin	1	1
wc1953	4 Oct	Dublin	3	5
wc1953	25 Nov	Paris	0	1
wc1972	15 Nov	Dublin	2	1
wc1973	19 May	Paris	1	1
wc1976	17 Nov	Paris	0	2
wc1977	30 Mar	Dublin	1	0
wc1980	28 Oct	Paris	0	2

v GERMANY

			RI	*G*
1935	8 May	Dortmund	1	3
1936	17 Oct	Dublin	5	2
1939	23 May	Bremen	1	1

v WEST GERMANY

			RI	*WG*
1951	17 Oct	Dublin	3	2
1952	4 May	Cologne	0	3
1955	28 May	Hamburg	1	2
1956	25 Nov	Dublin	3	0
1960	11 May	Dusseldorf	1	0
1966	4 May	Dublin	0	4
1970	9 May	Berlin	1	2
1979	22 May	Dublin	1	3
1981	21 May	Bremen	0	3†

†*v West Germany 'B'*

v HUNGARY

			RI	*H*
1934	15 Dec	Dublin	2	4
1936	3 May	Budapest	3	3
1936	6 Dec	Dublin	2	3
1939	19 Mar	Cork	2	2
1939	18 May	Budapest	2	2
wc1969	8 June	Dublin	1	2
wc1969	5 Nov	Budapest	0	4

v ICELAND

			RI	*I*
EC1962	12 Aug	Dublin	4	2
EC1962	2 Sept	Reykjavik	1	1

v LUXEMBOURG

			RI	*L*
1936	9 May	Luxembourg	5	1
wc1953	28 Oct	Dublin	4	0
wc1954	7 Mar	Luxembourg	1	0

v IRAN

			RI	*I*
1972	18 June	Recife	2	1

v N IRELAND

			RI	*NI*
EC1978	20 Sept	Dublin	0	0
EC1979	21 Nov	Belfast	0	1

v ITALY

			RI	*I*
1926	21 Mar	Turin	0	3
1927	23 Apr	Dublin	1	2
EC1970	8 Dec	Rome	0	3
EC1971	10 May	Dublin	1	2

v NETHERLANDS

			RI	N
1932	8 May	Amsterdam	2	0
1934	8 Apr	Amsterdam	2	5
1935	8 Dec	Dublin	3	5
1955	1 May	Dublin	1	0
1956	10 May	Rotterdam	4	1
WC1980	10 Sept	Dublin	2	1

v NORWAY

			RI	N
WC1937	10 Oct	Oslo	2	3
WC1937	7 Nov	Dublin	3	3
1950	26 Nov	Dublin	2	2
1951	30 May	Oslo	3	2
1954	8 Nov	Dublin	2	1
1955	25 May	Oslo	3	1
1960	6 Nov	Dublin	3	1
1964	13 May	Oslo	4	1
1973	6 June	Oslo	1	1
1976	24 Mar	Dublin	3	0
1978	21 May	Oslo	0	0

v POLAND

			RI	P
1938	22 May	Warsaw	0	6
1938	13 Nov	Dublin	3	2
1958	11 May	Katowice	2	2
1958	5 Oct	Dublin	2	2
1964	10 May	Cracow	1	3
1964	25 Oct	Dublin	3	2
1968	15 May	Dublin	2	2
1968	30 Oct	Katowice	0	1
1970	6 May	Dublin	1	2
1970	23 Sept	Dublin	0	2
1973	16 May	Wroclaw	0	2
1973	21 Oct	Dublin	1	0
1976	26 May	Posnan	2	0
1977	24 Apr	Dublin	0	0
1978	12 Apr	Lodz	0	3
1981	23 May	Bydgoszcz	0	3

v PORTUGAL

			RI	P
1946	16 June	Lisbon	1	3
1947	4 May	Dublin	0	2
1948	23 May	Lisbon	0	2
1949	22 May	Dublin	1	0
1972	25 June	Recife	1	2

v SCOTLAND

			RI	S
WC1961	3 May	Glasgow	1	4
WC1961	7 May	Dublin	0	3
1963	9 June	Dublin	1	0
1969	21 Sept	Dublin	1	1

v SPAIN

			RI	S
1931	26 Apr	Barcelona	1	1
1931	13 Dec	Dublin	0	5
1946	23 June	Madrid	1	0
1947	2 Mar	Dublin	3	2
1948	30 May	Barcelona	1	2
1949	12 June	Dublin	1	4
1952	1 June	Madrid	0	6
1955	27 Nov	Dublin	2	2
EC1964	11 Mar	Seville	1	5
EC1964	8 Apr	Dublin	0	2
WC1965	5 May	Dublin	1	0
WC1965	27 Oct	Seville	1	4
WC1965	10 Nov	Paris	0	1
EC1966	23 Oct	Dublin	0	0
EC1966	7 Dec	Valencia	0	2
1977	9 Feb	Dublin	0	1

v SWEDEN

			RI	S
WC1949	2 June	Stockholm	1	3
WC1949	13 Nov	Dublin	1	3
1959	1 Nov	Dublin	3	2
1960	18 May	Malmo	1	4
EC1970	14 Oct	Dublin	1	1
EC1970	28 Oct	Malmo	0	1

v SWITZERLAND

			RI	S
1935	5 May	Basle	0	1
1936	17 Mar	Dublin	1	0
1937	17 May	Berne	1	0
1938	18 Sept	Dublin	4	0
1948	5 Dec	Dublin	0	1
EC1975	11 May	Dublin	2	1
EC1975	21 May	Berne	0	1
1980	30 Apr	Dublin	2	0

v TURKEY

			RI	T
EC1966	16 Nov	Dublin	2	1
EC1967	22 Feb	Ankara	1	2
EC1974	20 Nov	Izmir	1	1
EC1975	29 Oct	Dublin	4	0
1976	13 Oct	Ankara	3	3
1978	5 Apr	Dublin	4	2

v URUGUAY

			RI	U
1974	8 May	Montevideo	0	2

v USA

			RI	USA
1979	29 Oct	Dublin	3	2

v USSR

			RI	USSR
WC1972	18 Oct	Dublin	1	2
WC1973	13 May	Moscow	0	1
EC1974	30 Oct	Dublin	3	0
EC1975	18 May	Kiev	1	2

v WALES

			RI	W
1960	28 Sept	Dublin	2	3
1979	11 Sept	Swansea	1	2
1981	24 Feb	Dublin	1	3

v YUGOSLAVIA

			RI	Y
1955	19 Sept	Dublin	1	4

ENGLAND v YOUNG ENGLAND

			E	YE
1954	30 April	Highbury	2	1
1955	6 May	Highbury	5	0
1957	3 May	Highbury	1	2
1958	2 May	Stamford Bridge	4	1
1959	1 May	Highbury	3	3
1960	6 May	Highbury	2	1
1961	5 May	Stamford Bridge	1	1
1962	4 May	Highbury	3	2
1963	24 May	Highbury	3	2
1964	1 May	Stamford Bridge	3	0
1965	30 April	Highbury	2	2
1966	13 May	Stamford Bridge	1	1
1967	19 May	Highbury	0	5
1968	17 May	Highbury	1	4
1969	25 April	Stamford Bridge	0	0

BRITISH INTERNATIONAL MATCHES 1980–81

Southampton, 9 September, 1980
UNDER-21 INTERNATIONAL
England (3) 3 (*Eggan og, Goddard 2*)
Norway (0) 0 6973
England: Lukic; Dennis, Gilbert, Dyson, Fenwick, Baker, Johnston, Hodgson (Moses), Goddard (Fashanu), Hilaire, Allen.
Norway: Haugvaldstad; Roed, Herlovsen, Kojedal, Iversen, Gran, Giske, Soler, Eggan, Hjort, Osvold.

Degerfors, 9 September, 1980
UNDER-21 INTERNATIONAL
Sweden (1) 2 (*Sandberg, Nilsson*)
Scotland (0) 0 2140
Sweden: Revelli T.; Weidenstolpe, Revelli A., Hysen, Dennerby, Stromberg, Prytz (Hansson), Kindvall, Hohnquist (Ohlsson), Nilsson, Sandberg.
Scotland: McCulloch; Nicol, Connor, Blair, Paterson, Fulton, Nicholas, Watson, Brazil, Bett, MacDonald (Redford).

Dordrecht, 9 September, 1980
UNDER-21 INTERNATIONAL
Netherlands (0) 0
Wales (1) 2 (*Lowndes, Rush*) 800
Netherlands: Metgod; van der Merr (Scheve), Balkestein, Bosveld, Zondervan, Lokhoff, Weiysters, de Leeuw, Carvo (Koolhof), Valke, Kaiser.
Wales: Thomas; Jones V., Ratcliffe, Jones F., Price, Jackett, Lowndes, Charles, Rush, Giles, Aizlewood.

Dublin, 10 September, 1980
WORLD CUP
European Group Two
Eire (0) 2 (*Daly, Lawrenson*)
Netherlands (0) 1 (*Tahamata*) 32,000
Eire: Peyton; Langan, Hughton, O'Leary P., O'Leary D., Brady, Daly, Lawrenson, Stapleton, Grealish, Givens.
Netherlands: Hiele; Wijnstekers, Spelbos, Van der Korput (Metgod), Brandts, van Mierlo, Thijssen, Schoenmaker (van der Kerkhof W.), Peters, van Diensen, Tahamata.

Wembley, 10 September, 1980
WORLD CUP
European Group Four
England (1) 4 (*McDermott 2* [1 pen], *Woodcock, Mariner*)
Norway (0) 0 48,200
England: Shilton; Anderson, Sansom, Thompson, Watson, Robson, Gates, McDermott, Mariner, Woodcock, Rix.
Norway: Jacobsen T.; Berntsen, Kordahl, Aas, Grondalen, Albertsen, Hareide, Dokken, Larsen-Okland, Jacobsen P., Erlandsen (Ottesen).

Stockholm, 10 September, 1980
WORLD CUP
European Group Six
Sweden (0) 0
Scotland (0) 1 (*Strachan*) 39,831
Sweden: Hellstroem; Gustavsson, Borg, Bild, Arvidsson, Erlandsson, Ramberg, Nordgren, Nilsson, Sjoberg, Ohlsson.
Scotland: Rough, McGrain, Gray F., Miller, McLeish, Hansen, Dalglish (Archibald), Strachan, Gray A., Gemmill, Robertson.

Ploesti, 14 October, 1980
UEFA UNDER-21 CHAMPIONSHIP
Rumania (0) 4 (*Terhes 3, Dyson og*)
England (0) 0 10,000
Rumania: Speriatu; Vlad, Soloman, Rednik, Iouan, Pop, Zamfir (Geolgau), Suciv, Terhes, Bozesan, Klein.
England: Lukic; Fenwick, Dennis (Ranson), Baker, Gilbert, Dyson, Hilaire, Fashanu, Allen, Cowans, Dillon (Hodgson).

Old Trafford, 14 October, 1980
England 'B' (0) 1 (*Statham*)
USA (0) 0 7176
England 'B': Bailey; Batson, Statham, Talbot, Osman, Elliott, Barnes, Williams, Regis (Ward), Sunderland (Reeves), Armstrong.
USA: Mausser; Crudo (Fowles), Keough, Pecher, Macowski, Di Bernado, Cantilla (Van der Beck), Bandov (Huker), Nanchoff, Davis, Liveridge (Moyers).

Dublin, 15 October, 1980
WORLD CUP
European Group Two
Eire (1) 1 (*Grealish*)
Belgium (1) 1 (*Cluytens*) 40,000
Eire: Peyton; Hughton, Langan, Moran, Lawrenson, a1Daly, Grealish, Brady, Stapleton, Heighway, Givens (McGee).
Belgium: Pfaff; Gerets, Millecamps (De Wolfe), Meeuws, Renquin, Cluytens, Van der Eycken, Van Moer (Heyligan), Van den Bergh, Coeck, Ceulemans.

Cardiff, 15 October, 1980
WORLD CUP
European Group Three
Wales (2) 4 (*Flynn, James L. 2* [1 pen], *Walsh*)
Turkey (0) 0 11,770
Wales: Davies; Nicholas, Jones, Phillips, Price, Yorath, Flynn, Giles, Harris, Walsh, James L.
Turkey: Senol; Tungay, Cem, Husnu, Fatih, Erhan, Necdet (Serrdar), Gungor, Tuncay, Sedat, Halil.

Bucharest, 15 October, 1980
WORLD CUP
European Group Four
Rumania (1) 2 (*Raducanu, Iordanescu* pen)
England (0) 1 (*Woodcock*) 75,000
Rumania: Iordache; Negrila, Munteanu, Sames, Stefanescu, Beldeanu, Crisan, Iordanescu, Camataru, Ticleanu (Dumitru), Raducanu.
England: Clemence; Neal, Sansom, Thompson, Watson, Robson, Rix, McDermott, Birtles (Cunningham), Woodcock, Gates (Coppell).

Belfast, 15 October, 1980
WORLD CUP
European Group Six
Northern Ireland (3) 3 (*Brotherston, McIlroy, Nicholl J.*)
Sweden (0) 0 20,000
Northern Ireland: Platt; Nicholl J., Nicholl C., McClelland, Donaghy, Brotherston, O'Neill, Cassidy (McCreery), McIlroy, Hamilton (Cochrane), Armstrong.
Sweden: Moller; Borg, Borgesson, Arvidson, Larsson, Ramberg (Erlandsson), Nilsson P., Halmgren, Nilsson T., Edstrom, Ohlsson (Sjoberg).

Glasgow, 15 October, 1980
WORLD CUP
European Group Six
Scotland (0) 0
Portugal (0) 0 60,765

Scotland: Rough; McGrain, Gray F., Souness, Hansen, Miller, Strachan, Dalglish, Gray A., Gemmill, Robertson.
Portugal: Bento; Gabriel, Pietra, Simoes, Laranjeira, Fernandes, Eurico, Costa, Chalana, Dos Santos, Jordao (Nene).

Paris, 28 October, 1980
WORLD CUP
European Group Two
France (1) 2 (*Platini, Zimako*)
Eire (0) 0 46,300

France: Dropsy; Battison, Specht, Lopes, Bossis, Larios, Tigana, Platini (Petit), Rocheteau, Lacombe (Zimako), Six.
Eire: Peyton; Langan, Lawrenson, Moran, Hughton, Martin (Ryan), Brady, Grealish, Heighway, Stapleton, Robinson.

Birmingham, 17 November, 1980
England 'B' (0) 1 (*Sunderland*)
Australia (0) 0 3292

England 'B': Bailey G.; Batson (Bond), Bailey J., Williams, Gallagher, Wright, Sunderland, Mortimer, Regis (Morley), Cowans, Ward.
Australia: Maher; Perry (Felemidis), Tansey, Barnes, Prskaio, Henderson, Sharne, Boden (Jankovics), Cole (Bertogna), Davidson (Hogg), Krnevic.

Ipswich, 18 November, 1980
UEFA UNDER-21 CHAMPIONSHIP
England (4) 5 (*In-Albon og, Owen, Fashanu, Goddard, Hodgson*)
Switzerland (0) 0 3808

England: Woods; Ranson, Fenwick, Curbishley, Gilbert, Dyson, Goddard, Fashanu, Hodgson, Owen (Duxbury), Moses (Hilaire).
Switzerland: Mellacina (Bockli); Lauper, Schallibaum, Dutoit, Andermatt, In-Albon, Swicker, Kundert, Mauron, Perret, Koller.

Aberdeen, 18 November, 1980
UEFA UNDER-21 CHAMPIONSHIP
Scotland (1) 2 (*Watson, Gillespie*)
Denmark (0) 1 (*Eriksen*) 10,000

Scotland: Brough; Doyle, Stewart, Gillespie, McLaughlin, Bett, McGhee, Watson, Archibald, Bell (Fulton), McBride.
Denmark: Nielsen; Olczyk, Weber, Christensen, Busk (Jensen M.), Nedergaard, Sivebak (Johanssen), Helt, Olsen, Eriksen, Therkelssen.

Dublin, 19 November, 1980
WORLD CUP
European Group Two
Eire (4) 6 (*Daly 2* [1 pen], *Grealish, Robinson, Stapleton, Hughton*)
Cyprus (0) 0 20,000

Eire: Peyton; Hughton, Langan, Lawrenson, Moran, Daly, Grealish, Brady, Stapleton, Robinson (Givens), Heighway.
Cyprus: Constantino; Kalotheou, Loucia, Lysandrou, Pantziaras, Erotokiou, Theofamous, Ylagoudakis, Kalafas (Kouis), Tsingis, Miamiliotis (Maroudis).

Cardiff, 19 November, 1980
WORLD CUP
European Group Three
Wales (1) 1 (*Giles*)
Czechoslovakia (0) 0 20,175

Wales: Davies; Price, Ratcliffe, Nicholas, Yorath, Phillips, Thomas, Flynn, Walsh, Giles (Harris C.), Charles.
Czechoslovakia: Hruska; Barmos, Vojacek, Jurkemik, Macela, Radimec, Kozak, Panenka, Vizek, Masny, Nehoda.

Wembley, 19 November, 1980
WORLD CUP
European Group Four
England (2) 2 (*Tanner og, Mariner*)
Switzerland (0) 1 (*Pfister*) 70,000

England: Shilton; Neal, Sansom, Robson, Watson, Mills, Coppell, McDermott, Mariner, Brooking (Rix), Woodcock.
Switzerland: Burgener; Wehrli, Hermann, Ludi, Geiger, Barberis, Pfister, Tanner (Egli), Schonenberger (Marti), Elsener, Botteron.

Lisbon, 19 November, 1980
WORLD CUP
European Group Six
Portugal (0) 1 (*Jordao*)
Northern Ireland (0) 0 50,000

Portugal: Bento; Gabriel, Simoes, Laranjeira, Pietra, Sheu, Carlos Manuel (Nene), Alves (Texeira), Chalana, Jordao, Costa.
Northern Ireland: Platt; Nicholl J., O'Neill J., Nicholl C., Donaghy, O'Neill M., Cassidy (McCreery), McIlroy, Brotherston, Armstrong, Hamilton (Cochrane).

Dublin, 24 February, 1981
Eire (1) 1 (*Grealish*)
Wales (2) 3 (*Price, Boyle, Yorath*) 15,000

Eire: McDonagh; Langan, O'Callaghan, Holmes, Hughton, Daly, Grealish, Waddock, O'Keefe, Givens (Moran), Heighway.
Wales: Davies; Nicholas, Price, Jones, Ratcliffe, Boyle, Yorath, Flynn, James, Walsh, Harris.

Tel Aviv, 25 February, 1981
WORLD CUP
European Group Four
Israel (0) 0
Scotland (0) 1 (*Dalglish*) 35,000

Israel: Mizrahi; Machness, Cohen J., Ekhois, Cohen A., Bar, Shum, Cohen N., Sinai, Damti, Tarak.
Scotland: Rough, McGrain, Gray F., Souness, McLeish, Burns, Wark (Miller), Dalglish (Gray A.), Archibald, Gemmill, Robertson.

Anfield, Liverpool, 25 February, 1981
UNDER-21 INTERNATIONAL
England (1) 1 (*Shaw*)
Eire (0) 0 5882

England: Lukic (Hesford); Thomas, Dyson (Duxbury), Smith, Fenwick, Moses (Proctor), Johnston, McMahon, Shaw (Goddard), Chapman (Fashanu), Hodgson.
Eire: Bonner; Whelan A., McDonagh, Anderson, Hughton, Atkinson, Whelan R., Sheedy (Kinsella), O'Connor (Buckley), Donovan, McGee.

Brussels, 25 March, 1981
WORLD CUP
European Group Two
Belgium (0) 1 (*Ceulemans*)
Eire (0) 0 42,000
Belgium: Preud'Homme; Gerets, Millecamps, Meeuws, Renquin, Mommens (Vercauteren), Van der Eycken, Cluytens, Van den Bergh, Coeck (Wellens), Ceulemans.
Eire: McDonagh; Langan, Martin, Moran, Hughton, Daly, Grealish, Brady, Stapleton (Walsh), Robinson, Heighway.

Ankara, 25 March, 1981
WORLD CUP
European Group Three
Turkey (0) 0
Wales (0) 1 (*Harris*) 35,000
Turkey: Senol; Onur, Necati, Husnu, Gelik-Sedat, Gungor, Sedat, Volkan, Necdet, Tuncay, Halil (Sinan).
Wales: Davies; Jones, Price, Phillips, Ratcliffe, Flynn, Nicholas, Yorath, James, Harris (Giles), Walsh (Charles).

Glasgow, 25 March, 1981
WORLD CUP
European Group Six
Scotland (0) 1 (*Wark*)
Northern Ireland (0) 1 (*Hamilton*) 78,444
Scotland: Rough (Thomson); McGrain, Gray F., Burns (Hartford), McLeish, Miller, Wark, Archibald, Gray A., Gemmill, Robertson.
Northern Ireland: Jennings; Nicholl J., Nicholl C., O'Neill J., Nelson, McCreery, McIlroy, McClelland, Cochrane, Armstrong, Hamilton (Spence).

Wembley, 25 March, 1981
England (1) 1 (*Hoddle*)
Spain (2) 2 (*Satrustegui, Zamora*) 71,840
England: Clemence; Neal, Sansom, Robson, Butcher, Osman, Keegan, Francis (Barnes), Mariner, Brooking (Wilkins), Hoddle.
Spain: Arconada; Camacho, Gordillo, Maceda, Tendillo, Munoz (Montero), Juanito (Dani), Alonso, Satrustegui, Zamora, Marcos.

Granada, 25 March, 1981
Spain 'B' (2) 3 (*Alonso, Rubio* pen, *Santillana*)
England 'B' (0) 2 (*Statham, Martin*) 18,000
Spain 'B': Urruti; Gerardo (Alberto), Jiminez, Alvarez, Cundi, Diego (Fernandez), Alonso, Suara, Moran, Santillana, Rubio (Esteban).
England 'B': Corrigan; Batson, Statham, Williams, Martin, Elliott, MacKenzie (Power), Reeves, Morley, Sunderland, Rix.

Dublin, 15 April, 1981
INTER-LEAGUE
League of Ireland ( ) 1(*Davis* pen)
Irish League (0) 0
League of Ireland: Blackmore; Fenuik, Keely, Dunning, Lawlor, Flanagan, Walsh (O'Connor P.), Fagan, Devlin, Davis, Fairclough (Eviston).
Irish League: Dunlop; Smyth, Stitt, Dornan (McCurry), McKeown, Cleary, Anderson, Malone, Blackledge, Sloan, Worthington.

Glasgow, 28 April, 1981
WORLD CUP
European Group Six
Scotland (2) 3 (*Robertson 2* [2 pens], *Provan*)
Israel (0) 1 (*Sinai*) 61,489
Scotland: Rough; McGrain, Gray F., Hansen, McLeish, Souness, Provan, Archibald, Jordan, Hartford, Robertson.
Israel: Mizrahi; Machness, Cohen J., Ekhois, Cohen A., Bar, Shum, Zeitouni, Sinai, Damti, Tabak.

Swindon, 28 April, 1981
UEFA UNDER-21 CHAMPIONSHIP
England (1) 3 (*Heath 2, Thompson*)
Rumania (0) 0 8739
England: Lukic; Ranson (Duxbury), Fenwick, Moses, Gilbert, Smith, Mills, Lee, Thompson, Owen, Heath.
Rumania: Alexa; Vlad, Iovan, Rednic, Boldovan, Soloman, Soiman, Cimpeanu, Terhes, Klein, Geolgau.

Wembley, 29 April, 1981
WORLD CUP
European Group Four
England (0) 0
Rumania (0) 0 62,500
England: Shilton; Anderson, Sansom, Robson, Watson, Osman, Wilkins, Brooking (McDermott), Coppell, Francis, Woodcock.
Rumania: Iordache; Negrila, Munteanu, Sames, Stefanescu, Beldeanu, Crisan, Iordanescu, Camataru, Stoica, Balaci.

Belfast, 29 April, 1981
WORLD CUP
European Group Six
Northern Ireland (0) 1 (*Armstrong*)
Portugal (0) 0 25,000
Northern Ireland: Jennings; Nicholl J., Nicholl C., O'Neill J., Nelson, O'Neill M., McCreery, McIlroy, Armstrong, Hamilton, Cochrane.
Portugal: Bento; Gabriel, Humberto, Simoes, Pietra, Sheu, Manuel, Alves, Jordao, Oliveira (Nene), Costa.

Dublin, 29 April, 1981
Eire (1) 3 (*Moran 2, Stapleton*)
Czechoslovakia (0) 1 (*Masny*) 8000
Eire: McDonagh; Langan, Devine, Daly (Whelan), O'Leary D., Moran, Grimes, Martin, Stapleton, Walsh, O'Callaghan.
Czechoslovakia: Seman; Barmos, Macela (Jurkemik), Radimec, Jakubec, Kozak, Nemec (Bicovsky), Berger, Masny, Licka, Nehoda.

Wembley, 12 May, 1981
England (0) 0
Brazil (1) 1 (*Zico*) 75,000
England: Clemence; Neal, Sansom, Robson, Martin, Wilkins, Coppell, McDermott, Withe, Rix, Barnes.
Brazil: Valdir; Edevaldo, Isidoro, Luisinho, Cerezo, Junior, Oscar, Socrates, Reinaldo, Zico, Eder.

Swansea, 16 May, 1981
BRITISH INTERNATIONAL CHAMPIONSHIP
Wales (2) 2 (*Walsh 2*)
Scotland (0) 0 18,985
Wales: Davies; Ratcliffe, Jones (Boyle), Price, Phillips, Nicholas, Flynn, Harris, Thomas, Walsh (Charles), James L.
Scotland: Rough; Burns, Stewart, Gray F. (McGrain), McQueen, Miller, Hartford, Narey, Provan, Jordan, Graham (Sturrock).

Glasgow, 19 May, 1981
BRITISH INTERNATIONAL CHAMPIONSHIP
Scotland (1) 2 (*Stewart, Archibald*)
Northern Ireland (0) 0 25,448
Scotland: Thomson; McGrain, Gray F., Stewart, McLeish, Miller, Hartford, Sturrock, Archibald, Burns T., Robertson.
Northern Ireland: Jennings; Nicholl J., Nelson (Donaghy), McClelland, Nicholl C., O'Neill J., Cochrane, O'Neill M., Armstrong, McIlroy, Hamilton.

Wembley, 20 May, 1981
BRITISH INTERNATIONAL CHAMPIONSHIP
England (0) 0
Wales (0) 0 34,280
England: Corrigan; Anderson, Sansom, Robson, Watson, Wilkins, Coppell, Hoddle, Withe (Woodcock), Rix, Barnes.
Wales: Davies; Jones, Ratcliffe, Nicholas, Phillips, Price, Harris (Giles), Flynn, Walsh, Thomas, James L. (Rush).

Bremen, 21 May, 1981
West Germany 'B' (0) 3 (Del'Haye, Moran og, Schroder)
Eire (0) 0
West Germany 'B': Nigburg (Junghans); Koch, Geils, Steiner, Fleer, Bittcher, Funkel (Gross), Schroder, Del'Haye, Dieter Muller, Wilmer (Pinkall).
Eire: McDonagh; Langan, Moran, O'Leary D., Devine, Martin (Grimes), Grealish, Daly, Robinson (Donovan), Stapleton, O'Callaghan K. (Ryan).

Wembley, 23 May, 1981
BRITISH INTERNATIONAL CHAMPIONSHIP
England (0) 0
Scotland (0) 1 (*Robertson* pen) 90,000
England: Corrigan; Anderson, Sansom, Wilkins, Watson (Martin), Robson, Coppell, Hoddle, Withe, Rix, Woodcock (Francis).
Scotland: Rough; Stewart, Gray F., McGrain, McLeish, Miller, Provan (Sturrock), Archibald, Jordan, Hartford (Narey), Robertson.

Bydgoszcz, 23 May, 1981
Poland (2) 3 (*Iwan, O'Leary og, Ogaza*)
Eire (0) 0
Poland: Mowlik (Kostrzewa); Dziuba (Milewski), Janas (Skrobowski), Zmuda, Jalocha, Buncol, Kupcewicz, Buda (Kapka), Iwan, Ogaza, Smolarek (Okonski).
Eire: Bonner; Langan, Hughton, Grimes (Daly), O'Leary, Lawrenson, Moran (Waddock), Grealish, Robinson, Stapleton, O'Callaghan K. (Ryan).

Wrexham, 30 May, 1981
WORLD CUP
European Group Three
Wales (0) 0
USSR (0) 0 29,366
Wales: Davies; Jones, Price, Phillips, Ratcliffe, Flynn, Yorath, Nicholas, Thomas, Walsh (Charles), Harris (Giles).
USSR: Dasaev; Sulakvelidze, Chivadze, Blatcha, Burovsky, Buriak, Bessonov, Oganisian, Andreev, Kipiani (Gavrilov), Blokhin.

Basle, 30 May, 1981
WORLD CUP
European Group Four
Switzerland (2) 2 (*Scheiwiler, Sulser*)
England (0) 1 (*McDermott*) 40,000
Switzerland: Burgener; Ludi, Zappa, Egli, Hermann (Weber), Wehrli, Barberis, Botteron, Scheiwiler, Sulser, Elsener (Maissen).
England: Clemence; Mills, Osman, Watson (Barnes), Sansom, Coppell, Wilkins, Robson, Keegan, Mariner, Francis (McDermott).

Neuchatel, 31 May, 1981
UEFA UNDER-21 CHAMPIONSHIP
Switzerland (0) 0
England (0) 0 1500
Switzerland: Rurbuchen; Zeender, Dutoit, Schalibaum, Geiger, Kundert, Zahnd, Andermatt, Luthi (Saunier), Faure, Perret.
England: Lukic; Duxbury (Ranson), McCall, Moses, Gilbert, Smith, Heath, Shaw, Thompson, Lee, Proctor.

Stockholm, 3 June, 1981
WORLD CUP
European Group Six
Sweden (0) 1 (*Borg* pen)
Northern Ireland (0) 0 21,431
Sweden: Ravelli; Frederiksson, Hysen, Borjesson, Erlandsson, Persson, Borg, Nilsson P., Thomas Nilsson (Torbjorn Nilsson), Sjoberg, Svensson.
Northern Ireland: Jennings; Nicholl J. (McClelland), Nicholl C., O'Neill J., Nelson, O'Neill M., McCreery, McIlroy, Cochrane, Armstrong, Hamilton (Spence).

Keszthely, 5 June, 1981
UEFA UNDER-21 CHAMPIONSHIP
Hungary (1) 1 (*Mortel*)
England (1) 2(*Shaw, Fashanu*) 8000
Hungary: Disztl; Kerepeczky, Hires, Vadaz, Pesztor, Kardos, Melin (Fecsky), Salai, Mortel, Poloska, Rixer.
England: Lukic; Ranson, McCall, Lee, Gilbert, Smith, Moses, Fashanu, Thompson (Reid), Shaw, Heath.

Budapest, 6 June, 1981
WORLD CUP
European Group Four
Hungary (1) 1 (*Garaba*)
England (1) 3 (*Brooking 2, Keegan* pen) 65,000
Hungary: Katzirz; Martos, Garaba, Balint, Varga, Muller (Komjati), Nyilasi, Mucha, Fazekas (Bodonyi), Kiss, Torocsik.
England: Clemence; Neal, Thompson, Watson, Mills, McDermott, Robson, Brooking (Wilkins), Coppell, Mariner, Keegan.

INTERNATIONAL APPEARANCES

This is a list of full international appearances by Englishmen, Irishmen, Scotsmen and Welshmen in matches against the Home Countries and against foreign nations. It does not include unofficial matches against Commonwealth and Empire countries. The year indicated refers to the season; ie 1981 is the 1980-81 season.

Explanatory code for matches played by all five countries: A represents Austria; Alb, Albania; Arg, Argentina; Aus, Australia; B, Bohemia; Bel, Belgium; Br, Brazil; Bul, Bulgaria; Ch, Chile; Co, Colombia; Cy, Cyprus; Cz, Czechoslovakia; D, Denmark; Ec, Ecuador; Ei, Eire; EG, East Germany; F, France; Fi, Finland; G, Germany (pre-war); Gr, Greece; H, Hungary; Ho, Holland; I, Italy; Ic, Iceland; Ir, Iran; Is, Israel; K, Kuwait; L, Luxembourg; M, Mexico; Ma, Malta; N, Norway; Ni, Northern Ireland; P, Portugal; Par, Paraguay; Pe, Peru; Pol, Poland; R, Rumania; R of E, Rest of Europe; R of W, Rest of World; S, Scotland; Se, Sweden; Sp, Spain; Sw, Switzerland; T, Turkey; U, Uruguay; UK, Rest of United Kingdom; US, United States of America; USSR; W, Wales; WG, West Germany; Y, Yugoslavia.

(Note: For purposes of this code, and in order to distinguish from Eire, Northern Ireland is given throughout the series as Ni).

ENGLAND

Abbott, W. (Everton), 1902 v W (1)
A'Court, A. (Liverpool), 1958 v Ni, Br, A, USSR; 1959 v W (5)
Adcock, H. (Leicester C), 1929 v F, Bel, Sp; 1930 v Ni, W (5)
Alcock, C. W. (Wanderers), 1875 v S (1)
Alderson, J. T. (C Palace), 1923 v F (1)
Aldridge, A. (WBA), 1888 v Ni; (with Walsall Town Swifts), 1889 v Ni (2)
Allen, A. (Stoke C) 1960 v Se, W, Ni (3)
Allen, A. (Aston Villa), 1888 v Ni (1)
Allen, H. (Wolverhampton W), 1888 v S, W, Ni; 1889 v S; 1890 v S (5)
Allen, J. P. (Portsmouth), 1934 v Ni, W (2)
Allen, R. (WBA), 1952 v Sw; 1954 v Y, S; 1955 v WG, W (5)
Alsford, W. J. (Tottenham H), 1935 v S (1)
Amos, A. (Old Carthusians), 1885 v S; 1886 v W (2)
Anderson, R. D. (Old Etonians), 1879 v W (1)
Anderson, S. (Sunderland), 1962, v A, S (2)
Anderson, V. (Nottingham F), 1979 v Cz, Se; 1980 v Bul, Sp; 1981 v N, R, W, S (8)
Angus, J. (Burnley), 1961 v A (1)
Armfield, J. C. (Blackpool), 1959 v Br, Pe, M, US; 1960 v Y, Sp, H, S; 1961 v L, P, Sp, M, L, A, W, Ni, S; 1962 v A, Sw, Pe, W, Ni, S, L, P, H, Arg, Bul, Br; 1963 v F (2), Br, EG, Sw, Ni, W, S; 1964 v R of W, W, Ni, S; 1966 v Y, Fi (43)
Armitage, G. H. (Charlton Ath), 1926 v Ni (1)
Armstrong, D. (Middlesbrough), 1980 v Aus (1)
Armstrong, K. (Chelsea), 1955 v S (1)
Arnold, J. (Fulham), 1933 v S (1)
Arthur, J. W. H. (Blackburn R), 1885 v S, W, Ni; 1886 v S, W; 1887 v W, Ni (7)
Ashcroft, J. (Woolwich Arsenal), 1906 v Ni, W, S (3)
Ashmore, G. S. (WBA), 1926 v Bel (1)
Ashton, C. T. (Corinthians), 1926 v Ni (1)
Ashurst, W. (Notts Co), 1923 v Se (2); 1925 v S, W, Bel (5)
Astall, G. (Birmingham C), 1956 v Fi, WG (2)
Astle, J. (WBA), 1969 v W; 1970 v S, P, Br (sub), Cz (5)
Aston, J. (Manchester U), 1949 v S, W, D, Sw, Se, N, F; 1950 v S, W, Ni, Ei, I, P, Bel, Ch, US; 1951 v Ni (17)
Athersmith, W. C. (Aston Villa), 1892 v Ni, 1897 v S, W, Ni; 1898 v S, W, Ni; 1899 v S, W, Ni; 1900 v S, W (12)
Atyeo, P. J. W. (Bristol C), 1956 v Br, Se, Sp; 1957 v D, Ei (2) (6)
Austin, S. W. (Manchester C), 1926 v Ni (1)

Bach, P. (Sunderland), 1899 v Ni (1)
Bache, J. W. (Aston Villa), 1903 v W; 1904 v W, Ni; 1905 v S; 1907 v Ni; 1910 v Ni; 1911 v S (7)
Baddeley, T. (Wolverhampton W), 1903 v S, Ni; 1904 v S, W, Ni (5)
Bagshaw, J. J. (Derby Co), 1920 v Ni (1)
Bailey, H. P. (Leicester Fosse), 1908 v W, A (2), H, B (5)
Bailey, M. A. (Charlton Ath), 1964 v US; 1965 v W (2)
Bailey, N. C. (Clapham Rovers), 1878 v S; 1879 v S, W; 1880 v S; 1881 v S; 1882 v S, W; 1883 v S, W; 1884 v S, W, Ni; 1885 v S, W, Ni; 1886 v S, W; 1887 v S, W (19)
Baily, E. F. (Tottenham H), 1950 v Sp; 1951 v Y, Ni, W; 1952 v A (2), Sw, W; 1953 v Ni (9)
Bain, J. (Oxford University), 1887 v S (1)
Baker, A. (Arsenal), 1928 v W (1)
Baker, B. H. (Everton), 1921 v Bel; (with Chelsea), 1926 v Ni (2)
Baker, J. H. (Hibernian), 1960 v Y, Sp, H, Ni, S; (with Arsenal) 1966 v Sp, Pol, Ni (8)
Ball, A. J. (Blackpool), 1965 v Y, WG, Se; 1966 v S, Sp, Fi, D, U, Arg, P, WG (2), Pol (2); (with Everton), 1967 v W, S, Ni, A, Cz, Sp; 1968 v W, S, USSR, Sp (2), Y, WG; 1969 v Ni, W, S, R (2), M, Br, U; 1970 v P, Co, Ec, R, Br, Cz (sub), WG, W, S, Bel; 1971 v Ma, EG, Gr, Ma (sub), Ni, S; 1972 v Sw, Gr; (with Arsenal) WG (2), S; 1973 v W (3), Y, S (2), Cz, Ni, Pol; 1974 v P (sub); 1975 v WG, Cy (2), Ni, W, S (72)
Ball, J. (Bury), 1928 v Ni (1)
Balmer, W. (Everton), 1905 v Ni (1)
Bamber, J. (Liverpool), 1921 v W (1)
Bambridge, A. L. (Swifts), 1881 v W; 1883 v W; 1884 v Ni (3)
Bambridge, E. C. (Swifts), 1879 v S; 1880 v S; 1881 v S; 1882 v S, W, Ni; 1883 v W; 1884 v S, W, Ni; 1885 v S, W, Ni; 1886 v S, W; 1887 v S, W, Ni (18)
Bambridge, E. H. (Swifts), 1876 v S (1)
Banks, G. (Leicester C), 1963 v S, Br, Cz, EG; 1964 v W, Ni, S, R of W, U, P (2), US, Arg; 1965 v Ni, S, H, Y, WG, Se; 1966 v Ni, S, Sp, Pol (2), WG (2), Y, Fi, U, M, F, Arg, P; 1967 v Ni, W, S, Cz; (with Stoke C), 1968 v W, Ni, S, USSR (2), Sp, WG, Y; 1969 v Ni, S, R (2), F, U, Br; 1970 v W, Ni, S, Ho, Bel, Co, Ec, R, Br, Cz; 1971 v Gr, Ma (2), Ni, S; 1972 v Sw, Gr, WG (2), W, S (73)
Banks, H. E. (Millwall), 1901 v Ni (1)
Banks, T. (Bolton W), 1958 v USSR (3), Br, A; 1959 v Ni (6)
Bannister, W. (Burnley), 1901 v W; (with Bolton W), 1902 v Ni (2)
Barclay, R. (Sheffield W), 1932 v S; 1933 v Ni; 1936 v S (3)
Barkas, S. (Manchester C), 1936 v Bel; 1937 v S; 1938 v W, Ni, Cz (5)
Barker, J. (Derby Co), 1935 v I, Ho, S, W, Ni; 1936 v G, A, S, W, Ni; 1937 v W (11)
Barker, R. (Herts Rangers), 1872 v S (1)
Barker, R. R. (Casuals), 1895 v W (1)
Barlow, R. J. (WBA), 1955 v Ni (1)
Barnes, P. S. (Manchester C), 1978 v I, WG, Br, W, S, H; 1979 v D, Ei, Cz, Ni (2), S, Bul, A; (with WBA), 1980 v D, W; 1981 v Sp (sub), Br, W, Sw (sub) (20)
Barnet, H. H. (Royal Engineers), 1882 v Ni (1)

Barrass, M. W. (Bolton W), 1952 v W, Ni; 1953 v S (3)
Barrett, A. F. (Fulham), 1930 v Ni (1)
Barrett, J. W. (West Ham U), 1929 v Ni (1)
Barry, L. (Leicester C), 1928 v F, Bel; 1929 v F, Bel, Sp (5)
Barson, F. (Aston Villa), 1920 v W (1)
Barton, J. (Blackburn R), 1890 v Ni (1)
Barton, P. H. (Birmingham), 1921 v Bel; 1922 v Ni; 1923 v F; 1924 v Bel, S, W; 1925 v Ni (7)
Bassett, W. I. (WBA), 1888 v Ni, 1889 v S, W; 1890 v S, W; 1891 v S, Ni; 1892 v S; 1893 v S, W; 1894 v S; 1895 v S, Ni; 1896 v S, W, Ni (16)
Bastard, S. R. (Upton Park), 1880 v S (1)
Bastin, C. S. (Arsenal), 1932 v W; 1933 v I, Sw; 1934 v S, Ni, W, H, Cz; 1935 v S, Ni, I; 1936 v S, W, G, A; 1937 v W, Ni; 1938 v S, G, Sw, F (21)
Baugh, R. (Stafford Road), 1886 v Ni; (with Wolverhampton W) 1890 v Ni (2)
Bayliss, A. E. J. M. (WBA), 1891 v Ni (1)
Baynham, R. L. (Luton T), 1956 v Ni, D, Sp (3)
Beasley, A (Huddersfield T), 1939 v S (1)
Beats, W. E. (Wolverhampton W), 1901 v W; 1902 v S (2)
Beattie, T. K. (Ipswich T), 1975 v Cy (2), S; 1976 v Sw, P; 1977 v Fi, I (sub), Ho; 1978 v L (sub) (9)
Becton, F. (Preston NE), 1895 v Ni; (with Liverpool), 1897 v W (2)
Bedford, H. (Blackpool), 1923 v Se; 1925 v Ni (2)
Bell, C. (Manchester C), 1968 v Se, WG; 1969 v W, Bul, F, U, Br; 1970 v Ni (sub), Ho (2), P, Br (sub), Cz, WG (sub); 1972 v Gr, WG (2), W, Ni, S; 1973 v W (3), Y, S (2), Ni, Cz, Pol; 1974 v A, Pol, I, W, Ni, S, Arg, EG, Bul, Y; 1975 v Cz, P, WG, Cy (2), Ni, S; 1976 v Sw, Cy (48)
Bennett, W. (Sheffield U), 1901 v S, W (2)
Benson, R. W. (Sheffield U), 1913 v Ni (1)
Bentley, R. T. F. (Chelsea), 1949 v Se; 1950 v S, P, Bel, Ch, USA; 1953 v W, Bel; 1955 v W, WG, Sp, P (12)
Beresford, J. (Aston Villa), 1934 v Cz (1)
Berry, A. (Oxford University), 1909 v Ni (1)
Berry, J. J. (Manchester U), 1953 v Arg, Ch, U; 1956 v Se (4)
Bestall, J. G. (Grimsby T), 1935 v Ni (1)
Betmead, H. A. (Grimsby T), 1937 v Fi (1)
Betts, M. P. (Old Harrovians), 1877 v S (1)
Betts, W. (Sheffield W), 1889 v W (1)
Beverley, J. (Blackburn R), 1884 v S, W, Ni (3)
Birkett, R. H. (Clapham Rovers), 1879 v S (1)
Birkett, R. J. E. (Middlesbrough), 1936 v Ni (1)
Birley, F. H. (Oxford University), 1874 v S; (with Wanderers), 1875 v S (2)
Birtles, G. (Nottingham F), 1980 v Arg (sub), I; 1981 v R (3)
Bishop, S. M. (Leicester C), 1927 v S, Bel, L, F (4)
Blackburn, F. (Blackburn R), 1901 v S; 1902 v Ni; 1904 v S (3)
Blackburn, G. F. (Aston Villa), 1924 v F (1)
Blenkinsop, E. (Sheffield W), 1928 v F, Bel; 1929 v S, W, Ni, F, Bel, Sp; 1930 v S, W, Ni, G, A; 1931 v S, W, Ni, F, Bel; 1932 v S, W, Ni, Sp; 1933 v S, W, Ni, A (26)
Bliss, H. (Tottenham H), 1921 v S (1)
Blockley, J. P. (Arsenal), 1973 v Y (1)
Bloomer, S. (Derby Co), 1895 v S, Ni; 1896 v W, Ni; 1897 v S, W, Ni; 1898 v S; 1899 v S, W, Ni; 1900 v S; 1901 v S, W; 1902 v S, W, Ni; 1904 v S; 1905 v S, W, Ni; (with Middlesbrough), 1907 v S, W (23)
Blunstone, F. (Chelsea), 1955 v W, S, F, P; 1957 v Y (5)
Bond, R. (Preston NE), 1905 v Ni, W; 1906 v S, W, Ni; (with Bradford C), 1910 v S, W, Ni (8)
Bonetti, P. P. (Chelsea), 1966 v D; 1967 v Sp, A; 1968 v Sp; 1970 v Ho, P, WG (7)
Bonsor, A. G. (Wanderers), 1873 v S; 1875 v S (2)
Booth, F. (Manchester C), 1905 v Ni (1)
Booth, T. (Blackburn R.), 1898 v W; (with Everton), 1903 v S (2)
Bowden, E. R. (Arsenal), 1935 v W, I; 1936 v W, Ni, A; 1937 v H (6)
Bower, A. G. (Corinthians), 1924 v Ni, Bel; 1925 v W, Bel; 1927 v W (5)
Bowers, J. W. (Derby Co), 1934 v S, Ni, W (3)
Bowles, S. (QPR), 1974 v P, W, Ni; 1977 v I, Ho (5)
Bowser, S. (WBA), 1920 v Ni (1)
Boyer, P. J. (Norwich C), 1976 v W (1)
Boyes, W. (WBA), 1935 v Ho; (with Everton), 1939 v W, R of E (3)
Boyle, T. W. (Burnley), 1913 v Ni (1)
Brabrook, P. (Chelsea), 1958 v USSR; 1959 v Ni; 1960 v Sp (3)
Bradford, G. R. W. (Bristol R), 1956 v D (1)
Bradford, J. (Birmingham), 1924 v Ni; 1925 v Bel; 1928 v S; 1929 v Ni, W, F, Sp; 1930 v S, Ni, G, A; 1931 v W (12)
Bradley, W. (Manchester U), 1959 v I, US, M (sub) (3)
Bradshaw, F. (Sheffield W), 1908 v A (1)
Bradshaw, T. H. (Liverpool), 1897 v Ni (1)
Bradshaw, W. (Blackburn R), 1910 v W, Ni; 1912 v Ni; 1913 v W (4)
Brann, G. (Swifts), 1886 v S, W; 1891 v W (3)
Brawn, W. F. (Aston Villa), 1904 v W, Ni (2)
Bray, J. (Manchester C), 1935 v W; 1936 v S, W, Ni, G; 1937 v S (6)
Brayshaw, E. (Sheffield W), 1887 v Ni (1)
Bridges, B. J. (Chelsea), 1965 v S, H, Y; 1966 v A (4)
Bridgett, A. (Sunderland), 1905 v S; 1908 v S, A (2), H, B; 1909 v Ni, W, H (2), A (11)
Brindle, T. (Darwen), 1880 v S, W (2)
Brittleton, J. T. (Sheffield W), 1912 v S, W, Ni; 1913 v S; 1914 v W (5)
Britton, C. S. (Everton), 1935 v S, W, Ni, I; 1937 v S, Ni, H, N, Se (9)
Broadbent, P. F. (Wolverhampton W), 1958 v USSR; 1959 v S, W, Ni, I, Br; 1960 v S (7)
Broadis, I. A. (Manchester C), 1952 v S, A, I; 1953 v S, Arg, Ch, U, US; (with Newcastle U), 1954 v S, H, Y, Bel, Sw, U (14)
Brockbank, J. (Cambridge University), 1872 v S (1)
Brodie, J. B. (Wolverhampton W), 1889 v S, Ni; 1891 v Ni (3)
Bromilow, T. G. (Liverpool), 1921 v W; 1922 v S, W; 1923 v Bel; 1926 v Ni (5)
Bromley-Davenport, W. E. (Oxford University), 1884 v S, W (2)
Brook, E. F. (Manchester C), 1930 v Ni; 1933 v Sw: 1934 v S, W, Ni, F, H, Cz; 1935 v S, W, Ni, I; 1936 v S, W, Ni; 1937 v H; 1938 v W, Ni (18)
Brooking, T. D. (West Ham U), 1974 v P, Arg, EG, Bul, Y; 1975 v Cz (sub), P; 1976 v P, W, Br, I, Fi; 1977 v Ei, Fi, I, Ho, Ni, W; 1978 v I, WG, Br, W, S (sub), H; 1979 v D, Ei, Ni, W (sub), S, Bul, Se (sub), A; 1980 v D, Ni, Arg (sub), W, Ni, S, Bel, Sp; 1981 v Sw, Sp, R, H (44)
Brooks, J. (Tottenham H), 1957 v W, Y, D (3)
Broome, F. H. (Aston Villa), 1938 v G, Sw, F; 1939 v N, I, R, Y (7)
Brown, A. (Aston Villa), 1882 v S, W, Ni (3)
Brown, A. S. (Sheffield U), 1904 v W; 1906 v Ni (2)
Brown, A. (WBA), 1971 v W (1)
Brown, G. (Huddersfield T), 1927 v S, W, Ni, Bel, L, F; 1928 v W; 1929 v S; (with Aston Villa), 1933 v W (9)
Brown, J. (Blackburn R), 1881 v W; 1882 v Ni; 1885 v S, W, Ni (5)
Brown, J. H. (Sheffield W), 1927 v S, W, Bel, L, F; 1930 v Ni (6)
Brown, K. (West Ham U), 1960 v Ni (1)
Brown, W. (West Ham U), 1924 v Bel (1)
Bruton, J. (Burnley), 1928 v F, Bel; 1929 v S (3)

Bryant, W. I. (Clapton), 1925 v F (1)
Buchan, C. M. (Sunderland), 1913 v Ni; 1920 v W; 1921 v W, Bel; 1923 v F; 1924 v S (6)
Buchanan, W. S. (Clapham R), 1876 v S (1)
Buckley, F. C. (Derby Co), 1914 v Ni (1)
Bullock, F. E. (Huddersfield T), 1921 v Ni (1)
Bullock, N. (Bury), 1923 v Bel; 1926 v W; 1927 v Ni (3)
Burgess, H. (Manchester C), 1904 v S, W, Ni; 1906 v S (4)
Burgess, H. (Sheffield W), 1931 v S, Ni, F, Bel (4)
Burnup, C. J. (Cambridge University), 1896 v S (1)
Burrows, H. (Sheffield W), 1934 v H, Cz; 1935 v Ho (3)
Burton, F. E. (Nottingham F), 1889 v Ni (1)
Bury, L. (Cambridge University), 1877 v S; (with Old Etonians), 1879 v W (2)
Butcher, T. (Ipswich T), 1980 v Aus; 1981 v Sp (2)
Butler, J. D. (Arsenal), 1925 v Bel (1)
Butler, W. (Bolton W), 1924 v S (1)
Byrne, G. (Liverpool), 1963 v S; 1966 v N (2)
Byrne, J. J. (C Palace), 1962 v Ni; (with West Ham U), 1963 v Sw; 1964 v S, U, P (2), Ei, Br, Arg; 1965 v W, S (11)
Byrne, R. W. (Manchester U), 1954 v S, H, Y, Bel, Sw, U; 1955 v S, W, Ni, WG, F, Sp, P; 1956 v S, W, Ni, Br, Se, Fi, WG, D, Sp; 1957 v S, W, Ni, Y, D (2), Ei (2); 1958 v W, Ni, F (33)

Callaghan, I. R. (Liverpool), 1966 v Fi, F; 1978 v Sw, L (4)
Calvey, J. (Nottingham F), 1902 v Ni (1)
Campbell, A. F. (Blackburn R), 1929 v W, Ni; (with Huddersfield T), 1931 v W, S, Ni; 1932 v W, Ni, Sp (8)
Camsell, G. H. (Middlesbrough), 1929 v F, Bel; 1930 v Ni, W; 1934 v F; 1936 v S, G, A, Bel (9)
Capes, A. J. (Stoke C), 1903 v S (1)
Carr, J. (Middlesbrough), 1920 v Ni; 1923 v W (2)
Carr, J. (Newcastle U), 1905 v Ni; 1907 v Ni (2)
Carr, W. H. (Owlerton, Sheffield), 1875 v S (1)
Carter, H. S. (Sunderland), 1934 v S, H; 1936 v G; 1937 v S, Ni, H; (with Derby Co), 1947 v S, W, Ni, Ei, Ho, F, Sw (13)
Carter, J. H. (WBA), 1926 v Bel; 1929 v Bel, Sp (3)
Catlin, A. E. (Sheffield W), 1937 v W, Ni, H, N, Se (5)
Chadwick, A. (Southampton), 1900 v S, W (2)
Chadwick, E. (Everton), 1891 v S, W; 1892 v S; 1893 v S; 1894 v S; 1896 v Ni; 1897 v S (7)
Chambers, H. (Liverpool), 1921 v S, W, Bel; 1923 v S, W, Ni, Bel; 1924 v Ni (8)
Channon, M. R. (Southampton), 1973 v Y, S (2), Ni, W, Cz, USSR, I; 1974 v A, Pol, I, P, W, Ni, S, Arg, EG, Bul, Y; 1975 v Cz, P, WG, Cy (2), Ni (sub), W, S; 1976 v Sw, Cz, P, W, Ni, S, Br, I, Fi; 1977 v Fi, I, L, Ni, W, S, Br (sub), Arg, U; (with Manchester C), 1978 v Sw (46)
Charlton, J. (Leeds U), 1965 v S, H, Y, WG, Se; 1966 v W, Ni, S, A, Sp, Pol (2), WG (2), Y, Fi, D, U, M, F, Arg, P; 1967 v W, S, Ni, Cz; 1968 v W, Sp; 1969 v W, R, F; 1970 v Ho (2), P, Cz (35)
Charlton, R. (Manchester U), 1958 v S, P, Y; 1959 v S, W, Ni, USSR, I, Br, Pe, M, US; 1960 v W, S, Se, Y, Sp, H; 1961 v Ni, W, S, L, P, Sp, M, I, A; 1962 v W, Ni, S, A, Sw, Pe, L, P, H, Arg, Bul, Br; 1963 v S, F, Br, Cz, EG, Sw; 1964 v S, W, Ni, R of W, U, P, Ei, Br, Arg, US (sub); 1965 v Ni, S, Ho; 1966 v W, Ni, S, A, Sp, WG (2), Y, Fi, N, Pol, U, M, F, Arg, P; 1967 v Ni, W, S, Cz; 1968 v W, Ni, S, USSR (2), Sp (2), Se, Y; 1969 v S, W, Ni, R (2), Bul, M, Br; 1970 v W, Ni, Ho (2), P, Co, Ec, Cz, R, Br, WG (106)
Charnley, R. O. (Blackpool), 1963 v F (1)
Charsley, C. [illegible] (Small Heath), 1893 v Ni (1)
Chedgzoy, S. (Everton), 1920 v W; 1921 v W, S, Ni; 1922 v Ni; 1923 v S; 1924 v W; 1925 v Ni (8)
Chenery, C. J. (C Palace), 1872 v S; 1873 v S; 1874 v S (3)
Cherry, T. J. (Leeds U), 1976 v W, S (sub), Br, Fi; 1977 v Ei, I, L, Ni, S (sub), Br, Arg, U; 1978 v Sw, L, I, Br, W; 1979 v Cz, W, Se; 1980 v Ei, Arg (sub), W, Ni, S, Aus, Sp (sub) (27)
Chilton, A. (Manchester U), 1951 v Ni; 1952 v F (2)
Chippendale, H. (Blackburn R), 1894 v Ni (1)
Chivers, M. (Tottenham H), 1971 v Ma (2), Gr, Ni, S; 1972 v Sw (1+1 sub), Gr, WG (2), Ni (sub), S; 1973 v W (3), S (2), Ni, Cz, Pol, USSR, I; 1974 v A, Pol (24)
Christian, E. (Old Etonians), 1879 v S (1)
Clamp, E. (Wolverhampton W), 1958 v USSR (2), Br, A (4)
Clapton, D. R. (Arsenal), 1959 v W (1)
Clare, T. (Stoke C), 1889 v Ni; 1892 v Ni; 1893 v W; 1894 v S (4)
Clarke, A. J. (Leeds U), 1970 v Cz; 1971 v EG, Ma, Ni, W (sub), S (sub); 1973 v S (2), W, Cz, Pol, USSR, I; 1974 v A, Pol, I; 1975 v P; 1976 v Cz, P (sub) (19)
Clarke, H. A. (Tottenham H), 1954 v S (1)
Clay, T. (Tottenham H), 1920 v W; 1922 v W, S, Ni (4)
Clayton, R. (Blackburn R), 1956 v Ni, Br, Se, Fi, WG, Sp; 1957 v S, W, Ni, Y, D (2), Ei (2); 1958 v S, W, Ni, F, P, Y, USSR; 1959 v S, W, Ni, USSR, I, Br, Pe, M, US; 1960 v W, Ni, S, Se, Y (35)
Clegg, J. C. (Sheffield W), 1872 v S (1)
Clegg, W. E. (Sheffield W), 1873 v S; (with Sheffield Albion), 1879 v W (2)
Clemence, R. N. (Liverpool), 1973 v W (2); 1974 v EG, Bul, Y; 1975 v Cz, P, WG, Cy, Ni, W, S; 1976 v Sw, Cz, P, W (2), Ni, S, Br, Fi; 1977 v Ei, Fi, I, Ho, L, S, Br, Arg, U; 1978 v Sw, L, I, WG, Ni, S; 1979 v D, Ei, Ni (2), S, Bul, A (sub); 1980 v D, Bul, Ei, Arg, W, S, Bel, Sp; 1981 v R, Sp, Br, Sw, H (56)
Clement, D. T. (QPR), 1976 v W (sub), W, I; 1977 v I, Ho (5)
Clough, B. H. (Middlesbrough), 1960 v W, Se (2)
Coates, R. (Burnley), 1970 v Ni; 1971 v Gr (sub); (with Tottenham H), Ma, W (4)
Cobbold, W. N. (Cambridge University), 1883 v S, Ni; 1885 v S, Ni; 1886 v S, W; (with Old Carthusians), 1887 v S, W, Ni (9)
Cock, J. G. (Huddersfield T), 1920 v Ni; (with Chelsea), v S (2)
Cockburn, H. (Manchester U), 1947 v W, Ni, Ei; 1948 v S, I; 1949 v S, Ni, D, Sw, Se; 1951 v Arg, P; 1952 v F (13)
Cohen, G. R. (Fulham), 1964 v U, P, Ei, US, Br; 1965 v W, S, Ni, Bel, H, Ho, Y, WG, Se; 1966 v W, S, Ni, A, Sp, Pol (2), WG (2), N, D, U, M, F, Arg, P; 1967 v W, S, Ni, Cz, Sp; 1968 v W, Ni (37)
Coleclough, H. (C Palace), 1914 v W (1)
Coleman, E. H. (Dulwich Hamlet), 1921 v W (1)
Coleman, J. (Woolwich Arsenal), 1907 v Ni (1)
Common, A. (Sheffield U), 1904 v W, Ni; (with Middlesbrough), 1906 v W (3)
Compton, L. H. (Arsenal), 1951 v W, Y (2)
Conlin, J. (Bradford C), 1906 v S (1)
Connelly, J. M. (Burnley), 1960 v W, N, S, Se; 1962 v W, A Sw, P; 1963 v W, F; (with Manchester U), 1965 v H, Y, Se; 1966 v W, Ni, S, A, N, D, U (20)
Cook, T. E. R. (Brighton), 1925 v W (1)
Cooper, N. C. (Cambridge University), 1893 v Ni (1)
Cooper, T. (Derby Co), 1928 v Ni; 1929 v W, Ni, S, F, Bel, Sp; 1931 v F; 1932 v W, Sp; 1933 v S; 1934 v S, H, Cz; 1935 v W (15)
Cooper, T. (Leeds U), 1969 v W, S, F, M; 1970 v Ho, Bel, Co, Ec, R, Cz, Br, WG; 1971 v EG, Ma, Ni, W, S; 1972 v Sw (2); 1975 v P (20)
Coppell, S. J. (Manchester U), 1978 v I, WG, Br, W, Ni, S, H; 1979 v D, Ei, Cz, Ni (2), W (sub), S, Bul, A; 1980 v D, Ni, Ei (sub), Sp, Arg, W, S, Bel, I; 1981 v R (sub), Sw, R, Br, W, S, Sw, H (33)

Copping, W. (Leeds U), 1933 v I, Sw; 1934 v S, Ni, W, F; (with Arsenal), 1935 v Ni, I; 1936 v A, Bel; 1937 v N, Se, Fi; 1938 v S, W, Ni, Cz; 1939 v W, R of E; (with Leeds U), R (20)
Corbett, B. O. (Corinthians), 1901 v W (1)
Corbett, R. (Old Malvernians), 1903 v W (1)
Corbett, W. S. (Birmingham), 1908 v A, H, B (3)
Corrigan, J. T. (Manchester C), 1976 v I (sub), Br; 1979 v W; 1980 v Ni, Aus; 1981 v W, S (7)
Cotterill, G. H. (Cambridge University), 1891 v Ni; (with Old Brightonians), 1892 v W; 1893 v S, Ni (4)
Cottle, J. R. (Bristol C), 1909 v Ni (1)
Cowan, S. (Manchester C), 1926 v Bel; 1930 v A; 1931 v Bel (3)
Cowell, A. (Blackburn R), 1910 v Ni (1)
Cox, J. (Liverpool), 1901 v Ni; 1902 v S; 1903 v S (3)
Cox, J. D. (Derby Co), 1892 v Ni (1)
Crabtree, J. W. (Burnley), 1894 v Ni; 1895 v Ni, S; (with Aston Villa), 1896 v W, S, Ni; 1899 v S, W, Ni; 1900 v S, W, Ni; 1901 v W; 1902 v W (14)
Crawford, J. F. (Chelsea), 1931 v S (1)
Crawford, R. (Ipswich T), 1962 v Ni, A (2)
Crawshaw, T. H. (Sheffield W), 1895 v Ni; 1896 v S, W, Ni; 1897 v S, W, Ni; 1901 v Ni; 1904 v W, Ni (10)
Crayston, W. J. (Arsenal), 1936 v S, W, G, A, Bel; 1938 v W, Ni, Cz (8)
Creek, F. N. S. (Corinthians), 1923 v F (1)
Cresswell, W. (South Shields), 1921 v W; (with Sunderland), 1923 v F; 1924 v Bel; 1925 v Ni; 1926 v W; 1927 v Ni; (with Everton), 1930 v Ni (7)
Crompton, R. (Blackburn R), 1902 v S, W, Ni; 1903 v S, W; 1904 v S, W, Ni; 1906 v S, W, Ni; 1907 v S, W, Ni; 1908 v S, W, Ni, A (2), H, B; 1909 v S, W, Ni, H (2), A; 1910 v S, W; 1911 v S, W, Ni; 1912 v S, W, Ni; 1913 v S, W, Ni; 1914 v S, W, Ni (41)
Crooks, S. D. (Derby Co), 1930 v S, G, A; 1931 v S, W, Ni, F, Bel; 1932 v S, W, Ni, Sp; 1933 v Ni, W, A; 1934 v S, Ni, W, F, H, Cz; 1935 v Ni; 1936 v S, W; 1937 v W, H (26)
Crowe, C. (Wolverhampton W), 1963 v F (1)
Cuggy, F. (Sunderland), 1913 v Ni; 1914 v Ni (2)
Cullis, S. (Wolverhampton W), 1938 v S, W, Ni, F, Cz; 1939 v S, Ni, R of E, N, I, R, Y (12)
Cunliffe, A. (Blackburn R), 1933 v Ni, W (2)
Cunliffe, D. (Portsmouth), 1900 v Ni (1)
Cunliffe, J. N. (Everton), 1936 v Bel (1)
Cunningham, L. (WBA), 1979 v W, Se, A (sub); (with Real Madrid), 1980 v Ei, Sp (sub); 1981 v R (sub) (6)
Currey, E. S. (Oxford University), 1890 v S, W (2)
Currie, A. W. (Sheffield U), 1972 v Ni; 1973 v USSR, I; 1974 v A, Pol, I; 1976 v Sw; (with Leeds U), 1978 v Br, W (sub), Ni, S, H (sub); 1979 v Cz, Ni (2), W, Se (17)
Cursham, A. W. (Notts Co), 1876 v S; 1877 v S; 1878 v S; 1879 v W; 1883 v S, W (6)
Cursham, H. A. (Notts Co), 1880 v W; 1882 v S, W, Ni; 1883 v S, W, Ni; 1884 v Ni (8)

Daft, H. B. (Notts Co), 1889 v Ni; 1890 v S, W; 1891 v Ni; 1892 v Ni (5)
Danks, T. (Nottingham F), 1885 v S (1)
Davenport, J. K. (Bolton W), 1885 v W; 1890 v Ni (2)
Davis, G. (Derby Co), 1904 v W, Ni (2)
Davis, H. (Sheffield W), 1903 v S, W, Ni (3)
Davison, J. E. (Sheffield W), 1922 v W (1)
Dawson, J. (Burnley), 1922 v S, Ni (2)
Day, S. H. (Old Malvernians), 1906 v Ni, W, S (3)
Dean, W. R. (Everton), 1927 v S, W, F, Bel, L; 1928 v S, W, Ni, F, Bel; 1929 v S, W, Ni; 1931 v S; 1932 v Sp; 1933 v Ni (16)
Deeley, N. V. (Wolverhampton W), 1959 v Br, Pe (2)
Devey, J. H. G. (Aston Villa), 1892 v Ni; 1894 v Ni (2)
Devonshire, A. (West Ham U), 1980 v Aus (sub), Ni (2)
Dewhurst, F. (Preston NE), 1886 v W, Ni; 1887 v S, W, Ni; 1888 v S, W, Ni; 1889 v W (9)
Dewhurst, G. P. (Liverpool Ramblers), 1895 v W (1)
Dickinson, J. W. (Portsmouth), 1949 v N, F; 1950 v S, W, Ei, P, Bel, Ch, US, Sp; 1951 v Ni, W, Y; 1952 v W, Ni, S, A (2), I, Sw; 1953 v W, Ni, S, Bel, Arg, Ch, U, US; 1954 v W, Ni, S, R of E, H (2), Y, Bel, Sw, U; 1955 v Sp, P; 1956 v W, Ni, S, D, Sp; 1957 v W, Y, D (48)
Dimmock, J. H. (Tottenham H), 1921 v S; 1926 v W, Bel (3)
Ditchburn, E. G. (Tottenham H), 1949 v Sw, Se; 1953 v US; 1957 v W, Y, D (6)
Dix, R. W. (Derby Co), 1939 v N (1)
Dixon, J. A. (Notts Co), 1885 v W (1)
Dobson, A. T. C. (Notts Co), 1882 v Ni; 1884 v S, W, Ni (4)
Dobson, C. F. (Notts Co), 1886 v Ni (1)
Dobson, J. M. (Burnley), 1974 v P, EG, Bul, Y; (with Everton), 1975 v Cz (5)
Doggart, A. G. (Corinthians), 1924 v Bel (1)
Dorrell, A. R. (Aston Villa), 1925 v W, Bel, F; 1926 v Ni (4)
Douglas, B. (Blackburn R), 1958 v S, W, Ni, F, P, Y, USSR (2), Br, A; 1959 v S, USSR; 1960 v Y, H; 1961 v Ni, W, S, L, P, Sp, M, I, A; 1962 v W, Ni, S, Pe, L, P, H, Arg, Bul, Br; 1963 v S, Br, Sw (36)
Downs, R. W. (Everton), 1921 v Ni (1)
Doyle, M. (Manchester C), 1976 v W, S (sub), Br, I; 1977 v Ho (5)
Drake, E. J. (Arsenal), 1935 v Ni, I; 1936 v W; 1937 v H; 1938 v F (5)
Ducat, A. (Woolwich Arsenal), 1910 v S, W, Ni; (with Aston Villa), 1920 v S, W; 1921 v Ni (6)
Dunn, A. T. B. (Cambridge University), 1883 v Ni; 1884 v Ni; (with Old Etonians), 1892 v S, W (4)

Earle, S. G. J. (Clapton), 1924 v F; (with West Ham U), 1928 v Ni (2)
Eastham, G. (Arsenal), 1963 v Br, Cz, EG; 1964 v W, Ni, S, R of W, U, P, Ei, US, Br, Arg; 1965 v H, WG, Se; 1966 v Sp, Pol, D (19)
Eastham, G. R. (Bolton W), 1935 v Ho (1)
Eckersley, W. (Blackburn R), 1950 v Sp; 1951 v S, Y, Arg, P; 1952 v A (2), Sw; 1953 v Ni, Arg, Ch, U, US; 1954 v W, Ni, R of E, H (17)
Edwards, D. (Manchester U), 1955 v S, F, Sp, P; 1956 v S, Br, Se, Fi, WG; 1957 v S, Ni, Ei (2), D (2); 1958 v W, Ni, F (18)
Edwards, J. H. (Shropshire Wanderers), 1874 v S (1)
Edwards, W. (Leeds U), 1926 v S, W; 1927 v W, Ni, S, F, Bel, L; 1928 v S, F, Bel; 1929 v S, W, Ni; 1930 v W, Ni (16)
Ellerington, W. (Southampton), 1949 v N, F (2)
Elliott, G. W. (Middlesbrough), 1913 v Ni; 1914 v Ni; 1920 v W (3)
Elliott, W. H. (Burnley), 1952 v I, A; 1953 v Ni, W, Bel (5)
Evans, R. E. (Sheffield U), 1911 v S, W, Ni; 1912 v W (4)
Ewer, F. H. (Casuals), 1924 v F; 1925 v Bel (2)

Fairclough, P. (Old Foresters), 1878 v S (1)
Fairhurst, D. (Newcastle U), 1934 v F (1)
Fantham, J. (Sheffield W), 1962 v L (1)
Felton, W. (Sheffield W), 1925 v F (1)
Fenton, M. (Middlesbrough), 1938 v S (1)
Field, E. (Clapham Rovers), 1876 v S; 1881 v S (2)
Finney, T. (Preston NE), 1947 v W, Ni, Ei, Ho, F, P; 1948 v S, W, Ni, Bel, Se, I; 1949 v S, W, Ni, Se, N, F; 1950 v S, W, Ni, Ei, I, P, Bel, Ch, US, Sp; 1951 v W, S, Arg, P; 1952 v W, Ni, S, F, I, Sw, A; 1953 v W, Ni, S, Bel, Arg, Ch, U, US; 1954 v W, S, Bel, Sw, U, H, Y; 1955 v WG;

1956 v S, W, Ni, D, Sp; 1957 v S, W, Y, D (2), Ei (2); 1958 v W, S, F, P, Y, USSR (2); 1959 v Ni, USSR (76)
Fleming, H. J. (Swindon T), 1909 v S, H (2); 1910 v W, Ni; 1911 v W, Ni; 1912 v Ni; 1913 v S, W; 1914 v S (11)
Fletcher, A. (Wolverhampton W), 1889 v W; 1890 v W (2)
Flowers, R. (Wolverhampton W), 1955 v F; 1959 v S, W, I, Br, Pe, US, M (sub); 1960 v W, Ni, S, Se, Y, Sp, H; 1961 v Ni, W, S, L, P, Sp, M, I, A; 1962 v W, Ni, S, A, Sw, Pe, L, P, H, Arg, Bul, Br; 1963 v Ni, W, S, F (2), Sw; 1964 v Ei, US, P; 1965 v W, Ho, WG; 1966 v N (49)
Forman, Frank (Nottingham F), 1898 v S, Ni; 1899 v S, W, Ni; 1901 v S; 1902 v S, Ni; 1903 v W (9)
Forman, F. R. (Nottingham F), 1899 v S, W, Ni (3)
Forrest, J. H. (Blackburn R), 1884 v W; 1885 v S, W, Ni; 1886 v S, W; 1887 v S, W, Ni; 1889 v S; 1890 v Ni (11)
Fort, J. (Millwall), 1921 v Bel (1)
Foster, R. E. (Oxford University), 1900 v W; (with Corinthians), 1901 v W, Ni, S; 1902 v W (5)
Foulke, W. J. (Sheffield U), 1897 v W (1)
Foulkes, W. A. (Manchester U), 1955 v Ni (1)
Fox, F. S. (Gillingham), 1925 v F (1)
Francis, G. C. J. (QPR), 1975 v Cz, P, W, S; 1976 v Sw, Cz, P, W, Ni, S, Br, Fi (12)
Francis, T. (Birmingham C), 1977 v Ho, L, S, Br; 1978 v Sw, L, I (sub), WG (sub), Br, W, S, H; (with Nottingham F), 1979 v Bul (sub), Se, A (sub); 1980 v Ni, Bul, Sp; 1981 v Sp, R, S (sub), Sw (22)
Franklin, C. F. (Stoke C), 1947 v S, W, Ni, Ei, Ho, F, Sw, P; 1948 v S, W, Ni, Bel, Se, I; 1949 v S, W, Ni, D, Sw, N, F, Se; 1950 v W, S, Ni, Ei, I (27)
Freeman, B. C. (Everton), 1909 v S, W; (with Burnley), 1912 v S, W, Ni (5)
Froggatt, J. (Portsmouth), 1950 v Ni, I; 1951 v S; 1952 v S, A (2), I, Sw; 1953 v Ni, W, S, Bel, US (13)
Froggatt, R. (Sheffield W), 1953 v W, S, Bel, US (4)
Fry, C. B. (Corinthians), 1901 v Ni (1)
Furness, W. I. (Leeds U), 1933 v I (1)

Galley, T. (Wolverhampton W), 1937 v N, Se (2)
Gardner, T. (Aston Villa), 1934 v Cz; 1935 v Ho (2)
Garfield, B. (WBA), 1898 v Ni (1)
Garratty, W. (Aston Villa), 1903 v W (1)
Garrett, T. (Blackpool), 1952 v S, I; 1954 v W (3)
Gates, E. (Ipswich T), 1981 v N, R (2)
Gay, L. H. (Cambridge University), 1893 v S; (with Old Brightonians), 1894 v S, W (3)
Geary, F. (Everton), 1890 v Ni; 1891 v S (2)
Geaves, R. L. (Clapham Rovers), 1875 v S (1)
Gee, C. W. (Everton), 1932 v W, Sp; 1937 v Ni (3)
Geldard, A. (Everton), 1933 v I, Sw; 1935 v S; 1938 v Ni (4)
George, C. (Derby Co), 1977 v Ei (1)
George, W. (Aston Villa), 1902 v S, W, Ni (3)
Gibbins, W. V. T. (Clapton), 1924 v F; 1925 v F (2)
Gidman, J. (Aston Villa), 1977 v L (1)
Gillard, I. T. (QPR), 1975 v WG, W; 1976 v Cz (3)
Gilliat, W. E. (Old Carthusians), 1893 v Ni (1)
Goodall, F. R. (Huddersfield T), 1926 v S; 1927 v S, F, Bel, L; 1928 v S, W, F, Bel; 1930 v S, G, A; 1931 v S, W, Ni, Bel; 1932 v Ni; 1933 v W, Ni, A, I, Sw; 1934 v W, Ni, F (25)
Goodall, J. (Preston NE), 1888 v S, W; 1889 v S, W; (with Derby Co), 1891 v S, W; 1892 v S; 1893 v W; 1894 v S; 1895 v S, Ni; 1896 v S, W; 1898 v W (14)
Goodhart, H. C. (Old Etonians), 1883 v S, W, Ni (3)
Goodwyn, A. G. (Royal Engineers), 1873 v S (1)
Goodyer, A. C.(Nottingham F), 1879 v S (1)
Gosling, R. C. (Old Etonians), 1892 v W; 1893 v S; 1894 v W; 1895 v W, S (5)
Gosnell, A. A. (Newcastle U), 1906 v Ni (1)
Gough, H. C. (Sheffield U), 1921 v S (1)
Goulden, L. A. (West Ham U), 1937 v Se, N; 1938 v W, Ni, Cz, G, Sw, F; 1939 v S, W, R of E, I, R, Y (14)
Graham, L. (Millwall), 1925 v S, W (2)
Graham, T. (Nottingham F), 1931 v F; 1932 v Ni (2)
Grainger, C. (Sheffield U), 1956 v Br, Se, Fi, WG; 1957 v W, Ni; (with Sunderland), 1957 v S (7)
Greaves, J. (Chelsea), 1959 v Pe, M, US; 1960 v W, Se, Y, Sp; 1961 v Ni, W, S, L, P, Sp, I, A; (with Tottenham H), 1962 v S, Sw, Pe, H, Arg, Bul, Br; 1963 v Ni, W, S, F (2), Br, Cz, Sw; 1964 v W, Ni, R of W, P (2), Ei, Br, U, Arg; 1965 v Ni, S, Bel, Ho, H, Y; 1966 v W, A, Y, N, D, Pol, U, M, F; 1967 v S, Sp, A (57)
Green, F. T. (Wanderers), 1876 v S (1)
Green, G. H. (Sheffield U), 1925 v F; 1926 v S, Bel, W; 1927 v W, Ni; 1928 v F, Bel (8)
Greenhalgh, E. H. (Notts Co), 1872 v S; 1873 v S (2)
Greenhoff, B. (Manchester U), 1976 v W, Ni; 1977 v Ei, Fi, I, Ho, Ni, W, S, Br, Arg, U; 1978 v Br, W, Ni, S (sub), H (sub); (with Leeds U), 1980 v Aus (sub) (18)
Greenwood, D. H. (Blackburn R), 1882 v S, Ni (2)
Grimsdell, A. (Tottenham H), 1920 v S, W; 1921 v S, Ni; 1923 v W, Ni (6)
Grosvenor, A. T. (Birmingham), 1934 v Ni, W, F (3)
Gunn, W. (Notts Co), 1884 v S, W (2)
Gurney, R. (Sunderland), 1935 v S (1)

Hacking, J. (Oldham Ath), 1929 v S, W, Ni (3)
Hadley, N. (WBA), 1903 v Ni (1)
Hagan, J. (Sheffield U), 1949 v D (1)
Haines, J. T. W. (WBA), 1949 v Sw (1)
Hall, A. E. (Aston Villa), 1910 v Ni (1)
Hall, G. W. (Tottenham H), 1934 v F; 1938 v S, W, Ni, Cz; 1939 v S, Ni, R of E, I, Y (10)
Hall, J. (Birmingham C), 1956 v S, W, Ni, Br, Se, Fi, WG, D, Sp; 1957 v S, W, Ni, Y, D (2), Ei (2) (17)
Halse, H. J. (Manchester U), 1909 v A (1)
Hammond, H. E. D. (Oxford University), 1889 v S (1)
Hampson, J. (Blackpool), 1931 v Ni, W; 1933 v A (3)
Hampton, H. (Aston Villa), 1913 v S, W; 1914 v S, W (4)
Hancocks, J. Wolverhampton W), 1949 v Sw; 1950 v W; 1951 v Y (3)
Hapgood, E. (Arsenal), 1933 v I, Sw; 1934 v S, Ni, W, H, Cz; 1935 v S, Ni, W, I, Ho; 1936 v S, Ni, W, G, A, Bel; 1937 v Fi; 1938 v S, G, Sw, F; 1939 v S, W, Ni, R of E, N, I, Y (30)
Hardinge, H. T. W. (Sheffield U), 1910 v S (1)
Hardman, H. P. (Everton), 1905 v W; 1907 v S, Ni; 1908 v W (4)
Hardwick, G. F. M. (Middlesbrough), 1947 v S, W, Ni, Ei, Ho, F, Sw, P; 1948 v S, W, Ni, Bel, Se (13)
Hardy, H. (Stockport Co), 1925 v Bel (1)
Hardy, S. (Liverpool), 1907 v S, W, Ni; 1908 v S; 1909 v S, W, Ni, H (2), A; 1910 v S, W, Ni; 1912 v Ni; (with Aston Villa), 1913 v S; 1914 v Ni, W, S; 1920 v S, W, Ni (21)
Hargreaves, F. W. (Blackburn R), 1880 v W; 1881 v W; 1882 v Ni (3)
Hargreaves, J. (Blackburn R), 1881 v S, W (2)
Harper, E. C. (Blackburn R), 1926 v S (1)
Harris, G. (Burnley), 1966 v Pol (1)
Harris, P. P. (Portsmouth), 1950 v Ei; 1954 v H (2)
Harris, S. S. (Cambridge University), 1904 v S; (with Old Westminsters), 1905 v Ni, W; 1906 v S, W, Ni (6)
Harrison, A. H. (Old Westminsters), 1893 v S, Ni (2)
Harrison, G. (Everton), 1921 v Bel; 1922 v Ni (2)
Harrow, J. H. (Chelsea), 1923 v Ni, Se (2)
Hart, E. (Leeds U), 1929 v W; 1930 v W, Ni; 1933 v S, A; 1934 v S, H, Cz (8)
Hartley, F. (Oxford C), 1923 v F (1)
Harvey, A. (Wednesbury Strollers), 1881 v W (1)
Harvey, J. C. (Everton), 1971 v Ma (1)

Hassall, H. W. (Huddersfield T), 1951 v S, Arg, P; 1952 v F; (with Bolton W), 1954 v Ni (5)
Haworth, G. (Accrington), 1887 v Ni, W, S; 1888 v S; 1890 v S (5)
Hawtrey, J. P. (Old Etonians), 1881 v S, W (2)
Hawkes, R. M. (Luton T), 1907 v Ni; 1908 v A (2), H, B (5)
Haygarth, E. B. (Swifts), 1875 v S (1)
Haynes, J. N. (Fulham), 1955 v Ni; 1956 v S, Ni, Br, Se, Fi, WG, Sp; 1957 v W, Y, D, Ei (2); 1958 v W, Ni, S, F, P, Y, USSR (3), Br, A; 1959 v S, Ni, USSR, I, Br, Pe, M, US; 1960 v Ni, Y, Sp, H; 1961 v Ni, W, S, L, P, Sp, M, I, A; 1962 v W, Ni, S, A, Sw, Pe, P, H, Arg, Bul, Br (56)
Healless, H. (Blackburn R), 1925 v Ni; 1928 v S (2)
Hector, K. J. (Derby Co), 1974 v Pol (sub), I (sub), (2)
Hedley, G. A. (Sheffield U), 1901 v Ni (1)
Hegan, K. E. (Corinthians), 1923 v Bel, F; 1924 v Ni, Bel (4)
Hellawell, M. S. (Birmingham C), 1963 v Ni, F (2)
Henfrey, A. G. (Cambridge University), 1891 v Ni; (with Corinthians), 1892 v W; 1895 v W; 1896 v S, W (5)
Henry, R. P. (Tottenham H), 1963 v F (1)
Heron, F. (Wanderers), 1876 v S (1)
Heron, G. H. H. (Uxbridge), 1873 v S; 1874 v S; (with Wanderers), 1875 v S; 1876 v S; 1878 v S (5)
Hibbert, W. (Bury), 1910 v S (1)
Hibbs, H. E. (Birmingham), 1930 v S, W, A, G; 1931 v S, W, Ni; 1932 v W, Ni, Sp; 1933 v S, W, Ni, A, I, Sw; 1934 v Ni, W, F; 1935 v S, W, Ni, Ho; 1936 v G, W (25)
Hill, F. (Bolton W), 1963 v Ni, W (2)
Hill, J. H. (Burnley), 1925 v W; 1926 v S; 1927 v S, Ni, Bel, F; 1928 v Ni, W; 1929 v F, Bel, Sp (11)
Hill, G. A. (Manchester U), 1976 v I; 1977 v Ei (sub), Fi (sub), L; 1978 v Sw (sub), L (6)
Hill, R. H. (Millwall), 1926 v Bel (1)
Hillman, J. (Burnley), 1899 v Ni (1)
Hills, A. F. (Old Harrovians), 1879 v S (1)
Hilsdon, G. R. (Chelsea), 1907 v Ni; 1908 v S, W, Ni, A, H, B; 1909 v Ni (8)
Hine, E. W. (Leicester C), 1929 v W, Ni; 1930 v W, Ni; 1932 v W, Ni (6)
Hinton, A. T. (Wolverhampton W), 1963 v F; (with Nottingham F), 1965 v W, Bel (3)
Hitchens, G. A. (Aston Villa), 1961 v M, I, A; (with Inter-Milan), 1962 v Sw, Pe, H, Br (7)
Hobbis, H. H. F. (Charlton Ath), 1936 v A, Bel (2)
Hoddle, G. (Tottenham H), 1980 v Bul, W, Aus, Sp; 1981 v Sp, W, S (7)
Hodgetts, D. (Aston Villa), 1888 v S, W, Ni; 1892 v S, Ni; 1894 v Ni (6)
Hodgkinson, A. (Sheffield U), 1957 v S, Ei (2), D; 1961 v W (5)
Hodgson, G. (Liverpool), 1931 v S, Ni, W (3)
Hodkinson, J. (Blackburn R), 1913 v W, S; 1920 v Ni (3)
Hogg, W. (Sunderland), 1902 v S, W, Ni (3)
Holdcroft, G. H. (Preston NE), 1937 v W, Ni (2)
Holden, A. D. (Bolton W), 1959 v S, I, Br, Pe, M (5)
Holden, G. H. (Wednesday OA), 1881 v S; 1884 v S, W, Ni (4)
Holden-White, C. (Corinthians), 1888 v W, S (2)
Holford, T. (Stoke), 1903 v Ni (1)
Holley, G. H. (Sunderland), 1909 v S, W, H (2), A; 1910 v W; 1912 v S, W, NI; 1913 v S (10)
Holliday, E. (Middlesbrough), 1960 v W, Ni, Se (3)
Hollins, J. W. (Chelsea), 1967 v Sp (1)
Holmes, R. (Preston NE), 1888 v Ni; 1891 v S; 1892 v S; 1893 v S, W; 1894 v Ni; 1895 v Ni (7)
Holt, J. (Everton), 1890 v W; 1891 v S, W; 1892 v S, Ni; 1893 v S; 1894 v S, Ni; 1895 v S; (with Reading), 1900 v Ni (10)
Hopkinson, E. (Bolton W), 1958 v W, Ni, S, F, P, Y; 1959 v S, I, Br, Pe, M, US; 1960 v W, Se (14)
Hossack, A. H. (Corinthians), 1892 v W; 1894 v W (2)
Houghton, W. E. (Aston Villa), 1931 v Ni, W, F, Bel; 1932 v S, Ni; 1933 v A (7)
Houlker, A. E. (Blackburn R), 1902 v S; (with Portsmouth), 1903 v S, W; (with Southampton), 1906 v W, Ni (5)
Howarth, R. H. (Preston NE), 1887 v Ni; 1888 v S, W; 1891 v S; (with Everton), 1894 v Ni (5)
Howe, D. (WBA), 1958 v S, W, Ni, F, P, Y, USSR (3), Br, A; 1959 v S, W, Ni, USSR, I, Br, Pe, M, US; 1960 v W, Ni, Se (23)
Howe, J. R. (Derby Co), 1948 v I; 1949 v S, Ni (3)
Howell, L. S. (Wanderers), 1873 v S (1)
Howell, R. (Sheffield U), 1895 v Ni; (with Liverpool) 1899 v S (2)
Hudson, A. A. (Stoke C), 1975 v WG, Cy (2)
Hudson, J. (Sheffield), 1883 v Ni (1)
Hudspeth, F. C. (Newcastle U), 1926 v Ni (1)
Hufton, A. E. (West Ham U), 1924 v Bel; 1928 v S, Ni; 1929 v F, Bel, Sp (6)
Hughes, E. W. (Liverpool), 1970 v W, Ni, S, Ho, P, Bel; 1971 v EG, Ma (2), Gr, W; 1972 v Sw, Gr, Wg (2), W, Ni, S; 1973 v W (3), S (2), Pol, USSR, I; 1974 v A, Pol, I, W, Ni, S, Arg, EG, Bul, Y; 1975 v Cz, P, Cy (sub), Ni; 1977 v I, L, W, S, Br, Arg, U; 1978 v Sw, L, I, WG, Ni, S, H; 1979 v D, Ei, Ni, W, Se; (with Wolverhampton W), 1980 v Sp (sub), Ni, S (sub) (62)
Hughes, L. (Liverpool), 1950 v Ch, US, Sp (3)
Hulme, J. H. A. (Arsenal), 1927 v S, Bel, F; 1928 v S, Ni, W; 1929 v Ni, W; 1933 v S (9)
Humphreys, P. (Notts Co), 1903 v S (1)
Hunt, G. S. (Tottenham H), 1933 v I, Sw, S (3)
Hunt, Rev K. R. G. (Leyton), 1911 v S, W (2)
Hunt, R. (Liverpool), 1962 v A; 1963 v EG; 1964 v S, US, P; 1965 v W; 1966 v S, Sp, Pol (2), WG (2), Fi, N, U, M, F, Arg, P; 1967 v Ni, W, Cz, Sp, A; 1968 v W, Ni, USSR (2), Sp (2), Se, Y; 1969 v R (2) (34)
Hunter, J. (Sheffield Heeley), 1878 v S; 1880 v S, W; 1881 v S, W; 1882 v S, W (7)
Hunter, N. (Leeds U), 1966 v WG, Y, Fi, Sp (sub); 1967 v A; 1968 v Sp, Se, Y, WG, USSR; 1969 v R, W; 1970 v Ho, WG (sub); 1971 v Ma; 1972 v WG (2), W, Ni, S; 1973 v W (2) USSR (sub); 1974 v A, Pol, Ni (sub), S; 1975 v Cz (28)
Hurst, G. C. (West Ham U), 1966 v S, WG (2), Y, Fi, D, Arg, P; 1967 v Ni, W, S, Cz, Sp, A; 1968 v W, Ni, S, Se (sub), WG, USSR (2); 1969 v Ni, S, R (2), Bul, F, M, U, Br; 1970 v W, Ni, S, Ho (1 + 1 sub), Bel, Co, Ec, R, Br, WG; 1971 v EG, Gr, W, S; 1972 v Sw (2), Gr, WG (49)

Iremonger, J. (Nottingham F), 1901 v S; 1902 v Ni (2)

Jack, D. N. B. (Bolton W), 1924 v S, W; 1928 v F, Bel; (with Arsenal), 1930 v S, G, A; 1933 v W, A (9)
Jackson, E. (Oxford University), 1891 v W (1)
Jarrett, B. G. (Cambridge University), 1876 v S; 1877 v S; 1878 v S (3)
Jefferis, F. (Everton), 1912 v S, W (2)
Jezzard, B. A. G. (Fulham), 1954 v H; 1956 v Ni (2)
Johnson, D. E. (Ipswich T), 1975 v W, S; 1976 v Sw; (with Liverpool), 1980 v Ei, Arg, Ni, S, Bel (8)
Johnson, E. (Saltley College), 1880 v W; (with Stoke C), 1884 v Ni (2)
Johnson, J. A. (Stoke C), 1937 v N, Se, Fi, S, Ni (5)
Johnson, T. C. F. (Manchester C), 1926 v Bel; 1930 v W; (with Everton), 1932 v S, Sp; 1933 v Ni (5)
Johnson, W. H. (Sheffield U), 1900 v S, W, Ni; 1903 v S, W, Ni (6)

Johnston, H. (Blackpool), 1947 v S, Ho; 1951 v S; 1953 v Arg, Ch, U, US; 1954 v W, Ni, H (10)
Jones, A. (Walsall Town Swifts), 1882 v S, W; (with Great Lever), 1883 v S (3)
Jones, H. (Blackburn R), 1927 v S, Bel, L, F; 1928 v S, Ni (6)
Jones, H. (Nottingham F), 1923 v F (1)
Jones, M. D. (Sheffield U), 1965 v WG, Se; (with Leeds U), 1970 v Ho (3)
Jones, W. (Bristol C), 1901 v Ni (1)
Jones, W. H. (Liverpool), 1950 v P, Bel (2)
Joy, B. (Casuals), 1936 v Bel (1)

Kail, E. I. L. (Dulwich Hamlet), 1929 v F, Bel, Sp (3)
Kay, A. H. (Everton), 1963 v Sw (1)
Kean, F. W. (Sheffield W), 1923 v S, Bel; 1924 v W; 1925 v Ni; 1926 v Ni, Bel; 1927 v L; (with Bolton W), 1929 v F, Sp (9)
Keegan, J. K. (Liverpool), 1973 v W (2); 1974 v W, Ni, Arg, EG, Bul, Y; 1975 v Cz, WG, Cy (2), Ni, S; 1976 v Sw, Cz, P, W (2), Ni, S, Br, Fi; 1977 v Ei, Fi, I, Ho, L; (with SV Hamburg), W, Br, Arg, U; 1978 v Sw, I, WG, Br, H; 1979 v D, Ei, Cz, Ni, W, S, Bul, Se, A; 1980 v D, Ni, Ei, Sp (2), Arg, Bel, I; (with Southampton), 1981 v Sp, Sw, H (57)
Keen, E. R. L. (Derby Co), 1933 v A; 1937 v W, Ni, H (4)
Kelly, R. (Burnley), 1920 v S; 1921 v S, W, Ni; 1922 v S, W; 1923 v S; 1924 v Ni; 1925 v W, Ni, S; (with Sunderland), 1926 v W; (with Huddersfield T), 1927 v L; 1928 v S (14)
Kennedy, R. (Liverpool), 1976 v W (2), Ni, S; 1977 v L, W, S, Br (sub), Arg (sub); 1978 v Sw, L; 1980 v Bul, Sp, Arg, W, Bel (sub), I (17)
Kenyon-Slaney, W. S. (Wanderers), 1873 v S (1)
Kevan, D. T. (WBA), 1957 v S; 1958 v W, Ni, S, P, Y, USSR (3), Br, A; 1959 v M, US; 1961 v M (14)
Kidd, B. (Manchester U), 1970 v Ni, Ec (sub) (2)
King, R. S. (Oxford University), 1882 v Ni (1)
Kingsford, R. K. (Wanderers), 1874 v S (1)
Kingsley, M. (Newcastle U), 1901 v W (1)
Kinsey, G. (Wolverhampton W), 1892 v W; 1893 v S; (with Derby Co), 1896 v W, Ni (4)
Kirchen, A. J. (Arsenal), 1937 v N, Se, Fi (3)
Kirton, W. J. (Aston Villa), 1922 v Ni (1)
Knight, A. E. (Portsmouth), 1920 v Ni (1)
Knowles, C. (Tottenham H), 1968 v USSR, Sp, Se, WG (4)

Labone, B. L. (Everton), 1963 v Ni, W, F; 1967 v Sp, A; 1968 v S, Sp, Se, Y, USSR, Wg; 1969 v Ni, S, R, Bul, M, U, Br; 1970 v S, W, Bel, Co, Ec, R, Br, WG (26)
Lampard, F. R. G. (West Ham U), 1973 v Y; 1980 v Aus (2)
Langley, E. J. (Fulham), 1958 v S, P, Y (3)
Langton, R. (Blackburn R), 1947 v W, Ni, Ei, Ho, F, Sw; 1948 v Se; (with Preston NE), 1949 v D, Se; (with Bolton W), 1950 v S; 1951 v Ni (11)
Latchford, R. D. (Everton), 1978 v I, Br, W; 1979 v D, Ei, Cz (sub), Ni (2), W, S, Bul, A (12)
Latheron, E. G. (Blackburn R), 1913 v W; 1914 v Ni (2)
Lawler, C. (Liverpool), 1971 v Ma, W, S; 1972 v Sw (4)
Lawton, T. (Everton), 1939 v S, W, Ni, R of E, N, I, R, Y; (with Chelsea), 1947 v S, W, Ni, Ei, Ho, F, Sw, P; 1948 v W, Ni, Bel; (with Notts Co), 1948 v S, Se, I; 1949 v D (23)
Leach, T. (Sheffield W), 1931 v W, Ni (2)
Leake, A. (Aston Villa), 1904 v S, Ni; 1905 v S, W, Ni (5)
Lee, E. A. (Southampton), 1904 v W (1)
Lee, F. H. (Manchester C), 1969 v Ni, W, S, Bul, F, M, U; 1970 v W, Ho (2), P, Bel, Co, Ec, R, Br, WG; 1971 v EG, Gr, Ma, Ni, W, S; 1972 v Sw (2), Gr, WG (27)
Lee, J. (Derby Co), 1951 v Ni (1)
Leighton, J. E. (Nottingham F), 1886 v Ni (1)
Lilley, H. E. (Sheffield U), 1892 v W (1)
Linacre, H. J. (Nottingham F), 1905 v W, S (2)
Lindley, T. (Cambridge University), 1886 v S, W, Ni, 1887 v S, W, Ni; 1888 v S, W, Ni; (with Nottingham F), 1889 v S; 1890 v S, W; 1891 v Ni (13)
Lindsay, A. (Liverpool), 1974 v Arg, EG, Bul, Y (4)
Lindsay, W. (Wanderers), 1877 v S (1)
Lintott, E. H. (QPR), 1908 v S, W, Ni; (with Bradford C), 1909 v S, Ni, H (2) (7)
Lipsham, H. B. (Sheffield U), 1902 v W (1)
Little, B. (Aston Villa), 1975 v W (sub) (1)
Lloyd, L. V. (Liverpool), 1971 v W; 1972 v Sw, Ni; (with Nottingham F), 1980 v W (4)
Lockett, A. (Stoke C), 1903 v Ni (1)
Lodge, L. V. (Cambridge University), 1894 v W; 1895 v S, W; (with Corinthians), 1896 v S, Ni (5)
Lofthouse, J. M. (Blackburn R), 1885 v S, W, Ni; 1887 v S, W; (with Accrington), 1889 v Ni; (with Blackburn R), 1890 v Ni (7)
Lofthouse, N. (Bolton W), 1951 v Y; 1952 v W, Ni, S, A (2), I, Sw; 1953 v W, Ni, S, Bel, Arg, Ch, U, US; 1954 v W, Ni, R of E, Bel, U; 1955 v Ni, S, F, Sp, P; 1956 v W, S, Sp, D, Fi (sub); 1959 v W, USSR (33)
Longworth, E. (Liverpool), 1920 v S; 1921 v Bel; 1923 v S, W, Bel (5)
Lowder, A. (Wolverhampton W), 1889 v W (1)
Lowe, E. (Aston Villa), 1947 v F, Sw, P (3)
Lucas, T. (Liverpool), 1922 v Ni; 1924 v F; 1926 v Bel (3)
Luntley, E. (Nottingham F), 1880 v S, W (2)
Lyttelton, Hon. A. (Cambridge University), 1877 v S (1)
Lyttelton, Hon. E. (Cambridge University), 1878 v S (1)

McCall, J. (Preston NE), 1913 v S, W; 1914 v S; 1920 v S; 1921 v Ni (5)
McDermott, T. (Liverpool), 1978 v Sw, L; 1979 v Ni, W, Se; 1980 v D, Ni (sub), Ei, Ni, S, Bel (sub), Sp; 1981 v N, R, Sw, R (sub), Br, Sw (sub), H (19)
McDonald, C. A. (Burnley), 1958 v USSR (3), Br, A; 1959 v W, Ni, USSR (8)
McFarland, R. L. (Derby Co), 1971 v Gr, Ma (2), Ni, S; 1972 v Sw, Gr, WG, W, S; 1973 v W (3), Ni, S, Cz, Pol, USSR, I; 1974 v A, Pol, I, W, Ni; 1976 v Cz, S; 1977 v Ei, I (28)
McGarry, W. H. (Huddersfield T), 1954 v Sw, U; 1956 v W, D (4)
McGuinness, W. (Manchester U), 1959 v Ni, M (2)
McInroy, A. (Sunderland), 1927 v Ni (1)
McNab, R. (Arsenal), 1969 v Ni, Bul, R (1 + 1 sub) (4)
McNeal, R. (WBA), 1914 v S, W (2)
McNeil, M. (Middlesbrough), 1961 v W, Ni, S, L, P, Sp, M, I; 1962 v L (9)
Macaulay, R. H. (Cambridge University), 1881 v S (1)
Macdonald, M. (Newcastle U), 1972 v W, Ni, S (sub); 1973 v USSR (sub); 1974 v P, S (sub), Y (sub); 1975 v WG, Cy (2), Ni; 1976 v Sw (sub), Cz, P (14)
Macrae, S. (Notts Co), 1883 v S, W, Ni; 1884 v S, W, Ni (6)
Maddison, F. B. (Oxford University), 1872 v S (1)
Madeley, P. E. (Leeds U), 1971 v Ni; 1972 v Sw (2), Gr, WG (2), W, S; 1973 v S, Cz, Pol, USSR, I; 1974 v A, Pol, I; 1975 v Cz, P, Cy; 1976 v Cz, P, Fi; 1977 v Ei, Ho (24)
Magee, T. P. (WBA), 1923 v W, Se; 1925 v S, Bel, F (5)
Makepeace, H. (Everton), 1906 v S; 1910 v S; 1912 v S, W (4)
Male, C. G. (Arsenal), 1935 v S, Ni, I, Ho; 1936 v S, W, Ni, G, A, Bel; 1937 v S, Ni, H, N, Se, Fi; 1939 v I, R, Y (19)
Mannion, W. J. (Middlesbrough), 1947 v S, W, Ni, Ei, Ho, F, Sw, P; 1948 v W, Ni, Bel, Se, I; 1949 v N, F;

1950 v S, Ei, P, Bel, Ch, US; 1951 v Ni, W, S, Y; 1952 v F (26)
Mariner, P. (Ipswich T), 1977 v L (sub), Ni; 1978 v L, W (sub), S; 1980 v W, Ni (sub), S, Aus, I (sub), Sp (sub); 1981 v N, Sw, Sp, Sw, H (16)
Marsden, J. T. (Darwen), 1891 v Ni (1)
Marsden, W. (Sheffield W), 1930 v W, S, G (3)
Marsh, R. W. (QPR), 1972 v Sw (sub); (with Manchester C), WG (sub + 1), W, Ni, S; 1973 v W (2), Y (9)
Marshall, T. (Darwen), 1880 v W; 1881 v W (2)
Martin, A. (West Ham U), 1981 v Br, S (sub) (2)
Martin, H. (Sunderland), 1914 v Ni (1)
Maskrey, H. M. (Derby Co), 1908 v Ni (1)
Mason, C. (Wolverhampton W), 1887 v Ni; 1888 v W; 1890 v Ni (3)
Matthews, R. D. (Coventry C), 1956 v S, Br, Se, WG; 1957 v Ni (5)
Matthews, S. (Stoke C), 1935 v W, I; 1936 v G; 1937 v S; 1938 v S, W, Cz, G, Sw, F; 1939 v S, W, Ni, R of E, N, I, Y; 1947 v S; (with Blackpool), 1947 v Sw, P; 1948 v S, W, Ni, Bel, I; 1949 v S, W, Ni, D, Sw; 1950 v Sp; 1951 v Ni, S; 1954 v Ni, R of E, H, Bel, U; 1955 v Ni, W, S, F, WG, Sp, P; 1956 v W, Br; 1957 v S, W, Ni, Y, D (2) Ei (54)
Matthews, V. (Sheffield U), 1928 v F, Bel (2)
Maynard, W. J. (1st Surrey Rifles), 1872 v S; 1876 v S (2)
Meadows, J. (Manchester C), 1955 v S (1)
Medley, L. D. (Tottenham H), 1951 v Y, W; 1952 v F, A, W, Ni (6)
Meehan, T. (Chelsea), 1924 v Ni (1)
Melia, J. (Liverpool), 1963 v S, Sw (2)
Mercer, D. W. (Sheffield U), 1923 v Ni, Bel (2)
Mercer, J. (Everton), 1939 v S, Ni, I, R, Y (5)
Merrick, G. H. (Birmingham C), 1952 v Ni, S, A (2), I, Sw; 1953 v Ni, W, S, Bel, Arg, Ch, U; 1954 v W, Ni, S, R of E, H (2), Y, Bel, Sw, U (23)
Metcalfe V. (Huddersfield T), 1951 v Arg, P (2)
Mew, J. W. (Manchester U), 1921 v Ni (1)
Middleditch, B. (Corinthians), 1897 v Ni (1)
Milburn, J. E. T. (Newcastle U), 1949 v S, W, Ni, Sw; 1950 v W, P, Bel, Sp; 1951 v W, Arg, P; 1952 v F; 1956 v D (13)
Miller, B. G. (Burnley), 1961 v A (1)
Miller, H. S. (Charlton Ath), 1923 v Se (1)
Mills, G. R. (Chelsea), 1938 v W, Ni, Cz (3)
Mills, M. D. (Ipswich T), 1973 v Y; 1976 v W (2), Ni, S, Br, I (sub), Fi; 1977 v Fi (sub), I, Ni, W, S; 1978 v WG, Br, W, Ni, S, H; 1979 v D, Ei, Ni (2), S, Bul, A; 1980 v D, Ni, Sp (2); 1981 v Sw (2), H (33)
Milne, G. (Liverpool), 1963 v Br, Cz, EG; 1964 v W, Ni, S, R of W, U, P, Ei, Br, Arg; 1965 v Ni, Bel (14)
Milton, C. A. (Arsenal), 1952 v A (1)
Milward, A. (Everton), 1891 v S, W; 1897 v S, W (4)
Mitchell, C. (Upton Park), 1880 v W; 1881 v S; 1883 v S, W; 1885 v W (5)
Mitchell, J. F. (Manchester C), 1925 v Ni (1)
Moffat, H. (Oldham Ath), 1913 v W (1)
Molyneux, G. (Southampton), 1902 v S; 1903 v S, W, Ni (4)
Moon, W. R. (Old Westminsters), 1888 v S, W; 1889 v S, W; 1890 v S, W; 1891 v S (7)
Moore, H. T. (Notts Co), 1883 v Ni; 1885 v W (2)
Moore, J. (Derby Co), 1923 v Se (1)
Moore, R. F. (West Ham U), 1962 v Pe, H, Arg, Bul, Br; 1963 v W, Ni, S, F (2), Br, Cz, EG, Sw; 1964 v W, Ni, S, R of W, U, P (2), Ei, Br, Arg; 1965 v Ni, S, Bel, H, Y, WG, Se; 1966 v W, Ni, S, A, Sp, Pol (2), WG (2), N, D, U, M, F, Arg, P; 1967 v W, Ni, S, Cz, Sp, A; 1968 v W, Ni, S, USSR (2), Sp (2), Se, Y, WG; 1969 v Ni, W, S, R, Bul, F, M, U, Br; 1970 v W, Ni, S, Ho, P, Bel, Co, Ec, R, Br, Cz, WG; 1971 v EG, Gr, Ma, Ni, S; 1972 v Sw (2), Gr, WG (2), W, S; 1973 v W (3), Y, S (2), Ni, Cz, Pol, USSR, I; 1974 v I (108)
Moore, W. G. B. (West Ham U), 1923 v Se (1)
Mordue, J. (Sunderland), 1912 v Ni; 1913 v Ni (2)
Morice, C. J. (Barnes), 1872 v S (1)
Morley, H. (Notts Co), 1910 v Ni (1)
Morren, T. (Sheffield U), 1898 v Ni (1)
Morris, F. (WBA), 1920 v S; 1921 v Ni (2)
Morris, J. (Derby Co), 1949 v N, F; 1950 v Ei (3)
Morris, W. W. (Wolverhampton W), 1939 v S, Ni, R (3)
Morse, H. (Notts Co), 1879 v S (1)
Mort, T. (Aston Villa), 1924 v W, F; 1926 v S (3)
Morten, A. (C Palace), 1873 v S (1)
Mortensen, S. H. (Blackpool), 1947 v P; 1948 v W, S, Ni, Bel, Se, I; 1949 v S, W, Ni, Se, N; 1950 v S, W, Ni, I, P, Bel, Ch, US, Sp; 1951 v S, Arg; 1954 v R of E, H (25)
Morton, J. R. (West Ham U), 1938 v Cz (1)
Mosforth, W. (Sheffield W), 1877 v S; (with Sheffield Albion), 1878 v S; 1879 v S, W; 1880 v S, W; (with Sheffield W), 1881 v W; 1882 v S, W (9)
Moss, F. (Arsenal), 1934 v S, H, Cz; 1935 v I (4)
Moss, F. (Aston Villa), 1922 v S, Ni; 1923 v Ni; 1924 v S, Bel (5)
Mosscrop, E. (Burnley), 1914 v S, W (2)
Mozley, B. (Derby Co), 1950 v W, Ni, Ei (3)
Mullen, J. (Wolverhampton W), 1947 v S; 1949 v N, F; 1950 v Bel (sub), Ch, US; 1954 v W, Ni, S, R of E, Y, Sw (12)
Mullery, A. P. (Tottenham H), 1965 v Ho; 1967 v Sp, A; 1968 v W, Ni, S, USSR, Sp (2), Se, Y; 1969 v Ni, S, R, Bul, F, M, U, Br; 1970 v W, Ni, S (sub), Ho (sub), Bel, P, Co, Ec, R, Cz, WG, Br; 1971 v Ma, EG, Gr; 1972 v Sw (35)

Neal, P. G. (Liverpool), 1976 v W, I; 1977 v W, S, Br, Arg, U; 1978 v Sw, I, WG, Ni, S, H; 1979 v D, Ei, Ni (2), S, Bul, A; 1980 v D, Ni, Sp, Arg, W, Bel, I; 1981 v R, Sw, Sp, Br, H (32)
Needham, E. (Sheffield U), 1894 v S; 1895 v S; 1897 v S, W, Ni; 1898 v S, W; 1899 v S, W, Ni; 1900 v S, Ni; 1901 v S, W, Ni; 1902 v W (16)
Newton, K. R. (Blackburn R), 1966 v S, WG; 1967 v Sp, A; 1968 v W, S, Sp, Se, Y, WG; 1969 v Ni, W, S, R, Bul, M, U, Br, F; (with Everton), 1970 v Ni, S, Ho, Co, Ec, R, Cz, WG (27)
Nicholls, J. (WBA), 1954 v S, Y (2)
Nicholson, W. E. (Tottenham H), 1951 v P (1)
Nish, D. J. (Derby Co), 1973 v Ni; 1974 v P, W, Ni, S (5)
Norman, M. (Tottenham H), 1962 v Pe, H, Arg, Bul, Br; 1963 v S, F, Br, Cz, EG; 1964 v W, Ni, S, R of W, U, P (2), US, Br, Arg; 1965 v Ni, Bel, Ho (23)
Nuttall, H. (Bolton W), 1928 v W, Ni; 1929 v S (3)

Oakley, W. J. (Oxford University), 1895 v W; 1896 v S, W, Ni; (with Corinthians), 1897 v S, W, Ni; 1898 v S, W, Ni; 1900 v S, W, Ni; 1901 v S, W, Ni (16)
O'Dowd, J. P. (Chelsea), 1932 v S; 1933 v Ni, Sw (3)
O'Grady, M. (Huddersfield T), 1963 v Ni; (with Leeds U), 1969 v F (2)
Ogilvie, R. A. M. M. (Clapham R), 1874 v S (1)
Oliver, L. F. (Fulham), 1929 v Bel (1)
Olney, B. A. (Aston Villa), 1928 v F, Bel (2)
Osborne, F. R. (Fulham), 1923 v Ni, F; (with Tottenham H), 1925 v Bel; 1926 v Bel (4)
Osborne, R. (Leicester C), 1928 v W (1)
Osgood, P. L. (Chelsea), 1970 v Bel, R (sub), Cz (sub), 1974 v I (4)
Osman, R. (Ipswich T), 1980 v Aus; 1981 v Sp, R, Sw (4)
Ottaway, C. J. (Oxford University), 1872 v S; 1874 v S (2)
Owen, J. R. B. (Sheffield), 1874 v S (1)
Owen, S. W. (Luton T), 1954 v H, Y, Bel (3)

Page, L. A. (Burnley), 1927 v S, W, Bel, L, F; 1928 v W, Ni (7)
Paine, T. L. (Southampton), 1963 v Cz, EG; 1964 v W, Ni, S, R of W, U, US, P; 1965 v Ni, H, Y, WG, Se; 1966 v W, A, Y, N, M (19)
Pantling, H. H. (Sheffield U), 1924 v Ni (1)
Paravacini, P. J. de (Cambridge University), 1883 v S, W, Ni (3)
Parker, T. R. (Southampton), 1925 v F (1)
Parkes, P. B. (QPR), 1974 v P (1)
Parkinson, J. (Liverpool), 1910 v S, W (2)
Parr, P. C. (Oxford University), 1882 v W (1)
Parry, E. H. (Old Carthusians), 1879 v W; 1882 v W, S (3)
Parry, R. A. (Bolton W), 1960 v Ni, S (2)
Patchitt, B. C. A. (Corinthians), 1923 v Se (2)
Pawson, F. W. (Cambridge University), 1883 v Ni; (with Swifts), 1885 v Ni (2)
Payne, J. (Luton T), 1937 v Fi (1)
Peacock, A. (Middlesbrough), 1962 v Arg, Bul; 1963 v Ni, W; (with Leeds U), 1966 v W, Ni (6)
Peacock, J. (Middlesbrough), 1929 v F, Bel, Sp (3)
Pearson, H. F. (WBA), 1932 v S (1)
Pearson, J. H. (Crewe Alex), 1892 v Ni (1)
Pearson, J. S. (Manchester U), 1976 v W, Ni, S, Br, Fi; 1977 v Ei, Ho (sub), W, S, Br, Arg, U; 1978 v I (sub), WG, Ni (15)
Pearson, S. C. (Manchester U), 1948 v S; 1949 v S, Ni; 1950 v Ni, I; 1951 v P; 1952 v S, I (8)
Pease, W. H. (Middlesbrough), 1927 v W (1)
Pegg, D. (Manchester U), 1957 v Ei (1)
Pejic, M. (Stoke C), 1974 v P, W, Ni, S (4)
Pelly, F. R. (Old Foresters), 1893 v Ni; 1894 v S, W (3)
Pennington, J. (WBA), 1907 v S, W; 1908 v S, W, Ni, A; 1909 v S, W, H (2), A; 1910 v S, W; 1911 v S, W, Ni; 1912 v S, W, Ni; 1913 v S, W; 1914 v S, Ni; 1920 v S, W (25)
Pentland, F. B. (Middlesbrough), 1909 v S, W, H (2), A (5)
Perry, C. (WBA), 1890 v Ni; 1891 v Ni; 1893 v W (3)
Perry, T. (WBA), 1898 v W (1)
Perry, W. (Blackpool), 1956 v Ni, S, Sp (3)
Peters, M. (West Ham U), 1966 v Y, Fi, Pol, M, F, Arg, P, WG; 1967 v Ni, W, S, Cz; 1968 v W, Ni, S, USSR (2), Sp (2), Se, Y; 1969 v Ni, S, R, Bul, F, M, U, Br; 1970 v Ho (2), P (sub), Bel; (with Tottenham H), W, Ni, S, Co, Ec, R, Br, Cz, WG; 1971 v EG, Gr, Ma (2), Ni, W, S; 1972 v Sw, Gr, WG (1 + 1 sub) Ni (sub) 1973 v S (2), Ni, W, Cz, Pol, USSR, I; 1974 v A, Pol, I, P, S (67)
Phillips, L. H. (Portsmouth), 1952 v Ni; 1955 v W, WG (3)
Pickering, F. (Everton), 1964 v US; 1965 v Ni, Bel (3)
Pickering, J. (Sheffield U), 1933 v S (1)
Pike, T. M. (Cambridge University), 1886 v Ni (1)
Pilkington, B. (Burnley), 1955 v Ni (1)
Plant, J. (Bury), 1900 v S (1)
Plum, S. L. (Charlton Ath), 1923 v F (1)
Pointer, R. (Burnley), 1962 v W, L, P (3)
Porteous, T. S. (Sunderland), 1891 v W (1)
Priest, A. E. (Sheffield U), 1900 v Ni (1)
Prinsep, J. F. M. (Clapham Rovers), 1879 v S (1)
Puddefoot, S. C. (Blackburn R), 1926 v S, Ni (2)
Pye, J. (Wolverhampton W), 1950 v Ei (1)
Pym, R. H. (Bolton W), 1925 v S, W; 1926 v W (3)

Quantrill, A. (Derby Co), 1920 v S, W; 1921 v W, Ni (4)
Quixall, A. (Sheffield W), 1954 v W, Ni, R of E; 1955 v Sp, P (sub) (5)

Radford, J. (Arsenal), 1969 v R; 1972 v Sw (sub) (2)
Raikes, G. B. (Oxford University), 1895 v W; 1896 v W, Ni, S (4)
Ramsey, A. E. (Southampton), 1949 v Sw; (with Tottenham H), 1950 v S, I, P, Bel, Ch, US, Sp; 1951 v S, Ni, W, Y, Arg, P; 1952 v S, W, Ni, F, A (2), I, Sw; 1953 v Ni, W, S, Bel, Arg, Ch, U, US; 1954 v R of E, H (32)
Rawlings, A. (Preston NE), 1921 v Bel (1)
Rawlings, W. E. (Southampton), 1922 v S, W (2)
Rawlinson, J. F. P. (Cambridge University), 1882 v Ni (1)
Rawson, H. E. (Royal Engineers), 1875 v S (1)
Rawson, W. S. (Oxford University), 1875 v S; 1877 v S (2)
Read, A. (Tufnell Park), 1921 v Bel (1)
Reader, J. (WBA), 1894 v Ni (1)
Reaney, P. (Leeds U), 1969 v Bul (sub); 1970 v P; 1971 v Ma (3)
Reeves, K. (Norwich C), 1980 v Bul; (with Manchester C), Ni (2)
Revie, D. G. (Manchester C), 1955 v Ni, S, F; 1956 v W, D; 1957 v Ni (6)
Reynolds, J. (WBA), 1892 v S; 1893 v S, W; (with Aston Villa), 1894 v S, Ni; 1895 v S; 1897 v S, W (8)
Richards, C. H. (Nottingham F), 1898 v Ni (1)
Richards, G. H. (Derby Co), 1909 v A (1)
Richards, J. P. (Wolverhampton W), 1973 v Ni (1)
Richardson, J. R. (Newcastle U), 1933 v I, Sw (2)
Richardson, W. G. (WBA), 1935 v Ho (1)
Rickaby, S, (WBA), 1954 v Ni (1)
Rigby, A. (Blackburn R), 1927 v S, Bel, L, F; 1928 v W (5)
Rimmer, E. J. (Sheffield W), 1930 v S, G, A; 1932 v Sp (4)
Rimmer, J. J. (Arsenal), 1976 v I (1)
Rix, G. (Arsenal), 1981 v N, R, Sw (sub), Br, W, S (6)
Robb, G. (Tottenham H), 1954 v H (1)
Roberts, C. (Manchester U), 1905 v Ni, W, S (3)
Roberts, F. (Manchester C), 1925 v S, W, Bel, F (4)
Roberts, H. (Arsenal), 1931 v S (1)
Roberts, H. (Millwall), 1931 v Bel (1)
Roberts, R. (WBA), 1887 v S; 1888 v Ni; 1890 v Ni (3)
Roberts, W. T. (Preston NE), 1924 v W, Bel (2)
Robinson, J. (Sheffield W), 1937 v Fi; 1938 v G, Sw; 1939 v W (4)
Robinson, J. W. (Derby Co), 1897 v S, Ni; (with New Brighton Tower), 1898 v S, W, Ni; (with Southampton), 1899 v W, S; 1900 v S, W, Ni; 1901 v Ni (11)
Robson, B. (WBA), 1980 v Ei, Aus; 1981 v N, R, Sw, Sp, R, Br, W, S, Sw, H (12)
Robson, R. (WBA), 1958 v F, USSR (2), Br, A; 1960 v Sp, H; 1961 v Ni, W, S, L, P, Sp, M, I; 1962 v W, Ni, Sw, L, P (20)
Rose, W. C. (Wolverhampton W), 1884 v S, W, Ni; (with Preston NE), 1886 v Ni; (with Wolverhampton W), 1891 v Ni (5)
Rostron, T. (Darwen), 1881 v S, W (2)
Rowe, A. (Tottenham H), 1934 v F (1)
Rowley, J. F. (Manchester U), 1949 v Sw, Se, F; 1950 v Ni, I; 1952 v S (6)
Rowley, W. (Stoke C), 1889 v Ni; 1892 v Ni (2)
Royle, J. (Everton), 1971 v Ma; 1973 v Y; (with Manchester C), 1976 v Ni (sub), I; 1977 v Fi, L (6)
Ruddlesdin, H. (Sheffield W), 1904 v W, Ni; 1905 v S (3)
Ruffell, J. W. (West Ham U), 1926 v S; 1927 v Ni; 1929 v S, W, Ni; 1930 v W (6)
Russell, B. B. (Royal Engineers), 1883 v W (1)
Rutherford, J. (Newcastle U), 1904 v S; 1907 v S, Ni, W; 1908 v S, Ni, W, A (2), H, B (11)

Sadler, D. (Manchester U), 1968 v Ni, USSR; 1970 v Ec (sub); 1971 v EG (4)
Sagar, C. (Bury), 1900 v Ni; 1902 v W (2)
Sagar, E. (Everton), 1936 v S, Ni, A, Bel (4)
Sandford, E. A. (WBA), 1933 v W (1)

Sandilands, R. R. (Old Westminsters), 1892 v W; 1893 v Ni; 1894 v W; 1895 v W; 1896 v W (5)
Sands, J. (Nottingham F), 1880 v W (1)
Sansom, K. (C Palace), 1979 v W; 1980 v Bul, Ei, Arg, W (sub), Ni, S, Bel, I; (with Arsenal), 1981 v N, R, Sw, Sp, R, Br, W, S, Sw (18)
Saunders, F. E. (Swifts), 1888 v W (1)
Savage, A. H. (C Palace), 1876 v S (1)
Sayer, J. (Stoke C), 1887 v Ni (1)
Scattergood, E. (Derby Co), 1913 v W (1)
Schofield, J. (Stoke C), 1892 v W; 1893 v W; 1895 v Ni (3)
Scott, L. (Arsenal), 1947 v S, W, Ni, Ei, Ho, F, Sw, P; 1948 v S, W, Ni, Bel, Se, I; 1949 v W, Ni, D (17)
Scott, W. R. (Brentford), 1937 v W (1)
Seddon, J. (Bolton W), 1923 v F, Se (2); 1924 v Bel; 1927 v W; 1929 v S (6)
Seed, J. M. (Tottenham H), 1921 v Bel: 1923 v W, Ni, Bel; 1925 v S (5)
Settle, J. (Bury), 1899 v S, W, Ni; (with Everton), 1902 v S, Ni; 1903 v Ni (6)
Sewell, J. (Sheffield W), 1952 v Ni, A, Sw; 1953 v Ni; 1954 v H (2) (6)
Sewell, W. R. (Blackburn R), 1924 v W (1)
Shackleton, L. F. (Sunderland), 1949 v W, D; 1950 v W; 1955 v W, WG (5)
Sharp, J. (Everton), 1903 v Ni; 1905 v S (2)
Shaw, G. E. (WBA), 1932 v S (1)
Shaw, G. L. (Sheffield U), 1959 v S, W, USSR, I; 1963 v W (5)
Shea, D. (Blackburn R), 1914 v W, Ni (2)
Shellito, K. J. (Chelsea), 1963 v Cz (1)
Shelton A. (Notts Co), 1889 v Ni; 1890 v S, W; 1891 v S, W; 1892 v S (6)
Shelton, C. (Notts Rangers), 1888 v Ni (1)
Shepherd, A. (Bolton W), 1906 v S; (with Newcastle U), 1911 v Ni (2)
Shilton, P. L. (Leicester C), 1971 v EG, W; 1972 v Sw, Ni; 1973 v Y, S (2), Ni, W, Cz, Pol, USSR, I; 1974 v A, Pol, I, W, Ni, S, Arg; (with Stoke C), 1975 v Cy; 1977 v Ni, W; (with Nottingham F), 1978 v W, H; 1979 v Cz, Se, A; 1980 v Ni, Sp, I; 1981 v N, Sw, R (34)
Shimwell, E. (Blackpool), 1949 v Se (1)
Shutt, G. (Stoke C), 1886 v Ni (1)
Silcock, J. (Manchester U), 1921 v S, W; 1923 v Se (3)
Sillett, R. P. (Chelsea), 1955 v F, Sp, P (3)
Simms, E. (Luton T), 1922 v Ni (1)
Simpson, J. (Blackburn R), 1911 v S, W, Ni; 1912 v S, W, Ni; 1913 v S; 1914 v W (8)
Slater, W. J. (Wolverhampton W), 1955 v W, WG; 1958 v S, P, Y, USSR (3), Br, A; 1959 v USSR; 1960 v S (12)
Smalley, T. (Wolverhampton W), 1937 v W (1)
Smart, T. (Aston Villa), 1921 v S; 1924 v S, W; 1926 v Ni; 1930 v W (5)
Smith, A. (Nottingham F), 1891 v S, W; 1893 v Ni (3)
Smith, A. K. (Oxford University), 1872 v S (1)
Smith, B. (Tottenham H), 1921 v S; 1922 v W (2)
Smith, C. E. (C Palace), 1876 v S (1)
Smith, G. O. (Oxford University), 1893 v Ni; 1894 v W, S; 1895 v W; 1896 v Ni, W, S; (with Old Carthusians), 1897 v Ni, W, S; 1898 v Ni, W, S; (with Corinthians), 1899 v Ni, W, S; 1899 v Ni, W, S; 1901 v S (20)
Smith, H. (Reading), 1905 v W, S; 1906 v W, Ni (4)
Smith, J. (WBA), 1920 v Ni; 1923 v Ni (2)
Smith, Joe (Bolton W), 1913 v Ni; 1914 v S, W; 1920 v W, Ni (5)
Smith, J. C. R. (Millwall), 1939 v Ni, N (2)
Smith, J. W. (Portsmouth), 1932 v Ni, W, Sp (3)
Smith, Leslie (Brentford), 1939 v R (1)
Smith, Lionel (Arsenal), 1951 v W; 1952 v W, Ni; 1953 v W, S, Bel (6)
Smith, R. A. (Tottenham H), 1961 v Ni, W, S, L, P, Sp; 1962 v S; 1963 v S, F, Br, Cz, EG; 1964 v W, Ni, R of W (15)
Smith, S. (Aston Villa), 1895 v S (1)
Smith, S. C. (Leicester C), 1936 v Ni (1)
Smith, T. (Birmingham C), 1960 v W, Se (2)
Smith, T. (Liverpool), 1971 v W (1)
Smith, W. H. (Huddersfield T), 1922 v W, S; 1928 v S (3)
Sorby, T. H. (Thursday Wanderers, Sheffield), 1879 v W (1)
Southworth, J. (Blackburn R), 1889 v W; 1891 v W; 1892 v S (3)
Sparks, F. J. (Herts Rangers), 1879 v S; (with Clapham Rovers), 1880 v S, W (3)
Spence, J. W. (Manchester U), 1926 v Bel; 1927 v Ni (2)
Spence, R. (Chelsea), 1936 v A, Bel (2)
Spencer, C. W. (Newcastle U), 1924 v S; 1925 v W (2)
Spencer, H. (Aston Villa), 1897 v S, W; 1900 v W; 1903 v Ni; 1905 v W, S (6)
Spiksley, F. (Sheffield W), 1893 v S, W; 1894 v S, Ni; 1896 v Ni; 1898 v S, W (7)
Spilsbury, B. W. (Cambridge University), 1885 v Ni; 1886 v Ni, S (3)
Spouncer, W. A. (Nottingham F), 1900 v W (1)
Springett, R. D. G. (Sheffield W), 1960 v Ni, S, Y, Sp, H; 1961 v Ni, S, L, P, Sp, M, I, A; 1962 v W, Ni, S, A, Sw, Pe, L, P, H, Arg, Bul, Br; 1963 v Ni, W, F (2), Sw; 1966 v W, A, N (33)
Sproston, B. (Leeds U), 1937 v W; 1938 v S, W, Ni, Cz, G, Sw, F; (with Tottenham H), 1939 v W, R of E; (with Manchester C), N (11)
Squire, R. T. (Cambridge University), 1886 v S, W, Ni (3)
Stanbrough, M. H. (Old Carthusians), 1895 v W (1)
Staniforth, R. (Huddersfield T), 1954 v S, H, Y, Bel, Sw, U; 1955 v W, WG (8)
Starling, R. W. (Sheffield W), 1933 v S; (with Aston Villa), 1937 v S (2)
Steele, F. C. (Stoke C), 1937 v S, W, Ni, N, Se, Fi (6)
Stephenson, C. (Huddersfield T), 1924 v W (1)
Stephenson, G. T. (Derby Co), 1928 v F, Bel; (with Sheffield W), 1931 v F (3)
Stephenson, J. E. (Leeds U), 1938 v S; 1939 v Ni (2)
Stepney, A. C. (Manchester U), 1968 v Se (1)
Stewart, J. (Sheffield W), 1907 v S, W; (with Newcastle U), 1911 v S (3)
Stiles, N. P. (Manchester U), 1965 v S, H, Y, Se; 1966 v W, Ni, S, A, Sp, Pol (2), WG (2), N, D, U, M, F, Arg, P; 1967 v Ni, W, S, Cz; 1968 v USSR; 1969 v R; 1970 v Ni, S (28)
Stoker, J. (Birmingham), 1933 v W; 1934 v S, H (3)
Storer, H. (Derby Co), 1924 v F; 1928 v Ni (2)
Storey, P. E. (Arsenal), 1971 v Gr, Ni, S; 1972 v Sw, WG, W, Ni, S; 1973 v W (3), Y, S (2), Ni, Cz, Pol, USSR, I (19)
Storey-Moore, I. (Nottingham F), 1970 v Ho (1)
Strange, A. H. (Sheffield W), 1930 v S, A, G; 1931 v S, W, Ni, F, Bel; 1932 v S, W, Ni, Sp; 1933 v S, Ni, A, I, Sw; 1934 v Ni, W, F (20)
Stratford, A. H. (Wanderers), 1874 v S (1)
Streten, B. (Luton T), 1950 v Ni (1)
Sturgess, A. (Sheffield U), 1911 v Ni; 1914 v S (2)
Summerbee, M. G. (Manchester C), 1968 v S, Sp, WG; 1972 v Sw, WG (sub), W, Ni; 1973 v USSR (sub) (8)
Sunderland, A. (Arsenal), 1980 v Aus (1)
Sutcliffe, J. W. (Bolton W), 1893 v W; 1895 v S, Ni; 1901 v S; (with Millwall), 1903 v W (5)
Swan, P. (Sheffield W), 1960 v Y, Sp, H; 1961 v Ni, W, S, L, P, Sp, M, I, A; 1962 v W, Ni, S, A, Sw, L, P (19)
Swepstone, H. A. (Pilgrims), 1880 v S; 1882 v S, W; 1883 v S, W, Ni (6)
Swift, F. V. (Manchester C), 1947, v S, W, Ni, Ei, Ho, F, Sw, P; 1948 v S, W, Ni, Bel, Se, I; 1949 v S, W, Ni, D, N (19)

Tait, G. (Birmingham Excelsior), 1881 v W (1)
Talbot, B. (Ipswich T), 1977 v Ni (sub), S, Br, Arg, U; (with Arsenal), 1980 v Aus (6)
Tambling, R. V. (Chelsea), 1963 v W, F; 1966 v Y (3)
Tate, J. T. (Aston Villa), 1931 v F, Bel; 1933 v W (3)
Taylor, E. (Blackpool), 1954 v H (1)
Taylor, E. H. (Huddersfield T), 1923 v S, W, Ni, Bel; 1924 v S, Ni, F; 1926 v S (8)
Taylor, J. G. (Fulham), 1951 v Arg, P (2)
Taylor, P. J. (C Palace), 1976 v W (sub), W, Ni, S (4)
Taylor, P. H. (Liverpool), 1948 v W, Ni, Se (3)
Taylor, T. (Manchester U), 1953 v Arg, Ch, U; 1954 v Bel, Sw; 1956 v S, Br, Se, Fi, WG; 1957 v Ni, Y (sub), D (2), Ei (2); 1958 v W, Ni, F (19)
Temple, D. W. (Everton), 1965 v WG (1)
Thickett, H. (Sheffield U), 1899 v S, W (2)
Thomas, D. (QPR), 1975 v Cz (sub), P, Cy (sub + 1), W, S (sub); 1976 v Cz (sub), P (sub) (8)
Thompson, P. (Liverpool), 1964 v P (2), Ei, US, Br, Arg; 1965 v Ni, W, S, Bel, Ho; 1966 v Ni; 1968 v Ni, WG; 1970 v S, Ho (sub) (16)
Thompson, P. B. (Liverpool), 1976 v W (2), Ni, S, Br, I, Fi; 1977 v Fi; 1979 v Ei (sub), Cz, Ni, S, Bul, Se (sub), A; 1980 v D, Ni, Bul, Ei, Sp (2), Arg, W, S, Bel, I; 1981 v N, R, H (29)
Thompson, T. (Aston Villa), 1952 v W; (with Preston NE), 1957 v S (2)
Thomson, R. A. (Wolverhampton W), 1964 v Ni, US, P, Arg; 1965 v Bel, Ho, Ni, W (8)
Thornewell, G. (Derby Co), 1923 v Se (2); 1924 v F; 1925 v F (4)
Thornley, I. (Manchester C), 1907 v W (1)
Tilson, S. F. (Manchester C), 1934 v H, Cz; 1935 v W; 1936 v Ni (4)
Titmuss, F. (Southampton), 1922 v W; 1923 v W (2)
Todd, C. (Derby Co), 1972 v Ni; 1974 v P, W, Ni, S, Arg, EG, Bul, Y; 1975 v P (sub), WG, Cy (2), Ni, W, S; 1976 v Sw, Cz, P, Ni, S, Br, Fi; 1977 v Ei, Fi, Ho (sub), Ni (27)
Toone, G. (Notts Co), 1892 v S, W (2)
Topham, A. G. (Casuals), 1894 v W (1)
Topham, R. (Wolverhampton W), 1893 v Ni; (with Casuals) 1894 v W (2)
Towers, M. A. (Sunderland), 1976 v W, Ni (sub), I (3)
Townley, W. J. (Blackburn R), 1889 v W; 1890 v Ni (2)
Townrow, J. E. (Clapton Orient), 1925 v S; 1926 v W (2)
Tremelling, D. R. (Birmingham), 1928 v W (1)
Tresadern, J. (West Ham U), 1923 v S, Se (2)
Tueart, D. (Manchester C), 1975 v Cy (sub), Ni; 1977 v Fi, Ni, W (sub), S (sub) (6)
Tunstall, F. E. (Sheffield U), 1923 v S; 1924 v S, W, Ni, F; 1925 v Ni, S (7)
Turnbull, R. J. (Bradford), 1920 v Ni (1)
Turner, A. (Southampton), 1900 v Ni; 1901 v Ni (2)
Turner, H. (Huddersfield T), 1931 v F, Bel (2)
Turner, J. A. (Bolton W), 1893 v W; (with Stoke C) 1895 v Ni; (with Derby Co) 1898 v Ni (3)
Tweedy, G. J. (Grimsby T), 1937 v H (1)

Ufton, D. G. (Charlton Ath), 1954 v R of E (1)
Underwood A. (Stoke C), 1891 v Ni; 1892 v Ni (2)
Urwin, T. (Middlesbrough), 1923 v Se (2); (with Newcastle U) 1924 v Bel; 1926 v W (4)
Utley, G. (Barnsley), 1913 v Ni (1)

Vaughton, O. H. (Aston Villa), 1882 v S, W, Ni; 1884 v S, W (5)
Veitch, C. C. M. (Newcastle U), 1906 v S, W, Ni; 1907 v S, W; 1909 v W (6)
Veitch, J. G. (Old Westminsters), 1894 v W (1)
Venables, T. F. (Chelsea), 1965 v Ho, Bel (2)
Vidal, R. W. S. (Oxford University), 1873 v S (1)
Viljoen, C. (Ipswich T), 1975 v Ni, W (2)
Viollet, D. S. (Manchester U), 1960 v H; 1962 v L (2)
Von Donop (Royal Engineers), 1873 v S; 1875 v S (2)

Wace, H. (Wanderers), 1878 v S; 1879 v S, W (3)
Wadsworth, S. J. (Huddersfield T), 1922 v S; 1923 v S, Bel; 1924 v S, Ni; 1925 v S, Ni; 1926 v W; 1927 v Ni (9)
Wainscoat, W. R. (Leeds U), 1929 v S (1)
Waiters, A. K. (Blackpool), 1964 v Ei, Br; 1965 v W, Bel, Ho (5)
Walden, F. I. (Tottenham H), 1914 v S; 1922 v W (2)
Walker, W. H. (Aston Villa), 1921 v Ni; 1922 v Ni, W, S; 1923 v Se (2); 1924 v S; 1925 v Ni, W, S, Bel, F; 1926 v Ni, W, S; 1927 v Ni, W; 1933 v A (18)
Wall, G. (Manchester U), 1907 v W; 1908 v Ni; 1909 v S; 1910 v W, S; 1912 v S; 1913 v Ni (7)
Wallace, C. W. (Aston Villa), 1913 v W; 1914 v Ni; 1920 v S (3)
Walters, A. M. (Cambridge University), 1885 v S, N; 1886 v S; 1887 v S, W; (with Old Carthusians) 1889 v S, W; 1890 v S, W (9)
Walters, P. M. (Oxford University), 1885 v S, Ni; (with Old Carthusians), 1886 v S, W, Ni; 1887 v S, W; 1888 v S, Ni; 1889 v S, W; 1890 v S, W (13)
Walton, N. (Blackburn R) 1890 v Ni (1)
Ward, J. T. (Blackburn Olympic), 1885 v W (1)
Ward, P. (Brighton & HA), 1980 v Aus (sub) (1)
Ward, T. V. (Derby Co), 1948 v Bel; 1949 v W (2)
Waring, T. (Aston Villa), 1931 v F, Bel; 1932 v S, W, Ni (5)
Warner, C. (Upton Park), 1878 v S (1)
Warren, B. (Derby Co), 1906 v S, W, Ni; 1907 v S, W, Ni; 1908 v S, W, Ni, A (2), H, B; 1909 v S, Ni, W, H (2), A; 1911 v S, Ni, W (22)
Waterfield, G. S. (Burnley), 1927 v W (1)
Watson, D. V. (Sunderland), 1974 v P, S (sub), Arg, EG, Bul, Y; 1975 v Cz, P, WG, Cy (2), Ni, W, S; (with Manchester C) 1976 v Sw, Cz (sub), P; 1977 v Ho, L, Ni, W, S, Br, Arg, U; 1978 v Sw, L, I, WG, Br, W, Ni, S, H; 1979 v D, Ei, Cz, Ni (2), W, S, Bul, Se, A; (with Werder Bremen), 1980 v D; (with Southampton) Ni, Bul, Ei, Sp (2), Arg, Ni, S, Bel, I; 1981 v N, R, Sw, R, W, S, Sw, H (63)
Watson, V. M. (West Ham U), 1923 v W, S; 1930 v S, G, A (5)
Watson, W. (Burnley), 1913 v S; 1914 v Ni; 1920 v Ni (3)
Watson, W. (Sunderland), 1950 v Ni, I; 1951 v W, Y (4)
Weaver, S. (Newcastle U), 1932 v S, 1933 v S, Ni (3)
Webb, G. W. (West Ham U), 1911 v S, W (2)
Webster, M. (Middlesbrough), 1930 v S, A, G (3)
Wedlock, W. J. (Bristol C), 1907 v S, Ni, W; 1908 v S, Ni, W, A (2), H, B; 1909 v S, W, Ni, H (2), A; 1910 v S, W, Ni; 1911 v S, W, Ni; 1912 v S, W, Ni; 1914 v W (26)
Weir, D. (Bolton W), 1889 v S, Ni (2)
Welch, R. de C. (Wanderers), 1872 v S; (with Harrow Chequers) 1874 v S (2)
Weller, K. (Leicester C), 1974 v W, Ni, S, Arg (4)
Welsh, D. (Charlton Ath), 1938 v G, Sw; 1939 v R (3)
West, G. (Everton), 1969 v W, Bul, M (3)
Westwood, R. W. (Bolton W), 1935 v S, W, Ho; 1936 v Ni, G; 1937 v W (6)
Whateley, O. (Aston Villa), 1883 v S, Ni (2)
Wheeler, J. E. (Bolton W), 1955 v Ni (1)
Wheldon, G. F. (Aston Villa), 1897 v Ni; 1898 v S, W, Ni (4)
White, T. A. (Everton), 1933 v I (1)
Whitehead, J. (Accrington), 1893 v W; (with Blackburn R) 1894 v Ni (2)
Whitfeld, H. (Old Etonians), 1879 v W (1)
Whitham, M. (Sheffield U), 1892 v Ni (1)
Whitworth, S. (Leicester C), 1975 v WG, Cy, Ni, W, S; 1976 v Sw, P (7)
Whymark, T. J. (Ipswich T), 1978 v L (sub) (1)
Widdowson, S. W. (Nottingham F), 1880 v S (1)
Wignall, F. (Nottingham F), 1965 v W, Ho (2)
Wilkes, A. (Aston Villa), 1901 v S, W; 1902 v S, W, Ni (5)

Wilkins, R. G. (Chelsea), 1976 v I; 1977 v Ei, Fi, Ni, Br, Arg, U; 1978 v Sw (sub), L, I, WG, W, Ni, S, H; 1979 v D, Ei, Cz, Ni, W, S, Bul, Se (sub), A; (with Manchester U) 1980 v D, Ni, Bul, Sp (2), Arg, W (sub), Ni, S, Bel, I; 1981 v Sp (sub), R, Br, W, S, Sw, H (sub) (42)
Wilkinson, B. (Sheffield U), 1904 v S (1)
Wilkinson, L. R. (Oxford University), 1891 v W (1)
Williams, B. F. (Wolverhampton W), 1949 v F; 1950 v S, W, Ei, I, P, Bel, Ch, US, Sp; 1951 v Ni, W, S, Y, Arg, P; 1952 v W, F; 1955 v S, WG, F, Sp, P; 1956 v W (24)
Williams, O. (Clapton Orient), 1923 v W, Ni (2)
Williams, W. (WBA), 1897 v Ni; 1898 v W, Ni, S; 1899 v W, Ni (6)
Williamson, E. C. (Arsenal), 1923 v Se (2) (2)
Williamson, R. G. (Middlesbrough), 1905 v Ni; 1911 v Ni, S, W; 1912 v S, W; 1913 v Ni (7)
Willingham, C. K. (Huddersfield T), 1937 v Fi; 1938 v S, G, Sw, F; 1939 v S, W, Ni, R of E, N, I, Y (12)
Willis, A. (Tottenham H), 1952 v F (1)
Wilshaw, D. J. (Wolverhampton W), 1954 v W; Sw, U; 1955 v S, F, Sp, P; 1956 v W, Ni, Fi, WG; 1957 v Ni (12)
Wilson, C. P. (Hendon), 1884 v S, W (2)
Wilson, C. W. (Oxford University), 1879 v W; 1881 v S (2)
Wilson, G. (Sheffield W), 1921 v S, W, Bel; 1922 v S, Ni; 1923 v S, W, Ni, Bel; 1924 v W, Ni, F (12)
Wilson, G. P. (Corinthians), 1900 v S, W (2)
Wilson, R. (Huddersfield T), 1960 v S, Y, Sp, H; 1962 v W, Ni, S, A, Sw, Pe, P, H, Arg, Bul, Br; 1963 v Ni, F, Br, Cz, EG, Sw; 1964 v W, S, R of W, U, P (2), Ei, Br, Arg; (with Everton), 1965 v S, H, Y, WG, Se; 1966 v WG (sub), W, Ni, A, Sp, Pol (2), Y, Fi, D, U, M, F, Arg, P, WG; 1967 v Ni, W, S, Cz, A; 1968 v Ni, S, USSR (2), Sp (2), Y (63)
Wilson, T. (Huddersfield T), 1928 v S (1)
Winckworth, W. N. (Old Westminsters), 1892 v W; 1893 v Ni (2)
Windridge, J. E. (Chelsea), 1908 v S, W, Ni, A (2), H, B; 1909 v Ni (8)
Wingfield-Stratford, C. V. (Royal Engineers), 1877 v S (1)
Withe, P. (Aston Villa), 1981 v Br, W, S (3)
Wollaston, C. H. R. (Wanderers), 1874 v S; 1875 v S; 1877 v S; 1880 v S (4)
Wolstenholme, S. (Everton), 1904 v S; (with Blackburn R), 1905 v W, Ni (3)
Wood, H. (Wolverhampton W), 1890 v S, W; 1896 v S (3)
Wood, R. E. (Manchester U), 1955 v Ni, W; 1956 v Fi (3)
Woodcock, T. (Nottingham F), 1978 v Ni; 1979 v Ei (sub), Cz, Bul (sub), Se; 1980 v Ni; (with Cologne), Bul, Ei, Sp (2), Arg, Bel, I; 1981 v N, R, Sw, R, W (sub), S (19)
Woodger, G. (Oldham Ath), 1911 v Ni (1)
Woodhall, G. (WBA), 1888 v S, W (2)
Woodley, V. R. (Chelsea), 1937 v S, N, Se, Fi; 1938 v S, W, Ni, Cz, G, Sw, F; 1939 v S, W, Ni, R of E, N, I, R, Y (19)
Woodward, V. J. (Tottenham H), 1903 v S, W, Ni; 1904 v S, Ni; 1905 v S, W, Ni; 1907 v S; 1908 v S, W, Ni, A (2), H, B; 1909 v W, Ni, H (2), A; (with Chelsea), 1910 v Ni; 1911 v W (23)
Woosnam, M. (Manchester C), 1922 v W (1)
Worrall, F. (Portsmouth), 1935 v Ho; 1937 v Ni (2)
Worthington, F. S. (Leicester C), 1974 v Ni (sub), S, Arg, EG, Bul, Y; 1975 v Cz, P (sub) (8)
Wreford-Brown, C. (Oxford University), 1889 v Ni; (with Old Carthusians), 1894 v W; 1895 v W; 1898 v S (4)
Wright, E. G. D. (Cambridge University), 1906 v W (1)
Wright, J. D. (Newcastle U), 1939 v N (1)
Wright, T. J. (Everton), 1968 v USSR; 1969 v R (2), M (sub), U, Br; 1970 v W, Ho, Bel, R (sub), Br (11)
Wright, W. A. (Wolverhampton W), 1947 v S, W, Ni, Ei, Ho, F, Sw, P; 1948 v S, W, Ni, Bel, Se, I; 1949 v S, W, Ni, D, Sw, Se, N, F; 1950 v S, W, Ni, Ei, I, P, Bel, Ch, US, Sp; 1951 v Ni, S, Arg; 1952 v W, Ni, S, F, A (2), I, Sw; 1953 v Ni, W, S, Bel, Arg, Ch, U, US; 1954 v W, Ni, S, R of E, H (2), Y, Bel, Sw, U; 1955 v W, Ni, S, WG, F, Sp, P; 1956 v Ni, W, S, Br, Se, Fi, WG, D, Sp; 1957 v S, W, Ni, Y, D (2), Ei (2); 1958 v W, Ni, S, P, Y, USSR (3), Br, A, F; 1959 v W, Ni, S, USSR, I, Br, Pe, M, US (105)
Wylie, J. G. (Wanderers), 1878 v S (1)

Yates, J. (Burnley), 1889 v Ni (1)
York, R. E. (Aston Villa), 1922 v S; 1926 v S (2)
Young, A. (Huddersfield T), 1933 v W; 1937 v S, H, N, Se; 1938 v G, Sw, F; 1939 v W (9)
Young, G. M. (Sheffield W), 1965 v W (1)

R. E. Evans also played for Wales against E, Ni, S; J. Reynolds also played for Ireland against E, W, S.

NORTHERN IRELAND

Aherne, T. (Belfast C), 1947 v E; 1948 v S; 1949 v W; (with Luton T), 1950 v W (4)
Alexander, A. (Cliftonville), 1895 v S (1)
Allen, C. A. (Cliftonville), 1936 v E (1)
Allen, J. (Limavady), 1887 v E (1)
Anderson, T. (Manchester U), 1973 v Cy, E, S, W; 1974 v Bul, P; (with Swindon T), 1975 v S (sub); 1976 v Is; 1977 v Ho, Bel, WG, E, S, W, Ic; 1978 v Ic, Ho, Bel; (with Peterborough U), S, E, W; 1979 v D (22)
Anderson, W. (Linfield), 1898 v W, E, S; 1899 v S (4)
Andrews, W. (Glentoran), 1908 v S; (with Grimsby T), 1913 v E, S (3)
Armstrong, G. (Tottenham H), 1977 v WG, E, W (sub), Ic (sub); 1978 v Bel, S, E, W; 1979 v Ei, D, Bul, E, Bul, E, S, W, D; 1980 v E, Ei, Is, S, E, W, Aus (3); 1981 v Se; (with Watford), P, S, P, S, Se (32)

Baird, G. (Distillery), 1896 v S, E, W (3)
Baird, H. (Huddersfield T), 1939 v E (1)
Balfe, J. (Shelbourne), 1909 v E; 1910 v W (2)
Bambrick, J. (Linfield), 1929 v W, S, E; 1930 v W, S, E; 1932 v W; (with Chelsea), 1935 v W; 1936 v E, S; 1938 v W (11)
Banks, S. J. (Cliftonville), 1937 v W (1)
Barr, H. H. (Linfield), 1962 v E; (with Coventry C), 1963 v E, Pol (3)
Barron, H. (Cliftonville), 1894 v E, W, S; 1895 v S; 1896 v S; 1897 v E, W (7)
Barry, H. (Bohemians), 1900 v S (1)
Baxter, R. A. (Cliftonville), 1887 v S, W (2)
Bennett, L. V. (Dublin University), 1889 v W (1)
Berry, J. (Cliftonville), 1888 v S, W; 1889 v E (3)
Best, G. (Manchester U), 1964 v W, U; 1965 v E, Ho (2), S, Sw (2), Alb; 1966 v S, E, Alb; 1967 v E; 1968 v S; 1969 v E, S, W, T; 1970 v S, E, W, USSR; 1971 v Cy (2), Sp, E, S, W; 1972 v USSR, Sp; 1973 v Bul; 1974 v P; (with Fulham), 1977 v Ho, Bel, WG; 1978 v Ic, Ho (37)
Bingham, W. L. (Sunderland), 1951 v F; 1952 v E, S, W; 1953 v E, S, F, W; 1954 v E, S, W; 1955 v E, S, W; 1956 v E, S, W; 1957 v E, S, W, P (2), I; 1958 v S, E, W, I (2), Arg, Cz (2), WG, F; (with Luton T), 1959 v E, S, W, Sp; 1960 v S, E, W; (with Everton), 1961 v E, S, WG (2), Gr, I; 1962 v E, Gr; 1963 v E, S, Pol (2), Sp; (with Port Vale), 1964 v S, E, Sp (56)
Black, J. (Glentoran), 1901 v E (1)
Blair, H. (Portadown), 1931 v S; 1932 v S; (with Swansea), 1934 v S (3)
Blair, J. (Cliftonville), 1907 v W, E, S; 1908 v E, S (5)
Blair, R. V. (Oldham Ath), 1975 v Se (sub), S (sub), W; 1976 v Se, Is (5)
Blanchflower, R. D. (Barnsley), 1950 v S, W; 1951 v E, S; (with Aston Villa), F; 1952 v W; 1953 v E, S, W, F; 1954 v E, S, W; (with Tottenham H), 1955 v E, S, W;

1956 v E, S, W; 1957 v E, S, W, I, P (2); 1958 v E, S, W, I (2), Cz (2), Arg, F, WG; 1959 v E, S, W, Sp; 1960 v E, S, W; 1961 v E, S, W, WG (2); 1962 v E, S, W, Gr, Ho; 1963 v E, S, Pol (2) (56)
Blanchflower, J. (Manchester U), 1954 v W; 1955 v E, S; 1956 v S, W; 1957 v S, E, P; 1958 v S, E, I (2) (12)
Bookman, L. O. (Bradford C), 1914 v W; (with Luton T), 1921 v S, W; 1922 v E (4)
Bothwell, A. W. (Ards), 1926 v S, E, W; 1927 v E, W (5)
Bowler, G. C. (Hull C), 1950 v E, S, W (3)
Boyle, P. (Sheffield U), 1901 v E; 1902 v E; 1903 v S, W; 1904 v E (5)
Braithwaite, R. S. (Linfield), 1962 v W; 1963 v P, Sp; (with Middlesbrough), 1964 v W, U; 1965 v E, S, Sw (2), Ho (10)
Breen, T. (Belfast C), 1935 v E, W; 1937 v E, S; (with Manchester U), 1937 v W; 1938 v E, S; 1939 v W, S (9)
Brennan, B. (Bohemians), 1912 v W (1)
Brennan, R. A. (Luton T), 1949 v W; (with Birmingham C), 1950 v E, S, W; (with Fulham), 1951 v E (5)
Briggs, W. R. (Manchester U), 1962 v W; (with Swansea T), 1965 v Ho (2)
Brisby, D. (Distillery), 1891 v S (1)
Brolly, T. (Millwall), 1937 v W; 1938 v W; 1939 v E, W (4)
Brookes, E. A. (Shelbourne), 1920 v S (1)
Brotherston, N. (Blackburn R), 1980 v S, E, W, Aus (3); 1981 v Se, P (8)
Brown, J. (Glenavon), 1921 v W; (with Tranmere R), 1924 v E, W (3)
Brown, J. (Wolverhampton W), 1935 v E, W; 1936 v E; (with Coventry C), 1937 v E, W; 1938 v S, W; (with Birmingham C), 1939 v E, S, W (10)
Brown, W. G. (Glenavon), 1926 v W (1)
Brown, W. M. (Limavady), 1887 v E (1)
Browne, F. (Cliftonville), 1887 v E, S, W; 1888 v E, S (5)
Browne, R. J. (Leeds U), 1936 v E, W; 1938 v E, W; 1939 v E, S (6)
Bruce, W. (Glentoran), 1961 v S; 1967 v W (2)
Buckle, H. (Cliftonville), 1882 v E (1)
Buckle, H. R. (Sunderland), 1904 v E; (with Bristol R), 1908 v W (2)
Burnett, J. (Distillery), 1894 v E, W, S; (with Glentoran), 1895 v E, W (5)
Burnison, J. (Distillery), 1901 v E, W (2)
Burnison, S. (Distillery), 1908 v E; 1910 v E, S; (with Bradford), 1911 v E, S, W; (with Distillery), 1912 v E; 1913 v W (8)
Burns, J. (Glenavon), 1923 v E (1)
Butler, M. P. (Blackpool), 1939 v W (1)

Campbell, A. C. (Crusaders), 1963 v W; 1965 v Sw (2)
Campbell, J. (Cliftonville), 1896 v W; 1897 v E, S, W; (with Distillery), 1898 v E, S, W; (with Cliftonville), 1899 v E; 1900 v E, S; 1901 v S, W; 1902 v S; 1903 v E; 1904 v S (15)
Campbell, J. P. (Fulham), 1951 v E, S (2)
Campbell, W. G. (Dundee), 1968 v S, E; 1969 v T; 1970 v S, W, USSR (6)
Carey, J. J. (Manchester U), 1947 v E, S, W; 1948 v E; 1949 v E, S, W (7)
Carroll, E. (Glenavon), 1925 v S (1)
Casey, T. (Newcastle U), 1955 v W; 1956 v W; 1957 v E, S, W, I, P (2); 1958 v WG, F; (with Portsmouth), 1959 v E, Sp (12)
Cashin, M. (Cliftonville), 1898 v S (1)
Caskey, W. (Derby Co), 1979 v Bul, E, Bul, E, D (sub); 1980 v E (sub) (6)
Cassidy, T. (Newcastle U), 1971 v E (sub); 1972 v USSR (sub); 1974 v Bul (sub), S, E, W; 1975 v N; 1976 v S, E, W; 1977 v WG (sub); 1980 v E, Ei (sub), Is, S, E, W, Aus (3); (with Burnley), 1981 v Se, P (22)
Chambers, J. (Distillery), 1921 v W; (with Bury), 1928 v E, S, W; 1929 v E, S, W; 1930 v S, W; (with Nottingham F), 1932 v E, S, W (12)
Chatton, H. A. (Partick T), 1925 v E, S; 1926 v E (3)
Christian, J. (Linfield), 1889 v S (1)
Clarke, R. (Belfast C), 1901 v E, S (2)
Clements, D. (Coventry C), 1965 v W, Ho; 1966 v M; 1967 v S, W; 1968 v S, E; 1969 v T (2), S, W; 1970 v S, E, W, USSR (2); 1971 v Sp, E, S, W, Cy; (with Sheffield W), 1972 v USSR (2), Sp, E, S, W; 1973 v Bul, Cy (2), P, E, S, W; (with Everton), 1974 v Bul, P, S, E, W; 1975 v N, Y, E, S, W; 1976 v Se, Y; (with New York Cosmos), E, W (48)
Clugston, J. (Cliftonville), 1888 v W; 1889 v W, S, E; 1890 v E, S; 1891 v E, W; 1892 v E, S, W; 1893 v E, S, W (14)
Cochrane, D. (Leeds U), 1939 v E, W; 1947 v E, S, W; 1948 v E, S, W; 1949 v S, W; 1950 v S, E (12)
Cochrane, M. (Distillery), 1898 v S, W, E; 1899 v E; 1900 v E, S, W; (with Leicester Fosse), 1901 v S (8)
Cochrane, T. (Coleraine), 1976 v N; (with Burnley), 1978 v S (sub), E (sub), W (sub); 1979 v Ei (sub); (with Middlesbrough), D, Bul, E, Bul, E; 1980 v Is, E (sub), W (sub), Aus (1+2 sub); 1981 v Se (sub), P (sub), S, P, S, Se (22)
Collins, F. (Glasgow C), 1922 v S (1)
Condy, J. (Distillery), 1882 v W; 1886 v E, S (3)
Connell, T. (Manchester U), 1978 v W (sub) (1)
Connor, J. (Glentoran), 1901 v S, E; (with Belfast C), 1905 v E, S, W; 1907 v E, S; 1908 v E, S; 1909 v W; 1911 v S, E, W (13)
Connor, M. J. (Brentford), 1903 v S, W; (with Fulham), 1904 v E (3)
Cook, W. (Celtic), 1933 v E, W, S; (with Everton), 1935 v E; 1936 v S, W; 1937 v E, S, W; 1938 v E, S, W; 1939 v E, S, W (15)
Cooke, S. (Belfast YMCA), 1889 v E; (with Cliftonville), 1890 v E, S (3)
Coulter, J. (Belfast C), 1934 v E, S, W; (with Everton), 1935 v E, S, W; 1937 v S, W; (with Grimsby T), 1938 v S, W; (with Chelmsford C), 1939 v S (11)
Cowan, J. (Newcastle U), 1970 v E (sub) (1)
Cowan, T. S. (Queen's Island), 1925 v W (1)
Coyle, F. (Coleraine), 1956 v E, S; 1957 v P (with Nottingham F), 1958 v Arg (4)
Coyle, R. I. (Sheffield W), 1973 v P, Cy (sub), W (sub); 1974 v Bul (sub), P (sub) (5)
Craig, A. B. (Rangers), 1908 v E, S, W; 1909 v S; (with Morton), 1912 v S, W; 1914 v E, S, W (9)
Craig, D. J. (Newcastle U), 1967 v W; 1968 v W; 1969 v T (2), E, S, W; 1970 v E, S, W, USSR; 1971 v Cy (2), S, S (sub); 1972 v USSR, S (sub); 1973 v Cy (2), E, S, W; 1974 v Bul, P; 1975 v N (25)
Crawford, S. (Distillery), 1889 v E, W; (with Cliftonville), 1891 v E, S, W; 1893 v E, W (7)
Croft, T. (Queen's Island), 1924 v E (1)
Crone, R. (Distillery), 1889 v S; 1890 v E, S, W (4)
Crone, W. (Distillery), 1882 v W; 1884 v E, S, W; 1886 v E, S, W; 1887 v E; 1888 v E, W; 1889 v S; 1890 v W (12)
Crooks, W. (Manchester U), 1922 v W (1)
Crossan, E. (Blackburn R), 1950 v S; 1951 v E; 1955 v W (3)
Crossan, J. A. (Sparta-Rotterdam), 1960 v E; (with Sunderland), 1963 v W, P, Sp; 1964 v E, S, W, U, Sp; 1965 v E, S, Sw (2); (with Manchester C), W, Ho (2), Alb; 1966 v S, E, Alb, WG; 1967 v E, S; (with Middlesbrough), 1968 v S (24)
Crothers, C. (Distillery), 1907 v W (1)
Cumming, L. (Huddersfield T), 1929 v W, S; (with Oldham Ath), 1930 v E (3)
Cunningham, R. (Ulster), 1892 v S, E, W; 1893 v E (4)

Cunningham, W. E. (St Mirren), 1951 v W; 1953 v E; 1954 v S; 1955 v S; (with Leicester C), 1956 v E, S, W; 1957 v E, S, W, I, P (2); 1958 v S, W, I, Cz (2), Arg, WG, F; 1959 v E, S, W; 1960 v E, S, W; (with Dunfermline Ath), 1961 v W; 1962 v W, Ho (30)
Curran, S. (Belfast C), 1926 v S, W; 1928 v S (3)
Curran, J. J. (Glenavon), 1922 v W; (with Pontypridd), 1923 v E, S; (with Glenavon), 1924 v E (4)
Cush, W. W. (Glenavon), 1951 v E, S; 1954 v S, E; 1957 v W, I, P (2); (with Leeds U), 1958 v I (2), W, Cz (2), Arg, WG, F; 1959 v E, S, W, Sp; 1960 v E, S, W; (with Portadown), 1961 v WG, Gr; 1962 v Gr (26)

Dalton, W. (YMCA), 1888 v S; (with Linfield), 1890 v S, W; 1891 v S, W; 1892 v E, S, W; 1894 v E, S, W (11)
D'Arcy, S. D. (Chelsea), 1952 v W; 1953 v E; (with Brentford), 1953 v S, W, F (5)
Darling, J. (Linfield), 1897 v E, S; 1900 v S; 1902 v E, S, W; 1903 v E, S, W; 1905 v E, S, W; 1906 v E, S, W; 1908 v W; 1909 v E; 1910 v E, S, W; 1912 v S (21)
Davey, H. H. (Reading), 1926 v E; 1927 v E, S; 1928 v E; (with Portsmouth), 1928 v W (5)
Davis, T. L. (Oldham Ath), 1937 v E (1)
Davison, J. R. (Cliftonville), 1882 v E, W; 1883 v E, W; 1884 v E, W, S; 1885 v E (8)
Devine, W. (Limavady), 1886 v E, W; 1887 v W; 1888 v W (4)
Dickson, D. (Coleraine), 1970 v S (sub), W; 1973 v Cy, P (4)
Dickson, T. A. (Linfield), 1957 v S (1)
Dickson, W. (Chelsea), 1951 v W, F; 1952 v E, S, W; 1953 v E, S, W, F; (with Arsenal), 1954 v E, W; 1955 v E (12)
Diffin, W. (Belfast C), 1931 v W (1)
Dill, A. H. (Knock and Down Ath), 1882 v E, W; (with Cliftonville), 1883 v W; 1884 v E, S, W; 1885 v E, S, W (9)
Doherty, I. (Belfast C), 1901 v E (1)
Doherty, J. (Cliftonville), 1933 v E, W (2)
Doherty, M. (Derry C), 1938 v S (1)
Doherty, P. D. (Blackpool), 1935 v E, W; 1936 v E, S; (with Manchester C), 1937 v E, W; 1938 v E, S; 1939 v E, W; (with Derby Co), 1947 v E; (with Huddersfield T), 1947 v W; 1948 v E, W; 1949 v S; (with Doncaster R), 1951 v S (16)
Donaghy, M. (Luton T), 1980 v S, E, W; 1981 v Se, P, S (sub) (6)
Donnelly, L. (Distillery), 1913 v W (1)
Doran, J. F. (Brighton), 1921 v E; 1922 v E, W (3)
Dougan, A. D. (Portsmouth), 1958 v Cz; (with Blackburn R), 1960 v S; 1961 v E, W, I, Gr; (with Aston Villa), 1963 v S, P (2); (with Leicester C), 1966 v S, E, W, M, Alb, WG; 1967 v E, S; (with Wolverhampton W), 1967 v W; 1968 v S, W, Is; 1969 v T (2), E, S, W; 1970 v S, E, USSR (2); 1971 v Cy (2), Sp, E, S, W; 1972 v USSR (2), E, S, W; 1973 v Bul, Cy (43)
Douglas, J. P. (Belfast C), 1947 v E (1)
Dowd, H. O. (Glenavon), 1974 v W; 1975 v N (sub), Se (3)
Duggan, H. A. (Leeds U), 1930 v E; 1931 v E, W; 1933 v E; 1934 v E; 1935 v S, W; 1936 v S (8)
Dunne, J. (Sheffield U), 1928 v W; 1931 v W, E; 1932 v E, S; 1933 v E, W (7)

Eames, W. L. E. (Dublin U), 1885 v E, S, W (3)
Eglington, T. J. (Everton), 1947 v S, W; 1948 v E, S, W; 1949 v E (6)
Elder, A. R. (Burnley), 1960 v W; 1961 v S, E, W, WG (2), Gr; 1962 v E, S, Gr; 1963 v E, S, W, P (2), Sp; 1964 v W, U; 1965 v E, S, W, Sw (2), Ho (2), Alb; 1966 v E, S, W, M, Alb; 1967 v E, S, W; (with Stoke C), 1968 v E, W; 1969 v E (sub), S, W; 1970 v USSR (40)
Elleman, A. R. (Cliftonville), 1889 v W; 1890 v E (2)
Elwood, J. H. (Bradford), 1929 v W; 1930 v E (2)
Emerson, W. (Glentoran), 1920 v E, S, W; 1921 v E; 1922 v E, S; (with Burnley), 1922 v W; 1923 v E, S, W; 1924 v E (11)
English, S. (Glasgow R), 1933 v W, S (2)
Enright, J. (Leeds C), 1912 v S (1)

Falloon, E. (Aberdeen), 1931 v S; 1933 v S (2)
Farquharson, T. G. (Cardiff C), 1923 v S, W; 1924 v E, S, W; 1925 v E, S (7)
Farrell, P. (Distillery), 1901 v S, W (2)
Farrell, P. (Hibernian), 1938 v W (1)
Farrell, P. D. (Everton), 1947 v S, W; 1948 v E, S, W; 1949 v E, W (7)
Feeney, J. M. (Linfield), 1947 v S; (with Swansea T), 1950 v E (2)
Feeney, W. (Glentoran), 1976 v Is (1)
Ferguson, W. (Linfield), 1966 v M; 1967 v E (2)
Ferris, J. (Belfast Celtic), 1920 v E, W; (with Chelsea), 1921 v S, E; (with Belfast C), 1928 v S (5)
Ferris, R. O. (Birmingham), 1950 v S; 1951 v F; 1952 v S (3)
Finney, T. (Sunderland), 1975 v N, E (sub), S, W; 1976 v N, Y, S; (with Cambridge U), 1980 v E, Is, S, E, W, Aus (2) (14)
Fitzpatrick, J. C. (Bohemians), 1896 v E, S (2)
Flack, H. (Burnley), 1929 v S (1)
Forbes, G. (Limavady), 1888 v W; (with Distillery), 1891 v E, S (3)
Forde, J. T. (Ards), 1959 v Sp; 1961 v E, S, WG (4)
Foreman, T. A. (Cliftonville), 1899 v S (1)
Forsyth, J. (YMCA), 1888 v E, S (2)
Fox, W. (Ulster), 1887 v E, S (2)
Fulton, R. P. (Belfast C), 1930 v W; 1931 v E, S, W; 1932 v W, E; 1933 v E, S; 1934 v E, W, S; 1935 v E, W, S; 1936 v S, W; 1937 v E, S, W; 1938 v W (20)

Gaffikin, J. (Linfield Ath), 1890 v S, W; 1891 v S, W; 1892 v E, S, W; 1893 v E, S, W; 1894 v E, S, W; 1895 v E, W (15)
Galbraith, W. (Distillery), 1890 v W (1)
Gallagher, P. (Celtic), 1920 v E, S; 1922 v S; 1923 v S, W; 1924 v S, W; 1925 v S, W, E; (with Falkirk), 1927 v S (11)
Gallogly, C. (Huddersfield T), 1951 v E, S (2)
Gara, A. (Preston NE), 1902 v E, S, W (3)
Gardiner, A. (Cliftonville), 1930 v S, W; 1931 v S; 1932 v E, S (5)
Garrett, J. (Distillery), 1925 v W (1)
Gaston, R. (Oxford U), 1969 v Is (sub) (1)
Gaukrodger, G. (Linfield), 1895 v W (1)
Gaussen, A. W. (Moyola Park), 1884 v E, S; 1888 v E, W; 1889 v E, W (6)
Geary, J. (Glentoran), 1931 v S; 1932 v S (2)
Gibb, J. T. (Wellington Park) 1884 v S, W; 1885 v S, E, W; 1886 v S; 1887 v S, E, W; 1889 v S (10)
Gibb, T. J. (Cliftonville), 1936 v W (1)
Gibson W. K. (Cliftonville), 1894 v S, W, E; 1895 v S; 1897 v W; 1898 v S, W, E; 1901 v S, W, E; 1902 v S, W (13)
Gillespie, R. (Hertford), 1886 v E, S, W; 1887 v E, S, W (6)
Gillespie, W. (Sheffield U), 1913 v E, S; 1914 v E, W; 1920 v S, W; 1921 v E; 1922 v E, S, W; 1923 v E, S, W; 1924 v E, S, W; 1925 v E, S; 1926 v S, W; 1927 v E, W; 1928 v E; 1929 v E; 1931 v E (25)
Gillespie, W. (West Down), 1889 v W (1)
Goodall, A. L. (Derby Co), 1899 v S, W; 1900 v E, W; 1901 v E; 1902 v S; 1903 v E, W; (with Glossop), 1904 v E, W (10)

Goodbody, M. F. (Dublin University), 1889 v E; 1891 v W (2)
Gordon, H. (Linfield), 1891 v S; 1892 v E, S, W; 1893 v E, S, W; 1895 v E, W; 1896 v E, S (11)
Gordon, T. (Linfield), 1894 v W; 1895 v E (2)
Gorman, W. C. (Brentford), 1947 v E, S, W; 1948 v W (4)
Gowdy, J. (Glentoran), 1920 v E; (with Queen's Island), 1924 v W; (with Falkirk), 1926 v E, S; 1927 v E, S (6)
Gowdy, W. A. (Hull C), 1932 v S; (with Sheffield W), 1933 v S; (with Linfield), 1935 v E, S, W; (with Hibernian), 1936 v W (6)
Graham, W. G. L. (Doncaster R), 1951 v W, F; 1952 v E, S, W; 1953 v S, F; 1954 v E, W; 1955 v S, W; 1956 v E, S; 1959 v E (14)
Greer, W. (QPR), 1909 v E, S, W (3)
Gregg, H. (Doncaster R), 1954 v W; 1957 v E, S, W, I, P (2); 1958 v E, I; (with Manchester U), 1958 v Cz, Arg, WG, F, W; 1959 v E, W; 1960 v S, E, W; 1961 v E, S; 1962 v S, Gr; 1964 v S, E (25)

Hall, G. (Distillery), 1897 v E (1)
Halligan, W. (Derby Co), 1911 v W; (with Wolverhampton W), 1912 v E (2)
Hamill, M. (Manchester U), 1912 v E; 1914 v E, S; (with Belfast C), 1920 v E, S, W; (with Manchester C), 1921 v S (7)
Hamilton, B. (Linfield), 1969 v T; 1971 v Cy (2), E, S, W; (with Ipswich T), 1972 v USSR (1+1 sub), Sp; 1973 v Bul, Cy (2), P, E, S, W; 1974 v Bul, S, E, W; 1975 v N, Se, Y, E; 1976 v Se, N, Y; (with Everton), Is, S, E, W; 1977 v Ho, Bel, WG, E, S, W, Ic; (with Millwall), 1978 v S, E, W; 1979 v Ei (sub); (with Swindon T), Bul (2), E, S, W, D; 1980 v Aus (2 sub) (50)
Hamilton, J. (Knock), 1882 v E, W (2)
Hamilton, R. (Distillery), 1908 v W (1)
Hamilton, R. (Glasgow R), 1928 v S; 1929 v E; 1930 v S, E; 1932 v S (5)
Hamilton, W. (QPR), 1978 v S (sub); (with Burnley), 1980 v S, E, W, Aus (2); 1981 v Se, P, S, P, S, Se (12)
Hamilton, W. D. (Dublin Association), 1885 v W (1)
Hamilton, W. J. (Dublin Association), 1885 v W (1)
Hampton, H. (Bradford C), 1911 v E, S, W; 1912 v E, W; 1913 v E, S, W; 1914 v E (9)
Hanna, D. R. A. (Portsmouth), 1899 v W (1)
Hanna, J. (Nottingham F), 1912 v S, W (2)
Hannon, D. J. (Bohemian), 1908 v E, S; 1911 v E, S; 1912 v W; 1913 v E (6)
Harkin, J. T. (Southport), 1968 v W; 1969 v T; (with Shrewsbury T), W (sub); 1970 v USSR; 1971 v Sp (5)
Harland, A. I. (Linfield), 1923 v E (1)
Harris, J. (Cliftonville), 1921 v W (1)
Harris, V. (Shelbourne), 1906 v E; 1907 v E, W; 1908 v E, W, S; (with Everton), 1909 v E, W, S; 1910 v E, S, W; 1911 v E, S, W; 1912 v E; 1913 v E, S; 1914 v S, W (20)
Harvey, M. (Sunderland), 1961 v I; 1962 v Ho; 1963 v W, Sp; 1964 v S, E, W, U, Sp; 1965 v E, S, W, Sw (2), Ho (2), Alb; 1966 v S, E, W, M, Alb, WG; 1967 v E, S; 1968 v E, W; 1969 v Is, T (2), E; 1970 v USSR; 1971 v Cy, W (sub) (33)
Hastings, J. (Knock), 1882 v E, W; (with Ulster), 1883 v W; 1884 v E, S; 1886 v E, S (7)
Hatton, S. (Linfield), 1963 v S, Pol (2)
Hayes, W. E. (Huddersfield T), 1938 v E, S; 1939 v E, S (4)
Hegan, D. (WBA), 1970 v USSR; (with Wolverhampton W), 1972 v USSR, E, S, W; 1973 v Bul, Cy (7)
Henderson, A. W. (Ulster), 1885 v E, S, W (3)
Hewison, G. (Moyola Park), 1885 v E, S (2)
Hill, M. J. (Norwich C), 1959 v W; 1960 v W; 1961 v WG; 1962 v S; (with Everton), 1964 v S, E, Sp (7)
Hinton, E. (Fulham), 1947 v S, W; 1948 v S, E, W; (with Millwall), 1951 v W, F (7)
Hopkins, J. (Brighton), 1926 v E (1)
Houston, J. (Linfield), 1912 v S, W; 1913 v W; (with Everton), 1913 v E, S; 1914 v S (6)
Houston, W. (Linfield), 1933 v W (1)
Houston, W. G. (Moyola Park), 1885 v E, S (2)
Hughes, W. (Bolton W), 1951 v W (1)
Humphries, W. (Ards), 1962 v W; (with Coventry C), 1962 v Ho; 1963 v E, S, W, Pol, Sp; 1964 v S, E, Sp; 1965 v S; (with Swansea T), 1965 v W, Ho, Alb (14)
Hunter, A. (Blackburn R), 1970 v USSR; 1971 v Cy (2), E, S, W; (with Ipswich T), 1972 v USSR (2), Sp, E, S, W; 1973 v Bul, Cy (2), P, E, S, W; 1974 v Bul, S, E, W; 1975 v N, Se, Y, E, S, W; 1976 v Se, N, Y, Is, S, E, W; 1977 v Ho, Bel, WG, E, S, W, Ic; 1978 v Ic, Ho, Bel; 1979 v Ei, D, S, W, D; 1980 v E, Ei (53)
Hunter, A. (Distillery), 1905 v W; 1906 v W, E, S; (with Belfast C), 1908 v W; 1909 v W, E, S (8)
Hunter, R. J. (Cliftonville), 1884 v E, S, W (3)
Hunter, V. (Coleraine), 1962 v E; 1964 v Sp (2)

Irvine, R. W. (Everton), 1922 v S; 1923 v E, W; 1924 v E, S; 1925 v E; 1926 v E; 1927 v E, W; 1928 v E, S; (with Portsmouth), 1929 v E; 1930 v S; (with Connah's Quay), 1931 v E; (with Derry C), 1932 v W (15)
Irvine, R. J. (Linfield), 1962 v Ho; 1963 v E, S, W, Pol (2), Sp; (with Stoke C), 1965 v W (8)
Irvine, W. J. (Burnley), 1963 v W, Sp; 1965 v S, W, Sw, Ho (2), Alb; 1966 v S, E, W, M, Alb; 1967 v E, S; 1968 v E, W; (with Preston NE), 1969 v Is, T, E; (with Brighton), 1972 v E, S, W (23)
Irving, S. J. (Dundee), 1923 v S, W; 1924 v S, E, W; 1925 v S, E, W; 1926 v S, W; (with Cardiff C), 1927 v S, E, W; 1928 v S, E, W; (with Chelsea), 1929 v E; 1931 v W (18)

Jackson, T. (Everton), 1969 v Is, E, S, W; 1970 v USSR (1+1 sub); (with Nottingham F), 1971 v Sp; 1972 v E, S, W; 1973 v Cy, E, S, W; 1974 v Bul, P, S (sub), E (sub), W (sub); 1975 v N (sub), Se, Y, E, S, W; (with Manchester U); 1976 v Se, N, Y; 1977 v Ho, Bel, WG, E, S, W, Ic (35)
Jamison, J. (Glentoran), 1976 v N (1)
Jennings, P. A. (Watford), 1964 v W, U; (with Tottenham H), 1965 v E, S, Sw (2), Ho, Alb; 1966 v S, E, W, Alb, WG; 1967 v E, S; 1968 v S, E, W; 1969 v Is, T (2), E, S, W; 1970 v S, E, USSR (2); 1971 v Cy (2), E, S, W; 1972 v USSR, Sp, S, E, W; 1973 v Bul, Cy, P, E, S, W; 1974 v P, S, E, W; 1975 v N, Se, Y, E, S, W; 1976 v Se, N, Y, Is, S, E, W; 1977 v Ho, Bel, WG, E, S, W, Ic; (with Arsenal), 1978 v Ic, Ho, Bel; 1979 v Ei, D, Bul, E, Bul, E, S, W, D; 1980 v E, Ei, Is; 1981 v S, P, S, Se (87)
Johnston, H. (Portadown), 1927 v W (1)
Johnston, R. (Old Park), 1885 v S, W (2)
Johnston, S. (Distillery), 1882 v W; 1884 v E; 1886 v E, S (4)
Johnston, S. (Linfield), 1890 v W; 1893 v S, W; 1894 v E (4)
Johnston, S. (Distillery), 1905 v W (1)
Johnston, W. C. (Glenavon), 1962 v W; (with Oldham Ath), 1966 v M (sub) (2)
Jones, J. (Linfield), 1930 v S, W; 1931 v S, W, E; 1932 v S, E; 1933 v S, E, W; 1934 v S, E, W; 1935 v S, E, W; 1936 v E, S; (with Hibernian), 1936 v W; 1937 v E, W, S; (with Glenavon), 1938 v E (23)
Jones, J. (Glenavon), 1956 v W; 1957 v E, W (3)
Jones, S. (Distillery), 1934 v E; (with Blackpool), 1934 v W (2)
Jordan, T. (Linfield), 1895 v E, W (2)

Kavanagh, P. J. (Glasgow C), 1930 v E (1)

Keane, T. R. (Swansea T), 1949 v S (1)
Kearns, A. (Distillery), 1900 v E, S, W; 1902 v E, S, W (6)
Keith, R. M. (Newcastle U), 1958 v E, W, Cz (2), Arg, I, WG, F; 1959 v E, S, W, Sp; 1960 v S, E; 1961 v S, E, W, I, WG (2), Gr; 1962 v W, Ho (23)
Kelly, H. R. (Fulham), 1950 v E, W; (with Southampton), 1951 v E, S (4)
Kelly, J. (Glentoran), 1896 v E (1)
Kelly, J. (Derry C), 1932 v E, W; 1933 v E, W, S; 1934 v W; 1936 v E, S, W; 1937 v S, E (11)
Kelly, P. (Manchester C), 1921 v E (1)
Kelly, P. M. (Barnsley), 1950 v S (1)
Kennedy, A. L. (Arsenal), 1923 v W; 1925 v E (2)
Kernaghan, N. (Belfast C), 1936 v W; 1937 v S; 1938 v E (3)
Kirkwood, H. (Cliftonville), 1904 v W (1)
Kirwan, J. (Tottenham H), 1900 v W; 1902 v E, W; 1903 v E, S, W; 1904 v E, S, W; 1905 v E, S, W; (with Chelsea), 1906 v E, S, W; 1907 v W; (with Clyde), 1909 v S (17)

Lacey, W. (Everton), 1909 v E, S, W; 1910 v E, S, W; 1911 v E, S, W; 1912 v E; (with Liverpool), 1913 v W; 1914 v E, S, W; 1920 v E, S, W; 1921 v E, S, W; 1922 v E, S; (with New Brighton), 1925 v E (23)
Lawther, W. I. (Sunderland), 1960 v W; 1961 v I; (with Blackburn R), 1962 v S, Ho (4)
Leatham, J. (Belfast C), 1939 v W (1)
Ledwidge, J. J. (Shelbourne), 1906 v S, W (2)
Lemon, J. (Glentoran), 1886 v W; 1888 v S; (with Belfast YMCA), 1889 v W (3)
Leslie, W. (YMCA), 1887 v E (1)
Lewis, J. (Glentoran), 1899 v S, E, W; (with Distillery), 1900 v S (4)
Little, J. (Glentoran), 1898 v W (1)
Lockhart, H. (Rossall School), 1884 v W (1)
Lockhart, N. (Linfield), 1947 v E; (with Coventry C), 1950 v W; 1951 v W; 1952 v W; (with Aston Villa), 1954 v S, E; 1955 v W; 1956 v W (8)
Lowther, R. (Glentoran), 1888 v E, S (2)
Loyal, J. (Clarence), 1891 v S (1)
Lutton, R. J. (Wolverhampton W), 1970 v S, E; (with West Ham U), 1973 v Cy (sub), S (sub), W (sub); 1974 v P (6)
Lyner, D. (Glentoran), 1920 v E, W; 1922 v S, W; (with Manchester U), 1923 v E; (with Kilmarnock), 1923 v W (6)

McAdams, W. J. (Manchester C), 1954 v W; 1955 v S; 1957 v E; 1958 v S, I; (with Bolton W), 1961 v E, S, W, I, WG (2), Gr; 1962 v E, Gr; (with Leeds U), Ho (15)
McAlery, J. M. (Cliftonville), 1882 v E, W (2)
McAlinden, J. (Belfast C), 1938 v S; 1939 v S; (with Portsmouth), 1947 v E; (with Southend U), 1949 v E (4)
McAllen, J. (Linfield), 1898 v E; 1899 v E, S, W; 1900 v E, S, W; 1901 v W; 1902 v S (9)
McAlpine, W. J. (Cliftonville), 1901 v S (1)
McArthur, A. (Distillery), 1886 v W (1)
McAuley, J. L. (Huddersfield T), 1911 v E, W; 1912 v E, S; 1913 v E, S (6)
McAuley, P. (Belfast C), 1900 v S (1)
McCabe, J. J. (Leeds U), 1949 v S, W; 1950 v E; 1951 v W; 1953 v W; 1954 v S (6)
McCabe, W. (Ulster), 1891 v E (1)
McCambridge, J. (Ballymena), 1930 v S, W; (with Cardiff C), 1931 v W; 1932 v E (4)
McCandless, J. (Bradford), 1912 v W; 1913 v W; 1920 v W, S; 1921 v E (5)
McCandless, W. (Linfield), 1920 v E, W; 1921 v E; (with Rangers), 1921 v W; 1922 v S; 1924 v W, S; 1925 v S; 1929 v W (9)
McCann, P. (Belfast C), 1910 v E, S, W; 1911 v E; (with Glentoran), 1911 v S; 1912 v E; 1913 v W (7)
McCashin, J. (Cliftonville), 1896 v W; 1898 v S, W; 1899 v S (4)
McCavana, W. T. (Coleraine), 1955 v S; 1956 v E, S (3)
McCaw, D. (Distillery), 1882 v E (1)
McCaw, J. H. (Linfield), 1927 v W; 1930 v S; 1931 v E, S, W (5)
McClatchey, J. (Distillery), 1886 v E, S, W (3)
McClatchey, R. (Distillery), 1895 v S (1)
McCleary, J. W. (Cliftonville), 1955 v W (1)
McCleery, W. (Cliftonville), 1922 v N; 1930 v E, W; 1931 v E, S, W; 1932 v S, W; 1933 v E, W (10)
McClelland, J. (Arsenal), 1961 v W, I, WG (2), Gr; (with Fulham), 1967 v M (6)
McClelland, J. (Mansfield T), 1980 v S (sub), Aus (3); 1981 v Se, S (with Rangers), S, Se (8)
McCluggage, A. (Bradford), 1924 v E; (with Burnley), 1927 v S, W; 1928 v S, E, W; 1929 v S, E, W; 1930 v W; 1931 v E, W (14)
McClure, G. (Cliftonville), 1907 v S, W; 1908 v E; (with Distillery), 1909 v E (4)
McConnell, E. (Cliftonville), 1904 v S, W; (with Glentoran), 1905 v S; (with Sunderland), 1906 v E; 1907 v E; 1908 v S, W; (with Sheffield W), 1909 v S, W; 1910 v S, W, E (12)
McConnell, P. (Doncaster R), 1928 v W; (with Southport), 1932 v E (2)
McConnell, W. G. (Bohemians), 1912 v W; 1913 v E, S; 1914 v E, S, W (6)
McConnell, W. H. (Reading), 1925 v W; 1926 v E, W; 1927 v E, S, W; 1928 v E, W (8)
McCourt, F. J. (Manchester C), 1952 v E, W; 1953 v E, S, W, F (6)
McCoy, J. (Distillery), 1896 v W (1)
McCracken, R. (C Palace), 1921 v E; 1922 v E, S, W (4)
McCracken, W. (Distillery), 1902 v E, W; 1903 v E; 1904 v E, S, W; (with Newcastle U), 1905 v E, S, W; 1907 v E; 1920 v E; 1922 v E, S, W; (with Hull C), 1923 v S (15)
McCreery, D. (Manchester U), 1976 v S (sub), E, W; 1977 v Ho, Bel, WG, E, S, W, Ic; 1978 v Ic, Ho, Bel, S, E, W; 1979 v Ei, D, Bul, E, Bul, W, D; (with QPR), 1980 v E, Ei, S (sub), E (sub), W (sub), Aus (1+ sub); 1981 v Se (sub), P (sub); (with Tulsa R), S, P, Se (35)
McCrory, S. (Southend U), 1958 v E (1)
McCullough, K. (Belfast C), 1935 v W; 1936 v E; (with Manchester C), 1936 v S; 1937 v E, S (5)
McCullough, W. J. (Arsenal), 1961 v I; 1963 v Sp; 1964 v S, E, W, U, Sp; 1965 v E, Sw; (with Millwall), 1967 v E (10)
McCurdy, C. (Linfield), 1980 v Aus (sub) (1)
McDonald, R. (Glasgow R), 1930 v S; 1932 v E (2)
McDonnell, J. (Bohemians), 1911 v E, S; 1912 v W; 1913 v W (4)
McFaul, W. S. (Linfield), 1967 v E (sub); (with Newcastle U), 1970 v W; 1971 v Sp; 1972 v USSR; 1973 v Cy; 1974 v Bul (6)
McGarry, J. K. (Cliftonville), 1951 v W, F, S (3)
McGee, G. (Wellington Park), 1885 v E, S, W (3)
McGrath, R. C. (Tottenham H), 1974 v S, E, W; 1975 v N; 1976 v Is (sub); (with Manchester U), 1977 v Ho, Bel, WG, E, S, W, Ic; 1978 v Ic, Ho, Bel, S, E, W; 1979 v Bul (sub), E (sub), E (sub) (21)
McGregor, S. (Glentoran), 1921 v S (1)
McGrillen, J. (Clyde), 1924 v S; (with Belfast C), 1927 v S (2)
McGuire, E. (Distillery), 1907 v S (1)
McIlroy, H. (Cliftonville), 1906 v E (1)
McIlroy, J. (Burnley), 1952 v E, S, W; 1953 v E, S, W; 1954 v E, S, W; 1955 v E, S, W; 1956 v E, S, W; 1957 v E, S, W, I, P (2); 1958 v E, S, W, I (2), Cz (2), Arg,

WG, F; 1959 v E, S, W, Sp; 1960 v E, S, W; 1961 v E, W, WG (2), Gr; 1962 v E, S, Gr, Ho; 1963 v E, S, Pol (2); (with Stoke C), 1963 v W; 1966 v S, E, Alb (55)
McIlroy, S. B. (Manchester U), 1972 v Sp, S (sub); 1974 v S, E, W; 1975 v N, Se, Y, E, S, W; 1976 v Se, N, Y, S, E, W; 1977 v Ho, Bel, E, S, W, Ic; 1978 v Ic, Ho, Bel, S, E, W; 1979 v Ei, D, Bul, E, Bul, E, S, W, D; 1980 v E, Ei, Is, S, E, W; 1981 v Se, P, S, P, S, Se (50)
McIlvenny, J. (Distillery), 1890 v E; 1891 v E (2)
McIlvenny, P. (Distillery), 1924 v W (1)
McKeag, W. (Glentoran), 1968 v S, W (2)
McKee, F. W. (Cliftonville), 1906 v S, W; (with Belfast C), 1914 v E, S, W (5)
McKelvie, H. (Glentoran), 1901 v W (1)
McKenna, J. (Huddersfield), 1950 v E, S, W; 1951 v E, S, F; 1952 v E (7)
McKenzie, H. (Distillery), 1923 v S (1)
McKenzie, R. (Airdrie), 1967 v W (1)
McKeown, H. (Linfield), 1892 v E, S, W; 1893 v S, W; 1894 v S, W (7)
McKie, H. (Cliftonville), 1895 v E, S, W (3)
McKinney, D. (Hull C), 1921 v S; (with Bradford C), 1924 v S (2)
McKinney, V. J. (Falkirk), 1966 v WG (1)
McKnight, J. (Preston NE), 1912 v S; (with Glentoran), 1913 v S (2)
McLaughlin, J. C. (Shrewsbury T), 1962 v E, S, W, Gr; 1963 v W; (with Swansea T), 1964 v W, U; 1965 v E, W, Sw (2); 1966 v W (12)
McLean, T. (Limavady), 1885 v S (1)
McMahon, J. (Bohemians), 1934 v S (1)
McMaster, G. (Glentoran), 1897 v E, S, W (3)
McMichael, A. (Newcastle U), 1950 v E, S; 1951 v E, S, F; 1952 v E, S, W; 1953 v E, S, W, F; 1954 v E, S, W; 1955 v E, W; 1956 v W; 1957 v E, S, W, I, P (2); 1958 v E, S, W, I (2), Cz (2), Arg, WG, F; 1959 v S, W, Sp; 1960 v E, S, W (40)
McMillan, G. (Distillery), 1903 v E; 1905 v W (2)
McMillan, S. (Manchester U), 1963 v E, S (2)
McMillen, W. S. (Manchester U), 1934 v E; 1935 v S; 1937 v S; (with Chesterfield), 1938 v S, W; 1939 v E, S (7)
McMordie, A. S. (Middlesbrough), 1969 v Is, T (2), E, S, W; 1970 v E, S, W, USSR; 1971 v Cy (2), E, S, W; 1972 v USSR, Sp, E, S, W; 1973 v Bul (21)
McMorran, E. J. (Belfast C), 1947 v E; (with Barnsley), 1951 v E, S, W; 1952 v E, S, W; 1953 v E, S, F; (with Doncaster R), 1953 v W; 1954 v E; 1956 v W; 1957 v I, P (15)
McMullan, D. (Liverpool), 1926 v E, W; 1927 v S (3)
McNinch, J. (Ballymena), 1931 v S; 1932 v S, W (3)
McParland, P. J. (Aston Villa), 1954 v W; 1955 v E, S; 1956 v E, S; 1957 v E, S, W, P; 1958 v E, S, W, I (2), Cz (2), Arg, WG, F; 1959 v E, S, W, Sp; 1960 v E, S, W; 1961 v E, S, W, I, WG (2), Gr; (with Wolverhampton W), 1962 v Ho (34)
McShane, J. (Cliftonville), 1899 v S; 1900 v E, S, W (4)
McVickers, J. (Glentoran), 1888 v E; 1889 v S (2)
McWha, W. B. R. (Knock), 1882 v E, W; (with Cliftonville), 1883 v E, W; 1884 v E; 1885 v E, W (7)
Macartney, A. (Ulster), 1903 v S, W; (with Linfield), 1904 v S, W; (with Everton), 1905 v E, S; (with Belfast C), 1907 v E, S, W; 1908 v E, S, W; (with Glentoran), 1909 v E, S, W (15)
Mackie, J. (Arsenal), 1923 v W; (with Portsmouth), 1935 v S, W (3)
Madden, O. (Norwich C), 1938 v E (1)
Magill, E. J. (Arsenal), 1962 v E, S, Gr; 1963 v E, S, W, Pol (2), Sp; 1964 v E, S, W, U, Sp; 1965 v E, S, Sw (2), Ho, Alb; 1966 v S, Alb; (with Brighton), 1966 v E, W, WG, M (26)
Maginnis, H. (Linfield), 1900 v E, S, W; 1903 v S, W; 1904 v E, S, W (8)
Maguire, E. (Distillery), 1907 v S (1)
Mahood, J. (Belfast C), 1926 v S; 1928 v E, S, W; 1929 v E, S, W; 1930 v W; (with Ballymena), 1934 v S (9)
Manderson, R. (Glasgow R), 1920 v W, S; 1925 v S, E; 1926 v S (5)
Mansfield, J. (Dublin Freebooters), 1901 v E (1)
Martin, C. J. (Glentoran), 1947 v S; (with Leeds U), 1948 v E, S, W; (with Aston Villa), 1949 v E; 1950 v W (6)
Martin, D. (Bo'ness), 1925 v S (1)
Martin, D. C. (Cliftonville), 1882 v E, W; 1883 v E (3)
Martin, D. K. (Belfast C), 1934 v E, S, W; 1935 v S; (with Wolverhampton W), 1935 v E; 1936 v W; (with Nottingham F), 1937 v S; 1938 v E, S; 1939 v S (10)
Mathieson, A. (Luton T), 1921 v W; 1922 v E (2)
Maxwell, J. (Linfield), 1902 v W; 1903 v W, E; (with Glentoran), 1905 v W, S; (with Belfast C), 1906 v W; 1907 v S (7)
Meek, H. L. (Glentoran), 1925 v W (1)
Mehaffy, J. A. C. (Queen's Island), 1922 v W (1)
Meldon, J. (Dublin Freebooters), 1899 v S, W (2)
Mercer, H. V. A. (Linfield), 1908 v E (1)
Mercer, J. T. (Distillery), 1898 v E, S, W; 1899 v E; (with Linfield), 1902 v E, W; (with Distillery), 1903 v S, W; (with Derby Co), 1904 v E, W; 1905 v S (11)
Millar, W. (Barrow), 1932 v W; 1933 v S (2)
Miller, J. (Middlesbrough), 1929 v W, S; 1930 v E (3)
Milligan, D. (Chesterfield), 1939 v W (1)
Milne, R. G. (Linfield), 1894 v E, S, W; 1895 v E, W; 1896 v E, S, W; 1897 v E, S; 1898 v E, S, W; 1899 v E, W; 1901 v W; 1902 v E, S, W; 1903 v E, S; 1904 v E, S, W; 1906 v E, S, W (27)
Mitchell, C. (Glentoran), 1934 v W (1)
Mitchell, E. J. (Cliftonville), 1933 v S (1)
Mitchell, W. (Distillery), 1932 v E, W; 1933 v E, W; (with Chelsea), 1934 v W, S; 1935 v S, E; 1936 v S, E; 1937 v E, S, W; 1938 v E, S (15)
Molyneux, T. B. (Ligoniel), 1883 v E, W; (with Cliftonville), 1884 v E, W, S; 1885 v E, W; 1886 v E, W, S; 1888 v S (11)
Montgomery, F. J. (Coleraine), 1955 v E (1)
Moore, C. (Glentoran), 1949 v W (1)
Moore, J. (Linfield Ath), 1891 v E, S, W (3)
Moore, P. (Aberdeen), 1933 v E (1)
Moore, T. (Ulster), 1887 v S, W (2)
Moore, W. (Falkirk), 1923 v S (1)
Moorhead, F. W. (Dublin University), 1885 v E (1)
Moorhead, G. (Linfield), 1923 v S; 1928 v S; 1929 v S (3)
Moran, J. (Leeds C), 1912 v S (1)
Moreland, V. (Derby Co), 1979 v Bul (sub), Bul (sub), E, S; 1980 v E, Ei (6)
Morgan, F. G. (Linfield), 1923 v E; (with Nottingham F), 1924 v S; 1927 v E; 1928 v E, S, W; 1929 v E (7)
Morgan, S. (Port Vale), 1972 v Sp; 1973 v Bul (sub), P, Cy, E, S, W; (with Aston Villa), 1974 v Bul, P, S, E; 1975 v Se; 1976 v Se (sub), N, Y; (with Brighton & HA), S, W (sub); (with Sparta Rotterdam), 1979 v D (18)
Morrison, J. (Linfield Ath), 1891 v E, W (2)
Morrison, T. (Glentoran), 1895 v E, S, W; (with Burnley), 1899 v W; 1900 v W; 1902 v E, S (7)
Morrogh, E. (Bohemians), 1896 v S (1)
Morrow, W. J. (Moyola Park), 1883 v E, W; 1884 v S (3)
Muir, R. (Oldpark), 1885 v S, W (2)
Mulholland, S. (Celtic), 1906 v S, E (2)
Mulligan, J. (Manchester C), 1921 v S (1)
Murphy, J. (Bradford C), 1910 v E, S, W (3)
Murphy, N. (QPR), 1905 v E, S, W (3)
Murray, J. M. (Motherwell), 1910 v E, S; (with Sheffield W), 1910 v W (3)

Napier, R. J. (Bolton W), 1966 v WG (1)
Neill, W. J. T. (Arsenal), 1961 v I, Gr, WG; 1962 v E, S, W, Gr; 1963 v E, W, Pol, Sp; 1964 v S, E, W, U, Sp; 1965 v E, S, W, Sw, Ho (2), Alb; 1966 v S, E, W, Alb, WG, M; 1967 v S, W; 1968 v S, E; 1969 v E, S, W, Is, T (2); 1970 v S, E, W, USSR (2); (with Hull C), 1971 v Cy, Sp; 1972 v USSR (2), Sp, S, E, W; 1973 v Bul, Cy (2), P, E, S, W (59)
Nelis, P. (Nottingham F), 1923 v E (1)
Nelson, S. (Arsenal), 1970 v W, E (sub); 1971 v Cy, Sp, E, S, W; 1972 v USSR (2), Sp, E, S, W; 1973 v Bul, Cy, P; 1974 v S, E; 1975 v Se, Y; 1976 v Se, N, Is, E; 1977 v Bel (sub), WG, W, Ic; 1978 v Ic, Ho, Bel; 1979 v Ei, D, Bul, E, Bul, E, S, W, D; 1980 v E, Ei, Is; 1981 v S, P, S, Se (47)
Nicholl, C. J. (Aston Villa), 1975 v Se, Y, E, S, W; 1976 v Se, N, Y, S, E, W; 1977 v W; (with Southampton), 1978 v Bel (sub), S, E, W; 1979 v Ei, Bul, E, Bul, E, W; 1980 v Ei, Is, S, E, W, Aus (3); 1981 v Se, P, S, P, S, Se (36)
Nicholl, J. M. (Manchester U), 1976 v Is, W (sub); 1977 v Ho, Bel, E, S, W, Ic; 1978 v Ic, Ho, Bel, S, E, W; 1979 v Ei, D, Bul, E, Bul, E, S, W, D; 1980 v E, Ei, Is, S, E, W, Aus (3); 1981 v Se, P, S, P, S, Se (38)
Nicholl, H. (Belfast C), 1902 v E, W; 1905 v E (3)
Nicholson, J. J. (Manchester U), 1961 v S, W; 1962 v E, W, Gr, Ho; 1963 v E, S, Pol (2); (with Huddersfield T), 1965 v W, Ho (2), Alb; 1966 v S, E, W, Alb, M; 1967 v S, W; 1968 v S, E, W; 1969 v S, E, W, T (2); 1970 v S, E, W, USSR (2); 1971 v Cy (2), E, S, W; 1972 v USSR (2) (41)
Nixon, R. (Linfield), 1914 v S (1)
Nolan-Whelan, J. V. (Dublin Freebooters), 1901 v E, W; 1902 v S, W (4)

O'Brien, M. T. (QPR), 1921 v S; (with Leicester C), 1922 v S, W; 1924 v S, W; (with Hull C), 1925 v S, E, W; 1926 v W; (with Derby Co), 1927 v W (10)
O'Connell, P. (Sheffield W), 1912 v E, S; (with Hull C), 1914 v E, S, W (5)
O'Doherty, A. (Coleraine), 1970 v E, W (sub) (2)
O'Driscoll, J. F. (Swansea T), 1949 v E, S, W (3)
O'Hagan, C. (Tottenham H), 1905 v S, W; 1906 v S, W, E; (with Aberdeen), 1907 v E, S, W; 1908 v S, W; 1909 v E (11)
O'Hagan, W. (St Mirren), 1920 v E, W (2)
O'Hehir, J. C. (Bohemians), 1910 v W (1)
O'Kane, W. J. (Nottingham F), 1970 v E, W, S (sub); 1971 v Sp, E, S, W; 1972 v USSR (2); 1973 v P, Cy; 1974 v Bul, P, S, E, W; 1975 v N, Se, E, S (20)
O'Mahoney, M. T. (Bristol R), 1939 v S (1)
O'Neill, J. (Leicester C), 1980 v Is, S, E, W, Aus (3); 1981 v P, S, P, S, Se (12)
O'Neill, J. (Sunderland), 1962 v W (1)
O'Neill, M. H. (Distillery), 1972 v USSR (sub), (with Nottingham F), Sp (sub), W (sub); 1973 v P, Cy, E, S, W; 1974 v Bul, P, E (sub), W; 1975 v Se, Y, E, S; 1976 v Y; 1977 v E (sub), S; 1978 v Ic, Ho, S, E, W; 1979 v Ei, D, Bul, E, Bul, D; 1980 v Ei, Is, Aus (3); 1981 v Se, P (with Norwich C), P, S, Se (40)
O'Reilly, H. (Dublin Freebooters), 1901 v S, W; 1904 v S (3)

Parke, J. (Linfield), 1964 v S; (with Hibernian), 1964 v E, Sp; (with Sunderland), 1965 v Sw, S, W, Ho (2), Alb; 1966 v WG; 1967 v E, S; 1968 v S, E (14)
Peacock, R. (Celtic), 1952 v S; 1953 v F; 1954 v W; 1955 v E, S; 1956 v E, S; 1957 v W, I, P; 1958 v S, E, W, I (2), Arg, Cz (2), WG; 1959 v E, S, W; 1960 v S, E; 1961 v E, S, I, WG (2), Gr; (with Coleraine), 1962 v S (31)
Peden, J. (Linfield), 1887 v S, W; 1888 v W, E; 1889 v S, E; 1890 v W, S; 1891 v W, E; 1892 v W, E; 1893 v E, S, W; (with Distillery), 1896 v W, E, S; 1897 v W, S; 1898 v W, E, S; (with Linfield), 1899 v W (24)
Percy, J. C. (Belfast YMCA), 1889 v W (1)
Platt, J. A. (Middlesbrough), 1976 v Is (sub); 1978 v S, E, W; 1980 v S, E, W, Aus (3); 1981 v Se, P (12)
Ponsonby, J. (Distillery), 1895 v S; 1896 v E, S, W; 1897 v E, S, W; 1899 v E (8)
Potts, R. M. C. (Cliftonville), 1883 v E, W (2)
Priestley, T. J. (Coleraine), 1933 v S; (with Chelsea), 1934 v E (2)
Pyper, Jas. (Cliftonville), 1897 v S, W; 1898 v S, E, W; 1899 v S; 1900 v E (7)
Pyper, John (Cliftonville), 1897 v E, S, W; 1899 v E, W; 1900 v E, W, S; 1902 v S (9)
Pyper, M. (Linfield), 1932 v W (1)

Rafferty, P. (Linfield), 1980 v E (sub) (1)
Rankine, J. (Alexander), 1883 v E, W (2)
Raper, E. O. (Dublin University), 1886 v W (1)
Rattray, D. (Avoniel), 1882 v E; 1883 v E, W (3)
Rea, B. (Glentoran), 1901 v E (1)
Redmond, J. (Cliftonville), 1884 v W (1)
Reid, G. H. (Cardiff C), 1923 v S (1)
Reid, J. (Ulster), 1883 v E; 1884 v W; 1887 v S; 1889 v W; 1890 v S, W (6)
Reid, S. E. (Derby Co), 1934 v E, W; 1936 v E (3)
Reid, W. (Hearts), 1931 v E (1)
Reilly, J. (Portsmouth), 1900 v E; 1902 v E (2)
Renneville, W. T. (Leyton), 1910 v S, E, W; (with Aston Villa), 1911 v W (4)
Reynolds, J. (Distillery), 1890 v E, W; (with Ulster), 1891 v E, S, W (5)
Reynolds, R. (Bohemians), 1905 v W (1)
Rice, P. J. (Arsenal), 1969 v Is; 1970 v USSR; 1971 v E, S, W; 1972 v USSR, Sp, E, S, W; 1973 v Bul, Cy, E, S, W; 1974 v Bul, P, S, E, W; 1975 v N, Y, E, S, W; 1976 v Se, N, Y, Is, S, E, W; 1977 v Ho, Bel, WG, E, S, Ic; 1978 v Ic, Ho, Bel; 1979 v Ei, D, E (2), S, W, D; 1980 v E (49)
Roberts, F. C. (Glentoran), 1931 v S (1)
Robinson, P. (Distillery), 1920 v S; (with Blackburn R), 1921 v W (2)
Rollo, D. (Linfield), 1912 v W; 1913 v W; 1914 v W, E; (with Blackburn R), 1920 v S, W; 1921 v E, S, W; 1922 v E; 1923 v E; 1924 v S, W; 1925 v W; 1926 v E; 1927 v E (16)
Rosbotham, A. (Cliftonville), 1887 v E, S, W; 1888 v E, S, W; 1889 v E (7)
Ross, W. E. (Newcastle U), 1969 v Is (1)
Rowley, R. W. M. (Southampton), 1929 v S, W; 1930 v W, E; (with Tottenham H), 1931 v W; 1932 v S (6)
Russell, A. (Linfield), 1947 v E (1)
Russell, S. R. (Bradford C), 1930 v E, S; (with Derry C), 1932 v E (3)
Ryan, R. A. (WBA), 1950 v W (1)

Scott, E. (Liverpool), 1920 v S; 1921 v E, S, W; 1922 v E; 1925 v W; 1926 v E, S, W; 1927 v E, S, W; 1928 v E, S, W; 1929 v E, S, W; 1930 v E; 1931 v E; 1932 v W; 1933 v E, S, W; 1934 v E, S, W; (with Belfast C), 1935 v S; 1936 v E, S, W (30)
Scott, J. (Grimsby), 1958 v Cz, F (2)
Scott, J. E. (Cliftonville), 1901 v S (1)
Scott, L. J. (Dublin University), 1895 v S, W (2)
Scott, P. W. (Everton), 1975 v W; 1976 v Y; (with York C), Is, S, E (sub), W; 1978 v S, E, W; (with Aldershot), 1979 v S (sub) (10)
Scott, T. (Cliftonville), 1894 v E, S; 1895 v S, W; 1896 v S, E, W; 1897 v E, W; 1898 v E, S, W; 1900 v W (13)
Scott, W. (Linfield), 1903 v E, S, W; 1904 v E, S, W; (with Everton), 1905 v E, S; 1907 v E, S; 1908 v E, S, W; 1909

v E, S, W; 1910 v E, S; 1911 v E, S, W; 1912 v E; (with Leeds City), 1913 v E, S, W (25)
Scraggs, M. J. (Glentoran), 1921 v W; 1922 v E (2)
Seymour, H. C. (Bohemians), 1914 v W (1)
Seymour, J. (Cliftonville), 1907 v W; 1909 v W (2)
Shanks, T. (Woolwich Arsenal), 1903 v S; 1904 v W; (with Brentford), 1905 v E (3)
Sharkey, P. (Ipswich T), 1976 v S (1)
Sheehan, Dr G. (Bohemians), 1899 v S; 1900 v E, W (3)
Sheridan, J. (Everton), 1903 v W, E, S; 1904 v E, S; (with Stoke C), 1905 v E (6)
Sherrard, J. (Limavady), 1885 v S; 1887 v W; 1888 v W (3)
Sherrard, W. (Cliftonville), 1895 v E, W, S (3)
Sherry, J. J. (Bohemians), 1906 v E; 1907 v W (2)
Shields, J. (Southampton), 1957 v S (1)
Silo, M. (Belfast YMCA), 1888 v E (1)
Simpson, W. J. (Glasgow R), 1951 v W, F; 1954 v E, S; 1955 v E; 1957 v I, P; 1958 v S, E, W, I; 1959 v S (12)
Sinclair, J. (Knock), 1882 v E, W (2)
Slemin, J. C. (Bohemians), 1909 v W (1)
Sloan, A. S. (London Caledonians), 1925 v W (1)
Sloan, D. (Oxford U), 1969 v Is; 1971 v Sp (2)
Sloan, H. A. de B. (Bohemians), 1903 v E; 1904 v S; 1905 v E; 1906 v W; 1907 v E, W; 1908 v W; 1909 v S (8)
Sloan, J. W. (Arsenal), 1947 v W (1)
Sloan, T. (Cardiff C), 1926 v S, W, E; 1927 v W, S; 1928 v E, W; 1929 v E; (with Linfield), 1930 v W, S; 1931 v S (11)
Sloan, T. (Manchester U), 1979 v S, W (sub), D (sub) (3)
Small, J. (Clarence), 1887 v E (1)
Small, J. M. (Cliftonville), 1893 v E, S, W (3)
Smith, E. E. (Cardiff C), 1921 v S; 1923 v W, E; 1924 v E (4)
Smith, J. (Distillery), 1901 v S, W (2)
Smyth, R. H. (Dublin University), 1886 v W (1)
Smyth, S. (Wolverhampton W), 1948 v E, S, W; 1949 v S, W; 1950 v E, S, W; (with Stoke C), 1952 v E (9)
Smyth, W. (Distillery), 1949 v E, S; 1954 v S, E (4)
Snape, A. (Airdrie), 1920 v E (1)
Spence, D. W. (Bury), 1975 v Y, E, S, W; 1976 v Se, Is, E, W, S (sub); (with Blackpool), 1977 v Ho (sub), WG (sub), E (sub), S (sub), W (sub), Ic (sub); 1979 v Ei, D (sub), E (sub), Bul (sub), E (sub), S, W, D; 1980 v Ei; (with Southend U), Is (sub), Aus (sub); 1981 v S (sub), Se (sub) (28)
Spencer, S. (Distillery), 1890 v E, S; 1892 v E, S, W; 1893 v E (6)
Spiller, E. A. (Cliftonville), 1883 v E, W; 1884 v E, W, S (5)
Stanfield, O. M. (Distillery), 1887 v E, S, W; 1888 v E, S, W; 1889 v E, S, W; 1890 v E, S; 1891 v E, S, W; 1892 v E, S, W; 1893 v E, W; 1894 v E, S, W; 1895 v E, S; 1896 v E, S, W; 1897 v E, S, W (30)
Steele, A. (Charlton Ath), 1926 v W, S; (with Fulham), 1929 v W, S (4)
Stevenson, A. E. (Rangers), 1934 v E, S, W; (with Everton), 1935 v E, S; 1936 v S, W; 1937 v E, W; 1938 v E, W; 1939 v E, S, W; 1947 v S, W; 1948 v S (17)
Stewart, A. (Glentoran), 1967 v W; 1968 v S, E; (with Derby Co), 1968 v W; 1969 v Is, T (1+1 sub) (7)
Stewart, D. C. (Hull C), 1978 v Bel (1)
Stewart, R. H. (St Columb's Court), 1890 v E, S, W; (with Cliftonville), 1892 v E, S, W; 1893 v E, W; 1894 v E, S, W (11)
Stewart, T. C. (Linfield), 1961 v W (1)
Swan, S. (Linfield), 1899 v S (1)

Taggart, J. (Walsall), 1899 v W (1)
Thompson, F. W. (Cliftonville), 1910 v E, S, W; (with Bradford C), 1911 v E; (with Linfield), v W; 1912 v E, W; 1913 v E, S, W; (with Clyde), 1914 v E, S (12)
Thompson, J. (Distillery), 1897 v S (1)
Thompson, J. (Belfast Ath), 1889 v S (1)
Thunder, P. J. (Bohemians), 1911 v W (1)
Todd, S. J. (Burnley), 1966 v M (sub); 1967 v E; 1968 v W; 1969 v E, S, W; 1970 v S, USSR; (with Sheffield W), 1971 v Cy (2), Sp (sub) (11)
Toner, J. (Arsenal), 1922 v W; 1923 v W; 1924 v W, E; 1925 v E, S; (with St Johnstone), 1927 v E, S (8)
Torrans, R. (Linfield), 1893 v S (1)
Torrans, S. (Linfield), 1889 v S; 1890 v S, W; 1891 v S, W; 1892 v E, S, W; 1893 v E, S; 1894 v E, S, W; 1895 v E; 1896 v E, S, W; 1897 v E, S, W; 1898 v E, S; 1899 v E, W; 1901 v S, W (26)
Trainor, D. (Crusaders), 1967 v W (1)
Tully, C. P. (Glasgow C), 1949 v E; 1950 v E; 1952 v S; 1953 v E, S, W, F; 1954 v S; 1956 v E; 1959 v Sp (10)
Turner, E. (Cliftonville), 1896 v E, W (2)
Turner, W. (Cliftonville), 1886 v E; 1886 v S; 1888 v S (3)
Twoomey, J. F. (Leeds U), 1938 v W; 1939 v E (2)

Uprichard, W. N. M. C. (Swindon T), 1952 v E, S, W; 1953 v E, S; (with Portsmouth), 1953 v W, F; 1955 v E, S, W; 1956 v E, S, W; 1958 v S, I, Cz; 1959 v S, Sp (18)

Vernon, J. (Belfast C), 1947 v E, S; (with WBA), 1947 v W; 1948 v E, S, W; 1949 v E, S, W; 1950 v E, S; 1951 v E, S, W, F; 1952 v S, E (17)

Waddell, T. M. R. (Cliftonville), 1906 v S (1)
Walker, J. (Doncaster R), 1955 v W (1)
Walker, T. (Bury), 1911 v S (1)
Walsh, D. J. (WBA), 1947 v S, W; 1948 v E, S, W; 1949 v E, S, W; 1950 v W (9)
Walsh, W. (Manchester C), 1948 v E, S, W; 1949 v E, S (5)
Waring, R. (Distillery), 1899 v E (1)
Warren, P. (Shelbourne), 1913 v E, S (2)
Watson, J. (Ulster), 1883 v E, W; 1886 v E, S, W; 1887 v S, W; 1889 v E, W (9)
Watson, P. (Distillery), 1971 v Cy (sub) (1)
Watson, T. (Cardiff C), 1926 v S (1)
Wattle, J. (Distillery), 1899 v E (1)
Webb, C. G. (Brighton), 1909 v S, W; 1911 v S (3)
Weir, E. (Clyde), 1939 v W (1)
Welsh, E. (Carlisle U), 1966 v W, WG, M; 1967 v W (4)
Whiteside, T. (Distillery), 1891 v E (1)
Whitfield, E. R. (Dublin University), 1886 v W (1)
Williams, J. R. (Ulster), 1886 v E, S (2)
Williamson, J. (Cliftonville), 1890 v E; 1892 v S; 1893 v S (3)
Willigham, T. (Burnley), 1933 v W; 1934 v S (2)
Willis, G. (Linfield), 1906 v S, W; 1907 v S; 1912 v S (4)
Wilson, H. (Linfield), 1925 v W (1)
Wilson, M. (Distillery), 1884 v E, S, W (3)
Wilson, R. (Cliftonville), 1888 v S (1)
Wilson, S. J. (Glenavon), 1962 v S; 1964 v S; (with Falkirk), 1964 v E, W, U, Sp; 1965 v E, Sw; (with Dundee), 1966 v W, WG; 1967 v S; 1968 v E (12)
Wilton, J. M. (St Columb's Court), 1888 v E, W; 1889 v S, E; (with Cliftonville), 1890 v E; (with St Columb's Court), 1892 v W; 1893 v S (7)
Wright, J. (Cliftonville), 1906 v E, S, W; 1907 v E, S, W (6)

Young, S. (Linfield), 1907 v E, S; 1908 v E, S; (with Airdrie), 1909 v E; 1912 v S; (with Linfield), 1914 v E, S, W (9)

SCOTLAND

Adams, J. (Hearts), 1889 v Ni; 1892 v W; 1893 v Ni (3)
Agnew, W. B. (Kilmarnock), 1907 v Ni; 1908 v W, Ni (3)

Aird, J. (Burnley), 1954 v N (2), A, U (4)
Aitken, A. (Newcastle U), 1901 v E; 1902 v E; 1903 v E, W; 1904 v E; 1905 v E, W; 1906 v E; (with Middlesbrough), 1907 v E, W; 1908 v E; (with Leicester Fosse), 1910 v E; 1911 v E, Ni (14)
Aitken, G. G. (East Fife), 1949 v E, F; 1950 v W, Ni, Sw; (with Sunderland), 1953 v W, Ni; 1954 v E (8)
Aitken, R. (Dumbarton), 1886 v E; 1888 v Ni (2)
Aitken, R. (Celtic), 1980 v Pe (sub), Bel, W (sub), E, Pol (5)
Aitkenhead, W. A. C. (Blackburn R), 1912 v Ni (1)
Alexander, D. (East Stirlingshire), 1894 v W, Ni (2)
Allan, D. S. (Queen's Park), 1885 v E, W; 1886 v W (3)
Allan, G. (Liverpool), 1897 v E (1)
Allan, H. (Hearts), 1902 v W (1)
Allan, J. (Queen's Park), 1887 v E, W (2)
Allan, T. (Dundee), 1974 v WG, N (2)
Ancell, R. F. D. (Newcastle U), 1937 v W, Ni (2)
Anderson, A. (Hearts), 1933 v E; 1934 v A, E, W, Ni; 1935 v E, W, Ni; 1936 v E, W, Ni; 1937 v G, E, W, Ni, A; 1938 v E, W, Ni, Cz, Ho; 1939 v W, H (23)
Anderson, F. (Clydesdale), 1874 v E (1)
Anderson, G. (Kilmarnock), 1901 v Ni (1)
Anderson, H. A. (Raith R), 1914 v W (1)
Anderson, J. (Leicester C), 1954 v Fi (1)
Anderson, K. (Queen's Park), 1896 v Ni; 1898 v E, Ni (3)

Anderson, W. (Queen's Park), 1882 v E; 1883 v E, W; 1884 v E; 1885 v E, W (6)
Andrews, P. (Eastern), 1875 v E (1)
Archibald, A. (Rangers), 1921 v W; 1922 v W, E; 1923 v Ni; 1924 v E, W; 1931 v E; 1932 v E (8)
Archibald, S. (Aberdeen), 1980 v P (sub); (with Tottenham H), Ni, Pol, H; 1981 v Se (sub), Is, Ni, Is, Ni, E (10)
Armstrong, M. W. (Aberdeen), 1936 v W, Ni; 1937 v G (3)
Arnott, W. (Queen's Park), 1883 v W; 1884 v E, Ni; 1885 v E, W; 1886 v E; 1887 v E, W; 1888 v E; 1889 v E; 1890 v E; 1891 v E; 1892 v E; 1893 v E (14)
Auld, J. R. (Third Lanark), 1887 v E, W; 1889 v W (3)
Auld, R. (Celtic), 1959 v H, P; 1960 v W (3)

Baird, A. (Queen's Park), 1892 v Ni; 1894 v W (2)
Baird, D. (Hearts), 1890 v Ni; 1891 v E; 1892 v W (3)
Baird, H. (Airdrie), 1956 v A (1)
Baird, J. C. (Vale of Leven), 1876 v E; 1878 v W; 1880 v E (3)
Baird, S. (Rangers), 1957 v Y, Sp (2), Sw, WG; 1958 v F, Ni (7)
Baird, W. U. (St Bernard), 1897 v Ni (1)
Bannon, E. (Dundee U), 1980 v Bel (1)
Barbour, A. (Renton), 1885 v Ni (1)
Barker, J. B. (Rangers), 1893 v W; 1894 v W (2)
Barrett, F. (Dundee), 1894 v Ni; 1895 v W (2)
Battles, B. (Celtic), 1901 v E, W, Ni (3)
Battles, B. jun. (Hearts), 1931 v W (1)
Bauld, W. (Hearts), 1950 v E, Sw, P (3)
Baxter, J. C. (Rangers), 1961 v Ni, Ei (2), Cz; 1962 v Ni, W, E, Cz (2), U; 1963 v W, Ni, E, A, N, Ei, Sp; 1964 v W, E, N, WG; 1965 v W, Ni, Fi; (with Sunderland), 1966 v P, Br, Ni, W, E, I; 1967 v W, E, USSR; 1968 v W (34)
Baxter, R. D. (Middlesbrough), 1939 v E, W, H (3)
Beattie, A. (Preston NE), 1937 v E, A, Cz; 1938 v E; 1939 v W, Ni, H (7)
Beattie, R. (Preston NE), 1939 v W (1)
Begbie, I. (Hearts), 1890 v Ni; 1891 v E; 1892 v W; 1894 v E (4)
Bell, A. (Manchester U), 1912 v Ni (1)
Bell, J. (Dumbarton), 1890 v Ni; 1892 v E; (with Everton), 1896 v E; 1897 v E; 1898 v E; (with Celtic), 1899 v E, W, Ni; 1900 v E, W (10)
Bell, M. (Hearts), 1901 v W (1)
Bell, W. J. (Leeds U), 1966 v P, Br (2)
Bennett, A. (Celtic), 1904 v W; 1907 v Ni; 1908 v W; (with Rangers), 1909 v W, Ni, E; 1910 v E, W; 1911 v E, W; 1913 v Ni (11)
Bennie, R. (Airdrieonians), 1925 v W, Ni; 1926 v Ni (3)
Berry, D. (Queen's Park), 1894 v W; 1899 v W, Ni (3)
Berry, W. H. (Queen's Park), 1888 v E; 1889 v E; 1890 v E; 1891 v E (4)
Beveridge, W. W. (Glasgow University), 1879 v E, W; 1880 v W (3)
Black, A. (Hearts), 1938 v Cz, Ho; 1939 v H (3)
Black, D. (Hurlford), 1889 v Ni (1)
Black, I. H. (Southampton), 1948 v E (1)
Blackburn, J. E. (Royal Engineers), 1873 v E (1)
Blacklaw, A. S. (Burnley), 1963 v N, Sp; 1966 v I (3)
Blackley, J. (Hibernian), 1974 v Cz, E, Bel, Z; 1976 v Sw; 1977 v W, Se (7)
Blair, D. (Clyde), 1929 v W, Ni; 1931 v E, A, I; 1932 v W, Ni; (with Aston Villa), 1933 v W (8)
Blair, J. (Sheffield W), 1920 v E, Ni; (with Cardiff C), 1921 v E; 1922 v E; 1923 v E, W, Ni; 1924 v W (8)
Blair, J. (Motherwell), 1934 v W (1)
Blair, J. A. (Blackpool), 1947 v W (1)
Blair, W. (Third Lanark), 1896 v W (1)
Blessington J. (Celtic), 1894 v E, Ni; 1896 v E, Ni (4)
Blyth, J. A. (Coventry C), 1978 v Bul, W (2)
Bone, J. (Norwich C), 1972 v Y (sub); 1973 v D (2)
Bowie, J. (Rangers), 1920 v E, Ni (2)
Bowie, W. (Linthouse), 1891 v Ni (1)
Bowman, G. A. (Montrose), 1892 v Ni (1)
Boyd, J. M. (Newcastle U), 1934 v Ni (1)
Boyd, R. (Mossend Swifts), 1889 v Ni; 1891 v W (2)
Boyd, W. G. (Clyde), 1931 v I, Sw (2)
Brackenbridge, T. (Hearts), 1888 v Ni (1)
Bradshaw, T. (Bury), 1928 v E (1)
Brand, R. (Rangers), 1961 v Ni, Cz, Ei (2); 1962 v Ni, W, Cz, U (8)
Branden, T. (Blackburn R), 1896 v E (1)
Brazil, A. (Ipswich T), 1980 v Pol (sub), H (2)
Bremner, D. (Hibernian), 1976 v Sw (sub) (1)
Bremner, W. J. (Leeds U), 1965 v Sp; 1966 v E, Pol, P, Br, I (2); 1967 v W, Ni, E; 1968 v W, E; 1969 v W, E, Ni, D, A, WG, Cy (2); 1970 v Ei, WG, A; 1971 v W, E; 1972 v P, Bel, Ho, Ni, W, E, Y, Cz, Br; 1973 v D (2), E (2), Ni (sub), Sw, Br; 1974 v Cz, WG, Ni, W, E, Bel, N, Z, Br, Y; 1975 v Sp (2); 1976 v D (54)
Brennan, F. (Newcastle U), 1947 v W, Ni; 1953 v W, Ni, E; 1954 v Ni, E (7)
Breslin, B. (Hibernian), 1897 v W (1)
Brewster, G. (Everton), 1921 v E (1)
Brogan, J. (Celtic), 1971 v W, Ni, P, E (4)
Brown, A. (Middlesbrough), 1904 v E (1)
Brown, A. (St Mirren), 1890 v W; 1891 v W (2)
Brown, A. D. (East Fife), 1950 v Sw, P, F; (with Blackpool), 1952 v USA, D, Se; 1953 v W; 1954 v W, E, N (2), Fi, A, U (14)
Brown, G. C. P. (Rangers), 1931 v W; 1932 v E, W, Ni; 1933 v E; 1935 v A, E, W; 1936 v E, W; 1937 v G, E, W, Ni, Cz; 1938 v E, W, Cz, Ho (19)
Brown, H. (Partick T), 1947 v W, Bel, L (3)
Brown, J. (Cambuslang), 1890 v W (1)
Brown, J. B. (Clyde), 1939 v W (1)
Brown, J. G. (Sheffield U), 1975 v R (1)
Brown, R. (Dumbarton), 1884 v W, Ni (2)
Brown, R. (Rangers), 1947 v Ni; 1949 v Ni; 1952 v E (3)
Brown, R. jun. (Dumbarton), 1885 v W (1)
Brown, W. D. F. (Dundee), 1958 v F; 1959 v E, W, Ni; (with Tottenham H), 1960 v W, Ni, Pol, A, H, T; 1962

v Ni, W, E, Cz; 1963 v W, Ni, E, A; 1964 v Ni, W, N; 1965 v E, Fi, Pol, Sp; 1966 v Ni, Pol, I (28)
Browning, J. (Celtic), 1914 v W (1)
Brownie, J. (Hibernian), 1971 v USSR; 1972 v Pe, Ni, E; 1973 v D (2); 1976 v R (7)
Brownlie, J. (Third Lanark), 1909 v E, Ni; 1910 v E, W, Ni; 1911 v W, Ni; 1912 v W, Ni, E; 1913 v W, Ni, E; 1914 v W, Ni, E (16)
Bruce, D. (Vale of Leven), 1890 v W (1)
Bruce, R. F. (Middlesbrough), 1934 v A (1)
Buchan, M. M. (Aberdeen), 1972 v P (sub), Bel; (with Manchester U), W, Y, Cz, Br; 1973 v D (2), E; 1974 v WG, Ni, W, N, Br, Y; 1975 v EG, Sp, P; 1976 v D, R; 1977 v Fi, Cz, Ch, Arg, Br; 1978 v EG, W (sub), Ni, Pe, Ir, Ho; 1979 v A, N, P (34)
Buchanan, J. (Cambuslang), 1889 v Ni (1)
Buchanan, J. (Rangers), 1929 v E; 1930 v E (2)
Buchanan, P. S. (Chelsea), 1938 v Cz (1)
Buchanan, R. (Abercorn), 1891 v W (1)
Buckley, P. (Aberdeen), 1954 v N; 1955 v W, Ni (3)
Buick, A. (Hearts), 1902 v W, Ni (2)
Burley, G. (Ipswich T), 1979 v W, Ni, E, Arg, N; 1980 v P, Ni, E (sub), Pol (9)
Burns, F. (Manchester U), 1970 v A (1)
Burns, K. (Birmingham C), 1974 v WG; 1975 v EG (sub), Sp (2); 1977 v Cz (sub), W, Se, W (sub); (with Nottingham F), 1978 v Ni (sub), W, E, Pe, Ir; 1979 v N; 1980 v Pe, A, Bel; 1981 v Is, Ni, W (20)
Burns, T. (Celtic), 1981 v Ni (1)
Busby, M. W. (Manchester C), 1934 v W (1)

Cairns, T. (Rangers), 1920 v W; 1922 v E; 1923 v E, W; 1924 v Ni; 1925 v W, E, Ni (8)
Calderhead, D. (Queen of the South), 1889 v Ni (1)
Calderwood, R. (Cartvale), 1885 v Ni, E, W (3)
Caldow, E. (Rangers), 1957 v Sp (2), Sw, WG, E; 1958 v Ni, W, Sw, Par, H, Pol, Y, F; 1959 v E, W, Ni, WG, Ho, P; 1960 v E, W, Ni, A, H, T; 1961 v E, W, Ni, Ei (2), Cz; 1962 v Ni, W, E, Cz (2), U; 1963 v W, Ni, E (40)
Callaghan, P. (Hibernian), 1900 v Ni (1)
Callaghan, W. (Dunfermline Ath), 1970 v Ei (sub), W (2)
Cameron, J. (St Mirren), 1904 v Ni; (with Chelsea), 1909 v E (2)
Cameron, J. (Queen's Park), 1896 v Ni (1)
Cameron, J. (Rangers), 1886 v Ni (1)
Campbell, C. (Queen's Park), 1874 v E; 1876 v W; 1877 v E, W; 1878 v E; 1879 v E; 1880 v E; 1881 v E; 1882 v E, W; 1884 v E; 1885 v E; 1886 v E (13)
Campbell, H. (Renton), 1889 v W (1)
Campbell, Jas. (Sheffield W), 1913 v W (1)
Campbell, J. (South Western), 1880 v W (1)
Campbell, J. (Kilmarnock), 1891 v Ni; 1892 v W (2)
Campbell, John (Celtic), 1893 v E, Ni; 1898 v E, Ni; 1900 v E, Ni; 1901 v E, W, Ni; 1902 v W, Ni; 1903 v W (12)
Campbell, John (Rangers), 1899 v E, W, Ni; 1901 v Ni (4)
Campbell, K. (Liverpool), 1920 v E, W, Ni; (with Partick T), 1921 v W, Ni; 1922 v W, Ni, E (8)
Campbell, P. (Rangers), 1878 v W; 1879 v W (2)
Campbell, P. (Morton), 1898 v W (1)
Campbell, R. (Chelsea), 1947 v Bel, L; 1950 v Sw, P, F (5)
Campbell, W. (Morton), 1947 v Ni; 1948 v E, Bel, Sw, F (5)
Carabine, J. (Third Lanark), 1938 v Ho; 1939 v E, Ni (3)
Carr, W. M. (Coventry C), 1970 v Ni, W, E; 1971 v D; 1972 v Pe; 1973 v D (sub) (6)
Cassidy, J. (Celtic), 1921 v W, Ni; 1923 v Ni; 1924 v W (4)
Chalmers, S. (Celtic), 1965 v W, Fi; 1966 v P (sub), Br; 1967 v Ni (5)
Chalmers, W. (Rangers), 1885 v Ni (1)
Chalmers, W. S. (Queen's Park), 1929 v Ni (1)
Chambers, T. (Hearts), 1894 v W (1)
Chaplin, G. D. (Dundee), 1908 v W (1)
Cheyne, A. G. (Aberdeen), 1929 v E, N, G, Ho; 1930 v F (5)
Christie, A. J. (Queen's Park), 1898 v W; 1899 v E, Ni (3)
Christie, R. M. (Queen's Park), 1884 v E (1)
Clark, J. (Celtic), 1966 v Br; 1967 v W, Ni, USSR (4)
Clark, R. B. (Aberdeen), 1968 v W, Ho; 1970 v Ni; 1971 v W, Ni, E, D, P, USSR; 1972 v Bel, Ni, W, E, Cz, Br; 1973 v D, E (17)
Cleland, J. (Royal Albert), 1891 v Ni (1)
Clements, R. (Leith Ath), 1891 v Ni (1)
Clunas, W. L. (Sunderland), 1924 v E; 1926 v W (2)
Collier, W. (Raith R), 1922 v W (1)
Collins, R. Y. (Celtic), 1951 v W, Ni, A; 1955 v Y, A, H; 1956 v Ni, W; 1957 v E, W, Sp (2), Sw, WG; 1958 v Ni, W, Sw, H, Pol, Y, F, Par; (with Everton), 1959 v E, W, Ni, WG, Ho, P; (with Leeds U), 1965 v E, Pol, Sp (31)
Collins, T. (Hearts), 1909 v W (1)
Colman, D. (Aberdeen), 1911 v E, W, Ni; 1913 v Ni (4)
Colquhoun, E. P. (Sheffield U), 1972 v P, Ho, Pe, Y, Cz, Br; 1973 v D (2), E (9)
Combe, J. R. (Hibernian), 1948 v E, Bel, Sw (3)
Conn, A. (Hearts), 1956 v A (1)
Conn, A. (Tottenham H), 1975 v Ni (sub), E (2)
Connachan, E. D. (Dunfermline Ath), 1962 v Cz, U (2)
Connelly, G. (Celtic), 1974 v Cz, WG (2)
Connolly, J. (Everton), 1973 v Sw (1)
Connor, J. (Airdrieonians), 1886 v Ni (1)
Connor, J. (Sunderland), 1930 v F; 1932 v Ni; 1934 v E; 1935 v Ni (4)
Cook, W. L. (Bolton W), 1934 v E; 1935 v W, Ni (3)
Cooke, C. (Dundee), 1966 v W, I; (with Chelsea), P, Br; 1968 v E, Ho; 1969 v W, Ni, A, WG (sub), Cy (2); 1970 v A; 1971 v Bel; 1975 v Sp, P (16)
Cooper, D. (Rangers), 1980 v Pe, A (sub) (2)
Cormack, P. B. (Hibernian), 1966 v Br; 1969 v D (sub); 1970 v Ei, WG; (with Nottingham F), 1971 v D (sub), W, P, E; 1972 v Ho (sub) (9)
Cowan, J. (Aston Villa), 1896 v E; 1897 v E; 1898 v E (3)
Cowan, J. (Morton), 1948 v Bel, Sw; F; 1949 v E, W, F; 1950 v E, W, Ni, Sw, P, F; 1951 v E, W, Ni, A (2), D, F, Bel; 1952 v Ni, W, USA, D, Se (25)
Cowan, W, D. (Newcastle U), 1924 v E (1)
Cowie, D. (Dundee), 1953 v E, Se; 1954 v Ni, W, Fi, N, A, U; 1955 v W, Ni, A, H; 1956 v W, A; 1957 v Ni, W; 1958 v H, Pol, Y, Par (20)
Cox, C. J. (Hearts), 1948 v F (1)
Cox, S. (Rangers), 1949 v E, F; 1950 v E, F, W, Ni, Sw, P; 1951 v E, D, F, Bel, A; 1952 v Ni, W, USA, D, Se; 1953 v W, Ni, E; 1954 v W, Ni, E (24)
Craig, A. (Motherwell), 1929 v N, Ho; 1932 v E (3)
Craig, J. (Celtic), 1977 v Se (sub) (1)
Craig, J. P. (Celtic), 1968 v W (1)
Craig, T. (Rangers), 1927 v Ni; 1928 v Ni; 1929 v N, G, Ho; 1930 v Ni, E, W (8)
Craig, T. B. (Newcastle U), 1976 v Sw (1)
Crapnell, J. (Airdrieonians), 1929 v E, N, G; 1930 v F; 1931 v Ni, Sw; 1932 v E, F; 1933 v Ni (9)
Crawford, D. (St Mirren), 1894 v W, Ni; 1900 v W (3)
Crawford, J. (Queen's Park), 1932 v F, Ni; 1933 v E, W, Ni (5)
Crerand, P. T. (Celtic), 1961 v Ei (2), Cz; 1962 v Ni, W, E, Cz (2), U; 1963 v W, Ni; (with Manchester U), 1964 v Ni; 1965 v E, Pol, Fi; 1966 v Pol (16)
Cringan, W. (Celtic), 1920 v W; 1922 v E, Ni; 1923 v W, E (5)
Crosbie, J. A. (Ayr U), 1920 v W; (with Birmingham), 1922 v E (2)
Croal, J. A. (Falkirk), 1913 v Ni; 1914 v E, W (3)
Cropley, A. J. (Hibernian), 1972 v P, Bel (2)
Cross, J. H. (Third Lanark), 1903 v Ni (1)

Cruickshank, J. (Hearts), 1964 v WG; 1970 v W, E; 1971 v D, Bel; 1976 v R (6)
Crum, J. (Celtic), 1936 v E; 1939 v Ni (2)
Cullen, M. J. (Luton T), 1956 v A (1)
Cumming, D. S. (Middlesbrough), 1938 v E (1)
Cumming, J. (Hearts), 1955 v E, H, P, Y; 1960 v E, Pol, A, H, T (9)
Cummings, G. (Partick T), 1935 v E; 1936 v W, Ni; (with Aston Villa), E; 1937 v G; 1938 v W, Ni, Cz; 1939 v E (9)
Cunningham, A. N. (Rangers), 1920 v Ni; 1921 v W, E; 1922 v Ni; 1923 v E, W; 1924 v E, Ni; 1926 v E, Ni; 1927 v E, W (12)
Cunningham, W. C. (Preston NE), 1954 v N (2), U, Fi, A; 1955 v W, E, H (8)
Curran, H. P. (Wolverhampton W), 1970 v A; 1971 v Ni, E, D, USSR (sub) (5)

Dalglish, K. (Celtic), 1972 v Bel (sub), Ho; 1973 v D (1+1 sub), E (2), W, Ni, Sw, Br; 1974 v Cz (2), WG (2), Ni, W, E, Bel, N (sub), Z, Br, Y; 1975 v EG, Sp (sub+1), Se, P, W, Ni, E, R; 1976 v D (2), R, Sw, Ni, E; 1977 v Fi, Cz, W (2), Se, Ni, E, Ch, Arg, Br; (with Liverpool), 1978 v EG, Cz, W, Bul, Ni (sub), W, E, Pe, Ir, Ho; 1979 v A, N, P, W, Ni, E, Arg, N; 1980 v Pe, A, Bel (2), P, Ni, W, E, Pol, H; 1981 v Se, P, Is (78)
Davidson, D. (Queen's Park), 1878 v W; 1879 v W; 1880 v W; 1881 v E, W (5)
Davidson, J. A. (Partick T), 1954 v N (2), A, U; 1955 v W, Ni, E, H (8)
Davidson, S. (Middlesbrough), 1921 v E (1)
Dawson, A. (Rangers), 1980 v Pol (sub), H (2)
Dawson, J. (Rangers), 1935 v Ni; 1936 v E; 1937 v G, E, W, Ni, A, Cz; 1938 v W, Ho, Ni; 1939 v E, Ni, H (14)
Deans, J. (Celtic), 1975 v EG, Sp (2)
Delaney, J. (Celtic), 1936 v W, Ni; 1937 v G, E, A, Cz; 1938 v Ni; 1939 v W, Ni; (with Manchester U), 1947 v E; 1948 v E, W, Ni (13)
Devine, A. (Falkirk), 1910 v W (1)
Dewar, G. (Dumbarton), 1888 v Ni; 1889 v E (2)
Dewar, N. (Third Lanark), 1932 v E, F; 1933 v W (3)
Dick, J. (West Ham U), 1959 v E (1)
Dickie, M. (Rangers), 1897 v Ni; 1899 v Ni; 1900 v W (3)
Dickson, W. (Kilmarnock), 1970 v Ni, W, E; 1971 v D, USSR (5)
Dickson, W. (Dumbarton), 1888 v Ni (1)
Divers, J. (Celtic), 1895 v W (1)
Divers, J. (Celtic), 1939 v Ni (1)
Docherty, T. H, (Preston NE), 1952 v W; 1953 v E, Se; 1954 v N (2), A, U; 1955 v W, E, H (2), A; 1957 v E, Y, Sp (2), Sw, WG; 1958 v Ni, W, E, Sw; (with Arsenal), 1959 v W, E, Ni (25)
Dodds, J. (Celtic), 1914 v E, W, Ni (3)
Doig, J. E. (Arbroath), 1887 v Ni; 1889 v Ni; (with Sunderland), 1896 v E; 1899 v E; 1903 v E (5)
Donachie, W. (Manchester C), 1972 v Pe, Ni, E, Y, Cz, Br; 1973 v D, E, W, Ni; 1974 v Ni; 1976 v R, Ni, W, E; 1977 v Fi, Cz, W (2), Se, Ni, E, Ch, Arg, Br; 1978 v EG, W, Bul, W, E, Ir, Ho; 1979 v A, N, P (sub) (35)
Donaldson, A. (Bolton W), 1914 v E, Ni, W; 1920 v E, Ni; 1922 v Ni (6)
Donnachie, J. (Oldham Ath), 1913 v E; 1914 v E, Ni (3)
Dougall, C. (Birmingham C), 1947 v W (1)
Dougall, J. (Preston NE), 1939 v E (1)
Dougan, R. (Hearts), 1950 v Sw (1)
Douglas, A. (Chelsea), 1911 v Ni (1)
Douglas, J. (Renfrew), 1880 v W (1)
Dowds, P. (Celtic), 1892 v Ni (1)
Downie, R. (Third Lanark), 1892 v W (1)
Doyle, D. (Celtic), 1892 v E; 1893 v W; 1894 v E; 1895 v E, Ni; 1897 v E; 1898 v E, Ni (8)
Doyle, J. (Ayr U), 1976 v R (1)
Drummond, J. (Falkirk), 1892 v Ni; (with Rangers), 1894 v Ni; 1895 v Ni, E; 1896 v E, Ni; 1897 v Ni; 1898 v E; 1900 v E; 1901 v E; 1902 v E, W, Ni; 1903 v Ni (14)
Dunbar, M. (Cartvale), 1886 v Ni (1)
Duncan, A. (Hibernian), 1975 v P (sub), W, Ni, E, R; 1976 v D (6)
Duncan, D. (Derby Co), 1933 v E, W; 1934 v A, W; 1935 v E, W; 1936 v E, W, Ni; 1937 v G, E, W, Ni; 1938 v W (14)
Duncan, D. M. (East Fife), 1948 v Bel, Sw, F (3)
Duncan, J. (Alexandra Ath), 1878 v W; 1882 v W (2)
Duncan, J. (Leicester C), 1926 v W (1)
Duncanson, J. (Rangers), 1947 v Ni (1)
Dunlop, J. (St Mirren), 1890 v W (1)
Dunlop, W. (Liverpool), 1906 v E (1)
Dunn, J. (Hibernian), 1925 v W, Ni; 1927 v Ni; 1928 v Ni, E; (with Everton), 1929 v W (6)
Dykes, J. (Hearts), 1938 v Ho; 1939 v Ni (2)

Easson, J. F. (Portsmouth), 1931 v A, Sw; 1934 v W (3)
Ellis, J. (Mossend Swifts), 1892 v Ni (1)
Evans, R. (Celtic), 1949 v E, W, Ni, F; 1950 v W, Ni, Sw, P; 1951 v E, A; 1952 v Ni; 1953 v Se; 1954 v Ni, W, E, N, Fi; 1955 v Ni, P, Y, A, H; 1956 v E, Ni, W, A; 1957 v WG, Sp; 1958 v Ni, W, E, Sw, H, Pol, Y, Par, F; 1959 v E, WG, Ho, P; 1960 v E, Ni, W, Pol; (with Chelsea), 1960 v A, H, T (48)
Ewart, J. (Bradford C), 1921 v E (1)
Ewing, T. (Partick T), 1958 v W, E (2)

Farm, G. N. (Blackpool), 1953 v W, Ni, E, Se; 1954 v Ni, W, E; 1959 v WG, Ho, P (10)
Ferguson, J. (Vale of Leven), 1874 v E; 1876 v E, W; 1877 v E, W; 1878 v W (6)
Ferguson, R. (Kilmarnock), 1966 v W, E, Ho, P, Br; 1967 v W, Ni (7)
Fernie, W. (Celtic), 1954 v Fi, A, U; 1955 v W, Ni; 1957 v E, Ni, W, Y; 1958 v W, Sw, Par (12)
Findlay, R. (Kilmarnock), 1898 v W (1)
Fitchie, T. T. (Woolwich Arsenal), 1905 v W; 1906 v W, Ni; (with Queen's Park), 1907 v W (4)
Flavell, R. (Airdrieonians), 1947 v Bel, L (2)
Fleming, C. (East Fife), 1954 v Ni (1)
Fleming, J. W. (Rangers), 1929 v G, Ho; 1930 v E (3)
Fleming, R. (Morton), 1886 v Ni (1)
Forbes, A. R. (Sheffield U), 1947 v Bel, L, E; 1948 v W, Ni; (with Arsenal), 1950 v E, P, F; 1951 v W, Ni, A; 1952 v W, D, Se (14)
Forbes, J. (Vale of Leven), 1884 v E, W, Ni; 1887 v W, E (5)
Ford, D. (Hearts), 1974 v Cz (sub), WG (sub), W (3)
Forrest, J. (Rangers), 1966 v W, I; (with Aberdeen), 1971 v Bel (sub), D, USSR (5)
Forrest, J. (Motherwell), 1958 v E (1)
Forsyth, A. (Partick T), 1972 v Y, Cz, Br; 1973 v D; (with Manchester U), E; 1975 v Sp, Ni (sub), R, EG; 1976 v D (10)
Forsyth, C. (Kilmarnock), 1964 v E; 1965 v W, Ni, Fi (4)
Forsyth, T. (Motherwell), 1971 v D; (with Rangers), 1974 v Cz; 1976 v Sw, Ni, W, E; 1977 v Fi, Se, W, Ni, E, Ch, Arg, Br; 1978 v Cz, W, Ni, W (sub), E, Pe, Ir (sub), Ho (22)
Foyers, R. (St Bernards), 1893 v W; 1894 v W (2)
Fraser, D. M. (WBA), 1968 v Ho; 1969 v Cy (2)
Fraser, J. (Moffat), 1891 v Ni (1)
Fraser, M. J. E. (Queen's Park), 1880 v W; 1882 v W, E; 1883 v W, E (5)
Fraser, J. (Dundee), 1907 v Ni (1)
Fraser, W. (Sunderland), 1955 v W, Ni (2)
Fulton, W. (Abercorn), 1884 v Ni (1)
Fyfe, J. H. (Third Lanark), 1895 v W (1)

Gabriel, J. (Everton), 1961 v W; 1964 v N (sub) (2)
Gallacher, H. K. (Airdrieonians), 1924 v Ni; 1925 v E, W, Ni; 1926 v W; (with Newcastle U), 1926 v E, Ni; 1927 v E,

W, Ni; 1928 v E, W; 1929 v E, W, Ni; 1930 v W, Ni, F; (with Chelsea), 1934 v E; (with Derby Co), 1935 v E (20)
Gallacher, P. (Sunderland), 1935 v Ni (1)
Galt, J. H. (Rangers), 1908 v W, Ni (2)
Gardiner, I. (Motherwell), 1958 v W (1)
Gardner, D. R. (Third Lanark), 1897 v W (1)
Gardner, R. (Queen's Park), 1872 v E; 1873 v E; (with Clydesdale), 1874 v E; 1875 v E; 1878 v E (5)
Gemmell, T. (St Mirren), 1955 v P, Y (2)
Gemmell, T. (Celtic), 1966 v E; 1967 v W, Ni, E, USSR; 1968 v Ni, E; 1969 v W, Ni, E, D, A, WG, Cy; 1970 v E, Ei, WG; 1971 v Bel (18)
Gemmill, A. (Derby Co), 1971 v Bel; 1972 v P, Ho, Pe, Ni, W, E; 1976 v D, R, Ni, W, E; 1977 v Fi, Cz, W (2), Ni (sub), E (sub), Ch (sub), Arg, Br; 1978 v EG (sub); (with Nottingham F), Bul, Ni, W, E (sub), Pe (sub), Ir, Ho; 1979 v A, N, P, N; (with Birmingham C), 1980 v A, P, Ni, W, E, H; 1981 v Se, P, Is, Ni (43)
Gibb, W. (Clydesdale), 1873 v E (1)
Gibson, D. W. (Leicester C), 1963 v A, N, Ei, Sp; 1964 v Ni; 1965 v W, Fi (7)
Gibson, J. D. (Partick T), 1926 v E; 1927 v E, W, Ni; (with Aston Villa), 1928 v E, W; 1930 v W, Ni (8)
Gibson, N. (Rangers), 1895 v E, Ni; 1896 v E, Ni; 1897 v E, Ni; 1898 v E; 1899 v E, W, Ni; 1900 v E, Ni; 1901 v W; (with Partick T), 1905 v Ni (14)
Gilchrist, J. E. (Celtic), 1922 v E (1)
Gilhooley, M. (Hull C), 1922 v W (1)
Gillespie, G. (Rangers), 1880 v W; 1881 v E, W; 1882 v E; (with Queen's Park), 1886 v W; 1890 v W; 1891 v Ni (7)
Gillespie, Jas. (Third Lanark), 1898 v W (1)
Gillespie, John. (Queen's Park), 1896 v W (1)
Gillespie, R. (Queen's Park), 1927 v W; 1931 v W; 1932 v F; 1933 v E (4)
Gillick, T. (Everton), 1937 v A, Cz; 1939 v W, Ni, H (5)
Gilmour, J. (Dundee), 1931 v W (1)
Gilzean, A. J. (Dundee), 1964 v W, E, N, WG; 1965 v Ni, (with Tottenham H), Sp; 1966 v Ni, W, Pol, I; 1968 v W; 1969 v W, E, WG, Cy (2), A (sub); 1970 v Ni, E (sub), WG, A; 1971 v P (22)
Glavin, R. (Celtic), 1977 v Se (1)
Glen, A. (Aberdeen), 1956 v E, Ni (2)
Glen, R. (Renton), 1895 v W; 1896 v W; (with Hibernian), 1900 v Ni (3)
Gordon, J. E. (Rangers), 1912 v E, Ni; 1913 v E, Ni, W; 1914 v E, Ni; 1920 v W, E, Ni (10)
Gossland, J. (Rangers), 1884 v Ni (1)
Goudle, J. (Abercorn), 1884 v Ni (1)
Gourlay, J. (Cambuslang), 1886 v Ni; 1888 v W (2)
Govan, J. (Hibernian), 1948 v E, W, Bel, Sw, F; 1949 v Ni (6)
Gow, D. R. (Rangers), 1888 v E (1)
Gow, J. J. (Queen's Park), 1885 v E (1)
Gow, J. R. (Rangers), 1888 v Ni (1)
Graham, A. (Leeds U), 1978 v EG (sub); 1979 v A (sub), N, W, Ni, E, Arg, N; 1980 v A; 1981 v W (10)
Graham, G. (Arsenal), 1972 v P, Ho, Ni, Y, Cz, Br; 1973 v D (2); (with Manchester U), E, W, Ni, Br (sub) (12)
Graham, J. (Annbank), 1884 v Ni (1)
Graham, J. A. (Arsenal), 1921 v Ni (1)
Grant, J. (Hibernian), 1959 v W, Ni (2)
Gray, A. (Hibernian), 1903 v Ni (1)
Gray, A. M. (Aston Villa), 1976 v R, Sw; 1977 v Fi, Cz; 1979 v A, N; (with Wolverhampton W), 1980 v P, E (sub); 1981 v Se, P, Is (sub), Ni (12)
Gray, D. (Rangers), 1929 v W, Ni, G, Ho; 1930 v W, E, Ni; 1931 v W; 1933 v W, Ni (10)
Gray, E. (Leeds U), 1969 v E, Cy; 1970 v WG, A; 1971 v W, Ni; 1972 v Bel, Ho; 1976 v W, E; 1977 v Fi, W (12)
Gray, F. T. (Leeds U), 1976 v Sw; 1979 v N, P, W, Ni, E, Arg (sub); (with Nottingham F) 1980 v Bel (sub); 1981 v Se, P, Is, Ni, Is, W, (with Leeds U) Ni, E (16)
Gray, W. (Pollokshields Ath), 1886 v E (1)
Green, A. (Blackpool), 1971 v Bel (sub), P (sub), Ni, E; 1972 v W, E (sub) (6)
Greig, J. (Rangers), 1964 v E, WG; 1965 v W, Ni, E, Fi (2), Sp, Pol; 1966 v Ni, W, E, Pol, I (2), P, Ho, Br; 1967 v W, Ni, E; 1968 v Ni, W, E, Ho; 1969 v W, Ni, E, D, A, WG, Cy (2); 1970 v W, E, Ei, WG, A; 1971 v D, Bel, W (sub), Ni, E; 1976 v D (44)
Groves, W. (Hibernian), 1888 v W; (with Celtic), 1889 v Ni; 1890 v E (3)
Guilliland, W. (Queen's Park), 1891 v W; 1892 v Ni; 1894 v E; 1895 v E (4)

Haddock, H. (Clyde), 1955 v E, H (2), P, Y; 1958 v E (6)
Haddow, D. (Rangers), 1894 v E (1)
Haffey, F. (Celtic), 1960 v E; 1961 v E (2)
Hamilton, A. (Queen's Park), 1885 v E, W; 1886 v E; 1888 v E (4)
Hamilton, A. W. (Dundee), 1962 v Cz, U, W, E; 1963 v W, Ni, E, A, N, Ei; 1964 v Ni, W, E, N, WG; 1965 v Ni, W, E, Fi (2), Pol, Sp; 1966 v Pol, Ni (24)
Hamilton, G. (Aberdeen), 1947 v Ni; 1951 v Bel, A; 1954 v N (2) (5)
Hamilton, G. (Port Glasgow Ath), 1906 v Ni (1)
Hamilton, J. (Queen's Park), 1892 v W; 1893 v E, Ni (3)
Hamilton, J. (St Mirren), 1924 v Ni (1)
Hamilton, R. C. (Rangers), 1899 v E, W, Ni; 1900 v W; 1901 v E, Ni; 1902 v W, Ni; 1903 v E; 1904 v Ni; (with Dundee), 1911 v W (11)
Hamilton, T. (Hurlford), 1891 v Ni (1)
Hamilton, T. (Rangers), 1932 v E (1)
Hamilton, W. M. (Hibernian), 1965 v Fi (1)
Hannah, A. B. (Renton), 1888 v W (1)
Hannah, J. (Third Lanark), 1889 v W (1)
Hansen, A. D. (Liverpool), 1979 v W, Arg; 1980 v Bel, P; 1981 v Se, P, Is (7)
Hansen, J. (Partick T), 1972 v Bel (sub), Y (sub) (2)
Harkness, J. D. (Queen's Park), 1927 v E, Ni; 1928 v E; (with Hearts), 1929 v W, E, Ni; 1930 v E, W; 1932 v W, F; 1934 v Ni (11)
Harper, J. M. (Aberdeen), 1973 v D (1+1 sub); (with Hibernian), 1976 v D; (with Aberdeen), 1978 v Ir (sub) (4)
Harper, W. (Hibernian), 1923 v E, Ni, W; 1924 v E, Ni, W; 1925 v E, Ni, W; (with Arsenal), 1926 v E, Ni (11)
Harris, J. (Partick T), 1921 v W, Ni (2)
Harris, N. (Newcastle U), 1924 v E (1)
Harrower, W. (Queen's Park), 1882 v E; 1884 v Ni; 1886 v W (3)
Hartford, R. A. (WBA), 1972 v Pe, W (sub), E, Y, Cz, Br; (with Manchester C), 1976 v D, R, Ni (sub); 1977 v Cz (sub), W (sub), Se, W, Ni, E, Ch, Arg, Br; 1978 v EG, Cz, W, Bul, W, E, Pe, Ir, Ho; 1979 v A, N, P, W, Ni, E, Arg, N; (with Everton), 1980 v Pe, Bel; 1981 v Ni (sub), Is, W, Ni, E (42)
Harvey, D. (Leeds U), 1973 v D; 1974 v Cz, WG, Ni, W, E, Bel, Z, Br, Y; 1975 v EG, Sp (2); 1976 v D (2); 1977 v Fi (sub) (16)
Hastings, A. C. (Sunderland), 1936 v Ni; 1938 v Ni (2)
Haughney, M. (Celtic), 1954 v E (1)
Hay, D. (Celtic), 1970 v Ni, W, E; 1971 v D, Bel, W, P, Ni; 1972 v P, Bel, Ho; 1973 v W, Ni, E, Sw, Br; 1974 v Cz (2), WG, Ni, W, E, Bel, N, Z, Br, Y (27)
Hay, J. (Celtic), 1905 v Ni; 1909 v Ni; 1910 v W, Ni, E; 1911 v Ni, E; (with Newcastle U), 1912 v E, W; 1914 v E, Ni (11)
Hegarty, P. (Dundee U), 1979 v W, Ni, E, Arg, N (sub); 1980 v W, E (7)
Heggie, C. (Rangers), 1886 v Ni (1)
Henderson, G. H. (Rangers), 1904 v Ni (1)
Henderson, J. G. (Portsmouth), 1953 v Se; 1954 v Ni, E, N; 1956 v W; (with Arsenal), 1959 v W, Ni (7)
Henderson, W. (Rangers), 1963 v W, Ni, E, A, N, Ei, Sp; 1964 v W, Ni, E, N, WG; 1965 v Fi, Pol, E, Sp; 1966 v Ni,

W, Pol, I, Ho; 1967 v W, Ni; 1968 v Ho; 1969 v Ni, E, Cy; 1970 v Ei; 1971 v P (29)
Hepburn, J. (Alloa Ath), 1891 v W (1)
Hepburn, R. (Ayr U), 1932 v Ni (1)
Herd, A. C. (Hearts), 1935 v Ni (1)
Herd, D. G. (Arsenal), 1959 v E, W, Ni; 1961 v E, Cz (5)
Herd, G. (Clyde), 1958 v E; 1960 v H, T; 1961 v W, Ni (5)
Herriot, J. (Birmingham C), 1969 v Ni, E, D, Cy (2), W (sub); 1970 v Ei (sub), WG (8)
Hewie, J. D. (Charlton Ath), 1956 v E, A; 1957 v E, Ni, W, Y, Sp (2), Sw, WG; 1958 v Pol, Y, F; 1959 v Ho, P; 1960 v Ni, W, Pol (18)
Higgins, A. (Kilmarnock), 1885 v Ni (1)
Higgins, A. (Newcastle U), 1910 v E, Ni; 1911 v E, Ni (4)
Highet, T. C. (Queen's Park), 1875 v E; 1876 v E, W; 1878 v E (4)
Hill, D. (Rangers), 1881 v E, W; 1882 v W (3)
Hill, D. A. (Third Lanark), 1906 v Ni (1)
Hill, F. R. (Aberdeen), 1930 v F; 1931 v W, Ni (3)
Hill, J. (Hearts), 1891 v E; 1892 v W (2)
Hogg, G (Hearts), 1896 v E, Ni (2)
Hogg, J. (Ayr U), 1922 v Ni (1)
Hogg, R. M. (Celtic), 1937 v Cz (1)
Holm, A. H. (Queen's Park), 1882 v W; 1883 v E, W (3)
Holt, D. D. (Hearts), 1963 v A, N, Ei, Sp; 1964 v WG (sub) (5)
Holton, J. A. (Manchester U), 1973 v W, Ni, E, Sw, Br; 1974 v Cz, WG, Ni, W, E, N, Z, Br, Y; 1975 v EG (15)
Hope, R. (WBA), 1968 v Ho; 1969 v D (2)
Houliston, W. (Queen of the South), 1949 v E, Ni, F (3)
Houston, S. M. (Manchester U), 1976 v D (1)
Howden, W. (Partick T), 1905 v Ni (1)
Howe, R. (Hamilton A), 1929 v N, Ho (2)
Howie, J. (Newcastle U), 1905 v E; 1906 v E; 1908 v E (3)
Howie, H. (Hibernian), 1949 v W (1)
Howieson, J. (St Mirren), 1927 v Ni (1)
Hughes, J. (Celtic), 1965 v Pol, Sp; 1966 v Ni, I (2); 1968 v E; 1969 v A; 1970 v Ei (8)
Hughes, W. (Sunderland), 1975 v Se (sub) (1)
Humphries, W. (Motherwell), 1952 v Se (1)
Hunter, A. (Kilmarnock), 1972 v Pe, Y; (with Celtic), 1973 v E; 1974 v Cz (4)
Hunter, J. (Dundee), 1909 v W (1)
Hunter, J. (Third Lanark), 1874 v E; (with Eastern), 1875 v E; (with Third Lanark), 1876 v E; 1877 v W (4)
Hunter, R. (St Mirren), 1890 v Ni (1)
Hunter, W. (Motherwell), 1960 v H, T; 1961 v W (3)
Husband, J. (Partick T), 1947 v W (1)
Hutchison, T. (Coventry C), 1974 v Cz (2), WG (2), Ni, W, Bel (sub), N, Z (sub), Y (sub); 1975 v EG, Sp (2), P, E (sub), R (sub); 1976 v D (17)
Hutton, J. (Aberdeen), 1923 v E, W, Ni; 1924 v Ni; 1926 v W, E, Ni; (with Blackburn R), 1927 v Ni; 1928 v W, Ni (10)
Hutton, J. (St Bernards), 1887 v Ni (1)
Hyslop, T. (Stoke C), 1896 v E; (with Rangers), 1897 v E (2)

Imlach, J. J. S. (Nottingham F), 1958 v H, Pol, Y, F (4)
Imrie, W. N. (St Johnstone), 1929 v N, G (2)
Inglis, J. (Kilmarnock Ath), 1884 v Ni (1)
Inglis, J. (Rangers), 1883 v E, W (2)
Irons, J. H. (Queen's Park), 1900 v W (1)

Jackson, A. (Cambuslang), 1886 v W; 1888 v Ni (2)
Jackson, A. (Aberdeen), 1925 v E, W, Ni; (with Huddersfield T), 1926 v E, W, Ni; 1927 v W, Ni; 1928 v E, W; 1929 v E, W, Ni; 1930 v E, W, Ni, F (17)
Jackson, C. (Rangers), 1975 v Se, P (sub), W; 1976 v D, R, Ni, W, E (8)
Jackson, J. (Partick T), 1931 v A, I, Sw; 1933 v E; (with Chelsea), 1934 v E; 1935 v E; 1936 v W, Ni (8)
Jackson, T. A. (St Mirren), 1904 v W, E, Ni; 1905 v W; 1907 v W, Ni (6)
James, A. W. (Preston NE), 1926 v W; 1928 v E; 1929 v E, Ni; (with Arsenal), 1930 v E, W, Ni; 1933 v W (8)
Jardine, A. (Rangers), 1971 v D (sub); 1972 v P, Bel, Ho; 1973 v E, Sw, Br; 1974 v Cz (2), WG (2), Ni, W, E, Bel, N, Z, Br, Y; 1975 v EG, Sp (2), Se, P, W, Ni, E; 1977 v Se (sub), Ch (sub), Br (sub); 1978 v Cz, W, Ni, Ir; 1980 v Pe, A, Bel (2) (38)
Jarvie, A. (Airdrieonians), 1971 v P (sub), Ni (sub), E (sub) (3)
Jenkinson, T. (Hearts), 1887 v Ni (1)
Johnston, L. H. (Clyde), 1948 v Bel, Sw (2)
Johnston, R. (Sunderland), 1938 v Cz (1)
Johnston, W. (Rangers), 1966 v W, E, Pol, Ho; 1968 v W, E; 1969 v Ni (sub); 1970 v Ni; 1971 v D; (with WBA), 1977 v Se, W (sub), Ni, E, Ch, Arg, Br; 1978 v EG, Cz, W, W, E, Pe (22)
Johnstone, D. (Rangers), 1973 v W, Ni, E, Sw, Br; 1975 v EG (sub), Se (sub); 1976 v Sw, Ni (sub), E (sub); 1978 v Bul (sub), Ni, W; 1980 v Bel (14)
Johnstone, J. (Abercorn), 1888 v W (1)
Johnstone, J. (Celtic), 1965 v W, Fi; 1966 v E; 1967 v W, USSR; 1968 v W; 1969 v A, WG; 1970 v E, WG; 1971 v D, E; 1972 v P, Bel, Ho, Ni, E (sub); 1974 v W, E, Bel, N; 1975 v EG, Sp (23)
Johnstone, Jas (Kilmarnock), 1894 v W (1)
Johnstone, J. A. (Hearts), 1930 v W; 1933 v W, Ni (3)
Johnstone, R. (Hibernian), 1951 v E, D, F; 1952 v Ni, E; 1953 v E, Se; 1954 v W, E, N, Fi; 1955 v Ni, H; (with Manchester C), 1955 v E; 1956 v E, Ni, W (17)
Johnstone, W. (Third Lanark), 1887 v Ni; 1889 v W; 1890 v E (3)
Jordan, J. (Leeds U), 1973 v E (sub), Sw (sub), Br; 1974 v Cz (sub+1), WG (sub), Ni (sub), W, E, Bel, N, Z, Br, Y; 1975 v EG, Sp (2); 1976 v Ni, W, E; 1977 v Cz, W, Ni, E; 1978 v EG, Cz, W; (with Manchester U), Bul, Ni, E, Pe, Ir, Ho; 1979 v A, P, W (sub), Ni, E, N; 1980 v Bel, Ni (sub), W, E, Pol; 1981 v Is, W, E (47)

Kay, J. L. (Queen's Park), 1880 v E; 1882 v E, W; 1883 v E, W; 1884 v W (6)
Keillor, A. (Montrose), 1891 v W; 1892 v Ni; (with Dundee), 1894 v Ni; 1895 v W; 1896 v W; 1897 v W (6)
Keir, L. (Dumbarton), 1885 v W; 1886 v Ni; 1887 v E, W; 1888 v E (5)
Kelly, H. T. (Blackpool), 1952 v USA (1)
Kelly, J. (Renton), 1888 v E; (with Celtic), 1889 v E; 1890 v E; 1892 v E; 1893 v E, Ni; 1894 v W; 1896 v Ni (8)
Kelly, J. C. (Barnsley), 1949 v W, Ni (2)
Kelso, R. (Renton), 1885 v W, Ni; 1886 v W; 1887 v E, W; 1888 v E, Ni; (with Dundee), 1898 v Ni (8)
Kelso, T. (Dundee), 1914 v W (1)
Kennaway, J. (Celtic), 1934 v A, W (2)
Kennedy, A. (Eastern), 1875 v E; 1876 v E, W; (with Third Lanark), 1878 v E; 1882 v W; 1884 v W (6)
Kennedy, J. (Celtic), 1964 v W, E, WG; 1965 v W, Ni, Fi (6)
Kennedy, J. (Hibernian), 1897 v W (1)
Kennedy, S. (Aberdeen), 1978 v Bul, W, E, Pe, Ho; 1979 v A, P (7)
Kennedy, S. (Partick T), 1905 v W (1)
Kennedy, S. (Rangers), 1975 v Se, P, W, Ni, E (5)
Ker, G. (Queen's Park), 1880 v E; 1881 v E, W; 1882 v W, E (5)
Ker, W. (Granville), 1872 v E; (with Queen's Park), 1873 v E (2)
Kerr, A. (Partick T), 1955 v A, H (2)
Kerr, P. (Hibernian), 1924 v Ni (1)
Key, G. (Hearts), 1902 v Ni (1)
Key, W. (Queen's Park), 1907 v Ni (1)
King, A. (Hearts), 1896 v E, W; (with Celtic), 1897 v Ni; 1898 v Ni; 1899 v Ni, W (6)

King, J. (Hamilton A), 1933 v Ni; 1934 v Ni (2)
King, W. S. (Queen's Park) 1929 v W (1)
Kinloch, J. D. (Partick T), 1922 v Ni (1)
Kinnaird, A. F. (Wanderers), 1873 v E (1)
Kinnear, D. (Rangers), 1938 v Cz (1)

Lambie, J. A. (Queen's Park), 1886 v Ni; 1887 v Ni; 1888 v E (3)
Lambie, W. A. (Queen's Park), 1892 v Ni; 1893 v W; 1894 v E; 1895 v E, Ni; 1896 v E, Ni; 1897 v E, Ni (9)
Lamont, D. (Pilgrims), 1885 v Ni (1)
Lang, A. (Dumbarton), 1880 v W (1)
Lang, J. J. (Clydesdale), 1876 v W; (with Third Lanark), 1878 v W (2)
Latta, A. (Dumbarton), 1888 v W; 1889 v E (2)
Law, D. (Huddersfield T), 1959 v W, Ni, Ho, P; 1960 v Ni, W; (with Manchester C), 1960 v E, Pol, A; 1961 v E, Ni; (with Torino), 1962 v Cz (2) E; (with Manchester U), 1963 v W, Ni, E, A, N, Ei, Sp; 1964 v W, E, N, WG; 1965 v W, Ni, E, Fi (2), Pol, Sp; 1966 v Ni, E, Pol; 1967 v W, E, USSR; 1968 v Ni; 1969 v Ni, A, WG; 1972 v Pe, Ni, W, E, Y, Cz, Br; (with Manchester C), 1974 v Cz (2), WG (2), Ni, Z (55)
Law, G. (Rangers), 1910 v E, Ni, W (3)
Law, T. (Chelsea), 1928 v E; 1930 v E (2)
Lawrence, J. (Newcastle U), 1911 v E (1)
Lawrence, T. (Liverpool), 1963 v Ei; 1969 v W, WG (3)
Lawson, D. (St Mirren), 1923 v E (1)
Leckie, R. (Queen's Park), 1872 v E (1)
Leggat, G. (Aberdeen), 1956 v E; 1957 v W; 1958 v Ni, H, Pol, Y, Par; (with Fulham), 1959 v E, W, Ni, WG, Ho; 1960 v E, Ni, W, Pol, A, H (18)
Lennie, W. (Aberdeen), 1908 v W, Ni (2)
Lennox, R. (Celtic), 1967 v Ni, E, USSR; 1968 v W, L; 1969 v D, A, WG, Cy (sub); 1970 v W (sub) (10)
Leslie, L. G. (Airdrieonians), 1961 v W, Ni, Ei (2), Cz (5)
Liddell, W. (Liverpool), 1947 v W, Ni; 1948 v E, W, Ni; 1950 v E, W, P, F; 1951 v W, Ni, E, A; 1952 v W, Ni, E, USA, D, Se; 1953 v W, Ni, E; 1954 v W; 1955 v P, Y, A, H; 1956 v Ni (28)
Liddle, D. (East Fife), 1931 v A, I, Sw (3)
Lindsay, D. (St Mirren), 1903 v Ni (1)
Lindsay, J. (Dumbarton), 1880 v W; 1881 v W, E; 1884 v W, E; 1885 v W, E; 1886 v E (8)
Lindsay, J. (Renton), 1888 v E; 1893 v E, Ni (3)
Linwood, A. B. (Clyde), 1950 v W (1)
Little, R. J. (Rangers), 1953 v Se (1)
Livingstone, G. T. (Manchester C), 1906 v E; (with Rangers), 1907 v W (2)
Lochhead, A. (Third Lanark), 1889 v W (1)
Logan, J. (Ayr U), 1891 v W (1)
Logan, T. (Falkirk), 1913 v Ni (1)
Logie, J. T. (Arsenal), 1953 v Ni (1)
Loney, W. (Celtic), 1910 v W, Ni (2)
Long, H. (Clyde), 1947 v Ni (1)
Longair, W. (Dundee), 1894 v Ni (1)
Lorimer, P. (Leeds U), 1970 v A (sub); 1971 v W, Ni; 1972 v Ni (sub), W, E; 1973 v D (2), E (2); 1974 v WG (sub), E, Bel, N, Z, Br, Y; 1975 v Sp (sub); 1976 v D (2), R (sub) (21)
Love, A. (Aberdeen), 1931 v A, I, Sw (3)
Low, A. (Falkirk), 1934 v Ni (1)
Low, T. P. (Rangers), 1897 v Ni (1)
Low, W. L. (Newcastle U), 1911 v E, W; 1912 v Ni; 1920 v E, Ni (5)
Lowe, J. (Cambuslang), 1891 v Ni (1)
Lowe, J. (St Bernards), 1887 v Ni (1)
Lundie, J. (Hibernian), 1886 v W (1)
Lyall, J. (Sheffield W), 1905 v E (1)

McAdam, J. (Third Lanark), 1880 v W (1)
McArthur, D. (Celtic), 1895 v E, Ni; 1899 v W (3)
McAtee, A. (Celtic), 1913 v W (1)
McAulay, J. (Dumbarton), 1882 v W; (with Arthurlie), 1884 v Ni (2)
McAulay, J. (Dumbarton), 1883 v E, W; 1884 v E; 1885 v E, W; 1886 v E; 1887 v E, W (8)
McAuley, R. (Rangers), 1932 v Ni, W (2)
McBain, E. (St Mirren), 1894 v W (1)
McBain, N. (Manchester U), 1922 v E; (with Everton), 1923 v Ni; 1924 v W (3)
McBride, J. (Celtic), 1967 v W, Ni (2)
McBride, P. (Preston NE), 1904 v E; 1906 v E; 1907 v E, W; 1908 v E; 1909 v W (6)
McCall, J. (Renton), 1886 v W; 1887 v E, W; 1888 v E; 1890 v E (5)
McCalliog, J. (Sheffield W), 1967 v E, USSR; 1968 v Ni; 1969 v D; (with Wolverhampton W), 1971 v P (5)
McCallum, N. (Renton), 1888 v Ni (1)
McCann, R. J. (Motherwell), 1959 v WG; 1960 v E, Ni, W; 1961 v E (5)
McCartney, W. (Hibernian), 1902 v Ni (1)
McClory, A. (Motherwell), 1927 v W; 1928 v Ni; 1935 v W (3)
McCloy, P. (Ayr U), 1924 v E; 1925 v E (2)
McCloy, P. (Rangers), 1973 v W, Ni, Sw, Br (4)
McColl, A. (Renton), 1888 v Ni (1)
McColl, I. M. (Rangers), 1950 v E, F; 1951 v W, Ni, Bel; 1957 v E, Ni, W, Y, Sp, Sw, WG; 1958 v Ni, E (14)
McColl, R. S. (Queen's Park), 1896 v W, Ni; 1897 v Ni; 1898 v Ni; 1899 v Ni, E, W; 1900 v E, W; 1901 v E, W; (with Newcastle U), 1902 v E; (with Queen's Park), 1908 v Ni (13)
McColl, W. (Renton), 1895 v W (1)
McCombie, A. (Sunderland), 1903 v E, W; (with Newcastle U), 1905 v E, W (4)
McCorkindale, J. (Partick T), 1891 v W (1)
McCormick, R. (Abercorn), 1886 v W (1)
McCrae, D. (St Mirren), 1929 v N, G (2)
McCreadie, A. (Rangers), 1893 v W; 1894 v E (2)
McCreadie, E. G. (Chelsea), 1965 v E, Sp, Fi, Pol; 1966 v P, Ni, W, Pol, I; 1967 v E, USSR; 1968 v Ni, W, E, Ho; 1969 v W, Ni, E, D, A, WG, Cy (2) (23)
McCulloch, D. (Hearts), 1935 v W; (with Brentford), 1936 v E; 1937 v W, Ni; 1938 v Cz; (with Derby Co), 1939 v H, W (7)
MacDonald, A. (Rangers), 1976 v Sw (1)
McDonald, J. (Edinburgh University), 1886 v E (1)
McDonald, J. (Sunderland), 1956 v W, Ni (2)
MacDougall, E. J. (Norwich C) 1975 v Se, P, W, Ni, E; 1976 v D, R (7)
McDougall, J. (Liverpool), 1931 v I, A (2)
McDougall, J. (Airdrieonians), 1926 v Ni (1)
McDougall, J. (Vale of Leven), 1877 v E, W; 1878 v E; 1879 v E, W (5)
McFadyen, W. (Motherwell), 1934 v A, W (2)
Macfarlane, A. (Dundee), 1904 v W; 1906 v W; 1908 v W; 1909 v Ni; 1911 v W (5)
McFarlane, R. (Greenock Morton), 1896 v W (1)
Macfarlane, W. (Hearts), 1947 v L (1)
McGarr, E. (Aberdeen), 1970 v Ei, A (2)
McGarvey, F. P. (Liverpool), 1979 v Ni (sub), Arg (2)
McGeoch, A. (Dumbreck), 1876 v E, W; 1877 v E, W (4)
McGhee, J. (Hibernian), 1886 v W (1)
McGonagle, W. (Celtic), 1933 v E; 1934 v A, E, Ni; 1935 v Ni, W (6)
McGrain, D. (Celtic), 1973 v W, Ni, E, Sw, Br; 1974 v Cz (2), WG, W (sub), E, Bel, N, Z, Br, Y; 1975 v Sp, Se, P, W, Ni, E, R; 1976 v D (2), Sw, Ni, W, E; 1977 v Fi, Cz, W (2), Se, Ni, E, Ch, Arg, Br; 1978 v EG, Cz, 1980 v Bel, P, Ni, W, E, Pol, H; 1981 v Se, P, Is, Ni, Is, W (sub), Ni, E (55)
McGregor, J. C. (Vale of Leven), 1877 v E, W; 1878 v E; 1880 v E (4)
McGrory, J. E. (Kilmarnock), 1965 v Ni, Fi; 1966 v P (3)

McGrory, J. (Celtic), 1928 v Ni; 1931 v E; 1932 v Ni, W; 1933 v E, Ni; 1934 v Ni (7)
McGuire, W. (Beith), 1881 v E, W (2)
McGurk, F. (Birmingham), 1934 v W (1)
McHardy, H. (Rangers), 1885 v Ni (1)
McInally, T. B. (Celtic), 1926 v Ni; 1927 v W (2)
McInnes, T. (Cowlairs), 1889 v Ni (1)
McIntosh, W. (Third Lanark), 1905 v Ni (1)
McIntyre, A. (Vale of Leven), 1878 v E; 1882 v E (2)
McIntyre, H. (Rangers), 1880 v W (1)
McIntyre, J. (Rangers), 1884 v W (1)
McKay, D. (Celtic), 1959 v E, WG, Ho, P; 1960 v E, Pol, A, H, T; 1961 v W, Ni; 1962 v Ni, Cz, U (sub) (14)
Mackay, D. C. (Hearts), 1957 v Sp; 1958 v F; 1959 v W, Ni; (with Tottenham H), 1959 v WG, E; 1960 v W, Ni, A, Pol, H, T; 1961 v W, Ni, E; 1963 v E, A, N; 1964 v Ni, W, N; 1966 v Ni (22)
McKay, J. (Blackburn R), 1924 v W (1)
McKay, R. (Newcastle U), 1928 v W (1)
McKean, R. (Rangers), 1976 v Sw (1)
McKenzie, D. (Brentford), 1938 v Ni (1)
Mackenzie, J. A. (Partick T), 1954 v W, E, N, Fi, A, U; 1955 v E, H; 1956 v A (9)
McKeown, M. (Celtic), 1889 v Ni; 1890 v E (2)
McKie, J. (East Stirling), 1898 v W (1)
McKillop, T. R. (Rangers), 1938 v Ho (1)
McKinlay, D. (Liverpool), 1922 v W, Ni (2)
McKinnon, A. (Queen's Park), 1874 v E (1)
McKinnon, R. (Rangers), 1966 v W, E, I (2), Ho, Br; 1967 v W, Ni, E; 1968 v Ni, W, E, Ho; 1969 v D, A, WG, Cy; 1970 v Ni, W, E, Ei, WG, A; 1971 v D, Bel, P, USSR, D (28)
MacKinnon, W. (Dumbarton), 1883 v E, W; 1884 v E, W (4)
McKinnon, W. W. (Queen's Park), 1872 v E; 1873 v E; 1874 v E; 1875 v E; 1876 v E, W; 1877 v E; 1878 v E; 1879 v E (9)
McLaren, A. (St Johnstone), 1929 v N, G, Ho; 1933 v W, Ni (5)
McLaren, A. (Preston NE), 1947 v E, Bel, L; 1948 v W (4)
McLaren, J. (Hibernian), 1888 v W; (with Celtic), 1889 v E; 1890 v E (3)
McLean, A. (Celtic), 1926 v W, Ni; 1927 v W, E (4)
McLean, D. (St Bernards), 1896 v W; 1897 v Ni (2)
McLean, D. (Sheffield W), 1912 v E (1)
McLean, G. (Dundee), 1968 v Ho (1)
McLean, T. (Kilmarnock), 1969 v D, Cy, W; 1970 v Ni, W; 1971 v D (6)
McLeish, A. (Aberdeen), 1980 v F, Ni, W, E, Pol, H; 1981 v Se, Is, Ni, Is, Ni, E (12)
McLeod, D. (Celtic), 1905 v Ni; 1906 v E, W, Ni (4)
McLeod, J. (Dumbarton), 1888 v Ni; 1889 v W; 1890 v Ni; 1892 v E; 1893 v W (5)
MacLeod, J. M. (Hibernian), 1961 v E, Ei (2), Cz (4)
McLeod, W. (Cowlairs), 1886 v Ni (1)
McLintock, A. (Vale of Leven), 1875 v E; 1876 v E; 1880 v E (3)
McLintock, F. (Leicester C), 1963 v N (sub), Ei, Sp; (with Arsenal), 1965 v Ni; 1967 v USSR; 1970 v Ni; 1971 v W, Ni, E (9)
McLuckie, J. S. (Manchester C), 1934 v W (1)
McMahon, A. (Celtic), 1892 v E; 1893 v E, Ni; 1894 v E; 1901 v Ni; 1902 v W (6)
McMenemy, J. (Celtic), 1905 v Ni; 1909 v Ni; 1910 v E, W; 1911 v Ni, W, E; 1912 v W; 1914 v W, Ni, E; 1920 v Ni (12)
McMenemy, J. (Motherwell), 1934 v W (1)
McMillan, J. (St Bernards), 1897 v W (1)
McMillan, I. L. (Airdrieonians), 1952 v E, USA, D; 1955 v E; 1956 v E; (with Rangers), 1961 v Cz (6)
McMillan, T. (Dumbarton), 1887 v Ni (1)
McMullan, J. (Partick T), 1920 v W; 1921 v W, Ni, E; 1924 v E, Ni; 1925 v E; 1926 v W; (with Manchester C), 1926 v E; 1927 v E, W; 1928 v E, W; 1929 v W, E, Ni (16)
McNab, A. (Morton), 1921 v E, Ni (2)
McNab, A. (Sunderland), 1937 v A; (with WBA), 1939 v E (2)
McNab, C. D. (Dundee), 1931 v E, W, A, I, Sw; 1932 v E (6)
McNab, J. S. (Liverpool), 1923 v W (1)
McNair, A. (Celtic), 1906 v W; 1907 v Ni; 1908 v E, W; 1909 v E; 1910 v W; 1912 v E, W, Ni; 1913 v E; 1914 v E, Ni; 1920 v E, W, Ni (15)
McNaught, W. (Raith R), 1951 v A, W, Ni; 1952 v E; 1955 v Ni (5)
McNeil, H. (Queen's Park), 1874 v E; 1875 v E; 1876 v E, W; 1877 v W; 1878 v E; 1879 v E, W; 1881 v E, W (10)
McNeil, M. (Rangers), 1876 v W; 1880 v E (2)
McNeill, W. (Celtic), 1961 v E, Ei (2), Cz; 1962 v Ni, E, Cz, U; 1963 v Ei, Sp; 1964 v W, E, WG; 1965 v E, Fi, Pol, Sp; 1966 v Ni, Pol; 1967 v USSR; 1968 v E; 1969 v Cy, W, E, Cy (sub); 1970 v WG; 1972 v Ni, W, E (29)
McPhail, J. (Celtic), 1950 v W; 1951 v W, Ni, A; 1954 v Ni (5)
McPhail, R. (Airdrieonians), 1927 v E; (with Rangers), 1929 v W; 1931 v E, Ni; 1932 v W, Ni, F; 1933 v E, Ni; 1934 v A, Ni; 1935 v E; 1937 v G, E, Cz; 1938 v W, Ni (17)
McPherson, D. (Kilmarnock), 1892 v Ni (1)
McPherson, J. (Kilmarnock), 1888 v W; (with Cowlairs), 1889 v E; 1890 v Ni, E; (with Rangers), 1892 v W; 1894 v E; 1895 v E, Ni; 1897 v Ni (9)
McPherson, J. (Clydesdale), 1875 v E (1)
McPherson, J. (Vale of Leven), 1879 v E, W; 1880 v E; 1881 v W; 1883 v E, W; 1884 v E; 1885 v N (8)
McPherson, J. (Hearts), 1891 v E (1)
McPherson, R. (Arthurlie), 1882 v E (1)
McQueen, G. (Leeds U), 1974 v Bel; 1975 v Sp (2), P, W, Ni, E, R; 1976 v D; 1977 v Cz, W (2), Ni, E; 1978 v EG, Cz, W; (with Manchester U), Bul, Ni, W; 1979 v A, N, P, Ni, E, N; 1980 v Pe, A, Bel; 1981 v W (30)
McQueen, M. (Leith Ath), 1890 v W; 1891 v W (2)
McRorie, D. M. (Morton), 1931 v W (1)
McSpadyen, A. (Partick T), 1939 v E, H (2)
McStay, W. (Celtic), 1921 v W, Ni; 1925 v E, Ni, W; 1926 v E, Ni, W; 1927 v E, Ni, W; 1928 v W, Ni (13)
McTavish, J. (Falkirk), 1910 v Ni (1)
McWhattie, G. C. (Queen's Park), 1901 v W, Ni (2)
McWilliam, P. (Newcastle U) 1905 v E; 1906 v E; 1907 v E, W; 1909 v E, W; 1910 v E; 1911 v W (8)
Macari, L. (Celtic), 1972 v W (sub), E, Y, Cz, Br; 1973 v D; (with Manchester U), E (2), W (sub), Ni (sub); 1975 v Se, P (sub), W, E (sub), R; 1977 v Ni (sub), E (sub), Ch, Arg; 1978 v EG, W, Bul, Pe (sub), Ir (24)
Macauley, A. R. (Brentford), 1947 v E; (with Arsenal), 1948 v E, W, Ni, Bel, Sw, F (7)
Madden, J. (Celtic), 1893 v W; 1895 v W (2)
Main, F. R. (Rangers), 1938 v W (1)
Main, J. (Hibernian), 1909 v Ni (1)
Maley, W. (Celtic), 1893 v E, Ni (2)
Marshall, H. (Celtic), 1899 v W; 1900 v Ni (2)
Marshall, J. (Rangers), 1932 v E; 1933 v E; 1934 v E (3)
Marshall, J. (Middlesbrough), 1921 v E, W, Ni; 1922 v E, W, Ni; (with Llanelly), 1924 v W (7)
Marshall, J. (Third Lanark), 1885 v Ni; 1886 v W; 1887 v E, W (4)
Marshall, R. W. (Rangers), 1892 v Ni; 1894 v Ni (2)
Martin, F. (Aberdeen), 1954 v N (2), A, U; 1955 v E, H (6)
Martin, N. (Hibernian), 1965 v Fi, Pol; (with Sunderland), 1966 v I (3)
Martis, J. (Motherwell), 1961 v W (1)
Mason, J. (Third Lanark), 1949 v E, W, Ni; 1950 v Ni; 1951 v Ni, Bel, A (7)
Massie, A. (Hearts), 1932 v Ni, W, F; 1933 v Ni; 1934 v E, Ni; 1935 v E, Ni, W; 1936 v W, Ni; (with Aston Villa), 1936 v E; 1937 v G, E, W, Ni, A; 1938 v W (18)
Masson, D. S. (QPR), 1976 v Ni, W, E; 1977 v Fi, Cz, W, Ni, E, Ch, Arg, Br; 1978 v EG, Cz, W; (with Derby Co), Ni, E, Pe (17)

Mathers, D. (Partick T), 1954 v Fi (1)
Maxwell, W. S. (Stoke C), 1898 v E (1)
May, J. (Rangers), 1906 v W, Ni; 1908 v E, Ni; 1909 v W (5)
Meechan, P. (Celtic), 1896 v Ni (1)
Meiklejohn, D. D. (Rangers), 1922 v W; 1924 v W; 1925 v W, Ni, E; 1928 v W, Ni; 1929 v E, Ni; 1930 v E, Ni; 1931 v E; 1932 v W, Ni; 1934 v A (15)
Menzies, A. (Hearts), 1906 v E (1)
Mercer, R. (Hearts), 1912 v W; 1913 v Ni (2)
Middleton, R. (Cowdenbeath), 1930 v Ni (1)
Millar, J. (Rangers), 1897 v E; 1898 v E, W (3)
Millar, J. (Rangers), 1963 v A, Ei (2)
Millar, A. (Hearts), 1939 v W (1)
Miller, J. (St Mirren), 1931 v E, I, Sw; 1932 v F; 1934 v E (5)
Miller, P. (Dumbarton), 1882 v E; 1883 v E, W (3)
Miller, T. (Liverpool), 1920 v E; (with Manchester U), 1921 v E, Ni (3)
Miller, W. (Third Lanark), 1876 v E (1)
Miller, W. (Celtic), 1947 v E, W, Bel, L; 1948 v W, Ni (6)
Miller, W. (Aberdeen), 1975 v R; 1978 v Bul; 1980 v Bel, W, E, Pol, H; 1981 v Se, P, Is (sub), Ni, W, Ni, E (14)
Mills, W. (Aberdeen), 1936 v W, Ni; 1937 v W (3)
Milne, J. V. (Middlesbrough), 1938 v E; 1939 v E (2)
Mitchell, D. (Rangers), 1890 v Ni; 1892 v E; 1893 v E, Ni; 1894 v E (5)
Mitchell, J. (Kilmarnock), 1908 v Ni; 1910 v Ni, W (3)
Mitchell, R. C. (Newcastle U), 1951 v D, F (2)
Mochan, N. (Celtic), 1954 v N, A, U (3)
Moir, W. (Bolton W), 1950 v E (1)
Moncur, R. (Newcastle U), 1968 v Ho; 1970 v Ni, W, E, Ei; 1971 v D, Bel, W, P, Ni, E, D; 1972 v Pe, Ni, W, E (16)
Morgan, H. (St Mirren), 1898 v W; (with Liverpool), 1899 v E (2)
Morgan, W. (Burnley), 1968 v Ni; (with Manchester U) 1972 v Pe, Y, Cz, Br; 1973 v D (2), E (2), W, Ni, Sw, Br; 1974 v Cz (2), WG (2), Ni, Bel (sub), Br, Y (21)
Morris, D. (Raith R), 1923 v Ni; 1924 v E, Ni; 1925 v E, W, Ni (6)
Morris, H. (East Fife), 1950 v Ni (1)
Morrison, T. (St Mirren), 1927 v E (1)
Morton, A. L. (Queen's Park), 1920 v W, Ni; (with Rangers), 1921 v E; 1922 v E, W; 1923 v E, W, Ni; 1924 v E, W, Ni; 1925 v E, W, Ni; 1927 v E, Ni; 1928 v E, W, Ni; 1929 v E, W, Ni; 1930 v E, W, Ni; 1931 v E, W, Ni; 1932 v E, W, F (31)
Morton, H. A. (Kilmarnock), 1929 v G, Ho (2)
Mudie, J. K. (Blackpool), 1957 v W, Ni, E, Y, Sw, Sp (2), WG; 1958 v Ni, E, W, Sw, H, Pol, Y, Par, F (17)
Muir, W. (Dundee), 1907 v Ni (1)
Muirhead, T. A. (Rangers), 1922 v Ni; 1923 v E; 1924 v W; 1927 v Ni; 1928 v Ni; 1929 v W, Ni; 1930 v W (8)
Mulhall, G. (Aberdeen), 1960 v Ni; (with Sunderland), 1963 v Ni; 1964 v Ni (3)
Munro, A. D. (Hearts), 1937 v W, Ni; (with Blackpool), 1938 v Ho (3)
Munro, F. M. (Wolverhampton W), 1971 v Ni (sub), E (sub), D, USSR; 1975 v Se, W (sub), Ni, E, R (9)
Munro, I. (St Mirren), 1979 v Arg, N; 1980 v Pe, A, Bel, W, E (7)
Munro, N. (Abercorn), 1888 v W; 1889 v E (2)
Murdoch, J. (Motherwell), 1931 v Ni (1)
Murdoch, R. (Celtic), 1966 v W, E, I (2); 1967 v Ni; 1968 v Ni; 1969 v W, Ni, E, WG, Cy; 1970 v A (12)
Murphy, F. (Celtic), 1938 v Ho (1)
Murray, J. (Renton), 1895 v W (1)
Murray, J. (Hearts), 1958 v E, H, Pol, Y, F (5)
Murray, J. W. (Vale of Leven), 1890 v W (1)
Murray, P. (Hibernian), 1896 v Ni; 1897 v W (2)
Murray, S. (Aberdeen), 1972 v Bel (1)
Mutch, G. (Preston NE), 1938 v E (1)

Napier, C. E. (Celtic), 1932 v E; 1935 v E, W; (with Derby Co), 1937 v Ni, A (5)
Narey, D. (Dundee U), 1977 v Se (sub); 1979 v P, Ni (sub), Arg; 1980 v P, Ni, Pol, H; 1981 v W, E (sub) (10)
Neil, R. G. (Hibernian), 1896 v W; (with Rangers), 1900 v W (2)
Neill, R. W. (Queen's Park), 1876 v W; 1877 v E, W; 1878 v W; 1880 v E (5)
Neilles, P. (Hearts), 1914 v W, Ni (2)
Nelson, J. (Cardiff C), 1925 v W, Ni; 1928 v E; 1930 v F (4)
Niblo, T. D. (Aston Villa), 1904 v E (1)
Nibloe, J. (Kilmarnock), 1929 v E, N, Ho; 1930 v W; 1931 v E, Ni, A, I, Sw; 1932 v E, F (11)
Nisbet, J. (Ayr U), 1929 v N, G, Ho (3)
Niven, J. B. (Moffatt), 1885 v Ni (1)

O'Donnell, F. (Preston NE), 1937 v E, A, Cz; 1938 v E, W; (with Blackpool), Ho (6)
Ogilvie, D. H. (Motherwell), 1934 v A (1)
O'Hare, J. (Derby Co), 1970 v W, Ni, E; 1971 v D, Bel, W, Ni; 1972 v P, Bel, Ho (sub), Pe, Ni, W (13)
Ormond, W. E. (Hibernian), 1954 v E, N, Fi, A, U; 1959 v E (6)
O'Rourke, F. (Airdrieonians), 1907 v Ni (1)
Orr, J. (Kilmarnock), 1892 v W (1)
Orr, R. (Newcastle U), 1902 v E; 1904 v E (2)
Orr, T. (Morton), 1952 v Ni, W (2)
Orr, W. (Celtic), 1900 v Ni; 1903 v Ni; 1904 v W (3)
Orrock, R. (Falkirk), 1913 v W (1)
Oswald, J. (Third Lanark), 1889 v E; (with St Bernards), 1895 v E; (with Rangers), 1897 v W (3)

Parker, A. H. (Falkirk), 1955 v P, Y, A; 1956 v E, Ni, W, A; 1957 v Ni, W, Y; 1958 v Ni, W, E, Sw; (with Everton), Par (15)
Parlane, D. (Rangers), 1973 v W, Sw, Br; 1975 v Sp (sub), Se, P, W, Ni, E, R; 1976 v D (sub); 1977 v W (12)
Parlane, R. (Vale of Leven), 1878 v W; 1879 v E, W (3)
Paterson, G. D. (Celtic), 1939 v Ni (1)
Paterson, J. (Leicester C), 1920 v E (1)
Paterson, J. (Cowdenbeath), 1931 v A, I, Sw (3)
Paton, A. (Motherwell), 1952 v D, Se (2)
Paton, D. (St Bernards), 1896 v W (1)
Paton, M. (Dumbarton), 1883 v E; 1884 v W; 1885 v W, E; 1886 v E (5)
Paton, R. (Vale of Leven), 1879 v E, W (2)
Patrick, J. (St Mirren), 1897 v E, W (2)
Paul, H. McD. (Queen's Park), 1909 v E, W, Ni (3)
Paul, W. (Partick T), 1888 v W; 1889 v W; 1890 v W (3)
Paul, W. (Dykebar), 1891 v Ni (1)
Pearson, T. (Newcastle U), 1947 v E, Bel (2)
Penman, A. (Dundee), 1966 v Ho (1)
Pettigrew, W. (Motherwell), 1976 v Sw, Ni, W; 1977 v W (sub), Se (5)
Phillips, J. (Queen's Park), 1877 v E, W; 1878 v W (3)
Plenderleith, J. B. (Manchester C), 1961 v Ni (1)
Porteous, W. (Hearts), 1903 v Ni (1)
Pringle, C. (St Mirren), 1921 v W (1)
Provan, D. (Rangers), 1964 v Ni, N; 1966 v I (2), Ho (5)
Provan, D. (Celtic), 1980 v Bel (2 sub), P (sub), Ni (sub); 1981 v Is, W, E (7)
Pursell, P. (Queen's Park), 1914 v W (1)

Quinn, J. (Celtic), 1905 v Ni; 1906 v Ni, W; 1908 v Ni, E; 1909 v E; 1910 v E, Ni, W; 1912 v E, W (11)
Quinn, P. (Motherwell), 1961 v E, Ei (2); 1962 v U (4)

Rae, J. (Third Lanark), 1889 v W; 1890 v Ni (2)
Raeside, J. S. (Third Lanark), 1906 v W (1)
Raisbeck, A. G. (Liverpool), 1900 v E; 1901 v E; 1902 v E; 1903 v E, W; 1904 v E; 1906 v E; 1907 v E (8)
Rankin, G. (Vale of Leven), 1890 v Ni; 1891 v E (2)

Rankin, R. (St Mirren), 1929 v N, G, Ho (3)
Redpath, W. (Motherwell), 1949 v W, Ni; 1951 v E, D, F, Bel, A; 1952 v Ni, E (9)
Reid, J. G. (Airdrieonians), 1914 v W; 1920 v W; 1924 v Ni (3)
Reid, R. (Brentford), 1938 v E, Ni (2)
Reid, W. (Rangers), 1911 v E, W, Ni; 1912 v Ni; 1913 v E, W, Ni; 1914 v E, Ni (9)
Reilly, L. (Hibernian), 1949 v E, W, F; 1950 v W, Ni, Sw, F; 1951 v W, E, D, F, Bel, A; 1952 v Ni, W, E, USA, D, Se; 1953 v Ni, W, E, Se; 1954 v W; 1955 v H (2), P, Y, A, E; 1956 v E, W, Ni, A; 1957 v E, Ni, W, Y (38)
Rennie, H. G. (Hearts), 1900 v E, Ni; (with Hibernian), 1901 v E; 1902 v E, Ni, W; 1903 v Ni, W; 1904 v Ni; 1905 v W; 1906 v Ni; 1908 v Ni, W (13)
Renny-Tailyour, H. W. (Royal Engineers), 1873 v E (1)
Rhind, A. (Queen's Park), 1872 v E (1)
Richmond, A. (Queen's Park), 1906 v W (1)
Richmond, J. T. (Clydesdale), 1877 v E; (with Queen's Park), 1878 v E; 1882 v W (3)
Ring, T. (Clyde), 1953 v Se; 1955 v W, Ni, E, H; 1957 v E, Sp (2), Sw, WG; 1958 v Ni, Sw (12)
Rioch, B. D. (Derby Co), 1975 v P, W, Ni, E, R; 1976 v D (2), R, Ni, W, E; 1977 v Fi, Cz, W; (with Everton), W, Ni, E, Ch, Br; 1978 v Cz; (with Derby Co), Ni, E, Pe, Ho (24)
Ritchie, A. (East Stirlingshire), 1891 v W (1)
Ritchie, H. (Hibernian), 1923 v W; 1928 v Ni (2)
Ritchie, J. (Queen's Park), 1897 v W (1)
Ritchie, W. (Rangers), 1962 v U (sub) (1)
Robb, D. T. (Aberdeen), 1971 v W, E, P, D (sub), USSR (5)
Robb, W. (Rangers), 1926 v W; (with Hibernian), 1928 v W (2)
Robertson, A. (Clyde), 1955 v P, A, H; 1958 v Sw, Par (5)
Robertson, G. (Motherwell), 1910 v W; (with Sheffield W), 1912 v W; 1913 v E, Ni (4)
Robertson, G. (Kilmarnock), 1938 v Cz (1)
Robertson, H. (Dundee), 1962 v Cz (1)
Robertson, J. (Dundee), 1931 v A, I (2)
Robertson, J. (Nottingham F), 1978 v Ni, Ir; 1979 v P, N; 1980 v Pe, A, Bel (2), P; 1981 v Se, P, Is, Ni, Is, Ni, E (16)
Robertson, J. G. (Tottenham H), 1965 v W (1)
Robertson, J. T. (Everton), 1898 v E; (with Southampton), 1899 v E; (with Rangers), 1900 v E, W; 1901 v W, Ni, E; 1902 v W, Ni, E; 1903 v E, W; 1904 v E, W, Ni; 1905 v W (16)
Robertson, P. (Dundee), 1903 v Ni (1)
Robertson, T. (Queen's Park), 1889 v Ni; 1890 v E; 1891 v W; 1892 v Ni (4)
Robertson, T. (Hearts), 1898 v Ni (1)
Robertson, W. (Dumbarton), 1887 v E, W (2)
Robinson, R. (Dundee), 1974 v WG (sub); 1975 v Se, Ni, R (sub) (4)
Rough, A. (Partick T), 1976 v Sw, Ni, W, E; 1977 v Fi, Cz, W (2), Se, Ni, E, Ch, Arg, Br; 1978 v Cz, W, Ni, E, Pe, Ir, Ho; 1979 v A, P, W, Arg, N; 1980 v Pe, A, Bel (2), P, W, E, Pol, H; 1981 v Se, P, Is, Ni, Is, W, E (42)
Rowan, A. (Caledonian), 1880 v E; (with Queen's Park), 1882 v W (2)
Russell, D. (Hearts), 1895 v E, Ni; (with Celtic), 1897 v W; 1898 v Ni; 1901 v W, Ni (6)
Russell, J. (Cambuslang), 1890 v Ni (1)
Russell, W. F. (Airdrieonians), 1924 v W; 1925 v E (2)
Rutherford, E. (Rangers), 1948 v F (1)

St John, I. (Motherwell), 1959 v WG; 1960 v E, Ni, W, Pol, A; 1961 v E; (with Liverpool), 1962 v Ni, W, E, Cz (2), U; 1963 v W, Ni, E, N, Ei (sub), Sp; 1964 v Ni; 1965 v E (21)
Sawers, W. (Dundee), 1895 v W (1)
Scarff, P. (Celtic), 1931 v Ni (1)
Schaedler, E. (Hibernian), 1974 v WG (1)
Scott, A. S. (Rangers), 1957 v Ni, Y, WG; 1958 v W, Sw; 1959 v P; 1962 v Ni, W, E, Cz, U; (with Everton), 1964 v W, N; 1965 v Fi; 1966 v P, Br (16)
Scott, J. (Hibernian), 1966 v Ho (1)
Scott, J. (Dundee), 1971 v D (sub), USSR (2)
Scott, M. (Airdrieonians), 1898 v W (1)
Scott, R. (Airdrieonians), 1894 v Ni (1)
Scoular, J. (Portsmouth), 1951 v D, F, A; 1952 v E, USA, D, Se; 1953 v W, Ni (9)
Sellar, W. (Battlefield), 1885 v E; 1886 v E; 1887 v E, W; 1888 v E; (with Queen's Park), 1891 v E; 1892 v E; 1893 v E, Ni (9)
Semple, W. (Cambuslang), 1886 v W (1)
Shankly, W. (Preston NE), 1938 v E; 1939 v E, W, Ni, H (5)
Sharp, J. (Dundee), 1904 v W; (with Woolwich Arsenal), 1907 v W, E; 1908 v E; (with Fulham), 1909 v W (5)
Shaw, D. (Hibernian), 1947 v W, Ni; 1948 v E, Bel, Sw, F; 1949 v W, Ni (8)
Shaw, F. W. (Pollokshields Ath), 1884 v E, W (2)
Shaw, J. (Rangers), 1947 v E, Bel, L; 1948 v Ni (4)
Shearer, R. (Rangers), 1961 v E, Ei (2), Cz (4)
Sillars, D. C. (Queen's Park), 1891 v Ni; 1892 v E; 1893 v W; 1894 v E; 1895 v W (5)
Simpson, J. (Third Lanark), 1895 v E, W, Ni (3)
Simpson, J. (Rangers), 1935 v E, W, Ni; 1936 v E, W, Ni; 1937 v G, E, W, Ni, A, Cz; 1938 v W, Ni (14)
Simpson, R. C. (Celtic), 1967 v E, USSR; 1968 v Ni, E; 1969 v A (5)
Sinclair, G. L. (Hearts), 1910 v Ni; 1912 v W, Ni (3)
Sinclair, J. W. E. (Leicester C), 1966 v P (1)
Skene, L. H. (Queen's Park), 1904 v W (1)
Sloan, T. (Third Lanark), 1904 v W (1)
Smellie, R. (Queen's Park), 1887 v Ni; 1888 v W; 1889 v E; 1891 v E; 1893 v E, Ni (6)
Smith, A. (Rangers), 1898 v E; 1900 v E, Ni, W; 1901 v E, Ni, W; 1902 v E, Ni, W; 1903 v E, Ni, W; 1904 v Ni; 1905 v W; 1906 v E, Ni; 1907 v W; 1911 v E, Ni (20)
Smith, D. (Aberdeen), 1966 v Ho; (with Rangers), 1968 v Ho (2)
Smith, G. (Hibernian), 1947 v E, Ni; 1948 v W, Bel, Sw, F; 1952 v E, USA; 1955 v P, Y, A, H; 1956 v E, Ni, W; 1957 v Sp (2), Sw (18)
Smith, J. (Rangers), 1935 v Ni; 1938 v Ni (2)
Smith, J. (Ayr U), 1924 v E (1)
Smith, J. (Aberdeen), 1968 v Ho (sub); (with Newcastle U), 1974 v WG, Ni (sub), W (sub) (4)
Smith, J. E. (Celtic), 1959 v H, P (2)
Smith, Jas. (Queen's Park), 1872 v E (1)
Smith, John. (Mauchline), 1877 v E, W; 1879 v E, W; (with Edinburgh University), 1880 v E; (with Queen's Park), 1881 v W, E; 1883 v E, W; 1884 v E (10)
Smith, N. (Rangers), 1897 v E; 1898 v W; 1899 v E, W, Ni; 1900 v E, W, Ni; 1901 v Ni, W; 1902 v E, Ni (12)
Smith, R. (Queen's Park), 1872 v E; 1873 v E (2)
Smith, T. M. (Kilmarnock), 1934 v E; (with Preston NE), 1938 v E (2)
Somers, P. (Celtic), 1905 v E, Ni; 1907 v Ni; 1909 v W (4)
Somers, W. S. (Third Lanark), 1879 v E, W; (with Queen's Park), 1880 v W (3)
Somerville, G. (Queen's Park), 1886 v E (1)
Souness, G. J. (Middlesbrough), 1975 v EG, Sp, Se; (with Liverpool), 1978 v Bul, W, E (sub), Ho; 1979 v A, N, W, Ni, E; 1980 v Pe, A, Bel, P, Ni; 1981 v P, Is (2) (20)
Speedie, F. (Rangers), 1903 v E, W, Ni (3)
Speirs, J. H. (Rangers), 1908 v W (1)
Stanton, P. (Hibernian), 1966 v Ho; 1969 v Ni; 1970 v Ei, A; 1971 v D, Bel, P, USSR, D; 1972 v P, Bel, Ho, W; 1973 v W, Ni; 1974 v WG (16)
Stark, J. (Rangers), 1909 v E, Ni (2)
Steel, W. (Morton), 1947 v E, Bel, L; (with Derby Co), 1948 v F, E, W, Ni; 1949 v E, W, Ni, F; 1950 v E, W, Ni, Sw, P, F; (with Dundee), 1951 v W, Ni, E, A (2), D, F, Bel; 1952 v W; 1953 v W, E, Ni, Se (30)

Steele, D. M. (Huddersfield), 1923 v E, W, Ni (3)
Stein, C. (Rangers), 1969 v W, Ni, D, E, Cy (2); 1970 v A (sub), Ni (sub), W, E, Ei, WG; 1971 v D, USSR, Bel, D; 1972 v Cz (sub); (with Coventry C), 1973 v E (2 sub), W (sub), Ni (21)
Stephen, J. F. (Bradford), 1947 v W; 1948 v W (2)
Stevenson, G. (Motherwell), 1928 v W, Ni; 1930 v Ni, E, F; 1931 v E, W; 1932 v W, Ni; 1933 v Ni; 1934 v E; 1935 v Ni (12)
Stewart, A. (Queen's Park), 1888 v Ni; 1889 v W (2)
Stewart, A. (Third Lanark), 1894 v W (1)
Stewart, D. (Dumbarton), 1888 v Ni (1)
Stewart, D. (Queen's Park), 1893 v W; 1894 v Ni; 1897 v Ni (3)
Stewart, D. S. (Leeds U), 1978 v EG (1)
Stewart, G. (Hibernian), 1906 v W, E; (with Manchester C), 1907 v E, W (4)
Stewart, J. (Kilmarnock), 1977 v Ch (sub); (with Middlesbrough), 1979 v N (2)
Stewart, R. (West Ham U), 1981 v W, Ni, E (3)
Stewart, W. E. (Queen's Park), 1898 v Ni; 1900 v Ni (2)
Storrier, D. (Celtic), 1899 v E, W, Ni (3)
Strachan, G. (Aberdeen), 1980 v Ni, W, E, Pol, H (sub); 1981 v Se, P (7)
Sturrock, P. (Dundee U), 1981 v W (sub), Ni, E (sub) (3)
Summers, W. (St Mirren), 1926 v E (1)
Symon, J. S. (Rangers), 1939 v H (1)

Tait, T. S. (Sunderland), 1911 v W (1)
Taylor, J. (Queen's Park), 1872 v E; 1873 v E; 1874 v E; 1875 v E; 1876 v E, W (6)
Taylor, J. D. (Dumbarton), 1892 v W; 1893 v W; 1894 v Ni; (with St Mirren), 1895 v Ni (4)
Taylor, W. (Hearts), 1892 v E (1)
Telfer, W. (Motherwell), 1933 v Ni; 1934 v Ni (2)
Telfer, W. D. (St Mirren), 1954 v W (1)
Templeton, R. (Aston Villa), 1902 v E; (with Newcastle U), 1903 v E, W; 1904 v E; (with Woolwich Arsenal), 1905 v W; (with Kilmarnock), 1908 v Ni; 1910 v E, Ni; 1912 v E, Ni; 1913 v W (11)
Thomson, A. (Arthurlie), 1886 v Ni (1)
Thomson, A. (Airdrieonians), 1909 v Ni (1)
Thomson, A. (Celtic), 1926 v E; 1932 v F; 1933 v W (3)
Thomson, A. (Third Lanark), 1889 v W (1)
Thomson, C. (Hearts), 1904 v Ni; 1905 v E, Ni, W; 1906 v W, Ni; 1907 v E, W, Ni; 1908 v E, W, Ni; (with Sunderland), 1909 v W; 1910 v E; 1911 v Ni; 1912 v E, W; 1913 v E, W; 1914 v E, Ni (21)
Thomson, C. (Sunderland), 1937 v Cz (1)
Thomson, D. (Dundee), 1920 v W (1)
Thomson, J. (Celtic), 1930 v F; 1931 v E, W, Ni (4)
Thomson, J. J. (Queen's Park), 1872 v E; 1873 v E; 1874 v E (3)
Thomson, J. R. (Everton), 1933 v W (1)
Thomson, R. (Celtic), 1932 v W (1)
Thomson, R. W. (Falkirk), 1927 v E (1)
Thomson, S. (Rangers), 1884 v W, Ni (2)
Thomson, W. (Dumbarton), 1892 v W; 1893 v W; 1898 v Ni, W (4)
Thomson, W. (Dundee), 1896 v W (1)
Thomson, W. (St Mirren), 1980 v Ni; 1981 v Ni (sub), Ni (3)
Thornton, W. (Rangers), 1947 v W, Ni; 1948 v E, Ni; 1949 v F; 1952 v D, Se (7)
Toner, W. (Kilmarnock), 1959 v W, Ni (2)
Townsley, T. (Falkirk), 1926 v W (1)
Troup, A. (Dundee), 1920 v E; 1921 v W, Ni; 1922 v Ni; (with Everton), 1926 v E (5)
Turnbull, E. (Hibernian), 1948 v Bel, Sw; 1951 v A; 1958 v H, Pol, Y, Par, F (8)
Turner, T. (Arthurlie), 1884 v W (1)
Turner, W. (Pollokshields), 1885 v Ni; 1886 v Ni (2)

Ure, J. F. (Dundee), 1962 v W, Cz; 1963 v W, Ni, E, A, N, Sp; (with Arsenal), 1964 v Ni, N; 1968 v Ni (11)
Urquhart, D. (Hibernian), 1934 v W (1)

Vallance, T. (Rangers), 1877 v E, W; 1878 v E; 1879 v E, W; 1881 v E, W (7)
Venters, A. (Cowdenbeath), 1934 v Ni; (with Rangers), 1936 v E; 1939 v E (3)

Waddell, T. S. (Queen's Park), 1891 v Ni; 1892 v E; 1893 v E, Ni; 1895 v E, Ni (6)
Waddell, W. (Rangers), 1947 v W; 1949 v E, W, Ni, F; 1950 v E, Ni; 1951 v E, D, F, Bel, A; 1952 v Ni, W; 1954 v Ni; 1955 v W, Ni (17)
Wales, H. M. (Motherwell), 1933 v W (1)
Walker, F. (Third Lanark), 1922 v W (1)
Walker, G. (St Mirren), 1930 v F; 1931 v Ni, A, Sw (4)
Walker, J. (Hearts), 1895 v Ni; 1897 v W; 1898 v Ni; (with Rangers), 1904 v W, Ni (5)
Walker, J. (Swindon T), 1911 v E, W, Ni; 1912 v E, W, Ni; 1913 v E, W, Ni (9)
Walker, R. (Hearts), 1900 v E, Ni; 1901 v E, W; 1902 v E, W, Ni; 1903 v E, W, Ni; 1904 v E, W, Ni; 1905 v E, W, Ni; 1906 v Ni; 1907 v E, Ni; 1908 v E, W, Ni; 1909 v E, W; 1912 v E, W, Ni; 1913 v E, W (29)
Walker, T. (Hearts), 1935 v E, W; 1936 v E, W, Ni; 1937 v G, E, W, Ni, A, Cz; 1938 v E, W, Ni, Cz, Ho; 1939 v E, W, Ni, H (20)
Walker, W. (Clyde), 1909 v Ni; 1910 v Ni (2)
Wallace, I. A. (Coventry C), 1978 v Bul (sub); 1979 v P (sub), W (3)
Wallace, W. S. B. (Hearts), 1965 v Ni; 1966 v E, Ho; (with Celtic), 1967 v E, USSR (sub); 1968 v Ni; 1969 v E (sub) (7)
Wardhaugh, J. (Hearts), 1955 v H; 1957 v Ni (2)
Wark, J. (Ipswich T), 1979 v W, Ni, E, Arg, N (sub); 1980 v Pe, A, Bel (2); 1981 v Is, Ni (11)
Watson, A. (Queen's Park), 1881 v E, W; 1882 v E (3)
Watson, J. (Sunderland), 1903 v E, W; 1904 v E; 1905 v E; (with Middlesbrough), 1909 v E, Ni (6)
Watson, J. (Motherwell), 1948 v Ni; (with Huddersfield T), 1954 v Ni (2)
Watson, J. A. K. (Rangers), 1878 v W (1)
Watson, P. R. (Blackpool), 1934 v A (1)
Watson, R. (Motherwell), 1971 v USSR (1)
Watson, W. (Falkirk), 1898 v W (1)
Watt, F. (Kilbirnie), 1889 v W, Ni; 1890 v W; 1891 v E (4)
Watt, W. W. (Queen's Park), 1887 v Ni (1)
Waugh, W. (Hearts), 1938 v Cz (1)
Weir, A. (Motherwell), 1959 v WG; 1960 v E, P, A, H, T (6)
Weir, J. (Third Lanark), 1887 v Ni (1)
Weir, J. B. (Queen's Park), 1872 v E; 1874 v E; 1875 v E; 1878 v W (4)
Weir, P. (St Mirren), 1980 v N (sub), W, Pol (sub), H (4)
White, John (Albion R), 1922 v W; (with Hearts), 1923 v Ni (2)
White, J. A. (Falkirk), 1959 v WG, Ho, P; 1960 v Ni; (with Tottenham H), 1960 v W, Pol, A, T; 1961 v W; 1962 v Ni, W, E, Cz (2); 1963 v W, Ni, E; 1964 v Ni, W, E, N, WG (22)
White, W. (Bolton W), 1907 v E; 1908 v E (2)
Whitelaw, A. (Vale of Leven), 1887 v Ni; 1890 v W (2)
Wilson, A. (Sheffield W), 1907 v E; 1908 v E; 1912 v E; 1913 v E, W; 1914 v Ni (6)
Wilson, A. (Portsmouth), 1954 v Fi (1)
Wilson, A. N. (Dunfermline), 1920 v E, W, Ni; 1921 v E, W, Ni; (with Middlesbrough), 1922 v E, W, Ni; 1923 v E, W, Ni (12)
Wilson, D. (Queen's Park), 1900 v W (1)
Wilson, D. (Oldham Ath), 1913 v E (1)
Wilson, D. (Rangers), 1961 v E, W, Ni, Ei (2), Cz; 1962 v Ni,

W, E, Cz, U; 1963 v W, E, A, N, Ei, Sp; 1964 v E, WG; 1965 v Ni, E, Fi (22)

Wilson, G. W. (Hearts), 1904 v W; 1905 v E, Ni; 1906 v W; (with Everton), 1907 v E; (with Newcastle U), 1909 v E (6)

Wilson, Hugh, (Newmilns), 1890 v W; (with Sunderland), 1897 v E; (with Third Lanark), 1902 v W; 1904 v Ni (4)

Wilson, J. (Vale of Leven), 1888 v W; 1889 v E; 1890 v E; 1891 v E (4)

Wilson, P. (Celtic), 1926 v Ni; 1930 v F; 1931 v Ni; 1933 v E (4)

Wilson, P. (Celtic), 1975 v Sp (sub) (1)

Wilson, R. P. (Arsenal), 1972 v P, Ho (2)

Wiseman, W. (Queen's Park), 1927 v W; 1930 v Ni (2)

Wood, G. (Everton), 1979 v Ni, E, Arg (sub) (3)

Woodburn, W. A. (Rangers), 1947 v E, Bel, L; 1948 v W, Ni; 1949 v E, F; 1950 v E, W, Ni, P, F; 1951 v E, W, Ni, A (2), D, F, Bel; 1952 v E, W, Ni, USA (24)

Wotherspoon, D. N. (Queen's Park), 1872 v E; 1873 v E (2)

Wright, T. (Sunderland), 1953 v W, Ni, E (3)

Wylie, T. G. (Rangers), 1890 v Ni (1)

Yeats, R. (Liverpool), 1965 v W; 1966 v I (2)

Yorston, B. C. (Aberdeen), 1931 v Ni (1)

Yorston, H. (Aberdeen), 1955 v W (1)

Young, A. (Hearts), 1960 v E, A (sub), H, T; 1961 v W, Ni; (with Everton), Ei; 1966 v P (8)

Young, A. (Everton), 1905 v E; 1907 v W (2)

Young, G. L. (Rangers), 1947 v E, Ni, Bel, L; 1948 v E, Ni, Bel, Sw, F; 1949 v E, W, Ni, F; 1950 v E, W, Ni, Sw, P, F; 1951 v E, W, Ni, A (2), D, F, Bel; 1952 v E, W, Ni, USA, D, Se; 1953 v W, E, Ni, Se; 1954 v Ni, W; 1955 v W, Ni, P, Y; 1956 v Ni, W, E, A; 1957 v E, Ni, W, Y, Sp, Sw (53)

Young, J. (Celtic), 1906 v Ni (1)

Younger, T. (Hibernian), 1955 v P, Y, A, H; 1956 v E, Ni, W, A; (with Liverpool), 1957 v E, Ni, W, Y, Sp (2), Sw, WG; 1958 v Ni, W, E, Sw, H, Pol, Y, Par (24)

WALES

Adams, H. (Berwyn R), 1882 v Ni, E; (with Druids), 1883 v Ni, E (4)

Allchurch, I. J. (Swansea T), 1951 v E, Ni, P, Sw; 1952 v E, S, Ni, R of UK; 1953 v S, E, Ni, F, Y; 1954 v S, E, Ni, A; 1955 v S, E, Ni, Y; 1956 v E, S, Ni, A; 1957 v E, S; 1958 v Ni, Is (2), H (2), M, Sw, Br; (with Newcastle U), 1959 v E, S, Ni; 1960 v E, S; 1961 v Ni, H, Sp (2); 1962 v E, S, Br (2), M; (with Cardiff C), 1963 v S, E, Ni, H (2); 1964 v E; 1965 v S, E, Ni, Gr, I, USSR; 1966 (with Swansea T), v USSR, E, S, D, Br (2), Ch (68)

Allchurch, L. (Swansea T), 1955 v Ni; 1956 v A; 1958 v S, Ni, EG, Is; 1959 v S; (with Sheffield U), 1962 v S, Ni, Br; 1964 v E (11)

Allen, B. W. (Coventry C), 1951 v S, E (2)

Arridge, S. (Bootle), 1892 v S, Ni; (with Everton), 1894 v Ni; 1895 v Ni; 1896 v E; (with New Brighton Tower), 1898 v E, Ni; 1899 v E (8)

Astley, D. J. (Charlton Ath), 1931 v Ni; (with Aston Villa), 1932 v E; 1933 v E, S, Ni; 1934 v E, S; 1935 v S; 1936 v E, Ni; (with Derby Co), 1939 v E, S; (with Blackpool), F (13)

Atherton, R. W. (Hibernian), 1899 v E, Ni; 1903 v E, S, Ni; (with Middlesbrough), 1904 v E, S, Ni; 1905 v Ni (9)

Bailiff, W. E. (Llanelly), 1913 v E, S, Ni; 1920 v Ni (4)

Baker, C. W. (Cardiff C), 1958 v M; 1960 v S, Ni; 1961 v S, E, Ei; 1962 v S (7)

Baker, W. G. (Cardiff C), 1948 v Ni (1)

Bamford, T. (Wrexham), 1931 v E, S, Ni; 1932 v Ni; 1933 v F (5)

Barnes, W. (Arsenal), 1948 v E, S, Ni; 1949 v E, S, Ni; 1950 v E, S, Ni, Bel; 1951 v E, S, Ni, P; 1952 v E, S, Ni, R of UK; 1954 v E, S; 1955 v S, Y (22)

Bartley, T. (Glossop NE), 1898 v E (1)

Beadles, G. H. (Cardiff C), 1925 v E, S (2)

Bell, W. S. (Shrewsbury Engineers), 1881 v E, S; (with Crewe Alex), 1886 v E, S, Ni (5)

Bennion, S. R. (Manchester U), 1926 v S; 1927 v S; 1928 v S, E, Ni; 1929 v S, E, Ni; 1930 v S; 1932 v Ni (10)

Berry, G. F. (Wolverhampton W), 1979 v WG; 1980 v Ei, WG (sub), T (4)

Blew, H. (Wrexham), 1899 v E, S, Ni; 1902 v S, Ni; 1903 v E, S; 1904 v E, S, Ni; 1905 v S, Ni; 1906 v E, S, Ni; 1907 v S; 1908 v E, S, Ni; 1909 v E, S; 1910 v E (22)

Boden, T. (Wrexham), 1880 v E (1)

Bostock, A. M. (Shrewsbury), 1892 v Ni (1)

Boulter, L. M. (Brentford), 1939 v Ni (1)

Bowdler, H. E. (Shrewsbury), 1893 v S (1)

Bowdler, J. C. H. (Shrewsbury), 1890 v Ni; (with Wolverhampton W), 1891 v S; 1892 v Ni; (with Shrewsbury), 1894 v E (4)

Bowen, D. L. (Arsenal), 1955 v S, Y; 1957 v Ni, Cz, EG; 1958 v E, S, Ni, EG, Is (2), H (2), M, Se, Br; 1959 v E, S, Ni (19)

Bowen, E. (Druids), 1880 v S; 1883 v S (2)

Bowsher, S. J. (Burnley), 1929 v Ni (1)

Boyle, T. (C Palace), 1981 v Ei, S (sub) (2)

Britten, T. J. (Parkgrove), 1878 v S; (with Presteigne), 1880 v S (2)

Brookes, S. J. (Llandudno), 1900 v E, Ni (2)

Brown, A. I. (Aberdare Ath), 1926 v Ni (1)

Bryan, T. (Oswestry), 1886 v E, Ni (2)

Buckland, T. (Bangor), 1899 v E (1)

Burgess, W. A. R. (Tottenham H), 1947 v E, S, Ni; 1948 v E, S; 1949 v E, S, Ni, P, Bel, Sw; 1950 v E, S, Ni, Bel; 1951 v S, Ni, P, Sw; 1952 v E, S, Ni, R of UK; 1953 v S, E, Ni, F, Y; 1954 v S, E, Ni, A (32)

Burke, T. (Wrexham), 1883 v E; 1884 v S; 1885 v E, S, Ni; (with Newton Heath), 1887 v E, S; 1888 v S (8)

Burnett, T. B. (Ruabon), 1877 v S (1)

Burton, A. D. (Norwich C), 1963 v Ni, H; (with Newcastle U), 1964 v E; 1969 v S, E, Ni, I, EG; 1972 v Cz (9)

Butler, A. (Druids), 1900 v S, Ni (2)

Butler, J. (Chirk), 1893 v E, S, Ni (3)

Cartwright, L. (Coventry C), 1974 v E (sub), S, Ni; 1976 v S (sub); 1977 v WG (sub); (with Wrexham), 1978 v Ir (sub); 1979 v Ma (7)

Carty, T. (Wrexham), 1889 v Ni (1)

Challen, J. B. (Corinthians), 1887 v E, S; 1888 v E; (with Wellingborough GS), 1890 v E (4)

Chapman, T. (Newtown), 1894 v E, S, Ni; 1895 v S, Ni; (with Manchester C), 1896 v E; 1897 v E (7)

Charles, J. (Swansea C), 1981 v Cz, T (sub), S (sub), USSR (sub) (4)

Charles, M. (Swansea T), 1955 v Ni; 1956 v E, S, A; 1957 v E, Ni, Cz (2), EG; 1958 v E, S, EG, Is (2), H (2), M, Se, Br; 1959 v E, S; (with Arsenal), 1961 v Ni, H, Sp (2); 1962 v E, S; (with Cardiff C), 1962 v Br, Ni; 1963 v S, H (31)

Charles, W. J. (Leeds U), 1950 v Ni; 1951 v Sw; 1953 v Ni, F, Y; 1954 v E, S, Ni, A; 1955 v S, E, Ni, Y; 1956 v E, S, A, Ni; 1957 v E, S, Ni, Cz (2), EG; (with Juventus), 1958 v Is (2), H (2) M, Se; 1960 v S; 1962 v E, Br (2), M; (with Leeds U), 1963 v S; (with Cardiff C), 1964 v S; 1965 v S, USSR (38)

Clarke, R. J. (Manchester C), 1949 v E; 1950 v S, Ni, Bel; 1951 v E, S, Ni, P, Sw; 1952 v S, E, Ni, R of UK; 1953 v S, E; 1954 v E, S, Ni; 1955 v Y, S, E; 1956 v Ni (22)

Collier, D. J. (Grimsby T), 1921 v S (1)

Collins, W. S. (Llanelly), 1931 v S (1)
Conde, C. (Chirk), 1884 v E, S, Ni (3)
Cook, F. C. (Newport Co), 1925 v E, S; (with Portsmouth), 1928 v E, S; 1930 v E, S, Ni; 1932 v E (8)
Crompton, W. (Wrexham), 1931 v E, S, Ni (3)
Cross, E. A. (Wrexham), 1876 v S; 1877 v S (2)
Cross, K. (Druids), 1879 v S; 1881 v E, S (3)
Crowe, V. H. (Aston Villa), 1959 v E, Ni; 1960 v E, Ni; 1961 v S, E, Ni, Ei, H, Sp (2); 1962 v E, S, Br, M; 1963 v H (16)
Cumner, R. H. (Arsenal), 1939 v E, S, Ni (3)
Curtis, A. (Swansea C), 1976 v E, Y (sub), S, Ni, Y (sub), E; 1977 v WG, S (sub), Ni (sub); 1978 v WG, E, S; 1979 v WG, S; (with Leeds U), E, Ni, Ma; 1980 v Ei, WG, T (20)
Curtis, E. R. (Cardiff C), 1928 v S; (with Birmingham), 1932 v S; 1934 v Ni (3)

Daniel, R. W. (Arsenal), 1951 v E, Ni, P; 1952 v E, S, Ni, R of UK; 1953 v S, E, Ni, F, Y; (with Sunderland), 1954 v E, S, Ni; 1955 v E, Ni; 1957 v S, E, Ni, Cz (21)
Darvell, S. (Oxford University), 1897 v S, Ni (2)
Davies, A. (Wrexham), 1876 v S; 1877 v S (2)
Davies, A. (Shrewsbury), 1891 v Ni (1)
Davies, A. (Druids), 1904 v S; (with Middlesbrough), 1905 v S (2)
Davies, A. O. (Barmouth), 1885 v Ni; 1886 v E, S; (with Swifts), 1887 v E, S; 1888 v E, Ni; (with Wrexham), 1889 v S; (with Crewe Alex), 1890 v E (9)
Davies, C. (Brecon), 1899 v Ni; (with Hereford), 1900 v Ni (2)
Davies, C. (Charlton Ath), 1972 v R (sub) (1)
Davies, D. (Bolton W), 1904 v S, Ni; 1908 v E (sub) (3)
Davies, D. W. (Treharris), 1912 v Ni; (with Oldham Ath), 1913 v Ni (2)
Davies, E. Lloyd, (Stoke C), 1904 v E; 1907 v E, S, Ni; (with Northampton T), 1908 v S; 1909 v Ni; 1910 v Ni; 1911 v E, S; 1912 v E, S; 1913 v E, S; 1914 v Ni, E, S (16)
Davies, E. R. (Newcastle U), 1953 v S, E; 1954 v E, S; 1958 v E, EG (6)
Davies, G. (Fulham), 1980 v T, Ic (2)
Davies, Rev. H. (Wrexham), 1928 v Ni (1)
Davies, Idwal (Liverpool Marine), 1923 v S (1)
Davies, J. E. (Oswestry), 1885 v E (1)
Davies, Jas. (Wrexham), 1878 v S (1)
Davies, John. (Wrexham), 1879 v S (1)
Davies, Jos. (Everton), 1889 v S, Ni; (with Chirk), 1891 v Ni; (with Ardwick), v E, S; (with Sheffield U), 1895 v E, S, Ni; (with Manchester C), 1896 v E; (with Millwall), 1897 v E; (with Reading), 1900 v E (11)
Davies, Jos. (Newton Heath), 1888 v E, S, Ni; 1889 v S; 1890 v E; (with Wolverhampton W), 1892 v E; 1893 v E (7)
Davies, J. P. (Druids), 1883 v E, Ni (2)
Davies, Ll. (Wrexham), 1907 v Ni; 1910 v Ni, S, E; (with Everton), 1911 v S, Ni; 1912 v Ni, S, E; 1913 v Ni, S, E; 1914 v Ni (13)
Davies, L. S. (Cardiff C), 1922 v E, S, Ni; 1923 v E, S, Ni; 1924 v E, S, Ni; 1925 v S, Ni; 1926 v E, Ni; 1927 v E, Ni; 1928 v S, Ni, E; 1929 v S, Ni, E; 1930 v E, S (23)
Davies, O. (Wrexham), 1890 v S (1)
Davies, R. (Wrexham), 1883 v Ni; 1884 v Ni; 1885 v Ni (3)
Davies, R. (Druids), 1885 v E (1)
Davies, R. L. (Wrexham), 1892 v Ni (1)
Davies, R. O. (Wrexham), 1892 v Ni, E (2)
Davies, R. T. (Norwich C), 1964 v Ni; 1965 v E; 1966 v Br (2), Ch; (with Southampton), 1967 v S, E, Ni; 1968 v S, Ni, WG; 1969 v S, E, Ni, I, WG, R of UK; 1970 v E, S, Ni; 1971 v Cz, S, E, Ni; 1972 v R, E, S, N; (with Portsmouth), 1974 v E (29)
Davies, R. W. (Bolton W), 1964 v E; 1965 v E, S, Ni, D, Gr, USSR; 1966 v E, S, Ni, USSR, D, Br (2), Ch (sub); 1967 v S; (with Newcastle U), E; 1968 v S, Ni, WG; 1969 v S, E, Ni, I; 1970 v EG; 1971 v R, Cz; (with Manchester C), 1972 v E, S, Ni; (with Manchester U), 1973 v E, S (sub), Ni; (with Blackpool), 1974 v Pol (34)
Davies, Stanley (Preston NE), 1920 v E, S, Ni; (with Everton), 1921 v E, S, Ni; (with WBA), 1922 v E, S, Ni; 1923 v S; 1925 v S, Ni; 1926 v S, E, Ni; 1927 v S; 1928 v S; (with Rotherham U), 1930 v Ni (18)
Davies, T. (Oswestry), 1886 v E (1)
Davies, T. (Druids), 1903 v E, Ni, S; 1904 v S (4)
Davies, W. (Swansea T), 1924 v E, S, Ni; (with Cardiff C), 1925 v E, S, Ni; 1926 v E, S, Ni; 1927 v S; 1928 v Ni; (with Notts Co), 1929 v E, S, Ni; 1930 v E, S, Ni (17)
Davies, W. (Wrexham), 1884 v Ni (1)
Davies, William (Wrexham), 1903 v Ni; 1905 v Ni; (with Blackburn R), 1908 v E, S; 1909 v E, S, Ni; 1911 v E, S, Ni; 1912 v Ni (11)
Davies, W. C. (C Palace), 1908 v S; (with WBA), 1909 v E; 1910 v S; (with C Palace), 1914 v E (4)
Davies, W. D. (Everton), 1975 v H, L, S, E, Ni; 1976 v Y (2), E, Ni; 1977 v WG, S (2), Cz, E, Ni; 1978 v K; (with Wrexham), S, Cz, WG, Ir, E, S, Ni; 1979 v Ma, T, WG S, E, Ni, Ma; 1980 v Ei, WG, T, E, S, Ni, Ic; 1981 v T, Cz, Ei, T, S, E, USSR (44)
Davies, W. H. (Oswestry), 1876 v S; 1877 v S; 1879 v E; 1880 v E (4)
Davies, W. O. (Millwall Ath), 1913 v E, S, Ni; 1914 v S, Ni (5)
Davis, G. (Wrexham), 1978 v Ir, E (sub), Ni (3)
Day, A. (Tottenham H), 1934 v Ni (1)
Deacy, N. (PSV Eindhoven), 1977 v Cz, S, E, Ni; 1978 v K (sub), S (sub), Cz (sub), WG, Ir, S (sub), Ni; (with Beringen), 1979 v T (12)
Dearson, D. J. (Birmingham), 1939 v S, Ni, F (3)
Derrett, S. C. (Cardiff C), 1969 v S, WG; 1970 v I; 1971 v Fi (4)
Dewey, F. T. (Cardiff Corinthians), 1931 v E, S (2)
Doughty, J. (Druids), 1886 v S; (with Newton Heath), 1887 v S, Ni; 1888 v E, S, Ni; 1889 v S (7)
Doughty, R. (Newton Heath and Druids), 1888 v S, Ni; 1890 v E (3)
Durban, A. (Derby Co), 1966 v Br (sub); 1967 v Ni; 1968 v E, S, Ni, WG; 1969 v EG, S, E, Ni, WG; 1970 v E, S, Ni, EG, I; 1971 v R, S, E, Ni, Cz, Fi; 1972 v Fi, Cz, E, S, Ni (27)
Dwyer, P. (Cardiff C), 1978 v Ir, E, S, Ni; 1979 v T, S, E, Ni, Ma (sub); 1980 v WG (10)

Edwards, C. (Wrexham), 1878 v S (1)
Edwards, G. (Birmingham C), 1947 v E, S, Ni; 1948 v E, S, Ni; (with Cardiff C), 1949 v Ni, P, Bel, Sw; 1950 v E, S (12)
Edwards, H. (Wrexham Civil Service), 1878 v S; 1880 v E; 1882 v E, S; 1883 v S; 1884 v Ni; 1887 v Ni (7)
Edwards, R. I. (Chester), 1978 v K (sub); 1979 v Ma, WG; (with Wrexham), 1980 v T (sub) (4)
Edwards, J. H. (Oswestry), 1895 v Ni; 1897 v E, Ni; (with Aberystwyth), 1898 v Ni (4)
Edwards, J. H. (Wanderers), 1876 v S (1)
Edwards, L. T. (Charlton Ath), 1957 v Ni, EG (2)
Edwards, T. (Linfield), 1932 v S (1)
Egan, W. (Chirk), 1892 v S (1)
Ellis, B. (Motherwell), 1932 v E; 1933 v E, S; 1934 v S; 1936 v E; 1937 v S (6)
Ellis, E. (Nunhead), 1931 v E; (with Oswestry), S; 1932 v Ni (3)
Emanuel, W. J. (Bristol C), 1973 v E (sub), Ni (sub) (2)
England, H. M. (Blackburn R), 1962 v Ni, Br, M; 1963 v Ni, H; 1964 v E, S, Ni; 1965 v E, D, Gr (2), USSR, Ni, I; 1966 v E, S, Ni, USSR, D; (with Tottenham H), 1967

v S, E; 1968 v E, Ni, WG; 1969 v EG; 1970 v R of UK, EG, E, S, Ni, I; 1971 v R; 1972 v Fi, E, S, Ni; 1973 v E (3), S; 1974 v Pol; 1975 v H, L (44)
Evans, B. C. (Swansea C), 1972 v Fi, Cz; 1973 v E (2), Pol, S; (with Hereford U), 1974 v Pol (7)
Evans, D. G. (Reading), 1926 v Ni; 1927 v Ni, E; (with Huddersfield T), 1929 v S (4)
Evans, H. P. (Cardiff C), 1922 v E, S, Ni; 1924 v E, S, Ni (6)
Evans, I. (Crystal Palace), 1976 v A, E, Y (2), E, Ni; 1977 v WG, S (2), Cz, E, Ni; 1978 v K (13)
Evans, J. (Cardiff C), 1912 v Ni; 1913 v Ni; 1914 v S; 1920 v S, Ni; 1922 v Ni; 1923 v E, Ni (8)
Evans, J. (Oswestry), 1893 v Ni; 1894 v E, Ni (3)
Evans, J. H. (Southend U), 1922 v E, S, Ni; 1923 v S (4)
Evans, Len (Cardiff C), 1931 v E, S; (with Birmingham), 1934 v Ni (3)
Evans, L. H. (Aberdare Ath), 1927 v Ni (1)
Evans, M. (Oswestry), 1884 v E (1)
Evans, R. (Clapton), 1902 v Ni (1)
Evans, R. E. (Wrexham), 1906 v E, S; (with Aston Villa), Ni; 1907 v E; 1908 v E, S; (with Sheffield U), 1909 v S; 1910 v E, S, Ni (10)
Evans, R. O. (Wrexham), 1902 v Ni; 1903 v E, S, Ni; (with Blackburn R), 1908 v Ni; (with Coventry C), 1911 v E, Ni; 1912 v E, S, Ni (10)
Evans, R. S. (Swansea T), 1964 v Ni (1)
Evans T. J. (Clapton Orient), 1927 v S; 1928 v E, S; (with Newcastle U), Ni (4)
Evans, W. (Tottenham H), 1933 v Ni; 1934 v E, S; 1935 v E; 1936 v E, Ni (6)
Evans, W. A. W. (Oxford University), 1876 v S; 1877 v S (2)
Evans, W. G. (Bootle), 1890 v E; 1891 v E; (with Aston Villa), 1892 v E (3)
Evelyn, E. C. (Crusaders), 1887 v E (1)
Eyton-Jones, J. A. (Wrexham), 1883 v Ni; 1884 v Ni, E, S (4)

Farmer, G. (Oswestry), 1885 v E, S (2)
Finnigan, R. J. (Wrexham), 1930 v Ni (1)
Flynn, B. (Burnley), 1975 v L (2 sub), H (sub), S, E, Ni; 1976 v A, E, Y (2), E, Ni; 1977 v WG (sub), S (2), Cz, E, Ni; 1978 v K (2), S; (with Leeds U), Cz, WG, Ir (sub), E, S, Ni; 1979 v Ma, T, S, E, Ni, Ma; 1980 v Ei, WG, E, S, Ni, Ic; 1981 v T, Cz, Ei, T, S, E, USSR (46)
Ford, T. (Swansea T), 1947 v S; (with Aston Villa), 1947 v Ni; 1948 v S, Ni; 1949 v E, S, Ni, P, Bel, Sw; 1950 v E, S, Ni, Bel; 1951 v S; (with Sunderland), 1951 v E, Ni, P, Sw; 1952 v E, S, Ni, R of UK; 1953 v S, E, Ni, F, Y; (with Cardiff C), 1954 v A; 1955 v S, E, Ni, Y; 1956 v S, Ni, E, A; 1957 v S (38)
Foulkes, H. E. (WBA), 1932 v Ni (1)
Foulkes, W. I. (Newcastle U), 1952 v E, S, Ni, R of UK; 1953 v E, S, F, Y; 1954 v E, S, Ni (11)
Foulkes, W. T. (Oswestry), 1884 v Ni; 1885 v S (2)
Fowler, J. (Swansea T), 1925 v E; 1926 v E, Ni; 1927 v S; 1928 v S; 1929 v E (6)

Garner, J. (Aberystwyth), 1896 v S (1)
Giles, D. (Swansea C), 1980 v E, S, Ni, Ic; 1981 v T, Cz, T (sub), E (sub), USSR (sub) (9)
Gillam, S. G. (Wrexham), 1889 v S, Ni; (with Shrewsbury), 1890 v E, Ni; (with Clapton), 1894 v S (5)
Glascodine, G. (Wrexham), 1879 v E (1)
Glover, E. M. (Grimsby T), 1932 v S; 1934 v Ni; 1936 v S; 1937 v E, S, Ni; 1939 v Ni (7)
Godding, G. (Wrexham), 1923 v S, Ni (2)
Godfrey, B. C. (Preston NE), 1964 v Ni; 1965 v D, I (3)
Goodwin, U. (Ruthin), 1881 v E (1)
Gough, R. T. (Oswestry White Star), 1883 v S (1)
Gray, A. (Oldham Ath), 1924 v E, S, Ni; 1925 v E, S, Ni; 1926 v E, S; 1927 v S; (with Manchester C), 1928 v E, S; 1929 v E, S, Ni; (with Manchester Central), 1930 v S; (with Tranmere R), 1932 v E, S, Ni; (with Chester), 1937 v E, S, Ni; 1938 v E, S, Ni (24)
Green, A. W. (Aston Villa), 1901 v Ni; (with Notts Co), 1903 v E; 1904 v S, Ni; 1906 v Ni, E; (with Nottingham F), 1907 v E; 1908 v S (8)
Green, C. R. (Birmingham C), 1965 v USSR, I; 1966 v E, S, USSR, Br (2); 1967 v E; 1968 v E, S, Ni, WG; 1969 v S, I, Ni (sub) (15)
Green, G. H. (Charlton Ath), 1938 v Ni; 1939 v E, Ni, F (4)
Grey, Dr W. (Druids), 1876 v S; 1878 v S (2)
Griffiths, A. T. (Wrexham), 1971 v Cz (sub); 1975 v A, H (2), L (2), E, Ni; 1976 v A, E, S, E (sub), Ni, Y (2); 1977 v WG, S (17)
Griffiths, F. J. (Blackpool), 1900 v E, S (2)
Griffiths, G. (Chirk), 1887 v Ni (1)
Griffiths, J. H. (Swansea T), 1953 v Ni (1)
Griffiths, M. W. (Leicester C), 1947 v Ni; 1949 v P, Bel; 1950 v E, S, Bel; 1951 v E, Ni, P, Sw; 1954 v A (11)
Griffiths, P. (Chirk), 1884 v E, Ni; 1888 v E; 1890 v S, Ni; 1891 v Ni (6)
Griffiths, S. (Wrexham), 1902 v S (1)
Griffiths, T. P. (Everton), 1927 v E, Ni; 1929 v E; 1930 v E; 1931 v Ni; 1932 v Ni, S, E; (with Bolton W), 1933 v F, E, S, Ni; (with Middlesbrough), 1934 v E, S; 1935 v E, Ni; 1936 v S; (with Aston Villa), Ni; 1937 v E, S, Ni (21)

Hallam, J. (Oswestry), 1889 v E (1)
Hanford, H. (Swansea T), 1934 v Ni; 1935 v S; 1936 v E; (with Sheffield W), 1936 v Ni; 1938 v E, S; 1939 v F (7)
Harrington, A. C. (Cardiff C), 1956 v Ni; 1957 v E, S; 1958 v S, Ni, Is (2); 1961 v S, E; 1962 v E, S (11)
Harris, C. S. (Leeds U), 1976 v E, S; 1978 v WG, Ir, E, S, Ni; 1979 v Ma, T, WG, E (sub), Ma; 1980 v Ni (sub), Ic (sub); 1981 v T, Cz (sub), Ei, T, S, E, USSR (21)
Harris, W. C. (Middlesbrough), 1954 v A; 1957 v EG, Cz; 1958 v E, S, EG (6)
Harrison, W. C. (Wrexham), 1899 v E; 1900 v E, S, Ni; 1901 v Ni (5)
Hayes, A. (Wrexham), 1890 v Ni; 1894 v Ni (2)
Hennessey, W. T. (Birmingham C), 1962 v Ni, Br (2); 1963 v S, E, H (2); 1964 v E, S; 1965 v S, E, D, Gr, USSR; 1966 v E, USSR; (with Nottingham F), 1966 v S, Ni, D, Br (2), Ch; 1967 v S, E; 1968 v E, S, Ni; 1969 v WG, EG, R of UK, EG; (with Derby Co), 1970 v E, S, Ni; 1972 v Fi, Cz, E, S; 1973 v E (39)
Hersee, A. M. (Bangor), 1886 v S, Ni (2)
Hersee, R. (Llandudno), 1886 v Ni (1)
Hewitt, R. (Cardiff C), 1958 v Ni, Is, Se, H, Br (5)
Hewitt, T. J. (Wrexham), 1911 v E, S, Ni; (with Chelsea), 1913 v E, S, Ni; (with South Liverpool), 1914 v E, S (8)
Heywood, D. (Druids), 1879 v E (1)
Hibbott, H. (Newtown Excelsior), 1880 v E, S (2)
Hibbott, R. (Newtown), 1885 v S (1)
Higham, G. G. (Oswestry), 1878 v S; 1879 v E (2)
Hill, M. R. (Ipswich T), 1972 v Cz, R (2)
Hockey, T. (Sheffield U), 1972 v Fi, R; 1973 v E (2); (with Norwich C), Pol, S, E, Ni; (with Aston Villa), 1974 v Pol (9)
Hoddinott, T. F. (Watford), 1921 v E, S (2)
Hodgkinson, A. V. (Southampton), 1908 v Ni (1)
Hole, B. G. (Cardiff C), 1963 v Ni; 1964 v Ni; 1965 v S, E, Ni, D, Gr (2), USSR, I; 1966 v E, S, Ni, USSR, D, Br (2), Ch; (with Blackburn R), 1967 v S, E, Ni; 1968 v E, S, Ni, WG; (with Aston Villa), 1969 v I, WG, EG; 1970 v I; (with Swansea C), 1971 v R (30)
Hole, W. J. (Swansea T), 1921 v Ni; 1922 v E; 1923 v E, Ni; 1928 v E, S, Ni; 1929 v E, S (9)

Hollins, D. M. (Newcastle U), 1962 v Br (sub), M; 1963 v Ni, H; 1964 v E; 1965 v Ni, Gr, I; 1966 v S, D, Br (11)
Hopkins, I. J. (Brentford), 1935 v S, Ni; 1936 v E, Ni; 1937 v E, S, Ni; 1938 v E, Ni; 1939 v E, S, Ni (12)
Hopkins, M. (Tottenham H), 1956 v Ni; 1957 v Ni, S, E, Cz (2), EG; 1958 v E, S, Ni, EG, Is (2), H (2), M, Se, Br; 1959 v E, S, Ni; 1960 v E, S; 1961 v Ni, H, Sp (2); 1962 v Ni, Br (2), M; 1963 v S, Ni, H (34)
Howell, E. G. (Builth), 1888 v Ni; 1890 v E; 1891 v E (3)
Howells, R. G. (Cardiff C), 1954 v E, S (2)
Hugh, A. R. (Newport Co), 1930 v Ni (1)
Hughes, A. (Rhos), 1894 v E, S (2)
Hughes, A. (Chirk), 1907 v Ni (1)
Hughes, A. J. (Aberystwyth), 1879 v S (1)
Hughes, E. (Everton), 1899 v S, Ni; (with Tottenham H), 1901 v E, S; 1902 v Ni; 1904 v E, Ni, S; 1905 v E, Ni, S; 1906 v E, Ni; 1907 v E (14)
Hughes, E. (Wrexham), 1906 v S; (with Nottingham F), 1906 v Ni; 1908 v S, E; 1910 v Ni, E, S; 1911 v Ni, E, S; (with Wrexham), 1912 v Ni, E, S; (with Manchester C), 1913 v E, S; 1914 v N (16)
Hughes, F. W. (Northwich Victoria), 1882 v E, Ni; 1883 v E, Ni, S; 1884 v S (6)
Hughes, I. (Luton T), 1951 v E, Ni, P, Sw (4)
Hughes, J. (Cambridge University), 1877 v S (1)
Hughes, J. (Liverpool), 1905 v E, S, Ni (3)
Hughes, J. I. (Blackburn R), 1935 v Ni (1)
Hughes, P. W. (Bangor), 1887 v Ni; 1889 v Ni, E (3)
Hughes, W. (Bootle), 1891 v E; 1892 v S, Ni (3)
Hughes, W. A. (Blackburn R), 1949 v E, Ni, P, Bel, Sw (5)
Hughes, W. M. (Birmingham), 1938 v E, Ni, S; 1939 v E, Ni, S, F; 1947 v E, S, Ni (10)
Humphreys, J. V. (Everton), 1947 v Ni (1)
Humphreys, R. (Druids), 1888 v Ni (1)
Hunter, W. H. (North End, Belfast), 1887 v Ni (1)

Jackson, W. (St Helens Rec), 1899 v Ni (1)
James, E. (Chirk), 1893 v E, Ni; 1894 v E, S, Ni; 1898 v E; 1899 v Ni (7)
James, E. G. (Blackpool), 1966 v Br (2), Ch; 1967 v Ni; 1968 v S; 1971 v Cz, S, E, Ni (9)
James, L. (Burnley), 1972 v Cz, R, S (sub); 1973 v E (3), Pol, S, Ni; 1974 v Pol, E, S, Ni; 1975 v A, H (2), L (2), S, E, Ni; 1976 v A; (with Derby Co), S, E, Y (2), Ni; 1977 v WG, S (2), Cz, E, Ni; 1978 v K (2); (with QPR), WG; (with Burnley) 1979 v T; 1980 (with Swansea C), v E, S, Ni, Ic; 1981 v T, Ei, T, S, E (46)
James, R. (Swansea C), 1979 v Ma, WG (sub), S, E, Ni, Ma; 1980 v WG (7)
James, W. (West Ham U), 1931 v Ni; 1932 v Ni (2)
Jarrett, R. H. (Ruthin), 1889 v Ni; 1890 v S (2)
Jarvis, A. L. (Hull C), 1967 v S, E, Ni (3)
Jenkins, E. (Lovell's Ath), 1925 v E (1)
Jenkins, J. (Brighton), 1924 v Ni, E, S; 1925 v S, Ni; 1926 v E, S; 1927 v S (8)
Jenkins, R. W. (Rhyl), 1902 v Ni (1)
Jenkyns, C. A. L. (Small Heath), 1892 v E, S, Ni; 1895 v E; (with Woolwich Arsenal), 1896 v S; (with Newton Heath), 1897 v Ni; (with Walsall), 1898 v S, E (8)
Jennings, W. (Bolton W), 1914 v E, S; 1920 v S; 1923 v Ni, E; 1924 v E, S, Ni; 1927 v S, Ni; 1929 v S (11)
John, R. F. (Arsenal), 1923 v S, Ni; 1925 v Ni; 1926 v E; 1927 v E; 1928 v E, Ni; 1930 v E, S; 1932 v E; 1933 v F, Ni; 1935 v Ni; 1936 v S; 1937 v E (15)
John, W. R. (Walsall), 1931 v Ni; (with Stoke C), 1933 v E, S, Ni, F; 1934 v E, S; (with Preston NE), 1935 v E, S; (with Sheffield U), 1936 v E, S, Ni; (with Swansea T), 1939 v E, S (14)
Johnson, M. G. (Swansea T), 1964 v Ni (1)
Jones, A. F. (Oxford University), 1877 v S (1)
Jones, A. T. (Nottingham F), 1905 v E; (with Notts Co), 1906 v E (2)
Jones, Bryn (Wolverhampton W), 1935 v Ni; 1936 v E, S, Ni; 1937 v E, S, Ni; 1938 v E, S, Ni; (with Arsenal), 1939 v E, S, Ni; 1947 v S, Ni; 1948 v E; 1949 v S (17)
Jones, B. S. (Swansea T), 1963 v S, E, Ni, H (2); 1964 v S, Ni; (with Plymouth Arg), 1965 v D; (with Cardiff C), 1969 v S, E, Ni, I (sub), WG, EG, R of UK (15)
Jones, Charlie (Nottingham F), 1926 v E; 1927 v S, Ni; 1928 v E; (with Arsenal), 1930 v E, S; 1932 v E; 1933 v F (7)
Jones, Cliff (Swansea T), 1954 v A; 1956 v E, Ni, S, A; 1957 v E, S, Ni, Cz (2), EG; 1958 v EG, E, S, Is (2); (with Tottenham H), 1958 v Ni, H (2), M, Se, Br; 1959 v Ni; 1960 v E, S, Ni; 1961 v S, E, Ni, Sp, H, Ei; 1962 v E, Ni, S, Br (2), M; 1963 v S, Ni, H; 1964 v E, S, Ni; 1965 v E, S, Ni, D, Gr (2), USSR, I; 1967 v S, E; 1968 v E, S, WG; (with Fulham), 1969 v I, R of UK (59)
Jones, C. W. (Birmingham), 1935 v Ni; 1939 v F (2)
Jones, D. (Chirk), 1888 v S, Ni; (with Bolton W), 1889 v E, S, Ni; 1890 v E, Ni; 1891 v S; 1892 v Ni; 1893 v E; 1894 v E; 1895 v E; 1898 v S; (with Manchester C), 1900 v E, Ni (15)
Jones, D. E. (Norwich C), 1976 v S, E (sub); 1978 v S, Cz, WG, Ir, E; 1980 v E (8)
Jones, D. O. (Leicester C), 1934 v E, Ni; 1935 v E, S; 1936 v E, Ni; 1937 v Ni (7)
Jones, Evan (Chelsea), 1910 v S, Ni; (with Oldham Ath), 1911 v E, S; 1912 v E, S; (with Bolton W), 1914 v Ni (7)
Jones, F. R. (Bangor), 1885 v E, Ni; 1886 v S (3)
Jones, F. W. (Small Heath), 1893 v S (1)
Jones, G. P. (Wrexham), 1907 v S, Ni (2)
Jones, H. (Aberaman), 1902 v Ni (1)
Jones, Humphrey (Bangor), 1885 v E, Ni, S; 1886 v E, Ni, S; (with Queen's Park), 1887 v E; (with East Stirlingshire), 1889 v E, Ni; 1890 v E, S, Ni; (with Queen's Park), 1891 v E, S (14)
Jones, Ivor (Swansea T), 1920 v S, Ni; 1921 v Ni, E; 1922 v S, Ni; (with WBA), 1923 v E, Ni; 1924 v S; 1926 v Ni (10)
Jones, J. (Druids), 1876 v S (1)
Jones, J. (Berwyn Rangers), 1883 v S, Ni; 1884 v S (3)
Jones, J. (Wrexham), 1925 v Ni (1)
Jones, Jeffrey (Llandrindod Wells), 1908 v Ni; 1909 v Ni; 1910 v S (3)
Jones, J. L. (Sheffield U), 1895 v E, S, Ni; 1896 v Ni, S, E; 1897 v Ni, S, E; (with Tottenham H), 1898 v Ni, E, S; 1899 v S, Ni; 1900 v S; 1902 v E, S, Ni; 1904 v E, S, Ni (21)
Jones, J. Love (Stoke C), 1906 v S; (with Middlesbrough), 1910 v Ni (2)
Jones, J. O. (Bangor), 1901 v S, Ni (2)
Jones, J. P. (Liverpool), 1976 v A, E, S; 1977 v WG, S (2), Cz, E, Ni; 1978 v K (2), S, Cz, WG, Ir, E, S, Ni; (with Wrexham), 1979 v Ma, T, WG, S, E, Ni, Ma; 1980 v Ei, WG, T, E, S, Ni, Ic; 1981 v T, Ei, T, S, E, USSR (38)
Jones, J. T. (Stoke C), 1912 v E, S, Ni; 1913 v E, Ni; 1914 v S, Ni; 1920 v E, S, Ni; (with C Palace), 1921 v E, S; 1922 v E, S, Ni (15)
Jones, K. (Aston Villa), 1950 v S (1)
Jones, Leslie J. (Cardiff C), 1933 v F; (with Coventry C), 1935 v Ni; 1936 v S; 1937 v E, S, Ni; (with Arsenal), 1938 v E, S, Ni; 1939 v E, S (11)
Jones, P. W. (Bristol R), 1971 v Fi (1)
Jones, R. (Bangor), 1887 v S; 1889 v E; (with Crewe Alex), 1890 v E (3)
Jones, R. (Bangor), 1900 v S, Ni (2)
Jones, R. (Druids), 1899 v S; (with Millwall), 1906 v S, Ni (3)
Jones, R. A. (Druids), 1884 v E, Ni, S; 1885 v S (4)
Jones, R. S. (Everton), 1894 v Ni; (with Leicester Fosse), 1898 v S (2)
Jones, S. (Wrexham), 1887 v Ni; (with Chester), 1890 v S (2)
Jones, S. (Wrexham), 1893 v S, Ni; (with Burton Swifts), 1895 v S; 1896 v E, Ni (5)
Jones, T. (Manchester U), 1926 v Ni; 1927 v E, Ni; 1930 v Ni (4)
Jones, T. D. (Aberdare), 1908 v Ni (1)
Jones, T. G. (Everton), 1938 v Ni; 1939 v E, S, Ni; 1947 v E,

S; 1948 v E, S, Ni; 1949 v E, Ni, P, Bel, Sw; 1950 v E, S, Bel (17)
Jones, T. J. Sheffield W), 1932 v Ni; 1933 v F (2)
Jones, W. (Druids), 1899 v E (1)
Jones, W. E. A. (Swansea T), 1947 v E, S; (with Tottenham H), 1949 v E, S (4)
Jones, W. J. (Aberdare), 1901 v E, S; (with West Ham U), 1902 v E, S (4)
Jones, W. Lot (Manchester C), 1905 v E, Ni; 1906 v E, S, Ni; 1907 v E, S, Ni; 1908 v S; 1909 v E, S, Ni; 1910 v E; 1911 v E; 1913 v E, S; 1914 v S, Ni; (with Southend U), 1920 v E, Ni (20)
Jones, W. P. (Druids), 1889 v E, Ni; (with Wynstay), 1890 v S, Ni (4)
Jones, W. R. (Aberystwyth), 1897 v S (1)

Keenor, F. C. (Cardiff C), 1920 v E, Ni; 1921 v E, Ni, S; 1922 v Ni; 1923 v E, Ni, S; 1924 v E, Ni, S; 1925 v E, Ni, S; 1926 v S; 1927 v E, Ni, S; 1928 v E, Ni, S; 1929 v E, Ni, S; 1930 v E, Ni, S; 1931 v E, Ni, S; (with Crewe Alex), 1933 v S (32)
Kelly, F. C. (Wrexham), 1899 v S, Ni; (with Druids), 1902 v Ni (3)
Kelsey, A. J. (Arsenal), 1954 v Ni, A; 1955 v S, Ni, Y; 1956 v E, Ni, S, A; 1957 v E, Ni, S, Cz (2), EG; 1958 v E, S, Ni, Is (2), H (2), M, Se, Br; 1959 v E, S; 1960 v E, Ni, S; 1961 v E, Ni, S, H, Sp (2); 1962 v E, S, Ni, Br (2) (41)
Kenrick, S. L. (Druids), 1876 v S; 1877 v S; (with Oswestry), 1879 v E, S; (with Shropshire Wanderers), 1881 v E (5)
Ketley, C. F. (Druids), 1882 v Ni (1)
King, J. (Swansea T), 1955 v E (1)
Kinsey, N. (Norwich C), 1951 v Ni, P, Sw; 1952 v E; (with Birmingham C), 1954 v Ni; 1956 v E, S (7)
Krzywicki, R. L. (Huddersfield T), 1970 v E, S; (with WBA), Ni, EG, I; 1971 v R, Fi; 1972 v Cz (sub) (8)

Lambert, R. (Liverpool), 1947 v S; 1948 v E; 1949 v P, Bel, Sw (5)
Lathom, G. (Liverpool), 1905 v E, S; 1906 v S; 1907 v E, S, Ni; 1908 v E; 1909 v Ni; (with Southport Central), 1910 v E; (with Cardiff C), 1913 v Ni (10)
Lawrence, E. (Clapton Orient), 1930 v Ni; (with Notts Co), 1932 v S (2)
Lawrence, S. (Swansea T), 1932 v Ni; 1933 v F; 1934 v S, E, Ni; 1935 v E, S; 1936 v S (8)
Lea, A. (Wrexham), 1889 v E; 1891 v S, Ni; 1893 v Ni (4)
Lea, C. (Ipswich T), 1965 v Ni, I (2)
Leary, P. (Bangor), 1889 v Ni (1)
Leek, K. (Leicester C), 1961 v S, E, Ni, H, Sp (2); (with Newcastle U), 1962 v S; (with Birmingham C), v Br (sub), M; 1963 v E; 1965 v S, Gr; (with Northampton T), 1965 v Gr (13)
Lever, A. R. (Leicester C), 1953 v S (1)
Lewis, B. (Wrexham), 1891 v Ni; 1892 v S, E, Ni; (with Middlesbrough), 1893 v S, E; (with Wrexham), 1894 v S, E, Ni; 1895 v S (10)
Lewis, D. (Arsenal), 1927 v E; 1928 v Ni; 1930 v E (3)
Lewis, D. J. (Swansea T), 1933 v E, S (2)
Lewis, J. (Bristol R), 1906 v E (1)
Lewis, J. (Cardiff C), 1926 v S (1)
Lewis, T. (Wrexham), 1881 v E, S (2)
Lewis, W. L. (Swansea T), 1927 v E, Ni; 1928 v E, Ni; 1929 v S; (with Huddersfield T), 1930 v E (6)
Lewis, W. (Bangor), 1885 v E; 1886 v E, S; 1887 v E, S; 1888 v E; 1889 v E, Ni, S; (with Crewe Alex), 1890 v E, Ni, S; 1891 v E, Ni, S; 1892 v E, S, Ni; 1894 v E, S, Ni; (with Chester), 1895 v S, Ni, E; 1896 v E, S, Ni; (with Manchester C), 1897 v E, S; (with Chester), 1898 v Ni (30)
Lloyd, B. W. (Wrexham), 1976 v A, E, S (3)
Lloyd, J. W. (Wrexham), 1879 v S; (with Newtown), 1885 v S (2)
Lloyd, R. A. (Ruthin), 1891 v Ni; 1895 v S (2)
Lockley, A. (Chirk), 1898 v Ni (1)
Lowrie, G. (Coventry C), 1948 v E, S, Ni; (with Newcastle U), 1949 v P (4)
Lucas, P. M. (Leyton Orient), 1962 v Ni, M; 1963 v S, E (4)
Lucas, W. H. (Swansea T), 1949 v S, Ni, P, Bel, Sw; 1950 v E; 1951 v E (7)
Lumberg, A. (Wrexham), 1929 v Ni; 1930 v E, S; (with Wolverhampton W), 1932 v S (4)

McMillan, R. (Shrewsbury Engineers), 1881 v E, S (2)
Mahoney, J. F. (Stoke C), 1968 v E; 1969 v EG; 1971 v Cz; 1973 v E (3), Pol, S, Ni; 1974 v Pol, E, S, Ni; 1975 v A, H (2), L (2), S, E, Ni; 1976 v A, Y (2), E, Ni; 1977 v WG, Cz, S, E, Ni; (with Middlesbrough), 1978 v K (2), S, Cz, Ir, E (sub), S, Ni; 1979 v WG, S, E, Ni, Ma; (with Swansea C), 1980 v Ei, WG, T (sub) (47)
Martin, T. J. (Newport Co), 1930 v Ni (1)
Mates, J. (Chirk), 1891 v Ni; 1897 v E, S (3)
Mathews, R. W. (Liverpool), 1921 v Ni; (with Bristol C), 1923 v E; (with Bradford), 1926 v Ni (3)
Matthews, W. (Chester), 1905 v Ni; 1908 v E (2)
Matthias, J. S. (Brymbo), 1896 v S, Ni; (with Shrewsbury), 1897 v E, S; (with Wolverhampton W), 1899 v S (5)
Matthias, T. J. (Wrexham), 1914 v S, E; 1920 v Ni, S, E; 1921 v S, E, Ni; 1922 v S, E, Ni; 1923 v S (12)
Mays, A. W. (Wrexham), 1929 v Ni (1)
Medwin, T. C. (Swansea T), 1953 v Ni, F, Y; (with Tottenham H), 1957 v E, S, Ni, Cz (2), EG; 1958 v E, S, Ni, Is (2), H (2), M, Br; 1959 v E, S, Ni; 1960 v E, S, Ni; 1961 v S, Ei, Sp; 1963 v E, H (30)
Meredith, S. (Chirk), 1900 v S; 1901 v S, E, Ni; (with Stoke C), 1902 v E; 1903 v Ni; 1904 v E; (with Leyton), 1907 v E (8)
Meredith, W. H. (Manchester C), 1895 v E, Ni; 1896 v E, Ni; 1897 v E, Ni, S; 1898 v E, Ni; 1899 v E; 1900 v E, Ni; 1901 v E, Ni; 1902 v E, S; 1903 v E, S, Ni; 1904 v E; 1905 v E, S; (with Manchester U), 1907 v E, S, Ni; 1908 v E, Ni; 1909 v E, S, Ni; 1910 v E, S, Ni; 1911 v E, S, Ni; 1912 v E, S, Ni; 1913 v E, S, Ni; 1914 v E, S, Ni; 1920 v E, S, Ni (48)
Mielczarek, R. (Rotherham U), 1971 v Fi (1)
Millership, H. (Rotherham Co), 1920 v E, S, Ni; 1921 v E, S, Ni (6)
Millington, A. H. (WBA), 1963 v S, E, H; (with C Palace), 1965 v E, USSR; (with Peterborough U), 1966 v Ch, Br; 1967 v E, Ni; 1968 v Ni, WG; 1969 v I, EG; (with Swansea) 1970 v E, S, Ni; 1971 v Cz, Fi; 1972 v Fi (sub), Cz, R (21)
Mills, T. J. (Clapton Orient), 1934 v E, Ni; (with Leicester C), 1935 v E, S (4)
Mills-Roberts, R. H. (St Thomas' Hospital), 1885 v E, S, Ni; 1886 v E; 1887 v E; (with Preston NE), 1888 v E, Ni; (with Llanberis), 1892 v E (8)
Moore, G. (Cardiff C), 1960 v E, S, Ni; 1961 v Ei, Sp; (with Chelsea), 1962 v Br; 1963 v Ni, H; (with Manchester U), 1964 v S, Ni; (with Northampton T), 1966 v Ni, Ch; (with Charlton Ath), 1969 v S, E, Ni, R of UK; 1970 v E, S, Ni, I; 1971 v R (21)
Morgan, J. R. (Cambridge University), 1877 v S; (with Swansea), 1879 v S; (with Derby School Staff), 1880 v E, S; 1881 v E, S; 1882 v E, S, Ni; (with Swansea), 1883 v E (10)
Morgan, J. T. (Wrexham), 1905 v Ni (1)
Morgan-Owen, H. (Oxford University), 1901 v E, S; 1902 v S; 1906 v E, Ni; (with Welshpool), 1907 v S (6)
Morgan-Owen, M. M. (Oxford University), 1897 v S, Ni; 1898 v E, S; 1899 v S; 1900 v E; (with Corinthians), 1903 v S; 1906 v S, E, Ni; 1907 v E (11)
Morley, E. J. (Swansea T), 1925 v E; (with Clapton Orient), 1929 v E, S, Ni (4)
Morris, A. G. (Aberystwyth), 1896 v E, Ni, S; (with Swindon T), 1897 v E; 1898 v S; (with Nottingham F), 1899 v E, S; 1903 v E, S; 1905 v E, S; 1907 v E, S; 1908 v E; 1910 v E, S, Ni; 1911 v E, S, Ni; 1912 v E (21)
Morris, C. (Chirk), 1900 v E, S, Ni; (with Derby Co), 1901 v

E, S, Ni; 1902 v E, S; 1903 v E, S, Ni; 1904 v Ni; 1905 v E, S, NI; 1906 v S; 1907 v S; 1908 v E, S; 1909 v E, S, Ni; 1910 v E, S, Ni; (with Huddersfield T), 1911 v E, S, Ni (28)
Morris, E. (Chirk), 1893 v E, S, Ni (3)
Morris, H. (Sheffield U), 1894 v S; (with Manchester C), 1896 v E; (with Grimsby T), 1897 v E (3)
Morris, J. (Oswestry), 1887 v S (1)
Morris, J. (Chirk), 1898 v Ni (1)
Morris, R. (Chirk), 1900 v E, Ni; 1901 v Ni; 1902 v S; (with Shrewsbury T), 1903 v E, Ni (6)
Morris, R. (Druids), 1902 v E, S; (with Newtown), 1902 v Ni; (with Liverpool), 1903 v S, Ni; 1904 v E, S, Ni; (with Leeds C), 1906 v S; (with Grimsby T), 1907 v Ni; (with Plymouth Arg), 1908 v Ni (11)
Morris, S. (Birmingham), 1937 v E, S; 1938 v E, S; 1939 v F (5)
Morris, W. (Burnley), 1947 v Ni; 1949 v E; 1952 v S, Ni, R of UK (5)
Moulsdale, J. R. B. (Corinthians), 1925 v Ni (1)
Murphy, J. P. (WBA), 1933 v F, E, Ni; 1934 v E, S; 1935 v E, S, Ni; 1936 v E, S, Ni; 1937 v S, Ni; 1938 v E, S (15)

Nardiello, D. (Coventry C), 1978 v Cz, WG (sub) (2)
Neal, J. E. (Colwyn Bay), 1931 v E, S (2)
Newnes, J. (Nelson), 1926 v Ni (1)
Newton, L. F. (Cardiff Corinthians), 1912 v Ni (1)
Nicholas, D. S. (Stoke C), 1923 v S; (with Swansea T), 1927 v E, Ni (3)
Nicholas, P. (C Palace), 1979 v S (sub), Ni (sub), Ma; 1980 v Ei, WG, T, E, S, Ni, Ic; 1981 v T, Cz, E; (with Arsenal), T, S, E, USSR (17)
Nicholls, J. (Newport Co), 1924 v E, Ni; (with Cardiff C), 1925 v E, S (4)
Nock, W. (Newtown), 1897 v Ni (1)
Nurse, M. T. G. (Swansea T), 1960 v E, Ni; 1961 v S, E, H, Ni, Ei, Sp (2); (with Middlesbrough), 1963 v E, H; 1964 v S (12)
O'Callaghan, E. (Tottenham H), 1929 v Ni; 1930 v S; 1932 v S, E; 1933 v Ni, S, E; 1934 v Ni, S, E; 1935 v E (11)
Oliver, A. (Blackburn R), 1905 v E; (with Bangor), S (2)
O'Sullivan, P. A. (Brighton), 1973 v S (sub); 1976 v S; 1979 v Ma (sub) (3)
Owen, D. (Oswestry), 1879 v E (1)
Owen, E. (Ruthin Grammar School), 1884 v E, Ni, S (3)
Owen, G. (Chirk), 1888 v S; (with Newton Heath), 1889 v S, Ni; 1892 v E; 1893 v Ni (5)
Owen, T (Oswestry), 1879 v E (1)
Owen, Trevor (Crewe Alex), 1899 v E, S (2)
Owen, W. (Chirk), 1884 v E; 1885 v Ni; 1887 v E; 1888 v E; 1889 v E, Ni, S; 1890 v S, Ni; 1891 v E, S, Ni; 1892 v E, S; 1893 v S, Ni (16)
Owen, W. P. (Ruthin), 1880 v E, S; 1881 v E, S; 1882 v E, S, Ni; 1883 v E, S; 1884 v E, S, Ni (12)
Owens, J. (Wrexham), 1902 v S (1)

Page, M. E. (Birmingham C), 1971 v Fi; 1972 v S, Ni; 1973 v E (1 + 1 sub), Ni; 1974 v S, Ni; 1975 v H, L, S, E, Ni; 1976 v E, Y (2), E, Ni; 1977 v WG, S; 1978 v K (sub + 1), WG, Ir, E, S; 1979 v Ma, WG (28)
Palmer, D. (Swansea T), 1957 v Cz; 1958 v E, EG (3)
Parris, J. E. (Bradford), 1932 v Ni (1)
Parry, B. J. (Swansea T), 1951 v S (1)
Parry, C. (Everton), 1891 v E, S; 1893 v E; 1894 v E; 1895 v E, S; (with Newtown), 1896 v E, S, Ni; 1897 v Ni; 1898 v E, S, Ni (13)
Parry, E. (Liverpool), 1922 v S; 1923 v E, Ni; 1925 v Ni; 1926 v Ni (5)
Parry, H. (Newtown), 1895 v Ni (1)
Parry, M. (Liverpool), 1901 v E, S, Ni; 1902 v E, S, Ni; 1903 v E, S; 1904 v E, Ni; 1906 v E; 1908 v E, S, Ni; 1909 v E, S (16)
Parry, T. D. (Oswestry), 1900 v E, S, Ni; 1901 v E, S, Ni; 1902 v E (7)
Paul, R. (Swansea T), 1949 v E, S, Ni, P, Sw; 1950 v E, S, Ni, Bel; (with Manchester C), 1951 v S, E, Ni, P, Sw; 1952 v E, S, Ni, R of UK; 1953 v S, E, Ni, F, Y; 1954 v E, S, Ni; 1955 v S, E, Y; 1956 v E, Ni, S, A (33)
Peake, E. (Aberystwyth), 1908 v Ni; (with Liverpool), 1909 v Ni, S, E; 1910 v S, Ni; 1911 v Ni; 1912 v E; 1913 v E, Ni; 1914 v Ni (11)
Peers, E. J. (Wolverhampton W), 1914 v Ni, S, E; 1920 v E, S; 1921 v S, Ni, E; (with Port Vale), 1922 v E, S, Ni; 1923 v E (12)
Perry, E. (Doncaster R), 1938 v E, S, Ni (3)
Phennah, E. (Civil Service), 1878 v S (1)
Phillips, C. (Wolverhampton W), 1931 v Ni; 1932 v E; 1933 v S; 1934 v E, S, Ni; 1935 v E, S, Ni; 1936 v S; (with Aston Villa), 1936 v E, Ni; 1938 v S (13)
Phillips, L. (Cardiff C), 1971 v Cz, S, E, Ni; 1972 v Cz, R, S, Ni; 1973 v E; 1974 v Pol (sub), Ni; 1975 v A; (with Aston Villa), H (2), L (2), S, E, Ni; 1976 v A, E, Y (2), E, Ni; 1977 v WG, S (2), Cz, E; 1978 v K (2), S, Cz, WG, E, S; 1979 v Ma; (Swansea C), T, WG, S, E, Ni, Ma; 1980 v Ei, WG, T, S (sub), Ni, Ic; 1981 v T, Cz, T, S, E, USSR (56)
Phillips, T. J. S. (Chelsea), 1973 v E; 1974 v E; 1975 v H (sub); 1978 v K (4)
Phoenix, H. (Wrexham), 1882 v S (1)
Poland, G. (Wrexham), 1939 v Ni, F (2)
Pontin, K. (Cardiff C), 1980 v E (sub), S (2)
Powell, A. (Leeds U), 1947 v E, S; 1948 v E, S, Ni; (with Everton), 1949 v E; 1950 v Bel; (with Birmingham C), 1951 v S (8)
Powell, D. (Wrexham), 1968 v WG; (with Sheffield U), 1969 v S, E, Ni, I, WG; 1970 v E, S, Ni, EG; 1971 v R (11)
Powell, I. V. (QPR), 1947 v E; 1948 v E, S, Ni; (with Aston Villa), 1949 v Bel; 1950 v S, Bel; 1951 v S (8)
Powell, J. (Druids), 1878 v S; 1880 v E, S; 1882 v E, S, Ni; 1883 v E, S, Ni; (with Bolton W), 1884 v E; (with Newton Heath), 1887 v E, S; 1888 v E, S, Ni (15)
Powell, Seth (WBA), 1885 v S; 1886 v E, Ni; 1891 v E, S; 1892 v E, S (7)
Price, H. (Aston Villa), 1907 v S; (with Burton U), 1908 v Ni; (with Wrexham), 1909 v S, E, Ni (5)
Price, J. (Wrexham), 1877 v S; 1878 v S; 1879 v E; 1880 v E, S; 1881 v E, S; (with Druids), 1882 v S, E, Ni; 1883 v S, Ni (12)
Price, P. (Luton T), 1980 v E, S, Ni, Ic; 1981 v T, Cz, Ei, T, S, E, USSR (11)
Pring, K. D. (Rotherham U), 1966 v Ch, D; 1967 v Ni (3)
Pryce-Jones, A. W. (Newtown), 1895 v E (1)
Pryce-Jones, W. E. (Cambridge University), 1887 v S; 1888 v S, E, Ni; 1890 v Ni (5)
Pugh, A. (Rhostyllen), 1889 v S (sub) (1)
Pugh, D. H. (Wrexham), 1896 v S, Ni; 1897 v S, Ni; (with Lincoln C), 1900 v S; 1901 v S, E (7)
Pugsley, J. (Charlton Ath), 1930 v Ni (1)
Pullen, W. J. (Plymouth Arg), 1926 v E (1)

Rankmore, F. E. J. (Peterborough), 1966 v Ch (sub) (1)
Ratcliffe, K. (Everton), 1981 v Cz, Ei, T, S, E, USSR (6)
Rea, J. C. (Aberystwyth), 1894 v Ni, S, E; 1895 v S; 1896 v S, Ni; 1897 v S, Ni; 1898 v Ni (9)
Reece, G. I. (Sheffield U), 1966 v E, S, Ni, USSR; 1967 v S; 1969 v R of UK (sub); 1970 v I (sub); 1971 v S, E, Ni, Fi; 1972 v Fi, R, E (sub), S, Ni; (with Cardiff C), 1973 v E (sub), Ni; 1974 v Pol (sub), E, S, Ni; 1975 v A, H (2), L (2), S, Ni (29)
Reed, W. G. (Ipswich T), 1955 v S, Y (2)
Rees, R. R. (Coventry C), 1965 v S, E, Ni, D, Gr (2), I, R; 1966 v E, S, Ni, R, D, Br (2), Ch; 1967 v E, Ni; 1968 v E, S, Ni; (with WBA), WG; 1969 v I; (with Nottingham F), 1969 v WG, EG, S (sub), R of UK; 1970 v E, S, Ni, EG, I; 1971 v Cz, R, E (sub), Ni (sub), Fi; 1972 v Cz (sub), R (39)

Rees, W. (Cardiff C), 1949 v Ni, Bel, Sw; (with Tottenham H), 1950 v Ni (4)
Richards, A. (Barnsley), 1932 v S (1)
Richards, D. (Wolverhampton W), 1931 v Ni; 1933 v E, S, Ni; 1934 v E, S, Ni; 1935 v E, S, Ni; 1936 v S; (with Brentford), 1936 v E, Ni; 1937 v S, E; (with Birmingham), 1937 v Ni; 1938 v E, S, Ni; 1939 v E, S (21)
Richards, G. (Druids), 1899 v E, S, Ni; (with Oswestry), 1903 v Ni; (with Shrewsbury), 1904 v S; 1905 v Ni (6)
Richards, R. W. (Wolverhampton W), 1920 v E, S; 1921 v Ni; 1922 v E, S; (with West Ham U), 1924 v E, S, Ni; (with Mold), 1926 v S (9)
Richards, S. V. (Cardiff C), 1947 v E (1)
Richards, W. E. (Fulham), 1933 v Ni (1)
Roach, J. (Oswestry), 1885 v Ni (1)
Robbins, W. W. (Cardiff C), 1931 v E, S; 1932 v Ni, E, S; (with WBA), 1933 v F, E, S, Ni; 1934 v S; 1936 v S (11)
Roberts, D. F. (Oxford U), 1973 v Pol, E (sub), Ni; 1974 v E, S; 1975 v A; (with Hull C), L, Ni; 1976 v S, Ni, Y; 1977 v E (sub), Ni; 1978 v K (1 + sub), S, Ni (18)
Roberts, J. G. (Arsenal), 1971 v S, E, Ni, Fi; 1972 v Fi, E, Ni; (with Birmingham C), 1973 v E (2), Pol, S, Ni; 1974 v Pol, E, S, Ni; 1975 v A, H, S, E; 1976 v E, S (22)
Roberts, J. H. (Bolton), 1949 v Bel (1)
Roberts, J. (Corwen), 1879 v S; 1880 v E, S; 1882 v E, S, Ni; (with Berwyn R), 1883 v E (7)
Roberts, J. (Ruthin), 1881 v S; 1882 v S (2)
Roberts, J. (Bradford C), 1906 v Ni; 1907 v Ni (2)
Roberts, Jas. (Chirk), 1898 v S (1)
Roberts, Jas (Wrexham), 1913 v S, Ni (2)
Roberts, P. S. (Portsmouth), 1974 v E; 1975 v A, H, L (4)
Roberts, R. (Rhos), 1891 v Ni; (with Crewe Alex), 1893 v E (2)
Roberts, R. (Druids), 1884 v S; (with Bolton W), 1887 v S; 1888 v S, E; 1889 v S, E; 1890 v S; 1892 v Ni; (with PNE), S (9)
Roberts, R. (Wrexham), 1886 v Ni; 1887 v Ni; 1891 v Ni (3)
Roberts, W. (Llangollen), 1879 v E, S; 1880 v E, S; (with Berwyn R), 1881 v S; 1883 v E, S (7)
Roberts, W. (Wrexham), 1886 v E, S, Ni; 1887 v Ni (4)
Roberts, W. H. (Ruthin), 1882 v E, S; 1883 v E, S, Ni; (with Rhyl), 1884 v S (6)
Rodrigues, P. J. (Cardiff C), 1965 v Ni, Gr (2); 1966 v USSR, E, S, D; (with Leicester C), v Ni, Br (2), Ch; 1967 v S; 1968 v E, S, Ni; 1969 v E, Ni, EG, R of UK; 1970 v E, S, Ni, EG; (with Sheffield W), 1971 v R, E, S, Cz, Ni; 1972 v Fi, Cz, R, E, Ni (sub); 1973 v E (3), Pol, S, Ni; 1974 v Pol (40)
Rogers, J. P. (Wrexham), 1896 v E, S, Ni (3)
Rogers, W. (Wrexham), 1931 v E, S (2)
Roose, L. R. (Aberystwyth), 1900 v Ni; (with London Welsh), 1901 v E, S, Ni; (with Stoke C), 1902 v E, S; 1904 v E; (with Everton), 1905 v S, E; (with Stoke C), 1906 v E, S, Ni; 1907 v E, S, Ni; (with Sunderland), 1908 v E, S; 1909 v E, S, Ni; 1910 v E, S, Ni; 1911 v S (24)
Rouse, R. V. (C Palace), 1959 v Ni (1)
Rowlands, A. C. (Tranmere R), 1914 v E (1)
Rowley, T. (Tranmere R), 1959 v Ni (1)
Rush, I. (Liverpool), 1980 v S (sub), Ni; 1981 v E (sub) (3)
Russell, M. R. (Merthyr T), 1912 v S, Ni; 1914 v E; (with Plymouth Arg), 1920 v E, S, Ni; 1921 v E, S, Ni; 1922 v E, Ni; 1923 v E, S, Ni; 1924 v E, S, Ni; 1925 v E, S; 1926 v E, S; 1928 v S; 1929 v E (23)

Sabine, H. W. (Oswestry), 1887 v Ni (1)
Savin, G. (Oswestry), 1878 v S (1)
Sayer, P. (Cardiff C), 1977 v Cz, S, E, Ni; 1978 v K (2), S (7)
Scrine, F. H. (Swansea T), 1950 v E, Ni (2)
Sear, C. R. (Manchester C), 1963 v E (1)
Shaw, E. G. (Oswestry), 1882 v Ni; 1884 v S, Ni (3)
Sherwood, A. T. (Cardiff C), 1947 v E, Ni; 1948 v S, Ni; 1949 v E, S, Ni, P, Sw; 1950 v E, S, Ni, Bel; 1951 v E, S, Ni, P, Sw; 1952 v E, S, Ni, R of UK; 1953 v S, E, Ni, F, Y; 1954 v E, S, Ni, A; 1955 v S, E, Y, Ni; 1956 v E, S, Ni, A; (with Newport Co), 1957 v E, S (41)
Shone, W. W. (Oswestry), 1879 v E (1)
Shortt, W. W. (Plymouth Arg), 1947 v Ni; 1950 v Ni, Bel; 1952 v E, S, Ni, R of UK; 1953 v S, E, Ni, F, Y (12)
Showers, D. (Cardiff C), 1975 v E (sub), Ni (2)
Sidlow, C. (Liverpool), 1947 v E, S; 1948 v E, S, Ni; 1949 v S; 1950 v E (7)
Sisson, H. (Wrexham Olympic), 1885 v Ni; 1886 v S, Ni (3)
Smallman, D. P. (Wrexham), 1974 v E (sub), S (sub), Ni; (with Everton), 1975 v H (sub), E, Ni (sub); 1976 v A (7)
Sprake, G. (Leeds U), 1964 v S, Ni; 1965 v S, D, Gr; 1966 v E, Ni, USSR; 1967 v S; 1968 v E, S; 1969 v S, E, Ni, WG, R of UK; 1970 v EG, I; 1971 v R, S, E, Ni; 1972 v Fi, E, S, Ni; 1973 v E (2), Pol, S, Ni; 1974 v Pol; (with Birmingham C), S, Ni; 1975 v A, H, L (37)
Stansfield, F. (Cardiff C), 1949 v S (1)
Stevenson, B. (Leeds U), 1978 v Ni; 1979 v Ma, T, S, E, Ni, Ma; 1980 v WG, T, Ic (sub) (10)
Stitfall, R. F. (Cardiff C), 1953 v E; 1957 v Cz(2)
Sullivan, D. (Cardiff C), 1953 v Ni, F, Y; 1954 v Ni; 1955 v E, Ni; 1957 v E, S; 1958 v Ni, H (2), Se, Br; 1959 v S, Ni; 1960 v E, S (17)

Tapscott, D. R. (Arsenal), 1954 v A; 1955 v S, E, Ni, Y; 1956 v E, Ni, S, A; 1957 v Ni, Cz, EG; (with Cardiff C), 1959 v E, Ni (14)
Taylor, J. (Wrexham), 1898 v E (1)
Taylor, O. D. S. (Newtown), 1893 v S, Ni; 1894 v S, Ni (4)
Thomas, C. (Druids), 1899 v Ni; 1900 v S (2)
Thomas, D. A. (Swansea T), 1957 v Cz; 1958 v EG (2)
Thomas, D. S. (Fulham), 1948 v E, S, Ni; 1949 v S (4)
Thomas, E. (Cardiff Corinthians), 1925 v E (1)
Thomas, G. (Wrexham), 1885 v E, S (2)
Thomas, H. (Manchester U), 1927 v E (1)
Thomas, M. (Wrexham), 1977 v WG, S (1 + 1 sub), Ni (sub); 1978 v K (sub), S, Cz, Ir, E, Ni (sub); 1979 v Ma; (with Manchester U), T, WG, Ma (sub); 1980 v Ei, WG (sub), T, E, S, Ni; 1981 v Cz, S, E, USSR (24)
Thomas, R. J. (Swindon T), 1967 v Ni; 1968 v WG; 1969 v E, Ni, I, WG, R of UK; 1970 v E, S, Ni, EG, I; 1971 v S, E, Ni, R, Cz; 1972 v Fi, Cz, R, E, S, Ni; 1973 v E (3), Pol, S, Ni; 1974 v Pol; (with Derby Co), E, S, Ni; 1975 v H (2), L (2), S, E, Ni; 1976 v A, Y, E; 1977 v Cz, S, E, Ni; 1978 v K, S; (with Cardiff C), Cz (50)
Thomas, T. (Bangor), 1898 v S, Ni (2)
Thomas, W. R. (Newport Co), 1931 v E, S (2)
Thomson, D. (Druids), 1876 v S (1)
Thomson, G. F. (Druids), 1876 v S; 1877 v S (2)
Toshack, J. B. (Cardiff C), 1969 v S, E, Ni, WG, EG, R of UK; 1970 v EG, I; (with Liverpool), 1971 v S, E, Ni, Fi; 1972 v Fi, E; 1973 v E (3), Pol, S; 1975 v A, H (2), L (2), S, E; 1976 v Y (2), E; 1977 v S; 1978 v K (2), S, Cz; (Swansea C), 1979 v WG (sub), S, E, Ni, Ma; 1980 v WG (40)
Townsend, W. (Newtown), 1887 v Ni; 1893 v Ni (2)
Trainer, H. (Wrexham), 1895 v E, S, Ni (3)
Trainer, J. (Bolton W), 1887 v S; (with Preston NE), 1888 v S; 1889 v E; 1890 v S; 1891 v S; 1892 v Ni, S; 1893 v E; 1894 v Ni, E; 1895 v Ni, E; 1896 v S; 1897 v Ni, S, E; 1898 v S, E; 1899 v Ni, S (20)
Turner, H. G. (Charlton Ath), 1937 v E, S, Ni; 1938 v E, S, Ni; 1939 v Ni, F (8)
Turner, J. (Wrexham), 1892 v E (1)
Turner, R. E. (Wrexham), 1891 v E, Ni (2)
Turner, W. H. (Wrexham), 1887 v E, Ni; 1890 v S; 1891 v E, S (5)

Vaughan, Jas (Druids), 1893 v E, S, Ni; 1899 v E (4)
Vaughan, John (Oswestry), 1879 v S; 1880 v S; 1881 v E, S; 1882 v E, S, Ni; 1883 v E, S, Ni; (with Bolton W), 1884 v E (11)
Vaughan, J. O. (Rhyl), 1885 v Ni; 1886 v Ni, E, S (4)

Vaughan, T. (Rhyl), 1885 v E (1)
Vearncombe, G. (Cardiff C), 1958 v EG; 1961 v Ei (2)
Vernon, T. R. (Blackburn R), 1957 v Ni, Cz (2), EG; 1958 v E, S, EG, Se; 1959 v S; (with Everton), 1960 v Ni; 1961 v S, E, Ei; 1962 v Ni, Br (2), M; 1963 v S, E, H; 1964 v E, S; (with Stoke C), 1965 v Ni, Gr, I; 1966 v E, S, Ni, USSR, D; 1967 v Ni; 1968 v E (32)
Villars, A. K. (Cardiff C), 1974 v E, S, Ni (sub) (3)
Vizard, E. T. (Bolton W), 1911 v E, S, Ni; 1912 v E, S; 1913 v S; 1914 v E, Ni; 1920 v E; 1921 v E, S, Ni; 1922 v E, S; 1923 v E, Ni; 1924 v E, S, Ni; 1926 v E, S; 1927 v S (22)

Walley, J. T. (Watford), 1971 v Cz (1)
Walsh, I. (C Palace), 1980 v Ei, T, E, S, Ic; 1981 v T, Cz, Ei, T, S, E, USSR (12)
Ward, D. (Bristol R), 1959 v E; (with Cardiff C), 1962 v E (2)
Warner, J. (Swansea T), 1937 v E; (with Manchester U), 1939 v F (2)
Warren, F. W. (Cardiff C), 1929 v Ni; (with Middlesbrough), 1931 v Ni; 1933 v F, E; (with Hearts), 1937 v Ni; 1938 v Ni (6)
Watkins, A. E. (Leicester Fosse), 1898 v E, S; (with Aston Villa), 1900 v E, S; (with Millwall), 1904 v Ni (5)
Watkins, W. M. (Stoke C), 1902 v E; 1903 v E, S; (with Aston Villa); 1904 v E, S, Ni; (with Sunderland), 1905 v E, S, Ni; (with Stoke C), 1908 v Ni (10)
Webster, C (Manchester U), 1957 v Cz; 1958 v H, M, Br (4)
Whatley, W. J. (Tottenham H), 1939 v E, S (2)
White, P. F. (London Welsh), 1896 v Ni (1)
Wilcocks, A. R. (Oswestry), 1890 v Ni (1)
Wilding, J. (Wrexham O), 1885 v E, S, Ni; 1886 v E, Ni; (with Bootle), 1887 v E; 1888 v S, Ni; (with Wrexham), 1892 v S (9)
Williams, A. L. (Wrexham), 1931 v E (1)
Williams, B. D. (Swansea T), 1928 v Ni, E; 1930 v E, S; (with Everton), 1931 v Ni; 1932 v E; 1933 v E, S, Ni; 1935 v Ni (10)
Williams, B. (Bristol C), 1930 v Ni (1)
Williams, D. R. (Merthyr T), 1921 v E, S; (with Sheffield W), 1923 v S; 1926 v S; 1927 v E, Ni; (with Manchester U), 1929 v E, S (8)
Williams, E. (Crewe Alex), 1893 v E, S (2)
Williams, E. (Druids), 1901 v E, Ni, S; 1902 v E, Ni (5)
Williams, G. (Chirk), 1893 v S; 1894 v S; 1895 v E, S, Ni; 1898 v Ni (6)
Williams, G. E. (WBA), 1960 v Ni; 1961 v S, E, Ei; 1963 v Ni, H; 1964 v E, S, Ni; 1965 v S, E, Ni, D, Gr (2), USSR, I; 1966 v Ni, Br (2), Ch; 1967 v S, E, Ni; 1968 v Ni; 1969 v I (26)
Williams, G. G. (Swansea T), 1961 v Ni, H, Sp (2); 1962 v E (5)
Williams, G. J. J. (Cardiff C), 1951 v Sw (1)
Williams, G. O. (Wrexham), 1907 v Ni (1)
Williams, H. J. (Swansea), 1965 v Gr (2); 1972 v R (3)
Williams, H. T. (Newport Co), 1949 v Ni, Sw; (with Leeds U), 1950 v Ni; 1951 v S (4)
Williams, J. H. (Oswestry), 1884 v E (1)
Williams, J. T. (Wrexham), 1939 v F (1)
Williams J. T. (Middlesbrough), 1925 v Ni (1)
Williams, J. W. (C Palace), 1912 v S, Ni (2)
Williams, R. (Newcastle U), 1935 v S, E (2)
Williams, R. P. (Caernarvon), 1886 v S (1)
Williams, S. G. (WBA), 1954 v A; 1955 v E, Ni; 1956 v E, S, A; 1958 v E, S, Ni, Is (2), H (2), M, Se, Br; 1959 v E, S, Ni; 1960 v E, S, Ni; 1961 v Ni, Ei, H, Sp (2); 1962 v E, S, Ni, Br (2), M; (with Southampton), 1963 v S, E, H (2); 1964 v E, S; 1965 v S, E, D; 1966 v D (43)
Williams, W. (Druids), 1876 v S; 1878 v S; (with Oswestry), 1879 v E, S; (with Druids), 1880 v E, S; 1881 v E, S; 1882 v E, S, Ni; 1883 v Ni (12)
Williams, W. (Northampton T), 1925 v S (1)
Witcomb, D. F. (WBA), 1947 v E, S; (with Sheffield W), 1947 v Ni (3)
Woosnam, A. P. (Leyton Orient), 1959 v S; (with West Ham U), v E; 1960 v E, S, Ni; 1961 v S, E, Ni, Ei, Sp, H; 1962 v E, S, Ni, Br, (with Aston Villa), 1963 v Ni, H (17)
Woosnam, G. (Newton White Star), 1879 v S (1)
Worthington, T. (Newtown), 1894 v S (1)
Wynn, G. A. (Chirk), 1903 v Ni; (with Wrexham), 1909 v E, S, Ni; (with Manchester C), 1910 v E; 1911 v Ni; 1912 v E, S; 1913 v E, S; 1914 v E, S (12)

Yorath, T. C. (Leeds U), 1970 v I; 1971 v S, E, Ni; 1972 v Cz, E, S, Ni; 1973 v E, Pol, S; 1974 v Pol, E, S, Ni; 1975 v A, H (2), L (2), S; 1976 v A, E, S, Y (2), E, Ni; (with Coventry C), 1977 v WG, S (2), Cz, E, Ni; 1978 v K (2), S, Cz, WG, Ir, E, S, Ni; 1979 v T, WG, S, E, Ni; (with Tottenham H), 1980 v Ei, T, E, S, Ni, Ic; 1981 v T, Cz; (with Vancouver W), Ei, T, USSR (59)

REPUBLIC OF IRELAND

Aherne, T. (Belfast Celtic), 1946 v P, Sp; (with Luton T), 1950 v Fi, E, Fi, Se, Bel; 1951 v N, Arg, N; 1952 v WG (2), A, Sp; 1953 v F; 1954 v F (16)
Ambrose, P. (Shamrock R), 1955 v N, Ho; 1964 v Pol, N, E (5)
Anderson, J. (Preston NE), 1980 v Cz (sub), US (sub) (2)
Andrews, P. (Bohemians), 1936 v Ho (1)
Arrigan, T. (Waterford), 1938 v N (1)

Bailham, E. (Shamrock R), 1964 v E (1)
Barber, E. (Shelbourne), 1966 v Sp; (with Birmingham C), 1966 v Bel (2)
Barry, P. (Fordsons), 1928 v Bel; 1929 v Bel (2)
Bermingham, J. (Bohemians), 1929 v Bel (1)
Bermingham, P. (St James' Gate), 1935 v H (1)
Braddish, S. (Dundalk), 1978 v Pol (1)
Bonner, P. (Celtic), 1981 v Pol (1)
Bradshaw, P. (St James' Gate), 1939 v Sw, Pol, H (2), G (5)
Brady, F. (Fordsons), 1926 v I; 1927 v I (2)
Brady, T. R. (QPR), 1964 v A (2), Sp (2), Pol, N (6)
Brady, W. L. (Arsenal), 1975 v USSR, T, Sw, USSR, Sw; 1976 v T, N, Pol; 1977 v E, T, F (2), Sp, Bul; 1978 v Bul, N; 1979 v Ni, E, D, Bul, WG, Arg; 1980 v W, Bul, E, Cy; (with Juventus), 1981 v Ho, Bel, F, Cy, Bel (31)
Breen, T. (Manchester U), 1937 v Sw, F; (with Shamrock R), 1947 v E, Sp, P (5)
Brennan, F. (Drumcondra), 1965 v Bel (1)
Brennan, S. A. (Manchester U), 1965 v Sp; 1966 v Sp, A, Bel; 1967 v Sp, T, Sp; 1969 v Cz, D, H; 1970 v S, Cz, D, H, Pol (sub), WG; (with Waterford), 1971 v Pol, Se, I (19)
Brown, J. (Coventry C), 1937 v Sw, F (2)
Browne, W. (Bohemians), 1964 v A, Sp, E (3)
Burke, F. (Cork), 1934 v Bel (1)
Burke, F. (Cork Ath), 1952 v WG (1)
Burke, J. (Shamrock R), 1929 v Bel (1)
Byrne, A. B. (Southampton), 1970 v D, Pol, WG; 1971 v Pol, Se (2), I (2), A; 1973 v F, USSR (sub), F, N; 1974 v Pol (14)
Byrne, D. (Shelbourne), 1929 v Bel; (with Shamrock R), 1932 v Sp; (with Coleraine), 1934 v Bel (3)
Byrne, J. (Bray Unknowns), 1928 v Bel (1)
Byrne, P. (Shelbourne), 1931 v Sp; 1932 v Ho; (with Drumcondra), 1934 v Ho (3)
Byrne, S. (Bohemians), 1931 v Sp (1)

Campbell, N. (St Patrick's Ath), 1971 v A (sub); (with Fortuna, Cologne), 1972 v Ir, Ec, Ch, P; 1973 v USSR, F (sub); 1976 v N; 1977 v Sp, Bul (sub) (10)

Cannon, H. (Bohemians), 1926 v I; 1928 v Bel (2)
Cantwell, N. (West Ham U), 1954 v L; 1956 v Sp, Ho; 1957 v D, WG, E (2); 1958 v D, Pol, A; 1959 v Pol, Cz (2); 1960 v Se, Ch, Se; 1961 v N; (with Manchester U), 1961 v S (2); 1962 v Cz (2), A; 1963 v Ic (2), S; 1964 v A, Sp, E; 1965 v Pol, Sp; 1966 v Sp (2), A, Bel; 1967 v Sp, T (36)
Carey, J. J. (Manchester U), 1938 v N, Cz, Pol; 1939 v Sw, Pol, H (2), G; 1946 v P, Sp; 1947 v E, Sp, P; 1948 v P, Sp; 1949 v Sw, Bel, P, Se, Sp; 1950 v Fi, E, Fi, Se; 1951 v N, Arg, N; 1953 v F, A (29)
Carolan, J. (Manchester U), 1960 v Se, Ch (2)
Carroll, B. (Shelbourne), 1949 v Bel; 1950 v Fi (2)
Carroll, T. R. (Ipswich T), 1968 v Pol; 1969 v Pol, A, D; 1970 v Cz, Pol, WG; 1971 v Se; (with Birmingham C), 1972 v Ir, Ec, Ch, P; 1973 v USSR (2), Pol, F, N (17)
Chandler, J. (Leeds U), 1980 v Cz (sub), US (2)
Chatton, H. A. (Shelbourne), 1931 v Sp; (with Dumbarton), 1932 v Sp; (with Cork), 1934 v Ho (3)
Clarke, J. (Drogheda U), 1978 v Pol (sub) (1)
Clarke, K. (Drumcondra), 1948 v P, Sp (2)
Clarke, M. (Shamrock R), 1950 v Bel (1)
Clinton, T. J. (Everton), 1951 v N; 1954 v F, L (3)
Coad, P. (Shamrock R), 1947 v E, Sp, P; 1948 v P, Sp; 1949 v Sw, Bel, P, Se; 1951 v N (sub); 1952 v Sp (11)
Coffey, T. (Drumcondra), 1950 v Fi (1)
Colfer, M. D. (Shelbourne), 1950 v Bel; 1951 v N (2)
Collins, F. (Jacobs), 1927 v I (1)
Conmy, O. M. (Peterborough U), 1965 v Bel; 1967 v Cz; 1968 v Cz, Pol; 1970 v Cz (5)
Connolly, J. (Fordsons), 1926 v I (1)
Connolly, N. (Cork), 1937 v G (1)
Conroy, G. A. (Stoke C), 1970 v Cz, D, H, Pol, WG; 1971 v Pol, Se (2), I; 1973 v USSR, F, USSR, N; 1974 v Pol, Br, U, Ch; 1975 v T, Sw, USSR, Sw; 1976 v T (sub), Pol; 1977 v E, T, Pol (26)
Conway, J. P. (Fulham), 1967 v Sp, T, Sp; 1968 v Cz; 1969 v A (sub), H; 1970 v S, Cz, D, H, Pol, WG; 1971 v I, A; 1974 v U, Ch; 1976 v N, Pol; (with Manchester C), 1977 v Pol (19)
Corr, P. J. (Everton), 1949 v P, Sp; 1950 v E, Se (4)
Courtney, E. (Cork U), 1946 v P (1)
Cummins, G. P. (Luton T), 1954 v L (2); 1955 v N (2), WG; 1956 v Y, Sp; 1958 v D, Pol, A; 1959 v Pol, Cz (2); 1960 v Se, Ch, WG, Se; 1961 v S (2) (19)
Cuneen, T. (Limerick), 1951 v N (1)
Curtis, D. P. (Shelbourne), 1957 v D, WG; (with Bristol C), 1957 v E (2); 1958 v D, Pol, A; (with Ipswich T), 1959 v Pol; 1960 v Se, Ch, WG, Se; 1961 v N, S; 1962 v A; 1963 v Ic (with Exeter C), 1964 v A (17)
Cusack, S. (Limerick), 1953 v F (1)

Daly, G. A. (Manchester U), 1973 v Pol (sub), N; 1974 v Br (sub), U (sub); 1975 v Sw (sub); 1977 v E, T, F; (with Derby Co), F, Bul; 1978 v Bul, T, D; 1979 v Ni, E, D, Bul; 1980 v Ni, E, Cy, Sw, Arg; (with Coventry C), 1981 v Ho, Bel, Cy, W, Bel, Cz, WG 'B', Pol (sub) (30)
Daly, J. (Shamrock R), 1932 v Ho; 1935 v Sw (2)
Daly, M. (Wolverhampton W), 1978 v T, Pol (2)
Daly, P. Shamrock R), 1950 v Fi (sub) (1)
Davis, T. L. (Oldham Ath), 1937 v G, H; (with Tranmere R), 1938 v Cz, Pol (4)
Dempsey, J. T. (Fulham), 1967 v Sp, Cz; 1968 v Cz, Pol; 1969 v Pol, A, D; (with Chelsea), 1969 v Cz, D; 1970 v H, WG; 1971 v Pol, Se (2), I; 1972 v Ir, Ec, Ch, P (19)
Dennehy, J. (Cork Hibernians), 1972 v Ec (sub), Ch; (with Nottingham F), 1973 v USSR (sub), Pol, F, N; 1974 v Pol (sub); 1975 v T (sub); (with Walsall), 1976 v Pol (sub); 1977 v Pol (sub) (10)
Desmond, P. (Middlesbrough), 1950 v Fi, E, Fi, Se (4)
Devine, J. (Arsenal), 1980 v Cz, Ni; 1981 v Cz, WG 'B' (4)
Donnelly, J. (Dundalk), 1935 v H, Sw, G; 1936 v Ho, Sw, H, L; 1937 v G, H; 1938 v N (10)
Donnelly, T. (Drumcondra), 1938 v N; (Shamrock R), 1939 v Sw (2)
Donovan, D. C. (Everton), 1955 v N, Ho, N, WG; 1957 v E (5)
Donovan, T. (Aston Villa), 1980 v Cz; 1981 v WG 'B' (sub) (2)
Dowdall, C. (Fordsons), 1928 v Bel; (with Barnsley), 1929 v Bel; (with Cork), 1931 v Sp (3)
Doyle, C. (Shelbourne), 1959 v Cz (1)
Doyle, D. (Shamrock R), 1926 v I (1)
Doyle, L. (Dolphin), 1932 v Sp (1)
Duffy, B. (Shamrock R), 1950 v Bel (1)
Duggan, H. A. (Leeds U), 1927 v I; 1930 v Bel; 1936 v H, L; (with Newport Co), 1938 v N (5)
Dunne, A. P. (Manchester U), 1962 v A; 1963 v Ic, S; 1964 v A, Sp, Pol, N, E; 1965 v Pol, Sp; 1966 v Sp (2), A, Bel; 1967 v Sp, T, Sp; 1969 v Pol, D, H; 1970 v H; 1971 v Se, I, A; (with Bolton W), 1974 v Br (sub), U, Ch; 1975 v T, Sw, USSR, Sw; 1976 v T (32)
Dunne, J. (Sheffield U), 1930 v Bel; (with Arsenal), 1936 v Sw, H, L; (with Southampton), 1937 v Sw, F; (with Shamrock R), 1938 v N (2), Cz, Pol; 1939 v Sw, Pol, H (2), G (15)
Dunne, J. C. (Fulham), 1971 v A (1)
Dunne, L. (Manchester C), 1935 v Sw, G (2)
Dunne, P. A. J. (Manchester U), 1965 v Sp; 1966 v Sp (2), WG; 1967 v T (5)
Dunne, S. (Luton T), 1953 v F, A; 1954 v F, L; 1956 v Sp, Ho; 1957 v D, WG, E; 1958 v D, Pol, A; 1959 v Pol; 1960 v WG, Se (15)
Dunne, T. (St Patrick's Ath), 1956 v Ho; 1957 v D, WG (3)
Dunning, P. (Shelbourne), 1971 v Se, I (2)
Dunphy, E. M. (York C), 1966 v Sp; (with Millwall), 1966 v WG; 1967 v T, Sp, T, Cz; 1968 v Cz, Pol; 1969 v Pol, A, D (2), H; 1970 v D, H, Pol, WG (sub); 1971 v Pol, Se (2), I (2), A (23)
Dwyer, N. M. (West Ham U), 1960 v Se, Ch, WG, Se; (with Swansea T), 1961 v W, N, S (2); 1962 v Cz (2); 1964 v Pol (sub), N, E; 1965 v Pol (14)

Egan, R. (Dundalk), 1929 v Bel (1)
Eglington, T. J. (Shamrock R), 1946 v P, Sp; (with Everton), 1947 v E, Sp, P; 1948 v P; 1949 v Sw, P, Se; 1951 v N, Arg; 1952 v WG (2), A, Sp; 1953 v F, A; 1954 v F, L, F; 1955 v N, Ho, WG; 1956 v Sp (24)
Ellis, P. (Bohemians), 1935 v Sw, G; 1936 v Ho, Sw, L; 1937 v G, H (7)

Fagan, E. (Shamrock R), 1973 v N (sub) (1)
Fagan, F. (Manchester C), 1955 v N; 1960 v Se; (with Derby Co), 1960 v Ch, WG, Se; 1961 v W, N, S (8)
Fagan, K. (Shamrock R), 1926 v I (1)
Fallon, S. (Celtic), 1951 v N; 1952 v WG (2), A, Sp; 1953 v F; 1955 v N, WG (8)
Fallon, W. J. (Notts Co), 1935 v H; 1936 v H; 1937 v H, Sw, F; 1939 v Sw, Pol; (with Sheffield W), 1939 v H, G (9)
Farquharson, T. G. (Cardiff C), 1929 v Bel; 1930 v Bel; 1931 v Sp; 1932 v Sp (4)
Farrell, P. (Hibernian), 1937 v Sw, F (2)
Farrell, P. D. (Shamrock R), 1946 v P, Sp; (with Everton), 1947 v Sp, P; 1948 v P, Sp; 1949 v Sw, P (sub), Sp; 1950 v E, Fi, Se; 1951 v Arg, N; 1952 v WG (2), A, Sp; 1953 v F, A; 1954 v F (2); 1955 v N, Ho, WG; 1956 v Y, Sp; 1957 v E (28)
Feenan, J. J. (Sunderland), 1937 v Sw, F (2)

Finucane, A. (Limerick), 1967 v T, Cz; 1969 v Cz, D, H; 1970 v S, Cz; 1971 v Se, I, I (sub); 1972 v A (11)
Fitzgerald, F. J. (Waterford), 1955 v Ho; 1956 v Ho (2)
Fitzgerald, P. J. (Leeds U), 1961 v W, N, S; 1962 v Cz (2) (5)
Fitzpatrick, K. (Limerick), 1970 v Cz (1)
Fitzsimons, A. G. (Middlesbrough), 1950 v Fi, Bel; 1952 v WG (2), A, Sp; 1953 v F, A; 1954 v F, L, F; 1955 v Ho, N, WG; 1956 v Y, Sp, Ho; 1957 v D, WG, E (2); 1958 v D, Pol, A; 1959 v Pol; (with Lincoln C), 1959 v Cz (26)
Flood, J. J. (Shamrock R), 1926 v I; 1929 v Bel; 1930 v Bel; 1931 v Sp; 1932 v Sp (5)
Fogarty, A. (Sunderland), 1960 v WG, Se; 1961 v S; 1962 v Cz (2); 1963 v Ic (2), S (sub); 1964 v A (2); (with Hartlepools U), Sp (11)
Foley, J. (Cork), 1934 v Bel, Ho; (with Celtic), 1935 v H, Sw, G; 1937 v G, H (7)
Foley, M. (Shelbourne), 1926 v I (1)
Foley, T. C. (Northampton T), 1964 v Sp, Pol, N; 1965 v Pol, Bel; 1966 v Sp (2), WG; 1967 v Cz (9)
Foy, T. (Shamrock R), 1938 v N; 1939 v H (2)
Fullam, J. (Preston NE), 1961 v N; (with Shamrock R), 1964 v Sp, Pol, N; 1966 v A, Bel; 1968 v Pol; 1969 v Pol, A, D; 1970 v Cz (sub) (11)
Fullam, R. (Shamrock R), 1926 v I; 1927 v I (2)

Gallagher, C. (Celtic), 1967 v T, Cz (2)
Gallagher, M. (Hibernian), 1954 v L (1)
Gallagher, P. (Falkirk), 1932 v Sp (1)
Gannon, E. (Notts Co), 1949 v Sw; (with Sheffield W), 1949 v Bel, P, Se, Sp; 1950 v Fi; 1951 v N; 1952 v G, A; 1954 v L, F; 1955 v N; (with Shelbourne), 1955 v N, WG (14)
Gannon, M. (Shelbourne), 1972 v A (1)
Gaskins, P. (Shamrock R), 1934 v Bel, Ho; 1935 v H, Sw, G; (with St James' Gate), 1938 v Cz, Pol (7)
Gavin, J. T. (Norwich C), 1950 v Fi (2); 1953 v F; 1954 v L; (with Tottenham H), 1955 v Ho, WG; (with Norwich C), 1957 v D (7)
Geoghegan, M. (St James' Gate), 1937 v G; 1938 v N (2)
Gibbons, A. (St Patrick's Ath), 1952 v WG; 1954 v L; 1956 v Y, Sp (4)
Gilbert, R. (Shamrock R), 1966 v WG (1)
Giles, C. (Doncaster R), 1951 v N (1)
Giles, M. J. (Manchester U), 1960 v Se, Ch; 1961 v W, N, S (2); 1962 v Cz (2), A; 1963 v Ic, S; (with Leeds U), 1964 v A (2), Sp (2), Pol, N, E; 1965 v Sp; 1966 v Sp (2), A, Bel; 1967 v Sp, T (2); 1969 v A, D, Cz; 1970 v S, Pol, WG; 1971 v I; 1973 v F, USSR; 1974 v Br, U, Ch; 1975 v USSR, T, Sw, USSR, Sw; (with WBA), 1976 v T; 1977 v E, T, F (2), Pol, Bul; (with Shamrock R), 1978 v Bul, T, Pol, N, D; 1979 v Ni, D, Bul, WG, Arg (60)
Givens, D. J. (Manchester U), 1969 v D, H; 1970 v S, Cz, D, H; (with Luton T), 1970 v Pol, WG; 1971 v Se, I (2), A; 1972 v Ir, Ec, P; 1973 v F, USSR, Pol, F, N; (with QPR), 1974 v Pol, Br, U, Ch; 1975 v USSR, T, Sw, USSR, Sw; 1976 v T, N, Pol; 1977 v E, T, F (2), Sp, Bul; 1978 v Bul, N, D; (with Birmingham C), 1979 v Ni (sub), E, D, Bul, WG, Arg; 1980 v US (sub), Ni (sub), Sw, Arg; 1981 v Ho, Bel, Cy (sub), W (55)
Glen, W. (Shamrock R), 1927 v I; 1929 v Bel; 1930 v Bel; 1932 v Sp; 1936 v Ho, Sw, H, L (8)
Glynn, D. (Drumcondra), 1952 v WG; 1955 v N (2)
Godwin, T. F. (Shamrock R), 1949 v P, Se, Sp; 1950 v Fi, E; (with Leicester C), 1950 v Fi, Se, Bel; 1951 v N; (with Bournemouth & Boscombe Ath), 1956 v Ho; 1957 v E; 1958 v D, Pol (13)
Golding, L. (Shamrock R), 1928 v Bel; 1930 v Bel (2)
Gorman, W. C. (Bury), 1936 v Sw, H, L; 1937 v G, H; 1938 v N, Cz, Pol; 1939 v Sw, Pol, H; (with Brentford); 1947 v E, P (13)
Grace, J. (Drumcondra), 1926 v I (1)
Grealish, A. (Orient), 1976 v N, Pol, N, D; 1979 v Ni, E, WG, Arg; (with Luton T), 1980 v W, Cz, Bul, US, Ni, E, Cy, Sw, Arg; 1981 v Ho, Bel, F, Cy, W, Bel, WG 'B', Pol (25)
Gregg, E. (Bohemians), 1978 v Pol, D (sub); 1979 v E (sub), D, Bul, WG, Arg; 1980 v W, Cz (9)
Griffith, R. (Walsall), 1935 v H (1)
Grimes, A. A. (Manchester U), 1978 v T, Pol, N (sub); 1980 v Bul, US, Ni, E, Cy; 1981 v Cz, WG 'B' (sub), Pol (11)

Hale, A. (Aston Villa), 1962 v A; (with Doncaster R), 1963 v Ic; 1964 v Sp (2); (with Waterford), 1967 v Sp; 1968 v Pol (sub); 1969 v Pol, A, D; 1970 v S, Cz; 1971 v Pol (sub); 1972 v A (sub) (13)
Hamilton, T. (Shamrock R), 1959 v Cz (2) (2)
Hand, E. K. (Portsmouth), 1969 v Cz (sub); 1970 v Pol, WG; 1971 v Pol, A; 1973 v USSR, F, USSR, Pol, F; 1974 v Pol, Br, U, Ch; 1975 v T, Sw, USSR, Sw; 1976 v T (19)
Harrington, W. (Cork), 1936 v Ho, Sw, H, L (4)
Hartnett, J. B. (Middlesbrough), 1949 v Sp; 1954 v L (2)
Haverty, J. (Arsenal), 1956 v Ho; 1957 v D, WG, E (2); 1958 v D, Pol, A; 1959 v Pol; 1960 v Se, Ch; 1961 v W, N, S (2); (with Blackburn R), 1962 v Cz (2); (with Millwall), 1963 v S; 1964 v A, Sp, Pol, N, E; (with Celtic), 1965 v Pol; (with Bristol R), 1965 v Sp; (with Shelbourne), 1966 v Sp (2), WG, A, Bel; 1967 v T, Sp (32)
Hayes, A. W. P. (Southampton), 1979 v D (1)
Hayes, W. E. (Huddersfield T), 1947 v E, P (2)
Hayes, W. J. (Limerick), 1949 v Bel (1)
Healey, R. (Cardiff C), 1977 v Pol; 1980 v E (sub) (2)
Heighway, S. D. (Liverpool), 1971 v Pol, Se (2), I, A; 1973 v USSR; 1975 v USSR, T, USSR; 1976 v T, N; 1977 v E, F (2), Sp, Bul; 1978 v Bul, N, D; 1979 v Ni, Bul; 1980 v Bul, US, Ni, E, Cy, Arg; 1981 v Bel, F, Cy, W, Bel (32)
Henderson, B. (Drumcondra), 1948 v P, Sp (2)
Hennessy, J. (Shelbourne), 1956 v Pol, B, Sp; 1966 v WG; (with St Patrick's Ath), 1969 v A (5)
Herrick, J. (Cork Hibernians), 1972 v A, Ch (sub); (with Shamrock R), 1973 v F (sub) (3)
Higgins, J. (Birmingham C), 1951 v Arg (1)
Holmes, J. (Coventry C), 1971 v A (sub); 1973 v F, USSR, Pol, F, N; 1974 v Pol, Br; 1975 v USSR, Sw; 1976 v T, N, Pol; 1977 v E, T, F, Sp; (with Tottenham H), F, Pol, Bul; 1978 v Bul, T, Pol, N, D; 1979 v Ni, E, D, Bul; 1981 (with Vancouver W), v W (30)
Horlecher, A. F. (Bohemians), 1930 v Bel; 1932 v Sp, Ho; 1935 v H; 1936 v Ho, Sw (6)
Hoy, M. (Dundalk), 1938 v N; 1939 v Sw, Pol, H (2), G (6)
Hughton, C. (Tottenham H), 1980 v US, E, Sw, Arg; 1981 v Ho, Bel, F, Cy, W, Bel, Pol (11)
Hurley, C. J. (Millwall), 1957 v E; 1958 v D, Pol, A; (with Sunderland), 1959 v Cz (2); 1960 v Se, Ch, WG, Se; 1961 v W, N, S (2); 1962 v Cz (2), A; 1963 v Ic (2), S; 1964 v A (2), Sp (2), Pol, N; 1965 v Sp; 1966 v WG, A, Bel; 1967 v T, Sp, T, Cz; 1968 v Cz, Pol (2); (with Bolton W), 1969 v D, Cz, H (40)
Hutchinson, F. (Drumcondra), 1935 v Sw, G (2)

Jordan, D. (Wolverhampton W), 1937 v Sw, F (2)
Jordan, W. (Bohemians), 1934 v Ho; 1938 v N (2)

Kavanagh, P. J. (Celtic), 1931 v Sp; 1932 v Sp (2)
Keane, T. R. (Swansea T), 1949 v Sw, P, Se, Sp (4)
Kearin, M. (Shamrock R), 1972 v A (1)

Kearns, F. T. (West Ham U), 1954 v L (1)
Kearns, M. (Oxford U), 1970 v Pol (sub); (with Walsall), 1974 v Pol (sub), U, Ch; 1976 v N, Pol; 1977 v E, T, F (2), Sp, Bul; 1978 v N, D; 1979 v Ni, E; (with Wolverhampton W), 1980 v US, Ni (18)
Kelly, J. (Derry C), 1932 v Ho; 1934 v Bel; 1936 v Sw, L (4)
Kelly, J. A. (Drumcondra), 1957 v WG, E; (with Preston NE), 1962 v A; 1963 v Ic (2), S; 1964 v A (2), Sp (2), Pol; 1965 v Bel; 1966 v A, Bel; 1967 v Sp (2), T, Cz (2), Pol; 1968 v Pol, A, D, Cz, D, H; 1970 v S, D, H, Pol, WG; 1971 v Pol, Se (2), I (2), A; 1972 v Ir, Ec, Ch, P; 1973 v USSR, F, USSR, Pol, F, N (47)
Kelly, J. P. V. (Wolverhampton W), 1961 v W, N, S· 1962 v Cz (2) (5)
Kelly, N. (Nottingham F), 1954 v L (1)
Kendrick, J. (Everton), 1927 v I; 1934 v Bel, Ho; 1936 v Ho (4)
Kennedy, W. (St James' Gate), 1932 v Ho; 1934 v Bel, Ho (3)
Keogh, J. (Shamrock R), 1966 v WG (sub) (1)
Keogh, S. (Shamrock R), 1959 v Pol (1)
Kiernan, F. W. (Shamrock R), 1951 v Arg, N; (with Southampton), 1952 v WG (2), A (5)
Kinnear, J. P. (Tottenham H), 1967 v T; 1968 v Cz, Pol; 1969 v A; 1970 v Cz, D, H, Pol; 1971 v Se (sub), I; 1972 v Ir, Ec, Ch, P; 1973 v USSR, F; 1974 v Pol, Br, U, Ch; 1975 v USSR, T, Sw, USSR; (with Brighton), 1976 v T (sub) (25)
Kinsella, J. (Shelbourne), 1928 v Bel (1)
Kinsella, P. (Shamrock R), 1932 v Ho; 1938 v N (2)
Kirkland, A. (Shamrock R), 1927 v I (1)

Lacey, W. (Shelbourne), 1927 v I; 1928 v Bel; 1930 v Bel (3)
Langan, D. (Derby Co), 1978 v T, N; 1980 v Sw, Arg; (with Birmingham C), 1981 v Ho, Bel, F, Cy, W, Bel, Cz, WG 'B', Pol (13)
Lawler, J. F. (Fulham), 1953 v A; 1954 v L, F; 1955 v N, H, N, WG; 1956 v Y (8)
Lawlor, J. C. (Drumcondra), 1949 v Bel; (with Doncaster R), 1951 v N, Arg (3)
Lawlor, M. (Shamrock R), 1971 v Pol, Se (2), I (sub); 1973 v Pol (5)
Lawrenson, M. (Preston NE), 1977 v Pol; (with Brighton), 1978 v Bul, Pol, N (sub); 1979 v Ni, E; 1980 v E, Cy, Sw; 1981 v Ho, Bel, F, Cy, Pol (14)
Leech, M. (Shamrock R), 1969 v Cz, D, H; 1972 v A, Ir, Ec, P; 1973 v USSR (sub) (8)
Lennon, C. (St James' Gate), 1935 v H, Sw, G (3)
Lennox, G. (Dolphin), 1931 v Sp; 1932 v Sp (2)
Lowry, D. (St Patrick's Ath), 1962 v A (sub) (1)
Lunn, R. (Dundalk), 1939 v Sw, Pol (2)
Lynch, J. (Cork Bohemians), 1934 v Bel (1)

McAlinden, J. (Portsmouth), 1946 v P, Sp (2)
McCann, J. (Shamrock R), 1957 v WG (1)
McCarthy, J. (Bohemians), 1926 v I; 1928 v Bel; 1930 v Bel (3)
McCarthy, M. (Shamrock R), 1932 v Ho (1)
McConville, T. (Dundalk), 1972 v A; (with Waterford), 1973 v USSR, F, USSR, Pol, F (6)
McDonagh, J. (Everton), 1981 v W, Bel, Cz, WG 'B' (4)
McEvoy, M. A. (Blackburn R), 1961 v S (2); 1963 v S; 1964 v A, Sp (2), Pol, N, E; 1965 v Pol, Bel, Sp; 1966 v Sp (2); 1967 v Sp, T, Cz (17)
McGee, P. (QPR), 1978 v T, N (sub), D (sub); 1979 v Ni, E, D (sub), Bul (sub), Arg (sub); 1980 v Cz, Bul; (with Preston NE), US, Ni, Cy, Sw, Arg; 1981 v Bel (sub) (16)
McGowan, D. (West Ham U), 1949 v P, Se, Sp (3)
McGowan, J. (Cork U), 1947 v Sp (1)
McGrath, M. (Blackburn R), 1958 v A; 1959 v Pol, Cz (2); 1960 v Se, WG, Se; 1961 v W; 1962 v C (2); 1963 v S; 1964 v A (2), E; 1965 v Pol, Bel, Sp; 1966 v Sp; (with Bradford), 1966 v WG, A, Bel; 1967 v T (22)
McGuire, W. (Bohemians), 1936 v Ho (1)
McKenzie, G. (Southend U), 1938 v N (2), Cz, Pol; 1939 v Sw, Pol, H (2), G (9)
Mackey, G. (Shamrock R), 1957 v D, WG, E (3)
McLoughlin, F. (Fordsons), 1930 v Bel; (with Cork), 1932 v Sp (2)
McMillan, W. (Belfast Celtic), 1946 v P, Sp (2)
McNally, J. B. (Luton T), 1959 v Cz; 1961 v Sp; 1963 v Ic (3)
Macken, A. (Derby Co), 1977 v Sp (1)
Madden, O. (Cork), 1936 v H (1)
Maguire, J. (Shamrock R), 1929 v Bel (1)
Malone, G. (Shelbourne), 1949 v Bel (1)
Mancini, T. J. (QPR), 1974 v Pol, Br, U, Ch; (with Arsenal), 1975 v USSR (5)
Martin, C. (Bo'ness), 1927 v I (1)
Martin, C. J. (Glentoran), 1946 v P (sub), Sp; 1947 v E; (with Leeds U), 1947 v Sp; 1948 v P, Sp; (with Aston Villa), 1949 v Sw, Bel, P, Se, Sp; 1950 v Fi, E, Fi, Se, Bel; 1951 v Arg; 1952 v WG, A, Sp; 1954 v F (2), L; 1955 v N, Ho, N, WG; 1956 v Y, Sp, Ho (30)
Martin, M. P. (Bohemians), 1972 v A, Ir, Ec, Ch, P; 1973 v USSR; (with Manchester U), 1973 v USSR, Pol, F, N; 1974 v Pol, Br, U, Ch; 1975 v USSR, T, Sw, USSR, Sw; (with WBA), 1976 v T, N, Pol; 1977 v E, T, F (2), Sp, Pol, Bul; (with Newcastle U), 1979 v D, Bul, WG, Arg; 1980 v W, Cz, Bul, US, Ni; 1981 v F, Bel, Cz, WG 'B' (42)
Meagan, M. K. (Everton), 1961 v S; 1962 v A; 1963 v Ic; 1964 v Sp; (with Huddersfield T), 1965 v Bel; 1966 v Sp (2), A, Bel; 1967 v Sp, T, Sp, T, Cz; 1968 v Cz, Pol; (with Drogheda), 1970 v S (17)
Meehan, P. (Drumcondra), 1934 v Ho (1)
Monahan, P. (Sligo R), 1935 v Sw, G (2)
Mooney, J. (Shamrock R), 1965 v Pol, Bel (2)
Moore, P. (Shamrock R), 1931 v Sp; 1932 v Ho; (with Aberdeen), 1934 v Bel, Ho; 1935 v H, G; (with Shamrock R), 1936 v Ho; 1937 v G, H (9)
Moran, K. (Manchester U), 1980 v Sw, Arg; 1981 v Bel, F, Cy, W (sub), Bel, Cz, WG 'B', Pol (10)
Moroney, T. (West Ham U), 1948 v Sp; 1949 v P, Se, Sp; 1950 v Fi, E, Fi, Bel; 1951 v N (2); 1952 v WG; 1954 v F (12)
Moulson, C. (Lincoln C), 1936 v H, L; (with Notts Co), 1937 v H, Sw, F (5)
Moulson, G. B. (Lincoln C), 1948 v P, Sp; 1949 v Sw (3)
Mucklan, C. (Drogheda U), 1978 v Pol (1)
Muldoon, T. (Aston Villa), 1927 v I (1)
Mulligan, P. M. (Shamrock R), 1969 v Cz, D, H; 1970 v S, Cz, D; (with Chelsea), 1970 v H, Pol, WG; 1971 v Pol, Se, I; 1972 v A, Ir, Ec, Ch, P; 1973 v F, USSR, Pol, F, N; 1974 v Pol, Br, U, Ch; 1975 v USSR, T, Sw, USSR, Sw; (with WBA), 1976 v T, Pol; 1977 v E, T, F (2), Pol, Bul; 1978 v Bul, N, D; 1979 v E, D, Bul (sub), WG, Arg; (with Shamrock R) 1980 v W, Cz, Bul, US (sub) (51)
Munroe, L. (Shamrock R), 1954 v L (1)
Murphy, A. (Clyde), 1956 v Y (1)
Murphy, J. (C. Palace), 1980 v W, US, Cy (3)
Murray, T. (Dundalk), 1950 v Bel (1)

Newman, W. (Shelbourne), 1969 v D (1)
Nolan, R. (Shamrock R), 1957 v D, WG, E; 1958 v Pol; 1960 v Ch, WG, Se; 1962 v Cz (2); 1963 v Ic (10)

O'Brien, F. (Philadelphia F), 1980 v Cz, E, Cy (sub), Arg (4)
O'Brien, M. T. (Derby Co), 1927 v I; (with Walsall), 1929

v Bel; (with Norwich C), 1930 v Bel; (with Watford), 1932 v Ho (4)
O'Brien, R. (Notts Co), 1976 v N, Pol; 1977 v Sp, Pol (4)
O'Byrne, L. B. (Shamrock R), 1949 v Bel (1)
O'Callaghan, B. R. (Stoke C), 1979 v WG (sub), Arg (sub); 1980 v W, US; 1981 v W (5)
O'Callaghan, K. (Ipswich T), 1981 v Cz, WG 'B', Pol (3)
O'Connell, A. (Dundalk), 1967 v Sp; (with Bohemians), 1971 v Pol (sub) (2)
O'Connor, T. (Shamrock R), 1950 v Fi, E, Fi, Se (4)
O'Connor, T. (Fulham), 1968 v Cz; (with Dundalk), 1972 v A, Ir (sub), Ec (sub), Ch; (with Bohemians), 1973 v F (sub), Pol (sub) (7)
O'Driscoll, J. F. (Swansea T), 1949 v Sw, Bel, Se (3)
O'Farrell, F. (West Ham U), 1952 v A; 1953 v A; 1954 v F; 1955 v Ho, N; 1956 v Y, Ho; (with Preston NE), 1958 v D; 1959 v Cz (9)
O'Flanagan, K. P. (Bohemians), 1938 v N, Cz, Pol, H (2), G; (with Arsenal), 1947 v E, Sp, P (10)
O'Flanagan, M. (Bohemians), 1947 v E (1)
O'Kane, P. (Bohemians), 1935 v H, Sw, G (3)
O'Keefe, E. (Everton), 1981 v W (1)
O'Keefe, T. (Cork), 1934 v Bel; (with Waterford), 1938 v Cz, Pol (3)
O'Leary, D. (Arsenal), 1977 v E, F (2), Sp, Bul; 1978 v Bul, N, D; 1979 v E, Bul, WG, Arg; 1980 v W, Bul, Ni, E, Cy; 1981 v Ho, Cz, WG 'B', Pol (21)
O'Leary, P. (Shamrock R), 1980 v Bul, US, NI, E (sub), Cz, Arg; 1981 v Ho (7)
O'Mahoney, M. T. (Bristol R), 1938 v Cz, Pol; 1939 v Sw, Pol, H, G (6)
O'Neill, F. S. (Shamrock R), 1962 v Cz (2); 1965 v Pol, Bel, Sp; 1966 v Sp (2), WG, A; 1967 v Sp, T, Sp, T; 1969 v Pol, A, D, Cz, D (sub), H (sub); 1972 v A (20)
O'Neill, J. (Everton), 1952 v Sp; 1953 v F, A; 1954 v F, L, F; 1955 v N, Ho, N, WG; 1956 v Y, Sp; 1957 v D; 1958 v M; 1959 v Pol, Cz (2) (17)
O'Neill, J. (Preston NE), 1961 v W (1)
O'Neill, W. (Dundalk), 1936 v Ho, Sw, H, L; 1937 v G, H, Sw, F; 1938 v N; 1939 v H, G (11)
O'Reilly, J. (Brideville), 1932 v Ho; (with Aberdeen), 1934 v Bel, Ho; (with Brideville), 1936 v Ho; Sw, H, L; (with St James' Gate), 1937 v G, H, Sw, F; 1938 v N (2), Cz, Pol; 1939 v Sw, Pol, H (2), G (20)
O'Reilly, J. (Cork U), 1946 v P, Sp (2)

Peyton, G. (Fulham), 1977 v Sp (sub); 1978 v Bul, T, Pol; 1979 v D, Bul, WG, Arg; 1980 v W, Cz, Bul, E, Cy, Sw, Arg; 1981 v Ho, Bel, F, Cy (19)
Peyton, N. (Shamrock R), 1957 v WG; (with Leeds U), 1960 v WG, Se (sub); 1961 v W; 1963 v Ic, S (6)

Reid, C. (Brideville), 1931 v Sp (1)
Richardson, D. J. (Shamrock R), 1972 v A (sub); (with Gillingham), 1973 v N (sub); 1980 v Cz (3)
Rigby, A. (St James' Gate), 1935 v H, Sw, G (3)
Ringstead, A. (Sheffield U), 1951 v Arg, N; 1952 v WG (2), A, Sp; 1953 v A; 1954 v F; 1955 v N; 1956 v Y, Sp, Ho; 1957 v E (2); 1958 v D, Pol, A; 1959 v Pol, Cz (2) (20)
Robinson, J. (Bohemians), 1928 v Bel; (with Dolphin), 1931 v Sp (2)
Robinson, M. (Brighton), 1981 v F, Cy, Bel, WG 'B', Pol (5)
Roche, P. J. (Shelbourne), 1972 v A; (with Manchester U), 1975 v USSR, T, Sw, USSR, Sw; 1976 v T (7)
Rogers, E. (Blackburn R), 1968 v Cz, Pol; 1969 v Pol, A, D, Cz, D, H; 1970 v S, D, H; 1971 v I (2), A; (with Charlton Ath), 1972 v Ir, Ec, Ch, P; 1973 v USSR (19)
Ryan, G. (Derby Co), 1978 v T; (with Brighton), 1979 v E, WG; 1980 v W, Cy (sub), Sw, Arg (sub); 1981 v F (sub), WG 'B' (sub), Pol (sub) (10)
Ryan, R. A. (WBA), 1950 v Se, Bel; 1951 v N, Arg, N; 1952 v WG (2), A, Sp; 1953 v F, A; 1954 v F, L, F; 1955 v N; (with Derby Co), 1956 v Sp (16)

Saward, P. (Millwall), 1954 v L; (with Aston Villa), 1957 v E (2); 1958 v D, Pol, A; 1959 v Pol, Cz; 1960 v Se, Ch, WG, Se; 1961 v W, N; (with Huddersfield T), 1961 v S; 1962 v A; 1963 v Ic (2) (18)
Scannell, T. (Southend U), 1954 v L (1)
Sloan, J. W. (Arsenal), 1946 v P, Sp (2)
Smyth, M. (Shamrock R), 1969 v Pol (sub) (1)
Squires, J. (Shelbourne), 1934 v Ho (1)
Stapleton, F. (Arsenal), 1977 v T, F, Sp, Bul; 1978 v Bul, N, D; 1979 v Ni, E (sub), D, WG, Arg; 1980 v W, Bul, Ni, E, Cy; 1981 v Ho, Bel, F, Cy, Bel, Cz, WG 'B', Pol (25)
Stevenson, A. E. (Dolphin), 1932 v Ho; (with Everton), 1947 v E, Sp, P; 1948 v P, Sp; 1949 v Sw (7)
Strahan, F. (Shelbourne), 1964 v Pol, N, E; 1965 v Pol; 1966 v WG (5)
Sullivan, J. (Fordsons), 1928 v Bel (1)
Swan, M. M. G. (Drumcondra), 1960 v Se (sub) (1)
Synnott, N. (Shamrock R), 1978 v T, Pol; 1979 v Ni (3)

Thomas, P. (Waterford), 1974 v Pol, Br (2)
Traynor, T. J. (Southampton), 1954 v L; 1962 v A; 1963 v Ic (2), S; 1964 v A (2), Sp (8)
Treacy, R. C. P. (WBA), 1966 v WG; 1967 v Sp, Cz; 1968 v Cz; (with Charlton Ath), 1968 v Pol; 1969 v Pol, Cz, D; 1970 v S, D, H (sub), Pol (sub), WG (sub); 1971 v Pol, Se (sub), Se, I, A; (with Swindon T), 1972 v Ir, Ec, Ch, P; 1973 v USSR, F, USSR, Pol, F, N; 1974 v Pol; (with Preston NE), 1974 v Br; 1975 v USSR, Sw (2); 1976 v T, N (sub), Pol (sub); (with WBA), 1977 v F, Pol; 1978 (with Shamrock R), v T, Pol (2); 1980 v Cz (sub) (42)
Tuohy, L. (Shamrock R), 1956 v Y; 1959 v Cz (2); (with Newcastle U), 1962 v A; 1963 v Ic (2); (with Shamrock R), 1964 v A; 1965 v Bel (8)
Turner, A. (Celtic), 1963 v S; 1964 v Sp (2)
Turner, C. J. (Southend U), 1936 v Sw; 1937 v G, H, Sw, F; (with West Ham U), 1938 v N (2), Cz, Pol; 1939 v H (10)

Vernon, J. (Belfast Celtic), 1946 v P, Sp (2)

Waddock, G. (QPR), 1980 v Sw, Arg; 1981 v W, Pol (sub) (4)
Walsh, D. J. (WBA), 1946 v P, Sp; 1947 v Sp, P; 1948 v P, Sp; 1949 v Sw, P, Se, Sp; 1950 v E, Fi, Se; 1951 v N; (with Aston Villa), v Arg, N; 1952 v Sp; 1953 v A; 1954 v F (2) (20)
Walsh, M. (Blackpool), 1976 v N, Pol; 1977 v F (sub), Pol; (with Everton), 1979 v Ni (sub); (with QPR), D (sub), Bul, WG (sub), Arg; (with Porto), 1981 v Bel (sub), Cz (11)
Walsh, W. (Manchester C), 1947 v E, Sp, P; 1948 v P, Sp; 1949 v Bel; 1950 v E, Se, Bel (9)
Waters, J. (Grimsby T), 1977 v T; 1980 v Ni (sub) (2)
Watters, F. (Shelbourne), 1926 v I (1)
Weir, E. (Clyde), 1939 v H (2), G (3)
Whelan, R. (St.Patrick's Ath), 1964 v A, E (sub) (2)
Whelan, R. (Liverpool), 1981 v Cz (sub) (1)
Whelan, W. (Manchester U), 1956 v Ho; 1957 v D, E (2) (4)
White, J. J. (Bohemians), 1928 v Bel (1)
Whittaker, R. (Chelsea), 1959 v Cz (1)
Williams, J. (Shamrock R), 1938 v N (1)

ENGLAND INTERNATIONAL TEAMS 1872–1980

Substitute in brackets † World Cup final stages

1872 Scotland	**1873 Scotland**	**1874 Scotland**	**1875 Scotland**	**1876 Scotland**
1 Maynard	1 Morton	1 Welch	1 Carr	1 Savage
2 Greenhalgh	2 Greenhalgh	2 Ogilvie	2 Haygarth	2 Green
3 Welch	3 Howell	3 Stratford	3 Rawson	3 Field
4 Maddison	4 Goodwyn	4 Ottaway	4 Birley	4 Bambridge E.H.
5 Barker	5 Vidal	5 Birley	5 von Donop	5 Jarrett
6 Brockbank	6 von Donop	6 Wollaston	6 Wollaston	6 Heron H.
7 Clegg J.C.	7 Chenery	7 Kingsford	7 Alcock	7 Cursham A.W.
8 Smith A.K.	8 Clegg W.E.	8 Edwards	8 Rawson	8 Heron F.
9 Ottaway	9 Bonsor	9 Chenery	9 Bonsor	9 Smith C.E.
10 Chenery	10 Capt Kenyon-Slaney	10 Heron	10 Heron	10 Buchanan
11 Morice	11 Heron	11 Owen	11 Geaves	11 Maynard
Glasgow Nov 30: 0-0	Kennington Oval Mar 8: 4-2 *Kenyon-Slaney 2, Bonsor, Chenery*	Glasgow Mar 7: 1-2 *Kingsford*	Kennington Oval Mar 6: 2-2 *Wollaston, Alcock*	Glasgow Mar 4: 0-3

1877 Scotland	**1878 Scotland**	**1879 Wales**	**1879 Scotland**	**1880 Scotland**
1 Betts	1 Warner	1 Anderson	1 Birkett	1 Swepstone
2 Lindsay	2 Hon E. Lyttelton	2 Bury	2 Morse	2 Brindle
3 Bury	3 Hunter	3 Wilson	3 Christian	3 Luntley
4 Rawson	4 Bailey	4 Bailey	4 Bailey	4 Bailey
5 Jarrett	5 Jarrett	5 Clegg W.E.	5 Prinsep	5 Hunter
6 Wollaston	6 Cursham A.W.	6 Parry	6 Hills	6 Wollaston
7 Cursham A.W.	7 Fairclough	7 Sorby	7 Goodyer	7 Bastard
8 Hon A. Lyttelton	8 Wace	8 Cursham A.W.	8 Wace	8 Sparks
9 Wingfield-Stratford	9 Wylie	9 Wace	9 Sparks	9 Widdowson
10 Bain	10 Heron H.	10 Mosforth	10 Bambridge E.C.	10 Mosforth
11 Mosforth	11 Mosforth	11 Whitfield	11 Mosforth	11 Bambridge E.C.
Kennington Oval Mar 3: 1-3 *Lyttelton*	Glasgow Mar 2: 2-7 *Wylie, Cursham*	Kennington Oval Jan 18: 2-1 *Sorby, Whitfield*	Kennington Oval April 5: 5-4 *Mosforth, Bambridge 2, Goodyer, Bailey*	Glasgow Mar 13: 4-5 *Mosforth, Bambridge 2, Sparks*

1880 Wales	**1881 Wales**	**1881 Scotland**	**1882 Ireland**	**1882 Scotland**
1 Sands	1 Hawtrey	1 Hawtrey	1 Rawlinson	1 Swepstone
2 Luntley	2 Harvey	2 Field	2 Dobson	2 Greenwood
3 Brindle	3 Bambridge A.L.	3 Wilson	3 Greenwood	3 Jones A.
4 Hunter	4 Hunter	4 Bailey	4 Hargreaves	4 Bailey
5 Hargreaves	5 Hargreaves	5 Hunter	5 King	5 Hunter
6 Marshall	6 Marshall	6 Holden	6 Bambridge E.C.	6 Cursham H.A.
7 Cursham H.A.	7 Rostron	7 Rostron	7 Barnet	7 Parry
8 Sparks	8 Brown J.	8 Macauley	8 Brown A.	8 Brown A.
9 Mitchell	9 Tait	9 Mitchell	9 Brown J.	9 Vaughton
10 Johnson	10 Hargreaves	10 Bambridge E.C.	10 Vaughton	10 Mosforth
11 Mosforth	11 Mosforth	11 Hargreaves	11 Cursham H.A.	11 Bambridge E.C.
Wrexham Mar 15: 3-2 *Sparks 2, Brindle*	Blackburn Feb 26: 0-1	Kennington Oval Mar 12: 1-6 *Bambridge*	Belfast Feb 18: 13-0 *Vaughton 5, Brown A. 4, Brown J. 2, Cursham, Bambridge*	Glasgow Mar 11: 1-5 *Vaughton*

1882 Wales	**1883 Wales**	**1883 Ireland**	**1883 Scotland**	**1884 Ireland**
1 Swepstone	1 Swepstone	1 Swepstone	1 Swepstone	1 Rose
2 Hunter	2 Paravacini	2 Paravacini	2 Paravacini	2 Dobson
3 Jones A.	3 Russell	3 Moore	3 Jones A.	3 Beverley
4 Bailey	4 Bailey	4 Hudson	4 Bailey	4 Bailey
5 Bambridge E.C.	5 Macrae	5 Macrae	5 Macrae	5 Macrae
6 Parry	6 Cursham A.W.	6 Whateley	6 Cursham H.A.	6 Johnson
7 Cursham H.A.	7 Bambridge A.L.	7 Pawson	7 Cobbold	7 Holden
8 Parr	8 Mitchell	8 Goodhart	8 Mitchell	8 Bambridge A.L.
9 Brown A.	9 Goodhart	9 Dunn	9 Goodhart	9 Dunn
10 Vaughton	10 Cursham H.A.	10 Cobbold	10 Cursham A.W.	10 Bambridge E.C.
11 Mosforth	11 Bambridge E.C.	11 Cursham H.A.	11 Whateley	11 Cursham H.A.
Wrexham Mar 13: 3-5 *Mosforth, Parry, Cursham*	Kennington Oval Feb 3: 5-0 *Mitchell 3, Cursham A.W., Bambridge E.C.*	Liverpool Feb 24: 7-0 *Cobbold 2, Dunn 2, Whateley 2, Pawson*	Sheffield Mar 10: 2-3 *Mitchell, Cobbold*	Belfast Feb 25: 8-1 *Johnson 2, Bambridge E. C. 2, Cursham 3, Bambridge A.L.*

1884 Scotland	**1884 Wales**	**1885 Ireland**	**1885 Wales**	**1885 Scotland**
1 Rose	1 Rose	1 Arthur	1 Arthur	1 Arthur
2 Dobson	2 Dobson	2 Walters P.M.	2 Moore	2 Walters P.M.
3 Beverley	3 Beverley	3 Walters A.M.	3 Ward	3 Walters A.M.
4 Bailey	4 Bailey	4 Bailey	4 Bailey	4 Bailey
5 Macrae	5 Forrest	5 Forrest	5 Forrest	5 Forrest
6 Wilson C.P.	6 Wilson C.P.	6 Lofthouse	6 Lofthouse	6 Amos
7 Bromley-Davenport	7 Holden	7 Spilsbury	7 Davenport	7 Brown J.
8 Gunn	8 Vaughton	8 Brown J.	8 Brown J.	8 Lofthouse
9 Bambridge E.C.	9 Bromley-Davenport	9 Pawson	9 Mitchell	9 Danks
10 Vaughton	10 Gunn	10 Cobbold	10 Dixon	10 Bambridge E.C.
11 Holden	11 Bambridge E.C.	11 Bambridge E.C.	11 Bambridge E.C.	11 Cobbold
Glasgow Mar 15: 0-1	Wrexham Mar 17: 4-0 *Bromley-Davenport 2, Gunn, Bailey*	Manchester Feb 28: 4-0 *Bambridge E.C., Spilsbury, Brown, Lofthouse*	Blackburn Mar 14: 1-1 *Mitchell*	Kennington Oval Mar 21: 1-1 *Bambridge*

1886 Ireland	**1886 Wales**	**1886 Scotland**	**1887 Ireland**	**1887 Wales**
1 Rose	1 Arthur	1 Arthur	1 Arthur	1 Arthur
2 Walters P.M.	2 Squire	2 Walters A.M.	2 Howarth R.	2 Walters P.M.
3 Baugh	3 Walters P.M.	3 Walters P.M.	3 Mason	3 Walters A.M.
4 Shutt	4 Bailey	4 Bailey	4 Haworth G.	4 Haworth G.
5 Squire	5 Amos	5 Squire	5 Brayshaw	5 Bailey
6 Dobson	6 Forrest	6 Forrest	6 Forrest	6 Forrest
7 Leighton	7 Dewhurst	7 Cobbold	7 Sayer	7 Lofthouse
8 Dewhurst	8 Brann	8 Bambridge E.C.	8 Dewhurst	8 Dewhurst
9 Lindley	9 Lindley	9 Lindley	9 Lindley	9 Lindley
10 Spilsbury	10 Cobbold	10 Spilsbury	10 Cobbold	10 Cobbold
11 Pike	11 Bambridge E.C.	11 Brann	11 Bambridge E.C.	11 Bambridge E.C.
Belfast Mar 13: 6-1 *Spilsbury 4, Dewhurst, Lindley*	Wrexham Mar 29: 3-1 *Dewhurst, Bambridge, Lindley*	Glasgow Mar 31: 1-1 *Lindley*	Sheffield Feb 5: 7-0 *Cobbold 2, Lindley 3, Dewhurst 2*	Kennington Oval Feb 26: 4-0 *Cobbold 2, Lindley 2*

1887 Scotland	1888 Wales	1888 Scotland	1888 Ireland	1889 Wales
1 Roberts	1 Moon	1 Moon	1 Roberts	1 Moon
2 Walters A.M.	2 Howarth R.	2 Howarth R.	2 Aldridge	2 Walters A.M.
3 Walters P.M.	3 Mason	3 Walters P.M.	3 Walters P.M.	3 Walters P.M.
4 Bailey	4 Saunders	4 Allen H.	4 Holmes	4 Fletcher
5 Haworth G.	5 Allen H.	5 Haworth G.	5 Allen H.	5 Lowder
6 Forrest	6 Holden-White	6 Holden-White	6 Shelton	6 Betts
7 Bambridge E.C.	7 Woodhall	7 Woodhall	7 Bassett	7 Bassett
8 Cobbold	8 Goodall	8 Goodall	8 Dewhurst	8 Goodall
9 Lofthouse	9 Lindley	9 Lindley	9 Lindley	9 Southworth
10 Dewhurst	10 Dewhurst	10 Hodgetts	10 Allen A.	10 Dewhurst
11 Lindley	11 Hodgetts	11 Dewhurst	11 Hodgetts	11 Townley
Blackburn Mar 19: 2-3 *Dewhurst, Lindley*	Crewe Feb 4: 5-1 *Dewhurst 2, Woodhall, Goodall, Lindley*	Glasgow Mar 17: 5-0 *Lindley, Hodgetts, Dewhurst 2, Goodall*	Belfast Mar 31: 5-1 *Dewhurst, Allen A. 3, Lindley*	Stoke Feb 23: 4-1 *Bassett, Goodall, Southworth, Dewhurst*

1889 Ireland	1889 Scotland	1890 Wales	1890 Ireland	1890 Scotland
1 Rowley	1 Moon	1 Moon	1 Roberts	1 Moon
2 Clare	2 Walters A.M.	2 Walters A.M.	2 Baugh	2 Walters A.M.
3 Aldridge	3 Walters P.M.	3 Walters P.M.	3 Mason	3 Walters P.M.
4 Wreford-Brown	4 Hammond	4 Fletcher	4 Barton	4 Haworth G.
5 Weir	5 Allen	5 Holt	5 Perry	5 Allen
6 Shelton	6 Forrest	6 Shelton	6 Forrest	6 Shelton
7 Lofthouse	7 Brodie	7 Bassett	7 Lofthouse	7 Bassett
8 Burton	8 Goodall	8 Currey	8 Davenport	8 Currey
9 Brodie	9 Bassett	9 Lindley	9 Geary	9 Lindley
10 Daft	10 Weir	10 Daft	10 Walton	10 Wood
11 Yates	11 Lindley	11 Wood	11 Townley	11 Daft
Everton Mar 2: 6-1 *Weir, Yates 3, Lofthouse, Brodie*	Kennington Oval April 13: 2-3 *Bassett, Weir*	Wrexham Mar 15: 3-1 *Currey 2, Lindley*	Belfast Mar 15: 9-1 *Townley 2, Davenport 2, Geary 3, Lofthouse, Barton*	Glasgow April 5: 1-1 *Wood*

1891 Wales	1891 Ireland	1891 Scotland	1892 Wales	1892 Ireland
1 Wilkinson	1 Rose	1 Moon	1 Toone	1 Rowley
2 Porteous	2 Marsden	2 Howarth	2 Dunn	2 Underwood
3 Jackson	3 Underwood	3 Holmes	3 Lilley	3 Clare
4 Smith A.	4 Bayliss	4 Smith A.	4 Hossack	4 Cox
5 Holt	5 Perry	5 Holt	5 Winckworth	5 Holt
6 Shelton	6 Brodie	6 Shelton	6 Kinsey	6 Whitham
7 Brann	7 Bassett	7 Bassett	7 Gosling	7 Athersmith
8 Goodall	8 Cotterill	8 Goodall	8 Cotterill	8 Pearson
9 Southworth	9 Lindley	9 Geary	9 Henfrey	9 Devey
10 Milward	10 Henfrey	10 Chadwick	10 Schofield	10 Daft
11 Chadwick	11 Daft	11 Milward	11 Sandilands	11 Hodgetts
Sunderland Mar 7: 4-1 *Goodall, Southworth, Chadwick, Milward*	Wolverhampton Mar 7: 6-1 *Cotterill, Daft, Henfrey, Lindley 2, Bassett*	Blackburn April 6: 2-1 *Goodall, Chadwick*	Wrexham Mar 5: 2-0 *Henfrey, Sandilands*	Belfast Mar 5: 2-0 *Daft 2*

1892 Scotland	1893 Ireland	1893 Wales	1893 Scotland	1894 Ireland
1 Toone	1 Charsley	1 Sutcliffe	1 Gay	1 Reader
2 Dunn	2 Harrison	2 Clare	2 Harrison	2 Howarth
3 Holmes	3 Pelly	3 Holmes	3 Holmes	3 Holmes
4 Holt	4 Smith A.	4 Reynolds	4 Reynolds	4 Reynolds
5 Reynolds	5 Winckworth	5 Perry	5 Holt	5 Holt
6 Shelton	6 Cooper	6 Turner	6 Kingsley	6 Crabtree
7 Bassett	7 Topham	7 Bassett	7 Bassett	7 Chippendale
8 Goodall	8 Smith G.O.	8 Whitehead	8 Gosling	8 Whitehead
9 Chadwick	9 Cotterill	9 Goodall	9 Cotterill	9 Devey
10 Hodgetts	10 Gilliatt	10 Schofield	10 Chadwick	10 Hodgetts
11 Southworth	11 Sandilands	11 Spiksley	11 Spiksley	11 Spiksley
Glasgow April 2: 4-1 *Southworth, Goodall 2, Chadwick*	Birmingham Feb 25: 6-1 *Sandilands, Gilliatt 3, Winckworth, Smith G.O.*	Stoke Mar 13: 6-0 *Spiksley 2, Goodall, Bassett, Schofield, Reynolds*	Richmond April 1: 5-2 *Spiksley 2, Gosling, Cotterill, Reynolds*	Belfast Mar 1: 2-2 *Devey, Spiksley*

1894 Wales	1894 Scotland	1895 Ireland	1895 Wales	1895 Scotland
1 Gay	1 Gay	1 Sutcliffe	1 Raikes	1 Sutcliffe
2 Lodge	2 Clare	2 Crabtree	2 Lodge	2 Crabtree
3 Pelly	3 Pelly	3 Holmes	3 Oakley	3 Lodge
4 Hossack	4 Reynolds	4 Howell	4 Henfrey	4 Needham
5 Wreford-Brown	5 Holt	5 Crawshaw	5 Wreford-Brown	5 Holt
6 Topham A.G.	6 Needham	6 Turner	6 Barker	6 Reynolds
7 Topham R.	7 Bassett	7 Bassett	7 Stanbrough	7 Gosling
8 Gosling	8 Smith G.O.	8 Bloomer	8 Dewhurst	8 Smith S.
9 Smith G.O.	9 Goodall	9 Goodall	9 Smith G.O.	9 Goodall
10 Veitch	10 Chadwick	10 Becton	10 Gosling	10 Bassett
11 Sandilands	11 Spiksley	11 Schofield	11 Sandilands	11 Bloomer
Wrexham Mar 12: 5-1 *Veitch 3, Gosling, 1 og*	Glasgow April 7: 2-2 *Goodall, Reynolds*	Derby Mar 9: 9-0 *Bloomer 2, Goodall 2, Bassett, Howell, Becton 2, 1 og*	Queen's Club Mar 18: 1-1 *Smith*	Goodison Park April 6: 3-0 *Bloomer, Smith, Gibson og*

1896 Ireland	1896 Wales	1896 Scotland	1897 Ireland	1897 Wales
1 Raikes	1 Raikes	1 Raikes	1 Robinson	1 Foulke
2 Lodge	2 Oakley	2 Lodge	2 Oakley	2 Oakley
3 Oakley	3 Crabtree	3 Oakley	3 Williams	3 Spencer
4 Crabtree	4 Henfrey	4 Crabtree	4 Middleditch	4 Reynolds
5 Crawshaw	5 Crawshaw	5 Crawshaw	5 Crawshaw	5 Crawshaw
6 Kinsey	6 Kinsey	6 Henfrey	6 Needham	6 Needham
7 Bassett	7 Bassett	7 Goodall	7 Athersmith	7 Athersmith
8 Bloomer	8 Bloomer	8 Bassett	8 Bloomer	8 Bloomer
9 Smith G.O.	9 Smith G.O.	9 Smith G.O.	9 Smith G.O.	9 Smith G.O.
10 Chadwick	10 Goodall	10 Wood	10 Wheldon	10 Beeton
11 Spiksley	11 Sandilands	11 Burnup	11 Bradshaw	11 Milward
Belfast Mar 7: 2-0 *Bloomer, Smith*	Cardiff Mar 16: 9-1 *Bloomer 5, Smith 2, Goodall, Bassett*	Glasgow April 4: 1-2 *Bassett*	Nottingham Feb 20: 6-0 *Bloomer 2, Wheldon 3, Athersmith*	Sheffield Mar 29: 4-0 *Bloomer, Needham, Milward 2*

1897 Scotland	**1898 Ireland**	**1898 Wales**	**1898 Scotland**	**1899 Ireland**
1 Robinson	1 Robinson	1 Robinson	1 Robinson	1 Hillman
2 Oakley	2 Oakley	2 Oakley	2 Williams	2 Bach
3 Spencer	3 Williams	3 Williams	3 Oakley	3 Williams
4 Reynolds	4 Forman, Frank	4 Perry	4 Needham	4 Forman, Frank
5 Crawshaw	5 Morren	5 Booth	5 Wreford-Brown	5 Crabtree
6 Needham	6 Turner	6 Needham	6 Forman, Frank	6 Needham
7 Athersmith	7 Athersmith	7 Athersmith	7 Spiksley	7 Athersmith
8 Bloomer	8 Richards	8 Goodall	8 Wheldon	8 Bloomer
9 Smith G.O.	9 Smith G.O.	9 Smith G.O.	9 Smith G.O.	9 Smith G.O.
10 Chadwick	10 Garfield	10 Wheldon	10 Bloomer	10 Settle
11 Milward	11 Wheldon	11 Spiksley	11 Athersmith	11 Forman, Fred
Crystal Palace April 3: 1-2 *Bloomer*	Belfast Mar 5: 3-2 *Morren, Athersmith, Smith*	Wrexham Mar 28: 3-0 *Smith, Wheldon 2*	Glasgow April 2: 3-1 *Bloomer 2, Wheldon*	Sunderland Feb 18: 13-2 *Frank Forman, Bloomer 2, Athersmith, Settle 3, Smith 4, Fred Forman 2*

1899 Wales	**1899 Scotland**	**1900 Ireland**	**1900 Wales**	**1900 Scotland**
1 Robinson	1 Robinson	1 Robinson	1 Robinson	1 Robinson
2 Thickett	2 Thickett	2 Oakley	2 Spencer	2 Oakley
3 Williams	3 Crabtree	3 Crabtree	3 Oakley	3 Crabtree
4 Needham	4 Forman, Frank	4 Johnson	4 Johnson	4 Johnson
5 Crabtree	5 Howell	5 Holt	5 Chadwick A.	5 Chadwick A.
6 Forman, Frank	6 Needham	6 Needham	6 Crabtree	6 Needham
7 Athersmith	7 Athersmith	7 Turner	7 Athersmith	7 Athersmith
8 Bloomer	8 Bloomer	8 Cunliffe	8 Foster	8 Bloomer
9 Smith G.O.	9 Smith G.O.	9 Smith G.O.	9 Smith G.O.	9 Smith G.O.
10 Settle	10 Settle	10 Sagar	10 Wilson	10 Wilson
11 Forman, Fred	11 Forman, Fred	11 Priest	11 Spouncer	11 Plant
Bristol Mar 20: 4-0 *Bloomer 2, Fred Forman, Needham*	Birmingham April 8: 2-1 *Smith, Settle*	Dublin Mar 17: 2-0 *Johnson, Sagar*	Cardiff Mar 26: 1-1 *Wilson*	Glasgow April 7: 1-4 *Bloomer*

1901 Ireland	**1901 Wales**	**1901 Scotland**	**1902 Wales**	**1902 Ireland**
1 Robinson	1 Kingsley	1 Sutcliffe	1 George	1 George
2 Fry	2 Crabtree	2 Iremonger	2 Crompton	2 Crompton
3 Oakley	3 Oakley	3 Oakley	3 Crabtree	3 Iremonger
4 Jones W.	4 Wilkes	4 Wilkes	4 Wilkes	4 Wilkes
5 Crawshaw	5 Bannister	5 Forman, Frank	5 Abbott	5 Bannister
6 Needham	6 Needham	6 Needham	6 Needham	6 Forman, Frank
7 Turner	7 Bennett	7 Bennett	7 Hogg	7 Hogg
8 Foster	8 Bloomer	8 Bloomer	8 Bloomer	8 Bloomer
9 Hedley	9 Beats	9 Smith G.O.	9 Sagar	9 Calvey
10 Banks	10 Foster	10 Foster	10 Foster	10 Settle
11 Cox	11 Corbett	11 Blackburn	11 Lipsham	11 Blackburn
Southampton Mar 9: 3-0 *Foster 2, Crawshaw*	Newcastle Mar 18: 6-0 *Bloomer 4, Foster, Needham*	Crystal Palace Mar 30: 2-2 *Blackburn, Bloomer*	Wrexham Mar 3: 0-0	Belfast Mar 22: 1-0 *Settle*

1902 Scotland	**1903 Ireland**	**1903 Wales**	**1903 Scotland**	**1904 Wales**
1 George	1 Baddeley	1 Sutcliffe	1 Baddeley	1 Baddeley
2 Crompton	2 Spencer	2 Crompton	2 Crompton	2 Crompton
3 Molyneux	3 Molyneux	3 Molyneux	3 Molyneux	3 Burgess
4 Wilkes	4 Johnson	4 Johnson	4 Johnson	4 Lee
5 Forman, Frank	5 Holford	5 Forman, Frank	5 Booth	5 Crawshaw
6 Houlker	6 Hadley	6 Houlker	6 Houlker	6 Ruddlesdin
7 Hogg	7 Davis	7 Davis	7 Davis	7 Brawn
8 Bloomer	8 Sharp	8 Garraty	8 Humphreys	8 Common
9 Beats	9 Woodward	9 Woodward	9 Woodward	9 Brown A.
10 Settle	10 Settle	10 Bache	10 Capes	10 Bache
11 Cox	11 Lockett	11 Corbett	11 Cox	11 Davis
Birmingham May 3: 2-2 *Wilkes, Settle*	Wolverhampton Feb 14: 4-0 *Sharp, Davis, Woodward 2*	Portsmouth Mar 2: 2-1 *Bache, Woodward*	Sheffield April 4: 1-2 *Woodward*	Wrexham Feb 29: 2-2 *Common, Bache*

1904 Ireland	**1904 Scotland**	**1905 Ireland**	**1905 Wales**	**1905 Scotland**
1 Baddeley	1 Baddeley	1 Williamson	1 Linacre	1 Linacre
2 Crompton	2 Crompton	2 Balmer	2 Spencer	2 Spencer
3 Burgess	3 Burgess	3 Carr	3 Smith H.	3 Smith H.
4 Ruddlesdin	4 Wolstenholme	4 Wolstenholme	4 Wolstenholme	4 Ruddlesdin
5 Crawshaw	5 Wilkinson	5 Roberts	5 Roberts	5 Roberts
6 Leake	6 Leake	6 Leake	6 Leake	6 Leake
7 Brawn	7 Rutherford	7 Bond	7 Bond	7 Sharp
8 Common	8 Bloomer	8 Bloomer	8 Bloomer	8 Bloomer
9 Woodward	9 Woodward	9 Woodward	9 Woodward	9 Woodward
10 Bache	10 Harris	10 Harris	10 Harris	10 Bache
11 Davis	11 Blackburn	11 Booth	11 Hardman	11 Bridgett
Belfast Mar 12: 3-1 *Common, Bache, Davis*	Glasgow April 9: 1-0 *Bloomer*	Middlesbrough Feb 25: 1-1 *Bloomer*	Liverpool Mar 27: 3-1 *Woodward 2, Harris*	Crystal Palace April 1: 1-0 *Bache*

1906 Ireland	**1906 Wales**	**1906 Scotland**	**1907 Ireland**	**1907 Wales**
1 Ashcroft	1 Ashcroft	1 Ashcroft	1 Hardy	1 Hardy
2 Crompton	2 Crompton	2 Crompton	2 Crompton	2 Crompton
3 Smith H.	3 Smith H.	3 Burgess	3 Carr	3 Pennington
4 Warren	4 Warren	4 Warren	4 Warren	4 Warren
5 Veitch	5 Veitch	5 Veitch	5 Wedlock	5 Wedlock
6 Houlker	6 Houlker	6 Makepeace	6 Hawkes	6 Veitch
7 Bond	7 Bond	7 Bond	7 Rutherford	7 Rutherford
8 Day	8 Day	8 Day	8 Coleman	8 Bloomer
9 Brown A.	9 Common	9 Shepherd	9 Hilsdon	9 Thornley
10 Harris	10 Harris	10 Harris	10 Bache	10 Stewart
11 Gosnell	11 Wright	11 Conlin	11 Hardman	11 Wall
Belfast Feb 17: 5-0 *Bond 2, Day, Harris, Brown*	Cardiff Mar 19: 1-0 *Day*	Glasgow April 7: 1-2 *Shepherd*	Everton Feb 16: 1-0 *Hardman*	Fulham Mar 18: 1-1 *Stewart*

1907 Scotland	**1908 Ireland**	**1908 Wales**	**1908 Scotland**	**1908 Austria**
1 Hardy	1 Maskrey	1 Bailey	1 Hardy	1 Bailey
2 Crompton	2 Crompton	2 Crompton	2 Crompton	2 Crompton
3 Pennington	3 Pennington	3 Pennington	3 Pennington	3 Corbett
4 Warren	4 Warren	4 Warren	4 Warren	4 Warren
5 Wedlock	5 Wedlock	5 Wedlock	5 Wedlock	5 Wedlock
6 Veitch	6 Lintott	6 Lintott	6 Lintott	6 Hawkes
7 Rutherford	7 Rutherford	7 Rutherford	7 Rutherford	7 Rutherford
8 Bloomer	8 Woodward	8 Woodward	8 Woodward	8 Woodward
9 Woodward	9 Hilsdon	9 Hilsdon	9 Hilsdon	9 Hilsdon
10 Stewart	10 Windridge	10 Windridge	10 Windridge	10 Windridge
11 Hardman	11 Wall	11 Hardman	11 Bridgett	11 Bridgett
Newcastle April 6: 1-1 *Bloomer*	Belfast Feb 15: 3-1 *Woodward,* *Hilsdon 2*	Wrexham Mar 16: 7-1 *Wedlock,* *Windridge* *Hilsdon 2,* *Woodward 3*	Glasgow April 4: 1-1 *Windridge*	Vienna June 6: 6-1 *Hilsdon 2,* *Windridge 2,* *Bridgett,* *Woodward*

1908 Austria	**1908 Hungary**	**1908 Bohemia**	**1909 Ireland**	**1909 Wales**
1 Bailey	1 Bailey	1 Bailey	1 Hardy	1 Hardy
2 Crompton	2 Crompton	2 Crompton	2 Crompton	2 Crompton
3 Pennington	3 Corbett	3 Corbett	3 Cottle	3 Pennington
4 Warren	4 Warren	4 Warren	4 Warren	4 Warren
5 Wedlock	5 Wedlock	5 Wedlock	5 Wedlock	5 Wedlock
6 Hawkes	6 Hawkes	6 Hawkes	6 Lintott	6 Veitch
7 Rutherford	7 Rutherford	7 Rutherford	7 Berry	7 Pentland
8 Woodward	8 Woodward	8 Woodward	8 Woodward	8 Woodward
9 Bradshaw	9 Hilsdon	9 Hilsdon	9 Hilsdon	9 Freeman
10 Windridge	10 Windridge	10 Windridge	10 Windridge	10 Holley
11 Bridgett	11 Bridgett	11 Bridgett	11 Bridgett	11 Bridgett
Vienna June 8: 11-1 *Woodward 4, Bridgett,* *Bradshaw 3, Warren,* *Rutherford,* *Windridge*	Budapest June 10: 7-0 *Hilsdon 4,* *Windridge,* *Woodward,* *Rutherford*	Prague June 13: 4-0 *Hilsdon 2,* *Windridge,* *Rutherford*	Bradford Feb 13: 4-0 *Hilsdon 2,* *Woodward 2*	Nottingham Mar 15: 2-0 *Holley,* *Freeman*

1909 Scotland	**1909 Hungary**	**1909 Hungary**	**1909 Austria**	**1910 Ireland**
1 Hardy	1 Hardy	1 Hardy	1 Hardy	1 Hardy
2 Crompton	2 Crompton	2 Crompton	2 Crompton	2 Morley
3 Pennington	3 Pennington	3 Pennington	3 Pennington	3 Cowell
4 Warren	4 Warren	4 Warren	4 Warren	4 Ducat
5 Wedlock	5 Wedlock	5 Wedlock	5 Wedlock	5 Wedlock
6 Lintott	6 Lintott	6 Lintott	6 Richards	6 Bradshaw
7 Pentland	7 Pentland	7 Pentland	7 Pentland	7 Bond
8 Fleming	8 Fleming	8 Fleming	8 Halse	8 Fleming
9 Freeman	9 Woodward	9 Woodward	9 Woodward	9 Woodward
10 Holley	10 Holley	10 Holley	10 Holley	10 Bache
11 Wall	11 Bridgett	11 Bridgett	11 Bridgett	11 Hall
Crystal Palace April 3: 2-0 *Wall 2*	Budapest May 29: 4-2 *Woodward 2,* *Fleming, Bridgett*	Budapest May 31: 8-2 *Woodward 4,* *Fleming 2,* *Holley 2*	Vienna June 1: 8-1 *Woodward 3,* *Warren, Halse 2,* *Holley 2*	Belfast Feb 12: 1-1 *Fleming*

1910 **Wales**	**1910** **Scotland**	**1911** **Ireland**	**1911** **Wales**	**1911** **Scotland**
1 Hardy	1 Hardy	1 Williamson	1 Williamson	1 Williamson
2 Crompton	2 Crompton	2 Crompton	2 Crompton	2 Crompton
3 Pennington	3 Pennington	3 Pennington	3 Pennington	3 Pennington
4 Ducat	4 Ducat	4 Warren	4 Warren	4 Warren
5 Wedlock	5 Wedlock	5 Wedlock	5 Wedlock	5 Wedlock
6 Bradshaw	6 Makepeace	6 Sturgess	6 Rev Hunt	6 Rev Hunt
7 Bond	7 Bond	7 Simpson	7 Simpson	7 Simpson
8 Fleming	8 Hibbett	8 Fleming	8 Fleming	8 Stewart
9 Parkinson	9 Parkinson	9 Shepherd	9 Webb	9 Webb
10 Holley	10 Hardinge	10 Woodger	10 Woodward	10 Bache
11 Wall	11 Wall	11 Evans	11 Evans	11 Evans
Cardiff	Glasgow	Derby	Millwall	Everton
Mar 14: 1-0	April 2: 0-2	Feb 11: 2-1	Mar 13: 3-0	April 1: 1-1
Ducat		*Shepherd, Evans*	*Woodward 2, Webb*	*Stewart*

1912 **Ireland**	**1912** **Wales**	**1912** **Scotland**	**1913** **Ireland**	**1913** **Wales**
1 Hardy	1 Williamson	1 Williamson	1 Williamson	1 Scattergood
2 Crompton	2 Crompton	2 Crompton	2 Crompton	2 Crompton
3 Pennington	3 Pennington	3 Pennington	3 Benson	3 Pennington
4 Brittleton	4 Brittleton	4 Brittleton	4 Cuggy	4 Moffatt
5 Wedlock	5 Wedlock	5 Wedlock	5 Boyle	5 McCall
6 Bradshaw	6 Makepeace	6 Makepeace	6 Utley	6 Bradshaw
7 Simpson	7 Simpson	7 Simpson	7 Mordue	7 Wallace
8 Fleming	8 Jefferis	8 Jefferis	8 Buchan	8 Fleming
9 Freeman	9 Freeman	9 Freeman	9 Elliott	9 Hampton
10 Holley	10 Holley	10 Holley	10 Smith, Joe	10 Latheron
11 Mordue	11 Evans	11 Wall	11 Wall	11 Hodkinson
Dublin	Wrexham	Glasgow	Belfast	Bristol
Feb 10: 6-1	Mar 11: 2-0	Mar 23: 1-1	Feb 15: 1-2	Mar 17: 4-3
Fleming 3, Freeman, Holley, Simpson	*Holley, Freeman*	*Holley*	*Buchan*	*Fleming, McCall, Latheron, Hampton*

1913 **Scotland**	**1914** **Ireland**	**1914** **Wales**	**1914** **Scotland**	**1919** **Ireland**
1 Hardy	1 Hardy	1 Hardy	1 Hardy	1 Hardy
2 Crompton	2 Crompton	2 Crompton	2 Crompton	2 Smith, Joe (*WBA*)
3 Pennington	3 Pennington	3 Colclough	3 Pennington	3 Knight
4 Brittleton	4 Cuggy	4 Brittleton	4 Sturgess	4 Bagshaw
5 McCall	5 Buckley	5 Wedlock	5 McCall	5 Bowser
6 Watson	6 Watson	6 McNeal	6 McNeal	6 Watson
7 Simpson	7 Wallace	7 Simpson	7 Walden	7 Turnbull
8 Fleming	8 Shea	8 Shea	8 Fleming	8 Carr
9 Hampton	9 Elliott	9 Hampton	9 Hampton	9 Cock
10 Holley	10 Latheron	10 Smith, Joe	10 Smith, Joe	10 Smith, Joe (*Bolton W*)
11 Hodkinson	11 Martin	11 Mosscrop	11 Mosscrop	11 Hodkinson
Chelsea	Middlesbrough	Cardiff	Glasgow	Belfast
April 5: 1-0	Feb 14: 0-3	Mar 16: 2-0	April 4: 1-3	Oct 25: 1-1
Hampton		*Smith, Wedlock*	*Fleming*	*Cock*

1920 Wales	**1920 Scotland**	**1920 Ireland**	**1921 Wales**	**1921 Scotland**
1 Hardy	1 Hardy	1 Mew	1 Coleman	1 Gough
2 Clay	2 Longworth	2 Downs	2 Cresswell	2 Smart
3 Pennington	3 Pennington	3 Bullock	3 Silcock	3 Silcock
4 Ducat	4 Ducat	4 Ducat	4 Bamber	4 Smith B.
5 Barson	5 McCall	5 McCall	5 Wilson	5 Wilson
6 Grimsdell	6 Grimsdell	6 Grimsdell	6 Bromilow	6 Grimsdell
7 Chedgzoy	7 Wallace	7 Chedgzoy	7 Chedgzoy	7 Chedgzoy
8 Buchan	8 Kelly	8 Kelly	8 Kelly	8 Kelly
9 Elliott	9 Cock	9 Walker	9 Buchan	9 Chambers
10 Smith, Joe	10 Morris	10 Morris	10 Chambers	10 Bliss
11 Quantrill	11 Quantrill	11 Quantrill	11 Quantrill	11 Dimmock
Arsenal	Sheffield	Sunderland	Cardiff	Glasgow
Mar 15: 1-2	April 10: 5-4	Oct 23: 2-0	Mar 14: 0-0	April 9: 0-3
Buchan	*Kelly 2, Cock, Morris, Quantrill*	*Kelly, Walker*		

1921 Belgium	**1921 Ireland**	**1922 Wales**	**1922 Scotland**	**1922 Ireland**
1 Baker H.	1 Dawson	1 Davison	1 Dawson	1 Taylor
2 Fort	2 Clay	2 Clay	2 Clay	2 Smith, Joe (*WBA*)
3 Longworth	3 Lucas	3 Titmuss	3 Wadsworth	3 Harrow
4 Read	4 Moss	4 Smith B.	4 Moss	4 Moss
5 Wilson	5 Wilson	5 Woosnam	5 Wilson	5 Wilson
6 Barton	6 Barton	6 Bromilow	6 Bromilow	6 Grimsdell
7 Rawlings	7 Chedgzoy	7 Walden	7 York	7 Mercer
8 Seed	8 Kirton	8 Kelly	8 Kelly	8 Seed
9 Buchan	9 Simms	9 Rawlings	9 Rawlings	9 Osborne
10 Chambers	10 Walker	10 Walker	10 Walker	10 Chambers
11 Harrison	11 Harrison	11 Smith W.H.	11 Smith W.H.	11 Williams
Brussels	Belfast	Liverpool	Birmingham	West Bromwich
May 21: 2-0	Oct 22: 1-1	Mar 13: 1-0	April 8: 0-1	Oct 21: 2-0
Buchan, Chambers	*Kirton*	*Kelly*		*Chambers 2*

1923 Wales	**1923 Belgium**	**1923 Scotland**	**1923 France**	**1923 Sweden**
1 Taylor	1 Taylor	1 Taylor	1 Alderson	1 Williamson
2 Longworth	2 Longworth	2 Longworth	2 Cresswell	2 Ashurst
3 Titmuss	3 Wadsworth	3 Wadsworth	3 Jones H.	3 Harrow
4 Magee	4 Kean	4 Kean	4 Plum	4 Patchitt
5 Wilson	5 Wilson	5 Wilson	5 Seddon	5 Seddon
6 Grimsdell	6 Bromilow	6 Tresadern	6 Barton	6 Tresadern
7 Carr	7 Mercer	7 Chedgzoy	7 Osborne	7 Thornewell
8 Seed	8 Seed	8 Kelly	8 Buchan	8 Moore
9 Watson	9 Bullock	9 Watson	9 Creek	9 Bedford
10 Chambers	10 Chambers	10 Chambers	10 Hartley	10 Walker
11 Williams	11 Hegan	11 Tunstall	11 Hegan	11 Urwin
Cardiff	Arsenal	Glasgow	Paris	Stockholm
Mar 5: 2-2	Mar 19: 6-1	April 14: 2-2	May 10: 4-1	May 21: 4-2
Chambers, Watson	*Hegan 2, Chambers, Mercer, Seed, Bullock*	*Kelly, Watson*	*Hegan 2, Buchan, Creek*	*Walker 2, Moore, Thornewell*

1923 Sweden	1923 Ireland	1923 Belgium	1924 Wales	1924 Scotland
1 Williamson	1 Taylor	1 Hufton	1 Sewell	1 Taylor
2 Ashurst	2 Bower	2 Cresswell	2 Smart	2 Smart
3 Silcock	3 Wadsworth	3 Bower	3 Mort	3 Wadsworth
4 Magee	4 Pantling	4 Moss	4 Kean	4 Moss
5 Seddon	5 Wilson	5 Seddon	5 Wilson	5 Spencer
6 Patchitt	6 Meehan	6 Barton	6 Barton	6 Barton
7 Thornewell	7 Hegan	7 Hegan	7 Chedgzoy	7 Butler
8 Moore	8 Kelly	8 Brown W.	8 Jack	8 Jack
9 Walker	9 Bradford	9 Roberts	9 Roberts	9 Buchan
10 Miller	10 Chambers	10 Doggart	10 Stephenson	10 Walker
11 Urwin	11 Tunstall	11 Urwin	11 Tunstall	11 Tunstall
Stockholm May 24: 3-1 *Moore 2, Miller*	Belfast Oct 20: 1-2 *Bradford*	Antwerp Nov 1: 2-2 *Brown, Roberts*	Blackburn Mar 3: 1-2 *Roberts*	Wembley April 12: 1-1 *Walker*

1924 France	1924 Ireland	1924 Belgium	1925 Wales	1925 Scotland
1 Taylor	1 Mitchell	1 Hardy	1 Pym	1 Pym
2 Lucas	2 Cresswell	2 Ashurst	2 Ashurst	2 Ashurst
3 Mort	3 Wadsworth	3 Bower	3 Bower	3 Wadsworth
4 Ewer	4 Keen	4 Magee	4 Hill	4 Magee
5 Wilson	5 Healless	5 Butler	5 Spencer	5 Townrow
6 Blackburn	6 Barton	6 Ewer	6 Graham	6 Graham
7 Thornewell	7 Chedgzoy	7 Osborne	7 Kelly	7 Kelly
8 Earle	8 Kelly	8 Roberts	8 Roberts	8 Seed
9 Gibbins	9 Bedford	9 Bradford	9 Cook	9 Roberts
10 Storer	10 Walker	10 Walker	10 Walker	10 Walker
11 Tunstall	11 Tunstall	11 Dorrell	11 Dorrell	11 Tunstall
Paris May 17: 3-1 *Gibbins 2, Storer*	Everton Oct 22: 3-1 *Kelly, Bedford, Walker*	West Bromwich Dec 8: 4-0 *Bradford 2, Walker 2*	Swansea Feb 28: 2-1 *Roberts 2*	Glasgow April 4: 0-2

1925 France	1925 Ireland	1926 Wales	1926 Scotland	1926 Belgium
1 Fox	1 Baker H.	1 Pym	1 Taylor	1 Ashmore
2 Parker	2 Smart	2 Cresswell	2 Goodall	2 Lucas
3 Felton	3 Hudspeth	3 Wadsworth	3 Mort	3 Hill R.H.
4 Magee	4 Kean	4 Edwards	4 Edwards	4 Kean
5 Bryant	5 Armitage	5 Townrow	5 Hill	5 Cowan
6 Green	6 Bromilow	6 Green	6 Green	6 Green
7 Thornewell	7 Austin	7 Urwin	7 York	7 Spence
8 Roberts	8 Puddefoot	8 Kelly	8 Puddefoot	8 Carter J.H.
9 Gibbins	9 Ashton	9 Bullock	9 Harper	9 Osborne
10 Walker	10 Walker	10 Walker	10 Walker	10 Johnson
11 Dorrell	11 Dorrell	11 Dimmock	11 Ruffell	11 Dimmock
Paris May 21: 3-2 *Gibbins, Dorrell, 1 og*	Belfast Oct 24: 0-0	Selhurst Mar 1: 1-3 *Walker*	Manchester April 17: 0-1	Antwerp May 24: 5-3 *Osborne 3, Carter, Johnson*

1926 Ireland	**1927 Wales**	**1927 Scotland**	**1927 Belgium**	**1927 Luxembourg**
1 McInroy	1 Brown J.	1 Brown J.	1 Brown J.	1 Brown J.
2 Cresswell	2 Bower	2 Goodall	2 Goodall	2 Goodall
3 Wadsworth	3 Waterfield	3 Jones H.	3 Jones H.	3 Jones H.
4 Edwards	4 Edwards	4 Edwards	4 Edwards	4 Edwards
5 Hill	5 Seddon	5 Hill	5 Hill	5 Kean
6 Green	6 Green	6 Bishop	6 Bishop	6 Bishop
7 Spence	7 Pease	7 Hulme	7 Hulme	7 Kelly
8 Brown G.	8 Brown G.	8 Brown G.	8 Brown G.	8 Brown G.
9 Bullock	9 Dean	9 Dean	9 Dean	9 Dean
10 Walker	10 Walker	10 Rigby	10 Rigby	10 Rigby
11 Ruffell	11 Page	11 Page	11 Page	11 Page
Liverpool Oct 20: 3-3 *Brown, Spence, Bullock*	Wrexham Feb 12: 3-3 *Dean 2, Walker*	Glasgow April 2: 2-1 *Dean 2*	Brussels May 11: 9-1 *Dean 3, Brown 2, Rigby 2, Page, Hulme*	Luxembourg May 21: 5-2 *Dean 3, Kelly, Bishop*

1927 France	**1927 Ireland**	**1927 Wales**	**1928 Scotland**	**1928 France**
1 Brown J.	1 Hufton	1 Tremelling	1 Hufton	1 Olney
2 Goodall	2 Cooper	2 Goodall	2 Goodall	2 Goodall
3 Jones H.	3 Jones H.	3 Osborne	3 Jones H.	3 Blenkinsop
4 Edwards	4 Nuttall	4 Baker	4 Edwards	4 Edwards
5 Hill	5 Hill	5 Hill	5 Wilson	5 Matthews
6 Bishop	6 Storer	6 Nuttall	6 Healless	6 Green
7 Hulme	7 Hulme	7 Hulme	7 Hulme	7 Bruton
8 Brown G.	8 Earle	8 Brown G.	8 Kelly	8 Jack
9 Dean	9 Dean	9 Dean	9 Dean	9 Dean
10 Rigby	10 Ball	10 Rigby	10 Bradford	10 Stephenson
11 Page	11 Page	11 Page	11 Smith W.H.	11 Barry
Paris May 26: 6-0 *Dean 2, Brown 2, Rigby, Rollet og*	Belfast Oct 22: 0-2	Burnley Nov 28: 1-2 *Keenor og*	Wembley Mar 31: 1-5 *Kelly*	Paris May 17: 5-1 *Stephenson 2, Dean 2, Jack*

1928 Belgium	**1928 Ireland**	**1928 Wales**	**1929 Scotland**	**1929 France**
1 Olney	1 Hacking	1 Hacking	1 Hacking	1 Hufton
2 Goodall	2 Cooper	2 Cooper	2 Cooper	2 Blenkinsop
3 Blenkinsop	3 Blenkinsop	3 Blenkinsop	3 Blenkinsop	3 Cooper
4 Edwards	4 Edwards	4 Edwards	4 Edwards	4 Kean
5 Matthews	5 Barrett J.	5 Hart	5 Seddon	5 Hill
6 Green	6 Campbell	6 Campbell	6 Nuttall	6 Peacock
7 Bruton	7 Hulme	7 Hulme	7 Bruton	7 Adcock
8 Jack	8 Hine	8 Hine	8 Brown G.	8 Kail
9 Dean	9 Dean	9 Dean	9 Dean	9 Camsell
10 Stephenson	10 Bradford	10 Bradford	10 Wainscoat	10 Bradford
11 Barry	11 Ruffell	11 Ruffell	11 Ruffell	11 Barry
Antwerp May 19: 3-1 *Dean 2, Matthews*	Everton Oct 22: 2-1 *Hulme, Dean*	Swansea Nov 17: 3-2 *Hulme 2, Hine*	Glasgow April 13: 0-1	Paris May 9: 4-1 *Kail 2, Camsell 2*

1929 Belgium	1929 Spain	1929 Ireland	1929 Wales	1930 Scotland
1 Hufton	1 Hufton	1 Brown J.	1 Hibbs	1 Hibbs
2 Cooper	2 Cooper	2 Cresswell	2 Smart	2 Goodall
3 Blenkinsop	3 Blenkinsop	3 Blenkinsop	3 Blenkinsop	3 Blenkinsop
4 Oliver	4 Kean	4 Edwards	4 Edwards	4 Strange
5 Hill	5 Hill	5 Hart	5 Hart	5 Webster
6 Peacock	6 Peacock	6 Barrett A.	6 Marsden	6 Marsden
7 Adcock	7 Adcock	7 Adcock	7 Adcock	7 Crooks
8 Kail	8 Kail	8 Hine	8 Hine	8 Jack
9 Camsell	9 Bradford	9 Camsell	9 Camsell	9 Watson
10 Carter J.H.	10 Carter J.H.	10 Bradford	10 Johnson	10 Bradford
11 Barry	11 Barry	11 Brook	11 Ruffell	11 Rimmer
Brussels May 11: 5-1 *Camsell 4, Carter*	Madrid May 15: 3-4 *Carter 2, Bradford*	Belfast Oct 19: 3-0 *Camsell 2, Hine*	Chelsea Nov 20: 6-0 *Adcock, Camsell 3, Johnson 2*	Wembley April 5: 5-2 *Jack, Watson 2, Rimmer 2*

1930 Germany	1930 Austria	1930 Ireland	1930 Wales	1931 Scotland
1 Hibbs	1 Hibbs	1 Hibbs	1 Hibbs	1 Hibbs
2 Goodall	2 Goodall	2 Goodall	2 Goodall	2 Goodall
3 Blenkinsop	3 Blenkinsop	3 Blenkinsop	3 Blenkinsop	3 Blenkinsop
4 Strange	4 Strange	4 Strange	4 Strange	4 Strange
5 Webster	5 Webster	5 Leach	5 Leach	5 Roberts
6 Marsden	6 Cowan	6 Campbell	6 Campbell	6 Campbell
7 Crooks	7 Crooks	7 Crooks	7 Crooks	7 Crooks
8 Jack	8 Jack	8 Hodgson	8 Hodgson	8 Hodgson
9 Watson	9 Watson	9 Hampson	9 Hampson	9 Dean
10 Bradford	10 Bradford	10 Burgess	10 Bradford	10 Burgess
11 Rimmer	11 Rimmer	11 Houghton	11 Houghton	11 Crawford
Berlin May 10: 3-3 *Bradford 2, Jack*	Vienna May 14: 0-0	Sheffield Oct 20: 5-1 *Burgess 2, Crooks, Hampson, Houghton*	Wrexham Nov 22: 4-0 *Hodgson, Bradford, Hampson 2*	Glasgow Mar 28: 0-2

1931 France	1931 Belgium	1931 Ireland	1931 Wales	1931 Spain
1 Turner	1 Turner	1 Hibbs	1 Hibbs	1 Hibbs
2 Cooper	2 Goodall	2 Goodall	2 Cooper	2 Cooper
3 Blenkinsop	3 Blenkinsop	3 Blenkinsop	3 Blenkinsop	3 Blenkinsop
4 Strange	4 Strange	4 Strange	4 Strange	4 Strange
5 Graham	5 Cowan	5 Graham	5 Gee	5 Gee
6 Tate	6 Tate	6 Campbell	6 Campbell	6 Campbell
7 Crooks	7 Crooks	7 Crooks	7 Crooks	7 Crooks
8 Stephenson	8 Roberts	8 Smith J.	8 Smith J.	8 Smith J.
9 Waring	9 Waring	9 Waring	9 Waring	9 Dean
10 Burgess	10 Burgess	10 Hine	10 Hine	10 Johnson
11 Houghton	11 Houghton	11 Houghton	11 Bastin	11 Rimmer
Paris May 14: 2-5 *Crooks, Waring*	Brussels May 16: 4-1 *Burgess 2, Houghton, Roberts*	Belfast Oct 17: 6-2 *Waring 2, Smith, Hine, Houghton 2*	Liverpool Nov 18: 3-1 *Smith, Crooks, Hine*	Arsenal Dec 9: 7-1 *Smith 2, Johnson 2, Crooks 2, Dean*

1932 Scotland	1932 Ireland	1932 Wales	1932 Austria	1933 Scotland
1 Pearson	1 Hibbs	1 Hibbs	1 Hibbs	1 Hibbs
2 Shaw	2 Goodall	2 Goodall	2 Goodall	2 Cooper
3 Blenkinsop	3 Blenkinsop	3 Blenkinsop	3 Blenkinsop	3 Blenkinsop
4 Strange	4 Strange	4 Stoker	4 Strange	4 Strange
5 O'Dowd	5 O'Dowd	5 Young	5 Hart	5 Hart
6 Weaver	6 Weaver	6 Tate	6 Keen	6 Weaver
7 Crooks	7 Crooks	7 Crooks	7 Crooks	7 Hulme
8 Barclay	8 Barclay	8 Jack	8 Jack	8 Starling
9 Waring	9 Dean	9 Brown G.	9 Hampson	9 Hunt
10 Johnson	10 Johnson	10 Sandford	10 Walker	10 Pickering
11 Houghton	11 Cunliffe	11 Cunliffe	11 Houghton	11 Arnold
Wembley April 9: 3-0 *Waring, Crooks Barclay*	Blackpool Oct 17: 1-0 *Barclay*	Wrexham Nov 16: 0-0	Chelsea Dec 7: 4-3 *Hampson 2, Houghton, Crooks*	Glasgow April 1: 1-2 *Hunt*

1933 Italy	1933 Switzerland	1933 Ireland	1933 Wales	1933 France
1 Hibbs	1 Hibbs	1 Hibbs	1 Hibbs	1 Hibbs
2 Goodall	2 Goodall	2 Goodall	2 Goodall	2 Goodall
3 Hapgood	3 Hapgood	3 Hapgood	3 Hapgood	3 Fairhurst
4 Strange	4 Strange	4 Strange	4 Strange	4 Strange
5 White	5 O'Dowd	5 Allen	5 Allen	5 Rowe
6 Copping	6 Copping	6 Copping	6 Copping	6 Copping
7 Geldard	7 Geldard	7 Crooks	7 Crooks	7 Crooks
8 Richardson J.R.	8 Richardson J.R.	8 Grosvenor	8 Grosvenor	8 Grosvenor
9 Hunt	9 Hunt	9 Bowers	9 Bowers	9 Camsell
10 Furness	10 Bastin	10 Bastin	10 Bastin	10 Hall
11 Bastin	11 Brook	11 Brook	11 Brook	11 Brook
Rome May 13: 1-1 *Bastin*	Berne May 20: 4-0 *Bastin 2, Richardson 2*	Belfast Oct 14: 3-0 *Brook, Grosvenor Bowers*	Newcastle Nov 15: 1-2 *Brook*	Tottenham Dec 6: 4-1 *Camsell 2, Brook, Grosvenor*

1934 Scotland	1934 Hungary	1934 Czechoslovakia	1934 Wales	1934 Italy
1 Moss	1 Moss	1 Moss	1 Hibbs	1 Moss
2 Cooper	2 Cooper	2 Cooper	2 Cooper	2 Male
3 Hapgood	3 Hapgood	3 Hapgood	3 Hapgood	3 Hapgood
4 Stoker	4 Stoker	4 Gardner	4 Britton	4 Britton
5 Hart	5 Hart	5 Hart	5 Barker	5 Barker
6 Copping	6 Burrows	6 Burrows	6 Bray	6 Copping
7 Crooks	7 Crooks	7 Crooks	7 Matthews	7 Matthews
8 Carter H.S.	8 Carter H.S.	8 Beresford	8 Bowden	8 Bowden
9 Bowers	9 Tilson	9 Tilson	9 Tilson	9 Drake
10 Bastin	10 Bastin	10 Bastin	10 Westwood	10 Bastin
11 Brook	11 Brook	11 Brook	11 Brook	11 Brook
Wembley April 14: 3-0 *Brook, Bastin, Bowers*	Budapest May 10: 1-2 *Tilson*	Prague May 16: 1-2 *Tilson*	Cardiff Sept 29: 4-0 *Tilson 2, Brook, Matthews*	Arsenal Nov 14: 3-2 *Brook 2, Drake*

1935 Ireland	1935 Scotland	1935 Holland	1935 Ireland	1935 Germany
1 Hibbs	1 Hibbs	1 Hibbs	1 Sagar	1 Hibbs
2 Male	2 Male	2 Male	2 Male	2 Male
3 Hapgood	3 Hapgood	3 Hapgood	3 Hapgood	3 Hapgood
4 Britton	4 Britton	4 Gardner	4 Smith S.	4 Crayston
5 Barker	5 Barker	5 Barker	5 Barker	5 Barker
6 Copping	6 Alsford	6 Burrows	6 Bray	6 Bray
7 Crooks	7 Geldard	7 Worrall	7 Birkett	7 Matthews
8 Bestall	8 Bastin	8 Eastham	8 Bowden	8 Carter H.S.
9 Drake	9 Gurney	9 Richardson W.G.	9 Tilson	9 Camsell
10 Bastin	10 Westwood	10 Westwood	10 Westwood	10 Westwood
11 Brook	11 Brook	11 Boyes	11 Brook	11 Bastin
Everton	Glasgow	Amsterdam	Belfast	Tottenham
Feb 6: 2-1	April 6: 0-2	May 18: 1-0	Oct 19: 3-1	Dec 4: 3-0
Bastin 2		*Worrall*	*Tilson 2, Brook*	*Camsell 2, Bastin*

1936 Wales	1936 Scotland	1936 Austria	1936 Belgium	1936 Wales
1 Hibbs	1 Sagar	1 Sagar	1 Sagar	1 Holdcroft
2 Male	2 Male	2 Male	2 Male	2 Sproston
3 Hapgood	3 Hapgood	3 Hapgood	3 Hapgood	3 Catlin
4 Crayston	4 Crayston	4 Crayston	4 Crayston	4 Smalley
5 Barker	5 Barker	5 Barker	5 Joy	5 Barker
6 Bray	6 Bray	6 Copping	6 Copping	6 Keen
7 Crooks	7 Crooks	7 Spence	7 Spence	7 Crooks
8 Bowden	8 Barclay	8 Bowden	8 Barkas	8 Scott
9 Drake	9 Camsell	9 Camsell	9 Camsell	9 Steele
10 Bastin	10 Bastin	10 Bastin	10 Cunliffe	10 Westwood
11 Brook	11 Brook	11 Hobbis	11 Hobbis	11 Bastin
Wolverhampton	Wembley	Vienna	Brussels	Cardiff
Feb 5: 1-2	April 4: 1-1	May 6: 1-2	May 9: 2-3	Oct 17: 1-2
Bowden	*Camsell*	*Camsell*	*Camsell, Hobbis*	*Bastin*

1936 Ireland	1936 Hungary	1937 Scotland	1937 Norway	1937 Sweden
1 Holdcroft	1 Tweedy	1 Woodley	1 Woodley	1 Woodley
2 Male	2 Male	2 Male	2 Male	2 Male
3 Catlin	3 Catlin	3 Barkas	3 Catlin	3 Catlin
4 Britton	4 Britton	4 Britton	4 Britton	4 Britton
5 Gee	5 Young	5 Young	5 Young	5 Young
6 Keen	6 Keen	6 Bray	6 Copping	6 Copping
7 Worrall	7 Crooks	7 Matthews	7 Kirchen	7 Kirchen
8 Carter H.S.	8 Bowden	8 Carter H.S.	8 Galley	8 Galley
9 Steele	9 Drake	9 Steele	9 Steele	9 Steele
10 Bastin	10 Carter H.S.	10 Starling	10 Goulden	10 Goulden
11 Johnson	11 Brook	11 Johnson	11 Johnson	11 Johnson
Stoke	Arsenal	Glasgow	Oslo	Stockholm
Nov 18: 3-1	Dec 2: 6-2	April 17: 1-3	May 14: 6-0	May 17: 4-0
Carter, Bastin, Worrall	*Drake 3, Brook, Britton, Carter*	*Steele*	*Steele 2, Kirchen, Galley, Goulden, Holmsen og*	*Steele 3, Johnson*

1937 Finland	**1937 Ireland**	**1937 Wales**	**1937 Czechoslovakia**	**1938 Scotland**
1 Woodley	1 Woodley	1 Woodley	1 Woodley	1 Woodley
2 Male	2 Sproston	2 Sproston	2 Sproston	2 Sproston
3 Hapgood	3 Barkas	3 Barkas	3 Barkas	3 Hapgood
4 Willingham	4 Crayston	4 Crayston	4 Crayston	4 Willingham
5 Betmead	5 Cullis	5 Cullis	5 Cullis	5 Cullis
6 Copping	6 Copping	6 Copping	6 Copping	6 Copping
7 Kirchen	7 Geldard	7 Matthews	7 Matthews	7 Matthews
8 Robinson	8 Hall	8 Hall	8 Hall	8 Hall
9 Payne	9 Mills	9 Mills	9 Mills	9 Fenton
10 Steele	10 Goulden	10 Goulden	10 Goulden	10 Stephenson
11 Johnson	11 Brook	11 Brook	11 Morton	11 Bastin
Helsinki	Belfast	Middlesbrough	Tottenham	Wembley
May 20: 8-0	Oct 23: 5-1	Nov 17: 2-1	Dec 1: 5-4	April 9: 0-1
Payne 2, Steele 2, Kirchen, Willingham, Johnson, Robinson	*Mills 3, Hall, Brook*	*Matthews, Hall*	*Crayston, Morton, Matthews 3*	

1938 Germany	**1938 Switzerland**	**1938 France**	**1938 Wales**	**1938 FIFA**
1 Woodley	1 Woodley	1 Woodley	1 Woodley	1 Woodley
2 Sproston	2 Sproston	2 Sproston	2 Sproston	2 Sproston
3 Hapgood	3 Hapgood	3 Hapgood	3 Hapgood	3 Hapgood
4 Willingham	4 Willingham	4 Willingham	4 Willingham	4 Willingham
5 Young	5 Young	5 Young	5 Young	5 Cullis
6 Welsh	6 Welsh	6 Cullis	6 Copping	6 Copping
7 Matthews	7 Matthews	7 Broome	7 Matthews	7 Matthews
8 Robinson	8 Robinson	8 Matthews	8 Robinson	8 Hall
9 Broome	9 Broome	9 Drake	9 Lawton	9 Lawton
10 Goulden	10 Goulden	10 Goulden	10 Goulden	10 Goulden
11 Bastin	11 Bastin	11 Bastin	11 Boyes	11 Boyes
Berlin	Zurich	Paris	Cardiff	Arsenal
May 14: 6-3	May 21: 1-2	May 26: 4-2	Oct 22: 2-4	Oct 26: 3-0
Robinson 2, Bastin, Broome, Matthews, Goulden	*Bastin*	*Drake 2, Broome, Bastin*	*Lawton, Matthews*	*Hall, Lawton, Goulden*

1938 Norway	**1938 Ireland**	**1939 Scotland**	**1939 Italy**	**1939 Yugoslavia**
1 Woodley	1 Woodley	1 Woodley	1 Woodley	1 Woodley
2 Sproston	2 Morris	2 Morris	2 Male	2 Male
3 Hapgood	3 Hapgood	3 Hapgood	3 Hapgood	3 Hapgood
4 Willingham	4 Willingham	4 Willingham	4 Willingham	4 Willingham
5 Cullis	5 Cullis	5 Cullis	5 Cullis	5 Cullis
6 Wright D.	6 Mercer	6 Mercer	6 Mercer	6 Mercer
7 Matthews	7 Matthews	7 Matthews	7 Matthews	7 Matthews
8 Broome	8 Hall	8 Hall	8 Hall	8 Hall
9 Lawton	9 Lawton	9 Lawton	9 Lawton	9 Lawton
10 Dix	10 Stephenson	10 Goulden	10 Goulden	10 Goulden
11 Smith J.R.	11 Smith J.R.	11 Beasley	11 Broome	11 Broome
Newcastle	Manchester	Glasgow	Milan	Belgrade
Nov 9: 4-0	Nov 16: 7-0	April 15: 2-1	May 13: 2-2	May 18: 1-2
Smith 2, Dix, Lawton	*Hall 5, Lawton, Matthews*	*Beasley, Lawton*	*Lawton, Hall*	*Broome*

1939 Rumania	**1946 N Ireland**	**1946 Rep of Ireland**	**1946 Wales**	**1946 Netherlands**
1 Woodley	1 Swift	1 Swift	1 Swift	1 Swift
2 Male	2 Scott	2 Scott	2 Scott	2 Scott
3 Morris	3 Hardwick	3 Hardwick	3 Hardwick	3 Hardwick
4 Mercer	4 Wright W.	4 Wright W.	4 Wright W.	4 Wright W.
5 Cullis	5 Franklin	5 Franklin	5 Franklin	5 Franklin
6 Copping	6 Cockburn	6 Cockburn	6 Cockburn	6 Johnston
7 Broome	7 Finney	7 Finney	7 Finney	7 Finney
8 Goulden	8 Carter	8 Carter	8 Carter	8 Carter
9 Lawton	9 Lawton	9 Lawton	9 Lawton	9 Lawton
10 Welsh	10 Mannion	10 Mannion	10 Mannion	10 Mannion
11 Smith L.C.	11 Langton	11 Langton	11 Langton	11 Langton
Bucharest May 24: 2-0 *Goulden, Welsh*	Belfast Sept 28: 7-2 *Carter, Mannion 3, Finney, Lawton, Langton*	Dublin Sept 30: 1-0 *Finney*	Maine Road Oct 19: 3-0 *Mannion 2, Lawton*	Huddersfield Nov 27: 8-2 *Lawton 4, Carter 2, Mannion, Finney*

1947 Scotland	**1947 France**	**1947 Switzerland**	**1947 Portugal**	**1947 Belgium**
1 Swift	1 Swift	1 Swift	1 Swift	1 Swift
2 Scott	2 Scott	2 Scott	2 Scott	2 Scott
3 Hardwick	3 Hardwick	3 Hardwick	3 Hardwick	3 Hardwick
4 Wright W.	4 Wright W.	4 Wright W.	4 Wright W.	4 Ward
5 Franklin	5 Franklin	5 Franklin	5 Franklin	5 Franklin
6 Johnston	6 Lowe	6 Lowe	6 Lowe	6 Wright W.
7 Matthews S.	7 Finney	7 Matthews S.	7 Matthews S.	7 Matthews S.
8 Carter	8 Carter	8 Carter	8 Mortensen	8 Mortensen
9 Lawton	9 Lawton	9 Lawton	9 Lawton	9 Lawton
10 Mannion	10 Mannion	10 Mannion	10 Mannion	10 Mannion
11 Mullen	11 Langton	11 Langton	11 Finney	11 Finney
Wembley April 12: 1-1 *Carter*	Highbury May 3: 3-0 *Finney, Mannion, Carter*	Zurich May 18: 0-1	Lisbon May 27: 10-0 *Lawton 4 Mortensen 4, Finney, Matthews*	Brussels Sept 21: 5-2 *Lawton 2, Mortensen, Finney 2*

1947 Wales	**1947 N Ireland**	**1947 Sweden**	**1948 Scotland**	**1948 Italy**
1 Swift	1 Swift	1 Swift	1 Swift	1 Swift
2 Scott	2 Scott	2 Scott	2 Scott	2 Scott
3 Hardwick	3 Hardwick	3 Hardwick	3 Hardwick	3 Howe J.
4 Taylor P.	4 Taylor P.	4 Taylor P.	4 Wright W.	4 Wright W.
5 Franklin	5 Franklin	5 Franklin	5 Franklin	5 Franklin
6 Wright W.	6 Wright W.	6 Wright W.	6 Cockburn	6 Cockburn
7 Matthews S.	7 Matthews S.	7 Finney	7 Matthews S.	7 Matthews S.
8 Mortensen	8 Mortensen	8 Mortensen	8 Mortensen	8 Mortensen
9 Lawton	9 Lawton	9 Lawton	9 Lawton	9 Lawton
10 Mannion	10 Mannion	10 Mannion	10 Pearson	10 Mannion
11 Finney	11 Finney	11 Langton	11 Finney	11 Finney
Cardiff Oct 18: 3-0 *Finney, Mortensen, Lawton*	Everton Nov 5: 2-2 *Mannion, Lawton*	Highbury Nov 19: 4-2 *Mortensen 3, Lawton* (pen)	Glasgow April 10: 2-0 *Finney, Mortensen*	Turin May 16: 4-0 *Mortensen, Lawton, Finney 2*

1948 Denmark	1948 N Ireland	1948 Wales	1948 Switzerland	1948 Scotland
1 Swift	1 Swift	1 Swift	1 Ditchburn	1 Swift
2 Scott	2 Scott	2 Scott	2 Ramsey	2 Aston
3 Aston	3 Howe J.	3 Aston	3 Aston	3 Howe J.
4 Wright W.	4 Wright W.	4 Ward	4 Wright W.	4 Wright W.
5 Franklin	5 Franklin	5 Franklin	5 Franklin	5 Franklin
6 Cockburn	6 Cockburn	6 Wright W.	6 Cockburn	6 Cockburn
7 Matthews S.	7 Matthews S.	7 Matthews S.	7 Matthews S.	7 Matthews S.
8 Hagan	8 Mortensen	8 Mortensen	8 Rowley J.	8 Mortensen
9 Lawton	9 Milburn	9 Milburn	9 Milburn	9 Milburn
10 Shackleton	10 Pearson	10 Shackleton	10 Haines	10 Pearson
11 Langton	11 Finney	11 Finney	11 Hancocks	11 Finney
Copenhagen Sept 26: 0-0	Belfast Oct 9: 6-2 *Matthews S, Mortensen 3, Milburn, Pearson*	Villa Park Nov 10: 1-0 *Finney*	Highbury Dec 1: 6-0 *Haines 2, Hancocks 2 Rowley, Milburn*	Wembley April 9: 1-3 *Milburn*

1949 Sweden	1949 Norway	1949 France	1949 Rep of Ireland	1949 Wales
1 Ditchburn	1 Swift	1 Williams	1 Williams	1 Williams
2 Shinwell	2 Ellerington	2 Ellerington	2 Mozley	2 Mozley
3 Aston	3 Aston	3 Aston	3 Aston	3 Aston
4 Wright W.	4 Wright W.	4 Wright W.	4 Wright W.	4 Wright W.
5 Franklin	5 Franklin	5 Franklin	5 Franklin	5 Franklin
6 Cockburn	6 Dickinson	6 Dickinson	6 Dickinson	6 Dickinson
7 Finney	7 Finney	7 Finney	7 Harris P.	7 Finney
8 Mortensen	8 Morris	8 Morris	8 Morris	8 Mortensen
9 Bentley	9 Mortensen	9 Rowley J.	9 Pye	9 Milburn
10 Rowley J.	10 Mannion	10 Mannion	10 Mannion	10 Shackleton
11 Langton	11 Mullen	11 Mullen	11 Finney	11 Hancocks
Stockholm May 13: 1-3 *Finney*	Oslo May 18: 4-1 *Mullen, Finney, Spydevolde og, Morris*	Paris May 22: 3-1 *Morris 2 Wright*	Goodison Park Sept 21: 0-2	Cardiff Oct 15: 4-1 *Mortensen, Milburn 3*

1949 N Ireland	1949 Italy	1950 Scotland	1950 Portugal	1950 Belgium
1 Streten	1 Williams	1 Williams	1 Williams	1 Williams
2 Mozley	2 Ramsey	2 Ramsey	2 Ramsey	2 Ramsey
3 Aston	3 Aston	3 Aston	3 Aston	3 Aston
4 Watson	4 Watson	4 Wright W.	4 Wright W.	4 Wright W.
5 Franklin	5 Franklin	5 Franklin	5 Jones W.H.	5 Jones W.H.
6 Wright W.	6 Wright W.	6 Dickinson	6 Dickinson	6 Dickinson
7 Finney	7 Finney	7 Finney	7 Milburn	7 Milburn (Mullen)
8 Mortensen	8 Mortensen	8 Mannion	8 Mortensen	8 Mortensen
9 Rowley J.	9 Rowley J.	9 Mortensen	9 Bentley	9 Bentley
10 Pearson	10 Pearson	10 Bentley	10 Mannion	10 Mannion
11 Froggatt J.	11 Froggatt J.	11 Langton	11 Finney	11 Finney
Maine Road Nov 16: 9-2 *Rowley 4, Froggatt, Pearson 2, Mortensen 2*	Tottenham Nov 30: 2-0 *Rowley, Wright*	Glasgow April 15: 1-0 *Bentley*	Luton May 14: 5-3 *Finney 4 (2 pens), Mortensen*	Brussels May 18: 4-1 *Mullen, Mortensen, Mannion, Bentley*

1950 Chile †	1950 USA †	1950 Spain †	1950 N Ireland	1950 Wales
1 Williams	1 Williams	1 Williams	1 Williams	1 Williams
2 Ramsey	2 Ramsey	2 Ramsey	2 Ramsey	2 Ramsey
3 Aston	3 Aston	3 Eckersley	3 Aston	3 Smith L.
4 Wright W.	4 Wright W.	4 Wright W.	4 Wright W.	4 Watson
5 Hughes L.	5 Hughes L.	5 Hughes L.	5 Chilton	5 Compton L.
6 Dickinson	6 Dickinson	6 Dickinson	6 Dickinson	6 Dickinson
7 Finney	7 Finney	7 Matthews S.	7 Matthews S.	7 Finney
8 Mannion	8 Mannion	8 Mortensen	8 Mannion	8 Mannion
9 Bentley	9 Bentley	9 Milburn	9 Lee J.	9 Milburn
10 Mortensen	10 Mortensen	10 Baily E.	10 Baily E.	10 Baily E.
11 Mullen	11 Mullen	11 Finney	11 Langton	11 Medley
Rio de Janeiro June 15: 2-0 *Mortensen, Mannion*	Belo Horizonte June 29: 0-1	Rio de Janeiro July 2: 0-1	Belfast Oct 7: 4-1 *Baily 2, Lee, Wright*	Sunderland Nov 15: 4-2 *Baily 2, Mannion, Milburn*

1950 Yugoslavia	1951 Scotland	1951 Argentina	1951 Portugal	1951 France
1 Williams	1 Williams	1 Williams	1 Williams	1 Williams
2 Ramsey	2 Ramsey	2 Ramsey	2 Ramsey	2 Ramsey
3 Eckersley	3 Eckersley	3 Eckersley	3 Eckersley	3 Willis
4 Watson	4 Johnston	4 Wright W.	4 Nicholson	4 Wright W.
5 Compton L.	5 Froggatt J.	5 Taylor J.	5 Taylor J.	5 Chilton
6 Dickinson	6 Wright W.	6 Cockburn	6 Cockburn	6 Cockburn
7 Hancocks	7 Matthews S.	7 Finney	7 Finney	7 Finney
8 Mannion	8 Mannion	8 Mortensen	8 Pearson	8 Mannion
9 Lofthouse	9 Mortensen	9 Milburn	9 Milburn	9 Milburn
10 Baily E.	10 Hassall	10 Hassall	10 Hassall	10 Hassall
11 Medley	11 Finney	11 Metcalfe	11 Metcalfe	11 Medley
Highbury Nov 22: 2-2 *Lofthouse 2*	Wembley April 14: 2-3 *Hassall, Finney*	Wembley May 9: 2-1 *Mortensen 2*	Goodison Park May 19: 5-2 *Nicholson, Milburn 2, Finney, Hassall*	Highbury Oct 3: 2-2 *Firoud og, Medley*

1951 Wales	1951 N Ireland	1951 Austria	1952 Scotland	1952 Italy
1 Williams	1 Merrick	1 Merrick	1 Merrick	1 Merrick
2 Ramsey	2 Ramsey	2 Ramsey	2 Ramsey	2 Ramsey
3 Smith L.	3 Smith L.	3 Eckersley	3 Garrett	3 Garrett
4 Wright W.	4 Wright W.	4 Wright W.	4 Wright W.	4 Wright W.
5 Barrass	5 Barrass	5 Froggatt J.	5 Froggatt J.	5 Froggatt J.
6 Dickinson	6 Dickinson	6 Dickinson	6 Dickinson	6 Dickinson
7 Finney	7 Finney	7 Milton	7 Finney	7 Finney
8 Thompson T.	8 Sewell	8 Broadis	8 Broadis	8 Broadis
9 Lofthouse	9 Lofthouse	9 Lofthouse	9 Lofthouse	9 Lofthouse
10 Baily E.	10 Phillips	10 Baily E.	10 Pearson	10 Pearson
11 Medley	11 Medley	11 Medley	11 Rowley J.	11 Elliott
Cardiff Oct 20: 1-1 *Baily*	Villa Park Nov 14: 2-0 *Lofthouse 2*	Wembley Nov 28: 2-2 *Ramsey (pen), Lofthouse*	Glasgow April 5: 2-1 *Pearson 2*	Florence May 18: 1-1 *Broadis*

1952 Austria	1952 Switzerland	1952 N Ireland	1952 Wales	1952 Belgium
1 Merrick	1 Merrick	1 Merrick	1 Merrick	1 Merrick
2 Ramsey	2 Ramsey	2 Ramsey	2 Ramsey	2 Ramsey
3 Eckersley	3 Eckersley	3 Eckersley	3 Smith L.	3 Smith L.
4 Wright W.	4 Wright W.	4 Wright W.	4 Wright W.	4 Wright W.
5 Froggatt J.	5 Froggatt J.	5 Froggatt J.	5 Froggatt J.	5 Froggatt J.
6 Dickinson	6 Dickinson	6 Dickinson	6 Dickinson	6 Dickinson
7 Finney	7 Allen R.	7 Finney	7 Finney	7 Finney
8 Sewell	8 Sewell	8 Sewell	8 Froggatt R.	8 Bentley
9 Lofthouse	9 Lofthouse	9 Lofthouse	9 Lofthouse	9 Lofthouse
10 Baily E.	10 Baily E.	10 Baily E.	10 Bentley	10 Froggatt R.
11 Elliott	11 Finney	11 Elliott	11 Elliott	11 Elliott
Vienna May 25: 3-2 *Lofthouse 2, Sewell*	Zurich May 28: 3-0 *Sewell, Lofthouse 2*	Belfast Oct 4: 2-2 *Lofthouse, Elliott*	Wembley Nov 12: 5-2 *Finney, Lofthouse 2, Froggatt J., Bentley*	Wembley Nov 26: 5-0 *Elliott 2, Lofthouse 2, Froggatt R.*

1953 Scotland	1953 Argentina	1953 Chile	1953 Uruguay	1953 USA
1 Merrick	1 Merrick	1 Merrick	1 Merrick	1 Ditchburn
2 Ramsey	2 Ramsey	2 Ramsey	2 Ramsey	2 Ramsey
3 Smith L.	3 Eckersley	3 Eckersley	3 Eckersley	3 Eckersley
4 Wright W.	4 Wright W.	4 Wright W.	4 Wright W.	4 Wright W.
5 Barrass	5 Johnston	5 Johnston	5 Johnston	5 Johnston
6 Dickinson	6 Dickinson	6 Dickinson	6 Dickinson	6 Dickinson
7 Finney	7 Finney	7 Finney	7 Finney	7 Finney
8 Broadis	8 Broadis	8 Broadis	8 Broadis	8 Broadis
9 Lofthouse	9 Lofthouse	9 Lofthouse	9 Lofthouse	9 Lofthouse
10 Froggatt R.	10 Taylor T.	10 Taylor T.	10 Taylor T.	10 Froggatt R.
11 Froggatt J.	11 Berry	11 Berry	11 Berry	11 Froggatt J.
Wembley April 18: 2-2 *Broadis 2*	Buenos Aires May 17: 0-0 (*abandoned after 23 min.*)	Santiago May 24: 2-1 *Taylor, Lofthouse*	Montevideo May 31: 1-2 *Taylor*	New York June 8: 6-3 *Broadis, Finney 2, Lofthouse 2, Froggatt R.*

1953 Wales	1953 Rest of Europe	1953 N Ireland	1953 Hungary	1954 Scotland
1 Merrick	1 Merrick	1 Merrick	1 Merrick	1 Merrick
2 Garrett	2 Ramsey	2 Rickaby	2 Ramsey	2 Staniforth
3 Eckersley	3 Eckersley	3 Eckersley	3 Eckersley	3 Byrne R.
4 Wright W.	4 Wright W.	4 Wright W.	4 Wright W.	4 Wright W.
5 Johnston	5 Ufton	5 Johnston	5 Johnston	5 Clarke H.
6 Dickinson	6 Dickinson	6 Dickinson	6 Dickinson	6 Dickinson
7 Finney	7 Matthews S.	7 Matthews S.	7 Matthews S.	7 Finney
8 Quixall	8 Mortensen	8 Quixall	8 Taylor E.	8 Broadis
9 Lofthouse	9 Lofthouse	9 Lofthouse	9 Mortensen	9 Allen R.
10 Wilshaw	10 Quixall	10 Hassall	10 Sewell	10 Nicholls
11 Mullen	11 Mullen	11 Mullen	11 Robb	11 Mullen
Cardiff Oct 10: 4-1 *Wilshaw 2, Lofthouse 2*	Wembley Oct 21: 4-4 *Mullen 2, Mortensen, Ramsey* (pen)	Goodison Park Nov 11: 3-1 *Hassall 2, Lofthouse*	Wembley Nov 25: 3-6 *Sewell, Mortensen, Ramsey* (pen)	Glasgow April 3: 4-2 *Broadis, Nicholls, Allen, Mullen*

1954 **Yugoslavia**	1954 **Hungary**	1954 **Belgium †**	1954 **Switzerland †**	1954 **Uruguay †**
1 Merrick	1 Merrick	1 Merrick	1 Merrick	1 Merrick
2 Staniforth	2 Staniforth	2 Staniforth	2 Staniforth	2 Staniforth
3 Byrne R.	3 Byrne R.	3 Byrne R.	3 Byrne R.	3 Byrne R.
4 Wright W.	4 Wright W.	4 Wright W.	4 McGarry	4 McGarry
5 Owen	5 Owen	5 Owen	5 Wright W.	5 Wright W.
6 Dickinson	6 Dickinson	6 Dickinson	6 Dickinson	6 Dickinson
7 Finney	7 Harris P.	7 Matthews S.	7 Finney	7 Matthews S.
8 Broadis	8 Sewell	8 Broadis	8 Broadis	8 Broadis
9 Allen R.	9 Jezzard	9 Lofthouse	9 Taylor T.	9 Lofthouse
10 Nicholls	10 Broadis	10 Taylor T.	10 Wilshaw	10 Wilshaw
11 Mullen	11 Finney	11 Finney	11 Mullen	11 Finney
Belgrade May 16: 0-1	Budapest May 23: 1-7 *Broadis*	Basle June 17: 4-4 (aet) *Broadis 2, Lofthouse 2*	Berne June 20: 2-0 *Wilshaw, Mullen*	Basle June 26: 2-4 *Lofthouse, Finney*

1954 **N Ireland**	1954 **Wales**	1954 **W Germany**	1955 **Scotland**	1955 **France**
1 Wood	1 Wood	1 Williams	1 Williams	1 Williams
2 Foulkes	2 Staniforth	2 Staniforth	2 Meadows	2 Sillett P.
3 Byrne R.	3 Byrne R.	3 Byrne R.	3 Byrne R.	3 Byrne R.
4 Wheeler	4 Phillips	4 Phillips	4 Armstrong	4 Flowers
5 Wright W.	5 Wright W.	5 Wright W.	5 Wright W.	5 Wright W.
6 Barlow	6 Slater	6 Slater	6 Edwards	6 Edwards
7 Matthews S.	7 Matthews S.	7 Matthews S.	7 Matthews S.	7 Matthews S.
8 Revie	8 Bentley	8 Bentley	8 Revie	8 Revie
9 Lofthouse	9 Allen R.	9 Allen R.	9 Lofthouse	9 Lofthouse
10 Haynes	10 Shackleton	10 Shackleton	10 Wilshaw	10 Wilshaw
11 Pilkington	11 Blunstone	11 Finney	11 Blunstone	11 Blunstone
Belfast Oct 2: 2-0 *Haynes, Revie*	Wembley Nov 10: 3-2 *Bentley 3*	Wembley Dec 1: 3-1 *Bentley, Allen, Shackleton*	Wembley April 2: 7-2 *Wilshaw 4, Lofthouse 2, Revie*	Paris May 18: 0-1

1955 **Spain**	1955 **Portugal**	1955 **Denmark**	1955 **Wales**	1955 **N Ireland**
1 Williams	1 Williams	1 Baynham	1 Williams	1 Baynham
2 Sillet P.	2 Sillett P.	2 Hall	2 Hall	2 Hall
3 Byrne R.	3 Byrne R.	3 Byrne R.	3 Byrne R.	3 Byrne R.
4 Dickinson	4 Dickinson	4 McGarry	4 McGarry	4 Clayton
5 Wright W.	5 Wright W.	5 Wright W.	5 Wright W.	5 Wright W.
6 Edwards	6 Edwards	6 Dickinson	6 Dickinson	6 Dickinson
7 Matthews S.	7 Matthews S.	7 Milburn	7 Matthews S.	7 Finney
8 Bentley	8 Bentley	8 Revie	8 Revie	8 Haynes
9 Lofthouse	9 Lofthouse (Quixall)	9 Lofthouse	9 Lofthouse	9 Jezzard
10 Quixall	10 Wilshaw	10 Bradford	10 Wilshaw	10 Wilshaw
11 Wilshaw	11 Blunstone	11 Finney	11 Finney	11 Perry
Madrid May 18: 1-1 *Bentley*	Oporto May 22: 1-3 *Bentley*	Copenhagen Oct 2: 5-1 *Revie 2 (1 pen), Lofthouse 2, Bradford*	Cardiff Oct 22: 1-1 *Charles J. og*	Wembley Nov 2: 3-0 *Wilshaw 2, Finney*

1955 Spain	1956 Scotland	1956 Brazil	1956 Sweden	1956 Finland
1 Baynham	1 Matthews R.	1 Matthews R.	1 Matthews R.	1 Wood
2 Hall	2 Hall	2 Hall	2 Hall	2 Hall
3 Byrne R.	3 Byrne R.	3 Byrne R.	3 Byrne R.	3 Byrne R.
4 Clayton	4 Dickinson	4 Clayton	4 Clayton	4 Clayton
5 Wright W.	5 Wright W.	5 Wright W.	5 Wright W.	5 Wright W.
6 Dickinson	6 Edwards	6 Edwards	6 Edwards	6 Edwards
7 Finney	7 Finney	7 Matthews S.	7 Berry	7 Astall
8 Atyeo	8 Taylor T.	8 Atyeo	8 Atyeo	8 Haynes
9 Lofthouse	9 Lofthouse	9 Taylor T.	9 Taylor T.	9 Taylor T. (Lofthouse)
10 Haynes	10 Haynes	10 Haynes	10 Haynes	10 Wilshaw
11 Perry	11 Perry	11 Grainger	11 Grainger	11 Grainger
Wembley	Glasgow	Wembley	Stockholm	Helsinki
Nov 30: 4-1	April 14: 1-1	May 9: 4-2	May 16: 0-0	May 20: 5-1
Atyeo, Perry 2, Finney	*Haynes*	*Taylor 2, Grainger 2*		*Wilshaw, Haynes, Astall, Lofthouse 2*

1956 W Germany	1956 N Ireland	1956 Wales	1956 Yugoslavia	1956 Denmark
1 Matthews R.	1 Matthews R.	1 Ditchburn	1 Ditchburn	1 Ditchburn
2 Hall	2 Hall	2 Hall	2 Hall	2 Hall
3 Byrne R.	3 Byrne R.	3 Byrne R.	3 Byrne R.	3 Byrne R.
4 Clayton	4 Clayton	4 Clayton	4 Clayton	4 Clayton
5 Wright W.	5 Wright W.	5 Wright W.	5 Wright W.	5 Wright W.
6 Edwards	6 Edwards	6 Dickinson	6 Dickinson	6 Dickinson
7 Astall	7 Matthews S.	7 Matthews S.	7 Matthews S.	7 Matthews S.
8 Haynes	8 Revie	8 Brooks	8 Brooks	8 Brooks
9 Taylor T.	9 Taylor T.	9 Finney	9 Finney	9 Taylor T.
10 Wilshaw	10 Wilshaw	10 Haynes	10 Haynes (Taylor T.)	10 Edwards
11 Grainger	11 Grainger	11 Grainger	11 Blunstone	11 Finney
Berlin	Belfast	Wembley	Wembley	Wolverhampton
May 26: 3-1	Oct 6: 1-1	Nov 14: 3-1	Nov 28: 3-0	Dec 5: 5-2
Edwards, Grainger, Haynes	*Matthews S.*	*Haynes, Brooks, Finney*	*Brooks, Taylor 2*	*Taylor 3, Edwards 2*

1957 Scotland	1957 Rep of Ireland	1957 Denmark	1957 Rep of Ireland	1957 Wales
1 Hodgkinson	1 Hodgkinson	1 Hodgkinson	1 Hodgkinson	1 Hopkinson
2 Hall	2 Hall	2 Hall	2 Hall	2 Howe D.
3 Byrne R.	3 Byrne R.	3 Byrne R.	3 Byrne R.	3 Byrne R.
4 Clayton	4 Clayton	4 Clayton	4 Clayton	4 Clayton
5 Wright W.	5 Wright W.	5 Wright W.	5 Wright W.	5 Wright W.
6 Edwards	6 Edwards	6 Edwards	6 Edwards	6 Edwards
7 Matthews S.	7 Matthews S.	7 Matthews S.	7 Finney	7 Douglas
8 Thompson T.	8 Atyeo	8 Atyeo	8 Atyeo	8 Kevan
9 Finney	9 Taylor T.	9 Taylor T.	9 Taylor T.	9 Taylor T.
10 Kevan	10 Haynes	10 Haynes	10 Haynes	10 Haynes
11 Grainger	11 Finney	11 Finney	11 Pegg	11 Finney
Wembley	Wembley	Copenhagen	Dublin	Cardiff
April 6: 2-1	May 8: 5-1	May 15: 4-1	May 19: 1-1	Oct 19: 4-0
Kevan, Edwards	*Taylor 3, Atyeo 2*	*Haynes, Taylor 2, Atyeo*	*Atyeo*	*Hopkins og, Haynes 2, Finney*

1957 **N Ireland**	**1957** **France**	**1958** **Scotland**	**1958** **Portugal**	**1958** **Yugoslavia**
1 Hopkinson	1 Hopkinson	1 Hopkinson	1 Hopkinson	1 Hopkinson
2 Howe D.	2 Howe D.	2 Howe D.	2 Howe D.	2 Howe D.
3 Byrne R.	3 Byrne R.	3 Langley	3 Langley	3 Langley
4 Clayton	4 Clayton	4 Clayton	4 Clayton	4 Clayton
5 Wright W.	5 Wright W.	5 Wright W.	5 Wright W.	5 Wright W.
6 Edwards	6 Edwards	6 Slater	6 Slater	6 Slater
7 Douglas	7 Douglas	7 Douglas	7 Douglas	7 Douglas
8 Kevan	8 Robson R.	8 Charlton R.	8 Charlton R.	8 Charlton R.
9 Taylor T.	9 Taylor T.	9 Kevan	9 Kevan	9 Kevan
10 Haynes	10 Haynes	10 Haynes	10 Haynes	10 Haynes
11 A'Court	11 Finney	11 Finney	11 Finney	11 Finney
Wembley Nov 6: 2-3 *A'Court, Edwards*	Wembley Nov 27: 4-0 *Taylor 2,* *Robson 2*	Glasgow April 19: 4-0 *Douglas, Kevan 2,* *Charlton*	Wembley May 7: 2-1 *Charlton 2*	Belgrade May 11: 0-5

1958 **USSR**	**1958** **USSR †**	**1958** **Brazil †**	**1958** **Austria †**	**1958** **USSR †**
1 McDonald	1 McDonald	1 McDonald	1 McDonald	1 McDonald
2 Howe D.	2 Howe D.	2 Howe D.	2 Howe D.	2 Howe D.
3 Banks T.	3 Banks T.	3 Banks T.	3 Banks T.	3 Banks T.
4 Clamp	4 Clamp	4 Clamp	4 Clamp	4 Clayton
5 Wright W.	5 Wright W.	5 Wright W.	5 Wright W.	5 Wright W.
6 Slater	6 Slater	6 Slater	6 Slater	6 Slater
7 Douglas	7 Douglas	7 Douglas	7 Douglas	7 Brabrook
8 Robson R.	8 Robson R.	8 Robson R.	8 Robson R.	8 Broadbent
9 Kevan	9 Kevan	9 Kevan	9 Kevan	9 Kevan
10 Haynes	10 Haynes	10 Haynes	10 Haynes	10 Haynes
11 Finney	11 Finney	11 A'Court	11 A'Court	11 A'Court
Moscow May 18: 1-1 *Kevan*	Gothenburg June 8: 2-2 *Kevan, Finney* (pen)	Gothenburg June 11: 0-0	Boras June 15: 2-2 *Haynes, Kevan*	Gothenburg June 17: 0-1

1958 **N Ireland**	**1958** **USSR**	**1958** **Wales**	**1959** **Scotland**	**1959** **Italy**
1 McDonald	1 McDonald	1 McDonald	1 Hopkinson	1 Hopkinson
2 Howe D.	2 Howe D.	2 Howe D.	2 Howe D.	2 Howe D.
3 Banks T.	3 Shaw G.	3 Shaw G.	3 Shaw G.	3 Shaw G.
4 Clayton	4 Clayton	4 Clayton	4 Clayton	4 Clayton
5 Wright W.	5 Wright W.	5 Wright W.	5 Wright W.	5 Wright W.
6 McGuinness	6 Slater	6 Flowers	6 Flowers	6 Flowers
7 Brabrook	7 Douglas	7 Clapton	7 Douglas	7 Bradley
8 Broadbent	8 Charlton R.	8 Broadbent	8 Broadbent	8 Broadbent
9 Charlton R.	9 Lofthouse	9 Lofthouse	9 Charlton R.	9 Charlton R.
10 Haynes	10 Haynes	10 Charlton R.	10 Haynes	10 Haynes
11 Finney	11 Finney	11 A'Court	11 Holden	11 Holden
Belfast Oct 4: 3-3 *Charlton 2,* *Finney*	Wembley Oct 22: 5-0 *Haynes 3* *Charlton* (pen), *Lofthouse*	Villa Park Nov 26: 2-2 *Broadbent 2*	Wembley April 11: 1-0 *Charlton*	Wembley May 6: 2-2 *Charlton,* *Bradley*

1959 Brazil	**1959 Peru**	**1959 Mexico**	**1959 USA**	**1959 Wales**
1 Hopkinson	1 Hopkinson	1 Hopkinson	1 Hopkinson	1 Hopkinson
2 Howe D.	2 Howe D.	2 Howe D.	2 Howe D.	2 Howe D.
3 Armfield	3 Armfield	3 Armfield	3 Armfield	3 Allen A.
4 Clayton	4 Clayton	4 Clayton	4 Clayton	4 Clayton
5 Wright W.	5 Wright W.	5 Wright W.	5 Wright W.	5 Smith T.
6 Flowers	6 Flowers	6 McGuinness (Flowers)	6 Flowers	6 Flowers
7 Deeley	7 Deeley	7 Holden (Bradley)	7 Bradley	7 Connelly
8 Broadbent	8 Greaves	8 Greaves	8 Greaves	8 Greaves
9 Charlton R.	9 Charlton R.	9 Kevan	9 Kevan	9 Clough
10 Haynes	10 Haynes	10 Haynes	10 Haynes	10 Charlton R.
11 Holden	11 Holden	11 Charlton R.	11 Charlton R.	11 Holliday
Rio de Janeiro May 13: 0-2	Lima May 17: 1-4 *Greaves*	Mexico City May 24: 1-2 *Kevan*	Los Angeles May 28: 8-1 *Charlton 3, Flowers 2, Bradley, Kevan, Haynes*	Cardiff Oct 17: 1-1 *Greaves*

1959 Sweden	**1959 N Ireland**	**1960 Scotland**	**1960 Yugoslavia**	**1960 Spain**
1 Hopkinson	1 Springett R.	1 Springett R.	1 Springett R.	1 Springett R.
2 Howe D.	2 Howe D.	2 Armfield	2 Armfield	2 Armfield
3 Allen A.	3 Allen A.	3 Wilson	3 Wilson	3 Wilson
4 Clayton	4 Clayton	4 Clayton	4 Clayton	4 Robson R.
5 Smith T.	5 Brown	5 Slater	5 Swan	5 Swan
6 Flowers	6 Flowers	6 Flowers	6 Flowers	6 Flowers
7 Connelly	7 Connelly	7 Connelly	7 Douglas	7 Brabrook
8 Greaves	8 Haynes	8 Broadbent	8 Haynes	8 Haynes
9 Clough	9 Baker	9 Baker	9 Baker	9 Baker
10 Charlton R.	10 Parry	10 Parry	10 Greaves	10 Greaves
11 Holliday	11 Holliday	11 Charlton R.	11 Charlton R.	11 Charlton R.
Wembley Oct 28: 2-3 *Connelly, Charlton*	Wembley Nov 18: 2-1 *Baker, Parry*	Glasgow April 19: 1-1 *Charlton* (pen)	Wembley May 11: 3-3 *Douglas, Greaves, Baker*	Madrid May 15: 0-3

1960 Hungary	**1960 N Ireland**	**1960 Luxembourg**	**1960 Spain**	**1960 Wales**
1 Springett R.	1 Springett R.	1 Springett R.	1 Springett R.	1 Hodgkinson
2 Armfield	2 Armfield	2 Armfield	2 Armfield	2 Armfield
3 Wilson	3 McNeil	3 McNeil	3 McNeil	3 McNeil
4 Robson R.	4 Robson R.	4 Robson R.	4 Robson R.	4 Robson R.
5 Swan	5 Swan	5 Swan	5 Swan	5 Swan
6 Flowers	6 Flowers	6 Flowers	6 Flowers	6 Flowers
7 Douglas	7 Douglas	7 Douglas	7 Douglas	7 Douglas
8 Haynes	8 Greaves	8 Greaves	8 Greaves	8 Greaves
9 Baker	9 Smith R.	9 Smith R.	9 Smith R.	9 Smith R.
10 Viollet	10 Haynes	10 Haynes	10 Haynes	10 Haynes
11 Charlton R.	11 Charlton R.	11 Charlton R.	11 Charlton R.	11 Charlton R.
Budapest May 22: 0-2	Belfast Oct 8: 5-2 *Smith, Greaves 2, Charlton Douglas*	Luxembourg Oct 19: 9-0 *Greaves 3, Charlton 3, Smith 2, Haynes*	Wembley Oct 26: 4-2 *Greaves, Douglas, Smith 2*	Wembley Nov 23: 5-1 *Greaves 2, Charlton, Smith, Haynes*

1961 **Scotland**	1961 **Mexico**	1961 **Portugal**	1961 **Italy**	1961 **Austria**
1 Springett R.	1 Springett R.	1 Springett R.	1 Springett R.	1 Springett R.
2 Armfield	2 Armfield	2 Armfield	2 Armfield	2 Armfield
3 McNeil	3 McNeil	3 McNeil	3 McNeil	3 Angus
4 Robson R.	4 Robson R.	4 Robson R.	4 Robson R.	4 Miller
5 Swan	5 Swan	5 Swan	5 Swan	5 Swan
6 Flowers	6 Flowers	6 Flowers	6 Flowers	6 Flowers
7 Douglas	7 Douglas	7 Douglas	7 Douglas	7 Douglas
8 Greaves	8 Kevan	8 Greaves	8 Greaves	8 Greaves
9 Smith R.	9 Hitchens	9 Smith R.	9 Hitchens	9 Hitchens
10 Haynes	10 Haynes	10 Haynes	10 Haynes	10 Haynes
11 Charlton R.	11 Charlton R.	11 Charlton R.	11 Charlton R.	11 Charlton R.
Wembley April 15: 9-3 *Robson, Greaves 3, Douglas, Smith 2, Haynes 2*	Wembley May 10: 8-0 *Hitchens, Charlton 3, Robson, Douglas 2, Flowers (*pen*)*	Lisbon May 21: 1-1 *Flowers*	Rome May 24: 3-2 *Hitchens 2, Greaves*	Vienna May 27: 1-3 *Greaves*

1961 **Luxembourg**	1961 **Wales**	1961 **Portugal**	1961 **N Ireland**	1962 **Austria**
1 Springett R.	1 Springett R.	1 Springett R.	1 Springett R.	1 Springett R.
2 Armfield	2 Armfield	2 Armfield	2 Armfield	2 Armfield
3 McNeil	3 Wilson	3 Wilson	3 Wilson	3 Wilson
4 Robson R.	4 Robson R.	4 Robson R.	4 Robson R.	4 Anderson
5 Swan	5 Swan	5 Swan	5 Swan	5 Swan
6 Flowers	6 Flowers	6 Flowers	6 Flowers	6 Flowers
7 Douglas	7 Connelly	7 Connelly	7 Douglas	7 Connelly
8 Fantham	8 Douglas	8 Douglas	8 Byrne J.	8 Hunt
9 Pointer	9 Pointer	9 Pointer	9 Crawford	9 Crawford
10 Viollet	10 Haynes	10 Haynes	10 Haynes	10 Haynes
11 Charlton R.	11 Charlton R.	11 Charlton R.	11 Charlton R.	11 Charlton R.
Highbury Sept 28: 4-1 *Pointer, Viollet, Charlton 2*	Cardiff Oct 14: 1-1 *Douglas*	Wembley Oct 25: 2-0 *Connelly, Pointer*	Wembley Nov 22: 1-1 *Charlton*	Wembley April 4: 3-1 *Crawford, Flowers (*pen*), Hunt*

1962 **Scotland**	1962 **Switzerland**	1962 **Peru**	1962 **Hungary †**	1962 **Argentina †**
1 Springett R.	1 Springett R.	1 Springett R.	1 Springett R.	1 Springett R.
2 Armfield	2 Armfield	2 Armfield	2 Armfield	2 Armfield
3 Wilson	3 Wilson	3 Wilson	3 Wilson	3 Wilson
4 Anderson	4 Robson R.	4 Moore	4 Moore	4 Moore
5 Swan	5 Swan	5 Norman	5 Norman	5 Norman
6 Flowers	6 Flowers	6 Flowers	6 Flowers	6 Flowers
7 Douglas	7 Connelly	7 Douglas	7 Douglas	7 Douglas
8 Greaves	8 Greaves	8 Greaves	8 Greaves	8 Greaves
9 Smith R.	9 Hitchens	9 Hitchens	9 Hitchens	9 Peacock
10 Haynes	10 Haynes	10 Haynes	10 Haynes	10 Haynes
11 Charlton R.	11 Charlton R.	11 Charlton R.	11 Charlton R.	11 Charlton R.
Glasgow April 14: 0-2	Wembley May 9: 3-1 *Flowers, Hitchens, Connelly*	Lima May 20: 4-0 *Flowers (*pen*), Greaves 3*	Rancagua May 31: 1-2 *Flowers (*pen*)*	Rancagua June 2: 3-1 *Flowers (*pen*), Charlton, Greaves*

1962 Bulgaria †	**1962 Brazil †**	**1962 France**	**1962 N Ireland**	**1962 Wales**
1 Springett R.	1 Springett R.	1 Springett R.	1 Springett R.	1 Springett R.
2 Armfield	2 Armfield	2 Armfield	2 Armfield	2 Armfield
3 Wilson	3 Wilson	3 Wilson	3 Wilson	3 Shaw G.
4 Moore	4 Moore	4 Moore	4 Moore	4 Moore
5 Norman	5 Norman	5 Norman	5 Labone	5 Labone
6 Flowers	6 Flowers	6 Flowers	6 Flowers	6 Flowers
7 Douglas	7 Douglas	7 Hellawell	7 Hellawell	7 Connelly
8 Greaves	8 Greaves	8 Crowe	8 Hill F.	8 Hill F.
9 Peacock	9 Hitchens	9 Charnley	9 Peacock	9 Peacock
10 Haynes	10 Haynes	10 Greaves	10 Greaves	10 Greaves
11 Charlton R.	11 Charlton R.	11 Hinton A.	11 O'Grady	11 Tambling
Rancagua June 7: 0-0	Vinà del Mar June 10: 1-3 *Hitchens*	Hillsborough Oct 3: 1-1 *Flowers* (pen)	Belfast Oct 20: 3-1 *Greaves, O'Grady 2*	Wembley Nov 21: 4-0 *Connelly, Peacock 2, Greaves*

1963 France	**1963 Scotland**	**1963 Brazil**	**1963 Czechoslovakia**	**1963 E Germany**
1 Springett R.	1 Banks G.	1 Banks G.	1 Banks G.	1 Banks G.
2 Armfield	2 Armfield	2 Armfield	2 Shellito	2 Armfield
3 Henry	3 Byrne G.	3 Wilson	3 Wilson	3 Wilson
4 Moore	4 Moore	4 Milne	4 Milne	4 Milne
5 Labone	5 Norman	5 Norman	5 Norman	5 Norman
6 Flowers	6 Flowers	6 Moore	6 Moore	6 Moore
7 Connelly	7 Douglas	7 Douglas	7 Paine	7 Paine
8 Tambling	8 Greaves	8 Greaves	8 Greaves	8 Hunt
9 Smith R.	9 Smith R.	9 Smith R.	9 Smith R.	9 Smith R.
10 Greaves	10 Melia	10 Eastham	10 Eastham	10 Eastham
11 Charlton R.	11 Charlton R.	11 Charlton R.	11 Charlton R.	11 Charlton R.
Paris Feb 27: 2-5 *Smith, Tambling*	Wembley April 6: 1-2 *Douglas*	Wembley May 8: 1-1 *Douglas*	Bratislava May 20: 4-2 *Greaves 2, Smith, Charlton*	Leipzig June 2: 2-1 *Hunt, Charlton*

1963 Switzerland	**1963 Wales**	**1963 Rest of World**	**1963 N Ireland**	**1964 Scotland**
1 Springett R.	1 Banks G.	1 Banks G.	1 Banks G.	1 Banks G.
2 Armfield	2 Armfield	2 Armfield	2 Armfield	2 Armfield
3 Wilson	3 Wilson	3 Wilson	3 Thomson R.	3 Wilson
4 Kay	4 Milne	4 Milne	4 Milne	4 Milne
5 Moore	5 Norman	5 Norman	5 Norman	5 Norman
6 Flowers	6 Moore	6 Moore	6 Moore	6 Moore
7 Douglas	7 Paine	7 Paine	7 Paine	7 Paine
8 Greaves	8 Greaves	8 Greaves	8 Greaves	8 Hunt
9 Byrne J.	9 Smith R.	9 Smith R.	9 Smith R.	9 Byrne J.
10 Melia	10 Eastham	10 Eastham	10 Eastham	10 Eastham
11 Charlton R.	11 Charlton R.	11 Charlton R.	11 Charlton R.	11 Charlton R.
Basle June 5: 8-1 *Charlton 3, Byrne 2, Douglas, Kay, Melia*	Cardiff Oct 12: 4-0 *Smith 2, Greaves, Charlton*	Wembley Oct 23: 2-1 *Paine, Greaves*	Wembley (first by floodlight) Nov 20: 8-3 *Greaves 4, Paine 3, Smith*	Glasgow April 11: 0-1

1964 Uruguay	**1964 Portugal**	**1964 Rep of Ireland**	**1964 USA**	**1964 Brazil**
1 Banks G.	1 Banks G.	1 Waiters	1 Banks G.	1 Waiters
2 Cohen	2 Cohen	2 Cohen	2 Cohen	2 Cohen
3 Wilson	3 Wilson	3 Wilson	3 Thomson R.	3 Wilson
4 Milne	4 Milne	4 Milne	4 Bailey M.	4 Milne
5 Norman	5 Norman	5 Flowers	5 Norman	5 Norman
6 Moore	6 Moore	6 Moore	6 Flowers	6 Moore
7 Paine	7 Thompson P.	7 Thompson P.	7 Paine	7 Thompson P.
8 Greaves	8 Greaves	8 Greaves	8 Hunt	8 Greaves
9 Byrne J.	9 Byrne J.	9 Byrne J.	9 Pickering	9 Byrne J.
10 Eastham	10 Eastham	10 Eastham	10 Eastham (Charlton R.)	10 Eastham
11 Charlton R.	11 Charlton R.	11 Charlton R.	11 Thompson P.	11 Charlton R.
Wembley May 6: 2-1 *Byrne 2*	Lisbon May 17: 4-3 *Byrne 3, Charlton*	Dublin May 24: 3-1 *Eastham, Byrne, Greaves*	New York May 27: 10-0 *Hunt 4, Pickering 3, Paine 2, Charlton*	Rio de Janeiro May 30: 1-5 *Greaves*

1964 Portugal	**1964 Argentina**	**1964 N Ireland**	**1964 Belgium**	**1964 Wales**
1 Banks G.	1 Banks G.	1 Banks G.	1 Waiters	1 Waiters
2 Thomson R.	2 Thomson R.	2 Cohen	2 Cohen	2 Cohen
3 Wilson	3 Wilson	3 Thomson R.	3 Thomson R.	3 Thomson R.
4 Flowers	4 Milne	4 Milne	4 Milne	4 Bailey M.
5 Norman	5 Norman	5 Norman	5 Norman	5 Flowers
6 Moore	6 Moore	6 Moore	6 Moore	6 Young
7 Paine	7 Thompson P.	7 Paine	7 Thompson P.	7 Thompson P.
8 Greaves	8 Greaves	8 Greaves	8 Greaves	8 Hunt
9 Byrne J.	9 Byrne J.	9 Pickering	9 Pickering	9 Wignall
10 Hunt	10 Eastham	10 Charlton R.	10 Venables	10 Byrne J.
11 Thompson P.	11 Charlton R.	11 Thompson P.	11 Hinton A.	11 Hinton A.
Sao Paulo June 4: 1-1 *Hunt*	Rio de Janeiro June 6: 0-1	Belfast Oct 3: 4-3 *Pickering, Greaves 3*	Wembley Oct 21: 2-2 *Pickering, Hinton*	Wembley Nov 18: 2-1 *Wignall 2*

1964 Netherlands	**1965 Scotland**	**1965 Hungary**	**1965 Yugoslavia**	**1965 W Germany**
1 Waiters	1 Banks G.	1 Banks G.	1 Banks G.	1 Banks G.
2 Cohen	2 Cohen	2 Cohen	2 Cohen	2 Cohen
3 Thomson R.	3 Wilson	3 Wilson	3 Wilson	3 Wilson
4 Mullery	4 Stiles	4 Stiles	4 Stiles	4 Flowers
5 Norman	5 Charlton J.	5 Charlton J.	5 Charlton J.	5 Charlton J.
6 Flowers	6 Moore	6 Moore	6 Moore	6 Moore
7 Thompson P.	7 Thompson P.	7 Paine	7 Paine	7 Paine
8 Greaves	8 Greaves	8 Greaves	8 Greaves	8 Ball
9 Wignall	9 Bridges	9 Bridges	9 Bridges	9 Jones M.
10 Venables	10 Byrne J.	10 Eastham	10 Ball	10 Eastham
11 Charlton R.	11 Charlton R.	11 Connelly	11 Connelly	11 Temple
Amsterdam Dec 9: 1-1 *Greaves*	Wembley April 10: 2-2 *Charlton R., Greaves*	Wembley May 5: 1-0 *Greaves*	Belgrade May 9: 1-1 *Bridges*	Nuremberg May 12: 1-0 *Paine*

1965 Sweden	1965 Wales	1965 Austria	1965 N Ireland	1965 Spain
1 Banks G.	1 Springett R.	1 Springett R.	1 Banks G.	1 Banks G.
2 Cohen	2 Cohen	2 Cohen	2 Cohen	2 Cohen
3 Wilson	3 Wilson	3 Wilson	3 Wilson	3 Wilson
4 Stiles	4 Stiles	4 Stiles	4 Stiles	4 Stiles
5 Charlton J.	5 Charlton J.	5 Charlton J.	5 Charlton J.	5 Charlton J.
6 Moore	6 Moore	6 Moore	6 Moore	6 Moore
7 Paine	7 Paine	7 Paine	7 Thompson P.	7 Ball
8 Ball	8 Greaves	8 Greaves	8 Baker	8 Hunt
9 Jones M.	9 Peacock	9 Bridges	9 Peacock	9 Baker (Hunter)
10 Eastham	10 Charlton R.	10 Charlton R.	10 Charlton R.	10 Eastham
11 Connelly	11 Connelly	11 Connelly	11 Connelly	11 Charlton R.
Gothenburg	Cardiff	Wembley	Wembley	Madrid
May 16: 2-1	Oct 2: 0-0	Oct 20: 2-3	Nov 10: 2-1	Dec 8: 2-0
Ball, Connelly		*Charlton R., Connelly*	*Baker, Peacock*	*Baker, Hunt*

1966 Poland	1966 W Germany	1966 Scotland	1966 Yugoslavia	1966 Finland
1 Banks G.	1 Banks G.	1 Banks G.	1 Banks G.	1 Banks G.
2 Cohen	2 Cohen	2 Cohen	2 Armfield	2 Armfield
3 Wilson	3 Newton K. (Wilson)	3 Newton K.	3 Wilson	3 Wilson
4 Stiles	4 Moore	4 Stiles	4 Peters	4 Peters
5 Charlton J.	5 Charlton J.	5 Charlton J.	5 Charlton J.	5 Charlton J.
6 Moore	6 Hunter	6 Moore	6 Hunter	6 Hunter
7 Ball	7 Ball	7 Ball	7 Paine	7 Callaghan
8 Hunt	8 Hunt	8 Hunt	8 Greaves	8 Hunt
9 Baker	9 Stiles	9 Charlton R.	9 Charlton R.	9 Charlton R.
10 Eastham	10 Hurst G.	10 Hurst G.	10 Hurst G.	10 Hurst G.
11 Harris G.	11 Charlton R.	11 Connelly	11 Tambling	11 Ball
Liverpool	Wembley	Glasgow	Wembley	Helsinki
Jan 5: 1-1	Feb 23: 1-0	April 2: 4-3	May 4: 2-0	June 26: 3-0
Moore	*Stiles*	*Hurst, Hunt 2, Charlton R.*	*Greaves, Charlton R.*	*Peters, Hunt, Charlton J.*

1966 Norway	1966 Denmark	1966 Poland	1966 Uruguay †	1966 Mexico †
1 Springett R.	1 Bonetti	1 Banks G.	1 Banks G.	1 Banks G.
2 Cohen	2 Cohen	2 Cohen	2 Cohen	2 Cohen
3 Byrne G.	3 Wilson	3 Wilson	3 Wilson	3 Wilson
4 Stiles	4 Stiles	4 Stiles	4 Stiles	4 Stiles
5 Flowers	5 Charlton J.	5 Charlton J.	5 Charlton J.	5 Charlton J.
6 Moore	6 Moore	6 Moore	6 Moore	6 Moore
7 Paine	7 Ball	7 Ball	7 Ball	7 Paine
8 Greaves	8 Greaves	8 Greaves	8 Greaves	8 Greaves
9 Charlton R.	9 Hurst G.	9 Charlton R.	9 Charlton R.	9 Charlton R.
10 Hunt	10 Eastham	10 Hunt	10 Hunt	10 Hunt
11 Connelly	11 Connelly	11 Peters	11 Connelly	11 Peters
Oslo	Copenhagen	Chorzow	Wembley	Wembley
June 29: 6-1	July 3: 2-0	July 5: 1-0	July 11: 0-0	July 16: 2-0
Greaves 4, Connelly, Moore	*Charlton, Eastham*	*Hunt*		*Charlton R., Hunt*

1966 **France †**	**1966** **Argentina †**	**1966** **Portugal †**	**1966** **W Germany †**	**1966** **N Ireland**
1 Banks G.	1 Banks G.	1 Banks G.	1 Banks G.	1 Banks G.
2 Cohen	2 Cohen	2 Cohen	2 Cohen	2 Cohen
3 Wilson	3 Wilson	3 Wilson	3 Wilson	3 Wilson
4 Stiles	4 Stiles	4 Stiles	4 Stiles	4 Stiles
5 Charlton J.	5 Charlton J.	5 Charlton J.	5 Charlton J.	5 Charlton J.
6 Moore	6 Moore	6 Moore	6 Moore	6 Moore
7 Callaghan	7 Ball	7 Ball	7 Ball	7 Ball
8 Greaves	8 Hurst G.	8 Hurst G.	8 Hurst G.	8 Hurst G.
9 Charlton R.	9 Charlton R.	9 Charlton R.	9 Charlton R.	9 Charlton R.
10 Hunt	10 Hunt	10 Hunt	10 Hunt	10 Hunt
11 Peters	11 Peters	11 Peters	11 Peters	11 Peters
Wembley July 20: 2-0 *Hunt 2*	Wembley July 23: 1-0 *Hurst*	Wembley July 26: 2-1 *Charlton R. 2*	Wembley (*World Cup Final*) July 30: 4-2 (aet) *Hurst 3, Peters*	Belfast Oct 22: 2-0 *Hunt, Peters*

1966 **Czechoslovakia**	**1966** **Wales**	**1967** **Scotland**	**1967** **Spain**	**1967** **Austria**
1 Banks G.	1 Banks G.	1 Banks G.	1 Bonetti	1 Bonetti
2 Cohen	2 Cohen	2 Cohen	2 Cohen	2 Newton K.
3 Wilson	3 Wilson	3 Wilson	3 Newton K.	3 Wilson
4 Stiles	4 Stiles	4 Stiles	4 Mullery	4 Mullery
5 Charlton J.	5 Charlton J.	5 Charlton J.	5 Labone	5 Labone
6 Moore	6 Moore	6 Moore	6 Moore	6 Moore
7 Ball	7 Ball	7 Ball	7 Ball	7 Ball
8 Hurst G.	8 Hurst G.	8 Greaves	8 Greaves	8 Greaves
9 Charlton R.	9 Charlton R.	9 Charlton R.	9 Hurst G.	9 Hurst G.
10 Hunt	10 Hunt	10 Hurst G.	10 Hunt	10 Hunt
11 Peters	11 Peters	11 Peters	11 Hollins	11 Hunter
Wembley Nov 2: 0-0	Wembley Nov 16: 5-1 *Hurst 2,* *Charlton R.,* *Charlton J.,* *Hennessy og*	Wembley April 15: 2-3 *Charlton J., Hurst*	Wembley May 24: 2-0 *Greaves, Hunt*	Vienna May 27: 1-0 *Ball*

1967 **Wales**	**1967** **N Ireland**	**1967** **USSR**	**1968** **Scotland**	**1968** **Spain**
1 Banks G.	1 Banks G.	1 Banks G.	1 Banks G.	1 Banks G.
2 Cohen	2 Cohen	2 Knowles C.	2 Newton K.	2 Knowles C.
3 Newton K.	3 Wilson	3 Wilson	3 Wilson	3 Wilson
4 Mullery	4 Mullery	4 Mullery	4 Mullery	4 Mullery
5 Charlton J.	5 Sadler	5 Sadler	5 Labone	5 Charlton J.
6 Moore	6 Moore	6 Moore	6 Moore	6 Moore
7 Ball	7 Thompson P.	7 Ball	7 Ball	7 Ball
8 Hunt	8 Hunt	8 Hunt	8 Hurst G.	8 Hunt
9 Charlton R.	9 Charlton R.	9 Charlton R.	9 Summerbee	9 Summerbee
10 Hurst G.	10 Hurst G.	10 Hurst G.	10 Charlton R.	10 Charlton R.
11 Peters	11 Peters	11 Peters	11 Peters	11 Peters
Cardiff Oct 21: 3-0 *Peters, Charlton R.,* *Ball*	Wembley Nov 22: 2-0 *Hurst, Charlton*	Wembley Dec 6: 2-2 *Ball, Peters*	Glasgow Feb 24: 1-1 *Peters*	Wembley April 3: 1-0 *Charlton R.*

1968 **Spain**	**1968** **Sweden**	**1968** **W Germany**	**1968** **Yugoslavia**	**1968** **USSR**
1 Bonetti	1 Stepney	1 Banks G.	1 Banks G.	1 Banks G.
2 Newton K.	2 Newton K.	2 Newton K.	2 Newton K.	2 Wright T.
3 Wilson	3 Knowles C.	3 Knowles C.	3 Wilson	3 Wilson
4 Mullery	4 Mullery	4 Hunter	4 Mullery	4 Stiles
5 Labone	5 Labone	5 Labone	5 Labone	5 Labone
6 Moore	6 Moore	6 Moore	6 Moore	6 Moore
7 Ball	7 Bell	7 Ball	7 Ball	7 Hunter
8 Peters	8 Peters	8 Bell	8 Peters	8 Hunt
9 Charlton R.	9 Charlton R. (Hurst G.)	9 Summerbee	9 Charlton R.	9 Charlton R.
10 Hunt	10 Hunt	10 Hurst G.	10 Hunt	10 Hurst G.
11 Hunter	11 Hunter	11 Thompson P.	11 Hunter	11 Peters
Madrid May 8: 2-1 *Peters, Hunter*	Wembley May 22: 3-1 *Peters, Charlton,* *Hunt*	Hanover June 1: 0-1	Florence June 5: 0-1	Rome June 8: 2-0 *Charlton, Hurst*

1968 **Rumania**	**1968** **Bulgaria**	**1969** **Rumania**	**1969** **France**	**1969** **N Ireland**
1 Banks G.	1 West	1 Banks G.	1 Banks G.	1 Banks G.
2 Wright T. (McNab)	2 Newton K. (Reaney)	2 Wright T.	2 Newton K.	2 Newton K.
3 Newton K.	3 McNab	3 McNab	3 Cooper	3 McNab
4 Mullery	4 Mullery	4 Stiles	4 Mullery	4 Mullery
5 Labone	5 Labone	5 Charlton J.	5 Charlton J.	5 Labone
6 Moore	6 Moore	6 Hunter	6 Moore	6 Moore
7 Ball	7 Lee F.	7 Radford	7 Lee F.	7 Ball
8 Hunt	8 Bell	8 Hunt	8 Bell	8 Lee F.
9 Charlton R.	9 Charlton R.	9 Charlton R.	9 Hurst G.	9 Charlton R.
10 Hurst G.	10 Hurst G.	10 Hurst G.	10 Peters	10 Hurst G.
11 Peters	11 Peters	11 Ball	11 O'Grady	11 Peters
Bucharest Nov 6: 0-0	Wembley Dec 11: 1-1 *Hurst*	Wembley Jan 15: 1-1 *Charlton J.*	Wembley Mar 12: 5-0 *Hurst 3,* *O'Grady, Lee*	Belfast May 3: 3-1 *Peters, Lee,* *Hurst* (pen)

1969 **Wales**	**1969** **Scotland**	**1969** **Mexico**	**1969** **Uruguay**	**1969** **Brazil**
1 West	1 Banks G.	1 West	1 Banks G.	1 Banks G.
2 Newton K.	2 Newton K.	2 Newton K. (Wright T.)	2 Wright T.	2 Wright T.
3 Cooper	3 Cooper	3 Cooper	3 Newton K.	3 Newton K.
4 Moore	4 Mullery	4 Mullery	4 Mullery	4 Mullery
5 Charlton J.	5 Labone	5 Labone	5 Labone	5 Labone
6 Hunter	6 Moore	6 Moore	6 Moore	6 Moore
7 Lee F.	7 Lee F.	7 Lee F.	7 Lee F.	7 Ball
8 Bell	8 Ball	8 Ball	8 Bell	8 Bell
9 Astle	9 Charlton R.	9 Charlton R.	9 Hurst G.	9 Charlton R.
10 Charlton R.	10 Hurst G.	10 Hurst G.	10 Ball	10 Hurst G.
11 Ball	11 Peters	11 Peters	11 Peters	11 Peters
Wembley May 7: 2-1 *Charlton R., Lee*	Wembley May 10: 4-1 *Peters 2,* *Hurst 2* (1 pen)	Mexico City June 1: 0-0	Montevideo June 8: 2-1 *Lee, Hurst*	Rio de Janeiro June 12: 1-2 *Bell*

1969 **Netherlands**	**1969** **Portugal**	**1970** **Netherlands**	**1970** **Belgium**	**1970** **Wales**
1 Bonetti	1 Bonetti	1 Banks G.	1 Banks G.	1 Banks G.
2 Wright T.	2 Reaney	2 Newton K.	2 Wright T.	2 Wright T.
3 Hughes E.	3 Hughes E.	3 Cooper	3 Cooper	3 Hughes E.
4 Mullery	4 Mullery	4 Peters	4 Moore	4 Mullery
5 Charlton J.	5 Charlton J.	5 Charlton J.	5 Labone	5 Labone
6 Moore	6 Moore	6 Hunter	6 Hughes E.	6 Moore
7 Lee F. (Thompson P.)	7 Lee F.	7 Lee F. (Mullery)	7 Lee F.	7 Lee F.
8 Bell	8 Bell (Peters)	8 Bell	8 Ball	8 Ball
9 Charlton R.	9 Astle	9 Jones M. (Hurst G.)	9 Osgood	9 Charlton R.
10 Hurst G.	10 Charlton R.	10 Charlton R.	10 Hurst G.	10 Hurst G.
11 Peters	11 Ball	11 Moore I.	11 Peters	11 Peters
Amsterdam Nov 5: 1-0 *Bell*	Wembley Dec 10: 1-0 *Charlton J.*	Wembley Jan 14: 0-0	Brussels Feb 25: 3-1 *Ball 2, Hurst*	Cardiff April 18: 1-1 *Lee*

1970 **N Ireland**	**1970** **Scotland**	**1970** **Colombia**	**1970** **Ecuador**	**1970** **Rumania †**
1 Banks G.	1 Banks G.	1 Banks G.	1 Banks G.	1 Banks G.
2 Newton K. (Bell)	2 Newton K.	2 Newton K.	2 Newton K.	2 Newton K. (Wright T.)
3 Hughes E.	3 Hughes E.	3 Cooper	3 Cooper	3 Cooper
4 Mullery	4 Stiles	4 Mullery	4 Mullery	4 Mullery
5 Moore	5 Labone	5 Labone	5 Labone	5 Labone
6 Stiles	6 Moore	6 Moore	6 Moore	6 Moore
7 Coates	7 Thompson P. (Mullery)	7 Lee F.	7 Lee F. (Kidd)	7 Lee F. (Osgood)
8 Kidd	8 Ball	8 Ball	8 Ball	8 Ball
9 Charlton R.	9 Astle	9 Charlton R.	9 Charlton R. (Sadler)	9 Charlton R.
10 Hurst G.	10 Hurst G.	10 Hurst G.	10 Hurst G.	10 Hurst G.
11 Peters	11 Peters	11 Peters	11 Peters	11 Peters
Wembley April 21: 3-1 *Peters, Hurst, Charlton*	Glasgow April 25: 0-0	Bogota May 20: 4-0 *Peters 2, Charlton, Ball*	Quito May 24: 2-0 *Lee, Kidd*	Guadalajara June 2: 1-0 *Hurst*

1970 **Brazil †**	**1970** **Czechoslovakia †**	**1970** **W Germany †**	**1970** **E Germany**	**1971** **Malta**
1 Banks G.	1 Banks G.	1 Bonetti	1 Shilton	1 Banks G.
2 Wright T.	2 Newton K.	2 Newton K.	2 Hughes	2 Reaney
3 Cooper	3 Cooper	3 Cooper	3 Cooper	3 Hughes
4 Mullery	4 Mullery	4 Mullery	4 Mullery	4 Mullery
5 Labone	5 Charlton J.	5 Labone	5 Sadler	5 McFarland
6 Moore	6 Moore	6 Moore	6 Moore	6 Hunter
7 Lee F. (Astle)	7 Bell	7 Lee F.	7 Lee F.	7 Ball
8 Ball	8 Charlton R. (Ball)	8 Ball	8 Ball	8 Chivers
9 Charlton R. (Bell)	9 Astle (Osgood)	9 Charlton R. (Bell)	9 Hurst G.	9 Royle
10 Hurst G.	10 Clarke A.	10 Hurst G.	10 Clarke A.	10 Harvey
11 Peters	11 Peters	11 Peters (Hunter)	11 Peters	11 Peters
Guadalajara June 7: 0-1	Guadalajara June 11: 1-0 *Clarke* (pen)	Leon June 14: 2-3 (aet) *Mullery, Peters*	Wembley Nov 25: 3-1 *Lee, Peters, Clarke*	Valletta Feb 3: 1-0 *Peters*

1971 **Greece**	**1971** **Malta**	**1971** **N Ireland**	**1971** **Wales**	**1971** **Scotland**
1 Banks G.	1 Banks G.	1 Banks G.	1 Shilton	1 Banks G.
2 Storey	2 Lawler	2 Madeley	2 Lawler	2 Lawler
3 Hughes	3 Cooper	3 Cooper	3 Cooper	3 Cooper
4 Mullery	4 Moore	4 Storey	4 Smith	4 Storey
5 McFarland	5 McFarland	5 McFarland	5 Lloyd	5 McFarland
6 Moore	6 Hughes	6 Moore	6 Hughes	6 Moore
7 Lee F.	7 Lee F.	7 Lee F.	7 Lee F.	7 Lee F. (Clarke)
8 Ball (Coates)	8 Coates	8 Ball	8 Coates (Clarke)	8 Ball
9 Chivers	9 Chivers	9 Chivers	9 Hurst G.	9 Chivers
10 Hurst G.	10 Clarke	10 Clarke	10 Brown A.	10 Hurst G.
11 Peters	11 Peters (Ball)	11 Peters	11 Peters	11 Peters
Wembley April 21: 3-0 *Chivers, Hurst, Lee*	Wembley May 12: 5-0 *Chivers 2, Lee, Clarke (pen), Lawler*	Belfast May 15: 1-0 *Clarke*	Wembley May 19: 0-0	Wembley May 22: 3-1 *Peters, Chivers 2*

1971 **Switzerland**	**1971** **Switzerland**	**1971** **Greece**	**1972** **W Germany**	**1972** **W Germany**
1 Banks G.	1 Shilton	1 Banks G.	1 Banks G.	1 Banks G.
2 Lawler	2 Madeley	2 Madeley	2 Madeley	2 Madeley
3 Cooper	3 Cooper	3 Hughes	3 Hughes	3 Hughes
4 Mullery	4 Storey	4 Bell	4 Bell	4 Storey
5 McFarland	5 Lloyd	5 McFarland	5 Moore	5 McFarland
6 Moore	6 Moore	6 Moore	6 Hunter	6 Moore
7 Lee F.	7 Summerbee (Chivers)	7 Lee F.	7 Lee F.	7 Ball
8 Madeley	8 Ball	8 Ball	8 Ball	8 Bell
9 Chivers	9 Hurst G.	9 Chivers	9 Chivers	9 Chivers
10 Hurst G. (Radford)	10 Lee F. (Marsh)	10 Hurst G.	10 Hurst G. (Marsh)	10 Marsh (Summerbee)
11 Peters	11 Hughes	11 Peters	11 Peters	11 Hunter (Peters)
Basle Oct 13: 3-2 *Hurst, Chivers, Weibel og*	Wembley Nov 10: 1-1 *Summerbee*	Athens Dec 1: 2-0 *Hurst, Chivers*	Wembley April 29: 1-3 *Lee*	Berlin May 13: 0-0

1972 **Wales**	**1972** **N Ireland**	**1972** **Scotland**	**1972** **Yugoslavia**	**1972** **Wales**
1 Banks G.	1 Shilton	1 Banks G.	1 Shilton	1 Clemence
2 Madeley	2 Todd	2 Madeley	2 Mills	2 Storey
3 Hughes	3 Hughes	3 Hughes	3 Lampard	3 Hughes
4 Storey	4 Storey	4 Storey	4 Storey	4 Hunter
5 McFarland	5 Lloyd	5 McFarland	5 Blockley	5 McFarland
6 Moore	6 Hunter	6 Moore	6 Moore	6 Moore
7 Summerbee	7 Summerbee	7 Ball	7 Ball	7 Keegan
8 Bell	8 Bell	8 Bell	8 Channon	8 Chivers
9 Macdonald	9 Macdonald (Chivers)	9 Chivers	9 Royle	9 Marsh
10 Marsh	10 Marsh	10 Marsh (Macdonald)	10 Bell	10 Bell
11 Hunter	11 Currie (Peters)	11 Hunter	11 Marsh	11 Ball
Cardiff May 20: 3-0 *Hughes, Bell, Marsh*	Wembley May 23: 0-1	Glasgow May 27: 1-0 *Ball*	Wembley Oct 11: 1-1 *Royle*	Cardiff Nov 15: 1-0 *Bell*

1973 **Wales**	**1973** **Scotland**	**1973** **N Ireland**	**1973** **Wales**	**1973** **Scotland**
1 Clemence	1 Shilton	1 Shilton	1 Shilton	1 Shilton
2 Storey	2 Storey	2 Storey	2 Storey	2 Storey
3 Hughes	3 Hughes	3 Nish	3 Hughes	3 Hughes
4 Hunter	4 Bell	4 Bell	4 Bell	4 Bell
5 McFarland	5 Madeley	5 McFarland	5 McFarland	5 McFarland
6 Moore	6 Moore	6 Moore	6 Moore	6 Moore
7 Keegan	7 Ball	7 Ball	7 Ball	7 Ball
8 Bell	8 Channon	8 Channon	8 Channon	8 Channon
9 Chivers	9 Chivers	9 Chivers	9 Chivers	9 Chivers
10 Marsh	10 Clarke	10 Richards	10 Clarke	10 Clarke
11 Ball	11 Peters	11 Peters	11 Peters	11 Peters
Wembley Jan 24: 1-1 *Hunter*	Glasgow Feb 14: 5-0 *Lorimer og,* *Clarke 2,* *Channon, Chivers*	Goodison Park May 12: 2-1 *Chivers 2*	Wembley May 15: 3-0 *Chivers, Channon,* *Peters*	Wembley May 19: 1-0 *Peters*

1973 **Czechoslovakia**	**1973** **Poland**	**1973** **USSR**	**1973** **Italy**	**1973** **Austria**
1 Shilton	1 Shilton	1 Shilton	1 Shilton	1 Shilton
2 Madeley	2 Madeley	2 Madeley	2 Madeley	2 Madeley
3 Storey	3 Hughes	3 Hughes	3 Hughes	3 Hughes
4 Bell	4 Storey	4 Storey	4 Storey	4 Bell
5 McFarland	5 McFarland	5 McFarland	5 McFarland	5 McFarland
6 Moore	6 Moore	6 Moore	6 Moore	6 Hunter
7 Ball	7 Ball	7 Currie	7 Currie	7 Currie
8 Channon	8 Bell	8 Channon (Summerbee)	8 Channon	8 Channon
9 Chivers	9 Chivers	9 Chivers	9 Chivers	9 Chivers
10 Clarke	10 Clarke	10 Clarke (Macdonald)	10 Clarke	10 Clarke
11 Peters	11 Peters	11 Peters (Hunter)	11 Peters	11 Peters
Prague May 27: 1-1 *Clarke*	Chorzow June 6: 0-2	Moscow June 10: 2-1 *Chivers,* *Khurtislava og*	Turin June 14: 0-2	Wembley Sept 26: 7-0 *Channon 2,* *Clarke 2,* *Chivers, Currie,* *Bell*

1973 **Poland**	**1973** **Italy**	**1974** **Portugal**	**1974** **Wales**	**1974** **N Ireland**
1 Shilton	1 Shilton	1 Parkes	1 Shilton	1 Shilton
2 Madeley	2 Madeley	2 Nish	2 Nish	2 Nish
3 Hughes	3 Hughes	3 Pejic	3 Pejic	3 Pejic
4 Bell	4 Bell	4 Dobson	4 Hughes	4 Hughes
5 McFarland	5 McFarland	5 Watson	5 McFarland	5 McFarland (Hunter)
6 Hunter	6 Moore	6 Todd	6 Todd	6 Todd
7 Currie	7 Currie	7 Bowles	7 Keegan	7 Keegan
8 Channon	8 Channon	8 Channon	8 Bell	8 Weller
9 Chivers (Hector)	9 Osgood	9 Macdonald (Ball)	9 Channon	9 Channon
10 Clarke	10 Clarke (Hector)	10 Brooking	10 Weller	10 Bell
11 Peters	11 Peters	11 Peters	11 Bowles	11 Bowles (Worthington)
Wembley Oct 17: 1-1 *Clarke* (pen)	Wembley Nov 14: 0-1	Lisbon April 3: 0-0	Cardiff May 11: 2-0 *Bowles, Keegan*	Wembley May 15: 1-0 *Weller*

	1974 **Scotland**	**1974** **Argentina**	**1974** **E Germany**	**1974** **Bulgaria**	**1974** **Yugoslavia**
1	Shilton	Shilton	Clemence	Clemence	Clemence
2	Nish	Hughes	Hughes	Hughes	Hughes
3	Pejic	Lindsay	Lindsay	Todd	Lindsay
4	Hughes	Todd	Todd	Watson	Todd
5	Hunter (Watson)	Watson	Watson	Lindsay	Watson
6	Todd	Bell	Dobson	Dobson	Dobson
7	Channon	Keegan	Keegan	Brooking	Keegan
8	Bell	Channon	Channon	Bell	Channon
9	Worthington (Macdonald)	Worthington	Worthington	Keegan	Worthington (Macdonald)
10	Weller	Weller	Bell	Channon	Bell
11	Peters	Brooking	Brooking	Worthington	Brooking
	Glasgow May 18: 0-2	Wembley May 22: 2-2 *Channon, Worthington*	Leipzig May 29: 1-1 *Channon*	Sofia June 1: 1-0 *Worthington*	Belgrade June 5: 2-2 *Channon, Keegan*

	1974 **Czechoslovakia**	**1974** **Portugal**	**1975** **W Germany**	**1975** **Cyprus**	**1975** **Cyprus**
1	Clemence	Clemence	Clemence	Shilton	Clemence
2	Madeley	Madeley	Whitworth	Madeley	Whitworth
3	Hughes	Watson	Gillard	Watson	Beattie (Hughes)
4	Dobson (Brooking)	Hughes	Bell	Todd	Watson
5	Watson	Cooper (Todd)	Watson	Beattie	Todd
6	Hunter	Brooking	Todd	Bell	Bell
7	Bell	Francis G.	Ball	Ball	Thomas
8	Francis G.	Bell	Macdonald	Hudson	Ball
9	Worthington (Thomas)	Thomas	Channon	Channon (Thomas)	Channon
10	Channon	Channon	Hudson	Macdonald	Macdonald
11	Keegan	Clarke (Worthington)	Keegan	Keegan	Keegan (Tueart)
	Wembley Oct 30: 3-0 *Channon, Bell 2*	Wembley Nov 20: 0-0	Wembley Mar 12: 2-0 *Bell, Macdonald*	Wembley April 16: 5-0 *Macdonald 5*	Limassol May 11: 1-0 *Keegan*

	1975 **N Ireland**	**1975** **Wales**	**1975** **Scotland**	**1975** **Switzerland**	**1975** **Czechoslovakia**
1	Clemence	Clemence	Clemence	Clemence	Clemence
2	Whitworth	Whitworth	Whitworth	Whitworth	Madeley
3	Hughes	Gillard	Beattie	Todd	Gillard
4	Bell	Francis G.	Bell	Watson	Francis G.
5	Watson	Watson	Watson	Beattie	McFarland (Watson)
6	Todd	Todd	Todd	Bell	Todd
7	Ball	Ball	Ball	Currie	Keegan
8	Viljoen	Channon (Little)	Channon	Francis G.	Channon (Thomas)
9	Macdonald (Channon)	Johnson	Johnson	Channon	Macdonald
10	Keegan	Viljoen	Francis G.	Johnson (Macdonald)	Clarke
11	Tueart	Thomas	Keegan (Thomas)	Keegan	Bell
	Belfast May 17: 0-0	Wembley May 21: 2-2 *Johnson 2*	Wembley May 24: 5-1 *Francis 2, Beattie, Bell, Johnson*	Basle Sept 3: 2-1 *Keegan, Channon*	Bratislava Oct 30: 1-2 *Channon*

1975 **Portugal**	1976 **Wales**	1976 **Wales**	1976 **N Ireland**	1976 **Scotland**
1 Clemence	1 Clemence	1 Clemence	1 Clemence	1 Clemence
2 Whitworth	2 Cherry (Clement)	2 Clement	2 Todd	2 Todd
3 Beattie	3 Mills	3 Mills	3 Mills	3 Mills
4 Francis G.	4 Neal	4 Towers	4 Thompson	4 Thompson
5 Watson	5 Thompson	5 Greenhoff	5 Greenhoff	5 McFarland (Doyle)
6 Todd	6 Doyle	6 Thompson	6 Kennedy	6 Kennedy
7 Keegan	7 Keegan	7 Keegan	7 Keegan (Royle)	7 Keegan
8 Channon	8 Channon (Taylor)	8 Francis G.	8 Francis G.	8 Francis G.
9 Macdonald (Thomas)	9 Boyer	9 Pearson	9 Pearson	9 Pearson (Cherry)
10 Brooking	10 Brooking	10 Kennedy	10 Channon	10 Channon
11 Madeley (Clarke)	11 Kennedy	11 Taylor	11 Taylor (Towers)	11 Taylor
Lisbon Nov 19: 1-1 *Channon*	Wrexham Mar 24: 2-1 *Kennedy, Taylor*	Cardiff May 8: 1-0 *Taylor*	Wembley May 11: 4-0 *Francis,* *Channon 2* (1 pen), *Pearson*	Glasgow May 15: 1-2 *Channon*

1976 **Brazil**	1976 **Italy**	1976 **Finland**	1976 **Rep of Ireland**	1976 **Finland**
1 Clemence	1 Rimmer (Corrigan)	1 Clemence	1 Clemence	1 Clemence
2 Todd	2 Clement	2 Todd	2 Todd	2 Todd
3 Doyle	3 Neal (Mills)	3 Mills	3 Madeley	3 Beattie
4 Thompson	4 Thompson	4 Thompson	4 Cherry	4 Thompson
5 Mills	5 Doyle	5 Madeley	5 McFarland	5 Greenhoff
6 Francis G.	6 Towers	6 Cherry	6 Greenhoff	6 Wilkins
7 Cherry	7 Wilkins	7 Keegan	7 Keegan	7 Keegan
8 Brooking	8 Brooking	8 Channon	8 Wilkins	8 Channon
9 Keegan	9 Royle	9 Pearson	9 Pearson	9 Royle
10 Pearson	10 Channon	10 Brooking	10 Brooking	10 Brooking (Mills)
11 Channon	11 Hill	11 Francis G.	11 George (Hill)	11 Tueart (Hill)
Los Angeles May 23: 0-1	New York May 28: 3-2 *Channon 2,* *Thompson*	Helsinki June 13: 4-1 *Keegan 2, Channon,* *Pearson*	Wembley Sept 8: 1-1 *Pearson*	Wembley Oct 13: 2-1 *Tueart, Royle*

1976 **Italy**	1977 **Netherlands**	1977 **Luxembourg**	1977 **N Ireland**	1977 **Wales**
1 Clemence	1 Clemence	1 Clemence	1 Shilton	1 Shilton
2 Clement (Beattie)	2 Clement	2 Gidman	2 Cherry	2 Neal
3 Mills	3 Beattie	3 Cherry	3 Mills	3 Mills
4 Greenhoff	4 Doyle	4 Kennedy	4 Greenhoff	4 Greenhoff
5 McFarland	5 Watson	5 Watson	5 Watson	5 Watson
6 Hughes	6 Madeley (Pearson)	6 Hughes	6 Todd	6 Hughes
7 Keegan	7 Keegan	7 Keegan	7 Wilkins (Talbot)	7 Keegan
8 Channon	8 Greenhoff (Todd)	8 Channon	8 Channon	8 Channon
9 Bowles	9 Francis T.	9 Royle (Mariner)	9 Mariner	9 Pearson
10 Cherry	10 Bowles	10 Francis T.	10 Brooking	10 Brooking (Tueart)
11 Brooking	11 Brooking	11 Hill	11 Tueart	11 Kennedy
Rome Nov 17: 0-2	Wembley Feb 9: 0-2	Wembley Mar 30: 5-0 *Keegan, Francis,* *Kennedy,* *Channon 2* (1 pen)	Belfast May 28: 2-1 *Channon, Tueart*	Wembley May 31: 0-1

1977 **Scotland**	**1977** **Brazil**	**1977** **Argentina**	**1977** **Uruguay**	**1977** **Switzerland**
1 Clemence	1 Clemence	1 Clemence	1 Clemence	1 Clemence
2 Neal	2 Neal	2 Neal	2 Neal	2 Neal
3 Mills	3 Cherry	3 Cherry	3 Cherry	3 Cherry
4 Greenhoff (Cherry)	4 Greenhoff	4 Greenhoff (Kennedy)	4 Greenhoff	4 McDermott
5 Watson	5 Watson	5 Watson	5 Watson	5 Watson
6 Hughes	6 Hughes	6 Hughes	6 Hughes	6 Hughes
7 Francis T.	7 Keegan	7 Keegan	7 Keegan	7 Keegan
8 Channon	8 Francis T.	8 Channon	8 Channon	8 Channon (Hill)
9 Pearson	9 Pearson (Channon)	9 Pearson	9 Pearson	9 Francis T.
10 Talbot	10 Wilkins (Kennedy)	10 Wilkins	10 Wilkins	10 Kennedy
11 Kennedy (Tueart)	11 Talbot	11 Talbot	11 Talbot	11 Callaghan (Wilkins)
Wembley June 4: 1-2 *Channon* (pen)	Rio de Janeiro June 8: 0-0	Buenos Aires June 12: 1-1 *Pearson*	Montevideo June 15: 0-0	Wembley Sept 7: 0-0

1977 **Luxembourg**	**1977** **Italy**	**1978** **W Germany**	**1978** **Brazil**	**1978** **Wales**
1 Clemence	1 Clemence	1 Clemence	1 Corrigan	1 Shilton
2 Cherry	2 Neal	2 Neal	2 Mills	2 Mills
3 Watson (Beattie)	3 Cherry	3 Mills	3 Cherry	3 Cherry (Currie)
4 Hughes	4 Wilkins	4 Wilkins	4 Greenhoff	4 Greenhoff
5 Kennedy	5 Watson	5 Watson	5 Watson	5 Watson
6 Callaghan	6 Hughes	6 Hughes	6 Currie	6 Wilkins
7 McDermott (Whymark)	7 Keegan (Francis T.)	7 Keegan (Francis T.)	7 Keegan	7 Coppell
8 Wilkins	8 Coppell	8 Coppell	8 Coppell	8 Francis T.
9 Francis T.	9 Latchford (Pearson)	9 Pearson	9 Latchford	9 Latchford (Mariner)
10 Mariner	10 Brooking	10 Brooking	10 Francis T.	10 Brooking
11 Hill	11 Barnes	11 Barnes	11 Barnes	11 Barnes
Luxembourg Oct 12: 2-0 *Kennedy,* *Mariner*	Wembley Nov 16: 2-0 *Keegan,* *Brooking*	Munich Feb 22: 1-2 *Pearson*	Wembley April 19: 1-1 *Keegan*	Cardiff May 13: 3-1 *Latchford,* *Currie, Barnes*

1978 **N Ireland**	**1978** **Scotland**	**1978** **Hungary**	**1978** **Denmark**	**1978** **Rep of Ireland**
1 Clemence	1 Clemence	1 Shilton	1 Clemence	1 Clemence
2 Neal	2 Neal	2 Neal	2 Neal	2 Neal
3 Mills	3 Mills	3 Mills	3 Mills	3 Mills
4 Wilkins	4 Currie	4 Wilkins	4 Wilkins	4 Wilkins
5 Watson	5 Watson	5 Watson (Greenhoff)	5 Watson	5 Watson (Thompson)
6 Hughes	6 Hughes (Greenhoff)	6 Hughes	6 Hughes	6 Hughes
7 Currie	7 Wilkins	7 Keegan	7 Keegan	7 Keegan
8 Coppell	8 Coppell	8 Coppell	8 Coppell	8 Coppell
9 Pearson	9 Mariner (Brooking)	9 Francis T.	9 Latchford	9 Latchford
10 Woodcock	10 Francis T.	10 Brooking (Currie)	10 Brooking	10 Brooking
11 Greenhoff	11 Barnes	11 Barnes	11 Barnes	11 Barnes (Woodcock)
Wembley May 16: 1-0 *Neal*	Glasgow May 20: 1-0 *Coppell*	Wembley May 24: 4-1 *Barnes, Neal* (pen), *Francis, Currie*	Copenhagen Sept 20: 4-3 *Keegan 2,* *Latchford, Neal*	Dublin Oct 25: 1-1 *Latchford*

1978 Czechoslovakia	1979 N Ireland	1979 N Ireland	1979 Wales	1979 Scotland
1 Shilton	1 Clemence	1 Clemence	1 Corrigan	1 Clemence
2 Anderson	2 Neal	2 Neal	2 Cherry	2 Neal
3 Cherry	3 Mills	3 Mills	3 Sansom	3 Mills
4 Thompson	4 Currie	4 Thompson	4 Wilkins (Brooking)	4 Thompson
5 Watson	5 Watson	5 Watson	5 Watson	5 Watson
6 Wilkins	6 Hughes	6 Wilkins	6 Hughes	6 Wilkins
7 Keegan	7 Keegan	7 Coppell	7 Keegan (Coppell)	7 Keegan
8 Coppell	8 Coppell	8 McDermott	8 Currie	8 Coppell
9 Woodcock (Latchford)	9 Latchford	9 Latchford	9 Latchford	9 Latchford
10 Currie	10 Brooking	10 Currie	10 McDermott	10 Brooking
11 Barnes	11 Barnes	11 Barnes	11 Cunningham	11 Barnes
Wembley Nov 29: 1-0 *Coppell*	Wembley Feb 7: 4-0 *Keegan, Latchford 2, Watson*	Belfast May 19: 2-0 *Watson, Coppell*	Wembley May 23: 0-0	Wembley May 26: 3-1 *Barnes, Coppell, Keegan*

1979 Bulgaria	1979 Sweden	1979 Austria	1979 Denmark	1979 N Ireland
1 Clemence	1 Shilton	1 Shilton (Clemence)	1 Clemence	1 Shilton
2 Neal	2 Anderson	2 Neal	2 Neal	2 Neal
3 Mills	3 Cherry	3 Mills	3 Mills	3 Mills
4 Thompson	4 McDermott (Wilkins)	4 Thompson	4 Thompson	4 Thompson
5 Watson	5 Watson	5 Watson	5 Watson	5 Watson
6 Wilkins	6 Hughes	6 Wilkins	6 Wilkins	6 Wilkins
7 Keegan	7 Keegan	7 Keegan	7 Coppell	7 Keegan
8 Coppell	8 Currie (Brooking)	8 Coppell	8 McDermott	8 Coppell
9 Latchford (Francis T.)	9 Francis T.	9 Latchford (Francis T.)	9 Keegan	9 Francis T.
10 Brooking	10 Woodcock	10 Brooking	10 Brooking	10 Brooking (McDermott)
11 Barnes (Woodcock)	11 Cunningham	11 Barnes (Cunningham)	11 Barnes	11 Woodcock
Sofia June 6: 3-0 *Keegan, Watson, Barnes*	Stockholm June 10: 0-0	Vienna June 13: 3-4 *Keegan, Coppell, Wilkins*	Wembley Sept 9: 1-0 *Keegan*	Belfast Oct 17: 5-1 *Francis 2, Woodcock 2, Nicholl og*

1979 Bulgaria	1980 Rep of Ireland	1980 Spain	1980 Argentina	1980 Wales
1 Clemence	1 Clemence	1 Shilton	1 Clemence	1 Clemence
2 Anderson	2 Cherry	2 Neal (Hughes)	2 Neal (Cherry)	2 Neal (Sansom)
3 Sansom	3 Sansom	3 Mills	3 Sansom	3 Cherry
4 Thompson	4 Thompson	4 Thompson	4 Thompson	4 Thompson
5 Watson	5 Watson	5 Watson	5 Watson	5 Lloyd (Wilkins)
6 Wilkins	6 Robson	6 Wilkins	6 Wilkins	6 Kennedy
7 Reeves	7 Keegan	7 Keegan	7 Keegan	7 Coppell
8 Hoddle	8 McDermott	8 Coppell	8 Coppell	8 Hoddle
9 Francis T.	9 Johnson (Coppell)	9 Francis T. (Cunningham)	9 Johnson (Birtles)	9 Mariner
10 Kennedy	10 Woodcock	10 Kennedy	10 Woodcock	10 Brooking
11 Woodcock	11 Cunningham	11 Woodcock	11 Kennedy (Brooking)	11 Barnes
Wembley Nov 22: 2-0 *Watson, Hoddle*	Wembley Feb 6: 2-0 *Keegan 2*	Barcelona March 26: 2-0 *Woodcock, Francis*	Wembley May 13: 3-1 *Johnson 2, Keegan*	Wrexham May 17: 1-4 *Mariner*

1980 N Ireland	1980 Scotland	1980 Australia	1980 Belgium	1980 Italy
1 Corrigan	1 Clemence	1 Corrigan	1 Clemence	1 Shilton
2 Cherry	2 Cherry	2 Cherry	2 Neal	2 Neal
3 Sansom	3 Sansom	3 Lampard	3 Sansom	3 Sansom
4 Hughes	4 Thompson	4 Talbot	4 Thompson	4 Thompson
5 Watson	5 Watson	5 Osman	5 Watson	5 Watson
6 Wilkins	6 Wilkins	6 Butcher	6 Wilkins	6 Wilkins
7 Reeves (Mariner)	7 Coppell	7 Robson (Greenhoff)	7 Keegan	7 Keegan
8 McDermott	8 McDermott	8 Sunderland (Ward)	8 Coppell (McDermott)	8 Coppell
9 Johnson	9 Johnson	9 Mariner	9 Johnson (Kennedy)	9 Birtles (Mariner)
10 Brooking	10 Mariner (Hughes)	10 Hoddle	10 Woodcock	10 Kennedy
11 Devonshire	11 Brooking	11 Armstrong (Devonshire)	11 Brooking	11 Woodcock
Wembley May 20: 1-1 *Brotherston og*	Glasgow May 24: 2-0 *Brooking, Coppell*	Sydney May 31: 2-1 *Hoddle, Mariner*	Turin June 12: 1-1 *Wilkins*	Turin June 15: 0-1

1980 Spain
1 Clemence
2 Anderson (Cherry)
3 Mills
4 Thompson
5 Watson
6 Wilkins
7 McDermott
8 Hoddle (Mariner)
9 Keegan
10 Woodcock
11 Brooking
Naples June 18: 2-1 *Brooking, Woodcock*

ENGLAND'S WORST-EVER RUN

During the 1980–81 season, England suffered their worst run in international history. They completed six matches without a win, losing four times in this sequence. They had once gone seven games, between May 1958 and October 1958, without victory but in that run they drew five and lost only two. Between March and May 1981, England played five successive matches at Wembley, lost three, drew two and scored only one goal.

IRELAND INTERNATIONAL TEAMS 1882-1980

Substitutes in brackets †World Cup final stages

1882 England	1882 Wales	1883 England	1883 Wales	1884 Scotland
1 Hamilton	1 Hamilton	1 Rankine	1 Rankine	1 Hunter
2 McAlery	2 Crone W.	2 Watson	2 Watson	2 Wilson
3 Rattray	3 McAlery	3 Rattray	3 Rattray	3 Crone W.
4 Martin	4 Martin	4 Molyneux	4 Molyneux	4 Hastings
5 Hastings	5 Hastings	5 Martin	5 Hastings	5 Molyneux
6 Buckle	6 Davison	6 Morrow	6 Morrow	6 Dill
7 McWha	7 McWha	7 Potts	7 Potts	7 Spiller
8 Davison	8 Condy	8 McWha	8 McWha	8 Gibb
9 Sinclair	9 Sinclair	9 Davison	9 Davison	9 Morrow
10 Dill	10 Dill	10 Reid	10 Spiller	10 Davison
11 McCaw	11 Johnston	11 Spiller	11 Dill	11 Gaussen
Belfast Feb 18: 0-13	Wrexham Feb 25: 1-7 *Johnston*	Liverpool Feb 24: 0-7	Belfast Mar 17: 1-1 *Morrow*	Belfast Jan 26: 0-5

1884 Wales	1884 England	1885 England	1885 Scotland	1885 Wales
1 Hunter	1 Hunter	1 Henderson	1 Henderson	1 Henderson
2 Wilson	2 Wilson	2 Hewison	2 Hewison	2 Johnston
3 Crone W.	3 Crone W.	3 Moorhead	3 Johnston	3 Eames
4 Molyneux	4 Hastings	4 Molyneux	4 Muir	4 Molyneux
5 Lockhart	5 Molyneux	5 Houston	5 Houston	5 Muir
6 Redmond	6 Dill	6 Eames	6 Eames	6 McWha
7 Davison	7 Spiller	7 McWha	7 McLean	7 Hamilton W.J.
8 Gibb	8 McWha	8 Davison	8 Sherrard	8 Hamilton W.D.
9 Reid	9 Johnston	9 Gibb	9 Gibb	9 Gibb
10 Spiller	10 Davison	10 McGee	10 McGee	10 McGee
11 Dill	11 Gaussen	11 Dill	11 Dill	11 Dill
Wrexham Feb 9: 0-6	Belfast Feb 23: 1-8 *McWha*	Manchester Feb 28: 0-4	Glasgow Mar 14: 2-8 *Gibb 2*	Belfast April 11: 2-8 *Molyneux, Dill*

1886 Wales	1886 England	1886 Scotland	1887 England	1887 Scotland
1 Gillespie	1 Gillespie	1 Gillespie	1 Gillespie	1 Gillespie
2 Watson	2 Watson	2 Watson	2 Browne	2 Fox
3 Devine	3 Devine	3 Crone W.	3 Fox	3 Watson
4 Molyneux	4 Molyneux	4 Molyneux	4 Rosbotham	4 Moore
5 Crone W.	5 Crone W.	5 Williams	5 Leslie	5 Rosbotham
6 McArthur	6 Hastings	6 Hastings	6 Crone W.	6 Baxter
7 McClatchey	7 Turner	7 McClatchey	7 Allen	7 Reid
8 Smyth	8 Condy	8 Johnston	8 Gibb	8 Stanfield
9 Whitfield	9 Johnston	9 Gibb	9 Stanfield	9 Browne
10 Lemon	10 McClatchey	10 Condy	10 Small	10 Peden
11 Raper	11 Williams	11 Turner	11 Brown W.M.	11 Gibb
Wrexham Feb 27: 0-5	Belfast Mar 13: 1-6 *Williams*	Belfast Mar 20: 2-7 *Condy, Johnston*	Sheffield Feb 5: 0-7	Glasgow Feb 19: 1-4 *Browne*

1887 Wales	**1888 Wales**	**1888 Scotland**	**1888 England**	**1889 England**
1 Gillespie	1 Clugston	1 Lowther	1 Lowther	1 Clugston
2 Browne	2 Forbes	2 Wilson	2 McVickers	2 Goodbody
3 Watson	3 Crone W.	3 Browne	3 Browne	3 Watson
4 Sherrard	4 Sherrard	4 Forsyth	4 Forsyth	4 Crawford
5 Rosbotham	5 Rosbotham	5 Rosbotham	5 Rosbotham	5 Rosbotham
6 Devine	6 Devine	6 Molyneux	6 Crone W.	6 Cooke
7 Moore	7 Gaussen	7 Dalton	7 Gaussen	7 Gaussen
8 Baxter	8 Stanfield	8 Stanfield	8 Stanfield	8 Stanfield
9 Gibb	9 Berry	9 Berry	9 Silo	9 Berry
10 Stanfield	10 Wilton	10 Lemon	10 Wilton	10 Wilton
11 Peden	11 Peden	11 Turner	11 Peden	11 Peden
Belfast	Wrexham	Belfast	Belfast	Everton
Mar 12: 4-1	Mar 3: 0-11	Mar 24: 2-10	April 7: 1-5	Mar 2: 1-6
Stanfield, Browne, Peden, Sherrard		*Lemon, Dalton*	*Crone*	*Wilton*

1889 Scotland	**1889 Wales**	**1890 Wales**	**1890 England**	**1890 Scotland**
1 Clugston	1 Clugston	1 Galbraith	1 Clugston	1 Clugston
2 McVickers	2 Elleman	2 Crone R.	2 Stewart	2 Stewart
3 Crone R.	3 Watson	3 Stewart	3 Crone R.	3 Crone R.
4 Thompson	4 Crawford	4 Crone W.	4 Williamson	4 Reid
5 Christian	5 Bennett	5 Reynolds	5 Spencer	5 Spencer
6 Crone W.	6 Reid	6 Reid	6 Cooke	6 Cooke
7 Torrans S.	7 Gaussen	7 Dalton	7 Elleman	7 Dalton
8 Stanfield	8 Stanfield	8 Gaffikin	8 Stanfield	8 Gaffikin
9 Gibb	9 Percy	9 Johnston	9 Wilton	9 Stanfield
10 Wilton	10 Lemon	10 Torrans S.	10 McIlvenny	10 Torrans S.
11 Peden	11 Gillespie	11 Peden	11 Reynolds	11 Peden
Glasgow	Belfast	Shrewsbury	Belfast	Belfast
Mar 9: 0-7	April 27: 1-3	Feb 8: 2-5	Mar 15: 1-9	Mar 29: 1-4
	Lemon	*Dalton 2*	*Reynolds*	*Peden*

1891 Wales	**1891 England**	**1891 Scotland**	**1892 Wales**	**1892 England**
1 Clugston	1 Clugston	1 Loyal	1 Clugston	1 Clugston
2 Goodbody	2 Forbes	2 Gordon H.	2 Gordon H.	2 Gordon H.
3 Morrison	3 Morrison	3 Forbes	3 Stewart	3 Stewart
4 Crawford	4 Crawford	4 Crawford	4 McKeown	4 McKeown
5 Reynolds	5 Reynolds	5 Reynolds	5 Spencer	5 Spencer
6 Moore	6 Moore	6 Moore	6 Cunningham	6 Cunningham
7 Dalton	7 Whiteside	7 Dalton	7 Dalton	7 Dalton
8 Gaffikin	8 Stanfield	8 Gaffikin	8 Gaffikin	8 Gaffikin
9 Stanfield	9 McCabe	9 Stanfield	9 Stanfield	9 Stanfield
10 Torrans S.	10 McIlvenny	10 Brisby	10 Torrans S.	10 Torrans S.
11 Peden	11 Peden	11 Torrans S.	11 Peden	11 Peden
Belfast	Wolverhampton	Glasgow	Bangor	Belfast
Feb 7: 7-2	Mar 7: 1-6	Mar 28: 1-2	Feb 27: 1-1	Mar 5: 0-2
Dalton 3, Stanfield 2, Gaffikin 2	*Whiteside*	*Stanfield*	*Stanfield*	

1892 Scotland	1893 England	1893 Scotland	1893 Wales	1894 Wales
1 Clugston	1 Clugston	1 Clugston	1 Clugston	1 Gordon T.
2 Gordon H.	2 Gordon H.	2 Gordon H.	2 Gordon H.	2 Stewart
3 Stewart	3 Stewart	3 Torrans R.	3 Stewart	3 Torrans S.
4 McKeown	4 Crawford	4 McKeown	4 Crawford	4 McKeown
5 Spencer	5 Spencer	5 Johnston	5 McKeown	5 Burnett
6 Cunningham	6 Cunningham	6 Torrans S.	6 Johnston	6 Milne
7 Dalton	7 Small	7 Small	7 Small	7 Dalton
8 Gaffikin	8 Gaffikin	8 Gaffikin	8 Gaffikin	8 Gaffikin
9 Williamson	9 Stanfield	9 Williamson	9 Stanfield	9 Stanfield
10 Stanfield	10 Torrans S.	10 Wilton	10 Wilton	10 Gibson
11 Torrans S.	11 Peden	11 Peden	11 Peden	11 Barron
Belfast Mar 19: 2-3 *Williamson, Gaffikin*	Birmingham Feb 25: 1-6 *Gaffikin*	Glasgow Mar 25: 1-6 *Gaffikin*	Belfast April 5: 4-3 *Peden 3, Wilton*	Swansea Feb 24: 1-4 *Stanfield*

1894 England	1894 Scotland	1895 England	1895 Wales	1895 Scotland
1 Scott T.	1 Scott T.	1 Gordon T.	1 Scott T.	1 Scott T.
2 Stewart	2 Stewart	2 Gordon H.	2 Gordon H.	2 Ponsonby
3 Torrans S.	3 Torrans S.	3 Torrans S.	3 Scott L.J.	3 Scott L.J.
4 Johnston	4 McKeown	4 McKie	4 McKie	4 McKie
5 Burnett	5 Burnett	5 Milne	5 Milne	5 Alexander
6 Milne	6 Milne	6 Burnett	6 Burnett	6 McClatchey
7 Dalton	7 Dalton	7 Morrison	7 Morrison	7 Morrison
8 Gaffikin	8 Gaffikin	8 Gaffikin	8 Sherrard	8 Sherrard
9 Stanfield	9 Stanfield	9 Stanfield	9 Jordan	9 Stanfield
10 Gibson	10 Gibson	10 Sherrard	10 Gawkrodger	10 Gibson
11 Barron	11 Barron	11 Jordan	11 Gaffikin	11 Barron
Belfast Mar 3: 2-2 *Stanfield, Gibson*	Belfast Mar 31: 1-2 *Stanfield*	Derby Mar 9: 0-9	Belfast Mar 16: 2-2 *Gawkrodger, Sherrard*	Glasgow Mar 30: 1-3 *Sherrard*

1896 Wales	1896 England	1896 Scotland	1897 England	1897 Wales
1 Scott T.	1 Scott T.	1 Scott T.	1 Scott T.	1 Scott T.
2 Ponsonby	2 Ponsonby	2 Ponsonby	2 Ponsonby	2 Gibson
3 Torrans S.	3 Torrans S.	3 Torrans S.	3 Torrans S.	3 Torrans S.
4 McCoy	4 Fitzpatrick	4 Gordon H.	4 Pyper, John	4 Pyper, John
5 Milne	5 Milne	5 Milne	5 Milne	5 Ponsonby
6 Campbell	6 Gordon H.	6 Fitzpatrick	6 McMaster	6 McMaster
7 Turner	7 Baird	7 Baird	7 Campbell	7 Campbell
8 Baird	8 Kelly	8 Morrogh	8 Hall	8 Stanfield
9 Stanfield	9 Stanfield	9 Stanfield	9 Stanfield	9 Pyper, James
10 McCashin	10 Turner	10 Barron	10 Darling	10 Peden
11 Peden	11 Peden	11 Peden	11 Barron	11 Barron
Wrexham Feb 29: 1-6 *Turner*	Belfast Mar 7: 0-2	Belfast Mar 28: 3-3 *Barron 2, Milne* (pen)	Nottingham Feb 20: 0-6	Belfast Mar 6: 4-3 *Barron, Stanfield, John Pyper, Peden*

1897 Scotland	1898 Wales	1898 England	1898 Scotland	1899 England
1 Thompson	1 Scott T.	1 Scott T.	1 Scott T.	1 Lewis
2 Ponsonby	2 Gibson	2 Gibson	2 Gibson	2 Pyper, John
3 Torrans S.	3 Cochrane	3 Torrans S.	3 Torrans S.	3 Torrans S.
4 Pyper, John	4 Anderson	4 Anderson	4 Anderson	4 Ponsonby
5 Milne	5 Milne	5 Milne	5 Milne	5 Milne
6 McMaster	6 Little	6 Cochrane	6 Cochrane	6 Cochrane
7 Campbell	7 Campbell	7 Campbell	7 Campbell	7 Campbell
8 Stanfield	8 Mercer	8 Mercer	8 Mercer	8 Mercer
9 Pyper, James	9 Pyper, James	9 Pyper, James	9 Pyper, James	9 Waring
10 Darling	10 McCashin	10 Peden	10 McCashin	10 Wattie
11 Peden	11 Peden	11 McAllen	11 Peden	11 McAllen
Glasgow	Llandudno	Belfast	Belfast	Sunderland
Mar 27: 1-5	Feb 19: 1-0	Mar 5: 2-3	Mar 26: 0-3	Feb 18: 2-13
James Pyper	*Peden*	*Pyper, Mercer*		*McAllen, Campbell*

1899 Wales	1899 Scotland	1900 Wales	1900 Scotland	1900 England
1 Lewis	1 Lewis	1 Scott T.	1 Lewis	1 Reilly
2 Pyper, John	2 Swan	2 Pyper, John	2 Pyper, John	2 Pyper, John
3 Torrans S.	3 Foreman	3 Cochrane	3 Cochrane	3 Cochrane
4 Goodall	4 Anderson	4 McShane	4 McShane	4 McShane
5 Milne	5 Goodall	5 Goodall	5 Barry	5 Goodall
6 Taggart	6 McShane	6 Maginnis	6 Maginnis	6 Maginnis
7 Morrison	7 Sheehan	7 Sheehan	7 Campbell	7 Sheehan
8 Meldon	8 Meldon	8 Morrison	8 Darling	8 Campbell
9 Hanna	9 Pyer, James	9 Kirwan	9 McAuley	9 Pyper, James
10 McAllen	10 McCashin	10 Kearns	10 McAllen	10 McAllen
11 Peden	11 McAllen	11 McAllen	11 Kearns	11 Kearns
Belfast	Glasgow	Llandudno	Belfast	Dublin
Mar 4: 1-0	Mar 25: 1-9	Feb 24: 0-2	Mar 3: 0-3	Mar 17: 0-2
Meldon	*Goodall*			

1901 Scotland	1901 England	1901 Wales	1902 Wales	1902 Scotland
1 McAlpine	1 Nolan-Whelan	1 Nolan-Whelan	1 Nolan-Whelan	1 Nolan-Whelan
2 Gibson	2 Gibson	2 Gibson	2 Gibson	2 Gibson
3 Torrans S.	3 Boyle	3 Torrans S.	3 McCracken W.	3 Pyper, John
4 Farrell	4 Connor	4 Farrell	4 Darling	4 Darling
5 Connor	5 Goodall	5 Milne	5 Milne	5 Goodall
6 Cochrane	6 Burnison	6 Burnison	6 Nicholl	6 Milne
7 Scott J.	7 Black	7 Campbell	7 Mercer	7 Campbell
8 Smith J.	8 Rea	8 Smith J.	8 Maxwell	8 Morrison
9 Campbell	9 Mansfield	9 McKelvie	9 Gara	9 Gara
10 O'Reilly	10 Doherty	10 O'Reilly	10 Kearns	10 Kearns
11 Clarke	11 Clarke	11 McAllen	11 Kirwan	11 McAllen
Glasgow	Southampton	Belfast	Cardiff	Belfast
Feb 23: 0-11	Mar 9: 0-3	Mar 23: 0-1	Feb 22: 3-0	Mar 1: 1-3
			Gara 3	*Milne*

1902 England	1903 England	1903 Scotland	1903 Wales	1904 England
1 Reilly	1 Scott W.	1 Scott W.	1 Scott W.	1 Scott W.
2 McCracken W.	2 McCracken W.	2 McCartney	2 McCartney	2 McCracken W.
3 Boyle	3 McMillan	3 Boyle	3 Boyle	3 Boyle
4 Darling	4 Darling	4 Darling	4 Darling	4 Milne
5 Milne	5 Milne	5 Milne	5 Goodall	5 Goodall
6 Nicholl	6 Goodall	6 Maginnis	6 Maginnis	6 Maginnis
7 Mercer	7 Campbell	7 Mercer	7 Mercer	7 Mercer
8 Morrison	8 Maxwell	8 Sheridan	8 Maxwell	8 Sheridan
9 Gara	9 Sheridan	9 Connor	9 Connor	9 Connor
10 Kearns	10 Sloan	10 Shanks	10 Sheridan	10 Kirwan
11 Kirwan	11 Kirwan	11 Kirwan	11 Kirwan	11 Buckle
Belfast Mar 22: 0-1	Wolverhampton Feb 14: 0-4	Glasgow Mar 21: 2-0 *Connor, Kirwan*	Belfast Mar 28: 2-0 *Goodall, Sheridan*	Belfast Mar 12: 1-3 *Kirwan*

1904 Wales	1904 Scotland	1905 England	1905 Scotland	1905 Wales
1 Scott W.	1 Scott W.	1 Scott W.	1 Scott W.	1 Reynolds
2 McCracken W.	2 McCracken W.	2 McCracken W.	2 McCartney	2 McCracken W.
3 McCartney	3 McCartney	3 McCartney	3 McCracken W.	3 McMillan
4 McConnell E.	4 McConnell E.	4 Darling	4 Darling	4 Darling
5 Milne	5 Milne	5 Connor	5 Connor	5 Connor
6 Maginnis	6 Maginnis	6 Nicholl	6 McConnell E.	6 Johnston
7 Mercer	7 Campbell	7 Sloan	7 Mercer	7 Hunter
8 Shanks	8 Sheridan	8 Sheridan	8 Maxwell	8 Maxwell
9 Goodall	9 O'Reilly	9 Murphy	9 Murphy	9 Murphy
10 Kirkwood	10 Sloan	10 Shanks	10 O'Hagan	10 O'Hagan
11 Kirwan	11 Kirwan	11 Kirwan	11 Kirwan	11 Kirwan
Bangor Mar 21: 1-0 *McCracken* (pen)	Dublin Mar 26: 1-1 *Sheridan*	Middlesbrough Feb 25: 1-1 *Williamson og*	Glasgow Mar 18: 0-4	Belfast April 8: 2-2 *Murphy, O'Hagan*

1906 England	1906 Scotland	1906 Wales	1907 England	1907 Wales
1 Sherry	1 McKee	1 McKee	1 Scott W.	1 Sherry
2 Darling	2 Willis	2 Willis	2 McCracken W.	2 Seymour
3 McIlroy	3 Darling	3 Darling	3 McCartney	3 McCartney
4 Wright	4 Wright	4 Wright	4 Wright	4 Wright
5 Milne	5 Milne	5 Milne	5 Connor	5 Crothers
6 McConnell E.	6 Ledwidge	6 Ledwidge	6 McConnell E.	6 McClure
7 Hunter	7 Hunter	7 Hunter	7 Blair	7 Blair
8 Mulholland	8 Mulholland	8 Maxwell	8 Harris	8 Harris
9 Harris	9 Waddell	9 O'Hagan	9 Sloan	9 Sloan
10 O'Hagan	10 O'Hagan	10 Sloan	10 O'Hagan	10 O'Hagan
11 Kirwan	11 Kirwan	11 Kirwan	11 Young	11 Kirwan
Belfast Feb 17: 0-5	Dublin Mar 17: 0-1	Wrexham April 2: 4-4 *Maxwell 2, Sloan 2*	Everton Feb 16: 0-1	Belfast Feb 23: 2-3 *O'Hagan, Sloan*

1907 Scotland	**1908 England**	**1908 Scotland**	**1908 Wales**	**1909 England**
1 Scott W.	1 Scott W.	1 Scott W.	1 Scott W.	1 Scott W.
2 Willis	2 Craig	2 Craig	2 Craig	2 Balfe
3 McCartney	3 McCartney	3 McCartney	3 McCartney	3 McCartney
4 Wright	4 Harris	4 Harris	4 Darling	4 Harris
5 Connor	5 Connor	5 Connor	5 McConnell E.	5 Darling
6 McClure	6 McClure	6 McConnell E.	6 Harris	6 McClure
7 Blair	7 Blair	7 Blair	7 Hunter	7 Hunter
8 Maxwell	8 Hannon	8 Hannon	8 Hamilton	8 Lacey
9 McGuire	9 Mercer	9 Andrews	9 Sloan	9 Greer
10 O'Hagan	10 Burnison	10 O'Hagan	10 O'Hagan	10 O'Hagan
11 Young	11 Young	11 Young	11 Buckle	11 Young
Glasgow Mar 16: 0-3	Belfast Feb 15: 1-3 *Hannon*	Dublin Mar 14: 0-5	Aberdare April 11: 1-0 *Sloan*	Bradford Feb 13: 0-4

1909 Scotland	**1909 Wales**	**1910 England**	**1910 Scotland**	**1910 Wales**
1 Scott W.	1 Scott W.	1 Scott W.	1 Scott W.	1 O'Hehir
2 Craig	2 Seymour	2 Burnison	2 Burnison	2 Balfe
3 McCartney	3 McCartney	3 McCann	3 McCann	3 McCann
4 Harris	4 Harris	4 Harris	4 Harris	4 Harris
5 McConnell E.	5 Connor	5 McConnell E.	5 McConnell E.	5 McConnell E.
6 Sloan	6 McConnell E.	6 Darling	6 Darling	6 Darling
7 Hunter	7 Hunter	7 Renneville	7 Renneville	7 Renneville
8 Lacey	8 Lacey	8 Lacey	8 Lacey	8 Lacey
9 Greer	9 Greer	9 Murray	9 Murray	9 Murray
10 Webb	10 Webb	10 Murphy	10 Murphy	10 Murphy
11 Kirwan	11 Slemin	11 Thompson	11 Thompson	11 Thompson
Glasgow Mar 15: 0-5	Belfast Mar 20: 2-3 *Lacey, Hunter*	Belfast Feb 12: 1-1 *Thompson*	Belfast Mar 19: 1-0 *Thompson*	Wrexham April 11: 1-4 *Darling* (pen)

1911 Wales	**1911 England**	**1911 Scotland**	**1912 England**	**1912 Scotland**
1 Scott W.	1 Scott W.	1 Scott W.	1 Scott W.	1 Hanna
2 Burnison	2 Burnison	2 Burnison	2 Burnison	2 Willis
3 Thunder	3 McCann	3 McCann	3 McCann	3 Craig
4 Harris	4 Harris	4 Harris	4 Harris	4 Darling
5 Connor	5 Connor	5 Connor	5 O'Connell	5 O'Connell
6 Hampton	6 Hampton	6 Hampton	6 Hampton	6 Moran
7 Renneville	7 Lacey	7 Lacey	7 Lacey	7 Houston
8 Lacey	8 Hannon	8 Hannon	8 Hamill	8 McKnight
9 Halligan	9 McDonnell	9 McDonnell	9 Halligan	9 McAuley
10 McAuley	10 McAuley	10 Webb	10 McAuley	10 Enright
11 Thompson	11 Thompson	11 Walker	11 Thompson	11 Young
Belfast Jan 28: 1-2 *Halligan*	Derby Feb 11: 1-2 *McAuley*	Glasgow Mar 18: 0-2	Dublin Feb 10: 1-6 *Hamill*	Belfast Mar 16: 1-4 *McKnight* (pen)

1912 **Wales**	**1913** **Wales**	**1913** **England**	**1913** **Scotland**	**1914** **Wales**
1 Hanna	1 Scott W.	1 Scott W.	1 Scott W.	1 McKee
2 Craig	2 Burnison	2 McConnell W.G.	2 McConnell W.G.	2 McConnell W.G.
3 McConnell W.G.	3 McCann	3 Warren	3 Warren	3 Craig
4 Hampton	4 Rollo	4 Hampton	4 Andrews	4 Harris
5 Brennan	5 Donnelly	5 Harris	5 Harris	5 O'Connell
6 Rollo	6 Hampton	6 Andrews	6 Hampton	6 Rollo
7 Houston	7 Houston	7 Houston	7 Houston	7 Seymour
8 Hannon	8 Lacey	8 Hannon	8 McKnight	8 Young
9 McDonnell	9 McDonnell	9 Gillespie	9 Gillespie	9 Gillespie
10 McCandless J.	10 McCandless J.	10 McAuley	10 McAuley	10 Lacey
11 Thompson	11 Thompson	11 Thompson	11 Thompson	11 Bookman
Cardiff April 13: 3-2 *McCandless 2, Brennan*	Belfast Jan 18: 0-1	Belfast Feb 15: 2-1 *Gillespie 2*	Dublin Mar 15: 1-2 *McKnight*	Wrexham Jan 19: 2-1 *Young, Gillespie*

1914 **England**	**1914** **Scotland**	**1919** **England**	**1920** **Wales**	**1920** **Scotland**
1 McKee	1 McKee	1 O'Hagan	1 O'Hagan	1 Scott E.
2 McConnell W.G.	2 McConnell W.G.	2 McCandless W.	2 Manderson	2 Manderson
3 Craig	3 Craig	3 McCracken W.	3 Rollo	3 Rollo
4 Hampton	4 Harris	4 Emerson	4 McCandless W.	4 Hamill
5 O'Connell	5 O'Connell	5 Hamill	5 Hamill	5 Lacey
6 Hamill	6 Hamill	6 Lacey	6 Emerson	6 Emerson
7 Rollo	7 Houston	7 Ferris	7 Lyner	7 Robinson
8 Young	8 Nixon	8 Snape	8 Lacey	8 Gallagher
9 Gillespie	9 Young	9 Gowdy	9 Gillespie	9 Brookes
10 Lacey	10 Lacey	10 Gallagher	10 Ferris	10 Gillespie
11 Thompson	11 Thompson	11 Lyner	11 McCandless J.	11 McCandless J.
Middlesbrough Feb 14: 3-0 *Lacey 2, Gillespie*	Belfast Mar 14: 1-1 *Young*	Belfast Oct 25: 1-1 *Ferris*	Belfast Feb 14: 2-2 *McCandless J.* *Emerson*	Glasgow Mar 13: 0-3

1920 **England**	**1921** **Scotland**	**1921** **Wales**	**1921** **England**	**1922** **Scotland**
1 Scott E.	1 Scott E.	1 Scott E.	1 Scott E.	1 Collins
2 Rollo	2 Mulligan	2 Rollo	2 McCracken W.	2 McCracken W.
3 McCandless W.	3 Rollo	3 McCandless W.	3 Rollo	3 McCandless W.
4 McCracken R.	4 Lacey	4 Lacey	4 McCracken R.	4 McCracken R.
5 Lacey	5 Smith E.E.	5 Scraggs	5 Scraggs	5 O'Brien
6 Emerson	6 O'Brien	6 Harris J.	6 Emerson	6 Emerson
7 Kelly	7 McGregor	7 Robinson	7 Lacey	7 Lacey
8 Ferris	8 Ferris	8 Brown J.	8 Gillespie	8 Gallagher
9 Doran	9 McKinney	9 Chambers	9 Doran	9 Irvine
10 Gillespie	10 Hamill	10 Mathieson	10 Mathieson	10 Gillespie
11 McCandless J.	11 Bookman	11 Bookman	11 Bookman	11 Lyner
Sunderland Oct 23: 0-2	Belfast Feb 26: 0-2	Swansea April 9: 1-2 *Chambers*	Belfast Oct 22: 1-1 *Gillespie*	Glasgow Mar 4: 1-2 *Gillespie*

1922 Wales	1922 England	1923 Scotland	1923 Wales	1923 England
1 Mehaffy	1 Harland	1 Farquharson	1 Farquharson	1 Farquharson
2 McCracken W.	2 Rollo	2 McCracken W.	2 Mackie	2 McCluggage
3 Curran	3 Curran	3 Curran	3 Kennedy	3 Curran
4 McCracken R.	4 Emerson	4 Irving	4 Irving	4 Irving
5 O'Brien	5 Smith E.E.	5 Moorhead	5 Smith E.E.	5 Smith E.E.
6 Emerson	6 Morgan	6 Emerson	6 Emerson	6 Emerson
7 Lyner	7 Lyner	7 McKenzie	7 Lyner	7 Brown J.
8 Crooks	8 Irvine	8 Gallagher	8 Gallagher	8 Croft
9 Doran	9 Nelis	9 Reid	9 Irvine	9 Irvine
10 Gillespie	10 Gillespie	10 Gillespie	10 Gillespie	10 Gillespie
11 Toner	11 Burns	11 Moore	11 Toner	11 Toner
Belfast April 1: 1-1 *Gillespie*	West Bromwich Oct 21: 0-2	Belfast Mar 3: 0-1	Wrexham April 14: 3-0 *Irvine 2, Gillespie*	Belfast Oct 20: 2-1 *Gillespie, Croft*

1924 Scotland	1924 Wales	1924 England	1925 Scotland	1925 Wales
1 Farquharson	1 Farquharson	1 Farquharson	1 Farquharson	1 Scott E.
2 Rollo	2 Rollo	2 Manderson	2 Manderson	2 Rollo
3 McCandless W.	3 McCandless W.	3 Kennedy	3 McCandless W.	3 McConnell W.H.
4 Irving	4 Gowdy	4 Chatton	4 Chatton	4 Garrett
5 O'Brien	5 O'Brien	5 O'Brien	5 O'Brien	5 O'Brien
6 Morgan	6 Irving	6 Irving	6 Irving	6 Irving
7 McKinney	7 Brown J.	7 Lacey	7 Martin	7 Cowan
8 Gallagher	8 Gallagher	8 Gallagher	8 Gallagher	8 Gallagher
9 Irvine	9 McIlvenny	9 Irvine	9 Carroll	9 Sloan
10 Gillespie	10 Gillespie	10 Gillespie	10 Gillespie	10 Meek
11 McGrillen	11 Toner	11 Toner	11 Toner	11 Wilson
Glasgow Mar 1: 0-2	Belfast Mar 15: 0-1	Everton Oct 22: 1-3 *Gillespie*	Belfast Feb 28: 0-3	Wrexham April 18: 0-0

1925 England	1926 Wales	1926 Scotland	1926 England	1927 Scotland
1 Scott E.	1 Scott E.	1 Scott E.	1 Scott E.	1 Scott E.
2 Rollo	2 Brown W.G.	2 Manderson	2 Rollo	2 McCluggage
3 McConnell W.H.	3 McConnell W.H.	3 Watson	3 McConnell W.H.	3 McConnell W.H.
4 Gowdy	4 Irving	4 Irving	4 Gowdy	4 Gowdy
5 Chatton	5 O'Brien	5 Gowdy	5 Morgan	5 Sloan
6 Sloan	6 Sloan	6 Sloan	6 Irving	6 McMullan
7 Bothwell	7 Bothwell	7 Bothwell	7 Bothwell	7 McGrillen
8 Irvine	8 Steele	8 Steele	8 Irvine	8 Gallagher
9 Davey	9 Curran	9 Curran	9 Davey	9 Davey
10 Hopkins	10 Gillespie	10 Gillespie	10 Gillespie	10 Irving
11 McMullan	11 McMullan	11 Mahood	11 Toner	11 Toner
Belfast Oct 24: 0-0	Belfast Feb 13: 3-0 *Gillespie, Curran 2*	Glasgow Feb 27: 0-4	Liverpool Oct 20: 3-3 *Gillespie, Davey, Irvine*	Belfast Feb 26: 0-2

1927 Wales	1927 England	1928 Wales	1928 Scotland	1928 England
1 Scott E.	1 Scott E.	1 Scott E.	1 Scott E.	1 Scott E.
2 McCluggage	2 McCluggage	2 McCluggage	2 McCluggage	2 McCluggage
3 McConnell W.H.	3 McConnell W.H.	3 McConnell W.H.	3 Hamilton	3 Hamilton
4 Irving	4 Irving	4 Irving	4 Irving	4 Irving
5 Sloan	5 Morgan	5 Morgan	5 Moorhead	5 Sloan
6 O'Brien	6 Sloan	6 Sloan	6 Morgan	6 Morgan
7 Bothwell	7 Chambers	7 Chambers	7 Chambers	7 Chambers
8 Irvine	8 Irvine	8 Dunne	8 Irvine	8 Irvine
9 Johnston	9 Davey	9 Davey	9 Curran	9 Bambrick
10 Gillespie	10 Gillespie	10 McConnell P.	10 Ferris	10 Gillespie
11 McCaw	11 Mahood	11 Mahood	11 Mahood	11 Mahood
Cardiff	Belfast	Belfast	Glasgow	Everton
April 9: 2-2	Oct 22: 2-0	Feb 4: 1-2	Feb 25: 1-0	Oct 22: 1-2
Johnston 2	*Jones og, Mahood*	*Chambers*	*Chambers*	*Bambrick*

1929 Wales	1929 Scotland	1929 England	1930 Wales	1930 Scotland
1 Scott E.	1 Scott E.	1 Scott E.	1 Gardiner	1 Gardiner
2 McCluggage	2 McCluggage	2 Russell	2 McCluggage	2 Russell
3 McCandless W.	3 Flack	3 Hamilton	3 Fulton	3 Hamilton
4 Miller	4 Miller	4 Miller	4 McCleery	4 McDonald
5 Elwood	5 Moorhead	5 Elwood	5 Cpl J. Jones	5 Cpl J. Jones
6 Steele	6 Steele	6 McCleery	6 Sloan	6 Sloan
7 Chambers	7 Chambers	7 Duggan	7 Chambers	7 Chambers
8 Rowley	8 Rowley	8 Rowley	8 Rowley	8 Irvine
9 Bambrick	9 Bambrick	9 Bambrick	9 Bambrick	9 Bambrick
10 Cumming	10 Cumming	10 Cumming	10 McCambridge	10 McCambridge
11 Mahood	11 Mahood	11 Kavanagh	11 Mahood	11 McCaw
Wrexham	Belfast	Belfast	Belfast	Glasgow
Feb 2: 2-2	Feb 23: 3-7	Oct 19: 0-3	Feb 1: 7-0	Feb 22: 1-3
Mahood, McCluggage (pen)	*Bambrick 2, Rowley*		*Bambrick 6, McCluggage*	*McCaw*

1930 England	1931 Scotland	1931 Wales	1931 Scotland	1931 England
1 Scott E.	1 Gardiner	1 Diffin	1 Gardiner	1 Gardiner
2 McCluggage	2 McNinch	2 McCluggage	2 McNinch	2 Russell
3 Fulton	3 Fulton	3 Fulton	3 Hamilton R.	3 Fulton
4 Jones J.	4 McCleery	4 Irving	4 McCleery	4 McDonald
5 Reid	5 Jones J.	5 Jones J.	5 Jones J.	5 Jones J.
6 McCleery	6 Sloan	6 McCleery	6 Gowdy	6 Mitchell
7 Duggan	7 Blair	7 Duggan	7 Blair	7 Chambers
8 Irvine	8 Falloon	8 Rowley	8 Rowley	8 McConnell P.
9 Dunne	9 Roberts	9 Dunne	9 Dunne	9 Dunne
10 Gillespie	10 Geary	10 McCambridge	10 Geary	10 McCambridge
11 McCaw	11 McCaw	11 McCaw	11 Chambers	11 Kelly
Sheffield	Belfast	Wrexham	Glasgow	Belfast
Oct 20: 1-5	Feb 21: 0-0	April 22: 2-3	Sept 19: 1-3	Oct 17: 2-6
Dunne		*Dunne, Rowley*	*Dunne*	*Dunne, Kelly*

1931 Wales	**1932 Scotland**	**1932 England**	**1932 Wales**	**1933 Scotland**
1 Scott E.	1 Scott E.	1 Scott E.	1 Scott E.	1 Scott E.
2 McNinch	2 Cook	2 Cook	2 Cook	2 Willingham
3 Fulton	3 Fulton	3 Fulton	3 Willingham	3 Fulton
4 McCleery	4 Falloon	4 Mitchell W.	4 Mitchell W.	4 McMahon
5 Pyper	5 Jones J.	5 Jones J.	5 Jones J.	5 Jones J.
6 Mitchell W.	6 Gowdy	6 McCleery	6 McCleery	6 Mitchell W.
7 Chambers	7 Mitchell E.	7 Duggan	7 Houston	7 Blair
8 Irvine	8 Priestley	8 Moore	8 English	8 Stevenson
9 Bambrick	9 Millar	9 Dunne	9 Dunne	9 Martin
10 Millar	10 English	10 Doherty J.	10 Doherty J.	10 Coulter
11 Kelly	11 Kelly	11 Kelly	11 Kelly	11 Mahood
Belfast	Belfast	Blackpool	Wrexham	Glasgow
Dec 5: 4-0	Sept 12: 0-4	Oct 17: 0-1	Dec 7: 1-4	Sept 16: 2-1
Kelly 2, Millar, Bambrick			*English*	*Martin 2*

1933 England	**1933 Wales**	**1934 Scotland**	**1935 England**	**1935 Wales**
1 Scott E.	1 Scott E.	1 Scott E.	1 Breen	1 Breen
2 Reid	2 Reid	2 Mackie	2 Cook	2 Mackie
3 Fulton	3 Fulton	3 Fulton	3 Fulton	3 Fulton
4 McMillen	4 Mitchell W.	4 McMillen	4 Gowdy	4 McCullough
5 Jones J.	5 Jones J.	5 Jones J.	5 Jones J.	5 Jones J.
6 Jones S.	6 Jones S.	6 Mitchell W.	6 Mitchell W.	6 Gowdy
7 Duggan	7 Mitchell C.	7 Duggan	7 Brown J.	7 Duggan
8 Stevenson	8 Stevenson	8 Gowdy	8 Doherty P.	8 Brown J.
9 Martin	9 Martin	9 Martin	9 Martin	9 Bambrick
10 Coulter	10 Coulter	10 Stevenson	10 Stevenson	10 Doherty P.
11 Priestley	11 Kelly	11 Coulter	11 Coulter	11 Coulter
Belfast	Belfast	Belfast	Everton	Wrexham
Oct 14: 0-3	Nov 4: 1-1	Oct 20: 2-1	Feb 6: 1-2	Mar 27: 1-3
	Jones S.	*Martin, Coulter*	*Stevenson*	*Bambrick*

1935 England	**1935 Scotland**	**1936 Wales**	**1936 Scotland**	**1936 England**
1 Scott E.	1 Scott E.	1 Scott E.	1 Breen	1 Breen
2 Reid	2 Cook	2 Cook	2 Cook	2 Cook
3 Allen	3 Fulton	3 Fulton	3 Fulton	3 Fulton
4 Mitchell W.	4 McCullough	4 Gowdy	4 McMillen	4 McCullough
5 Jones J.	5 Jones J.	5 Jones J.	5 Jones J.	5 Jones J.
6 Browne R.	6 Mitchell W.	6 Browne R.	6 Mitchell W.	6 Mitchell W.
7 Brown J.	7 Duggan	7 Kernaghan	7 Kernaghan	7 Brown J.
8 McCullough	8 Stevenson	8 Gibb	8 McCullough	8 Stevenson
9 Bambrick	9 Bambrick	9 Martin	9 Martin	9 Davis
10 Doherty P.	10 Doherty P.	10 Stevenson	10 Coulter	10 Doherty P.
11 Kelly	11 Kelly	11 Kelly	11 Kelly	11 Kelly
Belfast	Edinburgh	Belfast	Belfast	Stoke
Oct 19: 1-3	Nov 13: 1-2	Mar 11: 3-2	Oct 31: 1-3	Nov 18: 1-3
Brown	*Kelly*	*Gibb, Stevenson, Kernaghan*	*Kernaghan*	*Davis*

1937 Wales	1937 England	1937 Scotland	1938 Wales	1938 Scotland
1 Breen	1 Breen	1 Breen	1 Twoomey	1 Breen
2 Cook	2 Hayes	2 Hayes	2 Cook	2 Hayes
3 Fulton	3 Cook	3 Cook	3 Fulton	3 Cook
4 Brolly	4 Mitchell W.	4 Doherty M.	4 Brolly	4 McMillen
5 Jones J.	5 Jones J.	5 McMillen	5 McMillen	5 O'Mahoney
6 Mitchell W.	6 Browne R.	6 Mitchell W.	6 Browne R.	6 Browne R.
7 Brown J.	7 Kernaghan	7 Brown J.	7 Brown J.	7 Brown J.
8 Doherty P.	8 Stevenson	8 McAlinden	8 Farrell	8 McAlinden
9 Banks	9 Martin	9 Martin	9 Bambrick	9 Martin
10 Stevenson	10 Doherty P.	10 Doherty P.	10 Stevenson	10 Stevenson
11 Coulter	11 Madden	11 Coulter	11 Coulter	11 Coulter
Wrexham Mar 17: 1-4 *Stevenson*	Belfast Oct 23: 1-5 *Stevenson*	Aberdeen Nov 10: 1-1 *Doherty P.*	Belfast Mar 16: 1-0 *Bambrick*	Belfast Oct 8: 0-2

1938 England	1939 Wales	1946 England	1946 Scotland	1947 Wales
1 Twoomey	1 Breen	1 Russell	1 Hinton	1 Hinton
2 Hayes	2 Cook	2 Gorman	2 Gorman	2 Gorman
3 Cook	3 Butler	3 Ahearne	3 Feeney	3 Carey
4 Brolly	4 Brolly	4 Carey	4 Martin	4 Sloan
5 McMillen	5 Leatham	5 Vernon	5 Vernon	5 Vernon
6 Browne R.	6 Weir	6 Douglas	6 Farrell	6 Farrell
7 Cochrane	7 Cochrane	7 Cochrane	7 Cochrane	7 Cochrane
8 Stevenson	8 Stevenson	8 McAlinden	8 Carey	8 Stevenson
9 Baird	9 Milligan	9 McMorran	9 Walsh D.	9 Walsh D.
10 Doherty P.	10 Doherty P.	10 Doherty P.	10 Stevenson	10 Doherty P.
11 Brown J.	11 Brown J.	11 Lockhart	11 Eglington	11 Eglington
Manchester Nov 16: 0-7	Wrexham Mar 15: 1-3 *Milligan*	Belfast Sept 28: 2-7 *Lockhart 2*	Hampden Nov 27: 0-0	Belfast April 16: 2-1 *Stevenson, Doherty*

1947 Scotland	1947 England	1948 Wales	1948 England	1948 Scotland
1 Hinton	1 Hinton	1 Hinton	1 Smyth W.	1 Smyth W.
2 Martin	2 Martin	2 Martin	2 Carey	2 Carey
3 Aherne	3 Carey	3 Gorman	3 Martin	3 Keane
4 Walsh W.	4 Walsh W.	4 Walsh W.	4 Walsh W.	4 McCabe
5 Vernon	5 Vernon	5 Vernon	5 Vernon	5 Vernon
6 Farrell	6 Farrell	6 Farrell	6 Farrell	6 Walsh W.
7 Cochrane	7 Cochrane	7 Cochrane	7 O'Driscoll	7 Cochrane
8 Smyth S.	8 Smyth S.	8 Smyth S.	8 McAlinden	8 Smyth S.
9 Walsh D.	9 Walsh D.	9 Walsh D.	9 Walsh D.	9 Walsh D.
10 Stevenson	10 Doherty P.	10 Doherty P.	10 Tully	10 Doherty P.
11 Eglington	11 Eglington	11 Eglington	11 Eglington	11 O'Driscoll
Belfast Oct 4: 2-0 *Smyth 2*	Everton Nov 5: 2-2 *Doherty, Walsh D.*	Wrexham Mar 10: 0-2	Belfast Oct 9: 2-6 *Walsh D. 2*	Hampden Nov 17: 2-3 *Walsh D. 2*

1949 Wales	1949 Scotland	1949 England	1950 Wales	1950 England
1 Moore	1 Kelly P.M	1 Kelly H.	1 Kelly H.	1 Kelly H.
2 Carey	2 Bowler	2 Feeney	2 Bowler	2 Gallogly
3 Aherne	3 McMichael	3 McMichael	3 Aherne	3 McMichael
4 McCabe	4 Blanchflower D.	4 Bowler	4 Blanchflower D.	4 Blanchflower D.
5 Vernon	5 Vernon	5 Vernon	5 Martin	5 Vernon
6 Farrell	6 Ferris	6 McCabe	6 Ryan	6 Cush
7 Cochrane	7 Cochrane	7 Cochrane	7 McKenna	7 Campbell
8 Smyth S.	8 Smyth S.	8 Smyth S.	8 Smyth S.	8 Crossan
9 Walsh D.	9 Brennan	9 Brennan	9 Walsh D.	9 McMorran
10 Brennan	10 Crossan	10 Tully	10 Brennan	10 Brennan
11 O'Driscoll	11 McKenna	11 McKenna	11 Lockhart	11 McKenna
Belfast Mar 9: 0-2	Belfast Oct 1: 2-8 *Smyth 2*	Maine Road Nov 6: 2-9 *Smyth, Brennan*	Wrexham Mar 8: 0-0	Belfast Oct 7: 1-4 *McMorran*

1950 Scotland	1951 Wales	1951 France	1951 Scotland	1951 England
1 Kelly H.	1 Hinton	1 Hinton	1 Uprichard	1 Uprichard
2 Gallogly	2 Graham	2 Graham	2 Graham	2 Graham
3 McMichael	3 Cunningham	3 McMichael	3 McMichael	3 McMichael
4 Blanchflower D.	4 McCabe	4 Blanchflower D.	4 Dickson	4 Dickson
5 Vernon	5 Vernon	5 Vernon	5 Vernon	5 Vernon
6 Cush	6 Dickson	6 Ferris	6 Ferris	6 McCourt
7 Campbell	7 Hughes	7 Bingham	7 Bingham	7 Bingham
8 McGarry	8 McMorran	8 McGarry	8 McIlroy	8 Smyth S.
9 McMorran	9 Simpson	9 Simpson	9 McMorran	9 McMorran
10 Doherty P.	10 McGarry	10 Dickson	10 Peacock	10 McIlroy
11 McKenna	11 Lockhart	11 McKenna	11 Tully	11 McKenna
Hampden Nov 1: 1-6 *McGarry*	Belfast Mar 7: 1-2 *Simpson*	Belfast May 12: 2-2 *Ferris, Simpson*	Belfast Oct 6: 0-3	Villa Park Nov 20: 0-2

1952 Wales	1952 England	1952 Scotland	1952 France	1953 Wales
1 Uprichard	1 Uprichard	1 Uprichard	1 Uprichard	1 Uprichard
2 Graham	2 Cunningham	2 Graham	2 Graham	2 McCabe
3 McMichael	3 McMichael	3 McMichael	3 McMichael	3 McMichael
4 Blanchflower D.	4 Blanchflower D.	4 Blanchflower D.	4 Blanchflower D.	4 Blanchflower D.
5 Dickson	5 Dickson	5 Dickson	5 Dickson	5 Dickson
6 McCourt	6 McCourt	6 McCourt	6 McCourt	6 McCourt
7 Bingham	7 Bingham	7 Bingham	7 Bingham	7 Bingham
8 D'Arcy	8 D'Arcy	8 D'Arcy	8 D'Arcy	8 McIlroy
9 McMorran	9 McMorran	9 McMorran	9 McMorran	9 McMorran
10 McIlroy	10 McIlroy	10 McIlroy	10 Peacock	10 D'Arcy
11 Lockhart	11 Tully	11 Tully	11 Tully	11 Tully
Swansea Mar 19: 0-3	Belfast Oct 4: 2-2 *Tully 2*	Hampden Nov 5: 1-1 *D'Arcy*	Paris Nov 11: 1-3 *Tully*	Belfast April 15: 2-3 *McMorran 2*

1953 Scotland	1953 England	1954 Wales	1954 England	1954 Scotland
1 Smyth W.	1 Smyth W.	1 Gregg	1 Uprichard	1 Uprichard
2 Cunningham	2 Graham	2 Graham	2 Montgomery	2 Graham
3 McMichael	3 McMichael	3 McMichael	3 McMichael	3 Cunningham
4 Blanchflower D.	4 Blanchflower D.	4 Blanchflower D.	4 Blanchflower D.	4 Blanchflower D.
5 McCabe	5 Dickson	5 Dickson	5 Dickson	5 McCavana
6 Cush	6 Cush	6 Peacock	6 Peacock	6 Peacock
7 Bingham	7 Bingham	7 Bingham	7 Bingham	7 Bingham
8 McIlroy	8 McIlroy	8 Blanchflower J.	8 Blanchflower J.	8 Blanchflower J.
9 Simpson	9 Simpson	9 McAdams	9 Simpson	9 McAdams
10 Tully	10 McMorran	10 McIlroy	10 McIlroy	10 McIlroy
11 Lockhart	11 Lockhart	11 McParland	11 McParland	11 McParland
Belfast Oct 3: 1-3 *Lockhart*	Everton Nov 11: 1-3 *McMorran*	Wrexham Mar 31: 2-1 *McParland 2*	Belfast Oct 2: 0-2	Hampden Nov 3: 2-2 *Bingham, McAdams*

1955 Wales	1955 Scotland	1955 England	1956 Wales	1956 England
1 Uprichard	1 Uprichard	1 Uprichard	1 Uprichard	1 Gregg
2 Graham	2 Graham	2 Cunningham	2 Cunningham	2 Cunningham
3 McMichael	3 Cunningham	3 Graham	3 McMichael	3 McMichael
4 Blanchflower D.	4 Blanchflower D.	4 Blanchflower D.	4 Blanchflower D.	4 Blanchflower D.
5 McCleary	5 McCavana	5 McCavana	5 Blanchflower J.	5 Blanchflower J.
6 Casey	6 Peacock	6 Peacock	6 Casey	6 Casey
7 Bingham	7 Bingham	7 Bingham	7 Bingham	7 Bingham
8 Crossan	8 Blanchflower J.	8 McIlroy	8 McIlroy	8 McIlroy
9 Walker	9 Coyle	9 Coyle	9 Jones J.	9 Jones J.
10 McIlroy	10 McIlroy	10 Tully	10 McMorran	10 McAdams
11 Lockhart	11 McParland	11 McParland	11 Lockhart	11 McParland
Belfast April 20: 2-3 *Crossan, Walker*	Belfast Oct 8: 2-1 *Blanchflower J., Bingham*	Wembley Nov 2: 0-3	Cardiff April 11: 1-1 *Jones*	Belfast Oct 6: 1-1 *McIlroy*

1956 Scotland	1957 Portugal	1957 Wales	1957 Italy	1957 Portugal
1 Gregg	1 Gregg	1 Gregg	1 Gregg	1 Gregg
2 Cunningham	2 Cunningham	2 Cunningham	2 Cunningham	2 Cunningham
3 McMichael	3 McMichael	3 McMichael	3 McMichael	3 McMichael
4 Blanchflower D.	4 Blanchflower D.	4 Blanchflower D.	4 Blanchflower D.	4 Blanchflower D.
5 Blanchflower J.	5 Blanchflower J.	5 Cush	5 Cush	5 Cush
6 Casey	6 Casey	6 Peacock	6 Casey	6 Casey
7 Bingham	7 Bingham	7 Bingham	7 Bingham	7 Bingham
8 McIlroy	8 McIlroy	8 McIlroy	8 Simpson	8 Simpson
9 Shields	9 Coyle	9 Jones	9 McMorran	9 McMorran
10 Dickson	10 Cush	10 Casey	10 McIlroy	10 McIlroy
11 McParland	11 McParland	11 McParland	11 Peacock	11 Peacock
Hampden Nov 7: 0-1	Lisbon Jan 16: 1-1 *Bingham*	Belfast April 10: 0-0	Rome April 25: 0-1	Belfast May 1: 3-0 *Simpson, McIlroy, Casey*

1957 Scotland	**1957 England**	**1957 Italy**	**1958 Italy**	**1958 Wales**
1 Uprichard	1 Gregg	1 Gregg	1 Uprichard	1 Gregg
2 Cunningham	2 Keith	2 Keith	2 Cunningham	2 Cunningham
3 McMichael	3 McMichael	3 McMichael	3 McMichael	3 McMichael
4 Blanchflower D.	4 Blanchflower D.	4 Blanchflower D.	4 Blanchflower D.	4 Blanchflower D.
5 Blanchflower J.	5 Blanchflower J.	5 Blanchflower J.	5 Blanchflower J.	5 Keith
6 Peacock	6 Peacock	6 Peacock	6 Peacock	6 Peacock
7 Bingham	7 Bingham	7 Bingham	7 Bingham	7 Bingham
8 Simpson	8 McCrory	8 McIlroy	8 Cush	8 Cush
9 McAdams	9 Simpson	9 McAdams	9 Simpson	9 Simpson
10 McIlroy	10 McIlroy	10 Cush	10 McIlroy	10 McIlroy
11 McParland	11 McParland	11 McParland	11 McParland	11 McParland
Belfast Oct 5: 1-1 *Bingham*	Wembley Nov 6: 3-2 *McIlroy, McCrory, Simpson*	Belfast Dec 4: 2-2 *Cush 2*	Belfast Jan 15: 2-1 *McIlroy, Cush*	Cardiff April 16: 1-1 *Simpson*

1958 Czechoslovakia †	**1958 Argentina †**	**1958 W Germany †**	**1958 Czechoslovakia †**	**1958 France †**
1 Gregg	1 Gregg	1 Gregg	1 Uprichard	1 Gregg
2 Keith	2 Keith	2 Keith	2 Keith	2 Keith
3 McMichael	3 McMichael	3 McMichael	3 McMichael	3 McMichael
4 Blanchflower D.	4 Blanchflower D.	4 Blanchflower D.	4 Blanchflower D.	4 Blanchflower D.
5 Cunningham	5 Cunningham	5 Cunningham	5 Cunningham	5 Cunningham
6 Peacock	6 Peacock	6 Peacock	6 Peacock	6 Cush
7 Bingham	7 Bingham	7 Bingham	7 Bingham	7 Bingham
8 Cush	8 Cush	8 Cush	8 Cush	8 Casey
9 Dougan	9 Coyle	9 Casey	9 Scott	9 Scott
10 McIlroy	10 McIlroy	10 McIlroy	10 McIlroy	10 McIlroy
11 McParland	11 McParland	11 McParland	11 McParland	11 McParland
Halmstad June 8: 1-0 *Cush*	Halmstad June 11: 1-3 *McParland*	Malmo June 15: 2-2 *McParland 2*	Malmo June 17: 2-1 *McParland 2*	Norrkoping June 19: 0-4

1958 England	**1958 Spain**	**1958 Scotland**	**1959 Wales**	**1959 Scotland**
1 Gregg	1 Uprichard	1 Uprichard	1 Gregg	1 Gregg
2 Keith	2 Keith	2 Keith	2 Keith	2 Keith
3 Graham	3 McMichael	3 McMichael	3 McMichael	3 McMichael
4 Blanchflower D.	4 Blanchflower D.	4 Blanchflower D.	4 Blanchflower D.	4 Blanchflower D.
5 Cunningham	5 Forde	5 Cunningham	5 Cunningham	5 Cunningham
6 Peacock	6 Casey	6 Peacock	6 Peacock	6 Peacock
7 Bingham	7 Bingham	7 Bingham	7 Bingham	7 Bingham
8 Cush	8 Cush	8 Cush	8 McIlroy	8 Cush
9 Casey	9 McParland	9 Simpson	9 Cush	9 Dougan
10 McIlroy	10 McIlroy	10 McIlroy	10 Hill	10 McIlroy
11 McParland	11 Tully	11 McParland	11 McParland	11 McParland
Belfast Oct 4: 3-3 *Cush, Peacock, Casey*	Madrid Oct 15: 2-6 *Bingham, McIlroy*	Hampden Nov 5: 2-2 *1 og, McIlroy*	Belfast April 22: 4-1 *McParland 2, Peacock, McIlroy*	Belfast Oct 3: 0-4

1959 England	1960 Wales	1960 England	1960 W Germany	1960 Scotland
1 Gregg	1 Gregg	1 Gregg	1 McClelland	1 Gregg
2 Keith	2 Elder	2 Keith	2 Keith	2 Keith
3 McMichael	3 McMichael	3 Elder	3 Elder	3 Elder
4 Blanchflower D.	4 Blanchflower D.	4 Blanchflower D.	4 Blanchflower D.	4 Blanchflower D.
5 Cunningham	5 Cunningham	5 Forde	5 Forde	5 Forde
6 Peacock	6 Cush	6 Peacock	6 Peacock	6 Peacock
7 Bingham	7 Bingham	7 Bingham	7 Bingham	7 Bingham
8 Crossan	8 McIlroy	8 McIlroy	8 McIlroy	8 Bruce
9 Cush	9 Lawther	9 McAdams	9 McAdams	9 McAdams
10 McIlroy	10 Hill	10 Dougan	10 Hill	10 Nicholson
11 McParland	11 McParland	11 McParland	11 McParland	11 McParland
Wembley Nov 18: 1-2 *Bingham*	Wrexham April 6: 2-3 *Bingham, Blanchflower*	Belfast Oct 8: 2-5 *McAdams 2*	Belfast Oct 26: 3-4 *McAdams 3*	Hampden Nov 9: 2-5 *Blanchflower, McParland*

1961 Wales	1961 Italy	1961 Greece	1961 W Germany	1961 Scotland
1 McClelland	1 McClelland	1 McClelland	1 McClelland	1 Gregg
2 Keith	2 Keith	2 Keith	2 Keith	2 Magill
3 Elder	3 McCullough	3 Elder	3 Elder	3 Elder
4 Blanchflower D.	4 Harvey	4 Cush	4 Blanchflower D.	4 Blanchflower D.
5 Cunningham	5 Neill	5 Neill	5 Neill	5 Neill
6 Nicholson	6 Peacock	6 Peacock	6 Peacock	6 Peacock
7 Stewart	7 Bingham	7 Bingham	7 Bingham	7 Wilson
8 Dougan	8 Dougan	8 McIlroy	8 Cush	8 McIlroy
9 McAdams	9 Lawther	9 McAdams	9 McAdams	9 Lawther
10 McIlroy	10 McAdams	10 Dougan	10 McIlroy	10 Hill
11 McParland	11 McParland	11 McParland	11 McParland	11 McLaughlin
Belfast April 12: 1-5 *Dougan*	Bologna April 25: 2-3 *Dougan, McAdams*	Athens May 3: 1-2 *McIlroy*	Berlin May 10: 1-2 *McIlroy*	Belfast Oct 7: 1-6 *McLaughlin*

1961 Greece	1961 England	1962 Wales	1962 Netherlands	1962 Poland
1 Gregg	1 Hunter	1 Briggs	1 Irvine R.	1 Irvine R.
2 Magill	2 Magill	2 Keith	2 Keith	2 Magill
3 Elder	3 Elder	3 Cunningham	3 Cunningham	3 Elder
4 Blanchflower D.	4 Blanchflower D.	4 Blanchflower D.	4 Harvey	4 Blanchflower D.
5 Neill	5 Neill	5 Neill	5 Blanchflower D.	5 Hatton
6 Nicholson	6 Nicholson	6 Nicholson	6 Nicholson	6 Nicholson
7 Bingham	7 Bingham	7 Humphries	7 Humphries	7 Humphries
8 McIlroy	8 Barr	8 Johnston W.	8 Lawther	8 Barr
9 McAdams	9 McAdams	9 O'Neill	9 McAdams	9 Dougan
10 Cush	10 McIlroy	10 McLaughlin	10 McIlroy	10 McIlroy
11 McLaughlin	11 McLaughlin	11 Braithwaite	11 McParland	11 Bingham
Belfast Oct 17: 2-0 *McLaughlin 2*	Wembley Nov 22: 1-1 *McIlroy*	Cardiff April 11: 0-4	Rotterdam May 9: 0-4	Katowice Oct 10: 2-0 *Dougan, Humphries*

1962 **England**	1962 **Scotland**	1962 **Poland**	1963 **Wales**	1963 **Spain**
1 Irvine R.	1 Irvine R.	1 Irvine R.	1 Irvine R.	1 Irvine R.
2 Magill	2 Magill	2 Magill	2 Magill	2 Magill
3 Elder	3 Elder	3 Elder	3 Elder	3 Elder
4 Blanchflower D.	4 Blanchflower D.	4 Blanchflower D.	4 Harvey	4 Harvey
5 Neill	5 Hatton	5 Neill	5 Campbell	5 Neill
6 Nicholson	6 Nicholson	6 Nicholson	6 Neill	6 McCullough
7 Humphries	7 Humphries	7 Bingham	7 Humphries	7 Bingham
8 Barr	8 McMillan	8 Crossan	8 Crossan	8 Humphries
9 McMillan	9 Dougan	9 Dougan	9 Irvine W.	9 Irvine W.
10 McIlroy	10 McIlroy	10 McIlroy	10 McIlroy	10 Crossan
11 Bingham	11 Bingham	11 Braithwaite	11 McLaughlin	11 Braithwaite
Belfast	Hampden	Belfast	Belfast	Bilbao
Oct 20: 1-3	Nov 7: 1-5	Nov 28: 2-0	April 3: 1-4	May 30: 1-1
Barr	*Bingham*	*Crossan, Bingham*	*Harvey*	*Irvine W.*

1963 **Scotland**	1963 **Spain**	1963 **England**	1964 **Wales**	1964 **Uruguay**
1 Gregg	1 Hunter	1 Gregg	1 Jennings	1 Jennings
2 Magill	2 Magill	2 Magill	2 Magill	2 Magill
3 Parke	3 Parke	3 Parke	3 Elder	3 Elder
4 Harvey	4 Harvey	4 Harvey	4 Harvey	4 Harvey
5 Neill	5 Neill	5 Neill	5 Neill	5 Neill
6 McCullough	6 McCullough	6 McCullough	6 McCullough	6 McCullough
7 Bingham	7 Bingham	7 Bingham	7 Best	7 Best
8 Humphries	8 Humphries	8 Humphries	8 Crossan	8 Crossan
9 Wilson	9 Wilson	9 Wilson	9 Wilson	9 Wilson
10 Crossan	10 Crossan	10 Crossan	10 McLaughlin	10 McLaughlin
11 Hill	11 Hill	11 Hill	11 Braithwaite	11 Braithwaite
Belfast	Belfast	Wembley	Swansea	Belfast
Oct 12: 2-1	Oct 30: 0-1	Nov 20: 3-8	April 15: 3-2	April 29: 3-0
Bingham, Wilson		*Crossan, Wilson 2*	*McLaughlin, Wilson, Harvey*	*Crossan 2, Wilson*

1964 **England**	1964 **Switzerland**	1964 **Switzerland**	1964 **Scotland**	1965 **Netherlands**
1 Jennings	1 Jennings	1 Jennings	1 Jennings	1 Briggs
2 Magill	2 Magill	2 Magill	2 Magill	2 Parke
3 Elder	3 Elder	3 Elder	3 Elder	3 Elder
4 Harvey	4 Harvey	4 Harvey	4 Harvey	4 Harvey
5 Neill	5 Neill	5 Campbell	5 Neill	5 Neill
6 McCullough	6 McCullough	6 Parke	6 Parke	6 Nicholson
7 Best	7 Best	7 Best	7 Best	7 Humphries
8 Crossan	8 Crossan	8 Crossan	8 Humphries	8 Crossan
9 Wilson	9 Wilson	9 Irvine W.	9 Irvine W.	9 Irvine W.
10 McLaughlin	10 McLaughlin	10 McLaughlin	10 Crossan	10 Clements
11 Braithwaite	11 Braithwaite	11 Braithwaite	11 Braithwaite	11 Best
Belfast	Belfast	Lausanne	Hampden	Belfast
Oct 3: 3-4	Oct 14: 1-0	Nov 14: 1-2	Nov 25: 2-3	Mar 17: 2-1
Wilson, McLaughlin 2	*Crossan*	*Best*	*Best, Irvine*	*Crossan, Neill*

1965 Wales	1965 Netherlands	1965 Albania	1965 Scotland	1965 England
1 Irvine R.	1 Jennings	1 Jennings	1 Jennings	1 Jennings
2 Parke	2 Magill	2 Magill	2 Magill	2 Magill
3 Elder	3 Elder	3 Elder	3 Elder	3 Elder
4 Harvey	4 Harvey	4 Harvey	4 Harvey	4 Harvey
5 Neill	5 Neill	5 Neill	5 Neill	5 Neill
6 Nicholson	6 Parke	6 Parke	6 Nicholson	6 Nicholson
7 Humphries	7 Best	7 Humphries	7 McIlroy	7 McIlroy
8 Crossan	8 Crossan	8 Crossan	8 Crossan	8 Crossan
9 Irvine W.	9 Irvine W.	9 Irvine W.	9 Irvine W.	9 Irvine W.
10 McLaughlin	10 Nicholson	10 Nicholson	10 Dougan	10 Dougan
11 Clements	11 Braithwaite	11 Best	11 Best	11 Best
Belfast March 31: 0-5	Rotterdam April 7: 0-0	Belfast May 7: 4-1 *Crossan 3, Best*	Belfast Oct 2: 3-2 *Dougan, Crossan, Irvine*	Wembley Nov 10: 1-2 *Irvine*

1965 Albania	1966 Wales	1966 W Germany	1966 Mexico	1966 England
1 Jennings	1 Jennings	1 Jennings	1 McClelland	1 Jennings (McFaul)
2 Magill	2 Magill	2 Magill	2 Magill	2 Parke
3 Elder	3 Elder	3 Parke	3 Elder	3 Elder
4 Harvey	4 Harvey	4 Harvey	4 Harvey	4 Todd
5 Neill	5 Neill	5 Napier	5 Neill	5 Harvey
6 Nicholson	6 Nicholson	6 Neill	6 Nicholson	6 McCullough
7 McIlroy	7 Welsh	7 Welsh	7 Welsh	7 Ferguson
8 Crossan	8 Wilson	8 Crossan	8 Ferguson	8 Crossan
9 Irvine W.	9 Irvine W.	9 Wilson	9 Irvine W. (Johnston)	9 Irvine W.
10 Dougan	10 Dougan	10 Dougan	10 Dougan	10 Dougan
11 Best	11 McLaughlin	11 McKinney	11 Clements (Todd)	11 Best
Tirana Nov 24: 1-1 *Irvine*	Cardiff Mar 30: 4-1 *Irvine, Wilson, Welsh, Harvey*	Belfast May 7: 0-2	Belfast June 22: 4-1 *Johnston, Elder, Nicholson, Ferguson*	Belfast Oct 22: 0-2

1966 Scotland	1967 Wales	1967 Scotland	1967 England	1968 Wales
1 Jennings	1 McKenzie	1 Jennings	1 Jennings	1 Jennings
2 Parke	2 Craig	2 McKeag	2 Parke	2 Craig
3 Elder	3 Elder	3 Parke	3 Elder	3 Elder
4 Harvey	4 Stewart	4 Stewart	4 Stewart	4 Harvey
5 Neill	5 Neill	5 Neill	5 Neill	5 Todd
6 Nicholson	6 Nicholson	6 Clements	6 Harvey	6 McKeag
7 Wilson	7 Welsh	7 Campbell	7 Campbell	7 Irvine
8 Crossan	8 Trainor	8 Crossan	8 Irvine W.	8 Stewart
9 Irvine W.	9 Dougan	9 Dougan	9 Wilson	9 Dougan
10 Dougan	10 Bruce	10 Nicholson	10 Nicholson	10 Nicholson
11 Clements	11 Clements	11 Best	11 Clements	11 Harkin
Hampden Nov 16: 1-2 *Nicholson*	Belfast April 12: 0-0	Belfast Oct 21: 1-0 *Clements*	Wembley Nov 22: 0-2	Wrexham Feb 28: 0-2

1968 Israel	**1968 Turkey**	**1968 Turkey**	**1969 England**	**1969 Scotland**
1 Jennings	1 Jennings	1 Jennings	1 Jennings	1 Jennings
2 Rice	2 Craig (Stewart)	2 Craig	2 Craig	2 Craig
3 Jackson	3 Harvey	3 Harvey	3 Harvey (Elder)	3 Elder
4 Stewart	4 Nicholson	4 Nicholson	4 Todd	4 Todd
5 Neill	5 Neill	5 Neill	5 Neill	5 Neill
6 Harvey	6 Clements	6 Stewart	6 Nicholson	6 Nicholson
7 Sloan	7 Campbell	7 Hamilton	7 McMordie	7 Best
8 McMordie	8 McMordie	8 McMordie	8 Jackson	8 McMordie
9 Dougan (Gaston)	9 Dougan	9 Dougan	9 Dougan	9 Dougan
10 Irvine W.	10 Irvine W.	10 Harkin	10 Irvine W.	10 Jackson
11 Ross	11 Best	11 Clements	11 Best	11 Clements
Jaffa Sept 10: 3-2 *Irvine 2, Dougan*	Belfast Oct 23: 4-1 *Best, McMordie, Dougan, Campbell*	Istanbul Dec 11: 3-0 *Harkin 2, Nicholson*	Belfast May 3: 1-3 *McMordie*	Hampden May 6: 1-1 *McMordie*

1969 Wales	**1969 USSR**	**1969 USSR**	**1970 Scotland**	**1970 England**
1 Jennings	1 Jennings	1 Jennings	1 Jennings	1 Jennings
2 Craig	2 Rice	2 Craig	2 Craig	2 Craig
3 Elder	3 Elder	3 Harvey	3 Clements	3 Clements
4 Todd	4 Todd	4 Hunter	4 Todd (O'Kane)	4 O'Kane
5 Neill	5 Neill	5 Neill	5 Neill	5 Neill
6 Nicholson	6 Nicholson	6 Nicholson	6 Nicholson	6 Nicholson
7 Best	7 Campbell	7 Hegan	7 Campbell (Dickson)	7 McMordie
8 McMordie	8 McMordie	8 Jackson	8 Lutton	8 Best
9 Dougan	9 Dougan	9 Dougan	9 Dougan	9 Dougan
10 Jackson	10 Clements (Jackson)	10 Harkin	10 McMordie	10 O'Doherty (Nelson)
11 Clements (Harkin)	11 Best	11 Clements	11 Best	11 Lutton (Cowan)
Belfast May 10: 0-0	Belfast Sept 10: 0-0	Moscow Oct 22: 0-2	Belfast April 18: 0-1	Wembley April 21: 1-3 *Best*

1970 Wales	**1970 Spain**	**1971 Cyprus**	**1971 Cyprus**	**1971 England**
1 McFaul	1 McFaul	1 Jennings	1 Jennings	1 Jennings
2 Craig	2 Craig	2 Craig	2 Craig	2 Rice
3 Nelson	3 Nelson	3 Nelson	3 Clements	3 Nelson
4 O'Kane	4 Jackson	4 Hunter	4 Harvey	4 O'Kane
5 Neill	5 Neill	5 Neill	5 Hunter	5 Hunter
6 Nicholson	6 O'Kane	6 Todd	6 Todd (Watson)	6 Nicholson
7 Campbell (O'Doherty)	7 Sloan	7 Hamilton	7 Hamilton	7 Hamilton
8 Best	8 Best	8 McMordie	8 McMordie	8 McMordie (Cassidy)
9 Dickson	9 Dougan (Todd)	9 Dougan	9 Dougan	9 Dougan
10 McMordie	10 Harkin	10 Nicholson	10 Nicholson	10 Clements
11 Clements	11 Clements	11 Best	11 Best	11 Best
Swansea April 25: 0-1	Seville Nov 11: 0-3	Nicosia Feb 3: 3-0 *Nicholson, Dougan, Best*	Belfast April 21: 5-0 *Dougan, Best 3, Nicholson*	Belfast May 15: 0-1

1971 **Scotland**	1971 **Wales**	1971 **USSR**	1971 **USSR**	1972 **Spain**
1 Jennings	1 Jennings	1 McFaul	1 Jennings	1 Jennings
2 Rice	2 Rice	2 Craig (Hamilton)	2 Rice	2 Rice
3 Nelson	3 Nelson	3 Neill	3 Nelson	3 Nelson
4 O'Kane	4 O'Kane	4 Hunter	4 Nicholson	4 Neill
5 Hunter	5 Hunter	5 Nelson	5 Hunter	5 Hunter
6 Nicholson	6 Nicholson (Harvey)	6 Hegan	6 O'Kane	6 Clements
7 Hamilton	7 Hamilton	7 Clements	7 McMordie	7 Hamilton (O'Neill)
8 McMordie (Craig)	8 McMordie	8 Nicholson	8 Hamilton (O'Neill)	8 McMordie
9 Dougan	9 Dougan	9 O'Kane	9 Neill	9 Morgan
10 Clements	10 Clements	10 Dougan	10 Dougan (Cassidy)	10 McIlroy
11 Best	11 Best	11 Best	11 Clements	11 Best
Hampden May 18: 1-0 *1 og*	Belfast May 22: 1-0 *Hamilton*	Moscow Sept 22: 0-1	Belfast Oct 13: 1-1 *Nicholson*	Hull Feb 16: 1-1 *Morgan*

1972 **Scotland**	1972 **England**	1972 **Wales**	1972 **Bulgaria**	1973 **Cyprus**
1 Jennings	1 Jennings	1 Jennings	1 Jennings	1 Jennings
2 Rice	2 Rice	2 Rice	2 Rice	2 Rice
3 Nelson	3 Nelson	3 Nelson	3 Nelson	3 Neill
4 Neill	4 Neill	4 Neill	4 Hunter	4 Hunter
5 Hunter	5 Hunter	5 Hunter	5 Neill	5 Craig
6 Clements (Craig)	6 Clements	6 Clements	6 Clements	6 Hegan
7 Hegan	7 Hegan	7 Hegan	7 Hamilton (Morgan)	7 Clements
8 McMordie (McIlroy)	8 McMordie	8 McMordie	8 Hegan	8 Hamilton
9 Dougan	9 Dougan	9 Dougan (O'Neill)	9 McMordie	9 Dickson
10 Irvine W.	10 Irvine W.	10 Irvine W.	10 Dougan	10 Dougan
11 Jackson	11 Jackson	11 Jackson	11 Best	11 Nelson
Hampden May 20: 0-2	Wembley May 23: 1-0 *Neill*	Wrexham May 27: 0-0	Sofia Oct 18: 0-3	Nicosia Feb 14: 0-1

1973 **Portugal**	1973 **Cyprus**	1973 **England**	1973 **Scotland**	1973 **Wales**
1 Jennings	1 McFaul	1 Jennings	1 Jennings	1 Jennings
2 O'Kane	2 O'Kane	2 Rice	2 Rice	2 Rice
3 Nelson	3 Hunter (Coyle)	3 Craig	3 Craig	3 Craig
4 Neill	4 Neill	4 Neill	4 Neill	4 Neill
5 Hunter	5 Craig	5 Hunter	5 Hunter	5 Hunter
6 Clements	6 Hamilton (Lutton)	6 Clements	6 Clements	6 Clements
7 Hamilton	7 Jackson	7 Hamilton	7 Hamilton	7 Hamilton (Lutton)
8 Coyle	8 Clements	8 Jackson	8 Jackson	8 Jackson
9 Morgan	9 Morgan	9 Morgan	9 Morgan	9 Morgan
10 Dickson	10 O'Neill	10 O'Neill	10 O'Neill	10 O'Neill
11 O'Neill	11 Anderson	11 Anderson	11 Anderson (Lutton)	11 Anderson (Coyle)
Coventry Mar 28: 1-1 *O'Neill*	London May 8: 3-0 *Morgan,* *Anderson 2*	Everton May 12: 1-2 *Clements* (pen)	Glasgow May 16: 2-1 *O'Neill, Anderson*	Everton May 19: 1-0 *Hamilton*

	1973 **Bulgaria**	1973 **Portugal**	1974 **Scotland**	1974 **England**	1974 **Wales**
1	McFaul	Jennings	Jennings	Jennings	Jennings
2	Rice	Rice	Rice	Rice	Rice
3	Craig	Craig	Nelson	Nelson (Jackson)	Dowd
4	O'Kane	Lutton	O'Kane	O'Kane	O'Kane
5	Hunter	O'Kane	Hunter	Hunter	Hunter
6	Clements	Clements	Clements	Clements	Clements
7	Hamilton	Jackson (Coyle)	Hamilton (Jackson)	Hamilton (O'Neill)	Hamilton (Jackson)
8	Jackson (Coyle)	O'Neill	Cassidy	Cassidy	Cassidy
9	Morgan	Morgan	Morgan	Morgan	McIlroy
10	Anderson	Anderson	McIlroy	McIlroy	McGrath
11	O'Neill (Cassidy)	Best	McGrath	McGrath	O'Neill
	Hillsborough Sept 26: 0-0	Lisbon Nov 14: 1-1 *O'Kane*	Hampden May 11: 1-0 *Cassidy*	Wembley May 15: 0-1	Wrexham May 18: 0-1

	1974 **Norway**	1974 **Sweden**	1975 **Yugoslavia**	1975 **England**	1975 **Scotland**
1	Jennings	Jennings	Jennings	Jennings	Jennings
2	Rice	O'Kane	Rice	Rice	Rice
3	Craig (Dowd)	Nelson (Blair)	Nelson	O'Kane	O'Kane
4	O'Kane	Dowd	Nicholl C.	Nicholl C.	Nicholl C.
5	Hunter	Hunter	Hunter	Hunter	Hunter (Blair)
6	Clements	Nicholl C.	Clements	Clements	Clements
7	Hamilton	Jackson	Hamilton	Hamilton (Finney)	Finney
8	Cassidy	O'Neill	O'Neill	O'Neill	O'Neill (Anderson)
9	Finney	Morgan	Spence	Spence	Spence
10	McIlroy	McIlroy	McIlroy	McIlroy	McIlroy
11	McGrath (Jackson)	Hamilton	Jackson	Jackson	Jackson
	Oslo Sept 4: 1-2 *Finney*	Solna Oct 30: 2-0 *O'Neill, Nicholl*	Belfast March 16: 1-0 *Hamilton*	Belfast May 17: 0-0	Hampden May 20: 0-3

	1975 **Wales**	1975 **Sweden**	1975 **Norway**	1975 **Yugoslavia**	1976 **Israel**
1	Jennings	Jennings	Jennings	Jennings	Jennings (Platt)
2	Scott	Rice	Rice	Rice	Scott
3	Rice	Nelson	Nelson	Scott	Nicholl J.
4	Nicholl C.	Clements	Nicholl C.	Nicholl C.	Hunter
5	Hunter	Hunter	Hunter	Hunter	Rice
6	Clements	Nicholl C.	Jackson	Clements	Blair
7	Blair	Blair	Hamilton	Hamilton	Nelson
8	Jackson	Hamilton (Morgan)	McIlroy	McIlroy	Hamilton
9	Spence	Spence	Morgan (Cochrane)	Morgan	Anderson (McGrath)
10	McIlroy	McIlroy	Jamison	Jackson (O'Neill)	Spence
11	Finney	Jackson	Finney	Finney	Finney
	Belfast May 23: 1-0 *Finney*	Belfast Sept 3: 1-2 *Hunter*	Belfast Oct 29: 3-0 *Morgan, McIlroy, Hamilton*	Belgrade Nov 19: 0-1	Tel Aviv Mar 24: 1-1 *Lev og*

1976 **Scotland**	1976 **England**	1976 **Wales**	1976 **Netherlands**	1976 **Belgium**
1 Jennings	1 Jennings	1 Jennings	1 Jennings	1 Jennings
2 Scott	2 Rice	2 Scott	2 Nicholl J.	2 Nicholl J.
3 Nicholl C.	3 Nelson (Scott)	3 Rice	3 Jackson	3 Rice (Nelson)
4 Hunter	4 Clements	4 Nicholl C.	4 Rice	4 Jackson
5 Rice	5 Hunter	5 Hunter	5 Hunter	5 Hunter
6 Hamilton B.	6 Nicholl C.	6 Clements	6 Hamilton B.	6 Hamilton B.
7 Cassidy	7 Hamilton B.	7 Hamilton B.	7 Best	7 Best
8 Sharkey (McCreery)	8 Cassidy	8 McIlroy	8 McIlroy	8 McIlroy
9 McIlroy	9 McCreery	9 Spence (Morgan)	9 McGrath (Spence)	9 McGrath
10 Morgan (Spence)	10 Spence	10 Cassidy (Nicholl J.)	10 McCreery	10 McCreery
11 Finney	11 McIlroy	11 McCreery	11 Anderson	11 Anderson
Hampden May 8: 0-3	Wembley May 11: 0-4	Swansea May 14: 0-1	Rotterdam Oct 13: 2-2 *McGrath, Spence*	Liège Nov 10: 0-2

1977 **W Germany**	1977 **England**	1977 **Scotland**	1977 **Wales**	1977 **Iceland**
1 Jennings	1 Jennings	1 Jennings	1 Jennings	1 Jennings
2 Rice	2 Nicholl J.	2 Nicholl J.	2 Nicholl J.	2 Rice
3 Nelson	3 Rice	3 Rice	3 Nelson	3 Nelson
4 Jackson	4 Jackson	4 Jackson	4 Nicholl C.	4 Nicholl J.
5 Hunter	5 Hunter	5 Hunter	5 Hunter	5 Hunter
6 McCreery (Cassidy)	6 Hamilton B.	6 Hamilton B.	6 Hamilton B.	6 Hamilton B.
7 Hamilton B.	7 McGrath	7 McGrath	7 McGrath	7 McGrath
8 Best	8 McIlroy	8 McIlroy	8 McIlroy	8 McIlroy
9 Armstrong (Spence)	9 Armstrong (O'Neill)	9 O'Neill (Spence)	9 Jackson	9 Jackson (Spence)
10 McGrath	10 McCreery	10 McCreery	10 McCreery (Armstrong)	10 McCreery
11 Anderson	11 Anderson (Spence)	11 Anderson	11 Anderson (Spence)	11 Anderson (Armstrong)
Cologne April 27: 0-5	Belfast May 28: 1-2 *McGrath*	Hampden June 1: 0-2	Belfast June 3: 1-1 *Nelson*	Reykjavik June 11: 0-1

1977 **Iceland**	1977 **Netherlands**	1977 **Belgium**	1978 **Scotland**	1978 **England**
1 Jennings	1 Jennings	1 Jennings	1 Platt	1 Platt
2 Rice	2 Rice	2 Rice	2 Hamilton B.	2 Hamilton B.
3 Nicholl J.	3 Nelson	3 Nelson	3 Scott	3 Scott
4 Nelson	4 Nicholl J.	4 Nicholl J.	4 Nicholl C.	4 Nicholl C.
5 Hunter	5 Hunter	5 Hunter (Nicholl C.)	5 Nicholl J.	5 Nicholl J.
6 McCreery	6 O'Neill	6 McIlroy	6 McIlroy	6 McIlroy
7 McGrath	7 McIlroy	7 McGrath	7 McCreery	7 McCreery
8 Best	8 Best	8 McCreery	8 O'Neill	8 O'Neill
9 McIlroy	9 McCreery	9 Armstrong	9 Anderson (Hamilton W.)	9 Anderson
10 O'Neill	10 McGrath	10 Stewart	10 Armstrong	10 Armstrong
11 Anderson	11 Anderson	11 Anderson	11 McGrath (Cochrane)	11 McGrath (Cochrane)
Belfast Sept 21: 2-0 *McGrath, McIlroy*	Belfast Oct 12: 0-1	Belfast Nov 16: 3-0 *Armstrong 2, McGrath*	Hampden May 13: 1-1 *O'Neill*	Wembley May 16: 0-1

	1978 **Wales**	1978 **Rep of Ireland**	1978 **Denmark**	1978 **Bulgaria**	1979 **England**
1	Platt	Jennings	Jennings	Jennings	Jennings
2	Hamilton B.	Rice	Rice	Hamilton B.	Rice
3	Scott (Connell)	Nelson	Nelson	Nelson	Nelson
4	Nicholl C.	Nicholl C.	Nicholl J.	Nicholl C.	Nicholl C.
5	Nicholl J.	Hunter (Hamilton B.)	Hunter	Nicholl J.	Nicholl J.
6	O'Neill	Nicholl J.	McCreery	McCreery	McCreery
7	McCreery	O'Neill	O'Neill	O'Neill	O'Neill
8	McIlroy	McCreery	McIlroy	McIlroy (Moreland)	McIlroy
9	Anderson (Cochrane)	Armstrong	Armstrong	Armstrong	Armstrong
10	Armstrong	McIlroy	Morgan (Spence) (Anderson)	Caskey	Caskey (Spence)
11	McGrath	Spence (Cochrane)	Cochrane	Cochrane (McGrath)	Cochrane (McGrath)
	Wrexham May 19: 0-1	Dublin Sept 20: 0-0	Belfast Oct 25: 2-1 *Spence, Anderson*	Sofia Nov 29: 2-0 *Armstrong, Caskey*	Wembley Feb 7: 0-4

	1979 **Bulgaria**	1979 **England**	1979 **Scotland**	1979 **Wales**	1979 **Denmark**
1	Jennings	Jennings	Jennings	Jennings	Jennings
2	Hamilton B.	Rice	Rice	Rice	Rice
3	Nelson	Nelson	Nelson	Nelson	Nelson
4	Nicholl C. (Moreland)	Nicholl C.	Nicholl J.	Nicholl C.	Nicholl J.
5	Nicholl J.	Nicholl J.	Hunter	Hunter	Hunter
6	McCreery	Moreland (McGrath)	Moreland	Nicholl J.	McCreery
7	O'Neill	Hamilton B.	Hamilton B.	McCreery	O'Neill
8	McIlroy	McIlroy	McIlroy (Scott)	McIlroy	McIlroy
9	Armstrong	Armstrong	Armstrong	Armstrong	Armstrong
10	Caskey (Spence)	Caskey	Sloan	Spence (Sloan)	Spence
11	Cochrane	Cochrane (Spence)	Spence	Hamilton B.	Hamilton B.
	Belfast May 2: 2-0 *Nicholl C., Armstrong*	Belfast May 19: 0-2	Hampden May 22: 0-1	Belfast May 25: 1-1 *Spence*	Copenhagen June 6: 0-4

	1979 **England**	1979 **Rep of Ireland**	1980 **Israel**	1980 **Scotland**	1980 **England**
1	Jennings	Jennings	Jennings	Platt	Platt
2	Rice	Nicholl J.	Nicholl J.	Nicholl J.	Nicholl J.
3	Nelson	Nelson	Nelson	Donaghy	Donaghy
4	Nicholl J.	Nicholl C.	Nicholl C.	Nicholl C.	Nicholl C.
5	Hunter (Rafferty)	Hunter	O'Neill J.	O'Neill J.	O'Neill J.
6	McCreery	McCreery	O'Neill M.	Cassidy (McCreery)	Cassidy (McCreery)
7	Cassidy	O'Neill M. (Cassidy)	McIlroy	McIlroy	McIlroy
8	McIlroy	McIlroy	Cassidy	Hamilton W. (McClelland)	Hamilton W. (Cochrane)
9	Armstrong	Armstrong	Armstrong	Armstrong	Armstrong
10	Finney (Caskey)	Spence	Finney (Spence)	Finney	Finney
11	Moreland	Moreland	Cochrane	Brotherston	Brotherston
	Belfast Oct 17: 1-5 *Moreland* (pen)	Belfast Nov 21: 1-0 *Armstrong*	Tel Aviv Mar 26: 0-0	Belfast May 16: 1-0 *Hamilton*	Wembley May 20: 1-1 *Cochrane*

1980 Wales	1980 Australia	1980 Australia	1980 Australia
1 Platt	1 Platt	1 Platt	1 Platt
2 Nicholl J.	2 Nicholl J.	2 Nicholl J.	2 Nicholl J.
3 Donaghy	3 Nicholl C.	3 Nicholl C.	3 Nicholl C.
4 Nicholl C.	4 O'Neill J.	4 O'Neill J.	4 O'Neill J.
5 O'Neill J.	5 McClelland	5 McClelland	5 McClelland
6 Cassidy (McCreery)	6 Cassidy (McCreery)	6 Cassidy	6 Cassidy (Hamilton B.)
7 McIlroy	7 Brotherston	7 Brotherston	7 Cochrane
8 Hamilton W. (Cochrane)	8 Hamilton W.	8 McCreery (Cochrane)	8 Hamilton W. (McCurdy)
9 Armstrong	9 Armstrong	9 Armstrong	9 Armstrong
10 Finney	10 Finney (Hamilton B.)	10 Finney	10 O'Neill M.
11 Brotherston	11 O'Neill M.	11 O'Neill M.	11 Brotherston
Cardiff May 23: 1-0 *Brotherston*	Sydney June 11: 2-1 *Nicholl C., O'Neill M.*	Melbourne June 15: 1-1 *O'Neill M.*	Adelaide June 18: 2-1 *Brotherston, McCurdy*

OLDEST SURVIVING FA CUP FINALIST

At the time of the 100th FA Cup Final in May 1981, the oldest surviving final player was Billy Gillespie, in his 90th year and living in Bexley, Kent. Sadly, he died later in the year, in July. He captained Sheffield United when they beat Cardiff City 1-0 at Wembley in 1925. Born in the village of Kerry Keel, County Donegal, he was capped 25 times by Ireland from 1913 to 1930 and scored 12 goals.

SCOTLAND INTERNATIONAL TEAMS 1872–1980

Substitutes in brackets †World Cup final stages

1872 England	**1873 England**	**1874 England**	**1875 England**	**1876 England**
1 Gardner	1 Gardner	1 Gardner	1 Gardner	1 McGeoch
2 Ker	2 Ker	2 Hunter	2 Hunter	2 Hunter
3 Taylor	3 Taylor	3 Taylor	3 Taylor	3 Taylor
4 Thomson	4 Gibb	4 Thomson	4 McLintock	4 McLintock
5 Smith, James	5 Smith, Robert	5 Campbell C.	5 Kennedy	5 Kennedy
6 Smith, Robert	6 Wotherspoon	6 Weir	6 Weir	6 McNeil H.
7 Leckie	7 Renny-Tailyour	7 McKinnon W.W.	7 McKinnon W.W.	7 Highet
8 Rhind	8 Kinnaird	8 Ferguson	8 Highet	8 McKinnon W.W.
9 McKinnon W.W.	9 Blackburn	9 McKinnon A.	9 McNeil H.	9 Miller
10 Weir	10 Thomson	10 McNeil H.	10 Andrews	10 Ferguson
11 Wotherspoon	11 McKinnon W.W.	11 Anderson	11 McPherson	11 Baird
Glasgow	London	Glasgow	London	Glasgow
Nov 30: 0-0	Mar 8: 2-4	Mar 7: 2-1	Mar 6: 2-2	Mar 4: 3-0
	Renny-Tailyour, Gibb	*McKinnon A., Anderson*	*McNeil, Andrews*	*McKinnon, McNeil Highet*

1876 Wales	**1877 England**	**1877 Wales**	**1878 England**	**1878 Wales**
1 McGeoch	1 McGeoch	1 McGeoch	1 Gardner	1 Parlane
2 Taylor	2 Neill	2 Neill	2 McIntyre	2 Neill
3 Neill	3 Vallance	3 Vallance	3 Vallance	3 Duncan
4 Kennedy	4 Campbell C.	4 Phillips	4 Campbell C.	4 Phillips
5 Campbell C.	5 Phillips	5 Campbell C.	5 Kennedy	5 Davidson
6 Highet	6 Richmond	6 Smith J.	6 Richmond	6 Lang
7 Ferguson	7 McKinnon W.W.	7 McGregor	7 McKinnon W.W.	7 Weir
8 Lang	8 McGregor	8 Ferguson	8 McGregor	8 Watson
9 McKinnon W.W.	9 McDougall	9 McDougall	9 McDougall	9 Campbell P.
10 McNeil M.	10 Smith J.	10 McNeil H.	10 Highet	10 Ferguson
11 McNeil H.	11 Ferguson	11 Hunter	11 McNeil H.	11 Baird
Glasgow	London	Wrexham	Glasgow	Glasgow
Mar 25: 4-0	Mar 3: 3-1	Mar 5: 2-0	Mar 2: 7-2	Mar 23: 9-0
Ferguson, Lang, McKinnon, McNeil H.	*Ferguson 2 Richmond*	*Campbell, Powell og*	*McDougall 3, McGregor, McNeil 2, McKinnon*	*Campbell, Weir 2, Ferguson 3, Baird, Watson and one other*

1879 Wales	**1879 England**	**1880 England**	**1880 Wales**	**1881 England**
1 Parlane	1 Parlane	1 Rowan	1 Gillespie	1 Gillespie
2 Vallance	2 Somers	2 Neill	2 Somers	2 Watson
3 Somers	3 Vallance	3 McLintock	3 Lang	3 Vallance
4 McPherson	4 Campbell C.	4 Campbell C.	4 Davidson	4 Campbell C.
5 Davidson	5 McPherson	5 McPherson	5 McIntyre	5 Davidson
6 McNeil H.	6 Beveridge	6 Smith J.	6 Douglas	6 McGuire
7 McDougall	7 Smith J.	7 McNeil M.	7 McAdam	7 Hill
8 Campbell P.	8 McDougall	8 Ker	8 Frazer	8 Ker
9 Paton	9 Paton	9 McGregor	9 Lindsay	9 Lindsay
10 Beveridge	10 McKinnon W.W.	10 Baird	10 Campbell J.	10 McNeil H.
11 Smith J.	11 McNeil H.	11 Kay	11 Beveridge	11 Smith J.
Wrexham	London	Glasgow	Glasgow	London
April 7: 3-0	April 5: 4-5	Mar 13: 5-4	Mar 27: 5-1	Mar 12: 6-1
Campbell, Smith 2	*McKinnon 2, McDougall, Smith*	*Ker 3, Baird, Kay*	*Davidson, Beveridge, Lindsay, McAdam, Campbell*	*Smith 3, Ker 2, McGuire*

1881 Wales	**1882 England**	**1882 Wales**	**1883 England**	**1883 Wales**
1 Gillespie	1 Gillespie	1 Rowan	1 McAulay (*Dumbarton*)	1 McAulay (*Dumbarton*)
2 Vallance	2 Watson	2 Holm	2 Holm	2 Arnott
3 Watson	3 McIntyre	3 Duncan	3 Paton	3 Holm
4 McPherson	4 Campbell C.	4 Kennedy	4 Miller	4 Miller
5 Davidson	5 Miller	5 Campbell C.	5 McPherson	5 McPherson
6 Smith J.	6 Fraser	6 Fraser	6 Fraser	6 Smith Dr J.
7 McNeil H.	7 Anderson	7 Hill	7 Anderson	7 Inglis
8 Lindsay	8 Ker	8 Ker	8 Smith Dr J.	8 Mackinnon W.
9 McGuire	9 Harrower	9 McAulay (*Dumbarton*)	9 Inglis	9 Anderson
10 Ker	10 Kay	10 Kay	10 Kay	10 Kay
11 Hill	11 McPherson	11 Richmond	11 Mackinnon W.	11 Fraser
Wrexham Mar 14: 5-1 *Smith 2, Ker 2, Lindsay*	Glasgow Mar 11: 5-1 *Harrower, Ker 2, Kay, McPherson*	Glasgow Mar 25: 5-0 *Kay, Ker, Fraser 2, McAulay*	Sheffield Mar 10: 3-2 *Smith 2, Fraser*	Wrexham Mar 12, 3-0 *Smith, Fraser, Anderson*

1884 Ireland	**1884 England**	**1884 Wales**	**1885 Ireland**	**1885 England**
1 Inglis	1 McAulay (*Dumbarton*)	1 Turner	1 Chalmers	1 McAulay (*Dumbarton*)
2 Forbes	2 Arnott	2 Forbes	2 Niven	2 Arnott
3 Arnott	3 Forbes	3 Paton	3 McHardy	3 Paton
4 Graham	4 Campbell C.	4 Kennedy	4 McPherson	4 Campbell C.
5 Fulton	5 McPherson	5 McIntyre	5 Kelso	5 Gow
6 Brown R.	6 Shaw	6 Kay	6 Turner	6 Anderson
7 Thomson	7 Anderson	7 Lindsay	7 Lamont	7 Hamilton
8 Gossland	8 Lindsay	8 Shaw	8 Barbour	8 Sellar
9 Goudie	9 Smith Dr J.	9 Mackinnon W.	9 Calderwood	9 Lindsay
10 Harrower	10 Christie	10 Thomson	10 Marshall	10 Allan
11 McAulay (*Arthurlie*)	11 Mackinnon W.	11 Brown R.	11 Higgins	11 Calderwood
Belfast Jan 26: 5-0 *Goudie, Harrower 2, Gossland 2*	Glasgow Mar 15: 1-0 *Smith*	Glasgow Mar 29: 4-1 *Kay 2, Lindsay, Shaw*	Glasgow Mar 14: 8-2 *Higgins 4, Kelso, Barbour, McPherson, Calderwood*	London Mar 21: 1-1 *Lindsay*

1885 Wales	**1886 Ireland**	**1886 England**	**1886 Wales**	**1887 Ireland**
1 McAulay (*Dumbarton*)	1 Connor	1 McAulay (*Dumbarton*)	1 Gillespie	1 Doig
2 Arnott	2 McLeod	2 Arnott	2 Lundie	2 Whitelaw
3 Paton	3 Thomson	3 Paton	3 Semple	3 Smellie
4 Kelso	4 Keir	4 Campbell C.	4 Kelso	4 Weir
5 Keir	5 Cameron	5 McDonald	5 McCall	5 McMillan
6 Hamilton	6 Turner	6 Sellar	6 Jackson	6 Hutton
7 Anderson	7 Heggie	7 Hamilton	7 McCormack	7 Jenkinson
8 Lindsay	8 Dunbar	8 Somerville	8 Marshall	8 Lambie
9 Calderwood	9 Fleming	9 Lindsay	9 Harrower	9 Watt
10 Brown R. jun	10 Lambie J.	10 Gray	10 McGhee	10 Lowe
11 Allan	11 Gourlay	11 Aitken	11 Allan	11 Johnstone
Wrexham Mar 23: 8-1 *Anderson 3, Lindsay 2, Allan 2, Calderwood*	Belfast Mar 20: 7-2 *Heggie 5, Dunbar, Gourlay*	Glasgow Mar 31: 1-1 *Somerville*	Glasgow April 10: 4-1 *Harrower 2, Allan 2*	Glasgow Feb 19: 4-1 *Watt, Jenkinson, Johnstone, Lowe*

1887 England	**1887 Wales**	**1888 Wales**	**1888 England**	**1888 Ireland**
1 McAulay (*Dumbarton*)	1 McAulay (*Dumbarton*)	1 Wilson	1 Lindsay	1 McLeod
2 Arnott	2 Arnott	2 Hannah	2 Arnott	2 Jackson
3 Forbes	3 Forbes	3 Smellie	3 Gow	3 Stewart D.
4 Kelso	4 Keir	4 Gourlay	4 Kelso	4 Stewart A.
5 Auld	5 Auld	5 Johnston J.	5 Kelly	5 Dewar
6 Keir	6 Kelso	6 McLaren	6 Keir	6 Kelso
7 Marshall	7 Robertson	7 Latta	7 Hamilton	7 Gow
8 Robertson	8 McCall	8 McPherson	8 Berry	8 Brackenridge
9 Sellar	9 Allan	9 Groves	9 Sellar	9 Dickson
10 Allan	10 Marshall	10 Paul	10 McCall	10 Aitken
11 McCall	11 Sellar	11 Munro	11 Lambie	11 McCallum
Blackburn Mar 19: 3-2 *McCall, Allan 2*	Wrexham Mar 21: 2-0 *Robertson, Marshall*	Edinburgh Mar 10: 5-1 *Paul 2, McPherson 2, Groves*	Glasgow Mar 17: 0-5	Belfast Mar 24: 10-2 *Dewar, Dickson, Aitken, McCallum, Brackenridge, Wilson og and 4 others*

1889 Ireland	**1889 England**	**1889 Wales**	**1890 Wales**	**1890 Ireland**
1 Doig	1 Wilson	1 McLeod	1 Gillespie	1 McLeod
2 Adams	2 Arnott	2 Thomson	2 Whitelaw	2 Hunter
3 McKeown	3 Smellie	3 Rae	3 Murray	3 Rae
4 Robertson	4 Kelly	4 Stewart	4 McQueen	4 Russell
5 Calderhead	5 Dewar	5 Auld	5 Brown A.	5 Begbie
6 Buchanan	6 McLaren	6 Lochead	6 Wilson	6 Mitchell
7 Watt	7 Latta	7 Watt	7 Watt	7 Wylie
8 McInnes	8 Berry	8 Campbell H.	8 Brown J.	8 Rankin
9 Groves	9 Oswald	9 Paul	9 Paul	9 McPherson
10 Boyd	10 McPherson	10 Johnstone	10 Dunlop	10 Bell
11 Black	11 Munro	11 Hannah	11 Bruce	11 Baird
Glasgow Mar 9: 7-0 *Watt, McInnes 2, Black, Groves 3*	London April 13: 3-2 *McLaren, Oswald, Munro*	Wrexham April 15: 0-0	Glasgow Mar 22: 5-0 *Paul 4, Wilson*	Belfast Mar 29: 4-1 *Wylie, Rankin 2, McPherson*

1890 England	**1891 Wales**	**1891 Ireland**	**1891 England**	**1892 Ireland**
1 Wilson	1 McCorkindale	1 Gillespie	1 Wilson	1 Baird
2 Arnott	2 Ritchie	2 Sillars	2 Arnott	2 Bowman
3 McKeown	3 Hepburn	3 Paul	3 Smellie	3 Drummond
4 Robertson	4 McQueen	4 Hamilton	4 Begbie	4 Marshall
5 Kelly	5 Brown A.	5 Cleland	5 McPherson	5 Robertson
6 McLaren	6 Robertson	6 Campbell (*Kilm'k*)	6 Hill	6 Dowds
7 Groves	7 Gulliland	7 Lowe	7 Rankin	7 Gulliland
8 Berry	8 Buchanan	8 Bowie	8 Watt	8 McPherson
9 Johnstone W.	9 Boyd	9 Fraser	9 Sellar	9 Ellis
10 McPherson	10 Logan	10 Clements	10 Berry	10 Keillor
11 McCall	11 Keillor	11 Waddell	11 Baird	11 Lambie
Glasgow April 5: 1-1 *McPherson*	Wrexham Mar 21: 4-3 *Logan, Buchanan, Boyd 2*	Glasgow Mar 28: 2-1 *Waddell, Lowe*	Blackburn April 6: 1-2 *Watt*	Belfast Mar 19: 3-2 *Keillor, Lambie, Ellis*

1892 Wales	1892 England	1893 Wales	1893 Ireland	1893 England
1 Downie	1 McLeod	1 McLeod	1 Lindsay	1 Lindsay
2 Adams	2 Doyle	2 Doyle	2 Adams	2 Arnott
3 Orr	3 Arnott	3 Foyers	3 Smellie	3 Smellie
4 Begbie	4 Kelly	4 Sillars	4 Maley	4 Maley
5 Campbell (*Kilm'k*)	5 Sillars	5 McCreadie	5 Kelly	5 Kelly
6 Hill	6 Mitchell	6 Stewart	6 Mitchell	6 Mitchell
7 Taylor	7 Sellar	7 Taylor	7 Waddell	7 Sellar
8 Thomson	8 Taylor	8 Thomson	8 Campbell (*Celtic*)	8 Waddell
9 Hamilton	9 Waddell	9 Madden	9 Hamilton	9 Hamilton
10 McPherson	10 McMahon	10 Lambie	10 Sellar	10 McMahon
11 Baird	11 Bell	11 Barker	11 McMahon	11 Campbell (*Celtic*)
Edinburgh	Glasgow	Wrexham	Glasgow	Richmond
Mar 26: 6-1	April 2: 1-4	Mar 18: 8-0	Mar 25: 6-1	April 1: 2-5
Thomson, Hamilton 2, McPherson, Baird 2	*Bell*	*Madden 4, Barker 3, Lambie*	*Sellar 2, Kelly, McMahon, Hamilton, 1 og*	*Sellar 2*

1894 Wales	1894 Ireland	1894 England	1895 Wales	1895 Ireland
1 Baird	1 Barrett	1 Haddow	1 Barrett	1 McArthur
2 Crawford	2 Crawford	2 Sillars	2 Sillars	2 Doyle
3 Foyers	3 Drummond	3 Doyle	3 Glen	3 Drummond
4 Johnstone	4 Marshall	4 Begbie	4 Simpson	4 Simpson
5 Kelly	5 Stewart	5 McCreadie	5 McColl	5 Russell
6 McBain	6 Longair	6 Mitchell	6 Keillor	6 Gibson
7 Chalmers	7 Taylor	7 Gulliland	7 Fyfe	7 Taylor
8 Stewart	8 Blessington	8 Blessington	8 Murray	8 Waddell
9 Alexander	9 Alexander	9 McMahon	9 Madden	9 McPherson
10 Berry	10 Scott	10 McPherson	10 Sawers	10 Walker J.
11 Barker	11 Keillor	11 Lambie	11 Divers	11 Lambie
Kilmarnock	Belfast	Glasgow	Wrexham	Glasgow
Mar 24: 5-2	Mar 31: 2-1	April 7: 2-2	Mar 23: 2-2	Mar 30: 3-1
Berry, Barker, Chalmers, Alexander, Johnstone	*Taylor, Torrans og*	*Lambie, McMahon*	*Madden, Divers*	*Lambie, Walker 2*

1895 England	1896 Wales	1896 Ireland	1896 England	1897 Wales
1 McArthur	1 McFarlane	1 Anderson	1 Doig	1 Patrick
2 Drummond	2 McLean	2 Meechan	2 Brandon	2 Ritchie
3 Doyle	3 Glen	3 Drummond	3 Drummond	3 Gardner
4 Russell	4 Gillespie	4 Gibson	4 Gibson	4 Breslin
5 Simpson	5 Neil	5 Kelly	5 Cowan	5 Russell
6 Gibson	6 Blair	6 Hogg	6 Hogg	6 Keillor
7 Lambie	7 Thomson	7 Murray	7 Bell	7 Kennedy
8 McPherson	8 Paton	8 Blessington	8 Blessington	8 Murray
9 Oswald	9 McColl	9 McColl	9 Hyslop	9 Oswald
10 Waddell	10 King	10 Cameron	10 King	10 McMillan
11- Gulliland	11 Keillor	11 Lambie	11 Lambie	11 Walker J.
Liverpool	Dundee	Belfast	Glasgow	Wrexham
April 6: 0-3	Mar 21: 4-0	Mar 28: 3-3	April 4: 2-1	Mar 20: 2-2
	Neil 2, Keillor 2	*McColl 2, Drummond*	*Lambie, Bell*	*Ritchie* (pen), *Jones og*

1897 **Ireland**	**1897** **England**	**1898** **Wales**	**1898** **Ireland**	**1898** **England**
1 Dickie	1 Patrick	1 Watson	1 Anderson	1 Anderson
2 McLean	2 Smith N.	2 Smith N.	2 Kelso	2 Drummond
3 Drummond	3 Doyle	3 Scott	3 Doyle	3 Doyle
4 Gibson	4 Gibson	4 Thomson	4 Thomson	4 Gibson
5 Stewart	5 Cowan	5 Christie	5 Russell	5 Cowan
6 Baird	6 Wilson	6 Campbell P.	6 King	6 Robertson
7 Low	7 Bell	7 Gillespie	7 Stewart	7 Bell
8 King	8 Miller	8 Miller	8 Campbell (*Celtic*)	8 Campbell (*Celtic*)
9 McColl	9 Allan	9 McKie	9 McColl	9 Maxwell
10 McPherson	10 Hyslop	10 Morgan	10 Walker J.	10 Miller
11 Lambie	11 Lambie	11 Findlay	11 Robertson	11 Smith A.
Glasgow Mar 27: 5-1 *McPherson 2, Gibson, McColl, King*	London April 3: 2-1 *Hyslop, Miller*	Motherwell Mar 19: 5-2 *Gillespie 3, McKie 2*	Belfast Mar 26: 3-0 *Robertson, McColl, Stewart*	Glasgow April 2: 1-3 *Miller*

1899 **Wales**	**1899** **Ireland**	**1899** **England**	**1900** **Wales**	**1900** **Ireland**
1 McArthur	1 Dickie	1 Doig	1 Dickie	1 Rennie
2 Smith N.	2 Smith N.	2 Smith N.	2 Smith N.	2 Smith N.
3 Storrier	3 Storrier	3 Storrier	3 Crawford	3 Glen
4 Gibson	4 Gibson	4 Gibson	4 Irons	4 Marshall
5 Marshall	5 Christie	5 Christie	5 Neil	5 Orr
6 King	6 King	6 Robertson	6 Robertson	6 Gibson
7 Campbell (*Rangers*)	7 Campbell (*Rangers*)	7 Campbell (*Rangers*)	7 Bell	7 Stewart
8 Hamilton	8 Hamilton	8 Hamilton	8 Wilson	8 Walker R.
9 McColl	9 McColl	9 McColl	9 McColl	9 Campbell (*Celtic*)
10 Bell	10 Bell	10 Morgan	10 Hamilton	10 Callaghan
11 Berry	11 Berry	11 Bell	11 Smith A.	11 Smith A.
Wrexham Mar 18: 6-0 *Campbell 2, McColl 3, Marshall*	Glasgow Mar 25: 9-1 *McColl 3, Hamilton 2, Campbell 2, Bell, Christie*	Birmingham April 8: 1-2 *Hamilton*	Aberdeen Feb 3: 5-2 *Bell, Wilson 2, Hamilton, Smith A.*	Belfast Mar 3: 3-0 *Campbell 2, Smith A.*

1900 **England**	**1901** **Ireland**	**1901** **Wales**	**1901** **England**	**1902** **Ireland**
1 Rennie	1 McWhattie	1 McWhattie	1 Rennie	1 Rennie
2 Smith N.	2 Smith N.	2 Smith N.	2 Battles	2 Smith N.
3 Drummond	3 Battles	3 Battles	3 Drummond	3 Drummond
4 Gibson	4 Russell	4 Gibson	4 Aitken	4 Key
5 Raisbeck	5 Anderson	5 Russell	5 Raisbeck	5 Buick
6 Robertson	6 Robertson	6 Robertson	6 Robertson	6 Robertson
7 Walker R.	7 Campbell (*Rangers*)	7 Bell	7 Walker R.	7 McCartney
8 Campbell (*Celtic*)	8 Campbell (*Celtic*)	8 Walker R.	8 Campbell (*Celtic*)	8 Walker R.
9 McColl	9 Hamilton	9 McColl	9 McColl	9 Hamilton
10 Bell	10 McMahon	10 Campbell (*Celtic*)	10 Hamilton	10 Campbell (*Celtic*)
11 Smith A.	11 Smith A.	11 Smith A.	11 Smith A.	11 Smith A.
Glasgow April 7: 4-1 *McColl 3, Bell*	Glasgow Feb 23: 11-0 *Campbell* (Celtic) *2, McMahon 4, Hamilton 4, Russell*	Wrexham Mar 2: 1-1 *Robertson*	London Mar 30: 2-2 *Campbell, Hamilton*	Belfast Mar 1: 5-1 *Hamilton 3, Buick, Walker*

1902 Wales	1902 England	1903 Wales	1903 Ireland	1903 England
1 Rennie	1 Rennie	1 Rennie	1 Rennie	1 Doig
2 Allan	2 Smith N.	2 McCombie	2 Gray	2 McCombie
3 Drummond	3 Drummond	3 Watson	3 Drummond	3 Watson
4 Wilson	4 Aitken	4 Aitken	4 Cross	4 Aitken
5 Buick	5 Raisbeck	5 Raisbeck	5 Robertson	5 Raisbeck
6 Robertson	6 Robertson	6 Robertson	6 Orr	6 Robertson
7 Campbell (*Celtic*)	7 Templeton	7 Templeton	7 Lindsay	7 Templeton
8 Walker R.	8 Walker R.	8 Walker R.	8 Walker R.	8 Walker R.
9 Hamilton	9 McColl	9 Campbell (*Celtic*)	9 Porteous	9 Hamilton
10 McMahon	10 Orr	10 Speedie	10 Speedie	10 Speedie
11 Smith A.	11 Smith A.	11 Smith A.	11 Smith A.	11 Smith A.
Greenock Mar 15: 5-1 *Smith 3, Buick, Drummond*	Birmingham May 3: 2-2 *Templeton, Orr*	Cardiff Mar 9: 1-0 *Speedie*	Glasgow Mar 21: 0-2	Sheffield April 4: 2-1 *Speedie, Walker*

1904 Wales	1904 Ireland	1904 England	1905 Wales	1905 Ireland
1 Skene	1 Rennie	1 McBride	1 Rennie	1 Howden
2 Jackson	2 Jackson	2 Jackson	2 McCombie	2 McLeod
3 Sharp	3 Cameron	3 Watson	3 Jackson	3 McIntosh
4 Orr	4 Henderson	4 Aitken	4 Aitken	4 Gibson
5 Sloan	5 Thomson	5 Raisbeck	5 Thomson	5 Thomson
6 Robertson	6 Robertson	6 Robertson	6 Robertson	6 Hay
7 Walker J.	7 Walker J.	7 Niblo	7 Templeton	7 McMenemy
8 Walker R.	8 Walker R.	8 Walker R.	8 Walker R.	8 Walker R.
9 Bennett	9 Hamilton	9 Brown A.	9 Kennedy	9 Quinn
10 McFarlane	10 Wilson	10 Orr	10 Fitchie	10 Somers
11 Wilson	11 Smith A.	11 Templeton	11 Smith A.	11 Wilson
Dundee Mar 12: 1-1 *Walker R.*	Dublin Mar 26: 1-1 *Hamilton*	Glasgow April 9: 0-1	Wrexham Mar 6: 1-3 *Robertson*	Glasgow Mar 18: 4-0 *Thomas 2 (2 pens), Walker, Quinn*

1905 England	1906 Wales	1906 Ireland	1906 England	1907 Wales
1 Lyall	1 Raeside	1 Rennie	1 McBride	1 McBride
2 McCombie	2 McLeod	2 McLeod	2 McLeod	2 Jackson
3 Watson	3 Richmond	3 Hill	3 Dunlop	3 Sharp
4 Aitken	4 McNair	4 Young	4 Aitken	4 Aitken
5 Thomson	5 Thomson	5 Thomson	5 Raisbeck	5 Thomson
6 McWilliam	6 Hay	6 Hay	6 McWilliam	6 McWilliam
7 Walker R.	7 Stewart	7 Hamilton	7 Stewart	7 Stewart
8 Howie	8 McFarlane	8 Walker R.	8 Howie	8 Livingstone
9 Young	9 Quinn	9 Quinn	9 Menzies	9 Young
10 Somers	10 Fitchie	10 Fitchie	10 Livingstone	10 Fitchie
11 Wilson	11 Wilson	11 Smith A.	11 Smith A.	11 Smith A.
London April 1: 0-1	Edinburgh Mar 3: 0-2	Dublin Mar 17: 1-0 *Fitchie*	Glasgow April 7: 2-1 *Howie 2*	Wrexham Mar 4: 0-1

1907 **Ireland**	**1907** **England**	**1908** **Wales**	**1908** **Ireland**	**1908** **England**
1 Muir	1 McBride	1 Rennie	1 Rennie	1 McBride
2 Jackson	2 Thomson	2 Agnew	2 Mitchell	2 McNair
3 Agnew	3 Sharp	3 Chaplin	3 Agnew	3 Sharp
4 Key	4 Aitken	4 McNair	4 May	4 Aitken
5 Thomson	5 Raisbeck	5 Thomson	5 Thomson	5 Thomson
6 McNair	6 McWilliam	6 Galt	6 Galt	6 May
7 Bennett	7 Stewart	7 Bennett	7 Templeton	7 Howie
8 Walker R.	8 Walker R.	8 Walker R.	8 Walker R.	8 Walker R.
9 O'Rourke	9 Wilson A.	9 Spiers	9 Quinn	9 Wilson A.
10 Somers	10 White	10 McFarlane	10 McColl	10 White
11 Fraser	11 Wilson G.	11 Lennie	11 Lennie	11 Quinn
Glasgow Mar 16: 3-0 *O'Rourke, Walker, Thomson* (pen)	Newcastle April 6: 1-1 *Crompton og*	Dundee Mar 7: 2-1 *Bennett, Lennie*	Dublin Mar 14: 5-0 *Quinn 4, Galt*	Glasgow April 4: 1-1 *Wilson*

1909 **Wales**	**1909** **Ireland**	**1909** **England**	**1910** **Wales**	**1910** **Ireland**
1 McBride	1 Brownlie	1 Brownlie	1 Brownlie	1 Brownlie
2 Collins	2 Main	2 Cameron	2 Law	2 Law
3 Sharp	3 Watson	3 Watson	3 Mitchell	3 Mitchell
4 May	4 Walker W.	4 McNair	4 McNair	4 Walker W.
5 Thomson	5 Stark	5 Stark	5 Loney	5 Loney
6 McWilliam	6 Hay	6 McWilliam	6 Hay	6 Hay
7 Bennett	7 Bennett	7 Bennett	7 Bennett	7 Sinclair
8 Hunter	8 McMenemy	8 Walker R.	8 McMenemy	8 McTavish
9 Walker R.	9 Thomson	9 Quinn	9 Quinn	9 Quinn
10 Somers	10 McFarlane	10 Wilson G.	10 Devine	10 Higgins
11 Paul	11 Paul	11 Paul	11 Robertson	11 Templeton
Wrexham Mar 1: 2-3 *Walker, Paul*	Glasgow Mar 15: 5-0 *McMenemy 2, McFarlane, Thomson, Paul*	London April 3: 0-2	Kilmarnock Mar 5: 1-0 *Devine*	Belfast Mar 19: 0-1

1910 **England**	**1911** **Wales**	**1911** **Ireland**	**1911** **England**	**1912** **Wales**
1 Brownlie	1 Brownlie	1 Brownlie	1 Lawrence	1 Brownlie
2 Law	2 Colman	2 Colman	2 Colman	2 McNair
3 Hay	3 Walker J.	3 Walker J.	3 Walker J.	3 Walker J.
4 Aitken	4 Tait	4 Aitken	4 Aitken	4 Mercer
5 Thomson	5 Low	5 Thomson	5 Low	5 Thomson
6 McWilliam	6 McWilliam	6 Hay	6 Hay	6 Hay
7 Bennett	7 Bennett	7 Douglas	7 Bennett	7 Sinclair
8 McMenemy	8 McMenemy	8 McMenemy	8 McMenemy	8 McMenemy
9 Quinn	9 Reid	9 Reid	9 Reid	9 Quinn
10 Higgins	10 McFarlane	10 Higgins	10 Higgins	10 Walker R.
11 Templeton	11 Hamilton	11 Smith A.	11 Smith A.	11 Robertson
Glasgow April 2: 2-0 *McMenemy, Quinn*	Cardiff Mar 6: 2-2 *Hamilton 2*	Glasgow Mar 18: 2-0 *Reid, McMenemy*	Liverpool April 1: 1-1 *Higgins*	Edinburgh Mar 2: 1-0 *Quinn*

1912 Ireland	**1912 England**	**1913 Wales**	**1913 Ireland**	**1913 England**
1 Brownlie	1 Brownlie	1 Brownlie	1 Brownlie	1 Brownlie
2 McNair	2 McNair	2 Orrock	2 Colman	2 McNair
3 Walker J.	3 Walker J.	3 Walker J.	3 Walker J.	3 Walker J.
4 Gordon	4 Gordon	4 Gordon	4 Mercer	4 Gordon
5 Low	5 Thomson	5 Thomson	5 Logan	5 Thomson
6 Bell	6 Hay	6 Campbell	6 Nellies	6 Wilson D.
7 Sinclair	7 Templeton	7 McAtee	7 Bennett	7 Donnachie
8 Walker R.	8 Walker R.	8 Walker R.	8 Gordon	8 Walker R.
9 Reid	9 McLean	9 Reid	9 Reid	9 Reid
10 Aitkenhead	10 Wilson A.	10 Wilson A.	10 Croal	10 Wilson A.
11 Templeton	11 Quinn	11 Templeton	11 Robertson	11 Robertson
Belfast Mar 16: 4-1 *Aitkenhead 2, Reid, Walker R.*	Glasgow Mar 23: 1-1 *Wilson*	Wrexham Mar 3: 0-0	Dublin Mar 15: 2-1 *Reid, Bennett*	Stamford Bridge April 5: 0-1

1914 Wales	**1914 Ireland**	**1914 England**	**1920 Wales**	**1920 Ireland**
1 Brownlie	1 Brownlie	1 Brownlie	1 Campbell	1 Campbell
2 Kelso	2 Dodds	2 McNair	2 McNair	2 McNair
3 Dodds	3 McNair	3 Dodds	3 Thomson	3 Blair
4 Nellies	4 Gordon	4 Gordon	4 Gordon	4 Bowie
5 Pursell	5 Thomson	5 Thomson	5 Cringen	5 Low
6 Anderson	6 Hay	6 Hay	6 McMullan	6 Gordon
7 Donaldson	7 Donaldson	7 Donaldson	7 Reid	7 Donaldson
8 McMenemy	8 McMenemy	8 McMenemy	8 Crosby	8 McMenemy
9 Reid	9 Reid	9 Reid	9 Wilson A.N.	9 Wilson A.N.
10 Croal	10 Wilson A.	10 Croal	10 Cairns	10 Cunningham
11 Browning	11 Donnachie	11 Donnachie	11 Morton	11 Morton
Glasgow Feb 28: 0-0	Belfast Mar 14: 1-1 *Donnachie*	Glasgow April 4: 3-1 *Thomson, McMenemy, Reid*	Cardiff Feb 26: 1-1 *Cairns*	Glasgow Mar 13: 3-0 *Wilson, Morton, Cunningham*

1920 England	**1921 Wales**	**1921 Ireland**	**1921 England**	**1922 Wales**
1 Campbell	1 Campbell	1 Campbell	1 Ewart	1 Campbell
2 McNair	2 Marshall	2 Marshall	2 Marshall	2 Marshall
3 Blair	3 McStay	3 McStay	3 Blair	3 McKinlay
4 Bowie	4 Harris	4 Harris	4 Davidson	4 Meiklejohn
5 Low	5 Pringle	5 Graham	5 Brewster	5 Gilhooley
6 Gordon	6 McMullan	6 McMullan	6 McMullan	6 Collier
7 Donaldson	7 Archibald	7 McNab	7 McNab	7 Archibald
8 Miller	8 Cunningham	8 Miller	8 Miller	8 White
9 Wilson A.N.	9 Wilson A.N.	9 Wilson A.N.	9 Wilson A.N.	9 Wilson A.N.
10 Paterson	10 Cassidy	10 Cassidy	10 Cunningham	10 Walker F.
11 Troup	11 Troup	11 Troup	11 Morton	11 Morton
Sheffield April 10: 4-5 *Miller 2, Wilson, Donaldson*	Aberdeen Feb 12: 2-1 *Wilson 2*	Belfast Feb 26: 2-0 *Wilson (pen), Cassidy*	Glasgow April 9: 3-0 *Wilson, Morton, Cunningham*	Wrexham Feb 4: 1-2 *Archibald*

1922 Ireland	1922 England	1923 Ireland	1923 Wales	1923 England
1 Campbell	1 Campbell	1 Harper	1 Harper	1 Harper
2 Marshall	2 Marshall	2 Hutton	2 Hutton	2 Hutton
3 McKinlay	3 Blair	3 Blair	3 Blair	3 Blair
4 Hogg	4 Gilchrist	4 Steele	4 McNab	4 Steele
5 Cringan	5 Cringan	5 Morris	5 Cringan	5 Cringan
6 Muirhead	6 McBain	6 McBain	6 Steele	6 Muirhead
7 Donaldson	7 Archibald	7 Archibald	7 Ritchie	7 Lawson
8 Kinloch	8 Crosbie	8 White	8 Cunningham	8 Cunningham
9 Wilson A.N.	9 Wilson A.N.	9 Wilson A.N.	9 Wilson A.N.	9 Wilson A.N.
10 Cunningham	10 Cairns	10 Cassidy	10 Cairns	10 Cairns
11 Troup	11 Morton	11 Morton	11 Morton	11 Morton
Glasgow Mar 4: 2-1 *Wilson 2*	Birmingham April 8: 1-0 *Wilson*	Belfast Mar 3: 1-0 *Wilson*	Glasgow Mar 17: 2-0 *Wilson 2*	Glasgow April 14: 2-2 *Cunningham, Wilson*

1924 Wales	1924 Ireland	1924 England	1925 Wales	1925 Ireland
1 Harper	1 Harper	1 Harper	1 Harper	1 Harper
2 Marshall	2 Hutton	2 Smith J.	2 Nelson	2 Nelson
3 Blair	3 Hamilton	3 McCloy	3 McStay	3 McStay
4 Meiklejohn	4 Kerr	4 Clunas	4 Meiklejohn	4 Meiklejohn
5 McBain	5 Morris	5 Morris	5 Morris	5 Morris
6 Muirhead	6 McMullan	6 McMullan	6 Bennie	6 Bennie
7 Archibald	7 Reid	7 Archibald	7 Jackson	7 Jackson
8 Russell	8 Cunningham	8 Cowan	8 Dunn	8 Dunn
9 Cassidy	9 Gallacher	9 Harris	9 Gallacher	9 Gallacher
10 McKay	10 Cairns	10 Cunningham	10 Cairns	10 Cairns
11 Morton	11 Morton	11 Morton	11 Morton	11 Morton
Cardiff Feb 16: 0-2	Glasgow Mar 1: 2-0 *Cunningham, Morris*	Wembley April 12: 1-1 *Taylor og*	Edinburgh Feb 14: 3-1 *Meiklejohn, Gallacher 2*	Belfast Feb 28: 3-0 *Meiklejohn, Gallacher, Dunn*

1925 England	1925 Wales	1926 Ireland	1926 England	1926 Wales
1 Harper	1 Robb	1 Harper	1 Harper	1 McClory
2 McStay	2 Hutton	2 Hutton	2 Hutton	2 McStay
3 McCloy	3 McStay	3 McStay	3 McStay	3 Wiseman
4 Meiklejohn	4 Clunas	4 Wilson	4 Gibson	4 Gibson
5 Morris	5 Townsley	5 McDougall	5 Summers	5 Gillespie
6 McMullan	6 McMullan	6 Bennie	6 McMullan	6 McMullan
7 Jackson	7 Jackson	7 Jackson	7 Jackson	7 Jackson
8 Russell	8 Duncan	8 Cunningham	8 Thomson	8 Cunningham
9 Gallacher	9 Gallacher	9 Gallacher	9 Gallacher	9 Gallacher
10 Cairns	10 James	10 McInally	10 Cunningham	10 McInally
11 Morton	11 McLean	11 McLean	11 Troup	11 McLean
Glasgow April 4: 2-0 *Gallacher 2*	Cardiff Oct 31: 3-0 *Duncan, McLean, Clunas*	Glasgow Feb 27: 4-0 *Gallacher 3, Cunningham*	Manchester April 17: 1-0 *Jackson*	Glasgow Oct 30: 3-0 *Gallacher, Jackson 2*

1927 Ireland	1927 England	1927 Wales	1928 Ireland	1928 England
1 Harkness	1 Harkness	1 Robb	1 McClory	1 Harkness
2 Hutton	2 McStay	2 Hutton	2 Hutton	2 Nelson
3 McStay	3 Thomson	3 McStay	3 McStay	3 Law
4 Muirhead	4 Morrison	4 Meiklejohn	4 Muirhead	4 Gibson
5 Gibson	5 Gibson	5 Gibson	5 Meiklejohn	5 Bradshaw
6 Craig	6 McMullan	6 McMullan	6 Craig	6 McMullan
7 Jackson	7 McLean	7 Jackson	7 Ritchie	7 Jackson
8 Dunn	8 Cunningham	8 McKay	8 Dunn	8 Dunn
9 Gallacher	9 Gallacher	9 Gallacher	9 McGrory	9 Gallacher
10 Howieson	10 McPhail	10 Stevenson	10 Stevenson	10 James
11 Morton	11 Morton	11 Morton	11 Morton	11 Morton
Belfast Feb 26: 2-0 *Morton 2*	Glasgow April 2: 1-2 *Morton*	Wrexham Oct 29: 2-2 *Gallacher, Hutton* (pen)	Glasgow Feb 25: 0-1	Wembley Mar 31: 5-1 *Jackson 3, James, Gibson*

1928 Wales	1929 Ireland	1929 England	1929 Norway	1929 Germany
1 Harkness	1 Harkness	1 Harkness	1 McLaren	1 McLaren
2 Gray	2 Gray	2 Crapnell	2 Crapnell	2 Gray
3 Blair	3 Blair	3 Nibloe	3 Nibloe	3 Crapnell
4 Muirhead	4 Muirhead	4 Buchanan	4 Imrie	4 Morton H.
5 King	5 Meiklejohn	5 Meiklejohn	5 Craig A.	5 Imrie
6 McMullan	6 McMullan	6 McMullan	6 Craig T.	6 Craig T.
7 Jackson	7 Jackson	7 Jackson	7 Nisbet	7 Nisbet
8 Dunn	8 Chalmers	8 Cheyne	8 Cheyne	8 Cheyne
9 Gallacher	9 Gallacher	9 Gallacher	9 McCrae	9 McCrae
10 McPhail	10 James	10 James	10 Rankin	10 Rankin
11 Morton	11 Morton	11 Morton	11 Howe	11 Fleming
Glasgow Oct 27: 4-2 *Gallacher 3, Dunn*	Belfast Feb 23: 7-3 *Gallacher 4, Jackson 2, James*	Glasgow April 13: 1-0 *Cheyne*	Bergen May 26: 7-3 *Cheyne 3, Nisbet 2, Craig T., Rankin*	Berlin June 1: 1-1 *Imrie*

1929 Netherlands	1929 Wales	1930 Ireland	1930 England	1930 France
1 McClaren	1 Harkness	1 Middleton	1 Harkness	1 Thomson
2 Gray	2 Gray	2 Gray	2 Gray	2 Nelson
3 Nibloe	3 Nibloe	3 Wiseman	3 Law	3 Crapnell
4 Morton H.	4 Gibson	4 Gibson	4 Buchanan	4 Wilson
5 Craig A.	5 Johnstone	5 Meiklejohn	5 Meiklejohn	5 Walker G.
6 Craig T.	6 Craig T.	6 Craig T.	6 Craig T.	6 Hill
7 Nisbet	7 Jackson	7 Jackson	7 Jackson	7 Jackson
8 Cheyne	8 Muirhead	8 Stevenson	8 James	8 Cheyne
9 Fleming	9 Gallacher	9 Gallacher	9 Fleming	9 Gallacher
10 Rankin	10 James	10 James	10 Stevenson	10 Stevenson
11 Howe	11 Morton	11 Morton	11 Morton	11 Connor
Amsterdam June 4: 2-0 *Fleming, Rankin*	Cardiff Oct 26: 4-2 *Gallacher 2, James, Gibson*	Glasgow Feb 22: 3-1 *Gallacher 2, Stevenson*	Wembley April 5: 2-5 *Fleming 2*	Paris May 18: 2-0 *Gallacher 2*

1930 Wales	**1931 Ireland**	**1931 England**	**1931 Austria**	**1931 Italy**
1 Thomson	1 Thomson	1 Thomson	1 Jackson	1 Jackson
2 Gray	2 Crapnell	2 Blair	2 Blair	2 Blair
3 Gilmour	3 Nibloe	3 Nibloe	3 Nibloe	3 Nibloe
4 McNab	4 Wilson P.	4 McNab	4 McNab	4 McNab
5 Gillespie	5 Walker G.	5 Meiklejohn	5 McDougall	5 McDougall
6 Hill	6 Hill	6 Miller	6 Walker G.	6 Miller
7 McRorie	7 Murdoch	7 Archibald	7 Love	7 Love
8 Brown G.	8 Scarff	8 Stevenson	8 Paterson	8 Paterson
9 Battles	9 Yorston	9 McGrory	9 Easson	9 Boyd
10 Stevenson	10 McPhail	10 McPhail	10 Robertson	10 Robertson
11 Morton	11 Morton	11 Morton	11 Liddell D.	11 Liddell D.
Glasgow Oct 25: 1-1 *Battles*	Belfast Feb 21: 0-0	Glasgow Mar 28: 2-0 *Stevenson, McGrory*	Vienna May 16: 0-5	Rome May 20: 0-3

1931 Switzerland	**1931 Ireland**	**1931 Wales**	**1932 England**	**1932 France**
1 Jackson	1 Hepburn	1 Harkness	1 Hamilton T.	1 Harkness
2 Crapnell	2 Blair	2 Blair	2 Crapnell	2 Crapnell
3 Nibloe	3 McAulay	3 McAulay	3 Nibloe	3 Nibloe
4 McNab	4 Massie	4 Massie	4 McNab	4 Massie
5 Walker G.	5 Meiklejohn	5 Meiklejohn	5 Craig A.	5 Gillespie
6 Miller	6 Brown G.	6 Brown G.	6 Brown G.	6 Miller
7 Love	7 Crawford	7 Thomson R.	7 Archibald	7 Crawford
8 Paterson	8 Stevenson	8 Stevenson	8 Marshall	8 Thomson A.
9 Boyd	9 McGrory	9 McGrory	9 Dewar	9 Dewar
10 Easson	10 McPhail	10 McPhail	10 Napier	10 McPhail
11 Liddell D.	11 Connor	11 Morton	11 Morton	11 Morton
Geneva May 24: 3-2 *Easson, Boyd, Love*	Glasgow Sept 19: 3-1 *Stevenson, McGrory, McPhail*	Wrexham Oct 31: 3-2 *Stevenson, Thomson, McGrory*	Wembley April 9: 0-3	Paris May 8: 3-1 *Dewar 3*

1932 Ireland	**1932 Wales**	**1933 England**	**1933 Ireland**	**1933 Wales**
1 McLaren	1 McLaren	1 Jackson	1 Harkness	1 Kennaway
2 Gray	2 Gray	2 Anderson	2 Anderson	2 Anderson
3 Crapnell	3 Blair	3 McGonagle	3 McGonagle	3 Urquhart
4 Massie	4 Wales	4 Wilson P.	4 Massie	4 Busby
5 Johnstone	5 Johnstone	5 Gillespie	5 Lowe	5 Blair
6 Telfer	6 Thomson J.	6 Brown G.	6 Telfer	6 McLuckie
7 Crawford	7 Crawford	7 Crawford	7 Boyd	7 McGurk
8 Stevenson	8 Thomson A.	8 Marshall	8 Venters	8 McMenemy
9 McGrory	9 Dewar	9 McGrory	9 McGrory	9 McFadyen
10 McPhail	10 James	10 McPhail	10 McPhail	10 Easson
11 King	11 Duncan	11 Duncan	11 King	11 Duncan
Belfast Sept 19: 4-0 *McPhail 2, King, McGrory*	Edinburgh Oct 26: 2-5 *Dewar, Duncan*	Glasgow April 1: 2-1 *McGrory 2*	Glasgow Sept 16: 1-2 *McPhail*	Cardiff Oct 4: 2-3 *Duncan, McFadyen*

1933 Austria	**1934 England**	**1934 Ireland**	**1934 Wales**	**1935 England**
1 Kennaway	1 Jackson	1 Dawson	1 McClory	1 Jackson
2 Anderson	2 Anderson	2 Anderson	2 Anderson	2 Anderson
3 McGonagle	3 McGonagle	3 McGonagle	3 McGonagle	3 Cummings
4 Meiklejohn	4 Massie	4 Massie	4 Massie	4 Massie
5 Watson P.	5 Smith T.	5 Simpson	5 Simpson	5 Simpson
6 Brown G.	6 Miller	6 Herd	6 Brown G.	6 Brown G.
7 Ogilvie	7 Cook	7 Cook	7 Cook	7 Napier
8 Bruce	8 Marshall	8 Stevenson	8 Walker T.	8 Walker T.
9 McFadyen	9 Gallacher	9 Smith J.	9 McCulloch	9 Gallacher
10 McPhail	10 Stevenson	10 Gallacher	10 Napier	10 McPhail
11 Duncan	11 Connor	11 Connor	11 Duncan	11 Duncan
Glasgow	Wembley	Belfast	Aberdeen	Glasgow
Nov 29: 2-2	April 14: 0-3	Oct 20: 1-2	Nov 21: 3-2	April 6: 2-0
Meiklejohn, McFadyen		*Gallacher*	*Duncan, Napier 2*	*Duncan 2*

1935 Wales	**1935 Ireland**	**1936 England**	**1936 Germany**	**1936 Ireland**
1 Jackson	1 Jackson	1 Dawson	1 Dawson	1 Dawson
2 Anderson	2 Anderson	2 Anderson	2 Anderson	2 Anderson
3 Cummings	3 Cummings	3 Cummings	3 Cummings	3 Ancell
4 Massie	4 Massie	4 Massie	4 Massie	4 Massie
5 Simpson	5 Simpson	5 Simpson	5 Simpson	5 Simpson
6 Brown G.	6 Hastings	6 Brown G.	6 Brown G.	6 Brown G.
7 Delaney	7 Delaney	7 Crum	7 Delaney	7 Munro
8 Walker T.	8 Walker T.	8 Walker T.	8 Walker T.	8 Walker T.
9 Armstrong	9 Armstrong	9 McCulloch	9 Armstrong	9 McCulloch
10 Mills	10 Mills	10 Venters	10 McPhail	10 Napier
11 Duncan	11 Duncan	11 Duncan	11 Duncan	11 Duncan
Cardiff	Edinburgh	Wembley	Glasgow	Belfast
Oct 5: 1-1	Nov 13: 2-1	April 4: 1-1	Oct 14: 2-0	Oct 31: 3-1
Duncan	*Walker, Duncan*	*Walker*	*Delaney 2*	*Napier, Munro, McCulloch*

1936 Wales	**1937 England**	**1937 Austria**	**1937 Czechoslovakia**	**1937 Wales**
1 Dawson	1 Dawson	1 Dawson	1 Dawson	1 Dawson
2 Anderson	2 Anderson	2 Anderson	2 Hogg	2 Anderson
3 Ancell	3 Beattie A.	3 Beattie A.	3 Beattie A.	3 Cummings
4 Massie	4 Massie	4 Massie	4 Thomson	4 Massie
5 Simpson	5 Simpson	5 Simpson	5 Simpson	5 Simpson
6 Brown G.	6 Brown G.	6 McNab	6 Brown G.	6 Brown G.
7 Munro	7 Delaney	7 Delaney	7 Delaney	7 Main
8 Walker T.	8 Walker T.	8 Walker T.	8 Walker T.	8 Walker T.
9 McCulloch	9 O'Donnell F.	9 O'Donnell F.	9 O'Donnell F.	9 O'Donnell F.
10 Mills	10 McPhail	10 Napier	10 McPhail	10 McPhail
11 Duncan	11 Duncan	11 Gillick	11 Gillick	11 Duncan
Dundee	Glasgow	Vienna	Prague	Cardiff
Dec 2: 1-2	April 17: 3-1	May 9: 1-1	May 22: 3-1	Oct 30: 1-2
Walker	*O'Donnell, McPhail 2*	*O'Donnell*	*Simpson, McPhail, Gillick*	*Massie*

1937 Ireland	**1937 Czechoslovakia**	**1938 England**	**1938 Netherlands**	**1938 Ireland**
1 Dawson	1 Waugh	1 Cumming	1 Dawson	1 Dawson
2 Anderson	2 Anderson	2 Anderson	2 Anderson	2 Carabine
3 Cummings	3 Cummings	3 Beattie A.	3 Carabine	3 Beattie A.
4 McKenzie	4 Robertson	4 Shankly	4 McKillop	4 Shankly
5 Simpson	5 Johnston	5 Smith T.	5 Dykes	5 Dykes
6 Hastings	6 Brown G.	6 Brown G.	6 Brown G.	6 Paterson
7 Delaney	7 Buchanan	7 Milne	7 Munro	7 Delaney
8 Walker T.	8 Walker T.	8 Walker T.	8 Walker T.	8 Walker T.
9 Smith J.	9 McCulloch	9 O'Donnell F.	9 O'Donnell F.	9 Crum
10 McPhail	10 Black	10 Mutch	10 Black	10 Divers
11 Reid	11 Kinnear	11 Reid	11 Murphy	11 Gillick
Aberdeen	Glasgow	Wembley	Amsterdam	Belfast
Nov 10: 1-1	Dec 8: 5-0	April 9: 1-0	May 21: 3-1	Oct 8: 2-0
Smith	*McCulloch 2, Black, Buchanan, Kinnear*	*Walker*	*Black, Murphy, Walker*	*Delaney, Walker*

1938 Wales	**1938 Hungary**	**1939 England**	**1946 Wales**	**1946 N Ireland**
1 Brown J.	1 Dawson	1 Dawson	1 Miller	1 Brown R.
2 Anderson	2 Anderson	2 Carabine	2 Stephen	2 Young
3 Beattie A.	3 Beattie A.	3 Cummings	3 Shaw D.	3 Shaw D.
4 Shankly	4 Shankly	4 Shankly	4 Brown	4 Campbell
5 Baxter	5 Baxter	5 Baxter	5 Brennan	5 Brennan
6 Miller	6 Symon	6 McNab	6 Husband	6 Long
7 Delaney	7 McSpadyen	7 McSpadyen	7 Waddell	7 Smith
8 Walker T.	8 Walker T.	8 Walker T.	8 Dougall	8 Hamilton
9 McCulloch	9 McCulloch	9 Dougall	9 Thornton	9 Thornton
10 Beattie R.	10 Black	10 Venters	10 Blair	10 Duncanson
11 Gillick	11 Gillick	11 Milne	11 Liddell	11 Liddell
Edinburgh	Glasgow	Glasgow	Wrexham	Hampden
Nov 9: 3-2	Dec 7: 3-1	April 15: 1-2	Oct 19: 1-3	Nov 27: 0-0
Walker 2, Gillick	*Black, Walker, Gillick*	*Dougall*	*Waddell*	

1947 England	**1947 Belgium**	**1947 Luxembourg**	**1947 N Ireland**	**1947 Wales**
1 Miller	1 Miller	1 Miller	1 Miller	1 Miller
2 Young	2 Young	2 Young	2 Young	2 Govan
3 Shaw J.	3 Shaw J.	3 Shaw J.	3 Shaw J.	3 Stephen
4 Macaulay	4 Brown	4 Brown	4 Macaulay	4 Macaulay
5 Woodburn	5 Woodburn	5 Woodburn	5 Woodburn	5 Woodburn
6 Forbes	6 Forbes	6 Forbes	6 Forbes	6 Forbes
7 Smith	7 Campbell	7 McFarlane	7 Delaney	7 Smith
8 McLaren	8 McLaren	8 McLaren	8 Watson	8 McLaren
9 Delaney	9 Flavell	9 Flavell	9 Thornton	9 Delaney
10 Steel	10 Steel	10 Steel	10 Steel	10 Steel
11 Pearson	11 Pearson	11 Campbell	11 Liddell	11 Liddell
Wembley	Brussels	Luxembourg	Belfast	Hampden
April 12: 1-1	May 18: 1-2	May 24: 6-0	Oct 4: 0-2	Nov 12: 1-2
McLaren	*Steel*	*McLaren 2, Steel 2, Flavell 2*		*McLaren*

1948 England	1948 Belgium	1948 Switzerland	1948 France	1948 Wales
1 Black	1 Cowan	1 Cowan	1 Cowan	1 Cowan
2 Govan	2 Govan	2 Govan	2 Govan	2 Howie
3 Shaw D.	3 Shaw D.	3 Shaw D.	3 Shaw D.	3 Shaw D.
4 Campbell	4 Campbell	4 Campbell	4 Campbell	4 Evans
5 Young	5 Young	5 Young	5 Young	5 Young
6 Macaulay	6 Macaulay	6 Macaulay	6 Macaulay	6 Redpath
7 Delaney	7 Smith	7 Smith	7 Rutherford	7 Waddell
8 Combe	8 Combe	8 Combe	8 Steel	8 Mason
9 Thornton	9 Johnstone	9 Johnstone	9 Smith	9 Reilly
10 Steel	10 Turnbull	10 Turnbull	10 Cox	10 Steel
11 Liddell	11 Duncan	11 Duncan	11 Duncan	11 Kelly
Hampden April 10: 0-2	Hampden April 28: 2-0 *Combe, Duncan*	Berne May 17: 1-2 *Johnstone*	Paris May 23: 0-3	Cardiff Oct 23: 3-1 *Howie, Waddell 2*

1948 N Ireland	1949 England	1949 France	1949 N Ireland	1949 Wales
1 Brown R.	1 Cowan	1 Cowan	1 Cowan	1 Cowan
2 Govan	2 Young	2 Young	2 Young	2 Young
3 Shaw D.	3 Cox	3 Cox	3 Cox	3 Cox
4 Evans	4 Evans	4 Evans	4 Evans	4 Evans
5 Young	5 Woodburn	5 Woodburn	5 Woodburn	5 Woodburn
6 Redpath	6 Aitken	6 Aitken	6 Aitken	6 Aitken
7 Waddell	7 Waddell	7 Waddell	7 Waddell	7 Liddell
8 Mason	8 Mason	8 Thornton	8 Mason	8 McPhail
9 Houliston	9 Houliston	9 Houliston	9 Morris	9 Linwood
10 Steel	10 Steel	10 Steel	10 Steel	10 Steel
11 Kelly	11 Reilly	11 Reilly	11 Reilly	11 Reilly
Hampden Nov 17: 3-2 *Houliston 2, Mason*	Wembley April 9: 3-1 *Mason, Steel Reilly*	Hampden April 27: 2-0 *Steel 2*	Belfast Oct 1: 8-2 *Morris 3, Waddell 2, Steel, Reilly, Mason*	Hampden Nov 9: 2-0 *McPhail, Linwood*

1950 England	1950 Switzerland	1950 Portugal	1950 France	1950 Wales
1 Cowan	1 Cowan	1 Cowan	1 Cowan	1 Cowan
2 Young	2 Young	2 Young	2 Young	2 Young
3 Cox	3 Cox	3 Cox	3 Cox	3 McNaught
4 McColl	4 Evans	4 Evans	4 McColl	4 McColl
5 Woodburn	5 Dougan	5 Woodburn	5 Woodburn	5 Woodburn
6 Forbes	6 Aitken	6 Forbes	6 Forbes	6 Forbes
7 Waddell	7 Campbell	7 Campbell	7 Campbell	7 Collins
8 Moir	8 Brown	8 Brown	8 Brown	8 McPhail
9 Bauld	9 Bauld	9 Bauld	9 Reilly	9 Reilly
10 Steel	10 Steel	10 Steel	10 Steel	10 Steel
11 Liddell	11 Reilly	11 Liddell	11 Liddell	11 Liddell
Hampden April 15: 0-1	Hampden April 26: 3-1 *Bauld, Campbell, Brown*	Lisbon May 25: 2-2 *Brown, Bauld*	Paris May 27: 1-0 *Brown*	Cardiff Oct 21: 3-1 *Reilly 2, Liddell*

1950 N Ireland	1950 Austria	1951 England	1951 Denmark	1951 France
1 Cowan	1 Cowan	1 Cowan	1 Cowan	1 Cowan
2 Young	2 Young	2 Young	2 Young	2 Young
3 McNaught	3 McNaught	3 Cox	3 Cox	3 Cox
4 McColl	4 Evans	4 Evans	4 Scoular	4 Scoular
5 Woodburn	5 Woodburn	5 Woodburn	5 Woodburn	5 Woodburn
6 Forbes	6 Forbes	6 Redpath	6 Redpath	6 Redpath
7 Collins	7 Collins	7 Waddell	7 Waddell	7 Waddell
8 Mason	8 Turnbull	8 Johnstone	8 Johnstone	8 Johnstone
9 McPhail	9 McPhail	9 Reilly	9 Reilly	9 Reilly
10 Steel	10 Steel	10 Steel	10 Steel	10 Steel
11 Liddell	11 Liddell	11 Liddell	11 Mitchell	11 Mitchell
Hampden Nov 1: 6-1 *McPhail 2, Steel 4*	Hampden Dec 13: 0-1	Wembley April 14: 3-2 *Johnstone, Reilly, Liddell*	Hampden May 12: 3-1 *Steel, Reilly, Mitchell*	Hampden May 16: 1-0 *Reilly*

1951 Belgium	1951 Austria	1951 N Ireland	1951 Wales	1952 England
1 Cowan	1 Cowan	1 Cowan	1 Cowan	1 Brown R.
2 Young	2 Young	2 Young	2 Young	2 Young
3 Cox	3 Cox	3 Cox	3 Cox	3 McNaught
4 McColl	4 Scoular	4 Evans	4 Docherty	4 Scoular
5 Woodburn	5 Woodburn	5 Woodburn	5 Woodburn	5 Woodburn
6 Redpath	6 Redpath	6 Redpath	6 Forbes	6 Redpath
7 Waddell	7 Waddell	7 Waddell	7 Waddell	7 Smith
8 Mason	8 Mason	8 Johnstone	8 Orr	8 Johnstone
9 Hamilton	9 Hamilton	9 Reilly	9 Reilly	9 Reilly
10 Steel	10 Steel	10 Orr	10 Steel	10 McMillan
11 Reilly	11 Reilly	11 Liddell	11 Liddell	11 Liddell
Brussels May 20: 5-0 *Hamilton 3, Mason, Waddell*	Vienna May 27: 0-4	Belfast Oct 6: 3-0 *Johnstone 2, Orr*	Hampden Nov 28: 0-1	Hampden April 5: 1-2 *Reilly*

1952 USA	1952 Denmark	1952 Sweden	1952 Wales	1952 N Ireland
1 Cowan	1 Cowan	1 Cowan	1 Farm	1 Farm
2 Young	2 Young	2 Young	2 Young	2 Young
3 Cox	3 Cox	3 Cox	3 Cox	3 Cox
4 Scoular	4 Scoular	4 Scoular	4 Scoular	4 Scoular
5 Woodburn	5 Paton	5 Paton	5 Brennan	5 Brennan
6 Kelly	6 Forbes	6 Forbes	6 Aitken	6 Aitken
7 Smith	7 Reilly	7 Reilly	7 Wright T.	7 Wright T.
8 McMillan	8 McMillan	8 Humphries	8 Brown	8 Logie
9 Reilly	9 Thornton	9 Thornton	9 Reilly	9 Reilly
10 Brown	10 Brown	10 Brown	10 Steel	10 Steel
11 Liddell	11 Liddell	11 Liddell	11 Liddell	11 Liddell
Hampden April 30: 6-0 *Reilly 3, McMillan 2, 1 og*	Copenhagen May 25: 2-1 *Thornton, Reilly*	Stockholm May 30: 1-3 *Liddell*	Cardiff Oct 15: 2-1 *Brown, Liddell*	Hampden Nov 5: 1-1 *Reilly*

1953 England	1953 Sweden	1953 N Ireland	1953 Wales	1954 England
1 Farm	1 Farm	1 Farm	1 Farm	1 Farm
2 Young	2 Young	2 Young	2 Young	2 Haughney
3 Cox	3 Little	3 Cox	3 Cox	3 Cox
4 Docherty	4 Evans	4 Evans	4 Evans	4 Evans
5 Brennan	5 Cowie	5 Brennan	5 Telfer	5 Brennan
6 Cowie	6 Docherty	6 Cowie	6 Cowie	6 Aitken
7 Wright T.	7 Henderson	7 Waddell	7 McKenzie	7 McKenzie
8 Johnstone	8 Johnstone	8 Fleming	8 Johnstone	8 Johnstone
9 Reilly	9 Reilly	9 McPhail	9 Reilly	9 Henderson
10 Steel	10 Steel	10 Watson	10 Brown	10 Brown
11 Liddell	11 Ring	11 Henderson	11 Liddell	11 Ormond
Wembley April 18: 2-2 *Reilly 2*	Hampden May 6: 1-2 *Johnstone*	Belfast Oct 3: 3-1 *Fleming 2, Henderson*	Hampden Nov 4: 3-3 *Brown, Johnstone, Reilly*	Hampden April 3: 2-4 *Brown, 1 og*

1954 Norway	1954 Norway	1954 Finland	1954 Austria †	1954 Uruguay †
1 Martin	1 Martin	1 Anderson	1 Martin	1 Martin
2 Cunningham	2 Cunningham	2 Wilson	2 Cunningham	2 Cunningham
3 Aird	3 Aird	3 Cunningham	3 Aird	3 Aird
4 Docherty	4 Docherty	4 Evans	4 Docherty	4 Docherty
5 Davidson	5 Davidson	5 Cowie	5 Davidson	5 Davidson
6 Evans	6 Cowie	6 Mathers	6 Cowie	6 Cowie
7 Johnstone	7 McKenzie	7 McKenzie	7 McKenzie	7 McKenzie
8 Hamilton	8 Hamilton	8 Johnstone	8 Fernie	8 Fernie
9 Buckley	9 Henderson	9 Brown	9 Mochan	9 Mochan
10 Brown	10 Brown	10 Fernie	10 Brown	10 Brown
11 Ormond	11 Mochan	11 Ormond	11 Ormond	11 Ormond
Hampden May 5: 1-0 *Hamilton*	Oslo May 19: 1-1 *McKenzie*	Helsinki May 25: 2-1 *Ormond, Johnstone*	Zurich June 16: 0-1	Basle June 19: 0-7

1954 Wales	1954 N Ireland	1954 Hungary	1955 England	1955 Portugal
1 Fraser	1 Fraser	1 Martin	1 Martin	1 Younger
2 Young	2 Young	2 Cunningham	2 Cunningham	2 Parker
3 Cunningham	3 McNaught	3 Haddock	3 Haddock	3 Haddock
4 Docherty	4 Evans	4 Docherty	4 Docherty	4 Evans
5 Davidson	5 Davidson	5 Davidson	5 Davidson	5 Young
6 Cowie	6 Cowie	6 Cumming	6 Cumming	6 Cumming
7 Waddell	7 Waddell	7 McKenzie	7 McKenzie	7 Smith
8 Yorston	8 Johnstone	8 Johnstone	8 Johnstone	8 Robertson
9 Buckley	9 Buckley	9 Reilly	9 Reilly	9 Reilly
10 Fernie	10 Fernie	10 Wardhaugh	10 McMillan	10 Gemmell
11 Ring	11 Ring	11 Ring	11 Ring	11 Liddell
Cardiff Oct 16: 1-0 *Buckley*	Hampden Nov 3: 2-2 *Davidson, Johnstone*	Hampden Dec 8: 2-4 *Ring, Johnstone*	Wembley April 2: 2-7 *Reilly, Docherty*	Hampden May 16: 3-0 *Reilly, Gemmell, Liddell*

1955 Yugoslavia	1955 Austria	1955 Hungary	1955 N Ireland	1955 Wales
1 Younger	1 Younger	1 Younger	1 Younger	1 Younger
2 Parker	2 Parker	2 Kerr	2 Parker	2 Parker
3 Haddock	3 Kerr	3 Haddock	3 McDonald	3 McDonald
4 Evans	4 Docherty	4 Docherty	4 Evans	4 Evans
5 Young	5 Evans	5 Evans	5 Young	5 Young
6 Cumming	6 Cowie	6 Cowie	6 Glen	6 Cowie
7 Smith	7 Smith	7 Smith	7 Smith	7 Smith
8 Collins	8 Collins	8 Collins	8 Collins	8 Johnstone
9 Reilly	9 Reilly	9 Reilly	9 Reilly	9 Reilly
10 Gemmell	10 Robertson	10 Robertson	10 Johnstone	10 Collins
11 Liddell	11 Liddell	11 Liddell	11 Liddell	11 Henderson
Belgrade May 15: 2-2 *Reilly, Smith*	Vienna May 19: 4-1 *Robertson, Smith, Liddell, Reilly*	Budapest May 29: 1-3 *Smith*	Belfast Oct 8: 1-2 *Reilly*	Hampden Nov 9: 2-0 *Johnstone 2*

1956 England	1956 Austria	1956 Wales	1956 N Ireland	1956 Yugoslavia
1 Younger	1 Younger	1 Younger	1 Younger	1 Younger
2 Parker	2 Parker	2 Parker	2 Parker	2 Parker
3 Hewie	3 Hewie	3 Hewie	3 Hewie	3 Hewie
4 Evans	4 Evans	4 McColl	4 McColl	4 McColl
5 Young	5 Young	5 Young	5 Young	5 Young
6 Glen	6 Cowie	6 Cowie	6 Cowie	6 Docherty
7 Leggat	7 McKenzie	7 Leggat	7 Scott	7 Scott
8 Johnstone	8 Conn	8 Mudie	8 Mudie	8 Mudie
9 Reilly	9 Reilly	9 Reilly	9 Reilly	9 Reilly
10 McMillan	10 Baird	10 Collins	10 Wardhaugh	10 Baird
11 Smith	11 Cullen	11 Fernie	11 Fernie	11 Fernie
Hampden April 14: 1-1 *Leggat*	Hampden May 2: 1-1 *Conn*	Cardiff Oct 20: 2-2 *Fernie, Reilly*	Hampden Nov 7: 1-0 *Scott*	Hampden Nov 21: 2-0 *Mudie, Baird*

1957 England	1957 Spain	1957 Switzerland	1957 W Germany	1957 Spain
1 Younger	1 Younger	1 Younger	1 Younger	1 Younger
2 Caldow	2 Caldow	2 Caldow	2 Caldow	2 Caldow
3 Hewie	3 Hewie	3 Hewie	3 Hewie	3 Hewie
4 McColl	4 McColl	4 McColl	4 McColl	4 Mackay
5 Young	5 Young	5 Young	5 Evans	5 Evans
6 Docherty	6 Docherty	6 Docherty	6 Docherty	6 Docherty
7 Collins	7 Smith	7 Smith	7 Scott	7 Smith
8 Fernie	8 Collins	8 Collins	8 Collins	8 Collins
9 Reilly	9 Mudie	9 Mudie	9 Mudie	9 Mudie
10 Mudie	10 Baird	10 Baird	10 Baird	10 Baird
11 Ring	11 Ring	11 Ring	11 Ring	11 Ring
Wembley April 6: 1-2 *Ring*	Hampden May 8: 4-2 *Mudie 3, Hewie* (pen)	Basle May 19: 2-1 *Mudie, Collins*	Stuttgart May 22: 3-1 *Collins 2, Mudie*	Madrid May 26: 1-4 *Smith*

1957 N Ireland	1957 Switzerland	1957 Wales	1958 England	1958 Hungary
1 Younger	1 Younger	1 Younger	1 Younger	1 Younger
2 Parker	2 Parker	2 Parker	2 Parker	2 Caldow
3 Caldow	3 Caldow	3 Caldow	3 Haddock	3 Hewie
4 McColl	4 Fernie	4 Docherty	4 McColl	4 Turnbull
5 Evans	5 Evans	5 Evans	5 Evans	5 Evans
6 Docherty	6 Docherty	6 Fernie	6 Docherty	6 Cowie
7 Leggat	7 Scott	7 Scott	7 Herd	7 Leggat
8 Collins	8 Collins	8 Collins	8 Murray	8 Murray
9 Mudie	9 Mudie	9 Gardiner	9 Mudie	9 Mudie
10 Baird	10 Robertson	10 Mudie	10 Forrest	10 Collins
11 Ring	11 Ring	11 Ewing	11 Ewing	11 Imlach
Belfast	Hampden	Hampden	Hampden	Hampden
Oct 5: 1-1	Nov 6: 3-2	Nov 13: 1-1	April 19: 0-4	May 7: 1-1
Leggat	*Robertson, Mudie, Scott*	*Collins*		*Mudie*

1958 Poland	1958 Yugoslavia †	1958 Paraguay †	1958 France †	1958 Wales
1 Younger	1 Younger	1 Younger	1 Brown	1 Brown
2 Caldow	2 Caldow	2 Parker	2 Caldow	2 Grant
3 Hewie	3 Hewie	3 Caldow	3 Hewie	3 Caldow
4 Turnbull	4 Turnbull	4 Turnbull	4 Turnbull	4 Mackay
5 Evans	5 Evans	5 Evans	5 Evans	5 Toner
6 Cowie	6 Cowie	6 Cowie	6 Mackay	6 Docherty
7 Leggat	7 Leggat	7 Leggat	7 Collins	7 Leggat
8 Murray	8 Murray	8 Collins	8 Murray	8 Collins
9 Mudie	9 Mudie	9 Mudie	9 Mudie	9 Herd
10 Collins	10 Collins	10 Robertson	10 Baird	10 Law
11 Imlach	11 Imlach	11 Fernie	11 Imlach	11 Henderson
Warsaw	Vasteraas	Norrkoping	Orebro	Cardiff
June 1: 2-1	June 8: 1-1	June 11: 2-3	June 15: 1-2	Oct 18: 3-0
Collins 2	*Murray*	*Mudie, Collins*	*Baird*	*Leggat, Law, Collins*

1958 N Ireland	1959 England	1959 W Germany	1959 Netherlands	1959 Portugal
1 Brown	1 Brown	1 Farm	1 Farm	1 Farm
2 Grant	2 McKay	2 McKay	2 McKay	2 McKay
3 Caldow	3 Caldow	3 Caldow	3 Caldow	3 Caldow
4 Mackay	4 Docherty	4 Mackay	4 Smith	4 Smith
5 Toner	5 Evans	5 Evans	5 Evans	5 Evans
6 Docherty	6 Mackay	6 McCann	6 Hewie	6 Hewie
7 Leggat	7 Leggat	7 Leggat	7 Leggat	7 Scott
8 Collins	8 Collins	8 White	8 Collins	8 Collins
9 Herd	9 Herd	9 St John	9 White	9 White
10 Law	10 Dick	10 Collins	10 Law	10 Law
11 Henderson	11 Ormond	11 Weir	11 Auld	11 Auld
Hampden	Wembley	Hampden	Amsterdam	Lisbon
Nov 5: 2-2	April 11: 0-1	May 6: 3-2	May 27: 2-1	June 3: 0-1
Herd, Collins		*White, Weir, Leggat*	*Collins, Leggat*	

1959 N Ireland	**1959 Wales**	**1960 England**	**1960 Poland**	**1960 Austria**
1 Brown	1 Brown	1 Haffey	1 Brown	1 Brown
2 Caldow	2 Caldow	2 McKay	2 McKay	2 McKay
3 Hewie	3 Mackay	3 Caldow	3 Hewie	3 Caldow
4 Mackay	4 Hewie	4 Cumming	4 Mackay	4 Mackay
5 Evans	5 Evans	5 Evans	5 Evans	5 Evans
6 McCann	6 McCann	6 McCann	6 Cumming	6 Cumming
7 Leggat	7 Leggat	7 Leggat	7 Leggat	7 Leggat
8 White	8 White	8 Young	8 White	8 White
9 St John	9 St John	9 St John	9 St John	9 St John
10 Law	10 Law	10 Law	10 Law	10 Law (Young)
11 Mulhall	11 Auld	11 Weir	11 Weir	11 Weir
Belfast Oct 3: 4-0 *Leggat, Hewie, White, Mulhall*	Hampden Nov 14: 1-1 *Leggat*	Hampden April 9: 1-1 *Leggat*	Hampden May 4: 2-3 *Law, St John*	Vienna May 29: 1-4 *Mackay*

1960 Hungary	**1960 Turkey**	**1960 Wales**	**1960 N Ireland**	**1961 England**
1 Brown	1 Brown	1 Leslie	1 Leslie	1 Haffey
2 McKay	2 McKay	2 McKay	2 McKay	2 Shearer
3 Caldow	3 Caldow	3 Caldow	3 Caldow	3 Caldow
4 Cumming	4 Mackay	4 Gabriel	4 Mackay	4 Mackay
5 Evans	5 Evans	5 Martins	5 Plenderleith	5 McNeill
6 Mackay	6 Cumming	6 Mackay	6 Baxter	6 McCann
7 Leggat	7 White	7 Herd	7 Herd	7 McLeod
8 Herd	8 Herd	8 White	8 Law	8 Law
9 Young	9 Young	9 Young	9 Young	9 St John
10 Hunter	10 Hunter	10 Hunter	10 Brand	10 Quinn
11 Weir	11 Weir	11 Wilson	11 Wilson	11 Wilson
Budapest June 5: 3-3 *Hunter, Herd, Young*	Ankara June 8: 2-4 *Caldow, Young*	Cardiff Oct 22: 0-2	Hampden Nov 9: 5-2 *Law, Caldow, Young, Brand 2*	Wembley April 15: 3-9 *Mackay, Wilson, Quinn*

1961 Rep of Ireland	**1961 Rep of Ireland**	**1961 Czechoslovakia**	**1961 Czechoslovakia**	**1961 N Ireland**
1 Leslie	1 Leslie	1 Leslie	1 Brown	1 Brown
2 Shearer	2 Shearer	2 Shearer	2 McKay	2 McKay
3 Caldow	3 Crerand	3 Caldow	3 Caldow	3 Caldow
4 Crerand	4 Caldow	4 Crerand	4 Crerand	4 Crerand
5 McNeill	5 McNeill	5 McNeill	5 McNeill	5 McNeill
6 Baxter	6 Baxter	6 Baxter	6 Baxter	6 Baxter
7 McLeod	7 McLeod	7 McLeod	7 Scott	7 Scott
8 Quinn	8 Quinn	8 McMillan	8 White	8 White
9 Herd	9 Young	9 Herd	9 St John	9 St John
10 Brand	10 Brand	10 Brand	10 Law	10 Brand
11 Wilson	11 Wilson	11 Wilson	11 Wilson	11 Wilson
Hampden May 3: 4-1 *Brand 2, Herd 2*	Dublin May 7: 3-0 *Young 2, Brand*	Bratislava May 14: 0-4	Hampden Sept 26: 3-2 *St John, Law 2*	Belfast Oct 7: 6-1 *Wilson, Scott 3 Brand 2*

1961 **Wales**	**1961** **Czechoslovakia**	**1962** **England**	**1962** **Uruguay**	**1962** **Wales**
1 Brown	1 Connachan	1 Brown	1 Connachan (Ritchie)	1 Brown
2 Hamilton	2 Hamilton	2 Hamilton	2 Hamilton	2 Hamilton
3 Caldow	3 Caldow	3 Caldow	3 Caldow	3 Caldow
4 Crerand	4 Crerand	4 Crerand	4 Crerand (McKay)	4 Crerand
5 Ure	5 Ure	5 McNeill	5 McNeill	5 Ure
6 Baxter	6 Baxter	6 Baxter	6 Baxter	6 Baxter
7 Scott	7 Brand	7 Scott	7 Scott	7 Henderson
8 White	8 White	8 White	8 Quinn	8 White
9 St John	9 St John	9 St John	9 St John	9 St John
10 Brand	10 Law	10 Law	10 Brand	10 Law
11 Wilson	11 Robertson	11 Wilson	11 Wilson	11 Wilson
Hampden Nov 8: 2-0 *St John 2*	Brussels Nov 29: 2-4 *St John 2*	Hampden April 14: 2-0 *Wilson, Caldow*	Hampden May 2: 2-3 *Baxter, Brand*	Cardiff Oct 20: 3-2 *Caldow, Law* *Henderson*

1962 **N Ireland**	**1963** **England**	**1963** **Austria**	**1963** **Norway**	**1963** **Rep of Ireland**
1 Brown	1 Brown	1 Brown	1 Blacklaw	1 Lawrence
2 Hamilton	2 Hamilton	2 Hamilton	2 Hamilton	2 Hamilton
3 Caldow	3 Caldow	3 Holt	3 Holt	3 Holt
4 Crerand	4 Mackay	4 Mackay	4 Mackay (McLintock)	4 McLintock
5 Ure	5 Ure	5 Ure	5 Ure	5 McNeill
6 Baxter	6 Baxter	6 Baxter	6 Baxter	6 Baxter
7 Henderson	7 Henderson	7 Henderson	7 Henderson	7 Henderson
8 White	8 White	8 Gibson	8 Gibson	8 Gibson
9 St John	9 St John	9 Millar	9 St John	9 Millar (St John)
10 Law	10 Law	10 Law	10 Law	10 Law
11 Mulhall	11 Wilson	11 Wilson	11 Wilson	11 Wilson
Hampden Nov 7: 5-1 *Law 4, Henderson*	Wembley April 6: 2-1 *Baxter 2*	Hampden May 8: 4-1 *Wilson 2, Law 2* (abandoned after 79 min.)	Bergen June 4: 3-4 *Law 3*	Dublin June 9: 0-1

1963 **Spain**	**1963** **N Ireland**	**1963** **Norway**	**1963** **Wales**	**1964** **England**
1 Blacklaw	1 Brown	1 Brown	1 Brown	1 Forsyth
2 McNeill	2 Hamilton	2 Hamilton	2 Hamilton	2 Hamilton
3 Holt	3 Provan	3 Provan	3 Kennedy	3 Kennedy
4 McLintock	4 Crerand	4 Mackay	4 Mackay	4 Greig
5 Ure	5 Ure	5 Ure	5 McNeill	5 McNeill
6 Baxter	6 Mackay	6 Baxter (Gabriel)	6 Baxter	6 Baxter
7 Henderson	7 Henderson	7 Scott	7 Henderson	7 Henderson
8 Gibson	8 White	8 White	8 White	8 White
9 St John	9 St John	9 Gilzean	9 Gilzean	9 Gilzean
10 Law	10 Gibson	10 Law	10 Law	10 Law
11 Wilson	11 Mulhall	11 Henderson	11 Scott	11 Wilson
Madrid June 13: 6-2 *St John, Wilson,* *Law, Henderson,* *Gibson, McLintock*	Belfast Oct 12: 1-2 *St John*	Hampden Nov 7: 6-1 *Law 4, Mackay 2*	Hampden Nov 20: 2-1 *White, Law*	Hampden April 11: 1-0 *Gilzean*

1964 W Germany	**1964 Wales**	**1964 Finland**	**1964 N Ireland**	**1965 England**
1 Cruickshank	1 Forsyth	1 Forsyth	1 Forsyth	1 Brown
2 Hamilton (Holt)	2 Hamilton	2 Hamilton	2 Hamilton	2 Hamilton
3 Kennedy	3 Kennedy	3 Kennedy	3 Kennedy	3 McCreadie
4 Greig	4 Greig	4 Greig	4 Greig	4 Crerand
5 McNeill	5 Yeats	5 McGrory	5 McGrory	5 McNeill
6 Baxter	6 Baxter	6 Baxter	6 McLintock	6 Greig
7 Henderson	7 Johnstone	7 Johnstone	7 Wallace	7 Henderson
8 White	8 Gibson	8 Gibson	8 Law	8 Collins
9 Gilzean	9 Chalmers	9 Chalmers	9 Gilzean	9 St John
10 Law	10 Law	10 Law	10 Baxter	10 Law
11 Wilson	11 Robertson	11 Scott	11 Wilson	11 Wilson
Hanover	Cardiff	Hampden	Hampden	Wembley
May 12: 2-2	Oct 3: 2-3	Oct 21: 3-1	Nov 25: 3-2	April 10: 2-2
Gilzean 2	*Chalmers, Gibson*	*Law, Chalmers, Gibson*	*Wilson 2, Gilzean*	*Law, St John*

1965 Spain	**1965 Poland**	**1965 Finland**	**1965 N Ireland**	**1965 Poland**
1 Brown	1 Brown	1 Brown	1 Brown	1 Brown
2 Hamilton	2 Hamilton	2 Hamilton	2 Hamilton	2 Hamilton
3 McCreadie	3 McCreadie	3 McCreadie	3 McCreadie	3 McCreadie
4 Bremner	4 Greig	4 Crerand	4 Mackay	4 Crerand
5 McNeill	5 McNeill	5 McNeill	5 McNeill	5 McNeill
6 Greig	6 Crerand	6 Greig	6 Greig	6 Greig
7 Henderson	7 Henderson	7 Henderson	7 Henderson	7 Henderson
8 Collins	8 Collins	8 Law	8 Law	8 Bremner
9 Law	9 Martin	9 Martin	9 Gilzean	9 Gilzean
10 Gilzean	10 Law	10 Hamilton	10 Baxter	10 Law
11 Hughes	11 Hughes	11 Wilson	11 Hughes	11 Johnston
Hampden	Chorzow	Helsinki	Belfast	Hampden
May 8: 0-0	May 23: 1-1	May 27: 2-1	Oct 2: 2-3	Oct 13: 1-2
	Law	*Wilson, Greig*	*Gilzean 2*	*McNeill*

1965 Italy	**1965 Wales**	**1965 Italy**	**1966 England**	**1966 Netherlands**
1 Brown	1 Ferguson	1 Blacklaw	1 Ferguson	1 Ferguson
2 Greig	2 Greig	2 Provan	2 Greig	2 Greig
3 Provan	3 McCreadie	3 McCreadie	3 Gemmell	3 Provan
4 Murdoch	4 Murdoch	4 Murdoch	4 Murdoch	4 Stanton
5 McKinnon	5 McKinnon	5 McKinnon	5 McKinnon	5 McKinnon
6 Baxter	6 Baxter	6 Greig	6 Baxter	6 Smith
7 Henderson	7 Henderson	7 Forrest	7 Johnstone	7 Henderson
8 Bremner	8 Cooke	8 Bremner	8 Law	8 Penman
9 Gilzean	9 Forrest	9 Yeats	9 Wallace	9 Scott
10 Martin	10 Gilzean	10 Cooke	10 Bremner	10 Wallace
11 Hughes	11 Johnston	11 Hughes	11 Johnston	11 Johnston
Hampden	Hampden	Naples	Hampden	Hampden
Nov 9: 1-0	Nov 24: 4-1	Dec 7: 0-3	April 2: 3-4	May 11: 0-3
Greig	*Murdoch 2, Henderson, Greig*		*Law, Johnston 2*	

1966 Portugal	1966 Brazil	1966 Wales	1966 N Ireland	1967 England
1 Ferguson	1 Ferguson	1 Ferguson	1 Ferguson	1 Simpson
2 Bell	2 Greig	2 Greig	2 Greig	2 Gemmell
3 McCreadie	3 Bell	3 Gemmell	3 Gemmell	3 McCreadie
4 Greig	4 Bremner	4 Bremner	4 Bremner	4 Greig
5 McGrory	5 McKinnon	5 McKinnon	5 McKinnon	5 McKinnon
6 Bremner	6 Clark	6 Clark	6 Clark	6 Bremner
7 Scott	7 Scott	7 Johnstone	7 Henderson	7 McCalliog
8 Cooke	8 Cooke	8 Law	8 Murdoch	8 Law
9 Young (Chalmers)	9 Chalmers	9 McBride	9 McBride	9 Wallace
10 Baxter	10 Baxter	10 Baxter	10 Chalmers	10 Baxter
11 Sinclair	11 Cormack	11 Henderson	11 Lennox	11 Lennox
Hampden June 18: 0-1	Hampden June 25: 1-1 *Chalmers*	Cardiff Oct 22: 1-1 *Law*	Hampden Nov 16: 2-1 *Murdoch, Lennox*	Wembley April 15: 3-2 *Law, Lennox, McCalliog*

1967 USSR	1967 N Ireland	1967 Wales	1968 England	1968 Netherlands
1 Simpson	1 Simpson	1 Clark	1 Simpson	1 Clark
2 Gemmell	2 Gemmell	2 Craig	2 Gemmell	2 Fraser
3 McCreadie	3 McCreadie	3 McCreadie	3 McCreadie	3 McCreadie
4 Clark	4 Greig	4 Greig	4 McNeill	4 Moncur
5 McNeill	5 McKinnon	5 McKinnon	5 McKinnon	5 McKinnon
6 Baxter	6 Ure	6 Baxter	6 Greig	6 Smith D.
7 Johnstone	7 Wallace	7 Johnstone	7 Cooke	7 Henderson
8 McLintock	8 Murdoch	8 Bremner	8 Bremner	8 Hope (Smith J.)
9 McCalliog	9 McCalliog	9 Gilzean	9 Hughes	9 McLean
10 Law (Wallace)	10 Law	10 Johnston	10 Johnston	10 Greig
11 Lennox	11 Morgan	11 Lennox	11 Lennox	11 Cooke
Hampden May 10: 0-2	Belfast Oct 21: 0-1	Hampden Nov 22: 3-2 *Gilzean 2, McKinnon*	Hampden Feb 24: 1-1 *Hughes*	Amsterdam May 30: 0-0

1968 Denmark	1968 Austria	1968 Cyprus	1969 W Germany	1969 Wales
1 Herriot	1 Simpson	1 Herriot	1 Lawrence	1 Lawrence (Herriot)
2 Gemmell	2 Gemmell	2 Fraser	2 Gemmell	2 Gemmell
3 McCreadie	3 McCreadie	3 McCreadie	3 McCreadie	3 McCreadie
4 Bremner	4 Bremner	4 Bremner	4 Murdoch	4 Bremner
5 McKinnon	5 McKinnon	5 McKinnon (McNeill)	5 McKinnon	5 McNeill
6 Greig	6 Greig	6 Greig	6 Greig	6 Greig
7 McLean	7 Johnstone	7 McLean	7 Johnstone	7 McLean
8 McCalliog (Cormack)	8 Cooke	8 Murdoch	8 Bremner	8 Murdoch
9 Stein	9 Hughes	9 Stein	9 Law	9 Stein
10 Hope	10 Law (Gilzean)	10 Gilzean	10 Gilzean	10 Gilzean
11 Lennox	11 Lennox	11 Cooke (Lennox)	11 Lennox (Cooke)	11 Cooke
Copenhagen Oct 16: 1-0 *Lennox*	Hampden Nov 6: 2-1 *Law, Bremner*	Nicosia Dec 11: 5-0 *Gilzean 2, Stein 2, Murdoch*	Hampden April 16: 1-1 *Murdoch*	Wrexham May 3: 5-3 *McNeill, Stein, Gilzean, Bremner, McLean*

1969 N Ireland	**1969 England**	**1969 Cyprus**	**1969 Rep of Ireland**	**1969 W Germany**
1 Herriot	1 Herriot	1 Herriot	1 McGarr (Herriot)	1 Herriot
2 McCreadie	2 McCreadie	2 McCreadie	2 Greig	2 Greig
3 Gemmell	3 Gemmell	3 Gemmell	3 Gemmell (Callaghan)	3 Gemmell
4 Bremner	4 Murdoch	4 Bremner	4 Stanton	4 Bremner
5 Greig	5 McNeill	5 McNeill	5 McKinnon	5 McKinnon
6 Stanton	6 Greig	6 Greig	6 Moncur	6 McNeill
7 Henderson	7 Henderson	7 Henderson	7 Henderson	7 Johnstone
8 Murdoch	8 Bremner	8 Cooke	8 Bremner	8 Cormack
9 Stein	9 Stein	9 Stein	9 Stein	9 Gilzean
10 Law	10 Gilzean (Wallace)	10 Gilzean	10 Cormack	10 Gray
11 Cooke (Johnston)	11 Gray	11 Gray	11 Hughes	11 Stein
Hampden May 6: 1-1 *Stein*	Wembley May 10: 1-4 *Stein*	Hampden May 12: 8-0 *Gray, McNeill, Stein 4, Henderson, Gemmell*	Dublin Sept 21: 1-1 *Stein*	Hamburg Oct 22: 2-3 *Johnstone, Gilzean*

1969 Austria	**1970 N Ireland**	**1970 Wales**	**1970 England**	**1970 Denmark**
1 McGarr	1 Clark	1 Cruickshank	1 Cruickshank	1 Cruickshank
2 Greig	2 Hay	2 Callaghan	2 Gemmell	2 Hay (Jardine)
3 Burns	3 Dickson	3 Dickson	3 Dickson	3 Greig
4 Murdoch	4 McLintock	4 Greig	4 Greig	4 Stanton
5 McKinnon	5 McKinnon	5 McKinnon	5 McKinnon	5 McKinnon
6 Stanton	6 Moncur	6 Moncur	6 Moncur (Gilzean)	6 Moncur
7 Cooke (Stein)	7 McLean	7 McLean (Lennox)	7 Johnstone	7 Johnstone
8 Bremner	8 Carr	8 Hay	8 Hay	8 Carr
9 Gilzean	9 O'Hare	9 O'Hare	9 Stein	9 Stein
10 Curran (Lorimer)	10 Gilzean (Stein)	10 Stein	10 O'Hare	10 O'Hare (Cormack)
11 Gray	11 Johnston	11 Carr	11 Carr	11 Johnston
Vienna Nov 5: 0-2	Belfast April 18: 1-0 *O'Hare*	Hampden April 22: 0-0	Hampden April 25: 0-0	Hampden Nov 11: 1-0 *O'Hare*

1971 Belgium	**1971 Portugal**	**1971 Wales**	**1971 N Ireland**	**1971 England**
1 Cruickshank	1 Clark	1 Clark	1 Clark	1 Clark
2 Hay	2 Hay	2 Hay	2 Hay	2 Greig
3 Gemmell	3 Brogan	3 Brogan	3 Brogan	3 Brogan
4 Stanton (Green)	4 Stanton (Green)	4 Bremner (Greig)	4 Greig	4 Bremner
5 McKinnon	5 McKinnon	5 McLintock	5 McLintock (Munro)	5 McLintock
6 Moncur	6 Moncur	6 Moncur	6 Moncur	6 Moncur
7 Gemmill	7 Henderson	7 Lorimer	7 Lorimer	7 Johnstone
8 Greig	8 McCalliog (Jarvie)	8 Robb	8 Green	8 Robb
9 Stein (Forrest)	9 Robb	9 O'Hare	9 O'Hare (Jarvie)	9 Curran (Munro)
10 O'Hare	10 Cormack	10 Cormack	10 Curran	10 Green (Jarvie)
11 Cooke	11 Gilzean	11 Gray	11 Gray	11 Cormack
Liège Feb 3: 0-3	Lisbon April 21: 0-2	Cardiff May 15: 0-0	Hampden May 18: 0-1	Wembley May 22: 1-3 *Curran*

1971 **Denmark**	1971 **USSR**	1971 **Portugal**	1971 **Belgium**	1971 **Netherlands**
1 Clark	1 Clark	1 Wilson	1 Clark	1 Wilson
2 Munro	2 Brownlie	2 Jardine	2 Jardine	2 Jardine
3 Dickson	3 Dickson	3 Colquhoun (Buchan)	3 Hay	3 Hay
4 Stanton	4 Munro	4 Stanton	4 Bremner	4 Bremner
5 McKinnon	5 McKinnon	5 Hay	5 Buchan	5 Colquhoun
6 Moncur	6 Stanton	6 Bremner	6 Stanton	6 Stanton
7 McLean	7 Forrest	7 Cropley	7 Johnstone (Hansen)	7 Johnstone (O'Hare)
8 Forsyth (Robb)	8 Watson	8 Graham	8 Murray	8 Gemmill
9 Stein	9 Stein (Curran)	9 Johnstone	9 O'Hare	9 Dalglish
10 Curran	10 Robb	10 O'Hare	10 Gray	10 Graham
11 Forrest (Scott)	11 Scott	11 Gemmill	11 Cropley (Dalglish)	11 Gray (Cormack)
Copenhagen June 9: 0-1	Moscow June 14: 0-1	Hampden Oct 13: 2-1 *O'Hare, Gemmill*	Aberdeen Nov 10: 1-0 *O'Hare*	Amsterdam Dec 1: 1-2 *Graham*

1972 **Peru**	1972 **N Ireland**	1972 **Wales**	1972 **England**	1972 **Yugoslavia**
1 Hunter	1 Clark	1 Clark	1 Clark	1 Hunter
2 Brownlie	2 Brownlie	2 Stanton	2 Brownlie	2 Forsyth A. (Hansen)
3 Donachie	3 Donachie	3 Buchan	3 Donachie (Green)	3 Buchan
4 Carr	4 Bremner	4 Bremner	4 Bremner	4 Colquhoun
5 Colquhoun	5 McNeill	5 McNeill	5 McNeill	5 Donachie
6 Moncur	6 Moncur	6 Moncur	6 Moncur	6 Bremner
7 Morgan	7 Johnstone (Lorimer)	7 Lorimer	7 Gemmill (Johnstone)	7 Hartford
8 Hartford	8 Gemmill	8 Green	8 Hartford	8 Graham
9 O'Hare	9 O'Hare	9 O'Hare (Macari)	9 Lorimer	9 Morgan
10 Law	10 Law	10 Law	10 Macari	10 Law (Bone)
11 Gemmill	11 Graham	11 Gemmill (Hartford)	11 Law	11 Macari
Hampden April 26:2-0 *O'Hare, Law*	Hampden May 20: 2-0 *Law, Lorimer*	Hampden May 24: 1-0 *Lorimer*	Hampden May 27: 0-1	Belo Horizonte June 29: 2-2 *Macari 2*

1972 **Czechoslovakia**	1972 **Brazil**	1972 **Denmark**	1972 **Denmark**	1973 **England**
1 Clark	1 Clark	1 Clark	1 Harvey	1 Clark
2 Forsyth A.	2 Forsyth A.	2 Brownlie	2 Brownlie	2 Forsyth A.
3 Colquhoun	3 Colquhoun	3 Forsyth A.	3 Donachie	3 Donachie
4 Buchan	4 Buchan	4 Bremner	4 Bremner	4 Bremner
5 Donachie	5 Donachie	5 Colquhoun	5 Colquhoun	5 Colquhoun
6 Bremner	6 Bremner	6 Buchan	6 Buchan	6 Buchan
7 Graham	7 Graham	7 Lorimer	7 Lorimer	7 Lorimer
8 Law (Stein)	8 Hartford	8 Macari) (Dalglish)	8 Dalglish (Carr)	8 Dalglish
9 Hartford	9 Morgan	9 Bone (Harper)	9 Harper	9 Macari
10 Morgan	10 Law	10 Graham	10 Graham	10 Graham
11 Macari	11 Macari	11 Morgan	11 Morgan	11 Morgan (Stein)
Porto Alegre July 2: 0-0	Rio de Janeiro July 5: 0-1	Copenhagen Oct 18: 4-1 *Macari, Bone, Harper, Morgan*	Glasgow Nov 15: 2-0 *Dalglish, Lorimer*	Glasgow Feb 14: 0-5

1973 Wales	**1973 N Ireland**	**1973 England**	**1973 Switzerland**	**1973 Brazil**
1 McCloy	1 McCloy	1 Hunter	1 McCloy	1 McCloy
2 McGrain	2 McGrain	2 Jardine	2 Jardine	2 Jardine
3 Donachie	3 Donachie	3 McGrain	3 McGrain	3 McGrain
4 Graham	4 Graham (Macari)	4 Bremner	4 Bremner	4 Bremner
5 Holton	5 Holton	5 Holton	5 Holton	5 Holton
6 Johnstone D.	6 Johnstone D.	6 Johnstone D.	6 Johnstone D.	6 Johnstone D.
7 Dalglish (Macari)	7 Dalglish	7 Morgan	7 Dalglish	7 Morgan
8 Stanton	8 Stanton (Bremner)	8 Macari (Jordan)	8 Hay	8 Hay
9 Parlane (Stein)	9 Stein	9 Dalglish	9 Parlane	9 Parlane
10 Hay	10 Hay	10 Hay	10 Connolly (Jordan)	10 Jordan
11 Morgan	11 Morgan	11 Lorimer (Stein)	11 Morgan	11 Dalglish (Graham)
Wrexham May 12: 2-0 *Graham 2*	Glasgow May 16: 1-2 *Dalglish*	Wembley May 19: 0-1	Berne June 22: 0-1	Glasgow June 30: 0-1

1973 Czechoslovakia	**1973 Czechoslovakia**	**1973 W Germany**	**1974 W Germany**	**1974 N Ireland**
1 Hunter	1 Harvey	1 Harvey	1 Allan	1 Harvey
2 Jardine	2 Jardine	2 Jardine	2 Jardine	2 Jardine
3 McGrain	3 McGrain	3 McGrain	3 Schaedler	3 Donachie (Smith)
4 Bremner	4 Forsyth T.	4 Bremner	4 Hay	4 Bremner
5 Holton	5 Blackley	5 Holton	5 Buchan	5 Holton
6 Connelly	6 Hay	6 Connelly	6 Stanton	6 Buchan
7 Hay	7 Morgan	7 Morgan	7 Morgan	7 Morgan
8 Law	8 Jordan	8 Smith (Lorimer)	8 Dalglish	8 Hay
9 Morgan	9 Law (Ford)	9 Law (Jordan)	9 Law (Ford)	9 Law (Jordan)
10 Dalglish (Jordan)	10 Dalglish	10 Dalglish	10 Hutchison	10 Dalglish
11 Hutchison	11 Hutchison	11 Hutchison	11 Burns (Robinson)	11 Hutchison
Hampden Sept 26: 2-1 *Holton, Jordan*	Bratislava Oct 17: 0-1	Hampden Nov 14: 1-1 *Holton*	Frankfurt March 27: 1-2 *Dalglish*	Hampden May 11: 0-1

1974 Wales	**1974 England**	**1974 Belgium**	**1974 Norway**	**1974 Zaire †**
1 Harvey	1 Harvey	1 Harvey	1 Allan	1 Harvey
2 Jardine	2 Jardine	2 Jardine	2 Jardine	2 Jardine
3 Hay	3 McGrain	3 McGrain	3 McGrain	3 McGrain
4 Bremner	4 Bremner	4 Bremner	4 Bremner	4 Bremner
5 Holton	5 Holton	5 McQueen	5 Holton	5 Holton
6 Buchan (McGrain)	6 Blackley	6 Blackley	6 Buchan	6 Blackley
7 Johnstone J.	7 Lorimer	7 Johnstone J. (Morgan)	7 Johnstone J. (Dalglish)	7 Dalglish (Hutchison)
8 Dalglish	8 Johnstone J.	8 Dalglish (Hutchison)	8 Lorimer	8 Hay
9 Ford	9 Jordan	9 Jordan	9 Jordan	9 Lorimer
10 Jordan	10 Dalglish	10 Hay	10 Hay	10 Jordan
11 Hutchison (Smith)	11 Hay	11 Lorimer	11 Hutchison	11 Law
Hampden May 14: 2-0 *Dalglish, Jardine*	Hampden May 18: 2-0 *Jordan, Todd og*	Bruges June 1: 1-2 *Johnstone*	Oslo June 6: 2-1 *Jordan, Dalglish*	Dortmund June 14: 2-0 *Lorimer, Jordan*

1974 Brazil †	**1974 Yugoslavia †**	**1974 E Germany**	**1974 Spain**	**1975 Spain**
1 Harvey	1 Harvey	1 Harvey	1 Harvey	1 Harvey
2 Jardine	2 Jardine	2 Jardine	2 Jardine	2 Jardine
3 McGrain	3 McGrain	3 Forsyth A.	3 Forsyth A.	3 McQueen
4 Holton	4 Holton	4 Souness	4 McQueen	4 Buchan
5 Buchan	5 Buchan	5 Holton (Burns)	5 Burns	5 McGrain
6 Bremner	6 Bremner	6 Buchan	6 Bremner	6 Bremner
7 Hay	7 Dalglish (Hutchison)	7 Johnstone J.	7 Souness	7 Cooke
8 Dalglish	8 Hay	8 Dalglish (Johnstone D.)	8 Hutchison (Dalglish)	8 Hutchison
9 Morgan	9 Morgan	9 Deans	9 Johnstone J.	9 Dalglish
10 Jordan	10 Jordan	10 Jordan	10 Deans (Lorimer)	10 Jordan (Parlane)
11 Lorimer	11 Lorimer	11 Hutchison	11 Jordan	11 Burns (Wilson)
Frankfurt June 18: 0-0	Frankfurt June 22: 1-1 *Jordan*	Hampden Oct 30: 3-0 *Hutchison* (pen), *Burns, Dalglish*	Hampden Nov 20: 1-2 *Bremner*	Valencia Feb 5: 1-1 *Jordan*

1975 Sweden	**1975 Portugal**	**1975 Wales**	**1975 N Ireland**	**1975 England**
1 Kennedy	1 Kennedy	1 Kennedy	1 Kennedy	1 Kennedy
2 Jardine	2 Jardine	2 Jardine	2 Jardine (Forsyth A.)	2 Jardine
3 McGrain	3 McGrain	3 McGrain	3 McGrain	3 McGrain
4 Munro	4 Buchan (Jackson)	4 Jackson (Munro)	4 Munro	4 Munro
5 Jackson	5 McQueen	5 McQueen	5 McQueen	5 McQueen
6 Robinson	6 Rioch	6 Rioch	6 Rioch	6 Rioch
7 Dalglish	7 Cooke (Macari)	7 Macari	7 Dalglish	7 Dalglish
8 Souness (Johnstone D.)	8 Dalglish	8 Dalglish	8 Robinson (Conn)	8 Conn
9 Parlane	9 Parlane	9 Parlane	9 Parlane	9 Parlane
10 MacDougall	10 MacDougall	10 MacDougall	10 MacDougall	10 MacDougall (Macari)
11 Macari (Hughes)	11 Hutchison (Duncan)	11 Duncan	11 Duncan	11 Duncan (Hutchison)
Gothenburg April 16: 1-1 *MacDougall*	Hampden May 13: 1-0 *Artur og*	Cardiff May 17: 2-2 *Jackson, Rioch*	Hampden May 20: 3-0 *MacDougall, Dalglish, Parlane*	Wembley May 24: 1-5 *Rioch* (pen)

1975 Rumania	**1975 Denmark**	**1975 Denmark**	**1975 Rumania**	**1976 Switzerland**
1 Brown	1 Harvey	1 Harvey	1 Cruickshank	1 Rough
2 McGrain	2 McGrain	2 McGrain	2 Brownlie	2 McGrain
3 Forsyth A.	3 Forsyth A.	3 Houston	3 Donachie	3 Gray F.
4 Munro	4 Bremner	4 Greig	4 Buchan	4 Forsyth T.
5 McQueen	5 McQueen	5 Jackson	5 Jackson	5 Blackley
6 Rioch (Hutchison)	6 Buchan	6 Rioch	6 Rioch	6 Craig
7 Dalglish	7 Lorimer	7 Lorimer	7 Doyle (Lorimer)	7 Dalglish (Bremner D.)
8 Miller	8 Dalglish	8 Dalglish	8 Hartford	8 Pettigrew (McKean)
9 Parlane	9 Harper	9 MacDougall (Parlane)	9 Gray A.	9 Gray A.
10 Macari (Robinson)	10 Rioch	10 Hartford	10 Dalglish (MacDougall)	10 MacDonald
11 Duncan	11 Hutchison (Duncan)	11 Gemmill	11 Gemmill	11 Johnstone D.
Bucharest June 1: 1-1 *McQueen*	Copenhagen Sept 3: 1-0 *Harper*	Glasgow Oct 29: 3-1 *Dalglish, Rioch, MacDougall*	Glasgow Dec 17: 1-1 *Rioch*	Glasgow April 7: 1-0 *Pettigrew*

	1976 **Wales**	**1976** **N Ireland**	**1976** **England**	**1976** **Finland**	**1976** **Czechoslovakia**
1	Rough	Rough	Rough	Rough (Harvey)	Rough
2	McGrain	McGrain	McGrain	McGrain	McGrain
3	Donachie	Donachie	Donachie	Donachie	Donachie
4	Forsyth T.	Forsyth T.	Forsyth T.	Rioch	Buchan
5	Jackson	Jackson	Jackson	Forsyth T.	McQueen
6	Rioch	Rioch (Hartford)	Rioch	Buchan	Rioch
7	Pettigrew	Masson	Masson	Dalglish	Dalglish (Burns)
8	Masson	Gemmill	Gemmill	Gemmill	Masson (Hartford)
9	Jordan	Pettigrew (Johnstone D.)	Dalglish	Gray A.	Jordan
10	Gemmill	Jordan	Jordan	Masson	Gray A.
11	Gray E.	Dalglish	Grey E. (Johnstone D.)	Gray E.	Gemmill
	Glasgow May 6: 3-1 *Pettigrew, Rioch, Gray*	Glasgow May 8: 3-0 *Gemmill, Masson, Dalglish*	Glasgow May 15: 2-1 *Masson, Dalglish*	Glasgow Sept 8: 6-0 *Rioch, Masson* (pen), *Dalglish, Gray A. 2, Gray E.*	Prague Oct 13: 0-2

	1976 **Wales**	**1977** **Sweden**	**1977** **Wales**	**1977** **N Ireland**	**1977** **England**
1	Rough	Rough	Rough	Rough	Rough
2	McGrain	McGrain	McGrain	McGrain	McGrain
3	Donachie	Forsyth T.	Donachie	Donachie	Donachie
4	Blackley	Blackley (Narey)	Rioch (Johnston)	Forsyth T.	Forsyth T.
5	McQueen	Donachie	McQueen	McQueen	McQueen
6	Rioch (Hartford)	Glavin (Jardine)	Forsyth T.	Rioch	Rioch
7	Burns	Dalglish	Masson	Masson	Masson (Gemmill)
8	Dalglish	Hartford	Gemmill	Hartford	Dalglish
9	Jordan	Burns (Craig J.)	Parlane (Burns)	Jordan (Macari)	Jordan (Macari)
10	Gemmill	Pettigrew	Dalglish	Dalglish	Hartford
11	Gray E. (Pettigrew)	Johnston	Hartford	Johnston (Gemmill)	Johnston
	Glasgow Nov 17: 1-0 *Evans og*	Glasgow April 27: 3-1 *Hartford, Dalglish, Craig*	Wrexham May 28: 0-0	Glasgow June 1: 3-0 *Dalglish 2, McQueen*	Wembley June 4: 2-0 *McQueen, Dalglish*

	1977 **Chile**	**1977** **Argentina**	**1977** **Brazil**	**1977** **E Germany**	**1977** **Czechoslovakia**
1	Rough (Stewart)	Rough	Rough	Stewart	Rough
2	McGrain	McGrain	McGrain	McGrain	Jardine
3	Donachie	Donachie	Donachie	Donachie	McGrain
4	Buchan	Gemmill	Rioch	Masson	Forsyth T.
5	Forsyth T.	Forsyth T.	Forsyth T.	McQueen	McQueen
6	Rioch (Gemmill)	Buchan	Buchan	Buchan	Rioch
7	Masson	Masson	Masson	Dalglish	Dalglish
8	Dalglish	Dalglish	Gemmill	Hartford (Gemmill)	Masson
9	Macari	Macari	Dalglish	Jordan	Jordan
10	Hartford (Jardine)	Hartford	Hartford	Macari	Hartford
11	Johnston	Johnston	Johnston (Jardine)	Johnston (Graham)	Johnston
	Santiago June 15: 4-2 *Dalglish, Macari 2, Hartford*	Buenos Aires June 18: 1-1 *Masson* (pen)	Rio de Janeiro June 23: 0-2	East Berlin Sept 7: 0-1	Glasgow Sept 21: 3-1 *Jordan, Hartford, Dalglish*

	1977 **Wales**	1978 **Bulgaria**	1978 **N Ireland**	1978 **Wales**	1978 **England**
1	Rough	Blyth	Rough	Blyth	Rough
2	Jardine (Buchan)	Kennedy	Jardine	Kennedy	Kennedy
3	Donachie	Donachie	Buchan (Burns)	Donachie	Burns
4	Masson	Souness	Forsyth T.	Burns	Forsyth T.
5	McQueen	McQueen	McQueen	McQueen (Forsyth T.)	Donachie
6	Forsyth T.	Miller	Rioch	Gemmill	Rioch (Souness)
7	Dalglish	Dalglish (Wallace)	Masson	Souness	Masson (Gemmill)
8	Hartford	Hartford	Gemmill	Hartford	Hartford
9	Jordan	Jordan (Johnstone D.)	Jordan (Dalglish)	Johnstone D.	Dalglish
10	Macari	Macari	Johnstone D.	Dalglish	Jordan
11	Johnston	Gemmill	Robertson	Johnston (Robertson)	Johnston
	Liverpool Oct 12: 2-0 *Masson* (pen), *Dalglish*	Glasgow Feb 22: 2-1 *Gemmill* (pen), *Wallace*	Glasgow May 13: 1-1 *Johnstone*	Glasgow May 17: 1-1 *Johnstone*	Glasgow May 20: 0-1

	1978 **Peru †**	1978 **Iran †**	1978 **Netherlands †**	1978 **Austria**	1978 **Norway**
1	Rough	Rough	Rough	Rough	Stewart
2	Burns	Buchan (Forsyth T.)	Donachie	Kennedy	Donachie
3	Kennedy	Jardine	Buchan	Donachie	Gray F.
4	Forsyth T.	Burns	Kennedy	Gemmill	Souness
5	Buchan	Donachie	Forsyth T.	McQueen	McQueen
6	Rioch (Macari)	Macari	Rioch	Buchan	Buchan
7	Masson (Gemmill)	Gemmill	Hartford	Dalglish	Dalglish
8	Hartford	Hartford	Gemmill	Hartford	Gemmill
9	Dalglish	Jordan	Souness	Jordan (Graham)	Gray A.
10	Jordan	Dalglish (Harper)	Dalglish	Gray A.	Hartford
11	Johnston	Robertson	Jordan	Souness	Graham
	Cordoba June 3: 1-3 *Jordan*	Cordoba June 7: 1-1 *Eskandarian og*	Mendoza June 11: 3-2 *Dalglish,* *Gemmill 2* (1 pen)	Vienna Sept 20: 2-3 *McQueen,* *Gray*	Glasgow Oct 25: 3-2 *Dalglish 2,* *Gemmill* (pen)

	1978 **Portugal**	1979 **Wales**	1979 **N Ireland**	1979 **England**	1979 **Argentina**
1	Rough	Rough	Wood	Wood	Rough (Wood)
2	Kennedy	Burley	Burley	Burley	Burley
3	Gray F. (Donachie)	Gray F.	Gray F.	Gray F.	Munro
4	Narey	Wark	Wark (Narey)	Wark	Narey
5	McQueen	Hegarty	McQueen	McQueen	Hegarty
6	Buchan	Hansen	Souness	Hegarty	Hansen
7	Dalglish	Dalglish	Dalglish	Dalglish	McGarvey
8	Hartford	Hartford	Hartford	Souness	Wark
9	Jordan (Wallace)	Wallace (Jordan)	Jordan	Jordan	Dalglish
10	Gemmill	Souness	Hegarty	Hartford	Hartford (Gray F.)
11	Robertson	Graham	Graham (McGarvey)	Graham	Graham
	Lisbon Nov 29: 0-1	Cardiff May 19: 0-3	Glasgow May 22: 1-0 *Graham*	Wembley May 26: 1-3 *Wark*	Glasgow June 2: 1-3 *Graham*

	1979 Norway	**1979 Peru**	**1979 Austria**	**1979 Belgium**	**1979 Belgium**
1	Rough	Rough	Rough	Rough	Rough
2	Burley (Hegarty) (Wark)	Jardine	Jardine	Jardine	Jardine
3	Munro	Munro	Munro	Munro (Gray F.)	McGrain
4	Burns	Souness	Souness	Wark	Wark
5	McQueen	McQueen	McQueen	Hansen	McQueen
6	Gemmill	Burns	Burns	Miller	Burns
7	Graham	Cooper (Wark)	Wark	Dalglish	Dalglish
8	Dalglish	Aitken	Gemmill	Souness	Aitken
9	Jordan	Dalglish	Dalglish	Jordan (Provan)	Johnstone D.
10	Hartford	Hartford	Graham (Cooper)	Hartford	Bannon (Provan)
11	Robertson	Robertson	Robertson	Robertson	Robertson
	Oslo June 7: 4-0 *Jordan, Dalglish, Robertson, McQueen*	Hampden Sept 12: 1-1 *Olaechea og*	Hampden Oct 17: 1-1 *Gemmill*	Brussels Nov 21: 0-2	Hampden Dec 19: 1-3 *Robertson*

	1980 Portugal	**1980 N Ireland**	**1980 Wales**	**1980 England**	**1980 Poland**
1	Rough	Thomson	Rough	Rough	Rough
2	Burley	Burley	McGrain	McGrain	Burley (Dawson)
3	McGrain	McGrain	Munro	Munro (Burley)	McGrain
4	Narey	Narey	Hegarty	Hegarty	Narey
5	McLeish	McLeish	McLeish	McLeish	McLeish
6	Hansen	Souness (Jordan)	Miller	Miller	Miller
7	Dalglish (Archibald)	Strachan	Strachan	Strachan	Strachan
8	Souness	Archibald	Gemmill	Aitken (Gray A.)	Aitken
9	Gray A.	Dalglish	Dalglish	Dalglish	Dalglish (Weir)
10	Gemmill	Gemmill	Jordan	Jordan	Archibald
11	Robertson (Provan)	Weir (Provan)	Weir (Aitken)	Gemmill	Jordan (Brazil)
	Hampden March 26: 4-1 *Dalglish, Gray, Archibald, Gemmill* (pen)	Belfast May 16: 0-1	Hampden May 21: 1-0 *Miller*	Hampden May 24: 0-2	Poznam May 28: 0-1

	1980 Hungary
1	Rough
2	McGrain
3	Dawson
4	Narey
5	McLeish
6	Miller
7	Brazil (Strachan)
8	Archibald
9	Dalglish
10	Gemmill
11	Weir
	Budapest May 31: 1-3 *Archibald*

WALES INTERNATIONAL TEAMS 1876-1980

Substitutes in brackets †World Cup final stages

1876 **Scotland**	**1877** **Scotland**	**1878** **Scotland**	**1879** **England**	**1879** **Scotland**
1 Thompson	1 Burnett	1 Phennah	1 Glascodine	1 Davies, John
2 Evans W.A.W.	2 Evans W.A.W.	2 Higham	2 Kenrick	2 Kenrick
3 Kenrick	3 Kenrick	3 Powell	3 Higham	3 Morgan J.R.
4 Cross	4 Morgan J.R.	4 Edwards H.	4 Williams W.	4 Cross
5 Williams W.	5 Cross	5 Williams W.	5 Owen T.	5 Williams W.
6 Dr Gray	6 Davies W.H.	6 Savin	6 Davies W.H.	6 Lloyd J.W.
7 Davies W.H.	7 Davies A.	7 Davies, James	7 Shone	7 Woosnam
8 Thomson	8 Price	8 Dr Gray	8 Heywood	8 Hughes A.J.
9 Edwards J.H.	9 Jones A.F.	9 Britten	9 Price	9 Roberts J.
10 Jones J.	10 Hughes J.	10 Price	10 Owen D.	10 Roberts W.
11 Davies A.	11 Thomson	11 Edwards C.	11 Roberts W.	11 Vaughan
Glasgow Mar 25: 0-4	Wrexham Mar 5: 0-2	Glasgow Mar 23: 0-9	London Jan 18: 1-2 *Davies*	Wrexham April 7: 0-3

1880 **England**	**1880** **Scotland**	**1881** **England**	**1881** **Scotland**	**1882** **Ireland**
1 Hibbott	1 Hibbott	1 McMillan	1 McMillan	1 Adams
2 Morgan J.R.	2 Morgan J.R.	2 Morgan J.R.	2 Morgan J.R.	2 Morgan J.R.
3 Powell	3 Powell	3 Kenrick	3 Roberts J. (*Ruthin*)	3 Powell
4 Edwards H.	4 Bowen	4 Williams W.	4 Williams W.	4 Hughes F.W.
5 Williams W.	5 Williams W.	5 Bell	5 Bell	5 Williams W.
6 Owen W.P.	6 Owen W.P.	6 Owen W.P.	6 Owen W.P.	6 Owen W.P.
7 Davies W.H.	7 Roberts W.	7 Lewis T.	7 Lewis T.	7 Shaw
8 Boden	8 Roberts J.	8 Cross	8 Price	8 Ketley
9 Price	9 Price	9 Price	9 Cross	9 Price
10 Roberts J.	10 Britten	10 Goodwin	10 Roberts W.	10 Roberts J.
11 Roberts W.	11 Vaughan	11 Vaughan	11 Vaughan	11 Vaughan
Wrexham Mar 15: 2-3 *Roberts J., Roberts W.*	Glasgow Mar 27: 1-5 *Roberts W.*	Blackburn Feb 26: 1-0 *Vaughan*	Wrexham Mar 14: 1-5 *Cross*	Wrexham Feb 25: 7-1 *Price 4, Morgan, Owen 2*

1882 **England**	**1882** **Scotland**	**1883** **England**	**1883** **Scotland**	**1883** **Ireland**
1 Adams	1 Phoenix	1 Adams	1 Gough	1 Adams
2 Morgan J.R.	2 Morgan J.R.	2 Powell	2 Powell	2 Powell
3 Powell	3 Powell	3 Morgan J.R.	3 Hughes F.W.	3 Hughes F.W.
4 Edwards H.	4 Edwards H.	4 Hughes F.W.	4 Bowen	4 Jones J.
5 Hughes F.W.	5 Williams W.	5 Burke	5 Jones J.	5 Williams W.
6 Williams W.	6 Roberts J. (*Ruthin*)	6 Roberts W.H.	6 Edwards H.	6 Eyton-Jones
7 Owen W.P.	7 Owen W.P.	7 Owen W.P.	7 Price	7 Price
8 Roberts W.H.	8 Roberts W.H.	8 Davies J.P.	8 Owen W.P.	8 Vaughan
9 Price	9 Price	9 Roberts W.	9 Roberts W.H.	9 Roberts W.H.
10 Roberts J.	10 Roberts J.	10 Roberts J.	10 Vaughan	10 Davies J.P.
11 Vaughan	11 Vaughan	11 Vaughan	11 Roberts W.	11 Davies R.
Wrexham Mar 13: 5-3 *Owen 2, Morgan, Vaughan, 1 og*	Glasgow Mar 25: 0-5	London Feb 3: 0-5	Wrexham Mar 12: 0-3	Belfast Mar 17: 1-1 *Roberts*

1884 Ireland	**1884 England**	**1884 Scotland**	**1885 England**	**1885 Scotland**
1 Owen E.	1 Owen E.	1 Owen E.	1 Mills-Roberts	1 Mills-Roberts
2 Conde	2 Powell	2 Roberts R.	2 Jones F.R.	2 Powell
3 Davies W.	3 Conde	3 Conde	3 Thomas G.	3 Thomas G.
4 Foulkes	4 Evans M.	4 Hughes F.W.	4 Davies R.	4 Burke
5 Griffiths	5 Williams J.H.	5 Burke	5 Jones H.	5 Jones H.
6 Edwards H.	6 Griffiths	6 Jones J.	6 Davies J.E.	6 Foulkes
7 Owen W.P.	7 Owen W.P.	7 Owen W.P.	7 Vaughan	7 Hibbott
8 Davies R.	8 Owen W.	8 Roberts W.H.	8 Farmer	8 Farmer
9 Shaw	9 Vaughan	9 Shaw	9 Lewis W.	9 Lloyd
10 Eyton-Jones	10 Eyton-Jones	10 Eyton-Jones	10 Burke	10 Jones R.A.
11 Jones R.A.	11 Jones R.A.	11 Jones R.A.	11 Wilding	11 Wilding
Wrexham	Wrexham	Glasgow	Blackburn	Wrexham
Feb 9: 6-0	Mar 17: 0-4	Mar 29: 1-4	Mar 14: 1-1	Mar 23: 1-8
Shaw 2, Owen W.P. 2, Jones, Eyton-Jones		*Roberts R.*	*Wilding*	*Jones R.A.*

1885 Ireland	**1886 Ireland**	**1886 England**	**1886 Scotland**	**1887 England**
1 Mills-Roberts	1 Hersee M.	1 Mills-Roberts	1 Hersee M.	1 Mills-Roberts
2 Jones F.R.	2 Roberts R. (*Wrexham*)	2 Davies A.O.	2 Davies A.O.	2 Davies A.O.
3 Davies A.O.	3 Powell	3 Powell	3 Jones F.R.	3 Powell
4 Burke	4 Vaughan	4 Vaughan	4 Vaughan	4 Jones H.
5 Vaughan	5 Bell	5 Bell	5 Bell	5 Burke
6 Jones H.	6 Jones H.	6 Jones H.	6 Jones H.	6 Evelyn
7 Davies R.	7 Wilding	7 Wilding	7 Williams R.P.	7 Challen
8 Owen W.	8 Roberts W.	8 Roberts W.	8 Roberts W.	8 Owen W.
9 Wilding	9 Sisson	9 Davies T.	9 Sisson	9 Wilding
10 Sisson	10 Bryan	10 Bryan	10 Lewis W.	10 Turner W.H.
11 Roach	11 Hersee R.	11 Lewis W.	11 Doughty J.	11 Lewis W.
Belfast	Wrexham	Wrexham	Glasgow	London
April 11: 8-2	Feb 27: 5-0	Mar 29: 1-3	April 10: 1-4	Feb 26: 0-4
Owen, Burke, Sisson 3, Roach 2, Jones H.	*Roberts, W., Wilding, Hersee R., Sisson, Bryan*	*Lewis*	*Lundie og*	

1887 Ireland	**1887 Scotland**	**1888 England**	**1888 Ireland**	**1888 Scotland**
1 Roberts R. (*Wrexham*)	1 Trainer	1 Mills-Roberts	1 Mills-Roberts	1 Trainer
2 Townsend	2 Davies A.O.	2 Davies A.O.	2 Davies A.O.	2 Jones D.
3 Jones S.	3 Powell	3 Roberts R.	3 Powell	3 Powell
4 Hughes P.W.	4 Morris	4 Powell	4 Jones D.	4 Burke
5 Hunter	5 Burke	5 Griffiths	5 Humphreys	5 Davies J. (*N Heath*)
6 Edwards H.	6 Roberts R.	6 Davies J. (*N Heath*)	6 Davies J. (*N Heath*)	6 Roberts R.
7 Sabine	7 Challen	7 Challen	7 Doughty J.	7 Doughty J.
8 Doughty J.	8 Doughty J.	8 Doughty J.	8 Howell	8 Doughty R.
9 Turner W.H.	9 Lewis W.	9 Lewis W.	9 Pryce-Jones	9 Pryce-Jones
10 Roberts W.	10 Pryce-Jones	10 Pryce-Jones	10 Doughty R.	10 Owen G.
11 Griffiths	11 Jones R.	11 Owen W.	11 Wilding	11 Wilding
Belfast	Wrexham	Crewe	Wrexham	Edinburgh
Mar 12: 1-4	Mar 21: 0-2	Feb 4: 1-5	Mar 3: 11-0	Mar 10: 1-5
Sabine		*Doughty J.*	*Wilding 2, Doughty J. 4, Howell 2, Doughty R. 2, Pryce-Jones*	*Doughty J.*

1889 **England**	**1889** **Scotland**	**1889** **Ireland**	**1890** **Ireland**	**1890** **England**
1 Trainer	1 Gillam (Pugh)	1 Gillam	1 Gillam	1 Gillam
2 Jones W.P.	2 Davies A.O.	2 Jones W.P.	2 Jones D.	2 Davies A.O.
3 Jones D.	3 Jones D.	3 Jones D.	3 Jones W.P.	3 Jones D.
4 Hughes P.W.	4 Roberts R.	4 Hughes P.W.	4 Griffiths	4 Davies J. (*N Heath*)
5 Jones H.	5 Davies J. (*N Heath*)	5 Carty	5 Hayes	5 Jones H.
6 Roberts R.	6 Jones H.	6 Leary	6 Jones H.	6 Evans W.G.
7 Hallam	7 Davies Jos	7 Davies Jos	7 Bowdler J.C.H.	7 Challen
8 Jones R.	8 Owen W.	8 Owen W.	8 Willcocks	8 Jones R.
9 Lewis W.	9 Doughty J.	9 Owen G.	9 Pryce-Jones	9 Doughty R.
10 Lea	10 Owen G.	10 Jarrett	10 Owen W.	10 Howell
11 Owen W.	11 Lewis W.	11 Lewis W.	11 Lewis W.	11 Lewis W.
Stoke Feb 23: 1-4 *Owen*	Wrexham April 15: 0-0	Belfast April 27: 3-1 *Jarrett 3*	Shrewsbury Feb 8: 5-2 *Lewis 2,* *Pryce-Jones 2, Owen*	Wrexham Mar 15: 1-3 *Lewis*

1890 **Scotland**	**1891** **Ireland**	**1891** **England**	**1891** **Scotland**	**1892** **Ireland**
1 Trainer	1 Turner R.E.	1 Turner R.E.	1 Trainer	1 Trainer
2 Jones W.P.	2 Roberts R. (*Wrexham*)	2 Evans W.G.	2 Powell	2 Arridge
3 Jones S.	3 Lloyd	3 Powell	3 Jones D.	3 Jones D.
4 Griffiths	4 Griffiths	4 Hughes W.	4 Lea	4 Hughes W.
5 Jones H.	5 Mates	5 Jones H.	5 Jones H.	5 Jenkyns
6 Roberts R.	6 Lea	6 Parry	6 Parry	6 Roberts R.
7 Lewis W.	7 Davies Jos	7 Davies Jos	7 Davies Jos	7 Davies R.O.
8 Davies O.	8 Owen W.	8 Owen W.	8 Owen W.	8 Bostock
9 Owen W.	9 Davies A.	9 Turner W.H.	9 Turner W.H.	9 Lewis B.
10 Jarrett	10 Roberts R. (*Rhos*)	10 Howell	10 Bowdler J.C.H.	10 Bowdler J.C.H.
11 Turner W.H.	11 Lewis W.	11 Lewis W.	11 Lewis W.	11 Lewis W.
Glasgow Mar 22: 0-5	Belfast Feb 7: 2-7 *Lewis 2*	Sunderland Mar 7: 1-4 *Howell*	Wrexham Mar 21: 3-4 *Bowdler 2, Owen*	Bangor Feb 27: 1-1 *Lewis B.*

1892 **England**	**1892** **Scotland**	**1893** **England**	**1893** **Scotland**	**1893** **Ireland**
1 Mills-Roberts	1 Trainer	1 Trainer	1 Jones S.	1 Jones S.
2 Evans	2 Arridge	2 Jones D.	2 Taylor	2 Townsend
3 Powell	3 Powell	3 Parry	3 Jones F.W.	3 Taylor
4 Davies J. (*Wolves*)	4 Hughes W.	4 Williams E.	4 Williams G.	4 Lea
5 Jenkyns	5 Jenkyns	5 Davies J. (*Wolves*)	5 Williams E.	5 Evans J.
6 Owen G.	6 Roberts R.	6 Morris E.	6 Morris E.	6 Morris E.
7 Owen W.	7 Wilding	7 Butler	7 Vaughan	7 Vaughan
8 Turner J.	8 Owen W.	8 Vaughan	8 Butler	8 Owen W.
9 Lewis B.	9 Lewis B.	9 James	9 Owen W.	9 Butler
10 Davies R.O.	10 Egan	10 Lewis B.	10 Lewis B.	10 Owen G.
11 Lewis W.	11 Lewis W.	11 Roberts R. (*Crewe Alex*)	11 Bowdler H.E.	11 James
Wrexham Mar 5: 0-2	Edinburgh Mar 26: 1-6 *Lewis B.*	Stoke Mar 13: 0-6	Wrexham Mar 18: 0-8	Belfast April 5: 3-4 *Owen G. 2,* *Stewart og*

1894 Ireland	1894 England	1894 Scotland	1895 Ireland	1895 England
1 Trainer	1 Trainer	1 Gillam	1 Trainer J.	1 Trainer J.
2 Arridge	2 Parry	2 Taylor	2 Arridge	2 Parry
3 Taylor	3 Jones D.	3 Hughes A.	3 Edwards	3 Jones D.
4 Jones R.S.	4 Evans J.	4 Williams G.	4 Williams G.	4 Williams G.
5 Chapman	5 Chapman	5 Chapman	5 Chapman	5 Jenkyns
6 Hayes	6 Hughes A.	6 Worthington	6 Jones J.L.	6 Jones J.L.
7 Evans J.	7 James	7 Morris H.	7 Meredith W.	7 Meredith W.
8 Lewis B.	8 Lewis B.	8 Lewis B.	8 Davies Jos	8 Davies Jos
9 Lewis W.	9 Lewis W.	9 Lewis W.	9 Trainer H.	9 Trainer H.
10 Rea	10 Rea	10 Rea	10 Parry	10 Pryce-Jones
11 James	11 Bowdler J.C.H.	11 James	11 Lewis W.	11 Lewis W.
Swansea Feb 24: 4-1 *Lewis W. 2, James 2*	Wrexham Mar 12: 1-5 *Bowdler*	Kilmarnock Mar 24: 2-5 *Morris 2*	Belfast Mar 16: 2-2 *Trainer H. 2*	London Mar 18: 1-1 *Lewis*

1895 Scotland	1896 Ireland	1896 England	1896 Scotland	1897 Ireland
1 Jones S.	1 Jones S.	1 Jones S.	1 Trainer	1 Trainer
2 Lloyd	2 Parry	2 Arridge	2 Parry	2 Edwards
3 Parry	3 Matthias	3 Parry	3 Matthias	3 Parry
4 Williams G.	4 Rogers	4 Rogers	4 Rogers	4 Darvell
5 Chapman	5 White	5 Chapman	5 Jenkyns	5 Jenkyns
6 Jones J.L.	6 Jones J.L.	6 Jones J.L.	6 Jones J.L.	6 Jones J.L.
7 Davies Jos	7 Meredith W.	7 Meredith W.	7 Pugh	7 Meredith W.
8 Lewis B.	8 Pugh	8 Davies Jos	8 Garner	8 Pugh
9 Trainer H.	9 Morris A.G.	9 Morris A.G.	9 Morris A.G.	9 Morgan-Owen
10 Lewis W.	10 Rea	10 Morris H.	10 Lewis W.	10 Rea
11 Rea	11 Lewis W.	11 Lewis W.	11 Rea	11 Nock
Wrexham Mar 23: 2-2 *Lewis W., Chapman*	Wrexham Feb 29: 6-1 *Lewis 2, Meredith 2, Pugh, Morris*	Cardiff Mar 16: 1-9 *Chapman*	Dundee Mar 21: 0-4	Belfast Mar 6: 3-4 *Meredith 2, Jenkyns*

1897 Scotland	1897 England	1898 Ireland	1898 Scotland	1898 England
1 Trainer	1 Trainer	1 Morris J.	1 Trainer	1 Trainer
2 Jones W.R.	2 Matthias	2 Parry	2 Parry	2 Parry
3 Matthias	3 Edwards	3 Arridge	3 Jones D.	3 Arridge
4 Darvell	4 Chapman	4 Williams G.	4 Jones R.S.	4 Taylor
5 Mates	5 Mates	5 Edwards	5 Jenkyns	5 Jenkyns
6 Jones J.L.	6 Jones J.L.	6 Jones J.L.	6 Jones J.L.	6 Jones J.L.
7 Meredith W.	7 Meredith W.	7 Meredith W.	7 Roberts J. (*Chirk*)	7 Meredith W.
8 Pugh	8 Davies Jos	8 Thomas	8 Thomas	8 Bartley
9 Morgan-Owen	9 Morris A.G.	9 Lewis W.	9 Morgan-Owen	9 Morgan-Owen
10 Rea	10 Morris H.	10 Lockley	10 Morris A.G.	10 Watkins
11 Lewis W.	11 Lewis W.	11 Rea	11 Watkins	11 James
Wrexham Mar 20: 2-2 *Pugh, Morgan-Owen*	Sheffield Mar 29: 0-4	Llandudno Feb 19: 0-1	Motherwell Mar 19: 2-5 *Thomas, Morgan-Owen*	Wrexham Mar 28: 0-3

1899 **Ireland**	**1899** **Scotland**	**1899** **England**	**1900** **Scotland**	**1900** **Ireland**
1 Trainer	1 Trainer	1 Jones W.	1 Griffiths	1 Roose
2 Blew	2 Matthias	2 Blew	2 Thomas	2 Jones D.
3 Thomas	3 Blew	3 Arridge	3 Morris C.	3 Morris C.
4 Richards	4 Richards	4 Richards	4 Meredith S.	4 Brookes
5 Jones J.L.	5 Jones J.L.	5 Buckland	5 Jones J.L.	5 Morris R. (*Chirk*)
6 Hughes E.	6 Hughes E.	6 Harrison	6 Harrison	6 Harrison
7 Kelly	7 Kelly	7 Vaughan	7 Pugh	7 Meredith W.
8 Atherton	8 Owen T.	8 Meredith W.	8 Butler	8 Butler
9 James	9 Morgan-Owen	9 Owen T.	9 Jones R.	9 Jones R.
10 Davies C.	10 Jones R.	10 Morris A.G.	10 Parry T.D.	10 Parry T.D.
11 Jackson	11 Morris A.G.	11 Atherton	11 Watkins	11 Davies C.
Belfast Mar 4: 0-1	Wrexham Mar 18: 0-6	Bristol Mar 20: 0-4	Aberdeen Feb 3: 2-5 *Butler, Parry*	Llandudno Feb 24: 2-0 *Parry,* *Meredith* (pen)

1900 **England**	**1901** **Scotland**	**1901** **England**	**1901** **Ireland**	**1902** **Ireland**
1 Griffiths	1 Roose	1 Roose	1 Roose	1 Evans R.O.
2 Jones D.	2 Meredith S.	2 Meredith S.	2 Meredith S.	2 Blew
3 Morris C.	3 Morris C.	3 Morris C.	3 Morris C.	3 Jones H.
4 Brookes	4 Parry M.	4 Parry M.	4 Parry M.	4 Parry M.
5 Morris R. (*Chirk*)	5 Jones W.J.	5 Jones W.J.	5 Morris R. (*Chirk*)	5 Hughes E.
6 Harrison	6 Hughes E.	6 Hughes E.	6 Harrison	6 Jones J.L.
7 Meredith W.	7 Pugh	7 Meredith W.	7 Meredith W.	7 Kelly
8 Davies Jos	8 Jones J.O.	8 Pugh	8 Jones J.O.	8 Jenkins
9 Morgan-Owen	9 Morgan-Owen	9 Morgan-Owen	9 Green	9 Evans R.
10 Watkins	10 Parry T.D.	10 Parry T.D.	10 Parry T.D.	10 Williams E.
11 Parry T.D.	11 Williams E.	11 Williams E.	11 Williams E.	11 Morris R.
Cardiff Mar 26: 1-1 *Meredith*	Wrexham Mar 2: 1-1 *Parry*	Newcastle Mar 18: 0-6	Belfast Mar 23: 1-0 *Jones*	Cardiff Feb 22: 0-3

1902 **England**	**1902** **Scotland**	**1903** **England**	**1903** **Scotland**	**1903** **Ireland**
1 Roose	1 Roose	1 Evans R.O.	1 Evans R.O.	1 Evans R.O.
2 Meredith S.	2 Blew	2 Blew	2 Blew	2 Meredith S.
3 Morris C.	3 Morris R. (*Chirk*)	3 Morris C.	3 Morris C.	3 Morris C.
4 Parry M.	4 Parry M.	4 Parry M.	4 Parry M.	4 Richards
5 Jones J.L.	5 Jones J.L.	5 Morris R. (*Shrewsbury T*)	5 Morgan-Owen	5 Morris R. (*Shrewsbury T*)
6 Jones W.J.	6 Jones W.J.	6 Davies T.	6 Davies T.	6 Davies T.
7 Meredith W.	7 Meredith W.	7 Meredith W.	7 Meredith W.	7 Meredith W.
8 Watkins W.M.	8 Griffiths	8 Watkins W.M.	8 Watkins W.M.	8 Wynn
9 Parry T.D.	9 Morgan-Owen	9 Green	9 Morris A.G.	9 Davies W.
10 Williams E.	10 Morris R.	10 Morris A.G.	10 Morris R.	10 Morris R.
11 Morris R.	11 Owens J.	11 Atherton	11 Atherton	11 Atherton
Wrexham Mar 3: 0-0	Greenock Mar 15: 1-5 *Meredith*	Portsmouth Mar 2: 1-2 *Watkins*	Cardiff Mar 9: 0-1	Belfast Mar 28: 0-2

1904 England	**1904 Scotland**	**1904 Ireland**	**1905 Scotland**	**1905 England**
1 Roose	1 Davies D.	1 Davies D.	1 Roose	1 Roose
2 Meredith S.	2 Blew	2 Blew	2 Blew	2 Jones A.T.
3 Blew	3 Davies T.	3 Morris C.	3 Morris C.	3 Morris C.
4 Parry M.	4 Richards	4 Parry M.	4 Lathom	4 Lathom
5 Hughes E.	5 Hughes E.	5 Hughes E.	5 Hughes E.	5 Hughes E.
6 Jones J.L.	6 Jones J.L.	6 Jones J.L.	6 Hughes J.	6 Hughes J.
7 Meredith W.	7 Davies A.	7 Watkins A.E.	7 Meredith W.	7 Meredith W.
8 Atherton	8 Watkins W.M.	8 Watkins W.M.	8 Davies A.	8 Jones W.L.
9 Watkins W.M.	9 Green	9 Green	9 Watkins M.	9 Watkins M.
10 Morris R.	10 Morris R.	10 Atherton	10 Morris A.G.	10 Morris A.G.
11 Davies Lloyd	11 Atherton	11 Morris R.	11 Oliver	11 Oliver
Wrexham Feb 29: 2-2 *Watkins, Davies*	Dundee Mar 12: 1-1 *Atherton*	Bangor Mar 21: 0-1	Wrexham Mar 6: 3-1 *Morris A.G., Meredith, Watkins*	Liverpool Mar 27: 1-5 *Morris A.G.*

1905 Ireland	**1906 Scotland**	**1906 England**	**1906 Ireland**	**1907 Ireland**
1 Morgan	1 Roose	1 Roose	1 Roose	1 Roose
2 Blew	2 Blew	2 Jones A.T.	2 Blew	2 Roberts
3 Morris C.	3 Morris C.	3 Blew	3 Roberts	3 Davies Lloyd
4 Richards	4 Hughes E. (*Wrexham*)	4 Parry M.	4 Hughes E. (*N Forest*)	4 Lathom
5 Hughes E.	5 Morgan-Owen M.M.	5 Morgan-Owen M.M.	5 Morgan-Owen M.M.	5 Williams G.O.
6 Hughes J.	6 Lathom	6 Hughes E.	6 Hughes E.	6 Davies Llew
7 Matthews	7 Jones W.L.	7 Jones W.L.	7 Jones W.L.	7 Meredith W.
8 Watkins	8 Morris R.	8 Morgan-Owen H.	8 Morgan-Owen H.	8 Jones W.L.
9 Davies W.	9 Jones J.L.	9 Green	9 Green	9 Hughes A.
10 Jones W.L.	10 Jones R.	10 Lewis	10 Jones R.	10 Morris R.
11 Atherton	11 Evans R.	11 Evans R.	11 Evans R.	11 Jones G.P.
Belfast April 8: 2-2 *Watkins, Atherton*	Edinburgh Mar 3: 2-0 *Jones W.L., Jones J.L.*	Cardiff Mar 19: 0-1	Wrexham April 2: 4-4 *Green 3, Morgan-Owen H.*	Belfast Feb 23: 3-2 *Morris, Meredith, Jones W.L.*

1907 Scotland	**1907 England**	**1908 Scotland**	**1908 England**	**1908 Ireland**
1 Roose	1 Roose	1 Roose	1 Roose (Davies D.)	1 Evans R.O.
2 Blew	2 Davies Lloyd	2 Blew	2 Blew	2 Blew
3 Morris C.	3 Meredith S.	3 Morris C.	3 Morris C.	3 Jones J.
4 Lathom	4 Hughes E.	4 Hughes E. (*N Forest*)	4 Hughes E. (*N Forest*)	4 Peake
5 Davies Lloyd	5 Morgan-Owen M.M.	5 Parry M.	5 Parry M.	5 Parry M.
6 Price	6 Lathom	6 Davies Lloyd	6 Lathom	6 Price
7 Meredith W.	7 Meredith W.	7 Davies W.C.	7 Meredith W.	7 Meredith W.
8 Jones W.L.	8 Jones W.L.	8 Jones W.L.	8 Matthews	8 Morris R.
9 Morgan-Owen H.	9 Green	9 Davies W.	9 Davies W.	9 Watkins W.M.
10 Morris A.G.	10 Morris A.G.	10 Green	10 Morris A.G.	10 Hodgkinson
11 Jones G.P.	11 Evans R.	11 Evans R.	11 Evans R.	11 Jones T.D.
Wrexham Mar 4: 1-0 *Morris A.G.*	Fulham Mar 18: 1-1 *Jones*	Dundee Mar 7: 1-2 *Jones*	Wrexham Mar 16:1-7 *Davies W.*	Aberdare April 11: 0-1

1909 **Scotland**	**1909** **England**	**1909** **Ireland**	**1910** **Scotland**	**1910** **England**
1 Roose	1 Roose	1 Roose	1 Roose	1 Roose
2 Blew	2 Blew	2 Morris C.	2 Jones J.	2 Blew
3 Morris C.	3 Morris C.	3 Jones J.	3 Morris C.	3 Morris C.
4 Parry M.	4 Parry M.	4 Lathom	4 Hughes E. (*N Forest*)	4 Hughes E. (*N Forest*)
5 Peake	5 Peake	5 Peake	5 Peake	5 Lathom
6 Price	6 Price	6 Davies Lloyd	6 Davies Llew	6 Davies Llew
7 Meredith W.	7 Meredith W.	7 Meredith W.	7 Meredith W.	7 Meredith W.
8 Wynn	8 Wynn	8 Wynn	8 Davies W.C.	8 Wynn
9 Davies W.	9 Davies W.	9 Davies W.	9 Jones E.	9 Jones W.L.
10 Jones W.L.	10 Jones W.L.	10 Jones W.L.	10 Morris A.G.	10 Morris A.G.
11 Evans R.	11 Davies W.C.	11 Price	11 Evans R.	11 Evans R.
Wrexham Mar 1: 3-2 *Davies 2, Jones*	Nottingham Mar 15: 0-2	Belfast Mar 20: 3-2 *Jones W.L., Wynn, Meredith*	Kilmarnock Mar 5: 0-1	Cardiff Mar 14: 0-1

1910 **Ireland**	**1911** **Ireland**	**1911** **Scotland**	**1911** **England**	**1912** **Scotland**
1 Roose	1 Evans R.O.	1 Roose	1 Evans R.O.	1 Evans R.O.
2 Davies Lloyd	2 Hewitt	2 Morris C.	2 Morris C.	2 Davies Llew
3 Morris C.	3 Morris C.	3 Hewitt	3 Hewitt	3 Davies Lloyd
4 Hughes E. (*N Forest*)	4 Hughes E. (*N Forest*)	4 Hughes E. (*N Forest*)	4 Hughes E. (*N Forest*)	4 Jones J.T.
5 Peake	5 Peake	5 Davies Lloyd	5 Davies Lloyd	5 Hughes E. (*Wrexham*)
6 Davies Llew	6 Davies Llew	6 Davies LLew	6 Jones W.L.	6 Russell
7 Meredith W.	7 Meredith W.	7 Meredith W.	7 Meredith W.	7 Meredith W.
8 Jones J.L.	8 Wynn	8 Jones E.	8 Jones E.	8 Wynn
9 Jones E.	9 Davies W.	9 Davies W.	9 Davies W.	9 Jones E.
10 Morris A.G.	10 Morris A.G.	10 Morris A.G.	10 Morris A.G.	10 Williams J.W.
11 Evans R.	11 Vizard	11 Vizard	11 Vizard	11 Vizard
Wrexham April 11: 4-1 *Evans 2, Morris A.G. 2*	Belfast Jan 28: 2-1 *Davies W., Morris A.G.*	Cardiff Mar 6: 2-2 *Morris A.G.2*	London Mar 13: 0-3	Edinburgh Mar 2: 0-1

1912 **England**	**1912** **Ireland**	**1913** **Ireland**	**1913** **Scotland**	**1913** **England**
1 Evans R.O.	1 Evans R.O.	1 Bailiff	1 Bailiff	1 Bailiff
2 Davies Llew	2 Davies Llew	2 Hewitt	2 Hewitt	2 Hewitt
3 Davies Lloyd	3 Russell	3 Davies Llew	3 Davies Llew	3 Davies Lloyd
4 Hughes E. (*Wrexham*)	4 Hughes E. (*Wrexham*)	4 Lathom	4 Hughes E. (*Man City*)	4 Hughes E. (*Man City*)
5 Peake	5 Newton	5 Peake	5 Davies Lloyd	5 Peake
6 Jones J.T.	6 Jones J.T.	6 Jones J.T.	6 Jones W.L.	6 Jones J.T.
7 Meredith W.	7 Meredith W.	7 Meredith W.	7 Meredith W.	7 Meredith W.
8 Wynn	8 Williams J.W.	8 Davies D.W.	8 Wynn	8 Wynn
9 Jones E.	9 Davies W.	9 Davies W.	9 Davies W.	9 Davies W.
10 Morris A.G.	10 Davies D.W.	10 Roberts	10 Roberts	10 Jones W.L.
11 Vizard	11 Evans J.	11 Evans J.	11 Vizard	11 Davies Llew
Wrexham Mar 11: 0-2	Cardiff April 13: 2-3 *Davies W., Davies D.W.*	Belfast Jan 18: 1-0 *Roberts*	Wrexham Mar 3: 0-0	Bristol Mar 17: 3-4 *Davies W., Meredith, Peake*

1914 Ireland	**1914 Scotland**	**1914 England**	**1920 Ireland**	**1920 Scotland**
1 Peers	1 Peers	1 Peers	1 Bailiff	1 Peers
2 Davies Llew	2 Hewitt	2 Hewitt	2 Millership	2 Millership
3 Davies Lloyd	3 Jennings	3 Russell	3 Russell	3 Russell
4 Hughes E. (*Man City*)	4 Matthias	4 Matthias	4 Matthias	4 Matthias
5 Peake	5 Davies Lloyd	5 Davies Lloyd	5 Jones J.T.	5 Jones J.T.
6 Jones J.T.	6 Jones J.T.	6 Jennings	6 Keenor	6 Jennings
7 Meredith W.	7 Meredith W.	7 Meredith W.	7 Meredith W.	7 Meredith W.
8 Jones E.	8 Wynn	8 Wynn	8 Jones W.L.	8 Jones I.
9 Davies W.	9 Davies W.	9 Rowlands	9 Davies S.	9 Davies S.
10 Jones W.L.	10 Jones W.L.	10 Davies W.C.	10 Jones I.	10 Richards
11 Vizard	11 Evans J.	11 Vizard	11 Evans J.	11 Evans J.
Wrexham Jan 19: 1-2 *Jones E.* (pen)	Glasgow Feb 28: 0-0	Cardiff Mar 16: 0-2	Belfast Feb 14: 2-2 *Davies 2*	Cardiff Feb 26: 1-1 *Evans*

1920 England	**1921 Scotland**	**1921 England**	**1921 Ireland**	**1922 Scotland**
1 Peers	1 Peers	1 Peers	1 Peers	1 Peers
2 Millership	2 Millership	2 Millership	2 Russell	2 Parry
3 Russell	3 Russell	3 Russell	3 Millership	3 Evans J.H.
4 Matthias	4 Keenor	4 Keenor	4 Keenor	4 Evans H.P.
5 Jones J.T.	5 Jones J.T.	5 Jones J.T.	5 Matthews	5 Jones J.T.
6 Keenor	6 Matthias	6 Matthias	6 Matthias	6 Matthias
7 Meredith W.	7 Williams R.	7 Williams R.	7 Hole	7 Davies S.
8 Jones W.L.	8 Collier	8 Jones I.	8 Jones I.	8 Jones I.
9 Davies S.	9 Hoddinott	9 Hoddinott	9 Davies S.	9 Davies L.
10 Richards	10 Davies S.	10 Davies S.	10 Richards	10 Richards
11 Vizard	11 Vizard	11 Vizard	11 Vizard	11 Vizard
London Mar 15: 2-1 *Davies* (pen), *Richards*	Aberdeen Feb 12: 1-2 *Collier*	Cardiff Mar 16: 0-0	Swansea April 9: 2-1 *Hole, Davies*	Wrexham Feb 4: 2-1 *Davies L., Davies S.*

1922 England	**1922 Ireland**	**1923 England**	**1923 Scotland**	**1923 Ireland**
1 Peers	1 Peers	1 Peers	1 Godding	1 Godding
2 Russell	2 Russell	2 Parry	2 Russell	2 Russell
3 Evans J.H.	3 Evans J.H.	3 Russell	3 Evans J.H.	3 Parry
4 Evans H.P.	4 Evans H.P.	4 Keenor	4 Matthias	4 John
5 Jones J.T.	5 Jones J.T.	5 Matthews	5 Keenor	5 Keenor
6 Matthias	6 Matthias	6 Jennings	6 John	6 Jennings
7 Hole	7 Davies S.	7 Hole	7 Williams R.	7 Hole
8 Davies S.	8 Keenor	8 Jones I.	8 Davies I.	8 Jones I.
9 Davies L.	9 Davies L.	9 Davies L.	9 Davies S.	9 Davies L.
10 Richards	10 Jones I.	10 Vizard	10 Davies L.	10 Vizard
11 Vizard	11 Evans J.	11 Evans J.	11 Nicholas	11 Evans J.
Liverpool Mar 13: 0-1	Belfast April 1: 1-1 *Davies L.*	Cardiff Mar 5: 2-2 *Keenor, Jones*	Glasgow Mar 17: 0-2	Wrexham April 14: 0-3

1924 Scotland	1924 England	1924 Ireland	1925 Scotland	1925 England
1 Gray	1 Gray	1 Gray	1 Gray	1 Gray
2 Russell	2 Russell	2 Russell	2 Jenkins	2 Morley
3 Jenkins	3 Jenkins	3 Jenkins	3 Russell	3 Russell
4 Evans H.P.	4 Evans J.P.	4 Evans H.P.	4 Davies S.	4 Jenkins E.
5 Keenor	5 Keenor	5 Keenor	5 Keenor	5 Keenor
6 Jennings	6 Jennings	6 Jennings	6 Williams W.	6 Thomas E.
7 Davies W.	7 Davies W.	7 Davies W.	7 Davies W.	7 Davies W.
8 Jones I.	8 Nicholls	8 Nicholls	8 Nicholls	8 Nicholls
9 Davies L.	9 Davies L.	9 Davies L.	9 Davies L.	9 Fowler
10 Richards	10 Richards	10 Richards	10 Beadles	10 Beadles
11 Vizard	11 Vizard	11 Vizard	11 Cook	11 Cook
Cardiff Feb 16: 2-0 *Davies W., Davies L.*	Blackburn Mar 3: 2-1 *Davies W., Vizard*	Belfast Mar 15: 1-0 *Russell* (pen)	Edinburgh Feb 14: 1-3 *Williams*	Swansea Feb 28: 1-2 *Bower og*

1925 Ireland	1925 Scotland	1926 Ireland	1926 England	1926 Scotland
1 Gray	1 Gray	1 Brown	1 Gray	1 Gray
2 Parry	2 Russell	2 Parry	2 Russell	2 Evans T.J.
3 Jenkins	3 Jenkins	3 Jones T.	3 Jenkins	3 Jenkins
4 Mousdale	4 Bennion	4 Newnes	4 Davies S.	4 Bennion
5 Keenor	5 Keenor	5 Matthews	5 Pullen	5 Keenor
6 John	6 Lewis	6 Evans D.	6 John	6 Jennings
7 Davies W.	7 Williams R.	7 Davies W.	7 Davies W.	7 Davies W.
8 Davies S.	8 Davies W.	8 Davies L.	8 Davies L.	8 Davies S.
9 Jones J.	9 Davies S.	9 Fowler	9 Fowler	9 Fowler
10 Davies L.	10 Richards	10 Davies S.	10 Jones C.	10 Jones C.
11 Williams J.	11 Vizard	11 Jones I.	11 Vizard	11 Vizard
Wrexham April 18: 0-0	Cardiff Oct 31: 0-3	Belfast Feb 13: 0-3	London Mar 1: 3-1 *Fowler 2, Davies W.*	Glasgow Oct 30: 0-3

1927 England	1927 Ireland	1927 Scotland	1927 England	1928 Ireland
1 Lewis D.	1 Evans L.	1 Gray	1 Gray	1 Lewis D.
2 Jones T.	2 Jones T.	2 Russell	2 Williams B.	2 Williams B.
3 John	3 Jennings	3 Evans T.J.	3 Evans T.J.	3 Evans T.J.
4 Keenor	4 Keenor	4 Bennion	4 Bennion	4 Bennion
5 Griffiths T.	5 Griffiths T.	5 Keenor	5 Keenor	5 Keenor
6 Evans D.	6 Evans D.	6 Davies S.	6 John	6 John
7 Williams R.	7 Williams R.	7 Hole	7 Hole	7 Hole
8 Lewis	8 Lewis	8 Davies L.	8 Davies L.	8 Davies W.
9 Davies L.	9 Davies L.	9 Fowler	9 Lewis	9 Lewis
10 Nicholas	10 Jones C.	10 Curtis	10 Jones C.	10 Davies L.
11 Thomas	11 Nicholas	11 Cook	11 Cook	11 Rev H. Davies
Wrexham Feb 14: 3-3 *Davies L. 2, Lewis*	Cardiff April 9: 2-2 *Williams 2*	Wrexham Oct 29: 2-2 *Curtis, Gibson og*	Burnley Nov 28: 2-1 *Lewis, Hill og*	Belfast Feb 4: 2-1 *Davies W., Lewis*

1928 Scotland	**1928 England**	**1929 Ireland**	**1929 Scotland**	**1929 England**
1 Gray	1 Gray	1 Gray	1 Gray	1 Lewis D.
2 Morley	2 Morley	2 Morley	2 Williams B.	2 Williams B.
3 Jennings	3 Russell	3 Lumberg	3 Lumberg	3 Lumberg
4 Bennion	4 Griffiths T.	4 Bennion	4 Bennion	4 Keenor
5 Keenor	5 Keenor	5 Keenor	5 Keenor	5 Griffiths T.
6 Evans D.	6 Bennion	6 Bowsher	6 John	6 John
7 Hole	7 Hole	7 Davies W.	7 Davies W.	7 Davies W.
8 Davies W.	8 Davies W.	8 O'Callaghan	8 O'Callaghan	8 Davies L.
9 Lewis	9 Fowler	9 Mays	9 Davies L.	9 Lewis
10 Davies L.	10 Davies L.	10 Davies L.	10 Jones C.	10 Jones C.
11 Williams R.	11 Williams R.	11 Warren	11 Cook	11 Cook
Glasgow Oct 27: 2-4 *Davies W. 2*	Swansea Nov 17: 2-3 *Fowler, Keenor*	Wrexham Feb 2: 2-2 *Mays, Warren*	Cardiff Oct 26: 2-4 *O'Callaghan* *Davies L.*	London Nov 20: 0-6

1930 Ireland	**1930 Scotland**	**1930 England**	**1931 Ireland**	**1931 Scotland**
1 Finnigan	1 Evans L.	1 Evans L.	1 John W.	1 Gray
2 Hugh	2 Dewey	2 Dewey	2 Williams B.	2 Richards
3 Jones T.	3 Crompton	3 Crompton	3 Crompton	3 Lumberg
4 Lawrence	4 Rogers	4 Rogers	4 Keenor	4 Edwards
5 Keenor	5 Keenor	5 Keenor	5 Griffiths T.	5 Griffiths T.
6 Pugsley	6 Ellis	6 Ellis	6 Richards	6 Lawrence
7 Davies W.	7 Collins	7 Williams L.	7 Phillips	7 Griffiths T.P.
8 Williams B.	8 Neal	8 Neal	8 Astley	8 O'Callaghan
9 Martin	9 Bamford	9 Bamford	9 Bamford	9 Glover
10 Davies S.	10 Robbins	10 Robbins	10 James	10 Robbins
11 Cook	11 Thomas	11 Thomas	11 Warren	11 Curtis
Belfast Feb 1: 0-7	Glasgow Oct 25: 1-1 *Bamford*	Wrexham Nov 22: 0-4	Wrexham April 22: 3-2 *Phillips, Griffiths,* *Warren*	Wrexham Oct 31: 2-3 *Curtis 2*

1931 England	**1931 Ireland**	**1932 Scotland**	**1932 England**	**1932 Ireland**
1 Gray	1 Gray	1 John W.	1 John W.	1 John W.
2 Williams B.	2 Lawrence	2 Williams B.	2 Williams B.	2 Williams B.
3 Ellis	3 Foulkes	3 Ellis	3 Ellis	3 John
4 Jones C.	4 Bennion	4 Keenor	4 Murphy	4 Murphy
5 Griffiths T.	5 Griffiths T.	5 Griffiths T.	5 Griffiths T.	5 Griffiths T.
6 John	6 Ellis	6 Richards	6 Richards	6 Richards
7 Phillips	7 Jones T.J.	7 Phillips	7 Warren	7 Richards W.
8 O'Callaghan	8 James	8 O'Callaghan	8 O'Callaghan	8 O'Callaghan
9 Astley	9 Bamford	9 Astley	9 Astley	9 Astley
10 Robbins	10 Robbins	10 Robbins	10 Robbins	10 Robbins
11 Cook	11 Parris	11 Lewis D.J.	11 Lewis D.J.	11 Evans W.
Liverpool Nov 18: 1-3 *Robbins*	Belfast Dec 5: 0-4	Edinburgh Oct 26: 5-2 *O'Callaghan 2,* *Griffiths, Astley* *Thomson J. og*	Wrexham Nov 16: 0-0	Wrexham Dec 7: 4-1 *Astley 2,* *Robbins 2*

1933 France	**1933 Scotland**	**1933 Ireland**	**1933 England**	**1934 England**
1 John W.	1 John W.	1 Evans L.	1 John W.	1 John W.
2 John	2 Lawrence	2 Lawrence	2 Lawrence	2 Lawrence
3 Lawrence	3 Ellis	3 Jones D.O.	3 Jones D.O.	3 Jones D.O.
4 Murphy	4 Murphy	4 Day	4 Murphy	4 Murphy
5 Griffiths T.	5 Griffiths T.	5 Hanford	5 Griffiths T.	5 Griffiths T.
6 Jones C.	6 Richards	6 Richards	6 Richards	6 Richards
7 Jones T.	7 Phillips	7 Phillips	7 Phillips	7 Phillips
8 Jones L.	8 O'Callaghan	8 O'Callaghan	8 O'Callaghan	8 O'Callaghan
9 Bamford	9 Astley	9 Glover	9 Astley	9 Williams R.
10 Robbins	10 Robbins	10 Mills	10 Mills	10 Mills
11 Warren	11 Evans W.	11 Curtis	11 Evans W.	11 Evans W.
Paris May 25: 1-1 *Griffiths*	Cardiff Oct 4: 3-2 *Evans, Robbins, Astley*	Belfast Nov 4: 1-1 *Glover*	Newcastle Nov 15: 2-1 *Mills, Astley*	Cardiff Sept 29: 0-4

1934 Scotland	**1935 Ireland**	**1935 Scotland**	**1936 England**	**1936 Ireland**
1 John W.	1 Hughes J.I.	1 John W.	1 John W.	1 John W.
2 Lawrence	2 Williams B.	2 Lawrence	2 Jones D.O.	2 Griffiths T.
3 Jones D.O.	3 John	3 John	3 Ellis	3 Jones D.O.
4 Murphy	4 Murphy	4 Murphy	4 Murphy	4 Murphy
5 Hanford	5 Griffiths T.	5 Griffiths T.	5 Hanford	5 Hanford
6 Richards	6 Richards	6 Richards	6 Richards	6 Richards
7 Hopkins	7 Hopkins	7 Phillips	7 Hopkins	7 Hopkins
8 Williams R.	8 Jones L.	8 Jones B.	8 Phillips	8 Phillips
9 Astley	9 Jones C.W.	9 Glover	9 Astley	9 Astley
10 Mills	10 Jones B.	10 Jones L.	10 Jones B.	10 Jones B.
11 Phillips	11 Phillips	11 Robbins	11 Evans W.	11 Evans W.
Aberdeen Nov 21: 2-3 *Phillips, Astley*	Wrexham Mar 27: 3-1 *Jones C.W., Phillips, Hopkins*	Cardiff Oct 5: 1-1 *Phillips*	Wolverhampton Feb 5: 2-1 *Astley, Jones B.*	Belfast Mar 11: 2-3 *Astley, Phillips*

1936 England	**1936 Scotland**	**1937 Ireland**	**1937 Scotland**	**1937 England**
1 Gray	1 Gray	1 Gray	1 Gray	1 Gray
2 Turner	2 Turner	2 Turner	2 Turner	2 Turner
3 John	3 Ellis	3 Jones D.	3 Hughes	3 Hughes
4 Warner	4 Murphy	4 Murphy	4 Murphy	4 Murphy
5 Griffiths T.	5 Griffiths T.	5 Griffiths T.	5 Hanford	5 Hanford
6 Richards	6 Richards	6 Richards	6 Richards	6 Richards
7 Hopkins	7 Hopkins	7 Hopkins	7 Phillips	7 Hopkins
8 Jones B.	8 Jones B.	8 Jones B.	8 Jones L.	8 Jones L.
9 Glover	9 Glover	9 Glover	9 Perry	9 Perry
10 Jones L.	10 Jones L.	10 Jones L.	10 Jones B.	10 Jones B.
11 Morris	11 Morris	11 Warren	11 Morris	11 Morris
Cardiff Oct 17: 2-1 *Morris, Glover*	Dundee Dec 2: 2-1 *Glover 2*	Wrexham Mar 17: 4-1 *Glover 2, Jones B., Warren*	Cardiff Oct 30: 2-1 *Jones B., Morris*	Middlesbrough Nov 17: 1-2 *Perry*

1938 Ireland	**1938 England**	**1938 Scotland**	**1939 Ireland**	**1939 France**
1 Gray	1 John W.	1 John W.	1 Poland	1 Poland
2 Turner	2 Whatley	2 Whatley	2 Turner	2 Turner
3 Hughes	3 Hughes	3 Hughes	3 Hughes	3 Hughes
4 Green	4 Green	4 Dearson	4 Green	4 Green
5 Jones T.G.	5 Jones T.G.	5 Jones T.G.	5 Jones T.G.	5 Hanford
6 Richards	6 Richards	6 Richards	6 Dearson	6 Warner
7 Hopkins	7 Hopkins	7 Hopkins	7 Hopkins	7 Williams J.
8 Jones L.	8 Jones L.	8 Jones L.	8 Boulter	8 Astley
9 Perry	9 Astley	9 Astley	9 Glover	9 Jones W.
10 Jones B.	10 Jones B.	10 Jones B.	10 Jones B.	10 Dearson
11 Warren	11 Cumner	11 Cumner	11 Cumner	11 Morris
Belfast	Cardiff	Edinburgh	Wrexham	Paris
Mar 16: 0-1	Oct 22: 4-2	Nov 9: 2-3	Mar 15: 3-1	May 20: 1-2
	Astley 2, Hopkins, Jones B.	*Astley, Jones L.*	*Cumner, Glover, Boulter*	*Astley*

1946 Scotland	**1946 England**	**1947 N Ireland**	**1947 England**	**1947 Scotland**
1 Sidlow	1 Sidlow	1 Shortt	1 Sidlow	1 Sidlow
2 Lambert	2 Sherwood	2 Sherwood	2 Lambert	2 Sherwood
3 Hughes	3 Hughes	3 Hughes	3 Barnes	3 Barnes
4 Witcomb	4 Witcomb	4 Whitcomb	4 Powell I.	4 Powell I.
5 Jones T.G.	5 Jones T.G.	5 Humphreys	5 Jones T.G.	5 Jones T.G.
6 Burgess	6 Burgess	6 Burgess	6 Burgess	6 Burgess
7 Jones E.	7 Jones E.	7 Griffiths	7 Thomas S.	7 Thomas S.
8 Powell A.	8 Powell A.	8 Morris	8 Powell A.	8 Powell A.
9 Ford	9 Richards	9 Ford	9 Lowrie	9 Ford
10 Jones B.	10 Powell I.	10 Jones B.	10 Jones B.	10 Lowrie
11 Edwards	11 Edwards	11 Edwards	11 Edwards	11 Edwards
Wrexham	Maine Road	Belfast	Cardiff	Hampden
Oct 19: 3-1	Nov 13: 0-3	April 16: 1-2	Oct 18: 0-3	Nov 12: 2-1
Jones B., Ford, Stephen og		*Ford*		*Ford, Lowrie*

1948 N Ireland	**1948 Scotland**	**1948 England**	**1949 N Ireland**	**1949 Portugal**
1 Sidlow	1 Sidlow	1 Hughes W.A.	1 Hughes W.A.	1 Hughes W.A.
2 Sherwood	2 Sherwood	2 Barnes	2 Barnes	2 Sherwood
3 Barnes	3 Barnes	3 Sherwood	3 Sherwood	3 Lambert
4 Powell I.	4 Paul	4 Paul	4 Paul	4 Paul
5 Jones T.G.	5 Stansfield	5 Jones T.G.	5 Jones T.G.	5 Jones T.G.
6 Baker	6 Burgess	6 Burgess	6 Burgess	6 Burgess
7 Thomas S.	7 Thomas S.	7 Jones E.	7 Williams H.T.	7 Griffiths
8 Powell A.	8 Lucas	8 Powell A.	8 Rees	8 Lucas
9 Ford	9 Ford	9 Ford	9 Ford	9 Ford
10 Lowrie	10 Jones B.	10 Morris	10 Lucas	10 Lowrie
11 Edwards	11 Jones E.	11 Clarke	11 Edwards	11 Edwards
Wrexham	Cardiff	Villa Park	Belfast	Lisbon
Mar 10: 2-0	Oct 23: 1-3	Nov 10: 0-1	Mar 9: 2-0	May 15: 2-3
Lowrie, Edwards	*Jones B.*		*Edwards, Ford*	*Ford 2*

1949 Belgium	**1949 Switzerland**	**1949 England**	**1949 Scotland**	**1949 Belgium**
1 Hughes W.A.	1 Hughes W.A.	1 Sidlow	1 Jones K.B.	1 Shortt
2 Roberts	2 Sherwood	2 Barnes	2 Barnes	2 Barnes
3 Lambert	3 Lambert	3 Sherwood	3 Sherwood	3 Sherwood
4 Powell I.	4 Paul	4 Paul	4 Powell I.	4 Powell I.
5 Jones T.G.	5 Jones T.G.	5 Jones T.G.	5 Jones T.G.	5 Jones T.G.
6 Burgess	6 Burgess	6 Burgess	6 Burgess	6 Burgess
7 Griffiths	7 Williams H.T.	7 Griffiths	7 Griffiths	7 Griffiths
8 Rees	8 Rees	8 Lucas	8 Paul	8 Paul
9 Ford	9 Ford	9 Ford	9 Ford	9 Ford
10 Lucas	10 Lucas	10 Scrine	10 Clarke	10 Powell A.
11 Edwards	11 Edwards	11 Edwards	11 Edwards	11 Clarke
Liège May 23: 1-3 *Ford*	Berne May 26: 0-4	Cardiff Oct 15: 1-4 *Griffiths*	Hampden Nov 9: 0-2	Cardiff Nov 23: 5-1 *Clarke, Paul,* *Ford 3*

1950 N Ireland	**1950 Scotland**	**1950 England**	**1951 N Ireland**	**1951 Portugal**
1 Shortt	1 Parry	1 Hughes I.	1 Hughes I.	1 Hughes I.
2 Barnes	2 Barnes	2 Barnes	2 Barnes	2 Barnes
3 Sherwood	3 Sherwood	3 Sherwood	3 Sherwood	3 Sherwood
4 Paul	4 Powell I.	4 Paul	4 Paul	4 Paul
5 Charles J.	5 Paul	5 Daniel	5 Daniel	5 Daniel
6 Burgess	6 Burgess	6 Lucas	6 Burgess	6 Burgess
7 Williams H.T.	7 Williams H.T.	7 Griffiths	7 Griffiths	7 Griffiths
8 Rees	8 Allen	8 Allen	8 Kinsey	8 Kinsey
9 Ford	9 Ford	9 Ford	9 Ford	9 Ford
10 Scrine	10 Powell A.	10 Allchurch I.	10 Allchurch I.	10 Allchurch I.
11 Clarke	11 Clarke	11 Clarke	11 Clarke	11 Clarke
Wrexham Mar 8: 0-0	Cardiff Oct 21: 1-3 *Powell A.*	Sunderland Nov 15: 2-4 *Ford 2*	Belfast Mar 7: 2-1 *Clarke 2*	Cardiff May 12: 2-1 *Griffiths, Ford*

1951 Switzerland	**1951 England**	**1951 Scotland**	**1951 Rest of UK**	**1952 N Ireland**
1 Hughes I.	1 Shortt	1 Shortt	1 Shortt	1 Shortt
2 Williams G. J.	2 Barnes	2 Barnes	2 Barnes	2 Barnes
3 Sherwood	3 Sherwood	3 Sherwood	3 Sherwood	3 Sherwood
4 Paul	4 Paul	4 Paul	4 Paul	4 Paul
5 Charles J.	5 Daniel	5 Daniel	5 Daniel	5 Daniel
6 Burgess	6 Burgess	6 Burgess	6 Burgess	6 Burgess
7 Griffiths	7 Foulkes	7 Foulkes	7 Foulkes	7 Foulkes
8 Kinsey	8 Kinsey	8 Morris	8 Morris	8 Morris
9 Ford	9 Ford	9 Ford	9 Ford	9 Ford
10 Allchurch I.	10 Allchurch I.	10 Allchurch I.	10 Allchurch I.	10 Allchurch I.
11 Clarke	11 Clarke	11 Clarke	11 Clarke	11 Clarke
Wrexham May 16: 3-2 *Ford 2, Burgess*	Cardiff Oct 20: 1-1 *Foulkes*	Hampden Nov 20: 1-0 *Allchurch*	Cardiff Dec 5: 3-2 *Allchurch 2, Ford*	Swansea Mar 19: 3-0 *Barnes, Allchurch,* *Clarke*

1952 Scotland	**1952 England**	**1953 N Ireland**	**1953 France**	**1953 Yugoslavia**
1 Shortt	1 Shortt	1 Shortt	1 Shortt	1 Shortt
2 Lever	2 Stitfall	2 Sullivan	2 Sullivan	2 Sullivan
3 Sherwood	3 Sherwood	3 Sherwood	3 Sherwood	3 Sherwood
4 Paul	4 Paul	4 Paul	4 Paul	4 Paul
5 Daniel	5 Daniel	5 Daniel	5 Daniel	5 Daniel
6 Burgess	6 Burgess	6 Burgess	6 Burgess	6 Burgess
7 Foulkes	7 Foulkes	7 Medwin	7 Medwin	7 Medwin
8 Davies R.	8 Davies R.	8 Charles J.	8 Charles J.	8 Charles J.
9 Ford	9 Ford	9 Ford	9 Ford	9 Ford
10 Allchurch I.	10 Allchurch I.	10 Allchurch I.	10 Allchurch I.	10 Allchurch I.
11 Clarke	11 Clarke	11 Griffiths J.H.	11 Foulkes	11 Foulkes
Cardiff Oct 18: 1-2 *Ford*	Wembley Nov 12: 2-5 *Ford 2*	Belfast April 15: 3-2 *Charles 2, Ford*	Paris May 14: 1-6 *Allchurch*	Belgrade May 21: 2-5 *Ford 2*

1953 England	**1953 Scotland**	**1954 N Ireland**	**1954 Austria**	**1954 Yugoslavia**
1 Howells	1 Howells	1 Kelsey	1 Kelsey	1 Kelsey
2 Barnes	2 Barnes	2 Sullivan	2 Williams S.	2 Barnes
3 Sherwood	3 Sherwood	3 Sherwood	3 Sherwood	3 Sherwood
4 Paul	4 Paul	4 Paul	4 Harris	4 Paul
5 Daniel	5 Daniel	5 Daniel	5 Charles J.	5 Charles J.
6 Burgess	6 Burgess	6 Burgess	6 Burgess	6 Bowen
7 Foulkes	7 Foulkes	7 Foulkes	7 Griffiths	7 Reed
8 Davies R.	8 Davies R.	8 Kinsey	8 Tapscott	8 Tapscott
9 Charles J.	9 Charles J.	9 Charles J.	9 Ford	9 Ford
10 Allchurch I.	10 Allchurch I.	10 Allchurch I.	10 Allchurch I.	10 Allchurch I.
11 Clarke	11 Clarke	11 Clarke	11 Jones C.	11 Clarke
Cardiff Oct 10: 1-4 *Allchurch*	Hampden Nov 4: 3-3 *Charles 2, Allchurch*	Wrexham Mar 31: 1-2 *Charles*	Vienna May 9: 0-2	Cardiff Sept 22: 1-3 *Allchurch*

1954 Scotland	**1954 England**	**1955 N Ireland**	**1955 England**	**1955 Scotland**
1 Kelsey	1 King	1 Kelsey	1 Kelsey	1 Kelsey
2 Barnes	2 Williams S.	2 Williams S.	2 Williams S.	2 Williams S.
3 Sherwood	3 Sherwood	3 Sherwood	3 Sherwood	3 Sherwood
4 Paul	4 Paul	4 Charles M.	4 Charles M.	4 Charles M.
5 Charles J.	5 Daniel	5 Daniel	5 Charles J.	5 Charles J.
6 Bowen	6 Sullivan	6 Sullivan	6 Paul	6 Paul
7 Reed	7 Tapscott	7 Tapscott	7 Tapscott	7 Tapscott
8 Tapscott	8 Ford	8 Ford	8 Kinsey	8 Kinsey
9 Ford	9 Charles J.	9 Charles J.	9 Ford	9 Ford
10 Allchurch I.	10 Allchurch I.	10 Allchurch I.	10 Allchurch I.	10 Allchurch I.
11 Clarke	11 Clarke	11 Allchurch L.	11 Jones C.	11 Jones C.
Cardiff Oct 16: 0-1	Wembley Nov 10: 2-3 *Charles 2*	Belfast April 20: 3-2 *Charles J. 3*	Cardiff Oct 22: 2-1 *Tapscott, Jones*	Hampden Nov 9: 0-2

1955 Austria	1956 N Ireland	1956 Scotland	1956 England	1957 N Ireland
1 Kelsey	1 Kelsey	1 Kelsey	1 Kelsey	1 Kelsey
2 Williams S.	2 Sherwood	2 Sherwood	2 Sherwood	2 Edwards
3 Sherwood	3 Hopkins	3 Hopkins	3 Hopkins	3 Hopkins
4 Charles M.	4 Harrington	4 Harrington	4 Harrington	4 Charles M.
5 Charles J.	5 Charles J.	5 Daniel	5 Daniel	5 Daniel
6 Paul	6 Paul	6 Sullivan	6 Sullivan	6 Bowen
7 Allchurch L.	7 Jones C.	7 Medwin	7 Medwin	7 Medwin
8 Tapscott	8 Tapscott	8 Charles J.	8 Charles M.	8 Tapscott
9 Ford	9 Ford	9 Ford	9 Charles J.	9 Charles J.
10 Allchurch I.	10 Allchurch I.	10 Allchurch I.	10 Allchurch I.	10 Vernon
11 Jones C.	11 Clarke	11 Jones C.	11 Jones C.	11 Jones C.
Wrexham Nov 23: 1-2 *Tapscott*	Cardiff April 11: 1-1 *Clarke*	Cardiff Oct 20: 2-2 *Ford, Medwin*	Wembley Nov 14: 1-3 *Charles J.*	Belfast April 10: 0-0

1957 Czechoslovakia	1957 E Germany	1957 Czechoslovakia	1957 E Germany	1957 England
1 Kelsey	1 Kelsey	1 Kelsey	1 Vearncombe	1 Kelsey
2 Stitfall	2 Edwards	2 Thomas	2 Thomas	2 Williams S.
3 Hopkins	3 Hopkins	3 Hopkins	3 Hopkins	3 Hopkins
4 Charles M.	4 Harris	4 Charles M.	4 Harris	4 Harris
5 Charles J.	5 Charles J.	5 Daniel	5 Charles M.	5 Charles M.
6 Bowen	6 Bowen	6 Harris	6 Bowen	6 Bowen
7 Medwin	7 Medwin	7 Medwin	7 Allchurch L.	7 Medwin
8 Tapscott	8 Tapscott	8 Palmer	8 Davies R.	8 Davies R.
9 Webster	9 Charles M.	9 Charles J.	9 Palmer	9 Palmer
10 Vernon	10 Vernon	10 Vernon	10 Vernon	10 Vernon
11 Jones C.	11 Jones C.	11 Jones C.	11 Jones C.	11 Jones C.
Cardiff May 1: 1-0 *Vernon*	Leipzig May 19: 1-2 *Charles M.*	Prague May 26: 0-2	Cardiff Sept 25: 4-1 *Palmer 3, Jones*	Cardiff Oct 19: 0-4

1957 Scotland	1958 Israel	1958 Israel	1958 N Ireland	1958 Hungary †
1 Kelsey	1 Kelsey	1 Kelsey	1 Kelsey	1 Kelsey
2 Williams S.	2 Williams S.	2 Williams S.	2 Williams S.	2 Williams S.
3 Hopkins	3 Hopkins	3 Hopkins	3 Hopkins	3 Hopkins
4 Harrington	4 Harrington	4 Harrington	4 Harrington	4 Sullivan
5 Charles M.	5 Charles M.	5 Charles M.	5 Sullivan	5 Charles M.
6 Bowen	6 Bowen	6 Bowen	6 Bowen	6 Bowen
7 Allchurch L.	7 Allchurch L.	7 Medwin	7 Allchurch L.	7 Webster
8 Harris	8 Charles J.	8 Hewitt	8 Hewitt	8 Medwin
9 Medwin	9 Medwin	9 Charles J.	9 Medwin	9 Charles J.
10 Vernon	10 Allchurch I.	10 Allchurch I.	10 Allchurch I.	10 Allchurch I.
11 Jones C.	11 Jones C.	11 Jones C.	11 Jones C.	11 Jones C.
Hampden Nov 13: 1-1 *Medwin*	Tel Aviv Jan 15: 2-0 *Allchurch I., Bowen*	Cardiff Feb 5: 2-0 *Allchurch, Jones*	Cardiff April 16: 1-1 *Hewitt*	Sandviken June 8: 1-1 *Charles*

1958 Mexico †	1958 Sweden †	1958 Hungary †	1958 Brazil †	1958 Scotland
1 Kelsey	1 Kelsey	1 Kelsey	1 Kelsey	1 Kelsey
2 Williams S.	2 Williams S.	2 Williams S.	2 Williams S.	2 Williams S.
3 Hopkins	3 Hopkins	3 Hopkins	3 Hopkins	3 Hopkins
4 Baker	4 Sullivan	4 Sullivan	4 Sullivan	4 Sullivan
5 Charles M.	5 Charles M.	5 Charles M.	5 Charles M.	5 Charles M.
6 Bowen	6 Bowen	6 Bowen	6 Bowen	6 Bowen
7 Webster	7 Vernon	7 Medwin	7 Medwin	7 Allchurch L.
8 Medwin	8 Hewitt	8 Hewitt	8 Hewitt	8 Vernon
9 Charles J.	9 Charles J.	9 Charles J.	9 Webster	9 Medwin
10 Allchurch I.	10 Allchurch I.	10 Allchurch I.	10 Allchurch I.	10 Allchurch I.
11 Jones C.	11 Jones C.	11 Jones C.	11 Jones C.	11 Woosnam
Stockholm June 11: 1-1 *Allchurch*	Stockholm June 15: 0-0	Stockholm June 17: 2-1 *Allchurch, Medwin*	Gothenburg June 19:0-1	Cardiff Oct 18: 0-3

1958 England	1959 N Ireland	1959 England	1959 Scotland	1960 N Ireland
1 Kelsey	1 Rouse	1 Kelsey	1 Kelsey	1 Kelsey
2 Williams S.	2 Williams S.	2 Williams S.	2 Williams S.	2 Williams S.
3 Hopkins	3 Hopkins	3 Hopkins	3 Hopkins	3 Williams G.
4 Crowe	4 Crowe	4 Crowe	4 Sullivan	4 Crowe
5 Charles M.	5 Sullivan	5 Nurse	5 Charles J.	5 Nurse
6 Bowen	6 Bowen	6 Sullivan	6 Baker	6 Baker
7 Medwin	7 Medwin	7 Medwin	7 Medwin	7 Medwin
8 Ward	8 Tapscott	8 Woosnam	8 Woosnam	8 Woosnam
9 Tapscott	9 Rowley	9 Moore	9 Moore	9 Moore
10 Allchurch I.	10 Allchurch I.	10 Allchurch I.	10 Allchurch I.	10 Vernon
11 Woosnam	11 Jones C.	11 Jones C.	11 Jones C.	11 Jones C.
Villa Park Nov 26: 2-2 *Tapscott, Allchurch*	Belfast April 22: 1-4 *Tapscott*	Cardiff Oct 17: 1-1 *Moore*	Hampden Nov 4: 1-1 *Charles*	Wrexham April 6: 3-2 *Medwin 2, Woosnam*

1960 Rep of Ireland	1960 Scotland	1960 England	1961 N Ireland	1961 Spain
1 Vearncombe	1 Kelsey	1 Kelsey	1 Kelsey	1 Kelsey
2 Williams S.	2 Harrington	2 Harrington	2 Williams S.	2 Williams S.
3 Williams G.	3 Williams G.	3 Williams G.	3 Hopkins	3 Hopkins
4 Crowe	4 Crowe	4 Crowe	4 Charles M.	4 Charles M.
5 Nurse	5 Nurse	5 Nurse	5 Nurse	5 Nurse
6 Baker	6 Baker	6 Baker	6 Crowe	6 Crowe
7 Medwin	7 Medwin	7 Medwin	7 Jones C.	7 Medwin
8 Woosnam	8 Woosnam	8 Woosnam	8 Woosnam	8 Woosnam
9 Moore	9 Leek	9 Leek	9 Leek	9 Leek
10 Vernon	10 Vernon	10 Vernon	10 Allchurch I.	10 Allchurch I.
11 Jones C.	11 Jones C.	11 Jones C.	11 Williams G.	11 Williams G.
Dublin Sept 28: 3-2 *Jones 2, Woosnam*	Cardiff Oct 22: 2-0 *Vernon, Jones*	Wembley Nov 23: 1-5 *Leek*	Belfast April 12: 5-1 *Charles, Jones 2, Allchurch, Leek*	Cardiff April 19: 1-2 *Woosnam*

1961 Spain	1961 Hungary	1961 England	1961 Scotland	1962 N Ireland
1 Kelsey	1 Kelsey	1 Kelsey	1 Kelsey	1 Kelsey
2 Williams S.	2 Williams S.	2 Harrington	2 Harrington	2 Williams S.
3 Hopkins	3 Hopkins	3 Williams S.	3 Williams S.	3 Hopkins
4 Charles M.	4 Charles M.	4 Charles M.	4 Crowe	4 Lucas
5 Nurse	5 Nurse	5 Charles J.	5 Charles M.	5 England
6 Crowe	6 Crowe	6 Crowe	6 Baker	6 Hennessey
7 Jones C.	7 Jones C.	7 Jones C.	7 Allchurch L.	7 Allchurch L.
8 Moore	8 Woosnam	8 Woosnam	8 Woosnam	8 Woosnam
9 Leek	9 Leek	9 Ward	9 Leek	9 Charles M.
10 Allchurch I.	10 Allchurch I.	10 Allchurch I.	10 Allchurch I.	10 Vernon
11 Williams G.	11 Williams G.	11 Williams G.	11 Jones C.	11 Jones C.
Madrid	Budapest	Cardiff	Hampden	Cardiff
May 18: 1-1	May 28: 2-3	Oct 14: 1-1	Nov 8: 0-2	April 11: 4-0
Allchurch	*Allchurch, Jones*	*Williams G.*		*Charles 4*

1962 Brazil	1962 Brazil	1962 Mexico	1962 Scotland	1962 Hungary
1 Kelsey	1 Kelsey (Hollins)	1 Hollins	1 Millington	1 Millington
2 Williams S.	2 Williams S.	2 Williams S.	2 Williams S.	2 Williams S.
3 Hopkins	3 Hopkins	3 Hopkins	3 Hopkins	3 Hopkins
4 Hennessey	4 England	4 Lucas	4 Hennessey	4 Hennessey
5 Charles J.	5 Charles J.	5 England	5 Charles J.	5 Nurse
6 Crowe	6 Hennessey	6 Crowe	6 Lucas	6 Crowe
7 Allchurch L.	7 Woosnam	7 Vernon	7 Jones B.	7 Medwin
8 Vernon	8 Vernon	8 Allchurch I.	8 Allchurch I.	8 Allchurch I.
9 Charles M.	9 Moore (Leek)	9 Charles J.	9 Charles M.	9 Charles M.
10 Allchurch I.	10 Allchurch I.	10 Leek	10 Vernon	10 Vernon
11 Jones C.	11 Jones C.	11 Jones C.	11 Jones C.	11 Jones B.
Rio de Janeiro	Sao Paulo	Mexico City	Cardiff	Budapest
May 12: 1-3	May 16: 1-3	May 22: 1-2	Oct 20: 2-3	Nov 7: 1-3
Allchurch I.	*Leek*	*Charles*	*Allchurch, Charles J.*	*Medwin*

1962 England	1963 Hungary	1963 N Ireland	1963 England	1963 Scotland
1 Millington	1 Hollins	1 Hollins	1 Hollins	1 Sprake
2 Williams S.	2 Williams S.	2 Hopkins	2 Williams S.	2 Williams S.
3 Sear	3 Williams G.	3 Williams G.	3 Williams G.	3 Williams G.
4 Hennessey	4 Hennessey	4 Burton	4 Hennessey	4 Hennessey
5 Nurse	5 England	5 England	5 England	5 England
6 Lucas	6 Burton	6 Hole	6 Burton	6 Nurse
7 Jones B.	7 Jones B.	7 Jones B.	7 Allchurch L.	7 Jones B.
8 Allchurch I.	8 Woosnam	8 Woosnam	8 Vernon	8 Moore
9 Leek	9 Moore	9 Moore	9 Davies W.	9 Charles J.
10 Vernon	10 Allchurch I.	10 Allchurch I.	10 Allchurch I.	10 Vernon
11 Medwin	11 Jones C.	11 Jones C.	11 Jones C.	11 Jones C.
Wembley	Cardiff	Belfast	Cardiff	Hampden
Nov 21: 0-4	Mar 20: 1-1	April 3: 4-1	Oct 12: 0-4	Nov 20: 1-2
	Jones C.	*Woosnam, Jones C. 3*		*Jones B.*

1964 N Ireland	1964 Scotland	1964 Denmark	1964 England	1964 Greece
1 Sprake	1 Sprake	1 Sprake	1 Millington	1 Sprake
2 Evans R.	2 Williams S.	2 Williams S.	2 Williams S.	2 Rodrigues
3 Williams G.	3 Williams G.	3 Williams G.	3 Williams G.	3 Williams G.
4 Johnson	4 Hole	4 Hennessey	4 Hennessey	4 Hennessey
5 England	5 Charles J.	5 England	5 England	5 England
6 Hole	6 Hennessey	6 Hole	6 Hole	6 Hole
7 Jones B.	7 Jones C.	7 Jones B.	7 Rees	7 Rees
8 Moore	8 Leek	8 Godfrey	8 Davies R.	8 Leek
9 Davies R.	9 Davies W.	9 Davies W.	9 Davies W.	9 Davies W.
10 Godfrey	10 Allchurch I.	10 Jones C.	10 Allchurch I.	10 Williams H.
11 Jones C.	11 Rees	11 Rees	11 Jones C.	11 Jones C.
Swansea April 15: 2-3 *Godfrey, Davies*	Cardiff Oct 3: 3-2 *Davies, Leek 2*	Copenhagen Oct 21: 0-1	Wembley Nov 18: 1-2 *Jones*	Athens Dec 9: 0-2

1965 Greece	1965 N Ireland	1965 Italy	1965 USSR	1965 England
1 Hollins	1 Hollins	1 Hollins	1 Millington	1 Sprake
2 Rodrigues	2 Rodrigues	2 Green	2 Green	2 Rodrigues
3 Williams G.	3 Williams G.	3 Williams G.	3 Williams G.	3 Green
4 Williams H.	4 Lea	4 Lea	4 Hennessey	4 Hennessey
5 England	5 England	5 England	5 England	5 England
6 Hole	6 Hole	6 Hole	6 Hole	6 Hole
7 Jones C.	7 Jones C.	7 Jones C.	7 Jones C.	7 Rees
8 Allchurch I.	8 Allchurch I.	8 Allchurch I.	8 Allchurch I.	8 Vernon
9 Leek	9 Davies W.	9 Godfrey	9 Davies W.	9 Davies W.
10 Vernon	10 Vernon	10 Vernon	10 Charles J.	10 Allchurch I.
11 Rees	11 Rees	11 Rees	11 Rees	11 Reece
Cardiff May 17: 4-1 *Allchurch 2, England, Vernon*	Belfast Mar 31: 5-0 *Vernon 2, Jones, Williams, Allchurch*	Florence May 1: 1-4 *Godfrey*	Moscow May 30: 1-2 *Davies*	Cardiff Oct 2: 0-0

1965 USSR	1965 Scotland	1965 Denmark	1966 N Ireland	1966 Brazil
1 Sprake	1 Hollins	1 Hollins	1 Sprake	1 Hollins
2 Rodrigues	2 Rodrigues	2 Rodrigues	2 Rodrigues	2 Green
3 Green	3 Green	3 Williams S.	3 Williams G.	3 Rodrigues
4 Hennessey	4 Hennessey	4 Hennessey	4 Hennessey	4 Hennessey
5 England	5 England	5 England	5 England	5 James
6 Hole	6 Hole	6 Hole	6 Hole	6 Hole
7 Rees	7 Rees	7 Rees	7 Rees	7 Rees
8 Vernon	8 Vernon	8 Vernon	8 Vernon	8 Davies R.
9 Davies W.	9 Davies W.	9 Davies W.	9 Davies W.	9 Davies W.
10 Allchurch I.	10 Allchurch I.	10 Allchurch I.	10 Moore	10 Allchurch I.
11 Reece	11 Reece	11 Pring	11 Reece	11 Williams G.
Cardiff Oct 27: 2-1 *Vernon, Allchurch*	Hampden Nov 24: 1-4 *Allchurch*	Wrexham Dec 1: 4-2 *Vernon 2, Davies, Rees*	Cardiff Mar 30: 1-4 *Davies*	Rio de Janeiro May 14: 1-3 *Davies R.*

1966 **Brazil**	**1966** **Chile**	**1966** **Scotland**	**1966** **England**	**1967** **N Ireland**
1 Millington	1 Millington	1 Sprake	1 Millington	1 Millington
2 Green	2 Rodrigues	2 Rodrigues	2 Green	2 Thomas
3 Rodrigues	3 Williams G.	3 Williams G.	3 Williams G.	3 Williams G.
4 Hennessey	4 Hennessey	4 Hennessey	4 Hennessey	4 Jarvis
5 James E.G.	5 James E.G. (Rankmore)	5 England	5 England	5 James E.G.
6 Hole	6 Hole	6 Hole	6 Hole	6 Hole
7 Rees (Durban)	7 Rees	7 Reece	7 Rees	7 Rees
8 Davies R.	8 Moore	8 Davies W.	8 Davies W.	8 Durban
9 Davies W.	9 Davies R.	9 Davies R.	9 Davies R.	9 Davies R.
10 Allchurch I.	10 Allchurch I.	10 Jones C.	10 Jones C.	10 Vernon
11 Williams G.	11 Pring (Davies W.)	11 Jarvis	11 Jarvis	11 Pring
Belo Horizonte May 18: 0-1	Santiago May 22: 0:2	Cardiff Oct 22: 1-1 *Davies R.*	Wembley Nov 16: 1-5 *Davies W.*	Belfast April 12: 0-0

1967 **England**	**1967** **Scotland**	**1968** **N Ireland**	**1968** **W Germany**	**1968** **Italy**
1 Sprake	1 Sprake	1 Millington	1 Millington	1 Millington
2 Rodrigues	2 Rodrigues	2 Rodrigues	2 Thomas	2 Thomas
3 Green	3 Green	3 Green	3 Green	3 Williams G.
4 Hennessey	4 Hennessey	4 Hennessey	4 Powell	4 Burton
5 England	5 James E.G.	5 England	5 England	5 Powell
6 Hole	6 Hole	6 Hole	6 Hole	6 Hole
7 Rees	7 Rees	7 Rees	7 Rees	7 Rees
8 Durban	8 Davies W.	8 Davies W.	8 Davies W.	8 Davies W.
9 Mahoney	9 Davies R.	9 Davies R.	9 Davies R.	9 Davies R.
10 Vernon	10 Durban	10 Durban	10 Durban	10 Green (Jones B.)
11 Jones C.	11 Jones C.	11 Williams G.	11 Jones C.	11 Jones C.
Cardiff Oct 21: 0-3	Hampden Nov 22: 2-3 *Davies R., Durban*	Wrexham Feb 28: 2-0 *Rees, Davies W.*	Cardiff May 8: 1-1 *Davies W.*	Cardiff Oct 23: 0-1

1969 **W Germany**	**1969** **E Germany**	**1969** **Scotland**	**1969** **England**	**1969** **N Ireland**
1 Sprake	1 Millington	1 Sprake	1 Sprake	1 Sprake
2 Thomas	2 Rodrigues	2 Derrett (Rees)	2 Rodrigues	2 Rodrigues (Green)
3 Derrett	3 Burton	3 Green	3 Thomas	3 Thomas
4 Powell	4 Hennessey	4 Durban	4 Durban	4 Durban
5 Hennessey	5 England	5 Burton	5 Powell	5 Powell
6 Hole	6 Hole	6 Powell	6 Burton	6 Burton
7 Jones B.	7 Jones B.	7 Moore	7 Jones B.	7 Jones B.
8 Durban	8 Durban	8 Toshack	8 Davies R.	8 Davies R.
9 Davies R.	9 Toshack	9 Davies R.	9 Toshack	9 Toshack
10 Toshack	10 Mahoney	10 Davies W.	10 Davies W.	10 Davies W.
11 Rees	11 Rees	11 Jones B.	11 Moore	11 Moore
Frankfurt Mar 26: 1-1 *Jones*	Dresden April 16: 1-2 *Toshack*	Wrexham May 3: 3-5 *Davies R. 2,* *Toshack*	Wembley May 7: 1-2 *Davies R.*	Belfast May 10: 0-0

1969 **Rest of UK**	**1969** **E Germany**	**1969** **Italy**	**1970** **England**	**1970** **Scotland**
1 Sprake	1 Sprake	1 Sprake	1 Millington	1 Millington
2 Rodrigues	2 Rodrigues	2 Thomas	2 Rodrigues	2 Rodrigues
3 Thomas	3 Thomas	3 Derrett	3 Thomas	3 Thomas
4 Hennessey	4 Hennessey	4 Durban	4 Hennessey	4 Hennessey
5 England	5 England	5 England	5 England	5 England
6 Moore	6 Powell	6 Moore	6 Powell	6 Powell
7 Jones B.	7 Durban	7 Yorath	7 Krzywicki	7 Krzywicki
8 Jones C.	8 Krzywicki	8 Toshack	8 Durban	8 Durban
9 Davies R.	9 Davies W.	9 Hole	9 Davies R.	9 Davies R.
10 Toshack	10 Toshack	10 Krzywicki	10 Moore	10 Moore
11 Rees (Reece)	11 Rees	11 Rees (Reece)	11 Rees	11 Rees
Cardiff July 28: 0-1	Cardiff Oct 22: 1-3 *Powell*	Rome Nov 4: 1-4 *England*	Cardiff April 18: 1-1 *Krzywicki*	Hampden April 22: 0-0

1970 **N Ireland**	**1970** **Rumania**	**1971** **Czechoslovakia**	**1971** **Scotland**	**1971** **England**
1 Millington	1 Sprake	1 Millington	1 Sprake	1 Sprake
2 Rodrigues	2 Rodrigues	2 Rodrigues	2 Rodrigues	2 Rodrigues
3 Thomas	3 Thomas	3 Thomas	3 Thomas	3 Thomas
4 Hennessey	4 Powell	4 Phillips	4 James E.G.	4 James E.G.
5 England	5 England	5 James E.G.	5 Roberts J.	5 Roberts J.
6 Powell	6 Hole	6 Walley	6 Yorath	6 Yorath
7 Krzywicki	7 Krzywicki	7 Rees	7 Phillips	7 Phillips
8 Durban	8 Durban	8 Durban	8 Durban	8 Durban
9 Davies R.	9 Davies W.	9 Davies R.	9 Davies R.	9 Davies R.
10 Moore	10 Moore	10 Davies W.	10 Toshack	10 Toshack
11 Rees	11 Rees	11 Mahoney (Griffiths)	11 Reece	11 Reece (Rees)
Swansea April 25: 1-0 *Rees*	Cardiff Nov 11: 0-0	Swansea April 21: 1-3 *Davies R.*	Cardiff May 15: 0-0	Wembley May 18: 0-0

1971 **N Ireland**	**1971** **Finland**	**1971** **Finland**	**1971** **Czechoslovakia**	**1971** **Rumania**
1 Sprake	1 Millington	1 Sprake (Millington)	1 Millington	1 Millington
2 Rodrigues	2 Page	2 Rodrigues	2 Rodrigues	2 Rodrigues
3 Thomas	3 Derrett	3 Thomas	3 Phillips	3 Thomas
4 James E.G.	4 Durban	4 Roberts J.	4 Burton	4 Phillips
5 Roberts J.	5 Roberts J.	5 England	5 Thomas	5 Williams H.
6 Yorath	6 Mielczarek	6 Hennessey	6 Yorath	6 Hockey
7 Phillips (Rees)	7 Krzywicki	7 Evans	7 Hennessey (Rees)	7 James
8 Durban	8 Jones W.	8 Reece	8 Durban	8 Hill (Davies C.)
9 Davies R.	9 Rees	9 Toshack	9 Evans (Krzywicki)	9 Davies R.
10 Toshack	10 Toshack	10 Durban	10 Hill	10 Reece
11 Reece	11 Reece	11 Hockey	11 James	11 Rees
Belfast May 22: 0-1	Helsinki May 26: 1-0 *Toshack*	Swansea Oct 13: 3-0 *Durban, Toshack, Reece*	Prague Oct 27: 0-1	Bucharest Nov 24: 0-2

1972 England	**1972 Scotland**	**1972 N Ireland**	**1972 England**	**1973 England**
1 Sprake	1 Sprake	1 Sprake	1 Sprake	1 Sprake
2 Rodrigues	2 Page	2 Page	2 Rodrigues (Reece)	2 Rodrigues (Page)
3 Thomas	3 Thomas	3 Thomas	3 Thomas	3 Thomas
4 Hennessey	4 Hennessey (James)	4 Yorath (Rodrigues)	4 Hennessey	4 Hockey
5 England	5 England	5 England	5 England	5 England
6 Roberts J. (Reece)	6 Yorath	6 Roberts J.	6 Hockey	6 Roberts J.
7 Yorath	7 Durban	7 Durban	7 Phillips	7 Evans
8 Davies R.	8 Davies W.	8 Davies W.	8 Mahoney	8 Mahoney
9 Davies W.	9 Reece	9 Reece	9 Davies W.	9 Toshack
10 Toshack	10 Davies R.	10 Davies R.	10 Toshack	10 Yorath
11 Durban	11 Phillips	11 Phillips	11 James	11 James
Cardiff May 20: 0-3	Hampden May 24: 0-1	Wrexham May 27: 0-0	Cardiff Nov 15: 0-1	Wembley Jan 24: 1-1 *Toshack*

1973 Poland	**1973 Scotland**	**1973 England**	**1973 N Ireland**	**1973 Poland**
1 Sprake	1 Sprake	1 Phillips J.	1 Sprake	1 Sprake
2 Rodrigues	2 Rodrigues	2 Rodrigues	2 Rodrigues	2 Rodrigues
3 Thomas	3 Thomas	3 Thomas	3 Thomas	3 Thomas
4 Roberts D.	4 Hockey	4 Hockey	4 Hockey (Emanuel)	4 Mahoney (Phillips)
5 Roberts J.	5 England	5 England (Roberts D.)	5 Roberts D.	5 England
6 Hockey	6 Roberts J.	6 Roberts J.	6 Roberts J.	6 Roberts J.
7 James	7 James	7 James	7 James	7 Evans (Reece)
8 Yorath	8 Mahoney	8 Mahoney	8 Mahoney	8 Yorath
9 Toshack	9 Toshack	9 Toshack	9 Reece	9 Davies W.
10 Mahoney	10 Yorath (Davies W.)	10 Page (Emanuel)	10 Page	10 Hockey
11 Evans	11 Evans (O'Sullivan)	11 Evans	11 Davies W.	11 James
Cardiff Mar 28: 2-0 *James, Hockey*	Wrexham May 12: 0-2	Wembley May 15: 0-3	Everton May 19: 0-1	Chorzow Sept 26: 0-3

1974 England	**1974 Scotland**	**1974 N Ireland**	**1974 Austria**	**1974 Hungary**
1 Phillips	1 Sprake	1 Sprake	1 Sprake	1 Sprake (Phillips J.)
2 Roberts P. (Cartwright)	2 Thomas	2 Page	2 Roberts P.	2 Thomas
3 Thomas	3 Page	3 Thomas	3 Phillips	3 Roberts P.
4 Mahoney	4 Mahoney	4 Mahoney	4 Roberts D.	4 Mahoney
5 Roberts J.	5 Roberts J.	5 Roberts J.	5 Roberts J.	5 England
6 Roberts D.	6 Roberts D.	6 Reece	6 Yorath	6 Phillips
7 Reece	7 Reece (Smallman)	7 Yorath	7 Mahoney	7 Griffiths
8 Villars	8 Villars	8 James	8 Griffiths	8 Yorath
9 Davies R. (Smallman)	9 Yorath	9 Smallman (Villars)	9 Reece	9 Reece
10 Yorath	10 Cartwright	10 Phillips	10 Toshack	10 Toshack
11 James	11 James	11 Cartwright	11 James	11 James
Cardiff May 11: 0-2	Hampden May 14: 0-2	Wrexham May 18: 1-0 *Smallman*	Vienna Sept 4: 1-2 *Griffiths*	Cardiff Oct 30: 2-0 *Griffiths, Toshack*

	1974 **Luxembourg**	**1975** **Hungary**	**1975** **Luxembourg**	**1975** **Scotland**	**1975** **England**
1	Sprake	Davies	Davies	Davies	Davies
2	Thomas	Thomas	Page	Thomas	Thomas
3	England	Page	Yorath	Page	Page
4	Roberts P.	Phillips	Thomas	Yorath	Mahoney
5	Phillips	Roberts J.	Roberts D.	Roberts J.	Roberts J.
6	Mahoney (Flynn)	Yorath	Mahoney	Phillips	Phillips
7	Yorath	Mahoney	Phillips	Mahoney	Griffiths
8	Griffiths	Griffiths	Griffiths (Flynn)	Flynn	Flynn
9	James	Reece (Smallman)	Reece	Reece	Smallman (Showers)
10	Reece	Toshack	Toshack	Toshack	Toshack
11	Toshack	James (Flynn)	James	James	James
	Swansea Nov 20: 5-0 *Toshack, England, Roberts P., Griffiths, Yorath*	Budapest April 16: 2-1 *Toshack, Mahoney*	Luxembourg May 1: 3-1 *Reece, James 2* (1 pen)	Cardiff May 17: 2-2 *Toshack, Flynn*	Wembley May 21: 2-2 *Toshack, Griffiths*

	1975 **N Ireland**	**1975** **Austria**	**1976** **England**	**1976** **Yugoslavia**	**1976** **Scotland**
1	Davies	Lloyd	Lloyd	Davies	Lloyd
2	Thomas	Thomas	Page	Thomas	Jones D.
3	Page	Jones J.	Jones J.	Page	Jones J.
4	Mahoney	Mahoney	Yorath	Mahoney	Roberts D.
5	Roberts D.	Evans	Phillips	Phillips	Roberts J.
6	Phillips	Phillips	Evans	Evans	Yorath
7	Griffiths	Griffiths	Harris	James (Curtis)	Griffiths
8	Flynn	Flynn	Flynn	Flynn	Harris (Cartwright)
9	Reece (Smallman)	Yorath	Curtis	Yorath	Curtis
10	Showers	Smallman	Roberts J.	Toshack	O'Sullivan
11	James	James	Griffiths	Griffiths	James
	Belfast May 23: 0-1	Wrexham Nov 19: 1-0 *Griffiths*	Wrexham Mar 24: 1-2 *Curtis*	Zagreb April 24: 0-2	Glasgow May 6: 1-3 *Griffiths* (pen)

	1976 **England**	**1976** **N Ireland**	**1976** **Yugoslavia**	**1976** **W Germany**	**1976** **Scotland**
1	Davies	Davies	Davies	Davies	Davies
2	Thomas (Jones D.)	Phillips	Phillips	Page (Cartwright)	Page
3	Page	Page	Roberts D.	Jones J.	Jones J.
4	Mahoney	Mahoney	Evans	Mahoney	Phillips
5	Phillips	Roberts D.	Page	Phillips	Evans
6	Evans	Evans	Griffiths (Curtis)	Evans	Griffiths
7	Yorath	Griffiths	Yorath	James	Thomas M.
8	Flynn	Flynn	Mahoney	Yorath	Flynn
9	Curtis (Griffiths)	Yorath	Flynn	Curtis	Yorath
10	Toshack	Curtis	Toshack	Thomas M.	Toshack
11	James	James	James	Griffiths (Flynn)	James (Curtis)
	Cardiff May 8: 0-1	Swansea May 14: 1-0 *James*	Cardiff May 22: 1-1 *Evans*	Cardiff Oct 6: 0-2	Glasgow Nov 17: 0-1

1977 Czechoslovakia	1977 Scotland	1977 England	1977 N Ireland	1977 Kuwait
1 Davies	1 Davies	1 Davies	1 Davies	1 Davies
2 Thomas	2 Thomas	2 Thomas	2 Thomas	2 Thomas (Page)
3 Jones J.	3 Jones J.	3 Jones J.	3 Jones J.	3 Jones J.
4 Mahoney	4 Mahoney	4 Mahoney	4 Mahoney	4 Mahoney
5 Phillips	5 Phillips	5 Phillips (Roberts D.)	5 Roberts D.	5 Phillips
6 Evans	6 Evans	6 Evans	6 Evans	6 Roberts D.
7 Sayer	7 Sayer	7 Sayer	7 Sayer (Curtis)	7 Sayer (Deacy)
8 Flynn	8 Flynn	8 Flynn	8 Flynn	8 Flynn
9 Yorath	9 Yorath	9 Yorath	9 Yorath	9 Yorath
10 Deacy	10 Deacy	10 Deacy	10 Deacy	10 Toshack
11 James	11 James (Thomas M.)	11 James	11 James (Thomas M.)	11 James
Wrexham Mar 30: 3-0 *James 2, Deacy*	Wrexham May 28: 0-0	Wembley May 31: 1-0 *James* (pen)	Belfast June 3: 1-1 *Deacy*	Wrexham Sept 6: 0-0

1977 Kuwait	1977 Scotland	1977 Czechoslovakia	1977 W Germany	1978 Iran
1 Phillips J.	1 Davies	1 Davies	1 Davies	1 Davies
2 Page	2 Thomas	2 Thomas	2 Page	2 Page
3 Jones J.	3 Jones J.	3 Jones J.	3 Jones J.	3 Jones J.
4 Mahoney	4 Mahoney	4 Mahoney	4 Jones D.	4 Davis
5 Phillips	5 Jones D.	5 Jones D.	5 Phillips	5 Jones D.
6 Evans	6 Phillips	6 Phillips	6 Harris	6 Mahoney (Flynn)
7 Sayer	7 Flynn	7 Nardiello	7 Flynn	7 Harris (Cartwright)
8 Flynn	8 Sayer	8 Flynn	8 Yorath	8 Yorath
9 Yorath (Roberts D.)	9 Yorath	9 Yorath	9 Deacy	9 Dwyer
10 Toshack (Edwards)	10 Toshack	10 Toshack	10 James	10 Deacy
11 James (Thomas M.)	11 Thomas M.	11 Thomas M. (Deacy)	11 Curtis (Nardiello)	11 Thomas M.
Kuwait Sept 20: 0-0	Liverpool Oct 12: 0-2	Prague Nov 16: 0-1	Dortmund Dec 14: 1-1 *Jones D.*	Teheran April 18: 1-0 *Dwyer*

1978 England	1978 Scotland	1978 N Ireland	1978 Malta	1978 Turkey
1 Davies	1 Davies	1 Davies	1 Davies	1 Davies
2 Page	2 Page (Deacy)	2 Jones J.	2 Stevenson	2 Stevenson
3 Jones J.	3 Jones J.	3 Stevenson	3 Jones J.	3 Jones J.
4 Phillips	4 Roberts D.	4 Roberts D.	4 Phillips	4 Phillips
5 Jones D. (Davis)	5 Phillips	5 Davis	5 Page	5 Yorath
6 Yorath (Mahoney)	6 Yorath	6 Mahoney	6 Thomas M.	6 Thomas M.
7 Harris	7 Mahoney	7 Yorath (Thomas M.)	7 Harris	7 Harris
8 Flynn	8 Flynn	8 Flynn	8 Flynn	8 Flynn
9 Curtis	9 Harris	9 Harris	9 Edwards	9 Deacy
10 Dwyer	10 Dwyer	10 Dwyer	10 James R.	10 Dwyer
11 Thomas M.	11 Curtis	11 Deacy	11 Cartwright (O'Sullivan)	11 James
Cardiff May 13: 1-3 *Dwyer*	Glasgow May 17: 1-1 *Donachie og*	Wrexham May 19: 1-0 *Deacy* (pen)	Wrexham Oct 25: 7-0 *Edwards 4,* *O'Sullivan,* *Thomas, Flynn*	Wrexham Nov 29: 1-0 *Deacy*

1979 **W Germany**	1979 **Scotland**	1979 **England**	1979 **N Ireland**	1979 **Malta**
1 Davies	1 Davies	1 Davies	1 Davies	1 Davies
2 Page	2 Stevenson	2 Stevenson	2 Stevenson	2 Stevenson
3 Jones J.	3 Jones J.	3 Jones J.	3 Jones J.	3 Jones J.
4 Phillips	4 Phillips	4 Phillips	4 Phillips	4 Phillips
5 Berry	5 Dwyer	5 Dwyer	5 Dwyer	5 Nicholas
6 Mahoney	6 Mahoney	6 Mahoney	6 Mahoney	6 Mahoney
7 Yorath (James R.)	7 Yorath (Nicholas)	7 Yorath	7 Yorath	7 Harris (Thomas M.)
8 Harris	8 Flynn	8 Flynn	8 Flynn	8 Flynn (Dwyer)
9 Edwards (Toshack)	9 James R.	9 James R.	9 James R.	9 James R.
10 Curtis	10 Toshack	10 Toshack	10 Toshack	10 Toshack
11 Thomas M.	11 Curtis	11 Curtis	11 Curtis (Nicholas)	11 Curtis
Wrexham May 2: 0-2	Cardiff May 19: 3-0 *Toshack 3*	Wembley May 23: 0-0	Belfast May 25: 1-1 *James*	Valetta June 2: 2-0 *Nicholas, Flynn*

1979 **Rep of Ireland**	1979 **W Germany**	1979 **Turkey**	1980 **England**	1980 **Scotland**
1 Davies	1 Davies	1 Davies	1 Davies	1 Davies
2 Nicholas	2 Stevenson	2 Stevenson	2 Nicholas	2 Nicholas
3 Jones J.	3 Jones J. (Berry)	3 Jones J.	3 Jones J.	3 Jones J.
4 Mahoney	4 Mahoney	4 Yorath	4 Yorath	4 Yorath
5 Berry	5 Phillips	5 Berry	5 Jones D. (Pontin)	5 Pontin (Phillips)
6 Phillips	6 Dwyer	6 Phillips	6 Price	6 Price
7 Yorath	7 Nicholas	7 Davies G. (Mahoney)	7 Giles	7 Giles
8 Flynn	8 Flynn	8 Nicholas	8 Flynn	8 Flynn
9 Walsh	9 Curtis	9 Curtis	9 Walsh	9 Walsh (Rush)
10 Curtis	10 Toshack (Thomas M.)	10 Walsh (Edwards)	10 James	10 James
11 Thomas M.	11 James R.	11 Thomas M.	11 Thomas M.	11 Thomas M.
Swansea Sept 11: 2-1 *Walsh, Curtis*	Cologne Oct 17: 1-5 *Curtis*	Izmir Nov 21: 0-1	Wrexham May 17: 4-1 *Thomas, Walsh, James, Thompson og*	Hampden May 21: 0-1

1980 **N Ireland**	1980 **Iceland**
1 Davies	1 Davies
2 Nicholas	2 Nicholas
3 Jones J.	3 Jones J.
4 Yorath	4 Yorath (Stevenson)
5 Phillips	5 Phillips
6 Price	6 Price
7 Giles	7 Giles
8 Flynn (Harris)	8 Flynn
9 Rush	9 Walsh
10 James	10 James
11 Thomas M.	11 Davies G. (Harris)
Cardiff May 23: 0-1	Reykjavik June 2: 4-0 *Walsh 2, Giles, Flynn* (pen)

UNDER-21 APPEARANCES 1976–1981

ENGLAND

Allen, C. (QPR), 1980 v EG (sub); 1981 (with C Palace) v N, R (3)
Anderson, V. A. (Nottingham F), 1978 v I (1)

Bailey, G. R. (Manchester U), 1979 v W, Bul; 1980 v D, S (2), EG (6)
Baker, G. E. (Southampton), 1981 v N, R (2)
Barnes, P. S. (Manchester C), 1977 v W (sub), S, Fi, N; 1978 v N, Fi, I (2), Y (9)
Bertschin, K. E. (Birmingham C), 1977 v S; 1978 v Y (2) (3)
Birtles, G. (Nottingham F), 1980 v Bul, EG (sub) (2)
Blissett, L. L. (Watford), 1979 v W, Bul (sub), Se; 1980 v D (4)
Bradshaw, P. W. (Wolverhampton W), 1977 v W, S; 1978 v Fi, Y (4)
Butcher, T. I. (Ipswich T), 1979 v Se; 1980 v D, Bul, S (2), EG (2) (7)

Chapman, L. (Stoke C), 1981 v Ei (1)
Corrigan, J. T. (Manchester C), 1978 v I (2), Y (3)
Cowans, G. S. (Aston Villa), 1979 v W, Se; 1980 v Bul, EG; 1981 v R (5)
Crooks, G. (Stoke C), 1980 v Bul, S (2), EG (sub) (4)
Cunningham, L. (WBA), 1977 v S, Fi, N (sub); 1978 v N, Fi, I (6)
Curbishley, L. C. (Birmingham C), 1981 v Sw (1)

Daniel, P. W. (Hull C), 1977 v S, Fi, N; 1978 v Fi, I, Y (2) (7)
Deehan, J. M. (Aston Villa), 1977 v N; 1978 v N, Fi, I; 1979 v Bul, Se (sub); 1980 v D (7)
Dennis, M. E. (Birmingham C), 1980 v Bul; 1981 v N, R (3)
Dillon, K. P. (Birmingham C), 1981 v R (1)
Duxbury, M. (Manchester U), 1981 v Sw (sub), Ei (sub), R (sub), Sw (4)
Dyson, P. I. (Coventry C), 1981 v N, R, Sw, Ei (4)

Fairclough, D. (Liverpool), 1977 v W (1)
Fashanu, J. (Norwich C), 1980 v EG; 1981 v N (sub), R, Sw, Ei (sub), H (6)
Fenwick, T. W. (C Palace), 1981 v N, R, Sw, Ei, (with QPR) R (5)
Foster, S. (Brighton & HA), 1980 v EG (sub) (1)
Futcher, P. (Luton T), 1977 v W, S, Fi, N; (with Manchester C), 1978 v N, Fi, I (2), Y (2); 1979 v D (11)

Gilbert, W. A. (C Palace), 1979 v W, Bul; 1980 v Bul; 1981 v N, R, Sw, R, Sw, H (9)
Goddard, P. (West Ham U), 1981 v N, Sw, Ei (sub) (3)

Haigh, P. (Hull C), 1977 v N (sub) (1)
Hazell, R. J. (Wolverhampton W), 1979 v D (1)
Heath, A. (Stoke C), 1981 v R, Sw, H (3)
Hesford, I. (Blackpool), 1981 v Ei (sub) (1)
Hilaire, V. (C Palace), 1980 v Bul, S (1+sub) EG (2); 1981 v N, R, Sw (sub) (8)
Hinshelwood, P. A. (C Palace), 1978 v N; 1980 v EG (2)
Hoddle, G. (Tottenham H), 1977 v W (sub); 1978 v Fi (sub), I (2), Y; 1979 v D, W, Bul; 1980 v S (2), EG (2) (12)
Hodgson, D. J. (Middlesbrough), 1981 v N, R (sub), Sw, Ei (4)

Johnston, C. P. (Middlesbrough), 1981 v N, Ei (2)
Jones, D. R. (Everton), 1977 v W (1)
Jones, C. H. (Tottenham H), 1978 v Y (sub) (1)

Keegan, G. A. (Manchester C), 1977 v W (1)
King, A. E. (Everton), 1977 v W; 1978 v Y (2)

Langley, T. W. (Chelsea), 1978 v I (sub) (1)
Lee, S. (Liverpool), 1981 v R, Sw, H (3)
Lukic, J. (Leeds U), 1981 v N, R, Ei, R, Sw, H (6)

McCall, S. H. (Ipswich T), 1981 v Sw, H (2)
McMahon, S. (Everton), 1981 v Ei (1)
Middleton, J. (Nottingham F), 1977 v Fi, N; (with Derby Co), 1978 v N (3)
Mills, G. R. (Nottingham F), 1981 v R (1)
Moses, R. M. (WBA), 1981 v N (sub), Sw, Ei, R, Sw, H (6)

Osman, R. C. (Ipswich T), 1979 v W (sub), Se; 1980 v D, S (2) EG (2) (7)
Owen, G. A. (Manchester C), 1977 v S, Fi, N; 1978 v N, Fi, I (2), Y; 1979 v D, W; (with WBA), Bul, Se (sub); 1980 v D, S (2), EG; 1981 v Sw, R (18)

Parkes, P. B. F. (QPR), 1979 v D (1)
Peach, D. S. (Southampton), 1977 v S, Fi, N; 1978 v N, I (2), Y (2) (8)
Proctor, M. (Middlesbrough), 1981 v Ei (sub), Sw (2)

Ranson, R. (Manchester C), 1980 v Bul, EG; 1981 v R (sub), R, Sw, Sw (sub), H (7)
Reeves, K. P. (Norwich C), 1978 v I, Y (2); 1979 v N, W, Bul, Se; 1980 v D, S; (with Manchester C), EG (10)
Regis, C. (WBA), 1979 v D, Bul, Se; 1980 v S, EG (5)
Reid, N. S. (Manchester C), 1981 v H (sub) (1)
Reid, P. (Bolton W), 1977 v S, Fi, N; 1978 v Fi, I, Y (6)
Richards, J. P. (Wolverhampton W), 1977 v Fi, N (2)
Rix, G. (Arsenal), 1978 v Fi (sub), Y; 1979 v D, Se; 1980 v D (sub), Bul, S (7)
Robson, B. (WBA), 1979 v W, Bul (sub), Se; 1980 v D, Bul, S (2) (7)
Rowell, G. (Sunderland), 1977 v Fi (1)

Sansom, K. G. (C Palace), 1979 v D, W, Bul, Se; 1980 v S (2), EG (2) (8)
Shaw, G. R. (Aston Villa), 1981 v Ei, Sw, H (3)
Sims, S. (Leicester C), 1977 v W, S, Fi, N; 1978 v N, Fi, I (2), Y (2) (10)
Smith, M. (Sheffield W), 1981 v Ei, R, Sw, H (4)
Statham, D. J. (WBA), 1978 v Fi; 1979 v W, Bul, Se; 1980 v D (5)
Sunderland, A. (Wolverhampton W), 1977 v W (1)
Swindlehurst, D. (C Palace), 1977 v W (1)

Talbot, B. (Ipswich T), 1977 v W (1)
Thomas, D. (Coventry C), 1981 v Ei (1)
Thompson, G. L. (Coventry C), 1981 v R, Sw, H (3)

Ward, P. D. (Brighton), 1978 v N; 1980 v EG (2)
Wilkins, R. C. (Chelsea), 1977 v W (1)
Williams, S. C. (Southampton), 1977 v S, Fi, N; 1978 v N, I (sub), I, Y (2); 1979 v D, Bul, Se (sub); 1980 v D, EG (2) (14)
Woodcock, A. S. (Nottingham F), 1978 v Fi, I (2)
Woods, C. C. E. (Nottingham F), 1979 v W (sub), Se; (with QPR), 1980 v Bul, EG; 1981 v Sw (5)
Wright, W. (Everton), 1979 v D, W, Bul; 1980 v D, S (2) (6)

SCOTLAND

Aitken, R. (Celtic), 1977 v Cz, W, Sw; 1978 v Cz, W; 1979 v P, N (2); 1980 v B, E (10)
Albiston, A. (Manchester U), 1977 v Cz, W, Sw; 1978 v Sw, Cz (5)
Archibald, S. (Aberdeen), 1980 v B, E (2), WG; (with Tottenham H), 1981 v D (5)

Bannon, E. J. P. (Hearts), 1979 v US, (with Chelsea), P, N (2); (with Dundee U), 1980 v B, WG, E (7)
Bell, D. (Aberdeen), 1981 v D (1)
Bett, J. (Rangers), 1981 v Se, D (2)
Blair, A. (Coventry C), 1980 v E; 1981 v Se (2)
Brazil, A. (Hibernian), 1978 v W (1)

Brazil, A. (Ipswich T), 1979 v N; 1980 v B (2), E (2), WG; 1981 v Se (7)
Brough, J. (Hearts), 1981 v D (1)
Burley, G. E. (Ipswich T), 1977 v Cz, W, Sw; 1978 v Sw, Cz (5)
Burns, T. (Celtic), 1977 v Cz, W, E; 1978 v Sw (4)

Casey, J. (Celtic), 1978 v W (1)
Clark, R. (Aberdeen), 1977 v Cz, W, Sw (3)
Connor, R. (Ayr U), 1981 v Se (1)
Cooper, D. (Clyde), 1977 v Cz, W, Sw, E; (with Rangers), 1978 v Sw, Cz (6)
Craig, T. (Newcastle U), 1977 v E (1)

Dawson, A. (Rangers), 1979 v P, N (2); 1980 v B (2), E (2) WG (8)
Dodds, D. (Dundee U), 1978 v W (1)
Doyle, J. (Partick T), 1981 v D (1)

Ferguson, R. (Hamilton A), 1977 v E (1)
Fitzpatrick, A. (St Mirren), 1977 v W (sub), Sw (sub), E; 1978 v Sw, Cz (5)
Fulton, M. (St Mirren), 1980 v B, WG, E; 1981 v Se, D (sub) (5)

Gillespie, G. (Coventry C), 1979 v US; 1980 v E; 1981 v D (3)

Hartford, R. A. (Manchester C), 1977 v Sw (1)

Jardine, I. (Kilmarnock), 1979 v US (1)

Lindsey, J. (Motherwell), 1979 v US (1)

MacDonald, J. (Rangers), 1980 v WG (sub); 1981 v Se (2)
MacLeod, A. (Hibernian), 1979 v P, N (2) (3)
MacLeod, M. (Dumbarton), 1979 v US; (with Celtic), P (sub), N (2); 1980 v B (5)
McBride, J. (Everton), 1981 v D (1)
McCulloch, A. (Kilmarnock), 1981 v Se (1)
McGarvey, F. (St Mirren), 1977 v E; 1978 v Cz (2)
McGhee, M. (Aberdeen), 1981 v D (1)
McLaughlin, J. (Morton), 1981 v D (1)
McLeish, A. (Aberdeen), 1978 v W; 1979 v US; 1980 v B, E (2) (5)
McNab, N. (Tottenham H), 1978 v W (1)
McNichol, J. (Brentford), 1979 v P, N (2); 1980 v B (2), WG, E (7)
McNiven, D. (Leeds U), 1977 v Cz, W (sub), Sw (sub) (3)
Melrose, J. (Partick T), 1977 v Sw; 1979 v US, P, N (2); 1980 v B (sub), WG, E (8)
Miller, W. (Aberdeen), 1978 v Sw, Cz (2)
Muir, L. (Hibernian), 1977 v Cz (sub) (1)
McCluskey, G. (Celtic), 1979 v US, P; 1980 v B (2) (4)

Narey, D. (Dundee U), 1977 v Cz, Sw; 1978 v Sw, Cz (4)
Nicholas, C. (Celtic), 1981 v Se (1)
Nicol, S. (Ayr U), 1981 v Se (1)

Orr, N. (Morton), 1978 v W (sub); 1979 v US, P, N (2); 1980 v B, E (7)

Parlane, D. (Rangers), 1977 v W (1)
Paterson, C. (Hibernian), 1981 v Se (1)
Payne, G. (Dundee U), 1978 v Sw, Cz, W (3)
Provan, D. (Kilmarnock), 1977 v Cz (sub) (1)

Redford, I. (Rangers), 1981 v Se (sub) (1)
Reid, R. (St Mirren), 1977 v W, Sw, E (3)
Richardson, L. (St Mirren), 1980 v WG, E (sub) (2)
Ritchie, A. (Morton), 1980 v B (1)
Robertson, C. (Rangers), 1977 v E (sub) (1)
Ross, T. W. (Arsenal), 1977 v W (1)
Russell, R. (Rangers), 1978 v W; 1980 v B (2)

Sinclair, G. (Dumbarton), 1977 v E (1)
Smith, G. (Rangers), 1978 v W (1)
Sneddon, A. (Celtic), 1979 v US (1)
Stanton, P. (Hibernian), 1977 v Cz (1)
Stevens, G. (Motherwell), 1977 v E (1)
Stewart, J. (Kilmarnock), 1978 v Sw, Cz; (with Middlesbrough), 1979 v P (3)
Stewart, R. (Dundee U), 1979 v P, N (2); (with West Ham U), 1980 v B (2), E (2), WG; 1981 v D (9)
Strachan, G. (Aberdeen), 1980 v B (1)
Sturrock, P. (Dundee U), 1977 v Cz, W, Sw, E; 1978 v Sw, Cz (6)

Thomson, W. (Partick T), 1977 v E (sub); 1978 v W; (with St Mirren), 1979 v US, N (2); 1980 v B (2), E (2), WG (10)
Tolmie, J. (Morton), 1980 v B (sub) (1)

Wallace, I. (Coventry C), 1978 v Sw (1)
Wark, J. (Ipswich T), 1977 v Cz, W, Sw; 1978 v W; 1979 v P; 1980 v E (2), WG (8)
Watson, A. (Aberdeen), 1981 v Se, D (2)
Watson, K. (Rangers), 1977 v E; 1978 v Sw (sub) (2)

WALES

Aizlewood, M. (Luton T), 1979 v E; 1981 v Ho (2)

Bater, P. T. (Bristol R), 1977 v E, S (2)

Cegielski, W. (Wrexham), 1977 v E (sub), S (2)
Charles, J. M. (Swansea C), 1979 v E; 1981 v Ho (2)
Clark, J. (Manchester U), 1978 v S; (with Derby Co), 1979 v E (2)
Curtis, A. T. (Swansea C), 1977 v E (1)

Davies, I. C. (Norwich C), 1978 v S (sub) (1)
Deacy, N. (PSV Eindhoven), 1977 v S (1)
Doyle, S. C. (Preston NE), 1979 v E (sub) (1)
Dwyer, P. J. (Cardiff C), 1979 v E (1)

Edwards, R. I. (Chester), 1977 v S; 1978 v W (2)
Evans, A. (Bristol R), 1977 v E (1)

Giles, D. C. (Cardiff C), 1977 v S; 1978 v S; 1981 (with Swansea C), v Ho (3)

Hughes, W. (WBA), 1977 v E, S; 1978 v S (3)

Jackett, K. (Watford), 1981 v Ho (1)
James, R. M. (Swansea C), 1977 v E, S; 1978 v S (3)
Jones, F. (Wrexham), 1981 v Ho (1)
Jones, V. (Bristol R), 1979 v E; 1981 v Ho (2)

Kendall, M. (Tottenham H), 1978 v S (1)

Letheran, G. (Leeds U), 1977 v E, S (2)
Lowndes, S. R. (Newport Co), 1979 v E; 1981 v Ho (2)

Nardiello, D. (Coventry C), 1978 v S (1)
Nicholas, P. (C Palace), 1978 v S; 1979 v E (2)

Phillips, L. (Swansea C), 1979 v E (1)
Pontin, K. (Cardiff C), 1978 v S (1)
Price, P. (Luton T), 1981 v Ho (1)

Ratcliffe, K. (Everton), 1981 v Ho (1)
Roberts, J. G. (Wrexham), 1977 v E (1)
Rush, I. (Liverpool), 1981 v Ho (1)

Sayer, P. A. (Cardiff C), 1977 v E, S (2)
Stevenson, W. B. (Leeds U), 1977 v E, S; 1978 v S (3)

Thomas, Martin, R. (Bristol R), 1979 v E; 1981 v Ho (2)
Thomas, Mickey, R. (Wrexham), 1977 v E; 1978 v S (2)
Thomas, D. G. (Leeds U), 1977 v E; 1979 v E (2)
Tibbott, L. (Ipswich T), 1977 v E, S (2)

Walsh, I. P. (C Palace), 1979 v E (1)

NORTHERN IRELAND

Team v Republic of Ireland 1978: Johnston; Nicholl, Hayes, Moreland, O'Neill, Donaghy, Sloan (sub), Harley, Brotherston, Blackledge, Hamilton, McCreery.

ENGLAND 'B' INTERNATIONAL MATCHES

v AUSTRALIA

			E	A
1980	17 Nov	Birmingham	1	0

v AUSTRIA

			E	A
*1979	12 June	Klagenfurt	1	0

Abandoned after an hour's play.

v CZECHOSLOVAKIA

			E	C
1978	28 Nov	Prague	1	0

v FINLAND

			E	F
1949	15 May	Helsinki	4	0

v FRANCE

			E	F
1952	22 May	Le Havre	1	7

v WEST GERMANY

			E	WG
1954	24 Mar	Gelsenkirchen	4	0
1955	23 Mar	Sheffield	1	1
1978	21 Feb	Augsburg	1	2

v ITALY

			E	I
1950	11 May	Milan	0	5

v LUXEMBOURG

			E	L
1950	21 May	Luxembourg	2	1

v MALAYSIA

			E	M
1978	30 May	Kuala Lumpur	1	1

v THE NETHERLANDS

			E	N
1949	18 May	Amsterdam	4	0
1950	22 Feb	Newcastle	1	0
1950	17 Mar	Amsterdam	0	3
1952	26 Mar	Amsterdam	1	0

v NEW ZEALAND

			E	NZ
1978	7 June	Christchurch	4	0
1978	11 June	Wellington	3	1
1978	14 June	Auckland	4	0
1979	17 Oct	Auckland	4	1

v SCOTLAND

			E	S
1953	11 Mar	Edinburgh	2	2
1954	3 Mar	Sunderland	1	1
1956	29 Feb	Dundee	2	2
1957	6 Feb	Birmingham	4	1

v SPAIN

			E	S
1980	26 Mar	Sunderland	1	0
1981	25 Mar	Granada	2	3

v SWITZERLAND

			E	S
1950	18 Jan	Sheffield	5	0
1954	22 May	Basle	0	2
1956	21 Mar	Southampton	4	1

v USA

			E	USA
1980	14 Oct	Manchester	1	0

v YUGOSLAVIA

			E	Y
1954	16 May	Lubljana	1	2
1955	19 Oct	Manchester	5	1

ENGLAND UNOFFICIAL INTERNATIONAL MATCHES

v SCOTLAND

			E	S
D1902	5 Apr	Glasgow	1	1
†1919	26 Apr	Everton	2	2
†1919	3 May	Glasgow	4	3
J1935	21 Aug	Glasgow	2	4
*1939	2 Dec	Newcastle	2	1
*1940	11 May	Glasgow	1	1
*1941	8 Feb	Newcastle	2	3
*1941	3 May	Glasgow	3	1
*1941	4 Oct	Wembley	2	0
*1942	17 Jan	Wembley	3	0
*1942	18 Apr	Glasgow	4	5
*1942	10 Oct	Wembley	0	0
*1943	17 Apr	Glasgow	4	0
*1943	16 Oct	Manchester	8	0
*1944	19 Feb	Wembley	6	2
*1944	22 Apr	Glasgow	3	2
*1944	14 Oct	Wembley	6	2
*1945	3 Feb	Aston Villa	3	2
*1945	14 April	Glasgow	6	1
†1946	13 Apr	Glasgow	0	1

v SWITZERLAND

			E	S
†1946	11 May	Chelsea	4	1

v FRANCE

			E	F
*1945	26 May	Wembley	2	2

v WALES

			E	W
†1919	11 Oct	Cardiff	1	2
†1919	18 Oct	Stoke	2	0
*1939	11 Nov	Cardiff	1	1
*1939	18 Nov	Wrexham	3	2
*1940	13 Apr	Wembley	0	1
*1941	26 Apr	Nottingham	4	1
*1941	7 June	Cardiff	3	2
*1941	25 Oct	Birmingham	2	1
*1942	9 May	Cardiff	0	1
*1942	24 Oct	Wolverhampton	1	2
*1943	27 Feb	Wembley	5	3
*1943	8 May	Cardiff	1	1
*1943	25 Sept	Wembley	8	3
*1944	6 May	Cardiff	2	0
*1944	16 Sept	Liverpool	2	2
*1945	5 May	Cardiff	3	2
†1945	20 Oct	West Bromwich	0	1

v IRELAND

			E	I
†1945	15 Sept	Belfast	1	0

v BELGIUM

			E	B
†1946	19 Jan	Wembley	2	0

v TEAM AMERICA

			E	TA
B1976	30 May	Philadelphia	3	1

D*Declared unofficial owing to disaster at ground.* †*Victory matches.* J*Jubilee match.* **War-time matches.* B*American Bicentennial Tournament.*

IRISH FOOTBALL 1980–81

By Malcolm Brodie

Only a year after winning the British Championship, Northern Ireland passed through one of its gravest crises when England and Wales decided not to fulfil their fixtures at Windsor Park, Belfast, because of the civil unrest prevalent in the province throughout May. It was a disastrous blow, taken against the advice of the Government and the security authorities and without consultation with the Irish FA. It meant a huge financial loss, but more important it dropped morale to zero point as World Cup interest reached its zenith.

Only one fixture was played – that against Scotland at Hampden Park, Glasgow – but the players, naturally, found it difficult to raise their game. Fortunately, World Cup prospects appear reasonably satisfactory with the final two matches at home against Scotland and Israel. Manager Billy Bingham remains confident that his side can be one of the two nations qualifying from what has been a fascinating Group Six. His approach to the series has been thorough and professional, with the advantages of a settled side always evident.

Domestically it was a season when Linfield found themselves with no major trophy, winning the County Antrim Shield as the consolation prize in their final fixture. Yet they revealed a progressive attitude by inviting Southampton, Manchester United, West Bromwich Albion, Blackburn Rovers and Tampa Bay Rowdies, as well as the Dutch second division club, Haarlem, who had provided facilities in Holland for the European game with Nantes – the second played away from home under the UEFA ban after their fans had rioted a year earlier at Dundalk.

The trophies were spread throughout the country, with Glentoran winning the Irish League and Ronnie McFall the 'Manager of the Year'; Ballymena United took the Irish Cup and the Ulster Cup under acting-manager Ivan Murray, who stood in for Alan Campbell, seriously injured in a car crash in August. Cliftonville, a team whose fortunes have revived over the last few years, won the Gold Cup but failed to make any impact in the other competitions.

For most of the season there was speculation that the Irish League would be increased from 12 to 14 clubs, with Derry City and possibly Newry Town re-admitted, but it was decided not to proceed with this at present. Carrick Rangers, Omagh Town and Ballyclare Comrades had also sought admission, but Distillery, who opened New Grosvenor Stadium near Lisburn at the start of the season, and Bangor, the two bottom clubs, were re-elected.

Because of fixture and other difficulties, the Tyler All-Ireland Cup was postponed and the next competition will not be played in the latter part of the 1981–82 season. However, to ensure continuity of involvement, Tylers sponsored in April the League of Ireland Irish League game at Tolka Park, Dublin, the first fixture of this nature since 1974.

Perhaps the most significant move was the resurgence of activity by the Northern Ireland Professional Footballers' Association under its secretary Peter Dornan, a Belfast solicitor and Linfield midfielder. With 100 per cent backing, they drew up a new form of contract which has been accepted by the soccer authorities and will be the subject of further discussion. Players had threatened to strike after they had reached deadlock, but fortunately this did not materialise. From now on, players' status will be considerably improved.

Although attendances increased, sponsorship, transfers – now much more limited than before – and social clubs provided the bulk of revenue, with every competition apart from the Irish League championship having its backer. Officials are hoping that the League championship, too, will soon be supported by commercial enterprise.

IRISH LEAGUE CHAMPIONSHIP

	P	*W*	*D*	*L*	*F*	*A*	*Pts*
Glentoran	22	15	7	0	59	26	37
Linfield	22	16	3	3	57	15	35
Ballymena	22	12	4	6	33	21	28
Crusaders	22	9	6	7	28	26	24
Ards	22	9	6	7	35	40	24
Glenavon	22	7	8	7	37	37	22
Larne	22	9	4	9	26	26	22
Portadown	22	8	5	9	30	34	21
Coleraine	22	8	5	9	28	36	21
Cliftonville	22	5	5	12	20	37	15
Bangor	22	4	5	13	35	54	13
Distillery	22	1	3	18	18	54	5

GUINNESS PLAYER OF THE MONTH

September	Gerry Mullan (Ballymena Utd)
October	Jim Smyth (Portadown)
November	Ciaran McCurry (Cliftonville)
December	Johnny Jamison (Glentoran)
January	Davy Neill (Ballymena Utd)
February	Gary Blackledge (Glentoran)
March	Brendan Tully (Glenavon)
April	Sammy Galway (Ards)

IRISH LEAGUE CHAMPIONSHIP WINNERS

1891	Linfield	1911	Linfield	1935	Linfield	1962	Linfield
1892	Linfield	1912	Glentoran	1936	Belfast Celtic	1963	Distillery
1893	Linfield	1913	Glentoran	1937	Belfast Celtic	1964	Glentoran
1894	Glentoran	1914	Linfield	1938	Belfast Celtic	1965	Derry City
1895	Linfield	1915	Belfast Celtic	1939	Belfast Celtic	1966	Linfield
1896	Distillery	1920	Belfast Celtic	1940	Belfast Celtic	1967	Glentoran
1897	Glentoran	1921	Glentoran	1948	Belfast Celtic	1968	Glentoran
1898	Linfield	1922	Linfield	1949	Linfield	1969	Linfield
1899	Distillery	1923	Linfield	1950	Linfield	1970	Glentoran
1900	Belfast Celtic	1924	Queen's Island	1951	Glentoran	1971	Linfield
1901	Distillery	1925	Glentoran	1952	Glenavon	1972	Glentoran
1902	Linfield	1926	Belfast Celtic	1953	Glentoran	1973	Crusaders
1903	Distillery	1927	Belfast Celtic	1954	Linfield	1974	Coleraine
1904	Linfield	1928	Belfast Celtic	1955	Linfield	1975	Linfield
1905	Glentoran	1929	Belfast Celtic	1956	Linfield	1976	Crusaders
1906	Cliftonville/Dist	1930	Linfield	1957	Glentoran	1977	Glentoran
1907	Linfield	1931	Glentoran	1958	Ards	1978	Linfield
1908	Linfield	1932	Linfield	1959	Linfield	1979	Linfield
1909	Linfield	1933	Belfast Celtic	1960	Glenavon	1980	Linfield
1910	Cliftonville	1934	Linfield	1961	Linfield	1981	Glentoran

MORANS ULSTER CUP

Winners – £1000; *Runners-up* – £600; *Third* – £400; *Fourth* – £300; *Fifth* – £200.

	P	*W*	*D*	*L*	*F*	*A*	*Pts*
Ballymena Utd	11	8	2	1	35	11	18
Linfield	11	6	4	1	28	9	16
Glentoran	11	6	4	1	20	10	16
Glenavon	11	5	2	4	16	22	12
Coleraine	11	3	5	3	20	21	11
Larne	11	4	3	4	11	16	11
Portadown	11	4	2	5	21	17	10
Bangor	11	3	4	4	19	25	10
Cliftonville	11	2	5	4	17	20	9
Crusaders	11	2	3	6	12	23	7
Distillery	11	2	3	6	10	22	7
Ards	11	1	3	7	8	21	5

Winners

1949	Linfield	1957	Linfield	1965	Coleraine	1973	Ards
1950	Larne	1958	Distillery	1966	Glentoran	1974	Linfield
1951	Glentoran	1959	Glenavon	1967	Linfield	1975	Coleraine
1952		1960	Linfield	1968	Coleraine	1976	Glentoran
1953	Glentoran	1961	Ballymena Utd	1969	Coleraine	1977	Linfield
1954	Crusaders	1962	Linfield	1970	Linfield	1978	Linfield
1955	Glenavon	1963	Crusaders	1971	Linfield	1979	Linfield
1956	Linfield	1964	Linfield	1972	Coleraine	1980	Ballymena Utd

HENNESSY GOLD CUP

Section A

	P	*W*	*D*	*L*	*F*	*A*	*Pts*
Linfield	5	4	1	0	14	4	9
Glenavon	5	4	1	0	13	3	9
Portadown	5	2	1	2	8	8	5
Bangor	5	2	0	3	6	10	4
Ards	5	1	0	4	2	12	2
Distillery	5	0	1	4	5	11	1

Section B

	P	*W*	*D*	*L*	*F*	*A*	*Pts*
Cliftonville	5	3	1	1	11	6	7
Glentoran	5	3	1	1	10	5	7
Ballymena Utd	5	1	3	1	11	10	5
Coleraine	5	1	3	1	8	10	5
Crusaders	5	1	1	3	8	10	3
Larne	5	1	1	3	3	10	3

Play-off (*at Windsor Park, Belfast, 2 December 1980*)
Cliftonville 3 (*Moffett, McCurry, Platt*), **Linfield 1** (*Feeney*)

Cliftonville: Johnston; Davey, Largey, Quinn, Platt, McCurry, Holden, Hewitt, Alexander, Mills, Moffett (Sub: McAteer, 77 min).
Linfield: Dunlop; Garrett, Parks, Hayes, Dornan, Mikeown, McKee, Murray, McCurdy, Feeney, Anderson (Sub: Rafferty, 55 min).

Manager of Tournament: Jim Brown (Cliftonville)
Player of Tournament: Ciaran McCurry (Cliftonville)

OTHER IRISH TROPHIES AND COMPETITIONS

	Winners	*Runners-up*
County Antrim Shield	Linfield	Glentoran
Irish League B Division		
Section 1	Newry Town	Duncannon Swifts
Section 2	Cliftonville Oly	Ballymena Utd Res
George Wilson Cup	Linfield Swifts	Crusaders Res
Steel Cup	Dundela	Killyleagh
Intermediate Cup	Newry Town	Chimney Corner
IFA Youth Cup	Glentoran Colts	Plunkett YC
IFA Junior Cup	Ballynafeigh Meth	Wakehurst
Irish Schools Cup	Orangefield	Deramore
County Antrim Junior Shield	1st Bangor OB	Cullybackey

Ulster Footballer of the Year (Promoted by Castlereagh Glentoran Supporters Club): George Dunlop (Linfield)
Northern Ireland Footballer of the Year (FWA): Gary Blackledge (Glentoran)
Young Footballer of the Year: Nigel Worthington (Ballymena United)
Ulster Personality of the Year: Eric Bowyer (Glenavon)
Manager of the Year (Coaches Association): Ronnie McFall (Glentoran)
NIPFA Player of the Year: Gary Blackledge (Glentoran)
Most Promising Newcomer: Nigel Worthington (Ballymena United)
Mullan-Stewart Award for Meritorious Service: Roy Marshall (Irish FA Administrative Staff)

BASS IRISH CUP 1980–81

Winners – £3000; *Runners-up* – £2000; *Defeated semi-finalists* – £1000 each; *Personality of each round* – £250 (First Round – Jimmy Todd [Carrick Rangers]; Second Round – Paul Malone [Ballymena United]; Semi-Finals – Billy Sinclair [Glenavon]; Final – Ivan Murray [act-mgr Ballymena United])

First Round (31 January)

Carrick Rangers v Larne	1-1, 0-1
Coleraine v Ballymena United	1-2
Crusaders v Glentoran	1-3
Ards v Ballyclare Comrades	3-0
Cliftonville v Chimney Corner	0-0, 2-1
Bangor v Newry Town	1-2
Glenavon v Distillery	3-2
Portadown v Linfield	0-0, 3-0

Second Round (21 February)

Cliftonville v Ballymena United	1-4
Glenavon v Carrick Rangers	2-1
Ards v Glentoran	1-3
Linfield v Newry Town	4-1

Semi-Finals (21 March)

Glenavon v Linfield (*at Oval*)	1-0
Ballymena United v Glentoran (*at Windsor Park*)	2-2, 2-0

Final (*at Windsor Park, 2 May. Attendance 8000.*)
Ballymena United 1 (*McQuiston*), **Glenavon 0**

Ballymena United: Matthews; Beattie, Worthington, Fox, R. McCullough, Smyth, Neill, Sloan, McQuiston, P. Malone, McCusker.
Glenavon: T. McCullough; Fielding, McGuckin, McGuigan, Stitt, Bowyer, Wilson, M. Malone, McDonald, Tully, Dennison.

IRISH CUP FINALS (from 1946–47)

1946–47	Belfast Celtic 1, Glentoran 0
1947–48	Linfield 3, Coleraine 0
1948–49	Derry City 3, Glentoran 1
1949–50	Linfield 2, Distillery 1
1950–51	Glentoran 3, Ballymena United 1
1951–52	Ards 1, Glentoran 0
1952–53	Linfield 5, Coleraine 0
1953–54	Derry City 1, Glentoran 0
1954–55	Dundela 3, Glenavon 0
1955–56	Distillery 1, Glentoran 0
1956–57	Glenavon 2, Derry City 0
1957–58	Ballymena United 2, Linfield 0
1958–59	Glenavon 2, Ballymena United 0
1959–60	Linfield 5, Ards 1
1960–61	Glenavon 5, Linfield 1
1961–62	Linfield 4, Portadown 0
1962–63	Linfield 2, Distillery 1
1963–64	Derry City 2, Glentoran 0
1964–65	Coleraine 2, Glenavon 1
1965–66	Glentoran 2, Linfield 0
1966–67	Crusaders 3, Glentoran 1
1967–68	Crusaders 2, Linfield 0
1968–69	Ards 4, Distillery 2
1969–70	Linfield 2, Ballymena United 1
1970–71	Distillery 3, Derry City 0
1971–72	Coleraine 2, Portadown 1
1972–73	Glentoran 3, Linfield 2
1973–74	Ards 2, Ballymena 1
1974–75	Coleraine 1:0:1, Linfield 1:0:0
1975–76	Carrick Rangers 2, Linfield 1
1976–77	Coleraine 4, Linfield 1
1977–78	Linfield 3, Ballymena United 1
1978–79	Cliftonville 3, Portadown 2
1979–80	Linfield 2, Crusaders 0
1980–81	Ballymena United 1, Glenavon 0

WELSH FOOTBALL 1980–81

WELSH FOOTBALL LEAGUE

PREMIER DIVISION

	P	W	D	L	F	A	Pts
Haverfordwest Co	34	19	10	5	61	39	48
Pontllanfraith	34	17	12	5	60	43	46
Ton Pentre	34	17	6	11	45	48	40
Maesteg Park	34	14	11	9	60	41	39
Milford U	34	13	11	10	50	49	37
Briton Ferry Ath	34	15	7	12	50	52	37
Swansea C	34	12	11	11	66	51	35
Caerleon	34	13	9	12	42	39	35
Barry Town	34	14	7	13	45	44	35
Newport Co	34	12	11	11	41	40	35
Pontlottyn	34	10	12	12	41	41	32
Merthyr Tydfil	34	11	9	14	53	50	31
Ammanford T	34	11	8	15	49	54	30
Cardiff Cor	34	12	6	16	47	55	30
Llanelli	34	9	11	14	36	41	29
Bridgend T	34	11	7	16	40	51	29
Pembroke Bor	34	8	11	15	44	52	27
Cardiff C	34	4	9	21	30	70	17

DIVISION 1

	P	W	D	L	F	A	Pts
Sully	34	22	6	6	75	26	50
Lake U	34	20	8	6	61	33	48
Newport YMCA	34	14	17	3	55	28	45
Spencer Works	34	16	13	5	57	36	45
South Glamorgan Inst	34	13	13	8	42	45	39
Blaenrhondda	34	14	9	11	40	43	37
Taffs Well	34	14	5	15	60	54	33
Brecon Cor	34	13	7	14	49	54	33
Tredomen Works	34	11	10	13	46	45	32
BP (Llandarcy)	34	12	7	15	42	43	31
Pontyclun	34	10	11	13	39	44	31
Carmarthen T	34	8	14	12	47	57	30
Abercynon Ath	34	10	9	15	38	41	29
Afan Lido	34	10	9	15	44	52	29
Caerau	34	7	12	15	47	54	26
Treharris Ath	34	7	12	15	36	63	26
Aberaman	34	9	7	18	41	62	25
Morriston T	34	8	7	19	32	71	23

DIVISION TWO

	P	W	D	L	F	A	Pts
Trelewis	38	28	6	4	120	40	62
Pontardawe Ath	38	28	6	4	93	28	62
Clydach United	38	26	7	5	99	37	59
Abergavenny Thursdays	38	26	4	8	115	54	56
Port Talbot Ath	38	25	5	8	82	37	55
Tonyrefail Welfare	38	23	6	9	79	50	52
Ebbw Vale	38	20	6	12	61	43	46
Garw	38	17	5	16	76	61	39
Ferndale Ath	38	15	8	15	71	58	38
Tondu Robins	38	14	7	17	66	71	35
Swansea Univ	38	14	6	18	58	58	34
Panteg	38	11	11	16	55	74	33
Skewen Ath	38	10	13	15	46	75	33
Seven Sisters	38	10	11	17	67	76	31
Tynte R	38	13	5	20	71	92	31
Cwmbran T	38	11	4	23	63	78	26
Ynysybwl	38	10	5	23	49	104	25
Blaina West Side	38	6	10	22	36	85	22
Blaenavon Blues	38	6	6	26	44	99	18
Lewistown	38	0	3	35	27	158	3

WELSH FOOTBALL LEAGUE (NORTH)

DIVISION ONE

	P	W	D	L	F	A	Pts
Colwyn Bay	22	17	5	0	48	16	39
Flint Town U	22	16	5	1	46	12	37
Pwllheli & District	22	13	4	5	48	18	30
Llandudno Amateurs	22	9	6	7	51	34	24
Porthmadog	22	8	5	9	43	34	21
Caernarfon T	22	6	9	7	32	28	21
Blaenau Ffestiniog	22	8	5	9	41	40	21
Conwy United	22	9	2	11	34	43	20
Holyhead U (J)	22	8	2	12	34	44	18
Bangor C	22	3	5	14	35	65	11
Rhyl	22	5	1	16	27	64	11
Menai Bridge (T)	22	4	3	15	19	60	11

HONOURS LIST

League champions: Colwyn Bay
runners-up: Flint Town United
Cookson Cup winners: Colwyn Bay
runners-up: Blaenau Ffestiniog
Alves Cup winners: Pwllheli & District
runners-up: Porthmadog
North Wales Coast FA Challenge Cup winners: Caernarfon Town
runners-up: Bangor City
Barritt Cup winners: Blaenau Ffestiniog
runners-up: Porthmadog

OTHER WELSH HONOURS

Welsh Youth Cup winners: Wrexham FC
Welsh National League (Mid-Wales): Llanidloes Town (*Champions* and *Challenge Cup winners*)
Welsh National League (Wrexham): Cefn Albion (*Champions*); Brymbo Steelworks (*Challenge Cup winners*)
South Wales Senior Challenge Cup winners: Sully FC
North Wales Coast Challenge Cup winners: Caernarvon Town FC
West Wales Senior Challenge Cup winners: Pembroke Borough FC
North-East Wales Challenge Cup winners: Buckley FC
Gwent County Senior Cup winners: Albion Rovers (Newport) FC
Central Wales Challenge Cup winners: Newtown FC

WELSH CUP 1980–81

First Round

Menai Bridge Tigers v Porthmadog	4-2
Conwy U v Caernarvon T	1-3
Abergele U v Llandudno A	0-4
Denbigh T v Pwllheli & District	1-3
Courtaulds Greenfield v Flint Town U	0-2
Buckley v Chirk AAA	0-1
Llay Welfare v Bala T	1-0
Mold Alex v Druids U	1-1, 2-1
Gresford Ath v Ruthin	0-0, 3-2
Montgomery T v Brierley Hill All	1-2
Bridgnorth T v Stourbridge	0-4
Ffostrasol W v Aberystwyth T	2-5
Llandrindod Wells v Knighton T	1-2
Aber AC v Talgarth	0-3
Llanidloes T wo Machynlleth (withdrew)	
Caersws v Welshpool	2-4
Towyn v Rhayader T	3-1
Aberaman v Cardiff Corinthians	0-2
Taffs Well v Bryntirion Ath	1-1, 2-1
South Glam Institute v Newport YMCA	1-1, 1-0
Afan Lido v Spencer Works	2-0
Sully v Caerleon	1-1, 0-1
Pontyclun v Ferndale Ath	1-2
Cwmbran Celtic v Abercynon Ath	0-4
Llanelli v Briton Ferry Ath	2-1
Pembroke Borough v Morriston T	2-0
Coedffranc v Pontardawe Ath	0-4
Milford U v Ammanford T	0-1

Second Round

Rhyl v Brymbo Steelworks	0-1
Welshpool v Oswestry T	2-1
Colwyn Bay v Menai Bridge Tigers	1-0
Flint Town U v Towyn	1-1, 0-1
Knighton T v Caernarvon T	1-1, 5-4
Chirk AAA v Pwllheli & District	1-1, 0-3
Aberystwyth T v Connah's Quay N	1-2
Blaenau Ffestiniog v Mold Alex	4-2
Gresford Ath v Llanidloes T	0-3
Newtown v Llay Welfare	7-1
Presteigne St Andrews wo Nantlle Vale (withdrew)	
Llandudno A v Berriew	5-1
Caerleon v Afan Lido	1-1, 2-0
Stourbridge v Pontllanfraith	1-1, 1-0
Caerau v Ammanford T	1-3
Bridgend T v South Glam Institute	0-1
Ton Pentre v Taffs Well	3-2
Maesteg Park v BP Llandarcy	2-2, 6-0
Pembroke Borough v Talgarth	4-3
Haverfordwest C v Ferndale Ath	7-0
Kidderminster H v Worcester C	0-2
Brierley Hill A v Cardiff Corinthians	1-1
(*Brierley Hill unable to fulfil replay fixture*)	
Abercynon Ath v Pontardawe Ath	4-1

Third Round

Brymbo Steelworks v Bangor C	1-4
Towyn v Presteigne St Andrews	2-2, 1-2
Llandudno A v Colwyn Bay	1-0
Wrexham v Pwllheli & District	6-0
Connah's Quay v Blaenau Ffestiniog	1-0
Hereford U v Newtown	1-0
Llanidloes T v Shrewsbury T (*at Shrewsbury*)	0-5
Knighton T v Welshpool	2-1
Abercynon Ath v Ammanford T	4-0
Cardiff Corinthians v Cardiff C (*at Ninian Park*)	0-6
Newport Co v Worcester C	2-2, 3-2
Caerleon v Swansea C (*at Vetch Field*)	1-5
Maesteg Park v South Glam Institute	5-2
Stourbridge v Ton Pentre	2-3
Merthyr Tydfil v Haverfordwest C	2-0
Barry T v Pembroke B	2-2, 2-1

Fourth Round

Presteigne St Andrews v Bangor C	0-2
Wrexham v Cardiff C	3-0
Llandudno A v Connah's Quay N	1-1, 1-2
Newport Co v Ton Pentre	3-0
Knighton T v Hereford U	1-4
Maesteg Park v Barry T	3-2
Shrewsbury T v Abercynon Ath	6-1
Merthyr Tydfil v Swansea C	0-2

Fifth Round

Swansea C v Maesteg Park	4-1
Shrewsbury T v Hereford U	2-2, 0-5
Wrexham v Connah's Quay N	2-1
Newport Co v Bangor C	3-1

Semi-Final

Hereford U v Newport Co	2-1, 1-1
Wrexham v Swansea C	2-2, 1-1
(*Swansea C won on away goals*)	

Final – First Leg: Swansea C 1, Hereford U 0

(*At Swansea, 4 May, 1981*)

Swansea C: Stewart; Evans, Hadziabdic, Robinson, Mahoney, Lewis, Curtis, James R., James L., Charles, Craig.

Hereford U: Cashley; Price, Bartley, Hicks, Cornes, Spiring, Harvey, Laidlaw, Showers, McGrellis, White.

Second Leg: Hereford U 1, Swansea C 1

(*At Hereford, 11 May 1981*)

Hereford U: Cashley; Price, Bartley, Hicks, Cornes, Spiring, Harvey, Laidlaw, Showers, McGrellis, White.

Swansea C: Stewart; Robinson, Attley, Evans, Mahoney, Lewis, Giles, James R., James L., Charles, Craig.

WELSH INTERMEDIATE CUP 1980–81

First Round

Menai Bridge Tigers v Holyhead	1-0
Rhostyllen Villa v Castell Alun Colts	4-2
Guilsfield v Waterloo R	2-3
Llangedwyn v Four Crosses	0-2
Shirenewton v Llantwit Major	1-8
Cwmbran Celtic v Cardiff Cosmos	1-3
Newport Corinthians v Bryntirion Ath	1-2
Llanelli Steel v Pontardulais T	3-0
Coedffranc v Carmarthen T	0-5

Second Round

Cemaes v Holywell T	1-0
Llanberis Ath v Menai Bridge T	1-1, 4-3
Cefn Albion v Rhos Aelwyd	4-2
Rhostyllen Villa v Lex XI	3-3, 2-1
Four Crosses v Llanfair C'ion	2-2, 5-4
Brecon Cor v Waterloo R	11-0
Welshpool R v Llanfyllin	2-3
Harlech T v Bow Street	3-0
Dolgellau Ath v Barmouth & Dyffryn	5-3
Aber AC v Newcastle Emlyn	2-1
Aberaeron v Bont	1-7
Penrhyncoch v Bargod R	6-1
Llantwit Major v Cardiff Cosmos	4-1
Alcan v Caldicot T	1-0
Tredomen Works v Bryntirion Ath	2-3
Carmarthen T v Abercynon Ath	3-2
Risca U v Fields Park	1-1, 1-2
Llanelli Steel v Ammanford T	0-1

Third Round

Flint Town U v Hawarden R	1-2
Conwy U v Connah's Quay N	0-3
Courtaulds Greenfield v Llanberis Ath	2-2, 4-7
Llandudno A v Abergele U	0-1
Cemaes v Blaenau Ffestiniog	0-4
Ruthin v Llay Welfare	2-2, 0-1
Cefn Albion v Denbigh T	2-2, 2-0
Bala T v Mold Alex	2-3
Rhostyllen Villa v Druids U	1-1, 0-1
Gresford Ath v Chirk AAA	1-1, 2-3
Brymbo Steelworks v Llangollen	5-0
Berriew v Buckley	1-1, 0-3
Penrhyncoch v Towyn	1-1, 0-4
UCW Aberystwyth v Caersws	1-2
Rhayader T v Newtown	0-2
Presteigne St Andrews v Bont	8-0
Harlech T v Welshpool	0-5
Llanfyllin wo Machynlleth (withdrew)	
Brecon Corinthians v Four Crosses	2-0
Aberystwyth T v Llanidloes T	0-2
Aber AC v Llandrindod Wells	2-4
Dolgellau Ath v Montgomery T	2-0
Briton Ferry Ath v South Glam Institute	4-1
Blaenrhondda v Treharris Ath	1-0
Sully v Dafen Welfare	2-0
Newport YMCA v Llantwit Major	3-0
Taffs Well v Carmarthen T	2-0
Bryntirion A v Abergavenny Thursdays	2-1
Cardiff Corinthians v Ammanford T	3-0
Afan Lido v Alcan	0-0, 1-4
Talgarth v Aberaman	1-2
Tonyrefail Welfare v Fields Park	2-3

Fourth Round

Dolgellau A v Connah's Quay N	1-3
Blaenau Ffestiniog v Caersws	1-2
Brymbo Steelworks v Mold Alex	1-1, 0-1
Abergele U v Buckley	2-3
Chirk AAA v Llay Welfare	0-1
Cefn Albion v Welshpool	2-1
Hawarden R v Llanberis Ath	3-1
Newtown v Druids U	1-1, 4-1
Towyn v Llanfyllin	1-1, 1-0
(*Towyn dismissed from competition following protest by Llanfyllin*)	
Blaenrhondda v Cardiff Corinthians	0-2
Taffs Well v Llanidloes T	1-0
Aberaman v Sully	2-2, 2-5
Alcan v Newport YMCA	1-3
Presteigne St Andrews v Bryntirion Ath	0-2
Briton Ferry Ath v Llandrindod Wells	2-1
Fields Park v Brecon Corinthians	2-3

Fifth Round

Cardiff Corinthians v Connah's Quay N	0-3
Buckley v Taffs Well	2-0
Briton Ferry Ath v Caersws	1-2
Hawarden R v Cefn Albion	2-3
Newport YMCA v Bryntirion Ath	1-0
Llay Welfare v Brecon Corinthians	1-3
Mold Alex v Newtown	5-2
Llanfyllin v Sully	1-2

Sixth Round

Brecon Corinthians v Newport YMCA	0-2
Connah's Quay N v Cefn Albion	3-0
Buckley v Sully	4-0, 1-0
(*First match abandoned after 72 mins; fog*)	
Caersws v Mold Alex	3-1

Semi-Final

Caersws v Connah's Quay N	1-2
Newport YMCA v Buckley	1-0

Final

Connah's Quay Nomads v Newport YMCA	1-0

WELSH INTERMEDIATE CUP 1975–80

(replacing Welsh Amateur Cup)

1975–76	Cardiff Coll of Ed 2, Shifnal T 1
1976–77	Welshpool 4, Whitchurch Alport 1
1977–78	Caernarvon T 1, Llanidloes T 0
1978–79	Flint Town U 0, Pontllanfraith 1
1979–80	Blaenau Ffestiniog 3:1, Brymbo Steelworks 3:0

THE WORLD CUP 1930–1978

URUGUAY 1930

Pool 1

France 4, Mexico 1
Argentina 1, France 0
Chile 3, Mexico 0
Chile 1, France 0
Argentina 6, Mexico 3
Argentina 3, Chile 1

	P	*W*	*D*	*L*	*F*	*A*	*Pts*
Argentina	3	3	0	0	10	4	6
Chile	3	2	0	1	5	3	4
France	3	1	0	2	4	3	2
Mexico	3	0	0	3	4	13	0

Pool 2

Yugoslavia 2, Brazil 1
Yugoslavia 4, Bolivia 0
Brazil 4, Bolivia 0

	P	*W*	*D*	*L*	*F*	*A*	*Pts*
Yugoslavia	2	2	0	0	6	1	4
Brazil	2	1	0	1	5	2	2
Bolivia	2	0	0	2	0	8	0

Pool 3

Rumania 3, Peru 1
Uruguay 1, Peru 0
Uruguay 4, Rumania 0

	P	*W*	*D*	*L*	*F*	*A*	*Pts*
Uruguay	2	2	0	0	5	0	4
Rumania	2	1	0	1	3	5	2
Peru	2	0	0	2	1	4	0

Pool 4

United States 3, Belgium 0
United States 3, Paraguay 0
Paraguay 1, Belgium 0

	P	*W*	*D*	*L*	*F*	*A*	*Pts*
United States	2	2	0	0	6	0	4
Paraguay	2	1	0	1	1	3	2
Belgium	2	0	0	2	0	4	0

Semi-Finals

Argentina 6, United States 1
Uruguay 6, Yugoslavia 1

Final (Montevideo, 30 July, 1930)

Uruguay (1) 4, Argentina (2) 2

Uruguay: Ballesteros; Nasazzi (capt), Mascheroni, Andrade, Fernandez, Gestido, Dorado, Scarone, Castro, Cea, Iriarte.

Argentina: Botasso; Della Torre, Paternoster, Evaristo J., Monti, Suarez, Peucelle, Varallo, Stabile, Ferreira (capt), Evaristo M.

Scorers: Dorado, Cea, Iriarte, Castro for Uruguay; Peucelle, Stabile for Argentina.

Leading scorer: Stabile (Argentina) 8.

ITALY 1934

First Round

Italy 7, United States 1
Czechoslovakia 2, Rumania 1
Germany 5, Belgium 2
Austria 3, France 2
Spain 3, Brazil 1
Switzerland 3, Holland 2
Sweden 3, Argentina 2
Hungary 4, Egypt 2

Second Round

Germany 2, Sweden 1
Austria 2, Hungary 1
Italy 1, Spain 1
Italy 1, Spain 0 *replay*
Czechoslovakia 3, Switzerland 2

Semi-Finals

Czechoslovakia 3, Germany 1 (in Rome)
Italy 1, Austria 0 (in Milan)

Third Place Match (Naples)

Germany 3, Austria 2

Final (Rome, 10 June, 1934)

Italy (0) (1) 2, Czechoslovakia (0) (1) 1 aet

Italy: Combi (capt); Monzeglio, Allemandi; Ferraris IV, Monti, Bertolini, Guaita, Meazza, Schiavio, Ferrari, Orsi.

Czechoslovakia: Planicka (capt); Zenisek, Ctyroky, Kostalek, Cambal, Krcil; Junek, Svoboda, Sobotka, Nejedly, Puc.

Scorers: Orsi, Schiavio for Italy; Puc for Czechoslovakia.

Leading scorers: Schiavio (Italy), Nejedly (Czechoslovakia), Conen (Germany) 4 each.

FRANCE 1938

First Round

Switzerland 1, Germany 1
Switzerland 4, Germany 2 *replay*
Cuba 3, Rumania 3
Cuba 2, Rumania 1 *replay*
Hungary 6, Dutch East Indies 0
France 3, Belgium 1
Czechoslovakia 3, Holland 0
Brazil 6, Poland 5
Italy 2, Norway 1

Second Round

Sweden 8, Cuba 0
Hungary 2, Switzerland 0
Italy 3, France 1
Brazil 1, Czechoslovakia 1
Brazil 2, Czechoslovakia 1 *replay*

Semi-Finals

Italy 2, Brazil 1 (in Marseilles)
Hungary 5, Sweden 1 (in Paris)

Third Place Match (Bordeaux)

Brazil 4, Sweden 2

Final (Paris, 19 June, 1938)

Italy (3) 4, Hungary (1) 2
Italy: Olivieri; Foni, Rava; Serantoni, Andreolo, Locatelli; Biavati, Meazza (capt), Piola, Ferrari, Colaussi.

Hungary: Szabo; Polgar, Biro; Szalay, Szucs, Lazar; Sas, Vincze, Sarosi (capt), Szengeller, Titkos.

Scorers: Colaussi 2, Piola 2 for Italy; Titkos, Sarosi for Hungary.

Leading Scorer: Leonidas (Brazil) 8.

BRAZIL 1950

Pool 1

Brazil 4, Mexico 0
Yugoslavia 3, Switzerland 0
Yugoslavia 4, Mexico 1
Brazil 2, Switzerland 2
Brazil 2, Yugoslavia 0
Switzerland 2, Mexico 1

	P	*W*	*D*	*L*	*F*	*A*	*Pts*
Brazil	3	2	1	0	8	2	5
Yugoslavia	3	2	0	1	7	3	4
Switzerland	3	1	1	1	4	6	3
Mexico	3	0	0	3	2	10	0

Pool 2

Spain 3, United States 1
England 2, Chile 0
United States 1, England 0
Spain 2, Chile 0
Spain 1, England 0
Chile 5, United States 2

	P	*W*	*D*	*L*	*F*	*A*	*Pts*
Spain	3	3	0	0	6	1	6
England	3	1	0	2	2	2	2
Chile	3	1	0	2	5	6	2
United States	3	1	0	2	4	8	2

Pool 3

Sweden 3, Italy 2
Sweden 2, Paraguay 2
Italy 2, Paraguay 0

	P	*W*	*D*	*L*	*F*	*A*	*Pts*
Sweden	2	1	1	0	5	4	3
Italy	2	1	0	1	4	3	2
Paraguay	2	0	1	1	2	4	1

Pool 4

Uruguay 8, Bolivia 0

	P	*W*	*D*	*L*	*F*	*A*	*Pts*
Uruguay	1	1	0	0	8	0	2
Bolivia	1	0	0	1	0	8	0

Final Pool

Final pool replaced knockout system.

Uruguay 2, Spain 2
Brazil 7, Sweden 1
Uruguay 3, Sweden 2
Brazil 6, Spain 1
Sweden 3, Spain 1

Uruguay (0) 2, Brazil (0) 1 (Rio de Janeiro, 16 July, 1950)

Uruguay: Maspoli; Matthias, Gonzales, Tejera; Gambetta, Varela (capt), Andrade; Ghiggia, Perez, Miguez, Schiaffino, Moran.

Brazil: Barbosa; Augusto (capt), Juvenal; Bauer, Danilo, Bigode; Friaça, Zizinho, Ademir, Jair, Chico.

Scorers: Schiffino, Ghiggia for Uruguay; Friaça for Brazil.

	P	*W*	*D*	*L*	*F*	*A*	*Pts*
Uruguay	3	2	1	0	7	5	5
Brazil	3	2	0	1	14	4	4
Sweden	3	1	0	2	6	11	2
Spain	3	0	1	2	4	11	1

Leading Scorer: Ademir (Brazil) 7

SWITZERLAND 1954

Group 1

Yugoslavia 1, France 0
Brazil 5, Mexico 0
France 3, Mexico 2
Brazil 1, Yugoslavia 1

	P	*W*	*D*	*L*	*F*	*A*	*Pts*
Brazil	2	1	1	0	6	1	3
Yugoslavia	2	1	1	0	2	1	3
France	2	1	0	1	3	3	2
Mexico	2	0	0	2	2	8	0

Group 2

Hungary 9, Korea 0
West Germany 4, Turkey 1
Hungary 8, West Germany 3
Turkey 7, Korea 0

	P	*W*	*D*	*L*	*F*	*A*	*Pts*
Hungary	2	2	0	0	17	3	4
West Germany	2	1	0	1	7	9	2
Turkey	2	1	0	1	8	4	2
Korea	2	0	0	2	0	16	0

Play-off: West Germany 7, Turkey 2

Group 3

Austria 1, Scotland 0
Uruguay 2, Czechoslovakia 0
Austria 5, Czechoslovakia 0
Uruguay 7, Scotland 0

	P	*W*	*D*	*L*	*F*	*A*	*Pts*
Uruguay	2	2	0	0	9	0	4
Austria	2	2	0	0	6	0	4
Czechoslovakia	2	0	0	2	0	7	0
Scotland	2	0	0	2	0	8	0

Group 4

England 4, Belgium 4
England 2, Switzerland 0
Switzerland 2, Italy 1
Italy 4, Belgium 1

	P	*W*	*D*	*L*	*F*	*A*	*Pts*
England	2	1	1	0	6	4	3
Italy	2	1	0	1	5	3	2
Switzerland	2	1	0	1	2	3	2
Belgium	2	0	1	1	5	8	1

Play-off: Switzerland 4, Italy 1

Quarter-Finals

West Germany 2, Yugoslavia 0
Hungary 4, Brazil 2
Austria 7, Switzerland 5
Uruguay 4, England 2

Semi-Finals

West Germany 6, Austria 1 (in Basle)
Hungary 4, Uruguay 2 (in Lausanne)

Third Place Match (Zurich)

Austria 3, Uruguay 1

Final (Berne, 4 July, 1954)

West Germany (2) 3, Hungary (2) 2

West Germany: Turek; Posipal, Kohlmeyer; Eckel, Liebrich, Mai; Rahn, Morlock, Walter O., Walter F. (capt), Schaefer.

Hungary: Grosics; Buzansky, Lantos; Bozsik, Lorant, Zakarias; Czibor, Kocsis, Hidegkuti, Puskas (capt), Toth J.

Scorers: Morlock, Rahn 2 for West Germany; Puskas, Czibor for Hungary.

Leading Scorer: Kocsis (Hungary) 11.

SWEDEN 1958

Group 1

West Germany 3, Argentina 1
Northern Ireland 1, Czechoslovakia 0
West Germany 2, Czechoslovakia 2
Argentina 3, Northern Ireland 1
West Germany 2, Northern Ireland 2
Czechoslovakia 6, Argentina 1

	P	*W*	*D*	*L*	*F*	*A*	*Pts*
West Germany	3	1	2	0	7	5	4
Czechoslovakia	3	1	1	1	8	4	3
Ireland	3	1	1	1	4	5	3
Argentina	3	1	0	2	5	10	2

Play-off: Northern Ireland 2, Czechoslovakia 1

Group 2

France 7, Paraguay 3
Yugoslavia 1, Scotland 1
Yugoslavia 3, France 2
Paraguay 3, Scotland 2
France 2, Scotland 1
Yugoslavia 3, Paraguay 3

	P	*W*	*D*	*L*	*F*	*A*	*Pts*
France	3	2	0	1	11	7	4
Yugoslavia	3	1	2	0	7	6	4
Paraguay	3	1	1	1	9	12	3
Scotland	3	0	1	2	4	6	1

Group 3

Sweden 3, Mexico 0
Hungary 1, Wales 1
Wales 1, Mexico 1
Sweden 2, Hungary 1
Sweden 0, Wales 0
Hungary 4, Mexico 0

	P	*W*	*D*	*L*	*F*	*A*	*Pts*
Sweden	3	2	1	0	5	1	5
Hungary	3	1	1	1	6	3	3
Wales	3	0	3	0	2	2	3
Mexico	3	0	1	2	1	8	1

Play-off: Wales 2, Hungary 1

Group 4

England 2, USSR 2
Brazil 3, Austria 0
England 0, Brazil 0
USSR 2, Austria 0
Brazil 2, USSR 0
England 2, Austria 2

	P	*W*	*D*	*L*	*F*	*A*	*Pts*
Brazil	3	2	1	0	5	0	5
England	3	0	3	0	4	4	3
USSR	3	1	1	1	4	4	3
Austria	3	0	1	2	2	7	1

Play-off: USSR 1, England 0

Quarter-Finals

France 4, Ireland 0
West Germany 1, Yugoslavia 0
Sweden 2, USSR 0
Brazil 1, Wales 0

Semi-Finals

Brazil 5, France 2 (in Stockholm)
Sweden 3, West Germany 1 (in Gothenburg)

Third Place Match (Gothenburg)

France 6, West Germany 3

Final (Stockholm, 29 June, 1958)

Brazil (2) 5, Sweden (1) 2

Brazil: Gilmar; Santos D., Santos N.; Zito, Bellini, Orlando, Garrincha, Didi, Vavà, Pelé, Zagalo.

Sweden: Svensson; Bergmark, Axbom; Boerjesson, Gustavsson, Parliag, Hamrin, Gren, Simonsson, Liedholm, Skoglund.

Scorers: Vavà 2, Pelé 2, Zagalo for Brazil; Liedholm, Simonsson for Sweden.

Leading Scorer: Fontaine (France) 13 (present record total).

CHILE 1962

Group 1

Uruguay 2, Colombia 1
USSR 2, Yugoslavia 0
Yugoslavia 3, Uruguay 1
USSR 4, Colombia 4
USSR 2, Uruguay 1
Yugoslavia 5, Colombia 0

	P	*W*	*D*	*L*	*F*	*A*	*Pts*
USSR	3	2	1	0	8	5	5
Yugoslavia	3	2	0	1	8	3	4
Uruguay	3	1	0	2	4	6	2
Colombia	3	0	1	2	5	11	1

Group 2

Chile 3, Switzerland 1
West Germany 0, Italy 0
Chile 2, Italy 0
West Germany 2, Switzerland 1
West Germany 2, Chile 0
Italy 3, Switzerland 0

	P	*W*	*D*	*L*	*F*	*A*	*Pts*
West Germany	3	2	1	0	4	1	5
Chile	3	2	0	1	5	3	4
Italy	3	1	1	1	3	2	3
Switzerland	3	0	0	3	2	8	0

Group 3

Brazil 2, Mexico 0
Czechoslovakia 1, Spain 0
Brazil 0, Czechoslovakia 0
Spain 1, Mexico 0
Brazil 2, Spain 1
Mexico 3, Czechoslovakia 1

	P	*W*	*D*	*L*	*F*	*A*	*Pts*
Brazil	3	2	1	0	4	1	5
Czechoslovakia	3	1	1	1	2	3	3
Mexico	3	1	0	2	3	4	2
Spain	3	1	0	2	2	3	2

Group 4

Argentina 1, Bulgaria 0
Hungary 2, England 1
England 3, Argentina 1
Hungary 6, Bulgaria 1
Argentina 0, Hungary 0
England 0, Bulgaria 0

	P	*W*	*D*	*L*	*F*	*A*	*Pts*
Hungary	3	2	1	0	8	2	5
England	3	1	1	1	4	3	3
Argentina	3	1	1	1	2	3	3
Bulgaria	3	0	1	2	1	7	1

Quarter-Finals

Yugoslavia 1, West Germany 0
Brazil 3, England 1
Chile 2, USSR 1
Czechoslovakia 1, Hungary 0

Semi-Finals

Brazil 4, Chile 2 (in Santiago)
Czechoslovakia 3, Yugoslavia 1 (in Viña del Mar)

Third Place Match (Santiago)

Chile 1, Yugoslavia 0

Final (Santiago, 17 June, 1962)

Brazil (1) 3, Czechoslovakia (1) 1

Brazil: Gilmar; Santos D., Mauro, Zozimo, Santos N.; Zito, Didi; Garrincha, Vavà, Amarildo, Zagalo.

Czechoslovakia: Schroiff; Tichy, Novak; Pluskal, Popluhar, Masopust, Pospichal, Scherer, Kvasniak, Kadraba, Jelinek.

Scorers: Amarildo, Zito, Vavà for Brazil; Masopust for Czechoslovakia.

Leading Scorer: Jerkovic (Yugoslavia) 5.

ENGLAND 1966

Group 1

England 0, Uruguay 0
France 1, Mexico 1
Uruguay 2, France 1
England 2, Mexico 0
Uruguay 0, Mexico 0
England 2, France 0

	P	*W*	*D*	*L*	*F*	*A*	*Pts*
England	3	2	1	0	4	0	5
Uruguay	3	1	2	0	2	1	4
Mexico	3	0	2	1	1	3	2
France	3	0	1	2	2	5	1

Group 2

West Germany 5, Switzerland 0
Argentina 2, Spain 1
Spain 2, Switzerland 1
Argentina 0, West Germany 0
Argentina 2, Switzerland 0
West Germany 2, Spain 1

	P	*W*	*D*	*L*	*F*	*A*	*Pts*
West Germany	3	2	1	0	7	1	5
Argentina	3	2	1	0	4	1	5
Spain	3	1	0	2	4	5	2
Switzerland	3	0	0	3	1	9	0

Group 3

Brazil 2, Bulgaria 0
Portugal 3, Hungary 1
Hungary 3, Brazil 1
Portugal 3, Bulgaria 0
Portugal 3, Brazil 1
Hungary 3, Bulgaria 1

	P	*W*	*D*	*L*	*F*	*A*	*Pts*
Portugal	3	3	0	0	9	2	6
Hungary	3	2	0	1	7	5	4
Brazil	3	1	0	2	4	6	2
Bulgaria	3	0	0	3	1	8	0

Group 4

USSR 3, North Korea 0
Italy 2, Chile 0
Chile 1, North Korea 1
USSR 1, Italy 0
North Korea 1, Italy 0
USSR 2, Chile 1

	P	*W*	*D*	*L*	*F*	*A*	*Pts*
USSR	3	3	0	0	6	1	6
North Korea	3	1	1	1	2	4	3
Italy	3	1	0	2	2	2	2
Chile	3	0	1	2	2	5	1

Quarter-Finals

England 1, Argentina 0
West Germany 4, Uruguay 0
Portugal 5, North Korea 3
USSR 2, Hungary 1

Semi-Finals

West Germany 2, USSR 1 (at Goodison Park)
England 2, Portugal 1 (at Wembley)

Third Place Match (Wembley)

Portugal 2, USSR 1

Final (Wembley, 30 July, 1966)

England (1) (2) 4, West Germany (1) (2) 2 aet

England: Banks; Cohen, Wilson; Stiles, Charlton J., Moore; Ball, Hurst, Hunt, Charlton R., Peters.

West Germany: Tilkowski; Hottges, Schulz, Weber, Schnellinger; Haller, Beckenbauer; Overath, Seeler, Held, Emmerich.

Scorers: Hurst 3, Peters for England; Haller, Weber for West Germany.

Leading Scorer: Eusebio (Portugal) 9.

MEXICO 1970

Group A

Mexico 0, USSR 0
Belgium 3, El Salvador 0
USSR 4, Belgium 1
Mexico 4, El Salvador 0
USSR 2, El Salvador 0
Belgium 0, Mexico 1

	P	*W*	*D*	*L*	*F*	*A*	*Pts*
USSR	3	2	1	0	6	1	5
Mexico	3	2	1	0	5	0	5
Belgium	3	1	0	2	4	5	2
El Salvador	3	0	0	3	0	9	0

Group B

Uruguay 2, Israel 0
Italy 1, Sweden 0
Uruguay 0, Italy 0
Israel 1, Sweden 1
Sweden 1, Uruguay 0
Israel 0, Italy 0

	P	*W*	*D*	*L*	*F*	*A*	*Pts*
Italy	3	1	2	0	1	0	4
Uruguay	3	1	1	1	2	1	3
Sweden	3	1	1	1	2	2	3
Israel	3	0	2	1	1	3	2

Group C

England 1, Rumania 0
Brazil 4, Czechoslovakia 1
Rumania 2, Czechoslovakia 1
Brazil 1, England 0
Brazil 3, Rumania 2
England 1, Czechoslovakia 0

	P	*W*	*D*	*L*	*F*	*A*	*Pts*
Brazil	3	3	0	0	8	3	6
England	3	2	0	1	2	1	4
Rumania	3	1	0	2	4	5	2
Czechoslovakia	3	0	0	3	2	7	0

Group D

Peru 3, Bulgaria 2
West Germany 2, Morocco 1
Peru 3, Morocco 0
West Germany 5, Bulgaria 2
West Germany 3, Peru 1
Bulgaria 1, Morocco 1

	P	*W*	*D*	*L*	*F*	*A*	*Pts*
West Germany	3	3	0	0	10	4	6
Peru	3	2	0	1	7	5	4
Bulgaria	3	0	1	2	5	9	1
Morocco	3	0	1	2	2	6	1

Quarter-Finals

Uruguay 1, USSR 0
Italy 4, Mexico 1
Brazil 4, Peru 2
West Germany 3, England 2

Semi-Finals

Italy 4, West Germany 3 (in Mexico City)
Brazil 3, Uruguay 1 (in Guadalajara)

Third Place Match (Mexico City)

West Germany 1, Uruguay 0

Final (Mexico City, 21 June, 1970)

Brazil (1) 4, Italy (1) 1

Brazil: Felix; Carlos Alberto, Brito, Piazza, Everaldo; Gerson, Clodoaldo; Jairzinho, Pelé, Tostão, Rivelino.

Italy: Albertosi; Burgnich, Cera, Rosato, Facchetti; Bertini (Juliano), Riva; Domenghini, Mazzola, De Sisti, Boninsegna (Rivera).

Scorers: Pelé, Gerson, Jairzinho, Carlos Alberto for Brazil; Boninsegna for Italy.

Leading Scorer: Müller (West Germany) 10.

WEST GERMANY 1974

Group 1

West Germany 1, Chile 0
East Germany 2, Australia 0
West Germany 3, Australia 0
East Germany 1, Chile 1
East Germany 1, West Germany 0
Chile 0, Australia 0

	P	*W*	*D*	*L*	*F*	*A*	*Pts*
East Germany	3	2	1	0	4	1	5
West Germany	3	2	0	1	4	1	4
Chile	3	0	2	1	1	2	2
Australia	3	0	1	2	0	5	1

Group 2

Brazil 0, Yugoslavia 0
Scotland 2, Zaire 0
Brazil 0, Scotland 0
Yugoslavia 9, Zaire 0
Scotland 1, Yugoslavia 1
Brazil 3, Zaire 0

	P	*W*	*D*	*L*	*F*	*A*	*Pts*
Yugoslavia	3	1	2	0	10	1	4
Brazil	3	1	2	0	3	0	4
Scotland	3	1	2	0	3	1	4
Zaire	3	0	0	3	0	14	0

Group 3

Holland 2, Uruguay 0
Sweden 0, Bulgaria 0
Holland 0, Sweden 0
Bulgaria 1, Uruguay 1
Holland 4, Bulgaria 1
Sweden 3, Uruguay 0

	P	*W*	*D*	*L*	*F*	*A*	*Pts*
Holland	3	2	1	0	6	1	5
Sweden	3	1	2	0	3	0	4
Bulgaria	3	0	2	1	2	5	2
Uruguay	3	0	1	2	1	6	1

Group 4

Italy 3, Haiti 1
Poland 3, Argentina 2
Argentina 1, Italy 1
Poland 7, Haiti 0
Argentina 4, Haiti 1
Poland 2, Italy 1

	P	*W*	*D*	*L*	*F*	*A*	*Pts*
Poland	3	3	0	0	12	3	6
Argentina	3	1	1	1	7	5	3
Italy	3	1	1	1	5	4	3
Haiti	3	0	0	3	2	14	0

Group A

Brazil 1, East Germany 0
Holland 4, Argentina 0
Holland 2, East Germany 0
Brazil 2, Argentina 1
Holland 2, Brazil 0
Argentina 1, East Germany 1

	P	*W*	*D*	*L*	*F*	*A*	*Pts*
Holland	3	3	0	0	8	0	6
Brazil	3	2	0	1	3	3	4
East Germany	3	0	1	2	1	4	1
Argentina	3	0	1	2	2	7	1

Group B

Poland 1, Sweden 0
West Germany 2, Yugoslavia 0
Poland 2, Yugoslavia 1
West Germany 4, Sweden 2
Sweden 2, Yugoslavia 1
West Germany 1, Poland 0

	P	*W*	*D*	*L*	*F*	*A*	*Pts*
West Germany	3	3	0	0	7	2	6
Poland	3	2	0	1	3	2	4
Sweden	3	1	0	2	4	6	2
Yugoslavia	3	0	0	3	2	6	0

Third Place Match (Munich)

Poland 1, Brazil 0

Final (Munich, 7 July, 1974)

West Germany (2) 2, Holland (1) 1

West Germany: Maier; Vogts, Schwarzenbeck, Beckenbauer, Breitner, Bonhof, Hoeness, Overath, Grabowski, Müller, Holzenbein.

Holland: Jongbloed; Suurbier, Rijsbergen (De Jong), Haan, Krol, Jansen, Van Hanegem, Neeskens, Rep, Cruyff, Rensenbrink (Van der Kerkhof R).

Scorers: Breitner (*pen*), Müller for West Germany; Neeskens (*pen*) for Holland.

Leading Scorer: Lato (Poland) 7.

ARGENTINA 1978

Group 1

Italy 2, France 1
Argentina 2, Hungary 1
Italy 3, Hungary 1
Argentina 2, France 1
France 3, Hungary 1
Italy 1, Argentina 0

	P	W	D	L	F	A	Pts
Italy	3	3	0	0	6	2	6
Argentina	3	2	0	1	4	3	4
France	3	1	0	2	5	5	2
Hungary	3	0	0	3	3	8	0

Group 2

West Germany 0, Poland 0
Tunisia 3, Mexico 1
Poland 1, Tunisia 0
West Germany 6, Mexico 0
Poland 3, Mexico 1
West Germany 0, Tunisia 0

	P	W	D	L	F	A	Pts
Poland	3	2	1	0	4	1	5
West Germany	3	1	2	0	6	0	4
Tunisia	3	1	1	1	3	2	3
Mexico	3	0	0	3	2	12	0

Group 3

Austria 2, Spain 1
Brazil 1, Sweden 1
Austria 1, Sweden 0
Brazil 0, Spain 0
Spain 1, Sweden 0
Brazil 1, Austria 0

	P	W	D	L	F	A	Pts
Austria	3	2	0	1	3	2	4
Brazil	3	1	2	0	2	1	4
Spain	3	1	1	1	2	2	3
Sweden	3	0	1	2	1	3	1

Group 4

Peru 3, Scotland 1
Holland 3, Iran 0
Scotland 1, Iran 1
Holland 0, Peru 0
Peru 4, Iran 1
Scotland 3, Holland 2

	P	W	D	L	F	A	Pts
Peru	3	2	1	0	7	2	5
Holland	3	1	1	1	5	3	3
Scotland	3	1	1	1	5	6	3
Iran	3	0	1	2	2	8	1

Group A

West Germany 0, Italy 0
Holland 5, Austria 1
Italy 1, Austria 0
Holland 2, West Germany 2
Holland 2, Italy 1
Austria 3, West Germany 2

	P	W	D	L	F	A	Pts
Holland	3	2	1	0	9	4	5
Italy	3	1	1	1	2	2	3
West Germany	3	0	2	1	4	5	2
Austria	3	1	0	2	4	8	2

Group B

Brazil 3, Peru 0
Argentina 2, Poland 0
Poland 1, Peru 0
Argentina 0, Brazil 0
Brazil 3, Poland 1
Argentina 6, Peru 0

	P	W	D	L	F	A	Pts
Argentina	3	2	1	0	8	0	5
Brazil	3	2	1	0	6	1	5
Poland	3	1	0	2	2	5	2
Peru	3	0	0	3	0	10	0

Third Place Match(Buenos Aires)

Brazil 2, Italy 1

Final (Buenos Aires, 25 June, 1978)

Argentina (1) (1) 3, Holland (0) (1) 1 aet

Argentina: Fillol; Passarella, Olquin, Galvan L., Tarantini, Ardiles (Larrosa), Gallego, Ortiz (Houseman), Bertoni, Luque, Kempes.

Holland: Jongbloed; Krol, Poortvliet, Brandts, Jansen (Suurbier), Haan, Neeskens, Van der Kerkhof W., Rep (Nanninga), Van der Kerkhof R., Resenbrink.

Scorers: Kempes 2, Bertoni for Argentina; Nanninga for Holland.

Leading Scorer: Kempes (Argentina) 6.

GOALSCORING AND ATTENDANCES IN WORLD CUP FINAL ROUNDS

	Matches	*Goals (avge)*	*Attendance (avge)*
1930, Uruguay	18	70 (3.8)	434,500 (24,138)
1934, Italy	17	70 (4.1)	395,000 (23,235)
1938, France	18	84 (4.6)	483,000 (26,833)
1950, Brazil	22	88 (4.0)	1,337,000 (60,772)
1954, Switzerland	26	140 (5.3)	943,000 (36,270)
1958, Sweden	35	126 (3.6)	868,000 (24,800)
1962, Chile	32	89 (2.7)	776,000 (24,250)
1966, England	32	89 (2.7)	1,614,677 (50,458)
1970, Mexico	32	95 (2.9)	1,673,975 (52,311)
1974, West Germany	38	97 (2.5)	1,774,022 (46,684)
1978, Argentina	38	102 (2.6)	1,610,215 (42,374)

WORLD CUP 1930–78 FINAL SERIES

	P	*W*	*D*	*L*	*F*	*A*
Brazil	52	33	10	9	119	56
West Germany	47	28	9	10	110	68
Italy	36	20	6	10	62	40
Uruguay	29	14	5	10	57	39
Argentina	29	14	5	10	55	43
Hungary	26	13	2	11	73	42
Sweden	28	11	6	11	48	46
England	24	10	6	8	34	28
Yugoslavia	25	10	5	10	45	34
USSR	19	10	3	6	30	21
Holland	16	8	3	5	32	19
Poland	14	9	1	4	27	17
Austria	18	9	1	8	33	36
Czechoslovakia	22	8	3	11	32	36
France	20	8	1	11	43	38
Chile	18	7	3	8	23	24
Spain	18	7	3	8	22	25
Switzerland	18	5	2	11	28	44
Portugal	6	5	0	1	17	8
Mexico	24	3	4	17	21	62
Peru	12	4	1	7	17	25
Scotland	11	2	4	5	12	21
East Germany	6	2	2	2	5	5
Paraguay	7	2	2	3	12	19

	P	*W*	*D*	*L*	*F*	*A*
United States	7	3	0	4	12	21
Wales	5	1	3	1	4	4
Northern Ireland	5	2	1	2	6	10
Rumania	8	2	1	5	12	17
Bulgaria	12	0	4	8	9	29
Tunisia	3	1	1	1	3	2
North Korea	4	1	1	2	5	9
Cuba	3	1	1	1	5	12
Belgium	9	1	1	7	12	25
Turkey	3	1	0	2	10	11
Israel	3	0	2	1	1	3
Morocco	3	0	1	2	2	6
Australia	3	0	1	2	0	5
Colombia	3	0	1	2	5	11
Iran	3	0	1	2	2	8
Norway	1	0	0	1	1	2
Egypt	1	0	0	1	2	4
Dutch East Indies	1	0	0	1	0	6
El Salvador	3	0	0	3	0	9
South Korea	2	0	0	2	0	16
Haiti	3	0	0	3	2	14
Zaire	3	0	0	3	0	14
Bolivia	3	0	0	3	0	16

Only six countries have won the World Cup: Brazil (1958, 1962 and 1970), Italy (1934 and 1938), Uruguay (1930 and 1950), West Germany (1954 and 1974), England (1966) and Argentina (1978).

1050 goals have been scored in 308 matches in the 11 final tournaments for an overall average of 3.4 per match.

EUROPEAN UNDER-21 CHAMPIONSHIP 1980–82

Group 1 results: Finland 0, Bulgaria 1; Finland 1, Austria 2; Bulgaria 1, West Germany 0; West Germany 4, Austria 0; Bulgaria 1, Finland 0; Finland 1, West Germany 2; Austria 1, Bulgaria 2; Austria 0, Finland 0.

	P	*W*	*D*	*L*	*F*	*A*	*Pts*
Bulgaria	4	4	0	0	5	1	8
West Germany	3	2	0	1	6	2	4
Austria	4	1	1	2	3	7	3
Finland	5	0	1	4	2	6	1

Fixtures: West Germany v Finland 22.9.81; Austria v West Germany 13.10.81; Bulgaria v Austria 10.11.81; West Germany v Bulgaria 21.11.81.

Group 2 results: France 3, Cyprus 1; Belgium 2, Cyprus 1; Cyprus 0, Belgium 1; France 1, Belgium 0.

	P	*W*	*D*	*L*	*F*	*A*	*Pts*
France	2	2	0	0	4	1	4
Belgium	3	2	0	1	3	2	4
Cyprus	3	0	0	3	2	6	0

Fixtures: Belgium v France 8.9.81; Cyprus v France 6.12.81.

Group 3 results: Czechoslovakia 3, Turkey 0; Turkey 2, Czechoslovakia 1.

	P	*W*	*D*	*L*	*F*	*A*	*Pts*
Czechoslovakia	2	1	0	1	4	2	2
Turkey	2	1	0	1	2	4	2

USSR have yet to play

Fixtures: USSR v Turkey 22.9.81; Turkey v USSR 6.10.81; USSR v Czechoslovakia 27.10.81; Czechoslovakia v USSR 28.11.81.

Group 4 results: Rumania 4, England 0; England 5, Switzerland 0; England 3, Rumania 0; Switzerland 0, Hungary 1; Hungary 4, Rumania 2; Switzerland 0, England 0; Hungary 1, England 2.

	P	*W*	*D*	*L*	*F*	*A*	*Pts*
England	5	3	1	1	10	5	7
Hungary	3	2	0	1	6	4	4
Rumania	3	1	0	2	6	7	2
Switzerland	3	0	1	2	0	6	1

Fixtures: Rumania v Hungary 22.9.81; Rumania v Switzerland 9.10.81; Hungary v Switzerland 13.10.81; Switzerland v Rumania 10.11.81; England v Hungary 17.11.81.

Group 5 results: Italy 1, Yugoslavia 0; Greece 1, Italy 3; Yugoslavia 1, Greece 1.

	P	*W*	*D*	*L*	*F*	*A*	*Pts*
Italy	2	2	0	0	4	1	4
Yugoslavia	2	0	1	1	1	2	1
Greece	2	0	1	1	2	4	1

Fixtures: Yugoslavia v Italy 16.10.81; Italy v Greece 13.11.81; Greece v Yugoslavia 28.11.81.

Group 6 results: Sweden 2, Scotland 0; Denmark 2, Sweden 1; Scotland 2, Denmark 1; Sweden 0, Denmark 0.

	P	*W*	*D*	*L*	*F*	*A*	*Pts*
Sweden	3	1	1	1	3	2	3
Denmark	3	1	1	1	3	3	3
Scotland	2	1	0	1	2	3	2

Fixtures: Scotland v Sweden 8.9.81; Denmark v Scotlanu 13.10.81

Group 7 results: Norway 0, Poland 1; East Germany 0, Norway 4; East Germany 2, Poland 3; Norway 1, East Germany 1.

	P	*W*	*D*	*L*	*F*	*A*	*Pts*
Poland	2	2	0	0	4	2	4
Norway	3	1	1	1	5	2	3
East Germany	3	0	1	2	3	8	1

Fixtures: Poland v East Germany 23.9.81; Poland v Norway 31.10.81.

Group 8 results: Netherlands 0, Spain 2; Spain 4, Luxembourg 1; Netherlands 1, Luxembourg 0.

	P	*W*	*D*	*L*	*F*	*A*	*Pts*
Spain	2	2	0	0	6	1	4
Netherlands	2	1	0	1	1	2	2
Luxembourg	2	0	0	2	1	5	0

Fixtures: Luxembourg v Spain 14.10.81; Luxembourg v Netherlands 28.10.81; Spain v Netherlands 18.11.81.

WORLD CUP 1982

EUROPE

Group 1

Results: Finland 0, Bulgaria 2; Albania 2, Finland 0; Finland 0, Austria 2; Bulgaria 2, Albania 1; Austria 5, Albania 0; Bulgaria 1, West Germany 3; Albania 0, Austria 1; Albania 0, West Germany 2; West Germany 2, Austria 0; Bulgaria 4, Finland 0; Austria 2, Bulgaria 0; Austria 5, Finland 1; Finland 0, West Germany 4.

	P	W	D	L	F	A	Pts
Austria	6	5	0	1	15	3	10
West Germany	4	4	0	0	11	1	8
Bulgaria	5	3	0	2	9	6	6
Albania	5	1	0	4	3	10	2
Finland	6	0	0	6	1	19	0

Group 2

Results: Cyprus 2, Eire 3; Eire 2, Netherlands 1; Cyprus 0, France 7; Eire 1, Belgium 1; France 2, Eire 0; Belgium 1, Netherlands 0; Eire 6, Cyprus 0; Cyprus 0, Belgium 2; Belgium 3, Cyprus 2; Netherlands 3, Cyprus 0; Netherlands 1, France 0; Belgium 1, Eire 0; France 3, Belgium 2; Cyprus 0, Netherlands 1.

	P	W	D	L	F	A	Pts
Belgium	6	4	1	1	10	6	9
Eire	6	3	1	2	12	7	7
France	4	3	0	1	12	3	6
Netherlands	5	3	0	2	6	3	6
Cyprus	7	0	0	7	4	25	0

Group 3

Results: Iceland 0, Wales 4; Iceland 1, USSR 2; Turkey 1, Iceland 3; USSR 5, Iceland 0; Wales 4, Turkey 0; Wales 1, Czechoslovakia 0; Czechoslovakia 2, Turkey 0; Turkey 0, Wales 1; Turkey 0, Czechoslovakia 3; Czechoslovakia 6, Iceland 1; Wales 0, USSR 0.

	P	W	D	L	F	A	Pts
Wales	5	4	1	0	10	0	9
Czechoslovakia	4	3	0	1	11	2	6
USSR	3	2	1	0	7	1	5
Iceland	5	1	0	4	5	18	2
Turkey	5	0	0	5	1	13	0

Group 4

Results: England 4, Norway 0; Norway 1, Rumania 1; Rumania 2, England 1; Switzerland 1, Norway 2; England 2, Switzerland 1; Switzerland 2, Hungary 2; England 0, Rumania 0; Hungary 1, Rumania 0; Norway 1, Hungary 2; Switzerland 2, England 1; Hungary 1, England 3; Rumania 1, Norway 0; Norway 1, Switzerland 1.

	P	W	D	L	F	A	Pts
England	6	3	1	2	11	6	7
Rumania	5	2	2	1	4	3	6
Hungary	4	2	1	1	6	6	5
Switzerland	5	1	2	2	7	8	4
Norway	6	1	2	3	5	10	4

Group 5

Results: Luxembourg 0, Yugoslavia 5; Yugoslavia 2, Denmark 1; Luxembourg 0, Italy 2; Denmark 0, Greece 1; Italy 2, Denmark 0; Italy 2, Yugoslavia 0; Denmark 5, Luxembourg 0; Greece 0, Italy 2; Greece 2, Luxembourg 0; Luxembourg 0, Greece 2; Luxembourg 1, Denmark 2; Yugoslavia 5, Greece 1; Denmark 3, Italy 1.

	P	W	D	L	F	A	Pts
Italy	5	4	0	1	9	3	8
Yugoslavia	4	3	0	1	12	4	6
Denmark	6	3	0	3	11	7	6
Greece	5	3	0	2	6	7	6
Luxembourg	6	0	0	6	1	18	0

Group 6

Results: Israel 0, Northern Ireland 0; Sweden 1, Israel 1; Sweden 0, Scotland 1; Northern Ireland 3, Sweden 0; Scotland 0, Portugal 0; Israel 0, Sweden 0; Portugal 1, Northern Ireland 0; Portugal 3, Israel 0; Israel 0, Scotland 1; Scotland 1, Northern Ireland 1; Scotland 3, Israel 1; Northern Ireland 1, Portugal 0; Sweden 1, Northern Ireland 0; Sweden 3, Portugal 0.

	P	W	D	L	F	A	Pts
Scotland	5	3	2	0	6	2	8
Northern Ireland	6	2	2	2	5	3	6
Sweden	6	2	2	2	5	5	6
Portugal	5	2	1	2	4	4	5
Israel	6	0	3	3	2	8	3

Group 7

Results: Malta 0, Poland 2 (abandoned after 82 mins; result stands); Malta 1, East Germany 2; Poland 1, East Germany 0.

	P	W	D	L	F	A	Pts
Poland	2	2	0	0	3	0	4
East Germany	2	1	0	1	2	2	2
Malta	2	0	0	2	1	4	0

AFRICA

First Round

Results: Zambia v Ethiopia 0-0, 4-0; Algeria v Sierra Leone 2-2, 3-1; Nigeria v Tunisia 0-2, 2-0 (4-3 on pens); Madagascar wo v Uganda (scr); Morocco v Senegal 1-0, 0-0; Zaire v Mozambique 5-2, 2-1; Cameroun v Malawi 3-0, 1-1; Guinea v Lesotho 3-1, 1-1; Libya v Gambia 2-1, 0-0; Niger v Somalia 0-0, 1-0; Egypt wo v Ghana (scr); Tanzania v Kenya 1-3, 5-0.

Second Round

Results: Egypt wo v Libya (scr); Algeria v Sudan 2-0, 1-1; Niger v Togo 0-1, 2-1 (Niger won on away goals); Guinea v Liberia 1-1, 1-0; Cameroun v Zimbabwe 2-0, 0-1; Morocco v Zambia 2-0, 0-2 (5-4 on pens); Nigeria v Tanzania 1-1, 2-0; Zaire v Madagascar 1-1, 3-2.

Third Round

Results: Nigeria v Guinea 1-1, 1-0; Morocco v Egypt 1-0, 0-0; Cameroun v Zaire 0-1, 6-1; Algeria v Niger 4-0, 0-1.

SOUTH AMERICA

Group 1

Results: Venezuela 0, Brazil 1; Bolivia 3, Venezuela 0; Bolivia 1, Brazil 2; Venezuela 1, Bolivia 0; Brazil 3, Bolivia 1; Brazil 5, Venezuela 0.
(Brazil qualified for finals.)

Group 2

Colombia, Peru and Uruguay to play.

Group 3

Results: Ecuador 1, Paraguay 0; Paraguay 3, Ecuador 1; Ecuador 0, Chile 0; Paraguay 0, Chile 1; Chile 2, Ecuador 0; Chile 3, Paraguay 0.
(Chile qualified for finals.)

NORTH AND CENTRAL AMERICA (CONCACAF)

Northern Zone

Results: Canada 1, Mexico 1; USA 0, Canada 0; Canada 2, USA 1; Mexico 5, USA 1; Mexico 1, Canada 1; USA 2, Mexico 1.
(Canada and Mexico qualified for play-off group.)

Central Zone

Results: Panama 0, Guatemala 2; Panama 0, Honduras 2; Panama 1, Costa Rica 1; Panama 1, El Salvador 3; Costa Rica 2, Honduras 3; El Salvador 4, Panama 1; Guatemala 0, Costa Rica 0; Honduras 2, El Salvador 0; Honduras 0, Guatemala 0; El Salvador 2, Costa Rica 0 (result awarded as Costa Rica refused to play in El Salvador); Costa Rica 2, Panama 0; Guatemala 0, El Salvador 0; Guatemala 5, Panama 0; Honduras 1, Costa Rica 1; El Salvador 2, Honduras 1; Costa Rica 0, Guatemala 3; Guatemala 0, Honduras 1; Costa Rica 0, El Salvador 0; Honduras 5, Panama 0; El Salvador 1, Guatemala 0.
(Honduras and El Salvador qualified for play-off group.)

CARIBBEAN ZONE

Group A

Results: Cuba 3, Surinam 0; Surinam 0, Cuba 0; Guyana 0, Surinam 1; Surinam 4, Guyana 0; Cuba 1, Guyana 0; Guyana 0, Cuba 3.

Group B

Results: Haiti 2, Trinidad & Tobago 0; Trinidad 1, Haiti 0; Netherlands Antilles 1, Haiti 1; Haiti 1, Netherlands Antilles 0; Trinidad 0, Netherlands Antilles 0; Netherlands Antilles 0, Trinidad 0.
(Cuba and Haiti qualified for play-off group.)

ASIA AND OCEANIA

Group 1

Results: New Zealand 3, Australia 3; Fiji 0, New Zealand 4; Taiwan 0, New Zealand 0; Indonesia 0, New Zealand 2; Australia 0, New Zealand 2; Australia 2, Indonesia 0; New Zealand 2, Taiwan 0; Fiji 0, Indonesia 0; Australia 3, Taiwan 2; Fiji 2, Taiwan 1; New Zealand 5, Indonesia 0; Indonesia 1, Taiwan 0; Taiwan 2, Indonesia 0.

Group 2

Results: Iraq 1, Qatar 0; Syria 0, Bahrain 1; Iraq 0, Saudi Arabia 1; Bahrain 0, Qatar 3; Syria 0, Saudi Arabia 2; Iraq 2, Bahrain 0; Syria 1, Qatar 2; Bahrain 0, Saudi Arabia 1; Iraq 2, Syria 1; Qatar 0, Saudi Arabia 1.
(Saudi Arabia qualified for play-off group.)

Group 3

Results: Malaysia 1, South Korea 2; Kuwait 6, Thailand 0; Thailand 1, South Korea 5; Kuwait 4, Malaysia 0; Thailand 2, Malaysia 2; Kuwait 2, South Korea 0.
(Kuwait qualified for play-off group.)

Group 4

First round: Hong Kong 0, China 1; Singapore 0, Japan 1; North Korea 3, Macao 0; Hong Kong 1, Singapore 1; China 3, Macao 0; North Korea 1, Singapore 0; China 1, Japan 0; Japan 3, Macao 0; North Korea 2, Hong Kong 2.
Semi-finals: North Korea 1, Japan 0 (aet); China 0, Hong Kong 0 (aet) – China won 5-4 on pens.
Final: China 4, North Korea 2 (aet).
(China qualified for play-off group.)

1982 WORLD CUP QUALIFYING COMPETITION – Remaining fixtures

EUROPE

Group 1

West Germany, Austria, Bulgaria, Finland, Albania.

2.9.81	Finland v Albania
23.9.81	West Germany v Finland
14.10.81	Austria v West Germany
14.10.81	Albania v Bulgaria
11.11.81	Bulgaria v Austria
18.11.81	West Germany v Albania
21/2.11.81	West Germany v Bulgaria

Group 2

Netherlands, France, Belgium, Eire, Cyprus

9.9.81	Netherlands v Eire
9.9.81	Belgium v France
14.10.81	Netherlands v Belgium
14.10.81	Eire v France
18.11.81	France v Netherlands
5.12.81	France v Cyprus

Group 3

Czechoslovakia, USSR, Wales, Turkey, Iceland

2.9.81	Iceland v Turkey
9.9.81	Czechoslovakia v Wales
23.9.81	USSR v Turkey
23.9.81	Iceland v Czechoslovakia
7.10.81	Turkey v USSR
14.10.81	Wales v Iceland
28.10.81	USSR v Czechoslovakia
28.11.81	USSR v Wales
30.11.81	Czechoslovakia v USSR

Group 4

England, Hungary, Switzerland, Rumania, Norway

9.9.81	Norway v England
23.9.81	Rumania v Hungary
10.10.81	Rumania v Switzerland
14.10.81	Hungary v Switzerland
31.10.81	Hungary v Norway
11.11.81	Switzerland v Rumania
18.11.81	England v Hungary

Group 5

Italy, Yugoslavia, Greece, Denmark, Luxembourg

9.9.81	Denmark v Yugoslavia
14.10.81	Greece v Denmark
17.10.81	Yugoslavia v Italy
14.11.81	Italy v Greece
21.11.81	Yugoslavia v Luxembourg
29.11.81	Greece v Yugoslavia
12.12.81	Italy v Luxembourg

Group 6

Scotland, Sweden, Portugal, Northern Ireland, Israel

9.9.81	Scotland v Sweden
14.10.81	Portugal v Sweden
14.10.81	Northern Ireland v Scotland
28.10.81	Israel v Portugal
18.11.81	Northern Ireland v Israel
18.11.81	Portugal v Scotland

Group 7

Poland, East Germany, Malta

10.10.81	East Germany v Poland
11.11.81	East Germany v Malta
15.11.81	Poland v Malta

WORLD CLUB CHAMPIONSHIP

Played annually up to 1974 and intermittently since then between the winners of the European Cup and the winners of the South American Champions Cup – known as the Copa Libertadores. In 1980 the winners were decided by one match arranged on neutral territory in February 1981.

1960 Real Madrid beat Penarol 0-0, 5-1
1961 Penarol beat Benfica 0-1, 5-0, 2-1
1962 Santos beat Benfica 3-2, 5-2
1963 Santos beat AC Milan 2-4, 4-2, 1-0
1964 Inter-Milan beat Independiente 0-1, 2-0, 1-0
1965 Inter-Milan beat Independiente 3-0, 0-0
1966 Penarol beat Real Madrid 2-0, 2-0
1967 Racing Club beat Celtic 0-1, 2-1, 1-0
1968 Estudiantes beat Manchester United 1-0, 1-1
1969 AC Milan beat Estudiantes 3-0,1-2
1970 Feyenoord beat Estudiantes 2-2, 1-0
1971 Nacional beat Panathinaikos 1-1, 2-1
1972 Ajax beat Independiente 1-1, 3-0
1973 Independiente beat Juventus 1-0
1974 Atlético Madrid beat Independiente 0-1, 2-0
1975 Independiente and Bayern Munich could not agree dates; no matches.
1976 Bayern Munich beat Cruzeiro 2-0, 0-0
1977 Boca Juniors beat Borussia Moenchengladbach 2-2, 3-0
1978 Not played
1979 Olimpia beat Malmö 1-0, 2-1

11 Feb 1981
Tokyo (National Stadium)

Nacional (Uruguay) (1) 1 (*Victorino*)
Nottingham Forest (0) 0 62,000

Nacional: Rodriguez; Moreira, Blanco, Enriquez, Gonzalez, Milar, Esparrago, Luzardo, Morales, Bica, Victorino.

Nottingham Forest: Shilton; Anderson, Gray F., Ponte (Ward), Lloyd, Burns, O'Neill, Gray S., Francis, Wallace, Robertson.

SOUTH AMERICAN CHAMPIONSHIPS

1916 Uruguay
1917 Uruguay
1919 Brazil
1920 Uruguay
1921 Argentina
1922 Brazil
1923 Uruguay
1924 Uruguay
1925 Argentina
1926 Uruguay
1927 Argentina
1929 Argentina
1935 Uruguay
1937 Argentina
1939 Peru
1941 Argentina
1942 Uruguay
1945 Argentina
1946 Argentina
1947 Argentina
1949 Brazil
1953 Paraguay
1955 Argentina
1956 Uruguay
1957 Argentina
1959 Argentina
1959 Uruguay
1963 Bolivia
1967 Uruguay
1975 Peru
1979 Paraguay

CHAMPIONSHIP RECORD 1917–1979

	P	*W*	*D*	*L*	*F*	*A*
Argentina	91	62	12	17	250	90
Uruguay	96	57	9	30	235	127
Brazil	82	45	11	26	210	115
Paraguay	97	46	13	38	177	182
Peru	75	31	14	30	124	127
Chile	90	27	18	45	142	186
Bolivia	52	13	6	33	60	164
Colombia	39	10	6	23	42	93
Ecuador	55	3	9	43	52	170
Venezuela	13	1	2	10	9	54

Table includes only 23 championships considered as 'official' tournaments.

COPA LIBERTADORES (South American Cup)

Year	*Winners*
1960	Penarol (Uruguay)
1961	Penarol
1962	Santos (Brazil)
1963	Santos
1964	Independiente (Argentina)
1965	Independiente
1966	Penarol
1967	Racing (Argentina)
1968	Estudiantes (Argentina)
1969	Estudiantes
1970	Estudiantes
1971	Nacional (Uruguay)
1972	Independiente
1973	Independiente
1974	Independiente
1975	Independiente
1976	Cruzeiro (Brazil)
1977	Boca Juniors (Argentina)
1978	Boca Juniors
1979	Olimpia (Paraguay)
1980	Nacional (Uruguay)

MUNDIALITO

Played in Montevideo, Uruguay, from December 1980 to January 1981 to celebrate the 50th anniversary of the first World Cup.

Group A

Uruguay 2, Holland 0
Uruguay 2, Italy 0
Holland 1, Italy 1

Group B

Argentina 2, West Germany 1
Argentina 1, Brazil 1
Brazil 4, West Germany 1

Final (attendance 71,000)

Uruguay 2, Brazil 1

NORTH AMERICAN SOCCER LEAGUE

Winners

1967 Oakland Clippers*
1968 Atlanta Chiefs
1969 Kansas City Spurs
1970 Rochester Lancers
1971 Dallas Tornado
1972 New York Cosmos
1973 Philadelphia Atoms
1974 Los Angeles Aztecs
1975 Tampa Bay Rowdies
1976 Toronto Metro-Croatia
1977 New York Cosmos
1978 New York Cosmos
1979 Vancouver Whitecaps
1980 New York Cosmos

* National Professional Soccer League.

Average crowds for 1980

New York	42,804
Tampa Bay	28,345
Vancouver	26,833
Seattle	24,247
Tulsa	19,787
Washington	19,205
Minnesota	18,278
Toronto	15,040
Fort Lauderdale	14,262
San Jose	13,168
San Diego	12,744
Los Angeles	12,057
Chicago	11,672
Detroit	11,193
Edmonton	10,926
Portland	10,178
Memphis	9864
New England	8744
Rochester	7756
California	7221
Dallas	6751
Houston	5818
Atlanta	4884
Philadelphia	4465

OLYMPIC FOOTBALL 1908–1980

LONDON 1908

Third Place Final: Holland v Sweden* 2-1
Final: Gt Britain v Denmark 2-0

**Sweden were nominated for the third-place final in preference to France 'A', who had been awarded a bye into the semi-finals.*

STOCKHOLM 1912

Third Place Final: Holland v Finland 9-0
Final: Gt Britain v Denmark 4-2

ANTWERP 1920

Play-off for Second and Third Places
Spain v Holland 2-0
Final: Belgium v Czechoslovakia 3-1

Czechoslovakia were disqualified for walking off during the final. Placings: Belgium – Olympic champions; Spain – Second; Holland – Third, France – Fourth.

PARIS 1924

Third Place Final: Sweden v Holland 1-1, 3-1
Final: Uruguay v Switzerland 3-0

AMSTERDAM 1928

Third Place Final: Italy v Egypt 11-3
Final: Uruguay v Argentina 1-1, 2-1

BERLIN 1936

Third Place Final: Norway v Poland 3-2
Final: Italy v Austria aet 2-1

LONDON 1948

Third Place Final: Denmark v Gt Britain 5-3
Final: Sweden v Yugoslavia 3-1

HELSINKI 1952

Third Place Final: Sweden v West Germany 2-0
Final: Hungary v Yugoslavia 2-0

MELBOURNE 1956

Third Place Final: Bulgaria v India 3-0
Final: USSR v Yugoslavia 1-0

ROME 1960

Third Place Final: Italy v Hungary 2-1
Final: Yugoslavia v Denmark 3-1

TOKYO 1964

Third Place Final: East Germany v UAR 3-1
Final: Hungary v Czechoslovakia 2-1

MEXICO CITY 1968

Third Place Final: Japan v Mexico 2-0
Final: Hungary v Bulgaria 4-1

MUNICH 1972

Third Place Final: USSR v East Germany 2-2
Final: Poland v Hungary 2-1

MONTREAL 1976

Third Place Final: USSR v Brazil 2-0
Final: East Germany v Poland 3-1

MOSCOW 1980

Group A	P	W	D	L	F	A	Pts
USSR	3	3	0	0	15	1	6
Cuba	3	2	0	1	3	9	4
Venezuela	3	1	0	2	3	7	2
Zambia	3	0	0	3	2	6	0

Group B	P	W	D	L	F	A	Pts
Czechoslovakia	3	1	2	0	4	1	4
Kuwait	3	1	2	0	4	2	4
Colombia	3	1	1	1	2	4	3
Nigeria	3	0	1	2	2	5	1

Group C	P	W	D	L	F	A	Pts
East Germany	3	2	1	0	7	1	5
Algeria	3	1	1	1	4	2	4
Spain	3	0	3	0	2	2	3
Syria	3	0	1	2	0	8	1

Group D	P	W	D	L	F	A	Pts
Yugoslavia	3	2	1	0	6	3	5
Iraq	3	1	2	0	4	1	4
Finland	3	1	1	1	3	2	3
Costa Rica	3	0	0	3	2	9	0

Quarter-Final: USSR 2, Kuwait 1; Czechoslovakia 3, Cuba 0; East Germany 4, Iraq 0; Yugoslavia 3, Algeria 0
Semi-Final: USSR 0, East Germany 1; Yugoslavia 0, Czechoslovakia 2
Third Place Final: USSR 2, Yugoslavia 0
Final: East Germany 0, Czechoslovakia 1

EUROPEAN FOOTBALL CHAMPIONSHIP

(formerly EUROPEAN NATIONS' CUP)

Year	*Winners*		*Runners-up*		*Venue*
1960	USSR	2	Yugoslavia	1	Paris
1964	Spain	2	USSR	1	Madrid
1968	Italy	2	Yugoslavia	0	Rome
			After 1-1 draw		
1972	West Germany	3	USSR	0	Brussels
1976	Czechoslovakia	2	West Germany	2	Belgrade
	Czechoslovakia won on penalties				
1980	West Germany	2	Belgium	1	Rome

EUROPEAN NATIONS' CUP 1958—60

Preliminary Round

Eire 2, Czechoslovakia 0
Czechoslovakia 4, Eire 0

First Round

France 7, Greece 1
Greece 1, France 1
USSR 3, Hungary 1
Hungary 0, USSR 1
Rumania 3, Turkey 0
Turkey 2, Rumania 0
Norway 0, Austria 1
Austria 5, Norway 2
Yugoslavia 2, Bulgaria 0
Bulgaria 1, Yugoslavia 1
Portugal 3, East Germany 2
East Germany 0, Portugal 2
Denmark 2, Czechoslovakia 2
Czechoslovakia 5, Denmark 1
Poland 2, Spain 4
Spain 3, Poland 0

Quarter-Finals

Portugal 2, Yugoslavia 1
Yugoslavia 5, Portugal 1
France 5, Austria 2
Austria 2, France 4
Rumania 0, Czechoslovakia 2
Czechoslovakia 3, Rumania 0
Russia w.o. Spain withdrew

Semi-Finals

Yugoslavia 5, France 4 (in Paris)
USSR 3, Czechoslovakia 0 (in Marseilles)

Third Place Match (Marseilles)

Czechoslovakia 2, France 0

Final (Paris, 10 July, 1960)

USSR (0) 2, Yugoslavia (1) 1 after extra time
USSR: Yachin; Tchekeli, Kroutikov; Voinov, Maslenkin, Netto; Metreveli, Ivanov, Ponedelnik, Bubukin, Meshki.
Yugoslavia: Vidinic; Durkovic, Jusufi; Zanetic, Miladinovic, Perusic; Sekularac, Jerkovic, Galic, Matus, Kostic.
Scorers: Metreveli, Ponedelnik for USSR; Netto og for Yugoslavia.

EUROPEAN NATIONS' CUP 1962–64

First Round

Spain 6, Rumania 0
Rumania 3, Spain 1
Poland 0, Northern Ireland 2
Northern Ireland 2, Poland 0
Denmark 6, Malta 1
Malta 1, Denmark 3
Eire 4, Iceland 2
Iceland 1, Eire 1
Greece withdrew against Albania
East Germany 2, Czechoslovakia 1
Czechoslovakia 1, East Germany 1
Hungary 3, Wales 1
Wales 1, Hungary 1
Italy 6, Turkey 0
Turkey 0, Italy 1
Holland 3, Switzerland 1
Switzerland 1, Holland 1
Norway 0, Sweden 2
Sweden 1, Norway 1
Yugoslavia 3, Belgium 2
Belgium 0, Yugoslavia 1
Bulgaria 3, Portugal 1
Portugal 3, Bulgaria 1
Bulgaria 1, Portugal 0
England 1, France 1
France 5, England 2

Second Round

Spain 1, Northern Ireland 1
Northern Ireland 0, Spain 1
Denmark 4, Albania 0
Albania 1, Denmark 0
Austria 0, Eire 0
Eire 3, Austria 2
East Germany 1, Hungary 2
Hungary 3, East Germany 3
USSR 2, Italy 0
Italy 1, USSR 1
Holland 1, Luxembourg 1
Luxembourg 2, Holland 1
Yugoslavia 0, Sweden 0
Sweden 3, Yugoslavia 2
Bulgaria 1, France 0
France 3, Bulgaria 1

Quarter-Finals

Luxembourg 2, Denmark 2
Denmark 3, Luxembourg 3
Denmark 1, Luxembourg 0
Spain 5, Eire 1
Eire 0, Spain 2
France 1, Hungary 3
Hungary 2, France 1
Sweden 1, USSR 1
USSR 3, Sweden 1

Semi-Finals

USSR 3, Denmark 0 (in Barcelona)
Spain 2, Hungary 1 (in Madrid)

Third Place Match (Barcelona)

Hungary 3, Denmark 1 after extra time

Final (Madrid, 21 June, 1964)

Spain (1) 2, USSR (1) 1

Spain: Iribar; Rivilla, Calleja; Fuste, Olivella, Zoco; Amancio, Pereda, Marcellino, Suarez, Lapetra.
USSR: Yachin; Chustikov, Mudrik, Voronin, Shesternjev, Anitchkin; Chislenko, Ivanov, Ponedelnik, Kornaev, Khusainov.
Scorers: Pereda, Marcellino for Spain; Khusainov for USSR.

EUROPEAN CHAMPIONSHIP 1966–68

Group 1

Eire 0, Spain 0
Eire 2, Turkey 1
Spain 2, Eire 0
Turkey 0, Spain 0
Turkey 2, Eire 1
Eire 0, Czechoslovakia 2
Spain 2, Turkey 0
Czechoslovakia 1, Spain 0
Spain 2, Czechoslovakia 1
Czechoslovakia 3, Turkey 0
Turkey 0, Czechoslovakia 0
Czechoslovakia 1, Eire 2

Group 2

Norway 0, Bulgaria 0
Portugal 1, Sweden 2
Bulgaria 4, Norway 2
Sweden 1, Portugal 1
Norway 1, Portugal 2
Sweden 0, Bulgaria 2
Norway 3, Sweden 1
Sweden 5, Norway 2
Bulgaria 3, Sweden 0
Portugal 2, Norway 1
Bulgaria 1, Portugal 0
Portugal 0, Bulgaria 0

Group 3

Finland 0, Austria 0
Austria 2, Finland 1
Greece 2, Finland 1
Greece 4, Austria 1
Finland 1, Greece 1
Austria 1, USSR 0
USSR 4, Austria 3
Greece 0, USSR 1
USSR 2, Finland 0
Austria 1, Greece 1
Finland 2, USSR 5
USSR 4, Greece 0

Group 4

Albania 0, Yugoslavia 2
West Germany 6, Albania 0
Yugoslavia 1, West Germany 0
West Germany 3, Yugoslavia 1
Yugoslavia 4, Albania 0
Albania 0, West Germany 0

Group 5

Holland 2, Hungary 2
Hungary 6, Denmark 0
Holland 2, Denmark 0
East Germany 4, Holland 3
Hungary 2, Holland 1
Denmark 0, Hungary 2
Denmark 1, East Germany 1
Holland 1, East Germany 0
Hungary 3, East Germany 1
Denmark 3, Holland 2
East Germany 3, Denmark 2
East Germany 1, Hungary 0

Group 6

Cyprus 1, Rumania 5
Rumania 4, Switzerland 2
Italy 3, Rumania 1
Cyprus 0, Italy 2
Rumania 7, Cyprus 0
Switzerland 7, Rumania 1
Italy 5, Cyprus 0
Switzerland 5, Cyprus 0
Switzerland 2, Italy 2
Italy 4, Switzerland 0
Cyprus 2, Switzerland 1
Rumania 0, Italy 1

Group 7

Poland 4, Luxembourg 0
France 2, Poland 1
Luxembourg 0, France 3
Luxembourg 0, Belgium 5
Luxembourg 0, Poland 0
Poland 3, Belgium 1
Belgium 2, France 1
Poland 1, France 4
Belgium 2, Poland 4
France 1, Belgium 1
Belgium 3, Luxembourg 0
France 3, Luxembourg 1

Group 8

Northern Ireland 0, England 2
Wales 1, Scotland 1
England 5, Wales 1
Scotland 2, Northern Ireland 1
Northern Ireland 0, Wales 0
England 2, Scotland 3
Wales 0, England 3
Northern Ireland 1, Scotland 0
England 2, Northern Ireland 0
Scotland 3, Wales 2
Scotland 1, England 1
Wales 2, Northern Ireland 0

Quarter-Finals

England 1, Spain 0
Spain 1, England 2
Bulgaria 3, Italy 2
Italy 2, Bulgaria 0
France 1, Yugoslavia 1
Yugoslavia 5, France 1
Hungary 2, USSR 0
USSR 3, Hungary 0

Semi-Finals

Yugoslavia 1, England 0 (in Florence)
Italy 0, USSR 0 (Italy won toss) (in Naples)

Third Place Match (Rome)

England 2, USSR 0

Final (Rome, 8 June, 1968)

Italy (0) 1, Yugoslavia (1) 1

Italy: Zoff; Burgnich, Facchetti; Ferrini, Guarneri, Castano; Domenghini, Juliano, Anastasi, Lodetti, Prati.
Yugoslavia: Pantelic; Fazlagic, Damjanovic; Pavlovic, Paunovic, Holcer; Petkovic, Acimovic, Musemic, Trivic, Dzajic.
Scorers: Domenghini for Italy; Dzajic for Yugoslavia.

Replayed Final (Rome, 10 June, 1968)

Italy (2) 2, Yugoslavia (0) 0

Italy: Zoff; Burgnich, Facchetti; Rosato, Guarneri, Salvadore; Domenghini, Mazzola, Anastasi, De Sisti, Riva.
Yugoslavia: Pantelic; Fazlagic, Damjanovic, Pavlovic, Paunovic, Holcer; Hosic, Acimovic, Musemic, Trivic, Dzajic.
Scorers: Riva, Anastasi for Italy.

EUROPEAN CHAMPIONSHIP 1970–72

Group 1

Czechoslovakia 1, Finland 1
Rumania 3, Finland 0
Wales 0, Rumania 0
Wales 1, Czechoslovakia 3
Finland 0, Wales 1
Czechoslovakia 1, Rumania 0
Finland 0, Czechoslovakia 4
Finland 0, Rumania 4
Wales 3, Finland 0
Czechoslovakia 1, Wales 0
Rumania 2, Czechoslovakia 1
Rumania 2, Wales 0

Group 2

Norway 1, Hungary 3
France 3, Norway 1
Bulgaria 1, Norway 1
Hungary 1, France 1
Bulgaria 3, Hungary 0
Norway 1, Bulgaria 4
Norway 1, France 3
Hungary 2, Bulgaria 0
France 0, Hungary 2
Hungary 4, Norway 0
France 2, Bulgaria 1
Bulgaria 2, France 1

Group 3

Greece 0, Switzerland 1
Malta 1, Switzerland 2
Malta 0, England 1
England 3, Greece 0
Switzerland 5, Malta 0
England 5, Malta 0
Malta 1, Greece 1
Switzerland 1, Greece 0
Greece 2, Malta 0
Switzerland 2, England 3
England 1, Switzerland 1
Greece 0, England 2

Group 4

Spain 3, Northern Ireland 0
Cyprus 0, Northern Ireland 3
Northern Ireland 5, Cyprus 0
Cyprus 1, USSR 3
Cyprus 0, Spain 2
USSR 2, Spain 1
USSR 6, Cyprus 1
USSR 1, Northern Ireland 0
Northern Ireland 1, USSR 1
Spain 0, USSR 0
Spain 7, Cyprus 0
Northern Ireland 1, Spain 1

Group 5

Denmark 0, Portugal 1
Scotland 1, Denmark 0
Belgium 2, Denmark 0
Belgium 3, Scotland 0
Belgium 3, Portugal 0
Portugal 2, Scotland 0
Denmark 1, Scotland 0
Portugal 5, Denmark 0
Denmark 1, Belgium 2
Scotland 2, Portugal 1
Scotland 1, Belgium 0
Portugal 1, Belgium 1

Group 6

Eire 1, Sweden 1
Sweden 1, Eire 0
Austria 1, Italy 2
Italy 3, Eire 0
Eire 1, Italy 2
Eire 1, Austria 4
Sweden 1, Austria 0
Sweden 0, Italy 0
Austria 1, Sweden 0
Italy 3, Sweden 0
Austria 6, Eire 0
Italy 2, Austria 2

Group 7

Holland 1, Yugoslavia 1
East Germany 1, Holland 0
Luxembourg 0, East Germany 5
Yugoslavia 2, Holland 0
East Germany 2, Luxembourg 1
Luxembourg 0, Yugoslavia 2
Holland 6, Luxembourg 0
East Germany 1, Yugoslavia 2
Holland 3, East Germany 2
Yugoslavia 0, East Germany 0
Yugoslavia 0, Luxembourg 0
Luxembourg 0, Holland 8

Group 8

Poland 3, Albania 0
West Germany 1, Turkey 1
Turkey 2, Albania 1
Albania 0, West Germany 1
Turkey 0, West Germany 3
Albania 1, Poland 1
West Germany 2, Albania 0
Poland 5, Turkey 1
Poland 1, West Germany 3
Albania 3, Turkey 0
West Germany 0, Poland 0
Turkey 1, Poland 0

Quarter-Finals

England 1, West Germany 3
Italy 0, Belgium 0
Hungary 1, Rumania 1
Yugoslavia 0, USSR 0
West Germany 0, England 0
Belgium 2, Italy 1
USSR 3, Yugoslavia 0
Rumania 2, Hungary 2
Play-off: Hungary 2, Rumania 1

Semi-Finals

USSR 1, Hungary 0 (in Brussels)
West Germany 2, Belgium 1 (in Antwerp)

Third Place Match (Liège)

Belgium 2, Hungary 1

Final (Brussels, 18 June, 1972)

West Germany (1) 3, USSR (0) 0

West Germany: Maier, Hottges, Schwarzenbeck, Beckenbauer, Breitner, Hoeness, Wimmer, Netzer, Heynkes, Müller, Kremers.
USSR: Rudakov, Dzodzuashvili, Khurtsilava, Kaplichny, Istomin, Troshkin, Kolotov, Baidachni, Konkov (Dolmatov), Banishevski (Kozinkievits), Onishenko.
Scorers: Müller 2, Wimmer for West Germany.

EUROPEAN CHAMPIONSHIP 1974–76

Group 1

England 3, Czechoslovakia 0
England 0, Portugal 0
England 5, Cyprus 0
Czechoslovakia 4, Cyprus 0

Czechoslovakia 5, Portugal 0
Cyprus 0, England 1
Cyprus 0, Portugal 2
Czechoslovakia 2, England 1
Portugal 1, Czechoslovakia 1
Portugal 1, England 1
Cyprus 0, Czechoslovakia 3
Portugal 1, Cyprus 0

Group 2

Austria 2, Wales 1
Luxembourg 2, Hungary 4
Wales 2, Hungary 0
Wales 5, Luxembourg 0
Luxembourg 1, Austria 2
Austria 0, Hungary 0
Hungary 1, Wales 2
Luxembourg 1, Wales 3
Hungary 2, Austria 1
Austria 6, Luxembourg 2
Hungary 8, Luxembourg 1
Wales 1, Austria 0

Group 3

Norway 2, Northern Ireland 1
Yugoslavia 3, Norway 1
Sweden 0, Northern Ireland 2
Northern Ireland 1, Yugoslavia 0
Sweden 1, Yugoslavia 2
Norway 1, Yugoslavia 3
Sweden 3, Norway 1
Norway 0, Sweden 2
Northern Ireland 1, Sweden 2
Yugoslavia 3, Sweden 0
Northern Ireland 3, Norway 0
Yugoslavia 1, Northern Ireland 0

Group 4

Denmark 1, Spain 2
Denmark 0, Rumania 0
Scotland 1, Spain 2
Spain 1, Scotland 1
Spain 1, Rumania 1
Rumania 6, Denmark 1
Rumania 1, Scotland 1
Denmark 0, Scotland 1
Spain 2, Denmark 0
Scotland 3, Denmark 1
Rumania 2, Spain 2
Scotland 1, Rumania 1

Group 5

Finland 1, Poland 2
Finland 1, Holland 3
Poland 3, Finland 0
Holland 3, Italy 1
Italy 0, Poland 0
Finland 0, Italy 1
Holland 4, Finland 1
Poland 4, Holland 1
Italy 0, Finland 0
Holland 3, Poland 0
Poland 0, Italy 0
Italy 1, Holland 0

Group 6

Eire 3, USSR 0
Turkey 1, Eire 1
Turkey 2, Switzerland 1
USSR 3, Turkey 0
Switzerland 1, Turkey 1
Eire 2, Switzerland 1
USSR 2, Eire 1
Switzerland 1, Eire 0
Switzerland 0, USSR 1
Eire 4, Turkey 0
USSR 4, Switzerland 1
Turkey 1, USSR 0

Group 7

Iceland 0, Belgium 2
East Germany 1, Iceland 1
Belgium 2, France 1
France 2, East Germany 2
East Germany 0, Belgium 0
Iceland 0, France 0
Iceland 2, East Germany 1
France 3, Iceland 0
Belgium 1, Iceland 0
Belgium 1, East Germany 2
East Germany 2, France 1
France 0, Belgium 0

Group 8

Bulgaria 3, Greece 3
Greece 2, West Germany 2
Greece 2, Bulgaria 1
Malta 0, West Germany 1
Malta 2, Greece 0
Bulgaria 1, West Germany 1
Greece 4, Malta 0
Bulgaria 5, Malta 0
West Germany 1, Greece 1
West Germany 1, Bulgaria 0
Malta 0, Bulgaria 2
West Germany 8, Malta 0

Quarter-Finals

Spain 1, West Germany 1
Yugoslavia 2, Wales 0
Czechoslovakia 2, USSR 0
Holland 5, Belgium 0
West Germany 2, Spain 0
USSR 2, Czechoslovakia 2
Wales 1, Yugoslavia 1
Belgium 1, Holland 2

Semi-Finals

Czechoslovakia 3, Holland 1 after extra time
(in Zagreb)
West Germany 4, Yugoslavia 2 after extra time
(in Belgrade)

Third Place Match (Zagreb)

Holland 3, Yugoslavia 2 after extra time

Final (Belgrade, 20 June, 1976)

Czechoslovakia (2) 2, West Germany (1) 2 (aet)
(*Czechoslovakia won 5-3 on penalties*)

Czechoslovakia: Viktor; Dobias (Vesely F.), Pivarnik, Ondrus, Capkovic, Gogh, Moder, Panenka, Svehlic (Jurkemik), Masny, Nehoda.
West Germany: Maier; Vogts, Beckenbauer, Schwarzenbeck, Dietz, Bonhof, Wimmer (Flohe), Müller D., Beer (Bongartz), Hoeness, Holzenbein.
Scorers: Svehlic, Dobias for Czechoslovakia; Müller, Holzenbein for West Germany.

EUROPEAN CHAMPIONSHIP 1978–80

Group 1

Denmark 3, Eire 3
Denmark 3, England 4
Eire 0, Northern Ireland 0

Denmark 2, Bulgaria 2
Eire 1, England 1
Northern Ireland 2, Denmark 1
Bulgaria 0, Northern Ireland 2
England 4, Northern Ireland 0
Northern Ireland 2, Bulgaria 0
Eire 2, Denmark 0
Bulgaria 1, Eire 0
Denmark 4, Northern Ireland 0
Bulgaria 0, England 3
England 1, Denmark 0
Eire 3, Bulgaria 0
Northern Ireland 1, England 5
Bulgaria 3, Denmark 0
Northern Ireland 1, Eire 0
England 2, Bulgaria 0
England 2, Eire 0

Group 2
Norway 0, Austria 2
Belgium 1, Norway 1
Austria 3, Scotland 2
Portugal 1, Belgium 1
Scotland 3, Norway 2
Austria 1, Portugal 2
Portugal 1, Scotland 0
Belgium 1, Austria 1
Austria 0, Belgium 0
Norway 0, Portugal 1
Norway 0, Scotland 4
Austria 4, Norway 0
Norway 1, Belgium 2
Belgium 2, Portugal 0
Scotland 1, Austria 1
Portugal 3, Norway 1
Belgium 2, Scotland 0
Portugal 1, Austria 2
Scotland 1, Belgium 3
Scotland 4, Portugal 1

Group 3
Yugoslavia 1, Spain 2
Rumania 3, Yugoslavia 2
Spain 1, Rumania 0
Spain 5, Cyprus 0
Cyprus 0, Yugoslavia 3
Rumania 2, Spain 2
Cyprus 1, Rumania 1
Spain 0, Yugoslavia 1
Yugoslavia 2, Rumania 1
Yugoslavia 5, Cyprus 0
Rumania 2, Cyprus 0
Cyprus 1, Spain 3

Group 4
Iceland 0, Poland 2
Holland 3, Iceland 0
East Germany 3, Iceland 1
Switzerland 1, Holland 3
Holland 3, East Germany 0
Poland 2, Switzerland 0
Holland 3, Switzerland 0
East Germany 2, Poland 1
Poland 2, Holland 0
Switzerland 0, East Germany 2
Switzerland 2, Iceland 0
Iceland 1, Switzerland 2
Iceland 0, Holland 4
Switzerland 0, Poland 2
Iceland 0, East Germany 3
Poland 1, East Germany 1
Poland 2, Iceland 0
East Germany 5, Switzerland 2
Holland 1, Poland 1
East Germany 2, Holland 3

Group 5
France 2, Sweden 2
Sweden 1, Czechoslovakia 3
Luxembourg 1, France 3
France 3, Luxembourg 0
Czechoslovakia 2, France 0
Luxembourg 0, Czechoslovakia 3
Sweden 3, Luxembourg 0
Sweden 1, France 3
Czechoslovakia 4, Sweden 1
Luxembourg 1, Sweden 1
France 2, Czechoslovakia 0
Czechoslovakia 4, Luxembourg 0

Group 6
Finland 3, Greece 0
Finland 2, Hungary 1
USSR 2, Greece 0
Hungary 2, USSR 0
Greece 8, Finland 1
Greece 4, Hungary 1
Hungary 0, Greece 0
USSR 2, Hungary 2
Finland 1, USSR 1
Greece 1, USSR 0
Hungary 3, Finland 1
USSR 2, Finland 2

Group 7
Wales 7, Malta 0
Wales 1, Turkey 0
Malta 0, West Germany 0
Turkey 2, Malta 1
Turkey 0, West Germany 0
Wales 0, West Germany 2
Malta 0, Wales 2
West Germany 5, Wales 1
Malta 1, Turkey 2
Turkey 1, Wales 0
West Germany 2, Turkey 0
West Germany 8, Malta 0

Final Tournament

Group 1
West Germany 1, Czechoslovakia 0
Greece 0, Holland 1
West Germany 3, Holland 2
Czechoslovakia 3, Greece 1
Czechoslovakia 1, Holland 1
West Germany 0, Greece 0

Group 2
Belgium 1, England 1
Spain 0, Italy 0
Spain 1, Belgium 2
Italy 1, England 0
England 2, Spain 1
Italy 0, Belgium 0

Third Place Match (Naples)
Italy 1, Czechoslovakia 1
(*Czechoslovakia won 9-8 on penalties*)

Final (Rome, 22 June, 1980)
West Germany (1) 2, Belgium (0) 1

West Germany: Schumacher; Briegel, Forster K., Dietz, Schuster, Rummenigge, Hrubesch, Müller, Aloffs, Stielike, Kaltz.
Belgium: Pfaff; Gerets, Millecamps, Meeuws, Renquin, Cools, Van der Eycken, Van Moer, Mommens, Van der Elst, Ceulemans.
Scorers: Hrubesch 2 for West Germany; Van der Eychen for Belgium.

EUROPEAN NATIONS SECTION

Details have been listed for all European footballing nations but unfortunately owing to some countries' seasons finishing at different times from the British season, not all league champions and cup winners are known for the current season. Total number of championship and cup wins is given with winners' present names, with previous names in brackets. In the tables of league champions and cup winners, contemporary names are used.

ALBANIA

President: Zyber Konci.
Secretary: Ilia Shuke.
Address of Association: Federation Albanaise de Football, Rruga, Kongresi I Permetit, 41 Tirana.
Telephone: 7256, 2426.
Cable: Albsport Tirana.
Area: 11,100 square miles.
Population: 2,405,000. *Number of Clubs:* 42.
Teams: 215.
Number of Players: 4,730.
Year of Formation: 1932.
National Colours: Red shirts, black shorts, black stockings with red stripe.
Second Choice of Colours: White shirts, white shorts, white stockings.
Name, Address and Capacity of National Stadium: Qemal Stafa, Tirana, 30,000.
Names and Capacity of Other Principal Football Grounds: Dinamo, 15,000; Shkodra, 13,000; Durresi, 15,000; Korca, 13,000; Fier, 10,000; Vlora, 13,000.
Season: September–May.

International matches 1980

3 Sept, Tirana: v Finland (h) won 2-0 (*Braho, Baci*)
19 Oct, Sofia: v Bulgaria (a) lost 1-2 (*Pernaska*)
15 Nov, Vienna: v Austria (a) lost 0-5
6 Dec, Tirana: v Austria (h) lost 0-1

League Championship wins (1945–81)

Dinamo Tirana 15; Partizan Tirana 12; 17 Nendori 5; Vlaznia 4.

Cup wins (1948–81)

Dinamo Tirana 12; Partizan Tirana 9; 17 Nendori 4; Vlaznia 3; Besa 1; Labinoti 1.

	League Champions	Cup Winners
1945	Vlaznia	
1946	Vlaznia	
1947	Partizan Tirana	
1948	Partizan Tirana	Partizan Tirana
1949	Partizan Tirana	Partizan Tirana
1950	Dinamo Tirana	Dinamo Tirana
1951	Dinamo Tirana	Dinamo Tirana
1952	Dinamo Tirana	Dinamo Tirana
1953	Dinamo Tirana	Dinamo Tirana
1954	Partizan Tirana	Dinamo Tirana
1955	Dinamo Tirana	*No competition*
1956	Dinamo Tirana	*No competition*
1957	Partizan Tirana	Partizan Tirana
1958	Partizan Tirana	Partizan Tirana
1959	Partizan Tirana	*No competition*
1960	Dinamo Tirana	Dinamo Tirana
1961	Partizan Tirana	Partizan Tirana
1963*	Dinamo Tirana	17 Nendori
1964	Partizan Tirana	Partizan Tirana
1965	17 Nendori	Dinamo Tirana
1966	17 Nendori	Dinamo Tirana
1967	Dinamo Tirana	Vlaznia
1968	17 Nendori	Dinamo Tirana
1969	17 Nendori	17 Nendori
1970	17 Nendori	Partizan Tirana
1971	Partizan Tirana	Dinamo Tirana
1972	Vlaznia	Besa
1973	Dinamo Tirana	Partizan Tirana
1974	Vlaznia	Dinamo Tirana
1975	Dinamo Tirana	Labinoti
1976	Dinamo Tirana	17 Nendori
1977	Dinamo Tirana	17 Nendori
1978	Dinamo Tirana	Dinamo Tirana
1979	Partizan Tirana	Vlaznia
1980	Dinamo Tirana	Partizan Tirana
1981	Partizan Tirana	Vlaznia

* *Changed from calendar season to overlapping season from autumn to spring.*

Final League Table 1980–81

	P	*W*	*D*	*L*	*F*	*A*	*Pts*
Partizan Tirana	26	15	7	4	36	17	37
Dinamo Tirana	26	14	8	4	32	17	36
17 Nendori	26	14	7	5	38	21	35
Vlaznia	26	9	9	8	30	33	27
Luftetari	26	10	5	11	25	24	25
Naftetari	26	10	5	11	24	32	25
Besa	26	7	10	9	28	25	24
Flamurtari	26	8	8	10	27	26	24
Labinoti	26	7	10	9	24	28	24
Beselidhija	26	6	11	9	21	25	23
Lokomotiva	26	6	11	9	20	24	23
Tomori	26	4	15	7	14	20	23
Skenderben	26	5	12	9	19	27	22
Traktori	26	4	8	14	17	36	16

AUSTRIA

President: Karl Sekanina.
Secretary: Otto Demuth.
Address of Association: Oesterreichischer Fussball-Bund, Mariahilferstrasse 99, Postfach 161, Wien A-1061.
Telephone: 57-15-36.
Cable: Football Wien.
Telex: 11919oefb a.
Area: 32,374 square miles.
Population: 7,457,000.
Number of Clubs: 2,041. *Teams:* 6,466.
Number of Players: 255,125.
Year of Formation: 1904.
National Colours: White shirt, black shorts, black stockings.
Second Choice of Colours: Red shirts, white shorts, red stockings.
Name, Address and Capacity of National Stadium: Wiener Stadion, Prater, Vienna, 70,714.
Names, Addresses and Capacities of Other Principal Football Grounds: Linzer Stadion, Linz, 22,000; Stadion Salzburger, Bundesstadion Liebenau, Graz, 19,000; Tivoli Stadion, Innsbruck, 14,400; Stadion, Wiener Neustadt, 12,600; Bodenseestadion, Bregenz, 12,000; Stadion Klagenfurt, Klagenfurt, 11,000; Hohe Warte, Vienna Weststadion, Vienna, 20,000; Bundesstadion Sudstadt, Maria Enzersdort, 15,600.
Season: August–December; February–June.

Principal Honours

Olympic Games: *runners-up* 1936.
European Cup-Winners' Cup: *runners-up* Austria/WAC (1978).

International matches 1980

2 April, Berlin: v West Germany (a) lost 0-1
21 May, Vienna: Argentina (h) lost 1-5 (*Jara*)
4 June, Budapest: v Hungary (a) drew 1-1 (*Jara*)
24 Sept, Helsinki: v Finland (a) won 2-0 (*Jara, Welzl*)
8 Oct, Vienna v Hungary (h) won 3-1 (*Welzl, Keglevits 2*)
15 Nov, Vienna: v Albania (h) won 5-0 (*Pezzey, Schachner 2, Welzl, Krankl*)
6 Dec, Tirana: v Albania (a) won 1-0 (*Welzl*)

League Championship wins (1912–81)

Rapid Vienna 25; Austria/Vienna (prev. Austria/WAC, FK Austria and WAC) 16; Admira-Energie-Wacker (prev. Sportklub Admira & Admira-Energie) 8; First Vienna 6; Tirol-Svarowski-Innsbruck (prev. Wacker Innsbruck) 5; Wiener Sportklub 3; FAC 1; Hakoah 1; Linz ASK 1; Wacker Vienna 1; WAF 1; Voest Linz 1.

Cup wins (1919–81)

Austria/WAC 20; Rapid Vienna 9; Admira-Energie-Wacker (prev. Sportklub Admira & Admira-Energie) 5; TS Innsbruck (prev. Wacker Innsbruck) 5; First Vienna 3; Linz ASK 1; Wacker Vienna 1; WAF 1; Wiener Sportklub 1, Graz AK 1.

	League Champions	Cup Winners
1946	Rapid Vienna	Rapid Vienna
1947	Wacker Vienna	Wacker Vienna
1948	Rapid Vienna	FK Austria
1949	FK Austria	FK Austria
1950	FK Austria	*No competition*
1951	Rapid Vienna	*No competition*
1952	Rapid Vienna	*No competition*
1953	FK Austria	*No competition*
1954	Rapid Vienna	*No competition*
1955	First Vienna	*No competition*
1956	Rapid Vienna	*No competition*
1957	Rapid Vienna	*No competition*
1958	Wiener Sportklub	*No competition*
1959	Wiener Sportklub	Wiener AC
1960	Rapid Vienna	FK Austria
1961	FK Austria	Rapid Vienna
1962	FK Austria	FK Austria
1963	FK Austria	FK Austria
1964	Rapid Vienna	Admira-Energie
1965	Linz ASK	Linz ASK
1966	Admira-Energie	Admira-Energie
1967	Rapid Vienna	FK Austria
1968	Rapid Vienna	Rapid Vienna
1969	FK Austria	Rapid Vienna
1970	FK Austria	Wacker Innsbruck
1971	Wacker Innsbruck	FK Austria
1972	TS Innsbruck	Rapid Vienna
1973	TS Innsbruck	TS Innsbruck
1974	Voest Linz	Austria/WAC
1975	TS Innsbruck	TS Innsbruck
1976	Austria/WAC	Rapid Vienna
1977	TS Innsbruck	Austria/WAC
1978	Austria/WAC	TS Innsbruck
1979	Austria/WAC	TS Innsbruck
1980	Austria/WAC	Austria/WAC
1981	Austria/Vienna	Graz AK

Final League Table 1980–81

	P	*W*	*D*	*L*	*F*	*A*	*Pts*
Austria/Vienna	36	20	6	10	77	46	46
Sturm Graz	36	17	11	8	58	39	45
Rapid Vienna	36	18	7	11	69	43	43
Admira Wacker	36	17	8	11	56	52	42
Graz AK	36	13	12	11	52	49	38
Voest Linz	36	12	12	12	44	40	36
Linz ASK	36	11	12	13	42	51	34
Wiener Sportklub	36	12	8	16	46	69	32
Austria Salzburg	36	10	3	23	40	61	23
SC Eisenstadt	36	6	9	21	25	59	21

BELGIUM

President: M. Louis Wouters.
Secretary: Albert Roosens.
Address of Association: Union Royale Belge des Sociétés de Football Association, Rue de la Loi 43, B-1040 Bruxelles.
Telephone: 02/230.07.30.
Telex: 23257 bvbfbfb.
Cable: UBSFA Bruxelles.
Area: 11,779 square miles.
Population: 9,250,000.
Number of Clubs: 3,071. *Teams:* 8,694.
Number of Players: 279,420.
Year of Formation: 1895.
National Colours: White shirts with tricoloured (black-yellow-red) collar and cuffs, white shorts, white stockings with tricoloured (black-yellow-red) tops.
Second Choice of Colours: Red shirts, black shorts, yellow stockings.
Name, Address and Capacity of National Stadium: Centenary Stadium, Marathon Avenue, Brussels (Heysel), 70,000.
Names, Addresses and Capacities of Other Principal Football Grounds: R. Antwerp FC-Bosuilbaan, at Deurne (Antwerp), 62,000; RFC Liégeois-Chaussée de Tongres, at Rocourt (Liège), 43,000; R. Standard C. Liégeois-2, rue de la Centrale at Sclessin (Liège), 43,000; RSC Anderlechtois-2, avenue Théo Verbeeck, Anderlecht (Brussels), 38,000.
Season: September–May.

Principal Honours

Olympic Games: *winners* 1920
European Championship: *runners-up* 1980
European Champions Cup: *runners-up* FC Bruges (1978)
European Cup-Winners' Cup: *winners* Anderlecht (1976, 1978); *runners-up* Anderlecht (1977)
Fairs Cup: *runners-up* Anderlecht (1970)
UEFA Cup: *runners-up* FC Bruges (1976)
Super Cup: Anderlecht (1978)

International matches 1980

27 Feb, Brussels: v Luxembourg (h) won 5-0 (*Van den Bergh 2, Van der Eycken, Van der Elst 2*)
18 March, Brussels: v Uruguay (h) won 2-0 (*Verheyen, Van der Elst*)
2 April, Brussels: v Poland (h) won 2-1 (*Coeck, Van den Bergh*)
6 June, Brussels: v Rumania (h) won 2-1 (*Ceulemans, Van der Elst*)
12 June, Turin: v England (a) drew 1-1 (*Ceulemans*)
15 June, Milan: v Spain (a) won 2-1 (*Gerets, Cools*)
18 June, Rome: v Italy (a) drew 0-0
22 June, Rome: v West Germany (a) lost 1-2 (*Van der Eycken* pen)
15 Oct, Dublin: v Republic of Ireland (a) drew 1-1 (*Cluytens*)
19 Nov, Brussels: v Netherlands (h) won 1-0 (*Van den Bergh*)
20 Dec, Nicosia: v Cyprus (a) won 2-0 (*Van den Bergh, Ceulemans*)

League Championship wins (1896–1981)

Anderlecht 17; Union St Gilloise 11; Beerschot 7; FC Bruges 6; Standard Liège 6; RC Brussels 6; FC Liège 5; Daring Brussels 5; Antwerp 4; Lierse SK 3; Malines 3; CS Bruges 3; RWD Molenbeek 1, Beveren 1.

Cup wins (1954–81)

Anderlecht 5; Standard Liège 4; FC Bruges 3; Beerschot 2; Antwerp 1; La Gantoise 1; Lierse SK 1; Tournai 1; Waregem 1; Beveren 1; Waterschei 1.

	League Champions	Cup Winners
1946	Malines	
1947	Anderlecht	
1948	Malines	
1949	Anderlecht	
1950	Anderlecht	
1951	Anderlecht	
1952	FC Liège	
1953	FC Liège	
1954	Anderlecht	Standard Liège
1955	Anderlecht	Antwerp
1956	Anderlecht	Tournai
1957	Antwerp	*No competition*
1958	Standard Liège	*No competition*
1959	Anderlecht	*No competition*
1960	Lierse SK	*No competition*
1961	Standard Liège	*No competition*
1962	Anderlecht	*No competition*
1963	Standard Liège	*No competition*
1964	Anderlecht	La Gantoise
1965	Anderlecht	Anderlecht
1966	Anderlecht	Standard Liège
1967	Anderlecht	Standard Liège
1968	Anderlecht	FC Bruges
1969	Standard Liège	Lierse SK
1970	Standard Liège	FC Bruges
1971	Standard Liège	Beerschot
1972	Anderlecht	Anderlecht
1973	FC Bruges	Anderlecht
1974	Anderlecht	Waregem
1975	RWD Molenbeek	Anderlecht
1976	FC Bruges	Anderlecht
1977	FC Bruges	FC Bruges
1978	FC Bruges	Beveren
1979	Beveren	Beerschot
1980	FC Bruges	Waterschei
1981	Anderlecht	Standard Liege

Final League Table 1980–81

	P	*W*	*D*	*L*	*F*	*A*	*Pts*
Anderlecht	34	26	5	3	83	24	57
Lokeren	34	20	6	8	74	36	46
Standard Liège	34	18	6	10	65	45	42
Beveren	34	16	9	9	48	31	41
Winterslag	34	16	6	12	46	43	38
FC Bruges	34	16	5	13	74	56	37
Lierse	34	12	11	11	58	49	35
RWD Molenbeek	34	14	7	13	49	50	35
Antwerp	34	11	11	12	42	53	33
La Gantoise	34	12	8	14	49	49	32
Waregem	34	11	10	13	40	47	32
FC Liege	34	11	9	14	53	44	31
Courtrai	34	11	8	15	42	55	30
CS Bruges	34	11	7	16	51	68	29
Beerschot	34	10	6	18	42	55	26
Waterschei	34	10	5	19	54	77	25
Beringen	34	8	8	18	35	62	24
Berchem	34	5	9	20	29	90	19

BULGARIA

President: Kroum Vassiltchev.
Secretary: Konstantin Stoytcheuski.
Address of Association: Federation Bulgare de Football, Boul. Tolboukhin 18, Sofia.
Telephone: 877490.
Cable: Besefese Sofia.
Area: 42,830 square miles.
Population: 9,000,000.
Number of Clubs: 3,923. *Teams:* 5,737.
Number of Players: 117,280.
Year of Formation: 1923.
National Colours: White shirts, green shorts, red stockings.
Second Choice of Colours: Red shirts, green shorts, white stockings.
Name, Address and Capacity of National Stadium: 'Vassil Levski', Sofia, 55,000.
Names, Addresses and Capacities of Other Principal Football Grounds: Stade Narodna Armia, Parc de la Liberté, Sofia, 43,000; Levski-Gerena, Sofia, 40,000; Stade Slavia, Ovtcha Koupel, Sofia, 35,000; Stade Rakovski, quartier Ivan Vasoc, Sofia, 29,000; Stade Guerena, quartier Podouene, Sofia, 33,000; Stade 9 Septembre, Plovdiv, 40,000; Stade Christo Botev, Plovdiv, 30,000; Stade Yuri Gagarine, Varna, 40,000; Stade de la ville de Rousse, 20,000; Stade 9 Septembre, Bourgass, 15,000.
Season: August–December; March–June.

Principal Honours

Olympic Games: *runners-up* 1968

International matches 1980

8 Feb, Damascus: v Syria (a) won 1-0.
26 March, Sofia: v USSR (h) lost 1-3 (*T. Tsvetkov*)
2 April, Kustentil: v Hungary (h) won 4-3 (*Jeliazkov 2, Kostadinov, P. Tsvetkov*)
14 May, Athens: v Greece (a) drew 0-0
22 May, Oslo: v Norway (a) lost 0-1
4 June, Helsinki: v Finland (a) won 2-0 (*Markov, Kostadinov*)
10 Sept, Varna: v Rumania (h) lost 1-2 (*Slavkov*)
24 Sept, Bourgas: v Sweden (h) lost 2-3 (*T. Tsvetkov, Markov*)
9 Oct, Buenos Aires: v Argentina (a) lost 0-2
19 Oct, Sofia: v Albania (h) won 2-1 (*Jeliaskov, Slavkov*)
3 Dec, Sofia: v West Germany (h) lost 1-3 (*Yonchev*)

League Championship wins (1925–81)

CSKA Sofia (prev. CDNA) 21; Levski Spartak (prev. Levski Sofia) 13; Slavia Sofia 6; Vladislav Varna 3; Lokomotiv Sofia 3; AS 23 Sofia 1; Botev Plovdiv 1; SC Sofia 1; Sokol Varna 1; Spartak Plovdiv 1; Tichka Varan 1; Trakia Plovdiv 1; ZSK Sofia 1.

Cup wins (1946–81)

Levski Spartak (prev. Levski Sofia) 13; CSKA Sofia (prev. CDNA) 10; Slavia Sofia 6; Lokomotiv Sofia 2; Botev Plovdiv 1; Spartak Plovdiv 1; Spartak Sofia 1; Marek Stanke 1, Trakia Plovdiv 1.

	League Champions	Cup Winners
1946	Levski Sofia	Levski Sofia
1947	Levski Sofia	Levski Sofia
1948	CDNA Sofia	Lokomotiv Sofia
1949	Levski Sofia	Levski Sofia
1950	Levski Sofia	Levski Sofia
1951	CDNA Sofia	CDNA Sofia
1952	CDNA Sofia	Slavia Sofia
1953	Levski Sofia	Lokomotiv Sofia
1954	CDNA Sofia	CDNA Sofia
1955	CDNA Sofia	CDNA Sofia
1956	CDNA Sofia	Levski Sofia
1957	CDNA Sofia	Levski Sofia
1958	CDNA Sofia	Spartak Plovdiv
1959	CDNA Sofia	Levski Sofia
1960	CDNA Sofia	CDNA Sofia
1961	CDNA Sofia	CDNA Sofia
1962	CDNA Sofia	Botev Plovdiv
1963	Spartak Plovdiv	Slavia Sofia
1964	Lokomotiv Sofia	Slavia Sofia
1965	Levski Sofia	CSKA Sofia
1966	CSKA Sofia	Slavia Sofia
1967	Trakia Plovdiv	Levski Sofia
1968	Levski Sofia	Spartak Sofia
1969	CSKA Sofia	CSKA Sofia
1970	Levski Spartak	Levski Spartak
1971	CSKA Sofia	Levski Spartak
1972	CSKA Sofia	CSKA Sofia
1973	CSKA Sofia	CSKA Sofia
1974	Levski Spartak	CSKA Sofia
1975	CSKA Sofia	Slavia Sofia
1976	CSKA Sofia	Levski Spartak
1977	Levski Spartak	Levski Spartak
1978	Lokomotiv Sofia	Marek Stanke
1979	Levski Spartak	Levski Spartak
1980	CSKA Sofia	Slavia Sofia
1981	CSKA Sofia	Trakia Plovdiv

Final League Table 1980–81

	P	*W*	*D*	*L*	*F*	*A*	*Pts*
CSKA Sofia	30	14	12	4	70	32	40
Levski Spartak	30	13	10	7	44	25	36
Trakia Plovdiv	30	15	5	10	64	40	35
Akademik	30	13	8	9	42	40	34
Spartak	30	12	7	11	38	41	31
Chernomore	30	8	13	9	36	37	29
Slavia Sofia	30	10	9	11	35	44	29
Lokomotiv Sofia	30	8	12	10	34	35	28
Marek Stanke	30	12	4	14	39	40	28
Beroe	30	11	6	13	45	49	28
Chernomorets	30	9	10	11	42	49	28
Botev Plovdiv	30	8	11	11	32	37	27
Belasitsa	30	11	5	14	38	47	27
Sliven	30	11	5	14	33	43	27
Minior	30	12	3	15	32	51	27
Pirin	30	6	14	10	33	47	26

CYPRUS

President: Michalakis Kyptianu.
General Secretary: Demetrakis Stephanides.
Address of Association: Cyprus Football Association, Stasinos Street 1, Engomi 114, PO Box 5071, Nicosia.
Telephone: 45341.
Telex: 3880 football cy.
Cable: Football Nicosia.
Area: 3,572 square miles.
Population: 630,000.
Number of Clubs: 41. *Teams:* 57.
Number of Players: 12,000.
Year of Formation: 1934.
National Colours: Sky blue shirts, white shorts, blue and white stockings.
Second Choice of Colours: White shirts, blue shorts, white stockings.
Name, Address and Capacity of National Stadium: GSP, Nicosia, 12,000.
Names, Addresses and Capacities of Other Principal Football Grounds: Tsition, Limassol, 20,000; GSE, Famagusta, 10,000; GSO Limassol, 10,000; GSj, Larnaca, 8,000.
Season: October–June.
All players are amateurs.

International matches 1980

16 Jan, Nicosia: v Greece (h) drew 1-1 (*Kitzas*)
26 March, Nicosia: v Republic of Ireland (h) lost 2-3 (*Pantziaras, Kaiafas* pen)
11 Oct, Limassol: v France (h) lost 0-7
19 Nov, Dublin: v Republic of Ireland (a) lost 0-6
20 Dec, Nicosia: v Belgium (h) lost 0-2

League Championship wins (1935–81)

Apoel 12; Omonia 10; Anorthosis 6; AEL 5; EPA 3; Olympiakos 3; Chetin Kayal 1; Pezoporikos 1; Trast 1.

Cup wins (1935–81)

Apoel 10; EPA 5; Omonia 4; AEL 3; Trast 3; Chetin Kaya 2; Apollon 2; Pezoporikos 2; Anorthosis 2; Paralimni 1; Olympiakos 1.

League Champions	Cup Winners
1946 EPA	EPA
1947 Apoel	Apoel
1948 Apoel	AEL
1949 Apoel	Anorthosis
1950 Anorthosis	EPA
1951 Chetin Kaya	Apoel
1952 Apoel	Chetin Kaya
1953 AEL	EPA
1954 Pezoporikos	Chetin Kaya
1955 AEL	EPA
1956 AEL	*No competition*
1957 Anorthosis	*No competition*
1958 Anorthosis	*No competition*
1959 *No competition*	*No competition*
1960 Anorthosis	*No competition*
1961 Omonia	*No competition*
1962 Anorthosis	Anorthosis
1963 Anorthosis	Apoel
1964 *No competition*	*No competition*
1965 Apoel	Omonia
1966 Omonia	Apollon
1967 Olympiakos	Apollon
1968 AEL	Apoel
1969 Olympiakos	Apoel
1970 EPA	Pezoporikos
1971 Olympiakos	Anorthosis
1972 Omonia	Omonia
1973 Apoel	Pezoporikos
1974 Omonia	Paralimni
1975 Omonia	Anorthosis
1976 Omonia	Apoel
1977 Omonia	Olympiakos
1978 Omonia	Apoel
1979 Omonia	Apoel
1980 Apoel	Omonia
1981 Omonia	Omonia

Final League Table 1980–81

	P	*W*	*D*	*L*	*F*	*A*	*Pts*
Omonia Nicosia	26	16	6	4	56	21	38
Apoel	26	13	10	3	41	16	36
Pezoporikos	26	14	6	6	45	33	34
Paralimni	26	11	10	5	32	21	32
Anorthosis	26	9	9	8	37	34	27
Apollon	26	10	6	10	32	32	26
NEA Salamina	26	8	8	10	29	32	24
Omonia Aradippou	26	7	9	10	30	41	23
Keravnos	26	8	7	11	27	41	23
EPA	26	6	9	11	25	27	21
Olympiakos	26	7	7	12	23	30	21
AEL	26	7	7	12	19	30	21
Alki	26	7	7	12	25	40	21
Aris	26	7	3	16	29	52	17

CZECHOSLOVAKIA

President: Jaromir Tomanek.
Secretary: Rudolf Bata.
Address of Association: Czechoslovak Football, 12, Na Porící, Prague, 1.
Telephone: 24 98 41, 22 58 36.
Cable: Sportsvaz.
Area: 49,370 square miles.
Population: 15,000,000.
Number of Clubs: 6,776. *Teams:* 26,847.
Number of Players: 352,227.
Year of Formation: 1906.
National Colours: Red shirts, white shorts, blue stockings.
Second Choice of Colours: White shirts, white shorts, white stockings.
Name, Address and Capacity of National Stadium: Stadion Ceskoslovenské Armády, Praha-Strahov, 60,000.
Names, Addresses and Capacities of Other Principal Football Grounds: Slovan Bratislava, Bratislava-Tehelné Pole, 63,000; Zbrojovka Brno, Brno, 70,000; Slavia Prague, Prague, 43,000; International, Bratislava, 40,000; Sparta Praha, Prague, 38,000.
Season: August–November; February–June.

Principal Honours

World Cup: *runners-up* 1934, 1962
European Championship: *winners* 1976
Olympic Games: *runners-up* 1964
European Cup-Winners' Cup: *winners* Slovan Bratislava (1969)

International matches 1980

23 Jan, Leon: v Mexico (a) lost 0-1
27 Jan, Canberra: v Australia (a) won 4-0 (*Jurkemik, Vizek, Nehoda, Krol*)
3 Feb, Sydney: v Australia (a) won 5-0 (*Masny 2, Gajdusek, Kroupa, Kozak*)
9 Feb, Melbourne: v Australia (a) drew 2-2 (*Dobias* pen, *Nehoda*)
26 March, Basle: v Switzerland (a) lost 0-2
16 April, Gijon: v Spain (a) drew 2-2 (*Nehoda 2*)
30 April, Kosice: v Hungary (h) won 1-0 (*Nehoda*)
16 May, Brno: v Rumania (h) won 2-1 (*Vizek 2*)
11 June, Rome: v West Germany (a) lost 0-1
14 June, Rome: v Greece (a) won 3-1 (*Panenka, Vizek, Nehoda*)
21 June, Naples: v Italy (a) drew 1-1 (*Jurkemik*) (Czechoslovakia won 9-8 on penalties)
17 June, Milan: v Netherlands (a) drew 1-1 (*Nehoda*)
24 Sept, Chorzow: v Poland (a) drew 1-1 (*Nehoda*)
8 Oct, Prague: v East Germany (h) lost 0-1
15 Oct, Buenos Aires: v Argentina (a) lost 0-1
19 Nov, Cardiff: v Wales (a) lost 0-1
3 Dec, Prague: v Turkey (h) won 2-0 (*Nehoda 2*)

League Championship wins (1926–81)
Sparta Prague 13; Slavia Prague 12; Dukla Prague (prev. UDA) 10; Slovan Bratislava 6; Spartak Trnava 5; Banik Ostrava 3; Inter-Bratislava 1; Spartak Hradec Kralove 1; Viktoria Zizkov 1; Zbrojovka Brno 1.

Cup wins (1961–81)
Dukla Prague 5; Slovan Bratislava 4; Sparta Prague 4; Spartak Trnava 3; Banik Ostrava 2; Lokomotiv Kosice 2; TJ Gottwaldov 1.

	League Champions	Cup Winners
1946	Sparta Prague	
1947	Slavia Prague	
1948	Sparta Prague	
1949	Slovan Bratislava	
1950	Slovan Bratislava	
1951	Slovan Bratislava	
1952	Sparta Prague	
1953	Dukla Prague	
1954	Sparta Prague	
1955	Slovan Bratislava	
1956	Dukla Prague	
1957	*No competition*	
1958	Dukla Prague	
1959	Inter-Bratislava	
1960	Hradec Kralove	
1961	Dukla Prague	Dukla Prague
1962	Dukla Prague	Slovan Bratislava
1963	Dukla Prague	Slovan Bratislava
1964	Dukla Prague	Sparta Prague
1965	Sparta Prague	Dukla Prague
1966	Dukla Prague	Dukla Prague
1967	Sparta Prague	Sparta Trnava
1968	Spartak Trnava	Slovan Bratislava
1969	Spartak Trnava	Dukla Prague
1970	Slovan Bratislava	TJ Gottwaldov
1971	Spartak Trnava	Spartak Trnava
1972	Spartak Trnava	Sparta Prague
1973	Spartak Trnava	Banik Ostrava
1974	Slovan Bratislava	Slovan Bratislava
1975	Slovan Bratislava	Spartak Trnava
1976	Banik Ostrava	Sparta Prague
1977	Dukla Prague	Lokomotiv Kosice
1978	Zbrojovka Brno	Banik Ostrava
1979	Dukla Prague	Lokomotiv Kosice
1980	Banik Ostrava	Sparta Prague
1981	Banik Ostrava	Dukla Prague

Final League Table 1980–81

	P	*W*	*D*	*L*	*F*	*A*	*Pts*
Banik Ostrava	**30**	**18**	**4**	**8**	**44**	**19**	**40**
Dukla Prague	**30**	**16**	**6**	**8**	**51**	**30**	**38**
Bohemians	**30**	**16**	**4**	**10**	**54**	**30**	**36**
Sparta Prague	**30**	**15**	**6**	**9**	**40**	**26**	**36**
Lokomotiv Kosice	**30**	**17**	**10**	**9**	**43**	**34**	**34**
RH Cheb	**30**	**12**	**8**	**10**	**43**	**36**	**32**
Slavia Prague	**30**	**13**	**6**	**11**	**40**	**48**	**32**
Tatran Presov	**30**	**12**	**5**	**13**	**47**	**44**	**29**
Slovan Bratislava	**30**	**12**	**5**	**13**	**40**	**38**	**29**
Spartak Trnava	**30**	**13**	**3**	**14**	**36**	**43**	**29**
Inter	**30**	**12**	**5**	**13**	**34**	**52**	**29**
Zbrojovka Brno	**30**	**10**	**8**	**12**	**42**	**45**	**28**
Plastika Nitra	**30**	**11**	**4**	**15**	**31**	**49**	**26**
Dukla Bystrica	**30**	**10**	**5**	**15**	**31**	**43**	**25**
Hradec Kralove	**30**	**10**	**5**	**15**	**31**	**43**	**25**
ZTS Kosice	**30**	**5**	**4**	**21**	**29**	**54**	**14**

DENMARK

President: Carl Nielsen.
Secretary: Erik Hyldstorp.
Address of Association: Dansk Boldspil – Union PW Ligns Alle 4, Copenhagen, 2100.
Telephone: 424540.
Cable: Danksboldspil.
Area: 17,159 square miles.
Population: 4,750,000.
Number of Clubs: 1,453. *Teams:* 7,400.
Number of Players: 208,000.
Year of Formation: 1889.
National Colours: Red shirts, white shorts, red stockings.
Second Choice of Colours: White shirts, white shorts, red stockings.
Name, Address and Capacity of National Stadium: Kobenhavns Idraetspark, PH-Lings-Alle 2, 50,000.
Names, Addresses and Capacities of Other Principal Football Grounds: Odense stadium, Odense, 20,000; Aarhus stadium, Aarhus, 24,000; Aalborg stadium, Aalborg, 22,000; Esbjerg stadium, Esbjerg, 18,000; Vejle stadium, Vejle, 18,000.
Season: April–November.

Principal Honours

Olympic Games: *runners-up* 1908, 1912, 1960

International matches 1980

7 May, Gothenburg: v Sweden (a) won 1-0 (*Steffensen*)
21 May, Copenhagen: v Spain (h) drew 2-2 (*Simonsen, Bastrup*)
4 June, Copenhagen: v Norway (h) won 3-1 (*B. Nielsen* pen, *Arnesen, Elkjaer*)
12 July, Moscow: v USSR (a) lost 0-2
27 Aug, Lausanne: v Switzerland (a) drew 1-1 (*Bastrup*)
27 Sept, Ljubljana: v Yugoslavia (a) lost 1-2 (*Arnesen* pen)
15 Oct, Copenhagen: v Greece (h) lost 0-1
1 Nov, Rome: v Italy (a) lost 0-2
19 Nov, Copenhagen: v Luxembourg (h) won 4-0 (*Arnesen 2*, [1 pen], *Elkjaer, Simonsen*)

League Championship wins (1913–80)

KB Copenhagen 15; B 93 Copenhagen 9; AB (Akademisk) 9; B 1903 Copenhagen 7; Frem 6; Esbjergs BK 5; AGF Aarhus 4; Vejle BK 4; B 1909 Odense 2; Hvidovre 2; Koge BK 2; Odense BK 1.

Cup wins (1955–81)

Vejle BK 6; Aarhus GF 5; BK 09 Odense 3; Randers Freja 3; Aalborg BK 2; Esbjerg BK 2; Frem 2; KB Copenhagen 1; Vanlose 1; B 1903 Copenhagen 1; Hvidovre 1.

	League Champions	Cup Winners
1946	BK 93	
1947	Akademisk	
1948	KB Copenhagen	
1949	KB Copenhagen	
1950	KB Copenhagen	
1951	Akademisk	
1952	Akademisk	
1953	KB Copenhagen	
1954	Koge BK	
1955	Aarhus GF	Aarhus GF
1956	Aarhus GF	Frem
1957	Aarhus GF	Aarhus GF
1958	Vejle	Vejle
1959	BK 09 Odense	Vejle
1960	Aarhus GF	Aarhus GF
1961	Esbjerg BK	Aarhus GF
1962	Esbjerg BK	BK Odense 09
1963	Esbjerg BK	BK Odense 09
1964	BK 09 Odense	Esbjerg
1965	Esbjerg BK	Aarhus GF
1966	Hvidovre	Aalborg BK
1967	Akademisk	Randers Freja
1968	KB Copenhagen	Randers Freja
1969	BK 03 Copenhagen	KB Copenhagen
1970	BK 03 Copenhagen	Aalborg BK
1971	Vejle	BK 09 Odense
1972	Vejle	Vejle
1973	Hvidovre	Randers Freja
1974	KB Copenhagen	Vanlose
1975	Koge BK	Vejle
1976	BK 03 Copenhagen	Esbjerg
1977	Odense BK	Vejle
1978	Vejle	Frem
1979	Esbjerg BK	B 1903 Copenhagen
1980	KB Copenhagen	Hvidovre
1981		Vejle

Final League Table 1980–81

	P	*W*	*D*	*L*	*F*	*A*	*Pts*
KB Copenhagen	30	16	8	6	59	35	40
Naestved	30	18	4	8	56	36	40
Odense	30	14	10	6	45	31	38
Aarhus	30	14	8	8	50	40	36
Ikast	30	16	3	11	43	42	35
B 93 Copenhagen	30	13	8	9	60	40	34
B 1903 Copenhagen	30	13	8	9	44	35	34
Vejle	30	14	5	11	63	50	33
Koge	30	12	8	10	39	39	32
Esbjerg	30	10	10	10	41	35	30
Hvidovre	30	11	8	11	47	48	30
Lyngby	30	11	5	14	52	48	27
Kastrup	30	9	9	12	34	35	27
Fremad	30	9	8	13	36	53	26
Frem	30	4	4	22	25	69	12
Aalborg	30	2	2	26	27	85	6

FINLAND

President: Jouko Loikkanen.
Secretary: Karl Salonen.
Address of Association: Suomen Palloliitto – Finlands Bollförbund, Stadion, 00250 Helsinki 25.
Telephone: 44 12 81, 49 93 99.
Cable: Suomifotboll.
Area: 130,119 square miles.
Population: 4,741,000.
Number of Clubs: 900. *Teams:* 2,437.
Year of Formation: 1907.
National Colours: White shirts, blue shorts, white stockings.
Second Choice of Colours: Blue shirts, white shorts, blue stockings.
Name, Address and Capacity of National Stadium: Olympiastadion, Helsinki, 50,000.
Names, Addresses and Capacities of Other Principal Football Grounds: Ratina, Tampere, 25,000; Urhei Lukeskus Kotka, 14,500; Kupittaa, Turku, 11,000; Vaino Lanniemi, Kuopio, 10,100.
All amateur players.
Season: April–October.

International matches 1980

22 May, Helsinki: v Sweden (h) lost 0-2
4 June, Helsinki: v Bulgaria (h) lost 0-2
25 June, Reykjavik: v Iceland (a) drew 1-1 (*Tissari*)
20 Aug, Oslo: v Norwav (a) lost 1-6 (*Himanka*)
3 Sept, Tirana: v Albania (a) lost 0-2
24 Sept, Helsinki v Austria (h) lost 0-2
30 Nov, La Paz: v Bolivia (a) lost 0-3
4 Dec, Santa Cruz: v Bolivia (a) drew 2-2 (*Bergvist, Jalasvaara*)
8 Dec, Montevideo: v Uruguay (a) lost 0-6

Championship wins (1949–80)

Turun Palloseura 5; Kupion Palloseura 5; Valkeakosken Haka 4; Helsinki JK 3; Lahden Reipas 3; IF Kamraterna 2; Kotkan TP 2; OPS Oulu 2; Turun Pyrkivä 1; IF Kronohagens 1; Helsinki PS 1; Ilves-Kissat 1; Kokkolan PV 1; IF Kamraterna I Vasa 1.

Cup wins (1955–80)

Lahden Reipas 7; Valkeakosken Haka 6; Kotkan TP 4; Mikkelin 2; IFK Abo 1; Drott 1; Helsinki JK 1; Helsinki PS 1; Kuopion Palloseura 1; Pallo-Peikot 1; Ilves Tampere 1.

	League Champions	Cup Winners
1949	Turun Palloseura	
1950	Ilves-Kissat	
1951	Kotkan TP	
1952	Kotkan TP	
1953	IF Kamraterna I	
1954	Turun Pyrkivä	
1955	IF Kronohagens	Valkaekosken Haka
1956	Kuopion Palloseura	Pallo-Peikot
1957	Helsinki PS	Drott
1958	Kuopion Palloseura	Kotkan TP
1959	IF Kamraterna	Valkeakosken Haka
1960	Valkeakosken Haka	Valkeakosken Haka
1961	IF Kamraterna	Kotkan TP
1962	Valkeakosken Haka	Helsinki PS
1963	Lahden Reipas	Valkeakosken Haka
1964	Helsinki JK	Lahden Reipas
1965	Valkeakosken Haka	IFK Abo
1966	Kuopion Palloseura	Helsinki JK
1967	Lahden Reipas	Kotkan TP
1968	Turun Palloseura	Kuopion Palloseura
1969	Kokkolan PV	Valkeakosken Haka
1970	Lahden Reipas	Mikkelin
1971	Turun Palloseura	Mikkelin
1972	Turun Palloseura	Lahden Reipas
1973	Helsinki JK	Lahden Reipas
1974	Kuopion Palloseura	Lahden Reipas
1975	Turun Palloseura	Lahden Reipas
1976	Kuopion Palloseura	Lahden Reipas
1977	Valkeakosken Haka	Valkeakosken Haka
1978	Helsinki JK	Lahden Reipas
1979	OPS Oulu	Ilves
1980	OPS Oulu	Kotkan TP

Qualifying series

	P	W	D	L	F	A	Pts
Oulun Palloseura	22	13	8	1	49	15	34
Turun Palloseura	22	12	7	3	38	17	31
HJK Helsinki	22	12	6	4	39	22	30
Haka Valkeakosken	22	13	4	5	41	30	30
KTP Kotka	22	7	10	5	24	23	24
Ilves	22	5	9	8	30	34	19
Sepsi-78	22	7	5	10	36	48	19
KuPS	22	7	3	12	28	45	17
OTP	22	6	4	12	24	47	16
Lahden Reipas	22	5	5	12	27	32	15
KPT	22	5	5	12	29	36	15
KPV	22	2	10	10	20	36	14

Final series

	P	W	D	L	F	A	Group Pts	Pts	Group Total
Oulun Palloseura	7	2	5	0	70	30	9	17	26
Haka Valkeakosken	7	3	4	0	57	37	10	15	25
HJK Helsinki	7	3	3	1	48	29	9	15	24
Turun Palloseura	7	2	3	2	49	29	7	16	23
KTP Kotka	7	2	3	2	36	39	7	12	19
Ilves	7	3	2	2	48	44	8	10	18
Sepsi-78	7	2	0	5	47	67	4	10	14
KuPS	7	0	2	5	35	63	2	9	11

Promotion/Relegation series

	P	W	D	L	F	A	Pts	Bonus Pts	Total
KPT	7	3	3	1	12	7	9	2	11
RoPS Rovaniemi	7	3	2	2	14	11	8	3	11
MP	7	3	1	3	12	9	7	4	11
MiPK	7	4	1	2	14	12	9	2	11
Kuusysi-69	7	3	2	2	16	10	8	1	9
KPV	7	4	0	3	11	15	8	1	9
OTP	7	2	1	4	9	16	5	4	9
Lahden Reipas	7	1	0	6	14	22	2	3	5

FRANCE

President: Fernand Sastre.
Secretary: Michel Cagnion (Dir Gen).
Address of Association: Fédération Française de Football, 60 bis, Avenue d'Iena, Paris 16e.
Telephone: 720 65–40.
Cable: Cefi Paris 034.
Telex: Fedfoot 620837 F.
Area: 209,454 square miles.
Population: 52,000,000.
Number of Clubs: 18,285. *Teams:* 52,000.
Number of Players: 1,194,189.
Year of Formation: 1919.
National Colours: Blue shirts, white shorts, red stockings.
Second Choice of Colours: Red shirts, white shorts, blue stockings.
Name, Address and Capacity of National Stadium: Stade du Parc des Princes, 24 rue du Commandant Guilbaud, 75, Paris 16ème, 50,000.
Names, Addresses and Capacities of Other Principal Football Grounds: Stade Vélodrome Jean Bouin, Marseilles, 45,000; Stade Municipal de Bordeaux, Avenue de la Côte d'Argent, 33, Bordeaux, 30,000; Stade Municipal de Gerland, Lyon, 45,000; Stade Geoffroy Guichard Saint Etienne, 42,000; Stade Marcel Saupin, Nantes, 33,000; Stade de la Meinau, Strasbourg, 30,000; Stadium Municipal de Toulouse, Parc des Sports, 31 Toulouse, 30,000.
Season: August–June.

Principal Honours

European Champions Cup: *runners-up* Stade de Reims (1956, 1959); St Etienne (1976)
UEFA Cup: *runners-up* Bastia (1978)

International matches 1980

27 Feb, Paris: v Greece (h) won 5-1 (*Bathenay* pen, *Platini 2, Christophe, Zimako*)
26 March, Paris: v Netherlands (h) drew 0-0
23 May, Moscow: v USSR (a) lost 0-1
11 Oct, Limassol: v Cyprus (a) won 7-0 (*Lacombe, Platini 2, Larios 2* pens, *Six, Zimako*)
28 Oct, Paris: v Republic of Ireland (h) won 2-0 (*Platini, Zimako*)
19 Nov, Hanover: v West Germany (a) lost 1-4 (*Larios* pen)

League Championship wins (1933–81)

Saint Etienne 10; Stade de Reims 6; Nantes 5; OGC Nice 4; Olympique Marseilles 4; Lille OSC 3; AS Monaco 3; FC Sete 2; Sochaux 2; Racing Club Paris 1; Roubaix-Tourcoing 1; Girondins Bordeaux 1; Strasbourg 1.

Cup wins (1918–81)

Olympique Marseilles 9; Saint Etienne 6; Lille OSC 5; Racing Club Paris 5; Red Star 5; AS Monaco 3; Olympique Lyon 3; CAS Genereaux 2; Nancy 2; OGC Nice 2; Racing Club Strasbourg 2; Sedan 2; FC Sete 2; Stade de Reims 2; Stade Rennes 2; AS Cannes 1; Club Français 1; Excelsior Roubaix 1; Girondins Bordeaux 1; Le Havre 1; SO Montpelier 1; Olympique de Pantin 1; CA Paris 1; Sochaux 1; Toulouse 1; Bastia 1; Nantes 1.

	League Champions	Cup Winners
1946	Lille OSC	Lille OSC
1947	Roubaix-Tourcoing	Lille OSC
1948	Ol Marseilles	Lille OSC
1949	Stade de Reims	Racing Paris
1950	Girondins Bordeaux	Stade de Reims
1951	OGC Nice	Racing Strasbourg
1952	OGC Nice	OGC Nice
1953	Stade de Reims	Lille OSC
1954	Lille OSC	OGC Nice
1955	Stade de Reims	Lille OSC
1956	OGC Nice	Sedan
1957	Saint Etienne	Toulouse
1958	Stade de Reims	Stade de Reims
1959	OGC Nice	Le Havre
1960	Stade de Reims	AS Monaco
1961	AS Monaco	Sedan
1962	Stade de Reims	Saint Etienne
1963	AS Monaco	AS Monaco
1964	Saint Etienne	Ol Lyon
1965	Nantes	Stade Rennes
1966	Nantes	Racing Club Strasbourg
1967	Saint Etienne	Ol Lyon
1968	Saint Etienne	Saint Etienne
1969	Saint Etienne	Ol Marseilles
1970	Saint Etienne	Saint Etienne
1971	Ol Marseilles	Stade Rennes
1972	Ol Marseilles	Ol Marseilles
1973	Nantes	Ol Lyon
1974	Saint Etienne	Saint Etienne
1975	Saint Etienne	Saint Etienne
1976	Saint Etienne	Ol Marseilles
1977	Nantes	Saint Etienne
1978	Monaco	Nancy
1979	Strasbourg	Nantes
1980	Nantes	Monaco
1981	Saint Etienne	Bastia

Final League Table 1980–81

	P	*W*	*D*	*L*	*F*	*A*	*Pts*
Saint Etienne	38	23	11	4	68	26	57
Nantes	38	22	11	5	74	36	55
Bordeaux	38	18	13	7	57	34	49
Monaco	38	19	11	8	58	41	49
Paris St Germain	38	17	12	9	62	50	46
Lyon	38	14	13	11	70	54	41
Strasbourg	38	14	12	12	44	47	40
Nancy	38	15	7	16	55	49	37
Metz	38	10	16	12	48	53	36
Auxerre	38	10	16	12	46	52	36
Valenciennes	38	12	12	14	51	70	36
Bastia	38	13	9	16	50	55	35
Lens	38	10	14	14	46	48	34
Sochaux	38	10	14	14	51	59	34
Nice	38	10	12	16	47	61	32
Laval	38	10	11	17	49	55	31
Lille	38	10	11	17	55	71	31
Tours	38	9	13	16	54	71	31
Nimes	38	6	14	18	46	66	26
Angers	38	5	14	19	33	66	24

EAST GERMANY

President: Gunter Schneider.
Secretary: Werner Lempert.
Address of Association: Deutscher Fussball-Verband, Storkower Strasse 118, 1055 Berlin.
Telephone: 438 43 88/91/93.
Cable: Fussball Verband Berlin.
Telex: 0112119. *Area:* 41,802 square miles.
Population: 17,000,000.
Number of Clubs: 4,981. *Teams:* 25,043.
Number of Players: 557,055.
Year of Formation: 1948.
National Colours: White shirts, blue shorts, white stockings.
Second Choice of Colours: Blue shirts, white shorts, blue stockings.
Name, Address and Capacity of National Stadium: Sportforum-Leipzig, 95,000.
Names, Addresses and Capacities of Other Principal Football Grounds: Festival Stadion, Berlin; Dynamo-Stadion, Dresden, 37,000; Ernst-Thälmann-Stadion, Karl-Marx-Stadt, 45,000; Georg-Dimitroff-Stadion, Erfurt, 50,000; Kurt-Wabbel-Stadion, Halle, 32,000; Ernest-Abbe-Stadion, Jena, 25,000; Ostsee-Stadion, Rostock, 30,000; Friedrich-Ludwig-Jahn-Sportpark, Berlin, 25,000; Ernest-Grube-Stadion, Magdeburg, 45,000.
Season: August–June (with winter break).

Principal Honours

Olympic Games: *winners* 1976
European Cup-Winners' Cup: *winners* FC Magdeburg (1974); *runners-up* Carl Zeiss Jena (1981)

International matches 1980

13 Feb, Malaga: v Spain (a) won 1-0 (*Streich*)
2 April, Bucharest: v Rumania (a) drew 2-2 (*Streich, Schmuck*)
16 April, Leipzig: v Greece (h) won 2-0 (*Weber, Streich*)
7 May, Rostock: v USSR (h) drew 2-2 (*Kuhn, Terletzki*)
8 Oct, Prague: v Czechoslovakia (a) won 1-0 (*Streich*)
15 Oct, Leipzig: v Spain (h) drew 0-0
19 Oct, Halle: v Hungary (h) won 2-0 (*Trocha, Streich*)

League Championship wins (1950–81)

ASK Vorwaerts 6; Dynamo Dresden 5; Wismut Karl-Marx-Stadt 4; FC Magdeburg 4; Carl Zeiss Jena (prev. Motor Jena) 3; Dynamo Berlin 3; Chemie Leipzig 2; Turbine Erfurt 2; Turbine Halle 1; Zwickau Horch 1; Empor Rostock 1.

Cup wins (1949–81)

Carl Zeiss Jena (prev. Motor Jena) 5; FC Magdeburg 3; Lokomotiv Leipzig 3; Dynamo Dresden 3; Chemie Leipzig 2; Magdeburg Aufbau 2; Motor Zwickau 2; ASK Vorwaerts 2; Dresden Einheit SC 1; Dresden VP 1; Dynamo Berlin 1; Halle Chemie SC 1; North Dessau Waggonworks 1; Thale EHW 1; Union East Berlin 1; Wismut Karl-Marx-Stadt 1; Sachsenring Zwickau 1.

	League Champions	Cup Winners
1949		North Dessau Waggonworks
1950	Zwickau Horch	Thale EHW
1951	Chemie Leipzig	*No competition*
1952	Halle Turbine	Dresden VP
1953	Dynamo Dresden	*No competition*
1954	Turbine Erfurt	ASK Vorwaerts
1955	Turbine Erfurt	Wismut Karl-Marx-Stadt
1956	Wismut Karl-Marx-Stadt	Chemie Leipzig
1957	Wismut Karl-Marx-Stadt	Lokomotiv Leipzig
1958	ASK Vorwaerts	Dresden Einheit SC
1959	Wismut Karl-Marx-Stadt	Dynamo Berlin
1960	ASK Vorwaerts	Motor Jena
1961	Empor Rostock	Motor Jena
1962	ASK Vorwaerts	Halle Chemie SC
1963	Motor Jena	Motor Zwickau
1964	Leipzig Chemie	Magdeburg Aufbau
1965	ASK Vorwaerts	Magdeburg Aufbau
1966	ASK Vorwaerts	Chemie Leipzig
1967	Wismut Karl-Marx-Stadt	Motor Zwickau
1968	Carl Zeiss Jena	Union East Berlin
1969	ASK Vorwaerts	FC Magdeburg
1970	Carl Zeiss Jena	ASK Vorwaerts
1971	Dynamo Dresden	Dynamo Dresden
1972	FC Magdeburg	Carl Zeiss Jena
1973	Dynamo Dresden	FC Magdeburg
1974	FC Magdeburg	Carl Zeiss Jena
1975	FC Magdeburg	Sachsenring Zwickau
1976	Dynamo Dresden	Lokomotiv Leipzig
1977	Dynamo Dresden	Dynamo Dresden
1978	FC Magdeburg	Dynamo Dresden
1979	Dynamo Berlin	FC Magdeburg
1980	Dynamo Berlin	Carl Zeiss Jena
1981	Dynamo Berlin	Lokomotiv Leipzig

Final League Table 1980–81

	P	*W*	*D*	*L*	*F*	*A*	*Pts*
Dynamo Berlin	**26**	**17**	**5**	**4**	**74**	**31**	**39**
Carl Zeiss Jena	**26**	**16**	**4**	**6**	**57**	**29**	**36**
FC Magdeburg	**26**	**15**	**4**	**7**	**58**	**35**	**34**
Dynamo Dresden	**26**	**16**	**2**	**9**	**49**	**37**	**34**
Vorwaerts Frankfurt	**26**	**13**	**5**	**8**	**58**	**40**	**31**
Lokomotiv Leipzig	**26**	**12**	**4**	**10**	**46**	**35**	**28**
Rot-Weiss Erfurt	**26**	**10**	**7**	**9**	**37**	**49**	**27**
Chemie Halle	**26**	**11**	**3**	**12**	**41**	**41**	**25**
Karl-Marx-Stadt	**26**	**6**	**9**	**11**	**37**	**54**	**21**
Hansa Rostock	**26**	**6**	**8**	**12**	**35**	**47**	**20**
Sachsenring Zwickau	**26**	**7**	**4**	**15**	**32**	**51**	**18**
Wismut Aue	**26**	**7**	**4**	**15**	**34**	**60**	**18**
Stahl Riesa	**26**	**6**	**5**	**15**	**38**	**64**	**17**
Chemie Bohlen	**26**	**5**	**6**	**15**	**25**	**48**	**16**

WEST GERMANY

President: Hermann Neuberger.
Secretary: Hans Passlack.
Address of Association: Deutscher Fussball-Bund, Otto-Fleck-Schneise 6, Frankfurt (Main) 71.
Telephone: (0611) 63 10 63.
Cable: Fussball, Frankfurt.
Telex: 41 6815 dfbd.
Area: 95,097 square miles.
Population: 61,510,000.
Number of Clubs: 17,549. *Teams:* 115,145.
Number of Players: 3,611,431.
Year of Formation: 1900.
National Colours: White shirts, black shorts, white stockings.
Second Choice of Colours: Green shirts, white shorts, white stockings.
Name, Address and Capacity of National Stadium: There is no stadium which could be considered as the National Stadium.
Names, Addresses and Capacities of Principal Football Grounds: Olympiastadion Berlin, 80,000 (61,800 seats); Olympiastadion München, 75,600 (44,200 seats); Neckarstadion Stuttgart, 72,200 (34,400 seats); Parkstadion Gelsenkirchen, 70,000 (36,000 seats); Rheinstadion Düsseldorf, 69,600 (31,800 seats); Waldstadion Frankfurt 61,000 (29,900 seats); Volksparkstadion Hamburg, 61,400 (27,800 seats); Niedersachsenstadion Hannover, 60,500 (39,000 seats); Westfalen Stadion Dortmund, 53,600 (16,600 seats), Müngersdorfer Stadion, Cologne 60,000 (28,000 seats).
Season: August–June.

Principal Honours

World Cup: *winners* 1954, 1974; *runners-up* 1966
European Championship: *winners* 1972, 1980; *runners-up* (1976)
World Club Champions: Bayern Munich (1976)
European Champions Cup: *winners* Bayern Munich (1974, 1975, 1976); *runners-up* Eintracht Frankfurt (1960), Borussia Moenchengladbach (1977), SV Hamburg (1980)
European Cup-Winners' Cup: *winners* Borussia Dortmund (1966), Bayern Munich (1967), SV Hamburg (1977); *runners-up* Munich 1860 (1965), SV Hamburg (1968), Fortuna Düsseldorf (1979)
UEFA Cup: *winners* Borussia Moenchengladbach (1975, 1979), Eintracht Frankfurt (1980); *runners-up* Borussia Moenchengladbach (1973, 1980)

International matches 1980

27 Feb, Bremen: v Malta (h) won 8-0 (*Klaus Allofs 2, Bonhof* pen, *Fischer 2, Kelsch, Rummenigge, Holland og*)
2 April, Berlin: v Austria (h) won 1-0 (*Hansi Muller*)
13 May, Frankfurt: v Poland (h) won 3-1 (*Rummenigge, Schuster, Klaus Allofs*)
11 June, Rome: v Czechoslovakia (a) won 1-0 (*Rummenigge*)
14 June, Naples: v Netherlands (a) won 3-2 (*Klaus Allofs 3*)
17 June, Turin: v Greece (a) drew 0-0
22 June, Rome: v Belgium (h) won 2-1 (*Hrubesch 2*)
10 Sept, Basle: v Switzerland (a) won 3-2 (*Hansi Muller 2, Magath*)
11 Oct, Eindhoven: v Netherlands (a) drew 1-1 (*Hrubesch*)
19 Nov, Hannover: v France (h) won 4-1 (*Kaltz* pen, *Briegel, Hrubesch, Klaus Allofs*)
3 Dec, Sofia: v Bulgaria (a) won 3-1 (*Kaltz 2* [1 pen], *Rummenigge*)

League Championship wins (1903–81)

IFC Nuremberg 9; Schalke 04 7; Bayern Munich 7; Borussia Moenchengladbach 5; SV Hamburg 4; VfB Leipzig 3; Sp Vgg Fürth 3; Borussia Dortmund 3; IFC Cologne 3; Viktoria Berlin 2; Hertha Berlin 2; Hanover 96 2; Dresden SC 2; VfB Stuttgart 2; IFC Kaiserslautern 2; Munich 1860 1; SV Werder Bremen 1; Union Berlin 1; FC Freibourg 1; Phoenix Karlsruhe 1; Karlsruher FV 1; Holstein Kiel 1; Fortuna Düsseldorf 1; Rapid Vienna 1; VfR Mannheim 1; Rot-Weiss Essen 1; Eintracht Frankfurt 1; Eintracht Brunswick 1.

Cup wins (1935–81)

Bayern Munich 5; IFC Nuremberg 3; IFC Cologne 3; Eintracht Frankfurt 3; Dresden SC 2; Fortuna Düsseldorf 2; Karlsruhe SC 2; Munich 1860 2; Schalke 04 2; VfB Stuttgart 2; Borussia Moenchengladbach 2; SV Hamburg 2; Borussia Dortmund 1; First Vienna 1; VfB Leipzig 1; Kickers Offenbach 1; Rapid Vienna 1; Rot-Weiss Essen 1; SW Essen 1; Werder Bremen 1.

	League Champions	**Cup Winners**
1948	IFC Nuremberg	
1949	VfR Mannheim	
1950	VfB Stuttgart	
1951	IFC Kaiserslautern	
1952	VfB Stuttgart	
1953	IFC Kaiserslautern	Rot-Weiss Essen
1954	Hanover 96	VfB Stuttgart
1955	Rot-Weiss Essen	Karlsruhe SC
1956	Borussia Dortmund	Karlsruhe SC
1957	Borussia Dortmund	Bayern Munich
1958	Schalke 04	VfB Stuttgart
1959	Eintracht Frankfurt	SW Essen
1960	SV Hamburg	Borussia Moenchengladbach
1961	IFC Nuremberg	Werder Bremen
1962	IFC Cologne	IFC Nuremberg
1963	Borussia Dortmund	SV Hamburg
1964	IFC Cologne	Munich 1860

1965	Werder Bremen	Borussia Dortmund
1966	Munich 1860	Bayern Munich
1967	Eintracht Brunswick	Bayern Munich
1968	IFC Nuremberg	IFC Cologne
1969	Bayern Munich	Bayern Munich
1970	Borussia Moenchengladbach	Kickers Offenbach
1971	Borussia Moenchengladbach	Bayern Munich
1972	Bayern Munich	Schalke 04
1973	Bayern Munich	Borussia Moenchengladbach
1974	Bayern Munich	Eintracht Frankfurt
1975	Borussia Moenchengladbach	Eintracht Frankfurt
1976	Borussia Moenchengladbach	SV Hamburg
1977	Borussia Moenchengladbach	IFC Cologne
1978	Cologne	Cologne
1979	SV Hamburg	Fortuna Düsseldorf
1980	Bayern Munich	Fortuna Düsseldorf
1981	Bayern Munich	Eintracht Frankfurt

Final League Table 1980–81

	P	*W*	*D*	*L*	*F*	*A*	*Pts*
Bayern Munich	**34**	**22**	**9**	**3**	**89**	**41**	**53**
SV Hamburg	**34**	**21**	**7**	**6**	**73**	**43**	**49**
VfB Stuttgart	**34**	**19**	**8**	**7**	**70**	**44**	**46**
IFC Kaiserslautern	**34**	**17**	**10**	**7**	**60**	**37**	**44**
Eintracht Frankfurt	**34**	**13**	**12**	**9**	**61**	**57**	**38**
Borussia Moenchengladbach	**34**	**15**	**7**	**12**	**68**	**64**	**37**
Borussia Dortmund	**34**	**13**	**9**	**12**	**69**	**59**	**35**
IFC Cologne	**34**	**12**	**10**	**12**	**54**	**55**	**34**
VFL Bochum	**34**	**9**	**15**	**10**	**53**	**45**	**33**
Karlsruhe SC	**34**	**9**	**14**	**11**	**56**	**63**	**32**
Bayer Leverkusen	**34**	**10**	**10**	**14**	**52**	**53**	**30**
MSV Duisburg	**34**	**10**	**9**	**15**	**45**	**59**	**29**
Fortuna Düsseldorf	**34**	**10**	**8**	**16**	**57**	**64**	**28**
IFC Nuremberg	**34**	**11**	**6**	**17**	**47**	**57**	**28**
Arminia Bielefeld	**34**	**10**	**6**	**18**	**46**	**65**	**26**
Munich 1860	**34**	**9**	**7**	**18**	**49**	**67**	**25**
Schalke 04	**34**	**8**	**7**	**19**	**43**	**88**	**23**
Bayer Uerdingen	**34**	**8**	**6**	**20**	**47**	**79**	**22**

RISE IN BUNDESLIGA ATTENDANCES

Attendances in the West German Bundesliga showed an increase in 1980–81 over the previous season. They rose to 7,050,274 from 6,938,832 in 1979–80. The average went up from 22,676 to 23,040.

GREECE

President: Dr Basile Hadzijannis.
Secretary: Chalambos David.
Address of Association: Federation Hellenique de Football Association, 93 Rue de L'Académie, Athenes.
Telephone: 362 22 02/03.
Cable: Football Athenes.
Telex: 215328.
Area: 50,547 square miles.
Population: 9,500,000.
Number of Clubs: 1,762.
Teams: 1,762.
Number of Players: 91,020.
Year of Formation: 1926.
National Colours: White shirts, blue shorts, white stockings.
Second Choice of Colours: Blue shirts, white shorts, blue stockings.
Name, Address and Capacity of National Stadium: Karaïskaki, Neon Faliron, 42,000.
Names, Addresses and Capacities of Other Principal Football Grounds: Kaftatzoglion, Salonika, 47,000; AEK, Athens, 35,000; Panathinaikos, Athenes, 25,000; PAOK, Salonika, 40,000; Aris, Salonika, 30,000.

Principal Honours

European Champions Cup: *runners-up* Panathinaikos (1971)

International matches 1980

16 Jan, Nicosia: v Cyprus (a) drew 1-1 (*Anastopoulos*)
27 Feb, Paris: v France (a) lost 1-5 (*Mavros*)
1 April, Zurich: v Switzerland (a) lost 0-2
16 April, Leipzig: v East Germany (a) lost 0-2
14 May, Athens: v Bulgaria (h) drew 0-0
11 June, Athens: v Netherlands (a) lost 0-1
14 June, Rome: v Czechoslovakia (a) lost 1-3 (*Anastopoulos*)
17 June, Turin: v West Germany (a) drew 0-0
15 Oct, Copenhagen: v Denmark (a) won 1-0 (*Kouis*)
11 Nov, Athens: v Australia (h) drew 3-3 (*Damanakis, Domazos, Delikaris* pen)
6 Dec, Athens: v Italy (h) lost 0-2

League Championship wins (1928–81)

Olympiakos 22; Panathinaikos 12; AEK Athens 7; Aris Salonika 3; PAOK Salonika 1.

Cup wins (1932–81)

Olympiakos 18; AEK Athens 8; Panathinaikos 6; PAOK Salonika 2; Aris Salonika 1; Ethnikos 1; Iraklis 1; Panionios 1; Kastoria 1.

	League Champions	Cup Winners
1946	Aris Salonika	
1947	Olympiakos	Olympiakos
1948	Olympiakos	Panathinaikos
1949	*No competition*	AEK Athens
1950	Panathinaikos	AEK Athens
1951	Olympiakos	Olympiakos
1952	*No competition*	Olympiakos
1953	Panathinaikos	Olympiakos
1954	Olympiakos	Olympiakos
1955	Olympiakos	Panathinaikos
1956	Olympiakos	AEK Athens
1957	Olympiakos	Olympiakos
1958	Olympiakos	Olympiakos
1959	Olympiakos	Olympiakos
1960	Panathinaikos	Olympiakos
1961	Panathinaikos	Olympiakos
1962	Panathinaikos	Olympiakos
1963	AEK Athens	Olympiakos
1964	Panathinaikos	AEK Athens
1965	Panathinaikos	Olympiakos
1966	Olympiakos	AEK Athens
1967	Olympiakos	Panathinaikos
1968	AEK Athens	Olympiakos
1969	Panathinaikos	Panathinaikos
1970	Panathinaikos	Aris Salonika
1971	AEK Athens	Olympiakos
1972	Panathinaikos	PAOK Salonika
1973	Olympiakos	Olympiakos
1974	Olympiakos	PAOK Salonika
1975	Olympiakos	Olympiakos
1976	PAOK Salonika	Iraklis
1977	Panathinaikos	Panathinaikos
1978	AEK Athens	AEK Athens
1979	AEK Athens	Panionios
1980	Olympiakos	Kastoria
1981	Olympiakos	Olympiakos

Final League Table 1980–81

	P	*W*	*D*	*L*	*F*	*A*	*Pts*
Olympiakos	34	20	9	5	47	18	49
AEK Athens	34	17	10	7	63	42	44
Aris Salonika	34	16	11	7	57	33	43
PAOK Salonika	34	15	12	7	52	31	42
Panathinaikos	34	13	13	8	44	21	39
Larissa	34	14	9	11	42	40	37
Ethnikos	34	11	12	11	45	32	34
Panserraikos	34	10	14	10	42	41	34
Doxa	34	10	13	11	38	42	33
OF Iraklion	34	11	10	13	33	37	32
Iannina	34	11	9	14	43	47	31
Apollon	34	12	7	15	31	47	31
Panionios	34	9	12	13	45	49	30
Kastoria	34	12	6	16	43	56	30
Kavala	34	10	9	15	28	47	29
Korinthos	34	9	9	16	27	42	27
Panachaiki	34	9	8	17	21	36	26
Atromitos	34	4	13	17	19	59	21

HUNGARY

President: Gyorgy Szepesi.
Secretary: Jozsef Krizsan.
Address of Association: Fédération Hongroise de Football, Népköztársaság utja 47, Budapest VI.
Telephone: 22 58 17, 42 13 16.
Cable: Misz-Budapest.
Area: 35,919 square miles.
Population: 10,500,000.
Year of Formation: 1901.
Number of Clubs: 2,440. *Teams:* 5,326.
Number of Players: 138,461.
National Colours: Red shirts, white shorts, green stockings.
Second Choice of Colours: All white.
Name, Address and Capacity of National Stadium: Népstadion Budapest XIV, István Mezei ut 3/5, 80,000.
Names, Addresses and Capacities of Other Principal Football Grounds: Ferencvaros, Budapest IX Ullöi-ut, 30,000; Bp Vasas SC Budapest XIII, Fay-u 58, 20,000; Ujpesti Dozsa SE Budapest IV, Mergyeri ut 13, 25,000; MTK-VM Budapest VIII, Hungaria krt 6, 20,000; Csepel SE Budapest XXI, Béke tér, 22,000; Györi Raba ETO Györ, 20,000; Pécs MSC, Pécs, 25,000; Szegedi Egyetemi OL Szeged, 25,000; Diösgyöri VTK, Diösgyör, 25,000; Bp Honved, Budapest, 30,000.
Season: September–December; March–June.

Principal Honours

World Cup: *runners-up* 1938, 1954
Olympic Games: *winners* 1952, 1964, 1968; *runners-up* 1972
European Cup-Winners' Cup: *runners-up* MTK Budapest (1964); Ferencvaros (1975)
Fairs Cup: *winners* Ferencvaros (1965); *runners-up* Ferencvaros (1968), Ujpest Dozsa (1969)

International matches 1980

26 March, Budapest: v Poland (h) won 2-1 (*Fazekas, Torocsik*)
2 April, Kustenil: v Bulgaria (a) lost 3-4 (*Kozma 3*)
30 April, Kosice: v Czechoslovakia (a) lost 0-1
31 May, Budapest: v Scotland (h) won 3-1 (*Torocsik 2, Kereki*)
4 June, Budapest: v Austria (h) drew 1-1 (*Soos*)
20 Aug, Budapest: v Sweden (h) won 2-0 (*Balint, Burcsa*)
27 Aug, Budapest: v USSR (h) lost 1-4 (*Pasztor*)
24 Sept, Budapest: v Spain (h) drew 2-2 (*Kiss, Bodonyi*)
8 Oct, Vienna: v Austria (a) lost 1-3 (*Bodonyi*)
19 Nov, Halle: v East Germany (a) lost 0-2

League Championship wins (1901–81)

Ferencvaros (prev. FTC) 23; MTK-VM Budapest (prev. Hungaria, Bastay and Vörös Lobogo) 18; Ujpest Dozsa 18; Vasas Budapest 6; Honved 6; Csepel 4; BTC 2; Nagyvarad 1; Vasas Györ 1.

Cup wins (1910–81)*

Ferencvaros (prev. FTC) 14; MTK-VM Budapest (prev. Hungaria, Bastya and Vörös Lobogo) 9; Ujpest Dozsa 4; Raba Györ (prev. Vasas Györ) 4; Diösgyör 2; Vasas Budapest 2; Bocskai 1; Honved 1; III Ker 1; Kispesti AC 1; Soroksar 1; Szolnoki MAV 1.
* *Cup not held regularly until 1964*

	League Champions	Cup Winners
1946	Ujpest Dozsa	
1947	Ujpest Dozsa	
1948	Vasas Csepel	
1949	Ferencvaros	
1950	Honved	
1950*	Honved	
1951	Bastya	
1952	Honved	Bastya
1953	Vörös Lobogo	
1954	Honved	
1955	Honved	Vasas Budapest
1956	Champ. abandoned	
1957	Vasas Budapest	
1958	MTK Budapest	Ferencvaros
1959	Vasas Csepel	
1960	Ujpest Dozsa	
1961	Vasas Budapest	
1962	Vasas Budapest	
1963	Ferencvaros	
1963*	Vasas Györ	
1964	Ferencvaros	Honved
1965	Vasas Budapest	Vasas Györ
1966	Vasas Budapest	Vasas Györ
1967	Ferencvaros	Vasas Györ
1968	Ferencvaros	MTK Budapest
1969	Ujpest Dozsa	Ujpest Dozsa
1970	Ujpest Dozsa	Ujpest Dozsa
1971	Ujpest Dozsa	Ujpest Dozsa
1972	Ujpest Dozsa	Ferencvaros
1973	Ujpest Dozsa	Vasas Budapest
1974	Ujpest Dozsa	Ferencvaros
1975	Ujpest Dozsa	Ujpest Dozsa
1976	Ferencvaros	Ferencvaros
1977	Vasas Budapest	Diösgyör
1978	Ujpest Dozsa	Ferencvaros
1979	Ujpest Dozsa	Raba Györ
1980	Honved	Diösgyör
1981	Ferencvaros	Vasas Budapest

* *Short season.*

Final League Table 1980–81

	P	W	D	L	F	A	Pts
Ferencvaros	34	21	9	4	75	33	51
Tatabanya	34	19	10	5	50	25	48
Vasas Budapest	34	18	10	6	68	38	46
Videoton	34	19	6	9	60	38	44
Honved	34	15	12	7	56	36	42
Debrecen	34	14	10	10	37	29	38
Nyireghyhaza	34	11	16	7	30	25	38
Ujpest Dozsa	34	10	16	8	53	49	36
Bekescsaba	34	13	10	11	51	48	36
Raba ETO	34	9	13	12	43	43	31
MSC Pecs	34	9	13	12	43	43	31
Csepel	34	6	15	13	34	38	27
Zalaegerszeg	34	10	7	17	52	70	27
Volan	34	8	11	15	39	57	27
Diösgyör	34	5	15	14	28	50	25
Kaposvar	34	6	12	16	34	67	24
MTK/VM	34	4	14	16	34	60	22
Dunaujvaros	34	4	11	19	34	72	19

ICELAND

President: Ellert B. Schram.
Secretary: K. T. Sigurdsson.
Address of Association: Football Association of Iceland, PO Box 1011, Reykjavik.
Telephone: 8–4444. *Cable:* KSI Reykjavik.
Telex: 2110 (att. E. Schram).
Area: 39,768 square miles.
Population: 222,055. *Number of Clubs:* 67.
Teams: 427. *Number of Players:* 13,856.
Year of Formation: 1929.
National Colours: Blue shirts, white shorts and blue stockings.
Second Choice of Colours: White shirts, blue shorts, white stockings.
Name, Address and Capacity of National Stadium: Laugardalsvöllur, Reykjavik, 14,800.
Names and Addresses of Other Principal Football Grounds: Melavöllur, Reykjavik; Ibróttavöllurinn, Akureyri; Ibróttavöllurinn, Akranesi; Ibróttavöllurinn, Keflavik, 10,000.
Season: April–October.

International matches 1980

2 June, Reykjavik: v Wales (h) lost 0-4
25 June, Reykjavik: v Finland (h) drew 1-1 (*Petursson*)
14 July, Oslo: v Norway (a) lost 1-3 (*Thorleifsson*)
17 July, Hamstad: v Sweden (a) drew 1-1 (*Thorbjornsson*)
3 Sept, Reykjavik: v USSR (h) lost 1-2 (*Sveinsson*)
24 Sept, Izmir: v Turkey (a) won 3-1 (*Gudlaugsson, Gudmundsson, Thordarson*)
15 Oct, Moscow: v USSR (a) lost 0-5

League Championship wins (1912–80)

KR 20; Valur 17; Fram 15; IA Akranes 10; IBK Keflavik 3; Vikingur 2; IBV Vestmann 2.

Cup wins (1960–80)

KR 7; Valur 4; Fram 4; IBV Vestmann 2; IBA Akureyri 1; Vikingur 1; IBK Keflavik 1; IA Akranes 1.

	League Champions	**Cup Winners**
1946	Fram	
1947	Fram	
1948	KR	
1949	KR	
1950	KR	
1951	IA Akranes	
1952	KR	
1953	IA Akranes	
1954	IA Akranes	
1955	KR	
1956	Valur	
1957	IA Akranes	
1958	IA Akranes	
1959	KR	
1960	IA Akranes	KR
1961	KR	KR
1962	Fram	KR
1963	KR	KR
1964	IBK Keflavik	KR
1965	KR	Valur
1966	Valur	KR
1967	Valur	KR
1968	KR	IBV Vestmann
1969	IBK Keflavik	IBV Akureyri
1970	IA Akranes	Fram
1971	IBV Vestmann	Vikingur
1972	Fram	IBV Vestmann
1973	IBK Keflavik	Fram
1974	IA Akranes	Valur
1975	IA Akranes	IBV Keflavik
1976	Valur	Valur
1977	IA Akranes	Valur
1978	Valur	IA Akranes
1979	IBV Vestmann	Fram
1980	Valur	Fram

Final League Table 1980–81

	P	*W*	*D*	*L*	*F*	*A*	*Pts*
Valur	**18**	**13**	**2**	**3**	**43**	**16**	**28**
Fram	**18**	**11**	**3**	**4**	**23**	**19**	**25**
IB Akranes	**18**	**8**	**4**	**6**	**29**	**20**	**20**
Vikingur	**18**	**7**	**6**	**5**	**24**	**23**	**20**
UBK	**18**	**8**	**1**	**9**	**25**	**22**	**17**
IBV	**18**	**5**	**7**	**6**	**26**	**28**	**17**
KR	**18**	**6**	**4**	**8**	**16**	**25**	**16**
FH	**18**	**5**	**5**	**8**	**24**	**34**	**15**
IBK	**18**	**3**	**7**	**8**	**16**	**26**	**13**
IL	**18**	**2**	**5**	**11**	**13**	**26**	**9**

REPUBLIC OF IRELAND

President: C. Cahill.
Secretary: P. J. O'Driscoll PC.
Address of Association: The Football Association of Ireland, 80 Merrion Square, Dublin 2.
Telephone: 76 68 64.
Cable: Soccer Dublin.
Population: 4,500,000.
Year of Formation: 1921.
Number of Clubs: 2,914. *Teams:* 2,928.
Number of Players: 54,596.
National Colours: Green shirts, white shorts, green stockings.
Second Choice of Colours: White.
Name, Address and Capacity of National Stadium: Dalymount Park, Dublin, 45,000; and Lansdowne Road, Dublin, 48,000.
Names, Addresses and Capacities of Other Principal Football Grounds: Glenmalure Park, Milltown, Dublin, 25,000; Flower Lodge, Cork, 25,000; Lourdes Stadium, Drogheda, 25,000; Tolka Park, Dublin, 20,000; Oriel Park, Dundalk, 15,000; Richmond Park, Dublin, 10,000; Markeis Field, Limerick, 10,000; Kilcohan Park, Waterford, 15,000.
Season: August–May.

International matches 1980

6 Feb, Wembley: v England (a) lost 0-2
26 March, Nicosia: v Cyprus (a) won 3-2 (*Lysandrou og, Lawrenson, McGee*)
30 April, Dublin: v Switzerland (h) won 2-0 (*Givens, Daly*)
16 May, Dublin: v Argentina (h) lost 0-1
10 Sept, Dublin: v Netherlands (h) won 2-1 (*Daly, Lawrenson*)
15 Oct, Dublin: v Belgium (h) drew 1-1 (*Grealish*)
28 Oct, Paris: v France (a) lost 0-2
19 Nov, Dublin: v Cyprus (h) won 6-0 (*Daly 2* [1 pen], *Grealish, Robinson, Stapleton, Hughton*)

League Championship wins (1922–81)

Shamrock Rovers 10; Shelbourne 7; Bohemians 7; Waterford 6; Cork United 5; Drumcondra 5; Dundalk 5; St Patrick's Athletic 3; St James's Gate 2; Cork Athletic 2; Sligo Rovers 2; Limerick 2; Dolphin 1; Cork Hibernians 1; Cork Celtic 1; Athlone Town 1.

Cup wins (1922–81)

Shamrock Rovers 21; Dundalk 7; Drumcondra 5; Bohemians 4; Shelbourne 3; Cork Athletic 2; Cork United 2; St James's Gate 2; St Patrick's Athletic 2; Cork Hibernians 2; Waterford 2; Alton United 1; Athlone Town 1; Cork 1; Fordsons 1; Limerick 1; Transport 1; Finn Harps 1; Home Farm 1.

	League Champions	Cup Winners
1946	Cork United	Drumcondra
1947	Shelbourne	Cork United
1948	Drumcondra	Shamrock Rovers
1949	Drumcondra	Dundalk
1950	Cork Athletic	Transport
1951	Cork Athletic	Cork Athletic
1952	St Patrick's Ath	Dundalk
1953	Shelbourne	Cork Athletic
1954	Shamrock Rovers	Drumcondra
1955	St Patrick's Ath	Shamrock Rovers
1956	St Patrick's Ath	Shamrock Rovers
1957	Shamrock Rovers	Drumcondra
1958	Drumcondra	Dundalk
1959	Shamrock Rovers	St Patrick's Ath
1960	Limerick	Shelbourne
1961	Drumcondra	St Patrick's Ath
1962	Shelbourne	Shamrock Rovers
1963	Dundalk	Shelbourne
1964	Shamrock Rovers	Shamrock Rovers
1965	Drumcondra	Shamrock Rovers
1966	Waterford	Shamrock Rovers
1967	Dundalk	Shamrock Rovers
1968	Waterford	Shamrock Rovers
1969	Waterford	Shamrock Rovers
1970	Waterford	Bohemians
1971	Cork Hibernians	Limerick
1972	Waterford	Cork Hibernians
1973	Waterford	Cork Hibernians
1974	Cork Celtic	Finn Harps
1975	Bohemians	Home Farm
1976	Dundalk	Bohemians
1977	Sligo Rovers	Dundalk
1978	Bohemians	Shamrock Rovers
1979	Dundalk	Dundalk
1980	Limerick	Waterford
1981	Athlone Town	Dundalk

Final League Table 1980–81

	P	*W*	*D*	*L*	*F*	*A*	*Pts*
Athlone Town	30	23	5	2	67	22	51
Dundalk	30	20	5	5	63	28	45
Limerick	30	17	7	6	47	25	41
Bohemians	30	10	16	4	38	25	36
Shamrock Rovers	30	14	8	8	37	29	36
Finn Harps	30	12	6	12	41	39	30
Waterford	30	11	8	11	32	35	30
St Patrick's Ath	30	11	6	13	45	48	28
Cork United	30	11	6	13	37	42	28
Drogheda	30	10	7	13	47	55	27
Sligo Rovers	30	12	2	16	45	57	26
UCD	30	8	9	13	37	49	25
Galway Rovers	30	6	9	15	26	39	21
Home Farm	30	7	6	17	34	55	20
Shelbourne	30	6	6	18	31	52	18
Thurles Town	30	7	4	19	38	65	18

President d'honneur: Dr Artemio Franchi.
President: Avv. Federico Sordillo.
Secretary: Dr Dario Borgogno.
Address of Association: Federazione Italiana Giuoco Calcio, via Gregorio Allegri 14, Rome.
Telephone: 84 91.
Cable: Federcalcio Roma.
Area: 97,068 square miles.
Population: 54,134,846.
Number of Clubs: 21,845. *Teams:* 22,132.
Number of Players: 833,564.
Year of Formation: 1898.
National Colours: Blue shirts, white shorts, blue stockings with white tops.
Second Choice of Colours: White with light blue stripe.
Name, Address and Capacity of National Stadium: Stadio Olimpico, Roma, 90,000.
Names, Addresses and Capacities of Other Principal Football Grounds: Bologna, Stadio Comunale, Via A. Costa 176, 50,000; Firenze, Stadio Comunale, Viale M. Fanti 4/6, 67,000; Milano, Stadio Comunale San Siro, Via Fetonte, 85,000; Torino, Stadio Comunale, Corso Sebatopoli 123, 71,000; Napoli, Stadio S. Paolo, Fuorigrotta, 82,000; Genova, Stadio Luigi, Ferraris, Via del Piano, 64,000.
Season: September–June.

Principal Honours

World Cup: *winners* 1934, 1938; *runners-up* 1970
European Championship: *winners* 1968
Olympic Games: *winners* 1936
World Club Champions: Inter-Milan (1964, 1965), AC Milan (1969)
European Champions Cup: *winners* AC Milan (1963, 1969), Inter-Milan (1964, 1965); *runners-up* Fiorentina (1957), AC Milan (1958), Inter-Milan (1967, 1972), Juventus (1973)
European Cup-Winners' Cup: *winners* Fiorentina (1961), AC Milan (1968, 1973); *runners-up* Fiorentina (1962), AC Milan (1974)
Fairs Cup: *winners* AS Roma (1961); *runners-up* Juventus (1965, 1971)
UEFA Cup: *winners* Juventus (1977)

International matches 1980

16 Feb, Naples: v Rumania (h) won 2-1 (*Collovati, Causio*)
15 March, Milan: v Uruguay (h) won 1-0 (*Graziani*)
19 April, Turin: v Poland (h) drew 2-2 (*Causio, Scirea*)
12 June, Milan: v Spain (h) drew 0-0
15 June, Turin: v England (h) won 1-0 (*Tardelli*)
18 June, Rome: v Belgium (h) drew 0-0
21 June, Naples: v Czechoslovakia (h) drew 1-1 (*Graziani*) (Czechoslovakia won 9-8 on penalties)
24 Sept, Genoa: v Portugal (h) won 3-1 (*Altobelli 2, Graziani*)
11 Oct, Luxembourg: v Luxembourg (a) won 2-0 (*Collovati, Bettega*)
1 Nov, Rome: v Denmark (h) won 2-0 (*Graziani 2*)
15 Nov, Turin: v Yugoslavia (h) won 2-0 (*Cabrini* pen, *Conti*)
6 Dec, Athens: v Greece (a) won 2-0 (*Antognoni, Scirea*)

League Championship wins (1898–1981)

Juventus 19; Inter-Milan 12; AC Milan 10; Genoa 9; Torino 8; Pro Vercelli 7; Bologna 7; Fiorentina 2; Casale 1; Novese 1; AS Roma 1; Cagliari 1; Lazio 1.

Cup wins (1922–81)

Juventus 6; Torino 4; Fiorentina 4; AC Milan 4; AS Roma 4; Napoli 2; Bologna 2; Inter-Milan 2; Atalanta 1; Genoa 1; Lazio 1; Vado 1; Venezia 1.

	League Champions	Cup Winners
1946	Torino	
1947	Torino	
1948	Torino	
1949	Torino	
1950	Juventus	
1951	AC Milan	
1952	Juventus	
1953	Inter-Milan	
1954	Inter-Milan	
1955	AC Milan	
1956	Fiorentina	
1957	AC Milan	
1958	Juventus	Lazio
1959	AC Milan	Juventus
1960	Juventus	Juventus
1961	Juventus	Fiorentina
1962	AC Milan	Napoli
1963	Inter-Milan	Atalanta
1964	Bologna	AS Roma
1965	Inter-Milan	Juventus
1966	Inter-Milan	Fiorentina
1967	Juventus	AC Milan
1968	AC Milan	Torino
1969	Fiorentina	AS Roma
1970	Cagliari	Bologna
1971	Inter-Milan	Torino
1972	Juventus	AC Milan
1973	Juventus	AC Milan
1974	Lazio	Bologna
1975	Juventus	Fiorentina
1976	Torino	Napoli
1977	Juventus	AC Milan
1978	Juventus	Inter-Milan
1979	AC Milan	Juventus
1980	Inter-Milan	AS Roma
1981	Juventus	AS Roma

Final League Table 1980–81

	P	*W*	*D*	*L*	*F*	*A*	*Pts*
Juventus	30	17	10	3	46	15	44
AS Roma	30	14	14	2	43	20	42
Napoli	30	14	10	6	31	21	38
Inter-Milan	30	14	8	8	41	24	36
Fiorentina	30	9	14	7	27	24	32
Cagliari	30	8	14	8	29	30	30
Bologna*	30	11	12	7	32	27	29
Catanzaro	30	6	17	7	24	27	29
Torino	30	8	10	12	26	29	26
Avellino*	30	10	10	10	35	32	25
Como	30	4	17	9	25	33	25
Udinese	30	8	9	13	24	39	25
Ascoli	30	6	13	11	18	34	25
Brescia	30	7	11	12	19	25	25
Perugia*	30	5	13	12	18	31	18
Pitroiese	30	6	4	20	19	46	16

*** Started season with 5 points deducted**

LIECHTENSTEIN

President: Hans Gassner.
Secretary: Werner Ospelt.
Address of Association: Liechtensteiner, Fussball-Verband, 9490 Vaduz.
Telephone: 23 879.
Year of Formation: 1933.
National Colours: Blue/red shirts, red shorts, blue stockings.
Second Choice of Colours: Yellow/red shirts, red shorts, yellow stockings.
Name, Address and Capacity of National Stadium: Landessportplatz, Vaduz, 10,000.
Population: 25,000.
Number of Clubs: 7. *Teams:* 60.
Number of Players: 1,200.
Liechtenstein has no national league. Teams compete in Swiss regional leagues.
Season: August–July.

LUXEMBOURG

President: M. Remy Wagner.
Secretary: Mlle Eliane Cremona.
Address of Association: Fédération Luxembourgeoise de Football, 50 Rue de Strasbourg, Luxembourg.
Telephone: 48–86–65.
Area: 999 square miles.
Population: 350,000.
Number of Clubs: 209. *Teams:* 532.
Number of Players: 15,730.
Year of Formation: 1908.
National Colours: Red shirts, white shorts, blue stockings.
Second Choice of Colours: Blue shirts, white shorts, blue stockings.
Name, Address and Capacity of National Stadium: City Stadium Luxembourg, 15,100.
Names, Addresses and Capacities of Other Principal Football Grounds: Stade Emile Mayrisch, Esch-sur-Alzette, 11,000; Stade Municipal, Differdange, 10,000.
Season: August–June.

International matches 1980

27 Feb, Brussels: v Belgium (a) lost 0-5
26 March, Esch: v Uruguay (h) lost 0-1
10 Sept, Luxembourg: v Yugoslavia (h) lost 0-5
4 Oct, Dudelingen: v USA (h) lost 0-2
11 Oct, Luxembourg: v Italy (h) lost 0-2
19 Nov, Copenhagen: v Denmark (a) lost 0-4

League Championship wins (1910–81)

Jeunesse Esch 17; Spora Luxembourg 10; Stade Dudelange 10; Red Boys Differdange 6; US Hollerich-Bonnevoie 5; Fola Esch 5; US Luxembourg 3; Aris Bonnevoie 3; Progres Niedercorn 3; Sporting Luxembourg 2; Racing Luxembourg 1; National Schiffige 1; Avenir Beggen 1.

Cup wins (1922–81)

Red Boys Differdange 14; Spora Luxembourg 8; Jeunesse Esch 8; US Luxembourg 6; Stade Dudelange 4; Progres Niedercorn 4; Fola Esch 3; Alliance Dudelange 2; US Rumelange 2; Aris Bonnevoie 1; US Dudelange 1; Jeunesse Hautcharage 1; National Schiffige 1; Racing Luxembourg 1; SC Tetange 1.

	League Champions	Cup Winners
1946	Stade Dudelange	Jeunesse Esch
1947	Stade Dudelange	US Luxembourg
1948	Stade Dudelange	Stade Dudelange
1949	Spora Luxembourg	Stade Dudelange
1950	Stade Dudelange	Spora Luxembourg
1951	Jeunesse Esch	SC Tetange
1952	National Schiffige	Red Boys Differdange
1953	Progres Niedercorn	Red Boys Differdange
1954	Jeunesse Esch	Jeunesse Esch
1955	Stade Dudelange	Fola Esch
1956	Spora Luxembourg	Stade Dudelange
1957	Stade Dudelange	Spora Luxembourg
1958	Jeunesse Esch	Red Boys Differdange
1959	Jeunesse Esch	US Luxembourg
1960	Jeunesse Esch	National Schiffige
1961	Spora Luxembourg	Alliance Dudelange
1962	US Luxembourg	Alliance Dudelange
1963	Jeunesse Esch	US Luxembourg
1964	Aris Bonnevoie	US Luxembourg
1965	Stade Dudelange	Spora Luxembourg
1966	Aris Bonnevoie	Spora Luxembourg
1967	Jeunesse Esch	Aris Bonnevoie
1968	Jeunesse Esch	US Rumelange
1969	Avenir Beggen	US Luxembourg
1970	Jeunesse Esch	US Luxembourg
1971	US Luxembourg	Jeunesse Hautcharage
1972	Aris Bonnevoie	Red Boys Differdange
1973	Jeunesse Esch	Jeunesse Esch
1974	Jeunesse Esch	Jeunesse Esch
1975	Jeunesse Esch	US Rumelange
1976	Jeunesse Esch	Jeunesse Esch
1977	Jeunesse Esch	Progres Niedercorn
1978	Progres Niedercorn	Progres Niedercorn
1979	Red Boys Differdange	Red Boys Differdange
1980	Jeunesse Esch	Spora Luxembourg
1981	Progres Niedercorn	Jeunesse Esch

Final League Table 1980–81

	P	*W*	*D*	*L*	*F*	*A*	*Pts*
Progres Niedercorn	22	17	1	4	68	25	35
Red Boys Differdange	22	15	4	3	60	24	34
Jeunesse Esch	22	14	3	5	48	23	31
Aris Bonnevoie	22	10	6	6	35	27	26
Avenir Beggen	22	9	4	9	29	33	22
Union	22	9	3	10	41	43	21
Eischen	22	8	4	10	27	32	20
Alliance	22	7	6	9	29	37	20
Grevenmacher	22	6	4	12	20	48	16
Spora Luxembourg	22	6	3	13	28	41	15
Etzella	22	5	4	13	22	41	14
Stade Dudelange	22	4	2	16	22	55	10

MALTA

President: Dr Giuseppe Mifsud Bonnici LLD.
Secretary: Frank Attard.
Address of Association: Malta Football Association, 84 Old Mint Street, Valletta, Malta.
Telephone: 22697, 67 43 72.
Cable: Football Malta Valletta.
Area: 122 square miles.
Population: 300,000.
Number of Clubs: 231.
Number of Players: 7,460. *Teams:* 362.
Year of Formation: 1900.
National Colours: Red.
Second Choice of Colours: White.
Name, Address and Capacity of National Stadium: The Stadium, Gzira, 30,000.
Name, Address and Capacity of Other Principal Football Grounds: Schreiber Sports Ground, Paola, 8,000; Manoel Island Upper Ground, 10,000.
Season: September–May.

International matches 1980

27 Feb, Bremen: v West Germany (a) lost 0-8
6 Dec, Valletta: v Poland (h) lost 0-2 (match abandoned after 82 minutes when the crowd rioted)

League Championship wins (1910–81)

Floriana 24; Sliema Wanderers 21; Valletta 11; Hibernians 5; Hamrum Spartans 3; St George's 1; KOMR 1.

Cup wins (1935–81)

Sliema Wanderers 16; Floriana 15; Valletta 5; Hibernians 4; Gzira United 1; Melita 1.

	League Champions	Cup Winners
1946	Valletta	Sliema W
1947	Hamrun Spart	Floriana
1948	Valletta	Sliema W
1949	Sliema W	Floriana
1950	Floriana	Floriana
1951	Floriana	Sliema W
1952	Floriana	Sliema W
1953	Floriana	Floriana
1954	Sliema W	Floriana
1955	Floriana	Floriana
1956	Sliema W	Sliema W
1957	Sliema W	Floriana
1958	Floriana	Floriana
1959	Valletta	Sliema W
1960	Valletta	Valletta
1961	Hibernians	Floriana
1962	Floriana	Hibernians
1963	Valletta	Sliema W
1964	Sliema W	Valletta
1965	Sliema W	Sliema W
1966	Sliema W	Floriana
1967	Hibernians	Floriana
1968	Floriana	Sliema W
1969	Hibernians	Sliema W
1970	Floriana	Hibernians
1971	Sliema W	Hibernians
1972	Sliema W	Floriana
1973	Floriana	Gzira
1974	Valletta	Sliema W
1975	Floriana	Valletta
1976	Sliema W	Floriana
1977	Floriana	Valletta
1978	Valletta	Valletta
1979	Hibernians	Sliema W
1980	Valletta	Hibernians
1981	Hibernians	Floriana

Final League Table 1980–81

	P	*W*	*D*	*L*	*F*	*A*	*Pts*
Hibernians	14	12	2	0	34	10	26
Sliema Wanderers	14	10	3	1	27	8	23
Hamrun	14	7	1	6	19	16	15
Floriana	14	5	5	4	17	13	15
Valletta	14	6	1	7	25	17	13
Zurrieq	14	4	4	6	15	18	12
Birkirkara	14	2	1	11	9	35	5
Marsa	14	1	1	12	5	34	3

NETHERLANDS

President: W. A. G. M. Meuleman.
Secretary/Treasurer: Drs E. J. Van Eijk.
Address of Association: Koninklijke Nederlandsche Voetbalbond, (KNVB) Woudenbergseweg 56–58, Zeist, Netherlands.
Telephone: 03439 922.
Cable: Voetbal Zeist.
Telex: 40497.
Area: 12,616 square miles.
Population: 13,000,000.
Number of Clubs: 7,635. *Teams:* 54,048.
Number of Players: 964,215.
Year of Formation: 1889.
National Colours: Orange shirts, white shorts, orange stockings.
Second Choice of Colours: All white.
Name, Address and Capacity of National Stadium: Olympisch Stadion, Stadionplein, 20, Amsterdam, 67,000.
Names, Addresses and Capacities of Other Principal Football Grounds: Stadion Feijenoord, Olympiaweg 50, Rotterdam, 67,000; Ground of Sparta, Spartastraat 5, Rotterdam, 30,000; Stadium De Goffert, Nijmegen, 30,000; Sportpark Diekman, J. J. van Deinselaan 30, Enschede, 27,564; PSV Eindhoven, Eindhoven, 27,500; Ajax Middemweg, Amsterdam, 29,000; AZ Alkmaar Dehout, 23,000.
Season: August–June.

Principal Honours

World Cup: *runners-up* 1974, 1978
World Club Champions: Feyenoord (1970), Ajax Amsterdam (1972)
European Champions Cup: *winners* Feyenoord (1970), Ajax Amsterdam (1971, 1972, 1973); *runners-up* Ajax Amsterdam (1969)
UEFA Cup: *winners* Feyenoord (1974), PSV Eindhoven (1978); *runners-up* Twente Enschede (1975); AZ 67 Alkmaar (1981)
Super Cup: Ajax Amsterdam (1972, 1973)

International matches 1980

23 Jan, Vigo: v Spain (a) lost 0-1
26 March, Paris: v France (a) drew 0-0
11 June, Naples: v Greece (a) won 1-0 (*Kist* pen)
14 June, Naples: v West Germany (a) lost 2-3 (*Rep* pen, *Willy Van der Kerkhof*)
17 June, Milan: v Czechoslovakia (a) drew 1-1 (*Kist*)
10 Sept, Dublin: v Republic of Ireland (a) lost 1-2 (*Tahamata*)
11 Oct, Eindhoven: v West Germany (h) drew 1-1 (*Brandts*)
19 Nov, Brussels: v Belgium (a) lost 0-1
30 Dec, Montevideo: v Uruguay (a) lost 0-2

League Championship wins (1898–1981)

Ajax Amsterdam 19; Feyenoord 12; HVV The Hague 8; PSV Eindhoven 7; Sparta Rotterdam 6; Go Ahead Deventer 4; HBS The Hague 3; Willem II Tilburg 3; RCH Haarlem 2; RAP 2; Heracles 2; ADO The Hague 2; Quick The Hague 1; BVV Scheidam 1; NAC Breda 1; Eindhoven 1; Enschede 1; Volewijckers Amsterdam 1; Limburgia 1; Rapid JC Haarlem 1; DOS Utrecht 1; DWS Amsterdam 1; Haarlem 1; Be Quick Groningen 1; SVV Scheidam 1; AZ 67 Alkmaar 1.

Cup wins (1899–1981)

Ajax Amsterdam 8; Feyenoord 5; Quick The Hague 4; PSV Eindhoven 4; HEC 3; Sparta Rotterdam 3; AZ 67 Alkmaar 2; DFC 2; Fortuna Geleen 2; Haarlem 2; HBS The Hague 2; RCH 2; VOC 2; Wageningen 2; Willem II Tilburg 2; FC Den Haag 2; Concordia Rotterdam 1; CVV 1; Eindhoven 1; HVV The Hague 1; Longa 1; Quick Njimegen 1; RAP 1; Roermond 1; Schoten 1; Velocitas Breda 1; Velocitas Groningen 1; VSV 1; VUC 1; VVV Groningen 1; ZFC 1; NAC Breda 1; Twente Enschede 1.

	League Champions	Cup Winners
1946	Haarlem	
1947	Ajax Amsterdam	
1948	BVV Scheidam	Wageningen
1949	SVV Scheidam	Quick Njimegen
1950	Limburgia	PSV Eindhoven
1951	PSV Eindhoven	*No competition*
1952	Willem II Tilburg	*No competition*
1953	RCH Haarlem	*No competition*
1954	Eindhoven	*No competition*
1955	Willem II Tilburg	*No competition*
1956	Rapid JC Haarlem	*No competition*
1957	Ajax Amsterdam	Fortuna Geleen
1958	DOS Utrecht	Sparta Rotterdam
1959	Sparta Rotterdam	VVV Groningen
1960	Ajax Amsterdam	*No competition*
1961	Feyenoord	Ajax Amsterdam
1962	Feyenoord	Sparta Rotterdam
1963	PSV Eindhoven	Willem II Tilburg
1964	DWS Amsterdam	Fortuna Geleen
1965	Feyenoord	Feyenoord
1966	Ajax Amsterdam	Sparta Rotterdam
1967	Ajax Amsterdam	Ajax Amsterdam
1968	Ajax Amsterdam	ADO The Hague
1969	Feyenoord	Feyenoord
1970	Ajax Amsterdam	Ajax Amsterdam
1971	Feyenoord	Ajax Amsterdam
1972	Ajax Amsterdam	Ajax Amsterdam
1973	Ajax Amsterdam	NAC Breda
1974	Feyenoord	PSV Eindhoven
1975	PSV Eindhoven	FC Den Haag
1976	PSV Eindhoven	PSV Eindhoven
1977	Ajax Amsterdam	Twente Enschede
1978	PSV Eindhoven	AZ 67 Alkmaar
1979	Ajax Amsterdam	Ajax Amsterdam
1980	Ajax Amsterdam	Feyenoord
1981	AZ 67 Alkmaar	AZ 67 Alkmaar

Final League Table 1980–81

	P	*W*	*D*	*L*	*F*	*A*	*Pts*
AZ 67 Alkmaar	34	27	6	1	101	30	60
Ajax Amsterdam	34	22	4	8	88	54	48
Utrecht	34	18	9	7	67	33	45
Feyenoord	34	18	9	7	74	48	45
PSV Eindhoven	34	18	8	8	62	31	44
Twente Enschede	34	16	7	11	60	49	39
Sparta Rotterdam	34	15	6	13	75	71	36
MVV	34	12	10	12	53	65	34
PEC Zwolle	34	10	10	14	42	49	30
Willem II Tilburg	34	11	7	16	49	69	29
Roda	34	9	10	15	67	75	28
Go Ahead Deventer	34	10	8	16	63	75	28
NAC Breda	34	9	9	16	46	66	27
FC Den Haag	34	12	3	19	53	79	27
Groningen	34	8	9	17	49	72	25
NEC Nijmegen	34	6	13	15	38	63	25
Excelsior	34	5	11	18	39	67	21
Wageningen	34	6	9	19	33	63	21

NORWAY

President: Einar Jorum.
Secretary: Nicolai Johansen.
Address of Associ tion: Norges Fotballforbund, Boks 3823, Ullevål Hageby, Oslo 8.
Telephone: 46.98.30. *Telex:* 71722 nff n.
Cable: Fotballforbund Oslo.
Area: 125,064 square miles.
Population: 4,000,000.
Number of Clubs: 3,100. *Teams:* 6,790.
Number of Players: 124,000.
Year of Formation: 1902.
National Colours: Red shirts, white shorts, blue and white stockings.
Second Choice of Colours: Blue shirts, white shorts, blue stockings.
Name, Address and Capacity of National Stadium: Ulleval Stadium, Sognsveien 75, Oslo, 24,500.
Names, Addresses and Capacities of Other Principal Football Grounds: Bislet Stadium, Oslo, 24,000; Brann Stadium, Bergen, 26,000; Lerkendal Stadium, Trondheim, 30,000; Stavanger Stadium, Stavanger, 19,800.
Season: April–November.

International matches 1980

22 May, Oslo: v Bulgaria (h) won 1-0 (*Jacobsen*)
4 June, Copenhagen: v Denmark (a) lost 1-3 (*Kollshaugen*)
14 July, Oslo: v Iceland (h) won 3-1 (*Kollshaugen, Jacobsen, Erlandsen*)
20 Aug, Oslo: v Finland (h) won 6-1 (*Jacobsen 4, Dokken, Aas*)
10 Sept, Wembley: v England (a) lost 0-4
24 Sept, Oslo: v Rumania (h) drew 1-1 (Hareide)
28 Oct, Berne: v Switzerland (a) won 2-1 (*Hareide, Mathisen*)

League Championship wins (1938–80)

Fredrikstad 9; Viking Stavanger 6; Rosenborg Trondheim 3; Larvik Turn 3; Lillestroem 3; Brann Bergen 2; Lyn Oslo 2; IK Start 2; Valerengen 1; Friedig 1; Fram 1; Skeid Oslo 1; Strömgodset Drammen 1.

Cup wins (1902–80)

Odds Bk, Skien 11; Fredrikstads 9; Lyn Oslo 8; Skeid Oslo 8; Sarpsborg FK 6; Orn F Horten 4; Brann Bergen 4; Mjondalens F 4; Rosenborg Trondheim 3; Strömgodset Drammen 3; Viking Stavanger 3; Mercantile 2; Lillestroem 2; Grane Nordstrand 1; Kvik Halden 1; Sparta 1; Gjovik 1; Bodo-Glimt 1; Valerengen 1.
(*Until* 1937 *the cup-winners were regarded as champions.*)

League Champions		Cup Winners
1946		Lyn Oslo
1947		Skeid Oslo
1948	Freidig	Sarpsborg FK
1949	Fredrikstad	Sarpsborg FK
1950	Fram	Fredrikstad
1951	Fredrikstad	Sarpsborg FK
1952	Fredrikstad	Sparta Sarpsborg
1953	Larvik Turn	Viking Stav
1954	Fredrikstad	Skeid Oslo
1955	Larvik Turn	Skeid Oslo
1956	Larvik Turn	Skeid Oslo
1957	Fredrikstad	Fredrikstad
1958	Viking Stav	Skeid Oslo
1959	Lillestroem	Viking Stav
1960	Fredrikstad	Rosenborg Tr
1961	Fredrikstad	Fredrikstad
1962	Brann Bergen	Gjovik Lyn
1963	Brann Bergen	Skeid Oslo
1964	Lyn Oslo	Rosenborg Tr
1965	Valerengen	Skeid Oslo
1966	Skeid Oslo	Fredrikstad
1967	Rosenborg Tr	Lyn Oslo
1968	Lyn Oslo	Lyn Oslo
1969	Rosenborg Tr	Strömgodset Dr
1970	Strömgodset Dr	Strömgodset Dr
1971	Rosenborg Tr	Rosenborg Tr
1972	Viking Stav	Brann Bergen
1973	Viking Stav	Strömgodset Dr
1974	Viking Stav	Skeid Oslo
1975	Viking Stav	Bodo-Glim
1976	Lillestroem	Brann Bergen
1977	Lillestroem	Lillestroem
1978	IK Start	Lillestroem
1979	Viking Stav	Viking Stav
1980	IK Start	Valerengen

Final League Table 1980–81

	P	*W*	*D*	*L*	*F*	*A*	*Pts*
IK Start	22	13	3	6	52	26	29
Bryne	22	12	5	5	44	22	29
Lillestroem	22	10	7	5	36	25	27
Viking Stavanger	22	10	5	7	34	27	25
Rosenborg Trondheim	22	9	5	8	42	36	23
Moss	22	8	7	7	33	27	23
Fredrikstad	22	9	5	8	35	39	23
Valerengen	22	6	8	8	26	26	20
Lyn Oslo	22	8	3	11	26	43	19
Molde	22	6	6	10	30	39	18
Skeid	22	4	8	10	21	39	16
Bodo/Glimt	22	5	2	15	13	43	12

POLAND

President: Dr Wlodzimierz Reczek.
General-Secretary: Zbigniew Kalinski.
Address of Association: Polish Football Association, Al. Ujazdowskie 22, Warszawa.
Telephone: 28–93–44: 29–24–89.
Area: 120,359 square miles.
Population: 34,528,000.
Number of Clubs: 5,334. *Teams:* 11,223.
Number of Players: 234,052.
Year of Formation: 1923.
National Colours: White shirts, red shorts, white and red stockings.
Second Choice of Colours: Red shirts, white shorts, red stockings.
Name, Address and Capacity of National Stadium: Stadium of the X Anniversary, Warszawa, 87,000.
Names, Addresses and Capacities of Other Principal Football Grounds: Stadium Slaski, Chorzow, 93,000; Stadium Warta, Poznan, 45,000; Stadium Olimpijski, Wroclaw, 72,000; Stadium Wisla Kraków, 45,000; Stadium Ruch, Chorzów, 40,000; Stadium Legia, Warszawa, 35,000; Stadium Piast, Gliwice, 55,000; Stadium Pgoon, Szczecin, 36,000; Stadium Polonia, Bytom, 35,000; Stade KS Zawisza, Bydgoszcz, 55,000.
Season: August–November; March–June.

Principal Honours

Olympic Games: *winners* 1972; *runners-up* 1976
European Cup-Winners' Cup: *runners-up* Gornik Zabrze (1970)

International matches 1980

26 March, Budapest: v Hungary (a) lost 1-2 (*Lato*)
2 April, Brussels: v Belgium (a) lost 1-2 (*Lato*)
19 April, Turin: v Italy (a) drew 2-2 (*Sybis, Szarmach* pen)
26 April, Borovo: v Yugoslavia (a) lost 1-2 (*Sybis*)
13 May, Frankfurt: v West Germany (a) lost 1-3 (*Boniek*)
28 May, Poznan: v Scotland (h) won 1-0 (*Boniek*)
22 June, Warsaw: v Iraq (h) won 3-0 (*Kmiecik, Lato, Iwan*)
29 June, Sao Paulo: v Brazil (a) drew 1-1 (*Lato*)
2 July, Santa Cruz: v Bolivia (a) won 1-0 (*Iwan*)
9 July, Bogota: v Colombia (a) won 4-1 (*Herrera og, Iwan 3*)
24 Sept, Chorzow: v Czechoslovakia (h) drew 1-1 (*Lubanski* pen)
12 Oct, Buenos Aires: v Argentina (a) lost 1-2 (*Zalezny* pen)
12 Nov, Barcelona: v Spain (a) won 2-1 (*Iwan 2*)
19 Nov, Warsaw: v Algeria (h) won 5-1 (*Kupcewicz, Ciolek, Iwan 2, Dziuba*)
6 Dec, Valletta: v Malta (a) won 2-0 (*Smolarek, Lipka*) (match abandoned after 82 mins when the crowd rioted)

League Championship wins (1921–81)

Ruch Chorzow 12; Gornik Zabrze 10; Wisla Krakow 6; Cracovia 5; Pogon Lwow 4; Legia Warsaw 4; Warta Poznan 2; Polonia Bytom 2; Stal Mielec 2; Garbarnia Krakow 1; Polonia Warsaw 1; LKS Lodz 1; Slask Wroclaw 1; Szombierki Bytom 1; Widzew Lodz 1.

Cup wins (1951–81)

Legia Warsaw 7; Gornik Zabrze 6; Zaglebie Sosnowiec 4; Ruch Chorzow 2; Gwardia Warsaw 1; LKS Lodz 1; Polonia Warsaw 1; Wisla Krakow 1; Stal Rzeszow 1; Slask Wroclaw 1; Arka Gdynia 1.

	League Champions	Cup Winners
1946	Polonia Warsaw	
1947	Warta Poznan	
1948	Cracovia	
1949	Wisla Krakow	
1950	Wisla Krakow	
1951	Wisla Krakow	Ruch Chorzow
1952	Ruch Chorzow	Polonia Warsaw
1953	Ruch Chorzow	*No competition*
1954	Polonia Bytom	Gwardia Warsaw
1955	Legia Warsaw	Legia Warsaw
1956	Legia Warsaw	Legia Warsaw
1957	Gornik Zabrze	LKS Lodz
1958	LKS Lodz	*No competition*
1959	Gornik Zabrze	*No competition*
1960	Ruch Chorzow	*No competition*
1961	Gornik Zabrze	*No competition*
1962	Polonia Bytom	Zaglebie Sosnowiec
1963	Gornik Zabrze	Zaglebie Sosnowiec
1964	Gornik Zabrze	Legia Warsaw
1965	Gornik Zabrze	Gornik Zabrze
1966	Gornik Zabrze	Legia Warsaw
1967	Gornik Zabrze	Wisla Krakow
1968	Ruch Chorzow	Gornik Zabrze
1969	Legia Warsaw	Gornik Zabrze
1970	Legia Warsaw	Gornik Zabrze
1971	Gornik Zabrze	Gornik Zabrze
1972	Gornik Zabrze	Gornik Zabrze
1973	Stal Mielec	Legia Warsaw
1974	Ruch Chorzow	Ruch Chorzow
1975	Ruch Chorzow	Stal Rzeszow
1976	Stal Mielec	Slask Wroclaw
1977	Slask Wroclaw	Zaglebie Sosnowiec
1979	Ruch Chorzow	Arka Gdynia
1980	Szombierki Bytom	Legia Warsaw
1981	Widzew Lodz	Legia Warsaw

Final League Table 1980–81

	P	*W*	*D*	*L*	*F*	*A*	*Pts*
Widzew Lodz	30	14	11	5	39	25	39
Wisla Krakow	30	15	7	8	51	30	37
Szombierki Bytom	30	15	6	9	51	33	36
Slask Wroclaw	30	13	10	7	32	28	36
Legia Warsaw	30	12	12	6	48	29	36
Baltyk	30	14	8	8	30	27	36
Ruch Chorzow	30	11	8	11	36	39	30
Lech	30	11	7	12	28	29	29
Stal Mielec	30	12	4	14	41	44	28
Motor Lublin	30	10	8	12	36	45	28
Arka Gdynia	30	9	10	11	40	42	28
Gornik Zabrze	30	9	9	12	20	27	27
LKS Lodz	30	8	9	13	24	38	25
Zaglebie Sosnowiec	30	7	10	13	22	27	24
Zawisza	30	9	5	16	25	43	23
Odra Opole	30	6	6	18	26	43	18

PORTUGAL

President: Romao Martins.
Secretary: Cesar Gracio.
Address of Association: Federação Portuguesa de Futebol, Praça de Alegria 25, Lisboa.
Telephone: 32 82 07/08/09, 32 82 00.
Cable: Futebol Lisboa.
Telex: 13 489 FPFP.
Area: 34,139 square miles.
Population: 8,668,267.
Number of Clubs: 880. *Teams:* 224.
Number of Players: 40,815.
Year of Formation: 1914.
National Colours: Red shirts, white shorts, green stockings.
Second Choice of Colours: White shirts, blue shorts, blue stockings.
Name, Address and Capacity of National Stadium: National Stadium, Lisbon, 51,000.
Names, Addresses and Capacities of Other Principal Football Grounds: Estadio de Luz, Lisbon, 69,000; Estadio Jose Alvalade, Lisbon, 47,000; Estadio do Restelo, Lisbon, 35,000; Estadio das Antas, Porto, 40,000; Estadio 28 de Maio, Braga, 30,000; Estadio Bonfim, Setubal, 20,000; Estadio Alfredo da Silva, 23,000; Estadio Municipal, Coimbra, 25,000; Estadio Municipal, Guimaraes, 25,000.
Season: September–July.

Principal Honours

European Champions Cup: *winners* Benfica (1961, 1962); *runners-up* Benfica (1963, 1965, 1968)
European Cup-Winners' Cup: *winners* Sporting Lisbon (1964)

International matches 1980

26 March, Glasgow: v Scotland (a) lost 1-4 (*Gomes*)
24 Sept, Genoa: v Italy (a) lost 1-3 (*Jordao*)
8 Oct, Lisbon: v USA (h) drew 1-1 (*C. Manuel*)
15 Oct, Glasgow: v Scotland (a) drew 0-0
19 Nov, Lisbon: v Northern Ireland (h) won 1-0 (*Jordao*)
17 Dec, Lisbon: v Israel (h) won 3-0 (*Humberto 2, Jordao*)

League Championship wins (1935–81)

Benfica 24; Sporting Lisbon 15; FC Porto 7; Belenenses 1.

Cup wins (1939–81)

Benfica 17; Sporting Lisbon 9; FC Porto 4; Boavista 3; Belenenses 2; Vitoria Setubal 2; Academica Coimbra 1; Leixoes Porto 1; Sporting Braga 1.

	League Champions	Cup Winners
1946	Belenenses	Sporting Lisbon
1947	Sporting Lisbon	*No competition*
1948	Sporting Lisbon	Sporting Lisbon
1949	Sporting Lisbon	Benfica
1950	Benfica	*No competition*
1951	Sporting Lisbon	Benfica
1952	Sporting Lisbon	Benfica
1953	Sporting Lisbon	Benfica
1954	Sporting Lisbon	Sporting Lisbon
1955	Benfica	Benfica
1956	FC Porto	FC Porto
1957	Benfica	Benfica
1958	Sporting Lisbon	FC Porto
1959	FC Porto	Benfica
1960	Benfica	Belenenses
1961	Benfica	Leixoes
1962	Sporting Lisbon	Benfica
1963	Benfica	Sporting Lisbon
1964	Benfica	Benfica
1965	Benfica	Vitoria Setubal
1966	Sporting Lisbon	Sporting Braga
1967	Benfica	Vitoria Setubal
1968	Benfica	FC Porto
1969	Benfica	Benfica
1970	Sporting Lisbon	Benfica
1971	Benfica	Sporting Lisbon
1972	Benfica	Benfica
1973	Benfica	Sporting Lisbon
1974	Sporting Lisbon	Sporting Lisbon
1975	Benfica	Boavista
1976	Benfica	Boavista
1977	Benfica	FC Porto
1978	FC Porto	Sporting Lisbon
1979	FC Porto	Boavista
1980	Sporting Lisbon	Benfica
1981	Benfica	Benfica

Final League Table 1980–81

	P	*W*	*D*	*L*	*F*	*A*	*Pts*
Benfica	30	22	6	2	72	14	50
FC Porto	30	21	6	3	53	18	48
Sporting Lisbon	30	14	9	7	48	28	37
Boavista	30	14	8	8	36	25	36
Guimaraes	30	11	9	10	38	30	31
Braga	30	10	10	10	34	39	30
Vitoria Setubal	30	9	11	10	29	30	29
Portimonense	30	12	5	13	34	36	29
Penafiel	30	11	5	14	28	38	27
Espinho	30	9	9	12	26	35	27
Belenenses	30	8	10	12	24	39	26
Amora	30	10	5	15	38	51	25
Viseu	30	8	9	13	24	40	25
Varzim	30	8	8	14	28	33	24
Maritimo Funchal	30	7	8	15	32	46	22
Coimbra	30	4	6	20	16	58	14

RUMANIA

President: Andrei Radulescu.
Secretaries: Daniel Lazarescu, Ion Alexandrescu, Iorian Dumitrescu.
Address of Association: Federatia Romana de Fotbal, Vasile Conta 16, Bucharest 6.
Telephone: 12–10–60, 12–09–40. *Cable:* Sportrom Bucaresti. *Telex:* 11180 Bucaresti.
Area: 91,699 square miles. *Population:* 23,000,000. *Number of Clubs:* 5,453. *Teams:* 5,577. *Number of Players:* 179,987.
Year of Formation: 1908.
National Colours: Yellow shirts, blue shorts, red stockings.
Second Choice of Colours: Blue shirts, yellow shorts, red stockings.
Name, Address and Capacity of National Stadium: 23 August, Bucharest, 95,000.
Names, Addresses and Capacities of Other Principal Football Grounds: Republicii, Bucharest, 37,000; Giulesti, Bucharest, 20,000; Municipal, Cluj, 40,000; 1 Mai, Timisoara, 30,000; 23 August, Iasi, 20,000; 1 Mai, Constanta, 20,000; Petrolul, Ploiesti, 20,000; 1 Mai, Pitesti, 20,000; Stade Central Craiova, 40,000.
Season: August–July (with winter break).

International matches 1980

17 Jan, Cali: v Colombia (a) drew 0-0
16 Feb, Naples: v Italy (a) lost 1-2 (*Boloni*)
30 Mar, Belgrade: v Yugoslavia (a) lost 0-2
2 April, Bucharest: v East Germany (h) drew 2-2 (*Mircea Sandu, Dorner og*)
16 May, Brno: v Czechoslovakia (a) lost 1-2 (*Ionescu*)
6 June, Brussels: v Belgium (a) lost 1-2 (*Camataru*)
27 Aug, Bucharest: v Yugoslavia (h) won 4-1 (*Iordanescu 3* [2 pens], *Camataru*)
10 Sept, Varna: v Bulgaria (a) won 2-1 (*Beldeanu, Iordanescu*)
24 Sept, Oslo: v Norway (a) drew 1-1 (*Iordanescu*)
15 Oct, Bucharest: v England (h) won 2-1 (*Raducanu, Iordanescu* pen)

League Championship wins (1910–81)

Dynamo Bucharest 9; Steaua Bucharest (prev. CCA) 9; Venus Bucharest 7; CSC Temesvar 6; UT Arad 6; Rapid Bucharest 4; Uni Craiova 3; Ripensia Temesvar 3; Petrolul Ploesti 3; Olimpia Bucharest 2; CAC Bucharest 2; Arges Pitesti 2; Soc RA Bucharest 1; Prahova Ploesti 1; CSC Brasov 1; Juventius Bucharest 1; SSUD Reita 1; Craiova Bucharest 1; Progresul 1; Ploesti United 1.

Cup wins (1934–81)

Steaua Bucharest (prev. CCA) 13; Rapid Bucharest 7; Dynamo Bucharest 3; Uni Craiova 3; UT Arad 2; CFR Bucharest 2; Progresul 2; RIP Timisoara 2; ICO Oradeo 1; Metal Ochimia Resita 1; Petrolul Ploesti 1; Stinta Cluj 1; Stinta Timisoara 1; Turnu Severin 1; Chimia Ramnicu 1; Jiul Petroseni 1; Poli Timisoara 1.

	League Champions	Cup Winners
1947	UT Arad	*No competition*
1948	UT Arad	UT Arad
1949	Progresul	CCA Bucharest
1950	UT Arad	CCA Bucharest
1951	CCA Bucharest	CCA Bucharest
1952	CCA Bucharest	CCA Bucharest
1953	CCA Bucharest	UT Arad
1954	UT Arad	Metal Och, Resitta
1955	Dynamo Bucharest	CCA Bucharest
1956	CCA Bucharest	ICO Oradea
1957	*No competition*	*No competition*
1958	Petrolul Ploesti	Stinta Timisoara
1959	Petrolul Ploesti	Dynamo Bucharest
1960	CCA Bucharest	Progresul
1961	CCA Bucharest	Progresul
1962	Dynamo Bucharest	Steaua Bucharest
1963	Dynamo Bucharest	Petrolul Ploesti
1964	Dynamo Bucharest	Dynamo Bucharest
1965	Dynamo Bucharest	Stinta Cluj
1966	Petrolul Ploesti	Steaua Bucharest
1967	Rapid Bucharest	Steaua Bucharest
1968	Steaua Bucharest	Dynamo Bucharest
1969	UT Arad	Steaua Bucharest
1970	UT Arad	Steaua Bucharest
1971	Dynamo Bucharest	Steaua Bucharest
1972	Arges Pitesti	Rapid Bucharest
1973	Dynamo Bucharest	Chimia Ramnicu
1974	Uni Craiova	Jiul Petroseni
1975	Dynamo Bucharest	Rapid Bucharest
1976	Steaua Bucharest	Steaua Bucharest
1977	Dynamo Bucharest	Uni Craiova
1978	Steaua Bucharest	Uni Craiova
1979	Arges Pitesti	Steaua Bucharest
1980	Uni Craiova	Poli Timisoara
1981	Uni Craiova	Uni Craiova

Final League Table 1980–81

	P	*W*	*D*	*L*	*F*	*A*	*Pts*
Uni Craiova	34	21	4	9	72	33	46
Dynamo Bucharest	34	18	7	9	57	34	43
Arges Pitesti	34	19	4	11	63	39	42
Steaua Bucharest	34	15	8	11	50	45	38
Sportul	34	17	2	15	54	35	36
Corvinul	34	16	3	15	72	48	35
Olt	34	14	7	13	44	49	35
Chimia RM Valcea	34	15	4	15	64	51	34
Brasov	34	14	6	14	35	41	34
Jiul Petroseni	34	14	5	15	44	41	33
SC Bacau	34	14	5	15	46	51	33
Poli Timisoara	34	13	7	14	34	46	33
Tirgu Mures	34	14	4	16	50	56	32
Stinta Cluj	34	14	4	16	47	57	32
Progresul	34	13	6	15	39	50	32
Iassy	34	12	6	16	44	53	30
Baia Mare	34	10	6	18	37	62	26
Galati	34	7	4	23	34	72	18

SPAIN

President: Pablo Porta Bussoms.
Secretary: Augustin Dominguez.
Address of Association: Real Federación Española de Futbol, Calle Alberto Bosch 13, Apartado 347, Madrid 14.
Telephone: 2391000, 2391008, 2391009.
Cable: Futbol.
Area: 190,115 square miles.
Population: 35,400,000.
Number of Clubs: 5,578. *Teams:* 5,578.
Number of Players: 202,574.
Year of Formation: 1913.
National Colours: Red shirts, dark blue shorts, black with yellow border stockings.
Second Choice of Colours: Blue shirts, dark blue shorts.
No National Stadium.
Names, Addresses and Capacities of Principal Football Grounds: Santiago Bernabeu, Madrid, 101,663; Campo Nuevo, Barcelona, 90,138; Manzanares, Madrid, 70,000; Mestalla, Valencia, 53,100; Sánchez Pizjuan, Sevilla, 46,000; San Mamés, Bilbao, 41,400; Sarriá, Barcelona, 38,295; Riazor, La Coruña, 35,860; La Romareda, Zaragoza, 32,416.
Season: September–June.

Principal Honours

European Nations Cup: *winners* 1964
Olympic Games: *runners-up* 1920
European Champions Cup: *winners* Real Madrid (1956, 1957, 1958, 1959, 1960, 1966); *runners-up* Real Madrid (1962, 1964, 1981), Barcelona (1961), Atlético Madrid (1974)
World Club Champions: Real Madrid (1960), Atlético Madrid (1975)
European Cup-Winners' Cup: *winners* Atlético Madrid (1962), Barcelona (1979), Valencia (1980); *runners-up* Atlético Madrid (1963), Barcelona (1969), Real Madrid (1971)
Fairs Cup: *winners* Barcelona (1958, 1960, 1966), Valencia (1962, 1963), Zaragoza (1964); *runners-up* Barcelona (1962), Valencia (1964), Zaragoza (1966)
UEFA Cup: *runners-up* Athletic Bilbao (1977)
Super Cup: *winners* Valencia (1981)

International matches 1980

23 Jan, Vigo: v Netherlands (h) won 1-0 (*Dani* pen)
13 Feb, Malaga: v East Germany (h) lost 0-1
26 March, Barcelona: v England (h) lost 0-2
16 April, Gijon: v Czechoslovakia (h) drew 2-2 (*Migueli, Quini*)
21 May, Copenhagen: v Denmark (a) drew 2-2 (*Saura, Alesanco*)
12 June, Milan: v Italy (a) drew 0-0
15 June, Milan: v Belgium (a) lost 1-2 (*Quini*)
18 June, Naples: v England (a) lost 1-2 (*Dani* pen)
24 Sept, Budapest: v Hungary (a) drew 2-2 (*Juanito, Satrustegui*)
15 Oct, Leipzig: v East Germany (a) drew 0-0
12 Nov, Barcelona: v Poland (h) lost 1-2 (*Dani* pen)

League Championship wins (1929–81)

Real Madrid 20; Barcelona 9; Atlético Madrid 8; Atlético Bilbao 6; Valencia 4; Real Betis 1; Seville 1; Real Sociedad 1.

Cup wins (1902–81)

Atlético Bilbao 22; Barcelona 19; Real Madrid 14; Atlético Madrid 5; Valencia 5; Real Union de Irun 3; Seville 3; Espanol 2; Real Zaragoza 2; Arenas 1; Ciclista Sebastian 1; Racing de Irun 1; Vizcaya Bilbao 1; Real Betis 1.

	League Champions	Cup Winners
1946	Seville	Real Madrid
1947	Valencia	Real Madrid
1948	Barcelona	Seville
1949	Barcelona	Valencia
1950	Atlético Madrid	Atlético Bilbao
1951	Atlético Madrid	Barcelona
1952	Barcelona	Barcelona
1953	Barcelona	Barcelona
1954	Real Madrid	Valencia
1955	Real Madrid	Atlético Bilbao
1956	Atlético Bilbao	Atlético Bilbao
1957	Real Madrid	Barcelona
1958	Real Madrid	Atlético Bilbao
1959	Barcelona	Barcelona
1960	Barcelona	Atlético Madrid
1961	Real Madrid	Atlético Madrid
1962	Real Madrid	Real Madrid
1963	Real Madrid	Barcelona
1964	Real Madrid	Real Zaragoza
1965	Real Madrid	Atlético Madrid
1966	Atlético Madrid	Real Zaragoza
1967	Real Madrid	Valencia
1968	Real Madrid	Barcelona
1969	Real Madrid	Atlético Bilbao
1970	Atlético Madrid	Real Madrid
1971	Valencia	Barcelona
1972	Real Madrid	Atlético Madrid
1973	Atlético Madrid	Atlético Bilbao
1974	Barcelona	Real Madrid
1975	Real Madrid	Real Madrid
1976	Real Madrid	Atlético Madrid
1977	Atlético Madrid	Real Betis
1978	Real Madrid	Barcelona
1979	Real Madrid	Valencia
1980	Real Madrid	Real Madrid
1981	Real Sociedad	Barcelona

Final League Table 1980–81

	P	*W*	*D*	*L*	*F*	*A*	*Pts*
Real Sociedad	34	19	8	7	52	29	45
Real Madrid	34	20	5	9	66	37	45
Atlético Madrid	34	16	10	8	46	39	42
Valencia	34	17	8	9	59	41	42
Barcelona	34	18	5	11	66	41	41
Betis	34	16	8	9	55	38	40
Gijon	34	15	9	10	58	40	37
Seville	34	14	9	11	34	42	37
Athletic Bilbao	34	14	7	13	64	53	35
Espanol	34	14	6	14	37	42	34
Osasuna	34	12	8	14	35	46	32
Valladolid	34	9	13	16	40	46	31
Hercules	34	10	10	14	42	48	30
Real Zaragoza	34	9	11	14	31	44	29
Las Palmas	34	12	4	18	47	61	28
Murcia	34	8	7	19	35	49	23
Salamanca	34	7	7	20	32	67	21
Almeria	34	6	7	21	30	66	19

SWEDEN

President: Tore Brodd.
Secretary: Robert Hernadi.
Address of Association: Svenska Fotbollförbundet, Box 1216 S-171 23, Solna.
Telephone: 08/27 25 00, 27 2900.
Cable: Fotball, Solna. *Telex:* 17711 Fotball s.
Area: 173,665 square miles.
Population: 8,268,086.
Number of Clubs: 3,220. *Teams:* 6,011.
Number of Players: 152,548.
Year of Formation: 1904.
National Colours: Yellow shirts, blue shorts, yellow and blue stockings.
Second Choice of Colours: Blue shirts, white shorts, yellow stockings.
Name, Address and Capacity of National Stadium: Fotbollstadion, Solna, 52,000.
Names, Addresses and Capacities of Other Principal Football Grounds: Nya Ullevi, Göteborg, 52,000; Malmö Stadion, Malmö, 35,000; Idrottsparken, Norrköping, 35,000; Olympia, Helsingborg, 25,000; Stadion, Stockholm, 25,000.
Season: April–October.

Principal Honours

Olympic Games: *winners* 1948
World Cup: *runners-up* 1958
European Champions Cup: *runners-up* Malmö FF (1979)

International matches 1980

28 April, Malmö: v USSR (h) lost 1-5 (*Nordgren*)
7 May, Gothenburg: v Denmark (h) lost 0-1
22 May, Helsinki: v Finland (a) won 2-0 (*Nordgren, Sjoberg*)
18 June, Stockholm: v Israel (h) drew 1-1 (*Ramberg*)
17 July, Hamstad: v Iceland (h) drew 1-1 (*Backe*)
20 Aug, Budapest: v Hungary (a) lost 0-2
10 Sept, Stockholm: v Scotland (h) lost 0-1
24 Sept, Bourgas: v Bulgaria (a) won 3-2 (*Ramberg, Billy Ohlsson, Holmgren*)
15 Oct, Belfast: v Northern Ireland (a) lost 0-3
12 Nov, Tel Aviv: v Israel (a) drew 0-0

League Championship wins (1896–1980)

Oergryte IS Gothenburg 13; Malmö FF 12; IFK Norrköping 11; Djurgaarden 8; IFK Gothenburg 8; AIK Stockholm 8; GAIS Gothenburg 4; Boras IF Elfsborg 4; IF Halsingborg 3; Oster Vaxjo 3; Halmstad 2; Atvidaberg 2; IFK Ekilstune 1; IF Gavle Brynas 1; IF Gothenburg 1; Fassbergs 1; Norrköping IK Sleipner 1.

Cup wins (1941–81)

Malmö FF 11; IFK Norrköping 3; AIK Stockholm 3; Atvidaberg 2; GAIS Gothenburg 1; IFK Halsingborg 1; Raa 1; Landskrona 1; IFK Gothenburg 1; Kalmar 1; Oster Vaxjo 1.

	League Champions	Cup Winners
1946	IFK Norrköping	Malmö FF
1947	IFK Norrköping	Malmö FF
1948	IFK Norrköping	Raa
1949	Malmö FF	AIK Stockholm
1950	Malmö FF	AIK Stockholm
1951	Malmö FF	Malmö FF
1952	IFK Norrköping	*No competition*
1953	Malmö FF	Malmö FF
1954	GAIS Gothenburg	*No competition*
1955	Djurgaarden	*No competition*
1956	IFK Norrköping	*No competition*
1957	IFK Norrköping	*No competition*
1958	IFK Gothenburg	*No competition*
1959	Djurgaarden	*No competition*
1960	IFK Norrköping	*No competition*
1961	Boras Elfsborg	*No competition*
1962	IFK Norrköping	*No competition*
1963	IFK Norrköping	*No competition*
1964	Djurgaarden	*No competition*
1965	Malmö FF	*No competition*
1966	Djurgaarden	*No competition*
1967	Malmö FF	Malmö FF
1968	Oster Vaxjo	*No competition*
1969	IFK Gothenburg	IFK Norrköping
1970	Malmö FF	Atvidaberg
1971	Malmö FF	Atvidaberg
1972	Atvidaberg	Landskrona
1973	Atvidaberg	Malmö FF
1974	Malmö FF	Malmö FF
1975	Malmö FF	Malmö FF
1976	Halmstad BK	AIK Stockholm
1977	Malmö FF	Malmö FF
1978	Oster Vaxjo	Oster Vaxjo
1979	Halmstad BK	IFK Gothenburg
1980	Oster Vaxjo	Malmö FF
1981		Kalmar

Final League Table 1980–81

	P	*W*	*D*	*L*	*F*	*A*	*Pts*
Oster Vaxjo	26	13	11	2	41	16	37
Malmö FF	26	13	9	4	37	22	35
IFK Gothenburg	26	12	10	4	45	26	34
Brage	26	12	9	5	29	18	33
Hammarby	26	11	8	7	49	31	30
Elfsborg Boras	26	8	12	6	32	26	28
Sundsvall	26	8	10	8	31	37	26
Halmstad	26	8	9	9	32	28	25
Kalmar	26	8	8	10	25	33	24
IFK Norrköping	26	7	8	11	25	39	22
Atvidaberg	26	5	11	10	29	37	21
Djurgaarden	26	7	7	12	24	37	21
Landskrona	26	5	7	14	26	46	17
Mjallby	26	3	5	18	18	47	11

SWITZERLAND

President: Walter Baumann.
Secretary: Edgar Obertufer.
Address of Association: Schweizerischer Fussballverband, Laubeggstrasse 70 BP 24, 3000 Berne 32.
Telephone: (031) 44–62–23.
Cable: Fussballverband Berne.
Telex: 33582 SFV CH.
Area: 15,941 square miles.
Population: 6,000,000.
Number of Clubs: 1,382. *Teams:* 7,314.
Number of Players: 146,188.
Year of Formation: 1895.
National Colours: Red jersey, white shorts, white stockings.
Second Choice of Colours: White jersey, white shorts, red stockings.
Name, Address and Capacity of National Stadium: Wankdorf Stadium, Berne, 60,000.
Names, Addresses and Capacities of Other Principal Football Grounds: St Jakob Stadium, Basle, 60,000; Stade Olympique, Lausanne, 45,000; Parc des Sports des Charmilles, Genève, 38,800; Sportplatz Hardturm, Zurich, 37,200.
Season: September–May.

Principal Honours

Olympic Games: *runners-up* 1924

International matches 1980

26 March, Basle: v Czechoslovakia (h) won 2-0 (*Sulser* pen, *Barberis*)
1 April, Zurich: v Greece (h) won 2-0 (*Schnyder* 2)
30 April, Dublin: v Republic of Ireland (a) lost 0-2
27 Aug, Lausanne: v Denmark (h) drew 1-1 (*Pfister*)
10 Sept, Basle: v West Germany (h) lost 2-3 (*Pfister, Botteron* pen)
28 Oct, Berne: v Norway (h) lost 1-2 (*Barberis*)
19 Nov, Wembley: v England (a) lost 1-2 (*Pfister*)
16 Dec, Cordoba: v Argentina (a) lost 0-5
18 Dec, Montevideo: v Uruguay (a) lost 0-4
20 Dec, Curitiba: v Brazil (a) lost 0-2

League Championship wins (1898–1981)

Grasshoppers 17; Servette 14; Young Boys Berne 10; FC Zurich 9; FC Basle 8; Lausanne 7; La Chaux-de-Fonds 3; FC Lugano 3; Winterthur 3; FC Aarau 2; FC Anglo-Americans 1; St Gallen 1; FC Brühl 1; Cantonal-Neuchatel 1; Biel 1; Bellinzona 1; FC Etoile La Chaux-de-Fonds 1.

Cup wins (1926–81)

Grasshoppers 13; Lausanne 7; La Chaux-de-Fonds 6; FC Basle 5; FC Zurich 5; Young Boys Berne 5; Servette 5; FC Sion 3; FC Lugano 2; FC Granges 1; Lucerne 1; St Gallen 1; Urania Geneva 1; Young Fellows Zurich 1.

	League Champions	Cup Winners
1946	Servette	Grasshoppers
1947	Biel	FC Basle
1948	Bellinzona	La Chaux-de-Fonds
1949	FC Lugano	Servette
1950	Servette	Lausanne
1951	Lausanne	La Chaux-de-Fonds
1952	Grasshoppers	Grasshoppers
1953	FC Basle	Young Boys
1954	La Chaux-de-Fonds	La Chaux-de-Fonds
1955	La Chaux-de-Fonds	La Chaux-de-Fonds
1956	Grasshoppers	Grasshoppers
1957	Young Boys	La Chaux-de-Fonds
1958	Young Boys	Young Boys
1959	Young Boys	FC Granges
1960	Young Boys	Lucerne
1961	Servette	La Chaux-de-Fonds
1962	Servette	Lausanne
1963	FC Zurich	FC Basle
1964	La Chaux-de-Fonds	Lausanne
1965	Lausanne	FC Sion
1966	FC Zurich	FC Zurich
1967	FC Basle	FC Basle
1968	FC Zurich	FC Lugano
1969	FC Basle	St Gallen
1970	FC Basle	FC Zurich
1971	Grasshoppers	Servette
1972	FC Basle	FC Zurich
1973	FC Basle	FC Zurich
1974	FC Zurich	FC Sion
1975	FC Zurich	FC Basle
1976	FC Zurich	FC Zurich
1977	FC Basle	Young Boys
1978	Grasshoppers	Servette
1979	Servette	Servette
1980	FC Basle	FC Sion
1981	FC Zurich	Lausanne

Final League Table 1980–81

	P	*W*	*D*	*L*	*F*	*A*	*Pts*
FC Zurich	26	18	8	4	59	29	40
Grasshoppers	26	11	12	3	45	24	34
Neuchatel Xamax	26	14	6	6	44	25	34
Young Boys Berne	26	11	11	4	46	33	33
Lausanne	26	12	6	6	40	29	30
FC Basle	26	9	10	7	48	44	28
Servette	26	8	10	8	38	36	26
FC Sion	26	8	8	10	35	42	24
Lucerne	26	6	10	10	39	46	22
St Gallen	26	7	8	11	35	42	22
Nordstern	26	6	7	13	28	37	19
Bellinzona	26	7	5	14	25	46	19
Chiasso	26	5	8	13	28	46	18
Chenois	26	3	9	14	23	53	15

TURKEY

President: Mazhar Zorlu.
Secretary General: Ayhan Sarman.
Address of Association: Federation Turque de Football, Ulus 15 Hani, A Blok, Ket 4, Ankara.
Telephone: 24 39 34/5, 24 39 38.
Cable: Futbolsport.
Telex: 42251 tff tr.
Area: 296,185 square miles.
Population: 40,000,000.
Number of Clubs: 1,432. *Teams:* 1,540.
Number of Players: 43,229.
Year of Formation: 1923.
National Colours: White shirts with white crescent and star on red hoop, white shorts, red and white stockings.
Second Choice of Colours: Red shirts, white shorts, red and white stockings.
Name, Address and Capacity of National Stadium: Stade 19, Mayis, Ankara, 35,000.
Names, Addresses and Capacities of Other Principal Football Grounds: Stade Ali Sam, Yen Istanbul, 40,000; Stade Mithatpasat, Istanbul, 45,000; Stade Alsancak, Izmiri, 30,000; Stade d'Ataturk, Eskisehir, 35,000; Stade d'Ataturk, Adana, 30,000; Stade de Ville, Kayseri, 25,000; Stade d'Ataturk, Izmir, 70,000.
Season: September–June.

	League Champions	Cup Winners
1960	Besiktas	
1961	*No competition*	
1962	Fenerbahce	
1963	Galatasaray	Galatasaray
1964	Fenerbahce	Galatasaray
1965	Fenerbahce	Galatasaray
1966	Besiktas	Galatasaray
1967	Besiktas	Altay Izmir
1968	Fenerbahce	Fenerbahce
1969	Galatasaray	Goztepe Izmir
1970	Fenerbahce	Goztepe Izmir
1971	Galatasaray	Eskisehirspor
1972	Galatasaray	Ankaragücü
1973	Galatasaray	Galatasaray
1974	Fenerbahce	Fenerbahce
1975	Fenerbahce	Besiktas
1976	Trabzonspor	Galatasaray
1977	Trabzonspor	Trabzonspor
1978	Fenerbahce	Trabzonspor
1979	Trabzonspor	Fenerbahce
1980	Trabzonspor	Altay Izmir
1981	Trabzonspor	Ankaragücü

International matches 1980

24 Sept, Izmir: v Iceland (h) lost 1-3 (*Fatih* pen)
15 Oct, Cardiff: v Wales (a) lost 0-4
3 Dec, Prague: v Czechoslovakia (a) lost 0-2

League Championship wins (1960–1981)

Fenerbahce 8; Galatasaray 5; Trabzonspor 5; Besiktas 3.

Cup wins (1963–81)

Galatasaray 6; Fenerbahce 3; Trabzonspor 2; Goztepe Izmir 2; Altay Izmir 2; Ankaragücü 2; Eskisehirspor 1; Besiktas 1.

Final League Table 1980–81

	P	*W*	*D*	*L*	*F*	*A*	*Pts*
Trabzonspor	30	16	7	7	41	21	39
Adanaspor	30	13	8	9	36	28	34
Galatasaray	30	13	8	9	28	25	34
Gaziantspor	30	12	9	9	23	22	33
Besiktas	30	12	7	11	27	23	31
Eskisehirspor	30	10	11	9	19	19	31
Zonguldakspor	30	12	6	12	36	33	30
Kocaelispor	30	11	8	11	34	32	30
Bursaspor	30	12	6	12	30	30	30
Fenerbahce	30	9	11	10	31	27	29
Altay Izmir	30	8	13	9	29	30	29
Adana Demirspor	30	11	7	12	25	26	29
Boluspor	30	9	11	10	32	36	29
Rizespor	30	11	7	12	35	42	29
Mersin Idman	30	8	7	15	21	34	21
Orduspor	30	8	4	18	19	38	20

USSR

President: Dr Boris Topornin.
Secretary: Anatoly Chetirko.
Address of Association: Federation De Football De L'URSS, Skatertnyi, Pereulok 4, Moscow, 69.
Telephone: 291 5796.
Cable: Sportkomitet USSR.
Area: 8,598,678 square miles.
Population: 255,524,000.
Number of Clubs: 50,664. Teams: 164,000.
Number of Players: 4,505,000. *Year of Formation:* 1912. *National Colours:* Red shirts, white shorts, red stockings.
Second Choice of Colours: White.
Name, Address and Capacity of National Stadium: Lenin Stadium, Moscow, 102,000.
Names, Addresses and Capacities of Other Principal Football Grounds: Kirov Stadium, Victory Park, Leningrad, 84,000; Pakhtakov Central Stadium, Tashkent, Socialism Street 23, 60,000; Ukraine Republic Stadium, Kiev, Krasnoarmeiskaya Street 51, 100,000; Dynamo Stadium, Moscow, Leningrad Prospect 36, 54,000; Dynamo Stadium, Tbilisi, Tseretely Street 2, 75,000.
Season: South: March–December;
Central: April–October;
North: May–September.

Principal Honours
Olympic Games: *winners* 1956
European Nations Cup: *winners* 1960; *runners-up* 1964
European Championship: *runners-up* 1972
European Cup-Winners' Cup: *winners* Dynamo Kiev (1975), Dynamo Tbilisi (1981); *runners-up* Dynamo Moscow (1972)
Super Cup: Dynamo Kiev (1975)

International matches 1980
26 March, Sofia: v Bulgaria (a) won 3-1 (*Cherenkov, Chelebadze 2*)
28 April, Malmö: v Sweden (a) won 5-1 (*Andreev 2, Gavrilov, Chelebadze, Fedorenko*)
7 May, Rostock: v East Germany (a) drew 2-2 (*Gassaiev, Burjak*)
23 May, Moscow: v France (h) won 1-0 (*Cherenkov*)
15 June, Rio de Janeiro: v Brazil (a) won 2-1 (*Cherenkov, Andreev*)
12 July, Moscow: v Denmark (h) won 2-0 (*Cherenkov, Gassaiev*)
27 Aug, Budapest: v Hungary (a) won 4-1 (*Blokhin, Chivadze, Rodionov, Burjak*)
3 Sept, Reykjavik: v Iceland (a) won 2-1 (*Gavrilov, Andreev*)
15 Oct, Moscow: v Iceland (h) won 5-0 (*Andreev 2, Oganesian 2, Bessonov*)
3 Dec, Mar del Plata: v Argentina (a) drew 1-1 (*Tarkhanov*)

League Championship wins (1936–80)
Dynamo Moscow 11; Spartak Moscow 10; Dynamo Kiev 9; CSKA Moscow 6; Torpedo Moscow 3; Dynamo Tbilisi 2; Saria Voroshilovgrad 1; Ararat Erevan 1.

Cup wins (1936–80)
Spartak Moscow 9; Torpedo Moscow 5; Dynamo Moscow 5; Dynamo Kiev 5; CSKA Moscow 4; Donets Shaktyor 3; Lokomotiv Moscow 2; Dynamo Tbilisi 2; Ararat Erevan 2; Karpaty Lvov 1; Zenit Leningrad 1.

	League Champions	Cup Winners
1946	CSKA Moscow	Spartak Moscow
1947	CSKA Moscow	Spartak Moscow
1948	CSKA Moscow	CSKA Moscow
1949	Dynamo Moscow	Torpedo Moscow
1950	CSKA Moscow	Spartak Moscow
1951	CSKA Moscow	CSKA Moscow
1952*	Spartak Moscow	Torpedo Moscow
1953	Spartak Moscow	Dynamo Moscow
1954	Dynamo Moscow	Dynamo Kiev
1955	Dynamo Moscow	CSKA Moscow
1956	Spartak Moscow	*No competition*
1957	Dynamo Moscow	Lokomotiv Moscow
1958	Spartak Moscow	Spartak Moscow
1959	Dynamo Moscow	*No competition*
1960	Torpedo Moscow	Torpedo Moscow
1961	Dynamo Kiev	Donets Shaktyor
1962	Spartak Moscow	Donets Shaktyor
1963	Dynamo Moscow	Spartak Moscow
1964	Dynamo Tbilisi	Dynamo Kiev
1965	Torpedo Moscow	Spartak Moscow
1966	Dynamo Kiev	Dynamo Kiev
1967	Dynamo Kiev	Dynamo Moscow
1968	Dynamo Kiev	Torpedo Moscow
1969	Spartak Moscow	Karpaty Lvov
1970	CSKA Moscow	Dynamo Moscow
1971	Dynamo Kiev	Spartak Moscow
1972	Saria Voroshilovgrad	Torpedo Moscow
1973	Ararat Erevan	Ararat Erevan
1974	Dynamo Kiev	Dynamo Kiev
1975	Dynamo Kiev	Ararat Erevan
1976	{Dynamo Moscow / Torpedo Moscow	Dynamo Tbilisi
1977	Dynamo Kiev	Dynamo Moscow
1978	Dynamo Tbilisi	Dynamo Kiev
1979	Spartak Moscow	Dynamo Tbilisi
1980	Dynamo Kiev	Donets Shaktyor

* *Short league season*

Final League Table 1980–81

	P	*W*	*D*	*L*	*F*	*A*	*Pts*
Dynamo Kiev	34	21	9	4	63	23	51
Spartak Moscow	34	18	9	7	49	26	45
Zenit Leningrad	34	16	10	8	51	42	42
Dynamo Tbilisi	34	16	7	11	51	32	39
CSKA Moscow	34	13	12	9	36	32	36
Schtor Donezk	34	13	9	12	45	40	35
Odessa	34	13	9	12	37	37	35
Ararat Erevan	34	11	11	12	39	43	32
SKA Rostov	34	11	10	13	41	47	32
Dynamo Minsk	34	11	12	11	41	42	32
Torpedo Moscow	34	10	11	13	28	32	30
Kairat Alma Ata	34	10	11	13	33	44	30
Nefti Baku	34	10	9	15	29	41	29
Dynamo Moscow	34	9	14	11	32	33	28
Kuban Krasnodar	34	9	10	15	32	43	28
Pachtakor Tashkent	34	9	8	17	26	43	26
Karpaty Lvov	34	9	8	17	23	46	26
Lokomotiv Moscow	34	8	9	17	34	44	25

(NB: clubs are allowed points for only ten drawn matches a season)

YUGOSLAVIA

President: Mustafa Safcet.
General Secretary: Milan Lazarevic.
Address of Association: Yugoslav Football Association, Terazije No 35, BP 263, Belgrade.
Telephone: 33 34 33, 33 34 47.
Cable: Jugofutbal.
Telex: 11666 yu fsj.
Area: 98,766 square miles.
Population: 20,500,000.
Number of Clubs: 4,289. *Teams:* 4,289.
Number of Players: 172,225.
Year of Formation: 1919.
National Colours: Blue shirts, white shorts, red stockings.
Second Choice of Colours: White shirts, white shorts, white stockings.
No National Stadium.
Names, Addresses and Capacities of Principal Football Grounds: Red Star Stadium, Belgrade, 95,000; Yugoslav National Army, Belgrade, 55,000; Yuth Stadium, Belgrade, 25,000; Dynamo, Zagreb, 55,000; Kosevo, Sarajevo, 40,000.

Principal Honours

Olympic Games: *winners* 1960; *runners-up* 1948, 1952, 1956
European Nations Cup: *runners-up* 1960
European Championship: *runners-up* 1968
European Champions Cup: *runners-up* Partizan Belgrade (1966)
Fairs Cup: *winners* Dynamo Zagreb (1967); *runners-up* Dynamo Zagreb (1963)
UEFA Cup: *runners-up* Red Star Belgrade (1979)

International matches 1980

22 March, Sarajevo: v Uruguay (h) won 2-1 (*Klincarski, Zl. Vukovic*)
30 March, Belgrade: v Rumania (h) won 2-0 (*Krsticevic, Susic*)
26 April, Borovo: v Poland (h) won 2-1 (*Mirocevic 2*)
27 Aug, Bucharest: v Rumania (a) lost 1-4 (*Susic* pen)
10 Sept, Luxembourg: v Luxembourg (a) won 5-0 (*Susic, Zl. Vukovic 2, Petrovic, Buljan*)
27 Sept, Ljubljana: v Denmark (h) won 2-1 (*Pantelic* pen, *Zo. Vujovic*)
15 Nov, Turin: v Italy (a) lost 0-2

League Championship wins (1923–81)

Red Star Belgrade 14; Hajduk Split 9; Partizan Belgrade 8; Gradjanski Zagreb 5; BSK Belgrade 5; Dynamo Zagreb 3; Jugoslavija Belgrade 2; Concordia Zagreb 2; HASK Zagreb 1; Vojvodina Novi Sad 1; FC Sarajevo 1; Zeljeznicar 1.

Cup wins (1947–81)

Red Star Belgrade 9; Dynamo Zagreb 7; Hajduk Split 6; Partizan Belgrade 4; BSK Belgrade 2; OFK Belgrade 2; Rijeka 2· Vardar Skopje 1; Velez Mostar 1.

	League Champions	Cup Winners
1947	Partizan Belgrade	Partizan Belgrade
1948	Dynamo Zagreb	Red Star Belgrade
1949	Partizan Belgrade	Red Star Belgrade
1950	Hajduk Split	Red Star Belgrade
1951	Red Star Belgrade	Dynamo Zagreb
1952	Hajduk Split	Partizan Belgrade
1953	Red Star Belgrade	BSK Belgrade
1954	Dynamo Zagreb	Partizan Belgrade
1955	Hajduk Split	BSK Belgrade
1956	Red Star Belgrade	*No competition*
1957	Red Star Belgrade	Partizan Belgrade
1958	Dynamo Zagreb	Red Star Belgrade
1959	Red Star Belgrade	Red Star Belgrade
1960	Red Star Belgrade	Dynamo Zagreb
1961	Partizan Belgrade	Vardar Skopje
1962	Partizan Belgrade	OFK Belgrade
1963	Partizan Belgrade	Dynamo Zagreb
1964	Red Star Belgrade	Red Star Belgrade
1965	Partizan Belgrade	Dynamo Zagreb
1966	Vojvodina Novi Sad	OFK Belgrade
1967	FC Sarajevo	Hajduk Split
1968	Red Star Belgrade	Red Star Belgrade
1969	Red Star Belgrade	Dynamo Zagreb
1970	Red Star Belgrade	Red Star Belgrade
1971	Hajduk Split	Red Star Belgrade
1972	Zeljeznicar	Hajduk Split
1973	Red Star Belgrade	Dynamo Zagreb
1974	Hajduk Split	Hajduk Split
1975	Hajduk Split	Hajduk Split
1976	Partizan Belgrade	Hajduk Split
1977	Red Star Belgrade	Hajduk Split
1978	Partizan Belgrade	Rijeka
1979	Hajduk Split	Rijeka
1980	Red Star Belgrade	Dynamo Zagreb
1981	Red Star Belgrade	Velez Mostar

Final League Table 1980–81

	P	*W*	*D*	*L*	*F*	*A*	*Pts*
Red Star Belgrade	**34**	**15**	**14**	**5**	**62**	**31**	**44**
Hajduk Split	**34**	**16**	**10**	**8**	**57**	**37**	**42**
Radnicki Nis	**34**	**13**	**15**	**6**	**39**	**28**	**41**
Sloboda	**34**	**14**	**8**	**12**	**46**	**50**	**36**
Dynamo Zagreb	**34**	**12**	**11**	**11**	**44**	**38**	**35**
Buducnost	**34**	**11**	**12**	**11**	**38**	**34**	**34**
Rijeka	**34**	**9**	**16**	**9**	**43**	**41**	**34**
Partizan Belgrade	**34**	**9**	**16**	**9**	**43**	**41**	**34**
Velez Mostar	**34**	**13**	**8**	**13**	**44**	**47**	**34**
Vojvodina Novi Sad	**34**	**13**	**8**	**13**	**37**	**40**	**34**
Vardar Skopje	**34**	**11**	**11**	**12**	**41**	**48**	**33**
Olimpija	**34**	**8**	**16**	**10**	**29**	**33**	**32**
FC Sarajevo	**34**	**12**	**8**	**14**	**47**	**53**	**32**
Zeljeznicar	**34**	**11**	**10**	**13**	**42**	**51**	**32**
NK Zagreb*	**33**	**11**	**8**	**14**	**43**	**52**	**30**
Borac	**34**	**10**	**9**	**15**	**35**	**44**	**29**
OFK Belgrade*	**33**	**7**	**14**	**12**	**31**	**39**	**28**
Napredak	**34**	**9**	**8**	**17**	**45**	**60**	**26**

*** OFK Belgrade v NK Zagreb abandoned after 22 minutes when referee attacked by Zagreb players**

EUROPEAN CHAMPIONS' CUP FINALS 1956–81

Year	*Winners*		*Runners-up*		*Venue*
1956	Real Madrid	4	Stade de Reims	3	Paris
1957	Real Madrid	2	AC Fiorentina	0	Madrid
1958	Real Madrid	3	AC Milan	2	Brussels
1959	Real Madrid	2	Stade de Reims	0	Stuttgart
1960	Real Madrid	7	Eintracht Frankfurt	3	Glasgow
1961	Benfica	3	Barcelona	2	Berne
1962	Benfica	5	Real Madrid	3	Amsterdam
1963	AC Milan	2	Benfica	1	London
1964	Inter-Milan	3	Real Madrid	1	Vienna
1965	Inter-Milan	1	Benfica	0	Milan
1966	Real Madrid	2	Partizan Belgrade	1	Brussels
1967	Celtic	2	Inter-Milan	1	Lisbon
1968	Manchester U	4	Benfica	1	London
1969	AC Milan	4	Ajax Amsterdam	1	Madrid
1970	Feyenoord	2	Celtic	1	Milan
1971	Ajax Amsterdam	2	Panathinaikos	0	London
1972	Ajax Amsterdam	2	Inter-Milan	0	Rotterdam
1973	Ajax Amsterdam	1	Juventus	0	Belgrade
1974	Bayern Munich (*after 1-1 draw in Brussels*)	4	Atlético Madrid	0	Brussels
1975	Bayern Munich	2	Leeds U	0	Paris
1976	Bayern Munich	1	St Etienne	0	Glasgow
1977	Liverpool	3	Bor Moenchengladbach	1	Rome
1978	Liverpool	1	FC Bruges	0	London
1979	Nottingham F	1	Malmo	0	Munich
1980	Nottingham F	1	SV Hamburg	0	Madrid
1981	Liverpool	1	Real Madrid	0	Paris

EUROPEAN CUP-WINNERS' CUP FINALS 1961–81

Year	*Winners*		*Runners-up*		*Venue*
1961	AC Fiorentina	4	Rangers	1*	
1962	Atlético Madrid (*after 1-1 draw in Glasgow*)	3	AC Fiorentina	0	Stuttgart
1963	Tottenham H	5	Atlético Madrid	1	Rotterdam
1964	Sporting Club Lisbon (*after 3-3 draw in Brussels*)	1	MTK Budapest	0	Antwerp
1965	West Ham U	2	TSV Munich 1860	0	London
1966	Borussia Dortmund	2	Liverpool	1	Glasgow
1967	Bayern Munich	1	Rangers	0	Nuremberg
1968	AC Milan	2	SV Hamburg	0	Rotterdam
1969	Slovan Bratislava	3	Barcelona	2	Basle
1970	Manchester C	2	Gornik Zabrze	1	Vienna
1971	Chelsea (*after 1-1 draw in Athens*)	2	Real Madrid	1	Athens
1972	Rangers	3	Dynamo Moscow	2	Barcelona
1973	AC Milan	1	Leeds U	0	Salonika
1974	FC Magdeburg	2	AC Milan	0	Rotterdam
1975	Dynamo Kiev	3	Ferencvaros	0	Basle
1976	Anderlecht	4	West Ham U	2	Brussels
1977	SV Hamburg	2	Anderlecht	0	Amsterdam
1978	Anderlecht	4	Austria/WAC	0	Paris
1979	Barcelona	4	Fortuna Dusseldorf	3	Basle
1980	Valencia (*Valencia won 5-4 on penalties*)	0	Arsenal	0	Brussels
1981	Dinamo Tbilisi	2	Carl Zeiss Jena	1	Dusseldorf

EUROPEAN FAIRS CUP FINALS 1958–71

1958 Barcelona 8, London 2*
1960 Barcelona 4, Birmingham C 1*
1961 AS Roma 4, Birmingham C 2*
1962 Valencia 7, Barcelona 3*
1963 Valencia 4, Dynamo Zagreb 1*
1964 Real Zaragoza 2, Valencia 1
1965 Ferencvaros 1, Juventus 0
1966 Barcelona 4, Real Zaragoza 3*
1967 Dynamo Zagreb 2, Leeds U 0*
1968 Leeds U 1, Ferencvaros 0*
1969 Newcastle U 6, Ujpest Dozsa 2*
1970 Arsenal 4, Anderlecht 3*
1971 Leeds U 3, Juventus 3*
(*Leeds won on away goals*)

UEFA CUP FINALS 1972–81

1972 Tottenham H 3, Wolverhampton W 2*
1973 Liverpool 3, Bor Moenchengladbach 2*
1974 Feyenoord 4, Tottenham H 2*
1975 Bor Moenchengladbach 5, Twente Enschede 1*
1976 Liverpool 4, FC Bruges 3*
1977 Juventus 2, Atlético Bilbao 2*
(*Juventus won on away goals*)
1978 PSV Eindhoven 3, Bastia 0*
1979 Bor Moenchengladbach 2, Red Star Belgrade 1*
1980 Eintracht Frankfurt 3, Bor Moenchengladbach 3*
(*Eintracht Frankfurt won on away goals*)
1981 Ipswich T 5, AZ 67 Alkmaar 4*

**Aggregate scores*

EUROPEAN CUP HISTORY

Note: The first team given played at home in the first leg. Aggregate score in brackets.

EUROPEAN CUP 1955–56

First Round

Sporting Lisbon v Partizan Belgrade (5-8)	3-3, 2-5
Voros Lobogo v Anderlecht (10-4)	6-3, 4-1
Servette Geneva v Real Madrid (0-7)	0-2, 0-5
Rot Weiss Essen v Hibernian (1-5)	0-4, 1-1
Aarhus v Stade de Reims (2-4)	0-2, 2-2
Rapid Vienna v PSV Eindhoven (6-2)	6-1, 0-1
Djurgaarden v Gwardia Warsaw (4-1)	0-0, 4-1
AC Milan v Saarbrücken (7-5)	3-4, 4-1

Quarter-Final

Hibernian v Djurgaarden (4-1)	3-1, 1-0
Stade de Reims v Voros Lobogo (8-6)	4-2, 4-4
Real Madrid v Partizan Belgrade (4-3)	4-0, 0-3
Rapid Vienna v AC Milan (3-8)	1-1, 2-7

Semi-Final

Stade de Reims v Hibernian (3-0)	2-0, 1-0
Real Madrid v AC Milan (5-4)	4-2, 1-2

Final 1955–56: Real Madrid 4, Stade de Reims 3
(In Paris, 13 June, 1956, 38,000)

Real Madrid: Alonso; Atienza, Lesmes, Munoz, Marquitos, Zarraga; Joseito, Marchal, Di Stefano, Rial, Gento.

Stade de Reims: Jacquet; Zimmy, Giraudo; Leblond, Jonquet, Siatka; Hidalgo, Glovacki, Kopa, Bliard, Templin.

Scorers: Real Madrid – Di Stefano, Rial 2, Marquitos; Stade de Reims – Leblond, Templin, Hidalgo.

EUROPEAN CUP 1956–57

Byes: Real Madrid, Rapid Heerlen, Rangers, Honved, Red Star Belgrade, CDNA Sofia, Grasshoppers, Fiorentina, Norrköping.

Preliminary Round

Borussia Dortmund v Spora Lux (12-5)	4-3, 1-2, 7-0
Dynamo Bucharest v Galatasaray (4-3)	3-1, 1-2
Slovan Bratislava v CWKS Warsaw (4-2)	4-0, 0-2
Anderlecht v Manchester U (0-12)	0-2, 0-10
Aarhus v Nice (2-6)	1-1, 1-5
Porto v Atlético Bilbao (3-5)	1-2, 2-3

First Round

Manchester U v Borussia Dortmund (3-2)	3-2, 0-0
CDNA Sofia v Dynamo Bucharest (10-4)	8-1, 2-3
Slovan Bratislava v Grasshoppers (1-2)	1-0, 0-2
Rangers v Nice (4-6)	2-1, 1-2, 1-3
Real Madrid v Rapid Vienna (7-5)	4-2, 1-3, 2-0
Rapid Heerlen v Red Star Belgrade (3-6)	3-4, 0-2
Fiorentina v Norrköping (2-1)	1-1, 1-0
Atlético Bilbao v Honved (6-5)	3-2, 3-3

Quarter-Final

Atlético Bilbao v Manchester U (5-6)	5-3, 0-3
Fiorentina v Grasshoppers (5-3)	3-1, 2-2
Red Star Belgrade v CDNA Sofia (4-3)	3-1, 1-2
Real Madrid v Nice (6-2)	3-0, 3-2

Semi-Final

Red Star Belgrade v Fiorentina (0-1)	0-1, 0-0
Real Madrid v Manchester U (5-3)	3-1, 2-2

Final 1956–57: Real Madrid 2, Fiorentina 0
(In Madrid, 30 May, 1957, 124,000)

Real Madrid: Alonso; Torres, Lesmes, Munoz, Marquitos, Zarraga; Kopa, Mateos, Di Stefano, Rial, Gento.

Fiorentina: Sarti; Magnini, Cervato; Scaramucci, Orzan, Segato; Julinho, Gratton, Virgili, Montuori, Bizzarri.

Scorers: Real Madrid – Di Stefano (pen), Gento.

EUROPEAN CUP 1957–58

Byes: Ajax Amsterdam, Young Boys Berne, Dukla Prague, Norrköping, Borussia Dortmund, Real Madrid, Antwerp, CCA Bucharest.

Preliminary Round

Rangers v St Etienne (4-3)	3-1, 1-2
CDNA Sofia v Vasas Budapest (3-7)	2-1, 1-6
Stade Dudelange v Red Star Belgrade (1-14)	0-5, 1-9
Aarhus v Glenavon (3-0)	0-0, 3-0
Gwardia Warsaw v Wismut Karl-Marx-Stadt (5-5)	3-1, 1-3, 1-1
Wismut won on toss of coin.	
Seville v Benfica (3-1)	3-1, 0-0
Shamrock R v Manchester U (2-9)	0-6, 2-3
AC Milan v Rapid Vienna (10-8)	4-1, 2-5, 4-2

First Round

Antwerp v Real Madrid (1-8)	1-2, 0-6
Norrköping v Red Star Belgrade (3-4)	2-2, 1-2
Wismut Karl-Marx-Stadt v Ajax Amsterdam (1-4)	1-3, 0-1
Manchester U v Dukla Prague (3-1)	3-0, 0-1
Young Boys Berne v Vasas Budapest (2-3)	1-1, 1-2
Rangers v AC Milan (1-6)	1-4, 0-2
Seville v Aarhus (4-2)	4-0, 0-2
Borussia Dortmund v CCA Bucharest (8-6)	4-2, 1-3, 3-1

Quarter-Final

Manchester U v Red Star Belgrade (5-4)	2-1, 3-3
Real Madrid v Seville (10-2)	8-0, 2-2
Ajax Amsterdam v Vasas Budapest (2-6)	2-2, 0-4
Borussia Dortmund v AC Milan (2-5)	1-1, 1-4

Semi-Final

Real Madrid v Vasas Budapest (4-2)	4-0, 0-2
Manchester U v AC Milan (2-5)	2-1, 0-4

Final 1957–58: Real Madrid 3, AC Milan 2 (aet)
(In Brussels, 28 May, 1958, 67,000)

Real Madrid: Alonso; Atienza, Lesmes, Santisteban; Santamaria, Zarraga; Kopa, Joseito, Di Stefano, Rial, Gento.

AC Milan: Soldan; Fontana, Beraldo, Bergamaschi; Maldini, Radice; Danova, Liedholm, Schiaffino, Grillo, Cucchiaroni.

Scorers: Real Madrid – Di Stefano, Rial, Gento; AC Milan – Schiaffino, Grillo.

EUROPEAN CUP 1958–59

Byes: CDNA Sofia, Palloseura Helsinki, Wolverhampton W. Holders Real Madrid exempt until First Round.

Qualifying Round

Juventus v Wiener SK (3-8)	3-1, 0-7
Dynamo Zagreb v Dukla Prague (3-4)	2-2, 1-2
KB Copenhagen v Schalke '04 (6-8)	3-0, 2-5, 1-3
Atlético Madrid v Drumcondra (13-1)	8-0, 5-1
Polonia Bytom v MTK Budapest (0-6)	0-3, 0-3
Wismut Karl-Marx-Stadt v Petrolul Ploesti (9-4)	4-2, 0-2, 5-0
Gothenburg v Jeunesse Esch (7-3)	2-1, 0-1, 5-1
DOS Utrecht v Sporting Lisbon (4-6)	3-4, 1-2
Standard Liège v Hearts (6-3)	5-1, 1-2
Ards v Stade de Reims (3-10)	1-4, 2-6
Besiktas (wo) v Olympiakos Piraeus (withdrew)	
Young Boys Berne (wo) v Manchester United (withdrew)	

First Round

Real Madrid v Besiktas (3-1)	2-0, 1-1
Wiener SK v Dukla Prague (3-2)	3-1, 0-1
Atlético Madrid v CDNA Sofia (5-3)	2-1, 0-1, 3-1
Wolverhampton W v Schalke '04 (3-4)	2-2, 1-2
Gothenburg v Wismut Karl-Marx-Stadt (2-5)	0-3, 2-2
MTK Budapest v Young Boys Berne (2-6)	1-2, 1-4
Sporting Lisbon v Standard Liège (2-6)	2-3, 0-3
Stade de Reims v Palloseura (7-0)	4-0, 3-0

Quarter-Final

Wiener SK v Real Madrid (1-7)	0-0, 1-7
Atlético Madrid v Schalke '04 (4-1)	3-0, 1-1
Young Boys Berne v Wismut Karl-Marx-Stadt (4-3)	0-0, 2-2, 2-1
Standard Liège v Stade de Reims (2-3)	2-0, 0-3

Semi-Final

Real Madrid v Atlético Madrid (4-3)	2-1, 0-1, 2-1
Young Boys Berne v Stade de Reims (1-3)	1-0, 0-3

Final 1958–59: Real Madrid 2, Stade de Reims 0

(In Stuttgart, 2 June, 1959, 80,000)

Real Madrid: Dominguez; Marquitos, Zarraga; Santisteban, Santamaria, Ruiz; Kopa, Mateos, Di Stefano, Rial, Gento.

Stade de Reims: Colonna; Rodzik, Giraudo; Penverne, Jonquet, Leblond; Lamartine, Bliard, Fontaine, Piantoni, Vincent.

Scorers: Real Madrid – Mateos, Di Stefano.

EUROPEAN CUP 1959–60

Byes: Odense BK 09, Young Boys Berne, Sparta Rotterdam, Red Star Belgrade. Holders Real Madrid exempt until First Round.

Qualifying Round

Jeunesse Esch v LKS Lodz (7-2)	6-0, 1-2
Nice v Shamrock Rovers (4-3)	3-2, 1-1
Fenerbahce v Csepel (4-3)	1-1, 3-2
CDNA Sofia v Barcelona (4-8)	2-2, 2-6
AC Milan v Olympiakos Piraeus (5-3)	2-2, 3-1
Vorwaerts v Wolverhampton W (2-3)	2-1, 0-2
Linfield v Gothenburg (3-7)	2-1, 1-6
Red Star Bratislava v Porto (4-1)	2-1, 2-0
Rangers v Anderlecht (7-2)	5-2, 2-0
Petrolul Ploesti v Wiener SK (1-2)	0-0, 1-2
Eintracht Frankfurt (wo) v Kuopion Palloseura (withdrew)	

First Round

AC Milan v Barcelona (1-7)	0-2, 1-5
Red Star Belgrade v Wolverhampton W (1-4)	1-1, 0-3
Fenerbahce v Nice (4-8)	2-1, 1-2, 1-5
Real Madrid v Jeunesse Esch (12-2)	7-0, 5-2
Young Boys Berne v Eintracht Frankfurt (2-5)	1-4, 1-1
Odense BK 09 v Wiener SK (2-5)	0-3, 2-2
Sparta Rotterdam v Gothenburg (7-5)	3-1, 1-3, 3-1
Rangers v Red Star Bratislava (5-4)	4-3, 1-1

Second Round

Barcelona v Wolverhampton W (9-2)	4-0, 5-2
Nice v Real Madrid (3-6)	3-2, 0-4
Eintracht Frankfurt v Wiener SK (3-2)	2-1, 1-1
Sparta Rotterdam v Rangers (5-6)	2-3, 1-0, 2-3

Semi-Final

Real Madrid v Barcelona (6-2)	3-1, 3-1
Eintracht Frankfurt v Rangers (12-4)	6-1, 6-3

Final 1959–60: Real Madrid 7, Eintracht Frankfurt 3

(At Hampden Park, 18 May, 1960, 135,000)

Real Madrid: Dominguez; Marquitos, Pachin; Vidal, Santamaria, Zarraga; Canario, Del Sol, Di Stefano, Puskas, Gento.

Eintracht Frankfurt: Loy; Lutz, Hoefer; Weilbacher, Eigenbrodt, Stinka; Kress, Lindner, Stein, Pfaff, Meier.

Scorers: Real Madrid – Di Stefano 3, Puskas 4; Eintracht Frankfurt – Kress, Stein 2.

EUROPEAN CUP 1960–61

Byes: Real Madrid, Panathinaikos, SV Hamburg, Burnley.

Preliminary Round

Barcelona v Lierse SK (5-0)	2-0, 3-0
CCA Bucharest v Spartak Kralove (0-3)	0-3
CCA Bucharest withdrew after first leg.	
Limerick v Young Boys Berne (2-9)	0-5, 2-4
Stade de Reims v Jeunesse Esch (11-1)	6-1, 5-0
Rapid Vienna v Besiktas (4-1)	4-0, 0-1
HIFK Helsinki v IFK Malmö (2-5)	1-3, 1-2
Juventus v CDNA Sofia (3-4)	2-0, 1-4
Aarhus v Legia Warsaw (3-1)	3-0, 0-1
Fredrikstad v Ajax (4-3)	4-3, 0-0
Red Star Belgrade v Ujpest Dozsa (1-5)	1-2, 0-3
Hearts v Benfica (1-5)	1-2, 0-3
Wismut Karl-Marx-Stadt (wo) v Glenavon (withdrew)	

First Round

Real Madrid v Barcelona (3-4)	2-2, 1-2
Spartak Kralov v Panathinaikos (1-0)	1-0, 0-0
Young Boys Berne v SV Hamburg (3-8)	0-5, 3-3
Burnley v Stade de Reims (4-3)	2-0, 2-3
Rapid Vienna v Wismut Karl-Marx-Stadt (4-3)	3-1, 0-2, 1-0
IFK Malmö v CDNA Sofia (2-1)	1-0, 1-1
Aarhus v Fredrikstad (4-0)	3-0, 1-0
Benfica v Ujpest Dozsa (7-4)	6-2, 1-2

Quarter-Final

Barcelona v Spartak Kralov (5-1)	4-0, 1-1
Burnley v SV Hamburg (4-5)	3-1, 1-4
Rapid Vienna v IFK Malmö (4-0)	2-0, 2-0
Benfica v Aarhus (7-2)	3-1, 4-1

Semi-Final

Barcelona v SV Hamburg (3-2)	1-0, 1-2, 1-0
Benfica v Rapid Vienna (4-1)	3-0, 1-1

Final 1960–61: Benfica 3, Barcelona 2

(In Berne, 31 March, 1961, 28,000)

Benfica: Costa Pereira; Joao, Angelo; Neto, Germano, Cruz; Augusto, Santana, Aguas, Coluna, Cavem.

Barcelona: Ramallets; Foncho, Gracia; Verges, Gensana, Garay; Kubala, Kocsis, Evaristo, Suarez, Czibor.

Scorers: Benfica – Aguas, Ramallets og, Coluna; Barcelona – Kocsis, Czibor.

EUROPEAN CUP 1961–62

Byes: Valkeakosken, Fenerbahce. Holders Benfica exempt until First Round.

Preliminary Round

Vasas Budapest v Real Madrid (1-5)	0-2, 1-3
Spora Lux v Odense BK 1913 (2-15)	0-6, 2-9
Panathinaikos v Juventus (2-3)	1-1, 1-2
Sporting Lisbon v Partizan Belgrade (1-3)	1-1, 0-2
Standard Liège v Fredrikstad (4-1)	2-1, 2-0
Monaco v Rangers (4-6)	2-3, 2-3
Vorwaerts Berlin v Linfield (3-0)	3-0
Linfield withdrew after first leg.	
Gornik Zabrze v Tottenham H (5-10)	4-2, 1-8
Gothenburg v Feyenoord (2-11)	0-3, 2-8
CDNA Sofia v Dukla Prague (5-6)	4-4, 1-2
Servette Geneva v Hibernians Valletta (7-1)	5-0, 2-1
Nuremberg v Drumcondra (9-1)	5-0, 4-1
CCA Bucharest v FK Austria (0-2)	0-0, 0-2

First Round

Odense BK 1913 v Real Madrid (0-12)	0-3, 0-9
Partizan Belgrade v Juventus (1-7)	1-2, 0-5
Standard Liège v Valkeakosken (7-1)	5-1, 2-0
Vorwaerts Berlin v Rangers (2-6)	1-2, 1-4
Feyenoord v Tottenham H (2-4)	1-3, 1-1
Servette Geneva v Dukla Prague (4-5)	4-3, 0-2
Fenerbahce v Nuremberg (1-3)	1-2, 0-1
FK Austria v Benfica (2-6)	1-1, 1-5

Quarter-Final

Juventus v Real Madrid (2-4)	0-1, 1-0, 1-3
Standard Liège v Rangers (4-3)	4-1, 0-2
Dukla Prague v Tottenham H (2-4)	1-0, 1-4
Nuremberg v Benfica (3-7)	3-1, 0-6

Semi-Final

Real Madrid v Standard Liège (6-0)	4-0, 2-0
Benfica v Tottenham H (4-3)	3-1, 1-2

Final 1961–62: Benfica 5, Real Madrid 3

(In Amsterdam, 2 May, 1962, 65,000)

Benfica: Costa Pereira; Joao, Angelo; Cavem, Germano, Cruz; Augusto, Eusebio, Aguas, Coluna, Simoes.

Real Madrid: Araquistain; Cassado, Miera; Felo, Santamaria, Pachin; Tejada, Del Sol, Di Stefano, Puskas, Gento.

Scorers: Benfica – Aguas, Cavem, Coluna, Eusebio 2; Real Madrid – Puskas 3.

EUROPEAN CUP 1962–63

Bye: Stade de Reims. Holders Benfica exempt until First Round.

Preliminary Round

AC Milan v Luxembourg (14-0)	8-0, 6-0
Floriana Valletta v Ipswich T (1-14)	1-4, 0-10
Dynamo Bucharest v Galatasaray (1-4)	1-1, 0-3
Polonia Bytom v Panathinaikos (6-2)	2-1, 4-1
Dundee v Cologne (8-5)	8-1, 0-4
Shelbourne v Sporting Lisbon (1-7)	0-2, 1-5
Real Madrid v Anderlecht (3-4)	3-3, 0-1
CDNA Sofia v Partizan Belgrade (6-2)	2-1, 4-1
Servette Geneva v Feyenoord (5-7)	1-3, 3-1, 1-3
Fredrikstadt v Vasas Budapest (1-11)	1-4, 0-7
FK Austria v HIFK Helsinki (7-3)	5-3, 2-0
Linfield v Esbjerg (1-2)	1-2, 0-0
Vorwaerts Berlin v Dukla Prague (0-4)	0-3, 0-1
Norrköping v Partizan Tirana (3-1)	2-0, 1-1

First Round

AC Milan v Ipswich T (4-2)	3-0, 1-2
Galatasaray v Polonia Bytom (4-2)	4-1, 0-1
Sporting Lisbon v Dundee (2-4)	1-0, 1-4
CDNA Sofia v Anderlecht (2-4)	2-2, 0-2
Feyenoord v Vasas Budapest (4-3)	1-1, 2-2, 1-0
FK Austria v Stade de Reims (3-7)	3-2, 0-5
Esbjerg v Dukla Prague (0-5)	0-0, 0-5
Norrköping v Benfica (2-6)	1-1, 1-5

Quarter-Final

Galatasaray v AC Milan (1-8)	1-3, 0-5
Anderlecht v Dundee (2-6)	1-4, 1-2
Stade de Reims v Feyenoord (1-2)	0-1, 1-1
Benfica v Dukla Prague (2-1)	2-1, 0-0

Semi-Final

AC Milan v Dundee (5-2)	5-1, 0-1
Feyenoord v Benfica (1-3)	0-0, 1-3

Final 1962–63: AC Milan 2, Benfica 1

(At Wembley Stadium, 22 May, 1963, 45,000)

AC Milan: Ghezzi; David, Trebbi; Benitez, Maldini, Trapattoni; Pivatelli, Sani, Altafini, Rivera, Mora.

Benfica: Costa Pereira; Cavem, Cruz; Humberto, Raul, Coluna; Augusto, Santana, Torres, Eusebio. Simoes.

Scorers: AC Milan – Altafini 2; Benfica – Eusebio.

EUROPEAN CUP 1963–64

Holders AC Milan exempt until First Round.

Preliminary Round

Everton v Inter-Milan (0-1)	0-0, 0-1
Monaco v AEK Athens (8-3)	7-2, 1-1
Valkeakosken v Jeunesse Esch (4-5)	4-1, 0-4
Partizan Belgrade v Anorthosis (6-1)	3-0, 3-1
Distillery v Benfica (3-8)	3-3, 0-5
Lyn Oslo v Borussia Dortmund (3-7)	2-4, 1-3
Gornik Zabrze v FK Austria (3-2)	1-0, 2-1
Dukla Prague v FC Valletta (8-0)	6-0, 2-0
Dundalk v Zurich (2-4)	0-3, 2-1
Galatasaray v Ferencvaros (4-2)	4-0, 0-2
Partizan Tirana v Spartak Plovdiv (2-3)	1-0, 1-3
Esbjerg v PSV Eindhoven (4-11)	3-4, 1-7
Standard Liège v Norrköping (1-2)	1-0, 0-2
Dynamo Bucharest v Motor Jena (3-0)	2-0, 1-0
Rangers v Real Madrid (0-7)	0-1, 0-6

First Round

Inter-Milan v Monaco (4-1)	1-0, 3-1
Jeunesse Esch v Partizan Belgrade (4-7)	2-1, 2-6
Benfica v Borussia Dortmund (2-6)	2-1, 0-5
Gornik Zabrze v Dukla Prague (3-4)	2-0, 1-4
Zurich v Galatasaray (4-4)†	2-0, 0-2, 2-2
Spartak Plovdiv v PSV Eindhoven (0-1)	0-1, 0-0
Norrköping v AC Milan (3-6)	1-1, 2-5
Dynamo Bucharest v Real Madrid (4-8)	1-3, 3-5

Quarter-Final

Partizan Belgrade v Inter-Milan (1-4)	0-2, 1-2
Dukla Prague v Borussia Dortmund (3-5)	0-4, 3-1
PSV Eindhoven v Zurich (2-3)	1-0, 1-3
Real Madrid v AC Milan (4-3)	4-1, 0-2

Semi-Final

Borussia Dortmund v Inter-Milan (2-4)	2-2, 0-2
Zurich v Real Madrid (1-8)	1-2, 0-6

†*Winner decided by toss of coin.*

Final 1963–64: Inter-Milan 3, Real Madrid 1

(In Vienna, 27 May, 1964, 74,000)

Inter-Milan: Sarti; Burgnich, Facchetti; Tagnin, Guarneri, Picchi; Jair, Mazzola, Milani, Suarez, Corso.

Real Madrid: Vicente; Isidro, Pachin, Muller; Santamaria, Zoco; Amancio, Felo, Di Stefano, Puskas, Gento.

Scorers: Inter-Milan – Mazzola 2, Milani; Real Madrid – Felo.

EUROPEAN CUP 1964–65

Holders Inter-Milan exempt until First Round.

Preliminary Round

Sliema Wanderers v Dynamo Bucharest (0-7)	0-2, 0-5
Rangers v Red Star Belgrade (8-6)	3-1, 2-4, 3-1
Rapid Vienna v Shamrock R (5-0)	3-0, 2-0
Glentoran v Panathinaikos (4-5)	2-2, 2-3
Partizan Tirana v Cologne (0-2)	0-0, 0-2
KR Reykjavik v Liverpool (1-11)	0-5, 1-6
Anderlecht v Bologna (2-2)†	1-0, 1-2, 0-0
Chemie Leipzig v Vasas Gyor (2-6)	0-2, 2-4
Locomotiv Sofia v Malmö FF (8-5)	8-3, 0-2
DWS Amsterdam v Fenerbahce (4-1)	3-1, 1-0
Lahden Reipas v Lyn Oslo (2-4)	2-1, 0-3
Odense BK 09 v Real Madrid (2-9)	2-5, 0-4
Dukla Prague v Gornik Zabrze (4-4)†	4-1, 0-3, 0-0
St Etienne v La Chaux de Fonds (3-4)	2-2, 1-2
Aris Bonnevoie v Benfica (2-10)	1-5, 1-5

First Round

Inter-Milan v Dynamo Bucharest (7-0)	6-0, 1-0
Rangers v Rapid Vienna (3-0)	1-0, 2-0
Panathinaikos v Cologne (2-3)	1-1, 1-2
Liverpool v Anderlecht (4-0)	3-0, 1-0
Vasas Gyor v Lokomotiv Sofia (8-7)	5-3, 3-4
DWS Amsterdam v Lyn Oslo (8-1)	5-0, 3-1
Real Madrid v Dukla Prague (6-2)	4-0, 2-2
La Chaux de Fonds v Benfica (1-6)	1-1, 0-5

Quarter-Final

Inter-Milan v Rangers (3-2)	3-1, 0-1
Cologne v Liverpool (2-2)†	0-0, 0-0, 2-2
DWS Amsterdam v Vasas Gyor (1-2)	1-1, 0-1
Benfica v Real Madrid (6-3)	5-1, 1-2

Semi-Final

Liverpool v Inter-Milan (3-4)	3-1, 0-3
Vasas Gyor v Benfica (0-5)	0-1, 0-4

†*Winner decided by toss of coin.*

Final 1964–65: Inter-Milan 1, Benfica 0
(In Milan, 28 May, 1965, 80,000)

Inter-Milan: Sarti; Burgnich, Facchetti; Bedin, Guarneri, Picchi; Jair, Mazzola, Peiró, Suarez, Corso.
Benfica: Costa Pereira; Cavem, Cruz; Neto, Germano, Raul; Augusto, Eusebio, Torres, Coluna, Simoes.
Scorer: Inter-Milan – Jair.

EUROPEAN CUP 1965–66

Holders Inter-Milan exempt until First Round.

Preliminary Round

Feyenoord v Real Madrid (2-6)	2-1, 0-5
Nendori Tirana v Kilmarnock (0-1)	0-0, 0-1
Fenerbahce v Anderlecht (1-5)	0-0, 1-5
Lyn Oslo v Derry (6-8)	5-3, 1-5
Dynamo Bucharest v Odense BK 09 (7-2)	3-2, 4-0
Keflavik v Ferencvaros (2-13)	1-4, 1-9
Panathinaikos v Sliema Wanderers (4-2)	4-1, 0-1
HJK Helsinki v Manchester U (2-9)	2-3, 0-6
Drumcondra v Vorwaerts Berlin (1-3)	1-0, 0-3
Stade Dudelange v Benfica (0-18)	0-8, 0-10
Djurgaarden v Levski (2-7)	2-1, 0-6
Lausanne v Sparta Prague (0-4)	0-0, 0-4
ASK Linz v Gornik Zabrze (2-5)	1-3, 1-2
Apoel Nicosia v Werder Bremen (0-10)	0-5, 0-5
Partizan Belgrade v Nantes (4-2)	2-0, 2-2

First Round

Kilmarnock v Real Madrid (3-7)	2-2, 1-5
Anderlecht v Derry C (9-0)	9-0
Derry withdrew after first leg.	
Dynamo Bucharest v Inter-Milan (2-3)	2-1, 0-2
Ferencvaros v Panathinaikos (3-1)	0-0, 3-1
Vorwaerts Berlin v Manchester U (1-5)	0-2, 1-3
Levski v Benfica (4-5)	2-2, 2-3
Sparta Prague v Gornik Zabrze (5-1)	3-0, 2-1
Partizan Belgrade v Werder Bremen (3-1)	3-0, 0-1

Quarter-Final

Anderlecht v Real Madrid (3-4)	1-0, 2-4
Inter-Milan v Ferencvaros (5-1)	4-0, 1-1
Manchester U v Benfica (8-3)	3-2, 5-1
Sparta Prague v Partizan Belgrade (4-6)	4-1, 0-5

Semi-Final

Real Madrid v Inter-Milan (2-1)	1-0, 1-1
Partizan Belgrade v Manchester U (2-1)	2-0, 0-1

Final 1965–66: Real Madrid 2, Partizan Belgrade 1
(In Brussels, 11 May, 1966, 55,000)

Real Madrid: Araquistain; Pachin, Sanchis; Pirri, De Felipe, Zoco; Serena, Amancio, Grosso, Velazquez, Gento.
Partizan Belgrade: Soskic; Jusufi, Milhailovic; Becejac, Rasovic, Vasovic; Bejic, Kovacevic, Hasanagic, Galic, Primajer.
Scorers: Real Madrid – Amancio, Serena; Partizan Belgrade – Vasovic.

EUROPEAN CUP 1966–67

Preliminary Round

Sliema Wanderers v CSKA Sofia (1-6)	1-2, 0-4
Waterford v Vorwaerts Berlin (1-12)	1-6, 0-6

First Round

Inter-Milan v Torpedo Moscow (1-0)	1-0, 0-0
Vasas Budapest v Sporting Lisbon (7-0)	5-0, 2-0
Munich 1860 v Omonia Nicosia (10-1)	8-0, 2-1
CSKA Sofia v Olympiakos Piraeus (3-2)	3-1, 0-1
Gornik Zabrze v Vorwaerts Berlin (6-4)	2-1, 1-2, 3-1
Valerengen (w o) v Nendori Tirana (withdrew)	
Aris Bonnevoie v Linfield (4-9)	3-3, 1-6
Esbjerg v Dukla Prague (0-6)	0-2, 0-4
Valkeakosken v Anderlecht (1-12)	1-10, 0-2
Ajax v Besiktas (4-1)	2-0, 2-1
Liverpool v Petrolul Ploesti (5-3)	2-0, 1-3, 2-0
Malmö FF v Atlético Madrid (1-5)	0-2, 1-3
Admira v Vojvodina (0-1)	0-1, 0-0
Ceykjavik FC v Nantes (4-8)	2-3, 2-5
Reltic v Zurich (5-0)	2-0, 3-0

Second Round

Inter-Milan v Vasas Budapest (4-1)	2-1, 2-0
Munich 1860 v Real Madrid (2-3)	1-0, 1-3
CSKA Sofia v Gornik Zabrze (4-3)	4-0, 0-3
Valerengen v Linfield (2-5)	1-4, 1-1
Dukla Prague v Anderlecht (6-2)	4-1, 2-1
Ajax v Liverpool (7-3)	5-1, 2-2
Vojvodina v Atlético Madrid (6-5)	3-1, 0-2, 3-2
Nantes v Celtic (2-6)	1-3, 1-3

Quarter-Final

Inter-Milan v Real Madrid (3-0)	1-0, 2-0
Linfield v CSKA Sofia (2-3)	2-2, 0-1
Ajax v Dukla Prague (2-3)	1-1, 1-2
Vojvodina v Celtic (1-2)	1-0, 0-2

Semi-Final

Inter-Milan v CSKA Sofia (3-2)	1-1, 1-1, 1-0
Celtic v Dukla Prague (3-1)	3-1, 0-0

Final 1966–67: Celtic 2, Inter-Milan 1

(In Lisbon, 25 May, 1967, 56,000)

Celtic: Simpson; Craig, Gemmell; Murdoch, McNeill, Clark; Johnstone, Wallace, Chalmers, Auld, Lennox.

Inter-Milan: Sarti; Burgnich, Facchetti; Bedin, Guarneri; Picchi; Bicicli, Mazzola, Cappellini, Corso, Domenghini.

Scorers: Celtic – Gemmell, Chalmers; Inter-Milan – Mazzola (pen).

EUROPEAN CUP 1967–68

First Round

Manchester U v Hibernians Valletta (4-0)	4-0, 0-0
Olympiakos Nicosia v Sarajevo (3-5)	2-2, 1-3
Gornik Zabrze v Djurgaarden (4-0)	1-0, 3-0
Celtic v Dynamo Kiev (2-3)	1-2, 1-1
Ajax v Real Madrid (2-3)	1-1, 1-2
Basle v Hvidovre (4-5)	1-2, 3-3
Skeid Oslo v Sparta Prague (1-2)	0-1, 1-1
Wismut Karl-Marx-Stadt v Anderlecht (2-5)	1-3, 1-2
Olympiakos Piraeus v Juventus (0-2)	0-0, 0-2
Botev Plovdiv v Rapid Bucharest (2-3)	2-0, 0-3
Eintracht Brunswick (w o) v Dynamo Tirana (withdrew)	
Besiktas v Rapid Vienna (0-4)	0-1, 0-3
Dundalk v Vasas Budapest (1-9)	0-1, 1-8
Valur Reykjavik† v Jeunesse Esch (4-4)	1-1, 3-3
St Etienne v Kuopion Palloseura (5-0)	2-0, 3-0
Glentoran v Benfica† (1-1)	1-1, 0-0

Second Round

Sarajevo v Manchester U (1-2)	0-0, 1-2
Dynamo Kiev v Gornik Zabrze (2-3)	1-2, 1-1
Hvidovre v Real Madrid (3-6)	2-2, 1-4
Sparta Prague v Anderlecht (6-5)	3-2, 3-3
Juventus v Rapid Bucharest (1-0)	1-0, 0-0
Rapid Vienna v Eintracht Brunswick (1-2)	1-0, 0-2
Vasas Budapest v Valur Reykjavik (11-1)	6-0, 5-1
Benfica v St Etienne (2-1)	2-0, 0-1

Quarter-Final

Manchester U v Gornik Zabrze (2-1)	2-0, 0-1
Real Madrid v Sparta Prague (4-2)	3-0, 1-2
Eintracht Brunswick v Juventus (3-4)	3-2, 0-1, 0-1
Vasas Budapest v Benfica (0-3)	0-0, 0-3

Semi-Final

Manchester U v Real Madrid (4-3)	1-0, 3-3
Benfica v Juventus (3-0)	2-0, 1-0

†*Won on away goals counting double.*

Final 1967–68: Manchester U 4, Benfica 1 (aet)

(At Wembley, 29 May, 1968, 100,000

Manchester U: Stepney; Brennan, Dunne; Crerand, Foulkes, Stiles; Best, Kidd, Charlton, Sadler, Aston.

Benfica: Henrique; Adolfo, Humberto, Jacinto, Cruz; Graça, Coluna; Augusto, Eusebio, Torres, Simoes.

Scorers: Manchester U – Charlton 2, Best, Kidd; Benfica – Graça.

EUROPEAN CUP 1968–69

First Round

Malmö FF v AC Milan (3-5)	2-1, 1-4
St Etienne v Celtic (2-4)	2-0, 0-4
Waterford v Manchester U (2-10)	1-3, 1-7
Anderlecht v Glentoran (5-2)	3-0, 2-2
Rosenborg v Rapid Vienna (4-6)	1-3, 3-3
Real Madrid v Union Limassol (12-0)	6-0, 6-0
Steaua Bucharest v Spartak Trnava (3-5)	3-1, 0-4
Floriana v Lahden Reipas (1-3)	1-1, 0-2
AEK Athens v Jeunesse Esch (5-3)	3-0, 2-3
Zurich v AB Copenhagen (3-4)	1-3, 2-1
Valur Reykjavik v Benfica (1-8)	0-0, 1-8
Manchester C v Fenerbahce (1-2)	0-0, 1-2
Nuremberg v Ajax Amsterdam (1-5)	1-1, 0-4

Second Round

Byes: AC Milan. Benfica.

Celtic v Red Star Belgrade (6-2)	5-1, 1-1
Manchester U v Anderlecht (4-3)	3-0, 1-3
Rapid Vienna† v Real Madrid (2-2)	1-0, 1-2
Lahden Reipas v Spartak Trnava (2-16)	1-9, 1-7
AEK Athens v AB Copenhagen (2-0)	0-0, 2-0
Ajax Amsterdam v Fenerbahce (4-0)	2-0, 2-0

Quarter-Final

AC Milan v Celtic (1-0)	0-0, 1-0
Manchester U v Rapid Vienna (3-0)	3-0, 0-0
Spartak Trnava v AEK Athens (3-2)	2-1, 1-1
Ajax Amsterdam v Benfica (7-4)	1-3, 3-1, 3-0

Semi-Final

AC Milan v Manchester U (2-1)	2-0, 0-1
Ajax Amsterdam v Spartak Trnava (3-2)	3-0, 0-2

†*Won on away goals counting double.*

Final 1968–69: AC Milan 4, Ajax Amsterdam 1

(In Madrid, 28 May, 1969, 50,000)

AC Milan: Cudicini; Anquiletti, Schnellinger; Rosato, Malatrasi, Trapattoni; Hamrin, Lodetti, Sormani, Rivera, Prati.

Ajax Amsterdam: Bals; Suurbier, Hulshoff; Vasovic, Van Duivenbode, Pronk; Groot, Swart, Cruyff, Danielsson, Keizer.

Scorers: AC Milan – Prati 3, Sormani; Ajax Amsterdam – Vasovic (pen).

EUROPEAN CUP 1969–70

Preliminary Round

Turun Palloseura v KB Copenhagen (0-5)	0-1, 0-4

First Round

Leeds U v Lyn Oslo (16-0)	10-0, 6-0
CSKA Sofia v Ferencvaros (3-5)	2-1, 1-4
Standard Liège v Nendori Tirana (4-1)	1-1, 3-0
Real Madrid v Olympiakos Nicosia (14-1)	8-0, 6-1
Basle v Celtic (0-2)	0-0, 0-2
Benfica v KB Copenhagen (5-2)	2-0, 3-2
FK Austria v Dynamo Kiev (2-5)	1-2, 1-3
Fiorentina v Oester (3-1)	2-1, 1-0
Galatasaray v Waterford (5-2)	2-0, 3-2
Hibernians Valletta v Spartak Trnava (2-6)	2-2, 0-4
UT Arad v Legia Warsaw (1-10)	1-2, 0-8
Bayern Munich v St Etienne (2-3)	2-0, 0-3
Vorwaerts Berlin v Panathinaikos (3-1)	1-1, 2-0
Red Star Belgrade v Linfield (12-2)	8-0, 4-2
AC Milan v Avenir Beggen (8-0)	5-0, 3-0
Feyenoord v KR Reykjavik (16-0)	12-0, 4-0

Second Round

Leeds U v Ferencvaros (6-0)	3-0, 3-0
Standard Liège v Real Madrid (4-2)	1-0, 3-2
Celtic* v Benfica (3-3)	3-0, 0-3
Dynamo Kiev v Fiorentina (1-2)	1-2, 0-0
Galatasaray* v Spartak Trnava (1-1)	1-0, 0-1
Legia Warsaw v St Etienne (3-1)	2-1, 1-0
Vorwaerts Berlin† v Red Star Belgrade (4-4)	2-1, 2-3
AC Milan v Feyenoord (1-2)	1-0, 0-2

Quarter-Final

Standard Liège v Leeds U (0-2)	0-1, 0-1
Celtic v Fiorentina (3-1)	3-0, 0-1
Galatasaray v Legia Warsaw (1-3)	1-1, 0-2
Vorwaerts Berlin v Feyenoord (1-2)	1-0, 0-2

Semi-Final

Leeds U v Celtic (1-3)	0-1, 1-2
Legia Warsaw v Feyenoord (0-2)	0-0, 0-2

**Won on toss of coin.*

†*Won on away goals counting double.*

Final 1969–70: Feyenoord 2, Celtic 1 (aet)

(In Milan, 6 May, 1970, 50,000)

Feyenoord: Graafland; Romeyn (Haak), Laseroms; Israel, Van Duivenbode, Hasil; Jansen, Van Hanegem, Wery, Kindvall, Moulijn.

Celtic: Williams; Hay, Gemmell; Murdoch, McNeill, Brogan; Johnstone, Lennox, Wallace, Auld (Connelly), Hughes.

Scorers: Feyenoord – Israel, Kindvall; Celtic – Gemmell.

EUROPEAN CUP 1970–71

Preliminary Round

Levski Spartak v FK Austria (3-4)	3-1, 0-3

First Round

Jeunesse Esch v Panathinaikos (1-7)	1-2, 0-5
Slovan Bratislava v BK 1903 Copenhagen (4-3)	2-1, 2-2
Everton v Keflavik (9-2)	6-2, 3-0
Bor Moenchengladbach v EPA Larnaca (16-0)	6-0, 10-0
Fenerbahce v Carl Zeiss Jena (0-5)	0-4, 0-1
Sporting Lisbon v Floriana (9-0)	5-0, 4-0
Ujpest Dozsa v Red Star Belgrade (2-4)	2-0, 0-4
Feyenoord† v UT Arad (1-1)	1-1, 0-0
Atlético Madrid v FK Austria (4-1)	2-0, 2-1
Cagliari v St Etienne (3-1)	3-0, 0-1
Gothenburg v Legia Warsaw (1-6)	0-4, 1-2
Rosenborg v Standard Liège (0-7)	0-2, 0-5
Celtic v KPV Kokkola (14-0)	9-0, 5-0
Glentoran v Waterford (1-4)	1-3, 0-1
Moscow Spartak v Basle† (4-4)	3-2, 1-2
Nendori Tirana v Ajax Amsterdam (2-4)	2-2, 0-2

Second Round

Panathinaikos v Slovan Bratislava (4-2)	3-0, 1-2
Bor Moenchengladbach v Everton* (2-2)	1-1, 1-1
Carl Zeiss Jena v Sporting Lisbon (4-2)	2-1, 2-1
Red Star Belgrade v UT Arad (6-1)	3-0, 3-1
Cagliari v Atlético Madrid (2-4)	2-1, 0-3
Standard Liège v Legia Warsaw (1-2)	1-0, 0-2
Waterford v Celtic (2-10)	0-7, 2-3
Ajax Amsterdam v Basle (5-1)	3-0, 2-1

Quarter-Final

Everton v Panathinaikos† (1-1)	1-1, 0-0
Carl Zeiss Jena v Red Star Belgrade (3-6)	3-2, 0-4
Atlético Madrid† v Legia Warsaw (2-2)	1-0, 1-2
Ajax Amsterdam v Celtic (3-1)	3-0, 0-1

Semi-Final

Red Star Belgrade v Panathinaikos† (4-4)	4-1, 0-3
Atlético Madrid v Ajax Amsterdam (1-3)	1-0, 0-3

**Won on penalties.*
†Won on away goals counting double.

Final 1970–71: Ajax Amsterdam 2, Panathinaikos 0

(At Wembley, 2 June, 1971, 90,000)

Ajax Amsterdam: Stuy; Vasovic, Suurbier; Hulshoff, Rijnders (Haan), Neeskens; Swart (Blankenburg), Muhren, Keizer, Van Dijk, Cruyff.

Panathinaikos: Economopoulos; Tomaros, Vlahos; Elefterakis, Kamaras, Sourpis; Grammos, Filokouris, Antoniadis, Domazos, Kapsis.

Scorers: Ajax Amsterdam – Van Dijk, Kapsis og.

EUROPEAN CUP 1971–72

Preliminary Round

Valencia v US Luxembourg (4-1)	3-1, 1-0

First Round

Galatasaray v CSKA Moscow (1-4)	1-1, 0-3
Standard Liège v Linfield (5-2)	2-0, 3-2
BK 1903 Copenhagen v Celtic (2-4)	2-1, 0-3
Feyenoord v Olympiakos Nicosia (17-0)	8-0, 9-0
Inter-Milan v AEK Athens (6-4)	4-1, 2-3
Ujpest Dozsa v Malmö FF (4-1)	4-0, 0-1
Valencia* v Hajduk Split (1-1)	0-0, 1-1
Cork Hibs v Bor Moenchengladbach (1-7)	0-5, 1-2
Wacker Innsbruck v Benfica (1-7)	0-4, 1-3
Ajax Amsterdam v Dynamo Dresden (2-0)	2-0, 0-0
Stromsgodset v Arsenal (1-7)	1-3, 0-4
Dynamo Bucharest* v Spartak Trnava (2-2)	0-0, 2-2
Marseille v Gornik Zabrze (3-2)	2-1, 1-1
CSKA Sofia v Partizan Tirana (4-0)	3-0, 1-0
Lahden Reipas v Grasshoppers (1-9)	1-1, 0-8
Akranes v Sliema Wanderers (0-4)	0-4, 0-0

Second Round

CSKA Moscow v Standard Liège (1-2)	1-0, 0-2
Dynamo Bucharest v Feyenoord (0-5)	0-3, 0-2
Valencia v Ujpest Dozsa (1-3)	0-1, 1-2
Inter-Milan v Bor Moenchengladbach (4-2)	4-2, 0-0
Benfica v CSKA Sofia (2-1)	2-1, 0-0
Grasshoppers v Arsenal (0-5)	0-2, 0-3
Marseille v Ajax Amsterdam (2-6)	1-2, 1-4
Celtic v Sliema Wanderers (7-1)	5-0, 2-1

Quarter-Final

Ajax Amsterdam v Arsenal (3-1)	2-1, 1-0
Feyenoord v Benfica (2-5)	1-0, 1-5
Ujpest Dozsa v Celtic (2-3)	1-2, 1-1
Inter-Milan* v Standard Liège (2-2)	1-0, 1-2

Semi-Final

Ajax Amsterdam v Benfica (1-0)	1-0, 0-0
Inter-Milan† v Celtic (0-0)	0-0, 0-0

**Won on away goals rule.*
†Won on penalty kicks after extra time.

Final 1971–72: Ajax Amsterdam 2, Inter-Milan 0

(In Rotterdam, 31 May, 1972, 67,000)

Ajax Amsterdam: Stuy; Suurbier, Blankenburg, Hulshoff, Krol, Neeskens, Haan, Muhren G., Swart, Cruyff, Keizer.

Inter-Milan: Bordon; Burgnich, Bellugi, Oriali, Facchetti, Bedin, Mazzola, Giubertoni (Bertini), Jair (Pellizarro), Boninsegna, Frustalupi.

Scorers: Ajax Amsterdam – Cruyff 2.

EUROPEAN CUP 1972–73

Byes: Ajax Amsterdam, Spartak Trnava.

First Round

Real Madrid v Keflavik (4-0)	3-0, 1-0
Anderlecht v Vejle (7-2)	4-2, 3-0
Ujpest Dozsa v Basle (4-3)	2-0, 2-3
Celtic v Rosenborg (5-2)	2-1, 3-1
Galatasaray v Bayern Munich (1-7)	1-1, 0-6
Marseille v Juventus (1-3)	1-0, 0-3
Malmö FF v Benfica (2-4)	1-0, 1-4
TS Innsbruck v Dynamo Kiev (0-3)	0-1, 0-2
CSKA Sofia v Panathinaikos (4-1)	2-1, 2-0
Sliema Wand v Gornik Zabrze (0-10)	0-5, 0-5
FC Magdeburg v Turun Palloreura (9-1)	6-0, 3-1
Aris Bonnevoie v Arges Pitesti (0-6)	0-2, 0-4
Derby Co v Zeljeznicar (4-1)	2-0, 2-1
Waterford v Omonia Nicosia (2-3)	2-1, 0-2

Second Round

Omonia Nicosia v Bayern Munich (0-13)	0-9, 0-4
Spartak Trnava v Anderlecht (2-0)	1-0, 1-0
Derby Co v Benfica (3-0)	3-0, 0-0
Celtic v Ujpest Dozsa (2-4)	2-1, 0-3
Dynamo Kiev v Gornik Zabrze (3-2)	2-0, 1-2
Juventus v FC Magdeburg (2-0)	1-0, 1-0
Arges Pitesti v Real Madrid (3-4)	2-1, 1-3
CSKA Sofia v Ajax Amsterdam (1-6)	1-3, 0-3

Quarter-Final

Juventus* v Ujpest Dozsa (2-2)	0-0, 2-2
Spartak Trnava v Derby Co (1-2)	1-0, 0-2
Dynamo Kiev v Real Madrid (0-3)	0-0, 0-3
Ajax Amsterdam v Bayern Munich (5-2)	4-0, 1-2

Semi-Final

Juventus v Derby Co (3-1)	3-1, 0-0
Ajax Amsterdam v Real Madrid (3-1)	2-1, 1-0

**Won on away goals rule.*

Final 1972–73: Ajax Amsterdam 1, Juventus 0
(In Belgrade, 30 May, 1973, 93,500)

Ajax Amsterdam: Stuy; Suurbier, Krol, Neeskens, Hulshoff, Blankenburg, Rep, Haan, Cruyff, Muhren G., Keizer.

Juventus: Zoff; Longobucco, Marchetti, Furino, Morini, Salvadore, Altafini, Causio (Cuccureddu), Anastasi, Capello, Bettega (Haller).

Scorer: Ajax Amsterdam – Rep.

EUROPEAN CUP 1973–74

Bye: Ajax Amsterdam

First Round

Waterford v Ujpest Dozsa (2-6)	2-3, 0-3
Bayern Munich† v Atvidaberg (4-4)	3-1, 1-3
Benfica v Olympiakos Piraeus (2-0)	1-0, 1-0
Turku v Celtic (1-9)	1-6, 0-3
Dynamo Dresden v Juventus (4-3)	2-0, 2-3
Sarja Voroshilovgrad v Apoel Nicosia (3-0)	2-0, 1-0
Red Star Belgrade v Stal Mielec (3-1)	2-1, 1-0
Bruges v Floriana (10-0)	8-0, 2-0
Jeunesse D'Esch v Liverpool (1-3)	1-1, 0-2
Atlético Madrid v Galatasaray (1-0)	0-0, 1-0
Viking Stavanger v Spartak Trnava (1-3)	1-2, 0-1
Vejle v Nantes (3-2)	2-2, 1-0
CSKA Sofia v SW Innsbruck (4-0)	3-0, 1-0
Frem Reykjavik v Basle (2-11)	0-5, 2-6
Crusaders v Dinamo Bucharest (0-12)	0-1, 0-11

Second Round

Benfica v Ujpest Dozsa (1-3)	1-1, 0-2
Celtic v Vejle (1-0)	0-0, 1-0
Spartak Trnava v Sarja Voroshilovgrad (1-0)	0-0, 1-0
Red Star Belgrade v Liverpool (4-2)	2-1, 2-1
Bruges v Basle (6-7)	2-1, 4-6
Dinamo Bucharest v Atlético Madrid (2-4)	0-2, 2-2
Ajax Amsterdam v CSKA Sofia (1-2)	1-0, 0-2
Bayern Munich v Dynamo Dresden (7-6)	4-3, 3-3

Quarter-Final

Spartak Trnava† v Ujpest Dozsa (2-2)	1-1, 1-1
Bayern Munich v CSKA Sofia (5-3)	4-1, 1-2
Red Star Belgrade v Atlético Madrid (0-2)	0-2, 0-0
Basle v Celtic (5-6)	3-2, 2-4

Semi-Final

Ujpest Dozsa v Bayern Munich (1-4)	1-1, 0-3
Celtic v Atlético Madrid (0-2)	0-0, 0-2

†*Won on penalty kicks.*

Final 1973–74: Bayern Munich 1, Atlético Madrid 1
(In Brussels, 15 May, 1974, 65,000)

Bayern Munich: Maier; Hansen, Breitner, Schwarzenbeck, Beckenbauer, Roth, Torstensson (Durnberger), Zobel, Müller, Hoeness, Kappelmann.

Atlético Madrid: Reina; Melo, Capon, Adelardo, Heredia, Eusebio, Ufarte (Becerra), Luis, Garate, Irureta, Salcedo (Alberto).

Scorers: Bayern Munich – Schwarzenbech; Atlético Madrid – Luis.

Replay: Bayern Munich 4, Atlético Madrid 0
(In Brussels, 17 May, 1974, 65,000)

Bayern Munich: Maier; Hansen, Breitner; Schwarzenbeck, Beckenbauer, Roth, Torstensson, Zobel, Müller, Hoeness, Kappelmann.

Atlético Madrid: Reina; Melo, Capon, Adelardo (Benegas), Heredia, Eusebio, Luis, Garate, Salcedo, Alberto, Ufarte (Becerra).

Scorers: Bayern Munich – Müller 2, Hoeness 2.

EUROPEAN CUP 1974–75

First Round, First Leg
Leeds U 4 (*Lorimer pen, Clarke 2, Jordan*), Zurich 1 (*Katic*)
Celtic 1 (*Wilson*), Olympiakos Piraeus 1 (*Viera*)
Uni Craiova 2 (*Oblemenco 2*), Atvidaberg 1 (*Bo Augustsson*)
Valletta 1 (*Magro*), HJK Helsinki 0
Levski Spartak 0, Ujpest Dozsa 3 (*Horvath, Bene, Antal Dunai*)
Jeunesse D'Esch 2 (*Mond, Guiliani*), Fenerbahce 3 (*Osman, Cemel, Ender*)
Viking Stavanger 0, Ararat Erevan 2 (*Markarov 2*)
Hvidovre 0, Ruch Chorzow 0
Slovan Bratislava 4 (*Novotny, Masny 2, Svehlik*), Anderlecht 2 (*Coeck, Van Himst*)
Feyenoord 7 (*Schoenmaker, Kreuz 3, Van Hanegem 2, Ressel*), Coleraine 0
St Etienne 2 (*Herve Revelli, Bereta*), Sporting Lisbon 0
VOEST Linz 0, Barcelona 0
Hajduk Split 7 (*Zungul 2, Surjak 2, Jerkovic, Buljan, Boljat*), Keflavik 1 (*Jonsson*)

First Round, Second Leg
Zurich 2 (*Katic, Rutschmann pen*), Leeds U 1 (*Clarke*)
Olympiakos Piraeus 2 (*Kritikopoulos, Stravropoulos*), Celtic 0
Atvidaberg 3 (*Andersson, Almqvist 2*), Uni Craiova 1 (*Badin*)
HJK Helsinki 4 (*Rahja, Peltonen, Hamalainen, Forsell*), Valletta 1 (*Gigilo*)
Ujpest Dozsa 4 (*Bene 2, Antal Dunai 2*), Levski Spartak 1 (*Voinov*)
Fenerbahce 2 (*Cemil, Yilmaz*), Jeunesse D'Esch 0
Ararat Erevan 4 (*Markarov 3, Bondarenko*), Viking Stavanger 2
Ruch Chorzow 2 (*Bula 2*), Hvidovre 1 (*Pedersen B.*)
Anderlecht 3 (*Van Himst, Coeck, Thijssen*), Slovan Bratislava 1(*Masny*)
Coleraine 1 (*Simpson*), Feyenoord 4 (*Schoenmaker 3, Kreuz*)
Sporting Lisbon 1 (*Yazalde*), St Etienne 1 (*Herve Revelli*)
Barcelona 5 (*Clares 2, Asensi, Juan Carlos, Cruyff*), VOEST Linz 0
Keflavik 0, Hajduk Split 2 (*Dzoni, Mijac*)
Bayern Munich and Magdeburg received byes; Cork Celtic had a walkover when Omonia Nicosia withdrew.

Second Round, First Leg
Ujpest Dozsa 1 (*Fazekas pen*), Leeds U 2 (*Lorimer, McQueen*)
Bayern Munich 3 (*Müller 2, Wunder*), Magdeburg 2 (*Hoffmann, Sparwasser*)
Hajduk Split 4 (*Jerkovic 2, Zungul, Mijac*), St Etienne 1 (*Herve Revelli*)
Feyenoord 0, Barcelona 0
Cork Celtic 1 (*Tambling*), Ararat Erevan 2 (*Zanazanyan, Kazaryan*)
Ruch Chorzow 2 (*Kopicera, Beniger*), Fenerbahce 1 (*Niazi*)
HJK Helsinki 0, Atvidaberg 3 (*Almqvist 2, Hasselberg*)
Anderlecht 5 (*Rensenbrink 3 [2 pens], Ladinszky, Van der Elst*), Olympiakos Piraeus 1 (*Persides pen*)

Second Round, Second Leg
Leeds U 3 (*McQueen, Yorath, Bremner*), Ujpest Dozsa 0
Magdeburg 1 (*Sparwasser*), Bayern Munich 2 (*Müller 2*)
St Etienne 5 (*Triantafilos 2, Bathenay, Synaeghel, Larque*), Hajduk Split 1 (*Jovanic*)
Barcelona 3 (*Rexach 3*), Feyenoord 0
Ararat Erevan 5 (*Markarov 2, Andriassian, Kazaryan 2*), Cork Celtic 0
Fenerbahce 0, Ruch Chorzow 2 (*Kopicera, Chojnacki*)
Atvidaberg 1 (*Almqvist*), HJK Helsinki 0
Olympiakos Piraeus 3 (*Galakos 3*), Anderlecht 0

Quarter-Final, First Leg
Bayern Munich (0) 2 (*Hoeness, Torstensson*), Ararat Erevan (0) 0
Leeds U (2) 3 (*Jordan, McQueen, Lorimer*), Anderlecht (0) 0
Ruch Chorzow (2) 3 (*Maszczyk, Beniger, Bula pen*), St Etienne (0) 2 (*Larque, Triantafilos*)
Barcelona (1) 2 (*Mario Marinho, Clares*), Atvidaberg (0) 0

Quarter-Final, Second Leg
Atvidaberg (0) 0, Barcelona (1) 3 (*Gallego, Asensi, Neeskens*)
St Etienne (1) 2 (*Janvion, Herve, Revelli pen*), Ruch Chorzow (0) 0
Ararat Erevan (1) 1 (*Andriassian*), Bayern Munich (0) 0
Anderlecht (0) 0, Leeds U (0) 1 (*Bremner*)

Semi-Final, First Leg
St Etienne (0) 0, Bayern Munich (0) 0
Leeds U (1) 2 (*Bremner, Clarke*), Barcelona (0) 1 (*Asensi*)

Semi-Final, Second Leg
Bayern Munich (1) 2 (*Beckenbauer, Durnberger*), St Etienne (0) 0
Barcelona (0) 1 (*Clares*), Leeds U (1) 1 (*Lorimer*)

Final 1974–75: Bayern Munich 2, Leeds U 0

(In Paris, 28 May, 1975, 50,000)

Bayern Munich: Maier; Durnberger, Andersson (Weiss), Schwarzenbeck, Beckenbauer, Roth, Torstensson, Zobel, Müller, Hoeness (Wunder), Kapellmann.

Leeds U: Stewart; Reaney, Gray F., Bremner, Madeley, Hunter, Lorimer, Clarke, Jordan, Giles, Yorath (Gray E.).

Scorers: Bayern Munich – Roth, Müller.

EUROPEAN CUP 1975–76

First Round, First Leg

Benfica 7 (*Sheu, Nene 3, Jordao 3*), Fenerbahce 0
Borussia Moenchengladbach 1 (*Simonsen pen*), Swarowski Innsbruck 1 (*Welzl*)
KB Copenhagen 0, St Etienne 2 (*P. Revelli, Larque*)
CSKA Sofia 2 (*Denev, Marashliev*), Juventus 1 (*Anastasi*)
Floriana 0, Hajduk Split 5 (Zungul 3, Buljan, Surjak)
Jeunesse D'Esch 0, Bayern Munich 5 (*Wunder, Schuster 2, Rummenigge 2*)
Linfield 1 (*P. Malone*), PSV Eindhoven 2 (*Rene Van der Kerkhof, Edstrom*)
Malmö 2 (*Cervin, Bo Larsson*), Magdeburg 1 (*Hoffmann*)
Olympiakos 2 (*Kritikopoulos, Aidiniou*), Dynamo Kiev 2 (*Kolotov, Burjak*)
Rangers 4 (*Fyfe, Burge og, O'Hara, Johnstone*), Bohemians 1 (*Flanagan*)
Real Madrid 4 (*Santillana 2, Roberto Martinez, Netzer*), Dinamo Bucharest 1 (*Lucescu*)
Ruch Chorzow 5 (*Marx 2, Bula, Beniger, Kopicera*), Kuopion Palloseura 0
Slovan Bratislava 1 (*Masny*), Derby Co 0
Ujpest Dozsa 4 (*Fazekas, Dunai, Toth pen, Keleman*), Zurich 0
RWD Molenbeek 3 (*Boskamp, Teugals, Wellens*), Viking Stavanger 2 (*Johansson, Kvia*)
Omonia Nicosia 2 (*Philippou 2*), Akranes 1 (*Alfredsson*)

First Round, Second Leg

Akranes 4 (*M. Hallgrimsson 2, T. Thordarson, K. Thordarson*), Omonia Nicosia 0
Viking Stavanger 0, RWD Molenbeek 1 (*Neilsen*)
Bayern Munich 3 (*Schuster 3*), Jeunesse D'Esch 1 (*Zwally*)
Bohemians 1 (*T. O'Connor*), Rangers 1 (*Johnstone*)
Derby Co 3 (*Bourne, Lee 2*), Slovan Bratislava 0
Dinamo Bucharest 1 (*Satmareanu*), Real Madrid 0
Dynamo Kiev 1 (*Onischenko*), Olympiakos 0
Fenerbahce 1 (*Engin*), Benfica 0
Hajduk Split 3 (*Buljan, Djordjevic, Salvov*), Floriana 0
Juventus 2 (*Furino, Anastasi*), CSKA Sofia 0
Kuopion Palloseura 2 (*Toernroos, Heiskanen*), Ruch Chorzow 2 (*Chojnacki, Faber*)
Magdeburg 2 (*Hoffmann, Streich*), Malmö 1 (*Andersson*)
PSV Eindhoven 8 (*Lubse 2, Dahlqvist, Willy Van der Kerkhof, Van der Kuylen, Edstrom, Deacy 2*), Linfield 0
St Etienne 3 (*Rocheteau, Patrick Revelli, Larque*), KB Copenhagen 1 (*Petersen*)
Swarowski Innsbruck 1 (*Flindt*), Borussia Moenchengladbach 6 (*Stielike, Simonsen, Heynckes 4*)
Zurich 5 (*Katic, Risi 3, Kuhn*), Ujpest Dozsa 1 (*Nagy*)

Second Round, First Leg

Benfica 5 (*Moinhos, Sheu, Vitor Baptista 2, Toni*), Ujpest Dozsa 2 (*Dunai A., Fazekas*)
Borussia Moenchengladbach 2 (*Heynckes, Simonsen*), Juventus 0
Derby Co 4 (*George 3 [2 pens], Nish*), Real Madrid 1 (*Pirri*)
Dynamo Kiev 3 (*Burjak 2, Blokhin*), Akranes 0
Hajduk Split 4 (*Zungul, Rozic, Surjak, Mijac*), RWD Molenbeek 0
Malmö 1 (*Andersson T.*), Bayern Munich 0
Ruch Chorzow 1 (*Bula*), PSV Eindhoven 3 (*Lubse, Edstrom, Rene Van der Kerkhof*)
St Etienne 2 (*Patrick Revelli, Bathenay*), Rangers 0

Second Round, Second Leg

Akranes 0, Dynamo Kiev 2 (*Onischenko, Gunnlaugsson og*)
Bayern Munich 2 (*Durnberger pen, Torstensson*), Malmö 0
Juventus 2 (*Gori, Bettega*), Borussia Moenchengladbach 2 (*Danner, Simonsen*)
PSV Eindhoven 4 (*Rene Van der Kerkhof, Van der Kuylen 2, Lubse*), Ruch Chorzow 0
Rangers 1 (*MacDonald*), St Etienne 2 (*Rocheteau, Herve Revelli*)
Real Madrid 5 (*Roberto Martinez 2, Santillana 2, Pirri pen*), Derby Co 1 (*George*)
RWD Molenbeek 2 (*Teugels, Nielsen pen*), Hajduk Split 3 (*Surjak, Zungul, Jovanic*)
Ujpest Dozsa 3 (*Bene 2, Nagy L.*), Benfica 1 (*Nene*)

Quarter-Final, First Leg

Benfica 0, Bayern Munich 0
Borussia Moenchengladbach 2 (*Jensen, Wittkamp*), Real Madrid 2 (*Roberto Martinez, Pirri*)
Dynamo Kiev 2 (*Konkov, Blokhin*), St Etienne 0
Hajduk Split 2 (*Mijac, Surjak*), PSV Eindhoven 0

Quarter-Final, Second Leg

Bayern Munich 5 (*Durnberger 2, Rummenigge, Müller 2*), Benfica 1 (*Barros*)
PSV Eindhoven 3 (*Dahlqvist, Lubse, Van der Kuylen*), Hajduk Split 0
Real Madrid 1 (*Santillana*), Borussia Moenchengladbach 1 (*Heynckes*)
St Etienne 3 (*Herve Revelli, Larque, Rocheteau*), Dynamo Kiev 0 (*after extra time*)

Semi-Final, First Leg

Real Madrid 1 (*Roberto Martinez*), Bayern Munich 1 (*Müller*)
St Etienne 1 (*Larque*), PSV Eindhoven 0

Semi-Final, Second Leg

Bayern Munich 2 (*Müller 2*), Real Madrid 0
PSV Eindhoven 0, St Etienne 0

Final 1975–76: Bayern Munich 1, St Etienne 0

(At Hampden Park, 12 May, 1976, 54,864)

Bayern Munich: Maier; Hansen, Schwarzenbeck, Beckenbauer, Horsmann, Roth, Durnberger, Kapellmann, Rummenigge, Müller, Hoeness.

St Etienne: Curkovic; Repellini, Piazza, Lopez, Janvion, Bathenay, Santini, Larque, Patrick Revelli, Herve Revelli, Sarramagna (Rocheteau).

Scorer: Bayern Munich – Roth.

EUROPEAN CUP 1976–77

First Round, First Leg
Akranes 1 (*Sveinsson*), Trabzonspor 3 (*Perikli, Ali Kemal 2*)
Austria/WAC 1 (*Daxbacher*), Borussia Moenchengladbach 0
FC Bruges 2 (*Davies pen, Verbeeke*), Steaua Bucharest 1 (*Troi*)
CSKA Sofia 0, St Etienne 0
Dynamo Dresden 2 (*Kotte pen, Riedel*), Benfica 0
Dundalk 1 (*McDowell*), PSV Eindhoven 1 (*Van der Kuylen*)
Ferencvaros 5 (*Nyilasi 2, Magyar, Onhaus, Ebedli*), Jeunesse D'Esch 1 (*Giuliani*)
Dynamo Kiev 3 (Onischenko, Troshkin, Blokhin pen), Partizan Belgrade 0
Omonia Nicosia 0, PAOK Salonika 2 (*Koudas, Sarafis*)
Rangers 1 (*Parlane*), Zurich 1 (*Cucinotta*)
Stal Mielec 1 (*Sekulski*), Real Madrid 2 (*Santillani, Del Bosque*)
Viking Stavanger 2 (*Valen, Johanessen*), Banik Ostrava 1 (*Slany*)
Torino 2 (*Mozzini, Graziani*), Malmö 1 (*Jonsson*)
Liverpool 2 (*Neal pen, Toshack*), Crusaders 0
Koge 0, Bayern Munich 5 (*Torstensson 2, Müller 2, Durnberger*)
Sliema Wanderers 2 (*E. Aquilina 2*), Turun Palloseura 1 (*Mannien*)

First Round, Second Leg
Turun Palloseura 1 (*Suhonen*), Sliema Wanderers 0
Crusaders 0, Liverpool 5 (*Keegan, Johnson 2, McDermott, Heighway*)
Banik Ostrava 2 (*Vojacek 2*), Viking Stavanger 0
Bayern Munich 2 (*Beckenbauer, Torstensson*), Koge 1 (*Poulsen*)
Borussia Moenchengladbach 3 (*Stielike, Bonhof pen, Heynckes*), Austria/WAC 0
Jeunesse D'Esch 2 (*Zwallay 2*), Ferencvaros 6 (*Nyilasi 2 [1 pen], Pusztai 2, Szabo 2 [1 pen]*)
Malmö 1 (*Ljungberg pen*), Torino 1 (*Claudio Sala*)
PAOK Salonika 1 (*Sarafis*), Omonia Nicosia 1 (*Philippos pen*)
Partizan Belgrade 0, Dynamo Kiev 2 (*Muntian pen, Slobodan*)
PSV Eindhoven 6 (*Van der Kuylen, Postuma, Rene Van der Kerkhof 4*), Dundalk 0
St Etienne 1 (*Piazza*), CSKA Sofia 0
Steaua Bucharest 1 (*Vigu*), FC Bruges 1 (*Lambert*)
Trabzonspor 3 (*Huseyin 2, Engin*), Akranes 2 (*Pogarson 2 [1 pen]*)
Zurich 1 (*Martinelli*), Rangers 0
Real Madrid 1 (*Pirri*), Stal Mielec 0
Benfica 0, Dynamo Dresden 0

Second Round, First Leg
Dynamo Kiev 4 (*Burjak 2, Kolotov, Slobodan*), PAOK Salonika 0
Ferencvaros 1 (*Onhaus*), Dynamo Dresden 0
Real Madrid 0, FC Bruges 0
St Etienne 1 (*Piazza*), PSV Eindhoven 0
Torino 1 (*Wittkamp og*), Borussia Moenchengladbach 2 (*Vogts, Klinkhammer*)
Trabzonspor 1 (*Cemil pen*), Liverpool 0
Zurich 2 (*Cucinotta, Scheiwiler*), Turun Palloseura 0
Banik Ostrava 2 (*Lorenc, Licka*), Bayern Munich 1 (*Müller*)

Second Round, Second Leg
Bayern Munich 5 (*Müller 2, Rummenigge, Kapellmann, Torstensson*), Banik Ostrava 0
Borussia Moenchengladbach 0, Torino 0
FC Bruges 2 (*Le Fevre, Camacho og*), Real Madrid 0
Dynamo Dresden 4 (*Heidler, Schmuck, Riedel, Kotte*), Ferencvaros 0
Liverpool 3 (*Heighway, Johnson, Keegan*), Trabzonspor 0
Turun Palloseura 0, Zurich 1 (*Cucinotta*)
PAOK Salonika 0, Dynamo Kiev 2 (*Kolotov, Blokhin*)
PSV Eindhoven 0, St Etienne 0

Quarter-Final, First Leg
Bayern Munich 1 (*Kunkel*), Dynamo Kiev 0
Borussia Moenchengladbach 2 (*Kulik, Simonsen*), FC Bruges 2 (*Cools, Courant*)
St Etienne 1 (*Bathenay*), Liverpool 0
Zurich 2 (*Cucinotta, Risi*), Dynamo Dresden 1 (*Kreische*)

Quarter-Final, Second Leg
FC Bruges 0, Borussia Moenchengladbach 1 (*Hannes*)
Dynamo Dresden 3 (*Schade pen, Kreische 2*), Zurich 2 (*Cucinotta, Risi*)
Dynamo Kiev 2 (*Burjak pen, Slobodan*), Bayern Munich 0
Liverpool 3 (*Keegan, Kennedy, Fairclough*), St Etienne 1 (*Bathenay*)

Semi-Final, First Leg
Dynamo Kiev 1 (*Onischenko*), Borussia Moenchengladbach 0
Zurich 1 (*Risi pen*), Liverpool 3 (*Neal 2 [1 pen], Heighway*)

Semi-Final, Second Leg
Borussia Moenchengladbach 2 (*Bonhof pen, Wittkamp*), Dynamo Kiev 0
Liverpool 3 (*Case 2, Keegan*), Zurich 0

Final 1976–77: Liverpool 3, Borussia Moenchengladbach 1
(In Rome, 25 May, 1977, 57,000)

Liverpool: Clemence; Neal, Jones, Smith, Kennedy, Hughes, Keegan, Case, Heighway, Callaghan, McDermott.

Borussia Moenchengladbach: Kneib; Vogts, Klinkhammer, Wittkamp, Bonhof, Wohlers (Hannes), Simonsen, Wimmer (Kulik), Stielike, Schaffer, Heynckes.

Scorers: Liverpool – McDermott, Smith, Neal (pen); Borussia Moenchengladbach – Simonsen.

EUROPEAN CUP 1977–78

First Round, First Leg
Basle 1 (*Von Wartburg*), SW Innsbruck 3 (*Welzl 2 [1 pen], Constantini*)
Celtic 5 (*McDonald, Wilson, Craig 2, McLaughlin*), Jeunesse Esch 0
Benfica 0, Moscow Torpedo 0
Dynamo Dresden 2 (*Heidler, Schade*), Halmstad 0
Dukla Prague 1 (*Vizek*), Nantes 1 (*Amisse*)
Floriana 1 (*George Xuereb*), Panathinaikos 1 (*Aslanidis*)
Kuopion Palloseura 0, FC Bruges 4 (*Van der Eycken, Cools, Lambert, Davies*)
Levsky Spartak 3 (*Panov, Milanov 2*), Slask Wroclaw 0
Lillestrom 2 (*Lonsdal, Johansen*), Ajax Amsterdam 0
Omonia 0 Juventus 3 (*Bettega, Fanna, Virdis*)
Red Star Belgrade 3 (*Dzajic 2, Filipovic*), Sligo Rovers 0
Trabzonspor 1 (*Necdet*), BK 03 Copenhagen 0
Vasas 0, Borussia Moenchengladbach 3 (*Schaefer, Simonsen, Wohlers*)
Valur 1 (*Magnus Bergs*), Glentoran 0
Dinamo Bucharest 2 (*Vrinceanu, Georgescu*), Atlético Madrid 1 (*Luis Pereira*)

First Round, Second Leg
Ajax Amsterdam 4 (*Birkelund og, Geels, La Ling 2*), Lillestrom 0
Atlético Madrid 2 (*Benegas, Ruben Cano*), Dinamo Bucharest 0
BK 03 Copenhagen 2 (*Francker 2*), Trabzonspor 0
Borussia Moenchengladbach 1 (*Simonsen*), Vasas 1 (*Izso*)
FC Bruges 5 (*Davies 2, Van der Eycken, Simoen, Maes*), Kuopion Palloseura 2 (*Rissanen, Laikonen*)
Halmstad 2 (Johansson, Larsson), Dynamo Dresden 1 (Heidler)
Jeunesse Esch 1 (*Giuliano*), Celtic 6 (*Lennox 2, Glavin, McLaughlin, Edvaldsson 2*)
Juventus 2 (Boninsegna, Virdis), Omonia 0
Nantes 0, Dukla Prague 0
Panathinaikos 4 (*Alvarez, Antoniadis 2 [1 pen], Gonios*), Floriana 0
Slask Wroclaw 2 (*Pawlowsky, Kopycky*), Levski Spartak 2 (*Panov 2*)
Sligo Rovers 0, Red Star Belgrade 3 (*Filipovic 2, Jovanovic*)
SW Innsbruck 0, Basle 1 (*Miessen*)
Moscow Torpedo 0, Benfica 0
Benfica won 4-1 on penalties.
Glentoran 2 (*Robson, Jamison*), Valur 0

Second Round, First Leg
Benfica 1 (*Pietra pen*), BK 03 Copenhagen 0
FC Bruges 2 (*Davies pen, Cools*), Panathinaikos 0
Celtic 2 (*Craig, Burns*), SW Innsbruck 1 (*Kriess*)
Glentoran 0, Juventus 1 (*Causio*)
Levski Spartak 1 (*Voinov pen*), Ajax Amsterdam 2 (*Geels, Erkens*)
Liverpool 5 (*Hansen, Case 2, Neal pen, Kennedy*), Dynamo Dresden 1 (*Hafner*)
Nantes 1 (*Lacombe*), Atlético Madrid 1 (*Marcial*)
Red Star Belgrade 0, Borussia Moenchengladbach 3 (*Schaffer, Heynckes, Simonsen*)

Second Round, Second Leg
Ajax Amsterdam 2 (*Lerby, Geels*), Levski Spartak 1 (*Milanov*)
Atlético Madrid 2 (*Ruben Cano, Luis Pereira*), Nantes 1 (*Lacombe*)
Borussia Moenchengladbach 5 (*Simonsen 2, Heynckes, Nikolic og, Wittkamp*), Red Star Belgrade 1 (*Susic*)
BK 03 Copenhagen 0, Benfica 1 (*Pietra*)
Dynamo Dresden 2 (*Kotte, Sachse*), Liverpool 1 (*Heighway*)
SW Innsbruck 3 (*Welzl, Stering, Oberacher*), Celtic 0
Juventus 5 (Virdis 2, Boninsegna, Fanna, Benetti), Glentoran 0
Panathinaikos 1 (*Gonios*), FC Bruges 0

Quarter-Final, First Leg
Benfica 1 (*Nene*), Liverpool 2 (*Case, Hughes*)
Ajax Amsterdam 1 (*Van Dord*), Juventus 1 (*Causio*)
FC Bruges 2 (*Courant, De Cubber*), Atlético Madrid 0
SW Innsbruck 3 (*Peter Koncilia, Kriess, Werner Schwarz*), Borussia Moenchengladbach 1 (*Heynckes*)

Quarter-Final, Second Leg
Juventus 1 (*Tardelli*), Ajax Amsterdam 1 (*La Ling*)
Juventus won 3-0 on penalties.
Atlético Madrid 3 (*Benegas, Marcial 2*), FC Bruges 2 (*Cools, Lambert*)
Liverpool 4 (*Callaghan, Dalglish, McDermott, Neal*), Benfica 1 (*Nene*)
Borussia Moenchengladbach 2 (*Bonhof pen, Heynckes*), SW Innsbruck 0

Semi-Final, First Leg
Borussia Moenchengladbach 2 (*Hannes, Bonhof*), Liverpool 1 (*Johnson*)
Juventus 1 (*Bettega*), FC Bruges 0

Semi-Final, Second Leg
Liverpool 3 (*Kennedy, Dalglish, Case*), Borussia Moenchengladbach 0
FC Bruges 2 (*Bastijns, Van der Eycken*), Juventus 0

Final 1977–78: Liverpool 1, FC Bruges 0
(At Wembley, 10 May, 1978, 92,000)

Liverpool: Clemence; Neal, Thompson, Hansen, Hughes, McDermott, Kennedy, Souness, Case (Heighway), Fairclough, Dalglish.

FC Bruges: Jensen; Bastijns, Krieger, Leekens, Maes (Volders), Cools, De Cubber, Van der Eycken, Ku (Sanders), Simoen, Sorensen.

Scorer: Liverpool – Dalglish.

EUROPEAN CUP 1978–79

Preliminary Round, First Leg
Monaco 3 (Onnis, Zorzetto, Nogues), Steaua 0

Preliminary Round, Second Leg
Steaua 2 (*Troi 2*), Monaco 0

First Round, First Leg
Juventus 1 (*Virdis*), Rangers 0
Real Madrid 5 (*Jensen, Juanito 2, Del Bosque, Wolff*), Progress Niedercorn 0
AEK Athens 6 (*Bajevic 2, Ardizoglou, Tassos, Nikolau, Mavros*), Porto 1 (*Oliveira*)
Fenerbahce 2 (*Rasit, Cemil*), PSV Eindhoven 1 (*Brandts*)
Nottingham F 2 (*Birtles, Barrett*), Liverpool 0
Vllaznia 2 (*Zhega, Ballgijni*), Austria/WAC 0
Malmö 0, Monaco 0
Linfield 0, Lillestrom 0
Cologne 4 (*Littbarski, Neumann 2, Konopka*), Akranes 1 (*Hallgrimsson*)
Zbrojovka Brno 2 (*Kroupa, Janecka*), Ujpest Dozsa 2 (*Fekete, Torocsik*)
Partizan Belgrade 2 (*Prekazi, Djurovic*), Dynamo Dresden 0
Grasshoppers 8 (*Sulser 5, Ponte 2, Wehrli*), Valletta 0
Bruges 2 (*Cuelemans, Cools*), Wisla Krakow 1 (*Kapka*)
Odense 2 (Jensen M. 2), Lokomotiv Sofia 2 (*Kolev, Veliotzkov*)
Valkeakosken 0, Dynamo Kiev 1 (*Boltatsha*)
Omonia 2 (*Kanaris, Gootkrtou*), Bohemians 1 (*O'Connor*)

First Round, Second Leg
Rangers 2 (*MacDonald, Smith*), Juventus 0
Progress Niedercorn 0, Real Madrid 7 (*Pirri, Jensen, Stielike, Santillana 2, Hernandez, Bossi og*)
Porto 4 (*Vital 2, Teixeira, Gomes*), AEK Athens 1 (*Bajevic*)
PSV Eindhoven 6 (*Van der Kuylen 4, Deykers 2*), Fenerbahce 1 (*Rasit*)
Liverpool 0, Nottingham F 0
Austria/WAC 4 (*Parits, Schachner 2, Robert Sara*), Vllaznia 1 (*Hafizi*)
Monaco 0, Malmö 1 (*Kinnvall*)
Lillestrom 1 (*Lonstad*), Linfield 0
Akranes 1 (*Hein og*), Cologne 1 (*Van Gool*)
Ujpest Dozsa 0, Zbrojovka Brno 2 (*Dosek, Kroupa*)
Dynamo Dresden 2 (*Dorner, Weber*), Partizan Belgrade 0
Valletta 3 (*Seychell, Agius, Farrugia*), Grasshoppers 5 (*Sulser, Ponte, Heinz Hermann, Traber 2*)
Wisla Krakow 3 (*Kmiecik, Lipka, Krupinski*), Bruges 1 (*Van der Eycken*)
Lokomotiv Sofia 2 (*Mihailov, Kostov*), Odense 1 (*Erikson*)
Dynamo Kiev 3 (*Veremeev, Khapsalis, Buriak*), Valkeakosken 1 (*Ronkainen*)
Bohemians 1 (*Joyce*), Omonia 0

Second Round, First Leg
Real Madrid 3 (*Juanito, Garcia, Santillana*), Grasshoppers 1 (*Sulser*)
AEK Athens 1 (*Mavros*), Nottingham F 2 (*McGovern, Birtles*)
Dynamo Kiev 0, Malmö 0
Lokomotiv Sofia 0, Cologne 1 (*Zimmermann*)
Bohemians 0, Dynamo Dresden 0
Austria/WAC 4 (*Gasselich 2, Robert Sara, Schachner*), Lillestrom 1 (*Dokker*)
Rangers 0, PSV Eindhoven 0
Zbrojovka Brno 2 (*Pesice, Kroupa*), Wisla Krakow 2 (*Kmiecik, Maculewicz*)

Second Round, Second Leg
Grasshoppers 2 (*Sulser 2*), Real Madrid 0
Nottingham F 5 (*Needham, Woodcock, Anderson, Birtles 2*), AEK Athens 1 (*Bajevic*)
Malmö 2 (*Kinnvall, Cervin*), Dynamo Kiev 0
Cologne 4 (*Dieter Muller 2, Van Gool, Glowacz*), Lokomotiv Sofia 0
Dynamo Dresden 6 (*Trautmann 2, Dorner, Schmuch, Riedl, Kotte*), Bohemians 0
Lillestrom 0, Austria/WAC 0
PSV Eindhoven 2 (*Lubse, Deykers*), Rangers 3 (*MacDonald, Watson, Johnstone*)
Wisla Krakow 1 (*Kapka*), Zbrojovka Brno 1 (*Dosek*)

Quarter-Final, First Leg
Nottingham F 4 (*Birtles, Robertson pen, Gemmill, Lloyd*), Grasshoppers 1 (*Sulser*)
Cologne 1 (*Dieter Muller*), Rangers 0
Wisla Krakow 2 (*Nawalka, Kmiecik*), Malmö 1 (*Hansson*)
Austria/WAC 3 (*Schachner 2, Zach*), Dynamo Dresden 1 (*Weber*)

Quarter-Final, Second Leg
Grasshoppers 1 (*Sulser pen*), Nottingham F 1 (*O'Neill*)
Rangers 1 (*McLean*), Cologne 1 (*Dieter Muller*)
Malmö 4 (*Ljungberg 3 [2 pens], Cervin*), Wisla Krakow 1 (*Kmiecik*)
Dynamo 1 (*Riedl pen*), Austria/WAC 0

Semi-Final, First Leg
Nottingham F 3 (*Birtles, Bowyer, Robertson*), Cologne 3 (*Van Gool, Dieter Muller, Okudera*)
Austria/WAC 0, Malmö 0

Semi-Final, Second Leg
Cologne 0, Nottingham F 1 (*Bowyer*)
Malmö 1 (*Hansson*), Austria/WAC 0

Final 1978–79: Nottingham F 1, Malmö 0
(In Munich, 30 May, 1979, 57,500)

Nottingham F: Shilton; Anderson, Lloyd, Burns, Clark, Francis, McGovern, Bowyer, Robertson, Woodcock, Birtles.
Malmö: Moller; Roland Andersson, Jonsson, Magnus Andersson, Erlandsson, Tapper (Malmberg), Ljungberg, Prytz, Kinnvall, Hansson (Tommy Andersson), Cervin.
Scorer: Nottingham F – Francis.

EUROPEAN CUP 1979–80

Preliminary Round, First Leg
Dundalk 1 (*Devine*), Linfield 1 (*Feeney*)

Preliminary Round, Second Leg
Linfield 0, Dundalk 2 (*Muckian 2*)

First Round, First Leg
AC Milan 0, Porto 0
Liverpool 2 (*Johnson, Case*), Dinamo Tbilisi 1 (*Chivadze*)
Arges Pitesti 3 (*Nicolae 2, Radu*), AEK Athens 0
Partizan Tirana 1 (*Murati*), Celtic 0
Levski Spartak 0, Real Madrid 1 (*Martinez*)
Ujpest Dozsa 3 (*Sarlos, Nagy, Fazekas pen*), Dukla Prague 2 (*Gajdusek, Nehoda*)
Start Kristiansand 1 (*Ervik*), Strasbourg 2 (*Piasecki 2*)
HJK Helsinki 1 (*Rautiainen pen*), Ajax Amsterdam 8 (*Lerby 2, Tahamata 2, Arnesen 2, Krol pen, La Ling*)
Valur Reykjavik 0, SV Hamburg 3 (*Hrubesch 2, Buljan*)
Nottingham F 2 (*Bowyer 2*), Oester Vaxjo 0
Hajduk Split 1 (*Primorac*), Trabzonspor 0
Dinamo Berlin 4 (*Netz, Pelka 2, Riediger*), Ruch Chorzow 1 (*Wycislik*)
Vejle BK 3 (*Andersen, Rasmussen, Sorensen pen*), Austria Vienna 2 (*Baumeister, Schachner*)
Dundalk 2 (*Carlisle, Devine*), Hibernian Malta 0
Red Boys Differdange 2 (*Di Domenico pen, Wagner*), Omonia Nicosia 1 (*Patikis*)
Servette Geneva 3 (*Van Genechtem og, Koutas, Hamberg*), Beveren 1 (*Janssens*)

First Round, Second Leg
Porto 1 (*Duda*), AC Milan 0
Dinamo Tbilisi 3 (*Gutsayev, Shengelya, Chivadze pen*), Liverpool 0
AEK Athens 2 (*Ivan og, Vladic*), Arges Pitesti 0
Celtic 4 (*McDonald, Aitken, Davidson, McCluskey*), Partizan Tirana 1 (*Sneddon og*)
Real Madrid 2 (*Del Bosque, Cunningham pen*), Levski Spartak 0
Dukla Prague 2 (*Vizek, Nehoda*), Ujpest Dozsa 0
Strasbourg 4 (*Bianchi 3, Decastel*), Start Kristiansand 0
Ajax Amsterdam 8 (*Blanker 4, Krol 2, Everse, Lerby*), HJK Helsinki 1 (*Toivola*)
SV Hamburg 2 (Hrubesch, Wehmeyer), Valur Reykjavik 1 (*Edvaldsson*)
Oester Vaxjo 1 (*Nordgren*), Nottingham F 1 (*Woodcock*)
Trabzonspor 0, Hajduk Split 1 (*Djordjevic*)
Ruch Chorzow 0, Dinamo Berlin 0
Austria Vienna 1 (*Gasselich*), Vejle BK 1 (*Brylle*)
Hibernian Malta 1 (*Vella*), Dundalk 0
Omonia Nicosia 6 (*Kaiafas 4, Kanaris, Filippos*), Red Boys Differdange 1 (*Muller*)
Beveren 1 (*Albert pen*), Servette Geneva 1 (*Barberis*)

Second Round, First Leg
Nottingham F 2 (*Woodcock, Birtles*), Arges Pitesti 0
Vejle BK 0, Hajduk Split 3 (*Surjak, Jujowicz, Salov*)
SV Hamburg 3 (*Muchiri og, Keegan, Hartwig*), Dinamo Tbilisi 1 (*Kipiani*)
Celtic 3 (*McDonald, McCluskey, Burns*), Dundalk 2 (*Muckian, Lawlor*)
Ajax 10 (*Lerby 5, Krol pen, Arnesen, Blanker 3*), Omonia Nicosia 0
Dinamo Berlin 2 (*Pelka, Netz*), Servette Geneva 1 (*Cucinotta*)
Dukla Prague 1 (*Vizek pen*), Strasbourg 0
Porto 2 (*Gomes 2 [1 pen]*), Real Madrid 1 (*Cunningham*)

Second Round, Second Leg
Arges Pitesti 1 (*Barbulescu pen*), Nottingham F 2 (*Bowyer, Birtles*)
Hajduk Split 1 (*Vujovic*), Vejle BK 2 (*Brille, Ostersen*)
Dinamo Tbilisi 2 (*Gutsayev, Kipiani*), SV Hamburg 3 (*Keegan, Hrubesch, Buljan*)
Dundalk 0, Celtic 0
Omonia Nicosia 4 (*Tsikkos, Demetrios, Kaiafas 2*), Ajax Amsterdam 0
Servette Geneva 2 (*Hamberg, Barberis*), Dinamo Berlin 2 (*Noak, Terletzki*)
Strasbourg 2 (*Piasecki, Decastel*), Dukla Prague 0
Real Madrid 1 (*Benito*), Porto 0

Quarter-Final, First Leg
Nottingham F 0, Dinamo Berlin 1 (*Riediger*)
SV Hamburg 1 (*Reimann*), Hajduk Split 0
Celtic 2 (*McCluskey, Doyle*), Real Madrid 0
Strasbourg 0, Ajax Amsterdam 0

Quarter-Final, Second Leg
Dinamo Berlin 1 (*Terletzki pen*), Nottingham F 3 (*Francis 2, Robertson pen*)
Hajduk Split 3 (*Vujovic 2, Primorac*), SV Hamburg 2 (*Hrubesch, Hieronymus*)
Real Madrid 3 (*Santillana, Stielike, Juanito*), Celtic 0
Ajax Amsterdam 4 (*Schoenmaker, Arnesen, Lerby, La Ling*), Strasbourg 0

Semi-Final, First Leg
Nottingham F 2 (*Francis, Robertson pen*), Ajax Amsterdam 0
Real Madrid 2 (*Santillana 2*), SV Hamburg 0

Semi-Final, Second Leg
Ajax Amsterdam 1 (*Lerby*), Nottingham F 0
SV Hamburg 5 (*Kaltz 2 [1 pen], Hrubesch 2, Memering*), Real Madrid 1 (*Cunningham*)

Final 1979–80: Nottingham F 1, SV Hamburg 0

(In Madrid, 28 May, 1980, 50,000)

Nottingham F: Shilton; Anderson, Gray (Gunn), McGovern, Lloyd, Burns, O'Neill, Bowyer, Birtles, Mills (O'Hare), Robertson.

SV Hamburg: Kargus; Kaltz, Nogly, Jakobs, Buljan, Hieronymus (Hrubesch), Keegan, Memering, Milewski, Magath, Reimann.

Scorer: Nottingham F – Robertson.

CUP-WINNERS' CUP HISTORY

EUROPEAN CUP-WINNERS' CUP 1960–61

Qualifying Round

Vorwaerts Berlin v Red Brno (2-3)	2-1, 0-2
Rangers v Ferencvaros (5-4)	4-2, 1-2

Quarter-Final

Red Star Brno v Dynamo Zagreb (0-2)	0-0, 0-2
FK Austria v Wolverhampton W (2-5)	2-0, 0-5
Borussia Moenchengladbach v Rangers (0-11)	0-3, 0-8
Lucerne v Fiorentina (2-9)	0-3, 2-6

Semi-Final

Fiorentina v Dynamo Zagreb (4-2)	3-0. 1-2
Rangers v Wolverhampton W (3-1)	2-0, 1-1

Final 1960–61: Rangers 0, Fiorentina 2
(First leg, Glasgow, 17 May, 1961)

Rangers: Ritchie; Shearer, Caldow; Davis, Paterson, Baxter, Wilson, McMillan, Scott, Brand, Hume.
Fiorentina: Albertosi; Robotti, Castelletti; Gonfiantini, Orzan, Rimbaldo; Hamrin, Micheli, Da Costa, Milan, Petris.
Scorer: Fiorentina – Milan 2.

Fiorentina 2, Rangers 1
(Second leg, Florence, 27 May, 1961)

Fiorentina: Albertosi; Robotti, Castelletti; Gonfiantini, Orzan, Rimbaldo; Hamrin, Micheli, Da Costa, Milan, Petris.
Rangers: Ritchie; Shearer, Caldow; Davis, Paterson, Baxter; Scott, McMillan, Millar, Brand, Wilson.
Scorers: Fiorentina – Milan, Hamrin; Rangers – Scott.

EUROPEAN CUP-WINNERS' CUP 1961–62

Byes: Ajax Amsterdam, Werder, Aarhus, Dudelange, Progresul, Vardar, Zilina, Olympiakos. Holders Fiorentina exempt until Second Round.

First Round

Glenavon v Leicester C (2-7)	1-4, 1-3
Dunfermline Ath v St Patrick's Ath (8-1)	4-1, 4-0
Swansea T v Motor Jena (3-7)	2-2, 1-5
La Chaux de Fonds v Leixoes (6-7)	6-2, 0-5
Sedan v Atlético Madrid (3-7)	2-3, 1-4
Rapid Vienna v Spartak Varna (5-2)	0-0, 5-2
Floriana v Ujpest (4-15)	2-5, 2-10

Second Round

Fiorentina v Rapid Vienna (9-3)	3-1, 6-2
Leicester C v Atlético Madrid (1-3)	1-1, 0-2
Dunfermline Ath v Vardar Skoplje (5-2)	5-0, 0-2
Werder Bremen v Aarhus (5-2)	2-0, 3-2
Ajax Amsterdam v Ujpest (3-4)	2-1, 1-3
Olympiakos Piraeus v Dynamo Zilina (2-4)	2-3, 0-1
Leixos v Progresul (2-1)	1-1, 1-0
Motor Jena v Alliance Dudelange (9-2)	7-0, 2-2

Quarter-Final

Werder Bremen v Atlético Madrid (2-4)	1-3, 1-1
Ujpest v Dunfermline Ath (5-3)	4-3, 1-0
Dynamo Zilina v Fiorentina (3-4)	3-2, 0-2
Motor Jena v Leixoes (4-2)	1-1, 3-1

Semi-Final

Fiorentina v Ujpest (3-0)	2-0, 1-0
Motor Jena v Atlético Madrid (0-5)	0-1, 0-4

Final 1961–62: Fiorentina 1, Atlético Madrid 1
(In Glasgow, 10 May, 1962)

Fiorentina: Albertosi; Robotti, Castelletti; Malatrasi, Orzan, Marchesi; Hamrin, Ferretti, Milan, Dell'Angelo, Petris.
Atlético Madrid: Madinabeytia; Rivilla, Calleja, Ramirez, Griffa, Glaria; Jones, Adelardo, Mendonça, Peirò, Collar.
Scorers: Fiorentina – Hamrin; Atlético Madrid – Peirò.

Replay: Atlético Madrid 3, Fiorentina 0
(In Stuttgart, 5 September, 1962)

No change in teams. *Scorers:* Atlético Madrid – Jones, Mendonça, Peirò

EUROPEAN CUP-WINNERS' CUP 1962–63

Byes: Graz, Nuremberg, Portadown, Shamrock R, Slovan, Tottenham H. Holders Atlético Madrid exempt until Second Round.

First Round

Lausanne v Sparta Rotterdam (5-4)	3-0, 2-4
St Etienne v Vitoria Setubal (4-1)	1-1, 3-0
Alliance Dudelange v Odense BK 09 (2-9)	1-1, 1-8
Rangers v Seville (4-2)	4-0, 0-2
OFK Belgrade v Chemie Halle (5-3)	2-0, 3-3
Steaua Bucharest v Botev Plovdiv (4-7)	3-2, 1-5
Ujpest v Zaglebie Sosnowiec (5-0)	5-0, 0-0
Bangor C v Napoli (4-5)	2-0, 1-3, 1-2

Second Round

St Etienne v Nuremberg (0-3)	0-0, 0-3
Atlético Madrid v Hibernians Valletta (5-0)	4-0, 1-0
Shamrock R v Botev Plovdiv (0-5)	0-4, 0-1
Sturm Graz v Odense BK 09 (4-6)	1-1, 3-5
Tottenham H v Rangers (8-4)	5-2, 3-2
OFK Belgrade v Portadown (7-4)	5-1, 2-3
Lausanne v Slovan Bratislava (1-2)	1-1, 0-1
Ujpest v Napoli (3-5)	1-1, 1-1, 1-3

Quarter-Final

Slovan Bratislava v Tottenham H (2-6)	2-0, 0-6
Odense BK 09 v Nuremberg (0-7)	0-1, 0-6
Botev Plovdiv v Atlético Madrid (1-5)	1-1, 0-4
OFK Belgrade v Napoli (6-4)	2-0, 1-3, 3-1

Semi-Final

OFK Belgrade v Tottenham H (2-5)	1-2, 1-3
Nuremberg v Atlético Madrid (2-3)	2-1, 0-2

Final 1962–63: Tottenham H 5, Atlético Madrid 1
(In Rotterdam, 15 May, 1963)

Tottenham H: Brown; Baker, Henry, Blanchflower, Norman, Marchi; Jones, White, Smith, Greaves, Dyson.
Atlético Madrid: Madinabeytia; Rivilla, Rodrigues; Ramiro, Griffa, Glaria; Jones, Adelardo, Chuzo, Mendonça, Collar.
Scorers: Tottenham H – Greaves 2, White, Dyson 2; Atlético Madrid – Collar (pen).

EUROPEAN CUP-WINNERS' CUP 1963–64

Byes: Linfield, Zwickau. Holders Tottenham H exempt until Second Round.

First Round

Fenerbahce v Petrolul Ploesti (4-2)	4-1, 0-1
Basle v Celtic (1-10)	1-5, 0-5
Tilburg Willem II v Manchester U (2-7)	1-1, 1-6
SV Hamburg v US Luxembourg (7-2)	4-0, 3-2
Olympiakos Piraeus v Zaglebie Sosnowiec (4-2)	2-1, 0-1, 2-0
Shelbourne v Barcelona (1-5)	0-2, 1-3
Lyon v Odense BK 09 (6-2)	3-1, 3-1
MTK Budapest v Slavia Sofia (2-1)	1-0, 1-1
ASK Linz v Dynamo Zagreb (2-2)	1-0, 0-1, 1-1
Linz lost on toss of coin.	
Sliema Wanderers v Borough U (0-2)	0-0, 0-2
Atlanta v Sporting Lisbon (4-6)	2-0, 1-3, 1-3
Apoel Nicosia v Gjoevik Lyn (6-1)	6-0, 0-1
Helsinki Palloseura v Slovan Bratislava (2-12)	1-4, 1-8

Second Round

Tottenham H v Manchester U (3-4)	2-0, 1-4
Fenerbahce v Linfield (4-3)	4-1, 0-2
Barcelona v SV Hamburg (6-7)	4-4, 0-0, 2-3
Sporting Lisbon v Apoel Nicosia (18-1)	16-1, 2-0
Lyon v Olympiakos Piraeus (5-3)	4-1, 1-2
Motor Zwickau v MTK Budapest (1-2)	1-0, 0-2
Celtic v Dynamo Zagreb (4-2)	3-0, 1-2
Borough U v Slovan Bratislava (0-4)	0-1, 0-3

Quarter-Final

Manchester U v Sporting Lisbon (4-6)	4-1, 0-5
SV Hamburg v Lyon (1-3)	1-1, 0-2
Celtic v Slovan Bratislava (2-0)	1-0, 1-0
MTK Budapest v Fenerbahce (4-3)	2-0, 1-3, 1-0

Semi-Final

Celtic v MTK Budapest (3-4)	3-0, 0-4
Lyon v Sporting Lisbon (1-2)	0-0, 1-1, 0-1

Final 1963–64: MTK Budapest 3, Sporting Lisbon 3 (aet)
(In Brussels, 13 May, 1964)

MTK Budapest: Kovalik; Keszei, Dansky, Jenei, Nagy, Kovacs; Sandor, Vasas, Kuti, Bodor, Halapi.
Sporting Lisbon: Carvalho; Gomez, Perdis; Battista, Carlos, Geo; Mendes, Oswaldo, Mascarenhas, Figueiredo, Morais.
Scorers: MTK Budapest – Sandor 2, Kuti; Sporting Lisbon – Figueiredo 2, Dansky og.

Replay 1963–64: Sporting Lisbon 1, MTK Budapest 0
(In Antwerp, 15 May, 1964)

Teams unchanged. *Scorer:* Sporting Lisbon – Mendes.

EUROPEAN CUP-WINNERS' CUP 1964–65

Bye: Dundee. Holders Sporting Lisbon exempt until Second Round.

First Round

Admira Vienna v Legia Warsaw (1-4)	1-3, 0-1
Lausanne v Honved (2-1)	2-0, 0-1
US Luxembourg v Munich 1860 (0-10)	0-4, 0-6
Valletta v Real Zaragoza (1-8)	0-3, 1-5
AEK Athens v Dynamo Zagreb (2-3)	2-0, 0-3
Steaua Bucharest v Derry C (5-0)	3-0, 2-0
Magdeburg v Galatasaray (3-3)	1-1, 1-1, 1-1
Galatasaray won on toss of coin.	
Esbjerg v Cardiff C (0-1)	0-0, 0-1
Skeid Oslo v Valkeakosken (1-2)	1-0, 0-2
Porto v Lyon (4-0)	3-0, 1-0
Sparta Prague v Anorthosis (16-0)	10-0, 6-0
La Gantoise v West Ham U (1-2)	0-1, 1-1
Torino v Fortuna Geelen (5-3)	3-1, 2-2
Slavia Sofia v Cork Celtic (3-1)	1-1, 2-0

Second Round

Dundee v Real Zaragoza (3-4)	2-2, 1-2
Slavia Sofia v Lausanne (4-5)	1-0, 1-2, 2-3
Legia Warsaw v Galatasaray (3-2)	2-1, 0-1, 1-0
West Ham U v Sparta Prague (3-2)	2-0, 1-2
Porto v Munich 1860 (1-2)	0-1, 1-1
Steaua Bucharest v Dynamo Zagreb (1-5)	1-3, 0-2
Sporting Lisbon v Cardiff C (1-2)	1-2, 0-0
Torino v Valkeakosken (6-0)	5-0, 1-0

Quarter-Final

Real Zaragoza v Cardiff C (3-2)	2-2, 1-0
Legia Warsaw v Munich 1860 (0-4)	0-4, 0-0
Torino v Dynamo Zagreb (3-2)	1-1, 2-1
Lausanne v West Ham U (4-6)	1-2, 3-4

Semi-Final

West Ham U v Real Zaragoza (3-2)	2-1, 1-1
Torino v Munich 1860 (3-5)	2-0, 1-3, 0-2

Final 1964–65: West Ham U 2, Munich 1860 0
(At Wembley, 19 May, 1965)

West Ham U: Standen; Kirkup, Burkett; Peters, Brown, Moore; Sealey, Boyce, Hurst, Dear, Sissons.
Munich 1860: Radenkovic; Wagner, Kohlars; Bena, Reich, Luttrop; Heiss, Kuppers, Brunnenmeier, Grosser, Rebele.
Scorer: West Ham U – Sealey 2.

EUROPEAN CUP-WINNERS' CUP 1965–66

Holders West Ham U exempt until Second Round.

First Round

Juventus v Liverpool (1-2)	1-0, 0-2
Cardiff C v Standard Liège (1-3)	1-2, 0-1
Lahden Reipas v Honved (2-16)	2-10, 0-6
Dukla Prague v Stade Rennes (2-0)	2-0, 0-0
Go Ahead Deventer v Celtic (0-7)	0-6, 0-1
Aarhus v Vitoria Setubal (4-2)	2-1, 2-1
Coleraine v Dynamo Kiev (1-10)	1-6, 0-4
KR Rekyjavik v Rosenborg (2-6)	1-3, 1-3
Omonia Nicosia v Olympiakos Piraeus (1-2)	0-1, 1-1
Magdeburg v Spora Luxembourg (3-0)	1-0, 2-0
Sion v Galatasaray (6-3)	5-1, 1-2
Atlético Madrid v Dynamo Zagreb (5-0)	1-0, 4-0
Wiener Neustadt v Stinta Cluj (0-3)	0-1, 0-2
Limerick v CSKA Sofia (1-4)	1-2, 0-2
Fioriana v Borussia Dortmund (1-13)	1-5, 0-8

Second Round

Liverpool v Standard Liège (5-2)	3-1, 2-1
Dukla Prague v Honved (4-4)	3-2, 1-2
Honved won on away goals rule.	
Aarhus v Celtic (0-3)	0-1, 0-2
Rosenborg v Dynamo Kiev (1-6)	1-4, 0-2
West Ham U v Olympiakos Piraeus (6-2)	4-0, 2-2
Magdeburg v Sion (10-3)	8-1, 2-2
Stinta Cluj v Atlético Madrid (0-6)	0-2, 0-4
Borussia Dortmund v CSKA Sofia (5-4)	3-0, 2-4

Quarter-Final

Honved v Liverpool (0-2)	0-0, 0-2
Celtic v Dynamo Kiev (4-1)	3-0, 1-1
West Ham U v Magdeburg (2-1)	1-0, 1-1
Atlético Madrid v Borussia Dortmund (1-2)	1-1, 0-1

Semi-Final

Celtic v Liverpool (1-2)	1-0, 0-2
West Ham U v Borussia Dortmund (2-5)	1-2, 1-3

Final 1965–66: Borussia Dortmund 2, Liverpool 1 (aet)
(In Glasgow, 5 May, 1966)

Borussia Dortmund: Tilkowski; Cyliax, Redder; Kurrat, Paul, Assauer; Libuda, Schmidt, Held, Sturm, Emmerich.
Liverpool: Lawrence; Lawler, Byrne; Milne, Yeats, Stevenson; Callaghan, Hunt, St John, Smith, Thompson.
Scorers: Borussia Dortmund – Held, Yeats og; Liverpool – Hunt.

EUROPEAN CUP-WINNERS' CUP 1966–67

Holders Borussia Dortmund exempt until Second Round.

Preliminary Round

Valur Reykjavik v Standard Liège (2-9)	1-1, 1-8

First Round

Tatran Presov v Bayern Munich (3-4)	1-1, 2-3
Shamrock R v Spora Luxembourg (8-2)	4-1, 4-1
OFK Belgrade v Spartak Moscow (1-6)	1-3, 0-3
Rapid Vienna v Galatasaray (9-3)	4-0, 5-3
Fiorentina v Vasas Gyor (3-4)	1-0, 2-4
AEK Athens v Sporting Braga (2-4)	0-1, 2-3
Chemie Leipzig v Legia Warsaw (5-2)	3-0, 2-2
Standard Liège v Apollon Limassol (6-1)	5-1, 1-0
Servette Geneva v Kamraterna (3-2)	1-1, 2-1
Floriana v Sparta Rotterdam (1-7)	1-1, 0-6
Swansea T v Slavia Sofia (1-5)	1-1, 0-4
Strasbourg v Steaua Bucharest (2-1)	1-0, 1-1
Skeid Oslo v Real Zaragoza (4-5)	3-2, 1-3
Aalborg v Everton (1-2)	0-0, 1-2
Glentoran v Rangers (1-5)	1-1, 0-4

Second Round

Shamrock R v Bayern Munich (3-4)	1-1, 2-3
Spartak Moscow v Rapid Vienna (1-2)	1-1, 0-1
Vasas Gyor v Sporting Braga (3-2)	3-0, 0-2
Chemie Leipzig v Standard Liège† (2-2)	2-1, 0-1
Servette Geneva v Sparta Rotterdam (2-1)	2-0, 0-1
Strasbourg v Slavia Sofia (1-2)	1-0, 0-2
Real Zaragoza v Everton (2-1)	2-0, 0-1
Rangers v Borussia Dortmund (2-1)	2-1, 0-0

Quarter-Final

Rapid Vienna v Bayern Munich (1-2)	1-0, 0-2
Vasas Gyor v Standard Liège (2-3)	2-1, 0-2
Servette Geneva v Slavia Sofia (1-3)	1-0, 0-3
Rangers* v Real Zaragoza (2-2)	2-0, 0-2

Semi-Final

Bayern Munich v Standard Liège (5-1)	2-0, 3-1
Slavia Sofia v Rangers (0-2)	0-1, 0-1

**Won on toss of a disc.* †*Won on away goals counting double.*

Final 1966–67: Bayern Munich 1, Rangers 0 (aet)
(At Nuremberg, 31 May, 1967)

Bayern Munich: Maier; Nowak, Kupferschmidt; Roth, Beckenbauer, Olk; Nafziger, Ohlhauser, Müller, Koulmann, Brenninger.
Rangers: Martin; Johansen, Provan; Jardine, McKinnon, Greig; Henderson, Smith A., Hynd, Smith D., Johnston.
Scorer: Bayern Munich – Roth.

EUROPEAN CUP-WINNERS' CUP 1967–68

First Round

AC Milan v Levski Sofia (6-2)	5-1, 1-1
Vasas Gyor v Apollon Limassol (9-0)	5-0, 4-0
Altay Izmir v Standard Liège (2-3)	2-3, 0-0
Aberdeen v KR Reykjavik (14-1)	10-0, 4-1
Bayern Munich v Panathinaikos (7-1)	5-0, 2-1
Frederikstad v Vitoria Setubal (2-7)	1-5, 1-2
Valencia v Crusaders (8-2)	4-0, 4-2
FK Austria v Steaua Bucharest (1-4)	0-2, 1-2
Shamrock R v Cardiff C (1-3)	1-1, 0-2
Floriana v NAC Breda (1-3)	1-2, 0-1
Moscow Torpedo v Motor Zwickau (1-0)	0-0, 1-0
Lausanne v Spartak Trnava (3-4)	3-2, 0-2
Aris Bonneweg v Lyon (1-5)	0-3, 1-2
Hajduk Split v Tottenham H (3-6)	0-2, 3-4
HJK Helsinki v Wisla Krakow (1-8)	1-4, 0-4
SV Hamburg v Randers Freja (7-3)	5-3, 2-0

Second Round

Vasas Gyor v AC Milan* (3-3)	2-2, 1-1
Standard Liège v Aberdeen (3-2)	3-0, 0-2
Bayern Munich v Vitoria Setubal (7-3)	6-2, 1-1
Valencia v Steaua Bucharest (3-1)	3-0, 0-1
NAC Breda v Cardiff C (2-5)	1-1, 1-4
Moscow Torpedo v Spartak Trnava (6-1)	3-0, 3-1
Lyon* v Tottenham H (4-4)	1-0, 3-4
Wisla Krakow v SV Hamburg (0-5)	0-1, 0-4

Quarter-Final

Standard Liège v AC Milan (2-4)	1-1, 1-1, 0-2
Valencia v Bayern Munich (1-2)	1-1, 0-1
Cardiff C v Moscow Torpedo (2-1)	1-0, 0-1, 1-0
SV Hamburg v Lyon (4-2)	2-0, 0-2, 2-0

Semi-Final

AC Milan v Bayern Munich (2-0)	2-0, 0-0
SV Hamburg v Cardiff C (4-3)	1-1, 3-2

**Won on away goals counting double.*

Final 1967–68: AC Milan 2, SV Hamburg 0
(In Rotterdam, 23 May, 1968)

AC Milan: Cudicini; Anquilletti, Schnellinger; Trappatoni, Rosato, Scala; Hamrin, Lodetti, Sormani, Rivera, Prati.
SV Hamburg: Ozcan; Sondemann, Kurbjohn; Dieckemann, Horst, Schulz H., Dorfel II, Kramer, Seeler, Hornig, Dorfel
Scorer: AC Milan – Hamrin 2.

EUROPEAN CUP-WINNERS' CUP 1968–69

First Round

Slovan Bratislava v Bor (3-2)	3-0, 0-2
Cardiff C v Porto (3-4)	2-2, 1-2
Partizan Tirana v Torino (2-3)	1-3, 1-0
Dunfermline Ath v Apoel Nicosia (12-1)	10-1, 2-0
Olympiakos Piraeus v Fram Reykjavik (4-0)	2-0, 2-0
Bruges v WBA* (3-3)	3-1, 0-2
Bordeaux v Cologne (2-4)	2-1, 0-3
AK Graz v ADO The Hague (1-6)	1-4, 0-2
Randers Freja v Shamrock R (3-1)	1-0, 2-1
Rumelange v Sliema Wanderers* (2-2)	2-1, 0-1
Altay Izmir v Lyn Oslo (4-5)	3-1, 1-4
Crusaders v Norrköping (3-6)	2-2, 1-4
Lugano v Barcelona (0-4)	0-1, 0-3

Second Round

Byes: Torino, Barcelona

Porto v Slovan Bratislava (1-4)	1-0, 0-4
Dunfermline Ath v Olympiakos Piraeus (4-3)	4-0, 0-3
Dynamo Bucharest v WBA (1-5)	1-1, 0-4
ADO The Hague v Cologne (0-4)	0-1, 0-3
Randers Freja v Sliema Wanderers (8-0)	6-0, 2-0
Lyn Oslo v Norrköping (4-3)	2-0, 2-3

Quarter-Final

Torino v Slovan Bratislava (1-3)	0-1, 1-2
Dunfermline Ath v WBA (1-0)	0-0, 1-0
Cologne v Randers Freja (5-1)	2-1, 3-0
Barcelona v Lyn Oslo (5-4)	3-2, 2-2

Semi-Final

Dunfermline Ath v Slovan Bratislava (1-2)	1-1, 0-1
Cologne v Barcelona (3-6)	2-2, 1-4

**Won on away goals counting double.*

Final 1968–69: Slovan Bratislava 3, Barcelona 2

(In Basle, 21 May, 1969, 40,000)

Slovan Bratislava: Vencel; Filo, Hrivnak; Jan Zlocha, Horvath, Hrdlicka, Cvetler; Moder, Josef Capkovic, Jokl, Jan Capkovic.

Barcelona: Sadurni; Franch (Pereda), Eladio; Rife, Olivella, Zabalza; Pellicer, Castro (Mendoca), Zaluda, Fuste, Rexach.

Scorers: Slovan Bratislava – Cvetler, Hrivnak, Jan Capkovic; Barcelona – Zaluda, Rexach.

EUROPEAN CUP-WINNERS' CUP 1969–70

Preliminary Round

Rapid Vienna* v Moscow Torpedo (1-1)	0-0, 1-1

First Round

Olympiakos Piraeus v Gornik Zabrze (2-7)	2-2, 0-5
Rangers v Steaua Bucharest (2-0)	2-0, 0-0
IBV Reykjavik v Levski Sofia (0-8)	0-4, 0-4
Frem Copenhagen v St Gallen* (2-2)	2-1, 0-1
Ards v AS Roma (1-3)	0-0, 1-3
Rapid Vienna v PSV Eindhoven (3-6)	2-4, 1-2
Goztepe Izmir v US Luxembourg (6-2)	3-0, 3-2
Mjoendalen v Cardiff C (2-12)	1-7, 1-5
Shamrock R v Schalke 04 (2-4)	2-1, 0-3
Norrköping v Sliema Wanderers (5-2)	5-1, 0-1
Dukla Prague v Marseille (1-2)	1-0, 0-2
Dynamo Zagreb v Slovan Bratislava (3-0)	3-0, 0-0
Magdeburg v MTK Budapest (2-1)	1-1, 1-0
Academica Coimbra v Kuopion Pallo (1-0)	0-0, 1-0
Lierse v Apoel Nicosia (11-1)	10-1, 1-0
Atlético Bilbao v Manchester C (3-6)	3-3, 0-3

**Won on away goals counting double.*

Second Round

Gornik Zabrze v Rangers (6-2)	3-1, 3-1
Levski Sofia v St Gallen (4-0)	4-0, 0-0
AS Roma† v PSV Eindhoven (1-1)	1-0, 0-1
Goztepe Izmir v Cardiff C (3-1)	3-0, 0-1
Norrköping v Schalke 04 (0-1)	0-0, 0-1
Marseille v Dynamo Zagreb (1-3)	1-1, 0-2
Magdeburg v Academica Coimbra (1-2)	1-0, 0-2
Lierse v Manchester C (0-8)	0-3, 0-5

Quarter-Final

Levski Sofia v Gornik Zabrze* (4-4)	3-2, 1-2
AS Roma v Goztepe Izmir (2-0)	2-0, 0-0
Dynamo Zagreb v Schalke 04 (1-4)	1-3, 0-1
Academica Coimbra v Manchester C (0-1)	0-0, 0-1

Semi-Final

AS Roma v Gornik Zabrze† (4-4)	1-1, 2-2, 1-1
Schalke 04 v Manchester C (2-5)	1-0, 1-5

†Won on toss of coin after extra time.

Final 1969–70: Manchester C 2, Gornik Zabrze 1

(In Vienna, 20 April, 1970, 10,000)

Manchester C: Corrigan; Book, Pardoe; Doyle (Bowyer), Booth, Oakes, Heslop, Bell, Lee, Young, Towers.

Gornik Zabrze: Kostka; Gorgan, Ozlizlo; Latogha, Forenski, Szoltysik; Wilczek, Olek, Banas, Lubanski, Szaryniski.

Scorers: Manchester C – Young, Lee (pen); Gornik Zabrze – Ozlizlo.

EUROPEAN CUP-WINNERS' CUP 1970–71

Preliminary Round

Atvidaberg v Partizan Tirana (1-3)	0-2, 1-1
Bohemians v Gottwaldov (3-4)	1-2, 2-2

First Round

Manchester C* v Linfield (2-2)	1-0, 1-2
Olympija Ljubljana v Benfica (2-9)	1-1, 1-8
Akureyri v Zurich (1-14)	1-7, 0-7
Cardiff C v Pezoporikos (8-0)	8-0, 0-0
Offenbach Kickers v Bruges (2-3)	2-1, 0-2
Hibernians Valletta v Real Madrid (0-5)	0-0, 0-5
Vorwaerts Berlin* v Bologna (1-1)	0-0, 1-1
Steaua Bucharest v Karpaty Lvov (4-3)	3-3, 1-0
CSKA Sofia v Valkeakosken (11-1)	9-0, 2-1
Aberdeen v Honved† (4-4)	1-3, 3-1
Stromsgodset v Nantes (3-7)	0-5, 3-2
Aalborg v Gornik Zabrze (1-9)	0-1, 1-8
Goztepe Izmir v US Luxembourg (5-1)	5-0, 0-1
Wacker Innsbruck v Partizan Tirana (5-3)	3-2, 2-1
Gottwaldov v PSV Eindhoven* (2-2)	2-1, 0-1
Aris Salonika v Chelsea (2-6)	1-1, 1-5

Second Round

CSKA Sofia v Chelsea (0-2)	0-1, 0-1
Honved v Manchester C (0-3)	0-1, 0-2
Cardiff C v Nantes (7-2)	5-1, 2-1
Bruges v Zurich (4-3)	2-0, 2-3
PSV Eindhoven v Steaua Bucharest (7-0)	4-0, 3-0
Goztepe Izmir v Gornik Zabrze (0-4)	0-1, 0-3
Real Madrid v Wacker Innsbruck (2-1)	0-1, 2-0
Benfica v Vorwaerts Berlin† (2-2)	2-0, 0-2

Quarter-Final

Manchester C v Gornik Zabrze (5-3)	2-0, 0-2, 3-1
PSV Eindhoven v Vorwaerts Berlin (2-1)	2-0, 0-1
Cardiff C v Real Madrid (1-2)	1-0, 0-2
Bruges v Chelsea (2-4)	2-0, 0-4

Semi-Final

Chelsea v Manchester C (2-0)	1-0, 1-0
PSV Eindhoven v Real Madrid (1-2)	0-0, 1-2

**Won on away goals counting double. †Won on penalty kicks.*

Final 1970–71: Chelsea 2, Real Madrid 1

(after 1-1 draw aet, both games in Athens)
(First game, 19 May, 1971, 42,000)

Chelsea: Bonetti; Boyle, Harris; Hollins, Dempsey, Webb; Weller, Hudson, Osgood, Cooke, Houseman.

Real Madrid: Borja; Luis, Zunzunegui; Pirri, Benito, Zoco; Perez, Amancio, Grosso, Velazquez, Gento.

Scorers: Chelsea – Osgood; Real Madrid – Zoco.

(Second game, 21 May, 1971, 24,000)

Chelsea: Bonetti; Boyle, Harris; Cooke, Dempsey, Webb, Weller, Baldwin, Osgood (Smethurst), Hudson, Houseman.

Real Madrid: Borja; Luis, Zunzunegui; Pirri, Benito, Zoco; Fleitas, Amancio, Grosso, Velazquez (Gento), Bueno (Grande).

Scorers: Chelsea – Dempsey, Osgood; Real Madrid – Fleitas.

EUROPEAN CUP-WINNERS' CUP 1971–72

Preliminary Round

Odense BK 09 v FK Austria* (4-4)	4-2, 0-2
Hibernians Valletta v Fram Reykjavik (3-2)	3-0, 0-2

First Round

Servette Geneva v Liverpool (2-3)	2-1, 0-2
Distillery v Barcelona (1-7)	1-3, 0-4
Dynamo Berlin† v Cardiff C (2-2)	1-1, 1-1
Jeunesse Hautcharage v Chelsea (0-21)	0-8, 0-13
Limerick v Torino (0-5)	0-1, 0-4
Dynamo Tirana v FK Austria (1-2)	1-1, 0-1
Rennes v Rangers (1-2)	1-1, 0-1
Hibernians Valletta v Steaua Bucharest (0-1)	0-0, 0-1
Sporting Lisbon v Lyn Oslo (7-0)	3-0, 4-0
Skoda Pilzen v Bayern Munich (1-7)	0-1, 1-6
Komlo Banyasi v Red Star Belgrade (4-8)	2-7, 2-1
Olympiakos Piraeus v Dynamo Moscow (2-3)	0-2, 2-1
Levski Sofia v Sparta Rotterdam (1-3)	1-1, 0-2
Zaglebie Sosnowiec v Atvidaberg (4-5)	3-4, 1-1
Mikkeli v Eskisehirspor (0-4)	0-0, 0-4
Beerschot v Famagusta (8-0)	7-0, 1-0

Second Round

Liverpool v Bayern Munich (1-3)	0-0, 1-3
Atvidaberg* v Chelsea (1-1)	0-0, 1-1
Torino v FK Austria (1-0)	1-0, 0-0
Rangers† v Sporting Lisbon (6-6)	3-2, 3-4
Beerschot v Dynamo Berlin (2-6)	1-3, 1-3
Sparta Rotterdam v Red Star Belgrade (2-3)	1-1, 1-2
Barcelona v Steaua Bucharest (1-3)	0-1, 1-2
Eskisehirspor v Dynamo Moscow (0-2)	0-1, 0-1

Quarter-Final

Torino v Rangers (1-2)	1-1, 0-1
Steaua Bucharest v Bayern Munich* (1-1)	1-1, 0-0
Atvidaberg v Dynamo Berlin (2-4)	0-2, 2-2
Red Star Belgrade v Dynamo Moscow (2-3)	1-2, 1-1

Semi-Final

Bayern Munich v Rangers (1-3)	1-1, 0-2
Dynamo Berlin v Dynamo Moscow† (2-2)	1-1, 1-1

**Won on away goals rule. †Won on penalty kicks.*

Final 1971-72: Rangers 3, Dynamo Moscow 2

(In Barcelona, 24 May, 1972, 35,000)

Rangers: McCloy; Jardine, Mathieson, Greig, Johnstone, Smith, McLean, Conn, Stein, MacDonald, Johnston.

Dynamo Moscow: Pilgui; Basalev, Dolmatov, Zykov, Dobbonosov (Gerschkovitch), Zhukov, Baidatchini, Jakubik (Estrekov), Sabo, Makovikov, Evryuzhikhin.

Scorers: Rangers – Stein, Johnston 2; Dynamo Moscow – Estrekov, Makovikov.

EUROPEAN CUP-WINNERS' CUP 1972–73

First Round

Bastia v Atlético Madrid (1-2)	0-0, 1-2
Floriana Valletta v Ferencvaros (1-6)	1-0, 0-6
Schalke 04 v Slavia Sofia (5-2)	2-1, 3-1
Standard Liège v Sparta Prague (3-4)	1-0, 2-4
Spartak Moscow v FC Den Haag (1-0)	1-0, 0-0
Vikingur Reykjavik v Legia Warsaw (0-11)	0-2, 0-9
Ankaragucu v Leeds U (1-2)	1-1, 0-1
Hajduk Split v Fredrikstad (2-0)	1-0, 1-0
Rapid Vienna* v PAOK Saloniki (2-2)	0-0, 2-2
Zurich v Wrexham (2-3)	1-1, 1-2
Sporting Lisbon v Hibernian (3-7)	2-1, 1-6
Rapid Bucharest v Landskrona (3-1)	3-0, 0-1
Pezoporikos v Cork Hibs (2-6)	1-2, 1-4
Fremad Amager v Besa* (1-1)	1-1, 0-0
Carl Zeiss Jena v Mikkeli (8-4)	6-1, 2-3
Red Boys Differdingen v AC Milan (1-7)	1-4, 0-3

Second Round

Rapid Vienna v Rapid Bucharest (2-4)	1-1, 1-3
Carl Zeiss Jena v Leeds U (0-2)	0-0, 0-2
Wrexham v Hajduk Split* (3-3)	3-1, 0-2
Cork Hibs v Schalke 04 (0-3)	0-0, 0-3
Atlético Madrid v Spartak Moscow* (5-5)	3-4, 2-1
Hibernian v Besa (8-2)	7-1, 1-1
Ferencvaros v Sparta Prague (3-4)	2-0, 1-4
Legia Warsaw v AC Milan (2-3)	1-1, 1-2

Quarter-Final

Leeds U v Rapid Bucharest (8-1)	5-0, 3-1
Hibernian v Hajduk Split (4-5)	4-2, 0-3
Schalke 04 v Sparta Prague (2-4)	2-1, 0-3
Spartak Moscow v AC Milan (1-2)	0-1, 1-1

Semi-Final

Leeds U v Hajduk Split (1-0)	1-0, 0-0
AC Milan v Sparta Prague (2-0)	1-0, 1-0

**Won on away goals rule.*

Final 1972–73: AC Milan 1, Leeds U 0

(In Salonika, 16 May, 1973, 45,000)

AC Milan: Vecchi; Sabadini, Zigno, Anquilletti, Turone, Rosato (Dolci), Sogliano, Benetti, Bigon, Rivera, Chiarugi.
Leeds U: Harvey; Reaney, Cherry, Bates, Madeley, Hunter, Lorimer, Jordan, Jones, Gray E., Yorath (McQueen).
Scorer: AC Milan – Chiarugi.

EUROPEAN CUP-WINNERS' CUP 1973–74

First Round

Legia Warsaw v PAOK Salonika (1-2)	1-1, 0-1
Anderlecht v Zurich* (3-3)	3-2, 0-1
Vestmannajar v Bor Moenchengladbach (1-16)	0-7, 1-9
Vasas Budapest v Sunderland (0-3)	0-2, 0-1
Ankaragucu v Rangers (0-6)	0-2, 0-4
AC Milan v Dynamo Zagreb (4-1)	3-1, 1-0
Torpedo Moscow v Atlético Bilbao (0-2)	0-0, 0-2
Gzira v Brann Bergen (0-9)	0-2, 0-7
NAC v Magdeburg (0-2)	0-0, 0-2
Randers Freja v Rapid Vienna (1-2)	0-0, 1-2
Chimia Ramnicu v Glentoran (2-4)	2-2, 0-2
Larnaca v Malmo (0-11)	0-0, 0-11
Fola Esch v Beroe Stara (1-11)	0-7, 1-4
Banik Ostrava v Cork Hibs (3-1)	1-0, 2-1
Reipas Lahti v Lyon (0-2)	0-0, 0-2
Cardiff C v Sporting Lisbon (1-2)	0-0, 1-2

Second Round

Lyon v PAOK Salonika (3-7)	3-3, 0-4
Bor Moenchengladbach v Rangers (5-3)	3-0, 2-3
Brann Bergen v Glentoran (2-4)	1-1, 1-3
Banik Ostrava v Magdeburg (2-3)	2-0, 0-3
Zurich* v Malmo (1-1)	0-0, 1-1
Beroe Stara v Atlético Bilbao (3-1)	3-0, 0-1
Sunderland v Sporting Lisbon (2-3)	2-1, 0-2
AC Milan v Rapid Vienna (2-0)	0-0, 2-0

Quarter Final

Magdeburg v Beroe Stara (3-1)	2-0, 1-1
Glentoran v Bor Moenchengladbach (0-7)	0-2, 0-5
Sporting Lisbon v Zurich (4-1)	3-0, 1-1
AC Milan v PAOK Salonika (5-2)	3-0, 2-2

Semi-Final

AC Milan v Bor Moenchengladbach (2-1)	2-0, 0-1
Sporting Lisbon v Magdeburg (2-3)	1-1, 1-2

**Won on away goals rule.*

Final 1973–74: FC Magdeburg 2, AC Milan 0

(In Rotterdam, 8 May, 1974, 5000)

FC Magdeburg: Schultz; Enge, Zapf, Gaube, Abraham, Tyll, Pommerenke, Seguin, Raugust, Sparwasser, Hoffman.
AC Milan: Pizzaballa; Anquilletti, Sabadini, Lanzi, Schnellinger, Maldera, Tresoldi, Benetti, Bigon, Rivera, Bergamaschi.
Scorers: FC Magdeburg – Lanzi og, Seguin.

EUROPEAN CUP-WINNERS' CUP 1974–75

First Round, First Leg

Liverpool 11 (*Lindsay pen, Boersma 2, Thompson 2, Heighway, Cormack, Hughes, Callaghan, Smith, Kennedy*), Stromsgodset 0
Dundee United 3 (*Narey, Copland, Gardener*), Jiul Petrosani 0
Ferencvaros 2 (*Nyilasi, Szabo*), Cardiff City 0
Bursapor 4 (*Turan 2, Ali, Sinan pen*), Finn Harps 2 (*Ferry, Bradley*)
Sliema Wanderers 2 (*Camilleri 2*), Reipas Lahti 0
Dynamo Kiev 1 (*Blokhin*), CSKA Sofia 0
Malmö 1 (*Cervin*), Sion 0
Gwardia Warsaw 2 (*Sroka, Kraska*), Bologna 1 (*Savoldi*)
Slavia Prague 1 (*Herda*), Carl Zeiss Jena 0
Waregem 2 (*Delesie 2*), Austria/WAC 1 (*Pirkner*)
PAOK Salonika 1 (*Terzanides*), Red Star Belgrade 0
PSV Eindhoven 10 (*Van der Kuylen 3, Lubse 3, Kemper, Deykers, Edstrom, Van Kraay*), Ards 0
Fram Reykjavik 0, Real Madrid 2 (*Roberto Martinez 2*)
Benfica 4 (*Jordao 2, Humberto, Nene*), Vanlose 0
Eintracht Frankfurt 3 (*Holzenbein 2, Rohrbach*), Monaco 0
Real Madrid 3 (*Krieger og, Santillana, Roberto Martinez*), Austria/WAC 0
Gwardia Warsaw 1 (*Malkiewicz*), PSV Eindhoven 5 (*Willy Van der Kerkhof, Kialak og, Deykers, Lubse, Van der Kuylen*)
Carl Zeiss Jena 1 (*Vogel*), Benfica 1 (*Nene*)
Red Star Belgrade 6 (*Sestic 3, Filipovic 2, Rajkovic*), Avenir Beggen 1 (*Sinner*)
Malmö 3 (*Larsson 2, Sjoberg*), Reipas Lahti 1 (*Kautonen*)
Eintracht Frankfurt 2 (*Nickel, Koerbel*), Dynamo Kiev 3 (*Kolotov, Blokhin, Muntian*)

First Round, Second Leg

Stromsgodset 0, Liverpool 1 (*Kennedy*)
Jiul Petrosani 2 (*Rosnai, Tonca*), Dundee United 0
Cardiff City 1 (*Dwyer*), Ferencvaros 4 (*Takacs, Szabo, Pusztai, Mate*)
Finn Harps 0, Bursaspor 0
Reipas Lahti 4 (*Salonen, Lahtanen, Sandberg 2*), Sliema Wanderers 1 (*Aquilina*)
CSKA Sofia 0, Dynamo Kiev 1 (*Blokhin*)
Sion 1 (*Suiza*), Malmö 0
Bologna 2 (*Savoldi 2*),Gwardia Warsaw 1 (*Terlecki*)
Carl Zeiss Jena 1 (*Stein*), Slavia Prague 0
Austria/WAC 4 (*Pirkner 2, Weigel, Fiala*), Waregem 1 (*Koudijzer*)
Red Star Belgrade 2 (*Petrovic V., Savic*), PAOK Salonika 0
Ards 1 (*Guy*), PSV Eindhoven 4 (*Van der Kuylen, Edstrom, Dahlqvist 2*)
Real Madrid 6 (*Pirri 2, Santillana, Netzer, Macanas, Aguilar*), Fram Reykjavik 0
Vanlose 1 (*Petersen*), Benfica 4 (*Nene, Jordao 2, Barros*)
Monaco 2 (*Onnis, Petit*), Eintracht Frankfurt 2 (*Beverungen, Nickel*)
Avenir Beggen had a walkover when Paralimni withdrew.

Second Round, First Leg

Liverpool 1 (*Keegan*), Ferencvaros 1 (*Mate*)
Dundee United 0, Bursaspor 0

Second Round, Second Leg

Ferencvaros 0, Liverpool 0
Bursaspor 1 (*Vahit*), Dundee United 0
Austria/WAC 2 (*Pirkner, Fiala*), Real Madrid 2 (*Roberto Martinez, Netzer*)
PSV Eindhoven 3 (*Van der Kuylen 2 [1 pen], Lubse*), Gwardia Warsaw 0
Benfica 0, Carl Zeiss Jena 0
Avenir Beggen 1 (*Dresch*), Red Star Belgrade 5 (*Rajkovic 2, Filipovic, Sestic, Savic*)
Reipas Lahti 0, Malmö 0
Dynamo Kiev 2 (*Onischenko 2*), Eintracht Frankfurt 1 (*Rohrbach*)

Quarter-Finals, First Leg

Real Madrid 2 (*Santillana, Netzer pen*), Red Star Belgrade 0
PSV Eindhoven 0, Benfica 0
Malmö 1 (*Sjoberg*), Ferencvaros 3 (*Nyilasi, Magyar, Mate*)
Bursaspor 0, Dynamo Kiev 1 (*Onischenko*)

Quarter-Finals, Second Leg

Benfica 1 (*Humberto*), PSV Eindhoven 2 (*Willy Van der Kerkhof, Quaars*)
Ferencvaros 1 (*Mate*), Malmö 1 (*Sjoberg*)
Dynamo Kiev 2 (*Kolotov pen, Muntian*), Bursaspor 0
Red Star Belgrade 2 (*Dzajic, Petrovic O. pen*), Real Madrid 0
Red Star Belgrade won on penalties.

Semi-Finals, First Leg

Ferencvaros 2 (*Branikovits, Magyar*), Red Star Belgrade 1 (*Savic*)
Dynamo Kiev 3 (*Kolotov, Onischenko, Blokhin*), PSV Eindhoven 0

Semi-Finals, Second Leg

Red Star Belgrade 2 (*Keri, Filipovic*), Ferencvaros 2 (*Pusztai, Megyesi pen*)
PSV Eindhoven 2 (*Edstrom 2*), Dynamo Kiev 1 (*Burjak*)

Final 1974–75: Dynamo Kiev 3, Ferencvaros 0
(at Basle, 14 May, 1975, 13,000)

Dynamo Kiev: Rudakov; Fomenko, Troshkin, Reshko, Matvienko, Muntian, Konkov, Burjak, Kolotov, Onischenko, Blokhin.

Ferencvaros: Geczi; Pataki, Martos, Rab, Megyesi, Nyilasi (Onhaus), Juhasz, Mucha, Szabo, Mate, Magyar.

Scorers: Dynamo Kiev – Onischenko 2, Blokhin.

EUROPEAN CUP-WINNERS' CUP 1975–76

First Round, First Leg

Ararat Erevan 9 (*Markarov 5 [1 pen], Oganiesian 2, Petrosian S., Bondarenko*), Anorthosis 0
Basle 1 (*Schoenberger*), Atlético Madrid 2 (*Garate, Ayala*)
Besiktas 0, Fiorentina 3 (*Caso 2, Casarsa*)
Borac Banja Luka 9 (*Cetina 3, Ibrahimbegovic 5, Jurkovic*), US Rumelange 0
Eintracht Frankfurt 5 (*Korbel, Beverungen, Holzenbein, Nickel 2*), Coleraine 1 (*Cochrane*)
Haladas Szombathely 7 (*Fedor 2, Horath 2, Frakas og, Halmosi*), Valletta 0
Home Farm 1 (*Brophy*), Lens 1 (*Hopquin*)
Lahden Reipas 2 (*Lindholm, Tupasela*), West Ham U 2 (*Brooking, Bonds*)
Panathinaikos 0, Sachsenring Zwickau 0
Rapid Bucharest 1 (*Thissen og*), Anderlecht 0
Spartak Trnava 0, Boavista 0
Skeid Oslo 1 (*Skjoensberg B.*), Stal Rzeszow 4 (*Kozierski 2, Curylo, Krawczyk*)
Sturm Graz 3 (*Stendal 2 pens, Kulmer*), Slavia Sofia 1 (*Kostov*)
Valur Reykjavik 0, Celtic 2 (*Dalglish, McDonald*)
Vejle 0, Den Haag 2 (*Jol, Van Leeuwen*)
Wrexham 2 (*Griffiths, Davis*), Djurgaardens 1 (*Krantz*)

First Round, Second Leg

Anderlecht 2 (*Van Binst, Rensenbrink*), Rapid Bucharest 0
Anorthosis 1 (*Fivos pen*), Ararat Erevan 1 (*Bondarenko*)
Atlético Madrid 1 (*Becerra*), Basle 1 (*Demarmels*)
Boavista 3 (*Mane, Celse, Salvador*), Spartak Trnava 0
Celtic 7 (*Edvaldsson, Dalglish, McCluskey pen, Hood 2, Deans, Callaghan*), Valur 0
Den Haag 2 (*Perazic, Mansveld*), Vejle 0
Djurgaarden 1 (*Lovfors*), Wrexham 1 (*Whittle*)
Lens 6 (*Northeaux, Mujica pen, Kaiser 3, Llorens*), Home Farm 0
Sachsenring Zwickau 2 (*Schykowski, Dietzsch pen*), Panathinaikos 0
Slavia Sofia 1 (*Kostov*), Sturm Graz 0
West Ham U 3 (*Robson 2, Jennings*), Reipas Landen 0
US Rumelange 1 (*Rohmann*), Borac Banja Luka 5 (*Smilevski, Reso, Kovahevic, Vidacek, Marjonaovic*)
Coleraine 2 (*McCurdy, Cochrane*), Eintracht Frankfurt 6 (*Grabowski 3, Nickel, Lorenz, Holzenbein*)
Valletta 1 (*Giglio*), Haladas Szombathely 1 (*Karaci*)
Fiorentina 3 (*Caso 2, Casarsa*), Besiktas 0
Stal Rzeszow 4 (*Kozierski, Miler, Krawczyk, Napieracz*), Skeid Oslo 0

Second Round, First Leg

Anderlecht 3 (*Rensenbrink 2, Coeck*), Borac Banja Luka 0
Ararat Erevan 1 (*Petrosian S.*), West Ham U 1 (*Taylor A.*)
Atlético Madrid 1 (*Bacerra*), Eintracht Frankfurt 2 (*Holzenbein 2*)
Boavista 0, Celtic 0
Den Haag 3 (*Schoenmaker, Van Vliet, Van Leeawen*), Lens 2 (*Zuraszek, Janovic*)
Fiorentina 1 (*Speggiorin*), Sachsenring Zwickau 0
Sturm Graz 2 (*Stendal, Stenier pen*), Haladas Szombathely 0
Wrexham 2 (*Ashcroft 2*), Stal Rzeszow 0

Second Round, Second Leg

Borac Banja Luka 1 (*Ibrahimbegovic*), Anderlecht 0
Celtic 3, (*Dalglish, Edvaldsson, Deans*), Boavista 1 (*Mane*)
Eintracht Frankfurt 1 (*Reichel*), Atlético Madrid 0
Haladas Szombathely 1 (*Horvath*), Sturm Graz 1 (*Jurtin*)
Lens 1 (*Mujica pen*), Den Haag 3 (*Shoenmaker 2, Van Leeuwen*)
Sachsenring Zwickau 1 (*Schykowski J.*), Fiorentina 0
Stal Rzeszow 1 (*Kozierski*), Wrexham 1 (*Sutton*)
West Ham U 3 (*Paddon, Robson, Taylor A.*), Ararat Erevan 1 (*Petrosian N.*)

Quarter-Finals, First Leg

Anderlecht 1 (*Van Binst*), Wrexham 0
Celtic 1 (*Dalglish*), Sachsenring Zwickau 1 (*Blank*)
Den Haag 4 (*Mansveld 3 [2 pens], Schoenmaker*), West Ham U 2 (*Jennings 2*)
Sturm Graz 0, Eintracht Frankfurt 2 (*Holzenbein, Wenzel*)

Quarter-Finals, Second Leg

Eintracht Frankfurt 1 (*Holzenbein*), Sturm Graz 0
Sachsenring Zwickau 1 (*Blank*), Celtic 0
West Ham U 3 (*Taylor A., Lampard, Bonds pen*), Den Haag 1 (*Schoenmaker*)
Wrexham 1 (*Lee*), Anderlecht 1 (*Rensenbrink*)

Semi-Finals, First Leg

Eintracht Frankfurt 2 (*Neuberger, Kraus*), West Ham U 1 (*Paddon*)
Sachsenring Zwickau 0, Anderlecht 3 (*Van der Elst 2, Rensenbrink*)

Semi-Finals, Second Leg

Anderlecht 2 (*Rensenbrink, Van der Elst*), Sachsenring Zwickau 0
West Ham U 3 (*Brooking 2, Robson*), Eintracht Frankfurt 1 (*Beverungen*)

Final 1976–76: Anderlecht 4, West Ham U 2

(At Heysel Stadium, Brussels, 5 May, 1976, 58,000)

Anderlecht: Ruiter; Lomme, Broos, Van Binst, Thissen, Dockx, Coeck (Vercauteren), Van der Elst, Ressel, Haan, Rensenbrink.

West Ham U: Day; Coleman, Bonds, Taylor T., Lampard (Taylor A.), McDowell, Brooking, Paddon, Holland, Jennings, Robson.

Scorers: Anderlecht – Rensenbrink 2 (1 pen), Van der Elst 2; West Ham U – Holland, Robson.

EUROPEAN CUP-WINNERS' CUP 1976–77

Preliminary Round, First Leg
Cardiff City 1 (*Evans*), Servette 0

Preliminary Round, Second Leg
Servette 2 (*Bizzini, Pfister*), Cardiff City 1 (*Showers*)

First Round, First Leg
Lierse 1 (*Ceulemans*), Hajduk Split 0
MTK Budape[illegible] (*Kunszt, Kovacs, Borso*), Sparta Prague 1 (*Cermak*)
AIK Stockholm 1 (*Wallgren*), Galatasaray 2 (*Gokmen, Nehmet*)
Anderlecht 2 (*Van der Elst, Rensenbrink*), Roda JC 1 (*Toonstra*)
Bodo Glimt 0, Napoli 2 (*Speggiorin 2*)
Bohemians 2 (*Ryan, Hansen B. og*), Esbjerg 1 (*Nielsen H.*)
Cardiff City 1 (*Alston*), Dynamo Tbilisi 0
Carrick Rangers 3 (*Prenter 2, Connor*), Aris Bonnevoie 1 (*Pissinger*)
Hamburg 3 (*Zaczyk, Reimann, Hidien*), Keflavik 0
Iraklis 0, Apoel Nicosia 0
Lokomotive Leipzig 2 (*Sekora, Fritsche*), He[illegible] 0
Southampton 4 (*Waldron, Channon 2 [1 pe[illegible]], Osgood*), Marseille 0
Levski Spartak 12 (*Yordanov 2, Milanov 6, Panov 2, Spassov 2*), Reipas Lahden 2 (*Sandberg, Tupasela*)
Floriana 1 (*Vassallo*), Slask Wroclaw 4 (*Gavslovski 2, Kwiatkowski, Farrugia og*)
Rapid Vienna 1 (*Krankl*), Atlético Madrid 2 (*Cano, Ayala*)
CSU Galati 2 (*Simionescu, Holzer*), Boavista 3 (*Mane 2, Salvador*)

First Round, Second Leg
Apoel Nicosia 2 (*Marcou 2*), Iraklis 0
Atlético Madrid 1 (*Leivinha*), Rapid Vienna 1 (*Krejcirik*)
Boavista 2 (*Mane 2*), CSU Galati 0
Esbjerg 0, Bohemians 1 (*Mitten*)
Galatasaray 1 (*Gokmen*), AIK Stockholm 1 (*Wallgren*)
Hajduk Split 3 (*Zungul 2, Jerkovic*), Lierse 0
Hearts 5 (*Kay, Gibson 2, Brown, Busby*), Lokomotive Leipzig 1 (*Fritsche*)
Keflavik 1 (*Johansson S.*), Hamburg 1 (*Hidien*)
Reipas Lahden 1 (*Sandberg*), Levski Spartak 7 (*Panov, Milanov 4 [2 pens], Spassov, Krastanov*)
Marseille 2 (*Nogues, Emon*), Southampton 1 (*Peach*)
Napoli 1 (*Massa*), Bodo Glimt 0
Roda JC 2 (*Vermeulen, Van der Lem pen*), Anderlecht 3 (*Rensenbrink, Van der Elst 2*)
Slask Wroclaw 2 (*Pawlowski, Ehrlich*), Floriana 0
Sparta Prague 1 (*Urban*), MTK Budapest 1 (*Kunszt*)
Dynamo Tbilisi 3 (*Gutsaev, Kipiani, Kandeladze pen*), Cardiff City 0
Aris Bonnevoie 2 (*Werner, Langers*), Carrick Rangers 1 (*Irwin*)

Second Round, First Leg
Anderlecht 5 (*Coeck, Vercauteren, Rensenbrink 2 [1 pen]*), Galatasaray 1 (*Ozdewak*)
Apoel Nicosia 1 (*Leonidas*), Napoli 1 (*Savoldi pen*)
Atlético Madrid 1 (*Cano*), Hajduk Split 0
Boavista 3 (*Celso 2, Mane*), Levski Spartak 1 (*Milanov*)
Carrick Rangers 2 (*Irwin, Prenter*), Southampton 5 (*Channon 2, Stokes, McCalliog, Osgood*)
Hamburg 4 (*Bjornmose, Eigl, Reimann, Gallacher og*), Hearts 2 (*Busby, Park*)
Dynamo Tbilisi 1 (*Macheidze*), MTK Budapest 4 (*Shyloshi, Takach 2, Kish*)
Slask Wroclaw 3 (*Kwiatkowski, Sybis 2*), Bohemians 0

Second Round, Second Leg
Bohemians 0, Slask Wroclaw 1 (*Pawlowski*)
Galatasaray 1 (*Gokmen*), Anderlecht 5 (*Rensenbrink 2, Haan, Ressel, Coeck*)
Hearts 1 (*Gibson*), Hamburg 4 (*Eigl 2, Magath 2*)
Levski Spartak 2 (*Panov, Milanov*), Boavista 0
MTK Budapest 1 (*Koritar*), Dynamo Tbilisi 0
Southampton 4 (*Williams, Hayes 2, Stokes*), Carrick Rangers 1 (*Reid*)
Napoli 2 (*Speggiorin, Massa*), Apoel Nicosia 0
Hajduk Split 1 (*Zungul*), Atlético Madrid 2 (*Ayala, Leal*)

Quarter-Finals, First Leg
Anderlecht 2 (*Ressel, Rensenbrink*), Southampton 0
Levski Spartak 2 (*Tsvetkov, Milanov*), Atlético Madrid 1 (*Ayala*)
MTK Budapest 1 (*Borso*), Hamburg 1 (*Volkert*)
Slask Wroclaw 0, Napoli 0

Quarter-Finals, Second Leg
Atlético Madrid 2 (*Ayala 2 pens*), Levski Spartak 0
Hamburg 4 (*Reimann 2, Kaltz pen, Zaczyk*), MTK Budapest 1 (*Siklosi*)
Napoli 2 (*Massa, Chiarugi*), Slask Wroclaw 0
Southampton 2 (*Peach pen, MacDougall*), Anderlecht 1 (*Van der Elst*)

Semi-Finals, First Leg
Napoli 1 (*Bruscolotti*), Anderlecht 0
Atlético Madrid 3 (*Cano 2, Leal*), Hamburg 1 (*Magath*)

Semi-Finals, Second Leg
Hamburg 3 (*Capon og, Reimann, Keller*), Atlético Madrid 0
Anderlecht 2 (*Thissen, Van der Elst*), Napoli 0

Final 1976–77: Hamburg 2, Anderlecht 0

(In Amsterdam, 11 May, 1977, 65,000)

Hamburg: Kargus; Kaltz, Ripp, Nogly, Hidien, Steffenhagen, Keller, Reimann, Memering, Magath, Volkert.

Anderlecht: Ruiter; Van Binst, Van den Daele, Broos, Thissen, Van der Elst, Coeck, Haan, Dockx (Van Poucke), Ressel, Rensenbrink.

Scorers: Hamburg – Volkert (pen), Magath.

EUROPEAN CUP-WINNERS' CUP 1977–78

Preliminary Round, First Leg
Rangers 1 (*Greig*), Young Boys 0

Preliminary Round, Second Leg
Young Boys 2 (*Jackson og, Leuzinger*), Rangers 2 (*Johnstone, Smith*)

First Round, First Leg
Lokomotiv Sofia 1 (*Kolev*), Anderlecht 6 (*Van der Elst 4 [1 pen], Nielsen, Van Poucke*)
Besiktas 2 (*Zeferiya Burth, Paunovic*), Diosgyor 0
Betis 2 (*Garcia Soriano, Eulate*), AC Milan 0
Brann Bergen 1 (*Aase*), IA Akranes 0
Cardiff City 0, Austria/WAC 0
Coleraine 1 (*Tweed*), Lokomotiv Leipzig 4 (*Eichhorn, Kuhn, Lowe 2*)
Dundalk 1 (*Flanagan*), Hajduk Split 0
Hamburg 8 (*Keller 4, Volkert pen, Buljan, Steffenhagen, Reimann*), Lahden Reipas 1 (*Riotto*)
FC Cologne 2 (*Lohr, Muller*), Porto 2 (*Gabriel, Octavio*)
Lokomotiv Kosice 0, Oster Vaxjo 0
PAOK Salonika 2 (*Pelios, Anastasiadis*), Zaglebie Sosnowiec 0
Progres Niedercorn 0, Vejle 1 (*Steen Tychosen*)
Rangers 0, Twente 0
St Etienne 1 (*Synaeghel*), Manchester U 1 (*Hill*)
Olympiakos Nicosia 1 (*Aristidou*), Uni Craiova 6 (*Balaci 2, Cirtsu, Marcu, Crisan, Irinescu*)
Valletta 0, Moscow Dynamo 2 (*Kazachenok, Maximenkov*)

First Round, Second Leg
IA Akranes 0, Brann Bergen 4 (*Aase 2, Dahlhaug, Tronstad*)
Anderlecht 2 (*Van der Elst, Bouvy*), Lokomotiv Sofia 0
Austria/WAC 1 (*Baumeister*), Cardiff City 0
Diosgyor 5 (*Fuko, Olah 2 [1 pen], Fekete 2), Besiktas 0*
Hajduk Split 4 (Vujovic, McManus og, Rukljac, McConville og), Dundalk 0
Lahden Reipas 2 (*Riotto 2*), Hamburg 5 (*Volkert pen, Keegan, Magath, Keller, Steffenhagen*)
Lokomotiv Leipzig 2 (*Altmann, Fritschepen*), Coleraine 2 (*Guy 2*)
AC Milan 2 (*Tosetto, Capello*), Betis 1 (*Lopez*)
Oster Vaxjo 2 (*Bild, Evesson*), Lokomotiv Kosice 2 (*Jozsa, Dobrovic*)
Porto 1 (*Murca*), FC Cologne 0
Twente 3 (*Gritter, Arnold Muhren, Van der Vall*), Rangers 0
Uni Craiova 2 (*Marcu, Cirtu*), Olympiakos Nicosia 0
Vejle 9 (*Sorensen, Ostergaard 2, Eg, Norgaard 3, Schacke, Tychosen*), Progres Niedercorn 0
Zaglebie Sosnowiec 0, PAOK Salonika 2 (*Kermanidis, Damanikis*)
Moscow Dynamo 5 (*Kolyesov 3, Jakubik, Kazachenkov*), Valletta 0
Manchester U 2 (*Pearson, Coppell*), St Etienne 0

Second Round, First Leg
Austria/WAC 0, Lokomotiv Kosice 0
Diosgyor 2 (*Tatar, Varadi*), Hajduk Split 1 (*Muzinic*)
Hamburg 1 (*Keller*), Anderlecht 2 (*Coeck, Rensenbrink*)
Lokomotiv Leipzig 1 (*Grobner*), Betis 1 (*Lopez*)
Moscow Dynamo 2 (*Kazachenov, Minaev*), Uni Craiova 0
Twente 2 (*Gritter 2*), Brann Bergen 0
Vejle 3 (*Eg, Jaquet, Ostergaard*), PAOK Salonika 0
Porto 4 (*Duda 3, Oliveira*), Manchester U 0

Second Round, Second Leg
Anderlecht 1 (*Van der Elst*), Hamburg 1 (*Keegan*)
Betis 2 (*Garcia Soriano 2*), Lokomotiv Leipzig 1 (*Liebers*)
Brann Bergen 1 (*Tronstad*), Twente 2 (*Gritter, Thoresen*)
Uni Craiova 2 (*Cirtu, Beideanu*), Moscow Dynamo 0
Dynamo won 3-0 on penalties
Hajduk Split 2 (*Vujovic, Rukljac pen*) Diosgyor 1 (*Tatar*)
Hajduk Split won 4-3 on penalties
Lokomotiv Kosice 1 (*Farkas pen*), Austria/WAC 1 (*Morales*)
Manchester U 5 (*Coppell 2, Murca 2 og, Nicholl*), Porto 2 (*Seninho 2*)
PAOK Salonika 2 (*Orfanos, Kermanides*), Vejle 1 (*Jaquet*)

Quarter-Finals, First Leg
Vejle 0, Twente 3 (*Arnold Muhren, Gritter, Thijssen*)
Austria/WAC 1 (*Parits*), Hajduk Split 1 (*Surjak*)
Betis 0, Moscow Dynamo 0
Porto 1 (*Gomes*), Anderlecht 0

Quarter-Finals, Second Leg
Hajduk Split 1 (*Cop*), Austria/WAC 1 (*Daxbacher*)
Austria/WAC won 3-0 on penalties.
Moscow Dynamo 3 (*Gershkovich, Kazachenov, Maximenkov*), Betis 0
Anderlecht 3 (*Rensenbrink pen, Nielsen, Vercauteren*), Porto 0
Twente 4 (*Thijssen, Overweg, Gritter, Van der Vall*), Vejle 0

Semi-Finals, First Leg
Moscow Dynamo 2 (*Tseretli, Gershkovich*), Austria/WAC 1 (*Baumeister*)
Twente 0, Anderlecht 1 (*Nielsen*)

Semi-Finals, Second Leg
Anderlecht 2 (*Haan, Rensenbrink pen*), Twente 0
Austria/WAC 2 (*Pirkner pen, Morales*), Moscow Dynamo 1 (*Yakubik*)

Final 1977–78: Anderlecht 4, Austria/WAC 0
(In Paris, 3 May, 1978, 48,679)

Anderlecht: De Bree; Van Binst, Broos, Dusbaba, Thissen, Van der Elst, Haan, Nielsen, Coeck, Vercauteren (Dockx), Rensenbrink.

Austria/WAC: Baumgartner; Robert Sara, Josef Sara, Obermayer, Baumeister, Prohaska, Daxbacher (Martinez), Gasselich, Morales (Drazen), Pirkner, Parits.

Scorers: Anderlecht – Rensenbrink 2, Van Binst 2.

EUROPEAN CUP-WINNERS' CUP 1978–79

First Round, First Leg
Floriana 1 (*Xuereb R.*), Inter-Milan 3 (*Altobelli 3*)
Valur 1 (*Albertsson*), Magdeburg 1 (*Steinbach*)
Sporting Lisbon 0, Banik Ostrava 1 (*Antalik*)
Beveren 3 (*Albert, Stevens, Schonberger*), Ballymena 0
Ferencvaros 2 (*Nyilasi, Major*), Kalmar 0
Marek Stanke Dimitrov 3 (*Petrov V., Petrov I. 2*), Aberdeen 2 (*Jarvie, Harper*)
Barcelona 3 (*Krankl 2, Sanchez*), Shakhtor 0
PAOK Salonika 2 (*Karmanides, Sarafis*), Servette 0
Uni Craiova 3 (*Camataru 2, Crisan*), Fortuna Dusseldorf 4 (*Fanz 2, Allofs, Zimmermann*)
Zaglebie Sosnowiec 2 (*Zarichta, Starinskj*), SW Innsbruck 3 (*Peter Koncilia, Oberacher, Brasoler*)
AZ 67 0, Ipswich T 0
Apoel 0
Shamrock Rovers 2 (*Giles, Lynex*)
Rijeka 3 (*Tomic, Durkalic, Curkov*), Wrexham 0
Bodo Glimt 4 (*Solhang 2, Berg, Hanssen*), Union Luxembourg 1 (*Teitgen*)
Frem 2 (*Jacobsen, Hansen*), Nancy 0

First Round, Second Leg
Inter-Milan 5 (*Muraro 2, Fedele 2, Chierico*), Floriana 0
Magdeburg 4 (*Seguin, Steinbach, Hoffmann, Streich*), Valur 0
Banik Ostrava 1 (*Licka*), Sporting Lisbon 0
Ballymena 0, Beveren 3 (*Jansen 2, Wissmann*)
Kalmar 2 (*Magnusson, Nyberg*), Ferencvaros 2 (*Ebedli, Szokolai*)
Aberdeen 3 (*Strachan, Jarvie, Harper*), Marek Stanke Dimitrov 0
Shakhtor 1 (*Resnik*), Barcelona 1 (*Krankl*)
Servette 4 (*Pfister, Hamberg, Elia 2*), PAOK Salonika 0
Fortuna Dusseldorf 1 (*Bommer*), Uni Craiova 1 (*Marcu*)
SW Innsbruck 1 (*Koterva og*), Zaglebie Sosnowiec 1 (*Dvorczik*)
Ipswich T 2 (*Mariner, Wark*), AZ 67 0
Shamrock Rovers 1 (*Lynex*), Apoel 0
Wrexham 2 (*McNeil, Cartwright*), Rijeka 0
Union Luxembourg 1 (*Teitgen*), Bodo Glimt 0
Nancy 4 (*Curbelo, Jeannol 2, Zenier*), Frem 0

Second Round, First Leg
Servette 2 (*Hamberg, Barberis*), Nancy 1 (*Robio*)
Banik Ostrava 3 (*Knapp, Radimec, Rygel*), Shamrock Rovers 0
Ipswich T 1 (*Wark*), SW Innsbruck 0
Anderlecht 3 (*Van der Elst 2, Coeck*), Barcelona 0
Inter-Milan 5 (*Beccalossi, Altobelli 3, Muraro*), Bodo Glimt 0
Fortuna Dusseldorf 3 (*Gunther 2, Zimmermann*), Aberdeen 0
Rijeka 0, Beveren 0
Magdeburg 1 (*Streich*), Ferencvaros 0

Second Round, Second Leg
Nancy 2 (*Zenier, Umpierrez*), Servette 2 (*Elia, Schnyder*)
Shamrock Rovers 1 (*Giles*), Banik Ostrava 3 (*Licka 2, Albrecht*)
SW Innsbruck 1 (*Oberacher*), Ipswich T 1 (*Burley*)
Barcelona 3 (*Krankl, Heredia, Zuviria*), Anderlecht 0
Bodo Glimt 1 (*Hansen*), Inter-Milan 2 (*Altobelli, Scanziani*)
Aberdeen 2 (*McLelland, Jarvie*), Fortuna Dusseldorf 0
Beveren 2 (*Baecke 2*), Rijeka 0
Ferencvaros 2 (*Pusztai, Szokolai*), Magdeburg 1 (*Stachmann*)

Quarter-Finals, First Leg
Inter-Milan 0, Beveren 0
Fortuna Dusseldorf 0, Servette 0
Ipswich T 2 (*Gates 2*), Barcelona 1 (*Esteban*)
Magdeburg 2 (*Streich 2*), Banik Ostrava 1 (*Antalik*)

Quarter-Finals, Second Leg
Beveren 1 (*Stevens*), Inter-Milan 0
Servette 1 (*Andrey*), Fortuna Dusseldorf 1 (*Bommer*)
Barcelona 1 (*Migueli*), Ipswich T 0
Banik Ostrava 4 (*Rygel 2, Albrecht, Nemec*), Magdeburg 2 (*Sparwasser, Pommerenke*)

Semi-Finals, First Leg
Fortuna Dusseldorf 3 (*Klaus Allofs 2, Thomas Allofs*), Banik Ostrava 1 (*Nemec*)
Barcelona 1 (*Rexach pen*), Beveren 0

Semi-Finals, Second Leg
Banik Ostrava 2 (*Licka, Antalik*), Fortuna Dusseldorf 1 (*Zewe*)
Beveren 0, Barcelona 1 (*Krankl pen*)

Final 1978–79: Barcelona 4, Fortuna Dusseldorf 3 aet
(In Basle, 16 May, 1979)

Barcelona: Artola; Zuviria, Migueli, Costas (Martinez), Albaladejo (De la Cruz), Sanchez, Neeskens, Asensi, Rexach, Krankl, Carrasco.

Fortuna Dusseldorf: Daniel; Baltes, Zewe, Zimmermann (Lund), Brei (Weikl), Kohnen, Bommer, Schmitz, Thomas Allofs, Klaus Allofs, Seel.

Scorers: Barcelona – Sanchez, Asensi, Rexach, Krankl; Fortuna Dusseldorf – Klaus Allofs, Seel 2.

EUROPEAN CUP-WINNERS' CUP 1979–80

Preliminary Round, First Leg
Rangers 1 (*Smith*), Lillestrom 0
B 1903 6 (*Haarby, Larsen, Kristiansen 2, Thygesen 2*), Apoel 0

Preliminary Round, Second Leg
Lillestrom 0, Rangers 2 (*MacDonald A., Johnstone*)
Apoel 0, B 1903 1 (*Larsen*)

First Round, First Leg
Juventus 2 (*Pozsgai og, Cabrini*), Raba Gyor 0
Reipas Lahti 0, Aris Bonnevoi 1 (*Schlitz*)
Arka Gdynia 3 (*Kwiatkovski, Kornynt 2*), Stara Zagora 2 (*Petkov, Lipenski*)
Panionios 4 (*Liolios 2, Pafiakakis, Anastopoulos*), Twente Enschede 0
Innsbruck 1 (*Poell pen*), Lokomotiv Kosice 2 (*Strapek, Jacko*)
Rangers 2 (*MacDonald, McLean*), Fortuna Dusseldorf 1 (*Wenzel*)
Arsenal 2 (*Sunderland, Young*), Fenerbahce 0
B 1903 2 (*Thycosen, Hansen*), Valencia 2 (*Arias, Castellanos*)
Wrexham 3 (*McNeil, Fox, Buxton*), Magdeburg 2 (*Streich, Steinbach*)
IFK Gothenburg 1 (*Holmgren*), Waterford 0
Beerschot 0, Rijeka Fiume 0
Young Boys Berne 2 (*Zwygart, Schoenenberger*), Steaua Bucharest 2 (*Soica, Jordanescu*)
Sliema Wanderers 2 (*Tortell 2 pens*), Boavista 1 (*Eliseu*)
Cliftonville 0, Nantes 1 (*Rampillon*)
IA Akranes 0, Barcelona 1 (*Rexach*)

First Round, Second Leg
Raba Gyor 2 (*Furino og, Poczik*), Juventus 1 (*Causio*)
Aris Bonnevoi 1 (*Colling*), Reipas Lahti 0
Stara Zagora 2 (*Stoyanov, Petkov*), Arka Gdynia 0
Twente Enschede 3 (*Bos pen, Linstadt, Otto*), Panionios 1 (*Anastopoulos*)
Lokomotiv Kosice 1 (*Kozak*), Innsbruck 0
Fortuna Dusseldorf 0, Rangers 0
Fenerbahce 0, Arsenal 0
Valencia 4 (*Felman, Kempes 2, Saura*), B 1903 0
Magdeburg 5 (*Hoffman 2, Newes, Steinbach pen, Streich*), Wrexham 2 (*Vinter, Hill*)
Waterford 1 (*Keane*), IFK Gothenburg 1 (*Holmgren*)
Rijeka Fiume 2 (*Radovic 2*), Beerschot 1 (*Demushel*)
Steaua Bucharest 6 (*Mitu, Sames 2, Aelenei, Raducanu, Zahlu*), Young Boys Berne 0
Boavista 8 (*Ailten, Julio 3, Moinhos, Salvador, Folha, Oscar*), Sliema Wanderers 0
Nantes 7 (*Pecout 3, Trossero 2, Rampillon, Rio*), Cliftonville 0
Barcelona 5 (*Krankl, Simonsen, Rexach, Carrasco, Asensi*), IA Akranes 0

Second Round, First Leg
Stara Zagora 1 (*Stojanov pen*), Juventus 0
Panionios 1 (*Anastopoulos*), IFK Gothenburg 0
Lokomotiv Kosice 2 (*Kozak 2*), Rijeka Fiume 0
Valencia 1 (*Kempes*), Rangers 1 (*McLean*)
Nantes 3 (*Pecout 2, Toure*), Steaua Bucharest 2 (*Raducanu 2 [1 pen]*)
Arsenal 2 (*Young, Sunderland*), Magdeburg 1 (*Pommerenke*)
Aris Bonnevoi 1 (*Mattes*), Barcelona 4 (*Simonsen 3, Rexach*)
Dynamo Moscow 0, Boavista 0

Second Round, Second Leg
Juventus 3 (*Scirea, Causio, Verza*), Stara Zagora 0
IFK Gothenburg 2 (*Nordin, Holmgren*), Panionios 0
Rijeka Fiume 3 (*Desnica 3*), Lokomotiv Kosice 0
Rangers 1 (*Johnstone*), Valencia 3 (*Bonhof, Kempes2*)
Steaua Bucharest 1 (*Jordanescu*), Nantes 2 (*Pecout, Amisse*)
Magdeburg 2 (*Streich, Stahmann*), Arsenal 2 (*Rice, Brady*)
Barcelona 7 (*Krankl 3, Heredia 2, Carrasco, Canito*), Aris Bonnevoi 1 (*Tuliuv*)
Boavista 1 (*Moinhos*), Dynamo Moscow 1 (*Minaev*)

Quarter-Finals, First Leg
Rijeka Fiume 0, Juventus 0
Arsenal 5 (*Sunderland 2, Price, Brady, Young*), IFK Gothenburg 1 (*Nilsson*)
Barcelona 0, Valencia 1 (*Pablo*)
Dynamo Moscow 0, Nantes 2 (*Tusseau, Pecout*)

Quarter-Finals, Second Leg
Juventus 2 (*Causio, Bettega*), Rijeka Fiume 0
IFK Gothenburg 0, Arsenal 0
Valencia 4 (*Saura 2, Bonhof, Kempes pen*), Barcelona 3 (*Canito 2, Landaburu*)
Nantes 2 (*Michel, Toure*), Dynamo Moscow 3 (*Minaev, Gatzaiev, Kolessov*)

Semi-Finals, First Leg
Arsenal 1 (*Bettega og*), Juventus 1 (*Cabrini*)
Nantes 2 (*Baronchelli 2*), Valencia 1 (*Kempes*)

Semi-Finals, Second Leg
Juventus 0, Arsenal 1 (*Vaessen*)
Valencia 4 (*Bonhof, Michel og, Kempes 2 [1 pen]*), Nantes 0

Final 1979–80: Valencia 0, Arsenal 0 (aet)
Valencia won 5-4 on penalties.
(In Brussels, 14 May, 1980, 40,000)

Valencia: Pereira; Carrette, Botubot, Arias, Tendillo, Solsona, Saura, Bonhof, Kempes, Subirates (Castellanos), Pablo.
Arsenal: Jennings; Rice, Nelson, Talbot, O'Leary, Young, Brady, Sunderland, Stapleton, Price (Hollins), Rix.

FAIRS & UEFA CUP HISTORY

FAIRS CUP 1955–58

Group A
Barcelona 6, Copenhagen 2
Copenhagen 1, Barcelona 1
Vienna withdrew

	P	*W*	*D*	*L*	*F*	*A*	*Pts*
Barcelona	2	1	1	0	7	3	3
Copenhagen	2	0	1	1	3	7	1

Group B
Inter-Milan 0, Birmingham C 0
Zagreb 0, Birmingham C 1
Zagreb 0, Inter-Milan 1
Birmingham C 3, Zagreb 0
Inter-Milan 4, Zagreb 0
Birmingham C 2, Inter-Milan 1

	P	*W*	*D*	*L*	*F*	*A*	*Pts*
Birmingham C	4	3	1	0	6	1	7
Inter-Milan	4	2	1	1	6	2	5
Zagreb	4	0	0	4	0	9	0

Group C
Leipzig 6, Lausanne 3
Lausanne 7, Leipzig 3
Cologne withdrew

	P	*W*	*D*	*L*	*F*	*A*	*Pts*
Lausanne	2	1	0	1	10	9	2
Leipzig	2	1	0	1	9	10	2

Group D
Basle 0, London 5
London 3, Frankfurt 2
London 1, Basle 0
Frankfurt 5, Basle 1
Frankfurt 1, London 0
Basle 6, Frankfurt 2

	P	*W*	*D*	*L*	*F*	*A*	*Pts*
London	4	3	0	1	9	3	6
Frankfurt	4	2	0	2	10	10	4
Basle	4	1	0	3	7	13	2

Semi-Final

Birmingham C v Barcelona (5-6)	4-3, 0-1, 1-2
Lausanne v London (2-3)	2-1, 0-2

Final

London v Barcelona (2-8)	**2-2, 0-6**

FAIRS CUP 1958–60

First Round

Basle v Barcelona (3-7)	1-2, 2-5
Inter-Milan v Lyon (8-1)	7-0, 1-1
Belgrade v Lausanne (11-4)	6-1, 5-3
Frem Copenhagen v Chelsea (2-7)	1-3, 1-4
Union St Gilloise v Leipzig (6-1)	6-0, 0-1
Hanover 96 v AS Roma (2-4)	1-3, 1-1
Zagreb v Ujpest Dozsa (4-3)	4-2, 0-1
Cologne v Birmingham C (2-4)	2-2, 0-2

Quarter-Final

Barcelona v Inter-Milan (8-2)	4-0, 4-2
Chelsea v Belgrade (2-4)	1-0, 1-4
Union St Gilloise v AS Roma (3-1)	2-0, 1-1
Birmingham C v Zagreb (4-3)	1-0, 3-3

Semi-Final

Belgrade v Barcelona (2-4)	1-1, 1-3
Union St Gilloise v Birmingham C (4-8)	2-4, 2-4

Final

Birmingham C v Barcelona (1-4)	**0-0, 1-4**

FAIRS CUP 1960–61

First Round

Union St Gilloise v AS Roma (1-4)	0-0, 1-4
Lyon v Cologne (3-4)	1-3, 2-1
Lausanne v Hibernian (0-2)	0-2

Lausanne withdrew after first leg.

Zagreb v Barcelona (4-5)	1-1, 3-4
Leipzig v Belgrade (6-8)	5-2, 1-4, 0-2
Inter-Milan v Hanover 96 (14-3)	8-2, 6-1
Copenhagen v Basle (11-4)	8-1, 3-3
Birmingham C v Ujpest Dozsa (5-3)	3-2, 2-1

Quarter-Final

Cologne v AS Roma (3-6)	0-2, 2-0, 1-4
Barcelona v Hibernian (6-7)	4-4, 2-3
Inter-Milan v Belgrade (5-1)	5-0, 0-1
Copenhagen v Birmingham C (4-9)	4-4, 0-5

Semi-Final

Hibernian v AS Roma (5-11)	2-2, 3-3, 0-6
Inter-Milan v Birmingham C (2-4)	1-2, 1-2

Final

Birmingham C v AS Roma (2-4)	**2-2, 0-2**

FAIRS CUP 1961–62

First Round

Valencia v Nottingham F (7-1)	2-0, 5-1
Lausanne	bye
Cologne v Inter-Milan (7-9)	4-2, 0-2, 3-5
Union St Gilloise v Hearts (1-5)	1-3, 0-2
Spartak Brno v Leipzig (3-6)	2-2, 1-4
Strasbourg v MTK Budapest (3-13)	1-3, 2-10
AC Milan v Novisad (0-2)	0-0, 0-2
Iraklis Salonika	bye
Basle v Red Star Belgrade (2-5)	1-1, 1-4
Hibernian v Belenenses (6-4)	3-3, 3-1
Hanover 96 v Espanol (0-3)	0-1, 0-2
Birmingham C	bye
Lyon v Sheffield W (6-7)	4-2, 2-5
AS Roma	bye
Copenhagen v Dynamo Zagreb (4-9)	2-7, 2-2
West Berlin v Barcelona (1-3)	1-0, 0-3

Second Round

Lausanne v Valencia (3-4)	3-4

Second leg not played.

Hearts v Inter-Milan (0-5)	0-1, 0-4
MTK Budapest v Leipzig (5-3)	3-0, 0-3, 2-0
Iraklis Salonika v Novisad (3-10)	2-1, 1-9
Red Star Belgrade v Hibernian (5-0)	4-0, 1-0
Espanol v Birmingham C (5-3)	5-2, 0-1
Sheffield W v AS Roma (4-1)	4-0, 0-1
Barcelona v Dynamo Zagreb (7-3)	5-1, 2-2

Quarter-Final

Valencia v Inter-Milan (5-3)	2-0, 3-3
Novisad v MTK Budapest (2-6)	1-4, 1-2
Espanol v Red Star Belgrade (2-6)	2-1, 0-5
Sheffield W v Barcelona (3-4)	3-2, 0-2

Semi-Final

Valencia v MTK Budapest (10-3)	3-0, 7-3
Red Star Belgrade v Barcelona (1-6)	0-2, 1-4

Final

Valencia v Barcelona (7-3)	**6-2, 1-1**

FAIRS CUP 1962–63

First Round

Valencia v Celtic (6-4)	4-2, 2-2
Everton v Dunfermline Ath (1-2)	1-0, 0-2
Hibernian v Copenhagen (7-2)	4-0, 3-2
DOS Utrecht v Tasmania Berlin (5-3)	3-2, 2-1
Altay Izmir v AS Roma (3-13)	2-3, 1-10
Glentoran v Real Zaragoza (2-8)	0-2, 2-6
Rapid Vienna v Red Star Belgrade (1-2)	1-1, 0-1
Barcelona v Belenenses (5-4)	1-1, 1-1, 3-2
Viktoria Cologne v Ferencvaros (5-7)	4-3, 1-4
Sampdoria v Aris Luxembourg (3-0)	1-0, 2-0
Petrolul Ploesti v Spartak Brno (4-3)	4-2, 0-1
Vojvodina v Leipzig (1-2)	1-0, 0-2
Basle v Bayern Munich (0-3)	0-3

Second leg not played.

Drumcondra v Odense BK 09 (6-5)	4-1, 2-4
Marseille v Union St Gilloise (3-4)	1-0, 2-4
Porto v Dynamo Zagreb (1-2)	1-2, 0-0

Second Round

Valencia v Dunfermline Ath (7-6)	4-0, 2-6, 1-0
DOS Utrecht v Hibernian (1-3)	0-1, 1-2
Real Zaragoza v AS Roma (3-6)	2-4, 1-2
Red Star Belgrade v Barcelona (4-3)	3-2, 0-1, 1-0
Sampdoria v Ferencvaros (1-6)	1-0, 0-6
Petrolul Ploesti v Leipzig (2-1)	1-0, 0-1, 1-0
Bayern Munich v Drumcondra (6-1)	6-0, 0-1
Dynamo Zagreb v Union St Gilloise (5-4)	2-1, 0-1, 3-2

Quarter-Final

Valencia v Hibernian (6-2)	5-0, 1-2
AS Roma v Red Star Belgrade (3-2)	3-0, 0-2
Ferencvaros v Petrolul Ploesti (2-1)	2-0, 0-1
Bayern Munich v Dynamo Zagreb (1-4)	1-4, 0-0

Semi-Final

Valencia v AS Roma (3-1)	3-0, 0-1
Ferencvaros v Dynamo Zagreb (1-3)	0-1, 1-2

Final

Dynamo Zagreb v Valencia (1-4)	**1-2, 0-2**

FAIRS CUP 1963–64

First Round

Real Zaragoza v Iraklis Salonika (9-1)	3-0, 6-1
Lausanne v Hearts (9-8)	2-2, 4-4, 3-2
Atlético Madrid v Porto (2-1)	2-1, 0-0
Juventus v OFK Belgrade (4-3)	2-1, 1-2, 1-0
Aris Luxembourg v Liège (0-2)	0-2, 0-0
Staevnet Copenhagen v Arsenal (4-9)	1-7, 3-2
Glentoran v Partick T (1-7)	1-4, 0-3
Spartak Brno v Servette Geneva (7-1)	5-0, 2-1
Cologne v La Gantoise (4-2)	3-1, 1-1
DOS Utrecht v Sheffield W (2-8)	1-4, 1-4
Hertha Berlin v AS Roma (1-5)	1-3, 0-2
Tresnjevka Zagreb v Belenenses (1-4)	0-2, 1-2
Ujpest Dozsa v Lokomotiv Leipzig (3-2)	0-0, 3-2
Red Flag Brasov v Lokomotiv Plovdiv (2-5)	1-3, 1-2
Rapid Vienna v Racing Club de Paris (4-2)	1-0, 3-2
Shamrock Rovers v Valencia (2-3)	0-1, 2-2

Second Round

Lausanne v Real Zaragoza (1-5)	1-2, 0-3
Juventus v Atlético Madrid (3-1)	1-0, 2-1
Arsenal v Liège (2-4)	1-1, 1-3
Partick T v Spartak Brno (3-6)	3-2, 0-4
Cologne v Sheffield W (5-3)	3-2, 2-1
AS Roma v Belenenses (3-1)	2-1, 1-0
Ujpest Dozsa v Lokomotiv Plovdiv (3-1)	0-0, 3-1
Rapid Vienna v Valencia (2-3)	0-0, 2-3

Quarter-Final

Real Zaragoza v Juventus (3-2)	3-2, 0-0
Liège v Spartak Brno (3-2)	2-0, 0-2, 1-0
AS Roma v Cologne (3-5)	3-1, 0-4
Valencia v Ujpest Dozsa (6-5)	5-2, 1-3

Semi-Final

Liège v Real Zaragoza (2-4)	1-0, 1-2, 0-2
Valencia v Cologne (4-3)	4-1, 0-2

Final (at Barcelona)

Real Zaragoza v Valencia	**2-1**

FAIRS CUP 1964–65

First Round

Union St Gilloise v Juventus (0-2)	0-1, 0-1
Betis v Stade Français (1-3)	1-1, 0-2
Goztepe Izmir v Petrolul Ploesti (1-3)	1-2, 0-1
Vojvodina v Lokomotiv Plovdiv (2-4)	1-1, 1-1, 0-2
KB Copenhagen v DOS Utrecht (4-6)	3-4, 1-2
Valencia v Liège (2-4)	1-1, 1-3
Belenenses v Shelbourne (2-3)	1-1, 0-0, 1-2
Servette Geneva v Atlético Madrid (3-8)	2-2, 1-6
Basle v Spora Luxembourg (2-1)	2-0, 0-1
Strasbourg v AC Milan (2-1)	2-0, 0-1
Barcelona v Fiorentina (2-1)	0-1, 2-0
Leixoes v Celtic (1-4)	1-1, 0-3
Borussia Dortmund v Bordeaux (4-3)	4-1, 0-2
Manchester U v Djurgaarden (7-2)	1-1, 6-1
Eintracht Frankfurt v Kilmarnock (4-5)	3-0, 1-5
Valerengen v Everton (4-9)	2-5, 2-4
Atlético Bilbao v OFK Belgrade (4-2)	2-2, 2-0
Hertha Berlin v Antwerp (2-3)	2-1, 0-2
Odense BK 13 v Stuttgart (1-4)	1-3, 0-1
Dunfermline Ath v Oergryte (4-2)	4-2, 0-0
Dynamo Zagreb v Graz (9-2)	3-2, 6-0
Aris Salonika v AS Roma (0-3)	0-0, 0-3
Wiener SK v Lokomotiv Leipzig (3-1)	2-1, 1-0
Ferencvaros v Spartak Brno (2-1)	2-0, 0-1

Second Round

Stade Français v Juventus (0-1)	0-0, 0-1
Petrolul Ploesti v Lokomotiv Plovdiv (1-2)	1-0, 0-2
DOS Utrecht v Liège (0-4)	0-2, 0-2
Shelbourne v Atlético Madrid (0-2)	0-1, 0-1
Basle v Strasbourg (2-6)	0-1, 2-5
Barcelona v Celtic (3-1)	3-1, 0-0
Borussia Dortmund v Manchester U (1-10)	1-6, 0-4
Kilmarnock v Everton (1-6)	0-2, 1-4
Atlético Bilbao v Antwerp (3-0)	2-0, 1-0
Dunfermline Ath v Stuttgart (1-0)	1-0, 0-0
Dynamo Zagreb v AS Roma (1-2)	1-1, 0-1
Ferencvaros v Wiener SK (4-2)	0-1, 2-1, 2-0

Third Round

Juventus v Lokomotiv Plovdiv (4-3)	1-1, 1-1, 2-1
Liège v Atlético Madrid (1-2)	1-0, 0-2
Strasbourg v Barcelona (2-2)	0-0, 2-2, 0-0
Strasbourg won on toss of coin.	
Manchester U v Everton (3-2)	1-1, 2-1
Atlético Bilbao v Dunfermline Ath (3-2)	1-0, 0-1, 2-1
AS Roma v Ferencvaros (1-3)	1-2, 0-1

Quarter-Final

Byes: Juventus, Atlético Madrid

Strasbourg v Manchester U (0-5)	0-5, 0-0
Ferencvaros v Atlético Bilbao (5-2)	1-0, 1-2, 3-0

Semi-Final

Atlético Madrid v Juventus (5-7)	3-1, 1-3, 1-3
Manchester U v Ferencvaros (4-5)	3-2, 0-1, 1-2

Final (in Turin)

Juventus v Ferencvaros	**0-1**

FAIRS CUP 1965–66

First Round

Byes: Hanover 96, Espanol, Red Flag Brasov, Goztepe Izmir, Servette Geneva, CUF, Lokomotiv Leipzig, Basle, Aris Salonika, Ujpest Dozsa, Dunfermline Ath, KB Copenhagen, Hearts, Valerengen, Shamrock Rovers, Real Zaragoza.

DOS Utrecht v Barcelona (1-7)	0-0, 1-7
Antwerp v Glentoran (4-3)	1-0, 3-3
Stade Français v Porto (0-1)	0-0, 0-1
Bordeaux v Sporting Lisbon (1-10)	0-4, 1-6
Liège v Dynamo Zagreb (1-2)	1-0, 0-2
Munich 1860 v Malmö FF (7-1)	4-1, 3-0
AIK Stockholm v Daring (3-1)	3-1, 0-0
AC Milan* v Strasbourg (3-3)	1-0, 1-2, 1-1
Wiener SK v PAOK Salonika (7-2)	6-0, 1-2
Chelsea v AS Roma (4-1)	4-1, 0-0
Leeds U v Torino (2-1)	2-1, 0-0
Hibernian v Valencia (2-5)	2-0, 0-2, 0-3
US Luxembourg v Cologne (0-17)	0-4, 0-13
Nuremberg v Everton (1-2)	1-1, 0-1
Red Star Belgrade v Fiorentina (1-7)	0-4, 1-3
Spartak Brno v Lokomotiv Plovdiv (2-1)	2-0, 0-1

Second Round

Antwerp v Barcelona (2-3)	2-1, 0-2
Hanover 96 v Porto (6-2)	5-0, 1-2
Sporting Lisbon v Espanol (6-7)	2-1, 3-4, 1-2
Dynamo Zagreb v Red Flag Brasov (2-3)	2-2, 0-1
Goztepe Izmir v Munich 1860 (3-10)	2-1, 1-9
AIK Stockholm v Servette Geneva (3-5)	2-1, 1-4
CUF v AC Milan (2-3)	2-0, 0-2, 0-1
Wiener SK v Chelsea (1-2)	1-0, 0-2
Lokomotiv Leipzig v Leeds U (1-2)	1-2, 0-0
Basle v Valencia (2-8)	1-3, 1-5
Aris Salonika v Cologne (2-3)	2-1, 0-2
Ujpest Dozsa v Everton (4-2)	3-0, 1-2
Dunfermline Ath v KB Copenhagen (9-2)	5-0, 4-2
Fiorentina v Spartak Brno (2-4)	2-0, 0-4
Hearts v Valerengen (4-1)	1-0, 3-1
Shamrock Rovers v Real Zaragoza (2-3)	1-1, 1-2

Third Round

Hanover 96 v Barcelona* (3-3)	2-1, 0-1, 1-1
Espanol v Red Flag Brasov (6-5)	3-1, 2-4, 1-0
Servette Geneva v Munich 1860 (2-5)	1-1, 1-4
AC Milan v Chelsea* (4-4)	2-1, 1-2, 1-1
Leeds U v Valencia (2-1)	1-1, 1-0
Cologne v Ujpest Dozsa (3-6)	3-2, 0-4
Dunfermline Ath v Spartak Brno (2-0)	2-0, 0-0
Hearts v Real Zaragoza (5-6)	3-3, 2-2, 0-1

Quarter-Final

Barcelona v Espanol (2-0)	1-0, 1-0
Munich 1860 v Chelsea (2-3)	2-2, 0-1
Leeds U v Ujpest Dozsa (5-2)	4-1, 1-1
Dunfermline Ath v Real Zaragoza (3-4)	1-0, 2-4

Semi-Final

Barcelona v Chelsea (7-2)	2-0, 0-2, 5-0
Real Zaragoza v Leeds U (5-3)	1-0, 1-2, 3-1

Final

Barcelona v Real Zaragoza (4-3)	**0-1, 4-2**

**Won on toss after extra time.*

EUROPEAN FAIRS CUP 1966–67

First Round

Byes: Leeds U, DWS Amsterdam, WBA, Sparta Prague, Liège, Benfica, Spartak Plovdiv, Kilmarnock, La Gantoise, Hvidovre, Lausanne, Odense BK 09, Vitoria Setubal, Dundee U, Barcelona, Toulouse.

Nuremberg v Valencia (1-4)	1-2, 0-2
Red Star Belgrade v Atlético Bilbao (5-2)	5-0, 0-2
DOS Utrecht v Basle (4-3)	2-1, 2-2
Bologna v Goztepe Izmir (5-2)	2-1, 3-1
Djurgaarden v Lokomotiv Leipzig (2-5)	1-3, 1-2
US Luxembourg v Antwerp (0-2)	0-1, 0-1
Porto v Bordeaux* (3-3)	2-1, 1-2
Drumcondra v Eintracht Frankfurt (1-8)	0-2, 1-6
Nice v Oergryte (3-4)	2-2, 1-2
Olympia Ljubljana v Ferencvaros (3-6)	3-3, 0-3
Stuttgart v Burnley (1-3)	1-1, 0-2
Wiener SK v Napoli (2-5)	1-2, 1-3
Juventus v Aris Salonika (7-0)	5-0, 2-0
Dynamo Pitesti v Seville (4-2)	2-0, 2-2
Frigg Oslo v Dunfermline Ath (2-6)	1-3, 1-3
Spartak Brno v Dynamo Zagreb* (2-2)	0-2, 2-0

Second Round

DWS Amsterdam v Leeds U (2-8)	1-3, 1-5
Valencia v Red Star Belgrade (3-1)	1-0, 2-1
WBA v DOS Utrecht (6-3)	5-2, 1-1
Sparta Prague v Bologna (3-4)	2-2, 1-2
Liège v Lokomotiv Leipzig (1-2)	0-0, 1-2
Spartak Plovdiv v Benfica (1-4)	1-1, 0-3
Antwerp v Kilmarnock (2-8)	0-1, 2-7
La Gantoise v Bordeaux (1-0)	1-0, 0-0
Eintracht Frankfurt v Hvidovre (7-3)	5-1, 2-2
Oergryte v Ferencvaros (1-7)	0-0, 1-7
Lausanne v Burnley (1-8)	1-3, 0-5
Odense BK 09 v Napoli (2-6)	1-4, 1-2
Juventus v Vitoria Setubal (5-1)	3-1, 2-0
Barcelona v Dundee U (1-4)	1-2, 0-2
Toulouse v Dynamo Pitesti (4-5)	3-0, 1-5
Dunfermline Ath v Dynamo Zagreb† (4-4)	4-2, 0-2

Third Round

Leeds U v Valencia (3-1)	1-1, 2-0
Bologna v WBA (6-1)	3-0, 3-1
Lokomotiv Leipzig v Benfica (4-3)	3-1, 1-2
Kilmarnock v La Gantoise (3-1)	1-0, 2-1
Eintracht Frankfurt v Ferencvaros (5-3)	4-1, 1-2
Burnley v Naples (3-0)	3-0, 0-0
Juventus v Dundee U (3-1)	3-0, 0-1
Dynamo Pitesti v Dynamo Zagreb (0-1)	0-1, 0-0

Quarter-Final

Bologna v Leeds U* (1-1)	1-0, 0-1
Lokomotiv Leipzig v Kilmarnock (1-2)	1-0, 0-2
Eintracht Frankfurt v Burnley (3-2)	1-1, 2-1
Juventus v Dynamo Zagreb (2-5)	2-2, 0-3

Semi-Final

Leeds U v Kilmarnock (4-2)	4-2, 0-0
Eintracht Frankfurt v Dynamo Zagreb (3-4)	3-0, 0-4

Final

Dynamo Zagreb v Leeds U (2-0)	**2-0, 0-0**

**Won on toss of coin.* †*Won on away goals rule.*

EUROPEAN FAIRS CUP 1967–68

First Round

Spora Luxembourg v Leeds U (0-16)	0-9, 0-7
PAOK Salonika v Liège (2-5)	0-2, 2-3
Wiener SK v Atlético Madrid (3-7)	2-5, 1-2
St Patrick's Athletic v Bordeaux (4-9)	1-3, 3-6
DOS Utrecht v Real Zaragoza (4-5)	3-2, 1-3
Napoli v Hanover 96 (5-1)	4-0, 1-1
Bologna v Lyn Oslo (2-0)	2-0, 0-0
Nice v Fiorentina (0-5)	0-1, 0-4
Dynamo Dresden v Rangers (2-3)	1-1, 1-2
Servette Geneva v Munich 1860 (2-6)	2-2, 0-4
Argesul Pitesti v Ferencvaros (3-5)	3-1, 0-4
Malmö FF v Liverpool (1-4)	0-2, 1-2
Hibernian v Porto (4-3)	3-0, 1-3
Eintracht Frankfurt v Nottingham F (0-5)	0-1, 0-4
Dynamo Zagreb v Petrolul Ploesti (5-2)	5-0, 0-2
Bruges v Sporting Lisbon (1-2)	0-0, 1-2
Frem Copenhagen v Atlético Bilbao (2-4)	0-1, 2-3
Zurich v Barcelona (3-2)	3-1, 0-1
Lokomotiv Leipzig v Linfield (5-2)	5-1, 0-1
DWS Amsterdam v Dundee (2-4)	2-1, 0-3
Partizan Belgrade v Lokomotiv Plovdiv (6-2)	5-1, 1-1
Vojvodina v CUF (4-1)	1-0, 3-1
Cologne v Slavia Prague (4-2)	2-0, 2-2
Antwerp v Goztepe Izmir (1-2)	1-2, 0-0

Second Round

Nottingham F v Zurich (2-2)	2-1, 0-1
Zurich won on away goals rule.	
Bordeaux v Atlético Bilbao (1-4)	1-3, 0-1
Dundee v Liège (7-2)	3-1, 4-1
Vojvodina v Lokomotiv Leipzig (2-0)	0-0, 2-0
Real Zaragoza v Ferencvaros (2-4)	2-1, 0-3
Liverpool v Munich 1860 (9-2)	8-0, 1-2
Rangers v Cologne (4-3)	3-0, 1-3
Bologna v Dynamo Zagreb (2-1)	0-0, 2-1
Napoli v Hibernian (4-6)	4-1, 0-5
Partizan Belgrade v Leeds U (2-3)	1-2, 1-1
Fiorentina v Sporting Lisbon (2-3)	1-1, 1-2
Atlético Madrid v Goztepe Izmir (2-3)	2-0, 0-3

Third Round

Byes: Atlético Bilbao, Bologna, Dundee, Rangers

Ferencvaros v Liverpool (2-0)	1-0, 1-0
Leeds U v Hibernian (2-1)	1-0, 1-1
Vojvodina v Goztepe Izmir (2-0)	1-0, 1-0
Zurich v Sporting Lisbon (3-1)	3-0, 0-1

Quarter-Final

Ferencvaros v Atlético Bilbao (4-2)	2-1, 2-1
Rangers v Leeds U (0-2)	0-0, 0-2
Dundee v Zurich (2-0)	1-0, 1-0
Bologna v Vojvodina (2-0)	0-0, 2-0

Semi-Final

Dundee v Leeds U (1-2)	1-1, 0-1
Ferencvaros v Bologna (5-4)	3-2, 2-2

Final

Leeds U v Ferencvaros (1-0)	**1-0, 0-0**

EUROPEAN FAIRS CUP 1968–69

First Round

Byes: Argesul, Leipzig, Ujpest

Chelsea v Morton (9-3)	5-0, 4-3
Newcastle U v Feyenoord (4-2)	4-0, 0-2
Atlético Bilbao* v Liverpool (3-3)	2-1, 1-2
Rangers v Vojvodina (2-1)	2-0, 0-1
Ljubljana v Hibernian (1-5)	0-3, 1-2
Rapid Bucharest v OFK Belgrade (4-7)	3-1, 1-6
Wiener SK v Slavia Prague (1-5)	1-0, 0-5
Skeid Oslo v AIK Stockholm (2-3)	1-1, 1-2
Trakia Plovdiv v Real Zaragoza† (3-3)	3-1, 0-2
Dynamo Zagreb v Fiorentina (2-3)	1-1, 1-2
Legia Warsaw v Munich 1860 (9-2)	6-0, 3-2
Daring v Panathinaikos (2-3)	2-1, 0-2
Wacker Innsbruck v Eintracht Frankfurt (2-5)	2-2, 0-3
Sporting Lisbon v Valencia (5-4)	4-0, 1-4
Bologna v Basle (6-2)	4-1, 2-1
Aris Salonika v Hibernians Valletta (7-0)	1-0, 6-0
DOS Utrecht v Dundalk (2-3)	1-1, 1-2
Atlético Madrid v Waregem* (2-2)	2-1, 0-1
Hansa Rostock v Nice (4-2)	3-0, 1-2
Goztepe Izmir* v Marseille (2-2)	2-0, 0-2
Metz v SV Hamburg (3-7)	1-4, 2-3
Lyon* v Academica Coimbra (1-1)	1-0, 0-1
Lausanne v Juventus (0-4)	0-2, 0-2
Beerschot v DWS Amsterdam (2-3)	1-1, 1-2
Hanover 96 v Odense BK 09 (4-2)	3-2, 1-0
Vitoria Setubal v Linfield (6-1)	3-0, 3-1
Standard Liège v Leeds U (2-3)	0-0, 2-3
Napoli v Grasshoppers (3-2)	3-1, 0-1
Slavia Sofia v Aberdeen (0-2)	0-0, 0-2

Second Round

Hibernian v Lokomotiv Leipzig (4-1)	3-1, 1-0
Leeds U* v Napoli (2-2)	2-0, 0-2
Rangers v Dundalk (9-1)	6-1, 3-0
Aberdeen v Real Zaragoza (2-4)	2-1, 0-3
Chelsea v DWS Amsterdam* (0-0)	0-0, 0-0
Sporting Lisbon v Newcastle U (1-2)	1-1, 0-1
Vitoria Setubal v Lyon (7-1)	5-0, 2-1
Goztepe Izmir v Argesul Pitesti (5-3)	3-0, 2-3
Hansa Rostock v Fiorentina† (4-4)	3-2, 1-2
SV Hamburg v Slavia Prague (5-4)	4-1, 1-3
Panathinaikos v Atlético Bilbao (0-1)	0-0, 0-1
OFK Belgrade v Bologna (2-1)	1-0, 1-1
Aris Salonika v Ujpest Dozsa (2-11)	1-2, 1-9
AIK Stockholm v Hanover 96 (6-7)	4-2, 2-5
Waregem v Legia Warsaw (1-2)	1-0, 0-2
Juventus v Eintracht Frankfurt (0-1)	0-0, 0-1

Third Round

Leeds U v Hanover 96 (7-2)	5-1, 2-1
SV Hamburg† v Hibernian (2-2)	1-0, 1-2
Legia Warsaw v Ujpest Dozsa (2-3)	0-1, 2-2
Real Zaragoza v Newcastle U† (4-4)	3-2, 1-2
OFK Belgrade v Goztepe Izmir† (3-3)	3-1, 0-2
Eintracht Frankfurt v Atlético Bilbao (1-2)	1-1, 0-1
DWS Amsterdam v Rangers (1-4)	0-2, 1-2
Vitoria Setubal v Fiorentina (4-2)	3-0, 1-2

Quarter-Final

Newcastle U v Vitoria Setubal (6-4)	5-1, 1-3
Rangers v Atlético Bilbao (4-3)	4-1, 0-2
Leeds U v Ujpest Dozsa (0-3)	0-1, 0-2
Goztepe Izmir v SV Hamburg	
Hamburg withdrew	

Semi-Final

Goztepe Izmir v Ujpest Dozsa (1-8)	1-4, 0-4
Rangers v Newcastle U (0-2)	0-0, 0-2

Final

Newcastle U v Ujpest Dozsa (6-2)	**3-0, 3-2**

**Won on toss of coin.*

†Won on away goals rule

EUROPEAN FAIRS CUP 1969–70

First Round

Arsenal v Glentoran (3-1)	3-0, 0-1
Dundee U v Newcastle U (1-3)	1-2, 0-1
Liverpool v Dundalk (14-0)	10-0, 4-0
Partizan Belgrade v Ujpest Dozsa (2-3)	2-1, 0-2
Sabadell v Bruges (3-5)	2-0, 1-5
Las Palmas v Hertha Berlin (0-1)	0-0, 0-1
Wiener SK v Ruch Chorzow (5-6)	4-2, 1-4
Rouen v Twente (2-1)	2-0, 0-1
Vitoria Guimaraes v Banik Ostrava (2-1)	1-0, 1-1
Sporting Lisbon v ASK Linz (6-2)	4-0, 2-2
Carl Zeiss Jena v Altay Izmir (1-0)	1-0, 0-0
Lausanne v Vasas Gyor (2-4)	1-2, 1-2
Rosenborg v Southampton (1-2)	1-0, 0-2
Hansa Rostock v Panionios (3-2)	3-0, 0-2
Dynamo Bacau v Floriana (7-0)	6-0, 1-0
Slavia Sofia v Valencia (3-1)	2-0, 1-1
Inter-Milan v Sparta Prague (4-0)	3-0, 1-0
Juventus v Lokomotiv Plovdiv (5-2)	3-1, 2-1
Stuttgart v Malmö FF (4-1)	3-0, 1-1
Hanover 96 v Ajax (2-4)	2-1, 0-3
Aris Salonika v Cagliari (1-4)	1-1, 0-3
Metz v Napoli (2-3)	1-1, 1-2
Barcelona v Odense BK 09 (6-0)	4-0, 2-0
Gwardia Warsaw v Vojvodina (2-1)	1-0, 1-1
Dunfermline Ath v Bordeaux (4-2)	4-0, 0-2
Zurich v Kilmarnock (4-5)	3-2, 1-3
Munich 1860 v Skeid Oslo (3-4)	2-2, 1-2
Valur Reykjavik v Anderlecht (0-8)	0-6, 0-2
SC Charleroi v ZNK Zagreb (5-2)	2-1, 3-1
Hvidovre v Porto (1-4)	1-2, 0-2
Jeunesse Esch v Coleraine (3-6)	3-2, 0-4
Vitoria Setubal v Rapid Bucharest (7-2)	3-1, 4-1

Second Round

Sporting Lisbon v Arsenal (0-3)	0-0, 0-3
SC Charleroi v Rouen† (3-3)	3-1, 0-2
Skeid Oslo v Dynamo Bacau (0-2)	0-0, 0-2
Kilmarnock v Slavia Sofia (4-3)	4-1, 0-2
Ajax v Ruch Chorzow (9-1)	7-0, 2-1
Stuttgart v Napoli (0-1)	0-0, 0-1
Carl Zeiss Jena v Cagliari (3-0)	2-0, 1-0
Bruges v Ujpest Dozsa† (5-5)	5-2, 0-3
Hansa Rostock v Inter-Milan (2-4)	2-1, 0-3
Vasas Gyor v Barcelona (2-5)	2-3, 0-2
Hertha Berlin v Juventus (3-1)	3-1, 0-0
Vitoria Setubal† v Liverpool (3-3)	1-0, 2-3
Porto v Newcastle U (0-1)	0-0, 0-1
Vitoria Guimaraes v Southampton (4-8)	3-3, 1-5
Dunfermline Ath v Gwardia Warsaw (3-1)	2-1, 1-0
Anderlecht v Coleraine (13-4)	6-1, 7-3

Third Round

Rouen v Arsenal (0-1)	0-0, 0-1
Kilmarnock v Dynamo Bacau (1-3)	1-1, 0-2
Napoli v Ajax (1-4)	1-0, 0-4
Carl Zeiss Jena v Ujpest Dozsa (4-0)	1-0, 3-0
Barcelona v Inter-Milan (2-3)	1-2, 1-1
Vitoria Setubal v Hertha Berlin (1-2)	1-1, 0-1
Newcastle U† v Southampton (1-1)	0-0, 1-1
Anderlecht† v Dunfermline Ath (3-3)	1-0, 2-3

Quarter-Final

Dynamo Bacau v Arsenal (1-9)	0-2, 1-7
Carl Zeiss Jena v Ajax (4-6)	3-1, 1-5
Hertha Berlin v Inter-Milan (1-2)	1-0, 0-2
Anderlecht† v Newcastle U (3-3)	2-0, 1-3

Semi-Final

Arsenal v Ajax (3-1)	3-0, 0-1
Anderlecht v Inter-Milan (2-1)	0-1, 2-0

† Won on away goals counting double.

Final 1969–70: Anderlecht 3, Arsenal 1
(At Brussels, 22 April, 1970, 37,000)

Anderlecht: Trappeniers; Heylens, Velkeneers; Nordahl, Kialunda, Cornelis (Peeters); Desanghere, Devrindt, Mulder, Van Himst, Puis.

Arsenal: Wilson; Storey, McNab; Kelly, McLintock, Simpson; Armstrong, Sammels, Radford, George (Kennedy), Graham.

Scorers: Anderlecht – Devrindt, Mulder 2; Arsenal – Kennedy.

Arsenal 3, Anderlecht 0
(At Highbury, 28 April, 1970, 51,612)

Arsenal: Wilson; Storey, McNab; Kelly, McLintock, Simpson; Armstrong, Sammels, Radford, George, Graham.

Anderlecht: Trappeniers; Heylens, Maartens; Nordahl, Velkeneers, Kialunda; Desanghere, Devrindt, Mulder, Van Himst, Puis.

Scorers: Arsenal – Kelly, Radford, Sammels.

EUROPEAN FAIRS CUP 1970–71

First Round

AEK Athens v Twente (0-4)	0-1, 0-3
Zeljeznicar v Anderlecht (7-9)	4-5, 3-4
La Gantoise v SV Hamburg (1-8)	0-1, 1-7
Seville v Eskisehirspor (2-3)	1-0, 1-3
Coleraine v Kilmarnock (4-3)	1-1, 3-2
Dundee U v Grasshoppers (3-2)	3-2, 0-0
Sarpsborg v Leeds U (0-6)	0-1, 0-5
Spartak Trnava* v Marseille (2-2)	2-0, 0-2
Cologne v Sedan (5-2)	5-1, 0-1
Lausanne v Vitoria Setubal (1-4)	0-2, 1-2
Hibernian v Malmo FF (9-2)	6-0, 3-2
Liverpool v Ferencvaros (2-1)	1-0, 1-1
Trakia Plovdiv v Coventry C (1-6)	1-4, 0-2
Lazio v Arsenal (2-4)	2-2, 0-2
Bayern Munich v Rangers (2-1)	1-0, 1-1
Dynamo Bucharest v PAOK Salonika (5-1)	5-0, 0-1
Uni Craiova v Pecs Dozsa (2-4)	2-1, 0-3
Katowice v Barcelona (2-4)	0-1, 2-3
Wiener SK v Beveren (0-5)	0-2, 0-3
Ilves Kissat v Sturm Graz (4-5)	4-2, 0-3
Barreirense v Dynamo Zagreb (3-6)	2-0, 1-6
Hajduk Split v Slavia Sofia (3-1)	3-0, 0-1
Cork Hibs v Valencia (1-6)	0-3, 1-3
Sparta Prague v Atletico Bilbao (3-1)	2-0, 1-1
Partizan Belgrade v Dynamo Dresden (0-6)	0-0, 0-6
AB Copenhagen v Sliema Wanderers (10-2)	7-0, 3-2
Juventus v Rumelange (11-0)	7-0, 4-0
Nykoping v Hertha Berlin (3-8)	2-4, 1-4
Ruch Chorzow v Fiorentina (1-3)	1-1, 0-2
Inter-Milan v Newcastle U (1-3)	1-1, 0-2
Sparta Rotterdam v Akranes (15-0)	6-0, 9-0
Vitoria Guimaraes v Angouleme (4-3)	3-0, 1-3

Second Round

Hibernian v Vitoria Guimaraes (3-2)	2-0, 1-2
Sparta Rotterdam v Coleraine (4-1)	2-0, 2-1
Bayern Munich v Coventry C (7-3)	6-1, 1-2
Barcelona v Juventus (2-4)	1-2, 1-2
Fiorentina v Cologne (1-3)	1-2, 0-1
Sturm Graz v Arsenal (1-2)	1-0, 0-2
Leeds U† v Dynamo Dresden (2-2)	1-0, 1-2
Liverpool v Dynamo Bucharest (4-1)	3-0, 1-1
AB Copenhagen v Anderlecht (1-7)	1-3, 0-4
Newcastle U v Pecs Dozsa* (2-2)	2-0, 0-2
Sparta Prague v Dundee U (3-2)	3-1, 0-1
Hertha Berlin v Spartak Trnava (2-3)	1-0, 1-3
Dynamo Zagreb v Hamburg (4-1)	4-0, 0-1
Vitoria Setubal v Hajduk Split (3-2)	2-0, 1-2
Valencia v Beveren (1-2)	0-1, 1-1
Eskisehir v Twente (4-8)	3-2, 1-6

Third Round

Spartak Trnava v Cologne (0-4)	0-1, 0-3
Bayern Munich v Sparta Rotterdam (5-2)	2-1, 3-1
Leeds U v Sparta Prague (9-2)	6-0, 3-2
Arsenal v Beveren (4-0)	4-0, 0-0
Pecs Dozsa v Juventus (0-3)	0-1, 0-2
Dynamo Zagreb v Twente (2-3)	2-2, 0-1
Anderlecht v Vitoria Setubal (3-4)	2-1, 1-3
Hibernian v Liverpool (0-3)	0-1, 0-2

Quarter-Final

Juventus v Twente (4-2)	2-0, 2-2
Arsenal v Cologne†(2-2)	2-1, 0-1
Leeds U v Setubal (3-2)	2-1, 1-1
Liverpool v Bayern Munich (4-1)	3-0, 1-1

Semi-Final

Liverpool v Leeds U (0-1)	0-1, 0-0
Cologne v Juventus (1-3)	1-1, 0-2

* *Won on penalty kicks.* † *Won on away goals rule.*

Final 1970–71: Juventus 2, Leeds U 2
(In Turin, 29 May, 1971, 45,000)

Juventus: Piloni; Spinosi, Marchetti, Furino, Morini, Salvadore, Haller, Causio, Anastasi (Novellini), Capello, Bettega.

Leeds U: Sprake; Reaney, Cooper, Bremner, Charlton, Hunter, Lorimer, Clarke, Jones (Bates), Giles, Madeley.

Scorers: Juventus – Bettega, Capello; Leeds U – Madeley, Bates.

Leeds U 1, Juventus 1
(At Leeds, 2 June, 1971, 42,483)

Leeds U: Sprake; Reaney, Cooper, Bremner, Charlton, Hunter, Lorimer, Clarke, Jones, Giles, Madeley (Bates).

Juventus: Tancredi; Spinosi, Marchetti, Furino, Morini, Salvadore, Haller, Causio, Anastasi, Capello, Bettega.

Scorers: Leeds U – Clarke; Juventus – Anastasi.

Leeds U won on away goals rule.

UEFA CUP 1971–72

First Round

Hertha Berlin v Elfsborg (7-2)	4-1, 3-1
Dundee v Akademisk Copenhagen (5-2)	4-2, 1-0
Rosenborg v IFK Helsinki (4-0)	3-0, 1-0
Vasas Budapest v Shelbourne (2-1)	1-0, 1-1
Glentoran v Eintracht Brunswick (1-7)	0-1, 1-6
Keflavik v Tottenham H (1-15)	1-6, 0-9
Celta Vigo v Aberdeen (0-3)	0-2, 0-1
FC Den Haag v Aris Luxembourg (6-1)	5-0, 1-1
Wolverhampton W v Academica Coimbra (7-1)	4-1, 3-0
St Etienne v Cologne (2-3)	1-1, 1-2
Lugano v Legia Warsaw (1-3)	1-3, 0-0
Porto v Nantes (1-3)	0-2, 1-1
SV Hamburg v St Johnstone (2-4)	2-1, 0-3
Southampton v Atlético Bilbao (2-3)	2-1, 0-2
Bologna v Anderlecht (3-1)	2-0, 1-1
Napoli v Rapid Bucharest (1-2)	1-0, 0-2
Vitoria Setubal* v Nimes (2-2)	1-0, 1-2
Atlético Madrid v Panionios* (2-2)	2-1, 0-1
Carl Zeiss Jena v Lokomotiv Plovdiv (4-3)	3-0, 1-3
Basle v Real Madrid (2-4)	1-2, 1-2
Marsa v Juventus (0-11)	0-6, 0-5
Dynamo Zagreb v Botev Vratza (8-2)	6-1, 2-1
UT Arad v Austria Salzburg (5-4)	4-1, 1-3
Fenerbahce v Ferencvaros (2-4)	1-1, 1-3
AC Milan v Dighenis (7-0)	4-0, 3-0
Spartak Moscow v VSS Kosice (3-2)	1-2, 2-0
OFK Belgrade v Djurgaarden (6-3)	2-2, 4-1
Rapid Vienna	Bye
Zeljeznicar v Bruges (4-3)	3-0, 1-3
Chemie Halle (withdrew) v PSV Eindhoven (0-0)	0-0, –
Zaglebie Walbrzych v Union Teplice (4-2)	1-0, 3-2
Lierse v Leeds U (4-2)	0-2, 4-0

Second Round

Rosenborg v Lierse* (4-4)	4-1, 0-3
Rapid Bucharest v Legia Warsaw (4-2)	4-0, 0-2
Cologne v Dundee (4-5)	2-1, 2-4
FC Den Haag v Wolverhampton W (1-7)	1-3, 0-4
Zeljeznicar* v Bologna (3-3)	1-1, 2-2
Nantes v Tottenham H (0-1)	0-0, 0-1
Eintracht Brunswick v Atlético Bilbao (4-3)	2-1, 2-2
St Johnstone v Vasas Budapest (2-1)	2-0, 0-1
Spartak Moscow v Vitoria Setubal (0-4)	0-0, 0-4
Hertha Berlin v AC Milan (4-5)	2-1, 2-4
OFK Belgrade v Carl Zeiss Jena (1-5)	1-1, 0-4
Zaglebie Walbrzych v UT Arad (2-3)	1-1, 1-2
Dynamo Zagreb v Rapid Vienna* (2-2)	2-2, 0-0
Real Madrid v PSV Eindhoven* (3-3)	3-1, 0-2
Juventus v Aberdeen (3-1)	2-0, 1-1
Ferencvaros v Panionios (6-0)	6-0, –
Panionios disqualified	

Third Round

AC Milan v Dundee (3-2)	3-0, 0-2
Carl Zeiss Jena v Wolverhampton W (0-4)	0-1, 0-3
Eintracht Brunswick v Ferencvaros (3-6)	1-1, 2-5
PSV Eindhoven v Lierse (1-4)	1-0, 0-4
Rapid Vienna v Juventus (1-5)	0-1, 1-4
St Johnstone v Zeljeznicar (2-5)	1-0, 1-5
Tottenham H v Rapid Bucharest (5-0)	3-0, 2-0
UT Arad v Vitoria Setubal (3-1)	3-0, 0-1

Quarter-Final

AC Milan v Lierse (3-1)	2-0, 1-1
UT Arad v Tottenham H (1-3)	0-2, 1-1
Ferencvaros† v Zeljeznicar (3-3)	1-2, 2-1
Juventus v Wolverhampton W (2-3)	1-1, 1-2

Semi-Final

Tottenham H v AC Milan (3-2)	2-1, 1-1
Ferencvaros v Wolverhampton W (3-4)	2-2, 1-2

* *Won on away goals rule.* † *Won on penalty kicks.*

Final 1971–72: Wolverhampton W 1, Tottenham H 2

(At Wolverhampton, 3 May, 1972, 45,000)

Wolverhampton W: Parkes; Shaw, Taylor, Hegan, Munro, McAlle, McCalliog, Hibbitt, Richards, Dougan, Wagstaffe.
Tottenham H: Jennings; Kinnear, Knowles, Mullery, England, Beal, Coates (Pratt), Perryman, Chivers, Peters, Gilzean.
Scorers: Wolverhampton W – McCalliog; Tottenham H – Chivers 2.

Tottenham H 1, Wolverhampton W 1

(At White Hart Lane, 17 May, 1972)

Tottenham H: Jennings; Kinnear, Knowles, Mullery, England, Beal, Coates, Perryman, Chivers, Peters, Gilzean.
Wolverhampton W: Parkes; Shaw, Taylor, Hegan, Munro, McAlle, McCalliog, Hibbitt (Bailey), Richards, Dougan (Curran), Wagstaffe.
Scorers: Tottenham H – Mullery; Wolverhampton W – Wagstaffe.

UEFA CUP 1972–73

First Round

Aberdeen v Bor Moenchengladbach (5-9)	2-3, 3-6
Atvidaberg v Bruges (5-6)	3-5, 2-1
Manchester C v Valencia (3-4)	2-2, 1-2
Lyn Oslo v Tottenham H (3-12)	3-6, 0-6
Cologne v Bohemians (5-1)	2-1, 3-0
Honved v Partick T (4-0)	1-0, 3-0
Viking Stavanger v IBV Vastmannejar (1-0)	1-0, 0-0
Feyenoord v US Rumelange (21-0)	9-0, 12-0
Liverpool v Eintracht Frankfurt (2-0)	2-0, 0-0
Grasshoppers v Nimes (4-2)	2-1, 2-1
Vitoria Setubal v Zaglebie Sosnowiec (6-2)	6-1, 0-1
Stoke C v Kaiserslautern (3-5)	3-1, 0-4
Racing White v CUF Barrierense (0-3)	0-1, 0-2
Torino v Las Palmas (2-4)	2-0, 0-4
Sochaux v Frem Copenhagen (2-5)	1-3, 1-2
Olympiakos Piraeus v Cagliari (3-1)	2-1, 1-0
Angers v Dynamo Berlin (2-3)	1-1, 1-2
Porto v Barcelona (4-1)	3-1, 1-0
Univ Cluj v Levski Sofia (5-6)	4-1, 1-5
Red Star Belgrade v Lausanne (7-4)	5-1, 2-3
Inter-Milan v FC Valetta (7-1)	6-1, 1-0
Beroe Stara v FK Austria (10-1)	7-0, 3-1
UT Arad v Norrköping (1-4)	1-2, 0-2
EPA Larna v Ararat Erevan (0-2)	0-1, 0-1
AEK Athens v Salgotarjan (4-2)	3-1, 1-1
Eskisehirspor v Fiorentina (1-5)	1-2, 0-3
Dukla Prague v OFK Belgrade (3-5)	2-2, 1-3
Slovan Bratislava v Vojvodina (8-1)	6-0, 2-1
Dynamo Tbilisi v FC Twente (3-4)	3-2, 0-2
Ruch Chorzow v Fenerbahce (3-1)	3-0, 0-1
Dynamo Dresden v Voest Linz (4-2)	2-0, 2-2
Hvidovre Copenhagen	bye

Second Round

Dynamo Berlin v Levski Sofia (3-2)	3-0, 0-2
Bor Moenchengladbach v Hvidovre Copenhagen (6-1)	3-0, 3-1
Porto v Bruges (5-3)	3-0, 2-3
Tottenham H v Olympiakos Piraeus (4-1)	4-0, 0-1
Red Star Belgrade v Valencia (4-1)	3-1, 1-0
Inter-Milan v Norrköping (4-2)	2-2, 2-0
Viking Stavanger v Cologne (2-9)	1-0, 1-9
Beroe Stara v Honved (3-1)	3-0, 0-1
Feyenoord v OFK Belgrade* (5-5)	4-3, 1-2
Liverpool v AEK Athens (6-1)	3-0, 3-1

Vitoria Setubal* v Fiorentina (2-2)	1-0, 1-2
Grasshoppers v Ararat Erevan (3-7)	1-3, 2-4
CUF Barreirense v Kaiserslautern (2-3)	1-3, 1-0
Las Palmas v Slovan Bratislava (3-2)	2-2, 1-0
Ruch Chorzow v Dynamo Dresden (0-4)	0-1, 0-3
Frem Copenhagen v FC Twente (0-9)	0-5, 0-4

Third Round

Ararat Erevan v Kaiserslautern† (2-2)	2-0, 0-2
Cologne v Bor Moenchengladbach (0-5)	0-0, 0-5
Tottenham H v Red Star Belgrade (2-1)	2-0, 0-1
FC Twente v Las Palmas (4-2)	3-0, 1-2
OFK Belgrade v Beroe Stara (3-1)	0-0, 3-1
Vitoria Setubal v Inter-Milan (2-1)	2-0, 0-1
Dynamo Berlin v Liverpool (1-3)	0-0, 1-3
Porto v Dynamo Dresden (1-3)	1-2, 0-1

Quarter-Final

Kaiserslautern v Bor Moenchengladbach (2-9)	1-2, 1-7
OFK Belgrade v FC Twente (3-4)	3-2, 0-2
Tottenham H* v Vitoria Setubal (2-2)	1-0, 1-2
Liverpool v Dynamo Dresden (3-0)	2-0, 1-0

Semi-Final

Liverpool* v Tottenham H (2-2)	1-0, 1-2
Bor Moenchengladbach v FC Twente (5-1)	3-0, 2-1

** Won on away goals rule.* † *Won on penalty kicks.*

Final 1972–73: Liverpool 3, Borussia Moenchengladbach 0
(At Liverpool, 10 May, 1973, 41,169)

Liverpool: Clemence; Lawler, Lindsay, Smith, Lloyd, Hughes, Keegan, Cormack, Toshack, Heighway (Hall), Callaghan.
Borussia Moenchengladbach: Kleff; Danner, Michallik, Vogts, Bonhof, Kulik, Jensen, Wimmer, Rupp (Simonsen), Netzer, Heynckes.
Scorers: Liverpool – Keegan 2, Lloyd.

Borussia Moenchengladbach 2, Liverpool 0
(At Moenchengladbach, 23 May, 1973, 35,000)

Borussia Moenchengladbach: Kleff; Vogts, Surau, Netzer, Bonhof, Danner, Wimmer, Kulik, Jensen, Rupp, Heynckes.
Liverpool: Clemence; Lawler, Lindsay, Smith, Lloyd, Hughes, Keegan, Cormack, Heighway (Boersma), Toshack, Callaghan.
Scorer: Bor Moenchengladbach – Heynckes 2.

UEFA CUP 1973–74

First Round

Fredrikstad v Dynamo Kiev (0-5)	0-1, 0-4
Ruch Chorzow v Wuppertal (8-6)	4-1, 4-5
BK 1903 Copenhagen v AIK (3-2)	2-1, 1-1
Carl Zeiss Jena v Mikkelin (6-0)	3-0, 3-0
Stroemgodset v Leeds U (2-7)	1-1, 1-6
Oesters v Feyenoord (2-5)	1-3, 1-2
Hibernian v Keflavik (3-1)	2-0, 1-1
Nice v Barcelona (3-2)	3-0, 0-2
Fortuna Dusseldorf v Naestved (3-2)	1-0, 2-2
Grasshoppers v Tottenham H (2-9)	1-5, 1-4
Aberdeen v Finn Harps (7-2)	4-1, 3-1
Dundee v FC Twente (3-7)	1-3, 2-4
Espanol v RWD Molenbeek (2-4)	0-3, 2-1
Belenenses v Wolverhampton W (1-4)	0-2, 1-2
US Luxembourg v Marseille (1-12)	0-5, 1-7
Setubal v Beerschot (4-0)	2-0, 2-0
Ipswich T v Real Madrid (1-0)	1-0, 0-0
Lazio v Sion (4-3)	3-0, 1-3
Sliema Wanderers v Lokomotiv Plovdiv (0-3)	0-2, 0-1
Fiorentina v Univ Craiova (0-1)	0-0, 0-1
Ferencvaros v Gwardia Warsaw (1-3)	0-1, 1-2
Stuttgart v Olympiakos Nicosia (13-0)	9-0, 4-0
Tatran Presov v Velez (5-3)	4-2, 1-1
Dynamo Tbilisi v Slavia Sofia (4-3)	4-1, 0-2
Panathinaikos v OFK Belgrade* (2-2)	1-2, 1-0
Admira-Wacker* v Inter-Milan (2-2)	1-0, 1-2
Fenerbahce v Agres Pitesti (6-2)	5-1, 1-1
VSS Kosice v Honved (3-5)	1-0, 2-5
Torino v Lokomotiv Leipzig (2-4)	1-2, 1-2
Eskisehirspor v Cologne (0-2)	0-0, 0-2
Panachaiki v AK Graz (3-1)	2-1, 1-0
Ards v Standard Liège (4-8)	3-2, 1-6

Second Round

Admira-Wacker v Fortuna Dusseldorf (2-4)	2-1, 0-3
Aberdeen v Tottenham H (2-5)	1-1, 1-4
Dynamo Tbilisi v OFK Belgrade (8-1)	3-0, 5-1
Nice v Fenerbahce (4-2)	4-0, 0-2
Lokomotiv Leipzig* v Wolverhampton W (4-4)	3-0, 1-4
Panachaiki v FC Twente (1-8)	1-1, 0-7
Setubal* v RWD Molenbeek (2-2)	1-0, 1-2
Marseille v Cologne (2-6)	2-0, 0-6
Ipswich T v Lazio (6-4)	4-0, 2-4
Dynamo Kiev v BK 1903 Copenhagen (3-1)	1-0, 2-1
Lokomotiv Plovdiv v Honved (5-7)	3-4, 2-3
Ruch Chorzow v Carl Zeiss Jena (3-1)	3-0, 0-1
Stuttgart v Tatran Presov (8-4)	3-1, 5-3
Leeds U† v Hibernian (0-0)	0-0, 0-0
Feyenoord v Gwardia Warsaw (3-2)	3-1, 0-1
Standard Liège v Univ Craiova (3-1)	2-0, 1-1

Third Round

Dynamo Kiev v Stuttgart (2-3)	2-0, 0-3
Dynamo Tbilisi v Tottenham H (2-6)	1-1, 1-5
Ipswich T v FC Twente (3-1)	1-0, 2-1
Honved v Ruch Chorzow (2-5)	2-0, 0-5
Leeds U v Setubal (2-3)	1-0, 1-3
Fortuna Dusseldorf v Lokomotiv Leipzig (2-4)	2-1, 0-3
Nice v Cologne (1-4)	1-0, 0-4
Standard Liège v Feyenoord* (3-3)	3-1, 0-2

Quarter-Final

Ipswich T v Lokomotiv Leipzig† (1-1)	1-0, 0-1
Cologne v Tottenham H (1-5)	1-2, 0-3
Stuttgart v Setubal (3-2)	1-0, 2-2
Ruch Chorzow v Feyenoord (2-4)	1-1, 1-3

Semi-Final

Lokomotiv Leipzig v Tottenham H (1-4)	1-2, 0-2
Feyenoord v Stuttgart (4-3)	2-1, 2-2

** Won on away goals.* † *Won on penalties.*

Final 1973–74: Tottenham Hotspur 2, Feyenoord 2
(At White Hart Lane, 21 May, 1974, 46,281)

Tottenham: Jennings; Evans, Naylor, Pratt, England, Beal, McGrath, Perryman, Chivers, Peters, Coates.
Feyenoord: Treytel; Rijsbergen, Van Daele, Israel, Vos, De Jong, Jansen, Van Hanegem, Ressel, Schoenmaker, Kristensen.
Scorers: Tottenham – England, Van Daele og; Feyenoord – Van Hanegem, De Jong.

Feyenoord 2, Tottenham Hotspur 0
(At Rotterdam, 29 May, 1974, 68,000)

Feyenoord: Treytel; Rijsbergen, Van Daele, Israel, Vos, Ramljak, Jansen, De Jong, Ressel, Schoenmaker, Kristensen (Boskamp) (Wery).
Tottenham: Jennings; Evans, Naylor, Pratt (Holder), England, Beal, McGrath, Perryman, Chivers, Peters, Coates.
Scorers: Feyenoord – Rijsbergen, Ressel.

UEFA CUP 1974–75

First Round, First Leg
Lyon 7 (*Lacombe 3, Maillard 3, Maniero*), Red Boys 0
Valur 0, Portadown 0
Derby Co 4 (*Hector 2, Daniel, Lee*), Servette 1 (*Petrovic*)
Ipswich T 2 (*Talbot, Hamilton*), Twente 2 (*Zuidema, Pahlplatz*)
Stoke C 1 (*Smith*), Ajax 1 (*Krol*)
RWD Molenbeek 1 (*Wellens*), Dundee 0
Rosenborg 2 (*Iversen 2*), Hibernian 3 (*Stanton, Gordon, Cropley*)
Porto 4 (*McAlle og, Cubillas, Flavio, Gomes*), Wolverhampton W 1 (*Bailey*)
Etar 0, Inter-Milan 0
Gornik Zabrze 2 (*Kurzeja, Kwasny*), Partizan Belgrade 2 (*Zavitic, Vukotic*)
Start 1 (*Mathiesen M.*), Djurgaarden 2 (*Svensson M., Skotte*)
Boluspor 0, Dynamo Bucharest 1 (*Deleanu*)
Spartak Moscow 3 (*Piscarov, Gladulin, Lovchev*), Velez Mostar 1 (*Bajevic*)
Besiktas 2 (*Sinan, Tezcan*), Steagul Brasov 0
SW Innsbruck 2 (*Flindt 2*), Borussia Moenchengladbach 1 (*Heynckes*)
Sturm Graz 2 (*Stendal, Kulmer*), Antwerp 1 (*Heyligen*)
Randers Freja 1 (*Nielsen*), Dynamo Dresden 1 (*Dorner*)
Hamburg 3 (*Volkert 2, Kaltz*), Bohemians 0
Rapid Vienna 3 (*Pajenk, Ritter, Krankl*), Aris Salonika 1 (*Alexiadis*)
Real Sociedad 0, Banik Ostrava 1 (*Micka*)
Lokomotiv Plovdiv 3 (*Kourbanov, Bonev, Stamboliev*), Raba ETO 1 (*Glazer*)
Oesters 3 (*Mattsson 2, Nordenberg pen*), Dynamo Moscow 2 (*Koslov, Pavlenkov*)
Nantes 2 (*Rampillon, Michel*), Legia Warsaw 2 (*Bialad 2*)
Napoli 2 (*Massa, Pogliana*), Videoton 0
Vorwaerts 2 (*Schutz, Krautzk*), Juventus 1 (*Capello*)
Grasshoppers 2 (*Elsener, Grahn*), Panathinaikos 0
Torino 1 (*Pulici*), Fortuna Dusseldorf 1 (*Zewe*)
Cologne 5 (*Muller 2, Flohe 2, Lohr*), Kokkolan 1 (*Makela*)
FC Amsterdam 5 (*Jansen 2, Otto, Koopman, Husers*), Hibernian Malta 0
KB Copenhagen 3 (*Sorensen, Holstrom, Bernborg*), Atlético Madrid 2 (*Ayala, Salcedo*)
Vitoria Setubal 1 (*Vicente*), Real Zaragoza 1 (*Arrua*)
Videoton 1 (*Wollek*), Napoli 1 (*Braglia*)
Juventus 3 (*Anastasi, Altafini, Hause og*), Vorwaerts 0
Panathinaikos 2 (*Antoniadis 2*), Grasshoppers 1 (*Santrac*)
Fortuna Dusseldorf 3 (*Zimmerman, Seel, Geye pen*), Torino 1 (*Agroppi*)
Kokkolan 1 (*Lamberg*), Cologne 4 (*Neumann, Lohr, Simmet 2*)
Hibernian Malta 0, FC Amsterdam 7 (*Karte 2, Jansen 2, Franz, Husers, Dekkers*)
Atlético Madrid 4 (*Leal, Garate, Irureta 2*), KB Copenhagen 0
Real Zaragoza 4 (*Arrua, Diarte, Castany, Leiros*), Vitoria Setubal 0
Dukla Prague had a walkover when Pezoporikos withdrew

First Round, Second Leg
Red Boys 1 (*Cristophe*), Lyon 4 (*Domenech 2, Mariot, Bernard*)
Portadown 2 (*McFaul, Morrison pen*), Valur 1 (*Albertson*)
Servette 1 (*Martin*), Derby Co 2 (*Lee, Hector*)
Twente 1 (*Bos*), Ipswich T 1 (*Hamilton*)
Ajax 0, Stoke C 0
Dundee 2 (*Duncan, Jocky Scott*), RWD Molenbeek 4 (*Teugels, Boskamp, Wellens 2*)
Hibernian 9 (*Harper 2, Munro 2, Stanton 2, Cropley 2, Gordon*), Rosenborg 1 (*Iversen*)
Wolverhampton W 3 (*Richards, Dougan, Daley*), Porto 1 (*Cubillas*)
Inter-Milan 3 (*Oriali, Boninsegna 2*), Etar 0
Partizan Belgrade 3 (*Dordevic, Vukotic, Todozevic*), Gornik Zabrze 0
Djurgaarden 5 (*Skotte, Stenbach, Karlsson 2, Samuelsson*) Start 1 (*Mathiesen*)
Dynamo Bucharest 3 (*Dinu, Dumitrache, Lucescu*), Boluspor 0
Velez Mostar 2 (*Colic, Popic*), Spartak Moscow 0
Steagul Brasov 3 (*Serbaniou 3*), Besiktas 0
Borussia Moenchengladbach 3 (*Heynckes, Jensen, Vogts*), SW Innsbruck 0
Antwerp 1 (*Kodat*), Sturm Graz 0
Dynamo Dresden 0, Randers Freja 0
Bohemians 0, Hamburg 1 (*Bertl*)
Aris Salonika 1 (*Alexiadis*), Rapid Vienna 0
Banik Ostrava 4 (*Vojacek, Slany, Albrecht, Kolecko*), Real Sociedad 0
Raba ETO 3 (*Sebo, Penzes, Proczik*), Lokomotiv Plovdiv 1 (*Kichekov*)
Dynamo Moscow 2 (*Evryuzhikhin, Petrushin*), Oesters 1 (*Svensson*)
Legia Warsaw 0, Nantes 1 (*Merigot*)

Second Round, First Leg
Derby Co 2 (*Nish, Rioch pen*), Atlético Madrid 2 (*Luis pen, Ayala*)
Hibernian 2 (*Stanton, Cropley*), Juventus 4 (*Gentile, Altafini 2, Cuccurredu*)
Partizan Belgrade 5 (*Kosic 2, Zavajic, Nikolic, Vukotic*), Portadown 0
Nantes 1 (*Bossis*), Banik Ostrava 0
Dynamo Bucharest 1 (*Dinu*), Cologne 1 (*Luscher*)
Raba ETO 2 (*Varsanyi, Stolz*), Fortuna Dusseldorf 0
Rapid Vienna 1 (*Ritter*), Velez Mostar 1 (*Halaldiz*)
Dynamo Dresden 1 (*Sasche*), Dynamo Moscow 0
Grasshoppers 2 (*Grahn, Santrac*), Real Zaragoza 1 (*Arrua*)
Borussia Moenchengladbach 1 (*Simonsen*), Lyon 0
Hamburg 8 (*Volkert 2, Bertl, Zaczyk, Memering, Nogly, Ripp, Krobach*), Steagul Brasov 0
Twente 2 (*Thijseen, Van der Vall*), RWD Molenbeek 1 (*Koens*)
Djurgaarden 0, Dukla Prague 2 (*Nehoda, Gajdusek*)
Inter-Milan 1 (*Boninsegna*), FC Amsterdam 2 (*Jansen 2*)
Napoli 1 (*Orlandini*), Porto 0
Ajax 1 (*Gerrie Muhren*), Antwerp 0

Second Round, Second Leg
Atlético Madrid 2 (*Luis 2*), Derby Co 2 (*Rioch, Hector*)
Derby won 7-6 on penalties
Juventus 4 (*Bettega, Anastasi 2, Altafini*), Hibernian 0
Portadown 1 (*Malcolmson*), Partizan Belgrade 1 (*Tordevic*)
Banik Ostrava (*Klement 2*), Nantes 0
Cologne 3 (*Overath, Muller, Neumann*), Dynamo Bucharest 2 (*Custov, Georgescu*)
Fortuna Dusseldorf 3 (*Herzog, Szernotzky, Brucken*), Raba ETO 0
Velez Mostar 1 (*Halaldiz*), Rapid Vienna 0
Dynamo Moscow 1 (*Korneev*), Dynamo Dresden 0
Real Zaragoza 5 (*Rubial 2, Soto, Oldhauser og, Niggl og*), Grasshoppers 0
Lyon 2 (*Valette, Domenech R.*), Borussia Moenchengladbach 5 (*Bonhof 2, Simonsen 2, Kulik*)
Steagul Brasov 1 (*Curbaniou*), Hamburg 2 (*Kaltz, Bjornmose*)
RWD Molenbeek 0, Twente 1 (*Zuidema*)
Dukla Prague 3 (*Nehoda 2, Macela*), Djurgaarden 1 (*Svensson*)
FC Amsterdam 0, Inter-Milan 0
Porto 0, Napoli 1 (*Juliano*)
Antwerp 2 (*Kodat, Riedl pen*), Ajax 1 (*Geels*)

Third Round, First Leg
Napoli 0, Banik Ostrava 2 (*Albrecht, Kolecko*)
Hamburg 4 (*Bjornmose 2, Volkert, Nogly*), Dynamo Dresden 1 (*Schmuck*)
Dukla Prague 3 (*Dvorak, Krumich, Nehoda*), Twente 1 (*Jeuring*)
Partizan Belgrade 1 (*Vukotic*), Cologne 0
Borussia Moenchengladbach 5 (*Heynckes 2, Simonsen 2, Bonhof*), Real Zaragoza 0
FC Amsterdam 3 (*Husers 2, Kriegler og*), Fortuna Dusseldorf 0

Juventus 1 (*Damiani*), Ajax 0
Derby Co 3 (*Bourne 2, Hinton*), Velez Mostar 1 (*Vladic*)

Third Round, Second Leg
Banik Ostrava 1 (*Slany*), Napoli 1 (*Ferrandini*)
Dynamo Dresden 2 (*Dorner, Hafner*), Hamburg 2 (*Bertl 2*)
Twente 5 (*Zuidema 3, Notten 2*), Dukla Prague 0
Cologne 5 (*Overath, Lohr, Muller, Glowacz, Flohe*), Partizan Belgrade 1 (*Povlovic*)
Real Zaragoza 2 (*Vileta, Galdos*), Borussia Moenchengladbach 4 (*Simonsen, Heynckes 2, Stielike*)
Fortuna Dusseldorf 1 (*Seel*), FC Amsterdam 2 (*Husers, Jansen*)
Ajax 2 (*Blankenburg, Gerrie Muhren*), Juventus 1 (*Damiani pen*)
Velez Mostar 4 (*Bajevic pen, Pecelj, Vladic, Primorac pen*), Derby Co 1 (*Hector*)

Quarter-Finals, First Leg
Juventus 2 (*Capello, Viola*), Hamburg 0
Cologne 5 (*Flohe 2 [1 pen], Muller 3*), FC Amsterdam 1 (*Visser*)
Velez Mostar 1 (*Kvesic*), Twente 0
Banik Ostrava 0, Borussia Moenchengladbach 1 (*Heynckes*)

Quarter-Finals, Second Leg
Hamburg 0, Juventus 0
Borussia Moenchengladbach 3 (*Micka og, Heynckes, Vogts*), Banik Ostrava 1 (*Hudecek*)
FC Amsterdam 2 (*Jansen 2*), Cologne 3 (*Strack, Muller, Lohr*)
Twente 2 (*Zuidema, Overweg*), Velez Mostar 0

Semi-Finals, First Leg
Twente 3 (*Jeuring, Zuidema 2*), Juventus 1 (*Altafini*)
Cologne 1 (*Lohr*), Borussia Moenchengladbach 3 (*Simonsen 2, Danner*)

Semi-Finals, Second Leg
Juventus 0, Twente 1 (*Zuidema*)
Borussia Moenchengladbach 1 (*Danner*), Cologne 0

Final 1974–75: Borussia Moenchengladbach 0, Twente Enschede 0
(At Dusseldorf, 7 May, 1975, 45,000)

Borussia Moenchengladbach: Kleff; Wittkamp, Stielike, Vogts, Surau, Bonhof, Wimmer, Danner (Del Haye), Kulik (Schaffer), Simonsen, Jensen.

Twente Enschede: Gross; Drost, Van Ierssel, Overweg, Oranen, Thijssen, Pahlplatz, Van der Vall, Bos, Jeuring (Achterberg), Zuidema.

Twente Enschede 1, Borussia Moenchengladbach 5
(At Enschede, 21 May, 1975, 24,500)

Twente Enschede: Gross; Drost, Van Ierssel, Overweg, Oranen, Bos (Muhren), Thijssen, Pahlplatz (Achterberg), Van der Vall, Jeuring, Zuidema.

Borussia Moenchengladbach: Kleff; Wittkamp, Vogts, Surau (Schafer), Klinkhammer, Bonhof, Wimmer (Koppel), Danner, Simonsen, Jensen, Heynckes.

Scorers: Borussia Moenchengladbach – Heynckes 3, Simonsen 2 (1 pen); Twente Enschede – Drost.

UEFA CUP 1975–76

First Round, First Leg

Duisburg 7 (*Mertakas og, Lehmann 3, Worm 2, Thies*), Paralimni 1 (*Chatzyannis*)
Glentoran 1 (*Jamieson*), Ajax 6 (*Geels 4, Meyer, Notten*)
Grasshoppers 3 (*Elsener, Santrac, Bosco*), Real Sociedad 3(*Satrustegui 2, Murillo*)
PAOK Salonika 1 (*Koudas*), Barcelona 0
AIK Stockholm 1 (*Leback pen*), Spartak Moscow 1 (*Lovchev*)
Antwerp 4 (*Heylingen, Kodat 3*), Aston Villa 1 (*Graydon*)
Bohemians Prague 1 (*Masnik*), Honved 2 (*Pinter, Toth*)
Carl Zeiss Jena 3 (*Sengewald 2, Kurbjuweit*), Marseille 0
Uni Craiova 1 (*Oblemenco*), Red Star Belgrade 3 (*Filipovic 2, Savic*)
Everton 0, AC Milan 0
Feyenoord 1 (*De Jong*), Ipswich T 2 (*Whymark, Johnson*)
GAIS Gothenburg 2 (*Palsson 2 [1 pen]*) Slask Wroclaw 1 (*Kwaitkowski*)
Hertha Berlin 4 (*Kostedde 2, Hoor 2*), HJK Helsinki 1 (*Kangaslorpi*)
Hibernian 1 (*Harper*), Liverpool 0
Holbaek 0, Stal Mielec 1 (*Domarski*)
Cologne 2 (*Glowacz, Lohr*), B 1903 Copenhagen 0
Lyon 4 (*Jodar, Millard 2, Mihajlovic*), Bruges 3 (*Van der Eycken 3 [1 pen]*)
Molde 1 (*Wetterdahl*), Oesters Vaxjo 0
Tirgu Mures 2 (*Muresan, Faxekas*), Dynamo Dresden 2 (*Schade, Heidler*)
Chernomonretz Odessa 1 (*Doroschenko*), Lazio 0
Porto 7 (*Julio, Cubillas 3 [1 pen], Oliveira, Octavio, Gomes*), Avenir Beggen 0
Rapid Vienna 1 (*Widmann*), Galatasaray 0
Roma 2 (*Pellegrini, Petrini*), Dounav Russe 0
Moscow Torpedo 4 (*Grishken 2, Sakharov pen, Belenkov*), Napoli 1 (*Savoldi*)
VOEST Linz 2 (*Scharmann, Stering*), Vasas Budapest 0
Vojvodina 0, AEK Athens 0
Young Boys 0, Hamburg 0
Athlone T 3 (*Martin, Davis 2*), Valerengen 1 (*Olsen*)
Inter Bratislava 5 (*Levicky, Luprich, Petras, Jurkemik, Sajanek*), Zaragoza 0
Keflavik 0, Dundee U 2 (*Narey 2*)
Levski Spartak 3 (*Spassov 2, Panov*), Eskisehirspor 0
Sliema Wanderers 1 (*Azzopardi*), Sporting Lisbon 2 (*Marinho, Fernandez*)
Red Star Belgrade 1 (*Filipovic pen*), Uni Craiova 1 (*Krizan*)
Real Sociedad 1 (*Urreisti*), Grasshoppers 1 (*Santrac*)
Slask Wroclaw 4 (*Sybis 3, Pawlowski*), GAIS Gothenburg 2 (*Hans Johanson 2*)
Moscow Spartak 1 (*Andreyev*), AIK Stockholm 0
Sporting Lisbon 3 (*Baltazar, Da Costa, Manuel Fernandes pen*), Sliema Wanderers 1 (*Loporto*)
Stal Mielec 2 (*Karas, Krawczyk*), Holbaek 1 (*Torben Hansen*)
Valerengen 1 (*Dag Olvavason*), Athlone T 1 (*Martin*)
Vasas Budapest 4 (*Varadi 2, Kovacs, Izso*), VOEST Linz 0
Zaragoza 2 (*Pepe Gonzalez pen, Arrua*), Inter Bratislava 3 (*Jurkemik, Petras, Mraz*)

First Round, Second Leg

Paralimni 2 (*Konstantinou A., Mertakas*), Duisburg 3 (*Dietz, Krause, Seliger*)
Dundee U 4 (*Hall 2, Hegarty pen, Sturrock*), Keflavik 0
Liverpool 3 (*Toshack 3*), Hibernian 1 (*Edwards*)
AEK Athens 3 (*Papaioannou, Papadopoulos, Wagner*), Vojvodina 1 (*Buikov*)
Ajax 8 (*Notten, Van Dord, Geels 3, Gerrie Muhren, Brokamp 2*), Glentoran 0
Aston Villa 0, Antwerp 1 (*Kodat*)
Barcelona 6 (*Neeskens 2 pens, Rexach 2, Cruyff*), PAOK Salonika 1 (*Anastasiadis*)
Bruges 3 (*Van der Eycken, Valette og, Chnier og*), Lyon 0
Avenir Beggen 0, Porto 3 (*Julio, Grilli og, Seninho*)
Marseille 0, Carl Zeiss Jena 1 (*Irmscher*)
B 1903 Copenhagen 2 (*Christiansen 2*), Cologne 3 (*Brucken 3*)
Dounav Russe 1 (*Ivanov*), Roma 0
Dynamo Dresden 4 (*Heidler 3, Kreische*), Tirgu Mures 1 (*Muresan*)
Eskisehirspor 1 (*Mehmet*), Levski Spartak 4 (*Spassov 2, Panov, Milanov*)
Galatasaray 3 (*Sevki, Gokmen 2*), Rapid Vienna 1 (*Krankl*)
Hamburg 4 (*Reimann, Bertl 2, Bjornmose*), Young Boys 2 (*Siegenthaler 2*)
HJK Helsinki 1 (*Salo*), Hertha Berlin 2 (*Sidka, Grau*)
Honved 1 (*Kocsis pen*), Bohemians Prague 1 (*Panenka*)
Ipswich T 2 (*Woods, Whymark*), Feyenoord 0
Lazio 3 (*Chinaglia 3 [1 pen]*), Chernomoretz Odessa 0
AC Milan 1 (*Calloni pen*), Everton 0
Napoli 1 (*Braglia*), Moscow Torpedo 1 (*Filatov*)
Oesters Vaxjo 6 (*Svensson, Matsson 2, Evesson, Ejderstedt, Isaxsson*), Molde 0

Second Round, First Leg

Duisburg 3 (*Schneider W., Worm, Krause*), Levski Spartak 2 (*Panov 2*)
Athlone 0, AC Milan 0
Carl Zeiss Jena 1 (*Kurbjuweit*), Stal Mielec 0
Dundee U 1 (*Rennie*), Porto 2 (*Oliveira, Seninho*)
Galatasaray 2 (*Sevki, Gokmen*), Moscow Torpedo 4 (*Enver og, Hrobroskin, Sakharov pen, Maksimenkov*)
Hertha Berlin 1 (*Kostedde*), Ajax 0
Honved 2 (*Weimper 2*), Dynamo Dresden 2 (*Heidler 2*)
Inter Bratislava 2 (*Luprich pen, Mraz*), AEK Athens 0
Ipswich T 3 (*Gates, Peddelty, Austin*), Bruges 0
Spartak Moscow 2 (*Lovchev 2*), Cologne 0
Oesters Vaxjo 1 (*Evansson*), Roma 0
Real Sociedad 1 (*Amas*), Liverpool 3 (*Heighway, Callaghan, Thompson*)
Red Star Belgrade 1 (*Susic*), Hamburg 1 (*Bjornmose*)
Slask Wroclaw 1 (*Pawlowski*), Antwerp 1 (*Houwaart*)
Vasas Budapest 3 (*Kovacs 2, Varad pen*), Sporting Lisbon 1 (*Chico*)
Lazio 0, Barcelona 3 (*Lazio refused to play because of possible political demonstrations against the Spaniards. FIFA thus awarded the game to Barcelona 3-0*).

Second Round, Second Leg

Levski Spartak 2 (*Ivkov, Panov pen*), Duisburg 1 (*Worm*)
Liverpool 6 (*Toshack, Kennedy 2, Fairclough, Heighway, Neal*), Real Sociedad 0
Ajax 4 (Brokamp, Geels 2 [1 pen], Meyer), Hertha Berlin 1 (*Kostedde*)
Antwerp 1 (*De Schrijver*), Slask Wroclaw 2 (*Sybis, Pawlowski*)
AEK Athens 3 (*Tassos 2 [1 pen], Wagner*), Inter Bratislava 1 (*Novotny*)
Barcelona 4 (*Sotil, Cruyff, Neeskens, Fortes*), Lazio 0
Bruges 4 (*Lambert 1 pen, De Cubber, Le Fevre, Van der Eycken*), Ipswich T 0
Dynamo Dresden 1 (*Dorner pen*), Honved 0
Hamburg 4 (*Reimann 2, Ettmayer, Memering*), Red Star Belgrade 0
Cologne 0, Moscow Spartak 1 (*Andreyev*)
AC Milan 3 (*Vincenzi, Benetti 2 [1 pen]*), Athlone T 0
Moscow Torpedo 3 (*Degtyarev, Sahkarov pen, Budulakin*), Galatasaray 0
Porto 1 (*Seninho*), Dundee U 1 (*Hegarty*)
Roma 2 (*Pellegrini, Boni*), Oesters Vaxjo 0
Sporting Lisbon 2 (*Manuel Fernandes 2*), Vasas Budapest 1 (*Grass*)
Stal Mielec 1 (*Karas*), Carl Zeiss Jena 0

Third Round, First Leg

Ajax 2 (*Geels, Steffenhagen*), Levski Spartak 1 (*Voinov*)
Barcelona 3 (*Migueli, Rexach, Neeskens*), Vasas Budapest 1 (*Muller*)
Bruges 1 (*Cools*), Roma 0
Dynamo Dresden 3 (*Riedel 2, Kreische*), Moscow Torpedo 0
Hamburg 2 (*Zaczyk, Volkert pen*), Porto 0
Inter Bratislava 1 (*Saljanek*), Stal Mielec 0
Slask Wroclaw 1 (*Pawlowski*), Liverpool 2 (*Faber og, Toshack*)

AC Milan 4 (*Calloni 2, Bigon, Maldera*), Moscow Spartak 0

Dynamo Dresden 0, Liverpool 0
Hamburg 1 (*Bertl*), Stal Mielec 1 (*Oratowski*)

Third Round, Second Leg
Levski Spartak 2 (*Panov 2*), Ajax 1 (*Geels*)
Liverpool 3 (*Case 3*), Slask Wroclaw 0
Moscow Spartak 2 (*Papayev, Ovchev*), AC Milan 0
Moscow Torpedo 3 (*Dedtyaryov 2, Petrenko*), Dynamo Dresden 1 (*Heidler*)
Porto 2 (*Julio, Cubillas*), Hamburg 1 (*Reimann*)
Roma 0, Bruges 1 (*Lambert*)
Stal Mielec 2 (*Sekulski, Karas*), Inter Bratislava 0
Vasas Budapest 0, Barcelona 1 (*Fortes*)

Quarter-Finals, First Leg
Barcelona 4 (*Neeskens pen, Marcial, Asensi, Heredia*), Levski Spartak 0
Bruges 2 (*Le Fevre, Krieger*), AC Milan 0

Quarter-Finals, Second Leg
Levski Spartak 5 (*Panov 2 [1 pen], Yordanov 2, Spassov*), Barcelona 4 (*Marcial, Asensi, Heredia, Neeskens pen*)
Liverpool 2 (*Case, Keegan*), Dynamo Dresden 1 (*Heidler*)
AC Milan 2 (*Chiarugi 2*), Bruges 1 (*Sanders*)
Stal Mielec 0, Hamburg 1 (*Nogly*)

Semi-Finals, First Leg
Barcelona 0, Liverpool 1 (*Toshack*)
Hamburg 1 (*Reimann*), Bruges 1 (*Lambert*)

Semi-Finals, Second Leg
Bruges 1 (*Kaltz og*), Hamburg 0
Liverpool 1 (*Thompson*), Barcelona 1 (*Rexach*)

Final 1975-76: Liverpool 3, Bruges 2

(At Anfield, 28 April, 1976, 56,000)

Liverpool: Clemence; Smith, Neal, Thompson, Kennedy, Hughes, Keegan, Fairclough, Heighway, Toshack (Case), Callaghan.

Bruges: Jensen; Bastyns, Krieger, Leekens, Volders, Cools, Van der Eycken, De Cubber, Van Gool, Lambert, Le Fevre.

Scorers: Liverpool – Kennedy, Case, Keegan (pen); Bruges – Lambert, Cools.

Bruges 1, Liverpool 1

(At Olympia Stadium, Bruges, 19 May, 1976, 32,000)

Bruges: Jensen; Bastyns, Krieger, Leekens, Volders, Cools, Van der Eycken, Van Gool, Lambert (Sanders), De Cubber (Hinderyckx), Le Fevre.

Liverpool: Clemence; Smith, Neal, Thompson, Kennedy, Hughes, Keegan, Case, Heighway, Toshack (Fairclough), Callaghan.

Scorers: Bruges – Lambert (pen); Liverpool – Keegan.

UEFA CUP 1976–77

First Round, First Leg

Porto 2 (*Rodolfo, Cubillas*), Schalke 04 2 (*Erwin Kremers, Fischer*)
Fram Reykjavik 0, Slovan Bratislava 3 (*Haraslin 2, Mrva*)
Glentoran 3 (*Feeney 2, Dickinson*), Basle 2 (*Maissen, Ramseier*)
Paralimni 1 (*Mertakas*), Kaiserslautern 3 (*Rinderl, Meier, Spiergeri*)
AEK Athens 2 (*Nikoloudis, Papaioannou*), Moscow Dynamo 0
Ajax 1 (*Krol*), Manchester U 0
Austria Salzburg 5 (*Schwarz 3 [1 pen], Haider 2*), Adanaspor 0
Belenenses 2 (*Quaresma, Horta*), Barcelona 2 (*Heredia 2*)
Celtic 2 (*McDonald, Dalglish*), Wisla Krakow 2 (*Kmiecik, Wrobel*)
Derby Co 12 (*Hector 5, Rioch, James 3, George 3*), Finn Harps 0
Dinamo Bucharest 0, AC Milan 0
Eintracht Brunswick 7 (*Hollmann, Stoltenburg 2, Frank 3, Gersdorff*), Holbaek 0
Espanol 3 (*Cuesta, Maranon, Caszely*), Nice 1 (*Toko*)
Feyenoord 3 (*Schneider pen, Kreuz, Vreysen*), Djurgaarden 0
Fenerbahce 2 (*Cemil 2*), Videoton 1 (*Nagy*)
Grasshoppers 7 (*Bosco, Ponte, Seller 2, Bauer, Cornioley 2 [1 pen]*), Hibernian Malta 0
Hibernian 1 (*Brownlie*), Sochaux 0
Internazionale 0, Honved 1 (*Kozma*)
Cologne 2 (*Flohe pen, Van Gool*), GKS Tychy 0
Kuopion Palloseura 3 (*Toernroos, Rissanen 2*), Oester Vaxjo 2 (*Stromberg, Ejderstedt*)
Magdeburg 3 (*Steinbach, Streich 2 [1 pen]*), Cesena 0
Manchester C 1 (*Kidd*), Juventus 0
Naestved 0, RWD Molenbeek 3 (*Boskamp, Wellens 2*)
QPR 4 (*Bowles 3, Masson*), Brann Bergen 0
Red Boys Differdange 0, Lokeren 3 (*Verheyen 2, Dalving*)
Slavia Prague 2 (*Herda, Radolsky*), Akademik Sofia 0
Schachtjor Donetzk 3 (*Rogovsky, Sokolvsky, Starukhin*), Dynamo Berlin 0
Sportul Studentesc 3 (*Grosu, Ionescu 2*), Olympiakos 0
SW Innsbruck 2 (*Sterig, Pezzey*), Start Kristiansand 1 (*Mathiesen pen*)
ASA Tirgu Mures 0, Dynamo Zagreb 1 (*Jurisic*)
Ujpest Dozsa 1 (*Dunai I.*), Atlético Bilbao 0
Lokomotiv Plovdiv 2 (*Fidanov, Bonev*), Red Star Belgrade 1 (*Filipovic*)

First Round, Second Leg

Adanaspor 2 (*Isa, Sener*), Austria Salzburg 0
Akademik Sofia 3 (*Dimitrov 2, Yankov*), Slavia Prague 0
Barcelona 3 (*Rexach, Asensi, Clares*), Belenenses 2 (*Vasques, Rocha*)
Basle 3 (*Nielsen, Mundschin, Demarmels*), Glentoran 0
Dynamo Berlin 1 (*Noak*), Schachtjor Donetzk 1 (*Rogowski*)
Atlético Bilbao 5 (*Rojo 2, Dani 3*), Ujpest Dozsa 0
Brann Bergen 0, QPR 7 (*Webb, Givens 2, Bowles 3, Thomas*)
Cesena 3 (*Mariani, Pepe, Macchi*), Magdeburg 1 (*Sparwasser*)
Djurgaarden 2 (*Karlsson K., Stenbaek*), Feyenoord 1 (*Nico Jansen*)
Dynamo Zagreb 3 (*Sensen 2, Bogdan*), ASA Tirgu Mures 0
Finn Harps 1 (*McFarland og*), Derby Co 4 (*Hector 2, George 2*)
Hibernian Malta 0, Grasshoppers 2 (*Sieler, Cornioley pen*)
Holbaek 1 (*Tofte*), Eintracht Brunswick 0
Honved 1 (*Poczik*), Internazionale 1 (*Mariani*)
Juventus 2 (*Scirea, Boninsegna*), Manchester C 0
Lokeren 3 (*Mommens, Hansen, Lubanski*), Red Boys Differdange 1 (*Flenghi pen*)
Manchester U 2 (*Macari, McIlroy*), Ajax 0
Moscow Dynamo 2 (*Bubnov, Yukubik pen*), AEK Athens 1 (*Tassos pen*)
Nice 2 (*Toko, Bjekovic*), Espanol 1 (*Aquino pen*)
Oester Vaxjo 2 (*Stromberg, Svensson*), Kuopion Palloseura 0
Olympiakos 2 (*Galakos, Karavitis pen*), Sportul Studentesc 1 (*Radacanu*)
RWD Molenbeek 4 (*Koons, Boskamp 2 [1 pen], Cordier*), Naestved 0
Schalke 04 3 (*Fichtel, Abramczik, Fischer*), Porto 2 (*Oliveira 2*)
Slovan Bratislava 5 (*Pekarik, Ondrus, Barto, Capkovic, Atlasson og*), Fram Reykjavik 0
Sochaux 0, Hibernian 0
Start Kristiansand 0, SW Innsbruck 5 (*Koncilia 2, Sterling 2 [1 pen], Witzl*)
GKS Tychy 1 (*Ogaza*), Cologne 1 (*Muller*)
Videoton 4 (*Wollek, Kovacs J., Szalmasy 2*), Fenerbahce 0
Wisla Krakow 2 (*Kmiecik 2*), Celtic 0
Kaiserslautern 8 (*Toppmuller 4, Pirrung 2, Meier, Riedl*), Paralimni 0
AC Milan 2 (*Calloni, Silva*), Dinamo Bucharest 1 (*Satmareanu*)
Red Star Belgrade 4 (*Bolicevic, Filipovic 2, Stamenkovic*), Lokomotiv Plovdiv 1 (*Bonev*)

Second Round, First Leg

AEK Athens 2 (*Wagner 2*), Derby Co 0
Akademik Sofia 4 (*Paunov 2, Manolov, Dimitrov*), AC Milan 3 (*Capello 2, Colovatti*)
Austria Salzburg 2 (*Schwarz P., Schwarz W. pen*), Red Star Belgrade 1 (*Filipovic*)
Barcelona 2 (*Cruyff, Clares*), Lokeren 0
Basle 1 (*Marti*), Atlético Bilbao 1 (*Madariaga*)
Eintracht Brunswick 2 (*Frank, Stolzenburg*), Espanol 1 (*Maranon*)
Hibernian 2 (*Blackley, Brownlie*), Oester Vaxjo 0
SW Innsbruck 1 (*Sterling*), Videoton 1 (*Czeczeli pen*)
Kaiserslautern 2 (*Briegel 2*), Feyenoord 2 (*De Jong, Nico Jansen*)
Cologne 2 (*Konopka, Muller*), Grasshoppers 0
Magdeburg 2 (*Steinbach, Zapf*), Dynamo Zagreb 0
Manchester U 1 (*Hill*), Juventus 0
Schachtjor Donetzk 3 (*Shevluch, Starukhin, Vasin*), Honved 0
Slovan Bratislava 3 (*Novotny, Haraslin, Ondrus*), QPR 3 (*Bowles 2, Givens*)
Sportul Studentesc 0, Schalke 04 1 (*Fischer*)
Wisla Krakow 1 (*Kapka*), RWD Molenbeek 1 (*Olsen*)

Second Round, Second Leg

Atlético Bilbao 3 (*Villar, Carlos, Rojo I*), Basle 1 (*Marti*)
Derby Co 2 (*George, Rioch*), AEK Athens 3 (*Nikoloudis, Tassos, Wagner*)
Dynamo Zagreb 2 (*Kranjcar 2*), Magdeburg 2 (*Streich, Pommerenke*)
Espanol 2 (*Jeremias, Ortiz Aquino pen*), Eintracht Brunswick 0
Feyenoord 5 (*Wim Jansen, Nico Jansen, De Jong, Van Deinsen, Schneider pen*), Kaiserslautern 0
Grasshoppers 2 (*Bauer pen, Bosco*), FC Cologne 3 (*Muller, Larsen 2*)
Honved 2 (*Kozma 2 [1 pen]*), Schachtjor Donetzk 3 (*Shevluik, Reznik 2*)
Juventus 3 (*Boninsegna 2, Benetti*), Manchester U 0
AC Milan 2 (*Calloni, Morini*), Akademik Sofia 0
Oester Vaxjo 4 (*Linderoth 2, Ejderstedt 2*), Hibernian 1 (*Smith*)
QPR 5 (*Givens 3 [1 pen], Bowles, Clement*), Slovan Bratislava 2 (*Ondrus, Jan Capkovic*)
Red Star Belgrade 1 (*Filipovic*), Austria Salzburg 0
RWD Molenbeek 1 (*Nielsen*), Wisla Krakow 1 (*Maculewicz*)
Schalke 04 4 (*Bongartz 2, Fischer 2*), Sportul Studentesc 0
Videoton 1 (*Nagy*), SW Innsbruck 0
Lokeren 2 (*Verheyen, Dalving*), Barcelona 1 (*Cruyff*)

Third Round, First Leg

AEK Athens 2 (*Papaioannou, Marvos*), Red Star Belgrade 0
Atlético Bilbao 4 (*Dani 2 [1 pen], Carlos 2*), AC Milan 1 (*Capello*)

Espanol 0, Feyenoord 1 (*De Felipe og*)
Juventus 3 (*Bettega, Tardelli, Boninsegna*), Schachtjor Donetzk 0
Magdeburg 5 (*Streich, Tyll 2, Mewes, Pommerenke*), Videoton 0
Oester Vaxjo 0, Barcelona 3 (*Clares 2, Neeskens*)
QPR 3 (*Givens, Webb, Bowles*), Cologne 0
RWD Molenbeek 1 (*Lafont*), Schalke 04 0

Third Round, Second Leg
Cologne 4 (*Muller 2, Lohr, Weber*), QPR 1 (*Masson*)
Barcelona 5 (*Clares, Cruyff, Asensi 2, Heredia*), Oester Vaxjo 1 (*Everson*)
Feyenoord 2 (*Krauz, Nico Jansen*), Espanol 0
AC Milan 3 (*Calloni 2 [1 pen], Biasiolo*), Atlético Bilbao 1 (*Madariaga pen*)
Red Star Belgrade 3 (*Baralic, Filipovic, Savic*), AEK Athens 1 (*Wagner*)
Schalke 04 1 (Abramczik), RWD Molenbeek 1 (*Teugels*)
Schachtjor Donetsk 1 (*Shevluk*), Juventus 0
Videoton 1 (*Nagy J.*), Magdeburg 0

Quarter-Final, First Leg
Atlético Bilbao 2 (*Churruca, Dani pen*), Barcelona 1 (*Asensi*)
Feyenoord 0, RWD Molenbeek 0
Magdeburg 1 (*Streich*), Juventus 3 (*Cuccureddu, Benetti, Boninsegna*)
QPR 3 (*Francis 2 pens, Bowles*), AEK Athens 0

Quarter-Final, Second Leg
AEK Athens 3 (*Mavros 2, Papaioannou*), QPR 0
Barcelona 2 (*Cruyff 2*), Atlético Bilbao 2 (*Irureta 2*)
Juventus 1 (*Cuccureddu*), Magdeburg 0
RWD Molenbeek 2 (*Wellens, Teugels pen*), Feyenoord 1 (*De Jong*)

Semi-Final, First Leg
RWD Molenbeek 1 (*Teugels*), Atlético Bilbao 1 (*Churruca*)
Juventus 4 (*Cuccureddu, Bettega 2, Causio*), AEK Athens 1 (*Papadopoulos*)

Semi-Final, Second Leg
AEK Athens 0, Juventus 1 (*Bettega*)
Atlético Bilbao 0, RWD Molenbeek 0

Final 1976–77: Juventus 1, Atlético Bilbao 0
(In Turin, 4 May, 1977, 75,000)

Juventus: Zoff; Cuccureddu, Gentile, Scirea, Morini, Tardelli, Furino, Benetti, Causio, Boninsegna (Gori), Bettega.
Atlético Bilbao: Iribar; Villar, Escalza, Guoicoechea, Guisasola, Quaderra, Irureta, Rojo II, Dani, Churruca, Rojo I.
Scorer: Juventus – Tardelli.

Atlético Bilbao 2, Juventus 1
(In Bilbao, 18 May, 1977, 43,000)

Atlético Bilbao: Iribar; Lasa (Carlos), Guisasola, Alesanco, Escalza, Villar, Churruca, Irureta, Amarrortu, Dani, Rojo I.
Juventus: Zoff; Cuccureddu, Morini, Scirea, Gentile, Causio, Tardelli, Furino, Benetti, Boninsegna (Spinosi), Bettega.
Scorers: Atlético Bilbao – Irureta, Carlos; Juventus – Bettega.
Juventus won on away goals rule.

UEFA CUP 1977–78

First Round, First Leg

Eintracht Frankfurt 5 (*Nickel 2, Wenzel, Kraus, Grabowski*), Sliema Wanderers 0
AZ 67 11 (*Van Hanegem, Arntz, Nygaard 3, Peters 4, Kist 2*), Red Boys 1 (*Christoph pen*)
Aston Villa 4 (*Gray, Deehan 2, Little*), Fenerbahce 0
Barcelona 5 (*Heredia 2, Cruyff pen, Clares, Zuviria*), Steaua 1 (*Nastase*)
Bastia 3 (*Felix 3*), Sporting Lisbon 2 (*Jordao pen, Fraguito*)
Bayern Munich 8 (*Oblak, Rummenigge 3, Hoeness, Müller 3*), Mjondalen 0
Boavista 1 (*Jorge Gomes*), Lazio 0
Bohemians 0, Newcastle U 0
Carl Zeiss Jena 5 (*Trocha 2, Vogel 2 [1 pen], Topfer*), Altay Izmir 1 (*Mustafa pen*)
Dundee U 1 (*Sturrock*), KB Copenhagen 0
Fiorentina 0, Schalke 04 0
Frem Copenhagen 0, Grasshoppers 2 (*Elsener, Becker*)
Glenavon 2 (*Malone pen, McDonald*), PSV Eindhoven 6 (*Van der Kuylen 2, Van Kraay, Deijkers, Deacy, Lubse*)
Gornik Zabrze 5 (*Gizil 3, Radecki, Wasilewski*), Haka Valkeakosken 3 (*Jarzyna og, Vimomen, Pivinen*)
Internazionale 0, Dynamo Tbilisi 1 (*Kipiani*)
Dynamo Kiev 1 (*Vermeeyev*), Eintracht Brunswick 1 (*Frank*)
Landskrona 0, Ipswich T 1 (*Whymark*)
Las Palmas 5 (*Maciel 2 [1 pen], Juani, Morete 2*), Sloboda Tuzla 0
Lens 4 (*Bosudira, Francoise, Djeballi, Elie*), Malmö FF 1 (*Sjoberg*)
Linz ASK 3 (*Koegelberger 2, Vokovic*), Ujpest Dozsa 2 (*Torocsik 2*)
Odra Opole 1 (*Decker*), Magdeburg 2 (*Sparwasser 2*)
Olympiakos Piraeus 3 (*Karavisis, Losanda, Galakos*), Dynamo Zagreb 1 (*Zedec*)
Manchester C 2 (*Barnes, Channon*), Widzew Lodz 2 (*Boniek 2 [1 pen]*)
Marek Stanke Dimitrov 3 (*Pargov, Petrov 2*), Ferencvaros 0
Rapid Vienna 1 (*Walzer*), Inter Bratislava 0
RWD Molenbeek 0, Aberdeen 0
Servette 1 (*Barberis*), Atlético Bilbao 0
Standard Liège 1 (*Nickel*), Slavia Prague 0
Start Kristiansand 6 (*Myhre, Skuse, Haugen 2, Mathisen 2 [1 pen]*), Fram Reykjavik 0
ASA Tirgu Mures 1 (*Fanici*), AEK Athens 0
Torino 3 (*Pulici 2, Claudio Sala*), Apoel 0
Zurich 1 (*Risi*), CSKA Sofia 0

First Round, Second Leg

Aberdeen 1 (*Jarvie*), RWD Molenbeek 2 (*Gores, Wellens*)
AEK Athens 3 (*Papaioannou, Viera, Moussouris*), ASA Tirgu Mures 0
Altay Izmir 4 (*Mustafa 2, Murat 2*), Carl Zeiss Jena 1 (*Lindemann*)
Apoel 1 (*Marcou*), Torino 1 (*Garritano*)
Atlético Bilbao 2 (*Dani, Amorrortu*), Servette 0
CSKA Sofia 1 (*Markov*), Zurich 1 (*Cuccinotta*)
Eintracht Brunswick 0, Dynamo Kiev 0
Fenebahce 0, Aston Villa 2 (*Deehan, Little*)
Ferencvaros 2 (*Pusztai, Ebedli pen*), Marek Stanke 0
Grasshoppers 6 (*Meyer 2, Becker, Elsener, Ponte 2*), Frem Copenhagen 1 (*Mikkelsen*)
Inter Bratislava 3 (*Novotny 2, Levicky 2*), Rapid Vienna 0
Ipswich T 5 (*Whymark 4 [1 pen], Mariner*), Landskrona 0
Lazio 5 (*Garlaschelli 2, Giordano 3*), Boavista 0
Magdeburg 1 (*Streich*), Odra Opole 1 (*Kiose*)
Malmö FF 2 (*Cervin, Ljungberg*), Lens 0
Mjondalen 0, Bayern Munich 4 (*Rausch, Gruber, Kunkel, Niedermaier*)
Newcastle U 4 (*Gowling 2, Craig T. 2*), Bohemians 0
PSV Eindhoven 5 (*Rene Van der Kerkhof, Lubse 2, Deijkers 2*), Glenavon 0
Schalke 04 2 (*Abramczik, Helmut Kremers*), Fiorentina 1 (*Desolati*)
Slavia Prague 3 (*Vesely, Notovy, Nachtman*), Standard Liège 2 (*Nickel, Sigurvinsson*)
Sliema Wanderers 0, Eintracht Frankfurt 0
Sloboda Tuzla 4 (*Gec, Kovacevic 2, Mulahasonovic*), Las Palmas 3 (*Morete 2, Maciel*)
Sporting Lisbon 1 (*Manuel Fernandes*), Bastia 2 (*Rep, Desvignes*)
Steaua 1 (*Dumitru pen*), Barcelona 3 (*Cruyff, Asensi, Sanchez*)
Dynamo Tbilisi 0, Internazionale 0
Ujpest Dozsa 7 (*Fazekas 2, Toth 2, Torocsik, Sarlos, Fekete*), Linz ASK 0
Valkeakosken 0, Gornik Zabrze 0
Widzew Lodz 0, Manchester C 0
Dynamo Zagreb 5 (*Cerin 2, Senzen, Zajec pen, Bonic*), Olympiakos Piraeus 1 (*Caravitis pen*)
Start Kristiansand 2 (*Skuseth, Ole Olsen*), Fram Reykjavik 0
Red Boys 0, AZ 67 5 (*Kist 3, Van Hanegem, Van Rijnsoer*)
KB Copenhagen 3 (*Andersen 3*), Dundee U 0

Second Round, First Leg

AEK Athens 2 (*Mavros, Nikoloudis*), Standard Liège 2 (*Sigurvinsson, Poul*)
AZ 67 1 (*Nygaard*), Barcelona 1 (*Neeskens*)
Aston Villa 2 (*McNaught 2*), Gornik Zabrze 0
Bastia 2 (*Papi 2*), Newcastle U 1 (*Cannell*)
Bayern Munich 3 (*Müller, Rummenigge 2*), Marek Stanke 0
Inter Bratislava 1 (*Sajanek*), Grasshoppers 0
Ipswich T 1 (*Gates*), Las Palmas 0
KB Copenhagen 1 (*Laudrup*), Dynamo Tbilisi 4 (*Chivadze, Kipiani, Chelebadze, Shengekiya*)
Lazio 2 (*Wilson, Giordano*), Lens 0
Magdeburg 4 (*Sparwasser 3, Steinbach*), Schalke 04 2 (*Demange, Abramczik*)
RWD Molenbeek 1 (*Wellens*), Carl Zeiss Jena 1 (*Lindemann*)
Start Kristiansand 1 (*Helge Haugen*), Eintracht Brunswick 0
Torino 3 (*Pulici, Patrizio Sala, Pecci*), Dynamo Zagreb 1 (*Cerin*)
Ujpest Dozsa 2 (*Torocsik, Viczko*), Atlético Bilbao 0
Widzew Lodz 3 (*Rozborsky, Kowenicki, Boniek*), PSV Eindhoven 5 (*Deijkers 2, Deacy, Van der Kuylen, Francois*)
Zurich 0, Eintracht Frankfurt 3 (*Holzenbein, Wenzel 2*)

Second Round, Second Leg

Barcelona 1 (*Rexach pen*), AZ 67 1 (*Kist*)
Barcelona won on penalties 5-4.
Atlético Bilbao 3 (*Dani 2, Tirapu*), Ujpest Dozsa 0
Eintracht Brunswick 4 (*Breitner, Handschuh, Hollman 2*), Start Kristiansand 0
Carl Zeiss Jena 1 (*Lindemann pen*), RWD Molenbeek 1 (*Alhino*)
Carl Zeiss Jena won on penalties 6-5.
Dynamo Zagreb 1 (*Senzen*), Torino 0
Eintracht Frankfurt 4 (*Kraus, Grabowski, Stepanovic, Krobach*), Zurich 3 (*Risi 2 [1 pen], Torstensson*)
Gornik Zabrze 1 (*Marcinkowski*), Aston Villa 1 (*Gray*)
Grasshoppers 5 (*Elsener 2, Ponte, Sulser, Hey*), Inter Bratislava 1 (*Jurkemik*)
Marek Stanke 2 (*Petrov, Pargov*), Bayern Munich 0
Las Palmas 3 (*Morete 2, Felix*), Ipswich T 3 (*Mariner 2, Tibbott*)
Lens 6 (*Six 3, Bousdira, Djebali 2*), Lazio 0
Newcastle U 1 (*Gowling*), Bastia 3 (*De Zerbi, Rep 2*)
PSV Eindhoven 1 (*Deijkers*), Widzew Lodz 0
Schalke 04 1 (*Kremers*), Magdeburg 3 (*Pommerenke 2, Steinbach*)
Standard Liège 4 (*Labarbe, Riedl, Nickel, Gorez*), AEK Athens 1 (*Ardizoglou*)
Dynamo Tbilisi 2 (*Kipiani, Chelebadze*), KB Copenhagen 1 (*Andersen*)

Third Round, First Leg

Aston Villa 2 (*Iribar og, Deehan*), Atlético Bilbao 0
Bastia 2 (*Papi, Rep*), Torino 1 (*Pulici*)
Carl Zeiss Jena 2 (*Schnuphase, Lindemann*), Standard Liège 0

Eintracht Frankfurt 4 (*Grabowski, Holzenbein, Kraus, Skala*), Bayern Munich 0
Ipswich T 3 (*Gates, Whymark, Talbot*), Barcelona 0
Magdeburg 4 (*Zapf, Pommerenke pen, Mewes, Steinbach*), Lens 0
PSV Eindhoven 2 (*Lubse, Van der Kuylen*), Eintracht Brunswick 0
Dynamo Tbilisi ! (*Shengelia*), Grasshoppers 0

Third Round, Second Leg
Atlético Bilbao 1 (*Dani*), Aston Villa 1 (*Mortimer*)
Barcelona 3 (*Cruyff 2, Rexach pen*), Ipswich T 0
Barcelona won on penalties 3-1.
Bayern Munich 1 (*Rummenigge*), Eintracht Frankfurt 2 (*Wenzel, Holzenbein*)
Eintracht Brunswick 1 (*Bruns*), PSV Eindhoven 2 (*Van Kraay, Deijkers*)
Grasshoppers 4 (*Sulser, Ponte 2 [1 pen], Elsener*), Dynamo Tbilisi 0
Lens 2 (*Bousdira 2*), Magdeburg 0
Standard Liège 1 (*Nickel*), Carl Zeiss Jena 2 (*Szengewald, Weise pen*)
Torino 2 (*Graziani 2*), Bastia 3 (*Larios, Krimau 2*)

Quarter-Final, First Leg
Aston Villa 2 (*McNaught, Deehan*), Barcelona 2 (*Cruyff, Zuviria*)
Bastia 7 (*Larios, Papi, Mariot, Felix 2, Cazes, Franceschetti*), Carl Zeiss Jena 2 (*Raab 2*)
Magdeburg 1 (Streich), PSV Eindhoven 0
Eintracht Frankfurt 3 (*Kraus, Holzenbein 2 [1 pen]*), Grasshoppers 2 (*Bosco, Ponte pen*)

Quarter-Final, Second Leg
Grasshoppers 1 (*Ponte pen*), Eintracht Frankfurt 0
Carl Zeiss Jena 4 (*Raab, Lindemann, Vogel, Topfer pen*), Bastia 2 (*Papi, Krimau*)
PSV Eindhoven 4 (*Brandst 2, Seguin og, Lubse*), Magdeburg 2 (*Hoffman, Pommerenke*)
Barcelona 2 (*Migueli, Asensi*), Aston Villa 1 (*Little*)

Semi-Final, First Leg
Grasshoppers 3 (*Hermann, Ponte pen, Montandon*), Bastia 2 (*Krimau, Papi pen*)
PSV Eindhoven 3 (*Olmo og, Lubse, Postuma*), Barcelona 0

Semi-Final, Second Leg
Barcelona 3 (*Rexach 2 pens, Fortes*), PSV Eindhoven 1 (*Deacy*)
Bastia 1 (*Papi*), Grasshoppers 0

Final 1977–78: Bastia 0, PSV Eindhoven 0
(In Corsica, 26 April, 1978, 15,000)

Bastia: Hiard; Burkhard, Guesdon, Orlanducci, Cazes, Papi, Lacuseta (Felix), Larios, Rep, Krimau, Mariot.
PSV Eindhoven: Van Beveren; Van Kraay, Krijgh, Stevens, Brandts, Poortvliet, Van der Kuylen, Willy Van der Kerkhof, Deijkers, Rene Van der Kerkhof, Lubse.

PSV Eindhoven 3, Bastia 0
(In Eindhoven, 9 May, 1978, 27,000)

PSV Eindhoven: Van Beveren; Krijgh, Stevens, Van Kraay (Deacy), Brandts, Willy Van der Kerkhof, Poortvliet, Van der Kuylen, Lubse, Deijkers, Rene Van der Kerkhof.
Bastia: Hiard (Weller); Marchioni, Orlanducci, Guesdon, Cazes, Lacuesta, Larios, Papi, Rep, Krimau, Mariot (De Zerbi).
Scorers: PSV Eindhoven – Willy Van der Kerkhof, Deijkers, Van der Kuylen.

UEFA CUP 1978–79

First Round, First Leg

Dukla Prague 1 (*Nehoda*), Lanerossi Vicenza 0
AC Milan 1 (*Novellino*), Lokomotiv Kosice 0
CSKA Sofia 2 (*Djevizov, Christov*), Valencia 1 (*Solsona*)
Borussia Moenchengladbach 5 (*Bruns 2, Gores, Nielsen, Simonsen*), Sturm Graz 1 (*Jurtin*)
Arges Pitesti 3 (*Toma, Moiceanu 2*), Panathinaikos 0
Atlético Bilbao 2 (*Van Dord og, Vidal*), Ajax 0
Everton 5 (*King 2, Thomas, Walsh, Latchford*), Finn Harps 0
Jeunesse Esch 0, Lausanne 0
Nantes 0, Benfica 2 (*Chalana, Nene*)
Gijon 3 (*Ferrero, Moran 2*), Torino 0
Sporting Braga 5 (*Chico Gordo 4, Lito*), Hibernians 0
Galatasaray 1 (*Fatih*), WBA 3 (*Robson, Regis, Cunningham*)
Dynamo Berlin 5 (*Riediger 3, Netz, Brillat*), Red Star Belgrade 2 (*Sestic, Savic*)
Palloseura 2 (*Monkkanen, Eiskanen*), 1903 Copenhagen 1 (*Haarby*)
Basle 2 (*Tanner, Stohler*), Stuttgart 3 (*Ohlicher 2, Dieter Hoeness*)
Torpedo Moscow 4 (*Vassilev, Mironov, Grijsin, Sutsijlin*), Molde 0
Elfsborg 2 (*Svensson, Magnusson*), Strasbourg 0
Duisburg 5 (*Jara, Alhaus, Bussers, Worm 2*), Lech Poznan 0
Standard Liège 1 (*Denier*), Dundee U 0
Start Kristiansand 0, Esbjerg 0
Arsenal 3 (*Stapleton 2, Sunderland*), Lokomotiv Leipzig 0
Carl Zeiss Jena 1 (*Topfer*), Lierse 0
Glentoran 0, IBV Vestmann 0
Twente 1 (*Thorsen*), Manchester C 1 (*Watson*)
Hibernian 3 (*Higgins 2, Temperley*), IFK Norrköping 2 (*Ohlsson, Andersson*)
Timisoara 2 (*Cotec, Paltinisan*), MTK Budapest 0
Pezoporikos 2 (*Teofonu 2*), Slask Wroclaw 2 (*Pawlowski, Sybis*)
Olympiakos 2 (Kritikopoulos, Kaltzas), Levski Spartak 1 (*Panov*)
Dynamo Tbilisi 2 (*Kipiani, Shengelja*), Napoli 0
Hajduk Split 2 (*Kop, Luchetin*), Rapid Vienna 0
Hertha Berlin 0, Trakia Plovdiv 0
Honved 6 (*Lukacs, Weimper 2, Gijmesi, Bodoyni, Nagy*), Adanaspor 0

First Round, Second Leg

Lanerossi Vicenza 1 (*Briaschi*), Dukla Prague 1 (*Roselli og*)
Lokomotiv Kosice 1 (*Kozak*), AC Milan 0
Valencia 4 (*Saura 2, Kempes, Felman*), CSKA Sofia 1 (*Christov*)
Sturm Graz 1 (*Schilcher*), Borussia Moenchengladbach 2 (*Simonsen, Bruns*)
Panathinaikos 1 (*Gonios*), Arges Pitesti 2 (*Duru, Radu*)
Ajax 3 (*Clarke 2, Lerby*), Atlético Bilbao 0
Finn Harps 0, Everton 5 (*King, Latchford, Walsh, Ross, Dobson*)
Lausanne 2 (*Dizerens, Sanpedro*), Jeunesse Esch 0
Benfica 0, Nantes 0
Torino 1 (*Graziani*), Gijon 0
Hibernians 3 (*Spiteri Gonzi, Mizzi 2*), Sporting Braga 2 (*Chico Gordo, Reinaldo*)
WBA 3 (*Robson, Cunningham, Trewick*), Galatasaray 1 (*Turgay*)
Red Star Belgrade 4 (*Borovnicka 2, Savic, Sestic*), Dynamo Berlin 1 (*Riediger*)
1903 Copenhagen 4 (*Christensen, Smidt, Larsen, Dam*), Palloseura 4 (*Eiskanen 2, Heinalainen, Rautio*)
Stuttgart 4 (*Kelsch 3, Hansi Muller*), Basle 1 (*Schonberger*)
Molde 3 (*Brakstad, Bjoraa, Fuglseth*), Torpedo Moscow 3 (*Vassilev 2, Zotijlin*)
Strasbourg 4 (*Piasecki, Tanter, Marx, Wagner*), Elfsborg 1 (*Ahlstrom*)
Lech Poznan 2 (*Kasalik, Okonski*), Duisburg 5 (*Bussers, Worm 2, Wenten, Buttgereit*)
Dundee U 0, Standard Liège 0
Esbjerg 1 (*Iversen*), Start Kristiansand 0
Lokomotiv Leipzig 1 (*Stapleton og*), Arsenal 4 (*Price, Sunderland, Stapleton 2*)
Lierse 2 (*Bosche, Van den Bergh*), Carl Zeiss Jena (*Schupase, Topfer*)
IBV Westmann 1 (*Oskarsson*), Glentoran 1 (*McFall*)
Manchester C 3 (*Kidd, Bell, Overweg og*), Twente (*Wildschut, Gritter*)
IFK Norrköping 0, Hibernian 0
MTK Budapest 2 (Koritar, Nadu og), Timisoara (*Petrescu*)
Slask Wroclaw 5 (*Garlowski, Faber, Olesiak, Kwiatkowski, Sybis*), Pezoporikos 1 (*Lambrou*)
Levski Spartak 3 (*Milkov, Panov, Voinov*), Olympiakos (*Kaltzas*)
Napoli 1 (*Savoldi*), Dynamo Tbilisi 1 (*Daraselia*)
Rapid Vienna 2 (*Krejcirik, Francker*), Hajduk Split (*Zungul*)
Trakia Plovdiv 1 (*Argirov*), Hertha Berlin 2 (*Granitza 2*)
Adanaspor 2 (*Irfan, Necip*), Honved 2 (*Sener og, Pinter*)

Second Round, First Leg

Ajax 1 (*Lerby*), Lausanne 0
Benfica 0, Borussia Moenchengladbach 0
Everton 2 (*Latchford, King*), Dukla Prague 1 (*Macela*)
Arges Pitesti 2 (*Dobrin, Moiceanu*), Valencia 1 (*Felman*)
Sporting Braga 0, WBA 2 (*Regis 2*)
Torpedo Moscow 2 (*Vassilev, Sakharov*), Stuttgart 1 (*Dieter Hoeness*)
Strasbourg 2 (*Gemmrich, Piasecki*), Hibernian 0
Gijon 0, Red Star Belgrade 1 (*Misa og*)
Carl Zeiss Jena 0, Duisburg 0
Palloseura 0, Esbjerg 2 (*Bach, Nielsen*)
IBV Westmann 0, Slask Wroclaw 2 (*Kwiatkowski, Halgrimsson og*)
Manchester C 4 (*Hartford, Palmer, Kidd 2*), Standard Liège 0
Honved 4 (*Weimper 2, Gijmesi, Pinter*), Timisoara 0
Hertha Berlin 2 (*Nussing, Granitza*), Dynamo Tbilisi 0
Hajduk Split 2 (*Kop, Djordjevic*), Arsenal 1 (*Brady*)
Levski Spartak 1 (*Milkov*), AC Milan 1 (*Chiodi*)

Second Round, Second Leg

WBA 1 (*Brown A.*), Sporting Braga 0
Stuttgart 2 (*Hansi Muller, Volkert*), Torpedo Moscow 0
Hibernian 1 (*MacLeod*), Strasbourg 0
Red Star Belgrade 1 (*Petrovic*), Gijon 1 (*Borovnika og*)
Duisburg 3 (*Dietz, Jara, Fruck*), Carl Zeiss Jena 0
Esbjerg 4 (*Berthelsen, Thoresen, Stergaard, Bach*), Palloseura 1 (*Loikkanen*)
Slask Wroclaw 2 (*Nocko, Kwiatkowski*), IBV Westmann 1 (*Halgrimsson*)
Standard Liège 2 (*Sigurvinsson 2*), Manchester C 0
Timisoara 2 (*Rosca, Paltinislan*), Honved 0
Dynamo Tbilisi 1 (*Shengelia*), Hertha Berlin 0
Arsenal 1 (*Young*), Hajduk Split 0
AC Milan 3 (*Maldera, Bigon, Chiodi*), Levski Spartak 0
Dukla Prague 1 (*Gajdusek*), Everton 0
Lausanne 0, Ajax 4 (*Erkens, Clarke 2, Arnesen*)
Valencia 5 (*Kempes 2, Bonhof, Saura, Solsona*), Arges Pitesti 2 (*Moiceanu, Doru Nicolae*)
Borussia Moenchengladbach 2 (*Bruns pen, Klinkhammer*), Benfica 0

Third Round, First Leg

Stuttgart 4 (*Volkert 2* [*1 pen*], *Kelsch, Ohlicher*), Dukla Prague 1 (*Gajdusek*)
Honved 4 (*Nagy 2, Lukacs, Weimper pen*), Ajax 1 (*Clarke pen*)
Red Star Belgrade 1 (*Blagojevic*), Arsenal 0
Esbjerg 2 (Hansen pen, Jaspersen), Hertha Berlin 1 (*Milewski*)
Borussia Moenchengladbach 1 (*Kulik pen*), Slask Wroclaw 1 (*Olesiak*)
Valencia 1 (*Felman*), WBA 1 (*Cunningham*)
Strasbourg 0, Duisburg 0
AC Milan 2 (*Bigon 2*), Manchester C 2 (*Kidd, Power*)

Third Round, Second Leg

Dukla Prague 4 (*Dieter Hoeness og, Vizek, Pelc pen, Gajdusek*), Stuttgart 0

Ajax 2 (*Clarke pen, Tahamata*), Honved 0
Arsenal 1 (*Sunderland*), Red Star Belgrade 1 (*Savic*)
Hertha Berlin 4 (*Milewski 4*), Esbjerg 0
Slask Wroclaw 2 (*Pawlowski 2 [1 pen]*), Borussia Moenchengladbach 4 (*Simonsen 3, Nielsen*)
WBA 2 (*Brown T. 2*), Valencia 0
Duisburg 4 (*Worm, Weber 2, Fruck*), Strasbourg 0
Manchester C 3 (*Booth, Hartford, Kidd*), AC Milan 0

Quarter-Finals, First Leg
Honved 2 (*Varga II, Weimper pen*), Duisburg 3 (*Worm 2, Seliger*)
Red Star Belgrade 1 (*Savic*), WBA 0
Manchester C 1 (*Channon*), Borussia Moenchengladbach 1 (*Lienen*)
Hertha Berlin 1 (*Nussing*), Dukla Prague 1 (*Pelc*)

Quarter-Finals, Second Leg
Duisburg 1 (*Bussers*), Honved 2 (*Karalyos, Pal*)
WBA 1 (*Regis*), Red Star Belgrade 1 (*Sestic*)
Borussia Moenchengladbach 3 (*Kulik, Bruns, Del Haye*), Manchester C 1 (*Deyna*)
Dukla Prague 1 (*Nehoda*), Hertha Berlin 2 (*Agerbeck, Milewski*)

Semi-Finals, First Leg
Red Star Belgrade 1 (*Savic*), Hertha Berlin 0
Duisburg 2 (*Worm, Fruck*), Borussia Moenchengladbach 2 (*Simonsen, Lausen*)

Semi-Finals, Second Leg
Hertha Berlin 2 (*Beer, Sidka*), Red Star Belgrade 1 (*Milosavljevic*)
Borussia Moenchengladbach 4 (*Simonsen 2, Kulik, Lienen*), Duisburg 1 (*Bussers*)

Final 1978–79: Red Star Belgrade 1, Borussia Moenchengladbach 1
(In Belgrade, 9 May, 1979, 87,500)

Red Star Belgrade: Stojanovic; Jovanovic, Miletovic, Jurisic, Jovin, Muslin (Krmpotic), Petrovic, Blagojevic, Milosavljevic (Milovanovic), Savic, Sestic.

Borussia Moenchengladbach: Kneib; Vogts, Hannes, Schaffer, Ringles, Schafer, Kulik, Nielsen (Danner), Wohlers (Gores), Simonsen, Lienen.

Scorers: Red Star Belgrade – Sestic; Borussia Moenchengladbach – Juristic og.

Borussia Moenchengladbach 1, Red Star Belgrade 0
(In Dusseldorf, 23 May, 1979, 45,000)

Borussia Moenchengladbach: Kneib; Vogts, Hannes, Schaffer, Ringles, Schafer, Kulik (Koppel), Gores, Wohlers, Simonsen, Lienen.

Red Star Belgrade: Stojanovic; Jovanovic, Miletovic, Jurisic, Jovin, Muslin, Petrovic, Blagojevic, Milovanovic (Sestic), Savic, Milosavljevic.

Scorer: Borussia Moenchengladbach – Simonsen (pen).

UEFA CUP 1979–80

First Round, First Leg
Perugia 1 (*Vujadinovic og*), Dinamo Zagreb 0
Inter-Milan 3 (*Muraro, Baresi, Marini*), Real Sociedad 0
Napoli 2 (*Damiani, Agostinelli*), Olympiakos 0
Stuttgart 1 (*Danova og*), Torino 0
Dundee U 0, Anderlecht 0
Glenavon 0, Standard Liège 1 (*Edstroem*)
Dinamo Kiev 2 (*Bessonov, Demianenko*), CSKA Sofia 1 (*Metodiev*)
Lokomotiv Sofia 3 (*Stankov, Velickov, Szokolov*), Ferencvaros 0
Kalmar 2 (*Sunesson, Sandberg*), IBK Keflavik 1 (*Mergeisson*)
KPT Kuopio 1 (*Pirinen*), Malmö 2 (*Andersson, Prytz pen*)
Dinamo Bucharest 3 (*Multescu, Georgescu, Vrinceanu*), Alki Larnaca 0
Bohemians Prague 0, Bayern Munich 2 (*Kraus, Rummenigge*)
Zbrojovka Brno 6 (*Mazura, Janecka 2, Kroupa, Jarusek 2*), Esbjerg 0
Valletta 0, Leeds U 4 (*Graham 3, Hart*)
Orduspor 2 (*Cihan, Arif*), Banik Ostrava 0
Wiener SK 0, Uni Craiova 0
Widzew Lodz 2 (*Boniek, Kowienicki*), St Etienne 1 (*Platini*)
Aris Salonika 3 (*Cuis, Pallas pen, Zindros*), Benfica 1 (*Reinaldo*)
Carl Zeiss Jena 2 (*Schnuphase, Lindemann*), WBA 0
Atlético Madrid 1 (*Ruben Cano*), Dinamo Dresden 2 (*Hafner, Weber*)
Aarhus 1 (*Olesen*), Stal Mielec 1 (*Karas*)
Feyenoord 1 (*Notten*), Everton 0
Skeid Oslo 1 (*Rein*), Ipswich T 3 (*Mills, Turner, Mariner*)
Gijon 0, PSV Eindhoven 0
Galatasaray 0, Red Star Belgrade 0
Aberdeen 1 (*Harper*), Eintracht Frankfurt 1 (*Bum Kun Cha*)
Rapid Vienna 0, Diosgyor 1 (*Fuko*)
Borussia Moenchengladbach 3 (*Lienen, Nickel pen, Kulik*), Viking 0
Sporting Lisbon 2 (*Fernandes 2*), Bohemians 0
Zurich 1 (*Zwicher*), Kaiserslautern 3 (*Neues, Bongartz, Wolff*)
Shakhtjor 2 (*Sokolovsky 2*), Monaco 1 (*Petit*)
Progres Niedercorn 0, Grasshoppers 2 (*Herbert Hermann, Egli*)
Eintracht Frankfurt 1 (*Holzenbein*), Aberdeen 0
Diosgyor 3 (*Szalai, Fekete, Tatar*), Rapid Vienna 2 (*Keglevits, Sallmayer*)
Viking 1 (*Bjensen*), Borussia Moenchengladbach 1 (*Kulik*)
Bohemians 0, Sporting Lisbon 0
Kaiserslautern 5 (*Melzer 2, Kaminke, Wendt, Geye*), Zurich 1 (*Zappa*)
Monaco 2 (*Onnis, Dalger*), Shakhtjor 0
Grasshoppers 4 (*Ponte, Pfister, Egli, Heinz Hermann*), Progres Niedercorn 0

First Round, Second Leg
Dinamo Zagreb 0, Perugia 0
Real Sociedad 2 (*Satrustegui 2*), Inter-Milan 0
Olympiakos 1 (*Karavitis*), Napoli 0
Torino 2 (*Sala, Graziani*), Stuttgart 1 (*Ohlicher*)
Anderlecht 1 (*Nielsen*), Dundee U 1 (*Kopel*)
Standard Liège 1 (*Edstrom*), Glenavon 0
CSKA Sofia 1 (*Metodiev pen*), Dinamo Kiev 1 (*Buryak*)
Ferencvaros 2 (*Pusztai, Pogany*), Lokomotiv Sofia 0
IBK Keflavik 1 (*Andreasson og*), Kalmar 0
Malmö 2 (*Arvidsson 2*), KPT Kuopio 0
Alki Larnaca 0, Dinamo Bucharest 9 (*Georgescu 3, Vrinceanu 2, Augustin, Talanar, Multescu, Moldovan*)
Bayern Munich 2 (*Rummenigge, Breitner pen*), Bohemians Prague 2 (*Ondrus, Prokas pen*)
Esbjerg 1 (*Bach*), Zbrojovka Brno 1 (*Jarusek*)
Leeds U 3 (*Curtis, Hankin, Hart*), Valletta 0
Banik Ostrava 6 (*Knapp, Vojacek, Nemec, Licka 2, Danek*), Orduspor 0
Uni Craiova 3 (*Camataru 2, Geolganu*), Wiener SK 1 (*Drabits*)
St Etienne 3 (*Rep 3 [1 pen]*), Widzew Lodz 0
Benfica 2 (*Reinaldo, Gomes*), Aris Salonika 1 (*Semertzidis*)
WBA 1 (*Wile*), Carl Zeiss Jena 2 (*Lindemann, Raab pen*)
Dinamo Dresden 3 (*Riedl, Ruiz og, Weber*), Atlético Madrid 0
Stal Mielec 0, Aarhus 1 (*Jensen*)
Everton 0, Feyenoord 1 (*Budding*)
Ipswich T 7 (*Wark, Muhren 2, McCall 2, Mariner, Thijssen*), Skeid Oslo 0
PSV Eindhoven 1 (*Van der Kerkhof W.*), Gijon 0
Red Star Belgrade 3 (*Savic 2, Milovanovic*), Galatasaray 1 (*Gungor*)

Second Round, First Leg
Aris Salonika 1 (*Semertzidis*), Perugia 1 (*Rossi*)
Standard Liège 2 (*Riedl, Sigurvinsson pen*), Napoli 1 (*Capone*)
Borussia Moenchengladbach 1 (*Hannes*), Inter-Milan 1 (*Altobelli*)
Dinamo Bucharest 2 (*Multescu pen, Augustin*), Eintracht Frankfurt 0
Uni Craiova 2 (*Balaci, Irimescu*), Leeds U 0
Zbrojovka Brno 3 (*Kotasek 2, Janecka*), IBK Keflavik 1 (*Georgsson*)
Red Star Belgrade 3 (*Savic pen, Muslin, Sestic*), Carl Zeiss Jena 2 (*Raab 2 [1 pen]*)
Lokomotiv Sofia 4 (*Mihailov 4 [2 pens]*), Monaco 2 (*Onnis 2 [1 pen]*)
Dundee U 0, Diosgyor 1 (*Fekete*)
Aarhus 1 (*Sander*), Bayern Munich 2 (*Rummenigge 2*)
Grasshoppers 0, Ipswich T 0
Feyenoord 4 (*Petursson 3 [1 pen], Van Diesen*), Malmö 0
PSV Eindhoven 2 (*Van der Kerkhof R., Moster*), St Etienne 0
Sporting Lisbon 1 (*Fernandes*), Kaiserslautern 1 (*Bongartz*)
Dinamo Dresden 1 (*Weber pen*), Stuttgart 1 (*Forster*)
Banik Ostrava 1 (*Nemec*), Dinamo Kiev 0

Second Round, Second Leg
Perugia 0, Aris Salonika 3 (*Cuis, Semertzidis, Zindros*)
Napoli 1 (*Damiani*), Standard Liège 1 (*Riedl*)
Inter-Milan 2 (*Altobelli 2*), Borussia Moenchengladbach 3 (*Nickel 2 [1 pen], Ringels*)
Eintracht Frankfurt 3 (*Bum Kun Cha, Holzenbein, Nickel*), Dinamo Bucharest 0
Leeds U 0, Uni Craiova 2 (*Cirtu, Beldeanu*)
IBK Keflavik 1 (*Olafsson*), Zbrojovka Brno 2 (*Kroupa, Kotasek*)
Carl Zeiss Jena 2 (*Trocha, Topfer*), Red Star Belgrade 3 (*Kurbjuweit og, Filipovic, Blagojevic*)
Monaco 2 (*Christophe, Onnis*), Lokomotiv Sofia 1 (*Mihailov*)
Diosgyor 3 (*Borostyan, Tatar 2 [1 pen]*), Dundee U 1 (*Kopel*)
Bayern Munich 3 (*Hoeness D. 2, Breitner*), Aarhus 1 (*Mickelsen*)
Ipswich T 1 (*Beattie*), Grasshoppers 1 (*Sulser*)
Malmö 1 (*Arvidsson*), Feyenoord 1 (*Petursson*)
St Etienne 6 (*Larios, Santini, Platini 2, Roussey, Rep pen*), PSV Eindhoven 0
Kaiserslautern 2 (*Bongartz, Neues pen*), Sporting Lisbon 0
Stuttgart 0, Dinamo Dresden 0
Dinamo Kiev 2 (*Demianenko, Kapsalis*), Banik Ostrava 0

Third Round, First Leg
Bayern Munich 2 (*Rummenigge, Janzon*), Red Star Belgrade 0
Grasshoppers 0, Stuttgart 2 (*Klotz, Hadewicz*)
Borussia Moenchengladbach 2 (*Nickel 2*), Uni Craiova 0
Diosgyor 0, Kaiserslautern 2 (*Wendt, Bongartz*)
Eintracht Frankfurt 4 (*Bum Kun Cha, Nickel, Muller, Lotterman*), Feyenoord 1 (*Stafleu*)
Standard Liège 1 (*Voordeckers*), Zbrojovka Brno 2 (*Svoboda, Dosek*)
St Etienne 4 (*Platini, Larios, Firos og, Roussey*), Aris Salonika 1 (*Semertzidis*)
Lokomotiv Sofia 1 (*Mihailov*), Dinamo Kiev 0

Third Round, Second Leg
Red Star Belgrade 3 (*Savic, Petrovic, Repcic*), Bayern Munich 2 (*Hoeness 2*)
Stuttgart 3 (*Muller, Martin, Kelsh*), Grasshoppers 0
Uni Craiova 1 (*Irimescu*), Borussia Moenchengladbach 0
Kaiserslautern 6 (*Neues, Melzer, Brummer, Kaminke, Bongartz, Stabel pen*), Diosgyor 1 (*Borostyan*)
Feyenoord 1 (*Peters*), Eintracht Frankfurt 0
Zbrojovka Brno 3 (*Jarusel, Kroupa, Janecka*), Standard Liège 2 (*Edstrom, De Matos*)
Aris Salonika 3 (*Larios og, Pallas pen, Venos*), St Etienne 3 (*Larios, Zimako, Rep*)
Dinamo Kiev 2 (*Blochin, Kapsalis*), Lokomotiv Sofia 1 (*Doychev*)

Quarter-Final, First Leg
St Etienne 1 (*Platini*), Borussia Moenchengladbach 4 (*Nielsen 2, Nickel, Lienen*)
Kaiserslautern 1 (*Brummer*), Bayern Munich 0
Eintracht Frankfurt 4 (*Nachtweih, Lorant pen, Nickel, Karger*), Zbrojovka Brno 1 (*Horny*)
Stuttgart 3 (*Muller, Volkert 2 [1 pen]*), Lokomotiv Sofia 1 (*Kolev*)

Quarter-Final, Second Leg
Borussia Moenchengladbach 2 (*Thychosen, Hannes*), St Etienne 0
Bayern Munich 4 (*Hoeness 2, Janzon, Breitner pen*), Kaiserslautern 1 (*Wendt*)
Zbrojovka Brno 3 (*Horny, Kotasek, Kopenec*), Eintracht Frankfurt 2 (*Karger, Neuberger*)
Lokomotiv Sofia 0, Stuttgart 1 (*Ohlicher*)

Semi-Final, First Leg
Stuttgart 2 (*Ohlicher, Volkert pen*), Borussia Moenchengladbach 1 (*Nickel*)
Bayern Munich 2 (*Hoeness, Breitner pen*), Eintracht Frankfurt 0

Semi-Final, Second Leg
Borussia Moenchengladbach 2 (*Matthaus, Schaefer*), Stuttgart 0
Eintracht Frankfurt 5 (*Pezzey 2, Karger 2, Lorant pen*), Bayern Munich 1 (*Dremmler*)

Final 1979–80: Borussia Moenchengladbach 3, Eintracht Frankfurt 2
(In Moenchengladbach, 7 May, 1980, 25,000)

Borussia Moenchengladbach: Kneib; Hannes, Schaefer, Schaeffer, Ringels, Matthaus, Kulik, Nielsen (Thychosen), Del'Haye (Boedeker), Harald Nickel, Lienen.

Eintracht Frankfurt: Pahl; Pezzey, Neuberger, Koerbel, Ehrmanntraut, Lorant, Holzenbein (Nachtweih), Borchers, Bernd Nickel, Tscha, Karger (Trapp).

Scorers: Borussia Moenchengladbach – Kulik 2, Matthaus; Eintracht Frankfurt – Karger, Holzenbein.

Eintracht Frankfurt 1, Borussia Moenchengladbach 0
(In Frankfurt, 21 May, 1980, 60,000)

Eintracht Frankfurt: Pahl; Pezzey, Neuberger, Koerbel, Ehrmanntraut, Lorant, Holzenbein, Borchers, Bernd Nickel, Tscha, Nachtweih (Schaub).

Borussia Moenchengladbach: Kneib; Hannes, Fleer, Schaefer, Ringels, Matthaus (Thychosen), Boedeker, Kulik, Nielsen (Del'Haye), Harald Nickel, Lienen.

Scorer: Eintracht Frankfurt – Schaub.

Eintracht Frankfurt won on away goals.

EUROPEAN CUP 1980–81

Preliminary Round
Honved 8 (*Bodonyi, Garaba, Esterhazy, Kocsis, Dajka 2, Varga 2 [1 pen]*), Valletta 0
Valletta 0, Honved 3 (*Esterhazy 2, Bodonyi*)

First Round, First Leg
Linfield 0, Nantes 1 (*Amisse*)
Aberdeen 1 (*McGhee*), Austria Vienna 0
FC Bruges 0, Basle 1 (*Maissen*)
CSKA Sofia 1 (*Yonchev*), Nottingham F 0
Dynamo Berlin 3 (*Terletzki, Trieloff, Schulz*), Apoel 0
Dynamo Tirana 0, Ajax 2 (*Arnesen 2*)
Inter-Milan 2 (*Altobelli 2 [1 pen]*), Uni Craiova 0
Jeunesse Esch 0, Moscow Spartak 5 (*Gavrilov 3, Khidiatulin, Yartsev*)
Limerick 1 (*Kennedy*), Real Madrid 2 (*Juanito pen, Pineda*)
Olympiakos 2 (*Galakos, Ahlstrom*), Bayern Munich 4 (*Dremmler 2, Rummenigge, Kraus*)
OPS Oulu 1 (*Puotiniemi*), Liverpool 1 (*McDermott*)
Sporting Club 0, Honved 2 (*Bodonyi, Nagy*)
Trabzonspor 2 (*Sinan, Tuncay*), Szombierki Bytom 1 (*Wazniewsky*)
Viking Stavanger 2 (*Svendsen, Sabo*), Red Star Belgrade 3 (*Petrovic, Brekke og, Repcic*)
IBV Vestmannayjar 1 (*Thorleifsson*), Banik Ostrava 1 (*Danek*)
Halmstad 0, Esbjerg 0

First Round, Second Leg
Nantes 2 (*Rampillon, Trossero E.*), Linfield 0
Honved 1 (*Dajka*), Sporting Club 0
Red Star Belgrade 4 (*Djurovski, Janjanin, Petrovic, Stamenkovic*), Viking Stavanger 1 (Brekke)
Uni Craiova 1 (*Beldeanu*), Inter-Milan 1 (*Muraro*)
Szombierki Bytom 3 (*Bys, Ogaza, Srodka pen*), Tranzonspor 0
Banik Ostrava 1 (*Vojacek*), IBV Vestmannayjar 0
Real Madrid 5 (*Santillana, Juanito 2, Cunningham, Pineda*), Limerick 1 (*Kennedy*)
Moscow Spartak 4 (*Pigat og, Rodionov, Gavrilov, Yartsev*), Jeunesse Esch 0
Nottingham Forest 0, CSKA Sofia 1 (*Kerimov*)
Bayern Munich 3 (*Hoeness, Rummenigge, Janzon pen*), Olympiakos 0
Basle 4 (*Tanner, Stohler pen, Von Wartburg, Gaisser*), FC Bruges 1 (*Ceulemans*)
Esbjerg 3 (*Iversen, Lauridsen, Nielsen*), Halmstad 2 (*Johansson, Larsson*)
Ajax 1 (*Lerby pen*), Dynamo Tirana 0
Austria Vienna 0, Aberdeen 0
Apoel 2 (*Hailis, Petrou*), Dynamo Berlin 1 (*Schnuphase*)
Liverpool 10 (*Souness 3, McDermott 2, Dalglish, Lee, Kennedy R., Fairclough 2*), OPS Oulu 1 (*Armstrong*)

Second Round, First Leg
Nantes 1 (*Rio pen*), Inter-Milan 2 (*Altobelli, Prohaska*)
Real Madrid 1 (*Santillana*), Honved 0
Bayern Munich 5 (*Durnberger, Rummenigge 2, Hoeness 2*), Ajax 1 (*Arnesen*)
Aberdeen 0, Liverpool 1 (*McDermott*)
CSKA Sofia 4 (*Yonchev 3, Zdranov*), Szombierki Bytom 0
Banik Ostrava 0, Dynamo Berlin 0
Moscow Spartak 3 (*Khidiatulin 2, Shavio*), Esbjerg 0
Basle 1 (*Lauscher*), Red Star Belgrade 0

Second Round, Second Leg
Honved 0, Real Madrid 2 (*Cunningham, Garcia Hernandez*)
Inter-Milan 1 (*Altobelli*), Nantes 1 (*Amisse*)
Ajax 2 (*Wiggemansen, Rijkaart*), Bayern Munich 1 (*Rummenigge*)
Red Star Belgrade 2 (*Repcic, Janjanin*), Basle 0
Liverpool 4 (*Miller og, Neal, Dalglish, Hansen*), Aberdeen 0
Dynamo Berlin 1 (*Troppa pen*), Banik Ostrava 1 (*Knapp pen*)
Esbjerg 2 (*Lauridsen, Iversen*), Moscow Spartak 0
Szombierki Bytom 0, CSKA Sofia 1 (*Djevisov*)

Quarter-Final, First Leg
Liverpool 5 (*Souness 3, Lee, McDermott*), CSKA Sofia 1 (*Yonchev*)
Bayern Munich 2 (*Janzon, Breitner pen*), Banik Ostrava 0
Inter-Milan 1 (*Caso*), Red Star Belgrade 1 (*Repcic*)
Moscow Spartak 0, Real Madrid 0

Quarter-Final, Second Leg
CSKA Sofia 0, Liverpool 1 (*Johnson*)
Banik Ostrava 2 (*Nemec, Licka*), Bayern Munich 4 (*Hoeness, Kraus, Rober, Durnberger*)
Red Star Belgrade 0, Inter-Milan 1 (*Muraro*)
Real Madrid 2 (*Isidro 2*), Moscow Spartak 0

Semi-Final, First Leg
Liverpool 0, Bayern Munich 0
Real Madrid 2 (*Santillana, Juanito*), Inter-Milan 0

Semi-Final, Second Leg
Bayern Munich 1 (*Rummenigge*), Liverpool 1 (*Kennedy R.*)
Inter-Milan 1 (*Bini*), Real Madrid 0

Final 1980–81: Liverpool (0) 1, Real Madrid (0) 0

(In Paris, 27 May 1981, 48,360)

Liverpool: Clemence; Neal, Kennedy A., Thompson, Kennedy R., Hansen, Dalglish (Case), Lee, Johnson, McDermott, Souness.

Real Madrid: Rodriguez; Garcia Cortes, Camacho, Stielike, Sabido (Pineda), Del Bosque, Juanito, De Los Santos, Santillana, Navajas, Cunningham.

Scorer: Liverpool – Kennedy A.

EUROPEAN CUP-WINNERS' CUP 1980–81

Preliminary Round
Celtic 6 (*McGarvey 2, McCluskey 2, Nedder og, Sullivan*), Diosgyor 0
Diosgyor 2 (*Gorgey 2*), Celtic 1 (*Nicholas*)
Altay Izmir 0, Benfica 0
Benfica 4 (*Chalana, Humberto, Nene, Cesar*), Altay Izmir 0

First Round, First Leg
Newport Co 4 (*Gwyther, Moore, Aldridge, Bruton*), Crusaders 0
Spora Luxembourg 0, Sparta Prague 6 (*Berger 2, Kotek, Chalana, Chaloupka 2*)
Slavia Sofia 3 (*Tsvetkov pen, Velichkov 2*), Legia Warsaw 1 (*Miloszewisz*)
Castilla 3 (*Paco, Balin, Cidon*), West Ham U 1 (*Cross*)
Celtic 2 (*Nicholas 2*), Poli Timisoara 1 (*Adrian*)
Dynamo Zagreb 0, Benfica 0
Fortuna Dusseldorf 5 (*Kohnen 2, Wenzel, Klaus Allofs, Theis*), Austria Salzburg 0
Hibernians Malta 1 (*Xuereb P.*), Waterford 0
Ilves Tampere 1 (*Uimonen*), Feyenoord 3 (*Notten pen, Van Deinsen, Troost*)
Hvidovre 1 (*Steen Hansen pen*), Fram Reykjavik 0
Kastoria 0, Dynamo Tbilisi 0
Malmö 1 (*McKinnon*), Partizan Tirana 0
Omonia Nicosia 1 (*Kanaris*), Waterschei 3 (*Van Pouche, Janssen, Meds*)
Roma 3 (*Pruzzo, Ancelotti, Falcao*), Carl Zeiss Jena 0
Sion 1 (*Brigger*), Haugar 1 (*Osborne*)
Valencia 2 (*Kempes, Morena pen*), Monaco 0

First Round, Second Leg
Monaco 3 (*Petit 2, Barberis*), Valencia 3 (*Morena, Kempes, Felman*)
Benfica 2 (*Nene, Cesar*), Dynamo Zagreb 0
Haugar 2 (*Nilsen, Kristophersen pen*), Sion 0
Partizan Tirana 0, Malmö 0
Poli Timisoara 1 (*Paltinisan*), Celtic 0
Waterford 4 (*Kirk 2, Finucane, Fitzpatrick*), Hibernians Malta 0
Sparta Prague 6 (*Pospisil, Slany, Jarohm 2, Berger, Horvath*), Spora Luxembourg 0
Dynamo Tbilisi 2 (*Shengelia, Gutsayev*), Kastoria 0
Legia Warsaw 1 (*Okonski pen*), Slavia Sofia 0
Austria Salzburg 0, Fortuna Dusseldorf 3 (*Thomas Allofs, Dusend 2*)
West Ham U 5 (*Pike, Cross 3, Goddard*), Castilla 1 (*Bernal*)
Feyenoord 4 (*Vermaulen, Nielsen, Troost, Notten*), Ilves Tampere 2 (Prinen pen, Wacklin)
Waterschei 4 (*Janssen, Plessers pen, Van Poucke, Grundel*), Omonia Nicosia 0
Fram Reykjavik 0, Hvidovre 2 (*Ambrose, Hansen*)
Crusaders 0, Newport Co 0
Carl Zeiss Jena 4 (*Krause, Lindeman, Bielau 2*) Roma 0

Second Round, First Leg
Carl Zeiss Jena 3 (*Sengewald, Schnuphase pen, Trocha*), Valencia 1 (*Morena*)
Malmö 1 (*Andersson M.*), Benfica 0
Waterschei 0, Fortuna Dusseldorf 0
Feyenoord 2 (*Wijnstekers, Bouwens*), Hvidovre 1 (*Mannicke*)
Sparta Prague 2 (*Vkovjak 2*), Slavia Sofia 0
Waterford 0, Dynamo Tbilisi 1 (*Shengelia*)
Haugar 0, Newport Co 0
West Ham U 4 (*Bonds, Goddard, Stewart pen, Cross*), Poli Timisoara 0

Second Round, Second Leg
Newport Co 6 (*Gwyther, Lowndes, Aldridge, Tynan 2, Moore*), Haugar 0
Valencia 1 (*Botubot*), Carl Zeiss Jena 0
Poli Timisoara 1 (*Paltinisan*), West Ham U 0
Dynamo Tbilisi 4 (*Daraselia 2, Chivadze, Chilaia*), Waterford 0
Fortuna Dusseldorf 1 (*Bansemer*), Waterschei 0
Feyenoord 1 (*Nielsen*), Hvidovre 0
Slavia Sofia 3 (*Velitchkov, Jeliazkov, Tsvetkov*), Sparta Prague 0
Benfica 2 (*Nene 2*), Malmö 0

Quarter-Final, First Leg
West Ham U 1 (*Cross*), Dynamo Tbilisi 4 (*Chivadze, Gutsayev, Shengelia 2*)
Carl Zeiss Jena 2 (*Raab 2*), Newport Co 2 (*Tynan 2*)
Slavia Sofia 3 (*Tsvetkov 2 [1 pen], Aliev*), Feyenoord 2 (*Nielsen, Vermeulen pen*)
Fortuna Dusseldorf 2 (*Wenzel, Dusend*), Benfica 2 (*Carlos Manuel, Humberto*)

Quarter-Final, Second Leg
Feyenoord 4 (*Notten, Van Deinsen, Vermeulen, Bouwens*), Slavia Sofia 0
Benfica 1 (*Chalana*), Fortuna Dusseldorf 0
Dynamo Tbilisi 0, West Ham U 1 (*Pearson*)
Newport Co 0, Carl Zeiss Jena 1 (*Kurbjuweit*)

Semi-Final, First Leg
Carl Zeiss Jena 2 (*Bielau, Raab*), Benfica 0
Dynamo Tbilisi 3 (*Sulakvelidze 2, Gutsayev*), Feyenoord 0

Semi-Final, Second Leg
Benfica 1 (*Reinaldo*), Carl Zeiss Jena 0
Feyenoord 2 (*Bouwens, Notten pen*), Dynamo Tbilisi 0

Final 1980–81: Dynamo Tbilisi (0) 2, Carl Zeiss Jena (0) 1
(In Dusseldorf, 13 May, 1981, 9000)

Dynamo Tbilisi: Gabelia; Kostava, Chivadze, Khisanishvili, Tavadze, Svanadze (Kakilashvili), Sulakvelidze, Daraselia, Gutsayev, Kipiani, Shengelia.

Carl Zeiss Jena: Grapenthin; Brauer, Kurbjuweit, Schnuphase, Schilling, Hoppe (Overmann), Krause, Lindemann, Bielau (Topfer), Raab, Vogel.

Scorers: Dynamo Tbilisi – Gutsayev, Daraselia; Carl Zeiss Jena – Hoppe.

UEFA CUP 1980–81

First Round, First Leg

AZ 67 Alkmaar 6 (*Hovenkamp, Nygaard, Peters 2, Welzl, Tol*), Red Boys 0
IA Akranes 0, Cologne 4 (*Kroth, Littbarski, Muller, Strack*)
Sliema Wanderers 0, Barcelona 2 (*Canito, Landaburu*)
Ujpest Dozsa 1 (*Kardos*), Real Sociedad 1 (*Alonso*)
Arges Pitesti 0, Utrecht 0
Ballymena U 2 (*McQuiston, Sloan*), Vorwaerts Frankfurt 1 (*Geyer*)
Bohemians Prague 3 (*Bicovsky 2, Levy*), Gijon 1 (*Ferrero*)
Dynamo Dresden 1 (*Weber*), Napredak 0
Elfsborg 1 (*Nilsson*), St Mirren 2 (*Somner, Abercromby*)
Grasshoppers 3 (*Meyer 3 [2 pens]*), KB Copenhagen 1 (*Eigenbrod*)
Hamburg 4 (*Kaltz, Hrubesch 2, Hartwig*), Sarajevo 2 (*Susic 2*)
Ipswich T 5 (*Wark 4 [3 pens], Mariner*), Aris Salonika 1 (*Pallas pen*)
Juventus 4 (*Scirea, Verza, Bettega, Cabrini pen*), Panathinaikos 0
Kaiserslautern 1 (*Funkel*), Anderlecht 0
Dynamo Kiev 1 (*Buryak pen*), Levski Spartak 1 (*Spassov*)
PSV Eindhoven 3 (*Brandts, Van Kraay, Van der Koylen pen*), Wolverhampton W 1 (*Gray*)
Kuopion Palloseura 0, St Etienne 7 (*Paganelli 2, Hyvarinen og, Platini 2, Roussey, Janvion*)
Linz ASK 1 (*Krieger*), Radnicki Nis 2 (*Stojlkovic, Pantelic pen*)
Lokeren 1 (*Verheyen pen*), Moscow Dynamo 1 (*Gassayev*)
Magdeburg 2 (*Hoffman, Pommerenke pen*), Moss 1 (*Henriksen*)
Manchester U 1 (*McIlroy*), Widzew Lodz 1 (*Surlit*)
Porto 1 (*Souza*), Dundalk 0
RWD Molenbeek 1 (*De Wolf*), Torino 2 (*Mariani, Graziani*)
Shakhtor Donetsk 1 (*Starukhin*), Eintracht Frankfurt 0
Slask Wroclaw 0, Dundee U 0
Sochaux 2 (*Jeskowiak, Ivezic pen*), Servette 0
Standard Liège 1 (*Dardenne*), Steaua Bucharest 1 (*Raducanu*)
Stuttgart 6 (*Klotz 3, Allgower 2, Kelsch*), Pezoporikos 0
Twente 5 (*Bos, Carlsson og, Kila 2, Jol*), IFK Gothenburg 1 (*Nilsson*)
Vasas 0, Boavista 2 (*Eliseu, Julio*)
Zbrojovka Brno 3 (*Kroupa, Mikulicka, Mazura*), Voest Linz 1 (*Haider*)
Fenerbahce 0, Beroe Stara Zagora 1 (*Peyev*)

First Round, Second Leg

St Etienne 7 (*Rep 4 [1 pen], Lestage, Paganelli, Lopez*), Kuopion Palloseura 0
Servette 2 (*Cuccinotta, Bizzini*), Sochaux 1 (*Genghini*)
Red Boys 0, AZ 67 Alkmaar 4 (*Kist 3 [1 pen], Welzl*)
Steaua Bucharest 1 (*Raducanu*), Standard Liège 2 (*Voordeckers, Edstrom*)
Aris Salonika 3 (*Tsirmokos, Drambis, Zeleidis*), Ipswich T 1 (*Gates*)
Radnicki Nis 4 (*Mitosevic, Stolijovic 2, Panajotovic*), Linz ASK 1 (*Siegl*)
Napredak 0, Dynamo Dresden 1 (*Muller pen*)
Moscow Dynamo 0, Lokeren 1 (*Verheyen*)
Vorwaerts Frankfurt 3 (*Conrad, Jarmuskiewicz, Krautzig*), Ballymena U 0
Boavista 0, Vasas 1 (*Kiss*)
IFK Gothenburg 2 (*Nilsson 2*), Twente 0
Sarajevo 3 (*Lukic, Pasic 2*), Hamburg 3 (*Hrubesch 3*)
Voest Linz 0, Zbrojovka Brno 2 (*Janecka, Kroupa*)
St Mirren 0, Elfsborg
Dundee U 7 (*Dodds 2, Hegarty, Pettigrew 2, Stark, Payne pen*), Slask Wroclaw 2 (*Pawlowski 2*)
Widzew Lodz 0, Manchester U 0
KB Copenhagen 2 (*Fossgaard, Hansen pen*), Grasshoppers 5 (*Heinz Hermann 3, Zanetti, Sulser*)
Moss 2 (*Kollshaugen 2*), Magdeburg 3 (*Streich, Mewes, Wildebrand*)
Levski Spartak 0, Kiev Dynamo 0
Beroe Stara Zagora 2 (*Petkov, Dragolov*), Fenerbahce 1 (*Selcuk*)
Anderlecht 3 (*Nielsen 3, [1 pen]*), Kaiserslautern 2 (*Gaye, Wendt*)
Real Sociedad 1 (*Satrustegui*), Ujpest Dozsa 0
Barcelona 1 (*Rexach pen*), Sliema Wanderers 0
Eintracht Frankfurt 3 (*Holzenbein, Cha Kun Bum 2*), Shakhtor Donetsk 0
Utrecht 2 (*Van der Lem, Carbo*), Arges Pitesti 0
Dundalk 0, Porto 0
Cologne 6 (*Engels, Muller 4, Okudera*), IA Akranes 0
Wolverhampton W 1 (*Eves*), PSV Eindhoven 0
Gijon 2 (*Ferrero, Jimenez*), Bohemians 1 (*Nemec*)
Panathinaikos 4 (*Gentile og, Andreucchi, Luvanthinos, Delikaris*), Juventus 2 (*Bettega, Fanna*)
Torino 2 (*D'Amico, Graziani*), RWD Molenbeek 2 (*De Bolle, Van de Korput og*)
Pezoporikos 1 (*Theophanous P.*), Stuttgart 4 (*Tuefekci 2, Klotz, Allgower*)

Second Round, First Leg

Sochaux 2 (*Genghini, Ravelli*), Boavista 2 (*Julio, Eliseu*)
St Mirren 0, St Etienne 0
Torino 3 (*Sala P., Pecci, Mewes og*), Magdeburg 1 (*Steinbach*)
Twente 1 (*Rohde*), Dynamo Dresden 1 (*Heidler*)
Widzew Lodz 3 (*Grebosz, Pieta, Smolarek*), Juventus 1 (Bettega)
Dundee U 1 (*Pettigrew*), Lokeren 1 (*Mommens*)
Utrecht 2 (*Carbo, Dr Kruyk pen*), Eintracht Frankfurt 1 (*Borchers*)
Ipswich T 3 (*Wark 2, Beattie*), Bohemians Prague 0
Levski Spartak 1 (*Spassov*), AZ 67 Alkmaar 1 (*Kist*)
PSV Eindhoven 1 (*Van der Kuylen*), Hamburg 1 (*Hrubesch*)
Cologne 0, Barcelona 1 (*Quini*)
Stuttgart 5 (*Tuefekci, Martin pen, Scuth og, Allgower, Klotz*), Vorwaerts Frankfurt 1 (*Krautzig*)
Kaiserslautern 1 (*Wendt*), Standard Liège 2 (*Wellens, Plessers*)
Beroe Stara Zagora 0, Radnicki Nis 1 (*Halilovic*)
Zbrojovka Brno 1 (*Murillo og*), Real Sociedad 1 (*Uraide*)
Porto 2 (*Teixeira, Albertino*), Grasshoppers 0

Second Round, Second Leg

AZ 67 Alkmaar 5 (*Tol 2, Nygaard pen, Kist, Peters*), Levski Spartak 0
Radnicki Nis 2 (*Stojikovic, Mitosevic*), Beroe Stara Zagora 1 (*Stojanov*)
Dynamo Dresden 0, Twente 0
St Etienne 2 (*Larios 2*), St Mirren 0
Boavista 0, Sochaux 1 (*Durkalic*)
Magdeburg 1 (*Tyll*), Torino 0
Juventus 3 (*Tardelli, Furino, Brady*), Widzew Lodz 1 (*Pieta*)
Eintracht Frankfurt 3 (*Karger, Nachtweih, Pezzey*), Utrecht 1 (*Neuberger og*)
Hamburg 2 (*Groh, Hrubesch*), PSV Eindhoven 1 (*Van der Kuylen*)
Standard Liège 2 (*Edström, Graf*), Kaiserslautern 1 (*Briegel*)
Barcelona 0, Cologne 4 (*Strack, Engels, Littbarski, Muller*)
Vorwaerts Frankfurt 1 (*Lindemann*), Stuttgart 2 (*Allgower, Hansi Muller pen*)
Real Sociedad 2 (*Satrustegui 2*), Zbrojovka Brno 1 (*Kotasek*)
Grasshoppers 3 (*Sulser, Koller, Pfister pen*), Porto 0
Lokeren 0, Dundee U 0
Bohemians 2 (*Micinec, Panenka*), Ipswich T 0

Third Round, First Leg

Eintracht Frankfurt 4 (*Neuberger, Borchers, Holzenbein, Nachtweih*), Sochaux 2 (*Genghini, Pezzey og*)
Hamburg 0, St Etienne 5 (*Hartwig og, Platini 2, Larios, Zimako*)
Stuttgart 3 (*Hansi Muller 2 [1 pen], Karl-Heinz Forster*), Cologne 1 (*Konopka*)

Lokeren 1 (*Lato*), Real Sociedad 0
Grasshoppers 2 (*Heinz Hermann, Koller*), Torino 1 (*Sclosa*)
Radnicki Nis 2 (*Pantelic pen, Panajotovic*), AZ 67 Alkmaar 2 (*Tol, Kist*)
Standard Liège 1 (*Plessers*), Dynamo Dresden 1 (*Heidler*)
Ipswich T 5 (*Wark 3, Brazil, Mariner*), Widzew Lodz 0

Third Round, Second Leg
Sochaux 2 (*Patrick Revelli 2*), Eintracht Frankfurt 0
St Etienne 1 (Paganelli), Hamburg 0
Cologne 4 (*Dieter Muller, Strack 2, Woodcock*), Stuttgart 1 (*Konopka og*)
Widzew Lodz 1 (*Pieta*), Ipswich T 0
Dynamo Dresden 1 (*Dorner*), Standard Liège 4 (*Sigurvinsson 3, Tahamata*)
Torino 2 (*Graziani, Pulici*), Grasshoppers 1 (*Terraneo og*)
Real Sociedad 2 (*Lopez Ufarte pen, Zamora*), Lokeren 2 (*Larsen 2*)
AZ 67 Alkmaar 5 (*Kist 3, Nygaard, Welzl*), Radnicki Nis 0

Quarter-Final, First Leg
Standard Liège 0, Cologne 0
AZ 67 Alkmaar 2 (*Tol, Welzl*), Lokeren 0
St Etienne 1 (*Rep*), Ipswich T 4 (*Mariner 2, Muhren, Wark*)
Grasshoppers 0, Sochaux 0

Quarter-Final, Second Leg
Ipswich T 3 (*Butcher, Wark pen, Mariner*), St Etienne 1 (*Zimako*)
Cologne 3 (*Dieter Muller, Bonhof pen, Littbarski*), Standard Liège 2 (*Graf, Vandersmissen*)
Sochaux 2 (*Durkalic, Genghini*), Grasshoppers 1 (*Koller*)
Lokeren 1 (*Verheyen*), AZ 67 Alkmaar 0

Semi-Final, First Leg
Ipswich T 1 (*Wark*), Cologne 0
Sochaux 1 (*Genghini*), AZ 67 Alkmaar 1 (*Arntz*)

Semi-Final, Second Leg
Cologne 0, Ipswich T 1 (*Butcher*)
AZ 67 Alkmaar 3 (*Metgod, Jonker, Peters*), Sochaux 2 (*Genghini, Meyer*)

Final 1980–81: Ipswich T (1) 3, AZ 67 Alkmaar (0) 0
(At Ipswich, 6 May, 1981, 27,532)

Ipswich T: Cooper; Mills, McCall, Thijssen, Osman, Butcher, Wark, Muhren, Mariner, Brazil, Gates.
AZ 67 Alkmaar: Treytel; Van der Meer, Spelbos, Metgod, Hovenkamp, Peters, Jonker, Arntz, Nygaard (Welzl), Kist, Tol.
Scorers: Ipswich T – Wark pen, Thijssen, Mariner.

AZ 67 Alkmaar (3) 4, Ipswich T (2) 2
(In Amsterdam, 20 May, 1981, 28,500)

AZ 67 Alkmaar: Treytel; Reynders, Spelbos, Metgod, Hovenkamp, Peters, Welzl (Kist), Arntz, Jonker, Nygaard, Tol.
Ipswich T: Cooper; Mills, McCall, Thijssen, Osman, Butcher, Wark, Muhren, Mariner, Brazil, Gates.
Scorers: AZ 67 Alkmaar – Welzl, Metgod, Tol, Jonker; Ipswich T – Thijssen, Wark.

GOLDEN BOOT AWARD

Winner of the Golden Boot Award for Europe's leading League goalscorer in 1980–81 was Georgi Slavkov, of Thrakia Plovdiv and Bulgaria, with 31 goals. Runner-up was Tibor Nyilasi of the Hungarian club, Ferencvaros, with 30 goals, followed by Karl-Heinz Rummenigge of West Germany's Bayern Munich with 29. Andrezj Szarmach, the Pole, was fourth with 28. Szarmach had started the season in his native Poland with Stal Mielec but joined the French club, Auxerre, halfway through the season.

BRITISH CLUBS IN EUROPE 1980–81

EUROPEAN CUP 1980–81

FIRST ROUND, FIRST LEG
16 SEPT
Linfield (0) 0
Nantes (1) 1 (*Amisse*) 600
At Haarlem, Holland
Linfield: Dunlop; Garrett, Dornan, McKeown, Frazer, Nixon (McGaughey), Hayes, McKee, Parks, McCurdy, Anderson.
Nantes: Bertrand-Demanes; Bossis, Rio, Michel, Tusseau, Muller (Toure), Poullain, Rampillon, Agerbeck (Pecout), Baronchelli, Amisse.

17 SEPT
Aberdeen (1) 1 (*McGhee*)
Austria Vienna (0) 0 20,000
Aberdeen: Leighton; Kennedy, Rougvie, Watson, McLeish, Miller, Strachan, McMaster, McGhee, Jarvie, Scanlon.
Austria Vienna: Koncilia; Sara R., Obermayer, Pospischil, Baumeister, Sara J., Dihanich, Daxbacher, Furst, Gasselich, Schachner.

CSKA Sofia (0) 1 (*Yonchev*)
Nottingham F (0) 0 70,000
CSKA Sofia: Velinov; Zafirov, Dimitrov D., Vasilev, Dimitrov G., Iliev, Yonchev, Kerimov, Djevizov, Markov, Velkov.
Nottingham F: Shilton; Anderson, Gray, McGovern, Lloyd, Needham, O'Neill, Bowyer (Ponte), Birtles, Wallace, Robertson.

OPS Oulu (0) 1 (*Puotineimi*)
Liverpool (1) 1 (*McDermott*) 14,000
OPS Oulu: Rantanen; Lahtinen, Ahonen, Hoikkinen, Houtsonen, Puotineimi, Jalasuaara, Kemppainen, Armstrong, Smith, Himanka.
Liverpool: Clemence; Neal, Cohen, Thompson, Kennedy R., Hansen, Dalglish, Lee, Fairclough, McDermott, Souness.

Limerick (0) 1 (*Kennedy*)
Real Madrid (0) 2 (*Juanito* pen, *Pineda*) 7000
Limerick: Fitzpatrick; Nolan, O'Mahony, Storan, Nodwell, Duggan (Morris), Hand (Meaney), Walsh, Hulmes, Kennedy, Matthews.
Real Madrid: Miguel Angel; Perez Garcia (Navajas), Benito (Pineda), Gallego, Camacho, Juan Angel, Garcia Hernandez, Stielike, Juanito, Isidro, Cunningham.

FIRST ROUND, SECOND LEG
30 SEPT
Nantes (0) 2 (*Rampillon, Trossero*)
Linfield (0) 0 12,000
Nantes: Bertrand-Demanes; Bossis, Rio, Michel, Tusseau (Ayache), Trossero, Baronchelli, Poullain, Toure, Rampillon, Amisse (Pecout).
Linfield: Dunlop; Garrett, Frazer, Hayes, Rafferty, McKeown, McKee, Dornan, McCurdy, Parks, Anderson.

1 OCT
Austria Vienna (0) 0
Aberdeen (0) 0 45,000
Austria Vienna: Koncilia; Sara R., Obermayer (Pfelier), Baumeister, Sara J., Dihanich, Daxbacher, Furst, Gasselich, Schachner, Zore (Borgan).
Aberdeen: Leighton; Kennedy, Rougvie, Miller, Watson, Strachan, McMaster, McGhee, Scanlon, Bell, Garner.

Nottingham F (0) 0
CSKA Sofia (1) 1 (*Kerimov*) 25,818
Nottingham F: Shilton; Anderson, Gray, McGovern, Needham, Burns (Lloyd), O'Neill, Bowyer, Birtles, Wallace, Robertson.
CSKA Sofia: Velinov; Zafirov, Dimitrov D., Vasilev, Rangelov, Iliev, Yonchev, Kerimov, Djevizov, Markov, Velkov.

Liverpool (4) 10 (*Souness 3* [1 pen], *Fairclough 2, McDermott 3, Lee, Kennedy R.*)
OPS Oulu (0) 1 (*Armstrong*) 21,013
Liverpool: Clemence; Neal, Cohen, Thompson, Kennedy R., Hansen, Dalglish, Lee, Fairclough, McDermott, Souness.
OPS Oulu: Rantanen; Lahtinen, Ahonen, Hoikkinen, Kemppainen (Juntunen), Puotineimi, Houtsonen, Smith, Jalasuaara (Matera), Armstrong, Himanka.

Real Madrid (2) 5 (*Santillana, Juanito, Angel, Cunningham, Pineda*)
Limerick (1) 1 (*Kennedy*) 50,000
Real Madrid: Remon; Isidro, Camacho, Gallego, Benito, Navajas A., Juanito (Pineda), Angel, Santillana, Steilike, Cunningham.
Limerick: Fitzpatrick; Nolan, O'Mahoney, Storan, Nodwell, Hand, Duggan, Walsh, Holmes (Morris), Kennedy, Matthews.

SECOND ROUND, FIRST LEG
22 OCT
Aberdeen (0) 0
Liverpool (1) 1 (*McDermott*) 24,000
Aberdeen: Leighton; Kennedy S., Rougvie, Watson, McLeish, Miller, Strachan, McMaster (Bell), McGhee, Jarvie (Hewitt), Scanlon.
Liverpool: Clemence; Neal, Kennedy A., Thompson, Kennedy R., Hansen, Dalglish, Lee (Case), Johnson, McDermott, Souness.

SECOND ROUND, SECOND LEG
5 NOV
Liverpool (2) 4 (*Miller og, Neal, Dalglish, Hansen*)
Aberdeen (0) 0 36,182
Liverpool: Clemence; Neal, Kennedy A. (Cohen), Thompson, Kennedy R., Hansen, Dalglish, Lee, Johnson, McDermott, Souness.
Aberdeen: Leighton; Dornan, Rougvie (Cooper), Watson, McLeish, Miller, Strachan, Bell (Hewitt), McGhee, Jarvie, Scanlon.

QUARTER-FINAL, FIRST LEG
4 MARCH
Liverpool (2) 5 (*Souness 3, Lee, McDermott*)
CSKA Sofia (0) 1 (*Yonchev*) 37,255
Liverpool: Clemence; Neal, Kennedy A., Thompson (Irwin), Kennedy R., Hansen, Dalglish, Lee, Heighway, McDermott, Souness.
CSKA Sofia: Velinov; Zafirov, Iliev (Dimitrov D.), Vasilev, Rangelov, Zdravkov, Yonchev, Kerimov (Vulkov), Djevizov, Markov, Velkov.

QUARTER-FINAL, SECOND LEG
18 MARCH
CSKA Sofia (0) 0
Liverpool (1) 1 (*Johnson*) 65,000
CSKA Sofia: Arsov; Iliev, Dimitrov D., Vasilev (Kalbourov), Rangelov, Zdravkov, Yonchev, Mladenov, Djevizov, Markov, Velkov.
Liverpool: Clemence; Neal, Kennedy A., Irwin, Kennedy R., Hansen, Dalglish, Lee, Johnson (Heighway), Case, Souness.

SEMI-FINAL, FIRST LEG
8 APRIL
Liverpool (0) 0
Bayern Munich (0) 0 44,543
Liverpool: Clemence; Neal, Kennedy A., Thompson, Kennedy R., Hansen, Dalglish, Lee, Rush, McDermott, Heighway (Case).
Bayern Munich: Junghans; Dremmier, Horsmann, Weiner, Augenthaler, Kraus, Durnberger, Breitner, Hoeness, Niedermayer, Rummenigge.

SEMI-FINAL, SECOND LEG
22 APRIL
Bayern Munich (0) 1 (*Rummenigge*)
Liverpool (0) 1 (*Kennedy R.*) 75,000
Bayern Munich: Junghans; Dremmler, Horsmann, Weiner, Augenthaler, Kraus, Durnberger (Janzon), Breitner, Hoeness, Del'Haye, Rummenigge.
Liverpool: Clemence; Neal, Money, Irwin, Kennedy R., Hansen, Dalglish (Gayle) (Case), Lee, Johnson, McDermott, Souness.

FINAL (Paris)
27 MAY
Liverpool (0) 1 (*Kennedy A.*)
Real Madrid (0) 0 48,360
Liverpool: Clemence; Neal, Kennedy A., Thompson, Kennedy R., Hansen, Dalglish (Case), Lee, Johnson, McDermott, Souness.
Real Madrid: Rodriguez; Garcia Cortes (Pineda), Camacho, Stielike, Sabido, Del Bosque, Juanito, De Los Santos, Santillana, Navajas, Cunningham.

EUROPEAN CUP-WINNERS' CUP 1980–81

PRELIMINARY ROUND, FIRST LEG
20 AUG
Celtic (0) 6 (*McGarvey 3, McCluskey 2, Sullivan*)
Diosgyör (0) 0 28,000
Celtic: Bonnar; Sneddon, McGrain, Aitken, McAdam, MacLeod (Doyle), Provan (Nicholas), Sullivan, McGarvey, Burns, McCluskey.
Diosgyör: Szabo; Szanto, Neder, Kadar, Olah, Kerekes, Szlifka (Teodoru V.), Fluko, Teodoru B, Gorgei, Borostyan.

PRELIMINARY ROUND, SECOND LEG
3 SEPT
Diosgyör (1) 2 (*Georgei 2*)
Celtic (1) 1 (*Nicholas*) 5000
Diosgyör: Szabo; Szanto, Neder, Kerekes, Teodoru B., Olah, Fluko, Georgei, Szlifka, Magyar, Borostyan.
Celtic: Bonnar; Sneddon, McGrain, Aitken, McAdam, MacLeod, Provan, Sullivan, McGarvey, Burns, Nicholas.

FIRST ROUND, FIRST LEG
16 SEPT
Newport Co (2) 4 (*Gwyther, Moore, Aldridge, Bruton*)
Crusaders (0) 0 6285
Newport Co: Dowler; Walden, Relish, Bruton, Oakes, Tynan, Bourne, Lowndes, Gwyther, Aldridge (Elsey), Moore.
Crusaders: McDonald; Thompson, Gorman, Mulhall, Gillespie, Whiteside, Jess, Fellowes, Byrne (King), Currie, Rice (Cromie).

17 SEPT
Castilla (0) 3 (*Paco, Ballin, Cicon*)
West Ham U (1) 1 (*Cross*) 40,000
Castilla: Miguel; Juanito (Chendo), Casimiro, Salguero, Espinosa, Sanchez Lorenzo, Balin, Alvarez, Paco, Bernal, Cidon (Blanco).
West Ham U: Parkes; Stewart, Lampard, Martin, Bonds, Devonshire (Brush), Morgan (Barnes), Brooking, Pike, Goddard, Cross.

Celtic (2) 2 (*Nicholas 2*)
Timisoara (0) 1 (*Adrian*) 30,000
Celtic: Bonnar; Sneddon, McGrain, Aitken, McAdam, MacLeod, Provan, Sullivan, McCluskey, Burns, Nicholas.
Timisoara: Moise; Nadu, Paltinisanu, Visan, Soandu, Serbanoiu, Cotec, Adrian, Nedelcu, Dumitru, Titi.

Hibernians (Malta) (0) 1 (*Xuereb*)
Waterford (0) 0 2000
Hibernians: Mizzi A.; Consiglio, Buttigeg, Zerafa, Mizzi R., Xuereb P., Mallia, Cauchi, Galea, Spiteri-Gonzi, Cumi.
Waterford: Thomas; Gardner, McQuaid, Finucane, Dunphy, Jackson, Kirk, Madigan, Meagan, McCarthy, Murray.

FIRST ROUND, SECOND LEG
1 OCT
Crusaders (0) 0
Newport Co (0) 0 2000
Crusaders: McDonald; Currie, Gorman, Mulhall, Gillespie, Thompson, Jess (Byrne), Followes, King, McPolin (Whiteside), Rice.
Newport Co: Plumley; Walden, Relish (Elsey), Bruton (Davies), Oakes, Tynan, Vaughan, Lowndes, Gwyther, Aldridge, Moore.

West Ham U (3) 5 aet (*Pike, Cross 3, Goddard*)
Castilla (0) 1 (*Bernal*) *262
(**Behind closed doors*)
West Ham U: Parkes; Stewart, Lampard, Bonds, Martin, Devonshire, Holland (Brush), Goddard (Morgan), Cross, Brooking, Pike.
Castilla: Miguel; Chendo, Casimiro, Salguero, Espinosa, Sanchez Lorenzo, Balin, Alvarez, Paco (Ramirez), Bernal, Cidon (Blanco).

Timisoara (0) 1 (*Paltinisan*)
Celtic (0) 0 50,000
Timisoara: Manea; Nadu, Serbanoiu, Paltinisanu, Sunda, Dumitru, Maned, Visan, Dembrovschi, Anghel, Nedelcu.
Celtic: Latchford; Sneddon, McAdam, McDonald, McGrain, Sullivan, Aitken, MacLeod, McGarvey, Nicholas, Provan.

Waterford (3) 4 (*Kirk 2, Finucane, Fitzpatrick*)
Hibernians (Malta) (0) 0 5000
Waterford: Thomas; O'Mahony (McQuaid), Finucane, Dunphy, Gardner, Madigan, Jackson, McCarthy, Murray (Meagan), Fitzpatrick, Kirk.
Hibernians: Mizzi A.; Consiglio (Campbell), Buttigeg, Zerafa, Mizzi R., Xuereb P., Mallia, Cauchi, Gallea, Spiteri-Gonzi, Cumi.

SECOND ROUND, FIRST LEG
22 OCT
Waterford (0) 0
Dynamo Tbilisi (0) 1 (*Shengelia*) 5000
Waterford: Thomas; O'Mahoney (Fitzpatrick), Gardner, Finucane, Dunphy, Jackson, Murray, Madigan, Kirk, McGrath (Kerry), Meagan.
Dynamo Tbilisi: Gabelia; Kostava, Chivadze, Khizanishvili, Mudzhiri, Daraselia, Sulakvelidze, Koridze, Gutsayev (Chelevadze), Kipiani, Shengelia (Kereselidze).

West Ham U (3) 4 (*Bonds, Goddard, Stewart* pen, *Cross*)
Timisoara (0) 0 27,157
West Ham U: Parkes; Stewart, Lampard, Bonds, Martin, Devonshire, Holland, Goddard (Morgan), Cross, Neighbour, Pike.
Timisoara: Moise; Nadu, Paltinisanu, Visan, Sunda, Murar, Anghel, Dembrowski (Titi), Nedelcu, Dumitru, Cotec.

Haugar (0) 0
Newport Co (0) 0 4522
Haugar: Sciefloe; Vikanes, Hestvik (Undahl), Sorensen, Solberg, Burnett, Christophersen, Heimdal, Nilsen, Osborne, Foleide.
Newport Co: Plumley; Walden, Bailey, Bruton, Oakes, Elsey, Vaughan, Lowndes, Gwyther, Aldridge, Moore.

SECOND ROUND, SECOND LEG
4 NOV
Newport Co (2) 6 (*Gwyther, Lowndes, Aldridge, Tynan 2, Moore*)
Haugar (0) 0 8855
Newport Co: Plumley; Walden, Bailey, Bruton, Oakes, Tynan, Vaughan, Lowndes, Gwyther, Aldridge, Moore.
Haugar: Sciefloe; Vikanes, Larsen, Sorensen, Solberg, Burnett, Heimdal, Christophersen (Undahl), Nilsen, Osborne, Foleide (Straume).

5 NOV
Dynamo Tbilisi (0) 4 (*Daraselia 2, Chivadze, Chilaia*)
Waterford (0) 0 45,000
Dynamo Tbilisi: Gabelia; Kostava, Chivadze, Khizanishvili, Mudzhiri (Chilaia), Daraselia, Sulakvelidze, Zhvania (Zhokadze), Chelevadze, Kipiani, Shengelia.
Waterford: Thomas; O'Mahoney, Gardner, Finucane, Dunphy, Jackson, Murray, Madigan, Kirk, McCarthy, Meagan.

Timisoara (0) 1 (*Paltinisanu*)
West Ham U (0) 0 25,000
Timisoara: Moise; Sunda, Paltinisanu, Visan, Titi, Serbanoiu, Anghel, Dembrowski (Sunda), Nedelcu, Dumitru, Cotec.
West Ham U: Parkes; Stewart (Brush), Lampard, Bonds, Martin, Allen, Holland, Goddard, Cross, Neighbour (Brooking), Pike.

QUARTER-FINAL, FIRST LEG
4 MARCH
Carl Zeiss Jena (1) 2 (*Raab 2*)
Newport Co (1) 2 (*Tynan 2*) 30,000
Carl Zeiss Jena: Grapenthin; Brauer, Schnuphase, Krause, Lindemann, Trocha, Schilling, Sengewald (Hoppe), Kurbjuweit, Raab, Vogel (Bielav).
Newport Co: Plumley; Walden, Relish, Davies, Oakes, Tynan, Vaughan, Lowndes, Gwyther, Elsey, Moore.

West Ham U (0) 1 (*Cross*)
Dynamo Tbilisi (2) 4 (*Chivadze, Gutsaev, Shengelia 2*) 34,957
West Ham U: Parkes; Stewart, Lampard, Bonds, Martin, Devonshire (Allen), Neighbour, Goddard, Cross, Brooking, Pike.
Dynamo Tbilisi: Gabelia; Khisanishvili, Chivadze, Khinchagashvili, Tavadze, Daraselia, Svanadze, Sulakvelidze, Gutsayev, Kipiani, Shengelia.

QUARTER-FINAL, SECOND LEG
18 MARCH
Newport Co (0) 0
Carl Zeiss Jena (1) 1 (*Kurbjuweit*) 18,000
Newport Co: Plumley; Walden, Relish, Davies, Oakes, Tynan, Vaughan, Lowndes, Gwyther, Elsey, Moore.
Carl Zeiss Jena: Grapenthin; Brauer, Schilling, Burow (Krause), Kurbjuweit, Schnuphase, Overman, Sengewald, Beilau, Rabb, Vogel.

Dynamo Tbilisi (0) 0
West Ham U (0) 1 (*Pearson*) 80,000
Dynamo Tbilisi: Gabelia; Chivadze, Khisanishvili, Khinchagashvili, Tavadze, Chilaya (Mudzhir), Svanadze, Sulakvelidze, Gutsayev, Kipiani, Shengelia.
West Ham U: Parkes; Stewart, Lampard, Bonds, Martin, Brush, Neighbour, Goddard (Pearson), Cross, Brooking, Pike.

UEFA CUP 1980–81

FIRST ROUND, FIRST LEG
17 SEPT
FC Porto (0) 1 (*Sousa*)
Dundalk (0) 0 57,000
FC Porto: Fonseca; Gabriel, Fernando, Freitas, Teixeira, Rodolfo, Frasco, Sousa, Niromar, Romeu, Costa.
Dundalk: Blackmore; McConville, Keely, Dunning, Lawlor, Doherty, Flanagan, McKenna, Clarke, Fairclough, Archbold.

Ballymena U (0) 2 (*McQuiston, Sloan*)
Vorwaerts Frankfurt (1) 1 (*Geyer*) 3000
Ballymena U: White; Beattie, Worthington, Fox, McCullough, McCall, Neill, Sloan, McQuiston, Malone, Bush.
Vorwaerts Frankfurt: Weinhild; Probst, Haust, Geyer, Schutch, Jarmuskiewicz, Handrich (Krautzig), Theuerkorn, Otto, Conrad, Piepsch.

Elfsborg (1) 1 (*Nilsson*)
St Mirren (1) 2 (*Somner, Abercromby*) 3776
Elfsborg: Svensson R.; Maalberg, Johansson L., Svensson T., Qvist, Andersen, Ahlstroem, Johansson T., Klarstroem, Gistafsson, Nilsson.
St Mirren: Thomson; Young, McCormach, Copland, Beckett, Richardson, Stark, Abercromby, McDougall, Somner, Weir.

Ipswich T (3) 5 (*Wark 4* [3 pens], *Mariner*)
Aris Salonika (0) 1 (*Pallas* pen) 20,842
Ipswich T: Cooper; Burley, Mills, Thijssen, Osman, Butcher, Wark, Muhren (Beattie), Mariner, Brazil (O'Callaghan), Gates.
Aris Salonika: Pantziaras; Mokalis, Pallas, Veenos, Firos, Kouis, Kindros, Balis, Tsirimokos (Drambis), Semertzidis, Zelidi.

Manchester U (1) 1 (*McIlroy*)
Widzew Lodz (1) 1 (*Surlit*) 38,037
Manchester U: Bailey; Nicholl (Duxbury), Albiston, McIlroy, Jovanovich, Buchan, Grimes, Greenhoff, Coppell, Macari, Thomas.
Widzew Lodz: Mlynarczyk; Plich, Grebosz, Mozejko, Zmuda, Tloninski, Pieta, Surlit, Boniek, Rozborski, Smolarek.

PSV Eindhoven (1) 3 (*Brandts, Van Kraay, Van der Kuylen* pen)
Wolverhampton W (0) 1 (*Gray*) 29,000
PSV Eindhoven: Doesburg; Wildschut, Maybank, Brandts, Stevens, Koster, Huh, Van der Kerkhof R., Van Kraay, Valke, Van der Kuylen (Jannse).
Wolverhampton W: Bradshaw; Palmer, Parkin (Brazier), Thomas, Hughes, Berry, Villazan, Carr, Gray, Richards (Clarke), Eves.

Slask Wroclaw (0) 0
Dundee U (0) 0 10,000
Slask Wroclaw: Kostezewa; Sobiesizk, Kowiczyk, Matys, Garlowski, Faber, Pawlowski, Woglicki, Szarak, Pakala, Nocko.
Dundee U: McAlpine; Stark, Kopel, Kirkwood, Hegarty, Narey, Bannon, Sturrock, Payne, Smith, Dodds.

FIRST ROUND, SECOND LEG
1 OCT
Aris Salonika (2) 3(*Tsirimokos, Drambis, Zeleelidis*)
Ipswich T (0) 1 (*Gates*) 25,000
Aris Salonika: Pantziaris; Mokalis, Chatziantonious, Michalistos, Venos, Kouis, Zeleelidis, Balis, Tsirimokos, Drambis, Semertzidis.
Ipswich T: Cooper; Burley, Mills, Thijssen, Osman, Butcher, Wark, Muhren (Beattie), Mariner, Brazil (McCall), Gates.

Dundee U (2) 7 (*Dodds 2, Pettigrew 2, Stark, Hegarty, Payne* pen)
Slask Wroclaw (1) 2 (*Pawlowski 2*) 8000
Dundee U: McAlpine; Stark, Kopel, Phillip, Hegarty, Narey, Pettigrew, Sturrock, Payne, Holt, Dodds.
Slask Wroclaw: Kostezewa; Sobiesizk, Kowiczyk, Kopyski, Garlowski, Wojaski, Pawlowski, Szarak, Bekala, Nocko, Sybis.

St Mirren (0) 0
Elfsborg (0) 0 8000
St Mirren: Thomson; Young, Beckett, Richardson (Logan), MacCormack, Copland, McDougall, Stark, Somner, Weir, Abercromby.
Elfsborg: Svensson R.; Gustavsson, Johansson L., Ahlstroem, Svensson T., Maalberg, Qvist, Nilsson, Larsson, Hansson (Klarstroem), Johansson T. (Andersen).

Dundalk (0) 0
FC Porto (0) 0 5000
Dundalk: Blackmore; McConville, Keely, Dunning, Lawlor, O'Doherty, McKenna (Duff), Flanagan, Clarke (Byrne), Fairclough, Archbold.
FC Porto: Fonseca; Gabriel, Simoes, Freitas, Pereira, Teixeira, Frasco, Sousa, Duda, Albertino, Costa.

Vorwaerts Frankfurt (2) 3 (*Conrad, Sloan og, Krautzig*)
Ballymena U (0) 0 15,000
Vorwaerts Frankfurt: Weinhild; Probst, Geyer, Ringk, Schutch, Jarmuskiewicz (Enzman), Handrich, Krautzig, Otto (Lindman), Conrad, Gramenz.
Ballymena U: White; Beattie, Worthington, Fox, McQuillan, McCall, Neill, Sloan, McQuiston, Malone, Mullen.

Widzew Lodz (0) 0
Manchester U (0) 0 40,000
Widzew Lodz: Mlynarczyk; Plich, Grebosz, Mozejko, Zmuda, Tloninski, Pieta, Surlit, Boniek, Rozborski, Smolarek.
Manchester U: Bailey; Nicholl, Albiston, McIlroy, Jovanovic, Buchan (Moran), Grimes, Coppell, Jordan, Duxbury, Thomas.

Wolverhampton W (0) 1 (*Eves*)
PSV Eindhoven (0) 0 20,000
Wolverhampton W: Bradshaw; Palmer, Parkin, Daniel, Hughes, Villazan, Hibbitt, Carr, Gray, Richards, Eves.
PSV Eindhoven: Doesburg; Wildschut, Brandts, Stevens, Van der Kerkhof R., Van Kraay, Valke, Poortvliet, Van der Kuylen, Koster, Postuma.

SECOND ROUND, FIRST LEG
22 OCT
Dundee U (0) 1 (*Pettigrew*)
Lokeren (0) 1 (*Mommens*) 7500
Dundee U: McAlpine; Stark, Kopel, Phillip, Hegarty, Narey, Pettigrew, Bannon, Payne, Sturrock, Campbell (Milne).
Lokeren: Hoggenbloom; Larsen, Snalders, Verbruggen, De Schrijver, Dalving, Verheyen, Somars, Lato, Mommens, Gudjohlsen.

Ipswich T (0) 3 (*Wark 2, Beattie*)
Bohemians (Prague) (0) 0 17,163
Ipswich T: Cooper; Burley, McCall, Mills, Osman, Butcher, Wark (Beattie), Muhren, Mariner, Brazil, Gates.
Bohemians: Hruska; Roubicek, Jakubec, Prokes, Ondra, Bicovski, Nemec, Panenka, Cermak, Chaloupka, Koukal.

St Mirren (0) 0
St Etienne (0) 0 11,471
St Mirren: Thomson; Young, Beckett, Richardson, McCormack, Copland, McDougall, Stark, Somner, Weir, Abercromby.
St Etienne: Castenada; Battiston, Janvion, Gardon, Lopez, Oleksian, Paganelli (Zimako), Larios, Roussey, Zanon, Rep.

SECOND ROUND, SECOND LEG
5 NOV
Bohemians (Prague) (1) 2 (*Micinec, Panenka*)
Ipswich T (0) 0 15,000
Bohemians: Postulka; Jakubec, Prokes, Koukal, Ondra, Bicovski, Nemec, Panenka, Chaloupka, Cermak, Micinec.
Ipswich T: Sivell; Burley, Butcher, Mills, Osman, Beattie, Wark, Muhren, Gates, Brazil (Turner), McCall.

Lokeren (0) 0
Dundee U (0) 0 12,000
Lokeren: Hoggenbloom; Larsen, Lato, Verbruggen, De Schrijver, Dalving, Verheyen, Somars, Lubanski, Mommens, Gudjohlsen.
Dundee U: McAlpine; Stark, Kopel, Phillip, Hegarty, Narey, Bannon, Kirkwood, Payne (Holt), Sturrock, Ward (Pettigrew).

St Etienne (1) 2 (*Larios 2*)
St Mirren (0) 0 20,000
St Etienne: Castenada; Battiston, Gardon, Lopez, Janvion, Larios, Elie, Platini, Zimako, Roussey, Rep.
St Mirren: Thomson; Young, Beckett, Copland, Dunlop (Richardson), Weir, Stark, McDougall, Somner, McCormack, Abercromby.

THIRD ROUND, FIRST LEG
26 NOV
Ipswich T (3) 5 (*Wark 3, Brazil, Mariner*)
Widzew Lodz (0) 0 20,445
Ipswich T: Cooper; Mills (Beattie), McCall, Thijssen, Osman, Butcher, Wark, Muhren, Mariner, Brazil (O'Callaghan), Gates.
Widzew Lodz: Mlynarczyk; Plich, Grebosz, Mozejko, Zmuda, Tlokinski, Pieta (Romke), Jezewski, Boniek, Rozborski, Smolarek.

THIRD ROUND, SECOND LEG
10 DEC
Widzew Lodz (0) 1 (*Pieta*)
Ipswich T (0) 0 9000
Widzew Lodz: Klepczynski; Plich, Grebosz, Mozejko, Romke, Tloninski, Pieta (Lisiak), Surlit, Jezewski, Rozborski, Smolarek.
Ipswich T: Cooper; Burley, McCall, Thijssen, Osman, Butcher, Wark, Muhren (Beattie), Mariner (O'Callaghan), Brazil, Gates.

QUARTER-FINAL, FIRST LEG
4 MARCH
St Etienne (1) 1 (*Rep*)
Ipswich T (1) 4 (*Mariner 2, Muhren, Wark*) 40,000
St Etienne: Castaneda; Battiston, Zanon, Gardon, Lopez, Janvion, Rep, Larios, Roussey (Zimako), Platini, Paganelli.
Ipswich T: Cooper; Mills, Butcher, Thijssen, Osman, Beattie, Wark, Muhren, Mariner, Brazil, Gates.

QUARTER-FINAL, SECOND LEG
18 MARCH
Ipswich T (0) 3 (*Butcher, Wark* pen, *Mariner*)
St Etienne (0) 1 (*Zimako*) 30,151
Ipswich T: Cooper; Steggles, McCall, Thijssen, Osman, Butcher, Wark, Muhren, Mariner, Brazil (O'Callaghan), Gates (D'Avray).
St Etienne: Castenada; Battiston, Zanon, Gardon, Lopez, Janvion, Zimako, Larios, Roussey, Platini, Rep.

SEMI-FINAL, FIRST LEG
8 APRIL
Ipswich T (1) 1 (*Wark*)
Cologne (0) 0 24,780
Ipswich T: Cooper; Mills, McCall (Beattie), Thijssen, Osman, Butcher, Wark, Muhren, Mariner, Brazil (O'Callaghan), Gates.
Cologne: Schumacher; Prestin, Konopka, Strack (Kroth), Gerber, Cullmann, Littbarski, Botteron, Muller (Willmer), Engels, Woodcock.

SEMI-FINAL, SECOND LEG
22 APRIL
Cologne (0) 0
Ipswich T (0) 1 (*Butcher*) 55,000
Cologne: Schumacher; Prestin, Konopka, Zimmermann (Kroth), Bonhof, Cullmann, Littbarski, Botteron, Muller, Engels, Woodcock.
Ipswich T: Cooper; Steggles, McCall, Thijssen, Osman, Butcher, Wark, Muhren, Mariner, Brazil, Mills.

FINAL, FIRST LEG
6 MAY
Ipswich T (1) 3 (*Wark* pen, *Thijssen, Mariner*)
AZ 67 Alkmaar (0) 0 27,532
Ipswich T: Cooper; Mills, McCall, Thijssen, Osman, Butcher, Wark, Muhren, Mariner, Brazil, Gates.
AZ 67 Alkmaar: Treytel; Van der Meer, Spelbos, Metgod, Hovenkamp, Peters, Jonker, Arntz, Nygaard (Welzl), Kist, Tol.

FINAL, SECOND LEG
20 MAY
AZ 67 Alkmaar (3) 4 (*Welzl, Metgod, Tol, Jonker*)
Ipswich T (2) 2 (*Thijssen, Wark*) 28,500
AZ 67 Alkmaar: Treytel; Reynders, Spelbos, Metgod, Hovenkamp, Peters, Welzl (Kist), Arntz, Jonker, Nygaard, Tol.
Ipswich T: Cooper; Mills, McCall, Thijssen, Osman, Butcher, Wark, Muhren, Mariner, Brazil, Gates.

SUPER CUP 1980

25 NOV
Nottingham F (0) 2 (*Bowyer 2*)
Valencia (0) 1 (*Felman*) 12,463
Nottingham F: Shilton; Anderson, Gray F., McGovern, Lloyd, Burns, Mills, Bowyer, Ward (Ponte), Wallace, Robertson.
Valencia: Pereira; Carrete, Cervero, Arias, Botubot, Castellanos, Saura, Solsona, Morena, Subirats, Felman (Gimenez).

17 DEC
Valencia (0) 1 (*Morena*)
Nottingham F (0) 0 40,000
Valencia: Sempere; Cervero, Botubot, Arias, Tendillo, Castellanos, Saura, Solsona, Morena, Subirats, Kempes.
Nottingham F: Shilton; Anderson, Gunn, McGovern, Lloyd, Burns, O'Neill, Ponte, Francis, Wallace, Walsh.

PREVIOUS MATCHES

1972 Ajax beat Rangers 3-1, 3-2
1973 Ajax beat AC Milan 0-1, 6-0
1974 Not contested
1975 Dynamo Kiev beat Bayern Munich 1-0, 2-0
1976 Anderlecht beat Bayern Munich 4-1, 1-2
1977 Liverpool beat Hamburg 1-1, 6-0
1978 Anderlecht beat Liverpool 3-1, 1-2
1979 Nottingham F beat Barcelona 1-0, 1-1

EUROPEAN FOOTBALLER OF THE YEAR 1980

If there needed to be any further reminder of the dearth of individual talent in Europe, then the overwhelmingly emphatic success of Karl-Heinz Rummenigge in becoming European Footballer of the Year provided it. He received 122 votes out of a possible 125 and was almost four times ahead of his nearest rival, fellow-countryman Bernd Schuster who finished second with 34 points.

Rummenigge, who was runner-up in 1979 to Kevin Keegan, is reported to be the highest-paid footballer in West Germany with an annual income of around £125,000, rather appropriate for a former bank clerk. The European award was one of half a dozen the Bayern Munich player picked up at home and abroad to underline the scarcity of first-class players.

Though Rummenigge picked up only one vote in 1978, he has since improved noticeably in the eyes of the panel. But if his rise has been dramatic, Keegan's demise has been just as sudden. After being a European super-star for two years, the Southampton and former Hamburg and Liverpool forward did not receive one vote in 1980. However, the West German Bundesliga has provided the last five winners, including Keegan in his stint with Hamburg.

Rummenigge, top scorer in the Bundesliga in 1979–80 with 26 goals and 29 in 1980–81, as well as being a regular choice for his country with 40 appearances up to the Copa de Oro competition in Uruguay in December 1980, has skill, speed and finishing ability – apparently qualities which are rare these days.

POINTS AWARDED

122 Karl-Heinz Rummenigge (Bayern Munich).
34 Bernd Schuster (Barcelona).
33 Michel Platini (St Etienne).
27 Wilfried Van Moer (Beveren).
20 Jan Ceulemans (FC Bruges).
18 Horst Hrubesch (Hamburg).
16 Herbert Prohaska (Inter-Milan).
11 Liam Brady (Juventus), Hansi Muller (Stuttgart).
10 Manfred Kaltz (Hamburg).
9 Erwin Van Den Bergh (Lierse), Luis Arconada (Real Sociedad), Dino Zoff (Juventus).
5 Kenny Dalglish (Liverpool).
4 Terry McDermott (Liverpool), Viv Anderson (Nottingham Forest), Rudi Krol (Napoli), Francesco Graziani (Torino).
3 Ladislav Vizek (Dukla Prague), Bruno Pezzey (Eintracht Frankfurt), Manuel Bento (Benfica).
2 Frank Arnesen (Ajax), Antonin Panenka (Bohemians Prague), David O'Leary (Arsenal), Vladimir Petrovic (Red Star Belgrade), Zbigniew Boniek (Widzew Lodz).
1 Giancarlo Antognoni (Fiorentina), Alessandro Altobelli (Inter-Milan), Marcel Raducanu (Steaua Bucharest), Trevor Francis (Nottingham Forest), Zdenek Nehoda (Dukla Prague), Peter Shilton (Nottingham Forest).

PAST WINNERS

1956 Stanley Matthews (Blackpool); 1957 Alfredo di Stefano (Real Madrid); 1958 Raymond Kopa (Real Madrid); 1959 Alfredo di Stefano (Real Madrid); 1960 Luis Suarez (Barcelona); 1961 Omar Sivori (Juventus); 1962 Josef Masopust (Dukla Prague); 1963 Lev Yashin (Dynamo Moscow); 1964 Denis Law (Manchester U); 1965 Eusebio (Benfica); 1966 Bobby Charlton (Manchester U); 1967 Florian Albert (Ferencvaros); 1968 George Best (Manchester U); 1969 Gianni Rivera (Milan); 1970 Gerd Muller (Bayern Munich); 1971 Johan Cruyff (Ajax); 1972 Franz Beckenbauer (Bayern Munich); 1973 Johan Cruyff (Barcelona); 1974 Johan Cruyff (Barcelona); 1975 Oleg Blokhin (Dynamo Kiev); 1976 Franz Beckenbauer (Bayern Munich); 1977 Allan Simonsen (B Moenchengladbach); 1978 Kevin Keegan (Hamburg); 1979 Kevin Keegan (Hamburg).

BRITISH AND IRISH CLUBS IN EUROPE

1955–56		
EUROPEAN CUP	**Hibernian** (Semi-Final)	
1955–58		
EUROPEAN INTER-CITIES FAIRS CUP	**London** beat Basle, Frankfurt and Lausanne before losing to Barcelona 2-2, 2-6 in the Final. **Birmingham C** knocked out Inter and Zagreb before losing to Barcelona 4-3, 0-1 and 1-2 at Basle.	
1956–57		
EUROPEAN CUP	**Manchester U** (Semi-Final)	**Rangers** (First Round Proper)
1957–58		
EUROPEAN CUP	**Manchester U** (Semi-Final) **Rangers** (First Round Proper)	**Glenavon** (Preliminary Round) **Shamrock R** (Preliminary Round)
1958–60		
FAIRS CUP	**Birmingham C** (Runners-Up)	**Chelsea** (Second Round)
1958–59		
EUROPEAN CUP	**Wolverhampton W** (First Round) **Ards** (Preliminary Round)	**Drumcondra** (Preliminary Round) **Hearts** (Preliminary Round)
	Manchester U were invited to compete, but were withdrawn by the Football League.	
1959–60		
EUROPEAN CUP	**Rangers** (Semi-Final) **Wolverhampton W** (Quarter-Final)	**Linfield** (Preliminary Round) **Shamrock R** (Preliminary Round)
1960–61		
EUROPEAN CUP	**Burnley** (Quarter-Final) **Hearts** (Preliminary Round)	**Limerick** (Preliminary Round) **Glenavon** – Withdrew
EUROPEAN CUP-WINNERS' CUP	**Rangers** (Runners-Up)	**Wolverhampton W** (Semi-Final)
FAIRS CUP	**Birmingham C** (Runners-Up)	**Hibernian** (Semi-Final)
1961–62		
EUROPEAN CUP	**Tottenham H** (Semi-Final) **Rangers** (Quarter-Final)	**Drumcondra** (Preliminary Round) **Linfield** (Preliminary Round)
EUROPEAN CUP-WINNERS' CUP	**Dunfermline Ath** (Quarter-Final) **Leicester C** (Second Round)	**Swansea T** (First Round) **Glenavon** (First Round) **St Patrick's Ath** (Preliminary Round)
FAIRS CUP	**Sheffield W** (Quarter-Final) **Hearts** (Second Round)	**Nottingham F** (First Round) **Birmingham C** (Second Round) **Hibernian** (Second Round)
1962–63		
EUROPEAN CUP	**Dundee** (Semi-Final) **Ipswich T** (First Round)	**Shelbourne** (Preliminary Round) **Linfield** (Preliminary Round)
EUROPEAN CUP-WINNERS' CUP	**Tottenham H**(Winners) **Rangers** (Second Round)	**Shamrock R** (Second Round) **Bangor C** (First Round) **Portadown** (First Round)
FAIRS CUP	**Hibernian** (Quarter-Final) **Dunfermline Ath** (Second Round) **Glentoran** (First Round)	**Everton** (First Round) **Celtic** (First Round) **Drumcondra** (Second Round)
1963–64		
EUROPEAN CUP	**Rangers** (Preliminary Round) **Everton** (Preliminary Round)	**Dundalk** (Preliminary Round) **Distillery** (Preliminary Round)
EUROPEAN CUP-WINNERS' CUP	**Celtic** (Semi-Final) **Manchester U** (Quarter-Final) **Linfield** (Second Round)	**Borough U** (Second Round) **Tottenham H** (Second Round) **Shelbourne** (First Round)
FAIRS CUP	**Partick T** (Second Round) **Arsenal** (Second Round) **Sheffield W** (Second Round)	**Hearts** (First Round) **Glentoran** (First Round) **Shamrock R** (First Round)

1964–65		
EUROPEAN CUP	**Liverpool** (Semi-Final) **Rangers** (Quarter-Final)	**Shamrock R** (Preliminary Round) **Glentoran** (Preliminary Round)
EUROPEAN CUP-WINNERS' CUP	**West Ham U** (Winners) **Cardiff C** (Quarter-Final) **Dundee** (Second Round)	**Cork Celtic** (First Round) **Derry C** (First Round)
FAIRS CUP	**Manchester U** (Semi-Final) **Dunfermline Ath** (Third Round) **Everton** (Third Round)	**Celtic** (Second Round) **Shelbourne** (Second Round) **Kilmarnock** (Second Round)
1965–66		
EUROPEAN CUP	**Manchester U** (Semi-Final) **Derry C** (First Round)	**Kilmarnock** (First Round) **Drumcondra** (Preliminary Round)
EUROPEAN CUP-WINNERS' CUP	**Liverpool** (Runners-Up) **Celtic** (Semi-Final) **West Ham U** (Semi-Final)	**Limerick** (First Round) **Cardiff C** (First Round) **Coleraine** (First Round)
FAIRS CUP	**Leeds U** (Semi-Final) **Chelsea** (Semi-Final) **Dunfermline Ath** (Quarter-Final) **Hearts** (Third Round)	**Everton** (Second Round) **Glentoran** (First Round) **Hibernian** (First Round) **Shamrock R** (Second Round)
1966–67		
EUROPEAN CUP	**Celtic** (Winners) **Linfield** (Quarter-Final)	**Liverpool** (First Round) **Waterford** (Preliminary Round)
EUROPEAN CUP-WINNERS' CUP	**Rangers** (Runners-Up) **Everton** (Second Round) **Shamrock R** (Second Round)	**Glentoran** (First Round) **Swansea T** (First Round)
FAIRS CUP	**Leeds U** (Runners-Up) **Kilmarnock** (Semi-Final) **Burnley** (Quarter-Final) **Dundee U** (Third Round)	**WBA** (Third Round) **Dunfermline Ath** (Second Round) **Drumcondra** (First Round)
1967–68		
EUROPEAN CUP	**Manchester U** (Winners) **Dundalk** (First Round)	**Celtic** (First Round) **Glentoran** (First Round)
EUROPEAN CUP-WINNERS' CUP	**Cardiff C** (Semi-Final) **Aberdeen** (Second Round) **Tottenham H** (Second Round)	**Crusaders** (First Round) **Shamrock R** (First Round)
FAIRS CUP	**Leeds U** (Winners) **Dundee** (Semi-Final) **Rangers** (Quarter-Final) **Hibernian** (Third Round)	**Liverpool** (Third Round) **Nottingham F** (Second Round) **Linfield** (First Round) **St Patrick's Ath** (First Round)
1968–69		
EUROPEAN CUP	**Manchester U** (Semi-Final) **Celtic** (Quarter-Final) **Manchester C** (First Round)	**Glentoran** (First Round) **Waterford** (First Round)
EUROPEAN CUP-WINNERS' CUP	**Dunfermline Ath** (Semi-Final) **WBA** (Quarter-Final) **Crusaders** (First Round)	**Cardiff C** (First Round) **Shamrock R** (First Round)
FAIRS CUP	**Newcastle U** (Winners) **Rangers** (Semi-Final) **Leeds U** (Quarter-Final) **Hibernian** (Third Round) **Aberdeen** (Second Round)	**Chelsea** (Second Round) **Dundalk** (Second Round) **Liverpool** (First Round) **Linfield** (First Round) **Morton** (First Round)
1969–70		
EUROPEAN CUP	**Celtic** (Runners-Up) **Leeds U** (Semi-Final)	**Waterford** (First Round) **Linfield** (First Round)
EUROPEAN CUP-WINNERS' CUP	**Manchester C** (Winners) **Rangers** (Second Round) **Cardiff C** (Second Round)	**Ards** (First Round) **Shamrock R** (First Round)
EUROPEAN FAIRS CUP	**Arsenal** (Winners) **Newcastle U** (Quarter-Final) **Dunfermline Ath** (Third Round) **Southampton** (Third Round) **Liverpool** (Second Round)	**Kilmarnock** (Third Round) **Dundee U** (First Round) **Coleraine** (Second Round) **Dundalk** (First Round) **Glentoran** (First Round)

1970–71 **EUROPEAN CUP**	**Celtic** (Quarter-Final) **Everton** (Quarter-Final)	**Waterford** (Second Round) **Glentoran** (First Round)
EUROPEAN CUP-WINNERS' CUP	**Chelsea** (Winners) **Manchester C** (Semi-Final) **Cardiff C** (Quarter-Final)	**Linfield** (First Round) **Aberdeen** (First Round) **Bohemians** (Preliminary Round)
EUROPEAN FAIRS CUP	**Leeds U** (Winners) **Arsenal** (Quarter-Final) **Liverpool** (Semi-Final) **Newcastle U** (Second Round) **Coleraine** (Second Round)	**Dundee U** (Second Round) **Coventry C** (Second Round) **Cork Hibs** (First Round) **Rangers** (First Round) **Kilmarnock** (First Round) **Hibernian** (Third Round)
1971–72 **EUROPEAN CUP**	**Arsenal** (Quarter-Final) **Celtic** (Semi-Final)	**Linfield** (First Round) **Cork Hibs** (First Round)
EUROPEAN CUP-WINNERS' CUP	**Liverpool** (Second Round) **Chelsea** (Second Round) **Cardiff C** (First Round)	**Rangers** (Winners) **Distillery** (First Round) **Limerick** (First Round)
UEFA CUP	**Tottenham H** (Winners) **Wolverhampton W** (Runners-Up) **Leeds U** (First Round) **Southampton** (First Round) **Shelbourne** (First Round) **Glentoran** (First Round)	**Dundee** (Third Round) **Aberdeen** (Second Round) **St Johnstone** (Third Round)
1972–73 **EUROPEAN CUP**	**Derby Co** (Semi-Final) **Celtic** (Second Round)	**Waterford** (First Round)
EUROPEAN CUP-WINNERS' CUP	**Leeds U** (Runners-Up) **Hibernian** (Quarter-Final)	**Wrexham** (Second Round) **Cork Hibs** (Second Round)
UEFA CUP	**Liverpool** (Winners) **Tottenham H** (Semi-Final) **Stoke C** (First Round) **Manchester C** (First Round)	**Aberdeen** (First Round) **Partick T** (First Round) **Bohemians** (First Round)
1973–74 **EUROPEAN CUP**	**Liverpool** (Second Round) **Celtic** (Semi-Final)	**Waterford** (First Round) **Crusaders** (First Round)
EUROPEAN CUP-WINNERS' CUP	**Sunderland** (Second Round) **Rangers** (Second Round) **Cardiff C** (First Round)	**Glentoran** (Quarter-Final) **Cork Hibs** (First Round)
UEFA CUP	**Tottenham H** (Runners-Up) **Ipswich T** (Quarter-Final) **Leeds U** (Third Round) **Wolverhampton W** (Second Round)	**Aberdeen**(Second Round) **Hibernian** (Second Round) **Finn Harps** (First Round) **Ards** (First Round)
1974–75 **EUROPEAN CUP**	**Leeds U** (Runners-Up) **Celtic** (First Round)	**Coleraine** (First Round) **Cork Celtic** (Second Round)
EUROPEAN CUP-WINNERS' CUP	**Liverpool** (Second Round) **Ards** (First Round) **Cardiff C** (First Round)	**Finn Harps** (First Round) **Dundee U** (Second Round)
UEFA CUP	**Derby Co** (Third Round) **Ipswich T** (First Round) **Stoke C** (First Round) **Wolverhampton W** (First Round)	**Bohemians** (First Round) **Dundee** (First Round) **Portadown** (Second Round) **Hibernian** (Second Round)
1975–76 **EUROPEAN CUP**	**Derby Co** (Second Round) **Linfield** (First Round)	**Rangers** (Second Round) **Bohemians** (First Round)
EUROPEAN CUP-WINNERS' CUP	**West Ham U** (Runners-Up) **Celtic** (Quarter-Final) **Home Farm** (First Round)	**Wrexham** (Quarter-Final) **Coleraine** (First Round)
UEFA CUP	**Liverpool** (Winners) **Aston Villa** (First Round) **Glentoran** (First Round) **Athlone T** (Second Round)	**Ipswich T** (Second Round) **Everton** (First Round) **Hibernian** (First Round) **Dundee U** (Second Round)

1976–77		
EUROPEAN CUP	**Liverpool** (Winners) **Crusaders** (First Round)	**Dundalk** (First Round) **Rangers** (First Round)
EUROPEAN CUP-WINNERS' CUP	**Southampton** (Quarter-Final) **Cardiff C** (First Round) **Hearts** (Second Round)	**Bohemians** (Second Round) **Carrick R** (Second Round)
UEFA CUP	**Manchester C** (First Round) **Derby Co** (Second Round) **Manchester U** (Second Round) **QPR** (Quarter-Final)	**Hibernian** (Second Round) **Glentoran** (First Round) **Celtic** (First Round) **Finn Harps** (First Round)
1977–78		
EUROPEAN CUP	**Liverpool** (Winners) **Sligo Rovers** (First Round)	**Celtic** (Second Round) **Glentoran** (Second Round)
EUROPEAN CUP-WINNERS' CUP	**Rangers** (First Round) **Dundalk** (First Round) **Coleraine** (First Round)	**Cardiff C** (First Round) **Manchester U** (Second Round)
UEFA CUP	**Aston Villa** (Quarter-Final) **Manchester C** (First Round) **Bohemians** (First Round) **Glenavon** (First Round)	**Ipswich T** (Third Round) **Newcastle U** (Second Round) **Dundee U** (First Round) **Aberdeen** (First Round)
1978–79		
EUROPEAN CUP	**Nottingham F** (Winners) **Liverpool** (First Round) **Linfield** (First Round)	**Rangers** (Quarter-Final) **Bohemians** (Second Round)
EUROPEAN CUP-WINNERS' CUP	**Ipswich T** (Quarter-Final) **Ballymena U** (First Round) **Wrexham** (First Round)	**Aberdeen** (Second Round) **Shamrock R** (Second Round)
UEFA CUP	**Manchester C** (Quarter-Final) **Arsenal** (Third Round) **Dundee U** (First Round) **Finn Harps** (First Round)	**WBA** (Quarter-Final) **Everton** (Second Round) **Hibernian** (Second Round) **Glentoran** (First Round)
1979–80		
EUROPEAN CUP	**Nottingham F** (Winners) **Liverpool** (First Round) **Celtic** (Quarter-Final)	**Dundalk** (Second Round) **Linfield** (Preliminary Round)
EUROPEAN CUP-WINNERS' CUP	**Arsenal** (Runners-Up) **Rangers** (Second Round) **Wrexham** (First Round)	**Waterford** (First Round) **Cliftonville** (First Round)
UEFA CUP	**Leeds U** (Second Round) **Ipswich T** (Second Round) **Dundee U** (Second Round) **Aberdeen** (First Round)	**Glenavon** (First Round) **Bohemians** (First Round) **WBA** (First Round) **Everton** (First Round)
1980–81		
EUROPEAN CUP	**Liverpool** (Winners) **Nottingham F** (First Round) **Aberdeen** (Second Round)	**Linfield** (First Round) **Limerick** (First Round)
EUROPEAN CUP-WINNERS' CUP	**West Ham U** (Quarter-Final) **Celtic** (First Round) **Newport Co** (Quarter-Final)	**Crusaders** (First Round) **Waterford** (Second Round)
UEFA CUP	**Ipswich T** (Winners) **Manchester U** (First Round) **Wolverhampton W** (First Round) **Dundee U** (Second Round)	**St Mirren** (Second Round) **Ballymena U** (First Round) **Dundalk** (First Round)

Summary of Appearances

EUROPEAN CUP (1955–81)

English clubs
8 Liverpool
5 Manchester U
2 Derby Co, Wolverhampton W, Everton, Leeds U, Nottingham F
1 Burnley, Tottenham H, Ipswich T, Manchester C, Arsenal

Scottish clubs
11 Celtic
9 Rangers
2 Hearts
1 Dundee, Kilmarnock, Hibernian, Aberdeen

Clubs from Northern Ireland
10 Linfield
5 Glentoran
2 Crusaders
1 Glenavon, Ards, Distillery, Derry C, Coleraine

Clubs from Eire
6 Waterford
4 Dundalk
3 Drumcondra, Shamrock R
2 Bohemians, Limerick
1 Shelbourne, Cork Hibs, Cork Celtic, Sligo Rovers

Winners: Celtic 1966–67; Manchester U 1967–68; Liverpool 1976–77, 1977–78, 1980–81; Nottingham F 1978–79, 1979–80

Finalists: Celtic 1969–70; Leeds U 1974–75

EUROPEAN CUP-WINNERS' CUP (1960–81)

English Clubs
4 West Ham U
3 Tottenham H, Liverpool
2 Chelsea, Manchester C, Manchester U
1 Wolverhampton W, Leicester C, Everton, WBA, Leeds U, Sunderland, Southampton, Ipswich T, Arsenal

Scottish clubs
8 Rangers
4 Celtic
3 Aberdeen
2 Dumfermline Ath
1 Dundee, Dundee U, Hibernian, Hearts

Welsh clubs
11 Cardiff C
4 Wrexham
2 Swansea T
1 Bangor C, Borough U, Newport Co

Clubs from Northern Ireland
3 Coleraine, Crusaders
2 Glentoran, Ards, Linfield
1 Glenavon, Derry C, Distillery, Portadown, Carrick Rangers, Ballymena U, Cliftonville

Clubs from Eire
6 Shamrock R
2 Limerick, Cork Hibs, Bohemians, Waterford
1 Shelbourne, Cork Celtic, St Patrick's Ath, Finn Harps, Home Farm, Dundalk

Winners: Tottenham H 1962–63; West Ham U 1964–65; Manchester C 1969–70; Chelsea 1970–71; Rangers 1971–72

Finalists: Liverpool 1965–66; Rangers 1960–61, 1966–67; Leeds U 1972–73; West Ham U 1975–76; Arsenal 1979–80

EUROPEAN FAIRS CUP & UEFA CUP (1955–81)

English clubs
8 Leeds U
6 Liverpool, Everton, Ipswich T
4 Arsenal, Manchester C, Birmingham C, Newcastle U, Wolverhampton W
3 Chelsea, Tottenham H, WBA, Manchester U
2 Sheffield W, Nottingham F, Southampton, Stoke C, Derby Co, Aston Villa
1 Burnley, Coventry C, London Rep XI, QPR

Scottish clubs
12 Hibernian
7 Dundee U
5 Dunfermline Ath, Aberdeen
4 Kilmarnock
3 Hearts, Rangers, Dundee, Celtic
2 Partick T
1 Morton, St Johnstone, St Mirren

Clubs from Northern Ireland
8 Glentoran
2 Linfield, Coleraine, Glenavon
1 Ards, Portadown, Ballymena U

Clubs from Eire
4 Bohemians
3 Finn Harps, Dundalk
2 Shelbourne, Shamrock R, Drumcondra
1 St Patrick's Ath, Cork Hibs, Athlone T

Winners: Leeds U 1967–68, 1970–71; Newcastle U 1968–69; Arsenal 1969–70; Tottenham H 1971–72; Liverpool 1972–73, 1975–76; Ipswich T 1980–81

Finalists: Birmingham C 1958–60, 1960-61; Leeds U 1966–67; Wolverhampton W 1971–72; Tottenham H 1973–74

RECORDS

Major British Records

No Scottish Premier Division records at present after only six seasons

HIGHEST SCORES

First-Class Match		Arbroath (*Scottish Cup 1st Round*)	36	Bon Accord	0	5.9.1885
International Match		England	13	Ireland	0	18.2.1882
FA Cup		Preston NE (*1st Round*)	26	Hyde U	0	15.10.1887
FOOTBALL LEAGUE						
Division 1	(*Home*)	WBA	12	Darwen	0	4.3.1892
		Nottingham F	12	Leicester Fosse	0	21.4.1909
	(*Away*)	Newcastle U	1	Sunderland	9	5.12.1908
		Cardiff C	1	Wolverhampton W	9	3.9.1955
Division 2	(*Home*)	Newcastle U	13	Newport Co	0	5.10.1946
	(*Away*)	Burslem PV	0	Sheffield U	10	10.12.1892
Division 3	(*Home*)	Tranmere R	9	Accrington S	0	18.4.1959
		Brentford	9	Wrexham	0	15.10.1963
	(*Away*)	Halifax T	0	Fulham	8	16.9.1969
		Brighton	2	Bristol R	8	1.12.1973
Division 3(S)	(*Home*)	Luton T	12	Bristol R	0	13.4.1936
	(*Away*)	Northampton T	0	Walsall	8	2.2.1947
Division 3(N)	(*Home*)	Stockport Co	13	Halifax T	0	6.1.1934
	(*Away*)	Accrington S	0	Barnsley	9	3.2.1934
Division 4	(*Home*)	Oldham Ath	11	Southport	0	26.12.1962
	(*Away*)	Crewe Alex	1	Rotherham U	8	8.9.1973
SCOTTISH LEAGUE						
Division 1	(*Home*)	Celtic	11	Dundee	0	26.10.1895
	(*Away*)	Airdrieonians	1	Hibernian	11	24.10.1959
Division 2	(*Home*)	East Fife	13	Edinburgh C	2	11.12.1937
	(*Away*)	Alloa Ath	0	Dundee	10	8.3.1947

MOST GOALS FOR IN A SEASON

FOOTBALL LEAGUE		*Goals*	*Games*	*Season*
Division 1	Aston V	128	42	1930–31
Division 2	Middlesbrough	122	42	1926–27
Division 3(S)	Millwall	127	42	1927–28
Division 3(N)	Bradford C	128	42	1928–29
Division 3	QPR	111	46	1961–62
Division 4	Peterborough U	134	46	1960–61
SCOTTISH LEAGUE				
Division 1	Hearts	132	34	1957–58
Division 2	Raith R	142	34	1937–38

FEWEST GOALS FOR IN A SEASON

FOOTBALL LEAGUE	(minimum 42 games)	*Goals*	*Games*	*Season*
Division 1	Leicester C	26	42	1977–78
Division 2	Watford	24	42	1971–72
Division 3(S)	Crystal Palace	33	42	1950–51
Division 3(N)	Crewe Alex	32	42	1923–24
Division 3	Stockport Co	27	46	1969–70
Division 4	Bradford	30	46	1967–68
	Workington	30	46	1975–76
	Gillingham	30	46	1963–64
SCOTTISH LEAGUE (minimum 30 games)				
Division 1	Stirling Alb	18	39	1980–81
Division 2	Lochgelly U	20	38	1923–24

MOST GOALS AGAINST IN A SEASON

FOOTBALL LEAGUE		Goals	Games	Season
Division 1	Blackpool	125	42	1930-31
Division 2	Darwen	141	34	1898–99
Division 3(S)	Merthyr T	135	42	1929–30
Division 3(N)	Nelson	136	42	1927–28
Division 3	Accrington S	123	46	1959–60
Division 4	Hartlepools U	109	46	1959–60
SCOTTISH LEAGUE				
Division 1	Leith Ath	137	38	1931–32
Division 2	Edinburgh C	146	38	1931–32

FEWEST GOALS AGAINST IN A SEASON

FOOTBALL LEAGUE	(minimum 42 games)	Goals	Games	Season
Division 1	Liverpool	16	42	1978–79
Division 2	Manchester U	23	42	1924–25
Division 3(S)	Southampton	21	42	1921–22
Division 3(N)	Port Vale	21	46	1953–54
Division 3	Rotherham U	32	46	1980–81
Division 4	Lincoln C	25	46	1980–81
SCOTTISH LEAGUE (minimum 30 games)				
Division 1	Celtic	14	38	1913–14
Division 2	Morton	20	38	1966–67

MOST POINTS IN A SEASON

FOOTBALL LEAGUE		Points	Games	Season
Division 1	Liverpool	68	42	1978–79
Division 2	Tottenham H	70	42	1919–20
Division 3	Aston Villa	70	46	1971–72
Division 3(S)	Nottingham F	70	46	1950–51
	Bristol C	70	46	1954–55
Division 3(N)	Doncaster R	72	42	1946–47
Division 4	Lincoln C	74	46	1975–76
SCOTTISH LEAGUE				
Division 1	Rangers	76	42	1920–21
Division 2	Morton	69	38	1966–67

FEWEST POINTS IN A SEASON

FOOTBALL LEAGUE	(minimum 34 games)	Points	Games	Season
Division 1	Leeds U	18	42	1946–47
	QPR	18	42	1968–69
	Glossop	18	34	1899–1900
	Notts Co	18	34	1904–05
	Woolwich Arsenal	18	38	1912–13
Division 2	Doncaster R	8	34	1904–05
	Loughborough T	8	34	1899–1900
Division 3	Rochdale	21	46	1973–74
Division 3(S)	Merthyr T	21	42	1924–25 & 1929–30
	QPR	21	42	1925–26
Division 3(N)	Rochdale	11	40	1931–32
Division 4	Bradford	20	46	1968–69
SCOTTISH LEAGUE (minimum 30 games)				
Division 1	Stirling A	6	30	1954–55

MOST WINS IN A SEASON

FOOTBALL LEAGUE		Wins	Games	Season
Division 1	Tottenham H	31	42	1960–61
Division 2	Tottenham H	32	42	1919–20
Division 3(S)	Millwall	30	42	1927–28
	Plymouth Arg	30	42	1929–30
	Cardiff C	30	42	1946–47
	Nottingham F	30	46	1950–51
	Bristol C	30	46	1954–55
Division 3(N)	Doncaster R	33	42	1946–47
Division 3	Aston Villa	32	46	1971–72
Division 4	Lincoln C	32	46	1975–76
SCOTTISH LEAGUE				
Division 1	Rangers	35	42	1920–21
Division 2	Morton	33	38	1966–67

RECORD HOME WINS IN A SEASON

Brentford won all 21 games in Division 3(S), 1929–30

RECORD AWAY WINS IN A SEASON

Doncaster R won 18 of 21 games in Division 3(N), 1946–47

FEWEST WINS IN A SEASON

FOOTBALL LEAGUE		Wins	Games	Season
Division 1	Stoke	3	22	1889–90
	Woolwich Arsenal	3	38	1912–13
Division 2	Loughborough T	1	34	1899–1900
Division 3(S)	Merthyr T	6	42	1929–30
Division 3(N)	Rochdale	4	40	1931–32
Division 3	Rochdale	2	46	1973–74
Division 4	Bradford	4	46	1967–68
SCOTTISH LEAGUE				
Division 1	Vale of Leven	0	22	1891–92
Division 2	East Stirlingshire	1	22	1905–06
	Forfar Ath	1	38	1974–75

MOST DEFEATS IN A SEASON

FOOTBALL LEAGUE		Defeats	Games	Season
Division 1	Leeds U	30	42	1946–47
	Blackburn R	30	42	1965–66
Division 2	Tranmere R	31	42	1938–39
Division 3	Newport Co	31	46	1961–62
Division 3(S)	Merthyr T	29	42	1924–25
Division 3(N)	Rochdale	33	40	1931–32
Division 4	Workington	32	46	1975–76
SCOTTISH LEAGUE				
Division 1	St Mirren	31	42	1920–21
Division 2	Lochgelly U	30	38	1923–24
	Brechin C	30	36	1962–63
	Forfar Ath	30	38	1974–75

FEWEST DEFEATS IN A SEASON

FOOTBALL LEAGUE		Defeats	Games	Season
Division 1	Preston NE	0	22	1888–89
	Leeds U	2	42	1968–69
Division 2	Liverpool	0	28	1893–94
	Burnley	2	30	1897–98
	Bristol C	2	38	1905–06
	Leeds U	3	42	1963–64
Division 3	QPR	5	46	1966–67
Division 3(S)	Southampton	4	42	1921–22
	Plymouth Arg	4	42	1929–30
Division 3(N)	Port Vale	3	46	1953–54
	Doncaster R	3	42	1946–47
	Wolverhampton W	3	42	1923–24
Division 4	Lincoln C	4	46	1975–76

SCOTTISH LEAGUE				
Division 1	Celtic	0	18	1897–98
	Rangers	0	18	1898–99
	Rangers	1	42	1920–21
	Hearts	1	34	1957–58
	Celtic	1	34	1967–68
	Rangers	1	34	1967–68
Division 2	Kilmarnock	0	18	1898–99
	Clyde	1	36	1956–57
	Morton	1	36	1963–64

MOST DRAWN GAMES IN A SEASON

FOOTBALL LEAGUE		*Draws*	*Games*	*Season*
Division 1	Norwich C	23	42	1978–79
SCOTTISH LEAGUE				
Division 1	Falkirk	17	42	1921–22
Division 1	Falkirk	17	38	1922–23
Division 2	Bo'ness	17	38	1922–23

MOST GOALS IN A GAME

FOOTBALL LEAGUE		
Division 1	Ted Drake (Arsenal) 7 goals v Aston Villa	14.12.1935
Division 2	Tommy Briggs (Blackburn R) 7 goals v Bristol R	5.2.1955
	Neville Coleman (Stoke C) 7 goals v Lincoln C	23.2.1957
Division 3(S)	Joe Payne (Luton T) 10 goals v Bristol R	13.4.1936
Division 3(N)	Robert Bell (Tranmere R) 9 goals v Oldham Ath	26.12.1935
Division 3	Steve Earle (Fulham) 5 goals v Halifax T	16.9.1969
	Barrie Thomas (Scunthorpe U) 5 goals v Luton T	24.4.1965
	Keith East (Swindon T) 5 goals v Mansfield T	20.11.1965
	Alf Wood (Shrewsbury T) 5 goals v Blackburn R	2.10.1971
Division 4	Herbert Lister (Oldham Ath) 6 goals v Southport	26.12.1962
SCOTTISH LEAGUE		
Division 1	Jimmy McGrory (Celtic) 8 goals v Dunfermline Ath	14.9.1928
Division 2	Owen McNally (Arthurlie) 8 goals v Armadale	1.10.1927
	Jim Dyet (King's Park) 8 goals v Forfar Ath	2.1.1930
	John Calder (Morton) 8 goals v Raith R	18.4.1936
FA CUP	Ted MacDougall (Bournemouth) 9 goals v Margate (*1st Round*)	20.11.1971
SCOTTISH CUP	John Petrie (Arbroath) 13 goals v Bon Accord (*1st Round*)	5.9.1885

MOST LEAGUE GOALS IN A SEASON

FOOTBALL LEAGUE		*Goals*	*Games*	*Season*
Division 1	Dixie Dean (Everton)	60	39	1927–28
Division 2	George Camsell (Middlesbrough)	59	37	1926–27
Division 3(S)	Joe Payne (Luton T)	55	39	1936–37
Division 3(N)	Ted Harston (Mansfield T)	55	41	1936–37
Division 3	Derek Reeves (Southampton)	39	46	1959–60
Division 4	Terry Bly (Peterborough U)	52	46	1960–61
SCOTTISH LEAGUE				
Division 1	William McFadyen (Motherwell)	52	34	1931–32
Division 2	Jim Smith (Ayr)	66	38	1927–28

MOST LEAGUE GOALS IN A CAREER

FOOTBALL LEAGUE		*Goals*	*Games*	*Season*
Arthur Rowley	WBA	4	24	1946–48
	Fulham	27	56	1948–50
	Leicester C	251	303	1950–58
	Shrewsbury T	152	236	1958–65
		434	619	
SCOTTISH LEAGUE				
Jimmy McGrory	Celtic	1	3	1922–23
	Clydebank	13	30	1923–24
	Celtic	396	375	1924–38
		410	408	

MOST GOALS IN AN INTERNATIONAL

England	Malcolm Macdonald (Newcastle U) 5 goals v Cyprus, at Wembley	16.4.1975
	Willie Hall (Tottenham H) 5 goals v Ireland, at Old Trafford	16.11.1938
	G. O. Smith (Corinthians) 5 goals v Ireland, at Sunderland	18.2.1899
	Steve Bloomer (Derby Co) 5 goals* v Wales, at Cardiff	16.3.1896
Scotland	Charles Heggie (Rangers) 5 goals v Ireland, at Belfast	20.3.1886
Ireland	Joe Bambrick (Linfield) 6 goals v Wales, at Belfast	1.2.1930
Wales	James Price (Wrexham) 4 goals v Ireland, at Wrexham	25.2.1882
	Mel Charles (Cardiff C) 4 goals v Ireland, at Cardiff	11.4.1962
	Ian Edwards (Chester) 4 goals v Malta, at Wrexham	25.10.78

* There are conflicting reports which make it uncertain whether Bloomer scored four or five goals in this game.

MOST GOALS IN AN INTERNATIONAL CAREER

		Goals	*Games*
England	Bobby Charlton (Manchester U)	49	106
Scotland	Denis Law (Huddersfield T, Manchester C, Torino, Manchester U)	30	55
Ireland	Billy Gillespie (Sheffield U)	13	25
Wales	Trevor Ford (Swansea T, Aston Villa, Sunderland, Cardiff C)	23	38

MOST CUP WINNERS' MEDALS

FA CUP – 5 medals each

James Forrest (Blackburn R) 1884, 1885, 1886, 1890, 1891
Hon. A. F. Kinnaird (Wanderers) 1873, 1877, 1878, (Old Etonians) 1879, 1882.
C. H. R. Wollaston (Wanderers) 1872, 1873, 1876, 1877, 1878.

SCOTTISH CUP – 7 medals each

Jimmy McMenemy (Celtic) 1904, 1907, 1908, 1911, 1912, 1914, (Partick T) 1921.
Bob McPhail (Airdieonians) 1924, (Rangers) 1928, 1930, 1932, 1934, 1935, 1936.
Billy McNeill (Celtic) 1965, 1967, 1969, 1971, 1972, 1974, 1975.

RECORD ATTENDANCES

Football League	83,260	Manchester U v Arsenal, Maine Road	17.1.1948
Scottish League	118,567	Rangers v Celtic, Ibrox Stadium	2.1.1939
FA Cup Final	126,047*	Bolton W v West Ham U, Wembley	28.4.1923
European Cup	135,826	Celtic v Leeds U, semi-final at Hampden Park	15.4.1970

* It has been estimated that as many as 70,000 more broke in without paying.

OTHER RECORDS

The oldest player to appear in the Football League was Neil McBain who played in goal for New Brighton v Hartlepools U, Division 3(N), 15 March, 1947. He was then aged 52 years 4 months.

The oldest player to appear for any of the home countries in a full international was Billy Meredith, who was nearly 46 years of age when he played for Wales v England, 15 March, 1920.

The record for most appearances in the Football League during one season by a player over 40 years of age was created by Bob McGrory. In his last season as a player with Stoke C (1934–35) he appeared in all 42 First Division games. Bob was then 43 years of age.

The record for most consecutive appearances in the Football League was created by Harold Bell, Tranmere R centre-half. From the opening game of season 1946–47 Bell did not miss a single game until August 1955 – a run of 401 consecutive Division 3(N) matches. Including FA Cup, Liverpool Senior Cup and Cheshire Bowl games, Bell enjoyed a run of 459 consecutive first team appearances.

John Trollope created a club record by making 770 League appearances for Swindon T between 1960 and 1980. In the Scottish League the record for most appearances for a single club was created by Bob Ferrier with 626 for Motherwell between 1918 and 1937.

Billy Wright (Wolverhampton W) set up a world record by playing in 70 consecutive internationals for England, from 1951 to 1959.

Since substitutes were introduced into League football in 1965, Bristol C is the club that has played through the longest spell without calling upon one of these players – a run of 52 League games, 4 FA Cup, and 2 League Cup ties from February 1966 to April 1967.

The shortest player to appear in the Football League is outside-right Fred le May, who was only 5ft tall. He played for Thames 1930–31, Watford 1931–32, and Clapton Orient 1932–33. The tallest was Albert Iremonger, Notts Co and Lincoln C goalkeeper 1904–27. He was 6ft 5in tall.

The longest FA Cup tie was the 4th qualifying round match between Alvechurch and Oxford C in 1971. It needed 11 hours (six games) before Alvechurch won 1-0.

The longest single game on record is that between Stockport Co and Doncaster R, 30 March, 1946. In an effort to reach a decisive result, this Third Division (N) Cup tie continued for 203 minutes before bad light forced an abandonment.

Rochdale suffered 14 consecutive home defeats in Division 3(N) in 1931–32. This is a Football League record. After beating New Brighton 3-2 on 7 November, 1931, they did not get another home point until holding Barrow to a goalless draw in their second home game of season 1932–33. During that same period Rochdale suffered one run of 17 consecutive defeats (home and away) – also a Football League record.

In season 1904–05 Manchester U won 14 consecutive Division 2 games. This Football League record was equalled by Bristol C and Preston NE in Division 2 in 1905–06 and 1950–51 respectively.

The Scottish League record for the longest run of consecutive victories was created by Morton in Division 2 in 1963–64 when they won 23 games in a row.

Nottingham F were undefeated in a run of 42 First Division games, November 1977 to December 1978. This is a Football League record.

The longest run without defeat in a single season of Football League games is one of 30 matches by Burnley in Division 1 in 1920–21.

In the Scottish League, Celtic created a record by remaining undefeated in a run of 62 games – November 1915 to April 1917.

Blackburn Rovers hold the record for the longest run of consecutive FA Cup ties without defeat. From December 1883 to December 1886 they were unbeaten in 24 Cup ties and won the trophy three times during this period.

Only two players have scored two goals for each side in a Football League game. Sam Wynne did so in a Division 2 game, 6 October, 1923, scoring twice for Oldham Ath as well as putting two through his own goal for Manchester U. Chris Nicholl (Aston Villa) scored all the goals in a 2-2 draw with Leicester C, Division 1, 20 March, 1976.

Jimmy Cookson reached a first century of Football League goals in the shortest time. He made his début for Chesterfield in 1925 and reached his century in December 1927 with West Bromwich A his 87th Football League game.

The record number of goals scored by a player making his Football League début is five – by George Hilsdon for Chelsea v Glossop, Division 2, 1 September, 1906.

The record for scoring the fastest goal in a Football League game is claimed by Jim Fryatt. According to referee Mr R. J. Simon this player scored for Bradford v Tranmere R only 4 seconds after the kick-off, 25 April, 1964. Fastest own goal was in 6 seconds by Pat Kruse (Torquay U) for Cambridge U, 3 January, 1977.

The fastest goals scored in the FA Cup Final at Wembley were obtained in the first minute. In 1928 John Roscamp put Blackburn R ahead when he charged both the Huddersfield goalkeeper and the ball into the net, and in 1955 Jackie Milburn headed Newcastle U into a first-minute lead over Manchester C.

John McIntyre scored four goals in 5 minutes for Blackburn R v Everton, Division 1, 16 September, 1922.

W. G. Richardson also scored four goals in 5 minutes for WBA, Division 1, 7 November, 1931, but this was even more remarkable because the feat was achieved in an away game – against West Ham U.

The record number of penalties missed by one side in a Football League Division 1 game is three: by Fletcher (2) and Thornley for Manchester C against Newcastle U, 27 January, 1912.

The most penalties scored by a player in a First Division game is three – Billy Walker for Aston Villa v Bradford C, 12 November, 1921; Charlie Mitten for Manchester U v Aston Villa, 8 March, 1950; and Ken Barnes for Manchester C v Everton, 7 December, 1957.

The record number of players from the same club in an England team is seven: Frank Moss, George Male, Eddie Hapgood, Wilf Copping, Raymond Bowden, Ted Drake and Clifford Bastin, all of Arsenal, played against Italy at Highbury, 14 November, 1934.

The England team twice included all Corinthian players in the 1890s but this cannot be considered a record because the Corinthians were a combined eleven, most of their players also appearing with other clubs.

The England team that won the 1966 World Cup created a record for the country by remaining unchanged in six consecutive games – the quarter-final, semi-final and final of the World Cup and their next three games.

England's longest run without defeat is one of 20 games between 1889 and 1896.

The biggest Championship-winning margin for any division of the Football League is 15 points; by Middlesbrough in Division 2 in 1973–74.

The smallest number of players called upon by a club to complete a season of Football League games is 14. Liverpool did so when winning the Championship in 1965–66, and Aston Villa equalled it in 1980–81 when they too won the Championship.

In the Scottish League, Dundee called upon only 15 players throughout season 1961–62, when they won the Championship.

The goalscoring record for a goalkeeper in a single season of Football League games is five (all from penalties) in 1923–24 by Arnold Birch of Chesterfield in Division 3(N).

Five men have both played in and managed Football League Championship winning teams: Ted Drake, Arsenal, centre-forward, 1933–34, 1934–35, 1937–38, Chelsea, manager, 1954–55. Bill Nicholson, Tottenham H, right half-back, 1950–51, manager, 1960–61. Alf Ramsey, right-back, Tottenham H, 1950–51, Ipswich T, manager, 1961–62. Joe Mercer, left-half, Everton 1938–39, Arsenal, 1947–48, 1952–53, Manchester C, manager, 1967–68. Dave Mackay, left-half, Tottenham H, 1960–61, Derby Co, manager, 1974–75. Bob Paisley, Liverpool, left half-back, 1946–47, manager, 1975–76, 1976–77, 1978–79, 1979–80.

In 1973–74 Leeds U created a Football League record for the longest run without defeat from the start of a season – 29 First Division games before losing 2-3 at Stoke. It could be said that this only equalled Liverpool's run in the Second Division in 1893–94 when they were unbeaten in all 28 games. Their 29th game that season was the extra 'Test Match' to decide promotion and relegation between the First and Second Divisions.

The youngest player to appear in the Football League is Albert Geldard who was aged 15 years 156 days when making his début for Bradford against Millwall, Division 2, 16 September, 1929.

The youngest player in an FA Cup Final is Paul Allen, who was aged 17 years 256 days when West Ham U beat Arsenal 1-0, 10 May, 1980.

The highest number of players ordered off in the Football League in a single day is eight, 5 October, 1974. This figure also represents the record for the FA Cup competition. Eight players were ordered off in 1st round matches, 9 January, 1915.

LEAGUE CUP ATTENDANCES

The attendances for the 1980–81 Football League Cup were:

Round 1	299,613	Semi-finals	83,456
Round 2	753,141		83,262
Round 3	298,431	Final	100,000
Round 4	238,996	Final Replay	36,693
Round 5	159,743	TOTAL	2,053,335

International Records

HIGHEST SCORES

World Cup Match	West Germany	12	Cyprus	0	1969
Olympic Games	Denmark	17	France	1	1908
	Germany	16	USSR	0	1912
International Match	Germany	13	Finland	0	1940
	Spain	13	Bulgaria	0	1933
European Cup	Feyenoord	12	Reykjavik	2	1969
European Cup-Winners' Cup	Sporting Lisbon	16	Apoel Nicosia	1	1963
Fairs & UEFA Cups	IFC Cologne	13	Union Luxembourg	0	1965

GOALSCORING RECORDS

World Cup Final	Geoff Hurst (England) 3 goals v West Germany	1966
World Cup Final tournament	Just Fontaine (France) 13 goals	1958
Major European Cup game	Lothar Emmerich (Borussia Dortmund) v Floriana in Cup-Winners' Cup – 6 goals	1965
Career	Arthur Friedenreich (Brazil) 1329 goals	1910–30
	Pelé (Brazil) 1281 goals	*1956–78
	Franz 'Bimbo' Binder (Austria, Germany) 1006 goals	1930–50

** Pelé has since scored two goals in Testimonial matches.*

MISCELLANEOUS

Brazil set up a record for undefeated matches in the World Cup in the 1958 and 1962 finals, playing 13, winning 11, and drawing two. Their run ended when they lost 3-1 to Hungary in the 1966 World Cup.

Hungary went 13 years undefeated at home. After losing 7-2 to Sweden in 1943 they were unbeaten at home until they lost 4-2 to Czechoslovakia in 1956. The Hungarians also had a run of 29 games before losing: from their 5-3 defeat against Austria in May 1950 until they lost the World Cup final 3-2 to West Germany in July 1954.

Real Madrid were undefeated in League matches at home from February 1957, when they lost 3-2 to Atlético Madrid, until beaten again by Atlético 1-0 in March 1965. Between these defeats they won 114 matches and drew eight.

Ferenc Deak was one of the most prolific goalscorers in League football in the years immediately after the war. In 1945–46 he scored 66 goals for Szentlorinci AC in Hungary, 48 in 1946–47, and 59 in 1948–49 when with Ferencvaros.

Players who have won international caps for three different countries are Ladislav Kubala, capped for Hungary, Czechoslovakia, and Spain, and Alfredo Di Stefano for Argentina, Colombia, and Spain.

The Nordahl brothers, Knut, Bertil, and Gunnar, won Olympic gold medals with Sweden in 1948.

In 1955–56 Fiorentina went 33 Italian League matches without defeat.

In what is thought to be the longest match on record, Santos (Brazil) and Penarol (Uruguay) played 3½ hours from 2 August to 3 August after kicking off at 9.30 p.m. The match ended 3-3 after interruptions during play.

The first international played in Europe, other than between British teams, was Austria 5 Hungary 0 on 12 October, 1902. The first match in South America was a 1-1 draw between Argentina and Uruguay in 1905.

The first transfer fee approaching £1 million was £922,300 for Johan Cruyff from Ajax (Holland) to Barcelona (Spain) in 1973.

Firsts in Football

Football League

The first five Football League games were played on 8 September, 1888. Bolton Wanderers were three goals up in about six minutes against Derby Co, but were eventually beaten 6-3. Cox of Aston Villa scored the first 'own goal', giving Wolverhampton W an early lead, but Villa recovered to draw 1-1.

Huddersfield T became the first team to complete a hat-trick of League Championships – 1924–25–26.

FA Cup

Tottenham H were the first Southern club to win the Cup when they beat Sheffield U in 1901. Spurs were then members of the Southern League and so were the first and only non-League club to carry off the trophy.

King George V was the first reigning monarch to attend a Cup Final. He saw Burnley beat Liverpool at the Crystal Palace in 1914.

David Jack (Bolton W) scored the first goal in a Wembley Cup Final. This was in 1923 when the crowd broke in to see the Wanderers beat West Ham U 2-0.

Extra time was first played in the Cup Final in 1877. Wanderers and Oxford University were drawing 1-1 at full-time; Wanderers won 2-1.

Internationals and representative games

The first representative game was played at Battersea Park, 31 March, 1866, London beating Sheffield by two goals and four touch-downs to nil.

The first official England v Scotland international was played at the West of Scotland Cricket Ground, Partick, 30 November, 1872, and resulted in a goalless draw.

Wales played their first international in 1876, losing 4-0 to Scotland in Glasgow.

Ireland's first international was against England at Bloomfield, Belfast, in 1882 when the visitors won 13-0.

Caps were first awarded for appearances in internationals in 1886.

The Football League played their first representative game in April 1891. It was against the Football Alliance at Sheffield and resulted in a 1-1 draw.

England's first defeat on foreign soil in a full international was 3-4 by Spain in Madrid in 1929.

England's first home defeat by a continental country was at Wembley in 1953 when Hungary won 6-3.

Scotland's first home defeat by a foreign team was at Hampden Park in 1950 when Austria won 1-0.

Billy Wright became the first international in Britain to gain 100 caps when he captained England against Scotland at Wembley in April 1959.

Terry Venables was the first player to win international honours for England at five levels – Schoolboy, Youth, Amateur, Under-23 and Full International. He gained his first full cap in October 1964.

Floodlit football

The first-ever game by floodlight was between two Sheffield Association teams at Bramall Lane, 14 October, 1878.

The first FA Cup tie under floodlights was a replay between Kidderminster Harriers and Brierley Hill Alliance, 14 September, 1955.

Floodlights were first switched on during an international match in England in November 1955 at Wembley – England v Spain.

The first Football League game under floodlights was Portsmouth v Newcastle U at Fratton Park, 22 February, 1956.

The first full international played entirely under floodlights in Britain took place at Wembley in 1963 when England beat N Ireland 8-3.

Hat-tricks

The first hat-trick in an FA Cup Final was scored by William Townley for Blackburn R v Sheffield Wednesday in 1890.

Equipment, etc.

Shinguards were first introduced and registered by Sam Widdowson of Nottingham F in 1874. The cross-bar first replaced the tape in 1875, and the whistle was used by the referee for the first time in 1878. Goalnets were invented and patented by J. A. Brodie of Liverpool in 1890 and were first used in the FA Cup Final in 1892.

Substitutes

First substitute in a Football League game was Keith Peacock of Charlton Ath, at Bolton, 21 August, 1965.

The first instance of a substitute in a Home International Championship game was at Wrexham in 1889 when Pugh of Rhostyllen took over from the injured S. G. Gillam in the Welsh goal against Scotland.

England's first substitute in a full international was Jimmy Mullen (Wolverhampton W) who took over from the injured Jackie Milburn after 10 minutes of the game against Belgium in Brussels, 18 May, 1950.

The first substitute to score in a Football League game was Bobby Knox (Barrow) v Wrexham, Division 4, 21 August, 1965.

Transfers

The first four, five, six and seven-figure transfer fees between British clubs were as follows:

£1000 – Alf Common, Sunderland to Middlesbrough, 1905.
£10,890 – David Jack, Bolton W to Arsenal, 1928.
£110,000 – Alan Ball, Blackpool to Everton, 1966.
£1,000,000 – Trevor Francis, Birmingham C to Nottingham F, 1979.

Radio and TV

The first match broadcast in England was the First Division game between Arsenal and Sheffield U at Highbury, 22 January, 1927.

The first Football League game to be televised was Blackpool v Bolton W, 10 September, 1960.

The first FA Cup tie to be televised – other than the final – was Charlton Ath v Blackburn R, 5th round, 8 February, 1947.

Corner kick

Billy Smith was the first player to score direct from a corner kick in a Football League game – Huddersfield T v Arsenal, 11 October, 1924.

Limited Company

The first football club to form itself into a limited liability company was Birmingham C in 1888. At that time they were known as Small Heath.

Penalty kick

The first player to score from a penalty kick in a Football League match was Heath of Wolverhampton W v Accrington, Division 1, 14 September, 1891.

Professional

The identity of the first professional footballer may never be definitely established, but it was probably J. J. Lang, a Scot who joined Sheffield Wednesday in 1876 after playing for Clydesdale and Glasgow Eastern.

Tour

Oxford University were the first to send a football team on an overseas tour when in 1875 they visited Germany.

Sunday football

The first Football League game to be played on a Sunday was between Millwall and Fulham on the morning of 20 January, 1974. Eleven other Football League games were played later the same day.

ANGLO-SCOTTISH CUP 1980–81

QUALIFYING COMPETITION

Group A	P	W	D	L	F	A	*Pts
Chesterfield	3	1	2	0	5	4	5
Grimsby T	3	1	1	1	4	4	4
Hull C	3	1	1	1	3	3	3
Sheffield U	3	1	0	2	2	3	2

Group B	P	W	D	L	F	A	Pts
Notts Co	3	1	2	0	4	3	4
Bristol C	3	1	1	1	3	2	3
Orient	3	1	1	1	4	4	3
Fulham	3	1	0	2	2	4	2

Group C	P	W	D	L	F	A	*Pts
Bury	3	2	0	1	5	6	5
Burnley	3	1	1	1	5	4	4
Shrewsbury T	3	1	1	1	5	5	4
Oldham Ath	3	1	0	2	7	7	3

Group D	P	W	D	L	F	A	*Pts
Blackpool	3	3	0	0	5	1	6
Blackburn R	3	2	0	1	5	3	5
Preston NE	3	0	1	2	0	2	1
Carlisle U	3	0	1	2	2	6	1

* Includes bonus point for scoring three or more goals in a match.

QUARTER-FINALS, FIRST LEG

9 SEPT

Airdrieonians (1) 2 (*Gordon, Thomson*)
Bury (1) 4 (*Mullen, Madden, Johnson 2* [1 pen]) 2500
Airdrieonians: Martin; Erwin, Rodger, Walker, March, Anderson, McKeown, Clark (Thomson), Russell (McCulloch), Gordon, McGuire.
Bury: Southall; Phillips, Kennedy, Madden, Bradley, Howard (Waddington), Mullen, Butler, Johnson, Waldron, Tully.

Blackpool (0) 2 (*MacDougall, Harrison*)
Kilmarnock (0) 1 (*Cramond*) 4904
Blackpool: Rush; Gardner, Williams, Doyle, McEwan, Sbragia, Morris, Hockaday (Collins), MacDougall, Deary (Seward), Harrison.
Kilmarnock: Brown; Morrison, Robertson, Mauchlen, Armstrong, McDicken, Gibson, Maxwell, McBride, Cramond, Hughes.

16 SEPT

Notts Co (1) 2 (*Christie, Hunt*)
Morton (0) 0 3558
Notts Co: Avramovic; Benjamin, O'Brien, Kelly, Kilcline, Richards, McCulloch, Masson, Christie, Hunt, Hooks.
Morton: Baines; Hayes, Holmes, Rooney, McLaughlin, Orr, McNeill, Cochrane, Thompson, Hutchinson, McLaren.

13 OCT

Rangers (1) 1 (*Dalziel*)
Chesterfield (1) 1 (*Walker*) 12,000
Rangers: McCloy; Jardine, Miller, Johnstone, Forsyth, Bett, McLean, Dalziel, McAdam, Redford, Johnston.
Chesterfield: Turner; Tartt, Pollard, Wilson, Green, Ridley, Birch, Moss, Bonnyman, Salmons, Walker.

QUARTER-FINALS SECOND LEG

30 SEPT

Morton (1) 1 (*Ritchie* pen)
Notts Co (0) 1 (*O'Brien*) 3500
Morton: Baines; Hayes, Holmes, Rooney, McLaughlin, Orr, McNeil, Cochrane, Thomson, Busby (McLaren), Ritchie (Tolmie).
Notts Co: Avramovic; Benjamin, O'Brien, Harkouk, Kilcline, Richards, McCulloch, Masson (Wood), Christie, Hunt, Hooks.

14 OCT

Bury (1) 1 (*Hilton*)
Airdrieonians (0) 0 2984
Bury: Southall; Phillips, Kennedy, Madden, Whitehead, Trainer, Mullen, Butler, Hilton, Jakub, Farley (Tully).
Airdrieonians: Martin; Walker, Rodger, McCluskey, March, Anderson, McKeown, Clark, McVeigh, Gordon, McGuire.

Kilmarnock (4) 4 (*Cramond 2, Burke, Maxwell*)
Blackpool (1) 2 (*Thompson, Hockaday*) 2700
Kilmarnock: Brown; Robertson, Cockburn, Clarke, Clark, McDicken, Houston, Maxwell, Bourke, Cramond, Gibson.
Blackpool: Rush; Simmonite, Williams, Doyle, Sbragia (Hendrick), Ashurst, Morris (Bamber), McEwan, Thompson, Hockaday, Deary.

28 OCT

Chesterfield (2) 3 (*Bonnyman 2, Moss*)
Rangers (0) 0 13,914
Chesterfield: Turner; Tartt, Pollard, Wilson, Green, Ridley, Birch, Moss, Bonnyman, Salmons, Walker.
Rangers: McCloy; Jardine, Dawson, Forsyth T., Jackson (MacDonald), Bett, McKay, Russell, McAdam, Redford, Johnstone.

SEMI-FINALS FIRST LEG

4 NOV

Kilmarnock (1) 1 (*McBride*)
Notts Co (2) 2 (*Robertson og, Harkouk*) 2900
Kilmarnock: Brown; McLean, Robertson, Clark, Clarke, McDicken, Houston, Mauchlen A., McBride, Mauchlen S. (Bourke), Cramond.
Notts Co: Avramovic; Benjamin, Wood, Kelly, Kilcline, Richards, McCulloch, Masson, Harkouk, Hunt, Hooks (Manns).

2 DEC

Bury (1) 1 (*Butler*)
Chesterfield (2) 2 (*Wilson, Crawford*) 3720
Bury: Southall; Phillips, Kennedy, Gore, Hilton, Howard, Mullen, Butler, Johnson, Jakub, Farley (Goodwin).
Chesterfield: Turner; Stirk, Kowalski, Wilson, Hunter, Tartt, Birch, Moss, Bonnyman, Salmons, Crawford (Windridge).

SEMI-FINALS SECOND LEG

18 NOV

Notts Co (2) 5 (*O'Brien* pen, *Harkouk, Kilcline, Christie, Hooks*)

Kilmarnock (0) 2 (*Street, McBride*) 4314

Notts Co: Avramovic; Benjamin, O'Brien (Manns), Kelly, Kilcline, Richards, Harkouk, Masson, Christie, Hunt, Hooks.
Kilmarnock: Brown; McLean, Robertson (Coburn), Clark, Clarke, McDicken, Street, Mauchlen A., Mauchlen S. (McBride), Maxwell, Cramond.

9 DEC

Chesterfield (1) 1 (*Stirk*)

Bury (0) 1 (*Johnson*) 6400

Chesterfield: Turner; Tartt, Stirk, Wilson, Green, Ridley, Birch, Moss, Bonnyman, Salmons, Crawford (Walwyn).
Bury: Southall; Howard, Kennedy, Cruickshank, Hilton, Whitehead, Mullen (Tully), Butler, Johnson, Jakub, Goodwin (Graham).

FINAL FIRST LEG

24 MAR

Chesterfield (1) 1 (*Moss*)

Notts Co (0) 0 10,190

Chesterfield: Turner; Stirk, O'Neill, Wilson (Tartt), Green, Ridley, Birch, Moss, Kowalski, Salmons, Walker.
Notts Co: Avramovic; Benjamin, O'Brien, Goodwin, Kilcline, Richards, McCulloch, Masson, Christie, Kelly, Hooks.

FINAL SECOND LEG

31 MAR

Notts Co (1) 1 (aet) (*Masson*)

Chesterfield (0) 1 (*Crawford*) 12,951

Notts Co: Avramovic; Benjamin, O'Brien, Goodwin, Kilcline, Richards, McCulloch, Masson, Christie (Harkouk), Hunt, Hooks.
Chesterfield: Gregory; Stirk (Tartt), O'Neill, Ridley, Green, Kowalski, Birch, Moss, Bonnyman (Crawford), Salmons, Walker.

UNIVERSITIES FOOTBALL 1980–81

UAU CHAMPIONSHIP

Quarter-Final

Swansea 1, Sheffield 1
Swansea eliminated on penalties.
Lancaster 1, Exeter 4
York 0, Loughborough 1
Hull 0, Leeds 3

Semi-Final

Sheffield 4, Exeter 2
(*at Bath University*)
Loughborough 2, Leeds 1
(*at Sheffield University*)

Final

(*at Nottingham University*)
Sheffield 1, Loughborough 1

Final Replay

(*at Alfreton FC*)
Sheffield 1, Loughborough 0

BRITISH UNIVERSITIES TOURNAMENT

(*at St Andrews University*)

Northern Ireland 1, Cambridge 0
Scotland 1, UAU II 0
London 2, Oxford 2
UAU I 2, Wales 0
Northern Ireland 1, Scotland 1
UAU II 2, Cambridge 1
Wales 2, Oxford 1
UAU I 1, London 1
Northern Ireland 1, UAU II 1
Scotland 2, Cambridge 1
UAU I 1, Oxford 0
Wales 9, London 0

Final UAU I 2, Scotland 0
3rd Place Match
Wales 2, Northern Ireland 0
5th Place Match
UAU II 3, London 1
7th Place Match
Oxford 2, Cambridge 0

UNIVERSITIES INTERNATIONAL TOURNAMENT

(*at The City University, London*)

West Germany 3, Belgium 1
Ireland 1, Great Britain 0
West Germany 3, Ireland 1
Great Britain 3, Belgium 1
West Germany 2, Great Britain 1
Ireland 1, Belgium 1

Placings 1 West Germany 6 pts
2 Ireland 3 pts
3 Great Britain 2 pts
4 Belgium 1 pt

REPRESENTATIVE FIXTURES

English Universities 1, Welsh Universities 0
UAU 5, British Polytechnics 1
UAU 1, York City 1
UAU 1, Dutch Universities 2

UNIVERSITY MATCH

(*at Wembley, 10 December, 1980*)
Oxford 2, Cambridge 0

YOUTH FOOTBALL 1980–81

FA YOUTH CHALLENGE CUP 1980–81

Preliminary Round

West End BC v York City	2-4
Bury v Preston North End	1-1
Chadderton v Rhyl	2-5
Barnsley v Southport	3-0
Bradford City v Wigan Athletic	2-0
Scunthorpe United v North Ferriby Utd	3-0
Boston v Mansfield Town	2-5
Chesterfield v Sutton Town	6-0
Bedworth United v Oldswinford	1-4
Desborough Town v Syston Juniors	1-4
Alvechurch v Kettering Town	1-3
Banbury United v Tamworth	0-1
Barking v Royston Town	5-0
Cambridge City v Welwyn Garden	6-0
Cambridge United v Tring Town	aet 4-3
Corby Town v Wellingborough Town	3-0
Dagenham v Rolenmil Youth	2-2
Epping Town v The '61'	4-2
Brentford v Walton & Hersham	2-3
Burnham v Windsor & Eton	1-1
Addlestone v Hendon	4-3
Baldock Town v Hounslow	1-2
Aldershot v Southall	10-2
Hillingdon Borough v Willesden	1-1
Sutton United v Molesey	2-2
Banstead Athletic v Maidstone United	2-3
Chatham Town v Welling United	0-0
Bromley v Ringmer	2-1
Dover v Shoreham	2-1
Camberley Town v Wokingham Town	1-2
Fareham Town v Worthing	1-1
Bournemouth v Exeter City	1-3
AFC Bournemouth v Swansea City	0-1

Preliminary Round – Replays

Preston North End v Bury	3-4
Rolenmil Youth v Dagenham	2-3
Windsor & Eton v Burnham	3-2
Willesden v Hillingdon Borough	1-3
Molesey v Sutton United	3-1
Welling United v Chatham Town	8-2
Worthing v Fareham Town	3-5

First Round Qualifying

York City v Tyne BC	12-0
Scarborough v Farsley Celtic	1-2
Bury v Marine	4–0
Formby v Rhyl	3-1
Barnsley v Halifax Town	7-1
Chorley v Bradford City	2-3
Scunthorpe United v Normanby PW	4-1
Louth United v Doncaster Rovers	1-4
Mansfield Town v Huncote Sports	1-0
Grantham v Chesterfield	1-2
Oldswinford w.o.; Mile Oak Rovers withdrew	
Hednesford Town v Syston Juniors	0-8
Kettering Town v Enderby Town	1-2
Coventry Sporting v Tamworth	5-2
Barking v Gorleston	2-1
Colchester United v Cambridge City	3-0
Cambridge United v Northampton Town	3-2
Milton Keynes City v Corby Town	1-3
Dagenham v Letchworth Garden City	4-2
Harefield United v Epping Town	1-1
Walton & Hersham v Harrow Borough	2-1
Enfield v Windsor & Eton	4-1
Addlestone v Hampton	3-0
Chalfont St Peter v Hounslow	1-3
Aldershot v Oxford City	0-2
Maidenhead United v Hillingdon Borough	2-4
Molesey v Ford United	2-1
Feltham v Dartford	2-2
Maidstone United v Leatherhead	5-0
Folkestone v Welling United	0-5
Bromley v Horley Town	2-0
Hastings United v Dover	1-1
Wokingham Town w.o.; Pagham withdrew.	
Gosport Borough v Fareham Town	0-1
Exeter City v Dorchester Town	5-0
Cheltenham Town v Swansea City	1-7

First Round Qualifying – Replays

Epping Town v Harefield United	0-1
Dartford v Feltham	5-2
Dover v Hastings United	5-1

Second Round Qualifying

York City v Farsley Celtic	10-0
Bury v Formby	3-0
Barnsley v Bradford City	2-0
Scunthorpe United v Doncaster Rovers	0-2
Mansfield Town v Chesterfield	2-4
Oldswinford v Syston Juniors	aet 3-1
Enderby Town v Coventry Sporting	aet 4-2
Barking v Colchester United	1-0
Cambridge United v Corby Town	3-1
Dagenham v Harefield United	14-1
Walton & Hersham v Enfield	2-0
Addlestone v Hounslow	4-0
Oxford City v Hillingdon Borough	2-2
Molesey v Dartford	2-5
Maidstone United v Welling United	1-3
Bromley v Dover	0-0
Wokingham Town v Fareham Town	0-1
Exeter City v Swansea City	0-3

Second Round Qualifying – Replays

Hillingdon Borough v Oxford City	0-1
Dover v Bromley	3-0

First Round

Burnley v Hull City	1-1
Huddersfield Town v Blackburn Rovers	0-1
Yorkshire Amateur v Rochdale	1-2
Hartlepool United v York City	2-1
Barnsley v Nunthorpe Athletic	3-0
Oldswinford v Shrewsbury Town	1-3
Port Vale v Oldham Athletic	3-1
Coventry City v Sutton Coldfield Town	5-0
Wolverhampton Wanderers v Bury	1-1
Stoke City v Tranmere Rovers	5-0
Liverpool v Wrexham	0-1
Walsall v Birmingham City	4-6
Grimsby Town v Doncaster Rovers	1-4
Sheffield United v Enderby Town	5-0
Chesterfield v Norwich City	0-1
Notts County v Nuneaton Borough	4-0
Queen's Park Rangers v Addlestone & W T	3-0
Fareham Town v Aylesbury United	1-1
Watford v Croydon	1-0
Welling United v Walton & Hersham	4-0
Oxford City v Wimbledon	2-2
Fulham v Gillingham	3-0
St Albans City v Dover	1-2
Cambridge United v Orient	1-2
Slough Town v West Ham United	0-4
Brighton & Hove Albion v Dagenham	2-2
Southend United v Reading	1-1
Redhill v Oxford United	0-5
Staines Town v Barking	1-1
Wealdstone v Dartford	1-3
Swindon Town v Portsmouth	0-1
Bristol Rovers v Torquay United	8-0
Newport County v Cardiff City	0-4
Swansea City v Plymouth Argyle	3-0

First Round – Replays

Hull City v Burnley	0-1
Bury v Wolverhampton Wanderers	1-2
Aylesbury United v Fareham Town	1-3
Wimbledon v Oxford City	2-0
Dagenham v Brighton & Hove Albion	2-3
Reading v Southend United	1-0
Barking v Staines Town	2-0

Second Round

Burnley v Rochdale	7-0
Doncaster Rovers v Middlesbrough	0-0
Blackpool v Leeds United	0-3
Blackburn Rovers v Newcastle United	0-4
Sunderland v Hartlepool United	4-2
Everton v Nottingham Forest	1-0
Birmingham City v Rotherham United	4-1
Leicester City v Shrewsbury Town	0-1
Bolton Wanderers v Notts County	4-0
Coventry City v Peterborough United	2-2
Stoke City v Wolverhampton Wanderers	2-2
West Bromwich Albion v Wrexham	0-0
Sheffield United v Aston Villa	2-2
Manchester City v Barnsley	2-1
Chester v Port Vale	0-0
Lincoln City v Derby County	2-5
Sheffield Wednesday v Manchester United	1-2
Welling United v Tottenham Hotspur	0-3
Barking v West Ham United	0-5
Orient v Dartford	1-1
Chelsea v Ipswich Town	3-2
Charlton Athletic v Dover	7-0
Luton Town v Queen's Park Rangers	3-4
Fulham v Norwich City	0-1
Arsenal v Wimbledon	6-0
Brighton & Hove Albion v Millwall	1-0
Watford v Crystal Palace	3-0
Southampton v Reading	3-1
Oxford United v Bristol Rovers	0-1
Portsmouth v Bristol City	4-1
Fareham Town v Swansea City	0-2
Hereford United v Cardiff City	0-0

Second Round – Replays

Middlesbrough v Doncaster Rovers	1-0
Peterborough United v Coventry City	3-3
Wolverhampton Wanderers v Stoke City	3-5
Wrexham v West Bromwich Albion	0-0
Aston Villa v Sheffield United	3-2
Port Vale v Chester	2-1
Dartford v Orient	0-2
Cardiff City v Hereford United	2-1

Second Round – Second Replays

Coventry City v Peterborough United (*at Coventry City*)	3-0
West Bromwich Albion v Wrexham (at West Bromwich Albion)	0-2

Third Round

Stoke City v Everton	1-3
Middlesbrough v Manchester City	0-3
Bolton Wanderers v Manchester United	2-4
Newcastle United v Burnley	2-0
Leeds United v Sunderland	1-0
Birmingham City v Norwich City	1-0
Chester v Derby County	2-3
Coventry City v Wrexham	4-1
Shrewsbury Town v Aston Villa	3-1
Brighton & Hove Albion v Orient	0-2
Swansea City v West Ham United	0-3
Portsmouth v Southampton	4-2
Arsenal v Queen's Park Rangers	1-1
Bristol Rovers v Watford	0-3
Cardiff City v Charlton Athletic	0-0
Chelsea v Tottenham Hotspur	1-1

Third Round – Replays

Queen's Park Rangers v Arsenal	2-2
Charlton Athletic v Cardiff City	2-3
Tottenham Hotspur v Chelsea	1-0

Third Round – Second Replay

Arsenal v Queen's Park Rangers (*at Arsenal*)	0-1

Fourth Round

Portsmouth v Tottenham Hotspur	2-4
Birmingham City v Orient	1-1
West Ham United v Cardiff City	6-0
Derby County v Manchester United	1-1
Everton v Watford	3-1
Coventry City v Queen's Park Rangers	2-2
Manchester City v Newcastle United	5-2
Shrewsbury Town v Leeds United	0-3

Fourth Round – Replays

Orient v Birmingham City	0-1
Manchester United v Derby County	2-1
Queen's Park Rangers v Coventry City	5-1

Fifth Round

West Ham United v Queen's Park Rangers	3-1
Leeds United v Tottenham Hotspur	1-3
Manchester City v Birmingham City	2-0
Everton v Manchester United	1-3

Semi-Finals – First Leg

West Ham United v Manchester City	5-0
Tottenham Hotspur v Manchester United	3-0

Semi-Finals – Second Leg

Manchester City v West Ham United	1-2
Manchester United v Tottenham Hotspur	1-0

Final – First Leg

West Ham United v Tottenham Hotspur	2-0

Final – Second Leg

Tottenham Hotspur v West Ham United	1-0

West Ham United won 2-1 on aggregate.

FA COUNTY YOUTH CUP 1980–81

First Round

North Riding v West Riding	4-4
Manchester v Durham	aet 2-4
Lincolnshire v Derbyshire	4-1
Leicestershire & Rutland v Worcestershire	0-1
Nottinghamshire v Northamptonshire	3-2
Herefordshire v Oxfordshire	1-3
Huntingdonshire v Berks & Bucks	2-1
Essex v Middlesex	1-4
Hertfordshire v RAF	5-1
London v Bedfordshire	2-1
Sussex v Hampshire	0-1
Army v Dorset	1-3
Somerset & Avon (S) v Gloucestershire	0-1
Wiltshire v Devon	0-3

First Round Replay

West Riding v North Riding	aet 2-1

Second Round

West Riding v Northumberland (*abandoned in extra time*)	1-0

Lancashire v Cumberland	2-0
Durham v Westmorland	5-0
Sheffield & Hallamshire v Liverpool	2-3
Lincolnshire v East Riding	0-1
Worcestershire v Cheshire	5-1
Nottinghamshire v Shropshire	3-3
Oxfordshire v Staffordshire	2-4
Huntingdonshire v Birmingham	1-0
Middlesex v Norfolk	2-1
Hertfordshire v Suffolk	6-0
London v Cambridgeshire	2-3
Hampshire v Kent	1-0
Dorset v Surrey	3-1
Gloucestershire v Royal Navy	2-0
Devon v Cornwall	1-0

Second Round Replays

West Riding v Northumberland	aet 1-3
Shropshire v Nottinghamshire	0-1

Third Round

Northumberland v East Riding	1-1
Durham v Lancashire	0-2
Liverpool v Worcestershire	0-1
Nottinghamshire v Staffordshire	1-2
Huntingdonshire v Cambridgeshire	4-0
Hertfordshire v Middlesex	1-3
Hampshire v Devon	2-4
Gloucestershire v Dorset	3-1

Third Round Replay

East Riding v Northumberland	3-1

Fourth Round

Staffordshire v East Riding	0-1
Huntingdonshire v Lancashire	aet 0-2
Devon v Worcestershire	0-1
Gloucestershire v Middlesex	aet 1-2

Semi-Finals

East Riding v Middlesex 2-0
(*at Hull City FC*)
Worcestershire v Lancashire 1-2
(*at Evesham United FC*)

Final

Lancashire v East Riding 3-2
(*at Leyland Motors FC*)

ENGLAND YOUTH INTERNATIONAL MATCHES 1980–81

YOUTH TOURNAMENT, YUGOSLAVIA

4 September, 1980, Rovinj
England 3 (*Walters, Kinsey, Webb*)
Switzerland 0
England: Westwood; Bennett, Corbett, Gernon, Cunningham, Webb, Martin, Wynn (Snodin), Walters, Schiavi (Barnes), Gibson (Kinsey).

6 September, 1980, Pazin
England 0
Austria 1 500
England: Naylor; Bennett, Nichols, Martin, Gernon, Webb, Corbett, Snodin, Walters (Gibson), Kinsey (Schiavi), Barnes.

8 September, 1980, Labin
England 6 (*Walters 2, Martin 2* (1 pen), *Kinsey, Barnes*)
Belgium 1 1000
England: Westwood; Bennett, Corbett, Gernon, Cunningham, Webb, Martin, Wynn, Gibson (Kinsey), Barnes, Walters (Schiavi).

FINAL.
11 September, 1980, Pula
England 1 (*Martin*)
Hungary 2 4000
England: Westwood; Bennett, Gernon, Corbett (Nichols), Cunningham, Webb (Gibson), Martin, Wynn (Snodin), Walters, Kinsey, Barnes.

EUROPEAN YOUTH CHAMPIONSHIP

QUALIFYING ROUND FIRST LEG

11 February, 1981, Walsall FC
England 1 (*Walsh*)
Northern Ireland 0 1575
England: Kite; Corbett, Hawker, Brooks, Gibson, Phelan, Allen, Walters, Walsh (Westwood), Barnes (Connor), Handysides.

QUALIFYING ROUND SECOND LEG

11 March, 1981, Crusaders FC
Northern Ireland 0
England 3 (*Connor 2, Handysides* pen)
England: Kite; Bennett, Hawker (Robson), Brooks, Gibson, Phelan, Walters, Connor (Kinsey), Walsh, Finnigan, Handysides.

EUROPEAN YOUTH CHAMPIONSHIP PROPER

25 May, 1981, Siegen
England 1 (*Connor*)
Spain 2 16,000
England: Kite; Gibson, Bennett, Finnigan, Slack, Phelan, Allen, Connor, Walsh (Barnes), Handysides, Walters (Pearson).

27 May, 1981, Aachen
England 0
Scotland 1 23,000
England: Kite; Walker, Slack, Phelan, Bennett, Finnigan, Brooks (Walters), Allen, Handysides, Pearson (Walsh), Connor.

29 May, 1981, Bonn
England 7 (*Connor, Brooks, Allen, Barnes, Walsh 3*)
Austria 0
England: Kite (Westwood); Walker, Bennett, Slack, Phelan, Finnigan (Barnes), Brooks, Allen, Handysides, Walsh, Connor.

ENGLAND YOUTH INTERNATIONAL MATCHES 1947–81

** Professionals. † Abandoned.* UYT *UEFA Youth Tournament.*

v SCOTLAND

				E	S
	1947	25 Oct	Doncaster	4	2
	1948	30 Oct	Aberdeen	1	3
UYT	1949	21 Apr	Utrecht	0	1
	1950	4 Feb	Carlisle	7	1
	1951	3 Feb	Kilmarnock	6	1
	1952	15 Mar	Sunderland	3	1
	1953	7 Feb	Glasgow	4	3
	1954	6 Feb	Middlesbrough	2	1
	1955	5 Mar	Kilmarnock	3	4
	1956	3 Mar	Preston	2	2
	1957	9 Mar	Aberdeen	3	1
	1958	1 Mar	Hull	2	0
	1959	28 Feb	Aberdeen	1	1
	1960	27 Feb	Newcastle	1	1
	1961	25 Feb	Elgin	3	2
	1962	24 Feb	Peterborough	4	2
*UYT	1963	19 Apr	White City	1	0
	1963	18 May	Dumfries	3	1
	1964	22 Feb	Middlesbrough	1	1
	1965	27 Feb	Inverness	1	2
	1966	5 Feb	Hereford	5	3
	1967	4 Feb	Aberdeen	0	1
*UYT	1967	1 Mar	Southampton	1	0
*UYT	1967	15 Mar	Dundee	0	0
	1968	3 Feb	Walsall	0	5
	1969	1 Feb	Stranraer	1	1
	1970	31 Jan	Derby	1	2
	1971	30 Jan	Greenock	1	2
	1972	30 Jan	Bournemouth	2	0
	1973	20 Jan	Kilmarnock	3	2
	1974	26 Jan	Brighton	2	2
*UYT	1981	27 May	Aachen	0	1

v WALES

				E	W
	1948	28 Feb	High Wycombe	4	2
UYT	1948	15 Apr	Shepherds Bush	4	0
	1949	26 Feb	Swansea	0	0
	1950	25 Feb	Worcester	1	0
	1951	17 Feb	Wrexham	1	1
	1952	23 Feb	Plymouth	6	0
	1953	21 Feb	Swansea	4	2
	1954	20 Feb	Derby	2	1
	1955	19 Feb	Milford Haven	7	2
	1956	18 Feb	Shrewsbury	5	1
	1957	9 Feb	Cardiff	7	1
	1958	15 Feb	Reading	8	2
	1959	14 Feb	Portmadoc	3	0
	1960	19 Mar	Canterbury	1	1
	1961	18 Mar	Newtown	4	0
	1962	17 Mar	Swindon	4	0
	1963	16 Mar	Haverfordwest	1	0
	1964	15 Mar	Leeds	2	1
	1965	20 Mar	Newport	2	2
	1966	19 Mar	Northampton	4	1
	1967	18 Mar	Cwmbran	3	3
	1968	16 Mar	Watford	2	3
	1969	15 Mar	Haverfordwest	3	1
*UYT	1970	25 Feb	Newport	0	0
*UYT	1970	18 Mar	Leyton	1	2
	1970	20 Apr	Reading	0	0
	1971	20 Feb	Aberystwyth	1	2
	1972	19 Feb	Swindon	4	0
	1973	24 Feb	Portmadoc	4	1
*UYT	1974	9 Jan	West Bromwich	1	0
	1974	2 Mar	Shrewsbury	2	1
*UYT	1974	13 Mar	Cardiff	0	1
*UYT	1976	11 Feb	Cardiff	1	0
*UYT	1976	3 Mar	Maine Rd	2	3
*UYT	1977	9 Mar	West Bromwich	1	0
*UYT	1977	23 Mar	Cardiff	1	1

v NORTHERN IRELAND

				E	NI
	1948	15 May	Belfast	2	2
UYT	1949	18 Apr	Haarlem	3	3
	1949	14 May	Hull	4	2
	1950	6 May	Belfast	0	1
	1951	5 May	Liverpool	5	2
	1952	19 Apr	Belfast	0	2
	1953	11 Apr	Wolverhampton	0	0
UYT	1954	10 Apr	Bruehl	5	0
	1954	8 May	Newtownards	2	2
	1955	14 May	Watford	3	0
	1956	12 May	Belfast	0	1
	1957	11 May	Leyton	6	2
	1958	10 May	Bangor	2	4
	1959	9 May	Liverpool	5	0
	1960	14 May	Portadown	5	2
	1961	13 May	Manchester	2	0
	1962	12 May	Londonderry	1	2
*UYT	1963	23 Apr	Wembley	4	0
	1963	11 May	Oldham	1	1
	1964	25 Jan	Belfast	3	1
	1965	22 Jan	Birkenhead	2	3
	1966	26 Feb	Belfast	4	0
	1967	25 Feb	Stockport	3	0
	1968	23 Feb	Belfast	0	2
	1969	28 Feb	Birkenhead	0	2
	1970	28 Feb	Lurgan	1	3
	1971	6 Mar	Blackpool	1	1
	1972	11 Mar	Chester	1	1
*UYT	1972	17 May	Sabadell	4	0
	1973	24 Mar	Telford	3	0
	1974	19 Apr	Birkenhead	1	2
*UYT	1975	13 May	Kriens	3	0
*UYT	1980	16 May	Arnstadt	1	0

v AUSTRIA

				E	A
UYT	1949	19 Apr	Zeist	4	2
UYT	1952	17 Apr	Barcelona	5	5
UYT	1957	16 Apr	Barcelona	0	3
	1958	4 Mar	Highbury	3	2
	1958	1 June	Graz	4	3
UYT	1960	20 Apr	Vienna	0	1
*UYT	1964	1 Apr	Rotterdam	2	1
	1980	6 Sept	Pazin	0	1
*UYT	1981	29 May	Bonn	7	0

v BELGIUM

				E	B
UYT	1948	16 Apr	West Ham	3	1
UYT	1951	22 Mar	Cannes	1	1
UYT	1953	31 Mar	Brussels	2	0
†	1956	7 Nov	Brussels	3	2
	1957	13 Nov	Sheffield	2	0
*UYT	1965	15 Apr	Ludwigshafen	3	0
*UYT	1969	11 Mar	West Ham	1	0

*UYT1969	26 Mar	Waregem	2	0
UYT1972	13 May	Palma	0	0
UYT1973	4 June	Viareggio	0	0
*UYT1977	19 May	Lokeren	1	0
1979	17 Jan	Brussels	4	0
1980	8 Sept	Labia	6	1

v BULGARIA

			E	B
UYT1956	28 Mar	Salgotarjan	1	2
UYT1960	16 Apr	Graz	0	1
UYT1962	24 Apr	Ploesti	0	0
*UYT1968	7 Apr	Nimes	0	0
*UYT1979	31 May	Vienna	0	1

v CZECHOSLOVAKIA

			E	C
UYT1955	7 Apr	Lucca	0	1
*UYT1966	21 May	Rijeka	2	3
*UYT1969	20 May	Leipzig	3	1
*UYT1979	24 May	Bischofshofen	3	0
1979	8 Sept	Pula	1	2

v DENMARK

			E	D
*1955	1 Oct	Plymouth	9	2
1956	20 May	Esbjerg	2	1
*UYT1979	31 Oct	Esbjerg	3	1
*UYT1980	26 Mar	Coventry	4	0

v FINLAND

			E	F
*UYT1975	19 May	Berne	1	1

v FRANCE

			E	F
1957	24 Mar	Fontainebleau	1	0
1958	22 Mar	Eastbourne	0	1
*UYT1966	23 May	Rijeka	1	2
*UYT1967	11 May	Istanbul	2	0
*1968	25 Jan	Paris	0	1
*UYT1978	8 Feb	Selhurst Park	3	1
*UYT1978	1 Mar	Paris	0	0
*UYT1979	2 June	Vienna	0	0

v EAST GERMANY

			E	EG
UYT1958	7 Apr	Neunkirchen	1	0
1959	8 Mar	Zwickau	3	4
1960	2 Apr	Portsmouth	1	1
*UYT1965	25 Apr	Essen	2	3
*UYT1969	22 May	Magdeburg	0	4
*UYT1973	10 June	Florence	3	2

v WEST GERMANY

			E	WG
UYT1953	4 Apr	Boom	3	1
UYT1954	15 Apr	Gelsenkirchen	2	2
UYT1956	1 Apr	Sztalinvaros	2	1
1957	31 Mar	Oberhausen	4	1
1958	12 Mar	Bolton	1	2
1961	12 Mar	Flensberg	0	2
*1962	31 Mar	Northampton	1	0
*1967	14 Feb	Moenchengladbach	1	0
UYT1972	22 May	Barcelona	2	0
1975	25 Jan	Las Palmas	4	2
1976	14 Nov	Monte Carlo	1	1
*UYT1979	28 May	Salzburg	2	0
1979	1 Sept	Pula	1	1

v GREECE

			E	G
UYT1957	18 Apr	Barcelona	2	3
UYT1959	2 Apr	Dimitrovo	4	0
UYT1977	23 May	Beveren	1	1

v HUNGARY

			E	H
UYT1954	11 Apr	Dusseldorf	1	3
UYT1956	31 Mar	Tatabanya	2	4
*1956	23 Oct	Tottenham	2	1
*1956	25 Oct	Sunderland	2	1
*UYT1965	21 Apr	Wuppertal	5	0
*UYT1975	16 May	Olten	3	1
*UYT1977	10 Oct	Las Palmas	3	0
1979	5 Sept	Pula	2	0
1980	11 Sept	Pula	1	2

v ICELAND

			E	I
*UYT1973	31 May	Viareggio	2	0
*UYT1977	21 May	Turnhout	0	0

v REPUBLIC OF IRELAND

			E	RI
UYT1953	5 Apr	Leuven	2	0
*UYT1964	30 Mar	Middleburg	6	0
*UYT1968	7 Feb	Dublin	0	0
*UYT1968	28 Feb	Portsmouth	4	1
*UYT1970	14 Jan	Dublin	4	1
*UYT1970	4 Feb	Luton	10	0
*UYT1975	9 May	Brunnen	1	0
*UYT1981	11 Feb	Walsall	1	0
*UYT1981	11 Mar	Belfast	3	0

v ISRAEL

			E	I
*1962	20 May	Tel Aviv	3	1
*1962	22 May	Haifa	1	2

v ITALY

			E	I
UYT1958	13 Apr	Luxembourg	0	1
UYT1959	25 Mar	Sofia	0	3
UYT1961	4 Apr	Braga	2	3
*UYT1965	23 Apr	Marl-Huels	3	1
*UYT1966	25 May	Rijeka	1	1
*UYT1967	5 May	Izmir	1	0
1973	14 Feb	Cava dei Tirreni	0	1
1973	14 Mar	Highbury	1	0
*UYT1973	6 June	Viareggio	1	0
1978	19 Nov	Monte Carlo	1	2
*UYT1979	28 Feb	Rome	1	0
*UYT1979	4 Apr	Villa Park	2	0

v LUXEMBOURG

			E	L
UYT1950	25 May	Vienna	1	2
UYT1954	17 Apr	Bad Neuenahr	0	2

1957	2 Feb	West Ham	7	1
1957	17 Nov	Luxembourg	3	0
UYT1958	9 Apr	Eschsalzette	5	0

v MALTA

			E	M
*UYT1969	18 May	Wolfen	6	0
*UYT1979	26 May	Salzburg	3	0

v NETHERLANDS

			E	N
UYT1948	17 Apr	Tottenham	3	2
UYT1951	26 Mar	Cannes	2	1
*1954	21 Nov	Arnhem	2	3
*1955	5 Nov	Norwich	3	1
1957	2 Mar	Brentford	5	5
UYT1957	14 Apr	Barcelona	1	2
1957	2 Oct	Amsterdam	3	2
1961	9 Mar	Utrecht	0	1
*1962	31 Jan	Brighton	4	0
UYT1962	22 Apr	Ploesti	0	3
*UYT1963	13 Apr	Wimbledon	5	0
*UYT1968	9 Apr	Nimes	1	0
*UYT1974	13 Feb	West Bromwich	1	1
*UYT1974	27 Feb	The Hague	1	0
*UYT1979	23 May	Halle	1	0

v POLAND

			E	P
UYT1960	18 Apr	Graz	4	2
*UYT1964	26 Mar	Breda	1	1
*UYT1971	26 May	Presov	0	0
UYT1972	20 May	Valencia	1	0
1975	21 Jan	Las Palmas	1	1
*UYT1978	9 May	Chorzow	0	2
1979	3 Sept	Porac	0	1
*UYT1980	25 May	Leipzig	2	1

v PORTUGAL

			E	P
UYT1954	18 Apr	Bonn	0	2
UYT1961	2 Apr	Lisbon	0	4
*UYT1964	3 Apr	The Hague	4	0
*UYT1971	30 May	Prague	3	0
1978	13 Nov	Monte Carlo	2	0
*UYT1980	18 May	Rosslau	1	1

v RUMANIA

			E	R
1957	15 Oct	Tottenham	4	2
UYT1958	11 Apr	Luxembourg	1	0
UYT1959	31 Mar	Pazardjic	1	2
*UYT1963	15 Apr	Highbury	3	0

v SAAR

			E	S
UYT1954	13 Apr	Dortmund	1	1
UYT1955	9 Apr	Prato	3	1

v SPAIN

			E	S
UYT1952	15 Apr	Barcelona	1	4
1957	26 Sept	Birmingham	4	4
UYT1958	5 Apr	Saarbrucken	2	2
*1958	8 Oct	Madrid	4	2
UYT1961	30 Mar	Lisbon	0	0
*1964	27 Feb	Murcia	2	1
*UYT1964	5 Apr	Amsterdam	4	0
*UYT1965	17 Apr	Heilbronn	0	0
*1966	30 Mar	Swindon	3	0
*UYT1967	7 May	Manisa	2	1
*1971	31 Mar	Pamplona	2	3
*1971	20 Apr	Luton	1	1
1972	9 Feb	Alicante	0	0
1972	15 Mar	Sheffield	4	1
*UYT1975	25 Feb	Bristol	1	1
*UYT1975	18 Mar	Madrid	1	0
1976	12 Nov	Monte Carlo	3	0
*UYT1978	7 May	Bukowno	1	0
1978	17 Nov	Monte Carlo	1	1
*UYT1981	25 May	Siegen	1	2

v SWEDEN

			E	S
*UYT1971	24 May	Poprad	1	0

v SWITZERLAND

			E	S
UYT1950	26 May	Stockerau	2	1
UYT1951	27 Mar	Nice	3	1
UYT1952	13 Apr	Barcelona	4	0
UYT1955	11 Apr	Florence	0	0
1956	11 Mar	Schaffhausen	2	0
1956	13 Oct	Brighton	2	2
1958	26 May	Zurich	3	0
*1960	8 Oct	Leyton	4	3
*†1962	22 Nov	Coventry	1	0
*1963	21 Mar	Bienne	7	1
*UYT1973	2 June	Forte dei Marim	2	0
*UYT1975	11 May	Buochs	4	0
1980	4 Sept	Rovinj	3	0

v TURKEY

			E	T
UYT1959	29 Mar	Dimitrovo	1	1
*UYT1978	5 May	Wodzislaw	1	1

v URUGUAY

			E	U
1977	9 Oct	Las Palmas	1	1

v USSR

			E	USSR
*UYT1963	17 Apr	Tottenham	2	0
*UYT1967	13 May	Istanbul	0	1
*UYT1968	11 Apr	Nimes	1	1
*UYT1971	28 May	Prague	1	1
1978	10 Oct	Las Palmas	1	0

v YUGOSLAVIA

			E	Y
UYT1953	2 April	Liège	1	1
1958	4 Feb	Chelsea	2	2
UYT1962	20 Apr	Ploesti	0	5
*UYT1967	9 May	Izmir	1	1
*UYT1971	22 May	Bardejor	1	0
UYT1972	18 May	Barcelona	1	0
1976	16 Nov	Monte Carlo	0	3
1978	15 Nov	Monte Carlo	1	1
*UYT1980	20 May	Altenburg	2	0

UEFA YOUTH TOURNAMENT 1980–81

Group A

Belgium v Greece	2-0
West Germany v Wales	5-0
Belgium v West Germany	2-3
Greece v Wales	0-1
Belgium v Wales	0-3
Greece v West Germany	0-1

Group B

Poland v Sweden	1-1
Rumania v Czechoslovakia	3-2
Poland v Rumania	3-1
Sweden v Czechoslovakia	3-1
Sweden v Rumania	1-1

Group C

Italy v France	0-0
Bulgaria v Denmark	2-2
Italy v Bulgaria	1-0
France v Denmark	2-1
Italy v Denmark	1-2
France v Bulgaria	3-0

Group D

Austria v Scotland	0-1
Spain v England	2-1
Austria v Spain	0-3
Scotland v England	1-0
Austria v England	0-7
Scotland v Spain	1-1

Semi-Finals

West Germany v France 1-1
(*West Germany won 4-3 on penalties*)
Poland v Spain 0-0
(*Poland won 5-4 on penalties*)

Third Place Play-Off

France v Spain 1-1
(*France won 2-1 on penalties*)

Final

West Germany v Poland 1-0

UEFA YOUTH TOURNAMENT FINALS 1948–81

Year	*Winners*		*Runners-up*		*Venue*
1948	England	3	Netherlands	2	London
1949	France	4	Netherlands	1	Rotterdam
1950	Austria	3	France	2	Vienna
1951	Yugoslavia	3	Austria	2	Cannes
1952	Spain*	0	Belgium	0	Barcelona
1953	Hungary	2	Yugoslavia	0	Brussels
1954	Spain*	2	West Germany	2	Cologne
1955–56	Played in groups only				
1957	Austria	3	Spain	2	Madrid
1958	Italy	1	England	0	Luxembourg
1959	Bulgaria	1	Italy	0	Sofia
1960	Hungary	2	Rumania	1	Vienna
1961	Portugal	4	Poland	0	Lisbon
1962	Rumania	4	Yugoslavia	1	Bucharest
1963	England	4	Northern Ireland	0	London
1964	England	4	Spain	0	Amsterdam
1965	East Germany	3	England	2	Essen
1966	Italy†	0	USSR	0	Belgrade
1967	USSR	1	England	0	Istanbul
1968	Czechoslovakia	2	France	1	Cannes
1969	Bulgaria*	1	East Germany	1	Leipzig
1970	East Germany*	1	Netherlands	1	Glasgow
1971	England	3	Portugal	0	Prague
1972	England	2	West Germany	0	Barcelona
1973	England	3	East Germany	2	Florence
1974	Bulgaria	1	Yugoslavia	0	Malmo
1975	England	1	Finland	0	Berne
1976	USSR	1	Hungary	0	Budapest
1977	Belgium	2	Bulgaria	1	Brussels
1978	USSR	3	Yugoslavia	0	Krakow
1979	Yugoslavia	1	Bulgaria	0	Vienna
1980	England	2	Poland	1	Leipzig
1981	West Germany	1	Poland	0	Dusseldorf

* *Won on toss of a coin.* † *Joint holders.*

NON-LEAGUE FOOTBALL 1980–81

FA CHALLENGE TROPHY 1980–81

Preliminary Round

Rossendale United v Accrington Stanley	1-1
Kirkby Town v Workington	0-1
Caernarvon Town v Colwyn Bay	1-4
Pwllheli & District v Rhyl	0-0
Belper Town v Curzon Ashton	3-2
Brereton Social v New Brighton	6-3
Alfreton Town v Sutton Town	2-0
Eastwood Town v Bridlington Trinity	1-2
Tamworth v Arnold	1-2
Sutton Coldfield Town v Ilkeston Town	2-1
Darlaston v Bilston	0-2
Highgate United v Heanor Town	4-1
Wellingborough Town v Wisbech Town	4-1
Bishop's Stortford v Spalding United	3-1
Cambridge City v Sudbury Town	2-3
Billericay Town v Lowestoft Town	0-0
Clapton v Wembley	1-0
Aveley v Clacton Town	5-1
Chesham United v St Albans City	2-1
Finchley v Corby Town	1-1
Ramsgate v Walton & Hersham	0-3
Horsham v Lewes	2-0
Canterbury City v Sheppey United	1-0
Sittingbourne v Kingstonian	1-3
Epsom and Ewell v Tilbury	2-5
Chatham Town v Tonbridge AFC	1-2
Hampton v Salisbury	2-2
Farnborough Town v Camberley Town	3-0
Basingstoke Town v Maidenhead United	2-1
Clandown v Moor Green	2-2
Keynsham Town v Dudley Town	2-4
Cinderford Town v Llanelli	0-0
Clevedon Town v Knighton Town	1-1
Welton Rovers v Pontllanfraith	0-2
Shepton Mallet Town v Maesteg Park	0-1
Bridport v Mangotsfield United	2-1
Dawlish v Paulton Rovers	6-3
Bideford v Saltash United	0-1
Glastonbury v Ilminster Town	4-1

Preliminary Round – Replays

Accrington Stanley v Rossendale United	1-0
Rhyl v Pwllheli & District	3-0
Lowestoft Town v Billericay Town	1-7
Corby Town v Finchley	4-0
Salisbury v Hampton	2-1
Moor Green v Clandown	5-3
Llanelli v Cinderford Town	1-0
Knighton Town v Clevedon Town	0-1

First Round Qualifying

Whitley Bay v Billingham Synthonia	2-2
Gateshead v Durham City	1-0
Ferryhill Athletic v Emley	3-2
Consett v Fleetwood Town	1-1
Bridlington Trinity v Darwen	4-0
Horwich RMI v Penrith	0-3
North Shields v Workington	2-5
Tow Law Town v South Bank	0-2
Netherfield v Mexborough Town Athletic	2-0
Accrington Stanley v St Helens Town	aet 4-1
Whitby Town v Ashton United	2-2
West Auckland Town v Shildon	1-2
Evenwood Town v Willington	1-3
Droylsden v Goole Town	1-3
Nantwich Town v Brereton Social	3-4
Bilston v South Liverpool	1-2
Rhyl v Hyde United	2-0
Southport v Burscough	1-0
Bootle v Colwyn Bay	2-1
Formby v Oswestry Town	0-3
Moor Green v AP Leamington	4-3
Alvechurch v Bromsgrove Rovers	2-2
Alfreton Town v Dudley Town	1-1
Macclesfield Town v Sutton Coldfield Town	3-4
Belper Town v Bedworth United	0-2
Lye Town v Leek Town	1-1
Worksop Town v Stourbridge	1-2
Hednesford Town v Arnold	2-0
Redditch United v Highgate United	1-0
Enderby Town v Long Eaton United	2-0
New Mills v Buxton	0-2
Leytonstone & Ilford v Hillingdon Borough	1-1
Chesham United v Witney Town	0-1
Banbury United v Hertford Town	2-0
Harwich & Parkeston v Harlow Town	1-2
Hitchin Town v Ware	3-1
Dunstable Town v Wellingborough Town	2-2
Wealdstone v Oxford City	2-4
Billericay Town v Milton Keynes City	6-0
Boreham Wood v Corby Town	0-0
Chelmsford City v Bishop's Stortford	1-2
Sudbury Town v King's Lynn	2-3
Margate v Metropolitan Police	4-1
Folkestone v Tilbury	2-1
Clapton v Farnborough Town	2-1
Ashford Town v Addlestone & Weybridge Town	0-3
Horsham v Bognor Regis Town	0-0
Waterlooville v Hayes	2-1
Canterbury City v Andover	3-1
Tonbridge AFC v Kingstonian	1-1
Walton & Hersham v Wokingham Town	1-1
Staines Town v Gosport Borough	2-2
Crawley Town v Fareham Town	3-2
Bromley v Carshalton Athletic	1-2
Croydon v Aveley	2-0
Basingstoke Town v Hounslow	2-2
Poole Town v Dawlish	0-1
Llanelli v Salisbury	1-2
Gloucester City v Glastonbury	3-1
Weston-super-Mare v Bridport	3-0
Taunton Town v Clevedon Town	3-0
Falmouth Town v Pontllanfraith	2-1
Bridgwater Town v Maesteg Park	2-2
Saltash United v Trowbridge Town	3-2

First Round Qualifying – Replays

Billingham Synthonia v Whitley Bay	8-2
Fleetwood Town v Consett	aet 2-3
Ashton United v Whitby Town	1-2
Bromsgrove Rovers v Alvechurch	0-2
Dudley Town v Alfreton Town	1-0
Leek Town v Lye Town	2-1
Hillingdon Borough v Leytonstone & Ilford	aet 1-3
Wellingborough Town v Dunstable Town	2-4
Corby Town v Boreham Wood	4-1
Bognor Regis Town v Horsham	4-2
Kingstonian v Tonbridge AFC	4-0
Wokingham Town v Walton & Hersham	3-0
Gosport Borough v Staines Town	1-0
Hounslow v Basingstoke Town	0-1
Maesteg Park v Bridgwater Town	0-1

Second Round Qualifying

Gateshead v Ferryhill Athletic	5-0
Consett v Accrington Stanley	0-1
Netherfield v Bridlington Trinity	0-0
Willington v Bootle	0-4
South Bank v Penrith	2-2
Billingham Synthonia v Goole Town	0-0
Workington v Whitby Town	1-2
Shildon v Southport	0-1
South Liverpool v Rhyl	5-1
Oswestry Town v Leek Town	2-1
Bedworth United v Moor Green	3-0
Redditch United v King's Lynn	3-0
Sutton Coldfield Town v Alvechurch	1-1
Brereton Social v Enderby Town	1-0
Dudley Town v Stourbridge	0-0

Hednesford Town v Buxton	3-2
Clapton v Wokingham Town	2-2
Gosport Borough v Canterbury City	4-1
Bishop's Stortford v Kingstonian	2-0
Waterlooville v Margate	1-1
Banbury United v Harlow Town	1-2
Basingstoke Town v Corby Town	1-0
Crawley Town v Bognor Regis Town	0-4
Hitchin Town v Billericay Town	3-0
Croydon v Oxford City	1-0
Witney Town v Carshalton Athletic	1-2
Folkestone v Leytonstone & Ilford	2-4
Addlestone & Weybridge T v Dunstable T	2-1
Weston-super-Mare v Taunton Town	3-2
Gloucester City v Bridgwater Town	1-0
Salisbury v Dawlish	2-1
Falmouth Town v Saltash United	1-3

Second Round Qualifying – Replays

Bridlington Trinity v Netherfield	1-1
Penrith v South Bank	2-1
Goole Town v Billingham Synthonia	1-2

Match awarded to Goole Town; Billingham Synthonia played an ineligible player.

Alvechurch v Sutton Coldfield Town	aet 3-1
Stourbridge v Dudley Town	3-2
Wokingham Town v Clapton	1-0
Margate v Waterlooville	3-1

Second Replay

Netherfield v Bridlington Trinity — aet 2-2
(*at Goole Town FC*)

Third Replay

Bridlington Trinity v Netherfield — aet 1-1
(*at Chorley FC*)

Fourth Replay

Netherfield v Bridlington Trinity — aet 1-1
(*at Chorley FC*)

Fifth Replay

Bridlington Trinity v Netherfield — aet 2-2
(*at Netherfield FC*)

Sixth Replay

Netherfield v Bridlington Trinity — 2-0
(*at Goole Town FC*)

Third Round Qualifying

Crook Town v Gateshead	1-3
Goole Town v Whitby Town	3-1
Bishop Auckland v Scarborough	1-1
Southport v Lancaster City	1-2
Horden Colliery Welfare v Penrith	0-1
Morecambe v Frickley Athletic	0-0
Stalybridge Celtic v Gainsboro' Trinity	3-0
Netherfield v Accrington Stanley	2-1
Hednesford Town v Winsford United	0-1
Redditch United v Kidderminster Harriers	1-2
Bootle v Oswestry Town	3-1
Burton Albion v Stourbridge	3-1
Witton Albion v Brereton Social	3-0
Bedworth United v Telford United	1-0
Northwich Victoria v Boston	2-1
Grantham v Gloucester City	1-3
South Liverpool v Alvechurch	0-3
Barnet v Harlow Town	0-1
Bognor Regis Town v Harrow Borough	2-1
Addlestone & Weybridge T v Carshalton Ath	2-5
Dover v Hitchin Town	2-5
Bishop's Stortford v Hendon	1-0
Hastings United v Basingstoke Town	2-1
Dartford v Margate	3-1
Aylesbury United v Gosport Borough	1-0
Slough Town v Wokingham Town	6-0
Leytonstone & Ilford v Croydon	2-0
Bath City v Merthyr Tydfil	1-1
Frome Town v Saltash United	0-0
Bridgend Town v Salisbury	2-0
Barnstaple Town v Dorchester Town	0-0
Weston-super-Mare v Minehead	1-1

Third Round Qualifying – Replays

Scarborough v Bishop Auckland	4-2
Frickley Athletic v Morecambe	0-2
Merthyr Tydfil v Bath City	1-3
Saltash United v Frome Town	2-4
Dorchester Town v Barnstaple Town	2-1
Minehead v Weston-super-Mare	aet 5-2

First Round

Runcorn v Stafford Rangers	0-1
Boston United v Gateshead	4-0
Stalybridge Celtic v Bootle	2-3
Nuneaton Borough v Ashington	1-2
Burton Albion v Blyth Spartans	0-2
Altrincham v Spennymoor United	3-2
Northwich Victoria v Barrow	3-0
Goole Town v Morecambe	2-0
Alvechurch v Penrith	4-2
Lancaster City v Winsford United	2-2
Marine v Matlock Town	2-0
Witton Albion v Bangor City	0-3
Kidderminster Harriers v Bedworth United	2-2
Chorley v Netherfield	1-2
Mossley v Scarborough	2-2
Dagenham v Bath City	4-0
Hitchin Town v Tooting & Mitcham U	2-1
Dorchester Town v Walthamstow Avenue	0-1
Woking v Sutton United	0-1
Carshalton Athletic v Barking	3-0
Cheltenham Town v Wycombe Wanderers	0-1
Bishop's Stortford v Bridgend Town	1-1
Hastings United v Maidstone United	1-1
Leytonstone & Ilford v Gloucester City	7-0
Aylesbury United v Enfield	2-2
Bedford Town v Dulwich Hamlet	3-1
Dartford v Slough Town	4-1
Frome Town v Yeovil Town	1-1
Gravesend & Northfleet v Kettering Town	2-3
Harlow Town v Bognor Regis Town	2-0
Minehead v Worcester City	1-3
Leatherhead v Weymouth	1-3

First Round – Replays

Winsford United v Lancaster City	aet 5-2
Bedworth United v Kidderminster Harriers	1-0
Scarborough v Mossley	0-1
Bridgend Town v Bishop's Stortford	1-2
Maidstone United v Hastings United	1-2
Enfield v Aylesbury United (*abandoned after 90 minutes*)	0-0
Yeovil Town v Frome Town	2-1

First Round – Second Replay

Aylesbury United v Enfield — 1-0
(*at Chesham United FC*)

Second Round

Alvechurch v Bedworth United	4-1
Aylesbury United v Netherfield	2-0
Sutton United v Wycombe Wanderers	5-1
Walthamstow Avenue v Bedford Town	0-0
Goole Town v Worcester City	1-4
Blyth Spartans v Stafford Rangers	1-0
Yeovil Town v Hastings United	1-1
Leytonstone & Ilford v Weymouth	1-1
Dagenham v Bishop's Stortford	1-1
Winsford United v Altrincham	0-2
Marine v Bangor City	0-1
Bootle v Carshalton Athletic	0-0
Harlow Town v Northwich Victoria	0-1
Boston United v Hitchin Town	0-1
Kettering Town v Mossley	0-1
Dartford v Ashington	1-0

Second Round – Replays

Bedford Town v Walthamstow Avenue	1-0
Hastings United v Yeovil Town	2-1
Weymouth v Leytonstone & Ilford	aet 3-4
Bishop's Stortford v Dagenham	3-1
Carshalton Athletic v Bootle	2-1

Third Round

Leytonstone & Ilford v Altrincham	0-1
Bishop's Stortford v Alvechurch	3-2
Sutton United v Bedford Town	2-0
Aylesbury United v Northwich Victoria	0-0
Hastings United v Worcester City	0-0
Carshalton Athletic v Mossley	0-3
Bangor City v Hitchin Town	1-0
Dartford v Blyth Spartans	1-0

Third Round – Replays

Northwich Victoria v Aylesbury United	1-1
Worcester City v Hastings United	2-1

Third Round – Second Replay

Aylesbury United v Northwich Victoria (*at Enderby Town FC*)	1-0

Fourth Round

Sutton United v Aylesbury United	0-0
Bishop's Stortford v Worcester City	4-0
Bangor City v Mossley	5-3
Dartford v Altrincham	3-1

Fourth Round – Replay

Aylesbury United v Sutton United	0-1

Semi-Finals – First Leg

Dartford v Bishop's Stortford	1-1
Bangor City v Sutton United	2-2

Semi-Finals – Second Leg

Bishop's Stortford v Dartford	2-1
Sutton United v Bangor City	4-1

Final (*at Wembley*)

Bishop's Stortford 1 (*Sullivan*) 22,578
Sutton United 0

Bishop's Stortford: Moore; Blackman, Brane, Smith (Worrell), Bradford, Avery, Sullivan, Knapman, Radford, Simmonds, Mitchell.

Sutton United: Collyer; Rogers, Green, Rains J., Rains T., Stephens (Sunnucks), Waldon, Pritchard, Cornwell, Parsons, Dennis.

Previous Finals

1970 Macclesfield T 2, Telford U 0 (28,000)
1971 Telford U 3, Hillingdon B 2 (29,500)
1972 Stafford R 3, Barnet 0 (24,000)
1973 Scarborough 2, Wigan Ath 1 (23,000)
1974 Morecambe 2, Dartford 1 (19,000)
1975 Matlock T 4, Scarborough 0 (21,000)
1976 Scarborough 3, Stafford R 2 (aet) (21,000)
1977 Scarborough 2, Dagenham 1 (20,000)
1978 Altrincham 3, Leatherhead 1 (19,999)
1979 Stafford R 2, Kettering T 0 (32,000)
1980 Dagenham 2, Mossley 1 (26,000)

ALLIANCE PREMIER LEAGUE CUP 1980–81

First Round

Byes: Altrincham, Automotive Products Leamington, Barnet, Barrow, Boston U, Frickley Ath, Kettering T, Northwich Victoria, Nuneaton Bor, Scarborough, Wealdstone, Yeovil T.

Bangor C v Worcester C 0-2, 3-4
Gravesend & Northfleet v Bath C 1-3, 1-1
Maidstone U v Weymouth 1-1, 3-3
After extra time. Score after 90 minutes 2-2. Weymouth won 4-3 on penalties. After the first 10 penalties the score was 1-1.
Telford U v Stafford Rangers 3-0, 4-2
Telford U were disqualified for playing an ineligible player in the first leg.

Second Round

Altrincham v Boston U	4-0, 2-1
Automotive Products Leamington v Barnet	3-1, 0-6
Bath C v Weymouth	0-0, 5-2
Frickley Ath v Stafford Rangers	1-1, 0-4
Nuneaton Bor v Wealdstone	0-1, 3-0
Scarborough v Barrow	0-0, 0-2
Worcester C v Northwich Victoria	0-0, 2-1
Yeovil T v Kettering T	0-1, 0-0

Third Round

Altrincham v Nuneaton Bor	2-0
Barrow v Stafford Rangers	2-0
Bath C v Worcester C	1-1
Kettering T v Barnet	1-1

Third Round Replays

Barnet v Kettering T	1-4
Worcester C v Bath C	2-1

Semi-Final

Barrow v Kettering T	0-2, 1-5
Worcester C v Altrincham	0-1, 1-2

Final – First Leg: Altrincham 2, Kettering T 0
(1887; 22 April 1981)

Altrincham: Connaughton; Allan, Davison; Bailey, Owens, Crossley; Barrow, Whitbread, Johnson, Heathcote, Howard.
Kettering T: Walters; Curtis, Forster; Clarke, Suddards, Guy; Phipps, Evans, Atkins, Duggan, Flannagan (Hofbauer).
Scorers: Altrincham – Bailey, Guy og.

Second Leg: Kettering T 2, Altrincham 1
(2092; 29 April 1981)

Kettering T: Walters; Curtis, Forster; Clarke, Suddards, Haverson; Phipps, Evans, Atkins, Hofbauer, Duggan (Guy).
Altrincham: Connaughton; Allan, Davison; Bailey, Owens, King; Barrow, Whitbread, Johnson, Heathcote, Howard.
Scorers: Kettering T – Atkins, Guy; Altrincham – Whitbread.

ALLIANCE PREMIER LEAGUE 1980–81

	Altrincham	Automotive Products Leamington	Bangor City	Barnet	Barrow	Bath City	Boston United	Frickley Athletic	Gravesend and Northfleet	Kettering Town	Maidstone United	Northwich Victoria	Nuneaton Borough	Scarborough	Stafford Rangers	Telford United	Wealdstone	Weymouth	Worcester City	Yeovil Town
Altrincham	—	4-1	2-0	2-0	2-2	3-1	2-0	2-0	2-1	4-1	2-1	1-1	0-3	4-3	4-2	0-2	2-0	1-2	1-0	2-1
Automotive Products Leamington	2-4	—	1-0	0-1	2-2	0-4	0-0	2-2	4-1	3-3	2-3	1-1	0-1	2-0	1-1	5-0	1-1	0-1	2-1	1-0
Bangor City	4-5	1-0	—	4-2	2-6	0-1	1-1	4-3	1-1	0-1	1-1	0-0	2-5	0-3	0-0	2-0	0-2	2-0	1-1	0-2
Barnet	3-2	1-0	0-1	—	0-0	1-5	2-2	2-0	1-1	0-1	4-1	1-0	1-0	1-2	1-1	2-1	3-0	0-3	0-2	4-4
Barrow	0-4	0-2	3-0	1-1	—	0-0	0-2	0-0	3-1	2-1	4-1	2-1	1-0	0-1	5-1	0-1	1-0	0-1	1-0	2-1
Bath City	0-1	5-0	0-0	1-0	2-1	—	2-0	3-0	1-0	0-0	0-0	0-0	0-0	0-1	0-0	0-1	2-0	2-3	3-0	2-1
Boston United	1-1	2-3	1-1	3-0	0-2	4-2	—	1-2	2-1	2-1	1-1	2-3	3-1	0-3	2-2	5-3	2-1	2-1	3-1	3-1
Frickley Athletic*	0-2	0-0	4-0	3-0	5-0	2-1	0-1	—	2-4	1-1	2-1	0-1	4-3	1-0	3-2	4-1	1-1	1-2	1-1	2-1
Gravesend and Northfleet	0-2	4-0	1-0	0-2	0-2	2-1	1-2	3-1	—	1-0	1-2	0-1	4-0	1-1	1-1	2-2	0-1	1-0	2-1	2-2
Kettering Town	1-1	3-0	3-1	2-1	0-1	2-2	0-0	6-1	2-0	—	3-0	3-3	3-0	1-0	1-0	2-1	0-1	1-0	1-0	4-0
Maidstone United	1-2	2-1	1-0	4-1	1-0	2-1	2-2	1-1	1-1	1-2	—	4-0	1-3	1-1	4-1	3-0	4-0	3-0	2-0	4-2
Northwich Victoria	1-0	2-0	2-1	4-1	0-0	3-1	3-1	1-3	4-0	1-1	2-1	—	2-0	0-1	2-1	1-0	0-0	0-0	3-0	1-2
Nuneaton Borough	0-0	3-0	3-2	0-1	3-1	0-0	0-2	0-1	1-2	1-5	1-1	2-0	—	0-4	2-2	3-3	2-0	1-4	2-3	3-0
Scarborough	1-0	0-0	1-1	3-0	0-0	1-0	3-2	2-1	1-0	1-2	1-2	0-0	2-1	—	0-0	1-1	4-0	2-0	0-0	2-1
Stafford Rangers	1-3	1-1	4-0	1-0	1-0	0-2	2-3	3-3	2-3	3-1	3-1	2-0	2-2	2-1	—	0-1	3-0	2-0	1-0	1-1
Telford United	3-2	2-3	1-1	0-0	5-2	2-1	2-0	1-0	0-0	0-2	1-2	1-3	2-2	0-0	1-1	—	2-1	1-0	1-2	0-1
Wealdstone	1-2	1-2	1-1	2-0	2-0	0-1	3-0	0-2	3-1	1-1	2-1	1-1	0-0	2-2	1-1	4-0	—	1-1	1-2	1-1
Weymouth	0-0	3-2	4-0	3-0	2-1	1-1	2-1	1-2	0-1	1-2	1-1	4-3	1-0	1-1	2-1	1-0	2-1	—	1-0	0-1
Worcester City	0-0	3-3	1-1	4-0	2-4	0-2	1-4	3-0	3-1	2-1	2-1	2-1	1-0	2-0	1-1	0-3	4-1	2-1	—	0-1
Yeovil Town	1-1	3-0	1-0	1-2	2-1	1-2	2-1	5-3	1-3	1-2	2-1	1-2	5-1	0-0	3-4	1-2	4-0	0-5	3-0	—

* *First season in the Alliance Premier League – promoted from Northern Premier League.*

ALLIANCE PREMIER LEAGUE CHALLENGE SHIELD 1980–81

Altrincham 0, Northwich Victoria 1

(At Altrincham, 18 August, 1980, attendance 1784)

Played between the 1979–80 League champions – Altrincham – and the League Cup winners – Northwich Victoria.

ALLIANCE PREMIER LEAGUE 1980–81

	P	W	D	L	F	A	Pts
Altrincham	38	23	8	7	72	41	54
Kettering T	38	21	9	8	66	37	51
Scarborough	38	17	13	8	49	29	47
Northwich Victoria	38	17	11	10	53	40	45
Weymouth	38	19	6	13	54	40	44
Bath City	38	16	10	12	51	32	42
Maidstone U	38	16	9	13	64	53	41
Boston U	38	16	9	13	63	58	41
Barrow	38	15	8	15	50	49	38
Frickley Ath	38	15	8	15	61	62	38
Stafford Rangers	38	11	15	12	56	56	37
Worcester C	38	14	7	17	47	54	35
Telford U	38	13	9	16	47	59	35
Yeovil T	38	14	6	18	60	64	34
Gravesend & Northfleet	38	13	8	17	48	55	34
AP Leamington	38	10	11	17	47	66	31
Barnet	38	12	7	19	39	64	31
Nuneaton Borough	38	10	9	19	49	65	29
Wealdstone	38	9	11	18	37	56	29
Bangor C	38	6	12	20	35	68	24

ALLIANCE PREMIER LEAGUE LEADING GOALSCORERS 1980–81

Note: Totals include goals scored in both the League and League Cup

26 Williams (Northwich Vic)
25 Evans (Kettering T)
19 Heathcote (Altrincham)
19 Rogers (Altrincham)
19 Withey (Bath C)
17 Ovard (Maidstone U)
16 Green (Yeovil T)
15 Cowperthwaite (Barrow)
13 Mather (Telford U)
12 Gardner (AP Leamington)
12 Hickton (AP Leamington)
12 Iannone (Weymouth)
12 Wadsworth (Frickley Ath)
12 Woodall (Frickley Ath)

BERGER ISTHMIAN LEAGUE 1980–81

PREMIER DIVISION

	P	W	D	L	F	A	Pts
Slough T	42	23	13	6	73	34	82
Enfield	42	23	11	8	81	43	80
Wycombe W	42	22	9	11	76	49	75
Leytonstone & Ilford	42	19	12	11	78	57	69
Sutton U	42	19	12	11	82	65	69
Hendon	42	18	10	14	66	58	64
Hayes	42	18	8	16	45	50	62
Dagenham	42	17	11	14	79	66	62
Harrow Bor	42	16	11	15	57	52	59
Bromley	42	16	9	17	63	69	57
Staines T	42	15	9	18	60	61	54
Tooting & Mitcham U	42	15	8	19	49	53	53
Hitchin T	42	14	10	18	64	52	52
Croydon	42	12	15	15	51	51	51
Dulwich H	42	13	12	17	62	67	51
Leatherhead	42	12	14	16	36	50	50
Carshalton Ath	42	14	8	20	57	82	50
Barking*	42	13	12	17	58	72	49
Harlow T	42	11	15	16	54	66	48
Walthamstow Ave	42	13	7	22	51	82	46
Boreham Wood	42	10	13	19	46	69	43
Woking†	42	11	7	24	40	70	37

** 2 points deducted.* *† 3 points deducted.*

DIVISION 1

	P	W	D	L	F	A	Pts
Bishop's Stortford	42	30	6	6	84	28	96
Billericay T	42	29	6	7	67	34	93
Epsom & Ewell	42	24	12	6	80	36	84
Farnborough T	42	23	11	8	75	39	80
St Albans C	42	24	5	13	85	61	77
Kingstonian*	42	20	9	13	63	51	66
Oxford C	42	18	9	15	71	48	63
Wokingham T	42	16	15	11	70	56	63
Metropolitan Police	42	18	7	17	61	58	61
Chesham U	42	17	7	18	64	64	58
Lewes	42	17	7	18	72	83	58
Maidenhead U	42	16	7	19	58	62	55
Walton & Hersham	42	12	15	15	46	53	51
Hertford T	42	13	11	18	46	65	50
Hampton	42	12	13	17	46	53	49
Aveley	42	13	9	20	54	55	48
Wembley	42	13	8	21	47	61	47
Clapton	42	12	8	22	53	86	44
Ware	42	9	13	20	50	69	40
Tilbury	42	10	8	24	42	84	38
Camberley T	42	8	7	27	42	88	31
Finchley	42	6	11	25	34	77	29

** 3 points deducted.*

DIVISION 2

	P	W	D	L	F	A	Pts
Feltham	38	24	10	4	65	30	82
Hornchurch	38	25	6	7	74	35	81
Hungerford T	38	23	10	5	84	29	79
Barton R	38	19	11	8	61	26	68
Worthing	38	19	11	8	74	43	68
Cheshunt	38	19	11	8	57	33	68
Letchworth Garden C	38	18	7	13	49	40	61
Southall	38	14	11	13	48	52	53
Dorking T	38	13	12	13	47	45	51
Horsham	38	16	3	19	47	47	51
Hemel Hempstead	38	14	7	17	49	55	49
Egham T	38	13	9	16	45	62	48
Harwich & Parkeston	38	12	11	15	57	58	47
Rainham T	38	11	13	14	44	45	46
Epping T	38	12	7	19	37	50	43
Eastbourne U	38	11	10	17	59	75	43
Willesden	38	11	8	19	57	68	41
Tring T	38	11	6	21	40	71	39
Molesey	38	4	9	25	31	83	21
Corinthian Casuals	38	1	8	29	17	95	11

JOHN SMITH'S NORTHERN PREMIER CHALLENGE CUP 1980–81

Byes: Burton A, Buxton, Grantham, Lancaster C, Macclesfield T, Matlock T, Mossley, Runcorn, Witton A, Worksop T.

First Round

Goole T v Tamworth	1-1, 1-2
King's Lynn v Gainsborough Trinity	1-1, 3-4
Marine v Southport	3-1, 5-0
Netherfield v Morecambe	4-0, 1-0
South Liverpool v Oswestry T	3-1, 2-3
After extra time. Score after 90 minutes 0-2.	
Workington v Gateshead	0-1, 2-2

Second Round

Grantham v Runcorn	0-1
Lancaster C v Burton A	1-2
Macclesfield T v Buxton	2-2
Marine v Gateshead	1-0
Netherfield v Mossley	2-2
Tamworth v Gainsborough Trinity	2-2
Witton A v Matlock T	3-0
Worksop T v South Liverpool	1-0

Second Round Replays

Buxton v Macclesfield T	1-0
Gainsborough Trinity v Tamworth	1-0
Mossley v Netherfield	1-3

Third Round

Burton A v Worksop T	1-2
Buxton v Marine	0-2
Gainsborough Trinity v Netherfield	2-1
Runcorn v Witton A	1-1

Third Round Replay

Witton A v Runcorn	aet 0-0

Third Round Second Replay

Witton A v Runcorn	1-2

Semi-Final

Marine v Gainsborough Trinity	2-1, 1-0
Runcorn v Worksop T	3-1, 0-1

Final: Marine 3, Runcorn 4

(At Maine Road, 28 April, 1981, attendance 1694)

Marine: Cunneely; Tym, Adams; Peter Smith, Johnson, Edwards; Hughes, Phil Smith, McClatchey, Meachin, Wagstaffe.

Runcorn: Holbrook; Roberts, Crompton; Seddon, Duff, Quinn (Kelly); Smith, Scott, Fraser, Lewis, Joel.

Scorers: Marine – Hughes, Meachin, Wagstaffe; Runcorn – Crompton, Joel, Fraser, Scott pen.

NORTHERN PREMIER LEAGUE CHALLENGE SHIELD 1980

Mossley 1, Runcorn 2

(*Score after 90 minutes 1-1*)

(At Mossley, 8 October, 1980, attendance 724)

Played between the 1979–80 League champions – Mossley – and the Cup winners – Runcorn.

NORTHERN PREMIER LEAGUE 1980–81

	P	*W*	*D*	*L*	*F*	*A*	*Pts*
Runcorn	42	32	7	3	99	22	71
Mossley	42	24	7	11	95	55	55
Marine	42	22	10	10	66	41	54
Buxton	42	21	7	14	64	50	49
Gainsborough Trinity	42	17	13	12	80	57	47
Burton Albion	42	19	8	15	63	54	46
Witton Albion	42	19	8	15	70	62	46
Goole T	42	14	16	12	56	50	44
South Liverpool	42	19	6	17	59	64	44
Workington	42	15	13	14	57	48	43
Gateshead	42	12	18	12	65	61	42
Worksop T	42	15	11	16	66	61	41
Macclesfield T	42	13	13	16	52	69	39
Grantham	42	14	9	19	57	74	37
Matlock T	42	12	12	18	57	80	36
Lancaster C	42	13	9	20	48	70	35
Netherfield	42	11	12	19	73	81	34
Oswestry T	42	13	8	21	54	67	34
King's Lynn	42	8	18	16	46	65	34
Southport	42	11	11	20	42	68	33
Morecambe	42	11	8	23	42	74	30
Tamworth	42	9	12	21	38	76	30

NORTHERN PREMIER LEAGUE 1980–81

	Burton Albion	Buxton	Gainsborough Trinity	Gateshead	Goole Town	Grantham	King's Lynn	Lancaster City	Macclesfield Town	Marine	Matlock Town	Morecambe	Mossley	Netherfield	Oswestry Town	Runcorn	South Liverpool	Southport	Tamworth	Witton Albion	Workington	Worksop Town
Burton Albion	—	2-0	0-1	1-0	2-2	2-0	4-1	2-1	1-1	0-0	3-0	3-1	1-5	1-1	2-1	0-1	0-1	5-2	3-0	0-0	5-0	1-1
Buxton	1-2	—	2-1	1-1	0-1	4-1	1-1	3-0	1-2	3-1	2-1	0-3	0-2	3-3	2-1	1-1	2-3	2-0	7-0	0-0	2-0	1-0
Gainsborough Trinity	2-0	0-0	—	2-1	2-1	1-1	6-0	6-0	6-1	0-2	3-2	2-0	1-1	4-3	3-2	0-2	3-0	0-0	2-3	3-1	1-1	1-1
Gateshead	1-0	2-0	2-2	—	0-0	1-1	3-2	2-2	0-0	0-1	5-0	2-1	1-5	0-0	2-2	1-1	2-0	0-2	0-0	1-2	1-0	1-2
Goole Town	0-1	2-4	1-1	2-2	—	0-1	2-2	1-1	3-1	0-0	3-0	1-0	3-4	2-0	3-0	1-2	2-1	2-1	2-2	0-2	1-0	3-0
Grantham	1-2	4-0	0-3	1-4	2-0	—	3-1	0-1	4-2	1-3	3-2	0-1	2-4	5-2	0-1	1-1	1-1	3-1	1-0	0-0	2-0	2-2
King's Lynn*	0-4	0-1	1-1	1-1	2-2	1-0	—	0-0	1-2	2-0	0-2	0-0	2-2	2-2	1-1	0-2	2-2	3-0	4-1	1-3	2-0	1-1
Lancaster City	2-0	0-1	1-5	3-2	0-0	2-0	1-0	—	1-1	1-2	1-3	1-1	1-2	4-1	4-2	0-2	0-3	0-1	1-1	3-0	2-3	2-2
Macclesfield Town	1-0	2-3	2-2	2-4	1-1	2-2	0-0	2-3	—	2-1	1-1	1-1	0-3	2-0	1-0	2-5	1-2	0-1	2-1	0-3	2-2	3-5
Marine	4-0	2-0	2-0	1-1	2-2	7-0	1-1	2-1	1-1	—	2-0	5-1	2-0	2-1	3-0	0-4	3-2	1-0	1-0	3-0	1-0	2-1
Matlock Town	3-1	0-1	2-1	2-4	3-2	2-3	3-3	2-0	0-1	0-0	—	2-1	1-4	1-1	1-3	0-4	4-2	1-1	0-0	0-0	0-4	3-3
Morecambe	2-3	2-1	2-0	1-0	0-0	1-4	0-1	1-3	2-1	0-0	2-1	—	1-3	1-4	2-0	0-2	2-1	1-2	4-0	0-2	2-3	1-1
Mossley	3-2	0-1	1-0	1-1	1-1	1-2	1-0	0-1	3-0	0-0	2-3	3-4	—	4-3	1-1	1-2	3-0	2-0	6-1	5-0	2-3	3-2
Netherfield	0-2	1-2	1-3	4-4	2-1	4-0	1-0	4-1	1-1	1-1	3-1	3-0	0-2	—	0-1	0-1	2-3	2-1	2-0	3-3	2-2	2-3
Oswestry Town	4-0	1-3	1-2	4-2	0-1	1-0	2-2	0-1	0-0	2-1	1-2	0-0	3-3	1-0	—	0-2	2-0	0-1	2-0	3-2	2-1	3-4
Runcorn	4-0	1-0	3-0	0-1	2-0	3-1	0-0	5-0	2-0	3-0	5-0	3-0	4-1	1-1	3-1	—	2-3	3-0	0-0	5-0	3-0	1-0
South Liverpool	2-1	1-4	1-1	2-1	2-3	4-0	0-2	1-0	2-1	2-0	0-0	1-0	0-1	4-3	2-0	2-4	—	2-0	1-3	1-0	1-0	1-0
Southport	1-1	0-2	4-2	1-1	0-0	0-3	2-0	1-2	0-1	2-3	2-2	1-1	1-3	0-0	3-2	1-3	2-0	—	2-2	2-2	0-0	2-1
Tamworth	0-2	0-1	1-1	1-1	0-2	1-1	2-0	1-0	0-3	3-2	2-2	2-0	0-5	4-3	0-2	1-4	0-0	1-0	—	2-0	0-1	2-3
Witton Albion	3-1	0-0	4-3	3-4	3-1	3-1	4-0	4-1	0-1	3-0	0-3	5-0	2-0	1-4	3-1	1-0	3-1	4-0	2-1	—	1-1	0-1
Workington	0-0	4-1	2-2	3-1	1-1	0-0	1-1	1-0	1-2	0-2	0-1	4-0	3-0	1-2	3-0	1-1	1-1	4-0	0-0	2-1	—	2-0
Worksop Town	1-3	2-1	2-1	2-2	0-1	3-0	1-3	0-0	0-1	1-0	1-1	3-0	0-2	6-1	1-1	1-2	3-1	1-2	1-0	4-0	0-2	—

* *Transferred from Southern League – Midland Division.*

SOUTHERN LEAGUE CUP 1980–81

First Round

Ashford T v Hastings U	1-4, 1-2
Alvechurch v Cheltenham T	3-2, 1-0
Banbury U v Enderby T	0-1, 1-2
Barry T v Trowbridge T	1-1, 0-2
Basingstoke T v Fareham T	2-1, 1-0
Bedworth U v Bromsgrove R	1-1, 1-2
Bognor Regis T v Waterlooville	2-0, 0-1
Bridgend T v Minehead	1-0, 0-2
Cambridge C v Wellingborough T	1-2, 2-4
Canterbury C v Addlestone & Weybridge T	1-1, 1-2
Chelmsford C v Milton Keynes C	1-0, 1-0
Corby T v Aylesbury U	1-0, 2-1
Dartford v Hillingdon Borough	3-0, 2-2
Dorchester T v Merthyr Tydfil	2-1, 3-2
Dunstable T v Bedford T	3-2, 2-4
Folkestone v Dover	0-5, 0-0
Gloucester C v Taunton T	5-1, 0-2
Gosport Borough v Poole T	0-1, 0-2
Hounslow v Margate	3-0, 1-1
Redditch U v Kidderminster Harriers	1-0, 0-1
Salisbury v Andover	6-1, 1-1
Tonbridge AFC v Crawley T	1-2, 0-4
Witney T v Stourbridge	1-2, 0-1

First Round Replay

Kidderminster Harriers v Redditch U	aet 2-1

Second Round

Byes: Alvechurch, Bognor Regis T, Corby T, Crawley T, Dartford, Dover, Gloucester C, Minehead, Salisbury.

Addlestone & Weybridge T v Hastings U	1-1
Bedford T v Enderby T	2-1
Chelmsford C v Hounslow	3-2
Dorchester T v Trowbridge T	3-1
Kidderminster Harriers v Bromsgrove R	0-0
Poole T v Basingstoke T	3-4
Wellingborough T v Stourbridge	0-1

Second Round Replays

Bromsgrove R v Kidderminster Harriers	0-2
Hastings U v Addlestone & Weybridge T	1-2

Third Round

Addlestone & Weybridge T v Dover	5-1
Alvechurch v Corby T	1-0
Bedford T v Stourbridge	5-1
Chelmsford C v Dartford	3-0
Crawley T v Basingstoke T	1-2
Gloucester C v Dorchester T	4-3
Kidderminster Harriers v Minehead	1-2
Salisbury v Bognor Regis T	0-2

Fourth Round

Basingstoke T v Chelmsford C	1-0
Bedford T v Minehead	2-0
Bognor Regis T v Addlestone & Weybridge T	2-0
Gloucester C v Alvechurch	2-1

Semi-Final

Basingstoke T v Bognor Regis T	1-0, 1-3
Gloucester C v Bedford T	1-3, 1-0

Final – First Leg: Bognor Regis T 1, Bedford T 2
(950; 28 March, 1981)

Bognor Regis T: Gilbert; Parslow, Pullein M.; Anderton, Legg, Hider; Clements, Burrows, Robson, Cooper (Poole), Pullein P.

Bedford T: Lane; Platnauer, James; Gould, Goodeve, Best; Kirkup, McGowan, Robinson, Campbell, Felton.

Scorers: Bognor Regis T – Robson; Bedford T – Kirkup, Campbell.

Second Leg: Bedford T 1, Bognor Regis T 0
(893; 11 April, 1981)

Bedford T: Lane; Platnauer, James; Gould, Goodeve, Best; Kirkup, McGowan, Robinson, Campbell, Felton.

Bognor Regis T: Gilbert; Parslow, Pullein M.; Anderton, Legg, Hider; Clements, Burrows, Musselwhite, Cooper, Manley (Robson).

Scorer: Bedford T – Campbell.

CHAMPIONSHIP MATCH

Bridgend T 3, Kidderminster Harriers 0
(At Bridgend, 2 September, 1980, attendance 211)

Played between the 1979–80 League champions – Bridgend T – and the Cup winners – Kidderminster Harriers.

The League champions are determined by matches played on a home and away basis between the winners of the Midland and Southern Divisions.

SOUTHERN LEAGUE – MIDLAND DIVISION 1980–81

	Alvechurch	Banbury United	Barry Town	Bedford Town	Bedworth United	Bridgend Town	Bromsgrove Rovers	Cambridge City	Cheltenham Town	Corby Town	Enderby Town	Gloucester City	Kidderminster Harriers	Merthyr Tydfil	Milton Keynes City	Minehead	Redditch United	Stourbridge	Taunton Town	Trowbridge Town	Wellingborough Town	Witney Town
Alvechurch	—	1-0	1-0	1-1	3-1	3-0	4-1	2-1	5-3	2-2	0-1	3-2	1-1	2-1	4-0	4-0	3-2	0-0	3-0	3-1	4-0	2-1
Banbury United	1-1	—	2-2	1-0	3-0	2-2	2-4	7-1	1-1	0-1	1-0	1-1	2-1	1-1	0-1	3-0	2-0	1-1	4-1	0-0	3-2	1-1
Barry Town	1-3	4-0	—	0-1	1-2	1-4	0-1	1-0	0-0	2-1	1-0	5-2	3-0	0-0	1-0	2-1	3-1	0-2	1-1	0-1	4-0	2-1
Bedford Town	1-0	2-1	1-0	—	1-0	2-2	0-0	4-1	2-0	1-0	2-2	3-2	2-0	0-1	4-0	0-0	1-0	3-1	2-1	0-2	1-0	2-2
Bedworth United	1-3	0-0	0-0	1-1	—	0-2	0-0	2-2	0-0	2-0	2-0	0-0	0-0	1-2	3-1	6-2	6-0	0-0	1-0	0-1	2-0	0-0
Bridgend Town	1-2	4-1	0-2	0-1	2-1	—	1-0	0-2	1-2	1-1	1-2	4-0	2-1	2-1	3-2	1-2	2-0	2-2	3-1	0-2	4-0	0-0
Bromsgrove Rovers	4-2	2-1	0-1	3-1	2-1	1-3	—	6-1	5-0	0-1	1-0	2-2	2-4	3-0	3-1	2-1	2-1	2-1	1-0	0-1	2-0	3-1
Cambridge City	0-0	1-1	1-1	1-3	1-3	1-1	3-0	—	2-1	0-0	1-1	1-3	2-2	2-2	1-0	0-3	0-5	0-4	2-0	2-1	3-0	1-3
Cheltenham Town	3-0	3-0	3-0	2-4	1-2	0-2	3-1	0-0	—	3-2	3-2	0-0	1-1	1-1	1-1	0-1	5-2	3-2	2-1	1-0	0-0	2-0
Corby Town	2-1	3-0	0-1	0-1	3-2	4-0	1-1	3-1	0-0	—	3-1	1-4	0-1	1-0	2-1	2-2	2-1	3-2	4-1	3-1	2-0	2-1
Enderby Town	0-1	2-0	2-2	0-2	1-1	2-0	1-1	2-0	1-2	4-1	—	2-1	0-1	3-1	4-0	0-0	4-2	3-2	2-1	1-1	4-1	1-0
Gloucester City	1-2	5-4	1-3	0-1	2-0	3-2	1-0	2-0	3-4	6-2	2-4	—	1-2	0-1	3-2	3-0	1-2	1-0	1-0	2-1	6-2	1-1
Kidderminster Harriers	3-2	1-0	0-1	2-0	1-0	3-4	1-1	3-0	1-0	1-0	2-1	3-1	—	0-3	1-0	4-0	2-0	2-3	0-0	2-0	4-0	0-0
Merthyr Tydfil	0-1	2-0	1-1	1-2	0-1	0-1	1-3	2-1	2-1	2-1	1-3	2-3	1-1	—	7-0	2-0	3-0	2-2	3-0	2-2	1-0	0-2
Milton Keynes City	0-1	0-1	0-2	0-0	2-3	1-2	1-1	4-1	0-5	1-7	0-3	0-3	0-1	2-1	—	0-1	2-2	0-1	1-1	0-0	0-2	1-4
Minehead	2-1	1-0	2-1	1-0	2-1	0-2	1-1	4-2	3-4	1-0	1-1	0-2	1-3	2-0	7-1	—	2-0	0-0	1-0	1-0	2-3	1-0
Redditch United*	1-2	2-1	1-2	0-4	2-1	1-1	1-0	0-0	0-2	3-1	1-2	1-3	2-3	1-1	3-2	0-2	—	1-4	1-4	2-3	2-0	3-2
Stourbridge	1-1	2-0	1-1	3-3	2-0	3-1	2-2	1-0	2-1	1-2	3-1	3-3	1-1	1-1	4-0	3-1	1-2	—	2-2	0-1	5-0	0-0
Taunton Town	0-1	2-0	0-2	1-1	1-1	2-4	2-1	1-1	1-1	0-3	0-2	2-0	0-3	0-4	2-0	1-2	4-2	1-1	—	3-1	6-0	2-0
Trowbridge Town	0-0	2-0	1-0	0-0	2-0	3-2	1-0	3-1	6-1	2-1	2-1	4-0	1-0	1-1	5-1	1-1	2-1	1-2	1-0	—	2-0	3-1
Wellingborough Town	0-1	3-0	1-3	0-1	0-1	4-3	1-0	3-5	1-1	1-1	0-3	2-1	1-5	2-2	0-0	3-0	4-1	0-2	3-1	2-2	—	1-1
Witney Town	0-0	2-3	1-3	0-2	0-1	3-2	0-1	3-1	1-4	3-1	0-2	0-4	2-0	0-1	3-0	1-0	1-2	1-2	0-2	2-5	0-1	—

* *Relegated from Alliance Premier League.*

SOUTHERN LEAGUE – SOUTHERN DIVISION 1980-81

	Addlestone and Weybridge Town	Andover	Ashford Town	Aylesbury United	Basingstoke Town	Bognor Regis Town	Canterbury City	Chelmsford City	Crawley Town	Dartford	Dorchester Town	Dover	Dunstable	Fareham Town	Folkestone	Gosport Borough	Hastings United	Hillingdon Borough	Hounslow	Margate	Poole Town	Salisbury	Tonbridge AFC	Waterlooville
Addlestone and Weybridge Town	—	3-0	1-0	1-0	0-2	3-2	1-0	3-2	3-1	1-3	2-2	5-0	2-0	1-2	1-0	1-1	4-0	1-1	2-1	0-0	1-1	2-0	0-1	1-1
Andover	2-4	—	3-1	2-0	0-2	1-6	0-0	0-1	2-1	0-0	2-2	1-3	2-0	2-0	0-3	0-1	3-3	0-1	0-1	2-3	1-1	0-0	0-0	1-1
Ashford Town	0-2	1-0	—	2-2	1-1	1-3	3-0	2-1	3-2	0-2	1-1	0-2	0-2	0-1	2-0	2-0	2-2	2-2	2-2	2-4	3-2	0-4	1-1	0-2
Aylesbury United	3-0	2-1	0-1	—	2-1	0-1	1-1	1-0	0-2	2-3	2-0	1-0	3-1	3-0	3-1	2-2	1-1	0-0	4-2	3-2	2-1	3-1	4-1	2-2
Basingstoke Town	1-2	2-0	2-1	1-1	—	1-4	0-2	0-1	0-1	1-3	2-2	0-0	2-2	3-0	2-0	2-2	2-2	1-2	3-0	3-2	2-3	1-0	6-0	2-3
Bognor Regis Town	1-0	2-0	6-0	0-0	1-1	—	0-0	4-0	3-0	2-2	1-0	2-1	2-2	4-0	3-1	2-0	0-1	0-1	1-1	3-0	3-1	2-0	1-1	0-1
Canterbury City	0-3	1-0	0-0	0-2	1-1	1-1	—	3-2	1-2	2-1	0-0	0-1	1-1	1-1	3-1	1-2	0-2	2-0	2-2	2-1	2-1	1-2	0-2	0-1
Chelmsford City	1-0	4-3	3-1	1-1	1-1	1-1	1-1	—	0-2	0-1	0-1	1-4	0-1	1-1	3-2	3-2	1-1	1-2	3-2	1-2	3-1	0-2	0-0	1-1
Crawley Town	1-1	2-0	1-1	1-3	1-0	4-3	3-2	5-1	—	1-2	0-6	5-2	0-3	3-0	2-1	0-4	1-0	2-1	0-3	8-1	1-2	1-2	0-1	0-3
Dartford	2-1	2-0	4-2	0-1	1-1	1-1	1-0	0-0	2-1	—	1-1	1-0	2-1	0-0	1-0	0-1	1-0	3-2	0-0	3-0	2-2	5-1	2-0	6-1
Dorchester Town	1-2	4-2	2-2	4-2	1-0	0-5	2-0	5-1	4-1	2-2	—	0-0	2-0	0-1	6-2	2-4	1-1	1-2	0-1	5-0	1-0	2-1	2-0	1-0
Dover	1-1	3-0	0-0	4-0	2-3	1-1	2-0	3-0	2-3	1-0	1-1	—	4-0	1-0	1-0	2-0	0-2	1-0	1-1	3-0	0-0	3-1	2-0	0-0
Dunstable	3-1	4-2	2-2	2-0	0-2	2-2	3-1	1-1	2-0	2-2	2-0	1-0	—	1-0	3-1	0-2	0-1	1-1	1-4	5-4	1-1	4-1	3-1	2-2
Fareham Town	1-3	1-3	1-3	0-2	0-4	1-4	1-1	0-1	0-0	0-0	0-1	1-3	1-2	—	1-0	2-4	0-2	1-1	1-1	1-1	1-1	1-1	0-1	0-1
Folkestone	2-1	2-2	0-1	1-0	1-0	0-1	3-1	3-1	0-0	1-0	0-2	4-2	3-2	0-0	—	1-0	1-1	1-2	0-3	1-2	0-1	0-0	2-3	1-1
Gosport Borough	2-0	5-0	3-2	3-0	2-1	1-0	4-1	3-1	1-0	1-3	1-3	2-1	1-1	1-1	1-1	—	0-2	1-0	5-3	1-1	1-1	3-0	3-1	7-2
Hastings United	1-1	3-0	2-1	4-0	4-0	2-1	2-0	2-1	4-0	2-1	4-1	2-0	0-0	0-0	1-4	2-0	—	1-1	3-0	1-2	3-0	6-0	1-1	6-0
Hillingdon Borough	0-1	2-1	0-1	1-0	0-1	2-3	0-0	0-2	3-0	1-1	0-2	4-2	0-0	2-2	0-0	0-0	4-2	—	0-0	3-1	0-3	1-0	2-0	1-1
Hounslow	5-1	1-0	3-0	0-1	1-1	2-3	1-2	2-0	2-1	0-2	1-1	1-2	1-0	0-2	2-1	0-1	1-1	1-2	—	3-1	1-0	5-1	0-0	0-1
Margate	4-1	4-1	1-4	3-2	1-4	0-0	0-1	2-3	2-1	1-2	0-5	0-1	1-3	2-0	1-1	3-2	1-3	1-3	1-3	—	2-5	0-0	1-3	2-2
Poole Town	1-0	5-0	0-0	2-2	1-1	2-1	1-0	1-2	1-0	1-2	2-1	1-3	2-3	1-1	1-0	0-0	1-1	1-0	1-0	4-2	—	2-0	5-0	3-3
Salisbury	2-1	3-1	2-0	1-3	2-0	1-3	0-2	3-1	0-3	0-1	1-2	4-2	1-2	2-2	0-0	0-2	0-2	2-0	0-1	7-1	1-2	—	3-0	0-0
Tonbridge AFC	0-1	1-1	0-0	2-0	1-2	2-4	0-1	1-1	0-1	2-3	3-1	0-2	4-2	2-2	1-1	1-1	2-1	0-0	0-0	3-2	0-1	1-3	—	0-0
Waterlooville	3-0	3-0	2-2	1-0	1-1	1-2	1-0	1-1	1-0	0-0	1-1	1-1	3-0	3-0	1-0	1-1	3-0	2-0	1-1	3-0	3-1	2-2	0-1	—

SOUTHERN LEAGUE 1980–81

SOUTHERN DIVISION

	P	W	D	L	F	A	Pts
Dartford	46	26	14	6	76	39	66
Bognor Regis Town	46	25	13	8	95	43	63
Hastings United	46	24	14	8	87	43	62
Gosport Borough	46	24	12	10	84	52	60
Waterlooville	46	19	21	6	67	50	59
Dorchester Town	46	21	13	12	84	56	55
Dover	46	22	10	14	70	50	54
Poole Town	46	19	14	13	70	56	52
Addlestone & Weybridge T	46	21	9	16	66	57	51
Dunstable	46	19	13	14	73	68	51
Aylesbury United	46	20	10	16	66	60	50
Hounslow	46	17	13	16	65	55	47
Hillingdon Borough	46	16	15	15	50	49	47
Basingstoke Town	46	16	14	16	69	58	46
Crawley Town	46	18	4	24	64	78	40
Ashford Town	46	12	15	19	55	76	39
Tonbridge AFC	46	12	15	19	44	68	39
Chelmsford City	46	13	12	21	54	78	38
Canterbury City	46	12	13	21	40	59	37
Salisbury	46	14	8	24	57	76	36
Folkestone	46	11	11	24	47	65	33
Margate	46	11	7	28	65	117	29
Fareham Town	46	5	18	23	31	73	28
Andover	46	6	10	30	41	94	22

Leading Goalscorers
(League and League Cup)
33 Finneston (Addlestone & Weybridge T)
28 Juliens (Dartford)
26 Batten (Hastings U)
25 Clements (Bognor Regis T)
23 Mulhern (Crawley T)
22 Cooper (Bognor Regis T)

MIDLAND DIVISION

	P	W	D	L	F	A	Pts
Alvechurch	42	26	9	7	76	40	61
Bedford Town	42	25	11	6	63	32	61
Trowbridge Town	42	24	9	9	69	39	57
Kidderminster Harriers	42	23	9	10	67	41	55
Barry Town	42	21	9	12	60	40	51
Stourbridge	42	17	16	9	75	49	50
Enderby Town	42	21	8	13	71	47	50
Cheltenham Town	42	18	12	12	70	59	48
Bromsgrove Rovers	42	19	9	14	65	50	47
Corby Town	42	19	7	16	69	58	45
Bridgend Town	42	19	7	16	74	64	45
Minehead	42	19	7	16	54	60	45
Gloucester City	42	19	6	17	82	72	44
Merthyr Tydfil	42	15	12	15	60	50	42
Bedworth United	42	14	12	16	49	46	40
Banbury United	42	11	11	20	51	65	33
Taunton Town	42	10	9	23	48	68	29
Cambridge City	42	8	12	22	46	87	28
Witney Town	42	9	9	24	44	65	27
Wellingborough Town	42	10	7	25	43	91	27
Redditch United	42	11	4	27	54	92	26
Milton Keynes City	42	3	7	32	28	103	13

Leading Goalscorers
(League and League Cup)
27 Lewis (Gloucester C)
26 Campbell (Bedford T)
23 Wright (Kidderminster Harriers)
22 Johnson (Enderby T)

OTHER LEAGUE TABLES 1980–81

ATHENIAN LEAGUE

	P	W	D	L	F	A	Pts
Windsor & Eton	38	27	6	5	100	32	60
Basildon U	38	24	11	3	71	24	59
Banstead Ath	38	23	10	5	73	32	56
Grays Ath	38	23	7	8	81	42	53
Edgware	38	20	8	10	77	38	48
Leyton-Wingate	38	18	12	8	72	46	48
Welling U	38	19	8	11	62	48	46
Woodford T	38	18	9	11	84	53	45
Burnham	38	20	4	14	62	45	44
Harefield U	38	16	10	12	67	51	42
Ruislip Manor	38	14	13	11	49	51	41
Uxbridge	38	11	13	14	38	39	35
Fleet T	38	8	13	17	50	65	29
Haringey Bor	38	9	10	19	41	68	28
Redhill	38	8	11	19	45	59	27
Hoddesdon T	38	10	6	22	53	80	26
Chertsey T	38	9	7	22	30	84	25
Marlow	38	7	10	21	43	85	24
Chalfont St Peter	38	5	5	28	39	89	15
Alton T	38	2	5	31	33	139	9

THE CENTRAL LEAGUE

	P	W	D	L	F	A	Pts
Liverpool	42	29	9	4	98	26	67
WBA	42	22	14	6	68	31	58
Newcastle U	42	23	9	10	74	40	55
Wolverhampton W	42	21	13	8	67	40	55
Manchester C	42	17	18	7	74	51	52
Aston Villa	42	20	11	11	79	54	51
Nottingham F	42	19	11	12	60	43	49
Everton	42	17	11	14	58	53	45
Burnley	42	16	12	14	45	45	44
Coventry C	42	16	10	16	75	74	42
Sheffield W	42	15	10	17	52	60	40
Leeds U	42	10	20	12	42	56	40
Bury	42	14	11	17	53	58	39
Stoke C	42	14	11	17	51	57	39
Manchester U	42	11	16	15	47	54	38
Preston NE	42	12	12	18	51	72	36
Huddersfield T	42	11	12	19	40	48	34
Sheffield U	42	9	16	17	44	61	34
Derby Co	42	9	14	19	57	65	32
Bolton W	42	9	9	24	40	85	27
Blackpool	42	6	12	24	28	85	24
Blackburn R	42	7	9	26	33	78	23

CHESHIRE COUNTY LEAGUE

DIVISION ONE

	P	W	D	L	F	A	Pts
Nantwich T	38	26	6	6	87	34	58
Hyde U	38	23	9	6	75	27	55
Winsford U	38	20	10	8	75	38	50
Formby	38	21	7	10	65	39	49
Stalybridge Celtic	38	16	15	7	62	50	47
Chorley	38	17	11	10	65	48	45
Bootle	38	18	7	13	68	53	43
Prescot Cables	38	16	9	13	60	46	41
Horwich RMI	38	15	9	14	53	49	39
Leek T	38	15	9	14	50	47	39
Ashton U	38	12	12	14	70	73	36
Curzon Ashton	38	14	8	16	48	63	36
St Helens T	38	14	7	17	63	82	35
Fleetwood T	38	9	13	16	33	53	31
Rossendale U	38	9	12	17	49	69	30
Burscough	38	11	6	21	52	62	28
Darwen	38	8	10	20	46	74	26
Droylsden	38	9	8	21	49	82	26
Kirkby T	38	6	11	21	30	65	23
New Mills	38	8	7	23	34	80	23

DIVISION TWO

	P	W	D	L	F	A	Pts
Accrington Stanley	38	26	3	9	73	20	55
Glossop	38	23	9	6	76	38	55
Leyland Motors	38	20	10	8	68	42	50
Middlewich Ath	38	20	10	8	56	32	50
Atherton LR	38	19	11	8	61	39	49
Prescot BI	38	20	5	13	59	40	45
Rhyl	38	20	5	13	69	57	45
Maghull	38	15	12	11	55	41	42
Ford Motors	38	16	9	13	49	52	41
Congleton T	38	16	8	14	67	55	40
Radcliffe Bor	38	15	10	13	58	48	40
Irlam T	38	15	6	17	49	51	36
Warrington T	38	15	5	18	59	78	35
Prestwich Heys	38	15	4	19	66	68	34
Salford	38	9	13	16	50	70	31
Eastwood (Hanley)	38	12	6	20	47	55	30
Skelmersdale U	38	9	10	19	51	68	28
Atherton Collieries	38	8	5	25	39	83	21
Ashton T	38	6	5	27	40	93	17
New Brighton	38	6	4	28	31	93	16

ESSEX SENIOR LEAGUE

	P	W	D	L	F	A	Pts
Bowers	32	22	8	2	73	31	52
Heybridge	32	20	7	5	69	27	47
Wivenhoe	32	20	5	7	67	34	45
Canvey Island	32	14	13	5	53	35	41
Witham	32	13	12	7	54	30	38
Brentwood	32	15	7	10	52	43	37
Maldon	32	13	7	12	48	47	33
Sawbridgeworth	32	10	11	11	45	41	31
Stansted	32	10	10	12	43	46	30
Ford	32	10	10	12	47	55	30
East Ham	32	8	11	13	33	48	27
East Thurrock	32	9	9	14	34	50	27
Brightlingsea	32	10	4	18	33	52	24
Coggeshall	32	9	5	18	44	71	23
Chelmsford	32	7	8	17	38	59	22
Halstead	32	6	7	19	42	82	19
Eton Manor	32	6	6	20	32	56	18

THE FOOTBALL COMBINATION

	P	W	D	L	F	A	Pts
Southampton	42	27	7	8	100	45	61
Tottenham H	42	22	13	7	99	56	57
Norwich C	42	23	10	9	77	43	56
Ipswich T	42	19	16	7	66	38	54
Plymouth Arg	42	21	12	9	73	54	54
Arsenal	42	20	13	9	68	48	53
Birmingham C	42	18	14	10	60	41	50
Chelsea	42	21	7	14	80	58	49
QPR	42	19	9	14	80	64	47
Leicester C	42	18	9	15	71	58	45
Crystal Palace	42	18	9	15	74	64	45
Luton T	42	17	10	15	63	55	44
West Ham U	42	15	10	17	81	63	40
Bristol R	42	11	12	19	45	63	34
Fulham	42	10	14	18	33	64	34
Oxford U	42	11	9	22	47	81	31
Bristol C	42	12	6	24	37	65	30
Orient	42	11	8	23	48	78	30
Reading	42	12	6	24	50	87	30
Hereford U	42	8	12	22	41	91	28
Swindon T	42	11	4	27	44	91	26
Cardiff C	42	6	12	24	39	69	24

GLOUCESTERSHIRE COUNTY LEAGUE

	P	W	D	L	F	A	Pts
Almondsbury Greenway	34	27	5	1	108	45	58
Shortwood U	34	23	3	8	73	37	49
Wilton R	34	22	4	8	72	43	48
Port of Bristol	34	17	9	8	65	45	43
Matson Ath	34	18	5	10	85	54	41
Sharpness	34	13	11	10	49	39	37
Imm Bristol St George	34	14	9	11	51	44	37
Lydbrook Ath	34	12	12	10	55	53	36
Gloucester City Res	34	16	4	14	63	71	36
Frampton U	34	15	5	14	59	56	35
Yate Town	34	15	4	15	62	55	34
Hambrook	34	15	4	15	52	51	34
Newent T	34	11	9	14	49	57	31
Oldland	34	8	12	14	39	57	28
Hanham Ath	34	9	2	23	47	79	20
Old Georgians	34	5	7	22	26	64	17
Cadbury Heath	34	5	7	22	27	68	17
Stonehouse	34	3	5	26	43	107	11

HAMPSHIRE LEAGUE

DIVISION ONE

	P	W	D	L	F	A	Pts
Newport	38	30	3	5	106	32	63
AFC Totton	38	21	9	8	81	33	51
Sholing Sports	38	20	11	7	56	24	51
Southampton A	38	18	14	6	70	45	50
Eastleigh	38	16	9	13	47	42	41
Horndean	38	15	10	13	51	60	40
Brockenhurst	38	16	7	15	52	50	39
Romsey	38	13	12	13	58	51	38
Havant T	38	13	10	15	50	65	36
Fareham T	38	12	11	15	54	51	35
Gosport Bor	38	11	13	14	46	52	35
Downton	38	12	11	15	48	63	35
Waterlooville	38	12	10	16	36	46	34
Pirelli General	38	14	6	18	51	62	34
Moneyfield Sports	38	12	10	16	50	69	34
East Cowes Vics	38	13	6	19	53	61	32
Brading T	38	11	10	17	40	69	32
Netley Central Sports	38	8	13	17	33	50	29
BAT	38	8	12	18	43	62	28
Bournemouth	38	5	13	20	43	81	23

HELLENIC LEAGUE

PREMIER DIVISION

	P	W	D	L	F	A	Pts
Newbury T	30	23	4	3	75	27	50
Thame U	30	17	8	5	51	22	42
Hazells	30	16	8	6	53	36	40
Moreton T	30	15	8	7	72	35	38
Flackwell Heath	30	13	8	9	47	30	34
Abingdon T	30	13	8	9	48	37	34
Forest Green R	30	14	6	10	57	53	34
Fairford T	30	15	2	13	47	42	32
Didcot T	30	9	9	12	36	47	27
Maidenhead T	30	10	5	15	42	48	25
Bicester T	30	7	11	12	41	60	25
Northwood	30	6	10	14	37	52	22
Kidlington	30	8	6	16	32	55	22
Wallingford T	30	8	5	17	43	73	21
Morris Motors	30	7	6	17	36	57	20
Abingdon U	30	5	4	21	31	74	14

KENT LEAGUE

	P	W	D	L	F	A	Pts
Cray Wanderers	32	24	5	3	92	27	53
Chatham T	32	22	6	4	61	23	50
Crockenhill	32	20	5	7	63	37	45
Erith & Belvedere	32	19	5	8	57	30	43
Sittingbourne	32	18	5	9	74	29	41
Hythe T	32	18	5	9	70	45	41
Sheppey U	32	16	9	7	45	33	41
Faversham T	32	12	11	9	36	28	35
Tunbridge Wells	32	10	9	13	33	49	29
Darenth Heathside	32	9	10	13	45	52	28
Deal T	32	10	7	15	46	49	27
Dartford Glentworth	32	11	3	18	40	60	25
Slade Green*	32	10	5	17	39	51	23
Whitstable T	32	7	7	18	33	58	21
Kent Police	32	5	9	18	43	67	19
Herne Bay	32	4	6	22	23	67	14
Ramsgate	32	2	3	27	26	121	7

** 2 points deducted for playing ineligible player.*

LANCASHIRE COMBINATION

	P	W	D	L	F	A	Pts
Wren R	34	24	7	3	75	25	55
Colne Dynamoes	34	21	5	8	57	30	47
Great Harwood T	34	18	7	9	68	42	43
Padiham*	34	16	11	7	57	40	41
Chorley Res	34	15	11	8	53	42	41
Caernarfon T	34	15	7	12	55	37	37
Vulcan Newton	34	15	6	13	53	44	36
Lytham	34	14	8	12	51	45	36
Clitheroe	34	14	7	13	42	36	35
Chadderton	34	14	7	13	58	64	35
Whitworth Valley	34	13	8	13	50	54	34
Wigan R	34	13	8	13	50	60	34
Daisy Hill	34	12	9	13	52	48	33
Bacup Bor	34	9	11	14	47	57	29
Ashton Ath	34	9	6	19	47	73	24
Blackpool Mechanics	34	6	11	17	32	57	23
Nelson	34	7	3	24	29	60	17
Manchester Poly	34	2	6	26	24	86	10

** 2 points deducted.*

LEICESTERSHIRE SENIOR LEAGUE

DIVISION ONE

	P	W	D	L	F	A	Pts
Shepshed Charterhouse	30	23	3	4	77	20	49
Anstey Nomads	30	22	3	5	83	24	47
Wigston Fields	30	21	5	4	66	27	47
Birstall U	30	17	5	8	64	29	39
Oadby Town	30	16	6	8	53	36	38
Melton Town	30	13	8	9	46	38	34
Earl Shilton A	30	12	9	9	68	42	33
Friar Lane OB	30	14	4	12	52	52	32
Enderby Res	30	10	9	11	45	49	29
Hinckley T	30	11	5	14	46	57	27
Harborough T	30	8	7	15	41	52	23
Stapenhill	30	7	7	16	43	59	21
Thringstone MW	30	8	4	18	22	46	20
Quorn	30	7	4	19	35	81	18
Newfoundpool WMC	30	6	4	20	29	69	16
Ibstock Pen R	30	2	3	25	15	104	7

LONDON SPARTAN LEAGUE

PREMIER DIVISION

	P	W	D	L	F	A	Pts
Fisher Ath	30	22	3	5	56	18	47
Malden Vale	30	18	7	5	63	30	43
Whyteleafe	30	14	12	4	59	31	40
Greenwich Bor	30	12	12	6	52	43	36
Kingsbury T	30	15	5	10	50	39	35
Merstham	30	12	10	8	39	33	34
Waltham Abbey	30	11	10	9	37	29	32
Berkhamsted T	30	10	11	9	40	42	31
Alma Swanley	30	13	3	14	52	56	29
Horley T	30	7	12	11	30	39	26
Beckton U	30	8	9	13	36	51	25
Swanley T	30	9	6	15	57	63	24
Amersham T	30	8	8	14	32	46	24
Beckenham T	30	8	6	16	32	48	22
Chingford	30	7	4	19	33	60	18
Chobham	30	4	6	20	23	63	14

MIDLAND COUNTIES LEAGUE

PREMIER DIVISION

	P	W	D	L	F	A	Pts
Boston FC	34	23	9	2	70	18	55
Alfreton T	34	16	10	8	73	40	42
Eastwood T	34	16	9	9	63	41	41
Bridlington Tr	34	15	10	9	62	40	40
Guisborough T	34	16	7	11	60	48	39
Belper T	34	15	8	11	44	43	38
Arnold FC	34	14	8	12	55	47	36
Heanor T	34	13	10	11	57	52	36
Skegness T	34	12	11	11	49	52	35
Long Eaton U	34	13	8	13	54	51	34
Appleby Frodingham	34	12	10	12	56	56	34
Sutton T	34	12	10	12	48	51	34
Mexborough T	34	12	5	17	42	67	29
Spalding U	34	10	7	17	28	47	27
Ashby FC	34	12	3	19	40	60	27
Ilkeston T	34	7	9	18	44	65	23
Brigg T	34	6	10	18	42	63	22
Kimberley T	34	6	8	20	34	81	20

MIDLAND FOOTBALL COMBINATION

DIVISION ONE

	P	W	D	L	F	A	Pts
Moor Green	38	28	7	3	109	30	63
Bridgnorth T	38	22	7	9	76	38	51
Mile Oak R	38	21	8	9	63	43	50
Cinderford T	38	22	5	11	68	30	49
Boldmere St Michaels	38	18	11	9	50	39	47
Oldbury U	38	18	10	10	65	47	46
Chipping Norton T	38	16	11	11	58	45	43
Racing Club Warwick	38	16	10	12	66	46	42
Knowle	38	16	10	12	50	42	42
Hurley Daw Mill	38	14	11	13	54	56	39
Highgate U	38	16	6	16	79	61	38
West Midlands Police	38	11	15	12	62	58	37
Paget R	38	13	11	14	42	41	37
Solihull Bor	38	13	10	15	58	69	36
Evesham U	38	10	10	18	57	81	30
Walsall Sportsco	38	8	12	18	49	69	28
Walsall Wood	38	10	8	20	42	71	28
Smethwick Highfield	38	8	10	20	37	74	26
Cradley T	38	5	4	29	33	100	14
Coleshill T	38	5	4	29	27	104	14

SOUTH MIDLANDS LEAGUE

PREMIER DIVISION

	P	W	D	L	F	A	Pts
Stotfold	34	19	11	4	64	32	49
Pirton	34	19	9	6	66	32	47
Baldock T	34	17	8	9	58	36	42
Vauxhall Motors	34	17	8	9	54	39	42
Arlesey T	34	16	9	9	54	38	41
Sandy Alb	34	15	9	10	60	45	39
Winslow U	34	15	9	10	53	45	39
Royston T	34	13	9	12	61	49	35
Shillington	34	13	8	13	52	49	34
Selby	34	9	14	11	49	55	32
Waterlows	34	12	6	16	50	48	30
Harpenden T	34	12	5	17	53	68	29
Walden R	34	11	6	17	51	61	28
Hatfield T	34	11	6	17	52	70	28
BAC	34	11	5	18	40	73	27
Biggleswade T	34	10	6	18	54	72	26
Leighton T	34	9	6	19	43	66	24
New Bradwell St Peter	34	5	10	19	37	73	20

WEST MIDLANDS (REGIONAL) LEAGUE

PREMIER DIVISION

	P	W	D	L	F	A	Pts
Shifnal T	42	31	7	4	89	33	69
Lye Town	42	27	9	6	80	36	63
Willenhall T	42	25	11	6	93	41	61
Brereton Social	42	22	8	12	74	51	52
Hednesford T	42	20	11	11	73	48	51
Coventry Sporting	42	19	12	11	75	54	50
Ledbury T	42	19	10	13	74	52	48
Dudley T	42	19	10	13	55	44	48
Sutton Coldfield T	42	18	10	14	71	56	46
Bilston	42	18	10	14	78	65	46
Armitage	42	20	5	17	58	59	45
Rushall Olympic	42	15	13	14	50	52	43
Blakenall	42	14	15	13	55	58	43
Darlaston	42	17	5	20	68	95	39
Gresley R	42	13	10	19	46	62	36
Halesowen T	42	10	15	17	53	67	35
Wednesfield Social	42	11	11	20	52	67	33
VS Rugby	42	9	10	23	50	80	28
Tividale	42	5	17	20	35	64	27
Malvern T	42	9	7	26	56	93	25
Brierley Hill All	42	6	8	28	33	85	20
Hinckley Ath	42	3	10	29	43	99	16

NORTHERN ALLIANCE

	P	W	D	L	F	A	Pts
Percy Main Amateurs	30	23	6	1	97	38	52
Ryhope CA	30	20	4	6	67	38	44
Bedlington Terriers	30	18	7	5	70	26	43
Forest Hall	30	19	5	6	67	33	43
Stockton Buffs	30	14	10	6	49	30	35
Dudley Welfare	30	13	9	8	58	48	35
Carlisle C	30	14	7	9	50	48	35
Wigton	30	11	8	11	46	37	30
High Pit SC	30	11	4	15	54	57	26
Stobswood Welfare	30	9	8	13	31	54	26
Sunderland Pyrex	30	6	10	14	40	62	22
Shotton Comrades	30	8	4	18	37	55	20
Cramlington Newtown	30	8	4	18	33	73	20
Alnwick T	30	3	12	15	44	66	18
Wallington	30	4	7	19	44	78	15
Morpeth T	30	5	2	23	41	93	13

NORTHERN LEAGUE

	P	W	D	L	F	A	Pts
Blyth Spartans	38	27	5	6	89	35	86
Spennymoor U	38	26	7	5	82	38	85
Bishop Auckland	38	22	7	9	68	36	73
Tow Law T	38	18	13	7	83	54	67
Ashington	38	17	12	9	95	66	63
Ferryhill Ath	38	17	10	11	71	49	61
Shildon	38	17	8	13	56	54	59
South Bank	38	16	9	13	55	44	57
Billingham Synthonia	38	13	15	10	52	51	54
Penrith	38	15	8	15	75	66	53
Whitby T	38	15	7	16	55	59	52
Horden Colliery Welfare	38	12	9	17	48	65	45
Consett	38	12	6	20	49	54	42
North Shields	38	10	10	18	56	71	40
Evenwood T	38	10	10	18	41	66	40
West Auckland T	38	10	10	18	40	67	40
Durham C	38	9	11	18	46	74	38
Crook T	38	10	8	20	47	79	38
Whitley Bay	38	9	7	22	53	72	34
Willington	38	6	6	26	41	102	24

SOUTH-EAST COUNTIES

SENIOR LEAGUE

	P	W	D	L	F	A	Pts
Tottenham H	30	23	3	4	96	40	49
Watford	30	18	7	5	62	41	43
Arsenal	30	15	7	8	49	35	37
Ipswich T	30	14	8	8	55	34	36
Charlton Ath	30	14	7	9	45	38	35
QPR	30	13	8	9	47	46	34
Norwich C	30	13	6	11	44	40	32
West Ham U	30	13	5	12	59	44	31
Chelsea	30	11	7	12	38	39	29
Gillingham*	30	10	6	14	31	42	24
Millwall	30	7	10	13	35	51	24
Fulham	30	8	7	15	39	51	23
Orient	30	9	4	17	41	61	22
Crystal Palace*	30	7	7	16	30	52	19
Portsmouth†	30	10	1	19	44	65	18
Southend U	30	5	7	18	32	68	17

** 2 points deducted.*
† 3 points deducted.

SOUTH-WESTERN LEAGUE

	P	*W*	*D*	*L*	*F*	*A*	*Pts*
St Blazey	38	26	8	4	71	24	60
Torrington	38	23	7	8	74	73	53
Newquay	38	20	10	8	67	38	50
Wadebridge	38	21	8	9	73	44	50
Plymouth Civil Service	38	17	12	9	69	44	46
Appledore	38	16	11	11	63	45	43
Torpoint	38	17	7	14	64	63	41
Penzance	38	16	7	15	77	62	39
Holsworthy	38	12	14	12	49	49	38
Millbrook	38	12	13	13	56	54	37
Bugle	38	14	9	15	58	58	37
Plymouth Arg	38	16	4	18	68	63	36
Truro C*	38	14	9	15	55	68	36
Newton Abbot	38	13	8	17	42	53	34
Launceston	38	12	7	19	60	65	31
Tavistock	38	10	10	18	40	63	30
Plymouth Command*	38	11	8	19	60	79	28
St Austell	38	7	10	21	49	90	24
Bodmin Town	38	6	10	22	41	77	22
Illogan RBL	38	6	10	22	36	90	22

* *Points adjusted.*

SUSSEX COUNTY LEAGUE

DIVISION ONE

	P	*W*	*D*	*L*	*F*	*A*	*Pts*
Pagham	30	18	9	3	52	22	45
Peacehaven & Telscombe	30	16	10	4	53	28	42
Steyning T	30	15	10	5	61	37	40
Hastings T	30	14	8	8	64	35	36
Southwick	30	10	13	7	42	35	33
Burgess Hill T	30	9	14	7	37	29	32
Three Bridges	30	12	7	11	44	39	31
Arundel	30	11	7	12	34	27	29
Shoreham	30	9	10	11	40	50	28
Chichester C	30	8	11	11	47	47	27
Littlehampton T	30	10	7	13	42	43	27
Ringmer	30	9	9	12	45	54	27
Eastbourne T	30	10	6	14	36	41	26
Horsham YMCA	30	8	9	13	35	55	25
Portfield	30	5	9	16	29	68	19
Bexhill T	30	5	3	23	23	74	13

TOWN AND COUNTRY LEAGUE

	P	*W*	*D*	*L*	*F*	*A*	*Pts*
Gorleston	42	32	7	3	98	33	71
Sudbury T	42	28	8	6	99	37	64
Tiptree U	42	23	10	9	81	52	56
Ely C	42	21	13	8	100	48	55
Great Yarmouth T	42	22	9	11	95	59	53
March Town U	42	20	12	10	63	47	52
Saffron Walden T	42	17	14	11	70	56	48
Lowestoft T	42	15	15	12	69	30	45
Bury T	42	16	11	15	66	62	43
Newmarket T	42	17	8	17	64	76	42
Wisbech T	42	16	9	17	73	74	41
Stowmarket	42	14	11	17	63	79	39
Colchester United Res	42	15	8	19	85	72	38
Brantham Ath	42	12	14	16	61	61	38
Clacton T	42	13	12	17	50	60	38
Felixstowe T	42	13	8	21	56	81	34
Braintree & Crittall Ath	42	12	10	20	43	74	34
Soham Town R	42	8	17	17	38	68	33
Thetford T	42	10	12	20	54	91	32
Haverhill R	42	9	12	21	44	55	30
Chatteris T	42	7	7	28	50	117	21
Histon	42	3	12	27	36	96	18

UNITED COUNTIES LEAGUE

PREMIER DIVISION

	P	*W*	*D*	*L*	*F*	*A*	*Pts*
Stamford AFC	34	22	9	3	76	36	53
Wootton Blue Cross	34	23	4	7	81	33	50
Kempston R	34	22	3	9	96	54	47
Holbeach U	34	21	5	8	59	43	47
Desborough T	34	18	9	7	79	55	45
Long Buckby AFC	34	15	12	7	70	54	42
Rushden T	34	16	7	11	57	33	39
Potton U	34	15	8	11	48	41	38
Irthlingborough Diamonds	34	15	5	14	60	54	35
Stewart & Lloyds (Corby)	34	13	9	12	53	51	35
Buckingham T	34	13	8	13	48	45	34
Wolverton T	34	11	9	14	49	70	31
St Neots T	34	9	6	19	35	61	24
Bourne T	34	7	9	18	41	64	23
Rothwell T	34	6	10	18	37	58	22
Ampthill T	34	6	10	18	39	69	22
Eymesbury R	34	7	7	20	37	71	21
Northampton Spencer	34	1	2	31	21	94	4

WEARSIDE LEAGUE

	P	*W*	*D*	*L*	*F*	*A*	*Pts*
Chester-le-Street	38	28	9	1	79	13	65
Whickham	38	29	6	3	95	33	64
Blue Star	38	25	8	5	94	40	58
Reyrolles	38	22	7	9	83	49	51
Peterlee Newtown	38	20	10	8	59	34	50
South Shields	38	17	9	12	97	58	43
Hartlepool Res	38	15	13	10	54	45	43
Seaham CW Red Star	38	17	6	15	61	48	40
Heaton Stannington	38	14	8	16	64	64	36
Wallsend T	38	11	10	17	63	73	32
Ryhope CW	38	12	8	18	47	68	32
Roker Zanussi	38	12	7	19	56	64	31
Annfield Plain	38	13	5	20	53	83	31
Wingate	38	10	10	18	49	73	30
Eppleton CW	38	9	10	19	37	59	28
Stockton FC	38	11	6	21	39	84	28
Murton FC	38	11	5	22	55	79	27
Boldon CA	38	8	11	19	39	65	27
Washington	38	6	13	19	38	86	25
Easington CW	38	8	3	27	41	85	19

WESTERN LEAGUE

PREMIER DIVISION

	P	*W*	*D*	*L*	*F*	*A*	*Pts*
Bridgwater T	38	25	6	7	54	25	56
Barnstaple T	38	22	6	10	58	40	50
Frome T	38	21	6	11	74	51	48
Falmouth T	38	18	9	11	71	53	45
Bideford	38	18	8	12	58	42	44
Saltash U	38	17	9	12	73	47	43
Portway-Bristol	38	16	11	11	55	45	43
Clevedon T	38	15	11	12	65	52	41
Clandown	38	16	9	13	60	53	41
Devizes T	38	14	13	11	61	56	41
Bridport	38	12	15	11	56	52	39
Keynsham T	38	12	15	11	33	34	39
Melksham T	38	13	11	14	45	49	37
Liskeard Ath	38	11	11	16	58	70	33
Mangotsfield U	38	8	15	15	43	66	31
Dawlish	38	7	16	15	40	50	30
Welton R	38	9	11	18	50	69	29
Weston-super-Mare	38	11	7	20	42	61	29
Paulton R	38	9	11	18	45	72	29
Tiverton T	38	1	10	27	23	77	12

FIRST DIVISION

	P	*W*	*D*	*L*	*F*	*A*	*Pts*
Chippenham T	36	25	8	3	76	24	58
Wellington	36	22	8	6	80	36	52
Exmouth T	36	22	7	7	74	37	51
Bath C	36	19	11	6	79	44	49
Odd Down*	36	20	8	8	59	41	47
Yeovil T	36	18	9	9	58	38	45
Torquay U	36	16	11	9	60	35	43
Swanage Town & Herston	36	13	11	12	58	55	37
Chard T	36	11	14	11	42	38	36
Bristol Manor Farm	36	14	8	14	53	57	36
Shepton Mallet T	36	13	8	15	68	75	34
Elmore	36	12	10	14	44	53	34
Glastonbury	36	9	10	17	44	60	28
Brixham U	36	11	5	20	50	70	27
Larkhall Ath	36	5	12	19	44	76	22
Ottery St Mary	36	7	8	21	37	77	22
Heavitree U	36	7	8	21	40	86	22
Ilminster T	36	7	6	23	39	70	20
Radstock T	36	8	4	24	47	80	20

** 1 point deducted for playing an ineligible player.*

YORKSHIRE LEAGUE

DIVISION ONE

	P	*W*	*D*	*L*	*F*	*A*	*Pts*
Leeds Ashley Road	30	18	8	4	58	25	44
Emley	30	17	8	5	61	36	42
North Ferriby U	30	16	8	6	40	23	40
Thackley	30	14	7	9	48	39	35
Guiseley	30	10	12	8	48	41	32
Winterton R	30	12	8	10	35	31	32
Scarborough	30	13	5	12	55	49	31
Frecheville CA	30	10	11	9	41	38	31
Hallam	30	11	7	12	42	39	29
Liversedge	30	11	7	12	35	49	29
Barton T	30	8	10	12	39	41	26
Sheffield	30	9	8	13	24	41	26
Bentley VW	30	9	7	14	47	47	25
Maltby MW	30	9	7	14	37	41	25
Kiveton Park	30	9	7	14	40	50	25
Bridlington T	30	1	6	23	12	72	8

DIVISION TWO

	P	*W*	*D*	*L*	*F*	*A*	*Pts*
Ossett Albion	30	15	8	7	46	30	38
York RI	30	13	10	7	52	46	36
Lincoln U	30	10	14	6	48	40	34
Farsley Celtic	30	12	10	8	36	28	34
Garforth Miners	30	12	9	9	49	42	33
Pilkington Recs	30	12	9	9	48	42	33
BSC (Parkgate)	30	11	9	10	31	35	31
Harworth CI	30	10	10	10	46	40	30
Norton Woodseats	30	11	7	12	34	31	29
Yorkshire Amateur	30	8	13	9	36	40	29
Hall Road R	30	7	14	9	37	44	28
Ossett T	30	11	5	14	37	41	27
Fryston CW	30	11	5	14	34	40	27
Hatfield Main	30	8	11	11	36	43	27
Thorne Colliery	30	9	5	16	44	53	23
Rawmarsh Welfare	30	4	13	13	27	46	21

FA VASE 1980–81

Preliminary Round

Percy Main Amateur v Darlington RA	0-1
Gretna v Annfield Plain	3-1
Wallsend Town v Carlisle City	1-0
Chester-le-Street v Billingham Social	3-1
Wingate v Ryhope CA	4-3
Teesside Poly v Cleator Moor Celtic	0-1
Washington v Eppleton CW	1-2
Stockton Buffs v Haig Colliery	aet 0-0
Heaton Stannington v Brandon United	1-1
South Shields v Nunthorpe Athletic	2-1
Peterlee Newtown v Appleby	6-1
Ryhope CW v Pickering Town	1-2
Redcar Albion v Boldon CA	1-2
Norton CCT v Harrogate Town	1-0
Hartlepool BW v Fryston Colliery	3-2
Old Blackburnians v Clitheroe	2-5
Guiseley v Dalton United	4-2
Yorkshire Amateur v Prestwich Heys	2-0
Wren Rovers v North Withington	4-0
Skelmersdale Utd v Blackpool Mechanics	4-0
HB & H Newtown v Atherton Collieries	0-1
Maghull v Blackpool Rangers	3-2
Brook Sports v Bacup Borough	0-1
Padiham v Hoylake Athletic	2-4
Leyland Motors v Chadderton	3-2
Salford v Linotype	2-0
Ossett Town v Burnley Belvedere	3-2
Wythenshawe Amateurs v Warrington Town	5-2
Waterloo Dock v Heswall	4-2
Whalley Range v Irlam Town	0-2
Stork v Abbey Hey WMC	aet 1-2
Rylands v Milton United	4-0
Prescot BI v GKN Sankey	5-1
Staveley Works v Birkenshaw Rovers	8-0
Kiveton Park v Barton Town	1-0
Retford Town v Bradley Rangers	
(*Retford Town withdrew, Bradley received w.o.*)	
Hall Road Rangers v Appleby Frodingham	1-2
Oakham United v Immingham Town	1-0
North Ferriby United v Hatfield Main	5-0
Woolley MW v Kimberley Town	1-6
Normanby PW v Harworth CI	1-2
Ruston Sports v Denaby United	1-3
Glossop v Arnold Kingswell	4-1
Louth United v Clay Cross Works	4-0
Clipstone Welfare v BSC (Parkgate)	2-1
Rainworth MW v Mile Oak Rovers & Youth	0-1
Newfoundpool WMC v Long Eaton Grange	2-3
Middlewich Ath v Boldmere St Michaels	2-0
Kidsgrove Athletic v Blakenall	0-2
Quorn v Gresley Rovers	0-2
Paget Rangers v Eastwood (Hanley)	0-1
Stapenhill v Bridgnorth Town	2-1
Rushall Olympic v Armitage	0-1
Shifnal Town v Northfield Town	3-1
Oadby Town v Gornal Athletic	4-0
Northampton Spencer v Brierley Hill All	0-2
Coleshill Town v Anstey Nomads	0-5
Moreton Town v Coventry Sporting	0-1
Knowle v Birstall United	0-2
Tividale v Mirrlees Blackstone	2-1
Oldbury United v Hinckley Town	0-1
Rothwell Town v Oldswinford	aet 1-0
Racing Club Warwick v Melton Town	aet 2-5
VS Rugby v Solihull Borough	0-2
Thringstone MW v Huntingdon United	2-1
Wednesfield Social v Pegasus Juniors	2-0
Walsall Wood v Lydney Town	aet 1-1
Watton Town v Holbeach United	3-2
Langford v Gorleston	0-7
Somersham Town v Diss Town	aet 0-0
Gt Yarmouth Town v Coggeshall Town	2-1
Wroxham v March Town United	1-2
Sandy Albions v Bourne Town	3-0
Soham Town Rangers v Brightlingsea U	2-3
Downham Town v Beccles	3-2
Stansted v Chatteris Town	1-3
Potton United v Bungay Town	3-0
Witham Town v Hadleigh United	5-2
Hoddesdon Town v Ely City	1-0
Wootton Blue Cross v Heybridge Swifts	aet 1-5
Newmarket Town v Baldock Town	0-1

Stowmarket v Letchworth GC	aet 3-4
Stotfold v Canvey Island	3-1
Woodford Town v Maldon Town	3-0
Selby v Felixstowe Town	0-1
Pirton v Brantham Athletic	aet 2-2
Hemel Hempstead v Bowers United	0-1
Sawbridgeworth T v Harpenden Town	5-0
Haverhill Rovers v Chingford	aet 1-1
Harefield United v Crown & Manor	5-1
Eton Manor v Braintree & Crittall Ath	3-1
Tiptree United v Ford United	2-1
Leighton Town v Berkhamsted Town	4-0
Saffron Walden Town v Beckton United	2-0
Hazells (Aylesbury) v Ampthill Town	2-0
Wolverton Town v Edgware	1-2
Thame United v Arlesey Town	2-0
Willesden v Chertsey Town	aet 1-1
Shillington v Amersham Town	4-1
Hornchurch v East Thurrock United	5-0
Fisher Athletic v Crockenhill	1-0
Tansley v Feltham	0-4
Flackwell Heath v Chalfont St Peter	1-2
Welling United v Hastings Town	5-2
Horley Town v Deal Town	aet 2-2
Sidley United v Merstham	1-2
Old Esthameians v Faversham Town	aet 1-1
Old Salesians v Bexhill Town	2-0
Herne Bay v Beckenham Town	0-3
Whitstable Town v Greenwich Borough	0-2
West Wickham v Eastbourne Town	2-0
Peacehave & Telscombe v Egham Town	0-1
Hythe Town v Banstead Athletic	0-2
Southwick v East Grinstead	3-0
Southall v Ash United	aet 3-1
Tunbridge Wells v Kew Association	2-3
Steyning v Chobham	4-1
Swanley Town v Corinthian-Casuals	1-0
Ringmer v Chessington United	1-2
Whyteleafe v Guildford & Worplesden	aet 2-2
Sholing Sports v Arundel	4-0
Malden Town v Darenth Heathside	0-2
Frimley Green v Burgess Hill Town	1-2
Ulysses v Chichester City	1-2
Cobham v Brading Town	2-3
Wick v Erith & Belvedere	1-2
Horsham YMCA v Dorking Town	0-5
Three Bridges v Dartford Glentworth	0-2
Farnham Town v Bracknell Town	3-1
Maidenhead T & Y v British Aerospace Wey.	1-0
Littlehampton Town v Alton Town	4-0
St Martins v Flight Refuelling	0-1
Portfield v Eastleigh	2-5
Thatcham Town v Brockenhurst	2-1
Wallingford Town v Kingsbury Town	1-3
Pagham v Amesbury	3-1
Worrall Hill v Odd Down	2-2
Peasedown Athletic v Calne Town	0-1
Yate Town v Malmesbury Victoria	3-2
Melksham Town v Imperial Bristol	2-1
Westbury United v Port of Bristol	2-6
Robinsons DRG v Clanfield	aet 3-1
Marlow v Avon Bradford	aet 2-1
Bristol Manor Farm v Abingdon Town	1-0
West Midlands Police v Ledbury Town	3-2
Matson Athletic v Bicester Town	2-1
Sharpness v Kidlington	2-1
Malvern Town v Evesham United	2-0
Shortwood United v Didcot Town	1-2
Glenside St Gabriels v Devizes Town	3-5
Forest Green Rovers v Chippenham Town	0-3
Chipping Norton Town v Cadbury Heath	3-0
Park v Fairford Town	2-0
Larkhall Athletic v Backwell United	3-2
Holsworthy v Bristol St George	1-0
Ottery St Mary v Appledore	1-0

Preliminary Round – Replays

Haig Colliery v Stockton Buffs	0-1
Brandon United v Heaton Stannington	0-1
Lydney Town v Walsall Wood	2-4
Diss Town v Somersham Town	2-1
Brantham Athletic v Pirton	1-3
Chingford v Haverhill Rovers	1-2
Chertsey Town v Willesden	aet 1-4
Deal Town v Horley Town	1-0
Faversham Town v Old Esthameians	3-1
Guildford & Worplesdon v Whyteleafe	0-3
Odd Down v Worrall Hill	aet 2-1

First Round

Stockton Buffs v Darlington RA	2-0
Seaham CW Red Star v Wallsend Town	aet 2-4
Heaton Stannington v Chester-le-Street	0-1
Guiseley v Smith's Dock	6-0
Hartlepool BW v Eppleton CW	2-1
Gretna v Peterlee Newtown	aet 3-1
Boldon CA v South Shields	0-3
Cleator Moor Celtic v Pickering Town	1-2
Tadcaster Albion v Norton CCT	4-2
Wingate v North Ferriby United	aet 3-5
Hallam v Yorkshire Amateur	1-0
Clitheroe v Maghull	aet 3-2
Waterloo Dock v Thackley	1-3
Wren Rovers v Salford	2-3
Wythenshawe Amateurs v Bacup Borough	0-1
Atherton Collieries v Leeds Ashley Road	1-3
Ossett Albion v Lytham	4-1
Hoylake Athletic v Abbey Hey WMC	5-1
Ossett Town v Leyland Motors	0-3
Skelmersdale United v Rylands	1-2
Prescot BI v Kiveton Park	0-1
Irlam Town v Bradley Rangers	aet 1-1
Gainsborough United v Appleby Frod'ham	3-2
Norton Woodseats v Harworth CI	2-0
Bentley Victoria v Denaby United	0-2
Ashby Institute v Staveley Works	0-1
Clipstone Welfare v Brigg Town	2-0
Sheffield v Louth United	1-3
Eastwood (Hanley) v Oakham United	0-1
Glossop v Stapenhill	3-0
Thringstone MW v Kimberley Town	0-3
Congleton Town v Gresley Rovers	3-2
Wednesfield Social v Armitage	aet 0-0
Middlewich Ath v Long Eaton Grange	4-1
Tividale v Shifnal Town	1-4
Mile Oak Rovers & Y v Anstey Nomads	aet 0-1
Rothwell Town v Birstall United	2-3
Brierley Hill All. v Solihull Borough	1-0
Desborough Town v Oadby Town	3-1
Blackenall v West Midlands Police	0-1
Chipping Norton Town v Hinckley Town	4-1
Coventry Sporting v Sandy Albions	1-0
Walsall Sportsco v Walsall Wood	aet 1-2
Halesowen Town v Matson Athletic	3-1
Watton Town v March Town United	aet 2-1
Melton Town v Diss Town	1-0
Baldock Town v Potton United	0-1
Wigston Fields v Chatteris Town	5-0
Royston Town v Downham Town	2-1
Gt Yarmouth Town v Brightlingsea United	3-0
Stotfold v Histon	2-0
Gorleston v Heybridge Swifts	1-0
Woodford Town v Felixstowe Town	1-3
St Neots Town v Bowers United	0-1
Edgware v Sawbridgeworth Town	aet 1-2
Pirton v Basildon United	0-1
Shillington v Witham Town	0-1
Hoddesdon Town v Tiptree United	1-2
Harefield Utd v Saffron Walden Town	2-1
Letchworth GC v Epping Town	2-1
Leighton Town v Haverhill Rovers	6-1
Rainham Town v Eton Manor	4-2
Kingsbury Town v Chalfont St Peter	0-1
Hornchurch v Willesden	6-1
Darenth Heathside v Deal Town	aet 4-3
Malden Vale v Welling United	2-1
Faversham Town v Feltham	aet 2-1
Fisher Athletic v Old Salesians	3-1
Chessington United v Chichester City	aet 3-1
Redhill v Burgess Hill Town	1-3
Egham Town v West Wickham	aet 2-2
Beckenham Town v Dartford Glentworth	1-0
Swanley Town v Dorking Town	aet 2-3
Erith & Belvedere v Southwick	1-0
Kew Association v Whyteleafe	1-4
Shoreham v Greenwich Borough	0-1
Banstead Athletic v Steyning	1-2
Southall v Merstham	1-0

Eastleigh v First Tower United	0-4
Worthing v Pagham	0-2
Hazells (Aylesbury) v Tring Town	2-3

Match awarded to Hazells (Aylesbury); Tring Town played an ineligible player.

Ruislip Manor v Didcot Town	aet 2-2
Park v Maidenhead Town & Youth	4-2
Uxbridge v Thame United	2-0
Brading Town v Farnham Town	0-2
Marlow v Littlehampton Town	aet 2-1
Thatcham Town v Sholing Sports	0-3
Newport IOW v Flight Refuelling	5-2
Robinsons DRG v Odd Down	3-0
Malvern Town v Melksham Town	1-0
Larkhall Athletic v Chippenham Town	aet 4-2
Sharpness v Port of Bristol	aet 1-4
Devizes Town v Calne Town	3-0
Yate Town v Bristol Manor Farm	aet 3-3
Illogan RBL v Ottery St Mary	0-3
Radstock Town v Holsworthy	aet 0-0

First Round – Replays

Bradley Rangers v Irlam Town	aet 2-2
Armitage v Wednesfield Social	0-2
West Wickham v Egham Town	aet 3-3
Didcot Town v Ruislip Manor	0-3
Bristol Manor Farm v Yate Town	0-2
Holsworthy v Radstock Town	1-2

First Round – Second Replays

Irlam Town v Bradley Rangers	0-1
Egham Town v West Wickham	2-0

Second Round

Chester-le-Street v Pickering Town	4-2
Gretna v Blue Star	aet 0-0
Hartlepool BW v Guiseley	2-4
Stockton Buffs v Whickham	0-1
Tadcaster Albion v South Shields	4-0
Clitheroe v Guiseborough Town	1-2
Bacup Borough v Thackley	aet 1-2
Leeds Ashley Road v Wallsend Town	4-2
Salford v Hoylake Athletic	2-1
Hallam v Prescot Cables	3-1
Rylands v Leyland Motors	2-0
Middlewich Athletic v Frecheville Com	3-0
Ossett Albion v Shepshed Charterhouse	5-1
Staveley Works v Bradley Rangers	2-1
Gainsborough United v North Ferriby Utd	1-2
Glossop v Winterton Rangers	3-0
Clipstone Welfare v Denaby United	aet 0-0
Birstall United v Lincoln United	aet 1-2
Kiveton Park v Louth United	4-1
Melton Town v Skegness Town	0-2
Oakham United v Norton Woodseats	0-2
Wednesfield Social v Friar Lane OB	aet 1-1
Kimberley Town v Congleton	3-5
Anstey Nomads v Hinckley Athletic	3-1
Wigston Fields v Walsall Wood	1-0
Desborough Town v Willenhall Town	aet 3-3
West Midlands Police v Shifnal Town	0-4
Leighton Town v Irthlingboro' Diamonds	1-2
Port of Bristol v Brierley Hill All	3-1
Halesowen Town v Buckingham Town	2-0
Great Yarmouth Town v Watton Town	aet 4-3
Stotfold v Stamford	0-1
Hazells (Aylesbury) v Coventry Sporting	1-3
Chalfont St Peter v Rushden Town	1-2
Witham Town v Gorleston	0-2
Royston Town v Kempston Rovers	2-4
Felixstowe Town v Haringey Borough	2-1
Bowers United v Barton Rovers	3-1
Harefield United v Tiptree United	3-2
Potton United v Cheshunt	aet 2-2
Sawbridgeworth Town v Letchworth GC	aet 1-1
Beckenham Town v Leyton-Wingate	2-0
Hornchurch v Grays Athletic	2-1
Greenwich Borough v East Ham United	3-2
Rainham Town v Basildon United	0-2
Fisher Athletic v Cray Wanderers	1-2
Darenth Heathside v Egham Town	0-2
Uxbridge v Alma Swanley	aet 1-2
Whyteleafe v Faversham Town	3-2
Burgess Hill Town v Eastbourne United	2-1
Erith & Belvedere v Malden Vale	aet 1-1
Marlow v Molesey	4-1
Southall v Chessington United	1-0
Steyning v Windsor & Eton	0-3
Pagham v First Tower United	aet 1-0
Sholing Sports v Dorking Town	3-2
Devizes Town v Newport IOW	aet 4-3
Farnham Town v Newbury Town	0-1
Ruislip Manor v Larkhall Athletic	aet 4-4
Park v Burnham	0-4
Chipping Norton Town v Malvern Town	3-2
Yate Town v Hungerford Town	aet 3-3
Radstock Town v Ottery St Mary	0-1
Robinsons DRG v Almondsbury Greenway	1-3

Second Round – Replays

Blue Star v Gretna	3-1
Denaby United v Clipstone Welfare	3-1
Friar Lane OB v Wednesfield Social	1-0
Willenhall Town v Desborough Town	1-0
Cheshunt v Potton United	3-1
Letchworth GC v Sawbridgeworth Town	0-1
Malden Vale v Erith & Belvedere	3-1
Larkhall Athletic v Ruislip Manor	1-2
Hungerford Town v Yate Town	3-0

Third Round

Tadcaster Albion v Chester-le-Street	0-1
Leeds Ashley Road v Guiseley	1-4
Thackley v Blue Star	4-0
Guisborough Town v Whickham	0-1
Norton Woodseats v Glossop	3-0
Rylands v Middlewich Athletic	0-1
Congleton Town v Ossett Albion	3-1
Salford v Staveley Works	2-1
Hallam v Denaby United	1-0
Kiveton Park v North Ferriby United	1-0
Anstey Nomads v Irthlingboro' Diamonds	3-4
Stamford v Skegness Town	aet 3-2
Wigston Fields v Lincoln United	1-1
Rushden Town v Chipping Norton Town	1-2
Friar Lane OB v Newbury Town	4-3
Coventry Sporting v Shifnal Town	1-0
Willenhall Town v Halesowen Town	1-0
Kempston Rovers v Sawbridgeworth Town	2-1

(*abandoned in extra time*)

Bowers United v Alma Swanley	2-3
Hornchurch v Basildon United	0-1
Gorleston v Great Yarmouth Town	2-3
Felixstowe Town v Cheshunt	0-2
Harefield United v Pagham	0-5
Marlow v Whyteleafe	1-4
Burnham v Malden Vale	aet 4-3
Windsor & Eton v Egham Town	6-0
Southall v Cray Wanderers	1-2
Beckenham Town v Ruislip Manor	aet 3-2
Burgess Hill Town v Greenwich Borough	2-1
Almondsbury Greenway v Ottery St Mary	2-1
Sholing Sports v Devizes Town	1-4
Hungerford Town v Port of Bristol	4-1

Third Round – Replays

Lincoln United v Wigston Fields	3-4
Sawbridgeworth Town v Kempston Rovers	1-2

Fourth Round

Salford v Whickham	0-2
Hallam v Chester-le-Street	3-0
Guiseley v Norton Woodseats	4-1
Thackley v Kiveton Park	3-1
Middlewich Athletic v Friar Lane OB	3-0
Wigston Fields v Irthlingborough Diamonds	0-4
Coventry Sporting v Stamford	1-0
Willenhall Town v Congleton Town	1-0
Great Yarmouth Town v Cray Wanderers	0-1
Cheshunt v Alma Swanley	1-3
Kempston Rovers v Burnham	2-1
Basildon United v Beckenham Town	2-0
Devizes Town v Chipping Norton Town	aet 2-1

Hungerford Town v Burgess Hill Town 3-0
Whyteleafe v Pagham aet 2-1
Windsor & Eton v Almondsbury Greenway 2-0

Fifth Round

Whickham v Thackley 2-0
Guiseley v Hallam 2-0
Willenhall Town v Middlewich Athletic 2-0
Alma Swanley v Coventry Sporting 2-0
Hungerford Town v Windsor & Eton 0-1
Whyteleafe v Basildon United 1-2
Devizes Town v Kempston Rovers 2-1
Cray Wanderers v Irthlingboro' Diamonds 0-0

Fifth Round – Replay

Irthlingboro' Diamonds v Cray Wanderers aet 6-0

Sixth Round

Basildon United v Irthlingboro' Diamonds aet 0-0
Whickham v Devizes Town 3-0
Alma Swanley v Windsor & Eton aet 2-2
Guiseley v Willenhall Town 2-4

Sixth Round – Replays

Irthlingboro' Diamonds v Cray Wanderers aet 6-4
Windsor & Eton v Alma Swanley 4-1

Semi-Finals – First Leg

Windsor & Eton v Whickham 1-1
Irthlingboro' Diamonds v Willenhall Town 1-1

Semi-Finals – Second Leg

Whickham v Windsor & Eton 1-0
Willenhall Town v Irthlingboro' Diamonds 2-0

Final (*at Wembley*)

Whickham 3 (*Scott, Williamson, Peck og*) aet
Willenhall Town 2 (*Smith, Stringer*) 12,000
Score after 90 minutes, 2-2.

Whickham: Thompson; Scott, Knox, Williamson, Cook, Ward, Carroll, Diamond, Cawchra, Roberton, Turnbull.

Willenhall Town: Newton (Trevor); White, Dams, Woodall, Heath, Fox, Peck, Price, Matthews, Smith, Stringer.

PREVIOUS FINALS

1975 Hoddesdon 2, Epsom 1 (10,000)
1976 Billericay T 1, Stamford 0 (12,000)
1977 Billericay T (1) 2, Sheffield (1) 1 (15,150)
1978 Blue Star 2, Barton R 1 (16,000)
1979 Billericay T 4, Almondsbury Greenway 1 (16,792)
1980 Stamford 2, Guisborough T 0 (11,500)

FA SUNDAY CUP 1980–81

First Round

Brompton Associated v Newbiggin Dolphin 1-4
Blue Star v Town End Farm 4-0
Morton Community Centre v Shildon Elm Road WMC 0-1
Sunderland Humbledon Plains WMC v Murton Victoria 4-0
Gillford Park v Aireville 4-2
Hartlepool Lion Hotel v Hartlepool WMC 0-2
Newbiggin Sports Centre v Carlisle United SC 4-2
Kendal Bowman v Winlaton West End 0-14
Finns (Steeplejacks) Knottingley v Esh Winning 'Pineapple' 0-1
Sportsco v Springfield Social aet 1-3
Bobbies Lane Sports v ASCH Hotel 2-3
Old Horns v Chorlton Olympic
Tie awarded to Chorlton Olympic
Red House v Brereton Town aet 1-0
Raysel & Lister Athletic v Jumbos XI 2-1
Slade Celtic v Hurst Rovers aet 2-2
East Levenshulme CC v Woodpecker 5-0
Bricklayers Sports v Marklynn Motors aet 1-1
Rose & Shamrock v Park Rangers (Wednesfield) aet 0-0
Dingle Rail v Shell (Carrington) 5-2
Lodge Cottrell v Fish Trades BC 9-0
Golden Cross United v Swanfield 0-1
Deborah United v Sleaford Rangers 2-1
Club Lafayette v Piper Club 1-2
Taverners v Byron Athletic 0-1
Swan Yardley v Hoyland Town Jaguars 1-3
Lion Rangers v Hoval-Farrar 5-1
Tabular-Beaufort v Bordesley Rovers 6-0
Backwell Sunday v Counts Promovere 1-3
Cowley Workers v Marston Sports 0-1
Laverstoke Park Albion v Undeb United 3-1
Black Horse v Rediffusion Bedminster Down Sunday 2-1
Quality Carpets v Newtown Unity 1-0
Cobblers v Robin Hoods Retreat 2-1
North Stoneham v Willmotts Sports 1-0
Olympic Star v Clyst Honiton SC 2-0
Hallen Sunday v Inter Volante 2-1
Loke United v Pools United
Tie awarded to Loke United
Rainham WMC v Girton Eagles 2-1
Coopers v Continental 2-3
Odhams OB v Mackintosh 1-2
Nicholas Breakspear OB v Arras 5-1
Sheffield House Rangers v Greenleys 0-2
Lakeside v Temperance United 4-3
Langleybury CC v Walmer 3-0
Croft City v Lee Chapel North 1-4
Glenn Sports v Brentford East 6-1
Road Sea v Temple Hill aet 1-1
Two-Seven-Nine v Troy Athletic 3-0
Elco v Thornton Heath United 4-1
Corby Kingfisher v Wrestlers 3-1

First Round – Replays

Hurst Rovers v Slade Celtic 2-4
Marklynn Motors v Bricklayers Sports 0-1
Park Rangers (Wednesfield) v Rose & Shamrock 4-0
Temple Hill v Road Sea 4-3

Byes to Second Round
Adelaide Park, Dudley & Weetslade Social, Sandwell, West Clandon RBL.

Exempt to Second Round
Cheshunt, Clifda, Croxteth & Gillmoss RBL, Evergreen, Fantail, Halesowen Harriers, Highgate, Langley Park Social Welfare, Ollis Transport Combined, Twin Foxes.

Second Round

Winlaton-West-End v Langley Park Social Welfare 1-1
Gillford Park v Highgate 2-0
Croxteth & Gillmoss RBL v Dudley & Weetslade Social 5-0
Shildon Elm Road WMC v Hartlepool WMC 1-1
Piper Club v ASCH Hotel 1-3
Deborah United v Blue Star 0-2
Esh Winning 'Pineapple' v Fantail 0-1
Swanfield v Newbiggin Dolphin aet 2-5
Sunderland Humbledon Plains WMC v Newbiggin Sports Centre 2-1
Dingle Rail v Hoyland Town Jaguars 3-1
Bricklayers Sports v Adelaide Park 0-1
Chorlton Olympic v Raysel & Lister Athletic 0-2
East Levenshulme Cricket Club v Red House 0-1
Halesowen Harriers v Cobblers 4-2
Lodge Cottrell v Slade Celtic 0-1
Park Rangers (Wednesfield) v Springfield Social aet 5-2
Hallen Sunday v Black Horse 3-0
Ollis Transport Combined v Lion Rangers 0-4
Byron Athletic v North Stoneham 1-0
Laverstoke Park Albion v West Clandon RBL 6-0

Quality Carpets v Lakeside 2-0
Tabular Beaufort v Temple Hill 6-0
Marston Sports v Sandwell 3-1
Olympic Star v Counts Promovere 2-4
Cheshunt v Loke United 2-1
Lee Chapel North v Langleybury CC 0-0
Nicholas Breakspear OB v Continental 2-3
Clifda v Evergreen 1-0
Corby Kingfisher v Rainham WMC 3-0
Two-Seven-Nine v Glenn Sports 2-1
Twin Foxes v Greenleys 1-0
Mackintosh v Elco 3-1

Second Round – Replays

Langley Park Social Welfare v Winlaton-West-End 1-4
Hartlepool WMC v Shildon Elm Road WMC aet 4-3
Langleybury CC v Lee Chapel North 1-3

Third Round

Raysel & Lister Athletic v Winlaton West End 4-2, 1-4
First match ordered to be replayed: Raysel & Lister Athletic included an ineligible player.
Red House v Dingle Rail 0-2
Sunderland Humbledon Plains WMC v Fantail 1-2
Newbiggin Dolphin v Gillford Park 5-2
Croxteth & Gillmoss RBL v ASCH Hotel 2-1
Blue Star v Hartlepool WMC 4-4
Hallen Sunday v Tabular-Beaufort 1-2
Quality Carpets v Twin Foxes 3-1
Adelaide Park v Laverstoke Park Albion 0-1
Park Rangers (Wednesfield) v Slade Celtic 2-0
Marston Sports v Halesowen Harriers 3-2
Mackintosh v Byron Athletic 3-2
Lee Chapel North v Lion Rangers aet 1-0
Counts Promovere v Corby Kingfisher 1-2
Two-Seven-Nine v Clifda 4-0
Cheshunt v Continental 2-3

Third Round – Replay

Hartlepool WMC v Blue Star 1-2

Fourth Round

Blue Star v Dingle Rail 3-0
Fantail v Newbiggin Dolphin 1-0
Croxteth & Gillmoss RBL v Winlaton West End 2-1
Laverstoke Park Albion v Lee Chapel North 0-2
Quality Carpets v Tabular-Beaufort 1-3
Park Rangers (Wednesfield) v Corby Kingfisher 1-0
Marston Sports v Mackintosh 0-3
Continental v Two-Seven-Nine 3-3

Fourth Round – Replay

Two-Seven-Nine v Continental 3-1

Fifth Round

Blue Star v Croxteth & Gillmoss RBL 3-2
Fantail v Park Rangers (Wednesfield) 3-0
Lee Chapel North v Tabular-Beaufort 2-1
Mackintosh v Two-Seven-Nine 1-0

Semi-Finals

Mackintosh v Lee Chapel North 1-0
(*at Great Yarmouth Town FC*)
Blue Star v Fantail 1-1
(*at North Shields FC*)

Semi-Final – Replay

Fantail v Blue Star 4-0
(*at Kirkby Town FC*)

Final (*at Tranmere Rovers FC*)

Fantail (Liverpool) v Mackintosh (Norwich) 1-0

AMATEUR FOOTBALL ALLIANCE 1980–81

CUP FINALS

Senior: West Wickham 4, Southbank Polytechnic 2.
Intermediate: Old Esthameians Res 2, Southgate Olympic 0.
Junior: Southgate Olympic 3rd 3, Old Finchleians 1.
Minor: Catford Wanderers 4th 2, Old Esthameians 4th 0.
Senior Novets: Midland Bank 5th 3, Old Actonians 5th 1.
Junior Novets: Catford Wanderers 6th 5, Old Actonians 6th 0.
Veterans: Corinthian Casuals 4, Old Uxonians 1.
Essex Senior: Old Parkonians 2, Old Parmiterians 0.
Middlesex Senior: Lensbury 1, Old Aloysians 0.
Surrey Senior: Policrom 1, Southbank Polytechnic 0.
Essex Intermediate: Old Parmiterians Res 3, Old Bealonians Res 1.
Kent Intermediate: Old Sedcopians 1st 1, West Wickham Res 0.
Middlesex Intermediate: Old Camdenians Res 2, Cardinal Manning OB 1st 1.
Surrey Intermediate: Southbank Polytechnic Res 2, Clapham OX Res 0.
W. E. Greenland Memorial: Old Ignatians 2, Old Bealonians 1.
Holders of Wilkinson Sword (Fair Play Trophy, Season 1979–80): Old Latymerians.

ARTHURIAN LEAGUE

DIVISION I

	P	*W*	*D*	*L*	*F*	*A*	*Pts*
Brentwoods	15	14	1	0	59	6	29
Lancing OB	15	10	3	2	46	15	23
Cholmeleians	15	9	4	2	48	19	22
Chigwellians	15	8	4	3	44	24	20
Carthusians	15	9	2	4	41	26	20
Wellingburians	15	8	1	6	45	35	17
Foresters	15	7	3	5	30	29	17
Malvernians	15	6	4	5	30	21	16
Harrovians	15	6	4	5	18	19	16
Aldenhamians	15	6	3	6	29	19	15
Wykehamists	15	5	2	8	20	30	12
Bradfieldians	15	3	4	8	28	35	10
Reptonians	15	3	3	9	25	43	9
Salopians	15	3	1	11	15	52	7
Etonians	15	1	2	12	22	59	4
Ardinians	15	1	1	13	10	78	3

DIVISION II

	P	*W*	*D*	*L*	*F*	*A*	*Pts*
Foresters	16	10	4	2	43	17	24
Lancing OB	16	9	2	5	49	38	20
Chigwellians	16	8	3	5	40	25	19
Westminsters	16	8	3	5	40	30	19
Cholmeleians II	16	7	2	7	31	38	16
Malvernians	16	4	7	5	26	28	15
Cholmeleians III	16	4	6	6	23	30	14
Aldenhamians	16	4	4	8	24	42	12
Carthusians	16	1	3	12	21	49	5

SOUTHERN AMATEUR LEAGUE

DIVISION ONE

	P	W	D	L	F	A	Pts
Old Esthameians	22	16	3	3	56	22	35
East Barnet OG	22	14	6	2	65	28	34
Kew Association	22	9	9	4	39	33	27
West Wickham	22	11	4	7	50	35	26
Midland Bank	22	8	5	9	44	40	21
South Bank Poly	22	7	7	8	30	35	21
Catford Wanderers	22	9	3	10	37	46	21
Lloyds Bank	22	5	8	9	37	45	18
Crouch End Vamps	22	7	3	12	24	45	17
Winchmore Hill	22	5	6	11	25	46	16
Nat West Bank	22	6	2	14	50	59	14
Southgate Olympic	22	5	4	13	28	51	14

DIVISION TWO

	P	W	D	L	F	A	Pts
Old Bromleians	22	15	4	3	60	20	34
Norsemen	22	15	3	4	56	28	33
Carshalton	22	13	4	5	42	21	30
Lensbury	22	11	5	6	38	25	27
Old Parkonians	22	7	7	8	37	31	21
Civil Service	22	9	3	10	35	40	21
Old Westminster Cits	22	7	6	9	39	42	20
Old Actonians Ass	22	6	6	10	29	47	18
Barclays Bank	22	6	5	11	41	41	17
Brentham	22	6	5	11	28	44	17
Merton	22	3	11	8	23	42	17
Broomfield	22	3	3	16	28	75	9

DIVISION THREE

	P	W	D	L	F	A	Pts
Britannic House	22	15	5	2	51	17	35
Polytechnic	22	13	8	1	39	10	34
Old Lyonians	22	11	3	8	44	29	25
Alleyn Old Boys	22	11	3	8	54	46	25
Alexandra Park	22	9	7	6	45	44	25
Old Stationers	22	8	4	10	39	34	20
Ibis	22	9	2	11	54	52	20
Bank of England	22	7	6	9	31	37	20
Old Latymerians	22	8	4	10	43	53	20
Cuaco	22	5	4	13	28	42	14
Reigate Priory	22	5	3	14	29	58	13
Pearl Assurance	22	4	5	13	29	64	13

NEMEAN AMATEUR LEAGUE

DIVISION ONE

	P	W	D	L	F	A	Pts
Albanian	22	16	2	4	62	33	34
Ealing Assoc	22	13	6	3	52	38	32
Tansley	22	13	5	4	62	31	31
Parkfield	22	11	7	4	52	36	29
Old Hamptonians	22	12	4	6	44	33	28
Hale End Ath	22	11	1	10	49	42	23
Wood Green OB	22	7	6	9	29	43	20
Old Tiffinians	22	7	5	10	31	40	19
Old Greenfordians	22	7	3	12	30	39	17
Old Isleworthians	22	6	1	15	35	47	13
Economicals	22	5	3	14	27	45	13
Old Hendonian	22	2	1	19	22	69	5

DIVISION TWO

	P	W	D	L	F	A	Pts
Albanian Res	22	14	5	3	76	48	33
Parkfield Res	22	14	4	4	66	27	32
London Airways	22	12	7	3	49	30	31
Duncombe Sports	22	12	3	7	56	39	27
Old Hamptonian Res	22	9	5	8	51	34	23
Ealing Assoc Res	22	8	7	7	45	38	23
Old Greenfordians Res	22	9	4	9	45	48	22
Tansley Res	22	9	3	10	45	41	21
Old Elysians	22	7	5	10	38	47	19
Old Isleworthians Res	22	6	5	11	38	50	17
Economical Res	22	4	2	16	35	67	10
Eastcote-Regeians	23	1	4	17	21	96	6

OLD BOYS' LEAGUE

PREMIER DIVISION

	P	W	D	L	F	A	Pts
Salesians	20	14	3	3	51	12	31
Ignatians	20	15	0	5	34	19	30
Camdenians	20	10	4	6	45	30	24
Minchendenians	20	9	5	6	37	35	23
Aloysians	20	8	4	8	36	26	20
Enfield	20	8	4	8	34	34	20
Wokingians	20	7	3	10	32	40	17
Meadonians	20	4	7	9	21	34	15
Suttonians	20	6	3	11	27	45	15
Westhamians	20	5	4	11	28	46	14
Tollingtonians	20	3	5	12	30	54	11

SENIOR DIVISION ONE

	P	W	D	L	F	A	Pts
Clapham	22	15	6	1	52	18	36
Strandians	22	14	3	5	51	26	31
Sinjuns	22	12	3	7	48	31	27
Highburians	22	12	2	8	41	31	26
Tenisonians	22	8	7	7	38	30	23
Fincunians	22	10	2	10	69	57	22
Josephians	22	9	4	9	44	37	22
O. Hill	22	9	4	9	33	30	22
Salesians Res	22	7	5	10	38	51	19
Leyton	22	6	4	12	36	55	16
Uxonians	22	7	2	13	29	55	16
Paludians	22	2	0	20	26	84	4

SENIOR DIVISION TWO

	P	W	D	L	F	A	Pts
Latymer	22	14	4	4	57	26	32
Glyn	22	13	5	4	54	35	31
Addeyans	22	12	6	4	50	24	30
Buckwellians	22	10	4	8	50	31	24
Pelhamians	21	9	5	7	50	46	23
Suttonians Res	22	8	5	9	43	42	21
Wokingians Res	22	8	4	10	37	52	20
Salvatorians	22	7	5	10	54	58	19
Vaughanians	22	7	4	11	38	41	18
Uffingtonians	22	7	4	11	28	46	18
Minchendenians Res	21	5	5	11	27	54	15
Shene	22	4	3	15	31	64	11

SOUTHERN OLYMPIAN LEAGUE

SENIOR SECTION

DIVISION ONE

	P	W	D	L	F	A	Pts
Old Parmiterians	22	17	2	3	82	36	36
Old Finchleians	22	16	3	3	65	26	35
Old Grammarians	22	12	8	2	51	21	32
Old Bealonians	22	12	3	7	64	36	27
Old Wilsonians	22	11	5	6	45	33	27
Old Monovians	22	8	6	8	51	43	22
Witan	22	7	8	7	36	37	22
Mill Hill Village	22	6	8	8	38	43	20
Mayfield Ath	22	9	0	13	43	65	18
Southgate County	22	6	3	13	46	71	15
Palmers Green Ath	22	2	3	17	12	50	7
Centymca	22	1	1	20	23	95	3

DIVISION TWO

	P	W	D	L	F	A	Pts
Old Fairlopians	24	15	5	4	87	39	35
Old Woodhouseians	24	15	4	5	67	28	34
Old Colfeians	24	13	5	6	58	42	31
Old Libertians	24	13	3	8	57	53	29
Old Owens	24	9	10	5	52	42	28
Colposa	24	12	4	8	51	43	28
Old Edmontonians	24	10	6	8	50	50	26
London Welsh	24	6	11	7	48	47	23
Wandsworth Borough	24	8	7	9	53	56	23
GWR	24	4	10	10	37	51	18
Inland Revenue	24	6	4	14	50	83	16
Fulham Compton Old Boys	24	3	9	12	37	68	15
Brent	24	1	4	19	19	64	6

FA REPRESENTATIVE MATCHES 1934–81

FA XI v ROYAL NAVY

			FA	RN
1934	Dec	Portsmouth	0	0
1935	Dec	Plymouth	3	4
1936	Dec	Chatham	7	0
1937	Dec	Devonport	5	0
1938	Dec	Portsmouth	6	2
1947	Feb	Portsmouth	3	0
1947	Dec	Portsmouth	4	0
1948	Dec	Plymouth	1	1
1949	Dec	Plymouth	4	1
1950	Dec	Portsmouth	1	2
1951	Dec	Portsmouth	4	1
1952	Dec	Plymouth	4	0
1953	Dec	Portsmouth	1	0
1954	Dec	Portsmouth	2	1
1955	Dec	Portsmouth	5	5
1957	Jan	Portsmouth	5	1
1957	Dec	Portsmouth	5	2
1958	Dec	Portsmouth	4	1
1959	Dec	Portsmouth	5	3
1960	Dec	Portsmouth	6	2
1961	Dec	Portsmouth	7	3
1962	Dec	Portsmouth	4	0
1963	Dec	Portsmouth	2	0
1964	Dec	Portsmouth	4	1
1965	Dec	Portsmouth	9	1
1966	Nov	Portsmouth	1	0
1967	Nov	Portsmouth	3	0
1968	Nov	Portsmouth	2	0
1969	Nov	Portsmouth	1	0
1970	Dec	Portsmouth	2	2
1971	Dec	Portsmouth	3	2
1972	Nov	Portsmouth	2	1
1973	Nov	Portsmouth	2	0

FA XI v THE ARMY

			FA	Army
1934	Nov	Tidworth	1	1
1935	Nov	Colchester	4	4
1936	Nov	Aldershot	6	3
1937	Nov	Aldershot	4	2
1938	Nov	Colchester	1	1
1946	Nov	Stoke	3	8
1947	Nov	Brighton	4	0
1948	Nov	Ipswich	0	2
1949	Nov	Charlton	4	1
1950	Nov	Highbury	3	2
1951	Nov	Highbury	4	2
1952	Nov	Leeds	4	1
1953	Nov	Newcastle	3	1
1954	Nov	Sheffield	1	1
1955	Nov	Newcastle	2	2
1956	Nov	Manchester	7	3
1957	Oct	Manchester	6	3
1958	Oct	Newcastle	4	1
1959	Oct	Newcastle	3	1
1960	Oct	Sheffield	2	1
1961	Oct	Sunderland	1	2
1962	Oct	Aldershot	6	2
1963	Oct	Aldershot	4	2
1964	Feb	Catterick	2	2
1964	Oct	Aldershot	1	4
1965	Feb	Catterick	1	2
1965	Oct	Aldershot	1	1
1966	Oct	Aldershot	1	1
1967	Oct	Aldershot	3	1
1968	Oct	Aldershot	1	1
1969	Oct	Aldershot	3	0
1970	Oct	Aldershot	2	0
1972	Oct	Aldershot	3	2
1973	Oct	Bordon	0	4

FA XI v OXFORD UNIVERSITY

			FA	OU
1934	Nov	Oxford	6	1
1935	Nov	Oxford	3	2
1936	Nov	Oxford	5	1
1937	Nov	Oxford	6	2
1938	Nov	Oxford	2	0
1945	Nov	Oxford	7	0
1946	Nov	Oxford	4	3
1947	Nov	Oxford	2	0
1948	Nov	Oxford	1	1
1949	Nov	Oxford	2	1
1950	Nov	Oxford	3	3
1951	Nov	Oxford	2	1
1952	Nov	Oxford	4	2
1953	Nov	Oxford	4	2
1954	Nov	Oxford	5	0
1955	Nov	Oxford	2	1
1956	Nov	Oxford	3	0
1957	Nov	Oxford	1	1
1958	Nov	Oxford	5	0
1959	Nov	Malvern	4	1
1960	Nov	Eastbourne	3	1
1961	Nov	Oxford	6	0
1962	Nov	Eastbourne	3	3
1963	Nov	Oxford	4	0
1964	Oct	Eastbourne	4	1
1965	Nov	Oxford	6	0
1966	Nov	Eastbourne	3	0
1967	Nov	Oxford	6	0
1968	Nov	Eastbourne	5	0
1969	Nov	Oxford	0	1
1970	Nov	Eastbourne	1	0
1971	Nov	Oxford	1	0
1972	Nov	Eastbourne	5	0
1973	Nov	Oxford	5	0
1976	Nov	Oxford	1	0
1977	Nov	Oxford	4	0
1978	Nov	Oxford	3	1
1979	Nov	Oxford	6	1
1980	Nov	Witney Town	3	1

FA XI v UNIVERSITIES ATHLETIC UNION

			FA	UAU
1934	Feb	Newcastle	5	2
1935	Feb	Manchester	0	5
1936	Feb	Manchester	2	2
1937	Feb	Exeter	1	4
1938	Feb	Leeds	4	1
1939	Feb	Southampton	0	2
1946	Feb	Darlington	10	1
1947	Feb	Southampton	4	1
1948	Feb	Bristol	2	1
1949	Feb	Sheffield	2	0
1950	Feb	Exeter	4	0
1951	Feb	Hull	2	1
1952	Mar	Doncaster	1	4
1953	Feb	Nottingham	4	1
1954	Feb	Bristol	3	1
1955	Feb	Sheffield	5	0
1956	Feb	Reading	0	3
1957	Mar	Stoke	4	1
1958	Mar	Leicester	1	1
1959	Mar	Peterborough	1	2
1960	Mar	Norwich	3	0
1961	Feb	Reading	1	2
1963	Apr	Sheffield	3	0
1964	Feb	Birmingham	8	0
1965	Mar	Coventry	1	3
1966	Mar	Rugby	5	0
1967	Mar	Sheffield	2	1
1968	Feb	Nottingham	1	1

1969	Apr	Sheffield	6	0
1970	Feb	Morecambe	3	1
1971	Apr	Durham	1	1
1971	Oct	Aldershot	0	2
1973	Feb	Newcastle	2	3
1974	Feb	Nuneaton	2	2
1976	Feb	York	2	2
1977	Mar	York	2	2
1978	Mar	Altrincham	2	1
1979	Mar	Altrincham	1	1
1980	Mar	Altrincham	4	2

FA XI v ROYAL AIR FORCE

			FA	*RAF*
1934	Jan	Cranwell	2	0
1935	Jan	Watford	4	0
1936	Jan	Uxbridge	3	3
1937	Jan	Uxbridge	9	1
1937	Nov	Uxbridge	4	4
1938	Dec	Cranwell	3	2
1946	Oct	Reading	4	1
1947	Oct	Highbury	3	0
1948	Oct	Highbury	9	2
1949	Oct	Fulham	2	1
1950	Oct	Fulham	6	1
1951	Oct	Stamford Bridge	4	0
1952	Oct	Stamford Bridge	8	1
1953	Oct	Tottenham	4	0
1954	Oct	Highbury	3	1
1955	Oct	Bristol	9	0
1956	Oct	Sheffield	2	1
1957	Oct	Nottingham	5	2
1958	Oct	Bristol	1	4
1959	Oct	Norwich	9	2
1960	Oct	Manchester	2	2
1961	Oct	Peterborough	13	0
1962	Oct	Uxbridge	4	2
1963	Oct	Uxbridge	4	2
1964	Sept	Uxbridge	5	1
1969	Oct	Halton	2	2
1970	Oct	Halton	5	0
1971	Oct	Halton	1	0
1972	Oct	Uxbridge	2	1
1973	Oct	Uxbridge	4	0
1976	Jan	Wealdstone	2	1

FA XI v CAMBRIDGE UNIVERSITY

			FA	*CU*
1934	Nov	Cambridge	5	0
1935	Nov	Cambridge	6	1
1936	Nov	Cambridge	5	0
1937	Nov	Cambridge	3	1
1938	Nov	Cambridge	6	2
1946	Feb	Cambridge	5	1
1946	Nov	Cambridge	3	2
1947	Nov	Cambridge	6	1
1948	Nov	Cambridge	7	1
1949	Nov	Cambridge	3	1
1950	Nov	Cambridge	4	2
1951	Nov	Cambridge	4	1
1952	Nov	Cambridge	8	0
1953	Nov	Cambridge	2	3
1954	Nov	Cambridge	4	2
1955	Nov	Cambridge	5	1
1956	Nov	Cambridge	6	1
1957	Nov	Cambridge	5	0
1958	Nov	Cambridge	1	1
1959	Nov	Eastbourne	1	2
1960	Nov	Cambridge	3	4
1961	Nov	Eastbourne	3	2
1962	Nov	Cambridge	abandoned	
1963	Oct	Eastbourne	2	0
1964	Nov	Cambridge	3	1
1965	Nov	Cambridge	5	1
1967	Nov	Eastbourne	1	1
1968	Nov	Cambridge	2	1
1969	Nov	Eastbourne	3	0
1970	Nov	Cambridge	7	0
1971	Nov	Eastbourne	4	0
1972	Nov	Cambridge	1	0
1973	Nov	Eastbourne	3	0
1976	Nov	Cambridge	1	0
1977	Nov	Cambridge	4	0
1978	Nov	Cambridge	6	1
1979	Nov	Cambridge	2	1
1980	Nov	Cambridge	1	1

FA XI v LONDON UNIVERSITY

			FA	*LU*
1958	Mar	Motspur Park	7	1
1959	Mar	Motspur Park	0	1
1960	Mar	Motspur Park	5	1
1961	Mar	Kingston	2	2
1962	Mar	Motspur Park	7	0
1964	Mar	Kingston	5	1
1965	Mar	Motspur Park	6	2
1966	Mar	Motspur Park	2	1
1967	Mar	Hayes	3	1
1968	Mar	Motspur Park	3	0
1969	Mar	Motspur Park	3	0
1970	Mar	Woking	9	0
1971	Mar	Motspur Park	4	0
1973	Mar	Motspur Park	4	1
1974	Mar	Motspur Park	8	1
1976	Mar	Kingston	4	1
1976	Dec	Wealdstone	3	0
1977	Dec	Metropolitan Police FC	2	0
1978	Dec	Harrow Borough FC	5	1
1979	Dec	Hayes	3	0
1980	Dec	Sutton United	3	1

FA XI v AMATEUR FOOTBALL ALLIANCE

			FA	*AFA*
1958	Jan	Maidstone	4	2
1959	Jan	Barking	3	1
1960	Feb	Maidstone	5	0
1961	Feb	Bromley	2	2
1962	Feb	Wimbledon	3	1
1963	Feb	Kingston	7	1
1964	Feb	Tooting	3	0
1965	Feb	Wealdstone	2	2
1966	Feb	Kingston	3	0
1967	Feb	Bromley	1	2
1968	Feb	Enfield	1	0
1969	Feb	Dulwich	Ground unfit	
1970	Feb	Clapton	2	2
1971	Feb	Tooting	4	0
1973	Feb	Bishop's Stortford	3	1
1974	Feb	Leytonstone	2	1
1976	Apr	Dulwich	4	0
1977	Mar	Leytonstone	2	2
1978	Feb	Wealdstone	4	1
1979	Feb	Metropolitan Police FC	5	2
1980	Jan	Metropolitan Police FC	2	1
1981	Feb	Metropolitan Police FC	5	1

FA XI v BERGER ISTHMIAN LEAGUE

			FA	*BIL*
1980	Mar		0	3

FA XI v BRITISH COLLEGES SPORTS ASSOCIATION

			FA	*BC*
1972	Dec	Chorley	2	1
1973	Dec	Spennymoor	0	1
1976	Mar	Cheltenham	0	1
1977	Feb	Cheltenham	4	0
1978	Feb	Cheltenham	0	1
1980	Feb	Stafford Rangers	2	0

FA XI v BRITISH POLICE

			FA	BP
1979	Oct		1	1
1980	Oct		1	0

FA XI v SUNDERLAND

			FA	Sund
1973	Dec	Sunderland	0	4

FA XI v COMBINED SERVICES

			FA	CS
1977	Apr	Aldershot	2	2
1978	Apr	Aldershot	1	1
1979	Apr	Aldershot	1	1
1980	Apr	Aldershot	1	2
1981	Apr	Aldershot	1	1

FA XI v NORTHERN LEAGUE

			FA	NL
1977	Mar	Blyth Spartans	2	3
1978	Apr	Consett	2	3
1979	Apr	North Shields	0	2
1980	Feb	Blyth Spartans	1	3
1981	Apr	Consett	0	0

FA XI v SOUTH-WEST COUNTIES

			FA	SWC
1977	Oct	Exeter City FC	0	1
1978	Oct	Southampton FC	1	1
1979	Oct	Bath City FC	5	1

FA XI v NORTHERN PREMIER LEAGUE

			FA	NPL
1980	Sept	Runcorn FC	0	0

FA XI v WESTERN LEAGUE

			FA	WL
1980	Sept	Frome Town FC	0	0

FA XI v JERSEY FA

			FA	J
1980	Oct	Springfield St Helier	3	0

International Semi-Professional Tournament 1981

Played in Italy.

9 JUNE
Italy 0
Scotland 0

England 2 (*Williams, Davison* pen)
Netherlands 0
England: Clarke; Thompson, Davison, Barrett, Jennings, Sellars, Finnigan, Watson, Howard, Williams, Rogers (Ovard).

11 JUNE
England 0
Scotland 0
England: Clarke; Thompson, Davison, Barrett, Jennings, Sellars, Finnigan (Johnson), Watson, Howard, Williams, Rogers (Ovard).

Italy 1
Netherlands 0

13 JUNE
England 1 (*Davison* pen)
Italy 1
England: Clarke; Thompson, Davison, Barrett, Jennings, Sellars, Watson, Johnson, Howard, Whitbread (Ovard), Rogers.

Scotland 2
Netherlands 2

FINAL TABLE

	P	W	D	L	F	A	Pts
England	3	1	2	0	3	1	4
Italy	3	1	2	0	2	1	4
Scotland	3	0	3	0	2	2	3
Netherlands	3	0	1	2	2	5	1

Previous winners: 1979 England; 1980 Scotland.

LAWS OF THE GAME

The Laws of the Game and Decisions of the International Board that follow are reproduced with the special permission of FIFA, and the text is the official text as published by FIFA.

LAW I
THE FIELD OF PLAY

The Field of Play and appurtenances shall be as shown in the following plan:

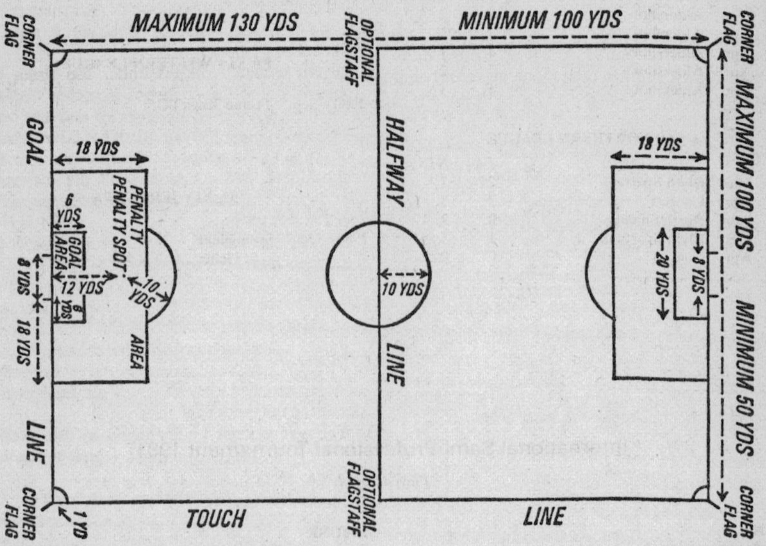

(1) **Dimensions.** The field of play shall be rectangular, its length being not more than 130 yards nor less than 100 yards and its breadth not more than 100 yards nor less than 50 yards. (In International Matches the length shall be not more than 120 yards nor less than 110 yards and the breadth not more than 80 yards nor less than 70 yards.) The length shall in all cases exceed the breadth.

(2) **Marking.** The field of play shall be marked with distinctive lines, not more than 5 inches in width, not by a V-shaped rut, in accordance with the plan, the longer boundary lines being called the touch-lines and the shorter the goal-lines. A flag on a post not less than 5ft high and having a non-pointed top, shall be placed at each corner; a similar flag-post may be placed opposite the halfway line on each side of the field of play, not less than 1 yard outside the touch-line. A halfway-line shall be marked out across the field of play. The centre of the field of play shall be indicated by a suitable mark and a circle with a 10 yards radius shall be marked round it.

(3) **The Goal-Area.** At each end of the field of play two lines shall be drawn at right-angles to the goal-line, 6 yards from each goal-post. These shall extend into the field of play for a distance of 6 yards and shall be joined by a line drawn parallel with the goal-line. Each of the spaces enclosed by these goal lines and the goal-line shall be called a goal-area.

(4) **The Penalty-Area.** At each end of the field of play two lines shall be drawn at right-angles to the goal-line, 18 yards from each goal-post. These shall extend into the field of play for a distance of 18 yards and shall be joined by a line drawn parallel with the goal-line. Each of the spaces enclosed by these lines and the goal-line shall be called a penalty-area. A suitable mark shall be made within each penalty-area, 12 yards from the mid-point of the goal-line, measured along an undrawn line at right-angles thereto. These shall be the penalty-kick marks. From each penalty-kick mark an arc of a circle, having a radius of 10 yards, shall be drawn outside the penalty-area.

(5) **The Corner-Area.** From each corner-flag post a quarter circle, having a radius of 1 yard, shall be drawn inside the field of play.

(6) **The Goals.** The goals shall be placed on the centre of each goal-line and shall consist of two upright posts, equidistant from the corner-flags and 8 yards apart (inside measurement), joined

by a horizontal cross-bar the lower edge of which shall be 8ft from the ground. The width and depth of the goal-posts and the width and depth of the cross-bars shall not exceed 5 inches (12cm). The goal-posts and the cross-bars shall have the same width.

Nets may be attached to the posts, cross-bars and ground behind the goals. They should be appropriately supported and be so placed as to allow the goal-keeper ample room.

Footnote

Goal nets. The use of nets made of hemp, jute or nylon is permitted. The nylon strings may, however, not be thinner than those made of hemp or jute.

Decisions of the International Board

(1) In International matches the dimensions of the field of play shall be: maximum 110×75 metres; minimum 100×64 metres.

(2) National Associations must adhere strictly to these dimensions. Each National Association organising an International Match must advise the visiting Association, before the match, of the place and the dimensions of the field of play.

(3) The Board has approved this table of measurements for the Laws of the Game:

130 yards	... 120 metres
120 yards	... 110
110 yards	... 100
100 yards	... 90
80 yards	... 75
70 yards	... 64
50 yards	... 45
18 yards	... 16.50
12 yards	... 11
10 yards	... 9.15
8 yards	... 7.32
6 yards	... 5.50
1 yard	... 1
8 feet	... 2.44
5 feet	... 1.50
28 inches	... 0.71
27 inches	... 0.68
9 inches	... 0.22
5 inches	... 0.12
¾ inch	... 0.019
½ inch	... 0.0127
⅜ inch	... 0.010
14 ounces	... 396 grams
16 ounces	... 453 grams
15 lb/sq in	... 1 kg/cm^2

(4) The goal-line shall be marked the same width as the depth of the goal-posts and the cross-bar, so that the goal-line and goal-post will conform to the same interior and exterior edges.

(5) The 6 yards (for the outline of the goal-area) and the 18 yards (for the outline of the penalty-area) which have to be measured along the goal-line, must start from the inner sides of the goal-posts.

(6) The space within the inside areas of the field of play includes the width of the lines marking these areas.

(7) All Associations shall provide standard equipment, particularly in International Matches, when the Laws of the Game must be complied with in every respect and especially with regard to the size of the ball and other equipment which must conform to the regulations. All cases of failure to provide standard equipment must be reported to FIFA.

(8) In a match played under the Rules of a Competition, if the cross-bar becomes displaced or broken, play shall be stopped and the match abandoned unless the cross-bar has been repaired and replaced in position or a new one provided without such being a danger to the players. A rope is not considered to be a satisfactory substitute for a cross-bar.

In a Friendly Match, by mutual consent, play may be resumed without the cross-bar provided it has been removed and no longer constitutes a danger to the players. In these circumstances, a rope may be used as a substitute for a cross-bar. If a rope is not used and the ball crosses the goal-line at a point which in the opinion of the Referee is below where the cross-bar should have been he shall award a goal.

The game shall be restarted by the Referee dropping the ball at the place where it was when play was stopped.

(9) National Associations may specify such maximum and minimum dimensions for the cross-bars and goal-posts, within the limits laid down in Law I, as they consider appropriate.

(10) Goal-posts and cross-bars must be made of wood, metal or other approved material as decided from time to time by the International FA Board. They may be square, rectangular, round, half-round or elliptical in shape. Goal-posts and cross-bars made of other materials and in other shapes are not permitted.

(11) 'Curtain-raisers' to International Matches should only be played following agreement on the day of the match, and taking into account the condition of the field of play, between representatives of the two Associations and the Referee (of the International Match).

(12) National Associations, particularly in International Matches, should

— restrict the number of photographers around the field of play,
— have a line ('photographers' line') marked behind the goal-lines at least two metres from the corner flag going through a point situated at least 3.5 metres behind the intersection of the goal-line with the line marking the goal area to a point situated at least six metres behind the goal-posts,
— prohibit photographers from passing over these lines,

— forbid the use of artificial lighting in the form of 'flashlights'.

LAW II – THE BALL

The ball shall be spherical; the outer casing shall be of leather or other approved materials. No material shall be used in its construction which might prove dangerous to the players.

The circumference of the ball shall not be more than 28in and not less than 27in. The weight of the ball at the start of the game shall not be more than 16oz nor less than 14oz. The pressure shall be equal to 0.6–0.7 atmosphere, which equals 9.0–10.5lb/sq in ($=600–700gr/cm^2$) at sea level. The ball shall not be changed during the game unless authorised by the Referee.

Decisions of the International Board

(1) The ball used in any match shall be considered the property of the Association or Club on whose ground the match is played, and at the close of play it must be returned to the Referee.

(2) The International Board, from time to time, shall decide what constitutes approved materials. Any approved material shall be certified as such by the International Board.

(3) The Board has approved these equivalents of the weights specified in the Law: 14 to 16 ounces = 396 to 453 grammes.

(4) If the ball bursts or becomes deflated during the course of a match, the game shall be stopped and restarted by dropping the new ball at the place where the first ball became defective.

(5) If this happens during a stoppage of the game (place-kick, goal-kick, corner-kick, free-kick, penalty-kick or throw-in) the game shall be restarted accordingly.

LAW III – NUMBER OF PLAYERS

(1) A match shall be played by two teams, each consisting of not more than eleven players, one of whom shall be the goalkeeper.

(2) Substitutes may be used in any match played under the rules of a competition, subject to the following conditions:

(a) that the authority of the international association(s) or national association(s) concerned, has been obtained,

(b) that, subject to the restriction contained in the following paragraph (c), the rules of a competition shall state how many, if any, substitutes may be used, and

(c) that a team shall not be permitted to use more than two substitutes in any match.

(3) Substitutes may be used in any other match, provided that the two teams concerned reach agreement on a maximum number, not exceeding five, and that the terms of such agreement are intimated to the Referee, before the match. If the Referee is not informed, or if the teams fail to reach agreement, no more than two substitutes shall be permitted.

(4) Any of the other players may change places with the goalkeeper, provided that the Referee is informed before the change is made, and provided also, that the change is made during a stoppage in the game.

(5) When a goalkeeper or any other player is to be replaced by a substitute, the following conditions shall be observed:

(a) the Referee shall be informed of the proposed substitution, before it is made,

(b) the substitute shall not enter the field of play until the player he is replacing has left, and then only after having received a signal from the Referee,

(c) he shall enter the field during a stoppage in the game, and at the half-way line.

Punishment:

(a) Play shall not be stopped for an infringement of paragraph 4. The players concerned shall be cautioned immediately the ball goes out of play.

(b) For any other infringement of this law, the player concerned shall be cautioned, and if the game is stopped by the Referee, to administer the caution, it shall be restarted by an indirect free-kick, to be taken by a player of the opposing team, from the place where the ball was, when play was stopped. If the free-kick is awarded to a side within its own goal-area, it may be taken from any point within that half of the goal-area in which the ball was when play was stopped.

Decisions of the International Board

(1) The minimum number of players in a team is left to the discretion of National Associations.

(2) The Board is of the opinion that a match should not be considered valid if there are fewer than seven players in either of the teams.

(3) A competition may require that the referee shall be informed, before the start of the match, of the names of not more than five players, from whom the substitutes (if any) must be chosen.

(4) A player who has been ordered off before play begins may be replaced only by one of the named substitutes. The kick-off must not be delayed to allow the substitute to join his team.

A player who has been ordered off after play has started may not be replaced.

A named substitute who has been ordered off, either before or after play has started, may not be replaced (this decision relates only to players who are ordered off under Law XII. It does not apply to players who have infringed Law IV).

(5) A player who has been replaced shall not take any further part in the game.

(6) A substitute shall be deemed to be a player and shall be subject to the authority and jurisdiction of the Referee whether called upon to play or not. For any offence committed on the field of play a substitute shall be subject to the same pun-

ishment as any other player whether called upon or not.

LAW IV – PLAYERS' EQUIPMENT

(1) A player shall not wear anything which is dangerous to another player.

(2) Footwear (boots or shoes) must conform to the following standard:

(a) Bars shall be made of leather or rubber and shall be transverse and flat, not less than half an inch in width and shall extend the total width of the sole and be rounded at the corners.

(b) Studs which are independently mounted on the sole and are replaceable shall be made of leather, rubber, aluminium, plastic or similar material and shall be solid. With the exception of that part of the stud forming the base, which shall not protrude from the sole more than one quarter of an inch, studs shall be round in plan and not less than half an inch in diameter. Where studs are tapered, the minimum diameter of any section of the stud must not be less than half an inch. Where metal seating for the screw type is used, this seating must be embedded in the sole of the footwear and any attachment screw shall be part of the stud. Other than the metal seating for the screw type of stud, no metal plates even though covered with leather or rubber shall be worn, neither studs which are threaded to allow them to be screwed on to a base screw that is fixed by nails or otherwise to the soles of footwear, nor studs which, apart from the base, have any form of protruding edge rim or relief marking or ornament should be allowed.

(c) Studs which are moulded as an integral part of the sole and are not replaceable shall be made of rubber, plastic, polyurethane or similar soft materials. Provided that there are no fewer than ten studs on the sole, they shall have a minimum diameter of three-eighths of an inch (10mm). Additional supporting material to stabilise studs of soft materials, and ridges which shall not protrude more than 5mm from the sole and moulded to strengthen it, shall be permitted provided that they are in no way dangerous to other players. In all other respects they shall conform to the general requirements of this Law.

(d) Combined bars and studs may be worn, provided the whole conforms to the general requirements of this Law. Neither bars nor studs on the soles shall project more than three-quarters of an inch. If nails are used they shall be driven in flush with the surface.

(3) The goalkeeper shall wear colours which distinguish him from the other players and from the Referee.

Punishment: For any infringement of this Law, the player at fault shall be sent off the field of play to adjust his equipment and he shall not return without first reporting to the Referee, who shall satisfy himself that the player's equipment is in order; the player shall only re-enter the game at a moment when the ball has ceased to be in play.

Decisions of the International Board

(1) The usual equipment of a player is a jersey or shirt, shorts, stockings and footwear. In a match played under the rules of a competition, players need not wear boots or shoes, but shall wear jersey or shirt, shorts, or track suit or similar trousers, and stockings.

(2) The Law does not insist that boots or shoes must be worn. However, in competition matches Referees should not allow one or a few players to play without footwear when all the other players are so equipped.

(3) In International Matches, International Competitions, International Club Competitions and friendly matches between clubs of different National Associations, the Referee, prior to the start of the game, shall inspect the players' footwear, and prevent any player whose footwear does not conform to the requirements of this Law from playing until such time as it does comply.

The rules of any competition may include a similar provision.

(4) If the Referee finds that a player is wearing articles not permitted by the Laws and which may constitute a danger to other players, he shall order him to take them off. If he fails to carry out the Referee's instruction, the player shall not take part in the match.

(5) A player who has been prevented from taking part in the game or a player who has been sent off the field for infringing Law IV must report to the Referee during a stoppage of the game and may not enter or re-enter the field of play unless and until the Referee has satisfied himself that the player is no longer infringing Law IV.

(6) A player who has been prevented from taking part in a game or who has been sent off because of an infringement of Law IV, and who enters or re-enters the field of play to join or rejoin his team, in breach of the conditions of Law XII, shall be cautioned. If the Referee stops the game to administer the caution, the game shall be restarted by an indirect free-kick, taken by a player of the opposing side, from the place where the ball was when the Referee stopped the game. If the free-kick is awarded to a side within its own goal-area, it may be taken from any point within that half of the goal-area in which the ball was when play was stopped.

LAW V – REFEREES

A Referee shall be appointed to officiate in each game. His authority and the exercise of the powers granted to him by the Laws of the Game commence as soon as he enters the field of play.

His power of penalising shall extend to offences committed when play has been temporarily suspended, or when the ball is out of play. His decision on points of fact connected with the play shall be final, so far as the result of the game is concerned. He shall:

(a) Enforce the Laws.

(b) Refrain from penalising in cases where he is satisfied that, by doing so, he would be giving an advantage to the offending team.

(c) Keep a record of the game, act as timekeeper and allow the full or agreed time, adding thereto all time lost through accident or other cause.

(d) Have discretionary power to stop the game for any infringement of the Laws and to suspend or terminate the game whenever, by reason of the elements, interference by spectators, or other cause, he deems such stoppage necessary. In such a case he shall submit a detailed report to the competent authority, within the stipulated time, and in accordance with the provisions set up by the National Association under whose jurisdiction the match was played. Reports will be deemed to be made when received in the ordinary course of post.

(e) From the time he enters the field of play, caution any player guilty of misconduct or ungentlemanly behaviour and, if he persists, suspend him from further participation in the game. In such cases the Referee shall send the name of the offender to the competent authority, within the stipulated time, and in accordance with the provisions set up by the National Association under whose jurisdiction the match was played. Reports will be deemed to be made when received in the ordinary course of post.

(f) Allow no person other than the players and linesmen to enter the field of play without his permission.

(g) Stop the game if, in his opinion, a player has been seriously injured; have the player removed as soon as possible from the field of play, and immediately resume the game. If a player is slightly injured, the game shall not be stopped until the ball has ceased to be in play. A player who is able to go to the touch or goal-line for attention of any kind, shall not be treated on the field of play.

(h) Send off the field of play, any player who, in his opinion, is guilty of violent conduct, serious foul play, or the use of foul or abusive language.

(i) Signal for recommencement of the game after all stoppages.

(j) Decide that the ball provided for a match meets with the requirements of Law II.

Decisions of the International Board

(1) Referees in International Matches shall wear a blazer or blouse the colour of which is distinct from the colours worn by the contesting teams.

(2) Referees for International Matches will be selected from a neutral country unless the countries concerned agree to appoint their own officials.

(3) The Referee must be chosen from the official list of International Referees. This need not apply to Amateur and Youth International Matches.

(4) The Referee shall report to the appropriate authority misconduct or any misdemeanour on the part of spectators, officials, players, named substitutes or other persons which take place either on the field of play or in its vicinity at any time prior to, during, or after the match in question so that appropriate action can be taken by the authority concerned.

(5) Linesmen are assistants of the Referee. In no case shall the Referee consider the intervention of a Linesman if he himself has seen the incident and from his position on the field, is better able to judge. With this reserve, and the Linesman neutral, the Referee can consider the intervention and if the information of the Linesman applies to that phase of the game immediately before the scoring of a goal, the Referee may act thereon and cancel the goal.

(6) The Referee, however, can only reverse his first decision so long as the game has not been restarted.

(7) If the Referee has decided to apply the advantage clause and to let the game proceed, he cannot revoke his decision if the presumed advantage has not been realised, even though he has not, by any gesture, indicated his decision. This does not exempt the offending player from being dealt with by the Referee.

(8) The Laws of the Game are intended to provide that games should be played with as little interference as possible, and in this view it is the duty of Referees to penalise only deliberate breaches of the Law. Constant whistling for trifling and doubtful breaches produces bad feeling and loss of temper on the part of the players and spoils the pleasure of spectators.

(9) By para. (d) of Law V the Referee is empowered to terminate a match in the event of grave disorder, but he has no power or right to decide, in such event, that either team is disqualified and thereby the loser of the match. He must send a detailed report to the proper authority who alone has power to deal further with this matter.

(10) If a player commits two infringements of a different nature at the same time, the Referee shall punish the more serious offence.

(11) It is the duty of the Referee to act upon the information of neutral Linesmen with regard to incidents that do not come under the personal notice of the Referee.

(12) The Referee shall not allow any person to enter the field until play has stopped, and only then, if he has given him a signal to do so, nor shall he allow coaching from the boundary lines.

LAW VI – LINESMEN

Two Linesmen shall be appointed, whose duty (subject to the decision of the Referee) shall be to indicate when the ball is out of play and which side is entitled to the corner-kick, goal-kick or throw-in. They shall also assist the Referee to control the game in accordance with the Laws. In the event of undue interference or improper conduct by a Linesman, the Referee shall dispense with his services and arrange for a substitute to be appointed. (The matter shall be reported by the Referee to the competent authority.) The Linesmen should be equipped with flags by the Club on whose ground the match is played.

Decisions of the International Board

(1) Linesmen, where neutral, shall draw the Referee's attention to any breach of the Laws of the Game of which they become aware if they consider that the Referee may not have seen it, but the Referee shall always be the judge of the decision to be taken.

(2) National Associations are advised to appoint official Referees of neutral nationality to act as Linesmen in International Matches.

(3) In International Matches, Linesmen's flags shall be of a vivid colour, bright reds and yellows. Such flags are recommended for use in all other matches.

(4) A Linesman may be subject to disciplinary action only upon a report of the Referee for unjustified interference or insufficient assistance.

LAW VII – DURATION OF THE GAME

The duration of the game shall be two equal periods of 45 minutes, unless otherwise mutually agreed upon, subject to the following: (a) Allowance shall be made in either period for all time lost through accident or other cause, the amount of which shall be a matter for the discretion of the Referee; (b) Time shall be extended to permit a penalty-kick being taken at or after the expiration of the normal period in either half.

At half-time the interval shall not exceed five minutes except by consent of the Referee.

Decisions of the International Board

(1) If a match has been stopped by the Referee, before the completion of the time specified in the rules, for any reason stated in Law V it must be replayed in full unless the rules of the competition concerned provide for the result of the match at the time of such stoppage to stand.

(2) Players have a right to an interval at half-time.

LAW VIII – THE START OF PLAY

(a) **At the beginning of the game,** choice of ends and the kick-off shall be decided by the toss of a coin. The team winning the toss shall have the option of choice of ends or the kick-off. The Referee having given a signal, the game shall be started by a player taking a place-kick (i.e., a kick at the ball while it is stationary on the ground in the centre of the field of play) into his opponents' half of the field of play. Every player shall be in his own half of the field and every player of the team opposing that of the kicker shall remain not less than 10 yards from the ball until it is kicked-off; it shall not be deemed in play until it has travelled the distance of its own circumference. The kicker shall not play the ball a second time until it has been touched or played by another player.

(b) **After a goal is scored,** the game shall be restarted in like manner by a player of the team losing the goal.

(c) **After half-time:** when restarting after half-time, ends shall be changed and the kick-off shall be taken by a player of the opposite team to that of the player who started the game.

Punishment: For any infringement of this Law, the kick-off shall be retaken, except in the case of the kicker playing the ball again before it has been touched or played by another player; for this offence, an indirect free-kick shall be taken by a player of the opposing team from the place where the infringement occurred, unless the offence is committed by a player in his opponent's goal-area, in which case the free-kick shall be taken from a point anywhere within that half of the goal-area in which the offence occurred. A goal shall not be scored direct from a kick-off.

(d) **After any other temporary suspension:** when restarting the game after a temporary suspension of play from any cause not mentioned elsewhere in these Laws, provided that immediately prior to the suspension the ball has not passed over the touch or goal-lines, the Referee shall drop the ball at the place where it was when play was suspended and it shall be deemed in play when it has touched the ground; if, however, it goes over the touch or goal-lines after it has been dropped by the Referee, but before it is touched by a player, the Referee shall again drop it. A player shall not play the ball until it has touched the ground. If this section of the Law is not complied with the Referee shall again drop the ball.

Decisions of the International Board

(1) If, when the Referee drops the ball, a player infringes any of the Laws before the ball has touched the ground, the player concerned shall be cautioned or sent off the field according to the seriousness of the offence, but a free-kick cannot be awarded to the opposing team because the ball was not in play at the time of the offence. The ball shall therefore be again dropped by the Referee.

(2) Kicking-off by persons other than the players competing in a match is prohibited.

LAW IX – BALL IN AND OUT OF PLAY

The ball is out of play:

(a) When it has wholly crossed the goal-line or touch-line, whether on the ground or in the air.

(b) When the game has been stopped by the Referee.

The ball is in play at all other times from the start of the match to the finish including:

(a) If it rebounds from a goal-post, cross-bar or corner-flag post into the field of play.

(b) If it rebounds off either the Referee or Linesmen when they are in the field of play.

(c) In the event of a supposed infringement of the Laws, until a decision is given.

Decisions of the International Board

---

(1) The lines belong to the areas of which they are the boundaries. In consequence, the touch-lines and the goal-lines belong to the field of play.

LAW X – METHOD OF SCORING

Except as otherwise provided by these Laws, a goal is scored when the whole of the ball has passed over the goal-line, between the goal-posts and under the cross-bar, provided it has not been thrown, carried or intentionally propelled by hand or arm, by a player of the attacking side, except in the case of a goalkeeper, who is within his own penalty-area.

The team scoring the greater number of goals during a game shall be the winner; if no goals, or an equal number of goals are scored, the game shall be termed a 'draw'.

Decisions of the International Board

---

(1) Law X defines the only method according to which a match is won or drawn; no variation whatsoever can be authorised.

(2) A goal cannot in any case be allowed if the ball has been prevented by some outside agent from passing over the goal-line. If this happens in the normal course of play, other than at the taking of a penalty-kick: the game must be stopped and restarted by the Referee dropping the ball at the place where the ball came into contact with the interference.

(3) If, when the ball is going into goal, a spectator enters the field before it passes wholly over the goal-line, and tries to prevent a score, a goal shall be allowed if the ball goes into goal unless the spectator has made contact with the ball or has interfered with play, in which case the Referee shall stop the game and restart it by dropping the ball at the place where the contact or interference occurred.

LAW XI – OFF-SIDE

(1) A player is in an off-side position if he is nearer to his opponents' goal-line than the ball, **unless:**

(a) He is in his own half of the field of play, or

(b) There are at least two of his opponents nearer their own goal-line than he is.

(2) A player shall only be declared off-side and penalised for being in an off-side position, if, at the moment the ball touches, or is played by, one of his team, he is, in the opinion of the referee

(a) interfering with play or with an opponent, or

(b) seeking to gain an advantage by being in that position.

(3) A player shall not be declared off-side by the referee

(a) merely because of his being in an off-side position, or

(b) if he receives the ball, direct, from a goal-kick, a corner-kick, a throw-in, or when it has been dropped by the referee.

(4) If a player is declared off-side, the referee shall award an indirect free-kick, which shall be taken by a player of the opposing team from the place where the infringement occurred, unless the offence is committed by a player in his opponents' goal-area, in which case, the free-kick shall be taken from a point anywhere within that half of the goal-area in which the offence occurred.

Decisions of the International Board

---

(1) Off-side shall not be judged at the moment the player in question receives the ball, but at the moment when the ball is passed to him by one of his own side. A player who is not in an off-side position when one of his colleagues passes the ball to him or takes a free-kick, does not therefore become off-side if he goes forward during the flight of the ball.

LAW XII – FOULS AND MISCONDUCT

A player who intentionally commits any of the following nine offences:

(a) Kicks or attempts to kick an opponent;

(b) Trips an opponent, i.e., throwing or attempting to throw him by the use of the legs or by stooping in front of or behind him;

(c) Jumps at an opponent;

(d) Charges an opponent in a violent or dangerous manner;

(e) Charges an opponent from behind unless the latter be obstructing;

(f) Strikes or attempts to strike an opponent;

(g) Holds an opponent;

(h) Pushes an opponent;

(i) Handles the ball, i.e., carries, strikes or propels the ball with his hand or arm. (This does not apply to the goalkeeper within his own penalty-area);

shall be penalised by the award of a direct free-kick to be taken by the opposing side from the place where the offence occurred, unless the offence is committed by a player in his opponents' goal-area in which case, the free-kick shall be taken from a point anywhere within that half of the goal-area in which the offence occurred.

Should a player of the defending side intentionally commit one of the above nine offences within the penalty-area he shall be penalised by a **penalty-kick.**

A penalty-kick can be awarded irrespective of the position of the ball, if in play, at the time an offence within the penalty-area is committed.

A player committing any of the five following offences:

(1) Playing in a manner considered by the Referee to be dangerous, e.g., attempting to kick the ball while held by the goalkeeper;

(2) Charging fairly, i.e., with the shoulder, when the ball is not within playing distance of the players concerned and they are definitely not trying to play it;

(3) When not playing the ball, intentionally obstructing an opponent, i.e. running between the opponent and the ball, or interposing the body so as to form an obstacle to an opponent;

(4) Charging the goalkeeper except when he

(a) is holding the ball;

(b) is obstructing an opponent;

(c) has passed outside his goal-area;

(5) When playing as goalkeeper,

(a) takes more than 4 steps whilst holding, bouncing or throwing the ball in the air and catching it again without releasing it so that it is played by another player, or

(b) indulges in tactics which, in the opinion of the Referee, are designed merely to hold up the game and thus waste time and so give an unfair advantage to his own team – shall be penalised by the award of an **indirect free-kick** to be taken by the opposing side from the place where the infringement occurred, unless the offence is committed by a player in his opponents' goal-area, in which case the free-kick shall be taken from a point anywhere within that half of the goal-area in which the offence occurred.

A player shall be **cautioned** if:

(j) he enters or re-enters the field of play to join or rejoin his team after the game has commenced, or leaves the field of play during the progress of the game (except through accident) without, in either case, first having received a signal from the Referee showing him that he may do so. If the Referee stops the game to administer the caution the game shall be restarted by an indirect free-kick taken by a player of the opposing team from the place where the ball was when the Referee stopped the game. If the free-kick is awarded to a side within its own goal-area it may be taken from any point within the half of the goal-area in which the ball was when play was stopped. If, however, the offending player has committed a more serious offence he shall be penalised according to that section of the law he infringed;

(k) he persistently infringes the Laws of the Game;

(l) he shows by word or action, dissent from any decision given by the Referee;

(m) he is guilty of ungentlemanly conduct.

For any of these last three offences, in addition to the caution, an **indirect free-kick** shall also be awarded to the opposing side from the place where the offence occurred unless a more serious infringement of the Laws of the Game was committed. If the offence is committed by a player in his opponents' goal-area, a free-kick shall be taken from a point anywhere within that half of the goal-area in which the offence occurred.

A player shall be **sent off** the field of play, if:

(n) in the opinion of the Referee he is guilty of violent conduct or serious foul play;

(o) he uses foul or abusive language;

(p) he persists in misconduct after having received a caution.

If play be stopped by reason of a player being ordered from the field for an offence without a separate breach of the Law having been committed, the game shall be resumed by an **indirect free-kick** awarded to the opposing side from the place where the infringement occurred, unless the offence is committed by a player in his opponents' goal-area, in which case, the free-kick shall be taken from a point anywhere within that half of the goal-area in which the offence occurred.

Decisions of the International Board

---

(1) If the goalkeeper either intentionally strikes an opponent by throwing the ball vigorously at him or pushes him with the ball while holding it, the Referee shall award a penalty-kick, if the offence took place within the penalty-area.

(2) If a player deliberately turns his back to an opponent when he is about to be tackled, he may be charged but not in a dangerous manner.

(3) In case of body-contact in the goal-area between an attacking player and the opposing goalkeeper not in possession of the ball, the Referee, as sole judge of intention, shall stop the game if, in his opinion, the action of the attacking player was intentional, and award an indirect free-kick.

(4) If a player leans on the shoulders of another player of his own team in order to head the ball, the Referee shall stop the game, caution the player for ungentlemanly conduct and award an indirect free-kick to the opposing side.

(5) A player's obligation when joining or rejoining his team after the start of the match to 'report to the Referee' must be interpreted as meaning 'to draw the attention of the Referee from the touch-line'. The signal from the Referee shall be made by a definite gesture which makes the player understand that he may come into the field of play; it is not necessary for the Referee to wait until the game is stopped (this does not apply in respect of an infringement of Law IV), but the Referee is the sole judge of the moment in which he gives his signal of acknowledgement.

(6) The letter and spirit of Law XII do not oblige the Referee to stop a game to administer a caution. He may, if he chooses, apply the advan-

tage. If he does apply the advantage, he shall caution the player when play stops.

(7) If a player covers up the ball without touching it in an endeavour not to have it played by an opponent, he obstructs but does not infringe Law XII para. 3 because he is already in possession of the ball and covers it for tactical reasons whilst the ball remains within playing distance. In fact, he is actually playing the ball and does not commit an infringement; in this case, the player may be charged because he is in fact playing the ball.

(8) If a player intentionally stretches his arms to obstruct an opponent and steps from one side to the other, moving his arms up and down to delay his opponent, forcing him to change course, but does not make 'bodily contact' the Referee shall caution the player for ungentlemanly conduct and award an indirect free-kick.

(9) If a player intentionally obstructs the opposing goalkeeper, in an attempt to prevent him from putting the ball into play in accordance with Law XII, 5(a), the Referee shall award an indirect free-kick.

(10) If after a Referee has awarded a free-kick a player protests violently by using abusive or foul language and is sent off the field, the free-kick should not be taken until the player has left the field.

(11) Any player, whether he is within or outside the field of play, whose conduct is ungentlemanly or violent, whether or not it is directed towards an opponent, a colleague, the Referee, a Linesman or other person, or who uses foul or abusive language, is guilty of an offence, and shall be dealt with according to the nature of the offence committed.

(12) If, in the opinion of the Referee a goalkeeper intentionally lies on the ball longer than is necessary, he shall be penalised for ungentlemanly conduct and

(a) be cautioned and an indirect free-kick awarded to the opposing team;

(b) in case of repetition of the offence, be sent off the field.

(13) The offence of spitting at opponents, officials or other persons, or similar unseemly behaviour shall be considered as violent conduct within the meaning of section (n) of Law XII.

(14) If, when a Referee is about to caution a player, and before he has done so, the player commits another offence which merits a caution, the player shall be sent off the field of play.

LAW XIII – FREE-KICK

Free-kicks shall be classified under two headings: 'Direct' (from which a goal can be scored direct against the offending side), and 'Indirect' (from which a goal cannot be scored unless the ball has been played or touched by a player other than the kicker before passing through the goal).

When a player is taking a direct or an indirect free-kick inside his own penalty-area, all of the opposing players shall remain outside the area, and shall be at least ten yards from the ball whilst the kick is being taken. The ball shall be in play immediately it has travelled the distance of its own circumference and is beyond the penalty-area. The goalkeeper shall not receive the ball into his hands, in order that he may thereafter kick it into play. If the ball is not kicked direct into play, beyond the penalty-area, the kick shall be retaken.

When a player is taking a direct or an indirect free-kick outside his own penalty-area, all of the opposing players shall be at least ten yards from the ball, until it is in play, unless they are standing on their own goal-line, between the goal-posts. The ball shall be in play when it has travelled the distance of its own circumference.

If a player of the opposing side encroaches into the penalty-area, or within ten yards of the ball, as the case may be, before a free-kick is taken, the Referee shall delay the taking of the kick, until the Law is complied with.

The ball must be stationary when a free-kick is taken, and the kicker shall not play the ball a second time, until it has been touched or played by another player.

Notwithstanding any other reference in these Laws to the point from which a free-kick is to be taken, any free-kick awarded to the defending side, within its own goal-area, shall be taken from any point within that half of the goal-area in which the free-kick has been awarded.

Punishment. If the kicker, after taking the free-kick, plays the ball a second time before it has been touched or played by another player an indirect free-kick shall be taken by a player of the opposing team from the spot where the infringement occurred.

Decisions of the International Board

(1) In order to distinguish between a direct and an indirect free-kick, the Referee, when he awards an indirect free-kick, shall indicate accordingly by raising an arm above his head. He shall keep his arm in that position until the kick has been taken and retain the signal until the ball has been played or touched by another player or goes out of play.

(2) Players who do not retire to the proper distance when a free-kick is taken must be cautioned and on any repetition be ordered off. It is particularly requested of Referees that attempts to delay the taking of a free-kick by encroaching should be treated as serious misconduct.

(3) If, when a free-kick is being taken, any of the players dance about or gesticulate in a way calculated to distract their opponents, it shall be deemed ungentlemanly conduct for which the offender(s) shall be cautioned.

LAW XIV – PENALTY-KICK

A penalty kick shall be taken from the penalty-mark and, when it is being taken, all players with the exception of the player taking the kick, and the opposing goal-keeper, shall be within the field of play but outside the penalty-area, and at least 10 yards from the penalty-mark. The opposing goalkeeper must stand (without moving his feet) on his own goal-line, between the goal-posts, until the ball is kicked. The player taking the kick must kick the ball forward; he shall not play the ball a second time until it has been touched or played by another player. The ball shall be deemed in play directly it is kicked, i.e., when it has travelled the distance of its circumference, and a goal may be scored direct from such a penalty-kick. If the ball touches the goalkeeper before passing between the posts, when a penalty-kick is being taken at or after the expiration of half-time or full-time, it does not nullify a goal. If necessary, time of play shall be extended at half-time or full-time to allow a penalty-kick to be taken.

Punishment

For any infringement of this Law:

(a) by the defending team, the kick shall be retaken if a goal has not resulted.

(b) by the attacking team other than by the player taking the kick, if a goal is scored it shall be disallowed and the kick retaken.

(c) by the player taking the penalty-kick, committed after the ball is in play, a player of the opposing team shall take an indirect free-kick from the spot where the infringement occurred. If, in the case of paragraph (c), the offence is committed by the player in his opponents' goal-area, the free-kick shall be taken from a point anywhere within that half of the goal-area in which the offence occurred.

Decisions of the International Board

---

(1) When the Referee has awarded a penalty-kick, he shall not signal for it to be taken, until the players have taken up position in accordance with the Law.

(2) (a) If, after the kick has been taken, the ball is stopped in its course towards goal, by an outside agent, the kick shall be retaken.

(b) If, after the kick has been taken, the ball rebounds into play, from the goalkeeper, the cross-bar or a goal-post, and is then stopped in its course by an outside agent, the Referee shall stop play and restart it by dropping the ball at the place where it came into contact with the outside agent.

(3) (a) If, after having given the signal for a penalty-kick to be taken, the Referee sees that the goalkeeper is not in his right place on the goal-line, he shall, nevertheless, allow the kick to proceed. It shall be retaken, if a goal is not scored.

(b) If, after the Referee has given the signal for a penalty-kick to be taken, and before the ball has been kicked, the goal-keeper moves his feet, the Referee shall, nevertheless, allow the kick to proceed. It shall be retaken, if a goal is not scored.

(c) If, after the Referee has given the signal for a penalty-kick to be taken, and before the ball is in play, a player of the defending team encroaches into the penalty-area, or within ten yards of the penalty-mark, the Referee shall, nevertheless, allow the kick to proceed. It shall be retaken, if a goal is not scored.

The player concerned shall be cautioned.

(4) (a) If, when a penalty-kick is being taken, the player taking the kick is guilty of ungentlemanly conduct, the kick, if already taken, shall be retaken, if a goal is scored.

The player concerned shall be cautioned.

(b) If, after the Referee has given the signal for a penalty-kick to be taken, and before the ball is in play, a colleague of the player taking the kick encroaches into the penalty-area or within ten yards of the penalty-mark, the Referee shall, nevertheless, allow the kick to proceed. If a goal is scored, it shall be disallowed, and the kick retaken.

The player concerned shall be cautioned.

(c) If, in the circumstances described in the foregoing paragraph, the ball rebounds into play from the goalkeeper, the crossbar or a goal-post, the Referee shall stop the game, caution the player and award an indirect free-kick to the opposing team from the place where the infringement occurred.

(5) (a) If, after the referee has given the signal for a penalty-kick to be taken, and before the ball is in play, the goalkeeper moves from his position on the goal-line, or moves his feet, and a colleague of the kicker encroaches into the penalty-area or within 10 yards of the penalty-mark, the kick, if taken, shall be retaken.

The colleague of the kicker shall be cautioned.

(b) If, after the Referee has given the signal for a penalty-kick to be taken, and before the ball is in play, a player of each team encroaches into the penalty-area, or within 10 yards of the penalty-mark, the kick, if taken, shall be retaken.

The players concerned shall be cautioned.

(6) When a match is extended, at half-time or full-time, to allow a penalty-kick to be taken or retaken, the extension shall last until the moment that the penalty-kick has been completed, i.e. until the Referee has decided whether or not a goal is scored.

A goal is scored when the ball passes wholly over the goal-line.

(a) direct from the penalty-kick,

(b) having rebounded from either goal-post or the cross-bar, or

(c) having touched or been played by the goalkeeper.

The game shall terminate immediately the Referee has made his decision.

(7) When a penalty-kick is being taken in extended time:

(a) the provisions of all of the foregoing paragraphs, except paragraphs (2)(b) and (4)(c) shall apply in the usual way, and

(b) in the circumstances described in paragraphs (2)(b) and (4)(c) the game shall terminate immediately the ball rebounds from the goalkeeper, the cross-bar or the goal-post.

LAW XV – THROW-IN

When the whole of the ball passes over a touch-line, either on the ground or in the air, it shall be thrown in from the point where it crossed the line, in any direction, by a player of the team opposite to that of the player who last touched it. The thrower at the moment of delivering the ball must face the field of play and part of each foot shall be either on the touch-line or on the ground outside the touch-line. The thrower shall use both hands and shall deliver the ball from behind and over his head. The ball shall be in play immediately it enters the field of play, but the thrower shall not again play the ball until it has been touched or played by another player. A goal shall not be scored direct from a throw-in.

Punishment:

(a) If the ball is improperly thrown in the throw-in shall be taken by a player of the opposing team.

(b) If the thrower plays the ball a second time before it has been touched or played by another player, an indirect free-kick shall be taken by a player of the opposing team from the place where the infringement occurred, unless the offence is committed by a player in his opponents' goal-area, in which case, the free-kick shall be taken from a point anywhere within that half of the goal-area in which the offence occurred.

Decisions of the International Board

(1) If a player taking a throw-in, plays the ball a second time by handling it within the field of play before it has been touched or played by another player, the Referee shall award a direct free-kick.

(2) A player taking a throw-in must face the field of play with some part of his body.

(3) If, when a throw-in is being taken, any of the opposing players dance about or gesticulate in a way calculated to distract or impede the thrower, it shall be deemed ungentlemanly conduct, for which the offender(s) shall be cautioned.

LAW XVI – GOAL-KICK

When the whole of the ball passes over the goal-line excluding that portion between the goal-posts, either in the air or on the ground, having last been played by one of the attacking team, it shall be kicked direct into play beyond the penalty-area from a point within that half of the goal-area nearest to where it crossed the line, by a player of the defending team. A goalkeeper shall not receive the ball into his hands from a goal-kick in order that he may thereafter kick it into play. If the ball is not kicked beyond the penalty-area, i.e., direct into play, the kick shall be retaken. The kicker shall not play the ball a second time until it has touched – or been played by – another player. A goal shall not be scored direct from such a kick. Players of the team opposing that of the player taking the goal-kick shall remain outside the penalty-area whilst the kick is being taken.

Punishment:

If a player taking a goal-kick plays the ball a second time after it has passed beyond the penalty-area, but before it has touched or been played by another player, an indirect free-kick shall be awarded to the opposing team, to be taken from the place where the infringement occurred, unless the offence is committed by a player in his opponents' goal-area, in which case, the free-kick shall be taken from a point anywhere within that half of the goal-area in which the offence occurred.

Decisions of the International Board

(1) When a goal-kick has been taken and the player who has kicked the ball touches it again before it has left the penalty-area, the kick has not been taken in accordance with the Law and must be retaken.

LAW XVII – CORNER-KICK

When the whole of the ball passes over the goal-line, excluding that portion between the goal-posts, either in the air or on the ground, having last been played by one of the defending team, a member of the attacking team shall take a corner-kick, i.e., the whole of the ball shall be placed within the quarter circle at the nearest corner-flag post, which must not be moved, and it shall be kicked from that position. A goal may be scored direct from such a kick. Players of the team opposing that of the player taking the corner-kick shall not approach within 10 yards of the ball until it is in play, i.e., it has travelled the distance of its own circumference, nor shall the kicker play the ball a second time until it has been touched or played by another player.

Punishment:

(a) If the player who takes the kick plays the ball a second time before it has been touched or played by another player, the Referee shall award an indirect free-kick to the opposing team, to be taken from the place where the infringement occurred, unless the offence is committed by a player in his opponents' goal-area, in which case the free-kick shall be taken from a point anywhere within that half of the goal-area in which the offence occurred.

(b) For any other infringement the kick shall be retaken.

SCHOOLS FOOTBALL 1980–81

ENGLISH SCHOOLS' INTER-ASSOCIATION TROPHY 1980–81

Fifth Round

Rotherham v Sunderland	1-3
Stafford v North Sefton	2-1
Middlesbrough v Gateshead	4-0
Chesterfield v Bolton Borough	0-2
Nottingham v Sheffield	1-1, 0-4
Blackpool v Blackburn	1-1, 0-4
Reading v Southampton	1-1, 1-5
Plymouth v South London	1-4
High Wycombe v North Herts	4-1
Redbridge v Bromley	4-2
Manchester v Kirkby	2-1
Brierley Hill v South Notts	3-0
Swindon v Swansea	1-3
East London v Havering	3-1
Bristol v Oxford	3-0
Enfield v Blackheath	0-3

Sixth Round

Sunderland v Stafford	3-1
Middlesbrough v Bolton Borough	5-3
Sheffield v Blackburn	1-2
Southampton v South London	1-2
High Wycombe v Redbridge	4-1
Manchester v Brierley Hill	1-2
Swansea v East London	2-3
Bristol v Blackheath	3-3, 0-4

Quarter-Finals

Sunderland v Middlesbrough	1-1, 3-1
Blackburn v South London	0-3
High Wycombe v Brierley Hill	2-0
East London v Blackheath	4-1

Semi-Finals

Sunderland v South London	5-0
High Wycombe v East London	3-1

Final

Sunderland v High Wycombe	0-1, 0-0

ENGLISH SCHOOLS' TROPHY FINALISTS 1905–81

	Winners	*Runners up*
1905	London	Sheffield
1906	Sheffield	Manchester
1907	West Ham	Sunderland
1908	Derby	Oxford
1909	Sheffield	Birmingham N
1910	Sunderland	Walsall
1911	Chester-le-Street	Tottenham
1912	West Ham	Birkenhead
1913	Watford	Sunderland
1914	Sheffield	West Ham
1915	Cardiff	Manchester
1916	Bradford	West Ham
1917	West Ham	Grimsby
1918	Liverpool	West Ham
1919	Grimsby	Sunderland
1920	Reading	Grimsby
1921	Liverpool	West Ham
1922	S London	Grimsby
1923	Sheffield	Birmingham
1924	N Staffs	Reading
1925	Sheffield	Brighton
1926	Grimsby	Liverpool
1927	E Northumberland	Rotherham
1928	N Staffordshire	Brighton
1929	S Northumberland	Southampton
1930	Newcastle	Chesterfield
1931	Islington	Wolverhampton
1932	Manchester*	Southampton*
1933	Sunderland	Edmonton
1934	Manchester	Swansea
1935	Manchester	Swansea
1936	Preston*	West Ham*
1937	Liverpool	Blyth (Northumberland)
1938	Manchester	Bootle
1939	Swansea	Chesterfield
1940	Abandoned	
1941–5	No Competition	
1946	Leicester	Stockton-on-Tees
1947	Salford	Leicester
1948	Stockport*	Liverpool*
1949	Barnsley	Derby County
1950	Swansea	Manchester
1951	Liverpool	Brierley Hill & Sedgeley
1952	Ilford	Swansea
1953	Swansea	Chesterfield
1954	Liverpool	Southampton
1955	Swansea	Manchester
1956	Liverpool	Brighton
1957	Southampton*	Barnsley*
1958	Bristol	Swansea
1959	Brierley Hill, Sedgeley & Tipton*	Doncaster*
1960	Manchester	East London
1961	Barnsley	Liverpool
1962	Stoke	Liverpool
1963	Stoke	Bristol
1964	Erdington and Saltley	Chester-le-Street
1965	Swansea*	Leicester*
1966	East London	Oxford
1967	Liverpool	East London
1968	Manchester*	Waltham Forest*
1969	Liverpool	Swindon
1970	Liverpool	East London
1971	Huyton	Stoke
1972	Chelmsford	Oxford
1973	Liverpool	Chelmsford
1974	Manchester	Oxford
1975	Barking	Havering
1976	Liverpool	Slough
1977	South London	Islington
1978	Newham	Ealing
1979	Bristol	Croydon
1980	Middlesbrough	Reading
1981	High Wycombe	Sunderland

**Joint winners.*

ESFA NATIONAL COMPETITIONS 1980–81

INTER-ASSOCIATION TROPHY

High Wycombe 1, Sunderland 0
(*30 April, Wycombe Wanderers FC*)
Sunderland 0, High Wycombe 0
(*6 May, Roker Park, Sunderland FC*)

ASSOCIATED BISCUITS TROPHY

Washwood Heath School (West Midlands) 2, City of Portsmouth High (Hampshire) 0
(*12 May, St Andrews, Birmingham City FC*)

DENTYNE COMPETITION

Clapham College (Inter-London) 2, St Cuthbert's High School (Northumberland) 2
(*8 May, Selhurst Park, London*)

BUKTA INTER-COUNTY

Merseyside 1, Middlesex 0
(*8 May, Anfield, Liverpool FC*)

SMITH'S FOOD GROUP 6-A-SIDE

Area Winners and Semi-Finalists

South-West Harewood Junior School, Tuffley, Gloucestershire
North-West Alvaston Junior School, Alvaston, Derby
North-East Bewley Junior School, Billingham, Cleveland
South-East Raglan Junior School, Enfield, Middlesex

ENGLISH SCHOOLS INTERNATIONALS

UNDER 15

Played 9: Won 7, Lost 2, Goals for 24, Goals against 6

28 March, Wembley
England 4 (Lambert 2, Sinton, Kerslake)
Northern Ireland 0

1 April, Cardiff
Wales 0
England 1 (Lambert)

14 April, Interlaken
Switzerland 1
England 7 (Kerslake 4, Lambert 2, Jones)

16 April, Burgdorf
Switzerland 0
England 4 (Cooper, Lambert, Kerslake, Neal)

27 April, Manchester
England 1 (Kerslake)
Scotland 0

4 May, Walsall
England 2 (Lambert 2)
Netherlands 0

16 May, Auxerre
France 3
England 0

13 June, Wembley
England 1 (West)
West Germany 2

16 June, Poole
England 4 (West, Lambert, Kerslake, Sinton)
West Germany 0

UNDER 18

Played 3: Drew 1, Lost 2, Goals for 6, Goals against 8.

21 March, Paisley
Scotland 2
England 1 (Steer)

11 April, Norwich
England 2 (Alexander, Farrelly)
Wales 3

2 May, Carlisle
England 3 (Maddock 3)
Scotland 3

COACHING AND THE COACHES

Coaching in England is organised by the English Football Association through their Coaching Department. All the official coaching awards emanate from there, and such available awards in descending order are: the Full Coaching Award, the Preliminary Coaching Badge, the Local Team Manager's Award, the Youth Team Manager's Certificate, and the School Team Manager's Certificate. In addition, the FA have devised with sponsorship from the Coca-Cola Company an award for schoolchildren of both sexes known as the Super Skills Awards.

On the administrative side there are additionally 43 County Coaching Associations plus the three Armed Services, all with County Secretaries who deal with the day-to-day running of coaching at the lower levels and various delegated aspects of the system.

The FA Coaching Headquarters are at the FA's offices at 16 Lancaster Gate, London W2 3LW, where the Director of Coaching, Mr Allen Wade, and his Assistant-Director of Coaching, Mr Charles Hughes, are situated.

Around the country there are various Regional Coaches supported by Coaching Organisers, and each Regional Coach or Organiser has under his control a number of Coaching Associations formed for the purpose of bringing coaches together to discuss fresh coaching ideas and to take part in refresher courses.

The Regional Coaches and Coaching Organisers are:

Regional Coaches

North-East Region: Mr Jack Detchon, 2nd Floor, 22 High Street, Sheffield S1 2GD.
North-West Region: Mr Richard Bate, 31a Wellington Street (St John's), Blackburn, Lancs BB1 8AU.
Midlands-West Region: Mr Kevin Verity, 25 Gresham Chambers, 14 Lichfield Street, Wolverhampton WV1 1DG, Staffs.
Midlands-East Region: Mr Keith Wright, 29b High Street, Oakham, Rutland.
London Region (North): Mr Colin Murphy, c/o The FA Regional Offices, 16 Lancaster Gate, London W2 3LW.
London Region (South): Mr Robin Russell, c/o The FA Regional Offices, 16 Lancaster Gate, London W2 3LW.

COACHING ORGANISERS

East Anglia Region: Mr Graham Morgan, Roundwell Cottage, 1 Grove Road, Hethersett, Norwich, Norfolk.
South-West Region: Mr Peter Amos, 20 Tuckers Meadow, Crediton, Devon.
Mid-West Region: Mr David Burnside, 3 Oakdale Avenue, Downend, Bristol, Glos.

The aforementioned are supplemented by the Staff Coaches who are awarded that status for their efforts and hard work in relation to coaching. The Staff Coaches are:
Adams, J. W.; Adamson, J.; Ainsley, G. E.; Allen, D.; Armfield, J.; Bate, R.; Beaglehole, E. W.; Blenkinsop, E. B.; Blunt, K. R. W.; Bond, C. E.; Bramley, J.; Brown, A.; Brown, A. W.; Burnside, D.; Burton, K.; Calvert, J. S.; Cann, S. T.; Cartwright, J.; Casey, T.; Charlton, J.; Churchill, T.; Curtis, G.; Detchon, J.; Dobson, C.; Ford, F.; Furphy, K.; Goodwin, J. W.; Gordon, J.; Gradi, D.; Greaves, I. C. R.; Greenwood, R.; Hardisty, J. R. E.; Hassall, H. W.; Henderson, J. R. E.; Hill, J. W. T.; Houghton, R.; Howe, D.; Hughes, C. F. C.; Jago, G.; Jarman, J. E.; Jones, C.; Kelly, M. J.; Lawrence, T. E.; Lee, B. R.; Lewin, R.; McCluskey, E.; McAnearney, J.; Mansel, J.; Megson, D. H.; Mercer, J.; Minshull, R.; Nicholson, W. E.; Powell, E. W.; Robson, R. W.; Saunders, T. W.; Sayer, C.; Sexton, D. J.; Shannon, L.; Shoulder, J.; Sirrell, J.; Slater, W. J.; Smith, G. C.; Smith, M. J.; Summers, G.; Taylor, G.; Tranter, T. G.; Truman, J. B.; Wade, A.; Waiters, A. K.; Walker, M.; Wardle, G.; Watson, T,; Welton, P.; Wigmore, S. T.; Wilkinson, H.; Williams, B.; Woosnam, P. A.; Worthington, E. S.; Wright, W. A.

ADDRESSES

The Football Association: 16 Lancaster Gate, London W2 3LW

Scotland: Ernie Walker, 6 Park Gardens, Glasgow G3 7YE

Northern Ireland (Irish FA): W. J. Drennan, J.P., M.B.E., 20 Windsor Avenue, Belfast BT9 6EG

Wales: Trevor Morris, O.B.E., 3 Fairy Road, Wrexham LL13 7PS

Republic of Ireland (FA of Ireland): P. J. O'Driscoll, 80 Merrion Square, Dublin 2

International Federation (FIFA): Dr H. Käser, FIFA House, Hitzigweg 11, CH-8032 Zurich, Switzerland

Union of European Football Associations: H. Bangerter, PO Box 16, CH-3000 Berne 15, Switzerland

THE LEAGUES

The Football League: R. H. G. Kelly, F.C.I.S., The Football League, Lytham St Annes, Lancs. FY8 1JG. *0253-729421. Telex 67675*

The Scottish League: J. Farry, 188 West Regent Street, Glasgow G2 4RY. *041-248 3844/5*

The Irish League: J. H. Long, 16 Donegall Square South, Belfast

Alliance Premier League: P. D. Hunter, 24 Barnehurst Road, Bexleyheath, Kent DA7 6EZ. *Crayford 22616*

Athenian League: G. G. Dell, 'Ardranech', Monument Lane, Chalfont St Peter, Bucks. *Chalfont St Giles 3819*

Central League: D. J. Grimshaw, 118 St Stephens Road, Deepdale, Preston, Lancs., PR1 6TD. *Preston 55898*

Cheshire County League: C. R. Mahood, Burscough Nurseries, Ring O'Bells Lane, Lathom, Ormskirk, Lancs L40 5US. *Rufford 822688*

Town & Country League: A. W. G. Rudd, 'Heathercliff', Gunton Cliff, Lowestoft. *Lowestoft 5996*

Football Combination: T. P. R. Kirkup, 15 Oulton Rise, Spinney Hill, Northampton NN3 1EW. *0604-47831*

Hellenic League: D. A. G. Harrison, 107 Thame Road, Haddenham, Aylesbury, Bucks. *Haddenham 290590*

Kent League: D. Baker, 17 Sterling Road, Sittingbourne, Kent. *Sittingbourne 25105*

Lancashire Amateur League: H. Heap, 'Maraldo', Carlton Road, Hale, Altrincham, Cheshire, WA15 8RH. *061-980 2344*

Lancashire Combination: K. H. Dean, 61 Queens Road, Blackburn, Lancs. BB1 1QF

Lancashire Football League: H. E. Lambert, 3 Cravans Avenue, Ewood, Blackburn BB2 4LB. *Blackburn 58561*

Leicestershire Senior League: P. Henwood, 63 Carisbrooke Rd, Leicester LE2 3PF. *Leicester 705475*

London Spartan: A. J. Stephens, 130 Torrington Park, London N12. *01-368 1959*

Manchester League: T. W. Gilgryst, 7 Bowlee Close, Unsworth, Bury, Lancs. *061-766 3082*

Midland Counties League: A. A. Ridsdale, 11 Eskdale Drive, Worksop, Notts. *Worksop 475008*

Midland Combination: L. W. James, 175 Barnet Lane, Kingswinford, Brierley Hill, West Midlands. *Kingswinford 3459*

Midland Intermediate: J. B. Holmes, 492 Melton Rd, Leicester LE4 7SP. *Leicester 63968*

Mid-Week Football League: Frank P. White, 11 Tulip Way, Clacton-on-Sea, Essex. *Clacton 32750*

Nemean Amateur League: W. Chivers, 58 Laurel Avenue, Potters Bar, Herts. EN6 2AB. *Potters Bar 54969*

Northern Intermediate League: F. R. Vicary, 12 Holmefield Avenue, Thornes, Wakefield, Yorks WF2 7AF. *Wakefield 75013*

Northern League: G. Nicholson, 99 Watling Road, Bishop Auckland, Co. Durham. *Bishop Auckland 2167*

Northern Premier League: R. D. Bayley, 22 Woburn Drive, Hale, Altrincham, Cheshire WA15. *061-980-7007*

North Midlands League: G. Thompson, 7 Wren Park Close, Ridgway, Sheffield

Old Boys Football League: B. Aldous, Clemitis Cottage, Ongar Road, White Roding, Dunmow, Essex. *White Roding 278*

Peterborough and District League: A. V. Brown, 27 Gloucester Road, Old Fletton, Peterborough

Isthmian League: A. C. F. Turvey, 'Ladymead', 18 Apple Way, Basing, Basingstoke, Hants. *Basingstoke 61789*

Southern Amateur League: F. J. Banner, 10 Oakwood Road, Orpington, Kent. *Farnborough 58720*

South-East Counties League: R. A. Bailey, 10 Highlands Road, New Barnet, Herts. EN5 5AB. *01-449 5131*

Southern League: W. E. Dellow, F.C.C.S., 1 Carmel Close, Great Tylers, Wray Common, Reigate, Surrey RH2 0LS. *Redhill 62585*

South Midlands League: C. Moyse, 33 Markham Crescent, Dunstable, Beds. LU5 4SS. *Dunstable 64682*

South Western League: G. Gazzard, 6 Coastguard Crescent, Penzance, Cornwall. *Penzance 61397*

United Counties League: G. Ellitson, 2 St Marks Close, Rushden, Northants. *Rushden 313106*

Wearside: J. R. Walsh, 85 Hartington St, Roker, Sunderland, Tyne & Wear. *Sunderland 75513*

Western League: J. Veale, 5 Everest Road, Bristol BS16 2BX. *0272-652699*

The Welsh League: Anthony W. Griffiths, 13 Llynfi Road, Maesteg, Bridgend, Mid Glamorgan CF34 9DS. *0656 734096*

West Midlands Regional League: K. H. Goodfellow, 152 Garrison Lane, Small Heath, Birmingham. *021-772-0375*

West Yorkshire League: W. Keyworth, 2 Hill Court Grove, Branley, Yorks. L13 2AP. *Pudsey 74465*

Yorkshire League: B. Wood, 5 Restmore Avenue, Guiseley, Nr Leeds, LS20 9DG. *Guiseley 4558 (home); Bradford 29595 (9 a.m. to 5 p.m.)*

COUNTY FOOTBALL ASSOCIATIONS

Bedfordshire: P. Burns, 13 Wendover Way, Luton, Beds. LU2 7LS. *Luton 30829*

Berks and Bucks: C. J. Twelftree, 42 Bourtonville, Buckingham, Bucks. *Buckingham 2137*

Birmingham County: W. F. Pennick, County F.A. Offices, Rayhall Lane, Great Barr, Birmingham B43 6JE *021-357-4278*

Cambridgeshire: R. E. Rogers, 20 Aingers Road, Histon, Cambridge. *Histon 2803*

Cheshire: F. Foden, 549 Crewe Road, Wistaston, Crewe, CW2 6PU. *Crewe 69429*

Cornwall: W. Parnell, 12 Higher Tremena, St Austell PL25 5QQ. *St Austell 3236*

Cumberland: R. Johnson, 72 Victoria Road, Workington, Cumberland. *Workington 3979*

Derbyshire: H. L. P. Holmes, 82 Friar Gate, Derby. *Derby 25835*

Devon County: C. H. Norsworthy, 8 Belair Road, Peverell, Plymouth PL2 3QH. *Plymouth 73550*

Dorset County: P. Hough, 110 Dorchester Rd, Oakdale, Poole, Dorset BH15 3SD *0202 746244*

Durham: R. D. Lyons, 'Codeslaw', Ferens Park, Durham DH1 1JZ. *Durham 3653*
East Riding County: C. Branton, 83 Belvedere Road, Hessel, Hull HU13 9JH *Hull 649294*
Essex County: M. S. Jeffers, 54A Eastwood Road, Goodmayes, Ilford, Essex. *01-590 7893*
Gloucestershire: E. J. Marsh, 46 Douglas Road, Horfield, Bristol BS7 0JD. *Bristol 46430*
Guernsey: Ritruslum, Carleeta, Marette Du Haut, St Martins, Guernsey C.I. *0481-36529*
Hampshire: R. G. Barnes, 367 Winchester Road, Southampton. *Southampton 766884*
Herefordshire: R. A. Doody, Longwynd, Paradise Green, Marden, Hereford. *Sutton St Nicholas 674*
Hertfordshire: F. Holloway, 115 Tile Kiln Lane, Leverstock Green, Hemel Hempstead HP3 8NX
Hunts County: M. M. Armstrong, 1 Chapel End, Great Giddings, Huntingdon, Cambs. *Winwick 262*
Isle of Man: Mrs R. Raley, 129 Bucks Road, Douglas, I.O.M.
Jersey: Miss S. Mourant, Racqueberg Farm, Samares Lane, St Clement, Jersey, C.I.
Kent County: K. T. Masters, 69 Maidstone Road, Chatham, Kent ME4 6DT. *Medway 43824*
Lancashire: J. Kenyon, 31A, Wellington St, St John's, Blackburn, Lancs. BB1 8AU *Blackburn 64333*
Lincolnshire: F. S. Richardson, 9 The Avenue, Lincoln. *Lincoln 24917*
Liverpool County: S. A. Rudd, 23 Greenfield Road, Old Swann, Liverpool 13. *051-526-9515*
London: A. F. Monger, 4 Aldworth Grove, London SE13 6HY. *01-690-9626*
Manchester County: S. Holliday, 87 Hart Road, Fallowfield, Manchester 14. *061-224-5185*
Middlesex County: A. L. Smith, 68 Squires Lane, London N3 2AP *01-346 7565*
Norfolk County: R. Kiddell, 39 Beaumont Road, Costessey, Norwich NR5 0HG. *Norwich 742421*
Northamptonshire: B. Walden, 37 Harding Terrace, Northampton. *Northampton 39584*
North Riding County: T. H. Harper, 125 Westbury Street, Thornaby-on-Tees, Cleveland TS17 6NF *Middlesbrough 67866*
Northumberland: J. A. Forster, 'Allenby', Woodside Lane, Ryton, Tyne & Wear. *089-422-2680*
Nottinghamshire: W. T. Annable, 7 Clarendon Street, Nottingham. *Nottingham 48954*
Oxfordshire: P. J. Ladbrook, 3 Wilkins Road, Cowley, Oxford
Sheffield and Hallamshire: G. Thompson, Clegg House, 253 Pittsmoor Road, Sheffield 3. *Sheffield 27817*
Shropshire: A. W. Brett, High Street Chambers, 10–11, High Street, Shrewsbury
Somerset County: L. G. Webb, 32 North Road, Midsomer Norton, Bath BA3 2QQ. *Midsomer Norton 3176*
Staffordshire: T. Myatt, County Offices, Miller Street, Newcastle-under-Lyme ST5 1HB. *Newcastle-under-Lyme 622585*
Suffolk County: B. A. H. Collings, 28 Burke Road, Ipswich IP1 6NL. *Ipswich 714676*
Surrey County: L. F. J. Smith, 2 Fairfield Avenue, Horley, Surrey RH6 7PD *Horley 4945*
Sussex County: R. F. Reeve, 56 Hawkins Crescent, Shoreham-by-Sea, Sussex BN4 6TP
Westmorland: J. R. Plumbe, 24 Crescent Green, Kendal LA9 6DR *Kendal 23227*
West Riding County: R. M. Robin, 77 Great George Street, Leeds LS1 3DR
Wiltshire: F. J. Peart, 161 Grange Drive, Stratton St Margaret, Swindon. *Stratton St Margaret 2239*
Worcestershire: P. Rushton, 84 Windermere Drive, Warndon, Worcester WR4 9JB. *Worcester 51166*

OTHER USEFUL ADDRESSES

Amateur Football Alliance: W. P. Goss, Room 33, 3rd Floor, 6 Langley Street, London WC2 *01-240 3837/8*
English Schools FA: A. Rice, 4A Eastgate Street, Stafford ST16 2NN. *0785-51142*
Oxford University: Sir Harold Thompson, C.B.E., F.R.S., St John's College, Oxford
Cambridge University: S. C. Aston, St Catherine's College, Cambridge
Army: Major A. Dobson, M.B.E., Ministry of Defence (A.S.C.B.), Clayton Barracks, Aldershot, Hants.
Royal Air Force: Flt/Lt C. P. Clayton, 79 Greenwoods, Walters Ash, High Wycombe, Bucks
Royal Navy: Lt-Cdr H. A. Sheppard, R.N. Sports Office, H.M.S. Nelson, Portsmouth, Hants. PO1 3HH
Universities Athletic Union: Alun Evans, U.A.U., 28 Woburn Square, London WC1 *01-637 4828*
Central Council of Physical Recreation: General Secretary, 70 Brompton Road, London, SW3 1HE. *01-584 6651*
British Olympic Association: 6 John Prince's Street, W1M 0DH *01-408 2029*
National Federation of Football Supporters' Clubs: Head Office: 1 Saville Row, Bath, Avon BA1 2QP *0225-318592*. General Secretary: Malcolm Gamlen, 69 Fourth Avenue, Chelmsford, Essex *0245-63305*
National Playing Fields Association: Col R. Satterthwaite, O.B.E., 578 Catherine Place, London, SW1
Professional Footballers' Association: C. Lloyd, 124 Corn Exchange Buildings, Hanging Ditch, Manchester M4 3BN. *061-834 7554*
Referees' Association: O. J. Venning, Summerhill, Kingswinford, West Midlands
The Association of Football League Referees and Linesmen: R. Hall, Secretary, 59 Woodcock Hill, Kenton, Harrow, Middlesex HA3 0JH
Women's Football Association: Miss P. Gregory, 7 Mayfield Road, London, N8
The Association of Provincial Football Supporters' Clubs in London: D. Leitch, 3 Pandora Court, Ewell Road, Surbiton, Surrey KT6 6HZ
The Association of Football League Commercial Managers: G. H. Dimbleby, Secretary WBA FC, The Hawthorns, Halfords Lane, West Bromwich B71 4LF
The Association of Football Statisticians: R. J. Spiller, 5 Hempstalls, Basildon, Essex. *0268 282556*
The Football Programme Directory: David Stacey, 'The Beeches', 66 Southend Road, Wickford, Essex SS11 8EN.
England Football Supporters Association: Hon. Publicity Officer, David Stacey, 66 Southend Road, Wickford, Essex SS11 8EN
The Football League Executive Staffs Association: Westwood House, 80 Warwick Street, Leamington Spa, Warwickshire CV32 4QG. *0926 313651/36418*

FOOTBALL LEAGUE FIXTURES 1981–82

These fixtures are the copyright of The Football League and may not be reproduced without permission. The Editor wishes to remind readers that these fixtures are subject to alteration and that it is advisable to check that a particular fixture still stands before travelling.

DIVISION ONE

ARSENAL

Date	Opponents	Venue
1981		
Aug 29	Stoke C	H
Sept 2	West Brom	A
Sept 5	Liverpool	A
Sept 12	Sunderland	H
Sept 19	Leeds U	A
Sept 22	Birmingham C	H
Sept 26	Manchester U	H
Oct 3	Notts Co	A
Oct 10	Swansea C	A
Oct 17	Manchester C	H
Oct 24	Ipswich T	A
Oct 31	Coventry C	H
Nov 7	Aston Villa	A
Nov 14	Wolverhampton W	H
Nov 21	Nottingham F	A
Nov 24	WBA	H
Nov 28	Everton	H
Dec 5	West Ham U	A
Dec 12	Middlesbrough	H
Dec 19	Southampton	A
Dec 26	Brighton & HA	H
Dec 28	Tottenham H	A
1982		
Jan 9	Liverpool	H
Jan 16	Stoke C	A
Jan 30	Leeds U	H
Feb 6	Sunderland	A
Feb 13	Notts Co	H
Feb 20	Manchester U	A
Feb 27	Swansea C	H
Mar 6	Manchester C	A
Mar 13	Ipswich T	H
Mar 20	Coventry C	A
Mar 27	Aston Villa	H
Apr 3	Wolverhampton W	A
Apr 10	Brighton & HA	A
Apr 12	Tottenham H	H
Apr 17	Nottingham F	H
Apr 24	Everton	A
May 1	West Ham U	H
May 4	Birmingham C	A
May 8	Middlesbrough	A
May 15	Southampton	H

ASTON VILLA

Date	Opponents	Venue
1981		
Aug 29	Notts Co	H
Sept 2	Sunderland	A
Sept 5	Tottenham H	A
Sept 12	Manchester U	H
Sept 19	Liverpool	A
Sept 23	Stoke C	H
Sept 26	Birmingham C	H
Oct 3	Leeds U	A
Oct 10	Coventry C	A
Oct 17	West Ham U	H
Oct 24	Wolverhampton W	A
Oct 31	Ipswich T	H
Nov 7	Arsenal	H
Nov 14	Swansea C	A
Nov 21	Middlesbrough	A
Nov 25	Tottenham H	H
Nov 28	Nottingham F	H
Dec 5	Manchester C	A
Dec 12	WBA	H
Dec 19	Everton	A
Dec 26	Southampton	H
Dec 28	Brighton & HA	A
1982		
Jan 9	Sunderland	H
Jan 16	Notts Co	A
Jan 30	Liverpool	H
Feb 6	Manchester U	A
Feb 13	Leeds U	H
Feb 20	Birmingham C	A
Feb 27	Coventry C	H
Mar 6	West Ham U	A
Mar 13	Wolverhampton W	H
Mar 20	Ipswich T	A
Mar 27	Arsenal	A
Apr 3	Swansea C	H
Apr 10	Southampton	A
Apr 12	Brighton & HA	H
Apr 17	Middlesbrough	H
Apr 24	Nottingham F	A
May 1	Manchester C	H
May 5	Stoke C	A
May 8	WBA	A
May 15	Everton	H

BIRMINGHAM CITY

Date	Opponents	Venue
1981		
Aug 29	Everton	A
Sept 1	Ipswich T	H
Sept 5	Nottingham F	H
Sept 12	Middlesbrough	A
Sept 19	Manchester C	H
Sept 22	Arsenal	A
Sept 26	Aston Villa	A
Oct 3	West Ham U	H
Oct 10	Southampton	H
Oct 17	Manchester U	A
Oct 24	Stoke C	A
Oct 31	WBA	H
Nov 7	Brighton & HA	A
Nov 14	Tottenham H	H
Nov 21	Wolverhampton W	H
Nov 24	Ipswich T	A
Nov 28	Swansea C	A
Dec 5	Notts Co	H
Dec 12	Liverpool	A
Dec 19	Coventry C	H
Dec 26	Leeds U	A
Dec 28	Sunderland	H
1982		
Jan 9	Nottingham F	A
Jan 16	Everton	H
Jan 30	Manchester C	A
Feb 6	Middlesbrough	H
Feb 13	West Ham U	A
Feb 20	Aston Villa	H
Feb 27	Southampton	A
Mar 6	Manchester U	H
Mar 13	Stoke C	H
Mar 20	WBA	A
Mar 27	Brighton & HA	H
Apr 3	Tottenham H	A
Apr 10	Leeds U	H
Apr 12	Sunderland	A
Apr 17	Wolverhampton W	A
Apr 24	Swansea C	H
May 1	Notts Co	A
May 4	Arsenal	H
May 8	Liverpool	H
May 15	Coventry C	A

BRIGHTON & HOVE A

Date	Opponents	Venue
1981		
Aug 29	West Ham U	A
Sept 1	Swansea C	H
Sept 5	Middlesbrough	H
Sept 12	Everton	A
Sept 19	Coventry C	H
Sept 22	Wolverhampton W	A
Sept 26	Nottingham F	A
Oct 3	Manchester C	H
Oct 10	WBA	A
Oct 17	Liverpool	H
Oct 24	Tottenham H	A
Oct 31	Stoke C	H
Nov 7	Birmingham C	H
Nov 14	Southampton	A
Nov 21	Notts Co	H
Nov 24	Swansea C	A
Nov 28	Manchester U	A
Dec 5	Sunderland	H
Dec 12	Ipswich T	A
Dec 19	Leeds U	H
Dec 26	Arsenal	A
Dec 28	Aston Villa	H
1982		
Jan 9	Middlesbrough	A
Jan 16	West Ham U	H
Jan 30	Coventry C	A
Feb 6	Everton	H
Feb 13	Manchester C	A
Feb 20	Nottingham F	H
Feb 27	WBA	H
Mar 6	Liverpool	A
Mar 13	Tottenham H	H
Mar 20	Stoke C	A
Mar 27	Birmingham C	A
Apr 3	Southampton	H
Apr 10	Arsenal	H
Apr 12	Aston Villa	A
Apr 17	Notts Co	A
Apr 24	Manchester U	H
May 1	Sunderland	A
May 4	Wolverhampton W	H
May 8	Ipswich T	H
May 15	Leeds U	A

DIVISION ONE

COVENTRY CITY

Date 1981		Opponents	Venue
Aug	29	Manchester U	H
Sept	2	Stoke C	A
Sept	5	Notts Co	A
Sept	12	Leeds U	H
Sept	19	Brighton & HA	A
Sept	22	Liverpool	H
Sept	26	Southampton	H
Oct	3	Sunderland	A
Oct	10	Aston Villa	H
Oct	17	Nottingham F	A
Oct	24	Swansea C	H
Oct	31	Arsenal	A
Nov	7	Wolverhampton W	A
Nov	14	Ipswich T	H
Nov	21	West Ham U	A
Nov	24	Stoke C	H
Nov	28	Middlesbrough	H
Dec	5	Tottenham H	A
Dec	12	Manchester C	H
Dec	19	Birmingham C	A
Dec	26	WBA	H
Dec	28	Everton	
1982			
Jan	9	Notts Co	H
Jan	16	Manchester U	A
Jan	30	Brighton & HA	H
Feb	6	Leeds U	A
Feb	13	Sunderland	H
Feb	20	Liverpool	A
Feb	27	Aston Villa	A
Mar	6	Nottingham F	H
Mar	13	Swansea C	A
Mar	20	Arsenal	H
Mar	27	Wolverhampton W	H
Apr	3	Ipswich T	A
Apr	10	WBA	A
Apr	13	Everton	H
Apr	17	West Ham U	H
Apr	24	Middlesbrough	A
May	1	Tottenham H	H
May	4	Southampton	A
May	8	Manchester C	A
May	15	Birmingham C	H

EVERTON

Date 1981		Opponents	Venue
Aug	29	Birmingham C	H
Sept	2	Leeds U	A
Sept	5	Southampton	A
Sept	12	Brighton & HA	H
Sept	19	Tottenham H	A
Sept	22	Notts Co	H
Sept	26	WBA	H
Oct	3	Stoke C	A
Oct	10	West Ham U	A
Oct	17	Ipswich T	H
Oct	24	Middlesbrough	A
Oct	31	Manchester C	H
Nov	7	Liverpool	A
Nov	14	Nottingham F	H
Nov	21	Sunderland	H
Nov	24	Notts Co	A
Nov	28	Arsenal	A
Dec	5	Swansea C	H
Dec	12	Wolverhampton W	A
Dec	19	Aston Villa	H
Dec	26	Manchester U	A
Dec	28	Coventry C	H
1982			
Jan	9	Southampton	H
Jan	16	Birmingham C	A
Jan	30	Tottenham H	H
Feb	6	Brighton & HA	A
Feb	13	Stoke C	H
Feb	20	WBA	A
Feb	27	West Ham U	H
Mar	6	Ipswich T	A
Mar	13	Middlesbrough	H
Mar	20	Manchester C	A
Mar	27	Liverpool	H
Apr	3	Nottingham F	A
Apr	10	Manchester U	H
Apr	13	Coventry C	A
Apr	17	Sunderland	A
Apr	24	Arsenal	H
May	1	Swansea C	A
May	4	Leeds U	H
May	8	Wolverhampton W	H
May	15	Aston Villa	A

IPSWICH TOWN

Date 1981		Opponents	Venue
Aug	29	Sunderland	H
Sept	1	Birmingham C	A
Sept	5	Manchester U	A
Sept	12	Liverpool	H
Sept	19	Notts Co	A
Sept	22	WBA	H
Sept	26	Leeds U	H
Oct	3	Southampton	A
Oct	10	Wolverhampton W	H
Oct	17	Everton	A
Oct	24	Arsenal	H
Oct	31	Aston Villa	A
Nov	7	Swansea C	H
Nov	14	Coventry C	A
Nov	21	Stoke C	A
Nov	24	Birmingham C	H
Nov	28	Manchester C	H
Dec	5	Middlesbrough	A
Dec	12	Brighton & HA	H
Dec	20	Nottingham F	A
Dec	26	Tottenham H	H
Dec	28	West Ham U	A
1982			
Jan	9	Manchester U	H
Jan	16	Sunderland	A
Jan	30	Notts Co	H
Feb	6	Liverpool	A
Feb	13	Southampton	H
Feb	20	Leeds U	A
Feb	27	Wolverhampton W	A
Mar	6	Everton	H
Mar	13	Arsenal	A
Mar	20	Aston Villa	H
Mar	27	Swansea C	A
Apr	3	Coventry C	H
Apr	10	Tottenham H	A
Apr	13	West Ham U	H
Apr	17	Stoke C	H
Apr	24	Manchester C	A
May	1	Middlesbrough	H
May	5	WBA	A
May	8	Brighton & HA	A
May	15	Nottingham F	H

LEEDS UNITED

Date 1981		Opponents	Venue
Aug	29	Swansea C	A
Sept	2	Everton	H
Sept	5	Wolverhampton W	H
Sept	12	Coventry C	A
Sept	19	Arsenal	H
Sept	23	Manchester C	A
Sept	26	Ipswich T	A
Oct	3	Aston Villa	H
Oct	10	Liverpool	A
Oct	17	WBA	H
Oct	24	Sunderland	H
Oct	31	Nottingham F	A
Nov	7	Notts Co	H
Nov	14	Manchester U	A
Nov	21	Southampton	A
Nov	25	Manchester C	H
Nov	28	West Ham U	H
Dec	5	Stoke C	A
Dec	12	Tottenham H	H
Dec	19	Brighton & HA	A
Dec	26	Birmingham C	H
Dec	28	Middlesbrough	A
1982			
Jan	9	Wolverhampton W	A
Jan	16	Swansea C	H
Jan	30	Arsenal	A
Feb	6	Coventry C	H
Feb	13	Aston Villa	A
Feb	20	Ipswich T	H
Feb	27	Liverpool	H
Mar	6	WBA	A
Mar	13	Sunderland	A
Mar	20	Nottingham F	H
Mar	27	Notts Co	A
Apr	3	Manchester U	H
Apr	10	Birmingham C	A
Apr	13	Middlesbrough	H
Apr	17	Southampton	H
Apr	24	West Ham U	A
May	1	Stoke C	H
May	4	Everton	A
May	8	Tottenham H	A
May	15	Brighton & HA	H

LIVERPOOL

Date 1981		Opponents	Venue
Aug	29	Wolverhampton W	A
Sept	1	Middlesbrough	H
Sept	5	Arsenal	H
Sept	12	Ipswich T	A
Sept	19	Aston Villa	H
Sept	22	Coventry C	A
Sept	26	West Ham U	A
Oct	3	Swansea C	H
Oct	10	Leeds U	H
Oct	17	Brighton & HA	A
Oct	24	Manchester U	H
Oct	31	Sunderland	A
Nov	7	Everton	H
Nov	14	Notts Co	A
Nov	21	WBA	A
Nov	24	West Ham U	H
Nov	28	Southampton	H
Dec	5	Nottingham F	A
Dec	12	Birmingham C	H
Dec	19	Tottenham H	A
Dec	26	Manchester C	H
Dec	28	Stoke C	A
1982			
Jan	9	Arsenal	A
Jan	16	Wolverhampton W	H
Jan	30	Aston Villa	A
Feb	6	Ipswich T	H
Feb	13	Swansea C	A
Feb	20	Coventry C	H
Feb	27	Leeds U	A
Mar	6	Brighton & HA	H
Mar	13	Manchester U	A
Mar	20	Sunderland	H
Mar	27	Everton	A
Apr	3	Notts Co	H
Apr	10	Manchester C	A
Apr	13	Stoke C	H
Apr	17	WBA	H
Apr	24	Southampton	A
May	1	Nottingham F	H
May	4	Middlesbrough	A
May	8	Birmingham C	A
May	15	Tottenham H	H

DIVISION ONE

MANCHESTER CITY

Date		Opponents	Venue
1981			
Aug	29	WBA	H
Sept	1	Notts Co	A
Sept	5	Stoke C	A
Sept	12	Southampton	H
Sept	19	Birmingham C	A
Sept	23	Leeds U	H
Sept	26	Tottenham H	H
Oct	3	Brighton & HA	A
Oct	10	Manchester U	H
Oct	17	Arsenal	A
Oct	24	Nottingham F	H
Oct	31	Everton	A
Nov	7	Middlesbrough	H
Nov	14	West Ham U	A
Nov	21	Swansea C	H
Nov	25	Leeds U	A
Nov	28	Ipswich T	A
Dec	5	Aston Villa	H
Dec	12	Coventry C	A
Dec	19	Sunderland	H
Dec	26	Liverpool	A
Dec	28	Wolverhampton W	H
1982			
Jan	9	Stoke C	H
Jan	16	WBA	A
Jan	30	Birmingham C	H
Feb	6	Southampton	A
Feb	13	Brighton & HA	H
Feb	20	Tottenham H	A
Feb	27	Manchester U	A
Mar	6	Arsenal	H
Mar	13	Nottingham F	A
Mar	20	Everton	H
Mar	27	Middlesbrough	A
Apr	3	West Ham U	H
Apr	10	Liverpool	H
Apr	12	Wolverhampton W	A
Apr	17	Swansea C	A
Apr	24	Ipswich T	H
May	1	Aston Villa	A
May	5	Notts Co	H
May	8	Coventry C	H
May	15	Sunderland	A

MANCHESTER UNITED

Date		Opponents	Venue
1981			
Aug	29	Coventry C	A
Aug	31	Nottingham F	H
Sept	5	Ipswich T	H
Sept	12	Aston Villa	A
Sept	19	Swansea C	H
Sept	22	Middlesbrough	A
Sept	26	Arsenal	A
Oct	3	Wolverhampton W	H
Oct	10	Manchester C	A
Oct	17	Birmingham C	H
Oct	21	Middlesbrough	H
Oct	24	Liverpool	A
Oct	31	Notts Co	H
Nov	7	Sunderland	A
Nov	14	Leeds U	H
Nov	21	Tottenham H	A
Nov	28	Brighton & HA	H
Dec	5	Southampton	A
Dec	12	West Ham U	H
Dec	19	Stoke C	A
Dec	26	Everton	H
Dec	28	WBA	A
1982			
Jan	9	Ipswich T	A
Jan	16	Coventry C	H
Jan	30	Swansea C	A
Feb	6	Aston Villa	H
Feb	13	Wolverhampton W	A
Feb	20	Arsenal	H
Feb	27	Manchester C	H
Mar	6	Birmingham C	A
Mar	13	Liverpool	H
Mar	20	Notts Co	A
Mar	27	Sunderland	H
Apr	3	Leeds U	A
Apr	10	Everton	A
Apr	12	WBA	H
Apr	17	Tottenham H	H
Apr	24	Brighton & HA	A
May	1	Southampton	H
May	5	Nottingham F	A
May	8	West Ham U	A
May	15	Stoke C	H

MIDDLESBROUGH

Date		Opponents	Venue
1981			
Aug	29	Tottenham H	H
Sept	1	Liverpool	A
Sept	5	Brighton & HA	A
Sept	12	Birmingham C	H
Sept	19	Southampton	A
Sept	22	Manchester U	H
Sept	26	Stoke C	H
Oct	3	WBA	A
Oct	10	Nottingham F	H
Oct	17	Wolverhampton W	A
Oct	21	Manchester U	A
Oct	24	Everton	H
Oct	31	West Ham U	A
Nov	7	Manchester C	A
Nov	14	Sunderland	H
Nov	21	Aston Villa	H
Nov	28	Coventry C	A
Dec	5	Ipswich T	H
Dec	12	Arsenal	A
Dec	19	Swansea C	H
Dec	26	Notts Co	A
Dec	28	Leeds U	H
1982			
Jan	9	Brighton & HA	H
Jan	16	Tottenham H	A
Jan	30	Southampton	H
Feb	6	Birmingham C	A
Feb	13	WBA	H
Feb	20	Stoke C	A
Feb	27	Nottingham F	A
Mar	6	Wolverhampton W	H
Mar	13	Everton	A
Mar	20	West Ham U	H
Mar	27	Manchester C	H
Apr	3	Sunderland	A
Apr	10	Notts Co	H
Apr	13	Leeds U	A
Apr	17	Aston Villa	A
Apr	24	Coventry C	H
May	1	Ipswich T	A
May	4	Liverpool	H
May	8	Arsenal	H
May	15	Swansea C	A

NOTTINGHAM FOREST

Date		Opponents	Venue
1981			
Aug	29	Southampton	H
Aug	31	Manchester U	A
Sept	5	Birmingham C	A
Sept	12	WBA	H
Sept	19	Stoke C	A
Sept	23	Sunderland	H
Sept	26	Brighton & HA	H
Oct	3	Tottenham H	A
Oct	10	Middlesbrough	A
Oct	17	Coventry C	H
Oct	24	Manchester C	A
Oct	31	Leeds U	H
Nov	7	West Ham U	H
Nov	14	Everton	A
Nov	21	Arsenal	H
Nov	25	Sunderland	A
Nov	28	Aston Villa	A
Dec	5	Liverpool	H
Dec	12	Swansea C	A
Dec	20	Ipswich T	H
Dec	26	Wolverhampton W	A
Dec	28	Notts Co	H
1982			
Jan	9	Birmingham C	H
Jan	16	Southampton	A
Jan	30	Stoke C	H
Feb	6	WBA	A
Feb	13	Tottenham H	H
Feb	20	Brighton & HA	A
Feb	27	Middlesbrough	H
Mar	6	Coventry C	A
Mar	13	Manchester C	H
Mar	20	Leeds U	A
Mar	27	West Ham U	A
Apr	3	Everton	H
Apr	10	Wolverhampton W	H
Apr	12	Notts Co	A
Apr	17	Arsenal	A
Apr	24	Aston Villa	H
May	1	Liverpool	A
May	5	Manchester U	H
May	8	Swansea C	H
May	15	Ipswich T	A

NOTTS COUNTY

Date		Opponents	Venue
1981			
Aug	29	Aston Villa	A
Sept	1	Manchester C	H
Sept	5	Coventry C	H
Sept	12	Swansea C	A
Sept	19	Ipswich T	H
Sept	22	Everton	A
Sept	26	Wolverhampton W	A
Oct	3	Arsenal	H
Oct	10	Sunderland	H
Oct	17	Southampton	A
Oct	24	West Ham U	H
Oct	31	Manchester U	A
Nov	7	Leeds U	A
Nov	14	Liverpool	H
Nov	21	Brighton & HA	A
Nov	24	Everton	H
Nov	28	Tottenham H	H
Dec	5	Birmingham C	A
Dec	12	Stoke C	H
Dec	19	WBA	A
Dec	26	Middlesbrough	H
Dec	28	Nottingham F	A
1982			
Jan	9	Coventry C	A
Jan	16	Aston Villa	H
Jan	30	Ipswich T	A
Feb	6	Swansea C	H
Feb	13	Arsenal	A
Feb	20	Wolverhampton W	H
Feb	27	Sunderland	A
Mar	6	Southampton	H
Mar	13	West Ham U	A
Mar	20	Manchester U	H
Mar	27	Leeds U	H
Apr	3	Liverpool	A
Apr	10	Middlesbrough	A
Apr	12	Nottingham F	H
Apr	17	Brighton & HA	H
Apr	24	Tottenham H	A
May	1	Birmingham C	H
May	5	Manchester C	A
May	8	Stoke C	A
May	15	WBA	H

DIVISION ONE

SOUTHAMPTON

Date		Opponents	Venue
1981			
Aug	29	Nottingham F	A
Sept	1	Wolverhampton W	H
Sept	5	Everton	H
Sept	12	Manchester C	A
Sept	19	Middlesbrough	H
Sept	22	West Ham U	A
Sept	26	Coventry C	A
Oct	3	Ipswich T	H
Oct	10	Birmingham C	A
Oct	17	Notts Co	H
Oct	24	WBA	A
Oct	31	Tottenham H	H
Nov	7	Stoke C	A
Nov	14	Brighton & HA	H
Nov	21	Leeds U	H
Nov	24	Wolverhampton W	A
Nov	28	Liverpool	A
Dec	5	Manchester U	H
Dec	12	Sunderland	A
Dec	19	Arsenal	H
Dec	26	Aston Villa	A
Dec	28	Swansea C	H
1982			
Jan	9	Everton	A
Jan	16	Nottingham F	H
Jan	30	Middlesbrough	A
Feb	6	Manchester C	H
Feb	13	Ipswich T	A
Feb	20	West Ham U	H
Feb	27	Birmingham C	H
Mar	6	Notts Co	A
Mar	13	WBA	H
Mar	20	Tottenham H	A
Mar	27	Stoke C	H
Apr	3	Brighton & HA	A
Apr	10	Aston Villa	H
Apr	13	Swansea C	A
Apr	17	Leeds U	A
Apr	24	Liverpool	H
May	1	Manchester U	A
May	4	Coventry C	H
May	8	Sunderland	H
May	15	Arsenal	A

STOKE CITY

Date		Opponents	Venue
1981			
Aug	29	Arsenal	A
Sept	2	Coventry C	H
Sept	5	Manchester C	H
Sept	12	West Ham U	A
Sept	19	Nottingham F	H
Sept	23	Aston Villa	A
Sept	26	Middlesbrough	A
Oct	3	Everton	H
Oct	10	Tottenham H	A
Oct	17	Swansea C	H
Oct	24	Birmingham C	H
Oct	31	Brighton & HA	A
Nov	7	Southampton	H
Nov	14	WBA	A
Nov	21	Ipswich T	H
Nov	24	Coventry C	A
Nov	28	Wolverhampton W	A
Dec	5	Leeds U	H
Dec	12	Notts Co	A
Dec	19	Manchester U	H
Dec	26	Sunderland	A
Dec	28	Liverpool	H
1982			
Jan	9	Manchester C	A
Jan	16	Arsenal	H
Jan	30	Nottingham F	A
Feb	6	West Ham U	H
Feb	13	Everton	A
Feb	20	Middlesbrough	H
Feb	27	Tottenham H	H
Mar	6	Swansea C	A
Mar	13	Birmingham C	A
Mar	20	Brighton & HA	H
Mar	27	Southampton	A
Apr	3	WBA	H
Apr	10	Sunderland	H
Apr	13	Liverpool	A
Apr	17	Ipswich T	A
Apr	24	Wolverhampton W	H
May	1	Leeds U	A
May	5	Aston Villa	H
May	8	Notts Co	H
May	15	Manchester U	A

SUNDERLAND

Date		Opponents	Venue
1981			
Aug	29	Ipswich T	A
Sept	2	Aston Villa	H
Sept	5	West Ham U	H
Sept	12	Arsenal	A
Sept	19	Wolverhampton W	H
Sept	23	Nottingham F	A
Sept	26	Swansea C	A
Oct	3	Coventry C	H
Oct	10	Notts Co	A
Oct	17	Tottenham H	H
Oct	24	Leeds U	A
Oct	31	Liverpool	H
Nov	7	Manchester U	H
Nov	14	Middlesbrough	A
Nov	21	Everton	A
Nov	25	Nottingham F	H
Nov	28	WBA	H
Dec	5	Brighton & HA	A
Dec	12	Southampton	H
Dec	19	Manchester C	A
Dec	26	Stoke C	H
Dec	28	Birmingham C	A
1982			
Jan	9	Aston Villa	A
Jan	16	Ipswich T	H
Jan	30	Wolverhampton W	A
Feb	6	Arsenal	H
Feb	13	Coventry C	A
Feb	20	Swansea C	H
Feb	27	Notts Co	H
Mar	6	Tottenham H	A
Mar	13	Leeds U	H
Mar	20	Liverpool	A
Mar	27	Manchester U	A
Apr	3	Middlesbrough	H
Apr	10	Stoke C	A
Apr	12	Birmingham C	H
Apr	17	Everton	H
Apr	24	WBA	A
May	1	Brighton & HA	H
May	4	West Ham U	A
May	8	Southampton	A
May	15	Manchester C	H

SWANSEA CITY

Date		Opponents	Venue
1981			
Aug	29	Leeds U	H
Sept	1	Brighton & HA	A
Sept	5	WBA	A
Sept	12	Notts Co	H
Sept	19	Manchester U	A
Sept	22	Tottenham H	H
Sept	26	Sunderland	H
Oct	3	Liverpool	A
Oct	10	Arsenal	H
Oct	17	Stoke C	A
Oct	24	Coventry C	A
Oct	31	Wolverhampton W	H
Nov	7	Ipswich T	A
Nov	14	Aston Villa	H
Nov	21	Manchester C	A
Nov	24	Brighton & HA	H
Nov	28	Birmingham C	H
Dec	5	Everton	A
Dec	12	Nottingham F	H
Dec	19	Middlesbrough	A
Dec	26	West Ham U	H
Dec	28	Southampton	A
1982			
Jan	9	WBA	H
Jan	16	Leeds U	A
Jan	30	Manchester U	H
Feb	6	Notts Co	A
Feb	13	Liverpool	H
Feb	20	Sunderland	A
Feb	27	Arsenal	A
Mar	6	Stoke C	H
Mar	13	Coventry C	H
Mar	20	Wolverhampton W	A
Mar	27	Ipswich T	H
Apr	3	Aston Villa	A
Apr	10	West Ham U	A
Apr	13	Southampton	H
Apr	17	Manchester C	H
Apr	24	Birmingham C	A
May	1	Everton	H
May	5	Tottenham H	A
May	8	Nottingham F	A
May	15	Middlesbrough	H

TOTTENHAM HOTSPUR

Date		Opponents	Venue
1981			
Aug	29	Middlesbrough	A
Sept	2	West Ham U	H
Sept	5	Aston Villa	H
Sept	12	Wolverhampton W	A
Sept	19	Everton	H
Sept	22	Swansea C	A
Sept	26	Manchester C	A
Oct	3	Nottingham F	H
Oct	10	Stoke C	H
Oct	17	Sunderland	A
Oct	24	Brighton & HA	H
Oct	31	Southampton	A
Nov	7	WBA	H
Nov	14	Birmingham C	A
Nov	21	Manchester U	H
Nov	25	Aston Villa	A
Nov	28	Notts Co	A
Dec	5	Coventry C	H
Dec	12	Leeds U	A
Dec	19	Liverpool	H
Dec	26	Ipswich T	A
Dec	28	Arsenal	H
1982			
Jan	9	West Ham U	A
Jan	16	Middlesbrough	H
Jan	30	Everton	A
Feb	6	Wolverhampton W	H
Feb	13	Nottingham F	A
Feb	20	Manchester C	H
Feb	27	Stoke C	A
Mar	6	Sunderland	H
Mar	13	Brighton & HA	A
Mar	20	Southampton	H
Mar	27	WBA	A
Apr	3	Birmingham C	H
Apr	10	Ipswich T	H
Apr	12	Arsenal	A
Apr	17	Manchester U	A
Apr	24	Notts Co	H
May	1	Coventry C	A
May	5	Swansea C	H
May	8	Leeds U	H
May	15	Liverpool	A

DIVISION ONE

WEST BROMWICH A

Date		Opponents	Venue
1981			
Aug	29	Manchester C	A
Sept	2	Arsenal	H
Sept	5	Swansea C	H
Sept	12	Nottingham F	A
Sept	19	West Ham U	H
Sept	22	Ipswich T	A
Sept	26	Everton	A
Oct	3	Middlesbrough	H
Oct	10	Brighton & HA	H
Oct	17	Leeds U	A
Oct	24	Southampton	H
Oct	31	Birmingham C	A
Nov	7	Tottenham H	A
Nov	14	Stoke C	H
Nov	21	Liverpool	H
Nov	24	Arsenal	A
Nov	28	Sunderland	A
Dec	5	Wolverhampton W	H
Dec	12	Aston Villa	A
Dec	19	Notts Co	H
Dec	26	Coventry C	A
Dec	28	Manchester U	H
1982			
Jan	9	Swansea C	A
Jan	16	Manchester C	H
Jan	30	West Ham U	A
Feb	6	Nottingham F	H
Feb	13	Middlesbrough	A
Feb	20	Everton	H
Feb	27	Brighton & HA	A
Mar	6	Leeds U	H
Mar	13	Southampton	A
Mar	20	Birmingham C	H
Mar	27	Tottenham H	H
April	3	Stoke C	A
Apr	10	Coventry C	H
Apr	12	Manchester U	A
Apr	17	Liverpool	A
April	24	Sunderland	H
May	1	Wolverhampton W	A
May	5	Ipswich T	H
May	8	Aston Villa	H
May	15	Notts Co	A

WEST HAM UNITED

Date		Opponents	Venue
1981			
Aug	29	Brighton & HA	H
Sept	2	Tottenham H	A
Sept	5	Sunderland	A
Sept	12	Stoke C	H
Sept	19	WBA	A
Sept	22	Southampton	H
Sept	26	Liverpool	H
Oct	3	Birmingham C	A
Oct	10	Everton	H
Oct	17	Aston Villa	A
Oct	24	Notts Co	A
Oct	31	Middlesbrough	H
Nov	7	Nottingham F	A
Nov	14	Manchester C	H
Nov	21	Coventry C	H
Nov	24	Liverpool	A
Nov	28	Leeds U	A
Dec	5	Arsenal	H
Dec	12	Manchester U	A
Dec	19	Wolverhampton W	H
Dec	26	Swansea C	A
Dec	28	Ipswich T	H
1982			
Jan	9	Tottenham H	H
Jan	16	Brighton & HA	A
Jan	30	WBA	H
Feb	6	Stoke C	A
Feb	13	Birmingham C	H
Feb	20	Southampton	A
Feb	27	Everton	A
Mar	6	Aston Villa	H
Mar	13	Notts Co	H
Mar	20	Middlesbrough	A
Mar	27	Nottingham F	H
Apr	3	Manchester C	A
Apr	10	Swansea C	H
Apr	13	Ipswich T	A
Apr	17	Coventry C	A
Apr	24	Leeds U	H
May	1	Arsenal	A
May	4	Sunderland	H
May	8	Manchester U	H
May	15	Wolverhampton W	A

WOLVERHAMPTON W

Date		Opponents	Venue
1981			
Aug	29	Liverpool	H
Sept	1	Southampton	A
Sept	5	Leeds U	A
Sept	12	Tottenham H	H
Sept	19	Sunderland	A
Sept	22	Brighton & HA	H
Sept	26	Notts Co	H
Oct	3	Manchester U	A
Oct	10	Ipswich T	A
Oct	17	Middlesbrough	H
Oct	24	Aston Villa	H
Oct	31	Swansea C	A
Nov	7	Coventry C	H
Nov	14	Arsenal	A
Nov	21	Birmingham C	A
Nov	24	Southampton	H
Nov	28	Stoke C	H
Dec	5	WBA	A
Dec	12	Everton	H
Dec	19	West Ham U	A
Dec	26	Nottingham F	H
Dec	28	Manchester C	A
1982			
Jan	9	Leeds U	H
Jan	16	Liverpool	A
Jan	30	Sunderland	H
Feb	6	Tottenham H	A
Feb	13	Manchester U	H
Feb	20	Notts Co	A
Feb	27	Ipswich T	H
Mar	6	Middlesbrough	A
Mar	13	Aston Villa	A
Mar	20	Swansea C	H
Mar	27	Coventry C	A
Apr	3	Arsenal	H
Apr	10	Nottingham F	A
Apr	12	Manchester C	H
Apr	17	Birmingham C	H
Apr	24	Stoke C	A
May	1	WBA	H
May	4	Brighton & HA	A
May	8	Everton	A
May	15	West Ham U	H

DIVISION TWO

BARNSLEY

Date		Opponents	Venue
1981			
Aug	29	Shrewsbury T	H
Sept	5	Norwich C	A
Sept	8	Leicester C	A
Sept	12	Bolton W	H
Sept	19	Cambridge U	A
Sept	22	Sheffield W	H
Sept	26	Cardiff C	H
Oct	3	Watford	A
Oct	10	Blackburn R	A
Oct	17	Newcastle U	H
Oct	24	Chelsea	A
Oct	31	Orient	H
Nov	7	Oldham Ath	H
Nov	14	Rotherham U	A
Nov	21	Wrexham	H
Nov	24	Sheffield W	A
Nov	28	Charlton Ath	A
Dec	5	Crystal Palace	H
Dec	12	QPR	A
Dec	19	Luton T	H
Dec	26	Derby Co	A
Dec	28	Grimsby T	H
1982			
Jan	9	Norwich C	H
Jan	16	Shrewsbury T	A
Jan	30	Cambridge U	H
Feb	6	Bolton W	A
Feb	13	Watford	H
Feb	20	Cardiff C	A
Feb	27	Blackburn R	H
Mar	6	Newcastle U	A
Mar	12	Chelsea	H
Mar	20	Orient	A
Mar	27	Oldham Ath	A
Apr	2	Rotherham U	H
Apr	9	Grimsby T	A
Apr	10	Derby Co	H
Apr	17	Wrexham	A
Apr	24	Charlton Ath	H
May	1	Crystal Palace	A
May	4	Leicester C	H
May	8	QPR	H
May	15	Luton T	A

BLACKBURN ROVERS

Date		Opponents	Venue
1981			
Aug	29	Sheffield W	H
Sept	1	Shrewsbury T	A
Sept	5	Charlton Ath	A
Sept	12	Orient	H
Sept	19	Cardiff C	A
Sept	23	Cambridge U	H
Sept	26	Leicester C	H
Oct	3	QPR	A
Oct	10	Barnsley	H
Oct	17	Derby Co	A
Oct	24	Grimsby T	A
Oct	31	Wrexham	H
Nov	7	Crystal Palace	A
Nov	14	Luton T	H
Nov	21	Watford	A
Nov	25	Shrewsbury T	H
Nov	28	Norwich C	H
Dec	5	Newcastle U	A
Dec	12	Rotherham U	H
Dec	19	Chelsea	A
Dec	26	Oldham Ath	H
Dec	28	Bolton W	A
1982			
Jan	9	Charlton Ath	H
Jan	16	Sheffield W	A
Jan	30	Cardiff C	H
Feb	6	Orient	A
Feb	13	QPR	H
Feb	20	Leicester C	A
Feb	27	Barnsley	A
Mar	6	Derby Co	H
Mar	13	Grimsby T	H
Mar	20	Wrexham	A
Mar	27	Crystal Palace	H
Apr	3	Luton T	A
Apr	10	Oldham Ath	A
Apr	12	Bolton W	H
Apr	17	Watford	H
Apr	24	Norwich C	A
May	1	Newcastle U	H
May	4	Cambridge U	A
May	8	Rotherham U	A
May	15	Chelsea	H

DIVISION TWO

BOLTON WANDERERS

Date	Opponents	Venue
1981		
Aug 29	Chelsea	A
Sept 5	Luton T	H
Sept 8	Newcastle U	H
Sept 12	Barnsley	A
Sept 19	Oldham Ath	H
Sept 23	Derby Co	A
Sept 26	Rotherham U	A
Oct 3	Grimsby T	H
Oct 10	Leicester C	H
Oct 17	Cardiff C	A
Oct 24	Cambridge U	H
Oct 31	Norwich C	A
Nov 7	Watford	H
Nov 14	Shrewsbury T	A
Nov 21	Orient	H
Nov 24	Luton T	A
Nov 28	Crystal Palace	A
Dec 5	QPR	H
Dec 12	Sheffield W	A
Dec 19	Charlton Ath	H
Dec 26	Wrexham	A
Dec 28	Blackburn R	H
1982		
Jan 9	Newcastle U	A
Jan 16	Chelsea	H
Jan 30	Oldham Ath	A
Feb 6	Barnsley	H
Feb 13	Grimsby T	A
Feb 20	Rotherham U	H
Feb 27	Leicester C	A
Mar 6	Cardiff C	H
Mar 13	Cambridge U	A
Mar 20	Norwich C	H
Mar 27	Watford	A
Apr 3	Shrewsbury T	H
Apr 10	Wrexham	H
Apr 12	Blackburn R	A
Apr 17	Orient	A
Apr 24	Crystal Palace	H
May 1	QPR	A
May 4	Derby Co	H
May 8	Sheffield W	H
May 15	Charlton Ath	A

CAMBRIDGE UNITED

Date	Opponents	Venue
1981		
Aug 29	Crystal Palace	A
Sept 1	Derby Co	H
Sept 5	Rotherham U	H
Sept 12	Newcastle U	A
Sept 19	Barnsley	H
Sept 23	Blackburn R	A
Sept 26	Oldham Ath	A
Oct 3	Chelsea	H
Oct 10	Grimsby T	A
Oct 17	Watford	H
Oct 24	Bolton W	A
Oct 31	Cardiff C	H
Nov 7	Shrewsbury T	H
Nov 14	Norwich C	A
Nov 21	Sheffield W	H
Nov 25	Derby Co	A
Nov 28	Leicester C	A
Dec 5	Wrexham	H
Dec 12	Charlton Ath	A
Dec 19	QPR	H
Dec 26	Luton T	A
Dec 28	Orient	H
1982		
Jan 9	Rotherham U	A
Jan 16	Crystal Palace	H
Jan 30	Barnsley	A
Feb 6	Newcastle U	H
Feb 13	Chelsea	A
Feb 20	Oldham Ath	H
Feb 27	Grimsby T	H
Mar 6	Watford	A
Mar 13	Bolton W	H
Mar 20	Cardiff C	A
Mar 27	Shrewsbury T	A
Apr 3	Norwich C	H
Apr 10	Luton T	H
Apr 12	Orient	A
Apr 17	Sheffield W	A
Apr 24	Leicester C	H
May 1	Wrexham	A
May 4	Blackburn R	H
May 8	Charlton Ath	H
May 15	QPR	A

CARDIFF CITY

Date	Opponents	Venue
1981		
Aug 29	Oldham Ath	A
Sept 5	Chelsea	H
Sept 12	Rotherham U	A
Sept 19	Blackburn R	H
Sept 22	Luton T	A
Sept 26	Barnsley	A
Oct 3	Newcastle U	H
Oct 10	Sheffield W	A
Oct 17	Bolton W	H
Oct 24	Shrewsbury T	H
Oct 31	Cambridge U	A
Nov 4	Wrexham	H
Nov 7	Norwich C	H
Nov 14	Watford	A
Nov 21	Leicester C	H
Nov 24	Wrexham	A
Nov 28	QPR	A
Dec 4	Derby Co	H
Dec 12	Crystal Palace	A
Dec 19	Grimsby T	H
Dec 26	Orient	A
Dec 28	Charlton Ath	H
1982		
Jan 9	Chelsea	A
Jan 16	Oldham Ath	H
Jan 30	Blackburn R	A
Feb 6	Rotherham U	H
Feb 13	Newcastle U	A
Feb 20	Barnsley	H
Feb 27	Sheffield W	H
Mar 6	Bolton W	A
Mar 13	Shrewsbury T	A
Mar 20	Cambridge U	H
Mar 27	Norwich C	A
Apr 3	Watford	H
Apr 10	Orient	H
Apr 13	Charlton Ath	A
Apr 17	Leicester C	A
Apr 24	QPR	H
May 1	Derby Co	A
May 5	Luton T	H
May 8	Crystal Palace	H
May 15	Grimsby T	A

CHARLTON ATHLETIC

Date	Opponents	Venue
1981		
Aug 29	Luton T	A
Sept 5	Blackburn R	H
Sept 12	Crystal Palace	A
Sept 19	Grimsby T	H
Sept 23	Chelsea	A
Sept 26	Wrexham	A
Oct 3	Derby Co	H
Oct 10	Shrewsbury Town	A
Oct 17	Sheffield W	H
Oct 20	Oldham Ath	H
Oct 25	Orient	A
Oct 31	QPR	H
Nov 7	Leicester C	H
Nov 14	Newcastle U	A
Nov 21	Rotherham U	A
Nov 24	Chelsea	H
Nov 28	Barnsley	H
Dec 5	Watford	A
Dec 12	Cambridge U	H
Dec 19	Bolton W	A
Dec 26	Norwich C	H
Dec 28	Cardiff C	A
1982		
Jan 9	Blackburn R	A
Jan 16	Luton T	H
Jan 30	Grimsby T	A
Feb 6	Crystal Palace	H
Feb 13	Derby Co	A
Feb 20	Wrexham	H
Feb 27	Shrewsbury T	H
Mar 6	Sheffield W	A
Mar 13	Orient	H
Mar 20	QPR	A
Mar 27	Leicester C	A
Apr 3	Newcastle U	H
Apr 10	Norwich C	A
Apr 13	Cardiff C	H
Apr 17	Rotherham U	H
Apr 24	Barnsley	A
May 1	Watford	H
May 4	Oldham Ath	A
May 8	Cambridge U	A
May 15	Bolton W	H

CHELSEA

Date	Opponents	Venue
1981		
Aug 29	Bolton W	H
Sept 5	Cardiff C	A
Sept 12	Watford	H
Sept 19	Shrewsbury T	A
Sept 23	Charlton Ath	H
Sept 26	Norwich City	H
Sept 29	Orient	A
Oct 3	Cambridge U	A
Oct 10	Wrexham	H
Oct 16	Leicester C	A
Oct 24	Barnsley	H
Oct 31	Rotherham U	A
Nov 7	Newcastle U	H
Nov 14	Oldham Ath	A
Nov 21	Grimsby T	H
Nov 24	Charlton Ath	A
Nov 28	Derby Co	A
Dec 5	Sheffield W	H
Dec 12	Luton T	A
Dec 19	Blackburn R	H
Dec 26	QPR	A
Dec 28	Crystal Palace	H
1982		
Jan 9	Cardiff C	H
Jan 16	Bolton W	A
Jan 30	Shrewsbury T	H
Feb 6	Watford	A
Feb 13	Cambridge U	H
Feb 20	Norwich C	A
Feb 27	Wrexham	A
Mar 6	Leicester C	H
Mar 12	Barnsley	A
Mar 20	Rotherham U	H
Mar 27	Newcastle U	A
Apr 3	Oldham Ath	H
Apr 10	QPR	H
Apr 12	Crystal Palace	A
Apr 17	Grimsby T	A
Apr 24	Derby Co	H
May 1	Sheffield W	A
May 5	Orient	H
May 8	Luton T	H
May 15	Blackburn R	A

DIVISION TWO

CRYSTAL PALACE

Date	Opponents	Venue
1981		
Aug 29	Cambridge U	H
Sept 2	Norwich C	A
Sept 5	Sheffield W	A
Sept 12	Charlton Ath	H
Sept 19	QPR	A
Sept 22	Orient	H
Sept 26	Shrewsbury T	H
Oct 3	Leicester C	A
Oct 10	Rotherham U	H
Oct 17	Wrexham	A
Oct 24	Derby Co	H
Oct 31	Luton T	A
Nov 7	Blackburn R	H
Nov 14	Grimsby T	A
Nov 21	Oldham Ath	A
Nov 24	Norwich C	H
Nov 28	Bolton W	H
Dec 5	Barnsley	A
Dec 12	Cardiff C	H
Dec 19	Newcastle U	A
Dec 26	Watford	H
Dec 28	Chelsea	A
1982		
Jan 9	Sheffield W	H
Jan 16	Cambridge U	A
Jan 30	QPR	H
Feb 6	Charlton Ath	A
Feb 13	Leicester C	H
Feb 21	Orient	A
Feb 27	Rotherham U	A
Mar 6	Wrexham	H
Mar 13	Derby Co	A
Mar 20	Luton T	H
Mar 27	Blackburn R	A
Apr 3	Grimsby T	H
Apr 9	Watford	A
Apr 12	Chelsea	H
Apr 17	Oldham Ath	H
Apr 24	Bolton W	A
May 1	Barnsley	H
May 4	Shrewsbury T	A
May 8	Cardiff C	A
May 15	Newcastle U	H

DERBY COUNTY

Date	Opponents	Venue
1981		
Aug 29	Orient	H
Sept 1	Cambridge U	A
Sept 5	Shrewsbury T	A
Sept 12	Leicester C	H
Sept 19	Sheffield W	A
Sept 23	Bolton W	H
Sept 26	QPR	H
Oct 3	Charlton Ath	A
Oct 10	Newcastle U	A
Oct 17	Blackburn R	H
Oct 24	Crystal Palace	A
Oct 31	Grimsby T	H
Nov 7	Luton T	A
Nov 14	Wrexham	H
Nov 21	Norwich C	A
Nov 25	Cambridge U	H
Nov 28	Chelsea	H
Dec 4	Cardiff C	A
Dec 12	Oldham Ath	H
Dec 19	Watford	A
Dec 26	Barnsley	H
Dec 28	Rotherham U	A
1982		
Jan 9	Shrewsbury T	H
Jan 16	Orient	A
Jan 30	Sheffield W	H
Feb 6	Leicester C	A
Feb 13	Charlton Ath	H
Feb 20	QPR	A
Feb 27	Newcastle U	H
Mar 6	Blackburn R	A
Mar 13	Crystal Palace	H
Mar 20	Grimsby T	A
Mar 27	Luton T	H
Apr 3	Wrexham	A
Apr 10	Barnsley	A
Apr 12	Rotherham U	H
Apr 17	Norwich C	H
Apr 24	Chelsea	A
May 1	Cardiff C	H
May 4	Bolton W	A
May 8	Oldham Ath	A
May 15	Watford	H

GRIMSBY TOWN

Date	Opponents	Venue
1981		
Aug 29	Leicester C	H
Sept 1	Watford	A
Sept 5	Orient	A
Sept 12	QPR	H
Sept 19	Charlton Ath	A
Sept 22	Norwich C	H
Sept 26	Sheffield W	H
Oct 3	Bolton W	A
Oct 10	Cambridge U	H
Oct 17	Luton T	A
Oct 24	Blackburn R	H
Oct 31	Derby Co	A
Nov 7	Wrexham	A
Nov 14	Crystal Palace	H
Nov 21	Chelsea	A
Nov 24	Watford	H
Nov 28	Newcastle U	H
Dec 5	Oldham Ath	A
Dec 12	Shrewsbury T	H
Dec 19	Cardiff C	A
Dec 26	Rotherham U	H
Dec 28	Barnsley	A
1982		
Jan 9	Orient	H
Jan 16	Leicester C	A
Jan 30	Charlton Ath	H
Feb 6	QPR	A
Feb 13	Bolton W	H
Feb 20	Sheffield W	A
Feb 27	Cambridge U	A
Mar 6	Luton Town	H
Mar 13	Blackburn R	A
Mar 20	Derby Co	H
Mar 27	Wrexham	H
Apr 3	Crystal Palace	A
Apr 9	Barnsley	H
Apr 10	Rotherham U	A
Apr 17	Chelsea	H
Apr 24	Newcastle U	A
May 1	Oldham Ath	H
May 5	Norwich C	A
May 8	Shrewsbury T	A
May 15	Cardiff C	H

LEICESTER CITY

Date	Opponents	Venue
1981		
Aug 29	Grimsby T	A
Sept 5	Wrexham	H
Sept 8	Barnsley	H
Sept 12	Derby Co	A
Sept 19	Luton T	H
Sept 22	Rotherham U	A
Sept 26	Blackburn R	A
Oct 3	Crystal Palace	H
Oct 10	Bolton W	A
Oct 16	Chelsea	H
Oct 24	QPR	A
Oct 31	Sheffield W	H
Nov 7	Charlton Ath	A
Nov 14	Orient	H
Nov 21	Cardiff C	A
Nov 24	Rotherham U	H
Nov 28	Cambridge U	H
Dec 5	Norwich C	A
Dec 12	Watford	H
Dec 19	Shrewsbury T	A
Dec 26	Newcastle U	H
Dec 28	Oldham Ath	A
1982		
Jan 9	Wrexham	A
Jan 16	Grimsby T	H
Jan 30	Luton T	A
Feb 6	Derby Co	H
Feb 13	Crystal Palace	A
Feb 20	Blackburn R	H
Feb 27	Bolton W	H
Mar 6	Chelsea	A
Mar 13	QPR	H
Mar 20	Sheffield W	A
Mar 27	Charlton Ath	H
Apr 3	Orient	A
Apr 10	Newcastle U	A
Apr 12	Oldham Ath	H
Apr 17	Cardiff C	H
Apr 24	Cambridge U	A
May 1	Norwich C	H
May 4	Barnsley	A
May 8	Watford	A
May 15	Shrewsbury T	H

LUTON TOWN

Date	Opponents	Venue
1981		
Aug 29	Charlton Ath	H
Sept 1	QPR	A
Sept 5	Bolton W	A
Sept 12	Sheffield W	H
Sept 19	Leicester C	A
Sept 22	Cardiff C	H
Sept 26	Watford	H
Oct 3	Orient	A
Oct 10	Oldham Ath	A
Oct 17	Grimsby T	H
Oct 24	Wrexham	A
Oct 31	Crystal Palace	H
Nov 7	Derby Co	H
Nov 14	Blackburn R	A
Nov 21	Newcastle U	A
Nov 24	Bolton W	H
Nov 28	Rotherham U	H
Dec 5	Shrewsbury T	A
Dec 12	Chelsea	H
Dec 19	Barnsley	A
Dec 26	Cambridge U	H
Dec 28	Norwich C	A
1982		
Jan 9	QPR	H
Jan 16	Charlton Ath	A
Jan 30	Leicester C	H
Feb 6	Sheffield W	A
Feb 13	Orient	H
Feb 20	Watford	A
Feb 27	Oldham Ath	H
Mar 6	Grimsby T	A
Mar 12	Wrexham	H
Mar 20	Crystal Palace	A
Mar 27	Derby Co	A
Apr 3	Blackburn R	H
Apr 10	Cambridge U	A
Apr 12	Norwich C	H
Apr 17	Newcastle U	H
Apr 24	Rotherham U	A
Apr 30	Shrewsbury T	H
May 5	Cardiff C	A
May 8	Chelsea	A
May 15	Barnsley	H

BRENTFORD

Date		Opponents	Venue
1981			
Aug	29	Fulham	A
Sept	5	Walsall	H
Sept	12	Portsmouth	A
Sept	19	Plymouth Arg	H
Sept	21	Gillingham	H
Sept	26	Doncaster R	A
Sept	29	Newport Co	A
Oct	3	Carlisle U	H
Oct	10	Exeter C	A
Oct	17	Lincoln C	H
Oct	19	Southend U	H
Oct	24	Chesterfield	A
Oct	31	Burnley	H
Nov	3	Swindon T	A
Nov	7	Bristol C	H
Nov	14	Oxford U	A
Nov	28	Chester	H
Dec	5	Preston NE	A
Dec	19	Reading	A
Dec	26	Wimbledon	H
Dec	28	Millwall	A
1982			
Jan	2	Huddersfield T	H
Jan	9	Walsall	A
Jan	16	Bristol R	H
Jan	23	Fulham	H
Jan	30	Plymouth Arg	A
Feb	6	Portsmouth	H
Feb	9	Gillingham	A
Feb	13	Carlisle U	A
Feb	20	Newport Co	H
Feb	27	Exeter C	H
Mar	6	Lincoln C	A
Mar	8	Southend U	A
Mar	13	Chesterfield	H
Mar	15	a1SwindonT	H
Mar	20	Burnley	A
Mar	27	Bristol C	A
Apr	3	Oxford U	H
Apr	9	Millwall	H
Apr	12	Wimbledon	A
Apr	17	Preston NE	H
Apr	24	Chester	A
May	1	Doncaster R	H
May	3	Bristol R	A
May	8	Huddersfield T	A
May	15	Reading	H

BRISTOL CITY

Date		Opponents	Venue
1981			
Aug	29	Carlisle U	A
Sept	5	Doncaster R	H
Sept	12	Fulham	A
Sept	19	Newport Co	H
Sept	22	Plymouth Arg	H
Sept	26	Portsmouth	A
Sept	29	Gillingham	A
Oct	3	Walsall	H
Oct	10	Preston NE	H
Oct	17	Oxford U	A
Oct	20	Reading	H
Oct	24	Lincoln C	A
Oct	31	Chesterfield	H
Nov	3	Millwall	A
Nov	7	Brentford	A
Nov	14	Southend U	H
Nov	28	Burnley	H
Dec	5	Swindon T	A
Dec	18	Chester	A
Dec	26	Exeter C	H
Dec	28	Bristol R	A
1982			
Jan	2	Wimbledon	H
Jan	9	Doncaster R	A
Jan	16	Huddersfield T	H
Jan	23	Carlisle U	H
Jan	30	Newport Co	A
Feb	6	Fulham	H
Feb	9	Plymouth Arg	A
Feb	13	Walsall	A
Feb	20	Portsmouth	H
Feb	27	Preston NE	A
Mar	6	Oxford U	H
Mar	10	Reading	A
Mar	13	Lincoln C	H
Mar	16	Millwall	H
Mar	20	Chesterfield	A
Mar	27	Brentford	H
Apr	3	Southend U	A
Apr	10	Exeter C	A
Apr	12	Bristol R	H
Apr	17	Swindon T	H
Apr	24	Burnley	A
May	1	Gillingham	H
May	4	Huddersfield T	A
May	8	Wimbledon	A
May	15	Chester	H

BRISTOL ROVERS

Date		Opponents	Venue
1981			
Aug	29	Chester	H
Sept	5	Chesterfield	A
Sept	12	Burnley	H
Sept	19	Reading	A
Sept	23	Exeter C	A
Sept	26	Lincoln C	H
Sept	29	Wimbledon	H
Oct	3	Preston NE	A
Oct	9	Southend U	A
Oct	17	Swindon T	H
Oct	21	Oxford U	A
Oct	24	Huddersfield T	H
Oct	31	Doncaster R	A
Nov	3	Newport Co	H
Nov	7	Gillingham	H
Nov	14	Millwall	A
Nov	28	Walsall	A
Dec	5	Fulham	H
Dec	19	Carlisle U	H
Dec	26	Portsmouth	A
Dec	28	Bristol C	H
1982			
Jan	2	Plymouth Arg	A
Jan	9	Chesterfield	H
Jan	16	Brentford	A
Jan	23	Chester	A
Jan	30	Reading	H
Feb	6	Burnley	A
Feb	9	Exeter C	H
Feb	13	Preston NE	H
Feb	20	Wimbledon	A
Feb	27	Southend U	H
Mar	6	Swindon T	A
Mar	9	Oxford U	H
Mar	13	Huddersfield T	A
Mar	16	Newport Co	A
Mar	20	Doncaster R	H
Mar	27	Gillingham	A
Apr	3	Millwall	H
Apr	10	Portsmouth	H
Apr	12	Bristol C	A
Apr	17	Fulham	A
Apr	24	Walsall	H
May	1	Lincoln C	A
May	3	Brentford	H
May	8	Plymouth Arg	H
May	15	Carlisle U	A

BURNLEY

Date		Opponents	Venue
1981			
Aug	29	Gillingham	A
Sept	5	Plymouth Arg	H
Sept	12	Bristol R	A
Sept	19	Huddersfield T	H
Sept	22	Doncaster R	H
Sept	26	Millwall	A
Sept	29	Carlisle U	A
Oct	3	Swindon T	H
Oct	10	Portsmouth	A
Oct	17	Exeter C	H
Oct	20	Preston NE	A
Oct	24	Fulham	H
Oct	31	Brentford	A
Nov	3	Chester	H
Nov	7	Wimbledon	H
Nov	14	Reading	A
Nov	28	Bristol C	A
Dec	5	Oxford U	H
Dec	19	Southend U	H
Dec	26	Lincoln C	A
Dec	28	Chesterfield	H
1982			
Jan	2	Walsall	A
Jan	9	Plymouth Arg	A
Jan	16	Newport Co	H
Jan	23	Gillingham	H
Jan	30	Huddersfield T	A
Feb	6	Bristol R	H
Feb	9	Doncaster R	A
Feb	13	Swindon T	A
Feb	20	Millwall	H
Feb	27	Portsmouth	H
Mar	6	Exeter C	A
Mar	9	Preston NE	H
Mar	13	Fulham	A
Mar	17	Chester	A
Mar	20	Brentford	H
Mar	27	Wimbledon	A
Apr	3	Reading	H
Apr	10	Lincoln C	H
Apr	12	Chesterfield	A
Apr	17	Oxford U	A
Apr	24	Bristol C	H
May	1	Newport Co	A
May	4	Carlisle U	H
May	8	Walsall	H
May	14	Southend U	A

CARLISLE UNITED

Date		Opponents	Venue
1981			
Aug	29	Bristol C	H
Sept	5	Exeter C	A
Sept	12	Southend U	H
Sept	19	Lincoln C	A
Sept	22	Chesterfield	A
Sept	26	Oxford U	H
Sept	29	Burnley	H
Oct	3	Brentford	A
Oct	10	Swindon T	A
Oct	17	Plymouth Arg	H
Oct	20	Huddersfield T	A
Oct	24	Walsall	H
Oct	31	Newport Co	A
Nov	3	Doncaster R	H
Nov	7	Fulham	H
Nov	14	Portsmouth	A
Nov	28	Gillingham	H
Dec	5	Millwall	A
Dec	19	Bristol R	A
Dec	26	Preston NE	H
Dec	28	Chester	A
1982			
Jan	2	Reading	H
Jan	9	Exeter C	H
Jan	16	Wimbledon	A
Jan	23	Bristol C	A
Jan	30	Lincoln C	H
Feb	6	Southend U	A
Feb	9	Chesterfield	H
Feb	13	Brentford	H
Feb	20	Oxford U	A
Feb	27	Swindon T	H
Mar	6	Plymouth Arg	A
Mar	9	Huddersfield T	H
Mar	13	Walsall	A
Mar	16	Doncaster R	A
Mar	20	Newport Co	H
Mar	27	Fulham	A
Apr	3	Portsmouth	H
Apr	10	Preston NE	A
Apr	13	Chester	H
Apr	17	Millwall	H
Apr	24	Gillingham	A
May	1	Wimbledon	H
May	4	Burnley	A
May	8	Reading	A
May	15	Bristol R	H

DIVISION THREE

CHESTER

Date	Opponents	Venue
1981		
Aug 29	Bristol R	A
Sept 5	Swindon T	H
Sept 12	Gillingham	A
Sept 19	Millwall	H
Sept 23	Walsall	H
Sept 26	Fulham	A
Sept 29	Huddersfield T	A
Oct 3	Doncaster R	H
Oct 10	Oxford U	H
Oct 17	Wimbledon	A
Oct 21	Chesterfield	H
Oct 24	Plymouth Arg	A
Oct 31	Reading	H
Nov 3	Burnley	A
Nov 7	Preston NE	A
Nov 14	Exeter C	H
Nov 28	Brentford	A
Dec 5	Southend U	H
Dec 18	Bristol C	H
Dec 26	Newport Co	A
Dec 28	Carlisle U	H
1982		
Jan 2	Lincoln C	A
Jan 10	Swindon T	A
Jan 16	Portsmouth	H
Jan 23	Bristol R	H
Jan 30	Millwall	A
Feb 6	Gillingham	H
Feb 9	Walsall	A
Feb 13	Doncaster R	A
Feb 20	Huddersfield T	H
Feb 27	Oxford U	A
Mar 6	Wimbledon	H
Mar 9	Chesterfield	A
Mar 13	Plymouth Arg	H
Mar 17	Burnley	H
Mar 20	Reading	A
Mar 27	Preston NE	H
Apr 3	Exeter C	A
Apr 10	Newport Co	H
Apr 13	Carlisle U	A
Apr 17	Southend U	A
Apr 24	Brentford	H
May 1	Portsmouth	A
May 5	Fulham	H
May 8	Lincoln C	H
May 15	Bristol C	A

CHESTERFIELD

Date	Opponents	Venue
1981		
Aug 29	Newport Co	A
Sept 5	Bristol R	H
Sept 12	Walsall	A
Sept 19	Fulham	H
Sept 22	Carlisle U	H
Sept 26	Plymouth Arg	A
Sept 29	Swindon T	A
Oct 3	Portsmouth	H
Oct 10	Reading	A
Oct 17	Southend U	H
Oct 21	Chester	A
Oct 24	Brentford	H
Oct 31	Bristol C	A
Nov 3	Huddersfield T	H
Nov 7	Oxford U	H
Nov 14	Lincoln C	A
Nov 28	Wimbledon	H
Dec 5	Exeter C	A
Dec 22	Gillingham	A
Dec 26	Doncaster R	H
Dec 28	Burnley	A
1982		
Jan 2	Preston NE	H
Jan 9	Bristol R	A
Jan 16	Millwall	H
Jan 23	Newport Co	H
Jan 30	Fulham	A
Feb 6	Walsall	H
Feb 9	Carlisle U	A
Feb 13	Portsmouth	A
Feb 20	Plymouth Arg	H
Feb 27	Reading	H
Mar 5	Southend U	A
Mar 9	Chester	H
Mar 13	Brentford	A
Mar 16	Huddersfield T	A
Mar 20	Bristol C	H
Mar 27	Oxford U	A
Apr 3	Lincoln C	H
Apr 10	Doncaster R	A
Apr 12	Burnley	H
Apr 17	Exeter C	H
Apr 24	Wimbledon	A
May 1	Swindon T	H
May 4	Millwall	A
May 8	Preston NE	A
May 15	Gillingham	H

DONCASTER ROVERS

Date	Opponents	Venue
1981		
Aug 29	Reading	H
Sept 5	Bristol C	A
Sept 11	Exeter C	H
Sept 19	Wimbledon	A
Sept 22	Burnley	A
Sept 26	Brentford	H
Sept 29	Preston NE	H
Oct 3	Chester	A
Oct 10	Newport Co	A
Oct 17	Millwall	H
Oct 20	Lincoln C	H
Oct 24	Swindon T	A
Oct 31	Bristol R	H
Nov 3	Carlisle U	A
Nov 6	Huddersfield T	H
Nov 14	Gillingham	A
Nov 28	Plymouth Arg	A
Dec 5	Portsmouth	H
Dec 19	Walsall	H
Dec 26	Chesterfield	A
Dec 29	Oxford U	H
1982		
Jan 2	Fulham	A
Jan 9	Bristol C	H
Jan 16	Southend U	A
Jan 23	Reading	A
Jan 29	Wimbledon	H
Feb 6	Exeter C	A
Feb 9	Burnley	H
Feb 13	Chester	H
Feb 20	Preston NE	A
Feb 27	Newport Co	H
Mar 6	Millwall	A
Mar 10	Lincoln C	A
Mar 12	Swindon T	H
Mar 16	Carlisle U	H
Mar 20	Bristol R	A
Mar 27	Huddersfield T	A
Apr 3	Gillingham	H
Apr 10	Chesterfield	H
Apr 12	Oxford U	A
Apr 17	Portsmouth	A
Apr 24	Plymouth Arg	H
May 1	Brentford	A
May 4	Southend U	H
May 8	Fulham	H
May 15	Walsall	A

EXETER CITY

Date	Opponents	Venue
1981		
Aug 29	Huddersfield T	A
Sept 5	Carlisle U	H
Sept 11	Doncaster R	A
Sept 19	Swindon T	H
Sept 23	Bristol R	H
Sept 26	Gillingham	A
Sept 29	Portsmouth	A
Oct 3	Millwall	H
Oct 10	Brentford	H
Oct 17	Burnley	A
Oct 20	Fulham	A
Oct 24	Preston NE	H
Oct 31	Wimbledon	A
Nov 4	Oxford U	H
Nov 7	Reading	H
Nov 14	Chester	A
Nov 28	Newport Co	A
Dec 5	Chesterfield	H
Dec 19	Lincoln C	H
Dec 26	Bristol C	A
Dec 28	Plymouth Arg	H
1982		
Jan 1	Southend U	A
Jan 9	Carlisle U	A
Jan 16	Walsall	H
Jan 23	Huddersfield T	H
Jan 31	Swindon T	A
Feb 6	Doncaster R	H
Feb 9	Bristol R	A
Feb 13	Millwall	A
Feb 20	Gillingham	H
Feb 27	Brentford	A
Mar 6	Burnley	H
Mar 10	Fulham	H
Mar 13	Preston NE	A
Mar 17	Oxford U	A
Mar 20	Wimbledon	H
Mar 27	Reading	A
Apr 3	Chester	H
Apr 9	Plymouth Arg	A
Apr 10	Bristol C	H
Apr 17	Chesterfield	A
Apr 24	Newport Co	H
May 1	Walsall	A
May 5	Portsmouth	H
May 8	Southend U	H
May 15	Lincoln C	A

FULHAM

Date	Opponents	Venue
1981		
Aug 29	Brentford	H
Sept 5	Lincoln C	A
Sept 12	Bristol C	H
Sept 19	Chesterfield	A
Sept 22	Wimbledon	A
Sept 26	Chester	H
Sept 29	Southend U	H
Oct 3	Oxford U	A
Oct 10	Huddersfield T	A
Oct 17	Newport Co	H
Oct 20	Exeter C	H
Oct 24	Burnley	A
Oct 31	Portsmouth	H
Nov 3	Plymouth Arg	A
Nov 7	Carlisle U	A
Nov 14	Walsall	H
Nov 28	Millwall	H
Dec 5	Bristol R	A
Dec 19	Preston NE	A
Dec 26	Gillingham	H
Dec 28	Swindon T	A
1982		
Jan 2	Doncaster R	H
Jan 9	Lincoln C	H
Jan 16	Reading	A
Jan 23	Brentford	A
Jan 30	Chesterfield	H
Feb 6	Bristol C	A
Feb 9	Wimbledon	H
Feb 13	Oxford U	H
Feb 19	Southend U	A
Feb 27	Huddersfield T	H
Mar 7	Newport Co	A
Mar 10	Exeter C	A
Mar 13	Burnley	H
Mar 16	Plymouth Arg	H
Mar 20	Portsmouth	A
Mar 27	Carlisle U	H
Apr 3	Walsall	A
Apr 10	Gillingham	A
Apr 13	Swindon T	H
Apr 17	Bristol R	H
Apr 24	Millwall	A
May 1	Reading	H
May 5	Chester	A
May 8	Doncaster R	A
May 15	Preston NE	H

DIVISION THREE

GILLINGHAM

Date		Opponents	Venue
1981			
Aug	29	Burnley	H
Sept	5	Reading	A
Sept	12	Chester	H
Sept	19	Preston NE	A
Sept	21	Brentford	A
Sept	26	Exeter C	H
Sept	29	Bristol C	H
Oct	3	Wimbledon	A
Oct	10	Plymouth Arg	A
Oct	17	Huddersfield T	H
Oct	20	Portsmouth	H
Oct	24	Millwall	A
Oct	31	Swindon T	H
Nov	2	Southend U	A
Nov	7	Bristol R	A
Nov	14	Doncaster R	H
Nov	28	Carlisle U	A
Dec	5	Walsall	H
Dec	22	Chesterfield	H
Dec	26	Fulham	A
Dec	28	Newport Co	H
1982			
Jan	2	Oxford U	A
Jan	9	Reading	H
Jan	16	Lincoln C	A
Jan	23	Burnley	A
Jan	30	Preston NE	H
Feb	6	Chester	A
Feb	9	Brentford	H
Feb	13	Wimbledon	H
Feb	20	Exeter C	A
Feb	27	Plymouth Arg	H
Mar	6	Huddersfield T	A
Mar	9	Portsmouth	A
Mar	12	Millwall	H
Mar	16	Southend U	H
Mar	20	Swindon T	A
Mar	27	Bristol R	H
Apr	3	Doncaster R	A
Apr	10	Fulham	H
Apr	12	Newport Co	A
Apr	17	Walsall	A
Apr	24	Carlisle U	H
May	1	Bristol C	A
May	4	Lincoln C	H
May	8	Oxford U	H
May	15	Chesterfield	A

HUDDERSFIELD TOWN

Date		Opponents	Venue
1981			
Aug	29	Exeter C	H
Sept	5	Oxford U	A
Sept	12	Wimbledon	H
Sept	19	Burnley	A
Sept	22	Preston NE	A
Sept	26	Southend U	H
Sept	29	Chester	H
Oct	3	Reading	A
Oct	10	Fulham	H
Oct	17	Gillingham	A
Oct	20	Carlisle U	H
Oct	24	Bristol R	A
Oct	31	Millwall	H
Nov	3	Chesterfield	A
Nov	6	Doncaster R	A
Nov	14	Swindon T	H
Nov	28	Portsmouth	A
Dec	5	Plymouth Arg	H
Dec	19	Newport Co	H
Dec	26	Walsall	A
Dec	28	Lincoln C	H
1982			
Jan	2	Brentford	A
Jan	9	Oxford U	H
Jan	16	Bristol C	A
Jan	23	Exeter C	A
Jan	30	Burnley	H
Feb	6	Wimbledon	A
Feb	9	Preston NE	H
Feb	13	Reading	H
Feb	20	Chester	A
Feb	27	Fulham	A
Mar	6	Gillingham	H
Mar	9	Carlisle U	A
Mar	13	Bristol R	H
Mar	16	Chesterfield	H
Mar	20	Millwall	A
Mar	27	Doncaster R	H
Apr	3	Swindon T	A
Apr	10	Walsall	H
Apr	12	Lincoln C	A
Apr	17	Plymouth Arg	A
Apr	24	Portsmouth	H
May	1	Southend U	A
May	4	Bristol C	H
May	8	Brentford	H
May	15	Newport Co	A

LINCOLN CITY

Date		Opponents	Venue
1981			
Aug	29	Portsmouth	A
Sept	5	Fulham	H
Sept	12	Plymouth Arg	A
Sept	19	Carlisle U	H
Sept	23	Millwall	H
Sept	26	Bristol R	A
Sept	29	Walsall	A
Oct	3	Newport Co	H
Oct	10	Wimbledon	H
Oct	17	Brentford	A
Oct	20	Doncaster R	A
Oct	24	Bristol C	H
Oct	31	Oxford U	A
Nov	4	Preston NE	H
Nov	7	Southend U	A
Nov	14	Chesterfield	H
Nov	28	Swindon T	H
Dec	5	Reading	A
Dec	19	Exeter C	A
Dec	26	Burnley	H
Dec	28	Huddersfield T	A
1982			
Jan	2	Chester	H
Jan	9	Fulham	A
Jan	16	Gillingham	H
Jan	23	Portsmouth	H
Jan	30	Carlisle U	A
Feb	6	Plymouth Arg	H
Feb	9	Millwall	A
Feb	13	Newport Co	A
Feb	20	Walsall	H
Feb	27	Wimbledon	A
Mar	6	Brentford	H
Mar	10	Doncaster R	H
Mar	13	Bristol C	A
Mar	16	Preston NE	A
Mar	20	Oxford U	H
Mar	27	Southend U	H
Apr	3	Chesterfield	A
Apr	10	Burnley	A
Apr	12	Huddersfield T	H
Apr	17	Reading	H
Apr	24	Swindon T	A
May	1	Bristol R	H
May	4	Gillingham	A
May	8	Chester	A
May	15	Exeter C	H

MILLWALL

Date		Opponents	Venue
1981			
Aug	29	Preston NE	H
Sept	5	Wimbledon	A
Sept	13	Reading	A
Sept	19	Chester	A
Sept	23	Lincoln C	A
Sept	26	Burnley	H
Sept	29	Oxford U	H
Oct	3	Exeter C	A
Oct	11	Walsall	H
Oct	17	Doncaster R	A
Oct	20	Newport Co	A
Oct	24	Gillingham	H
Oct	31	Huddersfield T	A
Nov	3	Bristol C	H
Nov	7	Swindon T	A
Nov	14	Bristol R	H
Nov	28	Fulham	A
Dec	5	Carlisle U	H
Dec	18	Plymouth Arg	H
Dec	26	Southend U	A
Dec	28	Brentford	H
1982			
Jan	2	Portsmouth	A
Jan	9	Wimbledon	H
Jan	16	Chesterfield	A
Jan	23	Preston NE	A
Jan	30	Chester	H
Feb	6	Reading	A
Feb	9	Lincoln C	H
Feb	13	Exeter C	H
Feb	20	Burnley	A
Feb	27	Walsall	A
Mar	6	Doncaster R	H
Mar	9	Newport Co	H
Mar	12	Gillingham	A
Mar	16	Bristol C	A
Mar	20	Huddersfield T	H
Mar	27	Swindon T	H
Apr	3	Bristol R	A
Apr	9	Brentford	A
Apr	12	Southend U	H
Apr	17	Carlisle U	A
Apr	24	Fulham	H
May	1	Oxford U	A
May	4	Chesterfield	H
May	8	Portsmouth	H
May	15	Plymouth Arg	A

NEWPORT COUNTY

Date		Opponents	Venue
1981			
Aug	29	Chesterfield	H
Sept	4	Southend U	A
Sept	12	Oxford U	H
Sept	19	Bristol C	A
Sept	23	Reading	A
Sept	26	Preston NE	H
Sept	29	Brentford	H
Oct	3	Lincoln C	A
Oct	10	Doncaster R	H
Oct	17	Fulham	A
Oct	20	Millwall	H
Oct	24	Portsmouth	A
Oct	31	Carlisle U	H
Nov	3	Bristol R	A
Nov	7	Walsall	A
Nov	14	Plymouth Arg	H
Nov	28	Exeter C	H
Dec	5	Wimbledon	A
Dec	19	Huddersfield T	A
Dec	26	Chester	H
Dec	28	Gillingham	A
1982			
Jan	2	Swindon T	H
Jan	9	Southend U	H
Jan	16	Burnley	A
Jan	23	Chesterfield	A
Jan	30	Bristol C	H
Feb	6	Oxford U	A
Feb	9	Reading	H
Feb	13	Lincoln C	H
Feb	20	Brentford	A
Feb	27	Doncaster R	A
Mar	7	Fulham	H
Mar	9	Millwall	A
Mar	13	Portsmouth	H
Mar	16	Bristol R	H
Mar	20	Carlisle U	A
Mar	27	Walsall	H
Apr	4	Plymouth Arg	A
Apr	10	Chester	A
Apr	12	Gillingham	H
Apr	17	Wimbledon	H
Apr	24	Exeter C	A
May	1	Burnley	H
May	4	Preston NE	A
May	8	Swindon T	A
May	15	Huddersfield T	H

DIVISION THREE

OXFORD UNITED

Date	Opponents	Venue
1981		
Aug 29	Plymouth Arg	A
Sept 5	Huddersfield T	H
Sept 12	Newport Co	A
Sept 19	Walsall	H
Sept 23	Portsmouth	H
Sept 26	Carlisle U	A
Sept 29	Millwall	A
Oct 3	Fulham	H
Oct 10	Chester	A
Oct 17	Bristol C	H
Oct 21	Bristol R	H
Oct 24	Southend U	A
Oct 31	Lincoln C	H
Nov 4	Exeter C	A
Nov 7	Chesterfield	A
Nov 14	Brentford	H
Nov 28	Preston NE	H
Dec 5	Burnley	A
Dec 19	Wimbledon	A
Dec 26	Reading	H
Dec 29	Doncaster R	A
1982		
Jan 2	Gillingham	H
Jan 9	Huddersfield T	A
Jan 17	Swindon T	H
Jan 23	Plymouth Arg	H
Jan 30	Walsall	A
Feb 6	Newport Co	H
Feb 9	Portsmouth	A
Feb 13	Fulham	A
Feb 20	Carlisle U	H
Feb 27	Chester	H
Mar 6	Bristol C	A
Mar 9	Bristol R	A
Mar 13	Southend U	H
Mar 17	Exeter C	H
Mar 20	Lincoln C	A
Mar 27	Chesterfield	H
Apr 3	Brentford	A
Apr 10	Reading	A
Apr 12	Doncaster R	H
Apr 17	Burnley	H
Apr 24	Preston NE	A
May 1	Millwall	H
May 4	Swindon T	A
May 8	Gillingham	A
May 15	Wimbledon	H

PLYMOUTH ARGYLE

Date	Opponents	Venue
1981		
Aug 29	Oxford U	H
Sept 5	Burnley	A
Sept 12	Lincoln C	H
Sept 19	Brentford	A
Sept 22	Bristol C	A
Sept 26	Chesterfield	H
Sept 29	Reading	H
Oct 3	Southend U	A
Oct 10	Gillingham	H
Oct 17	Carlisle U	A
Oct 20	Wimbledon	A
Oct 24	Chester	H
Oct 31	Walsall	A
Nov 3	Fulham	H
Nov 7	Portsmouth	H
Nov 14	Newport Co	A
Nov 28	Doncaster R	H
Dec 5	Huddersfield T	A
Dec 18	Millwall	A
Dec 26	Swindon T	H
Dec 28	Exeter C	A
1982		
Jan 2	Bristol R	H
Jan 9	Burnley	H
Jan 16	Preston NE	A
Jan 23	Oxford U	A
Jan 30	Brentford	H
Feb 6	Lincoln C	A
Feb 9	Bristol C	H
Feb 13	Southend U	H
Feb 20	Chesterfield	A
Feb 27	Gillingham	A
Mar 6	Carlisle U	H
Mar 9	Wimbledon	H
Mar 13	Chester	A
Mar 16	Fulham	A
Mar 20	Walsall	H
Mar 27	Portsmouth	A
Apr 4	Newport Co	H
Apr 9	Exeter C	H
Apr 10	Swindon T	A
Apr 17	Huddersfield T	H
Apr 24	Doncaster R	A
May 1	Preston NE	H
May 5	Reading	A
May 8	Bristol R	A
May 15	Millwall	H

PORTSMOUTH

Date	Opponents	Venue
1981		
Aug 29	Lincoln C	H
Sept 5	Preston NE	A
Sept 12	Brentford	H
Sept 19	Southend U	A
Sept 23	Oxford U	A
Sept 26	Bristol C	H
Sept 29	Exeter C	H
Oct 3	Chesterfield	A
Oct 10	Burnley	H
Oct 17	Walsall	A
Oct 20	Gillingham	A
Oct 24	Newport Co	H
Oct 31	Fulham	A
Nov 3	Wimbledon	H
Nov 7	Plymouth Arg	A
Nov 14	Carlisle U	H
Nov 28	Huddersfield T	H
Dec 5	Doncaster R	A
Dec 19	Swindon T	A
Dec 26	Bristol R	H
Dec 28	Reading	A
1982		
Jan 2	Millwall	H
Jan 9	Preston NE	H
Jan 16	Chester	A
Jan 23	Lincoln C	A
Jan 30	Southend U	H
Feb 6	Brentford	A
Feb 9	Oxford U	H
Feb 13	Chesterfield	H
Feb 20	Bristol C	A
Feb 27	Burnley	A
Mar 6	Walsall	H
Mar 9	Gillingham	H
Mar 13	Newport Co	A
Mar 16	Wimbledon	A
Mar 20	Fulham	H
Mar 27	Plymouth Arg	H
Apr 3	Carlisle U	A
Apr 10	Bristol R	A
Apr 12	Reading	H
Apr 17	Doncaster R	H
Apr 24	Huddersfield T	A
May 1	Chester	H
May 5	Exeter C	A
May 8	Millwall	A
May 15	Swindon T	H

PRESTON NORTH END

Date	Opponents	Venue
1981		
Aug 29	Millwall	A
Sept 5	Portsmouth	H
Sept 12	Swindon T	A
Sept 19	Gillingham	H
Sept 22	Huddersfield T	H
Sept 26	Newport Co	A
Sept 29	Doncaster R	A
Oct 3	Bristol R	H
Oct 10	Bristol C	A
Oct 17	Reading	H
Oct 20	Burnley	H
Oct 24	Exeter C	A
Oct 31	Southend U	H
Nov 4	Lincoln C	A
Nov 7	Chester	H
Nov 14	Wimbledon	A
Nov 28	Oxford U	A
Dec 5	Brentford	H
Dec 19	Fulham	H
Dec 26	Carlisle U	A
Dec 28	Walsall	H
1982		
Jan 2	Chesterfield	A
Jan 9	Portsmouth	A
Jan 16	Plymouth Arg	H
Jan 23	Millwall	H
Jan 30	Gillingham	A
Feb 6	Swindon T	H
Feb 9	Huddersfield T	A
Feb 13	Bristol R	A
Feb 20	Doncaster R	H
Feb 27	Bristol C	H
Mar 6	Reading	A
Mar 9	Burnley	A
Mar 13	Exeter C	H
Mar 16	Lincoln C	H
Mar 19	Southend U	A
Mar 27	Chester	A
Apr 3	Wimbledon	H
Apr 10	Carlisle U	H
Apr 13	Walsall	A
Apr 17	Brentford	A
Apr 24	Oxford U	H
May 1	Plymouth Arg	A
May 4	Newport Co	H
May 8	Chesterfield	H
May 15	Fulham	A

READING

Date	Opponents	Venue
1981		
Aug 29	Doncaster R	A
Sept 5	Gillingham	H
Sept 13	Millwall	A
Sept 19	Bristol R	H
Sept 23	Newport Co	H
Sept 26	Swindon T	A
Sept 29	Plymouth Arg	A
Oct 3	Huddersfield T	H
Oct 10	Chesterfield	H
Oct 17	Preston NE	A
Oct 20	Bristol C	A
Oct 24	Wimbledon	H
Oct 31	Chester	A
Nov 4	Walsall	H
Nov 7	Exeter C	A
Nov 14	Burnley	H
Nov 27	Southend U	A
Dec 5	Lincoln C	H
Dec 19	Brentford	H
Dec 26	Oxford U	A
Dec 28	Portsmouth	H
1982		
Jan 2	Carlisle U	A
Jan 9	Gillingham	A
Jan 16	Fulham	H
Jan 23	Doncaster R	H
Jan 30	Bristol R	A
Feb 6	Millwall	H
Feb 9	Newport Co	A
Feb 13	Huddersfield T	A
Feb 20	Swindon T	H
Feb 27	Chesterfield	A
Mar 6	Preston NE	H
Mar 10	Bristol C	H
Mar 13	Wimbledon	A
Mar 16	Walsall	A
Mar 20	Chester	H
Mar 27	Exeter C	H
Apr 3	Burnley	A
Apr 10	Oxford U	H
Apr 12	Portsmouth	A
Apr 17	Lincoln C	A
Apr 24	Southend U	H
May 1	Fulham	A
May 5	Plymouth Arg	H
May 8	Carlisle U	H
May 15	Brentford	A